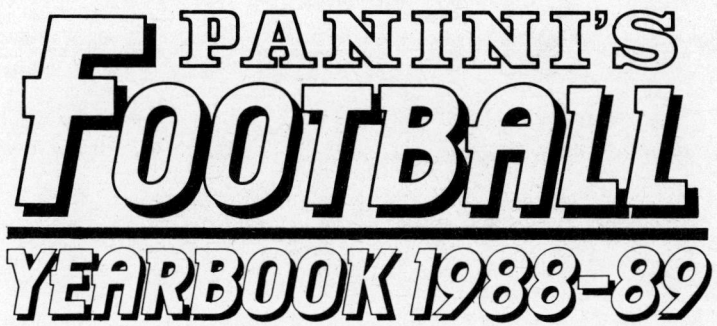

PANINI'S FOOTBALL YEARBOOK 1988-89

EDITOR: PETER DUNK

Panini Publishing Ltd · London

© Panini Publishing Limited 1988

First published in Great Britain in 1988 by
Panini Publishing Ltd
Panini House
116–120 Goswell Road
London EC1V 7QD

A subsidiary of Panini International SpA

Front cover: John Barnes (Liverpool & England)
Photo: Colorsport

British Library Cataloguing in Publication Data

Panini's football yearbook.—1st ed.
(1988–89)—
1. England. Football League football—
Serials
796.334′63′0942

ISBN 1–871178–00–2
(Paperback)

ISBN 1–871178–30–4
(Hardback)

Typeset, printed and bound in Great Britain by
Redwood Web Offset
Trowbridge, Wiltshire

CONTENTS

INTERNATIONAL FOOTBALL

MISCELLANEOUS

EDITORIAL

When this first edition of *Panini's Football Yearbook* was in the planning stages in the autumn of 1987, there was an air of genuine optimism about English football. The downward slide in attendance figures which had been a feature of our game for two decades seemed to have ended, the blight of hooliganism appeared to be fading, England had qualified in style for the final stages of the European Championship and there was a real hope that English clubs would be back in Europe next season.

By the time this editorial was written in July 1988, everything had changed for the worse. Violence accompanied the England fans on their journeys around West Germany during the summer, thus ending any hope of an immediate return by our clubs, and the England team was not only dumped out of the European Championships, but made to look decidedly second-rate in the process. As if this wasn't bad enough, there followed a bitter dispute between League clubs over TV revenues which threatened to break the League apart in its Centenary year, and the government announced legislation which would force the League to introduce a membership scheme by the beginning of the 1989–90 season.

To be fair to the England fans in West Germany, it seems that the trouble was usually started by German yobs who delighted in ambushing and provoking the English fans at every opportunity, but it is a great pity that the England followers did not have the necessary self-restraint to avoid the confrontations which were offered. Now, even though the German authorities went out of their way to point out that the English were largely not to blame, English football remains the loser.

It is an even greater pity that the British government has taken such a negative attitude to the problem of football-related violence. It is clear that the Prime Minister and her unimpressive Minister for Sport care little about the game, and have therefore dreamt up a scheme which puts the onus of responsibility for dealing with the problem on to the clubs, when what they should be doing is dealing with it themselves as a question of law and order. Considering that we have a government which has made great promises on the law and order issue in its various election manifestos, it is rather curious to see the buck being passed in this way.

The proposed membership scheme is ludicrous. Apart from the numerous practical difficulties involved, of which more later, the scheme must fail in its objectives for the simple reason that it does not address the problem which it seeks to solve. The problem, stated in its simplest terms, is that a very small minority of the people who attend football matches in this country are violent criminals. Therefore, instead of introducing a national membership scheme which will inconvenience the vast, innocent, majority, why does the government not ensure that these criminals are dealt with in an appropriate manner?

Unfortunately, we have seen the collapse of over 100 prosecutions against people accused of football-related violence during 1988, and although it would not be proper to comment on the specifics of these cases while internal police inquiries are in progress, we must all hope that the police are able to get their act together soon, and deal with the men of violence with considerably more success than hitherto. For their part, the government should be giving the police more support. Rather than imposing a membership scheme on the clubs, the government should be ensuring that adequate legislation is in place to control the people who are ruining our game. Crimes of violence should be punished by long prison sentences, especially where weapons such as knives, or worse, are involved. This would have the dual effect of removing the undesirables from the terraces and deterring others who might otherwise behave in the same way. And any conviction for a crime of violence, whether football-related or otherwise, should result in the automatic confiscation of passports. In this way, not only would the export of football-related violence be limited, but perhaps the beaches in the package holiday resorts would be safer, too.

The purely practical difficulties involved in the scheme are almost too numerous to mention, but those which would occur to even the simplest mind (which begs the question as to why they haven't occurred to anyone in the government) include cost, logistics and enforcement.

Although the costs will (presumably) be shared between the clubs, they will be considerable and ongoing. Therefore, it is safe to assume that they will be passed on to the consumers, which means that all those of us who like to go to football matches and behave ourselves are going to be penalised because the authorities are incompetent to deal with the trouble-makers in any other way.

The problems of logistics and enforcement are potentially appalling, and the main reason why even the police are opposed to the scheme. Checking identity cards through the expensive computer terminals which will have to be installed at every turnstile in the land, as well as relieving the customers of their money, will increase dramatically the time it takes to get people into the stadiums. Either we will all have to turn up an hour earlier than usual and stand in enormous queues, or the number of turnstiles (and computer terminals) will have to be increased, at huge expense.

And what happens when a card is rejected? Will there have to be a police officer on duty at every turnstile to remove the unwanted spectator? And remove him to where? And what happens if another card is rejected while the officer is busy escorting the previous unsuccessful applicant to we know not where? Perhaps we will need two police officers per turnstile, just in case. Or should the job be left to club stewards, assuming that the clubs have enough of them? If they haven't, will they be able to recruit them? But recruit them from where? And can these stewards, whose standards of training will necessarily be far below those of police officers, be trusted to enforce the scheme without running foul of the law themselves? And while all this is going on, the rest of us are waiting patiently in line . . .

Furthermore, the people responsible for dreaming up this wonderful scheme have forgotten all about the casual supporters such as overseas visitors who might want to take in a game while they are in town, and those of us who might want, for a variety of reasons, to attend only a handful of matches each season. Can people in these categories be expected to obtain identity cards on the off-chance that they might want to see a game? And how much will these identity cards cost? Will the cost of the scheme be recovered by charging for the cards, and if so, will there be relief for old age pensioners or the unwaged? Or will they simply be prohibited from attending at all? And when, eventually, English clubs are re-admitted to Europe, how will the scheme monitor foreign trouble-makers, of which there are many, when they follow their teams to our shores? Or will they simply be banned, thus destroying the atmosphere of the occasion?

Perhaps, during the months ahead, wiser counsel will prevail and the scheme be dropped, although it is difficult to be optimistic about this. We have a government which rarely changes its mind, and given that nobody in its ranks really cares about football, the chances of commonsense prevailing seem slim.

Meanwhile, the very structure of the game in this country has been threatened by an unseemly scramble on the part of television companies to get exclusive rights. For the time being, the formation of a so-called Super League has been postponed indefinitely, but one can't help wondering what makes the television people think that the domestic game is worth the incredible amounts of money that they are offering. There has been a noticeable growth of the greed factor throughout football in recent years, which is sad, and the money that television companies are now proposing to throw at the game can only make matters worse. Maybe it would be a good idea to have a small Premier Division. Such a device has been established in Scotland since the mid-seventies with considerable success. But it must be done for the right reasons, in other words for the benefit of the game as a whole, and not come about as the result of an acrimonious split which leaves ten or twelve clubs out on their own as the result of pure selfishness. A Premier Division should be the top of the pyramid, and cannot possibly succeed in isolation. On this matter, at least, there is still a good chance that commonsense will prevail. Let's hope so.

ACKNOWLEDGEMENTS

The Editor would like to thank the following people and organisations for their assistance in the compilation of this yearbook (and apologise to anybody who has been left out!) The Football League, The Scottish Football League, The Football Association, The Scottish Football Association, the Secretaries and Commercial Managers of all English and Scottish League clubs, Norman Barrett, Jim Bygrave, Jenny Dunk, Alan Elliott, Sherine Krause, Mike McNamara, Ken Scott, Juliet Scull, Margaret Stephens, and all the staff at Redwood Burn.

AN APPEAL FROM THE SCOTTISH FOOTBALL LEAGUE

The Scottish Football League will celebrate its centenary in 1990, and have commissioned Mr Bob Crampsey to write the official Centenary Book. No doubt many clubs and supporters are in possession of a wealth of pictorial material relating to the Scottish League. It would therefore be appreciated if anyone in possession of old photographs of teams, individuals, or stadiums would contact The Scottish Football League, 188 West Regent Street, Glasgow G2 4RY (Telephone 041–248 3844) with the details. Should the photograph be considered suitable for possible inclusion in the Centenary Book, arrangements will be made to uplift the photograph(s) and an acknowledgement of the source will be included in the book. Any other items, not necessarily photographs, will also be considered as part of a possible exhibition of football memorabilia which is also planned. Your co-operation is greatly appreciated, but please contact the Scottish Football League direct, and not Panini Publishing Ltd.

DAY-BY-DAY DIARY 1987–88

JULY 1987

1 FIFA confirm that the 46 African nations who advocated the amalgamation of the four British countries have withdrawn their proposal. Manchester United complete the transfers of Viv Anderson from Arsenal and Brian McClair from Celtic, the fees still to be agreed. Celtic sign a replacement striker, Andy Walker, from Motherwell for £350,000. Don Howe turns down a post with Turkish club Besiktas of Istanbul.

2 Kevin Bond is the new Southampton captain following the departure of Peter Shilton. Northampton sign Halifax striker David Longhurst for £40,000.

3 Celtic offer Arsenal striker Charlie Nicholas a lucrative contract. Brazil lose 4–0 to Chile in the South American Championship and are eliminated, leaving the country in a state of shock.

4 Gordon Milne accepts the Besiktas job.

6 Spurs sign Dutch midfielder Johnny Metgod from Forest for £250,000. Notts County sign West Ham's Geoff Pike for £35,000.

7 The FA refuse to sanction pre-season trips of Spurs to Holland, and Leeds to West Germany. Reading sign Wimbledon striker Colin Gordon for £80,000. Torquay ban away fans and threaten to punish any players who swear during a game.

8 Charlie Nicholas ends transfer speculation and re-signs for Arsenal, but only for one year. Former England captain Gerry Francis is appointed player-manager of Third Division Bristol Rovers.

9 Uruguay beat world champions Argentina at Buenos Aires in the semi-finals of the South American Championship. Millwall sign George Lawrence from Southampton for £160,000. Spurs have their £10,000 fine for fielding a weakened side against Everton in Cup final week halved on appeal.

11 Colombia beat Argentina 2–1 to win third place in the South American Championship.

12 Uruguay retain the South American Championship in Buenos Aires, beating Chile 1–0 with a goal from Bengoechea.

14 After a protracted negotiation, Liverpool sign Peter Beardsley from Newcastle for £1.8 million, but have to postpone their first home games because of a collapsed sewer under the Kop. Glasgow Rangers sign Watford striker Mark Falco for £300,000. Shrewsbury winger Gary Hackett joins Aberdeen for £100,000. Blackburn complete the signing of Chelsea defender John Miller. Injury forces former Southampton captain Nick Holmes, 32, to retire.

15 Coventry sign Chelsea striker David Speedie for a club record £750,000. Oxford announce a further £500,000 sponsorship deal with Wang.

16 Palace sign Neil Redfearn from Doncaster for £80,000.

18 Plymouth agree £100,000 sponsorship deal with local newspaper the *Sunday Independent*.

21 The FA pay Manchester United £300,000 compensation for keeper Gary Bailey, forced to retire through injury. Wimbledon pay Plymouth £150,000 for defender Clive Goodyear. Portsmouth sign midfielder Mike Fillery from QPR on a free transfer.

22 The FA impose a record £4,500 fine on Wimbledon for last season's poor disciplinary record. Blackpool received a £1,000 fine, Southend £500. Oxford sign Wednesday midfielder Gary Shelton for £155,000.

23 Bayern Munich beat Liverpool 3–2 in a testimonial for retired striker Dieter Hoeness. Leeds sign Villa defender Gary Williams, the fee to go to tribunal.

24 Everton's Adrian Heath and Kevin Sheedy are found guilty of making indecent gestures to the crowd at Anfield last April, but are let off with a warning. Watford sign Reading striker Trevor Senior for £325,000.

27 Ipswich sign Glasgow Rangers reserve striker Neil Woods for £120,000. Birmingham sign keeper Tony Godden from Chelsea for £35,000.

28 Villa sign striker Alan McInally from Celtic for £220,000.

29 Chelsea's new captain, Joe McLaughlin, 27, signs a six-year contract with the club.

30 Tribunal settle fee for Brian McClair at £850,000, more than twice what Manchester United offered, but Celtic are unhappy.

AUGUST 1987

1 League Champions Everton beat Coventry 1–0 in the Charity Shield with a goal from Wayne Clarke, but Kevin Sheedy injures an Achilles tendon. Arsenal thrash Celtic 5–1 in a friendly at Parkhead.

2 The Football League are shocked as the *Today* newspaper pulls out of their sponsorship deal.

4 Coventry management duo John Sillett and George Curtis receive the *Daily Telegraph* Football Sportsman Award. Despite his success in Spain, manager Colin Addison is sacked by Celta of Vigo.

5 São Paulo club Palmeiras announce the transfer of international striker Mirandinha to Newcastle for £600,000; he will be the first Brazilian to play English club football. QPR sign Israel international midfielder David Pisanti from Cologne for £150,000.

6 Glasgow Rangers sign Trevor Francis from Italian club Atalanta for £75,000 on a no-play no-pay contract, suggested by the 33-year-old ex-England international because of a recent shoulder operation. Aberdeen sign Welsh international Peter Nicholas from Luton for £350,000.

7 At an informal meeting in London between UEFA president Jacques Georges and Sports Minister Colin Moynihan, England's case for returning to European club competition is discussed and a review promised for next March. The FA slap a record £5,000 fine (£2,000 suspended for two years) on Portsmouth midfielder Mick Kennedy for bringing the game into disrepute with remarks made in a newspaper article.

8 The Football League launch their centenary season with a 3–0 win at Wembley over a star-studded Rest of World side managed by Terry Venables and including Maradona, Michel Platini, and Gary Lineker. The Scottish League season begins.

9 An American football game at Wembley draws 72,000 spectators, over 10,000 more than watched the previous day's Football League Centenary match.

11 Football League president Philip Carter warns the clubs against complacency in the battle against hooliganism.

12 The League tribunal settles Viv Anderson's transfer fee from Arsenal (asked for £450,000) to Manchester United (offered £100,000) at £250,000. Chris Fairclough is valued at £387,500 (Spurs offered £225,000, Forest wanted £477,500). Other fees settled by the tribunal include £285,000 for Ian Baird from Leeds (£500,000 valuation) to Portsmouth (£100,000). QPR sign Kevin Brock from Oxford, the fee to be decided. Welsh international back Joey Jones, 32, rejects a one-year contract at Huddersfield and returns to Wrexham for £7,000. Spurs' Clive Allen receives a disciplinary committee warning for a gesture he made to the crowd against QPR last season.

13 The Football League announce a new sponsorship deal—£4.5 million over three years by Barclays Bank—and drop their compensation claim against the *Today* newspaper.

15 The start of the League season, with two substitutes now allowed, is marred by crowd trouble caused by Wolves fans at new club Scarborough. The biggest gate of the day, 54,700 at Highbury, see Liverpool beat Arsenal 2–1. Peter Shilton makes his debut for Derby, who celebrate their return to the new 21-club Division I by beating Luton, who have Mick Harford sent off. Portsmouth's return after 28 years is spoilt as they lose 4–2 at Oxford. Injury-hit champions Everton

beat Norwich 1–0 at Goodison. Injury-prone Bryan Robson breaks his nose at Southampton. Watford's new manager Dave Bassett sees his team beat his old club, Wimbledon, 1–0 at Vicarage Road. The League's highest scorers are Fourth Division Torquay, who beat Wrexham 6–1, while in Division III Northampton win 5–0 at Chester, and Andy Jones scores all of Port Vale's goals in the 4–2 win over Aldershot. In Scotland, Rangers lose 2–0 at Aberdeen.

17 An FA emergency committee order Wolves' away matches to be all-ticket. The Football League appoint a security advisor, former Merseyside assistant chief constable Jack Crawford.

18 Southampton sign former England back Derek Statham from West Brom for £100,000. Portsmouth crash 3–0 at home to Chelsea.

19 Spurs beat Newcastle 3–1 but defender Gary Stevens limps off with a bad calf injury.

20 Villa sign keeper Lee Butler from non-League Lincoln City for £100,000. Former Spurs striker Terry Gibson is set to sign for Wimbledon from Manchester United for £200,000.

21 Wolves are fined £5,000 because of their fans' behaviour at Scarborough last Saturday, and a joint League and FA inquiry prohibits Wolves fans from obtaining tickets for six matches starting from 1 September.

22 After three matches, QPR, who beat Arsenal 2–0, and Forest, held at home by Everton, share top spot in Division I with 7 points, although Liverpool remain the only 100% side having played just one game. Brian McClair scores his first goal for Manchester United in their 2–0 win over Watford. In Scotland, Aberdeen take over from Celtic at the top. .

24 Arsenal sign ex-Everton midfielder Kevin Richardson from Watford for £250,000. Hibs sign Scottish midfielder Neil Orr from West Ham for £100,000.

25 Luton relax their ban on away fans for the Littlewoods Cup in time for the 2nd-round draw.

26 Spanish champions Real Madrid thrash injury-depleted Everton 6–1 in a friendly in Madrid. Portsmouth sign Oxford defender Malcolm Shotton for £70,000.

27 Barcelona name Gary Lineker and Bernd Schuster as their two foreign players, omitting Mark Hughes and Steve Archibald from their squad.

29 QPR and Forest stay top of Division I with away wins at Southampton and Newcastle respectively, but Liverpool's 4–1 defeat of Cup-holders Coventry at Highfield Road looks ominous. Arsenal, having dropped Charlie Nicholas, thrash Portsmouth 6–0 at Highbury for their first win and Alan Smith hits a hat-trick. Everton come back after their midweek debacle in Madrid with a 4–0 win over Sheffield Wed.

Everton get the domestic season under way by beating Coventry City 1–0 in the Charity Shield match at Wembley. Man-of-the-Match Peter Reid (*left*) and goalscorer Wayne Clarke display the trophy. *Photo: Bob Thomas Sports Photography.*

30 Plymouth lead Division II on goal difference, while Villa share bottom spot with Reading and West Brom. In Division III, the previously goalless Gillingham hammer Southend 8–1. Exeter, who have not conceded a goal in three matches, are the only 100% side apart from Liverpool in the League. In Scotland, Celtic beat Rangers, who have player-manager Graeme Souness sent off, and take over from Aberdeen at the top on goal difference. Hamilton top Division I with five wins in five games.

31 In a sizeable Bank Holiday programme except for Division I, Manchester United go top with a 3–1 win over Chelsea, and Portsmouth beat West Ham to chalk up their first win. With Anfield still not ready and Exeter losing, Liverpool are now the only 100% League club, having played only two games.

SEPTEMBER 1987

1 Spurs beat Oxford 3–0 and equal the club record of 12 consecutive home wins. Striker Mirandinha, who cost Newcastle over £1 million, makes a successful debut at Norwich. Brentford sign Chelsea midfielder Keith Jones, the fee to be agreed.

2 QPR beat Everton 1–0 at Loftus Road and go top. West Brom, bottom of Division II, announce the sacking yesterday of manager Ron Saunders.

3 Ron Atkinson is named new manager of West Brom. Chelsea announce a three-year, £1.25 million sponsorship with American-based computer giant Commodore, the biggest sponsorship in British club football. QPR confirm new shirt sponsorship, £200,000 from KLM and the Dutch Tourist Board.

4 Charlie Nicholas asks Arsenal for a transfer. Villa sign Derby striker Mark Lillis for £130,000.

5 QPR win 1–0 at Charlton and extend their lead to 4 points. Forest lose a 3–1 interval lead and go down 4–3 to Chelsea, who are the only First Division home winners and move into 3rd place. Liverpool, held at Upton Park, lose their first points. Luton win 5–2 at Oxford. Barnsley beat co-leaders Plymouth 2–1 and go top of Division II. Palace win 6–0 at Birmingham. The most extraordinary result, however, comes in Division III, where Gillingham swamp Chesterfield, who had previously not conceded a goal, by 10–0! Southend, who conceded 8 goals at Gillingham a week ago, go down 6–2 at Notts County. In Division IV, new club Scarborough join Exeter and Bolton at the top. Hearts join Celtic and Aberdeen at the top in Scotland.

8 West Ham striker Tony Cottee is sent off for the first time in his career in the Under-21 friendly with West Germany, which England lose 2–0. A Football League side, captained by Ossie Ardiles, scrapes a 2–2 draw with the Irish League in Belfast thanks to a late equalizer from Mirandhina.

9 Home countries go top of their respective qualifying groups in the European Championship, Mark Hughes giving Wales a 1–0 win over Denmark, and Ireland scraping through 2–1 over Luxembourg. In friendlies, Scotland beat Hungary 2–0 at Hampden, but England go down 3–1 in West Germany. Neil Webb (Forest), on for Hoddle after an hour, becomes England's 1,000th international.

12 QPR beat Chelsea 3–1 with a Gary Bannister hat-trick and go 5 points clear at the top of Division I. A last-minute Clive Allen penalty takes Spurs into second place as they beat Southampton 2–1 and chalk up their record 13th home win on the trot. Liverpool play their first home game of the season and beat Oxford 2–0. In Division II, Palace go top on goal difference. Walsall go top of Division III as Sunderland are held at home by Bury.

14 In Monday's only match, Port Vale beat Southend 4–1 and go top of Division III on goal difference. Gillingham sign keeper Tony Parks of Spurs on a month's loan.

15 Two late goals at Anfield give Liverpool a 3–2 win over struggling Charlton and take them into 3rd place with two games in hand. In Division II, Palace draw at Sheffield United but stay top. Notts County go top of Division III. Burnley, with an adverse goal difference (9–10), go top of Division IV. In the UEFA Cup 1st round, Celtic beat Borussia Dortmund by only 2–1 and Aberdeen can only draw in Dublin against part-timers Bohemians.

16 Welsh Cup-holders Merthyr beat Atalanta of Italy 2–1 in the Cup-Winners' Cup 1st round 1st leg. In the Champions' Cup, Rangers hold Dynamo Kiev to a single goal, a penalty, while in the clash of the giants in Spain, Real Madrid beat Napoli 2–0—behind closed doors because of crowd disturbances last season. In Division II, Bradford beat Plymouth 3–1 and go top. Arsenal grant Charlie Nicholas's transfer request.

17 Watford manager Dave Bassett transfers two more players, Richard Hill and David Bardsley, both to Oxford for £500,000.

18 Charlton sign Port Vale striker Andy Jones for £300,000.

19 It's 1–2–3 for London in Division I, with QPR top despite losing, followed by Spurs and Chelsea. Charlton beat Luton to chalk up their first win and push winless Wednesday into last place. Bradford stay top of Division II, but Wigan are

the new leaders of Division III. Scarborough go top of Division IV. Hearts go top of Scotland's Premier Division as Celtic draw with Aberdeen.

20 In the first televised League match of the season, a Steve Nicol hat-trick helps Liverpool cruise past Newcastle 4–1 at St James's Park and move into 3rd place. Everton sign Leicester midfielder Ian Wilson for £300,000 to ease their injury problems.

21 Albanian champions Partizan Tirana are banned from European competition for a year after having four players sent off last week in a tie against Benfica.

22 Notable performances in the 1st leg of the Littlewoods Cup 2nd round include Jimmy Quinn's hat-trick for Swindon, who beat Portsmouth 3–1, Bradford's 5–1 win at Fulham, and Wolves' 2–1 victory at Manchester City.

23 Intense speculation becomes reality as Barcelona manager Terry Venables is sacked after a disastrous start to the season. In the Littlewoods Cup, Division I teams fare poorly in the away leg, Chelsea losing 3–1 at Reading, Spurs 1–0 at Torquay, and Newcastle 1–0 at Blackpool, but Liverpool draw at Blackburn and holders Arsenal win 3–0 at Doncaster. At home, Oxford are held by Mansfield, while Manchester United and Forest have 5–0 wins. Manchester City sign reserve Liverpool defender Mark Seagraves for £100,000. Both Aberdeen and Rangers have two-goal victories in the Skol Cup semi-finals. In the European Championship, Bulgaria beat Belgium to leapfrog over Ireland into top place in Group 7.

24 Rangers player-manager Graeme Souness is suspended for five matches for his third sending-off in 14 months, against Celtic last month, and for his verbal abuse of the referee. Leeds sign Liverpool midfield reserve Ken De Mange for £75,000.

25 Exeter win 2–0 at Colchester and go top of Division IV.

26 QPR beat Luton 2–0 and consolidate their lead in Division I, while Chelsea move into 2nd place with a 3–0 win at Watford. With only 2 points separating the top 10 clubs in Division III, Northampton are the new leaders. In Scotland, leading clubs Hearts, Celtic, and Aberdeen all win away and Rangers thrash bottom club Morton 7–0 with hat-tricks from Mark Falco and Ally McCoist. In Division I, Hamilton lose their first game at home, to lowly East Fife, but retain their 5-point lead.

28 After just three months at Newcastle, Glyn Hodges joins Watford, signed by his former Wimbledon boss Dave Bassett for £300,000. Tommy Docherty takes over at GM Vauxhall club Altrincham with his usual enthusiasm. QPR's Irish international midfielder Gary Wad-

dock, 25, is forced to retire from first-class soccer for medical reasons.

29 John Aldridge scores a hat-trick as Liverpool beat Derby 4–0 and move into 2nd place. Celtic lose 2–0 to Borussia Dortmund and crash out of the UEFA Cup 3–2 on aggregate. Bristol City go top of Division III, Orient top of Division IV.

30 Rangers beat Dynamo Kiev 2–0 at Ibrox to win their 1st round European Cup tie 2–1 on aggregate, controversially but legally narrowing the pitch by 10 yards after the Soviet side practised on it last night. Real Madrid hold Diego Maradona's Naples in Italy to win the tie. Having drawn in Norway, Linfield lose 4–2 at home to Lillestrom, and the referee has to stop the game when missiles are thrown onto the pitch. Brave Merthyr go out of the Cup-Winners' Cup, beaten 2–0 at Atalanta, but St Mirren survive thanks to a goalless draw at Tromso. Aberdeen and Dundee United go through to the 2nd round of the UEFA Cup.

OCTOBER 1987

2 Richard Gough joins Rangers from Spurs for £1.5 million, a record between the two countries and a British record for a defender, and Gary Mabutt replaces him as Spurs captain. Frank McAvennie signs for Celtic from West Ham for £800,000. Cardiff go top of Division IV. Hereford and manager John Newman part company and Ian Bowyer is appointed caretaker-manager.

3 For the third time in seven days Liverpool, now the only unbeaten team in the League, win and score 4 goals. But QPR, 2–1 winners at Wimbledon, stay top. Everton also score 4, at Southampton, all from Graeme Sharp, his first hat-trick for the club. Bradford extend their Division II lead to 6 points over Hull, who lose their unbeaten record at Sheffield United. In Division III, Northampton beat leaders Bristol City 3–0 and take over at the top. Scarborough regain the lead in Division IV, beating Burnley 1–0, but away fans cause trouble for the third time this season. Aberdeen go top in Scotland as Celtic and Hearts draw at home.

6 Barnsley shock West Ham in the Littlewoods Cup, winning 5–2 at Upton Park with three goals in extra time, after being two down at half-time. Bournemouth hold Southampton at the Dell to go through to the 3rd round on aggregate. Liverpool and Everton both struggle to single-goal aggregate wins over lesser opposition, but Watford smash Darlington 8–0 at Vicarage Road for an 11–0 overall scoreline. Charlton agree to sign Forest midfielder David Campbell for £75,000.

'Who's he?' Pele seems to be asking as he chats to Michel Platini before the Centenary Match at Wembley (*above*). Afterwards, the crowd all want to touch Maradona's hand, but he looks a bit apprehensive. Understandable, perhaps. *Photos: Bob Thomas Sports Photography.*

7 More shocks for First Division sides in the Littlewoods Cup as Fourth Division Southend hold Derby at the Baseball Ground to win 1–0 and Second Division strugglers Reading, having lost their 3–1 first-leg lead to a hat-trick by Chelsea striker Gordon Durie at Stamford Bridge, come back to knock the Londoners out with two goals from Colin Gordon. Division II promotion hopefuls Swindon beat Portsmouth 3–1 at Fratton Park to win the tie 6–2. Hearts beat Aberdeen to top the Scottish League, while neighbours Hibs break the club transfer record, signing Scottish international keeper Andy Goram from Oldham for £325,000. Spurs reserve striker Mark Cooper signs for Gillingham for £105,000.

8 Luton, drawn at home to Coventry in the Littlewoods Cup, decide to play the tie at Craven Cottage rather than relax their members only rule. The FA ban West Ham striker Tony Cottee for three internationals. Leicester defender Steve Walsh is found guilty of violent conduct against Shrewsbury's David Geddis and is banned for six matches. Manchester United manager Alex Ferguson is fined £750 for using 'foul and abusive language' to the referee. The League fine Tranmere £2,000 and deduct 2 points because of the club's refusal to pay for extra policing against Bolton, which resulted in the postponement of the match. Palace sign Huddersfield left-back David Burke for £78,000, and sell midfielder Kevin Taylor to Scunthorpe for £20,000. Brian Eastick, former Charlton coach, is appointed Newport manager.

10 With QPR resting, Liverpool are denied the chance of going top of Division I when their game at Wimbledon is called off through water on the pitch. Arsenal's seventh win in a row takes them into 3rd place. In Division II, Villa register their sixth away win in a row, over Leeds at Elland Road. Sunderland beat Wigan 4–1 and shoot to the top of Division III on goal difference.

11 Northampton draw at Rotherham and go top of Division III on goal difference.

12 Luton transfer their home Littlewoods Cup tie with Coventry to Leicester because of the prohibitive cost of policing it at Craven Cottage. Malcolm Macdonald is appointed manager of bottom Division II club Huddersfield.

13 Turkey hold England 1–1 at Bramall Lane in the European Under-21 Championship, while Scotland beat Belgium 1–0. Jimmy Mullen, former England and Wolves winger, dies at 64.

14 Gary Lineker hits his fourth international hat-trick as England crush Turkey 8–0 at Wembley in the European Championship. Yugoslavia, who beat Northern Ireland 3–0, are 3 points behind England in Group 4 with a game in hand. Wales, without keeper Neville Southall, lose 1–0 in Denmark and must now win their remaining game in Czechoslovakia to qualify for the finals. The Republic of Ireland go top of Group 7, beating Bulgaria 2–0, but have Liam Brady sent off near the end. Scotland, with no chance themselves, do Ireland a favour by beating Belgium 2–0, but will have to win in Bulgaria if Ireland are to qualify.

15 Newcastle agree to pay Coleraine £80,000 for goalscoring winger Michael O'Neill, an 18-year-old schoolboy.

17 Liverpool demolish leaders QPR 4–0 at Anfield to go top with two games in hand. Who can stop them now? At the top of Division II, Bradford also win 4–0, against Birmingham, to maintain their 6-point lead. And Northampton's 4–0 defeat of Chesterfield keeps them at the top of Division III. At the top of Scotland's Premier Division, Hearts lose 2–1 at Hibs. Rangers hold Celtic at Ibrox; three men are sent off in this stormy Auld Firm encounter—Terry Butcher and keeper Chris Woods of Rangers and Frank McAvennie of Celtic—but with Graham Roberts in goal the 9-man Rangers side equalize in the last minute through Richard Gough.

18 Arsenal go 3rd by beating Spurs 2–1 at White Hart Lane. Liverpool sign Ray Houghton from Oxford for £825,000.

19 Cowdenbeath sack manager Dick Campbell and appoint former Hibs boss John Blackley. Colchester sign Northern Ireland international Colin Hill from Maritimo of Portugal.

20 A police report is ordered on Saturday's Rangers–Celtic brawl. It's all change in Division III as Sunderland win at Bristol City to go top. Mansfield sign defender John Ryan from Oldham for £25,000.

21 Glasgow Rangers recover their composure at Ibrox to beat Gornik 3–1 in the European Cup, while Real Madrid score twice in the last 10 minutes to beat champions Porto in their home tie played at Valencia. In the Cup-Winners' Cup, St Mirren earn a goalless draw with Mechelen in Belgium. In the UEFA Cup, Aberdeen fail to punish a Feyenoord side who have their captain Wijnstekers dismissed after 48 minutes and take a slender 2–1 lead to the away leg, while Dundee United lose at home to Czech side Vitkovice. The big shocks are home defeats for both Milan clubs, Inter beaten 1–0 by TPS of Finland and AC 2–0 by Español. Division II leaders Bradford, having conceded only 3 goals in 7 home games, lose 2–4 to Manchester City, previously winless away and with only 3 away goals to their credit; Paul Stewart scores a hat-trick for City. Mark Walters also hits a hat-trick as Villa score their first home win, 4–1 over Palace.

22 Reading pay a record £150,000 for Bristol City defender Keith Curle.
23 Spurs manager David Pleat resigns after 'kerb-crawling' allegations in the *Sun*.
24 Pleat denies the allegations, but says he had no alternative but to resign, while managerless Spurs go down 3–0 at Forest. Liverpool win 1–0 at Luton on the pitch they detest. In Division II, Bradford can only draw at Reading, but their immediate challengers also fail to win. Sunderland beat York 4–2 to consolidate their Division III lead, while Scarborough stay top of Division IV despite their third match running without a win. Hearts increase their lead in Scotland to 3 points as Celtic lose at home for the first time, 2–1 to Dundee United, who register their first away win.
25 A scintillating Skol Cup final is unsatisfactorily settled on penalties; Rangers, without the suspended Woods, Butcher, and Souness, beat Aberdeen by 5 spot-kicks to 3 after the scores were level at 3–3 after extra time.
27 Spurs announce that Terry Venables will take over as manager on 1 December. In the Littlewoods Cup 3rd round, Arsenal take their run of wins to 10 by beating Bournemouth 3–0, but QPR go down in a 1–0 shock at Bury and Forest are eliminated 3–0 by Manchester City. Other First Division losers are Charlton, beaten at home 1–0 by Bradford, and Norwich, who lose 2–1 at Stoke. In Scotland, Hearts win 3–0 at Motherwell to increase their Premier Division lead to 5 points.
28 Everton win 1–0 at Anfield to end Liverpool's unbeaten run and knock them out of the Littlewoods Cup thanks to an 83rd minute goal by Gary Stevens. Spurs lose 2–1 at Villa Park. Celtic scrape a 3–2 win at home to Falkirk to cut back Hearts' lead in Scotland's Premier Division.
29 Wimbledon's Vinny Jones is fined £250 by the FA for remarks in a newspaper article. Mark Hughes of Barcelona goes to Bayern Munich on loan.
30 Spurs replace coach and caretaker manager Trevor Hartley with reserve team manager Doug Livermore.
31 With Liverpool playing Sunday and QPR held at Norwich, Arsenal go top of Division I by winning 1–0 at Newcastle and notching their 11th consecutive victory. Below them, Forest draw at Old Trafford and Spurs crash 3–0 to Wimbledon at White Hart Lane. Bradford beat Palace 2–0 to restore their 6-point lead in Division II. Huddersfield and York chalk up their first wins. It gets tighter at the top of Division III as Notts Co beat Sunderland 2–1. Wolves take a 1-point lead in Division IV, where Halifax, in 16th place, are only 6 points behind. In Scotland, Celtic win 1–0

at Aberdeen, but make no impression on leaders Hearts, 4–2 winners over Dundee.

NOVEMBER

1 Liverpool beat Everton 2–0 at Anfield and go back on top.
2 Glasgow Rangers captain Terry Butcher becomes the fourth player charged by the police over incidents in the Celtic match. Colchester manager Mick Walker and assistant Allan Hunter resign on a matter of principle. Man Utd manager Alex Ferguson fines Graeme Hogg for newspaper comments and loans him to West Brom for a month.
3 Arsenal beat Chelsea 3–1 and leapfrog over Liverpool, who have three games in hand. In the lower divisions five players are sent off. Eric Gates scores 4 as Sunderland thrash Southend 7–0, but Walsall keep in touch thanks to 2 goals from David Kelly. In Division II, Ian Wright scores 3 as Palace beat Plymouth 5–1, and Villa, despite Mark Walters' dismissal, chalk up their 6th away win in 9 games to go 2nd. Watford beat Swindon 4–2 in a Littlewoods' Cup replay. In the UEFA Cup Werder Bremen beat Spartak Moscow 6–2 after extra time to go through 7–6.
4 Liverpool are held 1–1 at Wimbledon but go back on top on goal difference over Arsenal. Rangers draw at Gornik and go through to the 3rd round of the European Cup 4–2 on aggregate, but St Mirren lose at home to Mechelen 2–0 and are knocked out of the Cup Winners' Cup and both Aberdeen and Dundee Utd go out of the UEFA Cup. Oxford overcome a two-goal deficit to win their Littlewoods Cup replay 3–2 at Leicester. Colchester appoint former Fulham and Bournemouth central defender Roger Brown as manager. Wigan sign N. Ireland keeper Phil Hughes from Bury for £35,000.
5 Sports Minister Colin Moynihan names nine clubs who have failed to implement a 50% membership scheme and calls for League sanctions. UEFA fix Mo Johnstone's transfer fee from Celtic to Nantes at £373,600 and order Celtic to pay him about £5,000 back pay.
6 Colchester win at Halifax to go top of Division IV. Chelsea chairman Ken Bates demands an apology from the Sports Minister in the debate over membership schemes. UEFA president Jacques Georges threatens severe measures to stamp out football violence in Europe.
7 In a curtailed First Division programme because of Wednesday's international, QPR are held at home by Watford and fail to take advantage of the leaders' absence. In Division II, Bradford crash 3–0 at Barnsley and Middlesbrough, who

DAY-BY-DAY DIARY 1987-88

The England wall defends Herget's free kick in the friendly in Dusseldorf in September (*above*). Thon seems to have found something interesting in the grass. Howard Kendall, meanwhile, was experiencing life as the new manager of Athletic Bilbao. *Photos: Bob Thomas Sports Photography.*

win 2–0 at Sheff Utd, reduce their lead to 3 points. Villa's poor home form lets them down again as Millwall win 2–1. The day's highest attendance, 19,583, is at Maine Road, where Man City humiliate Huddersfield 10–1, with Stewart, Adcock, and White all scoring hat-tricks. Sunderland, in front of the day's next biggest gate in England, 18,197, are held at Roker Park by lowly Grimsby, but retain their 1-point lead in Division III. Wolves, with 10,000 at Molineux – more than four of the six Division I gates – beat Burnley 3–0 and go back to the top of Division IV. There is no change at the top of the Scottish Premier as Hearts are held 1–1 by Celtic.

9 Norwich sack manager Ken Brown after 14 years with the club, and appoint his assistant Dave Stringer as caretaker.

10 England's Under-21s cheer their seniors with a 5–1 win in Yugoslavia. Walsall's David Kelly hits a hat-trick on his international debut as ireland beat israel 5–0 in a friendly at Dalymount Park. Man City continue their scoring spree at Maine Road, beating Plymouth 6–2 in the Simod Cup, with Tony Adcock hitting another hat-trick.

11 A fine 4–1 win in Belgrade puts England through to the European Championship finals along with Ireland, who qualify thanks to Scotland's 1–0 win in Bulgaria. But Wales lose 2–0 in Czechoslovakia, allowing Denmark to qualify. N Ireland's consolation 1–0 win over Turkey is their only victory in the group and their first in 10 games. Bradford win 5–0 at Villa Park in the Simod Cup. Portsmouth manager Alan Ball puts 9 first-team players on the transfer list.

13 UEFA ban Liam Brady for four games after his sending-off against Bulgaria last month, virtually ruling him out of the European finals. Halifax are fined £500 and docked a League point for fielding an ineligible player against Darlington in August. Celtic sign striker Joe Miller from Aberdeen for £650,000.

14 With Liverpool playing tomorrow, Arsenal go back on top, beating Norwich 4–2 at Carrow Road, their 13th successive victory and a club record 10th League win on the trot. Peter Shilton makes his 800th League appearance as Derby draw 0–0 at Newcastle. QPR's Mark Dennis is dismissed for the 11th time in his career, but they hold Spurs 1–1 at White Hart Lane, and manager Jim Smith describes Ossie Ardiles as a 'professional con man' for his part in the sending off. In Division II, Bradford maintain their 3-point lead with a 2–0 home win over Sheff Utd, while Middlesbrough (2nd) beat Hull (3rd) 1–0 at Ayresome Park. Villa win 1–0 at Oldham, their 7th victory in 10 away games. In the 1st round of the FA Cup, Sutton Utd beat Aldershot 3–0, Macclesfield beat Carlisle 4–2

after being 2–0 down, Runcorn win 1–0 at Chester, and Lincoln beat Crewe 2–1. Steve Bull scores a hat-trick as Wolves dump Cheltenham 5–1, and so does Gary Penrice, for Bristol Rovers in their 6–0 thrashing of Merthyr, who lose their keeper with an injury and have a player sent off. In Scotland, Hearts draw 0–0 at Aberdeen and Celtic cut their lead to 2 points with a 5–0 win over Dundee. Italy beat Sweden 2–1 in Naples to secure their place in the European Championship finals.

15 Liverpool, with remarkably only one win over Man Utd in their last 14 League meetings, fail to improve this record as they draw 1–1 at Old Trafford and stay behind Arsenal at the top.

16 Sacked Spurs manager David Pleat is offered a job with Olympiakos, in Greece. QPR manager Jim Smith apologises for calling Spurs' Ossie Ardiles a 'con man'.

17 Arsenal, Everton, and Luton beat Second Division sides to go through to the last eight of the Littlewoods Cup but Watford lose 3–1 at Maine Road. In Scotland, Celtic win 2–0 at Motherwell to move level with Hearts, who have no game, and Aberdeen win 1–0 at Ibrox to go above Rangers into 3rd place. England centre-half Terry Butcher, back in the Rangers side after a three-match suspension, goes to hospital with a suspected broken leg. Aberdeen's Welsh midfielder Peter Nicholas is also carried off. Oxford's Jeremy Charles is forced to retire through injury.

18 In the Littlewoods Cup, Wednesday win at Villa Park and Man Utd at Bury, both by 2–1. Oxford knock out Wimbledon by the same score to chalk up their 25th successive home game without defeat in the tournament. Hearts win 3–0 at Dundee Utd to go back to the top of the Scottish Premier. Spain beat Albania 5–0 and qualify for the European Championship finals as Romania can only draw in Vienna. Terry Butcher has a clean break and is optimistic about returning to play for both Rangers and England in Europe. Thanks largely to the sale of players, Man Utd announce a profit of over £800,000 in the financial year. Strong rumours abound that Fosters are to sponsor the FA Cup for £12 million over three years.

19 European Champions France, ignominiously failing to qualify this year, decline an invitation to compete in the Rous Cup, leaving the tournament with problems after Scotland had vetoed Uruguay and the Government had disapproved of Argentina. Villa sign Palace midfielder Andy Gray for £150,000. Fulham sign Sheffield Utd central defender Jeff Eckhardt for £40,000. The Football League fine Peterborough £2,500 for irregularities over the signing of Rotherham's Mick Gooding.

20

DAY-BY-DAY DIARY 1987–88

20 Derby chairman Robert Maxwell, also Oxford's owner, has a takeover bid for Watford accepted, and will pay £3.5 million for Elton John's shares and outstanding loans; League secretary Graham Kelly says the League will not block the move. David Pleat turns down the job at Olympiakos. Orient win and go 2nd in Division IV.
21 Going for their 15th successive win, Arsenal lose 1–0 at home to Southampton, who had not won at Highbury for 20 years. They stay top, however, as Liverpool are held 0–0 by Norwich at Anfield. QPR are held at home by Newcastle, who have Paul Gascoigne dismissed, and Forest and Man Utd lose. Everton win 1–0 at Portsmouth, who have two players sent off. Luton's Mark Stein is also dismissed, but they beat Spurs 2–0. Robert Maxwell sees new club Watford draw at Oxford and expresses surprise that the League are now to investigate his triple involvement. In Division II, Bradford and Middlesbrough both win away. Notts County beat Walsall 3–1 and join Sunderland, held at Chesterfield, at the top of Division III. Wolves win 1–0 at Colchester to increase their lead in Division IV. Hearts are held at home by St Mirren, so Celtic, who slam Dunfermline 4–0, creep up to within a point, and Aberdeen and Rangers also win.
22 Maxwell will not go through with his Watford takeover if the League question his triple involvement, having a condition to this effect in his agreement with Elton John. UEFA allow Holland to replay their match with Cyprus, having originally reversed the result of their 8–0 victory, but increase the fine against the Dutch FA from £4,000 to £30,000 and halve the Cypriots' fine for leaving the field to £8,500.
23 Terry Venables takes over at Spurs. Bristol City assistant manager Clive Middlemass is appointed manager of Carlisle in place of Harry Gregg. Shrewsbury sack manager Chic Bates. Leeds sign Derby striker Bobby Davison for £350,000.
24 Liverpool beat Watford 4–0 to go back on top of Division I. Bradford beat Reading 1–0 in their Littlewoods Cup replay to go into the last eight. Hearts scrape through 3–2 at home to Dunfermline to extend their lead in Scotland as Celtic play tomorrow. Villa sign Barnsley midfielder Stuart Gray for £175,000. Oldham sign Man City defender Earl Barrett for £35,000.
25 Celtic just beat St Mirren 1–0 and keep the pressure on Hearts. Only 13,000 see Everton beat Bayern Munich 3–1 in the Mercantile Credit Centenary Challenge. Leicester defender Steve Walsh, whose booking on Saturday took him past the 21-point mark, receives a further 3-game ban to add to his 6-match suspension.

26 The League refuse to back Robert Maxwell's Watford takeover and ask him to withdraw. Maxwell accuses the League's 'mismanagement' committee of being 'frightened men', declaring: 'What we have is a professional game dominated by incompetent, selfish, bungling amateurs . . .' Elton John dispels rumours about manager Dave Bassett, saying he has the unanimous backing of the Watford board. Palace sign Southend captain and midfielder Glenn Pennyfather for £150,000. Spenders Reading put seven players up for sale to recoup some of the money they have laid out in transfer fees.
27 Arsenal manager George Graham slams the media for their treatment of Watford manager Dave Bassett. Knee trouble forces veteran Villa midfielder Steve Hunt to retire. Bristol City appoint Joe Jordan assistant manager, and he will continue to play for them. Norwich City's rebel shareholders present demands for an extraordinary general meeting designed to reinstate Ken Brown as manager.
28 Liverpool spoil Terry Venables' first game in charge, beating Spurs 2–0 at White Hart Lane and going 5 points clear as Arsenal lose by the same score at Watford and other leading clubs also falter. Spurs' Steve Hodge is sent off, along with Wimbledon's Brian Gayle and Carlton Fairweather and seven others from the lower divisions. Charlton's Colin Walsh breaks a leg as they lose at Newcastle. In Division II, Villa, with debutant Stuart Gray scoring two, beat leaders Bradford 4–2 away to go 3rd, and Middlesbro' go top, beating Barnsley 2–0. Sunderland beat Port Vale 2–1 and move 2 points clear in Division III as Notts Co are held at Brighton. Fourth Division leaders Wolves are shocked 2–0 at home by lowly Wrexham, but stay top as Cardiff are held at home by Hartlepool. Orient win 3–0 at Hereford and move into 2nd spot. Rangers, with £250,000 buy from Paris St Germain, Ray Wilkins, in the side only two hours after signing, help Celtic to the top of the Premier League by beating Hearts 3–2. Celtic win 1–0 at Hibs in a match stopped for 18 minutes after a gas canister is let off.
29 PFA spokesman Gordon Taylor calls for harsher action after yesterday's 10 dismissals takes the season's total to 118, suggesting managers should take more responsibility.
30 Mercantile Credit, sponsors of the League's centenary celebrations, are disappointed with events so far and call for a review of the position.

DECEMBER

1 Millwall beat Reading 3–0 and jump from 7th to 3rd in Division II. In the Simod Cup, Leicester

Men in the news during the season included new Spurs manager Terry Venables (*above, left*), Ted Croker, in his last season as FA Secretary, and (*below*) Manchester City's Tony Adcock, Paul Stewart and David White, who all scored hat-tricks in City's 10-1 drubbing of Huddersfield in November. *Photos: Bob Thomas Sports Photography.*

22

DAY-BY-DAY DIARY 1987–88

and Stoke notch away wins against First Division opposition, Charlton and Wednesday, respectively. Sacked Norwich manager Ken Brown agrees to take over as acting manager at Shrewsbury. Chelsea keeper Eddie Niedzwiecki and Everton defender Derek Mountfield are sidelined for months after knee operations.

2 In the last match of Group 7, under 2,000 see Scotland draw 0–0 in Luxembourg, who gain their first point. Bradford beat Newcastle 2–1 in the Simod Cup.

3 Striker Mark Falco turns down a move to Norwich, but Rangers agree a £400,000 fee with QPR and Falco signs on loan so that he can play on Saturday. Forest left-back Stuart Pearce signs a new 3½-year contract. Charlton vice-chairman Richard Collins denies Press rumours that the club are in financial trouble.

4 The League obtain a High Court ruling to prevent the Maxwell takeover of Watford. Clayton Blackmore is omitted from Man United's team after his ordeal in Bermuda, where he was accused of rape during the side's winter break.

5 Maxwell agrees to dispose of the family interests in Oxford, and the League abandon legal moves to block his Watford deal. Meanwhile Oxford manager Maurice Evans agrees a new 3-year contract but his side lose 3–1 at home to Newcastle, and Watford grab a welcome point at Derby, Maxwell's other club. Arsenal beat Wednesday 3–1 to keep the pressure on Liverpool, who play tomorrow. QPR lose at home 2–0 to Man Utd. In Division II, Bradford crash 4–0 at Ipswich, while Middlesbrough draw 0–0 at Leicester. Palace halt Man City's run with a 3–1 victory at Maine road, where City keeper Eric Nixon is sent off for violent conduct and referee John Deakin is hit by an object as he leaves the field. Villa gain a rare home win, but Millwall lose at Blackburn, unbeaten since late September. In the 2nd round of the FA Cup, Yeovil win 1–0 at Cambridge, Sutton 3–1 at Peterborough, while Scunthorpe come from behind to beat Sunderland 2–1. There is no change in the Scottish Premier League as all the leading clubs win.

6 Liverpool come from behind to beat Chelsea 2–1 at Anfield and restore their 5-point lead. In the Cup, Macclesfield slam Third Division Rotherham 4–0 thanks to a hat-trick from lorry driver Steve Burr.

7 QPR chairman David Bulstrode puts down a deposit of £290,000 on £7.6 million worth of Marler Estates' shares in the club, with the intention of offering them to the fans. Dave Mackay, after 9 years out of English football, succeeds Dave Cusack as Doncaster manager.

8 Australian brewers Elders, owners of Fosters lager, reduce their sponsorship offer to the FA,

who continue to make no comment. The High Court injunction against Maxwell still stands as League president Philip Carter is in Dubai with Everton; Maxwell gives the League a 48-hour deadline to complete the withdrawal. Gillingham manager Keith Peacock signs his son Gavin from QPR for £60,000. Cup winners Coventry and St Mirren fix dates for the new two-leg Anglo–Scottish Challenge Trophy. Norwich reject a £750,000 Man Utd bid for Steve Bruce.

9 Holland beat Cyprus 4–0 in their replayed match behind closed doors in Amsterdam and qualify for the European Championships at the expense of Greece. In the UEFA Cup, Bruge reverse a 3–0 first-leg deficit against Borussia Dortmund and win 5–0 after extra time. Greek side Panathinaikos, 5–2 down to Honved after the first leg, thrash the Hungarians 5–1 in front of 80,000 fans to go through 7–6 on aggregate. The League state they are taking no immediate action on Maxwell's ultimatum. Rotherham sack manager Norman Hunter after their ignominious Cup exit, and name former player John Breckin acting manager. Forest win the Guinness Soccer Six indoor tournament. Ken Brown resigns as Shrewsbury acting manager, fuelling speculation that a return to Norwich is on the cards, while former Chelsea assistant manager Ian McNeill takes over at Shrewsbury. Doncaster appeal successfully against the loss of 2 points for not fulfilling a fixture in October.

10 The FA impose a 53-day ban on Mark Dennis (QPR). Robert Maxwell and Elton John agree to delay completion of their deal until the League's management committee discuss it next week. England are seeded among the top 7 countries in the European section of the World Cup draw.

11 In Zurich for the World Cup draw, FA chairman Bert Millichip reveals that UEFA have made overtures concerning the return of English clubs to European competition. In Division IV, Colchester beat Bolton 3–0 and go top, above Wolves, on goal difference. Leicester dismiss manager Bryan Hamilton, and Exeter manager Colin Appleton resigns, John Delve taking over as caretaker.

12 England are drawn with Poland, Sweden, and Albania in the World Cup qualifying competition. Poor Wales face West Germany and Holland in their four-nation group. In five-nation groups, with two certain qualifiers, Scotland face France and Yugoslavia, while the two Irelands are in the same group with Spain and Hungary. There are 12 more dismissals in the League programme, including 4 in one incident between Brentford and Mansfield. Liverpool lose a 2–0 lead and almost lose their unbeaten record at the Dell, but increase their First Division lead to 6

points as Arsenal play tomorrow. In Division II, Middlesbrough and Bradford both win and Villa chalk up their 9th away victory in 12 games. Man City win 1–0 at Millwall and go 4th. Sunderland and Notts Co both have good away wins in Division II, but Walsall lose ground with a 0–0 home draw. Orient beat Tranmere 3–1 to go top of Division IV as Wolves are held at Hartlepool. Aberdeen and Rangers make up ground in Scotland as leaders Celtic and Hearts draw 2–2 at Parkhead, where Celtic come back from two down. Ian Rush is fined £2,500 by Juventus following his comments in the *Sun*.

13 European champions FC Porto beat Penarol of Uruguay 2–1 after extra time to win the Toyota Cup for the World Club Championship in Tokyo. Colombia agree to play England and Scotland in the Rous Cup. Nigel Clough scores 3 as Forest thrash QPR 4–0 and move up to 3rd in Division I, but Arsenal only draw at Coventry. Spurs crash at home 1–0 to bottom club Charlton. Palace beat Sheffield Utd 2–1 and move up to 4th in Division II. Roma keeper Franco Tancredi needs mouth-to-mouth resuscitation and heart massage and nearly dies after being hit by a firecracker in the match with AC Milan, and police use teargas to disperse rampaging fans.

14 UEFA president Jacques Georges expresses their desire to have English clubs back and sets up security planning talks with English officials for 13 January. League management committee opposition to Philip Carter's approval of Robert Maxwell's Watford deal is gathering. Struggling Morton sign three Danish players till the end of the season.

15 Carl Shutt scores 4 as Bristol City slam Fulham 4–0 and a player from each side is sent off. Norwich sign John O'Neill from QPR for £100,000. Yugoslavia Under-21s lose in Turkey, so England qualify for the finals of the European Under-21s.

16 Hearts are held at home by lowly Motherwell and miss a chance to go above Celtic, but Aberdeen beat St Mirren 2–1 and join the other two on 37 points. Norwich sign Robert Fleck from Rangers for £500,000. Wimbledon sign striker Robbie Turner from Bristol Rovers for £15,000. Maidstone beat Kidderminster 2–1 in the 3rd replay of their 2nd round Cup tie. Rangers are drawn against Steaua Bucharest in the European Cup.

17 UEFA reduce Liam Brady's ban to two matches, and Jack Charlton says he will be in Ireland's European squad. Dundee Utd fans win FIFA's first Fair Play Award, worth £21,000, for their 'model behaviour' in last season's two-legged UEFA Cup final, which they lost. Man Utd finally sign Norwich's Steve Bruce for £825,000. Chris Woods signs a new 5-year contract with Rangers. Sheffield United chairman Reg Brealey sacks himself and suggests a few more chairman should do the same. Angus Cook also decides to put his shares on the market only three months after taking control of Dundee. Blackburn sign Barcelona striker Steve Archibald on loan.

18 In Friday matches, QPR lose at home to Coventry and fall right out of contention, while a knee injury to debutant John O'Neill as Norwich lose at Wimbledon will keep him out for 10 weeks. Villa slip up again at home, held to 0–0 by West Brom. Walsall win at Gillingham and move 2nd in Division III. Colchester win at Tranmere and go top of Division IV. Spurs reject a £650,000 offer from Rangers for Nico Claesen.

19 Liverpool beat a defensive Sheff Wed 1–0 at Anfield to equal the club's record 19-match unbeaten league run. They go 7 points clear as Arsenal are held 1–1 by Everton at Highbury. Forest and Man Utd have away wins, although for the latter debutant Steve Bruce gives away a penalty and breaks his nose. In Division II, Middlesbrough are held 0–0 at Bournemouth, but go 2 points clear as Bradford play tomorrow. Millwall crash 4–1 at Barnsley. Notts Co beat Preston 4–2 and go top of Division III, as Sunderland play tomorrow. Wolves beat 2nd-place Orient 2–0 and go top of Division IV, above Colchester, while Cardiff move up to 4th. It's no change at the top in Scotland, where Aberdeen hold Celtic 0–0 at Parkhead and Hearts draw 0–0 at Dundee. Rangers win 2–0 at Motherwell and move to within 3 points of the joint leaders.

20 Robert Maxwell and Elton John finally call off Watford deal. Wales manager Mike England refuses to be drawn on alleged disparaging remarks made about him by Welsh FA secretary Alun Evans. Spurs win 2–1 at Derby. Charlton are held at home 2–2 by Chelsea but force Norwich to the bottom on goal difference. In Division II, Bradford lose at Plymouth and miss a chance to go top. An Eric Gates hat-trick gives Sunderland a 3–0 win over Rotherham and takes them back to the top of Division III. In the other Third Division game, Mansfield's Kevin Kent scores all their goals in a 4–0 win over Port Vale.

21 Reading come from behind to beat QPR 3–1 at Loftus Road in the Simod Cup. Spurs agree to pay £100,000 for non-League Weymouth keeper Peter Guthrie. Norwich's John O'Neill is now ruled out for the rest of the season and his career may be in danger. Alun Evans apologises to Mike England for his gratuitous remarks at a dinner.

22 Celtic win 2–0 at Falkirk and take a 2-point lead. St Mirren draw 1–1 at Coventry in the first leg of the Anglo-Scottish Challenge Trophy.

23 David Pleat accepts a severance payment from

24

John Barnes fires home England's second goal on the way to beating Yugoslavia 4-1 to clinch a place in West Germany (*above*), but new cap Gary Pallister wasn't so lucky in the friendly against Hungary, as he sees his header go fractionally wide. *Photos: Bob Thomas Sports Photography.*

Spurs and is set to join Leicester. The League agree to compromise over their pre-season knock-out tournament involving the top 8 Division I sides, part of their centenary celebrations, switching it to midweek in September and October. Brentford sign Arsenal's recouperating Graham Rix on loan. Sacked Doncaster manager Dave Cusack becomes Rotherham player-manager. Wigan sign former England and Liverpool back Alan Kennedy on trial. Swindon beat Derby 2–1 in the Simod Cup.

24 Pleat signs a 3¹/₂-year contract to manage Leicester.

26 Liverpool slam Oxford 3–0 at Manor Road to take a 10-point lead as Forest win 2–0 at Highbury and move above Arsenal into 2nd place. Charlton beat Portsmouth and move off the bottom. In Division II, Middlesbrough and Bradford are both held at home, while Palace win 3–2 at Ipswich and move above Villa into 3rd place. Teddy Sheringham hits a hat-trick for Millwall as they beat West Brom 4–1 at the Hawthorns. Sunderland, Notts Co, and Walsall all win and increase their lead in Division III. Wolves, without a game, lose the lead in Division IV as Colchester, chalking up their 8th away win, Orient, and Cardiff all overtake them. Celtic beat Dundee Utd 2–1, their first win at Tannadice for over 3 years, and maintain their 2-point lead, while Hearts can only draw at Morton and lose 2nd place to Aberdeen.

28 Liverpool and Forest both hit 4 goals, but faltering Arsenal go down 3–1 at Wimbledon. Norwich beat Chelsea 3–0 and move out of the last three. In Division II, Bradford, who draw at Blackburn, move closer to Middlesbrough, whose 14-match unbeaten run comes to an end at Leeds. Villa, held at home by lowly Huddersfield, and Palace, beaten at home by bottom club Reading, fail to take advantage, but Millwall beat Sheffield Utd 3–1 and move into 5th place. Not a good day for the Third Division's leading clubs either, as Sunderland are held at home by Preston, Notts Co are held by Blackpool, and Walsall lose 2–1 at Chesterfield. Bristol City smash Brighton 5–2 to end the Seagulls' club record 17-match unbeaten run and move above them into 4th place. Colchester beat Cardiff to stay top of Division IV, Wolves also win, but Orient lose two home points. Torquay's Dave Caldwell is sent off for the 4th time this season.

29 Gillingham, who lost 6–0 to Aldershot on Monday, sack manager Keith Peacock, whose assistant Paul Taylor takes over for the rest of the season. The FA express alarm at the sale of T-shirts with the slogan 'England Invasion of Germany 1988' and the England crest. Southampton take Yugoslav international Ljudomir Radanovic on trial.

30 Spurs sign Terry Fenwick on a 6-year contract from QPR for £550,000. Rangers beat Everton to the signature on Villa's Mark Walters for £500,000. West Brom sign Luton defender Stacey North for £100,000. Norwich confirm Dave Stringer as manager. The League reveal details, immediately renounced by Robert Maxwell, of stricter regulations to prevent one person, family, or associates from owning more than one club.

JANUARY

1 Liverpool beat Coventry 4–0 and go 13 points clear in Division I as Forest lose 2–0 at home to Newcastle. Watford physio Derek French is shown the red card at White Hart Lane, for allegedly swearing at a linesman. Villa slam Hull 5–0, only their 4th home win, and go top of Division II as Middlesbrough lose 3–1 at Oldham. Home wins for Palace and Millwall move them up in front of Bradford, who lose 2–0 at Leeds. Bottom club Reading win 3–1 at Plymouth to go ahead of Huddersfield, who lose 3–1 at Shrewsbury, who also leapfrog over Huddersfield. Sunderland beat Doncaster 3–1 to increase their lead in Division III to 4 points. York record their 2nd win of the season, beating Chester 2–0, and are now only 7 points adrift at the bottom. In Division IV, Wolves beat Hereford 2–0 and go top as Colchester lose 3–0 at home to Scunthorpe.

2 With many English clubs playing their 4th game in 8 days, about £7 million has been taken at the turnstiles. Liverpool's game at Derby is postponed, but they stay 13 points ahead as Forest do not play until tomorrow and Arsenal are held at Highbury by QPR. Wimbledon win 5–2 at Oxford and move into 5th place. Villa win 3–1 at Barnsley and go 3 points clear in Division II. Palace are held 4–4 at Leicester after leading 4–2 at the interval. Sheff Utd manager Billy McEwan resigns after his team lose 5–0 at home to Oldham. All the Division III leaders win, with Sunderland 3–2 victors at Bury. Wolves win 2–0 at Crewe and go 4 points clear of Orient as Colchester lose again. Frank McAvennie scores twice as Celtic beat Rangers 2–0 at Parkhead and go 3 points clear at the top, while both Aberdeen and Hearts are held 0–0 at home. Rangers and England keeper Chris Woods is carried off with broken ribs before McAvennie's 2nd goal.

3 Forest lose 1–0 at Everton. Portsmouth win 2–0 at Southampton and move out of the bottom three.

4 Bobby Charlton, Man Utd Director, advocates more full-time paid people in the game, in-

cluding a commissioner to run the Football League. John Wark returns to Ipswich on a £100,000 transfer from Liverpool. The threatened sponsorship of the FA Cup by Foster's appears to be receding as the Australian brewing company reveal there are no plans in the foreseeable future. Johan Cruyff resigns as manager of Ajax.

5 Aberdeen pay Arsenal £400,000 for Charlie Nicholas, who is believed to have taken a 50% cut in his £2,000 a week earnings. Bradford sign midfielder Mick Kennedy from Portsmouth for £250,000. Bradford chairman Stafford Heginbotham resigns through ill-health. Villa sign non-league striker Gareth Williams from Gosport Boro for £20,000. In Scotland's breach of the peace case, Butcher, Woods, Roberts, and McAvennie plead not guilty and are sent for trial on February 16. Former West Ham centre-half and Spurs chief scout Dick Walker dies, aged 75.

6 Torquay striker Dave Caldwell, sent off four times this season, is charged with bringing the game into disrepute, as is Watford physio Derek French, shown the red card at Spurs on Friday. FIFA fine Iraq $14,900 after the referee in their Olympic qualifying tie with Kuwait had to be preotected by security guards.

7 England manager Bobby Robson is forced to compromise in the Warsaw meeting to determine World Cup qualifying fixtures, reluctantly accepting a September fixture with Sweden. Wales manager Mike England complains that he was not consulted about their fixtures by the Welsh FA. Full-back Brian Borrows, who missed Coventry's triumph at Wembley last May through injury, is awarded an FA Cup medal after all.

9 For once, the FA Cup 3rd round produces no real surprises, although Stoke hold Liverpool 0–0 at the Victoria Ground and non-League Sutton Utd hold Middlesbrough 1–1. First Division sides that record good wins away to Second Division opponents include Spurs, 4–2 at Oldham, and Portsmouth, 2–1 at Blackburn. Chelsea win 3–1 at Derby. Arsenal beat Millwall 2–0 at Highbury, where there is fighting before and during the match: two local pubs are wrecked, 40 arrests made, and a policeman taken to hospital. Man City's Neil McNab is sent off in their 2–2 draw at Huddersfield and 6 players are booked. In Division III, Notts Co take advantage of gameless Sunderland to move within a point of the leaders. In Scotland, Aberdeen fail to take advantage of Celtic's draw at St Mirren, being held themselves 0–0 at Hibs, where debutant Charlie Nicholas twice hits the woodwork. Hearts win 4–0 at Dunfermline to leapfrog into 2nd place.

10 In Sunday's televised Cup game, Man Utd win 2–1 at Ipswich.

11 Watford manager Dave Bassett leaves the club by mutual consent. The FA unveil a new set of options available to discipline clubs with a history of crowd violence, including disqualification from cup competitions, deduction of League points, and even relegation.

12 In the European Championship draw, England, seeds along with hosts West Germany, will meet Ireland, Holland, and the USSR. In Cup replays, Sutton Utd take Middlesbrough to extra time before a Kerr goal puts them out, and Stoke also go down by a single goal at Anfield. Watford appoint Steve Harrison manager and he watches them come back from a 2–0 interval deficit at Hull to force another replay. Leicester sign winger Peter Weir from Aberdeen for £100,000. Spurs back Danny Thomas begins legal proceedings against Gavin Maguire and QPR over the injury that has ended his career.

13 Two headers from Swindon's Dave Bamber at Carrow Road are enough to knock out Norwich in their Cup replay, while Sheff Wed hold Everton 1–1 at Goodison. Elton John rejects a £2 million offer for Watford from impresario Paul Raymond and will probably stay on as chairman.

14 The FA confirm that the Cup will not be sponsored, the traditionalists within the organization having prevailed. Liverpool announce a new sponsorship deal worth £1 million over 3 years, Candy replacing Crown Paints. Dropped Oxford keeper Peter Hucker is transfer-listed at his own request. Shrewsbury sign Victor Kasule from Meadowbank for £30,000. Cardiff keeper Graham Moseley incurs broken limbs and ribs in a car crash.

15 Multi-millionaire property developer David Thompson, who owns a third of Marler Estates (who own Stamford Bridge and Craven Cottage), announces that he is outbidding Marler chairman David Bulstrode's offer for QPR. In Division IV, Colchester are held at home so make little impression on leaders Wolves.

16 Liverpool beat Arsenal 2–0 at Anfield and now lead by 15 points as Forest are held 2–2 at home by Charlton, who nevertheless go bottom as Watford win 2–1 at Wimbledon. Man Utd lose 2–0 to Southampton at Old Trafford. Everton win 3–0 at Norwich and move into 3rd place. Villa stay 3 points in front in Division II, beating Ipswich 1–0. Palace stay 2nd, but Middlesbrough lose 2–1 at Millwall, who leapfrog over them into 3rd place. Bradford, 3–0 down at Swindon, are saved by fog after 73 minutes. In Division III, Sunderland beat Brighton 1–0 at Roker Park, going 4 points ahead of Notts Co and 7 ahead of Walsall, who both lose. Division IV leaders Wolves are held 1–1 by lowly Roch-

Liverpool manager Kenny Dalglish and coach Ronnie Moran are warned by a senior police officer about their language during a match against QPR in March (*above*), and a couple of weeks later Liverpool suffered their first League defeat of the season when Everton's Wayne Clarke scored the only goal of the game at Goodison. *Photos: Bob Thomas Sports Photography.*

dale at Molineux, but Orient fail to take advantage, held themselves at home by Crewe. In Scotland, Celtic and Aberdeen both win, while Hearts and Rangers draw 1–1.

17 UEFA secretary Hans Bangerter, referring to Sports Minister Colin Moynihan's assertion yesterday that UEFA can only make their decision on whether English clubs return to European competition after the European Championships, says this will make it more certain that the decision will not be made, as speculated, at Monte Carlo this week. FA chairman Bert Millichip is nonplussed. PSV Eindhoven's 17-win start to the Dutch season is ended as they are held to a 2–2 draw at home by Twente Enschede.

18 Watford beat Hull 1–0 at Vicarage Road in the 2nd replay. Sports Minister Colin Moynihan warns football chiefs that he has ministerial backing for his position on the European situation, including that of the PM.

19 An emergency general meeting of League chairman passes a non-retrospective rule amendment prohibiting one person or his associates from being involved in the administration of more than one club, thus preserving the status quo of current multiple shareholdings but making it clear that Robert Maxwell would have to relinquish his interests in Oxford, Derby, and Reading if he pressed on with his intentions of purchasing the majority shareholding in Watford. Maxwell accepts this ruling and says that he is willing to sell his Reading shares and will stay as chairman of Derby while his son Kevin continues as chairman of Oxford. Luton beat Bradford 2–0 to win a place in the Littlewoods Cup semi-finals, but, with the club admitting substantial numbers of visiting supporters for the first time for 18 months, there are five arrests, a fan is stabbed and a policeman hurt before the match. In the Simod Cup 3rd round, Swindon beat Chelsea 4–0. Neil Webb signs a new 2-year contract with Forest, and Graham Roberts a new 3½-year contract with Rangers. AC Milan insure Ruud Gullit for £5 million.

20 In Monte Carlo, UEFA decide to defer any decision on the readmission of English clubs to their May 3 meeting in Scotland, stressing that the decision depends entirely on the subsequent behaviour of English fans. Oxford beat Man Utd 2–0 to reach the semi-finals of the Littlewoods Cup along with Arsenal, who beat Sheff Wed 1–0 at Hillsborough, and Everton, who beat Man City 2–0. Man City sign Northampton's Trevor Morley in an exchange deal valuing him at £235,000, while Tony Adcock makes the reverse journey at a value of £85,000. Mick Harford signs a new 3-year contract with Luton after rejecting a move to West Ham.

21 Dave Bassett becomes Sheff Utd manager. Leicester sign Walsall striker Nicky Cross for about £65,000.

22 Elton John decides to abandon his search for a buyer for his Watford shares.

23 The Pools Panel sits for the first time this season as snow and rain eat into the League programme. Only 15 goals are scored in the 12 games played. Liverpool win 2–0 at Charlton and, with Forest drawing 0–0 at Watford, go 17 points clear. Only three Division II games take place, but Villa, 2–0 winners at Maine Road, go 6 points clear as Palace lose 2–1 at Middlesbrough, who join them in 2nd place. At the bottom, Reading beat Shrewsbury 1–0. In the only Third Division game played, Wigan win 1–0 at Gillingham and go 3rd, while in Division IV Orient are held at home by Stockport so are still 3 points adrift of leaders Wolves. Rangers go 2nd in Scotland as they win and Aberdeen lose despite Charlie Nicholas scoring his first goal for them.

24 Man Utd win 2–1 at Highbury to go 3rd in Division I, while Arsenal sign Stoke right-back Lee Dixon for £400,000, 10 times what a League tribunal required Stoke to pay Bury for him at the start of last season.

25 In FA Cup 3rd-round 2nd replays, Sheff Wed hold Everton 1–1 at Goodison and Man City win 3–0 at Huddersfield. In the 3rd round of the Simod Cup, Second Division triumphs over First as Ipswich overcome a 2-goal deficit and slam Watford 5–2 after extra time and Bradford beat Southampton 1–0 . QPR full-back Mark Dennis has his 53-day ban changed, on his club's appeal, to an 8-game ban, which will probably cover a 61-day period, and is warned by QPR chairman David Bulstrode that if there is any more trouble he is unlikely to receive club support. Bulstrode confirms that he has reached an agreement with the group who blocked his £7 million bid for the club and will remain chairman.

26 Welsh manager Mike England's contract is in the balance as a meeting of the FA of Wales' finance committee is split 50-50 about his future. The FA clear Arsenal and Millwall of blame for the crowd trouble at their Cup tie.

27 Injury-hit Everton end the 3rd-round deadlock with a remarkable 5–0 win, scoring all the goals in the first half at Hillsborough in the 3rd replay, Graeme Sharp hitting a hat-trick and Paul Bracewell, on as a 73rd-minute sub, making his first appearance since the 1986 Cup final.

28 Villa sign Crewe striker David Platt for £200,000, with £40,000 going to Platt's first club Man Utd.

29 Palace lose 1–0 at Oldham.

30 Port Vale knock last year's beaten finalists Spurs

out of the FA Cup, winning 2–1 at Vale Park, while Cup holders Coventry are beaten 1–0 at home by Watford. There are no other 4th-round shocks, but Bradford beat Oxford 4–2 and Everton are held 1–1 by Middlesbrough at Goodison. Arsenal, Forest, and Wimbledon are all safely through 2–1, at Brighton, Orient, and Mansfield, respectively, while Man Utd beat Chelsea 2–0 at Old Trafford. QPR beat West Ham 3–1 at Loftus Road, where West German police, there to study crowd control, see an overcrowded section spill onto the field and the game held up for an hour, but are impressed with the crowd behaviour and the police methods used. In Division II, Blackburn move up to 2nd place with a 2–0 win at Ipswich, while at the other end Leicester win 2–1 at Reading to ease their problems while West Brom lose 4–1 to Leeds at the Hawthorns and sink to 3rd from bottom. In Division III, Sunderland, Notts Co, and Walsall all have home wins. Wolves win 1–0 at Scunthorpe and move 6 points clear of gameless Orient in Division IV. In the Scottish Cup, Celtic scrape a 1–0 home win over Stranraer, second bottom of Division 2. Dundee are held 0–0 at home by Second Division Brechin, but Dundee Utd have no trouble with Arbroath, winning 7–0 away. Chalfont St Peters' keeper Steven King collapses and dies during a Vauxhall-Opel Div. IIS match.

31 Liverpool win their 4th-round Cup match 2–0 at Villa Park. Derby sign former Rangers winger Ted McMinn from Seville for £300,000. Huddersfield sign Tow Law Town left-back Vince Chapman for an initial £5,000.

FEBRUARY

1 Two big plums come out of the FA Cup 5th-round draw: Arsenal v Man Utd and Everton or Middlesbrough v Liverpool. Millwall appoint John Stalker, former deputy chief constable of Greater Manchester, as part-time consultant to advise on crowd control. Wales manager Mike England returns from abroad furious to find not only that the FA of Wales is meeting tomorrow to discuss his contract, but also that he had not been informed of the meeting.

2 The FA of Wales meet in secret and do not disclose the result of their discussions on Mike England's contract. Brighton keeper Perry Digweed joins Chelsea on loan.

3 The Welsh FA announce the termination of Mike England's contract, which had 6 months still to run. In a 4th-round Cup replay, Everton force another match with a late equalizer in extra time at Ayrsome Park. Reading beat Forest 2–1 in the Simod Cup. The FA advertise for a 'chief

executive' to replace secretary Ted Croker when he retires next year. Former Spurs manager Keith Burkinshaw is sacked by Sporting Lisbon. Hearts' challenge in the Scottish Premier takes a further dive as they are held at home by Dundee Utd.

4 The Sports Minister accepts police-supported membership schemes for Southampton and Wimbledon below the 50% advocated by the government. Tommy Docherty parts company with Altincham after 19 weeks, as a new chairman takes over; it was his 14th managerial post. FA of Wales secretary Alun Evans denies reports that Brian Clough is to be offered the job as part-time manager.

5 There is to be a public inquiry into Chelsea's plans to develop Stamford Bridge. Notts Co, one down at half time and with a player sent off, win 2–1 at Southend to climb within a point of Sunderland at the top of Division III. Division IV promotion contenders Colchester crash 4–1 at home to Crewe.

6 Liverpool keep their 10th consecutive clean sheet but are held at Anfield by West Ham. Forest beat Chelsea 3–2 and cut the gap to 15 points. Mark Stein scores 3 as Luton beat their Littlewoods semi-final opponents Oxford 7–4. Division II also produces a high-scoring game as Bournemouth beat Hull 6–2. Leaders Villa beat Leicester 2–1 and Blackburn beat Man City by the same score, but Millwall lose 1–0 at home to Bradford, who chalk up their first win for 6 matches. Palace beat Birmingham 3–0 and go 3rd, above Middlesbrough, who draw at Swindon. In Division III, Walsall hold Sunderland 1–1 at Roker Park, and Wigan climb into 3rd place. In Division IV Wolves have their lead cut to 3 points by Cardiff, who thrash them 4–1 at Molineux. Bolton overtake Orient, who lose 2–0 at home to Hartlepool. In Scotland, Celtic again do just enough at Parkhead to beat a struggling side, Motherwell, 1–0 while Rangers win 2–1 at Aberdeen, despite having Richard Gough sent off, and Hearts win 6–0 at St Mirren.

7 A Perry Groves goal and a missed Trevor Steven penalty give Arsenal a 1–0 lead from the 1st leg of their Littlewoods Cup semi-final at Goodison.

8 Brian Clough expresses his eagerness to become part-time manager of Wales, against the wishes of Forest chairman Maurice Roworth, and is due to discuss terms with the Welsh FA subcommittee tomorrow. England manager Bobby Robson names Steve McMahon in the squad for the friendly with Israel on the 17th. Spurs' £600,000 bid for Norwich striker Kevin Drinkell is turned down. Rangers are held 0–0 at Raith in the Scottish Cup. Betis of Seville sack manager John Mortimore.

30

Kenny Dalglish celebrates Liverpool's FA Cup semi-final victory against Nottingham Forest (*above*), and not long afterwards his team were lining up behind yet another League Championship trophy. *Photos: Bob Thomas Sports Photography.*

9 Everton finally beat Middlesbrough in their Cup 2nd replay, winning 2–1 thanks to a late own goal, and they will meet Liverpool in the 5th round. Brian Clough is set to take the Welsh job on the 24th, although he still has not got the nod from Forest. Millwall's promotion hopes take another knock as they lose 1–0 at Birmingham. Walsall only draw at Bristol City but go 3rd. Coventry midfielder Lloyd McGrath breaks his leg as they beat Ipswich 2–0 in a Simod Cup quarter-final.

10 Luton gain a 1–1 draw at Oxford in the 1st leg of their Littlewoods Cup semi-final as Oxford's Dean Saunders scores one penalty and has another saved by Les Sealey. Man Utd win 2–1 at Derby and go 2nd in Division I, 12 points behind Liverpool, who have two games in hand. Rangers beat Raith 4–1 in a Scottish Cup replay. Reading beat Bradford 2–1 in a Simod Cup quarter-final and sign Oxford striker Billy Whitehurst for £120,000. Northampton sign Grimsby defender Trevor Slack for £10,000.

11 Forest refuse Brian Clough permission to manage Wales. Man City manager Mel Machin is fined £500 for using foul language to a referee. Southend sign Cambridge midfielder Peter Butler for £75,000.

12 Brian Clough says he will not resign from Forest over the Welsh job disappointment. Portsmouth, with a tax and VAT bill of over £700,000, have their assets frozen by their bank, and chairman John Deacon is paying the players out of his own pocket. Bolton win 2–1 at Stockport and go 2nd in Division IV.

13 Luther Blissett scores the first goal conceded by Liverpool in 11 matches, but Watford go down 4–1 at Vicarage Road. Man Utd win 2–1 at Chelsea and stay 12 points behind. Blackburn's 1–0 victory at Barnsley takes them within a point of Division II leaders Villa, who play at Middlesbrough tomorrow. Bradford come back into contention with another win, 5–3 over Oldham helped by a John Hendrie hat-trick, while Millwall win 3–2 at Reading, but Palace slip up 1–0 at West Brom. Sunderland, who have Steve Doyle sent off, draw 2–2 at Preston, but none of their Division III rivals takes advantage, as Notts Co lose 3–2 at home to Blackpool, Wigan 1–0 at Chester, and Walsall are held at home by Chesterfield. In Division IV, Wolves come back to form with a 4–2 win at Exeter thanks to a Steve Bull hat-trick, but Cardiff keep up their challenge, beating Colchester 1–0. Fourth-place Orient are dropping out of contention, losing 3–2 at Scunthorpe after leading 2–0 four-minutes from time! Burnley move up to 5th with the same number of points but still have a negative goal difference. Celtic and Rangers both win in Scotland, while Aberdeen draw at Hearts. In

the Scottish 2nd Division, Meadowbank beat Hamilton 2–0 and move to within 3 points of them at the top. Oxford sign Gillingham defender Colin Greenall for £235,000. In an FA Trophy match, Lincoln striker John McGinley is sent off for head-butting a team-mate following an argument over a bad pass!

14 Spurs sign Liverpool striker Paul Walsh for £500,000. Middlesbrough beat Division II leaders Villa 2–1 and move up to 3rd place.

15 Rangers sign St Mirren forward Ian Ferguson for £1 million, a record for a footballer in Scotland. Chelsea dismiss coach Ernie Walley over the head of manager John Hollins, who is not happy with the decision. Glenn Hoddle confirms his assertion that the technical standard of French football is higher than that in England by helping Monaco beat his former club Spurs 4–0 in a friendly at White Hart Lane.

16 Injured Bryan Robson flies home from Tel Aviv and an already depleted England squad due to play Israel tomorrow, with Steve McMahon winning his first cap in his place. England beat Scotland 1–0 in Aberdeen in the 1st leg of their UEFA Under-21s quarter-final. Fourth Division leaders Wolves lose 2–1 at Halifax. Everton's lowest ever first-team gate at Goodison, 5,204, see them lose 2–1 to Luton in the Simod Cup after leading at half-time, both Luton's goals being scored by David Oldfield, one of their four debutants.

17 England draw 0–0 with Israel in their first build-up match to the European Championships, played on a muddy pitch at Tel Aviv's Ramat Gan Stadium. N. Ireland lose 3–2 in Greece after twice leading, and Scotland draw 2–2 in Saudi Arabia. With chairman Ken Bates abroad, Chelsea announce the appointment of Bobby Campbell as first-team coach; manager John Hollins appears, ashen-faced, to announce that he has 'no comment' and then has a 3-hour meeting with director Graham Smith in a West London hotel after which all parties go home 'to sleep on it'. A High Court hearing is adjourned to give Portsmouth 14 days to pay off creditors, with debts of over £650,000 still outstanding. Watford sign Sheff Utd captain Martin Kuhl for £40,000 plus players Tony Agana and Peter Hetherston.

18 John Hollins announces his decision to stay at Chelsea and work with Bobby Campbell. The N. Ireland squad is stranded in Athens by an air traffic controllers' dispute and several English clubs anxiously await their return for Saturday's 5th round of the Cup. Brian Clough announces he is no longer interested in the Welsh job and hopes speculation will now cease. Portsmouth chairman John Deacon promises to pay their debts and save the club from a winding-up

order. Wimbledon receive international clearance to play former England winger Laurie Cunningham from the Belgian FA, where he was with Charleroi.

19 Scarborough hold Division IV leaders Wolves 0–0 at Molineux.

20 Wimbledon, with Laurie Cunningham making his debut, beat Newcastle 3–1 at St James's Park to reach the FA Cup quarter-finals. Arsenal also go through, beating Man Utd 2–1 at Highbury thanks in the end to a late penalty miss by Brian McClaire. Portsmouth transfer their recent League form to the Cup, beating Bradford 3–0, and Forest win 1–0 at Birmingham. In the battle of the 'plastic' clubs, Luton hold QPR 1–1 at Loftus Road. The only non-First Division side through are Man City, who beat Plymouth 3–1, but Port Vale live to fight another day, drawing 0–0 with Watford at Vale Park. The biggest Cup upset is in Scotland, where relegation-bound Dunfermline are 2–0 victors over Rangers, who have John Brown sent off. Aberdeen and Hearts are safely through. Charlton notch their first League victory this year and move off the bottom of Division I in England, beating Sheff Wed 3–1, while the Maxwell battle between relegation-haunted Oxford and Derby ends goalless but provides Derby's first point since December 5, after 8 consecutive defeats. Blackburn, with two goals from Steve Archibald, beat Division II leaders Aston Villa 3–2 and go top by 2 points. Millwall, at home, and Middlesbrough both draw. Sunderland beat Brentford 2–0 and increase their Division III lead to 6 points as Notts Co go down 2–1 at Wigan, who move into 3rd place above Walsall, defeated 2–0 at Fulham. In Division IV, Cardiff, whose fans cause more crowd trouble, crash 4–1 at Orient, who chalk up their first win for 7 weeks. Southampton chairman Alan Woodford, 65, collapses and dies.

21 A Ray Houghton goal breaks the deadlock at Goodison and Liverpool go through to the Cup quarter-finals at the expense of Everton. In Scotland, Hibs hold Celtic to a dull goalless draw at Parkhead. Rangers' leading scorer, Ally McCoist, must undergo cartilate surgery.

22 Spurs sign Everton reserve keeper Bobby Mimms for £400,000, initially on loan so that he can play against Man Utd tomorrow.

23 Watford beat Port Vale 2–0 in their Cup replay. Man Utd draw 1–1 at White Hart Lane and are now 11 points behind Liverpool, who have 3 games in hand. Notts Co and Walsall chalk up wins in Division III, but Division IV leaders Wolves are held at Torquay. Swindon beat Norwich 2–0 in their Simod Cup quarter-final. Southend sign Paul Brush from Palace for £10,000 after a month's loan, while Cardiff sign Palace keeper George Wood on a free transfer.

24 Luton beat QPR 1–0 in their FA Cup replay, thanks to a Warren Neill own goal. Celtic win 1–0 in their replay at Hibs to reach the Scottish Cup quarter-finals. Littlewoods Cup holders Arsenal reach the final again with a 3–1 victory over Everton for a 4–1 aggregate. Third Division leaders Sunderland are hammered 4–0 by lowly Bristol Rovers. Orient's brief revival in Division IV is dashed as they lose 3–1 at Scarborough. Swindon fine Chris Kamara £1,000 and suspend him for a month after an incident on Saturday when Shrewsbury striker Jim Melrose had his jaw broken; Shropshire police are to interview Kamara. Newcastle striker Mirandinha calls a Press conference to end reports that he is unhappy at St James's Park. Barnsley sign Darlington striker David Currie for £150,000. British Transport Police call on Cardiff to take action after their fans wrecked four trains on Saturday night. Spurs and England winger Chris Waddle undergoes a double hernia operation and will probably be out for 6 weeks.

25 Luton police clear the club from blame for the violence before Wednesday's Cup replay with QPR. Bristol Rovers are to send Sunderland a £200 bill for damage to their dressing room and player-coach Kenny Hibbitt considers sueing Sunderland's Gordon Armstrong after a tackle that broke his leg. Hearts transfer-list John Robertson. Doncaster manager Dave Mackay transfer-lists all his senior professionals.

26 Swansea sign Spurs reserve keeper Peter Guthrie on loan.

27 Goals from John Barnes give Liverpool a 2–0 victory at Portsmouth and stretch their Division I lead to 14 points and their unbeaten League run to 27 games. Derby win at last, 1–0 over West Ham, and threaten to move out of the relegation zone at the expense of Portsmouth. But Watford, who lose 1–0 at home to Coventry, and Charlton, 4–0 losers at Highbury, are in deeper trouble. Chelsea, 15 games without a win, are also dropping towards the danger zone, missing two penalties at St James's Park, where Newcastle win 3–1 despite having Ken Wharton sent off. Blackburn keep up their unbeaten run, recovering from 2–0 down to draw at Leeds, but they lose top place in Division II on goal difference to Villa, who beat Plymouth 5–2. Millwall win at Swindon to go above Middlesbrough, beaten 2–1 at home by Bradford who draw level with them in 4th place with two games in hand. Palace slip up badly, losing 2–1 at home to lowly Shrewsbury. Reading win their relegation battle 1–0 at West Brom. Sunderland's two-month reign at the top of Division III comes to an end as they lose 3–2 at Aldershot and Notts Co beat Chester 1–0 to go ahead on goal difference. Walsall and Wigan both lose, the latter 3–1 to

The body language experts might be interested in this shot of Brian Clough, as Forest were in all sorts of trouble and about to be dumped out of the FA Cup semi-final by Liverpool. *Photo: Bob Thomas Sports Photography.*

bottom club York, who end a run of 7 defeats. Steve Bull scores another two as Wolves beat Bolton 4–0 and go 7 points clear at the top of Division IV as Cardiff are held at home by Stockport. In Scotland, Celtic need a last-minute Roy Aitken penalty to beat bottom club Morton 1–0 at Parkhead, but increase their lead to 4 points as Rangers are held at Dundee Utd. Hearts, who lose 2–0 at Falkirk, are now 6 points adrift of the leaders, level with Aberdeen, now 12 points ahead of the rest of the field.

28 Luton beat Oxford 2–0 for a 3–1 aggregate and go through to meet Arsenal in the Littlewoods Cup final. West Ham's Liam Brady, stretchered off against Derby on Saturday with damaged knee ligaments, looks like missing Ireland's European Championship campaign after all.

29 Chris Kamara is in further trouble as Shrewsbury make an official complaint to the FA about the Jim Melrose incident. Chester sack trainer-coach Micky Clarke for allegedly spitting at a Notts Co player on Saturday, and Southend fine and transfer-list full back Chris Ramsey after an incident in a reserve game. Torquay's Dave Caldwell is charged for the second time this season with bringing the game into disrepute after his fifth dismissal.

MARCH 1988

1 Tottenham's lowest crowd of the season, 15,986, see Spurs play out a dull goalless draw with Derby at White Hart Lane. Luton beat Stoke 4–1 and move into the semi-finals of the Simod Cup. Sunderland beat Fulham 2–0 and return to the top of Division III. FIFA make the wearing of shin pads compulsory.

2 In the European Cup, Rangers return to Glasgow with a 2–0 deficit from Steaua Bucharest. In another quarter-final, Bayern Munich defensive errors give Real Madrid two late goals and the Spanish club return from Germany only 3–2 down. Over 15,000 at Elm Park see Reading beat Coventry 4–3 on penalties to reach the final of the Simod Cup. Charlton reveal plans to leave Selhurst Park and return to the borough of Greenwich, possibly to The Valley. Norwich sign defender Andy Linighan from Oldham. A winding-up order against Portsmouth by the Inland Revenue is withdrawn when chairman John Deacon pays about half the outstanding income tax bill of £626,000. The Football Trust announce that the cost of policing League matches in Britain in the 1986–87 season reached a record £3.65 million, of which they contributed 35%, or £1.28 million. The USA, Morocco, and Brazil have applied to host the 1994 World Cup.

3 Chelsea manager John Hollins puts projected transfers of both Kerry Dixon and Mike Hazard on ice because of injuries. Hull sign midfielder Ken De Mange from Leeds for £85,000 and much travelled ex-England winger Peter Barnes from Manchester City. West Brom sign forward Stewart Phillips from Hereford for £30,000. Darlington sign Norwich striker Paul Clayton for a club record £20,000.

4 Fourth Division leaders Wolves go down 3–0 at lowly Tranmere, but second-placed Cardiff are held at home by Peterborough. Portsmouth chairman John Deacon strips his deputy, John Parkhouse, of the vice-chairmanship in the wake of the recent High Court drama. Midfielder Paul Bodin joins Swindon from financially troubled Newport for £30,000, twice what the Welsh club paid Bath for him only six weeks earlier, while Chesterfield sign Leeds midfielder Nigel Thompson for £10,000.

5 Liverpool extend their unbeaten League run this season to within one of Leeds' record 29 by winning 1–0 on QPR's plastic and extend their lead to 17 points as Manchester United go down at Carrow Road. In Division II, Blackburn's 23-game unbeaten run comes to an end at Stoke, while Villa chalk up their 12th away win, 2–1 at Bournemouth, and go 3 points clear. In Division III, Sunderland are held at home by Blackpool while Notts Co leapfrog to the top by beating Doncaster. In Scotland, Rangers gain a measure of revenge over Cup conquerors Dunfermline with a 3–0 away win, but make up no ground on Celtic, still 6 points in front.

6 Arsenal beat Spurs 2–1 at Highbury, led by Tony Adams, who replaces Kenny Sansom as captain. Spurs chairman Irving Scholar refuses the Welsh FA permission to approach manager Terry Venables regarding the part-time job as Wales supremo.

7 Chelsea chairman Ken Bates returns from a holiday and creates a stir by doing nothing: the expected sacking of manager John Hollins and transfers of Kerry Dixon and Mike Hazard are not carried out, much to the consternation of the Press, who have been writing of little else for days. Wembley announces plans for more seating by next season, reducing the capacity to 87,000, including 63,000 seats, with the eventual object an all-seater stadium.

8 Reluctant Oxford manager Maurice Evans is allowed to step down: he will remain in charge until a successor is found. Kerry Dixon rejects a move to West Ham as his transfer to Arsenal is blocked by the Chelsea chairman. Luton beat Swindon after extra time in their Simod Cup semi-final to reach their second Wembley final of the season, but striker Brian Stein breaks a wrist in the last minutes. Forest midfielder Terry Wilson, 19, signs up for the club till 1992.

9 Portsmouth's boardroom drama continues as demoted director John Parkhouse resigns and chairman John Deacon takes over the day-to-day finances. Millwall sign former player Dean Horrix from Reading for £65,000.

10 Goal-starved Watford sign Chester striker and leading Division III goalscorer Stuart Rimmer for £200,000, prompting Trevor Senior (1 goal in 26 games) to ask for a transfer. QPR striker Gary Bannister returns to Coventry, his first club, for £300,000. Aberdeen transfer winger Gary Hackett to Stoke for £110,000 only eight months after they bought him from Shrewsbury.

11 Arsenal's David O'Leary is named in the Republic of Ireland's squad for the first time in nearly two years.

12 Two men are sent off in the FA Cup quarter-finals. Portsmouth's Mike Quinn gets his marching orders against Luton, who win 3–1, but it's a different story at Plough Lane, where Brian Gayle is shown the red card just before half-time, yet 10-man Wimbledon overcome a 1–0 deficit to beat Watford 2–1. The performance of the day, however, belongs to Forest, who beat Arsenal 2–1 in front of 50,000 at Highbury to take Brian Clough past the FA Cup quarter-finals for the first time as player or manager. In the Scottish quarter-finals, Aberdeen (with a Davie Dodds hat-trick), Hearts, and Celtic all have easy wins, while Dundee and Dundee United, who have Maurice Malpas sent off, will have to replay. In Division II, Blackburn's 3–1 home win over Bournemouth takes them level with leaders Villa, who lose 2–1 at home to Leeds. In Division III, leaders Notts County and Sunderland both draw away, while Wolves extend their lead in Division IV by 3 points. Newport, propping up the League, bid farewell to manager Brian Eastick, leaving for economic reasons.

13 With an awesome display of football, Liverpool sweep into the FA Cup semi-finals by brushing aside Manchester City 4–0 at Maine Road.

15 Eamonn Bannon puts Dundee United two up at half-time, but Dundee's sub Graham Harvey scores two to force another quarter-final replay. Swindon midfielder Chris Kamara is to be charged with causing grievous bodily harm, the first League player to face police proceedings over an on-field incident.

16 Liverpool draw at Derby and equal Leeds' record of starting a season with 29 games unbeaten, set in 1973–74. Rangers, the last British hope in Europe, are knocked out 3–2 on aggregate by Steaua Bucharest and are joined in the semi-finals by Benfica, PSV Eindhoven, and Real Madrid. Bristol City sack manager Terry Cooper after six years; Joe Jordan takes over until the end of the season.

17 Forest sign Preston striker Nigel Jemson, 18, for £150,000. Watford's Gary Chivers joins Brighton for £40,000, and Frank Stapleton joins Derby on loan from Ajax. Torquay striker Dave Caldwell is suspended for eight games after his fifth sending-off of the season.

18 West Ham sign Fulham striker Leroy Rosenior on loan for today's match with Watford and will complete the £275,000 transfer on Monday. Former wing-half Reg Halton dies, aged 71; he played for several clubs, including Manchester United and Bury.

19 Rosenior marks his West Ham debut with the winner against Watford. Derby win 3–0 at Coventry but Peter Shilton is carried off after a collision with Coventry sub Dave Bennett. Oxford hold Chelsea 4–4 after being 0–3 down at half-time. Charlton win at Southampton and climb out of the bottom three for the first time this season. Villa win at Reading to equal the Division II record of 13 away wins, while joint leaders Blackburn are held by Leicester at home. Joint Division III leaders Notts County and Sunderland draw 1–1 at Roker Park. In Scotland, relegation-bound Dunfermline put six past Dundee.

20 At Goodison, Everton end Liverpool's unbeaten League run as Wayne Clarke scores the only goal of the game. In Scotland, Celtic win 2–1 at Rangers and extend their lead to 6 points over their Glasgow rivals.

21 Shilton recovers from Saturday's injury, but Dave Bennett finds he has a broken leg. Everton defender Ian Marshall joins Oldham for £100,000. Sheffield United sign former Spurs defender Simon Webster from Huddersfield for £40,000.

22 Manager John Hollins finally leaves Chelsea, with an undisclosed settlement, and coach Bobby Campbell takes over as caretaker. Scotland are held to a 1–1 draw in Malta, while Under-21s lose 1–0 to England, who go into the European semi-finals 2–0 on aggregate. Wednesday sign Ipswich central defender Ian Cranson for £450,000, equalling the club record. Portsmouth manager Alan Ball is charged with bringing the game into disrepute after his booking in the Cup tie with Luton 10 days ago. Steaua players withdraw from Romania's international with the Republic of Ireland and president of the Romanian FA, Cornel Dragusin, puts it down to a 'very bad tackle by Souness' in the European Cup tie.

23 Centre-back Tony Adams scores for both sides as England and Holland draw 2–2 at Wembley, where Ruud Gullit stars for the Dutch before being substituted and Glenn Hoddle for England when he comes on. Mixed fortunes in the other friendlies as the Republic of Ireland

The Liverpool squad are presented to the Princess of Wales before the FA Cup final at Wembley (*above*), and a couple of hours later, Celtic were celebrating their Scottish Cup victory over Dundee United at Hampden Park (*below*). *Photos: Bob Thomas Sports Photography.*

beat Romania, Northern Ireland draw with Poland, and Wales lose to Yugoslavia. Signings before tomorrow's transfer deadline include winger Brian Marwood from Wednesday to Arsenal for £450,000, midfielder Garry Parker from Hull to Forest for £250,000, keeper Kevin Hitchcock from Mansfield to Chelsea for £250,000, and Northampton captain Phil Chard to Wolves for £45,000.

24 Some big names are involved in moves on transfer-deadline day and they don't cost a penny: Ossie Ardiles goes to Blackburn from Spurs on a loan transfer and Trevor Francis from Rangers to QPR on a free transfer. West Ham pay the biggest fee, £300,000, to Birmingham for left-back Julian Dicks, and Middlesbrough sign goal-starved striker Trevor Senior from Watford for £200,000. Other major transfers include Kevin Langley (Man City to Birmingham) and Ian Marshall (Everton to Oldham) both for £100,000. Newport County sell one of their few remaining assets, striker Gary Brook, to Scarborough for £10,000, barely enough to make a dent in their £200,000 debt, but they are saved from impending extinction after an all-day board meeting. The FA announce a four-year sponsorship by Coca-Cola Great Britain of the FA Coaching and Educational Programme.

25 Liverpool's Mark Lawrenson gives up his battle with injury and agrees to manage Oxford. Spurs and Bordeaux agree a £1 million close-season fee for striker Clive Allen.

26 Liverpool, with player-manager Kenny Dalglish making his first, brief appearance of the season as substitute, return to winning ways by beating Wimbledon at Anfield, but in Division II both leaders lose, Villa at home to Stoke and Blackburn 3–0 at Plymouth. Ardiles is injured on his debut for Blackburn. Division III leaders also go down, Notts County at home to Gillingham and Sunderland at York, where visiting fans invade the pitch, break the cross-bar, and fight with officials and police, who make 30 arrests. Wolves, helped by Steve Bull's fourth hat-trick of the season, stretch their lead in Division IV to 8 points with a 5–3 win over Darlington.

27 Reading, Division II relegation strugglers making their first appearance at Wembley, trounce Luton 4–1 in the Simod Cup final watched by a crowd of 61,740. Spurs and former Liverpool keeper Ray Clemence announces his retirement, after 23 years.

28 Manchester United's Norman Whiteside puts in a transfer request. Walsall chairman Terry Ramsden sells the club to a local consortium in a £1 million deal.

29 Vinny Jones is sent off at Goodison after 73 minutes, but Wimbledon hold on to draw 2–2. Blackburn manager Don Mackay condemns Plymouth's Nick Marker for his tackle on Ardiles and his remarks about the incident.

30 Arsenal manager George Graham is booked at the end of their goalless draw at Oxford, apparently for remarks made to a linesman. Chelsea players report Southampton's Graham Baker to the PFA for disparaging remarks alleged to have been made after Saturday's game. Celtic win at Aberdeen and extend their Premier League lead to 7 points. Barcelona win the Spanish Cup.

31 UEFA tell FA that no decision will be made on the return of English clubs to European competition until 25 June, the day of the European Championships final. Arsenal give Graham Rix, 30, a free transfer. Brian Hill (Kettering) is to referee the FA Cup final.

APRIL 1988

1 QPR inflict a fifth successive home defeat on Watford.

2 Liverpool, with Beardsley and Houghton on the subs bench, lose again, beaten 2–1 by Forest at the City Ground. A McClair hat-trick helps Manchester United to a 4–1 win over Derby. Portsmouth lift themselves out of the bottom three with a 1–0 win at Spurs. Michael O'Neill, 18, hits three for Newcastle. Villa lose 2–1 to Millwall, who move into 4th place in Division II. Middlesbrough, 6–0 victors over Sheffield Utd, move into 2nd. In Division III, Sunderland win at Grimsby and move ahead of Notts Co. In Scotland, Celtic move nearer to the title with a win at Hibs. Morton are the first side to be relegated. Sweden beat USSR 2–0 to win the international tournament in West Berlin.

4 In a full Easter Monday programme in England, Manchester Utd make a sensational comeback at Anfield, holding Liverpool 3–3 after being 3–1 down with Colin Gibson sent off. United manager Alex Ferguson alleges that the 'intimidating atmosphere' at Anfield gets to referees, and Liverpool manager Kenny Dalglish becomes involved in the argument. At the other end of the table, Charlton beat Watford 1–0. Villa crash 2–1 at home to Oldham. In Division III, Sunderland scrape a 3–2 home win over Chesterfield, while Notts Co suffer their third successive defeat. York are the first League side to be relegated this season. Steve Bull, with both goals in Wolves' 2–0 win over Colchester, takes his tally to 44 for a new club record.

5 Manchester Utd grant Norman Whiteside's transfer request.

6 In Wednesday's only League match, Millwall win 2–1 at Leeds and join Villa at the top of Division II with a game in hand. In the European

38

Cup semi-finals first leg, PSV gain a shock 1–1 draw at Real Madrid and Benfica hold Steaua 0–0 in Bucharest. Ajax virtually book their place in the Cup-Winners' Cup final with a 3–0 victory in Marseilles. Arsenal manager George Graham is to face a charge of bringing the game into disrepute following his booking at Oxford. Paul Gascoigne rejecs a lucrative five-year contract with Newcastle.

7 Portsmouth manager Alan Ball is fined £500 by the FA on a disrepute charge for an incident in the Cup quarter-final at Luton. Paul McGrath confirms that he has asked Manchester Utd for a transfer. Merseyside players fill 9 of the 11 places in the Division I side chosen by PFA members.

8 Derby chairman Robert Maxwell invites Johan Cruyff to become technical director. Swansea manager Terry Yorath is appointed caretaker manager of Wales for three matches.

9 Liverpool and Wimbledon are FA Cup finalists, 2–1 victors, respectively, over Forest and Luton. Chelsea beat Derby 1–0, their first win in 22 matches. Bottom club Watford beat fellow strugglers Oxford, now 21 games without a win. Alan Shearer, 17, scores a hat-trick in his first full match as Southampton beat Arsenal 4–2. Millwall go top of Division II, scoring 3 goals in 5 first-half minutes to beat Plymouth 3–2, while Villa, despite a draw at Palace, slip to 4th. Above them now, and with a game in hand, are Middlesbrough and Blackburn. In the Scottish Cup semi-finals, Celtic score 2 goals in the last 3 minutes to beat Hearts 2–1, while Aberdeen and Dundee Utd play out a goalless draw. In the League, bottom club Morton, who had gone eight matches without scoring, beat Rangers 3–2.

10 Wolves draw at Cambridge and extend their Division IV lead to 8 points.

11 John Barnes is voted PFA Player of the Year and Steve McMahon and Peter Beardsley make it a 1–2–3 for Liverpool. Newcastle's Paul Gascoigne is Young Player of the Year.

12 Brian McClair hits his 20th League goal, the first Manchester United player to do so since George Best (28) in 1967–68. Watford's survival hopes take a further dive at Newcastle, where 18-year-old Irish striker Michael O'Neill scores his 8th goal in 5 matches since coming in for the injured Mirandhina.

13 With John Barnes justifying his Player of the Year tag, Liverpool crush Forest 5–0 at Anfield with one of the best displays of football seen for years to move within a whisker of the title. Oxford look doomed after a 3–0 home defeat by Wednesday, for whom Lee Chapman scores his 100th League goal. Aberdeen and Dundee Utd, who have Paul Hegarty sent off, draw the re-

played Scottish Cup semi-final. In the Premier Division, Hearts score twice in the last four minutes to beat Dunfermline 2–1 and postpone Celtic's title celebrations. A depleted England Under-21 team lose 4–2 in France in the first leg of the European semi-finals.

14 Swindon's Chris Kamara is the first footballer in England to be punished (fined £1,200) in the civil courts for an on-field incident.

15 England internationals Terry Butcher and Chris Woods of Glasgow Rangers are found guilty in a Scottish court of disorderly conduct and breach of the peace on the field of play in a game against Celtic last October and are fined £250 and £500, respectively; the case against Graham Roberts is 'not proven' and Celtic's Frank McAvennie is found not guilty. Johan Cruyff announces that he will become Barcelona coach for a year, declining the offer from Derby. Watford win at Highbury to climb off the bottom, but their survival hopes are still dim.

16 There is no Saturday Football League programme owing to the Centenary festival at Wembley sponsored by Mercantile Credit. The first day of the festival attracts some 40,000 spectators to see a knock-out competition between 16 clubs (eight from Division I, four from Div II, and two each from Divs III & IV), who qualified on the results of 15 League matches between November and February. From 20-minute each way matches, the semi-finalists to emerge are Manchester Utd, Sheffield Wed, Forest, and, from a sector that contained Cup finalists Liverpool and Wimbledon, Fourth Division Tranmere. Tranmere are the heroes of the first day, beating Wimbledon 1–0 and Liverpool's conquerors Newcastle 2–0. Seven of the other 10 matches played are decided on penalties. Injuries to Liverpool's John Barnes and Luton's Mal Donaghy are unfortunate legacies of the tournament. In Scotland, Hearts again hold up the Celtic celebrations by beating them 2–1.

17 Forest win the League festival at Wembley. In the semi-finals they twice equalize against brave Tranmere before beating them on penalties, and in a dull, goalless final they beat Wednesday on penalties. Forest manager Brian Clough is conspicuous by his absence, as are the spectators, numbering only 17,000 on this second day.

18 Swindon's Chris Kamara, fined in the courts last week, is banned by FA for the rest of the season. Hearts striker John Robertson agrees to sign for Newcastle for £750,000. Torquay agree to let their youngest-ever player, YTS apprentice Lee Sharpe, go to Manchester Utd when he turns 17 on 27 May.

19 Portsmouth hold Wimbledon to a 2–2 draw at Plough Lane despite losing keeper Alan Knight

South American Footballer of the Year Carlos Valderrama, of Colombia, delights even his opponents during a practice match prior to facing England at Wembley. *Photo: Bob Thomas Sports Photography.*

in the second minute after a clash with John Fashanu. Millwall win 2–1 at Bournemouth to increase their lead in Division II to 4 points, and over 5,000 see the game on giant screens at The Den. Division IV leaders Wolves reach the final of the Sherpa Van Trophy by beating Notts County 3–0 (4–1 on aggregate) in the Southern final, while Burnley win 3–1 at Preston after extra time in the Northern final.

20 Norwich hold Liverpool to a goalless draw at Carrow Road to keep the champions elect waiting. In Division II, Bradford move into 2nd place by beating relegation-bound Reading. In the replayed Scottish Cup semi-final, Dundee United beat Aberdeen 1–0. St Mirren manager Alex Smith is sacked and chairman Jule Craig resigns. PSV beat Real Madrid on away goals and will meet Benfica in the European Cup final. In the Cup-Winners' Cup, Mechelen (Belgium) and Ajax both have 4–2 aggregate wins, and in the UEFA Cup Español overcome a 2–0 deficit to beat Bruges and will meet Bayer Leverkusen in the final.

21 The Football League and PFA put forward a plan designed to eradicate violence on the pitch next season by deducting points from clubs with poor disciplinary records and increasing the period of suspension for players sent off. Inter Milan sign Lothar Matthäus from Bayern Munich for £2.4 million.

23 Liverpool and Celtic clinch the League Championships of England and Scotland. Charlton's win consigns gameless Watford to Division II. Derby, with Peter Shilton equalling Terry Paine's 824 League appearances, beat Southampton 2–0. QPR play their last home game on plastic. In Division II, Villa scratch an untidy 1–0 win over Shrewsbury, but it takes them back to 2nd spot. Bradford recover from a 2–0 deficit and the dismissal of John Hendrie to salvage a point at Manchester City and stay above Middlesbrough, who crash 4–0 at Ipswich for whom transfer-listed Dalian Atkinson, 20, scores a hat-trick. Huddersfield lose 4–0 at Hull and are relegated. Sunderland show signs of nerves at the top of Division III, losing at home to Bristol City, while Notts Co move into 2nd place with a 4–0 win over strugglers Rotherham. Wolves beat Swansea and virtually clinch promotion from Division IV. Poor Newport, thrashed again, 6–0 at Bolton, lose their League status as Carlisle beat Colchester 4–0.

24 Luton beat holders Arsenal 3–2 at Wembley to win the Littlewoods Cup, their first ever major trophy.

25 Blackburn draw at home and miss their chance to go 2nd in Division II.

26 Steve Bull scores twice, to bring his seasonal tally to 50, as Wolves win 3–1 at Newport and clinch their place in Division III, where Sunderland's 4–0 win at Mansfield takes them 6 points clear at the top.

27 In a friendly international, England draw 0–0 in Hungary, Middlesbrough centre-back Gary Pallister making a promising debut. In Belfast, N. Ireland and France also draw 0–0, with Luton's young Littlewoods Cup star Kingsley Black making his debut as a 60th-minute substitute and thus settling the unedifying tug-of-war going on all week between Billy Bingham and Bobby Robson for his services. In Dublin, the Republic beat Yugoslavia 2–0, their 7th win in a row. In other friendlies, Scotland earn a creditable 0–0 draw in Spain, but Wales lose 4–1 in Sweden. In the European Under-21s semi-final second leg, France hold England 2–2 at Highbury, to win 6–4 on aggregate.

29 Over 6,000 at Doncaster for the 1st leg of the FA Youth Cup final see them go down 5–0 to Arsenal. Rotherham sack manager Dave Cusack only four months after his dismissal from Doncaster; he is replaced by Billy McEwan, who resigned as manager of Sheffield Utd in January.

30 Oxford lose at Newcastle and are relegated, although consolation for manager Mark Lawrenson is the League Championship medal he picks up for his contribution to Liverpool's campaign. Portsmouth lose at Coventry, while welcome draws are gained by Charlton at Everton, Chelsea at home to Liverpool thanks to a penalty save by Kevin Hitchcock, and Derby at Watford, where Peter Shilton makes his record 825th League appearance. John Barnes, back in the Liverpool side after injury, celebrates his selection as Footballer of the Year (Football Writers' version) with a goal. West Ham's defeat at Southampton pushes them into the relegation play-off place. Millwall, Bradford, and Middlesbrough consolidate their positions at the top of Division II with good home wins, the latter two leapfrogging over gameless Villa, while Palace beat Blackburn to challenge them for a play-off place. Reading hang on at the other end of the table by beating fellow strugglers Sheffield Utd. Sunderland win at Port Vale to clinch promotion from Division III, while Walsall overcome a half-time deficit to beat Notts Co 2–1 and move above them into 2nd place. Brighton's 6th win on the trot lifts them into 3rd place. Wolves fail to clinch the Division IV title, losing 4–2 at Wrexham. In the GM Vauxhall Conference, with only one game to go, Lincoln win and go top, above Barnet, who lose at home, while Kettering fade out of contention. In Scotland's Premier Division, all six home teams fail to score. Finnish international Mixu Paatelainen hits all 4 for Dundee Utd at Morton. In Division I, Hamilton lose but are promoted, as bottom club

Dumbarton win 4–2 at second-placed Meadowbank to keep their hopes of survival alive, while fellow-strugglers East Fife win 3–1 at Kilmarnock, the only other club in danger of relegation.

MAY

2 A full Bank Holiday programme in England sees Millwall gain promotion to Division I for the first time in their 103-year history with a 1–0 win at Hull. They go up as champions, as do Sunderland from Division III and Wolves from Division IV. A 29,000 crowd see Sunderland beat Northampton 3–1, while nearly 18,000 see Steve Bull score Wolves' goals in their 2–0 defeat of Hartlepool. Portsmouth lose 2–1 at home to Newcastle and return to Division II after just one season. West Ham, with Leroy Rosenior scoring twice and being sent off, beat Chelsea 4–1 and are safe, as are Spurs who draw 1–1 at Charlton. Now Chelsea must beat Charlton in their last match if they are to avoid the play-offs and force Charlton to suffer again. Liverpool are presented with the Championship trophy at Anfield but are held 1–1 by Southampton. Middlesbrough's 3–0 win at Barnsley moves them into 2nd place in Division II, needing only to win their last game, but Bradford lose 1–0 at Villa and look like meeting them again in the play-offs. Blackburn are held at home by Reading, but Palace lose at Leeds. Brighton draw at Chester, but move into 2nd place in Division III as Notts Co, at home, and Walsall both lose. Bristol City can now pip Northampton to reach the play-offs. Cardiff are promoted from Division IV, while Lincoln make a quick return as champions of the GM Vauxhall Conference.

3 UEFA set a limit of 4 foreign players per squad of 16 in UEFA competitions, a ruling that could seriously affect British clubs, as 'foreign' denotes players not qualified to represent the club's country. UEFA president Jacques Georges makes it clear, also, that any return of English clubs to European competition must have the backing of the British government. Arsenal win the FA Youth Cup 6–1 on aggregate after a 1–1 draw with Doncaster at Highbury. The Football League order Southend and Crewe to switch their last Friday fixtures to Saturday as they could effect outstanding issues. Coventry appoint Cyrille Regis and Trevor Peake as player-coaches and Terry Paine as youth coach.

4 Espanol of Barcelona beat Bayer Leverkusen 3–0 in the first leg of the UEFA Cup final. Malcolm Macdonald, unhappy with the efforts of others, resigns as manager of relegated Huddersfield after less than 7 months. Glasgow

Rangers' acting captain Graham Roberts is to be allowed to leave following a dressing-room row with player-manager Graeme Souness on Saturday. Johan Cruyff agrees to take over as Barcelona coach.

5 Spurs place Nico Claesen on the transfer list.

7 The last day of the League season sees Charlton stay up and Villa promoted. A draw at Stamford Bridge is enough to keep Charlton in Division I while Chelsea face the play-offs. West Ham make history by naming a keeper, Phil Parkes, as sub at Newcastle, to guard against a 7-goal defeat that could have put them in the play-offs; they lose 2–1. Liverpool climax their League season with another super show, beating Wednesday 5–1 at Hillsborough. Villa only manage a draw at Swindon, but Middlesbrough and Bradford both lose at home and go into the promotion play-offs with Blackburn, 4–1 winners at champions Millwall. Reading are relegated as Sheffield Utd win at Huddersfield and face the relegation play-offs. Brighton go up with Sunderland from Division III, while Bristol City leapfrog over Northampton for the last promotion play-off spot. At the bottom, Grimsby go down as they draw at home to Aldershot, who stay up. Southend, Chesterfield, and Mansfield escape, but Rotherham crash 4–1 at home to Sunderland and must play off to survive. Torquay lose at home to Scunthorpe in Division IV, and both must play off for promotion, while Bolton win at Wrexham and are promoted. Swansea clinch the last play-off spot as Orient lose at home to champions Wolves. In Scotland, Falkirk's relegation is confirmed as they go down 5–0 at home to Rangers while St Mirren win. In Division 1, Kilmarnock win at Partick to condemn East Fife and Dumbarton to Division 2. In the FA Trophy final, Enfield and Telford play a goalless draw at Wembley.

9 A draw at home to Luton in their last League game gives Liverpool 90 points, equalling Everton's Division I record, but a clash of heads between Gillespie and Spackman is a worry just five days before the Cup final. Aldridge scores to take his League tally to 26, top of the Division I scorers. Wimbledon lose at Old Trafford and injury to Terry Gibson gives them cause for concern, too. Chelsea caretaker-manager Bobby Campbell is given a two-year contract. Grimsby manager Bobby Roberts is dismissed, having taken the club from 2nd to 4th Division in two seasons. Terry Cooper is appointed Exeter manager, replacing caretaker John Delve.

10 Bristol City manager Joe Jordan signs a new two-year contract.

11 Mechelen from Belgium beat Ajax 1–0 in the Cup-Winners' Cup final after Ajax defender Danny Blind is sent off in the 16th minute. Man

DAY-BY-DAY DIARY 1987-88

It's a long time since Wolves have had anything to celebrate, but in 1987-88 they not only won the Fourth Division title but also the Sherpa Van Trophy at Wembley, where goalscorer Andy Mutch proudly displays the trophy. *Photo: Bob Thomas Sports Photography.*

Utd agree to pay £750,000 to Aberdeen for Scottish international Jim Leighton, a british record fee for a keeper. Arsenal manager George Graham is fined £250 for making 'improper comments' to a linesman at Oxford, Swindon manager Lou Macari £400 for remarks to a referee at Bradford, both on 30 March. Southampton manager Chris Nicholl gets a new two-year contract but his assistant Tony Barton is to be released. Former QPR chairman Jim Gregory is to take over at Portsmouth. Newport are saved from extinction by an unidentified benefactor.

12 The Football League agree a provisional deal with the new British Satellite Broadcasting (BSB) that would guarantee a minimum £9m per season and net football some £200m in 10 years; the BSB, with a 15-year franchise from the IBA and due to start operations in August 1989, would form a joint company with the League and the FA; but with the BBC and ITV possibly refusing to negotiate with a joint company, there may be no domestic football on TV next season. The Scottish League sign a two-year sponsorship deal worth £2m with DIY company B & Q, who will replace Fine Fare. Norwich sign Wigan midfielder Paul Cook for £73,000. Aldershot chairman Colin Hancock resigns and is replaced by 32-year-old Terry Lewis.

13 Kenny Dalglish wins the Bells Manager of the Year award. Wimbledon name their Cup team, with Gibson in and Clive Goodyear getting the nod over John Scales at right-back, while Dalglish reveals little about Liverpool's line-up except that both Gillespie and Spackman are fit.

14 A 38th minute goal by Lawrie Sanchez and a second-half penalty save by man-of-the-match Dave Beasant from John Aldridge give Wimbledon a sensational 1–0 victory over Liverpool at Wembley; Beasant is the first keeper to captain a Cup-winning team and Aldridge the first player to miss a penalty in a Wembley FA Cup final. Celtic chalk up another League and Cup double, coming from behind with two Frank McAvennie goals in the last 13 minutes to beat Dundee Utd 2–1 in the Scottish Cup final at Hampden. Sports Minister Colin Moynihan criticizes the West Germans' refusal to have all-ticket matches in the European Championships.

15 In the 1st and 2nd Division play-offs, Chelse win 2–0 at Blackburn, only their second victory in 27 matches, and Bradford will take a 2–1 lead over Middlesbrough to Ayrsome Park. In the other games, home sides Bristol City, Swansea, and Torquay all earn single-goal advantages, but Notts County lose 1–3 to Walsall. Scunthorpe defender Paul Nicol is sent off at Torquay, whose manager Cyril Knowles also gets his marching orders. AC Milan clinch the Italian

championship, Bruges the Belgian title.

16 Forest manager Brian Clough agrees a new two-year deal with the club. Luton give Brian Stein, 30, and Meka Nwajiobi, 29, free transfers. Aberdeen manager Ian Porterfield resigns. Portuguese club Vitoria Setubal sack manager Malcolm Allison. Newcastle's Paul Gascoigne is fined £200 for kicking over a bucket of water after being sent off at Derby. Guest Ian Rush scores twice in Liverpool's 3–2 win over an England XI in Alan Hansen's testimonial.

17 Colombia draw 0–0 with Scotland at Hampden in the first Rous Cup match. Cardiff beat Wrexham 2–0 at Swansea in the Welsh Cup final and earn their entry into Europe. AC Milan beat Manchester Utd 3–2 in a friendly at Old Trafford.

18 Chelsea beat Blackburn 4–1 (6–1 on aggregate) and will meet Middlesbrough, 2–0 victors over Bradford after extra time, for a First Division place. The other four play-offs finish 1–1, so Sheffield Utd go down, while Britsol City and Walsall meet for a place in Division II, and Rotherham are relegated, with Swansea and Torquay to play off for a place in Division III. There's a dramatic comeback for Bayer Leverkusen in the UEFA Cup, as three second-half goals cancel their first-leg deficit against Espanol and they win the trophy on penalties despite missing their first spot-kick. England manager Bobby Robson gives Arsenal centre-back Tony Adams a vote of confidence after a bout of uncertain form.

19 Provisional attendance figures of nearly 18 million for the four divisions of the League are 3.2% up on last season, despite the 2.7% decrease in First Division gates due to a 9% decrease in matches. An injury puts Mark Wright out of the Scotland match. West Ham make defender Steve Walford available for transfer.

20 The FA are to charge Cup-winners Wimbledon with bringing the game into disrepute after an incident during Alan Cork's testimonial just two days after the final in which eight players dropped their shorts to the crowd at half-time.

21 England win their Rous Cup match with Scotland at Wembley more easily than Beardsley's brilliant goal would indicate, Scots keeper Jim Leighton saving them from a more comprehensive defeat. Northern Ireland open up the World Cup qualifiers with a 3–0 win over Malta in Belfast. Portsmouth include Paul Mariner, Kenny Swain, and Noel Blake on their free transfer list.

22 The Republic of Ireland chalk up an impressive 8th successive victory, beating Poland 3–1 in a friendly at Lansdowne Road. FA chairman Bert Millichip feels that the 200 plus arrests inside and outside Wembley over the weekend cannot

have helped English clubs' chances of returning to Europe next season.

23 The England–Scotland fixture comes under threat as Sports Minister Colin Moynihan calls for a report on the weekend disturbances, while Scottish FA secretary Ernie Walker alleges an 'orchestrated campaign' by the English media against the Scotland fans. Bobby Robson makes four changes in the England team to meet Colombia tomorrow, Wright coming in for Watson, Anderson for Stephens, Waddle for Steven, and McMahon for Webb. Northern Ireland manager Billy Bingham signs a new 4-year contract.

24 Colombia hold England 1–1 at Wembley in an entertaining match watched by under 26,000; England win the Rous Cup.

25 PSV Eindoven take the European Cup on penalties after having the best of a disappointing goalless draw with Benfica. In the first legs of the League play-off finals, Middlesbrough beat Chelsea 2–0 at Ayrsome Park, two goals in the last 10 minutes from much-coveted Ireland striker David Kelly give Walsall a 3–1 lead over Bristol City to take to their home leg, and Swansea edge Torquay 2–1 at the Vetch Field. The FA are prepared to buy £34,000 worth of unsold European Championship tickets rather than let them go on sale in West Germany. Peterborough need a no-strings injection of £1 million to survive. Jimmy Case signs a new one-year contract with Southampton. Wimbledon's Dennis Wise is called into England's Under-21 squad as a replacement.

26 Manchester City's £2m rated striker Paul Stewart is suspended for four matches and fined £600 for exceeding 50 disciplinary points in the season. Aston Villa sign Derek Mountfield from Everton for £425,000 and full-back Chris Price from Blackburn for £150,000.

28 Chelsea win 1–0 at Stamford Bridge but are relegated and Middlesbrough promoted as crowd-trouble at the end of the game virtually scuppers any last remaining hopes of English clubs returning to Europe. The few hundred England fans who see Lineker score England's winner at Lausanne in their last international before the European Championships behave themselves, and the Under-21 game with Switzerland is drawn 1–1. Robson announces his squad, the only surprise being Chelsea left-back Tony Dorigo as cover for Kenny Sansom. In the other play-off games, Bristol City win 2–0 at Walsall to force a decider (Walsall win a penalty shoot-out to determine venue) and Swansea draw 3–3 at Torquay to claim the last promotion spot to Division III on aggregate.

29 Over 80,000 fans see two Fourth Division sides, Wolves and Burnley, contest the Sherpa Van Trophy final at Wembley, with Wolves triumphant 2–0.

30 Walsall beat Bristol City 4–0 in the replayed play-off to win promotion to Division II thanks largely to a David Kelly hat-trick. The whole Bristol Rovers youth team are held in police custody overnight in Mannheim, West Germany, after allegedly going on a drunken rampage. Jack Charlton names the Republic of Ireland squad for Europe and includes captain Frank Stapleton and Newcastle's John Anderson, after fitness tests, and John Byrne, just transferred from QPR to French club Le Havre for £175,000. The Scottish League agree to postpone fixtures on four Saturdays next season before World Cup qualifying ties.

31 England's matches in the European Championship are now to be all-ticket, after the Sports Minister's complaint to the German authorities. Ipswich sign defender David Linighan from Shrewsbury, who want £250,000.

JUNE

1 In pre-Championship internationals a Gullitless Holland impress with a 2–0 win over Romania, the USSR beat Poland 2–1, and Ireland are held 0–0 in Norway to halt their run of 8 successive victories. Denmark lose 1–0 at home to Czechoslovakia, Spain 3–1 at home to Sweden. Ian Rush scores the winner as Wales win 3–2 in Malta. Jim Gregory completes the takeover of Portsmouth.

3 The League's annual meeting comprehensively reject the PFA's plans, put forward by the League management committee, to deduct points for poor disciplinary records. Everton's Philip Carter is re-elected president, but Bobby Charlton fails to get on the management committee. The League limit the number of people on the trainers' bench to seven, and decree that from 1990–91 both sleeves of players' shirts will carry the League logo. Central defender Steve Bould joins Arsenal from Stoke for a fee to be decided. Hull sign Watford central defender Steve Terry for £100,000. Everton's Paul Power is forced to retire through a knee injury and becomes the youth team coach.

4 England win a full-scale work-out against Beazer Homes League champions Aylesbury 7–0, with Beardsley scoring 4. Ian Rush scores for Wales as they shock European finalists Italy 1–0 in Brescia. Chelsea keeper Eddie Niedzwiecki is forced to retire after a succession of knee operations and becomes youth team coach.

5 Cup-winners Wimbledon threaten to take UEFA to court if they fail to lift the ban on

Walsall's David Kelly celebrates after his hat-trick had clinched promotion in the play-off clash with Bristol City (*above*), while Middlesbrough dumped Chelsea into the Second Division in their play-off at Stamford Bridge. *Photos: Bob Thomas Sports Photography.*

English clubs. Former England international Gary Shaw joins BK Copenhagen on a free transfer from Villa. England beat Mexico 2–1 in the Toulon Under-21s tournament, but West Ham full-back Julian Dicks is sent off.

6 Inter Milan sign Porto's Algerian forward Rabah Madjer for over £2 million. Arthur Albiston joins West Brom on a free transfer from Man Utd. Alan Buckley is appointed manager of Grimsby. The Scottish FA tell training staff to remain seated following police complaints about the Celtic-Hearts Cup semi-final.

7 League secretary Graham Kelly is the surprise choice to succeed Ted Croker as chief executive of the FA. Newcastle sign Wimbledon Cup hero Dave Beasant for £850,000, a record fee for a keeper. England Under-21s beat USSR 1–0. Preston sign Blackburn midfielder Mark Patterson for £20,000.

8 Wimbledon are fined £5,000 and nine players £750 each for the 'mooning' incident at Alan Cork's testimonial. Wednesday sign Alan Harper from Everton for £275,000. Man City sign Luton's Littlewoods Cup hero goalkeeper Andy Dibble for a fee to be determined. Huddersfield appoint Eoin Hand as manager and Peter Withe as assistaqnt manager and coach. The Football League bar Coventry and Spurs from competing in a four-team tournament in Majorca in August.

9 England qualify for the Toulon Under-21 final by beating Morocco 1–0. Mark Wright limps off as England beat a local amateur side 4–0 in their last warm-up before the start of the European Championship. West German police stage a mock battle with colleagues shouting slogans in English! Spurs are favourites over Everton to sign Man City's £1.7 million rated striker Paul Stewart. Man City sign central defender Brian Gayle from Wimbledon, Southampton sign Russell Osman from Leicester, and Swindon's Jimmy Quinn agrees to join Leicester, all for fees to be determined. The High Court throw debt-ridden Peterborough a lifeline, allowing them time to raise new capital.

10 The European Championships open with a 1–1 draw between hosts West Germany and Italy. England are now anxious about Lineker's fitness as well as Wright's, while Ireland manager Jack Charlton appears to have no worries. Paul Stewart, on his wedding day, agrees to join Spurs. Consolation for Everton – they sign Bradford midfielder Stuart McCall for £850,000. Leeds sign Portsmouth captain Noel Blake on a free transfer, and Peter Osgood is made redundant as Portsmouth youth team coach. Scarborough appoint Sheffield United's Colin Morris as player-coach.

11 Spain beat a disappointing Denmark 3–2 with the help of a blatantly offside goal. Watford sign Willie Falconer from Aberdeen for £300,000.

12 Ireland shock a full-strength England 1–0 in Stuttgart as a shaky defence presents Ray Houghton with a 6th-minute goal and the forwards spurn chances galore. There is no crowd-trouble at the ground, but violence breaks out in the town after the match. In Cologne, a Rats goal and brilliant defence gives the USSR a surprise 1–0 victory over the disappointing Dutch. In Toulon, France twice equalize Michael Thomas goals for England to win the Under-21 tournament 4–2 after extra time.

13 England Under-21 players are officially congratulated for their behaviour on and off the pitch after the Toulon tournament, and Michael Thomas (Arsenal) is voted best player, Nigel Martyn (Bristol R.) best keeper. Hull appoint Eddie Gray as manager. The Scottish FA ban Leeds from a pre-season tournament in Perth because of their supporters' reputation.

14 West Germany outplay Denmark 2–0. In the best match so far, a Vialli goal gives Italy a well-deserved 1–0 win over Spain. British fans are involved in more violence, at night in Dusseldorf. Sports Minister Colin Moynihan's report to UEFA on last season's crowd behaviour inside English grounds presents a gloomy picture. The FA will stand by England manager Bobby Robson whatever tomorrow's result against Holland. Robson declines to announce his team, but media predictions are that Hoddle (for Webb) and possibly the fit again Steven will be in. The Irish have several injury problems.

15 Holland dump England out of the European Championships with a fine 3–1 win in Dusseldorf, thanks to a brilliantly taken hat-trick from Marco van Basten, who had almost walked out of the competition when omitted from their first game. The USSR are lucky to scrape a 1–1 draw with Ireland, who outplay them and score a spectacular goal through Ronnie Whelan. Home Secretary Douglas Hurd phones the West German Interior Ministry to apologise for the part played by English hooligans in the Dusseldorf violence last night. Meanwhile there are further clashes involving English, German, and Dutch mobs in Dusseldorf.

16 The FA withdraws its request to UEFA for the return of English clubs to European competition. And one of the points emerging from the Downing Street soccer summit is the possible withdrawal of the England team from international competition. Other measures being considered by the government, as announced by Home Secretary Mr Hurd, include new powers to impose restrictions on travel, and further restrictions on admission to grounds and on the sale of alcohol in the vicinity of grounds. English and German mobs create more night-time

disturbances, this time in Frankfurt. The FA cancel England's September trip to Italy, and will play Denmark at Wembley instead. The bookies give manager Bobby Robson only an even chance of still being in charge as media hysteria for his resignation grows. Watford sign Swindon striker Dave Bamber for a fee to be set. Chelsea sign a 5-year, £450,000 sponsorship deal with Umbro. Plymouth manager Dave Smith is set to manage home-team club Dundee. Paul Rideout is expected to join Southampton from Bari for £350,000.

17 West Germany and Italy go through to the semifinals of the European Championships, beating Spain and Denmark, respectively, 2–0.

18 The USSR beat England 3–1 in Frankfurt to qualify for the European semi-finals, but Ireland are denied by a fluke goal 8 minutes from time with a Dutchman blatantly offisde, so Holland also go through. Bobby Robson, who played five in midfield behind Gary Lineker, deflects calls for his resignation. There is more violence in Frankfurt during the night.

20 Bradford, having sold striker John Hendrie to Newcastle for £500,000, sign midfielder Andy Thomas from them for £80,000.

21 Justice is done in Hamburg when Holland beat West Germany 2–1 to reach the final of the European Championships. Outplayed in the first half, the Germans resort to dubious tactics in the second and their gamesmanships pays off when the rattled Dutch give away a penalty from which Matthäus scores. The referee later balances the books by awarding the Dutch a dubious penalty and Ronald Koeman equalizes. Van Basten scores a brilliant late winner. Gordon Cowans rejoins Villa on a £250,000 transfer from Italian club Bari.

22 The USSR beat Italy in the rain at Stuttgart to secure a place in the European final against Holland. England coach Don Howe is in hospital for tests after suffering chest pains soon after his return from West Germany. The League tribunal assess Steve Bould's transfer fee at £390,000, roughly midway between Arsenal's offer (£175,000) and Stoke's asking price (£650,000). Barcelona manager Johan Cruyff confirms that Gary Lineker will remain at Nou Camp.

23 Mark Hughes returns to Man Utd from Barcelona for £1.5 million, while United and England captain Bryan Robson is charged with drink-driving and failing to provide a specimen. French club Caen sign Graham Rix from Arsenal on a free transfer and Brian Stein from Luton.

24 FA chairman Bert Millichip is elected onto EUFA's executive committee. Next season's League fixture list includes full programmes for the Saturday's before England's World Cup qualifying matches. Colchester sign Dave Swindlehurst from Wimbledon on a free transfer.

25 Holland deservedly win the European Championship, beating the USSR 2–0 in the final, with a first-half header from Gullit from a van Basten headed pass and a spectacular far-post van Basten volley from an Arnold Muhren cross. The Dutch keeper van Breukelen saves a Belanov penalty to prevent the USSR getting back in the game.

26 UEFA suspend Michel and Hugo Sanchez for 9 and 3 games, respectively, for referee abuse after Real Madrid were knocked out of the European Cup.

27 The FA ban a proposed international tournament at Wembley in mid-August between Arsenal, Spurs, AC Milan, and Bayern Munich. Forest sign Middlesbrough full-back Brian Laws for a fee to be decided. Stoke sign Swindon's Chris Kamara.

28 Stoke sign Sheff Utd winger Peter Beagrie for £215,000, of which former club Middlesbrough get £60,000. Lee Chapman joins French club Chamois Niortass from Sheff Wed. Peterborough shareholders vote to accept constitutional changes that will allow control to be handed to a new owner by the end of the week and thus safeguard the club's future.

29 The FA charge Chelsea and Middlesbrough over the crowd-trouble at the end of their play-off match at Stamford Bridge, and the Police Federation launch a fierce attack on Chelsea chairman Ken Bates over his attitude towards their fans and call for the closure of Stamford Bridge for a season. The Football League name Holland, Spain, Belgium, and parts of Greece out-of-bounds for League clubs this summer in an attempt to pre-empt trouble. Rangers agree to pay Norwich £500,000 for striker Kevin Drinkell subject to a medical. Man City sign John Deehan from Ipswich.

30 Leicester sign Norwich back Tony Spearing for £100,000. Coventry captain Brian Kilcline signs a new 3-year contract. Liverpool sign Bristol Rovers defender Nick Tanner for £20,000. Oldham sign Sheff Utd striker Tony Philliskirk for £25,000. Doncaster sign former Irish international Gerry Daly, released by Stoke. Chelsea's Pat Nevin is thinking over a move to Everton. Middlesbrough ask for a personal FA hearing after the Stamford Bridge crowd-trouble charge and are confident of being cleared. Mexico will miss the 1990 World Cup after receiving a 2-year ban in all competitions for fielding four over-age players in the World Youth Championships qualifying tournament in April. England are to play a friendly international against Ireland in Dublin in May.

PLAYER DIRECTORY

INTRODUCTION

The following directory lists, in alphabetical order by surname, all those players listed as contract professionals by the Football League and the Scottish Football League (Premier Division) at the end of the 1987–88 season.

The information in each player's record is listed as follows: name, date of birth, place of birth, position (in brackets, GK = goalkeeper, DF = defender, MF = midfield, FW = forward), height, weight, and source. Then follow details of the player's League debut (LD), assuming that he has yet made a League appearance. The match, date and respective score are listed, with the team for which he made his first appearance underlined. For example, Cambridge U v Bolton W, 13.3.82, 2–1 means that he made his first appearance for Bolton away to Cambridge on 13.3.82, and Cambridge won 2–1.

Then follows a season-by-season listing, giving the team or teams for which he appeared each season, the Division, the number of League appearances and the number of League goals. Where the player was on loan, the team name is in italics, and appearances as substitutes have been amalgamated with full appearances. Appearances in end-of-season play-offs are not included, in accordance with Football League practice.

Unfortunately, in a very few cases, full details in the first two lines of data following each player's name have not been available at the time of going to press.

ABBOTT, Greg
14.12.63 Coventry (MF)
5.9 10.7 Apprentice
LD Plymouth Arg v <u>Bradford C</u>
19.2.83 3–1

1981–82 Coventry C	1	—	—
1982–83 Bradford C	3	11	—
1983–84 Bradford C	3	35	3
1984–85 Bradford C	3	42	6
1985–86 Bradford C	2	39	10
1986–87 Bradford C	2	33	7
1987–88 Bradford C	2	32	5

ABEL, Graham
17.9.60 Runcorn (DF)
6.2 13.0 Northwich V
and Runcorn
LD <u>Chester C</u> v Aldershot
2.11.85 1–0

1985–86 Chester C	4	23	2
1986–87 Chester C	3	41	1
1987–88 Chester C	3	45	2

ABERCROMBY, William
14.9.58 Glasgow (MF)
5.9 10.5 St Mirren BC
LD <u>St Mirren</u> v Arbroath
27.11.76 3–0

1975–76 St Mirren	1	—	—
1976–77 St Mirren	1	3	—
1977–78 St Mirren	P	30	3
1978–79 St Mirren	P	31	2
1979–80 St Mirren	P	15	—
1980–81 St Mirren	P	29	1
1981–82 St Mirren	P	30	—
1982–83 St Mirren	P	25	1
1983–84 St Mirren	P	34	4
1984–85 St Mirren	P	31	2
1985–86 St Mirren	P	23	1
1987–88 St Mirren	P	9	—

ABLETT, Gary
19.11.65 Liverpool (MF)
6.1¼ 10.11 Apprentice
LD <u>Derby Co</u> v Bournemouth
30.1.85 2–3

1983–84 Liverpool	1	—	—
1984–85 Liverpool	1	—	—
1984–85 Derby Co	3	6	—
1985–86 Liverpool	1	—	—
1986–87 Liverpool	1	5	1
1986–87 Hull C	2	5	—
1987–88 Liverpool	1	17	—

ABRAHAM, Gareth
13.2.69 Merthyr Tydfil (DF)
6.4 12.12 Apprentice
LD Wrexham v <u>Cardiff C</u>
12.9.87 3–0

1987–88 Cardiff C	4	2	1

ABRAHAMS, Antony
8.12.69 Liverpool (MF)
— — Apprentice
LD —

1987–88 Nottingham F	1	—	—

ACHAMPONG, Kenny
26.6.66 London (FW)
5.9 10.10 Apprentice
LD <u>Fulham</u> v Oxford U
19.2.85 1–0

1984–85 Fulham	2	10	3
1985–86 Fulham	2	35	3
1986–87 Fulham	3	21	6
1987–88 Fulham	3	15	3

ADAMS, Mick
8.11.61 Sheffield (MF)
5.8 11.6 Apprentice
LD Swindon T v <u>Gillingham</u>
19.4.80 3–0

1979–80 Gillingham	3	4	—
1980–81 Gillingham	3	13	—
1981–82 Gillingham	3	31	2
1982–83 Gillingham	3	44	3
1983–84 Coventry C	1	17	1
1984–85 Coventry C	1	31	3
1985–86 Coventry C	1	31	3
1986–87 Coventry C	1	11	2
1986–87 Leeds U	2	17	1
1987–88 Leeds U	2	40	—

ADAMS, Neil
23.11.65 Stoke (FW)
5.8 10.1 Local
LD Charlton Ath v <u>Stoke C</u>
21.9.85 2–0

1985–86 Stoke C	2	32	4
1986–87 Everton	1	12	—
1987–88 Everton	1	8	—

ADAMS, Tony
10.10.66 London (DF)
6.1 12.1 Apprentice
LD <u>Arsenal</u> v Sunderland
5.11.58 1–2

1983–84 Arsenal	1	3	—
1984–85 Arsenal	1	16	—
1985–86 Arsenal	1	10	—
1986–87 Arsenal	1	42	6
1987–88 Arsenal	1	39	2

ADCOCK, Tony
27.2.63 Bethnal Green (MF)
5.10 10.8 Apprentice
LD <u>Colchester U</u> v Carlisle U
2.5.81 1–0

1980–81 Colchester U	3	1	—
1981–82 Colchester U	4	40	5
1982–83 Colchester U	4	30	17
1983–84 Colchester U	4	43	26
1984–85 Colchester U	4	28	24
1985–86 Colchester U	4	33	15
1986–87 Colchester U	4	35	11
1987–88 Manchester C	2	15	5
1987–88 Northampton T	3	18	10

ADKINS, Nigel
11.3.65 Birkenhead (GK)
6.0 12.7 Apprentice
LD <u>Tranmere R</u> v Colchester U
13.11.82 2–4

1982–83 Tranmere R	4	10	—
1983–84 Tranmere R	4	4	—
1984–85 Tranmere R	4	38	—
1985–86 Tranmere R	4	34	—
1986–87 Wigan Ath	3	8	—
1987–88 Wigan Ath	3	2	—

AGANA, Tony
2.10.63 London (FW)
5.11 12.2 Apprentice
LD Watford v Wimbledon
15.8.87 1–0

1987–88	Watford	1	15	1
1987–88	Sheffield U	2	12	2

AGBOOLA, Reuben
30.5.62 London (DF)
5.9½ 11.0 Apprentice
LD Manchester U v Southampton
29.11.80 1–1

1979–80	Southampton	1	—	—
1980–81	Southampton	1	6	—
1981–82	Southampton	1	5	—
1982–83	Southampton	1	37	—
1983–84	Southampton	1	33	—
1984–85	Southampton	1	9	—
1984–85	Sunderland	1	8	—
1985–86	Sunderland	2	12	—
1986–87	Sunderland	2	11	—
1986–87	*Charlton Ath*	1	1	—
1987–88	Sunderland	3	38	—

AGNEW, Paul
15.8.65 Lisburn (DF)
5.9½ 10.4 Cliftonville
LD Oldham Ath v Grimsby T
7.5.84 2–1

1983–84	Grimsby T	2	1	—
1984–85	Grimsby T	2	12	—
1985–86	Grimsby T	2	16	—
1986–87	Grimsby T	2	29	—
1987–88	Grimsby T	2	38	1

AGNEW, Steve
9.11.65 Shipley (FW)
5.9 10.6 Apprentice
LD Barnsley v Charlton Ath
14.4.84 2–0

1983–84	Barnsley	2	1	—
1984–85	Barnsley	2	10	1
1985–86	Barnsley	2	2	—
1986–87	Barnsley	2	33	—
1987–88	Barnsley	2	25	6

AINSCOW, Alan
15.7.53 Bolton (FW)
5.8 11.5 Apprentice
LD Blackpool v Swindon T
14.8.71 4–1

1971–72	Blackpool	2	18	3
1972–73	Blackpool	2	37	10
1973–74	Blackpool	2	19	3
1974–75	Blackpool	2	31	4
1975–76	Blackpool	2	35	2
1976–77	Blackpool	2	17	2
1977–78	Blackpool	2	35	4
1978–79	Birmingham C	1	31	2
1979–80	Birmingham C	2	37	6
1980–81	Birmingham C	1	40	8
1981–82	Everton	1	17	2
1982–83	Everton	1	11	1
1982–83	*Barnsley*	2	2	—

Eastern (Hong Kong)

1984–85	Wolves	2	42	5
1985–86	Wolves	3	16	—
1985–86	Blackburn R	2	5	2
1986–87	Blackburn R	2	17	2
1987–88	Blackburn R	2	28	1

AINSCOW, Andrew
1.10.68 Orrell (MF)
— — YTS
LD Wigan Ath v Doncaster R
12.9.87 2–1

1987–88	Wigan Ath	3	15	4

AITKEN, Roy
24.11.58 Irvine (MF)
6.0 13.0 Celtic BC
LD Aberdeen v Celtic
21.2.76 0–1

1975–76	Celtic	P	12	—
1976–77	Celtic	P	33	5
1977–78	Celtic	P	33	2
1978–79	Celtic	P	36	5
1979–80	Celtic	P	35	3
1980–81	Celtic	P	33	4
1981–82	Celtic	P	33	3
1982–83	Celtic	P	33	6
1983–84	Celtic	P	31	5
1984–85	Celtic	P	33	3
1985–86	Celtic	P	36	—
1986–87	Celtic	P	42	1
1987–88	Celtic	P	43	1

AIZLEWOOD, Mark
1.10.59 Newport (DF)
6.0 12.8 Apprentice
LD Darlington v Newport Co
27.3.76 4–0

1975–76	Newport Co	4	6	—
1976–77	Newport Co	4	5	—
1977–78	Newport Co	4	27	1
1977–78	Luton T	2	—	—
1978–79	Luton T	2	39	—
1979–80	Luton T	2	10	—
1980–81	Luton T	2	23	—
1981–82	Luton T	2	26	3
1982–83	Luton T	1	—	—
1982–83	Charlton Ath	2	22	1
1983–84	Charlton Ath	2	31	1
1984–85	Charlton Ath	2	38	3
1985–86	Charlton Ath	2	35	3
1986–87	Charlton Ath	1	26	1
1987–88	Leeds U	2	15	—

ALDRIDGE, John
18.9.58 Liverpool (FW)
5.11 11.6 South Liverpool
LD Newport Co v Lincoln C
29.9.79 1–1

1978–79	Newport Co	4	—	—
1979–80	Newport Co	4	38	14
1980–81	Newport Co	3	27	7
1981–82	Newport Co	3	36	11
1982–83	Newport Co	3	41	17
1983–84	Newport Co	3	28	20
1983–84	Oxford U	3	8	4
1984–85	Oxford U	2	42	30
1985–86	Oxford U	1	39	23
1986–87	Oxford U	1	25	15
1986–87	Liverpool	1	10	2
1987–88	Liverpool	1	36	26

ALEXANDER, Ian
26.1.63 Glasgow (FW)
— — Leicester
LD C.Palace v Rotherham U
10.10.81 3–1

1981–82	Rotherham U	2	8	—
1982–83	Rotherham U	2	3	—
1983–84	Motherwell	P	16	1
1984–85	Motherwell	1	8	1
1984–85	Morton	P	7	1

1985–86 Pezoporikos (Cyprus)

1986–87	Bristol R	3	22	1
1987–88	Bristol R	3	45	1

ALLARDYCE, Sam
19.10.54 Dudley (DF)
6.1½ 14.0 Apprentice
LD Bolton W v Notts Co
17.11.73 1–3

1971–72	Bolton W	3	—	—
1972–73	Bolton W	3	—	—
1973–74	Bolton W	2	7	—
1974–75	Bolton W	2	18	3
1975–76	Bolton W	2	40	5
1976–77	Bolton W	2	41	6
1977–78	Bolton W	2	41	4
1978–79	Bolton W	1	20	1
1979–80	Bolton W	1	17	2
1980–81	Sunderland	2	25	2
1981–82	Sunderland	2	—	—
1981–82	Millwall	3	36	1
1982–83	Millwall	3	27	1
1983–84	Coventry C	1	28	1
1984–85	Huddersfield T	2	37	—
1985–86	Bolton W	3	14	—
1986–87	Preston NE	4	37	2
1987–88	Preston NE	3	39	—

PLAYER DIRECTORY

ALLEN, Clive
20.5.61 London (FW)
5.10 12.3 Apprentice
LD QPR v Chelsea
4.11.78 0–0

1978–79 QPR	1	10	4
1979–80 QPR	2	39	28
1980–81 Arsenal	1	—	—
1980–81 Crystal Palace	1	25	9
1981–82 QPR	2	37	13
1982–83 QPR	2	25	13
1983–84 QPR	1	25	14
1984–85 Tottenham H	1	13	7
1985–86 Tottenham H	1	19	9
1986–87 Tottenham H	1	39	33
1987–88 Tottenham H	1	34	11

ALLEN, Malcolm
21.3.67 Dioniolen (FW)
5.8½ 10.6 Apprentice
LD West Ham U v Watford
16.11.85 2–1

1984–85 Watford	1	—	—
1985–86 Watford	1	13	2
1986–87 Watford	1	4	—
1987–88 Watford	1	24	3
1986–87 *Aston Villa*	2	4	—

ALLEN, Martin
14.8.65 Reading (MF)
5.10 11.0 School
LD Luton T v QPR
23.3.85 2–0

1983–84 QPR	1	—	—
1984–85 QPR	1	5	—
1985–86 QPR	1	31	3
1986–87 QPR	1	32	5
1987–88 QPR	1	38	4

ALLEN, Paul
28.8.62 Aveley (MF)
5.7 10.10 Apprentice
LD West Ham U v Burnley
29.9.79 2–1

1979–80 West Ham U	2	31	2
1980–81 West Ham U	2	3	1
1981–82 West Ham U	1	28	—
1982–83 West Ham U	1	33	—
1983–84 West Ham U	1	19	—
1984–85 West Ham U	1	38	3
1985–86 Tottenham H	1	33	1
1986–87 Tottenham H	1	37	3
1987–88 Tottenham H	1	39	3

ALLEN, Sean
28.2.69 Preston (DF)
5.11 12.5 YTS
LD —

1987–88 Preston NE	3	—	—

ALLEYNE, Robert
27.9.68 Dudley (FW)
5.9 11.3 Apprentice
LD West Ham U v Leicester C
1.1.87 4–1

1986–87 Leicester C	1	3	—
1987–88 *Wrexham*	4	10	2
1987–88 Chesterfield	3	10	2

ALLINSON, Ian
1.10.57 Hitchin (FW)
5.10 11.0 Apprentice
LD Colchester U v Preston NE
19.4.75 2–2

1974–75 Colchester U	3	1	—
1975–76 Colchester U	3	5	—
1976–77 Colchester U	4	39	7
1977–78 Colchester U	3	45	6
1978–79 Colchester U	3	46	5
1979–80 Colchester U	3	38	2
1980–81 Colchester U	3	46	6
1981–82 Colchester U	4	42	21
1982–83 Colchester U	4	46	22
1983–84 Arsenal	1	9	—
1984–85 Arsenal	1	27	10
1985–86 Arsenal	1	33	6
1986–87 Arsenal	1	14	—
1987–88 Stoke C	2	9	—
1987–88 Luton T	1	27	3

ALLISON, Wayne
16.10.68 Huddersfield (MF)

LD Halifax T v Wolves
17.3.87 3–4

1986–87 Halifax T	4	8	3
1987–88 Halifax T	4	35	4

ALLON, Joe
12.11.66 Gateshead (FW)
5.11 11.2 YTS
LD Newcastle U v Stoke C
1.12.84 2–1

1984–85 Newcastle U	1	1	—
1985–86 Newcastle U	1	3	1
1986–87 Newcastle U	1	5	1
1987–88 Swansea C	4	32	12

ANDERSON, Colin
26.4.62 Newcastle (FW)
5.9 10.7 Apprentice
LD Fulham v Burnley
4.10.80 0–2

1979–80 Burnley	2	—	—
1980–81 Burnley	3	2	—
1981–82 Burnley	3	4	—

1982–83 Torquay U	4	42	5
1983–84 Torquay U	4	39	4
1984–85 Torquay U	4	28	2
1984–85 *QPR*	1	—	—
1984–85 WBA	1	—	—
1985–86 WBA	1	11	—
1986–87 WBA	2	28	1
1987–88 WBA	2	23	1

ANDERSON, Darren
6.9.66 Merton (DF)
6.1 13.5
Coventry C Apprentice
LD Leeds U v Charlton Ath
12.5.84 1–0

1983–84 Charlton Ath	2	1	—
1984–85 Charlton Ath	2	9	1
1985–86 Charlton Ath	2	—	—
1985–86 *Crewe Alex*	4	5	—
1986–87 Aldershot	4	24	—
1987–88 Aldershot	3	25	1

ANDERSON, Dougie
29.8.63 Hong Kong (FW)
6.0 10.5 Port Glasgow
LD Luton T v Oldham Ath
27.2.82 2–0

1980–81 Oldham Ath	2	—	—
1981–82 Oldham Ath	2	2	—
1982–83 Oldham Ath	2	5	—
1983–84 Oldham Ath	2	2	—
1984–85 Tranmere R	4	45	2
1985–86 Tranmere R	4	46	11
1986–87 Tranmere R	4	35	2
1987–88 Plymouth Arg	2	19	1

ANDERSON, John
7.11.59 Dublin (DF)
5.11 11.8 Apprentice
LD Preston NE v Fulham
12.1.80 3–2

1977–78 WBA	1	—	—
1978–79 WBA	1	—	—
1979–80 Preston	2	5	—
1980–81 Preston	2	8	—
1981–82 Preston	3	38	—
1982–83 Newcastle U	2	33	1
1983–84 Newcastle U	2	41	1
1984–85 Newcastle U	1	35	1
1985–86 Newcastle U	1	38	3
1986–87 Newcastle U	1	32	1
1987–88 Newcastle U	1	35	1

ANDERSON, Nicholas
29.3.69 Lincoln (DF)
— — YTS
LD Chester C v Mansfield T
18.10.86 1–1

1986–87 Mansfield T	3	7	—
1987–88 Mansfield T	3	12	—

ANDERSON, Viv
29.8.56 Nottingham (DF)
6.0 11.1 Apprentice
LD Sheffield W v Nottingham F
21.9.74 2–3

1974–75	Nottingham F	2	16	—
1975–76	Nottingham F	2	21	—
1976–77	Nottingham F	2	38	1
1977–78	Nottingham F	1	37	3
1978–79	Nottingham F	1	40	1
1979–80	Nottingham F	1	41	3
1980–81	Nottingham F	1	31	—
1981–82	Nottingham F	1	39	—
1982–83	Nottingham F	1	25	1
1983–84	Nottingham F	1	40	6
1984–85	Arsenal	1	41	3
1985–86	Arsenal	1	39	2
1986–87	Arsenal	1	40	4
1987–88	Manchester U	1	31	2

ANDREWS, Ian
1.12.64 Nottingham (GK)
6.1½ 12.6 Apprentice
LD Swindon T v Bristol C
24.1.84 1–1

1982–83	Leicester C	2	—	—
1983–84	Leicester C	1	2	—
1983–84	*Swindon T*	4	1	—
1984–85	Leicester C	1	31	—
1985–86	Leicester C	1	39	—
1986–87	Leicester C	1	42	—
1987–88	Leicester C	2	12	—

ANGELL, Brett
20.8.68 Marlborough (FW)
6.1 12.2 Cheltenham T
LD —

1987–88	Derby Co	1	—	—

ANGUS, Ian
19.11.61 Glasgow (MF)
5.10 10.3 Eastercraigs
LD Morton v Aberdeen
6.12.80 1–0

1979–80	Aberdeen	P	—	—
1980–81	Aberdeen	P	19	1
1981–82	Aberdeen	P	1	1
1982–83	Aberdeen	P	5	3
1983–84	Aberdeen	P	12	—
1984–85	Aberdeen	P	28	2
1985–86	Aberdeen	P	17	2
1986–87	Aberdeen	P	2	1
1986–87	Dundee	P	29	4
1987–88	Dundee	P	40	6

ANTHROBUS, Stephen
10.11.68 Lewisham (FW)
6.2 12.13 Apprentice
LD Plymouth Arg v Millwall
20.10.87 1–2

1987–88	Millwall	2	3	—

ARCHDEACON, Owen
4.3.66 Greenock (FW)
5.9 10.8 Gourock United
LD Celtic v Motherwell
10.4.84 4–2

1982–83	Celtic	P	—	—
1983–84	Celtic	P	1	—
1984–85	Celtic	P	3	1
1985–86	Celtic	P	23	3
1986–87	Celtic	P	29	2
1987–88	Celtic	‚P	10	1

ARMSTRONG, David
26.12.54 Durham (MF)
5.8 11.5 Apprentice
LD Blackpool v Middlesbrough
3.4.72 3–1

1971–72	Middlesbrough	2	6	—
1972–73	Middlesbrough	2	20	1
1973–74	Middlesbrough	2	42	5
1974–75	Middlesbrough	1	42	5
1975–76	Middlesbrough	1	42	6
1976–77	Middlesbrough	1	42	8
1977–78	Middlesbrough	1	42	6
1978–79	Middlesbrough	1	42	11
1979–80	Middlesbrough	1	42	11
1980–81	Middlesbrough	1	39	6
1981–82	Southampton	1	41	15
1982–83	Southampton	1	41	8
1983–84	Southampton	1	42	15
1984–85	Southampton	1	35	10
1985–86	Southampton	1	41	10
1986–87	Southampton	1	22	1
1987–88	Bournemouth	2	9	2

ARMSTRONG, Gordon
15.7.67 Newcastle (FW)
6.0 11.2 Apprentice
LD WBA v Sunderland
24.4.85 1–0

1984–85	Sunderland	1	4	—
1985–86	Sunderland	2	14	2
1986–87	Sunderland	2	41	5
1987–88	Sunderland	3	37	5

ARNOTT, Douglas
5.8.64 Lanark (FW)
5.7 10.7 Pollok Juniors
LD Motherwell v Hearts
15.4.87 0–1

1986–87	Motherwell	P	1	—
1987–88	Motherwell	P	2	—

ARNOTT, Kevin
28.9.58 Bensham (MF)
5.10 11.12 Apprentice
LD Leicester C v Sunderland
15.1.77 2–0

1976–77	Sunderland	1	20	3
1977–78	Sunderland	2	21	3
1978–79	Sunderland	2	15	—
1979–80	Sunderland	2	37	8
1980–81	Sunderland	1	34	2
1981–82	Sunderland	1	6	—
1981–82	*Blackburn R*	2	17	2
1982–83	Sheffield U	3	7	1
1982–83	*Blackburn R*	3	12	1
1982–83	*Rotherham U*	2	9	2
1983–84	Sheffield U	3	46	6
1984–85	Sheffield U	2	27	3
1985–86	Sheffield U	2	18	1
1986–87	Sheffield U	2	23	—
1987–88	Chesterfield	3	19	1

ASH, Mark
22.1.68 Sheffield (DF)
5.9½ 11.4 Apprentice
LD Rotherham U v Fulham
23.8.86 0–0

1985–86	Rotherham U	3	—	—
1986–87	Rotherham U	3	17	—
1987–88	Rotherham U	3	2	—

ASHLEY, Kevin
31.12.68 Birmingham (DF)
— — Apprentice
LD Birmingham C v WBA
12.4.87 0–1

1986–87	Birmingham C	2	7	—
1987–88	Birmingham C	2	1	—

ASHURST, Jack
12.10.54 Coatbridge (DF)
6.0 12.2 Apprentice
LD Millwall v Sunderland
9.9.72 0–1

1971–72	Sunderland	2	—	—
1972–73	Sunderland	2	11	—
1973–74	Sunderland	2	19	1
1974–75	Sunderland	2	6	—
1975–76	Sunderland	2	21	—
1976–77	Sunderland	1	31	—
1977–78	Sunderland	2	38	2
1978–79	Sunderland	2	11	1
1979–80	Sunderland	2	3	—
1979–80	Blackpool	3	25	—
1980–81	Blackpool	3	28	3
1981–82	Carlisle U	3	46	1
1982–83	Carlisle U	2	30	—
1983–84	Carlisle U	2	41	1
1984–85	Carlisle U	2	42	—
1985–86	Carlisle U	2	35	—
1986–87	Leeds U	2	41	1
1987–88	Leeds U	2	41	—

PLAYER DIRECTORY

ASKEW, Billy
2.10.59 Lumley (MF)
5.5 10.0 Apprentice
LD Middlesbrough v Arsenal
19.5.80 5–0

1977–78	Middlesbrough	1	—	—
1978–79	Middlesbrough	1	—	—
1979–80	Middlesbrough	1	1	—
1980–81	Middlesbrough	1	5	—
1981–82	Middlesbrough	1	6	—
1981–82	*Blackburn R*	2	—	—
1982–83	Hull C	4	36	6
1983–84	Hull C	3	33	1
1984–85	Hull C	3	46	6
1985–86	Hull C	2	33	2
1986–87	Hull C	2	27	—
1987–88	Hull C	2	30	3

ASPIN, Neil
12.4.65 Gateshead (DF)
6.1 12.3 Apprentice
LD Leeds U v Ipswich T
20.2.82 0–2

1981–82	Leeds U	1	1	—
1982–83	Leeds U	2	15	—
1983–84	Leeds U	2	21	1
1984–85	Leeds U	2	32	1
1985–86	Leeds U	2	38	2
1986–87	Leeds U	2	41	1
1987–88	Leeds U	2	26	—

ASPINALL, Warren
13.9.67 Wigan (MF)
5.8 10.6 Apprentice
LD Orient v Wigan Ath
2.3.85 1–1

1984–85	Wigan Ath	3	10	1
1985–86	Wigan Ath	3	—	—
1985–86	Everton	1	1	—
1985–86	*Wigan Ath*	3	41	21
1986–87	Everton	1	6	—
1986–87	Aston Villa	1	12	3
1987–88	Aston Villa	2	32	11

ASTBURY, Mike
22.1.64 Leeds (GK)
5.11 13.0 Apprentice
LD Tranmere R v York C
29.9.80 5–0

1980–81	York C	4	1	—
1981–82	York C	4	15	—
1982–83	York C	4	4	—
1983–84	York C	4	5	—
1984–85	York C	3	7	—
1985–86	York C	3	16	—
1985–86	*Peterborough U*	4	4	—
1985–86	Darlington	3	14	—
1986–87	Darlington	3	24	—
1987–88	Chester C	3	5	—

ATHERTON, Peter
65.4.70 Wigan (MF)
6.0 12.3 Apprentice
LD Blackpool v Wigan Ath
24.10.87 0–0

1987–88	Wigan Ath	3	16	—

ATKIN, Paul
3.9.69 Nottingham (MF)
6.1 12.10 Apprentice
LD —

1987–88	Notts Co	3	—	—

ATKINS, Bob
16.10.62 Leicester (DF)
6.0½ 12.1½ Local
LD Sheffield U v Gillingham
2.10.82 0–2

1982–83	Sheffield U	3	8	—
1983–84	Sheffield U	3	16	3
1984–85	Sheffield U	2	16	—
1984–85	*Preston NE*	4	4	—
1984–85	Preston NE	4	9	—
1985–86	Preston NE	4	34	2
1986–87	Preston NE	4	41	1
1987–88	Preston NE	3	45	1

ATKINS, Ian
16.1.57 Birmingham (MF)
6.0 11.13 Apprentice
LD Walsall v Shrewsbury T
22.9.75 2–0

1974–75	Shrewsbury T	4	—	—
1975–76	Shrewsbury T	3	32	4
1976–77	Shrewsbury T	3	43	7
1977–78	Shrewsbury T	3	41	10
1978–79	Shrewsbury T	3	44	11
1979–80	Shrewsbury T	2	39	3
1980–81	Shrewsbury T	2	39	6
1981–82	Shrewsbury T	2	40	17
1982–83	Sunderland	1	37	4
1983–84	Sunderland	1	40	2
1984–85	Sunderland	1	—	—
1984–85	Everton	1	6	1
1985–86	Everton	1	1	—
1985–86	Ipswich T	1	21	2
1986–87	Ipswich T	2	40	1
1987–88	Ipswich T	2	16	1
1987–88	*Birmingham C*	2	4	1
1987–88	Birmingham C	2	4	—

ATKINS, Mark
14.8.68 Doncaster (DF)
6.1 12.0 School
LD Scunthorpe U v Wolves
5.10.86 0–2

1986–87	Scunthorpe U	4	26	—
1987–88	Scunthorpe U	4	22	2

ATKINSON, Dalian
21.3.68 Shrewsbury (FW)
5.11 11.1
LD Newcastle U v Ipswich T
15.3.86 3–1

1985–86	Ipswich T	1	1	—
1986–87	Ipswich T	2	8	—
1987–88	Ipswich T	2	17	8

ATKINSON, Paul
19.1.66 Chester-le-Street (MF)
5.9¼ 10.2 Apprentice
LD Sunderland v Norwich C
27.8.83 1–1

1983–84	Sunderland	1	8	1
1984–85	Sunderland	1	9	1
1985–86	Sunderland	2	13	—
1986–87	Sunderland	2	8	—
1987–88	Sunderland	3	22	3

AYLOTT, Trevor
26.11.57 London (FW)
6.1½ 14.0 Apprentice
LD Newcastle U v Chelsea
22.10.77 1–0

1976–77	Chelsea	2	—	—
1976–77	*QPR*	1	—	—
1977–78	Chelsea	1	11	2
1978–79	Chelsea	1	15	—
1979–80	Chelsea	2	3	—
1979–80	Barnsley	3	18	4
1980–81	Barnsley	3	37	11
1981–82	Barnsley	2	41	11
1982–83	Millwall	3	32	5
1982–83	Luton T	1	12	2
1983–84	Luton T	1	20	8
1984–85	Crystal Palace	2	35	8
1985–86	Crystal Palace	2	18	4
1985–86	*Barnsley*	2	9	—
1986–87	Bournemouth	3	37	10
1987–88	Bournemouth	2	43	9

BAILEY, Dennis
13.11.65 Lambeth (FW)
5.10 10.10 Farnborough T
LD Hull C v C Palace
19.12.87 2–1

| 1987–88 | C Palace | 2 | 5 | 1 |

BAILIE, Colin
31.3.64 Belfast (DF)
5.11 10.11 Apprentice
LD Oxford U v Swindon T
7.4.82 5–0

1981–82	Swindon T	3	1	—
1982–83	Swindon T	4	26	1
1983–84	Swindon T	4	38	3
1984–85	Swindon T	4	42	—
1985–86	Reading	3	26	—
1986–87	Reading	2	37	1
1987–88	Reading	2	21	—

BAILLIE, Lex
6.7.66 Hamilton (DF)
6.2 12.0 Burnbank BC
LD Falkirk v Celtic
22.12.87 0–2

| 1987–88 | Celtic | P | 13 | — |

BAIRD, Ian
1.4.64 Rotherham (FW)
6.0 12.10 Apprentice
LD Southampton v Sunderland
19.2.83 2–0

1981–82	Southampton	1	—	—
1982–83	Southampton	1	11	2
1983–84	Southampton	1	6	1
1983–84	*Cardiff C*	2	12	6
1984–85	Southampton	1	5	2
1984–85	*Newcastle U*	1	5	1
1984–85	Leeds U	2	10	6
1985–86	Leeds U	2	35	12
1986–87	Leeds U	2	40	15
1987–88	Portsmouth	1	20	1
1987–88	Leeds U	2	10	3

BAKER, Clive
14.3.59 N. Walsham (GK)
5.9 11.0 Amateur
LD Newcastle U v Norwich C
26.4.78 2–2

1977–78	Norwich C	1	2	—
1978–79	Norwich C	1	2	—
1979–80	Norwich C	1	—	—
1980–81	Norwich C	1	10	—
1981–82	Norwich C	2	—	—
1982–83	Norwich C	1	—	—
1983–84	Norwich C	1	—	—
1984–85	Barnsley	2	37	—
1985–86	Barnsley	2	42	—
1986–87	Barnsley	2	39	—
1987–88	Barnsley	2	44	—

BAKER, Graham
3.12.58 Southampton (MF)
5.9 10.8 Apprentice
LD Southampton v Blackpool
12.11.77 2–0

1977–78	Southampton	2	3	1
1978–79	Southampton	1	22	5
1979–80	Southampton	1	23	4
1980–81	Southampton	1	39	8
1981–82	Southampton	1	26	4
1982–83	Manchester C	1	27	4
1983–84	Manchester C	2	36	8
1984–85	Manchester C	2	29	4
1985–86	Manchester C	1	10	—
1986–87	Manchester C	1	15	3
1987–88	Southampton	1	36	5

BAKER, Paul
5.1.63 Newcastle (MF)
6.1 12.10 Bishop Auckland
LD Carlisle U v Bradford C
17.8.85 1–2

1984–85	Southampton	1	—	—
1985–86	Carlisle U	2	35	2
1986–87	Carlisle U	3	36	9
1987–88	Hartlepool U	4	39	19

BAKER, Steve
16.6.62 Southampton (DF)
5.5 10.2 Apprentice
LD Ipswich T v Southampton
13.5.81 2–3

1979–80	Southampton	1	—	—
1980–81	Southampton	1	1	—
1981–82	Southampton	1	5	—
1982–83	Southampton	1	7	—
1983–84	Southampton	1	8	—
1983–84	*Burnley*	3	10	—
1984–85	Southampton	1	9	—
1985–86	Southampton	1	13	—
1986–87	Southampton	1	26	—
1987–88	Southampton	1	4	—
1987–88	Leyton Orient	4	9	2

BALL, Kevin
12.11.64 Hastings (DF)
5.9 11.6 Apprentice
LD Shrewsbury T v Portsmouth
2.1.84 2–0

1983–84	Portsmouth	2	1	—
1984–85	Portsmouth	2	—	—
1985–86	Portsmouth	2	9	—
1986–87	Portsmouth	2	16	—
1987–88	Portsmouth	1	29	1

BALL, Steven
2.9.69 Colchester (MF)
— — Apprentice
LD —

| 1987–88 | Arsenal | 1 | — | — |

BAMBER, Dave
1.2.59 St Helens (FW)
6.3 13.10 Manchester Univ
LD Mansfield T v Blackpool
1.12.79 1–1

| 1979–80 | Blackpool | 3 | 7 | 1 |
| 1980–81 | Blackpool | 3 | 15 | 3 |

1981–82	Blackpool	4	38	15
1982–83	Blackpool	4	26	10
1983–84	Coventry C	1	19	3
1983–84	Walsall	3	10	3
1984–85	Walsall	3	10	4
1984–85	Portsmouth	2	4	1
1985–86	Portsmouth	2	—	—
1985–86	Swindon T	4	23	9
1986–87	Swindon T	3	42	9
1987–88	Swindon T	2	41	13

BANKS, Ian
9.1.61 Mexborough (MF)
5.9 11.13 Apprentice
LD Wigan Ath v Barnsley
3.3.79 1–1

1978–79	Barnsley	4	2	—
1979–80	Barnsley	3	38	3
1980–81	Barnsley	3	45	14
1981–82	Barnsley	2	42	15
1982–83	Barnsley	2	37	5
1983–84	Leicester C	3	26	3
1984–85	Leicester C	3	33	9
1985–86	Leicester C	4	31	2
1986–87	Leicester C	1	3	—
1986–87	Huddersfield T	2	37	8
1987–88	Huddersfield T	2	41	9

BANNISTER, Gary
22.7.60 Warrington (FW)
5.8½ 11.3 Apprentice
LD Coventry C v Norwich C
26.8.78 4–1

1978–79	Coventry C	1	4	1
1979–80	Coventry C	1	7	—
1980–81	Coventry C	1	11	2
1981–82	Sheffield W	2	42	21
1982–83	Sheffield W	2	39	20
1983–84	Sheffield W	2	37	14
1984–85	QPR	1	42	17
1985–86	QPR	1	36	16
1986–87	QPR	1	34	15
1987–88	QPR	1	24	8
1987–88	Coventry C	1	8	1

BANNON, Eamonn
18.4.58 Edinburgh (MF)
5.9 11.11 Links B.C.
LD Hearts v Kilmarnock
5.2.77 4–0

1976–77	Hearts	P	13	1
1977–78	Hearts	1	39	12
1978–79	Hearts	P	19	5
1978–79	Chelsea	1	19	1
1979–80	Chelsea	2	6	—
1979–80	Dundee U	P	24	4
1980–81	Dundee U	P	34	8
1981–82	Dundee U	P	36	12
1982–83	Dundee U	P	32	10
1983–84	Dundee U	P	33	7
1984–85	Dundee U	P	35	10
1985–86	Dundee U	P	31	11
1986–87	Dundee U	P	39	9
1987–88	Dundee U	P	26	1

PLAYER DIRECTORY

BANTON, Dale
15.5.61 Kensington (MF)
5.10 10.10 Apprentice
LD West Ham U v Chelsea
20.8.79 0–1

1979–80	West Ham U	2	4	—
1980–81	West Ham U	2	—	—
1981–82	West Ham U	1	1	—
1982–83	Aldershot	4	45	24
1983–84	Aldershot	4	46	19
1984–85	Aldershot	4	15	4
1984–85	York C	3	30	12
1985–86	York C	3	35	10
1986–87	York C	3	29	7
1987–88	York C	3	33	16

BARBER, Fred
26.8.63 Ferryhill (GK)
5.11 11.7 Apprentice
LD Darlington v Stockport Co
26.3.83 3–1

1981–82	Darlington	4	—	—
1982–83	Darlington	4	12	—
1983–84	Darlington	4	46	—
1984–85	Darlington	4	45	—
1985–86	Darlington	3	32	—
1985–86	Everton	1	—	—
1986–87	Walsall	3	36	—
1987–88	Walsall	3	46	—

BARBER, Philip
10.6.65 Tring (FW)
5.11 12.6 Aylesbury
LD C Palace v Grimsby T
25.2.84 0–1

1983–84	Crystal Palace	2	9	2
1984–85	Crystal Palace	2	23	4
1985–86	Crystal Palace	2	39	9
1986–87	Crystal Palace	2	31	5
1987–88	Crystal Palace	2	37	7

BARDSLEY, David
11.9.64 Manchester (DF)
5.9 10.10 Apprentice
LD Bury v Blackpool
18.5.82 0–1

1981–82	Blackpool	4	1	—
1982–83	Blackpool	4	28	—
1983–84	Blackpool	4	16	—
1983–84	Watford	1	25	—
1984–85	Watford	1	17	—
1985–86	Watford	1	13	2
1986–87	Watford	1	41	5
1987–88	Watford	1	4	—
1987–88	Oxford U	1	34	1

BARHAM, Mark
12.7.62 Folkestone (MF)
5.7 11.0 Apprentice
LD Manchester U v Norwich C
24.11.79 5–0

1979–80	Norwich C	1	4	—
1980–81	Norwich C	1	35	1
1981–82	Norwich C	2	27	4
1982–83	Norwich C	1	38	4
1983–84	Norwich C	1	11	2
1984–85	Norwich C	1	14	1
1985–86	Norwich C	2	35	10
1986–87	Norwich C	1	13	2
1987–88	Huddersfield T	2	26	1

BARKER, Simon
4.11.64 Farnworth (MF)
5.9 10.11 Apprentice
LD Swansea C v Blackburn R
29.10.87 0–1

1982–83	Blackburn R	2	—	—
1983–84	Blackburn R	2	28	3
1984–85	Blackburn R	2	38	2
1985–86	Blackburn R	2	41	10
1986–87	Blackburn R	2	42	11
1987–88	Blackburn R	2	33	9

BARLOW, Andy
24.11.65 Oldham (DF)
5.9 11.1 Local
LD Oldham Ath v Birmingham C
25.8.84 0–1

1984–85	Oldham Ath	2	33	—
1985–86	Oldham Ath	2	26	—
1986–87	Oldham Ath	2	29	2
1987–88	Oldham Ath	2	26	—

BARNARD, Leigh
29.10.58 Worsley (MF)
5.8 11.7 Apprentice
LD Exeter C v Portsmouth
24.9.77 0–1

1977–78	Portsmouth	3	11	—
1978–79	Portsmouth	4	28	7
1979–80	Portsmouth	4	5	—
1980–81	Portsmouth	3	18	1
1981–82	Portsmouth	3	17	—
1981–82	Peterborough U	4	4	—
1982–83	Swindon T	4	46	4
1983–84	Swindon T	4	36	7
1984–85	Swindon T	4	32	2
1984–85	Exeter C	4	6	2
1985–86	Swindon T	4	38	3
1986–87	Swindon T	3	41	3
1987–88	Swindon T	2	17	2

BARNES, Bobby
17.12.62 Kingston (FW)
5.7 10.5 Apprentice
LD West Ham U v Watford
20.9.80 3–2

1980–81	West Ham U	2	6	1
1981–82	West Ham U	1	3	—
1982–83	West Ham U	1	—	—
1983–84	West Ham U	1	13	2
1984–85	West Ham U	1	20	2

1985–86	West Ham U	1	1	—
1985–86	Scunthorpe U	4	6	—
1985–86	Aldershot	4	14	8
1986–87	Aldershot	4	25	11
1987–88	Aldershot	3	10	—
1987–88	Swindon T	2	28	10

BARNES, David
16.11.61 London (DF)
5.10 11.1 Apprentice
LD Bolton W v Coventry C
15.4.80 1–1

1979–80	Coventry C	1	3	—
1980–81	Coventry C	1	—	—
1981–82	Coventry C	1	6	—
1981–82	Ipswich T	1	—	—
1982–83	Ipswich T	1	6	—
1983–84	Ipswich T	1	11	—
1984–85	Ipswich T	1	—	—
1984–85	Wolves	2	23	1
1985–86	Wolves	3	38	1
1986–87	Wolves	4	26	2
1987–88	Wolves	4	1	—
1987–88	Aldershot	3	30	7

BARNES, John
7.11.63 Jamaica (FW)
5.11 12.0 Sudbury Court
LD Watford v Oldham Ath
5.9.81 1–1

1981–82	Watford	2	36	13
1982–83	Watford	1	42	10
1983–84	Watford	1	39	11
1984–85	Watford	1	40	12
1985–86	Watford	1	39	9
1986–87	Watford	1	37	10
1987–88	Liverpool	1	38	15

BARNES, Paul
16.11.67 Leicester (FW)
5.10½ 10.2 Apprentice
LD Notts Co v Wigan Ath
4.2.86 1–1

1985–86	Notts Co	3	14	4
1986–87	Notts Co	3	—	—
1987–88	Notts Co	3	11	2

BARNETT, Gary
11.3.63 Stratford (MF)
5.5 9.4 Apprentice
LD Gillingham v Oxford U
28.8.82 0–1

1980–81	Coventry C	1	—	—
1981–82	Coventry C	1	—	—
1982–83	Oxford U	3	22	2
1982–83	Wimbledon	4	5	1
1983–84	Oxford U	3	19	7
1984–85	Oxford U	2	2	—
1984–85	Fulham	2	2	1
1985–86	Oxford U	1	2	—
1985–86	Fulham	2	36	6
1986–87	Fulham	3	42	9
1987–88	Fulham	3	42	9

BARNSLEY, Andy
9.6.62 Sheffield (DF)
6.0 11.11 Denaby U
LD Bolton W v Rotherham U
17.8.85 1–1

1984–85 Rotherham U	3	—	—
1985–86 Rotherham U	3	28	—
1986–87 Sheffield U	2	42	—
1987–88 Sheffield U	2	32	—

BARR, Billy
21.1.69 Halifax (DF)
— — Apprentice
LD Halifax T v Darlington
15.8.87 2–2

1987–88 Halifax T	4	30	—

BARR, Bobby
5.12.69 Halifax (DF)
— — Apprentice
LD Northampton T v Halifax T
27.2.87 1–0

1986–87 Halifax T	4	1	—
1987–88 Halifax T	4	—	—

BARR, Bobby
16.5.62 Lennoxtown (MF)
5.11 11.7
LD Queen's Park v Queen of the S
3.9.83 0–2

1983–84 Queen's Park	2	4	—
1983–84 Alloa	1	2	—
1984–85 Alloa	2	29	2
1985–86 Alloa	1	31	3
1986–87 Hamilton A	P	23	—
1987–88 Hamilton A	P	—	—

BARRATT, Tony
18.10.65 Salford (DF)
5.8 10.2 Billingham T
LD Grimsby T v Wimbledon
4.9.85 1–1

1985–86 Grimsby T	2	22	—
1986–87 Hartlepool U	4	23	—
1987–88 Hartlepool U	4	43	3

BARRETT, Earl
28.4.67 Rochdale (DF)
5.10 11.2 Apprentice
LD Manchester C v Luton T
3.5.86 1–1

1984–85 Manchester C	2	—	—
1985–86 Manchester C	1	1	—
1985–86 *Chester C*	4	12	—
1986–87 Manchester C	1	2	—
1987–88 Oldham Ath	2	18	—

BARRETT, Scott
2.4.63 Derby (GK)
6.0 12.11 Ilkeston T
LD Portsmouth v Wolves
27.10.84 0–1

1984–85 Wolves	2	4	—
1985–86 Wolves	3	21	—
1986–87 Wolves	4	5	—
1987–88 Stoke C	2	27	—

BARRICK, Dean
30.9.69 Pontefract (MF)
5.9 11.4 School
LD —

1987–88 Sheffield W	1	—	—

BARROW, Graham
13.6.54 Chorley (MF)
6.2 13.7 Altrincham
LD Bradford C v Wigan Ath
29.8.81 3–3

1981–82 Wigan Ath	4	41	12
1982–83 Wigan Ath	3	28	3
1983–84 Wigan Ath	3	42	5
1984–85 Wigan Ath	3	38	9
1985–86 Wigan Ath	3	30	7
1986–87 Chester C	3	41	5
1987–88 Chester C	3	38	4

BARTLETT, Kevin
12.10.62 Portsmouth (FW)
5.9 10.5 Apprentice
LD Portsmouth v Hull C
28.2.81 2–1

1980–81 Portsmouth	3	2	—
1981–82 Portsmouth	3	1	—
1982–86 Fareham			
1986–87 Cardiff C	4	23	4
1987–88 Cardiff C	4	37	12

BARTRAM, Vince
7.8.68 Birmingham (GK)
6.2 13.4 Local
LD Wolves v Cambridge U
23.8.86 1–2

1985–86 Wolves	3	—	—
1986–87 Wolves	4	1	—
1987–88 Wolves	4	—	—

BASTOCK, Paul
— Redditch (GK)
5.8 10.0 Coventry C
LD Colchester U v Cambridge U
25.3.88 0–0

1987–88 Cambridge U	4	10	—

BATER, Phil
26.10.55 Cardiff (DF)
5.10½ 12.12 Apprentice
LD Bristol R v Aston Villa
14.9.79 2–0

1973–74 Bristol R	3	—	—
1974–75 Bristol R	2	30	—
1975–76 Bristol R	2	17	—
1976–77 Bristol R	2	30	1
1977–78 Bristol R	2	41	—
1978–79 Bristol R	2	36	—
1979–80 Bristol R	2	34	1
1980–81 Bristol R	2	24	—
1981–82 Bristol R	3	—	—
1981–82 Wrexham	2	36	1
1982–83 Wrexham	3	37	—
1983–84 Wrexham	4	—	—
1983–84 Bristol R	3	32	1
1984–85 Bristol R	3	39	—
1985–86 Bristol R	3	27	—
1986–87 Brentford	3	19	2
1987–88 Cardiff C	4	40	—

BATES, Jamie
24.2.68 London (DF)
6.1 12.12 YTS
LD Carlisle U v Brentford
15.9.86 0–0

1986–87 Brentford	3	24	1
1987–88 Brentford	3	23	1

BATTY, David
2.12.68 Leeds (MF)
5.7 10.7 YTS
LD Leeds U v Swindon T
21.11.87 4–2

1987–88 Leeds U	2	23	1

BATTY, Laurence
15.2.64 London (GK)
6.0 13.7
LD Fulham v Grimsby T
26.8.85 2–1

1984–85 Fulham	2	—	—
1985–86 Fulham	2	2	—
1986–87 Fulham	3	2	—
1987–88 Fulham	3	—	—
1987–88 *Crystal Palace*	2	—	—

BATTY, Paul
9.1.64 Edington (MF)
5.7 10.7 Apprentice
LD Swindon T v Crewe Alex
25.9.82 1–0

1981–82 Swindon T	3	—	—
1982–83 Swindon T	4	39	1
1983–84 Swindon T	4	41	4
1984–85 Swindon T	4	28	2
1985–86 Chesterfield	3	26	—
1986–87 Exeter C	4	33	2
1987–88 Exeter C	4	32	6

BEAGRIE, Peter
28.11.65 Middlesbrough (DF)
5.8¼ 9.9¾ Local
LD Oldham Ath v Middlesbrough
2.10.84 2–0

1983–84 Middlesbrough	2	—	—
1984–85 Middlesbrough	2	7	1
1985–86 Middlesbrough	2	26	1
1986–87 Sheffield U	2	41	9
1987–88 Sheffield U	2	43	2

Peter Beardsley

Photo: Bob Thomas Sports Photography.

BEARDSLEY, Peter
18.1.61 Newcastle (FW)
5.8 11.4 Wallsend B.C.
LD Carlisle U v Blackburn R
21.8.79 1–1

1979–80	Carlisle U	3	37	8
1980–81	Carlisle U	3	43	10
1981–82	Carlisle U	3	22	4
Vancouver Whitecaps				
1982–83	Manchester U	1	—	—
Vancouver Whitecaps				
1983–84	Newcastle U	2	35	20
1984–85	Newcastle U	1	38	17
1985–86	Newcastle U	1	42	19
1986–87	Newcastle U	1	32	5
1987–88	Liverpool	1	38	15

BEARDSMORE, Russell
28.9.68 Wigan (DF)
5.6 8.10 Apprentice
LD —

1987–88	Manchester U	1	—	—

BEASANT, Dave
20.3.59 Willesden (GK)
6.4 13.0 Edgware T
LD Wimbledon v Blackpool
12.1.79 1–2

1979–80	Wimbledon	3	2	—
1980–81	Wimbledon	4	34	—
1981–82	Wimbledon	3	46	—
1982–83	Wimbledon	4	46	—
1983–84	Wimbledon	3	46	—
1984–85	Wimbledon	2	42	—
1985–86	Wimbledon	2	42	—
1986–87	Wimbledon	1	42	—
1987–88	Wimbledon	1	40	—

BEASLEY, Andy
5.2.64 Sedgley (GK)
6.2 12.2 Apprentice
LD Chesterfield v Mansfield T
26.12.84 0–0

1981–82	Luton T	2	—	—
1982–83	Luton T	1	—	—
1983–84	Luton T	1	—	—
1983–84	*Mansfield T*	4	—	—
1983–84	*Gillingham*	3	—	—
1984–85	Mansfield T	4	3	—
1985–86	Mansfield T	4	—	—
1986–87	*Peterborough U*	4	7	—
1987–88	Mansfield T	3	8	—
1987–88	*Scarborough*	4	4	—

BEATTIE, Stuart
10.7.67 Stevenston (DF)
6.2 11.10 Ardeer Recreation B.C.
LD Rangers v Hibernian
19.10.85 1–2

1985–86	Rangers	P	5	—
1986–87	Doncaster R	3	7	—
1987–88	Doncaster R	3	2	—

BEAUMONT, David
10.12.63 Edinburgh (DF)
5.10 11.5 'S' Form
LD St Johnstone v Dundee U
7.1.84 1–2

1980–81	Dundee U	P	—	—
1981–82	Dundee U	P	—	—
1982–83	Dundee U	P	—	—
1983–84	Dundee U	P	2	—
1984–85	Dundee U	P	18	1
1985–86	Dundee U	P	13	—
1986–87	Dundee U	P	28	—
1987–88	Dundee U	P	10	1

BEAUMONT, Robert
9.12.69 Sheffield (DF)
5.9 10.5 School
LD —

1987–88	Sheffield W	1	—	—

BEAVON, Stuart
30.11.58 Wolverhampton (MF)
5.6½ 10.4 Apprentice
LD Tottenham H v Manchester C
3.2.78 0–3

1976–77	Tottenham H	1	—	—
1977–78	Tottenham H	2	—	—
1978–79	Tottenham H	1	1	—
1979–80	Tottenham H	1	3	—
1979–80	*Notts Co*	2	6	—
1980–81	Reading	3	37	6
1981–82	Reading	3	40	5
1982–83	Reading	3	46	4
1983–84	Reading	4	36	7
1984–85	Reading	3	46	2
1985–86	Reading	3	44	3
1986–87	Reading	2	42	3
1987–88	Reading	2	34	2

BECK, John
25.5.54 Edmonton (MF)
5.10½ 11.9 Apprentice
LD Sheffield W v QPR
30.12.72 3–1

1972–73	QPR	2	1	—
1973–74	QPR	1	5	—
1974–75	QPR	1	29	1
1975–76	QPR	1	5	—
1976–77	Coventry C	1	40	3
1977–78	Coventry C	1	23	2
1978–79	Coventry C	1	6	1
1978–79	Fulham	2	32	2
1979–80	Fulham	2	40	2
1980–81	Fulham	3	37	8
1981–82	Fulham	3	5	1
1982–83	Fulham	2	—	—
1982–83	*Bournemouth*	3	4	1
1982–83	Bournemouth	3	11	3
1983–84	Bournemouth	3	45	3
1984–85	Bournemouth	3	36	1
1985–86	Bournemouth	3	41	5
1986–87	Cambridge U	4	35	5
1987–88	Cambridge U	4	35	2

BECKFORD, Darren
12.5.67 Manchester (FW)
6.1 11.1 Apprentice
LD Middlesbrough v Manchester C
20.10.84 2–1

1984–85	Manchester C	2	4	—
1985–86	Manchester C	1	3	—
1985–86	*Bury*	3	12	5
1986–87	Manchester C	1	4	—
1986–87	*Port Vale*	3	11	4
1987–88	Port Vale	3	40	9

BECKFORD, Jason
4.2.70 Manchester (FW)
5.9 12.4 Apprentice
LD Middlesbrough v Manchester C
9.4.88 2–1

1987–88	Manchester C	2	5	—

BEESLEY, Paul
21.7.65 Wigan (DF)
5.11 11.5 Local
LD Reading v Wigan Ath
3.10.84 0–1

1984–85	Wigan Ath	3	2	—
1985–86	Wigan Ath	3	17	—
1986–87	Wigan Ath	3	39	—
1987–88	Wigan Ath	3	42	1

BEESTON, Carl
30.6.67 Stoke (MF)
5.9 10.3 Apprentice
LD Stoke C v Coventry C
17.5.85 0–1

1984–85	Stoke C	1	1	—
1985–86	Stoke C	2	5	—
1986–87	Stoke C	2	—	—
1987–88	Stoke C	2	12	—

BEGLIN, Jim
29.7.63 Waterford (DF)
5.11 11.0 Shamrock R
LD Liverpool v Southampton
10.11.84 1–1

1982–83	Liverpool	1	—	—
1983–84	Liverpool	1	—	—
1984–85	Liverpool	1	10	1
1985–86	Liverpool	1	34	1
1986–87	Liverpool	1	20	—
1987–88	Liverpool	1	—	—

PLAYER DIRECTORY

BELL, Doug
5.9.59 Paisley (MF)
5.11 12.1 Cumbernauld
LD Partick Th v St Mirren
26.4.78 5-0

1977–78	St Mirren	P	2	1
1978–79	St Mirren	P	—	—
1979–80	Aberdeen	P	9	—
1980–81	Aberdeen	P	17	1
1981–82	Aberdeen	P	13	1
1982–83	Aberdeen	P	23	1
1983–84	Aberdeen	P	24	3
1984–85	Aberdeen	P	22	—
1985–86	Rangers	P	23	—
1986–87	*St Mirren*	P	4	—
1986–87	Rangers	P	12	1
1986–87	Hibernian	P	16	2
1987–88	Hibernian	P	16	1
1987–88	Shrewsbury T	2	15	2

BELL, Peter
23.12.65 Newcastle (FW)
5.11 11.5 Apprentice
LD —

1987–88	Bolton W	4	—	—

BELLAMY, Gary
4.7.62 Worksop (DF)
6.2 11.5 Apprentice
LD Millwall v Chesterfield
2.5.80 0-2

1980–81	Chesterfield	3	3	—
1981–82	Chesterfield	3	25	—
1982–83	Chesterfield	3	42	—
1983–84	Chesterfield	4	38	1
1984–85	Chesterfield	4	22	2
1985–86	Chesterfield	3	12	2
1986–87	Chesterfield	3	42	2
1987–88	Wolves	4	24	2

BENALI, Francis
30.12.68 Southampton
5.9½ 11.0 Apprentice
LD —

1987–88	Southampton	1	—	—

BENBOW, Ian
9.1.69 Hereford (MF)
5.10 12.4 YTS
LD Carlisle U v Hereford U
31.8.87 3-1

1987–88	Hereford U	4	21	2

BENJAMIN, Ian
11.12.61 Nottingham (MF)
5.11 12.0 Apprentice
LD Cardiff C v Sheffield U
21.4.79 4-0

1978–79	Sheffield U	2	2	2
1979–80	Sheffield U	3	3	1
1979–80	WBA	1	—	—
1980–81	WBA	1	2	—
1981–82	Notts Co	1	—	—
1982–83	Peterborough U	4	46	6
1983–84	Peterborough U	4	34	8
1984–85	Northampton T	4	44	18
1985–86	Northampton T	4	46	22
1986–87	Northampton T	4	46	18
1987–88	Northampton T	3	14	1
1987–88	Cambridge U	4	25	2

BENNETT, Dave
11.7.59 Manchester (FW)
6.0 11.2 Amateur
LD Manchester C v Everton
14.4.79 0-0

1978–79	Manchester C	1	1	—
1979–80	Manchester C	1	25	2
1980–81	Manchester C	1	26	7
1981–82	Manchester C	1	—	—
1981–82	Cardiff C	2	36	6
1982–83	Cardiff C	3	41	12
1983–84	Coventry C	1	34	6
1984–85	Coventry C	1	34	2
1985–86	Coventry C	1	38	6
1986–87	Coventry C	1	31	7
1987–88	Coventry C	1	28	4

BENNETT, Gary
4.12.61 Manchester (DF)
6.1 11.11½ Amateur
LD Cardiff C v Wrexham
4.11.81 3-2

1979–80	Manchester C	1	—	—
1980–81	Manchester C	1	—	—
1981–82	Cardiff C	2	19	1
1982–83	Cardiff C	3	36	8
1983–84	Cardiff C	2	32	2
1984–85	Sunderland	1	37	3
1985–86	Sunderland	2	28	3
1986–87	Sunderland	2	41	4
1987–88	Sunderland	3	38	3

BENNETT, Gary
20.9.63 Liverpool (MF)
6.1 12.6 Local
LD Cambridge U v Wigan Ath
19.10.84 1-1

1984–85	Wigan Ath	3	20	3
1985–86	Chester C	3	43	13
1986–87	Chester C	3	33	13
1987–88	Chester C	3	43	10

BENNETT, Martyn
4.8.61 Birmingham (DF)
6.0 12.12 Apprentice
LD WBA v Everton
7.4.79 1-0

1978–79	WBA	1	1	—
1979–80	WBA	1	4	—
1980–81	WBA	1	16	1
1981–82	WBA	1	23	2
1982–83	WBA	1	23	1
1983–84	WBA	1	29	—
1984–85	WBA	1	39	—
1985–86	WBA	1	25	2
1986–87	WBA	2	15	2
1987–88	WBA	2	6	1

BENNETT, Michael
27.7.69 London (MF)
5.10 11.11 Apprentice
LD Charlton Ath v West Ham U
7.3.87 2-1

1986–87	Charlton Ath	1	2	—
1987–88	Charlton Ath	1	16	1

BENNETT, Mike
24.12.62 Bolton (DF)
5.7 10.6 Apprentice
LD Manchester C v Bolton W
29.3.80 2-2

1979–80	Bolton W	1	8	—
1980–81	Bolton W	2	6	1
1981–82	Bolton W	2	35	—
1982–83	Bolton W	2	16	—
1983–84	Wolves	2	6	—
1983–84	Cambridge U	2	11	—
1984–85	Cambridge U	3	34	—
1985–86	Cambridge U	4	31	—
1986–87	Bradford C	2	—	—
1986–87	Preston NE	4	42	1
1987–88	Preston NE	4	34	—

BENNYWORTH, Ian
5.1.62 Hull (DF)
6.0 12.7 Apprentice
LD Hull C v Bury
5.5.80 0-1

1979–80	Hull C	3	1	—
1980–87	Non-League			
1987–88	Scarborough	4	39	1

BENSTEAD, Graham
20.8.63 Aldershot (GK)
6.1 12.11 Apprentice
LD Arsenal v Norwich C
6.4.85 2-0

1981–82	QPR	2	—	—
1982–83	QPR	2	—	—
1983–84	QPR	1	—	—
1984–85	QPR	1	—	—
1984–85	*Norwich C*	1	1	—
1985–86	Norwich C	2	—	—
1986–87	Norwich C	1	13	—
1987–88	Norwich C	1	2	—
1987–88	*Colchester U*	4	18	—
1987–88	*Sheffield U*	2	8	—

BENT, Junior
1.3.70 Huddersfield (FW)
5.11 11.5 Apprentice
LD Huddersfield T v
Middlesborough
10.10.87 1-4

1987–88	Huddersfield T	2	7	—

BERESFORD, John
4.9.66 Sheffield (MF)
5.5 10.4 Apprentice
LD Barnsley v Crystal Palace
23.8.86 2-3

1983–84	Manchester C	2	— —
1984–85	Manchester C	2	— —
1985–86	Manchester C	1	— —
1986–87	Barnsley	2	27 1
1987–88	Barnsley	2	34 3

BERESFORD, Marlon
2.9.69 Lincoln (GK)
6.1 11.10 Apprentice
LD —

1987–88	Sheffield W	1	— —

BERNAL, Andres
16.7.66 Canberra (Aus) (DF/MF)
5.10 12.5 —
LD Birmingham C v Ipswich T
28.11.87 1-0

1987–88	Ipswich T	2	9 —

BERRY, George
19.11.57 West Germany (DF)
6.0 13.4 Apprentice
LD Wolves v Chelsea
7.5.77 1-1

1975–76	Wolves	1	— —
1976–77	Wolves	2	1 —
1977–78	Wolves	1	7 —
1978–79	Wolves	1	30 3
1979–80	Wolves	1	41 —
1980–81	Wolves	1	25 1
1981–82	Wolves	1	20 —
1982–83	Stoke C	1	31 5
1983–84	Stoke C	1	8 —
1984–85	Stoke C	1	32 1
1984–85	*Doncaster R*	3	1 —
1985–86	Stoke C	2	41 3
1986–87	Stoke C	2	40 8
1987–88	Stoke C	2	36 5

BERRY, Les
4.5.56 Plumstead (DF)
6.2 11.13 Apprentice
LD Bristol C v Charlton Ath
11.10.75 4-0

1973–74	Charlton Ath	3	— —
1974–75	Charlton Ath	3	— —
1975–76	Charlton Ath	2	15 1
1976–77	Charlton Ath	2	39 2
1977–78	Charlton Ath	2	41 2
1978–79	Charlton Ath	2	38 1
1979–80	Charlton Ath	2	42 2
1980–81	Charlton Ath	3	44 2
1981–82	Charlton Ath	2	25 —
1982–83	Charlton Ath	2	39 1
1983–84	Charlton Ath	2	42 —
1984–85	Charlton Ath	2	26 —
1985–86	Charlton Ath	2	7 —
1986–87	Brighton & HA	2	23 —
1986–87	*Gillingham*	3	11 —
1987–88	Gillingham	3	20 —

BERRY, Neil
6.4.63 Edinburgh (DF)
6.0 12.0 Apprentice
LD Cambridge U v Bolton W
13.3.82 2-1

1980–81	Bolton W	2	— —
1981–82	Bolton W	2	3 —
1982–83	Bolton W	2	9 —
1983–84	Bolton W	3	14 —
1984–85	Bolton W	3	6 —
1984–85	Hearts	P	3 —
1985–86	Hearts	P	32 2
1986–87	Hearts	P	30 3
1987–88	Hearts	P	35 —

BERRY, Steve
4.4.63 Gosport (MF)
5.7 11.6 Apprentice
LD Portsmouth v Lincoln C
29.8.81 1-1

1980–81	Portsmouth	3	— —
1981–82	Portsmouth	3	27 2
1982–83	Portsmouth	3	1 —
1983–84	Portsmouth	2	— —
1983–84	*Aldershot*	4	7 —
1984–85	Sunderland	1	34 2
1985–86	Sunderland	2	1 —
1985–86	Newport Co	3	26 3
1986–87	Newport Co	3	34 3
1986–87	Swindon T	3	1 —
1987–88	Swindon T	2	3 —
1987–88	*Aldershot*	3	2 1
1987–88	Aldershot	3	34 5

BERTSCHIN, Keith
25.8.56 Enfield (FW)
6.1 11.8 Barnet
LD Arsenal v Ipswich T
17.4.76 1-2

1973–74	Ipswich T	1	— —
1974–75	Ipswich T	1	— —
1975–76	Ipswich T	1	3 2
1976–77	Ipswich T	1	29 6
1977–78	Birmingham C	1	42 11
1978–79	Birmingham C	1	9 2
1979–80	Birmingham C	2	37 12
1980–81	Birmingham C	1	30 4
1981–82	Norwich C	2	36 12
1982–83	Norwich C	1	40 8
1983–84	Norwich C	1	33 7
1984–85	Norwich C	1	5 2
1984–85	Stoke C	1	25 2
1985–86	Stoke C	2	42 19
1986–87	Stoke C	2	21 8
1986–87	Sunderland	2	11 2
1987–88	Sunderland	3	25 5

BETT, Jim
25.11.59 Hamilton (MF)
5.11 12.3 School
LD Airdrieonians v St Mirren
23.4.77 2-2

1976–77	Airdrieonians	1	1 —
1977–78	Airdrieonians	1	7 —

Iceland and Lokeren

1980–81	Rangers	P	34 4
1981–82	Rangers	P	35 11
1982–83	Rangers	P	35 6

Lokeren

1984–85	Rangers	P	— —
1985–86	Aberdeen	P	24 3
1986–87	Aberdeen	P	38 4
1987–88	Aberdeen	P	38 10

BIGGINS, Wayne
20.11.61 Sheffield (FW)
5.11 11.0 Apprentice
LD Lincoln C v Hartlepool U
21.3.81 2-0

1979–80	Lincoln C	4	— —
1980–81	Lincoln C	4	8 1
1981–83	Non-League		
1983–84	Burnley	3	20 8
1984–85	Burnley	3	46 18
1985–86	Burnley	4	12 3
1985–86	Norwich C	2	28 7
1986–87	Norwich C	1	31 4
1987–88	Norwich C	1	20 5

BILLINGE, Peter
24.10.64 Liverpool (DF)
6.2 12.7 South Liverpool
LD Everton v West Ham U
5.5.86 3-1

1985–86	Everton	1	1 —
1986–87	Crewe Alex	4	19 —
1987–88	Crewe Alex	4	32 —

BIRCH, Paul
20.11.62 West Bromwich (MF)
5.6 10.4 Apprentice
LD Aston Villa v Sunderland
29.8.83 1-0

1980–81	Aston Villa	1	— —
1981–82	Aston Villa	1	— —
1982–83	Aston Villa	1	— —
1983–84	Aston Villa	1	22 2
1984–85	Aston Villa	1	25 3
1985–86	Aston Villa	1	27 2
1986–87	Aston Villa	1	29 3
1987–88	Aston Villa	2	38 6

BIRCH, Paul
3.12.68 Reading (FW)
6.1 12.5 Portsmouth
LD York C v Brentford
18.12.87 1-1

1987–88	Portsmouth	1	— —
1987–88	*Brentford*	3	5 2
1987–88	Brentford	3	11 —

BIRD, Adrian
8.7.69 Bristol (DF)
6.1 11.7 School
LD Birmingham C v Millwall
29.12.86 1-1

1986–87	Birmingham C	2	6 —
1987–88	Birmingham C	2	9 —

PLAYER DIRECTORY

BIRTLES, Garry
27.7.56 Nottingham (FW)
6.0 12.0 Long Eaton U
LD Nottingham F v Hull C
12.3.77 2-0

1976–77 Nottingham F	2	1	—
1977–78 Nottingham F	1	—	—
1978–79 Nottingham F	1	35	14
1979–80 Nottingham F	1	42	12
1980–81 Nottingham F	1	9	6
1980–81 Manchester U	1	25	—
1981–82 Manchester U	1	33	11
1982–83 Manchester U	1	—	—
1982–83 Nottingham F	1	25	7
1983–84 Nottingham F	1	34	15
1984–85 Nottingham F	1	13	2
1985–86 Nottingham F	1	25	—
1986–87 Nottingham F	1	28	14
1987–88 Notts Co	3	43	7

BISHOP, Charles
12.2.68 Nottingham (DF)
6.0 12.11 Watford
LD Bury v Grimsby T
15.9.87 0-2

1987–88 Bury	3	17	—

BISHOP, Edward
28.11.62 Liverpool (MF)
5.8 11.7 Runcorn
LD Wrexham v Tranmere
2.4.88 3-0

1987–88 Tranmere R	4	5	1

BISHOP, Ian
29.5.65 Liverpool (MF)
5.9½ 10.6 Apprentice
LD Everton v Manchester U
5.5.84 1-1

1983–84 Everton	1	1	—
1983–84 *Crewe Alex*	4	4	—
1984–85 Everton	4	—	—
1984–85 Carlisle U	2	30	2
1985–86 Carlisle U	2	36	6
1986–87 Carlisle U	3	42	3
1987–88 Carlisle U	4	24	3

BLACK, Kenny
29.11.63 Stenhousemuir (DF)
5.8 10.11 Linlithgow Rose
LD Hibernian v Rangers
7.11.81 1-2

1980–81 Rangers	P	—	—
1981–82 Rangers	P	8	—
1982–83 Rangers	P	14	1
1983–84 Motherwell	P	17	—
1984–85 Hearts	P	32	7
1985–86 Hearts	P	29	2
1986–87 Hearts	P	42	1
1987–88 Hearts	P	42	4

BLACK, Kingsley
22.6.68 Luton (FW)
5.8 10.11 School
LD QPR v Luton T
26.9.87 2-0

1987–88 Luton T	1	13	—

BLACKMORE, Clayton
23.9.64 Neath (MF)
5.8 11.3 Apprentice
LD Nottingham F v Manchester U
16.5.84 2-0

1982–83 Manchester U	1	—	—
1983–84 Manchester U	1	1	—
1984–85 Manchester U	1	1	—
1985–86 Manchester U	1	12	3
1986–87 Manchester U	1	12	1
1987–88 Manchester U	1	22	3

BLACKWELL, Kevin
21.12.58 London (GK)
5.11 12.10 Barnet
LD Scarborough v Wolves
15.8.87 2-2

1987–88 Scarborough	4	21	—

BLADES, Paul
5.1.65 Peterborough (DF)
6.0 10.12 Apprentice
LD Leeds U v Derby C
18.9.82 2-1

1982–83 Derby Co	2	6	—
1983–84 Derby Co	2	4	—
1984–85 Derby Co	3	22	—
1985–86 Derby Co	3	30	—
1986–87 Derby Co	2	16	—
1987–88 Derby Co	1	31	—

BLAIR, Andy
18.12.59 Bedworth (MF)
5.8 10.4 Apprentice
LD Coventry C v Birmingham C
28.10.78 2-1

1977–78 Coventry C	1	—	—
1978–79 Coventry C	1	26	1
1979–80 Coventry C	1	32	1
1980–81 Coventry C	1	35	4
1981–82 Aston Villa	1	18	—
1982–83 Aston Villa	1	7	—
1983–84 Aston Villa	1	9	—
1983–84 *Wolves*	1	10	—
1984–85 Sheffield W	1	41	3
1985–86 Sheffield W	1	17	—
1985–86 Aston Villa	1	12	—
1986–87 Aston Villa	1	4	—
1987–88 Aston Villa	2	4	1
1987–88 *Barnsley*	2	6	—

BLAKE, Mark
19.12.67 Portsmouth (DF)
6.0 12.4 Apprentice
LD Tottenham H v Southampton
5.5.86 5-3

1985–86 Southampton	1	1	—
1986–87 Southampton	1	8	—
1987–88 Southampton	1	6	1

BLISSETT, Gary
29.6.64 Manchester (FW)
5.11 10.4 Altrincham
LD Rochdale v Crewe Alex
27.8.83 1-0

1983–84 Crewe Alex	4	22	3
1984–85 Crewe Alex	4	29	9
1985–86 Crewe Alex	4	38	11
1986–87 Crewe Alex	4	33	15
1986–87 Brentford	3	10	5
1987–88 Brentford	3	41	9

BLISSETT, Luther
1.2.58 W. Indies (FW)
5.11 12.0 Juniors
LD Watford v Barnsley
3.4.76 1-0

1975–76 Watford	4	3	1
1976–77 Watford	4	4	—
1977–78 Watford	4	33	6
1978–79 Watford	3	41	21
1979–80 Watford	2	42	10
1980–81 Watford	2	42	11
1981–82 Watford	2	40	19
1982–83 Watford	1	41	27
1983–84 AC Milan (I)	A	30	5
1984–85 Watford	1	41	21
1985–86 Watford	1	23	7
1986–87 Watford	1	35	11
1987–88 Watford	1	25	4

BLOOMER, Bob
21.6.66 Sheffield (MF)

LD Bournemouth v Chesterfield
31.1.86 3-2

1985–86 Chesterfield	3	6	—
1986–87 Chesterfield	3	31	3
1987–88 Chesterfield	3	38	1

BODAK, Peter
12.8.61 Birmingham (MF)
5.8 9.10 Apprentice
LD Coventry C v Crystal Palace
6.9.80 3-1

1980–81 Coventry C	1	23	3
1981–82 Coventry C	1	9	2
1982–83 Manchester U	1	—	—
1982–83 Manchester C	1	14	1
1983–86 Non-League			
1986–87 Crewe Alex	4	26	7
1987–88 Crewe Alex	4	27	—
1987–88 Swansea C	4	9	—

BODIN, Paul
13.9.64 Cardiff (MF)
6.0 12.1 Local
LD Stockport Co v Newport Co
29.1.88 5–1

1987–88 Newport Co	4	6	1
1987–88 Swindon T	2	5	1

BODLEY, Mike
14.9.67 Hayes (DF)
5.11 12.0 Apprentice
LD Chelsea v Norwich C
19.9.87 1–0

1985–86 Chelsea	1	—	—
1986–87 Chelsea	1	—	—
1987–88 Chelsea	1	6	1

BOGIE, Ian
6.12.67 Newcastle (MF)
5.7 10.2 Apprentice
LD Luton T v Newcastle U
30.8.86 0–0

1985–86 Newcastle U	1	—	—
1986–87 Newcastle U	1	1	—
1987–88 Newcastle U	1	7	—

BOLDER, Bob
2.10.58 Dover (GK)
6.1 14.8 Dover
LD Sheffield W v Rotherham U
27.12.77 1–0

1976–77 Sheffield W	3	—	—
1977–78 Sheffield W	3	23	—
1978–79 Sheffield W	3	19	—
1979–80 Sheffield W	3	31	—
1980–81 Sheffield W	2	39	—
1981–82 Sheffield W	2	42	—
1982–83 Sheffield W	2	42	—
1983–84 Liverpool	1	—	—
1984–85 Liverpool	1	—	—
1985–86 Liverpool	1	—	—
1985–86 Sunderland	2	22	—
1985–86 *Luton T*	1	—	—
1986–87 Charlton Ath	1	26	—
1987–88 Charlton Ath	1	35	—

BOND, Kevin
22.6.57 London (DF)
6.0 12.4 Bournemouth
LD Leicester C v Norwich C
10.4.76 0–0

1974–75 Norwich C	2	—	—
1975–76 Norwich C	1	1	—
1976–77 Norwich C	1	3	—
1977–78 Norwich C	1	28	—
1978–79 Norwich C	1	42	2
1979–80 Norwich C	1	40	9
1980–81 Norwich C	1	28	1

Seattle S

1981–82 Manchester C	1	33	3
1982–83 Manchester C	1	40	3
1983–84 Manchester C	2	34	4
1984–85 Manchester C	2	3	1
1984–85 Southampton	1	33	1
1985–86 Southampton	1	34	1
1986–87 Southampton	1	34	1
1987–88 Southampton	1	39	3

BONDS, Billy
17.9.46 Woolwich (DF)
6.0½ 13.7 Apprentice

1964–65 Charlton Ath	2	13	—
1965–66 Charlton Ath	2	40	—
1966–67 Charlton Ath	2	42	1
1967–68 West Ham U	1	37	1
1968–69 West Ham U	1	42	1
1969–70 West Ham U	1	42	3
1970–71 West Ham U	1	37	—
1971–72 West Ham U	1	42	3
1972–73 West Ham U	1	39	3
1973–74 West Ham U	1	40	13
1974–75 West Ham U	1	31	7
1975–76 West Ham U	1	18	1
1976–77 West Ham U	1	41	3
1977–78 West Ham U	1	29	1
1978–79 West Ham U	2	39	4
1979–80 West Ham U	2	34	1
1980–81 West Ham U	2	41	—
1981–82 West Ham U	1	29	1
1982–83 West Ham U	1	34	3
1983–84 West Ham U	1	27	—
1984–85 West Ham U	1	22	3
1985–86 West Ham U	1	—	—
1986–87 West Ham U	1	17	—
1987–88 West Ham U	1	22	—

BONNER, Pat
25.5.60 Donegal (GK)
6.2 13.1 Keadie Rovers
LD Celtic v Motherwell
17.3.79 2–1

1978–79 Celtic	P	2	—
1979–80 Celtic	P	—	—
1980–81 Celtic	P	36	—
1981–82 Celtic	P	36	—
1982–83 Celtic	P	36	—
1983–84 Celtic	P	33	—
1984–85 Celtic	P	34	—
1985–86 Celtic	P	30	—
1986–87 Celtic	P	43	—
1987–88 Celtic	P	32	—

BONNYMAN, Phil
6.2.54 Glasgow (MF)
5.10½ 12.4 Anniesland W
LD Cydebank v Hamilton A
27.10.73 1–1

1971–72 Rangers	1	—	—
1972–73 Rangers	1	—	—
1973–74 Hamilton A	2	13	—
1974–75 Hamilton A	2	35	5
1975–76 Hamilton A	1	23	2
1975–76 Carlisle U	2	9	—
1976–77 Carlisle U	2	37	1
1977–78 Carlisle U	3	33	8
1978–79 Carlisle U	3	45	7
1979–80 Carlisle U	3	28	10
1979–80 Chesterfield	3	11	3
1980–81 Chesterfield	3	42	8
1981–82 Chesterfield	3	46	14
1982–83 Grimsby T	2	40	1
1983–84 Grimsby T	2	29	3
1984–85 Grimsby T	2	37	8
1985–86 Grimsby T	2	29	3
1985–86 *Stoke C*	2	7	—
1986–87 Grimsby T	2	16	—
1987–88 Darlington	4	38	3

BOOKER, Bob
25.1.58 Watford (FW)
6.2½ 12.4 Bedmond Sports
LD Watford v Brentford
14.10.78 2–0

1978–79 Brentford	4	3	—
1979–80 Brentford	3	12	6
1980–81 Brentford	3	26	7
1981–82 Brentford	3	38	4
1982–83 Brentford	3	39	6
1983–84 Brentford	3	29	4
1984–85 Brentford	3	38	7
1985–86 Brentford	3	44	8
1986–87 Brentford	3	2	—
1987–88 Brentford	3	12	—

BOOTH, Dennis
9.4.49 Stanley (DF)
5.7½ 11.3 Apprentice

1965–66 Charlton Ath	2	—	—
1966–67 Charlton Ath	2	3	—
1967–68 Charlton Ath	2	17	—
1968–69 Charlton Ath	2	21	5
1969–70 Charlton Ath	2	30	—
1970–71 Charlton Ath	2	6	—
1971–72 Blackpool	2	12	—
1971–72 Southend U	4	16	—
1972–73 Southend U	3	43	—
1973–74 Southend U	3	19	1
1973–74 Lincoln C	4	16	3
1974–75 Lincoln C	4	46	2
1975–76 Lincoln C	4	42	1
1976–77 Lincoln C	3	45	2
1977–78 Lincoln C	3	13	1
1977–78 Watford	4	31	—
1978–79 Watford	3	37	—
1979–80 Watford	2	32	2
1980–81 Hull C	3	37	—
1981–82 Hull C	4	37	2
1982–83 Hull C	4	34	—
1983–84 Hull C	3	14	—
1984–85 Hull C	3	1	—
1985–86 Hull C	2	—	—
1986–87 Hull C	2	—	—
1987–88 Hull C	2	—	—

PLAYER DIRECTORY

BORROWS, Brian
20.12.60 Liverpool (DF)
5.10 10.12 Amateur
LD Everton v Stoke C
13.2.82 0–0

1979–80	Everton	1	—	—
1980–81	Everton	1	—	—
1981–82	Everton	1	15	—
1982–83	Everton	1	12	—
1982–83	Bolton W	2	9	—
1983–84	Bolton W	3	44	—
1984–85	Bolton W	3	42	—
1985–86	Coventry C	1	41	—
1986–87	Coventry C	1	41	1
1987–88	Coventry C	1	33	—

BORTHWICK, John
24.3.64 Hartlepool (FW)
5.10 10.12 Local
LD Colchester U v Hartlepool U
3.1.83 4–1

1982–83	Hartlepool U	4	2	—
1983–84	Hartlepool U	4	10	—
1984–85	Hartlepool U	4	6	1
1985–86	Hartlepool U	4	32	8
1986–87	Hartlepool U	4	14	—
1987–88	Hartlepool U	4	34	5

BOULD, Stephen
16.11.62 Stoke (DF)
6.3 12.8 Apprentice
LD Middlesbrough v Stoke C
26.9.81 3–2

1980–81	Stoke C	1	—	—
1981–82	Stoke C	1	2	—
1982–83	Stoke C	1	14	—
1982–83	Torquay U	4	9	—
1983–84	Stoke C	1	38	2
1984–85	Stoke C	1	38	3
1985–86	Stoke C	2	33	—
1986–87	Stoke C	2	28	1
1987–88	Stoke C	2	30	—

BOWDEN, John
21.1.63 Stockport (FW)
6.0 11.7 Local
LD Shrewsbury T v Oldham Ath
6.2.82 2–1

1979–80	Oldham Ath	2	—	—
1980–81	Oldham Ath	2	—	—
1981–82	Oldham Ath	2	5	2
1982–83	Oldham Ath	2	31	2
1983–84	Oldham Ath	2	31	1
1984–85	Oldham Ath	2	15	—
1985–86	Oldham Ath	2	—	—
1985–86	Port Vale	4	36	3
1986–87	Port Vale	3	34	4
1987–88	Wrexham	4	26	1

BOWEN, Mark
7.12.63 Neath (DF)
5.8 11.13 Apprentice
LD Tottenham H v Coventry C
29.8.83 1–1

1981–82	Tottenham H	1	—	—
1982–83	Tottenham H	1	—	—
1983–84	Tottenham H	1	7	—
1984–85	Tottenham H	1	6	—
1985–86	Tottenham H	1	2	1
1986–87	Tottenham H	1	2	1
1987–88	Norwich C	1	24	1

BOWMAN, David
10.3.60 Tunbridge Wells (MF)
5.10 11.2 Salvesen BC
LD Hearts v Airdrieonians
16.8.80 0–2

1980–81	Hearts	P	17	1
1981–82	Hearts	1	16	1
1982–83	Hearts	1	39	5
1983–84	Hearts	P	33	—
1984–85	Hearts	P	11	1
1984–85	Coventry C	1	10	—
1985–86	Coventry C	1	30	2
1986–87	Dundee U	P	29	—
1987–88	Dundee U	P	39	1

BOWYER, Ian
6.6.51 Ellesmere Port (MF)
5.10 11.11 Apprentice

1968–69	Manchester C	1	6	1
1969–70	Manchester C	1	34	12
1970–71	Manchester C	1	10	—
1971–72	Orient	2	42	14
1972–73	Orient	2	36	4
1973–74	Orient	2	—	—
1973–74	Nottingham F	2	28	6
1974–75	Nottingham F	2	32	6
1975–76	Nottingham F	2	40	13
1976–77	Nottingham F	2	41	12
1977–78	Nottingham F	1	29	4
1978–79	Nottingham F	1	29	4
1979–80	Nottingham F	1	19	1
1980–81	Nottingham F	1	21	3
1980–81	Sunderland	1	9	1
1981–82	Sunderland	1	6	—
1981–82	Nottingham F	1	24	1
1982–83	Nottingham F	1	40	4
1983–84	Nottingham F	1	42	6
1984–85	Nottingham F	1	39	2
1985–86	Nottingham F	1	26	3
1986–87	Nottingham F	1	35	3
1987–88	Hereford	4	29	1

BOYD, Charles
— Liverpool (FW)
5.6 9.4 School
LD —

1987–88	Liverpool	1	—	—

BOYD, Tom
24.11.65 Glasgow (DF)
5.11 11.4 'S' Form
LD Motherwell v Aberdeen
11.2.84 0–4

1983–84	Motherwell	P	13	—
1984–85	Motherwell	1	36	—
1985–86	Motherwell	P	31	—
1986–87	Motherwell	P	31	—
1987–88	Motherwell	P	42	2

BOYLE, Terry
29.10.58 Ammanford (DF)
5.10 12.8 Apprentice
LD Luton T v C Palace
27.3.78 1–0

1975–76	Tottenham H	1	—	—
1976–77	Tottenham H	1	—	—
1977–78	Tottenham H	2	—	—
1977–78	Crystal Palace	2	1	—
1978–79	Crystal Palace	2	—	—
1979–80	Crystal Palace	1	5	—
1980–81	Crystal Palace	1	20	1
1981–82	Wimbledon	3	5	1
1981–82	Bristol C	3	23	—
1982–83	Bristol C	4	14	—
1982–83	Newport Co	3	29	—
1983–84	Newport Co	3	45	1
1984–85	Newport Co	3	46	3
1985–86	Newport Co	3	46	7
1986–87	Cardiff C	4	46	1
1987–88	Cardiff C	4	46	4

BRACEWELL, Paul
19.7.62 Stoke (MF)
5.8 10.9 Apprentice
LD Wolves v Stoke C
22.3.80 3–0

1979–80	Stoke C	1	6	—
1980–81	Stoke C	1	40	2
1981–82	Stoke C	1	42	1
1982–83	Stoke C	1	41	2
1983–84	Sunderland	1	38	4
1984–85	Everton	1	37	2
1985–86	Everton	1	38	3
1986–87	Everton	1	—	—
1987–88	Everton	1	—	—

BRADLEY, Darren
24.11.65 Birmingham (DF)
5.10 11.4 Apprentice
LD Norwich C v Aston Villa
9.3.85 2–2

1983–84	Aston Villa	1	—	—
1984–85	Aston Villa	1	2	—
1985–86	Aston Villa	1	18	—
1985–86	WBA	1	10	—
1986–87	WBA	2	14	1
1987–88	WBA	2	19	—

BRADLEY, Russell

1987–88	Nottingham F	1	—	—

BRADSHAW, Carl
2.10.68 Sheffield (FW)
— — Apprentice
LD Barnsley v Crystal Palace
23.8.86 2–3

1986–87	Sheffield W	1	9	2
1986–87	Barnsley	2	6	1
1987–88	Sheffield W	1	20	2

BRADSHAW, Darren
19.3.67 Sheffield (MF)
5.10 11.3 Matlock T
LD Grimsby T v York C
21.11.87 5–1

1987–88 York C	3	25	1

BRADSHAW, Mark
7.6.69 Ashton (DF)
— — Trainee
LD Blackpool v Doncaster R
28.4.87 1–1

1986–87 Blackpool	3	4	—
1987–88 Blackpool	3	16	—

BRADY, Liam
13.2.56 Dublin (MF)
5.7 10.7 Apprentice
LD Arsenal v Birmingham C
6.10.73 1–0

1973–74 Arsenal	1	13	1
1974–75 Arsenal	1	32	3
1975–76 Arsenal	1	42	5
1976–77 Arsenal	1	38	5
1977–78 Arsenal	1	39	9
1978–79 Arsenal	1	37	13
1979–80 Arsenal	1	34	7
1980–81 Juventus (I)	A	28	8
1981–82 Juventus (I)	A	29	5
1982–83 Sampdoria (I)	A	29	2
1983–84 Sampdoria (I)	A	28	4
1984–85 Internazion. (I)	A	29	2
1985–86 Internazion. (I)	A	29	3
1986–87 Ascoli (I)	A	17	—
1986–87 West Ham U	1	12	2
1987–88 West Ham U	1	22	2

BRANAGAN, Jim
3.7.55 Barton (DF)
5.11 11.10 Amateur
LD Sheffield W v Oldham Ath
14.12.74 1–1

1973–74 Oldham Ath	3	—	—
1974–75 Oldham Ath	2	5	—
1975–76 Oldham Ath	2	13	—
1976–77 Oldham Ath	2	9	—
Cape Town C			
1977–78 Huddersfield T	4	24	—
1978–79 Huddersfield T	4	14	—
1979–80 Huddersfield T	4	—	—
1979–80 Blackburn R	3	31	1
1980–81 Blackburn R	2	42	—
1981–82 Blackburn R	2	40	1
1982–83 Blackburn R	2	37	1
1983–84 Blackburn R	2	41	—
1984–85 Blackburn R	2	40	1
1985–86 Blackburn R	2	33	—
1986–87 Blackburn R	2	30	1
1987–88 Preston NE	3	3	—
1987–88 York C	3	28	1

BRANAGAN, Keith
10.7.66 Fulham (GK)
6.0 11.10
LD Cambridge U v Carlisle U
14.1.84 0–2

1983–84 Cambridge U	2	1	—
1984–85 Cambridge U	3	19	—
1985–86 Cambridge U	4	9	—
1986–87 Cambridge U	4	46	—
1987–88 Cambridge U	4	35	—
1987–88 Millwall	2	—	—

BRAY, Ian
6.12.62 Neath (DF)
5.8 11.4½ Apprentice
LD Hereford U v Bury
5.9.81 3–0

1980–81 Hereford U	4	—	—
1981–82 Hereford U	4	16	2
1982–83 Hereford U	4	27	—
1983–84 Hereford U	4	23	1
1984–85 Hereford U	4	42	1
1985–86 Huddersfield T	2	32	1
1986–87 Huddersfield T	2	13	—
1987–88 Huddersfield T	2	30	—

BRAZIL, Derek
14.12.68 Dublin (DF)
6.0 12.0 Rivermount BC
LD —

1985–86 Manchester U	1	—	—
1986–87 Manchester U	1	—	—
1987–88 Manchester U	1	—	—

BRAZIL, Gary
19.9.62 Tunbridge Wells (FW)
5.11 9.12½ Crystal Palace
LD Sheffield U v Gillingham
17.1.81 0–1

1980–81 Sheffield U	3	3	—
1981–82 Sheffield U	4	1	—
1982–83 Sheffield U	3	33	5
1983–84 Sheffield U	3	19	2
1984–85 Sheffield U	2	6	2
1984–85 *Port Vale*	4	6	3
1984–85 Preston NE	3	17	3
1985–86 Preston NE	4	43	14
1986–87 Preston NE	4	45	17
1987–88 Preston NE	3	36	14

BREACKER, Tim
2.7.65 Bicester (DF)
6.0 12.6
LD Ipswich T v Luton T
31.3.84 3–0

1983–84 Luton T	1	2	—
1984–85 Luton T	1	35	—
1985–86 Luton T	1	36	—
1986–87 Luton T	1	29	1
1987–88 Luton T	1	40	1

BREMNER, Des
7.9.52 Aberchirder (MF)
5.9½ 11.11 Deveronvale
LD Dundee U v Hibernian
13.1.73 1–0

1972–73 Hibernian	1	11	—
1973–74 Hibernian	1	21	2
1974–75 Hibernian	1	30	2
1975–76 Hibernian	P	32	3
1976–77 Hibernian	P	36	4
1977–78 Hibernian	P	33	2
1978–79 Hibernian	P	31	5
1979–80 Hibernian	P	5	—
1979–80 Aston Villa	1	36	3
1980–81 Aston Villa	1	42	2
1981–82 Aston Villa	1	38	3
1982–83 Aston Villa	1	37	—
1983–84 Aston Villa	1	17	—
1984–85 Aston Villa	1	4	1
1984–85 Birmingham C	2	30	—
1985–86 Birmingham C	1	32	—
1986–87 Birmingham C	2	40	4
1987–88 Birmingham C	2	37	—

BREMNER, Kevin
7.10.57 Banff (FW)
5.10 12.3½ Keith
LD Colchester U v Barnsley
11.10.80 2–2

1980–81 Colchester U	3	34	8
1981–82 Colchester U	4	46	21
1982–83 Colchester U	4	15	2
1982–83 *Birmingham C*	1	4	1
1982–83 *Wrexham*	3	4	1
1982–83 *Plymouth Arg*	3	5	1
1982–83 Millwall	3	17	6
1983–84 Millwall	3	42	16
1984–85 Millwall	3	37	11
1985–86 Reading	3	22	7
1986–87 Reading	2	44	14
1987–88 Brighton & HA	3	44	8

BRENNAN, Mark
4.10.65 Rossendale (MF)
5.10 10.13 Apprentice
LD Ipswich T v Arsenal
2.11.83 1–0

1982–83 Ipswich T	1	—	—
1983–84 Ipswich T	1	19	1
1984–85 Ipswich T	1	36	2
1985–86 Ipswich T	1	40	3
1986–87 Ipswich T	2	37	7
1987–88 Ipswich T	2	36	6

BRIEN, Anthony
10.2.69 Dublin (DF)
5.11 11.9 Apprentice
LD Leicester C v Ipswich T
30.9.87 1–1

1987–88 Leicester C	2	15	1

PLAYER DIRECTORY

BRIGGS, Gary
8.5.58 Leeds (DF)
6.3 12.10 Apprentice
LD Oxford U v Cambridge U
11.1.78 2–3

1977–78	Middlesbrough	1	—	—
1977–78	Oxford U	3	20	2
1978–79	Oxford U	3	39	—
1979–80	Oxford U	3	46	1
1980–81	Oxford U	3	42	1
1981–82	Oxford U	3	45	1
1982–83	Oxford U	3	37	1
1983–84	Oxford U	3	38	3
1984–85	Oxford U	2	42	4
1985–86	Oxford U	1	38	—
1986–87	Oxford U	1	40	3
1987–88	Oxford U	1	18	1

BRIGHT, Mark
6.6.62 Stoke (FW)
6.0 11.0 Leek T
LD Port Vale v York C
1.5.82 0–0

1981–82	Port Vale	4	2	—
1982–83	Port Vale	4	1	1
1983–84	Port Vale	3	26	9
1984–85	Leicester C	1	16	—
1985–86	Leicester C	1	24	6
1986–87	Leicester C	1	2	—
1986–87	Crystal Palace	2	28	8
1987–88	Crystal Palace	2	38	25

BRIGHTWELL, David
7.1.71 Lutterworth
— — YTS
LD —

1987–88	Manchester C	2	—	—

BRIGHTWELL, Ian
9.4.68 Lutterworth (MF)
YTS
LD Manchester C v Wimbledon
23.8.86 3–1

1986–87	Manchester C	1	16	1
1987–88	Manchester C	2	33	5

BRILEY, Les
2.10.56 Lambeth (MF)
5.8 10.6 Apprentice
LD Hereford U v Burnley
4.9.76 3–0

1974–75	Chelsea	1	—	—
1975–76	Chelsea	2	—	—
1976–77	Hereford U	2	34	1
1977–78	Hereford U	3	27	1
1977–78	Wimbledon	4	14	1
1978–79	Wimbledon	4	26	1
1979–80	Wimbledon	3	21	—
1979–80	Aldershot	4	12	—
1980–81	Aldershot	4	44	—
1981–82	Aldershot	4	37	2
1982–83	Aldershot	4	28	—
1983–84	Aldershot	4	36	1
1984–85	Millwall	3	33	—
1985–86	Millwall	2	39	1
1986–87	Millwall	2	33	3
1987–88	Millwall	2	44	4

BRIMACOMBE, John
25.11.58 Plymouth (DF)
— — Liskeard and Saltash
LD Plymouth Arg v York C
18.1.86 2–2

1985–86	Plymouth Arg	3	1	1
1986–87	Plymouth Arg	2	11	—
1987–88	Plymouth Arg	2	42	1

BRINDLEY, Chris
5.7.69 Stoke (DF)
6.1 12.8 Hednesford
LD Hereford U v Wolves
26.12.86 2–0

1986–87	Wolves	4	7	—
1987–88	Wolves	4	—	—

BRISCOE, Robert
4.9.69 Derby (DF/MF)
5.8 10.13 Apprentice
LD —

1987–88	Derby Co	1	—	—

BRITTON, Ian
19.5.54 Dundee (MF)
5.5 9.7 Apprentice
LD Chelsea v Derby Co
30.12.72 1–1

1971–72	Chelsea	1	—	—
1972–73	Chelsea	1	14	—
1973–74	Chelsea	1	17	2
1974–75	Chelsea	1	15	1
1975–76	Chelsea	2	40	8
1976–77	Chelsea	2	37	10
1977–78	Chelsea	1	40	1
1978–79	Chelsea	1	13	—
1979–80	Chelsea	2	41	10
1980–81	Chelsea	2	28	1
1981–82	Chelsea	2	18	—
1982–83	Dundee U	P	10	1
1983–84	Blackpool	4	30	9
1984–85	Blackpool	4	46	5
1985–86	Blackpool	3	30	1
1986–87	Burnley	4	39	3
1987–88	Burnley	4	32	4

BROCK, Kevin
9.9.62 Middleton Stoney (MF)
5.9 10.10 Apprentice
LD Oxford U v Barnsley
1.9.79 1–0

1979–80	Oxford U	3	19	2
1980–81	Oxford U	3	26	5
1981–82	Oxford U	3	28	5
1982–83	Oxford U	3	37	4
1983–84	Oxford U	3	45	3
1984–85	Oxford U	2	37	6
1985–86	Oxford U	1	23	—
1986–87	Oxford U	1	31	1
1987–88	QPR	1	26	2

BROCKIE, Vincent
2.2.69 Greenock (DF)
5.8 10.10 YTS
LD Leeds U v C Palace
2.5.88 1–0

1987–88	Leeds U	2	2	—

BRODDLE, Julian
1.11.64 Laughton (MF)
5.9 11.3 Apprentice
LD Sheffield U v Halifax T
2.1.82 2–2

1981–82	Sheffield U	4	1	—
1982–83	Sheffield U	3	—	—
1983–84	Scunthorpe U	3	13	1
1984–85	Scunthorpe U	4	45	14
1985–86	Scunthorpe U	4	41	7
1986–87	Scunthorpe U	4	38	10
1987–88	Scunthorpe U	4	7	—
1987–88	Barnsley	2	19	1

BROMAGE, Russel
9.11.59 Stoke (DF)
5.11 11.5 Apprentice
LD Bradford C v Port Vale
8.3.78 1–1

1977–78	Port Vale	3	6	—
1978–79	Port Vale	4	20	2
1979–80	Port Vale	4	29	1
1980–81	Port Vale	4	45	4
1981–82	Port Vale	4	45	—
1982–83	Port Vale	4	46	2
1983–84	Port Vale	3	38	1
1983–84	Oldham Ath	2	2	—
1984–85	Port Vale	4	37	1
1985–86	Port Vale	4	40	1
1986–87	Port Vale	3	41	1
1987–88	Bristol C	3	30	—

BROOK, Gary
9.5.64 Dewsbury (FW)
5.10½ 10.6 Apprentice
LD Hereford U v Newport Co
26.12.87 4–2

1987–88	Newport Co	4	14	2
1987–88	Scarborough	4	5	—

BROOKMAN, Nick
28.10.68 Manchester (MF)
5.11 11.5 YTS
LD Bolton W v Carlisle U
18.4.87 2–0

1986–87	Bolton W	3	4	—
1987–88	Bolton W	4	26	6

BROOKS, Shaun
9.10.62 London (MF)
5.7 11.0 Apprentice
LD C Palace v Leeds U
12.4.80 1-0

1979–80	Crystal Palace	1	1	—
1980–81	Crystal Palace	1	17	—
1981–82	Crystal Palace	2	25	2
1982–83	Crystal Palace	2	7	2
1983–84	Crystal Palace	2	4	—
1983–84	Orient	3	36	9
1984–85	Orient	3	29	5
1985–86	Orient	4	38	7
1986–87	Orient	4	45	5
1987–88	Bournemouth	2	37	6

BROTHERSTON, Noel
18.11.56 Belfast (MF)
5.8 11.5 Apprentice
LD Tottenham H v Aston Villa
13.3.76 5-2

1973–74	Tottenham H	1	—	—
1974–75	Tottenham H	1	—	—
1975–76	Tottenham H	1	1	—
1976–77	Tottenham H	1	—	—
1977–78	Blackburn R	2	40	11
1978–79	Blackburn R	2	35	2
1979–80	Blackburn R	3	41	7
1980–81	Blackburn R	2	33	3
1981–82	Blackburn R	2	38	2
1982–83	Blackburn R	2	39	6
1983–84	Blackburn R	2	21	1
1984–85	Blackburn R	2	33	7
1985–86	Blackburn R	2	19	1
1986–87	Blackburn R	2	18	—
1987–88	Bury	3	36	4

BROWN, David
28.1.57 Hartlepool (GK)
6.1 12.8 Horden C.W.
LD Middlesbrough v Leicester C
27.3.78 0-1

1976–77	Middlesbrough	1	—	—
1977–78	Middlesbrough	1	10	—
1978–79	Middlesbrough	1	—	—
1979–80	Middlesbrough	1	—	—
1979–80	*Plymouth Arg*	3	5	—
1979–80	Oxford U	3	18	—
1980–81	Oxford U	3	3	—
1981–82	Oxford U	3	—	—
1981–82	Bury	4	27	—
1982–83	Bury	4	45	—
1983–84	Bury	4	28	—
1984–85	Bury	4	46	—
1985–86	Bury	3	—	—
1986–87	Preston NE	4	24	—
1987–88	Preston NE	3	27	—

BROWN, Gary
3.1.69 Beverly (DF)
5.10 11.2 Blackburn R
LD —

1987–88	Bolton W	4	—	—

BROWN, John
26.1.62 Stirling (MF)
5.11 11.2 Blantyre Welfare
LD Hamilton A v Clyde
28.11.79 3-1

1979–80	Hamilton A	1	19	—
1980–81	Hamilton A	1	38	6
1981–82	Hamilton A	1	28	5
1982–83	Hamilton A	1	9	—
1983–84	Hamilton A	1	39	—
1984–85	Dundee	P	34	7
1985–86	Dundee	P	29	11
1986–87	Dundee	P	31	10
1987–88	Dundee	P	20	3
1987–88	Rangers	P	9	2

BROWN, Kevan
2.1.66 Andover (MF) 5.9 11.8
LD Birmingham C v Brighton & HA
14.2.87 0-0

1983–84	Southampton	1	—	—
1984–85	Southampton	1	—	—
1985–86	Southampton	1	—	—
1986–87	Brighton & HA	2	15	—
1987–88	Brighton & HA	3	35	—

BROWN, Malcolm
13.12.56 Salford (DF)
6.2 13.0 Apprentice
LD Scunthorpe U v Bury
30.4.74 1-2

1973–74	Bury	4	1	—
1974–75	Bury	3	—	—
1975–76	Bury	3	5	—
1976–77	Bury	3	5	—
1977–78	Huddersfield T	4	30	1
1978–79	Huddersfield T	4	42	—
1979–80	Huddersfield T	4	46	2
1980–81	Huddersfield T	3	46	3
1981–82	Huddersfield T	3	46	1
1982–83	Huddersfield T	3	46	9
1983–84	Newcastle U	2	—	—
1984–85	Newcastle U	1	39	—
1985–86	Huddersfield T	2	37	—
1986–87	Huddersfield T	2	33	1
1987–88	Huddersfield T	2	25	—

BROWN, Mike
8.2.68 Birmingham (FW)
5.9 10.12 Apprentice
LD Shrewsbury T v Blackburn R
30.8.86 0-1

1985–86	Shrewsbury T	2	—	—
1986–87	Shrewsbury T	2	22	2
1987–88	Shrewsbury T	2	41	5

BROWN, Nicky
16.10.66 Hull (FW)
6.0 12.3 Local
LD Fulham v Hull C
12.4.86 1-1

1984–85	Hull C	3	—	—
1985–86	Hull C	2	1	—
1986–87	Hull C	2	—	—
1987–88	Hull C	2	10	—

BROWN, Phil
30.5.59 South Shields (DF)
5.11 11.6 Local
LD Hartlepool U v Peterborough U
1.3.80 1-2

1978–79	Hartlepool U	4	—	—
1979–80	Hartlepool U	4	10	—
1980–81	Hartlepool U	4	46	1
1981–82	Hartlepool U	4	44	4
1982–83	Hartlepool U	4	44	2
1983–84	Hartlepool U	4	31	—
1984–85	Hartlepool U	4	42	1
1985–86	Halifax T	4	46	2
1986–87	Halifax T	4	46	12
1987–88	Halifax T	4	44	5

BROWN, Tony
17.9.58 Bradford (DF)
6.2 12.10 Thackley
LD Leeds U v Leicester C
2.5.83 2-2

1982–83	Leeds U	2	1	—
1983–84	Leeds U	2	22	1
1984–85	Leeds U	2	1	—
1984–85	*Doncaster R*	3	14	—
1985–86	Doncaster R	3	38	2
1986–87	Doncaster R	3	35	—
1987–88	Scunthorpe U	4	22	—

BRUCE, Steve
31.12.60 Newcastle (MF)
6.0½ 12.6 Apprentice
LD Blackpool v Gillingham
18.8.79 2-1

1978–79	Gillingham	3	—	—
1979–80	Gillingham	3	40	6
1980–81	Gillingham	3	41	4
1981–82	Gillingham	3	45	6
1982–83	Gillingham	3	39	7
1983–84	Gillingham	3	40	6
1984–85	Norwich C	1	39	1
1985–86	Norwich C	2	42	8
1986–87	Norwich C	1	41	3
1987–88	Norwich C	1	19	2
1987–88	Manchester U	1	21	2

BRUSH, Paul
22.2.58 Plaistow (DF)
5.11 12.2 Apprentice
LD West Ham U v Norwich C
20.8.77 1-3

1976–77	West Ham U	1	—	—
1977–78	West Ham U	1	24	—
1978–79	West Ham U	2	42	—
1979–80	West Ham U	2	27	—
1980–81	West Ham U	1	11	—
1981–82	West Ham U	1	13	—
1982–83	West Ham U	1	6	—
1983–84	West Ham U	1	10	—
1984–85	West Ham U	1	18	1
1985–86	West Ham U	1	—	—
1985–86	Crystal Palace	2	26	2
1986–87	Crystal Palace	2	15	1
1987–88	Crystal Palace	2	9	—
1987–88	*Southend U*	2	4	1
1987–88	Southend U	2	10	—

PLAYER DIRECTORY

BUCKLEY, John
10.5.62 Glasgow (FW)
5.9 10.7
LD Partick Th v St Johnstone
2.4.83 2–1

1982–83	Partick T	1	8	1
1983–84	Partick T	1	37	4
1984–85	Doncaster R	3	39	6
1985–86	Doncaster R	3	45	5
1986–87	Leeds U	2	9	1
1986–87	*Leicester C*	1	5	—
1987–88	Leeds U	2	1	—
1987–88	*Doncaster R*	3	6	—
1987–88	Rotherham U	3	26	—

BUCKLEY, Neil
25.9.68 Hull (MF)
— — YTS
LD Plymouth Arg v Hull C
3.1.87 4–0

1986–87	Hull C	2	1	—
1987–88	Hull C	2	—	—

BULL, Gary
— — West Bromwich (FW)
5.9 11.2 Southampton
LD Cambridge U v Darlington
1.4.88 1–0

1987–88	Cambridge U	4	9	2

BULL, Steve
28.3.65 Tipton (FW)
5.11 11.4 Apprentice
LD QPR v WBA
12.4.86 1–0

1985–86	WBA	1	1	—
1986–87	WBA	2	3	2
1986–87	Wolves	4	30	15
1987–88	Wolves	4	44	34

BULLOCK, Steven
5.10.66 Stockport (MF)
5.8 11.1 School
LD Cardiff C v Oldham Ath
14.4.84 2–0

1983–84	Oldham Ath	2	1	—
1984–85	Oldham Ath	2	9	—
1985–86	Oldham Ath	2	8	—
1986–87	Tranmere R	4	30	1
1987–88	Stockport C	2	41	—

BUMSTEAD, John
27.11.58 Rotherhithe (MF)
5.7 10.5 Apprentice
LD Leeds U v Chelsea
22.11.78 2–1

1977–78	Chelsea	1	—	—
1978–79	Chelsea	1	8	1
1979–80	Chelsea	2	28	3
1980–81	Chelsea	2	41	1
1981–82	Chelsea	2	21	4
1982–83	Chelsea	2	36	4
1983–84	Chelsea	2	31	7
1984–85	Chelsea	1	25	3
1985–86	Chelsea	1	32	1
1986–87	Chelsea	1	29	8
1987–88	Chelsea	1	17	1

BUNN, Frankie
6.11.62 Birmingham (FW)
5.11 10.6 Apprentice
LD Luton T v Derby Co
23.8.80 1–2

1980–81	Luton T	2	3	1
1981–82	Luton T	2	2	—
1982–83	Luton T	1	4	—
1983–84	Luton T	1	30	3
1984–85	Luton T	1	20	5
1985–86	Hull C	2	42	14
1986–87	Hull C	2	35	4
1987–88	Hull C	2	18	5
1987–88	Oldham Ath	2	21	9

BURGESS, Dave
20.1.60 Liverpool (DF)
5.10 11.2 Local
LD Tranmere R v York C
29.8.81 0–2

1981–82	Tranmere R	4	46	1
1982–83	Tranmere R	4	46	—
1983–84	Tranmere R	4	44	—
1984–85	Tranmere R	4	41	—
1985–86	Tranmere R	4	41	—
1986–87	Grimsby T	2	31	—
1987–88	Grimsby T	3	38	—

BURGHER, Symon
— —

LD Exeter C v Aldershot
26.1.85 3–0

1984–85	Exeter C	4	14	—
1985–86	Exeter C	4	—	—
1986–87	Exeter C	4	—	—
1987–88	Exeter C	4	—	—

BURKE, David
6.8.60 Liverpool (DF)
5.10 11.1 Apprentice
LD Bolton W v Birmingham C
2.9.78 2–2

1977–78	Bolton W	2	—	—
1978–79	Bolton W	1	20	1
1979–80	Bolton W	1	27	—
1980–81	Bolton W	2	22	—
1981–82	Huddersfield T	3	41	1
1982–83	Huddersfield T	3	44	1
1983–84	Huddersfield T	2	42	—
1984–85	Huddersfield T	2	31	1
1985–86	Huddersfield T	2	—	—
1986–87	Huddersfield T	2	21	—
1987–88	Huddersfield T	2	10	—
1987–88	Crystal Palace	2	31	—

BURKE, Mark
12.2.69 Solihull (FW)
5.10 11.8½ Apprentice
LD Aston Villa v Everton
18.4.87 0–1

1986–87	Aston Villa	1	1	—
1987–88	Aston Villa	2	6	—
1987–88	*Middlesbrough*	3	1	—
1987–88	Middlesbrough	3	15	—

BURLEY, George
3.6.56 Cumnock (DF)
5.9½ 11.0 Apprentice
LD Manchester U v Ipswich T
29.12.73 2–0

1973–74	Ipswich T	1	20	—
1974–75	Ipswich T	1	31	—
1975–76	Ipswich T	1	42	—
1976–77	Ipswich T	1	40	2
1977–78	Ipswich T	1	31	1
1978–79	Ipswich T	1	38	1
1979–80	Ipswich T	1	38	—
1980–81	Ipswich T	1	23	—
1981–82	Ipswich T	1	29	—
1982–83	Ipswich T	1	31	1
1983–84	Ipswich T	1	28	—
1984–85	Ipswich T	1	37	—
1985–86	Ipswich T	1	6	—
1985–86	Sunderland	2	27	—
1986–87	Sunderland	2	27	—
1987–88	Sunderland	3	—	—

BURNS, Hugh
13.12.65 Lanark (DF)
6.0 11.7 Cambuslang Rangers
LD Hibernian v Rangers
27.12.83 0–2

1982–83	Rangers	P	—	—
1983–84	Rangers	P	5	—
1984–85	Rangers	P	15	—
1985–86	Rangers	P	28	3
1986–87	Rangers	P	3	—
1986–87	Hamilton A	P	5	1
1987–88	Hearts	P	24	—

BURNS, Tommy
16.2.56 Glasgow (MF)
5.11 11.3 Maryhill Juniors
LD Celtic v Dundee
19.4.75 1–2

1974–75	Celtic	1	1	—
1975–76	Celtic	P	5	—
1976–77	Celtic	P	22	1
1977–78	Celtic	P	23	3
1978–79	Celtic	P	29	3
1979–80	Celtic	P	15	—
1980–81	Celtic	P	33	4
1981–82	Celtic	P	33	9
1982–83	Celtic	P	17	7
1983–84	Celtic	P	33	9
1984–85	Celtic	P	27	7
1985–86	Celtic	P	34	5
1986–87	Celtic	P	17	—
1987–88	Celtic	P	27	2

BURNS, William
10.12.69 Motherwell
5.11½ 10.10 Apprentice
LD —

1987–88 Manchester C	2	—	—

BURRIDGE, John
3.12.51 Workington (GK)
5.11 12.11 Apprentice

1968–69 Workington	4	1	—
1969–70 Workington	4	—	—
1970–71 Workington	4	26	—
1970–71 Blackpool	1	3	—
1971–72 Blackpool	2	34	—
1972–73 Blackpool	2	22	—
1973–74 Blackpool	2	30	—
1974–75 Blackpool	2	38	—
1975–76 Blackpool	2	7	—
1975–76 Aston Villa	1	30	—
1976–77 Aston Villa	1	35	—
1977–78 Aston Villa	1	—	—
1977–78 *Southend U*	4	6	—
1977–78 Crystal Palace	2	10	—
1978–79 Crystal Palace	2	42	—
1979–80 Crystal Palace	1	36	—
1980–81 Crystal Palace	1	—	—
1980–81 QPR	2	19	—
1981–82 QPR	2	20	—
1982–83 Wolves	2	42	—
1983–84 Wolves	1	32	—
1984–85 Wolves	2	—	—
1984–85 *Derby Co*	3	6	—
1984–85 Sheffield U	2	30	—
1985–86 Sheffield U	2	42	—
1986–87 Sheffield U	2	37	—
1987–88 Southampton	1	31	—

BURROWS, Adrian
16.1.59 Sutton (DF)
5.11 12.0 Local
LD Sheffield U v Mansfield T
9.2.80 1–0

1979–80 Mansfield T	3	17	—
1980–81 Mansfield T	4	20	3
1981–82 Mansfield T	4	41	2
1982–83 Northampton T	4	43	4
1983–84 Northampton T	4	45	—
1984–85 *Plymouth Arg*	3	5	—
1984–85 Plymouth Arg	3	34	—
1985–86 Plymouth Arg	3	7	2
1986–87 Plymouth Arg	2	17	1
1987–88 Plymouth Arg	2	23	1
1987–88 *Southend U*	3	6	—

BURROWS, David
25.10.68 Dudley (DF)
5.11 11.5 Apprentice
LD WBA v Sheffield W
22.4.86 1–1

1985–86 WBA	1	1	—
1986–87 WBA	2	15	1
1987–88 WBA	2	21	—

BURVILL, Glen
26.10.62 Canning Town (FW)
5.9 10.5 Apprentice
LD Aldershot v Hereford U
27.8.83 1–4

1980–81 West Ham U	2	—	—
1981–82 West Ham U	1	—	—
1982–83 West Ham U	1	—	—
1983–84 Aldershot	4	38	12
1984–85 Aldershot	4	27	3
1984–85 Reading	3	14	—
1985–86 Reading	3	16	—
1985–86 *Fulham*	2	9	2
1986–87 Aldershot	4	36	2
1987–88 Aldershot	3	43	9

BUTCHER, Terry
28.12.58 Singapore (DF)
6.4 14.0 Amateur
LD Everton v Ipswich T
15.4.78 1–0

1976–77 Ipswich T	1	—	—
1977–78 Ipswich T	1	3	—
1978–79 Ipswich T	1	21	2
1979–80 Ipswich T	1	36	2
1980–81 Ipswich T	1	40	4
1981–82 Ipswich T	1	27	1
1982–83 Ipswich T	1	42	—
1983–84 Ipswich T	1	34	1
1984–85 Ipswich T	1	41	2
1985–86 Ipswich T	1	27	4
1986–87 Rangers	P	43	3
1987–88 Rangers	P	11	1

BUTLER, Barry
4.6.62 Farnworth (MF)
6.2 13.0 Atherton T
LD Chester C v Tranmere R
11.1.86 1–0

1985–86 Chester C	4	14	—
1986–87 Chester C	3	44	—
1987–88 Chester C	3	16	—

BUTLER, Brian
4.7.66 Salford (MF)
5.6 10.8 Apprentice
LD Darlington v Blackpool
26.8.85 2–1

1984–85 Blackpool	4	—	—
1985–86 Blackpool	3	19	1
1986–87 Blackpool	3	37	3
1987–88 Blackpool	3	18	1

BUTLER, John
7.2.62 Liverpool (MF)
5.11 11.0 Prescot Cables
LD Wigan Ath v Rochdale
24.4.82 1–0

1981–82 Wigan Ath	4	1	—
1982–83 Wigan Ath	3	40	5
1983–84 Wigan Ath	3	41	3
1984–85 Wigan Ath	3	45	3
1985–86 Wigan Ath	3	36	—
1986–87 Wigan Ath	3	36	—
1987–88 Wigan Ath	3	26	1

BUTLER, John
25.1.69 Bellshill (MF)
5.9 11.6 Orbiston BC
LD St Mirren v Motherwell
29.10.86 1–0

1986–87 St Mirren	P	3	—
1987–88 St Mirren	P	8	—

BUTLER, Lee
30.5.66 Sheffield (GK)
6.2 14.2 Haworth Colliery
LD Cambridge U v Lincoln C
27.9.86 1–1

1986–87 Lincoln C	4	30	—
1987–88 Aston Villa	2	—	—

BUTLER, Martin
3.3.66 Hull (FW)
5.8 10.9 YTS
LD York C v Millwall
20.10.84 1–1

1984–85 York C	3	19	3
1985–86 York C	3	14	—
1985–86 *Aldershot*	4	2	1
1986–87 York C	3	15	3
1986–87 *Exeter C*	4	4	1
1987–88 York C	3	5	—

BUTLER, Peter
27.8.66 Halifax (MF)
5.9 11.1 Apprentice
LD Huddersfield T v Oxford U
25.8.84 0–3

1984–85 Huddersfield T	2	4	—
1985–86 Huddersfield T	2	1	—
1985–86 *Cambridge U*	4	14	1
1986–87 Bury	3	11	—
1986–87 Cambridge U	4	29	4
1987–88 Cambridge U	4	—	—
1987–88 Southend U	3	15	3

BUTTERWORTH, Ian
25.1.65 Crewe (DF)
6.1 12.6 Apprentice
LD Swansea C v Coventry C
13.3.82 0–0

1981–82 Coventry C	1	14	—
1982–83 Coventry C	1	30	—
1983–84 Coventry C	1	24	—
1984–85 Coventry C	1	22	—
1985–86 Nottingham F	1	23	—
1986–87 Nottingham F	1	4	—
1986–87 Norwich C	1	28	—
1987–88 Norwich C	1	35	—

BUXTON, Steve
13.3.60 Birmingham (FW)
5.5 11.2 Amateur
LD Sheffield W v Wrexham
3.5.78 2–1

1977–78 Wrexham	3	1	—
1978–79 Wrexham	2	13	2
1979–80 Wrexham	2	13	1
1980–81 Wrexham	2	14	2
1981–82 Wrexham	2	9	3
1982–83 Wrexham	3	39	10
1983–84 Wrexham	4	20	3
1984–85 Stockport Co	4	18	1
1985–86 Torquay U	4	—	—
1985–86 Wrexham	4	5	3
1986–87 Wrexham	4	30	8
1987–88 Wrexham	4	35	6

BYRNE, David
5.3.61 London (FW)
5.8 11.0 Kingstonian
LD Gillingham v Darlington
24.8.85 1–1

1985–86 Gillingham	3	23	3
1986–87 Millwall	2	40	4
1987–88 Millwall	2	23	2

BYRNE, John
1.2.61 Manchester (FW)
5.11 11.6 Apprentice
LD York C v Lincoln C
25.8.79 0–2

1978–79 York C	4	—	—
1979–80 York C	4	9	2
1980–81 York C	4	38	6
1981–82 York C	4	29	6
1982–83 York C	4	43	12
1983–84 York C	4	46	27
1984–85 York C	4	10	2
1984–85 QPR	1	23	3
1985–86 QPR	1	36	12
1986–87 QPR	1	40	11
1987–88 QPR	1	27	4

BYRNE, Thomas
30.8.69 Dublin (MF)
5.8 10.4 Apprentice
LD —

1987–88 Chelsea	1	—	—

CADETTE, Richard
21.3.65 Hammersmith (FW)
5.8 11.7 Wembley
LD Brentford v Orient
25.8.84 0–1

1984–85 Orient	3	21	4
1985–86 Southend U	4	44	25
1986–87 Southend U	4	46	24
1987–88 Sheffield U	2	28	7

CAESER, Gus
5.3.66 London (DF)
6.0 12.0 Apprentice
LD Manchester U v Arsenal
21.12.85 0–1

1983–84 Arsenal	1	—	—
1984–85 Arsenal	1	—	—
1985–86 Arsenal	1	2	—
1986–87 Arsenal	1	15	—
1987–88 Arsenal	1	22	—

CALDERWOOD, Colin
20.1.65 Stranraer (DF)
6.0 11.9 Amateur
LD Crewe Alex v Mansfield T
13.3.82 0–2

1981–82 Mansfield T	4	1	—
1982–83 Mansfield T	4	28	—
1983–84 Mansfield T	4	30	1
1984–85 Mansfield T	4	41	—
1985–86 Swindon T	4	46	2
1986–87 Swindon T	3	46	1
1987–88 Swindon T	2	34	1

CALDWELL, Dave
31.7.60 Aberdeen (FW)
5.10 10.8 Inverness Caley
LD Reading v Mansfield T
29.9.79 1–0

1979–80 Mansfield T	3	3	—
1980–81 Mansfield T	4	28	8
1981–82 Mansfield T	4	33	9
1982–83 Mansfield T	4	35	10
1983–84 Mansfield T	4	38	21
1984–85 Mansfield T	4	20	9
1984–85 Carlisle U	2	4	—
1984–85 Swindon T	4	5	—
1985–86 Chesterfield	3	22	3
1986–87 Chesterfield	3	36	14
1987–88 Chesterfield	3	10	—
1987–88 Torquay U	4	24	4

CALDWELL, Tony
21.3.58 Salford (FW)
5.9 11.6 Horwich RMI
LD Bolton W v Wimbledon
27.8.83 2–0

1983–84 Bolton W	3	33	19
1984–85 Bolton W	3	31	18
1985–86 Bolton W	3	40	10
1986–87 Bolton W	3	35	11
1987–88 Bristol C	3	16	3
1987–88 Chester C	3	4	—

CALLAGHAN, Aaron
8.10.66 Dublin (DF)
5.11 11.2 Apprentice
LD Stoke C v Nottingham F
23.3.85 1–4

1984–85 Stoke C	1	5	—
1985–86 Stoke C	2	8	—
1985–86 Crewe Alex	4	8	—
1986–87 Stoke C	2	2	—
1986–87 Oldham Ath	2	5	—
1987–88 Oldham Ath	2	11	2

CALLAGHAN, Ian
5.8.69 Liverpool (MF)
5.7 10.11 YTS
LD Colchester U v Bolton W
11.12.87 3–0

1987–88 Bolton W	4	1	—

CALLAGHAN, Nigel
12.9.62 Singapore (MF)
5.9 10.9 Apprentice
LD Watford v Burnley
3.5.80 4–0

1979–80 Watford	2	1	—
1980–81 Watford	2	21	2
1981–82 Watford	2	37	5
1982–83 Watford	1	41	9
1983–84 Watford	1	41	10
1984–85 Watford	1	38	8
1985–86 Watford	1	23	4
1986–87 Watford	1	20	3
1986–87 Derby Co	2	18	4
1987–88 Derby Co	1	40	4

CAM, Scott
3.5.70 Sheffield (DF)
5.10 10.1 Apprentice
LD —

1987–88 Sheffield W	1	—	—

CAME, Mark
14.9.61 Exeter (DF)
6.1 13.0 Winsford U
LD Doncaster R v Bolton W
29.9.84 2–0

1983–84 Bolton W	3	—	—
1984–85 Bolton W	3	23	1
1985–86 Bolton W	3	35	1
1986–87 Bolton W	3	43	—
1987–88 Bolton W	4	43	5

CAMERON, Ian
24.8.66 Glasgow (MF)
5.9 10.4 'S' Form
LD St Mirren v Dundee
10.9.83 0–0

1983–84 St Mirren	P	8	—
1984–85 St Mirren	P	9	1
1985–86 St Mirren	P	12	—
1986–87 St Mirren	P	31	6
1987–88 St Mirren	P	41	8

PLAYER DIRECTORY

CAMPBELL, David
2.6.65 Eglinton (MF)
5.9 10.9 Oxford BC(NI)
LD Nottingham F v West Ham U
30.3.85 1-2

1983–84	Nottingham F	1	— —
1984–85	Nottingham F	1	1 —
1985–86	Nottingham F	1	18 3
1986–87	Nottingham F	1	14 —
1986–87	Notts Co	3	18 2
1987–88	Nottingham F	1	8 —
1987–88	Charlton Ath	1	21 1

CAMPBELL, Kevin
4.2.70 London (FW)
— — Apprentice
LD Everton v Arsenal
7.5.88 1-2

1987–88 Arsenal 1 1 —

CAMPBELL, Stephen
20.11.67 Dundee (MF)
5.9 11.2 Downfield B.C.
LD St Mirren v Dundee
22.2.86 2-1

1985–86 Dundee P 5 —
1986–87 Dundee P 4 —
1987–88 Dundee P 7 1

CANDLISH, Neil
2.6.68 Inverness (FW)
5.8 10.0 Wishaw J
LD Falkirk v Motherwell
6.12.86 1-0

1986–87 Motherwell P 2 —
1987–88 Motherwell P 9 —

CANHAM, Tony
8.6.60 Leeds (MF)
5.8 10.7 Harrogate Railway
LD York C v Brentford
2.3.85 1-0

1984–85 York C 3 3 1
1985–86 York C 3 41 13
1986–87 York C 3 38 9
1987–88 York C 3 18 2

CARR, Ashley
15.8.68 Crowland (MF)
5.9 10.10 YTS
LD Peterborough v Darlington
5.9.87 1-2

1987–88 Peterborough U 4 13 —

CARR, Cliff
19.6.64 London (MF)
5.5½ 10.4 Apprentice
LD Fulham v Burnley
23.10.82 3-1

1982–83 Fulham 2 6 1
1983–84 Fulham 2 41 4
1984–85 Fulham 2 38 4
1985–86 Fulham 2 35 4
1986–87 Fulham 3 25 1
1987–88 Stoke C 2 41 —

CARR, Darren
4.9.68 Bristol (DF)
6.2 13.0
LD Gillingham v Bristol R
3.5.86 2-0

1985–86 Bristol R 3 1 —
1986–87 Bristol R 3 20 —
1987–88 Bristol R 3 9 —
1987–88 Newport Co 4 4 —
1987–88 Newport Co 4 5 —
1987–88 Sheffield U 2 3 —

CARR, Franz
24.9.66 Preston (MF)
5.6 10.8½ Apprentice
LD Aston Villa v Nottingham F
12.10.85 1-2

1984–85 Blackburn R 2 — —
1985–86 Nottingham F 1 23 3
1986–87 Nottingham F 1 36 4
1987–88 Nottingham F 1 22 4

CARSON, Tom
26.3.59 Alexandria (GK)
6.0 12.0 Vale of Leven
LD Dumbarton v Motherwell
12.4.80 1-0

1978–79 Dumbarton 1 — —
1979–80 Dumbarton 1 3 —
1980–81 Dumbarton 1 33 —
1981–82 Dumbarton 1 39 —
1982–83 Dumbarton 1 37 —
1983–84 Dumbarton 1 37 —
1984–85 Dundee P 20 —
1985–86 Dundee P — —
1986–87 Hibernian P 2 —
1987–88 Partick Th 1 6 —
1987–88 Queen of the S 1 7 —
1987–88 Dunfermline Ath P 4 —
1987–88 Ipswich T 2 1 —
1987–88 Dunfermline Ath P 1 —
1987–88 Dundee P 6 —

CARTER, James
9.11.65 London (MF)
5.10 10.4 Apprentice
LD Millwall v Oldham Ath
14.3.87 0-0

1983–84 Crystal Palace 2 — —
1984–85 Crystal Palace 2 — —
1985–86 QPR 1 — —
1986–87 Millwall 2 12 1
1987–88 Millwall 2 26 —

CARTER, Mike
18.4.60 Warrington (FW)
5.9 10.7 Apprentice
LD Mansfield T v Blackpool
3.3.79 1-1

1977–78 Bolton W 2 — —
1978–79 Bolton W 1 — —
1978–79 Mansfield T 3 18 4
1979–80 Bolton W 1 22 5
1980–81 Bolton W 2 14 2
1981–82 Bolton W 2 13 1
1981–82 Swindon T 3 5 —
1982–83 Plymouth Arg 3 12 1
1982–83 Hereford U 4 10 —
1983–84 Hereford U 4 — —
1984–85 Hereford U 4 28 —
1985–86 Hereford U 4 31 9
1986–87 Hereford U 4 28 2
1987–88 Wrexham 4 21 6

CARTER, Tim
5.10.67 Bristol (GK)
6.1 12.0 Apprentice
LD Bristol R v Reading
28.12.85 0-2

1985–86 Bristol R 3 2 —
1986–87 Bristol R 3 38 —
1987–88 Bristol R 3 7 —
1987–88 Newport Co 4 1 —
1987–88 Sunderland 3 1 —
1987–88 Carlisle U 4 4 —

CASCARINO, Tony
1.9.62 St Paul's Cray (FW)
6.1½ 13.0 Crockenhill
LD Burnley v Gillingham
2.2.82 1-0

1981–82 Gillingham 3 24 5
1982–83 Gillingham 3 38 15
1983–84 Gillingham 3 37 12
1984–85 Gillingham 3 43 16
1985–86 Gillingham 3 34 14
1986–87 Gillingham 3 43 16
1987–88 Millwall 2 39 20

CASE, Jimmy
18.5.54 Liverpool (FW)
5.9 12.7 South Liverpool
LD Liverpool v QPR
26.4.75 3-1

1973–74 Liverpool 1 — —
1974–75 Liverpool 1 1 —
1975–76 Liverpool 1 27 6
1976–77 Liverpool 1 27 1
1977–78 Liverpool 1 33 5
1978–79 Liverpool 1 37 7
1979–80 Liverpool 1 37 3
1980–81 Liverpool 1 24 1
1981–82 Brighton & HA 1 33 3
1982–83 Brighton & HA 1 35 3
1983–84 Brighton & HA 2 35 4
1984–85 Brighton & HA 2 24 —
1984–85 Southampton 1 10 1
1985–86 Southampton 1 36 2
1986–87 Southampton 1 39 3
1987–88 Southampton 1 38 —

PLAYER DIRECTORY

CASS, David
27.3.62 Forest Gate (GK)
— Billericay
LD Northampton T v Orient
12.4.87 2–0

1986–87 Orient	4	7	—
1987–88 Leyton Orient	4	—	—

CASSELLS, Keith
10.7.57 London (FW)
5.10 11.12 Wembley T
LD Watford v Mansfield T
2.12.78 1–1

1977–78 Watford	4	—	—
1978–79 Watford	3	3	—
1979–80 Watford	2	7	—
1979–80 *Peterborough U*	4	8	—
1980–81 Watford	2	2	—
1980–81 Oxford U	3	18	3
1981–82 Oxford U	3	27	10
1981–82 Southampton	1	6	2
1982–83 Southampton	1	13	2
1982–83 Brentford	3	16	7
1983–84 Brentford	3	30	9
1984–85 Brentford	3	40	12
1985–86 Mansfield T	4	40	13
1986–87 Mansfield T	3	46	16
1987–88 Mansfield T	3	40	9

CASSERLEY, Dean
9.10.69 Swindon (MF)
5.7 10.6 Trainee
LD —

1987–88 Swindon T	2	—	—

CASTLE, Steve
17.5.66 Barkingside (DF)
— Apprentice
LD Orient v Bradford C
29.9.84 1–0

1984–85 Orient	3	21	1
1985–86 Orient	4	23	4
1986–87 Orient	4	24	5
1987–88 Leyton Orient	4	42	10

CATON, Tommy
6.10.62 Liverpool (DF)
6.2 13.0 Apprentice
LD Manchester C v C Palace
18.8.79 0–0

1979–80 Manchester C	1	42	—
1980–81 Manchester C	1	30	—
1981–82 Manchester C	1	39	1
1982–83 Manchester C	1	38	5
1983–84 Manchester C	2	16	2
1983–84 Arsenal	1	26	—
1984–85 Arsenal	1	35	1
1985–86 Arsenal	1	20	1
1986–87 Oxford U	1	17	2
1987–88 Oxford U	1	36	1

CAUGHEY, Mark
27.8.60 Belfast (FW)
5.11 12.9 Linfield
LD Dundee v Hibernian
16.8.86 3–0

1986–87 Hibernian	P	14	—
1986–87 Burnley	4	8	—
1986–87 Hamilton A	P	5	3
1987–88 Hamilton A	1	16	10
1987–88 Motherwell	P	15	—

CAWLEY, Peter
15.9.65 London (DF)
— Chertsey
LD Bristol R v Notts Co
28.2.87 0–0

1986–87 Wimbledon	1	—	—
1986–87 *Bristol R*	3	10	—
1987–88 Wimbledon	1	—	—

CECERE, Michele
4.1.68 Chester (FW)
6.0 11.4 Apprentice
LD Blackburn R v Oldham Ath
31.1.87 1–0

1985–86 Oldham Ath	2	—	—
1986–87 Oldham Ath	2	14	4
1987–88 Oldham Ath	2	25	2

CHALMERS, Paul
31.10.63 Glasgow (FW)
5.10 10.3 Eastercraigs
LD Celtic v Morton
19.2.85 4–0

1980–81 Celtic	P	—	—
1981–82 Celtic	P	—	—
1982–83 Celtic	P	—	—
1983–84 Celtic	P	—	—
1984–85 Celtic	P	1	1
1985–86 Celtic	P	3	—
1985–86 *Bradford C*	2	2	—
1986–87 St Mirren	P	23	2
1987–88 St Mirren	P	36	10

CHAMBERLAIN, Alec
20.6.64 March (GK)
6.2 11.11 Ramsey T
LD Darlington v Colchester U
27.8.83 0–2

1981–82 Ipswich T	1	—	—
1982–83 Colchester U	4	—	—
1983–84 Colchester U	4	46	—
1984–85 Colchester U	4	46	—
1985–86 Colchester U	4	46	—
1986–87 Colchester U	4	46	—
1987–88 Everton	1	—	—
1987–88 *Tranmere R*	4	15	—

CHAMBERLAIN, Mark
19.11.61 Stoke (FW)
5.8½ 10.7 Apprentice
LD Port Vale v Scunthorpe U
19.8.78 2–2

1978–79 Port Vale	4	8	—
1979–80 Port Vale	4	11	—

1980–81 Port Vale	4	31	9
1981–82 Port Vale	4	46	8
1982–83 Stoke C	1	37	6
1983–84 Stoke C	1	40	7
1984–85 Stoke C	1	28	1
1985–86 Stoke C	2	7	3
1985–86 Sheffield W	1	21	2
1986–87 Sheffield W	1	24	5
1987–88 Sheffield W	1	21	1

CHANDLER, Jeff
19.6.59 Hammersmith (MF)
5.6½ 10.0 Apprentice
LD Blackburn R v Blackpool
10.9.77 1–2

1976–77 Blackpool	2	—	—
1977–78 Blackpool	2	13	2
1978–79 Blackpool	3	24	5
1979–80 Blackpool	3	—	—
1979–80 Leeds U	1	17	2
1980–81 Leeds U	1	9	—
1981–82 Leeds U	1	—	—
1981–82 Bolton W	2	33	2
1982–83 Bolton W	2	37	4
1983–84 Bolton W	3	46	14
1984–85 Bolton W	3	41	16
1985–86 Derby Co	3	37	9
1986–87 Derby Co	2	9	—
1986–87 *Mansfield T*	3	6	—
1987–88 Bolton W	4	3	2

CHANNING, Justin
19.11.68 Reading (DF)
5.10 11.0 Apprentice
LD Luton T v QPR
1.11.86 1–0

1986–87 QPR	1	2	—
1987–88 QPR	1	14	1

CHAPMAN, Ian
31.5.70 Brighton (DF)

LD Birmingham C v Brighton & HA
14.2.87 0–0

1986–87 Brighton & HA	2	5	—
1987–88 Brighton & HA	3	—	—

CHAPMAN, Lee
5.12.59 Lincoln (FW)
6.1½ 13.5 Amateur
LD Plymouth Arg v Watford
9.12.78 1–1

1978–79 Stoke C	2	—	—
1978–79 *Plymouth Arg*	3	4	—
1979–80 Stoke C	1	17	3
1980–81 Stoke C	1	41	15
1981–82 Stoke C	1	41	16
1982–83 Arsenal	1	19	3
1983–84 Arsenal	1	4	1
1983–84 Sunderland	1	15	3
1984–85 Sheffield W	1	40	15
1985–86 Sheffield W	1	31	10
1986–87 Sheffield W	1	41	19
1987–88 Sheffield W	1	37	19

CHAPMAN, Les
27.9.48 Oldham (MF)
5.7 10.4 High Barn

Season	Club			
1966–67	Oldham Ath	3	16	—
1967–68	Oldham Ath	3	10	1
1968–69	Oldham Ath	3	41	7
1969–70	Oldham Ath	4	9	1
1969–70	Huddersfield T	2	10	—
1970–71	Huddersfield T	1	14	1
1971–72	Huddersfield T	1	39	3
1972–73	Huddersfield T	2	22	2
1973–74	Huddersfield T	3	33	1
1974–75	Huddersfield T	3	15	1
1974–75	Oldham Ath	2	24	—
1975–76	Oldham Ath	2	41	2
1976–77	Oldham Ath	2	42	2
1977–78	Oldham Ath	2	38	4
1978–79	Oldham Ath	2	42	3
1979–80	Stockport Co	4	32	1
1979–80	Bradford C	4	14	2
1980–81	Bradford C	4	45	—
1981–82	Bradford C	4	34	1
1982–83	Bradford C	3	46	—
1983–84	Rochdale	4	45	—
1984–85	Rochdale	4	43	—
1985–86	Stockport Co	4	38	3
1986–87	Preston NE	4	36	1
1987–88	Preston NE	3	17	—

CHAPMAN, Vince
5.12.67 Newcastle (DF)
— — Tow Law Town
LD Huddersfield T v Swindon T
13.2.88 0–3

Season	Club			
1987–88	Huddersfield T	2	6	—

CHAPPLE, Phil
26.11.66 Norwich (DF)
6.2 12.7 Apprentice
LD Rochdale v Cambridge U
4.4.88 2–1

Season	Club			
1984–85	Norwich C	1	—	—
1985–86	Norwich C	2	—	—
1986–87	Norwich C	1	—	—
1987–88	Norwich C	1	—	—
1987–88	Cambridge U	4	6	1

CHARD, Phil
16.10.60 Corby (MF)
5.8 11.12 Nottingham F Amateur
LD Peterborough U v Swindon T
24.4.79 2–1

Season	Club			
1978–79	Peterborough U	3	6	1
1979–80	Peterborough U	4	20	2
1980–81	Peterborough U	4	—	—
1981–82	Peterborough U	4	39	3
1982–83	Peterborough U	4	44	4
1983–84	Peterborough U	4	38	7
1984–85	Peterborough U	4	25	1
1985–86	Northampton T	4	41	7
1986–87	Northampton T	4	40	12
1987–88	Northampton T	3	34	8
1987–88	Wolves	4	9	2

CHARLES, Gary
13.4.70 London (DF)
— — Apprentice
LD —

Season	Club			
1987–88	Nottingham F	1	—	—

CHARLES, Steve
10.5.60 Sheffield (MF)
5.9 10.7 Sheffield University
LD Exeter C v Sheffield U
12.1.80 3–1

Season	Club			
1979–80	Sheffield U	3	14	1
1980–81	Sheffield U	3	31	6
1981–82	Sheffield U	4	30	1
1982–83	Sheffield U	3	35	—
1983–84	Sheffield U	3	11	1
1984–85	Sheffield U	2	2	1
1984–85	Wrexham	4	32	7
1985–86	Wrexham	4	40	20
1986–87	Wrexham	4	41	10
1987–88	Mansfield T	3	46	12

CHATTERTON, Nicky
18.5.54 Norwood (MF)
5.9½ 11.4 Amateur
LD C Palace v Notts Co
25.8.73 1–4

Season	Club			
1973–74	Crystal Palace	2	7	—
1974–75	Crystal Palace	3	25	6
1975–76	Crystal Palace	3	37	7
1976–77	Crystal Palace	3	37	6
1977–78	Crystal Palace	2	32	9
1978–79	Crystal Palace	2	13	3
1978–79	Millwall	2	27	4
1979–80	Millwall	3	43	10
1980–81	Millwall	3	40	8
1981–82	Millwall	3	45	12
1982–83	Millwall	3	32	9
1983–84	Millwall	3	27	6
1984–85	Millwall	3	33	3
1985–86	Millwall	2	17	4
1986–87	Colchester U	4	21	1
1987–88	Colchester U	4	26	7

CHERRY, Steve
5.8.60 Nottingham (GK)
5.11 11.0 Apprentice
LD Derby Co v Southampton
16.2.80 2–2

Season	Club			
1977–78	Derby Co	1	—	—
1978–79	Derby Co	1	—	—
1979–80	Derby Co	1	4	—
1980–81	Port Vale	4	4	—
1981–82	Derby Co	2	4	—
1982–83	Derby Co	2	31	—
1983–84	Derby Co	2	38	—
1984–85	Walsall	3	41	—
1985–86	Walsall	3	30	—
1986–87	Plymouth Arg	2	21	—
1987–88	Plymouth Arg	2	37	—

CHETTLE, Stephen
27.9.68 Nottingham (DF)
6.1 12.0 Apprentice
LD Chelsea v Nottingham F
5.9.87 4–3

Season	Club			
1987–88	Nottingham F	1	30	—

CHICK, Richard
30.9.70 Walthamstow (FW)
5.9½ 11.2 Apprentice
LD —

Season	Club			
1987–88	Millwall	2	—	—

CHILDS, Gary
19.4.64 Birmingham (MF)
5.7 10.9 Apprentice
LD WBA v Everton
20.2.82 0–0

Season	Club			
1981–82	WBA	1	2	—
1982–83	WBA	1	—	—
1983–84	WBA	1	1	—
1983–84	Walsall	3	30	2
1984–85	Walsall	3	40	2
1985–86	Walsall	3	33	5
1986–87	Walsall	3	28	8
1987–88	Birmingham C	2	32	1

CHISHOLM, Gordon
8.4.60 Glasgow (DF)
6.0¾ 12.0 Apprentice
LD Sunderland v Charlton Ath
19.8.78 1–0

Season	Club			
1977–78	Sunderland	2	—	—
1978–79	Sunderland	2	27	1
1979–80	Sunderland	1	13	—
1980–81	Sunderland	1	34	3
1981–82	Sunderland	1	22	—
1982–83	Sunderland	1	32	1
1983–84	Sunderland	1	36	4
1984–85	Sunderland	1	32	1
1985–86	Sunderland	2	1	—
1985–86	Hibernian	P	29	2
1986–87	Hibernian	P	23	2
1987–88	Hibernian	P	7	—
1987–88	Dundee	P	15	—

CHIVERS, Gary
15.5.60 Stockwell (DF)
5.11 11.5 Apprentice
LD Chelsea v Middlesbrough
21.4.79 2–1

Season	Club			
1978–79	Chelsea	1	5	—
1979–80	Chelsea	2	29	2
1980–81	Chelsea	2	40	2
1981–82	Chelsea	2	29	—
1982–83	Chelsea	2	30	—
1983–84	Swansea C	2	10	—
1983–84	QPR	1	—	—
1984–85	QPR	1	23	—
1985–86	QPR	1	14	—
1986–87	QPR	1	23	—
1987–88	Watford	1	14	—
1987–88	Brighton & HA	3	10	—

PLAYER DIRECTORY

CHRISTIE, Trevor
28.2.59 Newcastle (FW)
6.2 12.0 Apprentice
LD Leicester C v Wolves
25.2.78 1–0

1976–77	Leicester C	1	—	—
1977–78	Leicester C	1	5	—
1978–79	Leicester C	2	26	8
1979–80	Notts Co	2	41	9
1980–81	Notts Co	2	39	14
1981–82	Notts Co	1	35	13
1982–83	Notts Co	1	33	9
1983–84	Notts Co	1	39	19
1984–85	Nottingham F	1	14	5
1984–85	Derby Co	3	20	7
1985–86	Derby Co	3	45	15
1986–87	Manchester C	1	9	3
1986–87	Walsall	3	35	13
1987–88	Walsall	3	36	7

CLAESEN, Nico
1.10.62 Leut, Belgium (FW)
5.8 10.0 Standard Liege
LD Liverpool v Tottenham H
11.10.86 0–1

1986–87	Tottenham H	1	26	8
1987–88	Tottenham H	1	24	10

CLARK, Billy
19.5.67 Christchurch (DF)
5.11 11.8 Local
LD Bournemouth v Newport Co
13.5.85 3–0

1984–85	Bournemouth	3	1	—
1985–86	Bournemouth	3	1	—
1986–87	Bournemouth	3	—	—
1987–88	Bristol R	3	11	—
1987–88	Bristol R	3	20	1

CLARK, Howard
19.9.68 Coventry (DF)
— — Apprentice
LD —

1987–88	Coventry C	1	—	—

CLARK, John
22.9.64 Edinburgh (FW)
6.0 13.1 'S' Form
LD Dundee U v St Mirren
22.1.83 3–2

1981–82	Dundee U	P	—	—
1982–83	Dundee U	P	1	—
1983–84	Dundee U	P	9	1
1984–85	Dundee U	P	10	3
1985–86	Dundee U	P	11	1
1986–87	Dundee U	P	30	3
1987–88	Dundee U	P	28	3

CLARK, Jonathan
12.11.58 Swansea (MF)
5.10 11.10 Apprentice
LD Manchester U v Sunderland
10.11.76 3–3

1975–76	Manchester U	2	—	—
1976–77	Manchester U	1	1	—
1977–78	Manchester U	1	—	—
1978–79	Manchester U	1	—	—
1978–79	Derby Co	1	17	—
1979–80	Derby Co	1	14	1
1980–81	Derby Co	2	22	2
1981–82	Preston NE	3	18	—
1982–83	Preston NE	3	3	—
1983–84	Preston NE	3	31	5
1984–85	Preston NE	3	40	5
1985–86	Preston NE	4	6	—
1986–87	Preston NE	4	12	—
1986–87	Bury	3	14	—
1987–88	Carlisle U	4	41	1

CLARK, Paul
14.9.58 Benfleet (MF)
5.10 12.12 Apprentice
LD Southend U v Watford
21.8.76 2–1

1976–77	Southend U	4	25	—
1977–78	Southend U	4	8	1
1977–78	Brighton & HA	2	26	3
1978–79	Brighton & HA	2	33	4
1979–80	Brighton & HA	1	11	2
1980–81	Brighton & HA	1	9	—
1981–82	Reading	3	2	—
1982–83	Southend U	3	31	1
1983–84	Southend U	3	20	—
1984–85	Southend U	4	29	1
1985–86	Southend U	4	39	1
1986–87	Southend U	4	46	—
1987–88	Southend U	3	30	—

CLARK, Sandy
28.10.56 Airdrie (FW)
6.0 12.7 Aidrie BC
LD Dundee v Airdrieonians
28.12.74 1–0

1974–75	Airdrieonians	1	3	—
1975–76	Airdrieonians	1	20	7
1976–77	Airdrieonians	1	32	8
1977–78	Airdrieonians	1	38	7
1978–79	Airdrieonians	1	38	23
1979–80	Airdrieonians	1	37	22
1980–81	Airdrieonians	P	36	10
1981–82	Airdrieonians	P	30	15
1982–83	West Ham U	1	26	7
1982–83	Rangers	P	10	4
1983–84	Rangers	P	30	9
1984–85	Rangers	P	1	—
1984–85	Hearts	P	25	8
1985–86	Hearts	P	33	12
1986–87	Hearts	P	41	8
1987–88	Hearts	P	35	6

CLARKE, Brian
10.10.68 Eastbourne (DF)
6.2 11.7 YTS
LD —

1987–88	Gillingham	3	—	—

CLARKE, Colin
30.10.62 Newry (FW)
5.10 12.7 Apprentice
LD Halifax T v Peterborough U
5.9.81 1–1

1980–81	Ipswich T	1	—	—
1981–82	Peterborough U	4	27	4
1982–83	Peterborough U	4	37	9
1983–84	Peterborough U	4	18	5
1983–84	Gillingham	3	8	1
1984–85	Tranmere R	4	45	22
1985–86	Bournemouth	3	46	26
1986–87	Southampton	1	33	20
1987–88	Southampton	1	40	16

CLARKE, Michael
22.12.67 Birmingham (FW)
5.11 11.5.
LD Barnsley v WBA
29.11.86 2–2

1986–87	Barnsley	2	23	3
1987–88	Barnsley	2	14	—

CLARKE, Nicky
20.8.67 Walsall (DF)
5.11 11.10 Apprentice
LD Brentford v Wolves
17.8.85 2–1

1984–85	Wolves	2	—	—
1985–86	Wolves	3	23	1
1986–87	Wolves	4	24	—
1987–88	Wolves	4	8	—

CLARKE, Stephen
29.8.63 Saltcoats (DF)
5.10 10.2 Beith Juniors
LD Hibernian v St Mirren
4.9.82 0–0

1981–82	St Mirren	P	—	—
1982–83	St Mirren	P	31	—
1983–84	St Mirren	P	33	2
1984–85	St Mirren	P	33	—
1985–86	St Mirren	P	31	3
1986–87	St Mirren	P	23	1
1986–87	Chelsea	1	16	—
1987–88	Chelsea	1	38	1

CLARKE, Wayne
28.2.61 Wolverhampton (FW)
6.0 11.8 Apprentice
LD Ipswich T v Wolves
9.5.78 1–2

1977–78	Wolves	1	1	—
1978–79	Wolves	1	8	1
1979–80	Wolves	1	16	2
1980–81	Wolves	1	24	3
1981–82	Wolves	1	29	6
1982–83	Wolves	2	39	12
1983–84	Wolves	1	31	6
1984–85	Birmingham C	2	40	17
1985–86	Birmingham C	1	28	5
1986–87	Birmingham C	2	24	16
1986–87	Everton	1	10	5
1987–88	Everton	1	27	10

CLAYTON, Gary
2.2.63 Sheffield (MF)
5.11 12.8 Apprentice
Rotherham U & Burton A
LD Mansfield T v Doncaster R
23.8.86 2–1

1986–87	Doncaster R	3	35	5
1987–88	Cambridge U	4	45	5

CLAYTON, John
20.8.61 Elgin (FW)
5.11 11.7 Apprentice
LD Derby Co v Tottenham H
21.10.78 2–2

1978–79	Derby Co	1	1	—
1979–80	Derby Co	1	—	—
1980–81	Derby Co	2	9	1
1981–82	Derby Co	2	14	3
Bulova, Hong Kong				
1983–84	Chesterfield	4	33	5
1984–85	Tranmere R	4	44	31
1985–86	Tranmere R	4	3	4
1985–86	Plymouth Arg	3	36	12
1986–87	Plymouth Arg	2	21	3
1987–88	Plymouth Arg	2	20	7

CLAYTON, Paul
4.1.65 Dunstable (FW)
5.11 11.3 Apprentice
LD Norwich C v Coventry C
17.12.83 0–0

1982–83	Norwich C	1	—	—
1983–84	Norwich C	1	7	—
1984–85	Norwich C	1	5	—
1985–86	Norwich C	2	1	—
1986–87	Norwich C	1	—	—
1987–88	Norwich C	1	—	—
1987–88	Darlington	4	12	3

CLEGG, Tony
8.11.65 Keighley (DF)
6.0 11.5 Apprentice
LD Preston NE v Bradford C
5.5.84 1–2

1983–84	Bradford C	3	2	—
1984–85	Bradford C	3	7	—
1985–86	Bradford C	2	21	1
1986–87	Bradford C	2	18	1
1987–88	York C	3	37	3

CLELAND, Alec
10.12.70 Glasgow (DF)
5.8½ 10.0 'S' Form
LD Morton v Dundee
30.4.88 0–4

1987–88	Dundee	P	1	—

CLEMENT, Andy
12.11.67 Cardiff (DF)
5.8 11.0 Apprentice
LD Tottenham H v Wimbledon
1.11.86 1–2

1985–86	Wimbledon	2	—	—
1986–87	Wimbledon	1	4	—
1986–87	*Bristol R*	3	6	—
1987–88	Wimbledon	1	11	—
1987–88	*Newport Co*	4	5	1

CLEMENTS, Kenny
9.4.55 Manchester (DF)
6.1 12.6 Amateur
LD Aston Villa v Manchester C
27.8.75 1–0

1975–76	Manchester C	1	27	—
1976–77	Manchester C	1	35	—
1977–78	Manchester C	1	42	—
1978–79	Manchester C	1	15	—
1979–80	Manchester C	1	—	—
1979–80	Oldham Ath	2	36	1
1980–81	Oldham Ath	2	40	—
1981–82	Oldham Ath	2	27	1
1982–83	Oldham Ath	2	38	—
1983–84	Oldham Ath	2	41	—
1984–85	Oldham Ath	2	24	—
1984–85	*Manchester C*	2	12	1
1985–86	Manchester C	1	30	—
1986–87	Manchester C	1	39	—
1987–88	Manchester C	2	25	—
1987–88	Bury	3	9	1

CLOSE, Shaun
8.9.66 Islington (FW)
5.8 10.1 YTS
LD Tottenham H v Nottingham F
29.11.86 2–3

1984–85	Tottenham H	1	—	—
1985–86	Tottenham H	1	—	—
1986–87	Tottenham H	1	2	—
1987–88	Tottenham H	1	7	—
1987–88	*Bournemouth*	2	5	2
1987–88	Bournemouth	2	11	4

CLOUGH, Nigel
19.3.66 Sunderland (FW)
5.9 11.4 AC Hunters
LD Nottingham F v Ipswich T
26.12.84 2–0

1984–85	Nottingham F	1	9	1
1985–86	Nottingham F	1	39	15
1986–87	Nottingham F	1	42	14
1987–88	Nottingham F	1	34	18

COADY, John
25.8.60 Dublin (DF)
5.9 10.10 Shamrock R
LD QPR v Chelsea
18.4.87 1–1

1986–87	Chelsea	1	6	1
1987–88	Chelsea	1	10	1

COATSWORTH, Gary
7.10.68 Sunderland (DF)
6.1 11.6 Apprentice
LD Barnsley v Millwall
19.12.87 4–1

1987–88	Barnsley	2	6	—

COBB, Gary
6.8.68 Luton (MF)
5.8 11.6 Apprentice
LD Charlton Ath v Luton T
2.5.87 0–1

1986–87	Luton T	1	2	—
1987–88	Luton T	1	7	—

COCKERILL, Glenn
25.8.59 Grimsby (MF)
6.0 12.3½ Louth U
LD Lincoln C v Northampton T
5.2.77 5–4

1976–77	Lincoln C	3	4	—
1977–78	Lincoln C	3	13	1
1978–79	Lincoln C	3	35	6
1979–80	Lincoln C	4	19	3
1979–80	Swindon T	3	10	1
1980–81	Swindon T	3	16	—
1981–82	Lincoln C	3	44	11
1982–83	Lincoln C	3	38	8
1983–84	Lincoln C	3	33	6
1983–84	Sheffield U	3	10	1
1984–85	Sheffield U	2	40	7
1985–86	Sheffield U	2	12	2
1985–86	Southampton	1	30	7
1986–87	Southampton	1	42	7
1987–88	Southampton	1	39	2

COCKRAM, Allan
18.10.63 Kensington (MF)
5.9 11.5 St Alban's City
LD Brentford v Notts Co
2.4.88 1–0

1987–88	Brentford	3	7	2

COHEN, Avi
14.11.56 Cairo (DF)
5.11 12.4 Maccabi
LD Leeds U v Liverpool
15.9.79 1–1

1979–80	Liverpool	1	4	1
1980–81	Liverpool	1	14	—
1981–87	Maccabi			
1987–88	Rangers	P	7	—

COLE, David
28.9.62 Barnsley (DF)
6.0 11.10 Sunderland
LD Brentford v Swansea C
22.9.84 3–0

1984–85	Swansea C	3	8	—
1984–85	Swindon T	4	20	—
1985–86	Swindon T	4	44	3
1986–87	Swindon T	3	5	—
1986–87	Torquay U	4	29	—
1987–88	Torquay U	4	46	5

PLAYER DIRECTORY

COLE, Michael
3.9.66 Stepney (FW)
5.10½ 11.3½ Amateur
LD Stoke C v Ipswich T
8.12.84 0–2

1983–84 Ipswich T	1	—	—
1984–85 Ipswich T	1	2	—
1985–86 Ipswich T	1	18	1
1986–87 Ipswich T	2	16	2
1987–88 Ipswich T	2	2	—
1987–88 *Port Vale*	3	4	1
1987–88 Fulham	3	9	1

COLEMAN, Chris
10.6.70 Swansea (DF)
6.2½ 12.10 Apprentice
LD Stockport Co v Swansea C
15.8.87 0–2

1987–88 Swansea C	4	30	—

COLEMAN, David
8.4.67 Salisbury (MF)
5.7 10.8
LD Blackpool v Bournemouth
29.4.86 2–0

1985–86 Bournemouth	3	1	—
1986–87 Bournemouth	3	1	—
1987–88 Bournemouth	2	5	—
1987–88 *Colchester U*	4	6	1

COLEMAN, Nicky
6.5.66 Crayford (DF)
5.8 11.7 Apprentice
LD Brentford v Millwall
19.5.85 1–1

1983–84 Millwall	3	—	—
1984–85 Millwall	3	1	—
1985–86 Millwall	2	6	—
1985–86 *Swindon T*	4	13	4
1986–87 Millwall	2	42	—
1987–88 Millwall	2	36	—

COLEMAN, Simon
13.3.68 Worksop (MF)
6.0 10.8
LD Port Vale v Mansfield T
18.4.87 3–2

1985–86 Mansfield T	4	—	—
1986–87 Mansfield T	3	2	—
1987–88 Mansfield T	3	44	2

COLLINS, Eamonn
22.10.65 Dublin (MF)
5.6½ 8.13 Apprentice
LD Southampton v QPR
29.9.84 1–1

1982–83 Southampton	1	—	—
1983–84 Southampton	1	—	—
1984–85 Southampton	1	3	—
1985–86 Southampton	1	—	—
1986–87 Portsmouth	2	5	—
1987–88 Portsmouth	1	—	—
1987–88 *Exeter C*	4	9	—

COLLINS, Gerry
12.3.55 Glasgow (MF)
5.11 12.9 St Roch's
LD Albion R v Arbroath
22.9.81 2–0

1981–82 Albion R	2	32	1
1982–83 Albion R	2	35	—
1983–84 Albion R	2	1	—
1983–84 Ayr U	1	32	5
1984–85 Ayr U	1	34	8
1985–86 Ayr U	1	8	1
1985–86 Hamilton A	1	13	1
1986–87 Hamilton A	P	37	2
1987–88 Hamilton A	1	33	2

COLLINS, John
31.1.68 Galashiels (MF)
5.7 9.10 Hutchison Vale BC
LD Aberdeen v Hibernian
10.8.85 3–0

1984–85 Hibernian	P	—	—
1985–86 Hibernian	P	19	1
1986–87 Hibernian	P	30	1
1987–88 Hibernian	P	44	6

COLLINS, Steve
21.3.62 Stamford (DF)
5.8 12.4 Apprentice
LD Peterborough U v Blackpool
28.4.79 1–2

1978–79 Peterborough U	3	5	—
1979–80 Peterborough U	4	8	—
1980–81 Peterborough U	4	1	—
1981–82 Peterborough U	4	34	1
1982–83 Peterborough U	4	46	—
1983–84 Southend U	3	36	—
1984–85 Southend U	4	15	—
1984–85 *Lincoln C*	3	13	—
1985–86 Lincoln C	3	11	—
1985–86 Peterborough U	4	22	—
1986–87 Peterborough U	4	27	—
1987–88 Peterborough U	4	39	1

COLQUHOUN, John
14.7.63 Stirling (FW)
5.7 10.0 Grangemouth Inter
LD Dunfermline Ath v Stirling A
31.1.81 0–1

1980–81 Stirling Albion	1	13	—
1981–82 Stirling Albion	2	37	13
1982–83 Stirling Albion	2	39	21
1983–84 Stirling Albion	2	15	11
1983–84 Celtic	P	12	2
1984–85 Celtic	P	20	2
1985–86 Hearts	P	36	8
1986–87 Hearts	P	43	13
1987–88 Hearts	P	44	15

COLVILLE, Robert
27.4.63 Nuneaton (FW)
5.11 11.12 Rhos
LD Oldham Ath v Manchester C
20.4.84 2–2

1983–84 Oldham Ath	2	4	1
1984–85 Oldham Ath	2	7	1
1985–86 Oldham Ath	2	17	2
1986–87 Oldham Ath	2	4	—
1986–87 Bury	3	8	1
1987–88 Bury	3	3	—
1987–88 *Stockport Co*	4	15	2
1987–88 Stockport Co	4	25	12

COMFORT, Alan
8.12.64 Aldershot (MF)
5.7 11.2 Apprentice
LD Cambridge U v Bristol C
15.9.84 2–3

1982–83 QPR	2	—	—
1983–84 QPR	1	—	—
1984–85 QPR	1	—	—
1984–85 Cambridge U	3	33	2
1985–86 Cambridge U	4	30	3
1985–86 Orient	4	15	5
1986–87 Orient	4	45	11
1987–88 Leyton Orient	4	46	11

COMSTIVE, Paul
25.11.61 Southport (DF)
5.11 11.6 Amateur
LD Sheffield W v Blackburn R
7.10.80 2–1

1979–80 Blackburn R	3	—	—
1980–81 Blackburn R	2	3	—
1981–82 Blackburn R	2	2	—
1982–83 Blackburn R	2	1	—
1982–83 *Rochdale*	4	9	2
1983–84 Wigan Ath	3	29	2
1984–85 Wigan Ath	3	6	—
1984–85 Wrexham	4	28	3
1985–86 Wrexham	4	35	3
1986–87 Wrexham	4	36	2
1987–88 Burnley	4	44	8

CONEY, Dean
18.9.63 Dagenham (FW)
6.0 13.4 Apprentice
LD Fulham v Newport Co
28.3.81 2–1

1980–81 Fulham	3	7	3
1981–82 Fulham	3	42	13
1982–83 Fulham	2	37	4
1983–84 Fulham	2	27	7
1984–85 Fulham	2	24	7
1985–86 Fulham	2	37	12
1986–87 Fulham	3	37	10
1987–88 QPR	1	32	7

CONNELLY, Dino
6.1.70 Jersey (MF)
— — Apprentice
LD —

1987–88 Arsenal	1	—	—

CONNOR, Robert
4.8.60 Kilmarnock (MF)
5.11 11.4 Ayr U BC
LD Ayr U v Partick Th
15.3.78 1–3

1977–78 Ayr U	P	9	—
1978–79 Ayr U	1	29	—
1979–80 Ayr U	1	38	9
1980–81 Ayr U	1	39	8
1981–82 Ayr U	1	30	
1982–83 Ayr U	1	39	4
1983–84 Ayr U	1	39	7
1984–85 Dundee	P	34	7
1985–86 Dundee	P	35	2
1986–87 Dundee	P	2	—
1986–87 Aberdeen	P	32	4
1987–88 Aberdeen	P	34	1

CONNOR, Terry
9.11.62 Leeds (FW)
5.7 10.0 Apprentice
LD Leeds U v WBA
17.1.79 1–0

1979–80 Leeds U	1	23	6
1980–81 Leeds U	1	27	4
1981–82 Leeds U	1	27	4
1982–83 Leeds U	2	19	5
1982–83 Brighton & HA	1	7	1
1983–84 Brighton & HA	2	40	13
1984–85 Brighton & HA	2	38	14
1985–86 Brighton & HA	2	33	14
1986–87 Brighton & HA	2	38	9
1987–88 Portsmouth	1	19	4

CONROY, Michael
31.12.65 Glasgow (FW)
6.0 11.0 Apprentice
LD Partick Th v Clydebank
5.5.84 1–1

1983–84 Coventry C	1	—	—
1983–84 Clydebank	1	2	—
1984–85 Clydebank	1	26	11
1985–86 Clydebank	P	28	7
1986–87 Clydebank	P	36	9
1987–88 Clydebank	1	22	11
1987–88 St Mirren	P	10	1

COOK, Andrew
— Romsey (DF)
5.9 10.12 Apprentice
LD Southampton v Manchester U
15.8.87 2–2

1987–88 Southampton	1	2	—

COOK, Michael
— Coventry (MF)
— — YTS
LD York C v Walsall
31.8.87 1–3

1987–88 Coventry C	1	—	—
1987–88 York C	3	6	1

COOK, Mitchel
15.10.61 Scarborough (MF)
5.10 12.0 Scarborough
LD Aldershot v Darlington
29.9.84 3–4

1984–85 Darlington	4	31	3
1985–86 Darlington	3	3	1
1985–86 Middlesbrough	2	6	—
1986–87 Scarborough	—	—	—
1987–88 Scarborough	4	38	5

COOK, Paul
22.2.67 Liverpool (MF)
5.11 10.10
LD Wigan Ath v Reading
13.5.85 1–1

1984–85 Wigan Ath	3	2	—
1985–86 Wigan Ath	3	13	2
1986–87 Wigan Ath	3	27	4
1987–88 Wigan Ath	3	41	8

COOKE, Richard
4.9.65 Islington (FW)
5.6 9.0 Apprentice
LD Luton T v Tottenham H
19.11.83 2–4

1982–83 Tottenham H	1	—	—
1983–84 Tottenham H	1	9	1
1984–85 Tottenham H	1	—	—
1985–86 Tottenham H	1	2	1
1986–87 Birmingham C	2	5	—
1986–87 Bournemouth	3	23	7
1987–88 Bournemouth	2	34	5

COOKE, Robbie
16.2.57 Rotherham (FW)
5.9 10.8 Apprentice
LD Chester v Mansfield T
16.10.76 1–0

1976–77 Mansfield T	3	9	1
1977–78 Mansfield T	2	6	—
Grantham T			
1980–81 Peterborough U	4	46	22
1981–82 Peterborough U	4	46	24
1982–83 Peterborough U	4	23	5
1982–83 Luton T	1	—	—
1982–83 Cambridge U	2	12	2
1983–84 Cambridge U	2	37	6
1984–85 Cambridge U	3	16	6
1984–85 Brentford	3	24	12
1985–86 Brentford	3	44	17
1986–87 Brentford	3	40	20
1987–88 Brentford	3	16	4
1987–88 Millwall	2	4	1

COOPER, Colin
28.2.67 Durham (MF)
5.10 10.0
LD C Palace v Middlesborough
8.3.86 2–1

COOPER, Davie
25.2.56 Hamilton (FW)
5.8 12.5 Hamilton Avondale
LD Queen of the S v Clydebank
31.8.74 3–0

1974–75 Clydebank	2	26	4
1975–76 Clydebank	2	26	13
1976–77 Clydebank	1	38	11
1977–78 Rangers	P	35	6
1978–79 Rangers	P	30	5
1979–80 Rangers	P	30	2
1980–81 Rangers	P	25	3
1981–82 Rangers	P	30	3
1982–83 Rangers	P	31	5
1983–84 Rangers	P	34	6
1984–85 Rangers	P	32	5
1985–86 Rangers	P	32	4
1986–87 Rangers	P	42	8
1987–88 Rangers	P	33	1

COOPER, Geoff
27.12.66 Kingston-on-Thames (MF)
— — Bognor Regis T
LD Preston NE v Brighton & HA
5.3.88 3–0

1987–88 Brighton & HA	3	2	—

COOPER, Graham
18.11.65 Bolton (FW)
5.10 10.9 Amateur
LD Portsmouth v Huddersfield T
5.5.84 1–1

1983–84 Huddersfield T	2	3	1
1984–85 Huddersfield T	2	34	5
1985–86 Huddersfield T	2	—	—
1986–87 Huddersfield T	2	12	2
1987–88 Huddersfield T	2	25	5

COOPER, Leigh
7.5.61 Reading (MF)
5.8 10.9 Apprentice
LD Sheffield U v Plymouth Arg
1.12.79 3–2

1979–80 Plymouth Arg	3	14	—
1980–81 Plymouth Arg	3	28	3
1981–82 Plymouth Arg	3	43	5
1982–83 Plymouth Arg	3	45	4
1983–84 Plymouth Arg	3	43	2
1984–85 Plymouth Arg	3	21	—
1985–86 Plymouth Arg	3	40	1
1986–87 Plymouth Arg	2	35	—
1987–88 Plymouth Arg	2	37	—

1984–85 Middlesbrough	2	—	—
1985–86 Middlesbrough	2	11	—
1986–87 Middlesbrough	3	46	—
1987–88 Middlesbrough	2	43	2

PLAYER DIRECTORY

COOPER, Mark
18.12.68 Wakefield (MF)
5.8 11.4 Apprentice
LD —

1987–88 Bristol C	3	—	—

COOPER, Mark
5.4.67 Cambridge (MF)
6.1 13.0 Apprentice
LD Cambridge U v Barnsley
21.4.84 0–3

1983–84 Cambridge U	2	2	—
1984–85 Cambridge U	3	18	3
1985–86 Cambridge U	4	19	1
1986–87 Cambridge U	4	32	13
1987–88 Tottenham H	1	—	—
1987–88 *Shrewsbury T*	2	6	2
1987–88 Gillingham	3	31	8

COOPER, Neale
24.11.63 India (DF)
6.1 12.3 King St
LD Aberdeen v Kilmarnock
11.10.80 2–0

1979–80 Aberdeen	P	—	—
1980–81 Aberdeen	P	5	—
1981–82 Aberdeen	P	27	3
1982–83 Aberdeen	P	31	2
1983–84 Aberdeen	P	26	—
1984–85 Aberdeen	P	20	1
1985–86 Aberdeen	P	23	—
1986–87 Aston Villa	1	13	—
1987–88 Aston Villa	2	7	—

COOPER, Neil
12.8.59 Aberdeen (DF)
5.11 12.7 Hilton Academy
LD Airdrieonians v Aberdeen
4.3.75 2–2

1974–75 Aberdeen	1	1	—
1975–76 Aberdeen	P	2	—
1976–77 Aberdeen	P	—	—
1977–78 Aberdeen	P	1	—
1978–79 Aberdeen	P	7	1
1979–80 Aberdeen	P	1	—
1979–80 Barnsley	3	20	3
1980–81 Barnsley	3	30	2
1981–82 Barnsley	2	10	1
1981–82 Grimsby T	2	16	1
1982–83 Grimsby T	2	24	1
1983–84 Grimsby T	2	7	—
1983–84 St Mirren	P	25	—
1984–85 St Mirren	P	10	—
1985–86 St Mirren	P	30	—
1986–87 St Mirren	P	39	1
1987–88 St Mirren	P	27	1

COOPER, Paul
21.12.53 Brierley Hill (GK)
5.11 13.10 Apprentice
LD Birmingham C v Portsmouth
8.1.72 6–3

1971–72 Birmingham C	2	12	—
1972–73 Birmingham C	1	3	—
1973–74 Birmingham C	1	2	—
1973–74 Ipswich T	1	1	—
1974–75 Ipswich T	1	2	—
1975–76 Ipswich T	1	40	—
1976–77 Ipswich T	1	34	—
1977–78 Ipswich T	1	40	—
1978–79 Ipswich T	1	41	—
1979–80 Ipswich T	1	40	—
1980–81 Ipswich T	1	38	—
1981–82 Ipswich T	1	32	—
1982–83 Ipswich T	1	35	—
1983–84 Ipswich T	1	36	—
1984–85 Ipswich T	1	36	—
1985–86 Ipswich T	1	36	—
1986–87 Ipswich T	2	36	—
1987–88 Leicester C	2	32	—

COOPER, Richard
7.5.65 London (MF)
5.10 10.8 Amateur
LD Bradford C v Sheffield U
8.5.83 2–0

1982–83 Sheffield U	3	2	—
1983–84 Sheffield U	3	—	—
1984–85 Sheffield U	2	4	—
1985–86 Lincoln C	3	20	—
1986–87 Lincoln C	4	41	2
1987–88 Exeter C	4	33	1

COOPER, Steve
22.6.64 Birmingham (FW)
5.11½ 10.12 Apprentice
LD Halifax T v York C
26.12.83 1–2

1983–84 Birmingham C	1	—	—
1983–84 *Halifax T*	4	7	1
1984–85 *Mansfield T*	4	—	—
1984–85 Newport Co	3	38	11
1985–86 Plymouth Arg	3	38	8
1986–87 Plymouth Arg	2	12	4
1987–88 Plymouth Arg	2	23	3

CORK, Alan
4.3.59 Derby (FW)
6.0 12.0 Amateur
LD Oxford U v Lincoln C
14.9.77 1–0

1977–78 Derby Co	1	—	—
1977–78 *Lincoln C*	3	5	—
1977–78 Wimbledon	4	17	4
1978–79 Wimbledon	4	45	22
1979–80 Wimbledon	3	42	12
1980–81 Wimbledon	4	41	23
1981–82 Wimbledon	3	6	—
1982–83 Wimbledon	4	7	5
1983–84 Wimbledon	3	42	29
1984–85 Wimbledon	2	28	11
1985–86 Wimbledon	2	38	11
1986–87 Wimbledon	1	30	5
1987–88 Wimbledon	1	34	9

CORK, David
28.10.62 Doncaster (MF)
5.9 11.8 Apprentice
LD Arsenal v Watford
17.12.83 3–1

1980–81 Arsenal	1	—	—
1981–82 Arsenal	1	—	—
1982–83 Arsenal	1	—	—
1983–84 Arsenal	1	7	1
1984–85 Arsenal	1	—	—
1985–86 Huddersfield T	2	38	8
1986–87 Huddersfield T	2	36	9
1987–88 Huddersfield T	2	36	8

CORNER, David
15.5.66 Sunderland (DF)
6.2 12.7 Apprentice
LD Nottingham F v Sunderland
1.9.84 3–1

1983–84 Sunderland	1	—	—
1984–85 Sunderland	1	3	—
1985–86 Sunderland	2	9	—
1985–86 *Cardiff C*	3	6	—
1986–87 Sunderland	2	17	1
1987–88 Sunderland	3	4	—
1987–88 *Peterborough U*	4	9	—

CORNFORTH, John
7.10.67 Whitley Bay (DF)
6.1 11.5 Apprentice
LD Sunderland v Ipswich T
11.5.85 1–2

1984–85 Sunderland	1	1	—
1985–86 Sunderland	2	—	—
1986–87 *Doncaster R*	3	7	3
1987–88 Sunderland	3	12	2

CORNWELL, John
13.10.64 Bethnal Green (DF)
6.0 12.0 Apprentice
LD Norwich C v Orient
8.5.82 2–0

1981–82 Orient	2	3	—
1982–83 Orient	3	31	3
1983–84 Orient	3	42	7
1984–85 Orient	3	36	10
1985–86 Orient	4	44	8
1986–87 Orient	4	46	7
1987–88 Newcastle U	1	14	1

COTON, Tony
19.5.61 Tamworth (GK)
6.1 11.8 Mile Oak
LD Birmingham C v Sunderland
27.12.80 3–2

1978–79 Birmingham C	1	—	—
1979–80 Birmingham C	2	—	—
1979–80 *Hereford U*	4	—	—
1980–81 Birmingham C	1	3	—
1981–82 Birmingham C	1	15	—
1982–83 Birmingham C	1	28	—
1983–84 Birmingham C	1	41	—
1984–85 Birmingham C	2	7	—
1984–85 Watford	1	33	—
1985–86 Watford	1	40	—
1986–87 Watford	1	31	—
1987–88 Watford	1	37	—

Tony Cottee

Photo: *Bob Thomas Sports Photography*.

78

PLAYER DIRECTORY

COTTEE, Tony
11.7.65 West Ham (FW)
5.8 11.4 Apprentice
LD West Ham U v Tottenham H
1.1.83 3–0

1982–83 West Ham U	1	8	5
1983–84 West Ham U	1	39	15
1984–85 West Ham U	1	41	17
1985–86 West Ham U	1	42	20
1986–87 West Ham U	1	42	23
1987–88 West Ham U	1	40	13

COUGHLIN, Russell
15.2.60 Swansea (MF)
5.8 12.2 Apprentice
LD Blackburn R v Cambridge U
28.3.79 1–0

1977–78 Manchester C	1	—	—
1978–79 Manchester C	1	—	—
1978–79 Blackburn R	2	11	—
1979–80 Blackburn R	3	10	—
1980–81 Blackburn R	2	3	—
1980–81 Carlisle U	3	25	3
1981–82 Carlisle U	3	37	5
1982–83 Carlisle U	2	38	2
1983–84 Carlisle U	2	30	3
1984–85 Plymouth Arg	3	38	3
1985–86 Plymouth Arg	3	45	10
1986–87 Plymouth Arg	2	40	5
1987–88 Plymouth Arg	2	8	—
1987–88 Blackpool	3	24	2

COWAN, Steven
17.2.63 Paisley (FW)
5.11 11.4 Claremont HS
LD St Mirren v Aberdeen
9.8.80 0–1

1978–79 St Mirren	P	—	—
1979–80 Aberdeen	P	—	—
1980–81 Aberdeen	P	5	1
1981–82 Aberdeen	P	13	3
1982–83 Aberdeen	P	3	—
1983–84 Aberdeen	P	5	—
1984–85 Aberdeen	P	16	5
1985–86 Hibernian	P	36	19
1986–87 Hibernian	P	29	4
1987–88 Hibernian	P	5	—
1987–88 Motherwell	P	32	9

COXALL, Philip
29.1.69 Sunderland (DF)
5.10 11.5 Apprentice
LD —

1987–88 Newcastle U	1	—	—

COX, Brian
7.5.61 Sheffield (GK)
6.1 13.10 Apprentice
LD Sheffield W v Oxford U
17.10.78 1–1

COYNE, Peter
13.11.58 Hartlepool (FW)
5.9 10.7 Apprentice
LD Leicester C v Manchester U
24.4.76 2–1

1975–76 Manchester U	1	2	1
1976–77 Manchester U	1	—	—
Ashton U			
1977–78 Crewe Alex	4	41	16
1978–79 Crewe Alex	4	36	16
1979–80 Crewe Alex	4	25	2
1980–81 Crewe Alex	4	32	13
Hyde U			
1984–85 Swindon T	4	45	15
1985–86 Swindon T	4	31	10
1986–87 Swindon T	3	28	5
1987–88 Swindon T	2	5	—

COYNE, Tommy
14.11.62 Glasgow (FW)
6.0 10.7 Hillwood BC
LD Raith R v Clydebank
10.10.81 0–2

1981–82 Clydebank	1	31	9
1982–83 Clydebank	1	38	18
1983–84 Clydebank	1	11	10
1983–84 Dundee U	P	18	3
1984–85 Dundee U	P	21	3
1985–86 Dundee U	P	13	2
1986–87 Dundee U	P	10	1
1986–87 Dundee	P	20	9
1987–88 Dundee	P	43	33

CRABBE, Scott
12.8.68 Edinburgh (MF)
5.7 10.0 Tynecastle BC
LD Hearts v Clydebank
3.1.87 3–0

1986–87 Hearts	P	5	—
1987–88 Hearts	P	5	—

CRAIG, Albert
3.1.62 Glasgow (MF)
5.8 11.3
LD Newcastle U v Luton T
7.2.87 2–2

1986–87 Newcastle U	1	6	—
1987–88 Newcastle U	1	3	—
1987–88 *Hamilton A*	1	6	1

CRANSON, Ian
2.7.64 Easington (DF)
5.11¼ 12.4 Apprentice
LD Aston Villa v Ipswich T
17.12.83 4–0

1982–83 Ipswich T	1	—	—
1983–84 Ipswich T	1	8	—
1984–85 Ipswich T	1	20	1
1985–86 Ipswich T	1	42	1
1986–87 Ipswich T	2	32	2
1987–88 Ipswich T	2	29	1
1987–88 Sheffield W	1	4	—

CRIBLEY, Alex
1.4.57 Liverpool (DF)
5.11 12.9 Local
LD Bournemouth v Wigan Ath
1.11.80 3–0

1978–79 Liverpool	1	—	—
1979–80 Liverpool	1	—	—
1980–81 Liverpool	1	—	—
1980–81 Wigan Ath	4	30	—
1981–82 Wigan Ath	4	31	—
1982–83 Wigan Ath	3	41	1
1983–84 Wigan Ath	3	44	1
1984–85 Wigan Ath	3	31	1
1985–86 Wigan Ath	3	38	2
1986–87 Wigan Ath	3	45	8
1987–88 Wigan Ath	3	11	3

CRICHTON, Paul
3.10.65 Pontefract (GK)
6.1 12.5 Apprentice
LD Notts Co v Middlesbrough
21.10.86 1–0

1986–87 Nottingham F	1	—	—
1986–87 *Notts Co*	3	5	—
1986–87 *Darlington*	3	5	—
1986–87 *Peterborough U*	4	4	—
1987–88 Nottingham F	1	—	—
1987–88 *Darlington*	4	3	—
1987–88 *Swindon T*	2	4	—
1987–88 *Rotherham U*	3	6	—

CROFT, Brian
27.9.67 Chester (MF)
5.9 10.10
LD Peterborough U v Chester C
24.8.85 3–0

1984–85 Chester C	4	—	—
1985–86 Chester C	4	1	—
1986–87 Chester C	3	21	1
1987–88 Chester C	3	37	2

COX, Brian — Sheffield Wed/Huddersfield T records:

1978–79 Sheffield Wed	3	4	—
1979–80 Sheffield Wed	3	15	—
1980–81 Sheffield Wed	2	3	—
1981–82 Huddersfield T	3	14	—
1982–83 Huddersfield T	3	45	—
1983–84 Huddersfield T	2	23	—
1984–85 Huddersfield T	2	37	—
1985–86 Huddersfield T	2	37	—
1986–87 Huddersfield T	2	37	—
1987–88 Huddersfield T	2	20	—

CROMBIE, Dean
9.8.57 Lincoln (DF)
6.0 11.12 Ruston Sports
LD Lincoln C v Gillingham
26.3.77 4–0

1976–77	Lincoln C	3	13	—
1977–78	Lincoln C	3	20	—
1978–79	Grimsby T	4	46	1
1979–80	Grimsby T	3	39	—
1980–81	Grimsby T	2	33	—
1981–82	Grimsby T	2	38	—
1982–83	Grimsby T	2	32	1
1983–84	Grimsby T	2	40	—
1984–85	Grimsby T	2	39	—
1985–86	Grimsby T	2	34	1
1986–87	Grimsby T	2	19	—
1986–87	*Reading*	2	4	—
1987–88	Bolton W	4	24	—

CROOK, Ian
18.1.63 Romford (MF)
5.8 10.6 Apprentice
LD Coventry C v Tottenham H
1.5.82 0–0

1980–81	Tottenham H	1	—	—
1981–82	Tottenham H	1	4	—
1982–83	Tottenham H	1	4	—
1983–84	Tottenham H	1	3	—
1984–85	Tottenham H	1	5	1
1985–86	Tottenham H	1	4	—
1986–87	Norwich C	1	33	5
1987–88	Norwich C	1	23	1

CROOKS, Garth
10.3.58 Stoke (FW)
5.8 11.6 Apprentice
LD Stoke C v Coventry C
10.4.76 0–1

1975–76	Stoke C	1	2	—
1976–77	Stoke C	1	23	6
1977–78	Stoke C	2	42	18
1978–79	Stoke C	2	40	12
1979–80	Stoke C	1	40	12
1980–81	Tottenham H	1	40	16
1981–82	Tottenham H	1	27	13
1982–83	Tottenham H	1	26	8
1983–84	Tottenham H	1	10	1
1983–84	*Manchester U*	1	7	2
1984–85	Tottenham H	1	22	10
1985–86	WBA	1	19	5
1986–87	WBA	2	21	11
1986–87	Charlton Ath	1	7	2
1987–88	Charlton Ath	1	28	10

CROSBY, Gary
8.5.64 Sleaford (MF)
— — Grantham
LD Nottingham F v Charlton Ath
16.1.88 2–2

1987–88	Nottingham F	1	14	1

CROSBY, Phil
9.11.62 Leeds (DF)
5.9 10.8 Apprentice
LD Grimsby T v Blackburn R
12.1.80 1–2

1979–80	Grimsby T	3	4	—
1980–81	Grimsby T	2	10	—
1981–82	Grimsby T	2	15	1
1982–83	Grimsby T	2	10	—
1983–84	Rotherham U	3	39	—
1984–85	Rotherham U	3	33	—
1985–86	Rotherham U	3	12	—
1986–87	Rotherham U	3	34	—
1987–88	Rotherham U	3	28	—

CROSS, Nicky
7.2.61 Birmingham (FW)
5.9 11.1 Apprentice
LD Manchester U v WBA
18.4.81 2–1

1978–79	WBA	1	—	—
1979–80	WBA	1	—	—
1980–81	WBA	1	2	1
1981–82	WBA	1	22	2
1982–83	WBA	1	32	4
1983–84	WBA	1	25	3
1984–85	WBA	1	24	5
1985–86	Walsall	3	44	21
1986–87	Walsall	3	39	16
1987–88	Walsall	3	26	8
1987–88	Leicester C	2	17	6

CROSS, Paul
31.10.65 Barnsley (MF)
5.8 10.0 Apprentice
LD C Palace v Barnsley
7.10.84 0–1

1983–84	Barnsley	2	—	—
1984–85	Barnsley	2	1	—
1985–86	Barnsley	2	20	—
1986–87	Barnsley	2	18	—
1987–88	Barnsley	2	38	—

CROSS, Steve
22.12.59 Wolverhampton (DF)
5.10 10.8 Apprentice
LD Mansfield T v Shrewsbury T
12.4.77 1–0

1976–77	Shrewsbury T	3	5	—
1977–78	Shrewsbury T	3	1	—
1978–79	Shrewsbury T	3	19	2
1979–80	Shrewsbury T	2	19	—
1980–81	Shrewsbury T	2	35	2
1981–82	Shrewsbury T	2	34	3
1982–83	Shrewsbury T	2	33	5
1983–84	Shrewsbury T	2	41	9
1984–85	Shrewsbury T	2	40	5
1985–86	Shrewsbury T	2	35	8
1986–87	Derby Co	2	6	—
1987–88	Derby Co	1	15	3

CROSSLEY, Mark
16.6.69 Barnsley (GK)
— — Apprentice
LD —

1987–88	Nottingham F	1	—	—

CROWE, Mark
21.1.65 Southwold (DF)
5.10 10.10 Apprentice
LD Brighton & HA v Norwich C
11.12.82 3–0

1982–83	Norwich C	1	1	—
1983–84	Norwich C	1	—	—
1984–85	Norwich C	1	—	—
1985–86	Torquay U	4	45	2
1986–87	Torquay U	4	12	—
1986–87	Cambridge U	4	24	—
1987–88	Cambridge U	4	27	—

CROWN, David
16.2.58 Enfield (FW)
5.10 11.4 Walthamstow Ave
LD Charlton Ath v Brentford
16.8.80 3–1

1980–81	Brentford	3	38	6
1981–82	Brentford	3	8	2
1981–82	Portsmouth	3	27	2
1982–83	Portsmouth	3	1	—
1982–83	*Exeter C*	3	7	3
1983–84	Reading	4	45	7
1984–85	Reading	3	43	8
1985–86	Cambridge U	4	43	24
1986–87	Cambridge U	4	46	12
1987–88	Cambridge U	4	17	9
1987–88	Southend U	3	28	17

CRUDGINGTON, Geoff
14.2.52 Wolverhampton (GK)
6.0 12.12 Amateur
LD Bristol R v Aston Villa
9.1.71 1–2

1969–70	Aston Villa	2	—	—
1970–71	Aston Villa	3	3	—
1970–71	*Bradford C*	3	1	—
1971–72	Aston Villa	3	1	—
1971–72	Crewe Alex	4	14	—
1972–73	Crewe Alex	4	46	—
1973–74	Crewe Alex	4	20	—
1973–74	*Preston NE*	2	—	—
1974–75	Crewe Alex	4	46	—
1975–76	Crewe Alex	4	46	—
1976–77	Crewe Alex	4	32	—
1977–78	Crewe Alex	4	46	—
1978–79	Swansea C	3	46	—
1979–80	Swansea C	2	6	—
1979–80	Plymouth Arg	3	37	—
1980–81	Plymouth Arg	3	46	—
1981–82	Plymouth Arg	3	46	—
1982–83	Plymouth Arg	3	44	—
1983–84	Plymouth Arg	3	46	—
1984–85	Plymouth Arg	3	33	—
1985–86	Plymouth Arg	3	46	—
1986–87	Plymouth Arg	2	21	—
1987–88	Plymouth Arg	2	7	—

PLAYER DIRECTORY

CRUMPLIN, John
26.5.67 Bath (FW)
5.8½ 11.10 Bognor
LD Brighton & HA v Ipswich T
21.3.87 1–2

1986–87	Brighton & HA	2	5	—
1987–88	Brighton & HA	3	26	2

CULPIN, Paul
8.2.62 Kirby Muxloe (FW)
5.10 10.8
LD Coventry C v Oxford U
3.9.85 5–2

1981–82	Leicester C	2	—	—
Nuneaton				
1985–86	Coventry C	1	7	1
1986–87	Coventry C	1	2	1
1987–88	Northampton T	3	20	10

CULVERHOUSE, Ian
22.9.64 Bishop's Stortford (DF)
5.10 11.2 Apprentice
LD Notts Co v Tottenham H
21.2.84 0–0

1982–83	Tottenham H	1	—	—
1983–84	Tottenham H	1	2	—
1984–85	Tottenham H	1	—	—
1985–86	Tottenham H	1	—	—
1985–86	Norwich C	2	30	—
1986–87	Norwich C	1	25	—
1987–88	Norwich C	1	33	—

CUNNINGHAM, Tony
12.11.57 Jamaica (FW)
6.2 13.4 Stourbridge
LD Lincoln C v Peterborough U
18.8.79 0–1

1979–80	Lincoln C	4	38	12
1980–81	Lincoln C	4	34	6
1981–82	Lincoln C	3	46	11
1982–83	Lincoln C	3	5	3
1982–83	Barnsley	2	29	7
1983–84	Barnsley	2	13	4
1983–84	Sheffield W	2	28	5
1984–85	Manchester C	2	18	1
1984–85	Newcastle U	1	13	1
1985–86	Newcastle U	1	17	1
1986–87	Newcastle U	1	17	2
1987–88	Blackpool	3	40	10

CUNNINGTON, Edward
12.11.69 Kilbride (MF)
— — Trainee
LD —

1987–88	Chelsea	1	—	—

CUNNINGTON, Shaun
4.1.66 Bourne (DF)
5.8 10.4 Bourne T
LD Bristol R v Wrexham
18.12.83 4–0

1982–83	Wrexham	3	4	—
1983–84	Wrexham	4	42	—
1984–85	Wrexham	4	41	6
1985–86	Wrexham	4	42	2
1986–87	Wrexham	4	46	1
1987–88	Wrexham	4	24	3
1987–88	Grimsby T	3	15	2

CURBISHLEY, Alan
8.11.57 Forest Gate (MF)
5.10½ 11.4 Apprentice
LD West Ham U v Chelsea
29.3.75 0–1

1974–75	West Ham U	1	2	—
1975–76	West Ham U	1	14	2
1976–77	West Ham U	1	10	1
1977–78	West Ham U	1	32	1
1978–79	West Ham U	2	27	1
1979–80	Birmingham C	2	42	3
1980–81	Birmingham C	1	29	6
1981–82	Birmingham C	1	29	1
1982–83	Birmingham C	1	30	1
1982–83	Aston Villa	1	7	—
1983–84	Aston Villa	1	26	1
1984–85	Aston Villa	1	3	—
1984–85	Charlton Ath	2	23	2
1985–86	Charlton Ath	2	30	4
1986–87	Charlton Ath	1	10	—
1987–88	Brighton & HA	3	34	6

CURRAN, Henry
9.10.66 Glasgow (MF)
5.8 11.4 Eastercraigs
LD Dumbarton v Rangers
29.12.84 2–4

1984–85	Dumbarton	P	2	—
1985–86	Dumbarton	1	6	—
1986–87	Dumbarton	1	8	—
1986–87	Dundee U	P	3	—
1987–88	Dundee U	P	6	—

CURRIE, David
27.11.62 Stockton (FW)
6.0 11.13 Local
LD Swansea C v Middlesbrough
15.5.82 1–2

1981–82	Middlesbrough	1	1	—
1982–83	Middlesbrough	2	8	—
1983–84	Middlesbrough	2	39	15
1984–85	Middlesbrough	2	39	12
1985–86	Middlesbrough	2	26	4
1986–87	Darlington	3	45	12
1987–88	Darlington	4	31	21
1987–88	Barnsley	2	15	7

CURRY, Sean
13.11.66 Liverpool (FW)
5.8½ 10.11 Apprentice
LD Blackburn R v Millwall
21.2.87 1–0

1984–85	Liverpool	1	—	—
1985–86	Liverpool	1	—	—
1986–87	Blackburn R	2	11	2
1987–88	Blackburn R	2	20	4

CURTIS, Alan
16.4.54 Rhondda (FW)
5.11 12.7½ Amateur
LD Southend U v Swansea C
25.8.72 3–1

1972–73	Swansea C	3	13	—
1973–74	Swansea C	4	38	4
1974–75	Swansea C	4	37	—
1975–76	Swansea C	4	41	9
1976–77	Swansea C	4	46	14
1977–78	Swansea C	4	39	32
1978–79	Swansea C	3	34	13
1979–80	Leeds U	1	22	4
1980–81	Leeds U	1	6	1
1980–81	Swansea C	2	20	6
1981–82	Swansea C	1	40	10
1982–83	Swansea C	1	21	4
1983–84	Swansea C	2	9	1
1983–84	Southampton	1	9	—
1984–85	Southampton	1	30	4
1985–86	Southampton	1	11	1
1985–86	*Stoke C*	2	3	—
1986–87	Cardiff C	4	42	4
1987–88	Cardiff C	4	40	2

CUSACK, Nick
24.12.65 Rotherham (FW)
6.0 11.13 Alvechurch
LD Leicester C v Shrewsbury T
15.8.87 0–1

1987–88	Leicester C	2	16	1

CUTLER, Chris
7.4.64 Manchester (FW)
5.11 11.0 Amateur
LD Bury v York C
15.5.82 3–1

1981–82	Bury	4	2	—
1982–83	Bury	4	5	—
1983–84	Bury	4	12	2
1984–85	Bury	4	4	1
1985–86	Crewe Alex	4	28	6
1986–87	Crewe Alex	4	35	5
1987–88	Crewe Alex	4	36	6

DALE, Carl
24.9.66 Colwyn Bay (FW)
— — Bangor City
LD —
1987–88 Chester C 3 — —

DALEY, Tony
18.10.67 Birmingham (FW)
5.9 10.5 Apprentice
LD Southampton v Aston Villa
20.4.85 2–0

1984–85 Aston Villa 1 5 —
1985–86 Aston Villa 1 23 2
1986–87 Aston Villa 1 33 3
1987–88 Aston Villa 2 14 3

DALGLISH, Kenny
4.3.51 Glasgow (FW)
5.8 11.13 Cumbernauld U
LD Celtic v Raith R
4.10.69 7–1

1969–70 Celtic 1 2 —
1970–71 Celtic 1 3 —
1971–72 Celtic 1 31 17
1972–73 Celtic 1 32 23
1973–74 Celtic 1 33 18
1974–75 Celtic 1 33 16
1975–76 Celtic P 35 24
1976–77 Celtic P 35 14
1977–78 Liverpool 1 42 20
1978–79 Liverpool 1 42 21
1979–80 Liverpool 1 42 16
1980–81 Liverpool 1 34 8
1981–82 Liverpool 1 42 13
1982–83 Liverpool 1 42 18
1983–84 Liverpool 1 33 7
1984–85 Liverpool 1 36 6
1985–86 Liverpool 1 21 3
1986–87 Liverpool 1 18 6
1987–88 Liverpool 1 2 —

DALTON, Paul
25.4.67 —
— —
LD —
1987–88 Manchester U 1 — —

DANIEL, Peter
12.12.55 Hull (MF)
5.9 11.4 Amateur
LD WBA v Hull C
18.9.74 2–2

1973–74 Hull C 2 — —
1974–75 Hull C 2 19 —
1975–76 Hull C 2 27 2
1976–77 Hull C 2 41 6
1977–78 Hull C 2 26 1
1978–79 Wolves 1 40 5
1979–80 Wolves 1 37 6
1980–81 Wolves 1 28 —
1981–82 Wolves 1 20 2
1982–83 Wolves 2 13 —
1983–84 Wolves 1 19 —
1984–85 Sunderland 1 25 —
1985–86 Sunderland 2 9 —

1985–86 Lincoln C 3 16 2
1986–87 Lincoln C 4 39 —
1987–88 Burnley 4 27 —

DANIEL, Ray
10.12.64 Luton (MF)
5.10 11.0 Apprentice
LD Luton T v Sunderland
26.3.83 1–3

1982–83 Luton T 1 3 —
1983–84 Luton T 1 7 2
1983–84 *Gillingham* 3 5 —
1984–85 Luton T 1 7 1
1985–86 Luton T 1 5 1
1986–87 Hull C 2 9 —
1987–88 Hull C 2 26 2

DARBY, Julian
3.10.67 Bolton (DF)
— — School
LD Bolton W v Blackpool
31.3.86 1–3

1984–85 Bolton W 3 — —
1985–86 Bolton W 3 2 —
1986–87 Bolton W 3 28 —
1987–88 Bolton W 4 35 2

DARBY, Lee
20.9.69 Salford (MF)
5.11 12.0 Apprentice
LD Portsmouth v Oxford U
16.1.88 2–2

1987–88 Portsmouth 1 1 —

DAVENPORT, Peter
24.3.61 Birkenhead (FW)
5.11 11.3 Cammell Laird
LD Liverpool v Nottingham F
1.5.82 2–0

1981–82 Nottingham F 1 5 4
1982–83 Nottingham F 1 18 6
1983–84 Nottingham F 1 33 15
1984–85 Nottingham F 1 35 16
1985–86 Nottingham F 1 27 13
1985–86 Manchester U 1 11 1
1986–87 Manchester U 1 39 14
1987–88 Manchester U 1 34 5

DAVIES, Alan
5.12.61 Manchester (MF)
5.8 11.4 Apprentice
LD Manchester U v Southampton
1.5.82 1–0

1981–82 Manchester U 1 1 —
1982–83 Manchester U 1 3 —
1983–84 Manchester U 1 3 —
1984–85 Manchester U 1 — —
1985–86 Newcastle U 1 14 1
1985–86 *Charlton Ath* 2 1 —
1986–87 Newcastle U 1 7 —
1986–87 *Carlisle U* 3 4 1
1987–88 Swansea C 4 42 3

DAVIES, Billy
31.5.64 Glasgow (MF)
5.5 9.8 Pollok U BC
LD Rangers v Partick Th
20.3.82 4–1

1980–81 Rangers P — —
1981–82 Rangers P 4 —
1982–83 Rangers P 4 —
1983–84 Rangers P 3 1
1984–85 Rangers P — —
1985–86 Rangers P — —
1986–87 Elfsborg (Swe)
1987–88 St Mirren P 18 —

DAVIES, Gordon
3.8.55 Merthyr (FW)
5.7 10.12 Merthyr T
LD Fulham v Mansfield T
27.3.78 0–2

1977–78 Fulham 2 5 1
1978–79 Fulham 2 32 9
1979–80 Fulham 2 39 15
1980–81 Fulham 3 45 18
1981–82 Fulham 3 41 24
1982–83 Fulham 2 38 19
1983–84 Fulham 2 36 22
1984–85 Fulham 2 11 5
1984–85 Chelsea 1 12 6
1985–86 Chelsea 1 1 —
1985–86 Manchester C 1 26 9
1986–87 Manchester C 1 5 —
1986–87 Fulham 3 21 6
1987–88 Fulham 3 39 13

DAVIES, Michael
19.1.66 Stretford (MF)
5.8 10.0 Apprentice
LD Blackpool v Halifax T
7.5.84 4–0

1983–84 Blackpool 4 3 —
1984–85 Blackpool 4 17 —
1985–86 Blackpool 3 36 5
1986–87 Blackpool 3 42 6
1987–88 Blackpool 3 38 —

DAVIES, Stephen
16.7.60 Liverpool (FW)
6.0 11.9 Local
LD Port Vale v Preston NE
12.3.88 3–2

1987–88 Port Vale 3 6 —

DAVIS, Darren
5.2.67 Sutton-in-Ashfield (DF)
6.0 11.0 Apprentice
LD Sunderland v Notts Co
7.5.84 0–0

1983–84 Notts Co 1 1 —
1984–85 Notts Co 2 4 —
1985–86 Notts Co 3 22 1
1986–87 Notts Co 3 45 —
1987–88 Notts Co 3 20 —

DAVIS, Paul
9.12.61 London (MF)
5.8 9.7 Apprentice
LD Tottenham H v Arsenal
7.4.80 1–2

1979–80	Arsenal	1	2	—
1980–81	Arsenal	1	10	1
1981–82	Arsenal	1	38	4
1982–83	Arsenal	1	41	4
1983–84	Arsenal	1	35	1
1984–85	Arsenal	1	24	1
1985–86	Arsenal	1	29	4
1986–87	Arsenal	1	39	4
1987–88	Arsenal	1	29	5

DAVIS, Steve
— — Hexham (DF)
6.2 13.1 Apprentice
LD —

1987–88	Southampton	1	—	—

DAVIS, Steve
26.7.65 Birmingham (DF)
6.0 10.10 Stoke C
LD Rochdale v Crewe Alex
27.8.84 1–0

1983–84	Crewe Alex	4	24	—
1984–85	Crewe Alex	4	40	—
1985–86	Crewe Alex	4	45	1
1986–87	Crewe Alex	4	33	—
1987–88	Crewe Alex	4	3	—
1987–88	*Burnley*	4	10	1
1987–88	Burnley	4	23	4

DAVISON, Aidan
11.5.68 Sedgefield (GK)
6.1½ 13.2 Billingham Synth.
LD —

1987–88	Notts Co	3	—	—

DAVISON, Bob
17.7.59 S. Shields (FW)
5.8 11.8 Seaham CW
LD Rotherham U v Huddersfield T
30.8.80 0–0

1980–81	Huddersfield T	3	2	—
1981–82	Halifax T	4	46	20
1982–83	Halifax T	4	17	9
1982–83	Derby Co	2	26	8
1983–84	Derby Co	2	40	14
1984–85	Derby Co	3	46	24
1985–86	Derby Co	3	41	17
1986–87	Derby Co	2	40	19
1987–88	Derby Co	1	13	1
1987–88	*Leeds U*	2	1	1
1987–88	Leeds U	2	15	4

D'AVRAY, Mich
19.2.62 Johannesburg (FW)
6.1 13.2 Apprentice
LD Ipswich T v Southampton
24.11.79 3–1

1979–80	Ipswich T	1	2	—
1980–81	Ipswich T	1	5	1
1981–82	Ipswich T	1	13	2
1982–83	Ipswich T	1	17	2
1983–84	Ipswich T	1	23	6
1984–85	Ipswich T	1	33	6
1985–86	Ipswich T	1	26	5
1986–87	Ipswich T	2	19	
1986–87	*Leicester C*	1	3	—
1987–88	Ipswich T	2	29	7

DAWES, Ian
22.2.63 Croydon (DF)
5.7 11.11 Apprentice
LD Rotherham U v QPR
27.3.82 1–0

1980–81	QPR	2	—	—
1981–82	QPR	2	5	—
1982–83	QPR	2	42	—
1983–84	QPR	1	42	2
1984–85	QPR	1	42	—
1985–86	QPR	1	42	1
1986–87	QPR	1	23	—
1987–88	QPR	1	33	—

DAWKINS, Derek
29.11.59 Edmonton (DF)
5.10 11.1 Apprentice
LD Derby Co v Leicester C
22.4.78 4–1

1977–78	Leicester C	1	3	—
1978–79	Leicester C	2	—	—
1978–79	Mansfield T	3	26	—
1979–80	Mansfield T	3	35	—
1980–81	Mansfield T	4	12	—
1981–82	Bournemouth	4	5	—
1982–83	Bournemouth	3	3	—
1983–84	Torquay U	4	16	—
1984–85	Torquay U	4	46	—
1985–86	Torquay U	4	39	3
1986–87	Torquay U	4	24	1
1987–88	Torquay U	4	38	3

DAWS, Tony
10.9.66 Sheffield (MF)
5.8 10.8 Apprentice
LD Birmington C v Notts Co
9.3.85 2–1

1984–85	Notts Co	2	7	1
1985–86	Notts Co	3	1	—
1986–87	Sheffield U	2	11	3
1987–88	Scunthorpe U	4	10	3

DAWSON, Alistair
25.2.58 Glasgow (DF)
5.10 11.10 School
LD Dundee v Rangers
27.9.75 0–0

1975–76	Rangers	P	3	—
1976–77	Rangers	P	1	—
1977–78	Rangers	P	2	—
1978–79	Rangers	P	23	1
1979–80	Rangers	P	32	—
1980–81	Rangers	P	22	2
1981–82	Rangers	P	25	1
1982–83	Rangers	P	25	—
1983–84	Rangers	P	28	—
1984–85	Rangers	P	26	1
1985–86	Rangers	P	24	1
1986–87	Rangers	P	7	—
1987–88	Blackburn R	2	22	—

DAWSON, Robert
1.8.63 Stirling (DF)
5.9 10.10 Fallin Violet
LD Stirling A v Meadowbank Th
17.2.82 1–0

1981–82	Stirling A	2	18	—
1982–83	Stirling A	2	36	—
1983–84	Stirling A	2	33	2
1984–85	Stirling A	2	34	—
1985–86	Stirling A	2	39	—
1986–87	Stirling A	2	39	—
1987–88	St Mirren	P	24	—

DAY, Keith
29.11.62 Grays (DF)
6.1 13.0 Aveley
LD Colchester U v Southend U
25.8.84 3–3

1984–85	Colchester U	4	45	4
1985–86	Colchester U	4	30	5
1986–87	Colchester U	4	38	3
1987–88	Leyton Orient	4	41	3

DAY, Mervyn
26.6.55 Chelmsford (GK)
6.2 14.12 Apprentice
LD West Ham U v Ipswich T
27.8.73 3–3

1972–73	West Ham U	1	—	—
1973–74	West Ham U	1	33	—
1974–75	West Ham U	1	42	—
1975–76	West Ham U	1	41	—
1976–77	West Ham U	1	42	—
1977–78	West Ham U	1	23	—
1978–79	West Ham U	2	13	—
1979–80	Orient	2	42	—
1980–81	Orient	2	40	—
1981–82	Orient	2	42	—
1982–83	Orient	3	46	—
1983–84	Aston Villa	1	14	—
1984–85	Aston Villa	1	16	—
1984–85	Leeds U	2	18	—
1985–86	Leeds U	2	40	—
1986–87	Leeds U	2	34	—
1987–88	Leeds U	2	44	—

DEACY, Eamonn
1.10.58 Galway (DF)
5.8½ 10.8 Galway Rovers
LD Tottenham H v Aston Villa
15.12.79 1–2

1978–79	Aston Villa	1	—	—
1979–80	Aston Villa	1	3	—
1980–81	Aston Villa	1	9	—
1981–82	Aston Villa	1	4	—
1982–83	Aston Villa	1	4	1
1983–84	Aston Villa	1	13	—
1983–84	*Derby Co*	2	5	—
1984–85	Aston Villa	1	—	—
1985–86	Aston Villa	1	—	—
1986–87	Aston Villa	1	—	—
1987–88	Aston Villa	2	—	—

DEAKIN, Ray
19.6.59 Liverpool (DF)
5.8 11.1 Apprentice
LD Port Vale v Halifax T
29.8.81 0–0

1977–78	Everton	1	— —
1978–79	Everton	1	— —
1979–80	Everton	1	— —
1980–81	Everton	1	— —
1981–82	Port Vale	4	23 6
1982–83	Bolton W	2	30 1
1983–84	Bolton W	3	41 1
1984–85	Bolton W	3	34 —
1985–86	Burnley	4	46 3
1986–87	Burnley	4	46 —
1987–88	Burnley	4	37 3

DEANE, Brian
7.2.68 Leeds (FW)
6.3 12.7 Apprentice
LD Doncaster R v Swansea C
4.2.86 0–0

1985–86	Doncaster R	3	3 —
1986–87	Doncaster R	3	20 2
1987–88	Doncaster R	3	43 10

DEARY, John
18.10.62 Ormskirk (MF)
5.10 11.11 Apprentice
LD Fulham v Blackpool
5.9.80 1–2

1979–80	Blackpool	3	— —
1980–81	Blackpool	3	10 —
1981–82	Blackpool	4	27 —
1982–83	Blackpool	4	45 6
1983–84	Blackpool	4	31 6
1984–85	Blackpool	4	32 13
1985–86	Blackpool	3	40 7
1986–87	Blackpool	3	44 3
1987–88	Blackpool	3	37 3

DEEHAN, John
6.8.57 Solihull (FW)
6.0 11.3 Apprentice
LD Ipswich T v Aston Villa
1.11.75 3–0

1974–75	Aston Villa	2	— —
1975–76	Aston Villa	1	15 7
1976–77	Aston Villa	1	27 13
1977–78	Aston Villa	1	36 12
1978–79	Aston Villa	1	26 10
1979–80	Aston Villa	1	6 —
1979–80	WBA	1	28 3
1980–81	WBA	1	15 2
1981–82	WBA	1	4 —
1981–82	Norwich C	2	22 10
1982–83	Norwich C	1	40 20
1983–84	Norwich C	1	34 15
1984–85	Norwich C	1	40 13
1985–86	Norwich C	2	26 4
1986–87	Ipswich T	2	29 10
1987–88	Ipswich T	2	20 1

DE MANGE, Ken
3.9.64 Dublin (MF)
5.9½ 11.10 Home Farm
LD Colchester U v Scunthorpe U
3.1.87 1–0

1983–84	Liverpool	1	— —
1984–85	Liverpool	1	— —
1985–86	Liverpool	1	— —
1986–87	*Scunthorpe U*	4	3 2
1987–88	Leeds U	2	15 1
1987–88	Hull C	2	9 —

DEMPSEY, Mark
14.1.64 Manchester (MF)
5.7 9.4 Apprentice
LD Swindon T v Tranmere R
26.1.85 2–1

1981–82	Manchester U	1	— —
1982–83	Manchester U	1	— —
1983–84	Manchester U	1	— —
1984–85	Manchester U	1	— —
1984–85	*Swindon T*	4	5 —
1985–86	Manchester U	1	1 —
1986–87	Sheffield U	2	30 5
1987–88	Sheffield U	2	23 4

DENNIS, Mark
2.5.61 Streatham (DF)
5.9 10.8 Apprentice
LD Norwich C v Birmingham C
16.9.78 4–0

1978–79	Birmingham C	1	31 —
1979–80	Birmingham C	2	40 —
1980–81	Birmingham C	1	19 —
1981–82	Birmingham C	1	17 —
1982–83	Birmingham C	1	23 1
1983–84	Birmingham C	1	— —
1983–84	Southampton	1	20 —
1984–85	Southampton	1	31 —
1985–86	Southampton	1	24 —
1986–87	Southampton	1	20 2
1987–88	QPR	1	11 —

DENNISON, Robert
30.4.63 Banbridge (FW)
5.7 11.0 Glenavon
LD Newcastle U v WBA
14.9.85 4–1

1985–86	WBA	1	12 1
1986–87	WBA	2	4 —
1986–87	Wolves	4	10 3
1987–88	Wolves	4	43 3

DEVINE, Steve
11.12.64 Strabane (MF)
5.9 10.7 Apprentice.
LD Barnsley v Derby Co
31.3.84 5–1

1982–83	Wolves	2	— —
1983–84	Derby Co	2	10 —
1984–85	Derby Co	3	1 —
1985–86	Stockport Co	4	2 —
1985–86	Hereford U	4	11 1
1986–87	Hereford U	4	41 1
1987–88	Hereford U	4	43 —

DEVONSHIRE, Alan
13.4.56 London (MF)
5.10½ 11.0 Southall & Ealing Bor.
LD WBA v West Ham U
30.10.76 3–0

1976–77	West Ham U	1	28 —
1977–78	West Ham U	1	34 3
1978–79	West Ham U	2	41 5
1979–80	West Ham U	2	34 5
1980–81	West Ham U	2	39 6
1981–82	West Ham U	1	35 1
1982–83	West Ham U	1	39 3
1983–84	West Ham U	1	22 1
1984–85	West Ham U	1	— —
1985–86	West Ham U	1	38 3
1986–87	West Ham U	1	20 2
1987–88	West Ham U	1	1 —

DIAMOND, Tony
23.8.68 Rochdale (FW)
5.10 10.4 Apprentice
LD Blackburn R v Sunderland
6.9.86 6–1

1986–87	Blackburn R	2	8 2
1987–88	Blackburn R	2	7 —

DIBBLE, Andy
8.5.65 Cwmbran (GK)
6.0½ 13.7 Apprentice
LD Cardiff C v C Palace
8.5.82 0–1

1981–82	Cardiff C	2	1 —
1982–83	Cardiff C	3	20 —
1983–84	Cardiff C	2	41 —
1984–85	Luton T	1	13 —
1985–86	Luton T	1	7 —
1985–86	*Sunderland*	2	12 —
1986–87	Huddersfield T	2	5 —
1986–87	Luton T	1	1 —
1987–88	Luton T	1	9 —

DICKENS, Alan
3.9.64 Plaistow (MF)
5.11 12.1 Apprentice
LD Notts Co v West Ham U
18.12.82 1–2

1982–83	West Ham U	1	15 6
1983–84	West Ham U	1	10 —
1984–85	West Ham U	1	25 2
1985–86	West Ham U	1	41 4
1986–87	West Ham U	1	36 3
1987–88	West Ham U	1	28 3

PLAYER DIRECTORY

DICKENSON, Kevin
24.11.62 London (DF)
5.6 10.6 Apprentice
LD <u>Charlton Ath</u> v Swansea C
3.5.80 1–2

1979–80 Charlton Ath	2	1	—
1980–81 Charlton Ath	3	—	—
1981–82 Charlton Ath	2	7	—
1982–83 Charlton Ath	2	12	—
1983–84 Charlton Ath	2	42	1
1984–85 Charlton Ath	2	13	—
1985–86 Orient	4	46	1
1986–87 Orient	4	39	—
1987–88 Leyton Orient	4	22	1

DIGBY, Fraser
23.4.67 Sheffield (GK)
6.1½ 12.12 Apprentice
LD <u>Swindon T</u> v Rotherham U
27.9.86 2–0

1984–85 Manchester U	1	—	—
1985–86 Manchester U	1	—	—
1985–86 *Oldham Ath*	2	—	—
1985–86 *Swindon T*	4	—	—
1986–87 Swindon T	3	39	—
1987–88 Swindon T	2	31	—

DIGWEED, Perry
26.10.59 London (GK)
6.0 11.4 Apprentice
LD <u>Fulham</u> v Bolton W
3.1.77 0–2

1976–77 Fulham	2	1	—
1977–78 Fulham	2	—	—
1978–79 Fulham	2	2	—
1979–80 Fulham	2	11	—
1980–81 Fulham	3	1	—
1980–81 Brighton & HA	1	15	—
1981–82 Brighton & HA	1	12	—
1982–83 Brighton & HA	1	15	—
1983–84 Brighton & HA	2	4	—
1983–84 *WBA*	1	—	—
1984–85 Brighton & HA	2	—	—
1984–85 *Charlton Ath*	2	—	—
1985–86 Brighton & HA	2	33	—
1986–87 Brighton & HA	2	22	—
1987–88 Brighton & HA	3	—	—
1987–88 *Newcastle U*	1	—	—
1987–88 *Chelsea*	1	3	—

DILLON, Kevin
18.12.59 Sunderland (MF)
5.11 10.13 Apprentice
LD Middlesbrough v <u>Birmingham C</u>
10.9.77 1–2

1977–78 Birmingham C	1	17	1
1978–79 Birmingham C	1	36	2
1979–80 Birmingham C	2	31	6
1980–81 Birmingham C	1	39	2
1981–82 Birmingham C	1	36	1
1982–83 Birmingham C	1	27	3

1982–83 Portsmouth	3	11	5
1983–84 Portsmouth	2	36	9
1984–85 Portsmouth	2	37	9
1985–86 Portsmouth	2	31	5
1986–87 Portsmouth	2	39	8
1987–88 Portsmouth	1	32	9

DINEEN, Jack
23.9.70 Brighton (FW)
5.4 10.6 Local
LD —
1987–88 Brighton & HA 3 — —

DIXON, Andrew
19.4.68 Louth (DF)
6.1 10.11 Apprentice
LD Shrewsbury T v <u>Grimsby T</u>
4.10.86 4–1

1986–87 Grimsby T	2	1	—
1987–88 Grimsby T	3	32	—

DIXON, Kerry
24.7.61 Luton (FW)
6.0 13.0 Tottenham H
Apprentice and Dunstable
LD <u>Reading</u> v Walsall
16.8.80 2–0

1980–81 Reading	3	39	13
1981–82 Reading	3	42	12
1982–83 Reading	3	35	26
1983–84 Chelsea	2	42	28
1984–85 Chelsea	1	41	24
1985–86 Chelsea	1	38	14
1986–87 Chelsea	1	36	10
1987–88 Chelsea	1	33	11

DIXON, Kevin
27.7.60 Blackhill (FW)
5.10 10.6 Annfield Plain & Tow
Law T
LD <u>Carlisle U</u> v Cambridge U
27.8.83 0–0

1983–84 Carlisle U	2	9	—
1983–84 *Hartlepool U*	4	6	3
1984–85 Hartlepool U	4	42	12
1985–86 Hartlepool U	4	22	5
1985–86 *Scunthorpe U*	4	14	2
1986–87 Hartlepool U	4	43	9
1987–88 Scunthorpe U	4	41	4

DIXON, Lee
17.3.64 Manchester (DF)
5.9½ 10.12 Local
LD <u>Burnley</u> v QPR
10.5.83 2–1

1982–83 Burnley	2	3	—
1983–84 Burnley	3	1	—
1983–84 Chester C	4	16	1
1984–85 Chester C	4	41	—
1985–86 Bury	4	45	6
1986–87 Stoke C	2	42	3
1987–88 Stoke C	2	29	2
1987–88 Arsenal	1	6	—

DOBBIN, Jim
17.9.61 Dunfermline (MF)
5.8 10.7 Whitburn BC
LD St Johnstone v <u>Celtic</u>
3.12.83 0–3

1980–81 Celtic	P	—	—
1981–82 Celtic	P	—	—
1982–83 Celtic	P	—	—
1983–84 Celtic	P	2	—
1983–84 *Motherwell*	P	2	—
1983–84 Doncaster R	4	11	2
1984–85 Doncaster R	3	17	1
1985–86 Doncaster R	3	31	6
1986–87 Doncaster R	3	5	4
1986–87 Barnsley	2	30	4
1987–88 Barnsley	2	16	2

DOBBINS, Wayne
30.8.68 Bromsgrove (MF)
— — Apprentice
LD <u>WBA</u> v Sheffield U
25.8.86 1–0

1986–87 WBA	2	6	—
1987–88 WBA	2	10	—

DOBSON, Paul
17.12.62 Hartlepool (FW)
5.9 10.6 Newcastle U. Amateur
LD <u>Hartlepool U</u> v Scunthorpe U
10.2.82 3–3

1981–82 Hartlepool U	4	5	—
1982–83 Hartlepool U	4	26	8
Horden			
1983–84 Hartlepool U	4	27	12
1984–85 Hartlepool U	4	38	10
1985–86 Hartlepool U	4	15	2
1986–87 Torquay U	4	39	16
1987–88 Torquay U	4	38	22

DOBSON, Tony
5.2.69 Coventry (DF)
— — Apprentice
LD Aston Villa v <u>Coventry C</u>
23.3.87 1–0

1986–87 Coventry C	1	1	—
1987–88 Coventry C	1	1	—

DOCKER, Ian
12.9.69 Norwich (MF)
5.9 11.7 YTS
LD <u>Gillingham</u> v Preston NE
23.4.88 4–0

1987–88 Gillingham 3 1 —

DODDS, Billy
5.2.69 New Cummock (FW)
5.7 10.0 Apprentice
LD <u>Chelsea</u> v Arsenal
7.3.87 1–0

1986–87 Chelsea	1	1	—
1987–88 Chelsea	1	—	—
1987–88 *Partick Th*	1	30	9

DODDS, Davie
23.9.58 Dundee (FW)
5.11 11.5 'S' Form
LD Celtic v Dundee U
13.8.78 0–0

Season	Club	Div	Apps	Gls
1975–76	Dundee U	P	—	—
1976–77	Dundee U	P	—	—
1977–78	Dundee U	P	1	—
1977–78	*Arbroath*	1	6	1
1977–78	Dundee U	P	9	1
1978–79	Dundee U	P	27	10
1979–80	Dundee U	P	21	6
1980–81	Dundee U	P	24	14
1981–82	Dundee U	P	35	14
1982–83	Dundee U	P	36	22
1983–84	Dundee U	P	33	15
1984–85	Dundee U	P	26	8
1985–86	Dundee U	P	31	12
1986–87	Neuchatel Xamax (Swz)			
1986–87	Aberdeen	P	26	4
1987–88	Aberdeen	P	23	9

DOIG, Russell
17.1.64 Millport (MF)
5.8 10.9
LD East Stirling v Stirling A
20.8.83 0–1

Season	Club	Div	Apps	Gls
1983–84	East Stirling	2	38	3
1984–85	East Stirling	2	35	1
1985–86	East Stirling	2	36	5
1986–87	Leeds U	2	4	—
1986–87	*Peterborough U*	4	7	—
1987–88	Leeds U	2	2	—
1987–88	Hartlepool U	4	9	—

DOLAN, Eamonn
20.9.67 Dagenham (FW)
5.10 12.3 Apprentice
LD West Ham U v Manchester C
9.5.87 2–0

Season	Club	Div	Apps	Gls
1984–85	West Ham U	1	—	—
1985–86	West Ham U	1	—	—
1986–87	West Ham U	1	1	—
1987–88	West Ham U	1	4	—

DONACHIE, Willie
5.10.51 Glasgow (DF)
5.9 11.3 Juniors

Season	Club	Div	Apps	Gls
1968–69	Manchester C	1	—	—
1969–70	Manchester C	1	3	—
1970–71	Manchester C	1	11	—
1971–72	Manchester C	1	37	—
1972–73	Manchester C	1	40	1
1973–74	Manchester C	1	42	—
1974–75	Manchester C	1	40	1
1975–76	Manchester C	1	40	—
1976–77	Manchester C	1	42	—
1977–78	Manchester C	1	39	—
1978–79	Manchester C	1	38	—
1979–80	Manchester C	1	19	—
	Portland Timbers			
1981–82	Norwich C	2	11	—
	Portland Timbers			
1982–83	Burnley	2	23	—
1983–84	Burnley	3	37	3

Season	Club	Div	Apps	Gls
1984–85	Oldham Ath	2	39	—
1985–86	Oldham Ath	2	33	—
1986–87	Oldham Ath	2	33	—
1987–88	Oldham Ath	2	31	3

DONAGHY, Mal
13.9.57 Belfast (DF)
5.10 12.7 Larne
LD Luton T v Oldham Ath
19.8.78 6–1

Season	Club	Div	Apps	Gls
1978–79	Luton T	2	40	—
1979–80	Luton T	2	42	1
1980–81	Luton T	2	42	—
1981–82	Luton T	2	42	9
1982–83	Luton T	1	40	3
1983–84	Luton T	1	40	1
1984–85	Luton T	1	42	1
1985–86	Luton T	1	42	—
1986–87	Luton T	1	42	—
1987–88	Luton T	1	32	1

DONALD, Warren
7.10.64 Hillingdon (MF)
5.7 10.3 Apprentice
LD West Ham U v Southampton
26.12.83 0–1

Season	Club	Div	Apps	Gls
1982–83	West Ham U	1	—	—
1983–84	West Ham U	1	2	—
1984–85	West Ham U	1	—	—
1984–85	*Northampton T*	5	11	2
1985–86	West Ham U	1	—	—
1985–86	Northampton T	4	32	3
1986–87	Northampton T	4	41	3
1987–88	Northampton T	3	40	2

DONEGAL, Glenville
20.6.69 Northampton (FW)
6.2 12.8 Apprentice
LD Northampton T v Bury
28.12.87 0–0

Season	Club	Div	Apps	Gls
1987–88	Northampton T	3	10	1

DONNELLAN, Leo
19.1.65 Brent (MF)
5.10 11.5 Apprentice
LD Orient v Doncaster R
29.12.84 2–1

Season	Club	Div	Apps	Gls
1982–83	Chelsea	2	—	—
1983–84	Chelsea	2	—	—
1984–85	Chelsea	1	—	—
1984–85	*Orient*	3	6	—
1985–86	Fulham	2	23	—
1986–87	Fulham	3	30	4
1987–88	Fulham	3	11	—

DORIGO, Tony
31.12.65 Australia (DF)
5.8 9.11 Apprentice
LD Ipswich T v Aston Villa
12.5.84 2–1

Season	Club	Div	Apps	Gls
1983–84	Aston Villa	1	1	—
1984–85	Aston Villa	1	31	—
1985–86	Aston Villa	1	38	1
1986–87	Aston Villa	1	41	—
1987–88	Chelsea	1	40	—

DORNAN, Andy
19.8.61 Aberdeen (DF)
5.8 10.8 King St.
LD Aberdeen v Airdrieonians
1.11.80 4–1

Season	Club	Div	Apps	Gls
1978–79	Aberdeen	P	—	—
1979–80	Aberdeen	P	—	—
1980–81	Aberdeen	P	2	—
1981–82	Aberdeen	P	—	—
1982–83	Motherwell	P	19	—
1983–84	Motherwell	P	26	2
1984–85	Motherwell	1	21	1
1985–86	Motherwell	P	26	—
1986–87	Walsall	3	43	—
1987–88	Walsall	3	31	—

DOUGLAS, Colin
9.9.62 Hurlford (FW)
6.1 11.0 Celtic
LD Bristol C v Doncaster R
5.9.81 2–2

Season	Club	Div	Apps	Gls
1981–82	Doncaster R	3	42	3
1982–83	Doncaster R	3	38	7
1983–84	Doncaster R	4	44	15
1984–85	Doncaster R	3	46	10
1985–86	Doncaster R	3	42	13
1986–87	Rotherham U	3	43	3
1987–88	Rotherham U	3	40	1

DOWNES, Chris
17.1.69 Sheffield (DF)
5.10 10.8 Apprentice
LD Exeter C v Scarborough
12.3.88 1–0

Season	Club	Div	Apps	Gls
1987–88	Sheffield U	2	—	—
1987–88	*Scarborough*	4	2	—

DOWNING, Keith
23.7.65 Oldbury (FW)
5.8 10.9 Mile Oak R
LD Notts Co v Leeds U
25.8.84 1–2

Season	Club	Div	Apps	Gls
1984–85	Notts Co	2	12	—
1985–86	Notts Co	3	3	—
1986–87	Notts Co	3	8	1
1987–88	Wolves	4	34	1

DOWNS, Greg
13.12.58 Carlton (DF)
5.9½ 10.7 Apprentice
LD Ipswich T v Norwich C
27.3.78 4–0

Season	Club	Div	Apps	Gls
1976–77	Norwich C	1	—	—
1977–78	Norwich C	1	1	—
1977–78	*Torquay U*	4	1	1
1978–79	Norwich C	1	3	—
1979–80	Norwich C	1	18	—
1980–81	Norwich C	1	29	2
1981–82	Norwich C	2	28	1
1982–83	Norwich C	1	28	—
1983–84	Norwich C	1	42	4
1984–85	Norwich C	1	20	—
1985–86	Coventry C	1	41	—
1986–87	Coventry C	1	39	2
1987–88	Coventry C	1	27	2

PLAYER DIRECTORY

DOYLE, Steve
2.6.58 Neath (MF)
5.9½ 11.1 Apprentice
LD Tranmere R v Preston NE
15.11.74 3–1

1974–75	Preston NE	3	13	—
1975–76	Preston NE	3	24	1
1976–77	Preston NE	3	22	—
1977–78	Preston NE	3	32	1
1978–79	Preston NE	2	29	2
1979–80	Preston NE	2	14	—
1980–81	Preston NE	2	27	1
1981–82	Preston NE	3	36	3
1982–83	Huddersfield T	3	42	2
1983–84	Huddersfield T	2	36	2
1984–85	Huddersfield T	2	36	2
1985–86	Huddersfield T	2	42	—
1986–87	Huddersfield T	2	5	—
1986–87	Sunderland	2	33	—
1987–88	Sunderland	3	32	1

DOZZELL, Jason
9.12.67 Ipswich T (FW)
6.1 11.4 School
LD Ipswich T v Coventry C
4.2.84 3–1

1983–84	Ipswich T	1	5	1
1984–85	Ipswich T	1	14	2
1985–86	Ipswich T	1	41	3
1986–87	Ipswich T	2	42	2
1987–88	Ipswich T	2	39	1

DREYER, John
11.6.63 Alnwick (DF)
6.0 11.10 Wallingford T
LD Torquay U v Cambridge U
14.12.85 1–1

1984–85	Oxford U	2	—	—
1985–86	Oxford U	1	—	—
1985–86	Torquay U	4	5	—
1985–86	Fulham	2	12	2
1986–87	Oxford U	1	25	2
1987–88	Oxford U	1	35	—

DRINKELL, Kevin
18.6.60 Grimsby (FW)
5.10½ 12.6 Apprentice
LD Grimsby T v Gillingham
11.4.77 1–1

1976–77	Grimsby T	3	4	2
1977–78	Grimsby T	4	26	5
1978–79	Grimsby T	4	28	7
1979–80	Grimsby T	3	33	16
1980–81	Grimsby T	2	41	7
1981–82	Grimsby T	2	28	6
1982–83	Grimsby T	2	39	17
1983–84	Grimsby T	2	36	15
1984–85	Grimsby T	2	35	14
1985–86	Norwich C	2	41	22
1986–87	Norwich C	1	42	16
1987–88	Norwich C	1	38	12

DRYDEN, Richard
14.6.69 Stroud (MF)
— —
LD Brentford v Bristol R
28.12.86 1–2

1986–87	Bristol R	3	6	—
1987–88	Bristol R	3	6	—

DUBLIN, Keith
29.1.66 Wycombe (DF)
5.11 11.9 Apprentice
LD Chelsea v Barnsley.
7.5.84 3–1

1983–84	Chelsea	2	1	—
1984–85	Chelsea	1	11	—
1985–86	Chelsea	1	11	—
1986–87	Chelsea	1	28	—
1987–88	Brighton & HA	3	46	5

DUFFIELD, Peter
4.2.69 Middlesbrough (FW)
5.6½ 10.7 Middlesbrough
LD Sheffield U v Leicester C
17.10.87 2–1

1987–88	Sheffield U	2	11	1
1987–88	Halifax T	4	12	6

DUGGAN, Andy
19.9.67 Bradford (DF)
6.3 13.0 Apprentice
LD Ipswich T v Barnsley
22.11.86 1–0

1984–85	Barnsley	2	—	—
1985–86	Barnsley	2	—	—
1986–87	Barnsley	2	2	1
1987–88	Barnsley	2	—	—
1987–88	Rochdale	4	3	—

DUNCAN, Cameron
4.8.65 Lanark (GK)
6.1 11.0
LD Grimsby T v Sunderland
22.3.86 1–1

1983–84	Sunderland	1	—	—
1984–85	Sunderland	1	—	—
1985–86	Sunderland	2	1	—
1986–87	Sunderland	2	—	—
1987–88	Motherwell	P	43	—

DURIE, Gordon
6.12.65 Paisley (FW)
5.10 10.7 Hill of Beath Hawthorn
LD Stranraer v East Fife
20.2.82 1–1

1981–82	East Fife	2	13	1
1982–83	East Fife	2	25	2
1983–84	East Fife	2	34	16
1984–85	East Fife	1	9	7
1984–85	Hibernian	P	22	8
1985–86	Hibernian	P	25	6
1985–86	Chelsea	1	1	—
1986–87	Chelsea	1	25	5
1987–88	Chelsea	1	26	12

DURNIN, John
18.8.65 Bootle (FW)
5.10 11.4 Waterloo Dock
LD —

1985–86	Liverpool	1	—	—
1986–87	Liverpool	1	—	—
1987–88	Liverpool	1	—	—

DURRANT, Iain
29.10.66 Glasgow (MF)
5.8 9.7 Glasgow United
LD Morton v Rangers
20.4.85 0–3

1984–85	Rangers	P	5	—
1985–86	Rangers	P	30	2
1986–87	Rangers	P	39	4
1987–88	Rangers	P	40	10

DUXBURY, Mike
1.9.59 Accrington (DF)
5.10 10.12 Apprentice
LD Birmingham C v Manchester U
23.8.80 0–0

1976–77	Manchester U	1	—	—
1977–78	Manchester U	1	—	—
1978–79	Manchester U	1	—	—
1979–80	Manchester U	1	—	—
1980–81	Manchester U	1	33	2
1981–82	Manchester U	1	24	—
1982–83	Manchester U	1	42	1
1983–84	Manchester U	1	39	—
1984–85	Manchester U	1	30	1
1985–86	Manchester U	1	23	1
1986–87	Manchester U	1	32	1
1987–88	Manchester U	1	39	—

DYER, Alex
14.11.65 West Ham (MF)
5.11 11.12 Watford Apprentice
LD Blackpool v Rochdale
8.10.83 0–2

1983–84	Blackpool	4	9	—
1984–85	Blackpool	4	36	8
1985–86	Blackpool	3	39	8
1986–87	Blackpool	3	24	3
1986–87	Hull C	2	17	4
1987–88	Hull C	2	28	8

DYSON, Paul
27.12.59 Birmingham (DF)
6.2 13.6 Apprentice
LD Coventry C v Everton
23.12.78 3–2

1977–78	Coventry C	1	—	—
1978–79	Coventry C	1	2	—
1979–80	Coventry C	1	18	2
1980–81	Coventry C	1	41	2
1981–82	Coventry C	1	40	—
1982–83	Coventry C	1	39	1
1983–84	Stoke C	1	38	2
1984–85	Stoke C	1	37	3
1985–86	Stoke C	2	31	—
1985–86	WBA	1	11	—
1986–87	WBA	2	42	2
1987–88	WBA	2	8	2

EARLE, Robbie
27.1.65 Newcastle (FW)
5.9 10.10 Stoke C
LD Swindon T v Port Vale
28.8.82 1-0

1981–82 Port Vale	4	—	—
1982–83 Port Vale	4	8	1
1983–84 Port Vale	3	12	—
1984–85 Port Vale	4	46	15
1985–86 Port Vale	4	46	15
1986–87 Port Vale	3	35	6
1987–88 Port Vale	3	25	4

EBBRELL, John
1.10.69 Bromborough (MF)
5.7 9.12 Apprentice
LD —

1987–88 Everton	1	—	—

ECKHARDT, Jeff
7.10.65 Sheffield (DF)
5.11 11.6
LD C Palace v Sheffield U
30.3.85 1-3

1984–85 Sheffield U	2	7	—
1985–86 Sheffield U	2	33	2
1986–87 Sheffield U	2	22	—
1987–88 Sheffield U	2	12	—
1987–88 Fulham	3	29	1

EDMONDS, Neil
18.10.68 Accrington (MF
— — YTS
LD Shrewsbury T v Oldham Ath
5.5.87 2-0

1986–87 Oldham Ath	2	1	—
1987–88 Oldham Ath	2	4	—

EDWARDS, Dean
25.2.62 Wolverhampton (FW)
5.10 10.6 Apprentice
LD Cardiff C v Shrewsbury T
8.9.79 1-0

1979–80 Shrewsbury T	2	4	—
1980–81 Shrewsbury T	2	6	1
1981–82 Shrewsbury T	2	3	—
Palloseura and Telford U			
1985–86 Wolves	3	23	7
1986–87 Wolves	4	8	2
1986–87 Exeter C	4	11	5
1987–88 Exeter C	4	43	12

EDWARDS, Keith
16.7.57 Stockton (FW)
5.8 10.3
LD Sheffield U v QPR
28.2.76 0-0

1975–76 Sheffield U	1	3	—
1976–77 Sheffield U	2	31	18
1977–78 Sheffield U	2	36	11
1978–79 Hull C	3	46	24
1979–80 Hull C	3	41	19
1980–81 Hull C	3	40	13
1981–82 Hull C	4	5	1
1981–82 Sheffield U	4	41	35
1982–83 Sheffield U	3	42	13
1983–84 Sheffield U	3	44	33
1984–85 Sheffield U	2	29	13
1985–86 Sheffield U	2	35	20
1986–87 Leeds U	2	30	6
1987–88 Leeds U	2	8	—
1987–88 Aberdeen	P	9	2
1987–88 Hull C	2	9	3

EDWARDS, Paul
25.12.63 Birkenhead (DF)
5.11 11.2 Altrincham
LD Hartlepool U v Crewe Alex
27.2.88 2-1

1987–88 Crewe Alex	4	13	1

ELEY, Kevin
4.3.68 Mexborough (MF)
5.6 9.7 School
LD Rotherham U v Scunthorpe U
15.5.84 3-0

1983–84 Rotherham U	3	1	—
1984–85 Rotherham U	3	6	—
1985–86 Rotherham U	3	5	—
1986–87 Rotherham U	3	1	—
1987–88 Chesterfield	3	36	2

ELKINS, Gary
4.5.66 Wallingford (MF)
5.8½ 10.10 Apprentice
LD Fulham v Middlesbrough
22.9.84 2-1

1983–84 Fulham	2	—	—
1984–85 Fulham	2	21	—
1985–86 Fulham	2	13	—
1986–87 Fulham	3	9	—
1987–88 Fulham	3	29	—

ELLIOTT, Shaun
26.1.57 Hebden Bridge (MF)
6.0 11.6¼ Apprentice
LD Leicester C v Sunderland
15.1.77 2-0

1974–75 Sunderland	2	—	—
1975–76 Sunderland	2	—	—
1976–77 Sunderland	1	19	1
1977–78 Sunderland	2	29	3
1978–79 Sunderland	2	41	1
1979–80 Sunderland	2	41	4
1980–81 Sunderland	1	38	—
1981–82 Sunderland	1	36	—
1982–83 Sunderland	1	20	—
1983–84 Sunderland	1	33	—
1984–85 Sunderland	1	32	—
1985–86 Sunderland	2	32	2
1986–87 Norwich C	1	15	2
1987–88 Norwich C	1	16	—

ELLIOTT, Steve
15.9.58 Haltwistle (FW)
5.11½ 11.10 Apprentice
LD Coventry C v Nottingham F
22.8.78 0-0

1977–78 Nottingham F	1	—	—
1978–79 Nottingham F	1	4	—
1978–79 Preston NE	2	7	—
1979–80 Preston NE	2	42	16
1980–81 Preston NE	2	35	9
1981–82 Preston NE	3	35	10
1982–83 Preston NE	3	45	19
1983–84 Preston NE	3	44	16
1984–85 Luton T	1	12	3
1984–85 Walsall	3	28	5
1985–86 Walsall	3	41	16
1986–87 Bolton W	3	38	8
1987–88 Bolton W	4	19	2

ELLIOTT, Tony
30.11.69 Nuneaton (GK)
— — Apprentice
LD —

1987–88 Birmingham C	2	—	—

ELLIS, Mark
6.1.62 Bradford (FW)
5.9 10.9 Local
LD Bradford C v Wigan Ath
11.4.81 3-3

1980–81 Bradford C	4	4	1
1981–82 Bradford C	4	18	—
1982–83 Bradford C	3	25	3
1983–84 Bradford C	3	37	8
1984–85 Bradford C	3	45	7
1985–86 Bradford C	2	25	3
1986–87 Bradford C	2	31	5
1987–88 Bradford C	2	22	2

ELLIS, Tony
20.10.64 Salford (FW)
— — Northwich Vic
LD Oldham Ath v Stoke C
13.9.86 2-0

1986–87 Oldham Ath	2	5	—
1987–88 Oldham Ath	2	3	—
1987–88 Preston NE	3	24	4

PLAYER DIRECTORY

ELSEY, Karl
20.11.58 Swansea (MF)
5.10 12.6 Pembroke Boro
LD WBA v QPR
24.3.79 2–1

1978–79	QPR	1	3	—
1979–80	QPR	2	4	—
1980–81	Newport Co	3	34	2
1981–82	Newport Co	3	40	7
1982–83	Newport Co	3	42	5
1983–84	Newport Co	3	7	1
1983–84	Cardiff C	2	29	1
1984–85	Cardiff C	2	30	4
1985–86	Gillingham	3	46	5
1986–87	Gillingham	3	43	2
1987–88	Gillingham	3	39	6

EMERSON, Dean
27.12.62 Salford (MF)
5.8 10.8 Local
LD Bournemouth v Stockport Co
13.2.82 1–0

1981–82	Stockport Co	4	23	1
1982–83	Stockport Co	4	45	3
1983–84	Stockport Co	4	44	1
1984–85	Stockport Co	4	44	2
1985–86	Rotherham U	3	45	7
1986–87	Rotherham U	3	10	1
1986–87	Coventry C	1	19	—
1987–88	Coventry C	1	20	—

ENDERSBY, Scott
20.2.62 Lewisham (GK)
5.10 12.4 Apprentice
LD Tranmere R v Hereford U
12.9.81 0–0

1978–79	Ipswich T	1	—	—
1979–80	Ipswich T	1	—	—
1980–81	Ipswich T	1	—	—
1981–82	Tranmere R	4	43	—
1982–83	Tranmere R	4	36	—
1983–84	Swindon T	4	37	—
1984–85	Swindon T	4	46	—
1985–86	Swindon T	4	2	—
1985–86	Carlisle U	2	27	—
1986–87	Carlisle U	3	25	—
1987–88	York C	3	34	—
1987–88	*Cardiff C*	4	4	—

ENGLISH, Tony
10.10.66 Luton (MF)
5.11 11.2 Coventry C Apprentice
LD Southend U v Colchester U
29.1.85 2–5

1984–85	Colchester U	4	22	3
1985–86	Colchester U	4	45	13
1986–87	Colchester U	4	32	7
1987–88	Colchester U	4	43	2

ESQULANT, Danny
28.9.69 London (FW)
— — Apprentice
LD —
1987–88 Arsenal 1 — —

EVANS, Allan
12.10.56 Dunfermline (DF)
6.1 12.12½
LD Morton v Dumfermline Ath
27.10.73 1–2

1973–74	Dunfermline A	1	9	—
1974–75	Dunfermline A	1	26	—
1975–76	Dunfermline A	1	26	1
1976–77	Dunfermline A	2	37	13
1977–78	Aston Villa	1	9	1
1978–79	Aston Villa	1	37	6
1979–80	Aston Villa	1	35	8
1980–81	Aston Villa	1	39	7
1981–82	Aston Villa	1	38	2
1982–83	Aston Villa	1	40	4
1983–84	Aston Villa	1	36	7
1984–85	Aston Villa	1	38	6
1985–86	Aston Villa	1	35	3
1986–87	Aston Villa	1	26	6
1987–88	Aston Villa	2	20	1

EVANS, David
20.5.58 West Bromwich (DF)
5.11 12.5 Apprentice
LD Aston Villa v Everton
16.9.78 1–1

1975–76	Aston Villa	1	—	—
1976–77	Aston Villa	1	—	—
1977–78	Aston Villa	1	—	—
1978–79	Aston Villa	1	2	—
1979–80	Halifax T	4	45	3
1980–81	Halifax T	4	39	1
1981–82	Halifax T	4	46	2
1982–83	Halifax T	4	42	1
1983–84	Halifax T	4	46	2
1984–85	Bradford C	3	45	1
1985–86	Bradford C	2	35	—
1986–87	Bradford C	2	42	1
1987–88	Bradford C	2	43	1

EVANS, Gareth
14.1.67 Coventry (FW)
5.8 10.6 Apprentice
LD Manchester U v Coventry C
2.11.85 2–0

1984–85	Coventry C	1	—	—
1985–86	Coventry C	1	6	—
1986–87	Coventry C	1	1	—
1986–87	Rotherham U	3	34	9
1987–88	Rotherham U	3	39	4
1987–88	Hibernian	P	12	2

EVANS, Stewart
15.11.60 Maltby (FW)
6.4 11.5 Apprentice
LD Exeter C v Wimbledon
20.3.82 2–1

1978–79	Rotherham U	3	—	—
1979–80	Rotherham U	3	—	—
	Gainsborough T			
1980–81	Sheffield U	3	—	—
1981–82	Wimbledon	3	18	4
1982–83	Wimbledon	4	42	14
1983–84	Wimbledon	3	45	12
1984–85	Wimbledon	2	40	14
1985–86	Wimbledon	2	30	6
1986–87	WBA	2	14	1
1986–87	Plymouth Arg	2	5	—
1987–88	Plymouth Arg	2	37	10

John Fashanu

Photo: Bob Thomas Sports Photography.

PLAYER DIRECTORY

FAIRCLOUGH, Chris
12.4.64 Nottingham (DF)
5.11 11.2 Apprentice
LD Liverpool v Nottingham F
4.9.82 4–3

1981–82 Nottingham F	1	—	—
1982–83 Nottingham F	1	15	—
1983–84 Nottingham F	1	31	—
1984–85 Nottingham F	1	35	—
1985–86 Nottingham F	1	—	—
1986–87 Nottingham F	1	26	1
1987–88 Tottenham H	1	40	4

FAIRCLOUGH, Wayne
27.4.68 Nottingham (DF)
5.10 9.12 Apprentice
LD Darlington v Notts Co
22.9.85 2–3

1985–86 Notts Co	3	5	—
1986–87 Notts Co	3	9	—
1987–88 Notts Co	3	29	—

FAIRLIE, Jamie
1.5.57 Glasgow (MF)
5.8 10.2 Calderbank BC
LD Hamilton A v Forfar Ath
14.9.79 3–0

1974–75 Hamilton A	1	6	1
1975–76 Hamilton A	1	15	—
1976–77 Hamilton A	1	39	5
1977–78 Hamilton A	1	39	6
1978–79 Hamilton A	1	37	13
1979–80 Hamilton A	1	39	11
1980–81 Hamilton A	1	33	13
1981–82 Hamilton A	1	34	10
1982–83 Hamilton A	1	39	15
1983–84 Hamilton A	1	10	—
1983–84 Airdrieonians	1	18	1
1984–85 Airdrieonians	1	38	8
1985–86 Airdrieonians	1	35	2
1986–87 Airdrieonians	1	14	3
1986–87 Clydebank	P	27	1
1987–88 Motherwell	P	12	1
1987–88 Hamilton A	1	21	4

FAIRWEATHER, Carlton
22.9.61 London (FW)
5.11 11.0 Tooting & Mitcham
LD Brighton & HA v Wimbledon
29.12.84 2–1

1984–85 Wimbledon	2	13	2
1985–86 Wimbledon	2	20	7
1986–87 Wimbledon	1	26	8
1987–88 Wimbledon	1	21	4

FALCO, Mark
22.10.60 Hackney (FW)
6.0 12.0 Apprentice
LD Bolton W v Tottenham H
8.5.79 1–3

1978–79 Tottenham H	1	1	1
1979–80 Tottenham H	1	9	2
1980–81 Tottenham H	1	3	1
1981–82 Tottenham H	1	21	5
1982–83 Tottenham H	1	16	5
1982–83 *Chelsea*	2	3	—
1983–84 Tottenham H	1	36	13
1984–85 Tottenham H	1	42	22
1985–86 Tottenham H	1	40	18
1986–87 Tottenham H	1	6	—
1986–87 Watford	1	33	14
1987–88 QPR	1	19	5
1987–88 Rangers	P	14	5

FALCONER, Willie
5.4.66 Aberdeen (MF)
6.1 11.9 Lewis United
LD Aberdeen v Celtic
23.4.83 1–0

1982–83 Aberdeen	P	1	—
1983–84 Aberdeen	P	8	1
1984–85 Aberdeen	P	16	4
1985–86 Aberdeen	P	8	—
1986–87 Aberdeen	P	8	—
1987–88 Aberdeen	P	36	8

FARNABY, Craig
8.8.67 Hartlepool (FW)
— — —
LD Tranmere R v Hartlepool U
6.10.84 1–2

1984–85 Hartlepool U	4	5	—
1985–86 Hartlepool U	4	—	—
1985–86 Middlesbrough	2	—	—
1986–87 Halifax T	4	10	1
1987–88 Stockport Co	4	22	1

FARNINGHAM, Ray
10.4.61 Dundee (FW)
5.8 10.7 Dundee Celtic BC
LD Forfar Ath v Albion R
6.5.79 1–1

1978–79 Forfar Ath	2	1	—
1979–80 Forfar Ath	2	38	5
1980–81 Forfar Ath	2	34	4
1981–82 Forfar Ath	2	39	5
1982–83 Forfar Ath	2	21	3
1983–84 Forfar Ath	2	37	6
1984–85 Forfar Ath	1	31	4
1985–86 Forfar Ath	1	37	2
1986–87 Forfar Ath	1	2	—
1986–87 Motherwell	P	29	3
1987–88 Motherwell	P	29	6

FARNWORTH, Simon
28.10.63 Chorley (GK)
5.11 10.11 Apprentice
LD Bolton W v Wimbledon
27.8.83 2–0

1981–82 Bolton W	2	—	—
1982–83 Bolton W	2	—	—
1983–84 Bolton W	3	36	—
1984–85 Bolton W	3	46	—
1985–86 Bolton W	3	31	—
1986–87 *Tranmere R*	4	7	—
1986–87 *Stockport Co*	4	10	—
1986–87 Bury	3	14	—
1987–88 Bury	3	39	—

FARRELL, Andy
7.10.65 Colchester (DF)
5.11 11.7 School
LD Darlington v Colchester U
27.8.83 0–2

1983–84 Colchester U	4	15	—
1984–85 Colchester U	4	38	—
1985–86 Colchester U	4	24	1
1986–87 Colchester U	4	28	4
1987–88 Burnley	4	45	3

FARRELL, Sean
28.2.69 Watford (FW)
6.1 12.8 Apprentice
LD Colchester U v Cambridge U
25.3.88 0–0

1987–88 Luton T	1	—	—
1987–88 *Colchester U*	4	9	1

FASHANU, John
18.9.62 Kensington (FW)
6.1 11.12 Cambridge U Amateur
LD Norwich C v Shrewsbury T
17.10.81 2–1

1979–80 Norwich C	1	—	—
1980–81 Norwich C	1	—	—
1981–82 Norwich C	2	5	1
1982–83 Norwich C	1	2	—
1983–84 Norwich C	1	—	—
1983–84 *Crystal Palace*	2	1	—
1983–84 Lincoln C	3	26	7
1984–85 Lincoln C	3	10	4
1984–85 Millwall	3	25	4
1985–86 Millwall	2	25	8
1985–86 Wimbledon	2	9	4
1986–87 Wimbledon	1	37	11
1987–88 Wimbledon	1	38	14

FAZACKERLEY, Derek
5.11.51 Preston (DF)
5.11 11.2 Apprentice
LD Hull C v <u>Blackburn R</u>
23.2.71 0–0

1970–71	Blackburn R	2	14	—
1971–72	Blackburn R	3	39	—
1972–73	Blackburn R	3	46	2
1973–74	Blackburn R	3	46	2
1974–75	Blackburn R	3	23	4
1975–76	Blackburn R	2	42	1
1976–77	Blackburn R	2	38	—
1977–78	Blackburn R	2	28	—
1978–79	Blackburn R	2	37	3
1979–80	Blackburn R	3	46	1
1980–81	Blackburn R	2	38	—
1981–82	Blackburn R	2	39	1
1982–83	Blackburn R	2	38	—
1983–84	Blackburn R	2	39	4
1984–85	Blackburn R	2	39	4
1985–86	Blackburn R	2	37	1
1986–87	Blackburn R	2	7	1
1986–87	Chester C	3	23	—
1987–88	Chester C	3	43	—

FEARON, Ron
19.11.60 Romford (GK)
6.0 11.12 Sutton U
LD <u>Ipswich T</u> v Hull C
12.3.88 2–0

1987–88	Ipswich T	2	10	—

FEE, Gregory
24.6.64 Halifax (DF)
6.1 13.10 Boston U
LD Everton v <u>Sheffield W</u>
29.8.87 4–0

1987–88	Sheffield W	1	16	—

FEELEY, Andy
30.9.61 Hereford (MF)
5.9 12.7 Apprentice
LD <u>Hereford U</u> v Bournemouth
14.10.78 0–0

1978–79	Hereford U	4	26	—
1979–80	Hereford U	4	25	3
1979–80	*Chelsea*	2	—	—
1980–81	Hereford U	4	—	—
	Trowbridge T			
1983–84	Leicester C	1	3	—
1984–85	Leicester C	1	35	—
1985–86	Leicester C	1	26	—
1986–87	Leicester C	1	12	—
1987–88	Brentford	3	34	—

FELGATE, David
4.3.60 Blaenau Ffestiniog (GK)
6.2 13.10 Blaenau Ffestiniog
LD <u>Rochdale</u> v Halifax T
7.10.78 1–1

1978–79	Bolton W	1	—	—
1978–79	*Rochdale*	4	35	—
1979–80	Bolton W	1	—	—
1979–80	*Bradford C*	4	—	—
1979–80	*Crewe Alex*	4	14	—
1979–80	*Rochdale*	4	12	—
1980–81	Bolton W	2	—	—
1980–81	Lincoln C	4	42	—
1981–82	Lincoln C	3	43	—
1982–83	Lincoln C	3	46	—
1983–84	Lincoln C	3	46	—
1984–85	Lincoln C	3	21	—
1984–85	*Cardiff C*	2	4	—
1984–85	*Grimsby T*	2	12	—
1985–86	Grimsby T	2	12	—
1985–86	*Bolton W*	3	15	—
1986–87	Grimsby T	2	12	—
1986–87	*Rotherham U*	3	—	—
1986–87	Bolton W	3	20	—
1987–88	Bolton W	4	46	—

FENSOME, Andy
18.2.69 Northampton (MF)
5.8 11.2 Apprentice
LD —

1987–88	Norwich C	1	—	—

FENWICK, Terry
17.11.59 Camden,
Co. Durham (MF)
5.11 11.1 Apprentice
LD Tottenham H v <u>Crystal Palace</u>
17.12.77 2–2

1976–77	Crystal Palace	3	—	—
1977–78	Crystal Palace	2	10	—
1978–79	Crystal Palace	2	24	—
1979–80	Crystal Palace	1	15	—
1980–81	Crystal Palace	1	21	—
1980–81	QPR	2	19	2
1981–82	QPR	2	36	5
1982–83	QPR	2	39	3
1983–84	QPR	1	41	10
1984–85	QPR	1	41	2
1985–86	QPR	1	37	7
1986–87	QPR	1	21	1
1987–88	QPR	1	22	3
1987–88	Tottenham H	1	17	—

FERDINAND, Les
18.12.66 Acton (FW)
— — Hayes FC
LD Coventry C v <u>QPR</u>
20.4.87 4–0

1986–87	QPR	1	2	—
1987–88	QPR	1	1	—
1987–88	*Brentford*	3	3	—

FEREBEE, Stewart
6.9.60 Carshalton (FW)
5.10 11.5 Harrogate T
LD Lincoln C v <u>York C</u>
29.12.79 1–1

1979–80	York C	4	10	—
1980–81	York C	4	3	—
1981–83	Non League	—	—	—
1983–84	Bradford C	3	—	—
1984–86	Non League	—	—	—
1986–87	Darlington	3	8	—
1987–88	Whitley Bay	—	—	—
1987–88	Halifax T	4	12	—

FEREDAY, Wayne
16.6.63 Warley (MF)
5.9 11.0 Apprentice
LD <u>QPR</u> v Bristol R
19.8.80 4–0

1980–81	QPR	2	6	2
1981–82	QPR	2	4	—
1982–83	QPR	2	5	—
1983–84	QPR	1	17	4
1984–85	QPR	1	26	7
1985–86	QPR	1	34	2
1986–87	QPR	1	37	2
1987–88	QPR	1	37	4

FERGUSON, Allan
24.3.69 Lanark (GK)
5.10 11.3 Gartcosh &
Hamilton Th
LD <u>Hamilton A</u> v Clyde
6.2.88 2–0

1987–88	Hamilton A	1	6	—

FERGUSON, Derek
31.7.67 Glasgow (MF)
5.8 10.11 Gartcosh United.
LD <u>Rangers</u> v Hearts
8.12.84 1–1

1983–84	Rangers	P	1	—
1984–85	Rangers	P	8	—
1985–86	Rangers	P	19	—
1986–87	Rangers	P	30	1
1987–88	Rangers	P	32	4

FERGUSON, Iain
4.8.62 Newarthill (FW)
5.7 10.7 Fir Park BC
LD <u>Dundee</u> v Kilmarnock
15.12.79 3–1

1979–80	Dundee	P	13	5
1980–81	Dundee	1	11	1
1981–82	Dundee	P	34	12
1982–83	Dundee	P	29	9
1983–84	Dundee	P	33	12
1984–85	Rangers	P	28	6
1985–86	Rangers	P	4	—
1986–87	Dundee	P	3	2
1986–87	Dundee U	P	36	16
1987–88	Dundee U	P	39	11

PLAYER DIRECTORY

FERGUSON, Ian
15.3.67 Glasgow (MF)
5.10. 10.11 Clyde BC
LD Kilmarnock v <u>Clyde</u>
4.5.85 2–0

1984–85 Clyde	1	2	—
1985–86 Clyde	1	19	4
1986–87 Clyde	1	5	—
1986–87 St Mirren	P	35	4
1987–88 St Mirren	P	22	6
1987–88 Rangers	P	8	1

FILLERY, Mike
17.9.60 Mitcham (MF)
5.10 11.7 Apprentice
LD <u>Chelsea</u> v Derby Co
4.4.79 1–1

1978–79 Chelsea	1	7	—
1979–80 Chelsea	2	41	11
1980–81 Chelsea	2	36	6
1981–82 Chelsea	2	40	6
1982–83 Chelsea	2	37	9
1983–84 QPR	1	30	1
1984–85 QPR	1	32	6
1985–86 QPR	1	17	—
1986–87 QPR	1	18	2
1987–88 Portsmouth	1	18	—

FINNEY, Kevin
19.10.69 Newcastle-u-Lyme (MF)
6.0 12.0 Apprentice
LD Bristol C v <u>Port Vale</u>
31.8.87 1–0

1987–88 Port Vale	3	15	—

FINNIGAN, Tony
17.10.62 Wimbledon (FW)
6.0 12.0 Apprentice
LD Huddersfield T v <u>Crystal Palace</u>
16.2.85 2–0

1980–81 Fulham	3	—	—
1981–82 Fulham	3	—	—
1982–83 Fulham	2	—	—
1983–84 Fulham	2	—	—
1984–85 Crystal Palace	2	11	1
1985–86 Crystal Palace	2	36	3
1986–87 Crystal Palace	2	41	6
1987–88 Crystal Palace	2	17	—

FISHENDEN, Paul
2.8.63 Hillingdon (FW)
6.0 10.12 Local
LD Portsmouth v <u>Wimbledon</u>
3.11.81 1–0

1981–82 Wimbledon	4	5	1
1982–83 Wimbledon	3	9	4
1983–84 Wimbledon	2	23	8
1984–85 Wimbledon	2	20	10
1985–86 Wimbledon	1	18	2
1985–86 *Fulham*	2	3	—

1986–87 *Millwall*	2	3	—
1986–87 *Orient*	4	4	—
1987–88 *Crewe Alex*	4	6	1
1987–88 Crewe Alex	4	9	2

FITZGERALD, Thomas
2.1.70 Dublin (FW)
— — Trainee
LD —

1987–88 Tottenham H	1	—	—

FITZPATRICK, Paul
5.10.65 Liverpool (DF)
6.4 11.10
LD Millwall v <u>Bolton W</u>
4.5.85 5–2

1984–85 Tranmere R	4	—	—
1984–85 Liverpool	1	—	—
1984–85 Preston NE	3	—	—
1984–85 Bolton W	3	3	—
1985–86 Bolton W	3	11	—
1986–87 Bristol C	3	19	2
1987–88 Bristol C	3	24	5

FITZPATRICK, Tony
3.3.56 Glasgow (MF)
5.9 10.5 Possil YM
LD Stranraer v <u>St Mirren</u>
1.9.73 0–2

1973–74 St Mirren	2	9	—
1974–75 St Mirren	2	20	2
1975–76 St Mirren	1	24	—
1976–77 St Mirren	1	37	2
1977–78 St Mirren	P	34	2
1978–79 St Mirren	P	36	3
1979–80 St Mirren	P	41	—
1980–81 Bristol C	2	34	1
1981–82 St Mirren	P	24	1
1982–83 St Mirren	P	26	3
1983–84 St Mirren	P	28	—
1984–85 St Mirren	P	30	1
1985–86 St Mirren	P	29	3
1986–87 St Mirren	P	27	—
1987–88 St Mirren	P	26	1

FLECK, Robert
11.8.65 Glasgow (FW)
5.7 10.8 Possil YM
LD <u>Partick Th</u> v Clyde
2.1.84 1–2

1983–84 Partick T	1	2	1
1983–84 Rangers	P	1	—
1984–85 Rangers	P	8	—
1985–86 Rangers	P	15	3
1986–87 Rangers	P	40	19
1987–88 Rangers	P	21	7
1987–88 Norwich C	1	18	7

FLEMING, Gary
17.2.67 Londonderry (MF)
5.9½ 11.1 Apprentice
LD Arsenal v <u>Nottingham F</u>
13.4.85 1–1

1984–85 Nottingham F	1	2	—
1985–86 Nottingham F	1	16	—
1986–87 Nottingham F	1	34	—
1987–88 Nottingham F	1	22	—

FLEMING, Mark
— London (DF)
— — Apprentice
LD <u>QPR</u> v Wimbledon
27.2.88 1–0

1987–88 QPR	1	2	—

FLEMING, Paul
6.9.67 Halifax (DF)
LD Tranmere R v <u>Halifax T</u>
7.2.86 0–3

1985–86 Halifax T	4	13	—
1986–87 Halifax T	4	15	—
1987–88 Halifax T	4	9	—

FLETCHER, Jason
24.9.69 Nottingham (DF)
— — Apprentice
LD —

1987–88 Nottingham F	1	—	—

FLOUNDERS, Andy
13.12.63 Hull (FW)
5.11 11.6 Apprentice
LD <u>Hull C</u> v Oxford U
4.10.80 0–1

1980–81 Hull C	3	5	—
1981–82 Hull C	4	13	5
1982–83 Hull C	4	23	13
1983–84 Hull C	3	30	9
1984–85 Hull C	3	39	14
1985–86 Hull C	2	25	10
1986–87 Hull C	2	24	3
1986–87 Scunthorpe U	4	15	6
1987–88 Scunthorpe U	4	45	24

FLOWERS, Tim
3.2.67 Kenilworth (GK)
6.2 13.4 Apprentice
LD <u>Wolves</u> v Sheffield U
25.8.84 2–2

1984–85 Wolves	2	38	—
1985–86 Wolves	3	25	—
1985–86 *Southampton*	1	—	—
1986–87 Southampton	1	9	—
1986–87 *Swindon T*	3	2	—
1987–88 Southampton	1	9	—
1987–88 *Swindon T*	2	5	—

FLYNN, Michael
23.2.69 Oldham (FW)
— — YTS
LD Oldham Ath v Bradford C
18.8.87 0-2

1987-88 Oldham Ath	2	31	1

FOLEY, Steve
4.10.62 Liverpool (FW)
5.7 10.12 Apprentice
LD Oldham Ath v Fulham
17.12.83 3-0

1980-81 Liverpool	1	—	—
1981-82 Liverpool	1	—	—
1982-83 Liverpool	1	—	—
1983-84 Liverpool	1	—	—
1983-84 *Fulham*	2	3	—
1984-85 Grimsby T	2	31	2
1985-86 Sheffield U	2	28	5
1986-87 Sheffield U	2	38	9
1987-88 Swindon T	2	35	4

FORBES, Graeme
29.7.58 Forfar (MF)
5.11 11.0 Lochee U
LD Motherwell v Falkirk
16.8.80 3-0

1980-81 Motherwell	1	28	4
1981-82 Motherwell	P	31	6
1982-83 Motherwell	P	26	1
1983-84 Motherwell	1	32	1
1984-85 Motherwell	P	36	4
1985-86 Motherwell	P	27	—
1986-87 *Nottingham F*	1	—	—
1986-87 Walsall	3	40	3
1987-88 Walsall	3	44	3

FORD, Gary
8.2.61 York (MF)
5.8 11.10 Apprentice
LD Reading v York C
21.10.78 3-0

1978-79 York C	4	33	4
1979-80 York C	4	29	2
1980-81 York C	4	43	4
1981-82 York C	4	41	8
1982-83 York C	4	45	11
1983-84 York C	4	46	11
1984-85 York C	3	44	5
1985-86 York C	3	40	4
1986-87 York C	3	45	4
1987-88 Leicester C	2	16	2
1987-88 *Port Vale*	3	2	—
1987-88 Port Vale	3	21	3

FORD, Mike
9.2.66 Bristol (DF)
5.11½ 11.0 Apprentice
LD Leeds U v Cardiff C
29.12.84 1-1

1983-84 Leicester C	1	—	—

Devizes

1984-85 Cardiff C	2	20	1
1985-86 Cardiff C	3	44	4

1986-87 Cardiff C	4	36	1
1987-88 Cardiff C	4	45	7

FORD, Tony
14.5.59 Grimsby (FW)
5.9 12.8 Apprentice
LD Walsall v Grimsby T
4.10.75 2-0

1975-76 Grimsby T	3	14	—
1976-77 Grimsby T	3	6	—
1977-78 Grimsby T	4	34	2
1978-79 Grimsby T	4	45	15
1979-80 Grimsby T	3	37	5
1980-81 Grimsby T	2	28	4
1981-82 Grimsby T	2	35	7
1982-83 Grimsby T	2	37	4
1983-84 Grimsby T	2	42	8
1984-85 Grimsby T	2	42	6
1985-86 Grimsby T	2	34	3
1985-86 *Sunderland*	2	9	1
1986-87 Stoke C	2	41	6
1987-88 Stoke C	2	44	7

FOREMAN, Darren
12.2.68 Southampton (FW)
5.10 10.8
LD Barnsley v Plymouth Arg
20.9.86 1-1

1986-87 Barnsley	2	16	1
1987-88 Barnsley	2	9	7

FORREST, Craig
20.9.67 Vancouver (GK)
6.4 13.4 Apprentice
LD Colchester U v Wrexham
4.3.88 1-2

1985-86 Ipswich T	1	—	—
1986-87 Ipswich T	2	—	—
1987-88 Ipswich T	2	—	—
1987-88 *Colchester U*	4	11	—

FORREST, Gerry
21.1.57 Stockton (DF)
5.10 10.11 South Bank
LD Oxford U v Rotherham U
20.8.77 2-3

1976-77 Rotherham U	3	—	—
1977-78 Rotherham U	3	44	—
1978-79 Rotherham U	3	46	—
1979-80 Rotherham U	3	43	4
1980-81 Rotherham U	3	44	2
1981-82 Rotherham U	2	35	1
1982-83 Rotherham U	2	39	—
1983-84 Rotherham U	3	45	—
1984-85 Rotherham U	3	44	—
1985-86 Rotherham U	3	17	—
1985-86 Southampton	1	22	—
1986-87 Southampton	1	38	—
1987-88 Southampton	1	37	—

FORSYTH, Mike
20.3.66 Liverpool (DF)
5.11 11.0 Apprentice
LD Arsenal v WBA
3.12.83 0-1

1983-84 WBA	1	8	—
1984-85 WBA	1	10	—
1985-86 WBA	1	11	—
1985-86 *Northampton T*	4	—	—
1985-86 Derby Co	3	—	—
1986-87 Derby Co	2	41	1
1987-88 Derby Co	1	39	3

FORSYTH, Stewart
26.10.61 Insch (DF)
6.0 11.0 Middlefield BC
LD Arbroath v Hearts
11.8.79 1-2

1977-78 Arbroath	1	—	—
1978-79 Arbroath	1	—	—
1979-80 Arbroath	1	12	—
1980-81 Arbroath	2	28	1
1981-82 Arbroath	2	27	1
1982-83 Arbroath	2	33	—
1983-84 Arbroath	2	35	4
1984-85 Dundee	P	13	—
1985-86 Dundee	P	9	1
1986-87 Dundee	P	28	—
1987-88 Dundee	P	41	—

FOSTER, Colin
16.7.64 Chislehurst (DF)
6.4 13.10 Apprentice
LD Grimsby T v Orient
9.1.82 1-2

1981-82 Orient	2	23	2
1982-83 Orient	3	43	2
1983-84 Orient	3	11	1
1984-85 Orient	3	42	1
1985-86 Orient	4	36	2
1986-87 Orient	4	19	2
1986-87 Nottingham F	1	9	1
1987-88 Nottingham F	1	39	2

FOSTER, George
26.9.56 Plymouth (DF)
5.10 11.2 Apprentice
LD Hereford U v Plymouth Arg
20.2.79 0-1

1973-74 Plymouth Arg	3	5	—
1974-75 Plymouth Arg	3	—	—
1975-76 Plymouth Arg	2	16	1
1976-77 Plymouth Arg	2	15	2
1976-77 *Torquay U*	4	6	3
1977-78 Plymouth Arg	3	46	3
1978-79 Plymouth Arg	3	28	—
1979-80 Plymouth Arg	3	46	—
1980-81 Plymouth Arg	3	46	—
1981-82 Plymouth Arg	3	10	—
1981-82 *Exeter C*	3	28	—
1982-83 Derby Co	2	30	—
1983-84 Mansfield T	4	42	—
1984-85 Mansfield T	4	44	—
1985-86 Mansfield T	4	46	—
1986-87 Mansfield T	3	45	—
1987-88 Mansfield T	3	44	—

PLAYER DIRECTORY

FOSTER, Steve
24.9.57 Portsmouth (DF)
6.0 12.8 Apprentice
LD Orient v Portsmouth
29.8.75 0–1

1975–76 Portsmouth	2	11	—
1976–77 Portsmouth	3	31	1
1977–78 Portsmouth	3	31	3
1978–79 Portsmouth	4	36	2
1979–80 Brighton & HA	1	38	1
1980–81 Brighton & HA	1	42	1
1981–82 Brighton & HA	1	40	2
1982–83 Brighton & HA	1	36	1
1983–84 Brighton & HA	2	16	1
1983–84 Aston Villa	1	7	1
1984–85 Aston Villa	1	8	2
1984–85 Luton T	1	25	1
1985–86 Luton T	1	35	3
1986–87 Luton T	1	28	2
1987–88 Luton T	1	39	2

FOSTER, Wayne
11.9.63 Leigh (FW)
5.8½ 11.0 Apprentice
LD Bolton W v Cambridge U
24.10.81 3–4

1981–82 Bolton W	2	23	2
1982–83 Bolton W	2	24	4
1983–84 Bolton W	3	30	3
1984–85 Bolton W	3	28	4
1985–86 Preston NE	4	31	3
1986–87 Hearts	P	31	4
1987–88 Hearts	P	39	4

FOX, Peter
5.7.57 Scunthorpe (GK)
5.10½ 12.10 Apprentice
LD Sheffield W v Orient
31.3.73 2–0

1972–73 Sheffield W	2	1	—
1973–74 Sheffield W	2	—	—
1974–75 Sheffield W	2	20	—
1975–76 Sheffield W	3	27	—
1976–77 Sheffield W	3	1	—
1976–77 West Ham	1	—	—
1977–78 Sheffield W	3	—	—
1977–78 Barnsley	4	1	—
1977–78 Stoke C	2	—	—
1978–79 Stoke C	2	1	—
1979–80 Stoke C	1	23	—
1980–81 Stoke C	1	42	—
1981–82 Stoke C	1	38	—
1982–83 Stoke C	1	35	—
1983–84 Stoke C	1	42	—
1984–85 Stoke C	1	14	—
1985–86 Stoke C	2	37	—
1986–87 Stoke C	2	39	—
1987–88 Stoke C	2	17	—

FOX, Ruel
14.1.68 Ipswich (MF)
5.6 10.0 Apprentice
LD Norwich C v Oxford U
29.11.86 2–1

1985–86 Norwich C	2	—	—
1986–87 Norwich C	1	3	—
1987–88 Norwich C	1	34	2

FOYLE, Martin
2.5.63 Salisbury (FW)
5.9¾ 11.2 Amateur
LD Southampton v Coventry C
15.1.83 1–1

1980–81 Southampton	1	—	—
1981–82 Southampton	1	—	—
1982–83 Southampton	1	7	1
1983–84 Southampton	1	5	—
1983–84 Blackburn R	2	—	—
1984–85 Aldershot	4	44	15
1985–86 Aldershot	4	20	9
1986–87 Aldershot	4	34	11
1986–87 Oxford U	1	4	—
1987–88 Oxford U	1	33	10

FRAIN, John
8.10.68 Birmingham (FW)
— — Apprentice
LD Newcastle U v Birmingham C
12.4.86 4–1

1985–86 Birmingham C	1	3	—
1986–87 Birmingham C	2	3	1
1987–88 Birmingham C	2	14	2

FRANCE, Michael
10.9.68 Huddersfield (DF)
— — Apprentice
LD Shrewsbury T v Huddersfield T
1.1.88 3–1

1987–88 Huddersfield T	2	8	—

FRANCIS, Steve
29.5.64 Billericay (GK)
5.11 11.5 Apprentice
LD Oldham Ath v Chelsea
14.11.81 1–0

1981–82 Chelsea	2	29	—
1982–83 Chelsea	2	37	—
1983–84 Chelsea	2	—	—
1984–85 Chelsea	1	2	—
1985–86 Chelsea	1	3	—
1986–87 Reading	2	14	—
1987–88 Reading	2	34	—

FRANCIS, Trevor
19.4.54 Plymouth (FW)
5.10 11.7 Apprentice

1970–71 Birmingham C	2	22	15
1971–72 Birmingham C	2	39	12
1972–73 Birmingham C	1	31	6
1973–74 Birmingham C	1	37	6
1974–75 Birmingham C	1	23	13
1975–76 Birmingham C	1	35	17
1976–77 Birmingham C	1	42	21
1977–78 Birmingham C	1	42	25
Detroit E			
1978–79 Birmingham C	1	9	3
1978–79 Nottingham F	1	20	6
Detroit E			
1979–80 Nottingham F	1	30	14
1980–81 Nottingham F	1	18	6
1981–82 Nottingham F	1	2	2
1981–82 Manchester C	1	26	12
1982–83 Sampdoria (I)	A	14	7
1983–84 Sampdoria (I)	A	15	3
1984–85 Sampdoria (I)	A	24	6
1985–86 Sampdoria (I)	A	15	1
1986–87 Atalanta (I)	A	21	1
1987–88 Rangers	P	18	—
1987–88 QPR	1	9	—

FRANKLIN, Paul
5.10.63 Hainault (MF)
6.2 12.2 Apprentice
LD Watford v Liverpool
14.5.83 2–1

1981–82 Watford	2	—	—
1982–83 Watford	1	1	—
1983–84 Watford	1	24	—
1984–85 Watford	1	—	—
1985–86 Watford	1	4	—
1986–87 Watford	1	3	—
1986–87 Shrewsbury T	2	6	—
1986–87 Swindon T	3	5	1
1987–88 Reading	2	4	—

FRASER, Gary
1.11.65 Glasgow (MF)
5.7 9.8 Gartcosh
LD Berwick R v Queen's Park
20.8.83 3–0

1983–84 Queen's Park	2	15	3
1984–85 Queen's Park	2	28	5
1985–86 Queen's Park	2	37	11
1986–87 Motherwell	P	8	—
1987–88 Motherwell	P	14	—

FRASER, Sandy
31.8.67 Glasgow (FW)
5.8 10.0 Hamilton Thistle
LD Partick Th v Hamilton A

1985–86 Celtic	P	—	—
1986–87 Celtic	P	—	—
1987–88 Hamilton A	1	2	—

FREESTONE, Roger
19.8.68 Newport (GK)
6.2 12.3.
LD Port Vale v Newport Co
27.12.86 2–0

1986–87 Newport Co	3	13	—
1986–87 Chelsea	1	6	—
1987–88 Chelsea	1	15	—

FRENCH, Hamish
7.2.64 Aberdeen (MF)
5.10½ 11.4 Keith
LD Rangers v Dundee U
8.8.87 1–1

1987–88 Dundee U	P	20	2

FRIDGE, Les
27.8.68 Inverness (GK)
5.11 11.12 Inverness Thistle
LD Chelsea v Watford
5.5.86 1–5

1985–86 Chelsea	1	1	—
1986–87 St Mirren	P	1	—
1987–88 St Mirren	P	3	—
1987–88 *Stirling A*	2	1	—
1987–88 *Arbroath*	2	3	—

FRITH, Jim
28.12.69 Motherwell (FW)
5.7 9.2 Rangers Amateur BC
LD Partick Th v Hamilton A
17.10.87 1–0

1986–87 Rangers	P	—	—
1987–88 Hamilton A	1	4	1

FUTCHER, Paul
25.9.56 Chester (DF)
6.2 12.2 Apprentice
LD Cambridge U v Chester
24.3.73 1–0

1972–73 Chester	4	2	—
1973–74 Chester	4	18	—
1974–75 Luton T	1	19	—
1975–76 Luton T	2	41	—
1976–77 Luton T	2	40	1
1977–78 Luton T	2	31	—
1978–79 Manchester C	1	24	—
1979–80 Manchester C	1	13	—
1980–81 Oldham Ath	2	36	1
1981–82 Oldham Ath	2	37	—
1982–83 Oldham Ath	2	25	—
1982–83 Derby Co	2	17	—
1983–84 Derby Co	2	18	—
1983–84 Barnsley	2	10	—
1984–85 Barnsley	2	36	—
1985–86 Barnsley	2	37	—
1986–87 Barnsley	2	36	—
1987–88 Barnsley	2	41	—

FUTCHER, Ron
25.9.56 Chester (FW)
6.0 12.3 Apprentice
LD Workington v Chester
24.10.73 1–1

1973–74 Chester	4	4	—
1974–75 Luton T	1	17	7
1975–76 Luton T	2	31	10
1976–77 Luton T	2	33	13
1977–78 Luton T	2	39	10
1978–79 Manchester C	1	17	7
Minnesota K, Portland T, Tulsa R			
and NAC Breda			
1984–85 Barnsley	2	19	6
1985–86 Oldham Ath	2	40	17
1986–87 Oldham Ath	2	25	13
1986–87 Bradford C	2	10	4
1987–88 Bradford C	2	32	14

GABBIADINI, Marco
20.1.68 Nottingham (FW)
5.10 11.2 Apprentice
LD York C v Bolton W
29.3.85 0–3

1984–85 York C	3	1	—
1985–86 York C	3	22	4
1986–87 York C	3	29	9
1987–88 York C	3	8	1
1987–88 Sunderland	3	35	21

GAGE, Kevin
21.4.64 Chiswick (MF)
5.9 11.2 Apprentice
LD Wimbledon v Bury
2.5.81 2–4

1980–81 Wimbledon	4	1	—
1981–82 Wimbledon	3	21	1
1982–83 Wimbledon	4	26	4
1983–84 Wimbledon	3	24	4
1984–85 Wimbledon	2	37	2
1985–86 Wimbledon	2	29	1
1986–87 Wimbledon	1	30	3
1987–88 Aston Villa	2	44	2

GAGE, Wakeley
5.5.58 Northampton (DF)
6.4 13.7 Desborough T
LD Northampton T v Stockport Co
26.12.79 2–0

1979–80 Northampton T	4	21	1
1980–81 Northampton T	4	31	1
1981–82 Northampton T	4	43	2
1982–83 Northampton T	4	40	3
1983–84 Northampton T	4	40	6
1984–85 Northampton T	4	43	4
1985–86 Chester C	4	17	1
1985–86 Peterborough U	4	27	—
1986–87 Peterborough U	4	46	1
1987–88 Crewe Alex	4	40	1

GAHAGAN, John
24.8.58 Glasgow (FW)
5.9 10.7 Shettleston Juniors
LD Clydebank v Hibernian
18.3.78 0–3

1977–78 Clydebank	P	5	—
1978–79 Clydebank	1	—	—
1979–80 Motherwell	1	17	3
1980–81 Motherwell	1	34	1
1981–82 Motherwell	1	39	7
1982–83 Motherwell	P	28	4
1983–84 Motherwell	P	30	7
1984–85 Motherwell	1	31	5
1985–86 Motherwell	P	21	3
1986–87 Motherwell	P	19	—
1987–88 Motherwell	P	23	—

GALE, Tony
19.11.59 London (DF)
6.1½ 13.10 Apprentice
LD Fulham v Charlton Ath
20.8.77 1–1

1977–78 Fulham	2	38	8
1978–79 Fulham	2	36	2
1979–80 Fulham	2	42	4
1980–81 Fulham	3	40	1
1981–82 Fulham	3	44	1
1982–83 Fulham	2	42	2
1983–84 Fulham	2	35	1
1984–85 West Ham U	1	37	—
1985–86 West Ham U	1	42	—
1986–87 West Ham U	1	32	2
1987–88 West Ham U	1	18	—

GALLACHER, Bernard
22.3.67 Johnstone (DF)
5.8 11.2½ Apprentice
LD Manchester U v Aston Villa
9.5.87 3–1

1984–85 Aston Villa	1	—	—
1985–86 Aston Villa	1	—	—
1986–87 Aston Villa	1	1	—
1987–88 Aston Villa	2	43	—

GALLACHER, Kevin
23.11.66 Clydebank (FW)
5.6 8.8 Duntocher BC
LD Rangers v Dundee U
14.12.85 1–1

1983–84 Dundee U	P	—	—
1984–85 Dundee U	P	—	—
1985–86 Dundee U	P	20	3
1986–87 Dundee U	P	37	10
1987–88 Dundee U	P	26	4

GALLAGHER, Brian
8.9.58 Glasgow (FW)
5.9 11.1 Radnor Park Juveniles
LD Dumbarton v Hearts
13.8.77 2–2

1977–78 Dumbarton	1	34	10
1978–79 Dumbarton	1	32	8
1979–80 Dumbarton	1	39	11
1980–81 Dumbarton	1	33	14
1981–82 Kilmarnock	1	35	10
1982–83 Kilmarnock	P	34	9
1983–84 Kilmarnock	1	35	11
1984–85 St Mirren	P	32	9
1985–86 St Mirren	P	31	6
1986–87 St Mirren	P	23	1
1987–88 St Mirren	P	13	—

PLAYER DIRECTORY

Paul Gascoigne

Photo: Bob Thomas Sports Photography.

GALLAGHER, Jackie
6.4.58 Wisbech (FW)
5.10½ 12.9 March T
LD <u>Lincoln C</u> v Peterborough U
11.5.77 1–1

1975–76	Lincoln C	4	—	—
1976–77	Lincoln C	3	1	—
1977–78	Lincoln C	3	—	—
King's Lynn				
1979–80	Peterborough U	4	1	—
1980–81	Peterborough U	4	12	1
Wisbech T				
1982–83	Torquay U	4	42	7
Wisbech T				
1985–86	Peterborough U	4	42	11
1986–87	Peterborough U	4	40	8
1987–88	Wolves	4	19	3

GALLIERS, Steve
21.8.57 Fulwood (MF)
5.6 9.7 Chorley
LD <u>Wimbledon</u> v Halifax T
20.8.77 3–3

1977–78	Wimbledon	4	27	1
1978–79	Wimbledon	4	44	3
1979–80	Wimbledon	4	36	2
1980–81	Wimbledon	4	37	4
1981–82	Wimbledon	3	11	—
1981–82	Crystal Palace	2	13	—
1982–83	Wimbledon	4	34	2
1983–84	Wimbledon	3	36	1
1984–85	Wimbledon	2	29	1
1985–86	Wimbledon	2	32	1
1986–87	Wimbledon	1	14	—
1986–87	*Bristol C*	3	9	—
1987–88	Wimbledon	1	1	—
1987–88	Bristol C	3	35	6

GALLOWAY, Mick
30.5.65 Oswestry (DF)
5.11 11.7 Amateur
LD <u>Mansfield T</u> v Tranmere R
17.9.83 1–0

1983–84	Mansfield T	4	17	—
1984–85	Mansfield T	4	31	3
1985–86	Mansfield T	4	6	—
1985–86	Halifax T	4	19	—
1986–87	Halifax T	4	43	3
1987–88	Halifax T	4	17	2
1987–88	Hearts	P	25	6

GALVIN, Tony
12.7.56 Huddersfield (FW)
5.9 11.5 Goole T
LD <u>Tottenham H</u> v Manchester C
3.2.79 0–3

1977–78	Tottenham H	2	—	—
1978–79	Tottenham H	1	1	—
1979–80	Tottenham H	1	10	4
1980–81	Tottenham H	1	17	1
1981–82	Tottenham H	1	32	3
1982–83	Tottenham H	1	26	2
1983–84	Tottenham H	1	30	1
1984–85	Tottenham H	1	38	4
1985–86	Tottenham H	1	23	4
1986–87	Tottenham H	1	24	1
1987–88	Sheffield W	1	18	—

GANNON, John
18.12.66 Wimbledon (FW)
5.8 10.10 Apprentice
LD <u>Bradford C</u> v <u>Wimbledon</u>
8.5.86 1–1

1984–85	Wimbledon	2	—	—
1985–86	Wimbledon	2	1	1
1986–87	Wimbledon	1	2	—
1986–87	*Crewe Alex*	4	15	—
1987–88	Wimbledon	1	13	1

GARDNER, Stephen
— —
— —
LD <u>Burnley</u> v Colchester U
15.8.87 0–3

1987–88	Burnley	4	42	—

GARNER, Andy
8.3.66 Chesterfield (FW)
6.0 12.1 Apprentice
LD <u>Grimsby T</u> v <u>Derby Co</u>
21.2.84 2–1

1983–84	Derby Co	2	13	5
1984–85	Derby Co	3	16	3
1985–86	Derby Co	3	16	5
1986–87	Derby Co	2	2	—
1987–88	Derby Co	1	24	4

GARNER, Paul
1.12.55 Doncaster (DF)
5.8¾ 10.8 Apprentice
LD Hull C v <u>Huddersfield T</u>
23.4.73 0–0

1972–73	Huddersfield T	2	2	—
1973–74	Huddersfield T	3	43	—
1974–75	Huddersfield T	3	35	2
1975–76	Huddersfield T	4	16	—
1975–76	Sheffield U	1	25	1
1976–77	Sheffield U	2	40	—
1977–78	Sheffield U	2	3	—
1978–79	Sheffield U	2	19	1
1979–80	Sheffield U	3	36	1
1980–81	Sheffield U	3	35	3
1981–82	Sheffield U	4	34	—
1982–83	Sheffield U	3	35	—
1983–84	Sheffield U	3	24	1
1983–84	*Gillingham*	3	5	—
1984–85	Sheffield U	2	—	—
1984–85	Mansfield T	4	39	2
1985–86	Mansfield T	4	28	4
1986–87	Mansfield T	3	22	2
1987–88	Mansfield T	3	19	—

GARNER, Simon
23.11.59 Boston (FW)
5.10 11.4 Apprentice
LD Newcastle U v <u>Blackburn R</u>
9.9.78 3–1

1978–79	Blackburn R	2	25	8
1979–80	Blackburn R	3	28	6
1980–81	Blackburn R	2	33	7
1981–82	Blackburn R	2	36	14
1982–83	Blackburn R	2	41	22
1983–84	Blackburn R	2	42	19
1984–85	Blackburn R	2	37	12
1985–86	Blackburn R	2	38	12
1986–87	Blackburn R	2	40	10
1987–88	Blackburn R	2	40	14

GARTON, Billy
15.3.65 Salford (DF)
5.11 11.8 Apprentice
LD Leicester C v <u>Manchester U</u>
10.11.84 2–3

1982–83	Manchester U	1	—	—
1983–84	Manchester U	1	—	—
1984–85	Manchester U	1	2	—
1985–86	Manchester U	1	10	—
1985–86	*Birmingham C*	1	5	—
1986–87	Manchester U	1	9	—
1987–88	Manchester U	1	6	—

GARWOOD, Jason
23.3.69 Birmingham (FW)
5.7 10.2 Trainee
LD —

1987–88	Leicester C	2	—	—

GASCOIGNE, Paul
27.5.67 Gateshead (MF)
5.10 11.7 Apprentice
LD <u>Newcastle U</u> v QPR
13.4.85 1–0

1984–85	Newcastle U	1	2	—
1985–86	Newcastle U	1	31	9
1986–87	Newcastle U	1	24	5
1987–88	Newcastle U	1	35	7

GATES, Eric
28.6.55 Ferryhill (FW)
5.6 10.8 Apprentice
LD <u>Ipswich T</u> v Wolves
27.10.73 2–0

1972–73	Ipswich T	1	—	—
1973–74	Ipswich T	1	6	—
1974–75	Ipswich T	1	6	—
1975–76	Ipswich T	1	13	1
1976–77	Ipswich T	1	12	1
1977–78	Ipswich T	1	24	2
1978–79	Ipswich T	1	22	7
1979–80	Ipswich T	1	36	13
1980–81	Ipswich T	1	37	11
1981–82	Ipswich T	1	38	9
1982–83	Ipswich T	1	24	3
1983–84	Ipswich T	1	37	13
1984–85	Ipswich T	1	41	13
1985–86	Sunderland	2	39	9
1986–87	Sunderland	2	27	5
1987–88	Sunderland	3	42	19

PLAYER DIRECTORY

GATTING, Steve
29.5.59 Park Royal (DF)
5.11 11.11 Apprentice
LD Arsenal v Southampton
21.10.78 1-0

1976–77 Arsenal	1	—	—
1977–78 Arsenal	1	—	—
1978–79 Arsenal	1	21	1
1979–80 Arsenal	1	14	1
1980–81 Arsenal	1	23	3
1981–82 Arsenal	1	—	—
1981–82 Brighton & HA	1	39	3
1982–83 Brighton & HA	1	40	4
1983–84 Brighton & HA	2	35	4
1984–85 Brighton & HA	2	8	—
1985–86 Brighton & HA	2	17	—
1986–87 Brighton & HA	2	40	1
1987–88 Brighton & HA	3	46	3

GAVIN, Mark
10.12.63 Bailleston (MF)
5.7 10.8 Apprentice
LD Leeds U v Cambridge U
2.10.82 2-1

1981–82 Leeds U	1	—	—
1982–83 Leeds U	2	7	1
1983–84 Leeds U	2	12	1
1984–85 Leeds U	2	11	1
1984–85 *Hartlepool U*	4	7	—
1985–86 Carlisle U	2	13	1
1985–86 Bolton W	3	8	1
1986–87 Bolton W	3	41	2
1987–88 Rochdale	4	23	6
1987–88 Hearts	P	7	—

GAYLE, Brian
6.3.65 London (DF)
6.1 12.7
LD Wimbledon v Shrewsbury T
27.3.85 4-1

1984–85 Wimbledon	2	12	1
1985–86 Wimbledon	2	13	—
1986–87 Wimbledon	1	32	1
1987–88 Wimbledon	1	26	1

GAYLE, Howard
18.5.58 Liverpool (MF)
5.10 10.9 Local
LD Preston NE v Fulham
12.1.80 3-2

1977–78 Liverpool	1	—	—
1978–79 Liverpool	1	—	—
1979–80 Liverpool	1	—	—
1979–80 *Fulham*	2	14	—
1980–81 Liverpool	1	4	1
1981–82 Liverpool	1	—	—
1982–83 Liverpool	1	—	—
1982–83 *Birmingham C*	1	13	1
1982–83 *Newcastle U*	2	8	2
1983–84 Birmingham C	1	33	8
1984–85 Sunderland	1	25	2
1985–86 Sunderland	2	23	2
1986–87 Stoke C	2	6	2
1987–88 Blackburn R	2	13	1

GAYNOR, Tommy
29.1.63 Limerick (FW)
6.1 13.2 Limerick
LD Doncaster R v Swindon T
21.12.86 2-2

1986–87 Doncaster R	3	23	4
1987–88 Doncaster R	3	10	3
1987–88 Nottingham F	1	12	3

GEDDES, Bobby
12.8.60 Inverness (GK)
6.0 11.4 Ross County
LD Dunfermline Ath v Dundee
9.8.80 1-0

1977–78 Dundee	1	—	—
1978–79 Dundee	1	—	—
1979–80 Dundee	P	—	—
1980–81 Dundee	1	20	—
1981–82 Dundee	P	28	—
1982–83 Dundee	P	1	—
1983–84 Dundee	P	24	—
1984–85 Dundee	P	16	—
1985–86 Dundee	P	36	—
1986–87 Dundee	P	44	—
1987–88 Dundee	P	38	—

GEDDIS, David
12.3.58 Carlisle (FW)
5.10½ 12.12 Apprentice
LD Derby Co v Ipswich T
14.5.77 0-0

1975–76 Ipswich T	1	—	—
1976–77 Ipswich T	1	2	—
1976–77 *Luton T*	2	13	4
1977–78 Ipswich T	1	26	4
1978–79 Ipswich T	1	15	1
1979–80 Ipswich T	1	—	—
1979–80 Aston Villa	1	20	2
1980–81 Aston Villa	1	9	4
1981–82 Aston Villa	1	14	6
1982–83 Aston Villa	1	4	—
1982–83 *Luton T*	1	4	—
1983–84 Aston Villa	1	—	—
1983–84 Barnsley	2	31	14
1984–85 Barnsley	2	14	10
1984–85 Birmingham C	2	18	12
1985–86 Birmingham C	1	26	6
1986–87 Birmingham C	2	2	—
1986–87 *Brentford*	3	4	—
1986–87 Shrewsbury T	2	15	4
1987–88 Shrewsbury T	2	15	5

GEE, Phil
19.12.64 Pelsall (FW)
5.9 10.4 Gresley R
LD Derby Co v Walsall
12.3.86 3-1

1985–86 Derby Co	3	4	2
1986–87 Derby Co	2	41	15
1987–88 Derby Co	1	38	6

GENNOE, Terry
16.3.53 Shrewsbury (GK)
6.2 13.1 Bricklayers Sports
LD Workington v Bury
20.4.73 2-0

1972–73 Bury	4	1	—
1973–74 Bury	4	2	—
1973–74 *Blackburn R*	3	—	—
1974–75 Bury	3	—	—
1974–75 *Leeds U*	1	—	—
1975–76 Halifax T	3	26	—
1976–77 Halifax T	4	26	—
1977–78 Halifax T	4	26	—
1977–78 Southampton	2	—	—
1978–79 Southampton	1	23	—
1979–80 Southampton	1	13	—
1980–81 *Everton*	1	—	—
1980–81 *Crystal Palace*	1	3	—
1981–82 Blackburn R	2	35	—
1982–83 Blackburn R	2	33	—
1983–84 Blackburn R	2	30	—
1984–85 Blackburn R	2	37	—
1985–86 Blackburn R	2	32	—
1986–87 Blackburn R	2	11	—
1987–88 Blackburn R	2	39	—

GERNON, Irvin
30.12.62 Birmingham (DF)
6.2 12.1 Apprentice
LD Nottingham F v Ipswich T
17.3.82 1-1

1979–80 Ipswich T	1	—	—
1980–81 Ipswich T	1	—	—
1981–82 Ipswich T	1	4	—
1982–83 Ipswich T	1	26	—
1983–84 Ipswich T	1	19	—
1984–85 Ipswich T	1	13	—
1985–86 Ipswich T	1	11	—
1986–87 Ipswich T	2	3	—
1986–87 *Northampton T*	4	9	—
1986–87 Gillingham	3	14	—
1987–88 Gillingham	3	21	1

GIBBINS, Roger
6.9.55 Enfield (FW)
5.10½ 11.9 Apprentice
LD Carlisle U v Oxford U
16.8.75 1-1

1972–73 Tottenham H	1	—	—
1973–74 Tottenham H	1	—	—
1974–75 Tottenham H	1	—	—
1975–76 Oxford U	2	19	2
1976–77 Norwich C	1	20	5
1977–78 Norwich C	1	28	7
New England Tea Men (NASL)			
1979–80 Cambridge U	2	35	4
1980–81 Cambridge U	2	30	4
1981–82 Cambridge U	2	35	4
1982–83 Cardiff C	3	46	8
1983–84 Cardiff C	2	42	4
1984–85 Cardiff C	2	40	5
1985–86 Cardiff C	3	11	—
1985–86 Swansea C	3	35	6
1986–87 Newport Co	3	46	7
1987–88 Newport Co	4	33	1
1987–88 Torquay U	4	12	2

GIBBS, Nigel
20.11.65 St Albans (MF)
5.7 10.12 Apprentice
LD Watford v Wolves
5.5.84 0–0

1983–84	Watford	1	3	—
1984–85	Watford	1	12	—
1985–86	Watford	1	40	1
1986–87	Watford	1	15	—
1987–88	Watford	1	30	—

GIBSON, Colin
6.4.60 Bridport (DF)
5.8 10.8½ Apprentice
LD Aston Villa v Bristol C
18.11.78 2–0

1977–78	Aston Villa	1	—	—
1978–79	Aston Villa	1	12	—
1979–80	Aston Villa	1	31	2
1980–81	Aston Villa	1	21	—
1981–82	Aston Villa	1	23	—
1982–83	Aston Villa	1	23	1
1983–84	Aston Villa	1	28	1
1984–85	Aston Villa	1	40	4
1985–86	Aston Villa	1	7	2
1985–86	Manchester U	1	18	5
1986–87	Manchester U	1	24	1
1987–88	Manchester U	1	29	2

GIBSON, Terry
23.12.62 Walthamstow (FW)
5.5 10.0 Apprentice
LD Tottenham H v Stoke C
29.12.79 1–0

1979–80	Tottenham H	1	1	—
1980–81	Tottenham H	1	—	—
1981–82	Tottenham H	1	1	—
1982–83	Tottenham H	1	16	4
1983–84	Coventry C	1	36	17
1984–85	Coventry C	1	38	15
1985–86	Coventry C	1	24	11
1985–86	Manchester U	1	7	—
1986–87	Manchester U	1	16	1
1987–88	Wimbledon	1	17	6

GILBERT, Billy
10.11.59 Lewisham (DF)
5.11 12.0 Apprentice
LD Blackpool v C Palace
4.10.77 3–1

1976–77	Crystal Palace	3	—	—
1977–78	Crystal Palace	2	18	—
1978–79	Crystal Palace	2	41	1
1979–80	Crystal Palace	1	40	1
1980–81	Crystal Palace	1	39	—
1981–82	Crystal Palace	2	31	—
1982–83	Crystal Palace	2	34	—
1983–84	Crystal Palace	2	34	1
1984–85	Portsmouth	2	35	—
1985–86	Portsmouth	2	36	—
1986–87	Portsmouth	2	36	—
1987–88	Portsmouth	1	21	—

GILBERT, David
22.6.63 Lincoln (MF)
— — Boston U
LD Scunthorpe U v Northampton T
23.8.86 2–2

| 1986–87 | Northampton T | 4 | 45 | 8 |
| 1987–88 | Northampton T | 3 | 41 | 6 |

GILKES, Michael
20.7.65 Hackney (FW)
5.8 10.2
LD Lincoln C v Reading
27.10.84 5–1

1984–85	Reading	3	16	2
1985–86	Reading	3	9	2
1986–87	Reading	2	7	—
1987–88	Reading	2	39	4

GILL, Gary
28.11.64 Middlesbrough (DF)
5.10 11.9 Apprentice
LD Cardiff C v Middlesbrough
3.3.84 2–1

1982–83	Middlesbrough	2	—	—
1983–84	Middlesbrough	2	6	—
1983–84	Hull C	3	1	—
1984–85	Middlesbrough	2	14	—
1985–86	Middlesbrough	2	9	—
1986–87	Middlesbrough	3	36	2
1987–88	Middlesbrough	2	3	—

GILL, Tony
6.3.68 Bradford (DF)
5.9½ 10.0 Apprentice
LD Southampton v Manchester U
3.1.87 1–1

1985–86	Bradford C	2	—	—
1986–87	Manchester U	1	1	—
1987–88	Manchester U	1	—	—

GILLESPIE, Gary
5.7.60 Stirling (DF)
6.2 12.7 School
LD Falkirk v Berwick R
20.8.77 2–1

1977–78	Falkirk	2	22	—
1978–79	Coventry C	1	15	—
1979–80	Coventry C	1	38	1
1980–81	Coventry C	1	37	1
1981–82	Coventry C	1	40	2
1982–83	Coventry C	1	42	2
1983–84	Liverpool	1	—	—
1984–85	Liverpool	1	12	1
1985–86	Liverpool	1	14	3
1986–87	Liverpool	1	37	1
1987–88	Liverpool	1	35	4

GILLIGAN, Jimmy
24.1.64 London (FW)
6.2 13.2 Apprentice
LD Watford v Barnsley
3.10.81 3–1

1981–82	Watford	2	1	—
1982–83	Watford	1	4	2
1982–83	*Lincoln C*	3	3	—
1983–84	Watford	1	12	4
1984–85	Watford	1	10	—
1985–86	Grimsby T	2	25	4
1986–87	Swindon T	3	17	5
1986–87	Lincoln C	4	11	1
1986–87	*Newport Co*	3	5	1
1987–88	Cardiff C	4	46	18

GIPP, David
13.7.69 Forest Gate (FW)
5.7 9.12 Apprentice
LD Blackburn R v Brighton & HA
25.4.87 1–1

| 1986–87 | Brighton & HA | 2 | 3 | — |
| 1986–87 | Brighton & HA | 3 | 2 | — |

GITTENS, Jon
22.1.64 Moseley (DF)
5.11 12.6 Paget R
LD Birmingham C v Southampton
19.4.86 0–2

1985–86	Southampton	1	4	—
1986–87	Southampton	1	14	—
1987–88	Swindon T	2	29	—

GLEASURE, Peter
8.10.60 Luton (GK)
5.11 12.13 Apprentice
LD Millwall v Hull C
16.8.80 1–1

1978–79	Millwall	2	—	—
1979–80	Millwall	3	—	—
1980–81	Millwall	3	13	—
1981–82	Millwall	3	38	—
1982–83	Millwall	3	4	—
1982–83	*Northampton T*	4	11	—
1983–84	Northampton T	4	46	—
1984–85	Northampton T	4	43	—
1985–86	Northampton T	4	44	—
1986–87	Northampton T	4	46	—
1987–88	Northampton T	3	46	—

GLEGHORN, Nigel
12.8.62 Seaham (MF)
6.0 12.13 Seaham Red Star
LD Arsenal v Ipswich T
19.10.85 1–0

1985–86	Ipswich T	1	21	2
1986–87	Ipswich T	2	29	7
1987–88	Ipswich T	2	16	2

GLENN, David
30.11.62 Wigan (DF)
5.10 10.10 Apprentice
LD Wigan Ath v Port Vale
6.9.80 1–0

1980–81	Wigan Ath	4	11	2
1981–82	Wigan Ath	4	35	2
1982–83	Wigan Ath	3	26	—
1983–84	Blackburn R	2	22	—
1984–85	Blackburn R	2	2	—
1985–86	Chester C	4	33	1
1986–87	Chester C	3	1	—
1987–88	Chester C	3	21	—

PLAYER DIRECTORY

GLENNIE, Bobby
2.10.57 Dundee (DF)
5.11 11.4 St Columba's BC
LD Aberdeen v St Mirren
10.12.77 3–1

1974–75	Aberdeen	1	—	—
1975–76	Aberdeen	P	—	—
1976–77	Aberdeen	P	—	—
1977–78	Aberdeen	P	3	—
1977–78	Dundee	1	13	1
1978–79	Dundee	1	37	1
1979–80	Dundee	P	35	—
1980–81	Dundee	1	39	—
1981–82	Dundee	P	35	—
1982–83	Dundee	P	26	—
1983–84	Dundee	P	27	2
1984–85	Dundee	P	29	—
1985–86	Dundee	P	33	2
1986–87	Dundee	P	18	—
1987–88	Dundee	P	22	—

GLOVER, Dean
29.12.63 West Bromwich (DF)
5.9 11.2 Apprentice
LD Coventry C v Aston Villa
19.1.85 0–3

1981–82	Aston Villa	1	—	—
1982–83	Aston Villa	1	—	—
1983–84	Aston Villa	1	—	—
1984–85	Aston Villa	1	5	—
1985–86	Aston Villa	1	18	—
1986–87	Aston Villa	1	5	—
1986–87	*Sheffield U*	2	5	—
1987–88	Middlesbrough	2	38	4

GLOVER, Edward
24.4.70 Kettering (FW)
— — Apprentice
LD Charlton Ath v Nottingham F
15.8.87 1–0

1987–88	Nottingham F	1	20	3

GODDARD, Karl
29.12.67 Leeds (FW)
5.6 12.4 Apprentice
LD Bradford C v Birmingham C
3.1.87 0–0

1985–86	Manchester U	1	—	—
1986–87	Bradford C	2	20	—
1987–88	Bradford C	2	29	—

GODDARD, Paul
12.10.59 Harlington (FW)
5.8 12.0 Apprentice
LD QPR v Arsenal
11.4.78 2–1

1977–78	QPR	1	7	1
1978–79	QPR	1	23	6
1979–80	QPR	2	40	16
1980–81	West Ham U	2	37	17
1981–82	West Ham U	1	39	15
1982–83	West Ham U	1	39	10
1983–84	West Ham U	1	5	1
1984–85	West Ham U	1	40	9
1985–86	West Ham U	1	6	1
1986–87	West Ham U	1	4	1
1986–87	Newcastle U	1	26	11
1987–88	Newcastle U	1	35	8

GODDEN, Tony
2.8.55 Gillingham (GK)
6.1 12.4 Ashford T
LD Tottenham H v WBA
12.3.77 2–0

1975–76	WBA	2	—	—
1976–77	WBA	1	6	—
1976–77	*Preston NE*	3	—	—
1977–78	WBA	1	42	—
1978–79	WBA	1	42	—
1979–80	WBA	1	42	—
1980–81	WBA	1	42	—
1981–82	WBA	1	19	—
1982–83	WBA	1	12	—
1982–83	*Luton T*	1	12	—
1983–84	WBA	1	—	—
1983–84	*Walsall*	3	19	—
1984–85	WBA	1	41	—
1985–86	WBA	1	21	—
1985–86	*Chelsea*	1	8	—
1986–87	Chelsea	1	26	—
1987–88	Birmingham C	2	22	—

GODFREY, Peter
12.10.57 Falkirk (DF)
6.0 11.7 Linlithgow Rose
LD Stenhousemuir v Queen's Park
22.4.80 1–3

1979–80	Stenhousemuir	2	2	—
1980–81	Meadowbank T	2	2	—
1981–82	Meadowbank T	2	30	6
1982–83	Meadowbank T	2	38	3
1983–84	Meadowbank T	1	37	3
1984–85	Meadowbank T	1	19	—
1984–85	St Mirren	P	15	1
1985–86	St Mirren	P	34	3
1986–87	St Mirren	P	38	1
1987–88	St Mirren	P	24	—

GOODING, Mick
12.4.59 Newcastle (FW)
5.7 10.8 Bishop Auckland
LD Oxford U v Rotherham U
18.8.79 5–1

1979–80	Rotherham U	3	34	3
1980–81	Rotherham U	3	37	4
1981–82	Rotherham U	2	22	2
1982–83	Rotherham U	2	9	1
1982–83	Chesterfield	3	12	—
1983–84	Chesterfield	4	—	—
1983–84	Rotherham U	3	26	7
1984–85	Rotherham U	3	44	10
1985–86	Rotherham U	3	40	8
1986–87	Rotherham U	3	46	7
1987–88	Peterborough U	4	44	18

GOODISON, Wayne
23.9.64 Wakefield (DF)
5.8 11.7 Apprentice
LD Fulham v Barnsley
19.4.83 1–0

1982–83	Barnsley	2	3	—
1983–84	Barnsley	2	—	—
1984–85	Barnsley	2	12	—
1985–86	Barnsley	2	21	—
1986–87	Crewe Alex	4	35	—
1987–88	Crewe Alex	4	34	—

GOODMAN, Donald
9.5.66 Leeds (FW)
5.10 11.0 School
LD Bradford C v Newport Co
25.4.84 1–0

1983–84	Bradford C	3	2	—
1984–85	Bradford C	3	25	5
1985–86	Bradford C	2	20	4
1986–87	Bradford C	2	23	5
1986–87	WBA	2	10	2
1987–88	WBA	2	40	7

GOODWIN, Mark
23.2.60 Sheffield (MF)
5.10 10.9 Apprentice
LD Ipswich T v Leicester C
17.12.77 1–0

1977–78	Leicester C	1	14	3
1978–79	Leicester C	2	28	1
1979–80	Leicester C	2	30	4
1980–81	Leicester C	1	19	—
1980–81	Notts Co	2	10	2
1981–82	Notts Co	1	38	4
1982–83	Notts Co	1	34	4
1983–84	Notts Co	1	29	—
1984–85	Notts Co	2	38	4
1985–86	Notts Co	3	43	6
1986–87	Notts Co	3	45	4
1987–88	Walsall	3	36	2

GOODWIN, Shaun
14.6.69 Rotherham (MF)
5.7½ 8.10 Apprentice
LD Rotherham U v Aldershot
30.4.88 1–0

1987–88 Rotherham U	3	3	—

GOODYEAR, Clive
15.1.61 Lincoln (DF)
6.0 11.4 Local
LD Luton T v Wrexham
26.4.80 2–0

1979–80 Luton T	2	1	—
1980–81 Luton T	2	5	1
1981–82 Luton T	2	32	1
1982–83 Luton T	1	35	2
1983–84 Luton T	1	17	—
1984–85 Plymouth Arg	3	33	2
1985–86 Plymouth Arg	3	41	2
1986–87 Plymouth Arg	2	32	1
1987–88 Wimbledon	1	22	—

GORAM, Andy
13.4.64 Bury (GK)
5.11 11.6 WBA Apprentice
LD Oldham Ath v Charlton Ath
4.5.82 1–0

1981–82 Oldham Ath	2	3	—
1982–83 Oldham Ath	2	38	—
1983–84 Oldham Ath	2	22	—
1984–85 Oldham Ath	2	41	—
1985–86 Oldham Ath	2	41	—
1986–87 Oldham Ath	2	41	—
1987–88 Oldham Ath	2	9	—
1987–88 Hibernian	P	33	1

GORDON, Colin
17.1.63 Stourbridge (FW)
6.1 12.12 Oldbury U
LD Rochdale v Swindon T
3.11.84 0–1

1984–85 Swindon T	4	33	17
1985–86 Swindon T	4	39	17
1986–87 Wimbledon	1	3	—
1986–87 *Gillingham*	3	4	2
1987–88 Reading	2	20	8
1987–88 *Bristol C*	3	8	4

GORDON, Dale
9.1.67 Gt Yarmouth (FW)
5.10 11.8 Apprentice
LD Norwich C v Liverpool
25.8.84 3–3

1983–84 Norwich C	1	—	—
1984–85 Norwich C	1	23	3
1985–86 Norwich C	2	6	1
1986–87 Norwich C	1	41	5
1987–88 Norwich C	1	21	3

GORDON, Stuart
14.7.60 Glasgow (MF)
5.7 10.0 Pollok Juniors
LD Clydebank v Hibernian
15.3.86 1–3

1985–86 Clydebank	P	3	—
1986–87 Clydebank	P	29	9
1987–88 Clydebank	1	5	—
1987–88 Hamilton A	1	28	9

GORE, Ian
10.1.69 Liverpool (MF)
5.10 11.0 Southport
LD —

1987–88 Blackpool	3	—	—

GORE, Shaun
21.9.68 London (DF)
6.4 13.1
LD Fulham v Wimbledon
15.3.86 0–2

1985–86 Fulham	2	5	—
1986–87 Fulham	3	7	—
1987–88 Fulham	3	8	—

GORMAN, Paul
18.9.68 Doncaster (FW)
5.11 11.2 Trainee
LD Mansfield T v Doncaster R
29.9.87 2–0

1987–88 Doncaster R	3	7	1

GORMAN, Paul
6.8.63 Dublin (DF)
5.10 11.8 Apprentice
LD Manchester C v Arsenal
6.3.82 0–0

1980–81 Arsenal	1	—	—
1981–82 Arsenal	1	4	—
1982–83 Arsenal	1	—	—
1983–84 Arsenal	1	2	—

1984–85 Birmingham C	2	6	—
1984–85 Carlisle U	2	7	1
1985–86 Carlisle U	2	24	—
1986–87 Carlisle U	3	35	—
1987–88 Carlisle U	4	37	—

GORTON, Andy
23.9.66 Salford (GK)
5.11 11.4
LD Oldham Ath v Fulham
3.5.86 2–1

1984–85 Oldham Ath	2	—	—
1985–86 Oldham Ath	2	1	—
1986–87 Oldham Ath	2	1	—
1986–87 *Stockport Co*	4	14	—
1987–88 Oldham Ath	2	24	—
1987–88 *Tranmere R*	4	1	—

GOSNEY, Andy
8.11.63 Southampton (GK)
6.4 13.5 Apprentice
LD Millwall v Portsmouth
8.5.82 1–0

1981–82 Portsmouth	3	1	—
1982–83 Portsmouth	3	—	—
1983–84 Portsmouth	2	—	—
1984–85 Portsmouth	2	—	—
1985–86 Portsmouth	2	4	—
1986–87 Portsmouth	2	—	—
1987–88 Portsmouth	1	4	—

GOSS, Jeremy
11.5.65 Cyprus (MF)
5.9 10.9 Amateur
LD Coventry C v Norwich C
12.5.84 2–1

1982–83 Norwich C	1	—	—
1983–84 Norwich C	1	1	—
1984–85 Norwich C	1	5	—
1985–86 Norwich C	2	—	—
1986–87 Norwich C	1	1	—
1987–88 Norwich C	1	22	2

GOUGH, Richard
5.4.62 Stockholm (DF)
6.0 12.0 Witz University
LD Dundee U v Celtic
22.4.81 2–3

1980–81 Dundee U	P	4	—
1981–82 Dundee U	P	30	1
1982–83 Dundee U	P	34	8
1983–84 Dundee U	P	33	3
1984–85 Dundee U	P	33	6
1985–86 Dundee U	P	31	5
1986–87 Tottenham H	1	40	2
1987–88 Tottenham H	1	9	—
1987–88 Rangers	P	31	5

PLAYER DIRECTORY

GOULET, Brent
— Portland, USA
— — Seattle Sounders
LD Bournemouth v Huddersfield T
21.11.87 0–2

1987–88 Bournemouth	2	6	—
1987–88 *Crewe Alex*	4	3	3

GOURLAY, Archie
29.6.69 Greenock (MF)
5.8 10.0 Local
LD Morton v St Mirren
19.3.87 0–2

1987–88 Morton	P	2	—
1987–88 Newcastle U	1	—	—

GRAHAM, Arthur
26.10.52 Glasgow (FW)
5.8 11.0 Cambuslang R.
LD Aberdeen v Dunfermline Ath
21.3.70 2–0

1969–70 Aberdeen	1	5	1
1970–71 Aberdeen	1	31	5
1971–72 Aberdeen	1	29	7
1972–73 Aberdeen	1	23	—
1973–74 Aberdeen	1	32	3
1974–75 Aberdeen	1	34	11
1975–76 Aberdeen	P	35	—
1976–77 Aberdeen	P	35	5
1977–78 Leeds U	1	40	6
1978–79 Leeds U	1	39	8
1979–80 Leeds U	1	27	3
1980–81 Leeds U	1	40	3
1981–82 Leeds U	1	38	9
1982–83 Leeds U	2	39	5
1983–84 Manchester U	1	37	5
1984–85 Manchester U	1	—	—
1985–86 Bradford C	2	25	2
1986–87 Bradford C	2	6	—
1987–88 Bradford C	2	—	—

GRAHAM, Mike
24.2.59 Lancaster (DF)
5.9½ 11.7 Apprentice
LD Mansfield T v Bolton W
11.3.78 0–1

1976–77 Bolton W	2	—	—
1977–78 Bolton W	2	1	—
1978–79 Bolton W	1	9	—
1979–80 Bolton W	1	9	—
1980–81 Bolton W	2	27	—
1981–82 Swindon T	3	30	1
1982–83 Swindon T	4	46	—
1983–84 Swindon T	4	36	—
1984–85 Swindon T	4	29	—

1985–86 Mansfield T	4	45	—
1986–87 Mansfield T	3	41	—
1987–88 Mansfield T	3	46	1

GRAHAM, Milton
2.11.62 Tottenham (FW)
5.10½ 12.4 Local
LD Bournemouth v Bury
24.10.81 3–2

1981–82 Bournemouth	4	5	3
1982–83 Bournemouth	3	20	2
1983–84 Bournemouth	3	30	4
1984–85 Bournemouth	3	18	3
1985–86 Chester C	4	38	3
1986–87 Chester C	3	42	4
1987–88 Chester C	3	25	3

GRAHAM, Thomas
31.3.58 Glasgow (MF)
5.9 11.9 Arthurlie
LD Barnsley v Bradford C
18.11.78 0–1

1977–78 Aston Villa	1	—	—
1978–79 Aston Villa	1	—	—
1978–79 Barnsley	4	27	12
1979–80 Barnsley	3	11	1
1980–81 Barnsley	3	—	—
1980–81 Halifax T	4	34	9
1981–82 Halifax T	4	37	8
1982–83 Doncaster R	3	11	2
1982–83 Scunthorpe U	4	13	3
1983–84 Scunthorpe U	3	27	4
1984–85 Scunthorpe U	4	38	9
1985–86 Scunthorpe U	4	31	5
1986–87 Scarborough	—	—	—
1987–88 Scarborough	4	44	7

GRAINGER, Paul
28.1.68 Bloxwich (MF)
5.8 11.0 Mile Oak
LD —

1987–88 Wolves	4	—	—

GRANGER, Keith
5.10.68 Southampton (GK)
5.10 10.10 Apprentice
LD Everton v Southampton
3.5.86 6–1

1985–86 Southampton	1	2	—
1986–87 Southampton	1	—	—
1987–88 Southampton	1	—	—
1987–88 *Darlington*	4	9	—
1987–88 Darlington	4	14	—

GRANT, Brian
19.6.64 Bannockburn (MF)
5.9 10.7 Fallin Violet
LD Stirling A v Berwick R
15.5.82 0–0

1981–82 Stirling A	2	1	—
1982–83 Stirling A	2	1	—
1983–84 Stirling A	2	24	3
1984–85 Aberdeen	P	—	—
1985–86 Aberdeen	P	—	—
1986–87 Aberdeen	P	15	4
1987–88 Aberdeen	P	7	1

GRANT, Peter
30.8.65 Bellshill (MF)
5.9 10.3 Celtic BC
LD Rangers v Celtic
21.4.84 1–0

1982–83 Celtic	P	—	—
1983–84 Celtic	P	3	—
1984–85 Celtic	P	20	4
1985–86 Celtic	P	30	1
1986–87 Celtic	P	37	1
1987–88 Celtic	P	37	2

GRAY, Andy
30.11.55 Glasgow (FW)
5.11 11.10 Clydebank Strollers
LD Dumbarton v Dundee U
1.9.73 1–2

1973–74 Dundee U	1	26	16
1974–75 Dundee U	1	33	20
1975–76 Dundee U	P	3	—
1975–76 Aston Villa	1	30	10
1976–77 Aston Villa	1	36	25
1977–78 Aston Villa	1	32	13
1978–79 Aston Villa	1	15	6
1979–80 Aston Villa	1	—	—
1979–80 Wolves	1	35	12
1980–81 Wolves	1	27	9
1981–82 Wolves	1	29	5
1982–83 Wolves	2	33	10
1983–84 Wolves	1	9	2
1983–84 Everton	1	23	5
1984–85 Everton	1	26	9
1985–86 Aston Villa	1	35	5
1986–87 Aston Villa	1	19	—
1987–88 Aston Villa	2	—	—
1987–88 *Notts Co*	3	4	—
1987–88 *WBA*	2	7	4
1987–88 WBA	2	25	6

GRAY, Andy
22.2.64 Lambeth (FW)
5.10 11.6 Corinthian C.
and Dulwich H
LD C Palace v Cardiff C
9.12.84 1–1

1984–85 Crystal Palace	2	21	5
1985–86 Crystal Palace	2	30	10
1986–87 Crystal Palace	2	30	6
1987–88 Crystal Palace	2	17	6
1987–88 Aston Villa	2	19	1

GRAY, Frankie
27.10.54 Glasgow (DF)
5.10 11.10 Apprentice
LD Leicester C v Leeds U
10.2.73 2–0

1971–72	Leeds U	1	— —
1972–73	Leeds U	1	4 1
1973–74	Leeds U	1	6 —
1974–75	Leeds U	1	18 2
1975–76	Leeds U	1	42 2
1976–77	Leeds U	1	41 3
1977–78	Leeds U	1	41 3
1978–79	Leeds U	1	41 6
1979–80	Nottingham F	1	41 2
1980–81	Nottingham F	1	40 3
1981–82	Leeds U	1	37 —
1982–83	Leeds U	2	42 5
1983–84	Leeds U	2	24 4
1984–85	Leeds U	2	39 1
1985–86	Sunderland	2	34 4
1986–87	Sunderland	2	38 4
1987–88	Sunderland	3	34 —

GRAY, Philip
2.10.68 Belfast (FW)
5.10 11.7 Apprentice
LD Everton v Tottenham H
11.5.87 1–0

1986–87	Tottenham H	1	1 —
1987–88	Tottenham H	1	1 —

GRAY, Steven
7.2.67 Irvine (MF)
5.6 10.2 Kilmarnock BC
LD Aberdeen v St Mirren
7.9.85 1–1

1985–86	Aberdeen	P	13 1
1986–87	Aberdeen	P	13 1
1987–88	Aberdeen	P	7 —

GRAY, Stuart
19.4.60 Withernsea (DF)
5.10 10.9 Local
LD Manchester C v Nottingham F
7.2.81 1–1

1980–81	Nottingham F	1	14 1
1981–82	Nottingham F	1	33 2
1982–83	Nottingham F	1	2 —
1982–83	*Bolton W*	2	10 —
1983–84	Barnsley	2	17 8
1984–85	Barnsley	2	7 —
1985–86	Barnsley	2	36 2
1986–87	Barnsley	2	40 11
1987–88	Barnsley	2	20 2
1987–88	Aston Villa	2	20 5

GREALISH, Tony
21.9.56 Paddington (MF)
5.7 11.7 Apprentice
LD Orient v Sheffield W
28.9.74 1–0

1974–75	Orient	2	25 2
1975–76	Orient	2	38 1
1976–77	Orient	2	33 2
1977–78	Orient	2	36 —
1978–79	Orient	2	39 5
1979–80	Luton T	2	41 2
1980–81	Luton T	2	37 —
1981–82	Brighton & HA	1	37 1
1982–83	Brighton & HA	1	38 2
1983–84	Brighton & HA	2	25 3
1983–84	WBA	1	11 —
1984–85	WBA	1	38 4
1985–86	WBA	1	16 1
1986–87	Manchester C	1	11 —
1987–88	Rotherham U	3	38 3

GREEN, John
7.8.58 Rotherham (DF)
5.11 12.12 Apprentice
LD Southend U v Rotherham U
30.8.75 1–2

1975–76	Rotherham U	3	38 —
1976–77	Rotherham U	3	1 —
1977–78	Rotherham U	3	41 1
1978–79	Rotherham U	3	46 1
1979–80	Rotherham U	3	44 2
1980–81	Rotherham U	3	— —
1981–82	Rotherham U	2	41 3
1982–83	Rotherham U	2	36 1
1983–84	Rotherham U	3	1 —
1983–84	Scunthorpe U	3	45 2
1984–85	Scunthorpe U	4	46 1
1985–86	Scunthorpe U	4	9 1
1985–86	Darlington	3	30 1
1986–87	Darlington	3	15 1
1986–87	Rotherham U	3	27 —
1987–88	Rotherham U	3	37 2

GREEN, Richard
22.11.67 Wolverhampton (DF)
6.0 11.8
LD Shrewsbury T v Barnsley
13.9.86 1–0

1986–87	Shrewsbury T	2	15 —
1987–88	Shrewsbury T	2	31 2

GREENALL, Colin
30.12.63 Billinge (DF)
5.10 11.6 Apprentice
LD Huddersfield T v Blackpool
23.8.80 1–1

1980–81	Blackpool	3	12 —
1981–82	Blackpool	4	18 —
1982–83	Blackpool	4	24 1
1983–84	Blackpool	4	39 4
1984–85	Blackpool	4	44 3
1985–86	Blackpool	3	43 1
1986–87	Blackpool	3	3 —
1986–87	Gillingham	3	37 2
1987–88	Gillingham	3	25 2
1987–88	Oxford U	1	12 —

GREENOUGH, Ricky
30.5.61 Mexborough (FW)
6.1 13.4 Boston and Alfreton T
LD Chester C v Southend U
26.1.85 5–1

1984–85	Chester C	4	24 3
1985–86	Chester C	4	33 5
1986–87	Chester C	3	44 7
1987–88	Chester C	3	31 —

GREENWOOD, Nigel
27.11.66 Preston (FW)
5.11 12.0 Apprentice
LD Lincoln C v Preston NE
6.10.84 4–0

1984–85	Preston NE	3	15 5
1985–86	Preston NE	4	30 9
1986–87	Bury	3	37 14
1987–88	Bury	3	30 4

GREGORY, David
23.1.70 Sudbury (MF)
— — Trainee
LD —

1987–88	Ipswich T	2	— —

GREGORY, John
11.5.54 Scunthorpe (DF)
6.1 11.0 Apprentice
LD Northampton T v Gillingham
6.1.73 2–1

1972–73	Northampton T	4	9 —
1973–74	Northampton T	4	46 —
1974–75	Northampton T	4	41 1
1975–76	Northampton T	4	45 3
1976–77	Northampton T	3	46 4
1977–78	Aston Villa	1	26 3
1978–79	Aston Villa	1	39 7
1979–80	Brighton & HA	1	33 —
1980–81	Brighton & HA	1	39 7
1981–82	QPR	2	34 9
1982–83	QPR	2	42 15
1983–84	QPR	1	37 7
1984–85	QPR	1	37 5
1985–86	QPR	1	11 —
1985–86	Derby Co	3	22 4
1986–87	Derby Co	2	42 12
1987–88	Derby Co	1	39 6

PLAYER DIRECTORY

Bruce Grobbelaar   Photo: *Bob Thomas Sports Photography.*

GREGORY, Tony
21.3.68 Doncaster (MF)
5.8 10.10 Apprentice
LD Manchester C v Sheffield W
24.8.85 1–3

1985–86 Sheffield W	1	5	
1986–87 Sheffield W	1	10	1
1987–88 Sheffield W	1	—	—

GRENFELL, Steven
27.10.66 Enfield (DF)
5.9 10.11 Apprentice
LD Colchester U v Wolves
31.10.86 3–0

1984–85 Tottenham H	1	—	—
1985–86 Tottenham H	1	—	—
1986–87 Colchester U	4	23	1
1987–88 Colchester U	4	41	—

GREW, Mark
15.2.58 Bilston (GK)
5.10 11.2 Amateur
LD Halifax T v Wigan Ath
16.12.78 1–2

1976–77 WBA	1	—	—
1977–78 WBA	1	—	—
1978–79 WBA	1	—	—
1978–79 Wigan Ath	4	4	—
1978–79 Notts Co	2	—	—
1979–80 WBA	1	—	—
1980–81 WBA	1	—	—
1981–82 WBA	1	23	—
1982–83 WBA	1	10	—
1983–84 Leicester C	1	5	—
1983–84 Oldham Ath	2	5	—
1983–84 Ipswich T	1	—	—
1984–85 Ipswich T	1	6	—
1985–86 Ipswich T	1	—	—
1985–86 Fulham	2	4	—
1985–86 WBA	1	1	—
1985–86 Derby Co	3	—	—
1986–87 Port Vale	3	3	—
1987–88 Port Vale	3	41	—

GREWCOCK, Neil
26.4.62 Leicester (FW)
5.6 11.2 Apprentice
LD Leicester C v Cardiff C
3.3.79 1–2

1978–79 Leicester C	2	1	1
1979–80 Leicester C	2	—	—
1980–81 Leicester C	1	7	—
1981–82 Leicester C	2	—	—
1981–82 Gillingham	3	13	1

1982–83 Gillingham	3	21	3
Shepshed C			
1984–85 Burnley	3	46	6
1985–86 Burnley	4	38	7
1986–87 Burnley	4	36	9
1987–88 Burnley	4	32	—

GREYGOOSE, Dean
18.12.64 Thetford (GK)
5.11 11.5 Apprentice
LD Cambridge U v Chelsea
11.2.84 0–1

1983–84 Cambridge U	2	16	—
1984–85 Cambridge U	3	10	—
1984–85 Orient	3	—	—
1985–86 Cambridge U	4	—	—
1985–86 Lincoln C	3	6	—
1985–86 Orient	4	1	—
1986–87 Crystal Palace	2	—	—
1987–88 Crewe Alex	4	43	—

GRIFFIN, James
1.1.67 Hamilton (DF)
5.8 11.4 Fir Park BC
LD Hibernian v Motherwell
1.2.86 4–0

1985–86 Motherwell	P	1	—
1986–87 Motherwell	P	—	—
1987–88 Motherwell	P	6	—

GRIMES, Ashley
2.8.57 Dublin (MF)
6.0 11.0 Bohemians
LD Birmingham C v Manchester U
20.8.77 1–4

1976–77 Manchester U	1	—	—
1977–78 Manchester U	1	13	2
1978–79 Manchester U	1	16	—
1979–80 Manchester U	1	26	3
1980–81 Manchester U	1	8	2
1981–82 Manchester U	1	11	1
1982–83 Manchester U	1	16	2
1983–84 Coventry C	1	32	1
1984–85 Luton T	1	9	—
1985–86 Luton T	1	3	—
1986–87 Luton T	1	31	2
1987–88 Luton T	1	32	1

GRITT, Steve
31.10.57 Bournemouth (MF)
5.9 10.10 Apprentice
LD Rochdale v Bournemouth
2.10.76 0–0

1976–77 Bournemouth	4	6	3
1977–78 Charlton Ath	2	34	3
1978–79 Charlton Ath	2	39	3
1979–80 Charlton Ath	2	31	7
1980–81 Charlton Ath	3	40	—
1981–82 Charlton Ath	2	34	3

1982–83 Charlton Ath	2	27	1
1983–84 Charlton Ath	2	33	1
1984–85 Charlton Ath	2	35	1
1985–86 Charlton Ath	2	11	2
1986–87 Charlton Ath	1	14	1
1987–88 Charlton Ath	1	27	—

GROBBELAAR, Bruce
6.10.57 Durban (GK)
6.1 13.0 Vancouver Whitecaps
LD Wigan Ath v Crewe Ath
21.12.79 2–0

1979–80 Crewe Alex	4	24	1
Vancouver Whitecaps (NASL)			
1980–81 Liverpool	1	—	—
1981–82 Liverpool	1	42	—
1982–83 Liverpool	1	42	—
1983–84 Liverpool	1	42	—
1984–85 Liverpool	1	42	—
1985–86 Liverpool	1	42	—
1986–87 Liverpool	1	31	—
1987–88 Liverpool	1	38	—

GROCOCK, Chris
30.10.68 Grimsby (MF)
5.10½ 10.8 School
LD Blackburn R v Grimsby T
5.5.86 3–1

1985–86 Grimsby T	2	1	—
1986–87 Grimsby T	2	6	—
1987–88 Grimsby T	3	25	1

GROVES, Paul
28.2.66 Derby (MF)
5.11 11.5 Burton A
LD Leicester C v Huddersfield T
2.5.88 3–0

1987–88 Leicester C	2	1	1

GROVES, Perry
19.4.65 London (MF)
5.10 12.3 Apprentice
LD Colchester U v Bournemouth
10.4.82 1–2

1981–82 Colchester U	4	9	—
1982–83 Colchester U	4	17	2
1983–84 Colchester U	4	42	2
1984–85 Colchester U	4	44	10
1985–86 Colchester U	4	43	12
1986–87 Colchester U	4	1	—
1986–87 Arsenal	1	25	3
1987–88 Arsenal	1	34	6

PLAYER DIRECTORY

GUNN, Bryan
22.12.63 Thurso (GK)
6.2 12.5 Invergordon B.C
LD Hibernian v <u>Aberdeen</u>
30.10.82 1–1

Season	Club			
1980–81	Aberdeen	P	—	—
1981–82	Aberdeen	P	—	—
1982–83	Aberdeen	P	1	—
1983–84	Aberdeen	P	—	—
1984–85	Aberdeen	P	2	—
1985–86	Aberdeen	P	10	—
1986–87	Norwich C	1	29	—
1987–88	Norwich C	1	38	—

GUNN, Bryn
21.8.58 Kettering (DF)
6.2 13.7 Apprentice
LD <u>Nottingham F</u> v Notts Co
30.8.75 0–1

Season	Club			
1975–76	Nottingham F	2	11	—
1976–77	Nottingham F	2	—	—
1977–78	Nottingham F	1	—	—
1978–79	Nottingham F	1	1	—
1979–80	Nottingham F	1	2	—
1980–81	Nottingham F	1	26	—
1981–82	Nottingham F	1	37	—
1982–83	Nottingham F	1	33	1
1983–84	Nottingham F	1	4	—
1984–85	Nottingham F	1	17	—
1985–86	Nottingham F	1	—	—
1985–86	*Shrewsbury T*	2	9	—
1985–86	*Walsall*	3	6	—
1985–86	*Mansfield T*	4	5	—
1986–87	Peterborough U	4	39	7
1987–88	Peterborough U	4	46	—

GUTHRIE, Peter
10.10.61 Newcastle-upon-Tyne (GK)
— — Weymouth
LD Cambridge U v <u>Swansea C</u>
27.2.88 0–3

Season	Club			
1987–88	Tottenham H	1	—	—
1987–88	*Swansea C*	4	14	—

GWINNETT, Mel
14.5.63 Worcester (GK)
6.1½ 11.5½ Stourbridge
LD <u>Hereford U</u> v Mansfield T
18.9.82 0–2

Season	Club			
1981–82	Peterborough U	4	—	—
1982–83	Hereford U	4	1	—
1983–84	Bradford C	3	—	—
1984–85	Bradford C	3	—	—
1985–86	Exeter C	4	2	—
1986–87	Exeter C	4	3	—
1987–88	Exeter C	4	24	—

GYNN, Mick
19.8.61 Peterborough (MF)
5.5 10.6 Apprentice
LD Lincoln C v <u>Peterborough U</u>
14.4.79 0–1

Season	Club			
1978–79	Peterborough U	3	11	2
1979–80	Peterborough U	4	27	1
1980–81	Peterborough U	4	29	7
1981–82	Peterborough U	4	46	6
1982–83	Peterborough U	4	43	17
1983–84	Coventry C	1	23	2
1984–85	Coventry C	1	39	4
1985–86	Coventry C	1	12	1
1986–87	Coventry C	1	22	5
1987–88	Coventry C	1	25	3

HACKETT, Gary
11.10.62 Stourbridge (FW)
5.8 10.13 Bromsgrove R
LD Grimsby T v <u>Shrewsbury T</u>
27.8.83 1–1

Season	Club			
1983–84	Shrewsbury T	2	31	3
1984–85	Shrewsbury T	2	38	5
1985–86	Shrewsbury T	2	42	6
1986–87	Shrewsbury T	2	39	3
1987–88	Aberdeen	P	15	—
1987–88	Stoke C	2	1	—

HADDOCK, Peter
9.12.61 Newcastle (DF)
5.10 11.5 Apprentice
LD QPR v <u>Newcastle U</u>
5.9.81 3–0

Season	Club			
1979–80	Newcastle U	2	—	—
1980–81	Newcastle U	2	—	—
1981–82	Newcastle U	2	30	—
1982–83	Newcastle U	2	17	—
1983–84	Newcastle U	2	3	—
1984–85	Newcastle U	1	1	—
1985–86	Newcastle U	1	6	—
1985–86	*Burnley*	4	7	—
1986–87	Leeds U	2	11	—
1987–88	Leeds U	2	40	1

HAIGH, Paul
4.5.58 Scarborough (DF)
5.10 12.8 Apprentice
LD <u>Hull C</u> v Sheffield W
26.4.75 1–0

Season	Club			
1974–75	Hull C	2	1	—
1975–76	Hull C	2	7	—
1976–77	Hull C	2	42	2
1977–78	Hull C	2	38	1
1978–79	Hull C	3	45	1
1979–80	Hull C	3	29	2
1980–81	Hull C	3	18	2
1980–81	Carlisle U	3	28	—
1981–82	Carlisle U	3	23	—
1982–83	Carlisle U	2	40	1
1983–84	Carlisle U	2	34	—
1984–85	Carlisle U	2	36	2
1985–86	Carlisle U	2	28	—
1986–87	Carlisle U	3	44	1
1987–88	Hartlepool U	4	39	—

HALES, Kevin
13.1.61 Dartford (DF)
5.7 10.4 Apprentice
LD Orient v <u>Chelsea</u>
10.11.79 7–3

Season	Club			
1978–79	Chelsea	1	—	—
1979–80	Chelsea	2	7	—
1980–81	Chelsea	2	—	—
1981–82	Chelsea	2	10	2
1982–83	Chelsea	2	3	—
1983–84	Orient	2	43	2
1984–85	Orient	3	33	—
1985–86	Orient	4	31	2
1986–87	Orient	4	33	1
1987–88	Leyton Orient	4	42	6

HALL, Derek
5.1.65 Manchester (MF)
5.8½ 11.2 Apprentice
LD Birmingham C v Coventry C
18.9.82 1–0

1982–83 Coventry C	1	1	—
1983–84 Coventry C	1	—	—
1983–84 Torquay U	4	10	2
1984–85 Torquay U	4	45	4
1985–86 Swindon T	4	10	—
1986–87 Southend U	4	43	9
1987–88 Southend U	3	40	3

HALL, Gareth
20.3.69 Croydon (DF)
5.8 10.7
LD Wimbledon v Chelsea
5.5.87 2–1

1986–87 Chelsea	1	1	—
1987–88 Chelsea	1	13	—

HALLWORTH, Jon
26.10.65 Stockport (GK)
6.1 10.7 School
LD Reading v Bristol R
26.1.85 3–2

1983–84 Ipswich T	1	—	—
1984–85 Ipswich T	1	—	—
1984–85 Swindon T	4	—	—
1984–85 Fulham	2	—	—
1984–85 Bristol R	3	2	—
1985–86 Ipswich T	1	6	—
1986–87 Ipswich T	2	6	—
1987–88 Ipswich T	2	33	—

HALPIN, John
15.11.61 Broxburn (MF)
5.10 11.0 Celtic BC
LD Celtic v Hibernian
2.2.82 0–0

1981–82 Celtic	P	3	—
1982–83 Celtic	P	—	—
1983–84 Celtic	P	4	—
1984–85 Sunderland	1	—	—
1984–85 Carlisle U	2	19	1
1985–86 Carlisle U	2	33	5
1986–87 Carlisle U	3	7	—
1987–88 Carlisle U	4	23	3

HALSALL, Mick
21.7.61 Bootle (MF)
5.10 11.4 Apprentice
LD WBA v Birmingham C
19.3.83 2–0

1979–80 Liverpool	1	—	—
1980–81 Liverpool	1	—	—
1981–82 Liverpool	1	—	—
1982–83 Liverpool	1	—	—
1982–83 Birmingham C	1	12	1

1983–84 Birmingham C	1	21	2
1984–85 Birmingham C	2	3	—
1984–85 Carlisle U	2	26	5
1985–86 Carlisle U	2	41	4
1986–87 Carlisle U	3	25	2
1986–87 Grimsby T	2	12	—
1987–88 Peterborough U	4	45	4

HAMILL, Stewart
22.1.60 Glasgow (MF)
5.9 10.8 Pollok
LD Leicester C v Manchester C
8.11.80 1–1

1980–81 Leicester C	1	8	—
1981–82 Leicester C	2	2	2
1981–82 Scunthorpe U	4	4	—
Local			
1985–86 Northampton T	4	3	1
1986–87 Scarborough	—	—	—
1987–88 Scarborough	4	28	3

HAMILTON, Brian
5.8.67 Paisley (DF)
6.0 11.7 Pollok United BC
LD St Mirren v Aberdeen
15.3.86 1–1

1985–86 St Mirren	P	8	—
1986–87 St Mirren	P	28	3
1987–88 St Mirren	P	27	—

HAMILTON, David
7.11.60 South Shields (DF)
5.7 10.0 Apprentice
LD Blackburn R v Watford
10.1.81 0–0

1978–79 Sunderland	2	—	—
1979–80 Sunderland	2	—	—
1980–81 Sunderland	1	—	—
1980–81 Blackburn R	2	3	—
1981–82 Blackburn R	2	17	—
1982–83 Blackburn R	2	32	2
1983–84 Blackburn R	2	26	2
1984–85 Blackburn R	2	3	—
1984–85 Cardiff C	2	10	—
1985–86 Blackburn R	2	33	3
1986–87 Wigan Ath	3	41	3
1987–88 Wigan Ath	3	45	2

HAMILTON, Derek
26.8.58 Kilwinning (DF)
5.8 10.10 Beith Juniors
LD Aberdeen v Hibernian
7.4.79 0–0

1978–79 Aberdeen	P	10	—
1979–80 Aberdeen	P	13	3
1980–81 Aberdeen	P	8	—
1981–82 Aberdeen	P	1	—

1982–83 Aberdeen	P	2	—
1983–84 St Mirren	P	23	—
1984–85 St Mirren	P	13	—
1985–86 St Mirren	P	25	—
1986–87 St Mirren	P	36	—
1987–88 St Mirren	P	19	—

HAMILTON, Gary
27.12.65 Glasgow (FW)
5.9 11.2 Apprentice
LD Bolton W v Middlesbrough
26.2.83 3–1

1982–83 Middlesbrough	2	9	2
1983–84 Middlesbrough	2	31	3
1984–85 Middlesbrough	2	36	—
1985–86 Middlesbrough	2	33	4
1986–87 Middlesbrough	3	43	7
1987–88 Middlesbrough	2	41	6

HAMILTON, Ian
14.12.67 Stevenage (MF)
5.9 11.3 Apprentice
LD Cambridge U v Darlington
1.4.88 1–0

1985–86 Southampton	1	—	—
1986–87 Southampton	1	—	—
1987–88 Cambridge U	4	9	1

HAMMOND, Nicky
7.9.67 Essex (GK)
5.8 11.8 Apprentice
LD Bristol R v Blackpool
27.9.86 2–2

1985–86 Arsenal	1	—	—
1986–87 Bristol R	3	3	—
1986–87 Peterborough U	4	—	—
1986–87 Aberdeen	P	—	—
1987–88 Swindon T	2	4	—

HAMPTON, Peter
12.9.54 Oldham (DF)
5.7½ 11.2 Apprentice
LD Southampton v Leeds U
28.4.73 3–1

1971–72 Leeds U	1	—	—
1972–73 Leeds U	1	2	—
1973–74 Leeds U	1	—	—
1974–75 Leeds U	1	2	—
1975–76 Leeds U	1	1	1
1976–77 Leeds U	1	31	1
1977–78 Leeds U	1	11	—
1978–79 Leeds U	1	4	—
1979–80 Leeds U	1	17	—
1980–81 Stoke C	1	33	2
1981–82 Stoke C	1	33	—
1982–83 Stoke C	1	40	1
1983–84 Stoke C	1	32	1
1984–85 Burnley	3	45	1
1985–86 Burnley	4	40	1
1986–87 Burnley	4	33	—
1987–88 Carlisle U	4	12	—

PLAYER DIRECTORY

Alan Hansen

Photo: Bob Thomas Sports Photography.

HANDYSIDES, Ian
14.12.62 Jarrow (MF)
5.8 10.9 Apprentice
LD Birmingham C v Southampton
17.1.81 0–3

1979–80	Birmingham C	2	—	—
1980–81	Birmingham C	1	8	—
1981–82	Birmingham C	1	20	—
1982–83	Birmingham C	1	29	2
1983–84	Birmingham C	1	5	—
1983–84	Walsall	3	18	4
1984–85	Walsall	3	38	4
1985–86	Walsall	3	10	3
1985–86	Birmingham C	1	6	1
1986–87	Birmingham C	2	20	—
1986–87	*Wolves*	4	11	2
1987–88	Birmingham C	2	30	3

HANSBURY, Roger
26.1.55 Barnsley (GK)
5.11 12.0 Apprentice
LD Fulham v Norwich C
21.9.74 4–0

1972–73	Norwich C	1	—	—
1973–74	Norwich C	1	—	—
1974–75	Norwich C	2	4	—
1975–76	Norwich C	1	—	—
1976–77	Norwich C	1	4	—
1976–77	*Bolton W*	2	—	—
1977–78	Norwich C	1	14	—
1977–78	*Cambridge U*	3	11	—
1978–79	Norwich C	1	18	—
1978–79	*Orient*	2	—	—
1979–80	Norwich C	1	16	—
1980–81	Norwich C	1	22	—
1981–82	Norwich C	2	—	—
Eastern, Hong Kong				
1983–84	Burnley	3	46	—
1984–85	Burnley	3	37	—
1985–86	Cambridge U	4	37	—
1985–86	Birmingham C	1	—	—
1986–87	Birmingham C	2	31	—
1987–88	Birmingham C	2	22	—
1987–88	*Sheffield U*	2	5	—

HANSEN, Alan
13.6.55 Alloa (DF)
6.1 13.0 Sauchie BC
LD East Fife v Partick Th
27.10.73 2–1

1973–74	Partick T	1	1	—
1974–75	Partick T	1	29	—
1975–76	Partick T	1	21	2
1976–77	Partick T	P	35	4
1976–77	Liverpool	1	—	—
1977–78	Liverpool	1	18	—
1978–79	Liverpool	1	34	1
1979–80	Liverpool	1	38	4
1980–81	Liverpool	1	36	1
1981–82	Liverpool	1	35	—
1982–83	Liverpool	1	34	—
1983–84	Liverpool	1	42	1
1984–85	Liverpool	1	41	—
1985–86	Liverpool	1	41	—
1986–87	Liverpool	1	39	—
1987–88	Liverpool	1	39	1

HARBEY, Graham
29.8.64 Chesterfield (MF)
5.8 10.8 Apprentice
LD Charlton Ath v Derby Co
7.9.83 1–0

1982–83	Derby Co	2	—	—
1983–84	Derby Co	2	19	—
1984–85	Derby Co	3	4	1
1985–86	Derby Co	3	3	—
1986–87	Derby Co	2	14	—
1987–88	Ipswich T	2	35	1

HARDYMAN, Paul
11.3.64 Portsmouth (DF)
5.8½ 11.4 Local
LD Portsmouth v C Palace
24.3.84 0–1

1983–84	Portsmouth	2	3	—
1984–85	Portsmouth	2	15	—
1985–86	Portsmouth	2	21	1
1986–87	Portsmouth	2	33	—
1987–88	Portsmouth	1	20	1

HARFORD, Mick
12.2.59 Sunderland (FW)
6.2 12.9 Lambton St BC
LD Lincoln C v Gillingham
10.12.77 0–2

1977–78	Lincoln C	3	27	9
1978–79	Lincoln C	3	31	6
1979–80	Lincoln C	4	36	16
1980–81	Lincoln C	4	21	10
1980–81	Newcastle U	2	19	4
1981–82	Bristol C	3	30	11
1981–82	Birmingham C	1	12	9
1982–83	Birmingham C	1	29	6
1983–84	Birmingham C	1	39	8
1984–85	Birmingham C	2	12	2
1984–85	Luton T	1	22	15
1985–86	Luton T	1	37	22
1986–87	Luton T	1	18	4
1987–88	Luton T	1	25	9

HARLE, David
15.8.63 Denaby (MF)
5.9 10.7 Apprentice
LD Port Vale v Doncaster R
3.5.80 3–0

1979–80	Doncaster R	4	1	—
1980–81	Doncaster R	4	34	1
1981–82	Doncaster R	3	26	2
1982–83	Exeter C	3	37	6
1983–84	Exeter C	3	6	—
1983–84	Doncaster R	4	29	6
1984–85	Doncaster R	3	37	9
1985–86	Doncaster R	3	17	2
1985–86	Leeds U	2	3	—
1985–86	*Bristol C*	3	8	—

1986–87	Bristol C	3	15	2
1986–87	Scunthorpe U	4	26	2
1987–88	Scunthorpe U	4	45	6

HARPER, Alan
1.11.60 Liverpool (DF)
5.8 10.9 Apprentice
LD Everton v Stoke C
27.8.83 1–0

1977–78	Liverpool	1	—	—
1978–79	Liverpool	1	—	—
1979–80	Liverpool	1	—	—
1980–81	Liverpool	1	—	—
1981–82	Liverpool	1	—	—
1982–83	Liverpool	1	—	—
1983–84	Everton	1	29	1
1984–85	Everton	1	13	—
1985–86	Everton	1	21	—
1986–87	Everton	1	36	3
1987–88	Everton	1	28	—

HARPER, Steve
3.2.69 Stoke (FW)
5.10½ 11.5 Apprentice
LD Port Vale v Aldershot
15.8.87 4–2

1987–88	Port Vale	3	21	2

HARRIS, Colin
22.2.61 Sanquhar (FW)
5.11 10.10 Exit Th
LD Raith R v St Johnstone
10.11.79 1–2

1979–80	Raith R	1	3	—
1980–81	Raith R	1	25	9
1981–82	Raith R	1	22	1
1982–83	Raith R	1	36	18
1983–84	Raith R	*1	20	4
1983–84	Dundee	P	14	2
1984–85	Dundee	P	15	1
1984–85	Hibernian	P	7	2
1985–86	Hibernian	P	19	2
1986–87	Hibernian	P	—	—
1986–87	Raith R	2	27	22
1987–88	Raith R	1	33	14
1987–88	Hamilton A	1	8	6

HARRIS, Jamie
4.6.69 Exeter (MF)
— — YTS
LD Darlington v Exeter C
8.12.87 4–1

1987–88	Exeter C	4	9	1

HARRIS, Mark
15.7.63 Reading (DF)
6.1 13.0 Wokingham
LD —

1987–88	Crystal Palace	2	—	—

HARRISON, Frankie
19.9.63 Middlesbrough (FW)
— —
LD Wigan Ath v Lincoln C
30.11.85 3–2

1982–83 Middlesbrough	2	—	—
1983–85 Non-League			
1985–86 Lincoln C	3	1	—
1986–87 Halifax T	4	14	1
1987–88 Halifax T	4	18	—

HARRISON, Wayne
15.11.67 Stockport (FW)
5.8 10.7 Apprentice
LD Oldham Ath v Notts Co
27.10.84 3–2

1984–85 Oldham Ath	2	5	1
1984–85 Liverpool	1	—	—
1984–85 *Oldham Ath*	2	1	—
1985–86 Liverpool	1	—	—
1986–87 Liverpool	1	—	—
1987–88 Liverpool	1	—	—

HARROWER, Steven
9.10.61 Exeter (MF)
5.8 11.1 Local
LD Bournemouth v Exeter C
31.12.83 3–1

1983–84 Exeter C	3	13	1
1984–85 Exeter C	4	31	1
1985–86 Exeter C	4	38	6
1986–87 Exeter C	4	34	—
1987–88 Exeter C	4	46	2

HART, Nigel
1.10.58 Golborne (DF)
6.0 12.3 Local
LD Bournemouth v Wigan Ath
8.9.79 1–2

1978–79 Wigan Ath	4	—	—
1979–80 Wigan Ath	4	1	—
1979–80 Leicester C	2	—	—
1980–81 Leicester C	1	—	—
1981–82 Blackpool	4	28	—
1982–83 Blackpool	4	9	—
1982–83 Crewe Alex	4	28	—
1983–84 Crewe Alex	4	37	3
1984–85 Crewe Alex	4	44	6
1985–86 Crewe Alex	4	23	—
1986–87 Crewe Alex	4	10	1
1986–87 Bury	3	11	—
1987–88 Bury	3	34	2

HART, Paul
4.5.53 Manchester (DF)
6.2 12.8 Amateur
LD Stockport Co v Lincoln C
9.10.70 4–3

1970–71 Stockport Co	4	9	1
1971–72 Stockport Co	4	36	—
1972–73 Stockport Co	4	42	4
1973–74 Blackpool	2	3	—
1974–75 Blackpool	2	37	5
1975–76 Blackpool	2	33	3
1976–77 Blackpool	2	42	6
1977–78 Blackpool	2	28	3
1977–78 Leeds U	1	12	—
1978–79 Leeds U	1	40	5
1979–80 Leeds U	1	30	3
1980–81 Leeds U	1	38	4
1981–82 Leeds U	1	32	1
1982–83 Leeds U	2	39	3
1983–84 Nottingham F	1	36	—
1984–85 Nottingham F	1	34	1
1985–86 Sheffield W	1	34	1
1986–87 Sheffield W	1	18	—
1986–87 Birmingham C	2	1	—
1987–88 Notts Co	3	23	—

HART, Peter
14.8.57 Mexborough (DF)
5.10 12.7 Apprentice
LD Huddersfield T v Southend U
30.3.74 0–1

1973–74 Huddersfield T	3	1	—
1974–75 Huddersfield T	3	13	—
1975–76 Huddersfield T	4	19	1
1976–77 Huddersfield T	4	44	1
1977–78 Huddersfield T	4	41	—
1978–79 Huddersfield T	4	46	1
1979–80 Huddersfield T	4	46	4
1980–81 Walsall	3	45	5
1981–82 Walsall	3	45	1
1982–83 Walsall	3	45	—
1983–84 Walsall	3	45	3
1984–85 Walsall	3	46	—
1985–86 Walsall	3	44	2
1986–87 Walsall	3	46	—
1987–88 Walsall	3	37	1

HARTFORD, Asa
24.10.50 Clydebank (MF)
5.7 11.4 Amateur

1967–68 WBA	1	6	1
1968–69 WBA	1	26	7
1969–70 WBA	1	34	1
1970–71 WBA	1	34	2
1971–72 WBA	1	39	1
1972–73 WBA	1	41	3
1973–74 WBA	2	33	3
1974–75 Manchester C	1	30	2
1975–76 Manchester C	1	39	9
1976–77 Manchester C	1	40	4
1977–78 Manchester C	1	37	4
1978–79 Manchester C	1	39	3
1979–80 Nottingham F	1	3	—
1979–80 Everton	1	35	1
1980–81 Everton	1	39	5
1981–82 Everton	1	7	—

1981–82 Manchester C	1	30	3
1982–83 Manchester C	1	38	3
1983–84 Manchester C	2	7	1
Ft Lauderdale, (NASL)			
1984–85 Norwich C	1	28	2
1985–86 Bolton W	3	46	5
1986–87 Bolton W	3	35	3
1987–88 Stockport Co	4	31	—

HARVEY, Graham
23.4.61 Musselburgh (FW)
5.11 11.4 Ormiston Primrose
LD Hibernian v Morton
5.2.83 2–0

1982–83 Hibernian	P	14	1
1983–84 Hibernian	P	16	2
1984–85 Hibernian	P	3	—
1984–85 Dundee	P	7	2
1985–86 Dundee	P	30	5
1986–87 Dundee	P	33	12
1987–88 Dundee	P	29	4

HARVEY, Jimmy
2.5.58 Lurgan (MF)
5.9½ 11.4 Glenavon
LD Derby Co v Arsenal
9.5.78 3–0

1977–78 Arsenal	1	1	—
1978–79 Arsenal	1	2	—
1979–80 Arsenal	1	—	—
1979–80 *Hereford U*	4	11	—
1980–81 Hereford U	4	30	1
1981–82 Hereford U	4	42	5
1982–83 Hereford U	4	41	5
1983–84 Hereford U	4	44	9
1984–85 Hereford U	4	34	5
1985–86 Hereford U	4	42	9
1986–87 Hereford U	4	34	5
1986–87 Bristol C	3	2	—
1987–88 Bristol C	3	1	—
1987–88 *Wrexham*	4	6	—
1987–88 Tranmere R	4	33	3

HARVEY, Lee
21.12.66 Harlow (MF)
— — Local
LD Sheffield U v Orient
3.3.84 6–3

1983–84 Orient	3	4	—
1984–85 Orient	3	4	—
1985–86 Orient	4	12	2
1986–87 Orient	4	15	1
1987–88 Orient	4	23	1

HARVEY, Richard
17.4.69 Letchworth (DF)
5.9 11.10 Apprentice
LD Luton T v QPR
1.11.86 1–0

1986–87 Luton T	1	5	—
1987–88 Luton T	1	—	—

HASLEGRAVE, Sean
7.6.51 Stoke (MF)
5.8 10.7 Amateur
LD Stoke C v Derby Co
19.12.70 1-0

1968–69 Stoke C	1	—	—
1969–70 Stoke C	1	—	—
1970–71 Stoke C	1	15	—
1971–72 Stoke C	1	18	—
1972–73 Stoke C	1	6	2
1973–74 Stoke C	1	27	1
1974–75 Stoke C	1	19	1
1975–76 Stoke C	1	28	1
1976–77 Nottingham F	1	7	1
1977–78 Nottingham F	1	—	—
1977–78 Preston NE	3	38	—
1978–79 Preston NE	2	41	1
1979–80 Preston NE	2	25	—
1980–81 Preston NE	2	9	1
1981–82 Crewe Alex	4	40	1
1982–83 Crewe Alex	4	42	—
1983–84 York C	4	26	—
1984–85 York C	3	42	—
1985–86 York C	3	39	—
1986–87 York C	3	35	—
1987–88 Torquay U	4	34	1

HAWKER, Phil
7.12.62 Solihull (DF)
6.1 11.7 Apprentice
LD Birmingham C v Nottingham F
11.11.80 2-0

1980–81 Birmingham C	1	11	—
1981–82 Birmingham C	1	20	1
1982–83 Birmingham C	1	4	—
1982–83 Walsall	3	5	—
1983–84 Walsall	3	11	—
1984–85 Walsall	3	20	—
1985–86 Walsall	3	33	4
1986–87 Walsall	3	23	1
1987–88 Walsall	3	29	2

HAWKINS, Nigel
7.9.68 Bristol (FW)
5.9 10.7 Apprentice
LD Preston NE v Bristol C
9.1.88 2-0

1987–88 Bristol C	3	1	—

HAYES, Martin
21.3.66 Walthamstow (MF)
6.0 11.8 Apprentice
LD Arsenal v Oxford U
16.11.85 2-1

1983–84 Arsenal	1	—	—
1984–85 Arsenal	1	—	—
1985–86 Arsenal	1	11	2
1986–87 Arsenal	1	35	19
1987–88 Arsenal	1	27	1

HAYCOCK, Paul
8.7.62 Sheffield (FW)
6.1 12.0 Burton A
LD Port Vale v Rotherham U
30.8.86 1-1

1986–87 Rotherham U	3	26	6
1987–88 Rotherham U	3	35	12

HAYLOCK, Paul
24.3.63 Lowestoft (DF)
5.8 11.0 Apprentice
LD Norwich C v Bolton W
31.10.81 0-0

1980–81 Norwich C	1	—	—
1981–82 Norwich C	2	21	—
1982–83 Norwich C	1	42	1
1983–84 Norwich C	1	39	—
1984–85 Norwich C	1	41	1
1985–86 Norwich C	2	12	1
1986–87 Gillingham	3	45	—
1987–88 Gillingham	3	32	—

HAZARD, Mike
5.2.60 Sunderland (MF)
5.7 10.5 Apprentice
LD Tottenham H v Everton
19.4.80 3-0

1977–78 Tottenham H	2	—	—
1978–79 Tottenham H	1	—	—
1979–80 Tottenham H	1	3	—
1980–81 Tottenham H	1	4	—
1981–82 Tottenham H	1	28	5
1982–83 Tottenham H	1	18	1
1983–84 Tottenham H	1	11	2
1984–85 Tottenham H	1	23	4
1985–86 Tottenham H	1	4	1
1985–86 Chelsea	1	18	1
1986–87 Chelsea	1	18	6
1987–88 Chelsea	1	28	2

HAZEL, Desmond
15.7.67 Bradford (FW)
5.10 10.4 Apprentice
LD Grimsby T v Leeds U
25.10.86 0-0

1985–86 Sheffield W	1	—	—
1986–87 Sheffield W	1	—	—
1986–87 *Grimsby T*	2	9	2
1987–88 Sheffield W	1	6	—

HAZEL, Ian
1.12.67 London (MF)
5.10 10.4 Apprentice
LD Wimbledon v Liverpool
4.11.87 1-1

1985–86 Wimbledon	2	—	—
1986–87 Wimbledon	1	—	—
1987–88 Wimbledon	1	6	—

HAZELL, Bob
14.6.59 W Indies (DF)
6.2 14.6 Apprentice
LD Newcastle U v Wolves
17.12.77 4-0

1977–78 Wolves	1	20	1
1978–79 Wolves	1	13	—
1979–80 Wolves	1	—	—
1979–80 QPR	2	29	1
1980–81 QPR	2	8	2
1981–82 QPR	2	24	2
1982–83 QPR	2	39	3
1983–84 QPR	1	6	—
1983–84 Leicester C	1	27	—
1984–85 Leicester C	1	14	—
1985–86 Leicester C	1	—	—
1985–86 *Wolves*	3	1	—
1986–87 Leeds U	2	—	—
1986–87 Reading	2	4	1
1986–87 Port Vale	3	21	1
1987–88 Port Vale	3	43	—

HEALD, Paul
29.9.65 Wath-on-Dearne (GK)
6.2½ 12.5 Apprentice
LD —

1987–88 Sheffield U	2	—	—

HEATH, Adrian
11.1.61 Stoke (MF)
5.6 10.1 Apprentice
LD Fulham v Stoke C
7.10.78 2-0

1978–79 Stoke C	2	2	—
1979–80 Stoke C	1	38	5
1980–81 Stoke C	1	38	6
1981–82 Stoke C	1	17	5
1981–82 Everton	1	22	6
1982–83 Everton	1	38	10
1983–84 Everton	1	36	12
1984–85 Everton	1	17	11
1985–86 Everton	1	36	10
1986–87 Everton	1	41	11
1987–88 Everton	1	29	9

HEATH, Philip
24.11.64 Stoke (FW)
5.9 11.5 Apprentice
LD Stoke C v Coventry C
7.5.83 0-3

1982–83 Stoke C	1	1	—
1983–84 Stoke C	1	4	1
1984–85 Stoke C	1	36	2
1985–86 Stoke C	2	38	5
1986–87 Stoke C	2	38	1
1987–88 Stoke C	2	39	8

HEATHCOTE, Michael
10.9.65 Kellowe, Co Durham (DF)
6.1½ 12.7 Spennymore
LD Sunderland v Southend U
3.11.87 7-0

1987–88 Sunderland	3	1	—

PLAYER DIRECTORY

HEBBERD, Trevor
19.6.58 Winchester (MF)
5.11½ 11.4 Apprentice
LD Carlisle U v Southampton
22.1.77 0–6

1976–77 Southampton	2	12	2
1977–78 Southampton	2	12	1
1978–79 Southampton	1	22	2
1979–80 Southampton	1	36	2
1980–81 Southampton	1	11	—
1981–82 Southampton	1	4	—
1981–82 *Bolton W*	2	6	—
1981–82 *Leicester C*	2	4	1
1981–82 Oxford U	3	15	2
1982–83 Oxford U	3	39	10
1983–84 Oxford U	3	46	11
1984–85 Oxford U	2	42	6
1985–86 Oxford U	1	41	3
1986–87 Oxford U	1	38	2
1987–88 Oxford U	1	39	3

HEDMAN, Rudi
16.11.64 London (MF)
6.3 12.1 Local
LD Bury v Colchester U
3.3.84 1–1

1983–84 Colchester U	4	4	—
1984–85 Colchester U	4	30	2
1985–86 Colchester U	4	39	3
1986–87 Colchester U	4	44	4
1987–88 Colchester U	4	42	—

HEDWORTH, Chris
5.1.64 Newcastle (DF)
6.1 10.11 Apprentice
LD Leeds U v Newcastle U
30.10.82 3–1

1981–82 Newcastle U	2	—	—
1982–83 Newcastle U	2	4	—
1983–84 Newcastle U	2	—	—
1984–85 Newcastle U	1	1	—
1985–86 Newcastle U	1	4	—
1986–87 Barnsley	2	20	—
1987–88 Barnsley	2	5	—

HEGARTY, Paul
25.7.54 Edinburgh (DF)
5.10 11.4 Tynecastle BC
LD Forfar Ath v Hamilton A
2.9.72 1–0

1972–73 Hamilton A	2	36	7
1973–74 Hamilton A	2	31	10
1974–75 Hamilton A	2	12	5
1974–75 Dundee U	1	17	4
1975–76 Dundee U	P	33	8
1976–77 Dundee U	P	36	6
1977–78 Dundee U	P	36	4
1978–79 Dundee U	P	36	5
1979–80 Dundee U	P	27	—
1980–81 Dundee U	P	33	3
1981–82 Dundee U	P	36	2
1982–83 Dundee U	P	36	3
1983–84 Dundee U	P	36	4
1984–85 Dundee U	P	33	2
1985–86 Dundee U	P	36	5
1986–87 Dundee U	P	23	4
1987–88 Dundee U	P	41	1

HEGGARTY, Jim
4.8.65 Larne (DF)
6.2 13.8
LD Burnley v Northampton T
17.8.85 3–2

1984–85 Brighton & HA	2	—	—
1985–86 Burnley	4	36	1
1986–87 Burnley	4	—	—
1987–88 Burnley	4	—	—

HELLIWELL, Ian
7.12.62 Rotherham (FW)
6.3 13.12 Matlock T
LD Sunderland v York C
24.10.87 4–2

1987–88 York C	3	32	8

HEMMING, Chris
13.4.66 Newcastle (DF)
5.11 11.2 School
LD Tottenham H v Stoke C
3.3.84 1–0

1983–84 Stoke C	1	3	—
1984–85 Stoke C	1	16	1
1985–86 Stoke C	2	24	—
1986–87 Stoke C	2	22	—
1987–88 Stoke C	2	24	1

HENDERSON, Mick
31.3.56 Gosforth (DF)
5.10 11.4 Apprentice
LD York C v Sunderland
1.11.75 1–4

1973–74 Sunderland	2	—	—
1974–75 Sunderland	2	—	—
1975–76 Sunderland	2	13	1
1976–77 Sunderland	1	9	—
1977–78 Sunderland	2	32	1
1978–79 Sunderland	2	30	—
1979–80 Sunderland	2	—	—
1979–80 Watford	2	28	—
1980–81 Watford	2	19	—
1981–82 Watford	2	4	—
1981–82 Cardiff C	2	11	—
1982–83 Sheffield U	3	32	—
1983–84 Sheffield U	3	22	—
1984–85 Sheffield U	2	13	—
1984–85 Chesterfield	4	18	—
1985–86 Chesterfield	3	43	5
1986–87 Chesterfield	3	45	3
1987–88 Chesterfield	3	19	2

HENDRIE, John
24.10.63 Lennoxtown (FW)
5.7 11.4 Apprentice
LD Tottenham H v Coventry C
5.12.81 1–2

1981–82 Coventry C	1	6	—
1982–83 Coventry C	1	12	2
1983–84 Coventry C	1	3	—
1983–84 *Hereford U*	4	6	—
1984–85 Bradford C	3	46	9
1985–86 Bradford C	2	42	10
1986–87 Bradford C	2	42	14
1987–88 Bradford C	2	43	13

HENDRIE, Paul
27.3.54 Glasgow (MF)
5.6 10.3 Rob Roy
LD Birmingham C v Leeds U
30.4.73 2–1

1971–72 Birmingham C	2	—	—
1972–73 Birmingham C	1	1	—
1973–74 Birmingham C	1	5	—
1974–75 Birmingham C	1	12	1
1975–76 Birmingham C	1	5	—
From Portland Timbers			
1977–78 Bristol R	2	12	—
1978–79 Bristol R	2	18	1
1979–80 Halifax T	4	34	3
1980–81 Halifax T	4	34	4
1981–82 Halifax T	4	45	2
1982–83 Halifax T	4	34	1
1983–84 Halifax T	4	40	2
1984–85 Stockport Co	4	42	4
1985–86 Stockport Co	4	36	1
1986–87 Stockport Co	4	10	—
1987–88 Stockport Co	4	22	1

HENDRY, Colin
7.12.65 Keith (FW)
6.2 12.4 Islavale
LD Dundee v Hearts
7.1.84 4–1

1983–84 Dundee	P	4	—
1984–85 Dundee	P	4	—
1985–86 Dundee	P	20	—
1986–87 Dundee	P	13	2
1986–87 Blackburn R	2	13	3
1987–88 Blackburn R	2	44	12

HENRY, Charlie
13.2.62 Acton (FW)
5.11 12.8 Apprentice
LD Reading v Swindon T
30.8.80 4–1

1980–81 Swindon T	3	32	—
1981–82 Swindon T	3	42	3
1982–83 Swindon T	4	19	—
1983–84 Swindon T	4	29	—
1984–85 Swindon T	4	16	—
1985–86 Swindon T	4	38	18
1986–87 Swindon T	3	10	1
1986–87 *Torquay U*	4	6	1
1986–87 *Northampton T*	4	4	1
1987–88 Swindon T	2	15	1

HENRY, Liburd
29.8.67 Dominica (FW)
— — Leytonstone/Ilford
LD —

1987–88 Watford	1	—	—

HENRY, Nicholas
21.2.69 Liverpool (MF)
5.7 10.7 Apprentice
LD Hull C v Oldham Ath
19.9.87 1–0

1987–88 Oldham Ath	2	5	—
1987–88 *Halmstad* (Swe)			

HENRY, Tony
26.11.57 Newcastle (MF)
5.11 12.0 Apprentice
LD Sunderland v Manchester C
18.9.76 0–2

1974–75 Manchester C	1	—	—
1975–76 Manchester C	1	—	—
1976–77 Manchester C	1	2	—
1977–78 Manchester C	1	1	—
1978–79 Manchester C	1	15	—
1979–80 Manchester C	1	32	4
1980–81 Manchester C	1	27	2
1981–82 Manchester C	1	2	—
1981–82 Bolton W	2	39	13
1982–83 Bolton W	2	31	9
1982–83 Oldham Ath	2	11	1
1983–84 Oldham Ath	2	42	4
1984–85 Oldham Ath	2	40	3
1985–86 Oldham Ath	2	40	7
1987–88 Oldham Ath	2	21	4
1987–88 Stoke C	2	22	5

HENSHAW, Gary
18.2.65 Leeds (MF)
5.9½ 9.10 Apprentice
LD Grimsby T v Brighton & HA
15.10.83 5–0

1982–83 Grimsby T	2	—	—
1983–84 Grimsby T	2	4	—
1984–85 Grimsby T	2	7	1
1985–86 Grimsby T	2	10	4
1986–87 Grimsby T	2	29	4
1987–88 Bolton W	4	31	2

HEPPLE, John
12.3.70 Middlesbrough (FW)
5.6 9.12 Juniors
LD —

1987–88 Sunderland	3	—	—

HERRERA, Roberto
— — (DF)
— — Apprentice
LD —

1987–88 QPR	1	—	—

HESELTINE, Wayne
3.12.69 Bradford (DF)
5.9½ 11.6 Apprentice
LD —

1987–88 Manchester U	1	—	—

HESFORD, Iain
4.3.60 Zambia (GK)
6.2 14.6 Apprentice
LD Blackpool v Oldham Ath
20.8.77 1–1

1977–78 Blackpool	2	14	—
1978–79 Blackpool	3	33	—
1979–80 Blackpool	3	30	—
1980–81 Blackpool	3	42	—
1981–82 Blackpool	4	39	—
1982–83 Blackpool	4	44	—
1983–84 Sheffield W	2	—	—
1984–85 Sheffield W	1	—	—
1984–85 *Fulham*	2	3	—
1985–86 Sheffield W	1	—	—
1985–86 *Notts Co*	3	10	—
1986–87 Sunderland	2	38	—
1987–88 Sunderland	3	39	—

HETHERINGTON, Brent
6.12.61 Carlisle (FW)
5.8 11.10 Local
LD Peterborough U v Carlisle U
15.8.87 1–0

1987–88 Carlisle U	4	37	10

HETHERSTON, Peter
6.11.64 Belshill (MF)
5.10 11.5
LD Falkirk v East Fife
29.12.84 1–2

1984–85 Falkirk	1	12	2
1985–86 Falkirk	1	23	3
1986–87 Falkirk	P	36	3
1987–88 Watford	1	5	—
1987–88 Sheffield U	2	11	—

HETZKE, Steve
3.6.55 Marlborough (DF)
6.2 13.4 Apprentice
LD Darlington v Reading
4.12.71 0–1

1971–72 Reading	4	4	—
1972–73 Reading	4	1	—
1973–74 Reading	4	22	1
1974–75 Reading	4	15	—
1975–76 Reading	4	17	1
1976–77 Reading	3	24	3
1977–78 Reading	4	16	—
1978–79 Reading	4	42	9
1979–80 Reading	3	43	2
1980–81 Reading	3	45	5
1981–82 Reading	3	32	2

1982–83 Blackpool	4	42	2
1983–84 Blackpool	4	45	7
1984–85 Blackpool	4	30	5
1985–86 Blackpool	3	23	4
1985–86 Sunderland	2	8	—
1986–87 Sunderland	2	23	—
1987–88 Chester C	3	14	—
1987–88 Colchester U	4	5	—

HEWITT, Jamie
17.5.68 Chesterfield (DF)
5.10 10.8 School
LD Plymouth Arg v Chesterfield
2.11.85 0–0

1984–85 Chesterfield	4	—	—
1985–86 Chesterfield	3	17	—
1986–87 Chesterfield	3	42	2
1987–88 Chesterfield	3	28	2

HEWITT, John
9.2.63 Aberdeen (FW)
5.8 10.8 Middlefield Wasps
LD Aberdeen v St Mirren
15.12.79 2–0

1979–80 Aberdeen	P	4	—
1980–81 Aberdeen	P	21	2
1981–82 Aberdeen	P	25	11
1982–83 Aberdeen	P	16	4
1983–84 Aberdeen	P	32	12
1984–85 Aberdeen	P	21	3
1985–86 Aberdeen	P	23	6
1986–87 Aberdeen	P	34	11
1987–88 Aberdeen	P	37	1

HIBBITT, Kenny
3.1.51 Bradford (MF)
5.10½ 12.0 Apprentice

1967–68 Bradford PA	4	8	—
1968–69 Bradford PA	4	7	—
1968–69 Wolves	1	1	—
1969–70 Wolves	1	—	—
1970–71 Wolves	1	31	2
1971–72 Wolves	1	34	7
1972–73 Wolves	1	31	6
1973–74 Wolves	1	33	2
1974–75 Wolves	1	41	17
1975–76 Wolves	1	41	8
1976–77 Wolves	2	41	16
1977–78 Wolves	1	23	6
1978–79 Wolves	1	37	6
1979–80 Wolves	1	32	9
1980–81 Wolves	1	33	3
1981–82 Wolves	1	33	4
1982–83 Wolves	2	31	2
1983–84 Wolves	1	23	—
1984–85 Coventry C	1	33	3
1985–86 Coventry C	1	14	1
1986–87 Bristol R	3	28	3
1987–88 Bristol R	3	24	2

PLAYER DIRECTORY

HICKS, Martin
27.2.57 Stratford-on-Avon (DF)
6.3 13.6 Stratford T
LD Reading v Hartlepool U
18.2.78 2–3

1976–77	Charlton Ath	2	— —
1977–78	Charlton Ath	2	— —
1977–78	Reading	4	19 1
1978–79	Reading	4	46 1
1979–80	Reading	3	1 1
1980–81	Reading	3	27 2
1981–82	Reading	3	44 3
1982–83	Reading	3	32 1
1983–84	Reading	4	46 1
1984–85	Reading	3	40 2
1985–86	Reading	3	34 2
1986–87	Reading	2	34 3
1987–88	Reading	2	44 1

HIGGINS, David
19.8.69 Liverpool (DF)
6.0 11.0 Caernarfon T
LD Darlington v Tranmere R
3.10.87 0–0

1987–88	Tranmere R	4	33 1

HIGGINS, Mark
29.9.58 Buxton (DF)
6.1 13.5 Apprentice
LD Everton v Manchester C
5.10.76 2–2

1976–77	Everton	1	2 —
1977–78	Everton	1	26 1
1978–79	Everton	1	21 1
1979–80	Everton	1	19 —
1980–81	Everton	1	2 —
1981–82	Everton	1	29 3
1982–83	Everton	1	39 1
1983–84	Everton	1	14 —
Retired			
1985–86	Manchester U	1	6 —
1986–87	Bury	3	22 —
1987–88	Bury	3	41 —

HILAIRE, Vince
10.10.59 Forest Hill (FW)
5.6 10.0 Apprentice
LD Lincoln C v Crystal Palace
2.3.77 3–2

1976–77	Crystal Palace	3	3 —
1977–78	Crystal Palace	2	30 2
1978–79	Crystal Palace	2	31 6
1979–80	Crystal Palace	1	42 5
1980–81	Crystal Palace	1	31 4
1981–82	Crystal Palace	2	36 5
1982–83	Crystal Palace	2	42 5
1983–84	Crystal Palace	2	40 2
1984–85	Luton T	1	6 —
1984–85	Portsmouth	2	26 7
1985–86	Portsmouth	2	41 8
1986–87	Portsmouth	2	41 8
1987–88	Portsmouth	1	38 2

HILDITCH, Mark
20.8.60 Royton (FW)
5.11 11.8 Amateur
LD Rochdale v Scunthorpe U
15.4.78 1–1

1977–78	Rochdale	4	3 1
1978–79	Rochdale	4	27 3
1979–80	Rochdale	4	44 3
1980–81	Rochdale	4	44 12
1981–82	Rochdale	4	40 14
1982–83	Rochdale	4	39 7
1983–84	Tranmere R	4	39 8
1984–85	Tranmere R	4	3 1
1985–86	Tranmere R	4	7 3
1986–87	Wigan Ath	3	28 8
1987–88	Wigan Ath	3	29 8

HILL, Andy
20.1.65 Maltby (DF)
5.11 12.0 Apprentice
LD Darlington v Bury
25.8.84 1–1

1982–83	Manchester U	1	— —
1983–84	Manchester U	1	— —
1984–85	Bury	4	43 3
1985–86	Bury	3	35 2
1986–87	Bury	3	42 1
1987–88	Bury	3	43 2

HILL, Colin
12.11.63 Hillingdon (DF)
5.11 12.2 Apprentice
LD Norwich C v Arsenal
20.4.83 3–1

1982–83	Arsenal	1	7 —
1983–84	Arsenal	1	37 1
1984–85	Arsenal	1	2 —
1985–86	Brighton & HA	2	— —
1986–87	Maritime (Portugal)		
1987–88	Colchester U	4	25 —

HILL, David
6.6.66 Nottingham (MF)
5.9 10.3 Local
LD Scunthorpe U v Southend U
30.9.83 1–6

1983–84	Scunthorpe U	3	2 —
1984–85	Scunthorpe U	4	29 2
1985–86	Scunthorpe U	4	42 2
1986–87	Scunthorpe U	4	41 3
1987–88	Scunthorpe U	4	26 3

HILL, Ian
9.5.65 Dublin (DF)
5.11 11.6 Cherry Orchard
LD —

1987–88	Leicester C	2	— —

HILL, Keith
17.5.69 Bolton (DF)
6.0 11.3 Apprentice
LD Blackburn R v Middlesbrough
26.9.87 0–2

1987–88	Blackburn R	2	1 —

HILL, Ricky
5.3.59 London (MF)
5.11 13.0 Apprentice
LD Luton T v Bristol R
19.4.76 3–1

1975–76	Luton T	2	2 1
1976–77	Luton T	2	11 4
1977–78	Luton T	2	40 5
1978–79	Luton T	2	38 3
1979–80	Luton T	2	40 6
1980–81	Luton T	2	42 7
1981–82	Luton T	2	38 5
1982–83	Luton T	1	42 9
1983–84	Luton T	1	26 2
1984–85	Luton T	1	39 2
1985–86	Luton T	1	38 3
1986–87	Luton T	1	30 2
1987–88	Luton T	1	17 2

HILL, Richard
20.9.63 Hinckley (FW)
6.0 12.1 Forward
LD Burnley v Northampton T
17.8.85 3–2

1981–82	Leicester C	2	— —
From Grankulla, Nuneaton			
1985–86	Northampton T	4	41 17
1986–87	Northampton T	4	45 29
1987–88	Watford	1	4 —
1987–88	Oxford U	1	24 3

HILLIER, David
18.12.69 London (MF)
— — Apprentice
LD —

1987–88	Arsenal	1	— —

HILLYARD, Ron
31.3.53 Rotherham (GK)
5.11 11.4 Amateur

1969–70	York C	4	3 —
1970–71	York C	4	34 —
1971–72	York C	3	17 —
1971–72	Hartlepool U	4	23 —
1972–73	York C	3	4 —
1973–74	York C	3	3 —
1973–74	Bury	4	— —
1973–74	Brighton & HA	3	— —
1974–75	Gillingham	3	46 —
1975–76	Gillingham	3	44 —
1976–77	Gillingham	3	25 —
1977–78	Gillingham	3	44 —
1978–79	Gillingham	3	46 —
1979–80	Gillingham	3	46 —
1980–81	Gillingham	3	37 —
1981–82	Gillingham	3	44 —
1982–83	Gillingham	3	42 —
1983–84	Gillingham	3	8 —
1984–85	Gillingham	3	25 —
1985–86	Gillingham	3	46 —
1986–87	Gillingham	3	27 —
1987–88	Gillingham	3	18 —

HILTON, Paul
8.10.59 Oldham (DF)
6.1 11.6 Amateur
LD Swindon T v <u>Bury</u>
19.8.78 2–1

1978–79	Bury	3	9	1
1979–80	Bury	3	28	5
1980–81	Bury	4	32	13
1981–82	Bury	4	41	7
1982–83	Bury	4	19	7
1983–84	Bury	4	19	6
1983–84	West Ham U	1	8	2
1984–85	West Ham U	1	9	1
1985–86	West Ham U	1	2	—
1986–87	West Ham U	1	16	1
1987–88	West Ham U	1	14	3

HIMSWORTH, Gary
19.12.69 Appleton-le-Moors (FW)
5.7 9.8 Apprentice
LD Brighton & HA v <u>York C</u>
15.8.87 1–0

| 1987–88 | York C | 3 | 31 | 2 |

HINCHCLIFFE, Andy
5.2.69 Manchester (DF)
— — Apprentice
LD <u>Manchester C</u> v Plymouth Arg
15.8.87 2–1

| 1987–88 | Manchester C | 2 | 42 | 1 |

HINDMARCH, Rob
27.4.61 Stannington (DF)
6.1 13.5 Apprentice
LD Orient v <u>Sunderland</u>
14.1.78 2–2

1977–78	Sunderland	2	2	—
1978–79	Sunderland	2	—	—
1979–80	Sunderland	2	21	—
1980–81	Sunderland	1	29	—
1981–82	Sunderland	1	36	2
1982–83	Sunderland	1	14	—
1983–84	Sunderland	1	13	—
1983–84	*Portsmouth*	2	2	—
1984–85	Derby Co	3	22	1
1985–86	Derby Co	3	39	6
1986–87	Derby Co	2	33	2
1987–88	Derby Co	1	19	—

HINE, Mark
18.5.64 Middlesbrough (MF)
5.8 9.11 Local
LD Oldham v <u>Grimsby T</u>
23.3.85 2–0

1983–84	Grimsby T	2	—	—
1984–85	Grimsby T	2	9	—
1985–86	Grimsby T	2	13	1
1986–87	Darlington	3	43	2
1987–88	Darlington	4	45	4

HINNIGAN, Joe
3.12.55 Liverpool (DF)
6.0¼ 12.0 South Liverpool
LD Hereford U v <u>Wigan Ath</u>
19.8.78 0–0

1978–79	Wigan Ath	4	39	5
1979–80	Wigan Ath	4	27	5
1979–80	Sunderland	2	14	—
1980–81	Sunderland	1	16	4
1981–82	Sunderland	1	30	—
1982–83	Sunderland	1	3	—
1982–83	Preston NE	3	13	3
1983–84	Preston NE	3	39	5
1984–85	Gillingham	3	37	5
1985–86	Gillingham	3	39	2
1986–87	Gillingham	3	27	—
1987–88	Wrexham	4	29	1

HIRST, David
7.12.67 Barnsley (FW)
5.11 12.5 Apprentice
LD Charlton Ath v <u>Barnsley</u>
17.8.85 2–1

1985–86	Barnsley	2	28	9
1986–87	Sheffield W	1	21	6
1987–88	Sheffield W	1	24	3

HITCHCOCK, Kevin
5.10.62 Custom House (GK)
6.0 12.10 Barking
LD Colchester U v <u>Mansfield T</u>
10.3.84 1–0

1983–84	Nottingham F	1	—	—
1983–84	*Mansfield T*	4	14	—
1984–85	Mansfield T	4	43	—
1985–86	Mansfield T	4	46	—
1986–87	Mansfield T	3	46	—
1987–88	Mansfield T	3	33	—
1987–88	Chelsea	1	8	—

HOBSON, Gordon
27.11.57 Sheffield (FW)
5.9 10.7 Sheffield Rgrs
LD Cambridge U v <u>Lincoln C</u>
8.4.78 1–4

1977–78	Lincoln C	3	5	2
1978–79	Lincoln C	3	33	6
1979–80	Lincoln C	4	43	10
1980–81	Lincoln C	4	44	21
1981–82	Lincoln C	3	32	7
1982–83	Lincoln C	3	41	14
1983–84	Lincoln C	3	36	6
1984–85	Lincoln C	3	38	7
1985–86	Grimsby T	2	41	15
1986–87	Grimsby T	2	11	3
1986–87	Southampton	1	20	7
1987–88	Southampton	1	—	—

HOCKADAY, David
9.11.57 Billingham (FW)
5.10 10.9 Amateur
LD Notts Co v <u>Blackpool</u>
18.9.76 2–0

1975–76	Blackpool	2	—	—
1976–77	Blackpool	2	5	—
1977–78	Blackpool	2	—	—
1978–79	Blackpool	3	18	4
1979–80	Blackpool	3	7	1
1980–81	Blackpool	3	36	4
1981–82	Blackpool	4	41	7
1982–83	Blackpool	4	40	8
1983–84	Swindon T	4	36	3
1984–85	Swindon T	4	22	1
1985–86	Swindon T	4	37	1
1986–87	Swindon T	3	40	2
1987–88	Swindon T	2	43	—

HODDY, Kevin
6.1.68 Essex (MF)
5.10¼ 11.1 Apprentice
LD Notts Co v <u>Fulham</u>
20.9.86 2–3

1985–86	Fulham	2	—	—
1986–87	Fulham	3	15	1
1987–88	Fulham	3	5	—

HODGE, Martin
4.2.59 Southport (GK)
6.0 13.2 Apprentice
LD <u>Plymouth Arg</u> v Peterborough U
15.4.78 1–0

1976–77	Plymouth Arg	2	—	—
1977–78	Plymouth Arg	3	5	—
1978–79	Plymouth Arg	3	38	—
1979–80	Everton	1	23	—
1980–81	Everton	1	2	—
1981–82	*Preston NE*	3	28	—
1982–83	*Oldham Ath*	2	4	—
1982–83	*Gillingham*	3	4	—
1982–83	*Preston NE*	3	16	—
1983–84	Sheffield W	2	42	—
1984–85	Sheffield W	1	42	—
1985–86	Sheffield W	1	42	—
1986–87	Sheffield W	1	42	—
1987–88	Sheffield W	1	29	—

HODGE, Stephen
25.10.62 Nottingham (MF)
5.8 9.11 Apprentice
LD Ipswich T v <u>Nottingham F</u>
15.5.82 1–3

1980–81	Nottingham F	1	—	—
1981–82	Nottingham F	1	1	—
1982–83	Nottingham F	1	39	8
1983–84	Nottingham F	1	39	10
1984–85	Nottingham F	1	42	12
1985–86	Nottingham F	1	2	—
1985–86	Aston Villa	1	36	8
1986–87	Aston Villa	1	19	4
1986–87	Tottenham H	1	19	4
1987–88	Tottenham H	1	26	3

PLAYER DIRECTORY

HODGES, David
17.1.70 Hereford (MF)
— — Apprentice
LD Mansfield T v Bury
7.2.87 1–3

1986–87 Mansfield T	3	3	—
1987–88 Mansfield T	3	22	2

HODGES, Glyn
30.4.63 Streatham (FW)
6.0 12.3 Apprentice
LD Halifax T v Wimbledon
27.9.80 0–1

1980–81 Wimbledon	4	30	5
1981–82 Wimbledon	3	34	2
1982–83 Wimbledon	4	37	9
1983–84 Wimbledon	3	42	15
1984–85 Wimbledon	2	22	3
1985–86 Wimbledon	2	30	6
1986–87 Wimbledon	1	37	9
1987–88 Newcastle U	1	7	—
1987–88 Watford	1	24	3

HODGES, Kevin
12.6.60 Bridport (MF)
5.8 10.0 Apprentice
LD Bury v Plymouth Arg
12.9.78 1–2

1977–78 Plymouth Arg	3	—	—
1978–79 Plymouth Arg	3	12	—
1979–80 Plymouth Arg	3	44	5
1980–81 Plymouth Arg	3	41	5
1981–82 Plymouth Arg	3	46	11
1982–83 Plymouth Arg	3	46	11
1983–84 Plymouth Arg	3	43	4
1984–85 Plymouth Arg	3	45	10
1985–86 Plymouth Arg	3	46	16
1986–87 Plymouth Arg	2	35	5
1987–88 Plymouth Arg	2	37	6

HODKINSON, Andrew
4.11.65 Ashton (MF)
5.6 10.10 Bolton W Apprentice
LD Oldham Ath v Portsmouth
28.4.84 3–2

1983–84 Oldham Ath	2	4	1
1984–85 Oldham Ath	2	1	—
1985–86 Stockport Co	4	41	6
1986–87 Stockport Co	4	38	6
1987–88 Stockport Co	4	39	6

HODSON, Simeon
5.3.66 Lincoln (DF)
5.9 10.2 Apprentice
LD Norwich C v Notts Co
13.3.84 0–1

1983–84 Notts Co	1	13	—
1984–85 Notts Co	2	14	—
1984–85 Charlton Ath	2	5	—
1985–86 Charlton Ath	2	—	—
1985–86 Lincoln C	3	15	—
1986–87 Lincoln C	4	41	—
1987–88 Newport Co	4	34	1
1987–88 WBA	2	7	—

HOGG, Graeme
17.6.64 Aberdeen (DF)
6.1 12.12 Apprentice
LD QPR v Manchester U
13.1.84 1–1

1982–83 Manchester U	1	—	—
1983–84 Manchester U	1	16	1
1984–85 Manchester U	1	29	—
1985–86 Manchester U	1	17	—
1986–87 Manchester U	1	11	—
1987–88 Manchester U	1	10	—
1987–88 WBA	2	7	—

HOLDEN, Andrew
14.9.62 Flint (DF)
6.2 13.0 Rhyl
LD Chester C v Northampton T
27.8.83 1–1

1983–84 Chester C	4	44	7
1984–85 Chester C	4	38	6
1985–86 Chester C	4	10	2
1986–87 Chester C	3	8	2
1986–87 Wigan Ath	3	11	1
1987–88 Wigan Ath	3	15	2

HOLDEN, Richard
9.9.64 Skipton (MF)

LD Orient v Burnley
3.5.86 3–0

1985–86 Burnley	4	1	—
1986–87 Halifax T	4	32	2
1987–88 Halifax T	4	35	10
1987–88 Watford	1	10	2

HOLDSWORTH, David
8.11.68 London (DF)
5.11 11.4 Trainee
LD —

1987–88 Watford	1	—	—

HOLDSWORTH, Dean
8.11.68 London (FW)
5.11 11.4 Trainee
LD Watford v Luton T
12.12.87 0–1

1987–88 Watford	1	2	—
1987–88 Carlisle U	4	4	1
1987–88 Port Vale	3	6	2

HOLLOWAY, Ian
12.3.63 Kingswood (MF)
5.7 9.12 Apprentice
LD Wrexham v Bristol R
25.4.81 3–1

1980–81 Bristol R	2	1	—
1981–82 Bristol R	3	1	—
1982–83 Bristol R	3	31	7
1983–84 Bristol R	3	36	1
1984–85 Bristol R	3	42	6
1985–86 Wimbledon	2	19	2
1985–86 Brentford	3	13	2
1986–87 Brentford	3	16	—
1986–87 Torquay U	4	5	—
1987–88 Bristol R	3	43	5

HOLMES, Andy
7.1.69 Stoke (DF)
6.1 12.12 Apprentice
LD Shrewsbury T v Stoke C
28.11.87 0–3

1987–88 Stoke C	2	2	—

HOLMES, Paul
18.2.68 Wortley (DF)
5.10 11.0 Apprentice
LD Doncaster R v Wigan Ath
5.11.85 2–2

1985–86 Doncaster R	3	5	1
1986–87 Doncaster R	3	16	—
1987–88 Doncaster R	3	26	—

HOLSGROVE, Paul
26.8.69 Wellington (FW)
— — YTS
LD Aldershot v Notts Co
23.2.88 0–2

1987–88 Aldershot	3	2	—

HONE, Mark
31.3.68 Croydon (DF)
6.0 12.0
LD Crystal Palace v Millwall
10.10.87 1–0

1985–86 Crystal Palace	2	—	—
1986–87 Crystal Palace	2	—	—
1987–88 Crystal Palace	2	3	—

HONOR, Chris
5.6.68 Bristol (DF)
— — Apprentice
LD Darlington v Bristol C
15.5.86 1–1

1985–86 Bristol C	3	1	—
1986–87 Bristol C	3	2	—
1986–87 Torquay U	4	3	—
1987–88 Bristol C	3	17	—

HONOUR, Brian
16.2.64 Horden (MF)
5.7 12.5 Apprentice
LD Darlington v Crewe Alex
4.4.82 1–0

1981–82 Darlington	4	1	—
1982–83 Darlington	4	32	3
1983–84 Darlington	4	41	1
Peterlee			
1984–85 Hartlepool U	4	17	—
1985–86 Hartlepool U	4	46	8
1986–87 Hartlepool U	4	32	2
1987–88 Hartlepool U	4	44	—

Ray Houghton

Photo: Bob Thomas Sports Photography.

PLAYER DIRECTORY

HOOLICKIN, Gary
29.10.57 Middleton (DF)
5.11 11.1 Apprentice
LD Oldham Ath v Luton T
14.5.77 1–2

1975–76 Oldham Ath	2	—	—
1976–77 Oldham Ath	2	1	—
1977–78 Oldham Ath	2	17	—
1978–79 Oldham Ath	2	1	1
1979–80 Oldham Ath	2	4	—
1980–81 Oldham Ath	2	14	—
1981–82 Oldham Ath	2	28	—
1982–83 Oldham Ath	2	31	—
1983–84 Oldham Ath	2	34	1
1984–85 Oldham Ath	2	31	—
1985–86 Oldham Ath	2	32	—
1986–87 Oldham Ath	2	18	—
1987–88 Oldham Ath	2	—	—

HOOPER, Michael
10.2.64 Bristol (GK)
6.1 13.0
LD Bristol C v Lincoln C
1.12.84 2–1

1983–84 Bristol C	4	—	—
1984–85 Bristol C	3	1	—
1984–85 *Wrexham*	4	20	—
1985–86 Wrexham	4	14	—
1985–86 Liverpool	1	—	—
1986–87 Liverpool	1	11	—
1987–88 Liverpool	1	2	—

HOPKINS, Jeff
14.4.64 Swansea (DF)
6.1 11.11 Apprentice
LD Huddersfield T v Fulham
2.5.81 4–2

1980–81 Fulham	3	1	—
1981–82 Fulham	3	35	—
1982–83 Fulham	2	41	1
1983–84 Fulham	2	33	—
1984–85 Fulham	2	40	2
1985–86 Fulham	2	23	—
1986–87 Fulham	3	20	1
1987–88 Fulham	3	26	—

HOPKINS, Robert
25.10.61 Birmingham (MF)
5.7 10.5 Apprentice
LD Aston Villa v Norwich C
26.3.80 2–0

1979–80 Aston Villa	1	2	1
1980–81 Aston Villa	1	—	—
1981–82 Aston Villa	1	—	—
1982–83 Aston Villa	1	1	—
1982–83 Birmingham C	1	11	2
1983–84 Birmingham C	1	32	5
1984–85 Birmingham C	2	39	9
1985–86 Birmingham C	1	38	4
1986–87 Birmingham C	2	3	1
1986–87 Manchester C	1	7	1
1986–87 WBA	2	25	4
1987–88 WBA	2	29	2

HORNE, Barry
18.5.62 St Asaph (MF)
5.9 11.4 Rhyl
LD Swindon T v Wrexham
25.8.84 2–1

1984–85 Wrexham	4	44	6
1985–86 Wrexham	4	46	3
1986–87 Wrexham	4	46	8
1987–88 Portsmouth	1	39	3

HORNE, Brian
5.10.67 Billericay (GK)
5.10 12.4 Apprentice
LD Sheffield U v Millwall
2.9.86 2–1

1985–86 Millwall	2	—	—
1986–87 Millwall	2	32	—
1987–88 Millwall	2	43	—

HORRIX, Dean
21.11.61 Taplow (FW)
5.10 10.10 Apprentice
LD Millwall v Portsmouth
27.12.80 0–0

1978–79 Millwall	2	—	—
1979–80 Millwall	3	—	—
1980–81 Millwall	3	13	4
1981–82 Millwall	3	44	15
1982–83 Millwall	3	15	—
1982–83 Gillingham	3	14	—
1983–84 Reading	4	43	8
1984–85 Reading	3	43	19
1985–86 Reading	3	41	6
1986–87 Reading	2	18	—
1986–87 *Cardiff C*	4	9	3
1987–88 Reading	2	13	2
1987–88 Millwall	2	2	1

HOSKIN, Ashley
27.3.68 Accrington (MF)
5.2 8.5 Apprentice
LD Burnley v Southend
2.11.85 1–3

1985–86 Burnley	4	19	2
1986–87 Burnley	4	40	8
1987–88 Burnley	4	24	1

HOTTE, Tim
4.10.63 Bradford (MF)
5.6 11.7 North Ferriby U
LD Hull C v Huddersfield T
23.4.88 4–0

1987–88 Hull C	2	4	—

HOUCHEN, Keith
25.7.60 Middlesbrough (FW)
6.2 12.8 Chesterfield. Amateur
LD Hartlepool U v Crewe Alex
25.2.78 1–1

1977–78 Hartlepool U	4	13	4
1978–79 Hartlepool U	4	39	12
1979–80 Hartlepool U	4	41	14

1980–81 Hartlepool U	4	45	17
1981–82 Hartlepool U	4	32	18
1981–82 Orient	2	14	1
1982–83 Orient	3	32	10
1983–84 Orient	3	30	9
1983–84 York C	4	7	1
1984–85 York C	3	35	12
1985–86 York C	3	25	6
1985–86 Scunthorpe U	4	9	2
1986–87 Coventry C	1	20	2
1987–88 Coventry C	1	21	3

HOUGH, David
20.2.66 Crewe (MF)
5.10¼ 11.2 Apprentice
LD Swansea C v Leeds U
7.5.84 2–2

1983–84 Swansea C	2	2	—
1984–85 Swansea C	3	25	2
1985–86 Swansea C	3	31	3
1986–87 Swansea C	4	31	3
1987–88 Swansea C	4	20	—

HOUGHTON, Ray
9.1.62 Glasgow (MF)
5.7 10.10 Amateur
LD Arsenal v West Ham U
1.5.82 2–0

1979–80 West Ham U	2	—	—
1980–81 West Ham U	2	—	—
1981–82 West Ham U	1	1	—
1982–83 Fulham	2	42	5
1983–84 Fulham	2	40	3
1984–85 Fulham	2	42	8
1985–86 Fulham	2	5	—
1985–86 Oxford U	1	35	4
1986–87 Oxford U	1	37	5
1987–88 Oxford U	1	11	1
1987–88 Liverpool	1	28	5

HOWARD, Terence
26.2.66 Stepney (DF)
6.1 11.7 Apprentice
LD Chelsea v Aston Villa
16.4.85 3–1

1983–84 Chelsea	2	—	—
1984–85 Chelsea	1	4	—
1985–86 Chelsea	1	1	—
1985–86 *Crystal Palace*	2	4	—
1986–87 Chelsea	1	1	—
1986–87 Orient	4	12	2
1986–87 *Chester C*	3	2	—
1987–88 Leyton Orient	4	41	2

HOWELLS, David
15.12.67 Guildford (FW)
5.11 11.1 YTS
LD Sheffield W v Tottenham H
22.2.86 1–2

1984–85 Tottenham H	1	—	—
1985–86 Tottenham H	1	1	1
1986–87 Tottenham H	1	1	—
1987–88 Tottenham H	1	11	—

HOWEY, Lee
1.4.69 Sunderland (FW)
6.1 11.4 Apprentice
LD —

1987–88 Ipswich T	2	—	—

HOWLETT, Gary
2.4.63 Dublin (MF)
5.8 10.4 Home Farm
LD Brighton & HA v Liverpool
22.3.83 2–2

1980–81 Coventry C	1	—	—
1981–82 Coventry C	1	—	—
1982–83 Brighton & HA	1	9	1
1983–84 Brighton & HA	2	17	—
1984–85 Brighton & HA	2	6	1
1984–85 Bournemouth	3	17	2
1985–86 Bournemouth	3	20	2
1986–87 Bournemouth	3	23	3
1987–88 *Aldershot*	3	1	—
1987–88 *Chester C*	3	6	1
1987–88 York C	3	18	2

HOYLAND, Jamie
23.1.66 Sheffield (FW)
6.0 12.8½ Apprentice
LD Manchester C v Derby Co
26.11.83 1–1

1983–84 Manchester C	2	1	—
1984–85 Manchester C	2	1	—
1985–86 Manchester C	1	—	—
1986–87 Bury	3	36	2
1987–88 Bury	3	44	8

HUCKER, Peter
28.10.59 London (GK)
6.2 12.12 Apprentice
LD Shrewsbury T v QPR
2.5.81 3–3

1977–78 QPR	1	—	—
1977–78 *Cambridge U*	3	—	—
1978–79 QPR	1	—	—
1979–80 QPR	2	—	—
1980–81 QPR	2	1	—
1981–82 QPR	2	22	—
1982–83 QPR	2	42	—
1983–84 QPR	1	42	—
1984–85 QPR	1	42	—
1985–86 QPR	1	11	—
1986–87 Oxford U	1	5	—
1987–88 Oxford U	1	27	—
1987–88 *WBA*	2	7	—

HUGHES, Darren
6.10.65 Prescot (DF)
5.11 10.11½ Apprentice
LD Wolves v Everton
27.12.83 3–0

1983–84 Everton	1	1	—
1984–85 Everton	1	2	—
1985–86 Shrewsbury T	2	31	1
1986–87 Shrewsbury T	2	6	—
1986–87 Brighton & HA	2	26	2
1987–88 *Port Vale*	3	6	1
1987–88 Port Vale	3	37	—

HUGHES, Ken
9.1.66 Barmouth (GK)
— — Crystal Palace
LD Shrewsbury T v Huddersfield T
14.2.87 1–2

1986–87 Shrewsbury T	2	6	—
1987–88 Shrewsbury T	2	2	—

HUGHES, Mark
3.2.62 Port Talbot (DF)
5.11 11.8 Apprentice
LD Bristol R v West Ham U
3.5.80 0–2

1979–80 Bristol R	2	1	—
1980–81 Bristol R	2	38	1
1981–82 Bristol R	3	22	2
1982–83 Bristol R	3	4	—
1982–83 *Torquay U*	4	9	1
1983–84 Bristol R	3	9	—
1984–85 Swansea C	3	12	—
1984–85 Bristol C	3	20	—
1985–86 Bristol C	3	2	—
1985–86 Tranmere R	4	32	—
1986–87 Tranmere R	4	38	1
1987–88 Tranmere R	4	20	—

HUGHES, Philip
19.11.64 Manchester (GK)
5.11 12.7 Manchester U
Apprentice
LD Leeds U v Cardiff C
10.9.83 1–0

1982–83 Leeds U	2	—	—
1983–84 Leeds U	2	2	—
1984–85 Leeds U	2	4	—
1985–86 Bury	3	41	—
1986–87 Bury	3	32	—
1987–88 Bury	3	7	—
1987–88 *Wigan Ath*	3	1	—
1987–88 Wigan Ath	3	30	—

HUGHTON, Chris
11.12.58 West Ham U (DF)
5.7¼ 11.5 Amateur
LD Tottenham H v Manchester C
1.9.79 2–1

1977–78 Tottenham H	2	—	—
1978–79 Tottenham H	1	—	—
1979–80 Tottenham H	1	39	1
1980–81 Tottenham H	1	34	1
1981–82 Tottenham H	1	37	2
1982–83 Tottenham H	1	38	3
1983–84 Tottenham H	1	34	3
1984–85 Tottenham H	1	31	1
1985–86 Tottenham H	1	33	1
1986–87 Tottenham H	1	9	—
1987–88 Tottenham H	1	13	—

HULL, Alan
4.9.62 Rochford (FW)
— — Barkingside
LD Cardiff C v Leyton Orient
15.8.87 1–1

1987–88 Leyton Orient	4	36	5

HUMES, Anthony
19.3.66 Blyth (DF)
5.11 10.10 Apprentice
LD Blackburn R v Ipswich T
29.11.86 0–0

1983–84 Ipswich T	1	—	—
1984–85 Ipswich T	1	—	—
1985–86 Ipswich T	1	—	—
1986–87 Ipswich T	2	22	2
1987–88 Ipswich T	2	27	—

HUMPHREY, John
31.1.61 Paddington (DF)
5.10 11.1 Apprentice
LD Southampton v Wolves
7.4.80 0–3

1978–79 Wolves	1	—	—
1979–80 Wolves	1	2	—
1980–81 Wolves	1	12	—
1981–82 Wolves	1	23	—
1982–83 Wolves	2	42	3
1983–84 Wolves	1	28	—
1984–85 Wolves	2	42	—
1985–86 Charlton Ath	2	39	2
1986–87 Charlton Ath	1	39	—
1987–88 Charlton Ath	1	40	—

HUMPHRIES, Glenn
11.8.64 Hull (MF)
6.0 12.0 Apprentice
LD Mansfield T v Doncaster R
6.5.81 1–1

1980–81 Doncaster R	4	1	—
1981–82 Doncaster R	3	14	—
1982–83 Doncaster R	3	40	5
1983–84 Doncaster R	4	44	2
1984–85 Doncaster R	3	27	—
1985–86 Doncaster R	3	29	—
1986–87 Doncaster R	3	17	1
1986–87 *Lincoln C*	4	9	—
1987–88 Doncaster R	3	8	—
1987–88 Bristol C	3	24	—

HUNT, David
17.4.59 Leicester (MF)
5.11 11.0 Apprentice
LD Derby Co v Leeds U
17.9.78 2–2

1977–78 Derby Co	1	5	—
1977–78 Notts Co	2	12	—
1978–79 Notts Co	2	37	2
1979–80 Notts Co	2	38	4
1980–81 Notts Co	2	42	3
1981–82 Notts Co	1	30	3
1982–83 Notts Co	1	37	1
1983–84 Notts Co	1	39	2
1984–85 Notts Co	2	37	3
1985–86 Notts Co	3	34	8
1986–87 Notts Co	3	30	2
1987–88 Aston Villa	2	12	—

PLAYER DIRECTORY

HUNTER, Geoff
27.10.59 Hull (DF)
5.10 10.12 Apprentice
LD Bradford C v Crewe Alex
18.8.79 4–0

1976–77	Manchester U	1	— —
1977–78	Manchester U	1	— —
1978–79	Manchester U	1	— —
1979–80	Crewe Alex	4	41	4
1980–81	Crewe Alex	4	46	4
1981–82	Port Vale	4	41	3
1982–83	Port Vale	4	46	4
1983–84	Port Vale	3	42	1
1984–85	Port Vale	4	42	2
1985–86	Port Vale	4	45	5
1986–87	Port Vale	3	43	—
1987–88	Wrexham	4	39	4

HUNTER, Gordon
3.5.67 Wallyford (MF)
5.10 10.5 Musselburgh Windsor
LD Hibernian v Rangers
12.5.84 0–0

1983–84	Hibernian	P	1	—
1984–85	Hibernian	P	6	—
1985–86	Hibernian	P	25	—
1986–87	Hibernian	P	29	—
1987–88	Hibernian	P	35	—

HUNTER, Les
15.1.58 Middlesbrough (DF)
6.2 12.5 Apprentice
LD Swindon T v Chesterfield
16.8.76 0–1

1975–76	Chesterfield	3	45	2
1976–77	Chesterfield	3	16	—
1977–78	Chesterfield	3	17	2
1978–79	Chesterfield	3	40	—
1979–80	Chesterfield	3	22	1
1980–81	Chesterfield	3	13	2
1981–82	Chesterfield	3	12	1
1982–83	Scunthorpe U	4	46	8
1983–84	Scunthorpe U	3	15	—
1983–84	Chesterfield	4	21	2
1984–85	Chesterfield	4	46	3
1985–86	Chesterfield	3	32	4
1985–86	Scunthorpe U	4	12	1
1986–87	Scunthorpe U	4	37	4
1987–88	Chesterfield	3	25	3

HURLOCK, Terry
22.9.58 Hackney (MF)
5.9 13.2 Leytonstone and Ilford
LD Walsall v Brentford
30.8.80 2–3

1980–81	Brentford	3	42	4
1981–82	Brentford	3	40	2
1982–83	Brentford	3	39	3
1983–84	Brentford	3	32	4
1984–85	Brentford	3	40	3
1985–86	Brentford	3	27	2
1985–86	Reading	3	16	—

1986–87	Reading	2	13	—
1986–87	Millwall	2	13	1
1987–88	Millwall	2	28	4

HUTCHINGS, Chris
5.7.57 Winchester (DF)
5.10 11.0 Harrow Bor
LD Cardiff C v Chelsea
31.10.80 0–1

1980–81	Chelsea	2	12	1
1981–82	Chelsea	2	35	1
1982–83	Chelsea	2	36	—
1983–84	Chelsea	2	4	1
1983–84	Brighton & HA	2	26	1
1984–85	Brighton & HA	2	42	1
1985–86	Brighton & HA	2	29	1
1986–87	Brighton & HA	2	36	—
1987–88	Brighton & HA	3	20	1
1987–88	Huddersfield T	2	23	—

HUTCHINSON, Bobby
19.6.53 Glasgow (FW)
5.9 11.4 Aberdeen LCU
LD Berwick R v Montrose
15.4.72 1–2

1971–72	Montrose	2	3	—
1972–73	Montrose	2	10	1
1973–74	Montrose	2	28	7
1974–75	Dundee	P	23	7
1975–76	Dundee	1	21	5
1976–77	Dundee	1	35	12
1977–78	Dundee	1	9	1
1977–78	Hibernian	P	20	6
1978–79	Hibernian	P	22	4
1979–80	Hibernian	P	25	3
1980–81	Wigan Ath	4	35	3
1981–82	Tranmere R	4	29	4
1982–83	Tranmere R	4	6	2
1982–83	Mansfield T	4	25	3
1983–84	Mansfield T	4	10	—
1983–84	Tranmere R	4	21	4
1984–85	Bristol C	3	31	4
1985–86	Bristol C	3	42	4
1986–87	Bristol C	3	19	1
1986–87	Walsall	3	14	—
1987–88	Walsall	3	2	—
1987–88	*Blackpool*	3	6	—
1987–88	*Carlisle U*	4	13	2

HUTCHISON, Simon
24.9.69 Sheffield (MF)
5.10 11.12 Apprentice
LD —

1987–88	Manchester U	1	— —

INCE, Paul
21.10.67 Ilford (FW)
— — YTS
LD Newcastle U v West Ham U
30.11.86 4–0

1985–86	West Ham U	1	— —
1986–87	West Ham U	1	10	1
1987–88	West Ham U	1	28	3

IRVINE, Alan
12.7.58 Glasgow (FW)
5.8 11.4 Glasgow BC
LD Queen's Park v Raith R
24.9.77 0–3

1977–78	Queen's Park	1	4	—
1978–79	Queen's Park	1	8	—
1979–80	Queen's Park	2	38	5
1980–81	Queen's Park	2	38	4
1981–82	Everton	1	25	3
1982–83	Everton	1	14	1
1983–84	Everton	1	21	—
1984–85	Crystal Palace	2	35	5
1985–86	Crystal Palace	2	41	3
1986–87	Crystal Palace	2	33	4
1987–88	Dundee U	P	16	2
1987–88	Shrewsbury T	2	6	1

IRVINE, Brian
24.5.65 Bellshill (DF)
6.2 13.0 Victoria Park
LD Falkirk v Morton
21.4.84 0–1

1983–84	Falkirk	1	3	—
1984–85	Falkirk	1	35	—
1985–86	Aberdeen	P	1	—
1986–87	Aberdeen	P	20	3
1987–88	Aberdeen	P	16	1

IRWIN, Dennis
31.10.65 Cork (DF)
5.8 11.0 Apprentice
LD Leeds U v Fulham
21.1.84 1–0

1983–84	Leeds U	2	12	—
1984–85	Leeds U	2	41	1
1985–86	Leeds U	2	19	—
1986–87	Oldham Ath	2	41	1
1987–88	Oldham Ath	2	43	—

ISAAC, Robert
30.11.65 Hackney (DF)
5.11 12.7 Apprentice
LD Watford v Chelsea
16.3.85 1–3

1983–84	Chelsea	2	— —
1984–85	Chelsea	1	1	—
1985–86	Chelsea	1	3	—
1986–87	Chelsea	1	5	—
1986–87	Brighton & HA	2	11	—
1987–88	Brighton & HA	3	10	—

JACKETT, Kenny
5.1.62 Watford (DF)
5.10½ 11.2 Apprentice
LD Sunderland v <u>Watford</u>
26.4.80 5–0

1979–80 Watford	2	2	—
1980–81 Watford	2	42	3
1981–82 Watford	2	18	2
1982–83 Watford	1	41	4
1983–84 Watford	1	31	1
1984–85 Watford	1	36	4
1985–86 Watford	1	41	4
1986–87 Watford	1	32	6
1987–88 Watford	1	33	2

JACKSON, Craig
17.1.69 Rennishaw (MF)
— — YTS
LD <u>Notts Co</u> v Darlington
6.5.86 5–0

1985–86 Notts Co	3	1	—
1986–87 Notts Co	3	4	—
1987–88 Notts Co	3	—	—

JACKSON, Darren
25.7.66 Edinburgh (MF)
5.7 10.0 Broxburn Ath
LD Cowdenbeath v <u>Meadowbank</u>
10.8.85 3–1

1985–86 Meadowbank	2	39	17
1986–87 Meadowbank	2	9	5
1986–87 Newcastle U	1	23	3
1987–88 Newcastle U	1	31	2

JACKSON, Peter
6.4.61 Bradford (DF)
6.1 12.6 Apprentice
LD Hereford U v <u>Bradford C</u>
24.3.79 3–1

1978–79 Bradford C	4	9	1
1979–80 Bradford C	4	12	—
1980–81 Bradford C	4	45	1
1981–82 Bradford C	4	32	8
1982–83 Bradford C	3	41	3
1983–84 Bradford C	3	42	3
1984–85 Bradford C	3	45	8
1985–86 Bradford C	2	42	—
1986–87 Bradford C	2	10	—
1986–87 Newcastle U	1	31	1
1987–88 Newcastle U	1	28	2

JACOBS, Wayne
3.2.69 Sheffield (DF)
5.7½ 10.6 Apprentice
LD <u>Sheffield W</u> v Oxford U
18.8.87 1–1

1986–87 Sheffield W	1	—	—
1987–88 Sheffield W	1	6	—
1987–88 Hull C	2	6	—

JAMES, Robbie
23.3.57 Swansea (FW)
5.11 13.0 Apprentice
LD <u>Swansea C</u> v Charlton Ath
28.4.73 2–1

1972–73 Swansea C	3	1	—
1973–74 Swansea C	4	29	2
1974–75 Swansea C	4	42	8
1975–76 Swansea C	4	45	8
1976–77 Swansea C	4	46	14
1977–78 Swansea C	4	42	16
1978–79 Swansea C	3	43	14
1979–80 Swansea C	2	29	6
1980–81 Swansea C	2	35	8
1981–82 Swansea C	1	42	14
1982–83 Swansea C	1	40	9
1983–84 Stoke C	1	40	6
1984–85 Stoke C	1	8	—
1984–85 QPR	1	20	2
1985–86 QPR	1	28	1
1986–87 QPR	1	39	2
1987–88 Leicester C	2	23	—
1987–88 *Swansea C*	4	1	—
1987–88 Swansea C	4	15	3

JAMIESON, Willie
27.4.63 Barnsley (DF)
5.11 12.0 Tynecastle BC
LD <u>Hibernian</u> v Motherwell
6.9.80 1–0

1980–81 Hibernian	1	28	12
1981–82 Hibernian	P	12	5
1982–83 Hibernian	P	19	2
1983–84 Hibernian	P	33	4
1984–85 Hibernian	P	25	2
1985–86 Hamilton A	1	39	2
1986–87 Hamilton A	P	15	—
1987–88 Hamilton A	1	41	4

JARDINE, Iain
17.2.55 Irvine (MF)
5.10 12.0 Irvine Victoria
LD Partick Th v <u>Kilmarnock</u>
5.3.77 3–1

1976–77 Kilmarnock	P	12	—
1977–78 Kilmarnock	1	36	2
1978–79 Kilmarnock	1	29	2
1979–80 Kilmarnock	P	4	1
1979–80 Partick T	P	17	1
1980–81 Partick T	P	26	1
1981–82 Partick T	P	24	4
1982–83 Partick T	1	17	4
1983–84 Partick T	1	32	2
1984–85 Anorthosis		Not known	
1985–86 Hearts	P	22	7
1986–87 Hearts	P	15	1
1987–88 Hearts	P	18	2

JARDINE, Sandy
31.12.48 Edinburgh (DF)
5.9 11.5 Edinburgh Athletic

1965–66 Rangers	1	—	—
1966–67 Rangers	1	14	2
1967–68 Rangers	1	10	—
1968–69 Rangers	1	18	4
1969–70 Rangers	1	10	7
1970–71 Rangers	1	32	1
1971–72 Rangers	1	31	5
1972–73 Rangers	1	34	2
1973–74 Rangers	1	34	3
1974–75 Rangers	P	34	9
1975–76 Rangers	P	25	2
1976–77 Rangers	P	36	2
1977–78 Rangers	P	32	5
1978–79 Rangers	P	35	—
1979–80 Rangers	P	35	3
1980–81 Rangers	P	31	3
1981–82 Rangers	P	36	—
1982–83 Hearts	1	39	2
1983–84 Hearts	P	33	—
1984–85 Hearts	P	34	—
1985–86 Hearts	P	35	—
1986–87 Hearts	P	34	1
1987–88 Hearts	P	9	—

JEFFERS, John
Liverpool (FW)
5.10 10.10 School
LD —

1987–88 Liverpool	1	—	—

JEMSON, Nigel
10.8.69 Preston (MF)
— — YTS
LD Aldershot v <u>Preston NE</u>
3.5.86 0–4

1985–86 Preston NE	4	1	—
1986–87 Preston NE	4	4	3
1987–88 Preston NE	3	27	5
1987–88 Nottingham F	1	—	—

JENKINSON, Leigh
9.7.69 Thorne (FW)
6.0 12.2 Apprentice
LD <u>Hull C</u> v Sheffield U
27.2.88 1–2

1987–88 Hull C	2	3	1

JEWELL, Paul
28.9.64 Liverpool (FW)
5.8 10.8 Apprentice
LD Rotherham U v <u>Wigan Ath</u>
22.12.84 3–3

1982–83 Liverpool	1	—	—
1983–84 Liverpool	1	—	—
1984–85 Wigan Ath	3	26	9
1985–86 Wigan Ath	3	29	6
1986–87 Wigan Ath	3	39	9
1987–88 Wigan Ath	3	43	11

JOBLING, Kevin
1.1.68 Sunderland (MF)
5.9 10.13 Apprentice
LD Newcastle U v <u>Leicester C</u>
4.4.87 2–0

1985–86 Leicester C	1	—	—
1986–87 Leicester C	1	3	—
1987–88 Leicester C	2	6	—
1987–88 Grimsby T	3	15	1

PLAYER DIRECTORY

JOBSON, Richard
9.5.63 Hull (FW)
6.2 12.5 Burton A
LD Watford v Ipswich T
18.12.82 2-1

1982–83	Watford	1	13	1
1983–84	Watford	1	13	2
1984–85	Watford	1	2	1
1984–85	Hull C	3	8	—
1985–86	Hull C	2	36	7
1986–87	Hull C	2	40	5
1987–88	Hull C	2	44	2

JOHNS, Nicky
8.6.57 Bristol (GK)
6.2 11.5 Minehead
LD Carlisle U v Millwall
20.11.76 0-1

1975–76	Millwall	3	—	—
1976–77	Millwall	2	16	—
1977–78	Millwall	2	34	—
From Tampa Bay R, NASL				
1978–79	*Sheffield U*	2	1	—
1978–79	Charlton Ath	2	10	—
1979–80	Charlton Ath	2	34	—
1980–81	Charlton Ath	3	37	—
1981–82	Charlton Ath	2	40	—
1982–83	Charlton Ath	2	42	—
1983–84	Charlton Ath	2	36	—
1984–85	Charlton Ath	2	30	—
1985–86	Charlton Ath	2	38	—
1986–87	Charlton Ath	1	16	—
1987–88	Charlton Ath	1	5	—
1987–88	*QPR*	1	2	—
1987–88	QPR	1	5	—

JOHNSON, Ian
14.2.69 — (DF)
— — Apprentice
LD —

1987–88	Northampton T	3	—	—

JOHNSON, Marvin
29.10.68 Wembley (DF)
5.11½ 11.5 Apprentice
LD Wimbledon v Luton T
5.3.88 2-0

1987–88	Luton T	1	9	—

JOHNSON, Nigel
23.6.64 Rotherham (DF)
6.2½ 12.8 Apprentice
LD Middlesbrough v Rotherham U
12.3.83 1-1

1982–83	Rotherham U	2	11	—
1983–84	Rotherham U	3	43	1
1983–84	*Nottingham F*	1	—	—
1984–85	Rotherham U	3	35	—

1985–86	Manchester C	1	4	—
1986–87	Manchester C	1	—	—
1987–88	Rotherham U	3	23	—

JOHNSON, Paul
25.5.59 Stoke (DF)
5.9 11.3 Apprentice
LD Stoke C v Crystal Palace
30.9.78 1-1

1977–78	Stoke C	2	—	—
1978–79	Stoke C	2	8	—
1979–80	Stoke C	1	25	—
1980–81	Stoke C	1	1	—
1981–82	Shrewsbury T	2	41	1
1982–83	Shrewsbury T	2	33	1
1983–84	Shrewsbury T	2	18	—
1984–85	Shrewsbury T	2	36	1
1985–86	Shrewsbury T	2	13	—
1986–87	Shrewsbury T	2	39	—
1987–88	York C	3	39	—

JOHNSON, Peter
5.10.58 Harrogate (DF)
5.9½ 11.0 Apprentice
LD Birmingham C v Middlesbrough
4.2.78 1-2

1976–77	Middlesbrough	1	—	—
1977–78	Middlesbrough	1	4	—
1978–79	Middlesbrough	1	21	—
1979–80	Middlesbrough	1	18	—
1980–81	Newcastle U	2	16	—
1981–82	Newcastle U	2	—	—
1982–83	Newcastle U	2	—	—
1982–83	*Bristol C*	4	20	—
1982–83	Doncaster R	3	12	—
1983–84	Darlington	4	44	1
1984–85	Darlington	4	45	1
1985–86	Crewe Alex	4	8	—
1985–86	Exeter C	4	5	—
1986–87	Southend U	4	44	2
1987–88	Southend U	3	39	1

JOHNSON, Robert
22.2.62 Bedford (MF)
5.7 11.4 Apprentice
LD Oxford U v Lincoln C
27.8.83 3-0

1983–84	Luton T	1	2	—
1983–84	*Lincoln C*	3	4	—
1984–85	Luton T	1	—	—
1985–86	Luton T	1	15	—
1986–87	Luton T	1	34	—
1987–88	Luton T	1	25	—

JOHNSTON, Craig
8.12.60 S Africa (MF)
5.8½ 10.13 Apprentice
LD Birmingham C v Middlesbrough
4.2.78 1-2

1977–78	Middlesbrough	1	5	1
1978–79	Middlesbrough	1	2	—
1979–80	Middlesbrough	1	30	5
1980–81	Middlesbrough	1	27	10
1980–81	Liverpool	1	—	—
1981–82	Liverpool	1	18	6
1982–83	Liverpool	1	33	7
1983–84	Liverpool	1	29	2
1984–85	Liverpool	1	11	—
1985–86	Liverpool	1	41	7
1986–87	Liverpool	1	28	3
1987–88	Liverpool	1	30	5

JONES, Alex
27.11.64 Blackburn (DF)
6.0 11.6 Apprentice
LD Grimsby T v Oldham Ath
30.4.83 0-2

1982–83	Oldham Ath	2	2	—
1983–84	Oldham Ath	2	2	—
1984–85	Oldham Ath	2	5	—
1984–85	*Stockport Co*	4	3	—
1985–86	Oldham Ath	2	—	—
1986–87	Preston NE	4	46	1
1987–88	Preston NE	3	22	2

JONES, Andy
9.1.63 Wrexham (FW)
5.10 12.7 Rhyl
LD Exeter C v Port Vale
17.8.85 1-0

1985–86	Port Vale	4	41	12
1986–87	Port Vale	3	43	29
1987–88	Port Vale	3	6	6
1987–88	Charlton Ath	1	25	6

JONES, Joey
4.3.55 Llandudno (DF)
5.10 11.7 Amateur
LD Rotherham U v Wrexham
20.1.73 1-1

1972–73	Wrexham	3	17	—
1973–74	Wrexham	3	41	—
1974–75	Wrexham	3	40	2
1975–76	Liverpool	1	13	—
1976–77	Liverpool	1	39	3
1977–78	Liverpool	1	20	—
1978–79	Liverpool	1	—	—
1978–79	Wrexham	2	30	2
1979–80	Wrexham	2	36	3
1980–81	Wrexham	2	37	1
1981–82	Wrexham	2	36	—
1982–83	Wrexham	3	7	—
1982–83	Chelsea	2	28	1
1983–84	Chelsea	2	34	1
1984–85	Chelsea	1	16	—
1985–86	Huddersfield T	2	38	1
1986–87	Huddersfield T	2	30	2
1987–88	Wrexham	4	35	—

JONES, Keith
14.10.65 Dulwich (MF)
5.6½ 10.9 Apprentice
LD Chelsea v Barnsley
26.3.83 0–3

1982–83	Chelsea	2	2	—
1983–84	Chelsea	2	—	—
1984–85	Chelsea	1	19	2
1985–86	Chelsea	1	14	2
1986–87	Chelsea	1	17	3
1987–88	Chelsea	1	—	—
1987–88	Brentford	3	36	1

JONES, Linden
5.3.61 Tredegar (DF)
5.6 11.2 Apprentice
LD Cardiff C v Orient
24.2.79 1–0

1978–79	Cardiff C	2	14	—
1979–80	Cardiff C	2	17	1
1980–81	Cardiff C	2	29	1
1981–82	Cardiff C	2	36	—
1982–83	Cardiff C	3	43	—
1983–84	Cardiff C	2	6	—
1983–84	Newport Co	3	32	—
1984–85	Newport Co	3	44	4
1985–86	Newport Co	3	31	1
1986–87	Newport Co	3	34	—
1987–88	Reading	2	28	3

JONES, Mark
22.10.61 Warley (DF)
5.6 10.5½ Apprentice
LD Aston Villa v Coventry C
27.2.82 2–1

1979–80	Aston Villa	1	—	—
1980–81	Aston Villa	1	—	—
1981–82	Aston Villa	1	2	—
1982–83	Aston Villa	1	17	—
1983–84	Aston Villa	1	5	—
1983–84	Brighton & HA	2	6	—
1984–85	Brighton & HA	2	3	—
1984–85	Birmingham C	2	10	—
1985–86	Birmingham C	1	19	—
1986–87	Birmingham C	2	5	—
1987–88	Hereford U	4	28	—

JONES, Mark
26.9.61 Berinsfield (FW)
5.8 9.12 Apprentice
LD Oxford U v Exeter C
29.3.80 2–0

1979–80	Oxford U	3	2	—
1980–81	Oxford U	3	36	1
1981–82	Oxford U	3	21	3
1982–83	Oxford U	3	26	1
1983–84	Oxford U	3	20	2
1984–85	Oxford U	2	18	—
1985–86	Oxford U	1	6	—
1986–87	Swindon T	3	40	9
1987–88	Swindon T	2	—	—

JONES, Mark
4.1.68 Walsall (FW)
5.8 10.1 Apprentice
LD Blackpool v Walsall
22.8.87 1–2

1985–86	Walsall	3	—	—
1986–87	Walsall	3	—	—
1987–88	Walsall	3	8	—

JONES, Paul
6.9.65 Walsall (MF)
5.9 10.4 Apprentice
LD Walsall v Gillingham
5.2.83 0–0

1982–83	Walsall	3	2	—
1983–84	Walsall	3	4	—
1984–85	Walsall	3	22	—
1985–86	Walsall	3	26	1
1986–87	Walsall	3	27	3
1987–88	Walsall	3	43	11

JONES, Tom
7.10.64 Aldershot (MF)
5.10 11.7 Weymouth
LD Aberdeen v Dundee
10.10.87 0–0

1987–88	Aberdeen	P	28	3

JONES, Vaughan
2.9.59 Tonyrefail (DF)
5.8 12.0 Apprentice
LD Bristol R v Bolton W
17.5.77 2–2

1976–77	Bristol R	2	1	—
1977–78	Bristol R	2	—	—
1978–79	Bristol R	2	22	1
1979–80	Bristol R	2	23	1
1980–81	Bristol R	2	21	1
1981–82	Bristol R	3	34	—
1982–83	Newport Co	3	43	—
1983–84	Newport Co	3	25	4
1984–85	Cardiff C	2	11	—
1984–85	Bristol R	3	20	—
1985–86	Bristol R	3	32	—
1986–87	Bristol R	3	34	1
1987–88	Bristol R	3	46	3

JONES, Vince
5.1.65 Watford (MF)
5.10 11.10 Wealdstone
LD Nottingham F v Wimbledon
22.11.86 3–2

1986–87	Wimbledon	1	22	4
1987–88	Wimbledon	1	24	2

JONSSON, Siggi
27.9.66 Akranes (MF)
5.11 11.11 I A Akranes
LD Leicester C v Sheffield W
9.3.85 3–1

1984–85	Sheffield W	1	3	—
1985–86	Sheffield W	1	10	2
1985–86	*Barnsley*	2	5	—
1986–87	Sheffield W	1	13	—
1987–88	Sheffield W	1	13	1

JORDAN, Joe
15.12.51 Carlisle (FW)
6.0½ 12.3

1968–69	Morton	1	5	1
1969–70	Morton	1	5	1
1970–71	Morton	1	2	—
1970–71	Leeds U	1	—	—
1971–72	Leeds U	1	12	—
1972–73	Leeds U	1	26	9
1973–74	Leeds U	1	33	7
1974–75	Leeds U	1	29	4
1975–76	Leeds U	1	17	2
1976–77	Leeds U	1	32	10
1977–78	Leeds U	1	20	3
1977–78	Manchester U	1	14	3
1978–79	Manchester U	1	30	6
1979–80	Manchester U	1	32	13
1980–81	Manchester U	1	33	15
1981–82	AC Milan (I)	A	22	2
1982–83	AC Milan (I)	B	30	10
1983–84	Verona	A	12	1
1984–85	Southampton	1	34	12
1985–86	Southampton	1	12	—
1986–87	Southampton	1	2	—
1986–87	Bristol C	3	19	3
1987–88	Bristol C	3	28	4

JOSEPH, Francis
6.3.60 Kilburn (FW)
5.10 12.0 Hillingdon Bor
LD Wimbledon v Darlington
6.12.80 1–1

1980–81	Wimbledon	4	11	1
1981–82	Wimbledon	3	40	13
1982–83	Brentford	3	43	24
1983–84	Brentford	3	43	18
1984–85	Brentford	3	3	—
1985–86	Brentford	3	8	1
1986–87	Brentford	3	13	1
1986–87	*Wimbledon*	1	5	1
1987–88	Reading	2	11	—

JOSEPH, Roger
24.12.65 Paddington (DF)
6.0 12.0 Juniors
LD Brentford v Millwall
19.5.85 1–1

1984–85	Brentford	3	1	—
1985–86	Brentford	3	28	1
1986–87	Brentford	3	32	1
1987–88	Brentford	3	43	—

JOYCE, Joe
18.3.61 Consett (DF)
5.8 10.5 School
LD Reading v Barnsley
29.12.79 7–0

1979–80	Barnsley	3	8	—
1980–81	Barnsley	3	33	—
1981–82	Barnsley	2	20	—
1982–83	Barnsley	2	32	1
1983–84	Barnsley	2	40	1
1984–85	Barnsley	2	41	—
1985–86	Barnsley	2	40	—
1986–87	Barnsley	2	34	—
1987–88	Barnsley	2	38	2

PLAYER DIRECTORY

JOYCE, Warren
20.1.65 Oldham (MF)
5.8½ 11.5 Local
LD Carlisle U v <u>Bolton W</u>
5.4.83 5–0

1982–83 Bolton W	2	8	—
1983–84 Bolton W	3	45	3
1984–85 Bolton W	3	45	5
1985–86 Bolton W	3	31	4
1986–87 Bolton W	3	44	5
1987–88 Bolton W	4	11	—
1987–88 Preston NE	3	22	—

JUDGE, Alan
14.5.60 Kingsbury (GK)
5.11 11.5½ Amateur
LD Newcastle U v <u>Luton T</u>
3.5.80 2–2

1977–78 Luton T	2	—	—
1978–79 Luton T	2	—	—
1979–80 Luton T	2	1	—
1980–81 Luton T	2	2	—
1981–82 Luton T	2	4	—
1982–83 Luton T	1	4	—
1982–83 *Reading*	3	33	—
1983–84 Reading	4	41	—
1984–85 Reading	3	3	—
1984–85 Oxford U	2	—	—
1985–86 Oxford U	1	19	—
1985–86 *Lincoln C*	3	2	—
1986–87 Oxford U	1	9	—
1987–88 Oxford U	1	9	—
1987–88 *Cardiff C*	4	8	—

JURYEFF, Ian
24.11.62 Gosport (FW)
5.11 12.0 Apprentice
LD Coventry C v <u>Southampton</u>
26.11.84 0–0

1980–81 Southampton	1	—	—
1981–82 Southampton	1	—	—
1982–83 Southampton	1	—	—
1983–84 Southampton	1	2	—
1983–84 *Mansfield T*	4	12	5
1984–85 Southampton	1	—	—
1984–85 Reading	3	7	1
1984–85 Orient	3	19	7
1985–86 Orient	4	27	10
1986–87 Orient	4	13	2
1987–88 Leyton Orient	4	23	16

KAMARA, Alan
15.7.58 Sheffield (DF)
5.8½ 10.8 Burton A
LD Scunthorpe U v <u>Scarborough</u>
7.11.87 0–1

1987–88 Scarborough	4	29	—

KAMARA, Chris
25.12.57 Middlesbrough (MF)
6.1 12.0 Apprentice
LD <u>Portsmouth</u> v Luton T
6.9.75 0–2

1975–76 Portsmouth	2	24	4
1976–77 Portsmouth	3	39	3
1977–78 Swindon T	3	40	10
1978–79 Swindon T	3	28	2
1979–80 Swindon T	3	34	5
1980–81 Swindon T	3	45	4
1981–82 Portsmouth	3	11	—
1981–82 Brentford	3	31	5
1982–83 Brentford	3	44	11
1983–84 Brentford	3	38	6
1984–85 Brentford	3	39	6
1985–86 Swindon T	4	20	1
1986–87 Swindon T	3	42	3
1987–88 Swindon T	2	25	2

KANE, Paul
20.6.65 Edinburgh (MF)
5.8 9.9 Salvesen BC
LD Dundee U v <u>Hibernian</u>
10.9.83 5–0

1982–83 Hibernian	P	—	—
1983–84 Hibernian	P	13	1
1984–85 Hibernian	P	34	8
1985–86 Hibernian	P	32	5
1986–87 Hibernian	P	37	1
1987–88 Hibernian	P	44	10

KASULE, Victor
28.5.65 Glasgow (FW)
5.10 10.3
LD <u>Albion R</u> v Cowdenbeath
13.4.83 2–0

1982–83 Albion R	2	5	1
1983–84 Albion R	2	31	3
1984–85 Albion R	2	29	3
1985–86 Albion R	2	36	6
1986–87 Albion R	2	31	5
1986–87 Meadowbank	2	7	1
1987–88 Meadowbank	1	28	6
1987–88 Shrewsbury T	2	14	3

KAY, John
29.1.64 Sunderland (DF)
5.10 11.6 Apprentice
LD WBA v <u>Arsenal</u>
26.2.83 0–0

1981–82 Arsenal	1	—	—
1982–83 Arsenal	1	7	—
1983–84 Arsenal	1	7	—
1984–85 Wimbledon	2	21	1
1984–85 *Middlesbrough*	2	8	—
1985–86 Wimbledon	2	26	1
1986–87 Wimbledon	1	16	—
1987–88 Sunderland	3	46	—

KEANE, Tommy
16.9.68 Galway (FW)
5.6½ 10.4 Apprentice
LD <u>Bournemouth</u> v Walsall
3.5.86 0–1

1985–86 Bournemouth	3	1	—
1986–87 Bournemouth	3	—	—
1987–88 Bournemouth	2	2	—
1987–88 Colchester U	4	16	—

KEARNEY, Mark
12.6.62 Ormskirk (DF)
5.10 11.0 Marine
LD <u>Mansfield T</u> v Colchester U
19.3.83 1–1

1981–82 Everton	1	—	—
1982–83 Everton	1	—	—
1982–83 Mansfield T	4	11	1
1983–84 Mansfield T	4	17	2
1984–85 Mansfield T	4	38	4
1985–86 Mansfield T	4	31	7
1986–87 Mansfield T	3	43	10
1987–88 Mansfield T	3	4	—

KEARNS, Ollie
12.6.56 Banbury (FW)
6.0 12.0 Banbury U
LD <u>Reading</u> v Tranmere R
30.4.77 0–0

1976–77 Reading	3	5	2
1977–78 Reading	4	27	16
1978–79 Reading	4	27	11
1979–80 Reading	3	27	11
1980–81 Reading	3	—	—
1981–82 Oxford U	3	18	4
1982–83 Walsall	3	38	11
1983–84 Hereford U	4	41	10
1984–85 Hereford U	4	45	18
1985–86 Hereford U	4	33	13
1986–87 Hereford U	4	40	16
1987–88 Hereford U	4	11	1
1987–88 Wrexham	4	17	8

KEELEY, Glenn
1.9.54 Barking (DF)
6.2 13.1 Apprentice
LD <u>Ipswich T</u> v Manchester U
17.2.73 4–1

1972–73 Ipswich T	1	1	—
1973–74 Ipswich T	1	3	—
1974–75 Newcastle U	1	39	2
1975–76 Newcastle U	1	5	—
1976–77 Blackburn R	2	33	—
1977–78 Blackburn R	2	27	—
1978–79 Blackburn R	2	26	—
1979–80 Blackburn R	3	45	3
1980–81 Blackburn R	2	42	2
1981–82 Blackburn R	2	41	3
1982–83 Blackburn R	2	14	4
1982–83 *Everton*	1	1	—
1983–84 Blackburn R	2	35	4
1984–85 Blackburn R	2	41	2
1985–86 Blackburn R	2	31	4
1986–87 Blackburn R	2	35	1
1987–88 Oldham Ath	2	11	—
1987–88 *Colchester U*	4	4	—

PLAYER DIRECTORY

KEELEY, John
27.7.61 Plaistow (GK)
6.1 14.2 Apprentice
LD <u>Southend U</u> v Colchester U
12.10.79 0–1

1979–80	Southend U	3	4 —
1980–81	Southend U	4	— —
1981–82	Southend U	3	27 —
1982–83	Southend U	3	7 —
1983–84	Southend U	3	16 —
1984–85	Southend U	4	9 —
1985–86	Non–League	—	— —
1986–87	Brighton & HA	2	20 —
1987–88	Brighton & HA	3	46 —

KEEN, Kevin
25.2.67 Amersham (MF)
5.7 10.4 Wycombe W and
Apprentice
LD <u>West Ham U</u> v Liverpool
6.9.86 2–5

1983–84	West Ham U	1	— —
1984–85	West Ham U	1	— —
1985–86	West Ham U	1	— —
1986–87	West Ham U	1	13 —
1987–88	West Ham U	1	23 1

KELLY, Alan
11.8.68 Preston NE (GK)
6.2 12.5
LD Aldershot v <u>Preston NE</u>
3.5.86 4–0

1985–86	Preston NE	4	13 —
1986–87	Preston NE	4	22 —
1987–88	Preston NE	3	19 —

KELLY, David
25.11.65 Birmingham (FW)
5.11 11.1 Alvechurch
LD Millwall v <u>Walsall</u>
14.4.84 2–0

1983–84	Walsall	3	6 3
1984–85	Walsall	3	32 7
1985–86	Walsall	3	28 10
1986–87	Walsall	3	42 23
1987–88	Walsall	3	39 20

KELLY, Gary
3.8.66 Fulwood (GK)
5.10½ 12.3 Apprentice
LD <u>Newcastle U</u> v Wimbledon
20.9.86 1–0

1984–85	Newcastle U	1	— —
1985–86	Newcastle U	1	— —
1986–87	Newcastle U	1	3 —
1987–88	Newcastle U	1	37 —

KELLY, Gavin
29.9.68 Beverly (FW)
— — Apprentice
LD —

1987–88	Hull C	2	— —

KELLY, John
20.10.60 Bebbington (FW)
5.10 10.9 Cammell Laird
LD <u>Tranmere R</u> v Doncaster R
17.9.80 1–0

1979–80	Tranmere R	4	28 4
1980–81	Tranmere R	4	29 5
1981–82	Tranmere R	4	7 —
1981–82	Preston NE	3	30 5
1982–83	Preston NE	3	29 2
1983–84	Preston NE	3	34 13
1984–85	Preston NE	3	37 7
1985–86	Chester C	4	43 8
1986–87	Chester C	3	42 9
1987–88	Swindon T	2	7 1
1987–88	*Oldham Ath*	2	— —
1987–88	Oldham Ath	2	10 —

KELLY, Mark
27.11.69 Basingstoke (FW)
5.9 10.4 Apprentice
LD West Ham U v <u>Portsmouth</u>
13.2.88 1–1

1987–88	Portsmouth	1	3 —

KELLY, Mark
7.10.66 Blackpool (MF)
5.8 10.6
LD <u>Cardiff C</u> v Leyton Orient
15.8.87 1–1

1985–86	Shrewsbury T	2	— —
1986–87	Shrewsbury T	2	— —
1987–88	Cardiff C	4	36 1

KELLY, Robert
21.12.64 Birmingham (MF)
5.9½ 10.10 Apprentice
LD <u>Leicester C</u> v Sunderland
12.5.84 0–2

1982–83	Leicester C	2	— —
1983–84	Leicester C	1	1 —
1984–85	Leicester C	1	— —
1984–85	*Tranmere R*	4	5 2
1985–86	Leicester C	1	9 —
1986–87	Leicester C	1	14 1
1986–87	Wolves	4	14 2
1987–88	Wolves	4	— —

KELLY, Tom
28.3.64 Bellshill (DF)
5.10 11.10 Hibs
LD Cambridge U v <u>Hartlepool U</u>
17.8.86 4–2

1985–86	Hartlepool U	4	15 —
1986–87	Torquay U	4	38 —
1987–88	Torquay U	4	38 —

KELLY, Tony
1.10.64 Prescot (DF)
5.10 12.7 Liverpool Apprentice
LD <u>Wigan Ath</u> v Walsall
26.11.83 0–1

1983–84	Derby Co	2	— —
1983–84	Wigan Ath	3	29 2
1984–85	Wigan Ath	3	40 4
1985–86	Wigan Ath	3	32 9
1985–86	Stoke C	2	1 —
1986–87	Stoke C	2	35 4
1987–88	WBA	2	26 1

KENDALL, Mark
20.9.58 Blackwood (GK)
6.0 13.9 Apprentice
LD Norwich c v <u>Tottenham H</u>
4.11.78 2–2

1976–77	Tottenham H	1	— —
1977–78	Tottenham H	2	— —
1978–79	Tottenham H	1	23 —
1979–80	Tottenham H	1	2 —
1979–80	*Chesterfield*	3	9 —
1980–81	Tottenham H	1	4 —
1980–81	Newport Co	3	28 —
1981–82	Newport Co	3	46 —
1982–83	Newport Co	3	44 —
1983–84	Newport Co	3	43 —
1984–85	Newport Co	3	44 —
1985–86	Newport Co	3	46 —
1986–87	Newport Co	3	21 —
1986–87	Wolves	4	24 —
1987–88	Wolves	4	46 —

KENNEDY, Alex
25.6.63 Irvine (DF)
6.0 11.7 Craigmark Juniors
LD <u>Motherwell</u> v Aberdeen
11.2.84 0–4

1982–83	Motherwell	P	— —
1983–84	Motherwell	P	11 —
1984–85	Motherwell	1	16 2
1985–86	Motherwell	P	20 1
1986–87	Motherwell	P	26 1
1987–88	Motherwell	P	2 —

KENNEDY, Andy
8.10.64 Stirling (FW)
6.1 11.8 Sauchie Ath
LD <u>Rangers</u> v Motherwell
6.11.82 4–0

1982–83	Rangers	P	13 3
1983–84	Rangers	P	2 —
1984–85	Birmingham C	2	7 4
1985–86	Birmingham C	1	32 6
1986–87	Birmingham C	2	9 1
1986–87	*Sheffield U*	2	9 1
1987–88	Birmingham C	2	28 7

PLAYER DIRECTORY

KENNEDY, Mick
9.4.61 Salford (MF)
5.10 10.6· Apprentice
LD Bradford C v <u>Halifax T</u>
27.9.78 3–0

1978–79	Halifax T	4	30	—
1979–80	Halifax T	4	46	4
1980–81	Huddersfield T	3	42	2
1981–82	Huddersfield T	3	39	7
1982–83	Middlesbrough	2	38	5
1983–84	Middlesbrough	2	30	—
1984–85	Portsmouth	2	37	—
1985–86	Portsmouth	2	39	2
1986–87	Portsmouth	2	35	2
1987–88	Portsmouth	1	18	—
1987–88	Bradford C	2	15	1

KENT, Kevin
19.3.65 Stoke (FW)
5.10½ 11.0 Apprentice
LD <u>WBA</u> v Everton
11.2.84 1–1

1982–83	WBA	1	—	—
1983–84	WBA	1	2	—
1984–85	Newport Co	3	33	1
1985–86	Mansfield T	4	34	8
1986–87	Mansfield T	3	46	6
1987–88	Mansfield T	3	45	10

KENWORTHY, Tony
30.10.58 Leeds (DF)
5.10 10.7 Apprentice
LD Norwich C v <u>Sheffield U</u>
3.4.76 1–3

1975–76	Sheffield U	1	6	—
1976–77	Sheffield U	2	37	1
1977–78	Sheffield U	2	20	1
1978–79	Sheffield U	2	37	3
1979–80	Sheffield U	3	41	3
1980–81	Sheffield U	3	37	7
1981–82	Sheffield U	4	45	15
1982–83	Sheffield U	3	23	3
1983–84	Sheffield U	3	8	1
1984–85	Sheffield U	2	19	—
1985–86	Sheffield U	2	13	—
1985–86	*Mansfield T*	4	13	—
1986–87	Mansfield T	3	36	—
1987–88	Mansfield T	3	30	—

KEOWN, Martin
24.7.66 Oxford (DF)
6.1 12.4 Apprentice
LD Manchester C v <u>Brighton & HA</u>
23.2.85 2–0

1983–84	Arsenal	1	—	—
1984–85	Arsenal	1	—	—
1984–85	*Brighton & HA*	2	16	—
1985–86	Arsenal	1	22	—
1985–86	*Brighton & HA*	2	7	1
1986–87	Aston Villa	1	36	—
1987–88	Aston Villa	2	42	3

KERNAGHAN, Alan
25.4.67 Otley (FW)
6.1 12.12½ Apprentice
LD <u>Middlesbrough</u> v Notts Co
9.2.85 0–1

1984–85	Middlesbrough	2	8	1
1985–86	Middlesbrough	2	6	—
1986–87	Middlesbrough	3	13	—
1987–88	Middlesbrough	2	35	6

KERR, Jim
17.1.59 Hamilton (DF)
5.11 11.7 Stonehouse Violet
LD Morton v <u>Dundee U</u>
29.9.79 4–1

1978–79	Dundee U	P	—	—
1979–80	Dundee U	P	2	—
1980–81	Dundee U	P	—	—
1981–82	Airdrieonians	P	8	—
1982–83	Raith R	1	29	6
1983–84	Raith R	1	39	16
1984–85	Raith R	2	3	—
1984–85	Brechin C	1	31	3
1985–86	Brechin C	1	35	2
1986–87	Falkirk	P	36	2
1987–88	Falkirk	P	7	—
1987–88	Hamilton A	1	24	—

KERR, Paul
9.6.64 Portsmouth (FW)
5.8 11.11 Apprentice
LD Leicester C v <u>Aston Villa</u>
14.4.84 2–0

1982–83	Aston Villa	1	—	—
1983–84	Aston Villa	1	2	—
1984–85	Aston Villa	1	10	—
1985–86	Aston Villa	1	6	1
1986–87	Aston Villa	1	6	2
1986–87	Middlesbrough	3	20	—
1987–88	Middlesbrough	2	44	5

KERRINS, Wayne
5.8.65 Essex (FW)
5.8½ 11.2 Apprentice
LD Carlisle U v <u>Fulham</u>
20.11.84 3–0

1983–84	Fulham	2	—	—
1984–85	Fulham	2	2	—
1984–85	*Port Vale*	4	7	—
1985–86	Fulham	2	16	—
1986–87	Fulham	3	30	1
1987–88	Fulham	3	14	—

KERSLAKE, David
19.6.66 London (MF)
5.8 11.4 Apprentice
LD Newcastle U v <u>QPR</u>
13.4.85 1–0

1983–84	QPR	1	—	—
1984–85	QPR	1	1	—
1985–86	QPR	1	14	1
1986–87	QPR	1	3	—
1987–88	QPR	1	18	5

KETTERIDGE, Steve
7.11.59 Stevenage (MF)
5.8½ 10.7 Apprentice
LD <u>Wimbledon</u> v Wigan Ath
9.9.78 2–1

1977–78	Wimbledon	4	—	—
1978–79	Wimbledon	4	17	1
1979–80	Wimbledon	3	34	6
1980–81	Wimbledon	4	39	1
1981–82	Wimbledon	3	36	7
1982–83	Wimbledon	4	39	6
1983–84	Wimbledon	3	43	7
1984–85	Wimbledon	2	29	4
1985–86	Crystal Palace	2	33	4
1986–87	Crystal Palace	2	26	2
1987–88	Leyton Orient	4	26	1

KEVAN, David
31.8.68 Wigtown (MF)
Apprentice
LD Gillingham v <u>Notts Co</u>
1.2.86 4–0

1985–86	Notts Co	3	3	—
1986–87	Notts Co	3	33	1
1987–88	Notts Co	3	32	—

KIDD, Walter
10.3.58 Edinburgh (DF)
5.11 12.3 Newtongrange Star
LD Montrose v <u>Hearts</u>
19.10.77 3–1

1977–78	Hearts	1	23	—
1978–79	Hearts	P	30	—
1979–80	Hearts	1	34	2
1980–81	Hearts	P	25	1
1981–82	Hearts	1	30	—
1982–83	Hearts	1	37	—
1983–84	Hearts	P	31	1
1984–85	Hearts	P	33	1
1985–86	Hearts	P	28	—
1986–87	Hearts	P	35	—
1987–88	Hearts	P	18	—

KIELY, Dean
10.10.70 Manchester (GK)
— — Trainee
LD —

1987–88	Coventry C	1	—	—

KILCLINE, Brian
7.5.62 Nottingham (DF)
6.2 12.0 Apprentice
LD Bristol R v <u>Notts Co</u>
6.10.79 2–3

1979–80	Notts Co	2	16	1
1980–81	Notts Co	2	42	1
1981–82	Notts Co	1	36	3
1982–83	Notts Co	1	40	3
1983–84	Notts Co	1	24	1
1984–85	Coventry C	1	26	2
1985–86	Coventry C	1	32	7
1986–87	Coventry C	1	29	3
1987–88	Coventry C	1	28	8

KIMBLE, Alan
6.8.66 Poole (DF)
LD <u>Charlton Ath</u> v Sheffield U
16.4.85 0–0

1984–85 Charlton Ath	2	6	—
1985–86 Charlton Ath	2	—	—
1985–86 *Exeter C*	4	1	—
1986–87 Cambridge U	4	35	—
1987–88 Cambridge U	4	41	2

KIMBLE, Garry
6.8.66 Poole (FW)
LD <u>Charlton Ath</u> v Huddersfield T
28.8.84 2–2

1984–85 Charlton Ath	2	9	1
1985–86 Charlton Ath	2	—	—
1985–86 *Exeter C*	4	1	—
1986–87 Cambridge U	4	29	2
1987–88 Cambridge U	4	12	—
1987–88 Doncaster R	3	34	1

KING, Phil
28.12.67 Bristol (DF)
5.9 11.0 Apprentice
LD <u>Exeter C</u> v Halifax T
23.2.85 1–0

1984–85 Exeter C	4	16	—
1985–86 Exeter C	4	11	—
1986–87 Torquay U	4	24	3
1986–87 Swindon T	3	21	—
1987–88 Swindon T	2	44	1

KINNAIRD, Paul
11.11.66 Glasgow (FW)
5.8 10.10 Apprentice
LD <u>Dundee U</u> v Clydebank
18.10.86 2–0

1984–85 Norwich C	1	—	—
1985–86 Dundee U	P	—	—
1986–87 Dundee U	P	7	—
1987–88 Dundee U	P	11	—
1987–88 Motherwell	P	10	—

KIRK, Steve
3.1.63 Kirkcaldy (MF)
5.11 11.4 Buckhaven Hibs
LD Albion R v <u>East Fife</u>
22.10.83 1–2

1979–80 East Fife	2	25	2
1980–81 Stoke C	1	—	—
1981–82 Stoke C	1	12	—
1982–83 Partick Th	1	—	—
1982–83 East Fife	2	25	8
1983–84 East Fife	2	33	5
1984–85 East Fife	1	38	8
1985–86 East Fife	1	39	14
1986–87 Motherwell	P	35	10
1987–88 Motherwell	P	38	4

KIRKHAM, Paul
5.7.69 Manchester (FW)
— — Manchester U Apprentice
LD <u>Huddersfield T</u> v Ipswich T
8.4.88 1–2

1987–88 Huddersfield T	2	1	—

KIRKWOOD, Billy
1.9.58 Edinburgh (MF)
5.10 11.0 'S' Form
LD <u>Dundee U</u> v Hearts
20.4.77 1–2

1976–77 Dundee U	P	4	1
1977–78 Dundee U	P	27	4
1978–79 Dundee U	P	34	9
1979–80 Dundee U	P	28	3
1980–81 Dundee U	P	29	10
1981–82 Dundee U	P	32	2
1982–83 Dundee U	P	31	3
1983–84 Dundee U	P	26	9
1984–85 Dundee U	P	23	1
1985–86 Dundee U	P	15	1
1986–87 Dundee U	P	11	1
1986–87 Hibernian	P	26	1
1987–88 Dundee U	P	1	—
1987–88 Dumfermline A	P	24	—
1987–88 Dundee	P	9	—

KIRKWOOD, David
27.8.67 St Andrews (MF)
5.10 11.7 Leven Royal Colts
LD Albion R v <u>East Fife</u>
22.10.83 1–2

1983–84 East Fife	2	14	2
1984–85 East Fife	1	17	4
1985–86 East Fife	1	34	2
1986–87 East Fife	1	35	4
1987–88 Rangers	P	4	—

KITE, Phil
26.10.62 Bristol (GK)
6.1½ 14.7 Apprentice
LD Derby Co v <u>Bristol R</u>
10.1.81 2–1

1980–81 Bristol R	2	4	—
1981–82 Bristol R	3	27	—
1982–83 Bristol R	3	46	—
1983–84 Bristol R	3	19	—
1983–84 *Tottenham H*	1	—	—
1984–85 Southampton	1	1	—
1985–86 Southampton	1	3	—
1985–86 *Middlesbrough*	2	2	—
1986–87 Gillingham	3	17	—
1987–88 Gillingham	3	26	—

KIWOMYA, Andrew
1.10.67 Huddersfield (FW)
5.9 10.5 Apprentice
LD Grimsby T v <u>Barnsley</u>
22.4.86 1–2

1985–86 Barnsley	2	1	—
1986–87 Sheffield W	1	—	—
1987–88 Sheffield W	1	—	—

KIWOMYA, Chris
2.12.69 Huddersfield (FW)
5.9 10.7 Apprentice
LD —

1987–88 Ipswich T	2	—	—

KNIGHT, Alan
3.7.61 Balham (GK)
6.1 13.1½ Apprentice
LD Rotherham U v <u>Portsmouth</u>
29.4.78 0–1

1977–78 Portsmouth	3	1	—
1978–79 Portsmouth	4	—	—
1979–80 Portsmouth	4	8	—
1980–81 Portsmouth	3	1	—
1981–82 Portsmouth	3	45	—
1982–83 Portsmouth	3	46	—
1983–84 Portsmouth	2	42	—
1984–85 Portsmouth	2	42	—
1985–86 Portsmouth	2	38	—
1986–87 Portsmouth	2	42	—
1987–88 Portsmouth	1	36	—

KNIGHT, Ian
26.10.66 Hartlepool (DF)
6.2 12.4 Apprentice
LD <u>Sheffield W</u> v Aston Villa
19.4.86 2–0

1984–85 Barnsley	2	—	—
1985–86 Sheffield W	1	4	—
1986–87 Sheffield W	1	15	—
1987–88 Sheffield W	1	—	—

KNILL, Alan
8.10.64 Slough (DF)
6.2½ 10.9 Apprentice
LD <u>Halifax T</u> v Blackpool
25.8.85 0–2

1982–83 Southampton	1	—	—
1983–84 Southampton	1	—	—
1984–85 Halifax T	4	44	1
1985–86 Halifax T	4	33	2
1986–87 Halifax T	4	41	3
1987–88 Swansea C	4	46	1

KUHL, Martin
10.1.65 Frimley (MF)
5.11 11.13 Apprentice
LD WBA v <u>Birmingham C</u>
19.3.83 2–0

1982–83 Birmingham C	1	2	—
1983–84 Birmingham C	1	22	1
1984–85 Birmingham C	2	27	2
1985–86 Birmingham C	1	37	1
1986–87 Birmingham C	2	23	1
1986–87 Sheffield U	2	10	1
1987–88 Sheffield U	2	28	3
1987–88 Watford	1	4	—

PLAYER DIRECTORY

LAKE, Paul
28.10.68 Manchester (MF)
— — Trainee.
LD Wimbledon v Manchester C
24.1.87 0–0

1986–87 Manchester C	1	3	1
1987–88 Manchester C	2	33	3

LAMB, Alan
30.10.70 Gateshead (FW)
— — Apprentice
LD —

1987–88 Nottingham F	1	—	—

LAMBERT, Paul
7.8.69 Glasgow (MF)
5.8 9.8 Linwood Rangers BC
LD Motherwell v St Mirren
12.4.86 1–2

1985–86 St Mirren	P	1	—
1986–87 St Mirren	P	36	2
1987–88 St Mirren	P	36	2

LANE, Martin
12.4.61 Altrincham (DF)
5.9 11.3 Amateur
LD Chester C v Crewe Alex
28.8.82 1–0

1979–80 Manchester U	1	—	—
1980–81 Manchester U	1	—	—
1981–82 Manchester U	1	—	—
1982–83 Chester	4	41	2
1983–84 Chester C	4	38	—
1984–85 Chester C	4	31	—
1985–86 Chester C	4	44	1
1986–87 Chester C	3	21	—
1986–87 Coventry C	1	1	—
1987–88 Coventry C	1	2	—

LANGAN, David
15.2.57 Dublin (DF)
5.10 11.2 Apprentice
LD Derby Co v Leeds U
12.2.77 0–1

1976–77 Derby Co	1	21	—
1977–78 Derby Co	1	42	—
1978–79 Derby Co	1	40	—
1979–80 Derby Co	1	40	1
1980–81 Birmingham C	1	42	—
1981–82 Birmingham C	1	36	1
1982–83 Birmingham C	1	14	2
1983–84 Birmingham C	1	—	—
1984–85 Oxford U	2	39	1
1985–86 Oxford U	1	34	—
1986–87 Oxford U	1	39	—
1987–88 Oxford U	1	2	1
1987–88 *Leicester C*	2	5	—
1987–88 *Bournemouth*	2	3	—
1987–88 Bournemouth	2	17	—

LANGE, Tony
10.12.64 London (GK)
6.0 12.9 Apprentice
LD Fulham v Charlton Ath
10.12.83 0–1

1982–83 Charlton Ath	2	—	—
1983–84 Charlton Ath	2	6	—
1984–85 Charlton Ath	2	2	—
1985–86 Charlton Ath	2	4	—
1985–86 *Aldershot*	4	7	—
1986–87 Aldershot	4	45	—
1987–88 Aldershot	3	35	—

LANGLEY, Kevin
24.5.64 St Helens (DF)
6.1 10.5 Apprentice
LD Wigan v Northampton T
19.9.81 3–1

1981–82 Wigan Ath	4	2	—
1982–83 Wigan Ath	3	28	2
1983–84 Wigan Ath	3	44	1
1984–85 Wigan Ath	3	43	1
1985–86 Wigan Ath	3	43	2
1986–87 Everton	1	16	2
1986–87 *Manchester C*	1	9	—
1987–88 Manchester C	2	—	—
1987–88 *Chester C*	3	9	—
1987–88 Birmingham C	2	7	—

LANGLEY, Richard
20.3.65 London (DF)
5.7 11.5 Corinth.Cas.
LD Mansfield T v Fulham
9.5.87 1–1

1986–87 Fulham	3	1	—
1987–88 Fulham	3	15	—

LATCHFORD, Peter
27.9.52 Birmingham (GK)
6.0 14.2 Apprentice
LD WBA v Sheffield U
26.8.72 0–2

1971–72 WBA	1	—	—
1972–73 WBA	1	26	—
1973–74 WBA	1	42	—
1974–75 WBA	2	13	—
1974–75 Celtic	1	10	—
1975–76 Celtic	P	35	—
1976–77 Celtic	P	31	—
1977–78 Celtic	P	36	—
1978–79 Celtic	P	27	—
1979–80 Celtic	P	36	—
1980–81 Celtic	P	—	—
1981–82 Celtic	P	—	—
1982–83 Celtic	P	—	—
1983–84 Celtic	P	3	—
1984–85 Celtic	P	2	—
1985–86 Celtic	P	6	—
1986–87 Celtic	P	1	—
1987–88 Celtic	P	—	—

LAW, Brian
— — (DF) — School
LD QPR v Sheffield W
23.4.88 1–1

1987–88 QPR	1	1	—

LAW, Nicky
8.9.61 London (DF)
6.0 13.5 Apprentice
LD Shrewsbury T v Barnsley
2.2.82 0–2

1979–80 Arsenal	1	—	—
1980–81 Arsenal	1	—	—
1981–82 Barnsley	2	19	—
1982–83 Barnsley	2	28	—
1983–84 Barnsley	2	31	1
1984–85 Barnsley	2	35	—
1985–86 Barnsley	2	1	—
1985–86 Blackpool	2	39	1
1986–87 Blackpool	3	27	—
1986–87 Plymouth Arg	2	12	2
1987–88 Plymouth Arg	2	26	3

LAWRENCE, Alan
19.8.62 Edinburgh (FW)
5.7 10.0 Easthouses BC
LD Falkirk v Meadowbank Th
18.8.84 3–3

1984–85 Meadowbank	1	35	—
1985–86 Meadowbank	2	38	17
1986–87 Meadowbank	2	29	6
1986–87 Dundee	P	4	1
1987–88 Dundee	P	22	1

LAWRENCE, George
14.9.62 London (FW)
5.10 12.2 Apprentice
LD Southampton v Notts Co
17.10.81 3–1

1980–81 Southampton	1	—	—
1981–82 Southampton	1	4	—
1981–82 *Oxford U*	3	15	4
1982–83 Southampton	1	6	1
1982–83 Oxford U	3	22	9
1983–84 Oxford U	3	34	9
1984–85 Oxford U	2	7	3
1984–85 Southampton	1	11	1
1985–86 Southampton	1	21	2
1986–87 Southampton	1	36	8
1987–88 Millwall	2	17	4

LAWS, Brian
14.10.61 Wallsend (DF)
5.8 11.0 Apprentice
LD Watford v Burnley
3.5.80 4–0

1979–80 Burnley	2	1	—
1980–81 Burnley	3	42	2
1981–82 Burnley	3	44	6
1982–83 Burnley	2	38	4
1983–84 Huddersfield T	2	31	—
1984–85 Huddersfield T	2	25	1
1984–85 Middlesbrough	2	11	1
1985–86 Middlesbrough	2	42	2
1986–87 Middlesbrough	3	26	8
1987–88 Middlesbrough	2	28	1

LEABURN, Carl
30.3.69 Lewisham (FW)
6.3 11.2 Apprentice
LD Charlton Ath v Oxford U
24.3.87 0–0

1986–87 Charlton Ath	1	3	1
1987–88 Charlton Ath	1	12	—

LEANING, Andy
18.5.63 York (GK)
6.1 14.7 Rowntree Mackintosh
LD Newport Co v York C
6.11.85 1–1

1984–85 York C	3	—	—
1985–86 York C	3	30	—
1986–87 York C	3	39	—
1987–88 Sheffield U	2	21	—

LEE, Colin
12.6.56. Plymouth (FW)
6.1 11.9 Apprentice
LD Wrexham v Hereford U
9.11.74 2–1

1974–75 Bristol C	2	—	—
1974–75 *Hereford U*	3	9	—
1975–76 Hereford U	3	—	—
1976–77 Hereford U	2	—	—
1976–77 Torquay U	4	23	10
1977–78 Torquay U	4	12	4
1977–78 Tottenham H	1	25	11
1978–79 Tottenham H	2	27	7
1979–80 Tottenham H	1	10	—
1979–80 Chelsea	2	5	1
1980–81 Chelsea	2	35	15
1981–82 Chelsea	2	40	11
1982–83 Chelsea	2	35	5
1983–84 Chelsea	2	33	3
1984–85 Chelsea	1	22	1
1985–86 Chelsea	1	13	—
1986–87 Chelsea	1	2	—
1987–88 Brentford	3	22	1

LEE, Dave
5.11.67 Manchester (MF)
— — Blackburn Schools
LD Chesterfield v Bury
17.8.85 4–3

1984–85 Bury	4	—	—
1985–86 Bury	3	1	—
1986–87 Bury	3	30	4
1987–88 Bury	3	40	3

LEE, Robert
1.2.66 West Ham (FW)
5.8 10.12 ABTA
LD Charlton Ath v Grimsby T
10.3.84 3–3

1983–84 Charlton Ath	2	11	4
1984–85 Charlton Ath	2	39	10
1985–86 Charlton Ath	2	35	8
1986–87 Charlton Ath	1	33	3
1987–88 Charlton Ath	1	23	2

LEIGHTON, Jim
24.7.58 Johnstone (GK)
6.1 11.9 Dalry Thistle
LD Hearts v Aberdeen
12.8.78 1–4

1978–79 Aberdeen	P	11	—
1979–80 Aberdeen	P	1	—
1980–81 Aberdeen	P	35	—
1981–82 Aberdeen	P	36	—
1982–83 Aberdeen	P	35	—
1983–84 Aberdeen	P	36	—
1984–85 Aberdeen	P	34	—
1985–86 Aberdeen	P	26	—
1986–87 Aberdeen	P	42	—
1987–88 Aberdeen	P	44	—

LEMON, Paul
3.6.66 Middlesbrough (FW)
5.10 11.11 Apprentice
LD Aston Villa v Sunderland
1.12.84 1–0

1984–85 Sunderland	1	11	—
1984–85 *Carlisle U*	2	2	—
1985–86 Sunderland	2	5	—
1986–87 Sunderland	2	32	5
1987–88 Sunderland	3	41	9

LENNON, Daniel
6.4.69 Whitburn (MF)
5.5 9.5 Hutchison Vale BC
LD Hibernian v Morton
7.5.88 3–1

1985–86 Hibernian	P	—	—
1986–87 Hibernian	P	—	—
1987–88 Hibernian	P	1	—

LEONARD, Mark
27.9.62 St Helens (FW)
5.11 11.10 Witton Albion
LD Darlington v Tranmere R
15.2.83 1–0

1981–82 Everton	1	—	—
1982–83 Everton	1	—	—
1982–83 *Tranmere R*	4	7	—
1983–84 Crewe Alex	4	38	10
1984–85 Crewe Alex	4	16	5
1984–85 Stockport Co	4	23	4
1985–86 Stockport Co	4	44	19
1986–87 Stockport Co	4	6	—
1986–87 Bradford C	2	24	3
1987–88 Bradford C	2	28	10

LEONARD, Mick
9.5.59 Carshalton (GK)
5.11 11.0 Epsom & Ewell
LD Halifax T v Darlington
14.2.77 2–1

1976–77 Halifax T	4	19	—
1977–78 Halifax T	4	20	—
1978–79 Halifax T	4	25	—
1979–80 Halifax T	4	5	—
1979–80 Notts Co	2	9	—
1980–81 Notts Co	2	4	—
1981–82 Notts Co	1	—	—
1982–83 Notts Co	1	6	—
1983–84 Notts Co	1	18	—
1984–85 Notts Co	2	31	—
1985–86 Notts Co	3	23	—
1986–87 Notts Co	3	41	—
1987–88 Notts Co	3	45	—

LE SAUX, Graeme
17.10.68 Harrow (DF)
— — Apprentice
LD —

1987–88 Chelsea	1	—	—

LESTER, Mike
4.8.54 Manchester (MF)
5.10 11.7 Apprentice
LD Oldham Ath v York C
26.12.72 1–1

1972–73 Oldham Ath	3	16	1
1973–74 Oldham Ath	3	11	—
1973–74 Manchester C	1	1	—
1974–75 Manchester C	1	—	—
1975–76 Manchester C	1	—	—
1975–76 *Stockport Co*	4	9	1
1976–77 Manchester C	1	1	—
Washington D, NASL			
1977–78 Grimsby T	4	16	3
1978–79 Grimsby T	4	30	7
1979–80 Grimsby T	3	2	—
1979–80 Barnsley	3	33	6
1980–81 Barnsley	3	31	5
1981–82 Exeter C	3	19	6
1981–82 Bradford C	4	18	1
1982–83 Bradford C	3	31	1
1982–83 Scunthorpe U	4	11	3
1983–84 Scunthorpe U	3	33	3
1984–85 Scunthorpe U	4	44	3
1985–86 Scunthorpe U	4	18	—
1985–86 *Hartlepool U*	4	11	1
1986–87 Stockport Co	4	11	—
1987–88 Ludvik Fk (Swe)			
1987–88 Blackpool	3	11	1

LE TISSIER, Matthew
14.10.68 Guernsey (FW)
6.0 11.6 YTS
LD Norwich C v Southampton
30.8.86 4–3

1986–87 Southampton	1	24	6
1987–88 Southampton	1	19	—

LEVEIN, Craig
22.10.64 Dunfermline (DF)
6.0 11.4 Lochore Welfare
LD Cowdenbeath v Brechin C
13.2.82 0–0

1981–82 Cowdenbeath	2	15	—
1982–83 Cowdenbeath	2	30	—
1983–84 Cowdenbeath	2	15	—
1983–84 Hearts	P	22	—
1984–85 Hearts	P	36	1
1985–86 Hearts	P	33	2
1986–87 Hearts	P	12	—
1987–88 Hearts	P	21	—

PLAYER DIRECTORY

LEVITT, Simon
8.1.69 Newham (MF)
5.10 12.2 YTS
LD —

1987–88 West Ham U	1	—	—

LEWINGTON, Ray
7.9.56 Lambeth (MF)
5.6 11.8 Apprentice
LD Notts Co v Chelsea
21.2.76 3–2

1973–74 Chelsea	1	—	—
1974–75 Chelsea	1	—	—
1975–76 Chelsea	2	9	—
1976–77 Chelsea	2	42	2
1977–78 Chelsea	1	24	2
1978–79 Chelsea	1	10	—
Vancouver Whitecaps, NASL			
1979–80 *Wimbledon*	3	23	—
1979–80 Fulham	2	10	1
1980–81 Fulham	3	20	—
1981–82 Fulham	3	31	4
1982–83 Fulham	2	42	10
1983–84 Fulham	2	33	—
1984–85 Fulham	2	38	5
1985–86 Sheffield U	2	36	—
1986–87 Fulham	3	25	—
1987–88 Fulham	3	31	1

LEWIS, Dudley
17.11.62 Swansea (DF)
5.10¼ 10.9 Apprentice
LD Notts Co v Swansea C
7.2.81 2–1

1979–80 Swansea C	2	—	—
1980–81 Swansea C	2	12	—
1981–82 Swansea C	1	1	—
1982–83 Swansea C	1	23	1
1983–84 Swansea C	2	37	—
1984–85 Swansea C	3	43	1
1985–86 Swansea C	3	24	—
1986–87 Swansea C	4	32	—
1987–88 Swansea C	4	18	—

LEWIS, John
15.10.55 Tredegar (MF)
5.10 11.10 Pontllanfraith
LD Cardiff C v Blackburn R
23.9.78 2–0

1978–79 Cardiff C	2	16	—
1979–80 Cardiff C	2	28	2
1980–81 Cardiff C	2	32	1
1981–82 Cardiff C	2	19	1
1982–83 Cardiff C	3	39	5
1983–84 Cardiff C	2	6	—
1983–84 Newport Co	3	25	1
1984–85 Newport Co	3	33	2
1985–86 Newport Co	3	44	1
1986–87 Newport Co	3	43	4
1987–88 Newport Co	4	8	1
1987–88 Swansea C	4	25	—

LEWIS, Mickey
15.2.65 Birmingham (MF)
5.6 10.6 School
LD Coventry C v WBA
26.12.81 0–2

1981–82 WBA	1	4	—
1982–83 WBA	1	5	—
1983–84 WBA	1	14	—
1984–85 WBA	1	1	—
1984–85 Derby Co	2	22	—
1985–86 Derby Co	3	5	1
1986–87 Derby Co	2	—	—
1987–88 Derby Co	1	16	—

LEWORTHY, David
22.10.62 Portsmouth (FW)
5.8½ 11.11 Apprentice
LD Portsmouth v Newport Co
24.10.81 0–0

1980–81 Portsmouth	3	—	—
1981–82 Portsmouth	3	1	—
Fareham T			
1984–85 Tottenham H	1	6	3
1985–86 Tottenham H	1	5	—
1985–86 Oxford U	1	7	4
1986–87 Oxford U	1	18	3
1987–88 Oxford U	1	—	—
1987–88 *Shrewsbury T*	2	6	3

LILLIS, Jason
1.10.69 Chatham (FW)
6.1 12.10 Youth Scheme
LD Gillingham v Southend U
29.8.87 8–1

1987–88 Gillingham	3	7	—

LILLIS, Mark
17.1.60 Manchester (FW)
6.0 12.12 Local
LD Newport Co v Huddersfield T
14.10.78 2–1

1978–79 Huddersfield T	4	12	—
1979–80 Huddersfield T	4	—	—
1980–81 Huddersfield T	3	34	7
1981–82 Huddersfield T	3	42	5
1982–83 Huddersfield T	3	46	20
1983–84 Huddersfield T	2	37	11
1984–85 Huddersfield T	2	35	13
1985–86 Manchester C	1	39	11
1986–87 Derby Co	2	14	1
1987–88 Derby Co	1	1	—
1987–88 Aston Villa	2	29	4

LING, Martin
15.7.66 West Ham (FW)
5.7 9.12 Apprentice
LD Exeter C v Walsall
27.8.83 0–1

1983–84 Exeter C	3	29	—
1984–85 Exeter C	4	42	6
1985–86 Exeter C	4	45	8
1986–87 Swindon T	3	2	—
1986–87 Southend U	4	24	7
1987–88 Southend U	3	42	7

LINIGHAN, Andy
18.6.62 Hartlepool (DF)
6.2½ 12.6 Smiths BC
LD Hartlepool U v Stockport Co
28.3.81 1–0

1980–81 Hartlepool U	4	6	—
1981–82 Hartlepool U	4	17	—
1982–83 Hartlepool U	4	45	3
1983–84 Hartlepool U	4	42	1
1984–85 Leeds U	2	42	2
1985–86 Leeds U	2	24	1
1985–86 Oldham Ath	2	15	1
1986–87 Oldham Ath	2	40	3
1987–88 Oldham Ath	2	32	2
1987–88 Norwich C	1	12	2

LINIGHAN, David
9.1.65 Hartlepool (DF)
6.2 10.12 Local BC
LD Hartlepool U v Bradford C
27.3.82 0–2

1981–82 Hartlepool U	4	6	—
1982–83 Hartlepool U	4	6	1
1983–84 Hartlepool U	4	23	1
1984–85 Hartlepool U	4	17	2
1984–85 *Leeds U*	2	—	—
1985–86 Hartlepool U	4	39	1
1986–87 Derby Co	2	—	—
1986–87 Shrewsbury T	2	24	1
1987–88 Shrewsbury T	2	41	1

LISTER, Steve
18.11.61 Doncaster (MF)
6.1 11.0 Apprentice
LD Doncaster R v Reading
20.3.79 2–2

1978–79 Doncaster R	4	9	—
1979–80 Doncaster R	4	40	12
1980–81 Doncaster R	4	39	3
1981–82 Doncaster R	3	41	7
1982–83 Doncaster R	3	41	4
1983–84 Doncaster R	4	31	2
1984–85 Doncaster R	3	36	2
1985–86 Scunthorpe U	4	37	2
1986–87 Scunthorpe U	4	40	11
1987–88 Scunthorpe U	4	39	6

LITCHFIELD, Peter
27.7.56 Manchester (GK)
6.1 12.12 Droylsden
LD Preston NE v Chelsea
28.2.81 1–0

1978–79 Preston NE	2	—	—
1979–80 Preston NE	2	—	—
1980–81 Preston NE	2	3	—
1981–82 Preston NE	3	18	—
1982–83 Preston NE	3	23	—
1983–84 Preston NE	3	45	—
1984–85 Preston NE	3	18	—
1985–86 Bradford C	2	42	—
1986–87 Bradford C	2	39	—
1987–88 Bradford C	2	2	—

LIVINGSTONE, Steve
8.9.69 Middlesbrough (FW)
— — YTS
LD Luton T v Coventry C
18.4.87 2–0

1986–87 Coventry C	1	3	—
1987–88 Coventry C	1	4	—

LLEWELLYN, Andy
26.2.66 Bristol (MF)
5.7 11.12 Apprentice
LD Millwall v Bristol C
27.10.84 1–1

1983–84 Bristol C	4	—	—
1984–85 Bristol C	3	22	—
1985–86 Bristol C	3	38	1
1986–87 Bristol C	3	31	—
1987–88 Bristol C	3	42	1

LLOYD, Philip
26.12.64 Hemsworth (DF)
6.0 11.13 Apprentice
LD Chester C v Darlington
17.3.84 2–1

1982–83 Middlesbrough	2	—	—
1983–84 Barnsley	2	—	—
1983–84 Darlington	4	14	—
1984–85 Darlington	4	41	2
1985–86 Darlington	3	29	—
1986–87 Darlington	3	43	1
1987–88 Torquay U	4	46	2

LOGAN, David
5.12.63 Middlesbrough (DF)
5.9 10.9 Whitby
LD Halifax T v Mansfield T
10.11.84 1–0

1984–85 Mansfield T	4	17	—
1985–86 Mansfield T	4	24	1
1986–87 Mansfield T	3	26	—
1986–87 Northampton T	4	15	1
1987–88 Northampton T	3	26	—

LOMAX, Geoff
6.7.64 Manchester (DF)
5.8 11.5 Local
LD Southampton v Manchester C
19.3.83 4–1

1981–82 Manchester C	1	—	—
1982–83 Manchester C	1	1	—
1983–84 Manchester C	2	17	1
1984–85 Manchester C	2	7	—
1985–86 Manchester C	1	—	—
1985–86 *Wolves*	3	5	—
1985–86 Carlisle U	2	13	—
1986–87 Carlisle U	3	24	—
1987–88 Rochdale	4	44	—

LONGDEN, Paul
28.9.62 Wakefield (DF)
5.7 10.3 Apprentice
LD Barnsley v Grimsby T
23.3.82 3–2

1981–82 Barnsley	2	4	—
1982–83 Barnsley	2	1	—
1983–84 Scunthorpe U	3	43	—
1984–85 Scunthorpe U	4	14	—
1985–86 Scunthorpe U	4	31	—
1986–87 Scunthorpe U	4	42	—
1987–88 Scunthorpe U	4	44	—

LONGHURST, David
15.1.65 Northampton (FW)
5.8 10.12 Apprentice
LD Chester C v Halifax T
17.8.85 1–1

1982–83 Nottingham F	1	—	—
1983–84 Nottingham F	1	—	—
1984–85 Nottingham F	1	—	—
1985–86 Halifax T	4	44	14
1986–87 Halifax T	4	41	10
1987–88 Northampton T	3	35	7

LORAM, Mark
13.8.67 Brixham (MF)
6.0 12.0 Brixham
LD Torquay U v Rochdale
9.2.85 1–0

1984–85 Torquay U	4	14	2
1985–86 Torquay U	4	38	6
1985–86 *QPR*	1	—	—
1986–87 QPR	1	—	—
1986–87 *Torquay U*	4	13	4
1987–88 Torquay U	4	45	8

LORMOR, Anthony
29.10.70 Wallsend (FW)
6.1 12.3 Apprentice
LD Newcastle U v Tottenham H
23.1.88 2–0

1987–88 Newcastle U	1	5	2

LOVELL, Steve
16.7.60 Swansea (MF)
5.9 11.2 Apprentice
LD Stockport Co v Hereford U
5.10.79 2–1

1977–78 Crystal Palace	2	—	—
1978–79 Crystal Palace	2	—	—
1979–80 Crystal Palace	1	—	—
1979–80 *Stockport Co*	4	12	—
1980–81 Crystal Palace	1	25	2
1981–82 Crystal Palace	2	30	1
1982–83 Crystal Palace	2	19	—
1982–83 Millwall	3	17	1
1983–84 Millwall	3	46	7
1984–85 Millwall	3	41	22
1985–86 Millwall	2	42	14
1986–87 *Swansea C*	4	2	1
1986–87 Gillingham	3	6	1
1987–88 Gillingham	3	46	25

LOWE, David
30.8.65 Liverpool (FW)
5.10 9.3 Apprentice
LD Reading v Wigan Ath
23.10.82 2–1

1982–83 Wigan Ath	3	28	6
1983–84 Wigan Ath	3	40	8
1984–85 Wigan Ath	3	29	5
1985–86 Wigan Ath	3	46	5
1986–87 Wigan Ath	3	45	16
1987–88 Ipswich T	2	41	17

LOWE, Simon
26.12.62 London (FW)
5.10¼ 12.3
LD Fulham v Barnsley
14.1.84 1–0

1983–84 Barnsley	2	2	—
1984–85 Halifax T	2	42	12
1985–86 Halifax T	2	35	7
1986–87 Hartlepool U	4	14	1
1986–87 Colchester U	4	26	7
1987–88 Colchester U	4	10	1
1987–88 *Scarborough*	4	3	3
1987–88 Scarborough	4	10	—

LOWERY, Tony
6.7.61 Wallsend (MF)
5.9 11.1 Ashington
LD Manchester C v WBA
29.8.81 2–1

1980–81 WBA	1	—	—
1981–82 WBA	1	1	—
1981–82 *Walsall*	3	6	1
1982–83 Walsall	3	—	—
1982–83 Mansfield T	4	1	—
1983–84 Mansfield T	4	45	6
1984–85 Mansfield T	4	45	3
1985–86 Mansfield T	4	40	5
1986–87 Mansfield T	3	44	5
1987–88 Mansfield T	3	44	—

LOWNDES, Steve
17.6.60 Cwmbran (FW)
5.10 11.0 Amateur
LD Scunthorpe U v Newport Co
4.4.78 2–0

1977–78 Newport Co	4	5	—
1978–79 Newport Co	4	43	8
1979–80 Newport Co	4	46	7
1980–81 Newport Co	3	40	9
1981–82 Newport Co	3	31	3
1982–83 Newport Co	3	43	12
1983–84 Millwall	3	20	3
1984–85 Millwall	3	37	7
1985–86 Millwall	2	39	6
1986–87 Barnsley	2	15	1
1987–88 Barnsley	2	44	9

PLAYER DIRECTORY

LUKE, Noel
28.12.64 Birmingham (MF)
5.11 10.11 School
LD WBA v Norwich C
2.5.83 1–0

1981–82	WBA	1	— —
1982–83	WBA	1	1 —
1983–84	WBA	1	8 1
1984–85	Mansfield T	4	36 6
1985–86	Mansfield T	4	14 3
1986–87	Peterborough U	4	30 10
1987–88	Peterborough U	4	43 7

LUKIC, John
11.12.60 Chesterfield (GK)
6.4 13.7 Apprentice
LD Brighton & HA v Leeds U
13.10.79 0–0

1978–79	Leeds U	1	— —
1979–80	Leeds U	1	33 —
1980–81	Leeds U	1	42 —
1981–82	Leeds U	1	42 —
1982–83	Leeds U	2	29 —
1983–84	Arsenal	1	4 —
1984–85	Arsenal	1	27 —
1985–86	Arsenal	1	40 —
1986–87	Arsenal	1	36 —
1987–88	Arsenal	1	40 —

LUND, Gary
13.9.64 Grimsby (FW)
5.11 11.0 School
LD Barnsley v Grimsby T
27.9.83 3–1

1983–84	Grimsby T	2	7 4
1984–85	Grimsby T	2	24 12
1985–86	Grimsby T	2	29 8
1986–87	Lincoln C	4	44 13
1987–88	Notts Co	3	40 20

LUNDON, Sean
7.3.69 Liverpool (DF)
5.10 10.10 Apprentice
LD Bolton W v Chester C
25.10.86 1–1

1986–87	Chester C	3	12 —
1987–88	Chester C	3	22 2

LYNCH, Steve
— Belfast (MF)
— — Apprentice
LD —

1987–88	QPR	1	— —

MacAULEY, Steve
4.3.69 Lytham St
Annes (DF/MF)
5.11 11.6 Apprentice
LD —

1987–88	Manchester C	2	— —

MacDONALD, Gary
26.3.62 Middlesbrough (FW)
6.0 12.1 Apprentice
LD Brighton & HA v
Middlesbrough
8.11.80 0–1

1979–80	Middlesbrough	1	— —
1980–81	Middlesbrough	1	7 —
1981–82	Middlesbrough	1	8 1
1982–83	Middlesbrough	2	9 1
1983–84	Middlesbrough	2	29 3
1984–85	Carlisle U	2	9 —
1984–85	Darlington	4	33 4
1985–86	Darlington	3	36 16
1986–87	Darlington	3	10 3
1987–88	Darlington	4	42 7

MacDONALD, John
15.4.61 Glasgow (FW)
5.8 10.1 Clydebank Strollers
LD Hearts v Rangers
24.2.79 3–2

1978–79	Rangers	P	2	—
1979–80	Rangers	P	26	5
1980–81	Rangers	P	30	11
1981–82	Rangers	P	34	14
1982–83	Rangers	P	30	10
1983–84	Rangers	P	18	1
1984–85	Rangers	P	18	3
1985–86	Rangers	P	2	—
1986–87	Charlton Ath	1	2	—
1986–87	Barnsley	2	25	7
1987–88	Barnsley	2	33	7

MacDONALD, Kevin
22.12.60 Inverness (MF)
6.0¼ 11.11¼ Inverness Caley
LD Leicester C v Norwich C
29.11.80 1–2

1980–81	Leicester C	1	20	2
1981–82	Leicester C	2	25	1
1982–83	Leicester C	2	42	4
1983–84	Leicester C	1	38	1
1984–85	Leicester C	1	13	—
1984–85	Liverpool	1	13	—
1985–86	Liverpool	1	17	1
1986–87	Liverpool	1	6	—
1987–88	Liverpool	1	1	—
1987–88	*Leicester C*	2	3	—

MacFARLANE, David
16.1.67 Irvine (DF)
5.11½ 10.10 Ayr U BC
LD — Rangers v Dumbarton
2.3.85 3–1

1984–85	Rangers	P	2	—
1985–86	Rangers	P	—	2
1986–87	Rangers	P	4	—
1987–88	Rangers	P	1	—
1987–88	*Kilmarnock*	1	4	3
1987–88	*Dundee*	P	2	—

MACKAY, Gary
23.1.64 Edinburgh (MF)
5.9 10.5 Salvesen BC
LD Hearts v Dundee U
8.11.80 0–3

1980–81	Hearts	P	12	—
1981–82	Hearts	1	17	2
1982–83	Hearts	1	34	6
1983–84	Hearts	P	31	4
1984–85	Hearts	P	17	2
1985–86	Hearts	P	32	4
1986–87	Hearts	P	37	7
1987–88	Hearts	P	41	5

MACKENZIE, Steve
23.11.61 Romford (MF)
5.10 11.4 Apprentice
LD Manchester C v Crystal Palace
18.8.79 0–0

1979–80	Crystal Palace	1	—	—
1979–80	Manchester C	1	19	2
1980–81	Manchester C	1	39	6
1981–82	WBA	1	37	5
1982–83	WBA	1	1	—
1983–84	WBA	1	19	4
1984–85	WBA	1	38	8
1985–86	WBA	1	31	4
1986–87	WBA	2	30	2
1987–88	Charlton Ath	1	32	2

MacLAREN, Ross
14.4.62 Edinburgh (MF)
5.10 12.7 Glasgow Rangers
LD Shrewsbury T v Swansea C
11.11.80 0–0

1980–81	Shrewsbury T	2	4	—
1981–82	Shrewsbury T	2	35	—
1982–83	Shrewsbury T	2	40	5
1983–84	Shrewsbury T	2	40	7
1984–85	Shrewsbury T	2	42	6
1985–86	Derby Co	3	46	4
1986–87	Derby Co	2	42	—
1987–88	Derby Co	1	34	—

MacLEOD, Murdo
24.9.58 Glasgow (MF)
5.8 12.0 Glasgow Amateurs
LD Dumbarton v Queen of the S
25.10.75 2–1

1974–75	Dumbarton	1	— —
1975–76	Dumbarton	1	7 —
1976–77	Dumbarton	1	27 7
1977–78	Dumbarton	1	39 1
1978–79	Dumbarton	1	14 1
1978–79	Celtic	P	23 3
1979–80	Celtic	P	36 7
1980–81	Celtic	P	18 8
1981–82	Celtic	P	36 10
1982–83	Celtic	P	35 11
1983–84	Celtic	P	34 7
1984–85	Celtic	P	31 3
1985–86	Celtic	P	30 3
1986–87	Celtic	P	38 4
1987–88	Borussia Dortmund (FRG)		

MACOWAT, Ian
19.11.65 Oxford (FW)
5.9½ 11.10 Apprentice
LD Reading v Gillingham
14.5.85 0–2

1983–84	Everton	1	— —
1984–85	Everton	1	— —
1984–85	Gillingham	3	2 —
1985–86	Gillingham	3	3 —
1986–87	Crewe Alex	4	13 —
1987–88	Crewe Alex	4	29 —

MacPHAIL, John
7.12.55 Dundee (DF)
6.0 12.3 St Columba's
LD Rangers v Dundee
10.4.76 3–0

1975–76	Dundee	P	6 —
1976–77	Dundee	1	25 —
1977–78	Dundee	1	34 —
1978–79	Dundee	1	3 —
1978–79	Sheffield U	2	15 1
1979–80	Sheffield U	3	44 5
1980–81	Sheffield U	3	39 —
1981–82	Sheffield U	4	26 1
1982–83	Sheffield U	3	11 —
1982–83	York C	4	12 2
1983–84	York C	4	46 10
1984–85	York C	3	42 5
1985–86	York C	3	42 7
1986–87	Bristol C	3	26 1
1987–88	Sunderland	3	46 16

McADAM, Tom
9.4.54 Glasgow (DF)
6.0 12.9 Glasgow schools
LD Partick Th v Dumbarton
2.9.72 4–1

1971–72	Dumbarton	2	— —
1972–73	Dumbarton	1	17 9
1973–74	Dumbarton	1	19 5
1974–75	Dumbarton	1	33 11

1975–76	Dumbarton	1	6 4
1975–76	Dundee U	P	26 12
1976–77	Dundee U	P	33 9
1977–78	Dundee U	P	2 —
1977–78	Celtic	P	33 8
1978–79	Celtic	P	28 7
1979–80	Celtic	P	34 8
1980–81	Celtic	P	35 4
1981–82	Celtic	P	34 5
1982–83	Celtic	P	35 3
1983–84	Celtic	P	28 1
1984–85	Celtic	P	26 —
1985–86	Celtic	P	5 —
1986–87	*Stockport C*	4	5 1
1986–87	*Hamilton A*	P	3 —
1986–87	Motherwell	P	31 1
1987–88	Motherwell	P	34 1

McALISTER, Tom
10.12.52 Clydebank (GK)
6.1 12.13 Apprentice
LD Ipswich T v Sheffield U
15.4.72 0–0

1970–71	Sheffield U	2	— —
1971–72	Sheffield U	1	4 —
1972–73	Sheffield U	1	42 —
1973–74	Sheffield U	1	12 —
1974–75	Sheffield U	1	— —
1975–76	Sheffield U	1	5 —
1975–76	Rotherham U	3	22 —
1976–77	Rotherham U	3	46 —
1977–78	Rotherham U	3	46 —
1978–79	Rotherham U	3	45 —
1979–80	Blackpool	3	16 —
1980–81	Swindon T	3	1 —
1980–81	*Bristol R*	2	13 —
1981–82	West Ham U	1	3 —
1982–83	West Ham U	1	— —
1983–84	West Ham U	1	— —
1984–85	West Ham U	1	32 —
1985–86	West Ham U	1	— —
1986–87	West Ham U	1	9 —
1987–88	West Ham U	1	39 —

McALLISTER, Gary
25.12.64 Motherwell (MF)
5.10 9.6 Fir Park BC
LD Queen of the S v Motherwell
1.5.81 2–5

1981–82	Motherwell	1	1 —
1982–83	Motherwell	P	1 —
1983–84	Motherwell	P	21 —
1984–85	Motherwell	1	35 6
1985–86	Motherwell	P	1 —
1985–86	Leicester C	1	31 7
1986–87	Leicester C	1	39 9
1987–88	Leicester C	2	42 9

McALLISTER, Kevin
8.11.62 Falkirk (FW)
5.5 11.0
LD Falkirk v Raith R
3.9.83 2–1

1983–84	Falkirk	1	35 11
1984–85	Falkirk	1	29 7
1985–86	Chelsea	1	20 —
1986–87	Chelsea	1	8 —
1987–88	Chelsea	1	5 —
1987–88	*Falkirk*	P	6 3

McAUGHTRIE, David
30.1.63 Cumnock (DF)
6.2¼ 12.3 Apprentice
LD Nottingham F v Stoke C
30.8.80 5–0

1980–81	Stoke C	1	1 —
1981–82	Stoke C	1	13 —
1982–83	Stoke C	1	20 1
1983–84	Stoke C	1	17 —
1984–85	Carlisle U	2	28 1
1985–86	York C	3	41 1
1986–87	York C	3	23 —
1987–88	Darlington	4	19 —

McAVENNIE, Frank
22.11.59 Glasgow (FW)
5.9 11.0 Partick Th trialist
LD Airdrieonians v St Mirren
5.9.81 3–4

1981–82	St Mirren	P	31 13
1982–83	St Mirren	P	36 9
1983–84	St Mirren	P	34 12
1984–85	St Mirren	P	34 16
1985–86	West Ham U	1	41 26
1986–87	West Ham U	1	36 7
1987–88	West Ham U	1	8 —
1987–88	Celtic	P	32 15

McBRIDE, Joe
17.8.60 Glasgow (FW)
5.8 11.2 Apprentice
LD Bolton W v Everton
26.12.79 1–1

1978–79	Everton	1	— —
1979–80	Everton	1	18 1
1980–81	Everton	1	31 7
1981–82	Everton	1	8 1
1982–83	Rotherham U	2	42 11
1983–84	Rotherham U	3	3 1
1983–84	Oldham Ath	2	25 4
1984–85	Oldham Ath	2	11 1
1984–85	Hibernian	P	12 2
1985–86	Hibernian	P	14 1
1986–87	Hibernian	P	38 7
1987–88	Hibernian	P	13 1

McBRIDE, Martin
28.11.67 Bellshill (FW)
5.8 10.0 Wishaw Juniors
LD Motherwell v Hibernian
26.4.86 3–1

1984–85	Motherwell	P	— —
1985–86	Motherwell	P	1 —
1986–87	Motherwell	P	2 —
1987–88	Motherwell	P	10 —

PLAYER DIRECTORY

McCABE, Gerry
26.9.56 Hamilton (FW)
5.10 10.7 Windsor All-Stars
LD Brechin C v Clyde
   19.11.77 1–2

1977–78	Clyde	2	20	3
1978–79	Clyde	1	37	3
1979–80	Clyde	1	39	8
1980–81	Clydebank	1	38	1
1981–82	Clydebank	1	37	8
1982–83	Clydebank	1	37	4
1983–84	Clydebank	1	37	4
1984–85	Clydebank	1	33	4
1985–86	Clydebank	P	24	—
1986–87	Clydebank	P	10	—
1986–87	Hamilton A	P	24	2
1987–88	Hamilton A	1	33	7
1987–88	*Dumbarton*	1	6	1

McCAFFERY, Aidan
30.8.57 Newcastle (DF)
5.11 11.5 Apprentice
LD Ipswich T v Newcastle U
   15.3.75 5–4

1974–75	Newcastle U	1	3	—
1975–76	Newcastle U	1	4	—
1976–77	Newcastle U	1	38	3
1977–78	Newcastle U	1	14	1
1978–79	Derby Co	1	6	—
1979–80	Derby Co	1	31	4
1980–81	Bristol R	2	38	5
1981–82	Bristol R	3	25	3
1981–82	*Bristol C*	3	6	1
1981–82	Bristol R	3	4	—
1982–83	Bristol R	3	45	3
1983–84	Bristol R	3	45	—
1984–85	Bristol R	3	27	—
1984–85	*Torquay U*	4	6	—
1985–86	Exeter C	4	33	—
1986–87	Exeter C	4	25	—
1986–87	Hartlepool U	4	6	1
1987–88	Whitley Bay			
1987–88	Carlisle U	4	14	—

McCALL, Ian
30.9.64 Dumfries (FW)
5.9 11.7 Motherwell Tech
LD Queen's Park v Montrose
   6.3.84 3–0

1983–84	Queen's Park	2	3	1
1984–85	Queen's Park	2	28	—
1985–86	Queen's Park	2	35	8
1986–87	Dunfermline A	1	43	8
1987–88	Dunfermline A	P	4	—
1987–88	Rangers	P	12	1

McCALL, Steve
15.10.60 Carlisle (MF)
5.11 11.3 Apprentice
LD Ipswich T v Everton
   22.9.79 1–1

1978–79	Ipswich T	1	—	—
1979–80	Ipswich T	1	10	—
1980–81	Ipswich T	1	31	1
1981–82	Ipswich T	1	42	1
1982–83	Ipswich T	1	42	4
1983–84	Ipswich T	1	42	1
1984–85	Ipswich T	1	31	—
1985–86	Ipswich T	1	33	—
1986–87	Ipswich T	2	26	—
1987–88	Sheffield W	1	5	—

McCALL, Stuart
10.6.64 Leeds (MF)
5.6 10.1 Apprentice
LD Bradford C v Reading
   28.8.82 3–2

1982–83	Bradford C	3	28	4
1983–84	Bradford C	3	46	5
1984–85	Bradford C	3	46	8
1985–86	Bradford C	2	38	4
1986–87	Bradford C	2	36	7
1987–88	Bradford C	2	44	9

McCARRICK, Mark
4.2.62 Liverpool (DF)
5.8 10.8 Runcorn
LD Scunthorpe U v Tranmere R
   15.8.87 3–0

1987–88	Tranmere R	4	40	5

McCART, Chris
17.4.67 Motherwell (MF)
5.9 10.5 Fir Park BC
LD Celtic v Motherwell
   17.8.85 2–1

1984–85	Motherwell	1	—	—
1985–86	Motherwell	P	13	—
1986–87	Motherwell	P	—	—
1987–88	Motherwell	P	1	—

McCARTHY, Mike
7.2.59 Barnsley (DF)
6.1½ 13.3 Apprentice
LD Barnsley v Rochdale
   20.8.77 4–0

1977–78	Barnsley	4	46	1
1978–79	Barnsley	4	46	2
1979–80	Barnsley	3	44	1
1980–81	Barnsley	3	43	1
1981–82	Barnsley	2	42	1
1982–83	Barnsley	2	39	1
1983–84	Barnsley	2	12	—
1983–84	Manchester C	2	24	1
1984–85	Manchester C	2	39	—
1985–86	Manchester C	1	38	—
1986–87	Manchester C	1	39	1
1987–88	Celtic	P	22	—

McCARTHY, Sean
12.9.67 Bridgend (FW)
6.0 12.2
LD Swansea C v Bury
   2.11.85 1–0

1985–86	Swansea C	3	22	3
1986–87	Swansea C	4	44	14
1987–88	Swansea C	4	25	8

McCLAIR, Brian
8.12.63 Bellshill (FW)
5.10 10.6 Apprentice
LD Kilmarnock v Motherwell
   29.8.81 2–0

1980–81	Aston Villa	1	—	—
1981–82	Motherwell	1	11	4
1982–83	Motherwell	P	28	11
1983–84	Celtic	P	35	23
1984–85	Celtic	P	32	19
1985–86	Celtic	P	34	22
1986–87	Celtic	P	44	35
1987–88	Manchester U	1	40	24

McCLAREN, Steve
3.5.61 Fulford (MF)
5.9 10.7 Apprentice
LD Hull v Bury
   5.5.80 0–1

1978–79	Hull C	3	—	—
1979–80	Hull C	3	1	—
1980–81	Hull C	3	20	1
1981–82	Hull C	4	37	4
1982–83	Hull C	4	40	4
1983–84	Hull C	3	40	3
1984–85	Hull C	3	40	4
1985–86	Derby Co	3	23	—
1986–87	*Lincoln C*	4	8	—
1987–88	Derby Co	1	2	—
1987–88	Bristol C	3	16	1

McCLEAN, Chris
17.10.63 Colchester (DF/FW)
6.4 14.0 Clacton
LD Chesterfield v Bristol R
   2.4.88 0–1

1987–88	Bristol R	3	6	—

McCLELLAND, John
7.12.55 Belfast (DF)
6.1 11.4 Portadown
LD Cardiff C v Notts Co
   21.12.74 0–0

1973–74	Cardiff C	2	—	—
1974–75	Cardiff C	2	4	1
	Bangor			
1978–79	Mansfield T	3	36	1
1979–80	Mansfield T	3	43	1
1980–81	Mansfield T	4	46	6
1981–82	Rangers	P	14	—
1982–83	Rangers	P	35	2
1983–84	Rangers	P	36	2
1984–85	Rangers	P	11	—
1984–85	Watford	1	29	1
1985–86	Watford	1	31	1
1986–87	Watford	1	41	1
1987–88	Watford	1	40	—

McCLUSKEY, George
19.9.57 Hamilton (FW)
6.1 12.1 Celtic BC
LD Celtic v Rangers
1.11.75 1–1

1975–76	Celtic	P	4	—
1976–77	Celtic	P	—	—
1977–78	Celtic	P	15	6
1978–79	Celtic	P	21	5
1979–80	Celtic	P	23	10
1980–81	Celtic	P	22	10
1981–82	Celtic	P	35	21
1982–83	Celtic	P	10	2
1983–84	Leeds U	2	32	8
1984–85	Leeds U	2	19	5
1985–86	Leeds U	2	22	3
1986–87	Hibernian	P	35	9
1987–88	Hibernian	P	32	4

McCOIST, Ally
24.9.62 Bellshill (FW)
5.10 12.0 Fir Park BC
LD St Johnstone v Raith R
7.4.79 3–0

1978–79	St Johnstone	1	4	—
1979–80	St Johnstone	1	15	—
1980–81	St Johnstone	1	38	22
1981–82	Sunderland	1	28	2
1982–83	Sunderland	1	28	6
1983–84	Rangers	P	30	9
1984–85	Rangers	P	25	12
1985–86	Rangers	P	33	24
1986–87	Rangers	P	44	33
1987–88	Rangers	P	40	31

McCORD, Brian
24.8.68 Derby (MF)
5.10 11.6 Apprentice
LD Wimbledon v Derby Co
1.1.88 2–1

1987–88	Derby Co	1	1	—

McCREERY, David
16.9.57 Belfast (MF)
5.6 9.7 Apprentice
LD Portsmouth v Manchester U
15.10.74 0–0

1974–75	Manchester U	2	2	—
1975–76	Manchester U	1	28	4
1976–77	Manchester U	1	25	2
1977–78	Manchester U	1	17	1
1978–79	Manchester U	1	15	—
1979–80	QPR	2	42	4
1980–81	QPR	2	15	—
Tulsa R, NASL				
1982–83	Newcastle U	2	26	—
1983–84	Newcastle U	2	40	—
1984–85	Newcastle U	1	35	1
1985–86	Newcastle U	1	41	—
1986–87	Newcastle U	1	30	—
1987–88	Newcastle U	1	35	1

McDERMOTT, Brian
8.4.61 Slough (FW)
5.8 9.12 Apprentice
LD Arsenal v Bristol C
10.3.79 2–0

1978–79	Arsenal	1	2	—
1979–80	Arsenal	1	1	—
1980–81	Arsenal	1	23	5
1981–82	Arsenal	1	13	1
1982–83	Arsenal	1	9	4
1982–83	Fulham	2	3	—
1983–84	Arsenal	1	13	2
1984–85	Oxford U	2	18	2
1985–86	Oxford U	1	4	—
1986–87	Oxford U	1	2	—
1986–87	Huddersfield T	2	4	1
1987–88	Cardiff C	4	45	7

McDERMOTT, John
3.2.69 Middlesbrough (DF)
— —
LD Bradford C v Grimsby T
7.2.87 4–2

1986–87	Grimsby T	2	13	—
1987–88	Grimsby T	3	28	—

McDONALD, Alan
12.10.63 Belfast (DF)
6.2½ 12.7 Apprentice
LD Charlton Ath v Crystal Palace
4.4.83 2–1

1981–82	QPR	2	—	—
1982–83	QPR	2	—	—
1982–83	Charlton Ath	2	9	—
1983–84	QPR	1	5	—
1984–85	QPR	1	16	1
1985–86	QPR	1	42	—
1986–87	QPR	1	39	4
1987–88	QPR	1	36	3

McDONALD, Neil
2.11.65 Wallsend (MF)
5.11 11.4 Wallsend BC
LD Newcastle U v Barnsley
25.9.82 1–2

1982–83	Newcastle U	2	24	4
1983–84	Newcastle U	2	12	—
1984–85	Newcastle U	1	36	6
1985–86	Newcastle U	1	28	4
1986–87	Newcastle U	1	40	7
1987–88	Newcastle U	1	40	3

McDONALD, Paul
20.4.68 Motherwell (FW)
5.9 10.4 Fir Park BC
LD Hamilton A v Hibernian
4.10.86 1–4

1986–87	Hamilton A	P	5	—
1987–88	Hamilton A	P	18	—

McDONOUGH, Darron
7.11.62 Antwerp (FW)
5.11 11.7 Apprentice
LD Notts Co v Oldham Ath
13.12.80 0–2

1979–80	Oldham Ath	2	—	—
1980–81	Oldham Ath	2	15	3
1981–82	Oldham Ath	2	36	1
1982–83	Oldham Ath	2	38	10
1983–84	Oldham Ath	2	38	—
1984–85	Oldham Ath	2	32	—
1985–86	Oldham Ath	2	20	—
1986–87	Oldham Ath	2	4	—
1986–87	Luton T	1	18	1
1987–88	Luton T	1	27	4

McDONOUGH, Roy
16.10.58 Solihull (FW)
6.1 11.11 Apprentice
LD Sunderland v Birmingham C
7.5.77 1–0

1976–77	Birmingham C	1	2	1
1977–78	Birmingham C	1	—	—
1978–79	Birmingham C	1	—	—
1978–79	Walsall	3	34	7
1979–80	Walsall	4	42	7
1980–81	Walsall	3	6	1
1980–81	Chelsea	2	—	—
1980–81	Colchester U	3	12	2
1981–82	Colchester U	4	40	14
1982–83	Colchester U	4	41	8
1983–84	Southend U	3	22	4
1983–84	Exeter C	3	16	—
1984–85	Exeter C	4	4	1
1984–85	Cambridge U	3	32	5
1985–86	Southend U	4	38	7
1986–87	Southend U	4	33	4
1987–88	Southend U	3	42	9

McDOWALL, Kenny
29.7.63 Glasgow (FW)
5.10 10.3 Drumchapel Amateurs
LD Partick Th v Celtic
28.11.81 0–2

1980–81	Partick T	P	—	—
1981–82	Partick T	P	1	—
1982–83	Partick T	1	24	5
1983–84	Partick T	1	36	13
1984–85	Partick T	1	6	1
1984–85	St Mirren	P	23	3
1985–86	St Mirren	P	12	1
1986–87	St Mirren	P	19	1
1987–88	St Mirren	P	27	3

PLAYER DIRECTORY

McELHINNEY, Gerry
19.9.56 Londonderry (DF)
6.2 13.0 Distillery
LD Bolton W v Bristol R
6.9.80 2–0

1980–81	Bolton W	2	17	—
1981–82	Bolton W	2	19	1
1982–83	Bolton W	2	16	—
1982–83	Rochdale	4	20	1
1983–84	Bolton W	3	43	1
1984–85	Bolton W	3	14	—
1984–85	Plymouth Arg	3	21	—
1985–86	Plymouth Arg	3	44	2
1986–87	Plymouth Arg	2	20	—
1987–88	Plymouth Arg	2	6	—

McEWAN, Stan
8.6.57 Cambusrethan (FW)
6.0 12.7 Apprentice
LD WBA v Blackpool
28.12.74 2–0

1974–75	Blackpool	2	1	—
1975–76	Blackpool	2	17	—
1976–77	Blackpool	2	11	—
1977–78	Blackpool	3	39	1
1978–79	Blackpool	3	46	5
1979–80	Blackpool	3	39	12
1980–81	Blackpool	3	36	1
1981–82	Blackpool	4	25	5
1982–83	Exeter C	3	37	6
1983–84	Exeter C	3	28	9
1983–84	Hull C	3	16	1
1984–85	Hull C	3	37	11
1985–86	Hull C	2	42	10
1986–87	Hull C	2	17	3
1987–88	Hull C	2	1	—
1987–88	*Wigan Ath*	3	10	2
1987–88	Wigan Ath	3	13	2

McGARVEY, Frank
17.3.56 Glasgow (FW)
5.10 11.0 Kilsyth Rangers
LD East Stirling v St Mirren
26.4.74 5–0

1974–75	St Mirren	2	1	—
1975–76	St Mirren	1	25	5
1976–77	St Mirren	1	38	17
1977–78	St Mirren	P	35	17
1978–79	St Mirren	P	33	13
1979–80	Liverpool	1	—	—
1979–80	Celtic	P	12	2
1980–81	Celtic	P	34	23
1981–82	Celtic	P	26	10
1982–83	Celtic	P	34	17
1983–84	Celtic	P	30	10
1984–85	Celtic	P	33	15
1985–86	St Mirren	P	35	6
1986–87	St Mirren	P	40	10
1987–88	St Mirren	P	25	2

McGARVEY, Scott
22.4.63 Glasgow (FW)
6.0½ 11.5 Apprentice
LD Manchester U v Leicester C
13.9.80 5–0

1979–80	Manchester U	1	—	—
1980–81	Manchester U	1	2	—
1981–82	Manchester U	1	16	2
1982–83	Manchester U	1	7	1
1983–84	Manchester U	1	—	—
1983–84	*Wolves*	1	13	2
1984–85	Portsmouth	2	18	5
1985–86	Portsmouth	2	5	1
1985–86	*Carlisle U*	2	10	3
1986–87	Carlisle U	3	25	8
1986–87	Grimsby T	2	11	1
1987–88	Grimsby T	3	39	6

McGEACHIE, George
5.2.59 Skinflats (DF)
5.11 11.4 Bo'ness United
LD Dundee v Airdrieonians
13.8.77 3–0

1977–78	Dundee	P	15	2
1978–79	Dundee	P	5	—
1979–80	Dundee	P	28	1
1980–81	Dundee	P	30	2
1981–82	Dundee	P	29	3
1982–83	Dundee	P	22	—
1983–84	Dundee	P	23	—
1984–85	Dundee	P	35	1
1985–86	Dundee	P	2	—
1986–87	Dundee	P	28	—
1987–88	Dundee	P	14	1

McGEENEY, Pat
31.10.66 Sheffield (DF)
5.10½ 11.0 Apprentice
LD Sheffield U v Leeds U
23.3.85 2–1

1984–85	Sheffield U	2	10	—
1985–86	Sheffield U	2	6	—
1986–87	*Rochdale*	4	3	—
1987–88	Chesterfield	3	38	1

McGHEE, Mark
25.5.57 Glasgow (FW)
5.10 12.0 Apprentice
LD Kilmarnock v Morton
27.12.75 3–2

1974–75	Bristol C	2	—	—
1975–76	Morton	1	5	1
1976–77	Morton	1	39	20
1977–78	Morton	1	20	16
1977–78	Newcastle U	1	18	3
1978–79	Newcastle U	2	10	2
1978–79	Aberdeen	P	11	4
1979–80	Aberdeen	P	21	6
1980–81	Aberdeen	P	36	13
1981–82	Aberdeen	P	31	8
1982–83	Aberdeen	P	32	16
1983–84	Aberdeen	P	33	16
1984–85	SV Hamburg	1	26	6
1985–86	Celtic	P	18	4
1986–87	Celtic	P	17	1
1987–88	Celtic	P	24	6

McGINNIS, Gary
21.10.63 Dundee (DF)
5.11 10.3 Dundee BC
LD Dundee U v Rangers
1.10.83 0–2

1981–82	Dundee U	P	—	—
1982–83	Dundee U	P	—	—
1983–84	Dundee U	P	4	—
1984–85	Dundee U	P	10	—
1985–86	Dundee U	P	4	—
1986–87	Dundee U	P	20	—
1987–88	Dundee U	P	11	—

McGOLDRICK, Eddie
30.4.65 London (MF)
— — Nuneaton
LD Scunthorpe U v Northampton T
23.8.86 2–2

1986–87	Northampton T	4	39	5
1987–88	Northampton T	4	46	2

McGRATH, Lloyd
24.2.65 Birmingham (DF)
5.9 11.6 Apprentice
LD Southampton V Coventry C
28.4.84 8–2

1982–83	Coventry C	1	—	—
1983–84	Coventry C	1	1	—
1984–85	Coventry C	1	23	—
1985–86	Coventry C	1	32	—
1986–87	Coventry C	1	30	3
1987–88	Coventry C	1	17	—

McGRATH, Paul
4.12.59 Greenford (DF)
6.0½ 13.2 St Patrick's Ath
LD Manchester U v Tottenham H
13.11.82 1–0

1981–82	Manchester U	1	—	—
1982–83	Manchester U	1	14	3
1983–84	Manchester U	1	9	1
1984–85	Manchester U	1	23	—
1985–86	Manchester U	1	40	3
1986–87	Manchester U	1	35	2
1987–88	Manchester U	1	22	2

McGREGOR, John
5.1.63 Airdrie (DF)
5.11 12.0 School
LD Stenhousemuir v Queen's Park
22.9.79 0–1

1979–80	Queen's Park	2	30	2
1980–81	Queen's Park	2	38	13
1981–82	Queen's Park	2	37	4
1982–83	Liverpool	1	—	—
1983–84	Liverpool	1	—	—
1983–84	*St Mirren*	P	5	1
1984–85	Liverpool	1	—	—
1985–86	Liverpool	1	—	—
1985–86	*Leeds U*	2	5	—
1986–87	Liverpool	1	—	—
1987–88	Rangers	P	25	—

PLAYER DIRECTORY

McGUGAN, Paul
17.7.64 Glasgow (DF)
6.2 12.0 Eastercraigs
LD Celtic v Hibernian
28.4.84 3–2

1980–81	Celtic	P	—	—
1981–82	Celtic	P	—	—
1982–83	Celtic	P	—	—
1983–84	Celtic	P	1	—
1984–85	Celtic	P	3	—
1985–86	Celtic	P	21	2
1986–87	Celtic	P	22	—
1987–88	Celtic	P	2	—
1987–88	Barnsley	2	29	1

McILHARGEY, Stephen
28.8.63 Ferryhill (GK)
6.0 11.7 Blantyre Celtic
LD —

| 1987–88 | Walsall | 3 | — | — |

McINALLY, Alan
10.2.63 Ayr (FW)
6.1 11.6 Ayr U BC
LD Ayr U v Clydebank
21.2.81 4–1

1980–81	Ayr U	1	6	—
1981–82	Ayr U	1	17	9
1982–83	Ayr U	1	35	7
1983–84	Ayr U	1	35	16
1984–85	Celtic	P	11	1
1985–86	Celtic	P	16	1
1986–87	Celtic	P	38	15
1987–88	Aston Villa	2	25	4

McINALLY, Jim
19.2.64 Glasgow (MF)
6.0 12.0 Celtic BC
LD Celtic v Kilmarnock
26.2.83 4–0

1982–83	Celtic	P	1	—
1983–84	Celtic	P	—	—
1984–85	Nottingham F	1	24	—
1985–86	Nottingham F	1	12	—
1985–86	Coventry C	1	5	—
1986–87	Dundee U	P	32	1
1987–88	Dundee U	P	36	2

McINTYRE, Tommy
26.12.63 Bellshill (DF)
6.0 10.10 Fir Park BC
LD Aberdeen v St Mirren
8.10.83 5–0

1981–82	Aberdeen	P	—	—
1982–83	Aberdeen	P	—	—
1983–84	Aberdeen	P	10	—
1984–85	Aberdeen	P	—	—
1985–86	Aberdeen	P	5	—
1986–87	Aberdeen	P	4	—
1986–87	Hibernian	P	15	—
1987–88	Hibernian	P	25	—

McKEARNEY, David
20.6.68 Liverpool (MF)
5.10 11.2 Prescot Cables
LD —

| 1987–88 | Bolton W | 4 | — | — |

McKEE, Kevin
10.6.66 Edinburgh (DF)
5.9 11.4 Whitburn BC
LD Rangers v Hibernian
5.3.83 1–1

1982–83	Hibernian	P	4	—
1983–84	Hibernian	P	16	—
1984–85	Hibernian	P	17	—
1985–86	Hibernian	P	2	—
1986–87	Hamilton A	P	29	4
1987–88	Hamilton A	1	40	—

McKENNA, Ken
2.7.60 Birkenhead (FW)
5.10 12.0 Telford U
LD Scunthorpe U v Tranmere R
15.8.87 3–0

| 1987–88 | Tranmere R | 4 | 14 | 3 |

McKENZIE, Ian
22.8.66 Wallsend (MF)
— — Apprentice
LD Shrewsbury T v Barnsley
11.1.86 3–0

1985–86	Barnsley	2	1	—
1986–87	Stockport Co	4	30	—
1987–88	Stockport Co	4	12	—

McKENZIE, Paul
4.10.69 Aberdeen (MF/FW)
5.10 11.12 Youth Scheme
LD —

| 1987–88 | Sunderland | 3 | — | — |

McKENZIE, Stuart
19.9.67 Hull (DF)
5.11 11.0 Juniors
LD York C v Bristol R
12.3.86 4–0

1985–86	York C	3	4	—
1986–87	York C	3	15	—
1987–88	York C	3	13	—

McKEOWN, Kevin
12.10.67 Glasgow (GK)
6.1 11.7 Wishaw Juniors
LD Meadowbank T v Stenhousemuir
29.11.86 5–0

1986–87	Stenhousemuir	2	17	—
1986–87	Motherwell	P	1	—
1987–88	Motherwell	P	—	—

McKERNON, Craig
23.2.68 Gloucester (MF)
5.9 11.0 Apprentice
LD Torquay U v Mansfield T
19.3.85 1–0

1984–85	Mansfield T	4	2	—
1985–86	Mansfield T	4	11	—
1986–87	Mansfield T	3	18	—
1987–88	Mansfield T	3	14	—

McKIMMIE, Stuart
27.10.62 Aberdeen (DF)
5.8 10.7 Banks o' Dee
LD Dundee v Hamilton A
14.10.80 2–0

1980–81	Dundee	1	17	—
1981–82	Dundee	P	16	—
1982–83	Dundee	P	31	—
1983–84	Dundee	P	16	—
1983–84	Aberdeen	P	18	1
1984–85	Aberdeen	P	34	3
1985–86	Aberdeen	P	34	3
1986–87	Aberdeen	P	37	—
1987–88	Aberdeen	P	42	—

McKINLAY, Tosh
3.12.64 Glasgow (DF)
5.7 10.3 Celtic BC
LD St Mirren v Dundee
9.5.83 2–1

1981–82	Dundee	P	—	—
1982–83	Dundee	P	1	—
1983–84	Dundee	P	36	3
1984–85	Dundee	P	34	3
1985–86	Dundee	P	22	—
1986–87	Dundee	P	32	2
1987–88	Dundee	P	19	—

McKINLAY, Billy
22.4.69 Glasgow (MF)
5.9 9.13 Hamilton Thistle
LD Dundee U v Hibernian
22.11.86 1–0

| 1986–87 | Dundee U | P | 3 | — |

McKINNON, Rob
31.7.66 Glasgow (DF)
5.11 11.1 Rutherglen Glencairn
LD Tottenham H v Newcastle U
7.9.85 5–1

1984–85	Newcastle U	1	—	—
1985–86	Newcastle U	1	1	—
1986–87	Hartlepool U	4	45	—
1987–88	Hartlepool U	4	42	2

McKNIGHT, Allen
27.1.64 Antrim (GK)
6.1 12.0 Distillery
LD Albion R v Stenhousemuir
16.8.86 1–4

1986–87	Celtic	P	—	—
1986–87	*Albion R*	2	36	—
1987–88	Celtic	P	12	2

PLAYER DIRECTORY

McLAREN, Alan
4.1.71 Edinburgh (DF)
5.11 11.6 Cavalry Bank
LD Dundee U v Hearts
7.5.88 0–0

1987–88	Hearts	P	1	—

McLAUGHLIN, Joe
2.6.60 Greenock (DF)
6.1 12.0 School
LD Morton v Partick Th
18.8.79 2–1

1977–78	Morton	1	—	—
1978–79	Morton	P	—	—
1979–80	Morton	P	30	2
1980–81	Morton	P	34	1
1981–82	Morton	P	36	—
1982–83	Morton	P	34	—
1983–84	Chelsea	2	41	—
1984–85	Chelsea	1	36	1
1985–86	Chelsea	1	40	1
1986–87	Chelsea	1	36	2
1987–88	Chelsea	1	36	1

McLEARY, Alan
6.10.64 London (MF)
5.10½ 10.10 Apprentice
LD Exeter C v Millwall
16.10.82 2–1

1981–82	Millwall	3	—	—
1982–83	Millwall	3	3	1
1983–84	Millwall	3	30	—
1984–85	Millwall	3	21	—
1985–86	Millwall	2	35	3
1986–87	Millwall	2	42	—
1987–88	Millwall	2	31	—

McLEISH, Alex
21.1.59 Glasgow (DF)
6.1 12.4 Glasgow United
LD Aberdeen v Dundee U
2.1.78 1–0

1977–78	Aberdeen	P	1	—
1978–79	Aberdeen	P	19	1
1979–80	Aberdeen	P	35	2
1980–81	Aberdeen	P	32	3
1981–82	Aberdeen	P	32	5
1982–83	Aberdeen	P	34	2
1983–84	Aberdeen	P	32	2
1984–85	Aberdeen	P	30	1
1985–86	Aberdeen	P	34	3
1986–87	Aberdeen	P	40	3
1987–88	Aberdeen	P	36	1

McLEOD, Gordon
2.10.67 Edinburgh (MF)
5.8 10.4 Hutchison Vale BC
LD Dundee U v Dumbarton
23.2.85 4–0

1983–84	Dundee U	P	—	—
1984–85	Dundee U	P	3	—
1985–86	Dundee U	P	3	—
1986–87	Dundee U	P	8	—
1987–88	Dundee U	P	12	3

MacLEOD, Joe
30.12.67 Edinburgh (MF)
5.7 9.11 Hutchison Vale BC
LD Dumbarton v Montrose
21.2.87 2–1

1984–85	Dundee U	P	—	—
1985–86	Dundee U	P	—	—
1986–87	*Dumbarton*	1	5	—
1986–87	Dundee U	P	2	—
1987–88	Dundee U	P	10	1

McLOUGHLIN, Alan
20.4.67 Manchester (DF)
5.8½ 10.0 Local
LD Newport Co v Swindon T
6.9.86 2–2

1984–85	Manchester U	1	—	—
1985–86	Manchester U	1	—	—
1986–87	Swindon T	3	9	—
1986–87	Torquay U	4	16	—
1987–88	Swindon T	2	8	—
1987–88	*Torquay U*	4	8	3

McLOUGHLIN, Paul
—
—
LD Hereford U v Rochdale
15.8.87 0–0

1987–88	Hereford U	4	29	1

McLOUGHLIN, Stephen
21.11.69 Nottingham F (FW)
— — Apprentice
LD — —

1987–88	Nottingham F	1	—	—

McMAHON, Steve
20.8.61 Liverpool (MF)
5.7 10.9 Apprentice
LD Sunderland v Everton
16.8.80 3–1

1979–80	Everton	1	—	—
1980–81	Everton	1	34	5
1981–82	Everton	1	32	2
1982–83	Everton	1	34	4
1983–84	Aston Villa	1	37	5
1984–85	Aston Villa	1	35	2
1985–86	Aston Villa	1	3	—
1985–86	Liverpool	1	23	6
1986–87	Liverpool	1	37	5
1987–88	Liverpool	1	40	9

McMENEMY, Paul
5.11.66 Farnborough (FW)
5.10 11.12 Apprentice
LD Aldershot v Torquay U
29.3.86 1–1

1984–85	West Ham U	1	—	—
1985–86	West Ham U	1	—	—
1985–86	*Aldershot*	4	10	5
1986–87	*Northampton T*	4	4	2
1987–88	West Ham U	1	—	—

McMILLAN, Andy
22.6.68 S Africa (DF)
5.10 10.13 Apprentice
LD York C v Mansfield T
28.12.87 2–2

1987–88	York C	3	22	—

McMINN, Ted
28.9.62 Castle Douglas (FW)
5.11 11.2 Glenafton Athletic
LD East Stirling v Queen of the S
3.11.82 1–2

1982–83	Queen of the S	2	22	1
1983–84	Queen of the S	2	32	3
1984–85	Queen of the S	2	8	1
1984–85	Rangers	P	20	1
1985–86	Rangers	P	28	2
1986–87	Rangers	P	15	1
1987–88	Seville (Spain)			

McNAB, Neil
4.6.57 Greenock (MF)
5.7 10.10
LD Morton v Partick Th
14.4.73 5–0

1972–73	Morton	1	3	—
1973–74	Morton	1	11	—
1973–74	Tottenham H	1	1	—
1974–75	Tottenham H	1	2	—
1975–76	Tottenham H	1	15	—
1976–77	Tottenham H	1	10	—
1977–78	Tottenham H	2	42	3
1978–79	Tottenham H	1	2	—
1978–79	Bolton W	1	23	3
1979–80	Bolton W	1	12	1
1979–80	Brighton & HA	1	16	—
1980–81	Brighton & HA	1	33	1
1981–82	Brighton & HA	1	40	3
1982–83	Brighton & HA	1	14	—
1982–83	*Leeds U*	2	5	—
1982–83	*Portsmouth*	3	—	—
1983–84	Manchester C	2	33	1
1984–85	Manchester C	2	18	—
1985–86	Manchester C	1	37	4
1986–87	Manchester C	1	42	4
1987–88	Manchester C	2	37	2

McNALLY, Bernard
17.2.63 Shrewsbury (FW)
5.7 9.11 Apprentice
LD Shrewsbury T v Preston NE
21.2.81 3–0

1980–81	Shrewsbury T	2	1	—
1981–82	Shrewsbury T	2	33	1
1982–83	Shrewsbury T	2	25	1
1983–84	Shrewsbury T	2	41	4
1984–85	Shrewsbury T	2	42	2
1985–86	Shrewsbury T	2	35	6
1986–87	Shrewsbury T	2	40	5
1987–88	Shrewsbury T	2	43	2

McNAUGHT, John
19.6.64 Glasgow (DF)
5.11 11.12 Auchengill BC
LD St Johnstone v Hamilton A
4.9.82 3-0

1982–83	Hamilton A	1	27	1
1983–84	Hamilton A	1	28	3
1984–85	Hamilton A	1	27	4
1985–86	Hamilton A	1	24	11
1985–86	Chelsea	1	1	—
1986–87	Chelsea	1	8	2
1987–88	Chelsea	1	1	—
1987–88	Partick Th	1	10	3
1987–88	Hamilton A	1	4	1

McNICHOL, Jim
9.6.58 Glasgow (DF)
6.0 12.10 Ipswich T Apprentice
LD Luton T v Bolton W
7.5.77 1-1

1976–77	Luton T	2	2	—
1977–78	Luton T	2	12	—
1978–79	Luton T	2	1	—
1978–79	Brentford	3	32	4
1979–80	Brentford	3	31	8
1980–81	Brentford	3	14	—
1981–82	Brentford	3	26	3
1982–83	Brentford	3	32	3
1983–84	Brentford	3	20	4
1984–85	Exeter C	4	42	5
1985–86	Exeter C	4	45	5
1986–87	Torquay U	4	42	3
1987–88	Torquay U	4	46	6

McPARLAND, Ian
4.10.61 Edinburgh (MF)
5.8 10.8 Ormiston Primrose
LD Preston NE v Notts Co
27.12.80 2-2

1980–81	Notts Co	2	2	—
1981–82	Notts Co	1	12	—
1982–83	Notts Co	1	11	1
1983–84	Notts Co	1	21	2
1984–85	Notts Co	2	20	—
1985–86	Notts Co	3	44	15
1986–87	Notts Co	3	45	24
1987–88	Notts Co	3	43	21

McPHEE, Ian
31.1.61 Perth (MF)
5.8 9.13 Perth schools
LD Alloa v Forfar Ath
24.2.79 2-0

1978–79	Celtic	P	—	—
1978–79	Forfar Ath	2	12	1
1979–80	Forfar Ath	2	39	6
1980–81	Forfar Ath	2	35	1
1981–82	Forfar Ath	2	31	4
1982–83	Forfar Ath	2	39	6
1983–84	Forfar Ath	2	39	5
1984–85	Forfar Ath	1	39	3
1985–86	Forfar Ath	1	37	2
1986–87	Forfar Ath	1	41	4
1987–88	Forfar Ath	1	1	—
1987–88	Dundee U	P	10	1

McPHERSON, David
28.1.64 Paisley (DF)
6.3 11.11 Gartcosh United
LD Morton v Rangers
9.10.82 0-0

1980–81	Rangers	P	—	—
1981–82	Rangers	P	—	—
1982–83	Rangers	P	18	1
1983–84	Rangers	P	36	2
1984–85	Rangers	P	31	—
1985–86	Rangers	P	34	5
1986–87	Rangers	P	42	7
1987–88	Rangers	P	44	4

McPHERSON, Keith
11.9.63 Greenwich (DF)
5.11 10.11 Apprentice
LD West Ham U v Liverpool
20.5.85 0-3

1981–82	West Ham U	1	—	—
1982–83	West Ham U	1	—	—
1983–84	West Ham U	1	—	—
1984–85	West Ham U	1	1	—
1985–86	*Cambridge U*	4	11	1
1985–86	Northampton T	4	20	—
1986–87	Northampton T	4	46	5
1987–88	Northampton T	3	32	—

McPHILLIPS, Terry
1.10.68 Liverpool (FW)
— — Liverpool
LD Halifax T v Newport Co
5.9.87 3-1

1987–88	Halifax T	4	25	3

McQUEEN, Tommy
1.4.63 Bellshill (DF)
5.11 11.0 Gartcosh United
LD Clyde v Stenhousemuir
29.8.81 3-0

1981–82	Clyde	2	39	—
1982–83	Clyde	1	35	—
1983–84	Clyde	1	38	1
1984–85	Aberdeen	P	35	3
1985–86	Aberdeen	P	17	3
1986–87	Aberdeen	P	1	—
1986–87	West Ham U	1	9	—
1987–88	West Ham U	1	12	—

McSTAY, Paul
22.10.64 Hamilton (MF)
5.10 10.7 Celtic BC
LD Aberdeen v Celtic
30.1.82 1-3

1981–82	Celtic	P	10	1
1982–83	Celtic	P	36	6
1983–84	Celtic	P	34	3
1984–85	Celtic	P	32	4
1985–86	Celtic	P	34	8
1986–87	Celtic	P	43	3
1987–88	Celtic	P	44	5

McSTAY, Willie
26.11.61 Hamilton (DF)
5.11 10.7 Celtic BC
LD Celtic v Motherwell
2.4.83 3-0

1979–80	Celtic	P	—	—
1980–81	Celtic	P	—	—
1981–82	Celtic	P	—	—
1982–83	Celtic	P	1	—
1983–84	Celtic	P	19	1
1984–85	Celtic	P	14	1
1985–86	Celtic	P	18	—
1986–87	Celtic	P	16	—
1986–87	Huddersfield T	2	1	—
1987–88	Huddersfield T	2	8	—
1987–88	*Notts Co*	3	1	—
1987–88	Notts Co	3	8	—

McSWEGAN, Gary
24.9.70 Glasgow (FW)
5.7½ 10.9 Rangers Amateur BC
LD Rangers v Hibernian
16.4.88 1-1

1987–88	Rangers	P	1	—

McWALTER, Mark
20.6.68 Arbroath (FW)
5.11 10.9 Arbroath Lads Club
LD Arbroath v Montrose
18.8.84 0-3

1984–85	Arbroath	2	14	2
1985–86	Arbroath	2	37	14
1986–87	Arbroath	2	19	4
1987–88	St Mirren	P	4	—

McWHIRTER, Norman
4.9.69 Johnstone (DF)
5.9 9.6 Linwood Rangers BC
LD Aberden v St Mirren
28.3.87 0-1

1986–87	St Mirren	P	5	—
1986–87	St Mirren	P	24	1

MABBUTT, Gary
23.8.61 Bristol (MF)
5.9 10.10 Apprentice
LD Burnley v Bristol R
16.12.78 2-0

1978–79	Bristol R	2	11	—
1979–80	Bristol R	2	33	—
1980–81	Bristol R	2	42	5
1981–82	Bristol R	3	45	5
1982–83	Tottenham H	1	38	10
1983–84	Tottenham H	1	21	2
1984–85	Tottenham H	1	25	2
1985–86	Tottenham H	1	32	3
1986–87	Tottenham H	1	37	1
1987–88	Tottenham H	1	37	2

PLAYER DIRECTORY

MADDEN, Craig
25.9.58 Manchester (FW)
5.8 10.2 Northern Nomads
LD Chesterfield v Bury
18.3.87 2–1

1977–78 Bury	3	4	—
1978–79 Bury	3	13	1
1979–80 Bury	3	35	10
1980–81 Bury	4	30	10
1981–82 Bury	4	46	35
1982–83 Bury	4	43	20
1983–84 Bury	4	46	17
1984–85 Bury	4	46	22
1985–86 Bury	4	34	14
1985–86 WBA	1	9	2
1986–87 WBA	2	3	1
1986–87 Blackpool	3	19	5
1987–88 Blackpool	3	34	11

MADDEN, Lawrie
28.9.55 London (DF)
6.0 12.6 Arsenal Amateur
LD Mansfield T v Stockport Co
1.4.75 1–1

1974–75 Mansfield T	4	7	—
1975–76 Mansfield T	4	3	—
From Manchester Univ			
1977–78 Charlton Ath	2	4	—
1978–79 Charlton Ath	2	38	3
1979–80 ·Charlton Ath	3	36	1
1980–81 Charlton Ath	3	28	1
1981–82 Charlton Ath	2	7	2
1981–82 Millwall	3	10	—
1982–83 Millwall	3	37	2
1983–84 Sheffield W	2	38	1
1984–85 Sheffield W	1	19	—
1985–86 Sheffield W	1	25	—
1986–87 Sheffield W	1	35	1
1987–88 Sheffield W	1	38	—

MADDISON, Neil
— Darlington (MF)
5.9 11.8 Apprentice
LD —

1987–88 Southampton	1	—	—

MADDIX, Danny
11.10.67 Ashford (FW)
5.11 11.0 Apprentice
LD Southend U v Scunthorpe U
4.11.86 3–1

1985–86 Tottenham H	1	—	—
1986–87 Southend U	4	2	—
1987–88 QPR	1	9	—

MADDY, Paul
17.8.62 Cwmcarn (MF)
5.10 9.10½ Apprentice
LD Cardiff C v Bristol R
20.9.80 2–1

1980–81 Cardiff C	2	8	2
1981–82 Cardiff C	2	27	1
1982–83 Cardiff C	3	8	—

1982–83 Stoke C	1	—	—
1982–83 Hereford U	4	9	1
1983–84 Swansea C	2	20	3
1983–84 Hereford U	4	10	1
1984–85 Hereford U	4	34	8
1985–86 Hereford U	4	33	7
1986–87 Brentford	3	31	5
1987–88 Chester C	3	18	1
1987–88 Hereford U	4	8	—

MADRICK, Carl
20.9.68 Bolton (MF)
— — Apprentice
LD Huddersfield T v Birmingham C
27.2.88 2–2

1987–88 Huddersfield T	2	8	1

MAGILTON, James
— — Belfast (MF)
5.10½ 12.7 School
LD —

1987–88 Liverpool	1	—	—

MAGUIRE, Gavin
24.11.67 Hammersmith (MF)
5.10 11.8 Apprentice
LD Oxford U v QPR
27.12.86 0–1

1985–86 QPR	1	—	—
1986–87 QPR	1	14	—
1987–88 QPR	1	18	—

MAIL, David
12.9.62 Bristol (DF)
5.10 11.4 Apprentice
LD Derby Co v Blackburn R
25.9.82 1–2

1980–81 Aston Villa	1	—	—
1981–82 Blackburn R	2	—	—
1982–83 Blackburn R	2	34	—
1983–84 Blackburn R	2	11	1
1984–85 Blackburn R	2	4	—
1985–86 Blackburn R	2	18	1
1986–87 Blackburn R	2	38	—
1987–88 Blackburn R	2	36	—

MAIN, Alan
5.12.67 Elgin (GK)
5.11½ 12.3 Elgin City
LD Dundee U v Dundee
28.3.87 1–1

1986–87 Dundee U	P	2	—
1987–88 Dundee U	P	8	—

MAIR, Gordon
18.12.58 Bothwell (MF)
5.11 10.3 Apprentice
LD Fulham v Notts Co
20.11.76 1–5

1976–77 Notts Co	2	5	—
1977–78 Notts Co	2	—	—
1978–79 Notts Co	2	4	1
1979–80 Notts Co	2	42	5
1980–81 Notts Co	2	4	—
1981–82 Notts Co	1	34	9
1982–83 Notts Co	1	25	4
1983–84 Notts Co	1	17	—
1984–85 Lincoln C	3	31	—
1985–86 Lincoln C	3	26	3
1986–87 Motherwell	P	29	1

MALKIN, Chris
4.6.67 Bebington (FW)
6.0 10.12 Overpool
LD Tranmere R v Exeter C
31.8.87 2–1

1987–88 Tranmere R	4	5	—

MALPAS, Maurice
3.8.62 Dunfermline (DF)
5.8 10.11 'S' Form
LD Dundee U v Airdrieonians
21.11.81 4–0

1979–80 Dundee U	P	—	—
1980–81 Dundee U	P	—	—
1981–82 Dundee U	P	19	—
1982–83 Dundee U	P	34	1
1983–84 Dundee U	P	34	2
1984–85 Dundee U	P	35	2
1985–86 Dundee U	P	36	2
1986–87 Dundee U	P	36	—
1987–88 Dundee U	P	44	—

MANUEL, Billy
28.6.69 London (DF)
— — Trainee
LD —

1987–88 Tottenham H	1	—	—

MARDON, Paul
14.9.69 Bristol (DF)
6.0 11.10 Apprentice
LD Preston NE v Bristol C
9.1.88 2–0

1987–88 Bristol C	3	8	—

MARKER, Nick
3.5.65 Exeter (DF)
6.1 13.0 Apprentice
LD Burnley v Exeter C
17.10.81 3–3

1981–82 Exeter C	3	14	1
1982–83 Exeter C	3	18	1
1983–84 Exeter C	3	31	—
1984–85 Exeter C	4	45	—
1985–86 Exeter C	4	40	—
1986–87 Exeter C	4	43	1
1987–88 Exeter C	4	11	—
1987–88 Plymouth Arg	2	—	—
1987–88 Plymouth Arg	2	26	—

MARKS, Michael
23.3.68 Lambeth (FW)
— —
LD Reading v Millwall
23.8.86 0-1

1986–87 Millwall	2	36	10
1987–88 Millwall	2	—	—
1987–88 *Mansfield T*	3	1	—
1987–88 Leyton Orient	4	3	—

MARPLES, Chris
3.8.64 Chesterfield (GK)
5.11 11.12 Sutton T and Goole
LD Bury v Chesterfield
29.9.84 0-0

1984–85 Chesterfield	4	38	—
1985–86 Chesterfield	3	32	—
1986–87 Chesterfield	3	14	—
1986–87 Stockport Co	4	13	—
1987–88 Stockport Co	4	44	—

MARSH, Michael
— Kirby T (FW)
5.8 11.0 Apprentice
LD —

1987–88 Liverpool	1	—	—

MARSHALL, Colin
1.11.69 Glasgow (FW)
5.5 9.5 YTS
LD —

1987–88 Barnsley	2	—	—

MARSHALL, Gary
20.4.64 Bristol (FW)
5.11½ 10.10 Shepton Mallet
LD Bristol C v Chesterfield
26.11.83 2-0

1983–84 Bristol C	4	1	—
1984–85 Bristol C	3	5	2
1984–85 *Torquay U*	4	7	1
1985–86 Bristol C	3	19	2
1986–87 Bristol C	3	24	2
1987–88 Bristol C	3	19	1

MARSHALL, Ian
20.3.66 Oxford (DF)
6.1 12.12 Apprentice
LD Everton v WBA
20.8.85 2-0

1983–84 Everton	1	—	—
1984–85 Everton	1	—	—
1985–86 Everton	1	9	—
1986–87 Everton	1	2	1
1987–88 Everton	1	4	—
1987–88 *Oldham Ath*	2	2	—
1987–88 Oldham Ath	2	8	—

MARSHALL, John
18.8.64 Surrey (DF)
5.10 11.5 Apprentice
LD Fulham v Portsmouth
3.9.83 0-2

1982–83 Fulham	2	—	—
1983–84 Fulham	2	25	—
1984–85 Fulham	2	32	1
1985–86 Fulham	2	42	3
1986–87 Fulham	3	29	4
1987–88 Fulham	3	25	2

MARTIN, Alvin
29.7.58 Bootle (DF)
6.1 13.3 Apprentice
LD Aston Villa v West Ham U
18.3.78 4-1

1976–77 West Ham U	1	—	—
1977–78 West Ham U	1	7	1
1978–79 West Ham U	2	22	1
1979–80 West Ham U	2	40	2
1980–81 West Ham U	2	41	1
1981–82 West Ham U	1	28	4
1982–83 West Ham U	1	38	3
1983–84 West Ham U	1	29	3
1984–85 West Ham U	1	40	1
1985–86 West Ham U	1	40	4
1986–87 West Ham U	1	16	2
1987–88 West Ham U	1	15	—

MARTIN, Brian
24.2.63 Bellshill (DF)
6.0 13.0 Shotts Bon Accord
LD Airdrieonians v Falkirk
7.9.85 1-1

1985–86 Falkirk	1	25	1
1986–87 Falkirk	P	34	1
1986–87 Hamilton A	P	7	—
1987–88 Hamilton A	1	23	—
1987–88 St Mirren	P	12	1

MARTIN, David
25.4.63 East Ham (MF)
6.1 11.8 Apprentice
LD Rotherham U v Millwall
25.3.80 2-1

1979–80 Millwall	3	3	—
1980–81 Millwall	3	33	1
1981–82 Millwall	3	38	1
1982–83 Millwall	3	33	1
1983–84 Millwall	3	31	3
1984–85 Millwall	3	2	—
1984–85 Wimbledon	2	20	2
1985–86 Wimbledon	2	15	1
1986–87 Southend U	4	32	3
1987–88 Southend U	3	41	—

MARTIN, Dean
9.9.67 Halifax (MF)
5.10 10.2 Local
LD Halifax T v Northampton T
30.9.86 3-6

1984–85 Halifax T	4	—	—
1985–86 Halifax T	4	—	—
1986–87 Halifax T	4	16	1
1987–88 Halifax T	4	40	3

MARTIN, Lee
9.9.68 Huddersfield (GK)
— — Apprentice
LD WBA v Huddersfield T
24.10.87 3-2

1987–88 Huddersfield T	2	18	—

MARTIN, Lee
5.2.68 Hyde (DF)
5.11 11.5
LD Manchester U v Wimbledon
9.5.88 2-1

1987–88 Manchester U	1	1	—

MARTINDALE, David
9.4.64 Liverpool (MF)
5.11 11.10 Caernarfon
LD Scunthorpe U v Tranmere R
15.8.87 3-0

1987–88 Tranmere R	4	34	4

MARTYN, Tony
11.8.66 St Austell (GK)
6.2 14.0 St Blaizey
LD Bristol R v Rotherham U
15.8.87 3-1

1987–88 Bristol R	3	39	—

MARWOOD, Brian
5.2.60 Seaham Harbour (MF)
5.7½ 10.10 Apprentice
LD Hull C v Mansfield T
12.1.80 3-1

1977–78 Hull C	2	—	—
1978–79 Hull C	3	—	—
1979–80 Hull C	3	6	—
1980–81 Hull C	3	31	4
1981–82 Hull C	4	42	12
1982–83 Hull C	4	40	19
1983–84 Hull C	3	39	16
1984–85 Sheffield W	1	41	7
1985–86 Sheffield W	1	37	13
1986–87 Sheffield W	1	32	5
1987–88 Sheffield W	1	18	2
1987–88 Arsenal	1	4	1

MASKELL, Craig
10.4.68 Aldershot (MF)
5.9 10.5 Apprentice
LD Birmingham C v Southampton
19.4.86 0-2

1985–86 Southampton	1	2	1
1986–87 Southampton	1	4	—
1986–87 *Swindon T*	3	—	—
1987–88 Southampton	1	—	—

PLAYER DIRECTORY

MASON, Keith
19.7.58 Leicester (GK)
6.1 13.7
LD Huddersfield T v Cardiff C
23.10.82 4–0

1982–83	Huddersfield T	3	1	—
1983–84	Huddersfield T	2	19	—
1984–85	Huddersfield T	2	5	—
1985–86	Huddersfield T	2	5	—
1986–87	Huddersfield T	2	—	—
1987–88	Huddersfield T	2	—	—

MATTHEWS, John
1.11.55 London (DF)
6.0 12.6 Apprentice
LD Leicester C v Arsenal
17.8.74 0–1

1973–74	Arsenal	1	—	—
1974–75	Arsenal	1	20	—
1975–76	Arsenal	1	1	—
1976–77	Arsenal	1	17	2
1977–78	Arsenal	1	7	—
1978–79	Sheffield U	2	32	5
1979–80	Sheffield U	3	32	5
1980–81	Sheffield U	3	14	1
1981–82	Sheffield U	4	25	3
1982–83	Mansfield T	4	40	3
1983–84	Mansfield T	4	32	3
1984–85	Chesterfield	4	38	1
1985–86	Plymouth Arg	3	31	1
1986–87	Plymouth Arg	2	39	2
1987–88	Plymouth Arg	2	35	1

MATTHEWS, Mike
25.9.60 Hull (FW)
5.8 11.3 Apprentice
LD Wolves v Everton
4.5.81 0–0

1978–79	Wolves	1	—	—
1979–80	Wolves	1	—	—
1980–81	Wolves	1	1	—
1981–82	Wolves	1	32	2
1982–83	Wolves	2	40	5
1983–84	Wolves	1	3	—
1983–84	Scunthorpe U	3	25	1
1984–85	Scunthorpe U	4	22	3
1985–86	Scunthorpe U	4	11	1
1986–87	Halifax T	4	39	4
1987–88	Halifax T	4	45	3

MATTHEWS, Neil
3.12.67 Manchester (DF)
— — Apprentice
LD Darlington v Blackpool
26.8.85 2–1

1985–86	Blackpool	3	1	—
1986–87	Blackpool	3	22	—
1987–88	Blackpool	3	27	—

MATTHEWS, Neil
19.9.66 Grimsby (FW)
— —
LD Portsmouth v Grimsby T
13.10.84 3–2

1984–85	Grimsby T	2	4	1
1985–86	Grimsby T	2	4	—
1985–86	Scunthorpe U	4	1	—
1986–87	Grimsby T	2	3	—
1986–87	Halifax T	4	9	2
1986–87	Bolton W	3	1	—
1987–88	Halifax T	4	32	10

MAUCHLEN, Alister
29.6.60 Kilwinning (MF)
5.7 10.5 Irvine Meadow
LD Kilmarnock v Raith R
14.10.78 3–0

1978–79	Kilmarnock	1	20	—
1979–80	Kilmarnock	P	30	2
1980–81	Kilmarnock	P	31	3
1981–82	Kilmarnock	1	37	4
1982–83	Kilmarnock	P	2	1
1982–83	Motherwell	P	25	3
1983–84	Motherwell	P	20	—
1984–85	Motherwell	1	30	1
1985–86	Motherwell	P	1	—
1985–86	Leicester C	1	37	2
1986–87	Leicester C	1	30	1
1987–88	Leicester C	2	36	2

MAXWELL, Alistair
29.6.60 Hamilton (GK)
5.7 10.5 Fir Park BC
LD Aberdeen v Motherwell
7.4.84 2–1

1981–82	Motherwell	1	—	—
1982–83	Motherwell	P	—	—
1983–84	Motherwell	P	4	—
1984–85	Motherwell	1	15	—
1985–86	Motherwell	P	4	—
1986–87	Motherwell	P	21	—
1987–88	Clydebank	1	1	—
1987–88	Motherwell	P	1	—

MAY, Andy
26.2.64 Bury (DF)
5.8 10.10 Apprentice
LD Ipswich T v Manchester C
25.4.81 1–0

1980–81	Manchester C	1	1	—
1981–82	Manchester C	1	6	—
1982–83	Manchester C	1	8	—
1983–84	Manchester C	2	42	5
1984–85	Manchester C	2	39	3
1985–86	Manchester C	1	37	—
1986–87	Manchester C	1	17	—
1987–88	Huddersfield T	2	28	3
1987–88	Bolton W	4	10	2

MAY, Edward
30.8.67 Edinburgh (FW)
5.7 10.3 Hutchison Vale BC
LD Dundee v Hibernian
14.9.85 1–0

1983–84	Dundee U	P	—	—
1984–85	Dundee U	P	—	—
1984–85	Hibernian	P	—	—
1985–86	Hibernian	P	19	1
1986–87	Hibernian	P	30	5
1987–88	Hibernian	P	35	2

MAY, Larry
26.12.58 Sutton Coldfield (DF)
6.0½ 12.6 Apprentice
LD Leicester C v Bristol C
26.3.77 0–0

1976–77	Leicester C	1	1	—
1977–78	Leicester C	1	5	—
1978–79	Leicester C	2	36	4
1979–80	Leicester C	2	42	4
1980–81	Leicester C	1	34	—
1981–82	Leicester C	2	34	3
1982–83	Leicester C	2	35	1
1983–84	Barnsley	2	41	1
1984–85	Barnsley	2	23	1
1985–86	Barnsley	2	36	—
1986–87	Barnsley	2	22	1
1986–87	Sheffield W	1	13	—
1987–88	Sheffield W	1	18	1

MAZZON, Giorgio
4.9.60 Cheshunt (DF)
5.10 11.5 Hertford T
LD Tottenham H v Birmingham C
10.1.81 1–0

1978–79	Tottenham H	1	—	—
1979–80	Tottenham H	1	—	—
1980–81	Tottenham H	1	2	—
1981–82	Tottenham H	1	—	—
1982–83	Tottenham H	1	—	—
1983–84	Aldershot	4	45	3
1984–85	Aldershot	4	33	1
1985–86	Aldershot	4	44	—
1986–87	Aldershot	4	45	1
1987–88	Aldershot	3	—	—

MEACHAM, Jeff
6.2.62 Bristol (FW)
— —
LD Chesterfield v Bristol R
28.3.87 1–1

1986–87	Bristol R	3	12	5
1987–88	Bristol R	3	14	4

MEASHAM, Ian
14.12.64 Barnsley (DF)
5.11 11.1 Apprentice
LD Huddersfield T v Crystal Palace
16.2.85 2–0

1982–83	Huddersfield T	3	—	—
1983–84	Huddersfield T	2	—	—
1984–85	Huddersfield T	2	17	—
1985–86	Huddersfield T	2	—	—
1985–86	Lincoln C	3	6	—
1985–86	Rochdale	4	12	—
1986–87	Cambridge U	4	46	—
1987–88	Cambridge U	4	—	—

MEGSON, Gary
2.5.59 Manchester (MF)
5.10 11.6 Apprentice
LD Plymouth Arg v Portsmouth
29.10.77 3–1

1977–78	Plymouth Arg	3	24	2
1978–79	Plymouth Arg	3	42	8
1979–80	Plymouth Arg	3	12	—
1979–80	Everton	1	12	1
1980–81	Everton	1	10	1
1981–82	Sheffield W	2	40	5
1982–83	Sheffield W	2	41	4
1983–84	Sheffield W	2	42	4
1984–85	Nottingham F	1	—	—
1984–85	Newcastle U	1	20	1
1985–86	Newcastle U	1	4	—
1985–86	Sheffield W	1	20	3
1986–87	Sheffield W	1	35	6
1987–88	Sheffield W	1	37	2

MEHEW, David
29.10.67 Camberley (FW)
5.11 11.7
LD Bournemouth v Bristol R
26.10.85 6–1

1984–85	Leeds U	2	—	—
1985–86	Bristol R	3	4	—
1986–87	Bristol R	3	21	10
1987–88	Bristol R	3	18	8

MELROSE, Jim
7.10.58 Glasgow (FW)
5.8½ 11.2 Eastercraigs
LD Partick Th v Queen of the S
27.9.75 2–1

1975–76	Partick T	1	2	—
1976–77	Partick T	P	27	8
1977–78	Partick T	P	25	4
1978–79	Partick T	P	33	10
1979–80	Partick T	P	35	9
1980–81	Leicester C	1	32	9
1981–82	Leicester C	2	35	11
1982–83	Leicester C	2	5	1
1982–83	Coventry C	1	24	8
1983–84	Celtic	P	29	7
1984–85	Celtic	P	—	—
1984–85	*Wolves*	2	7	2
1984–85	Manchester C	2	24	7
1985–86	Manchester C	1	10	1
1985–86	Charlton Ath	2	11	5
1986–87	Charlton Ath	1	34	14
1987–88	Charlton Ath	1	3	—
1987–88	Leeds U	2	4	—
1987–88	*Shrewsbury T*	2	3	—
1987–88	Shrewsbury T	2	6	1

MELVILLE, Andy
29.11.68 Swansea (DF)
6.1 12.6 School
LD Swansea C v Bristol C
23.11.85 1–3

1985–86	Swansea C	3	5	—
1986–87	Swansea C	4	42	3
1987–88	Swansea C	4	37	4

MENDONCA, Clive
9.9.68 Tullington (FW)
— — Apprentice
LD Brighton & HA v Sheffield U
2.5.87 2–0

1986–87	Sheffield U	2	2	—
1987–88	Sheffield U	2	11	4
1987–88	*Doncaster R*	3	2	—
1987–88	Rotherham U	3	8	2

MENNIE, Vince
19.5.64 Dortmund (FW)
5.9 11.4 Borussia Lippstadt
LD Dundee v Celtic
1.2.86 1–3

1983–84	Cologne	1	17	1
1984–85	Cologne	1	7	1
1985–86	Cologne	1	5	—
1985–86	Dundee	P	11	1
1986–87	Dundee	P	20	1
1987–88	Dundee	P	29	1

MERCER, William
— Liverpool (GK)
6.1½ 11.0 School
LD —

1987–88	Liverpool	1	—	—

MERSON, Paul
20.3.68 London (FW)
5.10 11.9 Apprentice
LD Arsenal v Manchester C
22.11.86 3–0

1985–86	Arsenal	1	—	—
1986–87	Arsenal	1	7	3
1986–87	*Brentford*	3	7	—
1987–88	Arsenal	1	15	5

METGOD, Johnny
27.2.58 Amsterdam (MF)
6.4 13.6½ Real Madrid
LD Sheffield W v Nottingham F
25.8.84 3–1

1984–85	Nottingham F	1	40	6
1985–86	Nottingham F	1	39	6
1986–87	Nottingham F	1	37	3
1987–88	Tottenham H	1	12	—

METHVEN, Colin
10.12.55 India (DF)
6.2 12.7 Leven Royals
LD Stranraer v East Fife
26.4.75 2–1

1974–75	East Fife	2	1	—
1975–76	East Fife	1	26	1
1976–77	East Fife	1	39	—
1977–78	East Fife	1	39	2
1978–79	East Fife	2	39	11
1979–80	Wigan Ath	4	35	2
1980–81	Wigan Ath	4	46	2
1981–82	Wigan Ath	4	46	9
1982–83	Wigan Ath	3	44	1
1983–84	Wigan Ath	3	39	—
1984–85	Wigan Ath	3	43	—
1985–86	Wigan Ath	3	43	7
1986–87	Blackpool	3	46	5
1987–88	Blackpool	3	40	2

MICKLEWHITE, Gary
21.3.61 Manchester (FW)
5.7 10.4 Apprentice
LD QPR v Oldham Ath
15.11.80 2–0

1977–78	Manchester U	1	—	—
1978–79	Manchester U	1	—	—
1979–80	QPR	2	—	—
1980–81	QPR	2	1	—
1981–82	QPR	2	26	2
1982–83	QPR	2	34	6
1983–84	QPR	1	30	2
1984–85	QPR	1	15	1
1984–85	Derby Co	3	19	4
1985–86	Derby Co	3	46	11
1986–87	Derby Co	2	42	6
1987–88	Derby Co	1	16	1

MILLAR, John
8.12.66 Lanark (DF)
5.7 10.0
LD Chelsea v Oxford U
8.2.86 1–4

1984–85	Chelsea	1	—	—
1985–86	Chelsea	1	7	—
1986–87	Chelsea	1	4	—
1986–87	*Northampton T*	4	1	—
1986–87	*Hamilton A*	P	10	—
1987–88	Blackburn R	2	15	—

MILLEN, Keith
26.9.66 Croydon (DF)
6.1 12.5 Juniors
LD York C v Brentford
2.3.85 1–0

1984–85	Brentford	3	17	—
1985–86	Brentford	3	32	2
1986–87	Brentford	3	39	2
1987–88	Brentford	3	40	3

MILLER, Alan
29.3.70 Epping (GK)
— — Apprentice
LD —

1987–88	Arsenal	1	—	—

MILLER, David
8.1.64 Burnley (MF)
5.10½ 10.3 Apprentice
LD Burnley v Sheffield W
1.1.83 4–1

1981–82	Burnley	3	—	—
1982–83	Burnley	2	1	—
1982–83	*Crewe Alex*	4	3	—
1983–84	Burnley	3	17	2
1984–85	Burnley	3	14	1
1985–86	Tranmere R	4	29	1
1986–87	Preston NE	4	15	—
1987–88	Preston NE	3	28	2

PLAYER DIRECTORY

MILLER, Ian
13.5.55 Perth (FW)
5.9 11.7
LD Workington v Bury
1.9.73 0-0

1973-74 Bury	4	15	—
1974-75 Bury	3	—	—
1974-75 Nottingham F	2	—	—
1975-76 Doncaster R	4	43	9
1976-77 Doncaster R	4	46	5
1977-78 Doncaster R	4	35	—
1978-79 Swindon T	3	44	3
1979-80 Swindon T	3	40	2
1980-81 Swindon T	3	43	4
1981-82 Blackburn R	2	42	3
1982-83 Blackburn R	2	32	4
1983-84 Blackburn R	2	36	3
1984-85 Blackburn R	2	38	4
1985-86 Blackburn R	2	38	1
1986-87 Blackburn R	2	28	—
1987-88 Blackburn R	2	23	—

MILLER, Joe
8.12.67 Glasgow (FW)
5.8 9.12 'S' Form
LD Aberdeen v Dundee U
22.12.84 0-1

1984-85 Aberdeen	P	1	—
1985-86 Aberdeen	P	18	3
1986-87 Aberdeen	P	27	6
1987-88 Aberdeen	P	14	4
1987-88 Celtic	P	27	3

MILLER, Paul
11.10.59 London (DF)
6.1 12.2 Apprentice
LD Arsenal v Tottenham H
10.4.79 1-0

1977-78 Tottenham H	2	—	—
1978-79 Tottenham H	1	7	—
1979-80 Tottenham H	1	27	2
1980-81 Tottenham H	1	25	2
1981-82 Tottenham H	1	35	—
1982-83 Tottenham H	1	23	1
1983-84 Tottenham H	1	21	—
1984-85 Tottenham H	1	39	—
1985-86 Tottenham H	1	29	2
1986-87 Tottenham H	1	2	—
1986-87 Charlton Ath	1	14	1
1987-88 Charlton Ath	1	22	1

MILLER, Paul
—

— —

LD Watford v Wimbledon
15.8.87 1-0

1987-88 Wimbledon	1	5	—
1987-88 *Newport Co*	4	6	2

MILLER, Willie
2.5.55 Glasgow (DF)
5.10 11.8 Eastercraigs
LD Motherwell v Aberdeen
1.9.73 0-0

1971-72 Aberdeen	1	—	—
1972-73 Aberdeen	1	—	—
1973-74 Aberdeen	1	31	1
1974-75 Aberdeen	1	34	1
1975-76 Aberdeen	P	36	—
1976-77 Aberdeen	P	36	—
1977-78 Aberdeen	P	36	2
1978-79 Aberdeen	P	34	—
1979-80 Aberdeen	P	31	1
1980-81 Aberdeen	P	33	2
1981-82 Aberdeen	P	36	—
1982-83 Aberdeen	P	36	2
1983-84 Aberdeen	P	34	2
1984-85 Aberdeen	P	34	3
1985-86 Aberdeen	P	33	1
1986-87 Aberdeen	P	36	2
1987-88 Aberdeen	P	42	—

MILLIGAN, Mike
20.2.67 Manchester (MF)
5.8 11.0
LD Sheffield U v Oldham Ath
12.4.86 2-0

1984-85 Oldham Ath	2	—	—
1985-86 Oldham Ath	2	5	1
1986-87 Oldham Ath	2	38	2
1987-88 Oldham Ath	2	39	1

MILLIGAN, Terry
10.1.66 Manchester (MF)
5.10 9.5 Apprentice
LD Rochdale v Crewe Alex
23.8.86 1-1

1983-84 Manchester C	2	—	—
New Zealand			
1985-86 Oldham Ath	2	—	—
1986-87 Crewe Alex	4	40	3
1987-88 Crewe Alex	4	37	2

MILLS, Gary
11.11.61 Northampton (FW)
5.11 11.5 Apprentice
LD Nottingham F v Arsenal
9.9.78 2-1

1978-79 Nottingham F	1	4	1
1979-80 Nottingham F	1	13	1
1980-81 Nottingham F	1	27	5
1981-82 Nottingham F	1	14	1
Seattle S, NASL			
1982-83 Derby Co	2	18	1
Seattle S, NASL			
1983-84 Nottingham F	1	7	—
1984-85 Nottingham F	1	26	4
1985-86 Nottingham F	1	14	—
1986-87 Nottingham F	1	32	—
1987-88 Notts Co	3	46	5

MILLS, Scott
29.3.70 Sudbury (DF)
— — Trainee
LD

1987-88 Ipswich T	2	—	—

MILLS, Simon
16.8.64 Sheffield (MF)
5.11 10.12 Apprentice
LD Sheffield W v Charlton Ath
3.1.83 5-4

1982-83 Sheffield W	2	1	—
1983-84 Sheffield W	2	2	—
1984-85 Sheffield W	1	2	—
1985-86 York C	3	36	2
1986-87 York C	3	45	1
1987-88 York C	3	18	2
1987-88 Port Vale	3	19	—

MILNE, Callum
27.8.65 Edinburgh (DF)
5.8 10.7 Salvesen BC
LD Hibernian v Dundee
2.3.85 0-1

1983-84 Hibernian	P	—	—
1984-85 Hibernian	P	1	—
1985-86 Hibernian	P	7	—
1986-87 Hibernian	P	2	—
1987-88 Hibernian	P	3	—

MILNE, Ralph
13.5.61 Dundee (FW)
5.8 11.10 'S' Form
LD Celtic v Dundee U
8.9.79 2-2

1977-78 Dundee U	P	—	—
1978-79 Dundee U	P	—	—
1979-80 Dundee U	P	13	2
1980-81 Dundee U	P	21	7
1981-82 Dundee U	P	35	8
1982-83 Dundee U	P	34	16
1983-84 Dundee U	P	25	5
1984-85 Dundee U	P	19	4
1985-86 Dundee U	P	18	1
1986-87 Dundee U	P	14	1
1986-87 Charlton Ath	1	12	—
1987-88 Charlton Ath	1	10	—
1987-88 *Bristol C*	3	4	1
1987-88 Bristol C	3	15	3

MILLTON, Russell
12.1.69 Folkestone (MF)
— — YTS
LD —

1987-88 Arsenal	1	—	—

MILTON, Simon
23.8.63 London (MF)
5.10 10.9 Bury St Edmunds
LD Swindon T v Ipswich T
28.12.87 4-2

1987-88 Ipswich T	2	8	1

Mirandinha

Photo: Bob Thomas Sports Photography.

PLAYER DIRECTORY

MIMMS, Bobby
12.10.63 York (GK)
6.2½ 12.13 Halifax T Apprentice
LD Rotherham U v Blackburn R
8.5.82 4–1

1981–82 Rotherham U	2	2	—
1982–83 Rotherham U	2	13	—
1983–84 Rotherham U	3	22	—
1984–85 Rotherham U	3	46	—
1985–86 Everton	1	10	—
1985–86 *Notts Co*	3	2	—
1986–87 Everton	1	11	—
1986–87 *Sunderland*	2	4	—
1986–87 *Blackburn R*	2	6	—
1987–88 Everton	1	8	—
1987–88 *Manchester C*	2	3	—
1987–88 *Tottenham H*	1	1	—
1987–88 Tottenham H	1	12	—

MIRANDINHA, (Fransisco da Silva)
2.7.59 Sao Paulo, Brazil (FW)
5.8 11.0 Palmeiras
LD Norwich C v Newcastle U
1.9.87 1–1

1987–88 Newcastle U	1	26	11

MITCHELL, Brian
16.7.63 Stonehaven (DF)
6.1 13.1 King St
LD Hibernian v Aberdeen
10.4.82 0–3

1981–82 Aberdeen	P	1	—
1982–83 Aberdeen	P	1	—
1983–84 Aberdeen	P	9	—
1984–85 Aberdeen	P	14	1
1985–86 Aberdeen	P	23	—
1986–87 Aberdeen	P	17	—
1986–87 Bradford C	2	16	—
1987–88 Bradford C	2	42	6

MITCHELL, Graham
16.2.68 Shipley (DF)
6.0 11.5 Apprentice
LD Crystal Palace v Huddersfield T
9.9.86 1–0

1986–87 Huddersfield T	2	17	—
1987–88 Huddersfield T	2	29	1

MITCHELL, Graham
2.11.62 Glasgow (MF)
5.10 11.8 Auchengill BC
LD Hamilton A v Raith R
7.3.81 0–2

1980–81 Hamilton A	1	4	—
1981–82 Hamilton A	1	37	—
1982–83 Hamilton A	1	32	1
1983–84 Hamilton A	1	21	1
1984–85 Hamilton A	1	30	—
1985–86 Hamilton A	1	32	6
1986–87 Hamilton A	P	23	1
1986–87 Hibernian	P	17	1
1987–88 Hibernian	P	41	1

MOHAN, Nicholas
6.10.70 Middlesbrough (DF)
6.2 12.0 Apprentice
LD —

1987–88 Middlesbrough	2	—	—

MOLBY, Jan
4.7.63 Kolding (MF)
6.1 14.7 Kolding, Ajax
LD Norwich C v Liverpool
25.8.84 3–3

1984–85 Liverpool	1	22	1
1985–86 Liverpool	1	39	13
1986–87 Liverpool	1	34	7
1987–88 Liverpool	1	7	—

MONCUR, John
22.9.66 Stepney (DF)
5.7 9.10 Apprentice
LD Doncaster R v York C
27.9.86 3–1

1984–85 Tottenham H	1	—	—
1985–86 Tottenham H	1	—	—
1986–87 Tottenham H	1	1	—
1986–87 *Doncaster R*	3	4	—
1986–87 *Cambridge U*	4	4	—
1987–88 Tottenham H	1	5	—

MONEY, Campbell
31.8.60 Maybole (GK)
5.11 12.3 Dailly Ams
LD Aberdeen v St Mirren
14.4.82 4–1

1978–79 St Mirren	P	—	—
1979–80 St Mirren	P	—	—
1980–81 St Mirren	P	—	—
1981–82 St Mirren	P	1	—
1982–83 St Mirren	P	1	—
1983–84 St Mirren	P	6	—
1984–85 St Mirren	P	30	—
1985–86 St Mirren	P	33	—
1986–87 St Mirren	P	42	—
1987–88 St Mirren	P	41	—

MONEY, Richard
13.10.55 Lowestoft (DF)
5.11½ 11.5 Lowestoft T
LD Peterborough U v Scunthorpe U
8.8.73 1–0

1973–74 Scunthorpe U	4	29	1
1974–75 Scunthorpe U	4	43	—
1975–76 Scunthorpe U	4	45	3
1976–77 Scunthorpe U	4	38	—
1977–78 Scunthorpe U	4	18	—
1977–78 Fulham	2	23	2
1978–79 Fulham	2	42	1
1979–80 Fulham	2	41	—
1979–80 Liverpool	1	—	—
1980–81 Liverpool	1	14	—
1981–82 Liverpool	1	—	—
1981–82 *Derby Co*	2	5	—
1981–82 Luton T	2	13	1
1982–83 Luton T	1	31	—
1983–84 Portsmouth	2	16	—
1984–85 Portsmouth	2	—	—
1985–86 Portsmouth	2	1	—
1985–86 Scunthorpe U	4	25	—
1986–87 Scunthorpe U	4	42	—
1987–88 Scunthorpe U	4	32	—

MOONEY, Brian
2.2.66 Dublin (MF)
5.10½ 11.2 Home Farm
LD Stockport Co v Wrexham
13.12.85 2–0

1983–84 Liverpool	1	—	—
1984–85 Liverpool	1	—	—
1985–86 Liverpool	1	—	—
1985–86 *Wrexham*	4	9	2
1986–87 Liverpool	1	—	—
1987–88 Liverpool	1	—	—
1987–88 *Preston NE*	3	7	—
1987–88 Preston NE	3	27	3

MOORE, Allan
25.12.64 Glasgow (FW)
5.6. 9.10 Possil YM
LD Hamilton A v Dumbarton
17.12.83 4–1

1983–84 Dumbarton	1	4	—
1984–85 Dumbarton	P	4	—
1985–86 Dumbarton	1	33	4
1986–87 Dumbarton	1	18	3
1986–87 Hearts	P	10	—
1987–88 Hearts	P	7	1

MOORE, John
1.10.66 Consett (FW)
6.0 11.11 Apprentice
LD Sunderland v Chelsea
30.3.85 0–2

1984–85 Sunderland	1	4	1
1984–85 *St Patrick's*	1	—	—
1985–86 Sunderland	2	—	—
1985–86 *Newport Co*	3	2	—
1986–87 Sunderland	2	3	—
1986–87 *Darlington*	3	2	1
1986–87 *Mansfield T*	3	5	1
1987–88 Sunderland	3	9	—
1987–88 *Rochdale*	4	10	2

MOORE, Kevin
29.4.58 Grimsby (DF)
5.11 11.2 Local
LD Bury v Grimsby T
21.8.76 2–0

1976–77	Grimsby T	3	28	—
1977–78	Grimsby T	4	42	—
1978–79	Grimsby T	4	46	6
1979–80	Grimsby T	3	41	4
1980–81	Grimsby T	2	41	1
1981–82	Grimsby T	2	36	4
1982–83	Grimsby T	2	38	—
1983–84	Grimsby T	2	41	1
1984–85	Grimsby T	2	31	4
1985–86	Grimsby T	2	31	2
1986–87	Grimsby T	2	25	5
1986–87	Oldham Ath	2	13	1
1987–88	Southampton	1	35	3

MOORE, Ronnie
29.1.53 Liverpool (FW)
6.0 13.12 Amateur
LD Oldham Ath v Tranmere R
13.11.71 3–1

1971–72	Tranmere R	3	2	—
1972–73	Tranmere R	3	—	—
1973–74	Tranmere R	3	46	2
1974–75	Tranmere R	3	44	2
1975–76	Tranmere R	4	46	34
1976–77	Tranmere R	3	42	9
1977–78	Tranmere R	3	43	17
1978–79	Tranmere R	3	26	8
1978–79	Cardiff C	2	18	3
1979–80	Cardiff C	2	38	3
1980–81	Rotherham U	3	45	23
1981–82	Rotherham U	2	40	21
1982–83	Rotherham U	2	36	5
1983–84	Rotherham U	3	4	2
1983–84	Charlton Ath	2	28	8
1984–85	Charlton Ath	2	34	5
1985–86	Rochdale	4	43	9
1986–87	Tranmere R	4	35	6
1987–88	Tranmere R	4	30	—

MORAN, Paul
22.5.68 Enfield (FW)
5.10 11.0 YTS
LD Everton v Tottenham H
11.5.87 1–0

1984–85	Tottenham H	1	—	—
1985–86	Tottenham H	1	—	—
1986–87	Tottenham H	1	1	—
1987–88	Tottenham H	1	13	1

MORGAN, Darren
5.11.67 Camberwell (DF)
5.6½ 9.5 Apprentice
LD Millwall v Bradford C
13.9.86 1–2

1985–86	Millwall	2	—	—
1986–87	Millwall	2	21	1
1987–88	Millwall	2	4	—

MORGAN, Gary
1.4.61 Consett (DF)
5.8 12.0 Consett
LD Berwick R v Queen's Park
20.8.83 3–0

1983–84	Berwick R	2	37	3
1984–85	Berwick R	2	30	1
1985–86	Darlington	3	41	1
1986–87	Darlington	3	22	1
1987–88	Darlington	4	45	—

MORGAN, Nick
30.10.59 East Ham (FW)
5.10 12.8 Apprentice
LD West Ham U v Luton T
9.4.78 1–0

1977–78	West Ham U	1	—	—
1978–79	West Ham U	2	2	—
1979–80	West Ham U	2	6	1
1980–81	West Ham U	2	6	1
1981–82	West Ham U	1	—	—
1982–83	West Ham U	1	7	—
1982–83	Portsmouth	3	6	1
1983–84	Portsmouth	2	25	9
1984–85	Portsmouth	2	30	8
1985–86	Portsmouth	2	30	14
1986–87	Portsmouth	2	4	—
1986–87	Stoke C	2	29	9
1987–88	Stoke C	2	28	5

MORGAN, Simon
5.9.66 Birmingham (DF)
5.11 12.7
LD Coventry C v Leicester C
6.10.85 3–0

1984–85	Leicester C	1	—	—
1985–86	Leicester C	1	30	—
1986–87	Leicester C	1	41	2
1987–88	Leicester C	2	40	—

MORGAN, Steve
19.9.68 Oldham (DF)
5.11 12.0 Apprentice
LD Bristol R v Blackpool
12.4.86 1–0

1985–86	Blackpool	3	5	—
1986–87	Blackpool	3	11	—
1987–88	Blackpool	3	46	6

MORGAN, Trevor
30.9.56 Forest Gate (FW)
6.1 13.1 Leytonstone and Ilford
LD Bradford C v Bournemouth
6.9.80 1–1

1980–81	Bournemouth	4	42	10
1981–82	Bournemouth	4	11	3
1981–82	Mansfield T	4	12	6
1981–82	Bournemouth	4	14	4
1982–83	Bournemouth	3	45	16
1983–84	Bournemouth	3	29	13
1983–84	Bristol C	4	15	5
1984–85	Bristol C	3	17	3
1984–85	Exeter C	4	26	9
1985–86	Exeter C	4	4	—
1985–86	Bristol R	3	36	16
1986–87	Bristol R	3	19	8
1986–87	Bristol C	3	19	7
1987–88	Bolton W	4	38	7

MORLEY, Trevor
20.3.61 Nottingham (FW)
5.11 12.1 Nuneaton
LD Burnley v Northampton T
17.8.85 3–2

1985–86	Northampton T	4	43	13
1986–87	Northampton T	4	37	16
1987–88	Northampton T	3	27	10
1987–88	Manchester C	2	15	4

MORRELL, Paul
23.3.61 Poole (DF)
5.11 13.7 Weymouth
LD Bournemouth v Preston NE
27.8.83 0–1

1983–84	Bournemouth	3	22	2
1984–85	Bournemouth	3	44	1
1985–86	Bournemouth	3	38	1
1986–87	Bournemouth	3	45	2
1987–88	Bournemouth	2	42	—

MORRIS, Andy
17.11.67 Sheffield (FW)
6.5 15.0
LD Orient v Rotherham U
20.4.85 0–1

1984–85	Rotherham U	3	1	—
1985–86	Rotherham U	3	—	—
1986–87	Rotherham U	3	6	—
1987–88	Rotherham U	3	—	—
1987–88	Chesterfield	3	10	—

MORRIS, Chris
24.12.63 Newquay (MF)
5.10 10.8
LD Swansea C v Sheffield W
27.8.83 0–1

1982–83	Sheffield W	2	—	—
1983–84	Sheffield W	2	13	1
1984–85	Sheffield W	1	14	—
1985–86	Sheffield W	1	30	—
1986–87	Sheffield W	1	17	—
1987–88	Celtic	P	44	3

PLAYER DIRECTORY

MORRIS, Mark
26.9.62 Morden (DF)
6.0 11.10 Apprentice
LD Wimbledon v Exeter C
31.10.81 1–1

1980–81	Wimbledon	4	—	—
1981–82	Wimbledon	3	33	1
1982–83	Wimbledon	4	26	3
1983–84	Wimbledon	3	39	3
1984–85	Wimbledon	2	29	1
1985–86	Wimbledon	2	20	1
1985–86	*Aldershot*	4	14	—
1986–87	Wimbledon	1	21	—
1987–88	Watford	1	39	1

MORRIS, Mark
1.8.68 Chester (GK)
— — School
LD Exeter C v Wrexham
25.1.86 0–1

1985–86	Wrexham	4	3	—
1986–87	Wrexham	4	—	—
1987–88	Wrexham	4	6	—

MORRISSEY, John
8.3.65 Liverpool (MF)
5.5 9.11 Apprentice
LD Luton T v Everton
28.5.85 2–0

1982–83	Everton	1	—	—
1983–84	Everton	1	—	—
1984–85	Everton	1	1	—
1985–86	Wolves	3	10	1
1985–86	Tranmere R	4	32	5
1986–87	Tranmere R	4	38	7
1987–88	Tranmere R	4	39	4

MORROW, Stephen
2.7.70 Belfast (DF)
— — Apprentice
LD —

1987–88	Arsenal	1	—	—

MORTIMER, Paul
8.5.68 London (MF)
— — Fulham
LD Charlton Ath v Norwich C
7.11.87 2–0

1987–88	Charlton Ath	1	12	—

MORTON, Neil
21.12.68 Congleton (MF)
— — YTS
LD Peterborough U v Crewe Alex
20.9.86 1–2

1986–87	Crewe Alex	4	2	—
1987–88	Crewe Alex	4	24	1

MOSELEY, Graham
16.11.53 Manchester (GK)
6.0 11.8 Apprentice
LD Tottenham H v Derby Co
18.4.73 1–0

1971–72	Blackburn R	3	—	—
1971–72	Derby Co	1	—	—
1972–73	Derby Co	1	2	—
1973–74	Derby Co	1	—	—
1974–75	Derby Co	1	—	—
1974–75	*Aston Villa*	2	3	—
1975–76	Derby Co	1	18	—
1976–77	Derby Co	1	12	—
1977–78	Derby Co	1	—	—
1977–78	*Walsall*	3	3	—
1977–78	Brighton & HA	2	4	—
1978–79	Brighton & HA	2	17	—
1979–80	Brighton & HA	1	33	—
1980–81	Brighton & HA	1	26	—
1981–82	Brighton & HA	1	30	—
1982–83	Brighton & HA	1	27	—
1983–84	Brighton & HA	2	1	—
1983–84	*Ipswich T*	1	—	—
1984–85	Brighton & HA	2	42	—
1985–86	Brighton & HA	2	9	—
1986–87	Cardiff C	4	25	—
1987–88	Cardiff C	4	13	—

MOSES, Remi
14.11.60 Manchester (MF)
5.7 10.10 Apprentice
LD Crystal Palace v WBA
26.1.80 2–2

1978–79	WBA	1	—	—
1979–80	WBA	1	18	1
1980–81	WBA	1	41	4
1981–82	WBA	1	4	—
1981–82	Manchester U	1	21	2
1982–83	Manchester U	1	29	—
1983–84	Manchester U	1	35	2
1984–85	Manchester U	1	26	3
1985–86	Manchester U	1	4	—
1986–87	Manchester U	1	18	—
1987–88	Manchester U	1	17	—

MOULDEN, Paul
6.9.67 Farnworth (FW)
5.10 11.0 Apprentice
LD Aston Villa v Manchester C
1.1.86 0–1

1984–85	Manchester C	2	—	—
1985–86	Manchester C	1	2	—
1986–87	Manchester C	1	20	5
1987–88	Manchester C	2	6	—

MOUNTFIELD, Derek
2.11.62 Liverpool (DF)
6.1 12.7 Apprentice
LD Peterborough v Tranmere R
18.3.81 4–1

1980–81	Tranmere R	4	5	—
1981–82	Tranmere R	4	21	1
1982–83	Everton	1	1	—

1983–84	Everton	1	31	3
1984–85	Everton	1	37	10
1985–86	Everton	1	15	3
1986–87	Everton	1	13	3
1987–88	Everton	1	9	—

MOVERLEY, Robert
18.1.69 Leeds (GK)
6.2 13.7 YTS
LD —

1987–88	Bradford C	2	—	—

MOWBRAY, Tony
22.11.63 Saltburn (DF)
6.1 12.2 Apprentice
LD Newcastle U v Middlesbrough
8.9.82 1–1

1981–82	Middlesbrough	1	—	—
1982–83	Middlesbrough	2	26	—
1983–84	Middlesbrough	2	35	1
1984–85	Middlesbrough	2	40	2
1985–86	Middlesbrough	2	35	4
1986–87	Middlesbrough	3	46	7
1987–88	Middlesbrough	2	44	3

MOWER, Ken
1.12.60 Walsall (DF)
6.0 12.2 Apprentice
LD Rotherham U v Walsall
14.5.79 4–1

1978–79	Walsall	3	1	—
1979–80	Walsall	4	44	1
1980–81	Walsall	3	33	2
1981–82	Walsall	3	34	—
1982–83	Walsall	3	45	1
1983–84	Walsall	3	44	1
1984–85	Walsall	3	41	1
1985–86	Walsall	3	43	1
1986–87	Walsall	3	28	1
1987–88	Walsall	3	26	—

MUGGLETON, Carl
13.9.68 Leicester (GK)
6.1 11.13 Apprentice
LD —

1987–88	Leicester C	2	—	—

MUIR, Ian
5.5.63 Coventry (FW)
5.7 10.9 Apprentice
LD QPR v Cambridge U
25.4.81 5–0

1980–81	QPR	2	2	2
1981–82	QPR	2	—	—
1982–83	QPR	2	—	—
1982–83	*Burnley*	2	2	1
1983–84	Birmingham C	1	1	—
1983–84	Brighton & HA	2	2	—
1984–85	Brighton & HA	2	2	—
1984–85	*Swindon T*	4	2	—
1985–86	Tranmere R	4	32	13
1986–87	Tranmere R	4	46	20
1987–88	Tranmere R	4	43	—

MUMBY, Peter
22.2.69 Bradford (MF/FW)
5.9 11.5 YTS
LD–Huddersfield T v <u>Leeds U</u>
15.9.87 0–0

1987–88 Leeds U	2	5	—

MUNGALL, Steve
22.5.58 Bellshill (DF)
5.8 11.2
LD <u>Motherwell</u> v Aberdeen
23.4.77 1–3

1976–77 Motherwell	P	3	—
1977–78 Motherwell	P	13	—
1978–79 Motherwell	P	4	—
1979–80 Tranmere R	4	24	—
1980–81 Tranmere R	4	38	3
1981–82 Tranmere R	4	44	1
1982–83 Tranmere R	4	31	1
1983–84 Tranmere R	4	26	—
1984–85 Tranmere R	4	23	—
1985–86 Tranmere R	4	46	1
1986–87 Tranmere R	4	46	—
1987–88 Tranmere R	4	45	—

MUNRO, Stuart
15.9.62 Falkirk (DF)
5.8 10.5 Bo'ness United
LD Kilmarnock v <u>St Mirren</u>
4.10.86 1–6

1980–81 St Mirren	P	1	—
1981–82 St Mirren	P	—	—
1982–83 Alloa	1	39	5
1983–84 Alloa	1	21	1
1983–84 Rangers	P	5	—
1984–85 Rangers	P	13	—
1985–86 Rangers	P	29	—
1986–87 Rangers	P	43	—
1987–88 Rangers	P	17	—

MURPHY, Aidan
17.9.67 Manchester (MF)
5.10½ 10.10 Apprentice
LD <u>Lincoln C</u> v Hartlepool U
5.10.86 1–4

1984–85 Manchester U	1	—	—
1985–86 Manchester U	1	—	—
1986–87 *Lincoln C*	4	2	—
1986–87 *Oldham Ath*	2	—	—
1987–88 Crewe Alex	4	20	2

MURRAY, Derek
26.11.60 Dunfermline (DF)
5.8 10.8 Oakley
LD <u>Dundee U</u> v Aberdeen
25.4.81 0–0

1977–78 Dundee U	P	—	—
1978–79 Dundee U	P	—	—

1979–80 Dundee U	P	—	—
1980–81 Dundee U	P	1	—
1981–82 Dundee U	P	12	—
1982–83 Dundee U	P	1	—
1983–84 Dundee U	P	2	—
1984–85 Motherwell	1	34	5
1985–86 Motherwell	P	25	—
1986–87 Motherwell	P	7	—
1987–88 Motherwell	P	7	—

MURRAY, Eddie
10.7.62 Liverpool (FW)
5.10 11.0 Stork
LD <u>Tranmere R</u> v Hereford U
21.8.87 0–1

1987–88 Tranmere R	4	20	—

MURRAY, Jamie
27.12.58 Glasgow (DF)
5.9 10.12 Rivet Sports
LD <u>Cambridge U</u> v Crewe Alex
19.2.77 2–0

1976–77 Cambridge U	4	1	—
1977–78 Cambridge U	3	20	1
1978–79 Cambridge U	2	26	1
1979–80 Cambridge U	2	34	1
1980–81 Cambridge U	2	40	—
1981–82 Cambridge U	2	42	—
1982–83 Cambridge U	2	42	—
1983–84 Cambridge U	2	24	—
1983–84 *Sunderland*	1	1	—
1984–85 Brentford	3	46	—
1985–86 Brentford	3	45	3
1986–87 Brentford	3	39	—
1987–88 Brentford	3	4	—
1987–88 Cambridge U	4	13	—

MURRAY, Malcolm
26.7.64 Buckie (DF)
5.11 11.12 Buckie Thistle
LD Motherwell v <u>Hearts</u>
12.5.84 0–1

1983–84 Hearts	P	1	—
1984–85 Hearts	P	4	—
1985–86 Hearts	P	—	—
1986–87 Hearts	P	7	—
1987–88 Hearts	P	7	—

MURRAY, Paul
28.12.69 Ireland (MF)
— — Apprentice
LD —

1987–88 Charlton Ath	1	—	—

MURRAY, Shaun
17.10.70 Newcastle (MF)
— — Trainee
LD —

1987–88 Tottenham H	4	1	—

MUSTOE, Robbie
28.8.68 Oxford (MF)
— —
LD Norwich C v <u>Oxford U</u>
29.11.86 2–1

1986–87 Oxford U	1	3	—
1987–88 Oxford U	1	17	—

MUTCH, Andy
28.12.63 Liverpool (FW)
5.10½ 11.0 Southport
LD <u>Wolves</u> v Rotherham U
8.3.86 0–0

1985–86 Wolves	3	15	7
1986–87 Wolves	4	41	11
1987–88 Wolves	4	46	19

NARBETT, Jon
21.11.68 Birmingham (MF)
— — Apprentice
LD Sheffield U v <u>Shrewsbury T</u>
23.8.86 1–1

1986–87 Shrewsbury T	2	1	—
1987–88 Shrewsbury T	2	25	3

NAREY, Dave
21.6.56 Dundee (DF)
6.0 12.6 School
LD <u>Dundee U</u> v Falkirk
21.11.73 2–1

1973–74 Dundee U	1	12	—
1974–75 Dundee U	1	31	—
1975–76 Dundee U	P	33	6
1976–77 Dundee U	P	32	2
1977–78 Dundee U	P	35	—
1978–79 Dundee U	P	36	5
1979–80 Dundee U	P	35	1
1980–81 Dundee U	P	32	—
1981–82 Dundee U	P	34	1
1982–83 Dundee U	P	36	5
1983–84 Dundee U	P	34	1
1984–85 Dundee U	P	29	1
1985–86 Dundee U	P	35	—
1986–87 Dundee U	P	33	—
1987–88 Dundee U	P	39	—

NAUGHTON, Willie
20.3.62 Catrine (FW)
6.0 12.8 Apprentice
LD Wrexham v <u>Preston NE</u>
1.1.80 2–0

1979–80 Preston NE	2	3	—
1980–81 Preston NE	2	10	2
1981–82 Preston NE	3	33	3
1982–83 Preston NE	3	41	1
1983–84 Preston NE	3	42	3
1984–85 Preston NE	3	33	1
1984–85 Walsall	3	13	—
1985–86 Walsall	3	39	5
1986–87 Walsall	3	23	1
1987–88 Walsall	3	41	3

NAYLOR, Stuart
6.12.62 Wetherby (GK)
6.4 12.10 Yorkshire A
LD <u>Lincoln C</u> v Bristol C
24.10.81 2–1

1980–81 Lincoln C	4	—	—
1981–82 Lincoln C	3	3	—
1982–83 Lincoln C	3	1	—
1982–83 *Peterborough U*	4	8	—
1983–84 Lincoln C	3	—	—
1983–84 *Crewe Alex*	4	38	—
1984–85 *Crewe Alex*	4	17	—
1984–85 Lincoln C	3	25	—
1985–86 Lincoln C	3	20	—
1985–86 WBA	1	12	—
1986–87 WBA	2	42	—
1987–88 WBA	2	35	—

NEAL, Phil
20.2.51 Irchester (DF)
5.11 12.2 Apprentice

1968–69 Northampton T	3	21	4
1969–70 Northampton T	4	13	1
1970–71 Northampton T	4	17	2
1971–72 Northampton T	4	41	2
1972–73 Northampton T	4	38	9
1973–74 Northampton T	4	46	9
1974–75 Northampton T	4	10	2
1974–75 Liverpool	1	23	—
1975–76 Liverpool	1	42	6
1976–77 Liverpool	1	42	7
1977–78 Liverpool	1	42	4
1978–79 Liverpool	1	42	5
1979–80 Liverpool	1	42	1
1980–81 Liverpool	1	42	2
1981–82 Liverpool	1	42	2
1982–83 Liverpool	1	42	8
1983–84 Liverpool	1	41	1
1984–85 Liverpool	1	42	4
1985–86 Liverpool	1	13	—
1985–86 Bolton W	3	20	2
1986–87 Bolton W	3	28	1
1987–88 Bolton W	4	8	—

NEBBELING, Gavin
15.5.63 Johannesburg (DF)
6.0 12.4 Arcadia Shep.
LD <u>Crystal Palace</u> v Newcastle U
15.5.82 1–2

1981–82 Crystal Palace	2	1	—
1982–83 Crystal Palace	2	28	1
1983–84 Crystal Palace	2	16	—
1984–85 Crystal Palace	2	16	—
1985–86 Crystal Palace	2	14	—
1985–86 *Northampton T*	4	11	—
1986–87 Crystal Palace	2	23	—
1987–88 Crystal Palace	2	39	6

NEILL, Warren
21.11.62 Acton (DF)
5.8 11.10 Apprentice
LD Chelsea v <u>QPR</u>
30.8.80 1–1

1980–81 QPR	2	4	—
1981–82 QPR	2	11	—
1982–83 QPR	2	39	2
1983–84 QPR	1	41	1
1984–85 QPR	1	18	—
1985–86 QPR	1	16	—
1986–87 QPR	1	29	—
1987–88 QPR	1	23	—

NELSON, Garry
16.1.61 Braintree (FW)
5.10 11.4 Amateur
LD <u>Southend U</u> v Colchester U
12.10.79 0–1

1979–80 Southend U	3	22	2
1980–81 Southend U	4	22	3
1981–82 Southend U	3	40	4
1982–83 Southend U	3	45	8
1983–84 Swindon T	4	36	4
1984–85 Swindon T	4	43	3
1985–86 Plymouth Arg	3	42	13
1986–87 Plymouth Arg	2	32	7
1987–88 Brighton & HA	3	42	22

NELSON, Martin
9.5.67 Glasgow (MF)
5.7 10.4 Rutherglen Glencairn
LD Stirling Albion v <u>Alloa</u>
13.9.86 1–2

1986–87 Dumbarton	1	—	—
1986–87 Alloa	2	34	3
1987–88 Alloa	2	27	6
1987–88 Hamilton A	1	2	—

NEVILLE, Steve
18.9.57 Walthamstow (FW)
5.9 11.0 Apprentice
LD <u>Southampton</u> v Blackpool
12.11.77 2–0

1975–76 Southampton	2	—	—
1976–77 Southampton	2	—	—
1977–78 Southampton	2	5	1
1978–79 Southampton	1	—	—
1978–79 Exeter C	3	36	9
1979–80 Exeter C	3	43	8
1980–81 Exeter C	3	43	9
1980–81 Sheffield U	3	19	2
1981–82 Sheffield U	4	30	4
1982–83 *Exeter C*	3	33	17
1983–84 Exeter C	3	43	9
1984–85 Exeter C	4	16	1
1984–85 Bristol C	3	28	8
1985–86 Bristol C	3	46	19
1986–87 Bristol C	3	20	8
1987–88 Bristol C	3	40	5

NEVIN, Pat
6.9.63 Glasgow (FW)
5.6 10.0 Gartcosh U
LD <u>Clyde</u> v Stenhousemuir
29.8.81 3–0

1981–82 Clyde	2	34	12
1982–83 Clyde	1	39	5
1983–84 Chelsea	2	38	14
1984–85 Chelsea	1	41	4
1985–86 Chelsea	1	40	7
1986–87 Chelsea	1	37	5
1987–88 Chelsea	1	37	6

NEWCOMBE, Giles
9.7.68 Doncaster (GK)
— — YTS
LD <u>Rotherham U</u> v Bournemouth
13.12.86 4–2

1986–87 Rotherham U	3	6	—
1987–88 Rotherham U	3	—	—

NEWELL, Mike
27.1.65 Liverpool (FW)
6.0 12.0 Amateur
LD Crewe Alex v Swindon T
8.10.83 2–1

1983–84	Crewe Alex	4	3	—
1983–84	Wigan Ath	3	9	—
1984–85	Wigan Ath	3	39	9
1985–86	Wigan Ath	3	24	16
1985–86	Luton T	1	16	6
1986–87	Luton T	1	42	12
1987–88	Luton T	1	5	—
1987–88	Leicester C	2	36	8

NEWMAN, Rob
13.12.63 Bradford-on-Avon (DF)
6.0½ 12.0 Apprentice
LD Bristol C v Fulham
6.2.82 0–0

1981–82	Bristol C	3	21	3
1982–83	Bristol C	4	43	3
1983–84	Bristol C	4	30	1
1984–85	Bristol C	3	34	3
1985–86	Bristol C	3	39	3
1986–87	Bristol C	3	45	6
1987–88	Bristol C	3	44	11

NEWSON, Mark
7.12.60 Stepney (MF)
5.10 12.6 Apprentice
LD Derby Co v Bournemouth
17.8.85 3–0

1979–80	Charlton Ath	2	—	—
Maidstone U				
1985–86	Bournemouth	3	46	5
1986–87	Bournemouth	3	46	7
1987–88	Bournemouth	2	29	3

NICHOLAS, Charlie
30.12.61 Glasgow (FW)
5.10 11.0 Celtic BC
LD Kilmarnock v Celtic
16.8.80 0.3

1980–81	Celtic	P	29	16
1981–82	Celtic	P	10	3
1982–83	Celtic	P	35	29
1983–84	Arsenal	1	41	11
1984–85	Arsenal	1	38	9
1985–86	Arsenal	1	41	10
1986–87	Arsenal	1	28	4
1987–88	Arsenal	1	3	—
1987–88	Aberdeen	P	16	3

NICHOLL, Jimmy
28.2.56 Canada (DF)
5.9½ 11.8 Apprentice
LD Southampton v Manchester U
5.4.75 0–1

1973–74	Manchester U	1	—	—
1974–75	Manchester U	2	1	—
1975–76	Manchester U	1	20	—
1976–77	Manchester U	1	30	—
1977–78	Manchester U	1	37	2
1978–79	Manchester U	1	21	—
1979–80	Manchester U	1	42	—
1980–81	Manchester U	1	36	1
1981–82	Manchester U	1	1	—
1981–82	Sunderland	1	3	—
Toronto B, NASL				
1982–83	Sunderland	1	29	—
Toronto B, NASL				
1983–84	Rangers	P	17	—
1984–85	WBA	1	27	—
1985–86	WBA	1	29	—
1986–87	Rangers	P	42	—
1987–88	Rangers	P	22	—

NICOL, Paul
31.10.67 Scunthorpe (DF)
6.1 12.0
LD Scunthorpe U v Swansea C
11.10.86 2–1

1986–87	Scunthorpe U	4	9	—
1987–88	Scunthorpe U	4	25	—

NICOL, Steve
11.12.61 Irvine (MF)
5.10 12.0 Ayr UBC
LD Ayr U v Arbroath
20.10.79 2–1

1979–80	Ayr U	1	20	2
1980–81	Ayr U	1	39	3
1981–82	Ayr U	1	11	2
1981–82	Liverpool	1	—	—
1982–83	Liverpool	1	4	—
1983–84	Liverpool	1	23	5
1984–85	Liverpool	1	31	5
1985–86	Liverpool	1	34	4
1986–87	Liverpool	1	14	3
1987–88	Liverpool	1	40	6

NIEDZWIECKI, Eddie
3.5.59 Bangor (GK)
6.0 11.0 Amateur
LD Wrexham v Oxford U
22.8.77 2–2

1976–77	Wrexham	3	—	—
1977–78	Wrexham	3	15	—
1978–79	Wrexham	2	6	—
1979–80	Wrexham	2	6	—
1980–81	Wrexham	2	—	—
1981–82	Wrexham	2	42	—
1982–83	Wrexham	3	42	—
1983–84	Chelsea	2	42	—
1984–85	Chelsea	1	40	—
1985–86	Chelsea	1	30	—
1986–87	Chelsea	1	10	—
1987–88	Chelsea	1	14	—

NISBET, Scott
30.1.68 Edinburgh (DF)
6.1 11.8 Salvesen BC
LD Rangers v Motherwell
7.12.85 1–0

1985–86	Rangers	P	1	—
1986–87	Rangers	1	6	—
1986–87	Rangers	P	1	—
1986–87	East Fife	1	6	—
1987–88	Rangers	P	25	—

NIXON, Eric
4.10.62 Manchester (GK)
6.2½ 14.3 Curzon Ashton
LD Manchester C v West Ham U
21.9.85 2–2

1983–84	Manchester C	2	—	—
1984–85	Manchester C	2	—	—
1985–86	Manchester C	1	28	—
1986–87	Manchester C	1	—	—
1986–87	Wolves	4	16	—
1986–87	Bradford C	2	3	—
1986–87	Southampton	1	4	—
1986–87	Carlisle U	3	16	—
1987–88	Manchester C	2	25	—
1987–88	Tranmere R	4	8	—

NOBBS, Keith
19.9.61 Bishop Auckland (DF)
5.10 11.10 Apprentice
LD Middlesbrough v Coventry C
21.4.81 0–1

1979–80	Middlesbrough	1	—	—
1980–81	Middlesbrough	1	1	—
1981–82	Middlesbrough	1	—	—
1982–83	Halifax T	4	46	1
1983–84	Halifax T	4	41	—
Bishop Auckland				
1985–86	Hartlepool U	4	39	1
1986–87	Hartlepool U	4	40	—
1987–88	Hartlepool U	4	43	—

NOGAN, Lee
21.5.69 Cardiff (FW)
— — Apprentice
LD Brentford v Chester C
4.4.87 3–1

1986–87	Oxford U	1	—	—
1986–87	Brentford	3	11	2
1987–88	Oxford U	1	3	—
1987–88	Southend	3	6	1

NORMAN, Tony
24.2.58 Mancot (GK)
6.1¾ 12.8 Amateur
LD Hull C v Millwall
16.2.80 1–0

1976–77	Burnley	2	—	—
1977–78	Burnley	2	—	—
1978–79	Burnley	2	—	—
1979–80	Burnley	2	—	—
1979–80	Hull C	3	17	—
1980–81	Hull C	3	42	—
1981–82	Hull C	4	36	—
1982–83	Hull C	4	36	—
1983–84	Hull C	3	46	—
1984–85	Hull C	3	46	—
1985–86	Hull C	2	42	—
1986–87	Hull C	2	42	—
1987–88	Hull C	2	44	—

PLAYER DIRECTORY

NORTH, Mark
29.5.66 Ware (FW)
5.11 11.0 Apprentice
LD Lincoln C v Bristol C
27.4.85 1–1

1983–84	Luton T	1	—	—
1984–85	Luton T	1	—	—
1984–85	*Lincoln C*	3	4	—
1985–86	Luton T	1	13	3
1986–87	Luton T	1	5	—
1986–87	*Scunthorpe U*	4	5	2
1986–87	*Birmingham C*	2	5	1
1987–88	*Grimsby T*	2	4	—
1987–88	Grimsby T	2	34	11

NORTH, Stacey
25.11.64 Luton (DF)
6.0 12.0 Apprentice
LD WBA v Luton T
12.5.84 3–0

1982–83	Luton T	1	—	—
1983–84	Luton T	1	1	—
1984–85	Luton T	1	7	—
1985–86	Luton T	1	2	—
1985–86	*Wolves*	3	3	—
1986–87	Luton T	1	14	—
1987–88	Luton T	1	1	—
1987–88	*WBA*	2	2	—
1987–88	WBA	2	16	—

NORTON, David
3.3.65 Cannock (MF)
5.7½ 10.12 Apprentice
LD Coventry C v Aston Villa
19.1.85 0–3

1982–83	Aston Villa	1	—	—
1983–84	Aston Villa	1	—	—
1984–85	Aston Villa	1	2	—
1985–86	Aston Villa	1	20	2
1986–87	Aston Villa	1	20	—
1987–88	Aston Villa	2	2	—

NUGENT, Kevin
10.4.69 Edmonton (FW)
— — Trainee
LD Leyton Orient v Scarborough
22.8.87 3–1

1987–88	Leyton Orient	4	11	3

NUTTELL, Mike
22.11.68 Boston (FW)
— — YTS
LD Colchester U v Peterborough U
22.4.86 5–0

1985–86	Peterborough U	4	3	—
1986–87	Peterborough U	4	7	—
1987–88	Peterbouough U	4	11	—
1987–88	*Crewe Alex*	4	3	1

OAKES, Keith
3.7.56 Bedworth (DF)
6.1 13.1 Apprentice
LD Doncaster R v Peterborough U
9.3.73 1–1

1972–73	Peterborough U	4	4	—
1973–74	Peterborough U	4	4	—
1974–75	Peterborough U	3	12	—
1975–76	Peterborough U	3	9	1
1976–77	Peterborough U	3	23	1
1977–78	Peterborough U	3	10	—
1978–79	Peterborough U	3	—	—
1978–79	Newport Co	4	34	5
1979–80	Newport Co	4	45	11
1980–81	Newport Co	3	43	8
1981–82	Newport Co	3	45	1
1982–83	Newport Co	3	28	1
1983–84	Newport Co	3	37	1
1984–85	Gillingham	3	45	5
1985–86	Gillingham	3	40	2
1986–87	Gillingham	3	1	—
1986–87	Fulham	3	41	3
1987–88	Fulham	3	35	3

O'BRIEN, Liam
5.9.64 Dublin (MF)
6.1 13.3 Shamrock R.
LD Manchester U v Leicester C
20.12.86 2–0

1986–87	Manchester U	1	11	—
1987–88	Manchester U	1	17	2

O'BRIEN, Michael
28.11.70 Dublin (MF)
5.10½ 11.4 Apprentice
LD —

1987–88	Luton T	1	—	—

O'BRIEN, Steve
18.1.71 Dublin (GK)
5.7½ 10.0 Youth Scheme
LD —

1987–88	Gillingham	3	—	—

O'CALLAGHAN, Kevin
19.10.61 London (FW)
5.8½ 11.4 Apprentice
LD Charlton Ath v Millwall
10.3.79 2–4

1978–79	Millwall	2	10	—
1979–80	Millwall	3	10	3
1979–80	Ipswich T	1	4	—
1980–81	Ipswich T	1	24	—
1981–82	Ipswich T	1	19	1
1982–83	Ipswich T	1	28	—
1983–84	Ipswich T	1	25	2
1984–85	Ipswich T	1	15	—
1984–85	Portsmouth	2	15	2
1985–86	Portsmouth	2	39	11
1986–87	Portsmouth	2	33	3
1987–88	Millwall	2	22	7

O'CONNOR, Mark
10.3.63 Rochdale (MF)
5.7 10.2 Apprentice
LD QPR v Chelsea
26.12.81 0–2

1980–81	QPR	2	—	—
1981–82	QPR	2	1	—
1982–83	QPR	2	2	—
1983–84	QPR	1	—	—
1983–84	*Exeter C*	3	38	1
1984–85	Bristol R	3	46	8
1985–86	Bristol R	3	34	2
1985–86	Bournemouth	3	9	1
1986–87	Bournemouth	3	43	7
1987–88	Bournemouth	2	37	2

O'DOHERTY, Ken
30.3.63 Dublin (FW)
— — UCD
LD Crystal Palace v Blackburn R
26.10.85 2–0

1984–85	Crystal Palace	2	—	—
1985–86	Crystal Palace	2	13	—
1986–87	Crystal Palace	2	12	—
1987–88	Crystal Palace	2	17	—

O'DONNELL, Chris
26.5.68 Newcastle (DF)
5.9 12.0 Apprentice
LD Ipswich T v Sunderland
20.9.86 1–1

1985–86	Ipswich T	1	—	—
1986–87	Ipswich T	2	10	—
1987–88	Ipswich T	2	2	—
1987–88	*Northampton T*	3	1	—

O'DONNELL, Jim
23.7.69 Manchester (GK)
— — YTS
LD —

1987–88	Manchester U	1	—	—

O'DRISCOLL, Sean
1.7.57 Wolverhampton (MF)
5.8 11.3 Alvechurch
LD Notts Co v Fulham
1.3.80 1–1

1979–80	Fulham	2	10	1
1980–81	Fulham	3	42	2
1981–82	Fulham	3	42	7
1982–83	Fulham	3	42	3
1983–84	Fulham	2	12	—
1983–84	*Bournemouth*	3	19	1
1984–85	Bournemouth	3	44	1
1985–86	Bournemouth	3	46	5
1986–87	Bournemouth	3	46	5
1987–88	Bournemouth	2	39	4

OGHANI, George
2.9.60 Manchester (FW)
5.10 12.0 Hyde
LD Wimbledon v Bolton W
14.1.84 4-0

1983–84 Bolton W	3	3	—
1984–85 Bolton W	3	41	16
1985–86 Bolton W	3	36	7
1986–87 Bolton W	3	19	4
1986–87 *Wrexham*	4	7	—
1987–88 Burnley	4	37	14

OGLEY, Mark
10.3.67 Barnsley (DF)
5.10 11.2 Apprentice
LD Crystal Palace v Barnsley
23.11.85 1-0

1984–85 Barnsley	2	—	—
1985–86 Barnsley	2	2	—
1986–87 Barnsley	2	17	—
1987–88 Barnsley	2	—	—
1987–88 *Aldershot*	3	8	—
1987–88 Carlisle U	4	3	—

OGRIZOVIC, Steve
12.9.57 Mansfield (GK)
6.3 14.0 ONRYC
LD Port Vale v Chesterfield
20.8.77 1-3

1977–78 Chesterfield	3	16	—
1977–78 Liverpool	1	2	—
1978–79 Liverpool	1	—	—
1979–80 Liverpool	1	1	—
1980–81 Liverpool	1	1	—
1981–82 Liverpool	1	—	—
1982–83 Shrewsbury T	2	42	—
1983–84 Shrewsbury T	2	42	—
1984–85 Coventry C	1	42	—
1985–86 Coventry C	1	42	—
1986–87 Coventry C	1	42	1
1987–88 Coventry C	1	40	—

O'HANLON, Kelham
16.5.62 Saltburn (GK)
6.0 12.0 Apprentice
LD Middlesbrough v Sheffield W
15.1.83 1-1

1980–81 Middlesbrough	1	—	—
1981–82 Middlesbrough	1	—	—
1982–83 Middlesbrough	2	19	—
1983–84 Middlesbrough	2	30	—
1984–85 Middlesbrough	2	38	—
1985–86 Rotherham U	3	46	—
1986–87 Rotherham U	3	40	—
1987–88 Rotherham U	3	40	—

O'KEEFE, Vince
2.4.57 Birmingham (GK)
6.1½ 12.10 Local
LD Exeter C v Mansfield T
19.8.78 0-0

1975–76 Birmingham C	1	—	—
1975–76 *Peterborough U*	3	—	—
1976–77 Walsall	3	—	—
AP Leamington			
1978–79 Exeter C	3	33	—
1979–80 Exeter C	3	20	—
1979–80 Torquay U	4	16	—
1980–81 Torquay U	4	46	—
1981–82 Torquay U	4	46	—
1982–83 Blackburn R	2	9	—
1983–84 Blackburn R	2	12	—
1983–84 *Bury*	4	2	—
1984–85 Blackburn R	2	5	—
1985–86 Blackburn R	2	10	—
1986–87 Blackburn R	2	25	—
1986–87 *Blackpool*	3	1	—
1987–88 Blackburn R	2	5	—

OLDFIELD, David
30.5.68 Perth, Australia (FW)
6.1½ 12.6 Apprentice
LD Newcastle U v Luton T
2.4.88 4-0

1987–88 Luton T	1	8	3

O'LEARY, David
2.5.58 London (DF)
5.11 11.3 Apprentice
LD Burnley v Arsenal
16.8.75 0-0

1975–76 Arsenal	1	27	—
1976–77 Arsenal	1	33	2
1977–78 Arsenal	1	41	1
1978–79 Arsenal	1	37	2
1979–80 Arsenal	1	34	1
1980–81 Arsenal	1	24	1
1981–82 Arsenal	1	40	1
1982–83 Arsenal	1	36	1
1983–84 Arsenal	1	36	—
1984–85 Arsenal	1	36	—
1985–86 Arsenal	1	35	—
1986–87 Arsenal	1	39	—
1987–88 Arsenal	1	23	—

OLIVER, Gavin
6.9.62 Felling (DF)
5.11 13.2 Apprentice
LD Oldham Ath v Sheffield W
6.9.80 2-0

1980–81 Sheffield W	2	2	—
1981–82 Sheffield W	2	—	—
1982–83 Sheffield W	2	2	—
1982–83 *Tranmere R*	4	17	1
1983–84 Sheffield W	2	6	—
1984–85 Sheffield W	1	10	—
1985–86 Sheffield W	1	—	—
1985–86 *Brighton & HA*	2	16	—
1985–86 Bradford C	2	27	1
1986–87 Bradford C	2	40	—
1987–88 Bradford C	2	43	—

OLSEN, Jesper
20.3.61 Fakse (FW)
5.6 9.9 Ajax
LD Manchester U v Watford
25.8.84 1-1

1984–85 Manchester U	1	36	5
1985–86 Manchester U	1	28	11
1986–87 Manchester U	1	28	3
1987–88 Manchester U	1	37	2

O'NEILL, John
11.3.58 Derry (DF)
5.11¾ 13.3 Derry ABC
LD Burnley v Leicester C
19.8.78 2-2

1978–79 Leicester C	2	23	—
1979–80 Leicester C	2	33	—
1980–81 Leicester C	1	32	2
1981–82 Leicester C	2	41	—
1982–83 Leicester C	2	41	2
1983–84 Leicester C	1	31	2
1984–85 Leicester C	1	42	2
1985–86 Leicester C	1	41	—
1986–87 Leicester C	1	29	2
1987–88 QPR	1	2	—
1987–88 Norwich C	1	1	—

O'NEILL, Michael
5.7.69 Portadown (FW)
5.11 10.10 Coleraine
LD Luton T v Newcastle U
7.11.87 4-0

1987–88 Newcastle U	1	21	12

ORD, Richard
3.3.70 Easington, Co Durham (DF)
6.2 12.8 Youth Scheme
LD Sunderland v Southend U
3.11.87 7-0

1987–88 Sunderland	3	8	—

O'REGAN, Kieran
9.11.63 Cork (DF)
5.8 10.11 Tramore Ath
LD Norwich C v Brighton & HA
14.5.83 2-1

1982–83 Brighton & HA	1	1	—
1983–84 Brighton & HA	2	31	1
1984–85 Brighton & HA	2	15	—
1985–86 Brighton & HA	2	15	1
1986–87 Brighton & HA	2	24	—
1987–88 Swindon T	2	26	1

PLAYER DIRECTORY

O'REILLY, Gary
21.3.61 Isleworth (DF)
5.11 12.0 Amateur
LD Tottenham H v Southampton
26.12.80 4–4

1979–80	Tottenham H	1	—	—
1980–81	Tottenham H	1	2	—
1981–82	Tottenham H	1	5	—
1982–83	Tottenham H	1	26	—
1983–84	Tottenham H	1	12	—
1984–85	Brighton & HA	2	36	3
1985–86	Brighton & HA	2	35	—
1986–87	Brighton & HA	2	8	—
1986–87	Crystal Palace	2	13	—
1987–88	Crystal Palace	2	4	—

O'RIORDAN, Don
14.5.57 Dublin (DF)
6.0 11.12 Apprentice
LD Tottenham H v Derby Co
22.3.77 0–0

1975–76	Derby Co	1	—	—
1976–77	Derby Co	1	1	—
1977–78	Derby Co	1	5	1
1977–78	*Doncaster R*	4	2	—
Tulsa				
1978–79	Preston NE	2	32	—
1979–80	Preston NE	2	18	—
1980–81	Preston NE	2	21	—
1981–82	Preston NE	3	46	4
1982–83	Preston NE	3	41	4
1983–84	Carlisle U	2	42	8
1984–85	Carlisle U	2	42	10
1985–86	Middlesbrough	2	41	2
1986–87	Grimsby T	2	40	8
1987–88	Grimsby T	3	46	8

ORMONDROYD, Ian
22.9.64 Bradford (FW)
6.4 12.0 Thackley
LD Shrewsbury T v Bradford C
23.11.85 2–0

1985–86	Bradford C	2	12	3
1986–87	Bradford C	2	13	4
1986–87	*Oldham Ath*	2	10	1
1987–88	Bradford C	2	37	8

ORMSBY, Brendan
1.10.60 Birmingham (DF)
5.11 11.9½ Apprentice
LD Aston Villa v Derby Co
11.4.79 3–3

1978–79	Aston Villa	1	2	—
1979–80	Aston Villa	1	23	—
1980–81	Aston Villa	1	—	—
1981–82	Aston Villa	1	12	—
1982–83	Aston Villa	1	—	—
1983–84	Aston Villa	1	34	2
1984–85	Aston Villa	1	32	2
1985–86	Aston Villa	1	14	—
1985–86	Leeds U	2	12	1

1986–87	Leeds U	2	33	4
1987–88	Leeds U	2	—	—

ORR, Neil
13.5.59 Airdrie (DF)
5.10 12.2 Morton
LD Morton v Airdrieonians
22.11.75 1–0

1975–76	Morton	1	4	—
1976–77	Morton	1	24	—
1977–78	Morton	1	39	—
1978–79	Morton	P	35	—
1979–80	Morton	P	35	1
1980–81	Morton	P	33	—
1981–82	Morton	P	16	—
1981–82	West Ham U	1	24	1
1982–83	West Ham U	1	14	—
1983–84	West Ham U	1	29	—
1984–85	West Ham U	1	20	—
1985–86	West Ham U	1	36	2
1986–87	West Ham U	1	22	1
1987–88	West Ham U	1	1	—
1987–88	Hibernian	P	38	1

O'SHAUGHNESSY, Steve
13.10.67 Wrexham (DF)
6.1 12.0
LD Bradford C v Birmingham C
17.10.87 4–0

1984–85	Leeds U	2	—	—
1985–86	Leeds U	2	—	—
1985–86	Bradford C	2	—	—
1986–87	Bradford C	2	—	—
1987–88	Bradford C	2	1	—

O'SHEA, Danny
26.3.63 Kennington (DF)
6.0 12.8 Apprentice
LD Arsenal v Birmingham C
30.10.82 0–0

1980–81	Arsenal	1	—	—
1981–82	Arsenal	1	—	—
1982–83	Arsenal	1	6	—
1983–84	Arsenal	1	—	—
1983–84	*Charlton Ath*	2	9	—
1984–85	Exeter C	4	45	2
1985–86	Southend U	4	35	9
1986–87	Southend U	4	41	2
1987–88	Southend U	3	22	—

O'SHEA, Tim
12.11.66 London (DF)
5.11 11.4 Arsenal Schoolboy
LD Sheffield W v Tottenham H
7.4.87 0–1

1984–85	Tottenham H	1	—	—
1985–86	Tottenham H	1	—	—
1986–87	Tottenham H	1	2	—
1986–87	*Newport Co*	3	10	—
1987–88	Tottenham H	1	1	—

OSMAN, Russell
14.2.59 Repton (DF)
6.0 11.10 Apprentice
LD Ipswich T v Chelsea
3.9.77 1–0

1975–76	Ipswich T	1	—	—
1976–77	Ipswich T	1	—	—
1977–78	Ipswich T	1	28	—
1978–79	Ipswich T	1	39	2
1979–80	Ipswich T	1	42	2
1980–81	Ipswich T	1	42	1
1981–82	Ipswich T	1	39	2
1982–83	Ipswich T	1	38	4
1983–84	Ipswich T	1	37	3
1984–85	Ipswich T	1	29	3
1985–86	Leicester C	1	40	—
1986–87	Leicester C	1	31	3
1987–88	Leicester C	2	37	5

OUTTERSIDE, Mark
13.1.67 Hexham (DF)
5.11½ 11.8½ Apprentice
LD Sunderland v Oldham Ath
21.3.87 0–2

1984–85	Sunderland	1	—	—
1985–86	Sunderland	2	—	—
1985–86	*Blackburn R*	2	—	—
1986–87	Sunderland	2	—	—
1987–88	Darlington	4	38	—

OVERSON, Vince
15.5.62 Kettering (DF)
6.0 13.0 Apprentice
LD Burnley v Orient
3.11.79 1–2

1979–80	Burnley	2	22	—
1980–81	Burnley	3	39	1
1981–82	Burnley	3	36	4
1982–83	Burnley	2	6	—
1983–84	Burnley	3	38	—
1984–85	Burnley	3	42	1
1985–86	Burnley	4	28	—
1986–87	Birmingham C	2	34	1
1987–88	Birmingham C	2	37	—

OWERS, Adrian
26.2.65 Danbury, Essex (MF)
— — Chelmsford
LD Brentford v Brighton & HA
26.3.88 1–1

1987–88	Brighton & HA	3	9	2

OWERS, Gary
3.10.68 Newcastle-on-Tyne (MF)
5.10 11.10 Apprentice
LD Brentford v Sunderland
15.8.87 0–1

1987–88	Sunderland	3	37	4

Gary Pallister

Photo: Bob Thomas Sports Photography.

PLAYER DIRECTORY

PAATELAINAN, Mika-Matti
3.2.67 Helsinki (FW)
6.0 13.11 Valkeakosken Haka
LD Dundee U v St Mirren
31.10.87 2-3

1987–88 Dundee U	P	19	9

PALIN, Leigh
12.9.65 Worcester (MF)
5.9½ 10.3 Apprentice
LD Middlesbrough v Shrewsbury T
14.12.84 1-1

1983–84 Aston Villa	1	—	—
1984–85 Aston Villa	1	—	—
1984–85 *Shrewsbury T*	2	2	—
1985–86 Aston Villa	1	—	—
1985–86 Nottingham F	1	—	—
1986–87 Bradford C	2	21	3
1987–88 Bradford C	2	20	3

PALLISTER, Gary
30.6.65 Ramsgate (DF)
6.4 13.0
LD Wimbledon v Middlesbrough
17.8.85 3-0

1984–85 Middlesbrough	2	—	—
1985–86 Middlesbrough	2	20	—
1986–87 Middlesbrough	3	44	1
1987–88 Middlesbrough	2	44	3

PALMER, Carlton
5.12.65 West Bromwich (DF)
5.10 11.0 YTS
LD Newcastle U v WBA
14.9.85 4-1

1984–85 WBA	1	—	—
1985–86 WBA	1	20	—
1986–87 WBA	2	37	1
1987–88 WBA	2	38	3

PALMER, Charlie
10.7.63 Aylesbury (DF)
5.11 12.3 Apprentice
LD QPR v Watford
6.9.83 1-1

1981–82 Watford	2	—	—
1982–83 Watford	1	—	—
1983–84 Watford	1	10	1
1984–85 Derby Co	3	33	2
1985–86 Derby Co	3	18	—
1986–87 Hull C	2	17	—
1987–88 Hull C	2	35	—

PALMER, Roger
30.1.59 Manchester (FW)
5.10 10.10 Apprentice
LD Middlesbrough v Manchester C
27.12.77 0-2

1976–77 Manchester C	1	—	—
1977–78 Manchester C	1	5	3

1978–79 Manchester C	1	14	4
1979–80 Manchester C	1	7	1
1980–81 Manchester C	1	5	1
1980–81 Oldham Ath	2	21	6
1981–82 Oldham Ath	2	37	7
1982–83 Oldham Ath	2	42	15
1983–84 Oldham Ath	2	42	13
1984–85 Oldham Ath	2	36	9
1985–86 Oldham Ath	2	41	15
1986–87 Oldham Ath	2	46	16
1987–88 Oldham Ath	2	42	17

PARDEW, Alan
18.7.61 Wimbledon (FW)
— — Yeovil T
LD Crystal Palace v Stoke C
14.11.87 2-0

1987–88 Crystal Palace	2	20	—

PARIS, Alan
15.8.64 Slough (MF)
5.11 10.12 Slough T
LD Preston NE v Peterborough U
17.8.85 2-4

1982–83 Watford	1	—	—
1983–84 Watford	1	—	—
1984–85 Watford	1	—	—
1985–86 Peterborough U	4	46	—
1986–87 Peterborough U	4	45	—
1987–88 Peterborough U	4	46	2

PARKER, Garry
7.9.65 Oxford (MF)
5.8 11.0 Apprentice
LD Manchester U v Luton T
9.5.83 3-0

1982–83 Luton T	1	1	—
1983–84 Luton T	1	13	2
1984–85 Luton T	1	20	1
1985–86 Luton T	1	8	—
1985–86 Hull C	2	12	—
1986–87 Hull C	2	38	—
1987–88 Hull C	2	34	8
1987–88 Nottingham F	1	2	—

PARKER, Paul
4.4.64 Essex (DF)
5.7 10.9 Apprentice
LD Fulham v Reading
25.4.81 1-2

1980–81 Fulham	3	1	—
1981–82 Fulham	3	5	—
1982–83 Fulham	2	16	—
1983–84 Fulham	2	34	—
1984–85 Fulham	2	36	—
1985–86 Fulham	2	30	—
1986–87 Fulham	3	31	2
1987–88 QPR	1	40	—

PARKES, Phil
8.8.50 Sedgeley (GK)
6.3 15.1 Amateur

1967–68 Walsall	3	—	—
1968–69 Walsall	3	8	—
1969–70 Walsall	3	44	—
1970–71 QPR	2	41	—
1971–72 QPR	2	42	—
1972–73 QPR	2	41	—
1973–74 QPR	1	42	—
1974–75 QPR	1	41	—
1975–76 QPR	1	42	—
1976–77 QPR	1	40	—
1977–78 QPR	1	31	—
1978–79 QPR	1	24	—
1978–79 West Ham U	2	18	—
1979–80 West Ham U	2	40	—
1980–81 West Ham U	2	42	—
1981–82 West Ham U	1	39	—
1982–83 West Ham U	1	42	—
1983–84 West Ham U	1	42	—
1984–85 West Ham U	1	10	—
1985–86 West Ham U	1	42	—
1986–87 West Ham U	1	33	—
1987–88 West Ham U	1	1	—

PARKIN, Steve
7.11.65 Mansfield (DF)
5.6 10.7 Apprentice
LD Stoke C v Nottingham F
16.3.83 1-0

1982–83 Stoke C	1	2	—
1983–84 Stoke C	1	1	—
1984–85 Stoke C	1	13	1
1985–86 Stoke C	2	12	1
1986–87 Stoke C	2	38	—
1987–88 Stoke C	2	43	3

PARKIN, Tim
31.12.57 Penrith (DF)
6.2 13.3 Apprentice
LD Bristol R v Blackburn R
8.3.77 0-0

1976–77 Blackburn R	2	1	—
1977–78 Blackburn R	2	—	—
1978–79 Blackburn R	2	12	—
1979–80 Blackburn R	3	—	—
Malmo and Almondsbury Greenway			
1981–82 Bristol R	3	40	2
1982–83 Bristol R	3	41	3
1983–84 Bristol R	3	39	2
1984–85 Bristol R	3	43	3
1985–86 Bristol R	3	43	2
1986–87 Swindon T	3	32	2
1987–88 Swindon T	2	40	2

PARKINSON, Gary
10.1.68 Middlesbrough (DF)
— — Everton Amateur
LD Middlesbrough v Port Vale (at Hartlepool)
23.8.86 2-2

1985–86 Middlesbrough	2	—	—
1986–87 Middlesbrough	3	46	—
1987–88 Middlesbrough	2	38	—

PARKINSON, Philip
1.12.67 Chorley (MF)
5.10 10.11 Apprentice
LD Brentford v Bury
12.3.88 0–3

1985–86 Southampton	1	—	—
1986–87 Southampton	1	—	—
1987–88 Southampton	1	—	—
1987–88 Bury	3	8	1

PARKS, Tony
26.1.63 Hackney (GK)
5.10½ 10.8 Apprentice
LD West Ham U v Tottenham H
10.5.82 2–2

1980–81 Tottenham H	1	—	—
1981–82 Tottenham H	1	2	—
1982–83 Tottenham H	1	1	—
1983–84 Tottenham H	1	16	—
1984–85 Tottenham H	1	—	—
1985–86 Tottenham H	1	—	—
1986–87 Tottenham H	1	2	—
1986–87 *Oxford U*	1	5	—
1987–88 Tottenham H	1	16	—
1987–88 *Gillingham*	3	2	—

PARRIS, George
11.9.64 Ilford (MF)
5.9 12.0 Apprentice
LD West Ham U v Liverpool
20.5.85 0–3

1982–83 West Ham U	1	—	—
1983–84 West Ham U	1	—	—
1984–85 West Ham U	1	1	—
1985–86 West Ham U	1	26	1
1986–87 West Ham U	1	36	1
1987–88 West Ham U	1	30	1

PASCOE, Colin
9.4.65 Port Talbot (FW)
5.9½ 10.0 Apprentice
LD Swansea C v Brighton & HA
1.3.83 1–2

1982–83 Swansea C	1	7	1
1983–84 Swansea C	2	32	2
1984–85 Swansea C	3	41	9
1985–86 Swansea C	3	19	3
1986–87 Swansea C	4	41	11
1987–88 Swansea C	4	34	13
1987–88 Sunderland	3	9	4

PASHLEY, Terry
11.10.56 Chesterfield (DF)
5.8 12.0 Apprentice
LD Burnley v Birmingham C
10.4.76 1–0

1973–74 Burnley	1	—	—
1974–75 Burnley	1	—	—
1975–76 Burnley	1	1	—
1976–77 Burnley	2	11	—
1977–78 Burnley	2	6	—

1978–79 Blackpool	3	35	—
1979–80 Blackpool	3	44	3
1980–81 Blackpool	3	30	—
1981–82 Blackpool	4	46	1
1982–83 Blackpool	4	46	3
1983–84 Bury	4	40	—
1984–85 Bury	4	29	1
1985–86 Bury	3	39	1
1986–87 Bury	3	38	1
1987–88 Bury	3	46	1

PATERSON, Craig
2.10.59 South Queensferry (DF)
6.2 12.12 Bonnyrigg Rose
LD Hibernian v Rangers
11.8.79 1–3

1978–79 Hibernian	P	—	—
1979–80 Hibernian	P	30	—
1980–81 Hibernian	1	38	3
1981–82 Hibernian	P	36	1
1982–83 Rangers	P	20	—
1983–84 Rangers	P	21	1
1984–85 Rangers	P	22	2
1985–86 Rangers	P	18	1
1986–87 Rangers	P	2	—
1986–87 Motherwell	P	16	—
1987–88 Motherwell	P	44	2

PATES, Colin
10.8.61 Mitcham (DF)
5.11 11.0 Apprentice
LD Orient v Chelsea
10.11.79 3–7

1979–80 Chelsea	2	16	—
1980–81 Chelsea	2	15	—
1981–82 Chelsea	2	42	1
1982–83 Chelsea	2	35	4
1983–84 Chelsea	2	42	—
1984–85 Chelsea	1	36	1
1985–86 Chelsea	1	35	1
1986–87 Chelsea	1	33	2
1987–88 Chelsea	1	17	—

PATTERSON, Mark
24.5.65 Darwen (FW)
5.8 11.3 Apprentice
LD Manchester C v Blackburn R
17.9.83 6–0

1983–84 Blackburn R	2	29	7
1984–85 Blackburn R	2	9	—
1985–86 Blackburn R	2	26	10
1986–87 Blackburn R	2	24	1
1987–88 Blackburn R	2	13	2

PATTERSON, Mark
13.9.68 Leeds (MF)
— — YTS
LD Carlisle U v Mansfield T
27.9.86 1–2

1986–87 Carlisle U	3	6	—
1987–88 Carlisle U	4	13	—
1987–88 Derby Co	1	—	—

PAYTON, Andy
23.10.66 Burnley (MF)
5.9 10.6
LD Stoke C v Hull C
4.4.87 1–1

1986–87 Hull C	2	2	—
1987–88 Hull C	2	22	2

PEACOCK, Gavin
18.11.67 Kent (FW)
5.7 —
LD QPR v Sheffield W
29.11.86 2–2

1984–85 QPR	1	—	—
1985–86 QPR	1	—	—
1986–87 QPR	1	12	1
1987–88 QPR	1	5	—
1987–88 *Gillingham*	3	7	—
1987–88 Gillingham	3	19	2

PEAKE, Andy
11.1.61 Mkt Harborough (MF)
5.9½ 11.2½ Apprentice
LD Leicester C v Blackburn R
20.1.79 1–1

1978–79 Leicester C	2	18	2
1979–80 Leicester C	2	25	3
1980–81 Leicester C	1	24	1
1981–82 Leicester C	2	31	2
1982–83 Leicester C	2	4	—
1983–84 Leicester C	1	24	4
1984–85 Leicester C	1	21	1
1985–86 Grimsby T	2	36	4
1986–87 Grimsby T	2	3	—
1986–87 Charlton Ath	1	29	—
1987–88 Charlton Ath	1	16	—

PEAKE, Trevor
10.2.57 Nuneaton (DF)
6.0 12.9 Nuneaton Bor
LD Lincoln C v Peterborough U
18.8.79 0–1

1979–80 Lincoln C	4	45	1
1980–81 Lincoln C	4	43	1
1981–82 Lincoln C	3	37	4
1982–83 Lincoln C	3	46	1
1983–84 Coventry C	1	33	3
1984–85 Coventry C	1	35	1
1985–86 Coventry C	1	37	1
1986–87 Coventry C	1	39	—
1987–88 Coventry C	1	31	—

PEARCE, Alan
25.10.65 Middlesbrough (MF)
5.8 10.12 Apprentice
LD Hartlepool U v York C
26.11.83 2–3

1983–84 York C	4	18	5
1984–85 York C	3	23	4
1985–86 York C	3	7	—
1986–87 York C	3	30	—
1987–88 Torquay U	4	27	2

PLAYER DIRECTORY

PEARCE, Chris
7.8.61 Newport (GK)
6.0 11.4 Wolves Apprentice
LD Stockport Co v <u>Rochdale</u>
16.8.80 2–2

1979–80	Blackburn R	3	— —
1980–81	*Rochdale*	4	5 —
1981–82	*Barnsley*	2	— —
1982–83	Rochdale	4	36 —
1983–84	Port Vale	3	7 —
1984–85	Port Vale	4	36 —
1985–86	Port Vale	4	5 —
1986–87	Wrexham	4	25 —
1987–88	Burnley	4	46 —

PEARCE, Stuart
24.4.62 London (DF)
5.10 11.2 Wealdstone
LD <u>Coventry C</u> v QPR
12.11.83 1–0

1983–84	Coventry C	1	23	—
1984–85	Coventry C	1	28	4
1985–86	Nottingham F	1	30	1
1986–87	Nottingham F	1	39	6
1987–88	Nottingham F	1	34	5

PEARS, Steve
22.1.62 Brandon (GK)
5.11½ 12.2 Apprentice
LD <u>Middlesbrough</u> v Cardiff C
5.11.83 2–0

1978–79	Manchester U	1	— —
1979–80	Manchester U	1	— —
1980–81	Manchester U	1	— —
1981–82	Manchester U	1	— —
1982–83	Manchester U	1	— —
1983–84	Manchester U	1	— —
1983–84	*Middlesbrough*	2	12 —
1984–85	Manchester U	1	4 —
1985–86	Middlesbrough	2	38 —
1986–87	Middlesbrough	3	46 —
1987–88	Middlesbrough	2	43 —

PEARSON, John
1.9.63 Sheffield (FW)
6.2 13.1 Apprentice
LD <u>Sheffield W</u> v Bristol C
13.9.80 2–1

1980–81	Sheffield W	2	15	4
1981–82	Sheffield W	2	24	7
1982–83	Sheffield W	2	30	7
1983–84	Sheffield W	2	27	4
1984–85	Sheffield W	1	9	2
1985–86	Charlton Ath	2	42	14
1986–87	Charlton Ath	1	19	1
1986–87	Leeds U	2	18	4
1987–88	Leeds U	2	43	6

PEARSON, Nigel
21.8.63 Nottingham (DF)
6.0 12.10 Heanor T
LD Oldham Ath v <u>Shrewsbury T</u>
28.8.82 1–0

1981–82	Shrewsbury T	2	—	—
1982–83	Shrewsbury T	2	39	1
1983–84	Shrewsbury T	2	26	—
1984–85	Shrewsbury T	2	—	—
1985–86	Shrewsbury T	2	35	1
1986–87	Shrewsbury T	2	42	3
1987–88	Shrewsbury T	2	11	—
1987–88	Sheffield W	1	19	2

PEEBLES, Gary
6.2.67 Johnstone (MF)
6.0 11.0 Gleniffer Thistle
LD <u>St Mirren</u> v Hearts
6.12.86 0–0

1986–87	St Mirren	P	7	—
1987–88	St Mirren	P	1	—

PEER, Dean
8.8.69 Dudley (MF)
6.2 12.0 YTS
LD Hull C v <u>Birmingham C</u>
20.9.86 3–2

1986–87	Birmingham C	2	2	—
1987–88	Birmingham C	2	—	—

PEJIC, Mel
27.4.59 Chesterton (DF)
5.7½ 10.6 Local
LD <u>Stoke C</u> v Ipswich T
12.1.80 0–1

1977–78	Stoke C	2	— —
1978–79	Stoke C	2	— —
1979–80	Stoke C	1	1 —
1980–81	Hereford U	4	13 —
1981–82	Hereford U	4	27 —
1982–83	Hereford U	4	45 1
1983–84	Hereford U	4	44 —
1984–85	Hereford U	4	46 1
1985–86	Hereford U	4	45 1
1986–87	Hereford U	4	31 —
1987–88	Hereford U	4	44 1

PEMBERTON, John
18.11.64 Oldham (DF)
5.11 11.9
LD <u>Rochdale</u> v Aldershot
2.10.84 1–2

1984–85	Rochdale	4	1	—
1984–85	Crewe Alex	4	6	—
1985–86	Crewe Alex	4	41	—
1986–87	Crewe Alex	4	43	—
1987–88	Crewe Alex	4	31	1
1987–88	Crystal Palace	2	2	—

PENNEY, David
17.8.64 Wakefield (FW)
5.8 10.7 Pontefract
LD <u>Derby C</u> v Hull C
11.10.86 1–1

1985–86	Derby Co	3	— —
1986–87	Derby Co	2	1 —
1987–88	Derby Co	1	9 —

PENNEY, Steve
16.1.64 Ballymena (MF)
5.8 10.1 Ballymena U
LD Barnsley v <u>Brighton & HA</u>
26.11.83 3–1

1983–84	Brighton & HA	2	25	1
1984–85	Brighton & HA	2	26	4
1985–86	Brighton & HA	2	37	3
1986–87	Brighton & HA	2	27	3
1987–88	Brighton & HA	3	13	3

PENNYFATHER, Glenn
11.2.63 Billericay (MF)
5.8 10.10 Apprentice
LD <u>Southend U</u> v Doncaster R
27.2.81 0–0

1980–81	Southend U	4	1	—
1981–82	Southend U	3	33	4
1982–83	Southend U	3	34	1
1983–84	Southend U	3	33	4
1984–85	Southend U	4	41	7
1985–86	Southend U	4	41	7
1986–87	Southend U	4	38	10
1987–88	Southend U	3	17	3
1987–88	Crystal Palace	2	19	1

PENRICE, Gary
23.3.64 Bristol (FW)
5.7 10.0 Apprentice
LD <u>Bristol R</u> v Orient
27.4.85 0–1

1984–85	Bristol R	3	5	1
1985–86	Bristol R	3	39	5
1986–87	Bristol R	3	43	7
1987–88	Bristol R	3	46	18

PEPPER, Nigel
25.4.68 Rotherham (MF)
5.10 10.3 Apprentice
LD Wolves v <u>Rotherham U</u>
8.3.86 0–0

1985–86	Rotherham U	3	7 —
1986–87	Rotherham U	3	2 —
1987–88	Rotherham U	3	15 —

PERKS, Steve
19.4.63 Bridgnorth (GK)
6.0 11.0
LD Middlesbrough v <u>Shrewsbury T</u>
14.12.84 1–1

1980–81	Shrewsbury T	2	— —
1981–82	Shrewsbury T	2	— —
1982–83	Shrewsbury T	2	— —
1983–84	Shrewsbury T	2	— —
1984–85	Shrewsbury T	2	23 —
1985–86	Shrewsbury T	2	42 —
1986–87	Shrewsbury T	2	36 —
1987–88	Shrewsbury T	2	42 —

PERRY, Andrew
12.6.62 Dulwich (FW)
— — Local
LD <u>Portsmouth</u> v Oxford U
16.1.88 2–2

1987–88	Portsmouth	1	4 —

PERRY, Dave
17.5.67 Sheffield (MF)
— —
LD Bolton W v Chesterfield
14.12.85 2–1

1984–85	Chesterfield	4	— —
1985–86	Chesterfield	3	2 —
1986–87	Chesterfield	3	3 —
1987–88	Chesterfield	3	12 —

PERRY, Jason
2.4.70 Newport (DF)
— —
LD Cardiff C v Exeter C
31.3.87 0–0

1986–87	Cardiff C	4	1 —
1987–88	Cardiff C	4	3 —

PEYTON, Gerry
20.5.56 Birmingham (GK)
6.2 13.9 Atherstone T
LD Burnley v Liverpool
6.12.75 0–0

1975–76	Burnley	1	20	—
1976–77	Burnley	2	10	—
1976–77	Fulham	2	23	—
1977–78	Fulham	2	42	—
1978–79	Fulham	2	40	—
1979–80	Fulham	2	31	—
1980–81	Fulham	3	28	—
1981–82	Fulham	3	44	—
1982–83	Fulham	2	42	—
1983–84	Fulham	2	27	—
1983–84	*Southend U*	3	10	—
1984–85	Fulham	2	32	—
1985–86	Fulham	2	36	—
1986–87	Bournemouth	3	46	—
1987–88	Bournemouth	2	42	—

PHELAN, Mike
24.9.62 Nelson (DF)
5.10½ 11.1½ Apprentice
LD Chesterfield v Burnley
31.1.81 3–0

1980–81	Burnley	3	16	2
1981–82	Burnley	3	23	1
1982–83	Burnley	2	42	3
1983–84	Burnley	3	44	2
1984–85	Burnley	3	43	1
1985–86	Norwich C	2	42	3
1986–87	Norwich C	1	40	4
1987–88	Norwich C	1	37	—

PHELAN, Terry
16.3.67 Manchester (DF)
5.8 10.0
LD Shrewsbury T v Leeds U
7.9.85 1–3

1984–85	Leeds U	2	—	—
1985–86	Leeds U	2	14	—
1986–87	Swansea C	4	45	—
1987–88	Wimbledon	1	30	—

PHILLIBEN, John
14.3.64 Stirling (DF)
5.10 11.0 Gairdoch U
LD Stirling A v Clydebank
1.10.80 0–0

1980–81	Stirling A	1	15	—
1981–82	Stirling A	2	37	1
1982–83	Stirling A	2	34	—
1983–84	Stirling A	2	23	—
1983–84	Doncaster R	4	12	—
1984–85	Doncaster R	3	36	1
1985–86	Doncaster R	3	22	—
1985–86	*Cambridge U*	4	6	—
1986–87	Doncaster R	3	1	—
1986–87	Motherwell	P	37	—
1987–88	Motherwell	P	35	2

PHILLIPS, David
29.7.63 Wegberg (MF)
5.10 11.2 Apprentice
LD Plymouth Arg v Oxford U
29.8.81 0–1

1981–82	Plymouth Arg	3	8	1
1982–83	Plymouth Arg	3	23	8
1983–84	Plymouth Arg	3	42	6
1984–85	Manchester C	2	42	12
1985–86	Manchester C	1	39	1
1986–87	Coventry C	1	39	4
1987–88	Coventry C	1	35	2

PHILLIPS, Gary
20.9.61 St Albans (GK)
5.11 14.0
LD Brentford v Bristol R
26.12.84 0–3

1979–80	WBA	1	—	—
1980–81	WBA	1	—	—
From Barnet				
1984–85	Brentford	3	21	—
1985–86	Brentford	3	43	—
1986–87	Brentford	3	44	—
1987–88	Brentford	3	35	—

PHILLIPS, Ian
23.4.59 Edinburgh (DF)
5.10 12.0 Ipswich T Apprentice
LD Mansfield T v Millwall
10.9.77 0–0

1977–78	Mansfield T	2	18	—
1978–79	Mansfield T	3	5	—
1979–80	Peterborough U	4	39	1
1980–81	Peterborough U	4	41	—
1981–82	Peterborough U	4	17	2
1982–83	Northampton T	4	42	1
1983–84	Northampton T	4	—	—
1983–84	Colchester U	4	43	5
1984–85	Colchester U	4	37	1
1985–86	Colchester U	4	37	2
1986–87	Colchester U	4	33	2
1987–88	Aldershot	3	32	—

PHILLIPS, James
8.2.66 Bolton (DF)
6.0 12.0 Apprentice
LD Bolton W v Gillingham
7.4.84 0–1

1983–84	Bolton W	3	1	—
1984–85	Bolton W	3	40	1
1985–86	Bolton W	3	33	1
1986–87	Bolton W	3	34	—
1986–87	Rangers	P	6	—
1987–88	Rangers	P	19	—

PHILLIPS, Les
7.1.63 Lambeth (MF)
5.8 10.6 Apprentice
LD West Ham U v Birmingham C
13.2.82 2–2

1980–81	Birmingham C	1	—	—
1981–82	Birmingham C	1	11	1
1982–83	Birmingham C	1	13	2
1983–84	Birmingham C	1	20	—
1983–84	Oxford U	3	6	—
1984–85	Oxford U	2	3	—
1985–86	Oxford U	1	28	2
1986–87	Oxford U	1	35	—
1987–88	Oxford U	1	30	4

PHILLIPS, Stewart
30.12.61 Halifax (FW)
6.0½ 11.7 Amateur
LD Swindon T v Hereford U
22.4.78 1–0

1977–78	Hereford U	3	1	—
1978–79	Hereford U	4	8	—
1979–80	Hereford U	4	11	2
1980–81	Hereford U	4	8	1
1981–82	Hereford U	4	43	12
1982–83	Hereford U	4	41	13
1983–84	Hereford U	4	46	17
1984–85	Hereford U	4	46	19
1985–86	Hereford U	4	20	5
1986–87	Hereford U	4	39	11
1987–88	Hereford U	4	—	—
1987–88	WBA	2	10	2

PHILLISKIRK, Tony
10.2.65 Sunderland (FW)
6.1 11.3 Amateur
LD Sheffield U v Brentford
22.10.83 0–0

1983–84	Sheffield U	3	21	8
1984–85	Sheffield U	2	23	2
1985–86	Sheffield U	2	4	—
1986–87	Sheffield U	2	6	1
1986–87	*Rotherham U*	3	6	1
1987–88	Sheffield U	2	26	9

PLAYER DIRECTORY

PICKERING, Mike
29.9.56 Huddersfield (DF)
5.11 12.6 Local
LD Torquay U v Barnsley
11.1.75 1-1

1974–75	Barnsley	4	14	—
1975–76	Barnsley	4	41	—
1976–77	Barnsley	4	45	1
1977–78	Southampton	2	41	—
1978–79	Southampton	1	3	—
1978–79	Sheffield W	3	35	—
1979–80	Sheffield W	3	32	—
1980–81	Sheffield W	2	15	—
1981–82	Sheffield W	2	24	1
1982–83	Sheffield W	2	4	—
1983–84	Sheffield W	2	—	—
1983–84	*Norwich C*	1	1	—
1983–84	*Bradford C*	3	4	—
1983–84	*Barnsley*	2	3	—
1983–84	Rotherham U	3	24	—
1984–85	Rotherham U	3	32	1
1985–86	Rotherham U	3	46	—
1986–87	York C	3	32	1
1987–88	Stockport Co	4	8	—

PICKERING, Nick
4.8.63 Newcastle (DF)
6.0 11.10 Apprentice
LD Ipswich T v Sunderland
29.8.81 3-3

1981–82	Sunderland	1	37	3
1982–83	Sunderland	1	39	7
1983–84	Sunderland	1	42	1
1984–85	Sunderland	1	37	2
1985–86	Sunderland	2	24	5
1985–86	Coventry C	1	15	4
1986–87	Coventry C	1	36	5
1987–88	Coventry C	1	27	1

PIKE, Chris
19.10.61 Cardiff (FW)
6.2 13.3 Barry T
LD Fulham v Sheffield W
17.9.85 2-3

1984–85	Fulham	2	—	—
1985–86	Fulham	2	26	4
1986–87	Fulham	3	13	—
1986–87	*Cardiff C*	4	6	2
1987–88	Fulham	3	3	—

PIKE, Geoff
28.9.56 Clapton (MF)
5.6 11.0 Apprentice
LD West Ham U v Birmingham C
6.3.76 1-2

1975–76	West Ham U	1	3	—
1976–77	West Ham U	1	20	6
1977–78	West Ham U	1	28	2
1978–79	West Ham U	2	14	2
1979–80	West Ham U	2	31	4
1980–81	West Ham U	2	42	6
1981–82	West Ham U	1	34	2
1982–83	West Ham U	1	40	6
1983–84	West Ham U	1	28	2
1984–85	West Ham U	1	30	2
1985–86	West Ham U	1	10	—
1986–87	West Ham U	1	11	—
1987–88	Notts Co	3	46	14

PIKE, Martin
21.10.64 South Shields (MF)
5.9 11.4 Apprentice
LD Peterborough U v Hartlepool U
27.8.83 3-1

1982–83	WBA	1	—	—
1983–84	Peterborough U	4	35	2
1984–85	Peterborough U	4	45	4
1985–86	Peterborough U	4	46	2
1986–87	Sheffield U	2	42	—
1987–88	Sheffield U	2	39	—

PITCHER, Darren
12.10.69 London (DF)
— — Apprentice
LD —

1987–88	Charlton Ath	1	—	—

PIZANTI, David
— Tel Aviv (MF)
— — Cologne
LD Liverpool v QPR
17.10.87 4-0

1987–88	QPR	1	7	—

PLATNAUER, Nicky
10.6.61 Leicester (FW)
5.11 12.10 Bedford T
LD Bristol R v Lincoln C
18.9.82 1-2

1982–83	Bristol R	3	24	7
1983–84	Coventry C	1	34	6
1984–85	Coventry C	1	10	—
1984–85	Birmingham C	2	11	1
1985–86	Birmingham C	1	17	1
1985–86	*Reading*	3	7	—
1986–87	Cardiff C	4	38	3
1987–88	Cardiff C	4	38	1

PLATT, David
10.6.66 Chadderton (FW)
5.11 11.7 Chadderton
LD Crewe Alex v Mansfield T
26.1.85 1-1

1984–85	Manchester U	1	—	—
1984–85	Crewe Alex	4	22	5
1985–86	Crewe Alex	4	43	9
1986–87	Crewe Alex	4	43	22
1987–88	Crewe Alex	4	26	19
1987–88	Aston Villa	2	11	5

PLUMMER, Calvin
14.2.63 Nottingham (FW)
5.9 9.10 Apprentice
LD Brighton & HA v Nottingham F
20.2.82 0-1

1980–81	Nottingham F	1	—	—
1981–82	Nottingham F	1	9	2
1982–83	Nottingham F	1	3	—
1982–83	Chesterfield	3	28	7
1983–84	Derby Co	2	27	3
1983–84	Barnsley	2	2	1
1984–85	Barnsley	2	26	2
1985–86	Barnsley	2	23	3
1986–87	Barnsley	2	3	—
1987–88	Nottingham F	1	8	2
1987–88	*Derry Co*	—	—	—

POINTON, Neil
28.11.64 Church Warsop (DF)
5.10 10.10 Apprentice
LD Scunthorpe U v Torquay U
6.2.82 0-2

1981–82	Scunthorpe U	4	5	—
1982–83	Scunthorpe U	4	46	1
1983–84	Scunthorpe U	3	45	1
1984–85	Scunthorpe U	4	46	—
1985–86	Scunthorpe U	4	17	—
1985–86	Everton	1	15	—
1986–87	Everton	1	12	1
1987–88	Everton	1	33	3

POLSTON, John
10.6.68 London (DF)
— — Apprentice
LD Tottenham H v Coventry C
15.11.86 1-0

1985–86	Tottenham H	1	—	—
1986–87	Tottenham H	1	2	—
1987–88	Tottenham H	1	2	—

POOLE, Gary
11.9.67 Stratford (DF)
6.0 11.0 Arsenal schoolboy
LD Cambridge U v Cardiff C
1.9.87 0-0

1984–85	Tottenham H	1	—	—
1985–86	Tottenham H	1	—	—
1986–87	Tottenham H	1	—	—
1987–88	Cambridge U	4	42	—

POOLE, Kevin
21.7.63 Bromsgrove (GK)
5.10½ 11.6 Apprentice
LD Tottenham H v Aston Villa
30.3.85 0-2

1981–82	Aston Villa	1	—	—
1982–83	Aston Villa	1	—	—
1983–84	Aston Villa	1	—	—
1984–85	Aston Villa	1	7	—
1984–85	*Northampton T*	4	3	—
1985–86	Aston Villa	1	11	—
1986–87	Aston Villa	1	10	—
1987–88	Middlesbrough	2	1	—

PORTEOUS, Ian
21.11.64 Glasgow (MF)
5.9 10.3 Eastercraigs
LD Aberdeen v Kilmarnock
4.5.83 5-0

1981–82 Aberdeen	1	—	—
1982–83 Aberdeen	1	1	—
1983–84 Aberdeen	1	14	3
1984–85 Aberdeen	1	13	1
1985–86 Aberdeen	P	6	—
1986–87 Aberdeen	P	9	2
1987–88 Aberdeen	P	3	1

PORTER, Andy
17.9.68 Manchester
LD Port Vale v Blackpool
28.2.87 1-6

1986–87 Port Vale	3	1	—
1987–88 Port Vale	4	6	—

PORTER, Gary
6.3.66 Sunderland (MF)
5.6½ 9.10 Apprentice
LD Wolves v Watford
3.12.85 0-5

1983–84 Watford	1	2	—
1984–85 Watford	1	9	—
1985–86 Watford	1	8	1
1986–87 Watford	1	26	4
1987–88 Watford	1	40	3

POTTS, Steven
7.5.67 Hartford (USA) (DF)
5.8 10.5 Apprentice
LD West Ham U v QPR
1.1.85 1-3

1984–85 West Ham U	1	1	—
1985–86 West Ham U	1	1	—
1986–87 West Ham U	1	8	—
1987–88 West Ham U	1	8	—

POWELL, Cliff
21.2.68 Watford (DF)
5.11½ 11.3 Apprentice
LD Burnley v Hereford U
12.12.87 0-0

1985–86 Watford	1	—	—
1986–87 Watford	1	—	—
1987–88 Watford	1	—	—
1987–88 *Hereford U*	4	7	—
1987–88 Sheffield U	2	6	—

POWELL, Gary
2.4.69 Hoylake (FW)
5.10 10.2 Apprentice
LD —

1987–88 Everton	1	—	—

PRATLEY, Dick
12.1.63 Banbury (DF)
6.2 14.2 Banbury U
LD Derby Co v Oldham Ath
17.9.83 2-2

1983–84 Derby Co	2	2	—
1983–84 *Scunthorpe U*	3	10	—
1984–85 Derby Co	3	13	1
1985–86 Derby Co	3	7	—
1986–87 Derby Co	2	9	—
1987–88 Derby Co	1	—	—
1987–88 Shrewsbury T	2	11	—

PREECE, David
28.5.63 Bridgnorth (MF)
5.6 10.10 Apprentice
LD Walsall v Chester
17.1.81 2-1

1980–81 Walsall	3	8	—
1981–82 Walsall	3	8	—
1982–83 Walsall	3	42	2
1983–84 Walsall	3	41	3
1984–85 Walsall	3	12	—
1984–85 Luton T	1	21	2
1985–86 Luton T	1	41	2
1986–87 Luton T	1	14	—
1987–88 Luton T	1	13	—

PREECE, Roger
9.6.69 Much Wenlock (MF)
5.9 10.12 Apprentice
LD Exeter C v Wrexham
21.2.87 4-2

1986–87 Coventry C	1	—	—
1986–87 Wrexham	4	7	2
1987–88 Wrexham	4	40	4

PRESSMAN, Kevin
6.11.67 Fareham (GK)
6.1 13.0 Apprentice
LD Southampton v Sheffield W
5.9.87 1-1

1985–86 Sheffield W	1	—	—
1986–87 Sheffield W	1	—	—
1987–88 Sheffield W	1	11	—

PRESTON, Richard
10.6.67 Nottingham (FW)
6.2½ 13.6 Local
LD Halifax T v Scarborough U
4.4.88 2-2

1987–88 Scarborough U	4	4	—

PRICE, Chris
30.3.60 Hereford (DF)
5.7 10.2 Apprentice
LD Notts Co v Hereford U
1.4.77 3-2

1976–77 Hereford U	2	2	—
1977–78 Hereford U	3	13	—
1978–79 Hereford U	4	29	—
1979–80 Hereford U	4	42	—
1980–81 Hereford U	4	42	2
1981–82 Hereford U	4	41	10
1982–83 Hereford U	4	42	5
1983–84 Hereford U	4	37	1
1984–85 Hereford U	4	41	5
1985–86 Hereford U	4	41	4
1986–87 Blackburn R	2	40	1
1987–88 Blackburn R	2	43	10

PRIEST, Philip
9.9.66 Warley (FW)
5.7½ 10.6 School
LD Blackpool v Bury
13.12.86 1-1

1983–84 Chelsea	2	—	—
1984–85 Chelsea	1	—	—
1985–86 Chelsea	1	—	—
1986–87 *Blackpool*	3	1	—
1986–87 *Brentford*	3	5	1
1987–88 Shrewsbury T	2	21	2

PRITCHARD, Howard
18.10.58 Cardiff (FW)
5.10 12.0 Apprentice
LD Bristol C v Aston Villa
26.8.78 1-0

1976–77 Bristol C	1	—	—
1977–78 Bristol C	1	—	—
1978–79 Bristol C	1	1	—
1979–80 Bristol C	1	16	—
1980–81 Bristol C	2	21	2
1981–82 Swindon T	3	28	1
1982–83 Swindon T	4	37	10
1983–84 Bristol C	4	46	10
1984–85 Bristol C	3	39	6
1985–86 Bristol C	3	34	6
1986–87 Gillingham	3	46	12
1987–88 Gillingham	3	42	8

PROCTOR, Mark
30.1.61 Middlesbrough (MF)
5.9 11.10 Apprentice
LD Birmingham c v Middlesbrough
22.8.78 1-3

1978–79 Middlesbrough	1	33	9
1979–80 Middlesbrough	1	38	2
1980–81 Middlesbrough	1	38	1
1981–82 Nottingham F	1	37	1
1982–83 Nottingham F	1	27	4
1982–83 *Sunderland*	1	5	—
1983–84 Sunderland	1	41	2
1984–85 Sunderland	1	17	2
1985–86 Sunderland	2	19	7
1986–87 Sunderland	2	31	8
1987–88 Sunderland	3	4	—
1987–88 Sheffield W	1	35	2

PROUDLOCK, Paul
25.10.65 Hartlepool (FW)
5.9 10.5 Local
LD Colchester U v Hartlepool U
9.11.84 1-0

1984–85 Hartlepool U	4	14	—
1985–86 Hartlepool U	4	1	—
1986–87 Middlesbrough	3	3	1
1987–88 Middlesbrough	2	1	—

PLAYER DIRECTORY

PRUDHOE, Mark
8.11.63 Washington (GK)
6.0 12.12 Apprentice
LD WBA v Sunderland
11.12.82 3–0

1981–82 Sunderland	1	—	—
1982–83 Sunderland	1	7	—
1983–84 Sunderland	1	—	—
1983–84 *Hartlepool U*	4	3	—
1984–85 Sunderland	1	—	—
1984–85 Birmingham C	2	1	—
1985–86 Birmingham C	1	—	—
1985–86 Walsall	3	16	—
1986–87 Walsall	3	—	—
1986–87 *Doncaster R*	3	5	—
1986–87 *Sheffield W*	1	—	—
1986–87 *Grimsby T*	2	8	—
1987–88 *Hartlepool U*	4	13	—
1987–88 *Bristol C*	3	3	—
1987–88 *Carlisle U*	4	6	—
1987–88 Carlisle U	4	16	—

PUCKETT, David
29.10.60 Southampton (FW)
5.7 10.4 Apprentice
LD Southampton v Everton
17.3.81 3–0

1978–79 Southampton	1	—	—
1979–80 Southampton	1	—	—
1980–81 Southampton	1	7	—
1981–82 Southampton	1	17	3
1982–83 Southampton	1	25	3
1983–84 Southampton	1	18	3
1983–84 *Nottingham F*	1	—	—
1984–85 Southampton	1	13	1
1985–86 Southampton	1	15	4
1986–87 Bournemouth	3	19	10
1987–88 Bournemouth	2	12	4
1987–88 *Stoke*	2	7	—

PULIS, Tony
16.1.58 Newport (MF)
5.10 11.8 Apprentice
LD Bristol C v Bristol R
30.8.75 1–1

1975–76 Bristol R	2	4	—
1976–77 Bristol R	2	9	—
1977–78 Bristol R	2	23	—
1978–79 Bristol R	2	7	—
1979–80 Bristol R	2	34	3
1980–81 Bristol R	2	8	—
Happy Valley, Hong Kong			
1982–83 Bristol R	3	17	—
1983–84 Bristol R	3	28	2
1984–85 Newport C	3	37	—
1985–86 Newport C	3	40	—
1986–87 Bournemouth	3	35	—
1987–88 Bournemouth	2	29	3

PULLAN, Chris
14.12.67 Durham (MF)
5.8 10.12 School
LD Watford v Tottenham H
9.11.87 1–0

1986–87 Watford	1	1	—
1987–88 Watford	1	4	—

PURNELL, Philip
16.9.64 Bristol (FW)
— —
LD Bristol C v Bristol R
29.3.86 2–0

1985–86 Bristol R	3	11	2
1986–87 Bristol R	3	21	3
1987–88 Bristol R	3	41	8

PUTNEY, Trevor
11.2.61 Harold Hill (MF)
5.7 10.11 Brentwood & W
LD Ipswich T v Arsenal
9.10.82 0–1

1980–81 Ipswich T	1	—	—
1981–82 Ipswich T	1	—	—
1982–83 Ipswich T	1	20	3
1983–84 Ipswich T	1	35	2
1984–85 Ipswich T	1	27	2
1985–86 Ipswich T	1	21	1
1986–87 Norwich C	1	23	4
1987–88 Norwich C	1	26	1

QUINN, Jimmy
18.11.59 Belfast (FW)
6.1 12.0 Oswestry T
LD Swindon T v Walsall
9.3.82 2–2

1981–82 Swindon T	3	4	—
1982–83 Swindon T	4	13	3
1983–84 Swindon T	4	32	7
1984–85 Blackburn R	2	25	10
1985–86 Blackburn R	2	31	4
1986–87 Blackburn R	2	15	3
1986–87 Swindon T	3	22	9
1987–88 Swindon T	2	42	21

QUINN, Mike
2.5.62 Liverpool (FW)
5.9½ 12.0 Derby Co Apprentice
LD Wigan Ath v Halifax T
12.4.80 3–1

1979–80 Wigan Ath	4	4	1
1980–81 Wigan Ath	4	36	14
1981–82 Wigan Ath	4	29	4
1982–83 Stockport Co	4	39	24
1983–84 Stockport Co	4	24	15
1983–84 Oldham Ath	2	14	5
1984–85 Oldham Ath	2	40	18
1985–86 Oldham Ath	2	26	11
1985–86 Portsmouth	2	11	6
1986–87 Portsmouth	2	39	22
1987–88 Portsmouth	1	32	8

QUINN, Niall
6.10.66 Dublin (FW)
6.4 12.4
LD Arsenal v Liverpool
14.12.85 2–0

1983–84 Arsenal	1	—	—
1984–85 Arsenal	1	—	—
1985–86 Arsenal	1	12	1
1986–87 Arsenal	1	35	8
1987–88 Arsenal	1	11	2

QUOW, Trevor
28.9.60 Peterborough (FW)
5.7 10.12 Apprentice
LD Peterborough U v Sheffield W
19.8.78 2–0

1978–79 Peterborough U	3	8	—
1979–80 Peterborough U	4	29	3
1980–81 Peterborough U	4	44	4
1981–82 Peterborough U	4	10	1
1982–83 Peterborough U	4	18	1
1983–84 Peterborough U	4	28	1
1984–85 Peterborough U	4	36	1
1985–86 Peterborough U	4	30	3
1986–87 Gillingham	3	19	1
1987–88 Gillingham	3	40	1

RADFORD, Mark
20.12.68 Leicester (MF)
6.1 11.8 Trainee
LD Colchester U v Peterborough U
12.9.87 4–1

1987–88 Colchester U	4	14	—

RAE, Gordon
3.5.58 Edinburgh (DF)
6.0 13.5 Whitehill Welfare
LD Rangers v Hibernian
20.8.77 0–2

1977–78 Hibernian	P	2	1
1978–79 Hibernian	P	27	7
1979–80 Hibernian	P	33	4
1980–81 Hibernian	1	34	13
1981–82 Hibernian	P	29	11
1982–83 Hibernian	P	31	6
1983–84 Hibernian	P	16	—
1984–85 Hibernian	P	34	—
1985–86 Hibernian	P	32	2
1986–87 Hibernian	P	35	2
1987–88 Hibernian	P	40	—

RAFFERTY, Stuart
6.3.61 Port Glasgow (MF)
5.10 11.0 Port Glasgow
LD Partick Th v Motherwell
3.3.79 0–0

1978–79 Motherwell	P	5	—
1979–80 Motherwell	1	7	2
1980–81 Motherwell	1	5	2
1981–82 Motherwell	1	13	5
1982–83 Motherwell	P	33	4
1983–84 Motherwell	P	26	4
1984–85 Dundee	P	36	4
1985–86 Dundee	P	29	3
1986–87 Dundee	P	36	4
1987–88 Dundee	P	30	4

RAMSEY, Chris
28.4.62 Birmingham (DF)
5.9 10.12 Bristol C Amateur
LD C. Palace v Brighton & HA
18.4.81 0–3

1980–81 Brighton & HA	1	3	—
1981–82 Brighton & HA	1	—	—
1982–83 Brighton & HA	1	23	—
1983–84 Brighton & HA	2	4	—
1984–85 Swindon T	4	32	1
1985–86 Swindon T	4	43	3
1986–87 Swindon T	3	25	1
1987–88 Southend U	3	13	—

RAMSEY, Paul
3.9.62 Londonderry (DF)
5.10 12.0 Apprentice
LD Leicester C v Arsenal
7.3.81 1–0

1970–80 Leicester C	2	—	—
1980–81 Leicester C	1	3	—

1981–82 Leicester C	2	10	—
1982–83 Leicester C	2	40	1
1983–84 Leicester C	1	33	1
1984–85 Leicester C	1	39	—
1985–86 Leicester C	1	13	1
1986–87 Leicester C	1	29	6
1987–88 Leicester C	2	42	1

RANDALL, Adrian
10.11.68 Amesbury (FW)
5.11 10.11 Apprentice
LD Bournemouth v Doncaster R
19.4.86 1–1

1985–86 Bournemouth	3	2	—
1986–87 Bournemouth	3	—	—
1987–88 Bournemouth	2	1	—

RANSON, Ray
12.6.60 St Helens (DF)
5.9 11.13 Apprentice
LD Manchester C v Nottingham F
23.12.78 0–0

1978–79 Manchester C	1	8	—
1979–80 Manchester C	1	40	—
1980–81 Manchester C	1	33	1
1981–82 Manchester C	1	36	—
1982–83 Manchester C	1	40	—
1983–84 Manchester C	2	26	—
1984–85 Manchester C	2	—	—
1984–85 Birmingham C	2	28	—
1985–86 Birmingham C	1	37	—
1986–87 Birmingham C	2	17	—
1987–88 Birmingham C	2	38	—

RANTANEN, Jari
31.12.61 Finland (FW)
6.3 15.2 IFK Gothenburg
LD Crystal Palace v Leicester C
12.9.87 2–1

1987–88 Leicester C	2	13	3

RATCLIFFE, Kevin
12.11.60 Mancot (DF)
5.11 12.7 Apprentice
LD Manchester U v Everton
12.3.80 0–0

1978–79 Everton	1	—	—
1979–80 Everton	1	2	—
1980–81 Everton	1	21	—
1981–82 Everton	1	25	—
1982–83 Everton	1	29	1
1983–84 Everton	1	38	—
1984–85 Everton	1	40	—
1985–86 Everton	1	39	1
1986–87 Everton	1	42	—
1987–88 Everton	1	24	—

RATCLIFFE, Simon
8.2.67 Davyhulme (DF)
5.11 11.9 Apprentice
LD Norwich C v Newcastle U
1.9.87 1–1

1984–85 Manchester U	1	—	—
1985–86 Manchester U	1	—	—
1986–87 Manchester U	1	—	—
1987–88 Norwich C	1	9	—

RATHBONE, Mike
6.11.58 Birmingham (DF)
5.10 11.4 Apprentice
LD Tottenham H v Birmingham C
20.10.76 1–0

1976–77 Birmingham C	1	16	—
1977–78 Birmingham C	1	2	—
1978–79 Birmingham C	1	2	—
1978–79 Blackburn R	2	15	—
1979–80 Blackburn R	3	28	1
1980–81 Blackburn R	2	27	—
1981–82 Blackburn R	2	41	1
1982–83 Blackburn R	2	42	—
1983–84 Blackburn R	2	11	—
1984–85 Blackburn R	2	42	—
1985–86 Blackburn R	2	42	—
1986–87 Blackburn R	2	25	—
1987–88 Preston NE	3	36	1

RAYNOR, Paul
29.4.66 Nottingham (FW)
6.0 11.4½ Apprentice
LD Southampton v Nottingham F
3.11.84 1–0

1983–84 Nottingham F	1	—	—
1984–85 Nottingham F	1	3	—
1984–85 *Bristol R*	3	8	—
1985–86 Huddersfield T	2	30	5
1986–87 Huddersfield T	2	20	4
1986–87 Swansea C	4	12	1
1987–88 Swansea C	4	44	7

RECK, Sean
5.5.67 Oxford (MF)
5.10 12.7 Apprentice
LD Bournemouth v Newport Co
31.8.85 0–1

1984–85 Oxford U	2	—	—
1985–86 Oxford U	1	—	—
1985–86 *Newport Co*	3	15	—
1985–86 *Reading*	3	1	—
1986–87 Oxford U	1	6	—
1987–88 Oxford U	1	2	—

REDFEARN, Neil
20.6.65 Dewsbury (MF)
5.10 11.6 Nottingham F
Apprentice
LD Rotherham U v Bolton W
19.2.83 1–1

1982–83 Bolton W	2	10	—
1983–84 Bolton W	3	25	—
1983–84 *Lincoln C*	3	10	1
1984–85 Lincoln C	3	45	4
1985–86 Lincoln C	3	45	8
1986–87 Doncaster R	3	46	14
1987–88 Crystal Palace	2	42	8

PLAYER DIRECTORY

REDFORD, Ian
5.4.60 Perth (MF)
5.11 11.10 Errol Rovers
LD Dundee v East Fife
16.4.77 2–2

1976–77 Dundee	1	1	—
1977–78 Dundee	1	34	10
1978–79 Dundee	1	37	15
1979–80 Dundee	P	13	9
1979–80 Rangers	P	13	—
1980–81 Rangers	P	35	9
1981–82 Rangers	P	32	2
1982–83 Rangers	P	34	3
1983–84 Rangers	P	32	4
1984–85 Rangers	P	26	5
1985–86 Dundee U	P	30	4
1986–87 Dundee U	P	37	8
1987–88 Dundee U	P	25	6

REDMOND, Steven
2.11.67 Liverpool (DF)
— — Apprentice
LD Manchester C v QPR
8.2.86 2–0

1984–85 Manchester C	2	—	—
1985–86 Manchester C	1	9	—
1986–87 Manchester C	1	30	2
1987–88 Manchester C	2	44	—

REECE, Andrew
5.9.62 Shrewsbury (MF)
5.11 12.4 Willenhall
LD Bristol R v Rotherham U
15.8.87 3–1

1987–88 Bristol R	3	40	1

REED, Graham
24.6.61 Doncaster (FW)
5.11 12.7 Apprentice
LD Barnsley v Bradford C
18.11.78 0–1

1978–79 Barnsley	4	1	—
1979–80 Barnsley	3	2	—
Frickley Ath			
1985–86 Northampton T	4	36	1
1986–87 Northampton T	4	37	1
1987–88 Northampton T	3	31	—

REES, Mel
25.1.67 Cardiff (GK)
6.2 12.12 Plymouth Arg YTS
LD Cardiff C v Brighton & HA
8.9.84 2–4

1984–85 Cardiff C	2	1	—
1985–86 Cardiff C	3	9	—
1986–87 Cardiff C	4	21	—
1987–88 Watford	1	3	—

REES, Tony
1.8.64 Merthyr Tydfil (FW)
5.9 11.13 Apprentice
LD West Ham U v Birmingham C
27.8.83 4–0

1982–83 Aston Villa	1	—	—
1983–84 Birmingham C	1	25	2
1984–85 Birmingham C	2	9	2
1985–86 Birmingham C	1	8	—
1985–86 *Peterborough U*	4	5	2
1985–86 *Shrewsbury T*	2	2	—
1986–87 Birmingham C	2	30	4
1987–88 Birmingham C	2	23	4
1987–88 *Barnsley*	2	2	—
1987–88 Barnsley	2	12	2

REEVES, David
19.11.67 Birkenhead (FW)
— — Heswell
LD Scunthorpe U v Exeter C
19.12.86 3–1

1986–87 Sheffield W	1	—	—
1986–87 *Scunthorpe U*	4	4	2
1987–88 *Scunthorpe U*	4	6	4
1987–88 *Burnley*	4	16	8

REGIS, Cyrille
9.2.58 French Guyana (FW)
6.0 13.5 Hayes
LD WBA v Middlesbrough
3.9.77 2–1

1977–78 WBA	1	34	10
1978–79 WBA	1	39	13
1979–80 WBA	1	26	8
1980–81 WBA	1	38	14
1981–82 WBA	1	37	17
1982–83 WBA	1	26	9
1983–84 WBA	1	30	10
1984–85 WBA	1	7	1
1984–85 Coventry C	1	31	5
1985–86 Coventry C	1	34	5
1986–87 Coventry C	1	40	12
1987–88 Coventry C	1	31	10

REID, Mark
15.9.61 Kilwinning (DF)
5.8 11.5 Celtic BC
LD Airdrieonians v Celtic
15.11.80 1–4

1980–81 Celtic	P	22	—
1981–82 Celtic	P	36	2
1982–83 Celtic	P	26	1
1983–84 Celtic	P	24	2
1984–85 Celtic	P	16	—
1985–86 Charlton Ath	2	42	8
1986–87 Charlton Ath	1	42	—
1987–88 Charlton Ath	1	36	4

REID, Nicky
30.10.60 Ormston (DF)
5.9 12.1 Apprentice
LD Ipswich T v Manchester C
31.3.79 2–1

1978–79 Manchester C	1	8	—
1979–80 Manchester C	1	23	—
1980–81 Manchester C	1	37	—
1981–82 Manchester C	1	36	—
1982–83 Manchester C	1	25	—

1983–84 Manchester C	2	19	2
1984–85 Manchester C	2	32	—
1985–86 Manchester C	1	30	—
1986–87 Manchester C	1	7	—
1987–88 Blackburn R	2	44	1

REID, Paul
19.1.68 Warley (?)
5.5 10.2 Apprentice
LD Southampton v Leicester C
7.3.87 4–0

1985–86 Leicester C	1	—	—
1986–87 Leicester C	1	6	—
1987–88 Leicester C	2	26	5

REID, Shaun
13.10.65 Huyton (MF)
5.8 11.8 Local
LD Crewe Alex v Rochdale
14.1.84 0–1

1983–84 Rochdale	4	17	—
1984–85 Rochdale	4	21	1
1985–86 Rochdale	4	8	—
1985–86 *Preston NE*	4	3	—
1986–87 Rochdale	4	41	1
1987–88 Rochdale	4	28	—

REID, Wesley
10.9.68 Lewisham (MF)
5.8 11.3 Arsenal
LD —

1987–88 Millwall	2	—	—

REILLY, John
21.3.62 Dundee (FW)
5.7 10.1 'S' Form
LD Dundee U v Morton
23.8.80 1–1

1979–80 Dundee U	P	—	—
1980–81 Dundee U	P	1	—
1981–82 Dundee U	P	8	1
1982–83 Dundee U	P	17	7
1983–84 Dundee U	P	19	7
1984–85 Dundee U	P	10	4
1985–86 Motherwell	P	30	9
1986–87 Motherwell	P	26	3
1987–88 Motherwell	P	—	—

RENNIE, David
29.8.64 Edinburgh (DF)
5.11¾ 11.12 Apprentice
LD WBA v Leicester C
3.9.83 1–0

1982–83 Leicester C	2	—	—
1983–84 Leicester C	1	15	—
1984–85 Leicester C	1	3	1
1985–86 Leicester C	1	3	—
1985–86 Leeds U	2	16	2
1986–87 Leeds U	2	24	—
1987–88 Leeds U	2	28	2

RHOADES-BROWN, Peter
2.1.62 Hampton (FW)
5.9 11.4 Apprentice
LD Wrexham v Chelsea
29.12.79 2-0

1979–80 Chelsea	2	4	—
1980–81 Chelsea	2	34	1
1981–82 Chelsea	2	27	1
1982–83 Chelsea	2	25	1
1983–84 Chelsea	2	6	1
1983–84 Oxford U	3	20	4
1984–85 Oxford U	2	31	4
1985–86 Oxford U	1	17	3
1986–87 Oxford U	1	6	—
1987–88 Oxford U	1	31	2

RHODES, Andy
23.8.64 Doncaster (GK)
6.0 12.0 Apprentice
LD Crystal Palace v Barnsley
29.10.83 0-1

1982–83 Barnsley	2	—	—
1983–84 Barnsley	2	31	—
1984–85 Barnsley	2	5	—
1985–86 Barnsley	1	—	—
1985–86 Doncaster R	3	30	—
1986–87 Doncaster R	3	41	—
1987–88 Doncaster R	3	35	—
1987–88 Oldham Ath	2	11	—

RICE, Brian
11.10.63 Glasgow (MF)
6.0 11.10 Whitburn Central
LD Hibernian v Motherwell
6.9.80 1-0

1980–81 Hibernian	1	1	—
1981–82 Hibernian	P	1	—
1982–83 Hibernian	P	22	2
1983–84 Hibernian	P	25	5
1984–85 Hibernian	P	35	4
1985–86 Nottingham F	1	19	3
1986–87 Nottingham F	1	3	1
1986–87 *Grimsby T*	2	4	—
1987–88 Nottingham F	1	30	2

RICHARDS, Carl
12.1.60 Jamaica (FW)
6.0 13.0 Enfield FC
LD Brentford v Bournemouth
23.8.86 1-1

1986–87 Bournemouth	3	43	12
1987–88 Bournemouth	2	20	4

RICHARDS, Gary
2.8.63 Swansea (DF)
5.8½ 11.1½ Apprentice
LD Aston Villa v Swansea C
21.5.82 3-0

1981–82 Swansea C	1	1	—
1982–83 Swansea C	1	15	—
1983–84 Swansea C	2	34	1
1984–85 Swansea C	3	16	—
1985–86 Lincoln C	3	7	—
1985–86 Cambridge U	4	8	—
1986–87 Torquay U	4	25	1
1987–88 Torquay U	4	—	—

RICHARDSON, Barry
5.8.69 Willingtgon (GK)
6.1 12.1 Youth Scheme
LD —

1987–88 Sunderland	3	—	—

RICHARDSON, Ian
9.5.64 Ely (FW)
5.8 10.2 Apprentice
LD Hartlepool U v Blackpool
1.1.83 2-1

1981–82 Watford	2	—	—
1982–83 Watford	1	—	—
1982–83 *Blackpool*	4	5	2
1983–84 Watford	1	7	2
1984–85 Watford	1	1	—
1984–85 *Rotherham U*	3	5	2
1985–86 Watford	1	—	—
1985–86 Chester C	4	27	10
1986–87 Chester C	3	8	—
1986–87 Scunthorpe U	4	8	2
1987–88 Scunthorpe U	4	1	1

RICHARDSON, Kevin
14.8.69 Waltham Abbey (FW)
5.4½ 8.12 School
LD —

1986–87 Watford	1	—	—

RICHARDSON, Kevin
4.12.62 Newcastle (MF)
5.7 10.2 Apprentice
LD Everton v Sunderland
21.11.81 1-2

1980–81 Everton	1	—	—
1981–82 Everton	1	18	2
1982–83 Everton	1	29	3
1983–84 Everton	1	28	4
1984–85 Everton	1	15	4
1985–86 Everton	1	18	3
1986–87 Everton	1	1	—
1986–87 Watford	1	39	2
1987–88 Arsenal	1	29	4

RICHARDSON, Lee
12.3.69 Halifax (DF)
— — Apprentice
LD Halifax T v Darlington
15.8.87 2-2

1987–88 Halifax T	4	30	1

RICHARDSON, Steve
11.2.62 Slough (DF)
5.5 10.3 Apprentice
LD Reading v Plymouth Arg
4.9.82 3-2

1979–80 Southampton	1	—	—
1980–81 Southampton	1	—	—
1981–82 Southampton	1	—	—
1982–83 Reading	3	40	1
1983–84 Reading	4	34	—
1984–85 Reading	3	43	—
1985–86 Reading	3	32	—
1986–87 Reading	2	37	1
1987–88 Reading	2	27	—

RILEY, David
8.12.60 Northampton (FW)
5.7 10.10 Keyworth U
LD Nottingham F v WBA
7.4.84 3-1

1983–84 Nottingham F	1	1	—
1984–85 Nottingham F	1	10	2
1985–86 Nottingham F	1	—	—
1986–87 Nottingham F	1	1	—
1986–87 *Darlington*	3	6	2
1987–88 *Peterborough U*	4	12	2
1987–88 Port Vale	3	34	8

RIMMER, Neill
13.11.67 Liverpool (MF)
5.6½ 10.3 Apprentice
LD Luton T v Everton
28.5.85 2-0

1984–85 Everton	1	1	—
1985–86 Ipswich T	1	2	—
1986–87 Ipswich T	2	1	—
1987–88 Ipswich T	2	21	3

RIMMER, Stuart
12.10.64 Southport (FW)
5.7 9.4 Apprentice
LD Swansea C v Everton
1.5.82 1-3

1981–82 Everton	1	2	—
1982–83 Everton	1	—	—
1983–84 Everton	1	1	—
1984–85 Everton	1	—	—
1984–85 Chester C	4	24	14
1985–86 Chester C	4	18	16
1986–87 Chester C	3	38	13
1987–88 Chester C	3	34	24
1987–88 Watford	1	9	1

PLAYER DIRECTORY

RING, Mike
13.2.61 Brighton (FW)
5.10 10.6 Apprentice
LD Brighton & HA v Wolves
4.5.82 2–0

1978–79	Brighton & HA	2	— —
1979–80	Brighton & HA	1	— —
1980–81	Brighton & HA	1	— —
1981–82	Brighton & HA	1	1 —
1982–83	Brighton & HA	1	1 —
1983–84	Brighton & HA	2	3 —
1984–85	Hull C	3	15	1
1985–86	Hull C	2	9	1
1985–86	Bolton W	3	3	—
1986–87	Aldershot	4	33	8
1987–88	Aldershot	3	32	6

RIPLEY, Stuart
20.11.67 Middlesbrough (FW)
5.11 12.6 Apprentice
LD Middlesbrough v Oldham Ath
5.2.85 1–2

1984–85	Middlesbrough	2	1	—
1985–86	Middlesbrough	2	8	—
1985–86	Bolton W	3	5	1
1986–87	Middlesbrough	3	44	4
1987–88	Middlesbrough	2	43	9

RITCHIE, Andy
28.11.60 Manchester (FW)
5.10 11.7 Apprentice
LD Everton v Manchester U
26.12.77 2–6

1977–78	Manchester U	1	4	—
1978–79	Manchester U	1	17	10
1979–80	Manchester U	1	8	3
1980–81	Manchester U	1	4	—
1980–81	Brighton & HA	1	26	5
1981–82	Brighton & HA	1	39	13
1982–83	Brighton & HA	1	24	5
1982–83	Leeds U	2	10	3
1983–84	Leeds U	2	38	7
1984–85	Leeds U	2	28	12
1985–86	Leeds U	2	29	11
1986–87	Leeds U	2	31	7
1987–88	Oldham Ath	2	36	19

RITCHIE, Stuart
20.5.68 Southampton (MF)
5.10 11.0 Apprentice
LD Manchester U v Aston Villa
9.5.87 3–1

1986–87	Aston Villa	1	1	—
1987–88	Crewe Alex	4	18	—

RIX, Graham
23.10.57 Doncaster (MF)
5.9 11.0 Apprentice
LD Arsenal v Leicester C
2.4.77 3–0

1974–75	Arsenal	1	—	—
1975–76	Arsenal	1	—	—
1976–77	Arsenal	1	7	1
1977–78	Arsenal	1	39	2
1978–79	Arsenal	1	39	3
1979–80	Arsenal	1	38	4
1980–81	Arsenal	1	35	5
1981–82	Arsenal	1	39	9
1982–83	Arsenal	1	36	6
1983–84	Arsenal	1	34	4
1984–85	Arsenal	1	18	2
1985–86	Arsenal	1	38	3
1986–87	Arsenal	1	18	2
1987–88	Arsenal	1	10	—
1987–88	*Brentford*	3	6	—

ROBERTS, Alan
8.12.64 Newcastle (MF)
5.9 10.0 Apprentice
LD Rotherham U v Middlesbrough
30.10.82 1–1

1982–83	Middlesbrough	2	1	—
1983–84	Middlesbrough	2	7	1
1984–85	Middlesbrough	2	29	1
1985–86	Middlesbrough	2	1	—
1985–86	Darlington	3	38	4
1986–87	Darlington	3	43	7
1987–88	Darlington	4	38	7

ROBERTS, Anthony
— Anglesey (GK)
— — Holyhead Juniors
LD QPR v Coventry C
18.12.87 1–2

1987–88	QPR	1	1	—

ROBERTS, Brian
6.11.55 Manchester (DF)
5.8 11.7 Apprentice
LD Hereford U v Grimsby T
15.2.75 3–2

1974–75	Coventry C	1	—	—
1974–75	*Hereford U*	3	5	—
1975–76	Coventry C	1	2	—
1976–77	Coventry C	1	12	—
1977–78	Coventry C	1	26	—
1978–79	Coventry C	1	17	—
1979–80	Coventry C	1	14	—
1980–81	Coventry C	1	42	—
1981–82	Coventry C	1	34	—
1982–83	Coventry C	1	38	1
1983–84	Coventry C	1	30	—
1983–84	Birmingham C	1	11	—
1984–85	Birmingham C	2	41	—
1985–86	Birmingham C	1	33	—
1986–87	Birmingham C	2	24	—
1987–88	Birmingham C	2	27	—

ROBERTS, Iwan
26.6.68 Bangor (FW)
6.3 12.5
LD Watford v Ipswich T
29.3.86 0–0

1985–86	Watford	1	4	—
1986–87	Watford	1	3	1
1987–88	Watford	1	25	2

ROBERTS, Garreth
15.11.60 Hull (MF)
5.5 10.8 Apprentice
LD Hull C v Bury
10.3.79 4–1

1978–79	Hull C	3	19	3
1979–80	Hull C	3	44	2
1980–81	Hull C	3	20	3
1981–82	Hull C	4	29	6
1982–83	Hull C	4	44	6
1983–84	Hull C	3	38	9
1984–85	Hull C	3	29	3
1985–86	Hull C	2	33	4
1986–87	Hull C	2	35	5
1987–88	Hull C	2	44	3

ROBERTS, Graham
3.7.59 Southampton (DF)
5.10 12.12 Weymouth
LD Stoke C. v Tottenham H
4.10.80 2–3

1980–81	Tottenham H	1	24	—
1981–82	Tottenham H	1	37	6
1982–83	Tottenham H	1	24	2
1983–84	Tottenham H	1	35	6
1984–85	Tottenham H	1	40	7
1985–86	Tottenham H	1	32	1
1986–87	Tottenham H	1	17	1
1986–87	Rangers	P	18	2
1987–88	Rangers	P	37	1

ROBERTS, Jeremy
24.11.66 Middlesbrough (GK)
6.0 13.0 School
LD Chesterfield v Haartlepool U
7.4.84 4–1

1983–84	Hartlepool U	4	1	—
1984–85	Leicester C	1	—	—
1985–86	Leicester C	1	3	—
1986–87	Darlington	3	9	—
1987–88	Darlington	4	20	—

ROBERTS, Jonathan
30.12.68 Llwynpia (GK)
6.0 12.5 Apprentice
LD Newport Co v Cardiff C
21.11.87 1–2

1987–88	Cardiff C	4	8	—

ROBERTSON, Alistair
9.9.52 Philipstown (DF)
5.10 12.1 Apprentice
LD WBA v Manchester U
25.10.69 2–1

1969–70	WBA	1	10	—
1970–71	WBA	1	4	—
1971–72	WBA	1	31	—
1972–73	WBA	1	36	1
1973–74	WBA	2	40	—
1974–75	WBA	2	21	1
1975–76	WBA	2	42	1
1976–77	WBA	1	42	—
1977–78	WBA	1	42	1
1978–79	WBA	1	39	—
1979–80	WBA	1	38	1
1980–81	WBA	1	28	—
1981–82	WBA	1	33	1
1982–83	WBA	1	37	2
1983–84	WBA	1	6	—
1984–85	WBA	1	37	—
1985–86	WBA	1	20	—
1986–87	Wolves	4	31	—
1987–88	Wolves	4	41	—

ROBERTSON, David
17.10.68 Aberdeen (DF)
5.11 11.0 Deeside BC
LD Aberdeen v Hamilton A
16.8.86 2–0

1986–87	Aberdeen	P	34	—
1987–88	Aberdeen	P	23	—

ROBERTSON, Ian
14.10.66 Inverness (MF)
5.9 10.10 'S' Form
LD St Mirren v Aberdeen
12.5.84 3–2

1983–84	Aberdeen	P	—	—
1984–85	Aberdeen	P	—	—
1985–86	Aberdeen	P	4	—
1986–87	Aberdeen	P	4	—
1987–88	Aberdeen	P	—	—

ROBERTSON, John
2.10.64 Edinburgh (FW)
5.6 10.3 Edina Hibs
LD Hearts v Queen of South
17.2.82 4–1

1980–81	Hearts	P	—	—
1981–82	Hearts	1	1	—
1982–83	Hearts	1	23	19
1983–84	Hearts	P	15	15
1984–85	Hearts	P	33	8
1985–86	Hearts	P	35	20
1986–87	Hearts	P	37	16
1987–88	Hearts	P	39	26
1987–88	Newcastle U	1	—	—

ROBINS, Mark
22.12.69 Ashton-u-Lyme (FW)
5.7 10.1 Apprentice
LD —

1987–88	Manchester U	1	—	—

ROBINSON, Andy
10.3.66 Oldham (DF)
5.10 12.4 Apprentice
LD Burnley v Swindon T
12.10.85 0–2

1983–84	Manchester U	1	—	—
1984–85	Manchester U	1	—	—
1985–86	Manchester U	1	—	—
1985–86	*Burnley*	4	5	1
1985–86	Bury	3	10	—
1986–87	Bury	3	9	—
1986–87	Carlisle U	3	11	—
1987–88	Carlisle U	4	35	3

ROBINSON, Colin
15.5.60 Birmingham (FW)
5.10 10.12 Mile Oak Rovers
LD Leicester C v Shrewsbury T
22.2.83 3–2

1982–83	Shrewsbury T	2	12	3
1983–84	Shrewsbury T	2	30	4
1984–85	Shrewsbury T	2	42	14
1985–86	Shrewsbury T	2	42	10
1986–87	Shrewsbury T	2	41	9
1987–88	Shrewsbury T	2	27	1
1987–88	Birmingham C	2	4	1

ROBINSON, David
14.1.65 Cleveland (DF)
6.0 12.3
LD Northampton v Hartlepool U
10.4.84 1–1

1983–84	Hartlepool U	4	7	—
1984–85	Hartlepool U	4	38	—
1985–86	Hartlepool U	4	21	1
1986–87	Halifax T	4	10	—
1987–88	Halifax T	4	32	—

ROBINSON, Les
1.3.67 Mansfield (FW)
— — Local
LD Mansfield T v Hereford U
23.3.85 1–1

1984–85	Mansfield T	4	6	—
1985–86	Mansfield T	4	7	—
1986–87	Mansfield T	3	2	—
1986–87	Stockport Co	4	30	1
1987–88	Stockport Co	4	37	2
1987–88	Doncaster R	3	7	1

ROBINSON, Liam
29.12.65 Bradford (FW)
5.6 11.4 Nottingham F Schoolboy
LD Swansea C v Huddersfield T
18.1.83 2–2

1983–84	Huddersfield T	2	5	1
1984–85	Huddersfield T	2	15	1
1985–86	Huddersfield T	2	1	—
1985–86	*Tranmere R*	4	4	3
1986–87	Bury	3	33	13
1987–88	Bury	3	43	19

ROBINSON, Mark
21.11.68 Manchester (MF)
— — YTS
LD WBA v Sheffield W
22.4.86 1–1

1985–86	WBA	1	1	—
1986–87	WBA	2	1	—
1987–88	Barnsley	2	3	—

ROBINSON, Martin
17.7.57 Ilford (FW)
5.8½ 11.2 Apprentice
LD Tottenham H v Leicester C
28.2.76 1–1

1975–76	Tottenham H	1	2	1
1976–77	Tottenham H	1	—	—
1977–78	Tottenham H	2	4	1
1977–78	Charlton Ath	2	16	7
1978–79	Charlton Ath	2	35	15
1979–80	Charlton Ath	2	33	7
1980–81	Charlton Ath	3	40	10
1981–82	Charlton Ath	2	39	5
1982–83	Charlton Ath	2	32	4
1982–83	*Reading*	3	6	2
1983–84	Charlton Ath	2	27	8
1984–85	Charlton Ath	2	6	2
1984–85	Gillingham	3	33	10
1985–86	Gillingham	3	33	10
1986–87	Gillingham	3	30	4
1987–88	Southend U	3	37	8

ROBINSON, Philip
6.1.67 Stafford (DF)
5.9 10.10 Apprentice
LD Southampton v Aston Villa
21.3.87 5–0

1984–85	Aston Villa	1	—	—
1985–86	Aston Villa	1	—	—
1986–87	Aston Villa	1	3	1
1987–88	Wolves	4	41	5

ROBINSON, Ron
22.10.66 Sunderland (DF)
5.9 11.0
LD Carlisle U v Leeds U
23.11.85 1–2

1984–85	Ipswich T	1	—	—
Vaux Breweries				
1985–86	Leeds U	2	16	—
1986–87	Leeds U	2	—	—
1986–87	Doncaster R	3	12	—
1987–88	Doncaster R	3	37	1

PLAYER DIRECTORY

David Rocastle   *Photo: Bob Thomas Sports Photography.*

Bryan Robson

Photo: Bob Thomas Sports Photography.

PLAYER DIRECTORY

ROBSON, Bryan
11.1.57 Chester-le-Street (MF)
5.10½ 11.12 Apprentice
LD York C v <u>WBA</u>
12.4.75 1–3

1974–75 WBA	1	3	2
1975–76 WBA	1	16	1
1976–77 WBA	1	23	8
1977–78 WBA	1	35	3
1978–79 WBA	1	41	7
1979–80 WBA	1	34	8
1980–81 WBA	1	40	10
1981–82 WBA	1	5	—
1981–82 Manchester U	1	32	5
1982–83 Manchester U	1	33	10
1983–84 Manchester U	1	33	12
1984–85 Manchester U	1	33	9
1985–86 Manchester U	1	21	7
1986–87 Manchester U	1	30	7
1987–88 Manchester U	1	36	11

ROBSON, Gary
6.7.65 Durham (MF)
5.5 10.7 Apprentice
LD <u>WBA</u> v Southampton
7.5.83 1–0

1982–83 WBA	1	2	—
1983–84 WBA	1	7	—
1984–85 WBA	1	11	—
1985–86 WBA	1	14	—
1986–87 WBA	2	5	1
1987–88 WBA	2	31	1

ROBSON, Mark
22.5.69 Newham (MF)
— — YTS
LD <u>Exeter C</u> v Lincoln C
11.10.86 2–0

1986–87 Exeter C	4	26	7
1987–88 Tottenham H	1	—	—
1987–88 *Reading*	2	7	—

ROBSON, Stewart
6.11.64 Billericay (DF)
5.11 11.13 Apprentice
LD West Ham U v <u>Arsenal</u>
5.12.81 1–2

1981–82 Arsenal	1	20	2
1982–83 Arsenal	1	31	2
1983–84 Arsenal	1	28	6
1984–85 Arsenal	1	40	2
1985–86 Arsenal	1	27	4
1986–87 Arsenal	1	5	—
1986–87 West Ham U	1	18	1
1987–88 West Ham U	1	37	2

ROCASTLE, David
2.5.67 Lewisham (FW)
5.9 11.1 Apprentice
LD <u>Arsenal</u> v Newcastle U
28.9.85 0–0

1984–85 Arsenal	1	—	—
1985–86 Arsenal	1	16	1
1986–87 Arsenal	1	36	2
1987–88 Arsenal	1	40	6

ROCHE, Paddy
4.1.51 Dublin (GK)
6.1½ 11.4 Shelbourne
LD Oxford v <u>Manchester U</u>
8.2.75 1–0

1973–74 Manchester U	1	—	—
1974–75 Manchester U	2	2	—
1975–76 Manchester U	1	4	—
1976–77 Manchester U	1	2	—
1977–78 Manchester U	1	19	—
1978–79 Manchester U	1	14	—
1979–80 Manchester U	1	—	—
1980–81 Manchester U	1	2	—
1981–82 Manchester U	1	3	—
1982–83 Brentford	3	46	—
1983–84 Brentford	3	25	—
1984–85 Halifax T	4	43	—
1985–86 Halifax T	4	46	—
1986–87 Halifax T	4	24	—
1987–88 Halifax T	4	46	—

RODGER, Graham
1.4.67 Glasgow (DF)
— — Apprentice
LD <u>Wolves</u> v Ipswich T
21.4.84 0–3

1983–84 Wolves	1	1	—
1984–85 Coventry C	1	—	—
1985–86 Coventry C	1	10	—
1986–87 Coventry C	1	6	—
1987–88 Coventry C	1	12	1

RODGERSON, Ian
9.4.66 Hereford (MF)
5.8 10.7 Pegasus Juniors
LD Crewe Alex v <u>Hereford U</u>
27.8.85 2–0

1984–85 Hereford U	4	—	—
1985–86 Hereford U	4	19	2
1986–87 Hereford U	4	44	1
1987–88 Hereford U	4	37	3

ROEDER, Glenn
13.12.55 Woodford (DF)
6.0 12.13 Apprentice
LD <u>Orient</u> v Notts Co
8.3.75 0–1

1974–75 Orient	2	6	—
1975–76 Orient	2	25	2
1976–77 Orient	2	42	2
1977–78 Orient	2	42	—
1978–79 QPR	1	27	4
1979–80 QPR	2	40	9

1980–81 QPR	2	39	2
1981–82 QPR	2	41	2
1982–83 QPR	2	9	—
1983–84 QPR	1	1	—
1983–84 *Notts Co*	1	4	—
1983–84 Newcastle U	2	23	—
1984–85 Newcastle U	1	36	—
1985–86 Newcastle U	1	42	6
1986–87 Newcastle U	1	37	1
1987–88 Newcastle U	1	37	1

ROGAN, Anton
25.3.66 Belfast (DF)
5.11 12.6 Distillery
LD <u>Celtic</u> v Hamilton A
3.1.87 8–3

1986–87 Celtic	P	10	1
1987–88 Celtic	P	33	1

ROGERS, Lee
21.10.66 Doncaster (DF)
5.10 12.0 Doncaster R
LD Blackpool v <u>Chesterfield</u>
23.8.86 0–0

1986–87 Chesterfield	3	36	—
1987–88 Chesterfield	3	43	—

ROLPH, Darren
19.11.68 Romford (DF)
5.8½ 11.4 Apprentice
LD Shrewsbury T v <u>Barnsley</u>
30.4.88 1–1

1987–88 Barnsley	2	2	—

ROSARIO, Robert
4.3.66 Hammersmith (FW)
6.3 12.1 Hillingdon Bor
LD <u>Norwich C</u> v Watford
7.4.84 6–1

1983–84 Norwich C	1	8	1
1984–85 Norwich C	1	4	1
1985–86 Norwich C	2	8	2
1985–86 *Wolves*	3	2	1
1986–87 Norwich C	1	25	3
1987–88 Norwich C	1	14	2

ROSE, Kevin
23.11.60 Evesham (GK)
6.1 13.6 Ledbury T
LD <u>Hereford U</u> v Aldershot
3.1.83 2–1

1979–80 Lincoln C	4	—	—
1980–81 Lincoln C	4	—	—
From Ledbury T			
1982–83 Hereford U	4	15	—
1983–84 Hereford U	4	46	—
1984–85 Hereford U	4	46	—
1985–86 Hereford U	4	46	—
1986–87 Hereford U	4	46	—
1987–88 Hereford U	4	46	—

ROSENIOR, Leroy
24.3.64 London (FW)
6.1 11.10 School
LD Leicester C v Fulham
4.12.82 2–0

1982–83	Fulham	2	1 —
1983–84	Fulham	2	23 8
1984–85	Fulham	2	30 8
1985–86	QPR	1	18 3
1986–87	QPR	1	20 4
1987–88	Fulham	3	34 20
1987–88	*West Ham U*	1	1 1
1987–88	West Ham U	1	8 4

ROSTRON, Wilf
29.9.56 Sunderland (MF)
5.7 11.1½ Apprentice
LD Arsenal v Newcastle U
18.3.75 3–0

1973–74	Arsenal	1	— —
1974–75	Arsenal	1	6 2
1975–76	Arsenal	1	5 —
1976–77	Arsenal	1	6 —
1977–78	Sunderland	2	34 6
1978–79	Sunderland	2	34 11
1979–80	Sunderland	2	8 —
1979–80	Watford	2	31 3
1980–81	Watford	2	27 1
1981–82	Watford	2	27 2
1982–83	Watford	1	42 3
1983–84	Watford	1	39 4
1984–85	Watford	1	38 3
1985–86	Watford	1	30 5
1986–87	Watford	1	39 1
1987–88	Watford	1	37 —

ROUGVIE, Doug
24.5.56 Ballingry (DF)
6.2 13.8 Dumfermline YC
LD Rangers v Aberdeen
16.10.76 1–0

1976–77	Aberdeen	P	6 1
1977–78	Aberdeen	P	1 —
1978–79	Aberdeen	P	20 —
1979–80	Aberdeen	P	25 2
1980–81	Aberdeen	P	28 3
1981–82	Aberdeen	P	28 6
1982–83	Aberdeen	P	35 3
1983–84	Aberdeen	P	35 4
1984–85	Chelsea	1	27 1
1985–86	Chelsea	1	34 2
1986–87	Chelsea	1	13 —
1987–88	Brighton & HA	3	35 2

ROWBOTHAM, Darran
22.10.66 Cardiff (MF)
5.10 11.5 YTS
LD Plymouth Arg v Cambridge U
15.12.84 2–0

1984–85	Plymouth Arg	3	7 —
1985–86	Plymouth Arg	3	14 1
1986–87	Plymouth Arg	2	16 —
1987–88	Plymouth Arg	2	9 —
1987–88	*Exeter C*	4	1 —
1987–88	Exeter C	4	22 2

ROWBOTHAM, Jason
3.1.69 Cardiff (DF)
5.8 10.8 YTS
LD Stoke C v Plymouth Arg
10.10.87 1–0

1987–88	Plymouth Arg	2	4 —

RUDDOCK, Neil
9.5.68 London (DF)
6.2 12.6 Apprentice
LD Tottenham H v Charlton Ath
18.4.87 1–0

1985–86	Millwall	2	— —
1985–86	Tottenham H	1	— —
1986–87	Tottenham H	1	4 —
1987–88	Tottenham H	1	5 —

RUMBLE, Paul
14.3.69 Hemel Hempstead (DF)
5.11 11.5 Trainee
LD —

1987–88	Watford	1	— —

RUSSELL, Bobby
11.2.57 Glasgow (MF)
5.8 10.3 Shettleston
LD Aberdeen v Rangers
13.8.77 3–1

1976–77	Rangers	P	— —
1977–78	Rangers	P	33 3
1978–79	Rangers	P	36 4
1979–80	Rangers	P	23 7
1980–81	Rangers	P	28 6
1981–82	Rangers	P	32 6
1982–83	Rangers	P	21 4
1983–84	Rangers	P	31 4
1984–85	Rangers	P	18 —
1985–86	Rangers	P	27 —
1986–87	Rangers	P	1 —
1987–88	Motherwell	P	32 3

RUSSELL, Guy
28.9.67 Shirley (FW)
— — YTS
LD Birmingham C v Manchester C
19.3.85 0–0

1984–85	Birmingham C	2	1 —
1985–86	Birmingham C	1	1 —
1986–87	*Carlisle U*	3	12 2
1987–88	Birmingham C	2	9 —

RUSSELL, Kevin
6.12.66 Portsmouth (MF)
5.8 10.10 Apprentice
LD Portsmouth v Bradford C
3.5.86 4–0

1984–85	Portsmouth	2	— —
1985–86	Portsmouth	2	1 —
1986–87	Portsmouth	2	3 —
1987–88	Wrexham	4	38 21

RUSSELL, Martin
27.4.67 Dublin (MF)
5.10 11.0 Apprentice
LD WBA v Birmingham C
1.11.86 3–2

1984–85	Manchester U	1	— —
1985–86	Manchester U	1	— —
1986–87	*Birmingham C*	2	5 —
1986–87	Leicester C	1	5 —
1986–87	*Norwich C*	1	— —
1987–88	Leicester C	2	5 —

RYAN, John
18.2.62 Ashton (DF)
5.10 11.6 Apprentice
LD Oldham Ath v Cardiff C
29.8.81 2–2

1979–80	Oldham Ath	2	— —
1980–81	Oldham Ath	2	— —
1981–82	Oldham Ath	2	37 —
1982–83	Oldham Ath	2	40 8
1983–84	Newcastle U	2	22 1
1984–85	Newcastle U	1	6 —
1984–85	Sheffield W	1	8 1
1985–86	Oldham Ath	2	22 —
1986–87	Oldham Ath	2	1 —
1987–88	Oldham Ath	2	— —
1987–88	*Mansfield T*	3	5 —
1987–88	Mansfield T	3	27 —

RYAN, Laurie
15.10.63 Watford (FW)
5.10 11.12 Dunstable
LD Stockport Co v Cambridge U
2.5.88 0–2

1987–88	Cambridge U	4	2 —

RYAN, Vaughan
2.9.68 Westminster (MF)
— —
LD Wimbledon v Tottenham H
22.4.88 2–2

1986–87	Wimbledon	1	1 —
1987–88	Wimbledon	1	22 1

PLAYER DIRECTORY

Kenny Sansom

Photo: Bob Thomas Sports Photography.

SADDINGTON, Nigel
9.12.65 Sunderland (DF)
6.1 12.6
LD Doncaster R v Derby Co
22.2.85 2-1

1984–85	Doncaster R	3	5	—
1985–86	Doncaster R	3	—	—
1985–86	Sunderland	2	—	—
1986–87	Sunderland	2	3	—
1987–88	Sunderland	3	—	—
1987–88	Carlisle U	4	13	1

SAGE, Mel
24.3.64 Gillingham (DF)
5.8½ 10.10 Apprentice
LD Bristol C v Gillingham
1.5.82 2-1

1981–82	Gillingham	3	1	—
1982–83	Gillingham	3	9	—
1983–84	Gillingham	3	40	2
1984–85	Gillingham	3	36	1
1985–86	Gillingham	3	46	2
1986–87	Derby Co	2	26	2
1987–88	Derby Co	1	13	—

SALAKO, John
11.2.69 Nigeria (FW)
— — YTS
LD Crystal Palace v Barnsley
24.1.87 0-1

1986–87	Crystal Palace	2	4	—
1987–88	Crystal Palace	2	31	—

SALATHIEL, Neil
19.11.62 Wrexham (DF)
5.7 12.0 Sheffield W Amateur
LD QPR v Wrexham
25.10.80 0-1

1980–81	Wrexham	2	4	—
1981–82	Crewe Alex	4	44	—
1982–83	Crewe Alex	4	21	—
Arcadia Shepherds				
1983–84	Wrexham	4	29	—
1984–85	Wrexham	4	36	—
1985–86	Wrexham	4	42	1
1986–87	Wrexham	4	45	2
1987–88	Wrexham	4	24	—

SALMAN, Danis
12.3.60 Cyprus (DF)
5.10 11.8 Apprentice
LD Brentford v Watford
15.11.75 1-0

1975–76	Brentford	4	6	—
1976–77	Brentford	4	18	1
1977–78	Brentford	4	37	—
1978–79	Brentford	3	40	1
1979–80	Brentford	3	41	3
1980–81	Brentford	3	38	—
1981–82	Brentford	3	40	—
1982–83	Brentford	3	1	—
1983–84	Brentford	3	21	—
1984–85	Brentford	3	43	3
1985–86	Brentford	3	40	—
1986–87	Millwall	2	31	2
1987–88	Millwall	2	36	1

SALMON, Mike
14.6.74 Leyland (GK)
6.2 13.0 Local
LD Blackburn R v Chelsea
15.5.82 1-1

1981–82	Blackburn R	2	1	—
1982–83	Blackburn R	2	—	—
1982–83	*Chester*	4	16	—
1983–84	Stockport Co	4	46	—
1984–85	Stockport Co	4	46	—
1985–86	Stockport Co	4	26	—
1986–87	Bolton W	3	26	—
1986–87	*Wrexham*	4	17	—
1987–88	Wrexham	4	40	—

SAMWAYS, Vince
27.10.68 Bethnal Green (MF)
5.8 9.0 Apprentice
LD Nottingham F v Tottenham H
2.5.87 2-0

1985–86	Tottenham H	1	—	—
1986–87	Tottenham H	1	2	—
1987–88	Tottenham H	1	26	—

SANCHEZ, Lawrie
22.10.59 Lambeth (MF)
5.11 11.7 Amateur
LD Reading v Wimbledon
1.10.77 2-2

1977–78	Reading	4	8	1
1978–79	Reading	4	39	4
1979–80	Reading	3	46	5
1980–81	Reading	3	37	2
1981–82	Reading	3	35	3
1982–83	Reading	3	37	1
1983–84	Reading	4	45	10
1984–85	Reading	3	15	2
1984–85	Wimbledon	2	20	5
1985–86	Wimbledon	2	42	9
1986–87	Wimbledon	1	29	—
1987–88	Wimbledon	1	38	4

SANDFORD, Lee
22.4.68 Basingstoke (DF)
6.1 12.2 Apprentice
LD Millwall v Portsmouth
26.10.85 0-4

1985–86	Portsmouth	2	7	—
1986–87	Portsmouth	2	—	—
1987–88	Portsmouth	1	21	1

SANDISON, James
22.6.65 Edinburgh (MF)
6.0 11.2 Edinburgh Emmet
LD Rangers v Hearts
27.4.85 3-1

1983–84	Hearts	P	—	—
1984–85	Hearts	P	3	—
1985–86	Hearts	P	3	—
1986–87	Hearts	P	13	—
1987–88	Hearts	P	2	—

SANSOM, Kenny
26.9.58 Camberwell (DF)
5.6 11.8 Apprentice
LD Tranmere R v Crystal Palace
7.5.75 2-0

1974–75	Crystal Palace	3	1	—
1975–76	Crystal Palace	3	6	—
1976–77	Crystal Palace	3	46	—
1977–78	Crystal Palace	2	41	2
1978–79	Crystal Palace	2	42	—
1979–80	Crystal Palace	1	36	1
1980–81	Arsenal	1	42	3
1981–82	Arsenal	1	42	—
1982–83	Arsenal	1	40	—
1983–84	Arsenal	1	40	1
1984–85	Arsenal	1	39	1
1985–86	Arsenal	1	42	—
1986–87	Arsenal	1	35	—
1987–88	Arsenal	1	34	1

SANSOME, Paul
6.10.61 N Addington (GK)
6.0 12.6½ Apprentice
LD Millwall v Swindon T
28.3.82 0-0

1979–80	Millwall	3	—	—
1980–81	Millwall	3	—	—
1981–82	Millwall	3	8	—
1982–83	Millwall	3	24	—
1983–84	Millwall	3	31	—
1984–85	Millwall	3	46	—
1985–86	Millwall	2	36	—
1986–87	Millwall	2	10	—
1987–88	Millwall	2	1	—
1987–88	*Southend U*	3	1	—
1987–88	Southend U	3	5	—

SAUNDERS, Carl
26.11.64 Marston Green (FW)
5.8 10.12 Local
LD Everton v Stoke C
4.4.83 3-1

1982–83	Stoke C	1	1	—
1983–84	Stoke C	1	—	—
1984–85	Stoke C	1	23	2
1985–86	Stoke C	2	37	2
1986–87	Stoke C	2	31	13
1987–88	Stoke C	2	17	3

SAUNDERS, Dean
21.6.64 Swansea (FW)
5.8½ 10.0 Apprentice
LD Charlton Ath v Swansea C
22.10.83 2-2

1982–83	Swansea C	1	—	—
1983–84	Swansea C	2	19	3
1984–85	Swansea C	3	30	9
1984–85	*Cardiff C*	2	4	—
1985–86	Brighton & HA	2	42	14
1986–87	Brighton & HA	2	30	6
1986–87	Oxford U	1	12	6
1987–88	Oxford U	1	37	12

PLAYER DIRECTORY

SAUNDERS, Steve
12.9.64 Warrington (FW)
5.7½ 10.6 Apprentice
LD Bolton W v Wimbledon
27.8.83 2–0

1982–83 Bolton W	2	—	—
1983–84 Bolton W	3	3	—
1984–85 Bolton W	3	—	—
1985–86 Crewe Alex	4	22	1
1986–87 Preston NE	4	—	—
1987–88 Grimsby T	3	35	3

SAUNDERS, Wes
23.2.63 Sunderland (DF)
6.0 11.11 School
LD Chelsea v Newcastle U
7.11.81 2–1

1981–82 Newcastle U	2	29	—
1982–83 Newcastle U	2	13	—
1983–84 Newcastle U	2	16	—
1984–85 Newcastle U	1	21	—
1984–85 *Bradford C*	3	4	—
1985–86 Carlisle U	2	35	3
1986–87 Carlisle U	3	37	3
1987–88 Carlisle U	4	25	5
1987–88 Dundee	P	11	—

SAVAGE, Bob
8.1.60 Liverpool (MF)
5.7 11.1 Apprentice
LD Wrexham v Oxford U
23.10.82 1–1

1977–78 Liverpool	1	—	—
1978–79 Liverpool	1	—	—
1979–80 Liverpool	1	—	—
1980–81 Liverpool	1	—	—
1981–82 Liverpool	1	—	—
1982–83 Liverpool	1	—	—
1982–83 *Wrexham*	3	27	10
1983–84 Stoke C	1	7	—
1983–84 Bournemouth	3	23	5
1984–85 Bournemouth	3	43	9
1985–86 Bournemouth	3	—	—
1986–87 Bournemouth	3	16	4
1986–87 Bradford C	2	8	—
1987–88 Bradford C	2	3	—
1987–88 Bolton W	4	39	5

SAVILLE, Andrew
12.12.64 Hull (FW)
6.0 12.0 Local
LD Hull C v Port Vale
31.12.83 1–0

1983–84 Hull C	3	1	—
1984–85 Hull C	3	4	1
1985–86 Hull C	2	9	1
1986–87 Hull C	2	35	9
1987–88 Hull C	2	31	6

SAYER, Andy
6.6.66 Brent (FW)
5.9 10.12 Apprentice
LD Bolton W v Wimbledon
27.8.83 2–0

1983–84 Wimbledon	3	2	—
1984–85 Wimbledon	2	20	8
1985–86 Wimbledon	2	7	—
1986–87 Wimbledon	1	20	7
1987–88 Wimbledon	1	9	—
1987–88 *Cambridge U*	4	5	—

SCALES, John
4.7.66 Harrogate (DF)
6.0 12.2
LD Newport Co v Bristol R
7.9.85 3–0

1984–85 Leeds U	2	—	—
1985–86 Bristol R	3	29	1
1986–87 Bristol R	3	43	1
1987–88 Wimbledon	1	25	1

SCOTT, Gordon
19.7.60 Bath (FW)
5.9 11.0 Broxburn Ath
LD Forfar Ath v East Fife
11.8.79 1–0

1979–80 East Fife	2	27	3
1980–81 East Fife	2	35	7
1981–82 East Fife	2	34	16
1982–83 East Fife	2	34	12
1983–84 East Fife	2	17	1
1983–84 St Johnstone	P	15	3
1984–85 St Johnstone	1	33	7
1985–86 Forfar Ath	1	28	7
1986–87 Forfar Ath	1	25	10
1987–88 Forfar Ath	1	19	11
1987–88 Hamilton A	1	17	4

SCOTT, Ian
25.11.68 Luton (MF)
5.10 11.5 Apprentice

1987–88 Luton T	1	—	—

SCOTT, Ian
20.9.67 Radcliffe (FW)
— — Apprentice
LD Manchester C v Plymouth Arg
15.8.87 2–1

1985–86 Manchester C	1	—	—
1986–87 Manchester C	1	—	—
1987–88 Manchester C	2	23	3

SCOTT, Kevin
17.12.66 Easington (DF)
6.2 11.6
LD Newcastle U v Sheffield W
6.9.86 2–3

1984–85 Newcastle U	1	—	—
1985–86 Newcastle U	1	—	—
1986–87 Newcastle U	1	3	1
1987–88 Newcastle U	1	4	—

SCOTT, Martin
7.1.68 Sheffield (MF)
5.8 9.10 Apprentice
LD York C v Rotherham U
3.5.85 3–0

1984–85 Rotherham U	3	3	—
1985–86 Rotherham U	3	—	—
1986–87 Rotherham U	3	12	—
1987–88 Rotherham U	3	19	—
1987–88 *Nottingham F*	1	—	—

SCOTT, Peter
1.10.63 London (MF)
5.8 10.10 Apprentice
LD Huddersfield T v Fulham
10.10.81 1–0

1981–82 Fulham	3	1	—
1982–83 Fulham	2	—	—
1983–84 Fulham	2	32	4
1984–85 Fulham	2	19	1
1985–86 Fulham	2	32	5
1986–87 Fulham	3	30	6
1987–88 Fulham	3	23	2

SCULLY, Patrick
23.6.70 Dublin (DF)
— — Apprentice
LD —

1987–88 Arsenal	1	—	—

SEAGRAVES, Mark
22.10.66 Bootle (DF)
6.0½ 12.10
LD Coventry C v Norwich C
22.11.86 2–1

1983–84 Liverpool	1	—	—
1984–85 Liverpool	1	—	—
1985–86 Liverpool	1	—	—
1986–87 *Norwich C*	1	3	—
1987–88 Manchester C	2	17	—

SEALEY, Les
29.9.57 Bethnal Green (GK)
6.1 12.8 Apprentice
LD QPR v Coventry C
11.4.77 1–1

1975–76 Coventry C	1	—	—
1976–77 Coventry C	1	11	—
1977–78 Coventry C	1	2	—
1978–79 Coventry C	1	36	—
1979–80 Coventry C	1	20	—
1980–81 Coventry C	1	35	—
1981–82 Coventry C	1	15	—
1982–83 Coventry C	1	39	—
1983–84 Luton T	1	42	—
1984–85 Luton T	1	26	—
1984–85 *Plymouth Arg*	3	6	—
1985–86 Luton T	1	35	—
1986–87 Luton T	1	41	—
1987–88 Luton T	1	31	—

SEAMAN, David
19.9.63 Rotherham (GK)
6.3 13.0 Apprentice
LD Stockport Co v Peterborough U
28.8.82 1–1

1981–82	Leeds U	1	— —
1982–83	Peterborough U	4	38 —
1983–84	Peterborough U	4	45 —
1984–85	Peterborough U	4	8 —
1984–85	Birmingham C	2	33 —
1985–86	Birmingham C	1	42 —
1986–87	QPR	1	41 —
1987–88	QPR	1	32 —

SEDGLEY, Steve
26.5.68 Enfield (MF)
— — Apprentice
LD Coventry C v Arsenal
26.8.86 2–1

1986–87	Coventry C	1	26 —
1987–88	Coventry C	1	27 2

SEGERS, Hans
30.10.61 Eindhoven (GK)
5.11 12.7½ PSV Eindhoven
LD Coventry C v Nottingham F
17.11.84 1–3

1984–85	Nottingham F	1	28 —
1985–86	Nottingham F	1	11 —
1986–87	Nottingham F	1	14 —
1986–87	*Stoke C*	2	1 —
1987–88	Nottingham F	1	5 —
1987–88	Dunfermline A	P	4 —

SELLARS, Scott
27.11.65 Sheffield (MF)
5.6 10.0 Apprentice
LD Shrewsbury T v Leeds U
7.5.83 0–0

1982–83	Leeds U	2	1 —
1983–84	Leeds U	2	19 3
1984–85	Leeds U	2	39 7
1985–86	Leeds U	2	17 2
1986–87	Blackburn R	2	32 4
1987–88	Blackburn R	2	42 7

SEMLEY, Alan
21.2.66 Barnsley (FW)
6.0½ 11.0 Apprentice
LD Blackburn R v Barnsley
28.12.83 1–1

1983–84	Barnsley	2	4 —
1984–85	Barnsley	2	— —
1985–86	Barnsley	2	— —
1986–87	Barnsley	2	— —
1987–88	Barnsley	2	— —

SENIOR, Trevor
28.11.61 Dorchester (FW)
6.1½ 12.8 Dorchester T
LD Portsmouth v Fulham
20.3.82 1–1

1981–82	Portsmouth	3	9 2
1982–83	Portsmouth	3	2 —
1982–83	*Aldershot*	4	10 7
1983–84	Reading	4	45 36
1984–85	Reading	3	31 22
1985–86	Reading	3	46 27
1986–87	Reading	2	42 17
1987–88	Watford	1	24 1
1987–88	Middlesbrough	2	6 2

SHAKESPEARE, Craig
26.10.63 Birmingham (FW)
5.10 10.8 Apprentice
LD Huddersfield T v Walsall
11.9.82 2–2

1981–82	Walsall	3	— —
1982–83	Walsall	3	31 4
1983–84	Walsall	3	46 6
1984–85	Walsall	3	41 9
1985–86	Walsall	3	32 4
1986–87	Walsall	3	44 11
1987–88	Walsall	3	45 8

SHANKS, David
18.4.62 Bellshill (MF)
6.0 11.7 Broxburn Athletic
LD Stirling A v Cowdenbeath
2.4.83 3–1

1982–83	Cowdenbeath	2	2 1
1983–84	Cowdenbeath	2	29 2
1983–84	Clydebank	1	3 1
1984–85	Clydebank	1	34 2
1985–86	Clydebank	P	30 3
1986–87	Clydebank	P	41 1
1987–88	Clydebank	1	26 —
1987–88	Motherwell	P	7 —

SHANNON, Rab
20.4.66 Bellshill (DF)
5.11 11.8 St Columba's BC
LD Hibernian v Dundee
29.2.84 3–1

1982–83	Dundee	P	— —
1983–84	Dundee	P	6 —
1984–85	Dundee	P	3 —
1985–86	Dundee	P	33 —
1986–87	Dundee	P	39 5
1987–88	Dundee	P	41 —

SHARP, Graeme
16.10.60 Glasgow (FW)
6.1 11.8 Eastercraigs
LD Airdrieonians v Dumbarton
11.11.78 3–6

1978–79	Dumbarton	1	6 1
1979–80	Dumbarton	1	34 16
1979–80	Everton	1	2 —
1980–81	Everton	1	4 —
1981–82	Everton	1	29 15
1982–83	Everton	1	41 15
1983–84	Everton	1	28 7
1984–85	Everton	1	36 21
1985–86	Everton	1	37 19
1986–87	Everton	1	27 5
1987–88	Everton	1	32 13

SHAW, George
10.2.69 Glasgow (FW)
5.7 9.2 Ayresome N
LD St Mirren v Aberdeen
28.10.87 1–3

1987–88	St Mirren	P	2 —

SHAW, Graham
7.6.67 Stoke (FW)
5.7 10.3 Apprentice
LD Stoke C v Huddersfield T
2.11.85 3–0

1985–86	Stoke C	2	21 5
1986–87	Stoke C	2	18 2
1987–88	Stoke C	2	33 6

SHAW, Richard
11.9.68 Brentford (MF)
5.9 11.8 Apprentice
LD Reading v Crystal Palace
19.9.87 2–3

1987–88	Crystal Palace	2	3 —

SHEARER, Alan
— Newcastle-on-Tyne (FW)
5.11 11.3 Apprentice
LD Chelsea v Southampton
26.3.88 0–1

1987–88	Southampton	1	5 3

SHEARER, David
16.10.58 Fort William (FW)
5.10 12.0 Inverness Clach
LD Middlesbrough v Chelsea
4.4.78 2–0

1977–78	Middlesbrough	1	4 2
1978–79	Middlesbrough	1	5 1
1979–80	Middlesbrough	1	5 1
1979–80	*Wigan Ath*	4	11 9
1980–81	Middlesbrough	1	30 7
1981–82	Middlesbrough	1	24 3
1982–83	Middlesbrough	2	29 9
1983–84	Grimsby T	2	4 —
1984–85	Gillingham	3	23 12
1985–86	Gillingham	3	23 9
1986–87	Gillingham	3	36 16
1987–88	Gillingham	3	11 5
1987–88	Bournemouth	2	11 3
1987–88	Scunthorpe	4	15 7

PLAYER DIRECTORY

Peter Shilton.   *Photo: Bob Thomas Sports Photography.*

SHEARER, Duncan
28.8.62 Fort William (FW)
5.10 10.9 Inverness Clach
LD Chelsea v Leicester C
1.2.86 2–2

1983–84 Chelsea	2	—	—
1984–85 Chelsea	1	—	—
1985–86 Chelsea	1	2	1
1985–86 Huddersfield T	2	8	7
1986–87 Huddersfield T	2	42	21
1987–88 Huddersfield T	2	33	10

SHEEDY, Kevin
21.10.59 Builth Wells (MF)
5.9 10.11 Apprentice
LD Hereford U v Preston NE
28.4.76 3–1

1975–76 Hereford U	3	1	—
1976–77 Hereford U	2	16	1
1977–78 Hereford U	3	34	3
1978–79 Liverpool	1	—	—
1979–80 Liverpool	1	—	—
1980–81 Liverpool	1	1	—
1981–82 Liverpool	1	2	—
1982–83 Everton	1	40	11
1983–84 Everton	1	28	4
1984–85 Everton	1	29	11
1985–86 Everton	1	31	5
1986–87 Everton	1	28	13
1987–88 Everton	1	17	1

SHEFFIELD, Jonathan
1.2.69 Bulkington (GK)
5.11 11.7 Apprentice
LD —

1987–88 Norwich C	1	—	—

SHELTON, Gary
21.3.58 Nottingham (MF)
5.7 10.0 Apprentice
LD Southend U v Walsall
9.4.76 2–2

1975–76 Walsall	3	2	—
1976–77 Walsall	3	10	—
1977–78 Walsall	3	12	—
1977–78 Aston Villa	1	—	—
1978–79 Aston Villa	1	19	7
1979–80 Aston Villa	1	4	—
1979–80 Notts Co	2	8	—
1980–81 Aston Villa	1	—	—
1981–82 Aston Villa	1	1	—
1981–82 Sheffield W	2	9	1
1982–83 Sheffield W	2	40	4
1983–84 Sheffield W	2	40	5
1984–85 Sheffield W	1	41	4
1985–86 Sheffield W	1	31	1
1986–87 Sheffield W	1	37	3
1987–88 Oxford U	1	32	—

SHELTON, Richard
8.6.68 Sheffield (MF)
— — Apprentice
LD —

1987–88 Huddersfield T	2	—	—

SHEPHERD, Tony
16.11.66 Glasgow (MF)
5.9 10.7 Celtic BC
LD Celtic v Hearts
22.2.86 1–1

1983–84 Celtic	P	—	—
1984–85 Celtic	P	—	—
1985–86 Celtic	P	1	—
1986–87 Celtic	P	21	2
1987–88 Celtic	P	6	1

SHEPSTONE, Paul
8.11.70 Coventry (MF)
— — Trainee
LD —

1987–88 Coventry C	1	—	—

SHERIDAN, John
1.10.64 Manchester (MF)
5.9 10.8 Local
LD Leeds U v Middlesbrough
20.11.82 0–0

1981–82 Leeds U	1	—	—
1982–83 Leeds U	2	27	2
1983–84 Leeds U	2	11	1
1984–85 Leeds U	2	42	6
1985–86 Leeds U	2	32	4
1986–87 Leeds U	2	40	15
1987–88 Leeds U	2	38	12

SHERINGHAM, Teddy
2.4.66 Highams Park (FW)
5.8 11.7 Apprentice
LD Millwall v Brentford
15.1.84 1–2

1983–84 Millwall	3	7	1
1984–85 Millwall	3	—	—
1984–85 Aldershot	4	5	—
1985–86 Millwall	2	18	4
1986–87 Millwall	2	42	13
1987–88 Millwall	2	43	22

SHERWOOD, Steve
10.12.53 Selby (GK)
6.4 14.7 Apprentice
LD Derby Co v Chelsea
1.1.72 1–0

1970–71 Chelsea	1	—	—
1971–72 Chelsea	1	1	—
1972–73 Chelsea	1	3	—
1973–74 Chelsea	1	—	—
1973–74 Brighton & HA	3	—	—
1973–74 Millwall	2	1	—
1973–74 Brentford	4	16	—
1974–75 Chelsea	1	—	—
1974–75 Brentford	4	46	—
1975–76 Chelsea	2	12	—
1976–77 Chelsea	2	—	—
1976–77 Watford	4	8	—
1977–78 Watford	4	16	—
1978–79 Watford	3	16	—
1979–80 Watford	2	4	—
1980–81 Watford	2	22	—
1981–82 Watford	2	41	—
1982–83 Watford	1	42	—
1983–84 Watford	1	40	1
1984–85 Watford	1	9	—
1985–86 Watford	1	2	—
1986–87 Watford	1	11	—
1987–88 Grimsby T	3	46	—

SHERWOOD, Tim
6.2.69 St Albans (MF)
6.1 11.4 Apprentice
LD Sheffield W v Watford
12.9.87 2–3

1987–88 Watford	1	13	—

SHILTON, Peter
18.9.49 Leicester (GK)
6.0 14.0 Apprentice

1965–66 Leicester C	1	1	—
1966–67 Leicester C	1	4	—
1967–68 Leicester C	2	35	1
1968–69 Leicester C	2	42	—
1969–70 Leicester C	1	39	—
1970–71 Leicester C	1	40	—
1971–72 Leicester C	1	37	—
1972–73 Leicester C	1	41	—
1973–74 Leicester C	1	42	—
1974–75 Leicester C	1	5	—
1974–75 Stoke C	1	25	—
1975–76 Stoke C	1	42	—
1976–77 Stoke C	1	40	—
1977–78 Stoke C	2	3	—
1977–78 Nottingham F	1	37	—
1978–79 Nottingham F	1	42	—
1979–80 Nottingham F	1	42	—
1980–81 Nottingham F	1	40	—
1981–82 Nottingham F	1	41	—
1982–83 Southampton	1	39	—
1983–84 Southampton	1	42	—
1984–85 Southampton	1	41	—
1985–86 Southampton	1	37	—
1986–87 Southampton	1	29	—
1987–88 Derby Co	1	40	—

SHINNERS, Paul
8.1.59 Westminster (FW)
— — Fisher Ath
LD Gillingham v Plymouth Arg
2.10.84 3–3

1984–85 Gillingham	3	4	—
1984–85 Colchester U	4	6	1
1985–86 Orient	4	34	16
1986–87 Orient	4	13	5
1987–88 Leyton Orient	4	24	11

PLAYER DIRECTORY

SHIPLEY, George
7.3.59 Newcastle (MF)
5.8 10.8 Apprentice
LD Rochdale v Reading
24.3.79 1-0

1976–77 Southampton	2	—	—
1977–78 Southampton	2	—	—
1978–79 Southampton	1	—	—
1978–79 *Reading*	4	12	1
1979–80 Southampton	1	3	—
1979–80 *Blackpool*	3	—	—
1979–80 Lincoln C	4	23	2
1980–81 Lincoln C	4	46	8
1981–82 Lincoln C	3	43	11
1982–83 Lincoln C	3	38	7
1983–84 Lincoln C	3	42	4
1984–85 Lincoln C	3	31	7
1985–86 Charlton Ath	2	37	4
1986–87 Charlton Ath	1	24	2
1987–88 Gillingham	3	15	2

SHIRTLIFF, Peter
6.4.61 Barnsley (DF)
5.11 12.2 Apprentice
LD Peterborough v Sheffield W
19.8.78 2-0

1978–79 Sheffield W	3	26	1
1979–80 Sheffield W	3	3	—
1980–81 Sheffield W	2	28	—
1981–82 Sheffield W	2	31	2
1982–83 Sheffield W	2	8	—
1983–84 Sheffield W	2	36	1
1984–85 Sheffield W	1	35	—
1985–86 Sheffield W	1	21	—
1986–87 Charlton Ath	1	33	3
1987–88 Charlton Ath	1	36	2

SHORT, Craig
25.6.68 Bridlington (DF)
6.1 12.11 Local
LD Hereford U v Scarborough
21.10.87 1-1

1987–88 Scarborough	4	21	2

SHORT, Russell
4.9.68 Ilford (MF)
— — Trainee
LD Southend U v Colchester U
10.10.86 1-1

1986–87 Southend U	4	1	—
1987–88 Southend U	3	—	—

SHOTTON, Malcolm
16.2.57 Newcastle (DF)
6.3 13.12 Apprentice
LD Chester v Oxford U
16.8.80 0-1

1974–75 Leicester C	1	—	—
1975–76 Leicester C	1	—	—
Nuneaton Bor			
1980–81 Oxford U	3	38	5
1981–82 Oxford U	3	40	4
1982–83 Oxford U	3	46	1
1983–84 Oxford U	3	43	1
1984–85 Oxford U	2	42	1
1985–86 Oxford U	1	42	—
1986–87 Oxford U	1	11	—
1987–88 Portsmouth	1	10	—
1987–88 Huddersfield T	2	14	—

SHUTT, Carl
10.10.61 Sheffield (FW)
5.10 11.10 Spalding U
LD Oxford U v Sheffield W
31.8.85 0-1

1984–85 Sheffield W	1	—	—
1985–86 Sheffield W	1	19	9
1986–87 Sheffield W	1	20	7
1987–88 Sheffield W	1	1	—
1987–88 Bristol C	3	22	9

SIDDALL, Barry
12.9.54 Ellesmere Port (GK)
6.1 14.2 Apprentice
LD Walsall v Bolton W
7.10.72 3-2

1971–72 Bolton W	3	—	—
1972–73 Bolton W	3	4	—
1973–74 Bolton W	2	42	—
1974–75 Bolton W	2	42	—
1975–76 Bolton W	2	42	—
1976–77 Bolton W	2	7	—
1976–77 Sunderland	1	34	—
1977–78 Sunderland	2	42	—
1978–79 Sunderland	2	41	—
1979–80 Sunderland	2	12	—
1980–81 Sunderland	1	15	—
1980–81 *Darlington*	4	8	—
1981–82 Sunderland	1	23	—
1982–83 Port Vale	4	33	—
1983–84 Port Vale	3	39	—
1983–84 *Blackpool*	4	7	—
1984–85 Port Vale	4	9	—
1984–85 *Stoke C*	1	3	—
1984–85 Stoke C	1	15	—
1985–86 Stoke C	2	5	—
1985–86 *Tranmere R*	4	12	—
1985–86 *Manchester C*	1	6	—
1986–87 Blackpool	3	37	—
1987–88 Blackpool	3	38	—

SIMMONDS, Lyndon
11.11.66 Pontypool (FW)
5.4 9.10 Apprentice
LD Leeds U v Blackburn R
6.4.85 0-0

1984–85 Leeds U	2	1	—
1985–86 Leeds U	2	8	3
1986–87 *Swansea C*	4	8	1
1986–87 *Rochdale*	4	22	10
1987–88 Rochdale	4	43	12

SIMPSON, Neil
15.11.61 London (MF)
5.10 11.6 Middlefield Wasps
LD Partick Th v Aberdeen
20.12.80 1-1

1978–79 Aberdeen	P	—	—
1979–80 Aberdeen	P	—	—
1980–81 Aberdeen	P	16	2
1981–82 Aberdeen	P	29	4
1982–83 Aberdeen	P	33	5
1983–84 Aberdeen	P	24	2
1984–85 Aberdeen	P	33	4
1985–86 Aberdeen	P	22	1
1986–87 Aberdeen	P	9	—
1987–88 Aberdeen	P	15	1

SIMPSON, Paul
26.7.66 Carlisle (FW)
5.6 11.2½ Apprentice
LD Sheffield U v Manchester C
17.11.84 0-0

1983–84 Manchester C	2	—	—
1984–85 Manchester C	2	10	6
1985–86 Manchester C	1	37	8
1986–87 Manchester C	1	32	3
1987–88 Manchester C	2	38	1

SIMPSON, Wayne
19.9.68 Stoke (DF)
5.9 11.0 Apprentice
LD —

1987–88 Port Vale	3	—	—

SIMS, Steve
2.7.57 Lincoln (DF)
6.1½ 13.9 Apprentice
LD Manchester C v Leicester C
20.8.75 1-1

1974–75 Leicester C	1	—	—
1975–76 Leicester C	1	10	—
1976–77 Leicester C	1	32	1
1977–78 Leicester C	1	29	2
1978–79 Leicester C	2	8	—
1978–79 Watford	3	14	1
1979–80 Watford	2	34	2
1980–81 Watford	2	37	1
1981–82 Watford	2	17	—
1982–83 Watford	1	28	—
1983–84 Watford	1	22	—
1984–85 Watford	1	—	—
1984–85 Notts Co	2	34	2
1985–86 Notts Co	3	41	—
1986–87 Notts Co	3	10	3
1986–87 Watford	1	19	1
1987–88 Aston Villa	2	29	—

SINCLAIR, Ron
19.11.64 Stirling (GK)
5.10 11.9 Apprentice
LD Wrexham v Stockport Co
30.3.84 1-2

1982–83 Nottingham F	1	—	—
1983–84 Nottingham F	1	—	—
1983–84 *Wrexham*	4	11	—
1984–85 Nottingham F	1	—	—
1984–85 *Derby Co*	3	—	—
1985–86 Nottingham F	1	—	—
1985–86 *Sheffield U*	2	—	—
1985–86 *Leeds U*	2	—	—
1986–87 Leeds U	2	8	—
1986–87 *Halifax T*	4	4	—
1987–88 Leeds U	2	—	—

SINGLETON, Martin
2.8.63 Banbury (MF)
5.8 10.12 Apprentice
LD Coventry C v Everton
13.4.82 1–0

1980–81	Coventry C	1	—	—
1981–82	Coventry C	1	3	1
1982–83	Coventry C	1	5	—
1983–84	Coventry C	1	13	—
1984–85	Coventry C	1	2	—
1984–85	Bradford C	3	17	—
1985–86	Bradford C	2	36	2
1986–87	Bradford C	2	18	1
1986–87	WBA	2	7	—
1987–88	WBA	2	12	1
1987–88	*Northampton T*	3	1	—
1987–88	Northampton T	3	28	3

SINNOTT, Lee
12.7.65 Pelsall (DF)
6.1 11.9 Apprentice
LD Portsmouth v Walsall
6.3.82 1–0

1981–82	Walsall	3	4	—
1982–83	Walsall	3	32	2
1983–84	Walsall	3	4	—
1983–84	Watford	1	20	—
1984–85	Watford	1	30	—
1985–86	Watford	1	18	2
1986–87	Watford	1	10	—
1987–88	Bradford C	2	42	1

SINTON, Andy
19.3.66 Newcastle (MF)
5.7 10.7 Apprentice
LD Cambridge U v Wolves
2.11.82 2–1

1982–83	Cambridge U	2	13	5
1983–84	Cambridge U	2	34	6
1984–85	Cambridge U	3	26	2
1985–86	Cambridge U	4	20	—
1985–86	Brentford	3	26	3
1986–87	Brentford	3	46	5
1987–88	Brentford	3	46	11

SITTON John
21.10.59 Hackney (DF)
6.0½ 12.2 Apprentice
LD Chelsea v Coventry C
21.2.79 1–3

1978–79	Chelsea	1	12	—
1979–80	Chelsea	2	1	—
1979–80	Millwall	3	13	1
1980–81	Millwall	3	32	—
1981–82	Millwall	3	—	—
1981–82	Gillingham	3	30	2
1982–83	Gillingham	3	30	—
1983–84	Gillingham	3	42	3
1984–85	Gillingham	3	5	—
1985–86	Orient	4	39	—
1986–87	Orient	4	13	—
1987–88	Leyton Orient	4	20	1

SKINNER, Justin
30.1.69 London (MF)
5.10 11.1 Apprentice
LD Fulham v Rotherham U
17.2.87 1–1

1986–87	Fulham	3	3	—
1987–88	Fulham	3	32	6

SKIPPER, Peter
11.4.58 Hull (DF)
5.11 12.5 Local
LD Swansea C v Hull C
2.3.79 5–3

1978–79	Hull C	3	17	2
1979–80	Hull C	3	6	—
1979–80	*Scunthorpe U*	4	1	—
1980–81	Darlington	4	46	2
1981–82	Darlington	4	45	2
1982–83	Hull C	4	46	4
1983–84	Hull C	3	46	1
1984–85	Hull C	3	46	5
1985–86	Hull C	2	40	1
1986–87	Hull C	2	41	4
1987–88	Hull C	2	43	2

SLATER, Stuart
27.3.69 Sudbury (FW)
5.9 10.4 Apprentice
LD West Ham U v Derby Co
3.10.87 1–1

1987–88	West Ham	1	2	—

SLATTER, Neil
30.5.64 Cardiff (DF)
5.11 10.9 Apprentice
LD Bristol R v Shrewsbury T
11.4.81 1–1

1980–81	Bristol R	2	4	—
1981–82	Bristol R	3	28	1
1982–83	Bristol R	3	36	—
1983–84	Bristol R	3	43	1
1984–85	Bristol R	3	37	2
1985–86	Oxford U	1	22	2
1986–87	Oxford U	1	18	1
1987–88	Oxford U	1	16	3

SLAVEN, Bernie
13.11.60 Paisley (FW)
5.10 10.10
LD Morton v Airdrieonians
17.10.81 3–0

1981–82	Morton	P	13	1
1982–83	Morton	P	9	—
1983–84	Airdrie	1	2	—
1983–84	Queen of South	2	2	—
1983–84	Albion R	2	3	—
1984–85	Albion R	2	39	27
1985–86	Middlesbrough	2	32	8
1986–87	Middlesbrough	3	46	17
1987–88	Middlesbrough	2	44	21

SMALLEY, Mark
2.1.65 Newark (DF)
5.11 11.6 Apprentice
LD Ipswich T v Nottingham F
19.3.83 2–0

1982–83	Nottingham F	1	1	—
1983–84	Nottingham F	1	1	—
1984–85	Nottingham F	1	1	—
1985–86	Nottingham F	1	—	—
1985–86	*Birmingham C*	1	7	—
1986–87	*Bristol R*	3	10	—
1986–87	*Orient*	4	6	1
1986–87	Orient	4	16	—
1987–88	Leyton Orient	4	35	3

SMALLEY, Paul
17.11.66 Nottingham (DF)
5.11 11.0 Apprentice
LD Blackpool v Notts Co
24.8.85 1–3

1984–85	Notts Co	2	—	—
1985–86	Notts Co	3	26	—
1986–87	Notts Co	3	46	—
1987–88	Notts Co	3	46	—

SMART, Jason
15.2.69 Rochdale (DF)
6.0 12.00 YTS
LD Rochdale v Burnley
18.3.86 1–0

1985–86	Rochdale	4	1	—
1986–87	Rochdale	4	38	1
1987–88	Rochdale	4	36	3

SMILLIE, Neil
19.7.58 Barnsley (FW)
5.6 10.7 Apprentice
LD Crystal Palace v Oxford U
9.10.76 2–2

1975–76	Crystal Palace	3	—	—
1976–77	Crystal Palace	3	1	—
1976–77	*Brentford*	4	3	—
1977–78	Crystal Palace	2	1	—
1978–79	Crystal Palace	2	8	1
1979–80	Crystal Palace	1	8	1
1980–81	Crystal Palace	1	24	2
1981–82	Crystal Palace	2	41	3
1982–83	Brighton & HA	1	25	—
1983–84	Brighton & HA	2	26	2
1984–85	Brighton & HA	2	24	—
1985–86	Watford	1	16	3
1986–87	Reading	2	16	—
1987–88	Reading	2	23	—

SMITH, Alan
21.11.62 Birmingham (FW)
6.2½ 12.10 Alvechurch
LD Leicester C v Charlton Ath
28.8.82 1–2

1982–83	Leicester C	2	39	13
1983–84	Leicester C	1	40	15
1984–85	Leicester C	1	39	12
1985–86	Leicester C	1	40	19
1986–87	Leicester C	1	42	17
1987–88	Arsenal	1	39	11

PLAYER DIRECTORY

SMITH, Alan
7.12.66 Sheffield (DF)
6.0 11.2 Apprentice
LD Darlington v Bournemouth
4.10.86 0–3

1984–85	Sheffield W	1	— —
1985–86	Sheffield W	1	— —
1986–87	Darlington	3	16 1
1987–88	Darlington	4	— —

SMITH, Brian
27.10.66 Sheffield (DF)
5.9½ 11.2 Local
LD Shrewsbury T v Sheffield U
24.11.84 3–3

1984–85	Sheffield U	2	6 —
1985–86	Sheffield U	2	8 —
1986–87	Sheffield U	2	12 —
1986–87	Scunthorpe U	4	6 1
1987–88	Sheffield U	2	23 —

SMITH, Colin
3.11.58 Ruddington (DF)
6.0 12.10 Local
LD Arsenal v Norwich C
31.8.82 1–1

1981–82	Nottingham F	1	— —
1982–83	Norwich C	1	4 —
Sea Bee, Hong Kong			
1983–84	Cardiff C	2	34 2
1984–85	Cardiff C	2	16 1
1984–85	Aldershot	4	17 —
1985–86	Aldershot	4	34 1
1986–87	Aldershot	4	27 —
1987–88	Aldershot	3	42 1

SMITH, David
29.3.68 Gloucester (MF)
— — Local
LD Manchester U v Coventry C
6.2.88 1–0

1987–88	Coventry C	1	16 4

SMITH, David
25.6.61 Sidcup (MF)
— — Welling U
LD Gillingham v Middlesbrough
13.9.86 0–0

1986–87	Gillingham	3	27 1
1987–88	Gillingham	3	35 7

SMITH, Henry
10.3.56 Lanark (GK)
6.2 12.0 School
LD Dunfermline Ath v Hearts
29.8.81 1–1

1978–79	Leeds U	1	— —
1979–80	Leeds U	1	— —
1980–81	Leeds U	1	— —
1981–82	Hearts	1	33 —
1982–83	Hearts	1	39 —
1983–84	Hearts	P	36 —
1984–85	Hearts	P	36 —
1985–86	Hearts	P	36 —
1986–87	Hearts	P	43 —
1987–88	Hearts	P	44 —

SMITH, Jim
14.5.61 Elderslie (DF)
6.1 11.4 Greenock Juniors
LD Dundee v Rangers
17.10.81 2–3

1980–81	Dundee	1	— —
1981–82	Dundee	P	17 1
1982–83	Dundee	P	36 1
1983–84	Dundee	P	34 —
1984–85	Dundee	P	23 1
1985–86	Dundee	P	32 —
1986–87	Dundee	P	39 —
1987–88	Dundee	P	40 2

SMITH, John
23.7.70 Liverpool (MF)
5.7 10.2 Apprentice
LD —

1987–88	Tranmere R	4	— —

SMITH, Kevan
13.12.59 Eaglescliffe (DF)
6.3 11.9 Stockton
LD Torquay U v Darlington
29.9.79 4–0

1979–80	Darlington	4	35 1
1980–81	Darlington	4	39 2
1981–82	Darlington	4	45 1
1982–83	Darlington	4	46 3
1983–84	Darlington	4	44 2
1984–85	Darlington	4	36 2
1985–86	Rotherham U	3	43 3
1986–87	Rotherham U	3	16 1
1987–88	Coventry C	1	6 —
1987–88	York C	3	— —

SMITH, Lindsay
18.9.54 Enfield (DF)
5.11 12.0 Apprentice
LD Grimsby T v Colchester U
24.4.71 3–1

1970–71	Colchester U	4	1 —
1971–72	Colchester U	4	17 3
1972–73	Colchester U	4	31 1
1973–74	Colchester U	4	34 1
1974–75	Colchester U	4	43 1
1975–76	Colchester U	3	41 4
1976–77	Colchester U	3	45 6
1977–78	Colchester U	1	— —
1977–78	Charlton Ath	2	1 —
1977–78	Millwall	2	5 —
1977–78	Cambridge U	3	27 1
1978–79	Cambridge U	2	40 —
1979–80	Cambridge U	2	35 2
1980–81	Cambridge U	2	39 2
1981–82	Cambridge U	2	28 2
1981–82	Lincoln C	3	5 —
1982–83	Cambridge U	2	5 —
1982–83	Plymouth Arg	3	34 1
1983–84	Plymouth Arg	3	42 4
1984–85	Millwall	3	41 5
1985–86	Millwall	2	14 —
1986–87	Cambridge U	4	42 7
1987–88	Cambridge U	4	42 5

SMITH, Mark
21.3.60 Sheffield (DF)
6.1 12.2 Apprentice
LD Colchester U v Sheffield W
29.4.78 1–1

1977–78	Sheffield W	3	2 —
1978–79	Sheffield W	3	21 —
1979–80	Sheffield W	3	44 9
1980–81	Sheffield W	2	41 1
1981–82	Sheffield W	2	41 —
1982–83	Sheffield W	2	41 2
1983–84	Sheffield W	2	27 2
1984–85	Sheffield W	1	36 2
1985–86	Sheffield W	1	13 —
1986–87	Sheffield W	1	16 —
1987–88	Plymouth Arg	2	41 6

SMITH, Michael
19.2.69 Hull (FW)
5.8 10.9 Apprentice
LD —

1987–88	Hull C	2	— —

SMITH, Nick
28.1.69 (FW)
— —
LD Burnley v Southend U
2.5.87 2–1

1986–87	Southend U	4	1 —
1987–88	Southend U	3	34 5

SMITH, Tony
20.2.57 Sunderland (DF)
5.10 12.1 Amateur
LD Wolves v Newcastle U
12.11.77 1–0

1975–76	Newcastle U	1	— —
1976–77	Newcastle U	1	— —
1977–78	Newcastle U	1	2 —
1978–79	Newcastle U	2	— —
1978–79	Peterborough U	3	15 2
1979–80	Peterborough U	4	9 —
1980–81	Peterborough U	4	5 —
1981–82	Peterborough U	4	39 3
1982–83	Halifax T	4	44 2
1983–84	Halifax T	4	39 1
1984–85	Hartlepool U	4	44 2
1985–86	Hartlepool U	4	46 3
1986–87	Hartlepool U	4	45 1
1987–88	Hartlepool U	4	46 —

SMYTH, John
— Dublin (DF)
5.10 11.00 Dundalk
LD —

1987–88 Liverpool		1 — —

SNEDDON, Alan
12.3.58 Baillieston (DF)
5.11 12.3 Larkhall Thistle
LD Celtic v St Mirren
25.2.78 1–2

1977–78 Celtic	P	15	—
1978–79 Celtic	P	4	—
1979–80 Celtic	P	32	1
1980–81 Celtic	P	15	—
1980–81 Hibernian	1	14	—
1981–82 Hibernian	P	36	—
1982–83 Hibernian	P	36	—
1983–84 Hibernian	P	35	1
1984–85 Hibernian	P	36	2
1985–86 Hibernian	P	31	2
1986–87 Hibernian	P	26	—
1987–88 Hibernian	P	32	—

SNODIN, Glynn
14.2.60 Rotherham (FW)
5.6 9.5 Apprentice
LD Bradford C v Doncaster R
2.4.77 3–1

1976–77 Doncaster R	4	4	—
1977–78 Doncaster R	4	22	2
1978–79 Doncaster R	4	34	3
1979–80 Doncaster R	4	41	1
1980–81 Doncaster R	4	44	3
1981–82 Doncaster R	3	40	7
1982–83 Doncaster R	3	38	14
1983–84 Doncaster R	4	43	13
1984–85 Doncaster R	3	43	18
1985–86 Sheffield W	1	28	1
1986–87 Sheffield W	1	31	—
1987–88 Leeds U	2	35	7

SNODIN, Ian
15.8.63 Rotherham (MF)
5.7 8.11½ Apprentice
LD Doncaster R v Bournemouth
29.3.80 1–0

1979–80 Doncaster R	4	9	1
1980–81 Doncaster R	4	32	2
1981–82 Doncaster R	3	33	2
1982–83 Doncaster R	3	34	3
1983–84 Doncaster R	4	39	9
1984–85 Doncaster R	3	41	8
1985–86 Leeds U	2	37	5
1986–87 Leeds U	2	14	1
1986–87 Everton	1	16	—
1987–88 Everton	1	31	2

SNOOK, Eddie
18.10.68 Washington (FW)
5.7 10.1 Apprentice
LD —

1987–88 Notts Co		3 — —

SOUNESS, Graeme
6.5.53 Edinburgh (MF)
5.11 12.13 Apprentice
LD Fulham v Middlesbrough
6.1.73 2–1

1970–71 Tottenham H	1	—	—
1971–72 Tottenham H	1	—	—
1972–73 Tottenham H	1	—	—
1972–73 Middlesbrough	2	11	—
1973–74 Middlesbrough	2	35	7
1974–75 Middlesbrough	1	38	7
1975–76 Middlesbrough	1	35	3
1976–77 Middlesbrough	1	38	2
1977–78 Middlesbrough	1	19	3
1977–78 Liverpool	1	15	2
1978–79 Liverpool	1	41	8
1979–80 Liverpool	1	41	1
1980–81 Liverpool	1	37	6
1981–82 Liverpool	1	35	5
1982–83 Liverpool	1	41	9
1983–84 Liverpool	1	37	7
1984–85 Sampdoria (I)	A	28	5
1985–86 Sampdoria (I)	A	28	3
1986–87 Rangers	P	25	1
1987–88 Rangers	P	18	2

SOUTHALL, Neville
16.9.58 Llandudno (GK)
6.1 12.1 Winsford
LD Wigan Ath v Bury
20.9.80 2–1

1980–81 Bury	4	39	—
1981–82 Everton	1	26	—
1982–83 Everton	1	17	—
1982–83 Port Vale	4	9	—
1983–84 Everton	1	35	—
1984–85 Everton	1	42	—
1985–86 Everton	1	32	—
1986–87 Everton	1	31	—
1987–88 Everton	1	32	—

SPACKMAN, Nigel
2.12.60 Romsey (MF)
6.1 12.4 Andover
LD York C v Bournemouth
16.8.80 4–0

1980–81 Bournemouth	4	44	3
1981–82 Bournemouth	4	35	3
1982–83 Bournemouth	3	40	4
1983–84 Chelsea	2	40	3
1984–85 Chelsea	1	42	1
1985–86 Chelsea	1	39	7
1986–87 Chelsea	1	20	1
1986–87 Liverpool	1	12	—
1987–88 Liverpool	1	27	—

SPARHAM, Sean
4.12.68 Eltham (DF)
5.7 10.10 Apprentice
LD Middlesbrough v Millwall
15.8.87 1–1

1987–88 Millwall		2	7 —

SPEARING, Tony
7.10.64 Romford (DF)
5.9½ 10.12 Apprentice
LD Tottenham H v Norwich C
5.5.84 2–0

1982–83 Norwich C	1	—	—
1983–84 Norwich C	1	4	—
1984–85 Norwich C	1	—	—
1984–85 Stoke C	1	9	—
1984–85 Oxford U	2	5	—
1985–86 Norwich C	2	8	—
1986–87 Norwich C	1	39	—
1987–88 Norwich C	1	18	—

SPEEDIE, David
20.2.60 Glenrothes (MF)
5.7 11.0 Amateur
LD Barnsley v Wigan Ath
21.10.78 0–0

1978–79 Barnsley	4	10	—
1979–80 Barnsley	3	13	—
1980–81 Darlington	4	44	4
1981–82 Darlington	4	44	17
1982–83 Chelsea	2	34	7
1983–84 Chelsea	2	37	13
1984–85 Chelsea	1	35	10
1985–86 Chelsea	1	34	14
1986–87 Chelsea	1	22	3
1987–88 Coventry C	1	36	6

SPEIRS, Chico
22.3.66 Paisley (DF)
5.11 12.7 Glasgow Amateurs
LD Hamilton A v Queen's Park
8.9.82 2–2

1982–83 Hamilton A	1	3	—
1983–84 Hamilton A	1	28	1
1984–85 Hamilton A	1	33	1
1985–86 Hamilton A	1	24	—
1986–87 Hamilton A	P	14	1
1987–88 Hamilton A	1	9	1
1987–88 Queen of the S	1	3	—
1987–88 Hamilton A	1	9	—

SPEIRS, Gardner
14.4.63 Airdrie (FW)
5.8 10.0 St Mirren BC
LD St Mirren v Partick Th
13.12.80 1–0

1979–80 St Mirren	P	—	—
1980–81 St Mirren	P	2	—
1981–82 St Mirren	P	3	—
1982–83 St Mirren	P	1	—
1983–84 St Mirren	P	10	—
1984–85 St Mirren	P	17	6
1985–86 St Mirren	P	31	7
1986–87 St Mirren	P	26	2
1987–88 St Mirren	P	—	—

PLAYER DIRECTORY

SPINK, Nigel
8.8.58 Chelmsford (GK)
6.1 13.10 Chelmsford C
LD Nottingham F v <u>Aston Villa</u>
26.12.79 2-1

1976–77	Aston Villa	1	— —
1977–78	Aston Villa	1	— —
1978–79	Aston Villa	1	— —
1979–80	Aston Villa	1	1 —
1980–81	Aston Villa	1	— —
1981–82	Aston Villa	1	— —
1982–83	Aston Villa	1	22 —
1983–84	Aston Villa	1	28 —
1984–85	Aston Villa	1	19 —
1985–86	Aston Villa	1	31 —
1986–87	Aston Villa	1	32 —
1987–88	Aston Villa	2	44 —

SPOONER, Steve
25.1.61 London (MF)
5.11 12.3 Apprentice
LD Tottenham H v <u>Derby Co</u>
3.3.79 2-0

1978–79	Derby Co	1	1	—
1979–80	Derby Co	1	1	—
1980–81	Derby Co	2	2	—
1981–82	Derby Co	2	4	—
1981–82	Halifax T	4	29	2
1982–83	Halifax T	4	43	11
1983–84	Chesterfield	4	20	3
1984–85	Chesterfield	4	41	6
1985–86	Chesterfield	3	32	5
1986–87	Hereford U	4	42	11
1987–88	Hereford U	4	42	8

SPROSON, Phil
13.10.59 Trent Vale (DF)
6.0 12.0 Amateur
LD Peterborough U v <u>Port Vale</u>
17.3.78 1-1

1977–78	Port Vale	3	2	—
1978–79	Port Vale	4	23	—
1979–80	Port Vale	4	39	3
1980–81	Port Vale	4	44	1
1981–82	Port Vale	4	42	6
1982–83	Port Vale	4	42	4
1983–84	Port Vale	3	38	2
1984–85	Port Vale	4	44	3
1985–86	Port Vale	4	44	4
1986–87	Port Vale	3	44	5
1987–88	Port Vale	3	44	3

SPROTT, Adrian
23.3.62 Edinburgh (DF)
5.8 10.0 Merchiston BC
LD Albion R v <u>Meadowbank T</u>
24.8.80 3-1

1980–81	Meadowbank T	2	31	8
1981–82	Meadowbank T	2	39	9
1982–83	Meadowbank T	2	38	11
1983–84	Meadowbank T	1	37	6
1984–85	Meadowbank T	1	39	14
1985–86	Meadowbank T	2	13	3

1985–86	Hamilton A	1	17	3
1986–87	Hamilton A	P	26	2
1987–88	Hamilton A	1	41	6

STAINROD, Simon
1.2.59 Sheffield (FW)
5.10 12.9 Apprentice
LD Tottenham H v <u>Sheffield U</u>
27.3.76 5-0

1975–76	Sheffield U	1	7	2
1976–77	Sheffield U	2	21	3
1977–78	Sheffield U	2	25	6
1978–79	Sheffield U	2	14	3
1978–79	Oldham Ath	2	14	5
1979–80	Oldham Ath	2	37	11
1980–81	Oldham Ath	2	18	5
1980–81	QPR	2	15	4
1981–82	QPR	2	39	17
1982–83	QPR	2	31	9
1983–84	QPR	1	41	13
1984–85	QPR	1	19	5
1984–85	Sheffield W	1	9	1
1985–86	Sheffield W	1	6	1
1985–86	Aston Villa	1	30	10
1986–87	Aston Villa	1	29	6
1987–88	Aston Villa	2	4	—
1987–88	*Stoke C*	2	2	—
1987–88	Stoke C	2	10	2

STANCLIFFE, Paul
5.5.58 Sheffield (DF)
6.2 12.13 Apprentice
LD Brighton & HA v <u>Rotherham U</u>
16.8.75 3-0

1975–76	Rotherham U	3	42	2
1976–77	Rotherham U	3	46	—
1977–78	Rotherham U	3	32	3
1978–79	Rotherham U	3	33	—
1979–80	Rotherham U	3	33	1
1980–81	Rotherham U	3	44	—
1981–82	Rotherham U	2	42	2
1982–83	Rotherham U	2	13	—
1983–84	Sheffield U	3	43	1
1984–85	Sheffield U	2	33	1
1985–86	Sheffield U	2	40	1
1986–87	Sheffield U	2	36	2
1987–88	Sheffield U	2	41	3

STANISLAUS, Roger
2.11.68 Hammersmith (DF)
5.9 12.11 Arsenal
LD Preston NE v <u>Brentford</u>
29.9.87 1-2

1987–88	Brentford	3	37	2

STANNARD, Jim
6.10.62 London (GK)
6.0 13.6 Local
LD <u>Fulham</u> v Swindon T
31.1.81 2-0

1980–81	Fulham	3	17	—
1981–82	Fulham	3	2	—
1982–83	Fulham	2	—	—
1983–84	Fulham	2	15	—
1984–85	Fulham	2	7	—

1984–85	*Charlton Ath*	2	1	—
1984–85	*Southend U*	4	17	—
1985–86	Southend U	4	46	—
1986–87	Southend U	4	46	—
1987–88	Fulham	3	46	—

STANT, Phil
13.10.62 Bolton (FW)
— — Camberley
LD <u>Reading</u> v Newport Co
6.11.82 4-2

1982–83	Reading	3	4	2
Army				
1986–87	Hereford U	4	9	1
1987–88	Hereford U	4	39	9

STAPLETON, Frank
10.7.56 Dublin (FW)
5.11 13.2 Apprentice
LD <u>Arsenal</u> v Stoke C
29.3.75 1-1

1973–74	Arsenal	1	—	—
1974–75	Arsenal	1	1	—
1975–76	Arsenal	1	25	4
1976–77	Arsenal	1	40	13
1977–78	Arsenal	1	39	13
1978–79	Arsenal	1	41	17
1979–80	Arsenal	1	39	14
1980–81	Arsenal	1	40	14
1981–82	Manchester U	1	41	13
1982–83	Manchester U	1	41	14
1983–84	Manchester U	1	42	13
1984–85	Manchester U	1	24	6
1985–86	Manchester U	1	41	7
1986–87	Manchester U	1	34	7
1987–88	Ajax (Neth)	—	—	—
1987–88	Derby Co	1	10	1

STARBUCK, Philip
24.11.68 Nottingham (FW)
5.10 10.13 Apprentice
LD Newcastle U v <u>Nottingham F</u>
13.12.86 3-2

1986–87	Nottingham F	1	5	2
1987–88	*Nottingham F*	1	10	—
1987–88	*Birmingham C*	2	3	—

STARK, Billy
11.2.56 Glasgow (MF)
6.1 11.4 Anniesland W
LD Queen of the S v <u>St Mirren</u>
30.8.75 2-2

1975–76	St Mirren	1	21	6
1976–77	St Mirren	1	35	11
1977–78	St Mirren	P	33	7
1978–79	St Mirren	P	32	9
1979–80	St Mirren	P	36	8
1980–81	St Mirren	P	34	5
1981–82	St Mirren	P	33	10
1982–83	St Mirren	P	31	4
1983–84	Aberdeen	P	14	6
1984–85	Aberdeen	P	32	15
1985–86	Aberdeen	P	30	8
1986–87	Aberdeen	P	35	12
1987–88	Celtic	P	37	8

STATHAM, Brian
21.5.69 Zimbabwe (DF)
— — Trainee
LD Southampton v Tottenham H
26.12.87 2-1

1987-88	Tottenham H	1	18	—

STATHAM, Derek
24.3.59 Wolverhampton (DF)
5.5½ 11.0 Apprentice
LD Stoke C v WBA
18.12.76 0-2

1976-77	WBA	1	16	1
1977-78	WBA	1	40	—
1978-79	WBA	1	39	1
1979-80	WBA	1	16	—
1980-81	WBA	1	31	—
1981-82	WBA	1	35	—
1982-83	WBA	1	32	2
1983-84	WBA	1	16	—
1984-85	WBA	1	30	4
1985-86	WBA	1	37	—
1986-87	WBA	2	6	—
1987-88	Southampton	1	38	—

STAUNTON, Stephen
— Drogheda (DF)
5.11 11.2 Dundalk
LD Bradford C v Sheffield U
14.11.87 2-0

1987-88	Liverpool	1	—	—
1987-88	*Bradford C*	2	8	—

STEEL, Jim
4.12.59 Dumfries (FW)
6.3 14.0 Apprentice
LD Cardiff C v Oldham Ath
26.8.78 1-3

1978-79	Oldham Ath	2	7	4
1979-80	Oldham Ath	2	33	10
1980-81	Oldham Ath	2	24	3
1981-82	Oldham Ath	2	37	7
1982-83	Oldham Ath	2	7	—
1982-83	*Wigan Ath*	3	2	2
1982-83	*Wrexham*	3	9	6
1982-83	Port Vale	4	13	3
1983-84	Port Vale	3	15	3
1983-84	Wrexham	4	21	—
1984-85	Wrexham	4	45	14
1985-86	Wrexham	4	43	14
1986-87	Wrexham	4	37	17
1987-88	Wrexham	4	18	6
1987-88	Tranmere R	4	29	7

STEELE, Eric
14.5.54 Newcastle (GK)
6.0 12.8½ Amateur
LD Peterborough U v Chester
2.2.74 0-0

1972-73	Newcastle U	1	—	—
1973-74	Newcastle U	1	—	—
1973-74	Peterborough U	4	20	—
1974-75	Peterborough U	3	46	—
1975-76	Peterborough U	3	46	—
1976-77	Peterborough U	3	12	—
1976-77	Brighton & HA	3	15	—
1977-78	Brighton & HA	2	38	—
1978-79	Brighton & HA	2	25	—
1979-80	Brighton & HA	1	9	—
1979-80	Watford	2	28	—
1980-81	Watford	2	20	—
1981-82	Watford	2	1	—
1982-83	*Cardiff C*	3	7	—
1983-84	Watford	1	2	—
1984-85	Derby Co	3	26	—
1985-86	Derby Co	3	13	—
1986-87	Derby Co	2	8	—
1987-88	Southend U	3	27	—
1987-88	*Mansfield T*	3	5	—

STEELE, Tim
1.2.67 Coventry (FW)
5.9 11.0 Apprentice
LD Shrewsbury T v Fulham
8.3.86 2-1

1985-86	Shrewsbury T	2	2	—
1986-87	Shrewsbury T	2	11	1
1987-88	Shrewsbury T	2	33	3

STEIN, Mark
28.1.66 S Africa (MF)
5.6 10.0
LD Luton T v Everton
7.4.84 0-3

1983-84	Luton T	1	1	—
1984-85	Luton T	1	1	—
1985-86	Luton T	1	6	—
1985-86	*Aldershot*	4	2	1
1986-87	Luton T	1	21	8
1987-88	Luton T	1	25	11

STEPHENS, Archie
19.5.54 Liverpool (FW)
5.11 12.8 Melksham
LD Chesterfield v Bristol R
5.9.81 2-0

1981-82	Bristol R	3	39	11
1982-83	Bristol R	3	30	6
1983-84	Bristol R	3	34	13
1984-85	Bristol R	3	24	10
1984-85	Middlesbrough	2	9	2
1985-86	Middlesbrough	2	28	4
1986-87	Middlesbrough	3	44	16
1987-88	Middlesbrough	2	11	2
1987-88	Carlisle U	4	6	2

STEPHENSON, Paul
2.1.68 Wallsend (FW)
5.10 10.9 Apprentice
LD Newcastle U v Southampton
14.12.85 2-1

1985-86	Newcastle U	1	22	1
1986-87	Newcastle U	1	24	—
1987-88	Newcastle U	1	7	—

STERLAND, Mel
1.10.61 Sheffield (DF)
6.0 13.2 Apprentice
LD Sheffield W v Blackpool
17.5.79 2-0

1978-79	Sheffield W	3	2	1
1979-80	Sheffield W	3	2	—
1980-81	Sheffield W	2	22	2
1981-82	Sheffield W	2	27	—
1982-83	Sheffield W	2	35	—
1983-84	Sheffield W	2	39	8
1984-85	Sheffield W	1	24	2
1985-86	Sheffield W	1	38	8
1986-87	Sheffield W	1	30	2
1987-88	Sheffield W	1	38	8

STERLING, Worrell
8.6.65 Bethnal Green (MF)
5.6½ 10.11 Apprentice
LD Manchester U v Watford
23.4.83 2-0

1982-83	Watford	1	3	—
1983-84	Watford	1	10	1
1984-85	Watford	1	15	4
1985-86	Watford	1	24	3
1986-87	Watford	1	18	4
1987-88	Watford	1	21	2

STEVEN, Trevor
21.9.63 Berwick (MF)
5.8½ 10.9 Apprentice
LD Burnley v Huddersfield T
14.4.81 4-2

1980-81	Burnley	3	1	—
1981-82	Burnley	3	36	3
1982-83	Burnley	2	39	8
1983-84	Everton	1	27	1
1984-85	Everton	1	40	12
1985-86	Everton	1	41	9
1986-87	Everton	1	41	14
1987-88	Everton	1	36	6

STEVENS, Gary
30.3.62 Hillingdon (DF)
6.0 12.0 Apprentice
LD Brighton & HA v Ipswich T
15.9.79 2-0

1979-80	Brighton & HA	1	26	—
1980-81	Brighton & HA	1	34	1
1981-82	Brighton & HA	1	32	—
1982-83	Brighton & HA	1	41	—
1983-84	Tottenham H	1	40	4
1984-85	Tottenham H	1	28	—
1985-86	Tottenham H	1	29	2
1986-87	Tottenham H	1	20	—
1987-88	Tottenham H	1	18	—

PLAYER DIRECTORY

Gary Stevens

Photo: Bob Thomas Sports Photography.

STEVENS, Gary
27.3.63 Barrow (DF)
5.11 10.11 Apprentice
LD West Ham U v Everton
10.10.81 1-1

1980–81	Everton	1	— —
1981–82	Everton	1	19 1
1982–83	Everton	1	28 —
1983–84	Everton	1	27 1
1984–85	Everton	1	37 3
1985–86	Everton	1	41 1
1986–87	Everton	1	25 3
1987–88	Everton	1	31 —

STEVENS, Gary
30.8.54 Birmingham (FW)
6.1 12.4 Evesham
LD Cardiff C v Cambridge U
9.9.78 1-0

1978–79	Cardiff C	2	34 13
1979–80	Cardiff C	2	38 11
1980–81	Cardiff C	2	40 7
1981–82	Cardiff C	2	38 13
1982–83	Cardiff C	3	— —
1982–83	Shrewsbury T	2	35 4
1983–84	Shrewsbury T	2	38 1
1984–85	Shrewsbury T	2	39 20
1985–86	Shrewsbury T	2	38 4
1986–87	Brentford	3	32 10
1986–87	Hereford U	4	10 —
1987–88	Hereford U	4	45 7

STEVENS, Ian
21.10.66 Malta (FW)
5.11 12.0 YTS
LD Preston NE v Lincoln C
23.3.85 0-1

1984–85	Preston NE	3	4 1
1985–86	Preston NE	3	7 1
1986–87	Stockport Co	4	2 —
1986–87	Bolton W	3	8 2
1987–88	Bolton W	4	9 —

STEVENS, Keith
21.6.64 Merton (DF)
5.11¾ 12.½ Apprentice
LD Oxford U v Millwall
29.4.81 1-0

1980–81	Millwall	3	1 —
1981–82	Millwall	3	7 —
1982–83	Millwall	3	26 —
1983–84	Millwall	3	17 —
1984–85	Millwall	3	41 —
1985–86	Millwall	2	33 1
1986–87	Millwall	2	35 1
1987–88	Millwall	2	35 1

STEVENSON, Andy
29.9.67 Scunthorpe (MF)
6.0 12.3 School
LD Port Vale v Scunthorpe U

1985–86	Scunthorpe U	4	2 —
1986–87	Scunthorpe U	4	7 —
1987–88	Scunthorpe U	4	8 —

STEVENSON, Nigel
2.11.58 Swansea C (DF)
6.2 12.10 Apprentice
LD Swansea C v Southport
10.4.76 2-0

1975–76	Swansea C	4	2 —
1976–77	Swansea C	4	— —
1977–78	Swansea C	4	— —
1978–79	Swansea C	3	39 2
1979–80	Swansea C	2	34 3
1980–81	Swansea C	2	40 5
1981–82	Swansea C	1	20 —
1982–83	Swansea C	1	26 1
1983–84	Swansea C	2	37 3
1984–85	Swansea C	3	34 1
1985–86	Swansea C	3	12 —
1985–86	*Cardiff C*	3	14 —
1985–86	*Reading*	3	3 —
1986–87	Swansea C	4	15 —
1987–88	Cardiff C	4	36 1

STEWART, Billy
1.1.65 Liverpool (GK)
5.11 11.7 Apprentice
LD Wigan Ath v Millwall
9.2.85 0-1

1982–83	Liverpool	1	— —
1983–84	Liverpool	1	— —
1984–85	Wigan Ath	3	6 —
1985–86	Wigan Ath	3	8 —
1986–87	Chester C	3	29 —
1987–88	Chester C	3	27 —

STEWART, Ian
10.9.61 Belfast (FW)
5.7 10.9 Juniors
LD Blackburn R v QPR
4.10.80 2-1

1980–81	QPR	2	1 —
1981–82	QPR	2	3 —
1982–83	QPR	2	19 —
1982–83	*Millwall*	3	11 3
1983–84	QPR	1	31 2
1984–85	QPR	1	13 —
1985–86	Newcastle U	1	28 2
1986–87	Newcastle U	1	14 1
1987–88	Portsmouth	1	1 —
1987–88	*Brentford*	3	7 —

STEWART, Paul
7.10.64 Manchester (FW)
5.11 11.10 Apprentice
LD Blackpool v Rochdale
10.2.82 1-1

1981–82	Blackpool	4	14 3
1982–83	Blackpool	4	38 7
1983–84	Blackpool	4	44 10
1984–85	Blackpool	4	31 7
1985–86	Blackpool	3	42 8
1986–87	Blackpool	3	32 21
1986–87	Manchester C	1	11 2
1987–88	Manchester C	2	40 24

STEWART, Ray
7.9.59 Perth (DF)
5.11 11.11 Errol Rovers
LD Hibernian v Dundee U

1975–76	Dundee U	P	— —
1976–77	Dundee U	P	1 —
1977–78	Dundee U	P	6 1
1978–79	Dundee U	P	34 4
1979–80	Dundee U	P	3 —
1979–80	West Ham U	2	38 10
1980–81	West Ham U	2	41 5
1981–82	West Ham U	1	42 10
1982–83	West Ham U	1	39 8
1983–84	West Ham U	1	42 7
1984–85	West Ham U	1	37 6
1985–86	West Ham U	1	39 6
1986–87	West Ham U	1	23 4
1987–88	West Ham U	1	33 4

STILES, John
6.5.64 Manchester (MF)
5.9½ 10.12 Vancouver W
LD Middlesbrough v Leeds U
2.3.85 0-0

1984–85	Leeds U	2	1 —
1985–86	Leeds U	2	12 1
1986–87	Leeds U	2	29 —
1987–88	Leeds U	2	13 1

STIMSON, Mark
27.12.67 Plaistow (DF)
5.11 11.0 YTS
LD Everton v Tottenham H
11.5.87 1-0

1984–85	Tottenham H	1	— —
1985–86	Tottenham H	1	— —
1986–87	Tottenham H	1	1 —
1987–88	Tottenham H	1	— —
1987–88	*Leyton Orient*	4	10 —

STOCKWELL, Mike
14.2.65 Chelmsford (MF)
5.6½ 10.2 Apprentice
LD Coventry C v Ipswich T
26.12.85 0-1

1982–83	Ipswich T	1	— —
1983–84	Ipswich T	1	— —
1984–85	Ipswich T	1	— —
1985–86	Ipswich T	1	8 —
1986–87	Ipswich T	2	21 1
1987–88	Ipswich T	2	43 1

STOKES, Wayne
16.2.65 Birmingham (DF)
6.1 13.0 Apprentice
LD Gillingham v Bristol R
7.5.83 1-0

1982–83	Gillingham	3	2 —
1983–84	Gillingham	3	1 —
Non-league			
1986–87	Stockport Co	4	18 —
1987–88	Hartlepool U	4	24 —

PLAYER DIRECTORY

STONEHOUSE, Kevin
20.9.59 Bishop Auckland (FW)
5.11 11.1 Shildon
LD Blackburn R v Huddersfield T
29.9.79 0–3

1979–80	Blackburn R	3	7	2
1980–81	Blackburn R	2	26	10
1981–82	Blackburn R	2	37	11
1982–83	Blackburn R	2	15	4
1982–83	Huddersfield T	3	5	—
1983–84	Huddersfield T	2	17	4
1983–84	Blackpool	4	13	5
1984–85	Blackpool	4	26	11
1985–86	Blackpool	3	16	3
1986–87	Blackpool	3	—	—
1987–88	Darlington	4	43	13

STORER, Stuart
16.1.67 Harborough (FW)
5.11 11.8 Local
LD Mansfield T v Hartlepool U
22.10.83 5–0

1983–84	Mansfield T	4	1	—
1984–85	Birmingham C	2	—	—
1985–86	Birmingham C	1	2	—
1986–87	Birmingham C	2	6	—
1987–88	Everton	1	—	—
1987–88	*Wigan Ath*	3	12	—
1987–88	*Bolton W*	4	5	1
1987–88	Bolton W	4	10	—

STOWELL, Mike
19.4.65 Preston (GK)
6.2 11.10 Leyland Motors
LD Chester C v Aldershot
5.9.87 4–1

1984–85	Preston NE	3	—	—
1985–86	Preston NE	4	—	—
1985–86	Everton	1	—	—
1986–87	Everton	1	—	—
1987–88	Everton	1	—	—
1987–88	*Chester C*	3	14	—
1987–88	*York C*	3	6	—
1987–88	*Manchester C*	2	14	—

STRACHAN, Gordon
9.2.57 Edinburgh (MF)
5.6 10.3
LD Dundee v Hearts
23.4.76 2–0

1974–75	Dundee	1	1	—
1975–76	Dundee	P	23	6
1976–77	Dundee	1	36	7
1977–78	Aberdeen	P	12	2
1978–79	Aberdeen	P	31	5
1979–80	Aberdeen	P	33	10
1980–81	Aberdeen	P	20	6
1981–82	Aberdeen	P	30	7
1982–83	Aberdeen	P	32	12
1983–84	Aberdeen	P	25	13
1984–85	Manchester U	1	41	15
1985–86	Manchester U	1	28	5
1986–87	Manchester U	1	34	4
1987–88	Manchester U	1	36	8

STREETE, Floyd
5.5.59 W Indies (DF)
6.1 12.8 Rivet Sports
LD Cambridge U v Crewe Alex
19.2.77 2–0

1976–77	Cambridge U	4	3	1
1977–78	Cambridge U	3	21	3
1978–79	Cambridge U	2	13	1
1979–80	Cambridge U	2	21	1
1980–81	Cambridge U	2	22	4
1981–82	Cambridge U	2	31	5
1982–83	Cambridge U	2	14	4
Utrecht and SC Cambuur				
1984–85	Derby Co	3	30	—
1985–86	Derby Co	3	5	—
1985–86	Wolves	3	25	1
1986–87	Wolves	4	35	—
1987–88	Wolves	4	44	—

STRINGFELLOW, Ian
8.5.69 Nottingham (MF)
5.9 10.2 Apprentice
LD Mansfield T v Tranmere R
29.4.86 0–0

1985–86	Mansfield T	4	3	—
1986–87	Mansfield T	3	22	4
1987–88	Mansfield T	3	30	8

STRODDER, Gary
1.4.65 Leeds (DF)
6.1 11.3½ Apprentice
LD Lincoln C v Wigan Ath
28.8.82 2–1

1982–83	Lincoln C	3	8	—
1983–84	Lincoln C	3	22	1
1984–85	Lincoln C	3	26	2
1985–86	Lincoln C	3	43	1
1986–87	Lincoln C	4	33	2
1986–87	West Ham U	1	12	—
1987–88	West Ham U	1	30	1

STUART, Mark
15.12.66 Hammersmith (FW)
5.8½ 11.2 QPR Schoolboy
LD Charlton Ath v Manchester C
15.12.84 1–3

1984–85	Charlton Ath	2	6	1
1985–86	Charlton Ath	2	30	12
1986–87	Charlton Ath	1	36	9
1987–88	Charlton Ath	1	31	6

STUBBS, William
1.8.66 Hartlepool (FW)
— — Apprentice
LD —

1987–88	Nottingham F	1	—	—

STURROCK, Paul
10.10.56 Ellon (FW)
5.8 10.4 Bankfoot
LD Motherwell v Dundee U
28.12.74 0–1

1974–75	Dundee U	1	12	6
1975–76	Dundee U	P	17	3
1976–77	Dundee U	P	36	15
1977–78	Dundee U	P	33	3
1978–79	Dundee U	P	33	6
1979–80	Dundee U	P	33	4
1980–81	Dundee U	P	35	13
1981–82	Dundee U	P	31	15
1982–83	Dundee U	P	28	8
1983–84	Dundee U	P	17	4
1984–85	Dundee U	P	30	14
1985–86	Dundee U	P	31	8
1986–87	Dundee U	P	30	6
1987–88	Dundee U	P	9	3

SUCKLING, Perry
12.10.55 Leyton (GK)
6.0½ 12.1 Apprentice
LD Coventry C v Southampton
28.8.82 1–0

1982–83	Coventry C	1	3	—
1983–84	Coventry C	1	24	—
1984–85	Coventry C	1	—	—
1985–86	Coventry C	1	—	—
1986–87	Manchester C	1	37	—
1987–88	Manchester C	2	2	—
1987–88	*Chelsea*	1	—	—
1987–88	Crystal Palace	2	17	—

SULLEY, Chris
3.12.59 Camberwell (DF)
5.8 10.0 Apprentice
LD Bournemouth v Darlington
14.3.81 3–3

1978–79	Chelsea	1	—	—
1979–80	Chelsea	2	—	—
1980–81	Chelsea	2	—	—
1980–81	Bournemouth	4	8	—
1981–82	Bournemouth	4	46	—
1982–83	Bournemouth	3	46	1
1983–84	Bournemouth	3	46	2
1984–85	Bournemouth	3	23	—
1985–86	Bournemouth	3	37	—
1986–87	Dundee U	P	7	—
1986–87	Blackburn R	2	13	—
1987–88	Blackburn R	2	34	—

SUMMERFIELD, Kevin
7.1.59 Walsall (FW)
5.11 11.0 Apprentice
LD WBA v Derby Co
26.3.79 2–1

1976–77	WBA	1	—	—
1977–78	WBA	1	—	—
1978–79	WBA	1	2	1
1979–80	WBA	1	3	1
1980–81	WBA	1	—	—
1981–82	WBA	1	4	2
1982–83	Birmingham C	1	5	1
1982–83	Walsall	3	21	9
1983–84	Walsall	3	33	8
1984–85	Cardiff C	2	10	1
1984–85	Plymouth Arg	3	17	2
1985–86	Plymouth Arg	3	26	7
1986–87	Plymouth Arg	2	28	9
1987–88	Plymouth Arg	2	37	5

SUSSEX, Andy
23.11.64 Enfield (FW)
6.0 11.6 Apprentice
LD Orient v Sheffield W
7.11.81 3–0

1981–82	Orient	2	8	1
1982–83	Orient	3	24	2
1983–84	Orient	3	29	6
1984–85	Orient	3	19	2
1985–86	Orient	4	36	4
1986–87	Orient	4	20	1
1987–88	Leyton Orient	4	8	1

SUTTON, Steve
16.4.61 Hartington (GK)
6.0 12.12 Apprentice
LD Norwich C v Nottingham F
25.10.80 1–1

1980–81	Nottingham F	1	1	—
1980–81	*Mansfield T*	4	8	—
1981–82	Nottingham F	1	1	—
1982–83	Nottingham F	1	17	—
1983–84	Nottingham F	1	6	—
1984–85	Nottingham F	1	14	—
1984–85	*Derby Co*	3	14	—
1985–86	Nottingham F	1	31	—
1986–87	Nottingham F	1	28	—
1987–88	Nottingham F	1	35	—

SWAN, Peter
28.9.66 Leeds (FW)
6.0 11.12 Local
LD Leeds U v Oldham Ath
1.1.86 3–1

1984–85	Leeds U	2	—	—
1985–86	Leeds U	2	16	3
1986–87	Leeds U	2	7	—
1987–88	Leeds U	2	25	8

SWANN, Gary
11.4.62 York (DF)
5.9½ 11.2 Apprentice
LD Hull C v Exeter C
23.8.80 3–3

1980–81	Hull C	3	20	2
1981–82	Hull C	4	20	—
1982–83	Hull C	4	25	—
1983–84	Hull C	3	41	2
1984–85	Hull C	3	32	3
1985–86	Hull C	2	39	2
1986–87	Hull C	2	9	—
1986–87	Preston NE	4	30	5
1987–88	Preston NE	3	46	12

SWANNACK, Paul
10.5.69 Guildford (MF)
— Local
LD —

1987–88	Oxford U	1	—	—

TALBOT, Brian
21.7.53 Ipswich (MF)
5.10 12.0 Apprentice
LD Burnley v Ipswich T
9.2.74 0–1

1972–73	Ipswich T	1	—	—
1973–74	Ipswich T	1	15	3
1974–75	Ipswich T	1	40	8
1975–76	Ipswich T	1	19	2
1976–77	Ipswich T	1	42	5
1977–78	Ipswich T	1	40	4
1978–79	Ipswich T	1	21	3
1978–79	Arsenal	1	20	—
1979–80	Arsenal	1	42	1
1980–81	Arsenal	1	40	7
1981–82	Arsenal	1	42	7
1982–83	Arsenal	1	42	9
1983–84	Arsenal	1	27	6
1984–85	Arsenal	1	41	10
1985–86	Watford	1	41	7
1986–87	Watford	1	7	1
1986–87	Stoke C	2	32	3
1987–88	Stoke C	2	22	2
1987–88	WBA	2	15	2

TANNER, Nick
24.5.65 Bristol (DF)
6.2 13.7 Mangotsfield
LD Darlington v Bristol R
18.8.85 3–3

1984–85	Bristol R	3	—	—
1985–86	Bristol R	3	37	2
1986–87	Bristol R	3	44	1
1987–88	Bristol R	3	26	—

TAYLOR, Alex
13.6.62 Baillieston (MF)
5.7 10.11 Blantyre St J
LD Dundee U v Dundee
30.10.82 1–0

1982–83	Dundee U	P	3	—
1983–84	Dundee U	P	9	1
1984–85	Dundee U	P	21	5
1985–86	Dundee U	P	—	—
1986–87	Hamilton A	P	25	1
1987–88	Hamilton A	1	41	4

TAYLOR, Bob
3.2.67 Horden (FW)
5.10 11.2 Horden CW
LD Leeds U v Millwall
12.4.86 3–1

1985–86	Leeds U	2	2	—
1986–87	Leeds U	2	2	—
1987–88	Leeds U	2	32	9

TAYLOR, Kevin
22.1.61 Wakefield (MF)
5.8 11.11 Apprentice
LD Plymouth Arg v Sheffield W
27.1.79 2–1

1978–79	Sheffield W	3	5	—
1979–80	Sheffield W	3	21	6

1980–81	Sheffield W	2	30	5
1981–82	Sheffield W	2	35	7
1982–83	Sheffield W	2	29	3
1983–84	Sheffield W	2	5	—
1984–85	Derby Co	3	22	2
1984–85	Crystal Palace	2	13	—
1985–86	Crystal Palace	2	31	6
1986–87	Crystal Palace	2	41	8
1987–88	Crystal Palace	2	2	—
1987–88	Scunthorpe U	4	35	5

TAYLOR, Les
4.12.56 North Shields (MF)
5.8 11.7 Apprentice
LD Orient v Oxford U
31.3.75 1–1

1974–75	Oxford U	2	5	—
1975–76	Oxford U	2	35	—
1976–77	Oxford U	3	32	2
1977–78	Oxford U	3	46	6
1978–79	Oxford U	3	46	1
1979–80	Oxford U	3	36	6
1980–81	Oxford U	3	19	—
1980–81	Watford	2	24	1
1981–82	Watford	2	42	4
1982–83	Watford	1	39	5
1983–84	Watford	1	27	—
1984–85	Watford	1	39	3
1985–86	Watford	1	1	—
1986–87	Reading	2	31	1
1987–88	Reading	2	30	2

TAYLOR, Mark
20.11.64 Hartlepool (MF)
5.7 10.0 Local
LD Hartlepool U v Colchester U
14.4.84 0–0

1982–83	Hartlepool U	4	—	—
1983–84	Hartlepool U	4	6	—
1984–85	Hartlepool U	4	36	4
1985–86	Hartlepool U	4	5	—
1985–86	*Crewe Alex*	4	3	—
1986–87	Blackpool	3	40	14
1987–88	Blackpool	3	41	21

TAYLOR, Martin
9.12.66 Tamworth (GK)
5.11 12.9 Mile Oak R
LD Carlisle U v Scarborough
26.9.87 4–0

1987–88	Derby Co	1	—	—
1987–88	*Carlisle U*	4	10	—
1987–88	*Scunthorpe U*	4	4	8

TAYLOR, Robert
22.2.66 Walsall (MF)
5.10 11.0 Local
LD Hull C v Walsall
15.12.84 1–0

1984–85	Walsall	3	4	—
1985–86	Walsall	3	18	2
1986–87	Walsall	3	17	—
1987–88	Walsall	3	40	1

PLAYER DIRECTORY

TAYLOR, Shaun
26.3.63 Plymouth (DF)
— —
LD Wolves v Exeter C
27.12.86 2–2

1986–87 Exeter C	4	23	—
1987–88 Exeter C	4	41	1

TAYLOR, Steve
18.10.55 Royton (FW)
5.10 10.8 Apprentice
LD Bristol C v Bolton W
7.9.74 2–1

1974–75 Bolton W	2	5	—
1975–76 Bolton W	2	3	—
1975–76 *Port Vale*	3	4	2
1976–77 Bolton W	2	31	16
1977–78 Bolton W	1	2	—
1977–78 Oldham Ath	2	32	20
1978–79 Oldham Ath	2	15	5
1978–79 Luton T	2	20	1
1979–80 Mansfield T	3	37	7
1980–81 Burnley	3	38	16
1981–82 Burnley	3	22	9
1982–83 Burnley	2	26	12
1983–84 Wigan Ath	3	30	7
1983–84 Stockport Co	4	12	6
1984–85 Stockport Co	4	14	2
1984–85 Rochdale	4	30	12
1985–86 Rochdale	4	45	25
1986–87 Rochdale	4	9	5
1986–87 Preston NE	4	5	2
1987–88 Burnley	4	42	6

TEMPEST, Dale
30.12.63 Leeds (FW)
5.11 12.4 Apprentice
LD Burnley v Fulham
7.3.81 3–0

1980–81 Fulham	3	1	—
1981–82 Fulham	3	14	2
1982–83 Fulham	2	4	—
1983–84 Fulham	2	15	4
1984–85 Huddersfield T	2	35	15
1985–86 Huddersfield T	2	30	12
1985–86 Gillingham	3	9	4
1986–87 Lokeren (Bel)	—	—	—
1987–88 Colchester	4	44	11

TERRY, Steve
14.6.62 Clapton (DF)
6.1½ 13.3 Apprentice
LD Sunderland v Watford
26.4.80 5–0

1979–80 Watford	2	2	—
1980–81 Watford	2	5	—
1981–82 Watford	2	26	2
1982–83 Watford	1	7	1
1983–84 Watford	1	17	1
1984–85 Watford	1	38	4
1985–86 Watford	1	41	4
1986–87 Watford	1	18	2
1987–88 Watford	1	6	—

TESTER, Paul
10.3.59 Stroud (FW)
5.9 10.10 Cheltenham T
LD Cardiff C v Shrewsbury T
17.3.84 2–0

1983–84 Shrewsbury T	2	8	—
1984–85 Shrewsbury T	2	23	5
1984–85 *Hereford U*	4	4	—
1985–86 Shrewsbury T	2	9	1
1986–87 Shrewsbury T	2	29	5
1987–88 Shrewsbury T	2	29	1

THOMAS, Andy
16.12.62 Oxford (FW)
6.0 10.10 Apprentice
LD Oxford U v Chesterfield
6.9.80 0–3

1980–81 Oxford U	3	9	1
1981–82 Oxford U	3	39	14
1982–83 Oxford U	3	24	7
1982–83 Fulham	2	4	2
1982–83 *Derby Co*	2	1	—
1983–84 Oxford U	3	23	7
1984–85 Oxford U	2	4	1
1985–86 Oxford U	1	17	2
1986–87 Newcastle U	1	27	6
1987–88 Newcastle U	1	4	—

THOMAS, Geoff
5.8.64 Manchester (MF)
5.10 10.7 Local
LD Hereford U v Rochdale
30.10.82 1–0

1981–82 Rochdale	4	—	—
1982–83 Rochdale	4	1	—
1983–84 Rochdale	4	10	1
1983–84 Crewe Alex	4	8	1
1984–85 Crewe Alex	4	40	4
1985–86 Crewe Alex	4	37	6
1986–87 Crewe Alex	4	40	10
1987–88 Crystal Palace	2	41	6

THOMAS, Glen
6.10.67 Hackney (DF)
6.0½ 11.6 Apprentice
LD Swindon T v Fulham
21.3.87 2–0

1985–86 Fulham	2	—	—
1986–87 Fulham	3	1	—
1987–88 Fulham	3	27	—

THOMAS, Gwyn
26.9.57 Swansea (FW)
5.8 11.0 Apprentice
LD Wolves v Leeds
26.4.75 1–1

1974–75 Leeds U	1	1	—
1975–76 Leeds U	1	—	—
1976–77 Leeds U	1	7	1
1977–78 Leeds U	1	3	1
1978–79 Leeds U	1	2	—
1979–80 Leeds U	1	3	—
1980–81 Leeds U	1	2	—
1981–82 Leeds U	1	15	—
1982–83 Leeds U	2	39	1
1983–84 Leeds U	2	17	—
1983–84 Barnsley	2	13	—
1984–85 Barnsley	2	40	1
1985–86 Barnsley	2	39	5
1986–87 Barnsley	2	40	5
1987–88 Barnsley	2	42	4

THOMAS, John
5.8.58 Wednesbury (FW)
5.8 11.3
LD Tranmere R v Southend U
30.3.79 1–2

1978–79 Everton	1	—	—
1978–79 *Tranmere R*	3	11	2
1979–80 Everton	1	—	—
1979–80 *Halifax T*	4	5	—
1980–81 Bolton W	2	17	5
1981–82 Bolton W	2	5	1
1982–83 Chester	4	44	20
1983–84 Lincoln C	3	37	13
1984–85 Lincoln C	3	30	5
1985–86 Preston NE	4	40	17
1986–87 Preston NE	4	38	21
1987–88 Bolton W	4	44	22

THOMAS, Martin
28.11.59 Caerphilly (GK)
6.1 13.0 Apprentice
LD Charlton Ath v Bristol R
3.1.77 4–3

1976–77 Bristol R	2	1	—
1977–78 Bristol R	2	37	—
1978–79 Bristol R	2	42	—
1979–80 Bristol R	2	38	—
1980–81 Bristol R	2	25	—
1981–82 Bristol R	3	19	—
1982–83 *Cardiff C*	3	15	—
1982–83 *Tottenham H*	1	—	—
1982–83 *Southend U*	3	6	—
1982–83 *Newcastle U*	2	3	—
1983–84 Newcastle U	2	23	—
1984–85 Newcastle U	1	18	—
1984–85 *Middlesbrough*	2	4	—
1985–86 Newcastle U	1	32	—
1986–87 Newcastle U	1	39	—
1987–88 Newcastle U	1	3	—

THOMAS, Michael
24.8.67 Lambeth (DF)
5.10 12.4 Apprentice
LD Sheffield W v Arsenal
14.2.87 1–1

1985–86 Arsenal	1	—	—
1986–87 Arsenal	1	12	—
1986–87 *Portsmouth*	2	3	—
1987–88 Arsenal	1	37	9

THOMAS, Mitchell
2.10.64 Luton (DF)
6.0 12.0 Apprentice
LD West Ham U v <u>Luton T</u>
4.1.83 2–3

1982–83 Luton T	1	4	—
1983–84 Luton T	1	26	—
1984–85 Luton T	1	36	—
1985–86 Luton T	1	41	1
1986–87 Tottenham H	1	39	4
1987–88 Tottenham H	1	36	—

THOMAS, Rod
10.10.70 London
— —
LD Arsenal v <u>Watford</u>
15.4.88 0–1

1987–88 Watford	1	4	—

THOMPSON, Andy
9.11.67 Carnock (MF)
5.4 10.6 Apprentice
LD Liverpool v <u>WBA</u>
16.11.85 4–1

1985–86 WBA	1	15	1
1986–87 WBA	2	9	—
1986–87 Wolves	4	29	8
1987–88 Wolves	4	42	2

THOMPSON, David
15.4.69 Ashington (DF)
6.3 12.7 Apprentice
LD Barnsley v <u>Millwall</u>
19.12.87 4–1

1987–88 Millwall	2	5	—

THOMPSON, David
27.5.62 Manchester (FW)
5.10½ 12.4 Local
LD Hull C v <u>Rochdale</u>
8.5.82 2–1

1981–82 Rochdale	4	2	—
1982–83 Rochdale	4	46	5
1983–84 Rochdale	4	40	4
1984–85 Rochdale	4	40	4
1985–86 Rochdale	4	27	2
1985–86 *Manchester U*	1	—	—
1986–87 Notts Co	3	46	7
1987–88 Notts Co	3	—	—

THOMPSON, Garry
7.10.59 Birmingham (FW)
6.0 12.8 Apprentice
LD <u>Coventry C</u> v Aston Villa
21.3.78 2–3

1977–78 Coventry C	1	6	2
1978–79 Coventry C	1	20	8
1979–80 Coventry C	1	17	6
1980–81 Coventry C	1	35	8
1981–82 Coventry C	1	36	10
1982–83 Coventry C	1	20	4
1982–83 WBA	1	12	7
1983–84 WBA	1	37	13
1984–85 WBA	1	42	19
1985–86 Sheffield W	1	36	6
1986–87 Aston Villa	1	31	6
1987–88 Aston Villa	2	24	10

THOMPSON, Leslie
23.9.68 Cleethorpes (FW)
— — Local
LD <u>Hull C</u> v Ipswich T
10.10.87 1–0

1987–88 Hull	2	7	2

THOMPSON, Neil
2.10.63 Beverly (DF)
6.0 13.7 Nottingham F & Hull C
LD <u>Scarborough</u> v Wolves
15.8.87 2–2

1987–88 Scarborough	4	41	6

THOMPSON, Steve
21.1.64 Oldham (MF)
5.8½ 11.0 Apprentice
LD Derby Co v <u>Bolton W</u>
13.11.82 0–0

1982–83 Bolton W	2	3	—
1983–84 Bolton W	3	40	3
1984–85 Bolton W	3	34	4
1985–86 Bolton W	3	35	8
1986–87 Bolton W	3	44	8
1987–88 Bolton W	4	44	7

THOMPSON, Steve
28.7.55 Sheffield (MF)
6.1 14.4 Boston U
LD <u>Lincoln C</u> v Peterborough U
16.8.80 1–1

1979–80 Lincoln C	4	—	—
1980–81 Lincoln C	4	31	2
1981–82 Lincoln C	3	30	2
1982–83 Lincoln C	3	36	2
1983–84 Lincoln C	3	16	1
1984–85 Lincoln C	3	41	1
1985–86 Charlton Ath	2	38	—
1986–87 Charlton Ath	1	34	—
1987–88 Charlton Ath	1	23	—

THOMSON, Billy
10.2.58 Linwood (GK)
6.2 12.3 Glasgow United
LD Morton v <u>St Mirren</u>
26.8.78 1–3

1975–76 Partick T	1	—	—
1976–77 Partick T	P	—	—
1977–78 Partick T	P	—	—
1978–79 St Mirren	P	34	—
1979–80 St Mirren	P	36	—
1980–81 St Mirren	P	36	—
1981–82 St Mirren	P	35	—
1982–83 St Mirren	P	35	—
1983–84 St Mirren	P	30	—
1984–85 Dundee U	P	11	—
1985–86 Dundee U	P	28	—
1986–87 Dundee U	P	42	—
1987–88 Dundee U	P	36	—

THOMSON, Bobby
21.3.55 Glasgow (FW)
5.10 11.6
LD <u>St Johnstone</u> v Falkirk
23.2.74 2–0

1973–74 St Johnstone	1	6	—
1974–75 St Johnstone	1	14	—
1975–76 St Johnstone	P	26	3
1976–77 St Johnstone	1	36	7
1977–78 St Johnstone	1	36	7
1978–79 Morton	P	30	11
1979–80 Morton	P	27	11
1980–81 Morton	P	29	2
1981–82 Morton	P	4	1
1981–82 Middlesbrough	1	20	2
1982–83 Hibernian	P	30	6
1983–84 Hibernian	P	16	4
1984–85 Hibernian	P	16	3
1984–85 Morton	P	11	2
1985–86 Hibs	P	—	—
1985–86 Blackpool	3	16	2
1986–87 Blackpool	3	36	4
1987–88 Hamilton A	1	22	4

THORN, Andy
12.11.66 Carshalton (DF)
6.0 11.5 Apprentice
LD Notts Co v <u>Wimbledon</u>
6.4.85 2–3

1984–85 Wimbledon	2	10	—
1985–86 Wimbledon	2	28	—
1986–87 Wimbledon	1	34	2
1987–88 Wimbledon	1	35	—

THORNBER, Stephen
11.10.65 Dewsbury (FW)
5.9 10.11 Local
LD <u>Halifax T</u> v Chester C
14.2.84 2–2

1983–84 Halifax T	4	4	1
1984–85 Halifax T	4	31	3
1985–86 Halifax T	4	18	—
1986–87 Halifax T	4	16	—
1987–88 Halifax T	4	35	—

PLAYER DIRECTORY

THORPE, Adrian
20.11.63 Chesterfield (FW)
5.6 11.0 Heanor T
LD Carlisle U v Bradford C
17.8.85 1–2

1984–85	Bradford C	3	—	—
1985–86	Bradford C	2	10	1
1986–87	Bradford C	2	5	—
1986–87	*Tranmere R*	4	5	3
1987–88	Bradford C	2	2	—
1987–88	Notts Co	3	23	5

THORPE, Andy
15.9.60 Stockport (DF)
5.11 12.0 Amateur
LD Hartlepool U v Stockport Co
8.4.78 2–0

1977–78	Stockport Co	4	4	—
1978–79	Stockport Co	4	38	—
1979–80	Stockport Co	4	36	1
1980–81	Stockport Co	4	38	1
1981–82	Stockport Co	4	46	—
1982–83	Stockport Co	4	46	—
1983–84	Stockport Co	4	45	1
1984–85	Stockport Co	4	31	—
1985–86	Stockport Co	4	30	—
1986–87	Tranmere R	4	39	—
1987–88	Tranmere R	4	14	—
1987–88	*Stockport Co*	4	12	—
1987–88	Stockport Co	4	8	—

TIGHE, Aaron
11.7.69 Banbury (MF)
5.9 10.9 Apprentice
LD —

1987–88	Luton T	1	—	—

TINKLER, John
24.8.68 Trimdon (FW)

LD Cambridge U v Hartlepool U
24.1.87 3–0

1986–87	Hartlepool U	4	2	—
1987–88	Hartlepool U	4	20	—

TINNION, Brian
23.2.68 Stanley (DF)
6.0 11.5 Apprentice
LD Everton v Newcastle U
20.4.87 3–0

1985–86	Newcastle U	1	—	—
1986–87	Newcastle U	1	3	—
1987–88	Newcastle U	1	16	1

TODD, Mark
4.12.67 Belfast (MF)
5.5½ 8.3½ YTS
LD Blackburn R v Sheffield U
1.1.88 4–1

1985–86	Manchester U	1	—	—
1986–87	Manchester U	1	—	—
1987–88	Sheffield U	2	12	—

TOMAN, Andy
7.3.62 Northallerton (MF)
— — Bishop Auckland
LD Lincoln C v Gillingham
17.8.85 1–0

1985–86	Lincoln C	3	24	4
1986–87	Hartlepool U	4	21	5
1987–88	Hartlepool U	4	46	17

TOMLINSON, David
13.12.68 Rotherham (FW)
— — Apprentice
LD Leicester C v Sheffield W
3.1.87 6–1

1986–87	Sheffield W	1	1	—
1987–88	Rotherham U	3	9	—

TOMLINSON, Paul
2.22.64 Brierley Hill (GK)
6.2 12.10 Middlewood R
LD Sheffield U v Southend U
26.11.83 5–0

1983–84	Sheffield U	3	30	—
1984–85	Sheffield U	2	2	—
1985–86	Sheffield U	2	—	—
1986–87	Sheffield U	2	5	—
1986–87	*Birmingham C*	2	11	—
1987–88	Bradford C	2	42	—

TORTOLANO, Joe
6.4.66 Stirling (FW)
5.8 11.2 Apprentice
LD Clydebank v Hibernian
30.10.85 2–4

1983–84	WBA	1	—	—
1984–85	WBA	1	—	—
1985–86	Hibernian	P	20	3
1986–87	Hibernian	P	33	—
1987–88	Hibernian	P	21	4

TOWNSEND, Andy
23.7.63 Maidstone (MF)
5.10½ 12.7 Weymouth
LD Southampton v Aston Villa
20.4.85 2–0

1984–85	Southampton	1	5	—
1985–86	Southampton	1	27	1
1986–87	Southampton	1	14	—
1987–88	Southampton	1	37	3

TRACEY, Simon
9.12.67 Woolwich (GK)
6.0 12.0 Apprentice
LD —

1985–86	Wimbledon	2	—	—
1986–87	Wimbledon	1	—	—
1987–88	Wimbledon	1	—	—

TRAIN, Ray
Nuneaton 10251 5 5 10 5
(MF) Apprentice

1968–69	Walsall	3	18	4
1969–70	Walsall	3	18	3
1970–71	Walsall	3	24	3
1971–72	Walsall	3	13	1
1971–72	Carlisle U	2	20	—
1972–73	Carlisle U	2	42	1
1973–74	Carlisle U	2	27	3
1974–75	Carlisle U	1	42	2
1975–76	Carlisle U	2	24	2
1975–76	Sunderland	2	12	—
1976–77	Sunderland	1	20	1
1976–77	Bolton W	2	14	—
1977–78	Bolton W	2	32	—
1978–79	Bolton W	1	5	—
1978–79	Watford	3	21	1
1979–80	Watford	2	42	1
1980–81	Watford	2	29	1
1981–82	Watford	2	—	—
1981–82	Oxford U	3	15	—
1982–83	Oxford U	3	34	—
1983–84	Oxford U	3	1	—
1983–84	*Bournemouth*	3	7	—
1983–84	*Northampton T*	4	—	—
1984–85	Northampton T	4	46	1
1985–86	Tranmere R	4	36	—
1986–87	Walsall	3	16	—
1987–88	Walsall	3	—	—

TREVITT, Simon
20.12.67 Dewsbury (DF)
5.11 11.2 Apprentice
LD Huddersfield T v Derby Co
4.10.86 2–0

1986–87	Huddersfield T	2	11	—
1987–88	Huddersfield T	2	37	1

TROTTER, Michael
27.10.69 Hartlepool (DF)
6.3 12.2 Apprentice
LD —

1987–88	Middlesbrough	2	—	—

TRUSSON, Mike
26.5.59 Northolt (FW)
5.10 12.4 Apprentice
LD Bristol R v Plymouth Arg
23.10.76 1–1

1976–77	Plymouth Arg	2	4	—
1977–78	Plymouth Arg	3	15	2
1978–79	Plymouth Arg	3	27	5
1978–79	*Stoke C*	2	—	—
1979–80	Plymouth Arg	3	27	8
1980–81	Sheffield U	3	39	8
1981–82	Sheffield U	4	44	11
1982–83	Sheffield U	3	32	9
1983–84	Sheffield U	3	11	3
1983–84	Rotherham U	3	25	2
1984–85	Rotherham U	3	45	7
1985–86	Rotherham U	3	37	6
1986–87	Rotherham U	3	17	4
1987–88	Brighton & HA	3	15	2

TUCKER, Gordon
5.1.68 Manchester (DF)
— — Derby Co
LD Plymouth Arg v Huddersfield T
22.8.87 6–1

1987–88 Huddersfield T	2	23	—

TURNBULL, Lee
27.9.67 Teesside (FW)
6.0 11.9 Local
LD Middlesbrough v Millwall
26.4.86 3–0

1985–86 Middlesbrough	2	2	—
1986–87 Middlesbrough	3	14	4
1987–88 Aston Villa	2	—	—
1987–88 Doncaster R	3	30	1

TURNER, Chris
15.9.58 Sheffield (GK)
5.10½ 11.11 Apprentice
LD Sheffield W v Walsall
21.8.76 0–0

1976–77 Sheffield W	3	45	—
1977–78 Sheffield W	3	23	—
1978–79 Sheffield W	3	23	—
1978–79 Lincoln C	3	5	—
1979–80 Sunderland	2	30	—
1980–81 Sunderland	1	27	—
1981–82 Sunderland	1	19	—
1982–83 Sunderland	1	35	—
1983–84 Sunderland	1	42	—
1984–85 Sunderland	1	42	—
1985–86 Manchester U	1	17	—
1986–87 Manchester U	1	23	—
1987–88 Manchester U	1	24	—

TURNER, Phil
12.2.62 Sheffield (MF)
5.8 10.13 Apprentice
LD Lincoln C v Wigan Ath
29.2.80 4–0

1979–80 Lincoln C	4	14	1
1980–81 Lincoln C	4	38	4
1981–82 Lincoln C	3	28	1
1982–83 Lincoln C	3	40	3
1983–84 Lincoln C	3	42	3
1984–85 Lincoln C	3	36	3
1985–86 Lincoln C	3	43	4
1986–87 Grimsby T	2	34	4
1987–88 Grimsby T	3	28	5
1987–88 Leicester C	2	8	—

TURNER, Robert
18.9.66 Durham (FW)
6.3½ 14.1 Apprentice
LD Grimsby T v Huddersfield T
1.1.85 5–1

1984–85 Huddersfield T	2	1	—
1985–86 Cardiff C	3	34	7
1986–87 Cardiff C	4	5	1
1986–87 Hartlepool U	4	7	1
1986–87 Bristol R	3	17	1
1987–88 Bristol R	3	9	1
1987–88 Wimbledon	1	4	—

TURNER, Wayne
9.3.61 Luton (DF)
5.9 11.5 Apprentice
LD Wrexham v Luton T
7.5.79 2–0

1977–78 Luton T	2	—	—
1978–79 Luton T	2	1	—
1979–80 Luton T	2	2	—
1980–81 Luton T	2	1	—
1981–82 Luton T	2	7	1
1981–82 Lincoln C	3	16	—
1982–83 Luton T	1	30	1
1983–84 Luton T	1	19	—
1984–85 Luton T	1	24	—
1985–86 Coventry C	1	15	1
1986–87 Brentford	3	32	—
1987–88 Brentford	3	24	2

TUTILL, Stephen
1.10.69 York (DF)
6.0 11.0 Apprentice
LD Chester C v York C
29.8.87 1–0

1987–88 York C	3	21	—

TYNAN, Tommy
17.11.55 Liverpool (FW)
5.10½ 11.11 Apprentice
LD Doncaster R v Swansea C
18.10.75 2–1

1972–73 Liverpool	1	—	—
1973–74 Liverpool	1	—	—
1974–75 Liverpool	1	—	—
1975–76 Liverpool	1	—	—
1975–76 Swansea C	4	6	2
1976–77 Liverpool	1	—	—
1976–77 Sheffield W	3	39	14
1977–78 Sheffield W	3	44	16
1978–79 Sheffield W	3	8	1
1978–79 Lincoln C	3	9	1
1978–79 Newport Co	4	20	7
1979–80 Newport Co	4	34	8
1980–81 Newport Co	3	45	13
1981–82 Newport Co	3	38	13
1982–83 Newport Co	3	46	25
1983–84 Plymouth Arg	3	35	12
1984–85 Plymouth Arg	3	45	31
1985–86 Rotherham U	3	30	13
1985–86 Plymouth Arg	3	9	9
1986–87 Rotherham U	3	2	—
1986–87 Plymouth Arg	2	40	18
1987–88 Plymouth Arg	2	43	16

UNDERHILL, Philip
— Bristol (DF)
5.6 9.9 Apprentice
LD —

1987–88 Southampton	1	—	—

UZZELL, John
31.3.59 Plymouth (DF)
5.10 11.3 Apprentice
LD Plymouth Arg v Preston NE
20.8.77 0–0

1976–77 Plymouth Arg	2	—	—
1977–78 Plymouth Arg	3	44	1
1978–79 Plymouth Arg	3	21	—
1979–80 Plymouth Arg	3	1	—
1980–81 Plymouth Arg	3	16	—
1981–82 Plymouth Arg	3	35	2
1982–83 Plymouth Arg	3	42	1
1983–84 Plymouth Arg	3	42	—
1984–85 Plymouth Arg	3	29	1
1985–86 Plymouth Arg	3	8	—
1986–87 Plymouth Arg	2	21	—
1987–88 Plymouth Arg	2	10	1

PLAYER DIRECTORY

VALENTINE, Peter
16.6.63 Huddersfield (MF)
5.11 10.10 Apprentice
LD Huddersfield T v Gillingham
6.3.82 2–0

1980–81	Huddersfield T	3	— —
1981–82	Huddersfield T	3	14 1
1982–83	Huddersfield T	3	5 —
1983–84	Bolton W	3	42 1
1984–85	Bolton W	3	26 —
1985–86	Bury	3	46 3
1986–87	Bury	3	46 2
1987–88	Bury	3	42 2

VAN DEN HAUWE, Pat
16.12.60 Dendermonde (DF)
6.0 10.8 Apprentice
LD Birmingham C v Manchester C
7.10.78 1–2

1978–79	Birmingham C	1	8 —
1979–80	Birmingham C	2	1 —
1980–81	Birmingham C	1	4 —
1981–82	Birmingham C	1	31 —
1982–83	Birmingham C	1	31 1
1983–84	Birmingham C	1	42 —
1984–85	Birmingham C	2	6 —
1984–85	Everton	1	31 —
1985–86	Everton	1	40 1
1986–87	Everton	1	11 1
1987–88	Everton	1	28 —

VARADI, Imre
8.7.59 Paddington (FW)
5.8½ 11.1 Letchworth GC
LD Sheffield U v Crystal Palace
2.9.78 0–2

1977–78	Sheffield U	2	— —
1978–79	Sheffield U	2	10 4
1978–79	Everton	1	— —
1979–80	Everton	1	4 —
1980–81	Everton	1	22 6
1981–82	Newcastle U	2	42 18
1982–83	Newcastle U	2	39 21
1983–84	Sheffield W	2	38 17
1984–85	Sheffield W	1	38 16
1985–86	WBA	1	32 9
1986–87	Manchester C	1	30 9
1987–88	Manchester C	2	32 17

VAUGHAN, Nigel
20.5.59 Caerleon (MF)
5.5 8.9 Apprentice
LD Rochdale v Newport Co
13.11.76 0–0

1976–77	Newport Co	4	1 —
1977–78	Newport Co	4	11 —
1978–79	Newport Co	4	27 4
1979–80	Newport Co	4	46 12
1980–81	Newport Co	3	45 1
1981–82	Newport Co	3	44 3
1982–83	Newport Co	3	43 7

1983–84	Newport Co	3	7 5
1983–84	Cardiff C	2	36 8
1984–85	Cardiff C	2	38 16
1985–86	Cardiff C	3	43 12
1986–87	Cardiff C	4	32 6
1986–87	*Reading*	2	5 1
1987–88	Wolves	4	36 6

VENISON, Barry
16.8.64 Consett (MF)
5.9 11.9 Apprentice
LD Notts Co v Sunderland
10.10.81 2–0

1981–82	Sunderland	1	20 1
1982–83	Sunderland	1	37 —
1983–84	Sunderland	1	41 —
1984–85	Sunderland	1	39 1
1985–86	Sunderland	2	36 —
1986–87	Liverpool	1	33 —
1987–88	Liverpool	1	18 —

VENUS, Mark
6.4.67 Hartlepool (DF)
6.0 11.8
LD Bury v Hartlepool U
8.4.85 1–0

1984–85	Hartlepool U	4	4 —
1985–86	Leicester C	1	1 —
1986–87	Leicester C	1	39 —
1987–88	Leicester C	2	21 1
1987–88	*Wolves*	4	— —
1987–88	Wolves	4	4 —

VICKERS, Steve
13.10.67 Bishop Auckland (DF)
6.2 12.0 Spennymoor U
LD Tranmere R v Northampton T
4.4.86 1–3

1985–86	Tranmere R	4	3 —
1986–87	Tranmere R	4	36 2
1987–88	Tranmere R	4	46 1

VINEY, Keith
26.10.57 Portsmouth (DF)
5.11 11.11 Apprentice
LD Fulham v Portsmouth
6.3.76 0–1

1975–76	Portsmouth	2	7 —
1976–77	Portsmouth	3	35 1
1977–78	Portsmouth	3	4 —
1978–79	Portsmouth	4	39 2
1979–80	Portsmouth	4	16 —
1980–81	Portsmouth	3	41 —
1981–82	Portsmouth	3	24 —
1982–83	Exeter C	3	44 4
1983–84	Exeter C	3	42 —
1984–85	Exeter C	4	45 1
1985–86	Exeter C	4	45 2
1986–87	Exeter C	4	45 1
1987–88	Exeter C	4	46 —

WADDLE, Chris
14.12.60 Hepworth (FW)
6.0 11.5 Tow Law T
LD Newcastle U v Shrewsbury T
22.10.80 1–0

1980–81	Newcastle U	2	13 1
1981–82	Newcastle U	2	42 7
1982–83	Newcastle U	2	37 7
1983–84	Newcastle U	2	42 18
1984–85	Newcastle U	1	36 13
1985–86	Tottenham H	1	39 11
1986–87	Tottenham H	1	39 6
1987–88	Tottenham H	1	22 2

WADE, Bryan
25.6.63 Bath (FW)
5.8 11.5 Trowbridge T
LD Peterborough U v Swindon T
14.9.85 3–0

1985–86	Swindon T	4	34 10
1986–87	Swindon T	3	23 8
1987–88	Swindon T	2	3 —

WAKENSHAW, Robbie
22.12.65 Northumberland (FW)
5.10 11.10 Apprentice
LD Everton v Manchester U
5.5.84 1–1

1983–84	Everton	1	1 1
1984–85	Everton	1	2 —
1985–86	Everton	1	— —
1985–86	Carlisle U	2	8 2
1985–86	*Doncaster R*	3	8 3
1986–87	Rochdale	4	29 5
1987–88	Crewe Alex	4	20 1

WALFORD, Steve
5.1.58 Highgagte (DF)
6.1 11.7 Apprentice
LD Tottenham H v Liverpool
13.12.75 0–4

1974–75	Tottenham H	1	— —
1975–76	Tottenham H	1	2 —
1976–77	Tottenham H	1	— —
1977–78	Arsenal	1	5 —
1978–79	Arsenal	1	33 2
1979–80	Arsenal	1	19 1
1980–81	Arsenal	1	20 —
1980–81	Norwich C	1	10 —
1981–82	Norwich C	2	42 1
1982–83	Norwich C	1	41 1
1983–84	West Ham U	1	41 2
1984–85	West Ham U	1	33 —
1985–86	West Ham U	1	27 —
1986–87	West Ham U	1	14 —
1987–88	West Ham U	1	— —
1987–88	*Huddersfield T*	2	12 —

WALKER, Alan
17.12.59 Mossley (DF)
6.1 12.7 Telford U
LD Lincoln C v Burnley
22.10.83 3–1

1983–84	Lincoln C	3	33	2
1984–85	Lincoln C	3	42	2
1985–86	Millwall	2	26	3
1986–87	Millwall	2	40	1
1987–88	Millwall	2	26	4
1987–88	Gillingham	3	7	—

WALKER, Andy
6.4.65 Glasgow (FW)
5.8 10.7 Baillieston Juniors
LD Meadowbank Th v Motherwell
1.12.84 4–2

1984–85	Motherwell	1	11	3
1985–86	Motherwell	1	22	4
1986–87	Motherwell	P	43	10
1987–88	Celtic	P	42	16

WALKER, Clive
26.5.57 Oxford (FW)
5.8½ 11.4 Apprentice
LD Burnley v Chelsea
23.4.77 1–0

1974–75	Chelsea	1	—	—
1975–76	Chelsea	2	—	—
1976–77	Chelsea	2	1	—
1977–78	Chelsea	1	23	7
1978–79	Chelsea	1	30	4
1979–80	Chelsea	2	36	13
1980–81	Chelsea	2	37	11
1981–82	Chelsea	2	36	16
1982–83	Chelsea	2	29	6
1983–84	Chelsea	2	6	3
1984–85	Sunderland	1	38	10
1985–86	Sunderland	2	12	—
1985–86	QPR	1	5	1
1986–87	QPR	1	16	—
1987–88	QPR	1	—	—
1987–88	*Fulham*	3	1	2
1987–88	Fulham	3	25	6

WALKER, Des
26.11.65 Hackney (DF)
5.11 11.3 Apprentice
LD Nottingham F v Everton
13.3.84 1–0

1983–84	Nottingham F	1	4	—
1984–85	Nottingham F	1	3	—
1985–86	Nottingham F	1	39	—
1986–87	Nottingham F	1	41	—
1987–88	Nottingham F	1	35	—

WALKER, Gary
12.9.69 Billinge (DF)
6.1 12.5 Apprentice
LD —

1987–88	Preston NE	3	—	—

WALKER, Nicky
29.9.62 Aberdeen (GK)
6.2 11.12 Elgin C
LD Chelsea v Leicester C
9.3.82 4–1

1980–81	Leicester C	1	—	—
1981–82	Leicester C	2	6	—
1982–83	Motherwell	P	16	—
1983–84	Motherwell	P	15	—
1983–84	Rangers	P	8	—
1984–85	Rangers	P	14	—
1985–86	Rangers	P	34	—
1986–87	Rangers	P	2	—
1987–88	*Dumfermline Ath*	P	1	—
1987–88	Rangers	P	5	—

WALKER, Ray
28.9.63 North Shields (DF)
5.10 11.9 Apprentice
LD West Ham U v Aston Villa
23.4.83 2–0

1981–82	Aston Villa	1	—	—
1982–83	Aston Villa	1	1	—
1983–84	Aston Villa	1	8	—
1984–85	Aston Villa	1	7	—
1984–85	*Port Vale*	4	15	1
1985–86	Aston Villa	1	7	—
1986–87	Port Vale	3	45	4
1987–88	Port Vale	3	42	6

WALLACE, Danny
21.1.64 London (FW)
5.4½ 9.10 Apprentice
LD Manchester U v Southampton
29.11.80 1–1

1980–81	Southampton	1	2	—
1981–82	Southampton	1	7	—
1982–83	Southampton	1	35	12
1983–84	Southampton	1	41	11
1984–85	Southampton	1	35	7
1985–86	Southampton	1	35	8
1986–87	Southampton	1	31	8
1987–88	Southampton	1	35	11

WALLACE, Ray
— Lewisham (DF)
5.6 10.2 Apprentice
LD —

1987–88	Southampton	1	—	—

WALLACE, Rodney
— Lewisham (FW)
5.7 10.1 Apprentice
LD Newcastle U v Southampton
26.9.87 2–1

1987–88	Southampton	1	15	1

WALLER, David
20.12.63 Urmston (FW)
5.10 10.0 Local
LD Crewe Alex v Bournemouth
23.1.82 0–0

1981–82	Crewe Alex	4	1	—
1982–83	Crewe Alex	4	37	17
1983–84	Crewe Alex	4	42	10
1984–85	Crewe Alex	4	44	15
1985–86	Crewe Alex	4	44	13
1986–87	Shrewsbury T	2	11	—
1987–88	Chesterfield	3	40	19

WALLING, Dean
— — (FW)
— — Leeds U
LD Scunthorpe U v Rochdale
5.9.87 1–0

1987–88	Rochdale	4	12	2

WALLINGTON, Mark
17.9.52 Sleaford (GK)
6.1 14.2½
LD Torquay U v Walsall
11.9.71 2–2

1971–72	Walsall	3	11	—
1971–72	Leicester C	1	5	—
1972–73	Leicester C	1	1	—
1973–74	Leicester C	1	—	—
1974–75	Leicester C	1	30	—
1975–76	Leicester C	1	42	—
1976–77	Leicester C	1	42	—
1977–78	Leicester C	1	42	—
1978–79	Leicester C	2	42	—
1979–80	Leicester C	2	42	—
1980–81	Leicester C	1	42	—
1981–82	Leicester C	2	36	—
1982–83	Leicester C	2	42	—
1983–84	Leicester C	1	35	—
1984–85	Leicester C	1	11	—
1985–86	Derby Co	3	33	—
1986–87	Derby Co	2	34	—
1987–88	Derby Co	1	—	—

WALSH, Alan
9.12.56 Darlington (FW)
6.0 11.0 Horden CW
LD QPR v Middlesbrough
1.4.78 1–0

1976–77	Middlesbrough	1	—	—
1977–78	Middlesbrough	1	3	—
1978–79	Middlesbrough	1	—	—
1978–79	Darlington	4	33	9
1979–80	Darlington	4	43	15
1980–81	Darlington	4	46	22
1981–82	Darlington	4	45	13
1982–83	Darlington	4	46	18
1983–84	Darlington	4	38	10
1984–85	Bristol C	3	45	20
1985–86	Bristol C	3	44	18
1986–87	Bristol C	3	41	16
1987–88	Bristol C	3	42	12

PLAYER DIRECTORY

WALSH, Andrew
15.2.70 Preston (DF)
6.0 11.2 Local
LD Bury v Chester C
7.5.88 0–1

1987–88 Bury	3	1	—

WALSH, Colin
22.7.62 Hamilton (MF)
5.9 10.11 Apprentice
LD Coventry C v Nottingham F
29.11.80 1–1

1979–80 Nottingham F	1	—	—
1980–81 Nottingham F	1	16	4
1981–82 Nottingham F	1	15	3
1982–83 Nottingham F	1	37	5
1983–84 Nottingham F	1	38	13
1984–85 Nottingham F	1	13	1
1985–86 Nottingham F	1	20	6
1986–87 Charlton Ath	1	33	6
1987–88 Charlton Ath	1	11	3

WALSH, Gary
21.3.68 Wigan (GK)
6.1 12.12
LD Aston Villa v Manchester U
13.12.86 3–3

1984–85 Manchester U	1	—	—
1985–86 Manchester U	1	—	—
1986–87 Manchester U	1	14	—
1987–88 Manchester U	1	16	—

WALSH, Ian
4.9.58 St Davids (FW)
5.9½ 11.6 Apprentice
LD Crystal Palace v Chester
4.9.76 1–2

1975–76 Crystal Palace	3	—	—
1976–77 Crystal Palace	3	1	—
1977–78 Crystal Palace	2	16	2
1978–79 Crystal Palace	2	33	8
1979–80 Crystal Palace	1	29	6
1980–81 Crystal Palace	1	25	5
1981–82 Crystal Palace	2	13	2
1981–82 Swansea C	1	5	2
1982–83 Swansea C	1	8	3
1983–84 Swansea C	2	24	6
1984–85 Barnsley	2	16	—
1985–86 Barnsley	2	33	15
1986–87 Grimsby T	2	30	8
1987–88 Grimsby T	3	11	5
1987–88 Cardiff C	4	6	—

WALSH, Mario
19.1.66 Paddington (FW)
6.1 11.12 Apprentice
LD Port Vale v Torquay U
26.1.85 2–2

1983–84 Portsmouth	2	—	—
1984–85 Portsmouth	2	—	—
1984–85 Torquay U	4	21	5
1985–86 Torquay U	4	41	7
1986–87 Torquay U	4	38	6
1987–88 Colchester U	4	11	2

WALSH, Mick
20.6.56 Manchester (DF)
6.0 12.0
LD Nottingham F v Bolton W
8.2.75 2–3

1974–75 Bolton W	2	5	—
1975–76 Bolton W	2	9	—
1976–77 Bolton W	2	8	—
1977–78 Bolton W	2	41	1
1978–79 Bolton W	1	42	1
1979–80 Bolton W	1	42	1
1980–81 Bolton W	2	30	1
1981–82 Everton	1	18	—
1982–83 Everton	1	2	—
1982–83 *Norwich C*	1	5	—
1982–83 *Burnley*	2	3	—
Ft Lauderdale			
1983–84 Manchester C	2	4	—
1983–84 Blackpool	4	20	1
1984–85 Blackpool	4	35	1
1985–86 Blackpool	3	25	1
1986–87 Blackpool	3	34	2
1987–88 Blackpool	3	30	—

WALSH, Paul
1.10.62 Plumstead (FW)
5.7 10.8 Apprentice
LD Charlton Ath v Shrewsbury T
22.9.79 2–1

1979–80 Charlton Ath	2	9	—
1980–81 Charlton Ath	3	40	11
1981–82 Charlton Ath	2	38	13
1982–83 Luton T	1	41	13
1983–84 Luton T	1	39	11
1984–85 Liverpool	1	26	8
1985–86 Liverpool	1	20	11
1986–87 Liverpool	1	23	6
1987–88 Liverpool	1	8	—
1987–88 Tottenham H	1	11	1

WALSH, Steve
3.11.64 Fulwood (DF)
6.2 14.0 Local
LD Wigan Ath v Newport Co
330.10.82 0–1

1982–83 Wigan Ath	3	31	—
1983–84 Wigan Ath	3	42	1
1984–85 Wigan Ath	3	40	2
1985–86 Wigan Ath	3	13	1
1986–87 Leicester C	1	21	—
1987–88 Leicester C	2	32	7

WALTERS, Mark
12.1.61 Birmingham(FW)
5.9 10.12 Apprentice
LD Aston Villa v Leeds U
24.8.82 1–4

1981–82 Aston Villa	1	1	—
1982–83 Aston Villa	1	22	1
1983–84 Aston Villa	1	37	8
1984–85 Aston Villa	1	36	10
1985–86 Aston Villa	1	40	10
1986–87 Aston Villa	1	21	3
1987–88 Aston Villa	2	24	7
1987–88 Rangers	P	—	—

WALTON, Mark
1.6.69 Merthyr (GK)
6.2 13.12 Luton T
LD Colchester U v Wolves
21.11.87 0–1

1987–88 Luton T	1	—	—
1987–88 *Colchester U*	4	4	—
1987–88 Colchester U	4	13	—

WALWYN, Keith
17.2.56 W Indies (FW)
6.1 13.2 Winterton
LD Oxford U v Chesterfield
6.9.80 0–3

1979–80 Chesterfield	3	—	—
1980–81 Chesterfield	3	3	2
1981–82 York C	4	44	23
1982–83 York C	4	41	21
1983–84 York C	3	45	25
1984–85 York C	3	27	9
1985–86 York C	2	46	22
1986–87 York C	3	42	18
1987–88 Blackpool	3	39	13

WARBURTON, Ray
7.10.67 Rotherham (DF)
6.0 11.5 Apprentice
LD York C v Rotherham U
3.5.85 3–0

1984–85 Rotherham U	3	1	—
1985–86 Rotherham U	3	—	—
1986–87 Rotherham U	3	3	—
1987–88 Rotherham U	3	—	—

WARD, Mark
10.10.62 Prescot (MF)
5.6 9.12 Northwich Vic
LD Oldham Ath v Brighton & HA
27.8.83 1–0

1983–84 Oldham Ath	2	42	6
1984–85 Oldham Ath	2	42	6
1985–86 West Ham U	1	42	3
1986–87 West Ham U	1	37	1
1987–88 West Ham U	1	37	1

WARD, Paul
15.9.63 Sedgefield (DF)
5.11 12.5 Apprentice
LD Newcastle U v Middlesbrough
8.9.82 1–1

1981–82 Chelsea	1	—	—
1982–83 Middlesbrough	2	15	—
1983–84 Middlesbrough	2	28	1
1984–85 Middlesbrough	2	30	—
1985–86 Middlesbrough	2	3	—
1985–86 Darlington	3	35	2
1986–87 Darlington	3	44	1
1987–88 Darlington	4	45	6

WARD, Peter
15.10.64 Co Durham (FW)
6.0 11.10 Chester-le-Street
LD Oldham Ath v Huddersfield T
28.2.87 2–0

1986–87 Huddersfield T	2	7	—
1987–88 Huddersfield T	2	26	2

Neil Webb
Photo: Bob Thomas Sports Photography.

PLAYER DIRECTORY

WARK, John
4.8.57 Glasgow (MF)
5.10½ 11.12 Apprentice
LD Ipswich T v Leicester C
29.3.75 2-1

1974–75 Ipswich T	1	3	—
1975–76 Ipswich T	1	3	—
1976–77 Ipswich T	1	33	10
1977–78 Ipswich T	1	18	5
1978–79 Ipswich T	1	42	6
1979–80 Ipswich T	1	41	12
1980–81 Ipswich T	1	40	18
1981–82 Ipswich T	1	42	18
1982–83 Ipswich T	1	42	20
1983–84 Ipswich T	1	32	5
1983–84 Liverpool	1	9	2
1984–85 Liverpool	1	40	18
1985–86 Liverpool	1	9	3
1986–87 Liverpool	1	11	5
1987–88 Liverpool	1	1	—
1987–88 Ipswich	2	7	—

WARREN, Lee
— — (MF)
— — Leeds U
LD Cardiff C v Rochdale
31.10.87 1-0

1987–88 Rochdale	4	31	1

WASSALL, Darren
27.6.68 Edgbaston (DF)
— — Apprentice
LD Stockport Co v Hereford U
23.10.87 0-2

1987–88 Nottingham F	1	3	—
1987–88 *Hereford U*	4	5	—

WATSON, Alex
5.4.68 Liverpool (DF)
5.11½ 11.9 Apprentice
LD QPR v Liverpool
5.3.88 0-1

1984–85 Liverpool	1	—	—
1985–86 Liverpool	1	—	—
1986–87 Liverpool	1	—	—
1987–88 Liverpool	1	2	—

WATSON, Andy
3.9.59 Aberdeen (MF)
5.10 11.10 Sunnyside
LD Ayr U v Aberdeen
7.1.78 1-1

1976–77 Aberdeen	P	—	—
1977–78 Aberdeen	P	1	—
1978–79 Aberdeen	P	2	—
1979–80 Aberdeen	P	17	5
1980–81 Aberdeen	P	29	—
1981–82 Aberdeen	P	30	5
1982–83 Aberdeen	P	18	1
1983–84 Leeds U	2	31	7
1984–85 Leeds U	2	7	—

1984–85 Hearts	P	16	3
1985–86 Hearts	P	12	—
1986–87 Hearts	P	28	3
1987–88 Hibernian	P	30	3

WATSON, Dave
20.11.61 Liverpool (DF)
5.11½ 11.12 Amateur
LD Ipswich v Norwich C
26.12.80 2-0

1979–80 Liverpool	1	—	—
1980–81 Liverpool	1	—	—
1980–81 Norwich C	1	18	3
1981–82 Norwich C	2	38	3
1982–83 Norwich C	1	35	1
1983–84 Norwich C	1	40	1
1984–85 Norwich C	1	39	—
1985–86 Norwich C	2	42	2
1986–87 Everton	1	35	3
1987–88 Everton	1	37	4

WAUGH, Keith
27.10.56 Sunderland (GK)
5.11 12.2 Apprentice
LD Brighton & HA v Peterborough U
16.10.76 1-0

1974–75 Sunderland	2	—	—
1975–76 Sunderland	2	—	—
1976–77 Peterborough U	3	32	—
1977–78 Peterborough U	3	26	—
1978–79 Peterborough U	3	46	—
1979–80 Peterborough U	4	46	—
1980–81 Peterborough U	4	45	—
1981–82 Sheffield U	4	45	—
1982–83 Sheffield U	3	28	—
1983–84 Sheffield U	3	16	—
1984–85 Sheffield U	2	10	—
1984–85 *Bristol C*	3	3	—
1984–85 *Cambridge U*	3	4	—
1985–86 Bristol C	3	44	—
1986–87 Bristol C	3	46	—
1987–88 Bristol C	3	40	—

WEATHERLY, Mark
18.1.58 Ramsgate (DF)
6.0 12.0 Apprentice
LD Bournemouth v Gillingham
24.8.74 2-0

1974–75 Gillingham	3	5	1
1975–76 Gillingham	3	18	5
1976–77 Gillingham	3	17	2
1977–78 Gillingham	3	24	2
1978–79 Gillingham	3	46	2
1979–80 Gillingham	3	45	1
1980–81 Gillingham	3	43	1
1981–82 Gillingham	3	33	1
1982–83 Gillingham	3	43	10
1983–84 Gillingham	3	32	9
1984–85 Gillingham	3	35	2
1985–86 Gillingham	3	38	7
1986–87 Gillingham	3	44	4
1987–88 Gillingham	3	17	—

WEBB, Alan
1.1.63 Wellington (DF)
5.10 12.0 Apprentice
LD Brighton & HA v WBA
27.2.82 2-2

1979–80 WBA	1	—	—
1980–81 WBA	1	—	—
1981–82 WBA	1	6	—
1982–83 WBA	1	13	—
1983–84 WBA	1	5	—
1983–84 *Lincoln C*	3	11	—
1984–85 Port Vale	4	46	—
1985–86 Port Vale	4	39	1
1986–87 Port Vale	3	21	1
1987–88 Port Vale	3	26	—

WEBB, Jamie
— Portsmouth (MF)
5.8 10.6 Apprentice
LD —

1987–88 Southampton	1	—	—

WEBB, Neil
30.7.63 Reading (MF)
5.11 11.7 Apprentice
LD Mansfield T v Reading
16.2.80 2-2

1979–80 Reading	3	5	—
1980–81 Reading	3	27	7
1981–82 Reading	3	40	15
1982–83 Portsmouth	3	42	8
1983–84 Portsmouth	2	40	10
1984–85 Portsmouth	2	41	16
1985–86 Nottingham F	1	38	14
1986–87 Nottingham F	1	32	14
1987–88 Nottingham F	1	40	13

WEBSTER, Simon
20.1.64 Earl Shilton (DF)
6.0 11.7 Apprentice
LD Tottenham H v Everton
3.1.83 2-1

1981–82 Tottenham H	1	—	—
1982–83 Tottenham H	1	2	—
1983–84 Tottenham H	1	1	—
1983–84 *Exeter C*	4	26	—
1984–85 Tottenham H	1	—	—
1984–85 *Norwich C*	1	—	—
1984–85 Huddersfield T	2	16	1
1985–86 Huddersfield T	2	41	2
1986–87 Huddersfield T	2	39	1
1987–88 Huddersfield T	2	22	—
1987–88 *Sheffield U*	2	1	—
1987–88 Sheffield U	2	4	1

WEGERLE, Roy
19.3.64 South Africa (FW)
— — Tampa Bay R.
LD Everton v Chelsea
8.11.86 2-2

1986–87 Chelsea	1	12	2
1987–88 Chelsea	1	11	1
1987–88 *Swindon T*	2	7	1

WEIR, Jim
15.6.69 Motherwell (DF)
6.0 11.2 Motherwell Orbiston BC
LD Hibernian v <u>Hamilton A</u>
25.4.87 1-1

1986–87 Hamilton A	P	3	—
1987–88 Hamilton A	1	6	—

WEIR, Michael
16.1.66 Edinburgh (MF)
5.4 9.2 Portobello Thistle
LD <u>Hibernian</u> v Dumbarton
15.9.84 2-3

1982–83 Hibernian	P	—	—
1983–84 Hibernian	P	—	—
1984–85 Hibernian	P	—	—
1985–86 Hibernian	P	7	—
1986–87 Hibernian	P	24	4
1987–88 Hibernian	P	5	1
1987–88 Luton T	1	8	—
1987–88 Hibernian	P	13	2

WEIR, Peter
18.1.58 Johnstone (FW)
6.0 11.9 Neilston Juniors
LD Rangers v <u>St Mirren</u>
12.8.78 0-1

1978–79 St Mirren	P	6	—
1979–80 St Mirren	P	26	2
1980–81 St Mirren	P	28	2
1981–82 Aberdeen	P	25	2
1982–83 Aberdeen	P	31	6
1983–84 Aberdeen	P	27	5
1984–85 Aberdeen	P	16	3
1985–86 Aberdeen	P	22	5
1986–87 Aberdeen	P	34	2
1987–88 Aberdeen	P	5	—
1987–88 Leicester C	2	18	2

WELCH, Keith
3.10.68 Bolton (GK)
6.0 12.0 YTS
LD <u>Rochdale</u> v Orient
7.2.87 0-0

1986–87 Bolton W	3	—	—
1986–87 Rochdale	4	24	—
1987–88 Rochdale	4	46	—

WELLS, Peter
13.8.56 Nottingham (GK)
6.1 13.0 Apprentice
LD <u>Nottingham F</u> v York C
29.11.75 1-0

1974–75 Nottingham F	2	—	—
1975–76 Nottingham F	2	23	—
1976–77 Nottingham F	2	4	—
1976–77 Southampton	2	24	—

1977–78 Southampton	2	30	—
1978–79 Southampton	1	19	—
1979–80 Southampton	1	25	—
1980–81 Southampton	1	30	—
1981–82 Southampton	1	10	—
1982–83 Southampton	1	3	—
1982–83 *Millwall*	3	18	—
1983–84 Millwall	3	15	—
1984–85 Millwall	3	—	—
1985–86 Orient	4	45	—
1986–87 Orient	4	39	—
1987–88 Orient	4	46	—

WELSH, Brian
23.2.69 Edinburgh (DF)
6.2 12.1 Tynecastle BC
LD Hearts v <u>Dundee U</u>
11.5.87 1-1

1986–87 Dundee U	P	1	—
1987–88 Dundee U	P	1	1

WEST, Colin
19.9.67 Middlesbrough (FW)
5.7½ 11.0 Apprentice
LD East Fife v <u>Partick Th</u>
20.9.86 2-0

1985–86 Chelsea	1	—	—
1986–87 *Partick Th*	1	24	10
1986–87 Chelsea	1	7	1
1987–88 Chelsea	1	9	3

WEST, Colin
13.11.62 Wallsend (FW)
6.2 13.13 Apprentice
LD <u>Sunderland</u> v Tottenham H
17.10.81 0-2

1980–81 Sunderland	1	—	—
1981–82 Sunderland	1	18	6
1982–83 Sunderland	1	23	3
1983–84 Sunderland	1	38	9
1984–85 Sunderland	1	23	3
1984–85 Watford	1	12	7
1985–86 Watford	1	33	13
1986–87 Rangers	P	44	2
1987–88 Rangers	P	1	—
1987–88 Sheffield W	1	25	7

WEST, Gary
25.8.64 Scunthorpe (DF)
6.2 12.7 Apprentice
LD Exeter C v <u>Sheffield U</u>
23.10.82 0-3

1982–83 Sheffield U	3	26	1
1983–84 Sheffield U	3	24	—
1984–85 Sheffield U	3	25	—
1985–86 Lincoln C	3	38	2
1986–87 Lincoln C	4	45	2
1987–88 Gillingham	3	42	2

WESTLEY, Graham
4.3.68 London (FW)
5.9 10.11 QPR Apprentice
LD <u>Gillingham</u> v Bristol R
3.5.86 2-0

1985–86 Gillingham	3	1	—
1986–87 Gillingham	3	1	—
1987–88	1	—	—

WESTLEY, Shane
16.6.65 Canterbury (DF)
6.2 12.10 Apprentice
LD <u>Charlton Ath</u> v Crystal Palace
27.12.83 1-0

1983–84 Charlton Ath	2	8	—
1984–85 Charlton Ath	2	—	—
1984–85 Southend U	4	12	—
1985–86 Southend U	4	36	5
1986–87 Southend U	4	32	—
1987–88 Southend U	3	36	5

WESTON, Ian
6.5.68 Bristol (DF)
5.10 11.10 Apprentice
LD Brentford v <u>Bristol R</u>
28.12.86 1-2

1986–87 Bristol R	3	11	—
1987–88 Bristol R	3	5	—

WESTWOOD, Gary
3.4.63 Barrow (GK)
6.0 13.12 Apprentice
LD <u>Reading</u> v Darlington
1.10.83 1-0

1980–81 Ipswich T	1	—	—
1981–82 Ipswich T	1	—	—
1981–82 *Charlton Ath*	2	—	—
1982–83 Ipswich T	1	—	—
1982–83 *Crystal Palace*	2	—	—
1983–84 Ipswich T	1	—	—
1983–84 *Reading*	4	5	—
1983–84 *Peterborough U*	4	—	—
1984–85 Reading	3	43	—
1985–86 Reading	3	46	—
1986–87 Reading	2	24	—
1987–88 Reading	2	10	—

WHARTON, Ken
28.11.60 Newcastle (MF)
5.8 8.10 Grainger Park BC
LD West Ham U v <u>Newcastle U</u>
24.3.79 5-0

1978–79 Newcastle U	2	2	—
1979–80 Newcastle U	2	1	—
1980–81 Newcastle U	2	36	—
1981–82 Newcastle U	2	33	5
1982–83 Newcastle U	2	41	5
1983–84 Newcastle U	2	41	4
1984–85 Newcastle U	1	35	6
1985–86 Newcastle U	1	15	2
1986–87 Newcastle U	1	37	2
1987–88 Newcastle U	1	31	2

PLAYER DIRECTORY

WHEELER, Paul
3.1.65 Caerphilly (MF)
5.7½ 9.4 Apprentice
LD Cardiff C v Derby Co
28.9.85 0–2

1982–83 Bristol R	3	—	—
1983–84 Bristol R	3	—	—
Aberaman			
1985–86 Cardiff C	3	21	2
1986–87 Cardiff C	4	37	7
1987–88 Cardiff C	4	4	16

WHELAN, Ronnie
25.9.61 Dublin (MF)
5.9 10.13 Home Farm Eire
LD Liverpool v Stoke C
3.4.81 3–0

1979–80 Liverpool	1	—	—
1980–81 Liverpool	1	1	1
1981–82 Liverpool	1	32	10
1982–83 Liverpool	1	28	2
1983–84 Liverpool	1	23	4
1984–85 Liverpool	1	37	7
1985–86 Liverpool	1	39	10
1986–87 Liverpool	1	39	3
1987–88 Liverpool	1	28	1

WHELLANS, Robert
14.2.69 Harrogate (FW)
5.7 11.0 YTS
LD Rochdale v Hartlepool U
28.12.87 0–2

1987–88 Bradford C	2	—	—
1987–88 Hartlepool U	4	11	1

WHITE, David
30.10.67 Manchester (MF)
— —
LD Luton T v Manchester C
27.9.86 1–0

1985–86 Manchester C	1	—	—
1986–87 Manchester C	1	24	1
1987–88 Manchester C	2	44	13

WHITE, Devon
2.3.64 Nottingham (FW)
6.3 13.8 Boston
LD Bristol R v Aldershot
29.8.87 3–1

1987–88 Bristol R	3	39	15

WHITE, Steve
2.1.59 Chipping Sodbury (FW)
5.10½ 11.4 Mangotsfield U
LD Southampton v Bristol R
27.3.78 3–1

1977–78 Bristol R	2	8	4
1978–79 Bristol R	2	27	10
1979–80 Bristol R	2	15	6

1979–80 Luton T	2	9	—
1980–81 Luton T	2	21	7
1981–82 Luton T	2	42	18
1982–83 Charlton Ath	2	29	12
1982–83 Lincoln C	3	3	—
1982–83 Luton T	1	4	—
1983–84 Bristol R	3	43	9
1984–85 Bristol R	3	18	3
1985–86 Bristol R	3	40	12
1986–87 Swindon T	3	35	15
1987–88 Swindon T	2	25	11

WHITEHEAD, Clive
24.11.55 Birmingham (FW)
5.10½ 11.5 Northfield J
LD Millwall v Bristol C
13.10.73 0–2

1973–74 Bristol C	2	12	2
1974–75 Bristol C	2	14	—
1975–76 Bristol C	2	22	4
1976–77 Bristol C	1	41	—
1977–78 Bristol C	1	33	2
1978–79 Bristol C	1	30	2
1979–80 Bristol C	1	40	—
1980–81 Bristol C	2	31	—
1981–82 Bristol C	3	6	—
1981–82 WBA	1	8	1
1982–83 WBA	1	36	1
1983–84 WBA	1	34	1
1984–85 WBA	1	32	—
1985–86 WBA	1	24	—
1985–86 Wolves	3	2	—
1986–87 WBA	2	34	3
1987–88 Portsmouth	1	33	2

WHITEHURST, Billy
10.6.59 Thurnscoe (FW)
6.1½ 13.13 Mexborough
LD Gillingham v Hull C
25.10.80 2–0

1980–81 Hull C	3	26	1
1981–82 Hull C	4	36	6
1982–83 Hull C	4	36	3
1983–84 Hull C	3	37	10
1984–85 Hull C	3	40	20
1985–86 Hull C	2	18	7
1985–86 Newcastle U	1	20	7
1986–87 Newcastle U	1	8	—
1986–87 Oxford U	1	20	2
1987–88 Oxford U	1	20	—
1987–88 Reading	2	15	6

WHITESIDE, Norman
7.5.65 Belfast (FW)
6.0 12.8 Apprentice
LD Brighton & HA v Manchester U
24.4.82 0–1

1981–82 Manchester U	1	2	1
1982–83 Manchester U	1	39	8
1983–84 Manchester U	1	37	10
1984–85 Manchester U	1	27	9
1985–86 Manchester U	1	37	4
1986–87 Manchester U	1	31	8
1987–88 Manchester U	1	27	7

WHITLOCK, Mark
14.3.61 Portsmouth (DF)
5.11½ 12.2 Apprentice
LD Southampton v Wolves
1.9.81 4–1

1978–79 Southampton	1	—	—
1979–80 Southampton	1	—	—
1980–81 Southampton	1	—	—
1981–82 Southampton	1	9	1
1982–83 Grimsby T	2	8	—
1982–83 Aldershot	4	14	—
1983–84 Southampton	1	16	—
1984–85 Southampton	1	22	—
1985–86 Southampton	1	14	—
1986–87 Bournemouth	3	45	1
1987–88 Bournemouth	2	41	—

WHITTAKER, Brian
23.9.56 Glasgow (DF)
6.0 11.9 Sighthill Amateurs
LD Clyde v Partick Th
26.4.75 2–2

1974–75 Partick T	1	1	—
1975–76 Partick T	1	1	—
1976–77 Partick T	P	36	1
1977–78 Partick T	P	35	—
1978–79 Partick T	P	36	—
1979–80 Partick T	P	35	1
1980–81 Partick T	P	34	1
1981–82 Partick T	P	28	—
1982–83 Partick T	1	35	1
1983–84 Celtic	P	10	2
1984–85 Hearts	P	28	1
1985–86 Hearts	P	25	—
1986–87 Hearts	P	37	—
1987–88 Hearts	P	42	—

WHITTON, Steve
4.12.60 East Ham (MF)
6.0 12.7 Apprentice
LD Coventry C v Tottenham H
29.9.79 1–1

1978–79 Coventry C	1	—	—
1979–80 Coventry C	1	7	—
1980–81 Coventry C	1	1	—
1981–82 Coventry C	1	28	9
1982–83 Coventry C	1	38	12
1983–84 West Ham U	1	22	5
1984–85 West Ham U	1	17	1
1985–86 West Ham U	1	—	—
1985–86 Birmingham C	1	8	3
1986–87 Birmingham C	2	39	9
1987–88 Birmingham C	2	33	14

WHYTE, Derek
31.8.68 Glasgow (DF)
5.11 11.5 Celtic BC
LD Celtic v Hearts
22.2.86 1–1

1985–86 Celtic	P	11	—
1986–87 Celtic	P	42	—
1987–88 Celtic	P	41	3

WICKS, Steve
3.10.56 Reading (DF)
6.2 13.2 Apprentice
LD Chelsea v Ipswich T
31.3.75 0–0

1974–75 Chelsea	1	1	—
1975–76 Chelsea	2	19	—
1976–77 Chelsea	2	34	4
1977–78 Chelsea	1	41	—
1978–79 Chelsea	1	23	1
1978–79 Derby Co	1	19	—
1979–80 Derby Co	1	5	—
1979–80 QPR	2	35	—
1980–81 QPR	2	38	—
1981–82 Crystal Palace	2	14	1
1981–82 QPR	2	9	—
1982–83 QPR	2	14	1
1983–84 QPR	1	31	2
1984–85 QPR	1	33	2
1985–86 QPR	1	29	1
1986–87 Chelsea	1	15	1
1987–88 Chelsea	1	17	—

WIGLEY, Steve
15.10.61 Ashton (FW)
5.9 10.5 Curzon Ashton
LD Nottingham F v Arsenal
23.10.82 3–0

1980–81 *Nottingham F*	1	—	—
1981–82 Nottingham F	1	—	—
1982–83 Nottingham F	1	4	—
1983–84 Nottingham F	1	35	1
1984–85 Nottingham F	1	35	1
1985–86 Nottingham F	1	8	—
1985–86 Sheffield U	2	10	1
1986–87 Sheffield U	2	18	—
1986–87 Birmingham C	2	11	1
1987–88 Birmingham C	2	43	2

WIGNALL, Steve
17.9.54 Liverpool (DF)
5.11 11.11 Liverpool Amateur
LD Doncaster R v Crewe Alex
11.11.72 0–2

1971–72 Doncaster R	4	—	—
1972–73 Doncaster R	4	23	—
1973–74 Doncaster R	4	38	—
1974–75 Doncaster R	4	35	1
1975–76 Doncaster R	4	23	—
1976–77 Doncaster R	4	11	—
1976–77 Nottingham F	4	—	—
1977–78 Doncaster R	4	—	—
1977–78 Colchester U	3	34	2
1978–79 Colchester U	3	42	4
1979–80 Colchester U	3	40	3
1980–81 Colchester U	3	42	1
1981–82 Colchester U	4	43	—
1982–83 Colchester U	4	44	4
1983–84 Colchester U	4	36	8
1984–85 Brentford	3	36	—
1985–86 Brentford	3	28	2
1986–87 Brentford	3	3	—
1986–87 Aldershot	4	40	1
1987–88 Aldershot	3	37	1

WILCOX, Russell
25.3.64 Hemsworth (DF)
— — Apprentice
LD Mansfield T v Doncaster R
6.5.81 1–1

1980–81 Doncaster R	4	1	—
1981–82 Doncaster R	3	—	—
Frickley Ath			
1986–87 Northampton T	4	35	1
1987–88 Northampton	3	46	4

WILDER, Chris
23.9.67 Wortley (DF)
5.10 10.8 Apprentice
LD Shrewsbury T v Sheffield U
24.1.87 1–0

1985–86 Southampton	1	—	—
1986–87 Sheffield U	2	11	—
1987–88 Sheffield U	2	25	—

WILKINS, Dean
12.7.62 Hillingdon (MF)
5.9 11.10 Apprentice
LD Grimsby T v QPR
1.11.80 0–0

1980–81 QPR	2	2	—
1981–82 QPR	2	1	—
1982–83 QPR	2	3	—
1983–84 Brighton & HA	2	2	—
1983–84 *Orient*	3	10	—
1984–87 PEC Zwolle (Neth)			
1987–88 Brighton & HA	3	44	3

WILKINS, Ray
14.9.56 Hillingdon (MF)
5.8 11.2 Apprentice
LD Chelsea v Norwich C
26.10.73 3–0

1973–74 Chelsea	1	6	—
1974–75 Chelsea	1	21	2
1975–76 Chelsea	2	42	11
1976–77 Chelsea	2	42	7
1977–78 Chelsea	1	33	7
1978–79 Chelsea	1	35	3
1979–80 Manchester U	1	37	2
1980–81 Manchester U	1	13	—
1981–82 Manchester U	1	42	1
1982–83 Manchester U	1	26	1
1983–84 Manchester U	1	42	3
1984–85 AC Milan (I)	A	28	—
1985–86 AC Milan (I)	A	29	2
1986–87 AC Milan (I)	A	16	—
1987–88 Paris St Ger. (F)	1	—	—
1987–88 Rangers	P	24	1

WILKINS, Richard
28.5.65 London (MF)
6.0 12.0 Haverhill R
LD Colchester U v Preston NE
13.12.86 0–2

1986–87 Colchester U	4	23	2
1987–88 Colchester U	4	46	9

WILKINSON, Paul
30.10.64 Louth (FW)
5.11½ 11.0 Apprentice
LD Grimsby T v Charlton Ath
22.1.83 1–1

1982–83 Grimsby T	2	4	1
1983–84 Grimsby T	2	37	12
1984–85 Grimsby T	2	30	14
1984–85 Everton	1	5	2
1985–86 Everton	1	4	1
1986–87 Everton	1	22	3
1986–87 Nottingham F	1	8	—
1987–88 Nottingham F	1	26	6

WILKINSON, Steve
1.9.68 London (FW)
6.0 10.12 Apprentice
LD Leicester C v Manchester C
28.3.87 4–0

1986–87 Leicester C	1	1	—
1987–88 Leicester C	2	5	1

WILLIAMS, Andy
29.7.62 Birmingham (MF)
6.0 11.9 Dudley and Solihull B
LD Coventry C v Liverpool
9.11.85 0–3

1985–86 Coventry C	1	8	—
1986–87 Coventry C	1	1	—
1986–87 Rotherham U	3	36	4
1987–88 Rotherham U	3	36	6

WILLIAMS, Bill
7.10.60 Rochdale (DF)
6.1 12.11 Local
LD Hartlepool U v Rochdale
31.3.82 1–1

1981–82 Rochdale	4	6	—
1982–83 Rochdale	4	37	—
1983–84 Rochdale	4	27	2
1984–85 Rochdale	4	25	—
1985–86 Stockport Co	4	22	—
1986–87 Stockport Co	4	30	—
1987–88 Stockport Co	4	45	1

WILLIAMS, Brett
19.3.68 Dudley (DF)
5.10 11.11 Apprentice
LD Birmingham C v Nottingham F
26.12.85 0–1

1985–86 Nottingham F	1	11	—
1986–87 Nottingham F	1	3	—
1986–87 *Stockport Co*	4	2	—
1987–88 Nottingham F	1	4	—
1987–88 *Northampton T*	3	4	—

PLAYER DIRECTORY

WILLIAMS, Brian
5.11.55 Salford (DF)
5.9 12.1 Apprentice
LD Bury v Stockport Co
18.3.72 4-0

1971–72	Bury	4	1	—
1972–73	Bury	4	10	1
1973–74	Bury	4	35	9
1974–75	Bury	3	35	1
1975–76	Bury	3	46	5
1976–77	Bury	3	32	3
1977–78	QPR	1	19	—
1978–79	Swindon T	3	25	2
1979–80	Swindon T	3	43	3
1980–81	Swindon T	3	31	3
1981–82	Bristol R	3	37	4
1982–83	Bristol R	3	43	2
1983–84	Bristol R	3	46	10
1984–85	Bristol R	3	46	4
1985–86	Bristol C	3	36	1
1986–87	Bristol C	3	41	2
1987–88	Shrewsbury T	2	42	—

WILLIAMS, Darren
15.2.68 Birmingham (MF)
— — YTS
LD —

1987–88	Leicester C	2	—	—

WILLIAMS, David
11.3.55 Cardiff (MF)
5.10 11.8 Clifton Ath
LD Oldham Ath v Bristol R
16.8.75 2-0

1975–76	Bristol R	2	41	2
1976–77	Bristol R	2	39	10
1977–78	Bristol R	2	33	8
1978–79	Bristol R	2	42	10
1979–80	Bristol R	2	40	4
1980–81	Bristol R	2	25	3
1981–82	Bristol R	3	46	11
1982–83	Bristol R	3	25	9
1983–84	Bristol R	3	24	3
1984–85	Bristol R	3	37	6
1985–86	Norwich C	2	39	8
1986–87	Norwich C	1	12	3
1987–88	Norwich C	1	9	—

WILLIAMS, Gareth
12.3.67 Isle of Wight (FW)
— — —Gosport
LD Crystal Palace v Aston Villa
9.4.88 1-1

1987–88	Aston Villa	2	1	—

WILLIAMS, Gary
17.6.60 Wolverhampton (DF)
5.9 10.10 Apprentice
LD Aston Villa v Everton
16.9.78 1-1

1978–79	Aston Villa	1	23	—
1979–80	Aston Villa	1	2	—
1979–80	Walsall	3	9	—
1980–81	Aston Villa	1	22	—
1981–82	Aston Villa	1	28	—
1982–83	Aston Villa	1	36	—
1983–84	Aston Villa	1	40	—
1984–85	Aston Villa	1	38	—
1985–86	Aston Villa	1	25	—
1986–87	Aston Villa	1	26	—
1987–88	Leeds U	2	31	3

WILLIAMS, Gary
8.6.63 Bristol (DF)
5.8 10.11 Apprentice
LD Oldham Ath v Bristol C
2.5.81 2-0

1980–81	Bristol C	2	1	—
1981–82	Bristol C	3	33	1
1982–83	Bristol C	4	36	—
1983–84	Bristol C	4	30	—
1984–85	Portsmouth	2	—	—
1984–85	Swansea C	3	6	—
1984–85	Bristol R	3	—	—
1985–86	Oldham Ath	2	9	1
1986–87	Oldham Ath	2	32	9
1987–88	Oldham Ath	2	9	1

WILLIAMS, Gary
14.5.59 Nantwich (DF)
5.9½ 12.0 Amateur
LD Gillingham v Tranmere R
14.5.77 3-0

1976–77	Tranmere R	3	1	—
From Djurgaarden				
1980–81	Blackpool	3	31	2
1981–82	Swindon T	3	38	3
1982–83	Swindon T	4	—	—
1982–83	Tranmere R	4	13	—
1983–84	Tranmere R	4	37	3
1984–85	Tranmere R	4	32	6
1985–86	Tranmere R	4	25	4
1986–87	Tranmere R	4	35	3
1987–88	Tranmere R	4	24	—

WILLIAMS, Geraint
5.1.62 Treorchy (MF)
5.7 10.6 Apprentice
LD Bristol R v Sheffield W
18.10.80 3-3

1979–80	Bristol R	2	—	—
1980–81	Bristol R	2	28	1
1981–82	Bristol R	3	16	—
1982–83	Bristol R	3	35	3
1983–84	Bristol R	3	34	4
1984–85	Bristol R	3	28	—
1984–85	Derby Co	3	12	—
1985–86	Derby Co	3	40	4
1986–87	Derby Co	2	40	1
1987–88	Derby Co	1	40	1

WILLIAMS, Jeremy
24.3.60 Didcot (DF)
5.11 11.10 Apprentice
LD Reading v Bury
26.2.77 1-3

1976–77	Reading	3	5	—
1977–78	Reading	4	13	2
1978–79	Reading	4	1	—
1979–80	Reading	3	15	2
1980–81	Reading	3	27	3
1981–82	Reading	3	45	—
1982–83	Reading	3	41	2
1983–84	Reading	4	38	—
1984–85	Reading	3	38	1
1985–86	Reading	3	31	4
1986–87	Reading	2	34	2
1987–88	Reading	2	21	1

WILLIAMS, John
3.10.60 Liverpool (DF)
6.2 14.4 Amateur
LD Swindon T v Tranmere R
24.3.79 4-1

1978–79	Tranmere R	3	1	—
1979–80	Tranmere R	4	3	—
1980–81	Tranmere R	4	27	2
1981–82	Tranmere R	4	44	6
1982–83	Tranmere R	4	35	—
1983–84	Tranmere R	4	20	1
1984–85	Tranmere R	4	43	4
1985–86	Port Vale	4	36	3
1986–87	Port Vale	3	14	—
1986–87	Bournemouth	3	26	3
1987–88	Bournemouth	2	38	2

WILLIAMS, Keith
12.4.57 Burtwood (DF)
5.9 11.10 Apprentice
LD Northampton T v Shrewsbury T
26.2.77 5-3

1974–75	Aston Villa	1	—	—
1975–76	Aston Villa	1	—	—
1976–77	Aston Villa	1	—	—
1976–77	Northampton T	3	17	1
1977–78	Northampton T	4	28	1
1978–79	Northampton T	4	44	2
1979–80	Northampton T	4	3	—
1980–81	Northampton T	4	39	2
1981–82	Bournemouth	4	37	1
1982–83	Bournemouth	3	18	—
1983–84	Bournemouth	3	26	—
1984–85	Bournemouth	3	6	—
1985–86	Bournemouth	3	9	—
1986–87	Bournemouth	3	6	—
1987–88	Bath C	—	—	—
1987–88	Colchester U	4	10	—

WILLIAMS, Mike
6.2.65 Mancot (MF)
5.10 10.12 Apprentice
LD Chester v Lincoln C
8.5.82 1-2

1981–82	Chester	3	2	—
1982–83	Chester	4	12	2
1983–84	Chester	4	20	2
1984–85	Wrexham	4	27	—
1985–86	Wrexham	4	27	—
1986–87	Wrexham	4	42	1
1987–88	Wrexham	4	42	2

WILLIAMS, Oshor
21.4.58 Stockton (MF)
5.9½ 11.7 Middlesbrough
Apprentice
LD Southampton v Arsenal
3.3.79 2–0

1976–77 Manchester U	1	—	—
Gateshead			
1977–78 Southampton	2	—	—
1978–79 Southampton	1	5	—
1978–79 *Exeter C*	3	3	—
1979–80 Southampton	1	1	—
1979–80 Stockport Co	4	28	1
1980–81 Stockport Co	4	36	6
1981–82 Stockport Co	4	45	9
1982–83 Stockport Co	4	34	2
1983–84 Stockport Co	4	37	6
1984–85 Stockport Co	4	13	2
1984–85 Port Vale	4	17	3
1985–86 Port Vale	4	32	3
1986–87 Preston NE	4	29	10
1987–88 Preston NE	3	10	2

WILLIAMS, Paul
16.8.65 London (FW)
5.7 10.3 Woodford T
LD Wimbledon v Charlton Ath
1.9.87 4–1

| 1987–88 Charlton Ath | 1 | 12 | — |
| 1987–88 *Brentford* | 3 | 7 | 3 |

WILLIAMS, Steve
12.7.58 London (MF)
5.11 10.11 Apprentice
LD Portsmouth v Southampton
6.4.76 0–1

1974–75 Southampton	2	—	—
1975–76 Southampton	2	1	—
1976–77 Southampton	2	33	—
1977–78 Southampton	2	39	5
1978–79 Southampton	1	39	—
1979–80 Southampton	1	32	2
1980–81 Southampton	1	33	4
1981–82 Southampton	1	21	—
1982–83 Southampton	1	39	3
1983–84 Southampton	1	27	3
1984–85 Southampton	1	14	1
1984–85 Arsenal	1	15	1
1985–86 Arsenal	1	17	—
1986–87 Arsenal	1	34	2
1987–88 Arsenal	1	29	1

WILLIAMS, Wayne
17.11.63 Delford (DF)
5.10 10.10 Apprentice
LD Oldham Ath v Shrewsbury T
28.8.82 1–0

1981–82 Shrewsbury T	2	—	—
1982–83 Shrewsbury T	2	42	4
1983–84 Shrewsbury T	2	40	—
1984–85 Shrewsbury T	2	28	—
1985–86 Shrewsbury T	2	30	1
1986–87 Shrewsbury T	2	40	—
1987–88 Shrewsbury T	2	31	2

WILLIS, Jim
12.7.68 Liverpool (DF)
6.1 12.3 Apprentice
LD Tranmere R. Stockport Co
1.1.88 4–0

| 1987–88 Stockport Co | 4 | 10 | — |
| 1987–88 Darlington | 4 | 9 | — |

WILLIS, Paul
24.1.70 Liverpool (MF)
— — Apprentice
LD Halifax T v L. Orient
14.4.88 1–0

| 1987–88 Halifax T | 4 | 1 | — |

WILMOT, Rhys
21.2.62 Newport (GK)
6.1 12.0 Apprentice
LD Hereford U v Halifax T
19.3.83 2–0

1979–80 Arsenal	1	—	—
1980–81 Arsenal	1	—	—
1981–82 Arsenal	1	—	—
1982–83 Arsenal	1	—	—
1982–83 *Hereford U*	4	9	—
1983–84 Arsenal	1	—	—
1984–85 *Orient*	3	46	—
1985–86 Arsenal	1	2	—
1986–87 Arsenal	1	6	—
1987–88 Arsenal	1	—	—

WILSON, Barrie
— Newcastle-on-Tyne (FW)
5.9½ 10.2 Apprentice
LD —

| 1987–88 Southampton | 1 | — | — |

WILSON, Clive
13.11.61 Manchester (FW)
5.7 9.10 Local
LD Manchester C v Wolves
28.12.81 2–1

1979–80 Manchester C	1	—	—
1980–81 Manchester C	1	—	—
1981–82 Manchester C	1	4	—
1982–83 Manchester C	1	—	—
1982–83 *Chester*	4	21	2
1983–84 Manchester C	2	11	—
1984–85 Manchester C	2	27	4
1985–86 Manchester C	1	25	5
1986–87 Manchester C	1	42	—
1987–88 Chelsea	1	31	2

WILSON, Danny
1.1.60 Wigan (MF)
5.7 10.3 Wigan Ath
LD Cambridge U v Bury
8.11.77 3–0

1977–78 Bury	3	12	1
1978–79 Bury	3	46	7
1979–80 Bury	3	32	—
1980–81 Chesterfield	3	33	3
1981–82 Chesterfield	3	43	3
1982–83 Chesterfield	3	24	7
1982–83 Nottingham F	1	10	1
1983–84 *Scunthorpe U*	3	6	3
1983–84 Brighton & HA	2	26	10
1984–85 Brighton & HA	2	38	5
1985–86 Brighton & HA	2	33	11
1986–87 Brighton & HA	2	38	7
1987–88 Luton T	1	38	8

WILSON, David
20.3.69 Burnley (MF)
5.9 10.10 Apprentice
LD —
00.0.00

| 1987–88 Manchester U | 1 | — | — |

WILSON, Ian
27.3.58 Aberdeen (MF)
5.7½ 10.10 Elgin C
LD Leicester C v Watford
18.8.79 2–0

1978–79 Leicester C	2	—	—
1979–80 Leicester C	2	24	2
1980–81 Leicester C	1	40	1
1981–82 Leicester C	2	35	—
1982–83 Leicester C	2	36	8
1983–84 Leicester C	1	41	—
1984–85 Leicester C	1	39	1
1985–86 Leicester C	1	25	2
1986–87 Leicester C	1	37	1
1987–88 Leicester C	2	8	2
1987–88 Everton	1	16	—

WILSON, Kevin
18.4.61 Banbury (FW)
5.7 10.10 Banbury U
LD Liverpool v Derby Co
8.4.80 3–0

1979–80 Derby Co	1	4	—
1980–81 Derby Co	2	27	7
1981–82 Derby Co	2	24	9
1982–83 Derby Co	2	22	4
1983–84 Derby Co	2	32	2
1984–85 Derby Co	3	13	8
1984–85 Ipswich T	1	17	7
1985–86 Ipswich T	1	39	7
1986–87 Ipswich T	2	42	20
1987–88 Chelsea	1	25	5

WILSON, Paul
16.10.60 Hemsworth (DF)
5.10 10.12 Apprentice
LD Bury v Northampton T
13.22.88 0–0

1987–88 Norwich C	1	—	—
1987–88 *Northampton T*	3	11	—
1987–88 Northampton T	3	4	1

PLAYER DIRECTORY

WILSON, Phil
16.10.60 Hemsworth (MF)
5.6 11.3 Apprentice
LD Arsenal v Bolton W
23.2.80 2–0

1978–79	Bolton W	1	—	—
1979–80	Bolton W	1	17	1
1980–81	Bolton W	2	22	3
1981–82	Huddersfield T	3	34	2
1982–83	Huddersfield T	3	45	6
1983–84	Huddersfield T	2	41	3
1984–85	Huddersfield T	2	40	3
1985–86	Huddersfield T	2	35	1
1986–87	Huddersfield T	2	38	1
1987–88	York C	3	36	1

WILSON, Robert
5.6.61 Kensington (MF)
5.10 11.11 Apprentice
LD Preston NE v Fulham
12.1.80 3–2

1979–80	Fulham	2	2	—
1980–81	Fulham	3	35	4
1981–82	Fulham	3	43	5
1982–83	Fulham	2	40	11
1983–84	Fulham	2	16	3
1984–85	Fulham	2	39	11
1985–86	Millwall	2	28	12
1986–87	Luton T	1	21	1
1987–88	Luton T	1	3	—
1987–88	Fulham	3	20	3

WILSON, Terry
8.2.69 Broxburn (MF)
6.0 10.10 Apprentice
LD Nottingham F v Southampton
2.9.87 3–3

1987–88	Nottingham F	1	36	5

WILSON, Tommy
2.8.61 Paisley (DF)
5.8 9.7 School
LD Queen's Park v East Fife
26.1.80 3–1

1979–80	Queen's Park	2	1	—
1980–81	Queen's Park	2	1	—
1981–82	Queen's Park	2	30	—
1982–83	St Mirren	P	36	—
1983–84	St Mirren	P	1	—
1984–85	St Mirren	P	35	—
1985–86	St Mirren	P	27	—
1986–87	St Mirren	P	25	1
1987–88	St Mirren	P	35	—

WIMBLETON, Paul
13.11.64 Havant (MF)
5.8 10.6 Apprentice
LD Portsmouth v Fulham
20.3.82 1–1

1981–82	Portsmouth	3	8	—
1982–83	Portsmouth	3	—	—
1983–84	Portsmouth	2	2	—
1984–85	Portsmouth	2	—	—
1985–86	Portsmouth	2	—	—
1986–87	Cardiff C	4	46	8
1987–88	Cardiff C	4	37	9

WINNIE, David
26.10.66 Glasgow (DF)
5.11 10.7 'S' Form
LD St Mirren v Aberdeen
24.12.83 0–3

1983–84	St Mirren	P	8	—
1984–85	St Mirren	P	30	3
1985–86	St Mirren	P	20	1
1986–87	St Mirren	P	14	—
1987–88	St Mirren	P	26	2

WINSTANLEY, Mark
22.1.68 St Helens (DF)
— — YTS
LD Bournemouth v Bolton W
18.3.86 2–1

1984–85	Bolton W	3	—	—
1985–86	Bolton W	3	3	—
1986–87	Bolton W	3	13	—
1987–88	Bolton W	4	8	1

WINTER, Julian
6.9.65 Huddersfield (MF)
6.0 11.2 Local
LD Huddersfield T v Oxford
25.8.84 0–3

1983–84	Huddersfield T	2	—	—
1984–85	Huddersfield T	2	16	2
1985–86	Huddersfield T	2	4	—
1986–87	Huddersfield T	2	31	1
1987–88	Huddersfield T	2	7	—

WINTERBURN, Nigel
11.12.63 Nuneaton (DF)
5.10 10.7 Local
LD Bolton W v Wimbledon
27.8.83 2–0

1981–82	Birmingham C	1	—	—
1982–83	Birmingham C	1	—	—
1983–84	Oxford U	3	—	—
1983–84	Wimbledon	3	43	1
1984–85	Wimbledon	2	41	4
1985–86	Wimbledon	2	39	1
1986–87	Wimbledon	1	42	2
1987–88	Arsenal	1	17	—

WISE, Dennis
15.12.66 Kensington (FW)
5.6 9.5 Southampton Apprentice
LD Wimbledon v Cardiff C
11.5.85 2–1

1984–85	Wimbledon	2	1	—
1985–86	Wimbledon	2	4	—
1986–87	Wimbledon	1	28	4
1987–88	Wimbledon	1	30	10

WISHART, Fraser
1.3.65 Johnstone (DF)
5.8 10.0 Pollok
LD Celtic v Motherwell
10.4.82 4–2

1983–84	Motherwell	P	6	—
1984–85	Motherwell	1	—	—
1985–86	Motherwell	P	26	—
1986–87	Motherwell	P	44	3
1987–88	Motherwell	P	43	1

WITHE, Chris
25.9.62 Liverpool (DF)
5.10 11.3 Apprentice
LD Newcastle U v Shrewsbury T
22.10.80 1–0

1980–81	Newcastle U	2	2	—
1981–82	Newcastle U	2	—	—
1982–83	Newcastle U	2	—	—
1983–84	Bradford C	3	45	1
1984–85	Bradford C	3	45	—
1985–86	Bradford C	2	33	—
1986–87	Bradford C	2	18	1
1987–88	Bradford C	2	2	—
1987–88	Notts Co	3	35	2

WOOD, Darren
22.10.65 Derby (DF)
6.1 11.12
LD Chesterfield v Port Vale
12.9.87 1–3

1987–88	Chesterfield	3	35	1

WOOD, Darren
9.6.64 Scarborough (DF)
5.10 11.8 Apprentice
LD Southampton v Middlesbrough
19.9.81 2–0

1981–82	Middlesbrough	1	11	1
1982–83	Middlesbrough	2	42	3
1983–84	Middlesbrough	2	42	2
1984–85	Middlesbrough	2	6	—
1984–85	Chelsea	1	19	1
1985–86	Chelsea	1	28	—
1986–87	Chelsea	1	41	—
1987–88	Chelsea	1	34	1

WOOD, Nicky
11.1.66 Oldham (FW)
5.11½ 11.1 School
LD Everton v Manchester U
26.12.85 3–1

1983–84	Manchester U	1	—	—
1984–85	Manchester U	1	—	—
1985–86	Manchester U	1	1	—
1986–87	Manchester U	1	2	—
1987–88	Manchester U	1	—	—

WOOD, Paul
1.11.64 Middlesbrough (FW)
5.9 10.1 Apprentice
LD Middlesbrough v Portsmouth
14.1.84 0–0

1982–83	Portsmouth	3	—	—
1983–84	Portsmouth	2	8	1
1984–85	Portsmouth	2	6	1
1985–86	Portsmouth	2	25	4
1986–87	Portsmouth	2	8	—
1987–88	Brighton & HA	3	31	4

WOOD, Steve
2.2.63 Bracknell
6.0 11.9 Apprentice
LD Southend U v Reading
25.2.79 2-2

1979–80	Reading	3	2	—
1980–81	Reading	3	6	—
1981–82	Reading	3	32	—
1982–83	Reading	3	18	—
1983–84	Reading	4	37	3
1984–85	Reading	3	46	1
1985–86	Reading	3	46	4
1986–87	Reading	2	32	1
1987–88	Millwall	2	22	—

WOODS, Chris
14.11.59 Boston (GK)
6.2 12.8 Apprentice
LD QPR v Bristol R
18.8.79 2-0

1976–77	Nottingham F	2	—	—
1977–78	Nottingham F	1	—	—
1978–79	Nottingham F	1	—	—
1979–80	QPR	2	41	—
1980–81	QPR	2	22	—
1980–81	*Norwich*	1	10	—
1981–82	Norwich C	2	42	—
1982–83	Norwich C	1	42	—
1983–84	Norwich C	1	42	—
1984–85	Norwich C	1	38	—
1985–86	Norwich C	2	42	—
1986–87	Rangers	P	42	—
1987–88	Rangers	P	39	—

WOODS, Neil
30.7.66 York (FW)
6.0 12.11 Apprentice
LD Plymouth Arg v Doncaster R
19.3.83 1-2

1982–83	Doncaster R	3	4	—
1983–84	Doncaster R	4	7	1
1984–85	Doncaster R	3	6	2
1985–86	Doncaster R	3	30	7
1986–87	Doncaster R	3	18	6
1987–88	Rangers	P	—	—
1987–88	Ipswich T	2	19	4

WOODTHORPE, Colin
13.1.69 Ellesmere Port (DF)
5.11 11.8 Apprentice
LD Bury v Chester C
30.8.86 1-1

1986–87	Chester C	3	30	2
1987–88	Chester C	3	35	—

WORTHINGTON, Gary
10.11.66 Cleethorpes (FW)
5.10 10.5 Apprentice
LD Halifax T v Darlington
15.8.87 2-2

1984–85	Manchester U	1	—	—
1985–86	Manchester U	1	—	—
1986–87	Huddersfield T	2	—	—
1987–88	Darlington	4	9	3

WORTHINGTON, Nigel
4.11.61 Ballymena (DF)
5.10 12.0 Ballymena U
LD Wolves v Notts Co
26.9.81 3-2

1981–82	Notts Co	1	2	—
1982–83	Notts Co	1	41	3
1983–84	Notts Co	1	24	1
1983–84	Sheffield W	2	14	1
1984–85	Sheffield W	1	38	1
1985–86	Sheffield W	1	15	—
1986–87	Sheffield W	1	35	—
1987–88	Sheffield W	1	38	—

WRIGHT, Darren
14.3.68 West Bromwich (DF)
5.10 11.4 Apprentice
LD Plymouth Arg v Wolves
21.9.85 3-1

1984–85	Wolves	2	—	—
1985–86	Wolves	3	1	—
1986–87	Wrexham	4	14	—
1987–88	Wrexham	4	35	—

WRIGHT, Ian
3.11.63 Woolwich (FW)
5.8 11.0 Greenwich Bor
LD Crystal Palace v Huddersfield T
31.8.85 2-3

1985–86	Crystal Palace	2	32	9
1986–87	Crystal Palace	2	38	9
1987–88	Crystal Palace	2	41	20

WRIGHT, Keith
17.5.65 Edinburgh (FW)
5.11 11.0 Melbourne Thistle
LD Brechin C v Raith R
20.8.83 1-1

1983–84	Raith R	1	37	5
1984–85	Raith R	2	38	22
1985–86	Raith R	2	39	21
1986–87	Raith R	2	17	13
1986–87	Dundee	P	20	10
1987–88	Dundee	P	42	15

WRIGHT, Mark
1.8.63 Dorchester (DF)
6.3 12.1 Amateur
LD Oxford U v Bristol C
17.10.81 1-0

1980–81	Oxford U	3	—	—
1981–82	Oxford U	3	10	—
1981–82	Southampton	1	3	—
1982–83	Southampton	1	39	2
1983–84	Southampton	1	29	1
1984–85	Southampton	1	36	—
1985–86	Southampton	1	33	3
1986–87	Southampton	1	30	1
1987–88	Derby Co	1	38	3

WRIGHT, Paul
17.8.67 East Kilbride (FW)
5.8 10.8 'S' Form
LD Aberdeen v Hearts
2.4.84 1-1

1983–84	Aberdeen	P	1	—
1984–85	Aberdeen	P	—	—
1985–86	Aberdeen	P	10	2
1986–87	Aberdeen	P	25	4
1987–88	Aberdeen	P	9	4

WRIGHT, Steve
16.6.59 Clacton (DF)
6.0 11.0 Local
LD Swindon T v Colchester U
8.4.78 0-0

1977–78	Colchester U	3	1	—
1978–79	Colchester U	3	35	1
1979–80	Colchester U	3	26	1
1980–81	Colchester U	3	17	—
1981–82	Colchester U	4	38	—
HJK Helsinki				
1983–84	Wrexham	4	37	—
1984–85	Wrexham	4	39	—
1985–86	Torquay U	4	33	—
1986–87	Crewe Alex	4	34	—
1987–88	Crewe Alex	4	38	2

WRIGHT, Tommy
10.1.66 Dunfermline (FW)
5.9 11.0 Apprentice
LD Leeds U v Fulham
16.4.83 1-1

1982–83	Leeds U	2	4	1
1983–84	Leeds U	2	25	8
1984–85	Leeds U	2	42	14
1985–86	Leeds U	2	10	1
1986–87	Oldham Ath	2	28	7
1987–88	Oldham Ath	2	41	8

WRIGHT, Tommy
29.8.63 Belfast (GK)
6.1 13.5 Linfield
LD —

1987–88	*Newcastle U*	1	—	—
1987–88	Newcastle U.	1	—	—

WRIGHTSON, Jeff
18.5.68 Newcastle (DF)
5.11 11.0 Apprentice
LD Newcastle U v Everton
26.12.86 0-4

1986–87	Newcastle U	1	4	—
1987–88	Preston NE	3	25	—

PLAYER DIRECTORY

YALLOP, Frank
4.4.64 Watford (DF)
5.10½ 11.3 Apprentice
LD Everton v Ipswich T
17.3.84 1–0

1981–82	Ipswich T	1	—	—
1982–83	Ipswich T	1	—	—
1983–84	Ipswich T	1	6	—
1984–85	Ipswich T	1	10	—
1985–86	Ipswich T	1	34	—
1986–87	Ipswich T	2	31	—
1987–88	Ipswich T	2	41	2

YATES, Dean
26.10.67 Leicester (DF)
6.0 10.4 Apprentice
LD Notts Co v Wimbledon
6.4.85 2–3

1984–85	Notts Co	2	8	—
1985–86	Notts Co	3	44	4
1986–87	Notts Co	3	42	9
1987–88	Notts Co	3	46	2

YOUNG, Eric
25.3.60 Singapore (DF)
6.2 13.0 Slough Town
LD Blackburn R v Brighton & HA
24.9.83 2–2

1982–83	Brighton & HA	1	—	—
1983–84	Brighton & HA	2	30	4
1984–85	Brighton & HA	2	35	3
1985–86	Brighton & HA	2	32	2
1986–87	Brighton & HA	2	29	1
1987–88	Wimbledon	1	29	3

YOUNG, Richard
31.12.68 Nottingham (FW)
6.3 13.7 Apprentice
LD Notts Co v Wigan Ath
23.8.86. 2–0

1986–87	Notts Co	3	35	5
1987–88	Southend U	3	7	—

ZELEM, Peter
13.2.62 Manchester (DF)
6.0 11.3 Apprentice
LD Chester C v Carlisle U
23.8.80 1–0

1979–80	Chester	3	—	—
1980–81	Chester	3	6	—
1981–82	Chester	3	31	1
1982–83	Chester	4	35	3
1983–84	Chester	4	42	7
1984–85	Chester	4	15	4
1984–85	Wolves	2	16	—
1985–86	Wolves	3	14	—
1986–87	Wolves	4	15	1
1986–87	Preston NE	4	6	1
1987–88	Preston NE	1	—	—
1987–88	Burnley	4	10	1

ZONDERVAN, Romeo
4.3.59 Surinam (MF)
5.9½ 11.2 Den Haag and Twente
LD Middlesbrough v WBA
9.3.82 1–0

1981–82	WBA	1	14	—
1982–83	WBA	1	41	2
1983–84	WBA	1	29	3
1983–84	Ipswich T	1	8	2
1984–85	Ipswich T	1	41	1
1985–86	Ipswich T	1	28	2
1986–87	Ipswich T	2	39	1
1987–88	Ipswich T	2	29	4

ENGLISH
FOOTBALL

INTRODUCTION TO THE CLUB DIRECTORY

On the next 185 pages, you will find a directory of the 92 clubs which participated in the 1987–88 Barclays League programme, with two pages dedicated to each club. The clubs are arranged in strict alphabetical order, regardless of Division, although Lincoln City, who were promoted from the GM Vauxhall Conference at the end of the season, have been added at the end of the directory, as they have only one page, and had they been inserted in their 'proper' place it would have upset the balance of the directory. The Division printed at the top of each club's first page refers to the Division they will be playing in during season 1988–89.

The first page for each club lists all the basic information relating to that club, and is self-explanatory, although it should be noted that the team photographs are usually those taken at the beginning of the 1987–88 season. This is because the bulk of the statistics in this directory relate to that season, but there is another, practical reason – clubs do not usually hold photocalls for team photographs until immediately prior to the start of a new season, which is of course far too late for inclusion in the 1988–89 yearbook. All 93 clubs featured in the directory have been consulted about the content of this page, and every effort has been made to ensure that the information is correct and as up to date as possible.

The second page for each club is a complete statistical breakdown of their League programme for season 1987–88 (the various Cup competitions are dealt with later in the yearbook). Reading from the left on each line of the grid, you will find the match number, the opponents (an asterisk indicates that the team to which the page relates was playing at home), the date of the match, the shirt numbers of the players involved in each match (whose names run along the top of the grid) and finally, on the extreme right hand side of the grid, the full time score, the half-time score (in brackets), the attendance and the League position of the club following that particular match. The League position is not normally listed after mid-week games, or for the first couple of matches in the season.

It should be noted that the attendance figures quoted in this directory are those published in the Press at the time of the match, and will not necessarily be exactly the same as the official Football League attendance statistics which are published further on in the yearbook. There is also a note in the bottom right hand corner of each page showing the club's League position at the end of the season.

At the foot of each player's column are the totals of his full League appearances for the season, with substitute appearances in brackets, followed by his total of League goals. These substitute appearances are listed only if the player actually took part in a game. In the Player Directory starting on page 30, substitute appearances have been amalgamated with full appearances.

In the little boxes containing the shirt numbers, superior figures indicate goals scored in that match, while inferior figures indicate penalties scored. Note that the figures do not overlap, so a superior '1' together with an inferior '1' means that the player in question scored two goals, one of which was a penalty. A dagger indicates that the player was replaced during the match by substitute number 12, and a double dagger indicates he was replaced by substitute number 14. Own goals scored by opponents are listed separately at the foot of the page. As there is only room on the grid for a maximum of 30 players, any players used in excess of that number are also listed separately at the foot of the page.

Grids contained in the Scottish section of the yearbook conform to the same pattern.

DIVISION 3

ALDERSHOT

Recreation Ground, High Street, Aldershot GU11 1TW.

Back row (left to right): Paul Holsgrove, David Coles, Tommy Langley, Tony Lange, Darren Anderson. *Middle row:* Len Walker (Manager), Paul Davis, Glen Burvill, Paul Roberts, Andy King, Giorgio Mazzon, Colin Smith, Jim Lange (Physio). *Front row:* John Anderson (Trainer), Gary Howlett, Steve Wignall, Ian McDonald, Bobby Barnes, Mike Ring, Ian Phillips, Ian Gillard (Coach). Inset: David Barnes, Gary Johnson.

Stadium Capacity: 12,000.
Pitch Dimensions: 116 × 76yds.
Telephone: 0252–20211.
Chairman: C. Hancock.
Directors: T. Lewis, R. J. Driver, P. E. Hillman.
Manager: Len Walker
Post-War Managers: Bill McCracken, Gordon Clark, Harry Evans, Dave Smith, Tommy McAnearney, Jimmy Melia, Cliff Huxford, Tommy McAnearney, Len Walker, Ron Harris (10).
Physio: J. Lange MCSP, SRP.
Secretary: R. J. Driver.
Founded: 1926.
Turned Professional: 1927.
Nickname: The Shots.
Former Names: None.
Former Grounds: None.
Record Attendance: 19,138 v Carlisle U, FA Cup 4th Round replay, 28 January 1970.
Record Victory: 8–1 v Gateshead, Division 4, 13 September 1958.
Record Defeat: 0–9 v Bristol C, Division 3(S), 28 December 1946.
Most League Points: (3 for a win) 75, Division 4, 1983–84. (2 for a win) 57, Division 4, 1978–79.
Most League Goals: 83, Division 4, 1963–64.
Highest League Scorer in a Season: John Dungworth, 26, Division 4, 1978–79.
Highest Total of League Goals: Jack Howarth, 171, 1965–71 and 1972–77.
Most League Appearances: Murray Brodie, 461, 1964–83.
League History: 1932 Elected to Division 3(S), 1958–73 Division 4, 1973–76 Division 3, 1976–87 Division 4, 1987– Division 3.
Honours: None.
Colours: Red shirts with blue trim, blue shorts, red socks with two blue hoops. **Second strip:** All white with red and blue trim.

ALDERSHOT – LEAGUE RECORD 1987–88

Match no/Opp	Date	Langie	Roberts	Phillips	Anderson	Smith	Wignall	Barnes R	Howlett	Langley	McDonald	Ring	Barnes D	Johnson	Burvill	Coles	Davis	Berry	Riley	Ogler	Holsgrove	Bedford	Joseph	FT(HT):Att	Lge pos
1. Port Vale	15.8	1	2	3	4	5	6	7_1	8	9^1	10	11												2-4(1-1)3160	—
2. Bristol R	29.8	1		2	4	5	6	7		9	11	8^1	3	10†	12									1-3(0-3)3390	22
3. Doncaster*	31.8	1		2	12	5	6	7		8	10	11^2	3	9	4†									2-1(0-1)2598	—
4. Chester	5.9	1	12	2	14	5	6‡	7		8	10	11	3	9^1	4†									1-4(0-1)1700	21
5. Brighton*	12.9	1	12	2		5	6	7†		8	10	11	3	9	4									1-4(1-2)3970	21
6. Notts Co	15.9		4	2		5	6	7^1		8	10		3	9	11	1								1-2(1-1)4835	—
7. Bury	19.9		4	2	14	5	6	7†		8	10	12	3	9	11‡	1								0-1(0-1)1744	22
8. Brentford*	26.9		4	2		5	6	7^1		8^3	10		3	9	11	1								4-1(3-1)3651	21
9. Wigan*	29.9		4	2	14	5	6	7^{3+}		8	10	12	3‡	9	11	1								3-2(2-1)2529	—
10. Sunderland	3.10		4	3	14	5	6‡	7^1		9	10	12		8	11	1	2†							1-3(1-1)12,542	21
11. York	17.10		4	3	12	5	6			8^1	10	7^1		9†	11	1		2						2-2(0-1)1984	21
12. Chesterfield*	20.10		4	3		5	6			8	10	7		9	11^1	1	2^1							2-0(1-0)2054	—
13. Fulham	24.10		4	3	12	5	6			8	10^1	7^1†		9	11	1	2							2-1(0-1)6530	19
14. Nthampton*	31.10		4	3		5	6			8^1	10^1	7		9^1	11	1	2^1							4-4(1-3)3358	19
15. Walsall	3.11		4	3		5	6			8	10	7†		9	11	1	2	12						0-2(0-1)4816	—
16. Bristol C*	7.11		4	3	5		6			8^1	10	7†		9	11	1	2^1	12						2-1(1-0)4324	18
17. Southend	21.11	1	4	3		5	6			8	10			9	11		2	7^1						1-0(1-0)2362	17
18. Rotherham*	28.11	1	4	3	5^1	6				8	10	12		9†	11		2	7						1-3(0-2)2549	18
19. Preston	12.12	1	4	3	5		6			8	10	9†	7		11^2		2		12					2-0(2-0)4519	16
20. Grimsby*	19.12	1	4	3	5		6^1			8‡	10	9	7†		11^2		2	14	12					3-2(3-1)2405	14
21. Brentford	26.12	1	4	3	5		6			9	10				11		2	7	8					0-3(0-2)5578	15
22. Gillingham*	28.12	1	4	3	5	12	6			8^{1+}	10^1				11^1		2^1	9^2	7					6-0(5-0)4734	12
23. Bristol R*	1.1	1	4	3	5†	12	6			8^1_1	10		12		11^1		2	9	7					3-0(3-0)4593	11
24. Brighton	2.1	1				5	6				10	9	3		11		2	8	7					1-1(1-0)9420	11
25. Walsall*	9.1	1	4†		6	5				8	10	12	3		11		2	9	7					0-1(0-1)3270	11
26. Bury*	16.1	1	4	3		5	6			8†	10	12	7		11		2	9						0-2(0-0)2718	13
27. Doncaster	31.1	1	4	3	6	5				8	10		7		11		2	9						0-0(0-0)1908	—
28. Chester*	6.2	1	4	3		5				8	10^3	12^1	7		11		2	9†	6					4-1(1-1)2578	11
29. Gillingham	13.2	1	4	3		5	6			8	10	9	7		11^1		2							1-2(0-0)4001	11
30. Notts*	23.2	1	4	3		5	6†			8‡	10	9	7	12	11		2			14				0-2(0-0)2850	—
31. Sunderland*	27.2	1		3	6	5				4^1	10	7		8			2^1	9^1		11				3-2(2-2)5010	12
32. Wigan	1.3	1	4	3†	6	5					10	7		8			2	9	12	11				0-4(0-3)3017	—
33. York*	5.3	1	4†		6	5					10^1	11	3	8	12		7	9		2				1-2(0-1)2672	16
34. Blackpool	12.3	1	4		6	5				8	10^1		3		11^1		2	9		7				2-3(1-1)2661	16
35. Nthampton	19.3	1	4			5	6			8	10		3		11		2^1	9		7				1-1(1-0)4322	18
36. Mansfield	22.3	1	4			5	6			8	10		3		11		2	9		7				0-1(0-0)2344	—
37. Fulham*	26.3	1	4			5	6				10	12	3		11†		2	9		7	8			0-3(0-1)4448	19
38. Blackpool*	29.3	1	4			5	6			8	10	12	3		11†		2	9‡		7	14			0-0(0-0)2091	—
39. Bristol C	2.4	1		12	5	6				8		10†	3		11		2	9		7	4			0-2(0-1)8712	19
40. Southend*	4.4	1	4†		14	5	6				10	11‡	3		12		2	9		7	8			0-1(0-1)3436	21
41. Chesterfield	9.4	1			6	5				4	10		3		11		2	9		7	8			0-1(0-1)1900	21
42. Port Vale*	15.4	1				5	6			8^1	10		3		4		2	9^1		7	11^1			3-0(2-0)2257	11
43. Mansfield*	19.4	1		3	5^1	6				8^1†	10	12			4		2	9		7	11^1			3-0(2-0)2339	—
44. Rotherham	30.4	1	10	3		5	6			8					4		2	9		7	11			0-1(0-0)2818	18
45. Preston*	2.5	1	10			5	6			8		12	3		4		2	9†		7	11			0-0(0-0)3465	18
46. Grimsby	7.5	1	12			5	6			8^1	10†		3		4		2	9		7	11			1-1(1-1)5697	20
Apps(subs)/goals		35(0)0	36(3)0	32(0)0	16(9)1	40(2)1	37(0)1	10(0)7	10(0)0	41(0)14	43(0)8	21(11)6	29(1)10	20(1)2	40(3)9	11(0)0	10(0)0	36(0)6	24(3)5	6(2)0	0(2)0	16(0)1	9(1)2		

Final League Position: 20

Own goals: Brown, match 5. Trusson, match 24.

DIVISION 1

ARSENAL

Arsenal Stadium, Highbury, London N5 1BU.

Back row (left to right): Theo Foley (Ass. Manager), Martin Hayes, Alan Smith, Tony Adams, John Lukic, Rhys Wilmot, Perry Groves, Nigel Winterburn, Steve Williams, Gary Lewin (Physio). *Front row:* Paul Merson, Michael Thomas, Graham Rix, David O'Leary, Charlie Nicholas, George Graham (Manager), Paul Davis, Kenny Sansom, David Roecastle, Gus Caesar, Niall Quinn

Stadium Capacity: 57,000.
Pitch Dimensions: 110 × 71yds.
Telephone: 01–226 0304, **Recorded information:** 01–359 0131, **Clubcall:** 0898–121170.
Chairman: P. D. Hill–Wood.
Vice-Chairman: D. Dein. **Managing Director:** K. J. Friar.
Directors: Sir Robert Bellinger CBE, DSC, S. C. McIntyre MBE, FCIS, A. Wood, R. G. Gibbs, C. E. B. L. Carr, R. G. Gibbs, C. E. B. L. Carr, R. C. L. Carr.
Manager: George Graham.
Post-War Managers: George Allison, Tom Whittaker, Jack Crayston, George Swindin, Billy Wright, Bertie Mee, Terry Neill, Don Howe (8).
Assistant Manager: Theo Foley.
Physio: Gary Lewin.
Secretary: K. J. Friar
Assistant Secretary: David Miles.
Commercial Manager: Jack Kelsey.
Sponsors: JVC UK Ltd
Founded: 1886.
Turned Professional: 1891.
Nickname: The Gunners.
Former Names: Dial Square 1886, Royal Arsenal 1886–91, Woolwich Arsenal 1891–1914.
Former Grounds: Plumstead Common 1886–87, Sportsman Ground 1887–88, Manor Ground 1888–90, Invicta Ground 1890–93, Manor Ground 1893–1913.
Record Attendance: 73,295 v Sunderland, Division 1, 9 March 1935.
Record Victory: 12–0 v Loughborough T, Division 2, 12 March 1900.
Record Defeat: 0–8 v Loughborough T, Division 2, 12 December 1896.
Most League Points: (3 for a win) 71, Division 1, 1981–82. (2 for a win) 66, Division 1, 1930–31.
Most League Goals: 127, Division 1, 1930–31.
Highest League Scorer in a Season: Ted Drake, 42, 1934–35.
Highest Total of League Goals: Cliff Bastin, 150, 1930–47.
Most League Appearances: George Armstrong, 500, 1960–77.
League History: 1893 Elected to Division 2, 1904–13 Division 1, 1913–19 Division 2, 1919– Division 1.
Honours: Division 1 Champions 1930–31, 1932–33, 1933–34, 1934–35, 1937–38, 1947–48, 1952–53, 1970–71, runners-up 1925–26, 1931–32, 1972–73. Division 2 runners-up 1903–04. FA Cup winners 1930, 1936, 1950, 1971, 1979, runners-up 1927, 1932, 1952, 1978, 1980. League Cup winners 1987, runners-up 1968, 1969, 1988. European Fairs Cup winners 1970. European Cup-Winners' Cup runners-up 1980.
Colours: Red shirts with white sleeves, white shorts, red and white socks. **Second strip:** Yellow shirts, blue shorts, yellow socks.

ARSENAL – LEAGUE RECORD 1987–88

Match no/Opp/Date	Lukic	Thomas	Sansom	Williams	O'Leary	Adams	Rocastle	Davis	Smith	Nicholas	Hayes	Groves	Rix	Merson	Richardson	Caesar	Quinn	Winterburn	Dixon	Marwood	Campbell	FT(HT)Att Lge pos
1. Liverpool* 15.8	1	2	3	4	5	6	7†	8^1	9	10	11	12										1-2(1-1)54,703 —
2. Man Utd 19.8	1	2	3	4	5	6	7	8	9	10†	11	12										0-0(0-0)42,890 —
3. QPR 22.8	1	2	3	4	5	6	7†	8	9	10	11		12									0-2(0-1)15,981 19
4. Portsmouth* 29.8	1	2	3	4	5	6^1	7^1	8^1	9^3		10†	11‡	12	14								6-0(4-0)30,865 12
5. Luton 31.8	1	2	3	4	5	6	7	8^1	9		10	11										1-1(1-1)8745 —
6. Nottm F 12.9	1	2	3	4	5	6	7†	8	9^1	12	10	11										1-0(1-0)18,490 10
7. Wimbledon* 19.9	1	2_1	3	4‡	5	6	7	8	9^1		10†	11	12	14								3-0(3-0)27,752 9
8. West Ham* 26.9	1	2	3^1	4	5	6	7†	8	9	12	10	11										1-0(0-0)40,127 7
9. Charlton 3.10	1	2^1	3	4	5	6^1	7†	8	9	12	10^1	11										3-0(1-0)15,326 5
10. Oxford* 10.10	1	2	3	4^1	5	6	7†	8^1	9‡	12	10		11	14								2-0(1-0)25,244 3
11. Spurs 18.10	1	2^1	3	4	5	6	7†	8	9	12	10†		11									2-1(2-1)36,680 —
12. Derby* 24.10	1	2_1	3	4	5	6	7	8	9		10†		12	11^1								2-1(2-1)32,374 3
13. Newcastle 31.10	1	2	3	4†	5	6‡	7	8	9^1	12	10		11	14								1-0(0-0)23,662 1
14. Chelsea* 3.11	1	2	3	4	5	6	7	8	9		10			11^2								3-1(2-1)40,230 1
15. Norwich 14.11	1	2^1	3	4	5	6†	7^2	8	9		10^1		11	12								4-2(0-1)20,558 1
16. Sthampton* 21.11	1	2	3	4	5	6	7	8	9		10†		11			12‡	14					0-1(0-0)32,477 1
17. Watford 28.11	1	2	3	4	5	6	7	8	9	12	10		11†									0-2(0-1)19,598 2
18. Sheff Wed* 5.12	1	2	3	4	5	6	7	8†	9		10^1		12^1	11^1								3-1(0-1)23,670 2
19. Coventry 13.12	1	2	3	4	5	6	7		9	8†	10		12	11								0-0(0-0)17,557 —
20. Everton* 19.12	1	2	3	4	5	6	7^1	8	9		10		12	11†								1-1(0-1)34,857 2
21. Nottm F* 26.12	1	2	3	4	5‡	6	7		12		10		8†	11	14	9						0-2(0-1)31,211 3
22. Wimbledon 28.12	1	2	3	4		6	7		12	8†	10		11	5	9^1							1-3(1-0)12,473 3
23. Portsmouth 1.1	1	2				6	7		12^1	8	10‡		14	11	5	9†	3					1-0(1-0)17,366 3
24. QPR* 2.1	1		3	4		6	7		9	8	12		10†	11	5		2					0-0(0-0)28,271 3
25. Liverpool 16.1	1	12	3	4		6	7‡		9	8	14		11	5†	10	2						0-2(0-1)44,294 4
26. Man Utd* 24.1	1	2		4	5	6	7		9	12	8†		11	10^1	3							1-2(1-1)29,392 5
27. Luton* 13.1	1	4^1			5	6†	7^1		9	8	10		11	12		3	2					2-1(2-0)22,615 5
28. Charlton* 27.1	1	4^1	3			6	7	14	9^1	8	10^2†		11‡	5	12	2						4-0(1-0)25,394 5
29. Spurs* 6.2	1	4	3			6	7		9	8	10^1		11	5		2						2-1(1-0)37,143 5
30. Newcastle* 19.3	1	4				6	7	8	9†	11	10^1		5	12	3	2						1-1(0-0)25,889 5
31. Derby 26.3	1	4				6	7†	8	9‡	11	10		12	5	14	3	2					0-0(0-0)18,382 6
32. Oxford 30.3	1	4	3			6	7‡	8	9		10		12	5	14	2		11†				0-0(0-0)9088 —
33. Chelsea 2.4	1			4		6	7	8		11	10		5	9	3	2						1-1(0-0)26,034 6
34. Norwich* 4.4	1		3	4		6	7	8	9^1	11	10^1		5			2						2-0(1-0)19,341 6
35. Sthampton 9.4	1	6	3	4			7	8^1	9	11	10†	12			5	2						2-4(1-3)14,521 5
36. West Ham 12.4	1	4^1				6	7	8	9	12	10	11†	5			2						1-0(0-0)26,746 6
37. Watford* 15.4	1	4	3			6	7	8	9	12	10	11†	5			2						0-1(0-0)19,541 6
38. Sheff Wed 30.4	1	4	3			6	7	8‡	9^1	12	10^2	14	5			2†			11			3-3(1-3)16,681 6
39. Coventry* 2.5	1	4	3			6	7		9	12	14	10†	8‡		5			2	11_1			1-1(1-1)16,963 6
40. Everton 7.5	1	4^1	3			6	7		9	10‡	12		8		5†			2	11	14		2-1(2-1)22,445 6
Apps(subs)/goals	40(0)0	36(1)9	34(0)1	29(0)1	22(0)1	39(0)2	40(0)6	28(1)5	36(3)11	3(0)0	17(10)1	28(6)6	7(3)0	7(8)5	24(5)4	17(5)0	6(5)2	16(0)0	5(0)0	0(1)0		Final League Position: 6

Own goals: Thorn, match 7; Wegerle, match 14; McLaughlin, match 33; Bond, match 35.

DIVISION 1

ASTON VILLA

Villa Park, Trinity Road, Birmingham B6 6HE.

Back row (left to right): Martin Keown, Gary Shaw, Tommy Bennett, Mark Lillis, Gareth Williams, Garry Thompson, David Hunt, Kevin Gage, Stuart Gray. *Middle row:*, Jim Walker (Physio), Andy Blair, Anan McInally, John Ward (Ass. Manager), Nigel Spink, Lee Butler, Dave Richardson (Ass. Manager), Neale Cooper, Andy Gray, Bobby Downes (Youth Team Coach). *Front row:* Tony Daley, Paul Birch, Bernie Gallacher, Allan Evans, Graham Taylor (Manager), Steve Sims, Warren Aspinall, David Norton, David Platt.

Stadium Capacity: 48,000.
Pitch Dimensions: 155 × 75yds.
Telephone: 021–327 6604, **Recorded information:** 021–328 1722, **Commercial dept:** 021–327 5399, **Fax:** 021–322 2107, **Telex:** 334695, **Clubcall:** 0898–121148.
Chairman: H. D. Ellis.
Directors: J. A. Alderson, Dr D. H. Targett, P. D. Ellis.
Manager: Graham Taylor.
Post-War Managers: Alex Massie, George Martin, Eric Houghton, Joe Mercer, Dick Taylor, Tommy Cummings, Tommy Docherty, Vic Crowe, Ron Saunders, Tony Barton, Graham Turner, Billy McNeill (12). Assistant Managers: Dave Richardson, John Ward.
Physio: Jim Walker.
Secretary: Steven Stride.
Commercial Manager: John Dollimore.
Sponsors: Mita Copiers.
Founded: 1874.
Turned Professional: 1885.
Nickname: The Villans.
Former Names: None.
Former Grounds: Aston Park 1874–76, Perry Barr 1876–97.
Record Attendance: 76,588 v Derby Co. FA Cup 6th Round, 1st leg, 2 March 1946.
Record Victory: 13–0 v Wednesbury Old Athletic, FA Cup 1st Round, 1886.
Record Defeat: 1–8 v Blackburn R, FA Cup 3rd Round, 16 February 1889.
Most League Points: (3 for win) 78, Division 2, 1987–88. (2 for a win) 70, Division 3, 1971–72.
Most League Goals: 128, Division 1, 1930–31.
Highest League Scorer in a Season: Pongo Waring, 49, Division 1, 1930–31.
Highest Total of League Goals: Harry Hampton, 213, 1904–20 and Billy Walker, 213, 1919–34.
Most League Appearances: Charlie Aitken, 560, 1961–76.
League History: 1888 Founder Members of the League. 1936–38 Division 2, 1938–59 Division 1, 1959–60 Division 2, 1960–67 Division 1, 1967–70 Division 2, 1970–72 Division 3, 1972–75 Division 2, 1975–87 Division 1, 1987–88 Division 2, 1988– Division 1.
Honours: Division 1 Champions 1893–94, 1895–96, 1896–97, 1898–99, 1899–1900, 1909–10, 1980–81, runners-up 1888–89, 1902–03, 1907–08, 1910–11, 1912–13, 1913–14, 1930–31, 1932–33. Division 2 Champions 1937–38, 1959–60, runners-up 1974–75, 1987–88. Division 3 Champions 1971–72. FA Cup winners 1887, 1895, 1897, 1905, 1913, 1920, 1957 (7 wins – a record held jointly with Spurs), runners-up 1892, 1924. League Cup winners 1961, 1975, 1977, runners-up 1963, 1971. European Cup winners 1982, European Super Cup winners 1983.
Colours: Claret and blue shirts, claret shorts, blue socks. **Second strip:** All white with claret and blue trim.

212

ASTON VILLA – LEAGUE RECORD 1987–88

Match no/Opp/Date		Spink	Gage	Gallacher	Cooper	Sims	Keown	Birch	Aspinall	Stainrod	Hunt D	Walters	Hunt S	Daley	Burke	Allen	Lillis	McInally	Evans	Shaw	Blair	Gray A	Thompson	Gray S	Norton	Platt	Williams	FT(HT)Att Lge pos
1. Ipswich	15.8	1	2	3	4	5	6	7	8	9	10	11																1–1(1–1)14,508 —
2. Birmingham*	22.8	1	2	3	4	5	6	7	8	$9^‡$	$10^†$	11	12	14														0–2(0–0)30,870 19
3. Hull	29.8	1	2	3	4	5	6		8_1	9	10	11		$7^†$	12													1–2(1–1)8315 22
4. Man City*	31.8	1	2^1	3		5	6		8	9	4	11	10		7													1–1(1–0)16,282 —
5. Leicester	5.9	1	2	3		5	6			4	11^1	10		7	8	9^1												2–0(1–0)10,286 16
6. Middlesbro*	8.9	1	2	3	12	5	6		14		$4^†$	11	10	$7^‡$	8	9												0–1(0–0)12,665 —
7. Barnsley*	12.9	1	2	3	4	5	6	7	12		11	10		$8^†$	9													0–0(0–0)12,621 19
8. WBA	16.9	1	2	3	4	5	6	7	8^2		11	10		9														2–0(1–0)22,072 —
9. Huddersfield	19.9	1	2	3	$4^†$	5	6	7	8		12	11	10^1	9														1–0(1–0)6884 11
10. Sheff Utd*	26.9	1	2^1	3		5	6	7	8		4	11			12	$10^†$	9											1–1(1–0)14,761 10
11. Blackburn*	30.9	1	2	3		5	6	7	8^1		10	11				4	$9^†$	12										1–1(1–1)11,772 —
12. Plymouth	3.10	1	2	3		5	6	7	8		11^2	10				4^1	$9^†$	12										3–1(3–1)10,515 8
13. Leeds	10.10	1	2	3		5	6	7	8^2		11	10				4	9											3–1(1–1)20,741 6
14. Bournemouth*	17.10	1	2	3		5	6	7	$8^†$		11^1	10				4	9		12									1–1(1–0)15,145 7
15. C Palace	21.10	1	2	3		5	6	7	8	9	11^2	10^1				4												4–1(2–1)12,755 —
16. Stoke	24.10	1	2	3		5	6	7	$8^†$		10	11				4	9		12									0–0(0–0)13,494 4
17. Reading*	31.10	1	2	3		5	6	7	8	$10^†$		11				4^1	9				12^1							2–1(0–0)13,413 4
18. Shrewsbury	3.11	1	2	3		5	6^1	7	8^1			11				4	9			10								2–1(1–1)7089 —
19. Millwall*	7.11	1	2	3		5	6^1	7	8			11				4	9		12	$10^†$								1–2(1–2)13,255 5
20. Oldham	14.11	1	2	3		5	6	7	8			11				4	9^1			10								1–0(1–0)6469 4
21. Bradford	28.11	1	2	3		5	6	11^1	8									7			4	9^1	10^2					4–2(2–1)15,006 3
22. Swindon*	5.12	1	2	3		5	6	7	8			11									4	9^2	10					2–1(0–0)16,127 3
23. Birmingham	12.12	1	2	3		5	6	7	8			11				4						9^2	10					2–1(1–1)27,789 3
24. WBA*	18.12	1	2	3		5	6	7	$8^†$			11				4		12				9	10					0–0(0–0)24,437 4
25. Sheff Utd	26.12	1	2	3		5	6	7	8			11				4						9^1	10					1–1(0–0)15,809 4
26. Huddersfield*	28.12	1	2	3		5	6	7^1	$8^†$			11						12			4	9	10					1–1(1–1)20,948 3
27. Hull*	1.1	1	2	3			6	7	12^2							8	11^1	5			4^1	9	$10^†$					5–0(1–0)19,236 1
28. Barnsley	2.1	1	2	3			6	7^1	$10^†$							8	11^1	5			4	9		12				3–1(1–0)11,562 1
29. Ipswich*	16.1	1	2	3			6^1	7								8	11	5	10		4	9						1–0(1–0)20,201 1
30. Man City	23.1	1	2	3			6	7					10^1			8	11	5			4	9^1						2–0(1–0)24,668 1
31. Leicester*	6.2	1	2	3			6	7					10			8^1	11	5^1			4	9						2–1(2–0)18,867 1
32. Middlesbro	14.2	1	2	3			6	7					$10^†$			8	11	5			4	9	12					1–2(1–0)16,957 —
33. Blackburn	20.2	1	2	3			6	$7^†$					12			8		5			4	9	10	11^1				2–3(0–1)17,356 2
34. Plymouth*	27.2	1	2	3			6	7^2					8					5			4	9^1	10_1	11^1				5–2(3–1)16,142 1
35. Bournemouth	5.3	1	2	3			6	7					8^1					5			4	9	10	11^1				2–1(1–0)10,057 1
36. Leeds*	12.3	1	2	3			6	$7^†$					8					12^1	5		4	9	10	11				1–2(0–2)19,677 1
37. Reading	19.3	1	2	3			6	7^1					$8^†$					12	5		4	9^1	10	11				2–0(0–0)10,033 1
38. Stoke*	26.3	1	2	3			6	7					12		14	8		5			$4^‡$	$9^†$	10	11				0–1(0–0)20,392 1
39. Millwall	2.4	1	2	3			6	$7^†$	$8^‡$				14			4			12	5		9^1	10	11				1–2(1–1)13,697 —
40. Oldham*	4.4	1	2		3		6	$7^‡$	14				$8^†$							5		9	10^1	4	11			1–2(1–0)19,138 1
41. C Palace	9.4	1	2	3			6	7					12					5			4	9	10		8^1	$11^†$		1–1(1–0)16,476 4
42. Shrewsbury*	23.4	1	2	3			6		11^1				7			8		5			4	9	10					1–0(1–0)18,396 2
43. Bradford*	2.5	1	2	3		6			8							7		5			4	9	10	11^1				1–0(1,0–3,2)36,423 3
44. Swindon	7.5	1	2	3		5			7	8								6			4	9	10	11				0–0(0–0)10,959 2

Final League Position: 2

Apps(subs)/goals: Spink 44(0)0, Gage 44(0)2, Gallacher 43(0)0, Cooper 6(0)0, Sims 42(0)3, Keown 38(0)6, Birch 28(4)11, Aspinall 40(0)7, Stainrod 11(1)0, Hunt D 24(0)7, Walters 10(1)2, Hunt S 10(4)3, Daley 42(0)0, Burke 28(1)4, Allen 18(7)4, Lillis 18(2)1, McInally 13(0)1, Evans 19(0)1, Shaw 19(1)5, Blair 24(0)10, Gray A 19(1)5, Thompson 1(0)0, Gray S 11(0)5, Norton 1(0)0, Platt 1(0)0

Own goals: O'Donnell, match 1; Rennie, match 13; Hendry, match 33

DIVISION 2

BARNSLEY

Oakwell Ground, Grove Street, Barnsley S71 1ET.

Back row (left to right): Jim Dobbin, Darren Foreman, Mark Robinson, Clive Baker, Mark Ogley, Steve Agnew, Gary Coatsworth. *Middle row:*, Eric Winstanley, Paul Futcher, Ian Chandler, Chris Hedworth, Paul Malcolm, Simon Jeffels, Rodger Wylde, Andy Duggan, Norman Rimmington (Physio). *Front row:* John Beresford, Michael Clarke, Steve Lowndes, John Macdonald, Allan Clarke (Manager), Joe Joyce, Stuart Gray, Gwyn Thomas.

Stadium Capacity: 36,864.
Pitch Dimensions: 110 × 75yds.
Telephone: 0226–295353.
Chairman: G. Buckle LLB.
Vice-Chairman: C. B. Taylor.
Directors: R. F. Potter, J. A. Dennis, C. H. Harrison, M. R. Hayselden.
Manager: Allan Clarke.
Post-War Managers: Angus Seed, Tim Ward, Johnny Steele, John McSeveney, Jim Iley, Allan Clarke, Norman Hunter, Bobby Collins (8).
Assistant Manager:
Physio: Mark Nile.
Secretary: Michael Spinks.
Commercial Manager: G. Whewall.
Founded: 1887.
Turned Professional: 1888.
Nickname: The Tykes, Reds or Colliers.
Former Names: Barnsley St Peter's.
Former Grounds: None
Record Attendance: 40,255 v Stoke C, FA Cup 5th Round, 15 Feb 1936.
Record Victory: 9–0 v Loughborough T, Division 2, 28 January 1899 and v Accrington Stanley, Division 3 (N), 3 February 1934.
Record Defeat: 0–9 v Notts Co, Division 2, 19 November 1927.
Most League Points: (3 for a win) 67, Division 2, 1981–82. (2 for a win) 67, Division 3(N), 1938–39.
Most League Goals: 118, Division 3(N), 1933–34.
Highest League Scorer in a Season: Cecil McCormack, 33, Division 2, 1950–51.
Highest Total of League Goals: Ernest Hine, 123, 1921–26 and 1934–38.
Most League Appearances: Barry Murphy, 514, 1962–78.
League History: 1898 Elected to Division 2, 1932–34 Division 3(N), 1934–38 Division 2, 1938–39 Division 3(N), 1946–53 Division 2, 1953–55 Division 3(N), 1955–59 Division 2, 1959–65 Division 3, 1965–68 Division 4, 1968–72 Division 3, 1972–79 Division 4, 1979–81 Division 3, 1981– Division 2.
Honours: Division 3 runners-up 1980–81. Division 4 runners-up 1967–68. Division 3(N) Champions 1933–34, 1938–39, 1954–55, runners-up 1953–54. FA Cup winners 1912, runners-up 1910.
Colours: Red shirts, white shorts, white socks. **Second strip:** Yellow shirts, black shorts, yellow socks.

BARNSLEY – LEAGUE RECORD 1987–88

Match no/Opp/Date		Baker	Joyce	Beresford	Thomas	Gray	Futcher	Wylde	Agnew	Dobbin	MacDonald	Clarke	Lowndes	Jeffels	Cross	Robinson	Broddle	McGugan	Foreman	Coatsworth	Hedworth	Currie	Rees	Blair	Rolph	Tiler	FT(HT)Att Lge pos
1. Leeds*	16.8	1	2	3	4	5	6	7¹	8	9†	10	11	12														1–1(0–0)9778 —
2. Blackburn	18.8	1	2		4	5	6	7	8	10¹	11†	9	3	12													1–0(1–0)6708 —
3. Millwall	22.8	1	2		4	5	6	7	8	10	11†	9¹	3		12												1–3(0–0)6071 10
4. C Palace*	29.8	1	2	3†	4	5	6	7¹	8	10¹	11‡	9		12	14												2–1(0–1)4853 5
5. Bournemouth	31.8	1	2	3	4	5	6	7	8	10¹	11	9¹															2–1(1–1)7480 —
6. Plymouth*	5.9	1	2		4	5	6	7¹₁	8	10	11	9	3														2–1(0–0)6976 1
7. Aston Villa	12.9	1	2	12	4	5	6	7	8	10	11†	9	3														0–0(0–0)12,621 2
8. Swindon*	15.9	1	2		4	5	6	7	8	10	11	9	3														0–1(0–0)7773 —
9. Oldham	26.9	1	2	12	4	5	6	7	8	10‡	11†	9	3		14												0–1(0–0)5853 9
10. Sheff Utd*	29.9	1	2	12	4	5	6	7	8¹	10	11‡	9	3†		14												1–2(0–0)10,203 —
11. Ipswich	3.10	1	2	12	4	5	6	7†	8	14	10‡	9	3			11											0–1(0–1)10,992 13
12. Leicester	10.10	1	2	7	4	5	6		8		10	9	3			11											0–0(0–0)8669 13
13. Hull*	17.10	1	2	7	4	5	6		8		10	9¹	3			11†	12										1–3(0–1)7310 15
14. Reading*	20.10	1	2¹	11	4	5	6	7¹	8		10²	9	3														5–2(1–2)4396 —
15. Man City	24.10	1	2	11†	4¹	5	6	7	8	12	10	9	3														1–1(1–1)17,063 12
16. Stoke*	31.10	1	2		4	11	6	7²		8¹	10†	9¹	3				5	12									5–2(2–0)5908 11
17. Birmingham	3.11	1	2		4	11	6	7‡		8	10†	9	3		14	5	12										0–2(0–1)6622 —
18. Bradford*	7.11	1	2		4	11¹	6	7¹		8	10	9¹	3			5											3–0(1–0)11,569 10
19. Huddersfield	14.11	1	2		4	11¹	6	7		8	10¹	9	3			5											2–2(2–1)8629 11
20. Shrewsbury*	21.11	1	2	11	4¹	5	6	7	8		10	9¹	3														2–1(2–0)5364 11
21. Middlesbro	28.11	1	2	11	4		6		8	7	10		3				5										0–2(0–0)12,732 11
22. WBA*	5.12	1	2	11	4		6	8²			10	9	3†		12		5	7¹									3–1(1–0)5395 11
23. Millwall*	19.12	1			4		6	8¹₁		10†	12	9	3		11¹	5¹	7	2									4–1(2–1)5011 10
24. Oldham*	26.12	1		10†	4¹		6	14			12	9			11	5	7‡	2									1–1(1–1)8676 11
25. C Palace	1.1	1		10	4		6	8¹		9¹		3			11	5	7¹	2									2–3(0–1)8563 12
26. Aston Villa*	2.1	1		10	4		6	8		9		3			11	5	7¹	2									1–3(0–1)11,562 12
27. Leeds	16.1	1	2	12	4		6	8†	10	9		3			11	5	7²										2–0(1–0)19,028 12
28. Blackburn*	13.2	1	2	11	4		6	7	8	10†		9	3			12	5										0–1(0–0)8972 15
29. Sheff Utd	20.2	1	2	11‡	14		6		8†	4	12	9	3			10	5	7									0–1(0–0)11,861 15
30. Ipswich*	27.2	1	2	11	4		6		8†	10		9	3			12	5				7²						2–3(1–2)6482 15
31. Hull	5.3	1		4¹			6		8¹		10	9	12	3			5		2†		7	11					2–1(2–1)7622 13
32. Bournemouth*	8.3	1		4¹			6		8	10†	9¹	2	3			12	5				7	11					2–1(1–1)6140 —
33. Leicester*	12.3	1	2	4‡	14		6		8	10†	9		3			12	5				7	11¹					1–1(1–1)7447 12
34. Swindon	15.3	1	2		4		6		8	10†	9		3			12	5				7	11					0–3(0–1)7558 —
35. Stoke	19.3	1	2	10	4		6				9		3				5				7	11¹	8				1–3(0–0)8029 15
36. Man City*	26.3	1	2¹	10¹	4		6				9		3				5				7	11	8				3–1(2–1)9061 14
37. Bradford	2.4	1	2	10†	4¹		6				9		3				5		12		7¹	11	8				1–1(0–1)15,098 14
38. Huddersfield*	4.4	1	2	10†	4		6				9		3				5		12		7¹	11	8				1–0(1–0)7590 13
39. Reading	9.4	1	2	10	4		6				9		3				5			12	7	11	8†				1–2(0–1)4849 13
40. Plymouth	15.4	1	2	10	4		6				9	6	3				5		12		7	11¹	8				0–0(0–0)8059 —
41. Birmingham*	23.4	1	2	10†	4				8	12	9	6	3				5				7²	11					2–2(1–0)4949 13
42. Shrewsbury	30.4	1	2	3	4		6			10	11†	9¹					5	8‡			7	12		14			1–1(0–0)4712 13
43. Middlesbro	2.5	1	2	3	4		6			10†	11	9			14	5		8‡			7	12					0–3(0–2)13,240 15
44. WBA	7.5	1	2	10	4					9	6†		8			5					7²	11		3	12		2–2(0–1)8483 14

Apps(subs)/goals:
44(0) 0 | 38(0) 2 | 29(5) 3 | 40(2) 4 | 30(0) 2 | 41(0) 0 | 19(1) 8 | 25(0) 6 | 14(2) 2 | 31(2) 7 | 12(2) 0 | 43(1) 9 | 6(1) 0 | 36(2) 0 | 1(2) 0 | 9(0) 1 | 28(1) 1 | 7(2) 4 | 3(3) 0 | 40(1) 0 | 15(0) 7 | 12(2) 2 | 6(0) 0 | 0(1) 0 | 0(1) 0

Final League Position: 14

Own goals: Richardson, match 14; Hinchliffe, match 36; Hicks, match 39

DIVISION 2

BIRMINGHAM CITY

St Andrews, Birmingham B9 4NH.

Back row (left to right): Garry Pendrey (Manager), A. Kennedy, V. Overson, G. Russell, A. Bird, A. Godden, R. Hansbury, J. Frain, T. Williams, J. Dicks, P. Henderson (Physiotherapist), A. Brown (Coach). *Front row:* A. Rees, C. Robinson, G. Childs, I. Handysides, D. Bremner, S. Whitton, K. Ashley, S. Wigley, R. Ranson, B. Roberts, J. Trewick

Stadium Capacity: 38,408.
Pitch Dimensions: 115 × 75yds.
Telephone: 021-772 0101/2689, **Clubcall:** 0898–121188.
Chairman: K. E. Wheldon.
Vice-Chairman: T. W. J. Edmonds.
Directors: N. B. A. Bosworth LLB, H. Parkes, J. F. Wiseman.
Manager: Garry Pendrey
Post-War Managers: Ted Goodier, Harry Storer, Bob Brocklebank, Arthur Turner, Pat Beasley, Gil Merrick, Joe Mallett, Stan Cullis, Fred Goodwin, Willie Bell, Sir Alf Ramsey, Jim Smith, Ron Saunders, John Bond (14).
Physio: P. Henderson MCSP.
Secretary: H. J. Westmancoat FFA, MBIM.
Founded: 1875.
Turned Professional: 1888.
Nickname: The Blues.
Former Names: Small Heath Alliance 1875–88, Small Heath 1988, Birmingham 1905, Birmingham City 1945.
Former Grounds: Waste ground near Arthur Street 1875–77, Muntz Street, Small Heath 1877–1906.
Record Attendance: 66,844 v Everton, FA Cup 5th Round, 11 February 1939.
Record Victory: 12–0 v Walsall Town Swifts, Division 2, 17 December 1892 and v Doncaster R, Division 2, 11 April 1903.
Record Defeat: 1–9 v Sheffield W, Division 1, 13 December 1930 and v Blackburn R, Division 1, 5 January 1895.
Most League Points: (3 for a win) 82, Division 2, 1984–85. (2 for a win) 59, Division 2, 1947–48.
Most League Goals: 103, Division 2, 1893–94 (28 games).
Highest League Scorer in a Season: Joe Bradford, 29, Division 1, 1927–28.
Highest Total of League Goals: Joe Bradford, 249, 1920–35.
Most League Appearances: Gil Merrick, 486, 1946–60.
League History: 1892 Elected to Division 2. 1894–96 Division 1, 1896–1901 Division 2, 1901–02 Division 1, 1902–03 Division 2, 1903–08 Division 1, 1908–21 Division 2, 1921–39 Division 1, 1946–48 Division 2, 1948–50 Division 1, 1950–55 Division 2, 1955–65 Division 1, 1965–72 Division 2, 1972–79 Division 1, 1979–80 Division 2, 1980–84 Division 1, 1984–85 Division 2, 1985–86 Division 1, 1986– Division 2.
Honours: Division 2 Champions 1892–93, 1920–21, 1947–48, 1954–55, runners-up 1893–94, 1900–01, 1902–03, 1971–72, 1984–85. FA Cup runners-up 1931, 1956. League Cup winners 1963. European Fairs Cup runners-up, 1960, 1961.
Colours: Royal blue shirts, white shorts, blue socks with white hoops. **Second strip:** All yellow.

216

BIRMINGHAM CITY – LEAGUE RECORD 1987–88

Player columns (left to right): Gooddin, Ranson, Dicks, Overson, Williams, Handysides, Bremner, Kennedy, Whitton, Rees, Wigley, Roberts, Bird, Childs, Trewick, Hansbury, Frain, Wibe, Sproston, Russell, Robinson, Yates, Starbuck, Atkins, Langley, Ashley, Morris, Tait

Match no/Opp/Date		FT(HT)Att Lge pos
1. Stoke*	15.8	2–0(1–0)13,137
2. Aston Villa	22.8	2–0(0–0)30,870
3. Bournemouth*	29.8	1–1(0–0)8284
4. Millwall	1.9	1–3(1–1)6758
5. C Palace*	5.9	0–6(0–1)7011
6. Swindon	12.9	2–0(0–0)9128
7. Blackburn*	15.9	1–0(0–0)6032
8. Shrewsbury*	19.9	0–0(0–0)7183
9. Plymouth	26.9	1–1(1–1)8912
10. WBA	30.9	1–3(0–1)15,399
11. Huddersfield*	3.10	2–0(0–0)6282
12. Reading*	10.10	2–2(0–0)6147
13. Bradford	17.10	0–4(0–0)12,256
14. Sheff Utd	20.10	2–0(1–0)9287
15. Middlesbro*	24.10	0–0(0–0)7404
16. Oldham	31.10	2–1(1–0)5486
17. Barnsley*	3.11	2–0(1–0)6622
18. Hull	7.11	0–2(0–1)7901
19. Leicester*	14.11	2–2(1–1)8666
20. Man City	21.11	0–3(0–3)22,690
21. Ipswich*	28.11	1–0(0–0)6718
22. Leeds	5.12	1–0(0–0)15,977
23. Aston Villa*	12.12	1–2(1–2)27,789
24. Blackburn	19.12	0–2(0–0)8542
25. Plymouth*	26.12	0–1(0–0)9166
26. Shrewsbury	28.12	0–0(0–0)6397
27. Bournemouth	1.1	2–4(0–1)7963
28. Swindon*	2.1	1–1(0–0)7829
29. Stoke	16.1	1–3(1–1)10,076
30. C Palace	6.2	0–3(0–1)8809
31. Millwall*	9.2	1–0(0–0)5878
32. Huddersfield	27.2	2–2(2–1)5441
33. Bradford*	5.3	1–1(1–1)8101
34. WBA*	8.3	0–1(0–0)12,331
35. Reading	12.3	1–1(1–1)6285
36. Oldham*	19.3	1–3(0–0)6012
37. Middlesbro	26.3	1–0(0–1)15,465
38. Hull*	2.4	1–1(0–1)7059
39. Leicester	5.4	0–2(0–2)13,541
40. Sheff Utd*	9.4	1–0(1–0)7046
41. Barnsley	23.4	2–2(0–1)4949
42. Man City*	30.4	0–3(0–1)8014
43. Ipswich	2.5	0–1(0–0)11,067
44. Leeds*	6.5	0–0(0–0)6024

Final League Position: 19

Appearances (subs)/goals: 22(0) 0, 38(0) 0, 32(0) 1, 33(0) 1, 28(2) 3, 37(0) 0, 15(13) 7, 12(1) 1, 17(6) 4, 43(0) 2, 26(1) 0, 6(3) 0, 23(9) 1, 22(0) 0, 12(2) 2, 8(0) 2, 00(1) 0, 6(3) 0, 3(1) 1, 1(2) 0, 30(0) 0, 8(0) 0, 7(0) 0, 00(1) 0, 0(1) 0

Own goals: McElhinney, match 10; Jeffels, match 41.

BLACKBURN ROVERS

Ewood Park, Blackburn BB2 4JF.

Back row (left to right): Scott Sellars, Ally Dawson, Ian Miller, Colin Hendry, Keith Hill, David Mail. *Third row:* Jack Cunningham (Remedial Therapist), Jim Furnell (Reserve Team Manager), Chris Price, Simon Barker, Vince O'Keefe, Tony Diamond, Terry Gennoe, John Millar, Howard Gayle, Don S. Mackay (Manager), Tony Parkes (Ass. Manager). *Second row:* Sean Curry, Mark Patterson, Nicky Reid, William Fox (Chairman), John W. Howarth (Secretary), Chris Sulley, Alan Ainscow, Simon Garner. *Front row:* Ray Driver, Douglas Gornall, Jason Wilcox, Stephen Holmes, Craig Skinner, David Fantom, Len Johnrose, David May, Mark Lee, Micky Mylott, Paul Bolton

Stadium Capacity: 21,000
Pitch Dimensions: 116yd 2ft × 72yd 2ft.
Telephone: 0254–55432.
Chairman: W. Fox.
Vice-Chairman: R. D. Coar B. Sc.
Directors: T. W. Ibbotson LL. B. , K. C. Lee, L. Neale, I. R. Stanners, G. R. Root FCMA.
Manager: Donald Mackay.
Post-War Managers: Eddie Hapgood, Will Scott, Jack Bruton, Jackie Bestall, John Carey, Dally Duncan, Jack Marshall, Eddie Quigley, John Carey, Ken Furphy, Gordon Lee, Jim Smith, Jim Iley, Howard Kendall, Bobby Saxton (15).
Assistant Manager: T. Parkes.
Physio: J. Cunningham.
Secretary: John W. Howarth FAAI.
Commercial Manager: Ken Beamish.
Founded: 1875.
Turned Professional: 1880.
Nickname: The Blue and Whites.
Former Names: Blackburn Grammar School OB.
Former Grounds: Brookhouse Ground 1875–76, Alexandra Meadows 1876–81, Leamington Road 1881–90.
Record Attendance: 61,783 v Bolton W, FA Cup 6th Round, 2 March 1929.
Record Victory: 11–0 v Rossendale U, FA Cup 1st Round, 1884–85.
Record Defeat: 0–8 v Arsenal, Division 1, 25 February 1933.
Most League Points: (3 for a win) 77, Division 2, 1987–88. (2 for a win) 60, Division 3, 1974–75.
Most League Goals: 114, Division 2, 1954–55.
Highest League Scorer in a Season: Ted Harper, 43, Division 1, 1925–26.
Highest Total of League Goals: Tommy Briggs, 140, 1952–58.
Most League Appearances: Derek Fazackerley, 596, 1970–86.
League History: 1988 Founder Members of the League, 1936–39 Division 2, 1946–47 Division 1, 1947–57 Division 2, 1957–66 Division 1, 1966–71 Division 3, 1971–75 Division 3, 1975–79 Division 2, 1979–80 Division 3, 1980– Division 2.
Honours: Division 1 Champions 1911–12, 1913–14. Division 2 Champions 1938–39, runners-up 1957–58. Division 3 Champions 1974–75, runners-up 1979–80. FA Cup winners 1884, 1885, 1886, 1890, 1891, 1928, runners-up 1882, 1960. Full Members' Cup winners 1987.
Colours: Blue and white halved shirts, white shorts, blue socks with red and white tops. **Second strip:** All yellow.

BLACKBURN ROVERS – LEAGUE RECORD 1987–88

Match no/Opp/Date		O'Keefe	Price	Sulley	Barker	Hendry	Dawson	Gayle	Reid	Diamond	Garner	Paterson	Sellars	Ainscow	Curry	Gennoe	Miller	Mail	Hill	Millar	Johnrose	FT(HT)Att	Lge pos
1. Hull	15.8	1	2	3	4	5	6	7	8	9†	10^1	11^1	12									2-2(0-0)6426	—
2. Barnsley*	18.8	1	2	3	4	5	6	7	8	9†	10	11‡	12	14								0-1(0-1)6708	—
3. WBA*	22.8	1	2	3	4	5^1	6	7†	8		10^1	11	12	9^1								3-1(2-1)5619	7
4. Sheff Utd	29.8	1	2	3	4	5	6	7	8		10^1	11‡	14	12	9†							1-3(0-2)8540	14
5. Ipswich*	1.9	1‡	2	3	4	5^1	6	7	8		10	11†	14	12	9							1-0(0-0)6074	—
6. Man City	5.9		2	3	4	5	6		8	11‡	10	12	9^1		1		7					2-1(1-1)20,372	6
7. Huddersfield*	12.9		2	3	4_1	5	6†	11^1	8‡	14	10	9	12		1		7					2-2(2-2)7109	6
8. Birmingham	15.9		2	3	4	5		7	8	10	9	12	1	6	11†							0-1(0-0)6032	—
9. Bradford	19.9		2	3	4	5		7†	8	10	11	9^1	1	12	6							1-2(1-1)12,068	13
10. Middlesbro*	26.9		2†	3		9	6		8	10	11	12	1	7†	4‡	5	14					0-2(0-0)6879	16
11. Aston Villa	30.9		2	3	4^1	5	6		8	10	11		9	1	7							1-1(1-1)11,772	—
12. Leeds*	3.10		2	3	4	5	6		8	10^1	11	12	9	1	7†							1-1(0-0)7675	18
13. Bournemouth	10.10		2^1	3	4	5	6		8	10	11	12	9†	1	7							1-1(0-0)6789	16
14. Stoke*	17.10		2	3	4†	5			8	10^1	9	11^1	12		1		7	6				2-0(1-0)7280	12
15. Plymouth*	24.10		2	3		5			8	10	9†	11_1	4	12	1		7	6				1-1(0-0)6014	15
16. Leicester	31.10		2	3		5^1	12		8	10^1	$9‡$	11	4†	14	1		7	6				2-1(1-0)8650	12
17. Oldham*	7.11		2	3		5			8^1	$10†$	9	11	4	12	1		7	6				1-0(1-0)7519	12
18. Shrewsbury	14.11		2^1	3	4	5	7		8	10	11	9^1	1				6					2-1(0-0)3164	10
19. C Palace*	21.11		2^1	3	4^1	5	7		8	10	12	11	9†	1			6					2-0(0-0)6372	9
20. Reading	28.11		2	3	4	5	7		8	10	11	9	1				6					0-0(0-0)4535	10
21. Millwall*	5.12		2	3	4	5^1	7		8	10	11^1	9	1				6					2-1(1-0)6140	9
22. WBA	12.12		2^1	3	4	5	7†		8	10		11	9	1			6	12				1-0(1-0)7303	9
23. Birmingham*	19.12		2	3	4	5^1			8	10	11^1		1	7	6		9					2-0(0-0)8542	7
24. Middlesbro	26.12		2	3	4	5			8	10^1	11		1	7	6		9					1-1(1-1)23,536	8
25. Bradford*	28.12		2	3	4	5^1			8	10	11		1	7†	6	12	9					1-1(0-1)14,124	9
26. Sheff Utd*	1.1		2^1†		4_1	5^1	7‡	14	8	10^1	11	12	1	6	3		9					4-1(3-0)10,593	7
27. Huddersfield	2.1		2		4‡	5	7	14†	8	$10^1‡$	11	12	1	6	3		9					2-1(2-0)10,735	5
28. Hull*	16.1		2^1	3	4	5†			8	11	7	10	1	12	6		9^1					2-1(2-0)9692	4
29. Ipswich	30.1		2^1	3		5			8	10	11^1	4^1	1	7	6		9					2-0(2-0)12,406	2
30. Man City*	6.2		2^1	3		5			8	10^1	11	4	1	7	6		9					2-1(1-0)13,508	2
31. Barnsley	13.2		2	3		5			8	10	12	$11‡$	4	1	7	6	9					1-0(0-0)8972	2
32. Aston Villa*	20.2		2	3		5			8	10^1	11	4	1	7	6		9^2					3-2(1-0)17,356	1
33. Leeds	27.2		2	3	12	5^1	14		8	10^1	11	4‡	1	7‡	6		9					2-2(0-2)23,843	2
34. Stoke	5.3		2^1	3	4	5	7		8	10	11		1		6		9					1-2(0-1)14,100	2
35. Bournemouth*	12.3		2^1		4^1	5	7		8	10	11		1		6	3	9^1					3-1(1-0)10,807	2
36. Leicester*	19.3		2		4	5^1	12	8		10	11^1		1	7†	6	3	9					3-3(0-0)12,506	2
37. Plymouth	26.3		2	3	4	5		7		10	11	12	1	14	6‡		8	$9†$				0-3(0-1)12,359	2
38. Oldham	1.4		2	3	4^1	$5^1‡$	6	14		10	11	8	1	7†	12		9					2-4(2-2)14,853	—
39. Shrewsbury*	4.4		2		4^1†	5^1	7	12		10	11	9	1	6		3	8					2-2(2-0)13,741	3
40. Swindon	9.4				12	5	2			10	11	4	1	7	6	3	8^2	$9†$				2-1(0-1)9373	3
41. Swindon*	25.4		2			5	4			10	11	12	1	7†	6	3	8	9				0-0(0-0)13,563	—
42. C Palace	30.4		2		5†	4		14		$10‡$	11	7	1	12	6	3	8	9				0-2(0-1)13,059	5
43. Reading*	2.5		2		5^1	8	4	12		10	11	3	1	7†	6		9					1-0(0-0)11,373	5
44. Millwall	7.5		2^1		4^1	5	9	7		10^2	11	8	1	6	3							4-1(2-0)15,467	5
Apps(subs)/goals		5(0) 0	43(0) 10	31(2) 9	44(0) 12	20(2) 0	10(3) 1	2(5) 0	40(0) 14	11(2) 2	38(4) 7	16(12) 1	15(5) 4	5(4) 0	39(0) 0	19(4) 0	34(2) 0	10(1) 0	13(2) 0	20(0) 6	5(0) 0		

Final League Position: 5

Own goals: Walsh, match 36

DIVISION 3

BLACKPOOL

Bloomfield Road Ground, Blackpool FY 6JJ.

Back row (left to right): Bob Ward (Physiotherapist), Alan Hughes, Dean Kay, Ian Harrington, Sean Kellett, Jason Butcher, David Bailey, Mike McCarthy. *Middle row:* Mike Davies, John Deary, Andy McAteer, Richard Powell, Colin Methven, Tony Cunningham, Barry Siddall, Paul Jones, Neil Matthews, Mark Brashaw. *Front row:* Mark Taylor, Craig Madden, Steve Morgan, Mike Walsh, Keith Walwyn, Brian Butler, Carl Lancashire, Alan Mayes

Stadium Capacity: 12,696.
Pitch Dimensions: 111 × 73yds.
Telephone: 0253–404331.
Chairman: K. Chadwick LL. B.
Vice-Chairman: G. Bloor.
Directors: M. H. Melling, T. White, O. J. Oyston, J. Crowther, J. Wilde MBE, J. Allitt.
Manager: Sam Ellis.
Post-War Managers: Joe Smith, Ron Suart, Stan Mortensen, Les Shannon, Jimmy Meadows, Bob Stokoe, Harry Potts, Allan Brown, Jimmy Meadows, Bob Stokoe, Stan Ternent, Alan Ball Jnr, Allan Brown (13).
Assistant Manager: Mick Docherty.
Physio: Robert Ward MCSP SRP.
Secretary: David Johnson.
Commercial Manager: Geoffrey Warburton.
Sponsors: Harry Feeney for Nissan.
Founded: 1887.
Turned Professional: 1887.
Nickname: The Seasiders.
Former Names: Blackpool St John's prior to 1887. Combined with South Shore FC in 1899.
Former Grounds: Raikes Hall Gardens 1887–97, Athletic Grounds 1897–98.
Record Attendance: 39,118 v Man U, Division 1, April 1952.
Record Victory: 10–0 v Lanerossi Vicenza, Anglo–Italian Tournament, 10 June 1972.
Record Defeat: 1–10 v Small Heath, Division 2, 2 March 1901 and v Huddersfield T, Division 1, 13 December, 1930.
Most League Points: (3 for a win) 86, Division 4, 1984–85. (2 for a win) 58, Division 2, 1929–30.
Most League Goals: 98, Division 2, 1929–30.
Highest League Scorer in a Season: Jimmy Hampson, 45, Division 2, 1929–30.
Highest Total of League Goals: Jimmy Hampson, 247, 1927–38.
Most League Appearances: Jimmy Armfield, 568, 1952–71.
League History: 1896 Elected to Division 2, 1899 Failed re-election, 1900 Re–elected, 1900–30 Division 2, 1937–67 Division 1, 1967–70 Division 2, 1970–71 Division 1, 1971–78 Division 2, 1978–81 Division 3, 1981–85 Division 4, 1985– Division 3.
Honours: Division 1 runners-up 1955–56. Division 2 Champions 1929–30, runners-up 1936–37, 1969–70. Division 4 runners-up 1984–85. FA Cup winners 1953, runners-up 1948, 1951. Anglo-Italian Cup winners 1971, runners-up 1972.
Colours: All tangerine with white trim. **Second strip:** All blue.

BLACKPOOL – LEAGUE RECORD 1987–88

Match no/Opp/Date		Staddall	Davies	Morgan	Matthews	Methven	Jones	Cunningham	Madden	Welwyn	Dean	Taylor	Butler	Walsh	Rooney	Bradshaw	McAteer	Hutchinson	Lancashire	Coughlin	Lester	Shaw	Muggleton	Powell	Wright	FT(HT)Att Lge pos
1. Gillingham	15.8	1	2	3	4	5	6	7	8	9	10	11														0-0(0-0)4430 —
2. Walsall*	22.8	1	2	3	4	5	6†	7¹	8	9	10	11‡	12	14												1-2(0-1)4614 17
3. Bury	29.8	1	2	3	4	5	12		8‡	9¹	10	11†	7	6	14											1-3(0-3)3053 19
4. Bristol R*	31.8	1	2	3	4	5		7²		9	10	11	8	6												2-1(0-0)3319 —
5. Brighton	5.9	1	2	3	4	5		7²	8	9	10	11		6												3-1(1-0)7166 15
6. Chester*	12.9	1	2†	3	4	5	14	7	8	9	10	11	12‡	6												0-1(0-0)4035 16
7. Doncaster	15.9	1		3	4	5		7¹	8	9	10	11†		6	2	12										1-2(0-0)1558 —
8. Brentford	19.9	1	2	3	4	5†	10	7	8	9¹		11		6		12										1-2(0-1)3886 20
9. Preston*	26.9	1		3	4	12	10	7	8¹‡	9¹		11	6†		5	2	14									3-0(2-0)8406 16
10. York	29.9	1	2	3¹	4	12	10†	7‡	8¹			11	6		5	9	14									3-1(2-1)2559 —
11. Fulham*	3.10	1	2	3	4	5		7	8²	12		11	6		10	9†										2-1(1-0)4973 13
12. Sunderland*	17.10	1	2	3	4	5		7	8	9		11	6		10†	12										0-2(0-0)8476 14
13. Grimsby	20.10	1	2	3	4	5		7	12	9	8	11¹	6		10†											1-1(1-1)2260 —
14. Wigan*	24.10	1	2‡	3	4	5		7	8†	9		11	6		14	10	12									0-0(0-0)4821 18
15. Mansfield	31.10	1	2	3		5	6	7	8	9		11	4			10										0-0(0-0)3221 16
16. Bristol C*	3.11	1	2†	3¹	4	5		7	8‡	9		11¹	6			10	12									4-2(1-0)3140 —
17. Rotherham*	7.11	1	2	3	4	5			8¹	9		11¹	12	6¹		10		7†								3-0(1-0)3447 12
18. Port Vale	22.11	1	2	3	4	5		7	8†	9		11	12	6		10										0-0(0-0)3594 —
19. Nthampton*	28.11	1	2	3¹	4	5†	14	7¹	8	9¹		11	6‡			10	12									3-1(2-1)3593 10
20. Chesterfield	12.12	1	2	3	4	5			8	9		11¹	6			10			7							1-1(1-0)2279 11
21. Southend*	19.12	1	2‡	3	4†	5	6	7	12	9¹		11			14	10			8							1-1(1-0)3277 11
22. Preston	26.12	1	2¹	3	4	5	6	7	12	9†		11				10			8							1-2(1-0)11,155 12
23. Notts Co*	28.12	1	2	3	4†	5	6	7	12	9		11				10			8¹							1-0(0-0)4627 11
24. Bury*	1.1	1	12	3¹‡	4†	5	6	7¹	14¹	9¹		11			2¹	10			8							5-1(2-1)4240 9
25. Chester	2.1	1	12	3	4	5	6	7	14	9¹‡		11			2†	10			8							1-1(0-3)3093 9
26. Brentford*	16.1	1	2	3	4†	5	6	7	12	9	10	11							8							0-1(0-1)3911 12
27. Brighton*	6.2	1	2‡	3†		5	6		12	9	10	11			14				8	4¹	7					1-3(0-0)4081 14
28. Notts Co	13.2		2	3¹		5			12	9	10	11²		6†	14				8	4‡	7	1				3-2(0-1)5794 12
29. Gillingham*	20.2		2†	3		5‡			12	9¹	10	11¹		6	14				8¹	4	7	1				3-3(0-0)3045 12
30. Walsall	23.2	1	2	3		5	6		12	9†	10	11‡			14				8	4	7‡					2-3(0-0)4252 —
31. Fulham	27.2	1	2	3		5		7	12	9¹	10	11		6					8	4†						1-3(0-1)4072 15
32. York*	1.3	1	2	3		5¹		7	12	9	10	11¹		6					8	4†						2-1(1-1)2249 —
33. Sunderland	5.3	1	2	3		5		7	12	9	10	11¹		6					8	4†						2-2(1-2)15,513 14
34. Aldershot*	12.3	1	2	3	6	5			8	9¹	10¹	11¹								4	7					3-2(1-1)2661 12
35. Mansfield*	19.3	1	2	3	6	5			8†	9	10	11¹‡						12		4	7					2-0(1-0)2847 12
36. Wigan	25.3	1	2	3	6	5			8	9	10	11								4	7					0-0(0-0)4505 —
37. Aldershot	29.3	1	2	3	4	5			8	9	10	11	6								7					0-0(0-0)2091 —
38. Rotherham	2.4	1	2	3	4	5	6	7‡	12	9	10¹	11†			14				8							1-0(0-0)3001 9
39. Port Vale*	4.4	1	2	3	6	5			8†	9	10	11¹‡						12		4						1-2(0-2)5516 11
40. Bristol C	9.4	1		3‡	2	5			10	9	12	7	11¹‡			6	8	14		4						1-2(0-1)6460 12
41. Doncaster*	15.4		2	3	8	5			10	6¹	9¹	7†	11²					12		4				1		4-2(1-0)2291 —
42. Grimsby*	23.4		2	3	8	5			10	6†	9	7	11¹‡			12				4				1		3-0(1-0)2555 9
43. Bristol R	27.4		2	3	8	5			10	6†	9	7		12		11				4				1		0-2(0-2)3546 —
44. Nthampton	30.4		2‡	3¹	8	12¹			10	14	9¹	7			5	11	6†			4				1		3-3(0-0)5730 10
45. Chesterfield*	2.5		2	3	8	12			10		9¹	7			5†	11	6‡			4				1	14	1-0(1-0)2950 10
46. Southend	7.5		2	3	4				12	6	14	9†	7			5	8	11‡			10			1		0-4(0-1)5541 10

Final League Position: 10

Apps/(sub)/goals: 38(0)0 · 36(2)0 · 46(0)6 · 27(0)0 · 35(5)2 · 23(6)0 · 40(0)10 · 25(9)11 · 38(1)13 · 34(3)3 · 41(0)21 · 9(0)1 · 26(4)0 · 14(2)0 · 18(3)0 · 3(3)0 · 2(5)0 · 24(0)2 · 11(0)1 · 4(2)0 · 2(0)0 · 6(0)0 · 0(1)0

Own goal: Wrightson, match 9.

DIVISION 2

BOLTON WANDERERS

Burnden Park, Bolton BL3 2QR.

Back row (left to right): Neil Whatmore, Steve Elliot, John Thomas, Julian Darby, Steve Thompson, David Felgate, Ryan Price, Mark Came, Trevor Morgan, Dave Sutton, Dean Crombie, Mark Winstanley. *Middle row:* Peter Bell, Ian Stevens, Ian Callaghan, Jeff Chandler, Chris Banks, Paul Hughes, Nicky Brookman, Warren Joyce, Derek Scott, Gareth Henshaw, Derek Booth. *Front row (YTS):* Malcolm Jackson, Kevin Still, Patrick Halligan, Paul Gaskell, Dave Roberts, Pewter Nightingale (Physio), Phil Neil (Manager), Steve Carroll (Youth Coach), Neil Fisher, Mark Raben, Nicky Spooner, Mike Jeffery, Chris O'Brien.

Stadium Capacity: 2800.
Pitch Dimensions: 113 × 76yds.
Telephone: 0204–389200.
Chairman: B. Chaytow.
Vice-Chairman: S. Jones.
Directors: G. Hargreaves, G. Seymour, G. Warburton, G. Ball.
Manager: Phil Neal.
Post-War Managers: Walter Rowley, Bill Ridding, Nat Lofthouse, Jimmy McIlroy, Jimmy Meadows, Nat Lofthouse, Jimmy Armfield, Ian Greaves, Stan Anderson, George Mulhall, John McGovern, Charlie Wright (12).
Assistant Manager: Mick Brown.
Physio: Philip Stock.
Secretary: Des McBain.
Sponsors: Normid.
Founded: 1874.
Turned Professional: 1880.
Nickname: The Trotters.
Former Names: Christ Church FC 1874–77.
Former Grounds: Park Recreation Ground, then Cockle's Field. Moved to Pike's Lane 1881–95.
Record Attendance: 85,000 (estimated) v Stoke C. FA Cup 6th Round, 2nd leg, 9 March 1946.
Record Victory: 13–0 v Sheffield U, FA Cup 2nd Round, 1 February 1890.
Record Defeat: 0–7 v Manchester C, Division 1, 21 March 1936.
Most League Points: (3 for a win) 78, Division 4, 1987–88. (2 for a win) 61, Division 3, 1972–73.
Most League Goals: 96, Division 2, 1934–35.
Highest League Scorer in a Season: Joe Smith, 38, Division 1, 1920–21.
Highest Total of League Goals: Nat Lofthouse, 255, 1946–61.
Most League Appearances: Eddie Hopkinson, 519, 1956–70.
League History: 1888 Founder Members of the League, 1899–1900 Division 2, 1900–03 Division 1, 1903–05 Division 2, 1905–08 Division 1, 1908–09 Division 2, 1909–10 Division 1, 1910–11 Division 2, 1911–33 Division 1, 1933–35 Division 2, 1935–64 Division 1, 1964–71 Division 2 1971–73 Division 3, 1973–78 Division 2, 1978–80 Division 1, 1980–83 Division 2, 1983–87 Division 2, 1987–88 Division 4, 1988– Division 3.
Honours: Division 2 Champions 1908–09, 1977–78, runners-up 1899–1900, 1904–05, 1910–11, 1934–35. Division 3 Champions 1972–73. FA Cup winners 1923, 1926, 1929, 1958, runners-up 1894, 1904, 1953. Associate Members' Cup runners-up 1986.
Colours: White shirts, navy blue shorts, white socks. **Second strip:** Red shirts, white shorts, red socks.

BOLTON WANDERERS – LEAGUE RECORD 1987–88

Match no/Opp	Date	Felgate	Darby	Crombie	Thompson	Sutton	Came	Henshaw	Joyce	Morgan	Thomas	Chandler	Brookman	Scott	Elliott	Savage	Neal	Barnes	Stevens	Winstanley	Callaghan	Storer	Hughes	May	FT(HT)Att	Lge pos
1. Crewe*	15.8	1	2†	3	4	5	6	7¹	8	9	10	11	12												1-1(1-0)4792	—
2. Cardiff*	22.8	1	2	3	4	6	5	7	8	9	10	11¹													1-0(1-0)4530	5
3. Scarboro	29.8	1		3	4†	5	6	7	8	9	10			11	2	12									0-4(0-2)4462	16
4. Peterboro*	31.8	1		3	4¹	6	5	7	8	9	10			11	2										2-0(1-0)3746	—
5. Hereford	5.9	1		3	4	6	5	7	8	9¹	10²			11	2										3-0(2-0)2541	3
6. Halifax*	12.9	1		3	4	6	5	7¹	8	9	10				2	11									2-0(1-0)4445	2
7. Scunthorpe	15.9	1		3	4	6	5	7	8	9¹	10				2	11									1-1(1-0)2501	—
8. Torquay	19.9	1	2	3	4‡	6	5	7	8	9	10†	14		12	11¹1										1-2(0-2)2211	6
9. Hartlepool*	26.9	1	2‡	3			6	5¹	7	8	9†	10	4	12	11	14									1-2(0-0)4398	10
10. Wolves*	3.10	1		3	4	6	5	7	8	9	10₁				2	11									1-0(0-0)3833	9
11. Darlington	10.10	1		3	14	6	5	7‡	8	9†	12	2	10	4	11										0-1(0-1)1763	13
12. Carlisle*	17.10	1	14¹	3	8	6	5			10†	7²	2	9¹	4	11‡	12									5-0(2-0)4184	11
13. Exeter*	20.10	1	11	3†	8	6	5¹			9		7	2	10	4		12								1-0(0-0)4165	—
14. Rochdale	24.10	1	11	3†	8	6	5			9¹1		7	2	10	4		12								2-2(0-1)4294	8
15. Swansea*	31.10	1	11	3†	8¹	6	5		12	9		7	2	10	4										1-1(0-1)4607	10
16. Newport	3.11	1	11	3	8	5				9		7	2	10¹	4		6								1-0(1-0)1566	—
17. Orient*	7.11	1	11	3	8	5			12	9¹		7	2	10	4		6†								1-0(0-0)5189	3
18. Burnley	21.11	1	11	6	8	5	3†		12	9¹		7	2	10	4										1-2(0-0)7489	7
19. Cambridge*	28.11	1	11	3	8	5			12	9¹1		7	2	10	4		6†								2-2(1-1)4294	—
20. Colchester	11.12	1	11		6	5	12		14	9		7†	2	10	4	3			8‡						0-3(0-1)1725	—
21. Tranmere	15.12	1	11		8	6	5	7	12	9			2†	10	4			3							0-2(0-0)3064	—
22. Wrexham*	19.12	1	11		8¹	6	5	7	12¹	9		4	2	10†				3							2-0(1-0)3701	7
23. Hartlepool	26.12	1	11		8	6	5	4		10			2			3			7						0-0(0-0)4102	7
24. Stockport*	28.12	1	11		8	6	5	4		10¹†	9		3				12		7¹	2					2-1(1-0)6607	—
25. Scarboro*	1.1	1	11		8¹	6	5¹	4		10	9¹		2			3	12		7						3-1(1-0)6295	—
26. Halifax	12.1	1	11		8	6	5	4		10			2			3			9	7					0-0(0-0)2689	—
27. Torquay*	16.1	1	11			5¹	4†			10		12		3		6			9		7	2			1-2(1-1)5993	—
28. Peterboro	30.1	1			8	6	5	12		10	9¹2	11¹	3		4						7	2			4-0(2-0)3485	—
29. Hereford*	6.2	1			8	6	5			10	9	11	3		4¹						7	2			1-0(0-0)4559	—
30. Stockport	12.2	1	5		8	6				10¹	9	11¹	3		4						7	2			2-1(1-0)4814	—
31. Crewe	20.2	1			8	6	5	12		10¹	9	11	3		4						7†	2			1-2(1-0)4305	—
32. Wolves	27.2	1			8	6	5	12		10	9	11¹	3		4		14				7‡	2			0-4(0-4)12,430	—
33. Tranmere*	1.3	1	11		8¹	6	5	7		10	9¹					3	4			2					2-0(0-0)3979	—
34. Carlisle	5.3	1	11		8	6		7		10	9₁	5¹	3		4					2					2-0(1-0)2796	—
35. Darlington*	11.3	1	11		8	6		7†		10	9	5¹	3		4					12	2				1-1(1-0)4948	—
36. Swansea	18.3	1	11		8	6	5		12	10†	9		4		2	3					7				0-1(0-0)3980	—
37. Rochdale*	26.3	1	11		8	6	5		14	10†	9		4		2	3					7‡		12		0-0(0-0)4875	—
38. Orient	2.4	1	11¹	3	8	6	5			9			2	10	4								7¹		2-1(0-1)4537	—
39. Burnley*	4.4	1	11	3	8¹	6	5			9			2	10	4								7¹		2-1(1-1)9921	—
40. Exeter	9.4	1	11	3	8	6	5			9¹				10	4				2		7				1-0(1-0)1962	—
41. Cardiff	15.4	1	11	3‡	8	6†	5	14		10	9		2		4		12				7				0-1(0-0)6705	—
42. Scunthorpe*	19.4	1	11		8	5	4†			9			2	10		3		6			12		7		0-0(0-0)6669	—
43. Newport*	23.4	1	11‡	3	8¹	5	14			10¹	9²₁		2		4		12	6¹					7†		6-0(4-0)4357	—
44. Cambridge	29.4	1	11		8	5				10	9¹		2		4¹	3		6					7		2-2(1-1)2063	—
45. Colchester*	2.5	1	11		8	5¹				10	9¹†	12¹	2		4¹	3		6					7		4-0(2-0)5540	—
46. Wrexham	7.5	1	11		8	5				10	9		2		4¹	3		6					7		1-0(0-0)5977	—
Appearances(subs)/goals		46(0)0	34(1)2	24(0)0	43(1)7	38(0)0	43(0)5	23(0)2	11(0)0	31(2)7	45(1)22	22(3)2	23(5)6	40(0)0	16(5)2	39(0)5	2(0)0	2(7)0	8(0)1	1(0)0	12(3)1	11(0)0	9(1)2			Final League Position: 3

Own goals: Shaw, match 6; Wright, match 12.

DIVISION 2

AFC BOURNEMOUTH

Dean Court Ground, Bournemouth BH7 7AF.

Back row (left to right): Mark Whitlock, Billy Clark, John Williams, Carl Richards. *Middle row:* John Kirk (Physio/Trainer), Adrian Randall, David Coleman, Tony Pulis, Gerry Peyton, John Smeulders, Trevor Aylott, Tommy Heffernan, Paul Morrell, Jimmy Gabriel (Ass. Manager). *Front row:* Sean O'Driscoll, David Puckett, Tommy Keane, Mark Newson (Captain), Harry Redknapp (Manager), Richard Cooke, Mark O'Connor, Shaun Brooks, David Armstrong.

Stadium Capacity: 12,038.
Pitch Dimensions: 112 × 75yds.
Telephone: 0202–35381.
Chairman: J. P. Nolan.
Vice-Chairman: P. W. Hayward JP. **Managing Director:** B. Tiler.
Directors: E. G. Keep, G. P. Pound, J. P. Nolan, W. Oakley, T. E. A. Morey, G. M. C. Hayward, B. E. Willis.
Manager: Harry Redknapp.
Post-War Managers: Harry Kinghorn, Harry Lowe, Jack Bruton, Freddie Cox, Don Welsh, Bill McGarry, Reg Flewin, Freddie Cox, John Bond, Trevor Hartley, John Benson, Alec Stock, David Webb, Don Megson (14).
Assistant Manager: Jimmy Gabriel. Physios: J. Kirk & Brian Gant.
Secretary: B. Tiler.
Commercial Manager: B. Tiler.
Founded: 1899.
Turned Professional: 1912.
Nickname: The Cherries.
Former Names: Boscombe St Johns 1890–99, Boscombe 1899–1923, Bournemouth & Boscombe Athletic 1923–71.
Former Grounds: Castlemain Road, Pokesdown 1899–1910.
Record Attendance: 28,799 v Manchester U, FA Cup 6th Round, 2 March 1957.
Record Victory: 11–0 v Margate, FA Cup 1st Round, 20 November 1971.
Record Defeat: 0–9 v Lincoln C, Division 3, 18 December 1982.
Most League Points: (3 for a win) 97, Division 3, 1986–87. (2 for a win) 62, Division 3, 1971–72.
Most League Goals: 88, Division 3(S), 1956–57.
Highest League Scorer in a Season: Ted MacDougall, 42, 1970–71.
Highest Total of League Goals: Ron Eyre, 202, 1924–33.
Most League Appearances: Ray Bumstead, 412, 1958–70.
League History: 1923, Elected to Division 3(S). 1970–71 Division 4, 1971–75 Division 3, 1975–82 Division 4, 1982–87 Division 3, 1987– Division 2.
Honours: Division 3 Champions 1986–87. Division 3(S) runners-up 1947–48. Division 4 runners-up 1970–71. Associate Members' Cup winners 1984.
Colours: All red with white trim. **Second strip:** All sky blue.

BOURNEMOUTH – LEAGUE RECORD 1987–88

Match no/Opp	Date	Peyton	Newson	Morrell	Brooks	Williams	Whitlock	O'Driscoll	Richards	Aylott	Armstrong	O'Connor	Pulis	Smeulders	Cooke	Clark	Keane	Hefferman	Puckett	Shearer	Goulet	Langan	Coleman	Close	Randall	FT(HT)Att	Lge pos
1. Sheff Utd	15.8	1	2	3	4¹	5	6	7†	8	9	10	11	12													1-0(0-0)9757	—
2. Bradford*	22.8		2	3	4	5	6	7	8¹	9	10₁		1	11												2-0(0-0)7407	2
3. Birmingham	29.8	1	2	3	4	5	6	7	8	9	10¹			11												1-1(0-0)8284	3
4. Barnsley*	31.8	1	2	3	4†	5	6	7	8¹	9		12		11												1-2(1-1)7480	—
5. Hull	5.9	1	2	3	4¹†	5	6	7	8	9	10	11		12												1-2(0-1)5807	13
6. Reading*	12.9	1	2¹	3	4		6	7	8	9¹		11¹	10			5										3-0(1-0)7597	7
7. Middlesbro	15.9	1	2	3	4		6	7	8	9†		11	10		12	5										0-3(0-0)9660	—
8. WBA	19.9	1	2	3	4	5	6	7	12			11	10†	9		8										0-3(0-1)7749	15
9. Leicester*	26.9	1	2₁	3	4	5	6	7	8	9¹		11†		10		12										2-3(1-1)7969	18
10. Plymouth*	29.9	1	2	3	4¹	5	6	7		9¹		11†		10	12	8										2-2(1-1)6491	—
11. Stoke	3.10	1	2	3	4	5	6	7	8	9		12	10†	11												0-1(0-0)8104	21
12. Blackburn*	10.10	1	2	3	4†	5		7¹		9		11	10				6	12	8							1-1(0-0)6789	20
13. Aston Villa	17.10	1	2‡	3	12	5	6	7		9¹		11	4	10†			14		8							1-1(0-1)15,145	20
14. Shrewsbury*	20.10	1		3		5	6	7¹	12	9¹		11†	4	10			2		8							2-0(2-0)5587	—
15. Leeds	24.10	1		3	12	5	6	7	14¹	9		11	4†	10			2₁		8‡							2-3(0-3)15,253	19
16. Ipswich*	31.10	1		3	4¹	5	6	7	10†	9		11		8			2		12							1-0(1-0)8105	18
17. Millwall	3.11	1		3	4	5	6	7¹		9		11		8			2		10¹							2-1(0-0)5734	—
18. C Palace*	7.11	1		3	4‡	5¹	6	7¹		9		11		8	14		2	12	10†							2-3(2-3)9083	16
19. Huddersfield*	21.11	1		3	4	5	6	7		9		11	2†					8	12							0-2(0-1)6419	19
20. Swindon	28.11	1		3		5	6	7		9		11¹	4				2	8¹								2-4(1-2)7934	19
21. Man City*	1.12	1		3	14	5	6‡	7		9		11		12				8	10†	2	4					0-2(0-1)9499	—
22. Oldham*	5.12	1		3		5	6	7		9		11		12				8¹₁	10†	2	4					2-2(1-1)5777	19
23. Bradford	12.12	1				5	6	7		9		11	4†	10				8	12	2	3					0-2(0-0)10,763	19
24. Middlesbro*	19.12	1		3	4	5	6	7		9		11		10				8		2						0-0(0-0)6792	20
25. Leicester	26.12	1		3	4	5	6	7		9		11		10‡				8†	12	2						1-0(1-0)11,452	17
26. WBA*	28.12	1		3			6	7		9¹		11	4¹	10		5		8†	12¹	2						3-2(1-0)8969	16
27. Birmingham*	1.1	1		3	4†	5	6	7		9		11	12	10‡				14¹	8¹‡	2						4-2(1-0)7963	16
28. Sheff Utd*	16.1	1		3	4	5¹	6†	7		9‡		11	12	10				14		2	8					1-2(0-1)6466	17
29. Hull*	6.2	1	8	3	4¹	5	6	7		9¹				10₁						2	11²					6-2(3-1)5901	17
30. Man City	13.2	1	8	3	4	5	6†	7		9		12		10						2	11					0-2(0-1)16,161	17
31. Stoke*	27.2	1	8	3	4†	5	6	7		9		12		10						2	11†					0-0(0-0)6871	19
32. Aston Villa*	5.3	1	8	3	4	5	6	7‡		9	14	12		10						2	11†					1-2(0-1)10,057	20
33. Barnsley	8.3	1	8	3	4	5	6		11¹	9	10†	7							12	2						1-2(1-1)6140	—
34. Blackburn	12.3	1	8	3	4†	5	6		10‡	9		12	7					14		2	11¹					1-3(1-1)10,807	21
35. Ipswich	19.3	1	8	3	4	5			9¹	7	6			10						2	11¹					2-1(2-0)10,208	18
36. Leeds*	26.3	1	8	3	4	5			9	7	6			10						2	11					0-0(0-0)9147	18
37. C Palace	2.4	1	8		4	5			12	9	7	6†		10						2	3		11			0-3(0-2)9557	20
38. Shrewsbury	8.4	1	8	3	12	5		4	14	9	7†	6		10₁						2	11‡					1-2(0-1)7106	—
39. Reading	13.4	1	8	3		5		4		9	7	6		10						2	11†					0-0(0-0)10,037	—
40. Millwall*	19.4	1	8	3		5	6	4	12	9	7†	2¹		10							11					1-2(1-2)9204	—
41. Plymouth	26.4	1	8	3	4¹	5	6	7	12	9		2¹		10†					14		11‡					2-1(0-0)6310	—
42. Huddersfield	30.4	1	8	3	4	5	6	7		9¹	10	2									11¹					2-1(2-0)2794	18
43. Swindon*	2.5	1	8₁	3	4	5	6	7		9	10	2									11¹					2-0(2-0)5212	17
44. Oldham	7.5		8	3	4‡	5	6	7		9	10†		1						11		12	14	2			0-2(0-0)6009	17

Final League Position: 17

Appearances (subs)/goals: Peyton 42(0) 0; Newson 29(0) 3; Morrell 42(0) 0; Brooks 35(4) 6; Williams 38(0) 2; Whitlock 41(0) 0; O'Driscoll 39(0) 4; Richards 12(8) 4; Aylott 43(0) 9; Armstrong 34(3) 2; O'Connor 23(4) 3; Pulis 20(0) 0; Smeulders 29(5) 5; Cooke 20(0) 0; Clark 1(0) 0; Keane 9(2) 1; Hefferman 8(4) 4; Puckett 8(3) 3; Shearer 2(4) 0; Goulet 19(10) 0; Langan 4(1) 0; Coleman 15(1) 6; Close 10(0) 0.

Own goals: Norman, match 29; Gray A match 32.

DIVISION 2

BRADFORD CITY

Valley Parade Ground, Bradford BD8 7DY.

Back row (left to right): Brian Mitchell, Lee Sinnott, Ron Futcher, Mark Leonard, Ian Ormondroyd, Chris Withe. *Middle row:* Lee Sinnott, Ron Futcher, Mark Leonard, Ian Ormondroyd, Chris Withe. *Middle row:* Stan Ternent (Ass. Manager) Leigh Palin, Dave Evans, Paul Tomlinson, Peter Litchfield, Gavin Oliver, Mark Ellis, Bryan Edwards (Physiotherapist). *Front row:* Aidy Thorpe, Karl Goddard, Stuart McCall, Terry Dolan (Manager), John Hendrie, Greg Abbott, Rob Savage.

Stadium Capacity: 16,015.
Pitch Dimensions: 110 × 76yds.
Telephone: 0274–306062.
Chairman: Jack C. Tordoff.
Vice-Chairman: J. Terry Fountain.
Directors: D. Thompson, FCA.
Manager: Terry Dolan.
Post-War Managers: Jack Barker, John Milburn, David Steele, Ivor Powell, Peter Jackson, Bob Brocklebank, Bill Harris, Willie Watson, Grenville Hair, Jimmy Wheeler, Bryan Edwards, Bobby Kennedy, John Napier, George Mulhall, Roy McFarland, Trevor Cherry (16).
Assistant Manager: Stan Ternent.
Physio: Brian Edwards.
Secretary: T. F. Newman.
Commercial Manager: Tony Thornton.
Sponsors: Grattan plc.
Founded: 1903.
Turned Professional: 1903.
Nickname: The Bantams.
Former Names: None.
Former Grounds: None.
Record Attendance: 39,146 v Burnley, FA Cup 4th Round, 11 March 1911.
Record Victory: 11–1 v Rotherham U, Division 3(N), 25 August 1928.
Record Defeat: 1–9 v Colchester U, Division 4, 30 December 1961.
Most League Points: (3 for a win) 94, Division 3, 1984–85. (2 for a win) 63, Division 3(N), 1928–29.
Most League Goals: 128, Division 3(N), 1928–29.
Highest League Scorer in a Season: David Layne, 34, Division 4, 1961–62.
Highest Total of League Goals: Bobby Campbell, 121, 1981–84, 1984–86.
Most League Appearances: Cec Podd, 502, 1970–84.
League History: 1903 Elected to Division 2, 1908–22 Division 1, 1922–27 Division 2, 1927–29 Division 3(N), 1929–37 Division 2, 1937–61 Division 3, 1961–69 Division 4, 1969–72 Division 3, 1972–77 Division 4, 1977–78 Division 3, 1978–82 Division 4, 1982–85 Division 3, 1985– Division 2.
Honours: Division 2 Champions 1907–08. Division 3 Champions 1984–85. Division 3(N) Champions 1928–29. FA Cup winners 1911 (first holders of the current trophy).
Colours: Claret and amber shirts, black shorts, amber socks. **Second strip:** All white.

BRADFORD CITY – LEAGUE RECORD 1987–88

Match no/Opp/Date	Tomlinson	Mitchell	Goddard	McCall	Oliver	Savage	Sinnott	Fletcher	Abbott	Hendrie	Ellis	Leonard	Evans	Ormondroyd	Palin	Thorpe	Withe	Litchfield	O'Shaughnessy	Staunton	Kennedy	FT(HT)Att	Lge pos
1. Swindon* 15.8	1	2	3	4^1	5	6	7	$8{\uparrow}^1$	9	10	11	12										2-0(0-0)10,553	—
2. Oldham 18.8	1	2		4	5	3	8	9†	10_1	7↑	11‡	12	6	14								2-0(1-0)8087	—
3. Bournmouth 22.8	1	2†		4	5	3	8	9‡	10	7	11	12	6	14								0-2(0-0)7407	3
4. Leeds* 29.8	1	2	3	4	5		8	9†		7	11		6	12	10							0-0(0-0)11,428	4
5. Millwall* 5.9	1	2	3	4	5		8	9^1_1		7	11		6		10^1							3-1(0-0)8658	3
6. Stoke 12.9	1	2	3	4	5		8	9^1	12	7	11^1		6		10†							2-1(1-0)9571	3
7. Plymouth* 16.9	1	2	3‡	4	5		8	9	$10\frac12$	7	11†		6	14		12						3-1(1-0)11,009	—
8. Blackburn* 19.9	1	2^1	3	4	5		8	9	10	7^1			6	12		11†						2-1(1-1)12,068	1
9. Shrewsbury 26.9	1	2‡	3†	4	5		8	9^1	10	7		14	6	11^1			12					2-2(0-0)4247	1
10. Huddersfield 29.9	1	2^1	3	4^1	5		8	9‡	10†	7		14	6	11			12					2-1(1-0)11,671	1
11. Middlesbro* 3.10		2	3	4	5		8			7	9^1	6	11	10^1			1					2-0(0-0)14,222	1
12. WBA 10.10	1	2	3	4^1	5		8			7	9	6	11	10								1-0(1-0)12,241	1
13. Birmingham* 17.10	1		3‡	4^1	5		8		2†	7	12	9^2	6	11	10^1			14				4-0(0-0)12,256	1
14. Man City* 21.10	1	2^1		4	5		8	14	3†	7	12	9	6^1	11‡	10							2-4(0-1)14,818	—
15. Reading 24.10	1	2		4	5		8		3	7^1	12	9	6	11	10†							1-1(1-0)5920	1
16. C Palace* 31.10	1	2		4^1	5		8		3	7		9^1	6	11	10							2-0(0-1)13,012	1
17. Hull 3.11	1	2		4	5		8		3	7		9	6	11	10							0-0(0-0)15,443	1
18. Barnsley 7.11	1	2		4	5		8	12	3†	7	14	9	6	11‡	10							0-3(0-1)11,569	1
19. Sheff Utd* 14.11	1	2^1		4	5		8	9^1		7	11		6		10				3			2-0(1-0)13,694	1
20. Leicester 21.11	1	2		4	5		8	9^1	10	7^1	11		6						3			2-0(1-0)11,543	1
21. Aston Villa* 28.11	1	2†		4	5		8	9_2	14	7		12	6	11	10‡				3			2-4(1-2)15,006	2
22. Ipswich 5.12	1	2		4	5		8	9	12	7	14	11	6‡		10				3†			0-4(0-1)13,707	2
23. Bournemouth* 12.12	1	2		4	5		8	9	12	7		11^2	6		10†							2-2(0-0)10,763	2
24. Plymouth 20.12	1	2‡		4^1	5		8	9	12	7			6	14	10				3†			1-2(0-2)11,350	—
25. Shrewsbury* 26.12	1	2†		4	5		8	9‡	10	7	11^1	12	6	14					3			1-1(0-0)12,474	2
26. Blackburn 28.12	1	2^1	3	4	5		8	9‡	10	7	11		6	12								1-1(0-1)14,124	2
27. Leeds 1.1	1	2	3†	4	5		8	9^1	10	7	11	12	6	14								0-2(0-1)36,004	5
28. Stoke* 2.1	1	2		4	5		8		7†	11	9	6	3^1	10		12						1-4(0-3)12,223	6
29. Millwall 6.2		2	3	4	5			8	7	11		6	9^1		1		10					1-0(0-0)8201	6
30. Oldham* 13.2	1	2	3	4^1	5			8†	7^3	11		6	9	12			10_1					5-3(3-1)13,862	5
31. Middlesbro 27.2	1	2	3	4	5		11	8	7			6	9^2				10					2-1(0-0)21,079	5
32. Huddersfield* 1.3	1	2†	3	4	5		11	14	8	7	12		6	9	10‡							0-1(0-0)12,782	—
33. Birmingham 5.3	1		3	4	5		8	12	2	7^1	11†		6	9			10					1-1(1-1)8101	6
34. WBA* 12.3	1	5	3	4		8^1		2	7^1		11^2	6	9			10						4-1(1-0)12,502	4
35. C Palace 19.3	1	2	3†	4	5		8		11	7		6	9^1	12			10					1-1(0-0)9801	6
36. Swindon 30.3	1	2	3†	4	5		8	14^1	$11{\ddagger}^1$	7		12^1	6	9			10					2-2(0-0)8203	—
37. Barnsley* 2.4	1	2	3	4	5		8	12		7^1		11	6†	9			10					1-1(1-0)15,098	6
38. Sheff Utd 4.4	1	2	3†	4	5		8	12		7^1		11	6	9^1			10					2-1(0-1)13,888	5
39. Hull* 9.4	1	2	3	4	5		8	11_1		7		6	9^1				10					2-0(1-0)13,659	5
40. Reading* 20.4	1	2	3	4^1	5		8	11^1	12	7^1		6	9				10†					3-0(3-0)13,608	—
41. Man City 23.4	1	2	3	4	5		8	11_1		7		12^1	6†	9			10					2-2(1-2)20,335	3
42. Leicester* 30.4	1	2^1	3	4	5		8	11_1†		7^1		12	6	9^1			10					4-1(4-1)14,393	2
43. Aston Villa 2.5	1	2	3†	4	5		8	11		7		12	6	9			10					0-1(0-1)36,423	4
44. Ipswich* 7.5	1	2†	3	4^1	5		8	11	12^1		7	6	9				10					2-3(2-2)16,017	4
Apps(subs)/goals	42(0) 6	42(0) 0	29(0) 0	44(0) 9	43(0) 0	3(0) 0	42(0) 1	25(7) 14	25(2) 5	43(0) 13	16(6) 2	16(12) 10	28(9) 9	18(2) 3	1(1) 0	0(2) 0	0(1) 0	00(1) 0	7(1) 0	15(0) 1			

Final League Position: 4

BRENTFORD

DIVISION 3

Griffin Park, Braemer Road, Brentford, Middlesex TW8 0NT.

*Back row
(left to right):*
Roy Clare
Mark Gill
Paul Birch
Jamie Bates
Terry Evans
Gary Phillips
Bob Booker
Tony Oliver
Keith Millen
Gary Blissett
Colin Lee
Roger Stanislaus
Phil Holder
Front row:
Robbie Carroll
Keith Jones
Andy Feeley
Wayne Turner
Steve Perryman
Andy Sinton
Paul Smith
Roger Joseph
Alan Cockram

Stadium Capacity: 12,041.
Pitch Dimensions: 111 × 74yds.
Telephone: 01-847 2511, **Commercial dept:** 01-560 6062, **Press office:** 01-574 3047, **Clubcall:** 0898 121108.
Chairman: M. M. Lange.
Vice-Chairman: E. J. Radley Smith MS, FRCS, LRCP. Chief Executive: Keith Loring.
Directors: R. J. J. Blindell LL. B. , D. Tana, G. V. Potter.
Manager: Steve Perryman.
Post-War Managers: Harry Curtis, Jackie Gibbons, Jimmy Bain, Tom Lawton, Bill Dodgin (Snr), Malcolm McDonald, Tommy Cavanagh, Billy Gray, Jimmy Sirel, Frank Blunstone, Mike Everitt, John Docherty, Bill Dodgin (Jnr), Fred Callaghan, Frank McLintock (15).
Assistant Manager: Phil Holder.
Physio: Roy Clare.
Secretary: Royce Dickinson.
Marketing Manager: Polly Kater.
Sponsors: KLM Dutch Airlines.
Founded: 1889.
Turned Professional: 1899.
Nickname: The Bees.
Former Names: None.
Former Grounds: Clifden Road 1889–91, Benns Fields 1891–95, Shotters Field 1895–98, Cross Road 1898–1900, Boston Park 1900–04.
Record Attendance: 39,626 v Preston NE, FA Cup 6th Round, 5 March 1938.
Record Victory: 9–0 v Wrexham, Division 3, 15 October 1963.
Record Defeat: 0–7 v Swansea T, Division 3(S), 8 November 1924 and v Walsall, Division 3(S), 19 January 1957.
Most League Points: (3 for a win) 68, Division 3, 1981–82. (2 for a win) 62, Division 3(S), 1932–33 and Division 4, 1962–63.
Most League Goals: 98, Division 4, 1962–63.
Highest League Scorer in a Season: Jack Holliday, 38, Division 3(S), 1932–33.
Highest Total of League Goals: Jim Towers, 153, 1954–61.
Most League Appearances: Ken Coote, 514, 1949–64.
League History: 1920 Founder Members of Division 3, 1921–33 Division 3(S), 1933–35 Division 2, 1935–47 Division 1, 1947–54 Division 2, 1954–62 Division 3(S), 1962–63 Division 4, 1963–66 Division 3, 1966–72 Division 4, 1972–73 Division 3, 1973–78 Division 4, 1978– Division 3.
Honours: Division 2 Champions 1934–35. Division 4 Champions 1962–63. Division 3(S) Champions 1932–33, runners-up 1929–30, 1957–58. Associate Members' Cup runners-up 1985.
Colours: Red and white striped shirts, black shorts, red socks with white tops. **Second strip:** All blue.

BRENTFORD – LEAGUE RECORD 1987–88

Match no/Opp/Date		Phillips	Joseph	Murray	Millen	Lee	Priddle	Feeley	Sinton	Cooke	Blissett	Holloway	Carroll	Smith	Perryman	Bates	Jones	Booker	Gravette	Stanislaus	Williams	Evans	Thorne	Turner	Birch	Rix	Stewart	Oliver	Ferdinand	Cockram	Howard	FT(HT)Att Lge pos
1. Sunderland*	15.8	1	2	3	4	5	6†	7	8	9	10	11	12																			0–1(0–0)7559 —
2. Bristol*	29.8	1	2	3	4	5		6	8	9	10	11†		7	12																	0–2(0–0)4328 21
3. Grimsby	31.8	1		3	4	5		6	8	9†	10^1			7	11	2			12													1–0(1–0)3361 —
4. Rotherham*	5.9	1			3	4		6	8	9	10			7	11	2	5^1															1–1(0–0)3604 18
5. Nthampton	9.9	1	2		4	5		3	8	9_1	12			7	6†	10	11															1–2(0–0)5748 —
6. Southend	12.9	1	2		4		11	3	8^1	9^1	10^1			7		5	6†	12														3–2(3–1)2335 17
7. Chesterfield*	15.9	1	2		4	5†	11	3	8	9_1‡				7		10	6	12	14													2–0(2–0)3183 —
8. Blackpool*	19.9	1	2		4		11	3	8^1	9		7^1				5	6	10†	12													2–1(1–0)3886 11
9. Aldershot	26.9	1	2		4		11‡	3	8^1	9	10†		14	7	12	5	6															1–4(1–3)3651 13
10. Preston	29.9	1	2		4				8^1	9	10†	7^1		11	5	6																2–1(0–1)4241 —
11. Port Vale*	3.10	1	2		4	14			12	8^1	9			7‡	11†	5	6		3†													1–0(0–0)4130 6
12. Bury	10.10	1	2		4	5			8^1	9	10			11	6^1	7			3													2–2(1–1)2300 6
13. Walsall*	17.10	1	2		4				8	9	10	7†	12	11	5	6			3													0–0(0–0)5056 7
14. Chester*	20.10	1	2		4				12	8	9^1			11†	5	6			3	7												1–1(0–0)4027 —
15. Brighton	24.10	1	2		4				12	8	9‡	10		14	11	5†	6		3^1	7												1–2(1–0)7600 10
16. Bristol R*	31.10	1	2		4				8	12	10			7†	11	5	6		3	9^1												1–1(0–0)4487 12
17. Gillingham	3.11	1	2		4				12	8				11		6			3	9	5	7^1†										1–0(1–0)4529 —
18. Notts Co	7.11	1	2		4				7	8	10†			11		6	12		3	9	5											0–3(0–0)5634 11
19. Wigan*	21.11	1	2	9†				6	8^1					11	4		12		3	10^1	5	7										2–1(1–0)3625 9
20. Doncaster	28.11	1	2		12			6	8		10			11†	4				3	9^1	5	7										1–0(0–0)1360 7
21. Mansfield*	12.12	1	2			5		6	8		10^1		9^1	11	4				3			7										2–2(1–2)3729 8
22. York	18.12	1	2		11†			6	8		10		9		4				3			5	7^1	12								1–1(0–1)1801 —
23. Aldershot*	26.12	1	2	4^1				6	8^1		10			12			14		3			5	7	9^1†	11‡							3–0(2–0)5578 7
24. Fulham	28.12	1	2		4			6†	8		10			12					3			5^1	7	9^1	11							2–2(0–0)9340 7
25. Bristol C	1.1	1	2		4				8^1		10^2			12	14		6†		3			5	7	9‡	11							3–2(3–0)12,877 6
26. Southend*	2.1	1	2		4				8		10		12				6		3^1			5	7	9†	11							1–0(0–0)5752 6
27. Nthampton*	9.1	1	2		4	9		6‡	8		10†		12	14					3			5	7		11							0–1(0–0)6025 6
28. Blackpool	16.1	1	2		4^1	9		6	8								12		3			5	7	10†	11							1–0(1–0)3911 5
29. Fulham*	14.2	1	2		4^1				8		10^1		14	12	6				3			5	7	9†		11‡						3–1(1–0)8712 —
30. Rotherham	17.2	1	2		4				8		10						6		3			5	7	9		11						0–2(0–1)2572 —
31. Sunderland	20.2	1	2		4				8	12	10		14				6		3			5	7	9†		11‡						0–2(0–0)15,458 7
32. Grimsby*	23.2	1	2		4				9†	8			14			6	12		3			5	7	10		11‡						0–1(0–0)3534 —
33. Port Vale	27.2		2	4‡					11	8	10		14				6		3			5	7	9†			12	1				0–1(0–0)3876 7
34. Preston*	1.3		2		4				11	8†	10^1		12				6		3			5^1	7	9				1				2–0(1–0)3505 —
35. Walsall	5.3		2		4				11	8	10^1						6†		3			5^1	7	9‡		14	12	1				2–4(1–2)4494 7
36. Bury*	12.3		2		4				11	8	10						6		3			5	7	9†			12	1				0–3(0–1)3920 7
37. Bristol R	19.3				4	2			11	8	10						6	12	3	9†		5	7									0–0(0–0)3380 7
38. Brighton	26.3		2		4	14^1			11	8	10		12				6		3			5	7†					1	9‡			1–1(0–1)5331 8
39. Notts Co*	2.4		2		4	11			8		10^1					6	12		3			5						1	9†	7		1–0(1–0)4388 8
40. Wigan	4.4		2		4	11			8		10					6	12		3			5^1						1	9†	7		1–1(1–1)3597 8
41. Gillingham*	9.4		2		4	11†			8^2		10	9				6			3			5		12				1		7		2–2(0–0)3875 9
42. Chesterfield	19.4		2		4	11			8		10					6	12		3			5†	7^1			1			9			1–2(0–2)2010 —
43. Chester	23.4		2		4	11		3†	8		10					6		12		5	7							11	9^1			1–1(0–0)1777 10
44. Doncaster*	30.4	1	2		4	11‡			12	8	10					6†	14		3			5	7						9^1			1–1(0–3)3122 11
45. Mansfield	2.5	1	2			11‡			12	8	10	9^1			4	6			3			5	7	14†						11	12	1–2(1–0)2663 12
46. York*	7.5	1	2						7	8	10	9^1			4	6_1			3†	5										11	12	1–2(0–2)4180 12
Apps(subs)/goals		35(0)0	43(0)0	40(0)3	19(3)1	15(1)0	27(0)0	46(0)11	40(1)9	10(1)0	8(4)4	10(2)1	16(5)0	20(3)1	34(2)1	1(11)0	14(9)0	3(6)2	7(0)3	29(0)4	20(0)2	10(1)0	24(0)2	13(3)2	5(0)0	4(3)0	11(0)0	7(0)2	0(1)0	0(2)0	0(1)0	Final League Position: 12

Own goals: Benjamin, match 7, Elkins, match 29. Also played: Buckle, no 14, match 46.

DIVISION 2

BRIGHTON & HOVE ALBION

Goldstone Ground, Old Shoreham Road, Hove, Sussex BN3 7DE.

Back row (left to right): Mark Leather (Physio), Richard Tiltman, Trevor Wood, Steve March, Gerry Armstrong, Grant Horscroft, Sean McFadden, Mike Trusson, Garry Nelson, Dale Jasper, John Keeley, Damian Webber, Ted Streeter (Youth Development Officer). *Middle row:* Barry Lloyd (Team Manager), Jimmy Gibbins, Steve Gatting, Chris Hutchings, Robert Isaac, Perry Digweed, David Gipp, Ian Chapman, Chris Harris, John Crumplin, Martin Hinshelwood (Chief Coach). *Front row:* John Robinson, Jack Dineen, Kevan Brown, Darren Hughes, Kevin Bremner, Doug Rouvie, Gary Rowell, Dean Wilkins, Steve Penney, David Roberts, Darren Smith.

Stadium Capacity: 29,026.
Pitch Dimensions: 112 × 75yds.
Telephone: 0273–739535, Commercial Dept: 0273–778230.
Chairman: D. C. Sizen.
Vice-Chairman: J. L. Campbell.
Directors: B. S. Bedson, P. F. Kent, R. A. Bloom, G. Appleby, G. A. Stanley, F. Shannon FCA.
Manager: Barry Lloyd.
Post-War Managers: Charles Webb, Tommy Cook, Don Welsh, Billy Lane, George Curtis, Archie Macaulay, Freddie Goodwin, Pat Saward, Brian Clough, Peter Taylor, Alan Mullery MBE, Mike Bailey, Jimmy Melia, Chris Cattlin, Alan Mullery MBE (15). Coach: Martin Hinshelwood.
Physio: Mark Leather, MCSP, SRP.
Secretary: Stephen Rooke. Marketing Manager: Terry Gill.
Sponsors: NOBO Visual Aids Ltd.
Founded: 1900.
Turned Professional: 1900.
Nickname: The Seagulls.
Former Names: Brighton & Hove Rangers.
Former Grounds: Withdean 1900–01, County Ground 1901–02.
Record Attendance: 36,747 v Fulham, Division 2, 27 December 1958.
Record Victory: 10–1 v Wisbech, FA Cup 1st Round, 13 November 1965.
Record Defeat: 0–9 v Middlesbrough, Division 2, 23 August 1958.
Most League Points: (3 for a win) 84, Division 3, 1987–88. (2 for a win) 65, Division 3(S), 1955–56 and Division 3, 1971–72.
Most League Goals: 112, Division 3(S), 1955–56.
Highest League Scorer in a Season: Peter Ward, 32, Division 3, 1976–77.
Highest Total of League Goals: Tommy Cook, 113, 1922–29.
Most League Appearances: Tug Wilson, 509, 1922–36.
League History: 1920 Founder Members of Division 3, 1921–58 Division 3(S), 1958–62 Division 2, 1962–63 Division 3, 1963–65 Division 4, 1965–72 Division 3, 1972–73 Division 2, 1973–77 Division 3, 1977–79 Division 2, 1979–83 Division 1, 1983–87 Division 2, 1987–88 Division 3, 1988– Division 2.
Honours: Division 2 runners-up 1978–79. Division 3 runners-up 1971–72, 1976–77, 1987–88. Division 4 Champions 1964–65. Division 3(S) Champions 1957–58, runners-up 1953–54, 1955–56. FA Cup runners-up 1983.
Colours: Blue and white striped shirts, blue shorts and socks. **Second strip:** All yellow with blue trim.

BRIGHTON AND HOVE ALBION – LEAGUE RECORD 1987–88

Match no/Opp/Date		Keeley	Brown	Dublin	Rowell	Rougvie	Gatting	Penney	Hutchings	Bremner	Nelson	Wilkins	Curbishley	Crumplin	Tilman	Armstrong	Gipp	Wood	Jasper	Trusson	Horscroft	Cooper	Isaac	Chivers	Others	FT(HT)Att	Lge pos
1. York*	15.8	1	2	3	4	5	6	7	8	9	10¹	11														1–0(0–0)6068	—
2. Chesterfield	22.8	1	2	3		5	6		8			11	4	7	9†	12		10								0–0(0–0)2286	6
3. Fulham*	29.8	1	2	3		5	6		8	9²		11	4	7				10								2–0(1–0)8773	—
4. Nthampton	31.8	1	2	3		5	6		8	9		11	4	7†	12¹			10								1–1(0–0)7934	—
5. Blackpool*	5.9	1	2	3		5	6		8	9		11	4₁	7†	12			10								1–3(0–1)7166	10
6. Aldershot	12.9	1	2	3		5	6¹		8	9	7²	11	4					10								4–1(2–1)3970	5
7. Rotherham*	16.9	1	2	3		5	6		8	9¹	7‡	11	4	14		12		10†								1–0(1–0)6945	—
8. Sunderland*	19.9	1	2	3		5¹	6		8¹	9	7¹	11	4					10								3–1(2–0)8949	4
9. Southend	26.9	1	2†	3	12	5	6		8	9	7	11‡	4	14				10¹								1–2(0–0)3789	9
10. Port Vale	28.9	1	2	3		5	6		8	9	7	11†	4			12		10								0–2(0–0)3789	—
11. Bury*	3.10	1	2	3		5	6		8	9	7¹†	11	4₁			12		10								2–1(1–0)6509	8
12. Walsall	10.10	1	2	3		5	6		8	9	7¹	11†	4	14		12		10‡								1–0(1–0)5020	9
13. Preston*	17.10	1	2	3		5	6		8	9	7	11	4			12		10†								0–0(0–0)6043	10
14. Wigan	20.10	1	2	3		5	6		8	9²	7	11	4					10¹								3–3(0–1)2392	2
15. Brentford*	24.10	1	2	3		5†	6		8‡	9¹	7	11	4¹	14		12		10								2–1(0–1)7600	8
16. Grimsby	31.10	1	2	3		5	6		8	9¹	7	11	4					10								1–0(0–0)2711	5
17. Doncaster*	4.11	1	2	3		5	6		8	9	7²	11	4					10								2–0(1–0)7142	—
18. Gillingham	7.11	1	2	3¹		5	6		8	9	7	11	4					10								1–1(0–0)6437	5
19. Mansfield	21.11	1	2	3		5	6		8	9	7¹	11†	4			12										1–1(0–1)3284	6
20. Notts Co*	28.11	1	2	3¹		5	6		8	9	7	11	4					10								1–1(0–0)8725	6
21. Chester*	12.12	1	2	3		5	6			9	7	11	4					10	8¹							1–0(0–0)6738	4
22. Bristol R	19.12	1	2	3			6			9	7¹	11	4¹					10	8	5						2–1(1–1)3589	4
23. Southend*	26.12	1	2	3			6			9	7	11	4†			12		10	8	5						0–0(0–0)11,147	5
24. Bristol C	28.12	1	2	3		5	6			9	7¹	11¹	4					10	8¹							2–5(0–3)16,058	5
25. Fulham	10.1	1	2	3		5	6			9	7	11†	4¹			12		10	8¹							2–1(0–5)6530	5
26. Aldershot*	2.1	1	2	3¹		5	6			9	7	11	4					10	8							1–1(0–1)9420	5
27. Sunderland	16.1	1	2	3		5	6			9	7	11	4			12		10†	8							0–1(0–1)17,404	7
28. Blackpool	6.2	1	2	3		5	6			9	7²	11¹	4					10	8							3–1(0–0)4081	6
29. Bristol C*	13.2	1	2	3		5¹	6			9	7²	11	4					10	8							3–2(1–0)8781	5
30. Chesterfield	17.2	1	2	3		5	6			9	7¹	11	4			12¹		10	8†							2–2(1–1)8182	5
31. York	20.2	1	2	3		5	6			9	7¹	11†	4			12		10	8¹							2–0(1–0)2576	5
32. Bury	27.2	1	2	3		5	6			9	7¹	11†	4			12		10	8							1–2(0–0)2557	5
33. Port Vale*	2.3	1	2	3		5	6			9	7	11†	4₁			12¹		10	8							2–0(0–0)7296	—
34. Preston	5.3	1	2	3		5	6			9†	7	11	4			12		10‡	8		14					0–3(0–3)5834	6
35. Walsall*	12.3	1	2†	3¹		5	6	11		9¹	7	4				12		10	8							2–1(1–0)8345	6
36. Rotherham	16.3	1		3		5	6	11		9	7†	4				12		10	8				2			0–1(0–0)2562	6
37. Grimsby*	19.3	1		3			6	11†		9	7	4				12		10	8‡		14	5	2			0–0(0–0)7269	6
38. Brentford	26.3	1		3			6	11¹		9	7	4						10				5	2	8		1–1(0–5)5331	6
39. Gillingham*	2.4	1		3		5	6	11		9	7	4₁						10					2	8		2–0(2–0)9256	6
40. Notts Co	4.4	1		3		5		11		9	7¹	4						10				5	2	8¹		2–1(1–1)7522	6
41. Wigan*	9.4	1		3			6	11		9‡	7	4¹				12		10†			14	5	2	8		1–0(0–0)9423	4
42. Nthampton*	15.4	1		3			6¹	11		9	7¹	4†				12		10				5	2	8¹		3–0(1–0)14,421	4
43. Doncaster	23.4	1		3			6	11		9	7¹	4¹						10				5	2	8		2–0(0–0)1683	4
44. Mansfield*	30.4	1		3¹			6₁	11¹		9	7	4†				12		10				5	2	8		3–1(2–1)11,493	3
45. Chester	2.4	1		3			6	11		9†	7	4				12		10²				5	2	8		2–2(2–1)3345	3
46. Bristol R*	7.4	1		3			6	11		9¹	7¹	4†				12		10				5	2	8		2–1(1–0)19,800	2

Final League Position: 2

Apps(subs)/goals: 44(0) 0 · 35(0) 0 · 46(0) 5 · 1(1) 0 · 35(0) 2 · 46(0) 3 · 13(0) 3 · 20(0) 1 · 42(2) 8 · 42(0) 22 · 43(1) 3 · 34(0) 6 · 19(7) 2 · 10(0) 0 · 6(1) 1 · 1(1) 0 · 26(5) 4 · 22(2) 4 · 13(2) 2 · 2(0) 0 · 10(0) 0 · 10(0) 0 · 9(0) 2

Own goal: Smith, match 6.

DIVISION 3

BRISTOL CITY

Ashton Gate, Bristol BS3 2EJ.

Back row (left to right): L. Rogers, M. Tanner, G. Marshall, R. Newman, P. Fitzpatrick, K. Waugh, M. Coombe, Moyes, K. Curle, A. Walsh, C. Honor, R. Bromage. *Front row:* T. Caldwell, M. Cooper, N. Hawkins, S. Galliers, G. Owen, A. Llewellyn, S. Neville, J. Jordan

Stadium Capacity: 30,868.
Pitch Dimensions: 115 × 75yds.
Telephone: 0272–632812.
Chairman: D. T. Williams.
Vice-Chairman: L. J. Kew.
Directors: O. W. Newland, W. I. Williams, P. Manning, M. Fricker, K. Sage.
Manager: Joe Jordan.
Post-War Managers: Bob Hewison, Bob Wright, Pat Beasley, Peter Doherty, Fred Ford, Alan Dicks, Bob Houghton, Roy Hodgson, Terry Cooper (9).
Secretary: Miss J. Harrison.
Commercial Manager: D. Easton.
Sponsors: Hire–Rite.
Founded: 1894.
Turned Professional: 1897.
Nickname: The Robins.
Former Names: Bristol South End 1894–97.
Former Grounds: St John's Lane 1894–1904.
Record Attendance: 43,335 v Preston NE, FA Cup 5th Round, 16 February 1935.
Record Victory: 11–0 v Chichester, FA Cup 1st Round, 5 November 1960.
Record Defeat: 0–9 v Coventry C, Division 3(S), 28 April 1934.
Most League Points: (3 for a win) 82 Division 4, 1983–84. (2 for a win) 70, Division 3(S), 1954–55.
Most League Goals: 104, Division 3(S), 1926–27.
Highest League Scorer in a Season: Don Clark, 36, Division 3(S), 1946–47.
Highest Total of League Goals: John Atyeo, 315, 1951–66.
Most League Appearances: John Atyeo, 597, 1951–66.
League History: 1901 Elected to Division 2, 1906–11 Division 1, 1911–22 Division 2, 1922–23 Division 3(S), 1923–24 Division 2, 1924–27 Division 3(S), 1927–32 Division 2, 1932–55 Division 3(S), 1955–60 Division 2, 1960–65 Division 3, 1965–76 Division 2, 1976–80 Division 1, 1980–81 Division 2, 1981–82 Division 3, 1982–84 Division 4, 1984– Division 3.
Honours: Division 1 runners-up 1906–07. Division 2 Champions 1905–06, runners-up 1975–76. Division 3 runners-up 1964–65. Division 3(S) Champions 1922–23, 1926–27, 1954–55, runners-up 1937–38. FA Cup runners-up 1909. Welsh Cup winners 1934. Anglo-Scottish Cup winners 1978. Associate Members' Cup winners 1986, runners-up 1987.
Colours: Red shirts, white shorts, red socks. **Second strip:** Yellow shirts, green shorts, yellow socks.

BRISTOL CITY – LEAGUE RECORD 1987–88

Match no/Opp/Date	Waugh	Llewellyn	Bromage	Moyes	Newman	Tanner	Marshall	Fitzpatrick	Caldwell	Walsh	Jordan	Harvey	Owen	Neville	Galliers	Curle	Humphries	Honor	Pender	Shutt	Prudhoe	Hawkins	Mardon	Vaughan	Milne	McClaren	Gordon	FT(HT)Att	Lge pos
1. Mansfield 15.8	1	2	3	4	5	6	7	8†	9‡	10	11	12	14															0–2(0–2)5441	—
2. Preston* 22.8	1	2	3	4	5	6	7	8		10_1	11		9^2															3–1(1–0)7655	12
3. Brentford 29.8	1	2	3	4	5_1	6		8		10	11		9^1	7														2–0(0–0)4328	7
4. Port Vale* 31.8	1	2	3	4	5	6	7†	8	12	$10‡$	11		9	14^1														1–0(0–0)8716	—
5. Bury 5.9	1	2	3	4	5	6		8	9	10	11		7^1															1–1(1–1)2376	4
6. Bristol R* 12.9	1	2	3	4^1	5		7	8^1		10^1	11		9	6														3–3(1–1)14,746	
7. Walsall 15.9	1	2^1	3	4	5			8		10	11	7	9	6														1–1(0–0)6425	—
8. Notts Co 19.9	1	2	3	4	5_1			8		10	11	7	9	6														1–0(0–0)5705	5
9. Gillingham* 26.9	1	2	3	4	5			8^1	12	10	11†	9^2	7	6														3–3(1–2)10,070	6
10. Chesterfield* 29.9	1	2	3	4	5^1			8	12	10	11	$9†^1$	7	6														2–1(1–0)9088	—
11. Nthampton 3.10	1	2	3	4				8	12	$10‡$	11†	9	7	6														0–3(0–1)6234	7
12. Southend* 10.10	1	14	3	4	5^1_1		7†	8^1		$10‡$	11	9	12	6	2													3–2(1–1)8606	—
13. Grimsby 17.10	1	2	3	5	6^2	8	10†		12		11^1	9	7^1		4													4–1(4–0)3100	3
14. Sunderland 20.10	1	2	3	5	8	12			14	$10‡$	11	9	7	6†	4													0–1(0–1)15,109	—
15. Rotherham 24.10	1	2	3	4	5	7†		8‡	10^1	14	11	9			6	12												1–4(1–3)3397	6
16. Blackpool 3.11	1		3		2		10	8			11	7			6	4	5	9^2										2–4(1–1)3140	—
17. Aldershot 7.11	1	2	3				10†	8	12			7	11	6^1	4		5	9	1									1–2(0–1)4324	14
18. Chester* 21.11	1	2	3	5^1		11	8		12			7†	10	6	4			9^1	1									2–2(1–2)8103	12
19. Wigan 28.11	1	2	3	7				8		10^1	11		6		4		5	9	1									1–1(1–0)2879	13
20. York* 12.12	1		3				8^1		10†	12		7	11	6^2	4	2	5	9										3–2(2–1)6238	12
21. Fulham* 15.12	1	12	3				8†		10			7	11	6	4	2	5	9^4										4–0(3–0)6150	—
22. Doncaster 19.12	1	12	3	7			8†		10^1				11	6	4	2	5	9^1										2–1(1–1)1819	5
23. Gillingham 26.12	1	14	3_1	7†			8		10	12			$11‡$	6	4	2	5	9										1–1(0–0)6457	5
24. Brighton* 28.12	1	14	3^1	7†	8^1				10^1	12^1			11	6	4	2‡	5^1	9										5–2(3–0)16,058	4
25. Brentford* 1.1	1		3	8	7†				10	12			11	6^1	4		5	9^1										2–3(0–3)12,877	7
26. Preston 9.1	1	2	3	8	14				10	12			$11‡$	6	4			9	7†	5								0–2(0–1)5229	8
27. Notts Co* 16.1	1	14	3	8	7†				10^1	12^1			11	6	4‡	2	5	9										2–1(0–1)9558	8
28. Bury* 6.2	1		3	8					10^1				11	6^1	4	2	5	9			1		7^1					3–2(0–1)9158	8
29. Walsall* 9.2	1	2	3	8					12	10			11†	6‡	14	5	9		4	1		7						0–0(0–0)8454	—
30. Brighton 13.2	1	2	3	8					12^1	10^1			11		6	5	9†		4	1		7						2–3(0–1)8781	8
31. Mansfield* 20.2	1	2	3	8						9	10		11†		2	5			4			7	6					1–2(1–2)9528	8
32. Nthampton 27.2	1	2	3	8					12	9	10^1		11†		4	3	5					7	6					2–2(1–2)8578	9
33. Chesterfield 1.3	1	2		8					9^1	10^1		11			4	3	5^1					7^1	6					4–1(2–1)1657	—
34. Grimsby* 5.3	1	2	3						9	10^1		12	8‡		4	14	5	11†				7	6					1–1(0–0)8343	8
35. Southend 11.3	1	2	3				12	14	9			11†	8		4	10	5					$7‡$	6					0–2(0–1)3664	—
36. Fulham 19.3	1	2					10	12	9†			11	8		3	5			4			7	6					0–0(0–0)4896	8
37. Rotherham 26.3	1	2					12			10		11^1	6		4	3	5					7	8	$9^1†$				2–0(0–0)7517	
38. Aldershot 2.4	1	2	14	3					10^1			11	8		4		5	12				$7^1†$	6	9†				2–0(1–0)8712	7
39. Chester 4.4	1	2	3						10			11†	8		4	5	12					7	6					0–1(0–1)2849	
40. Blackpool* 9.4	1	2	3						10			11	6		4	5						7	8^1	9_1				2–1(1–0)6460	
41. Bristol R 12.4	1	2	3						10	12		11	8		4	5						7†	6	9				0–1(0–0)5947	—
42. Port Vale 18.4	1	2	3	11^1					10			8			4			12		5		7	6	9†				1–0(0–0)2671	—
43. Sunderland 23.4	1	2	14	3					10			$11‡$	8		4							7	6	$9^1†$				1–0(0–0)18,225	8
44. Wigan* 30.4	1	2	3	4	14^1				$10‡$	12^1		$11†$	8^1			5	9					7	6					4–1(2–1)7340	
45. York 2.5	1	2	3	4	10	14			12			$11‡$	8		5	9†						7^1	6					1–0(0–0)2616	
46. Doncaster* 7.5	1	2	3						10	12		$11†$	8		4							7	6	9^1				1–0(0–0)18,378	5
Apps(subs)/goals	40(0)0	36(6)1	28(2)0	44(0)11	10(2)0	13(6)1	22(2)5	8(9)3	39(3)12	17(11)4	9(1)0	17(0)16	37(0)5	35(0)6	30(0)0	24(0)0	14(3)0	28(4)9	18(4)9	30(0)0	1(0)0	10(0)0	8(0)0	3(0)0	19(0)4	8(0)4		Final League Position: 5	

Own goals: Foster, match 31; Reed, match 32.

DIVISION 3

BRISTOL ROVERS

Twerton Park, Bath, Avon BA2 1DB.

Back row (left to right): Phil Purnell, Andy Reece, Ian Alexander, Lee Portch, Nigel Martyn, Tim Carter, Ian Weston, Jason Eaton. *Centre row:* Ray Kendall (Kit Manager), Dave Wiffill, Jeff Meacham, Robbie Turner, David Mehew, Nicky Tanner, Darren Carr, Roy Dolling (Physiotherapist). *Front row:* Lee Howells, Vaughan Jones, Martin Boyle, Kenny Hibbitt (Ass. Manager), Gerry Francis (Player/Manager), Geoff Twentyman, Gary Penrice, Richard Dryden.

Stadium Capacity: 6,600.
Pitch Dimensions: 110 × 70yds.
Telephone: Match day: 0225–23087, Office: 0272–510363.
Chairman: D. H. A. Dunford.
Vice-Chairman: R. D. Redman.
Directors: R. Craig, G. M. H. Dunford, V. Stokes. **Associate Directors:** H. Draper, G. Francis.
Manager: Gerry Francis.
Post-War Managers: Brough Fletcher, Bert Tann, Fred Ford, Bill Dodgin (Snr), Don Megson, Bobby Campbell, Harold Jarman, Terry Cooper, Bobby Gould, David Williams (10).
Assistant Manager: Ken Hibbitt.
Physio: R. Dolling.
Secretary: R. C. Twyford.
Commercial Manager: A. Wood.
Sponsors: Design Windows.
Founded: 1883.
Turned Professional: 1897.
Nickname: The Pirates.
Former Names: Black Arabs 1883, 1884 Eastville Rovers, 1897 Bristol Eastville Rovers, 1898 Bristol Rovers.
Former Grounds: Purdown, Three Acres, Ashley Hill, Rudgeway, Eastville Stadium.
Record Attendance: 38,472 v Preston NE, FA Cup 4th Round, 30 January 1960.
Record Victory: 7–0 v Swansea T, Division 2, 2 October 1954 and v Brighton & HA, Division 3(S), 29 November 1952 and v Shrewsbury T, Division 3, 21 March 1964.
Record Defeat: 0–12 v Luton T, Division 3(S), 13 April, 1936.
Most League Points: (3 for a win) 79, Division 3, 1983–84. (2 for a win) 64, Division 3(S), 1952–53.
Most League Goals: 92, Division 3(S), 1952–53.
Highest League Scorer in a Season: Geoff Bradford, 33, Division 3(S), 1952–53.
Highest Total of League Goals: Geoff Bradford, 245, 1949–64.
Most League Appearances: Stuart Taylor, 545, 1966–80.
League History: 1920 Founder Members of Division 3, 1921–53 Division 3(S), 1953–62 Division 2, 1962–74 Division 3, 1974–81 Division 2, 1981– Division 3.
Honours: Division 3 runners-up 1973–74. Division 3(S) Champions 1952–53.
Colours: Blue and white quartered shirts, white shorts, blue socks. **Second strip:** Orange and yellow quartered shirts, orange shorts, yellow socks.

BRISTOL ROVERS – LEAGUE RECORD 1987–88

Match no/Opp/Date		Marrm	Alexander	Dryden	Hibbitt	Carr	Jones	Wiffill	Reece	Turner	Penrice	Purnell	Eaton	Holloway	Meacham	Twentyman	White	Weston	Carter	Tanner	Clark	Francis	Joseph	Mehew	McClean	FT(HT)Att Lge pos
1. Rotherham*	15.8	1	2	3	4	5	6	7†	8	9¹	10²	11	12													3-1(2-0)3399 —
2. Sunderland	22.8	1	2	3	4	5	6		8	9†	10¹	11		7	12											1-1(0-0)13,059 3
3. Aldershot*	29.8	1	2†	3	4	5	6		8		10¹	11			7¹	12	9¹									3-1(3-0)3390 1
4. Blackpool	31.8	1	2	3	4	5	6	8		12	10	11†			7		9¹									1-2(0-0)3319 —
5. Wigan*	5.9	1	2	3‡	4	5	6			12	10	11¹		7	14	9¹	8†									2-3(2-2)3168 12
6. Bristol C	12.9		2		4		6¹		8¹		10	11	7¹		5	9		1	3							3-3(1-1)14,764 14
7. York*	16.9		2		4		6¹		8	12	10¹	11	7		5	9†		1	3							2-1(1-0)3177 —
8. Nthampton*	19.9		2		4		6		8	12	10	11	7		5	9†		1	3							0-2(0-1)3655 14
9. Fulham	26.9		2		4†		6		8	12	10	11	7		5	9¹		1	3							1-3(0-1)4614 15
10. Notts Co	29.9		2			4	6		8		10¹	11	7		5	9		1	3							1-1(0-0)4334 —
11. Mansfield*	3.10		2			4†	6		8		10¹	11	7	12¹	5	9		1	3							2-1(1-0)2980 16
12. Gillingham	10.10		2			4†	6		8	12	10	11	7	9	5			1	3							0-3(0-0)4399 16
13. Chester*	17.10	1	2				6		8		10¹	11	7		5	9¹			3	4						2-2(2-1)3038 15
14. Port Vale	19.10	1		3			6		8	5†	10¹	11	7	12	9			2	4							1-2(1-1)3598 —
15. Doncaster*	24.10	1	2		5		6¹		8		10	11½	7†	12	9¹			3	4							4-0(3-0)2817 16
16. Brentford	31.10	1	2		5		6		8		10¹	11	7		9			3	4							1-1(0-1)4487 15
17. Preston*	4.11	1	2	5¹		6		8		10	11†	7	12		9			3	4							1-2(0-1)2804 —
18. Chesterfield*	7.11	1	2	5†		6		12		10	11½	7	8¹	3	9			4								2-0(2-0)2633 15
19. Bury	21.11	1	2	5¹		6				10	11	7	8	3	9			4								1-4(0-1)2356 16
20. Grimsby*	28.11	1	2	5		6				10¹	11¹	7	8¹	3	9¹			4								4-2(2-1)2787 15
21. Walsall	12.12	1	2	5†		6		8		10	11	7	12		9			3	4							0-0(0-0)4234 14
22. Brighton*	19.12	1	2	5		6		12		10	11	7¹	8†	14	9			3	4							1-2(1-1)3589 15
23. Fulham*	26.12	1	2	4	12	6				10¹	11	7¹		5†	9¹			3								3-1(1-1)4718 13
24. Southend	28.12	1	2†	4		6		8		10	11¹	12	7		5	9¹		3								2-4(1-2)4094 14
25. Aldershot	1.1	1	2	4†		6		12		10	11	7		5	9			3		8						0-3(0-3)4593 16
26. Northampton	16.1	1	2¹†		6				10	11	12	7		5	9	8		3	4							1-2(1-1)4473 19
27. Wigan	6.2	1	2†	8‡	6		14		10	11	7	12	5		3	4		9								0-1(0-0)3827 20
28. Southend*	13.2	1	2	5		6		8		10	11	7		3				4		9						0-0(0-0)3092 20
29. Rotherham	20.2	1	2	5		6				10	11	7		3	9¹			4	8†	12						1-1(0-0)2966 20
30. Sunderland*	24.2	1	2	5†		6		12		10†¹	11	7¹		3	9¹	14		4		8¹						4-0(1-0)4501 —
31. Mansfield	27.2	1	2		6		8		10	11	7		3	9			4		5							0-1(0-0)3191 20
32. Notts Co*	2.3	1	2		6		8		10	11	7		3¹	9			4		5							1-1(0-0)4075 —
33. Chester	5.3	1	2		6		8		10	11¹	7		3	9¹			4		5¹							3-0(2-0)2067 19
34. Gillingham*	12.3	1	2		6		8		10¹	11¹	7		3	9			4		5							2-0(0-0)3846 17
35. Brentford*	19.3	1	2		6		8		10	11	7		3	9			4		5							0-0(0-0)3380 19
36. Doncaster	25.3	1	2		6		8		10¹	11	7		3	9			4		5							1-0(1-0)1311 —
37. Chesterfield	2.4	1	2		6		8		10¹	11	7		3			12	4		5	9†						1-0(1-0)2208 15
38. Bury*	4.4	1	2		6		8		10	11	7		3				4		5	9						0-0(0-0)4264 16
39. Preston	8.4	1	2		6		8		10	11†	7		3	9			4		5¹	12						1-3(1-2)5386 —
40. Bristol C*	12.4	1	2		6		8		10¹	11	7		3	9			4		5							1-0(0-0)5947 —
41. York	15.4	1	2		6		8		10		7‡		3	9¹†	14		11	4		5³	12					4-0(2-0)1834 —
42. Port Vale*	23.4	1	2		6		8		10¹		7		3	9			11	4		5						1-0(0-0)3780 11
43. Blackpool*	27.4	1	2		6		8		10		7		3	9¹			11	4		5¹						2-0(2-0)3546 —
44. Grimsby	30.4	1	2		6		8		10	14	7		3	9†			11	4		5‡	12					0-0(0-0)2505 9
45. Walsall*	2.5	1	2		6		8		10		7¹		3	9¹			11	4		5¹						3-0(3-0)6328 8
46. Brighton	7.5	1	2		6		8		10		7		3	9	14		11¹	4		5	12					1-2(0-1)19,800 8

Final League Position: 8

Apps(subs)/goals: 39(0)0, 45(0)1, 4(0)0, 24(0)2, 8(1)0, 46(0)3, 2(0)0, 35(5)1, 36(1)9, 46(0)18, 40(1)8, 0(3)0, 43(0)5, 35(0)15, 39(0)0, 2(5)0, 7(0)0, 35(0)0, 39(0)0, 25(1)1, 31(0)0, 10(0)0, 38(0)0, 17(0)8, 24(0)0

DIVISION 4

BURNLEY

Turf Moor, Burnley BB10 4BX.

Back row
(left to right):
Phil Devaney
Steve Taylor
Andy Farrell
Steve Davis
Chris Pearce
George Oghani
Paul Comstive
Peter Zelem
Peter Daniel
Front row:
Ashley Hoskin
Neil Grewcock
Shaun McGrory
Steve Gardner
Ray Deakin (captain)
Phil Malley
Ian Britton
Peter Leebrook

Stadium Capacity: 25,000.
Pitch Dimensions: 115 × 73yds.
Telephone: 0282–27777/38021
Chairman: F. J. Teasdale.
Vice-Chairman: Dr R. D. Iven.
Directors: B. Dearing, J. Simmons.
Manager: Brian Miller.
Post-War Managers: Cliff Britton, Frank Hill, Alan Brown, Billy Dougall, Harry Potts, Jimmy Adamson, Joe Brown, Harry Potts, Brian Miller, Frank Casper (caretaker), John Bond, John Benson, Martin Buchan, Tommy Cavanagh (14).
Secretary: Robert Bradshaw.
Founded: 1882.
Turned Professional: 1883.
Nickname: The Clarets.
Former Names: Burnley Rovers 1881–82.
Former Grounds: Calder Vale 1881–82.
Record Attendance: 54,775 v Huddersfield T, FA Cup 3rd Round, 23 February 1924.
Record Victory: 9–0 v Darwen, Division 1, 9 January 1892; v Crystal Palace, FA Cup 2nd Round replay 1908–09; v Brighton, FA Cup 4th Round, 26 January 1957 and v Penrith, FA Cup 1st Round, 17 November 1984.
Record Defeat: 0–10 v Aston Villa, Division 1, 29 August 1925 and v Sheffield U, Division 1, 19 January 1929.
Most League Points: (3 for a win) 80, Division 3, 1981–82. (2 for a win) 62, Division 2, 1972–73.
Most League Goals: 102, Division 1, 1960–61.
Highest League Scorer in a Season: George Beel, 35, Division 1, 1927–28.
Highest Total of League Goals: George Beel, 178, 1923–32.
Most League Appearances: Jerry Dawson, 530, 1906–29.
League History: 1888 Founder Members of the Football League, 1897–98 Division 2, 1898–1900 Division 1, 1900–13 Division 2, 1913–30 Division 1, 1930–47 Division 2, 1947–71 Division 1, 1971–73 Division 2, 1973–76 Division 1, 1976–80 Division 2, 1980–82 Division 3, 1982–83 Division 2, 1983–85 Division 3, 1985– Division 4.
Honours: Division 1 Champions 1920–21, 1959–60, runners-up 1919–20, 1961–62. Division 2 Champions 1897–98, 1972–73, runners-up 1912–13, 1946–47. Division 3 Champions 1981–82. FA Cup winners 1914, runners-up 1947, 1962. Associate Members' Cup runners-up 1988. Anglo-Scottish Cup winners: 1979.
Colours: Claret shirts with light blue sleeves, white shorts and socks. **Second strip:** All yellow.

BURNLEY – LEAGUE RECORD 1987–88

Match no/Opp/Date		Pearce	Leebrook	McGrory	Daniel	Zelem	Deakin	Grewcock	Farrell	Oghani	Comstive	Britton	Gardner	Hoskin	Taylor	James	Malley	Davis	Reeves	Devaney	FT(HT)Att	Lge pos
1. Colchester*	15.8	1	2	3†	4	5	6	7	8	9	10	11‡	12	14							0–3(0–2)5369	—
2. Newport	22.8	1	2		4	5	6	7	8	9¹	10		3	11							1–0(0–0)2006	14
3. Carlisle*	29.8	1	2		4	5¹	3¹	7	8	9¹	10		6	11¹							4–3(3–1)5781	4
4. Orient	1.9	1	2		4	5	3	7	8¹	9	10†		6	12	11						1–4(0–1)3560	—
5. Swansea*	5.9	1	2		4	5	3	7	8	9¹	10		6	11							1–0(0–0)4778	6
6. Tranmere	11.9	1	2		4		3	7	8	9	10¹		6	11	5						1–0(0–0)4209	—
7. Wrexham*	15.9	1	2		4		3	7	8¹	9	10		6	11	5						1–0(0–0)5642	—
8. Cambridge*	19.9	1	2		4		3	7	8	9	10		6	11	5						0–2(0–2)5789	3
9. Rochdale	26.9	1	2†				3	8	7	9¹	10		6	12	11	5	4				1–2(0–1)4426	7
10. Crewe*	29.9	1	2†		14		3‡	8	7	9	10		6	12	11	5	4				0–0(0–0)5404	—
11. Scarboro	3.10	1	2					8	7	9	10		6	12	11	3	4†	5			0–1(0–1)4782	10
12. Hartlepool*	10.10	1	2	3				8	7	9	10¹		6		11	4		5			1–0(0–0)5215	6
13. Exeter	17.10	1		3	2			8	7	9¹₁	10		6		11	4					2–1(1–1)2780	4
14. Scunthorpe*	20.10	1		3	2			8	7	9	10		6		11¹	4		5			1–0(0–0)6323	—
15. Torquay	24.10	1		3†	2			8	7		10¹	9¹	6		11¹	4	12	5			3–1(1–0)2740	3
16. Stockport*	31.10	1			2	14		8	7‡	9	10	12	6		11	4	3†	5¹			1–1(1–1)6645	8
17. Halifax	3.11	1			2			8	7	9	10		6		11¹	4	3	5			1–2(1–1)3419	—
18. Wolves	7.11	1			2		3	8	7†	9	10	12	6		11	4		5			0–3(0–0)10,002	10
19. Bolton*	21.11	1				5	3	8	2		10	7¹	6		11		4	9¹			2–1(0–0)7489	9
20. Peterboro	28.11	1				5†	3	8	2		10	7	6	12	11		4	9			0–5(0–3)3550	10
21. Hereford*	12.12	1			2		3	8	7	9†	10	14	6		12	4‡	5	11			0–0(0–0)4216	12
22. Cardiff	19.12	1	2				3		7	9	10	4	6	11			5¹	8			1–2(0–0)3401	15
23. Rochdale*	26.12	1	2				3	8	7†¹	9¹	10¹	4¹	6	12	14		5	11‡			4–0(3–0)7013	9
24. Darlington	28.12	1	2				3	8	7	9†	10	4	6	12			5	11²			2–4(1–1)3325	14
25. Carlisle	1.1	1	2				3¹	8	7	9¹	10	4	6				5¹	11			4–3(2–2)4262	9
26. Tranmere*	2.1	1	2			6	3	8	7	9‡	10¹	4†		12	14		5	11			1–1(0–1)7317	10
27. Newport*	9.1	1	2†			6	3	8	2	7	10¹	4		12	9		5	11			2–0(0–0)5305	9
28. Cambridge	16.1	1	2				3	8	2			6	7	9			5	11			0–2(0–0)2148	9
29. Wrexham	2.2	1		10	2		3		7	9¹		4	6	11¹	8		5				3–1(0–0)1821	—
30. Swansea	6.2	1			2		3		7	9†	10	4	6	11			5	8		12	0–0(0–0)3498	8
31. Darlington*	13.2	1			2	12	3		7		10	4	6	11†	9		5	8²			2–1(1–0)6432	5
32. Colchester	19.2	1		2†		12	3		7		10	4	6		9		5	8¹			1–0(1–0)2520	—
33. Scarboro	27.2	1		3	2	12	14	7†			10	4	6	11	9‡	5		8			0–1(0–0)7845	7
34. Crewe*	1.3	1		3	2	12	14	7†			10	4	6	11†	9	5		8			1–0(0–0)3720	—
35. Exeter*	5.3	1			2		3	11	7		10	4	6		9¹		5¹	8¹			3–0(1–0)6052	4
36. Hartlepool*	12.3	1	2	3			10		7	8¹		4		11	9	6	5				1–2(0–2)2891	6
37. Stockport	18.3	1	2				3		7	8†	10	4	6	11	9		5			12	0–2(0–1)4423	—
38. Orient*	22.3	1	2				3		7	8¹₁	10	4	6	11	9		5				2–0(1–0)5878	—
39. Wolves*	2.4	1	2†				3		7	8	10	4	6	11	9		5			12	0–3(0–1)10,341	7
40. Bolton	4.4	1	2				3		7	8¹	10	4	6	9	11		5				1–2(1–1)9921	9
41. Halifax*	8.4	1	2				3		7	8	9	10	4	6	11		5¹				3–1(1–1)5766	—
42. Scunthorpe	23.4	1	3	2		6			8		10	4¹	11	9	7		5				1–1(0–0)5347	8
43. Peterboro*	30.4	1	2				3	7†	8‡	10₁	4	6	11	9	12	5		14			1–2(1–0)6305	11
44. Hereford	2.5	1	3	2		6¹		7	8	10	11	4		9		5					1–2(1–1)2304	13
45. Torquay*	4.5	1	11¹	2	3			7	8	10	4	6		9		5					1–0(1–0)5075	—
46. Cardiff*	7.5	1	11	2	5			7	8¹	10	4	6		9	3						1–2(0–0)8525	10

Apps(subs)/goals: Pearce 46(0)0, Leebrook 22(0)0, McGrory 16(0)1, Daniel 26(1)0, Zelem 9(1)1, Deakin 37(0)3, Grewcock 28(4)0, Farrell 45(0)3, Oghani 44(0)14, Comstive 44(0)8, Britton 29(3)4, Gardner 41(1)0, Hoskin 15(9)1, Taylor 38(4)6, James 6(2)0, Malley 33(0)5, Davis 16(6)8, Reeves 1(0)0, Devaney 0(4)0

Final League Position: 10

Own goals: Wright, match 25; Bowden, match 29; Gage, match 34.

DIVISION 3

BURY

Gigg Lane, Bury BL9 9HR.

Back row (left to right): Charlie Bishop, Peter Valentine, Phil Hughes, Mark Higgins, Simon Farnworth, Ian Fairbrother, Terry Pashley. *Middle row:* Frank Casper (Ass. Manager), Wilf McGuinness (Physio), Jimmy Collins, Bob Colville, Nigel Greenwood, Nigel Hart, Jamie Hoyland, Martin Dobson (Manager), Ray Pointer (Res. Team Coach). *Front row:* David Lee, Noel Brotherston, Andy Hill (Captain), Sammy McIlroy, Alan Taylor, Liam Robinson.

Stadium Capacity: 8,000.
Pitch Dimensions: 112 × 72yds.
Telephone: 061–764 4881, **Commercial dept:** 061–764 7475.
Chairman: T. Robinson.
Vice-Chairman: Canon J. R. Smith MA.
Directors: C. H. Eaves, R. Jacks, A. Metcalfe, I. Pickup, J. Smith.
Manager: Martin Dobson.
Post-War Managers: Norman Bullock, John McNeil, Dave Russell, Bob Stokoe, Bert Head, Les Shannon, Jack Marshall, Les Hart, Colin Mc Donald, Tommy McAnearney, Allan Brown, Bobby Smith, Bob Stokoe, Dave Hatton, Dave Connor, Jim Iley (16).
Assistant Manager: Frank Casper.
Physio: Wilf McGuiness.
Secretary: John Heap.
Commercial Manager: Neville Neville.
Sponsors: Macpherson Paints.
Founded: 1885.
Turned Professional: 1885.
Nickname: The Shakers.
Former Names: None.
Former Grounds: None.
Record Attendance: 35,000 v Bolton, FA Cup 3rd Round, 9 January 1960.
Record Victory: 21–1 v Stockton, FA Cup 1st Round replay, 1896–97.
Record Defeat: 0–10 V Blackburn R, FA Cup, preliminary Round, 1st October, 1887 and v West Ham U, Milk Cup, 2nd Round, 2nd leg, 25 October 1983.
Most League Points: (3 for a win) 84, Division 4, 1984–85. (2 for a win) 68, Division 3, 1960–61.
Most League Goals: 108, Division 3, 1960–61.
Highest League Scorer in a Season: Craig Madden, 35, Division 4, 1981–82.
Highest Total of League Goals: Craig Madden, 129, 1978–82.
Most League Appearances: Norman Bullock, 506, 1920–35.
League History: 1894 Elected to Division 2, 1895–1912 Division 1, 1912–24 Division 2, 1924–29 Division 1, 1929–57 Division 2, 1957–61 Division 3, 1961–67 Division 2, 1967–68 Division 3, 1968–69 Division 2, 1969–71 Division 3, 1971–74 Division 2, 1974–80 Division 3, 1980–85 Division 4, 1985– Division 3.
Honours: Division 2 Champions 1894–95, runners-up 1923–24. Division 3 Champions 1960–61, runners-up 1967–68. FA Cup winners 1900, 1903.
Colours: White shirts, navy blue shorts, white socks. **Second strip:** All red.

BURY – LEAGUE RECORD 1987–88

Match no/Opp/Date		Farnworth	Hill	Pashley	Hoyland	Valentine	Higgins	Lee	Greenwood	Cohille	McIlroy	Brotherston	Robinson	Hughes	Hart	Taylor	Fairbrother	Bishop	Collins	Parkinson	Clements	Walsh	FT(HT)Att Lge pos
1. Southend*	15.8	1	2	3	4¹	5	6	7	8	9†	10¹	11	12										2–2(1–0)1937 —
2. Rotherham	22.8		2	3	4	5		7	8		10	11	1		6	9¹							1–0(0–0)3017 4
3. Blackpool*	29.8		2	3	4	5		7	8†		10	11¹	1		6²	9	12						3–1(0–1)3053 2
4. Chesterfield	31.8		2	3	4	5		7	8†		10	11	12	1	6	9							0–1(0–0)2411 —
5. Bristol C*	5.9		2	3	4¹	5	12	7†	8‡	14	10	11	1		6	9							1–1(1–1)2376 9
6. Sunderland	12.9		2	3	4	5	7			12	10	11	8¹†	1	6	9							1–1(1–1)13,227 13
7. Grimsby*	15.9		2	3	4	5†		7			10	11	8	1	6	9‡	12	14					0–2(0–2)1899 —
8. Aldershot*	19.9	1	2	3	9	5	6	7†			10	11	8¹‡		4	14	12						1–0(1–0)1744 13
9. Wigan	26.9	1	2	3	9	5	6	7			10		8²			11	4						2–0(1–0)3664 10
10. Walsall*	29.9	1	2	3	9	5	6	7			10¹	11¹	8				4						2–2(1–2)2449 —
11. Brighton	3.10	1	2	3	9	5	6	7‡			10	11	8¹		12	14	4†						1–2(1–1)6509 14
12. Brentford*	10.10	1	2¹	3	9	5	6	7			10	11¹	8		4								2–2(1–1)2300 13
13. Port Vale	17.10		2	3	9	5	6	7	12		10	11	8	1	4†								0–1(0–1)3235 13
14. Notts Co	20.10	1	2	3†	9	5	6	7			10	11	8		4	12							0–3(0–1)4044 —
15. Preston*	24.10	1	2	3	4	5‡	6	7¹	9¹		10	11†	8₂		14	12							4–0(1–0)4316 12
16. Doncaster	31.10	1	2	3	4	5	6	7	9†		10	11¹	8¹		12								2–1(1–0)1403 10
17. Mansfield*	3.11	1	2	3	4¹	5	6	7	9†		10	11	8		12								1–0(1–0)2248 —
18. York	7.11	1	2	3‡	4	5	6	7	9†		10	11	8¹		14	12							1–1(1–0) 8
19. Bristol R*	21.11	1	2	3	4¹	5	6	7	9		10¹	11	8²										4–1(1–0)2356 7
20. Gillingham	28.11	1	2	3	4¹	5	6	7†	9		10₁	11	8₁		12								3–3(1–1)3981 8
21. Fulham*	12.12	1	2	3	4	5	6	7	9¹		10	11	8										1–1(1–1)2643 9
22. Chester	18.12	1	2	3	4	5¹	6	7‡	9†		10	11	8¹		14	12²							4–4(0–1)1772 —
23. Wigan*	26.12	1	2	3	4	5	6‡	7	12		10	11	8		14	9†							0–2(0–1)4555 10
24. Nthampton	28.12	1	2	3	4	5	6				10	11	8		7	9							0–0(0–0)6067 10
25. Blackpool	1.1	1	2	3	4¹	5‡	6	12			10	11	8		7	9‡	14						1–5(1–2)4240 13
26. Sunderland*	2.1	1	2†	3	4	5	6	7	9		10	11	8²		12								2–3(1–1)4883 13
27. Rotherham*	9.1	1	2	3	4		6	7	9‡		10	11†	8		5	12²	14						2–2(0–0)2320 13
28. Aldershot	16.1	1	2	3¹	4	5	6	7†			10		8¹		12	9	11						2–0(0–0)2718 10
29. Grimsby	26.1	1	2	3	4	5	6†	7‡				14	8		9	10	11	12					0–2(0–1)2525 —
30. Chesterfield*	30.1	1	2	3	4	5	6	7¹	12			8¹			9	10†	11						2–0(2–0)2071 9
31. Bristol C	6.2	1	2	3	4¹	5¹†	6	7‡	12			8			14	9	10	11					2–3(1–0)9158 10
32. Nthampton*	13.2	1	2	3	4		6	7	12			8			5	9†	10	11					0–0(0–0)2172 10
33. Southend	20.2	1	2	3		14	6	7	11			12			8	4†	9	10	5‡				0–1(0–1)3003 10
34. Brighton*	27.2	1	2	3		5	6	7	14			12	8²		4	9	10†	11‡					2–1(0–0)2557 10
35. Walsall	1.3	1	2	3	10	5	6	7¹				8			4	9		11					1–2(1–1)3920 —
36. Port Vale*	5.3	1	2	3	4	5	6	7	12			8			11†	9	10‡						0–1(0–0)2635 12
37. Brentford	12.3	1	2	3	4	5	6		10¹			8			11	9¹†	12		7¹				3–0(1–0)3920 11
38. Doncaster*	19.3	1	2	3†	4	12	6		10¹			8			11	9			7	5			2–1(1–0)2431 10
39. Preston	26.3	1	2	3	4		6‡	12	10†			8			11	9			7	5			0–1(0–1)6456 12
40. York*	2.4	1	2†	3	4		6	11‡	10			8			9	12			7	5			0–1(0–0)2277 13
41. Bristol R	4.4	1		3	4	6			10			11†	8		9	12	2		7	5			0–0(0–0)4664 13
42. Notts Co*	9.4	1		3	10	4	6					11	8		9	12	2†		7	5			0–1(0–0)2527 14
43. Mansfield	23.4	1	2	3	4	7	6	11				10	8		12	9†				5			0–0(0–0)2381 15
44. Gillingham*	30.4	1	2¹	3	4	7	6	11				10	8		12	9†			5¹				2–1(1–1)1433 15
45. Fulham	2.5	1	2†	3	4¹	10	6	7	12			8			11	9			9	5			1–0(1–0)5283 13
46. Chester*	7.5	1		3	4	7	6†	11	9†			8			2		14		10	5	12		0–1(0–0)1942 14

Final League Position: 14

Apps(subs)/goals: 39(0)/0, 43(0)/2, 44(0)/0, 40(2)/2, 40(1)/0, 38(2)/3, 22(6)/4, 1(2)/0, 28(0)/4, 30(6)/4, 41(2)/19, 7(0)/0, 23(1)/2, 23(7)/4, 8(9)/2, 13(4)/0, 0(1)/0, 8(0)/1, 9(0)/1, 0(1)/0

Own goal: Holmes, match 38.

CAMBRIDGE UNITED

Abbey Stadium, Newmarket Road, Cambridge CB5 8LL.

Back row (left to right): Gary Poole, Neil Horwood, Paul Casey, Roy Johnson (Physio), Keith Branagan, Gary Kimble, Alan Kimble. *Middle row:* Graham Scarff (Coach), Gary Clayton, Ian Measham, Lil Fuccillo, Jason Cowling, John Rigby, Gary Bratten, Wayne Ebanks, Malcolm Webster (Ass. Manager). *Front row:* Mark Crowe, Andy Beattie, Lindsay Smith, Chris Turner (Manager), Peter Butler, David Crown, John Beck.

Stadium Capacity: 10,150.
Pitch Dimensions: 110 × 74yds.
Telephone: 0223–241237.
Chairman: D. A. Ruston.
Vice-Chairman: R. H. Smart.
Directors: R. Stops, R. J. Smith, G. E. Taylor.
Manager: Chris Turner.
Post-War Managers: Bill Whittaker, Gerald Williams, Bert Johnson, Bill Craig, Roy Kirk, Alan Moore, Bill Leivers, Ron Atkinson, John Docherty, John Ryan, Ken Shellito (11).
Assistant Manager: J. Beck.
Physio: Roy F. Johnson.
Secretary: Roy F. Johnson.
Commercial Manager: John Carter.
Founded: 1919.
Turned Professional: 1946.
Nickname: United.
Former Names: Abbey United 1919–49.
Former Grounds: None.
Record Attendance: 14,000 v Chelsea, friendly, 1 May 1970.
Record Victory: 6–0 v Darlington, Division 4, 18 September 1971.
Record Defeat: 0–6 v Aldershot , Division 3, 13 April 1974 and v Darlington, Division 4, 28 September 1974 and v Chelsea, Division 2, 15 January 1983.
Most League Points: (3 for a win) 62, Division 4, 1986–87. (2 for a win) 65, Division 4, 1976–77.
Most League Goals: 87, Division 4, 1976–77.
Highest League Scorer in a Season: Craig Madden, 35, Division 4, 1981–82.
Highest Total of League Goals: Alan Biley, 74, 1975–80.
Most League Appearances: Steve Spriggs, 416, 1975–87.
League History: 1970 Elected to Division 4, 1973–74 Division 3, 1974–77 Division 4, 1924–29 Division 1, 1977–78 Division 3, 1978–84 Division 3, 1984–85 Division 3, 1985– Division 4.
Honours: Division 3 runners-up 1977–78. Division 4 Champions 1976–77.
Colours: Black and amber striped shirts, black shorts and socks. **Second strip:** All sky blue with amber and black trim.

CAMBRIDGE UNITED – LEAGUE RECORD 1987–88

Match no/Opp/Date		Bratgan	Ebanks	Kimble A	Crewe	Smith	Beck	Butler	Clayton	Horwood	Crown	Kimble G	Bratian	Rigby	Beattie	Poole	Turner	Murray	Purdie	Benjamin	Pugh	Neal	Hilderby	Fucillo	Sayer	Lawrence	Bastock	Hollis	Bull	Hamilton	Chapple	FT(HT)Att Lge pos
1. Exeter	15.8	1	2†	3	4	5	6	7	8	9	10	11	12																				0–3(0–2)2650 —
2. Crewe*	22.8	1	2	3	4	5	6	7	8¹		10³	11		9																			4–1(2–1)1523 11
3. Peterboro	29.8	1	2	3		5	6	7	8	12	10	11		9†	4																		0–1(0–0)4623 18
4. Cardiff*	1.9	1		3		5	6	7	8		10	11		9	4	2																	0–0(0–0)2079 —
5. Torquay	5.9	1		3		5	6	7	8		10¹	11		9	4	2																	1–0(0–0)2676 12
6. Scunthorpe*	12.9	1	14	3		5	6¹†		8	12	10¹	11	7	9²	4	2																	3–3(1–2)1830 13
7. Hartlepool	16.9	1		3		5			8		10¹	11	7	9	4	2	6																1–2(0–2)1376 —
8. Burnley	19.9	1		3		5		7	8	12	10¹	11	6	9†¹	4	2																	2–0(2–0)5789 13
9. Halifax*	26.9	1				5	6	7	8		10²	11		9	4	2		3															2–1(1–1)1805 9
10. Wrexham*	29.9	1		12		5	6	7	8†		10	11		9	4	2		3															0–1(0–0)2257 —
11. Swansea	3.10	1				5	6	7¹	8		10	11		9	4	2		3															1–1(0–0)3378 12
12. Newport*	10.10	1			5¹	6¹		8	12¹	10¹†	11	7	9	4	2			3															4–0(1–0)1874 9
13. Orient	17.10	1		12¹		5	6†	11¹	8		10		7	9	4	2		3															2–0(0–0)4059 7
14. Wolves	20.10	1		6		5		7	8†	12	10		11	9‡	4	2	14	3															0–3(0–3)6492 —
15. Colchester*	24.10	1				5		7	8	12	10		6	9†	4	2		3	11														0–1(0–0)2450 15
16. Tranmere	30.10	1			5		7	8¹		10			4	2	6	3	11	9															1–0(0–0)2240 —
17. Hereford*	3.11	1		14		5	6	7	8		10			4	2		3	11‡	9†														0–1(0–1)2257 —
18. Darlington*	8.11	1		11		5	6†	7¹	8	14			10‡	4	2	12	3		9														1–0(1–0)2463 —
19. Rochdale*	20.11	1		12		5	6‡	7	8	10†			4	2	14	3	11	9¹															1–2(1–2)2104 —
20. Bolton	28.11	1		11	4	5	6	7¹						2	8	3	9¹	10															2–2(1–1)4294 13
21. Stockport*	11.12	1		11	4	5	6	7	8					2	12	3†	12	10¹															2–0(2–0)1475 —
22. Carlisle	18.12	1		3	4	5¹	6†	7	8					2	12		9	10	11														1–2(0–2)1843 —
23. Halifax	26.12	1		3	4	5	6	7	8	9¹				2			10	11															1–1(1–3)1667 13
24. Scarboro*	28.12	1		3	4	5	6	7	8	12				2			10	11¹	9														1–0(0–0)3243 11
25. Peterboro*	1.1	1		3	4	5		7	8¹	12				2	6†		10	11	9														1–3(0–2)3975 13
26. Scunthorpe	2.1	1		3	4†	5‡		7	8				6¹	2	12		10	11	9														2–3(2–3)3252 14
27. Burnley*	16.1	1		3	4	5‡	6	7¹	8	12				2			10	11†	9														2–0(0–0)2148 11
28. Cardiff	30.1	1		3	4	5	6	7‡	8	9†			12	2			10			11	14												0–4(0–3)4012 13
29. Torquay*	6.2	1		3	4	5		7	8					2			10†			11¹	6	9	12										1–0(0–0)1948 13
30. Scarborough	13.2	1		3	4	5	6		8					2			7†			11	10	12	9										0–0(0–0)1879 14
31. Exeter*	19.2	1		3	4	5	6		8¹					2			7			11¹	10	6											2–1(0–0)1878 —
32. Swansea	27.2	1		3	4		14		8					5		2	7†			11	10	12	9										0–3(0–2)2080 14
33. Wrexham	1.3			3	4		6‡		8					5		2				11	10	7†	9										0–3(0–2)1025 —
34. Orient*	5.3	1		3	4	5	6		8				7¹			2				11¹	10		9										2–0(0–0)2500 13
35. Newport	12.3	1		3	4	5	6		8				7†			2				11	10	12	9										0–0(0–0)1208 13
36. Tranmere*	19.3	1		3	4	5‡	6		8				7			2				11	10		9										1–1(1–0)1514 13
37. Colchester	25.3			3	4	5	6		8				7†			2				12			10		9	1	11						1–0(0–0)2146 —
38. Darlington*	1.4			3	4	5	6		8							2							10		9	1		7	11¹				1–0(1–0)2249 —
39. Rochdale	4.4			3	4	5	6		8					2‡						12			10¹		9†	1		7	11	14			1–2(0–0)1596 15
40. Wolves*	10.4			3	4	5	6		8¹					2						12			10		9†	1		7‡	11	14			1–1(0–0)5017 —
41. Crewe	15.4			3	4	5	6		8							12				9†			10			1	2	7	11				0–0(0–0)1546 —
42. Hartlepool*	19.4			3	4	5	6		8					12						9			10¹			1	2†	7	11				1–1(0–1)1492 —
43. Hereford	23.4			3	4		6†		8					2	12					14			10			1		7‡	11	5			0–1(0–1)1666 15
44. Bolton*	29.4			3¹	4				8					2	6					9†			10			12	1	7¹	11	5			2–2(1–1)2063 —
45. Stockport	2.5			3			5			8				2	6								10			1		7¹	11	4¹			2–0(0–0)1842 15
46. Carlisle*	7.5			3		5			8					2	6								10			1		7‡	11	4			1–2(1–0)1738 15

Final League Position: 15

Apps(subs)/goals: 35(0) 0, 3(1) 0, 37(4) 2, 27(0) 0, 42(0) 5, 34(1) 2, 26(0) 5, 45(0) 5, 4(0) 2, 17(0) 9, 12(0) 0, 7(0) 1, 40(1) 14, 20(1) 1, 41(1) 0, 15(0) 0, 7(8) 0, 13(0) 0, 20(5) 2, 6(0) 1, 4(0) 0, 9(0) 3, 1(1) 0, 18(1) 2, 23(0) 0, 11(2) 0, 16(0) 0, 30(0) 5, 9(0) 3, 4(2) 1

Also played: Williams, match 43(9); Casey, match 33(1); Ryan, matches 45,46(9); groble, match 32(6‡), 33(14).

DIVISION 3

CARDIFF CITY

Ninian Park, Cardiff, CF1 8SX.

Back row
(left to right):
J. Gilligan
M. Ford
P. Wheeler
M. Kelly
Middle row:
S. Mardenborough
N. Stevenson
P. Sanderson
G. Moseley
J. Roberts
A. Curtis
N. Platnauer
P. Bater
Front row:
G. Abraham
J. Gummer
P. Wimbleton
T. Boyle
N. McDermott
K. Bartlett
J. Perry

Stadium Capacity: 39,900.
Pitch Dimensions: 114 × 78yds.
Telephone: 0222–398636.
Chairman: J. A. Clemo.
President: Lord Brooks of Tremorfa.
Directors: C. Bergin, Mrs L. Clemo, G. K. McCarthy.
Manager: Frank Burrows.
Post-War Managers: Bill McCandless, Cyril Spiers, Trevor Morris, Bill Jones, George Windin, Jimmy Scoular, Frank O'Farrell, Jimmy Andres, Richie Morgan, Len Ashurst, Jimmy Goodfellow, Alan Durban (12).
Assistant Manager: Jimmy Goodfellow.
Physio: J. Goodfellow.
Secretary: E. Harrison.
Commercial Manager: Mrs S. Wynne.
Sponsors: Buckleys Brewery.
Founded: 1899.
Turned Professional: 1910.
Nickname: The Bluebirds.
Former Names: Riverside 1899–1902, Riverside Albion 1902–06, Cardiff City 1906.
Former Grounds: Riverside, Sophia Gardens, Old Park and Fir Gardens. Ninian Park from 1910.
Record Attendance: 57,893 v Arsenal, Division 1, 22 April 1953.
Record Victory: 9–2 v Thames, Division 3(S), 6 February 1932.
Record Defeat: 2–11 v Sheffield U, Division 1, 1 January 1926.
Most League Points: (3 for a win) 86, Division 3, 1982–83. (2 for a win) 66, Division 3(S), 1946–47.
Most League Goals: 93, Division 3(S), 1946–47.
Highest League Scorer in a Season: Stan Richards, 31, Division 3(S), 1946–47.
Highest Total of League Goals: Len Davies, 128, 1920–31.
Most League Appearances: Phil Dwyer, 471, 1972–85.
League History: 1920 Elected to Division 2, 1921–29 Division 1, 1929–31 Division 2, 1931–47 Division 3(S), 1947–52 Division 2, 1952–57 Division 1, 1957–60 Division 2, 1960–62 Division 1, 1962–75 Division 2, 1975–76 Division 3, 1976–82 Division 2, 1982–83 Division 3, 1983–85 Division 2, 1985–86 Division 3, 1986–88 Division 4, 1988– Division 3.
Honours: Division 1 runners-up 1923–24. Division 2 runners-up 1920–21, 1951–52, 1959–60. Division 3 runners-up 1975–76, 1982–83. Division 4 runners-up 1987–88. Division 3(S) Champions 1946–47. FA Cup winners 1927, runners-up 1925. Welsh Cup winners 1912, 1920, 1922, 1923, 1927, 1928, 1930, 1956, 1959, 1964, 1965, 1967, 1968, 1969, 1970, 1971, 1973, 1974, 1976, 1988.
Colours: Royal blue shirts and socks, white shorts. **Second strip:** All red.

242

CARDIFF CITY – LEAGUE RECORD 1987–88

Match no/Opp/Date		Moseley	Perry	Ford	Gummer	Stevenson	Boyle	Curtis	Sanderson	Gilligan	McDermott	Kelly	Mardenborough	Wheeler	Platnauer	Bartlett	Bater	Wimbleton	Abrahams	Judge	Roberts	Enderby	Wood	Walsh	FT(HT)Att Lge pos
1. Orient*	15.8	1	2	3	4†	5	6	7	8	9¹	10	11	12												1–1(1–1)3357 —
2. Bolton	22.8	1	2†	3		5	6	7	8	9	10	11‡		12	4	14									0–1(0–1)4530 19
3. Swansea*	29.8	1		3		5	6	7	8	9	10	11	2		4										1–0(0–0)6010 13
4. Cambridge	1.9	1		3		5	6	7	8†	9	10	11	2		4	12									0–0(0–0)2079 —
5. Wolves*	5.9	1	5	2			6¹	7	12	9†	10¹	11	4		3	8¹									3–2(1–1)2258 10
6. Wrexham	12.9	1		2		6	7†	12	9	10	11	14			8	3	4‡	5							0–3(0–2)2212 15
7. Darlington*	15.9	1		2		6	7		9	10	11			8²	3	4	5¹								3–1(1–0)2201 —
8. Carlisle*	19.9	1		3¹		6¹	7	12	9¹	10	11			5	8†	2	4¹								4–2(1–2)2659 7
9. Tranmere	25.9	1		3		6	7		9	10	11	12	5	8†	2	4									1–0(0–0)2543 —
10. Halifax*	29.9	1		2		5	6	7	12	9	10	11†			3	8	4								0–0(0–0)3666 —
11. Stockport	2.10	1		3		5	6	7	12	9	10			11	8¹†	2	4								1–0(1–0)2332 —
12. Hereford*	10.10	1		11		5	6	7	14	9	10†	12		3‡	8	2	4								0–1(0–0)4420 4
13. Peterboro	17.10	1		11²			6	7	12	9	10‡	5	8†		3	14	2	4							3–4(2–1)3473 9
14. Torquay*	20.10			11¹	14		6	7		9¹	10‡	5	8†	12	3		2	4	1						2–1(0–1)3503 —
15. Scunthorpe	24.10			5		12	6		14¹	9	10	11	8‡	7†	3		2	4	1						1–2(0–2)2872 10
16. Rochdale*	31.10			4		5	6			9	10	11	8	7†	3	12	2	4	1						1–0(0–0)3046 7
17. Scarboro	4.11			8	5†	6	7		11	9	10	12			3		2	4¹	1						1–1(1–1)2599 —
18. Exeter*	7.11			8		6¹	7†	11‡	9²	10	5	14		3	12	2	4	1							3–2(1–1)3474 5
19. Newport	21.11			8			9	10	5	12		3‡	11¹†	2	4¹		1								2–1(0–0)4022 2
20. Hartlepool*	28.11			5		6	7	14	9	11¹	8†	12		3	10	2	4	1							1–1(0–1)3232 3
21. Crewe	12.12			5	8	6			9	10		7	11	3	2	4	1								0–0(0–0)2010 4
22. Burnley*	19.12			8	5†	6		9²	10	12	7‡	11	3	14	2	4	1								2–1(0–0)3401 4
23. Tranmere	26.12			8	5	6	7	14	9²	10†	12	11‡	3	2	4¹	1									3–0(1–0)5233 3
24. Colchester	28.12			8	5	6	7†	14	9	10‡	11¹	12	3	2	4	1									1–2(1–1)2599 4
25. Swansea	1.1			8¹	5	6	7		9¹	10‡	12	11†	3	14	2	4	1								2–2(0–0)10,300 4
26. Carlisle	16.1			8	5	6	7	12	9	10		3	11‡	2	4	1									0–0(0–0)2344 5
27. Cambridge*	30.1			8	5	6¹	7		9	10¹	14	12	3‡	11¹†	2	4₁	1								4–0(3–0)4012 3
28. Darlington	2.2			8	5	6		9	10		3	11¹†	2	4	1										0–0(0–0)2332 2
29. Wolves	6.2			8	5	6	7	9²		3	11	2	4²	1											4–1(0–0)10,077 2
30. Colchester*	13.2			8¹	5	6	7†	9	10	12	3	11	2	4	1										1–0(0–0)5458 2
31. Orient	20.2			8	5	6	7†	9	10‡	12	3	11¹	2	4	1	14									1–4(1–1)3523 2
32. Stockport*	27.2			8	5	6	7	12	9	10†	3	14	2	4	1	11‡									0–0(0–0)4008 2
33. Halifax	1.3			8	5	6		7	9	10	3	11¹	2	4	1										1–0(0–0)1128 2
34. Peterboro*	4.3			8	5	6		7†	9	10	3	12	14	11‡	2	4	1								0–0(0–0)4172 2
35. Hereford	13.3			8	5	6	7	9¹	10	3	11¹	2	4	1											2–1(1–1)3210 2
36. Wrexham*	16.3			8	5	6	7	9¹	10	3	11†	2	4	1	12										1–1(0–1)4083 2
37. Scunthorpe*	26.3			8	5	6	7†	9	10‡	14	3	11	2	4	1	12									0–1(0–0)4527 3
38. Rochdale	29.3			8	5	6	7	9	10	3	11¹†	2	4	1	12										2–2(0–1)1435 2
39. Exeter	2.4			8	5	6	7‡	9	10	14	3	11²†	2	4	1	12									2–0(2–0)2649 2
40. Newport*	4.4			8¹	5¹	6	7	9	10¹	12	3	11†	2	4¹	1										4–0(1–0)6536 2
41. Torquay	9.4			8	5	6	7	9†	10	14	12	3	11	2	4‡	1									0–2(0–2)3082 2
42. Bolton*	15.4			8	5	6	7	9¹	10	3	11	2	4	1											1–0(0–0)6705 2
43. Scarboro*	23.4			5	6	7¹	9	8₁	10	12	3	11	2	4†	1										2–0(1–0)5751 2
44. Hartlepool	30.4			4	5	6	7	9¹	8	10	3	11	2	1											1–0(1–0)1097 2
45. Crewe*	2.5			4	5	6	7	9	8¹	10	12	3	11¹†	2	1										2–0(2–0)10,125 2
46. Burnley	7.5			4	5	6	7¹	9¹	8	10	12	3	11†	2	1										2–2(0–2)8525 2
Apps(subs)/goals		13(0)0	3(0)0	45(0)7	1(0)0	35(1)1	46(0)4	40(0)2	8(13)1	46(0)19	45(0)7	28(8)1	6(12)0	41(0)0	46(0)1	30(7)12	40(0)0	37(0)9	20(1)0	8(0)0	8(0)0	4(0)0	13(0)0	1(5)0	Final League Position: 2

Own goal: Bramhall, match 38.

DIVISION 4

CARLISLE UNITED

Brunton Park, Carlisle CA1 1LL.

Back row
(left to right):
John Cooke
Mark Patterson
Malcolm Poskett
Paul Gorman
Steve Crompton
Brent Hetherington
Peter Harbach
Paul Tynan
Middle row:
Neil Wrightson
Ian Bishop
Bobby McNeil
Andy Robinson
Wes Saunders
Billy Wright
Ian Milburn
Front row (all YTS):
Alan Stewart
John McNamee
Jason Priestley
Jim Robertson
Brian Sweeney
Steve Harkness

Stadium Capacity: 18,035.
Pitch Dimensions: 117 × 78yds.
Telephone: 0228–26237.
Chairman: H. A. Jenkins.
Vice-Chairman: J. R. Sheffield. **Honorary Vice-President:** Dr T. Gardner MB,CHB.
Directors: R. S. Liddell, T. A. Bingley, C. J. Vasey, J. B. Lloyd, A. Liddell, A. Hodgkinson.
Manager: Clive Middlemass.
Post-War Managers: Willie Clark, Ivor Broadis, Bill Shankly, Fred Emery, Andy Beattie, Ivor Powell, Alan Ashman, Tim Ward, Bob Stokoe, Ian MacFarlane, Alan Ashman, Dick Young, Bobby Moncur, Martin Harvey, Bob Stokoe, Harry Gregg (16).
Assistant Manager: Peter Hampton.
Physio: Peter Hampton.
Secretary: Harold Wood.
Commercial Manager: Frank Layton.
Founded: 1904.
Turned Professional: 1921.
Nickname: The Cumbrians or The Blues.
Former Names: None.
Former Grounds: Milholme Bank 1903–5, Devonshire Park 1906–9.
Record Attendance: 27,500 v Birmingham C, FA Cup 3rd Round, 5 January 1957 and v Middlesbrough, FA Cup 5th Round, 7 February 1970.
Record Victory: 8–0 v Hartlepool U, Division 3(N), 1 September 1928 and v Scunthorpe U, Division 3(N), 25 December 1952.
Record Defeat: 1–11 v Hull C, Division 3(N), 14 January, 1939.
Most League Points: (3 for a win) 80, Division 3, 1981–82. (2 for a win) 62, Division 3(N), 1950–51.
Most League Goals: 113, Division 4, 1963–64.
Highest League Scorer in a Season: Jimmy McConnell, 42, Division 3(N), 1928–29.
Highest Total of League Goals: Jimmy McConnell, 126, 1928–32.
Most League Appearances: Alan Ross, 466, 1963–79.
League History: 1928 Elected to Division 3(N), 1958–62 Division 4, 1962–63 Division 3, 1963–64 Division 4, 1964–65 Division 3, 1965–74 Division 2, 1974–75 Division 1, 1975–77 Division 2, 1977–82 Division 3, 1982–86 Division 2, 1986–87 Division 3, 1987– Division 4.
Honours: Division 3 Champions 1964–65. Division 4 runners-up 1963–64.
Colours: All blue with red and white trim. **Second strip:** All red.

CARLISLE UNITED – LEAGUE RECORD 1987–88

Match no/Opp/Date		Crompton	Paterson	McNeil	Gorman	Wright	Saunders	Robinson	Cooke	Poskett	Bishop	Hetherington	Clark	Harbach	Taylor	Fulbrook	Tynan	Harrison	Houston	Mills	Robertson	Prudhoe	Hampton	Halpin	Stephens	McCaffery	Hutchinson	Saddington	Holdsworth	Fyfe	Rowell	FT(HT)Att Lge pos
1. Peterboro	15.8	1	2	3†	4	5	6	7	8	9	10	11	12																			0–1(0–1)4000 —
2. Scunthorpe*	22.8	1	2		4	5	6	7¹	8	9	10	11¹	3																			3–1(0–0)2074 10
3. Burnley	29.8	1	2		4	5	6	7	8¹	9	10	11†	3	12																		3–4(1–3)5781 17
4. Hereford*	31.8	1	2	3	4†	5	6		8	9	10	11¹	7	12																		3–1(1–1)2708 —
5. Stockport	4.9	1	2	3	4	5	6		8	9	10	11	7																			0–3(0–1)2257 —
6. Hartlepool*	12.9	1	2	3	4†	5	6		8	9	10¹	11	7	12																		1–3(0–2)2463 20
7. Exeter	16.9	1	2	3	4	5	6		8	9	10¹	11	7																			1–1(1–1)3347 —
8. Cardiff	19.9	1	2	3‡	4	5	6¹	14	8	9†	10	11¹	7	12																		2–4(2–1)2659 21
9. Scarboro*	26.9		2	3		5¹	6¹	4	8	9¹	10	11¹	7		1																	4–0(1–0)2693 18
10. Darlington*	29.9		2	3		5	6	4	8	9	10¹	11	7¹		1																	3–3(2–2)2996 16
11. Rochdale	3.10		2			5	6	4	8	9²	10	11	7		1	3																2–1(0–0)1940 16
12. Wolves*	10.10		2	3		5	6	4†	8	9	10	11	7		1		12															0–1(0–1)2620 18
13. Bolton	17.10		2	3	7	5		4	8	9		11			12	1	10†	6‡	14													0–5(0–2)4184 18
14. Colchester	20.10	1	2		3	5.		4	8	9		11	7	14			10‡	12	6†													0–1(0–0)1328 —
15. Tranmere*	24.10	1	2	3†	4	5		12	8¹	9	10	11¹	7					6¹														3–2(0–1)2160 19
16. Crewe	31.10	1	2			5	6		8	9	10	11¹	7			1	3	4														1–4(0–3)2124 20
17. Orient*	3.11			12	5	6	2	8	9	10	11	7				1	3	4†														1–2(1–1)2139 —
18. Newport*	7.11		2	12	5	6¹	3	8¹‡	9		11¹	7				1	10	14	4†													3–1(2–0)1766 20
19. Wrexham	21.11		2	4‡	5	6	7	8	9		11		12	1	3		10†		14													0–4(0–1)1485 21
20. Torquay*	28.11		2	4	5†	6	7¹	8	9¹		11¹			1	3	12	10															3–3(3–2)2017 21
21. Swansea	12.12		2		5	6	4¹	8	9		11	7							1	3	10											1–3(0–1)3876 21
22. Cambridge*	18.12		2		5	6¹	4	8	9		11	7			12				1	3	10¹											2–1(2–0)1843 —
23. Scarboro	26.12		2	6	5		4	8	12¹		11†	7							1	3	10	9										1–3(0–1)3261 20
24. Burnley*	1.1		2	6	5		4	8	11¹†		12	7							1	3	10†	9¹										3–4(2–2)4262 21
25. Hartlepool	2.1		2	5	6	4	8	11			7								1	3	10											0–0(0–0)3153 21
26. Darlington	9.1		2	5	6	4	8	11†		12									1	3	10	9¹	7									1–2(0–1)2517 21
27. Cardiff*	16.1		14	2	5	6	4	8		11‡				12					1	3	10	9†	7.									0–0(0–0)2344 21
28. Exeter*	23.1		2	5†	6	4	8			12	9								1	3	10		7	11								0–0(0–0)1699 21
29. Hereford	30.1		2	5	6	4			8	9				12					1	3	10		7†	11								0–2(0–2)1904 23
30. Stockport*	6.2		9	5₁	6¹	8			11	2									1	3	10		4	7								2–0(1–0)1842 22
31. Peterboro*	20.2		2	5		7			11	3				12					1		10			6	8	4	9†					0–2(0–2)2026 23
32. Rochdale*	27.2		2	5¹	8	7	11		3										1		10			6	8	4	9¹					2–0(2–0)1983 22
33. Bolton*	5.3		2	5	8†	7	11		3										1		10			6	12	4	9					0–2(0–1)2796 23
34. Wolves	12.3		2	5	12	7	11†		3										1		10			6	8¹	4	9					1–3(0–1)9262 23
35. Crewe*	19.3		9	5		7†			11	2									3		10			6	8	4		12				0–1(0–1)1834 23
36. Tranmere	25.3		9	5					11	3‡				14		2					10			6†	8.	4		12	7			0–3(0–2)3093 —
37. Newport	2.4			5			9²	11†	2										3		10			6	8	4		12	7			2–1(2–1)1376 23
38. Wrexham*	4.4			5				9	7	12	3										10			6†	8	4		14	11‡			0–4(0–2)2284 23
39. Orient	9.4		3	5	6		9†	7	12	2				14		1					10				8¹	4			11†			1–4(0–2)2861 23
40. Scunthorpe	12.4		3	5	6		9	7	12	2						1					10				8	4			11†			0–1(0–0)3514 —
41. Halifax*	19.4		3	5	6		9	7		2						1					10				8	4		12†	11†			1–0(0–0)1517 —
42. Colchester*	23.4		3	5	6	12	9	7		2											10¹					4¹		8²	11†			4–0(2–0)1496 23
43. Halifax	26.4		3	5	6	11¹	9	7		10						2	1									4		8				1–1(0–1)1002 —
44. Torquay	30.4		3	5	6	11†	9	7		2				12				10			4			8							0–1(0–1)3537 22
45. Swansea*	2.5		3	5	6		9†	7		10						2	1		12							8						0–1(0–1)1854 23
46. Cambridge	7.5		3	5	6†		9	7	11¹	10						2	1									8¹						2–1(0–1)1738 23

Final League Position: 23

App/(Subs)/goals: 10(0)0, 16(0)0, 18(1)0, 35(2)0, 40(0)3, 32(3)3, 36(1)5, 38(1)12, 24(0)3, 31(6)10, 40(1)1, 02(7)0, 09(0)0, 06(0)0, 23(0)0, 10(0)0, 8(6)1, 0(1)0, 40(0)0, 22(0)0, 12(0)0, 23(0)3, 5(1)2, 14(0)0, 12(0)2, 13(0)1, 40(1)0, 5(5)4, 7(0)0

Own goal: Atkins, match 2. Also played: Carter, matches 35,36,37,38(1); Ogley, match 38(2), 45(4), 46(4).

DIVISION 1 ————————— # CHARLTON ATHLETIC

Selhurst Park, London SE25 6PH.

Back row
(left to right):
Paul Williams
Andy Peake
Mark Stuart
John Humphrey
Micky Bennett
Ralph Milne
Mark Reid
Middle row:
Garth Crooks
John Pender
Carl Leaburn
Nicky Johns
Bob Bolder
Paul Miller
Steve MacKenzie
Robert Lee
Front row:
Colin Walsh
Steve Gritt
Peter Shirtliff
Lennie Lawrence
(Manager)
Steve Thompson
Alan Curbishley
Jim Melrose

Stadium Capacity: 36,000.
Pitch Dimensions: 110 × 74yds.
Telephone: 01–771 6321, **Clubcall:** 0898–121146.
Chairman: R. D. Collins.
Vice-Chairman: M. J. Norris.
Directors: R. N. Alwen, D. G. Ufton. **Presidents:** J. A. E. Fryer, J. B. Sunley.
Manager: Lennie Lawrence.
Post-War Managers: Jimmy Seed, Jimmy Trotter, Frank Hill, Bob Stokoe, Eddie Firmani, Theo Foley, Andy Nelson, Mike Bailey, Alan Mullery MBE, Ken Craggs (10).
Physio: Jimmy Hendry.
Secretary: Anne Payne.
Commercial Manager: Steve Sutherland.
Sponsors: The Woolwich Building Society.
Founded: 1905.
Turned Professional: 1920.
Nickname: The Haddicks, Robins or Valiants.
Former Names: None.
Former Grounds: Siemen's Meadow 1906–07, Woolwich Common 1907–09, Pound Park 1909–13, Horn Lane 1913–20, The Valley 1920–23, Catford (The Mount) 1923–24, The Valley 1924–85.
Record Attendance: 75,031 v Aston Villa, FA Cup 5th Round, 12 February 1938.
Record Victory: 8–1 v Middlesbrough, Division 1, 12 September 1953.
Record Defeat: 1–11 v Aston Villa, Division 2, 14 November 1959.
Most League Points: (3 for a win) 77, Division 2, 1985–86. (2 for a win) 61, Division 3(S), 1934–35.
Most League Goals: 107, Division 2, 1957–58.
Highest League Scorer in a Season: Ralph Allen, 32, Division 3(S), 1934–35.
Highest Total of League Goals: Stuart Leary, 153, 1953–62.
Most League Appearances: Sam Bartram, 583, 1934–56.
League History: 1921 Elected to Division 3(S), 1929–33 Division 2, 1933–35 Division 3(S), 1935–36 Division 2, 1936–57 Division 1, 1957–72 Division 2, 1972–75 Division 3, 1975–80 Division 2, 1980–81 Division 3, 1981–86 Division 2, 1986– Division 1.
Honours: Division 1 runners-up 1936–37. Division 2 runners-up 1935–36, 1985–86. Division 3(S) Champions 1928–29, 1934–35. FA Cup winners 1947, runners-up 1946. Full Members' Cup runners-up 1987.
Colours: Red shirts, white shorts and socks. **Second strip:** All silver grey.

CHARLTON ATHLETIC – LEAGUE RECORD 1987–88

Match no/Opp/Date		Bolder	Humphrey	Reid	MacKenzie	Thompson	Pender	Peake	Stuart	Melrose	Walsh	Crooks	Gritt	Milne	Miller	Lee	Williams	Johns	Shirtliff	Bennett	Jones	Campbell	Mortimer	Leaburn	FT(HT)Att Lge pos
1. Nottm F*	15.8	1	2	3₁	4	5†	6	7	8	9	10‡	11	12	14											1–2(1–0)6021 —
2. Man Utd*	29.8	1	2	3†	4	5		10	8¹	9		11	12		6	7									1–3(0–3)14,046 21
3. Wimbledon	1.9	1	2	3	10	5	6	7	8¹	9	11†						12								1–4(1–1)5184 —
4. QPR*	5.9		2	3	10			4†	8			11	12	7‡	6		9	1	5	14					0–1(0–1)7726 21
5. Portsmouth	12.9		2	3	10				8¹	9	11	4	7	6				1	5						1–1(1–0)13,136 21
6. Liverpool	15.9		2		10			4	8	9¹	11¹	3	7†	6			12	1	5						2–3(1–1)36,637 —
7. Luton*	19.9		2		10			4	8	9	11¹	3	7	6				1	5						1–0(1–0)5003 20
8. Sheff Wed	26.9		2	3	10			4		11		8	6	7			1	5	9						0–2(0–2)16,350 21
9. Arsenal*	3.10	1	2	3				4	10			11	7†	6	8		5	12	9						0–3(0–1)15,326 21
10. West Ham	10.10	1	2	3			6		4	7		11‡		8			5		9	10					1–1(1–1)15,757 21
11. Derby*	17.10	1	2	3	14	6†		4	8		11		12	7‡		5		9	10						0–1(0–1)5432 21
12. Oxford	24.10	1	2	3				4	8†	9	11		7	6		5		12¹	10						1–2(0–0)7325 21
13. Sthampton*	31.10	1	2		11			4		10¹		3	7	6		5		9	8						1–1(0–1)5158 21
14. Norwich*	7.11	1	2		11	6			10		3					5	7¹	9¹	8	4					2–0(2–0)5044 21
15. Watford	14.11	1	2	11		6		12	10¹		3					5	7	9	8	4†					1–2(0–1)12,093 21
16. Coventry*	21.11	1	2	3	11†	6		12¹	10	14	4					5	7	9¹	8‡						2–2(1–0)4936 21
17. Newcastle	28.11	1	2	3		6		14	12	10†		4	11			5	7‡	9	8						1–2(1–1)19,453 21
18. Everton*	5.12	1	2	3		6		7				4				9	5	10	8	11					0–0(0–0)7208 21
19. Spurs	13.12	1	2	3		6		7				4				9	5	10	8¹	11					1–0(0–0)20,392 —
20. Chelsea*	20.12	1	2	3		6		7	12¹			4				10	5¹	9	8	11†					2–2(0–1)10,893 —
21. Portsmouth*	26.12	1	2	3	7	6			11			4†				10	5¹	12	9¹	8					2–1(1–1)6686 19
22. Luton	28.12	1	2	3	4	6			7†					14	10‡		5	12	9	8	11				0–1(0–1)7243 20
23. Man Utd	1.1	1	2	3	4	6								10			5	7	9	8	11				0–0(0–0)37,257 20
24. Nottm F	16.1	1	2	3	4	6								10¹			5	7	9¹	8	11				2–2(0–0)15,363 21
25. Liverpool*	23.1	1	2	3	4	6					14	12		10			5	7†	9	8	11‡				0–2(0–1)28,095 21
26. QPR	6.2	1	2	3	4	6					14	12		10			5	7†	9‡	8	11				0–2(0–1)11,512 21
27. Wimbledon*	13.2	1	2	3₁	4	6			7		14			10‡	12		5		9	8	11†				1–1(1–0)5520 21
28. Sheff Wed*	20.2	1	2	3	4¹	6			7		11²			10			5		9	8					3–0(2–0)4517 20
29. Arsenal	27.2	1	2	3	4	6			7		11			12	10		5		9†	8‡	14				0–4(0–1)25,394 20
30. Derby	5.3	1	2	3¹	4	6†			7		11	9		8	10		5				12				1–1(0–1)16,139 20
31. West Ham*	12.3	1	2	3	4				7¹		11²	9		6	10		5				8				3–0(2–0)8118 19
32. Sthampton	19.3	1	2	3	4				7		11¹	9		6	10		5				8				1–0(0–0)12,103 18
33. Oxford*	26.3	1	2	3	4	5			7		11	9		6	10†	12					8				0–0(0–0)6245 18
34. Norwich	2.4	1	2	3	4				7‡		11	9		6		12		5	14	10	8†				0–2(0–0)15,015 19
35. Watford*	4.4	1	2	3	4				7		11	9		6	10‡†	12		5	14		8‡				1–0(1–0)6196 18
36. Coventry	9.4	1	2	3	4				7		11	9		6	10			5			8				0–0(0–0)14,313 18
37. Newcastle*	23.4	1	2	3	4				7		11²	9		6	10†			5	12		8				2–0(2–0)7482 18
38. Everton	30.4	1	2	3	4¹				7		11†	9		6	10†			5	12		8				1–1(0–0)20,372 17
39. Spurs*	2.5	1	2	3₁	4				7		11	9		6	10†			5	12		8				1–1(0–0)13,977 17
40. Chelsea	7.5	1	2	3	4				7‡		11			6¹	10			5	9†	12	14	8			1–1(0–0)33,701 17

Apps(subs)/goals: 35(0)0, 40(0)0, 36(0)4, 31(0)2, 21(0)0, 20(0)0, 15(0)0, 27(4)6, 30(0)0, 11(0)3, 24(4)10, 22(5)0, 9(1)0, 21(2)1, 22(0)2, 6(6)0, 5(0)0, 30(0)2, 9(7)1, 21(4)6, 21(0)1, 11(0)0, 10(2)0

Final League Position: 17

DIVISION 2

CHELSEA

Stamford Bridge, London SW6 1HS.

Back row (left to right): Eddie Niedzwiecki, John McNaught, Colin Pates, Steve Wicks, Joe McLaughlin, Kerry Dixon, Roy Wegerle, Micky Bodley, Roger Freestone. *Middle row:* Ernie Walley (Coach), Jerry Murphy, Gareth Hall, Darren Wood, Steve Clarke, Gordon Durie, John Coady, Tony Dorigo, John Bumstead, Norman Medhurst (Physio). *Front row:* Pat Nevin, Colin West, Clive Wilson, John Hollins (Manager), Billy Dodds, Mick Hazard, Kevin Wilson

Stadium Capacity: 43,900.
Pitch Dimensions: 114 × 71yds.
Telephone: 01–385 5545, **Information service:** 01–381 6221, **Clubcall:** 0898–121159.
Chairman: Ken W. Bates.
Directors: S. S. Tollman, R. M. Bates, G. W. C. Smith.
Manager: Bobby Campbell.
Post-War Managers: Billy Birrell, Ted Drake, Tommy Docherty, Dave Sexton, Ron Stuart, Eddie McCreadie, Ken Shellito, Danny Blanchflower, Geoff Hurst, John Neal, John Hollins (11).
Physio: Norman Medhurst.
Secretary: Janet Wayth.
Commercial Manager: John Shaw.
Sponsors: Commodore.
Founded: 1905.
Turned Professional: 1905.
Nickname: The Blues.
Former Names: None
Former Grounds: None.
Record Attendance: 82,905 v Arsenal, Division 1, 12 October 1935.
Record Victory: 13–0 v Jeunesse Hautcharage, European Cup-Winners' Cup 1st Round, 29 September 1971.
Record Defeat: 1–8 v Wolverhampton W, Division 1, 26 September 1953.
Most League Points: (3 for a win) 88, Division 2, 1983–84. (2 for a win) 57, Division 2, 1906–07.
Most League Goals: 98, Division 1, 1960–61.
Highest League Scorer in a Season: Jimmy Greaves, 41, 1960–61.
Highest Total of League Goals: Bobby Tambling, 164, 1958–70.
Most League Appearances: Ron Harris, 655, 1962–80.
League History: 1905 Elected to Division 2, 1907–10 Division 1, 1910–12 Division 2, 1912–24 Division 1, 1924–30 Division 2, 1930–62 Division 1, 1962–63 Division 2, 1963–75 Division 1, 1975–77 Division 2, 1977–79 Division 1, 1979–84 Division 2, 1984–88 Division 1, 1988– Division 2.
Honours: Division 1 Champions 1954–55. Division 2 Champions 1983–84, runners-up 1906–07, 1911–12, 1929–30, 1962–63, 1976–77. FA Cup winners 1970, runners-up 1915, 1967. League Cup winners 1965, runners-up 1972. Full Members' Cup winners 1986. European Cup-Winners' Cup winners 1971.
Colours: All royal blue. **Second strip:** All jade.

CHELSEA – LEAGUE RECORD 1987–88

Match no/Opp/Date	Niedzwiecki	Clarke	Dorigo	Wicks	McLaughlin	Wood	Nevin	Hazard	Dixon	Durie	Wilson C.	Wilson K.	Coady	McNaught	West	Bodley	Pates	Wegerle	Freestone	Hall	Murphy	McAllister	Bumstead	Digweed	Hitchcock	FT(HT)Att	Lge pos
1. Sheff Wed* 15.8	1	2	3	4	5	6	7	8†	9^1	10_1	11	12														2-1(1-0)21,929	—
2. Portsmouth 18.8	1	2	3	4	5	6	7^1	8	9^1	10	11^1															3-0(1-0)16,917	—
3. Spurs 22.8	1	2	3	4	5	6	7	8	9	10†	11	12														0-1(0-0)37,079	3
4. Luton* 29.8	1	2	3	4	5	6	7^1		9^1	10	8		11^1													3-0(1-0)16,075	3
5. Man Utd 31.8	1		3	4	5	2	7		9	10	8	12	11†	6												1-3(1-1)46,478	—
6. Nottm F* 5.9	1	2^1	3	4	5	6	7	8	9†	10^2	11^1	12														4-3(1-3)18,414	3
7. QPR 12.9	1	2	3	4	5	6	7	8		10^1	11	9														1-3(0-2)22,583	5
8. Norwich* 19.9	1	2†	3		5	6	7	8‡	9^1		11	10	14		12		4									1-0(1-0)15,242	3
9. Watford 26.9	1	2	3		5	6	7	8†	9^1	10‡	11				12		4									3-0(1-0)16,213	2
10. Newcastle* 3.10	1	2	3		5	6		8	9^1	10	11						4									2-2(2-1)22,071	4
11. Everton 10.10	1	2	3		5	6	7†	8‡	9^1	10	11	12	14				4									1-4(0-2)32,004	7
12. Coventry* 17.10	1	2	3		5	6	7	8	9^1†		11	10			12		4									1-0(0-0)16,699	5
13. Sthampton 24.10	1	2	3		5	6	7	8		10	11	9					4									0-3(0-0)11,890	7
14. Oxford* 31.10	1†	2	3		5	6	7^1		10	11	9				12		4	8^1								2-1(0-1)15,027	6
15. Arsenal 3.11		2	3		5	6	7^1		10	11	12	9					4	8†	1							1-3(1-2)40,230	—
16. Derby 22.11		2	3		5	6	7	8†	10	11	12	9‡	14				4		1							0-2(0-0)18,644	—
17. Wimbledon* 28.11		2†	3		5	6	7		9	10_1	11				12		4	8	1							1-1(0-0)15,608	7
18. Liverpool 6.12		2	3		5	6	7		9	10_1	11						4		1							1-2(1-0)31,211	—
19. West Ham* 12.12		2	3		5	6	7†	8	9	10^1	11				12		4		1							1-1(0-1)22,850	7
20. Charlton 20.12			3		5	6_1	7†		9	10	11		14				4^1	8‡	1	2	12					2-2(1-0)10,893	—
21. QPR* 26.12		4	3		5^1	6	7		9	10	11							8	1	2						1-1(0-0)18,020	8
22. Norwich 28.12		4	3†		5	6	7		10	11	9				12			8	1	2						0-3(0-0)19,668	8
23. Luton 1.1		4	3		5	2		8	9	10	11								1			7	6			0-3(0-1)8018	11
24. Spurs* 2.1		4	3		5	2		8	9	10	11				12				1			7†	6			0-0(0-2)29,317	11
25. Sheff Wed 16.1		4	3		5	2		8	9	10	11†				12				1			7	6			0-3(0-1)19,859	13
26. Portsmouth* 23.1		2	3		5	11	12	8	9†	10			14				4		1			7	6‡			0-0(0-0)15,856	13
27. Nottm F 6.2		2	3†		5	10	7	12	9^1		11						4	8^1	1				6			2-3(0-1)18,203	14
28. Man Utd* 13.2		2	3		5	10	7	8†	9		11	12^1					4		1				6			1-2(0-0)25,014	14
29. Newcastle 27.2		2†	3		5		7	8	9	10	11†	12^1	14	6			4		1							1-3(0-2)17,858	15
30. Coventry 5.3			3		5		7^1	8	9	10^2				6			4			2			11	1		3-3(2-2)16,816	16
31. Everton* 12.3		2	3		5	6	7	8	9	10							4						11	1		0-0(0-0)17,390	16
32. Oxford 19.3		2	3		5	6	7^1	8†	9^2	10‡			14				4					12	11^1	1		4-4(3-0)8468	17
33. Sthampton* 26.3		2	3		5	6	7	8	9	10‡			14				4†					12	11		1	0-1(0-1)15,380	17
34. Watford* 29.3		2	3	4	5	6	7	8	9	10^1													11		1	1-1(0-1)11,240	—
35. Arsenal 2.4		2	3	4	5	6	7	8^1	9†	10‡					12							14	11		1	1-1(0-0)26,084	16
36. Derby* 9.4		2	3	4	5	6	7	8^1		10†		9			12								11		1	1-1(0-1)16,996	15
37. Wimbledon 23.4		6	3	4	5		7	8	9	10^1										2			11		1	2-2(0-1)15,128	16
38. Liverpool* 30.4		6	3	4	5		7	8	9	10_1										2			11		1	1-1(0-3)35,625	16
39. West Ham 2.5		6	3	4	5		7	8†	9	10		12^1								2			11		1	1-4(0-2)28,521	18
40. Charlton* 7.5		2	3	4	5		7		9	10^1	11†			6	12			8							1	1-1(1-0)33,701	18
App(subs)/goals	14(0)0	38(0)1	40(0)0	17(0)0	36(0)1	34(0)1	36(1)6	28(0)2	33(0)11	26(0)12	27(4)2	16(9)5	4(6)1	10(0)0	3(6)3	6(0)1	16(1)0	8(5)1	15(6)0	8(5)0	2(0)0	4(1)0	17(0)1	3(0)0	8(0)0		

Final League Position: 18

Own goals: Walsh, match 5; McCreery, match 10.

DIVISION 3

CHESTER CITY

The Stadium, Sealand Road, Chester CH1 4LW.

Back row (left to right): Gary Bennett, Graham Abel, Ricky Greenough, Billy Steart, Steve Hetzke, Mike Astbury, Barry Butler, Peter Houghton, Colin Woodthorpe. *Front row:* Sean Lundon, David Glenn, Stuart Rimmer, Graham Barrow, Harry McNally (Manager), Derek Fazackerley, Paul Maddy, Brian Croft, Milton Graham

Stadium Capacity: 22,000.
Pitch Dimensions: 114 × 76yds.
Telephone: 0244–371376, **Commercial dept:** 0244–378162.
Chairman: A. E. Barnes JP, FCA.
Vice-Chairman: C. Thompson.
Directors: L. Lloyd, R. H. Crofts, F. Summers, H. McNally, D. Cross, D. Barker.
Manager: Harry McNally.
Post-War Managers: Frank Brown, Louis Page, John Harris, Stan Pearson, Bill Lambton, Peter Hauser, Ken Roberts, Alan Oakes, Cliff Sear, John Sainty, John McGrath (11).
Assistant Manager: Derek Fazackerley.
Secretary: J. A. Eckersley.
Founded: 1884.
Turned Professional: 1902.
Nickname: None.
Former Names: Chester until 1983.
Former Grounds: Faulkner Street, Old ShowgRound, Whipcord Lane 1904, Sealand Road 1906.
Record Attendance: 20,500 v Chelsea, FA Cup 3rd Round replay, 16 January 1987.
Record Victory: 12–0 v York C, Division 3(N), 1 February 1936.
Record Defeat: 2–11 v Oldham Athletic, Division 3(N), 19 January 1952.
Most League Points: (3 for a win) 84, Division 4, 1985–86. (2 for a win) 56, Division 3(N), 19 January 1952.
Most League Goals: 119, Division 4, 1964–65.
Highest League Scorer in a Season: Dick Yates, 36, Division 3(N), 1946–47.
Highest Total of League Goals: Gary Talbot, 83, 1963–67 and 1968–70.
Most League Appearances: Ray Gill, 408, 1951–62.
League History: 1931 Elected to Division 3(N), 1958–75 Division 4, 1975–82 Division 3, 1982–86 Division 4, 1986–Division 3.
Honours: Division 4 runners-up 1985–86. Division 3(N) runners-up 1935–36. Welsh Cup winners 1908, 1933, 1947.
Colours: Royal blue shirts, white shorts and socks. **Second strip:** Gold shirts and socks, black shorts.

CHESTER CITY – LEAGUE RECORD 1987–88

Match no/Opp/Date	Stewart	Greenough	Woodthorpe	Fazackerley	Abel	Henske	Butler	Lundon	Rimmer	Houghton	Graham	Moore	Croft	Parry	Barrow	Bennett	Stowell	Maddy	Lightfoot	Hawtin	Banks	Painter	Astbury	Howlett	Glenn	Caldwell	Langley	Lowey	Newhouse	FT(HT)Att Lge pos
1. Nthampton* 15.8	1	2	3	4	5	6	7†	8‡	9	10	11	12	14																	0-5(0-1)3458 —
2. Southend 19.8	1		3	4	2	6		5	9		11^1			7^1	8	10														2-2(1-1)2369 19
3. York* 29.8	1	4	3		2	6			9^1		11		5	7	8	10														1-0(0-0)2010 14
4. Rotherham 31.8	1	2	3		5	6			9^1		11^1		4	7	8	10														2-5(0-1)2551 —
5. Aldershot* 5.9		4	3	5	2	6			9‡		11		7^1		8	10^1	1													4-1(1-0)1700 16
6. Blackpool 12.9		4	3	5	2	6			9^1		11		7		8	10	1													1-0(0-0)4035 11
7. Fulham* 16.9	1	2	3	4	5				9		11^1		7		8	10		6												1-2(1-1)2469 —
8. Grimsby* 19.9		2	3	5	4				9^1		11		7	14	8	10‡	1		6†	12										1-0(0-0)1897 12
9. Sunderland 26.9		6	3	4	5				9^1				7^1		8	10	1	11		2										2-0(0-0)12,760 7
10. Gillingham 29.9		6	3	4	5				9^1				7		8	10	1	11		2										1-0(0-0)5193 —
11. Notts Co* 3.10		6	3	4	5				9^1				7		8	10	1	11		2										1-2(1-0)3365 7
12. Bristol R 17.10		2	3		5	4	6		9^1				12	7†	8	10^1	1	11												2-2(1-2)3038 11
13. Brentford 20.10		2	3	4	5	6	7		9^1				12		8	10	1	11†												1-1(0-0)4027 —
14. Mansfield* 24.10		2†	3	4	5	6	7		9				12		8	10	1	11												0-2(0-0)2453 11
15. Preston 31.10		2	3	4	5	6			9^1				7		8	10	1	11												1-1(0-1)5657 13
16. Port Vale* 4.11		10	3	4	5	6	2		9^1				7		8		1	11†		12										1-0(0-0)2789 —
17. Walsall* 7.11		10†	3	4		6	7		9				11		8	12	1		5^1	2										1-0(0-0)3269 10
18. Bristol C 21.11		2	3	4	6			5	9‡				11†		8	10	1	7			12									2-2(2-1)8103 10
19. Chesterfield* 28.11		2	3	4	5				9^1	8			11			10	1	7	6											1-1(1-0)1843 11
20. Doncaster* 5.12		2	3	4	5		6		9^1	8			11†			10		7			12	1								1-1(0-1)1853 11
21. Brighton 12.12		2	3	4	5		6		9	8†			12			10		7					1	11						0-1(0-0)6738 13
22. Bury* 18.12		2			4	5		3	9^2	11					8	10^1		7					1	6^1						4-4(1-0)1772 —
23. Sunderland* 26.12		2			4	5^1		3	9	11					8	10		7					1	6†	12					1-2(0-2)6663 14
24. Wigan 28.12		2			4	5		3	9	11†					8	10			6				1	7	12					0-1(0-0)4394 15
25. York 1.1	1	11			4	5		3	9				12		8	10			6†					7	2					0-2(0-1)2686 17
26. Blackpool* 2.1	1	10			4	5		3					11		8	9^1			6					7	2					1-0(1-0)3093 17
27. Southend* 9.1	1				4	5		3	9				11		8	12	7^1	6†						2	10					1-1(0-1)2065 16
28. Grimsby 16.1			12	4	5		6‡	3†	9^1	14	11				8			7						2	10					1-2(0-0)2594 16
29. Rotherham* 30.1			3	4	5				9		11†		12		8^1	6								2	10	7				1-0(0-0)2059 14
30. Aldershot 6.2			3	4	5				9		11		12		8^1	7	12							2	10†	6				1-4(1-1)2578 15
31. Wigan* 13.2			3	4	5	6			9^1		11				8	7								2	10					1-0(0-0)3088 14
32. Nthampton 20.2			3	4	5	6			9		11				8	7								2	10					0-2(0-0)4285 17
33. Notts Co 27.2			3	4	5		6		9		11				8	7								2	10					0-1(0-0)5868 18
34. Gillingham* 2.3	1	12	3	4	5		6†		9‡		11		14		8‡	7								2	10					3-1(0-0)1638 18
35. Bristol R* 5.3	1	12	3	4	5		6		9	14	11		8			7‡							2†		10					0-3(0-2)2067 18
36. Doncaster 11.3	1	12	3	4	5†		7				11‡	8			9^1				6					2	10					2-2(1-1)1482 17
37. Preston* 19.3	1		3	4	5		11				8		7			9^1			6					2	10					1-0(1-0)3724 17
38. Mansfield 26.3	1		3	4	5		7¹				11		10			9^1			6					2		8				2-1(1-2)2918 17
39. Walsall 2.4	1			4	5		12	7			11		10		8	9			6				2†			3				0-1(0-1)4978 17
40. Bristol C* 4.4	1			4	5			2	3		11		10		8	9^1			6						7					1-0(1-0)2849 15
41. Port Vale 9.4	1			4	5			2	3^1		11		10		8	9			6						7					1-1(1-1)4278 15
42. Fulham 15.4	1			4	5			2	3	12	11		10†		8	9			6						7					0-1(0-0)4131 —
43. Brentford* 23.4	1			4	10	5	3				11†		12		8	9			6					2	7					1-1(0-0)1777 17
44. Chesterfield 30.4	1	6	11	4	5		3			10†	12				8	9								2	7					0-0(0-0)2225 16
45. Brighton* 2.5	1	6	10	4	5^1		3				11				8	9		12						2	7					2-2(1-2)3345 16
46. Bury 7.5	1	6	3	4	5		10				11†				8	9¹‡		12						2	7				14	1-0(0-0)1942 —

Final League Position: 15

Apps(subs)/goals: 27(0)0 · 26(3)0 · 34(1)0 · 43(0)0 · 45(0)2 · 15(0)0 · 22(0)2 · 34(0)24 · 9(2)0 · 24(1)3 · 0(1)2 · 26(1)2 · 4(1)1 · 38(0)4 · 41(2)10 · 17(0)1 · 15(1)1 · 30(0) · 10(1)0 · 30(0) · 5(0)1 · 19(2)0 · 4(0)0 · 5(0)0 · 6(0)1 · 4(0)0 · 9(0)0 · 9(0)0 · 0(1)0

DIVISION 3

CHESTERFIELD

Recreation Ground, Chesterfield S40 4SX.

Back row (left to right): Paddy McGeeny, Dave Perry, Lee Rogers, Darren Wood, Simon Harrison, Jim Brown, Dave Caldwell, Darren Bradshaw, Jamie Hewitt, Tristan Benjamin. *Front row:* Bob Bloomer, Tony Reid, Dave Waller, Tony Coyle, Kevin Randall, Mick Henderson, Brian Ferguson, Kevin Eley, Andy Wood, Andy Taylor, Derek Walker.

Stadium Capacity: 11,210.
Pitch Dimensions: 112 × 72yds.
Telephone: 0246–209765, **Commercial dept:** 0246–31535.
Chairman: B. W. Hubbard.
Vice-Chairman: J. N. Lea.
Directors: P. Taylor.
Manager: Kevin Randall.
Post-War Managers: Bob Brocklebank, Bob Marshall, Ted Davison, Duggie Livingstone, Tony McShane, Jimmy McGuigan, Joe Shaw, Arthur Cox, Frank Barlow, John Duncan (10).
Physio: Tom Macdonald.
Secretary: Bob Pepper.
Commercial Manager: Jim Brown.
Sponsors: Coalite.
Founded: 1866.
Turned Professional: 1891.
Nickname: The Blues or Spireites.
Former Names: None.
Former Grounds: None.
Record Attendance: 30,968 v Newcastle U, Division 2, 7 April 1939.
Record Victory: 10–0 v Glossop North End, Division 2, 17 January 1903.
Record Defeat: 0–10 v Gillingham, Division 3, 5 September 1987.
Most League Points: (3 for a win) 91, Division 4, 1984–85. (2 for a win) 64, Division 4, 1969–70.
Most League Goals: 102, Division 3(N), 1930–31.
Highest League Scorer in a Season: Jimmy Cookson, 44, Division 3(N), 1925–26.
Highest Total of League Goals: Ernie Moss, 161, 1969–76, 1979–81 and 1984–86.
Most League Appearances: Dave Blakey, 613, 1948–67.
League History: 1888 Elected to Division 2, 1909 failed re-election, 1921–31 Division 3(N), 1931–33 Division 2, 1933–36 Division 3(N), 1936–51 Division 2, 1951–58 Division 3(N), 1958–61 Division 3, 1961–70 Division 4, 1970–83 Division 3, 1983–85 Division 4, 1985– Division 3.
Honours: Division 4 Champions 1969–70, 1984–85. Division 3(N) Champions 1930–31, 1935–36, runners-up 1933–34. Anglo-Scottish Cup winners 1981.
Colours: Royal blue shirts, white shorts and socks. **Second strip:** Red shirts, black shorts, red socks.

CHESTERFIELD – LEAGUE RECORD 1987-88

Match no/Opp/Date		Brown	Hewitt	Bloomer	Henderson	Benjamin	Brabham	Coyle	McGeeney	Walker	Eley	Taylor	Rogers	Travis	Caldwell	Perry	Muggleton	Wood	Walker	Reid	Arnott	Grayson	Hunter	Phillips	Morris	Thompson	Curran	Allerene	FT(HT)Att Lge pos
1. Preston	15.8	1	2	3	4	5	6	7	8	9	10	11¹																	1-0(0-0)6509
2. Brighton*	22.8	1		11	3	5	4	6	8	9	7	10	2																0-0(0-0)2286 7
3. Mansfield	29.8	1		11	3¹	5	4		8	9	7†	12	2	6	10														1-0(0-0)5224 5
4. Bury*	31.8	1		11	3	5	4		8	9¹	7	14	2	6†	10‡	12													1-0(0-0)2411 —
5. Gillingham	5.9	1	12	11	3	5	4		8	9	7†	10	2	6															0-10(0-5)4099 5
6. Port Vale*	12.9	1	6‡	11	3	5	4	10	8	9¹		12	2		14	1	7†												1-3(1-1)2406 12
7. Brentford	15.9	1		11	3	5	4		8	9	12	10‡	2	14		1	6	7†											0-2(0-2)3183 —
8. Doncaster	18.9	1		11	3	5	4‡		8	9	7		2	14	10†	1	6	12											0-1(0-1)1952 —
9. Notts Co*	26.9	1		11	3	5	4	7¹		9¹			2		10	1	6		8										2-0(1-0)3466 14
10. Bristol C	29.9			11	3	5	4	7		9¹			2		10	1	6		8										1-2(0-1)9088 —
11. Rotherham*	3.10			11‡	3	5	4	7	12	9³	14		2		10	1	6		8†										3-2(1-2)2993 15
12. Grimsby*	10.10		12	11		5	4	7‡	3	9	14		2		10‡	1	6		8										0-3(0-1)2072 15
13. Nthampton	17.10		10†	11	7‡	5	4	3		9	12	14	2			1	6		8										0-4(0-2)5073 16
14. Aldershot	20.10		10†	11‡		5	4	7	3	9	12		2		14	1	6		8										0-2(0-1)2054 —
15. Southend*	24.10		3	12		5	4	7		9¹	11¹		2		10†	1	6		8										3-1(2-0)1726 17
16. York	31.10		3	12		5	4	7		9	11†		2		10	1	6		8										0-1(0-1)2316 18
17. Wigan*	3.11		3	6		5	4	7		9	11		2	12	10	1			8†										0-1(0-1)1725 —
18. Bristol R	7.11		3	8		5	4	7	10	9	11		2			1	6												0-2(0-2)2633 19
19. Sunderland*	21.11		3¹	8				7	4	9	11		2		5	1	6				10								1-1(0-0)5700 19
20. Chester	28.11		3	6				7	4	9¹	11		2		5						10	8							1-1(0-1)1843 19
21. Blackpool*	12.12							7	4	9	11¹		2	6†	3	1	5			12	10	8							1-0(1-2)2279 19
22. Fulham	19.12							7†	4	9²	11	14	2		3	1	5			12	10‡	8	6						3-1(1-1)4006 17
23. Notts Co	26.12	1	12					7	4	9	11		2		3		5				10	8†							0-2(0-2)8675 19
24. Walsall*	28.12	1	12					7†	4	9¹	11		2		3		5				10	8	6¹						2-1(0-1)3916 18
25. Mansfield*	1.1	1	12¹					7	4	9¹	11		2		3		5				10	8†	6						3-1(1-0)5070 15
26. Port Vale	2.1	1	11					7	4	9			2		3		5				10₁	8	6						1-0(0-0)3495 14
27. Doncaster*	16.1	1	12					7	4		11		2	9‡	3		5	14			10	8†	6						0-1(0-0)2715 15
28. Bury	30.1	1	8†			12		7	4		11‡		2	14	3		5				10	6	9						0-2(0-2)2071 17
29. Gillingham*	6.2	1	12	3		5		7	4		11†		2				8¹				10	6	9						1-4(0-0)2141 17
30. Walsall	13.2	1	12	3	5†			7	8		11		2				4				10	6	9						0-0(0-0)4162 19
31. Brighton	17.2	1	12	3	5			7¹	8¹		11		2				4				10	6	9†						2-2(1-1)8182 —
32. Preston*	20.2	1	12	3	5†			7	8		11		2				4				10	6	9						0-0(0-0)2864 19
33. Rotherham	27.2	1		3	5			7†	8	12	11		2		4						10		6	9¹					1-1(0-0)3440 19
34. Bristol C*	1.3	1	12	3		5		7		9‡	11†		2		4						10	8¹	14						1-4(1-2)1657 —
35. Nthampton*	5.3	1	7	3		5†		12		9	11		2		4						10	8‡	14						0-2(0-2)2400 20
36. Grimsby	12.3	1		3		5				9	11		2		4						10	6¹	8†	7	12				1-0(0-0)3464 21
37. York*	19.3	1		3		5		12		9¹	11		2		4						10	6†		7		8¹			2-1(0-1)1966 20
38. Southend	25.3	1		3	5†			12	10	9	11		2		4						6			7		8			0-3(0-2)3315 —
39. Bristol R*	2.4	1		3		5		12	10	9	11		2	6†	4								14	7‡		8			0-1(0-1)2208 22
40. Sunderland	4.4	1		3	4	5		7	10	9²			2								6		11			8			2-3(2-2)21,886 22
41. Aldershot*	9.4	1		3	4	5†		7	10	9¹	12		2								6		11			8			1-0(0-0)1900 22
42. Brentford*	19.4	1		3	4¹	5		7	10	9			2								6¹		11			8			2-1(2-0)2010 —
43. Wigan	23.4	1		3¹	4	5		7	10	9†	12		2								6		11			8¹			2-1(1-1)3303 18
44. Chester*	30.4	1		3	4	5		7	10	9			2								6	12	11			8†			0-0(0-0)2225 17
45. Blackpool	2.5	1		3	4	5		7	10	9			2				2				6		11			8			0-1(0-1)2950 21
46. Fulham*	7.5	1		3	4	5		7	10	9¹			2				2				6		11			8			1-0(1-0)3084 18

Apps (sub)/goals: 29(0) 0 22(6) 2 32(6) 1 19(0) 2 32(2) 0 18(0) 0 35(5) 2 15(3) 1 39(1) 19 30(6) 2 16(5) 45(0) 43(0) 34(1) 1 1(3) 0 9(0) 0 17(0) 0 7(0) 23(0) 3 9(0) 2 7(3) 0 40(0) 0 00(1) 0 10(0) 2

Final League Position: 18

Own goals: Barnett, match 22; Coleman, match 25.

DIVISION 4

COLCHESTER UNITED

Layer Road Ground, Colchester CO2 7JJ.

Back row (left to right): John Chandler (Physio), Tony English, John Reeves, Mario Walsh, Rhys Jones, Roger Brown (Manager), Colin Hill, Richard Wilkins, Rudi Hedman, Terry Baker, Steve Foley (Coach). *Front row:* Stephen Grenfell, Nick Chatterton, Dale Tempest, Paul Hinshelwood, Gary Smith, Sean Norman, Simon Lowe, Winston White.

Stadium Capacity: 6,500
Pitch Dimensions: 110 × 71yds.
Telephone: 0206–574042.
Chairman: J. T. Crisp. **Deputy Chairman:** J. H. Schultz.
Directors: H. R. Carson, D. A. Johnson, G. H. Parker, H. R. Piper, R. Playdell.
Manager: Roger Brown.
Post-War Managers: Ted Fenton, Jimmy Allen, Jack Butler, Benny Fenton, Neil Franklin, Dick Graham, Jim Smith, Bobby Roberts, Allan Hunter, Cyril Lea, Mike Walker (11).
Physio: Charlie Simpson.
Secretary: Dee Elwood. **Sales & Marketing Director:** David Brimacombe.
Sponsors: Norcros Estates.
Founded: 1937.
Turned Professional: 1937.
Nickname: The U's.
Former Names: None.
Former Grounds: None.
Record Attendance: 19,072 v Reading, FA Cup 1st Round, 27 November 1948.
Record Victory: 9–1 v Bradford C, Division 4, 30 December 1961.
Record Defeat: 0–7 v Leyton Orient, Division 3(S), 5 January 1952 and v Reading, Division 3(S), 18 September 1957.
Most League Points: (3 for a win) 81, Division 4, 1982–83. (2 for a win) 60, Division 4, 1973–74.
Most League Goals: 104, Division 4, 1961–62. Highest League Scorer in Season: Bobby Hunt, 37, Division 4, 1961–62.
Highest Total of League Goals: Martyn King, 131, 1959–65.
Most League Appearances: Micky Cook, 613, 1969–84.
League History: 1950 Elected to Division 3(S), 1958–61 Division 3, 1961–62 Division 4, 1962–65 Division 3, 1965–66 Division 4, 1966–68 Division 3, 1968–74 Division 4, 1974–76 Division 3, 1976–77 Division 4, 1977–81 Division 3, 1981–Division 4.
Honours: Division 4 runners-up 1961–62.
Colours: Royal blue shirts, white shorts, royal blue socks. **Second strip:** Red shirts, white shorts, red socks.

COLCHESTER UNITED – LEAGUE RECORD 1987–88

Match no/Opp/Date	Benstead	Hinshelwood	Norman	Chatterton	Baker	Hedman	White	English	Walsh	Lowe	Wilkins	Reeves	Grenfell	Tempest	Radford	Hill	Smith	Walton	Williams	Angell	Keane	Ray	Keeley	Coleman	Hedzke	Forrest	Farrell	Hicks	Daniels	Hunter	FT(HT) Att Lge pos
1. Burnley 15.8	1	2	3	4	5	6	7	8¹	9¹	10¹	11																				3-0(2-0)5369 —
2. Torquay* 21.8	1	2	3	4	5	6	7	8	9†	10	11	12																			0-1(0-0)1372 —
3. Scunthorpe 29.8	1	2	3†	4	5	6	7¹	8		10	11¹			12	9																2-2(0-1)2003 9
4. Scarboro* 31.8	1	2		4	5	6	7	8		10	11			3	9¹																1-3(1-0)1525 —
5. Crewe 4.9	1	2†	12	4		5		14	10	8		11		3	9¹																0-0(0-0)1843 —
6. Peterboro* 12.9	1	2		4¹		6	7¹	5	12¹	10†	8			3	9¹	11															4-1(1-0)1164 —
7. Hereford 16.9	1	2		4		6	7	5	10		8			3	9	11															0-1(0-0)1951 —
8. Hartlepool 19.9	1	2¹		4		6	7	5	10†	12	8			11	3	9															1-3(0-1)1698 19
9. Exeter* 25.9	1	2	14	4		6	7†	5	12	10‡	8			11	3	9															0-2(0-1)1443 —
10. Swansea* 29.9	1	2¹	10	4		6	7	5		8				11	3	9¹															2-1(1-0)1140 —
11. Newport 3.10	1	2	10	4₁	5	6	7		12	8¹†				11	3	9															2-1(1-0)1200 17
12. Orient* 9.10	1	2	10	4	5	6	7			8				11	3	9															0-0(0-0)1665 —
13. Wrexham 17.10	1	2		4	5	6	7	10		12	8†	11¹		3	9																1-0(1-0)1493 15
14. Carlisle* 20.10	1	2		4	5	6	7	10		8		11		3	9¹																1-0(0-0)1328 —
15. Cambridge 24.10	1	2		4₁	5	6	7	10		8		11		3	9																1-0(0-0)2450 9
16. Darlington* 30.10	1	2		4¹	5	6	7†	10	12	8¹	11‡			3	9	14															2-1(0-0)1659 —
17. Rochdale 3.11	1	2¹		4₁†	5	6	7	10		8²	11			3	9	12															4-1(2-1)1399 —
18. Halifax 6.11	1	2		4₁	5		7	10		8¹	11			3	9		6														2-1(1-1)1432 —
19. Wolves* 21.11		6		4	5	2	7	10		8	11			3	9			1													0-1(0-0)2413 5
20. Stockport 27.11		6		4₁	5	2	7†	10	12	8	11		3‡	9		14		1													1-1(0-1)1703 —
21. Bolton* 11.12		2		4		3	7²	10		8¹			11	9		5		1	6												3-0(1-0)1725 —
22. Tranmere 18.12		2		4		3	7²	10		8			12	9		6		1	11	5†											2-0(1-0)2642 —
23. Exeter 26.12		2		4		3	7	10		8¹			11	9¹		5		1	6												2-0(0-0)2675 1
24. Cardiff* 28.12		2		4		3	7	10¹		8			11	9¹		5		1	6												2-1(1-1)2599 1
25. Scunthorpe* 1.1		2		4		3	7	10		8			11†	9		5		1	6		12										0-3(0-0)2287 2
26. Peterboro 2.1		2		4	5	3	7†			8			10	9		6		1	11		12										0-2(0-3)3665 3
27. Hartlepool* 15.1		2				3	7	6		8			11	9		5		1	4		10										0-0(0-0)1768 —
28. Scarboro 30.1	11¹				2	7	6†	14		8			3	9	4	5		1			10‡	12									1-3(0-0)2155 4
29. Crewe* 5.2		2			3	7	10			8			11	9¹	4†	6		1			12		5								1-4(0-2)1822 —
30. Cardiff 13.2		2			3	7	10			4			11	9		6		1			8	5									0-1(0-0)5458 6
31. Burnley* 19.2		4				14	7	10		8‡			11†	9		6	2	1			12	5	3								0-1(0-1)2520 —
32. Newport* 26.2		4					7	10		8			11	9		6	2	1				5	3								0-0(0-0)1784 —
33. Swansea 1.3		4					7¹	10		8†			11	9¹		6	2	1			12		3	5							2-1(0-0)4011 —
34. Wrexham* 4.3		4					7	10		8			11	9		6	2					3¹	5	1							1-2(1-2)1797 —
35. Orient 12.3		4			2			10		8			11	9		6					7		3	5	1						0-0(0-0)3125 12
36. Darlington 19.3		4			2			10		8			11	9		6					7		3	5	1						0-2(0-0)2034 12
37. Cambridge* 25.3		4			2			10		8			11	9	3	6					7†			5	1	12					0-0(0-0)2146 —
38. Halifax* 1.4		4¹			2		7	10		8			11	9	3	6			5†					1	12¹						2-1(0-1)1992 —
39. Wolves 4.4		4†			2		7	10		8			11	9	3	6			5					1	12						0-2(0-1)13,433 13
40. Rochdale* 8.4					2†			10		8	12	11‡	9¹	3	6	4		14						1	7	5					1-0(0-0)1864 —
41. Torquay 15.4	11‡				2	14	10			8			9	3†	6	4					12			1	7	5					0-0(0-0)3508 —
42. Hereford* 19.4					2			10		8	11		9¹	3	6	4					12			1	7†	5					1-0(0-0)1367 —
43. Carlisle 23.4				3	7	6		8		11			9	4‡		2					10†			1	12	5	14				0-4(0-2)1496 10
44. Stockport* 29.4				4	7	6		8¹†	11	3	9¹	12		2							10			1		5					2-0(0-0)1607 —
45. Bolton 2.5				4	7†	6		8	11‡	3	9	12		2	1						10				14	5					0-4(0-2)5540 10
46. Tranmere* 6.5				2	7	6		8		11	9	3		1							10	5					4				0-0(0-0)1704 9

Final League Position: 9

Apps (subs)/goals: 18(0) 5 · 40(0) 5 · 42(0) 0 · 25(0) 7 · 15(0) 0 · 41(1) 7 · 40(1) 0 · 43(0) 2 · 7(3) 1 · 46(0) 9 · 18(2) 1 · 39(2) 0 · 44(0) 11 · 22(3) 0 · 22(3) 0 · 11(0) 0 · 17(0) 0 · 9(1) 0 · 10(0) 0 · 9(2) 0 · 0(1) 0 · 40(0) 0 · 6(0) 1 · 5(0) 0 · 5(1) 0 · 4(5) 1 · 7(0) 0 · 0(1) 0 · 1(0) 0

DIVISION 1 COVENTRY CITY

Highfield Road Stadium, King Richard Street, Coventry CV2 4FW.

Back row (left to right): Trevor Peake, Graham Rodger, Keith Houchen, Brian Kilcline, Kevan Smith, Cyrille Regis, Paul Cuplin. *Middle row:* Mike Coop (Youth Team Coach), Neil Sillett (Ass. Physio), Brian Borrows, Steve Sedgley, Steve Ogrizovic, Jake Findlay, Nick Pickering, Martin Lane, Mick Kearns (Reserve Team Coach), George Dalton (Physio), *Front row:* David Phillips, Dave Bennett, Michael Gynn, John Sillett, (Team Manager) Greg Downs, Lloyd McGrath, David Speedie.

Stadium Capacity: 28,273.
Pitch Dimensions: 112 × 76yds.
Telephone: 0203–57171.
Chairman: J. Poynton.
Vice-Chairman: E. J. Stocker OBE. **Managing Director:** G. W. Curtis.
Directors: M. F. French FCA, J. F. W. Reason, D. W. Richardson.
Manager: John Sillet.
Post-War Managers: Dick Bayliss, Billy Frith, Harry Storer, Jack Fairbrother, Charlie Elliott, Jesse Carver, George Raynor, Harry Warren, Billy Frith, Jimmy Hill, Noel Cantwell, Bob Dennison, Gordon Milne, Dave Sexton, Bobby Gould, Don Mackay, George Curtis (17).
Physio: G. Dalton.
Secretary: G. P. Hover.
Founded: 1883.
Turned Professional: 1893.
Nickname: The Sky Blues.
Former Names: Singers FC 1883–98, Coventry City FC 1898.
Former Grounds: Binley Road 1883–87, Stoke Road 1887–99.
Record Attendance: 51,455 v Wolverhampton W, Division 2, 29 April 1967.
Record Victory: 9–0 v Bristol C, Division 3(S), 28 April 1934.
Record Defeat: 2–10 v Norwich C, Division 3(S), 15 March 1930.
Most League Points: (3 for a win) 63, Division 1, 1986–87. (2 for a win) 60, Division 4, 1958–59 and Division 3, 1963–64.
Most League Goals: 108, Division 3(S), 1931–32.
Highest League Scorer in a Season: Clarrie Bourton, 49, Division 3(S), 1931–32.
Highest Total of League Goals: Clarrie Bourton, 171, 1931–37.
Most League Appearances: George Curtis, 486, 1956–70.
League History: 1919 Elected to Division 2, 1925–26 Division 3(N), 1926–36 Division 3(S), 1936–52 Division 2, 1952–58 Division 3(S), 1958–59 Division 4, 1959–64 Division 3, 1964–67 Division 2, 1967– Division 1.
Honours: Division 2 Champions 1966–67. Division 3 Champions 1963–64. Division 4 runners-up 1958–59. Division 3(S) Champions 1935–36, runners-up 1933–34. FA Cup winners 1987.
Colours: All sky blue. **Second strip:** All yellow.

COVENTRY CITY – LEAGUE RECORD 1987–88

Match no/Opp/Date		Ogrizovic	Borrows	Downs	McGrath	Kilcline	Peake	Bennett	Gynn	Regis	Speedie	Pickering	Houchen	Phillips	Rodger	Sedgeley	Dobson	Emerson	Lane	Smith, K.	Livingstone	Smith, D.	Bannister	FT(HT)Att
1. Spurs*	15.8	1	2	3¹	4	5	6	7	8	9	10†	11	12											2-1(2-0)23,947
2. Luton	18.8	1	2	3	4	5₁	6	7	8		10	11	9											1-0(0-0)7506
3. Norwich	22.8	1	2‡	3	4	5₁	6	7	8	9†	10	11	12	14										1-3(0-1)13,726
4. Liverpool*	29.8	1	2	3‡	4	5	6	7	8†	9¹	10	11	12	14										1-4(0-1)27,637
5. Sheff Wed	31.8	1		3	4		6	7		10¹	11	9		2	5¹	8¹								3-0(2-0)17,171
6. Man Utd*	5.9	1		3	4		6	7	12	10†	11	9		2	5	8								0-0(0-0)27,125
7. Nottm F*	19.9	1	12	3†	4		6		14	9	10	8		2	5	7	11‡							0-3(0-1)17,519
8. Everton	26.9	1	2		4		6	7	11	9¹	10†		3	12	8¹	5								2-1(2-1)28,153
9. Watford*	3.10	1	2		4		6	7	11	9	10¹		3		8	5								1-0(0-0)16,111
10. Chelsea	17.10	1	2		4		6	7	11	9	12		3	10†	8	5								0-1(0-0)16,699
11. Sthampton*	20.10	1	2		4		6	7¹	11¹	9	10		3		8	5								2-3(2-1)14,522
12. Newcastle*	24.10	1	2	3	4		6	7		9¹	10	11	12		8	5†								1-3(1-2)18,585
13. Derby	31.10	1	2	3			6	7		9	10†	11	12		8	5	4							0-2(0-1)15,738
14. Oxford	7.11	1	2	3		5	6	7	14	9	10	11†	12		8‡		4							0-1(0-0)7856
15. Wimbledon*	14.11	1	2	3	8†	5₁	6	7	14¹	9‡	10¹	11	12				4							3-3(1-0)13,966
16. Charlton	21.11	1	2	3₁			6¹	7		9†	10	11	12		8	5	4							2-2(0-1)4936
17. West Ham*	28.11	1	2	3			6	7		9	10	11			8	5	4							0-0(0-0)16,740
18. Portsmouth	5.12	1	2	3		5	6	7	12	9	10†	11			8		4							0-0(0-0)13,002
19. Arsenal*	13.12	1	2	3		5	6	7	11	9					8		4				10			0-0(0-0)17,557
20. QPR	18.12	1	2	3		5	6	7†	11	9¹	12¹				8	14	4‡				10			2-1(0-1)7299
21. Nottm F	28.12	1	2	3	4	5	6	7	11	9¹	10				8									1-4(1-1)31,061
22. Liverpool	1.1	1	2	3	4	5	6	7†	11‡	9	10		12		8	14								0-4(0-1)38,790
23. Spurs	16.1	1	2	3	4	5	6	7¹	11	9¹					8						10			2-2(0-1)25,650
24. Man Utd	6.1	1	2	3			6		11	9	10			7	8†						12			0-1(0-1)37,144
25. Sheff Wed*	13.2	1	2	3		5	6	7²		9†	10		12	4			8¹				11			3-0(1-0)14,382
26. Norwich*	20.2	1	2	3		5	6‡	7			10		12	4			8	9†	14		11			0-0(0-0)15,577
27. Watford	27.2	1	2	3		5	6	7		9	10¹	11		4			8							1-0(1-0)12,052
28. Chelsea*	5.3	1		3		5¹	6	7		9	10¹	11†		4		2	8				12¹			3-3(2-3)16,816
29. Sthampton	12.3	1		3		5¹	5	7†		9	10			4		2	12				11¹	8		2-1(0-1)12,914
30. Luton*	15.3	1		3		5†↑	6			9¹	10			4¹		2	12				11	8¹		4-0(2-0)13,723
31. Derby*	19.3	1		3			6	12		9	10		14	7		5‡	4†				11	8		0-3(0-2)19,871
32. Newcastle	26.3	1				5	6	12		9	10¹	3		7		2	4				11¹	8†		2-2(0-0)19,050
33. Oxford*	2.4	1	2			5	6	12		9¹	10	3		7			8				11†			1-0(0-0)15,748
34. Wimbledon	5.4	1	2			5₁	6			9¹	10	3		7			8				11			2-1(2-1)5,920
35. Charlton*	9.4	1	2			5	6	7†		9	10	3					8				11	12		0-0(0-0)14,313
36. Everton*	19.4	1	2			5	6	7		9¹	10	3					8				11			1-2(1-0)15,641
37. West Ham	23.4	1	2			5	6	7		9¹	10	3					8				11			1-1(0-1)17,733
38. Portsmouth*	30.4	1	2			5₁	6	7		9	10	3		4			8				11			1-0(1-0)14,296
39. Arsenal	2.5	1	2			5	6	7		9	10	3	12	4			8†				11¹			1-1(1-1)16,963
40. QPR*	7.5	1	2			5	6	7		9	10	3		4			8				11			0-0(0-0)16,089
Apps(subs)/goals		40(0) 0	32(1) 0	27(0) 2	17(0) 0	28(0) 8	31(0) 0	27(1) 4	19(6) 3	30(1) 10	35(0) 6	24(0) 0	13(8) 3	32(0) 2	9(3) 1	25(2) 2	19(0) 0	0(2) 0	5(0) 0	3(0) 0	14(2) 4	7(0) 1		

Final League Position: 10

DIVISION 4

CREWE ALEXANDRA

Football Ground, Gresty Road, Crewe CW2 6EB.

Back row (left to right): Barry Bennall (Youth Manager), Jimmy Dyer (Physio), Geoff Parker, Steve Wright, Wakely Gage, Paul Edwards, Brian Parkin, Chris Cutler, Aiden Murphy, Peter Billing, Phil Blakemore (Trainer), Pat Slack (Ass. Manager). *Middle row:* Wayne Goodiston, John Gymer, Dave Platt, Dario Gradi (Manager), Peter Bodak, Terry Milligan, Steve Davis. *Front row:* Paul Allen, Ian Macowat, John Pemberton, Rob Wakenshaw, Stuart Ritchie

Stadium Capacity: 5,000.
Pitch Dimensions: 112 × 74yds.
Telephone: 0270–213014.
Chairman: John Bowler.
Managing Director: Hamilton Smith.
Directors: J. McHugh, K. Potts, H. Smith, D. Rowlinson, R. Clayton, J. McMillan, G. Basnet.
Manager: Dario Gradi.
Post-War Managers: George Lillycrop, Frank Hill, Arthur Turner, Harry Catterick, Ralph Ward, Maurice Lindley, Harry Ware, Jimmy McGuigan, Ernie Tagg, Dennis Viollet, Jimmy Melia, Ernie Tagg, Harry Gregg, Warwick Rimmer, Tony Waddington, Arfon Griffiths, Peter Morris (17).
Physio: Jim Dyer.
Secretary: Mrs Gill Palin.
Commercial Manager: Mike Bernard.
Sponsors: Bass.
Founded: 1877.
Turned Professional: 1893.
Nickname: The Railwaymen.
Former Names: None
Former Grounds: None.
Record Attendance: 20,000 v Tottenham H, FA Cup 4th Round, 30 January 1960.
Record Victory: 8–0 v Rotherham U, Division 3(N), 1 October 1932.
Record Defeat: 2–13 v Tottenham H, FA Cup 4th Round replay, 3 February 1960.
Most League Points: (3 for a win) 66, Division 4, 1984–85. (2 for a win) 59, Division 4, 1962–63.
Most League Goals: 95, Division 3(N), 1931–32.
Highest League Scorer in a Season: Terry Harkin, 35, Division 4, 1964–65.
Highest Total of League Goals: Bert Swindells, 126, 1928–37.
Most League Appearances: Tommy Lowry, 436, 1966–78.
League History: 1892 Founder Members of Division 2, 1896 failed re-election, 1921 re-entered Division 3(N), 1958–63 Division 4, 1963–64 Division 3, 1964–68 Division 4, 1968–69 Division 3, 1969– Division 4.
Honours: None.
Colours: Red shirts, white shorts, red socks. **Second strip:** White shirts, red shorts, white socks.

CREWE ALEXANDRA – LEAGUE RECORD 1987–88

Match no/Opp/Date	Parkin	Goodison	Pemberton	Milligan	Billing	Gage	Platt	Bodak	Cutler	Wright	Wakenshaw	Gyner	Murphy	Davis	Ritchie	Greygoose	Maconnat	Eli	Morton	Parker	Edwards R	Allatt	Nuttell	Healey	Goolet	Fiskenden	Jones	Harris	Doyle	Edwards P	FT(HT)Att	Lge pos
1. Bolton 15.8	1	2	3	4	5	6	7¹	8†	9‡	10	11	12		14																	1-1(0-1)4792	—
2. Cambridge 22.8	1	2†	3	4¹	5		7	8	9	6	11		10†	12	14																1-4(1-2)1523	23
3. Wrexham* 29.8		2		4		6	7¹	8	9	5	11‡	14		12	10†	1	3														2-0(1-0)2210	15
4. Rochdale 31.8		14		2	4	6	7²	8	9†	5	11	12			10‡	1	3														2-2(2-1)2346	—
5. Colchester* 4.9		10	2	4	6	7	8†	9‡	5	11	12		14			1	3														0-0(0-0)1843	—
6. Wolves 12.9			2	12	5	6	7²	8	9†	4	11	10				1	3														2-2(1-1)6285	17
7. Tranmere* 15.9			2	9†	5	6‡	7	8		4	11	10	14			1	3	12													0-0(0-0)1839	—
8. Orient* 18.9			2		5	6‡	7	8	12	4	11¹	10²	14			1	3†	9													3-3(1-0)2150	—
9. Swansea 26.9		3	2	14	5	6‡	7¹	8		4	11†	10¹				1		9¹‡													4-2(2-0)3832	13
10. Burnley 29.9		2	3	14	5	6	7	8†		12	4	11	10			1		9‡													0-0(0-0)5404	—
11. Hartlepool* 3.10		2	3	12	5	6	7₁	8	10	4	11†					1		9													1-1(0-0)2128	15
12. Torquay 10.10		2	3	12	5†	6		8‡	10	4	11	7	14			1		9													0-1(0-1)2499	17
13. Scarboro* 17.10	1	2	3		5	6	7¹	8	10	4		11	12					9†													1-0(1-0)2723	16
14. Stockport* 20.10		2	3		5	6	7²	8†	10¹	4			11		12	1		9													3-1(2-0)2251	—
15. Exeter 24.10		2	3		5	6	7¹	8	10	4		12	11†			1		9													1-3(0-1)2149	16
16. Carlisle* 31.10		2	3	12	5	6	7¹	8†	10¹	4		11²				1		9													4-1(3-0)2124	13
17. Darlington 3.11		2	3†	8	5	6	7		10	4		11				1	12	9													0-1(0-0)1720	—
18. Hereford 7.11		2	3	8	5	6	7		10†	4		11	9¹		12	1															1-1(0-0)2272	14
19. Scunthorpe* 21.11		2	3	10	5	6	7‡					4†		1	11	9	12	8													2-2(0-1)2045	15
20. Halifax 27.11		2	3	10	5	6	7¹	8†		14		4¹		1	11	12‡	9														2-1(0-0)1416	—
21. Cardiff* 12.12		2		10	5	6†	7		8			11		4	1	3	12		9												0-0(0-0)2010	13
22. Peterboro 18.12		2		10	5		7¹		6			14		1	3	9	4		11‡	8¹											4-0(3-0)2540	—
23. Swansea* 26.12		2	5	10		12	7¹		6					1	3†	9	4‡		11	8	14										2-2(1-0)2976	10
24. Newport 28.12		2	3	10	5		7		6					12	1		4†			14	8¹	9¹‡	11								2-1(1-0)1918	8
25. Wrexham 1.1		2	5¹	10			7	14	6						1	3†		4	12	9†	8		11								1-2(0-0)2939	10
26. Wolves* 2.1		2	3	10	5		7	14		6‡					1	11	9†				12	8	4								0-2(0-1)4629	12
27. Orient 16.1		2	6	4	5		7	8	9	14					1	3	12							11†	10¹‡						1-1(0-0)4082	14
28. Rochdale* 29.1		2	3	10	5	6		8	4		11†		9		1			7						12							0-1(0-1)2107	—
29. Colchester 5.2		2	3	10	5	6		8†	11				4		1			12							9²	7¹					4-1(2-0)1822	—
30. Newport* 13.2		2	3	10¹	5	6		8	11¹	12			4†		1		9	14								7‡					2-1(0-1)2080	12
31. Bolton* 20.2		2	3	10†	5	6		8	11¹		14		4		1	12	9¹									7‡					2-1(1-1)4305	11
32. Hartlepool 27.2				10	5	6		8	11¹	2‡			4		1	3	14	9†								7			12		1-2(1-2)2165	13
33. Burnley* 1.3		2		10	5	6		8‡	11†	14			4		1	3	12	9								7					0-1(0-0)3720	—
34. Scarboro 5.3		2		10	5	6			12	8			4		1	3	4†	9‡						14		7			11		0-2(0-1)2260	14
35. Torquay* 11.3			2	10	5	6		12	9		14		4		1	3		8†								7			11‡		0-1(0-1)1858	—
36. Carlisle 19.3			2	10					9	5	7		4		1	3		8						12					11‡	1-0(1-0)1834	14
37. Exeter* 26.3				10	5	6			7		11†		4		1	3	9	8	2										12		0-0(0-0)1665	16
38. Hereford* 1.4				10		6			9	5	11‡			4	1	3	2	8†						14					12		0-0(0-1)1313	—
39. Scunthorpe 4.4				10		6			9	5				4	1	3	2	12						8¹		7			11†		1-2(1-0)4091	17
40. Darlington* 9.4				10		6			9‡	5²				4	1	3	12	8	14					11¹		7	2†		16		3-1(1-1)1482	16
41. Cambridge* 15.4				10		6			9	5				4	1	3	12	14						11†		7	2	8‡			0-0(0-0)1546	—
42. Stockport 22.4		14			5†	6			12	9				4			10‡	8	11					7¹	2				3		1-1(0-0)2090	—
43. Tranmere 25.4		12			6				9¹	5				4	1		8†	11						7¹	2			10	3		2-2(1-2)2962	—
44. Halifax* 29.4		2			6				9	5				4	1	14		12	11‡					7		8†	10	3			0-0(0-0)1403	—
45. Cardiff 2.5		2			6				9					4	1	5	12	14	11‡					7		8†	10,125	3			0-2(0-2)10,125	17
46. Peterboro* 7.5		2			6				9	5				4†	1	3	8‡							7	14		12	11	3		0-1(0-1)1533	17

Apps(subs)/goals: 3(3)0, 31(3)0, 31(6)1, 31(6)2, 32(0)1, 39(0)1, 26(0)19, 24(3)0, 32(4)6, 17(3)1, 10(6)5, 15(6)2, 0(3)0, 15(5)0, 43(0)0, 26(9)0, 28(7)1, 17(2)0, 17(7)1, 7(2)0, 4(2)1, 4(0)2, 2(0)1, 7(3)2, 1(5)0, 4(1)0, 3(0)0, 10(3)1

Final League Position: 17

Own goals: Wright, match 3; Halsall, match 22, English, match 29. Also played: Walters, match 46(10).

DIVISION 2

CRYSTAL PALACE

Selhurst Park, London SE25 6PU.

Back row
(left to right):
Gary Stebbing
Mark Hone
Ian Wright
Gavin Nebbeling
Phil Barber
Middle row:
Ian Evans
(Ass. Manager)
Paul Hammond
Ken O'Doherty
Perry Suckling
Geoff Thomas
John Salako
Dennis Bailey
Jim Cannon
Front row:
Richard Shaw
Alan Pardew
Tony Finnigan
Steve Coppell
(Manager)
Glenn Pennyfather
David Burke
Neil Redfearn

Stadium Capacity: 36,000.
Pitch Dimensions: 110 × 74yds.
Telephone: 01–653 4462, **Clubcall:** 0898–121145.
President: S. Stephenson.
Chairman: R. G. Noades.
Directors: B. Coleman, A. S. C. De Souza, G. Geraghty, M. E. Lee, S. Hume-Kendall, P. H. N. Norman, C. D. Richards, K. A. Sinclair, B. O. Umunna.
Manager: Steve Coppell.
Post-War Managers: George Irwin, Jack Butler, Ronnie Rooke, Fred Dawes, Charlie Slade, Laurie Scott, Cyril Spiers, George Smith, Arthur Rowe, Dick Graham, Bert Head, Malcolm Allison, Terry Venables, Ernie Walley, Malcolm Allison, Dario Gradi, Steve Kember, Alan Mullery MBE (18).
Assistant Manager: Ian Evans.
Physio: David West MCSP, SRP.
Secretary: Alan Leather.
Commercial Manager: Graham Drew.
Marketing Manager: Mike Ryan.
Sponsors: Virgin Atlantic.
Founded: 1905.
Turned Professional: 1905.
Nickname: The Eagles.
Former Names: None.
Former Grounds: Crystal Palace 1905–15, Herne Hill 1915–19, The Nest 1919–24.
Record Attendance: 51,482 v Burnley, Division 2, 11 May 1979.
Record Victory: 9–0 v Barrow, Division 4, 10 October 1959.
Record Defeat: 4–11 v Manchester C, FA Cup 5th Round, 20 February 1926.
Most League Points: (3 for a win) 75, Division 2, 1987–88. (2 for a win) 64, Division 4, 1960–61.
Most League Goals: 110, Division 4, 1960–61.
Highest League Scorer in a Season: Peter Simpson, 46, Division 3(S), 1930–31.
Highest Total of League Goals: Peter Simpson, 154, 1930–36.
Most League Appearances: Jim Cannon, 572, 1973–88.
League History: 1920 Founder Members of Division 3, 1921–25 Division 2, 1925–58 Division 3(S), 1958–61 Division 4, 1961–64 Division 3, 1964–69 Division 2, 1969–73 Division 1, 1973–74 Division 2, 1974–77 Division 3, 1977–79 Division 2, 1979–81 Division 1, 1981– Division 2.
Honours: Division 2 Champions 1978–79, runners-up 1968–69. Division 3 runners-up 1963–64. Division 4 runners-up 1960–61. Division 3(S) Champions 1920–21, runners-up 1928–29, 1930–31, 1938–39.
Colours: Red and blue striped shirts, red shorts and socks. **Second strip:** All yellow.

CRYSTAL PALACE – LEAGUE RECORD 1987–88

Match no/Opp/Date		Wood	Stebbing	Brush	Gray	Nebbeling	Cannon	Redfearn	Thomas	Bright	Wright	Salako	Barber	Finnigan	O'Reilly	O'Doherty	Shaw	Taylor	Burke	Hone	Pardew	Pennyfather	Bailey	Suckling	Pemberton	FT(HT)Att Lge pos
1. Huddersfield	15.8	1	2	3	4	5	6	7	8	9²	10	11†	12													2-2(1-0)6132 —
2. Hull*	22.8	1	2	3	4₂	5	6	7	8	9	10	11														2-2(0-2)6688 15
3. Barnsley	29.8	1	2	3	4	5	6	7	8	9¹	10	11†		12												1-2(1-0)4853 18
4. Middlesbro*	1.9	1	2	3	4	5	6	7	8¹	9²	10	11														3-1(1-0)6866 —
5. Birmingham	5.9	1	2†	3	4¹₁	5	6¹	7¹	8¹	9¹†	10	11	12		14											6-0(1-0)7011 9
6. WBA*	8.9	1	2†	3	4	5	6	7¹	8	9²	10¹	11				12										4-1(1-0)8554 —
7. Leicester*	12.9	1		3	4	5	6	7	8¹	9	10¹	11†	12		2											2-1(1-1)8925 1
8. Sheff Utd	15.9	1		3	4	5	6	7	8	9	10¹	11			2†	12										1-1(0-0)7767 —
9. Reading	19.9	1	3‡		4	5¹	6†	7	8	9¹	10¹	11	12			2	14									3-2(0-1)6819 2
10. Ipswich*	26.9	1			4	5¹		7	8	9	10	11				2	3	6								1-2(0-0)10,828 7
11. Shrewsbury	3.10	1			4	5		7	3	9	10	11	12			6	2†	8								0-2(0-1)3999 4
12. Millwall*	10.10	1			4		6	7	8	9¹	10†	11	12			2			3	5						1-0(0-0)10,678 3
13. Aston Villa	21.10	1			4	5	6	7	8	9	10¹	11				2			3							1-4(1-2)12,755 —
14. Swindon*	24.10	1			4₁	5	6	7	8	9¹	10	11†	12			2			3							2-1(1-1)9077 6
15. Bradford	31.10	1			4	5	6	7	8	9	10	11†	12			2			3							0-2(0-0)13,012 8
16. Plymouth*	3.11	1	14		4¹	5¹	6	7	8	9	10³	11†	12			2‡			3							5-1(1-0)7424 —
17. Bournemouth	7.11	1	12		4	5	6	7	8¹	9²	10	11				2†			3							3-2(3-2)9083 6
18. Stoke*	14.11	1	2			5		7	8	9¹	10¹	11						6	3	4						2-0(0-0)8309 5
19. Blackburn	21.11	1	2			5		7	8	9	10	12	11†					6	3	4						0-2(0-0)6372 6
20. Leeds*	28.11	1	2			5	6	7	8	9¹	10¹	11							3	4						3-0(1-0)8749 5
21. Man City	5.12	1	2			5	6	7₁	8†	9²	10	11							3	4	12					3-1(0-0)23,161 4
22. Sheff Utd*	13.12	1	2			5	6	7₁	8		10	11†	9¹	12					3	4						2-1(0-1)8174 —
23. Hull	19.12	1	2			5	6	7	8		10		9¹						3	4†	11	12				1-2(1-2)6780 4
24. Ipswich	26.12	1	2			5	6	7₁†	8		10²	11	9						3	4	12					3-2(1-1)17,200 3
25. Reading*	28.12	1	2			5	6¹	7	8		10¹	11	9†						3	4	12					2-3(1-1)12,449 4
26. Barnsley*	1.1	1	2			5	6	7	8¹		10¹	11†	9						3	4	12¹					3-2(0-1)8563 3
27. Leicester	2.1	1	2			5	6	11	8		10²		9†						3	4¹	7	12				4-4(4-2)10,104 2
28. Huddersfield*	16.1		2			5	6¹	7		9	10	11¹							3	4	8			1		2-1(2-1)9013 2
29. Middlesbro	23.1		2				6	7		9	10¹	11				5			3	4	8			1		1-2(0-1)12,597 2
30. Oldham	29.1		2†				6	7		9	10	11			14	5			3	4†	8	12		1		0-1(0-0)6169 —
31. Birmingham*	6.2						6	11	8	9²	10¹		12			5	2		3	4	7†			1		3-0(1-0)8809 3
32. WBA	13.2						6	11	8	9	10	7				5	2		3	4†	12			1		0-1(0-0)8944 3
33. Shrewsbury*	27.2				14		6	7₁‡	8	9	10	12	11†			5	2		3	4				1		1-2(1-1)8210 6
34. Oldham*	5.3					5²	6	7	8	9	10¹	11					2		3	4				1		3-1(2-0)7032 4
35. Millwall	12.3					5	6¹	7	8	9	10	12	11†				2		3	4				1		1-0(0-0)12,815 6
36. Bradford*	19.3					5	6	7	8	9†	10	12	11¹				2		3	4				1		1-0(0-0)9801 5
37. Swindon	27.3					5	6		8	9¹	10¹	11					2		3	4	7			1		2-0(0-0)12,915 —
38. Bournemouth*	2.4					5	6	7₂	8	9¹	10	11					2		3	4				1		3-0(2-0)9557 5
39. Stoke	4.4					5	6	7†	8‡	9¹	10	12	11				2		3	4	14			1		1-1(0-1)9613 6
40. Aston Villa*	9.4					5	6	7†	8	9	10₁	11	22				2		3	4‡	14	1	1		12	1-1(0-1)16,476 6
41. Plymouth	23.4					5	6	7†	8	9²	10¹	1					2		3	4		1			12	3-1(1-0)8370 6
42. Blackburn*	30.4					5	6	7†	8¹	9	10	12	11				2		3	4		1				2-0(1-0)13,059 6
43. Leeds	2.5					5	6	7†	8	9	10	12	11				2		3	4		1				0-1(0-0)13,217 6
44. Man City*	7.5					5¹	6	7	8¹	9	10	11					2		3	4		1				2-0(0-0)17,555 6
Apps(subs)/goals		27(0)0	19(2)0	9(0)0	17(0)6	38(0)1	40(0)4	42(0)8	41(0)6	38(0)25	41(0)20	23(8)0	28(9)7	14(3)0	2(2)0	16(1)0	2(1)0	2(0)0	31(0)0	30(0)0	16(4)0	18(1)1	0(5)1	17(0)0	0(2)0	Final League Position: 6

Own goals: Ashurst, match 20; McGugan, match 26.

DIVISION 4

DARLINGTON

Feethams Ground, Darlington DL1 5JB.

Back row·
(left to right):
David Currie
Peter Robinson
David McAughtrie
Alan Smith
Gary Hinchley
Lew Clayton
(Physio)
Middle row:
Mark Hine
Gary Worthington
Jeremy Roberts
Garry Macdonald
Kevin Stonehouse
Gary Morgan
Front row:
Mark Outterside
Paul Ward
David Booth
(Manager)
Phil Bonnyman
(Ass. Manager)
Stephen Bell
Alan Roberts

Stadium Capacity: 13,511.
Pitch Dimensions: 110 × 74yds.
Telephone: 0325–465097, **Commercial dept:** 0325–481212.
Chairman: A. Heaton.
Vice-Chairman: J. B. Hadley.
Directors: D. Mason, A. Brown, A. Moore, C. H. Parias, P. Boddy, J. L. Moore, John Cheadle, Brian Sommerville.
Manager: David Booth.
Post-War Managers: Bill Forrest, George Irwin, Bob Gurney, Dick Duckworth, Eddie Carr, Lol Morgan, Jimmy Greenhalgh, Ray Yeoman, Len Richley, Frank Brennan, Allan Jones, Ralph Brand, Dick Conner, Billy Horner, Peter Madden, Len Walker, Billy Elliott, Cyril Knowles, Paul Ward (19).
Assistant Manager: Philip Bonnyman.
Physio: Lew Clayton.
Secretary: Brian Anderson.
Commercial Manager: Val Armstrong.
Founded: 1883.
Turned Professional: 1908.
Nickname: The Quakers.
Former Names: None.
Former Grounds: None.
Record Attendance: 21,023 v Bolton W, League Cup 3rd Round, 14 November 1960.
Record Victory: 9–2 v Lincoln C, Division 3(N), 7 January 1928.
Record Defeat: 0–10 v Doncaster R, Division 4, 25 January 1964.
Most League Points: (3 for a win) 85, Division 4, 1984–85. (2 for a win) 59, Division 4, 1965–66.
Most League Goals: 108, Division 3(N), 1929–30.
Highest League Scorer in a Season: David Brown, 39, Division 3(N), 1924–25.
Highest Total of League Goals: Alan Walsh, 90, 1978–84.
Most League Appearances: Ron Greener, 442, 1955–68.
League History: 1921 Founder Members of Division 3(N), 1925–27 Division 2, 1927–58 Division 3(N), 1958–66 Division 4, 1966–67 Division 3, 1967–85 Division 4, 1985–87 Division 3, 1987– Division 4.
Honours: Division 4 runners-up: 1965–66. Division 3(N) Champions 1924–25, runners-up 1921–22.
Colours: White shirts with black insert, white shorts with black side panels, white socks with three black hoops. **Second strip:** As main strip, but with yellow instead of white.

DARLINGTON – LEAGUE RECORD 1987–88

Match no/Opp/Date	Roberts J	Hinchley	Morgan	Hine	Robinson	McAughtrie	Outerside	Ward	MacDonald	Currie	Bell	Stonehouse	Worthington	Bonnyman	Roberts A	Crichton	Granger	O'Dell	Clayton	Willis	Anderson	Hyde	FT(HT)Att Lge pos
1. Halifax 15.8	1	2†	3	4	5	6	7	8	9¹	10¹	11‡	12	14										2-2(1-0)1342 —
2. Stockport* 22.8	1		3†	4‡	5	6	14	8	9¹	10	12	11		2	7								1-2(1-0)1744 17
3. Hartlepool 29.8	1		3	2	5	6		8¹	9	10²†	11	12			4	7²							5-2(1-0)2106 7
4. Torquay* 31.8	1		3	2	5	6		8	9	10	11				4	7							1-1(0-0)2251 —
5. Peterboro 5.9	1		3	2	5	6		8	9	10²	11				4	7							2-1(2-1)3200 8
6. Scarboro* 12.9	1		3	2	5	6		8	9	10¹	11†	12¹			4	7							2-1(1-0)3187 5
7. Cardiff 15.9	1		3	2	5	6		8	9	10	11‡	12			4	7							1-3(0-1)2201 —
8. Hereford 19.9	1	12	3	2	5	6		8	9	10	11				4	7†							0-1(0-1)2102 12
9. Scunthorpe* 26.9	1		3	2	5	6		8	9¹	10	11†	12			4	7							1-4(1-1)1638 15
10. Carlisle 29.9		2	3	4	5			8	9	10¹		11‡		6	7†			1	12				3-3(2-2)2996 —
11. Tranmere 3.10		2	3	4	5		7†	8	9	10	12	11		6		1							0-0(0-0)1612 18
12. Bolton* 10.10			3	4	5		2	8	9	10	12¹	11†		6	7	1							1-0(0-0)1763 14
13. Rochdale 17.10	1		3	4	5		2	8	9	10¹	7	11‡		6									3-1(1-1)1417 13
14. Wrexham 20.10	1		3	4	5		2	8	9	10¹	7	11		6									1-0(0-0)1278 —
15. Wolves* 24.10	1		3	4	5		2	8	9	10¹	7	11		6¹									2-2(2-2)2282 12
16. Colchester 30.10	1		3	4	5		2	8	9†	10	7	11	12¹	6									1-2(0-0)1659 —
17. Crewe* 3.11	1		3	4	5		2	8		10	7	11	9¹†	6	12								1-0(0-0)1720 —
18. Cambridge* 8.11	1		3	4	5	12	2	8		10	7	11†	9	6									0-1(0-1)2463 —
19. Orient 20.11	1		3	4¹	5	6	2	8	9	10	7	11‡											3-4(2-1)3644 —
20. Exeter* 8.12	1		3	4¹	5		2	8	9	10²		11		6	7¹								4-1(3-0)1107 —
21. Swansea* 19.12	1		3	4	5		2	8	9	10²		11		6	7								2-0(1-0)1726 9
22. Scunthorpe 26.12	1		3	4	5		2	8	9	10	12	11†		6	7								0-1(0-1)3140 12
23. Burnley* 28.12	1		3	4	5		2	8	9†	10²	11¹	12¹		6	7								4-2(1-1)3325 10
24. Hartlepool* 1.1			3	4¹	5		2	8	9		11			6	7	1							1-1(0-0)4735 11
25. Scarboro 2.1			3	4	5	12	2	8	9†	10¹	11			6	7	1							1-0(1-0)3371 8
26. Carlisle* 9.1			3	4	5		2	8	9†	10¹	11¹	12		6	7	1							2-1(1-0)2517 7
27. Newport 12.1			3	4	5		2	8	9	10	11			6	7	1							1-2(1-1)1402 —
28. Hereford* 17.1			3	4	5		2	8‡	9†	10²	11	12		6	7¹	1	14						3-1(0-0)2621 —
29. Cardiff* 2.2			3	4	5		2	8	9†	10	12	11		6	7	1							0-0(0-0)2332 —
30. Burnley 13.2			3	4	5			9	10¹		12	11†		6	7	1	8						1-2(0-1)6432 8
31. Halifax* 20.2			3	4	5		2	8²	9¹	10		11‡		6	7	1							4-1(2-1)1824 6
32. Tranmere 26.2			3	4	5		2	8¹	9		12	11	10†	6	7	1							1-2(0-1)2756 —
33. Rochdale* 5.3			3	4	5		2	8	9			11		6	7	1		10²					2-1(1-1)1773 8
34. Bolton 11.3			3	4	5		2	8	9			11		6	7¹	1		10					1-1(0-1)4948 —
35. Peterboro* 15.3			3	4¹	5		2	8	9		12	11‡		6	7†	1		10					2-1(2-1)1618 —
36. Colchester* 19.3			3	4	5		2	8	9¹			11		6¹	7	1		10					2-0(0-0)2034 4
37. Wolves 26.3			3		5		2	8	9¹		4	11‡		6	7	1		10¹					3-5(0-2)9349 7
38. Cambridge 1.4			3				2	8	9		12	11‡		6	7†	1		10	5				0-1(0-2)2249 —
39. Orient* 4.4			3	4			2	8	9†		12	11‡		6	7¹	1		10	5				2-2(1-1)2730 8
40. Crewe 9.4			3	4	10‡	9	2	8			12	11		6¹†	7	1			5	14			1-3(1-1)1482 10
41. Stockport 19.4			3	4	12	6	2	8¹†	9			11			7	1		10‡	5	14			1-0(0-1)1620 —
42. Wrexham* 23.4	3			4		6		8¹	9			11			7¹	1		10	5				2-1(1-0)1711 7
43. Torquay 27.4			3	4		6	2	8	9			11			7	1		10	5				0-0(0-0)3939 —
44. Exeter 30.4			3†	4	12	6	2	8	9‡	10		11			7	1			5	14			1-4(0-0)1515 9
45. Newport* 2.5			3	4		6	2	8	9	10‡		11			7	1		12	5†	14			0-2(0-2)1675 11
46. Swansea 7.5			3	4		6	2	8	9†			11			7	1		10‡	5	14			0-3(0-1)4071 13
Apps(subs)/goals	20(0) 0	4(1) 0	45(0) 4	45(0) 0	38(2) 0	17(2) 0	7(1) 0	45(0) 6	42(0) 7	31(0) 21	18(1) 12	38(5) 13	45(1) 3	38(0) 3	37(1) 7	30(0) 0	23(0) 0	1(2) 0	11(1) 3	9(0) 0	0(4) 0	0(2) 0	Final League Position: 13

Own goals: Mann, match 27; Carter, match 44.

DIVISION 1

DERBY COUNTY

Baseball Ground, Shaftesbury Crescent, Derby DE3 8NB.

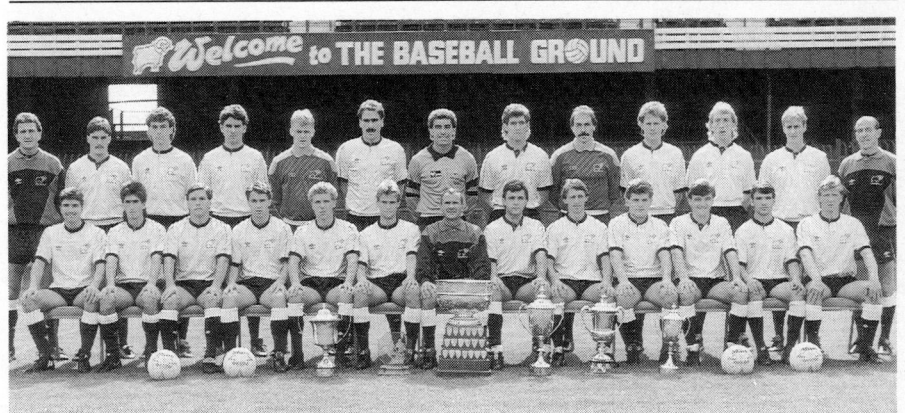

Back row (left to right): Roy McFarland (Ass. Manager), Ross MacLaren, Michael Forsyth, John Gregory, Martin Taylor, Richard Pratley, Peter Shilton, Rob Hindmarch, Mark Wallington, Andy Garner, Mark Lillis, Paul Blades, Gordon Guthrie (Physio). *Front row:* Brian McCord, Nigel Callaghan, Geraint Williams, Mel Sage, Steve Cross, Phil Gee, Arthur Cox (Manager), Bobby Davison, Gary Micklewhite, Mickey Lewis, David Penney, Robert Briscoe, Steve McClaren

Stadium Capacity: 26,500.
Pitch Dimensions: 110 × 75yds.
Telephone: 0332–40105, **Clubcall:** 0898–121187.
Chairman: Robert Maxwell.
Vice-Chairman: A. S. Webb.
Managing Director: A. S. Webb.
Directors: F. W. Fern, J. N. Kirkland, W. Hart, T. J. East, G. Glossop, C. R. Charlton, C. M. McKerrow, B. E. Fearn, M. McGarry.
Manager: Arthur Cox.
Post-War Managers: Stuart McMillan, Jack Barker, Harry Storer, Tim Ward, Brian Clough, Dave Mackay, Colin Murphy, Tommy Docherty, Colin Addison, John Newman, Peter Taylor, Roy McFarland (12).
Assistant Manager: Roy McFarland.
Physio: Gordon Guthrie.
Secretary: Michael Dunford.
Commercial Manager: Michael Dunford.
Sponsors: Maxwell Communications.
Founded: 1884.
Turned Professional: 1884.
Nickname: The Rams.
Former Names: None.
Former Grounds: Racecourse Ground 1884–95.
Record Attendance: 41,826 v Tottenham H, Division 1, 20 September 1969.
Record Victory: 12–0 v Finn Harps, UEFA Cup 3rd Round, 1st leg, 15 September 1976.
Record Defeat: 2–11 v Everton, FA Cup 1st Round, 1889–90.
Most League Points: (3 for a win) 84, Division 3, 1985–86 and Division 3, 1986–87. (2 for a win) 63, Division 2, 1968–69 and Division 3(N), 1955–56 and 1956–57.
Most League Goals: 111, Division 3(N), 1956–57.
Highest League Scorer in a Season: Jack Bowers, 37, Division 1, 1930–31 and Ray Straw, 37 Division 3(N), 1956–57.
Highest Total of League Goals: Steve Bloomer, 291, 1892–1906 and 1910–14.
Most League Appearances: Kevin hector, 486, 1966–78 and 1980–82.
League History: 1888 Founder Members of the League, 1904–12 Division 2, 1912–14 Division 1, 1914–15 Division 2, 1914–21 Division 1, 1921–26 Division 2, 1926–53 Division 1, 1953–55 Division 2, 1955–57 Division 3(N), 1957–69 Division 2, 1969–80 Division 1, 1980–84 Division 2, 1984–86 Division 3, 1986–87 Division 2, 1987– Division 1.
Honours: Division 1 Champions 1971–72, 1974–75, runners-up: 1895–96, 1929–30, 1935–36. Division 2 Champions 1911–12, 1914–15, 1968–69, 1986–87, runners-up 1925–26. Division 3(N) Champions 1956–57, runners-up 1955–56. FA Cup winners: 1946, runners-up: 1898, 1899, 1903.
Colours: White shirts, blue shorts and socks. **Second strip:** Blue shirts, white shorts and socks.

DERBY COUNTY – LEAGUE RECORD 1987–88

Match no/Opp/Date	Shilton	Sage	Forsyth	Williams	Hindmarch	MacLaren	Micklewhite	Gee	Davison	Gregory	Callaghan	Blades	Wright	Lillis	Garner	Cross	Lewis	Penney	McClaren	McCord	McMinn	Stapleton	FT(HT)Att Lge pos
1. Luton* 15.8	1	2	3	4	5	6	7	8	9	10^1	11												1–0(1–0)17,204 —
2. QPR 19.8	1	2	3	4	5	6	7	8^1	9	10	11												1–1(1–1)11,651 —
3. Wimbledon* 29.8	1	2	3	4	$5^{\dagger}$		7	8	$9^{\ddagger}$	10	11	12	6	14									0–1(0–0)15,165 13
4. Portsmouth* 5.9	1	2	3	4		6	7	$8^{\dagger}$	9	10	11		5		12								0–0(0–0)15,071 13
5. Norwich 12.9	1	2	3	4		6	7	$8^{\dagger}$	9^1	10^1	11		5		12								2–1(0–1)14,402 11
6. Sheff Wed* 19.9	1	7	3^1	4		6		$8^{\dagger}$	9	10^1	11	2	5		12								2–2(2–2)15,869 11
7. Oxford 26.9	1	7	3	4		6		$8^{\ddagger}$	$9^{\dagger}$	10	11	2	5		12	14							0–1(0–1)15,711 13
8. Liverpool 29.9	1	7	3	4		6		$8^{\dagger}$	9	10	11	2	5		12								0–4(0–1)43,405 —
9. West Ham 3.10	1	2	3	4		6		8^1	9	10	7		5			11							1–1(0–1)17,226 12
10. Nottm F* 10.10	1	$2^{\dagger}$	3	4		12		8		10	7	6	5		9	11							0–1(0–1)22,394 13
11. Charlton 17.10	1		3	4		2		9		10	7	6	5		8	11^1							1–0(1–0)5432 11
12. Arsenal 24.10	1		3	4		2	12	9		10^1	7	6	5		$8^{1\dagger}$	11	14						1–2(1–2)32,374 13
13. Coventry* 31.10	1		3	4		2		9		10	7	6	5		8^2	11							2–0(0–0)15,738 11
14. Newcastle 14.11	1		3	4		2	12	9		10	7	6	5		$8^{\dagger}$	11							0–0(0–0)21,698 13
15. Chelsea* 22.11	1		3	4		2		9		10^1	7	6	5		8	11^1							2–0(0–0)18,644 —
16. Sthampton 28.11	1		3	4		2		9^1		$10^{\ddagger}$	7	6	5		8^1	$11^{\dagger}$	14	12					2–1(0–1)15,201 10
17. Watford* 5.12	1		3	4		2		$9^{\dagger}$		$10^{\ddagger}$	7	6	5^1		8	11	14	12					1–1(1–0)14,516 9
18. Everton 12.12	1		3	4		2		9			$7^{\dagger}$	6	5		8	11	$10^{\ddagger}$	12	14				0–3(0–1)26,224 11
19. Spurs* 20.12	1		3	4		2		$9^{\ddagger}$		10^1	7	6	5		8	$11^{\dagger}$	14	12					1–2(1–0)17,593 —
20. Norwich* 26.12	1		3	4		2		9		10	7	6	5^1		8	11							1–2(0–1)15,452 14
21. Sheff Wed 28.12	1	12	3	4		2		9^1		10	7	6	5		$8^{\dagger}$	14	$11^{\ddagger}$						1–2(0–1)26,191 15
22. Wimbledon 1.1	1		3	4		2		9		10	7^1	6	5		8			11					1–2(1–1)5479 16
23. Luton 16.1	1		3	4		2		9		10	7	6	5		9			11					0–1(0–1)7175 17
24. Portsmouth 6.2	1		3	4		2		8		$10^{\ddagger}$	11	6	5^1		$9^{\dagger}$	14	12			7			1–2(0–1)14,790 18
25. Man Utd* 10.2	1		3	4	6	2		$9^{\dagger}$		10	$11^{\ddagger}$		5		14	8	12			7^1			1–2(0–0)20,016 —
26. Oxford 20.2	1		3	4	6			9		10	11	2	5			8				7			0–0(0–0)8924 18
27. West Ham* 27.2	1		3	4	6	14		9		10	11^1	$2^{\ddagger}$	5		12	$8^{\dagger}$				7			1–0(0–0)16,301 18
28. Spurs 1.3	1		3	4	6	14		9		$10^{\ddagger}$	11	2	5		12	$8^{\dagger}$				$7^{\dagger}$			0–0(0–0)15,968 —
29. Charlton* 5.3	1		3	4	6			9		10	$11^{\ddagger}$	2	5		12	$8^{\dagger}$				7			1–1(0–0)16,139 17
30. Liverpool* 16.3	1		3^1	4	6	12		9		10	11	2	5		14	$8^{\ddagger}$				$7^{\dagger}$			1–1(1–0)26,356 17
31. Coventry 19.3	$1^{\ddagger}$		3^1	4^1	6	14	12	9^1		10	11	2	5				8				$7^{\dagger}$		3–0(2–0)19,871 16
32. Arsenal* 26.3	1		3	4	6		12	$9^{\dagger}$		10	11	2	5				8				7		0–0(0–0)18,382 —
33. Nottm F 30.3	1		3	4	$6^{\ddagger}$	14	12	9		10	11	2	5				$8^{\dagger}$				7		1–2(0–1)25,017 —
34. Man Utd 2.4	1		3	4	6		7	$9^{\dagger}$		10	11	2	5		12^1							8	1–4(0–2)40,146 17
35. Newcastle* 4.4	1		3	4	6	12	7^1	9^1		10	11	$2^{\dagger}$	5									8	2–1(0–1)18,591 15
36. Chelsea 9.4	1		3	4	6	12	7	$9^{\ddagger}$		10	11	$2^{\dagger}$	5		14							8	0–1(0–1)16,996 16
37. QPR* 13.4	1		3	4	6	12	$7^{\ddagger}$	9		10	11	$2^{\dagger}$	5		14							8	0–2(0–1)14,214 —
38. Sthampton* 23.4	1	3		4	6	2	7	9		10^1	11		5									8^1	2–0(2–0)14,291 15
39. Watford 30.4	1	$2^{\dagger}$	3	4	6	12	7	9		10	11^1		5									8	1–1(1–1)14,181 15
40. Everton* 2.5	1		3	4	6	2	7	9		10	11		5									8	0–0(0–0)17,974 15
Appsubs/goals	40(0) 0	12(1) 0	39(0) 3	40(0) 1	19(0) 0	22(9) 0	12(4) 1	36(2) 6	13(0) 1	39(0) 6	40(0) 4	30(1) 0	38(0) 3	0(1) 0	14(10) 4	11(4) 3	10(6) 0	3(6) 0	1(0) 0	10(0) 0	7(0) 1	10(0) 1	Final League Position: 15

Own goal: Foster, match 33.

DIVISION 4

DONCASTER ROVERS

Belle Vue Ground, Doncaster DN4 5HT.

*Back row
(left to right):*
Colin Miller
Stewart Beattie
Andy Rhodes
Tommy Gaynor
Steve Burke
Middle row:
Tony Kinsella
Sean Joyce
Paul Holmes
Brian Dene
Micky Nesbitt
Ronnie Robinson
Front row:
Glenn Humphries
Micky Stead
Dave Cusack
Brian Carnaby
Steve Beaglehole
Colin Russell

Stadium Capacity: 6500
Pitch Dimensions: 110 × 74yds.
Telephone: 0302–539441, Commercial dept: 0302–531000.
Chairman: B. E. Boldry.
Vice-Chairman: M. J. H. Collett.
Vice-Presidents: R. Jones, K. Jackson.
Directors: P. Wetzel, J. J. Burke, I. M. Jones, T. C. Hamilton, K. Chappell.
Manager: Dave Mackay.
Post-War Managers: Bill Marsden, Jackie Bestall, Peter Doherty, Jack Hodgson, Syd Bycroft, Jack Crayston, Jack Bestall, Norman Curtis, Danny Malloy, Oscar Hold, Bill Leivers, Keith Kettleborough, George Raynor, Lawrie McMenemy, Maurice Setters, Stan Anderson, Billy Bremner, Dave Cusack (18).
Assistant Manager: Joe Kinnear.
Physio: G. Delahunt.
Secretary: K. J. Oldale.
Founded: 1879.
Turned Professional: 1885.
Nickname: The Rovers.
Former Names: None.
Former Grounds: Intake Ground 1880–1916, Benetthorpe Ground 1920–22.
Record Attendance: 37,149 v Hull C, Division 3(N), 2 October 1948.
Record Victory: 10–0 v Darlington, Division 4, 25 January 1964.
Record Defeat: 0–12 v Small Heath, Division 2, 11 April, 1903.
Most League Points: (3 for a win) 85, Division 4, 1983–84. (2 for a win) 72, Division 3(N), 1946–47.
Most League Goals: 123, Division 3(N), 1946–47.
Highest League Scorer in a Season: Clarrie Jordan, 42, Division 3(N), 1946–47.
Highest Total of League Goals: Tom Keetley, 180, 1923–29.
Most League Appearances: Fred Emery, 406, 1925–36.
League History: 1901 Elected to Division 2, 1903 Failed re-election, 1904 Re–elected, 1905 Failed re-election, 1923 Re–elected to Division 3(N), 1935–37 Division 2, 1937–47 Division 3(N), 1947–48 Division 2, 1948–50 Division 3(N), 1950–58 Division 2, 1958–59 Division 3, 1959–66 Division 4, 1966–67 Division 3, 1967–69 Division 4, 1969–71 Division 3, 1971–81 Division 4, 1981–83 Division 3, 1983–84 Division 4, 1984–88 Division 3, 1988– Division 4.
Honours: Division 4 Champions 1965–66, 1968–69, runners-up: 1983–84. Division 3(N) Champions 1934–35, 1946–47, 1949–50, runners-up 1937–38, 1938–39.
Colours: Red shirts, white shorts, red socks. **Second strip:** All white.

DONCASTER ROVERS – LEAGUE RECORD 1987–88

Match no/Opp/Date		Rhodes	Steed	Robinson R	Humphries	Flynn	Cusack	Russell	Chamberlain	Deane	Rankine	Kinsella	Burke	Joyce	Gaynor	Brevett	Nesbitt	Miller	Stubbs	Samways	Raffell	Buckley	Gorman	Kimble	Raven	Holmes	Robinson	Turnbull	James	Brannigan	Harbottle	FT(HT)Att Lge pos
1. **Grimsby***	15.8	1	2	3	4	5	6	7	8¹	9	10	11†	12																			1–0(1–0)2482 —
2. Fulham	22.8	1	2	3	4	5	6	7	8†	9		11	14	10‡	12																	0–4(0–3)4157 14
3. **Sunderland***	29.8	1	2	3		5	6	7‡	12	14		11†	9		10	4	8															0–2(0–1)2740 17
4. Aldershot	31.8	1	2	3		5	6	7	12	9¹	8†		11		10	4																1–2(1–0)2598 —
5. **Nthampton***	5.9	1	2	3	4	5	6	7		9			12	8	10	11†																0–2(0–0)1873 22
6. Wigan	12.9	1†	2	3	4	5	6	7		9¹			12	14	11		8	10‡														1–2(1–0)2764 22
7. **Blackpool***	15.9	1	2	3	4	5	6			9			12²	11†			8	10														2–1(0–0)1558 —
8. **Chesterfield***	18.9	1	2	3	4	5	6			9¹			11				8	10														1–0(1–0)1952 —
9. York	26.9	1	2	3		5	6			9		11¹		7			8	10	4													1–1(0–0)2702 19
10. Mansfield	29.9	1	2	3		5	6			9		11		7			8	10†		4		12										0–2(0–2)3159 —
11. **Gillingham***	3.10	1	2	3		5	6			9		11¹		7¹			8¹	10‡	4													4–2(2–0)1647 17
12. **Notts Co***	17.10	1	2	3	4	11	6			9							8	10†	5	7	12											0–1(0–1)2649 20
13. **Walsall***	20.10	1	2	3	4	5	6			9							8	10‡		7	12	11										0–4(0–1)1387 —
14. Bristol R	24.10	1	2	3		12	6†			9			4				8	14	5	7	10‡	11										0–4(0–3)2817 22
15. **Bury***	31.10	1	2	3		4	6			9¹							8		10	12	11	5	7†									1–2(0–1)1403 22
16. Brighton	4.11	1	2	3			6			9			4				8		7		11			10								0–2(0–1)7142 —
17. **Port Vale***	7.11	1	2	3		12				9¹			4				8		7†		11	6		10								1–1(1–0)1365 22
18. Preston	21.11	1	2	3		5	6¹			9	4						8				11¹	7		10								2–1(2–0)5178 22
19. **Brentford***	28.11	1	2†	3		5				9	4					14	8				11	6	12		10	7‡						0–1(0–0)1360 22
20. Chester	5.12	1			4¹		10†				6	12			3		8				11	5	2		9	7						1–1(0–1)1853 22
21. Southend	11.12	1			4					6¹	12			14	10‡	8		3‡			11	5	2		9	7						1–4(1–1)2268 —
22. **Bristol C***	19.12	1	2		12		14	9‡	8	5†			3			4				11					10	7	6					1–2(1–1)1819 23
23. **York***	26.12	1	2†			12	9¹	8	5				3							11	4¹				10		6					2–0(0–0)2409 21
24. Rotherham	28.12	1	2		12		14	9	8	5			3							11†	4				10	7‡	6					0–1(0–0)5840 23
25. Sunderland	1.1	1	2‡		12		14	9	8	5¹			3							11†	4				10	7	6					1–3(1–3)19,419 23
26. **Wigan***	2.1	1			12‡		7	9	8¹†	5			3							11	4¹	2			10	14	6¹					3–4(2–1)2464 23
27. **Fulham***	9.1	1					7	9	12	5			3							11	4¹	2		8¹			6	10†				2–2(0–1)1827 23
28. Chesterfield	16.1	1		5			7	9¹					4							11		2		8			6	10				1–0(0–0)2715 23
29. **Aldershot***	31.1	1		5			7	9	12				4							11	2			8			6	10†				0–0(0–0)1908 —
30. Nthampton	6.2	1		5			7	9	12				4						14	3				8‡			6	10†				0–1(0–1)4359 23
31. **Rotherham***	13.2	1		5			7†	9¹	10		12¹		4							3				8			6					2–2(1–1)2769 23
32. Grimsby	20.2	1		5				9	8		7		4							3				10			6					0–0(0–0)3890 23
33. Gillingham	27.2	1					14	9	8¹		7‡		4							3				11†	5	2	12		6			1–3(1–1)4041 23
34. **Mansfield***	1.3	1		5			7†	9	8				4							3				11	2		12		6			0–2(0–0)1987 —
35. Notts Co	5.3	1		5			7		8				10†		4‡				14	3				11	2		9		6			0–2(0–1)5816 23
36. **Chester***	11.3			5			7†	10	8¹		4							3	1				11	2	12	9‡		6			2–2(1–1)1482 —
37. Bury	19.3			5¹			7	10	8		4‡	9						3	1	6				11†	2		12		6			1–2(1–2)2431 23
38. **Bristol R***	25.3			5			10†	9	8		6	7						3	1				11	4	2		12					0–1(0–1)1311 —
39. Port Vale	2.4			5			10	9	8			7						3	1	12				11‡	6	2†	4					0–5(0–2)3680 23
40. **Preston***	4.4			5			10³	9†	8	7								3	1				11	6	2	4	12					3–2(0–1)2167 23
41. **Walsall***	9.4			5			10	9¹	8	7†								3	1				11	6	2	4	12					1–2(0–0)6631 23
42. Blackpool	15.4			5			10	9†		8		7¹						3	1				12¹	11		2‡	4	6				2–4(0–1)2291 —
43. **Brighton***	23.4			5			10	9	8	7				3		2	1	6					11			12	4†					0–2(0–0)1683 23
44. Brentford	30.4			5			10	9		7						3	1	6					11	6	2	4¹	8					1–1(0–1)3122 23
45. **Southend***	2.5			5			10	9		7‡		14				3	1	6				12	11†		2	4	8					0–1(0–1)1306 23
46. Bristol C	7.5			5			10	9	12	7‡				3		2	1	6					11‡		14	4	8					0–1(0–0)18,378 24

Final League Position: 24

Appearances/goals: 35(0)0, 23(0)0, 37(0)1, 8(0)0, 16(0)1, 17(0)0, 22(7)4, 42(1)10, 44(4)2, 21(0)3, 14(0)3, 10(2)1, 7(0)3, 16(1)0, 2(0)0, 41(0)1, 11(0)0, 11(3)0, 6(0)0, 1(0)1, 34(0)1, 17(0)3, 22(4)0, 7(0)1, 24(6)1, 7(0)1, 15(0)1, 4(0)0

Also played: Mendoca, match no 33(10), 34(10); Gaughan, match no 35(12), 36(14), 37(14), 39(14); Hall, match no 42(14); Peckett, match no 7(7), 8(7); Beatt match no 16(5), 17(5). Own goals: Langley, match 36

DIVISION 1

EVERTON

Goodison Park, Liverpool L4 4EL.

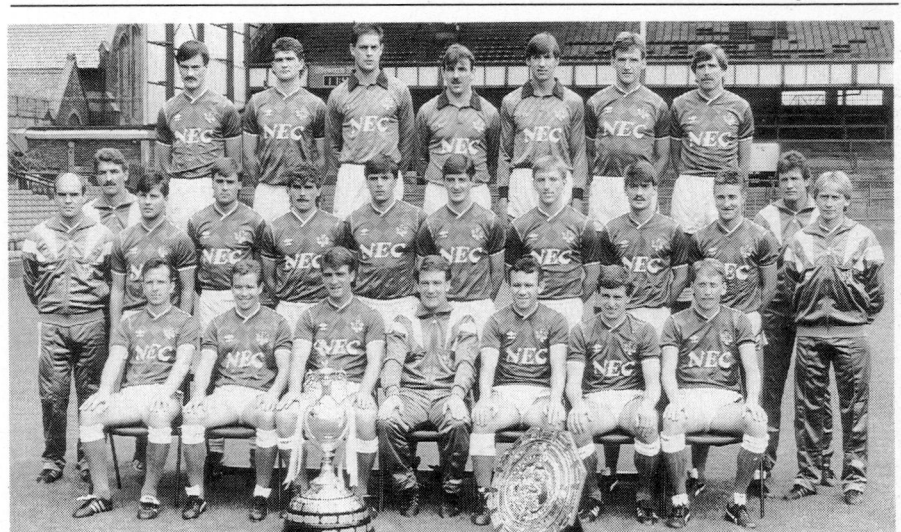

Back row (left to right): Derek Mountfield, Ian Marshall, Bobby Mimms, Neville Southall, Alec Chamberlaine, Dave Watson, Paul Power. *Middle row:* Jerry Darracot (Ass. Manager), John Clinkard, Paul Bracewell, Pat Van Den Hauwe, Neil Pointon, Graeme Sharpe, Wayne Clarke, Gary Stevens, Ian Snodin, Neil Adams, Mick Lyons, Graham Smith (Youth Development). *Front row:* Trevor Steven, Adrian Heath, Kevin Ratcliffe, Colin Harvey, Peter Reid, Kevin Sheedy, Alan Harper.

Stadium Capacity: 52,691.
Pitch Dimensions: 112 × 78yds.
Telephone: 051–521 2020, **Clubcall:** 0898–121199.
Chairman: P. D. Carter CBE.　　**Vice-Chairman:** T. H. W. Scott.
Directors: A. W. Waterworth, K. M. Tamlin, D. A. B. Newton, D. H. Pitcher, D. M. Marsh.
Manager: Colin Harvey.
Post-War Managers: Theo Kelly, Cliff Britton, Ian Buchan, John Carey, Harry Catterick, Billy Bingham, Gordon Lee, Howard Kendall (8).
Assistant Manager: Terry Darracott.　　**Physio:** C. Goodson.
Secretary/Chief Executive: J. Greenwood.
Marketing Manager: Derek Johnston.
Sales Promotion Manager: Nigel Coates.
Sponsors: N. E. C.
Founded: 1878.
Turned Professional: 1885.　　**Nickname:** The Toffeemen.　　**Former Names:** St Domingo FC, 1878–79.
Former Grounds: Stanley Park 1878–82, Priory Road 1882–84, Anfield 1884–92.
Record Attendance: 78,299 v Liverpool, Division 1, 18 September 1948.
Record Victory: 11–2 v Derby Co, FA Cup 1st Round, 1889–90.
Record Defeat: 4–10 v Tottenham H, Division 1, 11 October 1958.
Most League Points: (3 for a win) 90, Division 1, 1984–85. (2 for a win) 66, Division 1, 1969–70.
Most League Goals: 121, Division 2, 1930–31.
Highest League Scorer in a Season: William Ralph Dixie Dean, 60, Division 1, 1927–28 (League record).
Highest Total of League Goals: William Ralph Dixie Dean, 349, 1925–37.
Most League Appearances: Ted Sagar, 465, 1929–53.
League History: 1888 Founder Members of the League, 1930–31 Division 2, 1931–51 Division 1, 1951–54 Division 2, 1954– Division 1.
Honours: Division 1 Champions 1890–01, 1914–15, 1927–28, 1931–32, 1938–39, 1962–63, 1969–70, 1984–85, 1986–87, runners-up 1889–90, 1894–95, 1904–05, 1908–09, 1911–12, 1985–86. Division 2 Champions 1930–31, runners-up 1953–54. FA Cup winners 1906, 1933, 1966, 1984, runners-up 1893, 1897, 1907, 1968, 1985, 1986. League Cup runners-up 1977, 1984. European Cup-Winners' Cup winners 1985.
Colours: Royal blue shirts, white shorts, blue socks with white turnovers. **Second strip:** Yellow shirts, blue shorts, yellow socks.

EVERTON – LEAGUE RECORD 1987–88

Match no/Opp/Date	Date	Mimms	Van Den Hauwe	Pointon	Ratcliffe	Watson	Harper	Steven	Clarke	Sharp	Adams	Power	Marshall	Mountfield	Reid	Snodin	Sheedy	Heath	Southall	Wilson	Stevens	Jones	FT(HT)Att Lge pos
1. Norwich*	15.8	1	2	3	4	5	6	7	8	9	10	11^1											1-0(1-0)31,728 —
2. Wimbledon	18.8	1	2	3	4	5	6		8	9^1	7	11	10†	12									1-0(0-1)7763 —
3. Nottm F	22.8	1	2	3	4	5		7	8	9†		11	12		6	10							0-0(0-0)20,445 9
4. Sheff Wed*	29.8	1			4	5	2	7‡	8^2	9		11†			6	10		12					4-0(1-0)29,649 4
5. QPR	2.9	1		3	4	5	2	7	8†	9		11‡	12		6	10		14					0-1(0-1)15,380 —
6. Spurs*	5.9	1	3	11	4	5	2	7	8†	9					6	10	12						0-1(0-1)32,389 8
7. Luton	12.9		3	11†	4	5	2	7		9‡		14	12		6	10		8	1				1-2(1-1)8124 9
8. Manchester*	19.9		3	11	4	5	2	7		9^2					6	10		8	1				2-1(1-0)38,439 7
9. Coventry*	26.9		2†	3	4	5	6‡	7	8^1	9					14	10		12	1	11			1-2(1-2)28,153 9
10. Sthampton	3.10		3		4	5	12	7	8†	9^4					6	10		14	1	11†	2		4-0(3-0)15,719 9
11. Chelsea*	10.10	1	3		4	5				9^2					6	10	8^2		1		2		4-1(2-0)32,004 8
12. Newcastle	17.10	1	3		4	5	12	7		9					6	10^1		8		11	2†		1-1(1-1)20,266 8
13. Watford*	24.10		3		4	5		7		9^1					6	10		8^1	1	11	2		2-0(1-0)25,501 6
14. Liverpool	1.11		3		4	5		7	8†	9				12	6	10			1	11	2		0-2(0-1)44,760 —
15. West Ham*	14.11		3		4	5^1	12	7†		9^1					6^1	10	11‡	8	1	14	2		3-1(3-0)29,405 5
16. Portsmouth	21.11		3	12	4	5		7	14	9^1					6	10	11‡	8†	1		2		1-0(0-1)17,724 5
17. Oxford*	28.11		3		4	5		7							6	10†	11	8	1	12	2		0-0(0-0)25,443 5
18. Charlton	5.12		3		4	5		7		9	12				6	10	11	8†	1		2		0-0(0-0)7208 5
19. Derby*	12.12		3		4	5		7^1		9					6	10^1	11	8^1	1		2		3-0(1-0)26,224 3
20. Arsenal	19.12		3		4	5^1		7		9					6	10	11†	8	1	12	2		1-1(0-0)34,857 5
21. Luton*	26.12		3		4	5		7		9					6	10		8^2	1	11	2		2-0(1-0)32,242 4
22. Man Utd	28.12		3		4	5^1		7	12	9					6	10		8	1	11†	2		1-2(0-0)47,024 5
23. Sheff Wed	1.1		3		4	5		7	12	9					6	10		8†	1	11	2		0-1(0-1)26,433 6
24. Nottm F*	3.1		3		4	5		7		9^1					6	10		8	1	11	2		1-0(1-0)21,680 —
25. Norwich	16.1		4	3		5	12	7		9^2					6†			8^1	1	11	2		3-0(1-0)15,750 3
26. QPR*	13.2		4	3^1		5	12	7†		9	11	14			6	10†		8	1	11	2		2-0(1-0)24,724 4
27. Sthampton*	27.2		3		4	5			8	9	11^1	7†			6	10			1		2	12	1-0(1-0)20,764 4
28. Newcastle*	5.3		4	3		5	6	7	8^1	9						10	11		1		2		1-0(1-0)25,674 4
29. Spurs	9.3		4	3		5	6	7	8	9	10‡	14					11	12	1		2†		1-2(0-1)18,662 —
30. Chelsea	12.3		4	3		5	6	7	8	9							11		1		2		0-0(0-0)17,390 3
31. Liverpool*	20.3		4	3		5	10	7	8†	9		14			6		11‡	12	1		2		1-0(1-0)44,162 —
32. Watford	26.3		4	3			6	7	8^1	9	10			5			11^1		1		2		2-1(1-0)13,503 3
33. Wimbledon*	29.3		3^1		4		7^1		8		10			5	6		11	9	1		2		2-2(2-2)20,351 —
34. West Ham	4.4		4	3			10	7	8†					5	6	12	11	9	1		2		0-0(0-0)21,195 4
35. Portsmouth*	9.4		4	3		5	10	7^1							6	8	11	9^1	1		2		2-1(1-1)21,292 3
36. Coventry	19.4		4	3		5		7	8	9^1					6	10†	12^1		1	11	2		2-0(1-0)15,641 —
37. Oxford	23.4		4	3		5	14	7	8^1	9					6	12	10‡		1	11†	2		1-1(1-1)7619 3
38. Charlton*	30.4		4	3		5	10	7^1		9					6		11	8	1		2		1-0(0-0)20,372 3
39. Derby	2.5		3			5	8	7		9	11			4	6	10			1		2		0-0(0-0)17,974 3
40. Arsenal*	7.5		4	3		5^1	12	7	8†	9		11			6	10‡	14		1		2		1-2(1-2)22,445 4
Apps(subs)/goals		8(0) 0	28(0) 0	32(1) 3	24(0) 0	37(0) 4	21(7) 0	36(0) 6	24(3) 10	32(0) 13	7(1) 0	12(2) 2	1(3) 0	4(5) 0	32(0) 1	29(2) 2	14(3) 1	23(6) 9	23(0) 0	13(3) 0	31(0) 0	0(1) 0	Final League Position: 4

Own goals: Parker, match 26; Fenwick, match 29.

DIVISION 4

EXETER CITY

St James Park, Exeter EX4 6PX.

Back row (left to right): Mike Radford (Youth Development Officer), Melvyn Gwinnett, Richard Massey, Roy Carter, Nick Marker, Shaun Taylor, Paul Williams, Andrew Watson, Paul Olsson, Richard Cooper, John Shaw, Colin Appleton. *Front row:* Jamie Harris, Steve Harrower, Brendon O'Connell, Tony Kellow, Keith Viney, Gordon Nisbet, Dean Edwards, Paul Batty, Scot Hiley

Stadium Capacity: 17,086.
Pitch Dimensions: 114 × 73yds.
Telephone: 0392–54073, Commercial dept: 0392–59466.
Chairman: A. I. Doble.
President: W. C. Hill.
Directors: I. M. Couch, A. Gooch JP, M. Holladay, G. Vece, P. Carter, B. Snell.
Manager: Terry Cooper.
Post-War Managers: George Roughton, Norman Kirkman, Norman Dodgin, Bill Thompson, Frank Broome, Glen Wilson, Cyril Spiers, Jack Edwards, Ellis Stuttard, Jock Basford, Frank Broome, John Newman, Bobby Saxton, Brian Godfrey, Gerry Francis, Jim Iley, Colin Appleton (17).
Secretary: Stuart Brailey.
Commercial Manager: Tony Kellow.
Sponsors: Facer Books.
Founded: 1904.
Turned Professional: 1908.
Nickname: The Grecians.
Former Names: None.
Former Grounds: None.
Record Attendance: 20,984 v Sunderland, FA Cup 6th Round replay, 4 March 1931.
Record Victory: 8–1 v Coventry C, Division 3(S), 16 October, 1948 and v Northampton T, Division 3(S), 12 April, 1958.
Record Defeat: 0–9 v Notts Co, Division 3(S), 16 October, 1948 and v Northampton T, Division 3(S), 12 April, 1958.
Most League Points: (3 for a win) 57, Division 3, 1981–82. (2 for a win) 62, Division 4, 1976–77.
Most League Goals: 88, Division 3(S), 1932–33.
Highest League Scorer in a Season: Fred Whitlow, 34, Division 3(S), 1932–33.
Highest Total of League Goals: Tony Kellow, 125, 1976–78, 1980–83, 1985–87.
Most League Appearances: Arnold Mitchell, 495, 1952–66.
League History: 1920 Elected to Division 3, 1921–1958 Division 3(S), 1958–64 Division 4, 1964–66 Division 3, 1966–77 Division 4, 1977–84 Division 3, 1984– Division 4.
Honours: Division 4 runners-up 1976–77. Division 3(S) runners-up 1923–33. Division 3(S) Cup winners 1934.
Colours: Red and white striped shirts, black shorts, black socks with red turnovers. **Second strip:** All light blue with dark blue trim.

EXETER CITY – LEAGUE RECORD 1987-88

Match no/Opp	Date	Shaw	Nisbet	Viney	Marker	Taylor	Carter	Batty	Edwards	O'Connell	Olsson	Harrower	Cooper	Kellow	Massey	Williams	Watson	Phillips	Gwinnett	Hiley	Delve	Rowbotham	Collins	Milton	Harris	FT(HT)Att Lge pos
1. Cambridge*	15.8	1	2	3	4	5	6²	7	8	9¹	10†	11	12													3–0(2–0)2650 —
2. Swansea	22.8	1	2	3	4		6	7	8		10†	11	5	12¹												2–0(1–0)5557 2
3. Newport*	29.8	1	2	3	4		6	7¹	8	9†	10	11¹	5¹	12												3–0(0–0)2628 1
4. Tranmere	31.8	1	2	3	4		6	7	8	9¹	10	11	5†	12												1–2(0–1)3107 —
5. Wrexham*	5.9	1	2	3	4		6	7¹	8	9‡	10	11†	12	5	14											1–1(0–0)2719 1
6. Orient	12.9	1	2	3‡	4	5	6	7	8²	9	10†	14	12¹			11										3–2(1–0)3613 1
7. Carlisle*	16.9	1	2	3	4	5	6	7	8	9†	11‡	14	12		10¹											1–1(1–1)3347 —
8. Rochdale*	19.9	1	2	3	4	5	6	7	8†	9‡		14	12₁		10	11										1–1(0–1)2628 2
9. Colchester	25.9	1	2	3	4		6	7¹	8¹		10	11	5				9									2–0(1–0)1443 —
10. Hartlepool	30.9	1	2	3	4	5	6	7	8¹		10†	11			12	9										1–3(1–1)2973 —
11. Torquay*	3.10	1	2	3	4	5		7	8		10‡	11	14	12		6†	9									0–1(0–1)6281 5
12. Scarboro	10.10	1	2†	3		5	14	8	12	11	7	4	10	6‡	9¹											1–3(1–1)2472 7
13. Burnley*	17.10			3	5	4	7‡	8¹	6†	11	2	10	12		9			1	14							1–2(1–1)2780 14
14. Bolton	20.10			3	5	4	7	8		11	2	9	6					1	10							0–1(0–0)4165 —
15. Crewe*	24.10			3	5	4	7¹	8†		11	2	9¹	6¹		12	1			10							3–1(1–0)2149 14
16. Hereford	31.10	1		3	5	4	7†	8	9¹	11	2		12						10	6						1–1(0–0)2200 15
17. Cardiff	7.11	1		3	5	4	7¹	8†	9	12	11	2							10	6¹						2–3(1–1)3474 18
18. Stockport*	21.11	1		3	5	4		8	9	11	2		6						7	10²						2–1(1–0)2217 14
19. Darlington	8.12	1		3	5	4	7	8	9‡	11	12	2†								6	10¹	14				1–4(0–3)1107 —
20. Scunthorpe*	12.12	1		3	5	4	7	9	10₁	2	8	6									11					1–1(0–0)1831 17
21. Halifax	18.12	1		3	5	4	7‡	9	10	12	2	8	6†							14	11					0–2(0–1)1302 —
22. Colchester*	26.12	1		3	5	4	7	9	10	2	8		6						11†			12				0–2(0–0)2675 18
23. Wolves	28.12	1		3	5	4	7	9	10	12	2	8	11‡		6†					14						0–3(0–1)15,588 18
24. Newport	1.1	1		3	5	4	7	10	6¹	2	8	9								11						1–1(1–1)1691 20
25. Orient*	2.1	1		3	5	4	7¹	9¹	10	6	2	8								11						2–3(1–1)2568 20
26. Swansea*	9.1			3	5	4	7	9¹	10¹	6¹	2	12	14	1	8‡				11†							3–1(1–0)2225 18
27. Rochdale	16.1			3	5	4	7	9†	10	6	2	12		1	8				11							0–0(0–0)1431 20
28. Carlisle	23.1			3	5	4	7	9	10	6	2	12		1	8†	11										0–0(0–0)1699 19
29. Tranmere*	30.1			3†	5	4	7‡	9	10	6	2	8	14	12	1	11										0–1(0–1)2261 19
30. Wolves*	13.2			3	5	4	7	9	10²	6	2	12		1	8†	11										2–4(0–2)3483 21
31. Cambridge	19.2			3	5	7	11	9¹‡	10	6	2	4	8†	1	12	14										1–2(0–0)1878 —
32. Torquay	27.2			3	5¹	7	9	10	2	8	4	6	1	11†	12											1–1(0–1)3383 21
33. Hartlepool*	2.3			3	5	7	9	10₁	2	8	4	6	1	11												1–0(0–0)1573 —
34. Burnley	5.3			3	5	7	9	10	12	2	8	4	6†	1	11											0–3(0–1)6052 20
35. Peterboro*	9.3			3	5	7†	9	10‡	6	2	8	4	1	11	12		14									0–1(0–0)1584 —
36. Scarboro*	12.3			3	5	10	2	8	6	1	7	4	11	9¹												1–0(0–0)1738 20
37. Hereford*	19.3			3	5	12	10	8	2	6	1	7¹	4‡	11	9											2–2(0–2)1628 20
38. Wrexham	22.3			3	5	12	14	10	8	2	6†	1	7	4	11	9‡										0–3(0–0)963 —
39. Crewe	26.3			3	5	12	10	8	2	6	4	1	7	11	9†											0–0(0–0)1665 21
40. Cardiff*	2.4			3	5	12	10	8	2	6	4	1	7	11	9†											0–2(0–2)2649 22
41. Stockport	4.4			3†	5	12	9	10	8	2	6	4	1	7	11¹											1–2(1–0)2161 22
42. Bolton*	9.4			3	5	12	9	10₁	8	2	6	4	1	7†	11											1–1(1–0)1962 22
43. Peterboro	23.4			3	5	4	9‡	10	8	2¹	6	12	1	7†	11	14										1–2(0–1)2278 22
44. Darlington*	30.4			3	5	4	9³	10¹	7	2	6	1	12	8†	11											4–1(0–0)1515 21
45. Scunthorpe	2.5			3	5	4	12	9¹	10	8	2	6	1	7†	11											1–0(0–0)6736 21
46. Halifax*	7.5			3	5	4	12	9	10	7	2	6	1	8¹†	11											1–2(1–0)1602 22

Final League Position: 22

Apps(subs)/goals: 22(0)0 | 12(0)0 | 46(0)0 | 11(0)1 | 41(0)1 | 37(4)2 | 29(3)6 | 40(3)12 | 39(0)11 | 30(5)2 | 30(3)1 | 5(11)4 | 17(6)1 | 4(2)1 | 12(1)0 | 5(0)1 | 24(0)0 | 12(3)1 | 12(3)1 | 20(3)2 | 8(1)0 | 2(0)3 | 5(4)1

Own goal: Stevens, match 37.

DIVISION 3

FULHAM

Craven Cottage, Stevenage Road, Fulham, London SW6 6HH.

Back row (left to right): John Marshall, Jeff Hopkins, Glen Thomas, Justin Skinner, Shaun Gore, Jim Hicks, Keith Oakes, Leroy Rosenoir, Leo Donnellan, *Third row:* Terry Bullivant (First Team Coach), Rod Brathwaite, Laurence Batty, Kevin Hoddy, Jim Stannard, Brian Cottington, John Vaughan, Kenny Achampong, Jack Burkett (Ass. Manager). *Second row:* Peter Scott, Gordon Davies, Wayne Kerrins, Ray Lewington (Player/Manager), Richard Langley, Gary Elkins, Gary Barnett. *Front row:* Kevin Caskey, Paul Donovan, Sean Tobin, Jason Howes, Trevor Jones, Nicky Eaton, Terry Gale, Gavin French, Steven Greaves.

Stadium Capacity: 25,680.
Pitch Dimensions: 110 × 75yds.
Telephone: 01–736 6561, **Recorded information:** 01–736 7035.
Chairman: Jimmy Hill.
Vice-Chairman: W. F. Muddyman.
Directors: D. J. Gardner, C. A. Swain, A. Muddyman.
Manager: Ray Lewington.
Post-War Managers: Jack Peart, Frank Osborne, Bill Dodgin (Snr), Doug Livingstone, Bedford Jezzard, Vic Buckingham, Bobby Robson, Johnny Haynes, Bill Dodgin (Jnr), Alec Stock, Bobby Campbell, Malcolm Macdonald, Ray Harford (13).
Assistant Manager: Jack Burkett.
Physio: David Sharp.
Secretary: Mrs Yvonne Haines.
Commercial Director: D. J. Gardner.
Founded: 1879.
Turned Professional: 1898.
Nickname: Cottagers.
Former Names: Fulham St Andrew's 1879–98.
Former Grounds: Lille Road, Fulham Cross; Barn Elms, Barnes; Ranelagh House; Stansfields;s Field, Fulham Road; Half–Moon Cricket Ground, Putney; 1896 Craven Cottage.
Record Attendance: 49,335 v Millwall, Division 2, 8 October 1938.
Record Victory: 10–1 v Ipswich T, Division 1, 26 December, 1963.
Record Defeat: 0–10 v Liverpool, League Cup 2nd Round, 1st Leg, 23 September 1986.
Most League Points: (3 for a win) 78, Division 3, 1981–82. (2 for a win) 60, Division 2, 1958–59 and Division 3, 1970–71.
Most League Goals: 111, Division 3(S), 1931–32.
Highest League Scorer in a Season: Frank Newton, 43, Division 3(S), 1931–32.
Highest Total of League Goals: Bedford Jezzard, 154, 1948–56.
Most League Appearances: Johnny Haynes, 594, 1952–70.
League History: 1907 Elected to Division 2, 1928–32 Division 3(S), 1943–49 Division 2, 1949–52 Division 1, 1952–59 Division 2, 1959–68 Division 1, 1968–69 Division 2, 1969–71 Division 3, 1971–80 Division 2, 1980–82 Division 3, 1982–86 Division 2, 1986– Division 3.
Honours: Division 2 Champions 1948–49, runners-up 1958–59. Division 3 runners-up 1970–71. Division 3(S) Champions 1931–32. FA Cup runners-up 1975.
Colours: White shirts with black trim, black shorts, white socks.
Second strip: All red.

FULHAM – LEAGUE RECORD 1987–88

Match no/Opp/Date		Stannard	Langley	Thomas	Lewington	Oakes	Hopkins	Marshall	Skinner	Rosenior	Davies	Barnett	Kerrins	Donnellan	Achampong	Hicks	Elkins	Wilson	Walker	Eckhardt	Pike	Hoddy	Scott	Gore	Cole	Greaves	FT(HT)Att	Lge pos
1. Walsall	15.8	1	2	3	4†	5	6	7	8	9¹	10	11	12														1-0(0-0)4691	—
2. Doncaster*	22.8	1	2	3	4†	5	6	7‡	8	9²	10²	11	12	14													4-0(3-0)4157	1
3. Brighton	29.8	1	2	3	4	6	5	7	8†	9	10‡	11	12	14													0-2(0-1)8773	6
4. Notts Co*	1.9	1	2	3	4	6	5	7	8†	9‡	10	11	12	14													0-0(0-0)4767	—
5. Mansfield	4.9	1		3	4†	6	5	7	8	9¹	10¹	11	2	12													2-0(0-0)3536	—
6. Gillingham*	12.9	1		3	4†	6	5	7	8‡	9	10	11	2	12	14												0-2(0-0)7404	10
7. Chester	16.9	1		3	4	6	5	7	8	9²	10†	11	2	12													2-1(1-1)2469	—
8. Port Vale*	19.9	1		3	4		5	7	8¹	9	10†	11	2	12	6												1-1(1-0)3894	8
9. Bristol R*	26.9	1		3	4†	6	5		8	9¹	10¹	11¹	12				2	7									3-1(0-1)4614	2
10. Sunderland*	29.9	1		3	4†	6	5		8†	9	10	11	12				2	7									0-2(0-1)6996	—
11. Blackpool	3.10	1		3	4	6	5		8	9	10	11					2	7¹									1-2(0-1)4973	11
12. York*	10.10	1		3	4	6	5	8		9	10†	12					2	7	11²								3-1(2-1)4057	5
13. Wigan	17.10	1		3	4	6	5	8		9²	10						2	7	11¹								3-1(2-0)2806	5
14. Southend	20.10	1		3	4	5	6	8		9¹	10¹						2	7	11								2-0(1-0)3419	—
15. Aldershot*	24.10	1			4†	5	6‡	8	12	9	10¹			3	14		2	7	11								1-2(1-0)6530	5
16. Grimsby*	3.11	1	3†		4‡	5		7	8₂	9¹	10¹	11¹	12	14		6	2										5-0(3-0)3493	—
17. Nthampton	7.11	1	2	3	4	5		7	8	9	10	11				6											0-0(0-0)6717	6
18. Rotherham	21.11	1	2	3	4†				12	9	10¹	7				6	8		11¹	5							2-0(1-0)3427	5
19. Preston*	28.11	1	2	3	4†					9	10	7		12		6	8		11	5							0-1(0-1)5324	5
20. Bury	12.12	1	2	3	4					9¹	10	7				6	8		11	5							1-1(1-1)2643	5
21. Bristol C	15.12	1	2	3	4			7†		9	10					6	8		11	5	12						0-4(0-3)6150	—
22. Chesterfield*	19.12	1	2	3	4†			10	9		7¹			12	6		8		11	5							1-3(1-1)4006	7
23. Bristol R	26.12	1	2	3	4†				9¹	10	7			6	8		11	5			12						1-3(1-1)4718	9
24. Brentford*	28.12	1	2	3	4†				9	10	12			6	8¹	11	5			7¹							2-2(0-0)9340	9
25. Brighton*	1.1	1	2	3	4				9	10¹	7			12		6	8†		5	14	11						1-2(1-0)6530	10
26. Gillingham	2.1	1	2†	3	4				9²		7‡	8		10	12	6			5	14	11						2-2(1-2)6001	10
27. Doncaster	9.1	1		3	4				9¹	10¹	7	2		6			11	5			8						2-2(1-0)1827	9
28. Port Vale*	16.1	1		4¹	5			8		10†	7	6		12			11	2	9								1-2(1-0)3784	11
29. Notts Co	30.1	1		3	4	5		9		10†	7			12			11¹	2			8	6					1-5(1-2)6107	11
30. Mansfield*	6.2	1			4‡	5			12	9	10†	7				3	14	11	2		8	6					0-0(0-0)3330	12
31. Brentford	14.2	1			4‡	5		10†	9	12	7			3	14¹	11	2			8	6						1-3(0-1)8712	—
32. Walsall*	20.2	1			5				9¹	10¹	7			3	4	11	2			8	6						2-0(1-0)3718	11
33. Blackpool*	27.2	1			5			14	9¹	10†	7			12	3	4‡	11¹	2		8¹	6						3-1(1-0)4072	11
34. Sunderland	1.3	1			5				12	9	10†	7			3	4	11	2			8	6					0-2(0-2)11,379	—
35. Wigan*	5.3	1			5			4¹	9¹	10	7			3		11¹	2			8	6						3-2(3-2)3860	9
36. York	12.3	1			5	6	12	4	9¹	10¹	7†			3		11¹	2			8	6						3-1(2-1)2560	9
37. Bristol C*	19.3	1			5	6	9	4		7†		10		3		11‡	2		14	8	12						0-0(0-0)4896	10
38. Aldershot	26.3	1			5	6	11¹	4		7¹		10¹		3		2			12	8†	9						3-0(1-0)4448	10
39. Nthampton	2.4	1			5	6	9	4¹		12	7¹	10†		3		2			8	11							2-3(1-1)6211	11
40. Rotherham*	4.4	1			5	6	9	4¹			7²	10		3		2			8	11							3-1(2-0)4402	9
41. Grimsby	9.4	1			5	6	9¹				7	10¹		3		2		4	8	11							2-0(1-0)3123	8
42. Chester*	15.4	1			5	6	9	4†			7	10		3		12	2		8	11¹							1-0(0-0)4131	—
43. Southend*	23.4	1			5	6	9	4		12	7¹	10†		3		2¹			8	11							3-1(1-0)5043	7
44. Preston	30.4	1			5	6	9	4‡		12	14¹	10†		3		7	2		8	11							1-2(0-1)4192	8
45. Bury*	2.5	1			5	6	9			10†	7			3		4	2		12	8	11						0-1(0-1)5283	9
46. Chesterfield	7.5	1			5†	6	9			10	7			3		4	2		8	11	12						0-1(0-1)3084	9

Appearances/goals: 46(0) 0 · 15(0) 0 · 22(0) 0 · 31(0) 1 · 35(0) 0 · 24(1) 2 · 27(5) 6 · 34(0) 20 · 35(4) 13 · 39(3) 9 · 8(6) 0 · 0(1) 0 · 9(6) 3 · 9(0) 0 · 18(2) 3 · 25(1) 8 · 29(0) 1 · 0(3) 0 · 22(0) 2 · 7(1) 0 · 9(0) 1 · 0(1) 0

Final League Position: 9

DIVISION 3 | # GILLINGHAM

Priestfield Stadium, Gillingham ME7 4DD.

Back row (left to right): Mark Elsey, Howard Pritchard, Mel Eves, Ivan Haines, David Shearer, David Smith, Mark Westherly, Irvin Gernon. *Middle row:*. John Gorman (Ass. Manager), Brian Clarke, Phil Kite, Gary West, Paul Taylor (Manager), Colin Greenall, Ron Hillyard, Les Berry, Bill Collins (Physio). *Front row:* George Shipley, Steve Lovell, Paul Haylock, Keith Peacock, Neil Luff, Graham Pearce, Trevor Quow..

Stadium Capacity: 19,581.
Pitch Dimensions: 114 × 75yds.
Telephone: 0634–51854.
Chairman: R. J. Wood.
Vice-Chairman: The Rt. Hon. Earl Henry Sondes.
Directors: R. J. Wood, R. D. Welham, D. J. A. Berry.
Manager: Paul Taylor.
Post-War Managers: Archie Clark, Harry Barratt, Freddie Cox, Basil Hayward, Andy Nelson, Len Ashurst, Gerry Summers, Keith Peacock (8).
Assistant Manager: John Gorman.
Secretary: Harold Rumsey.
Commercial Manager: Kay Carver.
Sponsors: Chatham Maritime (English Estates Ltd).
Founded: 1893.
Turned Professional: 1894.
Nickname: The Gills.
Former Names: New Brompton 1893–1913.
Former Grounds: None.
Record Attendance: 23,002 v QPR, FA Cup 3rd Round, 19 January 1948.
Record Victory: 10–0 v Chesterfield, Division 3, 5 September 1987.
Record Defeat: 2–9 v Nottingham F, Division 3(S), 18 November 1950.
Most League Points: (3 for a win) 83, Division 3, 1984–85. (2 for a win) 62, Division 4, 1973–74.
Most League Goals: 90, Division 4, 1973–74.
Highest League Scorer in a Season: Ernie Morgan, 31, Division 3(S), 1954–55 and Brian Yeo, 31, Division 4, 1973–74.
Highest Total of League Goals: Brian Yeo, 135, 1963–75.
Most League Appearances: John Simpson, 571, 1957–72.
League History: 1920 Founder Members of Division 3, 1921 Division 3(S), 1938–44 Southern League, 1944–46 Kent League, 1946–50 Southern League, 1950 Re–elected to Division 3(S), 1958–64 Division 4, 1964–71 Division 3, 1971–74 Division 4, 1974– Division 3.
Honours: Division 4 Champions 1963–64, runners-up 1973–74.
Colours: Royal blue shirts, white shorts and socks with royal blue trim. **Second strip:** Red shirts, black shorts and socks.

GILLINGHAM – LEAGUE RECORD 1987–88

Match no/Opp	Date	Kite	Haylock	German	Shipley	West	Greenall	Pritchard	Shearer	Lovell	Elsey	Smith D	Quow	Eves	Pearce	Lillis	Hillyard	Parks	Berry	Cooper	Peacock	Weatherly	Luff	Haines	Walker	Docker	Smith M	Palmer	FT(HT)Att Lge pos
1. Blackpool*	15.8	1	2	3	4	5	6	7	8	9†	10	11	12																0-0(0-0)4430 —
2. Grimsby	22.8	1	2	3	4	5	6	7	8†	9	10		11	12															0-2(0-1)2901 18
3. Southend*	29.8	1	2		4	5	6	7¹	8¹†	9⁴	10‡	11²	14		3	12													8-1(4-0)4154 10
4. Wigan	31.8	1	2		4	5	6	7	8¹†	9	10	11			3														1-1(1-0)3412 —
5. Chesterfield*	5.9	1	2	4²‡		5	6¹	7²	8²	9†	10²	11¹	14		3	12													10-0(5-0)4099 7
6. Fulham	12.9		2		4	5	6	7	8¹	9¹	10	11			3		1												2-0(0-0)7404 4
7. Sunderland*	15.9		2		4	5	6	7	8	9	10	11			3			1											0-0(0-0)9184 —
8. York*	19.9		2	4†	5¹	6	7	8		9	10²	11	12		3			1											3-1(0-1)5507 2
9. Bristol C	26.9		2			5	6	7	8†	9¹‡	10¹	11¹	4	12	3				14										3-3(2-1)10,070 5
10. Chester*	29.9		2			5	6	7	8†	9	10	11	4		3				12										0-1(0-0)5193 —
11. Doncaster	3.10	1	2			5		7†	8‡	9¹	10	11	4	14¹	3	12			6										2-4(0-2)1647 12
12. Bristol R*	10.10	1	2			5		7¹		9¹		11¹	4		3				6	8	10								3-0(0-0)4399 7
13. Mansfield	17.10	1	2			5		7		9¹	8	11	4†		3				6	10									2-2(2-1)2957 8
14. Preston	20.10	1	2			5		7		9	6	12	4†		3				11	8¹	10								1-1(1-1)5676 —
15. Notts Co*	24.10	1	2			5	6	7		9²	4	11			3					8¹	10								3-1(0-1)5551 7
16. Port Vale	31.10	1	2			5	6	7		9	10				3					8	11								0-0(0-0)3495 7
17. Brentford*	3.11	1	2			5	6	7		9	10		4		3‡	12				8†	11	14							0-1(0-1)4529 —
18. Brighton*	7.11	1	2			5	6₁	7		9	10		4		3‡	11†				8	14	12							1-0(0-0)6437 —
19. Nthampton	21.11	1	2			5	6	7		9¹	3		4			11‡				8	12		14					10†	1-2(1-0)5151 11
20. Bury*	28.11	1	2		5¹		6	7		9	10		4		12²	3				8†	11								3-3(1-1)3981 12
21. Rotherham	12.12	1	2	12			6	7¹		9‡	10		4		8¹	3			14	11	5†								2-1(2-0)2557 10
22. Walsall*	18.12	1	2			5	6	7		9	10		4		8†	3			12	11									0-1(0-0)4020 —
23. Bristol C*	26.12	1	2			5	6	7		9‡	10	11¹			8†				12	4	14								1-1(0-1)6457 11
24. Aldershot	28.12	1		3		5	6	7		9	2	11	12							8	10	4†							0-6(0-5)4734 13
25. Southend	1.1		2	6		5		7		9¹	10	11†	12				1			8¹	4¹								3-1(2-0)5254 12
26. Fulham*	2.1		2	6		5		7		9	10	11			3		1			8²	4								2-2(2-1)6001 12
27. York	16.1		2	3	5‡	6		7¹		9¹	10	11	12				1			8†	4	14							2-0(0-0)2129 9
28. Wigan*	23.1		2	3†	5	6‡		7		9	10	11	8				1			12	4	14							0-1(0-1)4256 9
29. Sunderland	30.1				5	6	7			9	2	11	8		3		1		12	10¹	4								1-2(0-2)16,195 10
30. Grimsby*	2.2				5	6	7			9	2	11	8†		3		1		12	10¹	4								1-1(1-0)2993 —
31. Chesterfield	6.2				5	6	7			9³	2	11†	8		3		1		10	4	12								4-1(0-2)2141 9
32. Aldershot*	13.2		2	12¹		5				9₁	4	11	8		3		1		10		6†								2-1(0-0)4001 9
33. Blackpool	20.2		2	6				7		9²	4¹	11	8		3		1		10		5								3-3(0-0)3045 9
34. Doncaster*	27.2	1	2	6				7		9¹₁	4	11	8		3				12	10¹	5†								3-1(1-1)4041 8
35. Chester	2.3	1	2	6	11	5		7¹†		9	4		8		12	3‡			14	10									1-3(0-0)1638 —
36. Mansfield*	5.3	1	2†	6	11			7		9	4		8		12	3			5	10									0-0(0-0)3720 9
37. Bristol R	12.3	1		6	4	5		7		9	11		8		3				2	10†	12								0-2(0-0)3846 10
38. Port Vale*	19.3			6‡	10	5		7†		9	14	11	8		3		1		2		4	12							0-0(0-0)3459 9
39. Notts Co	26.3			3	7	5				9¹	11		8				1		2	10	4				6				1-0(0-0)6473 9
40. Brighton	2.4			3	7	5	12			9	11		8				1		2	10†	4				6				0-2(0-2)9256 10
41. Nthampton*	4.4			3	7†	5				9¹	14	11	8‡		10		1		2	12	4				6				1-2(0-0)4126 12
42. Brentford	9.4			3	5†					9	7	11	8		10¹		1		2		4¹				6				2-2(0-0)3875 11
43. Preston*	23.4			3†		5				9	11¹	8		10²	7‡	1			2		4	6			12	14			4-0(1-0)2721 12
44. Bury	30.4			3		5		7¹†		9	11	8			10		1		2	12	4				6				1-2(1-1)1433 13
45. Rotherham*	2.5					5		7		9	11†	8			10		1		2	12	4				6		3		0-2(0-1)3015 14
46. Walsall	7.5	1				5				9	3	8			10		2		11	4	7				6				0-0(0-0)8850 13
Apps(subs)/goals		26(0)0	32(0)0	19(2)1	15(0)2	42(0)2	25(0)2	40(2)8	11(0)5	46(0)25	37(2)6	34(4)7	33(7)1	3(2)0	32(0)0	3(4)0	18(0)0	2(0)0	15(5)0	24(7)8	26(0)2	8(9)0	0(1)0	0(0)0	7(0)0	0(1)0	1(0)0	10(0)0	Final League Position: 13

Own goal: Hunter, match 31.

DIVISION 4

GRIMSBY TOWN

Blundell Park, Cleethorpes, South Humberside DN35 7PY.

Back row (left to right): John McDermott, Steve Saunders, Andy Dixon, Neil Robinson, Dave Moore. *Third row:* John Frazer (Physio), Robert Thompson, Chris Grocock, Marc North, Steve Sherwood, Dave Burgess, Paul Agnew, Trevor Slack, Lee Pratt, Bobby Roberts (Manager). *Second row:* Dave Gamble (YTS), Peter Rawcliffe, Phil Turner, Don O'Riordan (Captain), Scott McGarvey, Ian Walsh, Ian Toale, Mark Lever. *Front row:* Marcus Newell (YTS), Geoff Stephenson, Tommy Watson, Lee Davies (YTS), Gary Curtis (YTS), Stephen Bell.

Stadium Capacity: 20,865.
Pitch Dimensions: 111 × 74yds.
Telephone: 0472–697111.
Chairman: P. W. Furneaux.
Vice-Chairman: T. Aspinall.
Directors: W. H. Carr, G. W. Duffield, B. Glover, T. J. Lindley, W. R. Ramsden, T. Wilkinson.
Manager:
Post-War Managers: Charlie Spencer, Bill Shankly, Billy Walsh, Allenby Chilton, Bill Lambton, Tim Ward, Tom Johnston, Jimmy McGuigan, Don McEvoy, Bill Harvey, Bobby Kennedy, Lawrie McMenemy, Ron Ashman, Tommy Casey, John Newman, George Kerr, David Booth, Mike Lyons, Robert Roberts (19).
Assistant Manager: D. O'Riordan.
Physio: J. Fraser.
Secretary: T. J. Lindley.
Founded: 1878. **Turned Professional:** 1890. **Nickname:** The Mariners.
Former Names: Grimsby Pelham.
Former Grounds: Clee Park, Abbey Park.
Record Attendance: 31,651 v Wolverhampton W, FA Cup 5th Round, 20 February 1937.
Record Victory: 9–2 v Darwen, Division 2, 15 April 1899.
Record Defeat: 1–9 v Arsenal, Division 1, 28 January 1931.
Most League Points: (3 for a win) 70, Division 2, 1983–84. (2 for a win) 68, Division 3(N), 1955–56.
Most League Goals: 103, Division 2, 1933–34.
Highest League Scorer in a Season: Pat Glover, 42, Division 2, 1933–34.
Highest Total of League Goals: Pat Glover, 182, 1930–39.
Most League Appearances: Keith Jobling, 448, 1953–69.
League History: 1892 Founder Members of Division 2, 1901–03 Division 1, 1903 Division 2, 1910 Failed Re-election, 1911 Re-elected Division 2, 1920–21 Division 3, 1921–26 Division 2(N), 1926–29 Division 2, 1929–32 Division 1, 1932–34 Division 2, 1934–38 Division 1, 1948–51 Division 2, 1951–56 Division 3(N), 1956–59 Division 2, 1959–62 Division 3, 1962–64 Division 2, 1964–68 Division 3, 1968–72 Division 4, 1972–77 Division 3, 1977–79 Division 4, 1979–80 Division 3, 1980–87 Division 2, 1987–88 Division 3, 1988– Division 4.
Honours: Division 2 Champions 1900–01, 1933–34, runners-up 1928–29. Division 3 Champions 1979–80, runners-up 1961–62. Division 4 Champions 1971–72, runners-up 1978–79. Division 3(N) Champions 1925–26, 1955–56, runners-up 1951–52. Associate Members' Cup winners 1982.
Colours: Black and white vertical striped shirts, black shorts, white socks. **Second strip:** Black and red striped shirts, black shorts, black socks with red turnover.

GRIMSBY TOWN – LEAGUE RECORD 1987–88

Match no/Opp/Date	Sherwood	McDermott	Agnew	Turner	Slack	Burgess	Robinson	Walsh	North	O'Riordan	McGarvey	Saunders	Toale	Watson	Grocock	Dixon	Rawcliffe	Curran	Moore	Lever	Cunningham	Jobling	Stubbs	FT(HT)Att Lge pos
1. Doncaster 15.8	1	2	3	4	5	6	7	8†	9	10	11	12												0-1(0-1)2482 —
2. Gillingham* 22.8	1	2†	3	7	5	6	4	8²	9	10	11			12										2-0(1-0)2901 11
3. Notts Co 29.8	1		3	4	5		7	8	9	10	11	6	2											0-0(0-0)5322 13
4. Brentford* 31.8	1		3	7	5	6	4	8	9	10	11			2										0-1(0-1)3361 —
5. Preston 5.9	1		3	4	5	6		8¹		10¹	11	7¹	2	9										3-1(2-0)5522 14
6. Mansfield* 12.9	1	12	3	4	5	6		8†	9	10¹	11‡		2	7	14¹									2-3(1-1)3410 15
7. Bury 15.9	1		3	4	5	6	9	12	8†	10	11½		2	7										2-0(2-0)1899 —
8. Chester 19.9	1		3	4	5	6	9	12	8	10	11†		2	7‡	14									0-1(0-0)1897 15
9. Walsall* 26.9	1	2	3	4	5	6		8	10	11	9†			12										0-2(0-1)3314 18
10. Rotherham 29.9	1	2		4	5	6		8	10	11	9		7		3									0-0(0-0)3375 ·
11. Southend* 3.10	1	2	3	4	5			12	8†	10¹	11	9	7	6†	14									1-3(0-3)2544 20
12. Chesterfield 10.10	1	2		4	5		6	8¹	9¹	10	11		3	7										3-0(1-0)2072 17
13. Bristol C* 17.10	1		3	4	5	6	8	9†		10	11¹		2	7	12									1-4(0-4)3100 17
14. Blackpool* 20.10	1		3	4¹	5	6	8		9	10	11		2†	7	12									1-1(1-1)2260 —
15. Nthampton 24.10	1		3	4‡¹	5	6	8		9	10	11		2†	7	12	14								1-2(1-1)5388 20
16. Brighton* 31.10	1	2			5	6‡	8		9	10	11	3		7†	4	14	12							0-1(0-1)2711 20
17. Fulham 3.11	1	2			5		4		9	10	11	8	6†	12	3		7							0-5(0-3)3493 —
18. Sunderland 7.11	1	2			5				9¹	10	11	8		4	6	3	12	7†						1-1(1-0)18,197 20
19. York* 21.11	1	2		4	5		6²		9²	10¹	11†	8		12	3		7							5-1(2-1)2200 20
20. Bristol R 28.11	1	2		4			6		9	10¹	11	8	7†		5	3			12					2-4(1-2)2787 20
21. Wigan* 12.12	1	2	3	4		5	6		9	10	11	8	7†			12								0-2(0-1)2196 —
22. Aldershot 19.12	1	2†	3	4¹	5	6			10	11	8¹	14		12	9	7‡								2-3(1-3)2405 20
23. Walsall 26.12	1		3	4	5†	6	7		9¹	10	11¹	8	14		2‡	12								2-3(1-0)6272 22
24. Port Vale* 28.12	1		3	4		5	6		9³	10	11	8			2	7								3-1(1-1)2941 21
25. Notts Co* 1.1	1		3	4		5	6		9†	10	11	8	12		2	7								0-0(0-0)5297 20
26. Mansfield 2.1	1		3	4		5	6			10	11	8	7†	14	12	2	9‡							0-1(0-1)3315 21
27. Chester* 16.1	1		3	4		5	6		9	10	11²	8		12	2	7†								2-1(0-0)2594 21
28. Bury* 26.1	1		3	4¹		5	6		10¹	11†	8		12	9	2	7								2-0(1-0)2525 —
29. Gillingham 2.2	1	7	3	4¹		5	6		9	10	11	8			2									1-1(0-1)2993 —
30. Preston* 6.2	1	7	3			5	6		9‡	10	11	8		14	12	2†								0-1(0-1)2907 21
31. Port Vale 13.2	1	3		4		5	7		9‡	10		8	6†	12	11	2			14					0-2(0-0)3417 21
32. Doncaster* 20.2	1	3			5	11			9	10		8		12	2	7†				4	6			0-0(0-0)3890 22
33. Brentford 23.2	1	12	3			5	7		9†	10	11	8¹			2					4	6¹			2-0(1-0)3534 —
34. Southend 26.2	1	9	3			5	7			10	11	8			2					4	6			0-0(0-0)3409 —
35. Bristol C 5.3	1	12	3			5	7		9†	10¹	11	8‡			2					4	6	14		1-1(0-0)8343 —
36. Rotherham* 8.3	1		3			5	7		9¹	10	11	8			2					4¹	6			2-1(1-0)3423 —
37. Chesterfield* 12.3	1	14	3			5	7		9†	10	11	8		2‡						4	6	12¹		1-0(0-0)3464 20
38. Brighton 19.3	1	14	3			5	7		9‡	10	11	8†			2					4	6	12		0-0(0-0)7269 21
39. Nthampton* 26.3	1	12	3			5	7¹		9	10		8		11	2					4‡†	6			2-2(2-0)3406 20
40. Sunderland* 2.4	1	14	3			5	7		9†	10		8‡		11	2					4	6	12		0-1(0-1)7001 21
41. York 4.4	1	9	3¹			5	7			10				11	2					4	6	8¹		2-0(1-0)3125 20
42. Fulham* 9.4	1	9	3			5	7			10		12		11	2†					4	6	8		0-2(0-1)3123 21
43. Blackpool 23.4	1		3			5	7		9†	10	11	8			2					4	6	12		0-3(0-1)2551 22
44. Bristol R* 30.4	1		3			5	7		9	10	12	8		11†‡	2					4	6			0-0(0-0)2505 22
45. Wigan 2.5	1	9†	3			5	7		12¹	10	11‡	8		14	2					4	6			1-0(0-2)2715 22
46. Aldershot* 7.5	1	11	3			5	7		9¹	10		8		12	2†					4	6			1-1(1-1)5697 22
Apps(subs)/goals	44(0)0	21(7)0	38(0)1	28(0)5	21(0)0	38(0)3	40(0)3	8(3)5	37(1)11	46(0)8	38(1)6	34(1)3	16(9)0	15(6)0	10(15)1	30(2)0	2(0)0	0(4)0	0(4)1	15(0)2	15(0)1	25(2)		

Final League Position: 22

DIVISION 4

HALIFAX TOWN

Shay Ground, Halifax HX1 2YS.

Back row (left to right): Billy Ayre (Manager), Wayne Allison, Phil Sharp, Stewart Ferebee, Jimmy Willis, Paddy Roche, Dave Robinson, Neil Matthews, Ricky Holden, Frankie Harrison, Gerry Brooke (Youth Coach). *Front row:* Paul Fleming, Billy Barr, Russell Black, Steve Thornber, Lee Richardson, Phil Brown, Mick Galloway, Adrian Shaw, Mick Matthews, Dean Martin, Tony Pearson..

Stadium Capacity: 4,021 (under review).
Pitch Dimensions: 110 × 70yds.
Telephone: 0422–53423, Promotions office: 0422–66593.
Chairman: Rod Thomas BEM.
Vice-Chairman: Jack Haymer.
President: John S. Crowther.
Vice-President: Frank Hinchcliffe.
Directors:
Manager: Bill Ayre.
Post-War Managers: Jack Breedon, Billy Wootton, Jimmy Thompson, Gerald Henry, Bobby Browne, Willie Watson, Bill Burnicle, Harry Hooper, Willie Watson, Vic Metcalfe, Alan Ball (Snr), George Kirby, Ray Henderson, George Mulhall, Johnny Quinn, Alan Ball (Snr), Jimmy Lawson, George Kirby, Micky Bullock, Mick Jones (20).
Physio: Gerry Brooke.
Secretary: Mrs Anne Pettifor.
Assistant Secretary: Miss Jeanette Magee.
Commercial Executive: Tony Thwaites.
Sponsors: G. H. Moody & Son.
Founded: 1911.
Turned Professional: 1911.
Nickname: The Shaymen.
Former Names: None.
Former Grounds: Sandhall, Exley.
Record Attendance: 36,885 v Tottenham H, FA Cup 5th Round, 14 February 1953.
Record Victory: 7–0 v Bishop Auckland, FA Cup 2nd Round replay, 10 January 1967.
Record Defeat: 0–13 v Stockport Co, Division 3(N), 6 January 1934.
Most League Points: (3 for a win) 60, Division 4, 1982–83. (2 for a win) 57, Division 4, 1968–69.
Most League Goals: 83, Division 3(N), 1957–58.
Highest League Scorer in a Season: Albert Valentine, 34, Division 3(N), 1934–35.
Highest Total of League Goals: Ernest Dixon, 129, 1922–30.
Most League Appearances: John Pickering, 367, 1965–74.
League History: 1921 Founder Members of Division 3(N), 1958–63 Division 3, 1963–69 Division 4, 1969–76 Division 3, 1976– Division 4.
Honours: Division 4 runners-up 1968–69. Division 3(N) runners-up 1934–35.
Colours: Blue and white striped shirts, white shorts, blue socks. **Second strip:** Yellow shirts, blue shorts, yellow socks.

HALIFAX TOWN – LEAGUE RECORD 1987–88

Match no/Opp/Date		Roche	Barr	Harrison	Matthews M	Robinson	Galloway	Richardson	Thornber	Freebee	Black	Holden	Allison	Matthews N	Brown	Martin	Shaw	McPhillips	Fleming	Heathcote	Blain	Dutfield	Kendall	Willis	FT(HT)Att Lge pos
1. Darlington*	15.8	1	2	3	4	5	6	7	8	9†	10‡	11	12‡	14¹											2-2(0-1)1342 —
2. Wolves	22.8	1		3	4	5	6¹	7	8		12	11	10†	9	2										1-0(0-0)7223 4
3. Rochdale*	28.8	1		3	4	5	6	7‡	8	14	12	11¹¹	10	9†	2										1-2(1-0)2275 —
4. Wrexham	31.8	1		3	4	5	6	7‡	8		10¹	11	12	9†	2₁	14									2-2(0-1)1661 —
5. Newport*	5.9	1		3	4		6		8	9‡		11¹	10	14²	2	7†	5	12							3-1(0-0)1095 9
6. Bolton	12.9	1		3	4		6	7†	8		12	11	10	9	2		5								0-2(0-1)4445 12
7. Swansea*	16.9	1		3	4¹			7	8		11¹	10†	9¹	2	5	6	12								3-1(2-0)1236 —
8. Tranmere*	18.9	1		3	4		6	7†	8		12	11	10‡	9¹	2¹		5	14							2-1(0-0)1754 —
9. Cambridge	26.9	1		3	4†		6	7	8	9‡	11¹	10		2	12	5	14								1-2(1-1)1805 8
10. Cardiff	29.9	1		3	4	7	6		8	9†	11		10	5	12										0-0(0-0)3666 —
11. Hereford*	3.10	1	12	3	4†	7	6		8		11¹		9‡¹	2	10	5	14								2-1(1-1)1414 7
12. Scunthorpe	10.10	1	12	3	4	7	6		8		11		9‡	2	10†	5	14								0-1(0-0)2105 11
13. Stockport*	17.10	1	12	3	4	5	6		8	9	11		2	7²		10†									2-0(2-0)1696 —
14. Hartlepool	21.10	1		3	4¹	5	6		8	9†	11	10	2	7		12									1-2(0-1)2768 —
15. Peterboro*	24.10	1		3	4	5	6		8	9†	11	10	2	7		12									0-0(0-0)1615 13
16. Orient	31.10	1		3	4	5	6		8	14	11¹	10†	9‡		7	2	12								1-4(1-3)3208 16
17. Burnley*	3.11	1		3	4		6		8	12	11	10†	9¹	2	7¹	5									2-1(1-1)3419 —
18. Colchester*	6.11	1		3†	4		6¹		8	10	11	12	9	2	7	5									1-2(1-1)1432 —
19. Scarboro	21.11	1	14		4	5			8	12	10¹	11		9	2	7†	6		3‡						1-0(0-1)2892 16
20. Crewe*	27.11	1			4	6			8	12	10†	11		9	2	7	5	3¹							1-2(0-0)1416 —
21. Torquay	12.12	1	3		4			14	8	12	10	11¹		9¹	2	7†	6	5‡							2-1(1-1)2422 16
22. Exeter*	18.12	1	3		4	5		14	8‡		10†	11	12	9	2		6			7¹					2-0(1-0)1302 —
23. Cambridge*	26.12	1	3		4‡	5		14	8		10†	11	12	9	2	7			6						1-1(1-1)1667 14
24. Rochdale	1.1	1	3		4‡	5		14	8		10†	11	12	9	2	7			6						0-0(0-0)2050 15
25. Bolton*	12.1	1	3		4	5		8			11	10	9	2	7			6							0-0(0-0)2689 —
26. Tranmere	15.1	1	3		4	5		8			11	10†	9‡	2	7		12	14	6						0-2(0-1)3317 —
27. Swansea	23.1	1	3		4		6	8			11	10¹	9	2	7			5							1-1(1-1)5064 16
28. Newport	5.2	1	3		4		6‡	8		10†	11		9	2	7		12	14	5						0-1(0-0)1509 —
29. Wolves*	16.2	1	3		4	5		8			11¹	10	9	2¹	7		6								2-1(1-1)2281 —
30. Darlington	20.2	1	3		4	5		8†		12	11	10¹		2	7		6								1-4(1-2)1824 17
31. Wrexham*	23.2	1	3		4¹	5		8			11¹	10†	9	2	7		12	6							2-0(1-0)1284 —
32. Hereford	27.2	1	3		4‡	5		14	8		12	11		9	2	7		10†	6						1-2(0-2)1905 18
33. Cardiff*	1.3	1	3		4	5		14	8‡		10	11†		9	2	7		12	6						0-1(0-0)1128 —
34. Stockport	4.3	1	3		4	5		6	8			11	10	9	2	7									0-1(0-1)2171 —
35. Scunthorpe*	12.3	1	3		4		6			11	10	2	7	5			8	9²							2-2(2-0)1807 17
36. Peterboro	26.3	1	3†		4	5		11	8			10	14	2	7	12		9‡	6						0-1(0-0)2308 19
37. Colchester	1.4	1			4	5		11	8			10	3¹	2	7†	6		9	12						1-2(1-0)1992 —
38. Scarboro*	4.4	1	3		4	5		11			12	10†	8¹	2	7	6		9¹							2-2(1-0)1747 21
39. Burnley	8.4	1	14			5†		11‡			12	10¹		2	7	6	8	3	9	4					1-3(1-1)5766 —
40. Orient*	14.4	1	3		4					11¹		10		2	7	6	8	9†	5	12					1-0(1-0)1006 —
41. Carlisle	19.4	1	3		4†			12			11		10	2	7	6	8¹	9	5						1-0(0-0)1517 —
42. Hartlepool*	23.4	1	3		4	5				11¹		10	2¹	7	12	8		9¹	6†						3-1(2-1)866 18
43. Carlisle*	26.4	1	3		4†	5		12			11		10	2	7		8¹	9	6						1-1(1-0)1002 —
44. Crewe	29.4	1	3		4	5†		12‡	14		11		10	2	7		8	9	6						0-0(0-0)1403 —
45. Torquay*	2.5	1	3		4					8	11†		10	2¹	7		6	12	9₁	5					2-2(1-1)1218 18
46. Exeter	7.5	1	3‡		4	5		12¹	8		11			2	7†	14	10	9¹	6						2-1(0-1)1602 18
App(subs)/goals		46(0)0	25(5)0	18(0)0	45(0)3	32(0)0	17(0)2	20(10)1	34(1)0	6(6)0	19(8)5	35(0)10	29(3)3	29(3)0	44(0)5	38(2)3	21(3)0	11(4)3	7(2)0	1(0)1	2(0)0	12(0)6	9(0)0	0(0)0	Final League Position: 18

Own goals: Collins, match 22

DIVISION 4

HARTLEPOOL UNITED

The Victoria Ground, Clarence Road, Hartlepool. TS24 8BZ

Back row (left to right): Paul Haigh, Paul Baker, Kevin Carr, Stuart Dawson, Dean Gibb, Wayne Stokes. *Middle row:* Andy Toman, Tony Barratt, Paul Butler, Andrew Dixon, John Timkler, John Borthwick, Rob McKinnon, Keith Nobbs. *Front row:* Alan Little, (Club Coach), Alan Shoulder, John Bird (Manager), Tony Smith, Brian Honour, Gary Henderson (Physio).

Stadium Capacity: 6,820.
Pitch Dimensions: 110 × 75yds.
Telephone: 0429–272584, Commercial dept: 0429–222077.
Chairman: J. W. Smart.
Vice-Chairman: D. Jukes.
Directors: A. Bamford ARICS, G. Lormor, P. Montgomery, W. Southeran, E. Egglestone.
Manager: John Bird.
Post-War Managers: Fred Westgarth, Ray Middleton, Bill Robinson, Allenby Chilton, Bob Gurney, Allan Williams, Geoff Twentyman, Brian Clough, Angus McLean, John Simpson, Len Ashurst, Ken Hale, Billy Horner, Mick Docherty, Billy Horner (15).
Physio: G. Henderson.
Secretary: M. Kirby.
Commercial Consultant: Eddie Barnett.
Founded: 1908.
Turned Professional: 1908.
Nickname: The Pool.
Former Names: Hartlepools United 1908–68, Hartlepool 1968–77.
Former Grounds: None.
Record Attendance: 17,426 v Manchester U, FA Cup 3rd Round, 5 January 1957.
Record Victory: 10–1 v Barrow, Division 4, 4 April 1959.
Record Defeat: 1–10 v Wrexham, Division 4, 3 March 1962.
Most League Points: (3 for a win) 70 Division 4, 1985–86. (2 for a win) 60, Division 4, 1967–68.
Most League Goals: 90, Division 3(N), 1956–57.
Highest League Scorer in a Season: William Robinson, 28, Division 3(N), 1949–64.
Highest Total of League Goals: Ken Johnson, 98, 1949–64.
Most League Appearances: Wattie Moore, 448, 1948–64.
League History: 1921 Founder Members of Division 3(N), 1958–68 Division 4, 1968–69 Division 3, 1969– Division 4.
Honours: Division 3(N) runners-up 1956–57.
Colours: Blue shirts, white shorts, blue socks. **Second strip:** All yellow.

HARTLEPOOL UNITED – LEAGUE RECORD 1987–88

Match no/Opp	Date	Owers	Barratt	Nobbs	Haigh	Smith	Stokes	Honour	Toman	Baker	Shoulder	Butler	Gibb	McKinnon	Borthwick	Prudhoe	Thomson	Dixon	Kennedy	Carr	Tinkler	Hall	Whellans	Danskin	Stokle	Doig	Grayson	McCarthy	FT(HT)Att Lge pos
1. Newport*	15.8	1	2	3	4	5	6	7	8	9	10	11†	12																0–0(0–0)1926 —
2. Wrexham	22.8	1	2		4	5	6	7	8	9	10†	11		3^1	12														1–2(0–0)1816 20
3. Darlington*	29.8	11	2		4	5	6	7	8‡	9^1			12	3†		1	10	14^1											2–5(0–1)2106 23
4. Swansea	31.8	12	2			5	6	7	8^1	9		11†		3		1	4	10											1–2(1–0)3569 —
5. Orient*	5.9	14	2		4	5	6	7	8^1	9^1	11	12		3‡		1	10†												2–2(1–1)1197 23
6. Carlisle	12.9	12	2		4	5	6	7	8^1	9^2	11			3†		1	14	10‡											3–1(2–0)2463 22
7. Cambridge*	16.9		2		4	5	6	7	8	9^2	11†	12		3	10	1													2–1(2–0)1376 —
8. Colchester*	19.9	11	2		4	5	6	7	8	9^1_2				3	10	1													3–1(1–0)1698 14
9. Bolton	26.9	11	2		4	5	6	7	8	9_1				3^1	10	1													2–1(0–0)4398 11
10. Exeter*	30.9	11	2		4	5	6	7	8	9^2				3	10	1													3–1(1–1)2973 —
11. Crewe	3.10	11	2		4	5	6	7	8	9_1				3	10	1													1–0(0–0)2128 6
12. Burnley	10.10	11‡	2		4	5	6	7	8	9			12	3	10†	1	14												0–0(0–0)5215 10
13. Torquay*	17.10		2		4		5	6	7	8	9			11	10	1	3												0–0(0–0)2870 12
14. Halifax*	21.10		2^1		4		5	6	7	8^1	9			11		1	10	3											2–1(1–0)2768 —
15. Scarboro	24.10		2	4	11	5	6	7	8_1	9†				10	3	12													1–1(0–0)3909 11
16. Scunthorpe*	31.10		4	2	5	6	7	8^1	9	11	10			3	1														1–0(1–0)2763 9
17. Stockport	3.11	11†	4	2	5	6	7	8	9				10	12		1													0–1(0–0)1408 —
18. Peterboro	7.11		4	2	5	6	7	8^1	9	11	10	3				1													1–0(0–0)3200 9
19. Tranmere*	21.11	14	4	2	5	6	7	8^1	9†	11‡	10	3	12			1													1–2(1–1)2507 10
20. Cardiff	28.11	11_1	4	2	5	6	7	8	9			12	3	10†		1													1–1(1–0)3232 9
21. Wolves*	12.12	11		2	5	6	7	8	9			3	10		1	4													0–0(0–0)2760 11
22. Hereford	19.12	11		2	5	6	7	8_1		12	3	10	9†	1	4‡	14													2–4(1–3)1655 14
23. Bolton*	26.12	11	4	2	5	6	7	8		9	3	10		1															0–0(0–0)4102 15
24. Rochdale	28.12	11	4	2	5	6	7	8	9^1		3			1					10^1										2–0(0–0)1851 12
25. Darlington	1.1	11	4	2	5		7	8	9^1	12	3			1	6		10†												1–0(0–0)4735 12
26. Carlisle*	2.1	11	4	2	5		7	8	9	12	3			1	6†		10												0–0(0–0)3153 11
27. Colchester	15.1		2	4	6	5		8	9		3	11		1	12		10	7†											0–0(0–0)1768 —
28. Wrexham*	26.1		2	4	6	5		8	9		3	11^1		1	12		10	7†											1–0(0–0)1692 —
29. Swansea*	30.1		2	4	6	5		14	8	9‡	10	3	11	1	12			7†											0–2(0–2)2092 11
30. Orient	6.2		2	4	6	5		7	8^1	9^1	3	11		1	10														2–0(1–0)4188 10
31. Rochdale*	13.2		2	4	6	5		7	8^1	9	3	11		1	10														1–0(0–0)2186 10
32. Newport	19.2		2	4	6	5		7	8_1	9†	3	11^2	12	1	10														3–2(2–1)1880 —
33. Crewe*	27.2		2	4	6†	5		7	8_1	9^1	3	11		1	10	12													2–1(2–1)2165 6
34. Exeter	2.3		2	4		5		7	8	9	12	3	11	1	6	10†													0–1(0–0)1573 —
35. Torquay	5.3		2^1	4		5		7	8	9	3	11		1	10							6							1–1(0–1)2857 10
36. Burnley*	12.3		2	4		5		7	8	9	3	11^1		1	10							6							2–1(2–0)2891 8
37. Scunthorpe	19.3		2	4		5		7†	8		12	3	11	14		1	10‡	9	6										0–3(0–3)3783 10
38. Scarboro*	26.3		2	4	6	5		7	8	9†	3	11^1		1	12							10							1–0(1–0)2443 9
39. Peterboro*	2.4		2	4‡	6	5		7	8	9†	3	11		1	14	12						10							0–1(0–1)2315 10
40. Tranmere	4.4		2	4	6	5		12	8^1	9	3	11		1	7†							10							1–3(0–1)3921 10
41. Stockport*	9.4		2	4	6	5		7	8^1	9†	3	11	12	1								10							1–3(1–2)1317 13
42. Cambridge	19.4		2	4	6	5		7	8	12	3	11		1		9						10†							1–1(1–0)1492 —
43. Halifax	23.4		2	14	6	5		7	8	9^1	3	11†	12	1	4‡							10							1–3(1–2)866 14
44. Cardiff*	30.4		2	4	6	5		7	8	9	3	12		10		1						11†							0–1(0–1)1097 15
45. Wolves	2.5		2	4	3	5		7	8		12	9		10		1	6					11†							0–2(0–1)17,895 16
46. Hereford*	7.5		2	4	3	5		7	8^1		10‡		12			1	6					11†			9		14		1–2(0–1)1002 16

Apps(subs)/goals: Owers 2(0)/0; Barratt 39(4)/3; Nobbs 42(0)/0; Haigh 39(0)/0; Smith 46(0)/0; Stokes 24(0)/0; Honour 42(2)/0; Toman 46(0)/17; Baker 38(1)/19; Shoulder 5(0)/0; Butler 6(3)/0; Gibb 9(0)/0; McKinnon 41(1)/2; Borthwick 13(0)/0; Prudhoe 25(0)/0; Thomson 7(6)/1; Dixon 4(1)/0; Kennedy 3(1)/0; Carr 16(4)/0; Tinkler 0(1)/0; Hall 8(3)/1; Whellans 3(0)/0; Danskin 9(4)/0; Stokle 10(0)/0; Doig 0(1)/0; Grayson 1(0)/0; McCarthy 0(1)/0

Final League Position: 16

Own goals: Nisbet, match 10; Crowe, match 42.

DIVISION 4 | # HEREFORD UNITED

Edgar Street, Hereford HR4 9JU.

Back row (left to right): Ian Bowyer (Manager), Sean Edwards, Ian Dalziel, Phil Start, Ollie Kearns, Kevin Rose, Gary Stevens, Chris Leadbitter, Steve Devine, Ian Benbow, Danny Corner, Peter Isaac (Physio). *Middle row:* Mark Jones, Steve Spooner, Ian Wells, Mel Rejic, Ian Rodgerson, Stewart Phillips, Paul McLoughlin. *Front row (YTS):* Jason Westmacott, Keith Holmans, Paul Mallender

Stadium Capacity: 11,914.
Pitch Dimensions: 111 × 74yds.
Telephone: 0432–276666, Commercial dept: 0432–273155.
Chairman: P. S. Hill.
Vice-Chairman: M. B. Roberts.
Directors: D. H. Vaughan, A. J. Phillips, G. R. E. Rivers, J. E. Jackson, G. C. E. Hales.
Manager: Ian Bowyer.
Post-War Managers: George Tranter, Alex Massie, Joe Wade, Ray Daniel, Bob Dennison, John Charles, Colin Addison, John Sillett, Tony Ford, Mike Bailey, Frank Lord, John Newman (12).
Physio: Peter Isaac.
Secretary: D. H. Vaughan.
Commercial Manager: Keith Butler.
Founded: 1924.
Turned Professional: 1924.
Nickname: United.
Former Names: None.
Former Grounds: None.
Record Attendance: 18,114 v Sheffield W, FA Cup 3rd Round, 5 January 1985.
Record Victory: 11–0 v Thynnes, FA Cup prelim Round, September 1947.
Record Defeat: 0–5 v Wrexham, Division 3, 22 December, 1973; 1–6 v Tranmere R, Division 3, 29 November, 1975; 1–6 v Wolverhampton W, Division 2, 2 October 1976, 2–7 v Arsenal, FA Cup, 3rd Round replay, 22 January 1985.
Most League Points: (3 for a win) 77 Division 4, 1984–85. (2 for a win) 63, Division 3, 1975–76.
Most League Goals: 86, Division 3, 1975–76.
Highest League Scorer in a Season: Dixie McNeil, 35, 1975–76.
Highest Total of League Goals: Dixie McNeil, 85, 1974–77.
Most League Appearances: Chris Price 330, 1976–86.
League History: 1972 Elected to Division 4, 1973–76 Division 3, 1976–77 Division 2, 1977–78 Division 3, 1978–Division 4.
Honours: Division 3 Champions 1975–76. Division 4 runners-up 1972–73. Welsh Cup runners-up 3 times.
Colours: White shirts with black pinstripe, black shorts white socks. **Second strip:** All red.

HEREFORD UNITED – LEAGUE RECORD 1987–88

Match no/Opp	Date	Rose	Jones	Devine	Stevens	Pejic	Spooner	McLoughlin	Bowyer	Phillips	Kearns	Dziuel	Leadbitter	Rodgerson	Stant	Benbow	Wassall	Powell	Campbell	Mallender	Maddy	Leonard	FT(HT)Att	Lge pos
1. Rochdale*	15.8	1	2	3	4	5	6	7	8	9	10	11†	12										0-0(0-0)2652	—
2. Tranmere	21.8	1	2	3	4	5	6	11¹	8	9	10			7									1-0(0-0)2824	—
3. Wolves*	29.8	1	2	3†	4	5			11	8	9	10	12	6	7‡	14¹							1-2(0-2)2628	14
4. Carlisle	31.8	1	2			4	5		7	6	9	10¹	3	11	8†		12						1-3(1-1)2708	—
5. Bolton*	5.9	1	2			4	5	6	11	8	9	10	3	12		7†							0-3(0-2)2541	22
6. Swansea	12.9	1	2			4	5	6	7	8	9†	10	3	11		12							0-3(0-0)3794	24
7. Colchester*	16.9	1	2	3	4	5	6			8	9		11	7	10¹								1-0(0-0)1951	—
8. Darlington*	19.9	1	2	3	4	5	6			8	9¹		11	7	10								1-0(1-0)2102	16
9. Newport	27.9	1	2	3	4	5	6	11	8	9	10		7										0-0(0-0)1480	—
10. Peterboro*	30.9	1	2	3	4	5	6	11	8	9‡	10†	12		7	14								0-1(0-1)2010	—
11. Halifax	3.10	1	2		4	10	5	6	11	8	9		3†	7¹		12							1-2(1-1)1414	20
12. Cardiff	10.10	1	2	3	4	5	6₁	11		9	12		7	10†	8								1-0(0-0)4420	19
13. Scunthorpe*	17.10	1	2	3	4¹	5	6	11		9			7¹	10	8								2-3(0-2)2092	19
14. Scarboro*	21.10	1	2	3	4	5	6	11	8¹	9			7	10									1-1(0-0)2359	—
15. Stockport	23.10	1	2	3	4		6	11		9†	12		7	10¹	8¹	5							2-0(1-0)1566	—
16. Exeter*	31.10	1	2†	3	4	12	6¹	11	8	9			7	10		5							1-1(0-0)2200	18
17. Cambridge	3.11	1		3	4	2	6		8	9¹		11	7	10		5							1-0(1-0)2257	—
18. Crewe*	7.11	1	2	3	4		6		8	9†		11	7¹	10	12	5							1-0(0-0)2272	17
19. Torquay	21.11	1	2	3	4	12	6		8			11	7†	10	9	5							0-1(0-1)2305	18
20. Orient*	28.11	1	2	3	4	5	6		8	9	10		11	7									0-3(0-2)1853	19
21. Burnley	12.12	1		3	5	2	6		8	9		7	11	10				4					0-0(0-0)4216	19
22. Hartlepool*	19.12	1	2	3	9¹	5	6¹		8			11	7	10²				4					4-2(3-1)1655	17
23. Newport*	26.12	1	2	3	9²	5	6		8		11¹		7	10				4					4-2(1-1)3203	16
24. Wrexham	28.12	1	2	3	9	5	6		8		11		7	10				4					0-0(0-0)2443	16
25. Wolves	1.1	1	2	3		5	6		12	9		11	7†	10	8			4					0-2(0-1)14,577	17
26. Swansea*	2.1	1		3	10	4	6		8	9	5†	11		7	12			2					0-0(0-0)3504	17
27. Tranmere*	9.1	1	2	3	10	5	6¹		8	9		11		7				4					1-1(1-0)2209	17
28. Darlington	17.1	1	2†	3	5	4	6		8	9		11¹		10	12		7						1-3(0-2)2621	—
29. Carlisle*	30.1	1		3	4	5	6¹		8	9¹		7	2	10			11						2-0(2-0)1904	16
30. Bolton	6.2	1		3	4	5	6		8	9†	12	7	2	10			11						0-1(0-2)4559	17
31. Wrexham*	13.2	1		3	4	5	6		8	9		11	2	10			7						0-2(0-2)2006	17
32. Rochdale	20.2	1	2	3	4¹	5	6	14	8‡	9		11	7	10†	12								1-3(0-2)1568	18
33. Peterboro	24.2	1		3	4	5	6¹	7		9		8	11	2	10¹								2-1(0-1)2065	—
34. Halifax*	27.2	1		3	4¹	5	6¹‡	7		9†		8	11	2	10	12			14				2-1(2-0)1905	16
35. Scunthorpe	5.3	1	12	3	4	5	6	7			8†	11	2	10	9								0-3(0-1)3413	17
36. Cardiff*	13.3	1	2	3	4	5		7				11		10¹	9					6	8		1-2(1-1)3210	19
37. ExeterR	19.3	1		3	4	5		7				11	2	10¹	9¹					6	8		2-2(2-0)1628	18
38. Stockport*	26.3	1		3	4	5					12	11	2	10	9†						8		1-0(1-0)1695	18
39. Crewe	1.4	1		3	4	5	6	7		8		11	2	9							10		0-0(0-0)1313	—
40. Torquay*	4.4	1		3	4	5	6	7		8		11	2	9							10		0-0(0-0)2425	19
41. Scarboro	9.4	1		3	4	5	6¹	7†		8	11‡	2	9	14						12	10		1-2(0-2)2154	19
42. Colchester	19.4	1		3	4	5	6	7		8		2	9†	10						12	11		0-1(0-1)1367	—
43. Cambridge*	23.4	1			4	9	5	8	11†		3	12	2		10					6	7		1-0(1-0)1666	20
44. Orient	30.4	1		4	10	5	8	7		3		2	9							6	11		0-4(0-3)3444	20
45. Burnley*	2.5	1		4	10	5¹	8	7		3		2	9							6	11¹		2-1(1-1)3204	19
46. Hartlepool	7.5	1		5†	10¹	4	8	7		3		2	9¹	12						6	11		2-1(1-0)1002	19
Apps(subs)/goals		46(0) 0	27(1) 0	43(0) 7	45(0) 7	42(2) 1	42(0) 8	28(0) 1	28(1) 1	30(0) 3	9(2) 1	21(4) 1	27(3) 1	37(0) 3	36(3) 9	12(9) 2	5(0) 0	7(0) 0	0(0)	0(0) 1	6(2) 0	11(0) 1		

Final League Position: 19

Own goals: Hodson, match 23; Chapple, match 43.

DIVISION 3

HUDDERSFIELD TOWN

Leeds Road, Huddersfield HF1 6PE.

Back row (left to right): Carl Madrick, John Clarke, David Cork, Andy May, Ian Banks, Malcolm Brown, Simon Trevitt, Gordon Tucker. *Third row:* Keith Mincher (Coach), Duncan Shearer, Paul France, Simon Webster, Graham Mitchell, Brian Cox, Lee Martin, Julian Winter, Willie McStay, Richard Shelton, George McAllister (Physio). *Second row:* Peter Ward, Graham Cooper, Mark Barham, Steve Smith (Youth, Coach/Chief Scout), Jimmy Robson (First Team Coach), David Burke, Ian Bray, Dave Cowling, *Front row:*, Adrian Boothroyd, Steven Donald, Sean Helliwell, Gary Haylock, Andrew Hirst, Marcus Pass, Shaun Weatherhead, Junior Bent, Richard Crossley.

Stadium Capacity: 32,000.
Pitch Dimensions: 115 × 75yds.
Telephone: 0484-20335, Lottery/souvenir shop: 0484-534867, **Clubcall:** 0898-121635.
Chairman: K. S. Longbottom.
Vice-Chairman: G. Headey.
Directors: C. Senior, E. A. Lodge, C. Hodgkinson, J. B. Buckley, F. L. Thewlis, R. B. Fielding, G. Headey.
Manager: Eoin Hand.
Post-War Managers: David Steele, George Stephenson, Andy Beattie, Bill Shankly, Eddie Boot, Tom Johnston, Ian Greaves, Bobby Collins, Tom Johnston, Mick Buxton, Stephen Smith, Malcolm Macdonald (12).
Assistant Manager: Peter Withe.
Physio: G. McAllister.
Secretary: G. S. Binns.
Commercial Executive: K. Hanvey.
Sponsors: Greenall Whitley plc.
Founded: 1908.
Turned Professional: 1908.
Nickname: The Terriers.
Former Names: None.
Former Grounds: None.
Record Attendance: 67,037 v Arsenal, FA Cup 6th Round, 27 February 1932.
Record Victory: 10–1 v Blackpool, Division 1, 13 December 1930.
Record Defeat: 1–10 v Manchester City, Division 2, 7 November 1987.
Most League Points: (3 for a win) 82, Division 3, 1982–83. (2 for a win) 66, Division 4, 1979–80.
Most League Goals: 101, Division 4, 1979–80.
Highest League Scorer in a Season: Sam Taylor, 35, Division 2, 1919–20; George Brown, 35, Division 1, 1925–26.
Highest Total of League Goals: George Brown, 142, 1921–29 and Jimmy Glazzard, 142, 1946–56.
Most League Appearances: Billy Smith, 520, 1914–34.
League History: 1910 Elected to Division 2, 1920–52 Division 1, 1952–53 Division 2, 1953–56 Division 1, 1956–70 Division 2, 1970–72 Division 1, 1972–73 Division 2, 1973–75 Division 3, 1975–80 Division 4, 1980–83 Division 3, 1983–88 Division 2, 1988– Division 3.
Honours: Division 1 Champions 1923–24, 1924–25, 1925–26, runners-up 1926–27, 1927–28, 1933–34. Division 2 Champions 1969–70, runners-up 1919–20, 1952–53. Division 4 Champions 1979–80. FA Cup winners 1922, runners-up 1920, 1928, 1930, 1938.
Colours: Blue and white striped shirts, white shorts and socks. **Second strip:** Yellow and black check shirts, black shorts, yellow and black socks.

HUDDERSFIELD TOWN – LEAGUE RECORD 1987–88

Match no/Opp/Date		Cox	Brown	Burke	Banks	Webster	Mitchell	Barham	May	Shearer	Cork	Cowling	Trevitt	Tucker	Bray	Ward	Cooper	McStay	Bent	Martin	Winter	Walford	Hutchings	France	McDonagh	Chapman	Shotton	Madrick	Kirkham	FT(HT)Att Lge pos
1. C Palace*	15.8	1	2	3	4	5	6	7†	8	9¹	10	11	12¹																	2–2(0–1)6132 —
2. Plymouth	22.8	1		3	4	5		7†	8	9	11	10‡	2	6	12	14¹														1–6(0–2)8811 21
3. Shrewsbury*	29.8	1		3	4	5			8	9	11†	7	6	2	10	12														0–0(0–0)4478 20
4. Oldham	31.8	1		3	4¹	5		7†	8	9¹		12	6	2	10	11														2–3(1–1)7377 —
5. Blackburn	12.9	1		3	4	5		7	8¹	9	11†		6	2	12	10¹														2–2(2–2)7109 23
6. Leeds*	15.9	1		3	4	5		7	8	9	10		12	6	2	11†														0–0(0–0)9085 —
7. Aston Villa*	19.9	1		3	4	5		7	8	9	11	12	10†	6	2															0–1(0–1)6884 23
8. Stoke	26.9	1		3	4	5		7†	8		11	12	6	2	10	9¹														1–1(1–0)8665 23
9. Bradford*	29.9	1		3	4	5		7	8‡	9¹	11	10†	12	6	2			14												1–2(0–1)11,671 —
10. Birmingham	3.10	1		3	4	5		12	8†	9	11	10		6	2			7‡	14											0–2(0–0)6282 23
11. Middlesbro*	10.10	1	2		4†	5			8	9¹	11	10‡	12			3		14	6	7										1–4(0–2)6169 23
12. Reading	17.10	1	2		4	5			8	9²	11		7‡	12	3			10	6†	14										2–3(0–2)4678 23
13. Hull*	20.10	1	2		4	5			8	9	11†		6	3	12	10		7												0–2(0–0)8033 —
14. WBA	24.10		2		4	5			8	9¹	11¹		6	3		10†		7	1	12										2–3(2–2)8450 23
15. Millwall*	31.10		2		4¹	5			12	8	9	11¹		3				7†	1	10	6									2–1(1–0)5504 23
16. Ipswich	3.11	1			4	5		7	8	9	11		12	3	2‡		14			10	6†									0–3(0–2)9984 —
17. Man City	7.11	1	2		4	5		7	8¹	9	11			3						10	6									1–0(0–4)19,583 23
18. Barnsley*	14.11				4¹		5		8	9†	11		2	3	10¹	12	7		1											2–2(1–2)8629 23
19. Bournemth	21.11				4¹		5		8		11¹		2	3	10	9	7†		1	12	6									2–0(1–0)6419 23
20. Leicester*	28.11				4		5		8		11		2	3	10	9¹			1	7	6									1–0(1–0)6704 22
21. Swindon	1.12				4		5		8†		11		2	3	10	9¹	12		1	7	6									1–4(2–0)6963 —
22. Sheff Utd	5.12				4¹		5	7	12		11		2	3	10†	9¹			1		6	8								2–2(1–1)9269 22
23. Plymouth*	12.12				4		5	7†	10		11²		2	3	12	9			1		6	8								2–1(1–0)5747 21
24. Leeds	12.12				4		5		10†	12	11		2	3	7	9			1		6	8								0–3(0–1)20,111 21
25. Stoke*	26.12			14	4		5		10	12	11		2	3	7†	9			1		6‡	8								0–3(0–0)9500 21
26. Aston Villa	28.12	1	12		4	7	5			9¹	11		2	3†		10					6	8								1–1(1–1)20,948 21
27. Shrewsbury	1.1	1	6		4	7	5			9	11¹‡		2	3	12	10†					8	14								1–3(0–1)5448 23
28. Blackburn*	2.1		6		4	7†	5		11₁	9			2	3	10	12					8									1–2(0–2)10,735 23
29. C Palace	16.1	1	4			5	6		8†	9¹	11		2	3	12					10	7									1–2(1–2)9013 23
30. Swindon*	13.2		2		4	5	6	7		9	11		10	3†						8		1	12							0–3(0–1)5458 —
31. Birmingham*	27.2		2		4¹		12	7¹		9	11‡		10							8	5	1	9†	6	14					2–2(1–2)5441 23
32. Bradford	1.3		2		4¹		3	7		9	11		10							8	5	1		6						1–0(0–0)12,782 —
33. Reading*	5.3		2†		4		3	7		9	11		10							8	5	1		6	12					0–2(0–2)6094 23
34. Middlesbro	12.3				4		3	7‡	2		11†		10	12		9				8		1	5	6	14					0–2(0–1)13,866 23
35. Millwall	19.3		2		4		3¹	7		9			10	12		11				8	5†	1		6						1–4(1–2)6181 23
36. WBA*	26.3	1			4	7			9	11¹		2	5	3†	10					8	12									1–3(1–0)4503 23
37. Man City*	2.4		3			4	7		9			2	5	10					1	8				6	11¹					1–0(0–0)7835 23
38. Barnsley	4.4		3		10	4		9‡				2	5	14					1	8	12			6†						0–1(0–1)7950 23
39. Ipswich*	8.4		3		10¹	4				9		2	5	7†					1	8				6	12	12				1–2(1–0)4023 —
40. Oldham*	19.4		3		10¹	4	7		9¹†			2	5		11				1	8				6	12					2–2(2–0)5547 —
41. Hull	23.4		3		10	4	7†			9		2	5		11				1	8				6	12					0–4(0–4)5221 23
42. Bournemouth*	30.4		3		10	4†	7			9¹		2	5		14	11‡			1	8				12	6					1–2(0–2)2794 23
43. Leicester	2.5		3		10	4						2	5	9					7	1		8		11	6					0–3(0–2)9803 23
44. Sheff Utd*	7.5	1	3		10	4	7			9		2			11					12		8		5†	6					0–2(0–0)8644 23
Apps(subs)/goals		20(0)0	23(2)0	10(0)0	41(0)9	22(0)0	28(0)1	24(2)1	27(1)3	31(2)10	36(0)8	5(1)0	31(6)1	19(4)0	29(2)1	19(7)2	20(1)5	4(4)0	5(2)0	18(0)0	12(0)0	23(0)0	5(3)0	6(0)0	4(2)0	14(0)0	3(5)1	0(1)0		

Final League Position: 23

DIVISION 2

HULL CITY

Boothferry Park, Hull HU4 6EU.

Back row (left to right): Les Thompson, Alex Dyer, Pat Heard, Leigh Jenkinson, Neil Buckley, Nicky Brown, Gary Parker, Charlie Palmer, Mike Smith. *Middle row:*, Tom Wilson (Reserve, Team Manager), Frankie Bunn, Gavin Kelly, Stan McEwan, Peter Skipper, Tony Norman, Richard Jobson, Andy Saville, Jeff Radcliffe (Physio). *Front row:* Steve Corkain, Neil Williams, Garreth Roberts, Brian Horton, (Manager), Billy Askew, Ray Daniel, Dennis Booth, (Ass. Manager).

Stadium Capacity: 20,059.
Pitch Dimensions: 112 × 75yds.
Telephone: 0482–51119/563750.
Chairman: D. Robinson.
Vice-Chairman: T. C. Waite FIM, MIRTE.
Directors: J. Johnson BA, G. H. C. Needler MA, ACA, R. Chetham, H. Bermitz, C. M. Thorpe LL. B. , M. W. Fish FCA.
Caretaker Managers: Dennis Booth, Tom Wilson.
Post-War Managers: Major Frank Buckley, Raich Carter, Bob Jackson, Bob Brocklebank, Cliff Britton, Terry Neill, John Kaye, Bobby Collins, Ken Houghton, Mike Smith, Colin Appleton, Brian Horton (12).
Physio: J. Radcliffe.
Secretary: K. Adamson
Marketing Executive: Paul Lofthouse.
Development Executive: Peter Roper.
Sponsors: Mansfield Brewery.
Founded: 1904.
Turned Professional: 1905.
Nickname: The Tigers.
Former Names: None.
Former Grounds: Boulevard Ground (Hull RFC) 1904–05, Anlaby Road (Hull CC) 1905–44, Boulevard Grounds 1944–46.
Record Attendance: 55,019 v Manchester U, FA Cup 6th Round, 26 February 1949.
Record Victory: 11–1 v Carlisle U, Division 3(N), 14 January 1939.
Record Defeat: 0–8 v Wolverhampton W, Division 2, 4 November 1911.
Most League Points: (3 for a win) 90, Division 4, 1982–83. (2 for a win) 69, Division 3, 1965–66.
Most League Goals: 109, Division 3, 1965–66.
Highest League Scorer in a Season: Bill McNaughton, 39, Division 3(N), 1932–33.
Highest Total of League Goals: Chris Chilton, 195, 1960–71.
Most League Appearances: Andy Davidson, 511, 1952–67.
League History: 1905 Elected to Division 2, 1930–33 Division 2(N), 1933–36 Division 2, 1936–49 Division 3(N), 1949–56 Division 2, 1956–58 Division 3(N), 1958–59 Division 3, 1959–60 Division 2, 1960–66 Division 3, 1966–78 Division 2, 1978–81 Division 3, 1981–83 Division 4, 1983–85 Division 3, 1985– Division 2.
Honours: Division 3 Champions 1965–66, runners-up 1958–59. Division 4 runners-up 1982–83. Division 3(N) Champions 1932–33, 1948–49. Associate Members' Cup runners-up 1984.
Colours: Amber shirts with black and red trim, black shorts with amber and red trim, red socks. **Second strip:** All white with red trim.

HULL CITY – LEAGUE RECORD 1987–88

Match no/Opp/Date	Norman	Palmer	Heard	Jobson	Skipper	McEwan	Parker	Burn	Dyer	Askew	Roberts	Saville	Daniel	Williams	Paxton	Thompson	Owen	Brown	Jenkinson	De Mange	Barnes	Jacobs	Edwards	Hotte	FT(HT)Att Lge pos
1. Blackburn* 15.8	1	2	3	4	5^1	6	7	8^1	9	10	11														2-2(0-0)6426 —
2. Stoke 18.8	1	2	3	4	5		6^1	8		10	7	9	11												1-1(1-0)9136 —
3. C Palace 22.8	1	2	3	4	5		6^1	8^1		10	7	9	11												2-2(2-0)6688 12
4. Aston Villa* 29.8	1	2	3_1	4	5	6		8	9^1	10	7		11												2-1(1-1)8315 7
5. Swindon 31.8	1	2	3	4	5	6		8	9	10	7		11												0-0(0-0)9600 —
6. Bournemouth* 5.9	1	2	3	4	5	6		8	9^1	10^1	7	12	11†												2-1(1-0)5807 4
7. Leeds 12.9	1	2	3	4	5		6^1	8	9^1	10	7		11												2-0(0-0)18,205 4
8. Shrewsbury* 15.9	1	2	3	4	5	6		8†	9	10	7^1	12	11												1-1(0-0)7939 —
9. Oldham* 19.9	1	2	3	4	5^1	6		8	9†	10	7	12	11‡	14											1-0(1-0)7183 3
10. Man City* 29.9	1	2	3	4	5†	6^1		8^2		10	7	9	11‡	14	12										3-1(2-0)9650 —
11. Sheff Utd 3.10	1	2	3	4	5	6		8^1		10	7	9		11											1-2(1-1)10,446 2
12. Ipswich* 10.10	1	2	3	4	5	6				10	7	9		11	8^1										1-0(0-0)6962 2
13. Barnsley 17.10	1	2	3_1	4	5	6				10^1	7	9^1		11	8										3-1(1-0)7310 2
14. Huddersfield 20.10	1	2	3	4	5	6^1			12	10	7	9		11	8^{1}†										2-0(0-0)8033 —
15. Leicester* 24.10	1	2	3	4	5	6		8	12	10	7^1	9†		11^1											2-2(1-1)8826 2
16. Plymouth 31.10	1	2	3	4	5	6			12	10	7	9^1		11	8†										1-3(1-3)8550 3
17. Bradford* 3.11	1	2	3	4	5	6		8	9	10	7			11											0-0(0-0)15,443 —
18. Birmingham 7.11	1	2	3	4	5	6		8	9	10	7			11^1											2-0(1-0)7901 —
19. Middlesbro 14.11	1	2		4	5	6		8	9	10	7		3	11†	12										0-1(0-1)15,709 3
20. WBA* 21.11	1	2		4	5	6		8	9	10^1	7		3	11											1-0(0-0)7654 3
21. Millwall 28.11	1	2		4	5	6		8	9	10	7		3	11†	12										0-2(0-0)6743 4
22. Reading* 5.12	1	2		4	5	6^1			9^1	10	7	8†	3	11	12										2-2(0-1)5797 7
23. Shrewsbury 12.12	1	2		4	5	6			9	10	7_1	8^1	3	11											2-2(2-1)2588 8
24. C Palace* 19.12	1	2		4	5	6^1			9^1	10	7	8†	3	12			11								2-1(2-1)6780 6
25. Oldham 28.12	1	2	10_1	4	5	6			9^1		7	8	3				11								2-1(0-1)8080 6
26. Aston Villa 1.1	1	2	11	4	5	6			9	10	7	8‡	3†	12	14										0-5(0-1)19,236 8
27. Leeds* 3.1	1	2	3	4^1	5	12			9^1	10	7	6	8^{1}†				11								3-1(3-1)14,694 —
28. Blackburn 16.1	1	2	3	4^1	5	6†			9	10	7	12	11	8											1-2(0-2)9692 7
29. Bournemouth 6.2	1	2‡	3	4	5	6			9^1	10†	7	12	11	8^1				14							2-6(1-3)5901 8
30. Stoke* 13.2	1	2	3	4	5	6			9	10	7	12	11†	8											0-0(0-0)6424 8
31. Sheff Utd* 27.2	1	2	3	4	5	6‡			9	10†	7	8^1	14	12					11						1-2(1-0)8832 9
32. Man City 2.3	1		3	4	5	6				10	7	8		11		2									0-2(0-0)16,040 —
33. Barnsley* 5.3	1		3	4	5	6			9		7	8^1		12		2				10†	11				1-2(1-2)7622 11
34. Ipswich 12.3	1			4	5				9‡		7	8	3	12	14	2	6†			10	11				0-2(0-1)9728 11
35. Plymouth* 19.3	1		3	4	5	6^1			9†		7	8		12		2				10	11				1-1(0-1)5172 11
36. Leicester 26.3	1	2		4	5						7	8		14			6†			10	11	3	9^1		1-2(0-1)10,353 11
37. Birmingham 2.4	1	2	6^1	4	5						7	8†		12						10	11	3	6		1-1(1-0)7059 13
38. Middlesbro* 4.4	1	2	6	4	5						7	8								10	11	3	9		0-0(0-0)10,758 15
39. Bradford 9.4	1	2†	6^1	4							7	12		8				5	14	10	11	3	6		0-2(0-1)13,659 15
40. Swindon* 12.4	1			4	5					14		12	8		10†		2‡	11^1	6	7	3	9			1-4(1-2)4583 —
41. Huddersfield* 23.4	1		3	4	5						7	8^1	10^1	12	6†		2				11‡	9^2	14		4-0(4-0)5221 14
42. WBA 30.4	1		3	4	5						7	8	10^1		6†		2				11	9	12		1-1(0-1)8004 14
43. Millwall* 2.5	1		3	4	5						7	8	10		6†		2			14	11‡	9	12		0-1(0-1)10,811 16
44. Reading 7.5	1		3	4	5						7	8	10	12			2					11	9†	6	0-0(0-0)6710 15
App(subs)/goals	44(0)/0	35(0)/0	35(0)/4	44(0)/2	1(0)/0	33(1)/8	16(2)/5	27(1)/8	20(0)/3	30(0)/3	43(1)/3	24(7)/6	23(3)/2	21(4)/2	11(11)/2	5(2)/2	3(6)/0	9(4)/0	2(1)/1	8(0)/0	11(0)/0	6(0)/3	9(0)/3	1(0)/0	Final League Position: 15

Own goal: Overson, match 18.

DIVISION 2

IPSWICH TOWN

Portman Road, Ipswich, Suffolk IP1 2DA.

Back row (left to right): Graham Harbey, David Lowe, Tony Humes, Nigel Gleghorn, Chris O'Donnell, Mick Stockwell. *Middle row:* Charlie Woods (Ass. Manager), Romeo Zondervan, Craig Forrest, John Deehan, Jon Hallworth, Michael Cole, John Duncan (Manager). *Front row:* Ian Cranson, Mich D'Avray, Ian Atkins, Jason Dozzell, Mark Brennan, Frank Yallop.

Stadium Capacity: 37,000.
Pitch Dimensions: 112 × 70yds.
Telephone: 0473–219211, Commercial dept: 0473–212202.
Chairman: P. M. Cobbold.
Directors: J. Kerr, H. R. Smith, J. M. Sangster, K. H. Brightwell, J. Kerridge, D. Sheepshanks.
Manager: John Duncan.
Post-War Managers: A. Scott Duncan, Alf Ramsey, Jackie Milburn, Bill McGarry, Bobby Robson, Bobby Ferguson (6).
Assistant Manager: Peter Trevivian.
Physio: David Bingham.
Secretary: David C. Rose.
Commercial Manager: Mike Noye.
Sponsors: Fisons.
Founded: 1878.
Turned Professional: 1936.
Nickname: The Blues or Town.
Former Names: None.
Former Grounds: None.
Record Attendance: 38,010 v Leeds U, FA Cup 6th Round, 8 March, 1975.
Record Victory: 10–0 v Floriana (Malta), European Cup 1st Round, 25 September 1962.
Record Defeat: 1–10 v Fulham, Division 1, 26 December 1963.
Most League Points: (3 for a win) 83, Division 1, 1981–82. (2 for a win) 64, Division 3(S), 1953–54 and 1955–56.
Most League Goals: 106, Division 3(S), 1955–56.
Highest League Scorer in a Season: Ted Phillips, 41, Division 3(S), 1956–57.
Highest Total of League Goals: Ray Crawford, 203, 1958–63 and 1966–69.
Most League Appearances: Mick Mills, 591, 1966–82.
League History: 1938 Elected to Division 3(S), 1954–55 Division 2, 1955–57 Division 3(S), 1957–61 Division 2, 1961–64 Division 1, 1964–68 Division 2, 1968–86 Division 1, 1986– Division 2.
Honours: Division 1 Champions 1961–62, runners-up 1980–81, 1981–82. Division 2 Champions 1960–61, 1967–68. Division 3(S) Champions 1953–54, 1956–57. FA Cup winners 1978. UEFA Cup winners 1981.
Colours: Blue shirts with white trim, white shorts, blue socks. **Second strip:** White shirts, blue shorts, red socks.

IPSWICH TOWN – LEAGUE RECORD 1987–88

Match no/Opp	Date	Hallworth	Yallop	Harbey	O'Donnell	Dozzell	Cranson	Lowe	Brennan	Woods	Zondervan	Gleghorn	Stockwell	D'Avray	Humes	Rimmer	Atkins	Atkinson	Dechan	Bernal	Cole	Wilson	Milton	Wark	Carson	Fearon	FT(HT)Att Lge pos
1. Aston Villa*	15.8	1	2	3	4†	5	6	7	8	9	10	11¹	12														1-1(1-1)14,508 —
2. Plymouth	18.8	1	4	3		5	6	7	8	9	10	11	2														0-0(0-0)11,901 —
3. Shrewsbury	22.8	1	4	3		5	6	7	8	9†	10	11	2	12													0-0(0-0)3610 14
4. Stoke*	29.8	1	4	3		5	6	7¹	8		10	11	2	9													2-0(1-0)11,149 6
5. Blackburn	1.9	1	4	3		5	6	7	8			11‡	2	9†	12	10	14										0-1(0-0)6074 —
6. Leeds*	5.9	1	4†	3		5	6	7¹	8			11	2	9	12	10											1-0(0-0)11,163 7
7. Millwall	12.9	1		3		5	6		8¹	14	7		2	9†	11	12	4‡	10									1-2(0-1)6356 11
8. Swindon*	19.9	1	2₁	3		5			8¹		10	11		9¹	6	4	7										3-2(3-1)10,460 10
9. C Palace	26.9	1	2	3		5	6¹	7¹	8		10	11		9	4												2-1(0-0)10,828 7
10. Leicester	30.9	1	2	3		5	6	7	8	9¹	10	11			4												1-1(1-1)11,533 —
11. Barnsley*	3.10	1	2	3		5‡	6	7¹	8	12	10†	11		9	4	14											1-0(1-0)10,992 3
12. Hull	10.10	1	2	3	12		6	7	8	14		11		9	4†	5‡	10										0-1(0-0)6962 7
13. Man City*	17.10	1	2	3¹		5	6	7	8	12	10	11		9†	4²												3-0(2-0)12,711 4
14. Middlesbro	20.10	1	2	3		5	6	7	8		10	11		9¹†	12	4											1-3(1-0)10,491 —
15. Sheff Utd*	24.10	1	2	3		5	6	7¹	8		10	12	11	9	4†												1-0(0-0)11,949 5
16. Bournemouth	31.10	1	2	3		5	6	7	8¹		10	14	9‡	12	4‡												1-1(1-0)8105 5
17. Huddersfield*	3.11	1		3		5	6	7¹	8¹	9¹	10		2		4												3-0(2-0)9984 —
18. Reading*	7.11	1		3		5	6	7²	8	9	10	11	2		4												2-1(0-1)11,508 4
19. WBA	14.11	1	2	3		5	6	7¹	8	9†	10				4¹			12									2-2(1-0)8457 6
20. Oldham*	21.11	1	2	3†		5	6	7¹	8¹		10	11		9‡	12	4		14									2-0(1-0)11,007 4
21. Birmingham	28.11	1	2	3‡		5†		7	8		10	11	12	6	4			9	14								0-1(0-0)6718 9
22. Bradford*	5.12	1	2	3				7	8	10₂	5¹	11¹		6	4			9†			12						4-0(1-0)13,707 5
23. Shrewsbury*	18.12	1	2	3					8	10₁	5	11		9¹	6	4											2-0(0-0)9930 —
24. C Palace*	26.12	1	2	3		10	4	7²	8		5	11			6‡			12	9†	14							2-3(1-2)17,200 5
25. Swindon	28.12	1	2	3‡		10	6	7¹	8¹	5		11	12					9	14	4†							2-4(0-2)12,429 8
26. Stoke	1.1	1	2	3		10	6	7¹	8			11		9¹	5	4											2-1(1-1)9976 6
27. Millwall*	2.1	1	2	3		10	6	7	8			11		9¹	5	4											1-0(0-0)13,710 7
28. Aston Villa	16.1	1	2	3	12		6	7	8			11		9	5†	4							10				0-1(0-1)20,201 8
29. Blackburn*	30.1	1	2	3			6	7	8	14		11†		9	5‡	4	12						10				0-2(0-2)12,406 9
30. Leeds	6.2	1	2	3†	14	6‡		7	8			11	12	5								9	10				0-1(0-1)19,564 9
31. Plymouth*	13.2	1	2	3		6‡		7	12	14	11			8	5†	4						9¹	10				1-2(1-1)10,476 9
32. Leicester*	20.2		2	12			6	7	8	14		3	5	11†	4	10	9‡					1					0-2(0-1)11,084 9
33. Barnsley	27.2	1	2		12		6	7¹	8				5	11	4₁	10²	9								3		3-2(2-1)6482 8
34. Man City	5.3	1	2		12		6	7	8¹				5	11	4	10	9‡	14							3		0-2(0-1)17,402 10
35. Hull*	12.3		2	3					8	7¹		9¹	4	11†	5					10	12	6				1	2-0(1-0)9728 9
36. Bournemouth*	19.3		2	3					8	7	9¹‡	4	14	11	5					10	12	6†				1	1-2(0-2)10,208 10
37. Sheff Wed	26.3		2	3					8	7	9†	4₁	11	14	5‡					10	6					1	1-4(1-2)8753 10
38. Reading	2.4		2					5	7¹	8†	9‡	4	11	5		14	10		3	12					1		1-0(0-0)9953 11
39. WBA*	4.4		2¹					8	7			4	11	5		9	10		3	6					1		1-1(0-1)10,665 11
40. Huddersfield	8.4		2					8	7			4	11	5		9²	10		3	6					1		2-1(0-1)4023 —
41. Middlesbro*	23.4		2					5	8			11†	9¹		10³	6	12	3	4						1		4-0(3-0)12,773 9
42. Oldham	30.4		2					5	7¹	14	8	11	9‡		10	6	12	3†	4						1		1-3(1-0)5018 11
43. Birmingham*	2.5		2					5	7		8	11	9	3	10¹	6				4†	12				1		1-0(0-0)11,067 9
44. Bradford	7.5		2					5¹	7		8	11	9¹†	3	10	6				4¹	12				1		3-2(2-2)16,017 8
Apps(subs)/goals		33(0)0	41(0)2	34(1)0	1(1)0	35(4)1	29(0)1	41(0)17	34(2)6	29(0)4	11(5)2	42(1)1	26(3)7	23(4)0	18(3)3	13(3)1	13(4)8	16(4)1	4(5)0	5(1)0	5(0)0	7(0)1	5(2)0	1(0)0		10(0)0	Final League Position: 8

Own goal: Hemming, match 4.

DIVISION 2   # LEEDS UNITED

Elland Road, Leeds LS11 0ES.

Back row (left to right): Jack Ashurst, David Rennie, John Pearson, Mervyn Day, Neil Aspin, Peter Swan, Peter Haddock. *Middle row:* David Bentley (Ass. Manager), Nigel Thompson, Bobby McDonald, John Buckley, John Sheridan, Ronnie Sinclair, Brendan Ormsby, Bob Taylor, Gary Williams, David Blakey (Chief Scout), Billy Bremner (Manager). *Front row:* Alan Sutton (Physio), John Stiles, Glynn Snodin, Micky Adams, Mark Aizlewood, David Batty, Russell Doig, Keith Edwards, Peter Gunby (Coach).

Stadium Capacity: 40,176.
Pitch Dimensions: 117 × 76yds.
Telephone: 0532–716037, **Clubcall:** 0898–121180.
Chairman: L. Silver OBE.
Deputy Chairman: J. W. G. Marjason.
Directors: R. Barker, G. M. Holmes B. Sc, P. J. Gilman, E. Carlile, M. J. Bedford, R. Feldman, A. Hudson.
Managing Director: W. J. Fotherby.
Manager: Billy Bremner.
Post-War Managers: Billy Hampson, Willis Edwards, Major Frank Buckley, Raich Carter, Bill Lambton, Jack Taylor, Don Revie OBE, Brian Clough, Jimmy Armfield, Jock Stein, Jimmy Adamson, Allan Clarke, Eddie Gray MBE (13).
Assistant Manager: Dave Bentley.
Physio: Alan Sutton.
Secretary: D. J. Dowse.
Commercial Manager: Bob Baldwin.
Sponsors: Burton Group.
Founded: 1904 as Leeds City. Reconstituted as Leeds United in 1919 after Leeds City were disbanded by order of the FA.
Turned Professional: 1920.
Nickname: United.
Former Names: Leeds City (see above).
Former Grounds: None.
Record Attendance: 57,892 v Sunderland, FA Cup 5th Round replay, 15 March 1967.
Record Victory: 10–0 v Lyn Oslo, European Cup 1st Round 1st leg, 17 September 1969.
Record Defeat: 1–8 v Stoke, Division 1, 27 August 1934.
Most League Points: (3 for a win) 69, Division 2, 1984–85 and Division 2, 1987–88. (2 for a win) 67, Division 1, 1968–69.
Most League Goals: 98, Division 2, 1927–28.
Highest League Scorer in a Season: John Charles, 42, Division 2, 1953–54.
Highest Total of League Goals: Peter Lorimer, 168, 1965–79 and 1983–86.
Most League Appearances: Jack Charlton, 629, 1953–73.
League History: 1920 Elected to Division 2, 1924–27 Division 1, 1927–28 Division 2, 1928–31 Division 1, 1931–32 Division 2, 1932–47 Division 1 1947–56 Division 2, 1956–60 Division 1, 1960–64 Division 2, 1964–82 Division 1, 1982–Division 2.
Honours: Division 1 Champions 1968–69, 1973–74, runners-up 1964–65, 1965–66, 1969–70, 1970–71, 1971–72. Division 2 Champions 1923–24, 1963–64, runners-up 1927–28, 1931–32, 1955–56. FA Cup winners 1972, runners-up 1965, 1970, 1973. League Cup winners 1968. European Cup runners-up 1975. European Cup-Winners' Cup runners-up 1973. European Fairs Cup winners 1968, 1971, runners-up 1967.
Colours: All white with blue and yellow trim. **Second strip:** All yellow with blue and white trim.

LEEDS UNITED – LEAGUE RECORD 1987–88

Match no/Opp/Date	Day	Aspin	Adams	Aizlewood	Ashurst	Rennie	Williams	Sheridan	Pearson	Taylor	Snodin	Edwards	Haddock	Buckley	Doig	Stiles	Grayson	Mumby	De Mange	Melrose	Swan	McDonald	Batty	Davison	Baird	Brockie	Maguire	Noteman	FT(HT)Att Lge pos
1. Barnsley 16.8	1	2	3	4	5	6	7	8	9	10†	11	12																	1–1(0–0)9778 —
2. Leicester* 19.8	1	2	3	4	5	6	7	8[1]	9	10†	11‡	12	14																1–0(0–0)21,034 —
3. Reading* 22.8	1	2	3	4	5	6	7	8	9†		10	11	12																0–0(0–0)19,286 4
4. Bradford 29.8	1	2	3	4	5	6	7	8	9	10		11																	0–0(0–0)11,428 9
5. WBA* 31.8	1	2	3	4	5	6	7†	8[1]	14	10	9‡	11		12															1–0(0–0)19,847 —
6. Ipswich 5.9	1	2	3	4	5	6	7	8	12	10†	9	11																	0–1(0–0)11,163 8
7. Hull* 12.9	1	2	3	4†	5	6		8	9		11	10	12			7													0–2(0–0)18,205 12
8. Huddersfield 15.9	1	2	3		5	6		8	9		7†	12	11	14	4‡	10													0–0(0–0)9085 —
9. Middlesbro 19.9	1	2	3		5	6		8	9	10†	11	12	4‡	14	7														0–2(0–1)12,051 16
10. Man City* 26.9	1	2	3		5	6†		8	14	10	11[1]		4			12	7[1]	9‡											2–0(1–0)25,358 11
11. Stoke* 30.9	1	2	3		5	6		8	12	10	11		4				7	9†											0–0(0–0)17,208 —
12. Blackburn 3.10	1	2	3		5	6		8	10	12[1]	11		4				7	9†											1–1(0–0)7675 12
13. Aston Villa* 10.10	1	14	3		5	6		8	9†		11	2			4‡		10	7	12										1–3(1–2)20,741 14
14. Plymouth 17.10	1	2	3†		5	6		8	10†	9[1]	11[2]	4					12	7		14									3–6(2–2)9358 16
15. Oldham 20.10	1	2	3		5			8	10†	9	11	6			4		7			12[1]									1–1(0–1)6312 —
16. Bournemouth* 24.10	1		3		5	6[1]	4	8	9[1]		11	2					7			10[1]									3–2(3–0)15,253 13
17. Sheff Utd 31.10	1		3		5			2	8	9	11[1]		7		6		4			10[1]									2–2(0–1)12,095 14
18. Shrewsbury* 7.11	1				5		7	2		9[1]	11				6	8[1]	4			10	3								2–1(1–0)13,760 13
19. Millwall 14.11	1				5		7	3	2	9	11				6	8	4			10									1–3(0–0)8014 13
20. Swindon* 21.11	1		3		5			8[1]	2†	9[1]	11	6[1]					12			4		7	10[1]						4–2(3–1)15,457 12
21. C Palace 28.11	1		3		5			8†	2	9	11									4		12	7	10					0–3(0–1)8749 13
22. Birmingham* 5.12	1	2	3		5		4	8[1]		9[1]	11											12[1]	7	10†					4–1(2–0)15,977 13
23. Reading 12.12	1	2	3		5			8[1]		9	6									4		11	7	10					1–0(0–0)6505 12
24. Huddersfield* 19.12	1	2	3		5		4	8[2]		9	6											11	7	10[1]					3–0(1–0)20,111 11
25. Man City 26.12	1	2	3		5		4	8			11†	6					12					9	7[1]	10					2–1(1–0)30,153 10
26. Middlesbro* 28.12	1	2	3		5		4	8			11	6					12					9[1]	7	10[1]					2–0(1–0)34,186 10
27. Bradford* 1.1	1	2	3		5		4[1]	8			11[1]	6										9	7	10					2–0(1–0)36,004 9
28. Hull 3.1	1	2	3		5		4	8†	14		11‡	6					12					9[1]	7	10					1–3(1–3)14,694 —
29. Barnsley* 16.1	1	2	3		5		4	8	9‡		6								14	12		11	7†	10					0–2(0–1)19,028 9
30. WBA 30.1	1	2	3		5		11†	4[1]	8[1]	9[1]	12	6								7			10†						4–1(2–0)9008 8
31. Ipswich* 6.2	1	2	3		5		7	4	9[1]		6												10						1–0(1–0)19,564 7
32. Leicester 13.2	1	2	3		5		7	4[1]	8[1]	9	12	6†											11	10					2–3(1–1)11,937 7
33. Stoke 23.2	1		3	4	5		2	8	9[1]		11												7	10					1–2(1–0)10,129 —
34. Blackburn* 27.2	1		3	4	5	12	2	8[1]	9	10	11[1]	6†											7						2–1(2–0)23,843 7
35. Plymouth* 5.3	1		3	4	5	12	2†	8	10		11									6			7		9[1]				1–0(0–0)18,115 7
36. Aston Villa 12.3	1			4†	5	12	2	10	8[1]		11	3								6[1]			7		9				2–1(2–0)19,677 7
37. Sheff Utd* 19.3	1			4†	5		2	12[1]	10[3]	8	11	3								6[1]			7		9				5–0(1–0)22,376 7
38. Bournemouth 26.3	1		3	4	5		2	12	10		11‡	8†								6			7	14	9				0–0(0–0)9147 6
39. Shrewsbury 2.4	1		3	4	5			2‡	8	10†	11	14								6			12		9				0–1(0–0)7369 7
40. Millwall* 6.4	1		3	4	5			8[1]	12	11‡	14									6			7	10†	9				1–2(0–1)24,241 —
41. Oldham* 23.4	1		3	4	5	10		8	12		11[1]									6†			7		9				1–1(0–0)13,442 7
42. Swindon 30.4	1		3			6		8	12	10†	11				4					5			7		9[2]				2–1(2–1)8299 7
43. C Palace* 2.5	1		3	14		6		8[1]	12		11				4†					5			7		9	2	10†		1–0(1–0)13,217 7
44. Birmingham 6.5	1		3†			6		8			11				4					5			7		9	2	10	12	0–0(0–0)6024 —
App(subs)/goals	44(0)0	25(1)0	40(0)0	16(1)0	41(0)0	25(3)2	31(0)3	21(0)6	27(5)9	33(2)7	38(2)1	4(1)0	2(0)1	7(6)1	2(0)0	3(2)0	14(1)1	2(1)0	1(0)0	21(4)8	1(0)0	22(1)1	15(0)5	10(0)3	2(0)0	2(0)0	0(1)0		Final League Position: 7

Own goals: McLeary, match 19; Redmond, match 25.

LEICESTER CITY

City Stadium, Filbert Street, Leicester LE2 7FL.

Back row (left to right): David Pleat (Manager), Ian Andrews, Peter Weir, Simon Morgan, Michael Newell, Steve Walsh, Gary McAllister, Nick Cusack, Steve Wilkinson, Tony Brien, Paul Cooper, Gordon Lee (Coach).
Front row: Nicky Cross, Martin Russell, Ali Mauchlen, Paul Ramsey, Russell Osman, Paul Reid, Phil Turner.

Stadium Capacity: 31,000.
Pitch Dimensions: 112 × 75yds.
Telephone: 0533–555000, **Fax:** 0533–470585, **Clubcall:** 0898–121185.
Chairman: T. W. Shipman.
Vice-Chairman: M. F. George.
Directors: W. G. Page, W. K. Shooter FCA, T. Smeaton, J. M. Elsom FCA.
Manager: David Pleat.
Post-War Managers: Johnny Duncan, Norman Bullock, David Halliday, Matt Gillies, Frank O'Farrell, Jimmy Bloomfield, Frank McLintock, Jock Wallace, Gordon Milne, Bryan Hamilton (10).
Physio: J. McVey.
Secretary: A. K. Bennett.
Commercial Manager: P. Hill.
Sponsors: Walkers Crisps.
Founded: 1884.
Turned Professional: 1894.
Nickname: The Filberts or Foxes.
Former Names: Leicester Fosse 1884–1919.
Former Grounds: Victoria Park 1884–87, Belgrave Road 1887–88, Victoria Park 1888–91.
Record Attendance: 47,298 v Tottenham H, FA Cup 5th Round, 18 February 1928.
Record Victory: 10–0 v Portsmouth, Division 1, 20 December 1928.
Record Defeat: 0–12 (as Leicester Fosse) v Nottingham F, Division 1, 21 April 1909.
Most League Points: (3 for a win) 70, Division 2, 1982–83. (2 for a win) 51, Division 2, 1956–57.
Most League Goals: 109, Division 2, 1956–57.
Highest League Scorer in a Season: Arthur Rowley, 44, Division 2, 1956–57.
Highest Total of League Goals: Arthur Chandler, 259, 1923–35.
Most League Appearances: Adam Black, 528, 1920–35.
League History: 1894 Elected to Division 2, 1908–09 Division 1, 1909–25 Division 2, 1925–35 Division 1, 1935–37 Division 2, 1937–39 Division 1, 1946–54 Division 2, 1954–55 Division 1, 1955–57 Division 2, 1957–69 Division 1, 1969–71 Division 2, 1971–78 Division 1, 1978–80 Division 2, 1980–81 Division 1, 1981–83 Division 2, 1983–87 Division 1, 1987– Division 2.
Honours: Division 1 runners-up 1928–29. Division 2 Champions 1924–25, 1936–37, 1953–54, 1956–57, 1970–71, 1979–80, runners-up 1907–08. FA Cup runners-up 1949, 1961, 1963, 1969. League Cup winners 1964, runners-up 1965.
Colours: Blue shirts, white shorts and socks with red, white and blue trim. **Second strip:** Red shirts, black shorts and socks with red, white and blue trim.

LEICESTER CITY – LEAGUE RECORD 1987–88

Match no/Opp/Date	Andrews	Morgan	James	Osman	Walsh	Ramsey	Ford	McAllister	Cusack	Wilson	Russell	Venus	Moran	Wilkinson	Horner	Reid	Cooper	Mauchlen	Rantanen	Newell	Breen	Langan	Jobling	Osvold	MacDonald	Prindiville	Weir	Cross	Turner	Brown	FT(HT)Att Lge pos
1. Shrewsbury* 15.8	1	2	3	4	5	6	7	8‡	9	10	11†	12	14																		0-1(0-0)8469 —
2. Leeds 19.8	1	12	2	4	5	6	7	10	9‡	11	3	8†	14																		0-1(0-0)21,034 —
3. Millwall* 29.8	1	12	2	4		6	7	10		11	3†	8¹		5	9																1-0(0-0)7559 17
4. Stoke 31.8	1	14	2	4		6‡	7	10¹		11	12	3	8	5	9†																1-2(1-2)9948 —
5. Aston Villa* 5.9	1	2	9	4	5	6	7	10†		11	14	3‡	8		12																0-2(0-1)10,286 22
6. C Palace 12.9		12	2†	4	5	6‡	14	10¹		11		3	8			1	7	9													1-2(1-1)8925 22
7. Oldham* 16.9		2	3	4	5	6	7¹	12	11¹			14				1	10†	9‡¹	8¹												4-1(4-0)7358 —
8. Plymouth* 19.9		2	3	4	5	6	7¹	12	11¹†			14				1	10	9‡¹	8¹												4-0(3-0)8872 17
9. Bournemouth 26.9		2	3	4¹		6		7		11†	12	14	5			1	10¹	9‡	8¹												3-2(1-1)7969 13
10. Ipswich* 30.9		2	3	4		6		7			11¹		5†			1	10	9	8	12											1-1(1-1)11,533 —
11. Man City 3.10		2‡	3	4		6		7			11	12		14		1	10	9‡†	8¹	5											2-4(1-1)16,481 15
12. Barnsley* 10.10		12	3†	4	5	6		7	14			9			11	1	10		8	2‡											0-0(0-0)8665 15
13. Sheff Utd 17.10		12	3‡	4	5	6		7¹			11	9			14	1	10		8	2†											1-2(0-2)10,593 17
14. WBA* 21.10		2	3†	4	5¹	6		7				9²			11	1	10		8	12											3-0(1-0)9262 —
15. Hull 24.10		3		4	5¹	6		7¹	12			9†			11	1	10		8		2										2-2(1-1)8826 14
16. Blackburn* 31.10		12	3	4	5	6‡		7				9¹			11†	1	10		8		2	14									1-2(0-0)8650 17
17. Swindon* 7.11			3	4	5¹	12¹	11	7			6¹					1	10†	9	8		2										3-2(0-1)8346 15
18. Birmingham 14.11		3		4	5¹	10	11	7	14¹		6					1	12	9†	8‡		2										2-2(1-1)8666 15
19. Bradford* 21.11		3†		4	5	10	11	7	14		6					1	12	9‡	8		2										0-2(0-1)11,543 15
20. Huddersfield 28.11		3†	12	4		10	11	7	9‡		6					1	2	14	8	5											0-1(0-1)6704 16
21. Middlesbro* 5.12			2	4			10	7	9		3					1	12	14	8‡	5	6	11†									0-0(0-0)9411 16
22. Oldham 12.12			2	4			10	7	9‡		3		14			1	6	8	5		12	11†									0-2(0-1)4785 16
23. Bournemouth* 26.12	1	4	2			10‡	11†	7	14		3				6	9		5									12	8			0-1(0-1)11,452 19
24. Plymouth 28.12	1	4	12			2	7‡	10	14		3				8	9	5										11	6†			0-4(0-0)15,581 19
25. Millwall 1.1	1		2				10	7			3		8	4	12	6	9	5				11†									0-1(0-1)7220 19
26. C Palace* 2.1	1	12	2†				10	7₁			3		8¹	4	11¹‡		14	9	5¹		6										4-4(2-4)10,104 12
27. Shrewsbury 16.1	1	2			4	6		7	12		3		8†				9	5		10‡			14	11							0-0(0-0)5052 21
28. Reading 30.1	1	2		4¹	5¹	6		7			3				10		9		12								11†	8			2-1(1-1)6645 19
29. Aston Villa 6.2	1	2		4	5	6		7							10	3†	9¹	12									11	8			1-2(0-2)18,867 20
30. Leeds* 13.2		3		4	5‡	6		7¹₁	12						10†	1	2	9	14								11	8¹			3-2(1-1)11,937 19
31. Ipswich 20.2		3		4	5	6		7							10¹	1	2	9¹									11	8			2-0(1-0)11,084 17
32. Man City* 27.2		3		4	5	6		7							10	1	2	9									11	8¹			1-0(0-0)13,852 17
33. Sheff Utd* 5.3		3		4	5	6		7							10	1	2	9									11	8¹			1-0(0-0)12,256 16
34. Barnsley 12.3		3		4	5¹	6		7	12						10	1	2										11	8†			1-1(1-1)7447 16
35. Stoke* 16.3		3		4	5	6		7							10	1	2¹	9									11	8			1-1(1-0)10,502 —
36. Blackburn 19.3		3		4	5	6		7							10²	1	2†	9¹									11	8	12		3-3(0-0)12,506 16
37. Hull* 26.3		3†		4	5	6		7							10	1	2	9¹									11₁	8	12		2-1(1-0)10,353 16
38. Swindon 2.4		3†		4¹	5	6		7¹	12						10	1	2										11	8	9		2-3(1-1)9450 16
39. Birmingham* 5.4		3		4²	5	6		7							10	1	2	9									11	8			2-0(2-0)13,541 —
40. WBA 9.4		3		4	5	6		7							10	1	2	9									11	8¹	7		1-1(1-1)11,013 16
41. Reading* 23.4		3		4†	5¹	6			12						10	1	2	9									11	8	7		1-0(1-0)9603 16
42. Bradford 30.4		3			5	6		7	12						10¹	1	2	9†									11₁	8	14	4	1-4(1-4)14,393 —
43. Huddersfield* 2.5		3†			5	6		7							10	1	2	9									11₁	8²	12	4	3-0(2-0)9803 13
44. Middlesbro 7.5		3		4	5	6		7¹								1	2	9									11¹	8	10		2-1(1-0)27,645 13
Apps(subs)/goals	12(0)0	32(8)0	21(2)0	37(0)5	32(0)7	44(1)1	15(1)2	40(2)9	5(11)1	8(0)2	23(0)10	19(2)1	11(5)5	3(2)1	6(1)0	23(3)5	22(0)0	33(3)2	10(3)3	16(0)8	11(4)1	5(0)0	3(1)0	3(0)0	3(0)0	0(1)0	18(0)2	17(0)6	4(0)0	2(0)0	

Final League Position: 13

Also played: Groves, no 14¹ match 43.

DIVISION 4

LEYTON ORIENT

Leyton Stadium, Brisbane Road, Leyton, London E10 5NE.

Back row (left to right): Bill Songhurst (Physio), Kevin Hales, Kevin Nugent, Ian Juryeff, Paul Shinners, David Cass, Keith Day, Peter Wells, Andy Sussex, John Sitton, Mike Conroy, Steve Ketteridge, Pat Holland (Coach). *Front row:* Kevin Dickenson, Kevin Godfrey, Terry Howard, Henry Hughton, Frank Clark (Manager), Lee Harvey, Steve Castle, Stephen John, Alan Comfort.

Stadium Capacity: 26,500.
Pitch Dimensions: 110 × 80yds.
Telephone: 01–539 2223.
Chairman: T. Woods.
Vice-Chairman: N. Ovenden.
Managing Director: F. Clark.
Directors: A. Pincus, D. L. Weinrabe, H. Linney, M. Ovenden.
Manager: Frank Clark.
Post-War Managers: Charles Hewitt, Neil McBain, Alec Stock, Les Gore, Alec Stock, John Carey, Benny Fenton, Dave Sexton, Dick Graham, Jimmy Bloomfield, George Petchey, Jimmy Bloomfield, Ken Knighton (13).
Physio: Bill Songhurst.
Secretary: Miss Carol Stokes.
Commercial Manager: Frank Woolf.
Sponsors: Comet Roofing.
Founded: 1881.
Turned Professional: 1903.
Nickname: The O's.
Former Names: Glyn Cricket and Football Club 1881–86, Eagle Football Club 1886–88, Orient Football Club 1888–98, Clapton Orient 1898–1946, Leyton Orient 1946–66, Orient 1966–87.
Former Grounds: Glyn Road 1884–96, Whittles Athletic Ground 1896–1900, Millfields Road 1900–30, Lea Bridge Road 1930–37.
Record Attendance: 34,345 v West Ham U, FA Cup 4th Round, 25 January 1964.
Record Victory: 9–2 v Aldershot, Division 3(S), 10 February 1934 and v Chester, League Cup 3rd Round, 15 October 1962.
Record Defeat: 0–8 v Aston Villa, FA Cup 4th Round 30 January 1929.
Most League Points: (3 for a win) 72, Division 4, 1985–86. (2 for a win) 66, Division 3(S), 1955–56.
Most League Goals: 106, Division 3(S), 1955–56.
Highest League Scorer in a Season: Tom Johnston, 35, Division 2, 1957–58.
Highest Total of League Goals: Tom Johnston, 121, 1956–58, 1959–61.
Most League Appearances: Peter Allen, 431, 1965–78.
League History: 1905 Elected to Division 2, 1929–56 Division 3(S), 1956–62 Division 2, 1962–63 Division 1, 1963–66 Division 2, 1966–70 Division 3, 1970–82 Division 2, 1982–85 Division 3, 1985– Division 4.
Honours: Division 2 runners-up 1961–62. Division 3 Champions 1969–70. Division 3(S) Champions 1955–56, runners-up 1954–55.
Colours: Red shirts with white trim, white shorts, red socks. **Second strip:** Yellow shirts with blue trim, blue shorts, yellow socks.

LEYTON ORIENT – LEAGUE RECORD 1987–88

Match no/Opp/Date		Wells	Howard	Hughton	Smalley	Day	Hales	Ketteridge	Castle	Juppelf	Godfrey	Comfort	Hull	Nugent	Shinners	Simon	Sussex	Harvey	Dickenson	Comroy	Marks	Stimson	Baker	FT(HT)Att Lge pos
1. Cardiff	15.8	1	2	3	4^1	5	6	7	8	9	10†	11	12											1-1(1-1)3357 —
2. Scarboro*	22.8	1	2		4	5^1	6	7	8	9†	10	11^1	12	3^1										3-1(0-1)3540 3
3. Torquay	29.8	1	2		4	5	6	7	8^1		10	11		3†	9	12								1-1(0-0)2705 5
4. Burnley*	1.9	1	2†	12	4	5	6	7	8		10^1	11^1	3^2											4-1(1-0)3560 4
5. Hartlepool	5.9	1		2	4	5	6	7	8		10^1	11	3	9†^{1}		12								2-2(1-1)1197 4
6. Exeter*	12.9	1		2	4	5^1	6	7	8		10^1	11	9	3										2-3(0-1)3613 7
7. Stockport	15.9	1	2		4	5^1	6	7	8		10†	11	3^1		9		12							2-1(2-1)2560 —
8. Crewe	18.9	1	2		4	5	6	7^1	8		10^2	11	3†		9		12							3-3(0-1)2150 —
9. Peterboro*	26.9	1	2		4^1	5	6	7	8		10†	11^1	3		9		12							2-0(0-0)3426 4
10. Newport*	29.9	1	2^1		4	5	6	7	8		10†	11	3^1	9†^{1}			12^1							4-1(3-1)3761 —
11. Wrexham	3.10	1	2		4	5		7	8		10	11	3†	9^1			12	6						2-2(1-1)2123 3
12. Colchester	9.10	1			4	5	2	7	8		10†	11	6		9		12	3						0-0(0-0)1665 —
13. Cambridge*	17.10	1			4	5	2	7	8		10†	11	6		9		12	3						0-2(0-0)4059 5
14. Rochdale*	20.10	1	2		4^1	5	7_1		8‡		10†	11^2	6	9^2		14	12	3^1						8-0(4-0)2995 —
15. Swansea	24.10	1	2		4	5	7		8		10	11	6†	9			12	3						0-3(0-1)3895 6
16. Halifax*	31.10	1	2		4	5	7_1		8		10	11	6^1	9^2				3						4-1(3-1)3208 2
17. Carlisle	3.11	1	2		4	5	7		8		12	11	6†	9^2		14	10‡	3						2-1(1-1)2139 —
18. Bolton	7.11	1	2		4	5	7		8		10†	11	6	9			12	3						0-1(0-0)5189 6
19. Darlington*	20.11	1	2		4	5	7_1				10	11^1	6	9^1		8^1		3						4-3(1-2)3644 —
20. Hereford	28.11	1	2		4	5	7		8^1		10^1	11	6	9^1				3						3-0(2-0)1853 2
21. Tranmere*	12.12	1	2		4	5	7		8^2		10	11	6†	9^1			12	3						3-1(1-0)3684 1
22. Wolves	19.12	1	2		4	5	7		8		10†	11	6	9			12	3						0-2(0-0)12,051 3
23. Peterboro	26.12	1	2		4	5	7_1		8^1		10†	11	6	9			12	3						2-1(1-0)3371 2
24. Scunthorpe*	28.12	1	2		4	5	7†	12	8	9¹‡		11	6	14			10	3						1-1(1-1)5542 3
25. Torquay*	1.1	1	2‡		4	5	7	14	8		10†	11	6	9			12	3						0-2(0-1)4839 3
26. Exeter	2.1	1			4	5	7	2	8	9^2		11^1	12	10†			6	3						3-2(1-1)2568 2
27. Crewe*	16.1	1	2		4	5	7	14	8‡	9	10†	11	6^1				12	3						1-0(0-0)4082 2
28. Stockport*	23.1	1	2‡			5	7		8	10^1		11	12	9	4		6†	3	14					1-0(0-1)4205 2
29. Hartlepool*	6.2	1	2		4			7	8	10	6	11	12			5	9	3						0-2(0-1)4188 4
30. Scunthorpe	13.2	1	2		14	5^1		7	8_1	10^1	6	11	9†				4	12	9					2-3(1-0)2951 4
31. Cardiff*	20.2	1	2^1		5		6_1	7	8^1	10^1		11	9				4	3						4-1(1-3)3523 4
32. Scarboro	24.2	1	2	12	5		6‡	7	8^1	10	14	11	9				4	3†						1-3(0-1)2116 —
33. Wrexham	27.2	1	2	3	12	5	6	7	8	10†		11^1	14		4^1			9†						2-1(2-0)3448 3
34. Newport	1.3	1	2	3	5		6	7†	8		12	11	9		4			10						0-0(0-0)1656 —
35. Cambridge	5.3	1	2	3	5			7	8		10	11	9		4		12	6†						0-2(0-0)2500 6
36. Colchester*	12.3	1	2		5	3	7		8		10	11	9		4			6						0-0(0-0)3125 7
37. Burnley	22.3	1	2		5	7		8	10	12	11		9	4	6†			3						0-2(0-1)5878 —
38. Swansea*	26.3	1	2		5	7		8	10^1		11^1		9	4			3	6						3-0(1-0)3390 6
39. Bolton*	2.4	1	2		5	7		8	10		11		9	4			3	6						1-2(1-0)4537 8
40. Darlington	4.4	1	2		5		7	8	10^2		11		9	4			3	6						2-2(1-1)2730 7
41. Carlisle*	9.4	1	2		5	7		8^1	10^2	12	11		9†	4			3	6^1						4-1(2-0)2861 6
42. Halifax	14.4	1	2		5	7		8	10	12	11	9		4			3	6†						0-1(0-1)1006 —
43. Rochdale	23.4	1	2		5	7		8^1	10^2		11		4			9	3	6						3-1(1-1)1390 6
44. Hereford*	30.4	1	2		5	7	12		10^2	9¹‡	11	14		4	8		3	6¹†						4-0(3-0)3444 6
45. Tranmere	2.5	1	2		5	7			10^1	9†	11	12		4	8		3	6						1-2(0-1)3604 6
46. Wolves*	7.5	1	2‡		5	7	12		10	9	11	14		4	8†		3	6						0-2(0-1)7738 8

Final League Position: 8

Appearances/goals:
Wells 46(0) 0; Howard 41(0) 2; Hughton 6(2) 0; Smalley 33(2) 3; Day 41(0) 3; Hales 21(5) 1; Ketteridge 42(0) 10; Castle 23(0) 16; Juppelf 28(6) 7; Godfrey 46(0) 11; Comfort 27(9) 5; Hull 10(1) 3; Nugent 24(0) 11; Shinners 19(1) 1; Simon 5(3) 1; Sussex 6(17) 1; Harvey 22(0) 1; Dickenson 21(0) 0; Comroy 3(0) 0; Marks 10(9) 0; Stimson 9(0) 2

Own goal: D. Lewis, match 38.

DIVISION 1

LIVERPOOL

Anfield Road, Liverpool L4 0TH.

Back row (left to right): Mark Lawrenson, Mike Hooper, Jan Molby, Bary Gillespie, Bruce Grobbelaar, Kevin MacDonald. *Middle row:* Ronnie Moran (Chief Coach), John Wark, Nigel Spackman, Alan Irvine, Gary Ablett, John Aldridge, Barry Venison, Roy Evans (1st Team Coach). *Front row:* John Barnes, Steve Nicol, Ronnie Whelan, Alan Hansen, Kenny Dalglish (Player/Manager), Craig Johnston, Paul Walsh, Steve McMahon, Peter Beardsley.

Stadium Capacity: 45,600. **Pitch Dimensions:** 110 × 75yds. **Telephone:** 051–263 2361, **Clubcall:** 0898–121184.
Chairman: J. W. Smith CBE, DL, JP. **Vice-Chairman:** W. D. Corkish FCA. **Vice-Presidents:** C. J. Hill, H. E. Roberts.
Directors: S. C. Reakes JP, J. T. Cross, S. T. Moss JP, W. D. Corkish FCA, R. Paisley OBE, M. Sc. (hon), G. A. Ensor LL. B., N. White FSCA.
Manager: Kenny Dalglish. **Post-War Managers:** George Kay, Don Welsh, Phil Taylor, Bill Shankly, Bob Paisley, Joe Fagan (6).
Chief Executive/General Secretary: P. B. Robinson.
Commercial Manager: K. Addison. **Sponsors:** Candy.
Founded: 1892. **Turned Professional:** 1892.
Nickname: The Reds or Pool. **Former Names:** None. **Former Grounds:** None.
Record Attendance: 61,905 v Wolverhampton W, FA Cup 4th Round, 2 February 1952.
Record Victory: 11–0 v Stromsgodset, European Cup-winners' Cup 1st Round 1st leg, 17 September 1974.
Record Defeat: 1–9 v Birmingham C, Division 2, 11 December 1954.
Most League Points: (3 for a win) 90, Division 1, 1987–88. (2 for a win) 68, Division 1, 1978–79.
Most League Goals: 106, Division 2, 1895–96.
Highest League Scorer in a Season: Roger Hunt, 41, Division 2, 1961–62.
Highest Total of League Goals: Roger Hunt, 245, 1959–69.
Most League Appearances: Ian Callaghan, 640, 1960–78.
League History: 1893 Elected to Division 2, 1894–95 Division 1, 1895–96 Division 2, 1896–1904 Division 1, 1904–05 Division 2, 1905–54 Division 1, 1954–62 Division 2, 1962– Division 1.
Honours: Division 1 Champions 1900–01, 1905–06, 1921–22, 1922–23, 1946–47, 1963–64, 1965–66, 1972–73, 1975–76, 1976–77, 1978–79, 1979–80, 1981–82, 1982–83, 1983–84, 1985–86, 1987–88, (17 League Championships – a record), runners-up 1898–99, 1909–10, 1968–69, 1973–74, 1974–75, 1977–78, 1984–85, 1986–87. Division 2 Champions 1893–94, 1895–96, 1904–05, 1961–62. FA Cup winners 1965, 1974, 1986, runners-up 1914, 1950, 1971, 1977, 1988. League Cup winners 1981, 1982, 1983, 1984, runners-up 1978, 1987. League Super Cup winners 1986. European Cup winners 1977, 1978, 1981, 1984, runners-up 1985. European Cup-Winners' Cup runners-up 1966. UEFA Cup winners 1973, 1976. European Super Cup winners 1977. World Club Championship runners-up 1981.
Colours: All red. **Second strip:** All silver grey.

LIVERPOOL – LEAGUE RECORD 1987–88

Match no/Opp/Date	Grobbelaar	Gillespie	Venison	Nicol	Whelan	Hansen	Beardsley	Aldridge	Johnston	Barnes	McMahon	Walsh	Spackman	Wark	Lawrenson	Houghton	Ablett	Hooper	Molby	Watson	Dalglish	MacDonald	FT(HT) Att	Lge pos
1. Arsenal 15.8	1	2	3	4¹	5	6	7†	8¹	9	10	11	12											2–1(1–1)54,703	—
2. Coventry 29.8	1	2	3	4²	5	6	7¹	8†₁	9	10	11	12											4–1(1–0)27,637	7
3. West Ham 5.9	1	2	3	4	5	6	7	8₁		10	11		9										1–1(0–0)29,865	9
4. Oxford* 12.9	1	2	3	4	5	6	7	8¹†		10¹	11‡	12	9	14									2–0(2–0)42,266	7
5. Charlton* 15.9	1	2	3	4	5	6¹	7	8₁		10	11¹		9†	12									3–2(1–0)36,637	7
6. Newcastle 20.9	1	2†	3	4³	5	6	7	8¹		10	11			12	9								4–1(2–0)24,141	—
7. Derby* 29.9	1	2	3	4‡	5	6	7¹	8½	9†	10	11	12		14									4–0(1–0)43,405	—
8. Portsmouth* 3.10	1	2	3	4	5¹	6	7¹	8₁	9†	10	11‡	12		14									4–0(1–0)44,366	2
9. QPR* 17.10	1	2	3	4	5	6	7	8₁	9¹‡	10²	11†	12		14									4–0(1–0)43,735	1
10. Luton 24.10	1	2¹	3	4	5	6	7	8		10	11		9										1–0(0–0)12,452	1
11. Everton* 1.11	1	2		4	5	6	7¹	8	9	10	11¹		3										2–0(1–0)44,760	—
12. Wimbledon 4.11	1	2		4	5	6	7¹	8	9†	10	11		3			12¹							1–0(0–0)13,454	—
13. Man Utd 15.11	1	2		4	5	6	7	8¹	9	10	11		3										1–1(1–0)47,106	—
14. Norwich* 21.11	1	2		4	5	6	7†	8	12	10	11		3			9							0–0(0–0)37,446	2
15. Watford* 24.11	1	2†		4	5	6	7	8¹‡	12	10¹	11¹		3		14	9¹							4–0(0–0)32,396	—
16. Spurs 28.11	1	2†		4	5	6	7‡	8	14¹	10	11¹	12	3			9							2–0(0–0)47,362	1
17. Chelsea* 6.12	1	2		4	5	6	7	8₁†	12	10	11¹		3			9							2–1(0–1)31,211	1
18. Sthampton 12.12	1	2		4	5	6	7	8		10²	11		3†		12	9							2–2(2–1)19,507	1
19. Sheff Wed* 19.12	1	2¹	3	4	5	6	7†	8	12	10	11					9							1–0(0–0)35,383	1
20. Oxford 26.12	1	2	3	4	5	6	7	8¹	12	10‡	11†				14	9							3–0(1–0)13,680	1
21. Newcastle* 28.12	1	2	3	4	5†	6	7	8½	12	10‡	11¹					9¹							4–0(1–0)44,637	1
22. Coventry* 1.1	1	2	3†	4	5	6	7²	8¹		10	11‡				14	9¹	12						4–0(1–0)38,790	1
23. Arsenal* 16.1			2	4	5	6	7¹	8¹		10	11	12	3†			9	1						2–0(1–0)44,294	1
24. Charlton 23.1		2‡	3	4	5	6	7¹	8†	12	10¹	11	14				9	1						2–0(1–0)28,095	1
25. West Ham* 6.2	1	2		4		6	7	8†	12	10	11		5			9	3						0–0(0–0)42,049	1
26. Watford 13.2	1	2		4		6	7²	8¹	12	10‡	11‡		5			9	3					14	4–1(1–0)23,838	1
27. Portsmouth 27.2	1	2		4		6	7	8		10²	11		5			9	3						2–0(0–0)28,197	1
28. QPR 5.3	1	2		4		6	7	8		10¹	11		5			9	3						1–0(1–0)26,171	1
29. Derby 16.3	1			4		6	7	8¹		10	11†		5			9	3		12				1–0(0–0)26,356	—
30. Everton 20.3	1			4		6	7	8		10	11		5†			9	3		12				0–1(0–1)44,162	—
31. Wimbledon* 26.3	1			4		6	7	8†¹	9	10¹	11‡		5				3		14			12	2–1(1–0)36,464	1
32. Nottm F 2.4	1			4		6	12	8†‡	9	10	11				14	3	7†						1–2(0–1)29,188	1
33. Man Utd* 4.4	1	2¹		4		6	7¹	8†	12	10	11‡		5			9	3						3–3(2–1)43,497	—
34. Nottm F* 13.4	1	2¹		4		6	7¹	8²	12	10	11‡		5		9†	3	14						5–0(2–0)39,535	—
35. Norwich 20.4	1	2		4		6	7	8	10		11		5			9	3						0–0(0–0)22,509	—
36. Spurs* 23.4	1	2		4		6	7¹	8	10		11		5			9	3						1–0(1–0)44,798	1
37. Chelsea 30.4	1			4	3	6	8†	7	10¹		11		5			9	2						1–1(0–1)35,625	1
38. Sthampton* 2.5	1	2		4	14	6	7	8¹	12	10	11†		5‡			9	3						1–1(1–0)37,610	1
39. Sheff Wed 7.5	1	2		4	12	6‡	7²	8²	10¹		11†		5			9	3		14				5–1(2–0)35,893	1
40. Luton* 9.5	1	2		4	6		8¹	7†	10		11		5†			9	3				12	14	1–1(1–1)30,374	—

Apps(subs)/goals:
Grobbelaar 38(0) 0 · Gillespie 35(0) 4 · Venison 18(0) 0 · Nicol 40(0) 6 · Whelan 26(2) 1 · Hansen 39(0) 1 · Beardsley 36(2) 15 · Aldridge 36(0) 26 · Johnston 18(12) 5 · Barnes 38(0) 15 · McMahon 40(0) 9 · Walsh 1(7) 0 · Spackman 19(0) 0 · Wark 0(1) 0 · Lawrenson 10(4) 0 · Houghton 24(2) 5 · Ablett 15(2) 0 · Hooper 2(0) 0 · Molby 1(6) 0 · Watson 2(0) 0 · Dalglish 0(2) 0 · MacDonald 0(15) 0

Final League Position: 1

DIVISION 1 LUTON TOWN

70–72 Kenilworth Road, Luton LU1 1DH.

Back row (left to right): Jim Ryan (Coach), John Faulkner (Coach), David Preece, Emeka Nwajiobi, Richard Harvey, Stacey North, Gary Cobb, Kingsley Black, Mark Stein. *Middle row:* Rob Johnson, Ashley Grimes, Les Sealey, Mick Harford, Andy Dibble, Darren McDonough, Robert Wilson, Micky Weir, Dave Kirby (Physio). *Front row:* Danny Wilson, Brian Stein, Steve Foster (Captain), Ray Harford (Manager), Mal Donaghy, Ricky Hill, Tim Breaker.

Stadium Capacity: 14,700.
Pitch Dimensions: 112 × 72yds.
Telephone: 0582–411622, Recorded information: 0582–423293, Ticket office: 0582–30748.
Chairman: David J. Evans MP.
President: Cecil Holloway.
Chief Executive Director: John R. Smith.
Directors: A. Aleyan, R. J. Smith, B. Cole, E. S. Pearson LL.M. , B.Sc. , T. W. Bailey, J. R. Smith, M. Watson Challis.
Manager: Ray Harford.
Post-War Managers: George Martin, Dally Duncan, Syd Owen, Sam Bartram, Bill Harvey, Allan Brown, Alec Stock, Harry Haslam, David Pleat, John Moore (10).
Physio: David Galley.
Secretary: Bill Tomlins.
Commercial Executive: Wendy Greaves.
Sponsors: Bedford Trucks.
Founded: 1885.
Turned Professional: 1890.
Nickname: The Hatters.
Former Names: None
Former Grounds: Excelsior, Dallow Lane 1885–97, Dunstable Road 1897–1905.
Record Attendance: 30,069 v Blackpool, FA Cup 6th Round replay, 4 March 1959.
Record Victory: 12–0 v Bristol R, Division 3(S), 13 April 1936.
Record Defeat: 0–9 v Small Heath, Division 2, 12 November 1898.
Most League Points: (3 for a win) 88, Division 2, 1981–82. (2 for a win) 66, Division 4, 1967–68.
Most League Goals: 103, Division 3(S), 1936–37.
Highest League Scorer in a Season: Joe Payne, 55, Division 3(S), 1936–37.
Highest Total of League Goals: Gordon Turner, 243, 1949–64.
Most League Appearances: Bob Morton, 494, 1948–64.
League History: 1897 Elected to Division 2, 1900 failed re-election, 1920 Elected to Division 3, 1921 Division 3(S), 1937–55 Division 2, 1955–60 Division 1, 1960–63 Division 2, 1963–65 Division 3, 1965–58 Division 4, 1968–70 Division 3, 1970–74 Division 2, 1974–75 Division 1, 1975–82 Division 2, 1982– Division 1.
Honours: Division 2 Champions 1981–82, runners-up 1954–55, 1973–74. Division 3 runners-up 1969–70. Division 4 Champions 1967–68. Division 3(S) Champions 1936–37, runners-up 1935–36. FA Cup runners-up 1959. League Cup winners 1988. Full Members' Cup runners-up 1988.
Colours: White shirts with navy and orange trim, navy shorts, white socks with orange and navy turnovers. **Second strip:** All royal blue with white trim.

LUTON TOWN – LEAGUE RECORD 1987–88

Match no/Opp/Date		Sealey	Breacker	Grimes	Hill	Foster	Donaghy	Wilson D	Stein B	Harford	Wilson R	Preece	Newell	McDonough	Nwajiobi	North	Cobb	Stein M	Johnson R	Weir	Black	Allinson	Johnson M	Oldfield	Dibble	James	FT(HT)Att Lge pos
1. Derby	15.8	1	2	3	4	5	6	7	8	9	10†	11‡	12	14													0–1(0–1)17,204 —
2. Coventry*	18.8	1	2	3	4	5		7		9	10†	11	8	6	12												0–1(0–0)7506 —
3. West Ham*	22.8	1	2	3	4	5		7		9²		11	10	6†			12	8									2–2(1–2)8073 16
4. Chelsea	29.8	1	2	3	7	5	4			6	11	9		10		8											0–3(0–1)16,075 18
5. Arsenal*	31.8	1	2	3	4	5	6	7₁	8		11	9†		10			12										1–1(1–1)8745 —
6. Oxford	5.9	1	2¹	3	4¹	5	6	7	8¹†	9¹		11‡		10¹			12	14									5–2(2–1)6804 14
7. Everton*	12.9	1	2	3	4¹	5	6	7	8¹	9		11‡		10†			12	14									2–1(1–1)8124 12
8. Charlton	19.9	1	2		4	5	6	7	8	9		11†		3‡			10	14	12								0–1(0–1)5003 12
9. QPR	26.9	1	2	3	4	5	6	7	8	9										10	11						0–2(0–1)11,175 14
10. Man Utd*	3.10	1	2	3	4	5	6	7	8	9¹			14				12		11†10‡								1–1(0–0)9137 14
11. Portsmouth	10.10	1	2	3	4	5	6	7	8	9₁			12	14				10†11‡									1–3(0–0)12,391 16
12. Wimbledon*	17.10	1	2	3		5	6	7¹	8¹	9		4					11	10†	12								2–0(1–0)7018 14
13. Liverpool*	24.10	1	2	3		5	6	7	8	9		4					11		10								0–1(0–0)12,452 16
14. Newcastle*	7.11	1	2	3		5	6	7	8¹			4	9¹			10²			11								4–0(1–0)7,638 14
15. Sheff Wed	14.11	1	2	3		5	6	7	8			4	9			10¹			11¹								2–0(1–0)16,960 12
16. Spurs*	21.11	1	2	3		5	6		8			4	9			10	7		11²								2–0(1–0)10,091 11
17. Norwich*	5.12	1	2	3	12	5	6	7	8¹			4	9†				10		11								1–2(1–0)7002 14
18. Watford	12.12	1	2	3	9	5¹	6	7	8			4					10		11								1–0(1–0)12,152 9
19. Sthampton*	18.12	1	2	3	9	5	6	7	8	12¹		4¹					10		11†								2–2(1–1)6618 —
20. Everton	26.12	1	2	3‡	10†	5	6	7	8	9		4					12	14	11								0–2(0–1)32,242 11
21. Charlton*	28.12	1	2			5	6	7¹	8	9		4		10	3				11								1–0(1–0)7243 9
22. Chelsea*	1.1	1	2			5	6	7	8¹	9¹		4		10¹	3				11								3–0(1–0)8013 8
23. West Ham	2.1	1	2			5	6	7	8	9		4		10¹	3				11								1–0(0–0)16,716 8
24. Derby*	16.1	1	2			5	6	7	8			4¹		10	3		9		11								1–0(0–0)7175 8
25. Oxford*	6.2	1	2	12		5	6	7	8¹	9²		4¹		10³	3†				11								7–4(3–2)8063 8
26. Arsenal	13.2	1	2	3		5	6	7	8	9		4		10¹					11								1–2(0–2)22,615 8
27. Wimbledon	5.3	1	2	3			6	7	8	9				10	4				11	5							0–2(0–1)5058 9
28. Coventry	15.3	1	2	3		5	6	7		9		4		12	10	8†		14	11‡								0–4(0–2)13,723 —
29. Portsmouth*	29.3	1	2	3		5	6	7¹	8¹			4		10¹	9				11								4–1(1–0)6740 —
30. Newcastle	2.4	1	2	3†		5	6	7		9		4		10‡	8		11	12		14							0–4(0–2)20,565 13
31. Sheff Wed*	5.4	1	2	3		5	6	7	8¹	9		4¹†		10	11		12										2–2(0–0)7337 —
32. Man Utd	12.4		2			5†	6	7	8	9				10	3		12	11			1				1		0–3(0–1)28,830 —
33. QPR*	19.4		2			5¹		7₁	8	9	11	4		10	3					6		1			1		2–1(1–1)6735 —
34. Norwich	30.4		2	10	4	5	6‡	7₁						8¹	3		11	9†	14	12	1				1		2–2(0–0)12,700 12
35. Watford*	2.5		2	3	10	5		7₁							4		11	8	6	9¹	1						1–2(2–1)10,409 11
36. Spurs	4.5		2	10¹		5		4		11†			7	12	3			9	6	8	1						1–2(1–1)15,437 —
37. Sthampton	7.5		2	3		5		7¹						10†	8‡		4	11	12	6	9	1			14		1–1(0–1)12,722 11
38. Liverpool	9.5		2	4		5		7			10				3‡		11	8†	6	9¹	1				14		1–1(1–3)30,374 —
39. Nottm F*	13.5		2	3		5	6¹†	7		9	10				4		11		12	8	1						1–1(1–0)9018 —
40. Nottm F	15.5		2			5		7			10†			4‡	8	3	12	11	6	9¹	1				14		1–1(1–0)13,106 9
Apps(subs)/goals		31(0)0	40(0)1	31(0)1	16(1)2	39(0)2	32(0)1	38(0)8	28(0)9	24(1)9	30(0)0	13(0)0	4(0)0	24(3)4	10(2)2	0(2)0	4(3)0	20(5)11	21(4)0	7(1)0	10(3)0	23(4)3	7(2)0	6(2)3	9(0)0	0(3)0	Final League Position: 9

Own goals: Mariner, match 29.

DIVISION 2 | **MANCHESTER CITY**

Maine Road, Moss Side, Manchester M14 7WN.

Back row (left to right): Paul Stewart, Steve Redmond, Tony Adcock, Ian Brightwell, John Gidman. *Middle row:* Mel Machin (Team Manager), Andy Hinchcliffe, David White, Eric Nixon, Perry Suckling, Paul Lake, Kevin Langley, Roy Bailey (Physio), Jimmy Frizzell (Manager). *Front row:* Ian Scott, Earl Barrett, Imre Varadi, Kenny Clements, Paul Simpson, Neil McNab, Paul Moulden

Stadium Capacity: 52,600. **Pitch Dimensions:** 119 × 79yds. **Telephone:** 061–226 1191, **Clubcall:** 0898–121191. **Chairman:** P. J. Swales. **Vice-Chairman:** F. Pye. **Directors:** C. B. Muir, I. L. G. Niven, M. T. Horwich, W. C. Adams, A. Thomas, G. Doyle, W. A. Miles, B. Turnbull, J. Greibach, J. K. White.
Manager: Jimmy Frizzell. **Team Manager:** Mel Machin. **Post-War Managers:** Wilf Wild, Sam Cowan, Jock Thomson, Les McDowall, George Poyser, Joe Mercer, Malcolm Allison, John Hart, Ron Saunders, Tony Book, Malcom Allison, John Bond, John Benson, Billy McNeill MBE (14). **Physio:** R. Bailey.
Secretary: J. B. Halford. **Commercial Manager:** P. Critchley. **Sponsors:** Brother.
Founded: 1887. **Turned Professional:** 1887. **Nickname:** City. **Former Names:** Ardwick FC 1887–95 (an amalgamation of West Gorton and Gorton Athletic). **Former Grounds:** Clowes Street 1880–81, Kirkmanshulme Cricket Ground 1882–84, Queens Road 1884–87, Pink Bank Lane 1887–1923, Hyde Road 1894–1923.
Record Attendance: 84,569 v Stoke C, FA Cup 6th Round, 3 March 1934.
(British record for games other than those played in London or Glasgow).
Record Victory: 10–1 v Huddersfield T, Division 2, 7 November 1987.
Record Defeat: 1–9 v Everton, Division 1, 3 September, 1906.
Most League Points: (3 for a win) 74, Division 2, 1984–85. (2 for a win) 62 Division 2, 1946–47.
Most League Goals: 108, ivision 2, 1926–27.
Highest League Scorer in a Season: Tommy Johnson, 158, 1919–30.
Highest Total of League Goals: Tommy Johson, 158, 1919–30.
Most League Appearances: Alan Oakes, 565, 1959–76.
League History: 1892 Founder Members of Division 2 (as Ardwick FC), 1894 Elected to Division 2 (as Manchester C), 1894–99 Division 2, 1899–1902 Division 1, 1902–03 Division 2, 1903–09 Division 1, 1909–10 Division 2, 1910–26 Division 1, 1926–28 Division 2, 1928–38 Division 1, 1938–47 Division 2, 1947–50 Division 1, 1950–51 Division 2, 1951–63 Division 1, 1963–66 Division 2, 1966–83 Division 1, 1983–85 Division 2, 1985–87 Division 1, 1987– Division 2.
Honours: Division 1 Champions 1936–37, 1967–68, runners-up 1903–04, 1920–21, 1976–77. Division 2 Champions 1898–99, 1902–03, 1909–10, 1927–28, 1946–47, 1965–66, runners-up 1895–96, 1950–51. FA Cup winners 1904, 1934, 1956, 1969, runners-up 1926, 1933, 1955, 1981. League Cup winners 1970, 1976, runners-up 1974. European Cup-Winners' Cup winners 1970. Full Members' Cup runners-up 1986.
Colours: Sky blue shirts, white shorts, navy blue socks. **Second strip:** Maroon shirts with blue and white stripes, maroon shorts, maroon socks.

MANCHESTER CITY – LEAGUE RECORD 1987–88

Match no/Opp/Date		Nixon	Gidman	Hinchliffe	Clements	Brightwell	Redmond	White	Stewart	Varadi	Scott	McNab	Adcock	Simpson	Lake	Mimms	Seagraves	Suckling	Morley	Stowell	Moulden	Beckford	Thompstone	Lennon	FT(HT)Att Lge pos
1. Plymouth*	15.8	1	2	3	4	5‡	6	7	8^1	9^1	10†	11	12	14											2-1(0-1)20,046 —
2. Oldham	22.8	1	2	3	4	5	6	7	8	9^1	10	11													1-1(1-1)15,984 8
3. Aston Villa	31.8	1	2	3	4	5	6	7	8		10^1	11	9												1-1(0-1)16,282 —
4. Blackburn*	5.9	1	2	3	4	5	6	7†	8		10^1	11	9	12											1-2(1-1)20,372 15
5. Shrewsbury	12.9	1	2	3		5†	6	7	8	9	10	11	12	4											0-0(0-0)6280 17
6. Millwall*	16.9	1	2^1	3			6	7^1	8^1	9	10^1	11	5	4											4-0(1-0)15,430 —
7. Stoke*	19.9	1	2	3			6	7	8	9^3	10	11	5	4											3-0(2-0)19,322 —
8. Leeds	26.9		2	3			6	7	8	9	10	11‡	14	5	4†	1	12								0-2(0-1)25,358 12
9. Hull	29.9		2	3	11		6	7‡	8_1	9	10	12	5†	14	1	4									1-3(0-2)9650 —
10. Leicester*	3.10		2	3	11		6	12	8^2	9^2	10†	7	5		1	4									4-2(1-1)16,481 11
11. Sheff Utd*	10.10	1	2	3†	14	11^1	6	9^1	8		10	7	12	5	4‡										2-3(2-1)18,377 11
12. Ipswich	17.10	1		3	4	5	6	2	8	12		7		10	9	11†									0-3(0-2)12,711 14
13. Bradford	21.10	1	2	3	4	5	6	12^1	8^2	9		10		11	7†										4-2(1-0)14,818 —
14. Barnsley*	24.10	1	2	3	4	5	6	12	8	9^1	7†	10		11											1-1(1-1)17,063 11
15. Swindon*	31.10	1	2	3	4	5	6	7^2	8	9^1	10		11¹‡	12											4-3(2-1)11,536 10
16. Middlesbro*	4.11	1	2	3^1	4	5†	6	7	8	9‡	10	14	11	12											1-1(0-1)18,434 —
17. Huddersfield*	7.11	1	2	3	4		6	7^3	8^3		10^1	9^3	11	5											10-1(4-0)19,583 9
18. Reading	14.11	1	2		4		3	6	7	8^2	12	10	9	11†	5										2-0(0-1)10,052 9
19. Birmingham*	21.11	1	2	3	4		6	7^2	8^1		10	9	11	5											3-0(3-0)22,690 8
20. WBA	28.11	1	2	3	4	12	6	7	8	14	10†	9^1	11‡	5											1-0(0-1)15,428 8
21. Bournemouth	1.12	1	2	3	4		6	7^1	8^1	12	10	9†	11	5											2-0(1-0)9499 —
22. C Palace*	5.12	1	2	3	4		6	7	8		10	9	11	5^1											1-3(0-0)23,161 8
23. Millwall	12.12	1	2	3			6	7	8		10	9^1	11	5	4										1-0(1-0)10,477 4
24. Oldham*	19.12		2	3	4		6	7†	8^1	12	10	9	11	5											1-2(0-1)22,518 8
25. Leeds*	26.12		2	3	4		6	7^1	8	9	10	11	5			1									1-2(1-1)30,153 9
26. Stoke	28.12	1		3	4	2^1	6	7	8^2	9†	12	10	11	5											3-1(2-0)18,020 7
27. Shrewsbury*	2.1	1		3	4	2	6	7		9‡	12	10	8	11†	5_1		14								1-3(1-0)21,455 10
28. Plymouth	16.1	1	2	3	4	5†	6	7	8^1	12	10^1	9‡	14	11											2-3(2-0)13,291 10
29. Aston Villa*	23.1	1	2	3	4	5†	6	7	8	12		11	9				10								0-2(0-1)24,668 10
30. Blackburn	6.2			3		2	6	7	8	9^1		4	11	5			10	1							1-2(0-1)13,508 10
31. Bournemouth*	13.2		2	3			6	7	8^1	9^1	10	4	11	5			10	1							2-0(1-0)16,161 10
32. Leicester	27.2		2	3			6	7	8	9	10	5†	11		4		12	1							0-1(0-0)13,852 11
33. Hull*	2.3			2	3		6	7	8	9^2	10†	4	11	5			12	1							2-0(0-0)16,040 —
34. Ipswich*	5.3			3	2	4	6	7		9^1	10		11	5			8^1	1							2-0(1-0)17,402 8
35. Sheff Utd	8.3			3	2†	4	6	7^1		9	10		11	5‡	14		8^1	1	12						2-1(0-1)13,906 —
36. Swindon*	19.3			3		2	6	7	8^1	9		10	11	4			5	1							1-1(0-0)17,022 8
37. Barnsley	26.3			3		2	6	7‡	8	9^1		10	1†	4	12		5	1	14						1-3(1-2)9061 9
38. Huddersfield	2.4		2†	3	5		6	7	8	9		12	10‡	4			11	1	14						0-1(0-0)7835 9
39. Reading*	4.4		2	3	5		6	7	8^1_1		10		11	4			9	1							2-0(0-0)15,172 8
40. Middlesbro	9.4		2	3	5		6	7				11		4			10†	1	8	9	12^1				1-2(0-1)19,443 8
41. Bradford*	23.4		14	3	5^1		6	7†	8		10		2‡	4			9^1	1	12	11					2-2(2-1)20,335 10
42. Birmingham	30.4			3	5^2	6	12	8		11^1	10			4			9	1		7		2†			3-0(1-0)8014 8
43. WBA*	2.5			3	5	6	2	8_2		11^1	10			4			9^1	1		7					4-2(2-1)16,490 8
44. C Palace	7.5	1		3	5†	6	2	8		12	10		14	4			9		11‡	7					0-2(0-0)17,555 9

Apps(subs)/goals: 25(0).0 30(1).1 42(0).1 24(1).0 32(1).0 44(0).0 40(4).13 40(0).24 26(0).17 19(4).3 36(1).2 12(3).5 31(7).1 30(3).3 30(0).0 13(4).0 2(0).0 14(0).0 2(4).0 5(0).0 0(1).1 1(0).0

Final League Position: 9

MANCHESTER UNITED

Old Trafford, Manchester M16 0RA.

Back row (left to right): Norman Whiteside, Chris Turner, Paul McGrath, Viv Anderson, Billy Garton, Graeme Hogg, Liam O'Brien, Gary Walsh, John Sivebaek. *Middle row:* Nicky Wood, Brian Whitehouse (Reserve Team Manager), Jim McGregor (Physio), Joe Brown (Youth, Development Officer), Archie Knox (Ass. Manager), Eric Harrison (Youth, Team Manager), Norman Davies (Kit, Manager), Jimmy Curran (Youth, Team Coach), Terry Gibson. *Front row:* Gordon Strachan, Peter Davenport, Mike Duxbury, Brian McClair, Kevin Moran, Alex Ferguson (Manager), Bryan Robson, Remi Moses, Colin Gibson, Arthur Albiston, Jesper Olsen.

Stadium Capacity: 56,385. **Pitch Dimensions:** 116 × 76yds.
Telephone: 061–872 1661, **Recorded information:** 061–872 0199, **Membership enquiries:** 061–872 5208, **Souvenir shop:** 061–872 0199, **Clubcall:** 0898–121161.
Chairman: C. M. Edwards. **Directors:** J. M. Edelson, R. Charlton CBE, E. M. Watkins LI. M. , A. M. Midani.
Manager: Alex Ferguson.
Post-War Managers: Matt Busby, Wilf McGuinness, Sir Matt Busby, Frank O'Farrell, Tommy Docherty, Dave Sexton, Ron Atkinson (7).
Assistant Manager: Archie Knox. **Physio:** J. McGregor.
Secretary: K. R. Merrett. **Commercial Manager:** D. McGregor.
Sponsors: Sharp UK Ltd.
Founded: 1878. **Turned Professional:** 1885.
Nickname: The Red Devils.
Former Names: Newton Heath LYR 1878–1902.
Former Grounds: North Road, Monsall Road 1880–93; Bank Street 1893–1910 (based at Maine Road 1941–49, due to war–time disruption at Old Trafford).
Record Attendance: 76,962 Wolverhampton W v Grimsby T, FA Cup semi–final, 25 March 1939.
Record Victory: 10–0 v Anderlecht, European Cup preliminary Round, 26 September 1956 (at Maine Road).
Record Defeat: 0–7 v Blackburn R, Division 1, 10 April 1926 and v Aston Villa, Division 1, 27 December 1930 and v Wolverhampton W, Division 2, 26 December 1931.
Most League Points: (3 for a win) 81, Division 1, 1987–88. (2 for a win) 64, Division 1, 1956–57.
Most League Goals: 103, Division 1, 1956–57 and 1958–59.
Highest League Scorer in a Season: Dennis Viollet, 32, 1959–60.
Highest Total of League Goals: Bobby Charlton, 198, 1956–73.
Most League Appearances: Bobby Charlton, 606, 1956–73.
League History: 1892 Newton Heath elected to Division 1, 1894–1906 Division 2, 1906–22 Division 1, 1922–25 Division 2, 1925–31 Division 1, 1931–36 Division 2, 1936–37 Division 1, 1937–38 Division 2, 1938–74 Division 1, 1974–75 Division 2, 1975– Division 1.
Honours: Division 1 Champions 1907–08, 1910–11, 1951–52, 1955–56, 1956–67, 1964–65, 1966–67, runners–up 1946–47, 1947–48, 1948–49, 1950–51, 1958–59, 1963–64, 1967–68, 1979–80, 1987–88. Division 2 Champions 1935–36, 1974–75, runners–up 1896–97, 1905–06, 1924–25, 1937–38. FA Cup winners 1909, 1948, 1963, 1977, 1983, 1985, runners–up 1957, 1958, 1976, 1979. League Cup runners–up 1982–83. European Cup winners 1968.
Colours: Red shirts with red, white and black trim, white shorts, black socks with red and white turnovers. **Second strip:** White shirts with black and red trim, black shorts with white trim, white socks with black hooped turnovers.

MANCHESTER UNITED – LEAGUE RECORD 1987–88

Match no/Opp/Date		Walsh	Anderson	Duxbury	Moses	McGrath	Moran	Robson	Strachan	McClair	Whiteside	Olsen	Albiston	Davenport	Gibson	Hogg	Garton	Blackmore	O'Brien	Graham	Turner	Bruce	Martin	FT(HT)Att Lge pos
1. Sthampton	15.8	1	2	3	4†	5	6	7	8	9	10²	11‡	12	14										2–2(2–1)21,214 —
2. Arsenal*	19.8	1	2	3	4	5	6	7	8	9	10	11												0–0(0–0)42,890 —
3. Watford*	22.8	1	2	3	4	5¹	6	7	8†	9¹	10	11‡	14	12										2–0(2–0)38,582 7
4. Charlton	29.8	1	2	3	4	5¹	6	7¹	8†	9¹	10	11‡		14	12									3–1(3–0)14,056 5
5. Chelsea*	31.8	1	2	7	4	5	6		8¹	9¹	10¹	11	3†		12									3–1(1–1)46,478 4
6. Coventry	5.9	1	2	7	4	5	6		8	9	10	11‡	3†	14	12									0–0(0–0)27,125 2
7. Newcastle*	12.9	1	2	3	4	5	6	7	8	9₁	10	11¹†	12											2–2(2–2)45,137 3
8. Everton	19.9	1	2	3	4	5		7	8‡	9	10¹	11		14		6†	12							1–2(0–1)38,439 6
9. Spurs*	26.9	1	2†	6		5		7	8‡	9₁	10	11		14	3		4	12						1–0(1–0)47,601 6
10. Luton	3.10	1		6		5		7	8	9¹	10	11			3		4	2†	12					1–0(1–0)9137 6
11. Sheff Wed	10.10	1		4		5	6†	7¹	8‡	9²	10	11		14	3		2	12¹						4–2(1–1)32,779 4
12. Norwich*	17.10	1		4		5	12	7¹		9	10	11		8¹	3		2†	6‡	14					2–1(0–1)39,345 4
13. West Ham	25.10	1	2	4		5	6	7	8†	9		11		10	3¹		12							1–1(1–0)19,863 —
14. Nottm F*	31.10	1	2	4			6	7¹	12	9	10¹†	11		8	3	5								2–2(0–1)44,669 5
15. Liverpool*	15.11	1	2	4			6†	7	8	9	10¹	11		12	3		5							1–1(0–1)47,106 6
16. Wimbledon	21.11	1	2	3†	4		6	7		9	10	11	12			5¹	14	8‡						1–2(0–0)11,532 6
17. QPR	5.12		2	4		5	7¹	8	9		11	3	10¹					6		1				2–0(1–0)20,632 6
18. Oxford*	12.12		2	4		5	7†	8²	9	10	11¹	12	6	3						1				3–1(2–0)34,709 4
19. Portsmouth	19.12		2	6		5	7¹	8	9¹	10	11†		12	3						1	4			2–1(1–0)22,207 4
20. Newcastle	26.12	12	2	6‡		5	7	8	9	10	14		11	3†						1	4			0–1(0–1)26,461 5
21. Everton*	28.12		2	6	12	5	7	8†	9‡	10‡	11		14	3						1	4			2–1(0–0)47,024 4
22. Charlton*	1.1		2	5	6†		7	8	9		11‡		10	3			14	12		1	4			0–0(0–0)37,257 4
23. Watford	2.1		2	6		5‡	7	8	9¹	10		3†	12	11			14			1	4			1–0(1–0)18,038 4
24. Sthampton*	16.1		2	8	6		5‡	7	12	9		11		10	3†		14			1	4			0–2(0–1)35,716 5
25. Arsenal	24.1		2	3			7	8¹	9¹	10	11			6		5†	12			1	4			2–1(1–1)29,392 4
26. Coventry*	6.2		2	3			7	8	9	10	11	12		6			5†¹			1	4			1–0(1–0)37,144 3
27. Derby	10.2		2	3†			7	8¹	9	10¹	11‡	12	14	6			5			1	4			2–1(0–0)20,016 —
28. Chelsea	13.2		2				7		9	10		3	8	11†	6		12	5¹		1	4¹			2–1(0–0)25,014 2
29. Spurs	23.2		2‡	3				12	9¹	10	14		7	11	6†		8	5		1	5			1–1(0–1)25,731 —
30. Norwich	5.3			3†			6	7	8	9		10	11				2	5		1	4			0–1(0–0)19,129 2
31. Sheff Wed*	12.3			5				7	8	9²		11†		10¹	3	6	2¹	12		1	4			4–1(2–0)33,318 2
32. Nottm F	19.3		2	5		14			9	7	8		10	11†	6‡		3	12		1	4			0–0(0–0)27,598 2
33. West Ham*	26.3		2¹	6		5		7¹	8†¹	9		12		10	11		3			1	4			3–1(0–0)37,269 2
34. Derby*	2.4		2	6		5‡		7	8	9³		12		10†11¹	4		3	14	1					4–1(2–0)40,146 2
35. Liverpool	4.4		2¹	6†		5		7²	8¹	9	14	12		10	11		3‡			1	4			3–3(1–2)43,497 2
36. Luton*	12.4		2	6		5		7¹	8	9¹		12		10¹	11†		3			1	4			3–0(1–0)28,830 —
37. QPR*	30.4		2	6		5		7	8	9		11		10			3†	12		1	4¹			2–1(1–0)35,733 2
38. Oxford	2.5		2¹†	6		5		7	8¹	9		11		10	3		12			1	4			2–0(2–0)8966 2
39. Portsmouth*	7.5		2‡	6		5†		7¹	8	9‡		11		10¹	3	12	14			1	4			4–1(3–0)35,105 2
40. Wimbledon*	9.5			2	6†	5		7	8	9‡				10	11		3			1	4	12		2–1(0–1)28,040 —

Apps(subs)/goals: 16(0)0, 30(1)2, 39(0)0, 16(1)0, 21(0)12, 20(0)0, 36(0)0, 33(3)8, 40(0)24, 26(0)7, 30(7)2, 21(13)5, 26(3)2, 9(1)0, 5(0)0, 15(0)3, 6(1)2, 10(0)0, 24(0)0, 21(0)2, 0(0)1, 0(1)0

Final League Position: 2

Own goals: Parker, match 37.

DIVISION 3

MANSFIELD TOWN

Field Mill Ground, Quarry Lane, Mansfield NG18 5DA.

Back row (left to right): Michael Graham, Tony Kenworthy, Andy Beasley, Kevin Hitchcock, Jason Pearcey, Steve Chambers, Paul Garner. *Third row:* Keith Cassells, Ian Stringfellow, Micky Anderson, David Hodges, Steve Williams, Glen Wathall, Jason Danskin, Simon Coleman. *Second row:* Kevin Kent, Tony Lowery, George Foster (Captain), John Jarman (Ass. Manager), Ian Greaves (Manager), Bill Dearden (Coach), Mark Kearney, Steve Charles, Craig McKernon. *Front row:* Martyn Evans, Richard Flint, Gareth Price, Paul Mackness, Shane Reddish, Sean Hood, Mark Place, John Blair, Tony Clarke, Dylan Jones.

Stadium Capacity: 10,468.
Pitch Dimensions: 115 × 72yds.
Telephone: 0623–23567.
Chairman: J. W. Pratt.
Vice-Chairman: J. B. Almond JP.
Directors: G. Hall, J. A. Brown.
Manager: Ian D. Greaves.
Post-War Managers: Roy Goodall, Freddie Steele, Stan Mercer, Charlie Mitten, Sam Weaver, Raich Carter, Tommy Cummings, Tommy Eggleston, Jock Basford, Danny Williams, Dave Smith, Peter Morris, Billy Bingham, Mick Jones, Stuart Boam (15).
Assistant Manager: John Jarman.
Physio: D. Pettet.
Secretary: J. D. Eaton.
Commercial Manager: Stuart Burgan.
Sponsors: Marksman Lager (Mansfield Brewery).
Founded: 1905.
Turned Professional: 1905.
Nickname: The Stags.
Former Names: None.
Former Grounds: None.
Record Attendance: 24,467 v Nottingham F, FA Cup 3rd Round, 10 January 1963.
Record Victory: 9–2 v Rotherham U, Division 3(N), 27 December 1932 and v Hounslow T, FA Cup 1st Round replay, 5 November 1962.
Record Defeat: 1–8 v Walsall, Division 3(N), 19 January 1933.
Most League Points: (3 for a win) 81, Division 4, 1985–86. (2 for a win) 68, Division 4, 1974–75.
Most League Goals: 108, Division 4, 1962–63.
Highest League Scorer in a Season: Ted Harston, 55, Division 3(N), 1936–37.
Highest Total of League Goals: Harry Johnson, 104, 1931–36.
Most League Appearances: Sandy Pate, 413, 1967–78.
League History: 1931 Elected to Division 3(S), 1932–37 Division 3(N), 1937–47 Division 3(S), 1947–58 Division 3(N), 1958–60 Division 3, 1960–63 Division 4, 1963–72 Division 3, 1972–75 Division 4, 1975–77 Division 3, 1977–78 Division 2, 1978–80 Division 3, 1980–86 Division 4, 1986– Division 3.
Honours: Division 3 Champions 1976–77. Division 4 Champions 1974–75. Division 3(N) runners-up 1950–51. Associate Members' Cup winners 1987.
Colours: All amber with blue trim. **Second strip:** All red.

MANSFIELD TOWN – LEAGUE RECORD 1987–88

Match no/Opp	Date	Hitchcock	Graham	Kearney	Lowery	Foster	Coleman	Kent	Hodges	Stringfellow	Cassells	Charles	Chambers	McKernon	Kenworthy	Anderson	Williams	Garner	Ryan	Eves	Whatmore	Beasley	Owen	Marks	Steele	FT(HT)Att	Lge pos
1. Bristol C*	15.8	1	2	3	4	5	6	7	8†	9[1]	10[1]	11	12													2-0(2-0)5441	—
2. Chesterfield*	29.8	1	2	3	4	5	6	7	8†	9	10	11		12												0-1(0-0)5224	16
3. Sunderland	31.8	1	2	3	4	5	6	7	8†	9[1]	10	11		12												1-4(1-0)13,994	—
4. Fulham*	4.9	1	2	3†	4	5		7	8	9‡	10	11		6	12	14										0-2(0-0)3586	—
5. Grimsby	12.9	1	2		4	5		7	8[1]	9	10[1]	11[1]		6				3								3-2(1-1)3410	18
6. Wigan*	15.9	1	2		4	5		7	8†	9‡	10	11		6	12	14										0-1(0-0)3261	—
7. Southend*	19.9	1	2		4	5	3	7	8†	9[1]	10	11	12	6												1-0(1-0)2857	17
8. Rotherham	26.9	1	2		4	5	3	7[1]	8†	9‡	10	11	12	14	6											1-2(1-1)3839	20
9. Doncaster*	29.9	1	2		4	5	3	10	8	9[2]		11	12	7	6†											2-0(2-0)3159	—
10. Bristol R	3.10	1	2		4	5	6	7	8†	9		11[1]		12				3								1-2(0-1)2980	18
11. Notts Co	11.10	1	2		4	5	6	7	8		10	11[1]		9				3								1-1(0-0)8564	—
12. Gillingham*	17.10	1	2		4	5	6	7	8†	14[1]	10[1]	11	12	9‡				3								2-2(1-2)2957	18
13. Nthampton*	20.10	1	2		4	5	6[1]		8[1]	9†	10	11[1]		7		12		3								3-1(2-1)3645	—
14. Chester	24.10	1	2		4	5	6	7	12	9†	10[1]	11[1]		8				3								2-0(0-0)2453	13
15. Blackpool*	31.10	1	2		4	5	6	7			10	11	12	8†				3	9							0-0(0-0)3221	14
16. Bury	3.11	1	2		4	5	6	7		12	10	11		8†				3	9							0-1(0-1)2248	—
17. Preston*	7.11	1	2		4	5	6	7			10	11	12	8†				3	9							0-0(0-0)3631	16
18. Brighton*	21.11	1	2		4	5	6	7[1]		9†	10	11[1]		8	12			3								1-1(1-0)3284	15
19. Walsall	28.11	1	2		4	5	6	7		9†	10	11[1]		8				3	12							1-2(0-1)4227	16
20. Brentford	12.12	1	2		4	5	6	7		9[1]†	10[1]	11		8	12			3								2-2(2-1)3729	17
21. Port Vale*	20.12	1	2		4	5	6	7[4]	9†	10‡		11		8	12	14		3								4-0(2-0)3173	—
22. Rotherham*	26.12		2		4		6	7	9‡		10	11		8	5†	14		3		12						0-1(0-1)4763	16
23. York	28.12		2		4		6	7[1]	9		10	11[1]		8†	12			3	5							2-2(2-1)2781	17
24. Chesterfield	1.1	1	2		4	5	6	7		9†	10[1]	11						3	8	12						1-3(0-1)5070	16
25. Grimsby*	2.1	1	2		4	5	6	7	9†		10	11	12					3	8[1]							1-0(0-1)3315	16
26. Southend	15.1	1	2		4	5	6	7			10[1]	11						3	9†			8	12			1-2(1-1)3091	—
27. Fulham	6.2	1	2		4	5	6	7			10	11		8				3	9							0-0(0-0)3330	18
28. York*	13.2	1	2	4†		5	6	8		12	10	11[1]						3	9			7[1]				2-1(0-1)2749	17
29. Bristol C	20.2	1	2[1]	4†		5	6	9[1]						8	12	3						7				2-1(2-1)9528	16
30. Bristol R*	27.2	1	2		4	5	6	9			10[1]	11		8				3				7				1-0(0-0)3191	14
31. Doncaster	1.3	1	2		4	5	6[1]	9			10[1]	11		8				3				7				2-0(0-0)1987	—
32. Gillingham	5.3	1	2		4	5	6	9		12	10	11		8				3				7†				0-0(0-0)3720	11
33. Notts Co*	12.3	1	2		4	5	6	9		12	10†	11		8				3				7[1]				1-1(1-1)7997	13
34. Blackpool	19.3	1	2		4	5	6	9‡		14	10	11		8	12			3†				7				0-2(0-1)2847	14
35. Aldershot*	22.3	1	2			5	6	9			10	11	4	8	12			3†				7				1-0(0-0)2344	—
36. Chester*	26.3		2†		4	5	6	9		12	10	11[1]		8	3†	14						7	1			1-2(1-1)2918	14
37. Wigan	28.3		2		4	5	6	9[1]			10	11		8				3				7	1			1-2(1-1)3217	—
38. Preston	2.4		2	4‡		5	6	9			10	11		8	3	14						7†	1			0-1(0-0)6254	16
39. Walsall*	5.4		2			5	6	4		9	10†	11[1]	12	8				3				7	1			1-3(1-2)4900	—
40. Nthampton	10.4		2		4	5	6	9			10†	11		8	12			3				7	1			0-2(0-0)6917	—
41. Aldershot	19.4		2		4	5	6	9	7		10†	11		8				3				12	1			0-3(0-2)2339	—
42. Bury*	23.4		2		4	5	6	10	7	9†		11		8				3				12			1	0-0(0-0)2381	19
43. Sunderland*	26.4		2		4	5	6	10	7	9		11		8	12			3†							1	0-4(0-2)6930	—
44. Brighton	30.4		2		4	5	6	9	7‡	10†		11		8	14	12		3							1	1-3(1-2)11,493	19
45. Brentford*	2.5		2		4	5	6	9[1]			10	11[1]		8	7†			3				12			1	2-1(0-1)2663	17
46. Port Vale	7.5		2		4	5	6				10	11		8				3				7[1]			1	1-0(1-0)3617	19

Final League Position: 19

Apps(subs)/goals: 33(0)0, 46(0)1, 40(0)0, 44(0)0, 44(0)0, 45(0)2, 45(5)10, 21(1)2, 22(8)8, 40(0)9, 46(0)12, 1(2)0, 9(5)0, 29(1)0, 3(0)0, 0(4)0, 14(5)0, 30(2)1, 0(4)0, 8(0)0, 15(2)3, 0(1)0, 5(0)0

305

DIVISION 1   MIDDLESBROUGH

Ayresome Park, Middlesbrough, Cleveland TS1 4PB.

Back row (left to right): Nicky Mohan, Gary Pallister, Kevin Poole, Stephen Pears, Bernie Slaven, Trevor Senior. *Middle row:* Paul Kerr, Dean Glover, Tony Mowbray, Stuart Ripley, Alan Kernaghan, Gary Gill, Mark Burke, Michael Trotter. *Front row:* Brian Laws, Gary Parkinson, Brian Little (Reserve, and Youth Team Coach), Bruce Rioch (Manager), Colin Todd (First, Team Coach), Gary Hamilton, Colin Cooper.

Stadium Capacity: 30,000.
Pitch Dimensions: 115 × 75yds.
Telephone: 0642–819659.
Chairman: M. C. Henderson.
Chief Executive: Keith Lamb
Directors: S. Gibson, G. Fordy, R. M. Corbridge.
Manager: Bruce Rioch.
Post-War Managers: David Jack, Walter Rowley, Bob Dennison, Raich Carter, Stan Anderson, Jack Charlton OBE, John Neal, Bobby Murdoch, Malcolm Allison, Willie Maddren (10).
Coach: Colin Todd.
Physio: Tommy Johnson.
Secretary: Tom Hughes.
Commercial Manager: Alan Murray.
Founded: 1876.
Turned Professional: 1889. Reverted to amateur status in 1892, and back to professional status in 1899.
Nickname: The Boro.   **Former Names:** None.
Former Grounds: Old Archery Ground, Linthorpe Road 1877–1903.
Record Attendance: 53,596 v Newcastle U, Division 1, 27 December 1949.
Record Victory: 9–0 v Brighton & HA, Division 2, 23 August 1958.
Record Defeat: 0–9 v Blackburn R, Division 2, 6 November 1954.
Most League Points: (3 for a win) 94, Division 3, 1986–87. (2 for a win) 65, Division 2, 1973–74.
Most League Goals: 122, Division 2, 1926–27.
Highest League Scorer in a Season: George Camsell, 59, Division 2, 1926–27 (Division 2 record).
Highest Total of League Goals: George Camsell, 326, 1925–39.
Most League Appearances: Tim Williamson, 563, 1902–23.
League History: 1899 Elected to Division 2, 1902–24 Division 1, 1924–27 Division 2, 1927–28 Division 1, 1928–29 Division 2, 1929–54 Division 1, 1954–66 Division 2, 1966–67 Division 3, 1967–74 Division 2, 1974–82 Division 1, 1982–86 Division 2, 1986–87 Division 3, 1987–88 Division 2, 1988– Division 1.
Honours: Division 2 Champions 1926–27, 1928–29, 1973–74, runners-up 1901–02. Division 3 runners-up 1966–67, 1986–87. Anglo–Scottish Cup winners 1976.
Colours: Red shirts with white chest panel, white shorts, red socks with blue and white hooped turnovers. **Second strip:** Navy blue shirts with sky blue chest panel, navy blue shorts, sky blue socks with navy blue hoops on turnovers.

MIDDLESBROUGH – LEAGUE RECORD 1987–88

Match no/Opp/Date		Pears	Glover	Cooper	Mowbray	Parkinson	Pallister	Slaven	Stephens	Hamilton	Kerr	Ripley	Kernaghan	Gill	Proudlock	Laws	Burke	Poole	Senior	FT(HT)Att	Lge pos
1. Millwall*	15.8	1	2	3	4	5	6	7	8^1	9	10	11								1–1(0–1)11,535	—
2. Stoke	22.8	1	2	3	4	5	6	7	8	9†	10	11	12							0–1(0–0)9345	18
3. Oldham	29.8	1	2	3	4	5	6	7^1	8	9	10	11†	12							1–2(0–0)10,551	13
4. C Palace	1.9	1		3	4	5	6	7^1	8	9	10	11								1–3(0–1)6866	—
5. Swindon*	5.9	1		3	4	5	6	7^1	8^1	9	10	11†	12	2†		14				2–3(1–2)9342	20
6. Aston Villa	8.9	1	2	3	4	5	6	7	8	9	10^1	11								1–0(0–0)12,665	—
7. Bournemouth*	15.9	1	2	3	4	5	6	7^1	8†	9^2	10	11	12							3–0(0–0)9660	—
8. Leeds	19.9	1	2	3	4	5	6^1	7	8†	9	10^1	11	12							2–0(1–0)12,051	6
9. Blackburn	26.9	1	2	3	4	5	6	7		9	10	11	8^1							2–0(0–0)6879	4
10. Reading*	29.9	1	2	3	4	5	6	7		9	10	11	8							0–0(0–0)10,903	—
11. Bradford	3.10	1	2	3	4	5	6	7	12	9†	10	11	8							0–2(0–0)14,222	9
12. Huddersfield	10.10	1	2	3	4	5	6	7^3		9	10	12	8†			11^1				4–1(2–0)6169	5
13. WBA*	17.10	1	2	3^1	4	5	6	7^1		9	10	12	8†			11				2–1(0–1)10,684	3
14. Ipswich*	20.10	1	2	3	4	5	6^1	7^1		9	10	12	8^1			11†				3–1(0–1)10,491	—
15. Birmingham	24.10	1	2	3	4	5	6	7		9	10	12	8†			12				0–0(0–0)7404	3
16. Shrewsbury*	31.10	1	2	3	4	5†	6	7^3		9	10	11	8^1			12				4–0(1–0)10,183	2
17. Man City	4.11	1	2^1	3	4	5	6	7		9	10	11	8							1–1(0–0)18,434	—
18. Sheff Utd	7.11	1	2	3	4	5	6	7^1		9	10	11^1	8							2–0(0–0)11,278	2
19. Hull*	14.11	1	2	3	4	5	6	7	12	9	10	11^1	8†							1–0(0–1)15,709	2
20. Plymouth	21.11	1	2	3	4	5	6	7		9^1	10	11	8							1–0(1–0)9428	2
21. Barnsley*	28.11	1	2	3	4	5†	6	7^1		9	10	11	8^1			12				2–0(0–0)12,732	1
22. Leicester	5.12	1	2	3	4		6	7	12	9	10	11	8†			5				0–0(0–0)9411	1
23. Stoke*	12.12	1	2	3	4	12	6	7		9^1	10	11†	8			5				2–0(0–0)12,289	1
24. Bournemouth	19.12	1	2	3	4		6	7†		9	10	11	8			5	12			0–0(0–0)6792	1
25. Blackburn*	26.12	1	2‡	3	4	14	6	7^1		9	10	11	8			5†	12			1–1(1–1)23,536	1
26. Leeds	28.12	1		3	4	12	6	7		9	10	11	8			5†	2			0–2(0–1)34,186	1
27. Oldham	1.1	1		3	4	5	6	7		9	10^1	11†	8	14		2‡	12			1–3(0–2)8181	2
28. Millwall	16.1		2	3	4	5	6	7^1		9	10		8			11		1		1–2(0–0)8517	5
29. C Palace*	23.1	1	2^1	3	4^1	5	6	7		9	10		8			11				2–1(1–0)12,597	3
30. Swindon	6.2	1	2	3	4^1	5	6	7†		9	10		8	12		11				1–1(1–1)9941	4
31. Aston Villa*	14.2	1	2	3	4^1	5	6	7		9	10†		8‡	12^1		11	14			2–1(0–1)16,957	—
32. Reading	20.2	1	2	3	4	5	6	7		9	10†		8‡	12		11	14			0–0(0–0)6446	3
33. Bradford*	27.2	1	2	3^1	4	5	6	7†		9	10‡		8	12		11	14			1–2(0–1)21,079	4
34. WBA	5.3	1	2	3	4	5†	6	7		9	10		8‡			11	12		14	0–0(0–0)8316	5
35. Huddersfield*	12.3	1	2_1	3	4	5	6	7			10^1		8			11	9			2–0(1–0)13,866	3
36. Shrewsbury	19.3	1	2_1	3	4	5	6	7		9	10†		8	12		11				1–0(0–0)5603	3
37. Birmingham*	26.3	1	2	3	4	5	6^1	7			10	12	8			11†	9			1–1(0–0)15,465	3
38. Sheff Utd*	2.4	1	2	3	4		6	7^1		10	8^3†		12	5		11			9^2	6–0(3–0)17,340	2
39. Hull	4.4	1	2	3	4		6	7		10	8			5		11			9	0–0(0–0)10,758	2
40. Man City*	9.4	1		3	4		6	7	2^1	10	8^1			5		11			9	2–1(1–0)19,443	2
41. Ipswich	23.4	1	2†	3	4		6	7	12	10	8			5		11			9	0–4(0–3)12,773	4
42. Plymouth*	30.4	1	12	3	4	2	6	7		5^1	10		8^1			11†			9^1	3–1(1–0)16,615	3
43. Barnsley	2.5	1		3	4	2	6	7^2		5	10		8^1†	12		11			9	3–0(2–0)13,240	2
44. Leicester*	7.5	1	14	3	4	2	6	7^1		5	10		8‡	12		11			9†	1–2(0–1)27,645	3

Final League Position: 3

Apps(subs)/goals: Pears 43(0)/0; Glover 36(2)/4; Cooper 43(0)/2; Mowbray 44(0)/3; Parkinson 35(3)/0; Pallister 44(0)/3; Slaven 44(0)/21; Stephens 8(3)/2; Hamilton 40(1)/6; Kerr 43(1)/5; Ripley 40(3)/8; Kernaghan 24(11)/6; Gill 2(1)/0; Proudlock 0(0)/0; Laws 24(4)/1; Burke 8(8)/0; Poole 1(0)/0; Senior 5(1)/2

DIVISION 1

MILLWALL

The Den, Cold Blow Lane, London, SE14 5RH.

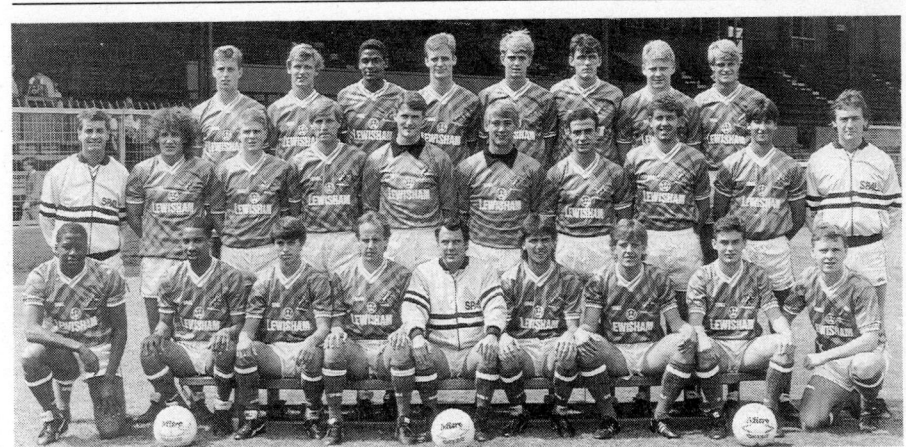

Back row (left to right): Keith Stevens, Teddy Sheringham, Steve Anthrobus, Alan Walker, David Thompson, Tony Cascarino, Michael Marks, Steve Wood. *Middle row:* Frank McLintock (Ass. Manager), Terry Hurlock, Dave Mehmet, Alan McLeary, Paul Sansome, Brian Horne, Denis Salman, Phil Coleman, Jimmy Carter, Roger Cross (Coach). *Front row:* George Lawrence, Wesley Reid, Darren Morgan, Les Briley, John Docherty (Manager), Dave Byrne, Nicky Coleman, Sean Sparham, Kevin O'Callaghan.

Stadium Capacity: 19,000.
Pitch Dimensions: 112 × 74yds.
Telephone: 01–639 3143, **Commercial dept:** 01–639 4590.
Chairman: R. I. Burr.
Vice-Chairman: P. W. Mead.
Directors: J. E. Burnige, B. E. Mitchell, Cllr D. Sullivan.
Manager: John Docherty.
Post-War Managers: Jack Cock, Charlie Hewitt, Ron Gray, Jimmy Seed, Reg Smith, Ron Gray, Billy Gray, Benny Fenton, Gordon Jago, George Petchey, Peter Anderson, George Graham (12).
Assistant Manager: Frank McLintock.
Physio: P. Melville.
Secretary: G. I. S. Hortop.
Commercial Manager: W. W. Neil.
Sponsors: Lewisham Council.
Founded: 1885.
Turned Professional: 1893.
Nickname: The Lions.
Former Names: Millwall Rovers 1885, Millwall Athletic 1889.
Former Grounds: Glengall Road, Millwall 1885–86, behind the Lord Nelson 1886–90, East Ferry Road 1890–1901, North Greenwich 1901–1910.
Record Attendance: 48,672 v Leicester C, FA Cup 5th Round, 20 February 1937.
Record Victory: 9–1 v Torquay U, Division 3(S), 29 August, 1927 and v Coventry C, Division 3(S), 19 November 1927.
Record Defeat: 1–9 v Aston Villa, FA Cup 4th Round, 28 January 1946.
Most League Points: (3 for a win) 90, Division 3, 1984–85. (2 for a win) 65, Division 3(S), 1927–28 an Division 3, 1965–66.
Most League Goals: 127, Division 3(S), 1927–28.
Highest League Scorer in a Season: Richard Parker, 37, Division 3(S), 1926–27.
Highest Total of League Goals: Derek Possee, 79. 1967–73.
Most League Appearances: Barry Kitchener, 523, 1967–82.
League History: 1920 Founder Members of Division 3, 1921 Division 3(S), 1928–34 Division 2, 1934–38 Division 3(S), 1938–48 Division 2, 1948–58 Division 3(S), 1958–62 Division 4, 1962–64 Division 3, 1964–65 Division 4, 1965–66 Division 3, 1966–75 Division 2, 1975–76 Division 3, 1976–79 Division 2, 1979–85 Division 3, 1985–88 Division 2, 1988– Division 1.
Honours: Division 2 Champions 1987–88. Division 3 runners-up 1965–66, 1984–85, Division 4 Champions 1961–62, runners-up 1964–65. Division 3(S) Champions 1927–28, 1937–38. Associate Members' Cup winners 1983.
Colours: Blue shirts, white shorts, blue socks. **Second strip:** Yellow shirts, black shorts and socks.

MILLWALL – LEAGUE RECORD 1987–88

Match no/Opp/Date		Home	Stevens	Sparham	Horlock	Walker	McLeary	Lawrence	Mehmet	Sheringham	Cascarino	Byrne	Briley	Wood	Salman	O'Callaghan	Coleman	Anthrobus	Carter	Cooke	Sansome	Thompson	Morgan	Horrix	FT(HT)Att	Lge pos
1. Middlesbro	15.8	1	2	3	4	5	6	7	8†	9^1	10	11	12												1-1(1-0)11,535	—
2. Barnsley*	22.8	1	2	3	4	5	6	7^1	8	9^1	10^1	11													3-1(1-0)6017	6
3. Leicester	29.8	1	2	3	4	5	6	7	8	9	10	11													0-1(0-0)7559	11
4. Birmingham	1.9	1	2^1	3	4	5^1	6	7^1	8	9	10	11													3-1(1-1)6758	—
5. Bradford	5.9	1	2	3	4^1	5	6	7	8	9	10	11													1-3(0-1)8658	12
6. Ipswich*	12.9	1	2	3	4	5^1		7	8	9	10	11	6_1												2-1(1-0)6356	8
7. Man. City	16.9	1	2	3	4	5	6	7	8	9†	10	12	11												0-4(0-2)15,430	—
8. Sheffield Utd	19.9	1			4	5	6	7^1	8	9	10			2	11^1	3									2-1(1-1)8048	8
9. WBA*	26.9	1			4	5	6		8	9^1	10^1		2		11	3									2-0(1-0)6564	6
10. Oldham	29.9	1	12		4	5	6†		8	9	10		2		11	3									0-0(0-0)4840	6
11. Swindon*	3.10	1			4	5	6	7^1	8	9^1			2		11	3									2-2(1-0)7018	6
12. C Palace	10.10	1			4	5	6	7	8	9	10		2		11	3									0-1(0-0)10,678	10
13. Shrewsbury*	17.10	1			4	5	6	7	8	9^1	10^1	12	2		11†	3									4-1(2-1)5202	8
14. Plymouth	20.10	1			4	5	6	7	8	9^1	10^1		2		3	11									2-1(1-1)8958	8
15. Huddersfield	31.10	1			4	5^1	6	7	8	9	10	12	2		3	11†									1-2(0-1)5504	9
16. Bournemouth*	3.11	1	4			5	6	7	8	9	10^1	12	2		3	11†									1-2(0-0)5734	—
17. Aston Villa	7.11	1	4			5	6		7	9	10^1	8^1	2		3		11								2-1(2-1)13,255	8
18. Leeds*	14.11	1	4			5	6		7	9	10^2	8	2		3		11								3-1(1-0)8014	7
19. Stoke	21.11	1	4			5	6		7	9	10^2	8	2		3		11								2-1(0-1)7998	7
20. Hull*	28.11	1	4			5	6		7^1	9^1	10	8	2		3		11								2-0(0-0)6743	7
21. Reading*	1.12	1	4			5	6	12^1	$7†$	9	10^2	8	2		3		11								3-0(2-0)6762	6
22. Blackburn	5.12	1	4	12		5	6	7		9	10^{1+}	8	2		3		11								1-2(0-1)6140	6
23. Man City*	12.12	1	4	10		5	6			9		8	2		3		11	7							0-1(0-1)10,477	7
24. Barnsley	19.12		4				6			9^1	10	8	2		3		11	7	1	5					1-4(1-2)5011	9
25. WBA	26.12		4							9^3	12	8^1	6	2	10†	3	11	7	5						4-1(2-1)9291	7
26. Sheff Utd*	28.12		4							9^1		7	8^1	6	2	3	11	10^1	5						3-1(3-0)7255	5
27. Leicester*	1.1	1	4							9	10	7	8^1		2	3	11			5	6				1-0(1-0)7220	4
28. Ipswich	9.1	1	4							9	10^1	7	8		2	3	11			5	6				1-1(0-1)13,710	4
29. Middlesbro*	16.1	1	4		5^1	6				9^1	10	7	8		2	3	11								2-1(0-0)8517	3
30. Bradford*	6.2	1	4			5	6			9	10	7	8		2	3	11								0-1(0-0)8201	5
31. Birmingham	9.2	1	4			5	6			9	10	7	8		2	3	11								0-1(0-0)5878	—
32. Reading	13.2	1	4		7^1	6				9^2	10		8	5	2	11	3								3-2(1-2)6050	4
33. Oldham*	20.2	1			4	6				9	10^1	12	8	5	2	11	3	7†							1-1(0-0)6839	4
34. Swindon	27.2	1			4†	6				9	10^1		8	5	2	11	3	7				12			1-0(1-0)9570	3
35. Shrewsbury	5.3	1	7		4	6				9	10		8	5	2	11	3								0-0(0-0)5408	3
36. C Palace*	12.3	1	4			6				9^1	10		8	5	2	11	3	7							1-1(0-0)12,815	5
37. Huddersfield*	19.3	1	4			6				9^2	10^1		8	5	2	11†	3	7					12^1		4-1(2-1)6181	4
38. Aston Villa*	2.4	1	4		7	6				9^1	10		8	5	2^{1+}	11	3	12							2-1(1-1)13,697	4
39. Leeds	6.4	1	2		4^1	6				9	10^1		8	5		11	3	7							2-1(1-0)24,241	—
40. Plymouth*	9.4	1	2		4	6				9^1	10^1		8	5		11†	3	7				12			3-2(3-2)11,052	1
41. Bournemouth	19.4	1	2		4^1	6				9	10		8	5		11_1		7				3			2-1(2-1)9204	1
42. Stoke*	30.4	1	2		4	6				9^1	10		8	5		11_1	3	7							2-0(0-0)12,636	1
43. Hull	2.5	1	2		4	6				9	10		8	5		11_1	3	7							1-0(1-0)10,811	1
44. Blackburn*	7.5	1	2		4	6				9^1	10		8	5		11	3	7							1-4(0-2)15,467	1
Apps(subs)/goals		43(0)/1	34(1)/1	7(0)/0	27(1)/4	24(0)/4	31(0)/0	16(1)/4	10(0)/0	43(0)/22	39(0)/20	17(6)/2	43(0)/14	22(0)/0	36(0)/1	22(0)/7	30(0)/0	25(1)/0	40(0)/1	10(0)/0	5(0)/0	3(1)/0	0(2)/1			

Final League Position: 1

Own goal: Griffin, match 13.

DIVISION 1

NEWCASTLE UNITED

St James' Park, Newcastle-upon-Tyne NE1 4ST.

Back row (left to right): Martin Thomas, Ian Bogie, Ken Wharton, Andy Thomas, Brian Tinnion, Paul Stephenson, Garry Kelly. *Middle row:* Paul Gascoigne, Neil McDonald, John Cornwell, Kevin Scott, Peter Jackson, John Anderson. *Front row:* Darren Jackson, Paul Goddard, Glen Roeder, Mirandinha, David McCreery.

Stadium Capacity: 36,585.
Pitch Dimensions: 115 × 75yds.
Telephone: 091–232 8361, **Commercial dept:** 091–232 2285, **Club shop:** 091–261 6357, **Recorded information:** 091–261 1571, **Clubcall:** 0898–121190.
Chairman: W. G. McKeag.
Directors: J. Rush AFC, R. Mackenzie, Sir George Bowman JP, G. R. Forbes, E. Dunn, G. R. Dickson, S. Seymour.
Manager: Willie McFaul.
Post-War Managers: George Martin, Duggie Livingstone, Charlie Mitten, Norman Smith, Joe Harvey, Gordon Lee, Richard Dinnis, Bill McGarry, Arthur Cox, Jack Charlton OBE (10).
Assistant Manager: Joe Harvey.
Physio: Derek Wright.
General Manager/Secretary: R. Cushing.
Commercial Manager: G. McDonnell.
Founded: 1882.
Turned Professional: 1889.
Nickname: The Magpies.
Former Names: Newcastle East End 1882–92.
Former Grounds: Chillingham Road, Heaton 1882–92.
Record Attendance: 68,386 v Chelsea, Division 1, 3 September 1930.
Record Victory: 13–0 v Newport Co, Division 2, 5 October 1946.
Record Defeat: 0–9 v Burton Wanderers, Division 2, 15 April 1895.
Most League Points: (3 for a win) 80, Division 2, 1983–84. (2 for a win) 57, Division 2, 1964–65.
Most League Goals: 98, Division 1, 1951–52.
Highest League Scorer in a Season: Hughie Gallacher, 36, Division 1, 1926–27.
Highest Total of League Goals: Jackie Milburn, 178, 1946–57.
Most League Appearances: Jim Lawrence, 432, 1904–22.
League History: 1893 Elected to Division 2, 1898–1934 Division 1, 1934–48 Division 2, 1948–61 Division 1, 1961–65 Division 2, 1965–78 Division 1, 1978–84 Division 2, 1984– Division 1.
Honours: Division 1 Champions 1904–05, 1906–07, 1908–09, 1926–27.
Division 2 Champions 1964–65, runners-up 1897–98, 1947–48. FA Cup winners 1910, 1924, 1932, 1951, 1952, 1955, runners-up 1905, 1908, 1911, 1974. League Cup runners-up 1976. European Fairs Cup winners 1969. Anglo–Italian Cup winners 1973. Texaco Cup winners 1974, 1975.
Colours: Black and white striped shirts, black shorts and socks. **Second strip:** Yellow and green striped shirts, green shorts, yellow socks.

NEWCASTLE UNITED – LEAGUE RECORD 1987–88

Match no/Opp/Date	Kelly	McDonald	Bailey	McCreery	Jackson P	Roeder	Jackson D	Gascoigne	Goddard	Wharton	Hodges	Thomas A	Scott	Thomas M	Anderson	Mirandinha	Tinnion	Stephenson	Cornwell	O'Neill	Bogie	Craig	Lormor	FT(HT)Att Lge pos
1. Spurs 19.8	1	2	3	4¹	5	6	7†	8	9	10	11	12												1–3(0–3)26,261 —
2. Sheff Wed 22.8	1	2	3	4	5		7¹	8	9	10	11		6											1–0(1–0)22,031 13
3. Nottm F* 29.8	1	2	3	4	5	6	7	8	9‡	10†	11	14	1	12										0–1(0–1)20,111 17
4. Norwich 1.9		2		4	5¹	6	7	8	3	11			1	10	9									1–1(0–0)16,636 —
5. Wimbledon* 5.9	1	2₁		4	5	6		8	9	3	11		1	7	10									1–2(0–2)22,684 18
6. Man Utd 12.9	1	2		4‡	5	6	12	9	8	11†				3		10²	14	7						2–2(2–2)45,137 18
7. Liverpool* 20.9	1	2₁		4	5	6	12	9	8	11†				3		10	7							1–4(0–2)24,141 —
8. Sthampton* 26.9	1	7		4	5	6	12	8	9¹					2†	10¹	3		11						2–1(0–0)18,093 15
9. Chelsea 3.10	1	7‡		4	5	6	12	8	9¹	14¹				2	10	3		11†						2–2(1–2)22,071 15
10. Everton* 17.10	1	2		4†	5	6		8	9	12					10¹	3		11						1–1(0–1)20,266 16
11. Coventry 24.10	1	2		4	5	6	7¹	8¹	9¹	14				12	10†	3		11‡						3–1(2–1)18,585 12
12. Arsenal* 31.10	1	7		4	5	6	10	8	9					2			3	11						0–1(0–0)23,662 15
13. Luton 7.11	1	7			5	6	11	8	9	4				2	10	3†			12					0–4(0–1)7638 18
14. Derby* 14.11	1	7†			5	6	10	8	9	4				2		3		11	12					0–0(0–0)21,698 17
15. QPR 21.11	1	7		4	5¹	6		8		3				2	9					10	11			1–1(0–1)11,794 16
16. Charlton* 28.11	1	7		4	5	6		8		3				2	10¹			11¹	9					2–1(1–1)19,453 16
17. Oxford 5.12	1	7₁		4	5	6				3				2	10¹			11	9¹	8				3–1(1–0)8190 15
18. Portsmouth* 12.12	1	7		4	5	6			9	3				2	10¹			11		8				1–0(1–0)20,455 14
19. West Ham 19.12	1	7		4	5	6	12	8	9					2	10¹	3†		11						1–2(0–0)18,679 15
20. Man Utd* 26.12	1	2		4		6¹	7‡	8	9	3†				5	10			11		14	12			1–0(1–0)26,461 12
21. Liverpool 28.12	1	2		4		6	7†	8	9	3				5	10			11		12				0–4(0–1)44,637 14
22. Nottm F 1.1	1	7		4	5	6		8¹	9	3				2	10¹			11						2–0(1–0)28,583 13
23. Sheff Wed* 2.1	1	7		4	5	6	11	8	9²‡	3				2†	10¹			12		14				2–2(0–0)25,503 12
24. Spurs* 23.1	1	7			5	6	4	8²	9	3				2	10†			11			12			2–0(1–0)24,616 12
25. Wimbledon 6.2	1	7			5	6	4†	8	9	3				2	10			11						0–0(0–0)10,505 10
26. Norwich* 13.2	1	7			5	6	4†	8¹	9	3				2	10			12	11					1–3(1–1)21,068 12
27. Chelsea* 27.2	1	2		4	5	6	12	8¹	9	3					10²‡			7	11					3–1(2–0)17,858 11
28. Sthampton 1.3	1	2		4	5	6		8	9	3					10			7	11¹					1–1(0–0)13,380 —
29. Everton 5.3	1	7		4†	5	6	12	8	9					2	10	3								0–1(0–1)25,674 11
30. Arsenal 19.3	1	2		4		6	10	8	9¹					5		3	12	7†						1–0(1–0)25,889 13
31. Coventry* 26.3	1	2		4		6	10	8	9					5		3	7†		11²	12				2–2(0–0)19,050 12
32. Luton* 2.4	1	2		4		6		8	9¹	11				5		3	7		10³					4–0(2–0)20,565 11
33. Derby 4.4	1	2‡		4		6		8	9	11				5	14	3	7†	12	10¹					1–2(1–0)18,591 11
34. QPR* 9.4	1	7		4	5	6	11	8	9	3				2					10¹					1–1(1–1)18,403 11
35. Watford* 12.4	1	2		4		6	7†	8	9	11¹				5		3¹	12		10¹					3–0(1–0)16,318 —
36. Watford 19.4	1	2		4		6	8		9	3		7†		5¹	10‡			12	11			14		1–1(0–1)12,075 —
37. Charlton 23.4	1	2		4		6	8	12	9	11				5		3†	7		10					0–2(0–2)7482 10
38. Oxford* 30.4	1	2		4		6	7†	8	9¹			12		5		3		10¹	11¹					3–1(1–0)16,617 10
39. Portsmouth 2.5	1	2	12	4			7	8		9	6¹			5		3		10†	11¹					2–1(1–0)12,468 8
40. West Ham* 7.5	1	2		4			7	8¹	9		6			5		3		10¹†	12	11				2–1(0–1)23,731 8
Apps(subs)/goals	37(0)0	40(0)3	3(1)0	35(0)1	28(0)2	37(0)1	24(1)7	34(1)17	35(0)8	28(3)2	7(0)0	1(3)0	4(0)1	30(0)0	33(2)1	25(0)11	15(0)1	5(2)0	20(4)1	19(2)12	3(4)0	1(2)0	3(2)2	

Final League Position: 8

GM Vauxhall Conference

NEWPORT COUNTY
Somerton Park, Newport, Gwent NP1 0HZ.

*Back row
(left to right):*
Dr D. G. Jones
(Medical Officer)
Richard Jones
Kevin Hamer
Darren Peacock
Richard Thompson
Paul Bradshaw
Steve Tupling
Dean Boughen
Glynne Millett
David Williams
(Caretaker Manager)
Dr D. T. Heffernan
(Medical Officer)
Front row:
Tony Gilbert (Trainer)
Andy Thackeray
Roy Davis
Norman Parselle
David Abbruzzese
Robbie Taylor
Sean Bennett

Stadium Capacity: 6,000.
Pitch Dimensions: 110 × 75 yds.
Telephone: 0633–277543.
Chairman:
Directors: J. Dickie, J. B. Henderson, T. D. Woods.
Manager:
Post-War Managers: Billy McCandless, Tom Bromilow, Fred Stansfield, Bill Lucas, Bobby Evans, Bill Lucas, Trevor Morris, Les Graham, Bob Ferguson, Bill Lucas, Brian Harris, Dave Elliot, Jimmy Scoular, Colin Addison, Len Ashurst, Colin Addison, Bobby Smith, John Relish, Jimmy Mullen, John Lewis (20).
Assistant Manager: David Williams.
Physio: David Williams.
Secretary: K. L. Saunders.
Sponsors: South Wales Argus.
Founded: 1912.
Turned Professional: 1912.
Nickname: The Ironsides.
Former Names: None.
Former Grounds: None.
Record Attendance: 24,268 v Cardiff C, Division 3 (S), 16 October 1937.
Record Victory: 10–0 v Merthyr Town, Division 3(S), 10 April, 1930.
Record Defeat: 0–13 v Newcastle U, Division 2, 5 October 1946.
Most League Points: (3 for a win) 78, Division 3, 1982–83. (2 for a win) 61, Division 4, 1979–80.
Most League Goals: 85, Division 4, 1964–65.
Highest League Scorer in a Season: Tudor Martin, 34, Division 3(S), 1929–30.
Highest Total of League Goals: Reg Parker, 99, 1948–54.
Most League Appearances: Len Weare, 526, 1955–70.
League History: 1920 Founder Members of Division 3, 1921 Division 3(S), left the League in 1931, re-elected in 1932, 1932–39 Division 3(S), 1946–47 Division 2, 1947–58 Division 3(S), 1958–62 Division 3, 1962–80 Division 4, 1980–87 Division 3, 1987–88 Division 4.
Honours: Division 3(S) Champions 1938–39. Welsh Cup winners 1980, runners-up 1963.
Colours: Amber shirts, black shorts, amber socks. **Second strip:** White shirts, black shorts, white socks.

NEWPORT COUNTY – LEAGUE RECORD 1987–88

Match no/Opp/Date		Bradshaw	Hodson	Lewis	Gibbins	Williams	Giles	Thackeray	Taylor	Evans	Tupling	Millett	Sherlock	Collins	Hamer	Parselle	Withers	Abruzzese	Jones	Hobbin	Preece	Thompson	Miller	Carr	Osborne	Mann	Downes	Brook	Clement	Coles	Bodin	FT(HT)Att	Lge pos
1. Hartlepool	15.8	1	2	3	4	5		7	8	9	10	11																				0-0(0-0)1926	—
2. Burnley*	22.8	1	2	3	4	5		7	8	9	10†	11	12																			0-1(0-0)2006	21
3. Exeter	29.8	1	2	3	4	5		7	8	9	10‡	11		12	14																	0-3(0-2)2628	24
4. Stockport*	31.8	1	2		4	5	7₁		8	9	10‡	11	12	3	14		6†															1-2(1-0)1626	—
5. Halifax	5.9	1	2		6	5	7	4	8	9¹	10	11	12	3																		1-3(0-0)1095	24
6. Torquay*	12.9	1	2	11	4	5			10¹	8				3¹	9†	12¹	6	7														3-1(2-1)1368	23
7. Scarboro	16.9	1	2	11†	4	5	14	12	10¹	8				3		9	6	7‡														1-3(1-1)2345	—
8. Scunthorpe	19.9	1	2		4	5			8	9‡	10†	11¹		3	14	12	6	7														1-3(1-2)2004	24
9. Hereford*	27.9	1	2	11		5		7	8	9†	10	12		3					4	6												0-0(0-0)1480	—
10. Orient	29.9	1	2¹	11	8	5	4	7		9‡		12		3	14		6			8†												1-4(1-3)3761	—
11. Colchester*	3.10		2	11	10	5	7	4	9	8								6†	3	12¹												1-2(0-1)1200	24
12. Cambridge	10.10	1	2		5	4†	6	8	11	7	10					12	9	3														0-4(0-1)1874	24
13. Swansea	17.10	1	2		5	3	7	4	11²	12	8	10†		6			14	9‡														2-1(1-0)3739	24
14. Peterboro	21.10	1	2		5	3	7	4	11	8		12					6		10				9									0-3(0-2)3163	—
15. Wrexham*	24.10	1	2		5	3	7	4¹	11†	8		12		6				14		9¹‡	10											2-0(1-0)1470	22
16. Wolves	31.10	1	2			3	7	4	11	8		12		6				14		9†	10¹		5									1-2(0-0)6467	22
17. Bolton*	3.11	1	2	3			7	4	12	8		9		6					11†		10		5									0-1(0-1)1566	—
18. Carlisle	7.11	1	2	3			7	4	12	8†		9†		6					14¹		10		5	11								1-3(0-2)1766	23
19. Cardiff*	21.11	1	2	3			7	4	9†	8		6	12				5		14		10¹			11‡								1-2(0-0)4022	24
20. Tranmere	27.11			3			7	4		8†		6	9‡				2	12			14		5	11	10							0-4(0-3)3252	—
21. Rochdale	19.12				4	3‡			8		10†	14		5			2	9	12				11	6	7							0-3(0-2)1491	24
22. Hereford	26.12		2	8†	5¹	12	4							3				14	7				11	10†		6¹	9					2-4(1-3)3203	24
23. Crewe*	28.12		2		5		4	11						3				12	7				8†	10		6¹	9					1-2(0-1)1918	24
24. Exeter*	1.1		2	8¹	5		4					11							7				6		10†		9	3				1-1(1-1)1691	24
25. Burnley	9.1		2	8	5†		4					11	12						7				6		10		9	3	1			0-2(0-0)5305	24
26. Darlington*	12.1		2	8	5		4					11							7				6		10		9¹	3¹	1			2-1(1-1)1402	—
27. Scunthorpe*	16.1		2	8	5		4	12				11¹							7				6†		10		9	3	1			1-1(1-0)1760	—
28. Stockport	29.1		2	8	5		4	12				14							7¹			5	6‡		10		9	3	1	11		1-5(1-2)2509	—
29. Halifax*	5.2		2	8	5		4												7			5	6		10¹		9		1	11		1-0(0-0)1509	—
30. Crewe	13.2		2	8	5			12						3					7				6		10†		9		1	11¹		1-2(1-0)2080	24
31. Hartlepool*	19.2		2	8	5²	4†		12						3					7				6		10		9		1	11¹		2-3(1-2)1880	—
32. Colchester	26.2		2	8	5									3					7				6	4	10		9		1	11		0-0(0-0)1784	—
33. Orient*	1.3		2	8	5									3					7				6	4	10		9		1	11		0-0(0-0)1656	—
34. Swansea*	5.3		2	8	5	11								3					7				6	4	10†		9¹		1			1-2(1-0)2235	24
35. Cambridge*	12.3		2		5		4	8	6		11			3					7			12			10†		9		1			0-0(0-0)1208	24
36. Wrexham	26.3			8	10				6	7¹		3									4			2	5	11	9†				1	1-4(1-1)1627	24
37. Carlisle*	2.4			8	10¹				6	7	3†			4	12									2	5	11	9‡				1	1-2(1-2)1376	24
38. Cardiff	4.4			8	10				6	7				4	11†									2	5	3	9‡				1	0-4(0-1)6536	24
39. Peterboro*	9.4			8	10				6	7	9			4	14									2	5	3†	12				1	0-4(0-1)988	24
40. Scarboro*	12.4			8	10				6	7				4	3									2	5		9					0-4(0-1)1025	24
41. Torquay	19.4	1		8†	10				6	7		4¹	11	3		2	5‡								9							1-6(1-2)3416	—
42. Bolton	23.4	1		8	10				6	7		4	11†			2	5								9‡							0-6(0-4)4357	—
43. Wolves*	26.4	1		8	10				6¹	7		4				2	5								9							1-3(0-2)3409	—
44. Tranmere*	30.4	1		8†	10				6	7		4				2	5								9							0-3(0-1)1110	24
45. Darlington	2.5	1		8	10¹				6	7		4				2	11								9¹							2-0(2-0)1675	24
46. Rochdale*	7.5	1		8	10				6	7		4†	12			2									9							0-1(0-0)2560	24
Appearances/goals		23(0)0	34(0)1	8(0)0	33(0)1	26(0)3	15(0)1	42(1)1	46(2)4	9(0)2	30(3)2	18(10)1	31(2)1	5(2)1	12(1)1	46(0)	4(0)3	21(1)0	28(3)1	7(3)0	10(3)2	6(0)2	9(0)0	15(0)0	17(0)1	7(1)0	40(2)2	14(0)2	5(0)1	14(0)0	6(0)1	Final League Position: 24	

Also played: Boughen, match 46(11), Griffiths, match 36(12), Carter, match 21(1), Davies, match 40(12), 42(14), Morgan, match 37(14), 38(14), O'Hagan, mat[ch] 39(1), 40(1), 41(1), Brignull, match 1(6), 2(6), 3(6†), Bennett, match 41(14), 43(11), 44(11), 45(3), 46(3), Peacock, match 42(3), 43(3), 44(3), 45(5), 46(Hopkins, match 38(12), 39(11‡), 40(11†), 41(12), 44(12), Dillon, matches 11, 20, 22, 23, 24 (all at no. 1).

DIVISION 3

NORTHAMPTON TOWN

County Ground, Abington Avenue, Northampton NN1 4PS.

Back row (left to right): David Longhurst, Graham Reed, Ian Johnson, Tony Adcock, Eddie McGoldrick. *Middle row:* Dennis Casey (Physio), Paul Wilson, Paul Bunce, Glenville Donegal, Peter Gleasure, Keith McPherson, Trevor Slack, Paul Culpin, Clive Walker (Captain). *Front row:* David Gilbert, Russell Wilcox, Graham Carr (Manager), Martin Singleton, Warren Donald.

Stadium Capacity: 14,767
Pitch Dimensions: 112 × 75 yds.
Telephone: 0604–721103.
Chairman: D. Banks.
Vice-Chairman: D. Underwood.
Directors: S. Wilson, E. P. Northover, M. Deane, B. Church, G. Wilson, B. Stonhill, L. Banks, B. Blundell.
Manager: Graham Carr.
Post-War Managers: T. Smith, Bob Dennison, David Smith, Dave Bowen, Jack Jennings (caretaker), Dave Bowen, Tony Marchi, Ron Flowers, Dave Bowen, Bill Baxter, Bill Dodgin (Jnr), Pat Crerand, John Petts, Mike Keen, Clive Walker, Bill Dodgin (Jnr), Clive Walker, Tony Barton (18).
Physio: D. Casey.
Secretary: Dr John Evans.
Founded: 1897.
Turned Professional: 1901.
Nickname: The Cobblers.
Former Names: None.
Former Grounds: None.
Record Attendance: 24,523 v Fulham, Division 1, 23 April 1966.
Record Victory: 10–0 v Walsall, Division 3(S), 5 November 1927.
Record Defeat: 0–10 v Bournemouth, Division 3(S), 2 September 1939.
Most League Points: (3 for a win), 99, Division 4, 1986–87, (2 for a win) 68, Division 4, 1975–76.
Most League Goals: 109, Division 4, 1962–63 and Division 3(S), 1952–53.
Highest League Scorer in a Season: Cliff HOlton, 36, Division 3, 1961–62.
Highest Total of League Goals: Jack English, 135, 1947–60.
Most League Appearances: Tommy Fowler, 521, 1946–61.
League History: 1920 Founder Members of Division 3, 1921 Division 3(S), 1958–61 Division 4, 1961–63 Division 3, 1963–65 Division 2, 1965–66 Division 1, 1966–67 Division 2, 1967–69 Division 3, 1969–76 Division 4, 1976–77 Division 3, 1977–87 Division 4, 1987– Division 3.
Honours: Division 2 runners-up 1964–65. Division 3 Champions 1962–63. Division 4 Champions 1986–87, runners-up 1975–76. Division 3(S) runners-up 1927–28, 1949–50.
Colours: Claret shirts with shite shoulders, white shorts, claret socks. **Second strip:** All dark blue with white trim.

NORTHAMPTON TOWN – LEAGUE RECORD 1987–88

Match no/Opp/Date	Gleasure	Reed	Logan	Donald	Wilcox	McPherson	Longhurst	Benjamin	Morley	Chard	Gilbert	Senior	McGoldrick	Mann	Bunce	Cubin	Singleton	Donegal	Sandeman	O'Donnell	Williams	Adcock	Wilson	Slack	Carter	FT(HT)Att Lge pos
1. Chester 15.8	1	2	3†	4	5^1	6	7^1	8‡	9^1	10^1	11^1	12	14													5-0(1-0)3458 —
2. Walsall 29.8	1	2‡	3	4	5	6	7	8	10	11†	9	12	14													0-1(0-1)5993 15
3. Brighton* 31.8	1	2	3	4	5	6	7	8	10^1		9		11													1-1(0-0)7934 —
4. Doncaster 5.9	1	2	3	4	5	6	7^1	8	10^1		9		11													2-0(0-0)1873 11
5. Brentford* 9.9	1	2	3	4†	5	6	7^1	8	10	12	9^1		11													2-1(0-0)5748 —
6. Notts Co* 12.9	1	2	3		5	6		8†	10	4	9		11	7	12											0-1(0-1)6023 8
7. Preston 15.9	1	2	3		5	6		8	10	4	9	7	11													0-0(0-0)5179 —
8. Bristol R 19.9	1	2	3		5	6		8	10^1	4^1	9		11		7											2-0(1-0)3655 6
9. Port Vale* 26.9	1	2	3	12	5	6		8	10	4^1	9		11		7†											1-0(0-0)5072 1
10. Southend 29.9	1	2	3		5	6		8	10^1	4	9	12	11		7†											1-1(1-1)3407 —
11. Bristol C* 3.10	1	2	3		5	6		8	10	4^2	9		11		7^1											3-0(1-0)6234 1
12. Rotherham 11.10	1	2	3	4	5	6		12	10^1	11^1	9		7		8^1											2-2(2-0)5244 —
13. Chesterfield* 17.10	1	2	3	4	5	6		11^1	10^1		9		7		8^2											4-0(2-0)5073 1
14. Mansfield 20.10	1	2	3	4	5	6		11	10		9		7		8^1											1-3(1-2)3645 —
15. Grimsby* 24.10	1	2	3†	4	5	6	12		10	11	9_1		7		8^1											2-1(1-1)5388 3
16. Aldershot 31.10	1	2		4	5	6	11^1		10^1	3	9		7		8^1											4-4(3-1)3538 3
17. York* 4.11	1	2		4	5	6	11		10†	3	9		7	12	8											0-0(0-0)4950 —
18. Fulham 7.11	1	2	3†	4	5	6	11		10		9		12	8	7											0-0(0-0)6717 4
19. Gillingham* 21.11	1	2	12	4	5^1	6	11		10^1	3	9		8†		7											2-1(0-1)5151 3
20. Blackpool 28.11	1	2	14	4	5	6	11^1		10	3	9		8‡		12	7†										1-3(1-2)3593 4
21. Sunderland* 12.12	1	2‡	3	4	5	6	12		10	11	9†		7		8	14										0-2(0-0)7279 6
22. Wigan 19.12	1		3	4^1	5	6	11		10	2	9				8	7^1										2-2(1-1)2692 6
23. Port Vale 26.12	1		3	4	5	6	11		10	2	9			12	8†	7^1										1-1(0-1)4446 8
24. Bury* 28.12	1		3	4	5	6	11		10	2	9		8†		7	12										0-0(0-0)6067 8
25. Walsall* 1.1	1		3	4	5	6	11		10	2^1	9†		8‡	12	7	14^1										2-2(0-2)5832 8
26. Notts Co 2.1	1	12	3	4	5	6	11†		10_1	2			8		7	9										1-3(0-1)8149 8
27. Brentford 9.1	1	2†	3	4	5	6	11		10	9^1			8		7		12									1-0(0-0)6025 7
28. Bristol R* 16.1	1			4^1	5		11	10	6	9^1			8		7	12	2†	3								2-1(1-1)4473 6
29. Preston* 27.1	1			4	5	6	11†		2	9			8		7	12		3	10							0-1(0-1)5052 —
30. Wigan* 30.1	1		3	4	5	6			2	9			8†		7	11		12	10							1-0(1-0)4825 6
31. Doncaster* 6.2	1	2		4	5	6			11	9			8		7			3	10^1							1-0(1-0)4359 5
32. Bury 13.2	1	2		4	5		8†		11	9			12		7	14					10‡	3	6			0-0(0-0)2172 6
33. Chester* 20.2	1	2		4	5		8	11†	9				12		7						10^1	3	6^1			2-0(0-0)4285 6
34. Bristol C 27.2	1	2		4	5		8†	11^1	9				12		7						10^1	3	6			2-2(2-1)8578 6
35. Southend* 2.3	1			4	5^1		8^1		2	9			11^1		7						10^1	3	6			4-0(1-0)4249 —
36. Chesterfield 5.3	1			4	5		8		2	9^1			11^1		7						10	3	6			2-0(2-0)2400 5
37. Rotherham* 11.3	1			4	5		8		2	9			11		7						10	3	6			0-0(0-0)5432 —
38. Aldershot* 19.3	1	2†			5		8‡		4		9		11	14	7	12					10^1	3	6			1-0(1-1)4322 5
39. Grimsby 26.3	1	12		4†	5		11				9		2		8^1	7^1					10	3	6			2-2(0-2)3406 5
40. Fulham* 2.4	1	12		4	5	6	11†				9		2		8^1	7					10^1	3				3-2(1-1)6211 5
41. Gillingham 4.4	1			4	5	6†	11				9		2	12	8^1	7					10^1	3				2-1(0-0)4126 5
42. Mansfield* 10.4	1			4	5^1		11				9		2		8	7					10	3	6			2-0(0-0)6917 —
43. Brighton 15.4	1	12		4	5		11†				9		2		8‡	7	14				10	3	6			0-3(0-1)14,421 —
44. York 23.4	1			4	5		11†				9		2		8^1	7	12				10	3^1	6‡	14		2-2(0-1)2048 5
45. Blackpool* 30.4	1			4	5		11^1				9^1		2		8†	7	12				10^1	3	6			3-3(0-0)5730 5
46. Sunderland 2.5	1			4	5		11				9		2		8	7					10^1	3	6			1-3(1-3)29,454 5
Apps(subs)/goals	46(0)/0	27(1)/0	24(2)/0	39(1)/2	40(0)/4	32(0)/0	32(2)/7	13(1)/1	27(0)/10	4(0)/6	41(0)/6	4(0)/2	4(6)/2	10(0)/0	5(1)/1	18(2)/10	28(0)/3	2(0)/1	09(2)/0	01(0)/0	18(0)/10	150(0)/1	0(1)/0			Final League Position: 6

Own goals: Roberts, match 16; Stannard, match 40; Kenworthy, match 42.

DIVISION 1   # NORWICH CITY
Carrow Road, Norwich NR1 1JE.

Back row (left to right): Ian Butterworth, Robert Rosario, Graham Benstead, Bryan Gunn, Jon Sheffield, Phil Chapple, Paul Clayton. *Middle row:* Mile Walker (Reserve, Team Cocach), Tim Sheppard (Physio), Shaun Elliot, Dale Gordon, Simon Ratcliffe, Dave Stringer (Manager), Wayne Biggins, Paul Wilson, Trevor Putney, Mark Bowen, Keith Webb (Youth, Team Coach), David Williams (Player/Coach). *Front row:* Jeremy Goss, Robert Fleck, Ruel Fox, Andy Fensome, Kevin Drinkell, Michael Phelan, Kenny Brown, Ian Culverhouse, Tony Spearing, Ian Crook.

Stadium Capacity: 26,812.
Pitch Dimensions: 114 × 74 yds.
Telephone: 0603–612131, **Ticket office:** 0603–761661, **Clubcall:** 0898–121144.
Chairman: Robert T. Chase JP.
Vice-Chairman: J. A. Jones.
Directors: B. W. Lockwood, G. A. Paterson, A. Scholes, F. Kennedy.
Manager: Dave Stringer.
Post-War Managers: Cyril Spiers, Dugald Lockhead, Norman Low, Tom Parker, Archie Macauley, Willie Reid, George Swindin, Ron Ashman, Lol Morgan, Ron Saunders, John Bond, Ken Brown (12).
Player–Coach: Dave Williams.
Physio: Tim Sheppard MCSP SRP.
Secretary: A. R. W. Neville.
Commercial Manager: R. Cossey.
Sponsors: Fosters Lager.
Founded: 1902.
Turned Professional: 1905.
Nickname: The Canaries.
Former Names: None.
Former Grounds: Newmarket Road 1905–1908, The Nest, Rosary Road 1908–35.
Record Attendance: 43,984 v Leicester City, FA Cup 6th Round, 30 March, 1963.
Record Victory: 10–2 v Coventry City, Division 3(S), 15 March 1930.
Record Defeat: 2–10 v Swindon Town, Southern League, 5 September 1908.
Most League Points: (3 for a win) 84, Division 2, 1985–86. (2 for a win) 64, Division 3(S), 1950–51.
Most League Goals: 99, Division 3(S), 1952–53.
Highest League Scorer in a Season: Ralph Hunt, 31, Division 3(S), 1955–56.
Highest Total of League Goals: Johnny Gavin, 122, 1945–54, 1955–58.
Most League Appearances: Ron Ashman, 590, 1947–64.
League History: 1920 Founder Members of Division 3, 1921 Division 3, 1921 Division 3(S), 1934–39 Division 2, 1946–60 Division 3, 1960–72 Division 2, 1972–74Division 1, 1974–75 Division 2, 1975–81 Division 1, 1981–82 Division 2, 1982–85 Division 1, 1985–86 Division 2, 1986– Division 1.
Honours: Division 2 Champions 1971–72, 1985–86. Division 3 runners-up 1959–60. Division 3(S) Champions 1933–34. League Cup winners 1962, 1985, runners-up 1973, 1975.
Colours: Yellow shirts with green trim, green shorts, yellow socks. **Second strip:** White shirts with green trim, green shorts, white socks.

NORWICH CITY – LEAGUE RECORD 1987–88

Match no/Opp/Date		Gunn	Brown	Spearing	Bruce	Phelan	Butterworth	Gordon	Drinkell	Biggins	Williams	Putney	Crook	Culverhouse	Fox	Bowen	Rosario	Ratcliffe	Elliott	Gross	O'Neill	Fleck	Renstead	Linighan	FT(HT)Att Lge pos
1. Everton	15.8	1	2†	3	4	5	6	7	8	9	10	11	12												0–1(0–1)31,728 —
2. Sthampton*	19.8	1		3	4¹	5	6		8	9			10	2	7	11†	12								0–1(0–0)14,429 —
3. Coventry*	22.8	1		3	4¹	5	6		8²	9			10	2	7	11									3–1(1–0)13,726 12
4. West Ham	29.8	1		3	4	5	6	12	8	9			10	2	7	11†									0–2(0–0)16,394 16
5. Newcastle*	1.9	1		3	4	5	6†		8	9¹			10	2	7	11	12								1–1(0–0)16,636 —
6. Watford	5.9	1		3	4¹	5	6		8	9			10	2	7	11									1–0(0–0)11,724 11
7. Derby*	12.9	1		3	4	5	6		8	9			10	2	7	11†	12¹								1–2(0–0)14,402 14
8. Chelsea	19.9	1		3†	4	5	6		8	9			10	2	7‡	11	14	12							0–1(0–1)15,242 16
9. Nottm F*	26.9	1			4	5		14	8		12	11‡	10†	2	7		9	6	3						0–2(0–2)13,755 18
10. Oxford	3.10	1			4	5		7	8		10	11		2			9	6	3						0–3(0–1)6847 19
11. Spurs*	10.10	1			4	5			8¹	9¹	10†		12	2	7	11		6	3						2–1(1–1)18,669 18
12. Man Utd	17.10	1			4	5			8	9¹	10†		12	2	7	11		6	3						1–2(1–0)39,345 18
13. Sheff Wed	24.10	1			4†	5	12		8	9	10		14	2	7	11		6‡	3						0–1(0–0)15,861 18
14. QPR*	31.10	1	2	3	4	5	6		8	9¹	10	11			7										1–1(0–0)14,522 19
15. Charlton	7.11	1	2	3†	4	5	6		8	9	12	11			7	14	10‡								0–2(0–2)5044 19
16. Arsenal*	14.11	1	2		4	5	6	11	8²	12			7†			9			3	10					2–4(1–0)20,558 20
17. Liverpool	21.11	1	2		4	5	6	11	8				10		7	9			3						0–0(0–0)37,446 20
18. Portsmouth*	28.11	1	2†		4	5	6	11	8				10		7	12	9		3						0–1(0–1)13,099 20
19. Luton	5.12	1			4	5	6	11¹‡	8				10	7¹	2	12	9		3						2–1(1–0)7002 20
20. Wimbledon	18.12	1				5	6	11	8				10	7	2	12			3†	14	9	4‡			0–1(0–1)4026 —
21. Derby	26.12	1				5	6	11¹	8					2	7	3			10		9¹	4			2–1(1–0)15,452 20
22. Chelsea*	28.12	1				5	6	11	8¹	12				2	7¹	3	9		10¹			4†			3–0(0–1)19,668 18
23. West Ham*	1.1	1				5	6	11	8¹				4	2	7	3¹	9		10						4–1(0–1)20,059 15
24. Everton*	16.1	1				5	6	11	8				4	2	7†	3			12	10	9				0–3(0–1)15,750 18
25. Sthampton	23.1	1				5	6	11	8				4	2	7	3			10		9	1			0–0(0–0)12,002 16
26. Watford*	6.2	1				5	6	11†	8				4	2	7	3			12	10	9	1			0–0(0–0)13,316 16
27. Newcastle	13.2	1				5	6	11	8¹				4†	2	7	3			10	12	9²				3–1(1–1)21,068 16
28. Coventry	20.2	1				5	6	11	8				12	2	7†	3			10	4	9				0–0(0–0)15,577 15
29. Man Utd*	5.3	1				5		11†	8				6	12	2	7	3		10		9¹	4			1–0(0–0)19,129 14
30. Spurs	12.3	1				5	6		8¹				11	2	7	3			10¹		9¹	4			3–1(1–0)19,322 13
31. Oxford*	16.3	1				5	6		8¹				11	2	7	3			10		9²	4¹			4–2(1–0)12,260 —
32. QPR	19.3	1				5‡			8	12		11	14	2	7	3†			10		9	4			0–3(0–1)9033 10
33. Sheff Wed*	26.3	1		12		6		8			11	5†	2	7	3				10		9	4			0–3(0–1)13,280 13
34. Charlton*	2.4	1		3		6		8¹		5	11		2	7¹					10		9	4			2–0(0–0)15,015 12
35. Arsenal	4.4	1		3		6		8	12	5†	11		2	7					10		9	4			0–2(0–1)19,341 13
36. Liverpool*	20.4	1		3		5	6		8			11	2	7					10		9	4			0–0(0–0)22,509 —
37. Portsmouth	23.4	1		3		5	6	12		14¹		11	2	7†	8				10		9‡	4¹			2–2(1–0)12,762 13
38. Luton*	30.4	1		3		5	6		8¹†	12		11¹	2	7					10		9‡	4			2–2(0–0)12,700 13
39. Nottm F	4.5	1		3		5	6	12		8		11	2	7		14			10†		9‡	4			0–2(0–2)11,610 —
40. Wimbledon*	7.5	1		3		5	6	12	8	9		11	2	7					10†			4			0–1(0–0)11,782 14
Apps(subs)/goals		38(0)/0	7(0)/0	17(1)/0	19(0)/2	37(0)/0	34(1)/0	16(5)/3	38(0)/12	13(5)/5	7(2)/0	25(0)/1	14(7)/1	33(0)/2	23(0)/1	9(5)/2	6(3)/0	14(2)/0	20(2)/2	10(0)/0	18(0)/7	20(0)/0	12(0)/2		

Final League Position: 14

DIVISION 1

NOTTINGHAM FOREST

City Ground, Nottingham NG2 5FJ.

Back row (left to right): Philip Starbuck, Terry Wilson, Stephen Chattle, Neil Webb, Brian Rice, Lee Glover. *Middle row:* Liam O'Kane, Paul Wilkinson, Colin Foster, Stephen Sutton, Hans Segers, Billy Stubbs, David Campbell, Ron Fenton (Ass. Manager). *Front row:* Nigel Clough, Kjetil Osvold, Des Walker, Brian Clough (Manager), Stuart Pearce, Franz Carr, Gary Fleming.

Stadium Capacity: 35,417 (14,561 seats).
Pitch Dimensions: 115 × 78 yds.
Telephone: 0602–822202, **Clubcall:** 0898–121184.
Chairman: M. Roworth.
Vice-Chairman: F. T. C. Pell FCA.
Directors: G. E. MacPherson JP, F. Reacher, J. F. Hickling, I. I. Korn, J. M. Smith, C. Wooton.
Manager: Brian Clough.
Post-War Managers: Billy Walker, Andy Beattie, John Carey, Mat Gillies, Dave Mackay, Allan Brown (6).
Physio: G. Lyas.
Secretary: P. White.
Commercial Manager: Dave Pullan.
Sponsors: James Shipstones & Sons.
Founded: 1865.
Turned Professional: 1889.
Nickname: The Reds.
Former Names: None.
Former Grounds: Forest Racecourse 1865–79, The Meadows 1879–80, Trent Bridge Cricket Ground 1880–82, Parkside, Lenton 1882–85, Gregory, Lenton 1885–90, Town Grown 1890–98.
Record Attendance: 49,946 v Manchester United, Division 1, 28 October 1967.
Record Victory: 14–0 v Clapton, FA Cup 1st Round, 1890–91.
Record Defeat: 1–9 v Blackburn Rovers, Division 2, 10 April 1937.
Most League Points: (3 for a win) 74, Division 1, 1983–84, (2 for a win) 70, Division 3(S), 1950–51.
Most League Goals: 110, Division 3(S), 1950–51.
Highest League Scorer in a Season: Wally Ardron, 36,Division 3(S), 1950–51.
Highest Total of League Goals: Grenville Morris, 199, 1898–1913.
Most League Appearances: Bob McKinlay, 614, 1951–70.
League History: 1892 Elected to Division 1, 1906 Division 2, 1907 Division 1, 1911–22 Division 2, 1922–25 Division 1, 1925–49 Division 2, 1949–51 Division 3(S), 1951–57 Division 2, 1957–72 Division 1, 1972–77 Division 2, 1977– Division 1.
Honours: Division 1 Champions 1977–78, runners-up 1966–67, 1978–79. Division 2 Champions 1906–07, 1921–22, runners-up 1956–57. Division 3(S) Champions 1950–51. FA Cup winners 1898, 1959. Anglo-Scottish Cup winners 1977. League Cup winners 1978, 1979, runners-up 1980. European Cup winners 1979, 1980. European Super Cup winners 1980, runners-up 1981. World Club Championship runners-up 1981.
Colours: Red shirts with white pinstripe, white shorts, red socks. **Second strip:** White shirts, red shorts, white socks.

NOTTINGHAM FOREST – LEAGUE RECORD 1987–88

Match no/Opp	Date	Sutton	Fleming	Pearce	Walker	Foster	Campbell	Carr	Webb	Clough	Wilkinson	Glover	Segers	Wilson	Chettle	Rice	Osvold	Starbuck	Gaynor	Plummer	Crosby	Wassell	Williams	Parker	FT(HT)Att	Lge pos
1. Charlton	15.8	1	2	3	4	5	6	7	8	9^1	10	11^1													2–1(0–1)6021	—
2. Watford*	19.8	1	2	3_1	4	5	6	7	8	9	10	11													1–0(1–0)14,527	—
3. Everton*	22.8		2	3	4	5	6	7	8	9	10	11	1												0–0(0–0)24,445	2
4. Newcastle	29.8		2	3	4	5	6	7	8	9^1	10	11	1												1–0(1–0)20,111	—
5. Sthampton*	2.9		2†	3^1	4	5	6	7	8^1	9	10^1	11	1	12											3–3(2–1)14,173	—
6. Chelsea	5.9		2	3	4	5^1	6†	7	8	9^1	10^1	11^1	1	12	14										3–4(3–1)18,414	6
7. Arsenal*	12.9		2	3	4	5	6†	7	8	9	10‡	11	1	12					14						0–1(0–1)18,490	6
8. Coventry	19.9	1	2†	3_1	4	5	12	7^1	8	9	10			6^1		11									3–0(1–0)17,519	4
9. Norwich	26.9	1		3	4	5		7	8^2	9	10	12		6	2	11†									2–0(2–0)13,755	3
10. Derby	10.10	1		3	4	5		7	8	9	10			6	2	11									1–0(1–0)22,394	5
11. Sheff Wed*	17.10	1		3	4	5		7^1	8	9^1	10^1			6†	2	11	12								3–0(1–0)17,685	
12. Spurs*	24.10	1		3	4	5		7^1	8^1	9^1	10^1			6†	2	11	12								3–0(1–0)23,543	3
13. Man Utd	31.10	1		3^1	4	5		7	8	9	10^1			6	2	11									2–2(1–0)44,669	4
14. Portsmouth*	14.11	1		3	4	5		7	8^1	9_1	10^1	14		6^1†	2	11^1‡	12								5–0(3–0)15,851	4
15. West Ham	12.11	1		3	4	5		7†	8^1	9^1	10‡			6	2	11	12	14							2–3(1–1)17,216	4
16. Wimbledon	5.12	1		3	4	5			8	9^1				6	2	11	10	7							1–1(0–1)5170	
17. QPR*	13.12	1	2	3	4	5			8	9^2				6†		11	12	10^1	7						4–0(1–0)18,130	6
18. Oxford	19.12	1		3	4	5			8	9				6	2	11^1	12	10	7^1†						2–0(0–0)7891	
19. Arsenal	26.12	1		3_1	4	5			8	9†				6^1	2	11	12	10	7						2–0(0–1)31,211	2
20. Coventry*	28.12	1	14	3	4	5			8	9				6^1	2‡	11	12	10^2	7†						4–1(1–0)31,061	2
21. Newcastle*	1.1	1	14	3	4	5			8	9‡				6	2	11	12	10†	7						0–2(0–1)28,583	2
22. Everton	3.1	1	12	3	4	5		7†	8					6	2	11	9	10							0–1(0–1)21,680	—
23. Charlton*	16.1	1		3	4	5			8^1	12	9†			6	2	11		10‡	7^1	14					2–2(0–1)15,363	2
24. Watford*	23.1	1		3	4	5			8	10	9			6	2	11									0–0(0–0)13,158	2
25. Chelsea*	6.2	1	2	3	4	5^1†			8	9_1				6	12	11‡	14	10	7^1						3–2(1–0)18,203	2
26. Sthampton	13.2	1	2	3	4				8	9^1	10			6		11			7	5					1–1(1–1)13,315	3
27. Sheff Wed	5.3	1	2	3	4	5			8^1	9	10			6		11		12	7†						1–0(1–0)19,509	3
28. QPR	16.3	1		3	4	5			8	9	10			6	2	11			7						1–2(0–1)8316	—
29. Man Utd*	19.3	1		3	4	5			8	9	10			6	2	11			7						0–0(0–0)27,598	3
30. Spurs	26.3	1	2		4	5			8	9^1	10			6	3	11			7						1–1(0–2)25,306	5
31. Derby*	30.3	1		3	4	5			8	9^2	10			6	2	11			7						2–1(1–0)25,017	
32. Liverpool*	2.4	1		3	4	5			8^1	9	10			6	2	11			7						2–1(1–0)29,188	3
33. Portsmouth	4.4	1		3		5			8	9	10	11		6^1	2				7	4					1–0(0–0)17,528	3
34. Liverpool	13.4	1		3	4†	5			8	9		10		6	2	11			7	12					0–5(0–2)39,535	—
35. West Ham*	20.4	1	2	3		5		10	8	9				6	4	11			7						0–0(0–0)15,775	—
36. Wimbledon*	30.4	1	2			5		7	8					6	4	11		9†				3	10		0–0(0–0)14,341	5
37. Norwich*	4.5	1	2			5		7	8^1	9†	12	10^1		6‡	4	11						3	14		2–0(2–0)11,610	—
38. Oxford*	7.5	1	2			5		7^1	8^2	9^2				6	4	11						3			5–3(4–1)12,762	3
39. Luton	13.5	1	2		4	12		7	8	9	10^1			6	5				11	3†					1–1(0–1)9018	—
40. Luton*	15.5	1	2		4	5		7†	8^1	9	10			6	3	11				12					1–1(0–1)13,106	3

Apps(subs)/goals: 35(0)/0, 19(3)/0, 34(0)/5, 35(0)/0, 38(1)/2, 7(1)/0, 22(0)/4, 40(0)/13, 24(2)/6, 12(3)/3, 5(0)/0, 33(3)/5, 28(2)/0, 30(0)/2, 12(1)/0, 1(9)/0, 10(2)/3, 8(0)/2, 12(2)/1, 21(1)/0, 4(0)/0, 1(1)/0

Final League Position: 3

Own goals: Borrows, match 20; Maddix, match 28; Hansen, match 32

319

DIVISION 3

NOTTS COUNTY
County Ground, Meadow Lane, Nottingham NG2 3HJ.

**Back row
(left to right):**
Iain McParland
Willie McStay
Mick Leonard
Aiden Davison
Craig Jackson
Chris Withe
Middle row:
Wayne Jones (Physio)
David Kevan
Garry Birtles
Gary Lund
Dean Yates
Wayne Fairclough
David Kevan
Paul Hart
(Player/Coach)
Front row:
Adrian Thorpe
Geoff Pike (Captain)
Gary Mills
John Barnwell
(Manager)
Paul Smalley
Sean Kimberley
Mark Harbottle

Stadium Capacity: 24,045.
Pitch Dimensions: 114 × 74 yds.
Telephone: 0602–861155.
Chairman: D. C. Pavis
Vice-Chairman: J. Mounteney.
Directors: J. J. Dunnett MA, LL. M. , W. A. Hopcroft. .
Manager: John Barnwell.
Post-War Managers: Arthur Stollery, Eric Houghton, George Poyser, Tommy Lawton, Frank Hill, Tim Coleman, Eddie Lowe, Jack Burkitt, Andy Beattie, Billy Gray, Jimmy Sirrel, Ron Fenton, Larry Lloyd, Richie Barker, Jimmy Sirrel (15).
Player-Coach: Paul Hart.
Physio: Wayne Jones.
Secretary/Chief Executive: Neal Hook JP.
Commercial Manager: Elaine Howes.
Sponsors: Home Ales.
Founded: 1862 (Currently the oldest club in the Football League)
Turned Professional: 1885.
Nickname: The Magpies.
Former Names: None.
Former Grounds: The Park 1862–1864, The Meadows 1864–1877, Beeston Cricket Ground 1877–1880, Castle Ground 1880–1883, Trent Bridge 1883–1910.
Record Attendance: 47,310 v York City, FA Cup 6th Round, 12 March 1955.
Record Victory: 15–0 v Thornhill United, FA Cup 1st Round, 24 October 1885.
Record Defeat: 1–9 v Blackburn Rovers, Division 1, 16 November 1889 and v Aston Villa, Division 1, 29 September 1888 and v Portsmouth, Division 2, 9 April 1927.
Most League Points: (3 for a win) 81, Division 3, 1987–88. (2 for a win) 69, Division 4, 1970–71.
Most League Goals: 107, Division 4, 1959–60.
Highest League Scorer in a Season: Tom Keetley, 39, Division 3(S), 1930–31.
Highest Total of League Goals: Les Bradd, 125, 1967–78.
Most League Appearances: Albert Iremonger, 564, 1904–26.
League History: 1888 Founder Members of Football League, 1893–97 Division 2, 1897–1913 Division 1, 1913–14 Division 2, 1914–20 Division 1, 1920–23Division 2, 1923–26 Division 1, 1926–30 Division 2, 1930–31 Division 3(S), 1931–35 Division 2, 1935–50Division 3(S), 1950–58 Division 2, 1958–59Division 3, 1959–60 Division 4, 1960–64 Division 3, 1964–71 Division 4, 1971–73 Division 3, 1973–81 Division 2, 1981–84 Division 1, 1984 Division 2, 1985– Division 3.
Honours: Division 2 Champions 1896–97, 1913–14, 1922–23, runners-up 1894–95, 1980–81. Division 4 Champions 1970–71, runners-up 1959–60. Division 3(S) Champions 1930–31, 1949–50, runners-up 1936–37. FA Cup winners 1894, runners-up 1891.
Colours: Black and white striped shirts, black shorts and socks. **Second strip:** All gold.

NOTTS COUNTY – LEAGUE RECORD 1987–88

Match no/Opp	Date	Leonard	Smalley	Davis	Kevan	Yates	Gray	McParland	Lund	Birtles	Pike	Mills	Thompson	Belford	Hart	Fairclough	Barnes	Withe	Thorpe	McStay	FT(HT)Att Lge pos
1. Wigan*	15.8	1	2	3	4	5	6	7	8	9²	10½	11†	12								4-4(2-3)6344
2. York	22.8		2	3	4	5	6	8²†	12	9	10¹	7	11¹	1							5-3(4-2)2878
3. Grimsby*	29.8	1	2	3	4	5	12	8	9	6	10	7	11†								0-0(0-0)5322
4. Fulham	1.9	1	2	3	4	5	11†	8	12	9	10	7			6						0-0(0-0)4767
5. Southend*	5.9	1	2	3	4	5		8²	12¹	9†	10²↓	7	11‡		6	14					6-2(3-2)4166
6. Nthampton	12.9	1	2	3	4	5		8†	11½	9	10	7			6	14	12				1-0(1-0)6023
7. Aldershot*	15.9	1	2	3†	4	5		8	11¹	9	10¹	7			6	12					2-1(1-1)4835
8. Bristol C*	19.9	1	2		4	5		8	11†	9	10	7	12		6		3				0-1(0-0)5705
9. Chesterfield	26.9	1	2		4	5		8	12	9	10	7	11†		6		3				0-2(0-1)3466
10. Bristol R*	29.9	1	2		4	5		8		9¹	10	7	11		6		3				1-1(0-0)4334
11. Chester	3.10	1	2		4	5‡		8	12	9†	10¹	7¹	11		6	14	3				2-1(1-1)3365
12. Mansfield*	11.10	1	2		4‡	5		8	12¹	9†	10	7¹	11		6	14	3				1-1(0-0)8564
13. Doncaster	17.10	1	2		4	5		8¹		9	10	7			6		3	11			1-0(1-0)2649
14. Bury*	20.10	1	2		4	5		8²		9¹	10	7			6		3	11			3-0(1-0)4044
15. Gillingham	24.10	1	2		4	5	12	8		9	10	7†			6		3¹	11			1-3(1-0)5551
16. Sunderland*	31.10	1	2		4	5		8		9²	10	7			6		3	11			2-1(1-1)8854
17. Rotherham	3.11	1	2		4	5		8		9	10	7			6		3	11			1-1(1-1)4157
18. Brentford*	7.11	1	2		4	5		8²		9	10	7	12		6		3¹	11†			3-0(0-0)5634
19. Walsall*	21.11	1	2	12	4†	5		8²		9¹	10	7			6		3	11			3-1(2-1)7211
20. Brighton	28.11	1	2	12	4†	5¹		8‡	14	9	10	7			6		3	11			1-0(0-0)8725
21. Port Vale	12.12	1	2		4	5		8¹		9	10¹	7			6		3	11			3-1(0-0)3358
22. Preston*	19.12	1	2		4	5		8²		9	10²	7	12		6		3	11†			4-2(2-1)5730
23. Chesterfield*	26.12	1	2		4	5		8		9¹	10	7¹			6		3	11			2-0(2-0)8675
24. Blackpool	28.12	1	2		4	5		8		9¹	10	7			6		3	11			1-1(0-0)4627
25. Grimsby	1.1	1	2		4	5		8		9	10	7	12		6		3	11†			0-0(0-0)5297
26. Northampton*	2.1	1	2		4†	5		8‡		9¹	10	7	12		6	14	3	11²			3-1(1-0)8149
27. York*	9.1	1	2		4	5		8		9¹	10	7¹			6		3	11¹			3-0(1-0)5924
28. Bristol C	16.1	1	2		4	5		8		9¹	10†	7‡	12		6	14	3	11			1-2(1-0)9558
29. Fulham*	30.1	1	2	3	4	5¹		8²¹		9¹	10	7	12		6			11†			5-1(2-1)6107
30. Southend	5.2	1	2		4	5		8₁		9	10¹	7			6		3	11			2-1(0-1)3904
31. Blackpool*	13.2	1	2		4	5		8₁		9	10	7			6		3	11¹			2-3(1-0)5794
32. Wigan	20.2	1	2	3				8¹		9	10	7			6			11	4		1-2(1-1)5182
33. Aldershot	23.2	1	2			5		8²		9	10	7			6		3	11	4		2-0(0-0)2880
34. Chester*	27.2	1	2			5		8	12¹	9†	10	7			6	14	3	11	4‡		1-0(0-0)5868
35. Bristol R	2.3	1	2		4	5		8		9	10	7	12		6		3	11	4†		1-1(0-0)4075
36. Doncaster*	5.3	1	2		4	5		8		9²	10	7			6		3	11			2-0(1-0)5816
37. Mansfield	12.3	1	2	3	4	5		8†		9	10₁	7	12		6‡	14		11			1-1(1-1)7997
38. Sunderland	19.3	1	2		4	5		8†		9	10	7	12¹		6		3	11			1-0(1-0)24,071
39. Gillingham*	26.3	1	2	3†	4	5		8		9‡	10	7	12		6	14		11			0-1(0-0)6473
40. Brentford	2.4	1	2		4	5	11†	8		9	10	7	12		6		3				0-1(0-1)4388
41. Brighton*	4.4	1	2		4†	5		8		9‡	10	7	12		6		3	11¹	14		1-2(1-1)7522
42. Bury	9.4	1	2			5		8		9¹	10	7	12		6	11†	3		4		1-0(0-0)2527
43. Rotherham*	23.4	1	2		4	5				9³	10	7¹	12		6		3	11†		8	4-0(0-0)7021
44. Walsall	30.4	1	2		4†	5	14			9¹	10	7	12		6		3	11		8‡	1-2(1-0)11,913
45. Port Vale*	2.5	1	2‡		4†	5		8		9	10	7	12		6		3	11¹	14		1-2(0-1)7702
46. Preston	7.5	1	12			5		8¹		9	10¹	7	4		6		3†	11		2	2-1(0-0)5822

Apps(subs)/goals: Leonard 45(0)0; Smalley 45(1)0; Davis 18(2)0; Kevan 32(0)0; Yates 46(0)2; Gray 3(1)0; McParland 41(2)21; Lund 32(8)20; Birtles 43(0)14; Pike 46(0)5; Mills 7(2)1; Thompson 10(0)0; Belford 23(0)0; Hart 11(19)0; Fairclough 4(7)2; Barnes 35(0)2; Withe 22(1)5; Thorpe 5(3)0.

Final League Position: 4

Own goals: McKenzie, match 2; Green, match 17; Twentyman, match 35.

321

DIVISION 2

OLDHAM ATHLETIC

Boundary Park, Oldham OL1 2PA.

Back row (left to right): Andy Gorton, Bob Monaghan, Tony Ellis, Andy Ritchie, Andy Goram, Gary Hoolickin, Paul Atkinson, Mike Flynn, David Williams. *Middle row:* Ronnie Evans (Kit, Manager), Billy Urmson (Coach), Tony Henry, John Ryan, Glenn Keeley, Andy Linighan, Aaron Callaghan, Mike Cecere, Neil Edmonds, Ian Liversedge (Physio), Willie Donachie (Player/Coach). *Front row:* Andy Barlow, Mike Milligan, Gary Williams, Tommy Wright, Joe Royle (Team, Manager), Roger Palmer, Nick Henry, Denis Irwin, Brian Adams.

Stadium Capacity: 21,962.
Pitch Dimensions: 110 × 74 yds.
Telephone: 061–624 4972, **Commercial dept:** 061–652 0966, **Clubcall:** 0898–121142.
Chairman & Managing Director: I. H. Stott.
Vice-Chairman: D. A. Brierley.
Directors: G. T. Butterworth, R. Adams, D. R. Taylor, P. Chadwick, J. Slevin, N. Holden.
Manager: Joe Royle.
Post-War Managers: Bob Mellor, Frank Womack, Billy Wooton, George Hardwick, Ted Goodier, Peter McKennan, Norman Dodgin, Jack Rowley, Les McDowall, Gordon Hurst, Jimmy McIlroy, Jack Rowley, Jimmy Frizzell (13).
Player-Coach: Willie Donachie.
Physio: Ian Liversidge.
Secretary: P. M. Hough.
Commercial Manager: A. Hardy.
Founded: 1894.
Turned Professional: 1899.
Nickname: The Latics.
Former Names: Pine Villa 1894–1899.
Former Grounds: Sheepfoot Lane 1894–1905.
Record Attendance: 47,671 v Sheffield Wednesday, FA Cup 4th Round, 25 January 1930.
Record Victory: 11–0 v Southport, Division 4, 26 December 1962.
Record Defeat: 4–13 v Tranmere Rovers, Division 3(N), 26 December 1935.
Most League Points: (3 for a win) 75, Division 2, 1986–87. (2 for a win) 62 Division 3, 1973–74.
Most League Goals: 95, Division 4, 1962–63.
Highest League Scorer in a Season: Tom Davis, 33, Division 3(N), 1936–37.
Highest Total of League Goals: Eric Gemmell, 110, 1947–54.
Most League Appearances: Ian Wood, 525, 1966–80.
League History: 1907 Elected to Division 2, 1910–23 Division 1, 1923–35 Division 2, 1935–53 Division 3(N), 1953–54 Division 2, 1954–58 Division 3, 1958–63 Division 4, 1963–69 Division 3, 1969–71 Division 4, 1971–74 Division 3, 1974– Division 2.
Honours: Division 1 runners-up 1914–15. Division 2 runners-up 1909–10. Division 3 Champions 1973–74. Division 4 runners-up 1962–63. Division 3(N) Champions 1952–53.
Colours: All blue. **Second Strip:** All red.

OLDHAM ATHLETIC – LEAGUE RECORD 1987–88

Match no/Opp/Date		Goram	Irwin	Barlow	Keeley	Linighan	Milligan	Palmer	Henry A	Cecere	Wright	Ritchie	Flynn	Edmonds	Atkinson	Donachie	Ellis	Henry N	Gorton	Callaghan	Williams	Morgan	Kelly J	Barrett	Bunn	Rhodes	Marshall	Blundell	Kelly N	FT(HT)Att Lge pos
1. WBA	15.8	1	2	3	4	5	6	7	8	9	10	11																		0–0(0–0)8873 —
2. Bradford*	18.8	1	2	3	4	5†	6	7	8	9	10	11	12																	0–2(0–1)8087 —
3. Man City*	22.8	1	2	3	4	5¹	6	7	8	9	10	11																		1–1(1–1)15,985 16
4. Middlesbro	29.8	1	2		4†	5	6	7	8	9‡	10	11	12		14	3														0–1(0–0)10,551 19
5. Huddersfield*	31.8	1	2		4	5	6	7	8¹	9†	10	11²	12			3														3–2(1–1)7377 —
6. Reading	5.9	1	2		4	5	6	7	8	9‡	10	11	12			3														0–3(0–1)4798 18
7. Sheff Utd	12.9	1	2		4	5¹	6	7¹	8	9	10	11				3														3–2(2–2)5730 14
8. Leicester	16.9	1	2		4	5	6	7	8	9‡	10	11¹	12			3														1–4(0–4)7358 —
9. Hull	19.9	1	2			5	6	7	8	9	12	11	4			3		10†												0–1(0–1)7183 20
10. Barnsley*	26.9		2			5	6	7	8	12	10†	11				3	9		1	4¹										1–0(0–0)5853 17
11. Millwall*	29.9		2			5	6	7	8	12	10†	11				3	9		1	4										0–0(0–0)4840 —
12. Swindon	10.10		2			5	6	7	14	9	8‡	11	12			3	4		1	10†										0–2(0–0)8160 21
13. Leeds*	20.10		2	14		5	6	7	8¹	9†	10	11‡	12			3	4		1											1–1(1–0)6312 —
14. Shrewsbury	24.10		2	12		5	6	7³	8	9	10	11				3	4†		1											3–2(0–2)3337 20
15. Birmingham*	31.10		2	9		5	6	7	8	12	10	11¹				3	4†		1											1–2(0–1)5487 20
16. Blackburn	7.11		2	9†		5	6	7	8	12	10	11				3	4		1											0–1(0–1)7519 20
17. Aston Villa*	14.11		2			5	6	7	9	12	10	11†	4			3			1	8										0–1(0–1)6469 20
18. Ipswich	21.11		2			5	6†	7	9	12	10	11	4			3			1	8										0–2(0–1)11,007 21
19. Plymouth*	28.11		2			5	6	7	8	12	10	11†	4			3	9		1	6										0–1(0–0)4516 21
20. Bournemouth	5.12		2	12		5	6	7	8¹		10¹	11†				3	4		1					9						2–2(1–1)5777 20
21. Stoke	8.12		2	12		5	6	7	8¹		10	11				3	4		1					9¹†						2–2(1–1)6740 —
22. Leicester*	12.12		2	12		5	6	7¹‡	14		10¹	11				3	4		1	8				9†						2–0(1–0)4785 20
23. Man City	19.12		2	3		5	6	7			10¹	11					4		1	8				9						2–1(1–0)22,518 16
24. Barnsley	26.12		2	3		5	6	7			10	11					4		1	8				9¹						1–1(1–1)8676 18
25. Hull*	28.12		2	3		5	6	7¹			10	11					4		1	8				9						1–2(1–0)8080 18
26. Middlesbro*	1.1		2	3		5	6	7¹			10	11¹	12				4		1	8†				9						3–1(2–0)8181 17
27. Sheff Utd	2.1		2	3		5	6	7¹			10¹	11					4¹		1	8				9²						5–0(3–0)9574 16
28. WBA*	16.1		2	3		5		7	6		10¹	11¹					4		1	8				9						2–1(0–0)5557 16
29. C Palace*	29.1		2	3		5	6	7			10¹	11					4		1	8				9						1–0(0–0)6169 —
30. Reading*	6.2		2	3		5	6¹	7			10	11					4		1	8				9²						4–2(0–1)5388 13
31. Bradford	13.2		2	3		5	6	7			10	11²					4†		1	8¹			12	9						3–5(1–3)13,862 14
32. Millwall	20.2		2	3		5	6	7	14		10†	11					4‡		1	8			12	9¹						1–1(0–0)6839 14
33. C Palace	5.3		2	3			6	7	12¹		10	11					4		1	8†	5			9						1–3(0–2)7032 15
34. Swindon*	12.3		2	12			6	7¹			10†	11¹				3	4		1	8				9¹	5					4–3(0–1)5193 15
35. Birmingham	19.3		2				6	7¹			10	11²				3	4		1	8				9	5					3–1(0–0)6012 13
36. Shrewsbury*	26.3		2‡				6	7¹	14	12	10†	11				3	4		1	8¹				9	5					2–2(0–1)5379 15
37. Blackburn*	1.4		2				6	7²		12	10					3	4		1	8				9	5					4–2(2–2)14,853 —
38. Aston Villa	4.4		2	12			6†	7			10¹	11				3	4		1	8				9¹	5					2–1(0–1)19,138 12
39. Stoke*	9.4		2				6	7³			10	11¹				3	4	5¹	1	8†				9	5		12			5–1(2–1)6505 10
40. Huddersfield	19.4		2†	12			6	7			10‡	11¹				3	4		1	8	14			9	5					2–2(0–2)5547 —
41. Leeds	23.4		2				6	7	12¹		10	11				3	4		1	8				9†	5					1–1(0–0)13,442 11
42. Ipswich*	30.4		2	9			6	7¹			10	11¹				3	4		1	8¹					5					3–1(1–1)5018 9
43. Plymouth	2.5		2	9‡			6	7	12		10	11				3	4		1	8†	14				5					0–1(0–0)6084 10
44. Bournemouth*	7.5		2				6	7	9†		10	11₁				3	4		1	8					5		12			2–0(0–0)6009 10

Final League Position: 10

Apps/subs/goals: Goram 9(0)0 · Irwin 43(0)0 · Barlow 19(2)0 · Keeley 10(0)0 · Linighan 32(0)2 · Milligan 39(0)1 · Palmer 42(0)17 · Henry A 20(1)4 · Cecere 14(1)2 · Wright 40(1)8 · Ritchie 36(0)19 · Flynn 29(2)1 · Edmonds 2(2)0 · Atkinson 3(4)0 · Donachie 30(1)3 · Ellis 21(1)0 · Henry N 3(2)0 · Gorton 24(0)1 · Callaghan 10(0)2 · Williams 9(0)1 · Morgan 4(1)0 · Kelly J 10(1)0 · Barrett 26(0)9 · Bunn 11(0)0 · Rhodes 10(0)0 · Marshall 4(1)0 · Blundell 1(1)0 · Kelly N 0(1)0

Own goals: Wilder, match 7; Suckling, match 23; Williams, match 44.

DIVISION 2

OXFORD UNITED

Manor Ground, Headington, Oxford OX3 7RS.

Back row (left to right): John Dreyer, Alan Judge, Gary Briggs, Peter Hucker, Billy Whitehurst, Steve Hardwick, Trevor Hebberd. *Middle row:* David Leworthy, David Bardsley, Ken Fish (Physio), Sean Reck, David Fogg (Res. Team Manager), Robbie Mustoe, Ray Graydon, Paul Swannack, David Coates (Chief Scout), Peter Rhoades-Brown, David Langan. *Front row:* Les Phillips, Neil Slatter, Martin Foyle, Tommy Caton, Maurice Evans, Ray Houghton, Richard Hill, Dean Saunders, Gary Shelton.

Stadium Capacity: 14,374.
Pitch Dimensions: 110 × 75 yds.
Telephone: 0865–61503, **Clubcall:** 0898–121172.
Chairman: Kevin Maxwell.
Directors: G. E. Coppock, H. Kimber, P. Reeves, P. McGeough, Miss G. Maxwell, J. Devaney, P. J. Morrissey.
Manager: Mark Lawrenson.
Managers since 1962: Arthur Turner, Ron Saunders, Gerry Summers, Mike Brown, Bill Asprey, Ian Greaves, Jim Smith, Maurice Evans (8).
Assistant Manager: Brian Horton.
Physio: John Clinkard.
Secretary: Jim Hunt.
Commercial Manager: Nick Johnson.
Sponsors: Wang Computers.
Founded: 1893.
Turned Professional: 1949.
Nickname: The U's.
Former Names: Headington United 1893–1960.
Former Grounds: None.
Record Attendance: 22,730 v Preston NE, FA Cup 6th Round,19 February 1964.
Record Victory: 7–0 v Barrow, Division 4, 19 December 1964.
Record Defeat: 0–6 v Liverpool, Division 1, 22 March 1986.
Most League Points: (3 for a win) 95, Division 3, 1983–84. (2 for a win) 61, Division 4, 1964–65.
Most League Goals: 91, Division 3, 1983–84.
Highest League Scorer in a Season: John Aldridge, 30, Division 2, 1984–85.
Highest Total of League Goals: Graham Atkinson, 73, 1962–73.
Most League Appearances: John Shuker, 480, 1962–77.
League History: 1962 Elected to Division 4, 1965–68 Division 3, 1968–76 Division 2, 1976–84 Division 3, 1984–85 Division 2, 1985–88 Division 1, 1988– Division 2.
Honours: Division 2 Champions 1984–85. Division 3 Champions 1967–68, 1983–84. League Cup winners 1986.
Colours: Yellow shirts with navy blue trim, navy blue shorts and socks. **Second strip:** All red.

OXFORD UNITED – LEAGUE RECORD 1987–88

Match no/Opp/Date		Hucker	Langan	Slatter	Shelton	Briggs	Caton	Houghton	Foyle	Whitehurst	Hebberd	Rhoades-Brown	Dreyer	Trewick	Shotton	Saunders	Reck	Mustoe	Phillips	Bardsley	Hill	Hardwick	Judge	Greenall	Nogan	Denton	FT(HT)Att Lge pos
1. Portsmouth*	15.8	1	2[1]†	3	4	5	6[1]	7	8	9[2]	10	11	12														4-2(1-0)9174 —
2. Sheff Wed	18.8	1		2	4	5	6	7	8[1]	9	10		3	11													1-1(1-1)17,868 —
3. Wimbledon	22.8	1		2	4	5	6	7	8[1]	9	10†		3	11	12												1-1(1-0)4229 6
4. Spurs	1.9	1		2	4	5	6	7	8	9	10		3	11†		12											0-3(0-2)21,811 —
5. Luton*	5.9	1	2	5[1]			6	7	8[1]	9	10		12	3†	11	4‡		14									2-5(1-2)6804 16
6. Liverpool	12.9	1		2	4	5	6	7	8	9	10		3	11†			12										0-2(0-2)42,266 19
7. QPR*	19.9	1		5	4		6	7[1]	8†	9	10		3		12				2	11[1]							2-0(2-0)9800 14
8. Derby	26.9			5[1]	4		6	7	8		10		3		9				2	11	1						1-0(1-0)15,711 11
9. Norwich*	3.10			5[1]	4		6	7	8[1]				3		9			10	2	11[1]	1	1					3-0(1-0)6847 10
10. Arsenal	10.10	1		3	4‡		6	7	8†	12	11	14	5		9			10	2								0-2(0-1)25,244 10
11. West Ham*	17.10	1		5	4		6	7†	8[1]	14	11		3		9[1]			10	2	12							1-2(1-2)9092 10
12. Charlton*	24.10	1		5	4‡		6		8[1]	7	12		3		9[1]			10	2	11							2-1(0-0)7325 9
13. Chelsea	31.10	1		5	4		6		8	7[1]	11		3		9			10	2								1-2(1-0)15,027 10
14. Coventry*	7.11	1		5†	4		6		8	7	11		3		9		12	10	2								1-0(0-0)7856 9
15. Sthampton	14.11	1		5	4‡		6	12	8	7	11†		3		9			10	2	14							0-3(0-1)12,095 11
16. Watford*	21.11	1		5	4		6		8	7	11		3		9			10[1]	2								1-1(0-1)7811 12
17. Everton	28.11	1			4		6		8	7	11		3		9			10	2	5							0-0(0-0)25,443 12
18. Newcastle*	5.12	1			4		6	12	8	7	11		3		9[1]			10	2	5†							1-3(0-1)8190 13
19. Man Utd	12.12	1			4		6		8	7	11		3		9[1]			10	2	5							1-3(0-2)34,709 15
20. Nottm F*	19.12	1			4†		6	12	8	7	11		3		9	14	10[1]		2	5							0-2(1-0)7891 16
21. Liverpool*	26.12	1			4		6		8	7	11		3		9	12	10		2	5†							0-3(01)13,680 17
22. QPR	28.12	1			4		6	11	8	7	12[1]		3		9[1]	5†	10		2								2-3(0-2)9125 17
23. Wimbledon*	2.1	1			4		6		8[1]	5	7	11	3		9[1]			10	2								2-5(0-3)6926 18
24. Portsmouth	16.1				4	5[1]	6		8	7	11†		3		9[1]		10	2	12	1							2-2(1-0)13,417 19
25. Luton	6.2				4‡	5	6†		8[1]	12	7	11			9[1]	14	10[1]	2	3[1]	1							4-7(2-3)8063 20
26. Spurs*	13.2					5	6		8		7	11	3		9		10	2	4		1						0-0(0-0)9906 19
27. Derby*	20.2					5	6		8		7	11	3		9		10	2	4		1						0-0(0-0)8924 19
28. West Ham	5.3				4	5			8		7	12	3		9		10[1]	2	11		1	6†					1-1(0-0)14,980 19
29. Norwich	16.3				4	5	6		8	7[1]	12		3		9		10	2[1]	11†		1						2-4(0-1)12,260 —
30. Chelsea*	19.3					5	6†		8[1]	7	11[1]		3		9[2]	12	10	2			1	4					4-4(0-3)8468 20
31. Charlton	26.3	1			4	5†			8	7		3			9	11	10	2	12		6						0-0(0-0)6245 20
32. Arsenal*	30.3	1			4	5			8	7	11	3†			9	10		2	12		6						0-0(0-0)9088 —
33. Coventry	2.4	1			4	5			8†	7	11				9	10		2	3		6	12					0-1(0-0)15,748 20
34. Sthampton*	4.4	1			4	5‡	14			7	11				9	10	3	2	12		6	8†					0-0(0-0)7657 20
35. Watford	9.4	1			4	5	14			7	11‡				9	10	3	2	12		6	8†					0-3(0-2)10,045 20
36. Sheff Wed*	13.4	1			4‡	5	14		8	7	11				9	10†	3	2	12		6						0-3(0-2)5727 —
37. Everton*						5			8	7	11	3			9[1]	10	4	2			1	6					1-1(1-1)7619 21
38. Newcastle	30.4					5			8	7	11	3†			9	10[1]	4[1]	2	12		1	6		14			1-3(0-1)16,617 21
39. Man Utd*	2.5					5			8	7	11†	3			9	10	4	2			1	6		12			0-2(0-2)8966 21
40. Nottm For	7.5					5			8[2]	7[1]	11	3			9	10	4	2			1	6					3-5(1-4)12,762 21
Apps(subs)/goals		27(0) 0	24(0) 1	16(0) 3	32(0) 0	18(0) 1	33(5) 1	1(1) 0	30(3) 10	17(3) 2	39(0) 3	25(6) 2	34(1) 1	3(0) 0	0(1) 0	35(2) 12	1(1) 0	12(5) 0	29(1) 3	34(0) 1	15(9) 3	40(0) 0	9(0) 0	12(0) 0	2(1) 0	0(2) 0	

Final League Position: 21

PETERBOROUGH UNITED

London Road Ground, Peterborough PE2 8AL.

Back row (left to right): Mick Gooding, Ashley Carr, Bryn Gunn, Mark Nightingale, Mick Halsall, Noel Luke. *Middle row:* Mick Jones (Ass. Manager), Gary Pollard, Kevin Shoemake, Mick Nuttell, Joe Neenan, Les Lawrence, Bill Harvey (Physio). *Front row:* Alan Paris, David Riley, Paul Price, Noel Cantwell (Manager), Stephen Collins, Errington Kelly, Steve Phillips.

Stadium Capacity: 28,000.
Pitch Dimensions: 112 × 76 yds.
Telephone: 0733–63947.
Chairman: John Devaney.
Vice-Chairman: Steve Kendrick.
Directors: Rob Boverman, Martin Lewis, Mike Cooke.
Manager: Noel Cantwell.
Managers since 1960: Jimmy Hagan, Jack Fairbrother, Gordon Clark, Norman Rigby, Jim Iley, Noel Cantwell, John Barnwell, Billy Hails, Peter Morris, Martin Wilkinson, John Wile (11).
Assistant Manager: Mick Jones.
Physio: Bill Harvey.
Secretary: A. V. Blades.
Commercial Manager: Ellis Stafford.
Founded: 1934.
Turned Professional: 1934.
Nickname: The Posh.
Former Names: None.
Former Grounds: None.
Record Attendance: 30,096 v Swansea Town, FA Cup 5th Round, 20 February 1965.
Record Victory: 8–1 v Oldham Athletic, Division 4, 26 November 1969.
Record Defeat: 1–8 v Northampton Town, FA Cup 2nd Round 2nd replay, 18 December 1946.
Most League Points: (3 for a win) 82, Division 4, 1981–82. (2 for a win) 66, Division 4, 1960–61.
Most League Goals: 134, Division 4, 1960–61.
Highest League Scorer in a Season: Terry Bly, 52, Division 4, 1960–61.
Highest Total of League Goals: Jim Hall, 122, 1967–75.
Most League Appearances: Tommy Robson, 482, 1968–81.
League History: 1960 Elected to Division 4, 1961–68 Division 3, (then relegated for financial irregularities), 1968–74 Division 4, 1974–79 Division 3, 1979– Division 4.
Honours: Division 4 Champions 1960–61, 1973–74.
Colours: Blue shirts, white shorts, blue socks. **Second strip:** All white.

PETERBOROUGH UNITED -- LEAGUE RECORD 1987–88

Match no/Opp/Date		Neman	Paris	Gunn	Gooding	Pollard	Price	Kelly	Phillips	Riley	Halsall	Luke	Nightingale	Lawrence	Collins	Butterworth	Carr	Shoemake	Nuttell	White	Kerr	Corner	Fife	Benning	Genovese	Philpott	FT(HT)Att Lge pos
1. Carlisle*	15.8	1	2	3	4^1	5	6	7	8	9	10	11															1-0(1-0)4000 —
2. Rochdale	22.8	1	2	3	4	5	6	7‡	8‡	9^1	10	11	12	14													1-1(1-1)1808 6
3. Cambridge*	29.8	1	2	3	4	5	6	7	8^1	9	10	11															1-0(0-0)4623 3
4. Bolton	31.8	1	2	3	4		6		8	9	10	11†	12	14	5	7‡											0-2(0-1)3746 —
5. Darlington*	5.9	1	2	3	4	5	6		8†	9^1	10	11		12			7										1-2(1-2)3200 14
6. Colchester	12.9	1	2	3	4	5	6		8	9	10	11		7^1													1-4(0-1)1164 18
7. Wolves*	16.9	1	2	3	4_1	5	6†			9	10	11	12	7	8												1-1(0-1)3089 —
8. Wrexham*	19.9	1	2	3	4	5	6			9	10	11		7^1	8												1-0(1-0)2805 15
9. Orient	26.9	1	2	3	4	5	6			9	10	11†	12	7	8		1										0-2(0-3)3426 17
10. Hereford	30.9	1	2^1	3	4	5	6			9	10	11		7	8												1-0(1-0)2010 —
11. Scunthorpe*	3.10	1	2	3	4^1	5	6			9	10	11†	12	7	8												1-1(1-0)3594 14
12. Stockport	10.10	1	2	3	4	5	6			9	10	11		7^1	8												1-0(0-0)1594 12
13. Cardiff*	17.10	1	2	3	4^1	5†	6		8			7^2	12	9^1	11		14		$10‡$								4-3(1-2)3473 10
14. Newport*	21.10	1	2	3	4^3		6		8			11		7	5				10	9							3-0(2-0)3163 —
15. Halifax	24.10	1	2	3	4		6		8			11		7	5				10	9							0-0(0-0)1615 5
16. Torquay	31.10	1	2†	3	4		6		8			11	12	7	5		14		$10‡$	9							0-2(0-3)3500 11
17. Hartlepool*	7.11	1	2	3	4		6		8			11	12	7	5				10†	9							0-1(0-3)3200 13
18. Swansea	21.11	1	2	5	4		6		8^1		10	11	12	7‡			14			9		3†					1-2(1-1)4033 17
19. Burnley*	28.11	1	2^1	5	4^2		6		8		10	11		7^1						9		3^1					5-0(3-0)3550 14
20. Scarboro	12.12	1	2	5	4		6		8		10	11^1	12	7†						9	10						1-1(0-1)2525 15
21. Crewe*	18.12	1	2	5	4		6		8		10	11	12	7†			14			9	10	3‡					0-4(0-3)2540 —
22. Orient*	26.12	1	2	5	4^1		6†		8		10	11	12	7						9	10						1-2(0-1)3371 17
23. Tranmere	28.12	1	2	5	4		6		8^1		10	11	12	7						9†	10						1-3(0-1)3193 17
24. Cambridge	1.1	1	2	5	4		6				10	11^1		7	8^1					9		3					3-1(2-1)3975 16
25. Colchester*	2.1	1	2	5	4		6				10	11^1		7	8					9^1		3					2-0(0-0)3665 15
26. Rochdale*	9.1	1	2	5	4		6				10	11		7	8					9^1		3					1-1(1-1)3212 14
27. Wrexham	16.1	1	2	5	4		6				10^1	11		7	8					9		3					1-3(0-1)1506 15
28. Bolton*	30.1	1	2‡	5	4		6				10	11		7	8		14	1	12	9†		3					0-4(0-2)3485 15
29. Tranmere*	13.2		2	5	4		6				10	11†	12^1	7	8			1		9^1		3					2-1(1-1)2230 15
30. Carlisle	20.2		2	5	4^1		6				10	11†		7	8					9^1	12	3					2-0(2-0)2026 15
31. Hereford*	24.2		2	5	4^1		6				10†	11‡		7	8		14	1	12	9		3					1-2(1-0)2065 —
32. Scunthorpe	27.2		2	5	4		6				10†	11		7	8			1	12	9		3					0-5(0-1)3378 15
33. Cardiff	4.3	1	2	5	4		6				10	11		7	8					9		3					0-0(0-0)4172 —
34. Exeter	9.3	1	2	5	4^1		6				10	11		7	8					9		3					1-0(0-0)1584 —
35. Stockport*	12.3	1	2	5	4		6				10	11		7	8†		14			$9‡$	12	3					0-0(0-0)2193 14
36. Darlington	15.3	1	2	5	4^1		6				10	11	12	7	8†					9		3					1-2(1-2)1618 —
37. Torquay	19.3	1	2	5			6				10	11	12	7	8†					9		3					0-0(0-2)2544 15
38. Wolves	22.3	1	2	5	4^1		6				10	11†	12	7	8					9		3					1-0(0-0)8049 —
39. Halifax*	26.3	1	2	5	4_1		6				10	11	12	7	8^1		14			9		3†					1-0(1-0)2308 11
40. Hartlepool	2.4	1	2	5	4		6				10	11		7	8					9^1		3					1-0(1-0)2315 11
41. Swansea*	4.4	1	2	5	4		6				10	11		7	8					9†	12	3					0-1(0-0)3360 12
42. Newport	9.4	1	2	5	4		6				10	11†		7^1	8‡					9^3	12	3		14			4-0(1-0)988 11
43. Exeter*	23.4	1	2	5	4^1_1		6				10	11†		7	8					9	12			3	10		2-1(1-0)2278 8
44. Burnley	30.4	1	2	5	4		6					11^1		7	8^1					9	12	3			10†		2-1(0-1)6305 8
45. Scarboro*	2.5	1	2	5	4		6				10	11		7	8					9		3					0-0(0-0)3244 8
46. Crewe	7.5	1	2	5	4		6				10	11^1		7	8					9		3					1-0(1-0)1533 7

Apps(subs)/goals: 40(0)/0 · 46(0)/0 · 46(0)/0 · 44(0)/18 · 12(0)/0 · 44(0)/0 · 10(8)/2 · 16(2)/5 · 12(0)/2 · 45(0)/4 · 41(0)/7 · 15(5)/4 · 16(5)/4 · 39(0)/1 · 6(5)/0 · 8(5)/0 · 6(0)/0 · 6(5)/0 · 14(0)/4 · 10(0)/1 · 9(0)/0 · 0(1)/0 · 2(0)/0 · 1(0)/0 · 0(1)/0

Final League Position: 7

Own goal: Crowe, match 24.

PLYMOUTH ARGYLE

DIVISION 2

Home Park, Plymouth, Devon PL2 3DQ.

Back row (left to right:), Adrian Burrows, Stewart Evans, Gerry McElhinney, Steve Cherry, Geoff Crudging-ton, Eddie McElhinney, John Brimacombe, Jason Rowbotham. *Middle row:* Martin Harvey (Team Coach), Mark Smith, Russell Coughlin, John Uzzell, Kevin Summerfield, John Clayton, Paul Edwards, Kevin Hodges, Malcolm Musgrove (Physio). *Front row:* John Matthews, Steve Cooper, Nicky Law, Dave Smith (Team Manager), Tommy Tynan, Daren Rowbotham, Leigh Cooper.

Stadium Capacity: 30,000.
Pitch Dimensions: 112 × 75yds.
Telephone: 0752–562561.
Chairman: P. D. Bloom.
Directors: B. L. Hooper, R. Burroughs ARICS, G. E. Jasper, J. E. C. Kent, D. Forshaw, C. Hartley, S. W. Dawe.
Manager: Ken Brown.
Post-War Managers: Jack Tresadern, Jimmy Rae, Jack Rowley, Neil Dougall, Ellis Stuttard, Andy Beattie, Malcolm Allison, Derek Ufton, Billy Bingham, Ellis Stuttard, Tony Waiters, Mike Kelly, Malcolm Allison, Bobby Saxton, Bobby Moncur, John Hore, Dave Smith (17).
Physio: Malcolm Musgrove.
Secretary: Graham Little.
Commercial Manager: W. Pearce.
Founded: 1886.
Turned Professional: 1903.
Nickname: The Pilgrims.
Former Names: Argyle Athletic Club 1886–1903.
Former Grounds: None
Record Attendance: 43,596 v Aston Villa, Division 2, 10 October 1936.
Record Victory: 8–1 v Millwall, Division 2, 16 January 1932.
Record Defeat: 0–9 v Stoke City, Division 2, 17 December 1960.
Most League Points: (3 for a win) 87, Division 3, 1985–86. (2 for a win) 68, Division 3(S), 1929–30.
Most League Goals: 107, Division 3(S), 1925–26 and 1951–52.
Highest League Scorer in a Season: Jack Cock, 32, Division 3(S), 1925–26.
Highest Total of League Goals: Sammy Black, 180, 1924–38.
Most League Appearances: Sammy Black, 470, 1924–38.
League History: 1920 Founder Members of Division 3, 1921–30 Division 3(S), 1930–50 Division 2, 1950–52 Division 3(S), 1952–56 Division 2, 1956–58 Division 3(S), 1958–59 Division 3, 1959–68 Division 2, 1968–75 Division 3, 1975–77 Division 2, 1977–86 Division 3, 1985–87 Division 2.
Honours: Division 3 Champions 1958–59, runners-up 1974–75, 1985–86.
Division 3(S) Champions 1929–30, 1951–52, runners-up 1921–22, 1922–23, 1923–24, 1924–25, 1925–26, 1926–27.
Colours: Green shirts with black trim, black shorts, white socks. **Second strip:** All white.

PLYMOUTH ARGYLE – LEAGUE RECORD 1987–88

Match no/Opp/Date		Cherry	Brimacombe	Cooper L	Coughlin	Law	Smith	Matthews	Summerfield	Tynan	Evans	Furphy	Cooper S	Uzzell	Rowbotham D	Clayton	Hodges	Anderson	McElhinney	Crudgington	Rowbotham J	Marker	Burrows	Morrison	FT(HT)Att	Lge pos
1. Man City	15.8	1	2	3	4†	5^{1}	6	7	8	9	10	11‡	12	14											1–2(1–0)20,046	—
2. **Ipswich***	18.8	1	2	3		4	5	6	8	9	10	11‡	7†		12	14									0–0(0–0)11,901	—
3. **Huddersfield***	22.8	1	2	3		5^{1}	6	7	8^{1}	9^{2}	10^{1}	11^{1}			4										6–1(2–0)8811	5
4. Reading	29.8	1	2	3		5	6	7	8	9	10	11	12		4†										1–0(1–0)6658	1
5. **Sheff Utd***	31.8	1	2	3		5	6	7	8	9	10^{1}	11			4†		12								1–0(1–0)14,504	—
6. Barnsley	5.9	1	2	3	12	5‡	6	7	8	9^{1}	10	11†		14			4								1–2(0–0)6976	2
7. **WBA***	12.9	1	2	3		5	6	4	8	9^{2}	10		14		12	11^{1}‡		7†							3–3(0–1)10,578	5
8. Bradford	16.9	1	2	3		5	6‡	7^{1}	8†	9	10		12	14		11		4							1–3(0–1)11,009	—
9. Leicester	19.9	1	2	3		5		4‡		9	10			14	8†	11	12	7	6						0–4(0–3)8872	12
10. **Birmingham***	26.9		2	3		5	6	12	8	9^{1}	10					14	7	11‡	4†	1					1–1(1–1)8912	14
11. Bournemouth	29.9		2	3		5	6	4	8	9	10		11†			12^{1}	7^{1}			1					2–2(1–1)6491	—
12. **Aston Villa***	3.10		2	3		5	6^{1}	4	8		10				11†	9	7	12		1					1–3(1–3)10,515	17
13. Stoke	10.10		2	3		5	6		8	4	10					9	7	11†		1	12				0–1(0–1)8275	19
14. **Leeds***	17.10		11	3		5	6^{1}	4	8^{2}	9^{1}					12	10^{2}	7			1	2†				6–3(2–2)9352	13
15. **Millwall***	20.10		11	3		5	6	4†	8‡	9	14^{1}				12	10	7			1	2				1–2(1–1)8958	—
16. Blackburn	24.10	1		3		5	6	4		9	8^{1}		11			10	7				2				1–1(0–0)6014	17
17. **Hull***	31.10	1	2	3	8	5	6^{1}	4†	12	9_{1}	11					10^{1}	7								3–1(3–1)8550	13
18. C Palace	3.11	1	2^{1}	3	8	5	6	4	12	9	11					10†	7								1–5(0–1)7424	—
19. Swindon	14.11	1	2	3	8		6			9	10^{1}†		12				7	11	4			5			1–1(1–1)9616	16
20. **Middlesbro***	21.11	1	2‡	3	8		6		14	9	10†		12				7	11	4			5			0–1(0–1)9428	17
21. Oldham	28.11	1	2	3	8		6			9^{1}			10				7	11				5	4		1–0(0–0)4516	15
22. **Shrewsbury***	5.12	1	2	3	8†		6		12	9			10^{1}				7^{1}	11				5	4		2–0(0–0)7603	14
23. Huddersfield	12.12	1	2			3	6		8	9			10^{1}			12	7†	11				5	4		1–2(0–1)5747	14
24. **Bradford***	20.12		2			3	6^{1}		8	9	12		10^{1}				7	11†		1		5	4		2–1(2–0)11,350	—
25. Birmingham	26.12	1	2	12		3	6		8†	9_{1}			10				7	11				5	4		1–0(0–0)9166	13
26. **Leicester***	28.12	1	2			3	6^{1}		8	9^{1}			10				7	11^{1}				5	4		4–0(0–0)15,581	13
27. **Reading***	1.1	1	2	12		3†	6	8		9_{1}	14		10‡				7	11				5	4		1–3(0–0)13,289	13
28. WBA	2.1	1	2	3			6	8		9	10		12				7	11†				5	4		0–1(0–1)8445	13
29. **Man City***	16.1	1	2	3			6^{1}	8	12	9^{1}	14^{1}		10‡				7	11†				5	4		3–2(0–2)13,291	13
30. Ipswich	13.2	1		3		2^{1}		8	11^{1}	9	10						7		6			5	4		2–1(1–1)10,476	13
31. Aston Villa	27.2	1	2	3				8	11	9^{1}			10				7^{1}		6†			5	4	12	2–5(1–3)16,142	13
32. Leeds	5.3	1	2	3			6	8	11	9	12		10				7†					5	4		0–1(0–0)18,115	14
33. **Stoke***	12.3	1	2				6	8	11	9^{2}	10†			3^{1}		12	7‡	14				5	4		3–0(2–0)8749	14
34. Hull	19.3	1	2	14			6	8	11	9	10^{1}†			3		12	7‡					5	4		1–1(1–0)5172	14
35. **Blackburn***	26.3	1	2	12			6	8	11	9	10^{1}†			3			7^{1}					5	4^{1}		3–0(1–0)12,359	13
36. **Swindon***	4.4	1	2	3			6	8	11	9	10^{1}†					12	7					5	4		1–0(1–0)13,299	14
37. Millwall	9.4	1	2	3			6	8	11^{1}	9	10						7^{1}					5	4		2–3(2–3)11,052	14
38. **Barnsley***	15.4	1	2	3			6	8	11	9	10						7					5	4		0–0(0–0)8059	—
39. Sheff Utd	19.4	1	2	3			6	8	11	9	10						7					5	4		0–1(0–0)9052	—
40. **C Palace***	23.4	1	2	3			6	8	11	9	10^{1}		12					7†				5	4		1–3(0–1)8370	15
41. **Bournemouth***	26.4	1	2	3†		12	6	8	11	9	10						7^{1}					5	4		1–2(0–1)6310	—
42. Middlesbro	30.4	1	2				6	8	11	9	10			3		4^{1}	7					5			1–3(0–1)16,615	15
43. **Oldham***	2.5	1	2				6	8	11	9†	10‡		12	3		14	7					5^{1}	4		1–0(0–0)6084	14
44. Shrewsbury	7.5	1	2			11	6	8†		12	14		9†	3		10^{1}	7					5	4		1–2(0–1)4510	16
Apps(subs)/goals		37(0)0	42(0)1	33(4)0	7(1)0	25(1)3	41(0)6	34(0)1	32(5)5	42(1)16	31(6)10	6(0)1	14(9)1	6(4)1	5(4)0	12(8)7	35(2)6	17(2)1	6(0)0	7(0)0	3(1)0	26(0)1	23(0)1	0(1)0	Final League Position: 16	

Own goals: Peters, match 4; Ramsey, match 26.

DIVISION 2

PORTSMOUTH

Fratton Park, Frogmore Rd, Portsmouth PO4 8RA.

Back row (left to right): Mick Quinn, Malcolm Shotton, Lee Sandford, Noel Blake, Paul Mariner, Kevin Dillon, Barry Horne. *Middle row:* John Dickens (Physio), Terry Conner, Mick Fillery, Andy Gosney, Alan Knight, Billy Gilbert, Andy Perry, Gordon Neave (Trainer). *Bottom row:* Vince Hilaire, Mick Kennedy, Kevin Ball, Graham Paddon (Ass. Manager), Alan Ball (Manager), Peter Osgood (Youth Team Manager), Clive Whitehead, Kenny Swain, Paul Hardyman.

Stadium Capacity: 28,000.
Pitch Dimensions: 116 × 73 yds.
Telephone: 0705–731204, **Clubcall:** 0898–121182.
Chairman: B. J. Deacon CBE.
Vice-Chairman: J. R. Parkhouse.
Directors: D. K. Deacon, S. W. Sloan, Mrs J. Deacon.
Manager: Alan Ball.
Post-War Managers: Jack Tinn, Bob Jackson, Eddie Lever, Freddie Cox, George Smith, John Mortimore, Ron Tindall, Ian St John, Jimmy Dickinson MBE, Frank Burrows, Bobby Campbell (11).
Assistant Manager: Graham Paddon.
Physio: John Dickens.
Company Secretary: Mrs J. Deacon.
Commercial Manager: Les Allen.
Founded: 1898.
Turned Professional: 1898.
Nickname: Pompey.
Former Names: None.
Former Grounds: None.
Record Attendance: 51,385 v Derby County, FA Cup 6th Round, 26 February 1949.
Record Victory: 9–1 v Notts County, Division 2, 9 April, 1927.
Record Defeat: 0–10 v Leicester City, Division 1, 20 October, 1928.
Most League Points: (3 for a win) 91, Division 3, 1982–83. (2 for a win) 65, Division 3, 1961–62.
Most League Goals: 91, Division 4, 1979–80.
Highest League Scorer in a Season: Billy Haines, 40, Division 2, 1926–27.
Highest Total of League Goals: Peter Harris, 194, 1946–60.
Most League Appearances: Jimmy Dickinson, 764, 1946–65.
League History: 1920 Founder Members of Divisoin 3, 1921Division 3(S), 1924–27 Division 2, 1927–59Division 1, 1959–61 Division 2, 1961–62 Division 3, 1962–76 Division 2, 1976–78 Division 3, 1978–80Division 4, 1980–83 Division 3, 1983–87 Division 2, 1987–88 Division 1, 1988– Division 2.
Honours: Division 1 Champions 1948–49, 1949–50. Division 2 runners-up 1926–27, 1986–87. Division 3 Champions 1961–62, 1982–83. Division 3(S) Champions 1923–24. FA Cup winners 1939, runners-up 1929, 1934.
Colours: Royal blue shirts with white trim, white shorts, red socks. **Second strip:** Pink shirts, black shorts and socks.

PORTSMOUTH – LEAGUE RECORD 1987–88

Match no/Opp/Date	Date	Knight	Swain	Hardman	Dillon	Mariner	Gilbert	Whitehead	Kennedy	Kerr	Quinn	Fillery	Stewart	Horne	Sandford	Baird	Hilaire	Shotton	Ball	Connor	Blake	Darby	Perry	Kelly	Gosney	FT(HT)Att Lge pos
1. Oxford	15.8	1	2	3	4‡	5¹	6	7¹	8	9	10	11†	12	14												2-4(0-1)9174 —
2. Chelsea*	18.8	1	2	3		5	6	4	8	9	10	11†	12	7												0-3(0-1)16,917 —
3. Sthampton*	22.8	1	2	3	14	5	6	4¹	8		10†	7‡		12	9	11¹										2-2(1-1)20,161 20
4. Arsenal	29.8	1	2			10	6	4†	8			7	12	3	9	11	5									0-6(0-4)30,865 20
5. West Ham*	31.8	1	2		4¹₁	10	6		8			7		3	9	11	5									2-1(1-1)16,104 —
6. Derby	5.9	1	2		4	10	6		8			7		3	9	11	5									0-0(0-0)15,071 —
7. Charlton*	12.9	1	2		4	10†	6‡	14	8		12¹	7		3	9	11	5									1-1(0-1)13,136 17
8. Watford	19.9	1	2		4		6		8	14†	10	7		3	9‡	11	5	12								0-0(0-0)13,277 17
9. Wimbledon*	26.9	1	2			9	6	12	8		10¹	4†		7	3¹	11	5									2-1(1-1)13,088 12
10. Liverpool	3.10	1	2		14	9	6†		8		10	4‡		7	3	11	5	12								0-4(0-1)44,366 13
11. Luton*	10.10	1	2	3	4¹₁	12¹			8		10			7	9†	11	5	6								3-1(0-0)12,391 11
12. QPR	24.10	1	2	3	4	12		6	8		10†			7	9¹	11	5									1-2(0-1)13,171 14
13. Sheff Wed*	31.10	1	2	3	4₁	12		14			8‡			7	9	11	5	6	10†							1-2(1-1)13,582 16
14. Spurs*	4.11	1	2	3	4		5		8					7	9	11		6	10							0-0(0-0)15,302 —
15. Nottm F	14.11	1	2	3		5		4	8		12			7	9	11		6	10†							0-5(0-3)15,851 18
16. Everton*	21.11	1	2	3	4			6	8		10			7	9	11	5									0-1(0-0)17,724 18
17. Norwich	28.11	1	2	3	4			6	8		10			7¹	9	11	5									1-0(1-0)13,099 18
18. Coventry*	5.12	1	2	3				6			10	4		7	9	11	5		8							0-0(0-0)13,002 18
19. Newcastle	12.12	1	2	3¹	4		12	6			10†			7	9	11	5		8							1-1(1-0)20,455 18
20. Man Utd*	19.12	1	2	3	4₁			6	8		12			7	9†	11	5		10							1-2(0-1)22,207 18
21. Charlton	26.12	1	2	3†			12	6	8		10¹	14		7	9	11	5		4‡							1-2(1-1)6686 18
22. Watford*	28.12	1	2				12	3	8		10			7	9†	11		6	4¹	5						1-0(0-0)15,003 19
23. Arsenal*	1.1	1		3	4		12	2	8		9†			7		11		6	10¹	5						1-1(1-0)17,366 19
24. Sthampton	3.1	1		3	4			2	8		9			7¹		11		6	10¹	5						2-0(2-0)17,002 —
25. Oxford*	16.1	1		3	4			2			9¹	10		7		11		6¹		5	8†	12				2-2(0-1)13,417 19
26. Chelsea	23.1	1		3	4			2			10	8		7	9	11		6		5						0-0(0-0)15,856 19
27. Derby*	6.2	1			4			2			9¹	8		7	3	11¹		6	10	5						2-1(1-0)14,790 19
28. West Ham	13.2	1		3	4		12	2			7	8‡			9†	11		6	10¹	5			14			1-0(0-0)18,639 19
29. Liverpool*	27.2	1		12	4†			2			9	8		7	3	11		6	10	5						0-2(0-0)28,197 19
30. Sheff W	19.3	1		3	4‡		14	2			9	8†		7	12	11		6	10	5						0-1(0-1)13,731 19
31. QPR*	26.3	1			4	9		2				8		7	3	11		6	10†	5	12					0-1(0-1)13,041 19
32. Luton	29.3	1	2		4¹	9	6		12			8		7	3	11				5				10†		1-4(0-1)6740 19
33. Spurs	2.4	1	2		4	9	6		8			10		7¹	3	11				5						1-0(1-0)18,616 19
34. Nottm F*	4.4	1	2		4				8			9		7	3	11				5						0-1(0-0)17,528 19
35. Everton	9.4	1	2		4¹		14	12	8			9		7	3	11		6	10‡	5†						1-2(1-1)21,292 19
36. Wimbledon	19.4	1†	2			12¹	9¹	4	8			10		7	3	11		6		5						2-2(0-2)9009 19
37. Norwich*	23.4		2		4	9¹			8			10¹		7	3	11		6		5				1		2-2(0-1)12,762 19
38. Coventry	30.4		2		4	9			8			10†		7	3	11		6		5	12			1		0-1(0-0)14,296 19
39. Newcastle*	2.5		2		4				8			9¹		7	3	11		6	10	5				1		1-2(0-1)12,468 19
40. Man Utd	7.5			3				2			9₁	8			4	11†		6	10	5	12		7		1	1-4(0-3)35,105 19
Apps(subs)/goals		36(0) 0	32(0) 0	19(1) 1	29(3) 9	16(7) 4	17(4) 0	30(3) 2	18(0) 0	2(2) 0	29(3) 8	17(1) 0	0(1) 0	36(3) 3	19(2) 1	20(0) 1	38(0) 2	10(0) 0	27(2) 1	19(0) 4	19(0) 0	10(0) 0	3(1) 0	12(0) 0	4(0) 0	

Final League Position: 19

DIVISION 3

PORT VALE

Vale Park, Hamil Road, Burslem, Stoke-on-Trent ST6 1AW.

Back row (left to right): Darren Beckford, Kevin Steggles, Phil Sproson, Mark Grew, Kevin Finney, Michael Cole, Simon Mills. *Middle row:* Mick Pejic (Coach), Chris Banks, Darren Hughes, Alan Webb, Steve Davies, Robbie Earle, Martin Copeland (Physio) *Bottom row:* Paul Maguire, Dave Riley, Ray Walker, John Rudge (Manager), Andy Porter, Gary Ford, Steve Harper.

Stadium Capacity: 23,000. **Pitch Dimensions:** 116 × 76 yds. **Telephone:** 0782-814134, **Commercial dept:** 0782-85524.
Chairman: W. T. Bell. **Vice-Chairman:** D. P. McGrath. **Directors:** I. McPherson, A. Belfield, M. J. Thompstone.
Manager: John Rudge. **Post-War Managers:** Billy Frith, Gordon Hodgson, Ivor Powell, Freddie Steele, Norman Low, Freddie Steele, Jackie Mudie, Sir Stanley Matthews, Gordon Lee, Roy Sproson, Colin Harper, Bob Smith, Dennis Butler, Alan Bloor, John McGrath (15). **Coach:** Mike Pejic. **Physio:** Martin Copeland.
Secretary: D. E. Barber JP. **Commercial Manager:** Mrs M. Moran-Smith.
Sponsors: ABC Minolta.
Founded: 1876. **Turned Professional:** 1885. **Nickname:** The Valiants. **Former Names:** Burslem Port Vale 1876–1913.
Former Grounds: Limekin Lane, Longport 1876–1881, Westport 1881–1884, Moorland Road, Burslem 1884–86, Athletic Ground, Cobridge 1886–1913, Recreation Ground, Hanley 1913–50.
Record Attendance: 50,000 v Aston Villa, FA Cup 5th Round, 20 February 1960.
Record Victory: 9–1 v Chesterfield, Division 2, 24 September 1932.
Record Defeat: 0–10 v Sheffield United, Division 2, 10 December 1892 and v Notts County, Division 2, 26 February 1895.
Most League Points: (3 for a win) 88, Division 4, 1982–83. (2 for a win) 69, Division 3(N), 1953–54.
Most League Goals: 110, Division 4, 1958–59.
Highest League Scorer in a Season: Wilf Kirkham, 38, Division 2, 1926–27.
Highest Total of League Goals: Wilf Kirkham, 154, 1923–29, 1931–33.
Most League Appearances: Roy Sproson, 761, 1950–72.
League History: Founder Members Division 2 1892–96, not re-elected 1898, re-elected 1898, resigned 1907, returned in October 1919 when they replaced Leeds City, 1929–30 Division 3(N), 1930–36 Division 2, 1936–38 Division 3(N), 1938–52 Division 3(S), 1952–54 Division 3(N), 1954–57 Division 2, 1957–58 Division 3(S), 1958–59 Division 4, 1959–65 Division 3, 1965–70 Division 4, 1970–78 Division 3, 1978–83 Division 4, 1983–84 Division 3, 1984–86 Division 4, 1986–Division 3.
Honours: Division 4 Champions 1958–59. Division 3(N) Champions 1929–30, 1953–54, runners-up 1952–53.
Colours: White shirts with black trim, black shorts, white socks. **Second strip:** All yellow.

PORT VALE – LEAGUE RECORD 1987–88

Match no/Opp/Date		Williams	Banks	Pearson	Walker	Webb	Sproson	Smith	Earle	Jones	Beckford	Harper	Hazell	Maguire	Hanson	Finney	Hughes	O'Kelly	Grew	Porter	Riley	Simons	Steggles	Barnes	Mills	Ford	Cole	Davies	Holdsworth	FT(HT)Att Lge pos
1. Aldershot*	15.8	1	2	3	4	5	6	7	8	9³	10	11																		4-2(1-1)3160 —
2. Rotherham*	29.8	1		3	4	2	6	7	8	9	10	11†	5	12																0-0(0-0)2895 11
3. Bristol C	31.8	1	4†	3		2	6		8	8	9	10	14	5	7	11‡	12													0-1(0-0)8716 —
4. York*	5.9	1	10		4	2	6			9¹		11¹		5	7	3	8													2-1(0-0)2711 13
5. Chesterfield	12.9				4	2	6	8¹	9¹	12		11¹		5	7	3	10¹	1												3-1(1-1)2406 9
6. Southend*	14.9			4¹		2	6		8	9	12	11¹⁴		5	7²	3	10	1												4-1(1-0)3670 —
7. Fulham*	19.9				4	2	6		8		10	11		5	7₁	3	9	1												1-1(0-1)3894 7
8. Nthampton	26.9				4	2	6			10	12			5	·7	11†	3	9	1	8										0-1(0-0)5072 11
9. Brighton*	28.9				4	2	6			10¹	11			5	7	3¹	9	1	8											2-0(0-0)3789 —
10. Brentford	3.10				4	2	6			10¹	11‡		5	7	14	12	3¹	9	1	8†										0-1(0-0)4130 10
11. Preston	10.10				4²	2	6			10	11†		5	7	12	3	9	1	8											2-3(1-0)6274 12
12. Bury*	17.10		12		4	2	6			10¹	11		5	7†		8	3	9	1											1-0(1-0)3235 9
13. Bristol R*	19.10				4	2	6			10	11		5	7₁		8	3		1	9¹										2-1(1-1)3598 9
14. Walsall	24.10		11		4	2	6						5	7		8	3	10	1	9¹										1-2(1-1)6083 9
15. Gillingham*	31.10		14		4	2	6			10	11		5	7†		8‡	3	12	1	9										0-0(0-0)3495 9
16. Chester	4.11				4	2	6			10	11		5	12	7†	8	3		1	9										0-1(0-0)2789 —
17. Doncaster	7.11				4	2	6¹			10	14		5†	7‡	11	8	3	12		9	1									1-1(0-1)1365 13
18. Blackpool*	22.11				4	2	6			12	11		5	7†		8	3	10	1	9										0-0(0-0)3594 —
19. Sunderland	28.11		14		4	2‡	6			12			5	7	11	8†	3	10	1	9¹										1-2(0-2)15,655 14
20. Notts Co*	12.12		12		4		6			8	14		5	7†	11‡	3	10	1	9¹	2										1-3(0-0)3358 15
21. Mansfield	20.12		6		4					8			5	12	11‡	3	10†	1	14	9	2	7								0-4(0-2)3173 —
22. Nthampton*	26.12		14		4		6			8	7		5	12	11¹⁴	3		1	9	2‡		10								1-1(1-0)4446 17
23. Grimsby	28.12				4		6			8	7		5	12	11¹⁴	3		1	9	2		10								1-3(1-1)2941 19
24. Rotherham	1.1				4		6			8	12		5			3	1.	9†	2	11	10	7								0-0(0-0)3913 19
25. Chesterfield*	2.1		2		4		6			8†			5	12		3		1	11	10	7									0-1(0-0)3495 19
26. Fulham	16.1		6		4					10				8	3		1	9¹	2	5¹	7	11								2-1(0-1)3784 18
27. Southend	22.1		5†		4		6			10				3		1	12	9¹	2	8¹	7¹	11								3-3(1-2)3038 —
28. York	6.2				4	6¹	8				5	12		3		1	9†	2	10¹	7	11¹									3-2(1-2)2420 19
29. Grimsby*	13.2				4		6	8²		5				3		1	9	2	10	7	11									2-0(0-0)3417 16
30. Brentford*	27.2		12			6	8‡	10¹		5	11	14	3		1	9	2†	4	7											1-0(0-0)3876 16
31. Brighton	2.3					6	8	10		5	11		3		1	9	2	4	7											0-2(0-0)7296 —
32. Bury	5.3				4		6	8		10¹	5			3		1	9	2	11	7										1-0(0-0)2635 15
33. Preston*	12.3				4¹	6¹	8			10	5			3		1	9†	2	11	7	12									3-2(1-1)4647 14
34. Gillingham	19.3				4		6	8		10	5			3		1	9	2		7	12	11†								0-0(0-0)3459 13
35. Walsall*	26.3				4		6	8		10	5			3		1	9¹	2		7	12	11¹⁴								2-1(1-0)6347 13
36. Doncaster*	2.4				4¹	14	6	8		10²₁	5			3		1	9¹	2‡		7†	12	11								5-0(2-0)3680 12
37. Blackpool	4.4				4		6	8		10¹	5			3		1	9	2		7¹		11								2-1(2-0)5516 10
38. Chester*	9.4				4		6	8		10	5			3		1	9	2		7		11¹								1-1(1-1)4278 10
39. Wigan	12.4				4		6	8			5		10	3		1	9	2		7	12	11†								0-2(0-1)3750 —
40. Aldershot	15.4				4		6	8			5		12	3		1	9	2	10	7	11†									0-3(0-2)2257 —
41. Bristol C*	18.4				4	2	6	8		10	5			3		1	9			11¹	7									1-0(0-0)2671 —
42. Bristol R	23.4				4	2	6	8		10	5	12		3		1	9†			11	7									0-1(0-0)3780 13
43. Wigan*	25.4				4¹	2	6	8		10	5			3		1	9			11	7¹									2-1(1-1)3044 —
44. Sunderland*	30.4				4	2	6	8		10	5	12		3		1	9†			11	7									0-1(0-0)7569 12
45. Notts Co	2.5				4	2	6	8¹		10¹	5			3		1	9			11	7									2-1(1-0)7702 11
46. Mansfield*	7.5					2	6	8		10	5		4	3		1	9			11¹	7									1-1(0-0)3617 11
Apps(subs)/goals		4(0)0	8(6)0	3(0)0	42(0)6	25(1)0	44(0)3	20(0)0	25(0)4	36(4)9	16(5)2	43(0)0	10(9)4	9(2)2	11(4)0	43(0)1	14(2)1	41(0)0	42(0)0	34(0)8	20(0)0	30(0)5	19(0)3	21(0)3	6(0)0	1(5)0	15(0)0	6(0)2		Final League Position: 11

Own goal: Atkins, match 33.

DIVISION 3

PRESTON NORTH END
Deepdale, Preston PR1 6RU.

Back row (left to right): Frank Worthington, Jeff Wrightson, Bob Atkins, Sam Allardyce, Alan Kelly, David Brown, Alex Jones, David Miller, Jim Branagan, Steve Taylor. *Front row:* Ronnie Hildersley, Oshor Williams, Gary Swann, Mick Rathbone, Les Chapman, Gary Brazil, Nigel Jemson, Mick Bennett, Stephen Wilkes.

Stadium Capacity: 19,000.
Pitch Dimensions: 110 × 72 yds.
Telephone: 0772–795919, **Recorded information:** 0772–709170, **Commercial dept:** 0772–795465/795156.
Chairman: Keith Leeming.
Vice-Chairmen: J. T. Garratt, M. J. Woodhouse.
Managing Director: B. J. Campbell.
Directors: J. Francis, E. Griffith (Company secretary), J. E. Wignall, J. W. Wilding, J. T. Worden.
Manager: John McGrath.
Post-War Managers: Will Scott, Scot Symon, Frank Hill, Cliff Britton, Jimmy Milne, Bobby Seith, Alan Ball Snr, Bobby Charlton CBE, Harry Catterick, Nobby Stiles, Tommy Docherty, Gordon Lee, Alan Kelly, Tommy Booth, Brian Kidd, Jon Clark (16).
Assistant Manager: Les Chapman.
Physio: Andy Jones.
Secretary: D. J. Allan.
Promotions Manager: Wayne Dore.
Sponsors: Garratt, Son & Flowerdew Ltd.
Founded: 1881.
Turned Professional: 1885.
Nickname: The Lilywhites or North End.
Former Names: None.
Former Grounds: None.
Record Attendance: 42,684 v Arsenal, Division 1, 23 April 1938.
Record Victory: 26–0 v Hyde, FA Cup 1st series, 1st Round, 15 October, 1887 (Record for a first-class match in England).
Record Defeat: 0–7 v Blackpool, Division 1, 1 May, 1948.
Most League Points: (3 for a win) 90, Division 4, 1986–87. (2 for a win) 61, Division 3, 1970–71.
Most League Goals: 100, Division 2, 1927–28 and Division 1, 1957–58.
Highest League Scorer in a Season: Ted Harper, 37, Division 2, 1932–33.
Highest Total of League Goals: Tom Finney, 187, 1946–60.
Most League Appearances: Alan Kelly, 447, 1961–75.
League History: 1888 Founder Members of League, 1901–04 Division 2, 1904–12 Division 1, 1912–13 Division 2, 1913–14 Division 1, 1914–15 Division 2, 1919–25 Division 1, 1925–34 Division 2, 1934–49 Division 1, 1949–51 Division 2, 1951–61 Division 1, 1961–70 Division 2, 1970–71 Division 3, 1971–74 Division 2, 1974–78 Division 3, 1978–81 Division 2, 1981–85 Division 3, 1985–87 Division 4, 1987– Division 3.
Honours: Division 1 Champions 1888–89, 1889–90, runners-up 1890–91, 1891–92, 1892–93, 1905–06, 1952–53, 1957–58. Division 2 Champions 1903–04, 1912–13, 1950–51, runners-up 1914–15, 1933–34. Division 3 Champions 1970–71. Division 4 runners-up 1986–87. FA Cup winners 1889, 1938, runners-up 1888, 1922, 1937, 1954, 1964.
Colours: All white. **Second strip:** All yellow.

PRESTON NORTH END – LEAGUE RECORD 1987–88

Match no/Opp/Date		Kelly	Branagan	Rathbone	Atkins	Chapman	Allardyce	Miller	Swann	Lowey	Brazil	Hilderbey	Worthington	Brown	Wrighson	Bennett	Jones	Williams	Jemson	Wilkes	Jeffels	Mooney	Ellis	Joyce	Hughes	FT(HT)Att	Lge pos
1. Chesterfield*	15.8	1	2	3	4	5	6	7†	8	9	10	11	12													0–1(0–0)6509	—
2. Bristol C	22.8	2†	11‡		4		6	7	8	9	10¹		14		1	12	3	5								1–3(0–1)7655	23
3. Wigan*	29.8				4	5†	6		2	8	10	11	12	1			3	7	9							0–1(0–0)7057	24
4. Southend	1.9				4¹	5	6		2	8	10	11		1				7¹	9							2–1(1–0)2600	—
5. Grimsby*	5.9				4	5†	6		2	8¹	10	11	12	1			3	7	9							1–3(0–2)5522	20
6. York	12.9	1	11	3	4		6		2	8†	10¹	14	9‡			5	7	12								1–1(0–0)3237	20
7. Nthampton*	15.9	1		2	4		6	7	8		10	11				5	3	9								0–0(0–0)5179	—
8. Rotherham*	19.9	1		2	4		6	7	8		10	11	9			5	3									0–0(0–0)5124	21
9. Blackpool	26.9	1		2	4		6	7	8			11	9	5	3†		10	12								0–3(0–2)8406	22
10. Brentford*	29.9	1		2	4	14	6	7‡	8†	9¹		11	12	5	3		10									1–2(1–0)4241	—
11. Walsall	3.10			2	4	11	6		8	9		12		5	3		10†		7							0–1(0–1)5467	23
12. Port Vale*	10.10			2	4		6	7†	14		10⌊		12	1	11	3	5				8‡	9¹				3–2(0–1)6274	22
13. Brighton	17.10			2	4		6		11		10†		1	12	3	5		14			8	9‡	7			0–0(0–0)6043	22
14. Gillingham*	20.10	1		2	4		6		11				3	5	7¹			10	9	8						1–1(1–1)5676	—
15. Bury	24.10	1	2†		4		6		11			12	7	3	5			10	9	8						1–1(1–0)4316	21
16. Chester*	31.10	1		2	4		6		8¹				3	5	10			7	9							1–1(1–0)5657	21
17. Bristol R	4.11	1		2	4		6		8				3	5	10¹			7	9¹							2–1(1–0)2804	—
18. Mansfield	7.11	1			4		6	2	8				3	5	10			7	9							0–0(0–0)3631	21
19. Doncaster*	21.11	1		2†	4		6	12¹	8		10	11	3	5	9			7								1–2(0–2)5178	21
20. Fulham	28.11	1		2	4		6		8		10	11	3	5	9¹			7								1–0(1–0)5324	21
21. Aldershot*	12.12	1		2	4		6		8		10	11	3	5	9			7†	12							0–2(0–2)4519	21
22. Notts Co	19.12	1		2	4		6	12	8¹		10		3	5†	9¹			7		11						2–4(1–2)5730	21
23. Blackpool*	26.12	1		2	4		6		8¹		10¹	12	3	5				7†	9	11						2–1(0–1)11,155	20
24. Sunderland	28.12	1		2	4		6		8		10		3	5¹				7	9	11						1–0(0–0)24,814	20
25. Wigan	1.1	1			4	14	6	2	8		10	11	3	5‡				12		7	9†					0–2(0–2)6872	21
26. York*	2.1				4	5	6	2¹	8		10¹		1	3				9			7¹		11			3–0(2–0)6302	20
27. Bristol C*	9.1			2¹†	4	5	6	12	8		10¹		1	3							7	9	11			2–0(1–0)5229	19
28. Rotherham	16.1			2	4	5	6				10²			3							7	9	11			2–2(2–1)4011	20
29. Nthampton	27.1			2	4		6		8		10		1	5	3						9¹		7	11		1–0(1–0)5052	—
30. Southend*	30.1			2	4		6		8				1	5	3						9	7¹	11			1–1(1–1)6180	16
31. Grimsby	6.2			2	4		6		8		10¹		1	5	3						9		11			1–0(1–0)2907	13
32. Sunderland*	13.2			2	4		6		8¹		10		1	5	3						9	7¹	11			2–2(2–2)10,852	15
33. Chesterfield	20.2			2	4	6			8		10		1	5	3						9†	7	12	11		0–0(0–0)2864	15
34. Walsall*	27.2			2	4	6			8		10₁		1	5	3						9	7		11		1–0(1–0)6479	13
35. Brentford	1.3			2	4	6			12		10		1	3†	5			9¹			7	14		11		0–2(0–1)3505	—
36. Brighton*	5.3			2†	4	6			12	8²	10			3	5			9¹			7			11		3–0(3–0)5834	13
37. Port Vale	12.3				4		6	2	8¹		10¹		1		3						9	7		11		2–3(1–1)4647	15
38. Chester	19.3				4	6		2	8		10		1	3	5	11					7	9				0–1(0–1)3724	16
39. Bury*	26.3			3	4			2	8		10	11	1	6	5¹						7	9				1–0(1–0)6456	15
40. Mansfield*	2.4			3	4	12		2	8¹		10	11	1	6	5†						7	9				1–0(0–0)6254	14
41. Doncaster	4.4				4	3†	6	2	8²		10	11	1	5				14			7	9¹	12			2–3(1–0)2167	14
42. Bristol R*	8.4			3	4		6	2	8		10₁	11¹	1	5							7	9¹				3–1(2–1)5386	—
43. Gillingham	23.4				4	6			8		10	11	1	3	5	12	2				7	9†	3			0–4(0–1)2721	14
44. Fulham*	30.4			3	4		6	2	8¹		10¹		12	5				7				9†	11			2–1(1–0)4192	14
45. Aldershot	2.5			3	4		6	2	8		10¹	12		5				9			7†	14	11			0–0(0–0)3465	15
46. Notts Co*	7.5			3	4			2	8				1	5				9			7	10¹	11	6		1–2(0–0)5822	16
Apps(subs)/goals		19(0)/0	5(0)/0	36(0)/1	45(0)/1	15(2)/0	38(1)/0	22(5)/2	45(1)/12	40(0)/1	36(0)/14	21(4)/1	4(8)/0	27(0)/0	22(0)/0	34(0)/0	22(0)/2	9(1)/2	24(3)/5	1(2)/0	10(0)/0	34(0)/3	20(4)/4	21(1)/0	1(0)/0		

Final League Position: 16

DIVISION 1

QUEEN'S PARK RANGERS

South Africa Road, London W12 7PA.

Back row (left to right): Wayne Fereday, Peter Shreeve (Coach), Justin Channing, Ron Berry (Kit Manager), David Seaman, Bobby Campbell (Coach), John Byrne, Dave Butler (Physio), David Pezanti. *Middle row:* Gavin Peacock, David Kerslake, Dean Coney, Gary Waddock, Danny Maddix, Martin Allen, Leslie Ferdinand, Gavin Maguire, Mark Dennis, Warren Neill. *Front row:* Jim Smith (Manager), Ian Dawes, John O'Neill, Alan McDonald, Terry Fenwick, Gary Bannister, Paul Parker, Kevin Brock, Frank Sibley (Ass. Manager).

Stadium Capacity: 27,500. **Pitch Dimensions:** 112 × 72 yds. **Telephone:** 01-743 0262, **Clubcall:** 0898-121162. **Chairman:** David Bulstrode. **Vice-Chairman:** R. Noonan. **Directors:** B. P. D. Ellis, A. Ingham, A. Chandler, M. R. Turner.
Manager: Jim Smith. **Post-War Managers:** Dave Mangnall, Jack Taylor, Alec Stock, Tommy Docherty, Les Allen, Gordon Jago, Dave Sexton, Frank Sibley, Steve Burtenshaw, Tommy Docherty, Terry Venables, Alan Mullery MBE.
Assistant Manager: Peter Shreeve.
Secretary: R. J. Phillips. **Head of Marketing:** B. Rowe. **Sponsors:** KLM & The Netherlands Tourist Board.
Founded: 1885. **Turned Professional:** 1898. **Nickname:** Rangers or The R's. **Former Names:** St Jude's 1885-87.
Former Grounds: Welford's Fields 1885-88, London Scottish Ground, Brondesbury, Home Farm, Kensal Rise Green, Gun Club Wormwood Scrubs, Kilburn Cricket Ground 1888-89, Kensal Rise Athletic Ground 1889-1901, Latimer Road, Notting Hill 1901-04, Agricultrual Society, Park Royal 1904-07, Park Royal Ground 1907-17, Loftus Road 1917-31, White City 1931-33, Loftus Road 1933-62, White City 1962-63.
Record Attendance: 35,353 v Leeds United, Division 1, 27 April 1974.
Record Victory: 9-2 v Tranmere Rovers, Division 3, 3 December 1960.
Record Defeat: 1-8 v Mansfield Town, Division 3, 15 March 1965 and v Manchester United, Division 1, 19 March 1969.
Most League Points: (3 for a win) 85, Division 2, 1982-83. (2 for a win) 67, Division 3, 1966-67.
Most League Goals: 111, Division 3, 1961-62.
Highest League Scorer in a Season: George Goddard, 37, Division 3 (S), 1929-30.
Highest Total of League Goals: George Goddard, 172, 1926-34.
Most League Appearances: Tony Ingham, 519, 1950-63.
League History: 1920 Founder Members of Division 3, 1921 Division 3(S), 1948-52 Division 2, 1952-58 Division 3(S), 1958-67 Division 3, 1967-68 Division 2, 1968-69 Division 1, 1969-73 Divison 2, 1973-79 Division 1, 1979-83 Divison 2, 1983- Division 1.
Honours: Division 1 runners-up 1975-76. Division 2 Champions 1982-83, runners-up 1967-68, 1972-73. Divison 3 Champions 1966-67. Division 3(S) Champions 1947-48, runners-up 1946-47. FA Cup runners-up 1982. League Cup winners 1967, runners-up 1986.
Colours: Blue and white hooped shirts, white shorts, white socks with blue hoops on turnovers. **Second strip:** Red and black hooped shirts, black shorts, black socks with red hoops on turnovers.

QUEEN'S PARK RANGERS – LEAGUE RECORD 1987–88

Match no/Opp/Date		Seaman	Fereday	Dennis	Parker	McDonald	Fenwick	Allen	Coney	Bannister	Byrne	Brock	Peacock	Dawes	Neill	Maguire	Pizanti	O'Neill	Channing	Maddix	Falco	Roberts	Johns	Kerslake	Ferdinand	Fleming	Francis	Law	FT(HT)Att Lge pos
1. West Ham	15.8	1	2	3	4	5	6	7	8	9[1]	10	11[1]																	3–0(3–0)22,881 —
2. Derby*	19.8	1	2	3	4	5	6	7	8	9[1]	10	11																	1–1(1–1)11,651 —
3. Arsenal*	22.8	1	2	3	4	5[1]	6	7	8	9	10[1]†	11	12																2–0(1–0)18,981 1
4. Southampton	29.8	1	2		4	5	6	7	8	9	10	11[1]		3															1–0(0–0)15,532 1
5. Everton*	2.9	1	2		4	5	6	7[1]	8	9	10	11		3															1–0(1–0)15,380 —
6. Charlton	5.9	1	2		4	5	6	7	8[1]	9	10†	11	12	3															1–0(1–0)7726 1
7. Chelsea*	12.9	1	2		4	5	6	7	8	9[3]	10	11		3															3–1(0–0)22,583 1
8. Oxford	19.9	1	2		4	5	6	7	8	9	10†	11	12	3‡	14														0–2(0–2)9800 1
9. Luton*	26.9	1	2†		4	5	6[1]	7	8[1]	9	10	11		3	12														2–0(0–0)11,175 1
10. Wimbledon	3.10	1			4	5	6[1]	7	8	9[1]	10	11		3	2														2–1(0–0)8552 1
11. Liverpool	17.10	1			4	5	6	7	8†	9	10	11		3	2‡	14	12												0–4(0–1)43,735 2
12. Portsmouth*	24.10	1	12		4	5	6[1]	7	8	9	10[1]†	11‡		3	2	14													2–1(1–0)13,171 2
13. Norwich	31.10	1	9		4		6	7[1]	8		10†			3	2		12	5	11										1–1(0–0)14,522 2
14. Watford*	7.11	1	12		4	5	6	7	8		10	11		3	2†	14		9‡											0–0(0–0)12,101 3
15. Spurs	14.11	1	2	3	4	5	6	7	8[1]		10†	11	12						9										1–1(1–2)28,113 3
16. Newcastle*	21.11	1	2	3	4	5‡	6	7	8	9	10†	11					12												1–1(1–0)11,794 3
17. Sheff Wed	28.11	1	2‡		4		6	7	8	9[1]	12	11†		3				5	10	14									1–3(0–2)16,933 3
18. Man Utd*	5.12	1	2		4			6	7	12	9	10	11	3				5			8†								0–2(0–1)20,632 3
19. Nottm F	13.12	1	2	3	4	5	6	7	8†	9	10	11‡						14	12										0–4(0–1)18,130 —
20. Coventry*	18.12		2	3	4	5	6	7	12	9†	10	11							8[1]	1									1–2(1–0)7299 —
21. Chelsea	26.12				4	5	6	7		9		11		3	2		12		8			1	10[1]						1–1(0–0)18,020 6
22. Oxford*	28.12		12		4	5	6	7[1]		9†				3	2				8[2]			1	10‡						3–2(2–0)9125 6
23. Sthampton*	1.1		14[1]	3	4	5		7	12	9[1]		11			2		6		8[1]†			1	10‡						3–0(0–0)8631 5
24. Arsenal	2.1		10	3	4	5		7		9		11†			2		6			12	8	1							0–0(0–0)28,271 6
25. West Ham*	16.1		10†	3	4	5		7		9	12	11‡			2		6		8			1	14						0–1(0–0)14,909 7
26. Charlton*	6.2		10		4	5		7		9	12[1]	11‡			2		6	3†	8[1]			1	14						2–0(1–0)11,512 5
27. Everton	13.2		10		4	5		7		9	12	11		2‡	14	6	3†				1	8							0–2(0–1)24,724 6
28. Wimbledon*	27.2	1	10		4			7†		9[1]				2	3	6		5	8			11	12						1–0(0–0)9080 6
29. Liverpool*	5.3	1	10		4	5			12		9†			2	3	6	7‡	8			11	14							0–1(0–1)23,171 6
30. Nottm F*	16.3	1	10[1]		4	5		9[1]		8†			3	2	6	12	11		7										2–1(1–0)8316 —
31. Norwich*	19.3	1	10[1]	14	4	5	7‡	9[1]†		12			3	2	11[1]	6		8											3–0(1–0)9033 6
32. Portsmouth	26.3	1	10		4	5	7	9[1]					3	2	11†	6	12	8‡	14										1–0(0–0)13,041 4
33. Watford	1.4	1	10		4	5[1]	7	9					3	2	6	12	8†	11											1–0(0–0)16,083 —
34. Spurs*	4.4	1	10		4	5	7‡	12					3	2	6	14	9	8[2]	11†										2–0(0–0)14,738 5
35. Newcastle	9.4	1	10		4	5	7	12					3	2	6	14	9	8[1]†	11‡										1–1(1–1)18,403 5
36. Derby	13.4	1	10[1]		4	5	7[1]						3	2	6	12	9	8†	11										2–0(1–0)14,214 —
37. Luton	19.4	1	10		4	5	7	12					3	2	14	6	9	8[1]‡	11†										1–2(0–1)6735 —
38. Sheff Wed*	23.4	1	10		4	5	7	9[1]					3	2	6‡	12	8	11†	14										1–1(0–1)12,531 4
39. Man Utd	30.4	1	10‡		4	5[1]	7	9					3	2	12	14	6†	8	11										1–2(0–1)35,733 4
40. Coventry	7.5	1	10		4	5	7	9					3	2†	6‡	14	12	8	11										0–0(0–0)16,089 5
Apps/subs/goals		32(0)0	13(4)4	10(1)0	40(0)0	36(0)3	38(0)4	25(7)7	24(0)8	22(5)4	26(0)2	14(5)0	33(0)0	20(3)0	13(5)0	3(4)0	20(1)0	7(7)1	6(3)0	15(4)5	1(0)0	7(0)0	16(2)5	1(0)0	10(0)0	0(2)0	8(1)0	0(1)0	Final League Position: 5

Own goals: Stewart, match 1; Wharton, match 16

DIVISION 3
READING
Elm Park, Norfolk Road, Reading RG3 2EF.

Back row (left to right): Jerry Williams, Francis Joseph, Gary Westwood, Colin Bailie, Steve Francis, Mark White, Dean Horrix. *Middle row:* Stewart Henderson (Youth Development Officer/Coach), Paul Franklin, Martin Hicks (Captain), Paul Canoville, Colin Gordon, Gary Peters, John Haseldon (Physio/Coach). *Front row:* Michael Gilkes, Stuart Beavon, Linden Jones, Ian Branfoot (Manager), Neil Smillie, Les Taylor, Steve Richardson.

Stadium Capacity: 17,500.
Pitch Dimensions: 112 × 77 yds.
Telephone: 0734–507878.
Chairman: Roger Smee.
Life President: J. H. Brooks.
Managing Director: Mike Lewis.
Directors: M. J. Lewis, J. Campbell, C. M. Brooks.
Manager: Ian Branfoot.
Post-War Managers: Joe Edelston, Ted Drake, Jack Smith, Harry Johnston, Roy Bentley, Jack Mansell, Charlie Hurley, Maurice Evans (8).
Physio: John Hasleden.
Secretary: Mike Lewis.
Founded: 1871.
Turned Professional: 1895.
Nickname: The Royals or The Biscuitmen.   **Former Names:** None.
Former Grounds: Reading Recreation, Reading Cricket Ground 1871–1882, Coley Park 1882–1889, Caversham Cricket Ground 1889–1896.
Record Attendance: 33,042 v Brentford, FA Cup 5th Round, 19 February 1927.
Record Victory: 10–2 v Crystal Palace, Division 3(S), 4 September 1946.
Record Defeat: 0–18 v Preston NE, FA Cup 1st Round, 1893–94.
Most League Points: (3 for a win) 94, Division 3, 1985–86. (2 for a win) 65, Division 4, 1978–79.
Most League Goals: 112, Division 3(S), 1951–52.
Highest League Scorer in a Season: Ronnie Blackman, 39,Division 3(S),1951–52.
Highest Total of League Goals: Ronnie Blackman, 156, 1947–54.
Most League Appearances: Steve Death, 471, 1969–82.
League History: 1920 Founder members of Division 3, 1921–26 Division 2, 1931–58 Division 3(S), 1958–71 Division 3, 1971–76 Division 4, 1976–77 Division 3, 1977–79Division 4, 1979–83 Division 3, 1983–84 Division 4, 1984–86 Division 3, 1986–88 Division 2, 1988– Division 3.
Honours: Division 3 Champions 1985–86. Division 4 Champions 1978–79. Division 3(S) Champions 1925–26, runners-up 1931–32, 1934–35, 1948–49, 1951–52. Full Members' Cup winners 1988.
Colours: Sky blue shirts with white centre panel, sky blue shorts, navy socks. **Second strip:** All yellow.

READING – LEAGUE RECORD 1987–88

Match no/Opp/Date		Francis	Jones	Richardson	Beavon	Hicks	Peters	Williams	Taylor	Gernon	Horrix	Smillie	Joseph	White	Tait	Canoville	Gilkes	Bailie	Westwood	Franklin	Curle	Moran	Madden	Cowling	Whitehurst	Robson	FT(HT)Att Lge pos
1. Leeds	22.8	1	2	3	4	5	6	7‡	8	9	10†	11	12	14													0–0(0–0)19,286 17
2. Plymouth*	29.8	1	2	3	4‡	5	6			9†	10	11	12	14	7												0–1(0–1)6658 21
3. Shrewsbury	1.9	1	2	3	12	5	6		8	9	7†	10¹	11	4													1–0(1–0)3223 —
4. Oldham	5.9	1	2	3	4	5	6		8	9¹	7	10¹	12			11¹†											3–0(1–0)4798 11
5. Bournemouth	12.9	1	2	3		5	6		8	9	7	10		4	11												0–3(0–1)7597 15
6. Stoke*	16.9	1	2	3		5	6		8	9	7	10†		4	11	12											0–1(0–0)5349 —
7. C Palace	19.9	1	2	3		5	6		8¹	9‡	7	10†	14	4	11	12₁											2–3(1–0)6819 21
8. Swindon	26.9	1	2	3	4	5	6		8	9		12	7			10	11†										0–4(0–2)10,073 21
9. Middlesbro	29.9	1	2	3	12	5	6		8	9	7			4†	10	11											0–0(0–0)10,903 —
10. WBA*	3.10	1	2	3		5	6		8	9	7	12		4		10¹	11†										1–2(1–1)5543 22
11. Birmingham	10.10		2	3	4	5	6		8	9²		12	7		11	10†			1								2–2(0–0)6147 22
12. Huddersfield*	17.10		2	3		5	12¹	7	8	9¹†	4	11	10¹				6		1								3–2(2–0)4678 21
13. Barnsley	20.10		2	3		5			8	9²	7	12	4	11†	10		6		1								2–5(2–1)4396 —
14. Bradford*	24.10			3		5		7	8	9¹	10	11	4	2			6		1								1–1(0–1)5920 22
15. Aston Villa	31.10		2			5		7	8	9	10¹	11	4	3			6		1								1–2(0–0)13,413 22
16. Ipswich	7.11		2	12		5	14	7	8	9¹	10‡	11	4†	3			6		1								1–2(1–0)11,508 21
17. Man City*	14.11		2		4	5		7	8	9		11		3			6	10	1								0–2(0–0)10,052 22
18. Sheff Utd	21.11		2		4	5			8	9	12	11	7†	3			6	10¹	1								1–4(1–3)6977 22
19. Blackburn*	28.11		2		4	5		7	8	9†		12		3	11		6	10									0–0(0–0)4535 23
20. Millwall	1.12	1	2	11†	4	5		12	8					7	3	9	6	10									0–3(0–2)6762 —
21. Hull	5.12	1			4	5		7	8¹		11	9		3	2		6	10¹									2–2(1–0)5797 23
22. Leeds*	12.12	1			4	5		7	8‡	12	11†	9		3	2		6	10				14					0–1(0–0)6505 23
23. Stoke	19.12	1			4	5		7	12	11	9¹			3	2		6	10¹	8†								2–4(0–0)6968 23
24. Swindon*	26.12	1			4	5		7	9	12	11			3	2		6	10	8†								0–1(0–0)8939 23
25. C Palace	28.12	1	7¹	2	4¹	5			9					3			6	10	8¹	11							3–2(1–1)12,449 23
26. Plymouth	1.1	1	7¹		4	5		12	9					3¹	2		6	10¹	8	11†							3–1(0–0)13,298 22
27. Shrewsbury*	23.1	1			4¹	5		7	12	9		11		3	2		6	10	8†								1–0(0–0)5170 22
28. Leicester*	30.1	1			4	5		7¹	9†	12	11			3	2		6	10	8								1–2(1–1)6645 22
29. Oldham	6.2	1			4	5		7	8	10†	11	9		3	2		6	12¹									2–4(1–0)5388 22
30. Millwall*	13.2	1			4†	5¹		7	11	8¹				3	2		6	10	12	9							2–3(2–1)6050 22
31. Middlesbro*	20.2	1				5		7	12	11	8			3	2	14	6	10†	4‡	9							0–0(0–0)6446 22
32. WBA	27.2	1	7¹		4	5			11	8				3	2		6	10		9							1–0(0–0)8509 22
33. Huddersfield	5.3	1	7		4	5			11	8				3	2		6	10						9²			2–0(2–0)6094 22
34. Birmingham*	12.3	1	7		4	5		12	11	8				3	2†		6	10						9¹			1–1(1–1)6285 22
35. Aston Villa*	19.3	1		3	4	5		7‡	12	11		8	14	2			6	10†		9							0–2(0–0)10,033 22
36. Ipswich*	2.4	1	7†	3	4	5			11	8		10		2			6	12		9							1–0(0–0)9953 22
37. Man City	4.4	1	7†	3	4	5		12	8	11				2			6	10‡	14	9							0–2(0–0)15,172 22
38. Barnsley*	9.4	1	12	2	4	5			8					10‡	3		6	14		11¹				9¹	7†		2–1(1–0)4849 22
39. Bournemouth*	13.4	1		2	4	5		12	8‡					10	3		6	14		11				9	7†		0–0(0–0)10,037 —
40. Bradford	20.4	1	7†	2	4	5	12		8‡					3			6		10	11				9	14		0–3(0–3)13,608 —
41. Leicester	23.4	1		2	4	5	7†		8					3			6	10		11				9	12		0–1(0–1)9603 22
42. Sheff Utd*	30.4			2	4	5			8					3		1	6	10²		11				9	7		2–1(2–0)6680 22
43. Blackburn	2.5			2	4	5	12		8					3		1	6	10		11				9¹	7†		1–1(0–0)11,373 22
44. Hull*	7.5	1		2	4	5	12		8					3			6	10		11†				9	7		0–0(0–0)6710 22
Apps(subs)/goals		34(0) 0	27(1) 3	26(1) 0	22(2) 2	44(0) 1	12(4) 1	17(4) 1	26(4) 2	20(0) 8	8(5) 2	22(1) 0	5(6) 2	9(5) 0	35(0) 2	7(0) 1	36(3) 4	21(0) 0	10(0) 0	3(6) 0	30(0) 0	24(4) 7	7(2) 0	9(0) 1	15(0) 6	5(2) 0	

Final League Position: 22

DIVISION 4

ROCHDALE

Spotland, Willbuts Lane, Rochdale OL11 5DS

*Back row
(left to right):*
J. Seasman
D. Walling
K. Welch
J. Bramhall
D. Redfern
R. Coyle
J. Smart
Front row:
B. Stanton
L. Simmonds
P. Hampton
M. Gavin
S. Reid
S. Holden
G. Lomax

Stadium Capacity: 12,001.
Pitch Dimensions: 113 × 75 yds.
Telephone: 0706–44648.
Chairman: J. Marsh.
Vice-Chairman: C. D. Walkden.
Directors: W. A. C. Dronsfield, G. Morris, E. Lord, L. Hilton, G. R. Brierley.
Manager: Eddie Gray.
Post-War Managers: Ted Goodier, Jack Warner, Harry Catterick, Jack Marshall, Tony Collins, Bob Stokoe, Len Richley, Dick Conner, Walter Joyce, Brian Green, Mike Ferguson, Doug Collins, Bob Stokoe, Peter Madden, Jimmy Greenhoff, Vic Halom (16).
Secretary: Bill Kenyon JP.
Commercial Manager: Alex Stepney.
Founded: 1907.
Turned Professional: 1907.
Nickname: The Dale.
Former Names: None.
Former Grounds: None.
Record Attendance: 24,231 v Notts Co, FA Cup 2nd Round, 10 December 1949.
Record Victory: 8–1 v Chesterfield, Division 3(N), 18 December 1926.
Record Defeat: 0–9 v Tranmere Rovers, Division 3(N), 25 December 1931.
Most League Points: (3 for a win) 55, Division 4, 1985–86. (2 for a win) 65 Division 4, 1978–79.
Most League Goals: 105, Division 3 (N), 1926–27.
Highest League Scorer in a Season: Albert Whitehurst, 44,Division 3(N), 1926–27.
Highest Total of League Goals: Reg Jenkins, 119, 1964–73.
Most League Appearances: Graham Smith, 317, 1966–74.
League History: 1921 Elected to Division 3(N), 1958–59 Division 3, 1959–60 Division 4, 1969–74 Division 3, 1974–Division 4.
Honours: Division 3(N) runners-up 1923–24, 1926–27. League Cup runners-up 1962.
Colours: White shirts, navy shorts, white socks. **Second strip:** Blue shirts, white shorts, blue socks.

ROCHDALE – LEAGUE RECORD 1987–88

Match no/Opp/Date	Date	Welch	Lomax	Hampton	Reid	Bramhall	Seasman	Thompson	Simmonds	Parlane	Coyle	Gavin	Stanton	Smart	Walling	Holden	Hughes	Hunt	Parker	Mycock	Warren	Duggan	Moore	Harris	Mellish	Hancox	Moss	Crennand	FT(HT)Att	Lge pos
1. Hereford	15.8	1	2	3	4	5	6	7†	8	9	10	11	12																0-0(0-0)2652	—
2. Peterboro*	22.8	1	2	3	4	5	7		8	9^1	10	11		6															1-1(1-1)1808	16
3. Halifax	28.8	1	2	3	4	5	7		8^1_1	9	10	11		6															2-1(0-1)2275	—
4. Crewe*	31.8	1	2	3	4	5	7		8	9	10†	11^1	12^1	6															2-2(1-2)2346	—
5. Scunthorpe	5.9	1	2	3	4†	5	7	12		9	10	11‡	8	6	14														0-1(0-1)1969	15
6. Stockport*	12.9	1	2		4†	5	7	3		9	10	11	8	6			12												0-1(0-1)2700	19
7. Torquay	15.9	1	2	3	4	5	7	12	8	9‡	10	11		6†	14														0-5(0-3)1895	—
8. Exeter	19.9	1	2	3	4†		7		8		10	11	12	6	5	9^1													1-1(1-0)2628	22
9. Burnley*	26.9	1	2	3	4	5^1	7		8	9^1	10	11†	12	6															2-1(1-0)4426	19
10. Wolves	29.9	1		3	4†	5	2‡	11	8	9	10		7	6	14		12												0-2(0-1)5553	—
11. Carlisle*	3.10	1	2	3	4	5	7†		8	9	10	11	12	6^1															1-2(0-0)1940	22
12. Tranmere	9.10	1	2†	3	4	5^1	7		8	9	10		12	6					11										1-6(1-2)2303	—
13. Darlington*	17.10	1	2†	3		5			9	10	11	7	4	12			6			8^1									1-3(1-1)1417	22
14. Orient	20.10	1	2	3		5			8	9	10	11		6			12	7	4†										0-8(0-4)2995	—
15. Bolton*	24.10	1	2	3	4	5^1	11		8	9^1	10			6				7											2-2(1-0)4294	23
16. Cardiff	31.10	1	2	3	4	5			8	9	10			6				7	11										0-1(0-0)3046	—
17. Colchester*	3.11	1	2	3	4	5	12		8^1	9	10			6†				7	11										1-4(1-2)1399	—
18. Swansea*	7.11	1		3	4		2		8^1	9†	10	11^1		6					12	7	5								2-3(0-0)1243	24
19. Cambridge	21.11	1	6	3^1	4		2		8^1	9	10	11								7	5								2-1(2-1)2104	—
20. Scarboro*	28.11	1	6	3	4		2		8	9	10^1	11								7	5								1-1(0-0)1838	23
21. Wrexham	12.12	1	6		5^1	4			8^1			11^1	2	9	7				3	10									3-2(2-2)1409	23
22. Newport	19.12	1	6		5	4			8			11^2	2	9^1	7				3	10									3-0(2-0)1491	—
23. Burnley	26.12	1	6		5	4			8		12	11	2†	9	7				3	10									0-4(0-3)7013	23
24. Hartlepool*	28.12	1	6		4	5	2		8	7†	11	12		9					3	10									0-2(0-1)1851	23
25. Halifax*	1.1	1	6		4	5	2		8	7	11			9†	12				3	10									0-0(0-0)2050	23
26. Stockport	2.1	1	6		4	5			8	7	11^1	2		9					3	10									1-1(1-1)2441	23
27. Peterboro	9.1	1	6		4	5			8		11	3	2	7					10		9^1								1-1(1-1)3212	23
28. Exeter*	16.1	1	6		4†	5			8		11	3	2	12					10		9	7							0-0(0-0)1431	23
29. Torquay	26.1	1	6		4	5			8			3	2^1	11					10		9	7							1-0(1-1)1281	21
30. Crewe	29.1	1	6		4	5			8^1			3	2	11					10		9								1-0(1-0)2107	—
31. Scunthorpe*	6.2	1	6		4	5			8			3	2	11					10		9	7							2-1(0-0)1455	21
32. Hartlepool	13.2	1	6		4	5			8_1			3	2	7					10		9	11							1-0(0-0)2186	20
33. Hereford*	20.2	1	6		4	5			8^1			3	2	7^1					12	10	9^1	11†							3-1(2-0)1568	19
34. Carlisle	27.2	1	6						8			2	5	11‡	7				3	10	9			4	12				0-2(0-2)1983	19
35. Wolves*	1.3	1	6						8			2	5	11‡	7				3	10	9			4	12				0-1(0-1)2805	—
36. Darlington	5.3	1	6		5	7^1			8			3	2	11					10		9			4					1-2(1-1)1773	21
37. Tranmere*	12.3	1	6		5	7†			8			3	2	11					10					4			9		0-0(0-0)1621	21
38. Bolton	26.3	1	6		5	2			8			3†		7					12	10				11			9		0-0(0-0)4875	22
39. Cardiff*	29.3	1	6		5	7			8_1			3	2						10					11^1	4		9		2-2(1-0)1435	—
40. Swansea	2.4	1	6		5	7			8^2			3	2						10					11	4		9^1		3-0(1-0)5367	21
41. Cambridge*	4.4	1	6		5	7†			8			3	2^1	12^1					10					11	4		9		2-1(0-0)1596	20
42. Colchester	8.4	1	6		5	7†			8			3	2	12					10					11	4†		9		0-1(0-0)1864	—
43. Orient*	23.4	1	6		5	7†			8			3	2	11					10					11	4		9^1		1-3(1-1)1390	21
44. Scarboro	30.4	1	6		5	2			8			3	12						10					11^1	4†		9	7	1-2(1-2)1852	22
45. Wrexham*	2.5	1	6		5	2			8			3	4						10^1					11			9	7	1-2(1-0)1539	22
46. Newport	7.5	1	6		5†	2			8			3	12^1						10					11	4		9	7	1-0(0-0)2560	21
Apps(subs)/goals		46(0)/0	44(0)/0	19(0)/1	28(0)/0	40(0)/4	32(1)/0	3(2)/0	43(0)/12	19(0)/3	23(0)/5	25(0)/1	36(0)/3	8(4)/2	15(0)/2	2(0)/0	6(1)/1	9(2)/0	31(0)/1	3(0)/0	15(0)/2	12(0)/0	0(2)/1	15(0)/0	12(0)/0	0(2)/0	10(0)/2	3(0)/0		

Final League Position: 21

Own goals; Money, Russell, match 31.

DIVISION 4

ROTHERHAM UNITED

Millmoor Ground, Rotherham S60 1HR.

Back row (left to right): John Breckin (Youth Liaison Officer), Ray Warburton, Colin Douglas, John Dungworth, Paul Haycock, Kelham O'Hanlon, Andy Morris, Giles Newcombe, Nigel Johnson, John Green, Carl Airey, Andy Williams, Phil Chambers (Reserve and Youth Team Coach). *Middle row:* Mr N. Darnhill (Secretary), Winston Campbell, Martin Scott, Mr B. Peacock (Director), Mr K.F. Booth (Chairman), D. Cusack (Player/Manager), Mr R. Hull (Vice-Chairman), Mr C. A. Luckock (Director), Tony Grealish, Phil Crosby. *Front row:* Shaun Goodwin, Nigel Pepper, Gareth Evans, John Buckley, David Tomlinson, Mark Ash, Ian Dennis, Greg Burrows.

Stadium Capacity: 18,500.
Pitch Dimensions: 115 × 75 yds.
Telephone: 0709–562434.
Chairman: K. F. Booth.
Vice-Chairman: R. Hull.
Directors: B. J. Peacock, C. A. Luckock, D. J. Batty, Sir John Layden JP.
Manager: W. McEwan.
Post-War Managers: Reg Freeman, Andy Smailes, Tom Johnston, Danny Williams, Jack Mansell, Tommy Docherty, Jimmy McAnearney, Jimmy McGuigan, Ian Porterfield, Emlyn Hughes, George Kerr, Norman Hunter, Dave Cusack (13).
Secretary: N. Darnill.
Physio: I. Bailey.
Commercial Manager: D. Nicholls.
Sponsors: Parkgate Retail World.
Founded: 1884.
Turned Professional: 1905.
Nickname: The Merry Millers.
Former Names: Thornhill United 1884–1905, Rotherham County 1905–1925.
Amalgamated with Rotherham Town in 1925 to form Rotherham United.
Former Grounds: Red House Ground 1884–1907.
Record Attendance: 25,000 v Sheffield United, Division 2, 13 December 1952 and v Sheffield Wednesday, Division 2, 26 January 1952.
Record Victory: 8–0 v Oldham Athletic, Division 3(N), 26 May 1947.
Record Defeat: 1–11 v Bradford City, Division 3(N), 25 August 1928.
Most League Points: (3 for a win) 67, Division 3, 1981–82. (2 for a win) 71, Division 3(N) 1950–51.
Most League Goals: 114, Division 3(N), 1946–47.
Highest League Scorer in a Season: Wally Ardron, 38, Division 3 (N), 1946–47.
Highest Total of League Goals: Gladstone Guest, 130, 1946–56.
Most League Appearances: Danny Williams, 459, 1946–62.
League History: 1893 Elected to Division 2, 1896 not re-elected, 1919 Elected to Division 2, 1923–51 Division 3(N), 1951–68 Division 2, 1968–73 Division 3, 1973–75 Division 4, 1975–81 Division 3, 1981–83Division 2, 1983–88 Division 3, 1988– Division 4.
Honours: Division 3 Champions 1980–81. Division 3(N) Champions 1950–51, runners-up 1946–47, 1947–48, 1948–49. League Cup runners-up 1961.
Colours: Red shirts with white trim, white shorts and socks. **Second strip:** Yellow shirts, blue shorts, yellow socks.

ROTHERHAM UNITED – LEAGUE RECORD 1987–88

Match no/Opp/Date		O'Hanlon	Douglas	Scott	Campbell	Dungworth	Green	Tomlinson	Williams	Airey	Evans	Pugh	Haycock	Greatlidge	Pepper	Johnson	Crosby	Buckley	Cusack	Ash	Crichton	Wylde	Mendonca	Goodwin	FT(HT)Att Lge pos
1. Bristol R	15.8	1	2	3	4¹	5	6	7	8	9	10†	11	12												1-3(0-2)3399 —
2. Bury*	22.8	1	2	3		5	6	7	8	10	9	11		4											0-1(0-0)3017 24
3. Port Vale	29.8	1	2	3	11	5	6		8	10	9	7		4											0-0(0-0)2895 20
4. Chester*	31.8	1	2	3	11¹	5	6		8	10²	9	7†	12	4											5-2(1-0)2551 —
5. Brentford	5.9	1	2	3	11	5	6		8	10¹	9	7		4											1-1(0-0)3604 17
6. Walsall*	12.9	1	2	3	11	5	6		8	10	9	7†	12	4											0-1(0-0)3325 19
7. Brighton	16.9	1	2	3	11†	5	6		8	10	9		12	4	7										1-1(1-0)6945 —
8. Preston	19.9	1	2	3			6		8		9		11	4	7	5									0-0(0-0)5124 19
9. Mansfield*	26.9	1	2	3	12		6		8¹	10	9	7		4¹	11†	5	7								2-1(1-1)3839 17
10. Grimsby*	29.9	1	2	3	4		6	7	8	10	9	11			5										0-0(0-0)3375 —
11. Chesterfield	3.10	1	2†	3	11	12	6		8	10	9¹	7		4¹	5										2-3(2-1)2993 19
12. Nthampton*	11.10	1		3	11	2	6	12	8	10¹	9	7†		4¹	5										2-2(0-2)5244 —
13. Southend	16.10	1		3	11¹	2	6	7	8	10	14	12	9‡	4	5†										1-1(1-1)2217 —
14. York	20.10	1	2	3	11	5	6		8¹	10	9¹	7		4											2-1(1-0)1932 —
15. Bristol C**	24.10	1	2	3	11	5	6		8	10²	9¹	7	12	4†											4-1(3-1)3397 15
16. Wigan	31.10	1	2	3	11	5	6		8	10	9	7		4											0-3(0-1)3004 17
17. Notts Co*	3.11	1	2	3	11	5	6¹		8	10	9	7†	12	4‡		14									1-1(1-1)4157 —
18. Blackpool	7.11	1	2	3	11	4	6		8		9	7	10		5										0-3(0-1)3447 17
19. Fulham*	21.11	1	2			5	6		8	10	9	11†	12		4		3	7							0-2(0-1)3427 18
20. Aldershot	28.11	1	2		11¹		6		8¹	10₁	9			4		5	3	7							3-1(2-0)2549 17
21. Gillingham*	12.12	1	2		11	5	6¹	14	8	10	9†		12	4			3	7‡							1-2(0-2)2557 18
22. Sunderland	20.12	1	2		11	5	6	12	8	10	9			4	3†			7							0-3(0-2)20,168 —
23. Mansfield	26.12	1	2		11		5		8₁		9		10	4			3	7	6						1-0(1-0)4763 18
24. Doncaster*	28.12	1	2		11		5		8		9		10¹	4			3	7	6						1-0(0-0)5840 16
25. Port Vale*	1.1	1	2‡		11	14	5		8	12	9†		10¹	4			3	7	6						1-0(0-0)3913 14
26. Walsall	2.1	1			11	2	5		8	12¹	9		10¹†	4			3	7	6†	14					2-5(1-3)5051 15
27. Bury	9.1	1			11	2	5		8		9¹		10¹	4			3	7	6						2-2(0-2)2320 15
28. Preston*	16.1	1			11	2	5		8¹		9		10¹	4			3	7	6						2-2(1-2)4011 14
29. Chester	30.1	1			11	2	5		8	12	9†		10¹	4			3	7	6						0-1(0-0)2059 15
30. Doncaster	13.2	1	2					8	9		11	10²		4	5	3	7	6							2-2(1-1)2769 18
31. Brentford*	17.2	1	2					8	9		11¹	10¹		4	5	3	7	6							2-0(1-0)2572 —
32. Bristol R*	20.2	1	2		12	9		8			11†	10¹	4		5	3	7	6							1-0(0-0)2966 14
33. Chesterfield*	27.2	1	2		11	9		8₁			7	10	4		5	3		6							1-1(0-3)3440 17
34. Southend*	5.3	1	2		9†			8	12¹		11	10	4		5	3	7	6							1-1(0-0)2531 17
35. Grimsby	8.3	1	2					8	9		11†	10¹	4	12	5	3	7	6							1-2(0-1)3423 —
36. Nthampton	11.3	1		2		14	12		8			10¹	4	11	5	3	7†	6		1	9				0-0(0-0)5432 —
37. Brighton*	16.3	1		2				11			12	10¹	4		5	3	7†	6		1	9				1-0(0-2)2562 15
38. Wigan*	19.3	1		2				11				10	4	8	5	3	7	6		1	9¹				1-1(1-0)3288 15
39. Bristol C	26.3	1		2		11‡	6			12		10	4	8	5	3	7			1	9†	14			0-2(0-0)7517 18
40. Blackpool*	2.4	1		2			6			14	11	10†	4	8	5	3	7			1	9‡	12			0-1(0-0)3001 18
41. Fulham	4.4	1		2			6				11	10	4	8	5	3	7			1	9†	12¹			1-3(0-2)4402 18
42. York*	8.4	1		2		11				9		10	4	8	5	3	7†	6			12				0-1(0-0)2942 —
43. Notts Co	23.4	1	2			11	8†	5			12	10	4			3	7	6			9				0-4(0-0)7021 20
44. Aldershot*	30.4	1	2¹	11‡	8	6	5					7	10†			3	12	14		9	4				1-0(0-0)2818 20
45. Gillingham	2.5	1	2		11	8	6					7	10¹			5	3			9¹	4				2-0(1-0)3015 19
46. Sunderland*	7.5	1	2		11‡	8	6					7	10	4†		5	3	14		9	12				1-4(0-2)9374 21
Apps(sub)/goals		40(0) 0	40(0) 1	19(0) 0	31(2) 5	29(3) 0	36(1) 2	6(5) 0	36(0) 6	25(7) 11	28(1) 4	27(2) 1	27(8) 12	38(0) 3	14(1) 0	23(0) 0	27(2) 0	24(2) 0	18(0) 0	0(2) 0	6(0) 0	6(0) 1	4(4) 2	2(1) 0	

Final League Position: 21

Own goals: Humphries, match 15; Leman, match 46.

DIVISION 4 | # SCARBOROUGH

The Athletic Ground, Seamer Road, Scarborough YO12 4HF.

Back row (left to right): Alan Kamara, Tommy Graham, Ian Bennyworth, Mitch Cook, Steve Richards, Craig Short, Kevin Blackwell, Robert Preston, Neil Thompson, Doug Newton, Tony Outhart, Stewart Mell. *Front row:* Les McJannet, Steve Adams, Neil Warnock (Manager), Peter Gargett (Chairman), Paul Evans (Ass. Manager), Stewart Hamill, Gary Brook.

Stadium Capacity: 9950.
Pitch Dimensions: 110 × 79 yds.
Telephone: 0723-375094, **Club shop:** 0723-369211.
Chairman: G. Richmond.
Vice-Chairman: P. Gargett.
Directors: T. Farrant BA, A. Scott, M. Jones, A. J. Peers, D. S. Fordham.
Manager: Neil Warnock.
Post-War Managers: G. Hall, H. Taylor, F. Taylor, A. Bell, R. Halton, C. Robson, G. Higgins, A. Smailes, E. Brown, A. Frank, S. Myers, G. Shaw, C. Appleton, K. Houghton, C. Appleton, J. McAnearney, J. Cottam, H. Dunn (18).
Assistant Manager: P. Evans.
General Manager/Secretary: M. G. Dooley.
Commercial Manager: G. Butterfield.
Sponsors: Scarborough Building Society.
Founded: 1879.
Turned Professional: 1926.
Nickname: The Boro.
Former Names: None.
Former Grounds: Scarborough Cricket Ground 1879–87, Recreation Ground 1887–98.
Record Attendance: 11,130 v Luton Town, FA Cup 1938.
Record Victory: 16–1 v Leeds Amateurs, FA Amateur Cup, 9 November 1907.
Record Defeat: 1–16 v South Bank, Northern League, 15 November 1919.
Most League Points: 65, Division 4, 1987–88.
Most League Goals: 56, Division 4, 1987–88.
Highest League Scorer in a Season: Stewart Mell, 8, Division 4 1987–88.
Highest Total of League Goals: Stewart Mell, 8, 1987–88.
Most League Appearances: Tommy Graham, 44, 1987–88.
League History: 1987 Promoted to Division 4.
Honours: GM Vauxhall Conference Champions 1986–87.
Colours: All red. **Second strip:** White shirts and socks, black shorts.

SCARBOROUGH – LEAGUE RECORD 1987–88

Match no/Opp/Date		Blackwell	McJannet	Thompson	Bennyworth	Richards	Kendall	Hamill	Moss	McHale	Mell	Graham	Harrison	Cook	Walker	Adams	Bowman	Russell	Short	Kamara	McDonagh	Lowe S	Dodd	Neenan	Lowe K	Beasley	Downes	Oathart	Ironside	Brook	Preston	FT(HT)Att Lge pos
1. Wolves*	15.8	1	2	3	4	5	6	7	8	9¹	10¹	10	11																			2–2(1–2)7314 —
2. Orient	22.8	1	2	3¹	4	5	6	7	8	9†	10‡	11	12	14																		1–3(1–0)3540 22
3. Bolton*	29.8	1	2	3	4†	5¹‡	6	7¹	8	9	10¹	11		14	12																	4–0(2–0)4462 8
4. Colchester	31.8	1	2	3₁	4	5	6	7	8¹	9†	10¹	11		12																		3–1(0–1)1525 —
5. Tranmere*	5.9	1	2	3₁	4	5	6	7	8	9	10	11¹																				2–0(0–0)2882 2
6. Darlington	12.9	1	2	3	4	5	6	7†	8	9‡	10	11		14	12¹																	1–2(0–1)3187 6
7. Newport*	16.9	1	2	3₁1	4	5	6	7	8	9†		11	12					10¹														3–1(1–2)2345 —
8. Swansea*	19.9	1	2	3	4	5	6	7	8¹	9		11¹					12	10†														2–0(0–0)3033 1
9. Carlisle	26.9	1	2	3	4	5	6	7‡	8	9	10	11†	12	14																		0–4(0–1)2693 5
10. Torquay	29.9	1		3	4	5			8	9	12	6	2	10		7	11¹†															1–0(0–0)3255 —
11. Burnley*	3.10	1	2	3	4			7¹	8	9	11†	6		10	12																	1–0(1–0)4782 1
12. Exeter*	10.10	1	2	3	4¹	5			8¹	9	11¹	6		10		7																3–1(1–1)2472 1
13. Crewe	17.10	1	2†	3	4	5		7	8	9	12	6		10			11															0–1(0–1)2723 1
14. Hereford	21.10	1	2	3	4	5			8	9†	10	6	11					7¹	12													1–1(0–0)2359 —
15. Hartlepool*	24.10	1	2	3	4	5	12	11		9	10†	6						7¹	8													1–1(0–0)3909 1
16. Wrexham	31.10	1	2	3	4	5	11	12	8†	9		6						10	7													0–1(0–1)1860 4
17. Cardiff*	4.11	1	2	3†	4	5	6	11		9	10¹‡	8	12		14			7														1–1(1–1)2599 —
18. Scunthorpe	7.11	1†	2	3	4	5	12			9¹	10	8	11		7			6														1–0(0–0)4506 4
19. Halifax*	21.11			3	4	5	6	10		9		8						7			2	1	11¹									1–1(1–0)2892 6
20. Rochdale	28.11		2	3	4	5				9		8						10	7		6	1	11¹									1–1(0–0)1838 6
21. Peterboro*	12.12		2	3	4	5		12	14	9		8						10	7†		6	1	11¹‡									1–1(0–2)2525 6
22. Stockport	19.12			3	4	5¹		12	8	9	10†	11	2					7			6	1										1–1(1–1)1779 6
23. Carlisle*	26.12			3	4	5		12	8¹‡	9¹	10‡	11	2					7			6	1	14									3–1(1–0)3261 5
24. Cambridge	28.12		2‡	3	4	5		12	8	9†	10	11						7			6	1										0–1(0–1)3243 7
25. Bolton	1.1		2		4	5	12	7		9†	10‡	11	3₁		14			6			1	8										1–3(0–0)6295 8
26. Darlington*	2.1		2†		4	5	12		8	9	14	11	3					7			6	1	10‡									0–1(0–1)3371 9
27. Swansea	16.1				4		12	8‡		10	9	11	7†	14	5	3	1		2	6												0–3(0–2)4366 12
28. Colchester*	30.1				5	6		8	12	11¹	9‡		7	4	3	2	1		10†													3–1(0–2)2155 10
29. Tranmere	6.2				5	6†		8		11	9		7	4	3	12	2	1	10													1–0(0–4)4174 12
30. Cambridge*	13.2			3		5	6	7	8	12		11	9		4	2	1		10†													0–0(0–0)1879 13
31. Wolves	19.2			3	2	5	6			10	11	9			4	7		8		1												0–0(0–0)11,391 —
32. Orient*	24.2			3	2	5	6			10²	11¹	9			4	7		8		1												3–1(1–0)2116 —
33. Burnley	27.2			3¹	2	5	6			10	11	9			4	7		8		1												1–0(0–0)7845 10
34. Torquay*	2.3			3	2†	5	6¹	12		10‡	11	9		14	4	7		8			1											1–2(0–1)2182 —
35. Crewe*	5.3			3	2	5¹	6			10†	11	9		12¹	4	7		8			1											2–0(1–0)2260 9
36. Exeter	12.3			3	6	5				10‡	11	9		14	4	2		8†				1	7	12								0–1(0–1)1738 11
37. Wrexham*	19.3			3	6	5	8	12		10		9			7	4	2			1	11†											0–2(0–2)2090 11
38. Hartlepool	26.3		12	3	4†	5					11	8		10	7‡	6	2				14	1	9									0–1(0–1)2443 13
39. Scunthorpe*	2.4		2	3	6		7			10	11	8			5	4					1	9										0–0(0–0)4677 15
40. Halifax	4.4		2	3	6		7†			11¹	8¹	12	10	5	4					1	9‡	14										2–2(0–1)1747 14
41. Hereford*	9.4		2	3				11²			7	10	6	4						1	9†	14										2–1(2–0)2154 14
42. Newport	12.4			3		5¹				11	12¹	7†		6¹						10¹	1	9	14									4–0(1–0)1025 —
43. Cardiff	23.4		2	3	12	5				10	11	8		14	6	4				7‡	1	9†										0–2(0–1)5751 13
44. Rochdale*	30.4	1	2	3		5¹	12			10†	11			7	6¹	4			9													2–1(2–1)1852 13
45. Peterboro	2.5	1	12	3		5				10	11	2		7†	6	4			9													0–0(0–0)3244 12
46. Stockport*	7.5	1	2	3		5		14¹		11		8		7	6†	4			9			10‡										1–0(0–2)2236 12

Apps(subs)/goals: 21(0) 1, 29(2) 0, 41(0) 6, 38(1) 1, 42(0) 5, 19(9) 3, 22(1) 4, 25(0) 3, 29(4) 8, 44(0) 7, 3(1) 0, 28(10) 5, 9(1) 0, 17(1) 2, 40(2) 2, 12(1) 2, 20(1) 2, 29(0) 0, 9(0) 0, 14(2) 3, 30(0) 0, 6(0) 0, 4(0) 0, 4(0) 0, 2(0) 0, 3(2) 1, 6(0) 0, 5(0) 0, 3(0) 0, 1(3) 0

Final League Position: 12

Own goal: Sutton, match 3. Also played: Newton, match 41(8), 42(8‡), 44(8), 45(8), 46(12).

DIVISION 4

SCUNTHORPE UNITED

Glanford Park, Doncaster Road, Scunthorpe, South Humberside.

Back row (left to right): Bill Green (Ass. Manager), Alan Birch, Ian Richardson, Dave Harle, Billy Russell, Andy Flounders, Dave McLean, Julian Broddle, Paul Longden, Tony Daws, Phil McLoughlin (Physio). *Middle row:* Jason Talbot, Darren Mountain, Richard Huxford, Andy Stevenson, Paul Nicol, Mark Atkins, Nick Dunhill, Jimmy Shaw, Desmond Young. *Front row:* Richard Money, Darren Heyes, Steve Johnson, Tony Brown, Steve Lister, Ron Green, Dave Hill.

Stadium Capacity: 11,266.
Pitch Dimensions: 111 × 73 yds.
Telephone: 0724–848077.
Chairman: G. Pearson.
President: Sir Reginald Sheffield, Bt.
Vice-Chairman: G. J. Alston.
Deputy Chairman: T. E. Belton.
Directors: R. Garton, J. A. C. Godfrey, D. M. Fletton.
Manager: M. Buxton.
Post-War Managers: Leslie Jones, Bill Corkhill, Ron Suart, Tony McShane, Bill Lambton, Frank Soo, Dick Duckworth, Freddie Goodwin, Ron Ashman, Ron Bradley, Dickie Rooks, Ron Ashman, John Duncan, Allan Clarke, Frank Barlow (15).
Assistant Manager: W. Green.
Physio: P. McLoughlin.
Secretary: A. D. Rowing.
Commercial Manager: A. D. Rowing.
Sponsors: Brikenden.
Founded: 1904.
Turned Professional: 1912.
Nickname: The Iron.
Former Names: Merged with Lindsey United in 1910 to become Scunthorpe and Lindsey United. Scunthorpe United from 1958.
Former Grounds: The Old Showground, Scunthorpe 1904–88.
Record Attendance: 23,935 v Portsmouth, FA Cup 4th Round, 30 January 1954 (at The Old Showground).
Record Victory: 9–0 v Boston United, FA Cup 1st Round, 21 November 1953.
Record Defeat: 0–8 v Carlisle United, Division 3(N), 25 December 1952.
Most League Points: (3 for a win) 83, Division 4, 1982–83. (2 for a win) 66, Division 3(N), 1957–58.
Most League Goals: 88, Division 3(N), 1957–58.
Highest League Scorer in a Season: Barrie Thomas, 31, Division 2, 1961–62.
Highest Total of League Goals: Steve Cammack, 110, 1979–81, 1981–86.
Most League Appearances: Jack Brownsword, 600, 1950–65.
League History: 1950 Elected to Division 3(N), 1958–64 Division 2, 1964–68 Division 3, 1968–72 Division 4, 1972–73 Division 3, 1973–83 Division 4, 1983–84 Division 3, 1984– Division 4.
Honours: Division 3(N) Champions 1957–58.
Colours: All Claret and blue. **Second strip:** All white with claret and blue trim.

SCUNTHORPE UNITED – LEAGUE RECORD 1987–88

Match no/Opp/Date		Green	Russell	Longden	McLean	Brown	Nicol	Dixon	Harle	Daws	Flounders	Hill	Atkins	Johnson	Brodie	Stevenson	Lister	Heys	Money	Birch	Taylor K	Reeves	Cowling	Taylor M	Shearer	Richardson	FT(HT)Att Lge pos
1. Tranmere*	15.8	1	2¹	3	4	5	6	7	8	9	10²	11															3–0(0–0)2277 —
2. Carlisle	22.8	1	2	3	4		6	7	8		10†	11	5	9¹	12												1–3(0–0)2074 9
3. Colchester*	29.8	1	2	3	4	5	6	7†	8		10¹	11		9¹	12												2–2(1–0)2003 10
4. Wolves	31.8	1	2	3	4†	5	6	7	8		10¹			9	11	12											1–4(1–2)6672 —
5. Rochdale*	5.9	1	2	3		5		7¹	8		10	11	6	9	4												1–0(1–0)1969 13
6. Cambridge	12.9	1	2	3		5		7	8¹		10²		6	9	11	4											3–3(2–1)1830 14
7. Bolton*	15.9		2₁	3		5		7	8		10		6	9	11	4	1										1–1(0–1)2501 —
8. Newport*	19.9		2	3		5		7	8		10²		6†	9	11	4	1										3–1(2–1)2004 10
9. Darlington	26.9	1	2¹	3			5	7¹	8		10¹		6	9		4¹	11										4–1(1–1)1638 6
10. Stockport*	29.9	1	2	3			5†	7	8		10		6	9		4		11	12								0–0(0–0)2181 —
11. Peterboro	3.10	1	2	3†		5		7¹	8		10		6	9		4		11	12								1–0(1–3)3954 8
12. Halifax*	10.10	1	2					7	8		10	11	3	9¹		5		6		4							1–0(0–0)2105 5
13. Hereford	17.10	1	2	11				7	8		10		3			5		6		4	9³						3–2(2–0)2092 3
14. Burnley	20.10	1	2†	11				7	8		10¹		3		12	5				4	9						1–1(0–0)6323 —
15. Cardiff*	24.10	1	2	11				7	8		10		3		12	5		6†		4¹	9						2–1(0–2)2872 2
16. Hartlepool	31.10	1	2	11			6	7	8		10		3†	12		5				4	9						0–1(0–1)2763 5
17. Wrexham*	3.11	1	2	11		5	7	8		10²		3				6		4	9¹								3–1(1–1)2348 —
18. Scarboro*	7.11	1	2	3				7‡	8		10		14	12		5		6		4	9†	11					0–1(0–0)4506 8
19. Crewe	21.11	1	2	3				7	8		10¹		11¹	9		5		6		4							2–2(1–0)2045 8
20. Swansea*	28.11	1	2	3†				7	8	12	10¹		11	9		5		6		4							1–2(0–0)2309 8
21. Exeter	12.12	1	2	3				7	8	12	10		11†	9¹	14	5	1	6‡		4							1–0(0–1)1831 7
22. Torquay*	18.12		7¹	3‡					12	8	11	10	2†	9	14	5		6		4			1				2–3(1–3)2261 —
23. Darlington*	26.12		2	3		6		7	8	11	10¹		9			5				4			1				1–0(1–0)3140 8
24. Orient	28.12		2	3			9	7	8¹	11	10					5		6		4			1				1–1(1–1)5542 9
25. Colchester	1.1		2	3			9	7	8	11²	10					5¹		6		4			1				3–0(0–0)2287 7
26. Cambridge*	2.1		2	3	12	6†	7	8	9¹	10	11¹					5				4¹			1				3–2(3–2)3252 5
27. Newport	16.1			3		6		7		9†	10	11		12	8	5		2		4¹			1				1–0(1–0)1760 6
28. Wolves*	30.1	1	2	3		6		7	8		10	11		12		9		5		4			1				0–1(0–5)5476 8
29. Rochdale	6.2	9	3			6		7†	8		10¹	11		12		5		2		4			1				1–2(0–0)1455 11
30. Orient*	13.2	1	2	3		6			8²		10	11†		12		5		7		4				9¹			3–2(0–1)2951 7
31. Tranmere	20.2	1	2	3		6			8		10²	11		12		5¹		7		4				9†			3–1(1–1)2803 7
32. Peterboro*	27.2	1	2	3		6			8		10³	11		12		5		7		4				9¹			5–0(1–0)3378 4
33. Stockport	1.3	1	2	3		6	14	8		10	11†		12			5		7		4				9¹‡			1–0(1–0)1834 —
34. Hereford*	5.3	1	2	3		6	12	8		10	11¹					5¹†		7		4¹				9			3–0(1–0)3413 5
35. Halifax	12.3	1		3		12	6	8₁		10	11†		9			5¹		2		4				9			2–2(0–2)1807 4
36. Hartlepool*	19.3	1		3		6	7‡	8		10¹	11¹		12			5		2		4				9†			3–0(3–0)3783 3
37. Cardiff	26.3	1		3		14	6	7	8‡	10†	11	2	12			5		2		4				9¹			1–0(0–0)4527 2
38. Scarboro	2.4	1		3		6	7	8		10	11					5		2		4				9			0–0(0–0)4677 3
39. Crewe*	4.4	1		3		6	7	8		10¹†	11		12			5		2		4¹				9			2–1(0–1)4091 3
40. Wrexham	9.4	1		3	14	6	7	8			11‡		10		12	5		2†		4				9¹			1–2(1–0)2589 3
41. Carlisle*	12.4	1		3		6	7	8		10	11					5		2		4				9¹			1–0(0–0)3514 —
42. Bolton	19.4	1		3		6	7	8		10	11	3				5		2		4				9			0–0(0–0)6669 —
43. Burnley*	23.4	1		3†	5	6	7	8¹		10	11	2	12							4				9			1–1(0–0)5347 3
44. Swansea	30.4	1	7‡	3	14	6	12	8		10	11					5¹		2†		4				9			1–1(0–1)3482 3
45. Exeter*	2.5	1		3	7	6		8		10	11		12			5†		2		4				9¹			1–0(0–6)6736 5
46. Torquay	7.5	1		3		6		8†	9	10¹	11		12		14	5		2‡		4					7¹		2–1(1–0)4989 4

Apps(subs)/goals: 35(0) 0 · 39(0) 4 · 44(0) 0 · 17(5) 0 · 25(0) 0 · 37(4) 4 · 45(0) 23 · 8(2) 3 · 45(0) 24 · 26(0) 3 · 21(1) 2 · 19(13) 4 · 5(2) 0 · 1(7) 0 · 39(0) 6 · 3(0) 0 · 32(0) 0 · 0(2) 0 · 35(0) 5 · 6(0) 0 · 1(0) 0 · 8(0) 0 · 15(1) 7 · 1(0) 0 · 1(0) 1

Final League Position: 4

Own goals: Ford, match 15; Impey, match 22, Gunn, match 32.

DIVISION 3

SHEFFIELD UNITED

Bramall Lane Ground, Sheffield S2 4SU.

Back row (left to right): Richard Cadette, Chris Wilder, Clive Mendonca, Andy Leaning, Phil Henson (Coach), Paul Heald, Tony Philliskirk, Mark Dempsey, Peter Beagrie. *Middle row:* Ian Bailey (Physio), Chris France, Simon Copeland, Martin Pike, Andy Barnsley, Brian Smith, Simon Grayson, Chris Marsden, Chris Downes, Danny Bergara (Coach). *Front row:* Colin Morris, Mark Todd, Paul Stancliffe, Dave Bassett (Team Manager), Martin Kuhl, David Frain, Peter Duffield.

Stadium Capacity: 44,010 (13,297 seats).
Pitch Dimensions: 117 × 75 yds.
Telephone: 0742–738955.
Chairman: R. J. Brearley.
Managing Director: Derek Dooley.
Directors: A. H. Laver, M. Wragg, R. Wragg M INST BM, D. Dooley.
Manager: Dave Bassett.
Post-War Managers: Ted Davison, Reg Freeman, Joe Mercer, John Harris, Arthur Rowley, John Harris, Ken Furphy, Jimmy Sirrel, Harry Haslam, Martin Peters, Ian Porterfield, Billy McEwan (12).
Secretary: G. E. Smith.
Commercial Manager: Andy Daykin.
Sponsors: Arnold Laver & Co. Ltd.
Founded: 1889.
Turned Professional: 1889.
Nickname: The Blades.
Former Names: None.
Former Grounds: None.
Record Attendance: 68,287 v Leeds United, FA Cup 5th Round, 15 February 1936.
Record Victory: 10–0 v Port Vale, Division 2, 10 December 1892 and v Burnley, Division 1, 19 January 1929.
Record Defeat: 0–13 v Bolton Wanderers, FA Cup 2nd Round, 1 February 1890.
Most League Points: (3 for a win) 96, Division 4, 1981–82. (2 for a win) 60, Division 2, 1952–53.
Most League Goals: 102, Division 1, 1925–26.
Highest League Scorer in a Season: Jimmy Dunne, 41, Division 1, 1930–31.
Highest Total of League Goals: Harry Johnson, 205, 1919–30.
Most League Appearances: Joe Shaw, 629, 1948–66.
League History: 1892 Elected to Division 2, 1893–1934 Division 1, 1934–39 Division 2, 1946–49 Division 1, 1949–53 Division 2, 1953–56 Division 1, 1956–61Division 2, 1961–68 Division 1, 1968–71 Division 2, 1971–76 Division 1, 1976–79 Division 2, 1979–81 Division 3, 1981–82Division 4, 1982–84 Division 3, 1984–88 Division 2, 1988– Division 3.
Honours: Division 1 Champions 1897–98, runners-up 1896–97, 1899–1900. Division 2 Champions 1952–53, runners-up 1892–93, 1938–39, 1960–61, 1970–71. Division 4 Champions 1981–82. FA Cup winners 1899, 1902, 1915, 1925, runners-up 1901, 1936.
Colours: Red and white striped shirts, black shorts, red socks. **Second strip:** All yellow with red trim.

SHEFFIELD UNITED – LEAGUE RECORD 1987–88

Match no/Opp/Date	Leaning	Wilder	Pike	Kuhl	Stancliffe	Barnsley	Frain	Norris	Cadette	Dempsey	Beagrie	Philliskirk	Eckhardt	Withe	Marsden	Mendonca	Hansbury	Duffield	Smith	Seagers	Todd	Downes	Hetherson	Agana	Powell	Webster	Williams	Benstead	Carr	Wood	FT(HT)Att Lge pos
1. Bournemouth 15.8	1	2	3	4	5	6	7†	8	9	10	11	12																			0–1(0–0)9757 —
2. Swindon 22.8	1		3	4	5	2		7	9	10	11		6	8																	0–2(0–2)8637 23
3. Blackburn* 29.8	1		3	4	5	2	12		9¹	10¹	11†		6	8	7¹																3–1(2–0)8540 16
4. Plymouth 31.8	1	14	3	4	5	2			9	10	11	12	6	8†	7‡																0–1(0–1)14,504 —
5. Stoke* 5.9	1	14	3	4	5	2‡			9	10	11	12	6	8	7†																0–0(0–0)10,086 19
6. Oldham 12.9	1	2	3	4	5¹			9	10¹	11		6	8	7																	2–3(2–2)5730 21
7. C Palace* 15.9	1	2	3	4	5		12		9	10	11	8¹	6		7†																1–1(0–0)7767 —
8. Millwall 19.9	1	2	3	4	5		12		9¹	10	11	8	6		7†																1–2(0–1)8048 22
9. Aston Villa 26.9	1	2	3	4	5		11	7₁	9	10	12	8†	6																		1–1(0–1)14,761 22
10. Barnsley 29.9	1	2	3	4	5		11	7₁	9†	10	8	12¹	6																		2–1(0–1)10,203 —
11. Hull* 3.10	1	2	3	4	5	12	11¹	7		10	9	8¹‡	6			14¹															2–1(1–1)10,446 19
12. Man City 10.10	1	2	3	4	5	6	11¹	7₁		10	9	8¹																			3–2(1–2)18,377 12
13. Leicester* 17.10		2	3	4	5	6	11½	7		10	9	8²						1	12												2–1(2–0)10,593 11
14. Birmingham* 20.10		2†	3	4	5	6	11	7		10	9	8				12		1													0–2(0–1)9287 —
15. Ipswich* 24.10		2	3	4	5	6†	11	7		10	9	8				12		1													0–1(0–1)11,949 16
16. Leeds* 31.10		2	3	4¹	5	6		7		10	9	8¹		10	11†	1	12														2–2(1–0)12,095 11
17. WBA 4.11		2	3	4	5	6	14	7		9	8	12		10	11‡	1†															0–4(0–2)8072 —
18. Middlesbro* 7.11	1	2	3	4	5	6	11†	7		9	8			10	12																0–2(0–0)11,278 19
19. Bradford 14.11	1		3	4	5	2	6†	7		10	9	8		11		12															0–2(0–0)13,694 19
20. Shrewsbury 17.11	1		14	4		2		7‡		10	11†	12	5		6	9		8	3												0–2(0–1)2555 —
21. Reading* 21.11			3	4¹	5	2			7	11		8²	10	9¹			6	1													4–1(3–1)6977 16
22. Huddersfield* 5.12			3	4	5	2		7		10¹			8	11		9¹	6	1													2–2(1–1)9269 17
23. C Palace 13.12			3	4¹	5	2		7		10	11			9		8	6	1													1–2(1–0)8174 —
24. Swindon* 20.12			2	3	4	5		7	9¹	10	11	8					6	1													1–0(0–0)7248 —
25. Aston Villa* 26.12			2	3	4	5		7	9	10¹	11					8	6	1													1–1(0–0)15,809 16
26. Millwall 28.12			2	3	4	5		14	7	9†	10	11			12¹		8‡	6	1												1–3(0–3)7255 17
27. Blackburn 1.1	1		2†	3	4	5		7		9‡	10	11			8¹		14	6		12											1–4(0–3)10,593 18
28. Oldham* 2.1	1	14	3	4†	5		11	7		10	12	8†			9			6		12											0–5(0–3)9574 18
29. Bournemouth 16.1			3		5¹	2			9	10	11	8¹					7	6	1	4											2–1(1–0)6466 18
30. Stoke 6.2			3		5	2	10	12	9†		11	8‡					7	6	1	4	14										0–0(0–0)9344 18
31. Shrewsbury* 13.2			3		5	2		7		10	11	8		14	9†		6	1	4‡	12											0–1(0–1)8227 20
32. Barnsley* 20.2			3		5	2			9	10	11						6	1	4		7	8¹									1–0(0–1)11,381 19
33. Hull 27.2	1		3		5	2		12	9¹†	10	11¹						6		4		7	8									2–1(0–1)8832 18
34. Leicester 5.3	1		3		5	2		12	9	10‡	11						6		4	14	7†	8									0–1(0–0)12,256 19
35. Man City* 8.3	1	2	3		5			12		10	11	8					6		4		7	9¹†									1–2(1–0)13,906 —
36. Leeds 19.3	1	2	3					12		11							6		4‡	10	7	9†	14	5	8						0–5(0–1)22,376 21
37. Ipswich* 26.3			3			2			9²		11						6		4	10¹	7			5¹	8	1					4–1(2–1)8753 20
38. Middlesbro 2.4			3		5†	2			9	12	11						10		4	7‡	14		6	8	1						0–6(0–3)17,340 21
39. Bradford* 4.4			3		5	2			9		4₁						6			10	7	11		8	1						1–2(0–1)13,888 21
40. Birmingham 9.4		12			5	2†			9	4‡	11	14					6			10	7	8	3								0–1(0–1)7046 21
41. Plymouth* 19.4				5	4		12¹	9		10	7†						6				11	8	3			1	2				1–0(0–0)9052 —
42. WBA* 23.4				5	4	7	9‡		10								6†				11	8	2		12	1	3	14			0–0(0–0)12,091 20
43. Reading 30.4				5¹	6	7	12		11			14					10				8†	2	4	9‡	1	3					1–2(0–2)6680 21
44. Huddersfield 7.5		2		5	6		8¹		11	12¹		9†					10				7	3	4		1						2–0(0–0)8644 21

Apps(sub)/goals: 21(0)0 · 21(4)0 · 38(1)0 · 28(0)3 · 41(0)3 · 31(1)0 · 13(5)1 · 25(5)4 · 26(2)7 · 22(1)4 · 41(2)2 · 19(7)9 · 11(1)0 · 18(3)1 · 8(0)4 · 5(0)0 · 7(4)1 · 23(0)0 · 11(1)0 · 11(0)0 · 6(3)1 · 11(0)0 · 11(0)2 · 5(0)10 · 30(1)0 · 5(0)10 · 5(0)10 · 8(0)0 · 3(0)0 · 0(1)0

DIVISION 1

SHEFFIELD WEDNESDAY

Hillsborough, Sheffield S6 1SW.

Back row (left to right): Lawrie Madden, Colin West, Nigel Pearson, Martin Hodge, Kevin Pressman, Lee Chapman, Siggi Jonsson, Mel Sterland. *Centre row:* Peter Eustace, Brian Marwood, Gary Megson, Tony Galvin, Greg Fee, Nigel Worthington, Carl Bradshaw, Mark Proctor, Alan Smith. *Front row:* Steve McCall, David Hirst, Mark Chamberlain, Howard Wilkinson (Manager), Des Hazel, Gary Owen, Wayne Jacobs.

Stadium Capacity: 54,181.
Pitch Dimensions: 115 × 75 yds.
Telephone: 0742–343122, Ticket office: 0742–337233, **Clubcall:** 0898–121186, **Commercial dept:** 0742–337235.
Chairman: H. G. McGee.
Vice-Chairman: M. Sheppard JP, FCA.
Directors: S. L. Speight OBE, C. Woodward, K. T. Addy, E. Barron, G. K. Hulley.
Manager: Howard Wilkinson.
Post-War Managers: Eric Taylor, Harry Catterick, Vic Buckingham, Alan Brown, Jack Marshall, Danny Williams, Derek Dooley, Steve Burtenshaw, Len Ashurst, Jack Charlton OBE (10).
Assistant Manager: Peter Eustace.
Physio: A. Smith.
Secretary: G. H. Mackrell FCCA.
Commercial Manager: R. Gorrill.
Founded: 1867.
Turned Professional: 1887.
Nickname: The Owls.
Former Names: The Wednesday.
Former Grounds: Highfield 1867–69, Myrtle Road 1869–1877, Sheaf House 1877, Olive Grove 1887–1889, Owlerton (known as Hillsborough since 1912) 1889– . Some games were played at Endcliffe or Bramall Lane between 1880 and 1895.
Record Attendance: 72,841 v Manchester City, FA Cup 5th Round, 17 February, 1934.
Record Victory: 12–0 v Halliwell, FA Cup 1st Round, 17 January, 1891.
Record Defeat: 0–10 v Aston Villa, Division 1, 5 October 1912.
Most League Points: (3 for a win) 88, Division 2, 1983–84. (2 for a win) 62, Division 2, 1958–59.
Most League Goals: 106, Division 2, 1958–59.
Highest League Scorer in a Season: Derek Dooley, 46, Division 2, 1951–52.
Highest Total of League Goals: Andy Wilson, 200, 1900–20.
Most League Appearances: Andy Wilson, 502, 1900–20.
League History: 1892 Elected to Division 1, 1899–1900 Division 2, 1900–20 Division 1, 1920–26 Division 2, 1926–37 Division 1, 1937–50 Division 2, 1950–51Division 1, 1951–52 Division 2, 1952–55 Division 1, 1955–56 Division 2, 1956–58 Division 1, 1958–59 Division 2, 1959–70Division 1, 1970–75 Division 2, 1975–80 Division 3, 1980–84 Division 2, 1984– Division 1.
Honours: Division 1 Champions 1902–03, 1903–04, 1928–29, 1929–30, runners-up 1960–61. Division 2 Champions 1899–1900, 1925–26, 1951–52, 1955–56, 1958–59, runners-up 1949–50, 1983–84. Division 3 runners-up 1979–80. FA Cup winners 1896, 1907, 1935, runners-up 1890, 1966.
Colours: Blue and white striped shirts, blue shorts, white socks. **Second strip:** All green with blue and white trim.

SHEFFIELD WEDNESDAY – LEAGUE RECORD 1987–88

Match no/Opp/Date		Hodge	Sterland	McCall	Madden	May	Worthington	Marwood	Megson	Chapman	Hirst	Chamberlain	Bradshaw	Jacobs	Owen	Hazel	Fee	Jemson	Galvin	Pressman	Proctor	West	Shutt	Pearson	Cranson	FT(HT)Att Lge pos
1. Chelsea	15.8	1	2	3	4	5	6	7	8	9¹	10	11†	12													1-2(0-1)21,929 —
2. Oxford*	18.8	1	2	3	4	5	6	7†	8	9¹	10		12	11‡	14											1-1(1-1)17,868 —
3. Newcastle*	22.8	1	2	3	4	5	6		8	9	10	11				7										0-1(0-1)22,031 17
4. Everton	29.8	1	2	3	4		6		8	9	10					7	5	11								0-4(0-1)29,694 19
5. Coventry*	31.8	1	2	3†	4	5	6		8	9	10	12				7			11							0-3(0-2)17,171 —
6. Sthampton	5.9		2		4	3			8	9¹		12			10†	7‡	5	14	11	1	6					1-1(1-0)12,526 20
7. Watford*	12.9		2		4	3			8	9¹		12				7‡	5	14	11†	1	6	10¹				2-3(1-2)16,144 20
8. Derby	19.9	1	2¹		5	3			8¹	9	10	12			4				11		6	7†				2-2(0-2)15,869 21
9. Charlton*	26.9	1	2		4	5	3		8	9²		12	7						11		6	10†				2-0(2-0)16,350 20
10. Spurs	3.10	1	2		4	5	3	7	8	9		12							11†		6	10				0-2(0-0)24,311 20
11. Man Utd*	10.10	1	2¹		4	5	3		8	9	12	7†							11		6	10				2-4(1-1)32,779 20
12. Nottm F	17.10	1	2		5	3			8	9	7	12	11‡					14			6	10†		4		0-3(0-1)17,685 20
13. Norwich*	24.10	1	2		4	3			8	9	7†	12			14				11		6	10‡		5¹		1-0(1-0)15,861 19
14. Portsmouth	31.10	1	2†		4	3			8		10	7			12				11		6	9²		5		2-1(1-1)13,582 18
15. West Ham	7.11	1			4	3			8		7†	10¹‡	2	12				14	11		6	9		5		1-0(1-0)16,277 16
16. Luton*	14.11	1			4	3	12	8	9		7		2					11†			6	10		5		0-2(0-1)16,960 16
17. QPR*	28.11	1	2		4				8¹	9	7							11			6¹	10		5		3-1(2-0)16,933 17
18. Arsenal	5.12	1	2		4	3	11†		9	12	7	8									6	10¹		5		1-3(1-2)23,670 17
19. Wimbledon*	12.12	1	2		4	3	7†		9¹		11	12	8		14						6	10‡		5		1-0(0-0)14,289 16
20. Liverpool	19.12	1	2		4	14	3	11	10	9	7†				8¹						6	12		5		0-1(0-0)35,383 17
21. Watford	26.12	1	2		4		3	7	8	9¹†		12						11‡	14		6	10¹		5¹		3-1(3-1)12,026 16
22. Derby*	28.12	1	2		4		3	7†	8	9		12						11			6	10		5		2-1(2-0)26,191 12
23. Everton*	1.1	1	2		4	11	3	7†	8‡	9		12	14								6¹	10		5		1-0(1-0)26,433 10
24. Newcastle	2.1	1	2		4		3	7¹	8	9¹		12	11								6	10		5		2-2(0-0)25,503 10
25. Chelsea*	16.1	1	2‡		4	11¹	3	7¹		12	9¹	8†			14						6	10¹		5		3-0(1-0)19,859 9
26. Sthampton*	6.2	1	2¹		4		3	7	8	9¹	14		12						11		6	10‡		5†		2-1(0-1)14,769 9
27. Coventry	13.2	1	2			5	3	7	8	9			11		4						6	10				0-3(0-1)14,382 9
28. Charlton	20.2	1	2		4		3	7	8	9¹	10	11†						12			6			5		1-3(0-3)4517 9
29. Spurs*	27.2	1	2		4		3	7	8	9	10‡	11†			14			12			6			5		0-3(0-1)18,046 10
30. Nottm F*	5.3	1	2		4	11	3	7†	8	9	10	12									6			5		0-1(0-1)19,509 12
31. Man Utd	12.3	1	2		4		3		8	9¹	10	7						12	11		6			5†		1-4(0-2)33,318 12
32. Portsmouth*	19.3		2₁		4		3	12	8	9	10‡	7			14			5	11†		6					1-0(1-0)13,731 12
33. Norwich	26.3		2₁		4				8	9¹	10†	7	12					11¹			6				5	3-0(1-0)13,280 12
34. West Ham*	2.4		2		3				8	9	10¹‡	7†	12					14	11		6				5	2-1(1-0)18,435 10
35. Luton	5.4		2¹		4	7	3		8	9¹	10†							11	14	1	6‡	12		5		2-2(0-0)7337 —
36. Oxford	13.4		2¹		4		3		8	9²	10	7						11		1	6			5		3-0(2-0)5727 —
37. QPR	23.4		2		4	5	3		8	9	10†							11	12	1	6	7¹				1-1(1-0)12,531 8
38. Arsenal*	30.4		2¹		4	5			8	9¹	10¹	3†	14	12	11					1	6	7				3-3(3-1)16,681 8
39. Wimbledon	3.5		2		4	5			8	9¹	10	3						11		1	6	7				1-1(0-1)7854 —
40. Liverpool*	7.5				4	5	3		8	9	10¹							11	12	1	6	7†				1-5(0-2)35,893 10

Final League Position: 11

Apps(subs)/goals: 29(0) 0 | 38(0) 8 | 5(0) 0 | 38(0) 0 | 17(0) 1 | 8(0) 0 | 16(2) 2 | 37(0) 2 | 37(0) 0 | 19(5) 3 | 15(6) 1 | 5(4) 2 | 5(0) 0 | 12(2) 0 | 5(0) 0 | 7(9) 0 | 11(2) 1 | 12(6) 0 | 11(0) 0 | 25(2) 7 | 10(0) 0 | 19(0) 2 | 4(0) 0

Own goals: Robson, match 11; Fenwick, match 17

351

SHREWSBURY TOWN

Gay Meadow, Shrewsbury SY2 6AB.

Back row (left to right): Victor Kasule, Andy Crane, Richard Pratley, Alan Irvine, David Linighan, Wayne Williams. *Middle row:* Colin Griffin (Coach), Jon Narbett, Paul Tester, Steve Perks, Ken Hughes, Michael Brown, Dougie Bell, David Geddis, Les Helm (Physio). *Front row:* Jim Melrose, Philip Priest, Bernard McNally, Ian McNeill (Manager), Tim Steele, Brian Williams, Richard Green.

Stadium Capacity: 16,000.
Pitch Dimensions: 116 × 76 yds.
Telephone: 0743–60111.
Chairman: K. R. Woodhouse.
Vice-Chairman: P. W. Newbrook.
Directors: A. C. Williams, F. C. G. Fry, M. J. Starkey, R. Bailey, G. W. Nelson, W. H. Richards.
Manager: Ian McNeill.
Post-War Managers: Sam Crooks, Walter Rowley, Harry Potts, John Spuhler, Arthur Rowley, Harry Gregg, Maurice Evans, Alan Durban, Richie Barker, Graham Turner, Chic Bates (11).
Physio: L. Helm.
Secretary: M. J. Starkey.
Commercial Manager: I. Hookway.
Founded: 1886.
Turned Professional: 1905.
Nickname: Town or The Shrews.
Former Names: None.
Former Grounds: Old Shrewsbury Racecourse.
Record Attendance: 18,917 v Walsall, Division 3, 26 April 1961.
Record Victory: 7–0 v Swindon Town, Division 3(S), 6 May 1955.
Record Defeat: 1–8 v Norwich City, Division 3(S), 1952–53 and v Coventry City, Division 3, 22 October 1963.
Most League Points: (3 for a win) 70, Division 2, 1981–82. (2 for a win) 62, Division 4, 1974–75.
Most League Goals: 101, Division 4, 1958–59.
Highest League Scorer in a Season: Arthur Rowley, 38, Division 4, 1958–59.
Highest Total of League Goals: Arthur Rowley, 152, 1958–65 (part of his League record 434 goals).
Most League Appearances: Colin Griffin, 405, 1975–88.
League History: 1950 Elected to Division 3(N), 1951–58 Division 3(S), 1958–59 Division 4, 1959–74 Division 3, 1974–75 Division 4, 1975–79 Division 3, 1979– Division 2.
Honours: Division 3 Champions 1978–79. Division 4 runners-up 1974–75. Welsh Cup winners 1891, 1938, 1977, 1984, 1985, runners-up 3 times.
Colours: White shirts with blue trim, blue shorts, white socks with blue trim. **Second strip:** Red shirts, white shorts, red socks.

SHREWSBURY TOWN – LEAGUE RECORD 1987–88

Match no/Opp/Date	Perks	Williams W	Williams B	Narbett	Pearson	Lineham	Steele	McNally	Geddis	Robinson	Tester	Brown	Leonard	Green	Cooper	Griffin	Leworthy	Mores	Smith	Hughes	Priest	Bell	Kasule	Melrose	Pradley	Irvine	FT(HT)Att Lge pos
1. Leicester 15.8	1	2	3	4	5	6	7	8	9¹†	10	11	12															1-0(0-0)8469 —
2. Ipswich* 22.8	1	2	3	4	5	6	7	8		10	11	9															0-0(0-0)3610 9
3. Huddersfield 29.8	1	2	3	4	5	6		8		10	11	9	7														0-0(0-0)4478 10
4. Reading* 1.9	1	2	3	4	5	6	7	8	10†	11	9			12													0-1(0-1)3223 —
5. WBA 5.9	1	2	3	4¹	5	6	7	8		10	11	9															1-2(0-0)8560 17
6. Man City* 12.9	1	2	3	4	5	6	7	8		10	11†			12	9												0-0(0-0)6280 18
7. Hull City 15.9	1	2	3	4	5	6	7¹	8		10	11	12				9†											1-1(0-0)7939 —
8. Birmingham 19.9	1	2	3	4	5	6	7	8		10	11	12				9†											0-0(0-0)7183 18
9. Bradford* 26.9	1	2	3	4	5	6	7	8		11	10					9²											2-2(0-0)4247 19
10. Swindon 29.9	1	2	3	4	5	6	7₁	8†	14	11‡	10	12			9												1-1(0-0)8261 —
11. C Palace* 3.10	1	2	3	4	5	6¹	7¹	8	12	11	10†				9												2-0(1-0)3999 16
12. Millwall 17.10	1	2	3	4			7	8	12	11†	9			5		6	10¹										1-4(1-2)5202 19
13. Bournemouth 20.10	1	2	3	4			7†	8	12	11	9‡	14	5			6	10										0-2(0-2)5587 —
14. Oldham* 24.10	1	2¹†	3	4			7	8			11	9	12	5		6	10¹										2-3(2-0)3337 21
15. Middlesbro 31.10	1	2†	3			6	12	8‡	7	11	9	4	14				10	5									0-4(0-1)10,183 21
16. Aston Villa* 3.11	1		3	4			7	8	10			12	11†	2			9¹	5									1-2(1-1)7089 —
17. Leeds 7.11	1		3	4¹		6	7	8	9		12	11	2‡				10†	5	14								1-2(0-1)13,760 21
18. Blackburn* 14.11	1	2†	3	4			6	7	8	10	11	9¹	12				5										1-2(0-0)3164 21
19. Sheff Utd* 17.11	1		3	4¹		6	7		10	11	9¹	8	2				5		1								2-0(1-0)2555 —
20. Barnsley 21.11	1		3			6	7	8	10	11	9¹	4	2				5		1								1-2(0-2)5364 20
21. Stoke* 28.11	1		3			6	7	8	10	11	9	12	2				5			4†							0-3(0-3)5158 20
22. Plymouth 5.12	1		3	11†		6		8	10	12	9	4	2				5			7							0-2(0-2)7603 21
23. Hull* 12.12	1		3	14		6	7	8₁	10	12¹	9	4†	2				5			11‡							2-2(1-2)2588 22
24. Ipswich 18.12	1		3	14		6	7	8	10	11†	9	12	2				5			4‡							0-2(0-0)9930 —
25. Bradford 26.12	1		3	12		6	7	8	10	11†	9		2¹				5			4							1-1(0-0)12,474 22
26. Birmingham* 28.12	1	14	3			6	7	8	10	11†	9		2				5			4‡	12						0-0(0-0)6397 22
27. Huddersfield* 1.1	1	14	3‡			6	7†	8	10¹	12	9¹		2				5			4	11¹						3-1(1-0)5448 21
28. Man City 2.1	1		3	12		6	7	8	10†		9		5²							4	11¹						3-1(0-1)21,455 20
29. Leicester* 16.1	1	12	3			6	7	8	10†		9		2							4‡	11	14					0-0(0-0)5025 19
30. Reading 23.1	1	14	3			6		8	12		7	9	2							4‡	11	10†					0-1(0-0)5170 19
31. WBA* 6.2	1	2	3	14		6		8	10			12						5		4	7‡	11†	9				0-1(0-0)6360 21
32. Sheff Utd 13.2	1	2	3			6		8	10		11									4¹	7	9†	5	12			1-0(1-0)8227 21
33. Swindon* 20.2	1	11‡	3			6		8₁	10				2							4†	14	7¹	9	5		12	2-1(2-1)5649 20
34. C Palace 27.2	1	11	3			6		8			12	10	2†							4	7		5	9¹			2-1(1-1)8210 20
35. Millwall* 5.3	1		3			6		8	9		12	11	2							4	7		5	10†			0-0(0-0)5408 18
36. Middlesbro 19.3	1	3				6	12	8	9		11†	10	2							4¹	7¹		5				0-1(0-0)5603 19
37. Oldham 26.3	1	3				6	12	8	9			10	2							4†	11†	7¹		5			2-2(1-0)5379 21
38. Leeds* 2.4	1	2	3			6	11	8	9			10	5							4		7¹†	12				1-0(0-0)7369 19
39. Blackburn 4.4	1	2¹	3			6	11†	8	9			10	5¹		12					4		7					2-2(0-2)13,741 19
40. Bournemouth* 8.4	1	14	3			6	12	8	9¹			10	2‡							4	11†		7¹	5			2-1(1-0)7106 —
41. Aston Villa 23.4	1	12	3			6		8	9			11	2							4†	7	10‡	5	14			0-1(0-1)18,396 19
42. Barnsley* 30.4	1	14	3			6	12	8	9¹			10	2							4	11	7‡	5	10†			1-1(1-0)4712 20
43. Stoke 2.5	1		3			6		8	9		10¹		2							4†	11	7	12	5			1-1(0-0)7452 19
44. Plymouth* 7.5	1		3	14		6		8	9²		10†		2							4‡	11	7	12	5			2-1(1-0)4510 18

Final League Position: 21

Apps(subs)/goals: 42(0)/0 · 24(7)/2 · 42(0)/0 · 19(6)/3 · 11(0)/0 · 41(0)/1 · 28(5)/3 · 43(0)/2 · 23(4)/5 · 24(5)/1 · 35(6)/5 · 8(7)/0 · 29(2)/2 · 30(2)/2 · 5(1)/0 · 6(0)/3 · 17(0)/2 · 6(0)/0 · 2(1)/0 · 13(2)/1 · 13(1)/3 · 6(3)/1 · 11(0)/0 · 5(3)/1

Own goal: O'Doherty, match 34.

SOUTHAMPTON

The Dell, Milton Road, Southampton SO9 4XX.

Back row (left to right): Don Taylor (Physio), Gordon Hobson, Gerry Forrest, Francis Benali, Phillip Parkinson, Mark Blake, Steve Davis, Matthew Le Tissier, Craig Maskell, Andy Cook, Gary Bull, Dennis Rofe (First, Team Trainer). *Middle row:* Dave Merrington (Youth, Team Trainer), Allen Tankard, Kevin Moore, Keith Granger, Glenn Cockerill, Tim Flowers, Colin Clarke, John Burridge, Jimmy Case, Ian Hamilton, George Horsfall. *Front row:* Chris Nicholl (Manager), Andy Townsend, Danny Wallace, Kevin Bond, Mark Wright, Graham Baker, Steve Baker, Tony Barton (Ass. Manager).

Stadium Capacity: 25,175.
Pitch Dimensions: 110 × 72 yds.
Telephone: 0703–220505, Ticket office: 0703–228575, **Clubcall:** 0898–121178.
Chairman: F. G. L. Askham FCA.
Vice-Chairman: K. St. J. Wiseman.
Directors: J. Corbett, Lt-Col Sir George Meyrick (Bart) MC TD, E. T. Bates, I. L. Gordon, B. D. W. Hunt.
Manager: Chris Nicholl.
Post-War Managers: Bill Dodgin (Snr), Sid Cann, George Roughton, Ted Bates, Lawrie McMenemy (5).
Physio: Don Taylor.
Secretary: Brian Truscott.
Marketing Manager: Bob Britten.
Sponsors: Draper Tools.
Founded: 1885.
Turned Professional: 1894.
Nickname: The Saints.
Former Names: Southampton St Mary's prior to 1885 (hence the nickname).
Former Grounds: Antelope Ground 1885–97, County Cricket Ground 1897–98.
Record Attendance: 31,044 v Manchester United, Division 1, 8 October 1969.
Record Victory: 14–0 v Newbury, FA Cup 1st qualifying Round, 10 September 1894.
Record Defeat: 0–8 v Tottenham Hotspur, Division 2, 28 March 1936 and v Everton, Division 1, 20 November 1971.
Most League Points: (3 for a win) 77, Division 1, 1983–84. (2 for a win) 61, Division 3(S), 1921–22 and Division 3, 1959–60.
Most League Goals: 112, Division 3(S), 1957–58.
Highest League Scorer in a Season: Derek Reeves, 39, Division 3, 1959–60.
Highest Total of League Goals: Mick Channon, 182, 1966–67, 1979–82.
Most League Appearances: Terry Paine, 713, 1956–74.
League History: 1920 Founder Members of Division 3, 1921 Division 3(S), 1922–53 Division 2, 1953–58 Division 3(S), 1958–60 Division 3, 1960–66 Division 2, 1966–74Division 1, 1974–78 Division 2, 1978– Division 1.
Honours: Division 1 runners-up 1983–84. Division 2 runners-up 1965–66, 1977–78. Division 3 Champions 1959–60, runners-up 1920–21. Division 3(S) Champions 1921–22. FA Cup winners 1976, runners-up 1900, 1902. League Cup runners-up 1979.
Colours: Red and white shirts with black trim, black shorts, white socks. **Second strip:** Blue shirts and socks, white shorts.

SOUTHAMPTON – LEAGUE RECORD 1987–88

Match no/Opp	Date	Flowers	Forrest	Cook	Baker G	Moore	Bond	Townsend	Cockerill	Clarke	Hobson	Wallace D	Case	Statham	Le Tissier	Baker S	Wallace R	Burridge	Blake	Shearer	FT(HT)Att Lge pos
1. Man Utd*	15.8	1	2	3	4	5	6	7	8	9	10†	11^2	12								2–2(1–2)21,214 —
2. Norwich	19.8	1	2	3	11	5^1	6	7	8	9	10		4								1–0(0–0)14,429 —
3. Portsmouth	22.8	1	2		11	5	6	7	8	9^2	10		4	3							2–2(1–1)20,161 8
4. QPR*	29.8	1	2		11	5	6	7‡	8	9	10†	12	4	3	14						0–1(0–0)15,532 10
5. Nottm F	2.9	1	2		11†	5	6	7^1	8	9_1	10^1		4	3		12					3–3(1–2)14,173 —
6. Sheff Wed*	5.9	1	2			5	6	7	8†	9^1	10	11	4	3	12						1–1(0–1)12,526 10
7. Spurs	12.9	1	2		11†	5	6	7	8	9	10	12	4	3							1–2(1–1)24,728 13
8. Newcastle	26.9	1	2		10	5	6	7	8†	9^1		11	4	3		12					1–2(0–0)18,093 17
9. Everton*	3.10	1	2		10†	5	6	7	8	9		11	4	3	12						0–4(0–3)15,719 18
10. Watford*	17.10		2		10	5	6		8	9		11^1	4	3	7			1			1–0(0–0)11,933 17
11. Coventry	20.10		2		10^1	5	6^1		8	9		11^1	4	3	7†	12		1			3–2(1–2)14,522 —
12. Chelsea*	24.10		2		10^1	5	6		8	9^1		11^1	4	3	7			1			3–0(0–0)11,890 10
13. Charlton	31.10		2		10	5	6	12	8	9		11^1	4	3	7†			1			1–1(1–0)5158 9
14. Wimbledon	7.11		2		10†	5	6	7	8	9		11	4	3		12		1			0–2(0–1)5014 11
15. Oxford*	14.11		2		10	5	6	7†	8^1	9		11^2	4	3		12		1			3–0(1–0)12,095 10
16. Arsenal	21.11		2		10	5	6	7†	8	9		11^1	4	3		12		1			1–0(0–0)32,477 9
17. Derby*	28.11		2		10‡	5	6	7^1	8†	9	12	11	4	3		14		1			1–2(0–0)15,201 9
18. West Ham	5.12		2		10	5	6	7	8	9		11^1	4	3				1			1–2(1–1)15,375 10
19. Liverpool*	12.12		2		10‡	5	6	7^1	8	9^1†		11	4	3	12	14		1			2–2(1–2)19,507 10
20. Luton	18.12		2		10	5	6	7	8	9^1_1		11†	4	3	12			1			2–2(1–1)6618 —
21. Spurs*	26.12		2		10	5^1	6	7†	8	9^1	11		4	3		12		1			2–1(2–0)18,456 9
22. QPR	1.1				10	5	6	7	8	9	11†		4	3	12	2		1			0–3(0–0)8631 12
23. Portsmouth*	3.1				10†	5	6	7	8	9		11	4‡	3	12	2	14	1			0–2(0–2)17,002 —
24. Man Utd	16.1		2		10	5	6	7	12	9^2		11	4	3	8†			1			2–0(1–0)35,716 11
25. Norwich*	23.1		2		10	5	6	7	12	9		11	4‡	3	8			1			0–0(0–0)12,002 11
26. Sheff Wed	6.2		2		4	5		10	8	9_1	7	11		3				1	6		1–2(1–0)14,769 12
27. Nottm F*	13.2		2		4	5	6	10	8	9_1	7	11		3				1			1–1(1–1)13,315 11
28. Everton	27.2		2			5	6	10	8	9	7	11	4	3				1			0–1(0–1)20,764 12
29. Newcastle*	1.3		2			5	6	10	8	9^1		11	4	3	7			1			1–1(0–0)13,380 —
30. Watford	5.3		2			5^1	6	10	8	9		11	4	3	7			1			1–0(1–0)11,824 10
31. Coventry*	12.3		2		12	5†	6	10‡	8	9		11^1	4	3	7		14	1			1–2(1–0)12,914 10
32. Charlton*	19.3		2				6	10	8	9		11	4	3	7†		12	1	5		0–1(0–0)12,103 14
33. Chelsea	26.3		2		7^1		6	10	8	9		11†	4	3				1	5	12	1–0(0–0)15,380 10
34. Wimbledon*	2.4		2		7^1		6	10	8^1	9		11	4	3				1	5		2–2(0–1)13,036 14
35. Oxford	4.4		2		7		6	10	8	9		11†	4	3				1	5	12	0–0(0–0)7657 12
36. Arsenal*	9.4		2		7		6	10	8	9			4	3		12		1	5^1	11^3†	4–2(3–1)14,521 10
37. Derby	23.4		2		7	5	6	10	8†	9		12	4	3			14	1		11‡	0–2(0–2)14,291 12
38. West Ham*	30.4		2		8	5	6^2	10		9			4†	3	12		7	1		11	2–1(0–0)15,652 11
39. Liverpool	2.5		2		8	5	6	10†	12	9		11	4	3			7^1	1			1–1(0–1)37,610 12
40. Luton*	7.5		2		8	5	6	10†	12	9^1		11‡	4	3	14		7	1			1–1(0–1)12,722 12
Apps(subs)/goals		9(0) 0	37(0) 0	2(0) 0	35(1) 5	35(0) 3	39(0) 3	36(1) 3	35(4) 2	40(0) 16	12(1) 1	30(3) 11	37(0) 0	38(0) 0	10(9) 0	2(2) 0	3(12) 1	31(0) 0	6(0) 1	5(2) 3	Final League Position: 12

DIVISION 3

SOUTHEND UNITED

Roots Hall Football Ground, Victoria Avenue, Southend-on-Sea SS2 6NQ

Back row (left to right): Adrian Burrows, Shane Westley, Paul Newell, Eric Steele, Roy McDonough, David Martin. *Middle row:* Vic Jobson (Chairman), Buster Footman (Treatment of, injuries Officer), Russell Short, Andy Rogers, Dean Neal, Lee Nogan, Martin Robinson, Chris Ramsey, Frank Banks (Ass. Manager), Kevin Lock (Youth, Team Manager). *Front row:* Martin Ling, Nicky Smith, Paul Clark (Manager), Glenn Pennyfather, Derek Hall, Peter Johnson.

Stadium Capacity: 11,053.
Pitch Dimensions: 110 × 74 yds.
Telephone: 0702–340707, **Commercial dept:** 0702–332113.
Chairman: V. T. Jobson.
Vice-Chairman & Company Secretary: J. W. Adams.
Directors: W. E. Parsons, R. F. Moore OBE, M. Markscheffel, J. Foster.
Player–Manager: Paul Clark.
Post-War Managers: Harry Warren, Eddie Perry, Frank Broome, Ted Fenton, Alvan Williams, Ernie Shepherd, Geoff Hudson, Arthur Rowley, David Smith, Peter Morris, Bobby Moore OBE, David Webb, Paul Clark, Dick Bate (14).
Assistant Manager: F. Banks.
Treatment of Injuries Officer: B. Footman.
Secretary: Miss Jane Austen.
Sponsors: Firholm Builders.
Founded: 1906.
Turned Professional: 1906.
Nickname: The Shrimpers.
Former Names: None.
Former Grounds: Roots Hall, Prittlewell 1906–20, Kursaal 1920–34, Southend Stadium 1934–55.
Record Attendance: 31, 033 v Liverpool, FA Cup 3rd Round, 10 January 1979.
Record Victory: 10–1 v Golders Green, FA Cup 1st Round, 24 November 1934 and v Brentwood, FA Cup 2nd Round, 7 December 1968.
Record Defeat: 1–9 v Brighton & HA, Division 3, 27 November 1965
Most League Points: (3 for a win) 80, Division 4, 1986–87. (2 for a win), 67, Division 4, 1980–81.
Most League Goals: 92, Division 3(S), 1950–51.
Highest League Scorer in a Season: Jim Shankly, 31, 1928–29 and Sammy McCrory, 1957–58, both in Division 3(S).
Highest Total of League Goals: Roy Hollis, 122, 1953–60.
Most League Appearances: Sandy Anderson, 451, 1950–63.
League History: 1920 Founder Members of Division 3, 1921 Division 3(S), 1958–66 Division 3, 1966–72 Division 4, 1972–76 Division 3, 1976–78 Division 4, 1978–80 Division 3, 1980–81 Division 4, 1981–84 Division 3, 1984–87 Division 4, 1987– Division 3.
Honours: Division 4 Champions 1980–81, runners-up 1971–72, 1977–78.
Colours: Blue shirts, yellow shorts, blue socks. **Second strip:** All yellow.

SOUTHEND UNITED – LEAGUE RECORD 1987–88

Match no/Opp/Date	Steele	Ramsey	Johnson	Rogers	Martin	Hall	Clark P	Smith	Neal	McDonough	Robinson	Westley	Young	Pennyfather	Ling	Burrows	Nogan	Newell	O'Shea	Crown	Brush	Butler	Sansome	FT(HT)Att Lge pos
1. Bury 15.8	1	2	3	4	5	6	7	8	9	10	11^2													2-2(0-1)1937 —
2. Chester* 22.8	1	2		4	6	3	7	8^1	12	10†	11	5^1	9											2-2(1-1)2369 15
3. Gillingham 29.8	1	2		4	6	3	7	8†	9	10	11	5	12											1-8(0-4)4154 18
4. Preston* 1.9	1	2†		4	6	3	7	12	9†	10	11^1	5		8	14									1-2(0-1)2600 —
5. Notts Co 5.9	1			4^1	6	3	7		9	10_1	11	5†		8	12									2-6(2-3)4166 23
6. Brentford* 12.9	1	2		4		3	7	6	12	10	9	5		8^2	11†									2-3(1-3)2335 23
7. Port Vale 14.9	1	2	3	4			6	7	9†	10^1	11	5		8	12									1-4(0-1)3670 —
8. Mansfield 19.9	1		3	12	2	6				10	7	5		8	11†	4	9							0-1(0-1)2854 23
9. Brighton* 26.9	1		3		2	6†	12			10	7	5^1		8^1	11	4	9							2-1(0-0)3789 23
10. Nthampton* 29.9	1		3		2	6^1				10	7	5		8	11	4	9							1-1(1-1)3407 —
11. Grimsby 3.10	1		3		2	6				10^1	7	5		8	11^1	4	9^1							3-1(3-0)2544 22
12. Bristol C 10.10	1		3		2	6				10^1	7^1	5		8	11	4								2-3(1-1)8606 23
13. Rotherham* 16.10	1		3	14	2	6†	12			10	7^1	5		8	11	4	9‡							1-1(1-1)2217 —
14. Fulham* 20.10	1	14	3	12	2	6	7‡		9†	10	11	5		8	4									0-2(0-1)3419 —
15. Chesterfield 24.10	1	14	3	12	2	6	7†		9	10_1	11†	5		8	4									1-3(0-2)1726 23
16. Walsall* 30.10	1	2	3	11	5	6†	7	12_1		10	9			8	4									1-1(0-1)2692 —
17. Sunderland 3.11	1		3	11	2	6	7†	12		10	9	5		8	4									0-7(0-3)15,754 —
18. Wigan 7.11	1		3	11	5	6	7			10				8	4			1	2					0-1(0-0)3081 23
19. Aldershot* 21.11	1		3	11	5	6	7	12		14	9		8†		4			1	2	10‡				0-1(0-0)2362 23
20. York 28.11			3	11	5	6	7	8^1		10					4^1			1	2	9^1				3-0(1-0)2225 23
21. Doncaster* 11.12			3	11	5	6^1	7	8		10^2					4			1	2	9^1				4-1(1-1)2268 —
22. Blackpool 19.12			3	11	5	6	7	8		10					4			1	2	9^1				1-1(0-1)3277 22
23. Brighton 26.12			3	11	5	6	7	8		10					4			1	2	9				0-0(0-0)11,147 23
24. Bristol R* 28.12		3‡	11†	5	6	7		8^1		10_1	12	14^1			4			1	2	9^1				4-2(2-1)4094 22
25. Gillingham* 1.1			11†	5	6	7		8		10	12	3			4			1	2	9^1				1-3(0-2)5254 22
26. Brentford 2.1		12	3†	5	6					10	11	7			4			1	2	9^1				0-1(0-0)5752 22
27. Chester 9.1			3	5	6	7	11		12	10†	8				4			1	2	9^1				1-1(1-0)2065 22
28. Mansfield* 15.1			3			6^1	7	8		10	11	5			4			1	2	9^1				2-1(1-1)3091 —
29. Port Vale* 22.1	1		12	3	5	6†		8		10	11^1				4				2	9^2	7			3-3(2-1)3038 —
30. Preston 30.1	1		3		5	6		8			11		4	12	10†				2	9	7^1			1-1(1-1)6180 22
31. Notts Co* 5.2	1		14		3	5	6‡	8^1			11†		4	12	10				2	9	7			1-2(1-0)3904 —
32. Bristol R 13.2	1		3		5			8			11		4	10	7				2	9		6		0-0(0-0)3092 22
33. Bury* 20.2	1		3		5			8	12		11	4	10†		7				2	9^1		6		1-0(1-0)3003 21
34. Grimsby* 26.2	1		3		5			8	12		11	4	10†		7				2	9		6		0-0(0-0)3409 —
35. Nthampton 2.3	1		3		5	12	8†			10	11	4			7				2	9		6		0-4(0-1)4249 —
36. Rotherham 5.3	1		3		5	8	7†				11	4		10‡	14				2	9	12	6^1		1-1(0-0)2531 22
37. Bristol C* 11.3	1		3		5	8			11	10†	4^1				12				2	9^1	7	6		2-0(1-0)3664 —
38. Walsall 19.3	1				5	7	8‡	11	10	14	4				12				2	9^1	3	6		1-2(1-1)4479 22
39. Chesterfield* 25.3			3		5	8	12	11		10^2					12				2†	9	6	7^1	1	3-0(2-3)3315 —
40. Wigan 1.4			3		5	2	8	11‡	12_1	10†				14^1						9^1	6	7	1	3-2(0-1)5003 —
41. Aldershot 4.4			3		2	4	8†		10	12	5			11						9^1	6	7	1	1-0(0-0)3436 19
42. Sunderland* 9.4			3		2	4	8		10	12	5			11						9^1	6†	7	1	1-4(1-3)8109 19
43. Fulham 23.4		3	1†		5	2	4	8	10	12				11						9	6	7	1	1-3(0-1)5043 21
44. York* 29.4			3		4		6	8	10			5		11^2						9^1	2	7	1	3-1(2-1)3768 —
45. Doncaster 2.5			3		4		6	8	10		5^1			11			1			9	2	7		1-0(0-0)1306 20
46. Blackpool* 7.5			3		4		6	8	10		5			11^2			1			9^1	2	7^1		4-0(1-0)5541 17
Apps(subs)/goals	27(0)/0	8(5)/0	39(0)/1	17(4)/1	41(0)/0	39(1)/3	28(2)/0	29(5)/5	10(2)/0	37(5)/9	31(6)/8	5(1)/5	5(2)/0	16(1)/3	35(7)/7	6(0)/0	6(0)/0	22(0)/0	28(0)/0	13(1)/3	15(0)/0	6(0)/0	6(0)/0	

Final League Position: 17

Own goal: West, match 3.

DIVISION 4

STOCKPORT COUNTY

Edgeley Park, Hardcastle Road, Stockport, Cheshire SK3 9DD.

Back row (left to right):
Les Robinson
Alan Birch
Chris Marples
Craig Farnaby
Bill Williams
Ian MacKenzie
Middle row:
Len Cantello (Coach)
Andy Hodgekinson
Wayne Entwhistle
Jim Willis
Tommy Sword
Bob Colville
Stevie Bullock
Dave Hindley (Physio)
Front row:
Levi Edwards
Denis Cronin
Frank Worthington
Asa Hartford
(Player/Manager)
Mike Pickering
Paul Hendrie
Neil Bailey

Stadium Capacity: 7,800.
Pitch Dimensions: 110 × 75 yds.
Telephone: 061-480 8888.
Chairman: D. Hunt.
Vice-Chairman: J. R. G. White.
Directors: J. N. Lewis, D. G. Gardner, A. W. Butler, M. Baker, B. Taylor, M. Rains, B. Elwood.
Manager: Asa Hartford.
Post-War Managers: Bob Marshall, Andy Beattie, Dick Duckworth, Willie Moir, Reg Flewin, Trevor Porteous, Bert Trautmann, Eddie Quigley, Jimmy Meadows, Walter Galbraith, Mat Woods, Brian Doyle, Jimmy Meadows, Roy Chapman, Eddie Quigley, Alan Thompson, Mike Summerbee, Jimmy McGuigan, Eric Webster, Colin Murphy, Les Chapman, Jimmy Melia, Colin Murphy (23).
Assistant Manager: Len Cantello.
Physio: David Hindley B. Sc., MCSP, SRP.
Secretary: T. R. McCreery FAAI.
Commercial Manager: John Rutter.
Founded: 1883.
Turned Professional: 1891.
Nickname: County or The Hatters.
Former Names: Heaton Norris Rovers 1883–88, Heaton Norris 1888–90.
Former Grounds: Heaton Norris Recreation Ground 1883–1884, Heaton Norris Wanderers Cricket Ground 1884–1885, Chorlton's Farm, Chorlton's Lane 1885–1886, Heaton Norris Cricket Ground 1886–1887, Wilkes' Field, Belmont Street 1887–89, Nursery Inn, Green Lane 1889–1902.
Record Attendance: 27,833 v Liverpool, FA Cup 5th Round, 11 February 1950.
Record Victory: 13–0 v Halifax Town, Division 3(N), 6 January 1934.
Record Defeat: 1–8 V Chesterfield, Division 2, 19 April 1902.
Most League Points: (3 for a win) 64, Division 4, 1985–86. (2 for a win) 64, Division 4, 1966–67.
Most League Goals: 115, Division 3(N), 1933–34.
Highest League Scorer in a Season: Alf Lythgoe, 46, Division 3(N), 1933–34.
Highest Total of League Goals: Jack Connor, 132, 1951–56.
Most League Appearances: Bob Murray, 465, 1952–63.
League History: 1900 Elected to Division 2, 1904 not re-elected, 1905 Elected to Division 2, 1905–21 Division 2, 1921–22 Division 3(N), 1922–26 Division 2, 1926–37 Division 3(N), 1937–38 Division 2, 1938–58 Division 3(N), 1958–59 Division 3, 1959–67 Division 4, 1967–70 Division 3, 1970– Division 4.
Honours: Division 4 Champions 1966–67. Division 3(N) Champions 1921–22, 1936–37, runners-up 1928–29, 1929–30.
Colours: White shirts, royal blue shorts, white socks. **Second strip:** All red.

STOCKPORT COUNTY – LEAGUE RECORD 1987–88

Players (column headings, left to right): Maples, Evans, Bailey, Robinson, Sword, Williams, Bullock, Cronin, Linnisile, Hartford, Edwards, Sertori, McKenzie, Hoskinson, Chandler, Mills, Scott, Colville, Farnaby, Burke, Birch, Pickering, Worthington, Hendrie, Willis, Thorpe, Crompton, Howard

Match no/Opp/Date	Mpl	Evn	Bai	Rob	Swd	Wil	Bul	Cro	Lin	Har	Edw	Ser	McK	Hos	Cha	Mil	Sco	Col	Far	Bur	Bir	Pic	Wor	Hen	Wls	Tho	Cmp	How	FT(HT)Att	Lge pos
1. Swansea* 15.8	1	2	3	4†	5	6	7	8	9	10	11	12																	0-2(0-0)2482	–
2. Darlington 22.8	1	2²		4	5	6	10	8		11			3	7	9														2-1(0-1)1744	13
3. Tranmere* 28.8	1	2	4			6	5	8		10	11		3	7¹	9														1-2(1-1)2229	–
4. Newport 31.8	1	2¹	4			6	5	8		10	11		3	7¹	9														2-1(0-1)1626	–
5. Carlisle* 4.9	1	2¹	3	4		6	5	8¹		10	11			7¹	9														3-0(1-0)2257	–
6. Rochdale 12.9	1		3	4		6	5		9†	10	11¹			7	12	8	2												1-0(1-0)2700	3
7. Orient* 15.9	1		3	4		6	5			10	11			7¹	8	2	9												1-2(1-2)2560	–
8. Wolves* 19.9	1		3	4		6	5		10†	11				7	8	12	2	9											0-2(0-2)2233	11
9. Wrexham 26.9	1	7	4	8	6	5		12		11			3†		10	2	9¹												1-2(1-2)1841	14
10. Scunthorpe 29.9	1		3	4		6	5							7			8	2	9	10	11								0-0(0-0)2181	–
11. Cardiff* 2.10	1		3	4		6	5		9	11†							2	8	10										0-1(0-1)2332	–
12. Peterboro* 9.10	1		3	4		6	5		9	14				7			12	8	2†	10‡	11								0-1(0-0)1594	20
13. Halifax 16.10	1		3	4		6	5		9†	14				7			2	8	12	10	11‡								0-2(0-0)1696	–
14. Crewe 20.10	1		3	4		6	5							7		9		8¹	2	10	11								1-3(0-2)2251	21
15. Hereford* 23.10	1		3	4		6	2		14	10‡				7		9	12	8†	11	5									0-2(0-1)1566	–
16. Burnley 31.10	1		3	4					9¹	10				7		12		8		5	11†								1-1(1-1)6645	21
17. Hartlepool* 3.11	1		3	4					9	10†				7				8		5	11¹								1-0(0-0)1408	–
18. Torquay* 6.11	1	8	4¹	12		6	2			10				7						5†	11								2-1(1-0)1697	–
19. Exeter 21.11	1		3	4		6	2		9	10‡				7	14		12	8	11¹	5†									1-2(0-1)2217	20
20. Colchester* 27.11	1		3	4		6	2							7	5			8	10¹	11	9								1-1(1-1)1703	–
21. Cambridge 11.12	1		3	4		6	2		10†	14				7‡	5			8		11		9	12						0-2(0-2)1475	–
22. Scarboro* 19.12	1		3	4		6	2		12	10				7†	5			8		11‡		9¹	14						1-1(1-1)1779	21
23. Wrexham* 26.12	1		3	4		6	2							7	5			8¹	12	11†		9	10						1-0(1-0)2504	21
24. Bolton 28.12	1		3	4		6	2		14	12				7	5†			8	10	11‡		9¹							1-2(0-1)6607	22
25. Tranmere 1.1	1		3‡	4		6	2		12	14				7†	5			8		11		9	10						0-4(0-2)3670	22
26. Rochdale* 2.1	1		3	4		6	2		12	10				7‡	5			8†		11		9¹	14						1-1(1-1)2441	22
27. Wolves 16.1	1		3	4		6	2		12									8		11		9¹	7†	10	5				1-1(0-0)8872	22
28. Orient 23.1	1		3	4		6	2		12									8¹†		11		9	7	10	5				1-1(1-0)4205	22
29. Newport* 29.1	1		3	4¹		6	2		14	10‡		12						8²		11¹		9†	7¹		5				5-1(1-2)2509	–
30. Carlisle 6.2	1		3	4		6	2		12	10								8		11†		9	7		5				0-2(0-1)1842	23
31. Bolton* 12.2	1		3†	4		6	2		10				12					8		11		9¹	7		5				1-2(0-1)4814	–
32. Swansea 19.2	1		3	4		6	2		10				12					8				9‡†	7	11	5				1-1(1-0)4405	–
33. Cardiff 27.2	1		3	4		6	2		9	10†								8					7	12	11	5			0-0(0-0)4008	23
34. Scunthorpe* 1.3	1		3	4		6	2		9	10†								8¹					7	12	11	5			1-1(0-0)1834	–
35. Halifax* 4.3	1		3	4		6			9	10							2	8¹					7	11	5				1-0(1-0)2171	–
36. Peterboro 12.3	1		3	4		6			9†	10			12				2	8					7	11	5				0-0(0-0)2193	22
37. Burnley* 18.3	1		3	4		6			9†	10							2	8¹				12	7¹	14	5	11‡			2-0(1-0)4423	–
38. Hereford 26.3	1		3	4		6			9¹	10							2	8					7	11	5				1-0(1-0)1695	20
39. Torquay 2.4	1		3	4		6				10							2†	8				9	12	11	5				0-3(0-2)2919	20
40. Exeter* 4.4	1			4†		6	2		12	10								7₁				8¹	4†	9	11	5			2-1(0-1)2161	18
41. Hartlepool 9.4	1		3	4		6	5			10¹				7			2	8²				9		11	4				3-1(2-1)1317	18
42. Darlington* 19.4	1		3	4		6	5		12	10			7†				2	8¹				9		11	4				1-1(0-0)1620	–
43. Crewe 22.4	1		3	4		6	5		12	10				3			7	8¹	2†			9		11	4				1-0(0-0)2090	–
44. Colchester 29.4	1				5	6	9		10	3			7				2	8						11	4				0-2(0-0)1607	–
45. Cambridge* 2.5			3		6	5	9		12	10			7				8		14				11†	4‡		1	1	2	0-2(0-0)1842	20
46. Scarboro 7.5	1			6₁	5	7	9		10								8						11	4	1		1	2	1-0(0-2)2236	20

Apps (subs)/goals: Maples 44(0) 0; Evans 5(0) 4; Bailey 34(0) 0; Robinson 37(0) 2; Sword 3(1) 0; Williams 45(0) 1; Bullock 41(0) 0; Cronin 11(4) 1; Linnisile 15(10) 3; Hartford 30(1) 0; Edwards 12(7) 2; Sertori 0(1) 0; McKenzie 12(0) 0; Hoskinson 36(3) 6; Chandler 41(0) 0; Mills 5(2) 0; Scott 15(1) 0; Colville 40(0) 14; Farnaby 17(5) 1; Burke 30(0) 0; Birch 18(2) 3; Pickering 36(0) 0; Worthington 18(1) 6; Hendrie 17(5) 1; Willis 10(0) 0; Thorpe 20(0) 0; Crompton 2(0) 0; Howard 2(0) 0.

Final League Position: 20

DIVISION 2

STOKE CITY
Victoria Ground, Stoke-on-Trent ST4 4EG.

Back row (left to right): Terry Williams, Philip Heath, Lee Dixon, Nicky Morgan, Ian Allinson, Graham Shaw, Steve Parkin, CLiff Carr. *Middle row:* Keith Rowley (Physio), Brian Talbot, Gerry Daly, Peter Fox, Scott Barrett, Andy Holmes, Tony Ford, Tony Lacey (Youth & Reserve Team Coach). *Front row:* Mick Mills (Manager), Steve Bould, Chris Hemming, George Berry, Carl Beeston, Carl Saunders, Sammy Chung (Ass. Manager).

Stadium Capacity: 35,812.
Pitch Dimensions: 116 × 75 yds.
Telephone: 0782–413511.
Chairman: P. Coates.
Vice-Chairman: T. E. Weetman.
Directors: G. L. Manning, M. Nield, K. A. Humphreys, M. Loftus.
Manager: Mick Mills.
Post-War Managers: Bob McGrory, Frank Taylor, Tony Waddington, George Eastham, Alan A'Court, Alan Durban, Richie Barker, Bill Asprey (8).
Physio: K. Rowley.
Secretary: M. J. Potts.
Commercial Manager: M. J. Cullerton.
Sponsors: H. & R. Johnson Tiles Ltd.
Founded: 1863.
Turned Professional: 1885.
Nickname: The Potters.
Former Names: None.
Former Grounds: Sweeting's Field 1875–1878.
Record Attendance: 51,380 v Arsenal, Division 1, 29 March 1937.
Record Victory: 10–3 v WBA, Division 1, 4 February 1937.
Record Defeat: 0–10 v Preston NE, Division 1, 14 September 1889.
Most League Points: (3 for a win) 62, Division 2, 1987–88. (2 for a win) 63, Division 3(N), 1926–27.
Most League Goals: 92, Division 3(N), 1926–27.
Highest League Scorer in a Season: Freddie Steele, 33, Division 1, 1936–37.
Highest Total of League Goals: Freddie Steele, 142, 1934–49.
Most League Appearances: Eric Skeels, 506, 1958–76.
League History: 1888 Founder Members of Football League, 1890 not re-elected, 1891 re-elected, 1907–08 Division 2, 1908 resigned from the League for financial reasons, 1919 re-elected toDivision 2, 1922–23 Division 1, 1923–26 Division 2, 1926–27 Division 3(N), 1927–33 Division 2, 1933–53 Division 1, 1953–63 Division2, 1963–77 Division 1, 1977–79 Division 2, 1979–85 Division 1, 1985– Division 2.
Honours: Division 2 Champions 1932–33, 1962–63, runners-up 1921–22. Division 3(N) Champions 1926–27. League Cup winners 1972, runners-up 1964.
Colours: Red and white striped shirts, white shorts and socks. **Second strip:** Yellow shirts, black shorts, yellow socks.

STOKE CITY – LEAGUE RECORD 1987–88

Match no/Opp	Date	Fox	Dixon	Parkin	Talbot	Henning	Berry	Ford	Daly	Morgan	Saunders	Allinson	Heath	Carr	Barrett	Boold	Shaw	Mills	Holmes	Henry	Stainrod	Beeston	Hackett	Puckett	Gibbons	Fowler	Lewis	Ware	FT(HT)Att	Lge pos
1. Birmingham	15.8	1	2	3	4	5	6	7	8	9	10	11†	12																0–2(0–1)13,137	—
2. Hull*	18.8	1	2	3	4‡	5	6	7¹	8†	9	10	11	12	14															1–1(0–1)9139	—
3. Middlesbro*	22.8	1	2	12	4	5	6₁	7	8†	9	10	11		3															1–0(0–0)9345	15
4. Ipswich	29.8	1	2	8	4	5	6	7		9	10	11†	12	3															0–2(0–1)11,149	15
5. Leicester*	31.8	1	2	8	4	5	6	7		9	10¹		11¹	3															2–1(2–1)9948	—
6. Sheff Utd	5.9		2	8	4	5	6	7		9	10		11	3	1														0–0(0–0)10,086	10
7. Bradford*	12.9		2	8	4	5	6¹	7	12		10†	9	11	3	1														1–2(0–1)9571	13
8. Reading	16.9		2	8¹	4		6	7	10	9			11	3	1	5													1–0(0–0)5349	—
9. Man City	19.9		2	8	4		6	7	10†	9		11		3		5	12												0–3(0–2)19,322	14
10. Huddersfield*	26.9	1	2	8			6	7¹	4†	9		12	11	3		5	10												1–0(0–1)8665	15
11. Leeds	30.9	1	2	4			6	7		9	8		11	3		5	10												0–0(0–0)17,208	—
12. Bournemouth*	3.10	1	2	4			6	7¹	14	9†	8	12	11	3‡		5	10												1–0(0–0)8104	10
13. Plymouth*	10.10	1	2	4		14	6	7	8†		9‡	12	11¹	3		5	10												1–0(0–1)8275	9
14. Blackburn	17.10	1	2	8	4	9	6	7					11	3		5	10												0–2(0–1)7280	10
15. Swindon	20.10	1	2	8	4	6‡	14	7	10			12	11			5	9	3†											0–3(0–1)9160	—
16. Aston Villa*	24.10	1	2	8	4	5	6	7					11	3			9												0–0(0–0)13,494	10
17. Barnsley	31.10	1	2	3	4	5	6	7¹	8	9		11						10¹											2–5(0–2)5908	15
18. WBA*	7.11	1	2	4¹		5	6₁	7	8	9	12	11¹		3				10											3–0(2–0)9992	14
19. C Palace	14.11	1	2	8	12	5	6	7	4†	9	10			3															0–2(0–0)8309	14
20. Millwall*	21.11		2	3	4	5		6	8	9†	7	11¹	12	1			10												1–2(1–0)7998	14
21. Shrewsbury	28.11		2¹	11	4	5†	6	7¹	8	9	10¹			3	1		12												3–0(3–0)5158	14
22. Oldham*	8.12	1	2	11	4†		6	7	8	9			12¹	3			10¹	5											2–2(1–1)6740	—
23. Middlesbro	12.12	1	2	11	4†		6	7		9			12	3	1	5	10	8											1–2(0–0)12,289	15
24. Reading*	19.12		2	4	12¹		6	7¹		9¹		11		3	1	5		10†		8¹									4–2(0–0)6968	14
25. Huddersfield	26.12		2	4¹			6	7		9¹		11		3	1	5		10¹	8										3–0(0–0)9500	14
26. Man City*	28.12		2	4			6₁	7		9	12	11†		3	1	5		10	8										1–3(0–2)18,020	15
27. Ipswich*	1.1		2	4	12		6	7	14	9¹				3	1	5		11		8†	10‡								1–2(1–1)9976	15
28. Bradford	2.1		2¹	11	4		6	7¹		9¹				3	1	5				8¹	10								4–1(3–0)12,223	14
29. Birmingham*	16.1		2		4¹		6	7	14	9†		11‡		3	1	5		12		8²	10								3–1(1–1)10,076	14
30. Sheff Utd*	6.2		2					7	4¹			11		3	1	5		9	8	10	6								1–0(0–0)9344	12
31. Hull	13.2		2					7				11		3	1	5		9	8	10	6								0–0(0–0)6424	12
32. Leeds*	23.2			4			6¹	7	12			11¹		3	1	5		9	8	10†	2								2–1(1–0)10,129	—
33. Bournemouth	27.2			4			6	7	9†			11		3	1	5		12	8	10	2								0–0(0–0)6871	10
34. Blackburn*	5.3			4			6	7	9¹			11		3	1	5		10¹	8		2								2–1(1–0)14,100	9
35. Plymouth	12.3			4	14		6	7	9†			12		3	1	5		10	8		2	11‡							0–3(0–2)8749	10
36. Leicester	16.3			4	2		6	7				11		3	1	5		9¹	8	10									1–1(0–1)10,502	—
37. Barnsley*	19.3			4	2¹		6†	7	12¹			11		3	1	5		9	8¹	10									3–1(0–0)8029	9
38. Aston Villa	26.3		2					7	4†			11¹		3	1	5		10	8	12	6			10					1–0(0–0)20,392	8
39. WBA	2.4		2		12			7				11		3	1	5		10	8	9†	6			4					0–2(0–1)12,144	8
40. C Palace*	4.4		2		6			7				11		3	1	5		9¹†	8		4			10	12				1–1(1–0)9613	9
41. Oldham	9.4		2		6			7				11¹		3	1	5		9	8	4†				10		12			1–5(1–2)6505	9
42. Swindon*	23.4		2		12		6	7				11		3	1	5		9	8	10¹†				4					1–0(1–0)6293	8
43. Millwll	30.4		2		6			7				11		3†	1	5		9	8	10				4		12			0–2(0–1)12,636	10
44. Shrewsbury*	2.5		2	3				7				11			1	5		9	6	10¹				8			4		1–1(0–1)7452	11
Apps(subs)/goals		17(0)0	42(0)2	42(1)3	19(3)2	20(4)1	35(1)5	44(0)7	46(5)1	27(2)5	15(2)3	6(3)0	32(7)8	39(2)0	27(0)0	30(3)6	1(0)0	1(1)0	22(0)5	11(1)2	12(0)0	1(0)0	7(0)0	6(1)0	6(0)0	8(1)0	1(0)0	7(0)0		

Final League Position: 11

SUNDERLAND

Roker Park Ground, Sunderland SR6 9SW.

Back row (left to right): John McPhail, David Corner, Gary Bennett, Iain Hesford, Nigel Saddington, Gordon Armstrong, Keith Bertschin. *Third row:* Jim Morrow (Youth Development Officer), George Burley, Eric Gates, Frank Gray, Reuben Agboola, Mark Proctor, John Kay, Chris McMenemy (Youth Coach), Steve Smelt (Physio). *Second row:* Paul Lemon, Paul Atkinson, Viv Busby (Chief Coach), Denis Smith (Manager), John Moore, Dale White. *Front row:* Gary Owers, Steve Doyle, David Buchanan, John Cornforth..

Stadium Capacity: 37,875.
Pitch Dimensions: 113 × 74 yds.
Telephone: 091–5140332, **Commercial dept:** 091–5672275, **Clubcall:** 0898–121140.
Chairman: R. S. Murray FCCA.
Directors: G. W. Hodgson FCA, G. Davidson FCA.
Manager: Denis Smith.
Post-War Managers: Bill Murray, Alan Brown, George Hardwick, Ian McColl, Alan Brown, Bob Stokoe, Jimmy Adamson, Billy Elliot, Ken Knighton, Alan Durban, Len Ashurst, Lawrie McMenemy (12).
Physio: S. Smelt.
General Manager/Secretary: G. Davidson FCA.
Commercial Manager: A. E. King.
Sponsors: Vaux Breweries.
Founded: 1879.
Turned Professional: 1886.
Nickname: The Rokerites.
Former Names: Sunderland and District Teachers' AFC 1879–81.
Former Grounds: Blue House Field 1879–1881, Ashbrook 1881–1883, Cooper Street 1883–1884, Abbs Field, Fulwell 1884–1886, Newcastle Road 1886–1889.
Record Attendance: 75,118 v Derby County, FA Cup 6th Round replay, 8 March 1933.
Record Victory: 11–1 v Fairfield, FA Cup 1st Round, 1894–94.
Record Defeat: 0–8 v West Ham United, Division 1, 19 October 1968 and v Watford, Division 1, 25 September 1982.
Most League Points: (3 for a win) 93, Division 3, 1987–88. (2 for a win) 61, Division 2, 1963–64.
Most League Goals: 109, Division 1, 1935–36.
Highest League Scorer in a Season: Dave Halliday, 43, Division 1, 1928–29.
Highest Total of League Goals: Charlie Buchan, 209, 1911–25.
Most League Appearances: Jim Montgomery, 537, 1962–77.
League History: 1890 Elected to Division 1, 1958–64 Division 2, 1964–70Division 1, 1970–76 Division 2, 1976–77 Division 1, 1977–80 Division 2, 1980–85 Division 1, 1985–87 Division 2, 1987–88 Division 1, 1988– Division 2.
Honours: Division 1 Champions 1891–92, 1892–93, 1894–95, 1901–02, 1912–13, 1935–36, runners-up 1893–94, 1897–98, 1900–01, 1922–23, 1934–35. Division 2 Champions 1975–76, runners-up 1963–64, 1979–80. Division 3 Champions 1987–88. FA Cup winners 1937, 1973, runners-up 1913. League Cup runners-up 1985.
Colours: Red and white striped shirts, black shorts, white socks. **Second strip:** Blue shirts, white shorts, blue socks.

SUNDERLAND – LEAGUE RECORD 1987–88

Match no/Opp/Date		Hardwick	Kay	Agboola	Bennett	MacPhail	Armstrong	Lemon	Proctor	Bertschin	Gates	Owers	Moore	Gray	Atkinson	Doyle	Buchanan	Hesford	Gabbiadini	Cornforth	Corner	Ord	Heathcote	McGuire	Pascoe	Carter	FT(HT)Att Lge po
1. Brentford	15.8	1	2	3	4	5	6	7	8	9^1	10†	11‡	12	14													1-0(0-0)7559
2. Bristol R*	22.8	1	2	3	4	5	6	7^1	8	9	10†	11‡	12	14													1-1(0-0)13,059
3. Doncaster	29.8	1	2	3	4	5	6	7^1	8	9†	10	11‡	12	14													2-0(1-0)2740
4. Mansfield*	31.8	1	2	3	4	5_2	6^1	7	8	9	10					11^1											4-1(0-1)13,994
5. Walsall	5.9	1	2	3	4	5	6	7‡		9^2	10†	11	12	14		8											2-2(1-1)6909
6. Bury*	12.9	1	2	3	4	5	6	7‡		9		11^1	12	14		8	10†										1-1(1-1)13,227
7. Gillingham	15.9		2	3	4	5	6	7		9	10	11				8	1										0-0(0-0)9184
8. Brighton	19.9		2	3	4	5_1	6‡	7†		9	10	11	14	12		8	1										1-3(0-2)8949
9. Chester*	26.9		2	3†	4	5		7		9	6	12	11			8		1	10								0-2(0-0)12,760
10. Fulham	29.9		2	3	4	5		7			6	12	14	11‡	8			1	10^2								2-0(1-0)6996
11. Aldershot*	3.10		2	3	4‡	5^1		7†		9	6	12	14	11	8			1	10^2								3-1(1-1)12,542
12. Wigan*	17.10		2	3	4‡	5				9^2	6	12	11	8				1	10^2	7							4-1(3-1)13,974
13. Blackpool	20.10		2	3		5^1_1		12		9†	6	14	11‡	8				1	10	7	4						2-0(0-0)8476
14. Bristol C	24.10		2	3		5		12		9	6^1	14	11‡	8				1	10	7†	4						1-0(1-0)15,109
15. York*	31.10		2	3		5				9^1	6	12	11†	8				1	10^1	7^2	4						4-2(3-1)19,314
16. Notts Co	3.11		2	3‡		5^1		12	8	9	6	14	11					1	10	7†	4						1-2(1-1)8854
17. Southend*	7.11		2			5		8	12	9^4	6	3	11^2					1	10^1	7†		4‡	14				7-0(3-0)15,754
18. Grimsby*	21.11		2			5		7^1	12	14	9	6†	3	11				1	10‡			4					1-1(0-1)18,197
19. Chesterfield	28.11		2	3		5_1		7†	12	10	9		6	11				1				4					1-1(1-0)5700
20. Port Vale*	12.12		2	3	4	5_1			7	12	9^1	6		11				1	10†								2-1(2-0)15,655
21. Nthampton	12.12		2	3	4	5		11	7^1		9	6						1	10^1								2-0(0-0)7279
22. Rotherham*	20.12		2	3	4	5		11	7	9^3	6							1	10	8							3-0(2-0)20,168
23. Chester	26.12		2	3	4	5^1		11	7^1		9†	6						1	10								2-1(2-0)6663
24. Preston*	28.12		2	3	4	5_1		11	7	9†		6‡	12	14				1	10^1								1-1(0-0)24,814
25. Doncaster*	1.1		2	3	4	5		11‡	7^2	12	9†		14	6				1	10^1								3-1(3-1)19,419
26. Bury	2.1		2	3	4	5		11	7	12	9^1	6						8^1	1	$10^†$							3-2(1-1)4883
27. Brighton*	16.1		2	3‡	4	5		11	7^1	12	9	6†		14				1	10								1-0(1-0)17,404
28. Gillingham*	30.1		2	3	4^1	5		11	7	12	9			6	8			1	10‡								2-1(2-0)16,195
29. Walsall*	6.2		2	3	4^1	5		11	7		9			6	8			1	10								1-1(0-1)18,311
30. Preston	13.2		2	3	4	5_1		11	7‡	$9^{1†}$			14	6	8			1	10	12							2-2(2-2)10,852
31. Brentford	20.2		2	3	4	5		11		10^1	9	7^1		12	6†	8		1									2-0(2-0)15,458
32. Bristol R	24.2		2	3	4	5		11			10	9	7		14	6‡	8†	1		12							0-4(0-1)4501
33. Aldershot	27.2		2	3	4	5_1		11	12		9	7			6‡			1	10^1	8†		14					2-3(2-2)5010
34. Fulham*	1.3		2	3	4	5		11^1	8		9	7		6				1	10^1								2-0(2-0)11,379
35. Blackpool*	5.3		2	3	4	5		11^1	8	14	$9^{1‡}$	7		6†				1	10	12							2-2(2-1)15,513
36. Wigan	12.3		2	3	4	5		11	8	12	9^1	7		6				1	10^1								2-2(0-1)6949
37. Notts Co*	19.3		2	3	4	5			8		9	7	12		11	6		1	10††								1-1(1-0)24,071
38. York	26.3		2	3	4	5		11			9	7‡		14		6		1	10					8†	12^1		1-2(0-1)8878
39. Grimsby	2.4		2	3†	4	5		11	8‡		9	7		14				1	10^1	12					6		1-0(1-0)7001
40. Chesterfield*	4.4		2		4	5		11	$7^{1†}$		9	6		3				1	10^1			12			8^1		3-2(2-2)21,886
41. Southend	9.4		2		4	5_1		11	7^1		9	6		3				1	$10^{†‡}$			12			8^1		4-1(3-1)8109
42. Bristol C*	23.4		2			5		11†	7	14	9^1	6		3	12				10		4			8		1	0-1(0-1)18,225
43. Mansfield	26.4		2		4	5		11	7		9^2			3	6			1	10^1						8^1		4-0(2-0)6930
44. Port Vale	30.4		2	12	4‡	5		11	7		9^1			3	6			1	10					8			1-0(0-0)7569
45. Nthampton*	2.5		2		4	5_1		11^1	7		9^1			3	6			1	10					8			3-1(1-2)29,454
46. Rotherham	7.5		2		4	5_1		11	7†	14^1	9			3	6			1	10^2			12‡		8			4-1(2-0)9374

Appearances/goals: Hardwick 6(0)0, Kay 46(0)0, Agboola 37(1)0, Bennett 38(0)2, MacPhail 46(0)5, Armstrong 35(6)9, Lemon 40(0)0, Proctor 14(1)5, Bertschin 42(0)19, Gates 37(0)4, Owers 09(1)0, Moore 12(22)0, Gray 21(0)3, Atkinson 3(1)1, Doyle 1(0)0, Buchanan 39(0)0, Hesford 35(0)21, Gabbiadini 8(4)2, Cornforth 40(0)0, Corner 4(4)0, Ord 0(1)0, Heathcote 1(0)0, McGuire 8(1)0, Pascoe 1(0)0, Carter 1(0)0

Final League Position: 1

Own goal: Valentine, match 26.

DIVISION 3

SWANSEA CITY

Vetch Field, Swansea SA1 3SU.

Back row
(left to right):
Joe Allon
Phil Williams
Chris Harrison
Gary Emmanuel
Keri Andrews
Alan Davies
Middle row:
Paul Raynor
David Hough
Alan Knill
Mike Hughes
Andrew Melville
Jason Ball
Ian Love
Ron Watson
Front row:
Sean McCarthy
Terry Yorath
(Manager)
Dudley Lewis
Tommy Hutchinson
Colin Pascoe

Stadium Capacity: 26,237.
Pitch Dimensions: 112 × 74 yds.
Telephone: 0792–51311.
Chairman: D. J. Sharpe.
Directors: D. G. Hammond, M. Griffiths.
Manager: Terry Yorath.
Post-War Managers: Bill McCandless, Ron Burgess, Trevor Morris, Glyn Davies, Bill Lucas, Roy Bentley, Harry Griffiths, John Toshack, Doug Livermore, John Toshack, Colin Appleton, John Bond (13).
Player–Coach: Tommy Hutchison.
Physio: Ken Davey.
Secretary: George Taylor.
Commercial Manager: Peter Jones.
Founded: 1900.
Turned Professional: 1912.
Nickname: The Swans.
Former Names: Swansea Town 1900–1970.
Former Grounds: None.
Record Attendance: 32,796 v Arsenal, FA Cup 4th Round, 17 February 1968.
Record Victory: 12–0 v Sliema Wanderers, European Cup-winners' Cup 1st Round 1st leg, 15 September 1982.
Record Defeat: 1–8 v Fulham, Division 2, 22 January 1938.
Most League Points: (3 for a win) 70, Division 4, 1987–88. (2 for a win) 62, Division 3(S), 1948–49.
Most League Goals: 90, Division 2, 1956–57.
Highest League Scorer in a Season: Cyril Pearce, 35, Division 2, 1931–32.
Highest Total of League Goals: Ivor Allchurch, 166, 1949–58, 1965–68.
Most League Appearances: Wilfred Milne, 585, 1919–37.
League History: 1920 Founder Members of Division 3, 1921–25 Division 3(S), 1925–47 Division 2, 1947–49 Division 3(S), 1949–65 Division 2, 1967–70 Division 3, 1970–73 Division 2, 1973–78 Division 3, 1978–79 Division 3, 1979–81 Division 2, 1981–83 Division 1, 1983–84 Division 2, 1984–86 Division 3, 1986–88 Division 4, 1988– Division 3.
Honours: Division 3(S) Champions 1924–25, 1948–49. Welsh Cup winners 1913, 1932, 1950, 1961, 1966, 1981, 1982, 1983, runners-up 8 times.
Colours: All white. **Second strip:** All red.

SWANSEA CITY – LEAGUE RECORD 1987–88

Match no/Opp/Date		Hughes	Harrison	Coleman	Melville	Knill	Davies	Williams	McCarthy	Raynor	Pascoe	Hutchison	Hough	Allon	Andrews	D'Auria	Emmanuel	Lewis D.	Marsh	Lewis J.	James	Davey	Love	Guthrie	Bodak	FT(HT)Att	Lge pos
1. Stockport	15.8	1	2†	3	4	5	6	7	8¹	9¹	10	11‡	12	14												2-0(0-0)2482	—
2. Exeter*	22.8	1		3	4	5	6	7	8	9	10		2	11†	12											0-2(0-1)5557	12
3. Cardiff	29.8	1		3†	4	5	6	7	12	9	10		2	8	11											0-1(0-0)6010	19
4. Hartlepool*	31.8	1		3	4	5	6	7‡	12¹	9	10¹		2	8†	11	14										2-1(0-1)3569	—
5. Burnley	5.9	1	2	3	4	5	6	7	8	9	10		12	11†												0-1(0-0)4778	18
6. Hereford*	12.9	1	2	3	4	5	6	7	8¹	9	10²						11									3-0(0-0)3794	8
7. Halifax	16.9	1	2	3†	4	5	6	7	8	9¹	10		12		14		11‡									1-3(0-2)1236	—
8. Scarboro	19.9	1	2		4	5	7	3	8	9‡	10		12	14	11†	6										0-2(0-0)3033	18
9. Crewe*	26.9	1	2	3	4	5	7¹	12	8	10¹			9†			6	11									2-4(0-2)3832	21
10. Colchester	29.9	1	2¹	3	4	5	7	8‡		9	10		12		14	6	11†									1-2(0-1)1140	—
11. Cambridge*	3.10	1	2	3	4	5	6	7		9¹		8†		12			11									1-1(0-1)3378	21
12. Wrexham*	10.10	1	2₁	3	4	5	7			10		8	9¹	11		6										2-1(0-0)3741	21
13. Newport*	17.10	1	2‡	3	4	5	8			10	7	12	9¹	11†	14	6										1-2(0-1)3739	20
14. Tranmere	20.10	1		3	4	5	7		8¹†	10	11	2	9¹	12		6										2-1(2-0)2210	—
15. Orient*	24.10	1		3	4	5	7¹		8	10¹		2	9¹	11†	12	6										3-0(1-0)3895	17
16. Bolton	31.10	1		3	4	5	7	12	8	10		2	9¹†			6	11									1-1(1-0)4607	17
17. Wolves*	3.11	1		3	4	5	7	12	8†	10		2	9¹			6	11									1-2(0-1)5293	—
18. Rochdale	7.11	1		3	4	5	7	12¹	8	10²		2	9			6†	11									3-2(0-0)1243	16
19. Peterboro*	21.11	1		3	4¹	5	7		8	10¹		2	9			6	11†									2-1(1-1)4033	13
20. Scunthorpe	28.11	1		3	4	5	7		8¹	10		2	9¹			6	11									2-1(0-0)2309	11
21. Carlisle*	12.12	1		3	4¹	5	7		8	10		2	9²	11		6										3-1(1-0)3876	9
22. Darlington	19.12	1	12	3†	4	5	7		8	10		2	9			6	11									0-2(0-1)1726	11
23. Crewe	26.12	1	2	3	4¹	5	7		8†	10¹			9	12		6	11									2-2(0-1)2976	11
24. Torquay*	28.12	1	2	3	4	5	7		12	10¹			9	8		6	11†									1-1(0-0)6108	13
25. Cardiff*	1.1	1	2	12	4	5	7		8¹	10			9¹	11		6			3†							2-2(0-0)10,300	14
26. Hereford	2.1	1	2	3	4	5	7		8	10			9	11		6										0-0(0-0)3504	13
27. Exeter	9.1	1	2	3	4	5	7	12	8	10			9¹	11†		6										1-3(0-1)2225	13
28. Scarboro*	16.1	1	2			5	7		8¹	10¹							11¹		4	3	6	9				3-0(2-0)4366	10
29. Halifax*	23.1	1	2			5	7†		8	10¹			12				11		4	3	6	9				1-1(1-1)5064	10
30. Hartlepool	30.1	1	2	11		5	7						12						4	3	6¹	9†	10¹			2-0(2-0)2092	9
31. Burnley*	6.2	1	2	11		5	7		8	·			10	11‡					4	3†	6	9	12			0-0(0-0)3498	9
32. Stockport*	19.2	1	2	14¹		5	7	12	10	8			9†				11‡		4	3	6					1-1(0-1)4405	—
33. Cambridge	27.2		2¹			5	7	12	8	10			9‡	12					4	3	6†		11²	1		3-0(2-0)2030	11
34. Colchester*	1.3		2			5	7	9†	8	10				12					4	3	6		11¹	1		1-2(0-0)4011	—
35. Newport	5.3		2	14	5‡		7	12¹	8	10¹							9		4	3	6		11†	1		2-1(0-1)2235	11
36. Wrexham	12.3		2			5	7	9	8	10									4	3	6¹		11¹	1		2-1(1-0)1916	9
37. Bolton*	19.3		2	12		5	7	9†	8	10									4	3	6		11¹	1		1-0(0-0)3980	—
38. Orient	26.3		2	12		5	7	9†	8	10				14					4	3	6		11‡	1	10	0-3(0-1)3390	10
39. Torquay	29.3		2			5	7¹	9	8										4	3	6		11	1	10	0-0(0-0)3037	—
40. Rochdale*	2.4		2	12		5	7	9‡	8†					14					4	3	6		11	1	10	0-3(0-1)5367	6
41. Peterboro	4.4		2			5	7		8				9¹	12					4	3	6		11	1	10†	1-0(0-0)3360	5
42. Tranmere*	9.4		2	14		5	7	12	8				9						4	3‡	6₁		11†	1	10	1-2(0-2)4104	7
43. Wolves	23.4			3	4	5	7	12	8				9†	14			10‡		2		6		11	1		0-2(0-1)12,344	7
44. Scunthorpe*	30.4		2	3	4	5	6	9¹	8	11							12				10		7†	1		1-1(1-0)3482	10
45. Carlisle	2.5		2	3	4	5¹	7	9‡	8	11							12				6		10	1		1-0(1-0)1854	7
46. Darlington*	7.5		2	3	4	5	7¹	9¹	10†	8							12				6		11	1		3-0(1-0)4071	6

Final League Position: 6

Apps(subs)/goals: 22(0)/0 · 34(1)/3 · 29(1)/0 · 46(0)/1 · 42(0)/3 · 13(5)/1 · 17(8)/8 · 43(1)/7 · 44(0)/13 · 6(1)/0 · 14(6)/0 · 26(6)/12 · 18(6)/1 · 0(4)/0 · 22(5)/0 · 18(0)/0 · 1(0)/0 · 25(0)/0 · 19(0)/3 · 4(0)/0 · 11(1)/6 · 14(0)/0 · 9(0)/0

DIVISION 2

SWINDON TOWN

County Ground, Swindon, Wiltshire SN1 2ED.

Back row (left to right): Tim Parkin, Jimmy Quinn, Fraser Digby, Chris Kamara, Nicky Hammond, Charlie Henry, Colin Calderwood. *Middle row:* Andy Rowland (Coach), Dave Hockaday, Terry Merriman, Dave Bamber, Tom Gittens, John Kelly, Steve White, Steve Foley, Chris Ramsey, Kevin Morris (Physio). *Front row:* Alan McLoughlin, Brian Wade, Peter Coyne, Lou Macari (Manager), John Trollope (Ass. Manager), Steve Berry, Leigh Barnard, Mark Jones.

Stadium Capacity: 20,200.
Pitch Dimensions: 114 × 72 yds.
Telephone: 0793–642984, **Fax:** 642984.
Chairman: B. Hillier.
Vice-Chairman: G. Herbert.
Directors: T. J. R. Kearsey, L. Smart, N. Arkell, R. Mattick, C. J. Green, C. Howard, D. Alderton.
Manager: Lou Macari.
Post-War Managers: Louis Page, Maurice Lindley, Bert Head, Danny Williams, Fred Ford, Dave Mackay, Les Allen, Danny Williams, Bob Smith, John Trollope, Ken Beamish (11).
Assistant Manager: John Tollope.
Physio: Kevin Morris.
Secretary: D. G. King.
Commercial Manager: Doug Buswell.
Sponsors: Lowndes Lambert Group.
Founded: 1881.
Turned Professional: 1894.
Nickname: The Robins.
Former Names: None.
Former Grounds: The Croft 1881–96.
Record Attendance: 32,000 v Arsenal, FA cup 3rd Round, 15 Jan 1972.
Record Victory: 10–1 v Farnham United Breweries, FA Cup 1st Round, 28 November 1925.
Record Defeat: 1–10 v Manchester City, FA Cup 4th Round replay, 25 January 1930.
Most League Points: (3 for a win) 102, Division 4, 1985–86 (League record), (2 for a win) 64, Division 3, 1968–69.
Most League Goals: 100, Division 3(S), 1926–27.
Highest League Scorer in a Season: Harry Morris, 47,Division 3(S), 1926–27.
Highest Total of League Goals: Harry Morris, 216, 1926–33.
Most League Appearances: John Trollope, 770, 1960–80.
League History: 1920 Founder Members of Division 3, 1921–58 Division 3 (S), 1958–63 Division 3, 1963–65 Division 2, 1965–69 Division 3, 1969–74 Division 2, 1974–82 Division 2, 1982–86 Division 4, 1986–87 Division 3, 1987– Division 2.
Honours: Division 3 runners-up 1962–63, 1968–69. Division 4 Champions 1985–86 (League record 102 points). League Cup winners 1969. Anglo–Italian Cup winners 1970.
Colours: Red shirts with white pinstripe, white shorts, red socks. **Second strip:** Yellow shirts, blue shorts, yellow socks.

SWINDON TOWN – LEAGUE RECORD 1987–88

Match no/Opp/Date		Digby	Hockaday	King	Coyne	Parkin	Calderwood	Gittens	Kelly	Bamber	Quinn	Kamara	Henry	O'Regan	Berry	Barnard	Foley	White	Barnes	Hammond	Flowers	Wade	Crichton	McLoughlin	Bodin	Weggette	T(HT)Att Lge pos
1. Bradford	15.8	1	2	3	4	5	6	7	8+	9	10	11	12														0–2(0–0)10,553 —
2. Sheff Utd*	22.8	1			5	6¹		8	7	9¹	4		2	10	11												2–0(2–0)8637 13
3. WBA	29.8	1	2	3	12	5	6	8¹	7	9¹	4			10+	11												2–1(1–1)7503 8
4. Hull*	31.8	1	2	3	12	5	6		7	9	4		8+	11	10												0–0(0–0)9600 —
5. Middlesbro	5.9	1	2	3		5	6		7¹	9¹	4		8		11¹	10											3–2(2–1)9342 —
6. Birmingham*	12.9	1	2	3+	12	5	6		14	7	9	4		8‡	11	10											0–2(0–0)9128 9
7. Barnsley	15.9	1	2	3		5	6		12	7¹	9‡	4	14	8	11	10+											1–0(0–0)7773 —
8. Ipswich	19.9	1	2	3		5	6		12	7	9¹	4		8+	11¹	10											2–3(1–3)10,460 7
9. Reading*	26.9	1	2	3		5¹	6+	12		7	9₁	4²	8‡		11	10	14										4–0(2–0)10,073 5
10. Shrewsbury*	29.9	1	2	3		5	6	12		7	9¹	4	8+		11	10											1–1(0–0)8261 —
11. Millwall	3.10	1	2	3		5	6			7	12₁	4	9	8+	11	10¹											2–2(0–1)7018 5
12. Oldham*	10.10	1	2	3+		5	6		12	7¹	9	4			11	10	8¹										2–0(0–0)8160 4
13. Stoke*	20.10	1	2	3+		5‡	6			7	9¹	4	14		12	10	8²	11									3–0(1–0)9160 —
14. C Palace	24.10	1	2	3		5	6	9		7			12	4	10+		8¹	11									1–2(1–1)9077 7
15. Man City*	31.10		2	3		5	6			7¹	9‡		14	12	4	10¹	8+	11¹	1								3–4(1–2)11,536 7
16. Leicester	7.11		2	3		5	6			7	9₁	8			4	10		11¹	1								2–3(1–0)8346 11
17. Plymouth*	14.11		2	3		5	6			7	9‡	4		12	8	10+	14	11¹	1								1–1(1–1)9616 12
18. Leeds	21.11		2	3+	4		6	5		7	9		12	10	8			11²	1›								2–4(1–3)15,457 13
19. Bournemouth*	28.11		2	3			6	5		8	9¹			4		10	11²	7¹	1								4–2(2–1)7934 12
20. Huddersfield*	1.12		2	3			6	5		8	9¹	4				10²	11	7¹	1								4–1(2–0)6963 —
21. Aston Villa	5.12		2	3		12	6	5		8	9+₁	4				10‡	11	7	1	14							1–2(0–0)16,127 12
22. Sheff Utd	20.12		2	3			6	5		8	9	4				10	11+	7	1	12							0–1(0–0)7248 —
23. Reading	26.12		2	3		11	6	5		8	9¹	4				10		7			1						1–0(0–0)8939 12
24. Ipswich*	28.12		2	3¹		11	6	5		8¹	9¹	4				10		7			1						4–2(2–0)12,429 11
25. WBA*	1.1		2	3		11	6	5		8+	9‡	4	14			10	12²	7			1›						2–0(0–0)12,155 11
26. Birmingham	2.1		2	3		11	6	5		8+	9	4‡		14		10	12	7¹			1						1–1(0–0)7829 11
27. Middlesbro*	6.2	1	2	3		5	6	8		7¹	9+	4		11		10	12										1–1(1–1)9941 11
28. Huddersfield	13.2	1	2	3		5	6	8		7²	9	4		11¹			10										3–0(1–0)5458 11
29. Shrewsbury	20.2	1	2	3+		5	6	8		7¹	9	4		11		10	12										1–2(1–2)5649 11
30. Millwall*	27.2	1	2	3		5		6		7	9+		12	8		4	10	11									0–1(0–1)9570 12
31. Oldham	12.3	1	2	3		5		7			10¹	14¹	9			6‡	8+		12		4	11¹					3–4(1–0)5193 13
32. Barnsley*	15.3	1	2	3		5				9₁		6	4			10²	7			8	11						3–0(1–0)7558 —
33. Man City	19.3	1	2	3		5				7¹	10	4	9			8	6	12				11+					1–1(0–0)17,022 12
34. C Palace*	27.3	1	2	3		5¹		6		8	9		4			11	10¹							7			2–2(0–0)12,915 —
35. Bradford*	30.3	1	2	3		5		6		8¹	9		12	4		10					11+			7¹			2–2(0–0)8203 12
36. Leicester*	2.4	1	2	3		5		6		7	9²		4			10		8¹						11			3–2(1–1)9450 10
37. Plymouth	4.4	1	2	3		5		4		7	10		9			8	12	11						6+			0–1(0–1)13,299 10
38. Blackburn*	9.4	1	2	3		5		6			9		4+			10	8	7¹			12			11			1–2(1–0)9373 12
39. Hull	12.4		2	3‡		5+	12	8		7²	9¹₁					10		11	1		4	14	6				4–1(2–1)4583 —
40. Stoke	23.4	1	2	3		5		6		7	9					10	12	8			4			11+			0–1(0–1)6293 12
41. Blackburn	25.4	1	2	3		5	4	6		9						10	8	7			11						0–0(0–0)13,563 —
42. Leeds*	30.4	1	2	3+		5	6	8		7	9¹					10		11			4	12					1–2(1–2)8299 12
43. Bournemouth	2.5	1	2	3		5	4	6+		7	9			11		10	12	8									0–2(0–2)5212 12
44. Aston Villa*	7.5	1	2	3		5	6	8		7	9			4		10	11										0–0(0–0)10,959 12

Apps(subs)/goals: 31(0)0, 43(0)1, 44(0)0, 24(3)0, 39(1)2, 3(3)1, 27(2)0, 3(6)1, 41(0)13, 41(1)21, 25(0)2, 5(1)0, 23(3)1, 30(0)0, 16(1)2, 35(0)4, 17(8)11, 26(2)10, 40(0)0, 5(0)0, 0(3)0, 7(0)10, 7(0)1, 3(2)1, 7(0)1

Final League Position: 12

Own goals: Cranson, match 24.

TORQUAY UNITED

DIVISION 4

Plainmoor Ground, Torquay, Devon TQ1 3PS.

Back row (left to right): Alan Morris (Physio), Darren Cann, Jim McNichol, David Cole, Kenny Allen, John Impey, Derek Dawkins, Tom Kelly, John James (Reserve Coach). *Front row:* Chris Myers, Gerry Nardiello, Mark Loram, Cyril Knowles (Manager), Sean Haslegrave, Mark Gardiner, Paul Dobson.

Stadium Capacity: 4999.
Pitch Dimensions: 112 × 74 yds.
Telephone: 0803–38666.
Chairman: L. W. Pope.
Vice-Chairman: G. J. Harvey.
Directors: W. W. Rogers, R. Daniel, F. M. Mosley TD, R. Harvey, R. Mildon, M. Benney.
Manager: Cyril Knowles.
Post-War Managers: Jack Butler, John McNeil, Bob John, Alex Massie, Eric Webber, Frank O'Farrell, Allan Brown, Jack Edwards, Malcolm Musgrove, Frank O'Farrell, Mike Green, Frank O'Farrell, Bruce Rioch, David Webb, Stuart Morgan (15).
Assistant Manager: S. Haslegrave.
Physio: A. Morris.
Secretary: D. Turner.
Founded: 1898.
Turned Professional: 1921.
Nickname: The Gulls.
Former Names: Torquay Town 1910–1921.
Former Grounds: Teignmouth Road 1898–1901, Torquay Recreation Ground 1901–1905, Cricket Field Road 1905–07, Torquay Cricket Ground 1907–10.
Record Attendance: 21,908 v Huddersfield Town, FA Cup 4th Round, 29 Jan 1955.
Record Victory: 9–0 v Swindon Town, Division 3 (S), 8 March 1952.
Record Defeat: 2–10 v Fulham, Division 3(S), 7 September, 1931 and v Luton Town, Division 3 (S), 2 September 1933.
Most League Points: (3 for a win) 77, Division 4, 1987–88. (2 for a win) 60, Division 4, 1959–60.
Most League Goals: 89, Division 3(S), 1956–57.
Highest League Scorer in a Season: Sammy Collins, 40, Division 3 (S), 1955–56.
Highest Total of League Goals: Sammy Collins, 204, 1948–58.
Most League Appearances: Dennis Lewis, 443, 1947–59.
League History: 1927 Elected to Division 3, 1958–60 Division 4, 1960–62Division 3, 1962–66 Division 4, 1966–72 Division 3, 1972– Division 4.
Honours: Division 3(S) runners-up 1956–57.
Colours: All white with blue and yellow trim. **Second strip:** All yellow.

TORQUAY UNITED – LEAGUE RECORD 1987–88

Match no/Opp/Date		Allen	McVitchol	Kelley	Haslegrave	Cole	Impey	Gardiner	Lloyd	McLoughlin	Loram	Dobson	Musker	Nardiello	Smith	Pearce	Cann	Dawkins	Riley	Sharpe	Walker	Caldwell	Wright	Milton	Gibbins	FT(HT)Att	Lge pos
1. Wrexham*	15.8	1	2	3	4†	5^1	6	7	8	9^2	10‡	11^3	12	14												6–1(2–1)1731	—
2. Colchester	21.8	1	2	3	4	5	6	7	8	9†	10	11^1	12													1–0(0–0)1372	—
3. Orient*	29.8	1	2	3	4	5	6‡	7	8	9†	10	11^1	12		14											1–1(0–0)2705	2
4. Darlington	31.8	1	2	3	4	5	6	7	8	9‡	10^1	11†	12			14										1–1(0–0)2251	—
5. Cambridge*	5.9	1	2†	3	4	5		7	8	9	10	11	12			14	6‡									0–1(0–0)2676	7
6. Newport	12.9	1	2†	3	4	5	6	14	8	12	10^1‡	11							7	9						1–3(1–2)1368	10
7. Rochdale*	15.9	1	2‡	3	4	5^1			8	12^1	10	11^2	6				14		7†	9^1						5–0(3–0)1895	—
8. Bolton*	19.9	1	2	3	4	5	6		8	12	10^1‡	11_1	14						7‡	9						2–1(2–0)2211	4
9. Wolves	26.9	1	2†	3	4	5^1	6	14	8	10‡	11	12^1							7	9						2–1(0–0)7349	2
10. Scarboro*	29.9	1	2	3	4	5	6	12	8		10†	11	7‡				14			9						0–1(0–0)3255	—
11. Exeter	3.10	1	2^1		4	5	6	7	8		10	11					3		9†	12						1–0(1–0)6281	2
12. Crewe*	10.10	1	2	3†	4	5	6	12	8		10^1	11					7			9						1–0(1–0)2499	2
13. Hartlepool	17.10	1	2	3	4	5	6	12	8		10†	11	14				7		9‡							0–0(0–0)2870	2
14. Cardiff	20.10	1	2	3	4	5	6	10	8			11	12				7^1		9†							1–2(1–0)3503	—
15. Burnley*	24.10	1	2	3	4	5	6	9	8		10†	11				12^1	7									1–3(0–1)2740	7
16. Peterboro	31.10	1	2		4	5		9	8		10^1	11^1‡	6	12			3		7							2–0(0–0)3500	3
17. Tranmere*	3.11	1	2		4	5	6	9‡	8		10	11^1‡	7	12			3		14							1–0(1–0)2512	—
18. Stockport	6.11	1	2†		4	5	6	7	8		10^1	11					3		7		9					1–2(0–1)1697	—
19. Hereford*	21.11	1	2		4	5		3‡	8		10	11				6†	7		14		9^1	12				1–0(1–0)2305	4
20. Carlisle	28.11	1	2^1		4	5			8^1		10	11^1				3	7				9	6				3–3(2–3)2017	4
21. Halifax*	12.12	1	2		4	5	6		8		10^1	11	9			3	7									1–2(1–1)2422	5
22. Scunthorpe	18.12	1	2	3	4	5^1	6		8		10	11^2	9				7									3–2(3–1)2261	—
23. Swansea	28.12	1	2	3†	4‡	5	6	14	8		10		11			12	7^1				9					1–1(0–0)6108	6
24. Orient	1.1	1	2	3	4	5	6	12	8		10		11			14	7†				9^2‡					2–0(1–0)4839	6
25. Bolton	16.1	1	2	3	4	5	6	12^1	8		10		11	9^1†			7									2–1(1–1)5993	4
26. Rochdale	26.1	1	2	3	4	5		6	8^1		10		11	12			7				9†					1–1(1–0)1281	—
27. Cambridge	6.2	1	2	3	4‡	5		14	8		10†		11	12		6	7				9					0–1(0–0)1948	7
28. Wrexham	20.2	1	2	3	12	5^1			8		10	11_1	4			6†	7				9					3–2(2–0)1488	8
29. Wolves*	23.2	1	2	3		5			8		10	11	4			6	7									0–0(0–0)3803	—
30. Exeter*	27.2	1	2^1	3	12	5			8		14	11	4†			6	7	10‡								1–1(0–0)3383	8
31. Scarboro	2.3	1	2	3		5		9	8		10^1	11^1‡	4			6	7	12								2–1(1–0)2182	—
32. Hartlepool*	5.3	1	2	3		5	6	12	8		10	11				6^1	7				9†	4				1–1(0–2)2857	7
33. Crewe	11.3	1	2	3	7	5	6		8		10	11					9					4^1				1–0(1–0)1858	—
34. Peterboro*	19.3	1	2	3		5	6		8		10	11†					7	12			9	4				0–0(0–0)2544	6
35. Swansea*	29.3	1	2	3	12	5	6		8		10‡	14				4†				9	7		11			0–1(0–0)3037	—
36. Stockport*	2.4	1	2^1	3		5	6	14	8		10†					4	12		7	9^1‡			11^1			3–0(1–0)2919	5
37. Hereford	4.4	1	2	3		5	6	14	8		10					4†	12	7‡		9			11			0–0(0–0)2425	6
38. Cardiff*	9.4	1	2^1	3		5	6		8		10					4†	12	7_1		9			11			2–0(2–0)3082	5
39. Colchester*	15.4	1	2†	3		5	6		8		10‡	14				4	12	7		9			11			0–0(0–0)3508	—
40. Newport*	19.4	1	2^1			5	6	3	8		10‡	14^2				4†	12	7^2		9			11^1			6–1(2–1)3416	—
41. Tranmere	22.4	1	2	3	4^1	5			8		10†	12					7	14		9‡			11			1–1(0–0)6189	—
42. Darlington*	27.4	1	2	3		5			8		10†	12					4	7		9			11			0–0(0–0)3939	—
43. Carlisle*	30.4	1	2	3		5	6		8		12	10_1					4	7		9†			11			1–0(1–0)3537	3
44. Halifax	2.5	1	2	3	4†	5	6^1		8		12	10^1	14				7^1			9‡			11			3–2(1–1)1218	3
45. Burnley	4.5	1	2	3	4†	5		6†	8		14	10‡					7	12		9			11			0–1(0–0)5075	—
46. Scunthorpe*	7.5	1	2	3		5	6†		8		12	10_1					4	7		9			11			1–2(0–1)4989	5

Final League Position: 5

Apps(subs)/goals:
Allen 46(0)/0 · McVitchol 46(0)/6 · Kelley 38(0)/0 · Haslegrave 31(3)/1 · Cole 40(0)/5 · Impey 34(0)/1 · Gardiner 15(12)/1 · Lloyd 46(0)/2 · McLoughlin 5(3)/3 · Loram 40(5)/8 · Dobson 33(15)/22 · Musker 14(7)/0 · Nardiello 2(7)/1 · Smith 0(0)/0 · Pearce 20(2)/2 · Cann 30(8)/3 · Dawkins 9(5)/3 · Riley 5(0)/0 · Sharpe 24(0)/4 · Walker 41(0)/0 · Caldwell 4(0)/1 · Wright 12(0)/2

TOTTENHAM HOTSPUR

748 High Road, London N17 0AP.

Back row (left to right): Steve Hodge, Chris Fairclough, Ray Clemence, Chris Waddle, Tony Parks, Mitchell Thomas, Gary Stevens. *Middle row:* Danny Thomas, Nico Claesen, Ossie Ardiles, John Chiedozie, Chris Hughton, Doug Livermore (Reserves Manager). *Front row:* Alan Harris (First Team Coach), Clive Allen, Johnny Metgood, Terry Venables (Manager), Gary Mabutt (Captain), Paul Allen, John Sheridan (Physio).

Stadium Capacity: 48,200.
Pitch Dimensions: 110 × 73 yds.
Telephone: 01–808 8080, **Commercial dept:** 01–808 0281, **Recorded information:** 01–808 1020.
Chairman: I. A. Scholar.
Vice-Chairman: D. A. Alexiou.
Directors: F. P. Sinclair, P. A. Bobroff, A. G. Berry. (D. R. Peter, plc only).
Manager: Terry Venables.
Post-War Managers: Joe Hulme, Arthur Rowe, Jimmy Anderson, Bill Nicholson, Terry Neill, Keith Burkinshaw, Peter Shreeve, David Pleat (8).
Assistant Manager: Alan Harris.
Physio: J. M. Sheridan.
Secretary: Peter Barnes.
Commercial Manager: M. Rollo.
Sponsors: Holsten.
Founded: 1882.
Turned Professional: 1895.
Nickname: Spurs.
Former Names: Hotspur Football Club 1882–85.
Former Grounds: Tottenham Marshes 1882–85, Northumberland Park 1885–1898.
Record Attendance: 75,038 v Sunderland, FA Cup 6th Round, 5 March 1938.
Record Victory: 13–2 v Crewe Alex, FA Cup 4th Round replay, 3 February 1960.
Record Defeat: 0–7 v Liverpool, Division 1, 2 September 1978.
Most League Points: (3 for a win) 77, Division 1, 1984–85. (2 for a win) 70, Division 2, 1919–20.
Most League Goals: 115, Division 1, 1960–61.
Highest League Scorer in a Season: Jimmy Greaves, 37, Division 1, 1962–63.
Highest Total of League Goals: Jimmy Greaves, 220, 1961–70.
Most League Appearances: Steve Perryman, 655, 1969–86.
League History: 1908 Elected to Division 2, 1909–15 Division 1, 1919–20 Division 2, 1920–28 Division 1, 1928–33 Division 2, 1933–35 Division 1, 1935–50 Division 2, 1950–77 Division 1, 1977–78 Division 2, 1978– Division 1.
Honours: Division 1 Champions 1950–51, 1960–61, runners-up 1921–22, 1951–52, 1956–57, 1962–63. Division 2 Champions 1919–20, 1949–50, runners-up 1908–09, 1932–33. FA Cup winners 1901 (as a Southern League club), 1921, 1961, 1962, 1967, 1981, 1982 (7 wins – a record held jointly with Aston Villa), runners-up 1987. League Cup winners 1971, 1973, runners-up 1982. European Cup-Winners' Cup winners 1963, runners-up 1982. UEFA Cup winners 1972, 1984, runners-up 1974.
Colours: White shirts, dark blue shorts, white socks. **Second strip:** All yellow.

TOTTENHAM HOTSPUR – LEAGUE RECORD 1987–88

Match no/Opp/Date		Clemence	Stevens	Thomas M	Gough	Fairclough	Mabbutt	Allen C	Allen P	Waddle	Hodge	Claesen	Ardiles	Metgod	Polston	Moran	Samways	Close	Howells	Parks	Hughton	Moncur	Ruddock	O'Shea	Statham	Fenwick	Mimms	Walsh	Gray	FT(HT)Att Lge pos
1. Coventry	15.8	1	2	3	4	5	6¹	7	8‡	9	10	11†	12	14																1–2(0–2)23,947 —
2. Newcastle*	19.8	1	2†	3	4	5	6	7¹	8	9¹	10¹	11	12																	3–1(3–0)26,261 —
3. Chelsea*	22.8	1		3	4	5	6	7	8	9	10	12¹	2	11†																1–0(0–0)37,079 4
4. Watford	29.8	1		3	4	5	6	7₁	8	9	10	11	2																	1–1(0–0)19,073 6
5. Oxford*	1.9	1		3†	4	5	6	7¹	8‡	9	10	11²	2	14	12															3–0(2–0)21,811 —
6. Everton	5.9	1		3	4	5	6	7	8	9	10†	11	2	12																0–0(0–0)32,389 4
7. Sthampton*	12.9	1	2†	3	4	5	6	7₁	8		10	11¹	9	12																2–1(1–1)24,728 2
8. West Ham	19.9	1	2	3	4	5¹		7‡	8		10	11	9	12		6†	14													1–0(1–0)27,750 2
9. Man Utd	26.9	1	2	3	4	5	6				10	11	9†	12		7‡	14													0–1(0–1)47,601 4
10. Sheff Wed*	3.10	1	2	3		5	6	7†	8¹		10	11¹	9			4	12													2–0(0–2)24,311 3
11. Norwich	10.10	1	2	3		5	6		8		10	11¹	9†			4	7	12												1–2(1–1)18,699 6
12. Arsenal*	18.10		2	3		5	6	12	8	9	10†	11¹	4			14	7‡		1											1–2(1–2)36,680 —
13. Nottm F	24.10		10	3		5	6	7	8			11	9			4‡	12	1		2†	14									0–3(0–1)23,543 8
14. Wimbledon*	31.10		10	3†		5	6	7	8			11	9			4‡	12	1		2	14									0–3(0–3)22,282 8
15. Portsmouth	4.11		2			5	6	12	8			11	9		7†	10		1		3	4									0–0(0–0)15,302 —
16. QPR*	14.11			2		5	6	7	8†		10	11†	9			12		1		3	4									1–1(1–1)28,113 8
17. Luton	21.11		2†	12		5	6	7	8‡		10		9			4	14	11	1	3										0–2(0–1)10,091 10
18. Liverpool*	28.11		11	3		5	6	7	8	9	10	12						1	2†		4‡	14								0–2(0–0)47,362 11
19. Charlton*	13.12		10	3		5	6	7	8	9		11				4		1	2											0–1(0–0)20,392 —
20. Derby	20.12		2	3		5	6‡	7¹	8†	9		11¹	10			12	4	1	14											2–1(0–1)17,593 —
21. Sthampton	26.12		6	3		5¹		7‡		9	8		10			11	4†	14	1	2				12						1–2(0–2)18,456 13
22. West Ham*	28.12		6†	3		5¹			8	9¹	4		10			7‡		14	11	1	2			12						2–1(1–0)39,456 11
23. Watford*	1.1			3		5	6	7¹	8	9	4		10			11¹†			12	1					2					2–1(0–0)25,235 9
24. Chelsea	2.1			3		5	6	7¹	8†	9	10					11			14	1	2			12	4					0–0(0–0)29,317 9
25. Coventry*	16.1			3		5	6	7²	8	9		10†				11‡			14	1	2			12	4					2–2(1–0)25,650 10
26. Newcastle	23.1			3		5	6	7	8	9		10				11†			12	1	2‡	14			4					0–2(0–1)24,616 10
27. Oxford	13.2			3		5	6	7	8	9		11				10			1					2	4					0–0(0–0)9906 10
28. Man Utd*	23.2			3		5	6	7¹	8	9		10												2	4	1	11			1–1(1–1)25,731 —
29. Sheff Wed	27.2			3		5	6	7¹	8¹		12¹					10				9				2	4	1	11†			3–0(1–0)18,046 9
30. Derby*	1.3			3		5	6	7	8			12				10				9†				2	4	1	11			0–0(0–0)15,986 —
31. Arsenal	6.3			3		5	6	7¹	8							10								2	4	1	11			1–2(0–1)37,143 —
32. Everton*	9.3			3		5¹	6	7	8			9				10†			12					2	4	1	11¹			2–1(1–0)18,662 —
33. Norwich*	12.3			3		5	6	7	8		12¹	9				10†								2	4	1	11			1–3(0–1)19,322 8
34. Wimbledon	19.3			3		5	6	7	8		12	9†				10								2	4	1	11			0–3(0–0)8616 8
35. Nottm F*	26.3			3		5	6		8		9	11‡		12	10	14								2	4†	1	7			1–1(0–0)25,306 8
36. Portsmouth*	2.4					5	6		8		9‡	11		12	10	14			3†					2	4	1	7			0–1(0–1)18,616 10
37. QPR	4.4					5	6		8	14	9†		3	12	10	11‡								2	4	1	7			0–2(0–0)14,738 10
38. Liverpool	23.4			3		5	6	12	8	9		4†				10‡								2		1	7			0–1(0–1)44,798 14
39. Charlton	2.5			3		5	6	7†	8	9	11¹	12		14		10‡								2	4	1				1–1(0–0)13,977 14
40. Luton*	4.5			3		5	6¹	7‡	8	9	11¹					10								2	4†	1			14	2–1(1–1)15,437 —

Final League Position: 13

Apps(subs)/goals: Clemence 11(0)0, Stevens 18(0)0, Thomas M 35(0)0, Gough 9(0)0, Fairclough 40(0)4, Mabbutt 37(0)2, Allen C 31(3)11, Allen P 39(0)3, Waddle 21(0)2, Hodge 25(1)3, Claesen 19(5)10, Ardiles 24(2)0, Metgod 5(7)0, Polston 9(4)1, Moran 21(5)0, Samways 25(5)0, Close 3(8)0, Howells 16(0)0, Parks 21(0)0, Hughton 32(0)0, Moncur 0(1)0, Ruddock 14(4)0, O'Shea 17(0)0, Statham 11(0)1, Fenwick 11(0)0

Own goals: Foster, match 35

DIVISION 4

TRANMERE ROVERS

Prenton Park, Prenton Road West, Birkenhead L42 9PN.

Back row (left to right): Phill Pullen, Steve Kearns, Shaun Garnett, Billy O'Rourke, Gary Williams, Eddie Bishop, Tony Thomas, Kenny Irons. *Middle row:* Warwick Rimmer (Youth Development Officer), Jimmy Harvey, Kenny McKenna, Steve Vickers, Jim Steel, Ronnie Moore, Mark Hughes, Dave Higgins, John Norman, Mark Brady, Kenny Jones (Trainer), Norman Wilson (Secretary). *Front row:* Mark McCarrick, John Morrissey, Steve Mungall, John King (Manager), Ian Muir, Dave Martindale, Eddie Murray.

Stadium Capacity: 10,000.
Pitch Dimensions: 112 × 71 yds.
Telephone: 051–608 3677/4194.
Chairman: P. R. Johnson.
Vice-Chairman: F. Corfe.
Directors: A. J. Adams BDS, G. E. H. Jones LLB, F. J. Williams, J. J. Holsgrove, FCA, G. A. Higham MSC, TECH LRSC, M Inst PI.
Manager: John King.
Post-War Managers: Ernie Blackburn, Noel Kelly, Peter Farrell, Walter Galbraith, Dave Russell, Jackie Wright, Ron Yeats, John King, Bryan Hamilton, Frank Worthington, Ronnie Moore (11).
Assistant Manager: Kenny Jones.
Physio: Alec McClellan.
Secretary: Norman Wilson FAAI.
Founded: 1883.
Turned Professional: 1912.
Nickname: The Rovers.
Former Names: Belmont AFC 1883–84.
Former Grounds: Steeles Field, 1883–85, South Road 1885–87, Old Prenton Park (Temple Road) 1887–1912.
Record Attendance: 24,424 v Stoke City, FA Cup 4th Round, 5 February 1972.
Record Victory: 13–4 v Oldham Athletic, Division 3 (N), 26 December 1935.
Record Defeat: 1–9 v Tottenham Hotspur, FA Cup 3rd Round replay, 14 January 1953.
Most League Points: (3 for a win) 75, Division 4, 1984–85. 60,Division 4 1964–65.
Most League Goals: 111, Division 3 (N), 1930–31.
Highest League Scorer in a Season: Bunny Bell, 35, Division 3(N), 1933–34
Highest Total of League Goals: Bunny Bell, 104, 1931–36.
Most League Appearances: Harold Bell, 595, 1946–64.
League History: 1921 Founder Members of Division 3 (N), 1938–39Division 2, 1946–58 Division 3 (N), 1958–61Division 3, 1961–67 Division 4, 1967–75 Division 3, 1975–76 Division 4, 1976–79 Division 3, 1979– Division 4.
Honours: Division 3(N) Champions 1937–38. Welsh Cup winners 1935, runners-up 1934.
Colours: All white. **Second strip:** Claret shirts with sky blue sleeves, sky blue shorts and socks.

TRANMERE ROVERS – LEAGUE RECORD 1987–88

Match no/Opp/Date	O'Rourke	McCarrick	Williams	Hughes	Thorpe	Vickers	Martindale	Craven	Mungall	Muir	Morrissey	McKenna	Muray	Aspinall	Malkin	Hall	Higgins	Harvey	Moore	Chamberlain	Steel	Nixon	Bishop	Garnett	Gorton	FT(HT)Att Lge pos
1. Scunthorpe 15.8	1	2	3	4	5	6	7†	8	9	10	11	12														0-3(0-0)2277 —
2. Hereford* 21.8	1	2	3	4	5	6		8	7	10	11†	9	12													0-1(0-0)2824 —
3. Stockport 28.8	1	2	3	4	5	6		8	7	10_1		9^1	11													2-1(1-1)2229 —
4. Exeter* 31.8	1	2^1	3	4	5	6		8†	7	10		9‡	11	12	14											2-1(1-0)3107 —
5. Scarboro 5.9	1		3	4	5	6		8	2	10	9	11†	7	12												0-2(0-0)2882 19
6. Burnley* 11.9	1		3	4†	5	6		8	2	10	7	9	11	12												0-1(0-0)4209 —
7. Crewe 15.9	1		3	8	4	5	6		2	10	7	9	11													0-0(0-0)1839 —
8. Halifax 18.9	1		3	8	4	5	6		2	10	7	9^1	11													1-2(0-0)1754 —
9. Cardiff* 25.9	1		3	8	4	5	6		2	10	7	9†	12	11												0-1(0-0)2543 —
10. Darlington 3.10	1		3	4	5	6	8	14		10	7†		12	11	$9‡$	2										0-0(0-0)1612 23
11. Rochdale* 9.10	1		3	4	5	6^1		12	2	10^3	7^1		11	9†		8^1										6-1(2-1)2303 —
12. Wolves 17.10	1		3	4‡	5	6		12	2	10	7		11	9†	14	8										0-3(0-3)6608 23
13. Swansea* 20.10	1		3	4	5	6			2	10	7	9	11^1			8										1-2(0-2)2210 24
14. Carlisle 24.10	1		3	5	4		6		2	10_1	7^1	9	11			8										2-3(1-0)2160 24
15. Cambridge* 30.10	1		3	11	5‡		6	4	12	2	10	7				14	8	$9†$								0-1(0-0)2240 —
16. Torquay 3.11	1		3	14	5‡		6	4	12	7	10		11			2	8†	9								0-1(0-1)2512 —
17. Wrexham* 6.11	1		3	5			6	4^1		7	10		11	8		2	9									1-0(0-0)3271 —
18. Hartlepool 21.11			3				6	4^1		7	10	12	11†			2	8	5	1	9						2-1(1-1)2507 22
19. Newport* 27.11			3				6	4		7	10^2		11^1			2	8	5	1	9^1						4-0(3-0)3252 —
20. Orient 12.12			3				6	4		7		12	10^1	11†		2	8	5	1	9						1-3(0-1)3684 22
21. Bolton* 15.12			3				6	4	14	7		12	10†	11‡		2	8^1	5	1	9^1						2-0(0-0)3064 —
22. Colchester* 18.12			3				6	4	14	7		12	10†	11‡		2	8	5	1	9						0-2(0-1)2642 —
23. Cardiff 26.12			3		12		6	4†		7	10	11				2	8	5	1	9						0-3(0-1)5233 22
24. Peterboro* 28.12			3	12			6	$4^1†$		11	10^1	7^1				2	8	5	1	9						3-1(0-0)3193 20
25. Stockport* 1.1			3^1	12			6	4†		11	10_1	7				2	8	5	1	9^1						4-0(2-0)3670 19
26. Burnley 2.1			3				6	4^1		11	10	7				2	8	5	1	9						1-1(1-0)7317 19
27. Hereford 9.1			3				6	4		11	10^1	7				2	8	5	1	9						1-1(0-1)2209 19
28. Halifax* 15.1			3				6	4		11	10^1	7^1				2	8	5	1	9						2-0(1-0)3317 —
29. Exeter 30.1			3				6	4		11	10^1	7				2	8	5	1	9						1-0(1-0)2261 17
30. Scarboro* 6.2			3				6	4		11	10^1	7	12			2	8	5†	1	9						1-0(0-0)4174 15
31. Peterboro 13.2			3				6	4		11	10^1	7				2	8	5	1	9						1-2(1-0)2230 16
32. Scunthorpe* 20.2			3	12			6	4		11†	10^1		7			2	8	5	1	9						1-3(1-1)2803 16
33. Darlington* 26.2	1		3				6	4		11	10	7	12			2	8^1	5†		9						2-1(1-0)2756 —
34. Bolton 1.3	1		3	14			6	4‡		11	10	7	12			2	8	5†		9						0-2(0-0)3979 —
35. Wolves* 4.3	1		3^1				6	4		11	10_1	7				2	8	5		9^1						3-0(1-0)5007 16
36. Rochdale 12.3	1		3	12			6	4†		11	10	7				2	8	5		9						0-0(0-0)1621 16
37. Cambridge 19.3	1		3				6	4		11	10_1	7				2	8	5		9						1-1(0-1)1514 16
38. Carlisle* 25.3			3^1	12			6	4		11	10^1	7†				2	8	5		9^1	1					3-0(2-0)3093 —
39. Wrexham 2.4			3	12	2		6	4‡		11	10	7					8	5†	9		1	14				0-3(0-2)3134 17
40. Hartlepool* 4.4			3	12			6	4		11	10^2	7				2	8	5†		9^1	1					3-1(1-0)3921 16
41. Swansea 9.4			3^1				6	4		11	10^1	7				2	8	5		9	1					2-1(2-0)4104 15
42. Torquay* 22.4			3				6	4		11	10^1	7				2	8	5		9	1					1-1(0-0)6189 —
43. Crewe* 25.4			3				6	4		11	10_1	7	12			2	8^1	5†		9	1	14				2-2(1-2)2962 —
44. Newport 30.4			3		5		$6‡$	4		11†	10^2	7	12				9	1		8^1	14					3-0(1-0)1110 14
45. Orient* 2.5			3		5		6	4		11	10	7				2^1	8†	5		9^1	1	12				2-1(1-0)3604 14
46. Colchester 7.5			3		5		6	4		11	10	7†	12			2			9		8		1			0-0(0-0)1704 —
Appearances (subs)/goals	22(0) 0	4(4) 0	16(8) 0	19(1) 0	13(1) 0	40(0) 1	34(0) 4	6(7) 0	45(0) 4	34(4) 27	35(4) 4	11(9) 3	1(1) 0	1(1) 0	3(2) 0	31(2) 0	30(0) 3	15(0) 0	29(0) 7	8(0) 0	2(5) 1	1(0) 0	0(1) 0	1(0) 0	1(0) 0	Final League Position: 14

Own goals: Carter, match 4; Smith, match 18; Outterside, match 33.

DIVISION 2

WALSALL

Fellows Park, Walsall WS2 9DB.

Back row (left to right): K. Oliver (Physio), R. Hutchinson, A. Dornan, P. Hart, W. Naughton, F. Barber, K. Mower, M. Goodwin, G. Forbes, T. Christie, P. Jones, F. Pedley (Physio). *Front row:* D. Kelly, C. Shakespeare, N. Cross, M. Jones, G. Sweeney (Ass. Manager), T. Coakley (Manager), P. Hawker, M. Rees, M. Taylor, R. Train.

Stadium Capacity: 16,018
Pitch Dimensions: 113 × 73yds.
Telephone: 0922–22791.
Chairman: B. S. Blower.
President: T. P. Ramsden.
Managing Director: R. Cox.
Directors: J. Bonser, R. Clift, T. F. Hargreaves, M. Miller.
Manager: Tommy Coakley.
Post-War Managers: Harry Hibbs, Tony McPhee, Brough Fletcher, Major Buckley, John Love, Billy Moore, Alf Wood, Ray Shaw, Ron Lewin, Dick Graham, Billy Moore, John Smith, Ronnie Allen, Doug Fraser, Dave Mackay, Alan Ashman, Frank Sibley, Alan Buckley, Neil Martin, Alan Buckley (20).
Assistant Manager: G. Sweeney.
Physio: T. Bradley.
Secretary: K. R. Whalley.
Founded: 1888.
Turned Professional: 1888.
Nickname: The Saddlers.
Former Names: Walsall Switfts (founded 1877) and Walsall Town (founded 1879) merged in 1888 and were called Walsall Town Swifts until 1895.
Former Grounds: The Chuckery and West Bromwich Road.
Record Attendance: 25,453 v Newcastle United, Division 2, 29 August 1961.
Record Victory: 10–0 v Darwen, Division 2, 4 March 1899.
Record Defeat: 0–12 v Small Heath, Division 2, 17 December 1892 and v Darwen, Division 2, 26 December 1896.
Most League Points: (3 for a win) 82, Division 3, 1987–88. (2 for a win) 65, Division 4, 1959–60.
Most League Goals: 106, Division 4, 1959–60.
Highest League Scorer in a Season: Gilbert Alsop, 40,Division 3(N), 1933–34 and 1934–35.
Highest Total of League Goals: Tony Richards, 184, 1954–63, and Colin Taylor, 184, 1958–63, 1964–68, 1969–73.
Most League Appearances: Colin Harrison, 467, 1964–82.
League History: 1892 Elected to Division 2, 1895 not re-elected, 1896–1901 Division 2, 1901 not re-elected, 1921 Founder Members of Division 3 (N), 1927–31 Division 3(S), 1931–36 Division 3 (N), 1936–58 Division 3 (S), 1958–60 Division 3, 1961–63 Division 2, 1963–79 Division 3, 1979–80 Division 4, 1980–88 Division 3, 1988– Division 2.
Honours: Division 3 runners-up 1960–61, Division 4 Champions 1959–60, runners-up 1979–80.
Colours: All white. **Second strip:** All yellow.

WALSALL – LEAGUE RECORD 1987–88

Match no/Opp/Date		Barber	Dornan	Mower	Shakespeare	Forbes	Hart	Goodwin	Cross	Kelly	Jones P	Naughton	Palgrave	Jones M	Taylor	Rees	Hutchinson	Christie	Hawker	Marsh	O'Kelly	Sanderson	FT(HT)Att Lge pos
1. Fulham*	15.8	1	2	3	4†	5	6	7	8	9	10	11	12										0–1(0–0)4691 —
2. Blackpool	22.8	1	2	3†		5	6	7	8²	9	10	11		12	4								2–1(1–0)4614 13
3. Nthampton*	29.8	1	2		4	5	6	7	8	9†	10¹	11		3	12								1–0(1–0)5993 8
4. York	31.8	1	2		4	5¹	6	7	8¹		10	11¹		3	9†	12							3–1(1–0)2661 —
5. Sunderland*	5.9	1	2		4¹	5	6	7	8	9¹	10	11†		3			12						2–2(1–1)6909 3
6. Rotherham	12.9	1	2		4¹	5	6	7	8	9		11		3	12	10†							1–0(0–0)3325 1
7. Bristol C*	15.9	1	2		4	5	6	7	8	9¹		11		3		10							1–1(0–0)6425 —
8. Wigan*	19.9	1	2		4	5	6	7†	8	9¹		11		3		10	12						1–2(0–1)5353 9
9. Grimsby	26.9	1	2	9	4	5	6	7	8			11	10¹	3¹									2–0(1–0)3314 3
10. Bury	29.9	1	2	3	4	5¹	6	7	8			11¹	9			10							2–2(2–1)2449 —
11. Preston*	3.10	1	2	3	4	5†	6	7	8			11	10		12		9¹						1–0(1–0)5467 2
12. Brighton*	10.10	1	2		4	5	6		8	9	11	7		3			10						1–1(1–0)5020 2
13. Brentford	17.10	1	2	3	4	5	6	7	8	9	11†			12			10						0–0(0–0)5056 6
14. Doncaster	20.10	1	2	3	4¹	5	6†	12¹	8	9¹		14		7‡			10¹	11					4–0(1–0)1387 —
15. Port Vale*	24.10	1	2	3	4	5		6	8†	9²	12	14		7‡			10	11					2–1(1–1)6083 2
16. Southend	30.10	1	2	3	4¹	5	6	7	8‡	9	11†	14		12			10						1–1(0–0)2692 —
17. Aldershot*	3.11	1	2	3	4	5	6			9²	8	11		7			10						2–0(1–0)4816 —
18. Chester	7.11	1	2	3	4	5	6		12	9	8₁	11		7			10†						1–1(0–0)3269 2
19. Notts Co	21.11	1	2		4	5†	6¹	12	8	9	7			3			10	11					1–3(1–2)7211 4
20. Mansfield*	28.11			3	4²	5	6	12		9	7	8		2			10	11†					2–1(1–0)4227 3
21. Bristol R*	12.12	1	2	3	4	5	6		8†	9	7	11		14			12	10‡					0–0(0–0)4234 3
22. Gillingham	18.12	1	2	3	4	5	6		8	9	7₁	11					10						1–0(0–0)4020 —
23. Grimsby*	26.12	1	2		4	5‡	6	14	8¹	9²†	12	14		3			12	10					3–2(0–1)6272 3
24. Chesterfield	28.12	1	2		4	5	6		8		7	11		3			9	10					1–2(0–1)3916 3
25. Nthampton	1.1	1	2		4	5	6	10	8¹†	9	7¹	11‡		3			12	14					2–2(2–0)5832 3
26. Rotherham*	2.1	1			4¹	5	6	10	8³†	9¹	7‡	11		2			12	3	14				5–2(3–1)5051 3
27. Aldershot	9.1	1			4	5	6	10	8	9	7	11		2				3¹					1–0(1–0)3270 3
28. Wigan	16.1	1			4	5	6	10	8	9¹	7†	11‡		2			12	3	14				1–3(0–2)5063 3
29. York*	30.1	1			4	5	6	8†		11¹	7	10		2			9¹	3	12				2–1(1–1)4371 3
30. Sunderland	6.2	1		3	4	5	6	8¹		10	12	11		2†			9	7‡		14			1–1(0–0)18,311 4
31. Bristol C	9.2	1		3	4	5	6	8		10	7	11	2				9†			12			0–0(0–0)8454 —
32. Chesterfield*	13.2	1		3	4	5	6	8†		10	7	11	2				12	9					0–0(0–0)4162 3
33. Fulham	20.2	1	12	3	4	5†		8		10	6	11	2	7			9						0–2(0–1)3718 4
34. Blackpool*	23.2	1	2	3	4			8		10	6₂	11	7				9¹		5				3–2(0–0)4252 —
35. Preston	27.2	1	2		4			8		10	6	11‡	7†	3	14		9	5	12				0–1(0–0)6479 3
36. Bury*	1.3	1	2		4¹	5			8		6¹	11		3			9	7	10				2–1(1–1)3920 —
37. Brentford*	5.3	1	2†		4	5¹			8		6₁	11	12	3			9¹	7		10¹			4–2(2–1)4494 3
38. Brighton	12.3	1	2		4	5			8		6	11		3			9¹	7	10				1–2(0–1)8345 3
39. Southend*	19.3	1	2		4	5		12	8²		6	11		3			9†	7	10				2–1(1–1)4479 3
40. Port Vale	26.3	1		2	4	5		8			6¹	11†	9	3			7			10	12		1–2(0–1)6347 3
41. Chester*	2.4	1		2	4	5	8			10	6	11		3			9	7¹					1–0(1–0)4978 3
42. Mansfield	5.4	1		2	4	5	8			10³	6	11		3			9	7					3–1(2–1)4900 —
43. Doncaster*	9.4	1		2	4	5‡	8	14		10¹	6†	11		3			9¹	7		12			2–1(0–0)6631 2
44. Notts Co*	30.4	1		2	4	5	8	12		10¹	6†	11₁		3			9	7					2–1(0–1)11,913 2
45. Bristol R	2.5	1		2	4	5	8	6‡		10		11		3			9†	7		12	14		0–3(0–3)6328 3
46. Gillingham*	7.5	1		2	4	5	8	6		10		11†		3			9	7			12		0–0(0–0)8850 3
Apps(subs)/goals		46(0) 0	30(1) 0	26(0) 0	45(0) 8	44(0) 3	37(0) 1	29(7) 2	25(1) 8	39(0) 20	41(2) 11	38(3) 3	0(1) 0	6(2) 0	36(4) 1	12(0) 0	30(6) 7	26(3) 2	0(3) 0	7(5) 1	0(3) 0		

Final League Position: 3

Own goal: Bremner, match 12.

DIVISION 2 | # WATFORD
Vicarage Road Stadium, Watford WD1 8ER.

Back row (left to right): Kenny Jackett, Gary Chivers, Glyn Hodges, Tim Sherwood, Iwan Roberts, Trevor Senior, Steve Terry, Dean Holdsworth, Peter Hetherston. *Middle row:* Worrell Sterling, Malcolm Allen, Mark Morris, Cliff Powell, Tony Coton, David Holdsworth, Mel Rees, Paul Rumble, Luther Blissett, Chris Pullan, Nigel Gibbs. *Front row:* Kevin Richardson, Wilf Rostron, Tony Agana, Steve Harrison (Manager), John McClelland, Tom Walley (First, Team Coach), Gary Porter, Liburd Henry, Neil Doherty.

Stadium Capacity: 26,996.
Pitch Dimensions: 115 × 75 yds.
Telephone: 0923–30933.
Chairman: Elton John.
Vice-Chairman: G. A. Smith.
Directors: J. Harrowell, Bertie Mee OBE, J. Reid, H. M. Stratford JP, M. Winwood.
Manager: Steve Harrison.
Post-War Managers: Jack Bray, Eddie Hapgood, Haydn Green, Ron Gray, Len Goulden, Johnny Paton, Neil McBain, Ron Burgess, Bill McGarry, Ken Furphy, George Kirby, Mike Keen, Graham Taylor, Dave Bassett (14).
First Team Coach: Tom Walley.
Physio: Billy Hails.
Secretary/Chief Executive: Eddie Plumley FAAI.
Marketing Manager: Chris Childs.
Founded: 1891.
Turned Professional: 1897.
Nickname: The Hornets.
Former Names: West Herts, Watford St Mary's until 1898.
Former Grounds: 1889–1922 Cassio Road.
Record Attendance: 34,099 v Manchester United, FA Cup 4th Round, 3 February 1969.
Record Victory: 10–1 v Lowestoft Town, FA Cup 1st Round, 27 November 1926.
Record Defeat: 0–10 v Wolverhampton Wanderers, FA Cup 1st Round replay, 13 January 1912.
Most League Points: (3 for a win) 80, Division 2, 1981–82. (2 for a win) 71, Division 4, 1977–78.
Most League Goals: 92, Division 4, 1959–60.
Highest League Scorer in a Season: Cliff Holton, 42, Division 4, 1959–60.
Highest Total of League Goals: Luther Blisset, 139, 1975–83, 1984–88.
Most League Appearances: Duncan Welbourne, 411, 1963–74.
League History: 1920 Founder Members of Division 3, 1921–58Division 3(S), 1958–60 Division 4, 1960–69Division 3, 1969–72 Division 2, 1972–75 Division 2, 1976–78 Division 4, 1978–79 Division 3, 1979–82 Division 2, 1982–88 Division 1, 1988– Division 2.
Honours: Division 1 runners-up 1982–83. Division 2 runners-up 1981–82.Division 3 Champions 1968–69, runners-up 1978–79. Division 4 Champions 1977–78. FA Cup runners-up 1984.
Colours: Yellow shirts with red and black trim, black shorts with red and yellow trim, red socks with black and yellow trim.
Second strip: White shirts, black shorts, black socks with red and yellow tops.

WATFORD – LEAGUE RECORD 1987–88

Match no/Opp/Date	Coton	Gibbs	Roston	Jackett	Morris	McClelland	Bardsley	Blissett	Senior	Porter	Agana	Roberts	Allen	Hill	Sterling	Terry	Chivers	Sherwood	Hetherston	Hodges	Pullin	Holdsworth	Rees	Kuhl	Holden	Rimmer	Thomas	FT(HT)Att Lge pos
1. Wimbledon* 15.8	1	2	3	4	5	6	7	8¹†	9	10	11	12																1-0(1-0)15,344 —
2. Nottm F 19.8	1	2	3	4†	5	6	7‡	8	9	10	11		12	14														0-1(0-1)14,527 —
3. Man Utd 22.8	1	2	3‡	4	5	6		8	9	10	11	12		14	7†													0-2(0-2)38,582 14
4. Spurs* 29.8	1	2	14	3	5	6	7	8	9†	10¹	11	12			4‡													1-1(0-0)19,073 15
5. Norwich* 5.9	1	2	12	3†	5	6	7	8	9	10	11	14			4‡													0-1(0-0)11,724 19
6. Sheff Wed 12.9	1	2	3		4	6		9¹‡	10¹	14	8			11¹	5	7†	12											3-2(2-1)16,144 15
7. Portsmouth* 19.9	1	2	3	4†	6			12	9	10		8		11	5	7												0-0(0-0)13,277 13
8. Chelsea* 26.9	1	2	3†	4‡	6			12	9	10		8		11	5	7		14										0-3(0-1)16,213 16
9. Coventry 3.10	1	2	3	4	6				9†	10	8	12			7	5			11									0-1(0-1)16,111 16
10. Sthampton 17.10	1	2	3	14	4	6		8		10‡	12	9			5			7†	11									0-1(0-0)11,933 19
11. Everton 24.10	1	2	3	4	5	6		9	12	7	8†						10		11									0-2(0-1)28,501 20
12. West Ham* 31.10	1	2	3	4	5	6		9	10	7†			8¹				12		11									1-2(0-1)14,427 20
13. QPR 7.11	1	2		3	5	6			10	9	8			4	7				11									0-0(0-0)21,101 20
14. Charlton* 14.11	1	2	3	4	5	6			10	9¹	8¹				7				11									2-1(1-0)12,093 19
15. Oxford 21.11	1			3	5	6	7¹	12	10	9‡	8†		14		2	4			11									1-1(0-0)7811 19
16. Liverpool 24.11	1		12	3	5	6	7	9‡	10		8		14		2	4†			11									0-4(0-0)32,396 —
17. Arsenal* 28.11	1			3	4¹	5	6	7¹	9	10	8†		12		2				11									2-0(1-0)19,598 19
18. Derby 5.12	1			3	5	6	7	9	10	12	8		2						11	11†	4							1-0(0-1)14,516 19
19. Luton* 12.12	1			3	4	5	6	7	9†	10	8		14		2‡				11	12								0-1(0-1)12,152 19
20. Sheff Wed* 26.12	1	2	3	4	5	6	7	12	10	11	9†	8‡					14											1-3(1-3)12,026 21
21. Portsmouth 28.12			3	4	5	6		9	10	8¹		12		11	2			7†		1								1-1(0-0)15,003 21
22. Spurs 1.1			3	4	5¹	6		9	10	8		12		11†	2		14	7‡		1								1-2(0-0)25,235 21
23. Man Utd* 2.1			3	4	5	6		9‡	10†	8		14		2	12	7		11		1								0-1(0-1)18,038 21
24. Wimbledon 16.1	1		3		5	6	9		10		8₁		7¹		2	4			11									2-1(1-0)6848 20
25. Nottm F* 23.1	1		3	4	5	6	9		10		8		7		2				11									0-0(0-0)13,158 20
26. Norwich 6.2	1	2	3	4	5	6	12	9	10		8		7						11†									0-0(0-0)13,316 19
27. Liverpool* 13.2	1	2	3‡	4	5	6	12¹	9†	10		8		7				11			14								1-4(0-1)23,838 20
28. Coventry* 27.2	1	2	3	4	5	6	12	9	10		8†		7									11						0-1(0-1)12,052 21
29. Sthampton* 5.3	1	2	3	4	5	6	12	9†	10	8‡	14		7						11									0-1(0-1)11,824 21
30. West Ham 19.3	1	2	3	11			9		10		12	8†	7	5		4												0-1(0-0)16,015 21
31. Everton* 26.3	1	2	3	4	5	6	9		10¹		12	8†	7										11					1-2(0-1)13,503 21
32. Chelsea 29.3	1	2	3	4	5	6	12		10	9			7				14						11‡		8¹†			1-1(1-0)11,240 —
33. QPR* 1.4	1	2	3	4	5	6	12		10	9			7										11†		8			0-1(0-0)16,083 —
34. Charlton 4.4	1	2	14	3	5	6	9		10	12						7†						4	11‡		8			0-1(0-1)6196 21
35. Oxford* 9.4	1	2	3		5	6	10	9									7²				4	11¹		8				3-0(2-0)10,045 21
36. Newcastle 12.4	1	2	3		5	6	10	9								7	12				4†	11		8				0-3(0-1)16,318 —
37. Arsenal 15.4	1	2	3	4	5	6	10	9								7†						11¹	8	12				1-0(0-0)19,541 —
38. Newcastle* 19.4	1	2	3	4¹	5	6	10	9								7†						11	8	12				1-1(1-0)12,075 —
39. Derby* 30.4	1	2	3	4	5	6	10	9¹								7‡	12					11	8†	14				1-1(1-1)14,181 20
40. Luton 2.5	1	2	3†	4	5	6	10‡	9						14	12							11	8	7				1-2(0-2)10,409 20
Apps(subs)/goals	37(0)/0	30(0)/0	33(4)/0	22(1)/2	39(0)/1	40(0)/0	17(8)/4	22(2)/1	39(1)/3	12(3)/1	18(7)/2	15(6)/3	2(2)/0	17(4)/2	40(0)/0	14(0)/0	9(4)/0	25(3)/0	22(2)/3	2(2)/0	14(2)/0	40(0)/0	10(0)/2	9(0)/1	1(3)/0			

Final League Position: 20

Own goals: Sterland, match 20; Johnson M, match 40

WEST BROMWICH ALBION

The Hawthorns, West Bromwich B17 4LF.

Back row (left to right): Carlton Palmer, Andy Gray, Bobby Williamson, David Powell, Martyn Bennett, Stuart Naylor, Colin Anderson, Gary Robson, George Reilly. *Middle row:* Graham Doig (Physio), Wayne Dobbins, Don Goodman, Tony Kelly, Barry Cowdrill, Martin Dickinson, Darren Bradley, Kevin Steggles, Norman Bodell (Chief Scout). *Front row:* Paul Dyson, Steve Lynex, David Burrows, Colin Addison (Ass. Manager), Ron Atkinson (Manager), Tony Morley, Martin Singleton, Robert Hopkins.

Stadium Capacity: 33,565. **Pitch Dimensions:** 115 × 75 yds.
Telephone: 021–525 8888, Ticket office: 021–553 5472.
Chairman: J. S. Lucas. **Vice-Chairman:** D. B. Boundy.
Directors: J. W. Brandrick, M. C. McGinnity, T. Summers, J. Silk.
Manager: Ron Atkinson. **Post-War Managers:** Jack Smith, Vic Buckingham, Gordon Clark, Archie Macaulay, Jimmy Hagan, Alan Ashman, Don Howe, Johnny Giles, Ronnie Allen, Ron Atkinson, Ronnie Allen, Ron Wylie, Johnny Giles, Nobby Stiles, Ron Saunders (15).
Assistant Manager: Colin Addison. **Physio:** Graham Doig.
Secretary: Gordon Bennett.
Commercial Manager: Alan Stevenson.
Sponsors: Apollo 2000 Gas & Electrical Superstores.
Founded: 1879. **Turned Professional:** 1885.
Nickname: The Throstles, Baggies or Albion.
Former Names: West Bromwich Strollers 1879–81.
Former Grounds: Coopers Hill 1879, Dartmouth Park, 1879–81, Bunns Field, Wallsall Street 1881–1882, Four Acres (Dartmouth Cricket Club) 1882–85, Stoney Lane 1885–1900.
Record Attendance: 64,815 v Arsenal, FA Cup 6th Round, 6 March 1937.
Record Victory: 12–0 v Darwen, Division 1, 4 April 1892
Record Defeat: 3–10 v Stoke City, Division 1, 4 February 1937.
Most League Points: (3 for a win) 57, Division 1, 1982–83. (2 for a win) 60, Division 1, 1919–20.
Most League Goals: 105, Division 2, 1929–30.
Highest League Scorer in a Season: William 'Ginger' Richardson, 39, Division 1, 1935–36.
Highest Total of League Goals: Tony Brown, 218, 1963–79.
Most League Appearances: Tony Brown, 574, 1963–80.
League History: 1888 Founder Members of Football League, 1901–02 Division 2, 1902–04 Division 1, 1904–11 Division 2, 1911–27 Division 1, 1927–31 Division 2, 1931–38 Division 1, 1938–49 Division 2, 1949–73 Division 1, 1973–76 Division 2, 1976–86 Division 1, 1986– Division 2.
Honours: Division 1 Champions 1919–20, runners-up 1924–25, 1953–54. Division 2 Champions 1901–02, 1910–11, runners-up 1930–31, 1948–49. FA Cup winners 1888, 1892, 1931, 1954, 1968, runners-up 1886, 1887, 1895, 1912, 1935. League Cup winners 1966, runners-up 1967, 1970.
Colours: Navy blue and white striped shirts, navy shorts, white socks. **Second strip:** Green and yellow striped shirts, green shorts, yellow socks.

WEST BROMWICH ALBION – LEAGUE RECORD 1987–88

Match no/Opp/Date	Naylor	Robson	Statham	Bennett	Dickinson	Kelly	Hopkins	Goodman	Williamson	Bradley	Morley	Palmer	Burrows	Reilly	Dobbins	Singleton	Steggles	Cowdrill	Gray	Anderson	Lynex	Hogg	Powell	North	Hucker	Talbot	Swain	Phillips	Dyson	Hodson	FT(HT)Att	Lge pos
1. Oldham* 15.8	1	2†	3	4	5	6	7	8	9‡	10	11	12	14																		0-0(0-0)8873	—
2. Blackburn 22.8	1	10‡		4	5	6	7	8†		2	11	12	3	9	14																1-3(1-2)5619	20
3. Swindon* 29.8	1	9		4¹	5‡	6		8	12	14	11†	7	3		2	10															1-2(1-1)7503	23
4. Leeds 31.8	1	9			5	6		8	12	2	11	7†	3			10	4														0-1(0-0)19,847	—
5. Shrewsbury* 5.9	1	7			5	6		8¹	9	12	11	2				10	4†	3													2-1(0-0)8560	21
6. Crystal Palace 8.9	1	7‡			5	6	14	8	9¹	12	11	2				10	4†	3													1-4(0-1)8554	—
7. Plymouth 12.9	1		4†	14		7	8‡	12	6	11	2¹		5			10		3	9²												3-3(1-0)10,578	20
8. Aston Villa* 16.9	1		4		7	8†	12	6	11	2		5				10		3	9												0-2(0-1)22,072	—
9. Bournemouth* 19.9	1		4‡	14	6†		8		10	11²	2¹		5			12		3	9												3-0(1-0)7749	19
10. Millwall 26.9	1			4	6	7	8	12	10		2‡		5			14		3	9†	11											0-2(0-1)6564	20
11. Birmingham* 30.9	1			6	7	8	12	2		4¹	5			10¹		3	9¹†	11													3-1(1-0)15,399	—
12. Reading 3.10	1			6	7	8	12¹	2	11	4	5			10		3	9¹†														2-1(1-1)5543	14
13. Bradford* 10.10	1			6	7	8	12	2	11	4	5			10†		3	9														0-1(0-1)12,241	17
14. Middlesbro 17.10	1			6‡		7	8	11	2		4	5		12	10		3	9†													1-2(0-0)10,684	18
15. Leicester 21.10	1	10			6		14	8‡	2	11	4	5		12		3†	9			7											0-3(0-1)9262	—
16. Huddersfield* 24.10	1	10†			6			8	2	11³	4	3	5			9	12	7													3-2(2-2)8450	18
17. Sheff Utd* 4.11	1				6		8¹†	14¹	10‡	11¹	2	3	5			9¹	12	7	4												4-0(2-0)8072	—
18. Stoke 7.11	1	12			6			8†	10‡	11	2	3	5			9	14	7	4												0-3(0-2)9992	18
19. Ipswich* 14.11	1				6		8¹			11	5	3			2	9¹	10	7	4												2-2(0-1)8457	17
20. Hull 21.11	1	12			6		8		11	2	3	5				9	10	7†	4												0-1(0-0)7654	18
21. Man City* 28.11	1			5		7	8¹		11	2	3	10				9		6	4												1-1(0-1)15,425	17
22. Barnsley 5.12	1	10		5		7	8		12	2	14	11				9‡	3	6†	4												1-3(0-1)5395	18
23. Blackburn* 12.12	1	14			5	7	8	12		11	2	3	9	10‡			6†		4												0-1(0-1)7303	18
24. Aston Villa 18.12	1	12			5	7	8		11	4	2	9			3		10†	6													0-0(0-0)24,437	—
25. Millwall* 26.12	1	14		7	5		8		11¹	4	2	9†			3	12	10‡	6													1-4(1-2)9291	20
26. Bournemouth 28.12	1	10		2	6		8¹	14	11‡	4	12	5†			3	9¹		7													2-3(0-1)8969	20
27. Swindon 1.1	1	10		2	6	7	8	11		4					3	9								1	5						0-2(0-0)12,155	20
28. Plymouth* 2.1	1	10†		2	6	7	8†	14	11‡	4					3	9	12							1	5						1-0(1-0)8445	19
29. Oldham 16.1	1	10¹			6	2	12	8	11†	4					3	9	7						5								1-2(0-0)5557	20
30. Leeds* 30.1	7		12¹	10†	2	8		11	6					3	9				5	1	4										1-4(0-2)9008	21
31. Shrewsbury 6.2	7			8		6				3	9	11¹			5	1	4	2													1-0(0-0)6360	19
32. C Palace* 13.2	10			7	8¹		6			3	9	11			5	1	4	2													1-0(0-0)8944	18
33. Reading* 27.2	10			8	9	11†	6	12	14	3		7‡			5	1	4	2													0-1(0-0)8509	21
34. Middlesbro* 5.3	10			8		6		7		3	11			5	1	4	2	9													0-0(0-0)8316	21
35. Birmingham 8.3	10†			7¹	8		6	12		3	11			5	1	4	2	9													1-0(0-0)12,331	—
36. Bradford 12.3	10			7	8		6			3	12	11			5	1	4₁	2	9												1-4(0-1)12,502	19
37. Huddersfield 26.3	1			7	8†		11			12	3	9²	10		5		4	2¹		6											3-1(0-1)4503	19
38. Stoke* 2.4	1	12		7				10		3	9¹†	11		5	4₁				8	6	2										2-0(1-0)12,144	18
39. Ipswich 4.4	1			7	12			10†		3	9	11		5	4		8¹	6	2												1-1(0-0)10,665	17
40. Leicester* 9.4	1			12						3	9	11	7¹†	5	4		8	6	2												1-1(1-1)11,013	19
41. Sheff Utd 23.4	1	10†		12						3	9	11	7	5	4		8	6	2												0-0(0-0)12,091	18
42. Hull* 30.4	1	10		7	12					3	9¹†	11		5	4		8	6¹	2												1-1(1-0)8004	19
43. Man City 2.5	1	10		7‡	9		14			3	11†	12¹		5	4		8	6¹	2												2-4(1-2)16,490	20
44. Barnsley* 7.5	1	10		7¹						3	9	11†	12	5	4		8¹	6	2												2-2(1-0)8483	20

Final League Position: 20

Appearances(subs)/goals: 35(0)/0, 25(6)/1, 10(0)/0, 6(0)/1, 13(3)/1, 26(0)/1, 28(1)/2, 34(6)/7, 10(12)/3, 15(4)/0, 27(1)/7, 36(2)/3, 17(1)/0, 13(1)/0, 35(0)/0, 10(2)/1, 40(0)/0, 30(2)/10, 20(3)/1, 16(5)/2, 7(0)/0, 20(0)/0, 7(0)/0, 15(0)/2, 7(0)/1, 10(0)/2, 8(0)/2, 7(0)/0

Own goals: Sulley, match 2; Pearson, match 5; Futcher, match 22.

DIVISION 1

WEST HAM UNITED

Boleyn Ground, Green Street, Upton Park, London E13 9AZ.

Back row (left to right): Paul Hilton, Gary Strodder, Billy Bonds, Lee Bracey, Phil Parkes, Tom McAlister, Tony Gale, Eamonn Dolan, Alvin Martin. *Middle row:* Alan Dickens, Neil Orr, Simon Livett, George Parris, Alan Devonshire, Ray Stewart, Stewart Robson, Paul Ince, Steve Potts, Steve Walford. *Front row:* Kevin Keen, Tommy McQueen, Frank McAvennie, Liam Brady, Mark Ward, Tony Cottee, Stuart Slater, John Strain.

Stadium Capacity: 35,510.
Pitch Dimensions: 112 × 72 yds.
Telephone: 01–472 2740, **Recorded information:** 01–470 1325, **Hammer Line:** 01–475 0555, **Dial-a-seat:** 01–472 3322, **Clubcall:** 0898–121165.
Chairman: Leonard C. Cearns.
Vice-Chairman: William F. Cearns.
Directors: Brian R. Cearns FCIS, Jack Petchey, Martin W. Cearns AIB.
Manager: John Lyall.
Post-War Managers: Charlie Paynter, Ted Fenton, Ron Greenwood (3).
Secretary: Tom M. Finn.
Administration & Commercial Manager: Brian Blower.
Founded: 1895.
Turned Professional: 1900.
Nickname: The Hammers.
Former Names: Thames Ironworks FC 1895–1900.
Former Grounds: Memorial Recreation Ground, Canning Town, 1895–1904.
Record Attendance: 42,322 v Tottenham Hotspur, Division 1, 17 October 1970.
Record Victory: 10–0 Bury, Milk Cup, 2nd Round 2nd leg, 25 October 1983.
Record Defeat: 2–8 v Blackburn Rovers, Division 1, 26 December 1963.
Most League Points: (3 for a win) 84, Division 1, 1985–86. (2 for a win) 66, Division 2 1980–81.
Most League Goals: 101, Division 1, 1957–58.
Highest League Scorer in a Season: Vic Watson, 41, Division 1, 1929–30.
Highest Total of League Goals: Vic Watson, 306, 1920–35.
Most League Appearances: Billy Bonds MBE, 663, 1967–88.
League History: 1919 Elected to Division 2, 1923–32 Division 1, 1932–58 Division 2, 1958–78 Division 1, 1978–81 Division 2, 1981– Division 1.
Honours: Division 2 Champions 1957–58, 1980–81, runners-up 1922–23. FA Cup winners 1964, 1975, 1980, runners-up 1923. League Cup runners-up 1966, 1981. European Cup-Winners Cup winners 1965, runners-up 1976.
Colours: Claret shirts with blue trim, white shorts and socks. **Second strip:** White shirts, blue shorts and socks.

WEST HAM UNITED – LEAGUE RECORD 1987–88

Match no/Opp/Date	McAlister	Stewart	McQueen	Orr	Martin	Devonshire	Ward	McAvennie	Brady	Cottee	Robson	Strodder	Dickens	Ince	Parris	Hilton	Keen	Slater	Dolan	Bonds	Gale	Potts	Rosenior	Dicks	Parkes	FT(HT)Att Lge pos
1. QPR* 15.8	1	2†	3	4	5	6‡	7	8	9	10	11	12	14													0–3(0–3)22,881 —
2. Luton 22.8	1	2_1	3		5		7	8	6^1	10	11	4		9												2–2(2–1)8073 18
3. Norwich* 29.8	1	2	3		5		7	8	6	10^2	11	4		9												2–0(0–0)16,394 14
4. Portsmouth 31.8	1	2†	3		5		7	8	6	10	11	4^1		9	12											1–2(1–1)16,104 —
5. Liverpool* 5.9	1	2	3†		5		7	8	6	10^1	11	4		9	12											1–1(0–0)29,865 15
6. Wimbledon 12.9	1	2			5		7	8	6	10^1	11	4		9	3											1–1(0–1)8507 16
7. Spurs* 19.9	1	2			5		7	8	6	10	11	4†		9	3	12										0–1(0–1)27,750 18
8. Arsenal 26.9	1	2			5			8	6	10	11	4		9	3		7									0–1(0–0)40,127 19
9. Derby* 3.10	1	2‡	3†		5				6^1	10	11	4		9	8	12	7	14								1–1(1–1)17,226 17
10. Charlton* 10.10	1	2			5		7		6	10	11		8	9^1	3		4									1–1(1–1)15,757 17
11. Oxford 17.10	1	2			5		7		6	10^1	11		8	9	3		4									2–1(2–1)9092 15
12. Man Utd* 25.10	1	2_1	11		5		7		6	10			8	9	3		4									1–0(1–0)19,863 —
13. Watford 31.10	1	2			5		7		6	10^1	11		8^1	9	3		4									2–1(1–0)14,427 14
14. Sheff Wed* 7.11	1	2			5		7		6	10	11		8	9	3		4†	12								0–1(0–1)16,277 15
15. Everton 14.11	1			5‡			7		6	10	11	12	8	9	3†	4^1	14			2						1–3(0–3)29,405 15
16. Nottm F* 21.11	1	5_1					7			10^2	11		8	9	3	4	6			2						3–2(1–1)17,216 13
17. Coventry 28.11	1	5					7			10	11		8	9	3	4	6			2						0–0(0–0)16,740 14
18. Sthampton* 5.12	1	5								10	11	4	8^1	9	3		6^1			2						2–1(1–1)15,375 11
19. Chelsea 12.12	1	5								10	11	4	8		3^1	9	6			2						1–1(1–0)22,850 12
20. Newcastle* 19.12	1	5					7			10	11^1	4	8	9^1	3	12	6			2†						2–0(0–0)18,679 9
21. Wimbledon* 26.12	1	5_1					7		14	10	11	4	8‡	9	3†	12	6			2						1–2(0–2)18,605 10
22. Spurs 28.12	1	5					7†	8		10	11	12		9	3	4^1	6			2						1–2(0–1)39,456 13
23. Norwich 1.1	1	5					7			10^1	11		8	9‡	3	4	6†	12		2	14					1–4(1–0)20,059 14
24. Luton* 2.1	1	5					7			10	11	4		12^1	3†	9				2	8	6				1–1(0–1)16,716 14
25. QPR 16.1	1	2	3				7	8		10	11	5		9^1						4	6					1–0(0–0)14,909 12
26. Liverpool 6.2	1	2	12				7	8		10	11	5		9†	3					4	6					0–0(0–0)42,049 13
27. Portsmouth* 13.2	1	2					7	8		10^1	11	5		9	3					4	6					1–1(0–0)18,639 13
28. Derby 27.2	1	2	12				7	8‡		10	11	5		9†	3		14			4	6					0–1(0–0)16,301 13
29. Oxford* 5.3	1	2	3				7^1			10	11	5		9†	8		12			4	6					1–1(0–0)14,980 13
30. Charlton 12.3	1	2	3				7			10	11	5		8†			12		9	4	6					0–3(0–2)8118 15
31. Watford* 19.3	1	2					7			10	11†	5		12			8			4	6	3	9^1			1–0(0–0)16,015 15
32. Man Utd 26.3	1	2					7			10	11	5		12			8†			4	6	3	9^1			1–3(0–2)37,269 15
33. Sheff Wed 2.4	1	2					7			10	11	5‡		12			8			4†	6	14	9^1	3		1–2(0–1)18,435 15
34. Everton* 4.4	1	2†					7			10	11	5	8	12			4				6		9	3		0–0(0–0)21,195 16
35. Arsenal* 12.4		2					7			10	11	5		8			12			4	6	2†	9	3	1	0–1(0–0)26,746 —
36. Nottm F 20.4	1						7			10	11	5	8				2			4	6		9	3		0–0(0–0)15,775 —
37. Coventry* 23.4	1						7			10^1	11	5	8	9†	2	12	4‡	14			6			3		1–1(0–1)17,733 17
38. Sthampton 30.4	1						7			10^1	11	5	8			11				4	6	2	9	3		1–2(0–0)15,652 18
39. Chelsea* 2.5	1						7			10^1	11		8		2	5^1					6	4	9^2	3		4–1(2–0)28,521 16
40. Newcastle 7.5	1						7			10	11^1		8		2	5					6	4	9	3		1–2(1–1)23,731 16
Apps(subs)/goals	39(0)/0	33(0)/4	10(2)/0	1(0)/0	15(0)/0	1(0)/0	37(0)/1	8(0)/0	21(0)/2	40(0)/13	37(0)/2	27(3)/1	23(3)/3	26(2)/3	27(3)/1	9(5)/3	19(4)/1	0(2)/0		22(0)/0	17(0)/0	7(0)/0	9(0)/5	8(0)/0	1(0)/0	Final League Position: 16

Own goals: Caton, match 11

DIVISION 3

WIGAN ATHLETIC
Springfield Park, Wigan WN6 7BA.

Back row (left to right): Dave Philpotts (Coach), Chris Thompson, Mark Hilditch, Bobby Campbell, Nigel Adkins (Goalkeeper), Paul Beesley, Paul Cook, Roy Tunks (Ass. Manager), Andy Holder. *Front row:* Andy Ainscow, John Butler, Paul Jewell, David Hamilton, Ray Mathias (Manager), Alex Cribley, Ian Griffiths, Stuart Storer, Barry Knowles.

Stadium Capacity: 12,500.
Pitch Dimensions: 117 × 73 yds.
Telephone: 0942–44433.
Chairman: W. Kenyon.
Vice-Chairman: G. D. Gorner.
Directors: J. A. Bennett, J. D. Fillingham, T. Hitchen, W. Howard, S. Jackson, R. Pearce.
Manager: Ray Mathias.
Managers since 1978: Ted Goodier, Allan Brown, Gordon Milne, Ian McNeil, Larry Lloyd, Bobby Charlton (acting), Harry McNally, Bryan Hamilton (8).
Physio: D. Bingham.
Secretary: Lynda Fillingham.
Chief Executive: Bryan Hamilton.
Sponsors: H. J. Heinz.
Founded: 1932.
Turned Professional: 1932.
Nickname: The Latics.
Former Names: None.
Former Grounds: None.
Record Attendance: 27,500 v Hereford United, 12 December 1953.
Record Victory: 7–2 Scunthorpe United Division 4, 12 March 1982.
Record Defeat: 0–5 v Bristol Rovers, Division 3, 26 February 1983 and 0–5 v Chelsea, FA Cup 3rd Round replay, 26 January 1985.
Most League Points: (3 for a win) 91, Division 4, 1981–82. (2 for a win) 55, Division 4, 1978–79 and 1979–80.
Most League Goals: 80, Division 4, 1981–82.
Highest League Scorer in a Season: Les Bradd, 19, Division 4, 1981–82.
Highest Total of League Goals: Peter Houghton, 62, 1978–84.
Most League Appearances: Colin Methven, 296, 1979–86.
League History: 1978 Elected to Division 4, 1982– Division 3.
Honours: Associate Members' Cup winners 1985.
Colours: Royal blue shirts and shorts, white socks. **Second strip:** Yellow shirts and socks, red shorts.

WIGAN ATHLETIC – LEAGUE RECORD 1987–88

Match no/Opp/Date		Tunks	Butler	Knowles	Hamilton	Cribley	Beesley	Stowe	Thompson C	Campbell	Jewell	Cook	Hilditch	Atkinson	Griffiths	Holden	Redfern	Adkins	Thompson D	Atherton	Senior	Hughes	Pilling	Wilson	Smith	Kennedy	McEwan	FT(HT)Att Lge pos
1. Notts Co	15.8	1	2	3^1	4	5_1	6	7†	8^1	9^1	10	11	12															4–4(3–2)6344 —
2. Preston	29.8	1	2	3	4	5	6		8	9	10	11^1	7															1–0(0–0)7057 12
3. Gillingham*	31.8	1	2	3	4	5_1	6	12	8	9	10†	11	7															1–1(0–1)3412
4. Bristol R	5.9	1	2	3	4^1	5	6^1	7†	8	9^1	10	11	12															3–2(2–2)3168 8
5. Doncaster*	12.9	1	2	3	4	5	6	7	8‡	9^1	10	11†	12	14^1														2–1(1–1)2764 5
6. Mansfield	15.9	1	2	3	4	5_1	6	7		9	10	11	8															1–0(0–0)3261
7. Walsall	19.9	1	2	3	4	5	6	7		9	10_2	11	8															2–1(1–0)5353
8. Bury*	26.9	1	2	3	4	5	6	7	14	9	10	12	8‡			11†												0–2(0–1)3664 4
9. Aldershot	29.9	1	2	3†	4	5	6	7‡		9^1	10	11	8^1		14	12												2–3(1–2)2529
10. York*	3.10		2^1	12	4	5	3	7‡		9	10		8	14	11^1	6	1											1–1(0–0)2878 9
11. Sunderland	10.10		2	12	4	5†	3	7	8		10^1		9	14	11‡	6	1											1–4(1–3)13,974 11
12. Fulham	17.10		2	3	4		5	12	8	9^1	10		7	11†	6													1–3(0–2)2806 12
13. Brighton*	20.10		2	3	4		5	12	8^1	9	10		11^2	14	6		1‡	7†										3–3(1–2)2392 —
14. Blackpool	24.10	1	2	3	4		5		8	9	10		11		6				7									0–0(0–0)4821 14
15. Rotherham*	31.10		2	3	4		5		8	9^2	$10†$	12	11		6		1		7									3–0(1–0)3004 11
16. Chesterfield	3.11		2	3	4		5		8	9	10^1	11			6				7	1								1–0(1–0)1725
17. Southend*	7.11		2	3	4		5		8	9	12	10^1	$11†$		6				7	1								1–0(0–0)3081
18. Brentford	21.11		2	3	4		5			9	10	11	14	8‡				6†	7	1			12^1					1–2(0–1)3625 8
19. Bristol C*	28.11		2	3	4		5			9	10†	11	12			6^1			7	1	8							1–0(0–2)2879 9
20. Grimsby	12.12			3	4		5			10	11^1	2	9			6			7	1	8							2–0(1–0)2196 7
21. Nthampton*	19.12				4		5			10	11	9†						6^1	3	7	1	8^1	2	12				2–2(1–1)2692 8
22. Bury	26.12				4					10	11		9			6^1			7	2	1	8				3	5^1	2–0(1–0)4555
23. Chester*	28.12				4					11	10^1	9				6			7	12	2†	1	8			3	5	1–0(0–0)4394 5
24. Preston*	1.1				4				12		11	$10^{2}‡$	9			6			7	2		1	8			3	5	2–0(2–0)6872
25. Doncaster	2.1				4	12					10^1	11^1	9			$6†$			7^1	2		1	8			3	5	4–3(1–2)2464
26. Walsall*	16.1				4	5					10	11	9^2						7	2		1	8			3	6^1	3–1(2–0)5063 4
27. Gillingham	23.1				4^1	6				10	11	12	9†						7	2		1	8			3	5	1–0(1–0)4256 3
28. Nthampton	30.1				4	6		12		10	11	9†							7	2		1	8^1			3	5	1–1(1–0)4825 3
29. Bristol R*	6.2				4	6				10	11^1	9							7	2		1	8			3	5	1–0(0–0)3827 3
30. Chester	13.2				4	6		12		10	11	9							7	2		1	8†			3	5	0–1(0–0)3088 3
31. Notts Co*	20.2				4†	6		12		$10‡$	11	9							7^1	2	14	1	8			3	5	2–1(1–1)5182 3
32. York	27.2				4‡	6		12	14	10^1	11	9							7	2	5	1	8†			3		1–3(0–1)2366 4
33. Aldershot*	1.3				4	6		8	12	10^3	11	9^{1+}							7	2	5	1				3		4–0(0–0)3017 —
34. Fulham	5.3				4	6		8	12	10	$11‡$	9^{1+}		14					7^1	2		1				3	5	2–3(2–3)3860 4
35. Sunderland*	12.3	12			4	6		8	9†	10	$11‡$		14						7		2^1	1				3	5	2–2(1–0)6949 3
36. Rotherham	19.3	12			4	6		8	14	10	11	9†							7		2	1				3‡	5^1	1–1(0–1)3288 3
37. Blackpool*	25.3	2			4	6		8	9	10	$11+$		12						7			1				3	5	0–0(0–0)4505
38. Mansfield*	28.3	2			4			8	9	10	$11+$		12^1						7		6	1				3	5^1	2–1(1–1)3217 3
39. Southend	1.4				4	6		8	9^1	$10+$	11^1		14						$7‡$		2	1	12			3	5	2–3(1–0)5003
40. Brentford*	4.4					6		8	9^1	10	11		4						$7+$		2	1	12			3	5	1–1(1–3)3597 3
41. Brighton	9.4				4	6		8	$9+$	10	11		12						7		2	1				3	5	0–1(0–0)9423 3
42. Port Vale*	12.4				4	6		8^1	9^1	10	11								7		2	1				3	5	2–0(1–0)3750 3
43. Chesterfield*	23.4				4	6		8	9^1	10	$11+$		12						7	2		1				3	5	1–2(1–1)3303 6
44. Port Vale	25.4	14	3		4	6		$8+$	9	10	$11‡$								7		2	1	12				5	1–2(1–1)3044 —
45. Bristol C	30.4	11	3		4	6		$8‡$	12	10^1	14								7		$2+$	1	9				5	1–4(1–2)7340 6
46. Grimsby*	2.5	2	3	$4+$	6			12	9	10	11								7		14	1	8				$5‡$	0–1(0–0)2715 7
App(subs)/goals		10(0)0	23(3)1	21(2)1	45(0)2	11(0)3	41(1)1	9(3)0	25(0)3	28(0)11	42(1)11	38(5)8	25(0)8	9(6)4	5(8)1	14(1)2	3(0)0	2(0)0	27(0)4	15(1)0	20(2)1	31(0)0	16(4)3	10(1)0	0(1)0	22(0)0	23(0)4	Final League Position: 7

Own goals: O'Riordan, match 20; Hughes, match 44.

DIVISION 1

WIMBLEDON

Plough Lane Ground, Durnsford Road, Wimbledon, London SW19 8HG.

Back row (left to right): Paul Fishenden, Peter Cawley, Lawrie Sanchez, Dave Beasant, Brian Gayle, Andy Thorn, Alan Cork. *Middle row:* Sid Neal, Don Howe (Coach), Carlton Fairweather, Paul Miller, Mick Smith, Eric Young, Simon Tracey, John Fashanu, John Scales, Vince Jones, Clive Goodyear, David Kemp, Steve Allen, Ron Stuart. *Front row:* Wally Downes, Andy Clement, Andy Sayer, Terry Phelan, Steve Galliers, Bobby Gould (Manager), Dennis Wise, Vaughan Ryan, John Gannon, Kevin Bedford, Ian Hazel.

Stadium Capacity: 16,000
Pitch Dimensions: 110 × 73 yds
Telephone: 01–946 6311, **Clubcall:** 0898–121175.
Chairman: S. G. Reed.
Vice-Chairman: J. Lelliott.
President: Lord Havers.
Managing Director: S. Hammam.
Directors: P. Cork, Q. Spicer, P. R. Cooper.
Manager: Bobby Gould.
Managers since 1955: Les Henley, Mike Everitt, Dick Graham, Allen Batsford, Dario Gradi, Dave Bassett (6).
Coach: Don Howe.
Physio: Steve Allen.
Secretary: Adrian Cook.
Commercial Manager: Reg Davis.
Founded: 1889.
Turned Professional: 1964.
Nickname: The Dons.
Former Names: Wimbledon Old Centrals 1899–1905.
Former Grounds: None.
Record Attendance: 18,000 v HMS Victory, FA Amateur Cup 3rd Round, 1934–35.
Record Victory: 15–2 v Polytechnic, FA Cup Preliminary Round, 7 February 1929.
Record Defeat: 0–8 v Everton, League Cup 2nd Round, 29 August 1978.
Most League Points: (3 for a win) 98, Division 4, 1982–83. (2 for a win) 61, Division 4, 1978–79.
Most League Goals: 97, Division 3, 1983–84.
Highest League Scorer in a Season: Alan Cork, 29, 1983–84.
Highest Total of League Goals: Alan Cork, 131, 1977–88.
Most League Appearances: Alan Cork, 330, 1978–88.
League History: 1977 Elected to Division 4, 1977–79 Division 4, 1979–80 Division 3, 1980–81 Division 4, 1981–82 Division 3, 1982–83 Division 4, 1983–84, Division 3, 1984–86 Division 2, 1986– Division 1.
Honours: Division 3 runners-up 1983–84.
FA Cup winners 1988. **Associate Members' Cup runners-up 1982.**
Colours: All royal blue with yellow trim. **Second strip:** All red with green trim.

WIMBLEDON – LEAGUE RECORD 1987–88

Match no/Opp/Date		Beasant	Scales	Phelan	Cork	Young	Thorn	Galliers	Sayer	Fashanu	Sanchez	Fairweather	Ryan	Miller	Gannon	Wise	Gayle	Gibson	Goodyear	Clement	Jones	Bedford	Hazel	Turner	Cunningham	Swindlehurst	FT(HT)Att	Lge pos
1. Watford ·	15.8	1	2	3	4	5	6	7†	8‡	9	10	11	12	14													0–1(0–1)15,344	—
2. Everton*	18.8	1	2	3	7¹	5	6		8	9	10	11†	4		12												1–1(1–0)7763	—
3. Oxford*	22.8	1	2	3	11¹	5	6		8	9	10		4		12	7†											1–0(0–1)4229	15
4. Derby	29.8	1		3	11	5	6			9¹	10	14	4		7	2†	8‡	12									1–0(0–0)15,165	11
5. Charlton*	1.9	1	2	3	11¹	5	6			9²	10	12	4¹		7		8†										4–1(1–1)5184	—
6. Newcastle	5.9	1	2	3†	11¹‡	5	6		8	9¹	10		4		7	12			14								2–1(2–0)22,684	3
7. West Ham*	12.9	1	2	3	11	5†	6		8‡	9	10		4		7¹	12	14										1–1(1–0)8507	4
8. Arsenal	19.9	1		3		5	6			9	10	11†	4		7	2	8	12									0–3(0–3)27,752	8
9. Portsmouth	26.9	1	2	3		5				9	10¹	11	12		7	6	8		4†								1–2(1–1)13,088	10
10. QPR*	3.10	1	2	3	7	5	6			9¹	10‡	11†	12	14			8		4								1–2(0–0)8552	11
11. Luton	17.10	1		3	8		6			9	10	11†	2		7		5				12	4					0–2(0–1)7018	13
12. Spurs	31.10	1			12		6			9¹	10	11	4	7¹		5	8†¹	2			3						3–0(1–0)22,282	13
13. Liverpool*	4.11	1			12		6			9	10	7¹	11†		11†·	5	8‡	2			3	14					1–1(0–0)13,454	—
14. Sthampton*	7.11	1			12¹		6			9	10	7‡¹	4	11	8†	5		2			3	14					2–0(1–0)5014	10
15. Coventry	14.11	1	14		12		6			9²	10	7	11†	8¹	5		2			3‡	4						3–3(0–1)13,966	9
16. Man Utd*	21.11	1	3¹		8		6			9	10	7¹		11	5		2		4								2–1(0–0)11,532	8
17. Chelsea	28.11	1	3		8	2	6			9	10	7		11¹	5		2		4								1–0(0–0)15,608	8
18. Nottm F*	5.12	1	3		8†	14	6		12	9	10	7		11¹	5		2‡		4								1–0(0–1)5170	8
19. Sheff W	12.12	1	3	14	12	5	6			9¹	10		7†	11			2		4	8‡							0–1(0–0)14,289	8
20. Norwich*	18.12	1	3		8	5	6			9+¹	10	7		11			2		4		12						1–0(1–0)4026	—
21. West Ham	26.12	1	3		8†	5	6			9¹	10¹	7		11			2		4		12						2–1(2–0)18,605	7
22. Arsenal*	28.12	1	3		8¹	5	6			9	10	7		11¹			2	4¹									3–1(0–1)12,473	7
23. Derby*	1.1	1	3	12	8¹	5	6†			9¹	10	7		11			2		4								2–1(1–1)5479	7
24. Oxford	2.1	1	3†		8²	5				9¹	10¹	7¹	12	11	6		2		4								5–2(3–0)6926	7
25. Watford*	16.1	1	3	8	5¹					9	10	7†	12	11‡		6	2		4		14						1–2(0–0)6848	6
26. Newcastle*	6.2	1	3	8†		6				9	10			11	5	7	2	12	4								0–0(0–0)10,505	7
27. Charlton	13.2	1	3	8		6				9	10			11†	5	7¹	2	12	4								1–0(0–1)5520	7
28. QPR	27.2	1	3	12		6				9	10			5	7	2	8†	4			11						0–1(0–0)9080	7
29. Luton*	5.3	1	11	3	8†		6			9¹	10			5	7¹	2	12	4									2–0(1–0)5058	7
30. Spurs*	19.3	1	12	3	8	5	6			9¹	10			11¹		7	2†	4¹									3–0(0–0)8616	7
31. Liverpool	26.3	1	2	3	8†	5¹	6		12	9	10	4		11							7						1–2(0–1)36,464	7
32. Everton	29.3	1		3	8	5	6†			9	10	2		11¹			12	4			7‡						2–2(2–2)20,351	—
33. Sthampton	2.4	1	2	3	8‡	5	6			9	10†	4		11	12¹		14				7¹						2–2(1–0)13,036	7
34. Coventry*	5.4	1	2	3		5¹	6		14	9‡		8	10	11	12			7†	4								1–2(1–2)5920	7
35. Portsmouth*	19.4	1	2	3	8†	5				9		4		12	11²	6	7				10						2–2(1–0)9009	7
36. Chelsea*	23.4	1	2	3		5	6				10¹	4†	8	7‡	11¹	12		14					9				2–2(1–0)15,128	7
37. Nottm F	30.4	1	2†	3		5	6				10		8	7	11	12		4			14		9‡				0–0(0–0)14,341	7
38. Sheff Wed*	3.5	1		3	8†	5	6			9	10			12		7¹	2	4			11						1–1(0–0)7854	7
39. Norwich	7.5	1		3	8		6			9	10			11	5	7¹	2	4									1–0(0–0)11,782	7
40. Man Utd	9.5	1		3		5			12	9	10			8‡		6	7¹†	2			4	14	11				1–2(1–0)28,040	7

Final League Position: 7

Appearances/goals: 40(0) 0 · 23(2) 1 · 28(2) 0 · 28(6) 9 · 28(13) 0 · 35(0) 0 · 10(0) 0 · 5(4) 0 · 38(0) 14 · 38(0) 4 · 19(2) 4 · 17(5) 1 · 3(2) 0 · 10(3) 1 · 20(1) 10 · 16(1) 6 · 21(1) 0 · 29(0) 2 · 24(0) 2 · 40(0) 0 · 35(0) 0 · 0(4) 0 · 6(0) 2 · 2(0) 0

DIVISION 3

WOLVERHAMPTON WANDERERS
Molineux Grounds, Wolverhampton WV1 4QR.

Back row (left to right): Robert Kelly, Jackie Gallagher, Andy Mutch, Steve Bull, Phil Robinson, Michael Holmes, Robert Dennison, Steve Stoutt, Mark Smith. *Centre row:* Paul Darby (Physio), Mark Venus, Nicky Clarke, Mark Freeman, Mark Kendall, Alistair Robertson, Vince Bartram, Chris Brindley, Floyd Streete, Gary Bellamy, Barry Powell (Coach). *Front row:* Matt Forman, John Purdie, Andy Thompson, Graham Turner (Manager), Phil Chard, Nigel Vaughan, Keith Downing, Mark Jones.

Stadium Capacity: 28,051.
Pitch Dimensions: 115 × 72 yds.
Telephone: 0902–712181, Lottery shop: 0902–27524.
Chairman: R. Homden.
Vice-Chairman: J. Harris.
Manager: Graham Turner.
Post-War Managers: Ted Vizard, Stan Cullis, Andy Beattie, Ron Allen, Bill McGarry, Sammy Chung, John Barnwell, Ian Greaves, Graham Hawkins, Tommy Docherty, Bill McGarry, Sammy Chapman (acting), Brian Little (13).
Physio: Paul Darby.
Secretary: Keith Pearson ACIS.
Commercial Manager: J. Witherington.
Founded: 1877.
Turned Professional: 1888.
Nickname: The Wolves.
Former Names: St Luke's, Blakenhall combined with The Wanderers to become Wolverhampton Wanderers in 1880.
Former Grounds: Goldthorn Hill 1877–84, Dudley Road 1884–1889.
Record Attendance: 61,315 v Liverpool, FA Cup 5th Round, 11 February 1939.
Record Victory: 14–0 v Crosswell's Brewery, FA Cup 2nd Round, 1886–87.
Record Defeat: 1–10 v Newton Heath, Division 1, 15 October 1892.
Most League Points: (3 for a win) 90, Division 4, 1987–88. (2 for a win) 64, Division 1 1957–58.
Most League Goals: 115, Division 2, 1931–32.
Highest League Scorer in a Season: Dennis Westcott, 37,Division 1, 1946–47.
Highest Total of League Goals: Bill Hartill, 164, 1928–35.
Most League Appearances: Derek Parkin, 501, 1967–82.
League History: 1888 Founder Members of Football League, 1906–23 Division 2, 1923–24 Division 3 (N), 1924–32 Division 2, 1932–65 Division 1, 1965–67 Division 2, 1967–76 Division 1, 1976–77Division 2, 1977–82 Division 1, 1982–83 Division 2, 1983–84 Division 1, 1984–85 Division 2, 1985–86 Division 3, 1986–88 Division 4, 1988– Division 3.
Honours: Division 1 Champions 1953–54, 1957–58, 1958–59, runners-up 1937–38, 1938–39, 1949–50, 1954–55, 1959–60. Division 2 Champions 1931–32, 1976–77, runners-up 1966–67, 1982–83. Division 4 Champions 1987–88. Division 3(N) Champions 1923–24. FA Cup winners 1893, 1908, 1949, 1960, runners-up 1889, 1896, 1921, 1939. League Cup winners 1974, 1980. UEFA Cup runners-up 1972. Associate Members' Cup winners 1988.
Colours: Old gold shirts, with black collar and cuffs, black shorts, old gold socks. **Second strip:** All white.

WOLVERHAMPTON WANDERERS – LEAGUE RECORD 1987–88

Match no/Opp/Date		Kendall	Stoutt	Barnes	Streete	Robertson	Robinson	Thompson	Dennison	Bull	Mutch	Holmes	Downing	Clarke	Gallagher	Vaughan	Bellamy	Purdie	Powell	Edwards	McDonald	Venus	Chard	FT(HT)Att Lge pos
1. Scarboro	15.8	1	2^1	3	4	5	6	7	$8^\dagger$	9^1	10	11	12											2-2(2-1)7314 —
2. Halifax*	22.8	1	2		4	5	6	8	7	9	$10^\dagger$	11	3	12										0-1(0-0)7223 18
3. Hereford	29.8	1	2		4	5	6	8	7	9^1	10^1	11	3											2-1(2-0)2628 12
4. Scunthorpe*	31.8	1	2		4	5	6	8	7	9^2	10^2	11	$3^\dagger$	12										4-1(2-1)6672 —
5. Cardiff	5.9	1	2		4	5	6	7	$8^\dagger$	9^1	10	$11^\ddagger$	3	12	14^1									2-3(1-1)2258 11
6. Crewe*	12.9	1	14		4	$5^\ddagger$	6	3	7	9^1	$10^\dagger$	11	12^1			8	2							2-2(1-1)6285 11
7. Peterboro	16.8	1	2		4		6	3	7	9^1	10	11				8	5							1-1(1-0)3089 —
8. Stockport	19.8	1			4	5	6^1	3	7		10^1	11				8	2							2-0(2-0)2233 9
9. Torquay*	26.8	1			4	5	6	3	7	9^1	10		12			8	2	$11^\dagger$						1-2(0-0)7349 12
10. Rochdale*	29.8	1			4	5	6	3	$7^\dagger$	9^1	10^1	12				8	2	11						2-0(1-0)5553 —
11. Bolton	10.3	1			4	5	6	3	7	9	$10^\dagger$		12			8	2	11						0-1(0-0)3833 11
12. Carlisle	10.10	1			4	5	6	3	$7^\dagger$	9^1	10	11	12			8	2							1-0(1-0)2620 8
13. Tranmere*	17.10	1			4	5	6	3	7	9^1	$10^{4\dagger}$	11	12			8^1	2							3-0(3-0)6608 6
14. Cambridge*	20.10	1	2		4	5	$6^\dagger$	3	7	9^1	10^1	11	12			8^1								3-0(3-0)6492 —
15. Darlington	24.10	1	2		4	5		3	7	9	10^2	6	11			8^1								2-2(2-2)2282 4
16. Newport	31.10	1	2		4	5		3	7		10^1	$6^\dagger$	9	8^1				12	11					2-1(0-0)6467 1
17. Swansea	3.11	1	2		4	5		3	7	9^1	10	11	6^1	8										2-1(1-0)5293 —
18. Burnley*	7.11	1	2		4	5		3	7	9	10	11^1	6^1	8^1										3-0(0-0)10,002 1
19. Colchester	21.11	1	2		4		12	3_1	7	9	10	$11^\dagger$	5	6	8									1-0(0-0)2413 1
20. Wrexham*	28.11	1	2		$4^\dagger$	5	6	3	$7^\dagger$	9	10	14	12	11	8									0-2(0-1)8541 1
21. Hartlepool	12.12	1	2		4	5	6	3	7		10		11	9	8									0-0(0-0)2760 2
22. Orient*	19.12	1	2		4	5	6	3	7	9^2	10		11		8									2-0(0-0)12,051 1
23. Exeter*	28.12	1	2		4		6	3_1	7^1	9	10^1	11	5		8									3-0(1-0)15,588 2
24. Hereford*	1.1	1	2		4	5	6	3	7	9^2	10	11		8										2-0(1-0)14,577 1
25. Crewe	2.1	1	2		4	5	6	3	7	9	10^2	11		8										2-0(1-0)4,629 1
26. Stockport*	16.1	1	$2^\ddagger$		4	5	6	3	7	9	10	14	$11^\dagger$	12	8^1									1-1(1-0)8872 1
27. Scunthorpe	30.1	1			4	5	6	3	7	9	10^1	11		8	2									1-0(0-0)5476 1
28. Cardiff*	6.2	1				5	6	3	7	9^1	10	11	4	8	2									1-4(0-0)10,077 1
29. Exeter	13.2	1			4	5	6	3	7	$9^{3\dagger}$	10	11		8	2	12^1								4-2(2-0)3483 1
30. Halifax	16.2	1			4	5	6	3		9	10	14	11	12	8	$2^{1\ddagger}$	$7^\dagger$							1-2(1-1)2281 —
31. Scarboro*	19.2	1			4	5	6	2	7	9	10	$11^\dagger$	12		8			3						0-0(0-0)11,391 —
32. Torquay	23.2	1			4	5	6	2	7	9	10	11			8			3						0-0(0-0)3803 —
33. Bolton*	27.2	1			4	5	6^1	2	7^1	9^2	10	11	12		$8^\dagger$			3						4-0(4-0)12,430 1
34. Rochdale	1.3	1			4	$5^\dagger$	6	2	7	9	10	11^1	12		8			3						1-0(1-0)2805 —
35. Tranmere	4.3	1			4		6	$2^\dagger$	7	9	10	11	12		8	5		3						0-3(0-1)5007 —
36. Carlisle*	12.3	1			4	5	6		7	9	10^1	11			8	2^1		3						3-1(1-0)9262 1
37. Peterboro*	22.3	1	2			5	6		7	9	10	$11^\ddagger$	12	14	$8^\dagger$	4			3					0-1(0-0)8049 —
38. Darlington*	26.3	1			4	5	6^1		7	9^3	10	11			2					3		8^1		5-3(2-0)9349 1
39. Burnley	2.4	1			4	5	6	12	$7^\dagger$	9^1	10^1	11^1			2					3		8		3-0(1-0)10,341 1
40. Colchester*	4.4	1			4	5	$6^\dagger$		7	9^2	10	11	12		2					3		8		2-0(1-0)13,433 1
41. Cambridge	10.4	1			4	5		3		9	10^1	11	6		7	2						8		1-1(0-0)5017 —
42. Swansea*	23.4	1			4	5	6^1	3	$7^\ddagger$	9^1	10	12	$8^\dagger$		2	14						11		2-0(1-0)12,344 1
43. Newport	26.4	1	5		4		6	3		9^2	10^1	7			2							8		3-1(2-0)3409 1
44. Wrexham	30.4	1			4	5	$6^\dagger$	3	7	9	10^1	11	12		2							8^1		2-4(2-3)6898 1
45. Hartlepool*	2.5	1			4	5	6	3	7	9^2	10				11	2						8		2-0(1-0)17,895 1
46. Orient	7.5	1			4	5	$6^{1\dagger}$	3	11^1	9	10	7	$8^\ddagger$		14	2							12	2-0(1-0)7738 1

Apps(subs)/goals: 46(0)0 | 21(1)1 | 1(0)0 | 44(0)0 | 41(0)0 | 40(1)5 | 41(1)2 | 43(0)3 | 44(0)34 | 46(0)19 | 16(4)2 | 27(7)1 | 7(1)0 | 6(13)3 | 33(4)6 | 24(0)2 | 7(2)1 | 0(4)0 | 1(0)0 | 6(0)0 | 4(0)0 | 8(1)2

Final League Position: 1

Own goal: Clark, match 36.

DIVISION 4

WREXHAM

Racecourse Ground, Mold Road, Wrexham LL1 2AN.

Back row (left to right): Dixie McNeil (Manager), Paul Emson, Joe Hinnigan, Mike Williams, Mike Salmon, Jim Steel, Mark Morris, Jon Bowden, Jamie Slater, Darren Wright, George Showell (Ass. Manager/Physio).
Front row: Mike Carter, Steve Massey, Kevin Russell, Neil Salathiel, Joe Cooke, Geoff Hunter, Roger Preece, Shaun Cunnington, Steve Buxton, Nick Hencher.

Stadium Capacity: 22,500.
Pitch Dimensions: 111 × 71 yds.
Telephone: 0978–262129, **Commercial dept:** 0978–352536.
Chairman: G. Mytton.
Vice-Chairman: W. P. Griffiths.
Manager: Dixie McNeil.
Post-War Managers: Tom Williams, Les McDowell, Peter Jackson, Cliff Lloyd, John Love, Bill Morris, Ken Barnes, Bill Morris, Jack Rowley, Alvan Williams, John Neal, Arfon Griffiths MBE, Mel Sutton, Bobby Roberts (14).
Assistant Manager: G. Showell.
Physio: G. Showell.
Secretary: S. Gandy.
Commercial Manager: S. R. Slater.
Sponsors: Marstons Ales.
Founded: 1873
Turned Professional: 1912
Nickname: The Robins.
Former Names:
Former Grounds: Acton Park 1873–97.
Record Attendance: 34,445 v Manchester United, FA Cup 4th Round, 26 Jan 1957.
Record Victory: 10–1 v Hartlepool United, Division 4, 3 March 1962.
Record Defeat: 0–9 v Brentford, Division 3, 15 October 1963.
Most League Points: (3 for a win) 66, Division 4, 1987–88. (2 for a win) 61, Division 4, 1969–70 and Division 3, 1977–78.
Most League Goals: 106, Division 3(N), 1932–33.
Highest League Scorer in a Season: Tom Bamford, 44, Division 3(N), 1933–34.
Highest Total of League Goals: Tom Bamford, 175, 1928–34.
Most League Appearances: Arfon Griffiths, 592, 1959–61, 1962–79.
League History: 1921 Founder Members of Division 3(N), 1958–60 Division3, 1960–62 Division 4, 1962–64 Division 3, 1964–70 Division 4, 1970–78 Division 3, 1978–82 Division 2, 1982–83 Division 3, 1983– Division 4.
Honours: Division 3 Champions 1977–78. Division 4 runners-up 1969–70.
Division 3(N) runners-up 1932–33. Welsh Cup winners 1903, 1905, 1909, 1910, 1911, 1914, 1915, 1921, 1924, 1925, 1931, 1957, 1958, 1960, 1972, 1975, 1978, 1986, runners-up 19 times.
Colours: Red shirts with white trim, white shorts with red trim, red socks with white hoops. **Second strip:** White shirts, black shorts, white socks, or green shirts, yellow shorts, green socks.

WREXHAM – LEAGUE RECORD 1987–88

Match no/Opp/Date		Salmon	Saladhiel	Hinnigan	Williams	Cooke	Jones	Carter	Hunter	Steel	Russell	Cunnington	Buxton	Preece	Bowden	Wright	Harvey	Slater	Hencher	Emson	Alloyne	Fairbrother	Scott	Morris	Kearns	Flynn	Massey	FT(HT)Att Lge pos
1. Torquay	15.8	1	2	3	4	5†	6	7¹	8	9	10	11	12															1-6(1-2)1731 —
2. Hartlepool*	22.8	1		12	4†	5	3	7	8	9²	10‡	11	14	2	6													2-1(0-0)1816 15
3. Crewe	29.8	1		4	·	5	3		9	10	11	8	7	6	2													0-2(0-1)2210 22
4. Halifax*	31.8	1		4	2	5	3		14	9¹†	10	11¹	8	7‡	6	12												2-2(1-0)1661 —
5. Exeter	5.9	1	2	4	5		3†		9¹	10	11	7	8	6	12													1-1(0-0)2719 21
6. Cardiff*	12.9	1	2	4	5		3	8¹	9	10¹	11	7¹					6											3-0(0-0)2212 16
7. Burnley	15.9	1	2†		5		3	8	9	10	11	7	12	4			6											0-1(0-0)5642 —
8. Peterboro	19.9	1	2		5		3	8	9	10†	11	7	12	4			6											0-1(0-1)2805 20
9. Stockport*	26.9	1	2	4	5		3	8	9¹	10	11	7¹	12			6†												2-1(2-1)1841 16
10. Cambridge	29.9	1	2	4	5¹		3	14	9	10	11	7†	12	8‡			6											1-0(0-0)2257 —
11. Orient*	3.10	1	2	4	5			11	9¹	10‡	3		7¹	8†	12	6	14											2-2(1-1)2123 13
12. Swansea	10.10	1	2†	4	5		3	12‡	8	9		6	7¹	10				14	11									1-2(0-0)3741 16
13. Colchester*	17.10	1		4	5		3	10‡	8	9		6	7	2		14		12	11†									0-1(0-1)1493 17
14. Darlington*	20.10	1		4	5		3		8	9		6	7	10		2		12	11†									0-1(0-0)1278 —
15. Newport	24.10	1		4	5		3		8	9		6	2			11		12	7†	10								0-2(0-1)1470 20
16. Scarboro*	31.10	1		4	5		6		8	9			7†	2	3			11	12	10								1-0(1-0)1860 19
17. Scunthorpe	3.11	1		4	5				8	9		7¹†	2		3	12		11	10	6								1-3(1-2)2348 —
18. Tranmere	6.11	1		4	5				8	9		7	2		3	12		11	10†	6‡	14							0-1(0-0)3271 —
19. Carlisle*	21.11	1		4	5			11¹	8¹		10	7	2		3			9¹	6	12								4-0(1-0)1485 19
20. Wolves	28.11	1		4	5			11		10¹		7	2	8	3			9¹	6									2-0(1-0)8541 18
21. Rochdale*	12.12	1		4	5	12			10†	11¹	7	2	8¹	3			14	9	6‡									2-3(2-2)1409 18
22. Bolton	19.12	1		4	5	12		8		10	3	7	2	6			11	9†										0-2(0-1)3701 19
23. Stockport	26.12	1		4	2	5		8		10¹	3	7†		6			11	12					1	9				1-1(1-0)2504 19
24. Hereford	28.12	1		4	2	5		8		10	3	7	12	6			11†						1	9				0-0(0-0)2443 19
25. Crewe*	1.1	1		4†	2	5		8		10‡	11		7	6	3			12					1	9				2-1(0-0)2939 18
26. Peterboro*	16.1	1		4	2	5		12	8	10²	11¹		7†	6	3									9				3-1(1-0)1506 19
27. Hartlepool	26.1	1		4	2		3			11	8	7	9	6	5									10				0-1(0-0)1692 —
28. Burnley*	2.2	1		4	5		3			10	8	12	7	6	2			11¹						9†				1-3(0-0)1821 —
29. Hereford	13.2	1		4	5		3	6		10	8		7					11						9²				2-0(2-0)2006 19
30. Torquay*	20.2	1		4¹	5		3			10¹		12	7	2				11†						9	6			2-3(0-2)1488 20
31. Halifax	23.2	1		4		5	3	11	8	10		9	7	2										6				0-2(0-1)1284 —
32. Orient	27.2	1	2			5	4	11	8		10	7		3										9†	6	12¹		1-2(0-2)3448 20
33. Cambridge*	1.3	1	2			5‡	4	11¹	8	9¹	10‡†	7	14	3										6	12			3-0(2-0)1025 —
34. Colchester	4.3	1	2		5		4	11¹	8¹	10	9	7		3										6				2-1(2-1)1797 —
35. Swansea*	12.3	1	2		5		4	11		10₁		7	8	3										12	6	9†		1-2(0-1)1916 19
36. Cardiff	16.3	1	2		5		4	11	8	10		7¹	12	3										9	6†			1-1(1-0)4083 —
37. Scarboro	19.3	1	2		5		4	11	8	10¹		7¹		3									1	9	6			2-0(2-0)2090 17
38. Exeter*	22.3		2		5		4	11	8	10²		7†	12	3									1	9	6			3-0(0-0)963 —
39. Newport*	26.3		2		5		4	11	8	10¹	12			3									1	9³	6	7†		4-2(1-1)1627 14
40. Tranmere*	2.4	1	2		5		4	11¹	8	10¹†	12		14	3										9¹	6	7‡		3-0(2-0)3134 13
41. Carlisle	4.4	1	2		5		4	11¹†	8	10¹	12			3										9²	6	7		4-0(2-0)2284 11
42. Scunthorpe*	9.4	1	2		5		4		8	10¹	7¹	12	11†	3										9	6			2-1(0-1)2589 9
43. Darlington	23.4	1	2		5		4		8	10₁	7	12	11	3										6	9†			1-2(0-1)1711 12
44. Wolves*	30.4	1	2		5¹		4	11†	8¹	10₁	7	12	3											6¹	9			4-2(3-2)6898 12
45. Rochdale	2.5	1	2		5		4	11	8	10¹	7¹†	12	3											6	9			2-1(0-1)1539 9
46. Bolton*	7.5	1	2		5		4	11	8	10	12	7	3											6	9†			0-1(0-0)5977 11

Appearances/goals: 40(0)/0 24(0)/0 28(1)/1 42(0)/2 11(2)/0 35(0)/0 19(2)/6 37(2)/4 18(0)/6 38(0)/21 24(0)/3 27(8)/6 35(7)/4 20(6)/1 31(4)/0 9(0)/0 0(3)/0 12(2)/2 7(3)/2 7(0)/0 6(2)/0 6(0)/0 16(1)/8 17(0)/1 8(2)/1

Final League Position: 11

Own goal: Saunders, match 19.

YORK CITY

DIVISION 4

Bootham Crescent, York YO3 7AQ.

Back row (left to right): Paul Johnson, Tony Canham, Scott Endersby, Martin Butler, Simon Mills. *Middle row:* Gerry Delahunt (Physio), Tony Clegg, Phil Kitching, Neil Smallwood, Derek Hood, David Spofforth, Alan Whitehead, Ricky Sbragia (Reserve Team Coach). *Front row:* Nigel Costello, Dale Banton, Stuart McKenzie, Bobby Saxton (Manager), Mark Brown, Marco Gabbiadini, Phil Wilson.

Stadium Capacity: 14,109
Pitch Dimensions: 114x76yds
Telephone: 0904–624447.
Chairman: M. D. B. Sinclair.
Vice-Chairman: D. M. Craig OBE, JP.
Directors: B. A. Houghton, R. B. Strachan MA, LLB, FCIS, C. Webb, E. B. Swallow; J. E. H. Quickfall FCA.
Manager: Bobby Saxton.
Post-War Managers: Tom Mitchell, Dick Duckworth, Charlie Spencer, Jimmy McCormick, Sam Bartram, Tom Lockie, Joe Shaw, Tom Johnston, Wilf McGuinness, Charlie Wright, Barry Lyons, Denis Smith (12).
Assistant Manager: John Newman.
Physio: Jeff Miller.
Secretary: Keith Usher.
Commercial Manager: Mrs Sheila Smith.
Sponsors: Camerons Brewery.
Founded: 1922.
Turned Professional: 1922.
Nickname: The Minstermen.
Former Names: None.
Former Grounds: Fulfordgate 1922–1932.
Record Attendance: 28,123 v Huddersfield Town, FA Cup 6th Round, 5 March 1938
Record Victory: 9–1 v Southport, Division 3 (N), 2 February 1957
Record Defeat: 0–12 v Chester, Division 3 (N), 1 February 1936
Most League Points: (3 for a win) 101, Division 4, 1983–84. (2 for a win) 62, Division 4, 1964–65.
Most League Goals: 96, Division 4, 1983–84
Highest League Scorer in a Season: Bill Fenton, 31, Division 3 (N), 1951–52; Arthur Bottom, 31, Division 3 (N), 1954–55 and 1955–56.
Highest Total of League Goals: Norman Wilkinson, 125, 1954–66.
Most League Appearances: Barry Jackson, 481, 1958–70.
League History: 1929 Elected to Division 3 (N), 1958–59 Division 4, 1959–60 Division, 1960–65 Division 4, 1965–66 Division 3, 1966–71 Division 4, 1971–74Division 3, 1974–76 Division 2, 1976–77 Division 3, 1977–84 Division 4, 1984–88 Division 3, 1988– Division 4.
Honours: Division 4 Champions 1983–84.
Colours: Red shirts, navy blue shorts, white socks. **Second strip:** All sky blue.

YORK CITY – LEAGUE RECORD 1987–88

Match no/Opp/Date		Endersby	McKenzie	Johnson	Wilson	Whitehead	Clegg	Himsworth	Hood	Gabbiadini M	Butler	Canham	Kitching	Banton	Tuthill	Smallwood	Cook	Mills	Gabbiadini R	Branagan	Buchanan	Costello	Downing	Staniforth	Helliwell	Bradshaw	Howlett	Stowell	Spofforth	McMillan	Rogers	FT(HT)Att Lge pos
1. Brighton	15.8	1	2	3	4	5	6	7†	8	9	10‡	11	12	14																		0-1(0-0)6068 —
2. Notts Co*	22.8	1	2	3	4	5¹	6		8	9†	7	11¹	12	10¹																		3-5(2-4)2878 22
3. Chester	29.8	1	2	3	4	5	6		8	9	7	11†	10	12																		0-1(0-0)2010 23
4. Walsall*	31.8		2	3	4	5	6	12	9	7†	11		10¹			1	8															1-3(0-1)2661 —
5. Port Vale	5.9	1	7†	3	4	5	6		2	9		11¹	10			1	8	12														1-2(0-0)2711 24
6. Preston*	12.9	1		3	4	5	6		2‡	9		11	10				8	7														1-1(0-0)3237 24
7. Bristol R	16.9	1	7	3	4†	5	6		2	9		12	10¹				8	11														1-2(0-1)3177 24
8. Gillingham	19.9	1	11	3		5	6	12	2	9¹		4†	10				8	7														1-3(1-0)5507 24
9. Doncaster*	26.9	1	12	3	4	5		11					10†	6		7¹	8		2	9												1-0(0-0)2702 24
10. Blackpool*	29.9	1	9†	3	4	5		11	8			12		6			7		2	10¹												1-3(1-2)2559 —
11. Wigan	3.10	1		3	4	5	6					8	10₁	11			7		2	9												1-0(0-0)2878 24
12. Fulham	10.10	1		3	4	5	6				12		10	11			8		2	9¹	7†											1-3(1-2)4057 24
13. Aldershot*	17.10	1		3	4	5	6						10²	11			8		2	9				7								2-2(1-0)1984 24
14. Rotherham*	20.10	1	7	3	4		6		5₁				10	11			8		2	9												1-2(0-1)1932 —
15. Sunderland	24.10	1	7‡	3	4	5	6		12				10¹	11			8¹		2†						14	9						2-4(1-3)19,314 24
16. Chesterfield*	31.10	1		3	4	5	6						10¹	11			8		2						7	9						1-0(1-0)2316 24
17. Nthampton	4.11	1		3	4	5	6							11			8		2				10		7	9						0-0(0-0)4950 —
18. Bury*	7.11	1		3	4	5	6		2				10	11			8								7	9¹						1-0(1-0)2641 24
19. Grimsby	21.11	1				5	6	3†				4	10	11			8¹		2					7‡	9	12						1-5(1-2)2200 24
20. Southend*	28.11	1			4	5		11†	2				10	6					7					3	12	9	8					0-3(0-1)2225 24
21. Bristol C	12.12			3	4	5	12	14	2‡			11	10²	6†		1	7								9	8						2-3(1-2)6238 24
22. Brentford*	18.12		3†	4	5	6¹	14					11‡	10			1	8		12						7	9	2					1-1(1-0)1801 —
23. Doncaster	26.12				4	5	6	7	3			12	10						2						11	9	8†		1			0-2(0-0)2409 24
24. Mansfield*	28.12				4	5	6	7				8	10₁‡						2		14				11	9¹		1	3†	12		2-2(1-2)2781 24
25. Chester*	1.1			4¹	5†		6¹	7					10						2						11	9	8	1	12	3		2-0(1-0)2686 24
26. Preston	2.1				4		6	7†					10					12	2		14				11‡	9	8	1	5	3		0-3(0-2)6302 24
27. Notts Co	9.1				4	5	12	7					10						2						11	9	8	1	6	3†		0-3(0-1)5924 24
28. Gillingham*	16.1			3	4	5	6	7					10												11	9	8	1		2		0-2(0-0)2129 24
29. Walsall	30.1		3†		4	5		7				11	10¹			1									12	9	8‡	6		2	14	1-2(1-1)4371 24
30. Port Vale*	6.2			3	4	5		8¹				11†	14	10₁		1									12	9‡		7		2	6	2-3(2-1)2420 24
31. Mansfield	13.2	1		3	4	5		8	5			11	10													9¹		7		2	6	1-2(1-0)2749 24
32. Brighton	20.2	1		3	4‡	5		11†				12						6							9	8	7		2	14		0-2(0-1)2576 24
33. Wigan*	27.2	1		4				11	5			12	10²					3							9¹	8	7	6†	2			3-1(1-0)2366 24
34. Blackpool	1.3	1		3				11†	5			12	10					6							9	8¹	7	4	2			1-2(1-1)2249 —
35. Aldershot	5.3	1		3			4	11	5¹				10					6							9¹	8	7		2			2-1(1-0)2672 24
36. Fulham*	12.3	1		3			4	11	5¹				10					6							9	8	7		2			1-3(1-2)2560 24
37. Chesterfield	19.3	1		3	12		4	11¹	5†			14	10					6							9‡	8	7		2			1-2(1-0)1966 24
38. Sunderland*	26.3	1		3			4	11					10¹	5				6							9¹	8	7		2			2-1(1-0)8878 24
39. Bury	2.4	1		3	12		4¹	11	14		10			5‡				6							9	8†	7		2			1-0(0-0)2277 24
40. Grimsby*	4.4	1		3	12	14	4	11	5		10†							6							9	8‡	7		2			0-2(0-1)3215 24
41. Rotherham	8.4	1		3	10		4	11	5														6¹		9	8	7		2			1-0(0-0)2942 —
42. Bristol R*	15.4	1		3	10		4	11	12				5										6‡		9	8	7		2			0-4(0-2)1834 —
43. Nthampton*	23.4	1		3	10†		4	11	6			12	5						2						9	8	7²		2			2-2(1-0)2048 24
44. Southend	27.4	1		3			4	11					5						2					10	9¹	8	7		6			1-3(1-2)3764 —
45. Bristol C*	2.5	1	6	3			4	11					5											10	9	8	7		2			0-1(0-0)2616 24
46. Brentford	7.5	1	6	3			4	11					5											10¹	9¹	8	7		2			2-1(2-0)4180 23
Apps(subs)/Goals		34(1)0	12(1)0	39(0)0	33(3)1	20(1)3	35(2)3	28(3)2	24(4)4	8(0)1	4(1)0	13(5)2	32(1)16	20(1)0		6(0)0	6(0)1	17(0)2	27(0)1	7(0)2	21(0)0	10(0)0	15(4)1	32(0)8	24(1)1	18(0)2	6(0)0	3(0)0	3(0)0	2(0)0	5(25)0	Final League Position: 23

Also played: Brough, match 19(14).

DIVISION 4

LINCOLN CITY
Sincil Bank, Lincoln LN5 8LD.

Back row (left to right): Steve Buckley, Tony Simmons, Dave Mossman, Mark Sertori, Les Hunter, Nigel Batch, Mick Waitt, John McGinley, Trevor Matthewson, Andy Moore, Clive Evans. *Front row:* Dave Clarke, Neil Franklin, Shane Nicholson, Colin Murphy (Manager), Bob Cumming, Dick Bate (Ass. Manager), Phil Brown, Paul Smith, Willie Gamble.

Stadium Capacity: 9,499.
Pitch Dimensions: 110 × 75yds.
Telephone: 0522–22224/510263.
Chairman: K. J. Reames.
Vice-Chairman: M. B. Pryor.
President: H. Dove.
Managing Director: G. R. Davey.
Directors: G. D. Overton, R. Staples, D. Barron.
Manager: Colin Murphy.
Post-War Managers: Bill Anderson, Roy Chapman, Ron Gray, Bert Loxley, David Herd, Graham Taylor, George Kerr, Willie Bell, Colin Murphy, John Pickering, George Kerr, Peter Daniel (12).
Assistant Manager: Dick Bate.
Physio: Adrian Davies.
Secretary: G. R. Davey.
Commercial Manager: G. R. Davey.
Sponsors: F & T Tyres (Fossitt & Thorne).
Founded: 1883.
Turned Professional: 1892.
Nickname: The Red Imps.
Former Names: None.
Former Grounds: John O'Gaunt's 1883–94.
Record Attendance: 23,196 v Derby Co, League Cup 4th Round replay, 15 November 1967.
Record Victory: 11–1 v Crewe Alex, Division 3(N), 29 September 1951.
Record Defeat: 3–11 v Manchester C, Division 2, 23 March 1895.
Most League Points: (3 for a win) 77, Division 3, 1981–82. (2 for a win) 74, Division 4, 1975–76.
Most League Goals: 121, Division 3(N), 1951–52.
Highest League Scorer in a Season: Allan Hall, 42, Division 3(N), 1931–32.
Highest Total of League Goals: Andy Graver, 144, 1950–55 and 1958–61.
Most League Appearances: Tony Emery, 402, 1946–59.
League History: 1892 Founder Members of Division 2. Missed seasons 1908–09, 1911–12 and 1920–21 when they were not re-elected. Otherwise, in Division 2 until 1921–32 Division 3(N), 1932–34 Division 2, 1934–48 Division 3(N), 1948–49 Division 2, 1949–52 Division 3(N), 1952–61 Division 2, 1961–62 Division 3, 1962–76 Division 4, 1976–79 Division 3, 1979–81 Division 4, 1981–86 Division 3, 1986–87 Division 4, 1987–88 GM Vauxhall Conference, 1988– Division 4.
Honours: Division 4 Champions 1975–76, runners-up 1980–81. Division 3(N) Champions 1931–32, 1947–48, 1951–52, runners-up 1927–28, 1930–31, 1936–37. Associate Members' Cup runners-up 1983. GM Vauxhall Conference Champions 1987–88.
Colours: Red and white striped shirts, black shorts, red socks. **Second strip:** All blue.

END-OF-SEASON PLAY-OFFS 1987–88

DIVISIONS 1 & 2

Semi-finals, first leg
BLACKBURN ROVERS (0)0, CHELSEA (0)2 15.5.88, 16,568
Blackburn R: Gennoe; Price, Millar, Barker, Hendry, Mail, Reid, Ainscow (Ardiles), Gayle (Hill), Garner, Sellars.
Chelsea: Hitchcock; Clarke, Dorigo (McAllister), Pates, McLaughlin, Hall, Nevin, Bumstead (K. Wilson), Dixon, Durie, C. Wilson. **Scorers:** Durie, Nevin.

BRADFORD CITY (0)2, MIDDLESBROUGH (0)1 15.5.88, 16,017
Bradford C: Tomlinson; Abbott, Goddard, McCall, Oliver, Evans, Hendrie, Sinnott, Ormondroyd, Kennedy, Futcher (Leonard). **Scorers:** Goddard, McCall.
Middlesbrough: Pears; Parkinson, Laws, Mowbray, Hamilton, Pallister, Slaven, Ripley, Senior, Kerr, Glover. **Scorer:** Senior.

Semi-finals, second leg
CHELSEA (1)4, BLACKBURN ROVERS (0)1 18.5.88, 22,757
Chelsea: Hitchcock; Clarke, C. Wilson, Pates, McLaughlin, Hall, Nevin, Bumstead (McAllister), Dixon, Durie, K. Wilson. **Scorers:** K. Wilson 2, Dixon, Durie.
Blackburn R: Gennoe; Reid, Millar, Barker, Mail (Hill), Hendry, Gayle, Archibald, Ardiles, Garner, Sellars. **Scorer:** Sellars.

MIDDLESBROUGH (1)2, BRADFORD CITY (0)0 18.5.88, 25,868
Middlesbrough: Pears; Parkinson, Cooper, Mowbray, Hamilton, Pallister, Slaven, Ripley (Kernaghan), Senior, Glover, Kerr (Laws). **Scorers:** Slaven, Hamilton.
Bradford C: Tomlinson; Abbott, Goddard, McCall, Oliver, Evans (Leonard), Hendrie, Sinnott, Ormondroyd, Kennedy, Futcher (Palin).

Final, first leg
MIDDLESBROUGH (1)2, CHELSEA (0)0 25.5.88, 25,531
Middlesbrough: Pears; Parkinson, Cooper, Mowbray, Hamilton, Pallister, Slaven, Ripley, Senior, Kerr, Glover. **Scorers:** Senior, Slaven.
Chelsea: Hitchcock; Clarke, Dorigo, Wicks, McLaughlin, Pates, Nevin, Bumstead, Dixon, Durie, C. Wilson.

Final, second leg
CHELSEA (1)1, MIDDLESBROUGH (0)0 28.5.88, 40,550
Chelsea: Hitchcock; Clarke, Dorigo, Wicks, McLaughlin, Pates (Hall), Nevin, Bumstead, Dixon, Durie, K. Wilson (McAllister). **Scorer:** Durie.
Middlesbrough: Pears; Parkinson, Cooper, Mowbray, Hamilton, Pallister, Slaven, Ripley, Senior, Kerr, Glover.

Middlesbrough promoted to Division One.

DIVISIONS 2 & 3

Semi-finals, first leg
BRISTOL CITY (1)1, SHEFFIELD UNITED (0)0 15.5.88, 25,335
Bristol C: Waugh; Llewellyn, Newman, Humphries, Pender, McClaren, Milne, Galliers, Gordon (Shutt), Walsh, Neville (Jordan). **Scorer:** Walsh.
Sheffield U: Benstead; Wilder, Powell, Webster, Stancliffe, Barnsley, Hetherston (Pike), Withe (Philliskirk), Cadette, Downes, Beagrie.

NOTTS COUNTY (1)1, WALSALL (1)3 15.5.88, 11,522
Notts Co: Leonard; McStay, Withe, Fairclough, Yates, Birtles, Mills, McParland (Barnes), Lund, Pike, Thorpe. **Scorer:** Yates.
Walsall: Barber; Taylor, O'Kelly, Shakespeare, Forbes, Goodwin, Hawker, Hart, Christie, Kelly, Naughton. **Scorers:** Kelly 2, Shakespeare.

Semi-finals, second leg
SHEFFIELD UNITED (0)1, BRISTOL CITY (1)1 18.5.88, 19,066
Sheffield U: Benstead; Powell, Pike, Webster, Stancliffe, Barnsley (Agana), Morris, Cadette, Williams, Downes, Beagrie. **Scorer:** Morris.
Bristol C: Waugh; Llewellyn, Newman, Humphries, Pender, McClaren, Milne, Galliers, Gordon (Jordan), Walsh, Shutt. **Scorer:** Shutt.

WALSALL (0)1, NOTTS COUNTY (1)1 18.5.88, 8,901
Walsall: Barber; Taylor, O'Kelly, Shakespeare, Forbes, Goodwin, Hawker, Hart (Dornan), Christie, Kelly, Naughton. **Scorer:** Christie.
Notts Co: Leonard; McStay, Withe, Fairclough, Yates, Hart, Mills, Barnes (Lund), Birtles, Pike (McParland), Thorpe. **Scorer:** Yates.

END-OF-SEASON PLAY-OFFS 1987–88

Final, first leg
BRISTOL CITY (1)1, WALSALL (0)3 25.5.88, 25,128
Bristol C: Waugh; Llewellyn, Newman, Humphries, Pender, McClaren, Milne, Galliers, Shutt, Walsh, Neville (Jordan).
Scorer: Walsh.
Walsall: Barber; Taylor, O'Kelly (M.Jones), Shakespeare, Forbes, Goodwin, Hawker, Hart, Christie, Kelly, Naughton.
Scorers: Christie, Kelly 2.

Final, second leg
WALSALL (0)0, BRISTOL CITY (1)2 28.5.88, 13,941
Walsall: Barber; Taylor, Dornan, Shakespeare, Forbes, Goodwin, Hawker, Hart, Christie, Kelly, Naughton.
Bristol C: Waugh; Llewellyn, Newman, Humphries, Pender, McClaren, Milne, Galliers, Shutt (Caldwell), Walsh, Jordan.
Scorers: Newman, Shutt.

Final, replay
WALSALL (3)4, BRISTOL CITY (0)0 30.5.88, 13,007
Walsall: Barber; Taylor, Dornan (Sanderson), Shakespeare, Forbes, Goodwin (M. Jones), Hawker, Hart, Christie, Kelly, Naughton. **Scorers:** Kelly 3, Hawker.
Bristol C: Waugh; Llewellyn, Newman, Humphries, Pender, McClaren, Milne, Galliers, Shutt, Walsh, Jordan.

Walsall promoted to Division Two.

DIVISIONS 3 & 4

Semi-finals, first leg
SWANSEA CITY (0)1, ROTHERHAM UNITED (0)0 15.5.88, 9,148
Swansea C: Guthrie; Harrison, Coleman, Melville, Knill, James, Davies, Hutchison, McCarthy, Raynor, Bodak (Love).
Scorer: McCarthy.
Rotherham U: O'Hanlon; Douglas, Crosby, Goodwin, Johnson, Green, Buckley, Dungworth, Haycock, Mendonca, Pugh.

TORQUAY UNITED (2)2, SCUNTHORPE UNITED (0)1 15.5.88, 4,602
Torquay U: Allen; McNichol, Kelly, Dawkins, Cole, Impey, Sharpe, Lloyd, Caldwell (Loram), Dobson (Nardiello), Gibbins. **Scorers:** Caldwell, Dobson.
Scunthorpe U: Green; Stevenson, Longden, Taylor, Lister, Nicol, Richardson (Shearer), McLean, Daws, Flounders, Hill. **Scorer:** Flounders.

Semi-finals, second leg
ROTHERHAM UNITED (1)1, SWANSEA CITY (1)1 18.5.88, 5,568
Rotherham U: O'Hanlon; Douglas, Crosby, Goodwin, Johnson, Green, Campbell, Dungworth, Haycock (Grealish), Airey (Mendonca), Buckley. **Scorer:** Johnson.
Swansea C: Guthrie; Harrison, Coleman, Melville, Knill, James, Davies, Hutchison (Lewis), McCarthy, Raynor, Bodak.
Scorer: McCarthy.

SCUNTHORPE UNITED (0)1, TORQUAY UNITED (0)1 18.5.88, 6,482
Scunthorpe U: Green; Stevenson, Longden (Atkins), Taylor, Lister, McLean, Richardson (Dixon), Shearer, Daws, Flounders, Hill. **Scorer:** Lister, pen.
Torquay U: Allen; McNichol, Kelly, Haslegrave, Cole, Impey, Pearce (Sharpe) (Caldwell), Lloyd, Loram, Dobson, Gibbins. **Scorer:** Loram.

Final, first leg
SWANSEA CITY (0)2, TORQUAY UNITED (0)1 25.5.88, 10,825
Swansea C: Guthrie; Harrison, Coleman, Melville, Knill, James, Davies, Hutchison, McCarthy, Raynor, Bodak (Love).
Scorers: McCarthy, Love.
Torquay U: Allen; McNichol, Kelly, Haslegrave, Cole, Impey, Dawkins, Lloyd, Loram (Caldwell), Dobson, Gibbins (Gardiner). **Scorer:** McNichol.

Final, second leg
TORQUAY UNITED (2)3, SWANSEA CITY (3)3 28.5.88, 4,999
Torquay U: Allen; McNichol, Kelly, Dawkins, Cole, Impey (Sharpe), Caldwell, Lloyd, Loram, Dobson, Gibbins. **Scorers:** McNichol 2, Caldwell.
Swansea C: Guthrie; Harrison, Coleman, Melville, Knill, James, Davies, Love, McCarthy, Raynor, Hutchison (J. Lewis).
Scorers: Raynor, McCarthy pen, Davies.

Swansea City promoted to Division Three.

BARCLAY LEAGUE FINAL TABLES 1987–88

DIVISION 1

		Home					Away						
	P	W	D	L	F	A	W	D	L	F	A	GD	Pts
1 Liverpool	40	15	5	0	49	9	11	7	2	38	15	+63	90
2 Manchester U	40	14	5	1	41	17	9	7	4	30	21	+33	81
3 Nottingham F	40	11	7	2	40	17	9	6	5	27	22	+28	73
4 Everton	40	14	4	2	34	11	5	9	6	19	16	+26	70
5 QPR	40	12	4	4	30	14	7	6	7	18	24	+10	67
6 Arsenal	40	11	4	5	35	16	7	8	5	23	23	+19	66
7 Wimbledon	40	8	9	3	32	20	6	6	8	26	27	+11	57
8 Newcastle U	40	9	6	5	32	23	5	8	7	23	30	+2	56
9 Luton T	40	11	6	3	40	21	3	5	12	17	37	−1	53
10 Coventry C	40	6	8	6	23	25	7	6	7	23	28	−7	53
11 Sheffield W	40	10	2	8	27	30	5	6	9	25	36	−14	53
12 Southampton	40	6	8	6	27	26	6	6	8	22	27	−4	50
13 Tottenham H	40	9	5	6	26	23	3	6	11	12	25	−10	47
14 Norwich C	40	7	5	8	26	26	5	4	11	14	26	−12	45
15 Derby Co	40	6	7	7	18	17	4	6	10	17	28	−10	43
16 West Ham U	40	6	9	5	23	21	3	6	11	17	31	−12	42
17 Charlton Ath	40	7	7	6	23	21	2	8	10	15	31	−14	42
18 Chelsea	40	7	11	2	24	17	2	4	14	26	51	−18	42
19 Portsmouth	40	4	8	8	21	27	3	6	11	15	39	−30	35
20 Watford	40	4	5	11	15	24	3	6	11	12	27	−24	32
21 Oxford U	40	5	7	8	24	34	1	6	13	20	46	−36	31

DIVISION 2

		Home					Away						
	P	W	D	L	F	A	W	D	L	F	A	GD	Pts
1 Millwall	44	15	3	4	45	23	10	4	8	27	29	+20	82
2 Aston Villa	44	9	7	6	31	21	13	5	4	37	20	+27	78
3 Middlesbrough	44	15	4	3	44	16	7	8	7	19	20	+27	78
4 Bradford C	44	14	3	5	49	26	8	8	6	25	28	+20	77
5 Blackburn R	44	12	8	2	38	22	9	6	7	30	30	+16	77
6 Crystal Palace	44	16	3	3	50	21	6	6	10	36	38	+27	75
7 Leeds U	44	14	4	4	37	18	5	8	9	24	33	+10	69
8 Ipswich T	44	14	3	5	38	17	5	6	11	23	35	+9	66
9 Manchester C	44	11	4	7	50	28	8	4	10	30	32	+20	65
10 Oldham Ath	44	13	4	5	43	27	5	7	10	29	37	+8	65
11 Stoke C	44	12	6	4	34	22	5	5	12	16	35	−7	62
12 Swindon T	44	10	7	5	43	25	6	4	12	30	35	+13	59
13 Leicester C	44	12	5	5	35	20	4	6	12	27	41	+1	59
14 Barnsley	44	11	4	7	42	32	4	8	10	19	30	−1	57
15 Hull C	44	10	8	4	32	22	4	7	11	22	38	−6	57
16 Plymouth Arg	44	12	4	6	44	26	4	4	14	21	41	−2	56
17 Bournemouth	44	7	7	8	36	30	6	3	13	20	38	−12	49
18 Shrewsbury T	44	7	8	7	23	22	4	8	10	19	32	−12	49
19 Birmingham C	44	7	9	6	20	24	4	6	12	21	42	−25	48
20 WBA	44	8	7	7	29	26	4	4	14	21	43	−19	47
21 Sheffield U	44	8	6	8	27	28	5	1	16	18	46	−29	46
22 Reading	44	5	7	10	20	25	5	5	12	24	45	−26	42
23 Huddersfield T	44	4	6	12	20	38	2	4	16	21	62	−59	28

DIVISION 3

		P	W	D	L	F	A	W	D	L	F	A	GD	Pts
				Home						Away				
1	Sunderland	46	14	7	2	51	22	13	5	5	41	26	+44	93
2	Brighton & HA	46	15	7	1	37	16	8	8	7	32	31	+22	84
3	Walsall	46	15	6	2	39	22	8	7	8	29	28	+18	82
4	Notts Co	46	14	4	5	53	24	9	8	6	29	25	+33	81
5	Bristol C	46	14	6	3	51	30	7	6	10	26	32	+15	75
6	Northampton T	46	12	8	3	36	18	6	11	6	34	33	+19	73
7	Wigan Ath	46	11	8	4	36	23	9	4	10	34	38	+9	72
8	Bristol R	46	14	5	4	43	19	4	7	12	25	37	+12	66
9	Fulham	46	10	5	8	36	24	9	4	10	33	36	+9	66
10	Blackpool	46	13	4	6	45	27	4	10	9	26	35	+9	65
11	Port Vale	46	12	8	3	36	19	6	3	14	22	37	+2	65
12	Brentford	46	9	8	6	27	23	7	6	10	26	36	−6	62
13	Gillingham	46	8	9	6	45	21	6	8	9	32	40	+16	59
14	Bury	46	9	7	7	33	26	6	7	10	25	31	+1	59
15	Chester C	46	9	8	6	29	30	5	8	10	22	32	−11	58
16	Preston NE	46	10	6	7	30	23	5	7	11	18	36	−11	58
17	Southend U	46	10	6	7	42	33	4	7	12	23	50	−18	55
18	Chesterfield	46	10	5	8	25	28	5	5	13	16	42	−29	55
19	Mansfield T	46	10	6	7	25	21	4	6	13	23	38	−11	54
20	Aldershot	46	12	3	8	45	32	3	5	15	19	42	−10	53
21	Rotherham U	46	8	8	7	28	25	4	8	11	22	41	−16	52
22	Grimsby T	46	6	7	10	25	29	6	7	10	23	29	−10	50
23	York C	46	4	7	12	27	45	4	2	17	21	46	−43	33
24	Doncaster R	46	6	5	12	25	36	2	4	17	15	48	−44	33

DIVISION 4

		P	W	D	L	F	A	W	D	L	F	A	GD	Pts
				Home						Away				
1	Wolverhampton W	46	15	3	5	47	19	12	6	5	35	24	+39	90
2	Cardiff C	46	15	6	2	39	14	9	7	7	27	27	+25	85
3	Bolton W	46	15	6	2	42	12	7	6	10	24	30	+24	78
4	Scunthorpe U	46	14	5	4	42	20	6	12	5	34	31	+25	77
5	Torquay U	46	10	7	6	34	16	11	7	5	32	25	+25	77
6	Swansea C	46	9	7	7	35	28	11	3	9	27	28	+6	70
7	Peterborough U	46	10	5	8	28	26	10	5	8	24	27	−1	70
8	Leyton Orient	46	13	4	6	55	27	6	8	9	30	36	+22	69
9	Colchester U	46	10	5	8	23	22	9	5	9	24	29	−4	67
10	Burnley	46	12	5	6	31	22	8	2	13	26	40	−5	67
11	Wrexham	46	13	3	7	46	26	7	3	13	23	32	+11	66
12	Scarborough	46	12	8	3	38	19	5	6	12	18	29	+8	65
13	Darlington	46	13	6	4	39	25	5	5	13	32	44	+2	65
14	Tranmere R	46	14	2	7	43	20	5	7	11	18	33	+8	64*
15	Cambridge U	46	10	6	7	32	24	6	7	10	18	28	−2	61
16	Hartlepool U	46	9	7	7	25	25	6	7	10	25	32	−7	59
17	Crewe Alex	46	7	11	5	25	19	6	8	9	32	34	+4	58
18	Halifax T	46	11	7	5	37	25	3	7	13	17	34	−5	55†
19	Hereford U	46	8	7	8	25	27	6	5	12	16	32	−18	54
20	Stockport Co	46	7	7	9	26	26	5	8	10	18	32	−14	51
21	Rochdale	46	5	9	9	28	34	6	6	11	19	42	−29	48
22	Exeter C	46	8	6	9	33	29	3	7	13	20	39	−15	46
23	Carlisle U	46	9	5	9	38	33	3	3	17	19	53	−29	44
24	Newport Co	46	4	5	14	19	36	2	2	19	16	69	−70	25

*2 pts deducted for failing to meet a fixture.   †1 pt deducted for fielding an unregistered player.

FOOTBALL LEAGUE HONOURS SINCE 1888

Season	Max Pts	First	Pts	Second	Pts	Third	Pts
FOOTBALL LEAGUE							
1888–89	44	Preston NE	40	Aston Villa	29	Wolverhampton W	28
1889–90	44	Preston NE	33	Everton	31	Blackburn R	27
1890–91	44	Everton	29	Preston NE	27	Notts Co	26
1891–92	52	Sunderland	42	Preston NE	37	Bolton W	36
FIRST DIVISION							
1892–93	60	Sunderland	48	Preston NE	37	Everton	36
1893–94	60	Aston Villa	44	Sunderland	38	Derby Co	36
1894–95	60	Sunderland	47	Everton	42	Aston Villa	39
1895–96	60	Aston Villa	45	Derby Co	41	Everton	39
1896–97	60	Aston Villa	47	Sheffield U	36	Derby Co	36
1897–98	60	Sheffield U	42	Sunderland	37	Wolverhampton W	35
1898–99	68	Aston Villa	45	Liverpool	43	Burnley	39
1899–1900	68	Aston Villa	50	Sheffield U	48	Sunderland	41
1900–01	68	Liverpool	45	Sunderland	43	Notts Co	40
1901–02	68	Sunderland	44	Everton	41	Newcastle U	37
1902–03	68	The Wednesday	42	Aston Villa	41	Sunderland	41
1903–04	68	The Wednesday	47	Manchester C	44	Everton	43
1904–05	68	Newcastle U	48	Everton	47	Manchester C	46
1905–06	76	Liverpool	51	Preston NE	47	The Wednesday	44
1906–07	76	Newcastle U	51	Bristol C	48	Everton	45
1907–08	76	Manchester U	52	Aston Villa	43	Manchester C	43
1908–09	76	Newcastle U	53	Everton	46	Sunderland	44
1909–10	76	Aston Villa	53	Liverpool	48	Blackburn R	45
1910–11	76	Manchester U	52	Aston Villa	51	Sunderland	45
1911–12	76	Blackburn R	49	Everton	46	Newcastle U	44
1912–13	76	Sunderland	54	Aston Villa	50	Sheffield W	49
1913–14	76	Blackburn R	51	Aston Villa	44	Middlesbrough	43
1914–15	76	Everton	46	Oldham Ath	45	Blackburn R	43
1919–20	84	WBA	60	Burnley	51	Chelsea	49
1920–21	84	Burnley	59	Manchester C	54	Bolton W	52
1921–22	84	Liverpool	57	Tottenham H	51	Burnley	49
1922–23	84	Liverpool	60	Sunderland	54	Huddersfield T	53
1923–24	84	Huddersfield T*	57	Cardiff C	57	Sunderland	53
1924–25	84	Huddersfield T	58	WBA	56	Bolton W	55
1925–26	84	Huddersfield T	57	Arsenal	52	Sunderland	48
1926–27	84	Newcastle U	56	Huddersfield T	51	Sunderland	49
1927–28	84	Everton	53	Huddersfield T	51	Leicester C	48
1928–29	84	Sheffield W	52	Leicester C	51	Aston Villa	50
1929–30	84	Sheffield W	60	Derby Co	50	Manchester C	47
1930–31	84	Arsenal	66	Aston Villa	59	Sheffield W	52
1931–32	84	Everton	56	Arsenal	54	Sheffield W	50
1932–33	84	Arsenal	58	Aston Villa	54	Sheffield W	51
1933–34	84	Arsenal	59	Huddersfield T	56	Tottenham H	49
1934–35	84	Arsenal	58	Sunderland	54	Sheffield W	49
1935–36	84	Sunderland	56	Derby Co	48	Huddersfield T	48
1936–37	84	Manchester C	57	Charlton Ath	54	Arsenal	52
1937–38	84	Arsenal	52	Wolverhampton W	51	Preston NE	49
1938–39	84	Everton	59	Wolverhampton W	55	Charlton Ath	50
1946–47	84	Liverpool	57	Manchester U	56	Wolverhampton W	56
1947–48	84	Arsenal	59	Manchester U	52	Burnley	52
1948–49	84	Portsmouth	58	Manchester U	53	Derby Co	53
1949–50	84	Portsmouth*	53	Wolverhampton W	53	Sunderland	52
1950–51	84	Tottenham H	60	Manchester U	56	Blackpool	50
1951–52	84	Manchester U	57	Tottenham H	53	Arsenal	53
1952–53	84	Arsenal*	54	Preston NE	54	Wolverhampton W	51
1953–54	84	Wolverhampton W	57	WBA	53	Huddersfield T	51
1954–55	84	Chelsea	52	Wolverhampton W	48	Portsmouth	48
1955–56	84	Manchester U	60	Blackpool	49	Wolverhampton W	49
1956–57	84	Manchester U	64	Tottenham H	56	Preston NE	56

1957–58	84	Wolverhampton W	64	Preston NE	59	Tottenham H	51
1958–59	84	Wolverhampton W	61	Manchester U	55	Arsenal	50
1959–60	84	Burnley	55	Wolverhampton W	54	Tottenham H	53
1960–61	84	Tottenham H	66	Sheffield W	58	Wolverhampton W	57
1961–62	84	Ipswich T	56	Burnley	53	Tottenham H	52
1962–63	84	Everton	61	Tottenham H	55	Burnley	54
1963–64	84	Liverpool	57	Manchester U	53	Everton	52
1964–65	84	Manchester U*	61	Leeds U	61	Chelsea	56
1965–66	84	Liverpool	61	Leeds U	55	Burnley	55
1966–67	84	Manchester U	60	Nottingham F	56	Tottenham H	56
1967–68	84	Manchester C	58	Manchester U	56	Liverpool	55
1968–69	84	Leeds U	67	Liverpool	61	Everton	57
1969–70	84	Everton	66	Leeds U	57	Chelsea	55
1970–71	84	Arsenal	65	Leeds U	64	Tottenham H	52
1971–72	84	Derby Co	58	Leeds U	57	Liverpool	57
1972–73	84	Liverpool	60	Arsenal	57	Leeds U	53
1973–74	84	Leeds U	62	Liverpool	57	Derby Co	48
1974–75	84	Derby Co	53	Liverpool	51	Ipswich T	51
1975–76	84	Liverpool	60	QPR	59	Manchester U	56
1976–77	84	Liverpool	57	Manchester C	56	Ipswich T	52
1977–78	84	Nottingham F	64	Liverpool	57	Everton	55
1978–79	84	Liverpool	68	Nottingham F	60	WBA	59
1979–80	84	Liverpool	60	Manchester U	58	Ipswich T	53
1980–81	84	Aston Villa	60	Ipswich T	56	Arsenal	53
1981–82	126	Liverpool	87	Ipswich T	83	Manchester U	78
1982–83	126	Liverpool	82	Watford	71	Manchester U	70
1983–84	126	Liverpool	80	Southampton	77	Nottingham F	74
1984–85	126	Everton	90	Liverpool	77	Tottenham H	77
1985–86	126	Liverpool	88	Everton	86	West Ham U	84
1986–87	126	Everton	86	Liverpool	77	Tottenham H	71
1987–88	120	Liverpool	90	Manchester U	81	Nottingham F	73

*Won on goal average/difference

SECOND DIVISION

1892–93	44	Small Heath	36	Sheffield U	35	Darwen	30
1893–94	56	Liverpool	50	Small Heath	42	Notts Co	39
1894–95	60	Bury	48	Notts Co	39	Newton Heath	38
1895–96	60	Liverpool*	46	Manchester C	46	Grimsby T	42
1896–97	60	Notts Co	42	Newton Heath	39	Grimsby T	38
1897–98	60	Burnley	48	Newcastle U	45	Manchester C	39
1898–99	68	Manchester C	52	Glossop NE	46	Leicester Fosse	45
1899–1900	68	The Wednesday	54	Bolton W	52	Small Heath	46
1900–01	68	Grimsby T	49	Small Heath	48	Burnley	44
1901–02	68	WBA	55	Middlesbrough	51	Preston NE	42
1902–03	68	Manchester C	54	Small Heath	51	Woolwich A	48
1903–04	68	Preston NE	50	Woolwich A	49	Manchester U	48
1904–05	68	Liverpool	58	Bolton W	56	Manchester U	53
1905–06	76	Bristol C	66	Manchester U	62	Chelsea	53
1906–07	76	Nottingham F	60	Chelsea	57	Leicester Fosse	48
1907–08	76	Bradford C	54	Leicester Fosse	52	Oldham Ath	50
1908–09	76	Bolton W	52	Tottenham H	51	WBA	51
1909–10	76	Manchester C	54	Oldham Ath	53	Hull C	53
1910–11	76	WBA	53	Bolton W	51	Chelsea	49
1911–12	76	Derby Co*	54	Chelsea	54	Burnley	52
1912–13	76	Preston NE	53	Burnley	50	Birmingham	46
1913–14	76	Notts Co	53	Bradford PA	49	Woolwich A	49
1914–15	76	Derby Co	53	Preston NE	50	Barnsley	47
1919–20	84	Tottenham H	70	Huddersfield T	64	Birmingham	56
1920–21	84	Birmingham*	58	Cardiff C	58	Bristol C	51
1921–22	84	Nottingham F	56	Stoke C	52	Barnsley	52
1922–23	84	Notts Co	53	West Ham U	51	Leicester C	51
1923–24	84	Leeds U	54	Bury	51	Derby Co	51
1924–25	84	Leicester C	59	Manchester U	57	Derby Co	55
1925–26	84	Sheffield W	60	Derby Co	57	Chelsea	52
1926–27	84	Middlesbrough	62	Portsmouth	54	Manchester C	54
1927–28	84	Manchester C	59	Leeds U	57	Chelsea	54

FOOTBALL LEAGUE

1928–29	84	Middlesbrough	55	Grimsby T	53	Bradford PA	48
1929–30	84	Blackpool	58	Chelsea	55	Oldham Ath	53
1930–31	84	Everton	61	WBA	54	Tottenham H	51
1931–32	84	Wolverhampton W	56	Leeds U	54	Stoke C	52
1932–33	84	Stoke C	56	Tottenham H	55	Fulham	50
1933–34	84	Grimsby T	59	Preston NE	52	Bolton W	51
1934–35	84	Brentford	61	Bolton W	56	West Ham U	56
1935–36	84	Manchester U	56	Charlton Ath	55	Sheffield U	52
1936–37	84	Leicester C	56	Blackpool	55	Bury	52
1937–38	84	Aston Villa	57	Manchester U	53	Sheffield U	53
1938–39	84	Blackburn R	55	Sheffield U	54	Sheffield W	53
1946–47	84	Manchester C	62	Burnley	58	Birmingham C	55
1947–48	84	Birmingham C	59	Newcastle U	56	Southampton	52
1948–49	84	Fulham	57	WBA	56	Southampton	55
1949–50	84	Tottenham H	61	Sheffield W	52	Sheffield U	52
1950–51	84	Preston NE	57	Manchester C	52	Cardiff C	50
1951–52	84	Sheffield W	53	Cardiff C	51	Birmingham C	51
1952–53	84	Sheffield U	60	Huddersfield T	58	Luton T	52
1953–54	84	Leicester C*	56	Everton	56	Blackburn R	55
1954–55	84	Birmingham C*	54	Luton T	54	Rotherham U	54
1955–56	84	Sheffield W	55	Leeds U	52	Liverpool	48
1956–57	84	Leicester C	61	Nottingham F	54	Liverpool	53
1957–58	84	West Ham U	57	Blackburn R	56	Charlton Ath	55
1958–59	84	Sheffield W	62	Fulham	60	Sheffield U	53
1959–60	84	Aston Villa	59	Cardiff C	58	Liverpool	50
1960–61	84	Ipswich T	59	Sheffield U	58	Liverpool	52
1961–62	84	Liverpool	62	Leyton Orient	54	Sunderland	53
1962–63	84	Stoke C	53	Chelsea	52	Sunderland	52
1963–64	84	Leeds U	63	Sunderland	61	Preston NE	56
1964–65	84	Newcastle U	57	Northampton T	56	Bolton W	50
1965–66	84	Manchester C	59	Southampton	54	Coventry C	53
1966–67	84	Coventry C	59	Wolverhampton W	58	Carlisle U	52
1967–68	84	Ipswich T	59	QPR	58	Blackpool	58
1968–69	84	Derby Co	63	Crystal Palace	56	Charlton Ath	50
1969–70	84	Huddersfield T	60	Blackpool	53	Leicester C	51
1970–71	84	Leicester C	59	Sheffield U	56	Cardiff C	53
1971–72	84	Norwich C	57	Birmingham C	56	Millwall	55
1972–73	84	Burnley	62	QPR	61	Aston Villa	50
1973–74	84	Middlesbrough	65	Luton T	50	Carlisle U	49
1974–75	84	Manchester U	61	Aston Villa	58	Norwich C	53
1975–76	84	Sunderland	56	Bristol C	53	WBA	53
1976–77	84	Wolverhampton W	57	Chelsea	55	Nottingham F	52
1977–78	84	Bolton W	58	Southampton	57	Tottenham H	56
1978–79	84	Crystal Palace	57	Brighton & HA	56	Stoke C	56
1979–80	84	Leicester C	55	Sunderland	54	Birmingham C	53
1980–81	84	West Ham U	66	Notts Co	53	Swansea C	50
1981–82	126	Luton T	88	Watford	80	Norwich C	71
1982–83	126	QPR	85	Wolverhampton W	75	Leicester C	70
1983–84	126	Chelsea*	88	Sheffield W	88	Newcastle U	80
1984–85	126	Oxford U	84	Birmingham C	82	Manchester C	74
1985–86	126	Norwich C	84	Charlton Ath	77	Wimbledon	76
1986–87	126	Derby Co	84	Portsmouth	78	Oldham Ath	75
1987–88	132	Millwall	82	Aston Villa	78	Middlesbrough	78

*Won on goal average/difference

THIRD DIVISION

1920–21	84	Crystal Palace	59	Southampton	54	QPR	53
1958–59	92	Plymouth Arg	62	Hull C	61	Brentford	57
1959–60	92	Southampton	61	Norwich C	59	Shrewsbury T	52
1960–61	92	Bury	68	Walsall	62	QPR	60
1961–62	92	Portsmouth	65	Grimsby T	62	Bournemouth	59
1962–63	92	Northampton T	62	Swindon T	58	Port Vale	54
1963–64	92	Coventry C*	60	Crystal Palace	60	Watford	58
1964–65	92	Carlisle U	60	Bristol C	59	Mansfield T	59
1965–66	92	Hull C	69	Millwall	65	QPR	57
1966–67	92	QPR	67	Middlesbrough	55	Watford	54

FOOTBALL LEAGUE

1967–68	92	Oxford U	57	Bury	56	Shrewsbury	55
1968–69	92	Watford*	64	Swindon T	64	Luton T	61
1969–70	92	Orient	62	Luton T	60	Bristol R	56
1970–71	92	Preston NE	61	Fulham	60	Halifax T	56
1971–72	92	Aston Villa	70	Brighton & HA	65	Bournemouth	62
1972–73	92	Bolton W	61	Notts Co	57	Blackburn R	55
1973–74	92	Oldham Ath	62	Bristol R	61	York C	61
1974–75	92	Blackburn R	60	Plymouth Arg	59	Charlton Ath	55
1975–76	92	Hereford U	63	Cardiff C	57	Millwall	56
1976–77	92	Mansfield T	64	Brighton & HA	61	Crystal Palace	59
1977–78	92	Wrexham	61	Cambridge U	58	Preston NE	56
1978–79	92	Shrewsbury T	61	Watford	60	Swansea C	60
1979–80	92	Grimsby T	62	Blackburn R	59	Sheffield W	58
1980–81	92	Rotherham U	61	Barnsley	59	Charlton Ath	59
1981–82	138	Burnley*	80	Carlisle U	80	Fulham	78
1982–83	138	Portsmouth	91	Cardiff C	86	Huddersfield T	82
1983–84	138	Oxford U	95	Wimbledon	87	Sheffield U	83
1984–85	138	Bradford C	94	Millwall	90	Hull C	87
1985–86	138	Reading	94	Plymouth Arg	87	Derby Co	84
1986–87	138	Bournemouth	97	Middlesbrough	94	Swindon T	87
1987–88	138	Sunderland	93	Brighton & HA	84	Walsall	82

*Won on goal average/difference

FOURTH DIVISION

1958–59	92	Port Vale	64	Coventry C	60	York C	60	Shrewsbury T	58
1959–60	92	Walsall	65	Notts Co	60	Torquay U	60	Watford	57
1960–61	92	Peterborough U	66	Crystal Palace	64	Northampton T	60	Bradford PA	60
1961–62	88†	Millwall	56	Colchester U	55	Wrexham	53	Carlisle U	52
1962–63	92	Brentford	62	Oldham Ath	59	Crewe Alex	59	Mansfield T	57
1963–64	92	Gillingham*	60	Carlisle U	60	Workington T	59	Exeter C	58
1964–65	92	Brighton & HA	63	Millwall	62	York C	62	Oxford U	61
1965–66	92	Doncaster R*	59	Darlington	59	Torquay U	58	Colchester U	56
1966–67	92	Stockport Co	64	Southport	59	Barrow	59	Tranmere R	58
1967–68	92	Luton T	66	Barnsley	61	Hartlepools U	60	Crewe Alex	58
1968–69	92	Doncaster R	59	Halifax T	57	Rochdale	56	Bradford C	56
1969–70	92	Chesterfield	64	Wrexham	61	Swansea C	60	Port Vale	59
1970–71	92	Notts Co	69	Bournemouth	60	Oldham Ath	59	York C	56
1971–72	92	Grimsby T	63	Southend U	60	Brentford	59	Scunthorpe U	57
1972–73	92	Southport	62	Hereford U	58	Cambridge U	57	Aldershot	56
1973–74	92	Peterborough U	65	Gillingham	62	Colchester U	60	Bury	59
1974–75	92	Mansfield T	68	Shrewsbury T	62	Rotherham U	59	Chester	57
1975–76	92	Lincoln C	74	Northampton T	68	Reading	60	Tranmere R	58
1976–77	92	Cambridge U	65	Exeter C	62	Colchester U	59	Bradford C	59
1977–78	92	Watford	71	Southend U	60	Swansea C	56	Brentford	56
1978–79	92	Reading	65	Grimsby T	61	Wimbledon	61	Barnsley	61
1979–80	92	Huddersfield T	66	Walsall	64	Newport Co	61	Portsmouth	60
1980–81	92	Southend U	67	Lincoln C	65	Doncaster R	56	Wimbledon	55
1981–82	138	Sheffield U	96	Bradford C	91	Wigan Ath	91	Bournemouth	88
1982–83	138	Wimbledon	98	Hull C	90	Port Vale	88	Scunthorpe U	83
1983–84	138	York C	101	Doncaster R	85	Reading	82	Bristol C	82
1984–85	138	Chesterfield	91	Blackpool	86	Darlington	85	Bury	84
1985–86	138	Swindon T	102	Chester C	84	Mansfield T	81	Port Vale	79
1986–87	138	Northampton T	99	Preston NE	90	Southend U	80	Wolverhampton W	79
1987–88	138	Wolverhampton W	90	Cardiff C	85	Bolton W	78	Scunthorpe U	77

*Won on goal average/difference.
†Maximum points reduced by Accrington Stanley's mid-season resignation from the League.

THIRD DIVISION (SOUTH)

Season	Max Pts	First	Pts	Second	Pts	Third	Pts
1921–22	84	Southampton*	61	Plymouth Arg	61	Portsmouth	53
1922–23	84	Bristol C	59	Plymouth Arg	53	Swansea T	53
1923–24	84	Portsmouth	59	Plymouth Arg	55	Millwall	54
1924–25	84	Swansea T	57	Plymouth Arg	56	Bristol C	53
1925–26	84	Reading	57	Plymouth Arg	56	Millwall	53
1926–27	84	Bristol C	62	Plymouth Arg	60	Millwall	56

FOOTBALL LEAGUE

1927–28	84	Millwall	65	Northampton T	55	Plymouth Arg	53
1928–29	84	Charlton Ath*	54	Crystal Palace	54	Northampton T	52
1929–30	84	Plymouth Arg	68	Brentford	61	QPR	51
1930–31	84	Notts Co	59	Crystal Palace	51	Brentford	50
1931–32	84	Fulham	57	Reading	55	Southend U	53
1932–33	84	Brentford	62	Exeter C	58	Norwich C	57
1933–34	84	Norwich C	61	Coventry C	54	Reading	54
1934–35	84	Charlton Ath	61	Reading	53	Coventry C	51
1935–36	84	Coventry C	57	Luton T	56	Reading	54
1936–37	84	Luton T	58	Notts Co	56	Brighton & HA	53
1937–38	84	Millwall	56	Bristol C	55	QPR	53
1938–39	84	Newport Co	55	Crystal Palace	52	Brighton & HA	49
1946–47	84	Cardiff C	66	QPR	57	Bristol C	51
1947–48	84	QPR	61	Bournemouth	57	Walsall	51
1948–49	84	Swansea T	62	Reading	55	Bournemouth	52
1949–50	84	Notts Co	58	Northampton T	51	Southend U	51
1950–51	92	Nottingham F	70	Norwich C	64	Reading	57
1951–52	92	Plymouth Arg	66	Reading	61	Norwich C	61
1952–53	92	Bristol R	64	Millwall	62	Northampton T	62
1953–54	92	Ipswich T	64	Brighton & HA	61	Bristol C	56
1954–55	92	Bristol C	70	Leyton Orient	61	Southampton	59
1955–56	92	Leyton Orient	66	Brighton & HA	65	Ipswich T	64
1956–57	92	Ipswich T*	59	Torquay U	59	Colchester U	58
1957–58	92	Brighton & HA	60	Brentford	58	Plymouth Arg	58

*Won on goal average

THIRD DIVISION (NORTH)

1921–22	76	Stockport Co	56	Darlington	50	Grimsby T	50
1922–23	76	Nelson	51	Bradford PA	47	Walsall	46
1923–24	84	Wolverhampton W	63	Rochdale	62	Chesterfield	54
1924–25	84	Darlington	58	Nelson	53	New Brighton	53
1925–26	84	Grimsby T	61	Bradford PA	60	Rochdale	59
1926–27	84	Stoke C	63	Rochdale	58	Bradford PA	55
1927–28	84	Bradford PA	63	Lincoln C	55	Stockport Co	54
1928–29	84	Bradford C	63	Stockport Co	62	Wrexham	52
1929–30	84	Port Vale	67	Stockport Co	63	Darlington	50
1930–31	84	Chesterfield	58	Lincoln C	57	Wrexham	54
1931–32	80	Lincoln C*	57	Gateshead	57	Chester	50
1932–33	84	Hull C	59	Wrexham	57	Stockport Co	54
1933–34	84	Barnsley	62	Chesterfield	61	Stockport Co	59
1934–35	84	Doncaster R	57	Halifax T	55	Chester	54
1935–36	84	Chesterfield	60	Chester	55	Tranmere R	55
1936–37	84	Stockport Co	60	Lincoln C	57	Chester	53
1937–38	84	Tranmere R	56	Doncaster R	54	Hull C	53
1938–39	84	Barnsley	67	Doncaster R	56	Bradford C	52
1946–47	84	Doncaster R	72	Rotherham U	64	Chester	56
1947–48	84	Lincoln C	60	Rotherham U	59	Wrexham	50
1948–49	84	Hull C	65	Rotherham U	62	Doncaster R	50
1949–50	84	Doncaster R	55	Gateshead	53	Rochdale	51
1950–51	92	Rotherham U	71	Mansfield T	64	Carlisle U	62
1951–52	92	Lincoln C	69	Grimsby T	66	Stockport Co	59
1952–53	92	Oldham Ath	59	Port Vale	58	Wrexham	56
1953–54	92	Port Vale	69	Barnsley	58	Scunthorpe U	57
1954–55	92	Barsnley	65	Accrington S	61	Scunthorpe U	58
1955–56	92	Grimsby T	68	Derby Co	63	Accrington S	59
1956–57	92	Derby Co	63	Hartlepools U	59	Accrington S	58
1957–58	92	Scunthorpe U	66	Accrington S	59	Bradford C	57

*Won on goal average

LEAGUE TITLE WINS

DIVISION 1: 17 – Liverpool, 9 – Everton, 8 – Arsenal, 7 – Aston Villa, Manchester U, 6 – Sunderland, 4 – Newcastle U, Sheffield W, 3 – Huddersfield T, Wolverhampton W, 2 – Blackburn R, Burnley, Derby Co, Leeds U, Manchester C, Portsmouth, Preston NE, Tottenham H, 1 – Chelsea, Ipswich T, Nottingham F, Sheffield U, WBA.

DIVISION 2: 6 – Leicester C, Manchester C, 5 – Sheffield W, 4 – Birmingham C (once as Small Heath), Derby Co, Liverpool, 3 – Middlesbrough, Notts Co, Preston NE, 2 – Aston Villa, Bolton W, Burnley, Grimsby T, Ipswich T, Leeds U,

FOOTBALL LEAGUE

Manchester U, Norwich C, Nottingham F, Stoke C, Tottenham H, WBA, West Ham U, Wolverhampton W, 1 – Blackburn R, Blackpool, Bradford C, Brentford, Bristol C, Bury, Chelsea, Coventry C, Crystal Palace, Everton, Fulham, Huddersfield T, Luton T, Millwall, Newcastle U, Oxford U, QPR, Sheffield U, Sunderland.

DIVISION 3: 2 – Oxford U, Portsmouth, 1 – Aston Villa, Blackburn R, Bolton W, Bradford C, Bournemouth, Burnley, Bury, Carlisle U, Coventry C, Crystal Palace, Grimsby T, Hereford U, Hull C, Leyton Orient, Mansfield T, Northampton T, Oldham Ath, Plymouth Arg, Preston NE, QPR, Reading, Rotherham U, Shrewsbury T, Southampton, Sunderland, Watford, Wrexham.

DIVISION 4: 2 – Chesterfield, Doncaster R, Peterborough U, 1 – Brentford, Brighton & HA, Cambridge U, Gillingham, Grimsby T, Huddersfield T, Lincoln C, Luton T, Mansfield T, Millwall, Northampton T, Notts Co, Port Vale, Reading, Sheffield U, Southend U, Southport, Stockport Co, Swindon T, Walsall, Watford, Wimbledon, Wolverhampton W, York C.

DIVISION 3 (South): 3 – Bristol C, 2 – Charlton Ath, Ipswich T, Millwall, Notts Co, Plymouth Arg, Swansea T, 1 – Brentford, Brighton & HA, Bristol R, Cardiff C, Coventry C, Fulham, Leyton Orient, Luton T, Newport Co, Nottingham F, Norwich C, Portsmouth, QPR, Reading, Southampton.

DIVISION 3 (North): 3 – Barnsley, Doncaster R, Lincoln C, 2 – Chesterfield, Grimsby T, Hull C, Port Vale, Stockport Co, 1 – Bradford C, Bradford PA, Darlington, Derby Co, Nelson, Oldham Ath, Rotherham U, Scunthorpe U, Stoke C, Tranmere R, Wolverhampton W.

RELEGATION

1891	League extended from 12 to 14 teams.
1892	Second Division formed.
1893	After test matches, Notts County relegated and Accrington Stanley resigned. Sheffield United and Darwen promoted to Division 1.
1894	After test matches, Liverpool and Small Heath promoted, Newton Heath and Darwen relegated.
1895	After test matches, Bury promoted, Liverpool relegated.
1896	After test matches, Liverpool promoted, Small Heath relegated.
1897	After test matches, Notts County promoted, Burnley relegated.
1898	Test matches abolished. League extended to two divisions of 18. Automatic promotion and relegation introduced.

RELEGATED FROM DIVISION ONE TO DIVISION TWO

1898–99	Bolton W, Sheffield W	1937–38	Manchester C, WBA
1899–1900	Burnley, Glossop	1938–39	Birmingham C, Leicester C
1900–01	Preston NE, WBA	1946–47	Brentford, Leeds U
1901–02	Manchester C, Small Heath	1947–48	Blackburn R, Grimsby T
1902–03	Bolton W, Grimsby T	1948–49	Preston NE, Sheffield U
1903–04	Liverpool, WBA	1949–50	Birmingham C, Manchester C
1904–05	League extended, no relegation	1950–51	Everton, Sheffield W
1905–06	Nottingham F, Wolverhampton W	1951–52	Fulham, Huddersfield
1906–07	Derby Co, Stoke C	1952–53	Derby Co, Stoke C
1907–08	Birmingham C, Bolton W	1953–54	Liverpool, Middlesbrough
1908–09	Leicester Fosse, Manchester C	1954–55	Leicester C, Sheffield W
1909–10	Bolton W, Chelsea	1955–56	Huddersfield T, Sheffield U
1910–11	Bristol C, Nottingham F	1956–57	Cardiff C, Charlton Ath
1911–12	Bury, Preston NE	1957–58	Sheffield W, Sunderland
1912–13	Notts Co, Woolwich Arsenal	1958–59	Aston Villa, Portsmouth
1913–14	Derby Co, Preston NE	1959–60	Leeds U, Luton T
1914–15	Chelsea, Tottenham H	1960–61	Newcastle U, Preston NE
1919–20	Notts Co, Sheffield W	1961–62	Cardiff C, Chelsea
1920–21	Bradford PA, Derby Co	1962–63	Leyton Orient, Manchester C
1921–22	Bradford C, Manchester U	1963–64	Bolton W, Ipswich T
1922–23	Oldham Ath, Stoke C	1964–65	Birmingham C, Wolverhampton W
1923–24	Chelsea, Middlesbrough	1965–66	Blackburn R, Northampton T
1924–25	Nottingham F, Preston NE	1966–67	Aston Villa, Blackpool
1925–26	Manchester C, Notts Co	1967–68	Fulham, Sheffield U
1926–27	Leeds U, WBA	1968–69	Leicester C, QPR
1927–28	Middlesbrough, Tottenham H	1969–70	Sheffield W, Sunderland
1928–29	Bury, Cardiff C	1970–71	Blackpool, Burnley
1929–30	Burnley, Everton	1971–72	Huddersfield T, Nottingham F
1930–31	Leeds U, Manchester U	1972–73	Crystal Palace, WBA
1931–32	Grimsby T, West Ham U	1973–74	Manchester U, Norwuch C, Southampton
1932–33	Blackpool, Bolton W	1974–75	Carlisle U, Chelsea, Lution T
1933–34	Newcastle U, Sheffield U	1975–76	Burnley, Sheffield U, WolverhamptonW
1934–35	Leicester C, Tottenham H	1976–77	Stoke C, Sunderland, Tottenham H
1935–36	Aston Villa, Blackburn R	1977–78	Leicester C, Newcastle U, West Ham U
1936–37	Manchester U, Sheffield W	1978–79	Birmingham C, Chelsea, QPR

FOOTBALL LEAGUE

1979–80	Bolton W, Bristol C, Derby Co
1980–81	Crystal Palace, Leicester C, Norwich C
1981–82	Leeds U, Middlesbrough, Wolverhampton W
1982–83	Brighton & HA, Manchester C, Swansea C
1983–84	Birmingham C, Notts Co, Wolverhampton W
1984–85	Norwich C, Stoke C, Sunderland
1985–86	Birmingham C, Ipswich, WBA
1986–87	Aston Villa, Leicester C, Manchester C
1987–88	Chelsea*, Oxford U, Portsmouth, Watford

RELEGATED FROM DIVISION 2 TO DIVISION 3

1920–21	Stockport Co
1921–22	Bradford PA, Bristol C
1922–23	Rotherham Co, Wolverhampton W
1923–24	Bristol C, Nelson
1924–25	Coventry C, Crystal Palace
1925–26	Stockport Co, Stoke C
1926–27	Bradford C, Darlington
1927–28	Fulham, South Shields
1928–29	Clapton Orient, Port Vale
1929–30	Hull C, Notts Co
1930–31	Cardiff C, Reading
1931–32	Barnsley, BristolC
1932–33	Charlton Ath, Chesterfield
1933–34	Lincoln C, Millwall
1934–35	Notts Co, Oldham Ath
1935–36	Hull C, Port Vale
1936–37	Bradford C, Doncaster R
1937–38	Barnsley, Stockport Co
1938–39	Norwich C, Tranmere R
1946–47	Newport Co, Swansea T
1947–48	Doncaster R, Millwall
1948–49	Lincoln C, Nottingham F
1949–50	Bradford PA, Plymouth Arg
1950–51	Chesterfield, Grimsby T
1951–52	Coventry C, QPR
1952–53	Barnsley, Southampton
1953–54	Brentford, Oldham Ath
1954–55	Derby Co, IpswichT
1955–56	Hull C, Plymouth Arg
1956–57	Bury, Port Vale
1957–58	Doncaster R, Notts Co
1958–59	Barnsley, Grimsby T
1959–60	Bristol C, Hull C
1960–61	Lincoln C, Portsmouth
1961–62	Brighton & HA, Bristol R
1962–63	Luton T,Walsall
1963–64	Grimsby T, Scunthorpe U
1964–65	Swansea T, Swindon T
1965–66	Leyton Orient, Middlesbrough
1966–67	Bury, Northampton T
1967–68	Plymouth Arg, Rotherham U
1968–69	Bury, Fulham
1969–70	Aston Villa, Preston NE
1970–71	Blackburn R, BoltonW
1971–72	Charlton Ath, Watford
1972–73	Brighton & HA, Huddersfield T
1973–74	Crystal Palace, Preston NE, Swindon T
1974–75	Cardiff C, Millwall, Sheffield W
1975–76	Oxford U, Portsmouth, York C
1976–77	Carlisle U, Hereford U, Plymouth Arg
1977–78	Blackpool, Hull C, Mansfield T
1978–79	Blackburn R, Millwall, SheffieldU
1979–80	Burnley, Charlton Ath, Fulham
1980–81	Bristol C, Bristol R, Preston NE
1981–82	Cardiff C, Orient, Wrexham
1982–83	Bolton W, Burnley, Rotherham U
1983–84	Cambridge U, Derby Co, Swansea C
1984–85	Cardiff C, Notts Co, Wolverhampton W
1985–86	Carlisle U, Fulham, Middlesbrough
1986–87	Brighton & HA, Grimsby T, Sunderland*
1987–88	Huddersfield T, Reading, Sheffield U*

DIVISION 3 TO DIVISION 4

1958–59	Doncaster R, Notts Co, Rochdale, Stockport Co
1959–60	Accrington S, Mansfield T, Wrexham, York C
1960–61	Bradford C, Chesterfield, Colchester U, Tranmere R
1961–62	Brentford, Lincoln C, Newport Co, Torquay U
1962–63	Bradford PA, Brighton & HA, Carlisle U, Halifax T
1963–64	Crewe Alex, Millwall, Notts Co, Wrexham
1964–65	Barnsley, Colchester U, Luton T, PortVale
1965–66	Brentford, Exeter C, Southend U, York C
1966–67	Darlington, Doncaster R, Swansea T, Workington T
1967–68	Colchester U, Grimsby T, Peterborough U (demoted by League order), Scunthorpe U
1968–69	Crewe Alex, Hartlepool, Northampton T, Oldham Ath
1969–70	Barrow, Bournemouth, Southport, Stockport Co
1970–71	Bury, Doncaster R, Gillingham, Reading
1971–72	Barnsley, Bradford C, Mansfield T, Torquay U
1972–73	Brentford, Rotherham U, Scunthorpe U, Swansea C
1973–74	Cambridge U, Rochdale, Shrewsbury T, Southport
1974–75	Bournemouth, Huddersfield T, Tranmere R, Watford
1975–76	Aldershot, Colchester U, Halifax T, Southend U
1976–77	Grimsby T, Northampton T, Reading, York C
1977–78	Bradford C, Hereford U, Portsmouth, Port Vale
1978–79	Lincoln C, Peterborough U, Tranmere R, Walsall
1979–80	Bury, Mansfield, Southend U, Wimbledon
1980–81	Blackpool, Colchester U, Hull C, SheffieldU
1981–82	Bristol C, Chester, Swindon T, Wimbledon
1982–83	Chesterfield, Doncaster R, Reading, Wrexham
1983–84	Exeter C, Port Vale, Scunthorpe U, Southend U
1984–85	Burnley, Cambridge U, Orient, Preston NE
1985–86	Cardiff C, Lincoln C, Swansea C, Wolverhampton W
1986–87	Bolton W*, Carlisle U, Darlington, Newport Co
1987–88	Doncaster R, Grimsby T, Rotherham U*, York C

*Relegated after play-offs.

APPLICATIONS FOR RE-ELECTION TO FOURTH DIVISION
(1958–59 to 1985–86)
11 – Hartlepool U. 7 – Crewe Alex. 6 – Barrow (replaced by Hereford U in 1972), Halifax T, Rochdale, Southport (replaced by Wigan Ath in 1978), York C. 5 – Chester C, Darlington, Lincoln C, Stockport Co, Workington (replaced by Wimbledon in 1977). 4 – Bradford PA (replaced by Cambridge U in 1970), Newport Co, Northampton T. 3 – Doncaster R, Hereford U. 2 – Bradford C, Exeter C, Oldham Ath, Scunthorpe U, Torquay U. 1 –; Aldershot, Blackpool, Cambridge U, Colchester U, Gateshead (replaced by Peterborough U in 1960), Grimsby T, Preston NE, Swansea C, Tranmere R, Wrexham.
Accrington S resigned and were replaced by Oxford U in 1962.
Port Vale were forced to re-apply following expulsion in 1968.

TO THIRD DIVISIONS NORTH & SOUTH (1921–22 to 1957–58*)
7 – Walsall. 6 – Exeter C, Halifax T, Newport Co. 5 – Accrington S, Barrow, Gillingham, New Brighton (replaced by Workington in 1951), Southport. 4 – Rochdale, Norwich C. 3 – Crewe Alex, Crystal Palace, Darlington, Hartlepool, Merthyr T (replaced by Thames in 1930), Swindon T. 2 – Aberdare Ath (replaced by Torquay U in 1927), Aldershot, Ashington (replaced by York C in 1929), Bournemouth, Brentford, Chester, Colchester U, Durham C (replaced by Carlisle U in 1928), Millwall, Nelson (replaced by Chester in 1931), QPR, Rotherham U, Southend U, Tranmere R, Watford, Workington. 1 – Bradford C, Bradford PA, Brighton & HA, Bristol R, Cardiff C, Carlisle U, Charlton Ath, Gateshead, Grimsby T, Mansfield T, Shrewsbury T, Torquay U, York C.
*Including Division 3, 1920–21.

OTHER RESIGNATIONS AND EXPULSIONS
Accrington – not to be confused with Accrington Stanley, they failed re–election in 1893, having been founder members of the League in 1888.
Bootle – resigned in 1893 after only one season.
Burton United – sometimes known as Burton Swifts, they failed re–election in 1907.
Burton Wanderers – failed re–election in 1897.
Darwen – failed re–election in 1899.
Gainsborough Trinity – failed re–election in 1912.
Glossop North End – resigned in 1915, to be replaced by Stoke (see below).
Leeds City – expelled on 4 October 1919 for making illegal payments during the war. Leeds United were formed soon after, but are not the same club.
Loughborough Town – failed re–election 1900.
Middlesbrough Ironopolis – resigned in 1894 after one season.
Northwich Victoria – resigned in 1894 after two seasons.
Rotherham Town – resigned in 1896 after three seasons.
Rotherham County – elected to Division 2 in 1919. Combined with Rotherham Town to form Rotherham United in 1925.
Stalybridge Celtic – resigned in 1923.
Stoke – failed re–election in 1890. Re–elected in 1891. Resigned in 1908. A new club (no real connection) was formed soon afterwards, and replaced Glossop NE in 1915. Changed name to Stoke City in 1925.
Thames – did not apply for re–election in 1932. Replaced by Newport.
Wigan Borough – resigned on 26 October 1931. Wigan Ath formed in 1932, but is not the same club.
The following 12 clubs have returned to the League after being expelled: Blackpool, Chesterfield, Crewe, Doncaster, Gillingham, Grimsby, Lincoln, Luton, Newport, Port Vale, Stockport, Walsall. Gillingham (1950) are the only club to have achieved this since the Second World War.

NEW LEAGUE MEMBERS SINCE 1986–87

	Relegated	Promoted
1986–87	Lincoln C	Scarborough
1987–88	Newport Co	Lincoln C

LEADING SCORERS 1987–88

Listed in order of League goals. Columns indicate League, Littlewoods Cup, FA Cup, Total.

DIVISION 1

John Aldridge (Liverpool)	26	1	2	29
Brian McClair (Manchester United)	24	5	2	31
Lee Chapman (Sheffield Wednesday)	19	1	2	22
Nigel Clough (Nottingham Forest)	18	2	1	21
Colin Clarke (Southampton)	16	0	1	17
Peter Beardsley (Liverpool)	15	0	3	18
John Barnes (Liverpool)	15	0	2	17
John Fashanu (Wimbledon)	14	3	4	21
Graeme Sharp (Everton)	13	1	6	20
Tony Cottee (West Ham United)	13	0	2	15
Neil Webb (Nottingham Forest)	13	2	0	15
Dean Saunders (Oxford United)	12	6	2	20
Gordon Durie (Chelsea)	12	4	0	16
Michael O'Neill (Newcastle United)	12	0	1	13
Kevin Drinkell (Norwich City)	12	0	0	12
Alan Smith (Arsenal)	11	4	1	16
Clive Allen (Tottenham Hotspur)	11	0	2	13
Kerry Dixon (Chelsea)	11	0	1	12
Mirandinha (Newcastle United)	11	1	0	12
Mark Stein (Luton Town)	11	0	1	12
Bryan Robson (Manchester United)	11	0	0	11
Danny Wallace (Southampton)	11	0	0	11
Nico Claesen (Tottenham Hotspur)	10	2	0	12
Garth Crooks (Charlton Athletic)	10	2	0	12
Cyrille Regis (Coventry City)	10	1	1	12
Dennis Wise (Wimbledon)	10	0	2	12
Wayne Clarke (Everton)	10	1	0	11

DIVISION 2

Mark Bright (Crystal Palace)	25	1	0	26
Paul Stewart (Manchester City)	24	2	1	27
Teddy Sheringham (Millwall)	22	0	0	22
Jimmy Quinn (Swindon Town)	21	8	0	29
Bernie Slaven (Middlesbrough)	21	1	0	22
Ian Wright (Crystal Palace)	20	3	0	23
Tony Cascarino (Millwall)	20	0	0	20
Andy Ritchie (Oldham Athletic)	19	1	0	20
Roger Palmer (Oldham Athletic)	17	3	0	20
Imre Varadi (Manchester City)	17	2	1	20
David Lowe (Ipswich Town)	17	1	0	18
Tommy Tynan (Plymouth Argyle)	16	1	1	18
Ron Futcher (Bradford City)	14	2	0	16
Simon Garner (Blackburn Rovers)	14	0	1	15
Steve Whitton (Birmingham City)	14	1	0	15
Dave Bamber (Swindon Town)	13	3	2	18
John Hendrie (Bradford City)	13	1	2	16
David White (Manchester City)	13	2	1	16
John Sheridan (Leeds United)	12	2	0	14
Colin Hendry (Blackburn Rovers)	12	0	0	12
Warren Aspinall (Aston Villa)	11	2	0	13
Andy Gray (West Bromwich Albion)	11	0	1	12
(Inc. 1 League, 1 FA Cup for Aston Villa)				
Steve White (Swindon Town)	11	1	0	12
Duncan Shearer (Huddersfield Town)	10	4	2	16
Stewart Evans (Plymouth Argyle)	10	0	1	11
Garry Thompson (Aston Villa)	10	1	0	11
David Barnes (Swindon Town)	10	0	0	10
Mark Leonard (Bradford City)	10	0	0	10
Chris Price (Blackburn Rovers)	10	0	0	10

DIVISION 3

David Crown (Southend United)	26	3	0	29
(Inc. 9 League, 3 Littlewoods Cup for Cambridge United)				
Steve Lovell (Gillingham)	25	0	1	26
Leroy Rosenior (Fulham)	25	1	1	27
(Inc. 5 League on loan to West Ham United)				
Stuart Rimmer (Chester City)	24	1	0	25
Garry Nelson (Brighton & Hove Albion)	22	0	5	27
Marco Gabbiadini (Sunderland)	22	1	0	23
(Inc. 1 League, 1 Littlewoods Cup for York City)				
Ian McParland (Notts County)	21	0	1	22
Mark Taylor (Blackpool)	21	0	1	22
David Kelly (Walsall)	20	0	1	21
Gary Lund (Notts County)	20	0	0	20
Eric Gates (Sunderland)	19	1	1	21
Liam Robinson (Bury)	19	2	0	21
Dave Waller (Chesterfield)	19	1	1	21
Gary Penrice (Bristol Rovers)	18	1	5	24
Dale Banton (York City)	16	0	1	17
John MacPhail (Sunderland)	16	0	0	16
Devon White (Bristol Rovers)	15	0	3	18
Tony Adcock (Northampton Town)	15	1	0	16
(Inc. 5 League, 1 Littlewoods Cup for Manchester City)				
Gary Brazil (Preston North End)	14	2	1	17
Geoff Pike (Notts County)	14	0	1	15
Tommy Langley (Aldershot)	14	0	0	14
Gordon Davies (Fulham)	13	2	0	15
Keith Walwyn (Blackpool)	13	0	1	14
Steve Charles (Mansfield Town)	12	0	3	15
Paul Haycock (Rotherham United)	12	0	2	14
Gary Swann (Preston North End)	12	0	0	12
Alan Walsh (Bristol City)	12	0	0	12

DIVISION 4

Steve Bull (Wolverhampton Wanderers)	34	3	3	40
Ian Muir (Tranmere Rovers)	27	0	2	29
Andy Flounders (Scunthorpe United)	24	1	0	25
John Thomas (Bolton Wanderers)	22	1	3	26
Paul Dobson (Torquay United)	22	1	1	24
Kevin Russell (Wrexham)	21	1	0	22
David Currie (Darlington)	21	0	0	21
Paul Baker (Hartlepool United)	19	1	3	23
Andy Mutch (Wolverhampton Wanderers)	19	2	0	21
David Platt (Crewe Alexandra)	19	2	0	21
Jimmy Gilligan (Cardiff City)	19	1	0	20
Mike Gooding (Peterborough United)	18	2	2	22
Andy Toman (Hartlepool United)	17	0	3	20
Ian Juryeff (Leyton Orient)	16	0	2	18
Robert Colville (Stockport County)	14	1	3	18
(Inc. 1 Littlewoods Cup for Bury)				
George Oghani (Burnley)	14	2	0	16
Colin Pascoe (Swansea City)	13	0	1	14
Kevin Stonehouse (Darlington)	13	1	0	14
Kevin Bartlett (Cardiff City)	12	0	1	13
Malcolm Poskett (Carlisle United)	12	1	0	13
Lyndon Simmonds (Rochdale)	12	1	0	13
Dean Edwards (Exeter City)	12	0	0	12
Brendan O'Connell (Exeter City)	11	2	0	13
Paul Shinners (Leyton Orient)	11	0	2	13
Alan Comfort (Leyton Orient)	11	0	1	12
Dale Tempest (Colchester United)	11	0	1	12
Joe Allon (Swansea City)	11	0	0	11

LEADING LEAGUE SCORERS SINCE 1946–47

1946–47 Division 1: D. Westcott (Wolverhampton W) 37. Division 2: C. Wayman (Newcastle U) 30. Division 3(S): D. Clark (Bristol C) 36. C. Jordan (Doncaster R) 42.

1947–48 Division 1: R. Rooke (Arsenal) 33. Division 2: E. Quigley (Sheffield W) 23. Division 3(S): L. Townsend (Bristol C). Division 3(N): J. Hutchinson (Lincoln C) 32.

1948–49 Division 1: W. Moir (Bolton W) 25. Division 2: C. Wayman (Southampton) 32. Division 3(S): D. McGibbon (Bournemouth & BA) 30. Division 3(N): W. Ardron (Rotherham U) 29.

1949–50 Division 1: D. Davis (Sunderland) 25. Division 2: T. Briggs (Grimsby T) 35. Division 3(S): T. Lawton (Notts Co). Division 3(N): P. Doherty (Doncaster R) & R. Phillips (Crewe Alex) 26.

1950–51 Division 1: S. Mortensen (Blackpool) 30. Division 2: J. McCormack (Barnsley) 33. Division 3(S): W. Ardron (Nottingham F) 36. Division 3(N): J. Shaw (Rotherham U) 37.

1951–52 Division 1: G. Robledo (Newcastle U) 33. Division 2: D. Dooley (Sheffield W) 46. Division 3(S): R. Blackman (Reading) 39. Division 3(N): A. Graver (Lincoln C) 36.

1952–53 Division 1: C. Wayman (Preston NE) 24. Division 2: A. Rowley (Leicester C) 39. Division 3(S): G. Bradford (Bristol R) 33. Division 3(N): J. Whitehouse (Carlisle U) 29.

1953–54 Division 1: J. Glazzard (Huddersfield T) & J. Nicholls (WBA) 29. Division 2: J. Charles (Leeds U) 42. Division 3(S): J. English (Northampton T) 28. Division 3(N): J. Connor (Stockport Co) 31.

1954–55 Division 1: R. Allen (WBA) 27. Division 2: T. Briggs (Blackburn R) 33. Division 3(S): E. Morgan (Gillingham) 31. Division 3(N): A. Bottom (York C) & J. Connor (Stockport Co) & D. Travis (Oldham Ath) 30.

1955–56 Division 1: N. Lofthouse (Bolton W) 33. Division 2: W. Gardiner (Leicester C) 34. Division 3(S): R. Collins (Torquay U) 40. Division 3(N): R. Crosbie (Grimsby T) 36.

1956–57 Division 1: J. Charles (Leeds U) 38. Division 2: A. Rowley (Leicester C) 44. Division 3(S): E. Phillips (Ipswich T) 41. Division 3(N): R. Straw (Derby Co) 37.

1957–58 Division 1: R. Smith (Tottenham H) 36. Division 2: T. Johnston (Leyton O, inc. 8 for Blackburn R) 43. Division 3(S): S. McCrory (Southend U) & D. Reeves (Southampton) 31. Division 3(N): A. Ackerman (Carlisle U) 35.

1958–59 Division 1: J. Greaves (Chelsea) & R. Smith (Tottenham H) 32. Division 2: B. Clough (Middlesbrough) 42. Division 3: E. Towers (Brentford) 32. Division 4: A. Rowley (Shrewsbury T) 37.

1959–60 Division 1: D. Viollet (Manchester U) 32. Division 2: B. Clough (Middlesbrough) 39. Division 3: D. Reeves (Southampton) 39. Division 4: C. Holton (Watford) 42.

1960–61 Division 1: J. Greaves (Chelsea) 41. Division 2: R. Crawford (Ipswich T) 39. Division 3: A. Richards (Walsall) 36. Division 4: T. Bly (Peterborough U) 52.

1961–62 Division 1: R. Crawford (Ipswich T) & D. Kevan (WBA) 33. Division 2: R. Hunt (Liverpool) 41. Division 3: C. Holton (Northampton T, inc. 1 for Watford) 37. Division 4: R. Hunt (Colchester U) 37.

1962–63 Division 1: J. Greaves (Tottenham H) 37. Division 2: R. Tambling (Chelsea) 35. Division 3: G. Hudson (Coventry C) 30. Division 4: K. Wagstaff (Mansfield T) & C. Booth (Doncaster R) 34.

1963–64 Division 1: J. Greaves (Tottenham H) 35. Division 2: R. Saunders (Portsmouth) 33. Division 3: A. Biggs (Bristol R) 30. Division 4: H. McIlmoyle (Carlisle U) 39.

1964–65 Division 1: J. Greaves (Tottenham H) & A. McEvoy (Blackburn R) 29. Division 2: G. O'Brien (Southampton) 34. Division 3: K. Wagstaff (Hull C, inc. 8 for Mansfield T) 31. Division 4: A. Jeffrey (Doncaster R) 36.

1965–66 Division 1: R. Hunt (Liverpool) 30. Division 2: M. Chivers (Southampton) 30. Division 3: L. Allen (QPR) 30. Division 4: K. Hector (Bradford C) 44.

1966–67 Division 1: R. Davies (Southampton) 37. Division 2: R. Gould (Coventry C) 24. Division 3: R. Marsh (QPR) 30. Division 4: E. Pythian (Hartlepools U) 23.

1967–68 Division 1: G. Best (Manchester U) & R. Davies (Southampton) 28. Division 2: J. Hickton (Middlesbrough) 24. Division 3: D. Rogers (Swindon T) & R. Owen (Bury) 25. Division 4: R. Chapman (Port Vale) & L. Massie (Halifax T) 25.

1968–69 Division 1: J. Greaves (Tottenham H) 27. Division 2: J. Toshack (Cardiff C) 22. Division 3: B. Lewis (Luton T) & D. Rogers (Swindon T) 22. Division 4: G. Talbot (Chester) 22.

1969–70 Division 1: J. Astle (WBA) 25. Division 2: J. Hickton (Middlesbrough) 24. Division 3: G. Jones (Bury) 26. Division 4: A. Kinsey (Wrexham) 27.

1970–71 Division 1: A. Brown (WBA) 28. Division 2: J. Hickton (Middlesbrough) 25. Division 3: G. Ingram (Preston NE) & D. Roberts (Mansfield T) 22. Division 4: E. MacDougall (Bournemouth & BA) 42.

1971–72 Division 1: F. Lee (Manchester C) 33. Division 2: R. Latchford (Birmingham C) 23. Division 3: E. MacDougall (Bournemouth & BA) & A. Wood (Shrewsbury T) 35. Division 4: P. Price (Peterborough U) 28.

406

LEADING LEAGUE SCORERS SINCE 1946–47

1972–73 Division 1: B. Robson (West Ham U) 28. Division 2: D. Givens (QPR) 23. Division 3: B. Bannister (Bristol R) & A. Horsfield (Charlton Ath) 25. Division 4: F. Binney (Exeter C) 28.

1973–74 Division 1: M. Channon (Southampton) 21. Division 2: D. McKenzie (Nottingham F) 26. Division 3: W. Jennings (Watford) 26. Division 4: B. Yeo (Gillingham) 31.

1974–75 Division 1: M. Macdonald (Newcastle U) 21. Division 2: B. Little (Aston Villa) 20. Division 3: R. McNeil (Hereford T) 31. Division 4: R. Clarke (Mansfield T) 28.

1975–76 Division 1: E. MacDougall (Norwich C) 23. Division 2: D. Hales (Charlton Ath) 28. Division 3: R. McNeil (Hereford U) 35. Division 4: R. Moore (Tranmere R) 34.

1976–77 Division 1: A. Gray (Aston Villa) & M. Macdonald (Arsenal) 25. Division 2: M. Walsh (Blackpool) 26. Division 3: P. Ward (Brighton & HA) 32. Division 4: B. Joicey (Barnsley) 25.

1977–78 Division 1: R. Latchford (Everton) 30. Division 2: R. Hatton (Blackpool) 22. Division 3: A. Bruce (Preston NE) 27. Division 4: S. Phillips (Brentford) & A. Curtis (Swansea C) 32.

1978–79 Division 1: F. Worthington (Bolton W) 24. Division 2: B. Robson (West Ham U) 24. Division 3: R. Jenkins (Watford) 29. Division 4: J. Dungworth (Aldershot) 26.

1979–80 Division 1: P. Boyer (Southampton) 23. Division 2: C. Allen (QPR) 28. Division 3: T. Curran (Sheffield W) 22. Division 4: C. Garwood (Aldershot, inc. 17 for Portsmouth) 27.

1980–81 Division 1: S. Archibald (Tottenham H) & P. Withe (Aston Villa) 20. Division 2: D. Cross (West Ham U) 22. Division 3: A. Kellow (Exeter C) 25. Division 4: A. Cork (Wimbledon) 23.

1981–82 Division 1: K. Keegan (Southampton) 26. Division 2: R. Moore (Rotherham U) 22. Division 3: G. Davies (Fulham) 24. Division 4: K. Edwards (Sheffield U, inc. 1 for Hull C) 36.

1982–83 Division 1: L. Blissett (Watford) 27. Division 2: G. Lineker (Leicester C) 26. Division 3: K. Dixon (Reading) 26. Division 4: S. Cammack (Scunthorpe U) 25.

1983–84 Division 1: I. Rush (Liverpool) 32. Division 2: K. Dixon (Chelsea) 28. Division 3: K. Edwards (Sheffield U) 33. Division 4: T. Senior (Reading) 36.

1984–85 Division 1: K. Dixon (Chelsea) & G. Lineker (Leicester C) 24. Division 2: J. Aldridge (Oxford U) 30. Division 3: T. Tynan (Plymouth Arg) 31. Division 4: J. Clayton (Tranmere R) 31.

1985–86 Division 1: G. Lineker (Everton) 30. Division 2: K. Drinkell (Norwich C) 22. Division 3: T. Senior (Reading) 27. Division 4: R. Cadette (Southend U) & S. Taylor (Rochdale) 25.

1986–87 Division 1: C. Allen (Tottenham H) 33. Division 2: M. Quinn (Portsmouth) 22. Division 3: A. Jones (Port Vale) 29. Division 4: R. Hill (Northampton T) 29.

1987–88 Division 1: J. Aldridge (Liverpool) 26. Division 2: M. Bright (Crystal Palace) 25. Division 3: D. Crown (Southend U, inc. 9 for Cambridge U) 26. Division 4: S. Bull (Wolverhampton W) 34.

FOOTBALL LEAGUE ATTENDANCES 1987–88

DIVISION ONE

Club	League Position	Home Average 1987–88	Home Average 1986–87	Difference
Arsenal	6	29,910	29,022	+888
Charlton Ath	17	8,684	9,012	−328
Chelsea	18	20,117	17,694	+2,423
Coventry C	10	17,509	16,119	+1,390
Derby Co*	15	17,157	15,539	+1,618
Everton	4	27,770	32,935	−5,165
Liverpool	1	39,582	36,285	+3,297
Luton T	9	8,038	10,256	−2,218
Manchester U	2	39,151	40,594	−1,443
Newcastle U	8	21,058	24,791	−3,733
Norwich C	14	15,942	17,564	−1,622
Nottingham F	3	19,670	19,086	+584
Oxford U	21	8,355	10,357	−2,002
Portsmouth*	19	15,923	13,404	+2,519
QPR	5	13,267	11,753	+1,514
Sheffield W	11	19,796	23,147	−3,351
Southampton	12	14,543	14,949	−406
Tottenham H	13	25,921	25,881	+40
Watford	20	14,529	15,799	−1,270
West Ham U	16	19,802	20,607	−805
Wimbledon	7	7,994	7,810	+184

*Promoted at the end of the previous season.

DIVISION TWO

Club	League Position	Home Average 1987–88	Home Average 1986–87	Difference
Aston Villa*	2	17,544	18,171	−627
Barnsley	14	7,349	5,870	+1,479
Birmingham City	19	8,206	7,426	+780
Blackburn R	5	9,089	6,772	+2,317
AFC Bournemouth*	17	7,530	6,610	+920
Bradford C	4	12,344	8,246	+4,098
Crystal Palace	6	9,321	7,583	+1,738
Huddersfield T	23	6,544	6,617	−73
Hull C	15	7,781	6,674	+1,107
Ipswich T	8	11,293	12,123	−830
Leeds United	7	19,391	17,612	+1,779
Leicester C†	13	9,716	11,697	−1,981
Manchester C†	9	18,407	21,922	−3,515
Middlesbrough*	3	13,878	10,174	+3,704
Millwall	1	8,051	4,304	+3,747
Oldham Ath	10	6,823	6,883	−60
Plymouth Arg	16	9,833	12,387	−2,554
Reading	22	6,643	6,883	−240
Sheffield U	21	9,763	9,991	−228
Shrewsbury T	18	4,729	4,097	+632
Stoke C	11	9,188	9,987	−799
Swindon T*	12	9,525	7,708	+1,817
West Bromwich A	20	9,686	9,133	+553

*Promoted at the end of the previous season.
†Relegated at the end of the previous season.

DIVISION THREE

Club	League Position	Home Average 1987–88	Home Average 1986–87	Difference
Aldershot*	20	3,259	2,358	+901
Blackpool	10	4,078	3,866	+212
Brentford	12	4,581	3,918	+663
Brighton & HA†	2	8,965	8,293	+672
Bristol C	5	9,818	9,441	+377
Bristol R	8	3,653	3,245	+408
Bury	14	2,565	2,501	+64
Chester C	15	2,663	2,731	−68
Chesterfield	18	2,661	2,575	+86
Doncaster R	24	1,913	2,408	−495
Fulham	9	4,921	4,085	+836
Gillingham	13	4,596	4,971	−375
Grimsby T†	22	3,416	5,050	−1,634
Mansfield T	19	3,811	3,215	+596
Northampton T*	6	5,514	6,316	−802
Notts Co	4	6,336	4,728	+1,608
Port Vale	11	3,847	3,312	+535
Preston NE*	16	6,194	8,079	−1,885
Rotherham U	21	3,665	2,983	+682
Southend U*	17	3,621	3,686	−65
Sunderland†	1	17,425	13,600	+3,825
Walsall	3	5,598	5,312	+286
Wigan Ath	7	3,759	3,397	+362
York C	23	2,760	3,432	−672

*Promoted at the end of the previous season.
†Relegated at the end of the previous season.

DIVISION FOUR

Club	League Position	Home Average 1987–88	Home Average 1986–87	Difference
Bolton W†	3	5,018	4,851	+167
Burnley	10	6,282	3,342	+2,940
Cambridge U	15	2,264	2,779	−515
Cardiff C	2	4,390	2,826	+1,564
Carlisle U†	23	2,236	2,644	−408
Colchester U	9	1,754	2,740	−986
Crewe Alex	17	2,281	1,931	+350
Darlington†	13	2,191	2,036	+155
Exeter C	22	2,463	2,627	−164
Halifax T	18	1,595	1,327	+268
Hartlepool U	16	2,129	1,650	+479
Hereford U	19	2,257	2,583	−326
Leyton Orient	8	3,933	2,857	+1,076
Newport Co†	24	1,763	2,063	−300
Peterborough U	7	3,204	3,714	−510
Rochdale	21	1,939	2,151	−212
Scarborough*	12	3,003	N/a	N/a
Scunthorpe U	4	3,233	2,126	+1,107
Stockport Co	20	2,272	2,113	+159
Swansea C	6	4,471	5,169	−698
Torquay U	5	3,005	1,777	+1,228
Tranmere R	14	3,322	2,126	+1,196
Wolverhampton W	1	9,855	5,754	+4,101
Wrexham	11	2,195	2,521	−326

*Promoted to the Football League at the end of the previous season.
†Relegated at the end of the previous season.

LEAGUE ATTENDANCES SINCE 1946–47

Season	Matches	Div.1	Div.2	Div.3(S)	Div.3(N)	Total
1946–47	1848	15,005,316	11,071,572	5,664,004	3,863,714	35,604,606
1947–48	1848	16,732,341	12,286,350	6,653,610	4,586,829	40,259,130
1948–49	1848	17,914,667	11,353,237	6,998,429	5,005,081	41,271,414
1949–50	1848	17,278,625	11,694,158	7,104,155	4,440,927,	40,517,865
1950–51	2028	16,679,454	10,780,580	7,367,884	4,757,109	39,584,967
1951–52	2028	16,110,322	11,066,189	6,958,927	4,880,428	39,015,866
1952–53	2028	16,050,278	9,686,654	6,704,299	4,708,735	37,149,966
1953–54	2028	16,154,915	9,510,053	6,311,508	4,198,114	36,174,590
1954–55	2028	15,087,221	8,988,794	5,996,017	4,051,071	34,133,103
1955–56	2028	14,108,961	9,080,002	5,692,479	4,269,367	33,150,809
1956–57	2028	13,803,037	8,718,162	5,622,189	4,601,017	32,744,405
1957–58	2028	14,468,652	8,663,712	6,097,183	4,332,661	33,562,208
1958–59	2028	14,727,691	8,641,997	5,946,600	4,276,697	33,610,985
1959–60	2028	14,391,227	8,399,627	5,739,707	4,008,050	32,538,611
1960–61	2028	12,926,948	7,033,936	4,784,256	3,874,614	28,619,754
1961–62	2015	12,061,194	7,453,089	5,199,106	3,266,513	27,979,902
1962–63	2028	12,490,239	7,792,770	5,341,362	3,261,481	28,885,852
1963–64	2028	12,486,626	7,594,158	5,419,157	3,035,081	28,535,022
1964–65	2028	12,708,752	6,984,104	4,436,245	3,512,067	27,641,168
1965–66	2028	12,480,644	6,914,757	4,779,150	3,032,429	27,206,980
1966–67	2028	14,242,957	7,253,819	4,421,172	2,984,648	28,902,596
1967–68	2028	15,289,410	7,450,410	4,013,087	3,354,391	30,107,298
1968–69	2028	14,584,851	7,382,390	4,339,656	3,075,275	29,382,172
1969–70	2028	14,868,754	7,581,728	4,223,761	2,926,729	29,600,972
1970–71	2028	13,954,337	7,098,265	4,377,213	2,764,331	28,194,146
1971–72	2028	14,484,603	6,769,308	4,697,392	2,749,426	28,700,729
1972–73	2028	13,998,154	5,631,730	3,737,252	2,081,506	25,448,642
1973–74	2027	13,070,991	6,326,108	3,421,624	2,163,480	24,982,203
1974–75	2028	12,613,178	6,955,970	4,086,145	1,992,684	25,577,977
1975–76	2028	13,089,861	5,798,405	3,948,449	2,059,338	24,896,053
1976–77	2028	13,647,585	6,250,597	4,152,218	2,132,400	26,182,800
1977–78	2028	13,255,677	6,474,763	3,332,042	2,330,390	25,392,872
1978–79	2028	12,704,549	6,153,223	3,374,558	2,308,297	24,540,627
1979–80	2028	12,163,002	6,112,025	3,999,328	2,349,620	24,623,975
1980–81	2028	11,392,894	5,175,442	3,637,854	1,701,379	21,907,569
1981–82	2028	10,420,793	4,750,463	2,836,915	1,998,790	20,006,961
1982–83	2028	9,295,613	4,974,937	2,943,568	1,552,040	18,766,158
1983–84	2028	8,711,448	5,359,757	2,729,942	1,557,484	18,358,631
1984–85	2028	9,761,404	4,030,823	2,667,008	1,390,600	17,849,835
1985–86	2028	9,037,854	3,551,968	2,490,481	1,408,274	16,488,577
1986–87	2028	9,144,676	4,168,131	2,350,970	1,715,441	17,379,218
1987–88	2046	8,094,571	5,350,754	2,751,275	1,772,287	17,968,887

FA CUP 1987–88

FIRST ROUND

ALTRINCHAM (0)0 WIGAN ATH (1)2
(14.11.87, 4008)
Altrincham: Butcher; Farrelly, Edwards, Worrall, Fraser, Cuddy, Stewart, Smith, Timmons, Bishop, Ellis (Collins).
Wigan Ath: Hughes; Butler, Knowles, Hamilton, Beesley, Holden, Senior, Thompson, Campbell, Jewell, Cook.
Scorers: Campbell, Butler.

BARNET (0)0 HEREFORD U (0)1
(14.11.87, 2754)
Barnet: Humphries; Stephens, Brown, Millett, Creaser, Codner, Stein, Ironton (Bowen), Sansom, Evans, Alexander.
Hereford U: Rose; Jones, Devine (Pejic), Stevens, Wassell, Spooner, Rodgerson, Bowyer, Benbow, Stant, Leadbitter.
Scorer: Stant.

BILLINGHAM (1)2 HALIFAX T (1)4
(Hartlepool, 14.11.87, 1153)
Billingham: Davison; Parry, Strong, Granycome, Harbron, Coleby, McMullen (Sills), Kalone, Hewitt, Whetter, Allen. Scorers: Allen, Hewitt.
Halifax T: Roche; Brown, Fleming, M. Matthews, Robinson, Shaw, Martin, Thornber, N. Matthews, Black, Holden (Ferebee). Scorers: Black 2, Robinson, N. Matthews.

BISHOP AUCKLAND (1)1 BLACKPOOL (3)4
(14.11.87, 2462)
Bishop Auckland: Harrison; Lynch, Knox, Fothergill, Brown, Blair, Pearson, Charlton, Ord, Grady, Hinds. Scorer: Pearson.
Blackpool: Siddall; Davies, Morgan, Bradshaw, Methven, Jones, Deary, Madden (Rooney), Walwyn, McAteer (Butler), Taylor. Scorers: Morgan, Madden (pen), Taylor 2.

BOGNOR (0)0 TORQUAY U (2)3
(14.11.87, 3500)
Bognor: Steele; P. Pullen, Bird, Quinn, M. Pullen, Marriner (Price), Burtenshaw, Thomas, Poole, Clements, Cooper.
Torquay U: Allen; McNichol, Pearce (Kelly), Haslegrave, Cole, Impey, Dawkins, Lloyd, Gardiner, Loram (Nardiello), Dobson. Scorers: Dobson, Pearce, Gardiner.

BRENTFORD (0)0 BRIGHTON & HA (0)2
(14.11.87, 6358)
Brentford: Phillips; Joseph, Stanislaus, Feeley, Evans, Jones (Carroll), Thorne, Sinton, Cooke (Booker), Lee, Perryman.
Brighton & HA: Keeley; Brown, Dublin, Curbishley (Jasper), Rougvie, Gatting, Nelson, Hutchings, Bremner, Wilkins, Crumplin (Wood). Scorers: Nelson 2 (1 pen)

BRISTOL C (0)1 AYLESBURY (0)0
(14.11.87, 8263)
Bristol C: Coombe; Llewellyn, Bromage, Humphries, Pender, Galliers, Owen, Newman, Shutt, Walsh (Marshall), Caldwell. Scorer: Caldwell.
Alyesbury: Garner; Robinson, James, Hackett, Hutter, Botterill, McBean (Davie), Duggan, Hercules, Phillips, Harthill.

BRISTOL R (2)6 MERTHYR TYDFIL (0)0
(14.11.87, 4635)
Bristol R: Martyn; Alexander (Dryden), Tanner, Hibbitt, Twentyman, Jones, Holloway, Meacham, White, Penrice (Reece), Purnell. Scorers: Penrice 3, White, Meacham.
Merthyr Tydfil: Wager (Chris Williams) (S. Williams); Tong, Jones, Holvey, Evans, Mullen, French, Rogers, Green, Beattie, Ceri Williams.

BURNLEY (0)0 BOLTON W (0)1
(14.11.87, 10,641)
Burnley: Pearce; Daniel (Britton), Deakin, James, Zelem, Gardner, Farrell, Grewcock, Oghani (Hoskin), Comstive, Taylor.
Bolton W: Felgate; Scott, Henshaw, Savage, Came, Crombie, Brookman, Thompson, Thomas, Elliott, Darby. Scorer: Thomas (pen).

CAMBRIDGE U (2)2 FARNBOROUGH (1)1
(14.11.87, 2200)
Cambridge U: Branagan; Poole, Murray, Beattie, Smith, Beck, Butler, Clayton, Benjamin, Rigby (Horwood), Kimble. Scorers: Beattie, Benjamin.
Farnborough: Riley; Harlow, Baker, Fielder, Pratt, Gosnell, Turkington, Read, Bailey, Bolton, Groom. Scorer: Bailey.

CHELMSFORD (0)1 BATH (1)2
(14.11.87, 1721)
Chelmsford: Harrold; Lee, Wells, Entwhistle, Spittle (Wilkins), Devine, Owers, Foley, Lazarus, Bartley, Pountney. Scorer: Wilkins.
Bath: Bond; Stevens, Palmer, Bodin, Craig, Adams, Wiffill, Grimshaw, Singleton, Williams, Payne. Scorers: Payne, Grimshaw.

CHESTER C (0)0 RUNCORN (1)1
(14.11.87, 3533)
Chester C: Stewart; Banks (Bennett), Woodthorpe, Fazackerley, Abel, Lightfoot, Butler, Barrow, Rimmer, Greenough, Croft.
Runcorn: McBride; Stephens, Densmore, Miller, Carroll, Rowlands, Pugh, Rooney, Carter, Page (McMahon), Anderson. Scorer: Carter.

CHORLEY (0)0 HARTLEPOOL U (0)2
(14.11.87, 2462)
Chorley: Darcy; Lloyd, Peters (Marsden), Nicholl, Pawsey, Phillips, Buckley, Hughes, Moss, Redshaw, Brady (Edwards).
Hartlepool U: Carr; Haigh, McKinnon, Nobbs, Smith, Stokes, Honour, Toman, Baker, Gibb, Butler. Scorers: Gibb, Baker.

COLCHESTER U (0)3 TAMWORTH (0)0
(14.11.87, 3215)
Colchester U: Walton; Hedman, Grenfell, Chatterton, Baker, Hinshelwood, White, Wilkins, Tempest, English, Reeves. Scorers: Wilkins, Tempest, Chatterton (pen).
Tamworth: Hemming; Lockett, B. Brown, McCormack, Foote, Cartwright (G. Brown), Myers, Stanton, Maddocks, Rathbone (Haynes), Gilmour.

DAGENHAM (0)0 MAIDSTONE (1)2
(14.11.87, 1137)
Dagenham: Scott; Stacey, La Ronde, Bissett, Wiggins (Greenaway), Campbell, Fitt, Coles, Olaleye, Bolle, Dalorto.
Maidstone: Beeney; Roast, Harrison, Pamphlett, Hill, Risk, Donn, Higginbottom, Doherty, Butler, Roberts. Scorers: Butler (pen), Harrison.

DONCASTER R (1)1 ROTHERHAM U (0)1
(14.11.87, 3359)
Doncaster R: Rhodes; Stead, Robinson, Joyce, Raven, Cusack, Holmes, Miller, Deane, Turnbull, Kimble. Scorer: Holmes.
Rotherham U: O'Hanlon; Douglas, Scott, Dungworth, Johnson, Green, Pugh, Williams, Evans, Haycock, Campbell. Scorer: Dungworth (pen).

FA CUP

GILLINGHAM (2)2 FULHAM (0)1
(14.11.87, 6444)
Gillingham: Kite; Haylock, Elsey, Quow, West, Greenall, Pritchard, Cooper, Lovell, M. Smith (Weatherly), Lillis. **Scorers:** Lillis, Pritchard.
Fulham: Stannard; Langley, Thomas, Lewington, Oakes (Elkins), Hicks, Barnett, Wilson, Rosenior, Davies, Walker. **Scorer:** Rosenior.

HALESOWEN (0)2 KIDDERMINISTER (1)2
(14.11.87, 2932)
Halesowen: Pemberton; Penn, Sherwood, Moore, Guest, Sturgess, Hancox, Cunningham (Moss), Stringer, P. Joinson, L. Joinson. **Scorers:** L. Joinson, Moss.
Kidderminster: Arnold; Barton, Collins, Boxall, C. Jones, Woodhall, McKenzie, R. Jones (Casey), Davies, Tuohy, Hazelwood. **Scorers:** Hazelwood, Woodhall.

HAYES (0)0 SWANSEA C (1)1
(14.11.87, 2682)
Hayes: Hyde; Bolton, Churchouse (Walton), Hayward, Leather, Whisky, Payne, Forde, Kelly, Graves (Knowles), Clevereford.
Swansea C: Hughes; Hough, Coleman (Harrison), Melville, Knill, Emmanuel, Davies, Raynor, Allon, Pascoe (McCarthy), Lewis. **Scorer:** Pascoe.

LEYTON ORIENT (1)2 EXETER C (0)0
(14.11.87, 3787)
Leyton Orient: Wells; Howard, Dickenson, Smalley, Day, Hull, Hales, Castle, Shinners, Godfrey, Comfort. **Scorers:** Godfrey, Hull.
Exeter C: Shaw; Cooper, Viney, Carter, Taylor (Watson), Massey, Batty, Edwards, O'Connell, Rowbotham (Olsson), Harrower.

LINCOLN C (1)2 CREW ALEX (0)1
(14.11.87, 3892)
Lincoln C: Batch; Evans, Nicholson, Brown, Matthewson, Moore, Mossman, Cumming, Sertori, Smith, McGinley. **Scorers:** McGinley, Cumming.
Crewe Alex: Parkin; Goodison, Pemberton, Wright, Billing, Gage, Platt, Wakenshaw (Murphy) (Macowat), Milligan, Eli, Gymer. **Scorer:** Macowat.

MACCLESFIELD (0)4 CARLISLE U (1)2
(14.11.87, 2385)
Macclesfield: Zelem; Roberts, Shaw, Edwards, Tobin, Hardman, Askey, Hanlon, Lake, Burr, Mountford. **Scorers:** Hardman, Askey, Tobin, Burr.
Carlisle U: Taylor; McNeil, Robinson, Gorman, Wright, Saunders, Clark, Cooke, Poskett, Fulbrook, Hetherington. **Scorers:** Hetherington, Fulbrook.

NORTHAMPTON T (0)2 NEWPORT CO (0)1
(14.11.87, 4581)
Northampton T: Gleasure; Reed, Chard, Donald, Wilcox, McPherson, Singleton, Culpin (McGoldrick), Gilbert, Morley, Longhurst. **Scorers:** Chard, Morley.
Newport Co: Bradshaw; Hodson, Gibbins, Thackeray, Abruzzese, Sherlock, Giles, Tupling, Taylor, Preece (Holtham), Osborne (Thompson). **Scorer:** Holtham.

NORTHWICK (1)1 COLWYN BAY (0)0
(14.11.87, 1520)
Northwick: Ryan; Young (Wilson), Jones, McNelle, Parker, Gardner, Imrie, Sayer, Salmon (Bennett), Reid, Dunn. **Scorer:** Sayer (pen).
Colwyn Bay: K. Williams; Dean Martin, Darren Martin, T. Williams, B. Jones, Smith, D. Williams (Bickerstaffe), Brett, Evans, Turley (Rush), S. Jones.

PETERBOROUGH U (1)2 CARDIFF C (1)1
(14.11.87, 3600)
Peterborough U: Neenan; Paris, Collins, Gooding, Gunn, Price, Carr (Kelly), Halsall, Lawrence, Nightingale, Luke. **Scorer:** Gooding 2.
Cardiff C: Roberts; Bater, Platnauer, Wimbleton, Kelly (Sanderson), Boyle, Curtis, Ford, Gilligan, McDermott, Bartlett (Mardenborough). **Scorer:** Bartlett.

PRESTON NE (0)1 MANSFIELD T (0)1
(14.11.87, 7415)
Preston NE: Kelly; Rathbone, Bennett, Atkins, Jones, Allardyce, Mooney, Swann, Ellis, Brazil, Hildersley. **Scorer:** Atkins.
Mansfield T: Hitchcock; Graham, Ryan, Lowery, Foster, Coleman, Kent, Kenworthy, Stringfellow, Cassells, Charles. **Scorer:** Stringfellow.

ROCHDALE (0)0 WREXHAM (2)2
(14.11.87, 1831)
Rochdale: Welch; Seasman, Hampton, Reid, Duggan, Smart, Warren, Simmonds, Parlane, Coyle (Walling), Gavin.
Wrexham: Salmon; Preece (Scott), Wright, Hinnigan, Williams, Carter, Buxton, Hunter, Steel, Russell, Emson (Slater). **Scorers:** Carter, Buxton.

SCARBOROUGH (0)1 GRIMSBY T (1)2
(14.11.87, 3864)
Scarborough: Evans; McJannet (Adams), Thompson, Bennyworth, Richards, Kamara, Hamill, Graham, McHale, Mell, Cook (Russell). **Scorer:** Graham.
Grimsby T: Sherwood; McDermott, Dixon, Turner, Slack, Robinson, Curran (Grocock), Saunders, North, O'Riordan, McGarvey. **Scorers:** McGarvey, North.

SCUNTHORPE U (2)3 BURY (1)1
(14.11.87, 3151)
Scunthorpe U: Green; Russell, Longden, Taylor, Lister, Money, Dixon, Harle, Johnson, Flounders, Atkins. **Scorers:** Russell 3 (1 pen).
Bury: Farnworth; Hill, Pashley (Hart), Hoyland, Valentine, Higgins, Lee (Taylor), Robinson, Greenwood, McIlroy, Brotherston. **Scorer:** McIlroy.

SOUTHEND U (0)0 WALSALL (0)0
(14.11.87, 3053)
Southend U: Newell; O'Shea, Johnson, Ling, Martin, Hall (Smith), Clark, Pennyfather, Robinson, Crown, Rogers.
Walsall: Barber; Dornan, Hawker, Shakespeare, Forbes, Hart, Taylor, P. Jones, Kelly, Christie, Naughton.

SUNDERLAND (1)2 DARLINGTON (0)0
(14.11.87, 16,892)
Sunderland: Hesford; Kay, Agboola, Ord, MacPhail, Owers, Armstrong, Doyle, Gates, Gabbiadini (Lemon), Atkinson. **Scorer:** Atkinson 2.
Darlington: Roberts; Outterside, Morgan, Hine, Robinson, McAughtrie, Bell, Ward, Macdonald, Currie, Stonehouse (Worthington).

SUTTON (1)3 ALDERSHOT (0)0
(14.11.87, 3419)
Sutton: Roffey; Jones, Rains, M. Golley, Hemsley, Rogers, Stephens, Cornwell, Awaritefe, McKinnon, N. Golley. **Scorers:** McKinnon 2, Cornwell.
Aldershot: Coles; Berry, Phillips, Roberts, Anderson, Wignall, Ring (King) (Riley), Langley, Johnson, McDonald, Burvill.

TELFORD (1)1 STOCKPORT CO (0)1
(14.11.87, 2758)
Telford: Charlton; McGinty, Wiggins, Griffiths (Joseph), Nelson, Storton, Lee, Biggins, Norris, Sankey, Alcock. **Scorers:** Biggins.
Stockport Co: Marples; Bullock, Bailey, Robinson, Pickering, Williams, Hodkinson, Colville, Entwistle, Hartford, Birch. **Scorer:** Entwistle.

TRANMERE R (1)2 PORT VALE (2)2
(14.11.87, 4035)
Tranmere R: O'Rourke; Higgins, McCarrick, Martindale, Williams, Vickers, Mungall, Harvey, Moore, Muir, Murray. **Scorers:** Martindale, Muir.
Port Vale: Simons; Webb (Porter), Hughes, Walker, Hazell, Sproson, Maguire, Finney, Riley, Beckford (O'Kelly), Hamson. **Scorers:** Maguire, Harvey (og).

VS RUGBY (0)0 ATHERSTONE (0)0
(14.11.87, 1500)
VS Rugby: Marsden; Potter, Riley, Lane, Gethefield, Ingram (Knox), Halton, Geddes, Ebrey, Conway, Ross.
Atherstone: Spencer; Thurman, Montgomery, Olner, Haskins, Waters, Tedds, Brotherston, Bradder, Farmer, Kennell.

WOLVERHAMPTON W (2)5 CHELTENHAM (1)1
(14.11.87, 10,541)
Wolverhampton W: Kendall; Stoutt, Thompson, Streete, Robertson (Powell), Gallagher, Dennison, Vaughan, Bull, Mutch, Downing (Clarke). **Scorers:** Vaughan, Bull 3, Downing.
Cheltenham: Churchward; Baverstock, Willetts, Crowley, Vircavs, Buckland (Jordan), Brown, Boyland (Townsend), Angell, Brookes, Hughes. **Scorer:** Angell.

WORCESTER (1)1 YEOVIL (1)1
(14.11.87, 3080)
Worcester: Moore; Ridding (Kavanagh), McGrath, Shail, Tudor, Ledbury, Powell, Whitehouse, Knight, Gavin, Ferguson. **Scorer:** Ferguson.
Yeovil: Iles; Sherwood, Ferns, Ricketts, Rutter, Cordice, Noble, Wallace, McGinlay (Randall), Pearson, Donnellan. **Scorer:** Pearson.

YORK C (0)0 BURTON ALBION (0)0
(14.11.87, 3140)
York C: Endersby; Kitching, Johnson, Wilson, Hood, Clegg, Staniforth, Mills, Brough, Banton, Tuthill.
Burton Albion: New; Simms, Blower, Straw, Essex, S. Redfern, Groves, Bancroft, Land, Dorsett.

NOTTS CO (1)3 CHESTERFIELD (0)3
(15.11.87, 4850)
Notts Co: Leonard; Smalley, Withe, Kevan, Yates, Hunt, Mills, McParland, Birtles, Pike, Thorpe. **Scorers:** Kevan, McParland, Birtles.
Chesterfield: Brown; Rogers, Hewitt, McGeeney, Benjamin, Wood, Coyle, Bloomer, Waller, Walker (Travis), Eley. **Scorers:** Waller, Travis 2.

FIRST ROUND REPLAYS

KIDDERMINSTER (1)4 HALESOWEN (0)0
(16.11.87, 4011)
Kidderminster: Arnold; Barton, Collins, Weir, C. Jones, Woodhall, McKenzie, N. Jones, Davies (Casey), Tuohy, Hazelwood. **Scorers:** Tuohy 2, Davies, R. Jones.
Halesowen: Pemberton; Penn (Woodhouse), Sherwood, Moore, Guest (Lacey), Ford, Hancox, Moss, Stringer, P. Joinson, L. Joinson.

PORT VALE (1)3 TRANMERE R (0)1
(16.11.87, 4097)
Port Vale: Grew; Banks, Hughes, Walker, Hazell, Sproson, Maguire, Finney, Riley, O'Kelly, Hamson. **Scorers:** O'Kelly, Hamson, Riley.
Tranmere R: O'Rourke; Higgins, McCarrick, Martindale, Williams, Vickers, Mungall, Harvey, Moore, Muir, Murray. **Scorer:** Muir.

ATHERSTONE (0)0 VS RUGBY (0)2
(17.11.87, 2816)
Atherstone: Spencer; Thurman (Neale), Montgomery, Olner, Haskins, Waters, Tedds (Rammell), Brotherston, Bradder, Farmer, Kennell.
VS Rugby: Marsden; Potter, Riley, Lane, Holton, Gethefield, Ingram, Geddes (Shepherd), Ebrey, Conway, Ross. **Scorers:** Ross, Conway.

CHESTERFIELD (0)0 NOTTS CO (1)1
(17.11.87, 4482)
Chesterfield: Brown; Hewitt, Bloomer, Rogers, Wood, Coyle (Perry), Travis, McGeeney, Waller, Walker (Taylor), Eley.
Notts Co: Leonard; Smalley, Withe, Kevan, Yates, Birtles, Mills, McParland, Lund, Pike, Thorpe. **Scorer:** Pike (pen).

MANSFIELD T (2)4 PRESTON NE (1)2
(17.11.87, 4682)
Mansfield T: Hitchcock; Graham, Ryan, Lowery, Foster, Coleman, Kent, Kenworthy, Stringfellow, Cassells, Charles. **Scorers:** Cassells 2, Charles (pen), Kent.
Preston NE: Kelly; Rathbone, Bennett, Atkins, Mooney, Jones, Allardyce, Swann, Jemson, Brazil, Hildersley. **Scorers:** Brazil, Jemson.

ROTHERHAM U (0)2 DONCASTER R (0)0
(17.11.87, 4530)
Rotherham U: O'Hanlon; Douglas, Scott, Grealish, Johnson, Green (Dungworth), Pugh, Williams, Evans, Haycock, Campbell. **Scorer:** Haycock 2.
Doncaster R: Rhodes; Stead (Flynn), Robinson, Joyce, Raven, Cusack, Holmes, Miller, Deane, Turnbull, Kimble (Gorman).

STOCKPORT CO (2)2 TELFORD (0)0
(17.11.87, 3083)
Stockport Co: Marples; Bullock, Bailey, Robinson, Pickering, Williams, Hodkinson, Colville, Entwistle, Hartford, Birch. **Scorers:** Colville, Hodkinson (pen).
Telford: Charlton; McGinty (Stringer), Wiggins, Griffiths, Kerr, Storton, Joseph, Biggins, Norris, Lee, Alcock.

WALSALL (0)2 SOUTHEND U (0)1
(17.11.87, 5162)
Walsall: Barber; Dornan, Taylor, Shakespeare, Forbes, Hart, P. Jones, Cross, Kelly, Christie, Naughton. **Scorer:** P. Jones 2 (2 pens).
Southend U: Newell; O'Shea, Johnson, Ling, Martin, Hall, Clark, Pennyfather, Robinson, Crown (Neal), Rogers. **Scorer:** Hall (pen).

BURTON ALBION (1)1 YORK C (1)2
(18.11.87, 4381)
Burton Albion: New; Blower, Simms, Essex, Straw, Bancroft, S. Redfern, Hutchinson (Land), D. Redfern, Groves, Dorsett. **Scorer:** Groves (pen).
York C: Endersby; Branagan, Tuthill, Wilson, Clegg, Whitehead, Staniforth, Mills, Brough, Banton, Hood. **Scorers:** Hood (pen), Mills.

FA CUP

YEOVIL (1)1 WORCESTER (0)0
(18.11.87, 3913)
Yeovil: Iles; Sherwood, Ferns, Ricketts, Rutter, Cordice, Noble (Randall), Wallace, McGinlay, Pearson, Donnellan. **Scorer:** McGinlay.
Worcester: Moore; Ridding (Cavanagh), McGrath, Shail, Tudor, Ledbury, Powell, Whitehouse, Knight, Gavin, Ferguson.

FIRST ROUND

WELLING (1)3 CARSHALTON (0)2
(23.12.87, 2237)
Welling: Richardson; Sawyer, Horton, Crowe, Ransom, Burgess (Reynolds), White, Handford; Abbott (Haverson), Booker, Lindsay. **Scorers:** Gaston (og), Booker, Abbott.
Carshalton: Cleevely; Warmington, Riley, Raffington, Croad, Armitt (Wadden), Wilgoss, Gaston, Jones, Dibble (Flemington), Kane. **Scorers:** Kane, Riley.

SECOND ROUND

BRISTOL C (0)0 TORQUAY U (0)1
(5.12.87, 9027)
Bristol C: Waugh; Honor, Bromage, Humphries, Pender, Galliers, Newman, Fitzpatrick (Marshall), Jordan (Neville), Shutt, Walsh.
Torquay U: Allen; McNichol, Pearce, Haslegrave, Cole, Impey, Dawkins, Lloyd, Caldwell, Loram, Dobson. **Scorer:** Caldwell.

CAMBRIDGE U (0)0 YEOVIL (0)1
(5.12.87, 2588)
Cambridge U: Branagan; Poole, Murray, Crowe, Smith, Beck, Butler, Clayton, Purdie, Benjamin, Kimble.
Yeovil: Iles; Sherwood, Ferns, Ricketts, Rutter, Cordice, Donnellan (Noble), Wallace, McGinley, Randall, Pearson. **Scorer:** Wallace.

COLCHESTER U (2)3 HEREFORD U (1)2
(5.12.87, 2216)
Colchester U: Walton; Hinshelwood, Hedman, Chatterton, Baker, Hill, White, Wilkins (Walsh), Tempest, English, Grenfell. **Scorers:** Chatterton, Wilkins, Hill.
Hereford U: Rose; Jones, Devine, Stevens, Pejic, Spooner, Dalziel, Bowyer, Phillips, Stant, Leadbitter. **Scorers:** Stant, Phillips.

GILLINGHAM (2)2 WALSALL (1)1
(5.12.87, 4916)
Gillingham: Kite; Haylock (Gernon), Pearce, Quow, West, Greenall, Pritchard, Eves, Lovell, Elsey, Weatherly. **Scorers:** Lovell, Elsey.
Walsall: Barber; Taylor, Mower, Shakespeare, Forbes, Hart, P. Jones, Hawker, Kelly, Christie, Naughton (Cross). **Scorer:** Kelly.

GRIMSBY T (0)0 HALIFAX T (0)0
(5.12.87, 3227)
Grimsby T: Sherwood; McDermott, Agnew, Turner, D. Moore, Robinson, Grocock, Saunders, North, O'Riordan, McGarvey.
Halifax T: Roche; Brown, Barr, M. Matthews, Fleming, Shaw, Martin, Thornber, N. Matthews, Black, Holden.

LEYTON ORIENT (1)2 SWANSEA C (0)0
(5.12.87, 4668)
Leyton Orient: Wells; Howard, Dickenson, Smalley, Day, Hull, Hales, Castle, Shinners, Godfrey, Comfort. **Scorers:** Shinners, Comfort.
Swansea C: Hughes; D. Lewis (McCarthy), Coleman,

Melville, Knill, Emmanuel, Davies, Raynor (Andrews), Allon, Pascoe, J. Lewis.

MAIDSTONE (1)1 KIDDERMINSTER (0)1
(5.12.87, 1657)
Maidstone: Beeney; Roast, Harrison, Pamphlett, Hill, Risk, Donn, Glover, Parsons (Roberts), Butler, Rogers. **Scorer:** Rogers.
Kidderminster: Arnold; Barton, Pearson, Boxall, C. Jones, Woodhall, Hazlewood (Davies), Casey, R. Jones, Tuohy, Weir. **Scorer:** Davies.

MANSFIELD T (2)4 LINCOLN C (2)3 (5.12.87, 5671)
Mansfield T: Hitchcock; Graham, Ryan, Lowery (Anderson), Foster, Coleman, Kent, Kenworthy, Stringfellow (Hodges), Cassells, Charles. **Scorers:** Lowery, Foster, Cassells, Kent.
Lincoln C: Batch; Evans, Nicholson, Clarke, Matthewson, Moore, Mossman, Cumming, Brown, Smith, Gamble. **Scorers:** Smith, Brown, Clarke.

NORTHAMPTON T (0)1 BRIGHTON & HA (0)2
(5.12.87, 6444)
Northampton T: Gleasure; Reed, Chard, Donald, Wilcox, McPherson, Singleton (Logan), McGoldrick, Gilbert, Morley, Longhurst (Culpin). **Scorer:** Morley.
Brighton & HA: Keeley; Brown, Dublin, Jasper, Rougvie, Gatting, Nelson, Trusson, Bremner, Wilkins, Wood. **Scorers:** Bremner, Nelson.

PETERBOROUGH U (1)1 SUTTON (2)3
(5.12.87, 3800)
Peterborough U: Neenan; Paris, Collins (Nuttell), Nightingale, Gunn, Price, Kelly (Carr), Halsall, Lawrence, Phillips, Luke. **Scorer:** Lawrence.
Sutton: Roffey; Jones, M. Golley, Hemsley, Rains, Rogers, Cornwell (Dennis), Joyce, Stephens, Awaritefe, McKinnon. **Scorers:** Lawrence (og), Cornwell, Dennis.

PORT VALE (0)2 NOTTS CO (0)0 (5.12.87, 5039)
Port Vale: Grew; Steggles, Hughes, Walker, Hazell, Sproson, Maguire, Beckford, Riley, O'Kelly, Hamson. **Scorers:** Beckford, Sproson.
Notts Co: Leonard; Smalley, Withe, Fairclough, Yates, Hart, Mills, McParland (Barnes), Lund, Pike, Thorpe.

RUNCORN (0)0 STOCKPORT CO (0)1
(5.12.87, 3102)
Runcorn: McBride; Stephens (Barnett), Densmore, Miller, Carroll, Rowlands, Pugh, Rooney, Carter, McMahon, Anderson.
Stockport Co: Marples; Bullock, Bailey, Robinson, Scott, Williams, Hodkinson, Colville, Worthington, Hartford, Birch. **Scorer:** Colville.

SCUNTHORPE U (0)2 SUNDERLAND (1)1
(5.12.87, 7178)
Scunthorpe U: Green; Russell, Longden, Taylor, Lister, Money, Dixon, Harle, Johnson, Flounders, Atkins. **Scorers:** Taylor, Harle.
Sunderland: Hesford; Burley, Agboola, Bennett, MacPhail, Owers, Lemon, Doyle, Gates (Bertschin), Gabbiadini, Atkinson (Gray). **Scorer:** Gates.

VS RUGBY (0)1 BRISTOL R (0)1 (5.12.87, 3168)
VS Rugby: Marsden; Potter, Reilly, Lane, Holton, Geddes, Ingram, Butterworth, Ebrey, Conway (Shepherd), Ross. **Scorer:** Ingram.
Bristol R: Martyn; Alexander, Tanner, Hibbitt, Twentyman, Jones, Holoway, Meacham, White, Penrice, Purnell. **Scorer:** Meacham.

WELLING (0)0 BATH (0)1
(5.12.87, 2332)
Welling: Richardson; Friar (Robins), Horton, Crowe, Ransom, Burgess, White, Handford, Abbott, Booker, Lindsay. **Bath:** Bond; Stevens, Palmer, Bodin, Craig, Adams, Wiffill, Grimshaw, Singleton, Wiliams, Payne. **Scorer:** Singleton.

WIGAN ATH (1)1 WOLVERHAMPTON W (0)3
(5.12.87, 5879)
Wigan Ath: Hughes; Butler (Ainscow), Knowles, Hamilton, Beesley, Holden, Senior, Pilling, Campbell, Hilditch, Cook. **Scorer:** Hilditch.
Wolverhampton W: Kendall; Stoutt, Thompson, Streete, Robertson, Robinson, Dennison, Vaughan, Gallagher, Hutch, Downing. **Scorers:** Gallagher, Robinson, Dennison.

WREXHAM (1)1 BOLTON W (1)2
(5.12.87, 4703)
Wrexham: Salmon; Preece, Wright (Emson), Hinnigan, Williams, Fairbrother, Buxton, Bowden, Cunnington, Russell, Carter (Slater). **Scorer:** Hinnigan.
Bolton W: Felgate; Scott, Crombie, Savage, Came, Neal, Brookman, Callaghan, Thomas, Elliott, Darby. **Scorer:** Thomas 2.

YORK C (1)1 HARTLEPOOL U (0)1
(5.12.87, 3394)
York C: Smallwood; Branagan, Johnson, Wilson, Whitehead, Tuthill, Mills, Bradshaw, Brough, Banton, Staniforth. **Scorer:** Wilson.
Hartlepool U: Carr; Haigh, McKinnon, Nobbs (Hall), Smith, Stokes, Honour, Toman, Baker, Borthwick, Barratt. **Scorer:** Baker.

MACCLESFIELD (2)4 ROTHERHAM U (0)0
(6.12.87, 4000)
Macclesfield: Zelem; Roberts, Grant, Edwards, Tobin, Hanlon, Askew (Glendon), Shaw, Lake, Burr, Mountford. **Scorers:** Burr 3, Grant.
Rotherham U: O'Hanlon; Douglas, Crossley, Grealish, Johnson (Dungworth), Green, Buckley, Williams, Evans (Haycock), Airey, Campbell.

NORTHWICH (0)0 BLACKPOOL (0)2
(6.12.87, 2528)
Northwich: Ryan; Young, M. Jones, G. Jones, Parker, Gardiner, Imrie, Sayer (Bennett), Salmon, Reid, Dunn (Crompton).
Blackpool: Siddall; Davies (Butler), Morgan, Bradshaw, Jones, Walsh, Deary, Madden, Walwyn, McAteer, Taylor. **Scorers:** Madden, Walwyn.

SECOND ROUND REPLAYS

KIDDERMINSTER (1)2 MAIDSTONE (0)2 aet
(7.12.87, 3018)
Kidderminster: Arnold; Barton, Pearson, Boxall, C. Jones, Woodhall (Brazier), Hazelwood, Casey, R. Jones, Tuhoy (Davies), Weir. **Scorers:** Tuohy, Casey.
Maidstone: Beeney; Roast, Harrison (Doherty), Pamphlett, Hill (Roberts), Risk, Donn, Glover, Parsons, Butler, Rogers. **Scorers:** Doherty, Pamphlett.

HALIFAX T (1)2 GRIMSBY T (0)0
(8.12.87, 2633)
Halifax T: Roche; Brown, Barr, M. Matthews, Fleming

(Richardson), Shaw, Martin, Thornber, N. Matthews, Black, Holden. **Scorers:** M. Matthews, Thornber.
Grimsby T: Sherwood; McDermott, Agnew, Turner, Burgess, Robinson (Grocock), Toale, Saunders, North, O'Riordan, McGarvey.

HARTLEPOOL U (1)3 YORK C (1)1
(9.12.87, 4057)
Hartlepool U: Carr; Haigh, McKinnon, Honour, Smith, Stokes, Tinkler, Toman, Baker, Borthwick, Barratt. **Scorers:** Baker, Toman 2.
York C: Smallwood; Branagan (Hood), Johnson, Wilson, Whitehead, Tuthill, Mills, Bradshaw, Brough, Banton, Staniforth. **Scorer:** Banton.

SECOND ROUND, SECOND REPLAY

KIDDERMINSTER (0)0 MAIDSTONE (0)0 aet
(14.12.87, 3008)
Kidderminster: Arnold; Barton, Pearson, Boxall, C. Jones, Hazelwood, McKenzie (R. Jones), Casey, Davies, Tuohy, Weir.
Maidstone: Beeney; Roast, Glover, Pamphlett, Hill, Risk, Donn, Doherty, Parsons (Roberts), Butler, Rogers (Higginbottom).

SECOND ROUND THIRD REPLAY

MAIDSTONE (0)2 KIDDERMINSTER (0)1
(16.12.87, 2052)
Maidstone: Beeney; Roast, Hill (Roberts) (Higginbottom), Pamphlett, Risk, Glover, Donn, Doherty, Parsons, Butler, Rogers. **Scorers:** Butler 2 (1 pen).
Kidderminster: P. Jones; Barton, Pearson, Boxall, R. Jones, Brazier, McKenzie, Casey, Davies, Tuohy, Weir (O'Dowd). **Scorer:** Casey.

SECOND ROUND REPLAY

BRISTOL R (1)4 VS RUGBY (0)0
(17.12.87, 2846)
Bristol R: Martyn; Alexander, Tanner, Hibbitt (Reece), Twentyman, Jones, Holloway, Meacham (Dryden), White, Penrice, Purnell. **Scorers:** Penrice, Alexander, White, Reece.
VS Rugby: Marsden; Potter, Riley, Lane, Holton, Gethefield, Ingram, Butterworth, Ebrey, Ross, Kane (Conway).

THIRD ROUND

ARSENAL (2)2 MILLWALL (0)0
(9.1.88, 42,083)
Arsenal: Lukic; Winterburn, Sansom, Williams, O'Leary, Adams, Rocastle, Hayes, Smith, Merson (Groves), Richardson. **Scorers:** Hayes, Rocastle.
Millwall: Horne; Salman, Coleman, Stevens, Walker, McLeary, O'Callaghan, Briley, Sheringham, Cascarino, Carter.

BARNSLEY (0)3 BOLTON W (0)1
(9.1.88, 9667)
Barnsley: Baker; Joyce, Cross, Thomas, McGugan, Futcher, Foreman, Agnew, Lowndes, Beresford, Broddle. **Scorers:** Broddle 2, Beresford.
Bolton W: Felgate; Scott, Neal, Henshaw, Came, Sutton, Storer, Thompson, Stevens, Morgan, Darby. **Scorer:** Stevens.

FA CUP

BLACKBURN R (1)1 PORTSMOUTH (1)2
(9.1.88, 10,352)
Blackburn R: Gennoe; Price, Sulley (Patterson), Barker, Hill, Mail, Dawson, Reid, Archibald, Garner (Curry), Sellars. **Scorer:** Garner.
Portsmouth: Knight; Whitehead, Hardyman (Gilbert), Dillon, Blake, Ball, Horne, Darby, Quinn, Connor (Fillery), Hilaire. **Scorers:** Quinn, Dillon.

BRADFORD C (1)2 WOLVERHAMPTON W (1)1
(9.1.88, 13,344)
Bradford C: Tomlinson; Mitchell, Goddard, McCall, Oliver, Evans, Hendrie, Sinnott, Futcher, Palin, Ellis. **Scorers:** Hendrie, Ellis.
Wolverhampton W: Kendall; Stoutt, Thompson, Streete, Robertson, Robinson, Dennison, Vaughan, Bull, Mutch, Downing (Holmes). **Scorer:** Sinnott (og).

BRIGHTON & HA (0)2 BOURNEMOUTH (0)0
(9.1.88, 14,411)
Brighton & HA: Keeley; Brown, Dublin, Curbishley, Rougvie, Gatting, Nelson, Trusson, Bremner, Wilkins, Crumplin. **Scorers:** Rougvie, Nelson.
Bournemouth: Peyton; Langan, Morrell, Pulis (Heffernan), Williams, Whitlock, O'Driscoll, Shearer (Puckett), Aylott, O'Connor, Cooke.

COVENTRY C (0)2 TORQUAY U (0)0
(9.1.88, 16,815)
Coventry C: Ogrizovic; Borrows, Downs, McGrath, Kilcline, K. Smith, Bennett, Phillips, Regis, Speedie, Gynn. **Scorers:** Kilcline (pen), Regis.
Torquay U: Allen; McNichol, Kelly, Haslegrave, Cole, Impey (Pearce), Dawkins, Lloyd, Caldwell, Loram, Musker (Gardiner).

DERBY CO (1)1 CHELSEA (1)3
(9.1.88, 18,753)
Derby Co: Shilton; MacLaren, Forsyth, Williams, Wright, Blades, Callaghan, Penney, Gee (Garner), Gregory, McCord (Lewis). **Scorer:** Penney.
Chelsea: Freestone; Wood, Dorigo, Clarke, McLaughlin, Bumstead, McAllister, Hazard, Dixon, Durie (Wegerle), C. Wilson. **Scorers:** McAllister, Dixon, Wegerle.

GILLINGHAM (0)0 BIRMINGHAM C (2)3
(9.1.88, 9267)
Gillingham: Hillyard; Haylock, Pearce, Peacock, West, Greenall, Pritchard, Cooper, Lovell (Eves), Elsey, Smith.
Birmingham C: Hansbury; Ranson, Dicks, Roberts, Williams, Frain, Handysides, Childs, Whitton, Kennedy, Wigley. **Scorers:** Greenall (og), Williams, Handysides.

HALIFAX T (0)0 NOTTINGHAM F (2)4
(9.1.88, 4013)
Halifax T: Roche; Brown, Barr, M. Matthews (Richardson), Robinson, Heathcote, Martin, Thornber, N. Matthews, Black (Allison), Holden.
Nottingham F: Sutton; Chettle, Pearce, Walker, Foster, Wilson, Plummer (Fleming), Webb, Glover, Gaynor (Wilkinson), Rice. **Scorers:** Wilson, Pearce, Plummer, Wilkinson.

HARTLEPOOL U (0)1 LUTON T (0)2
(9.1.88, 6056)
Hartlepool U: Carr; Barratt, McKinnon, Nobbs, Smith, Haigh, Honour, Toman, Baker, Whellans, Gibb (Tinkler). **Scorer:** Toman.
Luton T: Sealey; Breacker, Johnson, McDonough, Foster, Donaghy, Wilson, B. Stein, Weir, M. Stein, Allinson. **Scorers:** Weir, McDonough.

HUDDERSFIELD T (0)2 MANCHESTER C (1)2
(9.1.88, 18,102)
Huddersfield T: Cox; Trevitt, Bray, Banks (Cooper), Webster, Mitchell, France, May, Shearer, Ward, Cork. **Scorer:** Shearer 2.
Manchester C: Nixon; Gidman, Hinchcliffe, Clements, Brightwell, Redmond, White (Simpson), Adcock, Varadi (Moulden), McNab, Scott. **Scorers:** Brightwell, Gidman.

LEEDS U (0)1 ASTON VILLA (1)2
(9.1.88, 29,002)
Leeds U: Day; Aspin, Adams, Williams, Ashurst, Haddock, Batty, Sheridan, Taylor, Davison, Snodin (Melrose). **Scorer:** Davison.
Aston Villa: Spink; Gage, Gallacher, A. Gray, Evans, Keown, Birch, Lillis, Thompson, Aspinall, McInally. **Scorers:** McInally, A. Gray.

MANSFIELD T (1)4 BATH (0)0
(9.1.88, 5080)
Mansfield T: Hitchcock; Graham, Garner, Lowery, Foster, Coleman, McKernon, Kent, Chambers, Charles, Ryan (Danskin). **Scorers:** Ryan, Withey (og), Charles 2.
Bath: Bond; Palmer, Bodin, Pratt, Craig, Grimshaw, Wiffil, Williams, Withey (Lilygreen), Singleton, Payne.

NEWCASTLE U (1)1 CRYSTAL PALACE (0)0
(9.1.88, 20,203)
Newcastle U: Kelly; Anderson, Wharton, Cornwell, P. Jackson, Roeder, McDonald, Gascoigne, Goddard, O'Neill (Craig), D. Jackson. **Scorer:** Gascoigne.
Crystal Palace: Wood; Stebbing, Burke, Pardew, Nebbeling, Cannon, O'Doherty (Bright), Thomas, Barber (Finnigan), Wright, Redfearn.

OLDHAM ATH (1)2 TOTTENHAM H (3)4
(9.1.88, 17,432)
Oldham Ath: Gorton; Irwin, Barlow, Flynn, Linighan, Cecere, Palmer, Donachie, Bunn, Wright, Ritchie. **Scorers:** Wright, Cecere.
Tottenham H: Parks; Hughton, Thomas, Hodge (Statham), Fairclough, Mabbutt, C. Allen, Fenwick, Waddle, Ardiles, Moran (Howells). **Scorers:** C. Allen 2, Thomas, Waddle.

OXFORD U (1)2 LEICESTER C (0)0
(9.1.88, 7557)
Oxford U: Hardwick; Bardsley, Dreyer, Shelton, Briggs, Caton, Hebberd, Foyle, Saunders, Phillips (Hill), Rhoades-Brown. **Scorers:** Foyle, Saunders.
Leicester C: Andrews; Morgan (Jobling), Venus, Osman, Brien (Cusack), Mauchlen, McAllister, Wilkinson, Newell, Ramsey, Reid.

READING (0)0 SOUTHAMPTON (1)1
(9.1.88, 11,319)
Reading; Francis; Bailie, Gilkes, Beavon, Hicks, Franklin, Jones (Williams), Madden, Tait, Moran, Taylor (Gordon).
Southampton: Burridge; Forrest, Statham, Case, Moore, Bond, Townsend, Le Tissier, Clarke, Baker, D. Wallace. **Scorer:** Le Tissier.

SCUNTHORPE U (0)0 BLACKPOOL (0)0
(9.1.88, 6217)
Scunthorpe U: P. Johnson; Russell, Longden, Taylor, Lister, Brown, Dixon, Harle, Daws, Flounders, Hill.
Blackpool: Siddall; Davies, Morgan, Lester, Walsh, Jones, Cunningham, Coughlin, Madden, Deary, Taylor.

SHEFFIELD U (0)1 MAIDSTONE (0)0
(9.1.88, 8907)
Sheffield U: Leaning; Barnsley, Pike, Kuhl (Smith), Stancliffe, Todd, Duffield, Philliskirk, Cadette, Dempsey, Beagrie. **Scorer:** Dempsey.
Maidstone: Cawston; Jacques, Harrison, Pamphlett, Glover, Risk, Donn, Hill, Higginbottom, Butler, Rogers (Stuart).

SHEFFIELD W (0)1 EVERTON (0)1
(9.1.88, 33,304)
Sheffield W: Hodge; Sterland, Worthington, Madden, Pearson, Proctor, Marwood, Megson, Chapman, West, May. **Scorer:** West.
Everton: Southall; Stevens, Van Den Hauwe, Ratcliffe (Harper), Watson, Reid, Steven, Clarke, Sharp, Snodin, Wilson (Heath). **Scorer:** Reid.

SHREWSBURY T (1)2 BRISTOL R (0)1
(9.1.88, 6554)
Shrewsbury T. Perks; Green, B. Williams, Priest (Tester), Moyes, Linighan, Narbett (W. Williams), McNally, Brown, Robinson, Bell. **Scorers:** Moyes, B. Williams.
Bristol R: Martyn; Alexander, Tanner, Carr (Eaton), Twentyman, Jones, Holloway, Reece, White, Penrice, Purnell. **Scorer:** Penrice.

STOCKPORT CO (1)1 LEYTON ORIENT (0)2
(9.1.88, 4243)
Stockport Co: Marples; Bullock, Bailey, Robinson, Thorpe, Williams, Hendrie, Colville, Worthington, Hartford (Entwistle), Birch. **Scorer:** Colville.
Leyton Orient: Wells; Howard, Dickenson, Smalley (Ketteridge), Day, Harvey (Godfrey), Hales, Castle, Shinners, Juryeff, Comfort. **Scorers:** Juryeff, Shinners.

STOKE C (0)0 LIVERPOOL (0)0
(9.1.88, 31,979)
Stoke C: Barrett; Dixon, Carr, Talbot, Bould, Berry, Ford, Henry, Morgan, Stainrod (Shaw), Parkin.
Liverpool: Hooper; Gillespie, Lawrenson, Nicol, Whelan, Hansen, Beardsley, Aldridge, Houghton, Barnes, McMahon.

SUTTON (0)1 MIDDLESBROUGH (0)1
(9.1.88, 6000)
Sutton: Roffey; Jones, Rains, Stephens, M. Golley, Hemsley, Rogers, Cornwell, Dennis, McKinnon (Awaritefe), Joyce (N. Golley). **Scorer:** M. Golley.
Middlesbrough: Pears; Laws, Cooper, Mowbray, Parkinson, Pallister, Slaven, Gill, Hamilton, Kerr, Ripley. **Scorer:** Pallister.

SWINDON T (0)0 NORWICH C (0)0
(9.1.88, 12,807)
Swindon T: Hammond; Hockaday, King, Kamara, Parkin, Calderwood, Bamber, Gittens, Quinn, Foley, White (Wade).
Norwich C: Gunn; Culverhouse, Bowen, Putney, Phelan, Butterworth, Fox, Drinkell, Rosario, Goss, Gordon.

WATFORD (0)1 HULL C (0)1
(9.1.88, 12,761)
Watford: Rees; Chivers, Rostron (Allen), Jackett, Morris, McClelland, Hetherston, Agana, Senior, Porter, Hodges. **Scorer:** Allen.
Hull C: Norman; Palmer, Heard, Jobson, Skipper, Parker, Roberts, Payton, Dyer, Askew, Williams. **Scorer:** Roberts.

WEST HAM U (0)2 CHARLTON ATH (0)0
(9.1.88, 22,043)
West Ham U: McAlister; Potts, Stewart, Bonds, Gale, Strodder, Ward, Brady (Ince), Hilton, Cottee, Robson. **Scorers:** Brady, Cottee.

Charlton Ath: Bolder; Humphrey, Reid, MacKenzie, Shirtliff, Thompson, Bennett, Campbell, Jones (Crooks), Lee (Williams), Mortimer.

WIMBLEDON (1)4 WBA (0)1
(9.1.88, 7252)
Wimbledon: Beasant; Goodyear, Phelan, Jones, Gayle, Thorn, Fairweather, Cork, Fashanu, Sanchez, Wise (Turner). **Scorers:** Fashanu, Wise, Turner, Fairweather.
WBA: Powell; Dickinson, Cowdrill, Palmer, North, Kelly, Hopkins, Goodman, Reilly, Burrows, Williamson. **Scorer:** Thorn (og).

YEOVIL (0)0 QPR (1)3
(9.1.88, 9717)
Yeovil: Iles; Sherwood, Ferns, Ricketts, Rutter, Cordice, Donnellan (Chandler), Wallace, McGinlay, Pearson (Noble), Randall.
QPR: Johns; Dawes, Dennis, Parker, McDonald, Maguire, Allen, Falco, Bannister (Coney), Fereday (Kerslake), Brock. **Scorers:** Falco 2, Brock.

IPSWICH T (1)1 MANCHESTER U (1)2
(10.1.88, 23,012)
Ipswich T: Hallworth; Yallop, Harbey, Atkins, Humes, Cranson, Lowe, Brennan, D'Avray, Dozzell (Stockwell), Zondervan (Gleghorn). **Scorer:** Humes.
Manchester U: Turner; Anderson, Duxbury, Bruce, Moran, Moses (Olsen), Robson, Strachan, McClair, Whiteside, Gibson (Davenport). **Scorers:** D'Avray (og), Anderson.

PORT VALE (0)1 MACCLESFIELD (0)0
(10.1.88, 10,808)
Port Vale: Grew; Steggles, Hughes, Walker, Banks, Sproson, Ford, Finney, Riley, Beckford (Earle), Hamson (Maguire). **Scorer:** Finney.
Macclesfield: Zelem; Roberts, Grant, Edwards, Tobin, Hanlon, J. Askey, Shaw, Lake, Burr, Mountford (R. Askey).

PLYMOUTH ARG (2)2 COLCHESTER U (0)0
(11.1.88, 10,351)
Plymouth Arg: Cherry; Brimacombe, L. Cooper, Burrows, Marker, Smith, Hodges, Matthews, Tynan, S. Cooper, Anderson. **Scorers:** S. Cooper, Matthews.
Colchester U: Walton; Hinshelwood, Hedman, Chatterton (Walsh), Hill, Keane, White, Wilkins, Tempest, English, Grenfell.

THIRD ROUND REPLAYS

BLACKPOOL (0)1 SCUNTHORPE U (0)0
(12.1.88, 6127)
Blackpool: Siddall; Davies, Morgan, Lester, Walsh, Jones, Cunningham, Coughlin, Madden, Deary, McAteer (Methven). **Scorer:** Madden.
Scunthorpe U: P. Johnson; Russell (Money), Longden, Taylor, Lister, Brown, Dixon (S. Johnson), Harle, Daws, Flounders, Hill.

HULL C (2)2 WATFORD (0)2
(12.1.88, 13,681)
Hull C: Norman; Palmer, Heard, Jobson, Skipper, Parker, Roberts, Payton, Dyer, Askew, Williams. **Scorers:** Williams, Dyer.
Watford: Coton; Chivers, Rostron, Jackett, Morris, McClelland, Sterling, Agana (Allen), Blissett, Porter, Hodges. **Scorers:** Jackett (pen), Allen.
(aet 90 mins: 2–2)

416

FA CUP

LIVERPOOL (1)1 STOKE C (0)0
(12.1.88, 39,147)
Liverpool: Hooper; Gillespie, Lawrenson, Nicol, Whelan, Hansen, Beardsley, Aldridge, Houghton (Johnston), Barnes, McMahon. **Scorer:** Beardsley.
Stoke C: Barrett; Dixon, Carr, Talbot, Bould, Berry, Ford, Henry, Morgan, Stainrod (Shaw), Parkin.

MANCHESTER C (0)0 HUDDERSFIELD T (0)0 aet
(12.1.88, 24,565)
Manchester C: Nixon; Gidman, Hinchcliffe, Clements, Brightwell (Simpson), Redmond, White, Stewart, Adcock (Varadi), McNab, Scott.
Huddersfield T: Cox; Trevitt, Bray (Tucker), Brown, Webster, Mitchell, France, May, Shearer, Ward, Cork (Cooper).

MIDDLESBROUGH (0)1 SUTTON (0)0 aet
(12.1.88, 17,932)
Middlesbrough: Poole; Glover, Cooper, Mowbray, Parkinson, Pallister, Slaven, Kernaghan, Hamilton (Laws), Kerr (Gill), Burke. **Scorer:** Kerr.
Sutton: Roffey; Jones, Rains, M. Golley, Hemsley, Rogers, Stephens, Cornwell (Joyce), Dennis, Awaritefe (Dawson), N. Golley.

EVERTON (0)1 SHEFFIELD W (1)1 aet
(13.1.88, 32,935)
Everton: Southall; Stevens, Pointon, Van Den Hauwe, Watson, Reid, Steven, Heath, Sharp, Snodin, Wilson (Clarke). **Scorer:** Sharp.
Sheffield W: Hodge; Sterland, Worthington, Madden, Pearson, Proctor, Marwood (Bradshaw), Megson, Chapman (Chamberlain), West, May. **Scorer:** Chapman.

NORWICH C (0)0 SWINDON T (0)2
(13.1.88, 12,501)
Norwich C: Gunn; Culverhouse, Bowen, Putney, Phelan, Butterworth, Fox, Drinkell, Rosario (Fleck), Goss, Gordon.
Swindon T: Hammond; Hockaday, King, Kamara, Parkin, Calderwood, Bamber, Gittens, Quinn, Barnes, O'Regan. **Scorer:** Bamber 2.

THIRD ROUND, SECOND REPLAYS

WATFORD (1)1 HULL C (0)0
(18.1.88, 15,261)
Watford: Coton; Chivers, Rostron, Sherwood, Morris, McClelland, Sterling, Allen, Blissett, Porter, Hodges. **Scorer:** Allen.
Hull C: Norman; Brown, Heard, Jobson, Skipper, Parker, Roberts, Payton (Saville), Dyer, Askew (Daniel), Williams.

EVERTON (0)1 SHEFFIELD W (0)1 aet
(25.1.88, 37,414)
Everton: Southall; Stevens, Pointon, Van Den Hauwe, Watson, Reid, Steven, Heath (Clarke), Sharp, Snodin, Wilson (Harper). **Scorer:** Steven.
Sheffield W: Hodge; Sterland, Worthington, Madden, Pearson, Proctor, Marwood, Megson (Owen), Chapman, West, May (Chamberlain): **Scorer:** Chapman.

HUDDERSFIELD T (0)0 MANCHESTER C (0)3
(25.1.88, 21,510)
Huddersfield T: Cox; Brown, Bray, Banks, Webster, Mitchell, France, May (Bent), Shearer, Trevitt, Cork.
Manchester C: Nixon; Gidman, Hinchcliffe, Clements, Lake (Brightwell), Redmond, White, Stewart, Varadi, McNab, Simpson. **Scorers:** Hinchcliffe, White, Varadi.

THIRD ROUND, THIRD REPLAY

SHEFFIELD W (0)0 EVERTON (5)5
(27.1.88, 38,953)
Sheffield W: Hodge; Sterland, Worthington, May, Pearson, Proctor, Marwood, Megson, Chapman (Owen), West, Chamberlain.
Everton: Southall; Stevens, Pointon, Van Den Hauwe, Watson, Reid, Steven, Heath, Sharp (Clarke), Snodin (Bracewell), Harper. **Scorers:** Sharp 3, Heath, Snodin.

FOURTH ROUND

BARNSLEY (0)0 BIRMINGHAM C (1)2
(30.1.88, 13,219)
Barnsley: Baker; Joyce, Cross, Thomas, McGugan, Futcher, Foreman (Macdonald), Agnew, Lowndes, Dobbin (Hedworth), Broddle.
Birmingham C: Hansbury; Ranson, Dicks, Williams, Overson, Trewick, Bremner, Childs, Rees, Handysides, Wigley. **Scorers:** Rees, Wigley.

BLACKPOOL (0)1 MANCHESTER C (0)1
(30.1.88, 10,835)
Blackpool: Siddall; Davies, Morgan, Lester, Walsh, Jones, Rooney (Sendall), Coughlin, Walwyn, Deary, Taylor. **Scorer:** Sendall.
Manchester C: Nixon; Gidman, Hinchcliffe, Clements, Lake, Redmond, White, Stewart, Moulden (Brightwell), McNab, Simpson. **Scorer:** Lake.

BRADFORD C (3)4 OXFORD U (1)2
(30.1.88, 13,653)
Bradford C: Litchfield; Abbott, Goddard, McCall, Oliver, Evans, Hendrie, Sinnott, Ormondroyd, Kennedy, Ellis. **Scorers:** Kennedy (pen), McCall, Evans, Hendrie.
Oxford U: Hardwick; Bardsley, Hill (Whitehurst), Shelton, Briggs, Caton, Hebberd, Foyle, Saunders, Phillips, Rhoades-Brown. **Scorers:** Rhoades-Brown, Saunders (pen).

BRIGHTON & HA (1)1 ARSENAL (1)2
(30.1.88, 26,467)
Brighton & HA: Keeley; Brown, Dublin, Curbishley, Rougvie, Gatting, Nelson, Trusson, Bremner, Wilkins, Crumplin. **Scorer:** Nelson.
Arsenal: Lukic; Winterburn, Sansom, Williams, O'Leary, Adams, Rocastle, Rix (Hayes), Groves, Quinn, Richardson. **Scorers:** Richardson, Groves.

COVENTRY C (0)0 WATFORD (0)1
(30.1.88, 22,479)
Coventry C: Ogrizovic; Borrows, Downs, McGrath, Kilcline, Peake, Bennett, Phillips, Regis, Sedgley (Speedie), Gynn.
Watford: Coton; Chivers (Gibbs), Rostron, Jackett, Morris, McClelland, Sterling, Allen, Blissett (Senior), Porter, Hodges. **Scorer:** Senior.

EVERTON (1)1 MIDDLESBROUGH (0)1
(30.1.88, 36,564)
Everton: Southall; Stevens, Pointon, Van Den Hauwe, Watson, Reid, Steven, Heath, Sharp, Snodin, Harper (Clarke). **Scorer:** Sharp.
Middlesbrough: Pears; Glover, Cooper, Mowbray, Parkinson, Pallister, Slaven, Ripley, Hamilton, Kerr, Laws. **Scorer:** Kerr.

LEYTON ORIENT (0)1 NOTTINGHAM F (0)2
(30.1.88, 19,212)
Leyton Orient: Wells; Howard, Dickenson, Smalley, Day, Godfrey, Hales (Sitton), Castle, Shinners (Hull), Juryeff, Comfort. **Scorer:** Juryeff.
Nottingham F: Sutton; Chettle, Pearce, Walker, Foster, Wilson, Plummer, Webb, Glover, Wilkinson, Gaynor. **Scorers:** Glover, Plummer.

LUTON T (0)2 SOUTHAMPTON (0)1
(30.1.88, 10,009)
Luton T: Sealey; Breacker, Johnson (Grimes), McDonough, Foster, Donaghy, Wilson, B. Stein, Harford, M. Stein, Allinson. **Scorers:** Statham (og), B. Stein.
Southampton: Burridge; Forrest, Statham, Baker, Moore, Blake, Hobson, Cockerill, Clarke, Townsend, D. Wallace. **Scorer:** Clarke.

MANCHESTER U (1)2 CHELSEA (0)0
(30.1.88, 50,716)
Manchester U: Turner; Anderson, Duxbury, Bruce, Blackmore (O'Brien), Hogg, Whiteside, McClair, Whiteside, Olsen. **Scorers:** Whiteside, McClair.
Chelsea: Freestone; Clarke, Dorigo, Pates, McLaughlin, Wood, McAllister (Nevin), Bumstead (Hazard), Dixon, K. Wilson, C. Wilson.

MANSFIELD T (0)1 WIMBLEDON (1)2
(30.1.88, 10,642)
Mansfield T: Hitchcock; Graham, Garner, Lowery, Foster, Coleman, McKernon (Stringfellow), Ryan, Kent, Cassells, Charles. **Scorer:** Kent.
Wimbledon: Beasant; Goodyear, Phelan, Jones, Gayle, Thorn, Wise, Cork, Fashanu, Sanchez, Scales. **Scorers:** Cork, Phelan.

NEWCASTLE U (2)5 SWINDON T (0)0
(30.1.88, 27,548)
Newcastle U: Kelly; Anderson, Wharton, D. Jackson P. Jackson, Roeder, McDonald, Gascoigne, Goddard, Mirandinha, O'Neill. **Scorers:** D. Jackson, Gascoigne 2 (1 pen), O'Neill, Goddard.
Swindon T: Hammond; Hockaday, King, Kamara, Parkin, Calderwood, Bamber, Gittens, Quinn, O'Regan, Foley.

PLYMOUTH ARG (1)1 SHREWSBURY T (0)0
(30.1.88, 12,749)
Plymouth Arg: Cherry; Law, L. Cooper, Burrows, Marker, Smith, Hodges, Matthews, Tynan, Evans, Summerfield (Clayton). **Scorer:** Evans.
Shrewsbury T: Perks; Green, B. Williams, Priest (Kasule), Moyes, Linighan, W. Williams, McNally, Brown (Tester), Geddis, Bell.

PORT VALE (2)2 TOTTENHAM H (0)1
(30.1.88, 20,045)
Port Vale: Grew; Steggles, Hughes, Walker, Hazell, Sproson, Ford, Earle, Riley, Beckford (Finney), Cole. **Scorers:** Walker, Sproson.
Tottenham H: Parks; Hughton (Howells), Thomas, Ruddock, Fairclough, Mabbutt, C. Allen, P. Allen, Waddle, Fenwick, Moran. **Scorer:** Ruddock.

QPR (0)3 WEST HAM U (0)1
(30.1.88, 23,651)
QPR: Johns; Dawes, Pizanti, Parker, McDonald, Maguire, Allen, Falco, Bannister, Fereday (Byrne), Brock. **Scorers:** Pizanti, Bannister, Allen.
West Ham U: McAlister; Stewart, McQueen (Hilton), Bonds, Strodder, Gale, Ward, Brady, Dickens, Cottee, Robson. **Scorer:** Cottee.

ASTON VILLA (0)0 LIVERPOOL (0)2
(31.1.88, 46,324)
Aston Villa: Spink; Gage, Gallacher, A. Gray, Evans, Keown, Birch, Lillis, Thompson, Daley (Aspinall), McInally.
Liverpool: Grobbelaar; Venison, Ablett, Nicol, Spackman, Hansen, Beardsley, Aldridge, Houghton, Barnes, McMahon. **Scorers:** Barnes, Beardsley.

PORTSMOUTH (2)2 SHEFFIELD U (1)1
(1.2.88, 13,388)
Portsmouth: Knight; Whitehead, Swain, Dillon, Blake, Ball, Horne, Fillery, Baird (Connor), Quinn, Hilaire. **Scorers:** Dillon, Quinn.
Sheffield U: Leaning; Barnsley (Downes), Pike, Todd, Stancliffe, Smith, Duffield (Morris), Philliskirk, Cadette, Dempsey, Beagrie. **Scorer:** Philliskirk.

FOURTH ROUND REPLAYS

MANCHESTER C (2)2 BLACKPOOL (1)1
(3.2.88, 26,503)
Manchester C: Nixon; Gidman, Hinchcliffe, Clements, Lake, Redmond, White, Stewart, Varadi, McNab, Simpson. **Scorers:** Stewart, Simpson.
Blackpool: Siddall; Davies, Morgan, Lester (Madden), Walsh, Jones, Butler, Coughlin, Walwyn, Deary, Taylor. **Scorer:** Deary.

MIDDLESBROUGH (0)2 EVERTON (0)2 aet
(3.2.88, 25,235)
Middlesbrough: Pears; Glover, Cooper, Mowbray, Parkinson, Pallister (Kernaghan), Slaven, Ripley, Hamilton, Kerr, Laws. **Scorers:** Mowbray, Kernaghan.
Everton: Southall; Stevens, Pointon, Van Den Hauwe, Watson, Reid, Steven, Heath, Sharp, Snodin, Harper (Clarke). **Scorers:** Watson, Steven.
90 mins 1–1

FOURTH ROUND, SECOND REPLAY

EVERTON (1)2 MIDDLESBROUGH (0)1
(10.2.88, 32,222)
Everton: Southall; Stevens, Pointon, Van Den Hauwe, Watson, Reid, Steven, Heath, Sharp, Snodin, Power (Clarke). **Scorers:** Sharp, Duxbury (og).
Middlesbrough: Pears; Glover (Burke), Cooper, Mowbray, Parkinson, Pallister, Slaven (Kernaghan), Ripley, Hamilton, Kerr, Laws. **Scorer:** Ripley.

FIFTH ROUND

ARSENAL (2)2 MANCHESTER U (0)1
(20.2.88, 54,161)
Arsenal: Lukic; Winterburn, Sansom, Thomas, O'Leary (Rix), Adams, Rocastle, Hayes, Smith, Groves, Richardson. **Scorers:** Smith, Duxbury (og).
Manchester U: Turner; Anderson, Gibson, Bruce, Duxbury, Hogg (O'Brien), Davenport, Strachan, McClair, Whiteside, Olsen (Blackmore). **Scorer:** McClair.

BIRMINGHAM C (0)0 NOTTINGHAM F (1)1
(20.2.88, 34,494)
Birmingham C: Hansbury; Ranson, Dicks, Williams, Overson, Handysides, Bremner, Childs, Whitton, Rees (Trewick), Wigley.
Nottingham F: Sutton; Fleming, Pearce, Walker, Foster, Wilson, Crosby, Webb, Clough, Wilkinson, Rice. **Scorer:** Crosby.

FA CUP

MANCHESTER C (1)3 PLYMOUTH ARG (0)1
(20.2.88, 29,206)
Manchester C: Nixon; Gidman, Hinchcliffe, Seagraves, McNab, Redmond, White, Stewart, Varadi (Moulden), Scott, Simpson. **Scorers:** Scott, Simpson, Moulden.
Plymouth Arg: Cherry; Law (Brimacombe), L. Cooper, Burrows, Marker, McElhinney, Hodges, Matthews, Tynan, Clayton (S. Cooper), Summerfield. **Scorer:** Tynan.

NEWCASTLE U (0)1 WIMBLEDON (1)3
(20.2.88, 28,796)
Newcastle U: Kelly; Anderson, Wharton, McCreery, P. Jackson, Roeder, McDonald, Gascoigne, Goddard, Mirandinha, D. Jackson (O'Neill). **Scorer:** McDonald.
Wimbledon: Beasant; Goodyear, Phelan, Jones, Gayle, Thorn, Gibson, Cunningham (Cork), Fashanu, Sanchez, Wise. **Scorers:** Gibson, Gayle, Fashanu.

PORTSMOUTH (1)3 BRADFORD C (0)0
(20.2.88, 19,324)
Portsmouth: Knight; Whitehead, Sandford, Dillon, Blake, Ball, Horne, Fillery, Connor, Quinn, Hilaire. **Scorers:** Blake, Quinn, Connor.
Bradford C: Tomlinson; Mitchell, Goddard (Ellis), McCall, Oliver, Evans, Hendrie, Abbott (Leonard), Ormondroyd, Kennedy, Sinnott.

PORT VALE (0)0 WATFORD (0)0
(20.2.88, 22,483)
Port Vale: Grew; Steggles, Hughes, Walker, Hazell, Sproson, Ford, Earle, Riley, Beckford, Cole.
Watford: Coton; Gibbs, Rostron, Jackett, Morris, McClelland, Sterling, Allen, Senior, Porter (Blissett), Sherwood.

QPR (0)1 LUTON T (0)1
(20.2.88, 15,856)
QPR: Johns; Dawes, Neill, Parker, McDonald, Maguire, Allen, Falco, Bannister (Byrne), Fereday, Brock. **Scorer:** Neill.
Luton T: Sealey; Breacker, Grimes, McDonough, Foster, Donaghy, Wilson, B. Stein, Harford, M. Stein, Allinson. **Scorer:** Harford.

EVERTON (0)0 LIVERPOOL (0)1
(21.2.88, 48,270)
Everton: Southall; Stevens, Pointon, Van Den Hauwe, Watson, Reid (Bracewell), Steven, Heath, Sharp, Snodin, Power (Harper).
Liverpool: Grobbelaar; Ablett, Venison, Nicol, Spackman, Hansen, Beardsley, Aldridge, Houghton, Barnes, McMahon. **Scorer:** Houghton.

FIFTH ROUND REPLAYS

WATFORD (1)2 PORT VALE (0)0
(23.2.88, 18,359)
Watford: Coton; Gibbs, Rostron, Jackett, Morris, McClelland, Sterling, Allen (Blissett), Senior, Porter, Sherwood.
Scorers: Senior, Porter.
Port Vale: Grew; Steggles, Hughes, Walker, Hazell, Sproson, Ford, Earle, Riley (Maguire), Beckford, Cole.

LUTON T (0)1 QPR (0)0
(24.2.88, 10,854)
Luton T: Sealey; Breacker, Grimes, McDonough, Foster, Donaghy, Wilson, B. Stein, Harford, M. Stein, Allinson.
Scorer: Neill (og)
QPR: Seaman; Dawes, Neill (Kerslake), Parker, McDonald, Maguire, Allen, Falco (Coney), Byrne, Fereday, Brock.

SIXTH ROUND

ARSENAL (0)1 NOTTINGHAM F (1)2
(12.3.88, 50,157)
Arsenal: Lukic; Winterburn, Sansom, Thomas, O'Leary (Davis), Adams, Rocastle, Hayes (Quinn), Smith, Groves, Richardson. **Scorer:** Rocastle.
Nottingham F: Sutton; Chettle, Pearce, Walker, Foster, Wilson, Crosby, Webb, Clough, Wilkinson, Rice. **Scorers:** Wilkinson, Rice.

LUTON T (2)3 PORTSMOUTH (1)1
(12.3.88, 12,857)
Luton T: Sealey; Breacker, Grimes, McDonough, Foster, Donaghy, Wilson, Johnson, Harford, M. Stein, Allinson. **Scorers:** Wilson, M. Stein, Harford.
Portsmouth: Knight; Gilbert, Hardyman (Mariner), Dillon, Blake, Ball, Horne, Fillery, Quinn, Connor, Hilaire. **Scorer:** Quinn.

WIMBLEDON(0)2 WATFORD (1)1
(12.3.88, 12,228)
Wimbledon: Beasant; Goodyear, Phelan, Jones, Gayle, Thorn, Gibson, Cork (Young), Fashanu, Sanchez, Wise. **Scorers:** Young, Fashanu.
Watford: Coton; Gibbs, Rostron, Jackett, Morris, McClelland, Sterling (Roberts), Allen, Blissett, Porter, Hodges. **Scorer:** Allen

MANCHESTER C (0)0 LIVERPOOL (1)4
(13.3.88, 44,047)
Manchester C: Stowell; Gidman, Hinchcliffe, Brightwell, Lake, Redmond, White, Stewart, Varadi, McNab, Simpson.
Liverpool: Grobbelaar; Gillespie, Ablett, Nicol, Spackman, Hansen, Beardsley, Johnston, Houghton, Barnes, McMahon. **Scorers:** Houghton, Beardsley (pen), Johnston, Barnes.

SEMI-FINALS

LIVERPOOL (1)2 NOTTINGHAM F (0)1
(Hillsborough, 9.4.88, 51,627)
Liverpool: Grobbelaar; Gillespie, Ablett,, Nicol, Spackman, Hansen, Beardsley, Aldridge, Houghton, Barnes, McMahon. **Scorer:** Aldridge 2 (1 pen).
Nottingham F: Sutton; Chettle, Pearce, Walker, Foster, Wilson, Crosby, Webb, Clough, Wilkinson, Rice. **Scorer:** Clough.

LUTON T (0)1 WIMBLEDON (0)2
(White Hart Lane, 9.4.88, 25,963)
Luton T: Dibble; Breacker, Grimes (Black), McDonough, Foster, Donaghy, Wilson, B. Stein, Harford, M. Stein, Johnson. **Scorer:** Harford.
Wimbledon: Beasant; Scales, Phelan, Jones, Young, Thorn, Gibson (Cunningham), Cork, Fashanu, Sanchez, Wise. **Scorers:** Fashanu (pen), Wise.

FINAL

WIMBLEDON (1)1 LIVERPOOL (0)0
(Wembley, 14.5.88, 98,203)
Wimbledon: Beasant; Goodyear, Phelan, Jones, Young, Thorn, Gibson (Scales), Cork (Cunningham), Fashanu, Sanchez, Wise. **Scorer:** Sanchez.
Liverpool: Grobbelaar; Gillespie, Ablett, Nicol, Spackman (Molby), Hansen, Beardsley, Aldridge (Johnston), Houghton, Barnes, McMahon.
Referee: B. Hill (Kettering).

Wimbledon's Lawrie Sanchez (number 10) has just scored the winning goal in the FA Cup final, much to the delight of team-mates Dennis Wise (arm aloft), Clive Goodgear and Alan Cork. *Photo: Bob Thomas Sports Photography.*

A happy Wimbledon team, led by goalkeeper and captain Dave Beasant, celebrate their shock victory over Liverpool in the 1988 FA Cup final. *Photo: Bob Thomas Sports Photography.*

FA CUP FINALS 1872–1988

Venues: 1872 & 1874–92 Kennington Oval; 1873 Lillie Bridge; 1893 Fallowfield, Manchester; 1894 Everton; 1895–1914 Crystal Palace; 1915 Old Trafford; 1920–22 Stamford Bridge; 1923 to date Wembley. All replays at Wembley, except: 1875, 1876 Kennington Oval, 1886 Racecourse Ground, Derby; 1901 Bolton; 1902 Crystal Palace, 1910 Everton, 1911 Old Trafford, 1912 Bramall Lane, 1970 Old Trafford.

1872	Wanderers 1, Royal Engineers 0	1928	Blackburn R 3, Huddersfield T 1
1873	Wanderers 2, Oxford University 0	1929	Bolton W 2, Portsmouth 0
1874	Oxford University 2, Royal Engineers 0	1930	Arsenal 2, Huddersfield T 0
1875	Royal Engineers 1, Old Etonians 1 (aet)	1931	WBA 2, Birmingham 1
Replay: Royal Engineers 2, Old Etonians 0		1932	Newcastle U 2, Arsenal 1
1876	Wanderers 1, Old Etonians 1 (aet)	1933	Everton 3, Manchester C 0
Replay: Wanderers 3, Old Etonians 0		1934	Manchester C 2, Portsmouth 1
1877	Wanderers 2, Oxford University 1 (aet)	1935	Sheffield W 4, WBA 2
1878	*Wanderers 3, Royal Engineers 1	1936	Arsenal 1, Sheffield U 0
1879	Old Etonians 1, Clapham R 0	1937	Sunderland 3, Preston NE 1
1880	Clapham R 1, Oxford University 0	1938	Preston NE 1, Huddersfield T 0 (aet)
1881	Old Carthusians 3, Old Etonians 0	1939	Portsmouth 4, Wolverhampton W 1
1882	Old Etonians 1, Blackburn R 0	1946	Derby Co 4, Charlton Ath 1 (aet)
1883	Blackburn Olympic 2, Old Etonians 1 (aet)	1947	Charlton Ath 1, Burnley 0 (aet)
1884	Blackburn R 2, Queen's Park (Glasgow) 1	1948	Manchester U 4, Blackpool 2
1885	Blackburn R 2, Queen's Park (Glasgow) 0	1949	Wolverhampton W 3, Leicester C 1
1886	Blackburn R 0, WBA 0	1950	Arsenal 2, Liverpool 0
Replay: †Blackburn R 2, WBA 0		1951	Newcastle U 2, Blackpool 0
1887	Aston Villa 2, WBA 0	1952	Newcastle U 1, Arsenal 0
1888	WBA 2, Preston NE 1	1953	Blackpool 4, Bolton W 3
1889	Preston NE 3, Wolverhampton W 0	1954	WBA 3, Preston NE 2
1890	Blackburn R 6, Sheffield W 1	1955	Newcastle U 3, Manchester C 1
1891	Blackburn R 3, Notts Co 1	1956	Manchester C 3, Birmingham C 1
1892	WBA 3, Aston Villa 0	1957	Aston Villa 2, Manchester U 1
1893	Wolverhampton W 1, Everton 0	1958	Bolton W 2, Manchester U 0
1894	Notts Co 4, Bolton W 1	1959	Nottingham F 2, Luton T 1
1895	Aston Villa 1, WBA 0	1960	Wolverhampton W 3, Blackburn R 0
1896	Sheffield W 2, Wolverhampton W 1	1961	Tottenham H 2, Leicester C 0
1897	Aston Villa 3, Everton 2	1962	Tottenham H 3, Burnley 1
1898	Nottingham F 3, Derby Co 1	1963	Manchester U 3, Leicester C 1
1899	Sheffield U 4, Derby Co 1	1964	West Ham U 3, Preston NE 2
1900	Bury 4, Southampton 0	1965	Liverpool 2, Leeds U 1 (aet)
1901	Tottenham H 2, Sheffield U 2	1966	Everton 3, Sheffield W 2
Replay: Tottenham H 3, Sheffield U 1		1967	Tottenham H 2, Chelsea 1
1902	Sheffield U 1, Southampton 1	1968	WBA 1, Everton 0 (aet)
Replay: Sheffield U 2, Southampton 1		1969	Manchester C 1, Leicester C 0
1903	Bury 6, Derby Co 0	1970	Chelsea 2, Leeds U 2 (aet)
1904	Manchester C 1, Bolton W 0	Replay: Chelsea 2, Leeds U 1 (aet)	
1905	Aston Villa 2, Newcastle U 0	1971	Arsenal 2, Liverpool 1 (aet)
1906	Everton 1, Newcastle U 0	1972	Leeds U 1, Arsenal 0
1907	Sheffield W 2, Everton 1	1973	Sunderland 1, Leeds U 0
1908	Wolverhampton W 3, Newcastle U 1	1974	Liverpool 3, Newcastle U 0
1909	Manchester U 1, Bristol C 0	1975	West Ham U 2, Fulham 0
1910	Newcastle U 1, Barnsley 1	1976	Southampton 1, Manchester U 0
Replay: Newcastle U 2, Barnsley 0		1977	Manchester U 2, Liverpool 1
1911	Bradford C 0, Newcastle U 0	1978	Ipswich T 1, Arsenal 0
Replay: Bradford C 1, Newcastle U 0		1979	Arsenal 3, Manchester U 2
1912	Barnsley 0, WBA 0	1980	West Ham U 1, Arsenal 0
Replay: Barnsley 1, WBA 0 (aet)		1981	Tottenham H 1, Manchester C 1 (aet)
1913	Aston Villa 1, Sunderland 0	Replay: Tottenham H 3, Manchester C 2	
1914	Burnley 1, Liverpool 0	1982	Tottenham H 1, QPR 1 (aet)
1915	Sheffield U 3, Chelsea 0	Replay: Tottenham H 1, QPR 0	
1920	Aston Villa 1, Huddersfield T 0 (aet)	1983	Manchester U 2, Brighton & HA 2 (aet)
1921	Tottenham H 1, Wolverhampton W 0	Replay: Manchester U 4, Brighton & HA 0	
1922	Huddersfield T 1, Preston NE 0	1984	Everton 2, Watford 0
1923	Bolton W 2, West Ham U 0	1985	Manchester U 1, Everton 0 (aet)
1924	Newcastle U 2, Aston Villa 0	1986	Liverpool 3, Everton 1
1925	Sheffield U 1, Cardiff C 0	1987	Coventry C 3, Tottenham H 2 (aet)
1926	Bolton W 1, Manchester C 0	1988	Wimbledon 1, Liverpool 0
1927	Cardiff C 1, Arsenal 0		

*Won outright but restored to the FA.   †Special trophy awarded for third consecutive win.

WINS

7 – Aston Villa, Tottenham H. 6 – Blackburn R, Manchester U, Newcastle U. 5 – Arsenal, The Wanderers, WBA. 4 – Bolton W, Everton, Manchester C, Sheffield U, Wolverhampton W. 3 – Liverpool, Sheffield W, West Ham U. 2 – Bury, Nottingham F, Old Etonians, Preston NE, Sunderland. 1 – Barnsley, Blackburn Olympic, Blackpool, Bradford C, Burnley, Cardiff C, Charlton Ath, Chelsea, Clapham R, Coventry C, Derby Co, Huddersfield T, Ipswich T, Leeds U, Notts Co, Old Carthusians, Oxford University, Portsmouth, Royal Engineers, Southampton, Wimbledon.

APPEARANCES IN FINAL

11 – Arsenal, Newcastle U. 10 – Everton, Manchester U, WBA. 9 – Aston Villa. 8 – Blackburn R, Liverpool, Manchester C, Tottenham H, Wolverhampton W. 7 – Bolton W, Preston NE. 6 – Old Etonians, Sheffield U. 5 – Huddersfield T, Sheffield W, *The Wanderers. 4 – Derby Co, Leeds U, Leicester C, Oxford University, Royal Engineers, West Ham U. 3 – Blackpool, Burnley, Chelsea, Portsmouth, Southampton, Sunderland. 2 – Barnsley, Birmingham C, *Bury, Cardiff C, Charlton Ath, Clapham R, *Nottingham F, Notts Co, Queen's Park (Glasgow). 1 – *Blackburn Olympic, *Bradford C, Brighton & HA, Bristol C, *Coventry C, Fulham, *Ipswich T, Luton T, *Old Carthusians, QPR, Watford, *Wimbledon. *Denotes undefeated

APPEARANCES IN SEMI–FINALS

21 – Everton. 19 – WBA. 17 – Aston Villa, Manchester U. 16 – Arsenal, Blackburn R, Liverpool. 15 – Sheffield W (inc.8 as The Wednesday). 13 – Derby Co, Newcastle U, Wolverhampton W. 12 – Bolton W, Tottenham H. 10 – Chelsea, Manchester C, Nottingham F, Preston NE, Sheffield U, Southampton, Sunderland. 9 – Birmingham C (inc.1 as Small Heath Alliance). 8 – Burnley, Leeds U. 7 – Huddersfield T, Leicester C. 6 – Old Etonians, Oxford University. 5 – Fulham, Notts Co, The Wanderers, West Ham U. 4 – Portsmouth, Queen's Park (Glasgow), Royal Engineers. 3 – Blackpool, Cardiff C, Clapham R, Ipswich T, Luton T, Millwall, Old Carthusians, Stoke C, The Swifts, Watford. 2 – Barnsley, Blackburn Olympic, Bristol C, Bury, Charlton Ath, Crystal Palace, Grimsby T, Swansea T, Swindon T. 1 – Bradford C, Brighton & HA, Cambridge University, Coventry C, Crewe Alex, Darwen, Derby Junction, Glasgow Rangers, Hull C, Great Marlow, Norwich C, Oldham Ath, Old Harrovians, Orient, Plymouth Arg, Port Vale, QPR, Reading, Shropshire W, Wimbledon, York C.

FA CUP FINALS SINCE 1872

1871–72: THE WANDERERS 1, ROYAL ENGINEERS 0 (Kennington Oval, 16.3.72, 2000)
Wanderers: Welch; Bowen, A. Thompson, E. Lubbock, Crake, Wollaston, Alcock, Hooman, Betts, Vidal, Bonsor. **Scorer:** A. H. Chequer (Betts).
Royal Engineers: Merriman; Marindin, Addison, Creswell, Mitchell, Renny-Tailyour, Rich, Goodwyn, Muirhead, Cotter, Bogle.

1872–73: THE WANDERERS 2, OXFORD UNIVERSITY 0 (Lillie Bridge, 29.3.73, 3000)
Wanderers: Welch; Bowen, Kinnaird, Howell, Wollaston, Sturgis, Stewart, Kenyon-Slaney, Kingsford, Bonsor, C. Thompson.
Scorers: Kinnaird, Wollaston.
Oxford: Leach; Kirke-Smith, Mackarness, Birley, Longman, Maddison, Dixon, W. Paton, Sumner, Vidal, Ottaway.

1873–74: OXFORD UNIVERSITY 2, ROYAL ENGINEERS 0 (Kennington Oval, 14.3.74, 2500)
Oxford: Neapean; Benson, Mackarness, Birley, Johnson, Maddison, Green, F. Patton, W. Rawson, Vidal, Ottaway. **Scorers:** Mackarness, Patton.
Royal Engineers: Merriman; Marindin, Addison, Onslow, Oliver, Digby, Renny-Tailyour, H. Rawson, Von Donop, Blackburn, Wood.

1874–75: ROYAL ENGINEERS 1, OLD ETONIANS 1 (aet, Kennington Oval, 13.3.75, 3000)
Royal Engineers: Merriman; Sim, Onslow, R. Ruck, Von Donop, Wood, H. Rawson, Stafford, Renny-Tailyour, Wingfield-Stratford, Mein. **Scorer:** Renny-Tailyour.
Etonians: A. Thompson; Benson, E. Lubbock, Wilson, Kinnaird, Stronge, F. Patton, Farmer, Bonsor, Ottaway, Kenyon-Slaney. **Scorer:** Bonsor.

REPLAY: ROYAL ENGINEERS 2, OLD ETONIANS 0 (Kennington Oval, 16.3.75, 3000)
Royal Engineers: Unchanged. **Scorers:** Renny-Tailyour, Stafford.
Etonians: Drummond-Moray; Farrer, E. Lubbock, Wilson, Kinnaird, Stronge, F. Patton, Farmer, Bonsor, A. Lubbock, Hammond.

1875–76: THE WANDERERS 1, OLD ETONIANS 1 (aet, Kennington Oval, 11.3.76, 3000)
Wanderers: Greig; Stratford, W. Lindsay, Maddison, Birley, Wollaston, H. Heron, Hughes, F. Heron, Edwards, Kenrick. **Scorer:** Edwards.
Etonians: Hogg; Kinnaird, Welldon, E.Lyttleton, A.Thompson, Meysey, Kenyon-Slaney, A. Lyttleton, Sturgis, Bonsor, Allene. **Scorer:** Bonsor.

REPLAY: THE WANDERERS 3, OLD ETONIANS 0 (Kennington Oval, 18.3.76, 3500)
Wanderers: Unchanged. **Scorers:** Hughes 2, Wollaston.
Etonians: Hogg; E. Lubbock, E. Lyttleton, M. Farrer, Kinnaird, Stronge, Kenyon-Slaney, A. Lyttleton, Sturgis, Bonsor, Allene.

1876–77: THE WANDERERS 2, OXFORD UNIVERSITY 1 (aet, Kennington Oval, 24.3.77, 3000)
Wanderers: Kinnaird; Stratford, W. Lindsay, Green, Birley, Wollaston, H. Heron, Hughes, Wace, Denton, Kenrick. **Scorers:** Heron, Kenrick.
Oxford: Alington; Bain, Donnell, Savory, Tod, Waddington, Fernandez, Hills, Otter, Parry, W. Rawson. **Scorer:** Kinnaird (og).

1877–78: THE WANDERERS 3, ROYAL ENGINEERS 1 (Kennington Oval, 23.3.78, 4500)
Wanderers: Kirkpatrick; Stratford, W. Lindsay, Kinnaird, Green, Wollaston, H.Heron, Wylie, Wace, Denton, Kenrick. **Scorers:** Kenrick 2, Kinnaird.
Royal Engineers: Friend; Cowan, Morris, Mayne, Heath, Haynes, M. Lindsay, Hedley, Bond, Barnet, O. Ruck. **Scorer:** Unknown.

1878–79: OLD ETONIANS 1, CLAPHAM ROVERS 0 (Kennington Oval, 29.3.79, 5000)
Etonians: Kinnaird; Hawtrey, Christian, Bury, E.Lubbock, Clarke, Pares, Goodhart, Whitfield, Chevalier, Beaufoy. **Scorer:** Clarke.
Clapham R: Birkett; Ogilvie, Field, Bailey, Prinsep, F. Rawson, Stanley, Scott, Bevington, Growse, Falconer.

1879–80: CLAPHAM ROVERS 1, OXFORD UNIVERSITY 0 (Kennington Oval, 10.4.80, 6000)
Clapham R: Birkett; Ogilvie, Field, Weston, Bailey, Brougham, Stanley, Lloyd-Jones, Ram, Barry, Sparks. **Scorer:** Lloyd-Jones.
Oxford: Parr; Wilson, King, Phillips, Rogers, Heygate, Childs, Eyre, Crowdy, Hill, J. Lubbock.

1880–81: OLD CARTHUSIANS 3, OLD ETONIANS 0 (Kennington Oval, 9.4.81, 4500)
Carthusians: Gillett; Norris, Colvin, Prinsep, Vincent, Hansell, Richards, Page, Wynyard, Parry, Todd. **Scorers:** Page, Wynyard, Parry.
Etonians: Kinnaird; Foley, French, Rawlinson, R.Farrer, Chevalier, Anderson, Goodhart, Macauley, Whitfield, Novelli.

1881–82: OLD ETONIANS 1, BLACKBURN ROVERS 0 (Kennington Oval, 25.3.82, 6500)
Etonians: Kinnaird; French, De Paravicini, Rawlinson, Foley, Chevalier, Dunn, Macauley, Goodhart, Anderson, Novelli. **Scorer:** Anderson.
Blackburn R: Howarth; McIntyre, Suter, Sharples, F. Hargreaves, Duckworth, Douglas, Strachan, Brown, Avery, J. Hargreaves.

1882–83: BLACKBURN OLYMPIC 2, OLD ETONIANS 1 (aet, Kennington Oval, 31.3.83, 8000)
Blackburn O: Hacking; Ward, Warburton, Gibson, Astley, Hunter, Dewhurst, Matthews, Wilson, Crossley, Yates. **Scorers:** Matthews, Crossley.
Etonians: Kinnaird; French, De Paravicini, Rawlinson, Foley, Chevalier, Anderson, Macauley, Goodhart, Dunn, Bainbridge. **Scorer:** Goodhart.

1883–84: BLACKBURN ROVERS 2, QUEEN'S PARK (Glasgow) 1 (Kennington Oval, 29.3.84, 4000)
Blackburn R: Arthur; Beverley, Suter, McIntyre, J. Hargreaves, Forrest, Lofthouse, Douglas, Sowerbutts, Inglis, Brown. **Scorers:** Brown, Forrest.
Queen's Park: Gillespie; Arnott, MacDonald, Campbell, Gow, Anderson, Watt, Smith, Harrower, Allan, Christie. **Scorer:** Christie.

1884–85: BLACKBURN ROVERS 2, QUEEN'S PARK (Glasgow) 0 (Kennington Oval, 4.4.85, 12,500)
Blackburn R: Arthur; Turner, Suter, McIntyre, Haworth, Forrest, Lofthouse, Douglas, Brown, Fecitt, Sowerbutts. **Scorers:** Forrest, Brown.
Queen's Park: Gillespie; Arnott, MacLeod, Campbell, MacDonald, Hamilton, Anderson, Sellar, Gray, McWhannel, Allan.

1885–86: BLACKBURN ROVERS 0, WEST BROMWICH ALBION 0 (Kennington Oval, 3.4.86, 15,000)
Blackburn R: Arthur; Turner, Suter, Douglas, Forrest, McIntyre, Heyes, Strachan, Brown, Fecitt, Sowerbutts.
WBA: Roberts; H. Green, H.Bell, Horton, Perry, Timmins, Woodhall, T. Green, Bayliss, Loach, G. Bell.

REPLAY: BLACKBURN ROVERS 2, WEST BROMWICH ALBION 0 (Racecourse Ground, Derby, 10.4.86, 12,000)
Blackburn R: Walton for Heyes. **Scorers:** Brown, Sowerbutts.
WBA: Unchanged.

1886–87: ASTON VILLA 2, WEST BROMWICH ALBION 0 (Kennington Oval, 2.4.87, 15,500)
Aston Villa: Warner; Coulton, Simmonds, Yates, Dawson, Burton, Davis, Brown, Hunter, Vaughton, Hodgetts. **Scorers:** Hunter, Hodgetts.
WBA: Roberts; H. Green, Aldridge, Horton, Perry, Timmins, Woodhall, T. Green, Bayliss, Paddock, Pearson.

1887–88: WEST BROMWICH ALBION 2, PRESTON NORTH END 1 (Kennington Oval, 24.3.88, 19,000)
WBA: Roberts; Aldridge, H. Green, Horton, Perry, Timmins, Bassett, Woodhall, Bayliss, Wilson, Pearson. **Scorers:** Woodall, Bayliss.
Preston NE: Mills-Roberts; Howarth, N. Ross, Holmes, Russell, Graham, Gordon, J. Ross, J. Goodall, Dewhurst, Drummond. **Scorer:** Dewhurst.

1888–89: PRESTON NORTH END 3, WOLVERHAMPTON WANDERERS 0 (Kennington Oval, 30.3.89, 22,000)
Preston NE: Mills-Roberts; Howarth, Holmes, Drummond, Russell, Graham, Gordon, J. Ross, J. Goodall, Dewhurst, Thompson. **Scorers:** Gordon, Goodall, Thompson.
Wolverhampton W: Baynton; Baugh, Mason, Fletcher, Allen, Lowder, Hunter, Wykes, Brodie, Wood, Knight.

1889–90: BLACKBURN ROVERS 6, THE WEDNESDAY 1 (Kennington Oval, 29.3.90, 20,000)
Blackburn R: Horne; James Southworth, Forbes, Barton, Dewar, Forrest, Lofthouse, Campbell, John Southworth, Walton, Townley. **Scorers:** Townley 3, Lofthouse, John Southworth, Walton.
Wednesday: Smith; Brayshaw, Morley, Dungworth, Betts, Waller, Ingram, Woodhouse, Bennett, Mumford, Cawley. **Scorer:** Bennett.

1890–91: BLACKBURN ROVERS 3, NOTTS COUNTY 1 (Kennington Oval, 21.3.91, 23,000)
Blackburn R: Pennington; Brandon, Forbes, Barton, Dewar, Forrest, Lofthouse, Walton, John Southworth, Hall, Townley. **Scorers:** Southworth, Dewar, Townley.
Notts Co: Thraves; Ferguson, Hendry, Osborne, Calderhead, Shelton, McGregor, McInnes, Oswald, Locker, Daft. **Scorer:** Oswald.

1891–92: WEST BROMWICH ALBION 3, ASTON VILLA 0 (Kennington Oval, 12.3.92, 25,000)
WBA: Reader; Nicholson, McCulloch, Reynolds, Perry, Groves, Bassett, McLeod, Nicholls, Pearson, Geddes. **Scorers:** Nicholls, Geddes, Reynolds.
Aston Villa: Warner; Evans, Cox, H. Devey, James, Cowan, Baird, Athersmith, J. Devey, Dickson, Campbell, Hodgetts.

1892–93: WOLVERHAMPTON WANDERERS 1, EVERTON 0 (Fallowfield, Manchester, 25.3.93, 45,000)
Wolverhampton W: Rose; Baugh, Swift, Malpass, Allen, Kinsey, Topham, Wykes, Butcher, Wood, Griffin. **Scorer:** Allen.
Everton: Williams; Howarth, Kelso, Stewart, Holt, Boyle, Latta, Gordon, Maxwell, Chadwick, Milward.

1893–94: NOTTS COUNTY 4, BOLTON WANDERERS 1 (Goodison Park, 31.3.94, 37,000)
Notts Co: Toone; Harper, Hendry, Bramley, Calderhead, Shelton, Watson, Donnelly, Logan, Bruce, Daft. **Scorers:** Logan 3, Watson.
Bolton W: Sutcliffe; Somerville, Jones, Gardiner, Paton, Hughes, Dickinson, Wilson, Tannahill, Bentley, Cassidy. **Scorer:** Cassidy.

1894–95: ASTON VILLA 1, WEST BROMWICH ALBION 0 (Crystal Palace, 20.4.95, 42,560)
Aston Villa: Wilkes; Spencer, Welford, Reynolds, James Cowan, Russell, Athersmith, Chatt, J. Devey, Hodgetts, Smith. **Scorer:** Devey.
WBA: Reader; Williams, Horton, Taggart, Higgins, Perry, Bassett, McLeod, Richards, Hutchinson, Banks.

1895–96: THE WEDNESDAY 2, WOLVERHAMPTON W 1 (Crystal Palace, 18.4.96, 48,836)
Wednesday: Massey; Earp, Langley, Brandon, Crawshaw, Petrie, Brash, Brady, Bell, Davis, Spiksley. **Scorer:** Spiksley 2.
Wolverhampton W: Tennant; Bough, Dunn, Owen, Malpass, Griffiths, Tonks, Henderson, Beats, Wood, Black. **Scorer:** Black.

1896–97: ASTON VILLA 3, EVERTON 2 (Crystal Palace, 10.4.97, 65,891)
Aston Villa: Whitehouse; Spencer, Evans, Reynolds, James Cowan, Crabtree, Athersmith, J. Devey, Campbell, Wheldon, John Cowan. **Scorers:** Devey, Campbell, Crabtree.
Everton: Menham; Meechem, Storrier, Boyle, Holt, Stewart, Taylor, Bell, Hartley, Chadwick, Milward. **Scorers:** Bell, Hartley.

1897–98: NOTTINGHAM FOREST 3, DERBY COUNTY 1 (Crystal Palace, 16.4.98, 62,017)
Nottingham F: Allsop; Ritchie, Scott, Frank Forman, McPherson, Wragg, McInnes, Richards, Benbow, Capes, Spouncer. **Scorers:** Capes 2, McPherson.
Derby Co: Fryer; Methven, Leiper, Cox, A. Goodall, Turner, J. Goodall, Bloomer, Boag, Stevenson, McQueen. **Scorer:** Bloomer.

424

FA CUP

1898–99: SHEFFIELD UNITED 4, DERBY COUNTY 1 (Crystal Palace, 15.4.99, 73,833)
Sheffield U: Foulke; Thickett, Boyle, Johnson, Morren, Needham, Bennett, Beers, Hedley, Almond, Priest. **Scorers:** Bennett, Priest, Beers, Almond.
Derby Co: Fryer; Methven, Staley, Cox, Paterson, May, Arkesden, Bloomer, Boag, McDonald, Allen. **Scorer:** Boag.

1899–1900: BURY 4, SOUTHAMPTON 0 (Crystal Palace, 21,4,1900, 68,945)
Bury: Thompson; Darrock, Davidson, Pray, Leeming, Ross, Richards, Wood, McLuckie, Sagar, Plant. **Scorers:** McLuckie 2, Wood, Plant.
Southampton: Robinson; Meehan, Durber, Meston, Chadwick, Petrie, Turner, Yates, Farrell, Wood, Milward.

1900–01: TOTTENHAM HOTSPUR 2, SHEFFIELD UNITED 2 (Crystal Palace, 20.4.01, 114,815)
Tottenham H: Clawley; Erentz, Tait, Norris, Hughes, Jones, Smith, Cameron, Brown, Copeland, Kirwan. **Scorer:** Brown 2.
Sheffield U: Foulke; Thickett, Boyle, Johnson, Morren, Needham, Bennett, Field, Hedley, Priest, Lipsham. **Scorers:** Bennett, Priest.

REPLAY: TOTTENHAM HOTSPUR 3, SHEFFIELD UNITED 1 (Burnden Park, Bolton, 27.4.01, 20,740)
Tottenham H: Unchanged. **Scorers:** Cameron, Smith, Brown.
Sheffield U: Unchanged. **Scorer:** Priest.

1901–02: SHEFFIELD UNITED 1, SOUTHAMPTON 1 (Crystal Palace, 19.4.02, 76,914)
Sheffield U: Foulke; Thickett, Boyle, Needham, Wilkinson, Johnson, Bennett, Common, Hedley, Priest, Lipsham. **Scorer:** Common.
Southampton: Robinson; Fry, Molyneux, Meston, Bowman, Lee, A. Turner, Wood, Brown, Chadwick, J. Turner. **Scorer:** Wood.

REPLAY: SHEFFIELD UNITED 2, SOUTHAMPTON 1 (Crystal Palace, 26.4.02, 33,068)
Sheffield U: Barnes for Bennett. **Scorers:** Hedley, Barnes.
Southampton: Unchanged. **Scorer:** Brown.

1902–03: BURY 6, DERBY COUNTY 0 (Crystal Palace, 18.4.03, 63,102)
Bury: Monteith; Lindsey, McEwen, Johnson, Thorpe, Ross, Richards, Wood, Sagar, Leeming, Plant. **Scorers:** Leeming 2, Ross, Sagar, Plant, Wood.
Derby Co: Fryer; Methven, Morris, Warrren, A. Goodall, May, Warrington, York, Boag, Richards, Davis.

1903–04: MANCHESTER CITY 1, BOLTON WANDERERS 0 (Crystal Palace, 23.4.04, 61,374)
Manchester C: Hillman; McMahon, Burgess, Frost, Hynds, Ashworth, Meredith, Livingstone, Gillespie, A. Turnbull, Booth. **Scorer:** Meredith.
Bolton W: Davies; Brown, Struthers, Clifford, Greenhaigh, Freebairn, Stokes, Marsh, Yenson, White, Taylor.

1904–05: ASTON VILLA 2, NEWCASTLE UNITED 0 (Crystal Palace, 15.4.05, 101,117)
Aston Villa: George; Spencer, Miles, Pearson, Leake, Windmill, Brawn, Garratty, Hampton, Bache, Hall. **Scorer:** Hampton 2.
Newcastle U: Lawrence; McCombie, Carr, Gardner, Aitken, McWilliam, Rutherford, Howie, Appleyard, Veitch, Gosnell.

1905–06: EVERTON 1, NEWCASTLE UNITED 0 (Crystal Palace, 21.4.06, 75,609)
Everton: Scott; W. Balmer, Crelly, Makepeace, Taylor, Abbott, Sharp, Bolton, Young, Settle, Hardman. **Scorer:** Young.
Newcastle U: Lawrence; McCombie, Carr, Gardner, Aitken, McWilliam, Rutherford, Howie, Veitch, Orr, Gosnell.

1906–07: THE WEDNESDAY 2, EVERTON 1 (Crystal Palace, 20.4.07, 84,584)
Wednesday: Lyall; Layton, Burton, Brittleton, Crawshaw, Bartlett, Chapman, Bradshaw, Wilson, Stewart, Simpson. **Scorers:** Stewart, Simpson.
Everton: Scott; W. Balmer, R. Balmer, Makepeace, Taylor, Abbott, Sharp, Bolton, Young, Settle, Hardman. **Scorer:** Sharp.

1907–08: WOLVERHAMPTON WANDERERS 3, NEWCASTLE UNITED 1 (Crystal Palace, 25.4.08, 74,967)
Wolverhampton W: Lunn; Jones, Collins, Hunt, Wooldridge, Bishop, Harrison, Shelton, Hedley, Radford, Pedley. **Scorers:** Hunt, Hedley, Harrison.
Newcastle U: Lawrence; McCracken, Pudan, Gardner, Veitch, McWilliam, Rutherford, Howie, Appleyard, Speedie, Wilson. **Scorer:** Howie.

1908–09: MANCHESTER UNITED 1, BRISTOL CITY 0 (Crystal Palace, 24.4.09, 71,401)
Manchester U: Moger; Stacey, Hayes, Duckworth, Roberts, Bell, Meredith, Halse, J. Turnbull, A. Turnbull, Wall. **Scorer:** A. Turnbull.
Bristol C: Clay; Annan, Cottle, Hanlin, Wedlock, Spear, Staniforth, Hardy, Gilligan, Burton, Hilton.

1909–10: NEWCASTLE UNITED 1, BARNSLEY 1 (Crystal Palace, 23.4.10, 77,747)
Newcastle U: Lawrence; McCracken, Whitson, Veitch, Low, McWilliam, Rutherford, Howie, Shepherd, Higgins, Wilson. **Scorer:** Rutherford.
Barnsley: Mearns; Downs, Ness, Glendinning, Boyle, Utley, Bartrop, Gadsby, Lillycrop, Tufnell, Forman. **Scorer:** Tufnell.

REPLAY: NEWCASTLE UNITED 2, BARNSLEY 0 (Goodison Park, 28.4.10, 69,000)
Newcastle U: Carr for Whitson. **Scorer:** Shepherd 2 (1 pen).
Barnsley: Unchanged.

1910–11: BRADFORD CITY 0, NEWCASTLE UNITED 0 (Crystal Palace, 22.4.11, 69,098)
Bradford C: Mellors; Campbell, Taylor, Robinson, Gildea, McDonald, Logan, Spiers, O'Rourke, Devine, Thompson.
Newcastle U: Lawrence; McCracken, Whitson, Veitch, Low, Willis, Rutherford, Jobey, Stewart, Higgins, Wilson.

REPLAY: BRADFORD CITY 1, NEWCASTLE UNITED 0 (Old Trafford, 26.4.11, 58,000)
Bradford C: Torrance for Gildea. **Scorer:** Spiers.
Newcastle U: Unchanged.

1911–12: BARNSLEY 0, WEST BROMWICH ALBION 0 (Crystal Palace, 20.4.12, 54,556)
Barnsley: Cooper; Downs, Taylor, Glendinning, Bratley, Utley, Bartrop, Tufnell, Lillycrop, Travers, Moore.
WBA: Pearson; Cook, Pennington, Baddeley, Buck, McNeal, Jephcott, Wright, Pailor, Bowser, Shearman.

REPLAY: BARNSLEY 1, WEST BROMWICH ALBION 0 (aet, Bramall Lane, 24.4.12, 38,555)
Barnsley: Unchanged. **Scorer:** Tufnell.
WBA: Unchanged.

1912–13: ASTON VILLA 1, SUNDERLAND 0 (Crystal Palace, 19.4.13, 120,081)
Aston Villa: Hardy; Lyons, Weston, Barber, Harrop, Leach, Wallace, Halse, Hampton, Stephenson, Bache. **Scorer:** Barber.
Sunderland: Butler; Gladwin, Ness, Cuggy, Thompson, Low, Mordue, Buchan, Richardson, Holley, Martin.

1913–14: BURNLEY 1, LIVERPOOL 0 (Crystal Palace, 25.4.14, 72,778)
Burnley: Sewell; Bamford, Taylor, Halley, Boyle, Watson, Nesbit, Lindley, Freeman, Hodgson, Mosscrop. **Scorer:** Freeman.
Liverpool: Campbell; Longworth, Pursell, Fairfoul, Ferguson, McKinlay, Sheldon, Metcalf, Miller, Lacey, Nicholl.

1914–15: SHEFFIELD UNITED 3, CHELSEA 0 (Old Trafford, 24.4.15, 49,557)
Sheffield U: Gough; Cook, English, Sturgess, Brelsford, Utley, Simmons, Fazackerley, Kitchen, Masterman, Evans. **Scorers:** Simmons, Kitchen, Fazackerley.
Chelsea: Molyneux; Bettridge, Harrow, Taylor, Logan, Walker, Ford, Halse, Thompson, Croal, McNeil.

1919–20: ASTON VILLA 1, HUDDERSFIELD TOWN 0 (aet, Stamford Bridge, 24.4.20, 50,018)
Aston Villa: Hardy; Smart, Weston, Ducat, Barson, Moss, Wallace, Kirton, Walker, Stephenson, Dorrell. **Scorer:** Kirton.
Huddersfield T: Mutch; Wood, Bullock, Slade, Wilson, Watson, Richardson, Mann, Taylor, Swan, Islip.

1920–21: TOTTENHAM HOTSPUR 1, WOLVERHAMPTON WANDERERS 0 (Stamford Bridge, 23.4.21, 72,805)
Tottenham H: Hunter; Clay, McDonald, Smith, Walters, Grimsdell, Banks, Seed, Cantrell, Bliss, Dimmock. **Scorer:** Dimmock.
Wolverhampton W: George; Woodward, Marshall, Gregory, Hodnett, Riley, Lea, Burrill, Edmonds, Potts, Brooks.

1921–22: HUDDERSFIELD TOWN 1, PRESTON NORTH END 0 (Stamford Bridge, 29.4.22, 53,000)
Huddersfield T: Mutch; Wood, Wadsworth, Slade, Wilson, Watson, Richardson, Mann, Islip, Stephenson, W. H. Smith. **Scorer:** Smith (pen).
Preston NE: Mitchell; Hamilton, Doolan, Duxbury, McCall, Williamson, Rawlings, Jefferis, Roberts, Woodhouse, Quinn.

1922–23: BOLTON WANDERERS 2, WEST HAM UNITED 0 (Wembley, 28.4.23, 126,047*)
Bolton W: Pym; Haworth, Finney, Nuttall, Seddon, Jennings, Butler, Jack, J. R. Smith, J. Smith, Vizard. **Scorers:** Jack, J. R. Smith.
West Ham U: Hufton; Henderson, Young, Bishop, Kay, Tresadern, Richards, Brown, Watson, Moore, Ruffell.
*Official figure. Actual attendance probably nearer 200,000.

1923–24: NEWCASTLE UNITED 2, ASTON VILLA 0 (Wembley, 26.4.24, 91,695)
Newcastle U: Bradley; Hampson, Hudspeth, Mooney, Spencer, Gibson, Low, Cowan, Harris, McDonald, Seymour. **Scorers:** Harris, Seymour.
Aston Villa: Jackson; Smart, Mort, Moss, Milne, Blackburn, York, Kirton, Capewell, Walker, Dorrell.

1924–25: SHEFFIELD UNITED 1, CARDIFF CITY 0 (Wembley, 25.4.25, 91,763)
Sheffield U: Sutcliffe; Cook, Milton, Pantling, King, Green, Mercer, Boyle, Johnson, Gillespie, Tunstall. **Scorer:** Tunstall.
Cardiff C: Farquharson; Nelson, Blair, Wake, Keenor, Hardy, W. Davies, Gill, Nicholson, Beadles, J. Evans.

1925–26: BOLTON WANDERERS 1, MANCHESTER CITY 0 (Wembley, 24.4.26, 91,447)
Bolton W: Pym; Haworth, Greenhalgh, Nuttall, Seddon, Jennings, Butler, Jack, J. R. Smith, J. Smith, Vizard. **Scorer:** Jack.
Manchester C: Goodchild; Cookson, McCloy, Pringle, Cowan, McMullan, Austin, Browell, Roberts, Johnson, Hicks.

1926–27: CARDIFF CITY 1, ARSENAL 0 (Wembley, 23.4.27, 91,206)
Cardiff C: Farquharson; Nelson, Watson, Keenor, Sloan, Hardy, Curtis, Irving, Ferguson, L. Davies, McLachlan. **Scorer:** Ferguson.
Arsenal: Lewis; Parker, Kennedy, Baker, Butler, John, Hulme, Buchan, Brain, Blyth, Hoar.

1927–28: BLACKBURN ROVERS 3, HUDDERSFIELD TOWN 1 (Wembley, 21.4.28, 92,041)
Blackburn R: Crawford; Hutton, Jones, Healless, Rankin, Campbell, Thornewell, Puddefoot, Roscamp, McLean, Rigby. **Scorers:** Roscamp 2, McLean.
Huddersfield T: Mercer; Goodall, Barkas, Redfern, Wilson, Steele, Jackson, Kelly, Brown, Stephenson, W. H. Smith. **Scorer:** Jackson.

1928–29: BOLTON WANDERERS 2, PORTSMOUTH 0 (Wembley, 27.4.29, 92,576)
Bolton W: Pym; Haworth, Finney, Kean, Seddon, Nuttall, Butler, McClelland, Blackmore, Gibson, W. Cook. **Scorers:** Butler, Blackmore.
Portsmouth: Gilfillan; Mackie, Bell, Nichol, McIlwaine, Thackeray, Forward, J. Smith, Weddle, Watson, F. Cook.

1929–30: ARSENAL 2, HUDDERSFIELD TOWN 0 (Wembley, 26.4.30, 92,448)
Arsenal: Preedy; Parker, Hapgood, Baker, Seddon, John, Hulme, Jack, Lambert, James, Bastin. **Scorers:** James, Lambert.
Huddersfield T: Turner; Goodall, Spence, Naylor, Wilson, Campbell, Jackson, Kelly, Davies, Raw, W. H. Smith.

FA CUP

1930–31: WEST BROMWICH ALBION 2, BIRMINGHAM 1 (Wembley, 25.4.31, 92,406)
WBA: Pearson; Shaw, Trentham, Magee, W. Richardson, Edwards, Glidden, Carter, W. G. Richardson, Sandford, Wood. **Scorer:** W. G. Richardson 2.
Birmingham: Hibbs; Liddell, Barkas, Cringan, Morrall, Leslie, Briggs, Crosbie, Bradford, Gregg, Curtis. **Scorer:** Bradford.

1931–32: NEWCASTLE UNITED 2, ARSENAL 1 (Wembley, 23.4.32, 92,298)
Newcastle U: McInroy; Nelson, Fairhurst, McKenzie, Davidson, Weaver, Boyd, Richardson, Allen, McMenemy, Lang. **Scorer:** Allen 2.
Arsenal: Moss; Parker, Hapgood, C. Jones, Roberts, Male, Hulme, Jack, Lambert, Bastin, John. **Scorer:** John.

1932–33: EVERTON 3, MANCHESTER CITY 0 (Wembley, 29.4.33, 92,950)
Everton: Sagar; Cook, Cresswell, Britton, White, Thomson, Geldard, Dunn, Dean, Johnson, Stein. **Scorers:** Stein, Dean, Dunn.
Manchester C: Langford; Cann, Dale, Busby, Cowan, Bray, Toseland, Marshall, Herd, McMullan, Brook.

1933–34: MANCHESTER CITY 2, PORTSMOUTH 1 (Wembley, 28.4.34, 93,258)
Manchester C: Swift; Barnett, Dale, Busby, Cowan, Bray, Toseland, Marshall, Tilson, Herd, Brook. **Scorer:** Tilson 2.
Portsmouth: Gilfillan, Mackie, W. Smith, Nicholl, Allen, Thackeray, Worral, J. Smith, Weddle, Easson, Rutherford. **Scorer:** Rutherford.

1934–35: SHEFFIELD WEDNESDAY 4, WEST BROMWICH ALBION 2 (Wembley, 27.4.35, 93,204)
Sheffield W: Brown; Nibloe, Catlin, Sharp, Millership, Burrows, Hooper, Surtees, Palethorpe, Starling, Rimmer. **Scorers:** Rimmer 2, Palethorpe, Hooper.
WBA: Pearson; Shaw, Trentham, Murphy, W. Richardson, Edwards, Glidden, Carter, W. G. Richardson, Sandford, Boyes. **Scorers:** Boyes, Sandford.

1935–36: ARSENAL 1, SHEFFIELD UNITED 0 (Wembley, 25.4.36, 93,384)
Arsenal: Wilson; Male, Hapgood, Crayston, Roberts, Copping, Hulme, Bowden, Drake, James, Bastin. **Scorer:** Drake.
Sheffield U: Smith; Hooper, Wilkinson, Jackson, Johnson, McPherson, Barton, Barclay, Dodds, Pickering, Williams.

1936–37: SUNDERLAND 3, PRESTON NORTH END 1 (Wembley, 1.5.37, 93,495)
Sunderland: Mapson; Gorman, Hall, Thomson, Johnson, McNab, Duns, Carter, Gurney, Gallacher, Burbanks. **Scorers:** Gurney, Carter, Burbanks.
Preston NE: Burns; Gallimore, A. Beattie, Shankly, Tremelling, Milne, Dougal, Beresford, F. O'Donnell, Fagan, H. O'Donnell. **Scorer:** F. O'Donnell.

1937–38: PRESTON NORTH END 1, HUDDERSFIELD T 0 (aet, Wembley, 30.4.38, 93,497)
Preston NE: Holdcroft; Gallimore, A. Beattie, Shankly, Smith, Batey, Watmough, Mutch, Maxwell, R. Beattie, H. O'Donnell. **Scorer:** Mutch (pen).
Huddersfield T: Hesford; Craig, Mountford, Willingham, Young, Boot, Hulme, Isaac, McFadyen, Barclay, Beasley.

1938–39: PORTSMOUTH 4, WOLVERHAMPTON WANDERERS 1 (Wembley, 29.4.39, 99,370)
Portsmouth: Walker; Morgan, Rochford, Guthrie, Rowe, Wharton, Worrall, McAlinden, Anderson, Barlow, Parker. **Scorers:** Parker 2, Barlow, Anderson.
Wolverhampton W: Scott; Morris, Taylor, Galley, Cullis, Gardiner, Burton, McIntosh, Westcott, Dorsett, Maguire. **Scorer:** Dorsett.

1945–46: DERBY COUNTY 4, CHARLTON ATHLETIC 1 (aet, Wembley, 27.4.46, 98,000)
Derby Co: Woodley; Nicholas, Howe, Bullions, Leuty, Musson, Harrison, Carter, Stamps, Doherty, Duncan. **Scorers:** H.Turner (og), Doherty, Stamps 2.
Charlton Ath: Bartram; Phipps, Shreeve, H. Turner, Oakes, Johnson, Fell, Brown, A. Turner, Welsh, Duffy. **Scorer:** H.Turner.

1946–47: CHARLTON ATHLETIC 1, BURNLEY 0 (aet, Wembley, 26.4.47, 99,000)
Charlton Ath: Bartram; Croker, Shreeve, Johnson, Phipps, Whittaker, Hurst, Dawson, Robinson, Welsh, Duffy. **Scorer:** Duffy.
Burnley: Strong; Woodruff, Mather, Attwell, Brown, Bray, Chew, Morris, Harrison, Potts, Kippax.

1947–48: MANCHESTER UNITED 4, BLACKPOOL 2 (Wembley, 24.4.48, 99,000)
Manchester U: Crompton; Carey, Aston, Anderson, Chilton, Cockburn, Delaney, Morris, Rowley, Pearson, Mitten. **Scorers:** Rowley 2, Pearson, Anderson.
Blackpool: Robinson; Shimwell, Crosland, Johnston, Hayward, Kelly, Matthews, Munro, Mortensen, Dick, Rickett. **Scorers:** Shimwell (pen), Mortensen.

1948–49: WOLVERHAMPTON WANDERERS 3, LEICESTER CITY 1 (Wembley, 30.4.49, 99,500)
Wolverhampton W: Williams; Pritchard, Springthorpe, Crook, Shorthouse, Wright, Hancocks, Smyth, Pye, Dunn, Mullen. **Scorers:** Pye 2, Smyth.
Leicester C: Bradley; Jelly, Scott, W.Harrison, Plummer, King, Griffiths, Lee, J. Harrison, Chisholm, Adam. **Scorer:** Griffiths.

1949–50: ARSENAL 2, LIVERPOOL 0 (Wembley, 29.4.50, 100,000)
Arsenal: Swindin; Scott, Barnes, Forbes, L. Compton, Mercer, Cox, Logie, Goring, Lewis, D. Compton. **Scorer:** Lewis 2.
Liverpool: Sidlow; Lambert, Spicer, Taylor, Hughes, Jones, Payne, Baron, Stubbins, Fagan, Liddell.

1950–51: NEWCASTLE UNITED 2, BLACKPOOL 0 (Wembley, 28.4.51, 100,000)
Newcastle U: Fairbrother; Cowell, Corbett, Harvey, Brennan, Crowe, Walker, Taylor, Milburn, G. Robledo, Mitchell. **Scorer:** Milburn 2.
Blackpool: Farm; Shimwell, Garrett, Johnston, Hayward, Kelly, Matthews, Mudie, Mortensen, Slater, Perry.

1951–52: NEWCASTLE UNITED 1, ARSENAL 0 (Wembley, 3.5.52, 100,000)
Newcastle U: Simpson; Cowell, McMichael, Harvey, Brennan, E. Robledo, Walker, Foulkes, Milburn, G. Robledo, Mitchell. **Scorer:** G. Robledo.
Arsenal: Swindin; Barnes, L. Smith, Forbes, Daniel, Mercer, Cox, Logie, Holton, Lishman, Roper.

1952–53: BLACKPOOL 4, BOLTON WANDERERS 3 (Wembley, 2.5.53, 100,000)
Blackpool: Farm; Shimwell, Garrett, Fenton, Johnston, Robinson, Matthews, Taylor, Mortensen, Mudie, Perry. **Scorers:** Mortensen 3, Perry.
Bolton W: Hanson; Ball, Banks, Wheeler, Barrass, Bell, Holden, Moir, Lofthouse, Hassall, Langton. **Scorers:** Lofthouse, Moir, Bell.

1953–54: WEST BROMWICH ALBION 3, PRESTON NORTH END 2 (Wembley, 1.5.54, 100,000)
WBA: Sanders; Kennedy, Millard, Dudley, Dugdale, Barlow, Griffin, Ryan, Allen, Nicholls, Lee. **Scorers:** Allen 2 (1 pen), Griffin.
Preston NE: Thompson; Cunningham, Walton, Docherty, Marston, Forbes, Finney, Foster, Wayman, Baxter, Morrison. **Scorers:** Morrison, Wayman.

1954–55: NEWCASTLE UNITED 3, MANCHESTER CITY 1 (Wembley, 7.5.55, 100,000)
Newcastle U: Simpson; Cowell, Batty, Scoular, Stokoe, Casey, White, Milburn, Keeble, Hannah, Mitchell. **Scorers:** Milburn, Mitchell, Hannah.
Manchester C: Trautmann; Meadows, Little, Barnes, Ewing, Paul, Spurdle, Hayes, Revie, Johnstone, Fagan. **Scorer:** Johnstone.

1955–56: MANCHESTER CITY 3, BIRMINGHAM CITY 1 (Wembley, 5.5.56, 100,000)
Manchester C: Trautmann; Leivers, Little, Barnes, Ewing, Paul, Johnstone, Hayes, Revie, Dyson, Clarke. **Scorers:** Hayes, Dyson, Johnstone.
Birmingham C: Merrick; Hall, Green, Newman, Smith, Boyd, Astall, Kinsey, Brown, Murphy, Govan. **Scorer:** Kinsey.

1956–57: ASTON VILLA 2, MANCHESTER UNITED 1 (Wembley, 4.5.57, 100,000)
Aston Villa: Sims; Lynn, Aldis, Crowther, Dugdale, Saward, Smith, Sewell, Myerscough, Dixon, McParland. **Scorer:** McParland 2.
Manchester U: Wood; Foulkes, Byrne, Colman, J. Blanchflower, Edwards, Berry, Whelan, T. Taylor, R. Charlton, Pegg. **Scorer:** Taylor.

1957–58: BOLTON WANDERERS 2, MANCHESTER UNITED 0 (Wembley, 3.5.58, 100,000)
Bolton W: Hopkinson; Hartle, Banks, Hennin, Higgins, Edwards, Birch, Stevens, Lofthouse, Parry, Holden. **Scorer:** Lofthouse 2.
Manchester U: Gregg; Foulkes, Greaves, Goodwin, Cope, Crowther, Dawson, E. Taylor, R. Charlton, Viollett, Webster.

1958–59: NOTTINGHAM FOREST 2, LUTON TOWN 1 (Wembley, 2.5.59, 100,000)
Nottingham F: Thomson; Whare, McDonald, Whitefoot, McKinlay, Burkitt, Dwight, Quigley, Wilson, Gray, Imlach. **Scorers:** Dwight, Wilson.
Luton T: Baynham; McNally, Hawkes, Groves, Owen, Pacey, Bingham, Brown, Morton, Cummins, Gregory. **Scorer:** Pacey.

1959–60: WOLVERHAMPTON WANDERERS 3, BLACKBURN ROVERS 0 (Wembley, 7.5.60, 100,000)
Wolverhampton W: Finlayson; Showell, Harris, Clamp, Slater, Flowers, Deeley, Stobart, Murray, Broadbent, Horne. **Scorers:** McGrath (og), Deeley 2.
Blackburn R: Leyland; Bray, Whelan, Clayton, Woods, McGrath, Bimpson, Dobing, Dougan, Douglas, McLeod.

1960–61: TOTTENHAM HOTSPUR 2, LEICESTER CITY 0 (Wembley, 6.5.61, 100,000)
Tottenham H: Brown; Baker, Henry, D. Blanchflower, Norman, Mackay, Jones, White, Smith, Allen, Dyson. **Scorers:** Smith, Dyson.
Leicester C: Banks; Chalmers, Norman, McLintock, King, Appleton, Riley, Walsh, McIlmoyle, Keyworth, Cheesebrough.

1961–62: TOTTENHAM HOTSPUR 3, BURNLEY 1 (Wembley, 5.5.62, 100,000)
Tottenham H: Brown; Baker, Henry, D. Blanchflower, Norman, Mackay, Medwin, White, Smith, Greaves, Jones. **Scorers:** Greaves, Smith, Blanchflower (pen).
Burnley: Blacklaw; Angus, Elder, Adamson, Cummings, Miller, Connelly, McIlroy, Pointer, Robson, Harris. **Scorer:** Robson.

1962–63: MANCHESTER UNITED 3, LEICESTER CITY 1 (Wembley, 25.5.63, 100,000)
Manchester U: Gaskell; Dunne, Cantwell, Crerand, Foulkes, Setters, Giles, Quixall, Herd, Law, R. Charlton. **Scorers:** Law, Herd 2.
Leicester C: Banks; Sjoberg, Norman, McLintock, King, Appleton, Riley, Cross, Keyworth, Gibson, Stringfellow. **Scorer:** Keyworth.

1963–64: WEST HAM UNITED 3, PRESTON NORTH END 2 (Wembley, 2.5.64, 100,000)
West Ham U: Standen; Bond, Burkett, Bovington, Brown, Moore, Brabrook, Boyce, Byrne, Hurst, Sissons. **Scorers:** Sissons, Hurst, Boyce.
Preston NE: Kelly; Ross, Smith, Lawton, Singleton, Kendall, Wilson, Ashworth, Dawson, Spavin, Holden. **Scorers:** Holden, Dawson.

FA CUP

1964–65: LIVERPOOL 2, LEEDS UNITED 1 (aet, Wembley, 1.5.65, 100,000)
Liverpool: Lawrence; Lawler, Byrne, Strong, Yeats, Stevenson, Callaghan, Hunt, St John, Smith, Thompson. **Scorers:** Hunt, St John.
Leeds U: Sprake; Reaney, Bell, Bremner, J. Charlton, Hunter, Giles, Storrie, Peacock, Collins, Johanneson. **Scorer:** Bremner.

1965–66: EVERTON 3, SHEFFIELD WEDNESDAY 2 (Wembley, 14.5.66, 100,000)
Everton: West; Wright, Wilson, Gabriel, Labone, Harris, Scott, Trebilcock, Young, Harvey, Temple. **Scorers:** Trebilcock 2, Temple.
Sheffield W: Springett; Smith, Megson, Eustace, Ellis, Young, Pugh, Fantham, McCalliog, Ford, Quinn. **Scorers:** McCalliog, Ford.

1966–67: TOTTENHAM HOTSPUR 2, CHELSEA 1 (Wembley, 20.5.67, 100,000)
Tottenham H: Jennings; Kinnear, Knowles, Mullery, England, Mackay, Robertson, Greaves, Gilzean, Venables, Saul. **Scorers:** Robertson, Saul.
Chelsea: Bonetti; A. Harris, McCreadie, Hollins, Hinton, R.Harris, Cooke, Baldwin, Hateley, Tambling, Boyle. **Scorer:** Tambling.

1967–68: WEST BROMWICH ALBION 1, EVERTON 0 (aet, Wembley, 18.5.68, 100,000)
WBA: Osborne; Fraser, Williams, Brown, Talbut, Kaye (Clarke), Lovett, Collard, Astle, Hope, Clark. **Scorer:** Astle.
Everton: West; Wright, Wilson, Kendall, Labone, Harvey, Husband, Ball, Royle, Hurst, Morrissey.

1968–69: MANCHESTER CITY 1, LEICESTER CITY 0 (Wembley, 26.4.69, 100,000)
Manchester C: Dowd; Book, Pardoe, Doyle, Booth, Oakes, Summerbee, Bell, Lee, Young, Coleman. **Scorer:** Young.
Leicester C: Shilton; Rodrigues, Nish, Roberts, Woollet, Cross, Fern, Gibson, Lochhead, Clarke, Glover (Manley).

1969–70: CHELSEA 2, LEEDS UNITED 2 (aet, Wembley, 11.4.70, 100,000)
Chelsea: Bonetti; Webb, McCreadie, Hollins, Dempsey, Harris (Hinton), Baldwin, Houseman, Osgood, Hutchinson, Cooke. **Scorers:** Houseman, Hutchinson.
Leeds U: Sprake; Madeley; Cooper, Bremner, J.Charlton, Hunter, Lorimer, Clarke, Jones, Giles, Gray. **Scorers:** Charlton, Jones.

REPLAY: CHELSEA 2, LEEDS UNITED 1 (aet, Old Trafford, 29.4.70, 62,000)
Chelsea: Unchanged. Hinton came on for Osgood. **Scorers:** Osgood, Webb.
Leeds U: Harvey for Sprake. **Scorer:** Jones.

1970–71: ARSENAL 2, LIVERPOOL 1 (aet, Wembley, 8.5.71, 100,000)
Arsenal: Wilson; Rice, McNab, Storey (Kelly), McLintock, Simpson, Armstrong, Graham, Radford, R.Kennedy, George. **Scorers:** Kelly, George.
Liverpool: Clemence; Lawler, Lindsay, Smith, Lloyd, Hughes, Callaghan, Evans (Peter Thompson), Heighway, Toshack, Hall. **Scorer:** Heighway.

1971–72: LEEDS UNITED 1, ARSENAL 0 (Wembley, 6.5.72, 100,000)
Leeds U: Harvey; Reaney, Madeley, Bremner, J. Charlton, Hunter, Lorimer, Clarke, Jones, Giles, E. Gray. **Scorer:** Clarke.
Arsenal: Barnett; Rice, McNab, Storey, McLintock, Simpson, Armstrong, Ball, George, Radford (R. Kennedy), Graham.

1972–73: SUNDERLAND 1, LEEDS UNITED 0 (Wembley, 5.5.73, 100,000)
Sunderland: Montgomery; Malone, Guthrie, Horswill, Watson, Pitt, Kerr, Hughes, Halom, Porterfield, Tueart. **Scorer:** Porterfield.
Leeds U: Harvey; Reaney, Cherry, Bremner, Madeley, Hunter, Lorimer, Clarke, Jones, Giles, E. Gray (Yorath).

1973–74: LIVERPOOL 3, NEWCASTLE UNITED 0 (Wembley, 4.5.74, 100,000)
Liverpool: Clemence; Smith, Lindsay, Phil Thompson, Cormack, Hughes, Keegan, Hall, Heighway, Toshack, Callaghan. **Scorers:** Keegan 2, Heighway.
Newcastle U: McFaul; Clark, A. Kennedy, McDermott, Howard, Moncur, Smith (Gibb), Cassidy, Macdonald, Tudor, Hibbitt.

1974–75: WEST HAM UNITED 2, FULHAM 0 (Wembley, 2.5.75, 100,000)
West Ham U: Day; McDowell, T. Taylor, Lock, Lampard, Bonds, Paddon, Brooking, Jennings, A. Taylor, Holland. **Scorer:** A. Taylor 2.
Fulham: Mellor; Cutbush, Lacy, Moore, Fraser, Mullery, Conway, Slough, Mitchell, Busby, Barrett.

1975–76: SOUTHAMPTON 1, MANCHESTER UNITED 0 (Wembley, 1.5.76, 100,000)
Southampton: Turner; Rodrigues, Peach, Holmes, Blyth, Steele, Gilchrist, Channon, Osgood, McCalliog, Stokes. **Scorer:** Stokes.
Manchester U: Stepney; Forsyth, Houston, Daly, B. Greenhoff, Buchan, Coppell, McIlroy, Pearson, Macari, Hill (McCreery).

1976–77: MANCHESTER UNITED 2, LIVERPOOL 1 (Wembley, 21.5.77, 100,000)
Manchester U: Stepney; Nicholl, Albiston, McIlroy, B. Greenhoff, Buchan, Coppell, J. Greenhoff, Pearson, Macari, Hill (McCreery). **Scorers:** Pearson, J. Greenhoff.
Liverpool: Clemence; Neal, Jones, Smith, R. Kennedy, Hughes, Keegan, Case, Heighway, Johnson (Callaghan), McDermott. **Scorer:** Case.

1977–78: IPSWICH TOWN 1, ARSENAL 0 (Wembley, 6.5.78, 100,000)
Ipswich T: Cooper; Burley, Mills, Osborne (Lambert), Hunter, Beattie, Talbot, Wark, Mariner, Geddis, Woods. **Scorer:** Osborne.
Arsenal: Jennings; Rice, Nelson, Price, O'Leary, Young, Brady (Rix), Hudson, Macdonald, Stapleton, Sunderland.

1978–79: ARSENAL 3, MANCHESTER UNITED 2 (Wembley, 12.5.79, 100,000)
Arsenal: Jennings; Rice, Nelson, Talbot, O'Leary, Young, Brady, Sunderland, Stapleton, Price (Walford), Rix. **Scorers:** Talbot, Stapleton, Sunderland.
Manchester U: Bailey; Nicholl, Albiston, McIlroy, McQueen, Buchan, Coppell, J. Greenhoff, Jordan, Macari, Thomas. **Scorers:** McQueen, McIlroy.

1979–80: WEST HAM UNITED 1, ARSENAL 0 (Wembley, 10.5.80, 100,000)
West Ham U: Parkes; Stewart, Lampard, Bonds, Martin, Devonshire, Allen, Pearson, Cross, Brooking, Pike. **Scorer:** Brooking.
Arsenal: Jennings; Rice, Devine (Nelson), Talbot, O'Leary, Young, Brady, Sunderland, Stapleton, Price, Rix.

1980–81: TOTTENHAM HOTSPUR 1, MANCHESTER CITY 1 (aet, Wembley, 9.5.81, 100,000)
Tottenham H: Aleksic; Perryman, Miller, Roberts, Houghton, Hoddle, Ardiles, Villa (Brooke), Crooks, Archibald, Galvin. **Scorer:** Hutchison (og).
Manchester C: Corrigan; Ranson, Reid, Caton, McDonald, Gow, Mackenzie, Power, Hutchison (Henry), Bennett, Reeves. **Scorer:** Hutchison.

REPLAY: TOTTENHAM HOTSPUR 3, MANCHESTER CITY 2 (Wembley, 14.5.81, 92,000)
Tottenham H: Unchanged (no subs used). **Scorers:** Villa 2, Crooks.
Manchester C: Unchanged. Tueart came on for McDonald. **Scorers:** Mackenzie, Reeves (pen).

1981–82: TOTTENHAM HOTSPUR 1, QUEEN'S PARK RANGERS 1 (aet, Wembley, 22.5.82, 100,000)
Tottenham H: Clemence; Hughton, Miller, Price, Hazard (Brooke), Perryman, Roberts, Archibald, Galvin, Hoddle, Crooks. **Scorer:** Hoddle.
QPR: Hucker; Fenwick, Gillard, Waddock, Hazell, Roeder, Currie, Flanagan, Allen (Micklewhite), Stainrod, Gregory. **Scorer:** Fenwick.

REPLAY: TOTTENHAM HOTSPUR 1, QUEEN'S PARK RANGERS 0 (Wembley, 27.5.82, 90,000)
Tottenham H: Unchanged. Brooke came on for Hazard. **Scorer:** Hoddle (pen).
QPR: Neill for Roeder, Micklewhite for Allen, Burke came on for Micklewhite.

1982–83: MANCHESTER UNITED 2, BRIGHTON & HOVE ALBION 2 (aet, Wembley, 26.5.83, 100,000)
Manchester U: Bailey; Duxbury, Moran, McQueen, Albiston, Davies, Wilkins, Robson, Muhren, Stapleton, Whiteside. **Scorers:** Stapleton, Wilkins.
Brighton & HA: Moseley; Ramsey (Ryan), Stevens, Gatting, Pearce, Smillie, Case, Grealish, Howlett, Robinson, Smith. **Scorers:** Smith, Stevens.

REPLAY: MANCHESTER UNITED 4, BRIGHTON & HOVE ALBION 0 (Wembley, 26.5.83, 100,000)
Manchester U: Unchanged. **Scorers:** Robson 2, Whiteside, Muhren (pen).
Brighton & HA: Foster for Ramsey.

1983–84: EVERTON 2, WATFORD 0 (Wembley, 19.5.84, 100,000)
Everton: Southall; Stevens, Ratcliffe, Mountfield, Bailey, Steven, Reid, Heath, Richardson, Sharp, Gray. **Scorers:** Sharp, Gray.
Watford: Sherwood; Bardsley, Terry, Sinnott, Price (Atkinson), Taylor, Jackett, Callaghan, Johnston, Reilly, Barnes.

1984–85: MANCHESTER UNITED 1, EVERTON 0 (aet, Wembley, 18.5.85, 100,000)
Manchester U: Bailey; Gidman, Albiston (Duxbury), Whiteside, McGrath, Moran, Robson, Strachan, Hughes, Stapleton, Olsen. **Scorer:** Whiteside.
Everton: Southall; Stevens, Van den Hauwe, Ratcliffe, Mountfield, Reid, Steven, Gray, Sharp, Bracewell, Sheedy.

1985–86: LIVERPOOL 3, EVERTON 1 (Wembley, 10.5.86, 98,000)
Liverpool: Grobbelaar; Lawrenson, Beglin, Nicol, Whelan, Hansen, Dalglish, Johnston, Rush, Molby, MacDonald. **Scorers:** Rush 2, Johnston.
Everton: Mimms; Stevens (Heath), Van den Hauwe, Ratcliffe, Mountfield, Reid, Steven, Lineker, Sharp, Bracewell, Sheedy. **Scorer:** Lineker.

1986–87: COVENTRY CITY 3, TOTTENHAM HOTSPUR 2 (aet, Wembley, 16.5.87, 98,000)
Coventry C: Ogrizovic; Phillips, Downs, McGrath, Kilcline (Rodger), Peake, Bennett, Gynn, Regis, Houchen, Pickering. **Scorers:** Bennett, Houchen, Mabbutt (og).
Tottenham H: Clemence; Hughton (Claesen), M. Thomas, Hodge, Gough, Mabbutt, C. Allen, P. Allen, Waddle, Hoddle, Ardiles (Stevens). **Scorers:** C. Allen, Kilcline (og).

1987–88: WIMBLEDON 1, LIVERPOOL 0 (Wembley, 14.5.88, 98,203)
Wimbledon: Beasant; Goodyear, Phelan, Jones, Young, Thorn, Gibson, (Scales), Cork (Cunningham), Fashanu, Sanchez, Wise. **Scorer:** Sanchez.
Liverpool: Grobbelaar; Gillespie, Ablett, Nicol, Spackman (Molby), Hansen, Beardsley, Aldridge (Johnston), Houghton, Barnes, McMahon.

430

LITTLEWOODS CHALLENGE CUP 1987–88

FIRST ROUND, FIRST LEG

PORT VALE (0)0 NORTHAMPTON T (1)1
(17.8.87, 3398)
Port Vale: Williams; Banks, Pearson, Walker, Sproson, Webb, Smith, Earle (Hamson), Jones, Beckford (Maguire), Harper.
Northampton T: Gleasure; Reed, Senior, Donald, Wilcox, McPherson, Longhurst, Benjamin, Gilbert, Morley, Chard. **Scorer:** Longhurst.

BLACKPOOL (1)2 CHESTER C (0)0 (18.8.87, 3114)
Blackpool: Siddall; Davies, Morgan, Matthews, Methven, Jones, Cunningham, Madden, Walwyn, Deary, Taylor (Butler). **Scorers:** Cunningham, Methven.
Chester C: Stewart; Moore, Woodthorpe, Fazackerley, Abel, Hetzke, Lundon, Croft, Rimmer, Houghton (Hawtin), Graham.

BOURNEMOUTH (1)1 EXETER C (0)1
(18.8.87, 4094)
Bournemouth: Peyton; Newson, Morrell, Brooks, Williams, Whitlock, Pulis (Cooke), Armstrong, Aylott, Richards, O'Connor. **Scorer:** Armstrong (pen).
Exeter C: Shaw; Nisbet, Viney, Marker, Taylor (Cooper), Carter, Batty, Edwards (Kellow), O'Connell, Olsson, Harrower. **Scorer:** O'Connell.

BRENTFORD (1)2 SOUTHEND U (0)1 (18.8.87, 2839)
Brentford: Phillips; Joseph, Murray, Millen, Lee, Perryman, Feeley, Sinton, Cooke, Blissett, Caroll. **Scorers:** Sinton, Blissett.
Southend U: Steele; Ramsey, Johnson, Rogers, Martin, Hall, Clark, Smith, Neal, McDonough, Robinson. **Scorer:** Neal.

BURY (1)2 PRESTON NE (1)2 (18.8.87, 2363)
Bury: Farnworth; Hill, Pashley, Hoyland, Valentine, Higgins, Lee, Greenwood, Colville, McIlroy, Brotherston. **Scorers:** Greenwood, Colville.
Preston NE: Brown; Branagan, Rathbone, Atkins, Chapman (Wrightson), Allardyce, Miller, Swann, Lowey, Brazil, Hildersley (Worthington). **Scorers:** Allardyce, Brazil.

CAMBRIDGE U (1)1 ALDERSHOT (1)1
(18.8.87, 2164)
Cambridge U: Branagan; Ebanks, A. Kimble, Crowe, Smith, Beck, Butler, Clayton, Horwood, Crown, G. Kimble. **Scorer:** Beck.
Aldershot: Coles; Roberts, Phillips, Anderson, Smith, Wignall, Barnes, Howlett, Langley, McDonald, Ring. **Scorer:** Wignall.

CHESTERFIELD (1)2 PETERBOROUGH U (1)1
(18.8.87, 1938)
Chesterfield: Brown; Hewitt, Henderson, Bradshaw, Benjamin, Coyle, Eley, McGeeney, Waller, Caldwell (Rogers), Bloomer. **Scorers:** Caldwell, Waller (pen).
Peterborough U: Neenan; Paris, Gunn, Gooding, Pollard, Price, Kelly, Phillips, Riley, Halsall, Luke. **Scorer:** Kelly.

FULHAM (0)3 COLCHESTER U (1)1 (18.8.87, 2782)
Fulham: Stannard; Langley, Thomas, Lewington, Hopkins, Oakes, Marshall, Skinner, Rosenior, Davies, Barnett. **Scorers:** Davies, Marshall, Rosenior.
Colchester U: Lake (Reeves); Hinshelwood, Norman, Chatterton, Baker, Hedman, White, A. English, Walsh, Lowe, Wilkins. **Scorer:** White.

GILLINGHAM (0)1 BRIGHTON & HA (0)0
(18.8.87, 4162)
Gillingham: Kite; Haylock, Gernon, Shipley, West, Greenall, Pritchard, Shearer, Lovell, Elsey, Smith. **Scorer:** Greenall.
Brighton & HA: Keeley; Brown, Dublin, Rowell (Jasper), Rougvie, Isaac, Penney, Hutchings, Bremner, Nelson (Crumplin), Wilkins.

GRIMSBY T (3)3 DARLINGTON (2)2 (18.8.87, 2248)
Grimsby T: Sherwood; McDermott, Agnew, Robinson, Slack, Burgess, Turner, Walsh, North, O'Riordan, McGarvey. **Scorers:** Walsh, McGarvey, North.
Darlington: Roberts; Outterside, Morgan, Hine, Robinson, McAughtrie, Stonehouse, Ward, Macdonald, Currie, Bell. **Scorers:** MacDonald, Stonehouse.

HALIFAX T (1)1 YORK C (0)1 (18.8.87, 1359)
Halifax T: Roche; Brown, Harrison, M. Matthews, Robinson, Galloway, Richardson (Black), Thornber, N. Matthews, Allison (Ferebee), Holden. **Scorer:** Allison.
York C: Endersby; McKenzie, Johnson, Kitching, Whitehead, Clegg, Butler, Hood, Gabbiadini, Banton, Canham. **Scorer:** Gabbiadini.

LEYTON ORIENT (1)1 MILLWALL (1)1
(18.8.87, 4389)
Leyton Orient: Wells; Howard, Hughton (Sitton), Smalley, Day, Hales, Ketteridge, Castle, Jureyeff, Godfrey, Comfort. **Scorer:** Hales (pen).
Millwall: Horne; Stevens, Sparham, Hurlock, Walker, McLeary (Morgan), Lawrence, Briley, Sheringham, Cascarino, Byrne. **Scorer:** Morgan.

MANSFIELD T (1)2 BIRMINGHAM C (1)2
(18.8.87, 4425)
Mansfield T: Hitchcock; Graham, Kearney, Lowery, Foster, Coleman, Kent, Chalmers (Danskin), Stringfellow, Cassells, Charles (McKernon). **Scorer:** Stringfellow 2.
Birmingham C: Godden; Roberts, Dicks, Williams, Overson, Handysides, Bremner, Kennedy, Whitton, Rees, Wigley. **Scorers:** Whitton, Handysides.

NEWPORT CO (1)2 CARDIFF C (0)1
(Cardiff, 18.8.87, 3383)
Newport Co: Bradshaw; Hodson, Lewis, Gibbins, Williams, Brignull, Giles, Thackeray, Taylor, Evans, Tupling. **Scorer:** Evans 2.
Cardiff C: Moseley; Perry, Ford, Mardenborough, Abrahams, Boyle, Curtis, Sanderson (Bartlett), Gilligan, McDermott, Kelly. **Scorer:** Curtis.

ROCHDALE (0)3 TRANMERE R (1)1 (18.8.87, 1598)
Rochdale: Welch; Lomax, Hampton, Reid, Bramhall, Smart, Seasman (Stanton), Simmonds, Parlane, Coyle, Gavin. **Scorers:** Reid, Coyle, Parlane.
Tranmere R: O'Rourke; McCarrick, Williams (McKenna), Hughes, Thorpe, Vickers, Martindale, Craven, Mungall, Muir, Morrissey. **Scorer:** Mungall.

ROTHERHAM U (3)4 HUDDERSFIELD T (1)4
(18.8.87, 3353)
Rotherham U: O'Hanlon; Douglas, Scott, Campbell, Johnson (Dungworth), Green, Tomlinson, Williams, Evans, Airey (Haycock), Pugh. **Scorers:** Scott, Evans 2, Airey (pen).
Huddersfield T: Cox; Brown, Burke, Banks, Webster, Tucker, Trevitt, May (Barnham), Shearer, Cowling, Cork. **Scorers:** Shearer 3, Barham.

SCUNTHORPE U (2)3 HARTLEPOOL U (1)1
(18.8.87, 1613)
Scunthorpe U: Green; Russell, Longden, McLean, Brown, Nicol, Dixon, Harle, Johnson, Flounders, Hill. **Scorers:** Hill, Nicol, Russell (pen).
Hartlepool U: Owers; Barratt, Nobbs, Haigh, Smith, Stokes, Honour, Toman (Dixon), Baker, Shoulder, Butler. **Scorer:** Baker.

STOCKPORT CO (0)0 CARLISLE U (1)1
(18.8.87, 1476)
Stockport Co: Marples; Evans, Bailey, Robinson, Sword, Williams, Hodkinson, Cronin, Sertori, Hartford, Edwards. **Carlisle U:** Crompton; Patterson, Clark, Gorman, Wright, Saunders, Robinson, Cooke, Poskett, Bishop, Hetherington. **Scorer:** Hetherington.

SUNDERLAND (1)1 MIDDLESBROUGH (0)0
(18.8.87, 15,770)
Sunderland: Hardwick; Kay, Agboola, Bennett, MacPhail, Armstrong, Lemon, Proctor, Bertschin, Gates, Owers. **Scorer:** Gates.
Middlesbrough: Pears; Glover, Cooper, Mowbray, Parkinson, Pallister (Kernaghan), Slaven, Stephens, Hamilton, Kerr, Ripley.

SWINDON T (0)3 BRISTOL C (0)0 (18.8.87, 6807)
Swindon T: Digby; O'Regan, King, Kamara, Parkin, Calderwood, Kelly, Gittens (Henry), Quinn, Bamber, Barnard. **Scorer:** Quinn 3.
Bristol C: Waugh; Llewellyn, Bromage, Moyes, Newman, Tanner, Marshall (Neville), Fitzpatrick, Owen, Walsh, Jordan.

TORQUAY U (0)2 SWANSEA C (0)1 (18.8.87, 1964)
Torquay U: Allen; McNichol, Kelly, Haslegrave, Cole, Impey, Gardiner (Nardiello), Lloyd, Musker (Dawkins), Loram, Dobson. **Scorers:** Nardiello, Cole.
Swansea C: Hughes; Hough, Coleman, Melville, Knill, Davies, Williams, McCarthy, Raynor, Pascoe, Allon. **Scorer:** Raynor.

WIGAN ATH (1)2 BOLTON W (0)3 (18.8.87, 4115)
Wigan Ath: Tunks; Butler, Knowles, Hamilton, Griffiths (Hilditch), Beesley, Storer, C. Thompson, Campbell, Jewell, Cook. **Scorers:** Campbell, Thompson.
Bolton W: Felgate; Darby, Crombie, Joyce, Came, Sutton, Henshaw, Thompson, Morgan, Thomas, Chandler. **Scorers:** Morgan 2, Storer (og).

WOLVERHAMPTON W (1)3 NOTTS CO (0)0
(18.8.87, 5980)
Wolverhampton W: Kendall; Stoutt, Barnes, Streete, Robertson, Robinson, Thompson, Dennison, Bull, Mutch, Holmes (Downing). **Scorers:** Yates (og), Mutch 2.
Notts Co: Leonard; Smalley, Davis, Kevan, Yates, Gray, McParland, Lund (Jackson), Birtles, Pike, Mills (Thompson).

WREXHAM (0)1 BURNLEY (0)0
(18.8.87, 2301)
Wrexham: Salmon; Preece, Jones, Williams, Cooke, Bowden, Carter, Hunter (Buxton), Steel, Russell, Cunnington. **Scorer:** Russell.
Burnley: Pearce; Leebrook, McGrory, Daniel, Zelem, Deakin, Grewcock, Farrell, Oghani, Comstive, Britton.

BRISTOL R (1)1 HEREFORD U (0)0 (19.8.87, 2725)
Bristol R: Martyn; Alexander, Dryden, Hibbitt, Twentyman (Carr), Jones, Wiffill (Meacham), Reece, Turner, Penrice, Purnell. **Scorer:** Penrice.
Hereford U: Rose; Jones, Devine, Stevens, Pejic, Spooner, Rodgerson, Bowyer, Phillips, Kearns, McLoughlin.

SCARBOROUGH (0)1 DONCASTER R (0)0
(19.8.87, 3128)
Scarborough: Blackwell; McJannet, Thompson, Bennyworth (Harrison), Richards, Kendall, Hamill (Cook), Moss, McHale, Mell, Graham. **Scorer:** Richards.
Doncaster R: Rhodes; Stead, Robinson, Humphries, Flynn, Cusack, Russell, Chamberlain (Gaynor), Deane, Joyce, Kinsella.

WBA (1)2 WALSALL (1)3 (19.8.87, 9605)
WBA: Naylor; Dobbins, Burrows, Bennett, Steggles (Lynex), Kelly, Hopkins, Goodman, Palmer, Bradley, Morley. **Scorers:** Forbes (og), Bradley.
Walsall: Barber; Dornan, Mower (M. Jones), Shakespeare (Taylor), Forbes, Hart, Goodwin, Cross, Kelly, P. Jones, Naughton. **Scorers:** Shakespeare, P. Jones, Forbes.

CREWE ALEX (1)3 SHREWSBURY T (1)3
(25.8.87, 1781)
Crewe Alex: Parkin; Pemberton, Macowat, Milligan, Wright, Gage, Platt, Bodak, Cutler, Ritchie (Billing), Wakenshaw. **Scorers:** Wakenshaw 2 (1 pen), Platt.
Shrewsbury T: Perks; W. Williams, B. Williams, Narbett, Green, Linighan, Leonard, McInally, Brown, Robinson, Tester. **Scorers:** Tester, Leonard, W. Williams.

FIRST ROUND, SECOND LEG

ALDERSHOT (0)1 CAMBRIDGE U (3)4
(25.8.87, 2217)
Aldershot: Lange; Roberts (Davis), Phillips, Anderson, Smith, Wignall, Barnes, Langley, Ring, McDonald, Howlett (Johnson). **Scorer:** Johnson.
Cambridge U: Branagan; Ebanks, A. Kimble, Beattie, Smith, Beck, Butler, Clayton, Rigby, Crown, G. Kimble. **Scorers:** Crown 2, Beck, Rigby.
Cambridge won 5–2 on aggregate.

BIRMINGHAM C (0)0 MANSFIELD T (0)1
(25.8.87, 6054)
Birmingham C: Godden; Roberts, Dicks, Williams, Bird, Handysides, Bremner, Kennedy (Childs), Whitton, Rees, Wigley.
Mansfield T: Hitchcock; Graham, Kearney, Lowery, Foster, Coleman, Kent, Hodges, Stringfellow, Cassells, Charles. **Scorer:** Cassells.
Mansfield T won 3–2 on aggregate.

BOLTON W (1)1 WIGAN ATH (0)3 (25.8.87, 5847)
Bolton W: Felgate; Scott, Crombie, Thompson, Came, Sutton, Henshaw, Joyce, Morgan, Thomas, Chandler (Neal). **Scorer:** Thomas.
Wigan Ath: Tunks; Butler, Knowles, Hamilton, Cribley, Beesley, Storer (Hilditch), C. Thompson, Campbell, Jewell, Cook (Griffiths). **Scorer:** Campbell 3.
Wigan Ath won 5–4 on aggregate.

BRISTOL C (3)3 SWINDON T (1)2 (25.8.87, 7013)
Bristol C: Waugh; Llewellyn, Bromage, Moyes, Newman, Tanner, Marshall (Caldwell), Fitzpatrick, Owen, Walsh, Jordan (Neville). **Scorers:** Owen 2, Tanner.
Swindon T: Digby; O'Regan, King, Kamara, Parkin, Calderwood, Coyne (Henry), Berry, Quinn, Bamber, Barnard. **Scorers:** Bamber, Berry (pen).
Swindon T won 5–3 on aggregate.

BURNLEY (0)3 WREXHAM (0)0 (25.8.87, 3738)
Burnley: Pearce; Leebrook, Deakin, Daniel, Zelem, Gardner, Grewcock, Farrell, Oghani, Comstive, Taylor. **Scorers:** Comstive, Oghani (pen), Farrell.
Wrexham: Salmon; Preece, Jones, Hinnigan, Cooke, Bowden, Carter (Buxton), Hunter, Steel, Russell, Cunnington.
Burnley won 3–1 on aggregate.

CARDIFF C (2)2 NEWPORT CO (1)2 (25.8.87, 3550)
Cardiff C: Moseley; Perry (Bartlett), Ford, Stevenson, Boyle, Platnauer, Curtis, Sanderson, Kelly, Gilligan, McDermott. **Scorers:** Gilligan, Sanderson.
Newport Co: Bradshaw; Hodson, Lewis, Gibbins, Williams, Brignull, Giles, Thackeray, Tupling (Millett), Taylor, Evans. **Scorers:** Taylor, Tupling.
Newport Co won 4–3 on aggregate.

CARLISLE U (0)3 STOCKPORT CO (0)0
(25.8.87, 2174)
Carlisle U: Crompton; Patterson (McNeil), Clark, Gorman, Wright, Saunders, Robinson, Cooke, Poskett, Bishop, Hetherington. **Scorers:** Hetherington 2, Cooke.
Stockport Co: Marples; Evans, McKenzie, Robinson, Bullock, Williams, Hodkinson, Cronin, Mossman, Bailey, Edwards.
Carlisle U won 4–0 on aggregate.

COLCHESTER U (0)0 FULHAM (0)2 (25.8.87, 1554)
Colchester U: Walton; Hinshelwood, Norman (Grenfell), Chatterton, Baker, Hedman, White, English, Walsh (Reeves), Lowe, Wilkins.
Fulham: Stannard; Langley, Thomas, Lewington (Kerrins), Hopkins, Oakes, Marshall, Skinner (Donnellan), Rosenior, Davies, Barnett. **Scorers:** Barnett (pen), Davies.
Fulham won 5–1 on aggregate.

DONCASTER R (0)3 SCARBOROUGH (1)1
(25.8.87, 2370)
Doncaster R: Rhodes; Stead, Robinson, Brevett, Flynn, Cusack, Russell, Burke, Chamberlain (Nesbitt), Gaynor, Kinsella. **Scorers:** Gaynor, Kinsella, Stead.
Scarborough: Blackwell; McJannet, Thompson (Bennyworth), Harrison, Richards, Kendall, Hamill, Moss, McHale (Cook), Bowman, Graham. **Scorer:** Hamill.
Doncaster R won 3–2 on aggregate.

HUDDERSFIELD T (0)1 ROTHERHAM U (1)3
(25.8.87, 4528)
Huddersfield T: Cox; Trevitt, Burke, Banks, Webster, Tucker, Barham, May, Shearer, Ward (Cooper), Cork. **Scorer:** Shearer.
Rotherham U: O'Hanlon; Douglas, Scott, Grealish, Dungworth, Green, Pugh, Williams, Evans, Airey, Campbell. **Scorers:** Airey, Evans, Douglas.
Rotherham U won 7–5 on aggregate.

MIDDLESBROUGH (1)2 SUNDERLAND (0)0
(25.8.87, 15,571)
Middlesbrough: Pears; Glover, Cooper, Mowbray, Parkinson, Pallister, Slaven, Stephens, Hamilton, Kerr (Gill), Ripley. **Scorers:** Slaven, Mowbray.
Sunderland: Hardwick; Kay, Agboola, Bennett, MacPhail, Armstrong, Lemon (Gray), Proctor, Bertschin, Gates (Moore), Owers.
Middlesbrough won 2–1 on aggregate.

MILLWALL (0)1 LEYTON ORIENT (0)0 (25.8.87, 4120)
Millwall: Horne; Stevens, Sparham, Hurlock, Walker, Wood, Lawrence, Briley, Sheringham, Cascarino (Carter) (Salman), Byrne. **Scorer:** Lawrence.
Leyton Orient: Wells; Howard, Sitton, Smalley, Day

(Hull), Hales, Ketteridge, Castle, Nugent, Godfrey, Comfort.
Millwall won 2–1 on aggregate.

NOTTS CO (0)1 WOLVERHAMPTON W (0)2
(25.8.87, 2730)
Notts Co: Leonard; Smalley, Davis, Kevan, Yates, Birtles, Mills, McParland, Gray, Pike, Thompson. **Scorer:** Gray.
Wolverhampton W: Kendall; Stoutt, Clarke, Streete, Robertson, Robinson, Dennison (Gallagher), Thompson, Bull, Mutch, Downing. **Scorer:** Bull 2.
Wolverhampton W won 5–1 on aggregate.

PRESTON NE (1)2 BURY (0)3 (25.8.87, 4923)
Preston NE: Brown; Branagan, Bennett, Atkins, Jones, Allardyce, Miller (Worthington), Swann, Lowey, Brazil, Rathbone. **Scorers:** Brazil, Hill (og).
Bury: Hughes; Hill, Pashley, Hoyland, Valentine, Hart, Lee, Greenwood, Taylor, McIlroy, Brotherston. **Scorers:** Hoyland, Taylor, Brotherston.
aet; 90 mins 2–2; Bury won 5–4 on aggregate.

SOUTHEND U (2)4 BRENTFORD (1)2 (25.8.87, 2111)
Southend U: Steele; Ramsey, Hall, Rogers, Westley, Martin, Clark, Smith, Young, McDonough (Neal), Robinson. **Scorers:** Westley, Robinson, Martin, Neal.
Brentford: Phillips; Joseph (Perryman), Murray, Millen, Lee, Bates, Feeley, Sinton, Cooke, Blissett, Carroll. **Scorers:** Carroll, Cooke.
Southend won 5–4 on aggregate.

SWANSEA C (0)1 TORQUAY U (1)1 (25.8.87, 3800)
Swansea C: Hughes; Hough, Coleman (Andrews), Melville, Knill, Davies, Williams, Allon, Raynor, Pascoe (McCarthy), Hutchison. **Scorer:** Raynor.
Torquay U: Allen; McNichol, Kelly, Haslegrave, Cole, Impey, Gardiner, Lloyd, Pearce (Musker), Loram, Dobson. **Scorer:** Dobson.
Torquay won 3–2 on aggregate.

TRANMERE R (0)1 ROCHDALE (0)0 (25.8.87, 2314)
Tranmere R: O'Rourke; McCarrick, Williams, Hughes, Thorpe, Vickers, Mungall, Craven, McKenna, Muir, Morrissey. **Scorer:** Thorpe.
Rochdale: Welch; Lomax, Hampton, Reid, Bramhall, Smart, Seasman, Simmonds, Parlane, Coyle, Gavin.
Rochdale won 3–2 on aggregate.

WALSALL (0)0 WBA (0)0 (25.8.87, 8965)
Walsall: Barber; Dornan, Taylor, Shakespeare, Forbes, Hart, Goodwin, Cross, Kelly, P. Jones, Naughton.
WBA: Naylor; Dobbins, Burrows, Bennett, Dickinson, Kelly, Palmer (Lynex), Goodman, Robson, Singleton, Morley.
Walsall won 3–2 on aggregate.

YORK C (0)1 HALIFAX T (0)0 (25.8.87, 2382)
York C: Endersby; McKenzie, Johnson, Wilson, Whitehead, Clegg, Butler, Hood, Gabbiadini, Banton, Canham. **Scorer:** Hood (pen).
Halifax T: Roche; Brown, Harrison, M. Matthews, Martin, Galloway, Richardson, Shaw (Barr), N. Matthews, Black (Ferebee), Holden.
York C won 2–1 on aggregate.

BRIGHTON & HA (1)1 GILLINGHAM (0)0
(26.8.87, 5479)
Brighton & HA: Keeley; Brown, Dublin, Curbishley, Rougvie, Gatting, Crumplin, Hutchings, Armstrong, Gipp (Tiltman), Wilkins. **Scorer:** Hutchings.
Gillingham: Kite; Haylock, Gernon (Quow), Shipley, West, Greenall, Pritchard, Shearer, Lovell (Eves), Elsey, Smith.
aet: 90 mins 1–0; Gillingham won 5–4 on penalties; aggregate 1–1.

CHESTER C (1)1 BLACKPOOL (0)0 (26.8.87, 2143)
Chester C: Stewart; Abel, Woodthorpe, Fazackerley, Lundon, Hetzke, Parry, Barrow, Rimmer, Bennett, Graham. **Scorer:** Rimmer.
Blackpool: Siddall; Davies, Morgan, Matthews, Methven, Walsh, Butler, Madden, Walwyn, Deary, Taylor.
Blackpool won 2–1 on aggregate.

DARLINGTON (0)2 GRIMSBY T (1)1 (26.8.87, 1237)
Darlington: J. Roberts; Hine, Morgan, Bonnyman, Robinson, McAughtrie, A. Roberts, Ward, Macdonald, Currie, Stonehouse (Bell). **Scorer:** Macdonald 2.
Grimsby T: Sherwood; Toale, Agnew, Turner, Slack, Burgess, Robinson, Walsh (Saunders), North, O'Riordan, McGarvey. **Scorer:** North.
aet; 90 mins 2–1; aggregate 4–4; Darlington won on away goals.

EXETER C (0)1 BOURNEMOUTH (0)3
(26.8.87, 4094)
Exeter C: Shaw; Nisbet, Viney, Marker, Cooper, Carter, Batty (Williams), Edwards (Kellow), O'Connell, Olsson, Harrower. **Scorer:** O'Connell.
Bournemouth: Peyton; Newson, Morrell, Brooks, Williams, Whitlock, O'Driscoll, Richards, Aylott, Armstrong, Cooke (O'Connor). **Scorers:** Cooke, Newson, Aylott.
aet; 90 mins 1–1; Bournemoutrh won 4–2 on aggregate.

HARTLEPOOL U (0)0 SCUNTHORPE U (1)1
(26.8.87, 872)
Hartlepool U: Owers; Barratt, McKinnon, Haigh, Smith, Stokes, Honour, Toman, Baker, Thompson, Butler (Dixon).
Scunthorpe U: Green; Russell, Longden, McLean, Brown, Nicol, Dixon, Harle, Johnson, Flounders, Hill. **Scorer:** Johnson.
Scungthorpe U won 4–1 on aggregate.

HEREFORD U (1)2 BRISTOL R (0)0 (26.8.87, 2963)
Hereford U: Rose; Jones, Devine, Stevens, Pejic, Leadbitter, Rodgerson, Bowyer, Phillips, Kearns, McLoughlin. **Scorers:** McLoughlin, Phillips.
Bristol R: Martyn; Alexander, Dryden, Hibbitt, Carr, Jones, Wiffill (Meacham), Reece, Turner, Penrice, Purnell.
Hereford U won 2–1 on aggregate.

PETERBOROUGH U (1)2 CHESTERFIELD (0)0
(26.8.87, 2994)
Peterborough U: Neenan; Paris, Gunn, Gooding, Pollard, Price, Kelly, Phillips, Riley, Halsall, Luke. **Scorers:** Gunn (pen), Benjamin (og).
Chesterfield: Brown; Rogers, Henderson, Bradshaw, Benjamin, Coyle (Travis), Eley, McGeeney, Waller, Caldwell, Bloomer.
Peterborough U won 3–2 on aggregate.

NORTHAMPTON T (2)4 PORT VALE (0)0
(2.9.87, 4748)
Northampton T: Gleasure; Reed, Logan, Donald, Wilcox, McPherson, Longhurst, Benjamin, Gilbert, Morley, McGoldrick. **Scorers:** Morley 3, McPherson.

Port Vale: Williams; Webb, Pearson, Banks, Hazell, Sproson, Maguire (O'Kelly), Porter, Jones, Beckford (Harper), Hamson.
Northampton T won 5–0 on aggregate.

SHREWSBURY T (1)4 CREWE ALEX (0)1 (8.9.87, 2824)
Shrewsbury T: Perks; W. Williams, B. Williams, Narbett, Pearson, Linighan, Steele, Leonard, Brown, Robinson, Tester. **Scorers:** Robinson 2, Brown, Steele (pen).
Crewe Alex: Parkin; Pemberton, Macowat (Ritchie), Milligan, Billing, Gage, Platt, Bodak, Cutler, Wright, Wakenshaw (Gymer). **Scorer:** Platt.
Shrewsbury T won 7–4 on aggregate.

SECOND ROUND, FIRST LEG

BARNSLEY (0)0 WEST HAM U (0)0 (22.9.87, 10,330)
Barnsley: Baker; Joyce, Cross, Thomas, Gray, Futcher, Wylde, Agnew, Lowndes, MacDonald, Clarke (Beresford).
West Ham U: McAlister; Potts (McQueen), Parris, Strodder, Martin, Brady, Ward, McAvennie, Ince, Cottee, Robson.

BOURNEMOUTH (0)1 SOUTHAMPTON (0)0
(22.9.87, 10,364)
Bournemouth: Peyton; Newson, Morrell, Brooks, Williams, Whitlock, O'Driscoll, Richards, Cooke (Pulis), Heffernan, O'Connor. **Scorer:** Cooke.
Southampton: Flowers; Forrest, Statham, Case, Moore, Bond, Townsend, Cockerill, Clarke, Hobson (G. Baker), D. Wallace.

BURNLEY (1)1 NORWICH C (1)1 (22.9.87, 7926)
Burnley: Pearce; Leebrook, Deakin, Malley, James, Gardner, Farrell, Grewcock, Oghani, Comstive, Taylor. **Scorer:** Oghani.
Norwich C: Gunn; Culverhouse, Elliott, Bruce, Phelan, Butterworth, Gordon, Drinkell, Biggins, Crook, Bowen. **Scorer:** Biggins.

BURY (1)2 SHEFFIELD U (0)1 (22.9.87, 2401)
Bury: Farnworth; Hill, Pashley, Hart, Valentine, Higgins, Lee, Robinson, Hoyland, McIlroy, Brotherston. **Scorers:** Hill, Hoyland.
Sheffield U: Leaning; Wilder, Pike, Kuhl, Stancliffe, Eckhardt, Marsden (Frain), Philliskirk, Cadette, Dempsey, Beagrie. **Scorer:** Dempsey.

CAMBRIDGE U (0)0 COVENTRY C (1)1 (22.9.87, 5166)
Cambridge U: Branagan; Poole, A. Kimble, Beattie, Smith, Brattan (Turner), Butler, Clayton, Horwood (Williams), Crown, G. Kimble.
Coventry C: Ogrizovic; Borrows, Downs, McGrath, Rodger, Peake, Bennett, Phillips, Regis, Speedie, Gynn. **Scorer:** Gynn.

CARLISLE U (1)4 OLDHAM ATH (1)3 (22.9.87, 2271)
Carlisle U: Crompton; Patterson, McNeil, Robinson, Wright, Saunders, Clark, Cooke, Poskett, Bishop, Hetherington. **Scorers:** Hetherington, Wright (pen), Poskett, Cooke.
Oldham Ath: Goram; Irwin, Donachie, Keeley, Linighan, Milligan, Palmer, A. Henry, Cecere (N. Henry), Wright, Ritchie. **Scorers:** A. Henry, Irwin, Ritchie.

CRYSTAL PALACE (1)4 NEWPORT CO (0)0
(22.9.87, 6085)
Crystal Palace: Wood; O'Doherty, Shaw, Gray (Pardew), Nebeling, Taylor, Redfearn, Thomas, Barber, Wright, Salako (Powell). **Scorers:** Wright 2, Salako, Barber.
Newport Co: Bradshaw; Hodson, Sherlock, Abruzzese, Gibbins, Lewis, Giles, Tupling, Withers, Evans (Thackeray), Preece (Holtham).

LEAGUE CUP

DARLINGTON (0)0 WATFORD (0)3
(22.9.87, 5005)
Darlington: J. Roberts; Hine, Morgan, Bonnyman, Robinson, McAughtrie, A. Roberts, Ward, Macdonald, Currie, Bell.
Watford: Coton; Gibbs, Rostron, Morris, Terry, McClelland, Chivers (Hetherston), Roberts, Senior (Blissett), Porter, Sterling. **Scorers:** Porter, Senior, Gibbs.

EVERTON (1)3 ROTHERHAM U (1)2
(22.9.87, 15,369)
Everton: Southall; Harper, Van Den Hauwe, Ratcliffe, Watson, Reid, Steven, Heath (Sharp), Clarke, Snodin, Wilson. **Scorers:**
Snodin, Wilson, Clarke (pen).
Rotherham U: O'Hanlon; Douglas, Scott, Grealish (Dungworth), Johnson, Green, Pepper, Williams, Evans, Airey, Haycock (Pugh). **Scorers:** Scott, Pepper.

FULHAM (0)1 BRADFORD C (2)5
(22.9.87, 4357)
Fulham: Stannard; Marshall, Brathwaite, Lewington (Achampong), Hicks, Elkins, Kerrins, Skinner, Rosenior, Donnellan, Barnett. **Scorer:** Skinner.
Bradford C: Tomlinson; Mitchell, Goddard, McCall, Oliver, Evans, Hendrie, Sinnott, Futcher, Withe, Ormondroyd (Leonard). **Scorers:** Ormondroyd, Oliver, Mitchell, Futcher 2.

IPSWICH T (1)1 NORTHAMPTON T (0)1
(22.9.87, 8645)
Ipswich T: Hallworth; Yallop, Harbey, Rimmer, Dozzell, Humes, Atkinson (Milton), Brennan, D'Avray, Zondervan, Stockwell. **Scorer:** Zondervan.
Northampton T. Gleasure; Reed, Logan, Chard (Bunce), Wilcox, McPherson, Longhurst, Benjamin, Gilbert, Morley, McGoldrick. **Scorer:** Gilbert (pen).

MANCHESTER C (1)1 WOLVERHAMPTON W (0)2
(22.9.87, 8551)
Manchester C: Nixon; Gidman, Hinchcliffe, Lake, Simpson (Barnes), Redmond, White, Adcock, Varadi, Scott, McNab. **Scorer:** Adcock.
Wolverhampton W: Kendall; Bellamy, Thompson, Streete, Robertson, Robinson, Dennison, Vaughan, Bull, Mutch, Purdie. **Scorers:** Bull, Dennison.

ROCHDALE (1)1 WIMBLEDON (1)1
(22.9.87, 2801)
Rochdale: Welch; Lomax, Hampton, Reid, Bramhall, Smart, Seasman, Simmonds, Hunt (Stanton), Coyle (Thompson), Gavin. **Scorer:** Simmonds (pen).
Wimbledon: Beasant; Gayle, Phelan, Ryan (Jones), Young, Thorn, Wise, Gibson, Fashanu, Sanchez, Fairweather. **Scorer:** Fashanu (pen).

SHREWSBURY T (1)1 SHEFFIELD W (1)1
(22.9.87, 4364)
Shrewsbury T: Perks; W. Williams, B. Williams, Narbett (Leonard), Pearson, Linighan, Steele, McNally, Brown, Robinson, Tester. **Scorer:** McInally.
Sheffield W: Hodge; Sterland, Worthington, Madden, Fee, Jacobs, Jonsson, Megson, Chapman, West, Galvin (Bradshaw). **Scorer:** Fee.

SOUTHEND U (1)1 DERBY CO (0)0
(22.9.87, 4605)
Southend U: Steele; Martin, Johnson, Burrows, Westley, Hall, Robinson, Pennyfather, Nogan, McDonough, Ling. **Scorer:** McDonough (pen).
Derby Co: Shilton; Blades, Forsyth, Williams, Wright, MacLaren, Sage, Gee (Garner), Davison, Gregory, Callaghan.

STOKE C (1)2 GILLINGHAM (0)0
(22.9.87, 7198)
Stoke C: Fox; Dixon, Carr, Daley, Bould, Berry, Allinson, Ford, Morgan, Shaw, Heath. **Scorer:** Shaw 2.
Gillingham: Kite; Haylock, Pearce, Quow, West, Greenall, Pritchard, Shearer, Lovell, Elsey, Smith (Eves).

SWINDON T (2)3 PORTSMOUTH (0)1
(22.9.87, 9878)
Swindon T: Digby; Hockaday, King, Kamara, Parkin, Calderwood, Bamber, White (O'Regan), Quinn, Foley, Barnard. **Scorer:** Quinn 3 (1 pen).
Portsmouth: Knight; Swain, Sandford, Dillon, Shotton, Gilbert, Horne, Whitehead (Ball), Mariner (Kerr), Quinn, Hilaire. **Scorer:** Quinn.

WIGAN ATH (0)0 LUTON T (1)1
(22.9.87, 5018)
Wigan Ath: Adkins; Butler, Knowles, Hamilton, Cribley, Beesley, Storer, Hilditch, Campbell, Jewell, Cook (Griffiths).
Luton T: Sealey; Breacker, Johnson, Hill, Foster, Donaghy, Wilson, B. Stein, Harford, Weir, Preece (Nwajiobi). **Scorer:** Weir.

BLACKBURN R (0)1 LIVERPOOL (1)1
(23.9.87, 13,924)
Blackburn R: Gennoe; Price, Sulley, Barker (Millar), Hill, Mail, Gayle (Miller), Reid, Curry, Garner, Sellars. **Scorer:** Sellars.
Liverpool: Grobbelaar; Spackman, Venison, Nicol, Whelan, Hansen, Beardsley (Walsh), Aldridge, Lawrenson, Barnes, McMahon. **Scorer:** Nicol.

BLACKPOOL (1)1 NEWCASTLE U (0)0
(23.9.87, 7691)
Blackpool: Siddall; Davies (Lancashire), Morgan, Matthews, McAteer, Walsh, Cunningham, Madden, Jones, Taylor, Walwyn. **Scorer:** Cunningham.
Newcastle U: Kelly; McDonald, Tinnion, McCreery, P. Jackson, Roeder, Stephenson, Gascoigne, Goddard, Mirandinha, D. Jackson.

CHARLTON ATH (0)3 WALSALL (0)0
(23.9.87, 2948)
Charlton Ath: Johns; Humphrey, Reid, Gritt, Shirtliff, Miller, Milne, Stuart (Lee), Walsh, MacKenzie, Crooks. **Scorers:** Walsh, Crooks 2.
Walsall: Barber; Dornan, Taylor, Shakespeare, Forbes, Hart, Goodwin, Cross, Kelly, Christie, P. Jones.

DONCASTER R (0)0 ARSENAL (0)3
(23.9.87, 5469)
Doncaster R: Rhodes; Stead, Robinson, Raffell, Flynn, Cusack, Peckett (Nesbitt), Miller, Deane, Stubbs, Gaynor.
Arsenal: Lukic; Thomas, Sansom, Williams, O'Leary, Adams, Rocastle, Davis, Smith, Groves (Quinn), Rix (Richardson). **Scorers:** Groves, Smith, Williams.

LEEDS U (0)1 YORK C (0)1
(23.9.87, 11,527)
Leeds U: Day; Aspin, Adams, Stiles, Ashurst, Rennie, Williams (Doig), Sheridan, Pearson (Mumby), Taylor, Snodin. **Scorer:** Snodin.
York C: Endersby; Hood, Johnson, Wilson, Whitehead, Tuthill, Kitching (Buchanan), Mills, McKenzie, Banton, Himsworth. **Scorer:** Buchanan.

LEICESTER C (0)2 SCUNTHORPE U (1)1
(23.9.87, 7718)
Leicester C: Cooper; Morgan, James, Osman, Horner (Moran), Ramsey, Ford (McAllister), Newell, Rantanen, Mauchlen, Russell. Scorers: McAllister, Newell.
Scunthorpe U: Heyes; Russell, Longden, Lister, Nicol, Atkins, Dixon (Birch), Harle, Johnson, Flounders, Money. Scorer: Flounders.

MANCHESTER U (1)5 HULL C (0)0 (23.9.87, 25,041)
Manchester U: Walsh; Anderson, Gibson, Moses (Garton), McGrath, Duxbury, Robson, Strachan, McClair, Whiteside, Davenport. Scorers: McGrath, Davenport, Whiteside, Strachan, McClair.
Hull C: Norman; Palmer, Heard, Jobson, Skipper, Parker, Roberts, Bunn, Saville, Askew, Daniel (Williams).

MIDDLESBROUGH (0)0 ASTON VILLA (1)1
(23.9.87, 11,424)
Middlesbrough: Pears; Glover, Cooper, Mowbray, Parkinson, Pallister, Slaven, Stephens (Kernaghan), Hamilton, Kerr, Ripley.
Aston Villa: Spink; Gage, Gallacher, D. Hunt, Sims, Keown, Birch, Aspinall, Lillis, S. Hunt, Walters. Scorer: Aspinall.

NOTTINGHAM F (1)5 HEREFORD U (0)0
(23.9.87, 11,617)
Nottingham F: Sutton; Fleming, Pearce, Walker, Foster, Wilson, Carr, Webb, Clough, Wilkinson, Rice. Scorers: Webb 2, Carr, Clough, Wilkinson.
Hereford U: Rose; Jones, Devine, Stevens, Pejic, Spooner, Rodgerson, Bowyer, Phillips, Kearns, Leadbitter.

OXFORD U (0)1 MANSFIELD T (0)1 (23.9.87, 4651)
Oxford U: Hucker; Bardsley, Dreyer, Shelton, Slatter, Caton, Houghton, Foyle, Whitehurst (Saunders), Hebberd, Hill. Scorer: Saunders.
Mansfield T: Hitchcock; Graham, Coleman, Lowery, Foster, Kenworthy, Kent, Anderson, Stringfellow (McKernon), Cassells, Charles. Scorer: Kent.

PETERBOROUGH U (3)4 PLYMOUTH ARG (0)1
(23.9.87, 3843)
Peterborough U: Shoemake; Paris, Gunn, Gooding, Pollard, Price, Lawrence, Collins, Riley, Halsall, Luke. Scorers: Lawrence, Gooding, Halsall, Riley.
Plymouth Arg: Crudgington; Brimacombe, L. Cooper, McElhinney, Law, Smith, Hodges, Matthews (S. Cooper), Tynan, Evans, Anderson (Clayton). Scorer: Tynan.

QPR (1)2 MILLWALL (0)1 (23.9.87, 11,865)
QPR: Seaman; Fereday, Dawes, Parker, McDonald, Fenwick, Allen, Coney, Bannister, Byrne, Brock. Scorers: Bannister, McDonald.
Millwall: Horne; Salman, Coleman, Hurlock, Walker, Wood, Lawrence, Briley, Sheringham (Byrne), Cascarino, O'Callaghan. Scorer: Walker.

READING (3)3 CHELSEA (0)1 (23.9.87, 11,034)
Reading: Francis; Jones, Richardson, Beavon, Hicks, Peters, Tait, Taylor, Horrix, Gilkes, Bailie. Scorers: Gilkes 2, Hicks.
Chelsea: Niedzwiecki; Clarke, Dorigo, Pates, McLaughlin, Wood, Nevin, Hazard, Dixon, Durie, C. Wilson. Scorer: Durie (pen).

TORQUAY U (0)1 TOTTENHAM H (0)0 (23.9.87, 5000)
Torquay U: Allen; McNichol, Kelly, Haslegrave, Cole, Impey, Dawkins, Lloyd, Riley, Loram (Gardiner), Dobson. Scorer: Dawkins.
Tottenham H: Clemence; Ardiles, M. Thomas, Gough, Fairclough, Mabbutt, Howells, P. Allen, Waddle, Hodge, Metgod (Moran).

SECOND ROUND, SECOND LEG

ARSENAL (1)1 DONCASTER R (0)0 (6.10.87, 18,321)
Arsenal: Lukic; Thomas, Sansom, Williams, Caesar, Adams, Rocastle, Davis, Smith, Groves, Hayes. Scorer: Rocastle.
Doncaster R: Rhodes; Stead, Robinson, Raffell, Flynn, Cusack, Chamberlain (Rankine), Miller, Deane, Stubbs, Kinsella (Gorman).
Arsenal won 4–0 on aggregate.

COVENTRY C (0)2 CAMBRIDGE U (0)1
(6.10.87, 10,096)
Coventry C: Ogrizovic; Borrows, Pickering, McGrath, Sedgley, Peake (Downs), Bennett, Phillips, Regis, Houchen (Livingstone), Gynn. Scorers: Gynn, Regis.
Cambridge U: Branagan; Poole, A. Kimble, Beattie, Smith, Brattan, Butler, Clayton, Rigby (Horwood), Crown, G. Kimble. Scorer: Crown.
Coventry C won 3–1 on aggregate.

GILLINGHAM (0)0 STOKE C (1)1 (6.10.87, 5039)
Gillingham: Kite; Haylock, Pearce, Quow, West, Berry, Pritchard, Shearer (Lillis), Lovell, Elsey, Smith (Eves).
Stoke C: Fox; Dixon, Carr, Parkin, Bould, Berry, Ford, Daly, Morgan, Shaw, Heath. Scorer: Morgan.
Stoke C won 3–0 on aggregate.

LIVERPOOL (0)1 BLACKBURN R (0)0
(6.10.87, 28,994)
Liverpool: Grobbelaar; Gillespie, Venison, Nicol, Whelan, Hansen, Beardsley, Aldridge, Johnston, Barnes, Wark (Lawrenson). Scorer: Aldridge.
Blackburn R: Gennoe; Price, Sulley, Barker, Hendry, Dawson, Mail, Reid, Curry, Garner, Sellars.
Liverpool won 2–1 on aggregate.

LUTON T (3)4 WIGAN ATH (0)2 (6.10.87, 4227)
Luton T: Sealey; Breacker, Grimes, McDonough, Foster, Donaghy, Wilson, B. Stein, Harford, Black, Weir. Scorers: Harford 3, McDonough.
Wigan Ath: Redfern; Butler, Beesley, Hamilton, Cribley, Holden, Storer, Hilditch, Campbell (Ainscow), Jewell, Griffiths. Scorers: Hamilton, Foster (og).
Luton T won 5–2 on aggregate.

MANSFIELD T (0)0 OXFORD U (0)2 (6.10.87, 6295)
Mansfield T: Hitchcock; Graham, Ryan, Lowery, Foster, Coleman, Kent, Hodges (Chambers), Stringfellow (McKernon), Cassells, Charles.
Oxford U: Hucker; Bardsley, Dreyer, Shelton, Slatter, Caton, Houghton, Foyle, Saunders, Phillips, Hill (Rhoades-Brown). Scorers: Charles (og), Saunders.
Oxford U won 3–1 on aggregate.

MILLWALL (0)0 QPR (0)0 (6.10.87, 11,225)
Millwall: Horne; Salman, Coleman, Hurlock, Walker, McLeary, Lawrence, Briley, Sheringham, Cascarino, O'Callaghan.
QPR: Seaman; Neill, Dawes, Parker, McDonald, Fenwick, Allen, Coney, Bannister, Byrne, Brock.
QPR won 2–1 on aggregate.

NEWPORT CO (0)0 CRYSTAL PALACE (0)2
(6.10.87, 1303)
Newport Co: Dillon; Hodson, Preece, Tupling, Gibbins, Holtham (Parselle), Giles, Thackeray, Thompson (Evans), Taylor, Lewis.
Crystal Palace: Wood; O'Doherty, Barber, Gray, Nebbeling, Thomas, Redfearn, Taylor (Pardew), Bright, Wright (Hone), Salako. Scorers: Wright, Bright.
Crystal Palace won 6–0 on aggregate.

LEAGUE CUP

OLDHAM ATH (1)4 CARLISLE U (0)1 (6.10.87, 4353)
Oldham Ath: Gorton; Irwin, Donachie, Callaghan, Linighan, Milligan, Palmer, A. Henry, Cecere, Williams (N. Henry), Atkins. **Scorers:** Palmer 3, Linighan.
Carlisle U: Taylor; Patterson, Fulbrook (Gorman), Robinson, Wright, Saunders, Clark, Cooke, Poskett, Bishop, Hetherington (Tynan). **Scorer:** Cooke.
aet; Oldham Ath won 7–5 on aggregate.

PLYMOUTH ARG (0)1 PETERBOROUGH U (0)1 (6.10.87, 5524)
Plymouth Arg: Crudgington; Brimacombe, L. Cooper, Law, Smith, Matthews (J. Rowbotham), Hodges, Summerfield, Clayton, Evans, D. Rowbotham. **Scorer:** Clayton.
Peterborough U: Neenan; Paris, Gunn, Gooding, Pollard, Price, Luke, Halsall, Lawrence, Riley, Collins. **Scorer:** Gooding.
Peterborough U won 5–2 on aggregate.

ROTHERHAM U (0)0 EVERTON (0)0 (6.10.87, 12,995)
Rotherham U: O'Hanlon; Dungworth, Scott, Grealish, Johnson, Green, Pugh (Tomlinson), Williams, Evans (Haycock), Airey, Campbell.
Everton: Southall; Stevens, Van Den Hauwe, Ratcliffe, Watson, Reid, Steven, Clarke (Heath), Sharp, Snodin, Wilson.
Everton won 3–2 on aggregate.

SCUNTHORPE U (1)1 LEICESTER C (0)2 (6.10.87, 4031)
Scunthorpe U: Green; Russell, Money, Lister, Brown (Longden), Atkins, Dixon, Harle, Johnson, Flounders, Birch. **Scorer:** Johnson.
Leicester C: Cooper; Brien, James, Osman, Walsh, Ramsey, McAllister, Newell, Rantanen (Moran), Mauchlen, Reid. **Scorers:** Reid, Rantanen.
Leicester C won 4–2 on aggregate.

SHEFFIELD W (1)2 SHREWSBURY T (0)1 (6.10.87, 8572)
Sheffield W: Hodge; Sterland, Worthington, Madden, May, Jacobs, Chamberlain (Hirst), Megson, Chapman, West, Galvin. **Scorer:** West 2.
Shrewsbury T: Perks; W. Williams, B. Williams, Leonard, Pearson, Linighan, Steele, McNally, Brown, Robinson, Tester. **Scorer:** McNally (pen).
Sheffield W won 3–2 on aggregate.

SOUTHAMPTON (2)2 BOURNEMOUTH (1)2 (6.10.87, 13,429)
Southampton: Flowers; Forrest, Statham, Case, Moore, Bond, Le Tissier, Cockderill, Clarke, Townsend, D. Wallace. **Scorers:** Le Tissier, Statham.
Bournemouth: Peyton; Newson, Morrell, Brooks, Williams, Whitlock, O'Driscoll, Richards, Aylott, Pulis, Cooke (O'Connor). **Scorers:** Newson, O'Driscoll.
Bournemouth won 3–2 on aggregate.

WALSALL (2)2 CHARLTON ATH (0)0 (6.10.87, 4099)
Walsall: Barber; Dornan, Taylor, Shakespeare, Forbes, Hart, Naughton, Cross, Kelly (Goodwin), Christie, P. Jones. **Scorers:** Christie, Forbes.
Charlton Ath: Bolder; Humphrey, Reid, Peake, Shirtliff, Miller, Stuart, Lee, Leaburn, MacKenzie, Bennett.
Charlton Ath won 3–2 on aggregate.

WATFORD (3)8 DARLINGTON (0)0 (6.10.87, 8186)
Watford: Coton; Gibbs, Rostron, Morris, Terry, McClelland, Hetherston, Blissett, Roberts (Agana), Porter, Hodges. **Scorers:** Terry, Roberts, Hetherston 2, Hodges, Agana, Gibbs, Blissett.
Darlington: Crichton; Hinchley, Morgan, Hine, Robinson, Bonnyman, Bell, Ward, McAughtrie, Currie, Stonehouse.
Watford won 11–0 on aggregate.

WEST HAM U (2)2 BARNSLEY (0)5 (6.10.87, 12,403)
West Ham U: McAlister; Parris (Dickens), McQueen (Hilton), Strodder, Martin, Brady, Ward, Keen, Ince, Cottee, Robson. **Scorers:** Robson, Keen.
Barnsley: Baker; Joyce, Cross, Thomas, Gray, Futcher, Beresford, Agnew, Lowndes, Macdonald, Broddle. **Scorers:** Agnew 2 (1 pen), Beresford, Lowndes, MacDonald.
aet; 90 mins 2–2; Barnsley won 5–2 on aggregate.

WIMBLEDON (0)2 ROCHDALE (0)1 (6.10.87, 2605)
Rochdale: Welch; Lomax, Hampton, Parker, Bramhall, Smart, Seasman, Simmonds (Stanton), Parlane, Coyle, Holden. **Scorer:** Parker.
Wimbledon won 3–2 on aggregate.

WOLVERHAMPTON W (0)0 MANCHESTER C (1)2 (6.10.87, 13,843)
Wolverhampton W: Kendall; Bellamy, Thompson, Streete, Robertson, Robinson, Dennison, Vaughan, Bull, Mutch, Downing.
Manchester C: Nixon; Gidman, Hinchcliffe, Seagraves, Lake, Redmond, McNab, Stewart, Varadi (Adcock), Scott (White), Brightwell. **Scorers:** Hinchcliffe, Gidman.
Manchester C won 3–2 on aggregate.

YORK C (0)0 LEEDS U (1)4 (6.10.87, 5996)
York C: Endersby; Wood, Johnson, Whitehead, Clegg, Tuthill, Kitching, Wilson, Mills, Buchanan, Banton.
Leeds U: Day; Haddock, Ashurst, Rennie, Adams, Stiles, De Mange, Sheridan, Snodin (Doig), Taylor, Pearson (Mumby). **Scorers:** Sheridan 2, Taylor, Mumby.
Leeds U won 5–1 on aggregate.

ASTON VILLA (1)1 MIDDLESBROUGH (0)0 (7.10.87, 11,762)
Aston Villa: Spink; Gage, Gallacher, Lillis, Sims, Keown, Birch, Aspinall (Evans), McInally, S. Hunt, Walters. **Scorer:** Birch.
Middlesbrough: Pears; GLover, Cooper, Mowbray, Parkinson, Pallister, Slaven, Kernaghan (Laws), Hamilton, Kerr, Ripley.
Aston Villa won 2–0 on aggregate.

BRADFORD C (1)2 FULHAM (1)1 (7.10.87, 6408)
Bradford C: Litchfield; Mitchell, Goddard, McCall, Oliver, Evans, Sinnott (O'Shaughnessy), Palin, Hendrie, Leonard, Ormondroyd (Ellis). **Scorers:** Hendrie, McCall.
Fulham: Stannard; Elkins, Thomas, Marshall, Hopkins, Oakes, Wilson, Skinner, Rosenior, Davies, Barnett. **Scorer:** Wilson.
Bradford C won 7–2 on aggregate.

CHELSEA (3)3 READING (1)2 (7.10.87, 15,469)
Chelsea: Niedzqiecki; Clarke, Dorigo, Bodley, McLaughlin, Wood, Nevin, Hazard, Dixon, Durie (K. Wilson), C. Wilson (Coady). **Scorer:** Durie 3 (1 pen).
Reading: Francis; Jones, Richardson, Beavon, Hicks, Peters, Tait, Taylor, Gordon, Gilkes, Bailie (Canoville). **Scorer:** Gordon 2.
Reading won 5–4 on aggregate.

DERBY CO (0)0 SOUTHEND U (0)0 (7.10.87, 12,118)
Derby Co: Shilton; Sage, Forsyth (Blades), Williams, Wright, MacLaren, Callaghan, Gee, Garner, Gregory, Cross (Penney).
Southend U: Steele; Martin, Johnson, Burrows, Westley, Hall, Robinson, Pennyfather, Nogan, McDonough, Ling.
Southend U won 1–0 on aggregate.

HEREFORD U (0)1 NOTTINGHAM F (0)1 (7.10.87, 3905)
Hereford U: Rose; Jones, Devine, Stevens, Pejic, Spooner, Rodgerson, Benbow, Phillips, Stant, McLoughlin. Scorer: Stant.
Nottingham F: Sutton; Chettle, Pearce, Walker, Foster, Wilson, Carr, Webb, Clough, Wilkinson, Rice.
Nottingham F won 6–1 on aggregate.

HULL C (0)0 MANCHESTER U (0)1 (7.10.87, 13,586)
Hull C: Norman; Palmer, Herd, Jobson, Skipper, Parker, Roberts, Thompson, Saville (Payton), Askew, Williams (Jenkinson).
Manchester U: Turner; Blackmore, Gibson (O'Brien), Garton, McGrath, Duxbury (Graham), Robson, Strachan, McClair, Whiteside, Olsen. Scorer: McClair.
Manchester U won 6–0 on aggregate.

NEWCASTLE U (2)4 BLACKPOOL (1)1
(7.10.87, 20,808)
Newcastle U: Thomas (Stephenson); McDonald, Tinnion, McCreery, P. Jackson, Roeder, D. Jackson, Gascoigne (Wharton), Goddard, Mirandinha, Cornwell.
Scorers: Goddard, Mirandinha, D. Jackson, Gascoigne.
Blackpool: Siddall; Davies, Morgan, Matthews (Hutchinson), Methven, Walsh, Cunningham, Madden, Walwyn, McAteer, Taylor. Scorer: Morgan.
Newcastle U won 4–2 on aggregate.

NORTHAMPTON T (1)2 IPSWICH T (0)4 (7.10.87, 8316)
Northampton T: Gleasure; Reed, Logan, Chard, Wilcox, McPherson, Bunce (Senior), Benjamin (Donegal), Gilbert, Morley, McGoldrick. Scorers: Morley, Donegal.
Ipswich T: Hallworth; Yallop, Harbey, Humes (Milton), Dozzell, Cranson, Lowe, Brennan, D'Avray, Atkins, Stockwell. Scorers: Harbey, D'Avray 2, Lowe.
aet; 90 mins 1–1; Ipswich T won 5–3 on aggregate.

NORWICH C (0)1 BURNLEY (0)0 (7.10.87, 6168)
Norwich C: Gunn; Culverhouse, Elliott, Bruce, Phelan, Ratcliffe, Fox, Drinkell, Biggins, Williams, Bowen. Scorer: Bowen.
Burnley: Pearce; Leebrook, McGrory, James, Davis, Gardner, Farrell, Grewcock, Oghani, Comstive, Taylor.
Norwich C won 2–1 on aggregate.

PORTSMOUTH (1)1 SWINDON T (1)3
(7.10.87, 8727)
Portsmouth: Knight; Swain, Sandford, Fillery (Whitehead), Shotton, Ball, Horne, Perry (Mariner), Baird, Quinn, Hilaire. Scorer: Perry.
Swindon T: Digby; Hockaday, King, Kamara, Parkin, Calderwood, Bamber, O'Regan, Quinn (White), Foley (Henry), Barnard. Scorers: Bamber 2, White.
Swindon T won 6–2 on aggregate.

SHEFFIELD U (1)1 BURY (1)1 (7.10.87, 6377)
Sheffield U: Leaning; Wilder, Pike, Kuhl, Stancliffe, Eckhardt, Morris, Philliskirk, Beagrie, Dempsey, Frain (Mendonca). Scorer: Philliskirk.
Bury: Farnworth; Hill, Pashley, Hart, Valentine, Higgins, Lee, Robinson, Hoyland, McIlroy, Brotherston. Scorer: Robinson.
Bury won 3–2 on aggregate.

TOTTENHAM H (2)3 TORQUAY U (0)0
(7.10.87, 20,981)
Tottenham H: Clemence; Stevens, M. Thomas, Samways (Moran), Fairclough, Mabbutt, Close, P. Allen, Ardiles, Hodge, Claesen. Scorers: Claesen 2, Cole (og).
Torquay U: Allen; McNichol, Kelly, Haslegrave, Cole, Impey, Dawkins, Lloyd, Gardiner, Loram, Dobson.
Tottenham H won 3–1 on aggregate.

THIRD ROUND

ARSENAL (1)3 BOURNEMOUTH (0)0
(27.10.87, 26,050)
Arsenal: Lukic; Thomas, Sansom, Williams, O'Leary, Adams, Rocastle, Davis, Smith, Groves (Merson), Richardson. Scorers: Thomas (pen), Smith, Richardson.
Bournemouth: Peyton; Heffernan, Morrell, Brooks, Williams, Whitlock, O'Driscoll, Puckett (Pulis), Aylott, Cooke (Richards), O'Connor.

BARNSLEY (1)1 SHEFFIELD W (1)2
(27.10.87, 19,439)
Barnsley: Baker; Joyce, Cross, Thomas, Gray, Futcher, Wylde, Agnew (McGugan), Lowndes, Macdonald, Beresford (Dobbin). Scorer: Agnew.
Sheffield W: Hodge; Sterland, Worthington, Madden, May (Fee), Jacobs, Chamberlain, Megson, Chapman, West (Hirst), Galvin. Scorers: Chamberlain, Hirst.

BURY (1)1 QPR (0)0 (27.10.87, 5384)
Bury: Farnworth; Hill, Pashley, Hoyland, Valentine, Higgins, Lee, Robinson, Greenwood (Taylor), McIlroy, Brotherston. Scorer: Robinson.
QPR: Seaman; Neill, Dawes, Parker, McDonald, Fenwick, Allen, Fereday (Ferdinand), Bannister (Channing), Byrne, Pizanti.

CHARLTON ATH (0)0 BRADFORD C (1)1
(27.10.87, 3629)
Charlton Ath: Bolder; Humphrey, Reid, Peake, Shirtliff, Miller, Milne, Lee, Walsh (Stuart), Campbell, Crooks.
Bradford C: Tomlinson; Mitchell, Abbott, McCall, Oliver, Evans, Hendrie, Sinnott, Futcher (Leonard), Palin, Ellis (Ormondroyd). Scorer: Abbott.

IPSWICH T (1)1 SOUTHEND U (0)0 (27.10.87, 13,444)
Ipswich T: Hallworth; Yallop, Harbey, Rimmer (Gleghorn), Dozzell, Cranson, Lowe, Brennan, D'Avray, Zondervan, Stockwell. Scorer: Harbey.
Southend U: Steele; Ramsey, Johnson, Ling, Martin, Hall, Clark, Pennyfather, Robinson (Westley), McDonough, Rogers.

LUTON T (1)3 COVENTRY C (0)1
(Leicester, 27.10.87, 8113)
Luton T: Sealey; Breacker, Grimes, McDonough, Foster, Donaghy, Wilson, B. Stein, Harford, Johnson, Weir. Scorers: Harford 2, Weir.
Coventry C: Ogrizovic; Borrows, Downs, McGrath (Cook), Rodger, Sedgley, Bennett, Gynn, Houchen, Speedie, Pickering. Scorer: Pickering.

MANCHESTER C (2)3 NOTTINGHAM F (0)0
(27.10.87, 15,168)
Manchester C: Nixon; Gidman, Hinchcliffe, Clements, Brightwell, Redmond, White, Stewart, Varadi, McNab, Simpson. Scorers: Varadi 2, Stewart.
Nottingham F: Sutton; Chettle, Pearce, Walker, Foster (Starbuck), Wilson, Carr, Webb, Clough, Wilkinson (Osvold), Rice.

STOKE C (2)2 NORWICH C (0)1 (27.10.87, 8603)
Stoke C: Fox; Dixon, Carr, Talbot, Hemming, Berry, Ford, Parkin, Shaw, Daly, Heath. Scorers: Daly, Talbot.
Norwich C: Gunn; Culverhouse, Elliott, Bruce, Phelan, Ratcliffe, Fox, Drinkell, Biggins, Williams (Crook), Bowen (Butterworth). Scorer: Bruce.

438

LEAGUE CUP

ASTON VILLA (1)2 TOTTENHAM H (0)1
(28.10.87, 29,114)
Aston Villa: Spink; Gage, Gallacher, Lillis, Sims, Keown, Birch, Aspinall, McInally, D. Hunt, Walters. **Scorers:** McInally, Aspinall.
Tottenham H: Parks; Stevens, M. Thomas, Samways (Moran), Fairclough, Mabbutt, C. Allen, P. Allen, Ardiles, Metgod (Hughton), Claesen. **Scorer:** Ardiles.

LEEDS U (1)2 OLDHAM ATH (0)2 (28.10.87, 15,600)
Leeds U: Day; Aspin (Stiles), Adams, Williams, Ashurst, Haddock, De Mange, Sheridan, Taylor, Swan, Snodin. **Scorer:** Swan 2.
Oldham Ath: Gorton; Irwin, Donachie, Callaghan, Linighan, Milligan, Palmer, A. Henry, Cecere (Keeley), N. Henry (Wright), Williams. **Scorers:** Wright, Williams (pen).

LIVERPOOL (0)0 EVERTON (0)1 (28.10.87, 44,071)
Liverpool: Grobbelaar; Gillespie, Lawrenson, Nicol, Whelan, Hansen, Beardsley, Aldridge, Johnston, Barnes, McMahon.
Everton: Southall; Stevens, Van Den Hauwe, Ratcliffe, Watson, Reid, Steven, Heath, Sharp, Snodin, Wilson. **Scorer:** Stevens.

MANCHESTER U (2)2 CRYSTAL PALACE (1)1
(28.10.87, 27,283)
Manchester U: Turner; Anderson, Gibson, Duxbury, Garton, Moran, Robson (Blackmore), Strachan, McClair, Whiteside, Davenport (Olsen). **Scorer:** McClair 2 (1 pen).
Crystal Palace: Wood; O'Doherty, Hone, Gray, Nebbeling (Stebbing), Cannon, Redfearn, Thomas, Bright, Wright, Salako (Barber). **Scorer:** O'Doherty.

OXFORD U (0)0 LEICESTER C (0)0 (28.10.87, 6171)
Oxford U: Hucker; Bardsley, Dreyer, Shelton (Whitehurst), Slatter, Caton, Hebberd, Foyle, Saunders, Phillips, Hill (Rhoades-Brown).
Leicester C: Cooper; Morgan, James, Osman, Walsh, Ramsey, McAllister, Newell, Moran, Mauchlen, Reid.

PETERBOROUGH U (0)0 READING (0)0
(28.10.87, 6300)
Peterborough U: Neenan; Paris, Gunn, Gooding, Nightingale, Price, Luke, Halsall, Lawrence, Carr, Collins.
Reading: Westwood; Jones, Gilkes, Tait, Hicks, Curle, Williams, Taylor, Gordon, Horrix, White.

SWINDON T (1)1 WATFORD (1)1 (28.10.87, 13,833)
Swindon T: Hammond; Hockaday (Henry), King, O'Regan (Gittens), Parkin, Calderwood, Bamber, White, Quinn, Foley, Barnard. **Scorer:** Quinn (pen).
Watford: Coton; Gibbs, Rostron, Jackett, Morris, McClelland, Agana (Porter), Allen, Senior, Sherwood (Roberts), Hodges. **Scorer:** Agana.

WIMBLEDON (1)2 NEWCASTLE U (1)1
(28.10.87, 6443)
Wimbledon: Beasant; Goodyear, Bedford, Ryan, Gayle, Thorn, Fairweather, Gibson, Fashanu, Sanchez, Cork (Gannon). **Scorers:** Fashanu, Gibson.
Newcastle U: Kelly; Anderson, Tinnion, McCreery, P. Jackson, Roeder, McDonald, Gascoigne, Goddard, D. Jackson, Cornwell. **Scorer:** McDonald (pen).

THIRD ROUND REPLAYS

WATFORD (1)4 SWINDON T (1)2 (3.11.87, 13,378)
Watford: Coton; Gibbs, Rostron, Jackett, Morris, McClelland, Sherwood, Allen, Senior (Blissett), Porter, Hodges. **Scorers:** Morris, Porter, Hodges, Allen.

Swindon T: Hammond; Hockaday, King, O'Regan (White), Parkin, Calderwood, Bamber, Kamara, Quinn, Foley, Barnard. **Scorers:** Quinn, Foley.

LEICESTER C (2)2 OXFORD U (1)3 (4.11.87, 10,476)
Leicester C: Cooper; Morgan, James, Osman, Walsh, Ramsey (Ford), McAllister, Newell, Moran (Rantanen), Mauchlen, Reid. **Scorer:** Newell 2.
Oxford U: Hucker; Bardsley, Slatter, Shelton, Caton, Dreyer, Hebberd, Whitehurst, Saunders, Phillips, Rhoades-Brown. **Scorers:** Saunders, Shelton 2.

OLDHAM ATH (0)4 LEEDS U (0)2 (4.11.87, 7058)
Oldham Ath: Gorton; Irwin, Donachie, Callaghan, Linighan, Milligan, Palmer, A. Henry (N. Henry), Keeley, Wright (Morgan), Williams. **Scorers:** Keeley, Williams, Irwin, Wright.
Leeds U: Day; Williams, McDonald, De Mange, Ashurst, Haddock, Doig (Stiles), Sheridan, Taylor, Swan (Melrose), Snodin. **Scorers:** Snodin, Taylor.

READING (1)1 PETERBOROUGH U (0)0
(4.11.87, 6030)
Reading: Westwood; Jones, Gilkes, Tait, Hicks, Curle, Williams, Taylor, Gordon (Peters), Horrix, Smillie. **Scorer:** Peters.
Peterborough U: Neenan; Paris, Gunn, Gooding, Nightingale (Carr), Price, Luke, Halsall, Lawrence, Phillips (Kelly), Collins.

FOURTH ROUND

ARSENAL (1)3 STOKE C (0)0 (17.11.87, 30,058)
Arsenal: Lukic; Thomas, Sansom, Williams, O'Leary, Adams, Rocastle, Davis, Smith, Groves (Hayes), Richardson. **Scorers:** O'Leary, Rocastle, Richardson.
Stoke C: Barrett; Dixon, Parkin, Daly, Hemming, Berry, Ford, Saunders, Morgan, Shaw, Heath.

EVERTON (0)2 OLDHAM ATH (1)1 (17.11.87, 23,315)
Everton: Southall; Stevens, Van Den Hauwe, Ratcliffe, Watson, Reid, Adams, Heath, Sharp, Snodin, Sheedy. **Scorers:** Watson, Adams.
Oldham Ath: Gorton; Irwin, Callaghan, Flynn, Linighan, Milligan, Palmer, A. Henry, Atkinson, Wright, Williams. **Scorer:** Irwin.

IPSWICH T (0)0 LUTON T (1)1 (17.11.87, 15,643)
Ipswich T: Hallworth; Yallop, Harbey, Rimmer, Dozzell, Cranson, Lowe, Brennan, D'Avray (Deehan), Zondervan, Stockwell.
Luton T: Sealey; Breacker, Harvey, McDonough, Foster, Donaghy, Wilson (Black), B. Stein, Nwajiobi, Johnson (Oldfield), M. Stein. **Scorer:** B. Stein.

MANCHESTER C (1)3 WATFORD (0)1
(17.11.87, 20,357)
Manchester C: Nixon; Gidman, Brightwell, Clements, Lake, Redmond, White, Stewart, Adcock (Varadi), McNab, Simpson. **Scorers:** White 2, Stewart.
Watford: Coton; Gibbs, Rostron (Senior), Jackett, Morris, McClelland, Sherwood (Sterling), Allen, Roberts, Porter, Hodges. **Scorer:** Allen.

ASTON VILLA (1)1 SHEFFELD W (1)2
(18.11.87, 25,302)
Aston Villa: Spink; Gage, Gallacher, Lillis, Sims, Keown, Birch, Aspinall, McInally, Blair, Thompson (Evans). **Scorer:** Thompson.
Sheffield W: Hodge; Sterland, Worthington, Fee, Madden, Owen, Chamberlain, Megson, Chapman, West, Galvin (Bradshaw). **Scorers:** Chapman, West.

BURY (0)1 MANCHESTER U (0)2
(Old Trafford, 18.11.87, 33,519)
Bury: Farnworth; Hill, Pashley, Hoyland, Valentine (Hart), Higgins, Lee (Taylor), Robinson, Greenwood, McIlroy, Brotherston. **Scorer:** Hoyland.
Manchester U: Walsh; Anderson, Gibson (O'Brien), Duxbury, Blackmore, Davenport (Moses), Robson, Strachan, McClair, Whiteside, Olsen. **Scorers:** Whiteside, McClair.

OXFORD U (1)2 WIMBLEDON (0)1 (18.11.87, 5516)
Oxford U: Hucker; Bardsley, Dreyer, Shelton, Slatter, Caton, Hebberd, Whitehurst, Saunders, Phillips, Rhoades-Brown. **Wimbledon:** Beasant; Goodyear, Scales, Hazel, Gayle, Thorn, Fairweather, Wise (Jones), Fashanu, Sanchez, Gannon (Cork). **Scorer:** Cork.

READING (0)0 BRADFORD C (0)0 (18.11.87, 6784)
Reading: Westwood; Jones, Gilkes, Beavon, Hicks, Curle, Tait, Taylor, Gordon, Joseph, Smillie.
Bradford C: Tomlinson; Mitchell, Staunton, McCall, Oliver, Evans, Hendrie, Sinnott, Futcher, Palin (Abbott), Ellis.

FOURTH ROUND REPLAY

BRADFORD C (0)1 READING (0)0 (24.11.87, 10,448)
Bradford C: Tomlinson; Mitchell, Staunton, McCall, Oliver, Evans, Hendrie (Leonard), Sinnott, Futcher, Abbott (Palin), Ormondroyd. **Scorer:** Ormondroyd.
Reading: Francis; Jones, Gilkes, Beavon, Franklin, Curle, Bailie, Taylor, Gordon, Richardson, Smillie.

QUARTER-FINALS

LUTON T (0)2 BRADFORD C (0)0 (19.1.88, 11,022)
Luton T: Sealey; Breacker, Johnson, McDonough, Foster, Donaghy, Wilson, B. Stein, Harford, M. Stein, Black. **Scorers:** Foster, Harford.
Bradford C: Tomlinson; Mitchell, Goddard (Ormondroyd), McCall, Abbott, Evans, Hendrie, Hendrie, Sinnott, Futcher, Kennedy, Ellis.

EVERTON (1)2 MANCHESTER C (0)0
(20.1.88, 40,014)
Everton: Southall; Stevens, Pointon, Van Den Hauwe, Watson, Reid, Steven, Heath, Sharp (Clarke), Snodin, Wilson. **Scorers:** Heath, Sharp.
Manchester C: Nixon; Gidman, Hinchcliffe, Clements (Scott), Brightwell, Redmond, White, Stewart, Lake (Varadi), McNab, Simpson.

OXFORD U (2)2 MANCHESTER U (0)0
(20.1.88, 12,658)
Oxford U: Judge; Bardsley, Dreyer, Shelton, Briggs, Caton, Hebberd, Foyle (Whitehurst), Saunders, Phillips, Rhoades-Brown. **Scorers:** Saunders, Briggs.
Manchester U: Turner; Anderson, Gibson, Blackmore, Moran (Hogg), Duxbury, Robson, Strachan (Davenport), McClair, Whiteside, Olsen.

SHEFFIELD W (0)0 ARSENAL (0)1 (20.1.88, 34,531)
Sheffield W: Hodge; Sterland, Worthington, Madden, Fee (Chamberlain), Owen, Marwood, Megson, Chapman, West, May.
Arsenal: Lukic; Winterburn, Sansom, Williams, O'Leary, Adams, Rocastle, Rix, Smith, Quinn (Groves), Richardson. **Scorer:** Winterburn.

SEMI-FINALS, FIRST LEG

EVERTON (0)0 ARSENAL (1)1 (7.2.88, 25,476)
Everton: Southall; Stevens, Pointon, Van Den Hauwe, Watson, Reid, Steven, Heath, Sharp, Snodin, Harper (Clarke).
Arsenal: Lukic; Winterburn, Sansom, Davis, O'Leary, Adams, Rocastle (Caesar), Hayes, Smith (Quinn), Groves, Richardson. **Scorer:** Groves.

OXFORD U (0)1 LUTON T (1)1 (10.2.88, 12,943)
Oxford U: Judge; Bardsley, Dreyer, Shelton (Hill), Briggs, Caton, Hebberd, Foyle, Saunders, Phillips, Rhoades-Brown. **Scorer:** Saunders (pen).
Luton T: Sealey; Breacker, Johnson, McDonough, Foster, Donaghy, Wilson, B. Stein, Harford, M. Stein, Grimes. **Scorer:** B. Stein.

SEMI-FINALS, SECOND LEG

ARSENAL (0)3 EVERTON (0)1 (24.2.88, 51,148)
Arsenal: Lukic; Winterburn, Sansom, Thomas, O'Leary (Davis), Adams, Rocastle, Hayes, Smith, Groves, Richardson. **Scorers:** Thomas, Rocastle, Smith.
Everton: Southall; Stevens, Pointon, Van Den Hauwe (Harper), Watson, Bracewell, Steven, Clarke, Sharp, Snodin (Heath), Power. **Scorer:** Heath.
Arsenal won 4–1 on aggregate.

LUTON T (2)2 OXFORD U (0)0 (28.2.88, 13,010)
Luton T: Sealey; Breacker, Grimes, McDonough, Foster, Donaghy, Wilson, B. Stein, Harford, M. Stein, Johnson. **Scorers:** B. Stein, Grimes.
Oxford U: Judge; Bardsley, Dreyer, Hill (Shelton), Briggs, Caton, Hebberd, Foyle, Saunders, Phillips, Rhoades-Brown (Leworthy).
Luton T won 3–1 on aggregate.

FINAL

ARSENAL (0)2
LUTON T (1)3 (Wembley, 24.4.88, 95,732)
Arsenal: Lukic; Winterburn, Sansom, Thomas, Caeser, Adams, Rocastle, Davis, Smith, Groves (Hayes), Richardson. **Scorers:** Hayes, Smith.
Luton T: Dibble; Breacker, Johnson, Hill, Foster, Donaghy, Wilson, B. Stein, Harford (M. Stein), Preece (Grimes), Black. **Scorers:** B. Stein 2, Wilson.
Referee: J. Worrall (Warrington).

LEAGUE CUP FINALS 1961–88

Played as two legs until 1966. All subsequent finals at Wembley. In two-leg finals, first-named team played first leg at home. 1977 first replay at Hillsborough, second at Old Trafford. 1978 replay at Old Trafford. 1981 replay at Villa Park. 1984 replay at Maine Road.

1960–61	Rotherham U 2,0, Aston Villa 0,3*	1974–75	Aston Villa 1, Norwich C 0
1961–62	Rochdale 0,0, Norwich C 3,1	1975–76	Manchester C 2, Newcastle U 1
1962–63	Birmingham C 3,0, Aston Villa 1,0	1976–77	Aston Villa 0,1,3, Everton 0,1*,2*
1963–64	Stoke C 1,2, Leicester C 1,3	1977–78	Nottingham F 0,1, Liverpool 0*,0
1964–65	Chelsea 3,0, Leicester C 2,0	1978–79	Nottingham F 3, Southampton 2
1965–66	West Ham U 2,1, WBA 1,4	1979–80	Wolverhampton W 1, Nottingham F 0
1966–67	QPR 3, WBA 2	1980–81	Liverpool 1,2, West Ham U 1*,1
1967–68	Leeds U 1, Arsenal 0	1981–82	Liverpool 3, Tottenham H 1*
1968–69	Swindon T 3, Arsenal 1*	1982–83	Liverpool 2, Manchester U 1*
1969–70	Manchester C 2, WBA 1	1983–84	Liverpool 0,1, Everton 0*,0
1970–71	Tottenham H 2, Aston Villa 0	1984–85	Norwich C 1, Sunderland 0
1971–72	Stoke C 2, Chelsea 1	1985–86	Oxford U 3, QPR 0
1972–73	Tottenham H 1, Norwich C 0	1986–87	Arsenal 2, Liverpool 1
1973–74	Wolverhampton W 2, Manchester C 1	1987–88	Luton T 3, Arsenal 2

*After extra time (in second leg prior to 1967)

The triumphant Luton team show off the Littlewoods Challenge Cup after their thrilling victory against Arsenal. *Photo: Bob Thomas Sports Photography.*

WINS

4 – Liverpool; 3 – Aston Villa; 2 – Manchester C, Norwich C, Nottingham F, Tottenham H, Wolverhampton W; 1 – Arsenal, Birmingham C, Chelsea, Leeds U, Leicester C, Luton T, Oxford U, QPR, Stoke C, Swindon T, WBA.

APPEARANCES IN FINAL

6 – Liverpool; 5 – Aston Villa; 4 – Arsenal, Norwich C; 3 – Manchester C, Nottingham F, Tottenham H, WBA; 2 – Chelsea, Everton, Leicester C, QPR, Stoke C, West Ham U, Wolverhampton W*; 1 – Birmingham C, Leeds U*, Luton T, Manchester U, Newcastle U, Oxford U, Rochdale, Rotherham U, Southampton, Sunderland, Swindon T*.
*Undefeated.

APPEARANCES IN SEMI-FINALS

8 – Aston Villa, Liverpool; 7 – Tottenham H; 6 – Arsenal; 5 – Manchester C, Norwich C, West Ham U; 4 – Chelsea, Manchester U, WBA; 3 – Burnley, Everton, Leeds U, Nottingham F, QPR, Wolverhampton W; 2 – Birmingham C, Ipswich T, Leicester C, Oxford U, Plymouth Arg, Southampton, Stoke C, Sunderland, Swindon T; 1 – Blackburn R, Blackpool, Bolton W, Bristol C, Bury, Cardiff C, Carlisle U, Chester C, Coventry C, Derby Co, Huddersfield T, Luton T, Middlesbrough, Newcastle U, Peterborough U, Rochdale, Rotherham U, Shrewsbury T, Walsall, Watford.

LEAGUE CUP FINALS SINCE 1961

Played as two legs up to 1966.

1960–61: ROTHERHAM UNITED 2, ASTON VILLA 0 (Rotherham, 22.8.61, 12,226)
Rotherham U: Ironside; Perry, Morgan, Lambert, Madden, Waterhouse, Webster, Weston, Houghton, Kirkman, Bambridge. **Scorers:** Webster, Kirkman.
Aston Villa: Sims; Lynn, Lee, Crowe, Dugdale, Deakin, McEwan, Thomson, Brown, Wylie, McParland.

2nd LEG: ASTON VILLA 3, ROTHERHAM UNITED 0 (aet, Villa Park, 5.9.61, 27,000)
Aston Villa: Sidebottom; Neal, Lee, Crowe, Dugdale, Deakin, McEwan, O'Neill, McParland, Thomson, Burrows.
Scorers: O'Neill, Burrows, McParland.
Rotherham U: Unchanged.

1961–62: ROCHDALE 0, NORWICH CITY 3 (Rochdale, 26.4.62, 11,123)
Rochdale: Burgin; Milburn, Winton, Bodell, Aspden, Thompson, Wragg, Hepton, Bimpson, Cairns, Whitaker.
Norwich C: Kennon; McCrohan, Ashman, Burton, Butler, Mullett, Mannion, Lythgoe, Scott, Hill, Punton. **Scorers:**
Lythgoe 2, Punton.

2nd LEG: NORWICH CITY 1, ROCHDALE 0 (Norwich, 1.5.62, 19,708)
Norwich C: Unchanged. **Scorer:** Hill.
Rochdale: Whyke for Wragg, Richardson for Hepton.

1962–63: BIRMINGHAM CITY 3, ASTON VILLA 1 (St Andrews, 23.5.63, 31,850)
Birmingham C: Schofield; Lynn, Green, Hennessy, Smith, Beard, Hellawell, Bloomfield, Harris, Leek, Auld. **Scorers:**
Leek 2, Bloomfield.
Aston Villa: Sims; Fraser, Aitken, Crowe, Sleeuwenhoek, Lee, Baker, Graham, Thomson, Wylie, Burrows. **Scorer:**
Thomson.

2nd LEG: ASTON VILLA 0, BIRMINGHAM CITY 0 (Villa Park, 27.5.63, 37,920)
Aston Villa: Unchanged.
Birmingham C: Unchanged.

1963–64: STOKE CITY 1, LEICESTER CITY 1 (Stoke, 15.4.64, 22,309)
Stoke C: Leslie; Asprey, Allen, Palmer, Kinnell, Skeels, Dobing, Viollet, Ritchie, McIlroy, Bebbington. **Scorer:**
Bebbington.
Leicester C: Banks; Sjoberg, Appleton, Heath, King, Cross, Riley, Dougan, Keyworth, Gibson, Stringfellow. **Scorer:**
Gibson.

2nd LEG: LEICESTER CITY 3, STOKE CITY 2 (Leicester, 22.4.64, 25,372)
Leicester C: Unchanged. **Scorers:** Stringfellow, Gibson, Riley.
Stoke C: Unchanged. **Scorers:** Viollet, Kinnell.

1964–65: CHELSEA 3, LEICESTER CITY 2 (Stamford Bridge, 15.3.65, 20,690)
Chelsea: Bonetti; Hinton, R. Harris, Hollins, Young, Boyle, Murray, Graham, McCreadie, Venables, Tambling. **Scorers:**
Tambling, Venables (pen), McCreadie.
Leicester C: Banks; Sjoberg, Norman, Chalmers, King, Appleton, Hodgson, Cross, Goodfellow, Gibson, Sweenie.
Scorers: Appleton, Goodfellow.

2nd LEG: LEICESTER CITY 0, CHELSEA 0 (Leicester, 5.4.65, 26,958)
Leicester C: Unchanged.
Chelsea: Bonetti; Hinton, McCreadie, Harris, Mortimore, Upton, Murray, Boyle, Bridges, Venables, Tambling.

1965–66: WEST HAM UNITED 2, WEST BROMWICH ALBION 1 (Upton Park, 9.3.66, 28,3431)
West Ham U: Standen; Burnett, Burkett, Peters, Brown, Moore, Brabrook, Boyce, Byrne, Hurst, Dear. **Scorers:** Moore,
Byrne.
WBA: Potter; Cram, Fairfax, Fraser, Campbell, Williams, T. Brown, Astle, Kaye, Lovett, Clark. **Scorer:** Astle.

2nd LEG: WEST BROMWICH ALBION 4, WEST HAM UNITED 1 (The Hawthorns, 23.3.66, 31,925)
WBA: Hope for Lovett. **Scorers:** Kaye, Brown, Clark, Williams.
West Ham U: Bovington for Burkett, Sissons for Dear. **Scorer:** Peters.

1966–67: QUEEN'S PARK RANGERS 3, WEST BROMWICH ALBION 2 (Wembley, 4.3.67, 97,952)
QPR: P. Springett; Hazell, Langley, Sibley, Hunt, Keen, Lazarus, Sanderson, Allen, Marsh, R. Morgan. **Scorers:**
R. Morgan, Marsh, Lazarus.
WBA: Sheppard; Cram, Williams, Collard, D. Clarke, Fraser, T. Brown, Astle, Kaye, Hope, C. Clark. **Scorer:** C.Clark 2.

LEAGUE CUP

1967–68: LEEDS UNITED 1, ARSENAL 0 (Wembley, 2.3.68, 97,887)
Leeds U: Sprake; Reaney, Cooper, Bremner, Charlton, Hunter, J. Greenhoff, Lorimer, Madeley, Giles, E. Gray (Belfitt).
Scorer: Cooper.
Arsenal: Furnell; Storey, McNab, McLintock, Ure (Neill), Simpson, Radford, Jenkins, Graham, Sammels, Armstrong.

1968–69: SWINDON TOWN 3, ARSENAL 1 (aet, Wembley, 15.3.69, 98,189)
Swindon T: Downsborough; Thomas, Trollope, Butler, Burrows, Harland, Heath, Smart, Smith (Penman), Noble, Rogers. **Scorers:** Smart, Rogers 2.
Arsenal: Wilson; Storey, McNab, McLintock, Ure, Simpson, Radford, Sammels, Court, Gould, Armstrong. **Scorer:** Gould.

1969–70: MANCHESTER CITY 2, WEST BROMWICH ALBION 1 (Wembley, 7.3.70, 97,963)
Manchester C: Corrigan; Book, Mann, Doyle, Booth, Oakes, Heslop, Bell, Summerbee (Bowyer), Lee, Pardoe. **Scorers:** Doyle, Pardoe.
WBA: Osborne; Fraser, Wilson, T. Brown, Talbut, Kaye, Cantello, Suggett, Astle, Hartford (Krzywicki), Hope. **Scorer:** Astle.

1970–71: TOTTENHAM HOTSPUR 2, ASTON VILLA 0 (Wembley, 27.2.71, 100,000)
Tottenham H: Jennings; Kinnear, Knowles, Mullery, Collins, Beal, Gilzean, Perryman, Chivers, Peters, Neighbour. **Scorer:** Chivers 2.
Aston Villa: Dunn; Bradley, Aitken, Godfrey, Turnbull, Tiler, McMahon, Rioch, Lochhead, Hamilton, Anderson.

1971–72: STOKE CITY 2, CHELSEA 1 (Wembley, 4.3.72, 100,000)
Stoke C: Banks; Marsh, Pejic, Bernard, Smith, Bloor, Conroy, J. Greenhoff (Mahoney), Ritchie, Dobing, Eastham. **Scorers:** Conroy, Eastham.
Chelsea: Bonetti; Mulligan (Baldwin), R. Harris, Hollins, Dempsey, Webb, Cooke, Garland, Osgood, Hudson, Houseman. **Scorer:** Osgood.

1972–73: TOTTENHAM HOTSPUR 1, NORWICH CITY 0 (Wembley, 3.3.73, 100,000)
Tottenham H: Jennings; Kinnear, Knowles, Pratt (Coates), England, Beal, Gilzean, Perryman, Chivers, Peters, Pearce. **Scorer:** Coates.
Norwich C: Keelan; Payne, Butler, Stringer, Forbes, Briggs, Livermore, Blair (Howard), Cross, Paddon, Anderson.

1973–74: WOLVERHAMPTON WANDERERS 2, MANCHESTER CITY 1 (Wembley, 2.3.74, 100,000)
Wolverhampton W: Pierce; Palmer, Parkin, Bailey, Munro, McAlle, Sunderland, Hibbitt, Richards, Dougan, Wagstaffe (Powell). **Scorers:** Hibbitt, Richards.
Manchester C: MacRae; Pardoe, Donachie, Doyle, Booth, Towers, Summerbee, Bell, Lee, Law, Marsh. **Scorer:** Bell.

1974–75: ASTON VILLA 1, NORWICH CITY 0 (Wembley, 1.3.75, 100,000)
Aston Villa: Cumbes; Robson, Aitken, Ross, Nicholl, McDonald, Graydon, Little, Leonard, Hamilton, Carrodus. **Scorer:** Graydon.
Norwich C: Keelan; Machin, Sullivan, Morris, Forbes, Stringer, Miller, MacDougall, Boyer, Suggett, Powell.

1975–76: MANCHESTER CITY 2, NEWCASTLE UNITED 1 (Wembley, 28.2.76, 100,000)
Manchester C: Corrigan; G. Keegan, Donachie, Doyle, Watson, Oakes, Barnes, Booth, Royle, Hartford, Tueart. **Scorers:** Barnes, Tueart.
Newcastle U: Mahoney; Nattrass, Kennedy, Barrowclough, Keeley, Howard, Burns, Cassidy, Macdonald, Gowling, Craig. **Scorer:** Gowling.

1976–77: ASTON VILLA 0, EVERTON 0 (Wembley, 12.3.77, 100,000)
Aston Villa: Burridge; Gidman, Robson, Phillips, Nicholl, Mortimer, Deehan, Little, Gray, Cropley, Carrodus.
Everton: Lawson; Jones, Darracott, Lyons, McNaught, King, Hamilton, Dobson, Latchford, McKenzie, Goodlass.

REPLAY: ASTON VILLA 1, EVERTON 1 (aet, Hillsborough, 16.3.77, 55,000)
Aston Villa: Cowans for Cropley. **Scorer:** Kenyon (og).
Everton: Bernard for Jones, Kenyon for Dobson, Pearson came on for Hamilton. **Scorer:** Latchford.

REPLAY: ASTON VILLA 3, EVERTON 2 (aet, Old Trafford, 13.4.77, 54,749)
Aston Villa: Burridge; Gidman (Smith), Robson, Phillips, Nicholl, Mortimer, Graydon, Little, Deehan, Cropley, Cowans. **Scorers:** Little 2, Nicholl.
Everton: Lawson; Robinson, Darracott, Lyons, McNaught, King, Hamilton, Dobson, Latchford, Pearson (Seargeant), Goodlass. **Scorers:** Latchford, Lyons.

1977–78: NOTTINGHAM FOREST 0, LIVERPOOL 0 (aet, Wembley, 18.3.78, 100,000)
Nottingham F: Woods; Anderson, Clark, McGovern (O'Hare), Lloyd, Burns, O'Neill, Bowyer, Withe, Woodcock, Robertson.
Liverpool: Clemence; Neal, Hughes, Smith, Thompson, R. Kennedy (Fairclough), Dalglish, Case, Heighway, McDermott, Callaghan.

REPLAY: NOTTINGHAM FOREST 1, LIVERPOOL 0 (Old Trafford, 22.3.78, 54,375)
Nottingham F: O'Hare for McGovern. **Scorer:** Robertson (pen).
Liverpool: Unchanged. Fairclough came on for Case.

1978–79: NOTTINGHAM FOREST 3, SOUTHAMPTON 2 (Wembley, 17.3.79, 100,000)
Nottingham F: Shilton; Barrett, Clark, McGovern, Lloyd, Needham, O'Neill, Gemmill, Birtles, Woodcock, Robertson.
Scorers: Birtles 2, Woodcock.
Southampton: Gennoe; Golac, Peach, Williams, Nicholl, Waldron, Ball, Boyer, Hayes (Sealy), Holmes, Curran. **Scorers:** Peach, Holmes.

1979–80: WOLVERHAMPTON WANDERERS 1, NOTTINGHAM FOREST 0 (Wembley, 15.3.80, 100,000)
Wolverhampton W: Bradshaw; Palmer, Parkin, Daniel, Berry, Hughes, Carr, Hibbitt, A. Gray, Richards, Eves. **Scorer:** Gray.
Nottingham F: Shilton; Anderson, F. Gray, McGovern, Needham, Burns, O'Neill, Bowyer, Birtles, Francis, Robertson.

1980–81: LIVERPOOL 1, WEST HAM UNITED 1 (aet, Wembley, 14.3.81, 100,000)
Liverpool: Clemence; Neal, Irwin, Hansen, A.Kennedy, Lee, McDermott, Souness, R. Kennedy, Dalglish, Heighway (Case). **Scorer:** A. Kennedy.
West Ham U: Parkes; Stewart, Bonds, Martin, Lampard, Pike, Devonshire, Brooking, Neighbour, Cross, Goddard (Pearson). **Scorer:** Stewart (pen).

REPLAY: LIVERPOOL 2, WEST HAM UNITED 1 (Villa Park, 1.4.81, 36,693)
Liverpool: Clemence; Neal, Thompson, Hansen, A. Kennedy, Lee, McDermott, Case, R. Kennedy, Dalglish, Rush.
Scorers: Dalglish, R.Kennedy.
West Ham U: Unchanged. Pearson came on for Pike. **Scorer:** Goddard.

1981–82: LIVERPOOL 3, TOTTENHAM HOTSPUR 1 (aet, Wembley, 13.3.82, 100,000)
Liverpool: Grobbelaar; Neal, A. Kennedy, Thompson, Whelan, Lawrenson, Dalglish, Lee, Rush, McDermott (D. Johnson), Souness. **Scorers:** Whelan 2, Rush.
Tottenham H: Clemence; Hughton, Miller, Price, Hazard (Villa), Perryman, Ardiles, Archibald, Galvin, Hoddle, Crooks. **Scorer:** Archibald.

1982–83: LIVERPOOL 2, MANCHESTER UNITED 1 (aet, Wembley, 26.3.83, 100,000)
Liverpool: Grobbelaar; Neal, A. Kennedy, Lawrenson, Whelan, Hansen, Dalglish, Lee, Rush, C. Johnston (Fairclough), Souness. **Scorers:** Kennedy, Whelan.
Manchester U: Bailey; Duxbury, Albiston, Moses, Moran (Macari), McQueen, Wilkins, Muhren, Stapleton, Whiteside, Coppell. **Scorer:** Whiteside.

1983–84: LIVERPOOL 0, EVERTON 0 (aet, Wembley, 25.3.84, 100,000)
Liverpool: Grobbelaar; Neal, Kennedy, Lawrenson, Hansen, Dalglish, Lee, Whelan, Souness, Rush, C. Johnston (Robinson).
Everton: Southall; Stevens, Bailey, Ratcliffe, Mountfield, Reid, Irvine, Heath, Sharp, Richardson, Sheedy (Harper).

REPLAY: LIVERPOOL 1, EVERTON 0 (Maine Road, 28.3.84, 52,089)
Liverpool: Unchanged. **Scorer:** Souness.
Everton: Harper for Sheedy. King came on for Irvine.

1984–85: NORWICH CITY 1, SUNDERLAND 0 (Wembley, 24.3.85, 100,000)
Norwich C: Woods; Haylock, Van Wyk, Bruce, Mendham, Watson, Barham, Channon, Deehan, Hartford, Donowa. **Scorer:** Chisholm (og).
Sunderland: Turner; Venison, Pickering, Bennett, Chisholm, Corner (Gayle), Daniel, Wallace, Hodgson, Berry, Walker.

1985–86: OXFORD UNITED 3, QUEEN'S PARK RANGERS 0 (Wembley, 20.4.86, 90,396)
Oxford U: Judge; Langan, Trewick, Phillips, Briggs, Shotton, Houghton, Aldridge, Charles, Hebberd, Brock. **Scorers:** Hebberd, Houghton, Charles.
QPR: Barron; McDonald, Dawes, Neill, Wicks, Fenwick, Allen (Rosenior), James, Bannister, Byrne, Robinson.

1986–87: ARSENAL 2, LIVERPOOL 1 (Wembley, 5.4.87, 96,000)
Arsenal: Lukic; Anderson, Sansom, Williams, O'Leary, Adams, Rocastle, Davis, Quinn (Groves), Nicholas, Hayes (Thomas). **Scorer:** Nicholas 2.
Liverpool: Grobbelaar; Gillespie, Venison, Spaclman, Whelan, Hansen, Walsh (Dalglish), Johnston, Rush, Molby, McMahon (Wark). **Scorer:** Rush.

SIMOD CUP 1987–88

FIRST ROUND

BLACKBURN R (1)1 SWINDON T (1)2
(10.11.87, 3638)
Blackburn R: Gennoe; Price (Dawson), Sulley, Ainscow, Hendry, Mail, Miller, Reid, Patterson, Curry (Diamond), Sellars. **Scorer:** Reid.
Swindon T: Hammond; Hockaday, King, Barnard, Parkin, Calderwood, Bamber, Kamara, White (Henry), Gittens (Foley), Barnes. **Scorers:** Gittens, Parkin.

CHARLTON ATH (0)1 HULL C (0)1
(10.11.87, 1338)
Charlton Ath: Bolder; Humphrey, Mortimer, Gritt, Shirtliff, Miller, Bennett (Mauge), Crooks, Lee, Walsh, Stuart. **Scorer:** Walsh.
Hull C: Kelly; Palmer, Heard (Daniel), Jobson, Skipper, Parker, Roberts, Bunn (Thompson), Saville, Askew, Williams. **Scorer:** Roberts (pen).
aet; 90 mins 1–1; Charlton won 5–4 on penalties.

IPSWICH T (1)1 MIDDLESBROUGH (0)0
(10.11.87, 6108)
Ipswich T: Hallworth; Yallop, Harbey, Humes (Rimmer), Dozzell, Cranson, Lowe, Brennan, Woods (Deehan), Gleghorn, Stockwell. **Scorer:** Woods.
Middlesbrough: Poole; Glover, Laws, Mowbray, Parkinson, Pallister, Slaven (Gill), Kernaghan (Proudlock), Hamilton, Kerr, Ripley.

LEICESTER C (0)1 HUDDERSFIELD T (0)0
(10.11.87, 3440)
Leicester C: Cooper; Brien, Morgan, Osman, Walsh, McAllister, Ford, Newell, Rantanen (Moran), Jobling, Venus. **Scorer:** Ford.
Huddersfield T: Martin; McStay, Bray, Banks, Webster, Walford (Tucker), Barham, May, Shearer (Winter), Ward, Cork.

MANCHESTER C (4)6 PLYMOUTH ARG (1)2
(10.11.87, 5051)
Manchester C; Nixon; Gidman (Brightwell), Hinchcliffe, Clements, Lake, Redmond, White, Stewart, Adcock, McNab (Scott), Simpson. **Scorers:** Hinchcliffe, Adcock 3, Lake, Stewart.
Plymouth Arg: Cherry; Brimacombe, L. Cooper, Matthews, Marker, Smith, Hodges (Laws), Coughlin, Tynan, Evans (Clayton), Anderson. **Scorers:** Tynan, Coughlin.

OLDHAM ATH (0)0 WBA (3)3
(10.11.87, 1841)
Oldham Ath: Gorton; Callaghan, Edmonds, Flynn, Linighan, N. Henry, Palmer, Kelly, Cecere (Keeley), Wright, Williams (A. Henry).
WBA: Naylor; Steggles, Anderson, Palmer, Burrows, Kelly, Lynex, Dobbins, Reilly (Williamson), Robson, Morley. **Scorers:** Williamson, Lynex, Morley.

PORTSMOUTH (0)0 STOKE C (2)3
(10.11.87, 3226)
Portsmouth: Knight; Swain, Hardyman, Dillon, Mariner, Gilbert, Whitehead, Fillery (Daish), Kerr, Quinn, Perry (Stewart).
Stoke C: Fox; Dixon, Carr, Daly, Hemming, Berry, Ford, Saunders, Morgan, Shaw, Heath. **Scorers:** Gilbert (og), Daly, Shaw.

SHEFFIELD W (0)2 BOURNEMOUTH (0)0
(10.11.87, 3756)
Sheffield W: Hodge; Fee, Jacobs, Pearson, Madden, Proctor, Chamberlain (Hazel), Megson, Bradshaw (Chapman), West, Galvin. **Scorers:** Galvin, West.
Bournemouth: Peyton; Coleman, Morrell, Pulis, Williams, Whitlock (Randall), O'Driscoll, Puckett, Goulet, Howlet, Cooke (Aylott).

WEST HAM U (0)1 MILLWALL (0)2
(10.11.87, 11,737)
West Ham U: McAlister; Potts (Keen), Parris, Hilton, Martin, Brady, Ward, Dickens, Ince, Dolan, Robson. **Scorer:** Dickens.
Millwall: Horne; Salman, Coleman, Stevens, Walker, McLeary, Byrne (Lawrence), Briley, Sheringham, Cascarino, Carter. **Scorers:** Cascarino, Sheringham.

ASTON VILLA (0)0 BRADFORD C (3)5
(11.11.87, 4217)
Aston Villa: Spink; Gage, Gallacher, Lillis, Sims, McInally, Birch, Shaw, Thompson (Burke), Blair, Walters.
Bradford C: Tomlinson; Mitchell, Abbott, McCall, Oliver, Evans, Futcher (O'Shaughnessy), Sinnott, Leonard, Palin (Ormondroyd), Ellis. **Scorers:** Futcher, Mitchell, Ormondroyd, O'Shaughnessy.

OXFORD U (1)1 CRYSTAL PALACE (0)0
(11.11.87, 1478)
Oxford U: Hucker; Bardsley, Dreyer, Shelton, Briggs (Hill), Caton, Hebberd, Whitehurst, Saunders, Phillips, Rhoades-Brown. **Scorer:** Saunders (pen).
Crystal Palace: Wood; Stebbing, Burke, Pardew, Nebbeling, Cannon (O'Doherty), Redfearn, Thomas, Bright, Wright, Barber.

CHELSEA (0)2 BARNSLEY (1)1
(18.11.87, 8501)
Chelsea: Freestone; Clarke, Dorigo, Pates, McLaughlin, Wood, Nevin, C. Wilson, K. Wilson, Dixon (Hazard), Coady. **Scorers:** Hazard, Coady.
Barnsley: Baker; Hedworth, Cross, Thomas, McGugan, Futcher, Wylde, Dobbin, Agnew, Macdonald, Gray. **Scorer:** Macdonald.

DERBY CO (0)3 BIRMINGHAM C (0)1
(25.11.87, 8277)
Derby Co: Shilton; MacLaren, Forsyth, Williams, Wright, Blades, Callaghan, Garner, Gee (Penney), Gregory (McCord), Cross. **Scorers:** Trewick (og), McCord, Garner.
Birmingham C: Godden; Ranson, Trewick, Williams, Frain, Bird, Bremner, Childs (Rees), Whitton, Kennedy (Ashley), Wigley. **Scorer:** Whitton.
aet; 90 mins 0–0

LEEDS U (0)3 SHEFFIELD U (0)0
(25.11.87, 4425)
Leeds U: Day; Grayson, Adams, De Mange, Ashurst, Haddock, Batty, Rennie, Taylor, Davison, Noteman. **Scorers:** Taylor, Noteman, Rennie.
Sheffield U: Segers; Barnsley, Pike, Kuhl, Stancliffe, Smith, Dempsey, Marsden (Todd), Withe, Mendonca, Beagrie (Philliskirk).

NEWCASTLE U (1)2 SHREWSBURY T (0)1
(25.11.87, 7787)
Newcastle U: Kelly; Anderson, Wharton, Cornwell, P. Jackson, Scott, McDonald, Gascoigne, Mirandinha, Bogie, Craig (O'Neill). Scorers: Bogie, Mirandinha.
Shrewsbury T: Hughes; Green, B. Williams, Leonard, Moyes, Linighan, Steele, Priest (Crane), Brown, Robinson, Tester. Scorer: Green.

SECOND ROUND

CHARLTON ATH (1)1 LEICESTER C (0)2
(1.12.87, 1327)
Charlton Ath: Bolder; Humphrey, Reid, Gritt (Peake), Shirtliff, Thompson, Bennett, Campbell, Milne, Jones, Stuart (MacKenzie). Scorer: Brien (og).
Leicester C: Cooper; James (Rantanen), Venus, Osman, Brien, Jobling, McAllister, Newell, Reid, Cusack, Ford (Ramsey). Scorer: Jobling 2.
aet; 90 mins 1–1

IPSWICH T (1)2 WBA (0)1
(1.12.87, 5308)
Ipswich T: Hallworth; Yallop, Harbey, Atkins (Bernal), Gleghorn, Humes (D'Avray), Deehan, Brennan, Woods, Zondervan, Stockwell. Scorers: Gleghorn, Zondervan (pen).
WBA: Naylor; Palmer, Anderson, Dickinson,Hogg, Lynex, Hopkins, Goodman, Reilly, Dobbins, Morley (Robson). Scorer: Lynex (pen).

SHEFFIELD W (0)0 STOKE C (0)1
(1.12.87, 5228)
Sheffield W: Hodge; Sterland, Worthington, Madden, Pearson, Proctor, Chamberlain, Megson (Marwood), Chapman, West, Owen.
Stoke C: Barrett; Dixon, Carr, Talbot, Holmes, Berry, Ford, Daly, Morgan, Saunders (Heath), Parkin. Scorer: Berry.

BRADFORD C (0)2 NEWCASTLE U (0)1
(2.12.87, 8886)
Bradford C: Tomlinson; Mitchell, Staunton, McCall (Abbott), Oliver, Evans (Ellis), Hendrie, Sinnott, Futcher, Palin, Leonard. Scorers: Futcher, Abbott.
Newcastle U: Kelly; McDonald, Wharton, Craig, P. Jackson, Scott, Bogie, Gascoigne, O'Neill, Mirandinha, Cornwell. Scorer: Scott.

MILLWALL (1)2 LEEDS U (0)0
(8.12.87, 5034)
Millwall: Horne; Salman, Coleman, Stevens, Walker (Wood), McLeary, Lawrence (Morgan), Briley, Sheringham, Hurlock, Carter. Scorers: Walker, Sheringham.
Leeds U: Day, Aspin, Swan, De Mange, Ashurst, Haddock (Stiles) (Pearson), Batty, Sheridan, Taylor, Davison, Snodin.

MANCHESTER C (0)0 CHELSEA (0)2
(16.12.87, 6406)
Manchester C: Nixon; Gidman, Hinchcliffe, Seagrave, Lake, Redmond, White (Scott), Stewart, Adcock (Varadi), McNab, Simpson.
Chelsea: Freestone; Hall, Dorigo, Bodley, McLaughlin, Wood, Nevin, Wegerle, Dixon, K. Wilson, C. Wilson. Scorers: K. Wilson, Dixon.

FIRST ROUND

QPR (1)1 READING (0)3
(21.12.87, 4004)
QPR: Johns; Channing, Dennis, Parker, McDonald, Fenwick, Allen, Dawes, Falco, Byrne (Kerslake), Brock. Scorer: Allen.
Reading: Francis; Bailie, Gilkes, Beavon, Hicks, Curle, Jones, Madden, Tait, Horrix, Smillie (Joseph). Scorers: Jones 2, Tait.

SECOND ROUND

SWINDON T (0)2 DERBY CO (0)1
(23.12.87, 8133)
Swindon T: Hammond; Hockaday, King, Kamara, Parkin, Calderwood, Bamber, Gittens, Quinn, Foley, Barnes. Scorers: Quinn, Hockaday.
Derby Co: Shilton; Sage, Forsyth, Williams, Hindmarch, Blades, Callaghan, Garner (Penney), Gee, Lewis, McClaren. Scorer: Penney.

READING (0)1 OXFORD U (0)0
(13.1.88, 5186)
Reading: Francis; Bailie, Gilkes, Beavon, Hicks, Franklin, Williams, Madden (Smillie), Gordon, Horrix, Tait (Taylor). Scorer: Horrix.
Oxford U: Judge; Bardsley, Dreyer, Mustoe, McDonald, Caton, Hebberd, Foyle, Saunders, Hill (Nogan), Rhoades-Brown.

THIRD ROUND

COVENTRY C (1)2 WIMBLEDON (1)1
(13.1.88, 5549)
Coventry C: Ogrizovic; Borrows, Downs, McGrath, Kilcline, Peake, Bennett, Phillips, Regis, Sedgley, Gynn. Scorer: Bennett 2.
Wimbledon: Beasant; Goodyear (Scales), Phelan, Jones, Young, Gayle, Downes, Turner, Fashanu (Cork), Ryan, Gannon. Scorer: Turner.

LEICESTER C (0)0 STOKE C (0)0
(13.1.88, 5161)
Leicester C: Cooper; Morgan, Prindiville, Brien, Walsh, Ramsey, Jobling (Venus), Rantanen (Cusack), Newell, McAllister, Weir.
Stoke C: Barrett; Dixon, Carr, Talbot, Bould, Berry, Ford, Daly (Shaw), Morgan, Stainrod (Saunders), Heath.

MILLWALL (1)2 NORWICH C (2)3
(13.1.88, 4654)
Millwall: Horne; Salman, Morgan, Stevens, Walker, Wood, Byrne (O'Callaghan), Briley, Sheringham, Cascarino, Carter (Cooke). Scorer: Cascarino 2.
Norwich C: Gunn (Rosario); Culverhouse, Bowen, Putney, Phelan, Butterworth, Fox, Drinkell, Fleck, Goss, Gordon. Scorers: Fleck 2, Goss.

SIMOD CUP

SWINDON T (3)4 CHELSEA (0)0
(13.1.88, 12,317)
Swindon T: Hammond; Hockaday, King, Kamara, Parkin, Calderwood, Bamber, Gittens, Quinn, O'Regan, White. Scorers: Parkin, White 2, Quinn.
Chelsea: Freestone; Clarke, Dorigo, Pates, McLaughlin, Bumstead (C. Wilson), McAllister (Wegerle), Hazard, Dixon, K. Wilson, Wood.

BRADFORD C (1)1 SOUTHAMPTON (0)0
(25.1.88, 7844)
Bradford C: Litchfield; Mitchell, Goddard, McCall, Abbott, Evans, Hendrie, Sinnott, Ormondroyd, Kennedy, Ellis. Scorer: McCall.
Southampton: Burridge; Forrest, Statham, Le Tissier (R. Wallace), Moore, Blake, Townsend, Cockerill, Hobson, Baker, D. Wallace.

IPSWICH T (2)5 WATFORD (2)2
(25.1.88, 7466)
Ipswich T: Hallworth; Yallop, Harbey, Atkins (Gleghorn), Humes, Cranson, Lowe, Brennan, D'Avray (Deehan), Wark, Stockwell. Scorers: Wark 2 (1 pen), D'Avray, Deehan, Lowe.
Watford: Rees; Gibbs, Rumble, Pullan (Powell), Terry, Dave Holdsworth, Hetherston (Dean Holdsworth), Roberts, Senior, Sherwood, Agana. Scorers: Atkins (og), Senior.
aet; 90 mins 2–2.

READING (1)2 NOTTINGHAM F (0)1
(3.2.88, 9096)
Reading: Francis; Bailie, Gilkes, Beavon, Hicks, Curle, Williams, Taylor, Tait, Horrix, Smillie. Scorers: Horrix, Beavon.
Nottingham F: Sutton; Chettle, Pearce, Walker, Foster, Wilson, Plummer (Fleming), Webb, Glover, Wilkinson (Starbuck), Rice. Scorer: Webb.

QUARTER-FINALS

COVENTRY C (2)2 IPSWICH T (0)0
(9.2.88, 7607)
Coventry C: Ogrizovic; Borrows, Downs, McGrath (Phillips), Kilcline, Peake, Bennett, D. Smith, Speedie, Sedgley, Gynn. Scorers: Gynn, Phillips.
Ipswich T: Hallworth; Yallop, Harbey, Atkins, Humes, Dozzell (Bernal), Lowe, Brennan, Deehan, Wark, Stockwell (Gleghorn).

READING (1)2 BRADFORD C (1)1
(10.2.88, 6424)
Reading: Francis; Butler, Gilkes, Beavon, Hicks, Curle, Williams, Taylor (Madden), Tait, Horrix, Smillie. Scorers: Bailie, Horrix.
Bradford C: Tomlinson; Mitchell, Goddard, McCall, Oliver, Evans (Futcher), Hendrie, Abbott, Ormondroyd, Kennedy, Ellis (Palin). Scorer: Hendrie.
aet; 90 mins 1–1

THIRD ROUND

EVERTON (1)1 LUTON T (0)2
(10.2.88, 5204)
Everton: Southall; Jones, Pointon, Van Den Hauwe, Harper, Sheedy, Adams, Heath, Marshall, Bracewell, Power. Scorer: Power.
Luton T: Dibble; Breacker, Johnson, McEvoy, Foster, Allinson, Cobb, Gray, Oldfield, Black, Grimes. Scorer: Oldfield 2.

QUARTER-FINALS

SWINDON T (0)2 NORWICH C (0)0
(23.2.88, 10,491)
Swindon T: Digby; Hockaday, King, O'Regan, Parkin, Calderwood, Bamber, Gittens, Quinn, Foley, White. Scorers: Elliott (og), Foley.
Norwich C: Gunn; Culverhouse, Bowen (Crook), Goss, Phelan, Butterworth, Fox, Drinkell, Fleck, Elliott, Biggins.

LUTON T (1)4 STOKE C (0)1
(1.3.88, 4580)
Luton T: Sealey; Breacker, Harvey, R. Johnson, M. Johnson, Donaghy, Black, B. Stein, Harford (Oldfield), M. Stein, Allinson. Scorers: B. Stein 2, Harford 2.
Stoke C: Barrett; Beeston, Carr, Parkin, Bould, Berry, Ford, Daly, Shaw, Stainrod, Heath. Scorer: Shaw.

SEMI-FINALS

READING (0)1 COVENTRY C (0)1
(2.3.88, 15,348)
Reading: Francis; Bailie, Gilkes, Beavon, Hicks, Curle, Jones (Williams), Taylor, Tait, Horrix, Smillie. Scorer: Smillie.
Coventry C: Ogrizovic; Borrows (Rodger), Downs, Sedgley, Kilcline, Peake, Bennett, Phillips, Regis, Speedie, Pickering (D. Smith). Scorer: Speedie.
aet; 90 mins 1–1; Reading won 4–3 on penalties.

LUTON T (1)2 SWINDON T (0)1
(8.3.88, 10,027)
Luton T: Sealey; Breacker, Grimes, Johnson (Black), McDonough, Donaghy, Wilson, B. Stein, Harford, M. Stein, Allinson. Scorers: B. Stein, M. Stein.
Swindon T: Digby; Hockaday, King, Foley, Parkin, Gittens, Bamber, O'Regan, Quinn, Barnes (White), Bodin. Scorer: O'Regan.
aet; 90 mins 1–1.

FINAL

LUTON T (1)1 READING (2)4
(Wembley, 27.3.88, 61,740)
Luton T: Sealey; Breacker, Grimes, McDonough, Foster, Donaghy, Wilson, B. Stein (Johnson), Harford, M. Stein (Black), Allinson. Scorer: Harford.
Reading: Francis; Bailie, Richardson, Beavon, Hicks, Curle, Jones (Williams), Taylor, Tait (Peters), Gilkes, Smillie. Scorers: Gilkes, Beavon (pen), Tait, Smillie.
Referee: J. Martin (Alton).

SHERPA VAN TROPHY 1987–88

SOUTHERN AREA

ALDERSHOT (0)3 GILLINGHAM (0)1
(13.10.87, 1810)
Aldershot: Coles; Berry, Phillips, Roberts, Smith, Anderson, R. Barnes (Ring), Langley, Johnson, McDonald, Burvill. **Scorers:** McDonald, Berry, Johnson.
Gillingham: Kite; Haylock, Pearce, Quow, Elsey, Berry, Pritchard, Cooper, Lovell, Peacock, D. Smith. **Scorer:** Lovell.

CARDIFF C (1)3 WREXHAM (1)2
(13.10.87, 1102)
Cardiff C: Moseley; Bater, Kelly, Platnauer, Gummer, Stevenson, Mardenborough, Wheeler (Bartlett), Gilligan (Sanderson), McDermott, Ford. **Scorers:** Wheeler, McDermott, Gilligan.
Wrexham: Salmon; Preece, Wright, Hinnigan, Jones, Cunnington, Carter (Hencher), Hunter, Steel, Slater, Emson. **Scorers:** Wright, Cunnington.

COLCHESTER U (2)3 PETERBOROUGH U (0)2
(13.10.87, 912)
Colchester U: Benstead; Hinshelwood, Grenfell, Chatterton, Baker, Hedman, White, Wilkins, Tempest, Norman, Reeves. **Scorers:** Tempest 2, Norman.
Peterborough U: Neenan; Paris, Gunn, Gooding, Nightingale, Price, Luke (Carr), Halsall, Lawrence (Butterworth), Nuttell, Collins. **Scorers:** Nuttell, Gooding.

NEWPORT CO (1)2 PORT VALE (0)0
(13.10.87, 569)
Newport Co: Dillon; Hodson, Williams, Thackeray, Gibbins, Parselle, Giles, Tupling, Withers (Sugrue), Millett (Evans), Taylor. **Scorers:** Gibbins, Giles.
Port Vale: Grew; Pearson, Hughes, Walker, Hazell, Banks, Maguire, Finney, O'Kelly, Beckford, Hamson (Harper).

NOTTS CO (0)1 NORTHAMPTON T (0)0
(13.10.87, 2351)
Notts Co: Leonard; Smalley, Withe, Davis, Yates, Hart, Mills, Lund, Birtles, Pike, Fairclough. **Scorer:** Withe.
Northampton T: Gleasure; Reed, Logan, Donald, Wilcox, McPherson, Benjamin, Culpin, Gilbert, Morley, McGoldrick.

SOUTHEND U (1)1 FULHAM (0)0
(13.10.87, 1442)
Southend U: Steele; Martin, Johnson, Rogers, Burrows, Hall, Clark, Pennyfather, Nogan, McDonough, Robinson. **Scorer:** Nogan.
Fulham: Stannard; Elkins, Thomas, Skinner, Hopkins, Kerrins, Marshall, Wilson, Rosenior, Donnellan (Barnett), Walker.

TORQUAY U (2)2 BRISTOL R (0)0
(13.10.87, 1677)
Torquay U: Allen; McNichol, Gardiner, Haslegrave (Musker), Cole, Impey, Dawkins, Lloyd, Walker (Myers), Loram, Dobson. **Scorers:** Impey, McNichol.
Bristol R: Martyn; Alexander, Dryden, Tanner, Twentyman, Jones, Holloway (Meacham), Reece, White, Penrice, Purnell.

NORTHERN AREA

BOLTON W (0)0 PRESTON NE (0)0
(13.10.87, 3478)

Bolton W: Felgate; Scott, Crombie, Savage, Came, Sutton, Darby, Thompson, Thomas, Elliott, Brookman.
Preston NE: Brown; Rathbone, Bennett, Atkins, Jones, Allardyce, Williams (Miller), Swann, Ellis (Worthington), Mooney, Wrightson.

CARLISLE U (0)2 CHESTER C (1)1 (13.10.87, 1418)
Carlisle U: Taylor; Patterson, McNeil, Tynan (Robinson), Wright, Saunders, Clark, Cooke, Poskett, Bishop, Hetherington. **Scorers:** Poskett, Saunders.
Chester C: Stowell; Greenough, Woodthorpe, Fazackerley, Abel, Butler, Croft, Barrow, Rimmer, Bennett, Maddy. **Scorer:** Rimmer

DONCASTER R (0)0 MANSFIELD T (1)1
(13.10.87, 1280)
Doncaster R: Rhodes; Stead, Robinson, Raffell, Flynn, Cusack, (Humphries), Russell, Miller, Deane, Stubbs (Gorman), Rankine.
Mansfield T: Hitchcock; Graham, Ryan, Lowery (Chambers), Foster, Coleman, Kent, Hodges, McKernon, Cassells, Charles. **Scorer:** Lowery.

ROCHDALE (0)0 TRANMERE R (0)0
(13.10.87, 920)
Rochdale: Welch; Stanton, Hampton, Reid (Walling), Bramhall, Hughes, Holden, Simmonds, Parker, Coyle, Mycock.
Tranmere R: O'Rourke; Mungall, Williams, Hughes, Thorpe, Vickers, Morrissey, Harvey, Malkin, (Craven), Muir, Aspinall.

ROTHERHAM U (0)1 SCARBOROUGH (0)0
(13.10.87, 2161)
Rotherham U: O'Hanlon; Dungworth, Scott, Grealish, Johnson, Green, Tomlinson, Williams, Haycock, Airey, Campbell. **Scorer:** Green.
Scarborough: Blackwell; McJannet, Thompson, Bennyworth, Richards, Graham, Adams (Bowman), Moss, McHale, Cook, Mell.

SCUNTHORPE U (0)2 GRIMSBY T (0)0
(13.10.87, 1710)
Scunthorpe U: Heyes; Russell, Atkins, Taylor, Lister, Money, Dixon, Harle, Johnson (Stevenson), Flounders, Longden. **Scorers:** Dixon, Stevenson.
Grimsby T: Sherwood; Toale, Stephenson, Turner, Slack, Burgess, Robinson, Walsh, North (Rawcliffe), Dixon, McGarvey (Grocock).

WIGAN ATH (1)2 CREWE ALEX (0)2
(13.10.87, 1552)
Wigan Ath: Adkins; Butler, Knowles, Hamilton, Beesley, Holden, Hilditch, Thompson, Campbell, Jewell, Griffiths. **Scorers:** Thompson, Hamilton (pen)
Crewe Alex: Greygoose; Goodison, Pemberton, Wright, Billing, Gage, Gymer (Ritchie), Bodak, Eli, Cutler, Murphy. **Scorers:** Eli, Cutler.

YORK C (1)3 DARLINGTON (2)4
(13.10.87, 1296)
York C: Endersby; Branagan, Johnson, Wilson, Whitehead, Clegg, Butler (Tuthill), Mills, Banton, Buchanan, Hood. **Scorers:** Mills, Banton, Whitehead.
Darlington: Crichton (McGughtrie); Outterside, Morgan, Hine, Robinson, Bonnyman, Bell, Ward, MacDonald, Currie, Stonehouse. **Scorers:** Currie, Robinson, Ward, MacDonald.

SHERPA VAN TROPHY

SOUTHERN AREA

PORT VALE (1)2 EXETER C (0)0
(26.10.87, 2176)
Port Vale: Grew; Banks, Hughes, Walker, Hazell, Sproson, Maguire, Finney, Riley, O'Kelly, Harper. Scorers: O'Kelly, Riley.
Exeter C: Shaw; Cooper, Viney, Massey, Taylor, Carter, Batty, Edwards (Williams), Kellow, Delve, Harrower.

FULHAM (0)1 BRIGHTON & HA (5)6
(27.10.87, 2272)
Fulham: Stannard; Elkins, Langley, Skinner, Oakes, Kerrins, Marshall, Wilson, Rosenior, Davies, Walker (Donnellan). Scorer: Davies.
Brighton & HA: Keeley; Brown, Dublin, Curbishley, Rougvie, Gatting, Nelson, Jasper, Bremner, Wilkins, Crumplin. Scorers: Bremner 2, Crumplin, Wilkins, Nelson 2.

GILLINGHAM (1)2 LEYTON ORIENT (2)2
(27.10.87, 2558)
Gillingham: Kite; Haylock (Lillis), Pearce, Elsey, West, Greenall, Pritchard, Cooper, Lovell, Peacock (Berry), D. Smith. Scorer: Greenall 2 (1 pen).
Leyton Orient: Wells; Howard, Hughton, John, Day, Hull (Juryeff), Hales, Harvey, Shinners, Sussex, Comfort. Scorers: Comfort, Hull.

SWANSEA C (0)1 WOLVERHAMPTON W (0)1
(27.10.87, 2886)
Swansea C: Hughes; Hough, Coleman, Melville, Knill, Emmanuel, Davies, Raynor, Allon, Pascoe, Andrews. Scorer: Allon.
Wolverhampton W: Kendall; Stoutt, Thompson, Streete, Robertson, Holmes, Dennison, Vaughan, Bull, Mutch, Downing (Gallagher). Scorer: Bull.

NORTHERN AREA

GRIMSBY T (2)2 HALIFAX T (1)1
(27.10.87, 1316)
Grimsby T: Sherwood; Rawcliffe, Agnew, Watson, Slack, Burgess, Grocock, Robinson, North, O'Riordan, McGarvey. Scorers: Grocock, McGarvey.
Halifax T: Roche; Barr, Harrison, M. Matthews, Robinson, Galloway, Martin, Thornber, Ferebee, Allison, Holden. Scorer: Robinson.

MANSFIELD T (0)3 HARTLEPOOL U (1)2
(27.10.87, 2170)
Mansfield T: Beasley; Graham, Ryan, Lowery, Foster, Coleman, Kent, McKernon (Hodges), Eves, Cassells, Charles. Scorers: Eves, Cassells, Smith (og).
Hartlepool U: Carr; Barratt (Kennedy), McKinnon, Nobbs, Smith, Stokes, Hall (Borthwick), Toman, Baker, Gibb, Haigh. Scorers: Smith, Kennedy.

PRESTON NE (3)5 STOCKPORT CO (0)2
(27.10.87, 1968)
Preston NE: Kelly; Miller, Wrightson, Atkins, Walker, Lowey, Mooney, Swann, Ellis, Jemson, Hildersley. Scorers: Jemson 2 (1 pen), Swann, Mooney, Ellis.
Stockport Co: Marples; Bullock, Bailey, Robinson, Pickering, Williams, Hodkinson, Colville, Entwistle, Hartford, Birch. Scorers: Birch, Colville.

TRANMERE R (0)1 BURNLEY (1)2
(27.10.87, 1801)
Tranmere R: O'Rourke; Mungall, McCarrick, Martindale, Hughes, Vickers, Morrissey, Harvey, Moore, Muir, Williams. Scorer: Moore.
Burnley: Pearce; Daniel, Malley, James, Zelem, Gardner, Farrell, Grewcock, Oghani, Comstive, Taylor (Britton). Scorers: Oghani, Grewcock.

WREXHAM (2)2 WALSALL (1)2
(27.10.87, 1039)
Wrexham: Salmon; Preece, Jones, Hinnigan, Williams, Cunnington (Wright), Alleyne, Hunter, Steel, Fairbrother, Emson. Scorers: Cunnington, Jones.
Walsall: Barber; Dornan, Taylor, Shakespeare, Forbes, Hart, Rees (Jones), Goodwin, Kelly, Christie (Cross), Naughton. Scorers: Kelly, Hart.

CHESTER C (2)2 BLACKPOOL (0)1
(28.10.87, 1226)
Chester C: Stowell; Greenough, Woodthorpe, Fazackerley, Abel, Hetzke, Butler, Croft, Rimmer, Bennett, Maddy. Scorers: Rimmer, Bennett.
Blackpool: Siddall; Butler, Morgan, Matthews (Madden), Methven, Walsh (Bradshaw), Cunningham, Deary, Walwyn, McAteer, Taylor. Scorer: Greenough (og).

SCARBOROUGH (0)0 SUNDERLAND (2)3
(28.10.87, 3887)
Scarborough: Blackwell; McJannet, Thompson (Hamill), Short, Richards, Graham, Barkway, Bowman, Mell (Kendall), McHale, Cook.
Sunderland: Hesford; Kay, Agboola, Corner (Gray), MacPhail, Owers, Cornforth, Lemon, Moore (Armstrong), White, Atkinson. Scorers: Lemon 2, Moore.

SOUTHERN AREA

BRISTOL R (0)0 HEREFORD U (1)2
(28.10.87, 2158)
Bristol R: Martyn; Alexander, Tanner, Clark, Hibbitt, Jones, Holloway, Reece (Meacham), White, Penrice, Purnell.
Hereford U: Rose; Jones, Devine, Stevens, Wassall, Spooner, Rodgerson, Benbow (Pejic), Phillips, Stant (Kearns), McLoughlin. Scorers: Benbow, Phillips.

NORTHAMPTON T (0)1 BRENTFORD (0)0
(28.10.87, 3076)
Northampton T: Gleasure; Reed, Chard, Donald, Wilcox, McPherson, McGoldrick, Culpin, Gilbert, Morley, Longhurst. Scorer: Longhurst.
Brentford: Phillips; Joseph, Stanislaus, Millen, Bates, Jones, Smith, Sinton, Cooke (Booker), Blissett, Perryman (Feeley).

BRISTOL C (2)2 SWANSEA C (0)0
(10.11.87, 5037)
Bristol C: Prudhoe; Llewellyn, Bromage, Newman, Pender, Galliers, Owen, Fitzpatrick, Shutt, Walsh, Neville (Caldwell). Scorers: Walsh, Shutt.
Swansea C: Hughes; Hough (Harrison), Coleman, Melville, Knill, Emmanuel (Williams), Davies, Raynor, Allon, Pascoe, McCarthy.

BRENTFORD (2)3 NOTTS CO (2)2
(24.11.87, 2005)
Brentford: Phillips; Joseph, Stanislaus, Bates, Evans, Feeley, Turner, Sinton, Williams, Blissett, Perryman (Smith).
Scorer: Williams 3.
Notts Co: Leonard; Smalley, Withe, Fairclough, Yates, Birtles, Mills, McParland, Lund, Pike, Thorpe. Scorers: Birtles, McParland.

CAMBRIDGE U (0)0 COLCHESTER U (0)0
(24.11.87, 857)
Cambridge U: Branagan; Poole, Murray, Crowe, Beattie, Turner, Butler, Clayton, Rigby (Horwood), Purdie, Kimble.
Colchester U: Walton; Hinshelwood, Grenfell, Chatterton, Baker, Hedman, White, Wilkins, Tempest, English, Reeves (Hill).

EXETER C (0)0 NEWPORT CO (0)1
(24.11.87, 1006)
Exeter C: Shaw; Cooper, Viney, Carter, Massey, Collins, Batty, Edwards (Watson), O'Connell (Hiley), Milton, Harrower.
Newport Co: Dillon; Williams, Hodson (Preece), Sherlock, Gibbins, Giles, Thackeray, Jones, Tupling, Thompson, Mann. Scorer: Thackeray.

LEYTON ORIENT (2)2 ALDERSHOT (1)2
(24.11.87, 1606)
Leyton Orient: Wells; Howard, Dickenson, Smalley, Day, Hull, Hales, Sussex, Nugent, Godfrey (Harvey), Comfort.
Scorers: Comfort, Hull.
Aldershot: Lange; Berry, Phillips, Roberts, Anderson, Smith, Riley, Langley, Johnson, McDonald, Cottington (Burvill). Scorer: Johnson 2.

WALSALL (1)3 CARDIFF C (1)1
(24.11.87, 2420)
Walsall: Barber; Taylor, Mower, Shakespeare, Forbes, Hart, P. Jones, Cross, Kelly, Christie, Hawker. Scorers: Kelly, Cross, Hawker.
Cardiff C: Judge; Bater, Platnauer, Wimbleton, Kelly, Boyle, Curtis, Ford, Gilligan, Bartlett (Mardenborough), Sanderson. Scorer: Gilligan.

WOLVERHAMPTON W (2)3 BRISTOL C (0)1
(24.11.87, 5174)
Wolverhampton W: Kendall; Stoutt, Thompson, Streete, Clarke, Robinson, Dennison, Vaughan, Bull (Holmes), Mutch, Gallagher. Scorers: Vaughan, Bull 2.
Bristol C: Prudhoe; Llewellyn, Bromage, Rogers, Newman, Galliers, Marshall, Fitzpatrick, Shutt, Walsh, Caldwell. Scorer: Shutt.

NORTHERN AREA

BLACKPOOL (0)0 CARLISLE U (0)1
(24.11.87, 1491)
Blackpool: Siddall; Davies, Morgan (Walsh), Bradshaw, Methven, Jones, Deary, Cunningham, Walwyn, Butler (Matthews), Taylor.
Carlisle U: Taylor; McNeil, Fulbrook, Gorman, Wright, Saunders, Robinson, Cooke, Poskett, Houston, Hetherington. Scorer: Cooke.

BURNLEY (2)3 ROCHDALE (0)2
(24.11.87, 2677)
Burnley: Pearce; Farrell, Deakin, Davis, Zelem, Gardner, Britton, Grewcock (Hoskin), Reeves, Comstive, Taylor (Devaney). Scorers: Grewcock, Reeves, Farrell.
Rochdale: Welch; Seasman, Hampton, Reid, Duggan, Lomax, Warren, Simmonds, Parlane, Coyle, Gavin. Scorers: Seasman, Simmonds (pen).

BURY (2)5 WIGAN ATH (0)2
(24.11.87, 1624)
Bury: Farnworth; Hill, Pashley, Hoyland, Bishop, Hart, Lee, Robinson, Taylor, McIlroy (Brown), Brotherston.
Scorers: Lee, Hoyland, Brotherston, McIlroy 2.
Wigan Ath: Hughes; Butler, Knowles, Hamilton, Beesley, Holden, Senior, Griffiths (Pilling), Campbell, Jewell, Cook.
Scorer: Jewell 2.

CHESTERFIELD (1)2 YORK C (0)0
(24.11.87, 1197)
Chesterfield: Muggleton; Rogers, Hewitt, McGeeney, Travis, Perry, Coyle, Bloomer, Waller, Arnott, Eley.
Scorers: Arnott, Waller.
York C: Endersby; Branagan, Tuthill, Wilson, Whitehead, Clegg, Bradshaw, Mills, Helliwell, Banton, Himsworth.

HALIFAX T (1)3 SCUNTHORPE U (0)0
(24.11.87, 686)
Halifax T: Roche; Brown, Ferebee (McPhillips), M. Matthews, Shaw, Robinson, Martin, Thornber (Barr), N. Matthews, Black, Holden. Scorers: M. Matthews, N. Matthews, Martin.
Scunthorpe U: Heyes; Russell, Longden, Nicol, Lister, Brown, Dixon, Harle, Daws (Johnson), Flounders, Atkins.

HARTLEPOOL U (1)1 DONCASTER R (0)0
(24.11.87, 782)
Hartlepool U: Carr; Haigh, McKinnon, Nobbs, Smith, Stokes, Honour, Toman, Baker, Borthwick (Gibb), Barratt.
Scorer: Stokes.
Doncaster R: Rhodes; Stead, Robinson, Kinsella, Flynn, Cusack, Holmes, Miller, Deane, Turnbull, Kimble (Burke).

STOCKPORT CO (1)1 BOLTON W (1)3
(24.11.87, 2123)
Stockport Co: Marples; Bullock, Bailey, Robinson, Scott, Williams, Edwards, Colville, Entwistle (Hodkinson), Farnaby (Hendry), Birch. Scorer: Farnaby.
Bolton W: Felgate; Scott, Crombie, Savage, Came, Sutton, Brookman, Thompson, Thomas, Elliott, Darby. Scorers: Brookman, Thomas 2.

SUNDERLAND (6)7 ROTHERHAM U (1)1
(24.11.87, 6750)
Sunderland: Hesford; Burley, Agboola, Corner, MacPhail (Heathcote), Owers, Lemon, Doyle, Gates (Moore), Bertschin, Atkinson. Scorers: Corner, Burley, Lemon, Owers, Bertschin 2, Moore.
Rotherham U: O'Hanlon; Douglas, Crosby, Campbell, Dungworth, Green (Pepper), Tomlinson, Williams, Evans, Airey, Pugh. Scorer: Dungworth.

SHERPA VAN TROPHY

SOUTHERN AREA

BRIGHTON & HA (3)3 SOUTHEND U (1)2
(25.11.87, 3565)
Brighton & HA: Keeley; Brown, Dublin, Jasper, Rougvie, Gatting, Nelson, Hutchings, Bremner, Wilkins, Wood. Scorers: Jasper, Bremner, Nelson.
Southend U: Steele; Ramsey (Martin), Edinburgh, Ling, Westley, Hall, Short, Smith, Crown, McDonough, Robinson. Scorers: Westley, Hall.

HEREFORD U (0)0 TORQUAY U (1)2
(25.11.87, 1357)
Hereford U: Rose; Jones, Devine, Stevens, Pejic, Spooner, Benbow, Kearns, Stant (Phillips), Dalziel, Leadbitter.
Torquay U: Veysey; McNichol, Pearce, Myers, Cole, Burt, Dawkins, Lloyd, Loram, Smith (Dobson), Sharp. Scorers: McNichol, Lloyd.

PETERBOROUGH U (1)3 CAMBRIDGE U (0)0
(1.12.87, 1200)
Peterborough U: Neenan; Paris, Collins, Nightingale, Price, Gunn, Kelly, Gooding, Nuttell, Phillips, Luke. Scorers: Nuttell, Crowe (og), Luke.
Cambridge U: Branagan; Poole, Murray, Crowe, Beattie, Turner (Cowling), Butler, Clayton, Horwood, Purdie, Kimble.

NORTHERN AREA

CREWE ALEX (0)0 BURY (0)0
(4.12.87, 1617)
Crewe Alex: Greygoose; Goodison, Pemberton, Ritchie (Edwards), Billing, Gage, Platt, Macowat, Parker (Wright), Milligan, Murphy.
Bury: Farnworth; Hill, Bishop, Hoyland, Hart, Higgins (Greenwood), Lee, Robinson, Taylor (Valentine), McIlroy, Brotherston.

DARLINGTON (1)2 CHESTERFIELD (0)1
(5.12.87, 888)
Darlington: J. Roberts; Outterside, Morgan, Hine, Robinson, Bonnyman, A. Roberts, Ward (O'Dell), MacDonald, Currie, Stonehouse (Worthington). Scorers: MacDonald, Stonehouse.
Chesterfield: Muggleton; Rogers, Perry, McGeeney, Wood, Travis (Walker), Coyle, Grayson, Waller, Arnott, Eley. Scorer: Arnott (pen).

NORTHERN AREA PLAY-OFF

GRIMSBY T (0)1 SCUNTHORPE U (2)2
(5.12.87, 970)
Grimsby T: Sherwood; McDermott, Agnew, Turner, Curran, Robinson, Toale, Saunders, North (Watson), O'Riordan, McGarvey. Scorer: Turner.
Scunthorpe U: Heyes; Stevenson, Longden, Taylor, Nicol, Money, Dixon, Harle, Johnson, Flounders, Daws. Scorers: Harle, Flounders.

FIRST ROUND, SOUTHERN AREA

ALDERSHOT (0)1 BRISTOL C (0)0 (aet)
(19.1.88, 2662)
Aldershot: Lange; Berry, Phillips, Roberts, Smith, Wignall (Anderson), D. Barnes, Ring, Riley, McDonald, Burvill. Scorer: Burvill.
Bristol C: Waugh; Llewellyn, Bromage, Mardon, Pender, Honor (Marshall) Tanner (Jordan), Newman, Shutt, Walsh, Neville.

COLCHESTER U (1)1 LEYTON ORIENT (1)1
(19.1.88, 1351)
Colchester U: Walton; Hinshelwood, Hedman, Radford, Hill, English, White, Wilkins, Tempest, Keane, Grenfell. Scorer: White.
Leyton Orient: Wells; Howard, Dickenson, Sitton, Day, Harvey, Hales, Ketteridge (Hull), Nugent (Conroy), Juryeff, Comfort. Scorer: Juryeff.

NEWPORT CO (1)2 HEREFORD U(3)3
(19.1.88, 1232)
Newport Co: Dillon; Hodson, Clement, Tupling, Thompson (Brook), Osborne (Thackeray), Jones, Gibbins, Taylor, Mann, Sherlock. Scorers: Tupling, Mann (pen).
Hereford U: Rose; Rodgerson, Devine, Stevens, Pejic, Spooner, Benbow, Bowyer, Phillips, Stant, Leadbitter. Scorers: Stant, Phillips 2.

TORQUAY U (1)1 PORT VALE (0)0 (19.1.88, 2624)
Torquay U: Allen; McNichol (Pearce), Kelly, Haslegrave, Cole, Impey, Dawkins, Lloyd, Caldwell, Loram, Musker. Scorer: Dawkins.
Port Vale: Grew; Steggles, Hughes, Walker, Porter, Banks, Ford, Finney (Maguire), Riley, Beckford, Cole.

WALSALL (0)1 PETERBOROUGH U (1)2
(19.1.88, 2894)
Walsall: Barber; Taylor, Hawker, Shakespeare, Forbes, Hart, Christie, Cross, Kelly, Goodwin, Naughton. Scorer: Christie.
Peterborough U: Shoemake; Paris, Collins, Gooding, Gunn, Price (Carr) Nightingale, Halsall, Phillips, Kerr, Luke. Scorers: Carr, Gooding.

WOLVERHAMPTON W (1)4 BRENTFORD (0)0
(19.1.88, 6298)
Wolverhampton W: Kendall; Bellamy, Thompson, Streete, Robertson, Robinson, Dennison, Vaughan, Bull, Mutch, Downing (Holmes). Scorers: Bull 3, Dennison.
Brentford: Phillips; Joseph, Stanislaus, Millen, Evans, Feeley, Turner (Caroll), Sinton, Lee, Birch (Booker), Perryman.

FIRST ROUND, NORTHERN AREA

BURNLEY (0)1 CHESTER C (0)0 (19.1.88, 3436)
Burnley: Pearce; Farrell, Deakin, Britton, Davis, Gardner, Hoskin, Grewcock, Oghani, Comstive, Taylor. Scorer: Oghani.
Chester C: Stewart; Glenn (Greenough), Woodthorpe, Fazackerley, Abel, Butler, Maddy, Barrow, Rimmer, Graham, Croft.

BURY (0)1 BOLTON W (0)0
(19.1.88, 3796)
Bury: Farnworth; Hill, Pashley, Hoyland, Valentine, Higgins (Brotherston), Lee, Robinson, Taylor, McIlroy, Bishop. Scorer: Taylor.
Bolton W: Felgate; Hughes, Scott, Savage, Came (Brookman), Sutton, Storer (Thomas), Thompson, Stevens, Morgan, Darby.

HALIFAX T (0)2 CHESTERFIELD (1)1 (aet)
(19.1.88, 1001)
Halifax T: Roche; Brown, Barr, M. Matthews, Fleming, Richardson, Martin, Thornber (Black), N. Matthews, McPhillips (Harrison), Holden. Scorers: Allison, Black.
Chesterfield: Brown; Rogers, Perry, McGeeney, Wood, Hunter, Coyle (Benjamin), Grayson, Walker, Arnott, Eley. Scorer: Grayson.

MANSFIELD T (1)1 SCUNTHORPE U (0)0
(19.1.88, 3637)
Mansfield T: Hitchcock; Graham, Garner, Lowery, Foster, Coleman, Kent, Marks (Stubbins), Ryan, Cassells, Charles. Scorer: Charles.
Scunthorpe U: P Johnson; Money, Longden, Taylor, Lister, Atkins (S. Johnson), Dixon, Harle, Daws, (Hill), Flounders, Stevenson

PRESTON NE (2)3 ROCHDALE (0)1
(19.1.88, 2983)
Preston NE: Brown; Rathbone, Bennett, Atkins, Wrightson, Allardyce, Miller, Swann, Ellis, Brazil, Joyce. Scorers: Atkins, Swann, Ellis.
Rochdale: Welch; Smart, Lomax, Reid, Bramhall, Hughes, Harris, Simmonds, Hunt (Holden), Warren, Gavin. Scorer: Simmonds.

SUNDERLAND (0)1 CREWE ALEX (0)0
(19.1.88, 8881)
Sunderland: Hesford; Kay, Agboola, Bennett, MacPhail, Atkinson, Lemon, Doyle, Gates, Gabbiadini, Armstrong. Scorer: Gabbiadini.
Crewe Alex: Greygoose; Goodison, Pemberton, Cutler, Billing, Gage, Platt, Bodak, Eli (Murphy), Milligan, Goulet (Edwards).

SOUTHERN AREA

BRIGHTON & HA (2)4 SOUTHEND U (2)2
(20.1.88, 6654)
Brighton & HA: Keeley; Brown, Dublin, Curbishley (Cooper), Rougvie, Gatting, Nelson, Trusson, Bremner, Wilkins, Crumplin. Scorers: Nelson 2, Wilkins, Bremner.
Southend U: Steele; O'Shea, Johnson (Ramsey), Ling, McDonough, Hall, Clark, (Shaw), Smith, Crown, Robinson, Rogers. Scorers: Ling, McDonough (pen).

NOTTS CO (1)2 CARDIFF C (0)0
(20.1.88, 2704)
Notts Co: Leonard; Smalley, Davis, Kevan, Yates, Birtles, Mills, Barnes (Fairclough), Lund, Withe, Thorpe (McParland). Scorers: Barnes, McParland.
Cardiff C: Roberts; Kelly, Platnauer, Wimbleton, Stevenson, Boyle, Curtis (Wheeler), Ford, Gilligan, McDermott, Bartlett (Sanderson).

NORTHERN AREA

DARLINGTON (2)3 ROTHERHAM U (1)2
(26.1.88, 1354)
Darlington: Granger; Outterside, Morgan, Hine, Robinson, Bonnyman, Roberts, Ward, MacDonald (O'Dell), Currie, Stonehouse. Scorers: Stonehouse 2, Currie.
Rotherham U: O'Hanlon; Dungworth (Pugh), Crosby, Grealish, Green, Johnson, Buckley (Douglas), Williams, Evans, Haycock, Campbell. Scorer: Williams 2 (1 pen).

CARLISLE U (0)0 HARTLEPOOL U (0)2
(3.2.88, 1433)
Carlisle U: Coombe; Gorman, Fulbrook, Robinson (McCaffery), Wright, Saunders, Clark, Cooke, Hutchinson, Halpin, Poskett (Hetherington).
Hartlepool U: Carr; Barratt, McKinnon, Nobbs, Smith, Haigh, Honour, Toman, Baker, Tinkler, Borthwick. Scorers: Baker, Borthwick.

QUARTER-FINALS, SOUTHERN AREA

COLCHESTER U (0)2 NOTTS CO (1)3
(9.2.88, 1564)
Colchester U: Walton; Smith, Hedman, Hinshelwood, Keeley, Hill, White, Keane, Tempest, English, Grenfell. Scorer: White 2.
Notts Co: Leonard; Smalley, Withe, Kevan, Yates, Birtles, Mills, McParland, Lund, Pike, Thorpe. Scorers: McParland, Thorpe, Lund.

WOLVERHAMPTON W (1)4 PETERBOROUGH U (0)0
(9.2.88, 6155)
Wolverhampton W: Kendall; Bellamy, Thompson, Brindley, Robertson, Robinson, Dennison, Vaughan, Bull (Gallagher), Mutch, Downing (Holmes). Scorers: Bull 2, Dennison, Mutch.
Peterborough U: Shoemake; Paris, Collins, Gooding, Gunn, Price, Nightingale (Benning), Halsall, Nuttell, Carr (Kelly), Luke.

HEREFORD U (0)0 BRIGHTON & HA (0)1 (aet)
(10.2.88, 2345)
Hereford U: Rose; Rodgerson, Devine, Stevens, Pejic, Spooner, Leadbitter, Bowyer, Phillips, Stant, Campbell.
Brighton & HA: Keeley; Brown (Armstrong), Dublin, Curbishley, Rougvie, Gatting, Nelson, Trusson (Jasper), Wood, Wilkins, Crumplin. Scorer: Armstrong.

ALDERSHOT (0)0 TORQUAY U (1)1
(16.2.88, 2526)
Aldershot: Lange; Berry, Phillips, Roberts, Smith, Wignall, D. Barnes, Langley, Ring, McDonald, Burvill.
Torquay U: Allen; McNichol, Kelly, Musker, Cole, Pearce, Dawkins, Loram, Dobson, Lloyd, Caldwell. Scorer: Loram.

452

SHERPA VAN TROPHY

QUARTER-FINALS, NORTHERN AREA

BURY (0)0 BURNLEY (1)1
(9.2.88, 4672)
Bury: Farnworth; Hill, Pashley, Hart, Valentine, Higgins, Lee, Robinson, Taylor, Brotherston (Greenwood), Bishop.
Burnley: Pearce; Daniel, Deakin, Britton, Davis, Gardner, Farrell, Reeves, Taylor, Comstive, Hoskin. **Scorer:** Comstive (pen).

SUNDERLAND (0)0 HARTLEPOOL U (0)1
(9.2.88, 8976)
Sunderland: Hesford; Kay, Agboola, Bennett, MacPhail, Atkinson, Lemon, Doyle, Gates (Bertschin), Gabbiadini, Armstrong.
Hartlepool U: Carr; Barratt, McKinnon, Nobbs, Smith, Haigh, Honour, Toman, Baker, Tinkler, Borthwick. **Scorer:** Honour.

PRESTON NE (0)2 MANSFIELD T (0)1
(16.2.88, 5332)
Preston NE: Brown; Rathbone, Bennett, Atkins, Wrightson, Chapman, Mooney, Swann, Jemson (Ellis), Brazil, Joyce. **Scorer:** Brazil 2.
Mansfield T: Hitchcock; Graham, Garner (Stringfellow), Lowery, Foster, Coleman, Kent, Kenworthy, Ryan, Cassells, Charles. **Scorer:** Kent.

DARLINGTON (1)1 HALIFAX T (1)2
(18.2.88, 1510)
Darlington: Granger; Outterside, Morgan, Hine, Robinson, Bonnyman, Roberts, Ward (Bell), Macdonald (Worthington), Currie, Stonehouse. **Scorer:** Macdonald.
Halifax T: Roche; Brown, Barr, M. Matthews, Richardson, Fleming, Martin, Thornber, N. Matthews, Allison, Holden. **Scorers:** M. Matthews, N. Matthews.

SEMI-FINALS, NORTHERN AREA

BURNLEY (0)0 HALIFAX T (0)0 (aet)
(8.3.88, 10,222)
Burnley: Pearce; Daniel, Deakin, Britton, Davis, Gardner (McGrory), Farrell, Oghani, Taylor, Comstive, Grewcock (Hoskin).
Halifax T: Roche; Brown, Barr, M. Matthews, Fleming (N. Matthews), Richardson, Martin, Thornber (McPhillips), Duffield, Allison, Holden.
Burnley won 5–3 on penalties.

HARTLEPOOL U (0)0 PRESTON NE (0)2
(9.3.88, 4989)
Hartlepool U: Carr; Barratt (Gibb), McKinnon, Nobbs, Smith, Stokle, Honour, Toman, Baker (Whellans), Tinkler, Borthwick.
Preston NE: Brown; Miller, Bennett, Atkins, Jones, Chapman, Mooney, Swann, Jemson, Brazil, Joyce. **Scorers:** Atkins, Jemson.

SEMI-FINALS, SOUTHERN AREA

WOLVERHAMPTON W (1)1 TORQUAY U (0)0
(8.3.88, 11,039)
Wolverhampton W: Kendall; Stoutt, McDonald, Streete, Bellamy, Robinson, Dennison, Vaughan, Bull, Mutch, Holmes. **Scorer:** Bull.
Torquay U: Allen; McNichol, Kelly, Haslegrave, Cole, Pearce, Dawkins, Lloyd, Musker (Sharpe), Loram, Dobson.

BRIGHTON & HA (1)1 NOTTS CO (3)5
(9.3.88, 8499)
Brighton & HA: Keeley; Brown, Dublin, Curbishley, Rougvie, Gatting, Nelson, Jasper (Penney), Bremner (Armstrong), Wilkins, Wood. **Scorer:** Gatting.
Notts Co: Leonard; Smalley, Withe, Kevan, Yates, Birtles, Mills, McParland (Barnes), Lund, Pike, Thorpe. **Scorers:** Thorpe, McParland 2, Barnes 2.

SEMI-FINALS, FIRST LEG

BURNLEY (0)0 PRESTON NE (0)0
(12.4.88, 15,680)
Burnley: Pearce; McGrory, Deakin, Britton, Davis, Gardner, Farrell, Oghani, Taylor, Comstive, Hoskin.
Preston NE: Brown; Miller, Rathbone, Atkins, Allardyce, Wrightson, Mooney, Swann, Ellis, Brazil, Hildersley.

NOTTS CO (0)1 WOLVERHAMPTON W (0)1
(12.4.88, 10,041)
Notts Co: Leonard; Smalley, Fairclough, Kevan (McStay), Yates, Hart, Mills, McParland, Birtles (Lund), Pike, Withe. **Scorer:** McParland.
Wolverhampton W: Kendall; Bellamy, Thompson, Streete, Robertson, Robinson, Dennison, Downing, Bull, Mutch, Holmes. **Scorer:** Bull.

SEMI-FINALS, SECOND LEG

PRESTON NE (0)1 BURNLEY (1)3 (aet)
(19.4.88, 17,592)
Preston NE: Brown; Miller (Chapman), Joyce (Williams), Atkins, Jones, Wrightson, Mooney, Swann, Ellis, Brazil, Hildersley. **Scorer:** Brazil.
Burnley: Pearce; McGrory, Deakin, Britton, Davis, Gardner, Farrell (Malley), Oghani, Taylor, Comstive, Hoskin. **Scorers:** Oghani, Hoskin, Comstive.
Burnley won 3–1 on aggregate.

WOLVERHAMPTON W (2)3 NOTTS CO (0)0
(19.4.88, 18,413)
Wolverhampton W: Kendall; Bellamy, Thompson, Streete, Robertson, Robinson, Dennison, Downing, Bull, Mutch, Holmes. **Scorers:** Bull 2, Downing.
Notts Co: Leonard; Smalley, Fairclough, McStay, Yates, Hart, Mills, McParland, Birtles, Pike, Withe (Lund).
Wolverhampton W won 4–1 on aggregate.

FINAL AT WEMBLEY

BURNLEY (0)0 WOLVERHAMPTON W (1)2
(Wembley, 29.5.88, 80,841)
Burnley: Pearce; Daniel, Deakin, Britton, Davis, Gardner, Farrell, Oghani, Taylor, Comstive, McGrory (James).
Wolverhampton W: Kendall; Bellamy, Thompson, Streete, Robertson (Gallagher), Robinson, Dennison, Downing, Bull, Mutch, Holmes (Vaughan). **Scorers:** Mutch, Dennison.

FOOTBALL LEAGUE COMPETITIONS PAST FINALS

SUPER CUP

1985–86 (SCREEN SPORT SUPER CUP)

First Leg: LIVERPOOL (1)3, EVERTON (1)1 (Anfield, 16.9.87, 20,660)
Liverpool: Hooper; Venison, Beglin, Lawrenson, Whelan (Molby), Gillespie, Dalglish, Nicol, Rush, MacDonald, McMahon. Scorers: Rush 2, McMahon.
Everton: Mimms; Billinge, Power, Ratcliffe, Marshall, Langley, Adams, Wilkinson, Sharp, Steven, Sheedy (Aspinall). Scorer: Sheedy.

Second Leg: EVERTON (0)1, LIVERPOOL (2)4 (Goodison, 30.9.87, 26,068)
Everton: Mimms; Billinge, Power, Ratcliffe, Mountfield, Steven, Adams, Heath (Aspinall) (Pointon), Sharp, Wilkinson, Sheedy. Scorer: Wilkinson.
Liverpool: Grobbelaar; Gillespie, Beglin, Lawrenson, Whelan, Hansen, Wark, Nicol (Venison), Rush, Molby, McMahon (Walsh). Scorers: Rush 3, Nicol.

FULL MEMBERS' CUP

1985–86 CHELSEA (2)5, MANCHESTER C (1)4 (Wembley, 23.3.86, 68,000)
Chelsea: Francis; Wood, Rougvie, Pates, McLaughlin, Bumstead, Nevin, Spackman, Lee, Speedie, McAllister. Scorers: Speedie 3, Lee 2.
Manchester C: Nixon; Reid (Simpson), Power, Redmond, McCarthy, Phillips (Baker), Lillis, May, Kinsey, McNab, Wilson. Scorers: Kinsey, Lillis 2 (1 pen), Rougvie.

1986–87 BLACKBURN R (0)1, CHARLTON ATH (0)0 (Wembley, 29.3.87, 40,000)
Blackburn R: O'Keefe; Price, Sulley, Barker, Keeley, Mail, Miller, Ainscow, Hendry, Garner, Sellars (Patterson). Scorer: Hendry.
Charlton Ath: Bolder; Humphrey, Reid, Peake, Thompson, Miller, Milne, Lee, Melrose, Walsh, Shipley.

ASSOCIATE MEMBERS' CUP

1981–82 (FOOTBALL LEAGUE GROUP CUP)

GRIMSBY T (2)3, WIMBLEDON (1)2 (Grimsby, 6.4.82, 3,423)
Grimsby T: Batch (Grotier); Waters, Crosby, O'Dell, D.Moore, K.Moore, Steeples (Brolly), Ford, Whymark. Mitchell, Cumming. Scorers: Cumming, Ford 2.
Wimbledon: Beasant; Brown, Armstrong, Smith, Morris, Downes, Ketteridge (Gage), Joseph, Lazarus, Hodges, Leslie (Elliott). Scorers: Elliott, Smith.

1982–83 (FOOTBALL LEAGUE TROPHY)

MILLWALL (0)3, LINCOLN C (1)2 (Lincoln, 20.4.83, 3,142)
Millwall: Sansome; Stevens, Stride, Madden, Allardyce, Roberts, Massey, Neal, Martin, Robinson, McLeary. Scorers: Martin 2, McLeary.
Lincoln C: Felgate; Carr, Simmonite, Brazier, Peake, Strodder, Burke, Turner, Hobson, Moss, Shipley. Scorer: Burke 2.

1983–84 AFC BOURNEMOUTH (1)2, HULL C (1)1 (Hull, 24.5.84, 6,544)
Bournemouth: Leigh; Nightingale, Sulley, Beck, Brown, Brignull, O'Driscoll, Savage, Graham, Morrell, Thompson. Scorers: Graham, Morrell.
Hull C: Norman; McNeil, Swann, D.Roberts (Askey), Skipper, McEwan, Marwood, McClaren, Whitehurst, Taylor (Flounders), G.Roberts. Scorer: McNeil.

1984–85 (FREIGHT ROVER TROPHY)

WIGAN ATH (2)3, BRENTFORD (0)1 (Wembley, 1.6.85, 39,897)
Wigan Ath: Tunks; Cribley, Knowles, Kelly, Walsh, Methven, Lowe, Barrow, Bennet (Aspinall), Newell (Jewell), Langley. Scorers: Newell, Kelly, Lowe.
Brentford: Phillips; Salman, Murray, Millen, Wignall, Hurlock, Kamara, Cooke, Booker (Bullivant), Cassells, G. Roberts. Scorer: Cooke.

454

FOOTBALL LEAGUE COMPETITIONS PAST FINALS

1985–86 (FREIGHT ROVER TROPHY)

BRISTOL C (1)3, BOLTON W (0)0 (Wembley, 24.5.86, 54,000)
Bristol C: Waugh; Newman, Williams, Curle, Moyes, Riley, Pritchard, Hutchinson, Harle, Walsh, Neville. **Scorers:** Riley 2, Pritchard.
Bolton W: Farnworth; Scott, Phillips, Sutton, Came, Thompson (Bell), Neal, Oghani, Caldwell, Hartford, Gavin.

1986–87 (FREIGHT ROVER TROPHY)

MANSFIELD T (0)1, BRISTOL C (0)1 (aet, Wembley, 24.5.87, 58,586)
Mansfield T: Hitchcock; Graham, Garner, Lowery, Foster, Kenworthy, Kent, Danskin (Pollard), Whatmore (Stringfellow), Cassells, Kearney. **Scorer:** Kent.
Bristol C: Waugh; Newman, Williams, Moyes, MacPhail, Llewellyn, Owen, Marshall (Fitzpatrick), Riley, Walsh (Curle), Jordan. **Scorer:** Riley.
90 mins 1–1, Mansfield T won 5–4 on penalties.

ABERDEEN

Pittodrie Stadium, Aberdeen AB2 1QH.

Back row (left to right): Stewart McKimmie, Peter Weir, David Dodds, Brian Irvine, Ian Robertson, Willie Falconer, Tom Jones, Brian Grant. *Middle row:* Teddy Scott, Robert Connor, Gary Riddell, Jim Leighton, Steven Becket, Alex McLeish, Jim Bett, David Wylie. *Front row:* Ian Porterfield, Joe Miller, David Robertson, Ian Porteous, John Hewitt, Willie Miller, Neil Simpson, Paul Wright, Gary Hackett, Steven Gray, Jimmy Mullen.

Stadium Capacity: 22,568 (all seated)
Pitch Dimensions: 110 × 72 yds
Telephone: 0224–632328
Chairman: R. M. Donald.
Vice-Chairman: I. R. Donald.
Directors: R. M. Morrison.
Managers: Alex Smith & Jocky Scott.
Managers since 1975: Ally MacLeod, Billy McNeill, Alex Ferguson, Ian Porterfield (4).
Assistant Manager: Drew Jarvie.
Secretary: I. J. Taggart.
Founded: 1903.
Nickname: The Dons.
Former Names: None.
Former Grounds: None.
Record Attendance: 45,061 v Hearts, Scottish Cup, 13 March 1954.
Record Victory: 13–0 v Peterhead, Scottish Cup, 9 February 1923.
Record Defeat: 0–8 v Celtic, Division 1, 30 January 1965.
Most League Points: 61, Division 1, 1935–36.
Most League Goals: 96, Division 1, 1935–36.
Highest League Scorer in a Season: Benny Yorston, 38, Division 1, 1929–30.
Highest Total of League Goals: 199, Joe Harper.
Most League Appearances: 522, Willie Miller, 1973–88.
League History: 1905–06 Division 2, 1906–75 Division 1, 1975– Premier Division.
Honours: Division 1 Champions 1954–55, runners-up 1910–11, 1936–37, 1955–56, 1970–71, 1971–72. Premier Division Champions 1979–80, 1983–84, 1984–85, runners-up 1977–78, 1980–81, 1981–82. Scottish Cup winners 1947, 1970, 1982, 1983, 1984, 1986, runners-up 1937, 1953, 1954, 1959, 1967, 1978. League Cup winners 1955–56, 1976–77, 1985–86, runners-up 1946–47, 1978–79, 1987–88. European Cup-Winners' Cup winners 1983. Dryborough Cup winners 1971, 1980.
Colours: All red with white trim.

PREMIER DIVISION

CELTIC

Celtic Park, 95 Kerrydale Street, Glasgow G40 3RE.

Back row (left to right): Jim Steele (Masseur), Brian Scott (Physio), Allen McKnight, Tony Shepherd, Peter Grant, Mick McCarthy, Derek Whyte, Pat Bonner, Anton Rogan, Mark McGhee, Neil Mochan (Trainer), Billy McNeill (Manager), Owen Archdeacon, Tommy Craig (Ass. Manager). *Front row:* Tommy Burns, Billy Stark, Chris Morris, Paul McStay, Joe Miller, Roy Aitken (Captain), Frank McAvennie, Andy Walker, Lex Baillie.

Stadium Capacity: 60,800
Pitch Dimensions: 115 × 75 yds
Telephone: 041–554 2710/556 2611
Chairman: John C. McGinn.
Vice-Chairman: Kevin Kelly.
Directors: James Farrell, Christopher D. White, Thomas J. Grant.
Manager: Billy McNeill MBE.
Managers since 1975: Jock Stein, Billy McNeill, David Hay (3).
Assistant Manager: Tommy Craig.
Secretary: Desmond White & Co.
Founded: 1888.
Nickname: The Bhoys.
Former Names: None.
Former Grounds: None.
Record Attendance: 92,000 v Rangers, Division 1, 1 January 1938.
Record Victory: 11–0 v Dundee, Division 1, 26 October 1895.
Record Defeat: 0–8 v Motherwell, Division 1, 30 April 1937.
Most League Points: 72, Premier Division 1987–88.
Most League Goals: 116, Division 1, 1916–17.
Highest League Scorer in a Season: James McGrory, 50, Division 1, 1935–36.
Highest Total of League Goals: 397, James McGrory, 1922–39.
Most League Appearances: 486, Billy McNeill, 1957–75.
League History: Founder Members of Division 1 1890. 1890–1975 Division 1, 1975– Premier Division.
Honours: Division 1 Champions 1892–93, 1893–94, 1895–96, 1897–98, 1904–05, 1905–06, 1906–07, 1907–08, 1908–09, 1909–10, 1913–14, 1914–15, 1915–16, 1916–17, 1918–19, 1921–22, 1925–26, 1935–36, 1937–38, 1953–54, 1965–66, 1966–67, 1967–68, 1968–69, 1969–70, 1970–71, 1971–72, 1972–73, 1973–74. Premier Division Champions 1976–77, 1978–79, 1980–81, 1981–82, 1985–86, 1987–88. League Championship runners-up 21 times. Scottish Cup winners 1892, 1899, 1900, 1904, 1907, 1908, 1911, 1912, 1914, 1923, 1925, 1927, 1931, 1933, 1937, 1951, 1954, 1965, 1967, 1969, 1971, 1972, 1974, 1975, 1977, 1980, 1985, 1988, runners-up 15 times. League Cup winners 1956–57, 1957–58, 1965–66, 1966–67, 1967–68, 1968–69, 1969–70, 1974–75, 1982–83, runners-up 8 times. European Cup winners 1967, runners-up 1970.
Colours: Green and white hooped shirts, white shorts and socks.

DUNDEE

Dens Park, Sandeman Street, Dundee DD3 7JY.

Back row (left to right): Ross Jack, Keith Wright, Jim Smith, Stewart Forsyth, Bobby Glennie, Vince Mennie.
Middle row: Eric Ferguson (Physio), Jocky Scott (Manager), Ian Angus, Tom Carson, John Brown, Bobby Geddes, George McGeachie, Drew Jarvey (Ass. Manager), Bert Slater (Chief Scout). *Front row:* Stuart Rafferty, Tosh McKinlay, Tommy Coyne, Jim Duffy (Captain), Rab Shannon, Graham Harvey, Alan Lawrence.

Stadium Capacity: 22,381
Pitch Dimensions: 113 × 73 yds
Telephone: 0382–826104
Chairman: Angus J. Cook.
Directors: Ian R. G. Gellatly, Ian C. R. Bett, James Strachan.
Manager: Dave Smith.
Managers since 1975: David Whyte, Tommy Gemmell, Donald Mackay, Archie Knox, Jocky Scott (5).
Secretary: E. David Johnston.
Founded: 1893.
Nickname: The Dark Blues or The Dee.
Former Names: None.
Former Grounds: Carolina Port 1893–98.
Record Attendance: 43,024 v Rangers, Scottish Cup, 1953.
Record Victory: 10–0 v Alloa, Division 2 9 March 1947, and v Dunfermline Ath, Division 2, 22 March 1947.
Record Defeat: 0–11 v Celtic, Division 1, 26 October 1895.
Most League Points: 57, First Division, 1977–78.
Most League Goals: 113, Division 2, 1946–47.
Highest League Scorer in a Season: Dave Halliday, 38, Division 1, 1923–24.
Highest Total of League Goals: 113, Alan Gilzean.
Most League Appearances: 341, Doug Cowie, 1945–61.
League History: 1894–1938 Division 1, 1938–47 Division 2, 1948–75 Division 1, 1975–76 Premier Division, 1976–79 First Division, 1979–80 Premier Division, 1980–81 First Division, 1981– Premier Division.
Honours: Division 1 Champions 1961–62, runners-up 1902–03, 1906–07, 1908–09, 1948–49. First Division Champions 1978–79, runners-up 1980–81. Division 2 Champions 1946–47. Scottish Cup winners 1910, runners-up 1925, 1952, 1964. League Cup winners 1951–52, 1952–53, 1973–74, runners-up 1967–68, 1980–81.
Colours: Dark blue shirts with red and white trim, white shorts, red socks.

PREMIER DIVISION

DUNDEE UNITED

Tannadice Park, Tannadice Street, Dundee DD3 7JW.

Back row (left to right): Ian Campbell (Coach), Kevin Gallacher, Dave Bowman, Hamish French, Mixu Paateleinen, Billy Thompson, John Clark, Dave Narey, Jim McInally, Billy McKinlay, Jim McLean (Manager). *Front row:* Gordon Wallace (Ass. Manager), Alan Irvine, Ian Fergusson, Paul Hegarty, Maurice Malpas, Paul Sturrock, Eamonn Bannon, Ian McPhee, Jimmy Bone (Coach).

Stadium Capacity: 22,310
Pitch Dimensions: 110 × 74 yds
Telephone: 0382–826289
Chairman: George F. Fox.
Vice-Chairman: George M. Grant.
Directors: James Y. McLean, Douglas B. Smith, Dr Harry Leadbitter, James Littlejohn.
Manager: Jim McLean.
Managers since 1975: Jim McLean (1).
Assistant Manager: James Bone.
Secretary: Mrs Ann Diamond.
Founded: 1909.
Nickname: The Terrors.
Former Names: Dundee Hibernian 1909–23.
Former Grounds: None.
Record Attendance: 28,000 v Barcelona, Fairs Cup, 16 November 1966.
Record Victory: 14–0 v Nithsdale Wanderers, Scottish Cup 1st Round, 17 January 1931.
Record Defeat: 1–12 v Motherwell, Division 2, 23 January 1954.
Most League Points: 60, Premier Division, 1986–87.
Most League Goals: 105, Division 2, 1934–35.
Highest League Scorer in a Season: John Coyle, 41, Division 2, 1955–56.
Highest Total of League Goals: 202, Peter Mackay, in 238 appearances.
Most League Appearances: 625, Hamish McAlpine, 1969–85.
League History: 1911–15 Division 2, 1921–22 Division 2, 1923–25 Division 2, 1925–27 Division 1, 1927–29 Division 2, 1929–30 Division 1, 1930–31 Division 2, 1931–32 Division 1, 1932–60 Division 2, 1960–75 Division 1, 1975– Premier Division.
Honours: Premier Division Champions 1982–83. Division 2 Champions 1924–25, 1928–29, runners-up 1930–31, 1959–60. Scottish Cup runners-up 1974, 1981, 1985, 1987, 1988. League Cup winners 1979–80, 1980–81, runners-up 1981–82, 1984–85. UEFA Cup runners-up 1986–87.
Colours: Tangerine shirts and socks with black trim, black shorts with tangerine trim.

PREMIER DIVISION

HAMILTON ACADEMICAL
Douglas Park, Douglas Park Lane, Hamilton ML3 0DF.

Back row
(left to right):
Willie Jamieson
Gerry McCabe
Kevin McKee
Alex Taylor
Mark Coughey
Bobby Barr
Derick Walsh
Middle row:
Jim Weir
Mark Fulton
Brian Martin
David McKellar
Ronnie Yule
Chico Speirs
Adrian Sprott
Front row:
John Lambie
(Manager)
Paul McDonald
Stevie Clarke
Gerry Collins
John Gibson
William Dunlop
Bobby Reid (Physio)

Stadium Capacity: 14,505
Pitch Dimensions: 110 × 71 yds
Telephone: 0698–286103
Chairman: James W. Watson.
Directors: William P. Davidson, George McLachlan, David S. Morrison, George J. Fulston, Andrew Dick, John Heeps, Alan C. Dick.
Manager: John Lambie.
Managers since 1975: J. Eric Smith, Dave McParland, John Blackley, Bertie Auld (4).
Assistant Manager: James Dempsey.
Secretary: Alan C. Dick.
Founded: 1875.
Nickname: The Accies.
Former Names: None.
Former Grounds: Bent Farm, South Avenue, South Haugh.
Record Attendance: 28,690 v Hearts, Scottish Cup 3rd Round, 3 March 1937.
Record Victory: 10–2 v Cowdenbeath, Division 1, 15 October 1932.
Record Defeat: 1–11 v Hibernian, Division 1, 6 November 1965.
Most League Points: 56, First Division, 1985–86 & 1987–88.
Most League Goals: 91, Division 1, 1936–37, Division 2, 1959–60.
Highest League Scorer in a Season: David Wilson, 34, Division 1, 1936–37.
Highest Total of League Goals: 246, David Wilson, 1928–39.
Most League Appearances: 447, Rikkie Ferguson, 1974–88.
League History: 1897–1906 Division 2, 1906–47 Division 1, 1947–53 Division 2, 1953–54 Division 1, 1954–65 Division 2, 1965–66 Division 1, 1966–75 Division 2, 1975–86 First Division, 1986–87 Premier Division, 1987–88 First Division, 1988– Premier Division.
Honours: First Division Champions 1985–86, 1987–88. Division 2 Champions 1903–04, runners-up 1952–53, 1964–65. Scottish Cup runners-up 1911, 1935.
Colours: Red and white hooped shirts, white shorts and socks.

HEART OF MIDLOTHIAN

Tynecastle Park, Gorgie Road, Edinburgh EH11 2NL.

Back row
(left to right):
Hugh Burns
Rory MacDonald
Craig Levein
Henry Smith
Dave McPherson
Andy Bruce
Brian Whittaker
Sandy Clark
Neil Berry
Ian Jardine
Andy Watson
Front row:
Sandy Jardine
(Co-manager)
Gary Mackay
John Robertson
Alan Moore
Kenny Black
Walter Kidd
Wayne Foster
Scott Crabbe
John Colquhoun
Alex MacDonald
(Manager)

Stadium Capacity: 29,000
Pitch Dimensions: 110 × 76 yds
Telephone: 031–337 6132
Chairman: A. Wallace Mercer.
Directors: Robert Parker, Pilmar Smith, Douglas Park.
Managers: Alex MacDonald & William Jardine.
Managers since 1975: J. Hagart, W. Ormond, R. Moncur, A. MacDonald (4).
Secretary: L. W. Porteous.
Founded: 1874.
Nickname: The Jam Tarts.
Former Names: None.
Former Grounds: The Meadows 1873–78, Powderhall 1878–81, Tyneside 1881–86.
Record Attendance: 53,496 v Rangers, Scottish Cup 3rd Round, 13 February 1932.
Record Victory: 18–0 v Vale of Lothian, Edinburgh Shield, 17 September 1887.
Record Defeat: 0–7 v Hibernian, Division 1, 1 January 1973.
Most League Points: 62, Division 1, 1957–58, Premier Division 1987–88.
Most League Goals: 132, Division 1, 1957–58.
Highest League Scorer in a Season: Barney Battles, 44, Division 1, 1930–31.
Highest Total of League Goals: 206, Jimmy Wardhaugh, 1946–59.
League History: Founder Members, Division 1 1890. 1890–1975 Division 1, 1975–77 Premier Division, 1977–78 First Division, 1978–79 Premier Division, 1979–80 First Division, 1980–81 Premier Division, 1981–83 First Division, 1983–Premier Division.
Honours: Division 1 Champions 1894–95, 1896–97, 1957–58, 1959–60, runners-up 1893–94, 1989–99, 1903–04, 1905–06, 1914–15, 1937–38, 1953–54, 1956–57, 1958–59, 1964–65. First Division Champions 1979–80, runners-up 1977–78, 1982–83. Premier Division runners-up 1985–86, 1987–88. Scottish Cup winners 1891, 1896, 1901, 1906, 1956, runners-up 1903, 1907, 1968, 1976, 1986. League Cup winners 1954–55, 1958–59, 1959–60, 1962–63, runners-up 1961–62.
Colours: Maroon shirts, white shorts, maroon socks with white turnovers.

PREMIER DIVISION

HIBERNIAN

Easter Road Stadium, Albion Road, Edinburgh EH7 5QG.

Back row (left to right): Graham Mitchell, Gordon Hunter, Tom McIntyre, Gordon Chisholm, George McCluskey, Alan Sneddon, Steve Cowan. *Middle row:* Martin Ferguson (Coach), Joe Tortolano, Eddie May, Alan Rough, Calumn Milne, Paul Kane. *Front row:* Alex Miller (Manager), Mickey Weir, John Collins, Gordon Rae, Bobby Smith, Joe McBride, Peter Cormack (Ass. Manager).

Stadium Capacity: 23,353
Pitch Dimensions: 112 × 74 yds
Telephone: 031–661 2159
Chairman: David F. Duff.
Directors: James C. Gray (Managing), Charles McCole, Gregor M. Cowan, Jeremy E. James, Sheila Rowland.
Manager: Alex Miller.
Managers since 1975: Eddie Turnbull, Willie Ormond, Bertie Auld, Pat Stanton, John Blackley (5).
Assistant Manager: Peter Cormack.
Secretary: C. F. Graham.
Founded: 1875.
Nickname: The Hibees.
Former Names: None.
Former Grounds: The Meadows 1875–78, Powderhall 1878–79, Mayfield 1879–80, First Easter Road 1880–92.
Record Attendance: 65,860 v Hearts, Division 1, 2 January 1950.
Record Victory: 22–1 v 42nd Highlanders, 3 September 1881.
Record Defeat: 0–10 v Rangers, Division 1, 24 December 1898.
Most League Points: 57, First Division, 1980–81.
Most League Goals: 106, Division 1, 1959–60.
Highest League Scorer in a Season: Joe Baker, 42, Division 1, 1959–60.
Highest Total of League Goals: 364, Gordon Smith.
Most League Appearances: 446, Arthur Duncan, 1970–84.
League History: 1893–95 Divisin 2, 1895–1931 Division 1, 1931–33 Division 2, 1933–75 Division 1, 1975–80 Premier Division, 1980–81 First Division, 1981– Premier Division.
Honours: Division 1 Champions 1902–03, 1947–48, 1950–51, 1951–52, runners-up 1896–97, 1946–47, 1949–50, 1952–53, 1973–74. First Division Champions 1980–81. Division 2 Champions 1893–94, 1894–95. Scottish Cup winners 1887, 1902, runners-up 1896, 1914, 1923, 1924, 1947, 1958, 1972, 1979. League Cup winners 1972–73, runners-up 1950–51, 1968–69, 1974–75.
Colours: Green shirts with white sleeves, white shorts, green socks with white trim.

MOTHERWELL

Fir Park, Motherwell ML1 2QN.

Back row (left to right): Brian Wright, Tony McAdam, Chris McCart, Craig Paterson, Alex Kennedy, Stevie Kirk, John Philliben. *Middle row:* John Gahagan, Ray Farningham, Paul Smith, Cammy Duncan, Alasdair Maxwell, Kevin McKeown, Gordon Mair, Derek Murray, John Reilly. *Front row:* Tom McLean (Manager), Gary Fraser, Jamie Fairlie, Tom Boyd (Captain), Fraser Wishart, Bobby Russell, Tom Forsyth (Coach),.

Stadium Capacity: 23,500
Pitch Dimensions: 110 × 75 yds
Telephone: 0698–61437
Chairman: John C. Chapman.
Vice-Chairman: William H. Dickie.
Directors: George Deans, Tommy McLean.
Manager: Tommy McLean.
Managers since 1975: Ian St John, Willie McLean, Roger Hynd, Ally MacLeod, David Hay, Jock Wallace, Bobby Watson (7).
Assistant Manager: Tom Forsyth.
Secretary: Ian Alexander QPM.
Founded: 1886.
Nickname: The Well.
Former Names: None.
Former Grounds: Roman Road 1886–95.
Record Attendance: 35,632 v Rangers, Scottish Cup 4th Round replay, 12 March 1952.
Record Victory: 12–1 v Dundee U, Division 2, 23 January 1954.
Record Defeat: 0–8 v Aberdeen, Premier Division, 26 March 1979.
Most League Points: 66, Division 1, 1931–32.
Most League Goals: 119, Division 1, 1931–32.
Highest League Scorer in a Season: Willie McFadyen, 52, Division 1, 1931–32.
Highest Total of League Goals: 283, Hugh Ferguson, 1916–25.
Most League Appearances: Bobby Ferrier.
League History: 1893–1903 Division 2, 1903–53 Division 1, 1953–54 Division 2, 1954–68 Division 1, 1968–69 Division 2, 1969–75 Division 1, 1975–79 Premier Division, 1979–82 First Division, 1982–84 Premier Division, 1984–85 First Division, 1985– Premier Division.
Honours: Division 1 Champions 1931–32, runners-up 1926–27, 1929–30, 1932–33, 1933–34. First Division Champions 1981–82, 1984–85. Champions 1953–54, 1968–69, runners-up 1894–95, 1902–03. Scottish Cup winners 1952, runners-up 1931, 1933, 1939, 1951. League Cup winners 1950–51, runners-up 1954–55.
Colours: Amber shirts with claret band, claret shorts, amber socks.

PREMIER DIVISION

RANGERS

Ibrox Stadium, Glasgow G51 2XD.

*Back row
(left to right):*
Jimmy Nicholl
Trevor Francis
Stuart Munro
Avi Cohen
Graham Roberts
Iain Durrant
David Kirkwood
Middle row:
Alistair McCoist
John McGregor
Chris Woods
Mark Falco
Colin West
Nicky Walker
Jimmy Phillips
Derek Ferguson
Front row:
Walter Smith
(Ass. Manager)
Robert Fleck
Phil Boersma
(Physio)
Terry Butcher
(Captain)
Graeme Souness
(Manager)
Dave Cooper
George Soutar
(Kit Man)

Stadium Capacity: 44,500 (36,500 seated)
Pitch Dimensions: 115 × 75 yds
Telephone: 041–427 5232
Chairman/Chief Executive: David S. Holmes.
Vice-Chairman: John Gillespie.
Directors: Hugh Adam, Alfred O. Fletcher.
Manager: Graeme Souness.
Managers since 1975: Jock Wallace, John Greig, Jock Wallace (3).
Assistant Manager: Walter Smith.
Secretary: R. Campbell Ogilvie.
Founded: 1873.
Nickname: The Gers.
Former Names: None.
Former Grounds: Flesher's Haugh, Kinning Park, Burnbank.
Record Attendance: 118,567 v Celtic, Division 1, 2 January 1939.
Record Victory: 14–2 v Blairgowrie, Scottish Cup 1st Round, 20 January 1934.
Record Defeat: 2–10 v Airdrieonians, 1886.
Most League Points: 76, Division 1, 1920–21.
Most League Goals: 118, Division 1, 1931–32, 1933–34.
Highest League Scorer in a Season: Sam English, 44, Division 1, 1931–32.
Highest Total of League Goals: 233, Bob McPhail, 1927–39.
Most League Appearances: 496, John Greig, 1962–78.
League History: Founder Members of Division 1 1890. 1890–1975 Division 1, 1975– Premier Division.
Honours: Division 1 Champions 1890–91 (shared with Dumbarton), 1898–99, 1899–1900, 1900–01, 1901–02, 1910–11, 1911–12, 1912–13, 1917–18, 1919–20, 1920–21, 1922–23, 1923–24, 1924–25, 1926–27, 1927–28, 1928–29, 1929–30, 1930–31, 1932–33, 1933–34, 1934–35, 1936–37, 1938–39, 1946–47, 1948–49, 1949–50, 1952–53, 1955–56, 1956–57, 1958–59, 1960–61, 1962–63, 1963–64, 1974–75. Premier Division Champions 1975–76, 1977–78, 1986–87. Runners-up 23 times. Scottish Cup winners 1894, 1897, 1898, 1903, 1928, 1930, 1932, 1934, 1935, 1936, 1948, 1949, 1950, 1953, 1960, 1962, 1963, 1964, 1966, 1973, 1976, 1978, 1979, 1981, runners-up 14 times. League Cup winners 1946–47, 1948–49, 1960–61, 1961–62, 1963–64, 1964–65, 1970–71, 1975–76, 1977–78, 1978–79, 1981–82, 1983–84, 1984–85, 1986–87, 1987–88, runners-up 6 times. European Cup-Winners' Cup winners 1971–72, runners-up 1960–61, 1966–67.
Colours: Royal blue shirts with red and white trim, white shorts, red socks.

ST MIRREN

St Mirren Park, Love Street, Paisley PA3 2EJ.

Back row (left to right): Eddie Kerr, George Shaw, James Kelly, Paul Lambert, Norrie McWhirter, Craig Burns, Peter Feeney, Tom Callaghan, Paul McLaughlin, Danny McGill, Ross Hunter, Alan Hendry, Danny McGreish. *Middle row:* Bobby McCulley (Coach), Mark McWalter, Brian Hamilton, Garry Peebles, Keith Walker, David Winnie, Campbell Money, John Hillicoat, Les Fridge, Peter Godfrey, Neil Cooper, Robert Dawson, John Butler, Derek Hamilton, Bobby Holmes (Physio). *Front row:* Jimmy Bone (Ass. Manager), Frank McGarvey, Ian Ferguson, Brian Gallagher, Tommy Wilson, Billy Abercromby, Alex Smith (Manager), Tony Fitzpatrick, Paul Chalmers, Kenny McDowall, Ian Cameron, Gardner Speirs, Archie Rose (2nd Team Manager).

Stadium Capacity: 25,344
Pitch Dimensions: 111 × 78 yds
Telephone: 041–889 2558
Chairman: Lewis Kane.
Directors: John Corson, John Gilmour, William Todd, Allan W. Marshall, William W. Waters, J. Yule Craig.
Manager: Tony Fitzpatrick.
Managers since 1975: Alex Ferguson, Jim Clunie, Rikki MacFarlane, Alex Miller, Alex Smith (5).
Assistant Manager: Frank McGarvey.
Secretary: Allan W. Marshall.
Founded: 1877.
Nickname: The Buddies or The Paisley Saints.
Former Names: None.
Former Grounds: Short Roods 1877–79, Thistle Park Greenhill 1879–83, Westmarch 1883–94.
Record Attendance: 47,438 v Celtic, Scottish Cup 4th Round, 7 March 1925.
Record Victory: 15–0 v Glasgow University, Scottish Cup 1st Round, 30 January 1960.
Record Defeat: 0–9 v Rangers, Division 1, 4 December 1897.
Most League Points: 62, Division 2, 1967–68, First Division 1976–77.
Most League Goals: 114, Division 2, 1935–36.
Highest League Scorer in a Season: Dunky Walker, 45, Division 1, 1921–22.
Most League Appearances: 287, Billy Abercromby, 1976–87.
League History: Founder Members of Division 1 1890. 1890–1935 Division 1, 1935–36 Division 2, 1936–67 Division 1, 1967–68 Division 2, 1968–71 Division 1, 1971–75 Division 2, 1975–77 First Division, 1977– Premier Division.
Honours: First Division Champions 1976–77. Division 2 Champions 1967–68, runners-up 1935–36. Scottish Cup winners 1926, 1959, 1987, runners-up 1908, 1934, 1962. League Cup runners-up 1955–56.
Colours: Narrow black and white striped shirts with white chest panel, black shorts and socks.

DIVISION 1

AIRDRIEONIANS

Broomfield Park, Gartlea Road, Airdrie ML6 9JL.

Stadium Capacity: 11,830
Pitch Dimensions: 112 × 86 yds
Telephone: 0236–62067
Chairman: Robert H. Davidson.
Vice-Chairman: Ian L. McMillan.
Directors: James M. Ferguson, John C. Dalziel, David W. Smith, Joseph M. Rowan, George W. Peat, Robert O. Smith, Douglas J. A. Watson.
Manager: Gordon McQueen.
Managers since 1975: I. McMillan, J. Stewart, R. Watson, W. Munro, A. MacLeod, D. Whiteford (6).
Assistant Manager: Jim Duffy.
Secretary: George W. Peat CA.
Founded: 1878.
Nickname: The Diamonds or The Waysiders.
Former Names: None.
Former Grounds: Mavisbank.
Record Attendance: 24,000 v Hearts, Scottish Cup, 8 March 1952.
Record Victory: 15–1 v Dundee Wanderers, Division 2, 1 December 1894.
Record Defeat: 1–11 v Hibernian, Division 1, 24 October 1959.
Most League Points: 60, Division 2, 1973–74.
Most League Goals: 108, Division 2, 1961–62.
Highest League Scorer in a Season: Bert Yarnell, 39, Division 1, 1916–17.
Highest Total of League Goals: Club unable to supply this data.
Most League Appearances: Paul Jonquin, 523, 1962–79.
League History: 1895–1903 Division 2, 1903–36 Division 1, 1936–47 Division 2, 1947–48 Division 1, 1948–50 Division 2, 1950–54 Division 1, 1954–55 Division 2, 1955–65 Division 1, 1965–66 Division 2, 1966–73 Division 1, 1973–74 Division 2, 1974–75 Division 1, 1975–80 First Division, 1980–82 Premier Division, 1982– First Division.
Honours: Division 2 Champions 1902–03, 1954–55, 1973–74. runners-up 1922–23, 1923–24, 1924–25, 1925–26. First Division runners-up 1979–80. Division 2 runners-up 1900–01, 1946–47, 1949–50, 1965–66. Scottish Cup winners 1924, runners-up 1975.
Colours: White shirts with red diamond, white shorts, red socks with white diamond tops.

DIVISION 2

ALBION ROVERS

Cliftonhill Stadium, Main Street, Coatbridge ML5 9XX.

Stadium Capacity: 878
Pitch Dimensions: 100 × 74 yds
Telephone: 0236–32350
Chairman: David Forrester CA.
Vice-Chairman: Jack McGoogan.
Directors: Robin W. Marwick, Samuel Goodwin, David Lyttle.
Manager: Davie Provan.
Managers since 1975: George Caldwell, Sam Goodwin, Harry Hood, Joe Baker, Derek Whiteford, Martin Ferguson, Billy Wilson, Benny Rooney, Andy Ritchie, Joe Baker, Ray Franchetti, Tommy Gemmell (12).
Secretary: David Forrester CA.
Founded: 1882.
Nickname: The Wee Rovers.
Former Names: None.
Former Grounds: Cowheath Park, Meadow Park, Whifflet.
Record Attendance: 27,381 v Rangers, Scottish Cup 2nd Round, 8 February 1936.
Record Victory: 12–0 v Airdriehill, Scottish Cup, 3 September 1887.
Record Defeat: 1–9 v Motherwell, Division 1, 2 January 1937.
Most League Points: 54, Division 2, 1929–30.
Most League Goals: 101, Division 2, 1929–30.
Highest League Scorer in a Season: John Renwick, 41, Division 2, 1932–33.
Highest Total of League Goals: 105, Bunty Weir, 1928–31.
Most League Appearances: 399, Murdy Walls, 1921–36.
League History: 1904–15 Division 2, 1920–23 Division 1, 1923–34 Division 2, 1934–37 Division 1, 1937–38 Division 2, 1938–39 Division 1, 1946–48 Division 2, 1948–49 Division 1, 1949–75 Division 2, 1975– Second Division.
Honours: Division 2 Champions 1933–34, runners-up 1913–14, 1937–38, 1947–48. Scottish Cup runners-up 1920.
Colours: Yellow shirts with red and white trim, red shorts, yellow socks with red band.

DIVISION 2   ALLOA

Recreation Park, Clackmannan Road, Alloa FK10 1RR.

Stadium Capacity: 3100
Pitch Dimensions: 110 × 75 yds
Telephone: 0259–722695
Chairman: George Ormiston.
Vice-Chairman: Robert J. Hopkins.
Directors: Patrick Lawlor, John M. Keddie, Ronald J. Todd.
Manager: Gregor Abel.
Managers since 1975: H. Wilson, A. Totten, W. Garner, J. Thomson, D. Sullivan (5).
Secretary: Ewen G. Cameron.
Founded: 1883.
Nickname: The Wasps.
Former Names: None.
Former Grounds: None.
Record Attendance: 13,000 v Dunfermline Ath. , Scottish Cup 3rd Round replay, 26 February 1939.
Record Victory: 9–2 v Forfar Ath, Division 2, 18 March 1933.
Record Defeat: 0–10 v Dundee, Division 2, 8 March 1947 and v Third Lanark, League Cup, 8 August 1953.
Most League Points: 60, Division 2, 1921–22.
Most League Goals: 92, Division 2, 1961–62.
Highest League Scorer in a Season: William Crilley, 49, Division 2, 1921–22.
Most League Appearances: 237, Lawrence Haggart, 1980–88.
League History: 1921–22 Division 2, 1922–23 Division 1, 1923–75 Division 2, 1975–77 Second Division, 1977–78 First Division, 1978–82 Second Division, 1982–84 First Division, 1984–85 Second Division, 1985–86 First Division, 1986– Second Division.
Honours: Division 2 Champions 1921–22, runners-up 1938–39. Second Division runners-up 1976–77, 1981–82, 1984–85.
Colours: Gold shirts with black trim, black shorts, gold socks.

DIVISION 2   ARBROATH

Gayfield Park, Arbroath DD11 1QB.

Stadium Capacity: 10,000
Pitch Dimensions: 115 × 71 yds
Telephone: 0241–72157
Chairman: Herbert B. Crockatt.
Vice-Chairman: Ronald McLeish.
Directors: Robert Ripley, David Kean, George Johnson, Charles Kinnear, Lindsay Wood, James King.
Manager: John Young.
Managers since 1975: A. Henderson, I. J. Stewart, G. Fleming, J. Bone (4).
Assistant Manager: George Mackie.
Secretary: Ronald McLeish.
Founded: 1878.
Nickname: The Red Lichties.
Former Names: None.
Former Grounds: None.
Record Attendance: 13,510 v Rangers, Scottish Cup 3rd Round, 23 February 1952.
Record Victory: 36–0 v Bon Accord, Scottish Cup 1st Round, 12 September 1885.
Record Defeat: 0–8 v Kilmarnock, Division 2, 3 January 1949.
Most League Points: 57, Division 2, 1966–67.
Most League Goals: 87, Division 2, 1967–68.
Highest League Scorer in a Season: Dave Easson, 45, Division 2, 1958–59.
Highest Total of League Goals: 120, Jimmy Jack, 1966–71.
Most League Appearances: 445, Tom Cargill, 1966–81.
League History: 1922–35 Division 2, 1935–39 Division 1, 1946–59 Division 2, 1959–60 Division 1, 1960–68 Division 2, 1968–69 Division 1, 1969–72 Division 2, 1972–75 Division 1, 1975–80 First Division, 1980– Second Division.
Honours: Division 2 runners-up 1934–35, 1958–59, 1967–68, 1071–72.
Colours: Maroon shirts with white trim, white shorts, maroon socks with white hooped turnovers.

AYR UNITED

Somerset Park, Tryfield Place, Ayr KA8 9NB.

Stadium Capacity: 18,500
Pitch Dimensions: 111 × 72 yds
Telephone: 0292–263435
Chairman: George H. Smith.
Vice-Chairman: Robert A. G. Louden CA.
Directors: William J. Barr, Michael S. Thomson, Thomas J. Clydesdale, Donald McK. MacIntyre, Myles J. Callaghan.
Manager: Ally MacLeod.
Managers since 1975: Alex Stuart, Ally MacLeod, Willie McLean, George Caldwell (4).
Assistant Manager: David Wells.
Secretary: William J. Barr.
Assistant Secretary: Mrs Helen Nelson.
Founded: 1910.
Nickname: The Honest Men.
Former Names: None.
Former Grounds: None.
Record Attendance: 25,225 v Rangers, Division 1, 13 September 1969.
Record Victory: 11–1 v Dumbarton, League Cup, 13 August 1952.
Record Defeat: 0–9 v Rangers, Division 1, 1929, v Hearts, Division 1, 1931, v Third Lanark, Division 1 1954.
Most League Points: 61, Second Division 1987–88.
Most League Goals: 122, Division 2, 1936–37.
Highest League Scorer in a Season: Jimmy Smith, 66, 1927–28.
Most League Appearances: 318, Ian McAllister, 1977–88.
League History: 1910–13 Division 2, 1913–25 Division 1, 1925–28 Division 2, 1928–36 Division 1, 1936–37 Division 2, 1937–39 Division 1, 1946–56 Division 2, 1956–57 Division 1, 1957–59 Division 2, 1959–61 Division 1, 1961–66 Division 2, 1966–67 Division 1, 1967–69 Division 2, 1969–75 Division 1, 1975–78 Premier Division, 1978–86 First Division, 1986–88 Second Division, 1988– First Division.
Honours: Division 2 Champions 1911–12, 1912–13, 1927–28, 1936–37, 1958–59, 1965–66, runners-up 1910–11, 1955–56, 1968–69. Second Division Champions 1987–88.
Colours: White shirts with broad black chest panel and pinstripe, black shorts, white socks with black diamond tops.

BERWICK RANGERS

Shielfield Park, Tweedmouth, Berwick-upon-Tweed, TD15 2EF.

Stadium Capacity: 10,673
Pitch Dimensions: 112 × 76 yds
Telephone: 0289–307424
Chairman: Michael G. Elliott.
Vice-Chairman: John H. Hush.
Directors: David E. Cochrane, Raymond K. Gilchrist, Peter McAskill.
Manager: Jimmy Thomson.
Managers since 1975: H. Melrose, G. Haig, D. Smith, F. Connor, J. McSherry, E. Tait (6).
Secretary: Allan W. Rodger CA.
Founded: 1881.
Nickname: The Borderers.
Former Names: None.
Former Grounds: Bull Stob Close, Pier Field, Meadow Field, Union Park, Old Shielfield.
Record Attendance: 13,365 v Rangers, Scottish Cup 1st Round, 28 January 1967.
Record Victory: 8–1 v Forfar Athletic, Division 2, 25 December 1965, and v Vale of Leithen, Scottish Cup, December 1966.
Record Defeat: 1–9 v Hamilton Acad, First Division, 9 August 1980.
Most League Points: 54, Second Division, 1978–79.
Most League Goals: 83, Division 2, 1961–62.
Highest League Scorer in a Season: Ken Bowron, 38, Division 2, 1963–64.
Highest Total of League Goals: 115, Eric Tait, 1970–87.
Most League Appearances: 435, Eric Tait, 1970–87.
League History: 1951–55 Division C, 1955–75 Division 2, 1975–79 Second Division, 1979–81 First Division, 1981– Second Division.
Honours: Second Division Champions 1978–79.
Colours: All black, with gold shadow pinstripe on shirts.

BRECHIN CITY

Glebe Park, Brechin, Angus DD9 6BJ.

Stadium Capacity: 3491
Pitch Dimensions: 110 × 67 yds
Telephone: 03562–2856
President: David W. Hill.
Vice-President: Ricardo Gallaccio.
Directors: George C. Johnston, William C. Robertson, George Grant, Martin Smith, David H. Birse, David K. Lindsay.
Manager: John Ritchie.
Managers since 1975: Charlie Dunn, Ian Stewart, Doug Houston, Ian Fleming (4).
Assistant Manager: Dick Campbell.
Secretary: George C. Johnston.
Founded: 1906.
Nickname: The City.
Former Names: None.
Former Grounds: Nursery Park.
Record Attendance: 8122 v Aberdeen, Scottish Cup 3rd Round, 3 February 1973.
Record Victory: 12–1 v Thornhill, Scottish Cup 1st Round, 28 January 1926.
Record Defeat: 0–10 v Airdrieonians, Albion R & Cowdenbeath, all in Division 2, 1937–38.
Most League Points: 55, Second Division, 1982–83.
Most League Goals: 80, Division 2, 1957–58.
Highest League Scorer in a Season: W. McIntosh, 26, 1959–60.
Most League Appearances: 451, David Watt, 1975–88.
League History: 1924–26 Division 3, 1930–39 Division 2, 1946–54 Division C, 1954–75 Division 2, 1975–83 Second Division, 1983–87 First Division, 1987– Second Division.
Honours: Second Division Champions 1982–83. Division C Champions 1953–54.
Colours: All red with white trim.

CLYDE

Firhill Park, 90 Firhill Road, Glasgow G20 7AL.

Stadium Capacity: 20,600
Pitch Dimensions: 106 × 72 yds
Telephone: 041–946 9000
Hon. President: Ian V. Paterson CBE, DL, JP.
Chairman: John McBeth FRICS.
Vice-Chairman: William J. Dunn.
Directors: Robert B. Jack, Gabriel Johnstone, Harry McCall, J. Sean Fallon.
Manager: John Clark.
Managers since 1975: S. Anderson, C. Brown (2).
Assistant Manager: John Cushley.
Secretary: John D. Taylor.
Founded: 1878.
Nickname: The Bully Wee.
Former Names: None.
Former Grounds: Borrowfield Park, Shawfield Stadium.
Record Attendance: 52,000 v Rangers, Division 1, 21 November 1908.
Record Victory: 11–1 v Cowdenbeath, Division 2, 6 October 1951.
Record Defeat: 0–11 v Dumbarton, Scottish Cup 4th Round, 22 November 1879 and v Rangers, Scottish Cup 13 November 1880.
Most League Points: 64, Division 2, 1956–57.
Most League Goals: 122, Division 2, 1956–57.
Highest League Scorer in a Season: Bill Boyd, 32, Division 1, 1932–33.
Most League Appearances: 428, Brian Ahern, 1971–81, 1984–87.
League History: 1891–93 Division 1, 1893–94 Division 2, 1894–1900 Division 1, 1901–06 Division 2, 1906–24 Division 1, 1924–26 Division 2, 1926–51 Division 1, 1951–52 Division 2, 1952–56 Division 1, 1956–57 Division 2, 1957–61 Division 1, 1961–62 Division 2, 1962–63 Division 1, 1963–64 Division 2, 1964–72 Division 1, 1972–73 Division 2, 1973–75 Division 1, 1975–76 First Division, 1976–78 Second Division, 1978–80 First Division, 1980–82 Second Division, 1982– First Division.
Honours: Division 2 Champions 1904–05, 1951–52, 1956–57, 1961–62, 1972–73, runners-up 1903–04, 1905–06, 1925–26, 1963–64. Second Division Champions 1977–78, 1981–82. Scottish Cup winners 1939, 1955, 1958, runners-up 1910, 1912, 1949.
Colours: White shirts with red and black trim, black shorts, white socks.

CLYDEBANK

Kilbowie Park, Arran Place, Clydebank G81 2PB.

Stadium Capacity: 9900 (all seated)
Pitch Dimensions: 110 × 68 yds
Telephone: 041–952 2887
Chairman: C. A. Steedman.
Vice-Chairman: James Heggie.
Directors: John S. Steedman, Ian C. Steedman, William Howat, Colin L. Steedman.
Manager: Sam Henderson.
Managers since 1975: William Munro (1).
Secretary: I. C. Steedman CA.
Founded: 1965.
Nickname: The Bankies.
Former Names: None.
Former Grounds: None.
Record Attendance: 14,900 v Hibernian, Scottish Cup 1st Round, 10 February 1965.
Record Victory: 8–1 v Arbroath, First Division, 3 January 1977.
Record Defeat: 1–9 v Gala Fairydean, Scottish Cup Qualifying Round, 15 September 1965.
Most League Points: 58, First Division, 1976–77.
Most League Goals: 89, First Division, 1976–77.
Highest League Scorer in a Season: Blair Millar, 28, First Division, 1978–79.
Highest Total of League Goals: 84, Blair Millar.
Most League Appearances: 775, Jim Fallon, 1968–86.
League History: 1965–75 Division 2, 1975–76 Second Division, 1976–77 First Division, 1977–78 Premier Division, 1978–85 First Division, 1985–87 Premier Division, 1987– First Division.
Honours: Second Division Champions 1975–76. First Division runners-up 1976–77, 1984–85.
Colours: White shirts with red zig-zag band, white shorts, white socks with red hooped turnovers.

COWDENBEATH

Central Park, Cowdenbeath, KY4 9EY.

Stadium Capacity: 7250
Pitch Dimensions: 110 × 70 yds
Telephone: 0383–511205
Chairman: Thomas Currie.
Vice-Chairman: John Marshall.
Directors: Harry Ewing MP, Eric Mitchell, James Malcolm.
Manager: John Blackley.
Managers since 1975: D. McLindon, F. Connor, P. Wilson, A. Rolland, H. Wilson, W. McCulloch, J. Clark, J. Craig, R. Campbell (9).
Assistant Manager: John Brownlie.
Secretary: William Foster.
Founded: 1881.
Nickname: Cowden.
Former Names: None.
Former Grounds: North End Park, Cowdenbeath.
Record Attendance: 25,586 v Rangers, League Cup Quarter-final, 21 September 1949.
Record Victory: 12–0 v St Johnstone, Scottish Cup 1st Round, 21 January 1928.
Record Defeat: 1–11 v Clyde, Division 2, 6 October 1951.
Most League Points: 60, Division 2, 1938–39.
Most League Goals: 120, Division 2, 1938–39.
Highest League Scorer in a Season: Willie Devlin, 40, Division 1, 1925–26.
Highest Total of League Goals: Club unable to supply this data.
Most League Appearances: Club unable to supply this data.
League History: 1906–15 Division 2, 1921–24 Division 2, 1924–34 Division 1, 1934–70 Division 2, 1970–71 Division 1, 1971–75 Division 2, 1975– Second Division.
Honours: Division 2 Champions 1913–14, 1914–15, 1938–39, runners-up 1921–22, 1923–24, 1969–70.
Colours: Royal blue shadow striped shirts with white chest band, white shorts, royal blue socks.

DIVISION 2

DUMBARTON

Boghead Park, Miller Street, Dumbarton G82 2JA.

Stadium Capacity: 10,700
Pitch Dimensions: 110 × 72 yds
Telephone: 0389–62569/67864
Chairman: George Crozier.
Directors: Alex D. Wright, R. Campbell Ward.
Manager: Bertie Auld.
Managers since 1975: A. Wright, D. Wilson, S. Fallon, W. Lamont, D. Wilson, D. Whiteford, A. Totten, M. Clougherty (8).
Secretary: C. Cleary & Co.
Founded: 1872.
Nickname: The Sons.
Former Names: None.
Former Grounds: None.
Record Attendance: 18,000 v Raith R, Scottish Cup, 2 March 1957.
Record Victory: 13–1 v Kirkintilloch Central, Scottish Cup 1st Round, 1 September 1888.
Record Defeat: 1–11 v Albion R, Division 2, 30 January 1926, and v Ayr U, League Cup, 13 August 1952.
Most League Points: 53, First Division, 1986–87.
Most League Goals: 101, Division 2, 1956–57.
Highest League Scorer in a Season: Kenny Wilson, 38, Division 2, 1971–72.
League History: Founder members Division 1 1890, 1896–97 Division 2, 1906–13 Divisin 2, 1913–22 Division 1, 1922–54 Division 2, 1954–55 Division C, 1955–72 Division 2, 1972–75 Division 1, 1975–84 First Division, 1984–85 Premier Division, 1985– First Division.
Honours: Division 1 Champions 1890–91 (shared with Rangers), 1891–92. Division 2 Champions 1910–11, 1971–72. First Division runners-up 1983–84. Division 2 runners-up 1907–08. Scottish Cup winners 1883, runners-up 1881, 1882, 1887, 1891, 1897.
Colours: Gold shirts with white chest band, black shorts, gold and black socks.

DIVISION 1

DUNFERMLINE ATHLETIC

East End Park, Halbeath Road, Dunfermline KY12 7RB.

Stadium Capacity: 27,500
Pitch Dimensions: 114 × 72 yds
Telephone: 0383–724295
Chairman: William M. Rennie.
Vice-Chairman: William H. Braisby.
Directors: Dr John C. Yellowley, C. Roy Woodrow, Blair Morgan, James Watters.
Manager: Jim Leishman.
Managers since 1975: A,Miller, H. Melrose, P. Stanton, T. Forsyth (4).
Secretary: James McConville JP.
Founded: 1885.
Nickname: The Pars.
Former Names: None.
Former Grounds: None.
Record Attendance: 27,816 v Celtic, Division 1, 1968.
Record Victory: 11–2 v Stenhousemuir, Division 2, 27 September 1930.
Record Defeat: 0–10 v Dundee, Division 2, 22 March 1947.
Most League Points: 59, Division 2, 1925–26.
Most League Goals: 120, Division 2, 1957–58.
Highest League Scorer in a Season: Bobby Skinner, 55, Division 2, 1925–26.
Highest Total of League Goals: 154, Charles Dickson.
Most League Appearances: 360, Bobby Robertson, 1977–88.
League History: 1912–15 Division 2, 1921–26 Division 2, 1926–28 Division 1, 1928–34 Division 2, 1934–37 Division 1, 1937–55 Division 2, 1955–57 Division 1, 1957–58 Division 2, 1958–72 Division 1, 1972–73 Division 2, 1973–75 Division 1, 1975–76 First Division, 1976–79 Second Division, 1979–83 First Division, 1983–86 Second Division, 1986–87 First Division, 1987–88 Premier Division, 1988– First Division.
Honours: Division 2 Champions 1925–26, runners-up 1912–13, 1933–34, 1954–55, 1957–58, 1972–73. First Division runners-up 1986–87. Second Division runners-up 1978–79. Scottish Cup winners 1961, 1968, runners-up 1965. League Cup runners-up 1949–50.
Colours: Broad black and white striped shirts, black shorts, black socks with red diamond tops.

EAST FIFE

Bayview Park, Methil, Fife KY8 3AG.

Stadium Capacity: 14,200
Pitch Dimensions: 110 × 71 yds
Telephone: 0333–26323
Chairman: James Baxter.
Vice-Chairman: William Johnston.
Directors: John Fleming, James Drysdale, James Taylor, Stephen Baxter, James Gibson.
Manager: Gavin Murray.
Managers since 1975: Frank Christie, Roy Barry, David Clarke (3).
Secretary: Mrs I. McCammon.
Founded: 1903.
Nickname: The Fifers.
Former Names: None.
Former Grounds: None.
Record Attendance: 22,515 v Raith R, Division 1, 2 January 1950.
Record Victory: 13–2 v Edinburgh City, Division 2, 11 December 1937.
Record Defeat: 0–9 v Hearts, Division 1, 5 October 1957.
Most League Points: 57, Division 2, 1929–30.
Most League Goals: 114, Division 2, 1929–30.
Highest League Scorer in a Season: J. Wood, 41, Division 1, 1926–27, and H. Morris, 41, Division 2, 1947–48.
Highest Total of League Goals: 149, G. Dewar.
Most League Appearances: 517, David Clarke, 1968–87.
League History: 1922–30 Division 2, 1930–31 Division 1, 1931–48 Division 2, 1948–58 Division 1, 1958–71 Division 2, 1971–74 Division 1, 1974–75 Division 2, 1975–78 First Division, 1978–84 Second Division, 1984–88 First Division, 1988– Second Division.
Honours: Division 2 Champions 1947–48, runners-up 1929–30, 1970–71. Second Division runners-up 1983–84. Scottish Cup winners 1938, runners-up 1927, 1950. League Cup winners 1947–48, 1949–50, 1953–54.
Colours: Black and gold striped shirts, black shorts with gold trim, black socks with gold and white tops.

EAST STIRLINGSHIRE

Firs Park, Firs Street, Falkirk, FK2 7AY.

Stadium Capacity: 6000
Pitch Dimensions: 112 × 72 yds
Telephone: 0324–23583
Chairman: John P. Turnbull.
Directors:
Manager: J. David Connell.
Managers since 1975: I. Ure, D. McLinden, W. P. Lamont, M. Ferguson, W. Little, D. Whiteford, D. Lawson (7).
Secretary: Peter I. McKay.
Founded: 1881.
Nickname: Shire.
Former Names: None.
Former Grounds: Burnhouse, Randyford Park, Merchiston Park, New Kilbowie Park.
Record Attendance: 11,500 v Hibernian, Scottish Cup, 10 February 1969.
Record Victory: 10–1 v Stenhousemuir, Scottish Cup 1st Round, 1 September 1888.
Record Defeat: 1–12 v Dundee U, Division 2, 13 April 1936.
Most League Points: 55, Division 2, 1931–32.
Most League Goals: 111, Division 2, 1931–32.
Highest League Scorer in a Season: Malcolm Morrison, 36, Division 2, 1938–39.
Most League Appearances: Gordon Simpson 1967–79 (Club unable to confirm total.)
League History: 1901–15 Division 2, 1921–23 Division 2, 1923–24 Division 3, 1924–32 Division 2, 1932–33 Division 1, 1933–39 Division 2, 1947–48 Division C, 1949–55 Division C, 1955–63 Division 2, 1963–64 Division 1, 1964–75 Division 2, 1975–80 Second Division, 1980–82 First Division, 1982– Second Division.
Honours: Division 2 Champions 1931–32, runners-up 1962–63. Second Division runners-up 1979–80.
Colours: White shirts with black band across chest, black shorts with white and orange trim, black socks.

FALKIRK

Brockville Park, Hope Street, Falkirk FK1 5AX.

Stadium Capacity: 18,000
Pitch Dimensions: 110 × 70 yds
Telephone: 0324–24121
Chairman: Edward Moffat.
Vice-Chairman: James Johnston.
Directors: Malcolm Allan, W. Barrie Scott, Alistair McKenzie, Dr R. Gillies Sinclair, James Allan.
Manager: David Clarke.
Managers since 1975: J. Prentice, G. Miller, W. Little, J. Hagart, A. Totten, G. Abel, W. Lamont (7).
Secretary: W. Barrie Scott CA.
Founded: 1876.
Nickname: The Bairns.
Former Names: None.
Former Grounds: None.
Record Attendance: 23,100 v Celtic, Scottish Cup 3rd Round, 21 February 1953.
Record Victory: 12–1 v Laurieston, Scottish Cup 2nd Round, 23 March 1893.
Record Defeat: 1–11 v Airdrieonians, Division 1, 28 April 1951.
Most League Points: 59, Division 2, 1935–36.
Most League Goals: 132, Division 2, 1935–36.
Highest League Scorer in a Season: Evelyn Morrison, 43, Division 1, 1928–29.
League History: 1902–05 Division 2, 1905–35 Division 1, 1935–36 Division 2, 1936–51 Division 1, 1951–52 Division 2, 1952–59 Division 1, 1959–61 Division 2, 1961–69 Division 1, 1969–70 Division 2, 1970–74 Division 1, 1974–75 Division 2, 1975–77 First Division, 1977–80 Second Division, 1980–86 First Division, 1986–88 Premier Division, 1988– First Division.
Honours: Division 2 Champions 1935–36, 1969–70, 1974–75, runners-up 1904–05, 1951–52, 1960–61. Second Division Champions 1979–80, runners-up 1907–08, 1909–10. First Division runners-up 1985–86.
Colours: Dark blue shirts with white trim, white shorts, red socks.

FORFAR ATHLETIC

Station Park, Carseview Road, Forfar DD8 3BT.

Stadium Capacity: 8732
Pitch Dimensions: 115 × 69 yds
Telephone: 0307–63576
Chairman: Gordon Webster.
Vice-Chairman: Gordon Lowson.
Directors: Bryan Harlock, Douglas Soutar, John Sherriff, David McGregor, James Robertson, George Enston.
Manager: Henry Hall.
Managers since 1975: Jerry Kerr, Archie Knox, Alex Rae, Doug Houston (4).
Secretary: David McGregor.
Founded: 1885.
Nickname: The Sky Blues.
Former Names: None.
Former Grounds: None.
Record Attendance: 10,780 v Rangers, Scottish Cup 2nd Round, 2 February 1970.
Record Victory: 14–1 v Lindertis, Scottish Cup 1st Round, 1 September 1888.
Record Defeat: 2–12 v King's Park, Division 2, 2 January 1930.
Most League Points: 63, Second Division 1983–84.
Most League Goals: 98, Division 2, 1929–30.
Highest League Scorer in a Season: Dave Kilgour, 45, Division 2, 1929–30.
Most League Appearances: 376, Alex Brash, 1974–86.
League History: 1921–25 Division 2, 1925–26 Division 3, 1926–39 Division 2, 1946–49 Division C, 1949–75 Division 2, 1975–84 Second Division, 1984– First Division.
Honours: Second Division Champions 1983–84. Division C Champions 1948–49.
Colours: Sky blue shirts and socks, white shorts.

DIVISION 1

KILMARNOCK

Rugby Park, Kilmarnock KA1 2DP.

Stadium Capacity: 17,528
Pitch Dimensions: 115 × 75 yds
Telephone: 0563–25184
Hon. President: Thomas M. Lauchlan OBE.
Chairman: Robert Lauchlan.
Vice-Chairman: Alaxander Leggate.
Directors: Brian Faulds, James Thompson, Ronald Hamilton, Thomas Murray, Ian Dey.
Manager: Eddie Morrison.
Managers since 1975: W. Fernie, D. Sneddon, J. Clunie (3).
Secretary/General Manager: Walter W. McCrae.
Founded: 1869.
Nickname: Killie.
Former Names: None.
Former Grounds: None.
Record Attendance: 34,246 v Rangers, League Cup, August 1963.
Record Victory: 13–2 v Saltcoats Victoria, Scottish Cup 2nd Round, 12 September 1896.
Record Defeat: 0–8 v Hibernian, Division 1, 22 August 1925, v Rangers, Division 1, 27 February 1937, v Queen's Park, Division 2, 1892–93.
Most League Points: 58, Division 2, 1973–74.
Most League Goals: 96, Division 2, 1973–74.
Highest League Scorer in a Season: H. Cunningham, 35, Division 1, 1927–28.
Highest Total of League Goals: 148, W. Culley, 1912–23.
Most League Appearances: 466, Alan Robertson, 1972–88.
League History: 1892–93, 1895–99 Division 2, 1899–1947 Division 1, 1947–54 Division 2, 1954–73 Division 1, 1973–74 Division 2, 1974–75 Division 1, 1975–76 First Division, 1976–77 Premier Division, 1977–79 First Division, 1979–81 Premier Division, 1981–82 First Division, 1982–83 Premier Division, 1983– First Division.
Honours: Division 1 Champions 1964–65, runners-up 1959–60, 1960–61, 1962–63, 1963–64. Division 2 Champions 1897–98, 1898–99, runners-up 1953–54, 1973–74. First Division runners-up 1975–76, 1978–79, 1981–82. Scottish Cup winners 1920, 1929, runners-up 1898, 1932, 1938, 1957, 1960. League Cup runners-up 1952–53, 1960–61, 1962–63.
Colours: Blue and white hooped shirts, blue shorts and socks.

DIVISION 1

MEADOWBANK THISTLE

Meadowbank Stadium, London Road, Edinburgh EH7 6AE.

Stadium Capacity: 16,500 (all seated)
Pitch Dimensions: 105 × 72 yds
Telephone: 031–661 5351
Chairman: John P. Blacklaw.
Vice-Chairman: William L. Mill.
Directors: Terry Christie.
Manager: Terry Christie.
Managers since 1975: John Bain, Alec Ness, Willie MacFarlane (3).
Assistant Manager: Lawrie Glasson.
Secretary: William L. Mill.
Founded: 1943.
Nickname: Thistle or The Wee Jags.
Former Names: Ferranti Thistle 1943–74.
Former Grounds: Crewe Toll, Powderhall, City Park.
Record Attendance: 4000 v Albion Rovers, League Cup, 9 September 1974.
Record Victory: 6–0 v Raith R, Second Division, 9 November 1985.
Record Defeat: 0–8 v Hamilton Acad, Division 2, 14 December 1974.
Most League Points: 55, Second Division, 1986–87.
Most League Goals: 70, First Division, 1987–88.
Highest League Scorer in a Season: John McGachie, 21, 1986–87.
Highest Total of League Goals: 63, Adrian Sprott, 1980–85.
Most League Appearances: 408, Walter Boyd, 1979–88.
League History: 1974–75 Division 2, 1975–83 Second Division, 1983–85 First Division, 1985–87 Second Division, 1987– First Division.
Honours: Second Division Champions 1986–87, runners-up 1982–83. First Division runners-up 1987–88.
Colours: Amber shirts with black trim, black shorts, amber socks.

MONTROSE

Links Park, Wellington Street, Montrose DD10 8QD.

Stadium Capacity: 6500
Pitch Dimensions: 113 × 70 yds
Telephone: 0674–73200
President: William Johnston MBE, JP.
Chairman: Forbes W. Inglis.
Vice-Chairman: Frederick B. Scott.
Directors: Alan Lumsden, Glenn Millar, John Paton, William Henderson.
Manager: Ian J. Stewart.
Managers since 1975: A. Stuart, K. Cameron, R. Livingstone, S. Murray,
D. D'Arcy (5).
Assistant Manager: John Smith.
Secretary: Malcolm J. Watters.
Founded: 1879.
Nickname: The Gable Endies.
Former Names: None.
Former Grounds: None.
Record Attendance: 8983 v Dundee, Scottish Cup 3rd Round, 17 March 1973.
Record Victory: 12–0 v Vale of Leithen, Scottish Cup 2nd Round, 4 January
1975.
Record Defeat: 0–13 v Aberdeen, Scottish Cup, 17 March 1951.
Most League Points: 53, Division 2, 1974–75, Second Division 1984–85.
Most League Goals: 82, Division 2, 1938–39 & 1972–73.
Highest League Scorer in a Season: B. Third, 28, Division 2, 1972–73.
League History: 1923–26 Division 3, 1929–39 Division 2, 1946–55 Division C, 1955–75 Division 2, 1975–79 First Division, 1979–85 Second Division, 1985–87 First Division, 1987– Second Division.
Honours: Second Division Champions 1984–85.
Colours: Blue shirts with white pinstripe, white shorts, red socks.

MORTON

Cappielow Park, Sinclair Street, Greenock PA15 2TY.

Stadium Capacity: 16,600
Pitch Dimensions: 110 × 71 yds
Telephone: 0475–23571
Chairman: John L. Macpherson.
Vice-Chairman: John Wilson.
Directors: Thomas Robertson, William J. Know, Douglas Rae, Kenneth Woods, Andrew Gemmell.
Manager: Allan McGraw.
Managers since 1975: Joe Gilroy, Benny Rooney, Alex Miller, Tommy McLean, Willie McLean (5).
Assistant Manager: Jackie McNamara.
Secretary: Henderson & Co CA.
Founded: 1874.
Nickname: The Ton.
Former Names: None.
Former Grounds: Grant Street 1874–75, Garvel Park 1875–79, Cappielow Park 1879–82, Ladyburn Park 1882–83.
Record Attendance: 23,000 v Celtic, 1922.
Record Victory: 11–0 v Carfin Shamrock, Scottish Cup 1st Round, 13 November 1886.
Record Defeat: 1–10 v Port Glasgow Ath, Division 2, 5 May 1894, v St Bernard's, Division 2, 14 October 1933.
Most League Points: 69, Division 2, 1966–67.
Most League Goals: 135, Division 2, 1963–64.
Highest League Scorer in a Season: Allan McGraw, 58, Division 2, 1963–64.
Most League Appearances: 358, David Hayes, 1969–84.
League History: 1893–1900 Division 2, 1900–27 Division 1, 1927–29 Division 2, 1929–33 Division 1, 1933–37 Division 2, 1937–38 Division 1, 1938–39 Division 2, 1946–49 Division 1, 1949–50 Division 2, 1950–52 Division 1, 1952–64 Division 2, 1964–66 Division 1, 1966–67 Division 2, 1967–75 Division 1, 1975–78 First Division, 1978–83 Premier Division, 1983–84 First Division, 1984–85 Premier Division, 1985–87 First Division, 1987–88 Premier Division, 1988– First Division.
Honours: First Division Champions 1977–78, 1983–84, 1986–87. Champions 1949–50, 1963–64, 1966–67. Scottish Cup winners 1922, runners-up 1948. League Cup runners-up 1963–64.
Colours: Blue and white hooped shirts, white shorts, blue socks.

PARTICK THISTLE

Firhill Park, 90 Firhill Road, Glasgow G20 7AL.

Stadium Capacity: 20,600
Pitch Dimensions: 106 × 72 yds
Telephone: 041–946 2673
Hon. President: James R. Aitken.
Chairman: T. Miller Reid.
Vice-Chairman: James Donald.
Directors: Barrie D. Spears, Kevin Moore.
Manager: William P. Lamont.
Managers since 1975: R. Auld, P. Cormack, B. Rooney, R. Auld, D. Johnstone (5).
Secretary: Leslie J. McIntyre CA.
Founded: 1876.
Nickname: The Jags.
Former Names: None.
Former Grounds: None.
Record Attendance: 49,838 v Rangers, Division 1, 18 February 1922.
Record Victory: 16–0 v Royal Albert, Scottish Cup 1st Round, 17 January 1931.
Record Defeat: 0–10 v Queen's Park, Scottish Cup, 3 December 1881.
Most League Points: 56, Division 2, 1970–71.
Most League Goals: 91, Division 1, 1928–29.
Highest League Scorer in a Season: Alec Hair, 41, Division 1, 1926–27.
Most League Appearances: 410, Alan Rough, 1969–82.
League History: 1893–97 Division 2, 1897–99 Division 1, 1899–1900 Division 2, 1900–01 Division 1, 1901–02 Division 2, 1902–70 Division 1, 1970–71 Division 2, 1971–75 Division 1, 1975–76 First Division, 1976–82 Premier Division, 1982– First Division.
Honours: First Division Champions 1975–76. Division 2 Champions 1896–97, 1899–1900, 1970–71, runners-up 1901–02. Scottish Cup winners 1921, runners-up 1930. League Cup winners 1971–72, runners-up 1953–54, 1956–57, 1058–59.
Colours: Amber shirts with red shoulders and sleeves, red shorts with amber stripe, red socks.

QUEEN OF THE SOUTH

Palmerston Park, Terregles Street, Dumfries DG2 9BA.

Stadium Capacity: 13,000
Pitch Dimensions: 125 × 72 yds
Telephone: 0387–54853
Chairman: William J. Harkness CBE.
Vice-Chairman: William Houliston.
Directors: Samuel C. Harkness, Lewis Russell, William Jardine.
Manager: David Wilson.
Managers since 1975: M. Jackson, G. Herd, A. Busby, R. Clark, M. Jackson (5).
Secretary: James Farrell.
Founded: 1919.
Nickname: The Doonhamers.
Former Names: None.
Former Grounds: None.
Record Attendance: 24,500 v Hearts, Scottish Cup 3rd Round, 23 February 1952.
Record Victory: 11–1 v Stranraer, Scottish Cup 1st Round, 16 January 1932.
Record Defeat: 2–10 v Dundee, Division 1, 1 December 1962.
Most League Points: 55, Second Division, 1985–86.
Most League Goals: 99, Division 2, 1931–32.
Highest League Scorer in a Season: Jimmy Gray, 33, Division 2, 1927–28.
Most League Appearances: 819, Allan Ball, 1963–82.
League History: 1923–25 Division 3, 1925–33 Division 2, 1933–50 Division 1, 1950–51 Division 2, 1951–59 Division 1, 1959–62 Division 2, 1962–64 Division 1, 1964–75 Division 2, 1975–79 First Division, 1979–81 Second Division, 1981–82 First Division, 1982–86 Second Division, 1986– First Division.
Honours: Division 2 Champions 1950–51, runners-up 1932–33, 1961–62, 1974–75. Second Division runners-up 1980–81, 1985–86.
Colours: Royal blue shirts, white shorts, royal blue socks with white turnovers.

DIVISION 2

QUEEN'S PARK
Hampden Park, Mount Florida, Glasgow G42 9BA.

Stadium Capacity: 74,730
Pitch Dimensions: 115 × 75 yds
Telephone: 041–632 1275
President: William G. N. Geddes CBE.
Directors: William L. Ross, Robert L. Cromar, Peter G. Buchanan, Thomas Barr, Martin B. Smith, William Omand Jnr, Ian G. Harnett, William S. Burgess, Austen Reilly.
Managers since 1975: D. McParland, J. Gilroy, E. Hunter (3).
Secretary: James C. Rutherford.
Founded: 1867.
Nickname: The Spiders.
Former Names: None.
Former Grounds: First Hampden (Titwood Park), Second Hampden, Third Hampden.
Record Attendance: 95,772 v Rangers, Scottish Cup, 18 January 1930. (Stadium record: 149,547 Scotland v England, 1937).
Record Victory: 16–0 v St Peter's, Scottish Cup 1st Round, 29 August 1885.
Record Defeat: 0–9 v Motherwell, Division 1, 1937–38.
Most League Points: 57, Division 2, 1922–23.
Most League Goals: 100, Division 1, 1928–29.
Highest League Scorer in a Season: William Martin, 30, Division 1, 1937–38.
Highest Total of League Goals: 163, J. B. McAlpine.
Most League Appearances: 473, J. B. McAlpine.
League History: 1900–22 Division 1, 1922–23 Division 2, 1923–48 Division 1, 1948–56 Division 2, 1956–58 Division 1, 1958–75 Division 2, 1975–81 Second Division, 1981–83 First Division, 1983– Second Division.
Honours: Division 2 Champions 1922–23, 1955–56. Second Division Champions 1980–81. Scottish Cup winners 1874, 1875, 1876, 1880, 1881, 1882, 1884, 1886, 1890, 1893, runners-up 1892, 1900. FA Cup (England) runners-up 1884, 1885.
Colours: White and black hooped shirts and socks, white shorts.

DIVISION 1

RAITH ROVERS
Stark's Park, Pratt Street, Kirkcaldy KY1 1SA.

Stadium Capacity: 9500
Pitch Dimensions: 113 × 67 yds
Telephone: 0592–263514
Chairman: John Urquhart.
Vice-Chairman: William Shedden.
Directors: Ian Watt, Alex Penman, Robert Paxton, Peter Campsie.
Manager: Frank Connor.
Managers since 1975: A. Matthew, R. Paton, W. McLean, G. Wallace, R. Wilson (5).
Secretary: Peter J. Campsie.
Founded: 1883.
Nickname: Rovers.
Former Names: None.
Former Grounds: Balwearie, Robbie's Park.
Record Attendance: 31,306 v Hearts, Scottish Cup 2nd Round, 7 February 1953.
Record Victory: 10–1 v Coldstream, Scottish Cup 2nd Round, 13 February 1954.
Record Defeat: 2–11 v Morton, Division 2, 18 March 1936.
Most League Points: 59, Division 2, 1937–38.
Most League Goals: 142, Division 2, 1937–38.
Highest League Scorer in a Season: Norman Haywood, Division 2, 1937–38.
Most League Appearances: 387, Donald Urquhart.
League History: 1902–10 Division 2, 1910–26 Division 1, 1926–27 Division 2, 1927–29 Division 1, 1929–38 Division 2, 1938–39 Division 1, 1946–49 Division 2, 1949–63 Division 1, 1963–67 Division 2, 1967–70 Division 1, 1970–75 Division 2, 1975–76 Second Division, 1976–77 First Division, 1977–78 Second Division, 1978–84 First Division, 1984–87 Second Division, 1987– First Division.
Honours: Division 2 Champions 1907–08, 1909–10 (shared with Leith), 1937–38, 1948–49, runners-up 1908–09, 1926–27, 1966–67. Second Division runners-up 1975–76, 1977–78, 1986–87. Scottish Cup runners-up 1913. League Cup runners-up 1948–49.
Colours: Navy blue shirts with white sleeves, white shorts, red socks.

DIVISION 1

ST JOHNSTONE

Muirton Park, Dunkeld Road, Perth PH1 5AP.

Stadium Capacity: 10,000
Pitch Dimensions: 109 × 74 yd
Telephone: 0738–26961
Chairman: Geoffrey S. Brown.
Vice-Chairman: Allan W. Campbell.
Directors: Douglas B. McIntyre, David S. Sidey, Henry S. Ritchie.
Manager: Alex Totten.
Managers since 1975: J. Stewart, J. Storrie, A. Stuart, A. Rennie, I. Gibson (5).
Assistant Manager: B. Paton.
Secretary: Stewart Duff.
Founded: 1884.
Nickname: The Saints.
Former Names: None.
Former Grounds: Recreation Grounds.
Record Attendance: 29,972 v Dundee, Scottish Cup 2nd Round, 10 February 1952.
Record Victory: 8–1 v Partick Th, League Cup 16 August 1969.
Record Defeat: 1–10 v Third Lanark, Scottish Cup 1st Round, 24 January 1903.
Most League Points: 59, Second Division 1987–88.
Most League Goals: 102, Division 2, 1931–32.
Highest League Scorer in a Season: Jimmy Benson, 36, Division 2, 1931–32.
Highest Total of League Goals: 140, John Brogan, 1977–83.
Most League Appearances: 298, Drew Rutherford.
League History: 1911–24 Division 2, 1924–30 Division 1, 1930–32 Division 2, 1932–39 Division 1, 1946–60 Division 2, 1960–62 Division 1, 1962–63 Division 2, 1963–75 Division 1, 1975–76 Premier Division, 1976–83 First Division, 1983–84 Premier Division, 1984–85 First Division, 1985– First Division.
Honours: First Division Champions 1982–83. Division 2 Champions 1923–24, 1959–60, 1962–63, runners-up 1931–32. Second Division runners-up 1987–88. League Cup runners-up 1969–70.
Colours: All royal blue with white semi–circular panel on chest.

DIVISION 2

STENHOUSEMUIR

Ochilview Park, Gladstone Road, Stenhousemuir FK5 5QL.

Stadium Capacity: 4000
Pitch Dimensions: 113 × 78 yds
Telephone: 0324–562992
President: John Cook.
Vice-President: John Jenkins.
Directors: Hugh Brown, Peter Cowan, Terry Bulloch, Greig Thomson, William Blackhall, Sidney Collumbine, Richard Wilson.
Manager: Alex Rennie.
Managers since 1975: H. Glasgow, J. Black, A. Rose, W. Henderson (4).
Secretary: A. T. Bulloch.
Founded: 1884.
Nickname: The Warriors.
Former Names: None.
Former Grounds: Tryst Ground 1884–86, Goschen Park 1886–90.
Record Attendance: 12,500 v East Fife, Scottish Cup 4th Round, 11 March 1950.
Record Victory: 9–2 v Dundee U, Division 2, 19 April 1937.
Record Defeat: 2–11 v Dunfermline Ath, Division 2, 27 September 1930.
Most League Points: 50, Division 2, 1960–61.
Most League Goals: 99, Division 2, 1960–61.
Highest League Scorer in a Season: Evelyn Morrison, 31, Division 2, 1927–28 and Robert Murray, 31, Division 2, 1936–37.
Most League Appearances: 189, T. Mullen.
League History: 1921–75 Division 2, 1975– Second Division.
Honours: None.
Colours: Maroon shirts with white pinstripe, white shorts, maroon socks with white hooped turnovers.

STIRLING ALBION

Annfield Park, St Ninian's Road, Stirling FK8 2HE.

Stadium Capacity: 4000
Pitch Dimensions: 110 × 74 yds
Telephone: 0786–50399
Chairman: Peter Gardiner.
Directors: Duncan MacGregor, Peter McKenzie, Duncan McCallum, John Loch, J. Smith.
Manager: Jim Fleeting.
Managers since 1975: F. Beattie, A. Smith, G. Peebles (3).
Assistant Manager: Frank Coulston.
Secretary: Duncan McCallum.
Founded: 1945.
Nickname: The Albion.
Former Names: None.
Former Grounds: None.
Record Attendance: 26,400 v Celtic, Scottish Cup 4th Round, 14 March 1959.
Record Victory: 20–0 v Selkirk, Scottish Cup 1st Round, 8 December 1984.
Record Defeat: 0–9 v Dundee U, Division 1, 30 December 1967.
Most League Points: 59, Division 2, 1964–65.
Most League Goals: 105, Division 2, 1957–58.
Highest League Scorer in a Season: Joe Hughes, 29, Division 2, 1969–70.
Highest Total of League Goals: 129, Billy Steele, 1971–83.
Most League Appearances: 504, Matt McPhee, 1967–81.
League History: 1946–47 Division C, 1947–49 Division 2, 1949–50 Division 1, 1950–51 Division 2, 1951–52 Division 1, 1952–53 Division 2, 1953–56 Division 1, 1956–58 Division 2, 1958–60 Division 1, 1960–61 Division 2, 1961–62 Division 1, 1962–65 Division 2, 1965–68 Division 1, 1968–75 Division 2, 1975–77 Second Division, 1977–81 First Division, 1981–Second Division.
Honours: Division 2 Champions 1952–53, 1957–58, 1960–61, 1964–65, runners-up 1948–49, 1950–51. Second Division Champions 1976–77.
Colours: Red shirts with white sleeves, white shorts and socks.

STRANRAER

Stair Park, London Road, Stranraer DG9 8BS.

Stadium Capacity: 4000
Pitch Dimensions: 110 × 70 yds
Telephone: 0776–3271
Chairman: Thomas Rice.
Vice-Chairman: Alex McKie.
Directors: Andrew Hannah, William T. Fullerton, Alex Clanachan, Alex Hadden, James Hannah, James Brown, George F. Compton, R. A. Graham Rodgers, Andrew Burgess, Robert Clanachan.
Manager: Alex McAnespie.
Managers since 1975: J. Hughes, N. Hood, G. Hamilton, D. Sneddon, J. Clark, R. Clark (6).
Secretary: R. A. Graham Rodgers.
Founded: 1870.
Nickname: The Blues.
Former Names: None.
Former Grounds: None.
Record Attendance: 6500 v Rangers, Scottish Cup 1st Round, 24 January 1948.
Record Victory: 7–0 v Brechin C, Division 2, 6 February 1965.
Record Defeat: 1–11 v Queen of the S, Scottish Cup 1st Round, 16 January 1932.
Most League Points: 46, Second Division, 1976–77.
Most League Goals: 83, Division 2, 1960–61.
Highest League Scorer in a Season: Derek Frye, 27, Second Division, 1977–78.
Most League Appearances: 256, Daniel McDonald.
League History: 1949–55 Division C, 1955–75 Division 2, 1975– Second Division.
Honours: None.
Colours: All royal blue with amber chest band.

ABERDEEN – LEAGUE RECORD 1987–88 (PREMIER DIVISION)

Match no/Opp/Date		J.Leighton	S.McKimmie	D.Robertson	N.Simpson	A.McLeish	W.Miller	G.Hackett	B.Grant	J.Miller	P.Nicholas	J.Hewitt	R.Connor	D.Dodds	J.Bett	B.Irvine	W.Falconer	I.Porteous	K.Edwards	T.Jones	P.Weir	P.Wright	S.Gray	C.Nicholas	L.Gardner	M.McArthur	S.Harvie	FT(HT)Att Lge pos
1. Dundee	8.8	1	2	3	4	5	6	7†	8‡	9	10	11	12	14¹														1–1(0–0)10,223
2. Morton*	12.8	1	2†	3	4¹	5	6	14	12	9¹‡	10	11		7¹	8													3–1(2–1)8000
3. Rangers*	15.8	1	2	3	4	5‡	6	14		9	10¹	11		7¹†	8	12												2–0(1–0)22,500
4. Motherwell	22.8	1	2	3	4		6			9	10	11		7¹	8	5												1–0(0–0)4858
5. Dundee U*	29.8	1	2	3	4†		6	11	12	9	10			7¹	8₁	5	14											1–1(1–0)16,000
6. Falkirk	5.9	1	2	3			6	11‡	12	9¹	10	7	4†		8	5	14¹											2–2(0–2)5327
7. St Mirren*	12.9	1	2	3		5	6	12		9	10	7†	4		8		11¹											2–0(2–0)11,000
8. Celtic	19.9	1	2	3‡		5	6	14		9¹	10¹	7	4		8	11†	12											2–2(0–1)38,944
9. Hibernian	29.9	1	2			5		14	3¹	9‡	10	7†	4		8	6	11¹	12										2–0(0–0)10,500
10. Dunfermline A*	3.10	1	2			5	6		3†	9	10¹	7	4		8		11¹		12¹									3–0(0–0)11,313
11. Hearts	7.10	1	2			5	6			9	10	7	4		8₁	3†	11		12									1–2(1–2)17,741
12. Dundee*	10.10	1	2			5	6	11‡		12	10	7	4		8¹₁		3¹		9†	14								0–0(0–0)12,500
13. Dundee U	17.10	1	2			5	6		4	7	10	11			8		3		9									0–0(0–0)11,281
14. St Mirren	28.10	1	2		4	5	6				10	7	3		8		9			11								3–1(2–0)4707
15. Celtic*	31.10	1	2		4	5	6			14	10	7†	3		8		9‡	12		11								0–1(0–0)21,000
16. Morton	7.11	1	2			5	6	14			10	7	3		8‡		11	4†	9	12								0–0(0–0)8000
17. Hearts*	14.11	1	2		4	5	6			10	9	11	7†		8		3		12									0–0(0–0)20,000
18. Rangers	17.11	1	2		12	5	6¹			10†	9	4	7		8		3		11									1–0(1–0)41,371
19. Motherwell*	21.11	1	2			5	6	12			11†	4	7¹		8		3		9	10								1–0(1–0)9700
20. Hibernian*	24.11	1	2			5	6	14			12	4	7		8		3		9¹†	10	11‡							1–1(1–1)9000
21. Dunfermline A	28.11	1	2			5	6				12	4	7		8		3		10¹	11	9²†							3–0(0–0)7500
22. Dundee*	5.12	1	2			5	6			10	14	4	7¹		8		3		12‡	11†	9¹							2–1(2–0)8799
23. Falkirk*	9.12	1	2	3		5	6			10		4	7¹†		8¹				11		12	9¹						3–1(2–0)8000
24. Morton*	12.12	1	2	3		5	6			10	12	4¹	7¹‡		8₂				11		14	9†						4–0(2–0)8000
25. St Mirren*	16.12	1	2	3		5	6¹			10	12	4	7		8¹				11†		9							2–1(1–0)6500
26. Celtic	19.12	1	2	3		5	6			10	12	4	7		8		11†		14		9‡							0–0(0–0)37,721
27. Falkirk	26.12	1	2	3		5¹	6			10	12¹	4	7		8				11†		9‡	14						2–0(0–0)5000
28. Dundee U*	2.1	1	2	3		5‡	6			10	11	4	7†		8				14		9	12						0–0(0–0)21,500
29. Hibernian	9.1	1	2	3		5	6			10	11†	4					12				8	7						0–0(0–0)16,000
30. Dunfermline A*	16.1	1	2	3			6			10	11†	4			5	9†			12		8	7						1–0(1–0)20,000
31. Motherwell	23.1	1	2	3†			6	11		10	12	4		8	5	9						7¹						1–2(0–2)6584
32. Rangers*	6.2	1	2			5	6	11‡		10	12	4		8¹	3†	9			14			7						1–2(0–2)22,500
33. Hearts	13.2	1	2	3		5	6	12		10		4	7†	8¹‡		11			14¹			9						2–2(1–1)18,817
34. Dundee*	27.2	1	2	3			6			10	12	4†	7¹		5		8			11	9							1–0(0–0)13,500
35. St Mirren	5.3	1	2	3			6			10		4†		8	5	12	7	14		11‡	9							0–0(0–0)4858
36. Dundee U	19.3	1	2		4	5	6			10			7	8		3			11¹			9¹						2–0(1–0)10,403
37. Falkirk*	26.3	1	2		4	5	6¹			10			7	8		3¹			11			9						2–0(1–0)9410
38. Celtic*	30.3	1	2		4	5	6			10	12		7	8		3			11†			9						0–1(0–0)22,700
39. Dunfermline A	2.4	1	2		4†	5	6			10‡	11		7	8		3¹			12		14	9						1–1(0–0)7132
40. Morton	16.4	1	2	3				11‡	10			5	6	14¹		4		8			9¹†	7	12					2–0(1–0)3200
41. Hearts*	23.4	1	2	3		5†	6			10		8		12	11	4						9	7					0–0(0–0)10,500
42. Rangers	30.4	1		3	4	5	6			10			8	2¹	11	7						9						1–0(0–0)36,010
43. Hibernian*	4.5	1			5	6		10	7‡	12		8	2	11	4†				9			14	3					0–2(0–1)7000
44. Motherwell*	7.5	1	2		4	5	6			10	7	3		8		11						9						0–0(0–0)5500

Apps(subs)/goals: 44(0)/0 · 42(0)/0 · 23(0)/0 · 14(1)/1 · 36(0)/1 · 42(0)/3 · 6(9)/0 · 4(3)/1 · 12(2)/4 · 39(0)/3 · 32(6)/1 · 22(2)/1 · 22(1)/9 · 38(0)/17 · 14(2)/1 · 32(4)/8 · 1(2)/1 · 14(1)/4 · 3 · 5(0)/2 · 9(0)/4 · 4(3)/0 · 16(0)/0 · 1(2)/0 · 1(0)/0

Final League Position: 4

AIRDRIEONIANS – LEAGUE RECORD 1987–88 (DIVISION ONE)

Match no/Opp/Date	J Martin	D MacKinnon	T Black	B McKeown	D Lawrie	C Lindsay	C Campbell	R Reilly	J Flood	V Moore	D MacCabe	M Hughes	C Mitchell	P Docherty	G Christie	J D McCormack	S Ross	D Young	I McDonald	D Parlane	C Harris	D Grant	B Ross	W Thomson	M Nelson	S Shirkie	C Moore	FT(HT)Att	Lge pos
1. East Fife* 8.8	1	2	3	4	5	6	7	8	9	10^1	11																	1-0(1-0)1050	—
2. Partick Th 11.8	1	2	3	4	5	6	7	8†	9^1	10	11^1	12																2-2(2-2)1900	—
3. Queen of South 15.8	1	2	3	4	5	6‡	7^1	8	9	11^1	10†	14	12															2-2(0-2)900	5
4. Dumbarton* 22.8	1	2	3‡	4		8	7	10	11†	6	9	14			5	12												0-1(0-0)1200	7
5. Hamilton A* 29.8	1	2		4	5	3	7	10‡		6	9	12	14	8†	11													0-3(0-0)1700	8
6. Clydebank 5.9	1	2		4		3^1	7	8	10	6$_1$	9				11^1	5												3-2(1-2)1024	6
7. Meadowbank Th 12.9	1	2		4	5	3	7	8	10	6	9^1				11^1													2-1(0-0)750	5
8. Clyde* 15.9	1	2^1		4	5	3	7	8	10	6$_1$	9^1				11^1													4-3(0-2)1150	—
9. Kilmarnock* 19.9	1	2		4	5	3	7^1	8†	10^1	6	9^1		12	11														3-2(1-1)1300	3
10. Raith R 26.9	1	2		4	5	3	7^1	8	10	6^1†	9		12	11														2-3(2-1)1972	5
11. Forfar Ath* 28.9	1	2	3	4	5	6	7^1	8	10		9				11													1-0(0-0)1000	—
12. East Fife 3.10	1	2	12	4	5	3	7^1	8	10^1		9^1‡				11†	6	14											3-1(1-1)756	2
13. Dumbarton 10.10	1	2		4	5	3	7	8	10	6	9				11													0-0(0-0)1200	4
14. Meadowbank T* 17.10	1	2†		4	12	3	7	8‡	14	6	9				11		5	10										0-0(0-0)1000	2
15. Clyde 20.10	1	2		4		3	7	8	11†	6	9				12		5	10										0-1(0-0)800	—
16. Queen of South* 24.10	1	2†		4	12	3	7^2	14	11	6‡	9^1				8		5	10										5-1(2-1)1500	2
17. Forfar Ath 27.10	1	2		4		3	7^2		11	6	9^2				8		5	10										4-4(1-3)660	—
18. Clydebank* 31.10	1	2		4		3	7	12	11	6	9				8†		5	10										0-2(0-1)1600	5
19. Hamilton A 7.11	1	2	14		4	3†	7^1	8‡	11	6	9				12^1		5	10										2-2(0-0)2405	6
20. Partick Th* 11.11	1	2		4		3	7^1	8†	11^1	6	9				12		5^1	10										3-1(0-0)1850	—
21. Kilmarnock 14.11	1	2		4	14	3	7	8†	11	6‡	9				12		5	10										0-1(0-1)1978	5
22. Raith R* 28.11	1	2	3^1	4	8		7		11	6	9^2						5	10										3-0(3-0)2322	3
23. East Fife* 28.11	1	2	3	4	8		7‡	14	11	6†	9^1				12		5	10										2-1(2-0)1500	2
24. Partick Th 5.12	1	2‡	3	4	8		7†	14	11		9	6			12		5	10										0-2(0-0)2300	4
25. Meadowbank Th 12.12	1	2	3	4	6		7†		11		9				12		5	10	8									0-0(0-0)600	4
26. Clyde* 19.12	1	2	3	4	6		7		11		9‡	14			12		5†	10	8									0-2(0-2)1800	4
27. Clydebank 19.12	1	2	3	4	5	12	7		11	6‡	9^1	14					10†	8										1-1(0-0)1497	4
28. Hamilton A* 2.1	1	2	3	4	5	14	7‡		6		9				12		10	8^1	11†									1-4(0-4)3400	4
29. Kilmarnock* 9.1	1	2		4		3	7†	12	6	9	11^1						5	10	8^2									3-3(1-1)1740	5
30. Raith R 16.1	1	2	3	4			7		6	9^1	8					11	10^1						5					2-2(1-1)4988	5
31. Queen of South 26.1	1	2	3	4			7^1		6	9^1	8				11		10						5					2-1(1-1)950	—
32. Dumbarton* 6.2	1	2	3	4	12		14		6	9^1	8		11†		10	7‡							5					1-1(1-1)1150	5
33. Forfar Ath* 13.2	1	2	3	4			12		8^1	6	9^2		11†		10	7							5					3-0(2-0)1050	4
34. East Fife 27.2	1	2	3	4†	12	8		14	6	9^1	7‡				11	10							5					1-3(1-1)791	4
35. Meadowbank T* 5.3	1	2	3		12		7		6†	9		8‡	4	11		10				5	14							0-1(0-1)800	5
36. Clydebank* 19.3	1	2	3				7		11	6	9		4			10				5	8							1-0(0-0)904	5
37. Clyde 22.3	1		3		2		7	10^1	6	9		4			11					5	8^1							2-4(2-2)780	—
38. Hamilton A 26.3	1	2	3				7		6	9^1		4			11					5	8							1-1(1-0)1839	4
39. Dumbarton 2.4	1	2	3				10^1	11	6	9		4			8					5	7							1-0(1-0)800	3
40. Queen of South* 9.4	1		3				7	10	6$_1$	9†	8	2	4		12	11				5								1-1(0-1)900	4
41. Raith R* 16.4	1				12	7	10^1	6	9	8†				11		5	2		4									1-2(1-1)1250	5
42. Kilmarnock 23.4	1			12	8	7^1	10	6	9‡	14	2†			11		5		4										1-4(0-1)1953	6
43. Partick Th* 30.4	1	2	3	6	11	8^1	10	9				7	5		4													1-0(1-0)950	6
44. Forfar Ath 7.5	1	2	3	6	8‡	10	7	9				11	5†		4										12	14		0-3(0-3)535	6
Apps(subs)/goals	44(0)/0	40(0)/0	27(2)/1	33(0)/0	26(3)/1	40(2)/15	18(4)/0	36(0)/7	36(0)/20	44(0)/20	9(6)/1	3(2)/0	8(3)/0	17(10)/4	2(0)/0	42(0)/0	14(0)/1	31(0)/0	9(0)/4	16(0)/1	15(0)/0	4(0)/1	40(0)/1	0(1)/0	0(4)/0	0(1)/0	0(1)/0		

Final League Position: 6

Own goals: S. Pittman, match 23; J. Maher, match 37.

ALBION ROVERS – LEAGUE RECORD 1987–88 (DIVISION TWO)

Match no/Opp/Date	R.McCulloch	J.Lennon	M.McGowan	B.Ahern	A.Gallagher	J.Chapman	J.Mearns	A.Rodgers	C.Wilson	T.McDonald	P.Teevan	D.Houston	B.Fairlie	D.Edgar	B.Black	A.Graham	S.Harvey	J.Greene	D.McGuire	D.McDonald	R.Tracey	A.Henderson	S.McTavish	S.Cadden	G.Walker	E.Watson	J.Campbell	R.Clark	A.Gilhooly	FT(HT)Att Lge pos
1. Stenhousemuir 8.8	1	2	3	4	5	6†	7‡	8^1	9	10	11	12	14																	1–3(1–2)300 —
2. East Stirling* 15.8	1	5	3^1	4		6		8	9†	7	10		2	11	12															1–1(0–0)450 10
3. Montrose 22.8	1		3	4	5	6†		8	11	12		10		2	7	9^2														2–1(0–1)300 9
4. Queen's Park* 29.8	1	2	3	4				8	11		7†	10		5	12	9	6													0–4(0–2)300 12
5. Arbroath 5.9	1	5	3	4		6		8		11	7			2	9			10												0–3(0–0)390 12
6. Stirling Albion* 12.9	1			4		3	11†	8		6	7^1	10	12^1	2		9			5											2–1(0–0)450 10
7. Ayr U 15.9	1		12	4		3	11	8		6	7‡	10†	14	2		9			5											0–3(0–2)2231 —
8. Cowdenbeath 19.9	1	5	3	4			7	8	6†			12	11^1	9^2	2			10												3–3(1–0)145 12
9. Alloa* 26.9	1	5		6		12	7	8	10†			3	11	9^1	2			4												1–0(1–0)400 10
10. Brechin C 3.10	1			10	5	6	7	8				3	11^1	9	2			4												1–2(0–0)400 10
11. Stranraer* 10.10	1			4	5^1	6		8		7	10	12	3	11†	9^1	2														2–1(1–1)250 8
12. Berwick R 17.10	1			4	5	6^2	7	8		11^1	10		3		9	2														3–0(1–0)319 8
13. St Johnstone* 24.10	1	2	3	4	5	6	7	8		9^1	11		10†	12																1–1(1–1)832 7
14. Stenhousemuir* 31.10	1	2†	3	4	5	6	7^1	8		11^1	10‡		14	9^1				12												3–2(1–0)300 6
15. East Stirling 7.11	1	2	3	4	5	6	7^1	8		11‡	10†	14		9^1				12												2–2(0–0)300 6
16. Montrose* 14.11	1	2	3	4	5†	6	7	8		11			12	9				10												0–1(0–0)275 7
17. Alloa 21.11	1		3	4	5	6	7	8		11		2		9				10												0–2(0–1)325 8
18. Cowdenbeath* 28.11		2	3	4	5	10	11	8			7‡			14†	6			9			12	1								0–0(0–0)250 8
19. Ayr U* 12.12	1	2	3	4	5	10	11	8					6	9^1									7							1–1(0–0)850 8
20. Stirling Albion 19.12	1	2		4	5	6	11†	8	3	14^1	10			9			12						7‡							1–1(0–0)310 7
21. Arbroath* 26.12	1	2		4	5	6	11	8	3‡	7†	10			9^1			14						12							1–1(1–0)400 7
22. Queen's Park 2.1	1	2		4	5	6	11	8	3	7†	10‡			9			14						12^1							1–1(0–0)829 7
23. Stranraer 16.1	1		2	3	4	5	6^1‡	12	7			9		14	10†‡			8					11							2–1(0–0)400 6
24. Brechin C* 23.1	1	2	3	4	5	6	7	8†		14	10		12	9‡								11^2								2–0(0–0)350 6
25. Berwick R* 30.1	1	2	3	4	5†	10	7	6		11‡	8		12	14								9								0–2(0–0)200 6
26. St Johnstone 6.2	1	2	3	4		10	7	6		12^1	8‡		14	9		5						11†								1–4(1–3)1606 7
27. Montrose 13.2	1	5	3	4		6†	7	2		14	8		12									11	9‡	10						0–0(0–0)150 8
28. Stenhousemuir* 20.2	1	14	3	4			8	7†	2		12			10								9	11‡	6	5					0–4(0–2)300 9
29. East Stirling* 27.2	1	5‡	3	4			11	7	8		12	10										9†	14	6		2				1–4(0–3)210 10
30. Arbroath 5.3	1	6				11	7	12		3‡	14	10	9	4										6		2†	5			0–4(0–1)265 10
31. Brechin C* 12.3	1	2	3^1	4				11‡	14		7	8	10†		9									6		12	5			1–5(0–2)200 10
32. Ayr U 19.3	1		5					9	12	14	10	8		3	11†				7^1					6		2‡		4		2–6(1–4)2688 10
33. Cowdenbeath 26.3	1		11				9‡	6	14	3	10	8	4†							2			7			12	5			0–1(0–0)150 12
34. Stirling Albion* 2.4	1		3			10^1	11†	2			12	8	4		9									6^1			5	7		3–1(1–1)310 11
35. Queen's Park* 9.4	1		3^1	8		10	11†	2			12	5			9									4			6	7		1–2(1–1)279 11
36. Stranraer 16.4	1		3			10^1		2			8	12	4		9									6	7†		5	11	4	2–2(2–0)350 11
37. Alloa* 23.4	1		3^1			10	11	2			8†		5		9	12								4			6	7		1–2(0–0)200 12
38. Berwick R 30.4	1		10	6		8	7†				11^1		2		9^1				3					4		5		12^1		3–1(2–0)250 12
39. St Johnstone 7.5	1		3	8		10	11†	4			7‡		5		9			2							14		6	12		0–2(0–0)1934 12
Apps(subs)/goals	38(0)0	23(1)0	29(1)4	35(0)0	18(0)1	35(0)7	30(1)2	37(0)1	3(3)0	12(2)0	22(8)7	24(0)10	28(1)0	23(0)0	11(0)4	24(2)10	5(0)0	10(0)0	5(5)0	9(3)1	10(0)0	9(2)4	21(0)0	12(0)1	4(3)0	3(0)0	7(0)0	4(2)1		

Final League Position: 12

Own goal: I. McAllister, match 32.

ALLOA – LEAGUE RECORD 1987–88 (DIVISION TWO)

Match no/Opp/Date	R Lowrie	L Haggart	J Love	K Thomson	J Donaldson	S Sullivan	S Wilkie	R Torrance	S Sophie	M Nelson	A MacDonald	D Macartney	A Marshall	A Smith	A Millen	P Rutherford	K McCulloch	J Fawcett	J MacLay	R Findlay	R Robertson	G Allan	P Lamont	S Kean	M Shiels	S Smith	FT(HT)Att Lge pos
1. Brechin C* 8.8	1	2	3†	4	5	6	7	8	9	10	11			12													0–1(0–0)620 —
2. Queen's Park 15.8	1	3	12	4	5	6		9	11	10	14	8†	2	7‡													0–2(0–1)486 12
3. Cowdenbeath* 22.8	1	3	14	2	4	6‡		10^3	11	7^1†	8		12	5	9^1												5–2(3–2)415 10
4. Stirling Albion* 29.8	1	3			4	6		11	10^1	7	8†		12^1	5	9^2	2											4–0(0–0)1000 6
5. Stranraer 5.9	1	3			4	6		12	8	10	11†		7^2	5	9^1	2											3–0(1–0)450 5
6. East Stirling* 12.9	1	3			4	6	9^1		10	11	8†	12		7	5	2											1–2(0–0)475 7
7. Montrose 15.9	1	3	14		4	6†	8‡		10	11		12		7	5	9	2										0–2(0–1)450 —
8. Arbroath* 19.9	1	3			4	6		9	11^1	8†		2	12	7^1	10^1	5											3–1(0–1)424 6
9. Albion R 26.9	1	3			4	6	14	12	9	11‡		2†	8	7	10	5											0–1(0–0)400 9
10. St Johnstone 3.10	1	3			4	6	7	8	9^1	11		12		10†	5	2											1–2(0–1)404 9
11. Stenhousemuir* 10.10	1	3	10‡		4	6†		8	9^1	11	12		7	2		5	14										1–1(1–0)250 9
12. Ayr U 17.10	1	3		6‡			12	9	10	11^1	8†		2	7	4	5	14										1–2(0–0)2673 10
13. Berwick R* 24.10	1	3		6			12^1	9	10	11	8		2	7†	4	5											1–0(0–0)365 9
14. Brechin C 31.10	1	3	14	8	6†			10	11	7		2‡	12	4	9^1	5											1–3(1–3)500 10
15. Queen's Park* 1.11	1	2	3		4		14	12	8	10	11‡			7†	6	9	5										0–3(0–2)398 10
16. Cowdenbeath 14.11	1	3	8		7		6¹		9^1	11				4	10	5		2									2–2(2–1)220 11
17. Albion R* 21.11	1	3	8		7		6†		10	11^1		2	12	4	9	5^1											2–0(1–0)325 10
18. Arbroath 28.11	1	3	8		7		6†		10	11^1		2	12	4	9	5											1–1(1–1)408 9
19. Montrose* 12.12	1	3		6		8			10	11	14	2	12	4	9^1	5†	7‡										1–0(1–0)348 9
20. East Stirling 19.12	1	14	3	5‡		8			10	11		2	12	4^1	9		7†	6									1–3(1–2)300 9
21. Stranraer* 30.12	1	3	12	6	7				10	11^1				4	9^1	5				8	2†						2–0(1–0)430 —
22. Stirling Albion 2.1	1	3		6	7				10	11	12			4	9	5				8†	2						0–2(0–1)1208 10
23. Stenhousemuir 16.1	1	3	6	8^1†					10	11				12	4	9	5		14	2	7‡						1–0(1–0)300 9
24. Brechin C* 13.2	1	3	6	8^1‡					10^1	11				12	4	9^1	5		14	2	7†						3–0(1–0)347 10
25. St Johnstone* 17.2	1	3	6	8					10^1	11				4	9	5				2		7					1–1(0–1)1093 —
26. Arbroath 20.2	1	3	6	8					10	11^1	12		7†	4	9	5				2							1–1(1–0)380 10
27. Berwick R 23.2	1	3	6	8					10^1	11†				12	4	5				2^1	7	9					2–1(2–0)279 —
28. Queen's Park* 27.2	1	3†	6	8					10		14		11‡	2^1	9	5	12	7		4							1–0(1–0)590 8
29. Ayr U* 1.3	1		3	8	12				10		14		11‡	2	9	5	6	7†		4							0–2(0–0)941 —
30. Stirling Albion 5.3	1		6	8	12				10		14	7		2	9^1	5	11‡			4†		3					1–4(1–3)506 8
31. Stenhousemuir 12.3	1	2	3	8					10		6		7	4	9	5	11‡		12								0–0(0–0)340 9
32. Stranraer* 22.3	1	3	6	8					10^1		8		7‡	4	9	5	14		12		11†	2					1–1(0–1)320 7
33. Montrose 26.3	1	3	6	8					10		7	2†		4	9_1	5				12					11^1		2–0(1–0)250 7
34. Berwick R* 2.4	1	3	6	7					10^2		8†		2	14	4	9_1	5					12		11			2–0(1–0)379 7
35. Cowdenbeath 9.4	1	3	6	8‡					10		14	7†	2	9^1			5					12	11				1–0(1–0)239 7
36. Ayr U* 16.4	1	3	6	12					10		14	7†	2	11	4	9_1	5			8‡							1–3(0–3)1501 7
37. Albion R 23.4	1	3	6	12					10		11	7†	2	4^1	9_1	5			14	8‡							2–1(0–0)200 6
38. St Johnstone* 30.4	1	3	6	7					10		12	2	11	4	9_1	5			8†								1–1(0–0)817 7
39. East Stirling* 7.5	1	3	6	4					10		7†	2	11	9	5		12							8			0–1(0–1)355 7
Apps(subs)/goals	39(0)0	34(1)0	26(5)0	30(0)0	34(2)2	14(0)0	9(4)1	6(5)2	39(0)12	27(0)6	11(1)2	14(2)0	17(1)0	18(13)4	36(0)4	31(0)14	35(0)1	5(4)0	10(0)0	5(8)0	7(0)1	10(1)0	3(0)0	10(0)0	1(0)0	3(0)1	Final League Position: 7

ARBROATH – LEAGUE RECORD 1987–88 (DIVISION TWO)

Match no/Opp/Date		D Jackson	A Duff	P Jack	I Phillip	A Hill	D Sted	F Morrison	B Mitchell	A McKenna	G Cumming	D Laing	J Fotheringham	A Anderson	A Brannigan	G Mackie	A Richardson	D Burnside	B Kerr	J Rae	P Fleming	R Forrest	P Anderson	L Fridge	D Todd	D Balfour	K Tindall	C Farnan	FT(HT)Att Lge pos
1. Queen's Park*	8.8	1	2	3	4	5	6	7	8¹	9†	10¹	11	12¹																3-1(2-0)500 —
2. Stranraer	15.8	1	2	3	4	5			12	9¹‡	10	11†	14	6	7	8													1-3(1-1)390 7
3. Stirling Albion*	22.8	1	2	3†	4	5		6		9½	14¹	12	10‡		7	8	11												3-2(1-2)581 5
4. St Johnstone	29.8	1		2	6‡	5		14		9¹	10†	3		4	7	8	11	12											1-3(0-1)1598 8
5. Albion R*	5.9	1	2	3	4	5	12	14	9²		10	6‡	8			11¹	7†												3-0(0-0)390 7
6. Montrose*	12.9	1	2	3‡		5		12	4	9		14	10	6	8		11	7†											0-0(0-0)866 6
7. Stenhousemuir	15.9	1	2	3		5		12	4	9†		10	6	8¹		11	7												1-1(0-1)250 —
8. Alloa	19.9	1	2	3†		5		12	4	9		10	6	8¹	14	11	7‡												1-3(1-0)424 7
9. Berwick R*	26.9	1		3	4	5		12	2	9¹‡		10¹	6	8¹		11	7†	14											3-1(1-0)413 6
10. East Stirling*	3.10	1		3	4	5			2	9		10¹	6	8		11	7												1-1(1-0)405 6
11. Ayr U	10.10	1		3	4	5		7	2	12		9	6	8		11	10†												0-2(0-0)2846 7
12. Cowdenbeath	17.10	1			4	5¹		7	2	9³		10¹	6	8	11			3											5-3(2-2)140 6
13. Brechin C*	24.10	1		4‡	5			7	2	9†		10	6	8	14	11	12	3¹											1-2(1-1)726 6
14. Queen's Park	31.6	1	2	3†	4	5		7		9		10	6	8¹	12	11													1-1(0-1)525 7
15. Stranraer*	7.11		2	3		5		7	4	9²		10	6	8¹		11			1										3-2(2-0)369 5
16. Stirling Albion	14.11		2†	3		5		7	4	9		10‡	6	8		11	12	14	1										0-3(0-3)434 6
17. Berwick R	21.11	1			8	5		12	2	9		10¹	6	7	4†	11²				3									3-3(2-1)317 6
18. Alloa*	28.11	1				5			2	9		10	4	8		11¹				7									1-1(1-1)408 7
19. Stenhousemuir*	12.12	1		3	6	5		14	2	9¹†		10¹		8¹		11		12		7	4‡								3-0(2-0)356 6
20. Albion R	26.12	1		3	6	5			2	9		10		8		11				7¹	4								1-0(0-1)300 6
21. Montrose	29.12	1		3	6	5		2†		9		10¹	12	8		11				7	4								1-1(0-1)900 —
22. St Johnstone*	2.1	1		3	6†	5			9‡			10	2	8		11	14	12		7	4								0-2(0-1)2640 6
23. Ayr U*	16.1	1		3				11¹	2	12		10	4	8	5		9¹†			7	6								2-4(1-1)772 8
24. East Stirling	23.1	1		3				11‡	2	12		10¹	4	8	5	14	9†			7	6								1-1(0-1)300 9
25. Cowdenbeath*	9.2			3				7	2	12	3	10	4	8	5		9†			11²	6	1							2-1(1-0)427 —
26. Stenhousemuir	13.2			3				7	2	9		10	6	8	5		12			11‡	4	1							1-1(1-0)200 7
27. Brechin C	16.2			3				11	2	9		10	4	8	5					7‡	6	1							1-1(0-0)200 —
28. Alloa*	20.2	1		3				11	2	9‡		10	4	8	5	14	12			7¹	6†								1-1(0-1)380 6
29. Stranraer	27.2			3†	5		4		2	9		10		8		11	12		1	7¹	6¹								3-0(1-0)300 6
30. Albion R*	5.3			3	5		4	12	2	9‡		10¹		8†		11	14¹		1	7²	6								4-0(1-0)265 7
31. Queen's Park*	12.3			3			4		2	9‡		10	8	5†	11		14		1	7¹	6		12						1-2(0-1)418 7
32. East Stirling	19.3			3					2			9	4		8	10	11			7¹	6	5	1						1-2(1-2)250 7
33. Brechin C*	26.3			3	14			12	2			9	4‡		8	10	11			7†	6	5‡	1						0-3(0-1)343 8
34. Ayr U	2.4			5				7	2	12		9†	6	8		10	11	3‡	1		4		14						0-3(0-2)3343 8
35. Montrose*	9.4			5	3			12	2	9			6‡	10	14	11			1	7¹	4		8†						1-1(0-1)443 8
36. St Johnstone	16.4			5				8	3	9		10†		6	2	11	12		1	7	4								0-4(0-2)2503 9
37. Stirling Albion	23.4			3				7†	2	9		10	6			11		5	1	8	4		12						0-2(0-0)375 9
38. Cowdenbeath*	30.4			4	10†			12	2			9	6			11			1	7	5	8		3					0-0(0-0)451 9
39. Berwick R	7.5			6	10			12	2			9	4			11			1	7		8†	1	3	5				0-4(0-0)270 9

Final League Position: 9

Apps(subs)/goals: 22(0)0, 10(0)0, 31(0)0, 24(1)0, 24(0)1, 40(0)0, 16(1)3, 34(2)1, 30(5)13, 3(1)2, 4(2)0, 30(3)9, 30(1)0, 33(0)6, 13(3)0, 26(2)4, 11(8)1, 9(7)1, 36(0)1, 100(0)0, 22(0)12, 20(0)1, 5(3)0, 3(0)0, 24(0)0, 1(0)0

Own goal: G. Hay, match 29.

AYR UNITED – LEAGUE RECORD 1987–88 (DIVISION TWO)

Match no/Opp/Date		G Watson	J Hughes	J McCann	W Furphy	I McAllister	S Evans	H Templeton	P McKenzie	T Walker	I Sludden	J Cowell	D McCracken	S McIntyre	R Scott	K Wilson	P Welsh	R Brown	FT(HT)Att Lge pos
1. St Johnstone	8.8	1	2	3	4	5	6	7	8	9	10	11							0-0(0-0)1536 —
2. Montrose*	15.8	1	2	3	4	5	6	7^1	8†	9^2	10	11	12						3-1(1-1)1587 4
3. Berwick R	22.8	1	3		4		6	7_1		9^1	10	11†	5	2	8	12			2-0(0-0)724 2
4. Stranraer*	29.8	1	3		4	5	6‡	7		9^2	10^3	11	14	2	8†	12			5-1(1-1)1948 1
5. Stirling Albion	5.9	1	3		4	5	6†	7^1		9	10	11		2	8	12			1-1(0-1)2170 1
6. Cowdenbeath	12.9	1	3^1		4	5	6‡	7^1		9^1	10^3	11	14	2	8†	12			6-1(2-0)484 1
7. Albion R*	15.9	1	3		4	5	6	7_1		9	10^1	11^1		2	8				3-0(2-0)2231 —
8. Brechin C	19.9	1	3		4	5	6	7_1		9^2	10	11		2	8				3-0(0-0)650 1
9. Queen's Park*	26.9	1	3		4	5	6	7_1		9	10^3	11		2	8				4-1(2-1)2805 1
10. Stenhousemuir	3.10	1	3		4	5‡	6	7_1		9^1	10^2	11^2	14	2	8†	12			6-0(2-0)700 1
11. Arbroath*	10.10	1	3		4	5‡	6	7_1		9^1	10	11	14	2	8†	12			2-0(0-0)2846 1
12. Alloa*	17.10	1	3	2	4		6	7_1	12^1	9†	10	11	5		8				2-1(0-0)2673 1
13. East Stirling	24.10	1	3		4		6	7^1			10^1	11	5	2	8	9			2-0(0-0)800 1
14. St Johnstone*	31.10	1	3		4		6	7		9	10	11	5	2	8				0-3(0-0)5168 1
15. Montrose	7.11	1	3^1		4		6	7^1		9^2	10	11	5	2	8				4-2(0-1)700 1
16. Berwick R*	14.11	1	3	14	4		6	7^1‡	12	9	10	11†	5	2	8				2-0(1-0)2596 1
17. Queen's Park	21.11	1	3		4		6	7^1		9	10^1	11	5	2	8				2-0(0-0)1792 1
18. Brechin C*	28.11	1	3		4		6	7		9	10^1	11	5	2	8				1-2(0-1)3017 1
19. Albion R	12.12	1	3		4		6	7		9	10	11	5	2	8^1				1-1(0-1)950 1
20. Cowdenbeath*	19.12	1	3	12	4		6	7^1		9†	10^1	11	5^1	2	8‡	14			3-1(1-0)2080 1
21. Stirling Albion*	26.12	1	3		4		6	7^1		9^2	10^1	11	5	2	8				4-0(3-0)3658 1
22. Stranraer	2.1	1	3	12	4		6	7		9	10^1	11	5^1	2	8†				2-1(1-1)2080 1
23. Arbroath	16.1	1	3	2	4	12	6†	7^1		9‡	10^2	11	5		8^1	14			4-2(1-1)772 1
24. Stenhousemuir*	23.1	1	3		4	5	6	7^1		10	11	9	2†	8^1	12				3-0(1-0)2714 1
25. East Stirling*	6.2	1	3	12	4	5^1	6	7^1		9	10	11		2†	8				2-0(1-0)2347 1
26. Berwick R	13.2	1	3	2	4	5	6	7		9†	10	11^1		8	12				1-0(0-0)1000 1
27. Queen's Park*	20.2	1	3	2	4	5	6	7		9^1‡	10	11†	14	8	12				1-1(0-0)2771 1
28. St Johnstone	27.2	1	3		4	5	6‡	7	8†	14	10	11	9	2	12				0-2(0-2)5109 1
29. Alloa	1.3	1	3	2	4	5	6	7		9	10^2	11		8					2-0(0-0)941 —
30. Cowdenbeath*	5.3	1	3	2	4	5^1	6	7^1		9	10^1	11		8^2					5-0(1-0)2244 1
31. Montrose	12.3	1	3	2	4	5	6	7		9^1	10	11		8					1-1(1-1)600 1
32. Albion R*	19.3	1	3	12	4†	5	6	7		9^1	10^2	11	2	8^2					6-2(4-1)2688 1
33. Stirling Albion	26.3	1	3		4	5	6	7_1		9	10^1	11	2	8					2-2(1-1)1796 1
34. Arbroath*	2.4	1	3		4	5	6	7†		9	10^2	11^1	2	8	12				3-0(2-0)3343 1
35. Stranraer*	9.4	1	3	14	4†	5	6	7^1		9^1	10^1	11	2‡	8	12				3-1(0-1)2967 1
36. Alloa	16.4	1	3	5		6	7†	14	9	10^1	11^1	2	12	8^1‡	4				3-1(3-0)1501 1
37. East Stirling*	23.4	1	3	4		5	6	7		9	10	11	2	8					0-0(0-0)3442 1
38. Stenhousemuir	30.4	1	3	12	4	5	6	7_1	14	9	10	11	2†	8					0-1(0-0)1130 1
39. Brechin C	7.5	1	3		4	5	6	7		9^1	10	11	2†	8					1-2(0-1) 800 1

Apps(subs)/goals: 39(0) 0 / 39(0) 2 / 11(8) 0 / 37(0) 0 / 25(1) 2 / 39(0) 23 / 34(1) 0 / 36(1) 19 / 39(0) 31 / 39(0) 6 / 15(5) 2 / 29(1) 0 / 23(1) 3 / 15(12) 5 / 0(2) 0 / 1(0) 0

Final League Position: 1

Own goal: A. Rodgers, match 32.

486

BERWICK RANGERS – LEAGUE RECORD 1987–1988 (DIVISION TWO)

Match no/Opp/Date		J Thomson	H McCann	J Fleming	H Douglas	B Marshall	N Oliver	G Alexander	M Main	G Buckley	P Cavanagh	T Graham	K Buckley	R Haig	J Sokoluk	G Leitch	M Thompson	E Tait	K Wood	D Moyes	D Sanderson	I Watson	C Lyswn	P Renton	K Shell	C Pearce	G Tait	B Donaldson	M Cameron	A Thomson	S Bickmore	FT(HT)Att	Lge pos
1. Stranraer*	8.8	1	2†	3	4	5	6	7	8	9	10‡	11	12	14																		0-1(0-1)440	—
2. Brechin C	15.8	1	2	3	4	5‡		8		9	10	12			7	11																0-4(0-2)592	14
3. Ayr U*	22.8	1	2†	3	4			8		9	10	12			7	11	5	6‡	14													0-2(0-0)724	14
4. Cowdenbeath*	29.8	1		3	4	5	2		9‡	10†		14	7			11₁	12‡			6												2-2(0-0)442	13
5. Queen's Park	5.9			3	4†	5	2			9			7	12	10	8‡	11¹		6	1												2-3(1-3)511	13
6. Stenhousemuir*	12.9			3	4	5		12	2			14		7†	9	10‡	8	11		6		1										1-3(0-1)267	13
7. East Stirling	15.9			3	4	5		11	8			9	14	10‡	7†	6	12		2		1											0-1(0-0)200	—
8. Montrose*	19.9			3	4	5		7	8	9¹†		12		10‡	11	6		2		1												2-1(1-1)310	14
9. Arbroath	26.9			3	4	5		7†	8	9¹		14	12	10	11‡	6		2		1												1-3(0-1)413	14
10. Stirling Albion	3.10	1		3	4			7	11†			12	14	10		8	6‡	5	2		9											0-1(0-1)628	14
11. St Johnstone*	10.10	1		3	4			7	8		12		11†	10		6		5	2		9											0-4(0-1)779	14
12. Albion R*	17.10			3	4			7			11		10	12		6†		5	2	14	9											0-3(0-1)319	14
13. Alloa	24.10			3	5	4		7			11	8†	6	10			2	1	9	12												0-1(0-0)365	14
14. Stranraer	31.10			6	5	4		8				10	12	11			2	1	9²	3	7†											2-0(1-0)250	14
15. Brechin C*	7.11			6	5	4		8			10†	12	11			2	1	9	3	7‡	14											0-2(0-2)420	14
16. Ayr U	14.11			6		4		8			10	12	11		5		2	1	9	3	7†											0-2(0-1)2596	14
17. Arbroath*	21.11			3	5	4‡		14			7	9¹	11¹†	10		2	1	8	12		6¹											3-3(2-1)317	14
18. Montrose	28.11			3		4		14			12	7	9	11	6		2	1	8†	5‡		10										0-4(0-2)300	14
19. Stenhousemuir	19.12			3	5¹	4		12				14	9	11	6		2							10‡	8¹	1	7†					2-1(1-0)250	14
20. Queen's Park*	26.12			3	5	4		12				14	9	11	6		2							10‡	8†	1	7					0-1(0-0)550	14
21. Cowdenbeath	2.1			3¹		5		8			14	12	11†	9	6	4		2						10‡		1	7²					3-5(2-4)200	14
22. St Johnstone	16.1			3	5	4		11†				6	10			8		2						12		1	7	9¹				1-2(0-1)3106	14
23. East Stirling*	19.1			3	5¹	4		12				6‡	11†			8		2		10		14			1	7	9					1-1(1-0)380	—
24. Stirling Albion*	23.1			4	5			11†			12	6	7			2		10	3		14			1	8	9‡						0-4(0-3)320	14
25. Albion R	30.1			3	5	4		8†			11	6	10‡			2		9		12			1	7¹								2-0(0-0)300	14
26. Ayr U*	13.2			3	5	4			11	6†	10‡		12	8		2		9			14	1	7									0-1(0-0)1000	14
27. Alloa*	23.2			3	5¹	4			11	6	10‡		12	8†		2		9	14			1	7									1-2(0-2)279	—
28. Brechin C*	27.2			3	5	4	14		11	10†	12		8			2		9	7‡			1	6									0-0(0-0)725	13
29. East Stirling	1.3			3	5	4	14		11	10†		12	6			2		9₁	7‡			1	8									1-2(1-1)201	—
30. Queen's Park	5.3			3		5	8			11†	9		6			4		10	14	7‡	12	1	2									0-2(0-0)350	13
31. Stirling Albion	12.3			3		5	2	14		11	10‡	12		6†			4		7			1	8		9							0-2(0-1)297	13
32. Stenhousemuir*	19.3				5	2	8		11	6			10			4		7			1	3		9¹								1-3(1-0)300	13
33. Stranraer*	26.3			3	5		2	7		11¹	6	10		8¹		4			1		9											2-0(1-0)300	13
34. Alloa	2.4			3	5	4	2	14		11†	7		12	8‡		6		10		1		9										0-2(0-1)379	13
35. St Johnstone*	9.4			3	5	4		11†	14		12	8		2		10			6	1	7‡		9									0-2(0-2)570	13
36. Montrose	16.4			3	5	4		11		10	6†	7		2				8	1	12		9										0-1(0-0)517	13
37. Cowdenbeath	23.4			3	5	4	7		11†	12	14		2				6	1	10‡		9											0-3(0-0)150	14
38. Albion R*	30.4			3	5	4		11	14	12		10†		8‡		6	1	7		9												1-3(0-2)250	13
39. Arbroath*	7.5			3	4			7¹		6†		5¹		8¹			1	2		9¹												4-0(0-0)270	13

Final League Position: 13

Appearances (subs)/goals: 6(0) 0 · 3(0) 0 · 38(0) 1 · 33(0) 3 · 32(0) 0 · 10(2) 0 · 20(8) 0 · 7(0) 0 · 7(0) 2 · 40(0) 0 · 17(6) 3 · 18(10) 0 · 19(4) 1 · 16(2) 2 · 14(4) 3 · 11(1) 0 · 4(1) 1 · 35(0) 0 · 7(0) 0 · 40(0) 0 · 19(0) 3 · 5(3) 0 · 9(2) 1 · 35(1) 0 · 8(1) 2 · 21(0) 0 · 9(1) 3 · 30(0) 1 · 9(0) 2

Also played: A. De Gaetano at 6† in match 2, N. Nisbet, at 14 in match 2, R. Gordon, at 1‡ in match 12, E. Ewing at 8 in match 12, S. Porteous at 10 in match 39, J. Kirkhope at 11 in match 39, B. Cordery at 12 in match 39.

BRECHIN CITY – LEAGUE RECORD 1987–88 (DIVISION TWO)

Match no/Opp	Date	D Lawrie	D Watt	C Candlish	J Inglis	G Stevens	K Taylor	W Gallacher	C Adam	C Lytwyn	D Scott	K Lyall	G Lees	R Brown	J Bourke	E Scrimgeour	J McLeod	I Paterson	G Buckley	A Reid	R Hamilton	S Davidson	S Wilkie	P Ritchie	M Harkins	B Smart	FT(HT)Att	Lge pos
1. Alloa	8.8	1	2	3_1	4	5	6	7	8‡	9†	10	11	12	14													1–1(0–0)620	—
2. Berwick R*	15.8	1	2	3_1	4^2	5	6	7‡	8^1		10	11	9†	12	14												4–0(2–0)592	1
3. St Johnstone	22.8	1	2	3	4	5	6^1	7	8†		10	14	11‡	12	9												1–1(1–1)1768	1
4. Montrose*	29.8	1	2	3	4	5	6	7^1	8†		10^1	11†	12	14	9												2–0(0–0)500	2
5. Cowdenbeath	5.9	1	2	3	4^1	5	6	7	8		10‡	11†	12	14	9												1–1(1–1)150	2
6. Queen's Park*	12.9	1	2		4	5	6‡	7	8†		10	11	12	9^1	3	14											1–1(1–0)400	2
7. Stirling Albion	15.9	1	2	6	4	5		7	8		10		3	9^1	11												1–2(0–0)584	—
8. Ayr U*	19.9	1	2	3	4	5	8	7	9		10		11	6													0–3(0–0)650	5
9. Stranraer	26.9	1	2	3^1	4	5	10‡	6	8		11	7‡				14	9										1–1(0–0)400	4
10. Albion R*	3.10	1	2	3	4	5		8†	6		10		7	14			12	9^1	11‡								2–1(0–0)400	4
11. East Stirling*	10.10	1	2	3		5	4	8			10		7	6				9	11								0–0(0–0)200	4
12. Stenhousemuir*	17.10	1	2	3		5		12^1	8^1		10		7	4				9	11	6†							2–0(0–0)350	4
13. Arbroath	24.10	1	2	3_1		5	12	6	8†		10		7	4				9	11^1								2–1(1–1)726	4
14. Alloa*	31.10	1	2	3		5		6	8		10		7^1†	4	12			9	11^2								3–1(3–1)500	4
15. Berwick R	7.11	1	2	3		5	12	6†	8		10		7‡	4	14			9	11^1								2–0(2–0)420	4
16. St Johnstone*	14.11	1	2	3		5†		7	8^1		10			4	14			9^1	11	6‡							2–1(2–1)1104	2
17. Stranraer*	21.11	1	2	3		5	12	7†	8		10			4	14			9	11^2		6‡						2–0(1–0)416	2
18. Ayr U	28.11	1	2	3		5	6	7	8^2		10			4	12			9	11†								2–1(1–0)3017	2
19. Stirling Albion*	12.12	1	2		3	5	12	6†	8		10		14	4	7‡			9	11^1								1–2(0–0)500	3
20. Queen's Park	19.12	1	2	3		5	6	7†	8		10		12	4				9	11								0–2(0–1)434	3
21. Cowdenbeath*	26.12	1	2	3	4	5		7	8		10		12^1					9	11†	6							1–0(0–0)350	3
22. Montrose	2.1	1	2	3	4	5		7	8		10		11†		12			9^1		6							1–0(1–0)800	3
23. East Stirling*	16.1	1	2	3	4	5	14	7†	8		12							9^1	11^1	10	6‡						2–3(1–1)300	3
24. Albion R	23.1	1	2	3	4	5					10		7		12			9	11†	8	6						0–2(0–0)350	4
25. Alloa	13.2	1		3‡	4	5	8	7†	14		10		12	2				9	11		6						0–3(0–1)347	4
26. Arbroath*	16.2	1	2	3	4	5			8		10		7^1					9	11		6						1–1(0–0)200	—
27. Stranraer*	20.2	1	2	3_2	4	5		12	8		7^1	14						9†	11^1	6	10‡						4–1(2–1)300	4
28. Stenhousemuir	24.2	1	2	3	4	5		14	8^2		7	12						9	11‡	6	10†						2–1(2–0)250	—
29. Berwick R	27.2	1	2	3	4	5		10	8		7	12						9	11	6†							0–0(0–0)725	3
30. Montrose*	8.3	1	2	3	5			7†	8		14	10	4					9	11	12	6‡						0–1(0–1)550	—
31. Albion R	12.3	1	2	3_1	6‡	5	14				10		12					9^1	11†	4	8	7^3					5–1(2–0)200	4
32. Cowdenbeath*	19.3	1	2	3	6	5					10		12					9	11†	4	8	7					0–3(0–2)350	4
33. Arbroath	26.3	1		4	3_1		8		10^1		12	5						9	11^1	2	6	7†					3–0(1–0)343	4
34. Queen's Park*	2.4	1	2	3			5		6			4						9	11^2	10	8	7					2–0(1–0)500	3
35. East Stirling*	9.4	1	2	3	14		5		8		12	4^1						9	11‡	10	6	7†					1–0(0–0)325	3
36. Stenhousemuir	16.4	1	2			4	8†		10		9	5^1							11	3	6‡	7	14				1–2(0–2)240	3
37. St Johnstone	23.4	1	2	3	4	5			8		6	7						9	11†	10		12					0–2(0–1)1689	4
38. Stirling Albion*	30.4	1	2	3	4	5		8‡	6		10	12						9^1	11	14	7†						1–1(0–1)400	4
39. Ayr U*	7.5		2	3		5		10	8†		7	4						9	11^2	6		12				1	2–1(1–0)800	4
Apps(subs)/goals		38(0)0	38(0)0	36(0)8	25(1)3	35(0)0	16(2)1	27(3)2	34(1)8	1(0)0	29(2)1	4(1)0	21(13)4	19(1)2	6(8)2	1(0)0	1(3)0	30(0)6	29(0)15	1(0)0	16(2)0	1(0)0	13(1)0	7(1)3	0(1)0	1(0)0		

Final League Position: 4

Own goal: B. Marshall, match 15.

CELTIC – LEAGUE RECORD 1987–88 (PREMIER DIVISION)

Match no/Opp/Date	P Bonner	C Morris	A Rogan	R Aitken	D Whyte	P Grant	W Stark	P McStay	M McGhee	A Walker	T Burns	P McGugan	O Archdeacon	A Shepherd	D McGuire	A McKnight	M McCarthy	F McAvennie	D McCarrison	J Miller	A Baillie	FT(HT) Att Lge pos
1. Morton 8.8	1	2	3	4	5	6	7^1	8	9^1	10^2	11†		12									4–0(1–0) 15,500 —
2. Hearts* 12.8	1	2	3	4	5	6	7	8	9^1	10	11											1–0(0–0) 29,815 —
3. Motherwell* 15.8	1	2	3	4	5		7^1†	8‡	9^1	10^2	11	6	12	14								4–1(2–0) 24,478 1
4. Dunfermline A 22.8	1	2	3	4	5†	6	7	8	9	10_1	11‡	12	14									1–2(1–1) 18,070 2
5. Rangers* 29.8		2	3	4	5	6	7^1	8	9	10	11					1						1–0(1–0) 60,800 1
6. Dundee U 5.9		2	3	4	5	6	7	8	9	10	11					1						0–0(0–0) 16,192 1
7. Falkirk 12.9		2	3	4	5	6	7	8	9	10	11^1					1						1–0(1–0) 17,500 1
8. Aberdeen* 19.9		2	3	4	5	6	7^1	8	9†	10	11^1			12		1						2–2(1–0) 38,944 2
9. St Mirren 26.9		2	3	4	5^1	6	7	8		10	11	9†		12		1						1–0(0–0) 18,011 1
10. Hibernian* 3.10		2	3	4	5	11	7	8		10^1		12				1	6†	9				1–1(0–0) 31,805 3
11. Dundee 7.10		2	3	4	5	11‡	7†	8		10_1		14	12			1	6	9				1–1(0–1) 13,238 —
12. Morton* 10.10		2		4	3†	6	7	8		10^1		11				1	5	9^1				3–1(3–1) 22,780 2
13. Rangers 17.10		2	12	4	3†	6	7	8		10^1	11‡	14				1	5	9				2–2(2–0) 44,000 2
14. Dundee U* 24.10	1	2		4	3	6	7†	8		10		11	12^1				5	9				1–2(0–0) 31,032 2
15. Falkirk* 28.10	1	2		4	3	6	7^2†	8	12	10‡	11^1	14					5	9				3–2(1–0) 11,381 —
16. Aberdeen 31.10	1	2		4	3	6	7	8	11	10							5	9^1				1–0(0–1) 21,000 2
17. Hearts 7.11	1	2	12	4	3	6†	7	8	11^1	10	14						5	9‡				1–1(0–1) 29,000 2
18. Dundee* 14.11	1	2	3	4	5	6		8		10^2	11							9^2		7^1		5–0(2–0) 31,664 2
19. Motherwell 17.11	1	2	14	4	3†	6		8	12	10‡†	11‡							9		7		2–0(1–0) 17,261 —
20. Dunfermline A* 21.11	1	2		4	3	6	11^1	8		10^2								9^1		7		4–0(3–0) 28,534 2
21. St Mirren* 25.11	1	2		4	3	6^1	11	8		10								9		7		1–0(0–0) 26,718 —
22. Hibernian 28.11	1	2	12	4	3	6	11†	8		10								9^1		7		1–0(1–0) 23,500 1
23. Morton 5.12	1	2		4	3	6	11	8		10								9^4		7		4–0(1–0) 14,500 1
24. Hearts* 12.12	1	2	14	4	3‡	6	11	8^1	12	10^1								9		7†		2–2(0–1) 43,968 1
25. Aberdeen* 19.12	1	2	3	4	5	6	11	8	12	10†								9		7		0–0(0–0) 37,721 1
26. Falkirk 22.12	1	2	3	4	5‡	6	11	8^1	12	10^1								9†		7	14	2–0(0–0) 12,000 —
27. Dundee U 26.12		2	3	4		6†	11	8		10_1	12					1		9		7^1	5	2–1(1–0) 18,458 1
28. Rangers* 2.1	1	2		4		6	11	8		10						1		9^2		7	5	2–0(1–0) 60,800 1
29. St Mirren 9.1		2	3	4		6		8	10		11					1		9		7	5	1–1(0–1) 19,030 1
30. Hibernian* 16.1	1	2		4	3	6		8^1		10	11							9		7^1	5	2–0(2–0) 34,886 1
31. Motherwell* 6.2	1	2		4	3	6		8		10^1	11						5	9		7		1–0(0–0) 25,035 1
32. Dundee 13.2	1	2^1	3	4			11		8	12	10†						5	9^1		7	6	2–1(0–0) 17,106 1
33. Morton* 27.2	1	2	4^1		3	6	7†	8		10		11					5	9		12		1–0(0–0) 23,120 1
34. Dunfermline A 2.3	1	2		4	3	6	11†‡	8	14	10‡	12						5	9^2		7		4–0(3–0) 17,448 —
35. Falkirk* 5.3	1	2	14	4	3	6	11	8‡	9^1	10^1	12						5			7†		2–0(2–0) 23,174 1
36. Rangers 20.3	1	2	12	4	3		7	8^1		10^1							6			11†	5	2–1(0–0) 43,650 —
37. Dundee U* 26.3	1	2	14	4	3	6	7†	8		10	11‡							9		12	5	0–0(0–0) 34,933 —
38. Aberdeen 30.3	1	2	3	4		6	7	8		10^1								9		11	5	1–0(0–0) 22,700 —
39. Hibernian 2.4	1	2	3	4		6	7^1	8	12	10^1								9		11†	5	2–0(1–0) 19,500 1
40. St Mirren* 5.4	1	2	3	4		6†	7‡	8^1	12	10^1	9							14		11	5	2–0(0–0) 45,465 —
41. Hearts 16.4	1	2	3	4	5		7†	8	11^1	10	6					9‡				14	12	1–2(0–1) 26,200 1
42. Dundee* 23.4	1	2^1	3	4		6	12	8	14	10^2	11						5	9‡		7†		3–0(1–0) 60,800 1
43. Motherwell 30.4	1	2	3^1	4		6	12	8		10†	6	14					5	9		11‡	4	1–0(0–1) 13,874 1
44. Dunfermline A* 7.5	1	2^1	3	4		6	14	7‡	8†	10	12						5	9		11		1–0(1–0) 44,482 1

Final League Position: 1

Apps(subs)/goals: 32(0)/0   44(0)/3   25(8)/0   43(0)/1   41(0)/3   36(0)/2   44(3)/8   44(0)/5   15(9)/6   42(0)/26   21(6)/2   1(0)/0   4(6)/1   0(6)/0   0(0)/0   12(0)/0   22(0)/0   32(0)/15   0(3)/0   24(5)/0   11(2)/0

Own goals: T. Butcher, match 13; C. Money, match 29.

CLYDE – LEAGUE RECORD 1987–88 (DIVISION ONE)

Match no/Opp/Date	P Latchford	C Napier	C Buchanan	D Walker	P Flexney	P McDowall	A Willock	S Millar	C McGlashan	J Mailer	D Henderson	W Watters	J Murphy	R McFarlane	K Housely	T Tait	D Atkins	R Donnelly	M Clark	T McElmaggart	S Quinn	N Anderson	J Devlin	K Knox	FT(HT)Att Lge pos
1. Dumbarton* 8.8	1	2	3¹	4¹	5	6	7	8	9¹	10¹	11¹														5-0(3-0)1000 —
2. Forfar Ath 11.8	1	2	3	4	5	6	7¹	8¹	9²	10¹	11														5-3(3-2)750 —
3. Hamilton A 15.8	1	2	3†	4₁	5	6	7	8	9¹	10	11‡	14		12											2-3(0-0)2311 3
4. East Fife* 22.8	1	3		4₁	5	6	7	8	12	10¹	11†	9		2											3-3(2-2)847 3
5. Partick Th* 29.8	1	3		4₁	5	6	7	8	9¹	10²	11			2											4-1(1-1)2700 3
6. Raith R 5.9	1	3		4¹	5	6	7¹‡	8	9	10	11‡	14	12	2											3-1(1-1)1612 3
7. Clydebank* 12.9	1	3		4³	5	6	7‡	8†	9	10²	11	14	12	2											5-1(1-1)1100 —
8. Airdrieonians 15.9	1	3		4¹	5	6	7		9²				2	8											3-4(2-0)1150 —
9. Meadowbank T* 19.9	1	2	3	4	5				9	10	11	7		6	8										0-0(0-0)600 2
10. Kilmarnock 26.9	1	3		4	5	6‡	7		9	10†	11	14	12	2	8										0-2(0-2)1750 2
11. Queen of South* 29.9	1	3		4	5		7¹		9	10†	11	12		6	2	8¹									2-3(0-0)900 —
12. Dumbarton 3.10		3		4	5		7		9¹	10	11			6	2	8	1								1-1(0-0)1200 5
13. Forfar Ath* 7.10		3		4	5¹		7		9	10	11†	12₁		2	8	6	1								2-2(1-0)600 —
14. East Fife 10.10		3		4	5		7¹		9¹	10†	11	12		2	8	6	1								2-0(2-0)718 5
15. Clydebank 17.10		3		4‡	5		7		9	10†	11	14	12	2	8	6	1								0-2(0-1)1124 6
16. Airdrieonians* 20.10		3		4	5¹		7	8	9	10	11			6	2		1								1-0(0-0)800 —
17. Hamilton A* 24.10		3		4	5		7	8	9	10	11	12		6†	2		1								0-3(0-1)1300 6
18. Queen of South 28.10		3		4	5		7†	8‡	9		11	10¹	12		2		1	6	14						1-3(1-2)700 —
19. Raith R* 31.10		3		4₁	5		7²	8	9	10	11†			2			1	6	12						3-2(1-1)950 6
20. Partick Th 7.11		3			5		7¹	8	9¹	10‡				2	4¹	1		6	11	12					4-1(2-1)2245 4
21. Meadowbank T* 14.11		3		4₁	5		7	8	9¹	10				2	12	1		6	11†						2-0(1-0)500 4
22. Kilmarnock* 21.11		3		4	5		7†	8	9¹	10¹				2			1	6	11	12					2-0(2-0)1145 2
23. Dumbarton* 28.11		3		4	5		7	8	9²	10¹				2‡			1	14	6	11	12				3-4(3-1)800 4
24. Forfar Ath 5.12	1	3		4			7	8	9²	10			12	2‡			5	6	11‡	14					2-4(1-1)620 —
25. Clydebank* 12.12		3	11				7	8	9		12	4		2‡			1	5	6						0-1(0-1)900 6
26. Airdrieonians 19.12		3		4			7¹‡	8†	9	10¹	11			2	12		1	5	6	14					2-0(2-0)1800 5
27. Raith R 26.12		3		4†			7		9	10	11‡	12		2	8		1	5	6	14					0-2(0-1)3129 6
28. Partick Th* 1.1		3		4	5		7		9	10		12		2‡	8		1	14	6	11†					1-2(0-1)2500 —
29. Kilmarnock 16.1		3		4	5		7		9	10				2	8†	12	1		6	11¹					1-3(1-2)1752 7
30. Meadowbank T* 26.1		3¹	10¹	5			7	8	9		11†			2‡			1	4	6	14	12				2-2(1-1)600 —
31. Hamilton A 6.2		3		5			7	8	9	10†				2		4	1		6	12	11				0-2(0-1)1709 7
32. East Fife* 24.2		3	10	5‡			7	8	9		12			2		4	1		6	14	11†				0-4(0-2)998 —
33. Dumbarton 27.2		3	10				7¹	8	9		11			2			1	5	6		4				1-0(0-0)750 8
34. Queen of South* 1.3		3	10¹				7¹	8	9		11			2			1	5	6		4				2-1(1-0)800 —
35. Clydebank 5.3		3	10				7¹	8‡	9		11†	12		2	14		1	5¹	6		4				2-1(1-0)1006 7
36. Raith R* 19.3		3	11				7	8¹	9					2				5	6	12	4†		10		1-2(1-0)700 7
37. Airdrieonians* 22.3		3					7²	8	9					2		4	1	5	6	11²			10		4-2(2-2)780 —
38. Partick Th 26.3		3					7	8	9					2		12	1	5	6	11	4†		10		0-1(0-1)2300 7
39. Hamilton A* 2.4		3	12	5				8	9			7		2		4	1	5		11†			10		0-4(0-1)1400 8
40. East Fife 9.4		3†	8‡				7		9					2		4	1	5	6	14	11	12	10		0-2(0-0)718 9
41. Kilmarnock* 16.4				5			9	7				12	2‡	4	1	8	6	11				3	10		0-1(0-1)1100 9
42. Meadowbank Th 23.4				4₁	5		7		9		11†			2	8	1		6	12			3	10		1-0(1-0)700 9
43. Forfar Ath* 30.4		8		4	5		7		9	11				2			1	6				3	10		0-1(0-0)600 9
44. Queen of South 7.5		2		4¹	5†		7		9					1		12	6	14	11‡	8	3	10			1-2(1-1)750 9

Final League Position: 9

Apps(subs)/goals: 12(0)0 / 42(0)1 / 40(1) / 3(0)16 / 33(0)2 / 9(0)0 / 40(0)13 / 29(0)2 / 42(1)16 / 33(0)11 / 25(0)(2) / 3(8)1 / 1(12) / 31(2)0 / 17(4)2 / 32(0)0 / 15(5)1 / 25(1)0 / 8(9)1 / 7(6)2 / 6(0)0 / 4(1)0 / 9(0)0

Own goal: R. Law, match 28.

490

CLYDEBANK – LEAGUE RECORD 1987–88 (DIVISION ONE)

Match no/Opp/Date		C Brodie	A Bain	J Rodger	S Murdoch	S Auld	D Irons	D Shanks	D Fourna	S Gordon	A Grant	T Bryce	C Gray	M Conroy	G McGurn	S Sweeney	J Dickson	D Fulton	J Gallacher	M Treanor	J Maher	P Harvey	H Caffrey	A Maxwell	J Chamley	B Wright	J Davies	E Ferguson	K Eadie	FT(HT)Att Lge pos
1. Queen of South*	8.8	1	2	3	4	5	6¹	7	8†	9	10	11‡	12	14																1–1(1–0)867 —
2. Hamilton A	11.8	1	12	3	8†	5		7		9‡	11²	14	6	10	2	4														2–3(2–2)1797
3. Forfar Ath	15.8	1	14	3		5		8		12	10		11	9	6‡	4	2	7†												0–3(0–1)746 11
4. Partick Th*	22.8			3		5	6	7		9†	10	11	12			8		1	2	4										0–2(0–1)2147 12
5. Dumbarton	29.8	1	9	3		5	6	7	8†		10			11¹			12		2	4										1–1(1–0)900 12
6. Airdrieonians*	5.9	1	9‡	3		5	6	7	8†	14	10			11²			12		2	4										2–3(2–1)1024 12
7. Clyde	12.9	1		3		5	6	7	12		10	9¹		11†		8‡			2	4	14									1–5(1–1)1100 12
8. Kilmarnock*	15.9		3†			5	6		12			9¹		10¹		8	14	1	2	4	7‡	11								2–0(2–0)880
9. Raith R*	19.9			3		5	6			9				10		8¹‡	12	1	2	4	7	11								1–2(0–1)1112 11
10. Meadowbank Th	26.9	11		3		5	6							10	9	8	12	1	2	4	7†									0–0(0–0)400 12
11. East Fife*	29.9	14	3†	5¹		6							10‡	9	12	8			2	4	7	1	11¹							2–1(2–0)600 —
12. Partick Th	3.10	1	11	3		5	6			14		7¹		9		12	10†		2	4	8‡									1–0(1–0)1799 9
13. Hamilton A*	6.10	1	9‡	3		5	6	7				10			12				2	4	8	11								0–2(0–2)950 —
14. Queen of South	10.10			3		5	6†	7		9								1	2	4	8	12		11	10					0–2(0–0)1400 11
15. Clyde*	17.10			3		5	6	7		9²								1	2	4	10			11	8					2–0(1–0)1124 11
16. Kilmarnock	20.10			3		5	6	7		10¹	12							1	2	4	9‡			11	8¹					3–1(2–0)1730
17. Forfar Ath*	24.10			3		5	6	7		14	10¹			12				1	2	4†	9‡			11	8					1–0(0–0)650
18. East Fife	28.10			3		5	6	7		12	10†							1	2	4	9			11¹	8¹					2–1(1–0)790 —
19. Airdrieonians	31.10			3		5	6	7†		14	10¹			12				1	2¹	4	9‡			11	8					2–0(1–0)1200 7
20. Dumbarton*	7.11			3		5	6			10¹				7				1	2	4	9			11²	8					3–1(2–1)1231 7
21. Raith R	14.11			3		5	6			12	10			7‡				1	2	4	9†			11	8	14				0–1(0–0)2140 7
22. Meadowbank T*	21.11			3		5	6¹	7‡		12	10¹			14				1	2	4	9‡			11	8					2–1(1–1)686 6
23. Partick Th*	28.11			3		5	6	14			10			7†				1	2	4	9‡			11	8	12				0–3(0–1)1892 7
24. Hamilton A	5.12			3		5	6	7			10			14				1	2‡	4	9			11†	8	12				0–4(0–2)1455 7
25. Clyde	12.12			3			6¹	7	9							5		1	2	4	10			11	8					1–0(1–0)900 7
26. Kilmarnock*	19.12			3		5	6	7†	10¹					9				1	2	4	11				8	12				1–0(0–0)1015 7
27. Airdrieonians	26.12					5	6¹	10			12						3	1	2	4	7†			11	8	9				1–0(0–0)1497 7
28. Dumbarton	2.1					5	6¹	7			10					2			3¹	4	11¹				8	9				3–1(0–1)1077 5
29. Raith R*	9.1	1				4	6¹	7			10¹					2	5				11			3	8¹	9				3–1(1–1)1383 4
30. Meadowbank Th	16.1		12			6	5	8		14						3†	2	5		11¹	4	7	10‡	9¹						2–3(0–3)600 6
31. Forfar Ath	27.1			3		5	6				7					2†	1	12	4		11	10¹	8		9¹					2–2(1–0)676 —
32. Queen of South*	6.2			3		5	6	2			9†						1	4	12		11	8	7	10¹						1–0(1–0)842 6
33. Partick Th	27.2			3		5	6	11			10†						1	2	4	12		8	7	9						0–3(0–0)2844 6
34. East Fife*	1.3			3			6				10¹			5			1	2¹	4	11		8	7	9						2–0(0–0)587 —
35. Clyde*	5.3	1		3	6	12				9¹				5			2	4	14	10†	11‡	8	7							1–2(0–1)1006 6
36. Kilmarnock	12.3		3‡	6	5			14		9				4		12	1	2	11†			8	7	10‡						2–2(1–1)1549 5
37. Airdrieonians	19.3		3	2				8	12	5		14	1		4	6		11†	10	7‡		9								0–1(0–0)904 6
38. Dumbarton*	26.3		3			5		11¹	6	12				1	2	4	8†		10	7	9									1–0(0–0)1088 4
39. Queen of South	2.4		3¹	5				9			2	11†	1	4	6		12	8	7	10										1–0(0–0)1050 4
40. Forfar Ath*	9.4		3	4				9			5			1	2	6	12	11³†	8	7	10									3–2(1–0)505 3
41. Meadowbank T*	16.4		3	4				9			5†			1	2	6	12	11	8	7	10									0–2(0–1)765 3
42. Raith R	23.4		6	4				9¹			5	2	1	3				11	8	7²	10									3–2(2–0)1057 3
43. Hamilton A*	30.4		3	4				9¹			5	2	1		6			11¹	8¹	7	10									3–1(2–0)1546 3
44. East Fife	7.5		3	4		5		9¹			2	1	6					11	8	7	10									1–0(1–0)1496 —
Apps(subs)/goals		10(0)/0	6(3)/0	37(1)/1	7(0)/0	41(1)/1	31(0)/6	25(1)/0	6(4)/1	3(2)/0	27(8)/10	2(1)/0	20(2)/11	2(3)/0	12(2)/0	20(6)/1	2(6)/0	33(0)/0	36(1)/3	37(0)/0	22(6)/1	4(1)/0	1(0)/0	27(0)/10	29(0)/4	18(4)/3	4(0)/0	14(0)/5		Final League Position: 3

COWDENBEATH – LEAGUE RECORD 1987–88 (DIVISION TWO)

Match no/Opp/Date		R Allan	R Baillie	P Kirkcaldy	L Muir	D Grant	D McGovern	G Proudfoot	W Paxton	R Grant	P Cherry	K Hepburn	K McCulloch	P Leetion	J Sinnet	S Lynch	M Cochrane	R Dall	W Herd	P Cavanagh	G Hutt	S Williamson	A MacKenzie	S Burnside	S McKean	D Young	D Taylor	J Reid	G Malone	D Walker	FT(HT)Att	Lge pos
1. East Stirling	8.8	1	2	3	4	5	6	7	8†	9^1	10	11		12																	1–0(1–0)634	—
2. St Johnstone*	15.8	1	3	11†	4	5	6		8	9	7		2	12	10																0–3(0–1)640	9
3. Alloa	22.8	1	2†	3	4	5	6^1		8	9	7^1	11	12	14	10‡																2–5(2–3)415	12
4. Berwick R	29.8	1	3†	12	4	5		8		9‡	10	6		7		2	11														2–2(0–0)442	11
5. Brechin C*	5.9	1		14	4	5	6			9	7^1	12		10†	2		3^1	8	11												1–1(1–1)150	11
6. Ayr U*	12.9	1			4	5	6			10		7			9	2	3	8^1	11												1–6(0–2)484	12
7. Stranraer	15.9	1			4	5	6			9	10	12		7^2	2		3		11	8†											2–2(1–1)450	—
8. Albion R*	19.9	1			4	5	6†			9	7^1			10^2	2		3	8	11	12											3–3(0–1)145	11
9. Stirling Albion	26.9	1			4	5	12			9	7			10	2			8	11†	6	3										0–2(0–1)668	12
10. Queen's Park*	3.10	1			4	5	12			9	7^1	8†			2			6^1	11	10	3										2–4(0–2)263	13
11. Montrose	10.10	1			6	8			9	10^1	7		12		2	2	5		11†	4	3										1–2(1–1)200	13
12. Arbroath*	17.10	1			6	10†			12	9^1	11^1			7^1	2	5	4		8	3											3–5(2–2)140	13
13. Stenhousemuir	24.10	1		6	5	12			14	7	11			9‡	4†	3			10	8	2										0–0(0–0)200	13
14. East Stirling*	31.10	1		6	5	4			10	9				3		7	8	2	11												0–0(0–0)210	13
15. St Johnstone	7.11	1		6	5	4			10	9	11			3			8^1	2		7											1–0(0–0)1664	13
16. Alloa*	14.11	1		6	5		9^1	10‡	11	12			3		7†	8	2	14	4												2–2(1–2)220	13
17. Stirling Albion*	21.11	1		14	6	5			9^2	11	12	4		3‡		8	2	10†	7												2–4(0–3)300	13
18. Albion R	28.11	1		6	5			9	7	11	4				8	2	10	3													0–0(0–0)250	12
19. Stranraer*	12.12	1		6	5	4^1		9	7		11				8†	2	10^1	3	12												2–0(2–0)160	12
20. Ayr U	19.12	1	12	6	5	4		9	7	11			8†	14		2	10^1‡	3													1–3(1–0)2080	12
21. Brechin C	26.12	1		6	5	8		9	7	11	12		4		2	10†	3														0–1(0–0)350	12
22. Berwick R*	2.1	1		6	5^1	8		9^3	7	11†		4	12		2	10^1	3														5–3(4–2)200	11
23. Montrose*	16.1	1		6		4		9‡	7	11^1		5†	14	8	2	10	3	12													1–1(0–1)160	11
24. Queen's Park	23.1	1	2	6		4		9	11†	14		8		7‡	10^1	3	5	12^1													2–3(0–2)504	11
25. Stenhousemuir	6.2	1		6		12		7†		2	8	4		10^1	3	5	11	9													1–1(0–0)200	11
26. Arbroath	9.2	1		6		8		12		2	4	14	7	10^1‡	3	5	11†	9^1													1–2(0–1)427	11
27. St Johnstone*	9.2	1		6		4		9^1	7			11	2		3	5	8	10													1–0(0–0)800	11
28. Stranraer	24.2	1		6		4‡		$9†^1$	7^1	2		5	8^1	14	12	3	11^1	10													4–0(2–0)250	—
29. Stirling Albion*	27.2	1		6		4		9†	7			8	12	5	3	14	11	10‡													0–1(0–1)300	11
30. Ayr U	5.3	1	14			11		7	12	6		4	8‡	2	10†	3	5	9													0–5(0–1)2244	12
31. East Stirling*	12.3	1	11	6		4		7				10	8	2	12	3	5	9†													0–0(0–0)240	12
32. Brechin C	19.3	1	3	6		4‡						10	8†	2^1	14	11	12	5	9^2	7											3–0(2–0)350	12
33. Albion R*	26.3	1	3	6				7		2‡		12	10†	8	4	9^1	11	14	5												1–0(0–0)150	12
34. Stenhousemuir	2.4	1	3	6		4		9‡	7			2	8	14	10†	11	5	12													0–2(0–1)200	12
35. Alloa*	9.4	1	3	6		4		9	12	11		8	14	2	5‡	10†	7														0–1(0–1)239	12
36. Queen's Park	16.4	1	3	6		4		9†	7‡	12	10	5	8	14	11^1	2															1–1(1–1)443	12
37. Berwick R*	23.4	1	3	6		4		14	10‡		7^1	5	12	11†	8^1	2													9^1		3–0(0–0)150	11
38. Arbroath	30.4	1	3	6		4		9	5	12	7	11	8	2	10†															10†	0–0(0–0)451	11
39. Montrose*	7.5	1	3	6		4^1		9	5	7	11	8^1	2	10																10	2–1(1–1)200	11

Final League Position: 11

Appearances/goals: 39(0)0 · 14(2)0 · 3(3)0 · 36(0)0 · 22(0)1 · 3(4)3 · 2(0)0 · 3(0)0 · 29(3)11 · 33(2)8 · 16(4)2 · 1(1)0 · 13(9)0 · 9(0)5 · 14(0)1 · 10(0)0 · 17(1)0 · 22(3)3 · 11(2)0 · 22(5)4 · 2(0)0 · 14(4)6 · 20(0)0 · 0(4)0 · 10(1)0 · 5(1)3 · 9(1)3 · 2(0)0 · 3(0)1

DUMBARTON – LEAGUE RECORD 1987–88 (DIVISION ONE)

Match no/Opp/Date	G Arthur	A Kay	D McNeil	M Clougherty	S McCahill	D Martin	P McGowan	J Rooney	O Coyle	P Houston	S Maclean	J McNeil	B Rooney	S Grow	T Coyle	C Cranmer	R Montgomerie	J Bell	G McCoy	J Creaney	R Docherty	H Stevenson	W Cairns	D McGuire	J Carson	G Doyle	W Blackie	G McCabe	FT(HT)Att Lge pos
1. Clyde 8.8	1	2	3	4	5	6†	7	8	9	10	11	12																	0–5(0–3)1000 —
2. Meadowbank* 11.8	1		5	4†	8	3^1	7	6	9	10	11^1	14			2‡	12													2–3(2–3)740 —
3. Kilmarnock* 15.8	1	2	5		4	3^1†	7	8	9	10	11	6			12														1–3(1–0)800 12
4. Airdrieonians 22.8	1		5		4	3	7	8	9^1	10	12	6	11†		2														1–0(0–0)1200 11
5. Clydebank* 29.8	1		5		4	3	7	8	9	10	11†	6	12^1		2														1–1(0–1)900 11
6. Hamilton A 5.9	1	11	2	4	5		7†	8	9	10^1		6	12		3														1–2(1–2)1765 11
7. Forfar Ath* 12.9	1	6	3	4†	5		7	8^1	9	10	11‡	12	14		2														1–1(1–1)700 10
8. Partick Th 15.9	1	3	4		5	6	7	8^1	9	10‡	11†	14	12		2														2–1(1–1)1140 —
9. East Fife 19.9	1	3^1†	4		5	6	7^1	8	9	10	11†	12		14	2														2–1(2–0)619 8
10. Queen of South* 26.9	1	3	4		5	6	7†	8	9^1	11^1		12			2					10									2–2(1–1)700 9
11. Raith R 29.9	1	11‡	4		5	6	3†	8	9	7^1	12	14			2					10									1–4(0–1)1713 —
12. Clyde* 3.10	1	11‡	4		5^1	6	3†	8	9	7	12	14			2					10									1–0(0–0)1200 —
13. Meadowbank Th 7.10	1	11	4		5	6	3	8	9	7†	12				2					10									0–0(0–0)650 —
14. Airdrieonians* 10.10	1	11	4		5	6	3	8	9	7	12				2					10†									0–0(0–0)1200 8
15. Forfar Ath 17.10	1	11†	4		5	6	3	8	9^1	7	12				2					10^1									2–0(1–0)671 8
16. Partick Th* 20.10	1	11	4		5	6	3	8†	9‡	7	12^1				2					10^1									4–2(1–1)800 —
17. Kilmarnock 24.10	1	11†	4		5	6	3	8	9	7	12				2					10^1									0–1(0–0)1571 8
18. Raith R* 27.10	1	11‡	4		5	6	3†	8	9^1	7	14			12	2					10									1–3(1–1)700 —
19. Hamilton A* 31.10	1	2			5	6	4	8	9^1	11	12						3	7†		10^1									2–1(2–0)900 9
20. Clydebank 7.11	1	2‡			5	6	4^1	8	9	11				14			3	7†		10			12						1–3(1–2)1231 9
21. East Fife* 14.11	1	4†			5	6		8	9	11	12^1				2		3	7		10									1–1(1–0)600 9
22. Queen of South 21.11	1		3		5	6	4	8	9†	7					2			12		10			11						0–2(0–1)1100 9
23. Clyde 28.11	1		3		5‡	4	7	8	9^1	11	14^1	12			2			6^2		10†									4–3(1–3)800 8
24. Meadowbank T* 5.12	1		5		14	4	3	8	11	6	12	9†			2‡			7	1	10									0–1(0–0)500 9
25. Forfar Ath* 12.12	1		5		4	4	6	8	9	2	10	11			3			7											0–1(0–0)610 10
26. Partick Th 19.12	1		6^1		5	4†	2	8	9^1	11	10†			14	3			7^1		12									3–1(2–0)1407 10
27. Hamilton A 26.12	1		6		5	4	2	8	9	11	10†				3			7		12									0–2(0–0)1764 10
28. Clydebank* 2.1	1	14			5	4	2‡	8†	9	11	12				3			7		10		6							1–3(1–0)1077 11
29. East Fife 9.1	1	12			5	4	7^1		14^1	9	11‡				3		2			10^2		6	8†						4–3(2–0)615 10
30. Queen of South* 16.1	1	12			5	4	7†			11‡	9			14	3		2			10		6	8						0–2(0–0)800 11
31. Kilmarnock* 23.1	1		5		4		8^1	11	9						3		2			10		7	6						1–0(0–0)950 9
32. Airdrieonians 6.2	1		5		4	14†	8	11	9^1	12					3		2			10^1		7	6						1–1(1–1)1150 9
33. Raith R 13.2	1		5		4		8	11							3		2			10		7	6	9					1–1(1–0)1802 9
34. Clyde* 27.2	1				4	12	8	11	14						3		2			10		7‡	6†	9	5				0–1(0–0)750 10
35. Forfar Ath 5.3	1				6	3	8	11	14								2†			10		9‡	4	7	5	12			0–4(0–1)507 10
36. Hamilton A* 19.3	1				5	4	3	11	9	8					12		2			10^1		7	1	6†					1–1(0–1)1250 10
37. Partick Th* 22.3	1				5	4	6	11	9^1	7‡					3†		2			10		12	1	8†		14			1–2(0–1)925 —
38. Clydebank 26.3	1				5	4	6	9	11	12					3†		2			10		7	1	8					0–1(0–0)1088 10
39. Airdrieonians* 2.4	1				5	6	2	8‡	12	9†					3					10		14	4			7	11		0–1(0–1)800 11
40. Kilmarnock 9.4	1				5	4	2	8	9	12					3					10^1		6‡		14	7†	11			1–3(0–0)2205 12
41. Queen of South 16.4	1				5	6	4	7		9†					3					10		8		2	11	12			0–0(0–0)1100 12
42. East Fife* 23.4	1				5	6	2	7	12	8					3					10†				4	9	11			0–0(0–0)700 12
43. Meadowbank Th 30.4	1				5	6	2^1	7	10^1						3							11	8		4		9^1		4–2(1–0)600 12
44. Raith R* 7.5	1				5	6	2	7^1†	10^1	12					3							11^1	8		4		9		3–0(2–0)800 12
App (subs)/goals	40(0)0	18(5)1	40(2)0	40(0)0	41(0)1	42(0)2	38(2)4	42(0)4	42(0)3	42(4)4	37(5)3	12(4)4	4(0)1	4(9)1	49(1)0	1(0)0	19(2)0	31(0)0	0(1)0	30(0)8	0(1)0	19(3)5	40(0)0	16(0)0	3(0)0	21(1)0	40(0)0	5(0)1	Final League Position: 12

Own goals: J. Dickson, match 28; A. MacLeod, match 33.

DUNDEE – LEAGUE RECORD 1987–88 (PREMIER DIVISION)

Match no/Opp/Date		R Geddes	S Forsyth	T McKinlay	R Shannon	R Glennie	J Duffy	V Mennie	J Brown	K Wright	T Coyne	I Angus	S Rafferty	A Lawrence	J Smith	R Jack	G McGeachie	G Harvey	G Chisholm	S Frail	D MacFarlane	W Saunders	W Kirkwood	G Rowell	S Campbell	T Carson	S McSkimming	FT(HT)Att	Lge pos
1. **Aberdeen***	8.8	1	2	3	4	5	6	7†	8	9	10	11^1		12														1–1(0–0)10,223	—
2. Falkirk	12.8	1	2	3	4	5	6	7†	8^2	9^1‡	10	11			12	14												3–0(1–0)2300	—
3. Hibernian	15.8	1	2	3	4	6			8^1‡	9^1	10$^1_1$	11	7†		5		12	14										4–0(4–0)8000	2
4. **St Mirren***	22.8	1	7	3	4		6	8		9	10	11‡		12	5		2†	14										0–2(0–2)5969	3
5. **Dunfermline A***	29.8	1	2	3	8	4	6	7		9†	10$^3_1$‡	11			5	14		12										5–0(3–0)7564	3
6. Rangers	5.9	1	2	3	8†	4	6‡	7		9	10	11			5	14		12^1										1–2(0–1)38,302	4
7. Morton	12.9	1	2	3	4	6		8‡		9	10$^1_1$	11^1		7†	5		12	14										3–4(1–3)3000	4
8. **Hearts***	19.9	1	2†	3	7	6			8	9	10	11		12	5^1		4											1–3(0–1)9199	7
9. Motherwell	26.9	1		3	11	6		7†	8		10^1				5	12	2	9^1	4									2–0(1–0)2656	5
10. **Dundee U***	3.10	1		3†	7	4			8	9	10^1	12		11	5		2‡	14	6									1–1(1–1)11,497	6
11. **Celtic***	7.10	1	2		7	4		12	8	9	10	3^1		11†	5				6									1–1(1–0)13,238	—
12. Aberdeen	10.10	1	2		7	4			8	9	10	3		11	5				6									0–0(0–0)12,500	6
13. Dunfermline A	17.10	1	2		7	4		12	8†	9	10	3		11^1‡	5			14	6									1–0(0–0)6890	5
14. **Morton***	28.10	1	2		4	3		7	8	11	10		12		5			9^1†	6									1–0(1–0)3829	—
15. Hearts	31.10	1	2		4	3†		7‡	8	9^1	10^1	11	12		5			14	6									2–4(0–3)13,806	7
16. **Falkirk***	7.11	1	2		4	3		7	8	9^1	10$^1_1$	11			5				6									3–1(1–0)4324	5
17. Celtic	14.11	1	2		4	3		7	8†	9	10	11	12		5				6									0–5(0–2)31,664	6
18. St Mirren	17.11	1	2		4			7		9	10$^1_1$	11	8		5^1		3		6									2–1(0–0)3328	—
19. **Hibernian***	21.11	1	2		4			7		9	10^2	11	8		5		3		6									2–1(1–0)6583	5
20. **Motherwell***	24.11	1	2†		4			7^1	12	9‡	10^1	11	8		5		3	14	6									2–0(2–0)3695	—
21. Dundee U	28.11	1	2		4			7		9^1	10^2	11	8		5		3		6									3–1(1–1)13,625	5
22. **Aberdeen***	5.12	1	2^1		4			7‡		9	10	11	8	14	5		3†	12	6									1–2(0–2)8799	5
23. Falkirk	12.12	1	2		4			7		9^2	10^2	11	8		5		3		6									6–0(2–0)4162	5
24. Morton	16.12	1	2		4			7†	8	9^2	10^3	11	6		5		3^1‡	14^1		12								7–1(4–1)3821	—
25. **Hearts***	19.12	1	2	3	4			7	8	9	10	11	6		5													0–0(0–0)10,806	5
26. Rangers	26.12	1	2	3	4				8	9	10	11	6		5		7†	12										0–2(0–2)40,938	5
27. **Dunfermline A***	1.1	1	2	3	4				8	9	10$^1_1$	11	6		5			7										2–0(0–0)8527	—
28. **Rangers***	6.1	1	2		4	3			8	9	10	11	6		5			7										0–1(0–1)17,450	—
29. Motherwell	9.1	1	2		4	3			8†	9	10$^1_1$	11^1	6	12	5			7										3–3(0–1)2785	5
30. **Dundee U***	16.1	1	2	3	4‡	6				9	10	11	8	12	5			7†			14							0–2(0–1)13,651	5
31. Hibernian	6.2	1		3	4			6		9^1	10	11	8		5			7			2							1–2(1–2)6000	5
32. **Celtic***	13.2	1	2	3	4			7		9	10	11^1	8		5			12				6†						1–2(0–0)17,106	5
33. Aberdeen	27.2	1	2	3				6		9	10	11	8	7†	5			12					4					0–1(0–0)13,500	6
34. **St Mirren***	1.3	1	2	3	4†			7		9	10$^1_1$	11	8		5								6	12				2–1(0–1)4265	—
35. **Morton***	5.3	1	2	3				7†		9‡	10^1	11	8	12	5			14				6	4					1–0(1–0)4319	5
36. Dunfermline A	19.3		2		4			7†		9^1		11	8	12	5			10				6	3			1		1–6(0–3)4985	5
37. **Rangers***	26.3	1	2		4						10^1	11^1	8	7	5			9				6	3					2–3(1–1)14,879	5
38. Hearts	30.3	1	2					4		9	10	3		7				12		8†		6	5		11			0–2(0–1)9649	—
39. Dundee U	2.4	1	5		4			11†		12	10		8	7				9				6	2		3			0–1(0–0)13,874	6
40. **Motherwell***	6.4		5		4					12	10		8	7†						9		6	2		11^1	1	3	1–2(0–1)3732	—
41. **Falkirk***	16.4		2		4					9^3	10^1	11	8	7	5							6			3	1		4–2(1–0)4970	6
42. Celtic	23.4		2		4‡					9	10	3	8	7†	5			14		12		6			11	1		0–3(0–1)60,800	6
43. **Hibernian***	30.4		2		4					9	10	3	8	7	5†			12				6			11	1		0–0(0–0)4471	6
44. St Mirren	7.5		2		4					9	10	3	8‡	7†	5			14				6	11		12	1		0–1(0–1)5798	7
Apps(subs)/goals		38(0)0	41(0)1	19(0)0	41(0)0	19(0)0	5(0)0	27(2)1	19(1)3	40(2)15	43(0)33	39(1)6	27(3)0	14(8)1	39(1)2	0(4)0	12(2)1	10(19)4	15(0)0	2(2)0	1(1)0	11(0)0	9(0)0	0(1)0	6(1)1	6(0)0	1(0)0	Final League Position: 7	

Own goals: R. Manley (2), match 23.

DUNDEE UNITED – LEAGUE RECORD 1987–88 (PREMIER DIVISION)

Match no/Opp/Date		W Thomson	J McInally	M Malpas	D Beaumont	P Hegarty	D Narey	J A Irvine	D Bowman	E Bannon	H French	I Redford	J Holt	P Kinnaird	K Gallacher	J Clark	I Ferguson	P Sturrock	W McKinlay	I McPhee	W Kirkwood	G McGinnis	A J Irvine	J McLeod	H Curran	M Paatelainen	A Main	A Cleland	B Welsh	A Preston	FT(HT)Att Lge pos
1. Rangers	8.8	1	2	3	4¹	5	6	7‡	8	9	10	11†	12	14																	1-1(1-0)39,120 —
2. Motherwell*	12.8	1	2	3	4†	5	6	7	12	9		11₁		10‡	8	14															1-1(0-0)6663 —
3. Morton*	15.8	1	4¹	3		5	6	12	8		10₁	2		9		7	11¹†														3-1(2-1)6641 4
4. Hearts	22.8	1	4	3		5	6	10‡	8†		11	2		9	12	7¹	14														1-4(0-2)14,548 7
5. Aberdeen	29.8	1		3		5	6		8		11₁	2		14		7	10	4†	12		9‡										1-0(0-1)16,000 —
6. Celtic*	5.9	1		3		5	6		12	8	11	2		9		7	10†	4													0-0(0-0)16,192 6
7. Hibernian*	12.9	1		3		5¹	6		12	9	11	2†		8		7	10	4													1-2(0-1)7920 8
8. St Mirren	19.9	1		3	12	5	6		4‡	8†	11			9		7			10	2		14									0-2(0-0)3807 9
9. Falkirk*	26.9	1		3		5	6	8†			12			4	7	10²‡		11		2	9¹	14									3-0(0-0)6240 8
10. Dundee	3.10	1		3	10†	5	6	8	2		12			4	7¹						9	11‡	14								1-1(1-1)11,497 8
11. Dunfermline A	6.10	1		3		5	6	8	2		11	10		4	7					12	9†										0-0(0-0)7558 —
12. Rangers	10.10	1	4	3		5	6		2	8	11	10			7¹					9											1-0(0-0)18,214 7
13. Aberdeen*	17.10	1	4‡	3		5	6		2	8	11†			10	14	7				9		12									0-0(0-0)11,281 6
14. Celtic	24.10	1	4	3		5	6		2†	8	10‡			14	9¹	7¹					11		12								2-1(0-3)31,032 6
15. Hibernian	28.10	1	4†	3		5	6			8				10	9	7		2¹			11		12								1-0(0-0)8400 —
16. St Mirren*	31.10	1	4	3	5†	6		12	8	11‡				14	9	7¹		2						10¹							2-3(2-1)7607 6
17. Motherwell	7.11	1	4	3	6	5			2					14	9	7¹				10‡		11†	12	8							1-2(0-0)2927 6
18. Dunfermline A*	14.11	1	4	3	10	5	6		2	8				11		7							9¹								1-0(0-0)8699 5
19. Hearts*	18.11	1	4	3	10	5	6		2	8†				11	14	7		9‡				12									0-3(0-2)14,258 —
20. Morton	21.11	1	4	3	12	5	6		2					9	7¹	10	8†			11											1-0(0-0)2000 6
21. Falkirk	24.11	1	4	3	12	5	6	9	2		10†			7		8‡				11¹	14										1-4(0-1)5000 —
22. Dundee*	28.11	1	4	3		5	6		2					8†	10¹	7				11	12	9									1-3(1-1)13,625 6
23. Rangers	5.12	1	4	3	6			7						8	5†	11		14	2	10	12	9‡									0-1(0-1)41,159 6
24. Motherwell*	12.12	1	4	3										9	5	11¹	7	6	2	8¹		10¹									3-1(2-0)5792 6
25. Hibernian*	16.12	1	4	3			12							9	5	11	7‡	6¹	2†	8	14	10									1-2(1-2)6195 —
26. St Mirren	19.12	1	4	3	9	6		2	7					8	5	11			10†		12										1-0(1-0)3517 6
27. Celtic*	26.12	1	4	3	9	6		2	7	10†				8	5	11¹						12									1-2(0-1)18,458 6
28. Aberdeen	2.1	1	4	3	9	6		2	7					8	5	11					10										0-0(0-0)21,500 6
29. Falkirk*	9.1	1	4	3	9	6	12	2	7					8	5‡	11¹				14		10									0-0(0-0)6617 6
30. Dundee	16.1	1	4	3	5	6		2	7¹	10	11			8‡	12	14						9¹†									2-0(1-0)13,651 6
31. Hearts	3.2	1	4	3	5	6		2	7	10	11₁			8	12							9†									1-1(0-0)13,710 6
32. Morton*	6.2	1	4	3	5	6	14	2	7	10	11₁			8†		12						9‡	1								2-0(2-0)6566 6
33. Dunfermline A	13.2		4	3	5	6		2	7	10	11			8³								9	1								3-0(2-0)7154 6
34. Rangers*	27.2		4	3	5	6		2	7	10†	11			8	12	14						9¹‡	1								1-1(1-0)20,846 5
35. Hibernian	5.3		4	3	5	6		2	7	10†	11‡			8	12	14						9	1								0-0(0-0)7000 6
36. Aberdeen*	19.3	1	4	9	5	6		2	7	10‡	11			8		14				3†		12	1								0-2(0-1)10,403 6
37. Celtic	26.3	1	4	3	12	6	10	2	7		11†			8‡	5	9					14										0-0(0-0)34,933 6
38. St Mirren*	30.3		4†	3		5	6	11²	2¹	7‡	10¹	14			9	8¹			12					1							5-1(4-1)6294 —
39. Dundee*	2.4		4	3		5	6	11‡	2	7	8¹	9			12	14						10‡		1							1-0(0-1)13,874 5
40. Motherwell	16.4		12	3	6			7		14	8			5¹	9		4†	10‡		2		11¹									2-4(1-1)3922 5
41. Dunfermline A*	23.4	1	4¹†	3		5	6	14	2	7		11‡		8		10¹		12			9										2-2(2-1)8263 5
42. Morton	30.4	1		3		5	6	14	2	7†					10‡	8	11				12	9⁴	4								4-0(2-0)2000 5
43. Falkirk	4.5	1	4	3		5	6		2		7			9¹		12					8†				10¹	11					2-1(1-1)4455 —
44. Hearts*	7.5	1	4	3		5	6		2		7‡			14		10†	8	11			9							12			0-0(0-0)9520 5
App(subs)/goals		36(0)0	35(1)2	44(0)0	40(0)1	40(0)1	39(0)0	11(5)2	34(5)1	20(0)2	22(3)6	5(1)0	7(4)0	24(2)4	19(9)3	33(6)11	8(2)1	10(2)1	9(1)0	0(0)0	9(2)0	10(2)3	4(3)0	46(1)0	15(5)0	17(2)9	8(0)0	10(0)0	10(0)1	11(1)0	Final League Position: 5

Own goal: P. Godfrey, match 26.

DUNFERMLINE ATHLETIC – LEAGUE RECORD 1987–88 (PREMIER DIVISION)

Match no/Opp/Date	I Westwater	G Robertson	A Williamson	N McCathie	D Young	C Robertson	S Beedie	S Morrison	E Ferguson	I McCall	G Jenkins	G Thompson	W Irvine	R Forrest	G Cowie	J Donnelly	R Smith	W Kirkwood	R Robertson	T Smith	G Riddell	J Holt	M Smith	J Watson	R Jack	V Andersen	T Carson	D McKellar	D Irons	W Callaghan	FT(HT)Att Lge pos
1. Hibernian* 8.8	1	2	3†	4	5²	6	7¹	8	9‡	10	11	12	14																		3-3(1-1)12,000 —
2. St Mirren 11.8	1	2		4	5	6	7	12	9¹	10	11‡	8	14	3																	1-1(0-0)4762
3. Falkirk 15.8	1	3		4	5	6	7	12	9†	10	11‡	8	14	2																	0-0(0-0)5000 6
4. Celtic* 22.8	1	2		4	5	6¹	7	12	9¹	10	11†			3	8																2-1(1-1)18,070 5
5. Dundee 29.8	1	2		4	5	6	7	8	9		11	12	14				3‡	10†													0-5(0-3)7564 7
6. Motherwell* 5.9	1	2		4	5†	10		6	9		11‡	8	14	7	12	3															0-1(0-0)5500 10
7. Rangers 12.9	1	2		4		6		5†	9‡	10				7	11	3	8	12	14												0-4(0-2)39,749 10
8. Morton* 19.9	1			4		10²		12	9²		11			7†		3	8	2		5	6										4-1(2-0)5460 8
9. Hearts* 26.9	1			4		10		14	9‡		11			7†		3	8	2	12	5	3										0-1(0-1)14,748 9
10. Aberdeen 3.10	1			4		6		7†	12		11			10	8	2	9	5‡	3												0-3(0-1)11,313 9
11. Dundee U* 6.10	1			4		10		9	12		11			7	6	8	2	5†	3												0-0(0-0)7558 —
12. Hibernian 10.10	1			4	5	10		9†	12		11			14	6	8	2‡		3	7											0-4(0-4)10,000 10
13. Dundee* 17.10	1	2		4		10	11‡			14				12	6†	8		5	3	7	9										0-1(0-0)6890 10
14. Motherwell 24.10	1			4		10¹	6†			12				2	3	11		5	7	9	8¹										2-3(1-1)3685 10
15. Rangers* 28.10	1			4		10	6	12						2	3	11†		5	7	9	8										0-4(0-1)18,000 —
16. Morton 31.10	1			4		10	6							3	11	2		5	7¹	9¹	8										2-1(2-0)2000 10
17. St Mirren* 7.11	1			4¹		10	6							3	11	2		5	7	9¹	8										2-0(2-0)5990 10
18. Dundee U 14.11	1			4		10	6	12			11†			3		2		5	7	9	8										0-1(0-0)8699 10
19. Falkirk* 17.11	1			4		10	6	11†		14			12	3		2		5	7	9	8‡										0-0(0-0)6679 10
20. Celtic 21.11	1			4		10	7	12		14				3	11	2		5		9	8‡	6†									0-4(0-3)28,534 9
21. Hearts 24.11	1			4		10²	6	12						3	7	2	14		5	9	8‡	11†									2-3(0-1)14,517 —
22. Aberdeen* 28.11	1			4		10†	6							3	8	2	12	5	7	9		11									0-3(0-0)7500 10
23. Hibernian* 5.12	1	2		4		10¹	6							3	11			5	7	9	8										1-0(0-0)7500 10
24. St Mirren 12.12		2		4		10	6							3	11	14	12	5	7‡	9†	8₁			1							1-4(0-3)4364 10
25. Rangers 15.12		2		4		10¹	11¹							3	9		12	5	6	7		8†		1							2-2(1-1)31,687 —
26. Morton* 19.12		2‡		4		10	11							3†	9		14	5	6	7¹	12	8		1							1-0(0-0)5000 10
27. Motherwell* 26.12				4		10	6							3	11			5	2	7	9	8¹		1							1-1(1-0)5500 10
28. Dundee 1.1		2†				10				14				3	11		9	5	6	7	12	8‡									0-2(0-0)8527 —
29. Hearts* 9.1	1			4		10	6							3	11			5	2	7	9	8									0-4(0-1)11,963 10
30. Aberdeen 16.1				4		10†				14				3‡	11		6†	5	2	7	12	8	9								0-1(0-1)20,000 11
31. Falkirk 6.2	1	2		4			6†							3	11		9	5	8	7	14	10‡									0-1(0-0)5000 11
32. Dundee U* 13.2				6		10	11		12					3	2		9†	5	4	7‡		8	14		1						0-3(0-2)7154 11
33. Hibernian 27.2		2		4		10	11	14	12					3‡				6	7	9	8†	5		1							0-2(0-2)10,000 11
34. Celtic* 2.3		2		4		10	11							3†				6	7	12	8	5	1			9					0-4(0-3)17,448 —
35. Rangers* 5.3		2	3	4		10	12	6								14		5	7	9	8‡				11†						0-3(0-2)19,017 11
36. Dundee* 19.3						10²	11	8¹†			12				2		5	4¹	7¹	14¹		3			6	9‡					6-1(3-0)4985 11
37. Morton 23.3						10	11	8¹†			12				2		5	4	7¹	14		3			6	9¹‡					3-0(2-0)4000 —
38. Motherwell 26.3						10¹	11	8†							2		5	4	7	12		3			6	9¹					2-3(2-0)8958 11
39. Aberdeen* 2.4	1			7		10¹	11	8						14	2†		5	4		12		3‡			6	9					1-1(0-0)7132 11
40. Hearts 13.4	1			4		10	11	8¹							2		5		7		12	3			6	9†					1-2(1-0)7307 —
41. St Mirren* 16.4						10¹	11	8						3	2		5		7		12	4		1	6¹	9†					2-1(0-1)4390 11
42. Dundee U 23.4						10	11	8						3	2		5	4	7¹		12¹			1	6	9†					2-2(1-2)8263 11
43. Falkirk* 30.4				4		10	11	8						3			5	2	7		12			1	6	9†					0-1(0-1)4900 11
44. Celtic 7.5				14		10	11	12						3	2		5‡	4	7	8				1	6						0-1(0-1)44,482 11

Final League Position: 11

Apps(subs)/goals:
28(0)/0, 17(0)/0, 2(0)/0, 38(1)/1, 7(0)/2, 42(0)/13, 35(1)/2, 17(12)/3, 9(5)/4, 40(0)/0, 12(4)/0, 3(2)/0, 0(5)/0, 30(1)/0, 10(4)/0, 2(0)/0, 33(2)/0, 24(0)/0, 20(2)/0, 5(8)/0, 22(0)/0, 30(0)/5, 16(9)/0, 21(4)/4, 13(1)/0, 5(0)/0, 6(0)/0, 11(0)/1, 8(0)/2

Also played: S. Wordell at 14 in match 10 and at 12 in match 31, N. Walker at 1 in match 28, S. Strang at 9† in match 44, H. Segers at 1 in matches 35, 36, 37, 38.

EAST FIFE – LEAGUE RECORD 1987-88 (DIVISION ONE)

Match no/Opp/Date	R Charles	J Connor	S Pitman	J Perry	K Halley	J McLaren	M Stead	T McCafferty	P Hunter	J Mitchell	G Smith	B Deas	G Burns	D Conroy	J Thorpe	A Banner	D Graham	G Fairley	R Blair	R Scott	C Scott	G Reid	S McElhone	P McDowall	J Moffat	J Donnelly	B McNaughton	FT(HT)Att Lge pos
1. Airdrieonians 8.8	1	2	3	4	5	6	7†	8	9	10‡	11	12	14															0-1(0-1)1050 —
2. Kilmarnock* 12.8	1‡	2	3	7	5	6	4	11^1	10†	9^1	8		12	14														2-1(0-1)657 —
3. Meadowbank T* 15.8		2	3†	7	5	6	4	11^2	10	9	8	12^1					1											3-3(1-2)692 6
4. Clyde 22.8			8^1		5	6	12	4	9		11†	7		3		1	10^2											3-3(2-2)847 6
5. Raith R* 29.8		2	14	7	5	6	4^1	9^1	11‡	8†	3	12				1	10											2-1(0-0)1942 5
6. Partick Th 5.9		2	14^1	7	5	6	11‡	4	9	8^2	3	12				1	10†											3-3(1-1)1610 5
7. Queen of South* 12.9	1	2	10‡	4	5	6		8	9	7	3						11‡	12	14									0-3(0-1)765 7
8. Forfar Ath 15.9	1	2	3		5	6	4	9	8		10						12	7	11†									0-4(0-0)706 —
9. Dumbarton* 19.9	1	2	3	7$_1$	5	6	4	10	9	14	8†		12				11‡											1-2(0-2)619 9
10. Hamilton A 26.9	1	2^1	3	7	5	6	4	9‡	11†	10	12		14	8														1-0(0-0)1656 8
11. Clydebank 29.9	1	2		7	5	6	4	9^1	8†	10	3		12				11											1-2(0-2)600 —
12. Airdrieonians* 3.10	1	2		7	5	6	4	10^1	9†		3	14					11^1	8	12									1-3(1-1)756 10
13. Kilmarnock 6.10	1	2	3		6		4	12	11		14			8‡			9	10	7†	5								0-2(0-1)1850 —
14. Clyde* 10.10	1	2	3	4‡	6		10		14		7†						12	11	8	5	9							0-2(0-2)718 12
15. Queen of South 17.10	1	2		4	6		10‡		9^1		3	7					11†	14		5	12	8						1-2(1-0)1200 12
16. Forfar Ath* 20.10	1	2		7	6			3	9			11†					10‡	8^2	14	5	12	4						2-3(2-2)668 —
17. Meadowbank Th 24.10	1	2		4	6		10	12^1	14	9†	3‡	7^1					11^1			5	8							3-2(1-0)479 12
18. Clydebank* 28.10	1	2		4	6			9	3	10		7†		14			11^1			5	12	8‡						1-2(0-1)790 —
19. Partick Th* 31.10	1	2		4				9^1	10	11†	6		3	12			7^1			5	8	1						2-1(1-1)780 11
20. Raith 7.11	1	2			6			9	3	10†	8‡		12		11^1	14	7			5	4							1-7(0-1)2958 12
21. Dumbarton 14.11	1	2	3	4†	6			9^1	10	7‡			14		8	12	11			5								1-1(1-0)600 12
22. Hamilton A* 21.11	1	2	3	4	6			9	10	11‡			12		8	14	7†			5								0-1(0-0)811 12
23. Airdrieonians 28.11	1	2	5	4$_1$	6			9	10	11†			12		8		7											1-2(0-2)1500 12
24. Kilmarnock 5.12	1	2	3	4				9†		12	6	7^1			8		11^1			5			10					2-1(0-1)571 12
25. Queen of South* 12.12	1	2	3	4^1				9†	14	12	6	7			8		11^1			5			10‡					2-2(1-1)460 12
26. Forfar Ath 19.12	1	2	3	4	6			9^1			12	14			11†		7‡			5	8		10					1-1(0-1)598 12
27. Partick Th 26.12	1	2	3	4	6			9^1		7^1					12	8‡	11			5	14		10†					2-4(1-3)1740 12
28. Raith R* 2.1	1	2	3	4	6			10	9^1†		12				11	14	8			7‡		5						1-2(0-0)4161 12
29. Dumbarton* 9.1	1	2	3	4				9^1	10†	7‡	8$_1$	14					11				12^1							3-4(0-2)615 12
30. Hamilton A 16.1	1	2		4	6			8	9		14			3	12		10‡			11†	7		5					0-1(0-1)1478 12
31. Meadowbank T* 6.2	1	2	3	8	6			10	9		12						14			7†	4‡		5			11		0-0(0-0)582 12
32. Clyde 24.2	1	2	3	4	6			9^1									7^1			10	5^1	8			11^1			4-0(2-0)998 —
33. Airdrieonians 27.2	1	2	3‡	4$_2$	6			8	9		12	14					7†			10	5				11^1			3-1(1-1)791 12
34. Clydebank 1.3	1	2		4	6			8	9‡		12	14		3			7			10†					11			0-2(0-0)587 —
35. Queen of South 5.3	1	2		4	6			8	9		12	14		3			7‡			10†					11			0-2(0-2)950 12
36. Forfar Ath* 12.3	1	2	3^1	4	6			4	9								7			10	5^1				11^2			4-0(1-0)622 12
37. Partick Th* 19.3	1	2	3	4	6			4	9^1	14	12						7†			10‡	5				11			1-0(1-0)978 12
38. Raith R 26.3	1	2	3†	8$_1$	6			4	9		12						7			10	5				11			1-0(0-0)2345 12
39. Meadowbank Th 2.4	1	2	3	8	6			4	9					12			10	7^1			5				11†			1-2(0-0)800 12
40. Clyde* 9.4	1	2	3	8	6			4	9	14				12			11†		7		5^1‡				10^1			2-0(0-0)718 11
41. Hamilton A* 16.4	1	2	3	8	6			4	9^1					12			7			10	5				11†			1-1(0-1)1378 11
42. Dumbarton 23.4	1	2	3	8†	6			4	9					12			14		7		10	5			11‡			0-0(0-0)700 11
43. Kilmarnock 30.4	1	2	3	8†	6			4	9^2					12			7			10	5				11^1			3-1(3-0)2488 11
44. Clydebank* 7.5	1	2	3	8‡	6			4	9					12			14		7		10†	5			11^1			1-1(0-0)1496 11

Final League Position: 11

Apps(subs)/goals: 39(0)/0, 44(0)/2, 30(2)/2, 40(0)/7, 12(0)/0, 41(0)/0, 32(0)/1, 38(1)/17, 15(5)/0, 23(0)/5, 6(4)/0, 0(2)/0, 7(2)/2, 40(0)/1, 14(9)/3, 5(6)/0, 37(1)/9, 32(0)/0, 14(2)/1, 25(0)/3, 1(3)/0, 14(1)/0, 40(0)/0, 14(0)/7

Own goal: M. Treanor, match 18.

EAST STIRLINGSHIRE – LEAGUE RECORD 1987–88 (DIVISION ONE)

Match no/Opp/Date		C Kelly	J MacKay	G Harvey	D Wilcox	I Rennie	J Woods	C Grant	G Wilson	T Ward	G Wylde	A McGonigal	I Tasker	A Gilchrist	P O'Brien	G McColl	C Wilson	S Gallacher	G Murray	R McConville	G Russell	J Gaffney	S Burnside	A McKenzie	D McIntyre	J Irvine	G Tulloch	A Grant	P Kelly	W McNeill	G Lauchlan	FT(HT) Att Lge pos
1. Cowdenbeath*	8.8	1	2	3	4	5	6	7†	8‡	9	10	11	12	14																		0-1(0-1) 634 —
2. Albion R	15.8	1	2	3	4	5	6		12	9	8‡	10	7†	11¹	14																	1-1(0-0) 450 11
3. Stranraer*	22.8	1			3₁	6	5†	11‡	4	9	8	10	2	7	12	14																1-1(1-1) 170 11
4. Stenhousemuir*	29.8	1	2		4¹†	5	6		12	9‡	8	11	14	3	7			10¹														2-0(2-0) 400 7
5. Montrose	5.9	1	2		8	5	6		12	9¹	10	14		3	7†			11²†	4													3-0(0-0) 150 6
6. Alloa	12.9	1	2		4	5	6			9¹	10	12		3	7†			11¹	8													2-1(0-0) 475 5
7. Berwick R*	15.9	1	2		4	5	6			9	10	12		3	7†			11¹	8													1-0(0-0) 200 5
8. Queen's Park	19.9	1	2‡		4¹	5	6		12	9	10	7†		3			14	11	8													1-2(1-2) 465 4
9. St Johnstone*	26.9	1	14		4	5‡	6	7†	9		10			2				12	11	8	3											0-2(0-0) 750 5
10. Arbroath	3.10	1			4	5	6	14	8‡	9	10	7†		2¹			12	11			3											1-1(0-1) 405 5
11. Brechin C*	10.10	1			4	5	6		8	9	10			2	7			11			3											0-0(0-0) 200 5
12. Stirling Albion	17.10	1		6	4	5†		12			14		2	7	8	10		11			3	9‡										0-3(0-1) 621 7
13. Ayr U*	24.10	1			5	4			9			14	2	7†	10‡			11			3			8	12							0-2(0-0) 800 8
14. Cowdenbeath	31.10	1			5	4	6		9			12	2	7†	10			11			3			8								0-0(0-0) 210 8
15. Albion R*	7.11	1			5	4	6		9			2	7¹	12	8†			3						10	11¹							2-2(0-0) 300 8
16. Stranraer	14.11	1			5	4	6	8¹	9¹		2	10¹					3								1	7						3-3(1-3) 350 8
17. St Johnstone	21.11	1			5	4	6		9		2	10	8	11¹			3							7								1-3(1-1) 1290 9
18. Queen's Park*	28.11	1		12	4		6		9‡		2	10	8	11			3			14	7	5†										0-1(0-1) 300 10
19. Alloa*	19.12	1		10	4	6¹	14		9		2¹	8	11¹	3			12	7†	5‡													3-3(2-1) 300 10
20. Montrose*	26.12	1		10†	4	6			9¹		2	8¹	11	3			12	7	5													2-2(0-1) 200 9
21. Stenhousemuir	2.1	1		10	4	6		9²			8¹	2	11	3			12	7†	5													3-2(1-0) 220 9
22. Brechin C	16.1	1		10‡	4₁	6	14	5	9		2	8	11¹†	3			12	7¹														3-2(1-1) 300 7
23. Berwick R	19.1	1		10	4₁	6		5†	9		2	8	11	3			12	7	6													1-1(0-0) 380 —
24. Arbroath*	23.1	1		10	4	6		14	9		2	8	11¹	3			12	7†	5‡													1-1(1-0) 300 7
25. Stirling Albion*	2.2	1		10	4	6		12	9		2	8	11	3			7¹		5¹†													2-1(1-0) 600 —
26. Ayr	6.2	1		10†	4	6		12	9		2	8	11	3			7		14	5‡												0-2(0-1) 2347 6
27. Queen's Park	13.2	1			4	6		10			2	8		3			11		7¹	5	12¹											2-1(1-0) 575 6
28. Albion R	27.2	1		12	4¹	6		10†			2	8	14	3			11¹		7	5¹	9¹‡											4-1(3-0) 210 7
29. Berwick R*	1.3	1		3	4	6		10	14¹		2	8	9				11¹		7‡	5¹	12											2-1(1-1) 201 —
30. Stranraer*	5.3	1		3	4	6		10	9		2	8‡	14				11¹		7†	5¹	12											2-0(0-0) 150 5
31. Cowdenbeath	12.3	1		10	4	6			9		2	8	12	3			11		7†	5‡	14											0-0(0-0) 240 5
32. Arbroath*	19.3	1		10	4	6		5	9¹		2	8‡		3¹			12		7	14	11¹†											2-1(2-1) 250 5
33. Stenhousemuir*	26.3	1		10	4	6		5¹†	9		2‡	8		3			11		7	12	14											1-2(1-2) 300 5
34. St Johnstone	2.4	1		10	4	6		5			2‡	8		3			12		7	14	11†	9										0-0(0-0) 1907 5
35. Brechin C	9.4	1		10†	4	6		5			2‡	8		3			11		7	12	14	9										0-1(0-0) 325 6
36. Stirling Albion*	16.4	1			4	6		10†			2	8	12	3			7		5¹	11	9											1-3(1-2) 363 6
37. Ayr U	23.4	1		10	4	6					2	8†	14	3			11		7	5	9‡	12										0-0(0-0) 3442 6
38. Montrose*	30.4	1		10	4	6					2			3			11¹		7	5¹	9¹											3-2(2-1) 300 6
39. Alloa	7.5	1		10	4	6	14				2	8‡		3			11		7¹	5	9†	12										1-0(1-0) 355 6

Final League Position: 6

Apps(subs)/goals: 37(0)0, 7(1)0, 26(2)0, 39(0)6, 12(0)0, 37(0)1, 3(5)1, 16(7)1, 29(1)8, 40(0)0, 11(0)0, 36(1)2, 34(0)5, 6(3)0, 2(4)0, 0(2)0, 2(3)0, 5(0)0, 29(0)1, 1(0)0, 2(0)0, 0(1)0, 13(0)6, 1(0)0, 22(1)3, 17(4)5, 7(6)3, 3(2)0

Also played: G. Kirkwood at 1 in match 17; D. Clabby† at 9 in match 27; M. Strain at 8 in match 38.

FALKIRK – LEAGUE RECORD 1987-88 (PREMIER DIVISION)

Match no/Opp/Date	G.Marshall	J.MacLeod	J.Kerr	A.Nicol	J.Dempsey	S.Burgess	J.Gilmour	H.Hill	K.Eadie	C.Baptie	S.Conn	R.Manley	R.Stewart	S.McGivern	B.Scrimgeour	A.Rae	J.McCormack	D.McWilliams	J.Gallacher	A.Grant	J.McVeigh	S.Romaines	C.McNair	B.McIntyre	J.Holmes	K.McAllister	J.Stewart	FT(HT)Att	Lge pos
1. Hearts 8.8	1	2	3	4	5	6^1	7	8	9	10^1	11†		12															2-4(0-3)12,163	—
2. Dundee* 12.8	1	2	12	4	3	5	7	10†	9	8		6†	14	11														0-3(0-1)2300	—
3. Dunfermline A* 15.8	1	2	12	8	5	6	10	4	9†	7		14				3	11†											0-0(0-0)5000	11
4. Rangers 22.8	1	2		7	12	6	11	4	9	8		5			3†		10											0-4(0-1)32,340	12
5. Motherwell 29.8	1	2	10	6	5	7	4	9^2	8†	3†	14						12	11										2-1(0-1)3132	11
6. Aberdeen* 5.9	1	2†	10	6	5^1	7	4	9†	8	3	12			14				11^1										2-2(2-0)5327	11
7. Celtic* 12.9	1	2	14	10	6	5	7	4	9†	8		12					3†	11										0-1(0-1)17,500	11
8. Hibernian 19.9	1	2	14	10	6	5	7	4	9†	8	3	12	11‡															0-1(0-1)6500	11
9. Dundee U 26.9	1	2	7‡	10	6†	5	11	4	9	8	3	12	14															0-3(0-0)6240	11
10. St Mirren* 3.10	1	2	10†		6	5	11‡	4	9		3	8	7		12		14											1-3(1-2)3500	11
11. Morton 7.10	1	2		3	5	14	12		10	6	9‡		7	4†	11^1		8											1-4(1-2)2300	11
12. Hearts* 10.10	1	2			5		4	12		3	6	11^1‡		7	10		9	8										1-5(0-4)7000	12
13. Motherwell* 17.10	1	2			5		12^1	9^1	4	10†	6	7^1		14	3		11			8‡								3-0(0-0)3000	12
14. Celtic 28.10	1	2		3	5		8	9†	4	10	6^1	12^1			14		11			7‡								2-3(0-1)11,381	11
15. Hibernian* 31.10	1	2		3	5^1		7		4	10	6	9†			12		11			8								1-1(0-0)6000	11
16. Dundee 7.11	1	2		3‡	5_1		7		4	10	6	9†					11		12	8	14							1-3(0-1)4324	12
17. Morton* 14.11	1	2		3	5		4		10	6		9^2					11			8	7							2-0(0-0)3000	11
18. Dunfermline A 17.11	1	2		3	5			12	4	10	6	9‡					11†		14	8	7							0-0(0-0)6679	11
19. Rangers* 21.11	1	2		3†	5				4	11	6	9					10		12	8	7							0-1(0-0)17,500	11
20. Dundee U* 24.11	1	2		3	5^1			12	4‡	11	6	9‡					10		14	8	7†							4-1(1-0)5000	—
21. St Mirren 28.11	1	2		3	5			12	4	11^1	6	9‡					10		14	8†	7^1							2-2(2-1)3691	11
22. Hearts 5.12	1	2		3	5				4	10	6	9‡					11		14	8†	7							0-1(0-1)12,729	11
23. Aberdeen 9.12	1	2†	8	3	5^1			12	4	11	6	14							10	9	7‡							1-3(0-2)8000	11
24. Dundee* 12.12	1	2	10	3	5			12	4	11‡	6	9							14	8	7†							0-6(0-2)4162	11
25. Hibernian 19.12	1	2	8		5			12		10‡	6	11	7†			3			9	14	4							0-0(0-0)5286	11
26. Celtic* 22.12	1	2	8		5					11	6		7		14	3	9†		10	4					12‡			0-2(0-1)12,000	11
27. Aberdeen* 26.12	1	2	8		5					10	6	11	7†		12	3			9	4								0-2(0-0)5000	11
28. Motherwell 1.1	1	2	8	3	5					10	6						11		9	4								0-0(0-0)4168	—
29. Dundee U 9.1	1	2	8	3				14	9	11‡	12							7†		4	5							0-0(0-0)6617	11
30. St Mirren* 16.1	1	2	8	3			14		9^1	10‡	5	12^1						11^1		7†	4	6						3-0(1-0)4750	10
31. Rangers 23.1	1	2	8	3		5			9^1	10	6	12						11			4†							1-3(0-1)41,088	10
32. Dunfermline A* 6.2	1	2	10	9		8				11†	5	12^1	7					3^1		14		4	6					1-0(0-0)5000	10
33. Morton 16.2	1	2	10		5	8		9			6	11‡	7					3		12		4						0-0(0-0)2412	—
34. Hearts* 27.2	1		10		5	8		9^1			6		11^1					3			7	4	2					2-0(0-0)9009	10
35. Celtic 5.3	1		10		5	8		9‡			6	11	7†					3	14	12	2	4						0-2(0-2)23,174	10
36. Hibernian* 12.3	1		2		5	8		9^1	10		6	12	11†					3			4	7						1-0(0-0)6000	10
37. Motherwell* 19.3	1			4	5	8		9			6		11†					3	12	10	7	2						0-0(0-0)5500	10
38. Aberdeen 26.3	1		8	14	5		12		10†		6	11						3		4	7	2‡	9					0-2(0-1)9410	10
39. St Mirren 2.4	1		10		5			9		12	6						11			4†	7		2	3	8			0-0(0-0)4694	10
40. Dundee 16.4	1		8		5		12		9	10‡	6	14^1								4†	7^1		2	3	11			2-4(0-1)4970	10
41. Morton* 23.4	1		8		5^1	4			9	10‡^{1}	6	12								7			2	3	11^2			4-1(3-0)4000	10
42. Dunfermline A 30.4	1		4		5				9^1	10	6†	11				12				7			2	3	8			1-0(0-0)4900	10
43. Dundee U* 4.5	1		4		5				9	12	6	11‡		14			10†			7			2	3	8^1			1-2(1-1)4455	10
44. Rangers* 7.5	1		4		5				9	10	6	11†					7					12	2	3	8			0-5(0-1)11,500	10
Apps(subs)/goals	44(0)0	33(0)0	31(0)0	25(2)0	42(0)7	10(0)1	22(12)1	12(3)3	35(0)9	34(2)2	37(6)1	25(11)17	9(0)1	3(0)9	5(0)1	31(0)4	0(2)0	5(1)0	20(11)0	27(2)2	6(0)0	7(0)0	6(0)0	6(0)3	0(1)0				

Final League Position: 10

FORFAR ATHLETIC – LEAGUE RECORD 1987–88 (DIVISION ONE)

Match no/Opp/Date	S Kennedy	A Brazil	A Hamill	R Morris	B Lyall	J Clark	W Blackie	M Bennett	G Scott	C Brewster	K Macdonald	W Bennett	G Mitchell	I McPhee	K Ward	P Smith	R Lorimer	I Stewart	S Clarke	J Morton	W Brown	S Taylor	FT(HT)Att Lge pos
1. Raith R 8.8	1	2	3	4	5	6	7¹	8	9†	10	11⅟	12											4-1(2-0)1624 —
2. Clyde* 11.8	1	2	3	4	5†		8	7	9	10	11₁		6	12¹									3-5(2-3)750 —
3. Clydebank* 15.8	1	4	3			6	7		9¹⅟	10	11¹	2		14¹	5†	12							3-0(1-0)746 4
4. Kilmarnock 22.8	1	4	3†			6	14	8	9¹⅟	10	11¹	2		7	5	12							2-2(2-1)1478 4
5. Meadowbank T* 29.8	1	4	3				12	8	9†	10	11	2		7	5	6							0-0(0-0)730 4
6. Queen of South 5.9	1	4	3				9	8¹		10	11	2		7	5	6							1-1(0-0)1700 4
7. Dumbarton 12.9	1	4	3			6	7¹	8	9†	10	11			12	5	2							1-1(1-1)700 4
8. East Fife* 15.9	1	4†	3			6	7²	8	9¹⅟	10¹	11	12		14	5	2							4-0(0-0)706 4
9. Hamilton A* 19.9	1	4	3			6	7	8	9¹†	10	11			12	5	2							1-1(0-0)1005 4
10. Partick Th 26.9	1	4	3			6	14	8†	9¹⅟	10	11	12		7	5	2							1-1(0-0)1285 3
11. Airdrieonians 28.9	1	4	3		12	6†	7⅟		9	10	11	2		14	5	8							0-1(0-0)1000 —
12. Raith R* 3.10	1	4	3			12	14	8	9²⅟	10	11₁	6		7†	5	2							3-0(2-0)1079 4
13. Clyde 7.10	1	4	3			12	14	8	9¹	10	11	2		7†	5¹		6⅟						2-2(0-1)600 —
14. Kilmarnock* 10.10	1	4	3				14	8†	9¹⅟	10	11	2		7¹	5	6	12						2-0(0-0)896 2
15. Dumbarton* 17.10	1	4	3				14	8	9	10	11⅟	2		7†	5	6	12						0-2(0-1)671 3
16. East Fife 20.10	1	4	3				12	8	9¹	10	11²	2		7†	5		6						3-2(2-2)668 —
17. Clydebank 24.10	1	4	3				12	8	9†	10	11	2		7	5	6							0-1(0-0)650 3
18. Airdrieonians* 27.10	1	4	3					10¹	8	9¹	6	11¹		7¹	5	2							4-4(3-1)660 —
19. Queen of South* 31.10	1	4	3					10¹	8	9†	6	11⅟	12	7	5	2							3-1(1-0)630 3
20. Meadowbank Th 7.11	1	4	3	5				10†	8	9	6⅟	11	12	14	7		2						0-3(0-2)650 5
21. Hamilton A 14.11	1	4†	3	5		9	7	8		10	11	2	14		6⅟	12							0-1(0-0)1465 6
22. Partick Th* 21.11	1		3	4	5	9	8			11	2†			7		6	10¹	12					1-4(1-1)764 7
23. Raith R 28.11	1		3	4		10	9	8†		11	2			7	5	6	4	12					0-0(0-0)1726 6
24. Clyde* 5.12	1		3			6¹	9	12¹		11¹	2			7†	5	8	4	10¹					4-2(1-1)620 6
25. Dumbarton 12.12	1	6	3			9	7¹			11	2			5	8	4	10						1-0(0-0)610 5
26. East Fife* 19.12	1	4	3			6¹	9†		10	11	2		12	5	8		7						1-1(1-0)598 6
27. Queen of South 26.12	1	4	3			6	9†	10	12	14	2‡		7	5¹	8		11						1-1(0-1)1100 5
28. Meadowbank T* 1.1	1	4	3			9	14	6‡	12	11	2		7¹	5	8		10†						1-2(1-1)920 —
29. Hamilton A* 9.1	1	4	3			9	12		6†	11			7	5	2		8	10					0-0(0-0)771 6
30. Partick Th 16.1	1					9	7	12	6	11₁			5	2	8	10†							1-0(1-0)1673 4
31. Clydebank* 27.1	1	4	3	5		9	7		6	11¹	2		8	10†	12								2-2(0-1)676 —
32. Kilmarnock 6.2	1	4	3			12	14		6	11			7†	5	2	8¹	10	9¹⅟					2-0(1-0)1283 4
33. Airdrieonians 13.2	1	4	3	5		10†			6	11	7‡		14	2	8	12	9						0-3(0-2)1050 5
34. Raith R* 27.2	1		3	4		12	11	6					7¹	5	2	8	10†	9₁					2-2(2-1)1056 5
35. Dumbarton* 5.3	1		3	4			11⅟	6	12	14¹			7¹	5	2¹	8	10†	9¹					4-0(1-0)507 4
36. East Fife 12.3	1		3	4		14		6⅟	12	11			7†	5	2	8	10	9					0-4(0-1)622 4
37. Queen of South* 19.3	1		3	4		8¹			10	11	2†		12	5	6		7		9				1-1(0-0)504 4
38. Meadowbank Th 26.3	1	6	3	4					10	11			12	5	2†		8	7	9				0-3(0-0)600 6
39. Kilmarnock* 2.4	1	4	3			8			10¹	11	2		12	5			6	7†	9				1-1(0-0)713 6
40. Clydebank 9.4	1	2	3	4		12			10	11	14			5	8	7†	6	9²⅟					2-3(0-1)505 7
41. Partick Th* 16.4	1		3	4		7			8	11¹	2			5	6		10	9					1-0(0-0)731 6
42. Hamilton A 23.4	1	2	3	4					10	11			12	5	7¹	8†	6	9					1-0(0-0)1727 4
43. Clyde 30.4	1	2	3	4		9			10	11¹			12	5		8	6		7†				1-0(0-0)600 4
44. Airdrieonians* 7.5	1	2†	3¹	4		9			10	11¹	12			14	5	7	8¹⅟	6					3-0(3-0)535 4
Apps(subs)/goals	44(0) 0	36(0) 0	44(0) 1	14(0) 0	5(1) 0	22(12) 8	26(2) 2	19(0) 11	35(0) 9	41(2) 20	26(2) 7	0(2) 0	1(0) 0	10(0) 0	23(14) 7	37(0) 2	34(2) 2	3(0) 0	19(0) 3	19(3) 1	11(1) 5	1(0) 0	

Final League Position: 4

HAMILTON ACADEMICAL – LEAGUE RECORD 1987–88 (DIVISION ONE)

Match no/Opp/Date		D McKellar	B Martin	A Sprott	G Collins	M Fulton	S Clarke	K McKee	A Taylor	W Jamieson	M Caughey	G McCabe	P McDonald	D Walsh	J Gibson	J Weir	C Speirs	D McGrain	S Gordon	R Docherty	J Kerr	J Frith	R Ferguson	J Fairlie	R Thomson	G Scott	A Ferguson	A Fraser	C Harris	A Craig	J McNaught	FT(HT)Att	Lge pos
1. Kilmarnock	8.8	1	2	3	4^1	5	6	7	8	9	10^1	11																				2–0(2–0)1909	—
2. Clydebank*	11.8	1	2	3	6	5			8^1	9	10^1_1	11	7‡	4†	12	14																3–2(2–2)1797	—
3. Clyde*	15.8	1	2	3	4^1	5	7		8	9	10^1	11^1	12				6†															3–2(0–0)2311	1
4. Raith R	22.8	1	6	3	4	5	7†	12	8	9^1	10	11^1						2														2–1(1–1)2069	1
5. Airdrieonians	29.8	1	6	3	4		7^1		8^1	9	10	11^1					5	2														3–0(0–0)1700	1
6. Dumbarton*	5.9	1	6‡	3	4		7	12	8	9	10^1_1	11	14				5†	2														2–1(2–1)1765	1
7. Partick Th*	12.9	1		3	4		8†	7	6	5	10^2	11^1	12					2	9^2													5–0(0–0)2421	1
8. Queen of South	15.9	1		3^1	4		8	7	6^1	5	10^1	11						2	9													3–0(0–0)2400	—
9. Forfar Ath	19.9	1		3	4		8	7	6	5	10	11						2	9^1													1–1(0–0)1005	1
10. East Fife*	26.9	1		3	4		8	7†	6	5	10	11‡	12				14	2	9													0–1(0–0)1656	1
11. Meadowbank Th	29.9	1		3	4		6†	12	8	5	10	7		11				2	9^1													1–1(0–1)900	—
12. Kilmarnock*	3.10	1		3	4		6†	7	8	5	10	11‡	12					2	9^1	14												1–1(1–1)3236	1
13. Clydebank	6.10	1					6^1	7	8	5	10^1	11					4	2	9		3											2–0(2–0)950	—
14. Raith R*	10.10	1		12			8	7	6	5	10†	11‡	14				4	2	9		3											0–2(0–0)1925	1
15. Partick Th	17.10	1	4	6	8		14	7‡	11	5	10†							2	9		3	12										0–1(0–1)2162	1
16. Queen of South*	20.10	1	6	3^1	7		4		8	5	10†		11					2	9^1		12											2–2(2–1)1566	—
17. Clyde	24.10		4	3	6			7	8	10^1		11					5^1	2	9^1				1									3–0(1–0)1300	1
18. Meadowbank T*	27.10		5	3	8†			7		6^1		11‡	14				4	2	9		12		1	10								1–5(1–2)1349	—
19. Dumbarton	31.10		4	11	8†			7		6		12	14				5	2	9		3‡		1	10								1–2(1–2)900	1
20. Airdrieonians*	7.11		5	3			12	8	4^1	10			11					2	9†				1	7	6^1							2–2(0–0)2405	1
21. Forfar Ath*	14.11		5	3			12	8	4	10^1			11					2	9				1	7	6†							1–0(0–0)1465	1
22. East Fife	21.11		5	3				8	4	10		11^1						2	9				1	7	6							1–0(0–0)811	1
23. Kilmarnock	28.11		5	3	12			7	4			11†	14					2	9‡			10	1	8	6							0–1(0–0)1922	1
24. Clydebank*	5.12			10^1†	4			2	8	5		11_1						12	9^1		3	14^1	1	7‡	6							4–0(2–0)1455	1
25. Partick Th*	12.12		14	10	4			2	8	5		11_1							9‡		3		1	7	6†	12						1–0(1–0)2356	1
26. Queen of South	19.12		6	10	4			2	8	5									12		3		1	7	11	9†						0–0(0–0)1150	1
27. Dumbarton*	26.12		12	10	4			2	8	5		14							11^1‡		3		1	7^1	6	9†						2–0(0–0)1764	1
28. Airdrieonians	2.1		4	3	6			2	8	5		12									11		1	7^2	10^1†	9^1						4–1(4–0)3400	1
29. Forfar Ath	9.1		4	10	6			2	8	5		12									3		1	7	11†	9						0–0(0–0)771	1
30. East Fife*	16.1		4†	10^1	6			2	8	5		11				14			12		3		1‡	7		9						1–0(1–0)1478	1
31. Clyde*	6.2		4	3	6			2	8	5		11†				12			14		10			7^1		9^1‡	1					2–0(1–0)1709	1
32. Meadowbank Th	13.2		4	11				2	8	5		12				14	6				3‡			7	10†	9	1					0–2(0–0)1315	1
33. Kilmarnock*	27.2			10	6			2	8	5		12	11†			4					3			7	9^1		1					1–0(0–0)2048	1
34. Raith R	2.3			4	6			2	8	5		11					12				3			7	10^1†	9	1					1–0(0–0)2468	—
35. Partick Th	5.3			8	6			2		5		11					4				3		1	7		9		10				0–0(0–0)3340	1
36. Queen of South*	12.3			11^1	6			2	8	5		12	14								3		1	7†	4‡	9		10				1–2(0–1)1682	1
37. Dumbarton	19.3			10	6			2	8	5		12					4		14		3†		1	7‡	11				9_1			1–1(0–1)1250	1
38. Airdrieonians*	26.3			10				2	8	5		11†							12		3		1		6	9			7^1	4		1–1(0–1)1839	1
39. Clyde	2.4			11				2	8†				12				5		14		3		1		6	9^1‡			7^1_1	10	4^1	4–0(1–0)1400	1
40. Raith R*	9.4			11^1				2	8†				12				5				3		1		6	9			7^1	10	4	2–1(2–1)1833	1
41. East Fife	16.4			3				2	8	4							5								6	9^1	1		7	11	10	1–1(0–1)1378	1
42. Forfar Ath*	23.4			11				2	8	5							12				3		1	7	6†	9			10	4		0–1(0–0)1727	1
43. Clydebank	30.4				6†			2	8	5							4		12				1		7	9			11	3^1		1–3(0–2)1546	1
44. Meadowbank T*	7.5				6			2	8	5			11‡			12			9			14			3		1		7^1_1		4†	1–1(0–1)5170	1
Apps(subs)/goals		16(0)0	21(2)0	40(1)6	32(1)2	4(0)0	14(3)2	37(3)0	41(0)4	41(0)4	16(0)10	25(8)7	6(12)0	2(0)0	0(1)0	1(5)0	15(3)1	20(1)0	21(7)9	0(1)0	22(2)0	1(3)1	22(0)0	21(0)4	22(0)4	16(1)4	6(0)0	2(0)0	8(0)6	6(0)1	4(0)1	Final League Position: 1	

Own goal: R. Montgomerie, match 19. Also played: M. Nelson at 10 in matches 43, 44.

HEART OF MIDLOTHIAN – LEAGUE RECORD 1987–88 (PREMIER DIVISION)

Match no/Opp/Date	H.Smith	W.Kidd	B.Whittaker	W.Jardine	N.Berry	D.McPherson	J.Colquhoun	K.Black	A.Clark	G.MacKay	J.Robertson	I.Jardine	W.Foster	A.Moore	S.Crabbe	H.Burns	C.Levein	M.Galloway	M.Murray	M.Gavin	J.Sandison	A.McLaren	FT(HT)Att Lge pos
1. Falkirk* 8.8	1	2	3	4	5	6	7^1	8	9^1†	10	11^2		12										4–2(3–0)12,163 —
2. Celtic 12.8	1	2	3	4	5	6	7	8	9	10	11†		12										0–1(0–0)29,815 —
3. St Mirren 15.8	1	2	3	4	5	6	7‡	8	9	10†	11_1	12	14										1–1(1–0)7408 5
4. Dundee U* 22.8	1	2	3	4	5	6	7		9^2†	10	11_1	8^1	12										4–1(2–0)14,548 4
5. Hibernian* 29.8	1	2†	3	4	5	6	7	12	9	10	11‡	8	14										1–0(1–0)24,496 4
6. Morton 5.9	1	2	3	4	5	6	9^1	8		10	11_1†			7	12								2–1(2–0)4000 2
7. Motherwell* 12.9	1	2	3	4	5	6	9‡	8		10	11	12	14	7^1†									1–0(1–0)11,488 2
8. Dundee 19.9	1	2	3	4	5	6	9^2†	8		10	11_1	12	7‡	14									3–1(1–0)9199 1
9. Dunfermline A 26.9	1	2	3†	4	5	6	9^1	8	14	10	11‡	12	7										1–0(1–0)14,748 1
10. Rangers* 3.10	1		3		5	6	9	8		10	11		7			2	4						0–0(0–0)29,000 2
11. Aberdeen* 7.10	1		3		5	6^1	9†	8	12	10	11^1		7			2	4						2–1(2–1)17,741 1
12. Falkirk 10.10	1		3	5†	6	9^2‡	8	14	10	11_1	12^1	7^1				2	4						5–1(4–0)7000 1
13. Hibernian 17.10	1	2	3		5	6	9	8†	14	10	11^1	12	7‡				4						1–2(1–2)23,396 1
14. Morton* 24.10	1		3		5	6	9	8^2	14	10_1†	11	12	7‡			2	4						3–0(2–0)11,516 1
15. Motherwell 27.10	1		3		5	6	9†	8	12	10	11^1		7^1			2	4						3–0(2–0)6699 —
16. Dundee* 31.10	1		3		5	6	9^1	8^1	12	10	11^2†		7			2	4						4–2(3–0)13,806 1
17. Celtic* 7.11	1		3		5	6	9^1†	8	12	10	11		7			2	4						1–1(0–0)29,000 1
18. Aberdeen 14.11	1	12	3		5†	6	9	8	14	10	11_1		7			2	4						0–0(0–0)20,000 1
19. Dundee U 18.11	1	5†	3			6	9	8	14	10	11^2		7^1‡			2	4	12					3–0(2–0)14,258 —
20. St Mirren* 21.11	1	5	3			6	9	8	12	10‡	11		7†			2	4	14					0–0(0–0)14,879 1
21. Dunfermline A* 24.11	1	5†	3			6†	9^1	8	12‡	10	11^1		7			2	4	14					3–2(1–0)14,517 —
22. Rangers 28.11	1	14	3			6	9	8‡	12	10	11_1		7			2	4†	5^1					2–3(1–2)43,557 2
23. Falkirk* 5.12	1		3			6	9†	8	12	10	11_1		7			2	4	5					1–0(1–0)12,729 1
24. Celtic 12.12	1	2	3	12		6	7	8		10	11^1†			9			4	5^1					2–2(1–0)43,968 2
25. Motherwell* 16.12	1	2	3			6	7	8	12	10	11_1†			9			4	5					1–1(0–0)9047 —
26. Dundee 19.12	1	2‡	3		14	6	7	8		10	11†			9	12		4	5					0–0(0–0)10,806 2
27. Morton 26.12	1		3		14	6	7	8		10	11		9‡	14		2†	4	5					0–0(0–0)4000 3
28. Hibernian* 2.1	1		3		12	6	7	8†	14	10	11‡			9		2	4	5					0–0(0–0)28,992 3
29. Dunfermline A 9.1	1		3			6	10^1	11		7	9^2		8†	12		2	4	5^1					4–0(0–0)11,963 2
30. Rangers* 16.1	1		3			11	6	10	8^1	7	9	12				2	4†	5					1–1(0–0)28,967 3
31. Dundee U* 3.2	1		3		4	6	10	8	12	7^1	9	14	11†			2‡		5					1–1(0–0)13,710 —
32. St Mirren 6.2	1		3		2	6	10^3†	4	12	7	9‡	8	11^1					5					6–0(3–0)6659 3
33. Aberdeen* 13.2	1		3		2	6	10	4	11^1	7	9_1	8						5					2–1(1–1)18,817 3
34. Falkirk 27.2	1		3		2	6	10	4	12	7	9†	11				8		5					0–2(0–0)9009 3
35. Motherwell 8.3	1		3		8	6	10^1†	4	12	7	9^1	14	11			2		5					2–0(1–0)5831 —
36. Hibernian 19.3	1		3		5	6	10	4‡	12	7	9†	14	11			2		8					0–0(0–0)23,395 3
37. Morton* 26.3	1		3			6	10‡	4		7	9	8†	11		12		5^2	2	14				2–0(0–0)8787 3
38. Dundee* 30.3	1		3		8	6	10^1	4^1	12	7	9	14	11†			2		5					2–0(1–0)9649 —
39. Rangers 2.4	1		3		8	6^1	10†	4	9	7	11_1						5	2	12				2–1(0–1)41,125 2
40. Dunfermline A* 13.4	1				5	4^1	14	3	9	12^1		8†	11‡			10		6	2	7			2–1(0–1)7307 —
41. Celtic* 16.4	1		3		5	6	11†	4	12^1	7^1		9				10^1	2	8					2–1(1–0)26,200 2
42. Aberdeen 23.4	1		3		10	6	7	4	12		9‡			14		5	2	11†	8				0–0(0–0)10,500 2
43. St Mirren* 30.4	1		3		10	6	7	4	9		8†	12				5	2	11					0–1(0–0)8570 2
44. Dundee U 7.5	1					6	7	8	9†			12	10	2		5	11	4	3				0–0(0–0)9520 2

Appsubs/goals: 44(0)/0 16(2)/0 42(0)/0 9(0)/0 31(4)/0 44(0)/4 43(1)/15 41(1)/4 11(24)/6 40(1)/5 39(0)/26 6(12)/2 33(6)/4 26(5)/1 2(3)/0 23(1)/0 21(0)/0 7(0)/0 5(2)/0 2(0)/0 1(0)/0

Final League Position: 2

Own goal: M. Caughey, match 15.

HIBERNIAN – LEAGUE RECORD 1987–88 (PREMIER DIVISION)

Match no/Opp/Date	A Rough	C Milne	T McIntyre	E May	G Rae	G Hunter	M Weir	P Kane	S Cowan	J Collins	J McBride	J Tortolano	P McGovern	G Chisholm	G Mitchell	A Sneddon	G McCluskey	D Bell	N Orr	A Watson	A Goram	G Evans	D Lennon	FT(HT)Att Lge pos
1. Dunfermline A 8.8	1	2	3	4	5	6	7	8¹	9	10¹	11¹†	12												3–3(1–1)12,000 —
2. Rangers* 12.8	1	2	3	4	5		7	8	9†	11¹			6	10		12								1–0(0–0)22,000 —
3. Dundee* 15.8	1		3†	8‡	5	2	7		9	10	11	14	4	6		12								0–4(0–4)8000 8
4. Morton 22.8	1	6	4‡	5	2		7¹	8₁	9†	11¹			10	3		12	14							3–3(2–1)3500 8
5. Hearts 29.8	1		3		2		7	10	9¹				5	6		12	4	8						0–1(0–1)24,496 8
6. St Mirren* 5.9	1	6†	4		2		7‡	10		12			5	3			9	14	8	11				1–1(0–0)5500 9
7. Dundee U 12.9	1		2	4			7		6	12	11		5	3			9¹†		8	10¹				2–1(1–0)7920 7
8. Falkirk* 19.9	1		2	4			7¹†		6	12	11		5	3			9		8	10				1–0(1–0)6500 6
9. Aberdeen* 26.9	1		2	4‡	5	6	7	10				14		3			9†	12	8	11				0–2(0–0)10,500 7
10. Celtic 3.10	1			4	5	6	7	10							2	3	9		8	11¹				1–1(0–1)31,805 7
11. Motherwell 6.10	1			4‡	5	6	7	10				14			2	3	9‡	12	8	11				0–1(0–1)4093 —
12. Dunfermline A* 10.10			4‡†		5	6	7¹			10¹		14			2	3	9¹‡	12	8	11	1			4–0(4–0)10,000 8
13. Hearts* 17.10			4¹†		5	6	7¹			10		14			2	3	9‡	12	8	11	1			2–1(2–1)23,396 7
14. St Mirren 24.10			4		5	6	7			10	9†		3¹		2			12	8	11¹	1			2–2(1–2)7014 7
15. Dundee U* 28.10			4		5	6	7			10					2	3	9		8	11	1			0–1(0–0)8400 —
16. Falkirk 31.10			4		5	6	7			10	11†	12			2	3	9¹		8		1			1–1(0–0)6000 8
17. Rangers 7.11			4		5	6	7			10		14			2	3	9†	12	8	11‡	1			0–0(0–0)37,517 8
18. Motherwell* 14.11			2		5	6	7¹	10								3	9	4	8		1			1–0(1–0)7000 8
19. Morton* 18.11			2		5	6	7	10		12						3	9	4	8	11†	1			0–0(0–0)6000 —
20. Dundee 21.11			3‡	4†	5		7	10¹		14			6		2		9	11	8	12	1			1–2(0–1)6583 8
21. Aberdeen 24.11			4†		5		9¹	10		11					2	3	12	7	6	8	1			1–1(1–1)9000 —
22. Celtic* 28.11			4		5		7	10		12	11				2	3	9†	8	6		1			0–1(0–0)23,500 8
23. Dunfermline A 5.12			4		5	6	7			11†	14				2	3	9‡	8	12		1			0–1(0–0)7500 8
24. Rangers* 12.12		6	4	5	2			9		10	7	12				3		8	11†		1			0–2(0–1)19,000 8
25. Dundee U 16.12		6	4	5	2		7¹	10			11	12			3		9¹†		8		1			2–1(2–1)6195 —
26. Falkirk* 19.12			4	5	6		7	10			11†				3	2	9	8	12		1			0–0(0–0)5286 7
27. St Mirren* 26.12	12	2‡	4	5	6		7	10	14					8	3	9†			11		1			0–0(0–0)5500 7
28. Hearts 2.1	12	4‡	5	2			7	10	14				6	3	9			8	11†		1			0–0(0–0)28,992 7
29. Aberdeen* 9.1			4	5	6		7	10	12					3	2	9		8	11†		1			0–0(0–0)16,000 7
30. Celtic 16.1			4	5	6	11	7	10†						3	2	9		8	12		1			0–2(0–2)34,886 7
31. Morton 23.1			4	5	6		7	9		12¹					3	2		8	11†		1			1–0(0–0)2800 7
32. Dundee* 6.2		2	4†	5	6	7	9		10	11¹				3			8				1	12¹		2–1(2–1)6000 7
33. Motherwell 13.2		4		5	6	7¹†	9		10¹	12				3	2					1	11			2–0(1–0)5421 7
34. Dunfermline A* 27.2		12	5	6	7¹	9‡	10		11				3	2	14†	4		1	8					2–0(2–0)10,000 7
35. Dundee U* 5.3			5	6	7	9†	10		11				3	2	12	4		1	8					0–0(0–0)7000 7
36. Falkirk 12.3		12	5	6	7†	9	10‡						3	2	11	4	14	1	8					0–1(0–0)6000 7
37. Hearts* 19.3			5	6	7	9	10						3	2	12	4	11	1	8†					0–0(0–0)23,395 7
38. St Mirren 26.3			5	6	7	9	10						3	2		4	11	1	8¹					1–1(1–1)4655 7
39. Celtic* 2.4		12	5	6	7	9	10						3	2		4	11†	1	8					0–2(0–1)19,500 7
40. Rangers 16.4		12	5	6	7	9₁	10	11‡					3	2		4	14	1	8†					1–0(1–0)32,218 7
41. Motherwell* 23.4		4		5	6‡	9	10	14¹	7†				3	2		8	12	1	11					1–1(0–0)5500 7
42. Dundee 30.4		6	4	5		9	10		12				3	2	11	8		1	7†					0–0(0–0)4471 7
43. Aberdeen 4.5		6	4	5	7†	9¹	10	14¹					3	2	11‡	8		1	12					2–0(1–0)7000 —
44. Morton* 7.5		6‡	4	5	7	9†	10	12¹					3	2	11	8¹		1¹			14			3–1(2–1)7000 6

Apps(subs)/goals: 1(10)0 · 2(1)0 · 21(4)0 · 32(2)2 · 40(0)0 · 35(0)0 · 44(0)3 · 35(0)0 · 44(0)12 · 43(1)0 · 5(0)0 · 42(1)6 · 5(8)1 · 11(10)4 · 1(5)1 · 20(0)0 · 41(0)1 · 32(0)0 · 24(8)4 · 8(8)1 · 36(0)1 · 23(7)3 · 33(0)1 · 10(2)2 · 0(2)0

Final League Position: 6

Own goal: R. Dawson, match 6.

KILMARNOCK – LEAGUE RECORD 1987–88 (DIVISION ONE)

Match no/Opp/Date	B Holland	G Millar	J Cockburn	A Robertson	J McVeigh	R Clark	R McConville	S McLean	C Harkness	I Reid	I Bryson	J McGuire	I McInnes	L Lowe	A Bell	D Cook	F Davidson	S Cuthbertson	P Martin	G Wylde	A McCulloch	J Gilmour	H Houston	D MacFarlane	S Kearney	S Marshall	N Candlish	J Bourke	FT(HT)Att Lge pos
1. Hamilton A* 8.8	1	2	3	4	5	6	7†	8‡	9	10	11	12	14																0-2(0-2)1909 —
2. East Fife 12.8	1			4	5		6	8	10†‡	11	9	7	2	3	12														1-2(1-0)657 —
3. Dumbarton 15.8	1		6	4			2	9¹	10	11		7¹		3		5	8¹												3-1(0-1)800 8
4. Forfar Ath* 22.8	1		6	4			2	9¹	12¹	10		7	14	3	11†		8‡	5											2-2(1-2)1478 8
5. Queen of South* 29.8	1		3	4	8‡		2	9	10	11†		7		6	12		14	5											0-2(0-0)1836 10
6. Meadowbank Th 5.9	1		4	6			2	9		10	12	7		3	11†‡		5	8											1-2(1-1)900 9
7. Raith R* 12.9	1		4	6			2	10¹	12	11	14	7¹		3	9‡		8¹†	5											3-4(2-2)1436 11
8. Clydebank 15.9			3	6	4		2	9†	10	11		7			12	5	8	1											0-2(0-2)880 —
9. Airdrieonians 19.9			3	6	4		2	9¹‡		11	12	7		14	8†	5	10	1											2-3(1-1)1300 12
10. Clyde* 26.9			3	14	4		2	9¹		11¹	12	7	6†		8‡	5	10	1											2-0(2-0)1750 11
11. Partick Th* 29.9			3		4		2	9¹		11		7	6		8	5	10	1											1-1(1-0)1500 —
12. Hamilton A 3.10		6	3	4			2	9¹‡		11†	12	7	14		8	5	10	1											1-1(1-1)3236 12
13. East Fife* 6.10			3	4		6†	2	9²		11	12	7			8	5	10	1											2-0(1-0)1850 —
14. Forfar Ath 10.10			3		4		2	9		11	12	7	6†		8	5	10	1											0-2(0-0)896 10
15. Raith R 17.10			3		4	12	2	9¹		11†		7			8	5	6	1	10₁										2-0(1-0)2187 10
16. Clydebank* 20.10			3		4	14	2	9		11	12¹	7			8‡	5	6†	1	10										1-3(0-2)1730 —
17. Dumbarton* 24.10			3		4	14	2	9		11†	12	7			8‡	5	6	1	10¹										1-0(0-0)1571 10
18. Meadowbank T* 31.10			3		4		2	9²		11	12	7			8†	5	6	1	10										2-4(1-2)1442 10
19. Partick Th 3.11		2				6	3	9			7		11†	4	12	5	8	1	10										0-1(0-1)1407 —
20. Queen of South 7.11		2				6	3	9²	11¹		7¹			4	12	5	8†	1	10										4-1(0-0)1479 10
21. Airdrieonians* 14.11		2					3	9¹	11†	12	7			4		5	8	1	10	6									1-0(1-0)1978 10
22. Clyde 21.11		2					3	9	11†	12	7			4		5	8	1	10	6									0-2(0-2)1145 10
23. Hamilton A* 28.11		2					3	8¹	9†		12	7		4		5	10	1	11	6									1-0(0-0)1922 10
24. East Fife 5.12		2					3	9	10†‡	11¹	12	7		4		5	6	1	8										1-2(1-0)571 11
25. Raith R* 12.12		2				6	3	9	12¹	11	10‡	7		14	4		5	8†	1										1-1(0-0)1654 11
26. Clydebank 19.12		2					10	3	9		12			4†		5	8	1	11	6									0-1(0-0)1015 11
27. Meadowbank Th 26.12			3				10	2	9²†	11			8	4		5	7	1	12	6¹									3-1(1-1)950 11
28. Queen of South* 2.1			3				10†	2	9			12	8	4		5	7	1		6									0-0(0-0)3230 10
29. Airdrieonians 9.1			3				10	2	9			12	8	4		5	7	1	11₁	6₂†									3-3(1-1)1740 11
30. Clyde* 16.1			3				6†	2	9¹		11¹			12	4	8¹	5	7	1	10									3-1(2-1)1752 9
31. Dumbarton 23.1		7‡	3				6	2	9		11†			4	8	5		1	10	14									0-1(0-1)950 10
32. Forfar Ath* 6.2							14	2	9		11‡		7	12	4	8	5		1	10	6†		3						0-2(0-1)1283 11
33. Partick Th* 13.2			3				8	2	9†		11		7		4			6	1	12				5	10				0-1(0-0)2432 11
34. Hamilton A 27.2			3				8	2			11		7†		4	12	5	6	1	10					9				0-1(0-0)2048 11
35. Raith R 5.3			3				6	2			11		7†		4¹	14¹	8	1	12			5		10‡	9				2-2(0-1)1462 11
36. Clydebank* 12.3			3					2			11		12		4	8	5¹	7†	1	10				6		9¹			2-2(1-1)1549 11
37. Meadowbank T* 19.3		2					3	12			11		14		4	7†	5	8	1	10‡				6		9			0-1(0-0)1662 11
38. Queen of South 26.3		2						14	3	9†	11	12			4	7	5	8‡	1	10				6					0-1(0-0)1650 11
39. Forfar Ath 2.4		2‡						3	12		11	14			4	7†	5	6	1	10₁				8		9			1-1(0-0)713 10
40. Dumbarton* 9.4		2						3			11¹	7¹†	12		4		5	8	1	10¹				6		9			3-1(0-0)2205 10
41. Clyde 16.4		2						3			11	7			4		5	8	1	10				6		9¹			0-0(0-0)1100 10
42. Airdrieonians* 23.4		2						3			11	7²†	14		4	12	5	8	1	10₁				6		9¹‡			4-1(1-0)1953 10
43. East Fife* 30.4		2						3			11	7‡	14		4	12	5	8	1	10¹				6†		9			1-3(0-3)2488 10
44. Partick Th 7.5		2						3			11	7†			4	12	5	8	1	10¹				6		9			1-0(0-0)3200 10

Final League Position: 10

Apps(subs)/goals: B Holland 7(0) 0; G Millar 18(0) 0; J Cockburn 3(0) 0; A Robertson 27(0) 0; J McVeigh 11(1) 0; R Clark 10(0) 0; R McConville 14(5) 0; S McLean 44(0) 0; C Harkness 30(2) 16; I Reid 11(3) 6; I Bryson 40(2) 5; J McGuire 7(17) 4; I McInnes 29(8) 3; L Lowe 1(1) 0; A Bell 10(1) 0; D Cook 6(6) 1; F Davidson 27(0) 1; S Cuthbertson 20(9) 4; P Martin 39(0) 1; G Wylde 36(0) 0; A McCulloch 37(0) 0; J Gilmour 25(3) 8; H Houston 4(1) 0; D MacFarlane 40(3); S Kearney 11(0) 0; S Marshall 3(0) 0; N Candlish 9(0) 2

Own goal: D. Lawrie, match 9.

MEADOWBANK THISTLE – LEAGUE RECORD 1987–88 (DIVISION ONE)

Match no/Opp/Date		M.McDermott	T.Hendrie	D.Roseburgh	W.Boyd	G.Tierney	R.Scott	D.Park	M.Lawson	I.Kasule	A.Prentice	J.McGachie	J.Liddle	J.Bowie	G.Armstrong	R.Callachan	J.McQueen	I.Stewart	S.Logan	A.McGonigal	N.Irvine	R.Reilly	J.McCormack	FT(HT)Att	Lge pos
1. Partick Th*	8.8	1	2	3¹	4	5	6†	7	8	9¹	10¹	11¹	12	14										3-2(1-1)1039	—
2. Dumbarton	11.8	1	2	3	4	5		7¹	12	10	11²	8			6	9†								2-2(3-2)740	—
3. East Fife	15.8	1	2	3	4	5		7	14	12	11²	8	10†	6₁	9‡									3-3(2-1)692	2
4. Queen of South*	22.8		2	3	4	5		7	8	12	11	10†		6	9¹	1								1-0(0-0)550	2
5. Forfar Ath	29.8		2	3	4	5	10	14	12	11	7‡	6	9	1	8†									0-0(0-0)730	2
6. Kilmarnock*	5.9		2	3‡	4	5	10	7	12	8†	11²	14		6	9	1								2-1(1-1)900	2
7. Airdrieonians*	12.9		2	3	4	5	7		10¹		11			6	9	1	8							1-2(0-0)750	3
8. Raith R	15.9		2	3†		5	14	7	8	10	12	11		6	9	1	4‡							0-2(0-1)1545	2
9. Clyde	19.9		2		4	5	7		10	8	11			6	9	1	3							0-0(0-0)600	5
10. Clydebank*	26.9		2		4	5	7		10	8	11			6	9	1	3							0-0(0-0)400	4
11. Hamilton A*	29.9		2		4	5	8		10¹	6	11			3	9	1	12	7†						1-1(1-0)900	2
12. Queen of South	3.10		2		4	5¹	8		10	6¹	11			3	9	1		7						2-0(1-0)1700	3
13. Dumbarton*	7.10		2		4	5	8		10	6	11			3	9	1		7						0-0(0-0)650	—
14. Partick Th	10.10		2		4	5	8	12	10	6†	11	9‡	14	3		1		7						0-1(0-1)1513	6
15. Airdrieonians	17.10		2		4	5	8		10	6	11	9	3			1		7						0-0(0-0)1000	5
16. Raith R*	20.10		2		4	5¹	8		10†	6	11	12	3			1		7	9²					4-3(3-1)760	—
17. East Fife*	24.10		2	12	4	5	8		10†	6	11¹		3			1		7	9¹					2-3(0-1)479	5
18. Hamilton A	27.10		2	10	4	5	8¹		12	6†‡	11		3			1		7	9³					5-1(2-1)1349	2
19. Kilmarnock	31.10	2¹		10	4	5‡	8	14	12¹		11¹		6†	3		1		7	9¹					4-2(2-1)1442	2
20. Forfar Ath*	7.11		2	10	4		8		5		11		6	3¹		1		7	9²					3-0(2-0)650	2
21. Clyde*	14.11		2	10	4		8	12	5†		11		6‡	3	14	1		7	9					0-2(0-1)500	3
22. Clydebank	21.11		2	10	4		8		5	6	11†	12‡	3	14	1	7	9							1-2(1-1)686	5
23. Queen of South*	28.11		2	10²	4		14	8	11²†	6¹‡		3	12	1	7	9	5†							5-0(3-0)550	3
24. Dumbarton	5.12		2	10	4		12	8	11	6		3		1	7	9¹	5†							1-0(0-0)500	2
25. Airdrieonians*	12.12		2	10	4		12	8	11†	6		3	14	1	7‡	9	5							0-0(0-0)600	2
26. Raith R	19.12		2	10	4		5	8	11	6		3		1	7	9†	12							0-4(0-1)1940	3
27. Kilmarnock*	26.12		2	10	4	5	11¹		12	6†		3	8†	1	7	9	14							1-3(1-1)950	3
28. Forfar Ath	1.1		2¹	4		8		10	6	11¹		3	9	1	7	5								2-1(1-1)920	—
29. Clydebank*	16.1	10†₁	4	5		8	12		6	11¹		3	9	1	7¹	2								3-2(3-0)600	3
30. Partick Th*	23.1	10₁	4	5		8			6	11¹		3	9	1	7¹	2								3-1(1-0)1100	3
31. Clyde	26.1	10¹	4	5		8			6	11¹		3	9	1	7	2								2-2(1-1)600	—
32. East Fife	6.2	10	4	5		8			6	11†		3	9	1	7	9	2	12						0-0(0-0)582	2
33. Hamilton A*	13.2	10	4	5				6	11		3	9	1	7¹	2¹	8								2-0(0-0)1315	2
34. Queen of South	27.2	10₁	4	5				6†	11		3	9	1	7	8	2	12							1-2(0-2)1000	2
35. Airdrieonians	5.3	10¹	4	5				6	11		3	9	1	7	8	2								1-0(1-0)800	2
36. Raith R*	12.3	10	4¹	5				6	11		3	9	1	7¹	8	9¹	2							3-0(2-0)750	2
37. Kilmarnock	19.3	10	4	5				6	11		3	9	1	7	12	2	8†							0-0(0-0)1662	2
38. Forfar Ath*	26.3	10¹	4	5				6²	11		3	9	1	7	8	2								3-0(0-0)600	2
39. East Fife*	2.4	10	4	5				6¹	11		3	12	1	7¹†	8	9	2							2-1(0-0)800	2
40. Partick Th	9.4	2†	10¹	4	5				6	11‡		3	9	1	7	14	8	12						1-2(0-0)1400	2
41. Clydebank	16.4	2	10	4	5				11		3	9†	1	7	6²	8	12							2-0(1-0)765	2
42. Clyde*	23.4	2	10	4	5			11†	12	3		1	7	9	8	6								0-1(0-1)700	2
43. Dumbarton*	30.4	2	10¹	4	5		14	11¹	3¹		9	1	7	6†‡	8	12								2-4(0-1)600	2
44. Hamilton A	7.5	2	10	4	5		8‡	11†	14		9	1	7	12	3	6¹								1-1(1-0)5170	2

Apps(subs)/goals:
| McDermott 3(0) 0 | Hendrie 32(0) 1 | Roseburgh 35(1) 12 | Boyd 43(0) 1 | Tierney 36(0) 2 | Scott 3(0) 0 | Park 27(4) 3 | Lawson 9(5) 0 | Kasule 20(8) 6 | Prentice 32(2) 7 | McGachie 39(0) 14 | Liddle 5(2) 0 | Bowie 42(0) 3 | Armstrong 26(5) 1 | Callachan 41(0) 0 | McQueen 5(0) 0 | Stewart 34(0) 5 | Logan 17(3) 12 | McGonigal 18(2) 1 | Irvine 8(4) 2 | Reilly 4(0) 0 |

Final League Position: 2

MONTROSE – LEAGUE RECORD 1987–88 (DIVISION TWO)

Match no/Opp/Date		D Larter	L Barr	C McLelland	D Paterson	J Sheean	A Wright	M Allan	G Robertson	I Paterson	G Wallace	I McDonald	D Lees	S King	N Forbes	A Lyons	K Brown	S Brown	H Mackay	K Halley	G S Murray	I Gardiner	C Maver	D Powell	F Wright	FT(HT)Att Lge pos
1. **Stirling Albion***	8.8	1	2	3	4‡	5	6†	7¹	8	9	10	11	12		14											1–3(0–2)771	
2. Ayr U	15.8	1	2	3	4	5	8	7	12	9‡		11¹	14			6	10†									1–3(1–1)1587	13
3. Albion R*	22.8	1	2	3		5	10‡	7	12	9¹		11	14			6	8†	4								1–2(1–0)300	13
4. Brechin C	29.8	1	2		6‡	5	8†	7	14	9	10	11				3	4	12								0–2(0–0)500	14
5. **East Stirling***	5.9	1	2		5		7‡	10	9	6†	11	12	3			8	4	14								0–3(0–0)150	14
6. Arbroath	12.9	1		2	5	9	7‡	12	10	11	14	3				8	6	4†								0–0(0–0)866	14
7. Alloa*	15.9	1		2	5¹	10	7	6	11¹	14	3	8‡	4	12	9†											2–0(1–0)450	–
8. Berwick R	19.9	1		2	5	8†	7	10	11	14	3	4	12	9‡	9¹											1–2(1–1)310	13
9. **Stenhousemuir***	26.9	1	2		5	10	14	11	8‡	3	6	12	4	7†	9¹											1–0(0–0)200	13
10. Stranraer	3.10	1	2		5	8‡	14	10¹	11	12	3	6	4	7†‡	9¹											3–1(3–1)342	11
11. **Cowdenbeath***	10.10	1	2		5	8‡	7¹	14	10†	11	3	6	4	12	9¹											2–0(1–1)200	10
12. St Johnstone	17.10	1	2¹		5	8	7	14	10	11†	3	6	4	12	9‡											1–1(1–1)1548	9
13. **Queen's Park***	24.10	1	2	3	5	8	7	12	10†	11‡	6	4	14	9												0–2(0–1)350	10
14. Stirling Albion	31.10	1	3	2	8¹	7¹	10	12	6	4	11†	9‡	5	14												2–0(1–0)587	9
15. **Ayr U***	7.11	1	3	2	8‡	7	10	12	6	11†	9¹	5	14													2–4(1–0)700	9
16. Albion R	14.11	1	12	3	2	4	7‡	10	6	14	8†	9	5	11¹												1–0(0–0)275	9
17. Stenhousemuir	21.11	1	3	2	4¹	7	10	6	12	8	9	5	11¹†													2–0(2–0)250	7
18. **Berwick R***	28.11	1	3	2‡	4	7†	10¹	6	12	8	14	9	5¹	11²												4–0(2–0)300	6
19. Alloa	12.12	1	3	2	4	7	10‡	6	14	8	12	9†	5	11												0–1(0–1)348	7
20. East Stirling	26.12	1	2	3	4	8¹	7‡	12	10	6	14	9¹	5	11¹†												2–2(1–0)200	8
21. Arbroath*	29.12	1	2	3		8	7†	10	6	4	12	9¹	5													1–1(0–0)900	–
22. Brechin C*	2.1	1	2	3		8	7†	6	10	11	2	4	12	9	5											0–1(0–1)800	8
23. Cowdenbeath	16.1	1	2	3	12	4	8†	14	10	6	7	9¹	5	11¹												1–1(1–0)200	10
24. Stranraer*	23.1	1	2	3	12	4	10¹	6†	7	8	9¹	5	11¹													3–1(0–0)200	8
25. Queen's Park	6.2		2	3	12	4	14	10	7	6	8†	9	5	11¹‡	1											1–1(0–0)425	8
26. Albion R*	13.2	1	2	3	4	12	14	7	6	8‡	9†	5	11													0–0(0–0)150	9
27. Stirling Albion	20.2	1	2	3	4	12	7	6	8	9¹†	5	11¹														2–0(1–0)381	8
28. St Johnstone*	23.2	1	2	3	4	12	10	14	7†	6	8‡	9	5													0–1(0–0)700	–
29. Stenhousemuir*	27.2	1	2	3	4	12	10	14	7†	6	8‡	9¹	5													1–0(0–0)250	9
30. Brechin C	8.3	1	2	3	4	10		7†	6	14	9	5	11	8¹‡												1–0(1–0)550	–
31. Ayr U*	12.3	1	2	3	4	14	10	7†	6	9	5	11‡	8	12												1–1(1–1)600	8
32. St Johnstone	19.3	1	2‡	3†	4	7	10	6	14	9	5	11‡	8	12												1–5(1–4)1803	8
33. Alloa*	26.3	1		4	10	14	12	7‡	3	6	2†	9	5	11	8											0–2(0–1)250	9
34. Stranraer	2.4	1		3	4	14	12	10	7‡	6	2	9	5	11†												1–1(1–0)400	9
35. Arbroath	9.4	1	2		4	10‡	9	7	14	3	6	12	5	11	8¹†											1–1(1–0)443	9
36. Berwick R*	16.4	1		4†	10	12	14¹	7‡	3	6	9	5	11	8	2											1–0(0–0)517	8
37. Queen's Park*	23.4	1	2₁	4	12	7‡	10†	3	6	14	9	5	11	8												1–2(1–2)200	8
38. East Stirling	30.4	1	2	4	10	7	11†	12	3	6	9	5	8¹													2–3(1–2)300	8
39. Cowdenbeath	7.5	1		4	2‡	10	14	3	6	12	9	5	11¹	8	7†											1–2(1–1)200	8

Apps(subs)/goals: 38(0) 0 · 25(1) 2 · 27(0) 0 · 29(3) 0 · 15(0) 2 · 25(2) 1 · 19(0) 3 · 24(1) 3 · 7(0) 1 · 19(5) 1 · 11(0) 2 · 17(15) 0 · 15(0) 0 · 28(0) 0 · 16(3) 0 · 17(3) 1 · 3(1) 1 · 33(0) 1 · 26(0) 1 · 22(2) 10 · 10(0) 0 · 10(0) 3 · 1(0) 0 · 1(0) 0 · 1(0) 0

Final League Position: 8

Own goals: W. Furphy, match 31; N. Watt, match 34; J. Woods, match 38.

MORTON – LEAGUE RECORD 1987–1988 (PREMIER DIVISION)

Match no/Opp/Date		D Wylie	I Clinging	J Holmes	J Hunter	M Doak	J McMaster	T Turner	J McNamara	R Alexander	J McVeil	J Robertson	D Robertson	Jim Boag	A O'Hara	John Boag	A Bateman	J Arthur	G Ronald	R MacDonald	D Collins	J Rogers	A McGeachy	L Christensen	C Margaard	D Verlaque	H Terkelsen	J Kristensen	A Gourlay	B Robinson	D McInnes	FT(HT)Att Lge pos	
1. Celtic*	8.8	1	2	3	4†	5	6	7	8	9	10	11	12																			0-4(0-1)15,500	—
2. Aberdeen	12.8	1	8	3		5	6¹	7	4	9	10†	11‡	12	14	2																	1-3(1-2)8000	—
3. Dundee U	15.8	1	10	3	4	5	6	7		9	12	11‡	7¹	14	2†																	1-3(1-2)6641	12
4. Hibernian*	22.8	1	10¹	3	4†	5	6¹		8	9		11‡	7	12¹		2	14															3-3(1-2)3500	11
5. St Mirren	29.8	1	10	3	12	5	6		4†	9		11		7¹	8	2																1-2(0-1)5271	12
6. Hearts*	5.9	1	10	3	4	5	6†	8		9₁	11		7	2		12																1-2(0-2)4000	12
7. Dundee*	12.9	1	10	3	4	5			6	9¹		11¹		7¹	2	8																4-3(3-1)3000	12
8. Dunfermline A	19.9	1	10	3	4	5			6	9¹		11		7†	2	8		12														1-4(0-2)5460	12
9. Rangers	26.9	1	10	3	14	4	8†	7		9		11		2‡		12	5															0-7(0-3)35,843	12
10. Motherwell*	3.10	1	10	3	4	6	11†	7		9				8¹		5	2															1-1(0-0)2000	12
11. Falkirk*	7.10	1	10	3	4			8		9	11‡	12¹	8²	2		5																4-1(2-1)2300	—
12. Celtic	10.10	1	10	3	4	6		8		9†		11	12	7	2¹	5																1-3(1-3)22,780	11
13. St Mirren*	17.10	1	10	3	4	6		8		9		11†	12	7	2	5																0-0(0-0)3500	11
14. Hearts	24.10	1	8	3	4	6	10					11†	7	9	2	12	5															0-3(0-2)11,516	11
15. Dundee	28.10	1	8	3	4		6	10			12	11		7	2	9†	5															0-1(0-1)3829	—
16. Dunfermline A*	31.10	1	8	3	4	10	6		9		11	7¹	2	5																		1-2(0-2)2000	12
17. Aberdeen*	7.11	1	10	3	4		6†		9	12	11	7	2		8																	0-0(0-0)3000	12
18. Falkirk	14.11	1	6	3	4			9	10	11‡	7	2	12	5	8																	0-2(0-0)3000	12
19. Hibernian	18.11	1	6	3	4		8	9	11†	12	7	2	5	10																		0-0(0-0)6000	—
20. Dundee U*	21.11	1	6‡	3	4	14	8	9†	11	7	2	12	5	10																		0-1(0-0)2000	12
21. Rangers*	24.11	1		3	4‡	14	8	9†	12	7	10	6	11	5	2																	0-3(0-1)15,500	—
22. Motherwell	28.11	1		3	6	10	11	7	2	4	9†	5	8	12																		0-1(0-1)3008	12
23. Celtic*	5.12	1		3	4	8	11	7	10	6	9	5	2																			0-4(0-1)14,500	12
24. Aberdeen	12.12	1		3	4	8	11	9	2	6	12	5	10	7†																		0-4(0-2)8000	12
25. Dundee*	16.12	1		3	4	6	11	9¹	7	2†	5	10	8	12																		1-7(1-4)3821	12
26. Dunfermline A	19.12	1		3	4	11	10	9¹	7	5	2	8	6																			1-1(0-0)5000	12
27. Hearts*	26.12	1		3	4	11	8	9†	7	2	5	10	6	12																		0-0(0-0)4000	12
28. St Mirren	2.1	1		3	4	10	11	9†	7	12	5	2	8	6																		0-0(0-0)7095	12
29. Rangers	9.1	1		3	4	10†	14	11	9	7‡	12	5	2	8	6																	0-5(0-3)38,349	12
30. Motherwell*	16.1	1		3	4	10†	9	7	12	5	2	8	6	11‡	14																	0-2(0-3)3000	12
31. Hibernian*	23.1	1		3	4	9	12	7	11¹	10	5	2†	8	6																		1-1(0-0)2800	12
32. Dundee U	6.2	1		3	10	12	9	11‡	7	2	5	4	14	8†	6																	0-2(0-2)6566	12
33. Falkirk*	16.2	1		3	10	12	9	14	7	8	4	5	2	11‡	6†																	0-0(0-0)2412	12
34. Celtic	27.2	1		3	4	14	10‡	7	9	12	8	6	5	2	11†																	0-1(0-0)23,120	12
35. Dundee	5.3	1		3	4	10‡	8	9	12	7	14	6	5	2	11†																	0-1(0-1)4319	12
36. St Mirren*	19.3	1		3	4	10	8	9	11	6	5	2	7																			0-2(0-3)3000	12
37. Dunfermline A*	23.3	1		3		6	8	11†	10	9‡	4	12	14	7																		0-3(0-2)2500	—
38. Hearts	26.3	1		3	4	10	7†	11	8	6	9	5	2	12																		0-2(0-0)8787	12
39. Motherwell	2.4	1			4	7	9	11	10	6	5	2	3	8																		0-1(0-0)4764	12
40. Rangers*	9.4	1			4	5	6‡	7¹	9¹	2	10	12	8¹	3	11†	14																3-2(0-0)11,000	12
41. Aberdeen*	16.4	1	8		4	7	9	11	5	6†	2	3	10	12																		0-2(0-1)3200	12
42. Falkirk	23.4	1	10	6	14	9¹	2	4	12	5	8	3‡	7	11†																		1-4(0-3)4000	12
43. Dundee U*	30.4	1	7	4	6‡	9	11	2	12	5	8	10†	3	10																		1-0(1-2)7000	12
44. Hibernian	7.5	1	6¹	4	9	7†	11	2	5	8	12	3	10																			0-3(1-2)7000	12
Apps(subs)/goals		44(0) 0	24(0) 2	38(0) 0	36(2) 0	19(1) 2	29(0) 1	7(0) 0	36(0) 7	12(4) 1	22(5) 2	8(5) 2	27(3) 8	35(5) 1	15(0) 0	3(2) 0	5(8) 0	02(0) 0	31(0) 1	28(0) 0	64(0) 0	72(0) 0	8(0) 0	8(1) 0	14(0) 0	10(0) 0	06(0) 0	20(0) 0	1(0) 0				

Final League Position: 12

MOTHERWELL – LEAGUE RECORD 1987–88 (PREMIER DIVISION)

Players (column order): C Duncan, F Wishart, D Murray, C Paterson, T McAdam, T Boyd, J Fairlie, S Kirk, P Smith, R Russell, G Mair, R Farningham, J Gahagan, B Wright, A Kennedy, J Philliben, N Cauldish, G Fraser, A Maxwell, S Cowan, M McBride, M Caughey, D Arnott, J Griffin, D Shanks, P Kinnaird, C McCart

Match no/Opp/Date	Dun	Wis	Mur	Pat	McA	Boy	Fai	Kir	Smi	Rus	Mai	Far	Gah	Wri	Ken	Phi	Cau	Fra	Max	Cow	McB	Cau	Arn	Gri	Sha	Kin	McC	FT(HT)Att	Lge pos
1. St Mirren* 8.8	1	2	3	4	5†	6	7¹‡	8	9	10¹	11	12	14															2–1(2–0)4131	—
2. Dundee U 12.8	1	2	3	4	5	6¹	7†	8¹	9	10	11	12		14														1–1(0–0)6663	—
3. Celtic 15.8	1	2	3†	4	5	6	7	8¹	9	10	11‡	12		14														1–4(0–2)24,478	7
4. Aberdeen* 22.8	1	2	3‡	4	5	6	7	8†	9	10	11			12	14													0–1(0–0)4858	10
5. Falkirk* 29.8	1	2		4	5†	6	7†	8	9	10	11¹			14	12			3										1–2(1–0)3132	10
6. Dunfermline A 5.9	1	2	3	4¹	5	6	14	12	9‡	10†	11	8	7															1–0(0–0)5500	8
7. Hearts 12.9	1	2		4	5	6	12	8	9‡	10	11	7			3													0–1(0–1)11,488	9
8. Rangers* 19.9	1	2		4	5	6	12	10‡	9	14	11	8†	7		3													0–1(0–1)19,480	10
9. Dundee* 26.9	1	2		4	5	6	7		9	10		8‡	11	12	3†	14												0–2(0–1)2656	10
10. Morton 3.10	1	2		4	5	6	7†	10‡	9	8	12	11			3¹	14												1–1(0–0)2000	10
11. Hibernian* 6.10	1	2¹		4	5	6		8‡	9	7	14	12			3	11†	10											1–0(1–0)4093	—
12. St Mirren 10.10	1	2		4	5	6	14	8‡	9	7	12				3†		10	1	11									0–1(0–1)4133	9
13. Falkirk 17.10	1	2		4	5	6	10	14	8†	7	11				3‡	12		9										0–3(0–0)3000	9
14. Dunfermline A* 24.10	1	2	3	4	5	6		8†	7²	12						11‡	10		9	14								3–2(1–1)3685	9
15. Hearts* 27.10	1	2	3†	4	5	6			7	8‡					14	11	10		9		12							0–3(0–2)6699	—
16. Rangers 31.10	1	2	3	4	5		12			8	11				6	10†			9	7								0–1(0–0)36,583	9
17. Dundee U* 7.11	1	2	3	4	5	6¹	12			7	11‡				8	10‡			9¹	14								2–1(0–2)2927	9
18. Hibernian 14.11	1	2	3‡	4	5†	6	10			11					8	14			9	7	12							0–1(0–1)7000	9
19. Celtic* 17.11	1	2	3	4		6	12			7		5†			8	11	10		9‡	14								0–2(0–1)17,261	—
20. Aberdeen 21.11	1	2	3	4		6	7		8			12			5	11†	10		9‡	14								0–1(0–1)9700	10
21. Dundee 24.11	1	2		4		6	12		10†	11‡	8				5				9	7	14	3						0–2(0–2)3695	—
22. Morton* 28.11	1	2	3	4		6	10†		8‡		7				5	11	14		9¹	12								1–0(1–0)3008	9
23. St Mirren* 5.12	1	2	3	4		6	12				8¹				5¹	10†			9	7	11							2–1(1–0)2928	9
24. Dundee U 12.12	1	2	3	4		6			10†		8				5	14	12		9¹	7‡	11							1–3(0–2)5792	9
25. Hearts 16.12	1	2	3	4		6	10†		8	7					5				9¹	12	11‡		14					1–1(0–1)9047	9
26. Rangers* 19.12	1	2	3	4		6	12	14	10†		8				5				9	7	11‡							0–2(0–0)15,346	9
27. Dunfermline A 26.12	1	2	3	4		6	10	7¹			8				5				9‡	12	11							1–1(0–0)5500	9
28. Falkirk* 1.1	1	2	3†	4		6	10	7			8				5				9‡	12	11		14					0–0(0–0)4168	—
29. Dundee* 9.1	1	2	3	4	14			10‡	7¹	11†	8¹	12			5				9¹					6				3–3(1–0)2785	9
30. Morton 16.1	1	2	3	4				10	7²	11‡	8	12			3				9									2–0(2–0)3000	9
31. Aberdeen* 23.1	1	2		4¹	5	6		10	7‡	12	11†	8¹		14	3				9									2–1(2–0)6584	9
32. Celtic 6.2	1	2	3	4	5	6†			7	10	11‡				8			12	9	14								0–1(0–0)25,035	9
33. Hibernian* 13.2	1	2	3	4	5	6			7	10†	8								9	11	12							0–2(0–1)5421	9
34. St Mirren 27.2	1	2		4	5	6	10	7	8‡	11							14		9†	12			3					0–0(0–0)5419	9
35. Hearts* 8.3	1	2		4	5	6		8	7		12								9†					3	10	11		0–2(0–1)5831	—
36. Rangers 12.3	1	2		4	5	6		8‡	9	7	12				3										10	11		0–1(0–0)39,650	9
37. Falkirk 19.3	1	2		4	5	6			8	7		12			3				9†						10	11		0–0(0–0)5500	9
38. Dunfermline A* 26.3	1	2		4	5	6		8‡	7		12¹	14			3				9²						10†	11		3–2(0–2)8958	9
39. Morton* 2.4	1	2		4	5	6		8‡	7†	10¹		14			3				9						12	11		1–0(0–0)4764	9
40. Dundee 6.4	1	2		4	5	6	12¹		8	11		14			3				9¹‡						10†	7		2–1(1–0)3732	—
41. Dundee U* 16.4	1	2		4	5¹	6		10²‡	12	8	11¹‡	14			3				9¹							7†		4–2(1–1)3922	8
42. Hibernian 23.4	1	2†		4	5	6		10	12	8		7¹			3				9							11		1–1(1–0)5500	8
43. Celtic* 30.4	1	2†		4	5	6		10	14	12		8	11		3				9							7‡		0–1(0–0)13,874	8
44. Aberdeen 7.5	1			4	5	2		10	12	8		7			3				9†					6	11‡	14		0–0(0–0)5500	8
Apps(subs)/goals	43(0)0	43(0)1	22(0)0	44(0)2	33(1)1	42(0)2	8(4)1	29(5)4	25(5)4	28(4)3	16(5)1	25(4)6	11(12)0	05(1)0	33(2)2	7(2)1	8(6)0	1(0)0	32(0)9	46(0)0	96(0)0	02(0)0	42(0)0	64(1)0	00(1)0	0(1)0	05(5)00		

Final League Position: 8

PARTICK THISTLE – LEAGUE RECORD 1987–88 (DIVISION ONE)

Match no/Opp/Date		J Brough	A Dinnie	J Spittal	R Law	W McGhie	K Watson	P Kelly	W McGuire	H Leyden	I McDonald	A Logan	C McAdam	J Mitchell	J Rafferty	E Gallagher	J Workman	T Carson	W Paxton	A Pirie	B Scrimgeour	W Dodds	J McCormack	J Doyle	T Elliott	D Haxton	A McLean	B Purdie	J McNaught	P Maher	J Thomson	FT(HT)Att Lge pos
1. Meadowbank Th	8.8	1	2	3	4	5	6	7	8²	9	10‡	11†	12	14																		2-3(1-1)1039 —
2. Airdrieonians*	11.8	1	10	3	4‡	5	6₁	7	9¹		14	11	12	8†	2																	2-2(2-2)1900 —
3. Raith R*	15.8	1	4	2‡		5	6	7	9	8†	10	11		3	12	14																0-0(0-0)1951 9
4. Clydebank	22.8	4	2	8	5		7‡	9		10	11†		3	12	6	1																2-0(1-0)2147 5
5. Clyde	29.8		2	4	5		7	8		10₁	11‡	14	3	9	12	1	6†															1-4(1-1)2700 6
6. East Fife*	5.9		2	12	5		7	10		6	11¹		4	9¹	3	1	8†															3-3(1-1)1610 7
7. Hamilton A	12.9			2‡	5		7	10†		6	11	4		14	9		1	8		3	12											0-5(0-0)2421 9
8. Dumbarton*	15.9		14	6†	5		7‡	10		11	12		8	4	9		1		2‡	3												1-2(1-1)1140 —
9. Queen of South	19.9	4			5		7	12		10	9	11†		3	1	8	2	6														0-0(0-0)2000 10
10. Forfar Ath*	26.9	1	4	5		7	5		8	9	11₁	10‡		12	3			2	6†	14												1-1(0-0)1285 10
11. Kilmarnock	29.9	1	4	5			7†	9		10₁	12		14		3		8‡	2	6	11												1-1(0-1)1500 —
12. Clydebank*	3.10	1	4		14	5	6		11		10	7†			8	9	3‡		2		12											0-1(0-1)1799 11
13. Meadowbank T*	10.10	1	10			5	6		8†		11	7			9¹		3		2	4	12											1-0(0-0)1513 9
14. Hamilton A*	17.10	1†	10			5	6	7	14		11¹	12			9	3				4		2	8‡									1-0(1-0)2162 9
15. Dumbarton	20.10		4			5		7‡			10¹	14	11	12	9	3		8†	6¹		2											2-4(1-1)800 —
16. Raith R	24.10		4		7	5			10		11	12¹			9²	3		8†		6		2										3-4(0-1)1998 11
17. East Fife	31.10		2	7‡	5	6		8		10	11			9¹	3				4			12										1-2(1-1)780 12
18. Kilmarnock*	3.11		2			5		7		10‡	11†		8		9	3		14	4	12			6									1-0(1-0)1407 —
19. Clyde*	7.11		2‡		5	7†			11₁			4		3	9	10		8	14	6	12			1								1-4(1-2)2245 11
20. Airdrieonians	11.11				5		12	7		10			6	9	3		8†	2	4	11¹				1								1-3(0-0)1850 11
21. Queen of South*	14.11		4¹			7	12		10			6	9	3		2†	5	11²	8		1											3-3(1-1)1427 11
22. Forfar Ath	21.11		2		5	6	7²		10		12	8†	9¹	3			4	11¹			1											4-1(1-1)764 11
23. Clydebank	28.11		2		5	6	7¹	12¹		10		8	9¹†	3‡		14	4	11			1											3-0(0-0)1892 11
24. Airdrieonians*	5.12		2		5	6	7†	12		10		8¹	9¹	3			4	11			1											2-0(0-0)2300 8
25. Hamilton A	12.12		2		5	7	12		10		8†	9	3		4	6	11			1												0-1(0-0)2356 9
26. Dumbarton*	19.12		2		5	7	12		10		3	9¹			6	11†			1	4	8											1-3(0-2)1407 10
27. East Fife*	26.12		2		5	14	12	11		3	9‡		10	6	7⁴			1	4	8†												4-2(3-1)1740 9
28. Clyde	1.1		2	7	5	14	12	11		3			10	6‡	9¹			1	4	8¹†												2-1(1-0)2500 —
29. Queen of South	9.1		2		5	7	10‡	11†		3		14	12		6	9			1	4	8											0-0(0-0)1521 8
30. Forfar Ath*	16.1		2		5	7	12	10‡		3		9†	6		8		11	14		1	4											1-3(0-1)1673 8
31. Meadowbank Th	23.1			14	5	7	12	10₁		3		9			2†	11‡	6		1	4	8											1-3(0-1)1100 11
32. Raith R*	6.2		2	8¹	5	7²	14	10‡		3		9²	12		11†	6			1	4												5-0(3-0)1703 8
33. Kilmarnock	13.2		2	10	5	7	12	14		3		9¹		8†	11‡	6			1	4												1-0(0-0)2432 7
34. Clydebank*	27.2		2		5	7‡	8‡			3		9	12	11†	14	6			1	4	10											3-0(0-0)2844 7
35. Hamilton A*	5.3		2	10	5		7			3		9			11	6			1	4												0-0(0-0)3340 7
36. East Fife	19.3		2	10	5		7		11	12	3				9	6			1	4	8†											0-1(0-1)978 9
37. Dumbarton	22.3		2	10	5		7		11		3	9¹				6			1	4	8₁											2-1(1-0)925 7
38. Clyde*	26.3		2	10	5	8	11	7		12	3				6			1		9₁	4†											1-0(1-0)2500 8
39. Raith R	2.4		2	3	10	5	6	7²	8	11‡	9†			14				12	4		1											2-1(1-0)1529 7
40. Meadowbank T*	9.4		2	5			6	7¹	8₁			10	9†	3		11			12	4		1										2-1(0-0)1400 6
41. Forfar Ath	16.4					4	7	8†		14		10	9	3		2			12	6		1					5	11‡				0-1(0-0)731 7
42. Queen of South*	23.4		2		12	5†	3‡	7	8			10	9	3				11	6		1	4										0-3(0-1)1500 7
43. Airdrieonians	30.4		2	14	11	5	10	7†	8‡		12			3				9	6		1	4										0-1(0-1)950 7
44. Kilmarnock*	7.5		2		11†	5	10‡	7				8		9	3			14	12	6		1	4									0-1(0-0)3200 8

Final League Position: 8

Apps(subs)/goals: 8(0)/0, 37(0)/1, 10(2)/0, 18(4)/1, 40(0)/0, 17(0)/1, 33(3)/10, 27(3)/8, 20(0)/1, 33(2)/8, 15(9)/3, 25(4)/1, 11(3)/0, 31(3)/13, 24(2)/0, 8(0)/0, 19(4)/0, 21(0)/1, 19(4)/9, 18(0)/0, 19(1)/1, 9, 10(1)/0, 25(0)/0, 15(0)/0, 10(0)/3, 10(0)/0, 1(0)/0

Own goal: D. Conrooy, match 6. Also played: R. Ferguson at 1 in match 15, M. McDermott at 1 in match 16, H. Stevenson at 1 in match 17, F. Jackson at 1 in match 18.

QUEEN OF THE SOUTH – LEAGUE RECORD 1987–88 (DIVISION ONE)

Match no/Opp/Date		A Davidson	J Sinclair	R Dickson	D Docherty	A Mackin	K Hetherington	J Pelosi	J Hughes	K Ashwood	S Robertson	J Doherty	N Anderson	J Frye	G Cloy	S Moore	W Sim	W Reid	M Shanks	A Bain	T Carson	W Cunningham	M Oliver	C Speirs	D Mills	G Telfer	FT(HT)Att	Lge pos
1. Clydebank	8.8	1	2	3	4	5	6	7	8_1†	9‡	10	11	12	14													1-1(0-1)867	—
2. Raith R*	12.8	1	2	3	4	5	6	7	8	9	10†	11	12														0-3(0-1)1500	—
3. Airdrieonians*	15.8	1	2	3	4	5	6	7	8_1	11†	10	9^1‡	12	14													2-2(2-0)900	10
4. Meadowbank Th	22.8	1	2	3	4	5	6	7†	8	9	10	11	12														0-1(0-0)550	10
5. Kilmarnock	29.8	1	2		4†	5	6		8^1	9‡	10	11	12	14^1			3	7									2-0(0-0)1836	7
6. Forfar Ath*	5.9	1	2		4	5	6	10	8_1	9‡		11	12	14			3	7†									1-1(0-0)1700	8
7. East Fife	12.9	1	2		4	5	6	7†	8^2		10	11^1‡	14		9		3	12									3-0(1-0)765	6
8. Hamilton A*	15.9	1	2			5	6‡	7	8		10	11	14		9		3	4†	12								0-3(0-0)2400	—
9. Partick Th*	19.9	1	2		4	5	6	7†	8		10	11	14		9‡		3	12									0-0(0-0)2000	7
10. Dumbarton	26.9	1	2		4	5^1	6	7†	8^1		10	11	14		9‡		3	12									2-2(1-1)700	7
11. Clyde	29.9	1	2		4	5	6		8		10	11^2		9†	12		3	7^1									3-2(0-0)900	—
12. Meadowbank T*	3.10	1	2		4	5	6		8		10†	11	9‡	14			3	7	12								0-2(0-1)1700	7
13. Raith R	7.10	1	2	3	4	5	6		8		11^1	14	10†				7	12	9‡								1-3(0-2)1106	—
14. Clydebank*	10.10		2	3	4	5	6		8^1	9†	11	12	10				7^1				1						2-0(0-0)1400	7
15. East Fife*	17.10		2	3	4	5	6		8	11	10†	12					7^2	9			1						2-1(0-1)1200	7
16. Hamilton A	20.10		2	3	4_1	5	6		8	11	12	10					7^1	9†			1						2-2(1-2)1566	—
17. Airdrieonians	24.10		2	3‡		5	6	4^1	8	11	14	10					7	12	9†		1						1-5(1-2)1900	7
18. Clyde*	28.10		2			5	6	4	8	10†	9^3		14	3			7	12	11^1‡		1						3-1(2-1)700	—
19. Forfar Ath	31.10		2			5	6	4	8	9				10			3	7	11^1‡		1						1-3(0-1)630	8
20. Kilmarnock*	7.11		2	3		5		4	8†	9^1		12	6	10			7		11		1						1-4(0-0)1479	8
21. Partick Th	14.11			3‡	4	5	6	7	8	11^1	9^2†	2	12	10				14		1							3-3(1-1)1427	8
22. Dumbarton*	21.11		2	3	4	5	6	7	8‡	14	11†		12	9^1	10^1				1								2-0(1-0)1100	8
23. Meadowbank Th	28.11		2	3†	4	5	6	7	8	11	14	12		9‡	10				1								0-5(0-3)550	9
24. Raith R*	5.12		2		4	5	6	12	7	8‡	11^1†			9^1	3			10	14	1							1-5(1-1)900	10
25. East Fife	12.12	1	8		4^1	5	6	7†		11		9^1	3		10	2	12										2-2(1-1)460	8
26. Hamilton A*	19.12	1	8		4	5	6	12	14	10	11^1‡	9	3		7	2†											0-0(0-0)1150	9
27. Forfar Ath*	26.12	1	8		4	5	6	12	10†	9^1	3‡	11			7	2		14									1-1(1-0)1100	8
28. Kilmarnock	2.1	1	8		4	5	6		10	9†	11	3			7	2	12										0-0(0-2)3230	9
29. Partick Th*	9.1	1	8		4	5	6		10	9†	11	3			7	2	12										0-0(0-0)1521	9
30. Dumbarton	16.1	1	8		4		6	12	14	10	11^1‡	3			7	2	9^1†					5					2-0(0-0)800	8
31. Airdrieonians*	26.1	1	8		4		6	12	10^1	11		3			7	9†			8	5							1-2(1-1)950	—
32. Clydebank	6.2	1	8		4			12	7	10		14	3†	11	2	9‡			5	6							0-1(0-1)842	10
33. Meadowbank T*	27.2	1		3	4	5	10†	8½	9‡	11	12	7	2										6	14			2-1(2-0)1000	9
34. Clyde	1.3	1		3‡	4†	5	10	12	8^1	9	11	7	2	14									6				1-2(0-1)800	—
35. East Fife*	5.3	1	2		4	5	10	12	8^1‡	14	11^1	7	3	9†									6				2-0(2-0)950	9
36. Hamilton A	12.3	1	2		4	5^2	10	12	8†	14	11	7	3	9‡									6				2-1(1-0)1682	8
37. Forfar Ath	19.3	1	2		4	5	10	8	12	11	7	3†	9										6^1				1-1(0-0)504	8
38. Kilmarnock*	26.3	1	2		4	5	10	8^1	12	11	7	3	9†										6				1-0(0-1)1650	9
39. Clydebank*	2.4	1	2		4	5	10	12	8	9†	14	11	7	3‡									6				0-1(0-1)1050	9
40. Airdrieonians	9.4	1	3		4	5	10	8	9^1	11†	7	2											6	12			1-1(0-0)900	8
41. Dumbarton*	16.4		2		4	5	10	12	8	9†	11‡	7	3								1		6	14			0-0(0-0)1100	8
42. Partick Th	23.4		2		4	5	10	12	8^2	14	11‡	3	7								1		6	9^1†			3-0(1-0)1500	8
43. Raith R	30.4		2†		4	5	10^1		8	12	11^1	3	7								1		6	9^1			2-4(0-1)899	8
44. Clyde*	7.5		2		4		10		8‡	9†	12	11	3	7							1		6	5			2-1(1-1)750	7

Apps(subs)/goals: A Davidson 29(0)/0 · J Sinclair 41(0)/0 · R Dickson 15(0)/0 · D Docherty 39(0)/2 · A Mackin 40(0)/3 · K Hetherington 41(0)/1 · J Pelosi 17(2)/2 · J Hughes 36(2)/17 · K Ashwood 3(0)/0 · S Robertson 19(3)/1 · J Doherty 34(5)/10 · N Anderson 2(2)/0 · J Frye 14(15)/7 · G Cloy 29(9)/3 · S Moore 19(1)/0 · W Sim 37(3)/6 · W Reid 46(0)/2 · M Shanks 16(5)/0 · A Bain 14(6)/2 · T Carson 30(0)/0 · W Cunningham 8(0)/0 · M Oliver 1(1)/0 · C Speirs 30(0)/0 · D Mills 13(0)/1 · G Telfer 3(3)/2

Final League Position: 7

QUEEN'S PARK – LEAGUE RECORD 1987–88 (DIVISION TWO)

Match no/Opp/Date	S Ross	J Boyle	P McLaughlin	P McVannee	G Elder	S McLean	R Caven	P McLean	K MacKenzie	M Hendry	G Crooks	S O'Brien	S McFinnegart	D Elliot	G Lennox	P Armstrong	I Brown	J Rodden	J Gardner	S McGregor	J Martin	M Monaghan	C Morton	S Jack	FT(HT)Att Lge pos
1. Arbroath 8.8	1	2	3	4†	5	6	7	8	9‡	10	11	12¹	14												1-3(0-2)500 —
2. Alloa* 15.8	1	4	3		5		8	2	10¹	11¹	14	9‡	12	6	7†										2-0(1-0)486
3. Stenhousemuir 22.8	1	4	3		5		8	2	11‡		7†	6¹	12	9	14										3-2(1-0)350
4. Albion R 29.8	1	4₂	3		5	12	7¹	2	11	10‡		9		6	8¹†	14									4-0(2-0)300
5. Berwick R* 5.9	1	4	3		5		7	2	10	11		9†	6²	12	8¹										3-2(3-1)511
6. Brechin C 12.9	1	2			5	4	8	7	10	11†		9	6¹		3	12									1-1(0-1)400
7. St Johnstone* 15.9	1	2			5	4	8	7†	10	11‡		9	6		3	14	12								0-1(0-1)627
8. East Stirling* 19.9	1	4	3		5†	12	7	2	10‡	11		6	9¹	8	14										2-1(2-1)465
9. Ayr U 26.9	1	4	3¹		5	12	7	2	10	11‡		6	9	8†	14										1-4(1-2)2805
10. Cowdenbeath 3.10	1	2¹	3		5	4	7	6	10		9³		11	8											4-2(2-0)263
11. Stirling Albion* 10.10	1	6¹	3		5	4	7	2	10		12	9		11†	8										1-0(0-0)631
12. Stranraer* 17.10	1	6²	3		5	4	7	2		12	11	9¹	10†		8										3-0(1-0)529
13. Montrose 24.10	1	6	3		5	4	7	2	10		12	9²	11†		8										2-0(1-0)350
14. Arbroath* 31.10	1	2	3		5	4	7	6	10‡		11†	9¹	12	14	8										1-1(1-0)525
15. Alloa 7.11	1	2₁	3	4	5‡	14	7	6¹	10†		12	9¹	11		8										3-0(2-0)398
16. Stenhousemuir* 14.11	1	2	3	5		4	10	7		11	9	6†	12		8										0-2(0-2)564
17. Ayr U* 21.11	1	2	3		5		7	4	10		11	9	12	6†	8										0-2(0-0)1792
18. East Stirling 28.11	1	2		5		4		8		7	11	9¹†		6	3	10	12								1-0(1-0)300
19. St Johnstone 12.12	1	2	3	5		4	10	6	7†	11‡	9		12	14	8										0-2(0-1)1429
20. Brechin C* 19.12	1	2	3	5			7¹	4		6	11¹		10†	9	8				12						2-0(1-0)434
21. Berwick R 26.12	1	2	3¹	5			7	4		6	10		11†	9	8				12						1-0(0-0)550
22. Albion R* 2.1	1	2	3	5			7	4	6¹	11	10		9†	8					12						1-1(0-0)829
23. Stirling Albion 16.1	1		4	3	5¹		7	2	10†	6¹	12		8						11	1					2-2(0-1)533
24. Cowdenbeath* 23.1	1	2	3	4	5		7	6		10	12	9³		8					11†	1					3-2(2-0)504
25. Montrose* 6.2	1	2	3	4	5		7	6	10¹	12	9		8						11†	1					1-0(0-0)425
26. East Stirling* 13.2	1	2	3		5	4	7¹	8	10	6‡	12	9	14						11†	1					1-2(0-1)575
27. Stranraer* 16.2	1	2	3		5	4	7	8	10¹		11	12	6†	9¹						1					2-0(1-0)394 —
28. Ayr U 20.2	1	2	3		5	4	7	8¹	10		11		6	9						1					1-1(0-0)2771
29. Alloa 27.2	1	2	3		5	4	7	8	10		12	11	14	6†	9‡					1					0-1(0-1)590
30. Berwick R* 5.3	1	2		4	5		7	6		12	10¹		9¹	8					11†	1	3				2-0(0-0)350
31. Arbroath 12.3	1	2		4	5		7¹		11‡	9	6‡	14		8					12		3				2-1(1-0)418
32. Stirling Albion* 19.3	1	2		4‡	5		7	10	11	9¹	14	6†		8					12		3				1-1(1-0)626
33. St Johnstone* 26.3	1	2	3	4	5		9	7	10	11	6‡†	12	8												2-1(0-0)1030
34. Brechin C 2.4	1	2	3	4	5		7	6	10	11		12	9†	8											0-2(0-1)500
35. Albion R 9.4	1	2	3		5	7¹†	4	10	9‡	6	12		8						14		11¹				2-1(1-1)270
36. Cowdenbeath* 16.4	1	2	3	4	5		9	7	10†	14	6		12	8							11‡				1-1(1-1)443
37. Montrose 23.4	1	2	3	4	5		7‡	6	10		9	11¹	8												2-1(2-1)200
38. Stranraer 30.4		2₁	3	5		7	4	10²	12	6		9	8						1		11‡†				4-1(3-0)200
39. Stenhousemuir* 7.5	1	2	3		7¹	4	10	12	6	14	9‡	8									11‡†	5			2-1(1-1)463

Final League Position: 3

Appearances/goals: 30(0) 0 · 39(0) 8 · 33(0) 2 · 19(0) 1 · 30(0) 0 · 15(4) 0 · 36(0) 6 · 39(0) 3 · 29(0) 7 · 8(0) 4 · 13(13) 1 · 37(1) 17 · 1(5) 0 · 22(8) 6 · 9(6) 1 · 3(0) 0 · 1(4) 0 · 0(3) 0 · 0(1) 0 · 9(6) 1 · 9(0) 0 · 8(0) 4 · 1(0) 0

Own goal: D. McVicar, match 33.

RAITH ROVERS – LEAGUE RECORD 1987–88 (DIVISION ONE)

Match no/Opp/Date		H McAlpine	W Herd	A MacLeod	G Kerr	A Brash	P Sweeney	J Marshall	J McStay	A Harrow	C Harris	G Dalziel	I Ferguson	E Archibald	G Fairgrieve	J Wright	I Gibson	S Simpson	B Purdie	D Lloyd	C Fraser	R Coyle	R McLafferty	W Spence	FT(HT)Att Lge pos
Forfar Ath*	8.8	1	2	3	4	5	6	7	8†	9	10	11	12‡	14											1-4(0-2)1624 —
Queen of South	12.8	1		3	4	5		7†	8†	9	11‡	10	2	6	12										3-0(1-0)1500 —
Partick	15.8	1	8	3	4	5	7	6		9	11	10													0-0(0-0)1951 7
Hamilton A*	22.8	1		3†	4	5	8	11‡	12	9	10¹		2		14	6	7								1-2(1-1)2069 9
East Fife	29.8	1		11	4	5	8	3†	12	9	10¹		2			6	7								1-2(0-0)1942 9
Clyde*	5.9	1		3	4	5	11		2	9	10¹				8	6	7								1-3(1-1)1612 10
Kilmarnock	12.9	1¹		3	4	5	11†		2	9₁	10			12	8	6¹	7								4-3(2-1)1436 8
Meadowbank T*	15.9	1		3	4	5	11		2	9¹†	10¹				8	6	7		12						2-0(1-0)1545 —
Clydebank	19.9	1		3	4	5	11		2†	14	10			12	8‡	6	7			9²					2-1(2-0)1112 6
Airdrieonians*	26.9	1		3	4	5	11				9‡	10	2	12		6¹	7²	8†	14						3-2(1-2)1972 6
Dumbarton*	29.9	1		3	4	5	11				9‡†	10²	2	12		6	7‡	8	14						4-1(1-0)1713 —
Forfar Ath	3.10	1		3†	4	5	11				9‡	10	2	12		6	7	8	14						0-3(0-2)1079 6
Queen of South*	7.10	1		3‡	4	5	11			14	9	10²†	2			6	7	8¹	12						3-1(2-0)1106 —
Hamilton A	10.10	1		3	4	5	11			14	9	10†	2			6¹‡	7¹	8	12						2-0(0-0)1925 3
Kilmarnock*	17.10	1		3	4	5	11			14	9	10¹	2			6†	7	8‡	12						0-2(0-1)2187 4
Meadowbank Th	20.10	1		3	4	5	11			6¹†	12	10¹	2		14		7¹	8‡		9					3-4(1-3)760 4
Partick Th*	24.10	1		3		5	11			6²	12	9	10²	2†		8‡		7		14	4				4-3(1-0)1998 4
Dumbarton	27.10	1		3		5	11	8‡	2	14	9₁	10†			6¹		7			12	4				3-1(1-1)700 —
Clyde	31.10	1		3		5¹	11	8‡	2	14	9†	10¹			6		7			12	4				2-3(1-1)950 4
East Fife*	7.11	1		3		5¹	11	8‡	2¹	14	9²	10³			6		7†			12	4				7-1(1-0)2958 3
Clydebank*	14.11	1				5	11	8	2	3	9†	10			6		7			12¹	4				1-0(0-0)2140 2
Airdrieonians	21.11	1				5	11	8	2	3	10†			14	6‡		7			12	4				0-3(0-3)2322 4
Forfar Ath*	28.11	1				5	11	8	2	3	9	10			6		7			12	4				0-0(0-0)1726 5
Queen of South	5.12	1				5	11¹		2¹	3	9¹	10²			6		7†	8	12		4				5-1(1-1)900 3
Kilmarnock	12.12	1				5	11	12	2	3	9	10			6			8†	7¹		4				1-1(0-0)1654 3
Meadowbank T*	19.12	1			12	5	11	8	2	3	9¹	10	14²		6		7‡				4†				4-0(1-0)1940 2
Clyde*	26.12	1			12	5	11	8¹	2	3	9	10	7‡		14	6¹					4†				2-0(1-0)3129 2
East Fife	2.1	1			4	5	11	8	2		9†	10¹			6		7¹		12						2-1(0-0)4161 2
Clydebank	9.1	1				5		3	8	2					12	6		9†			4			11¹	1-3(1-1)1383 2
Airdrieonians*	16.1	1				5		11		2	3	9₁	10¹			6	7				4			8	2-2(1-1)4988 2
Partick Th	6.2	1			14		11‡		2	3	9	10	5		6		7†		12		4			8	0-5(0-3)1703 3
Dumbarton*	13.2	1		3		5	11	12	2		9				6		7	10¹†			4			8	1-1(0-1)1802 3
Forfar Ath	27.2	1				5	11	8		3	9¹	10†			6		7		12		4¹	2			2-2(1-2)1056 3
Hamilton A*	2.3	1		14		5	11		2	3	9	10†			6‡		7		12		4			8	0-1(0-0)2468 —
Kilmarnock*	5.3	1		3		5	11		2	9¹			8			7	10				4	6¹			2-2(1-0)1462 3
Meadowbank Th	12.3			3		5	11†		9‡	14			8	12	7	10		4			6	1			0-3(0-2)750 3
Clyde	19.3			3		5	11	12	2		10¹			6	7¹	9†	4	8			1				2-1(1-0)700 3
East Fife*	26.3			3	12	5	11‡		2	14	10			6	7	9‡	4	8			1				0-1(0-0)2345 3
Partick Th*	2.4	1		3	4		11†		2		10¹	9‡	5	12	6	7			8			1	14		1-2(0-1)1529 5
Hamilton A	9.4	1		3	4		11		2¹	9†	10	12	5		6	7			8			1			1-2(1-2)1833 5
Airdrieonians	16.4	1			4		11		2	3	10¹	9	5	12	6	7†		8¹				1			2-1(1-1)1250 4
Clydebank*	23.4	1			14			2	3	10†	9¹	5	11‡	6	7		12¹	4	8			1			2-3(0-2)1057 5
Queen of South*	30.4	1		3	12	5	11	8†	2		10½‡	9¹			7¹			4	6	1				14	4-2(1-0)899 5
Dumbarton	7.5	1		3		5	11	8	2		10†	9			7¹			4	6	1				12	0-3(0-2)800 5
Apps(subs)/goals		35(0) 1	2(0) 0	29(1) 0	22(6) 0	37(0) 2	39(0) 2	3(8) 2	37(2) 6	18(0) 0	33(0) 14	41(1) 25	6(3) 4	17(0) 0	12(8) 1	30(1) 4	38(0) 7	9(0) 1	10(19) 6	24(0) 1	16(0) 3	9(0) 0	0(3) 0		

Final League Position: 5

Own goals: J. Clark, match 1; T. Hendrie, match 26.

RANGERS – LEAGUE RECORD 1987–88 (PREMIER DIVISION)

Match no/Opp/Date	C.Woods	J.Nicholl	S.Munro	D.Ferguson	J.McGregor	A.Cohen	D.Kirkwood	M.Falco	A.McCoist	J.Phillips	D.Cooper	T.Durrant	R.Fleck	D.MacFarlane	S.Nisbet	C.West	G.Roberts	T.Butcher	G.Souness	I.McCall	T.Francis	R.Gough	R.Wilkins	M.Walters	N.Walker	J.Brown	J.Barram	T.Ferguson	G.McSwegan	FT(HT)Att Lge p
1. **Dundee U*** 8.8	1	2	3	4	5	6	7†	8	9_1	10†	11	12	14																	1–1(0–1)39,120
2. Hibernian 12.8	1		3		5	6‡	4	8	9	11		10	7†	2	12	14														0–1(0–0)22,000
3. Aberdeen 15.8	1	2	3†		5		7‡	12	9	11		10	14				4	6	8											0–2(0–1)22,500
4. **Falkirk*** 22.8	1	2		7‡	12		8^1	9^3	3	11	10	14					4†	6	5											4–0(1–0)32,340
5. Celtic 29.8	1	2	3	7	6		8	9		11†	10						4		5	12										0–1(0–1)60,800
6. **Dundee*** 5.9	1	2			6			9^1	3	11	7	8^1					4		5	10										2–1(1–0)38,302
7. **Dunfermline A*** 12.9	1	2		5				9^3‡	3	14	10†	8					4	6	12^1	7	11									4–0(2–0)39,749
8. Motherwell 19.9	1	2			12			9	3	14	11†	8					4	6	5	10‡	7									1–0(1–0)19,480
9. **Morton*** 26.9	1	2		5	12		8^3	9^2‡	3		11‡	14^1					4†	6		10	7									7–0(3–0)35,843
10. Hearts 3.10	1	2	5		4		8‡	9	3	7	11	14					6		10†	12										0–0(0–0)29,000
11. **St Mirren*** 6.10	1	2		4			8^1	9	3†	11	10						6^1	5^1	12	7										3–1(2–1)39,298
12. Dundee U 10.10	1	11	3		7	5†		8^1	9				14				4	6		10	12	2								0–1(0–0)18,214
13. **Celtic*** 17.10	1			5	11	12	8†	9^1	3	14	10						4	6			7‡	2^1								2–2(0–2)44,000
14. Dunfermline A 28.10	1	2		5		14		12	9_1	3	11	7^2†	8				6‡		10^1		4									4–0(0–0)18,000
15. **Motherwell*** 31.10	1	2		11‡		3		14	9^1		12	10	8†				4		5		7	6								1–0(0–0)36,583
16. **Hibernian*** 7.11	1	2		7	3				9		11	10	8^1				4		5†		12	6								1–0(1–0)37,517
17. St Mirren 14.11	1	2			5				9^2	3	11	7	8				4			10†	12	6								2–2(1–2)20,469
18. Aberdeen 17.11	1		12	5	2			14	9		11	10	8				4	6†		7‡	3									0–1(0–1)41,371
19. Falkirk 21.11	1			7	5				9	3	11	10	8^1				2					4	6							1–0(0–1)17,500
20. Morton 24.11	1			7^1	5‡			14	9^1	3	11†	10	8^1				2					4	12	6						3–0(1–0)15,500
21. **Hearts*** 28.11	1			7	14				9	3	11†	10^1	8^1				2					4	12	6	5‡					3–2(2–1)43,557
22. **Dundee U*** 5.12	1			11					9_1	3	12	10	8				2					4	7†	6	5					1–0(1–0)41,159
23. Hibernian 12.12	1			11	3				9		7	10	8				2					4	6^1	5						2–0(1–0)19,000
24. **Dunfermline A*** 15.12	1			11‡†	3				9^1		7	10	8				2	4			12		6	5						2–2(1–1)31,667
25. Motherwell 19.12	1		3	11					9_1		7	10					2	4			8		6	5						2–0(0–0)15,346
26. **Dundee*** 26.12	1		3	11					9_1	7†	10						2	4			8		12	6	5					2–0(2–0)40,938
27. Celtic 2.1	1‡		3		14				9	11†	10						2	4			8		12	6	5	7				0–2(0–1)60,800
28. Dundee 6.1			3		7				9^1		10						2	4			8			6	5	11	1			1–0(1–0)17,450
29. **Morton*** 9.1		2‡	3	7†	8				9^3		10^2					14		4			12	6	5	11	1					5–0(0–0)38,349
30. Hearts 16.1	1		3		14				9		10_1†						2	4		7		12	6	5	11	1	8‡			1–1(0–0)28,967
31. **Falkirk*** 23.1	1			7					9		12	10_1					2	4†				6	5	11	1	8^1	3^1			3–1(1–0)41,088
32. Aberdeen 6.2	1			7‡	8†				9^1	14	10						4		12		2^1	5	11		6	3				2–1(2–0)22,500
33. **St Mirren*** 13.2	1	12		8‡					7^1	10†						2		4	9	14	6^1	5^1	11^1		3					4–0(2–0)41,664
34. Dundee U 27.2	1	2		8					12	10					9†	4					6	5	11^1		3	7				1–1(0–1)20,846
35. Dunfermline A 5.3	1			8					9_1†	12	10				2	4					6^1	5	11^1		3	7				3–0(2–0)19,017
36. **Motherwell*** 12.3	1			7					9‡	14	10^1				2	4		12			6	5	11		3†	8				1–0(0–0)39,650
37. **Celtic*** 20.3	1			7					9		10				2	4					6	5	11		3^1	8				1–2(0–0)43,650
38. Dundee 26.3	1			7					9†	12	10_1				2	4^1					6	5	11^1		3	8				3–2(1–1)14,879
39. **Hearts*** 2.4	1			7						10					2	4					6	5	11	9	3^1	8				1–2(1–0)41,125
40. Morton 9.4	1			12				9‡	8	10^1					2	4†		14			5	11	6	3		7^1				2–3(0–0)11,000
41. **Hibernian*** 16.4		2	3	7‡†					12	10				4					5	11	1	6†	8	9					14	1–1(1–0)32,218
42. St Mirren 23.4	1	2	3	7					9^1	11				4				6	5	8^1		10^1								3–0(1–0)13,809
43. **Aberdeen*** 30.4	1	2	3	7					9	11				12	4			6	5	8		10†								0–1(0–0)36,010
44. Falkirk 7.5	1	2	3	7^1		12			9_1	10				8†				4	5	11^2		6								5–0(1–0)11,500

Final League Position: 3

Apps(sub)/goals: 39(0)0 | 21(1)0 | 16(1)0 | 31(1)0 | 31(0)4 | 4(3)0 | 3(0)0 | 9(5)5 | 40(0)31 | 19(9)0 | 24(2)1 | 39(1)10 | 15(0)7 | 1(0)0 | 22(3)0 | 0(1)0 | 37(0)1 | 11(0)1 | 14(4)2 | 8(4)1 | 8(10)0 | 31(0)5 | 24(0)1 | 11(0)7 | 9(0)2 | 11(0)3 | 8(0)1 | 0(4)0 | 0(1)0

Own goals: J. Philliben, matches 8 and 25; C. Levein, match 21.

ST JOHNSTONE – LEAGUE RECORD 1987–88 (DIVISION TWO)

Match no/Opp/Date		J Balavage	K Wilson	D McVicar	D Barron	A McKillop	J McGurn	S Maskrey	S Johnston	D Powell	W Brown	I Heddle	D Lloyd	C Mailer	T Coyle	M Smith	K Thomson	G Thompson	S Gavin	W Watters	G Jenkins	J Butter	K Nicolson	FT(HT)Att Lge pos
1. Ayr U*	8.8	1	2	3	4	5	6	7	8‡	9†	10	11	12	14										0-0(0-0)1536 —
2. Cowdenbeath	15.8	1	2	3	4	5	6	7‡	9†		10	11	12^1	8^1	14									3-0(1-0)640 3
3. Brechin C*	22.8	1	2	3	4	5	6	7‡	9		10	11		8										1-1(1-1)1768 4
4. Arbroath*	29.8	1		3	4	5	6‡	7	9	12	10†	11	14	8^3		2								3-1(1-0)1598 4
5. Stenhousemuir	5.9	1		3	4	5	6	7	9		10†	11	12	8		2								0-0(0-0)600 4
6. Stranraer*	12.9	1	12	3	4	5	6	7	9	10^1		11†		8		2								1-0(1-0)1252 2
7. Queen's Park	15.9	1	12	3	4	5‡	6	7	9	10		11†		8		2								1-0(1-0)627 2
8. Stirling Albion*	19.9	1		3	4	5	6	7	9^1	10		11		8†		2	12							1-1(1-0)1521 2
9. East Stirling	26.9	1		3	4	5	6	7	9†	10‡	14^1	11^1		8		2	12							2-0(0-0)750 2
10. Alloa*	3.10	1		3	4	5	6‡	7	9†	12	10	11		8^1		2	14^1							2-1(1-0)1404 2
11. Berwick R	10.10	1		3	4	5^2	12	14	7	10‡	9^1	11†		8		2	6							4-0(1-0)779 2
12. Montrose*	17.10	1		3	4	5		10	7	12	9^1	11†		8		2	6							1-1(1-1)1548 2
13. Albion R	24.10	1		3	4	5	14	10	7	12	9	11^1‡		8†		2	6							1-1(1-1)832 2
14. Ayr U	31.10	1		3	4	5	12		10†		9‡	11^1		8^2		2	6	14						3-0(0-0)5168 2
15. Cowdenbeath*	7.11	1		3	4	5		10	7†		9	11		8		2	6	12						0-1(0-0)1664 2
16. Brechin C	14.11	1		3	4	5	6†	14	12		10	11		8		2		7‡	9^1					1-2(1-2)1104 3
17. East Stirling*	21.11	1		3	4	5	12	7	6	9†		11‡		8		2		14	10^3					3-1(1-1)1290 3
18. Stirling Albion	28.11	1			4	5^1		7	6	9^1		11^2		8_1	3	2		12^1	10†					6-0(4-0)1201 3
19. Queen's Park*	12.12	1		3	4	5^1		12	6^1	9		11		8		2		7	10†					2-0(1-0)1429 2
20. Stranraer	19.12	1		3	4	5		14	6^1	9‡		11^4		8	12	2		7	10					2-1(1-0)500 2
21. Stenhousemuir*	26.12	1		3	4	5		9	6^2†	12		11^1‡		8		2		7	14	10^1				4-1(1-0)2289 2
22. Arbroath	2.1	1		3	4	5		9	6^2			11		8		2		7	10					2-0(1-0)2640 2
23. Berwick R*	16.1	1		3	4	5		9	6^1	12		11‡		8		2		7	14	10^1†				2-1(1-0)3106 2
24. Albion R*	6.2	1		3‡	4	5		9^1†	6^1			11		8^1	14	2		7	12	10^1				4-1(3-1)1606 2
25. Alloa	17.2			3	4	5		9^1	6†			11^1		8	14	2		7	12	10	1			1-1(1-0)1093 —
26. Cowdenbeath	20.2	1		3	4	5		6	14			11		8	12	2	7†		9	$10‡$				0-1(0-0)800 2
27. Montrose	23.2	1		3	4	5		6				11		8	9^1	2		7		10	1			1-0(0-0)700 —
28. Ayr U*	27.2	1		3	4	5		6				11		8	9^1†	2^1	7		12	10				2-0(2-0)5109 2
29. Stirling Albion*	1.3	1		3	4^1	5		6				11		8	9†	2	7	14	12	$10‡$				1-0(0-0)1960 —
30. Stenhousemuir	5.3	1		3	4	5		6				11		8	9†	2	7		12	10				0-3(0-1)406 —
31. Stranraer	12.3	1		3	4	5		14	6			11†		8_1	12	2	7		9^1	$10‡$				3-1(0-1)900 2
32. Montrose*	19.3	1		3	4	5		$9‡^1$	6^1			11		8		2	7	14	10^3†	12				5-1(4-1)1803 2
33. Queen's Park	26.3	1		3	4	5		9	6			11‡		8	14	2	7†		10^1	12				1-2(0-1)1030 2
34. East Stirling*	2.4			3	4	5		9	6			8			11†	2	7		10	12				0-0(0-0)1907 —
35. Berwick R	9.4	1		3	4	5		9	6			8†			14	2	7	11‡	10†	12				2-0(2-0)570 2
36. Arbroath*	16.4	1		3	4	5		9	6^1			8†			11	2	7	12	10^3					4-0(2-0)2503 2
37. Brechin C*	23.4	1		3	4	5		9†^{1}	6	14		8‡			11	2	7		10^1	12				2-0(1-0)1689 2
38. Alloa	30.4	1		3^1	4	5			6			11		8†	9	2	7		10	12				1-1(0-0)817 2
39. Albion R*	7.5	1		3				9	6			11		8^1		4	2	7†	10^1	12		5		2-0(0-0)1934 2
Apps(subs)/goals		37(0) 0	3(2) 0	38(0) 1	38(0) 5	11(4) 0	28(5) 5	38(1) 11	10(7) 3	12(1) 3	35(1) 9	0(4) 1	0(1) 0	38(0) 13	9(8) 2	36(0) 1	26(3) 0	35(9) 1	18(5) 16	8(7) 1	2(0) 0	1(0) 0		

Final League Position: 2

ST MIRREN – LEAGUE RECORD 1987–88 (PREMIER DIVISION)

Players (column order): C. Money, T. Wilson, D. Hamilton, W. Abercromby, D. Winnie, N. Cooper, F. McGarvey, I. Ferguson, P. Chalmers, A. Fitzpatrick, B. Hamilton, P. Lambert, I. Cameron, K. McDowall, N. McWhirter, R. Dawson, K. Walker, B. Gallagher, J. Butler, P. Godfrey, W. Davies, G. Shaw, L. Fridge, M. Conroy, G. Peebles, M. McWalter, B. Martin

Match no/Opp/Date	Mon	Wil	DHa	Abe	Win	Coo	McG	Fer	Cha	Fit	BHa	Lam	Cam	McD	McW	Daw	Wal	Gal	But	God	Dav	Sha	Fri	Con	Pee	McWa	Mar	FT(HT)Att	Lge pos
1. Motherwell 8.8	1	2	3	4	5¹	6	7	8	9†	12	10	11‡			14													1–2(0–2)4131	—
2. Dunfermline A* 11.8	1	2	3	4	5	6	7	8		10‡	11†	12	14	9														1–1(1–1)4762	—
3. Hearts* 15.8	1	3		4	5	6	7	8	11‡		10	12₁	14	9†		2												1–1(0–1)7408	9
4. Dundee 22.8	1			4	5	6	12	8				11	10¹	3	2	7¹	9†											2–0(2–0)5969	6
5. Morton* 29.8	1	12		4	5	6	7¹	8¹	9‡		11†		3	2	10	14												2–1(1–0)5271	5
6. Hibernian 5.9	1	14		4	5	6	7		12		11	10	3¹	2	8‡	9†												1–1(0–0)5500	5
7. Aberdeen 12.9	1	3‡		4	5	6	7		12			10†	11	2	8	9	14											0–2(0–2)11,000	6
8. Dundee U* 19.9	1	12		4	3	6			9			7†	11¹	10¹	2‡		8	14		5								2–0(0–0)3807	5
9. Celtic* 26.9	1	2		4	3	6			9†			7‡	11	10		14	8	12		5								0–1(0–0)18,011	6
10. Falkirk 3.10	1	2		3¹		6			9²	4		7†	11		12	8‡	10	14		5								3–1(2–1)3500	5
11. Rangers 6.10	1	2		3		6		10	9¹	4		7‡	11		14	8†	12			5								1–3(1–2)39,298	—
12. Motherwell* 10.10	1	2		3		6	8	9		4		7‡	11₁	14	12		10†			5								0–0(1–0)4133	5
13. Morton 17.10	1	2		3		6	8				12	7	11	10		4	9†			5								0–0(0–0)3500	6
14. Hibernian* 24.10	1	2		3†		6	8²	9				10	7‡	11		12	14			5	4							2–2(2–1)7014	5
15. Aberdeen* 28.10	1	2				6¹	8	9†	4	10				3				5	7	12								1–3(0–2)4707	—
16. Dundee U 31.10	1‡	2				6	8²		4	9	12	14	10	3	11¹			5	7†									3–2(1–2)7607	5
17. Dunfermline A 7.11	1	2		3		6†	8		4	9		7‡	11	14	12			5	10									0–2(0–2)5990	—
18. Rangers* 14.11	1	2	3		5†	6	7¹	12	4	9			14	11₁	10			8‡										2–0(0–1)20,469	7
19. Dundee* 17.11		2	3			6†	7	12	4	9			14	11₁	10			5	8‡				1					1–2(0–0)3328	—
20. Hearts 21.11		2	3			6	8	12	4	9		7	11	10†				5					1					0–0(0–0)14,879	7
21. Celtic 25.11		2	3			6	8	12		9		7†	11	10†				5		14		4	1					0–1(0–0)26,718	—
22. Falkirk* 28.11		2	3			6			9‡			10	12	11¹	14			5	7	8†		4						2–2(1–2)3691	7
23. Motherwell 5.12		2	3			6			9			10	7‡	11			5†		8‡	12		4		14				1–2(0–1)2928	7
24. Dunfermline A* 12.12	1	2	3			6†	14¹		10²			7	11	4		12		5	8						9¹‡			4–1(3–0)4364	—
25. Aberdeen 16.12	1	2	3†			14			10	8		7	11₁	6				5	4						9‡			1–2(0–1)6500	—
26. Dundee U* 19.12	1	2	3		6‡		12		10		7		11†	14	4	8		5				9						0–1(0–1)3517	8
27. Hibernian 26.12	1	14	3				12	8	5			7	11	10‡	4	2			6			9†						0–0(0–0)5500	8
28. Morton* 2.1	1	2					14	8	12		5	7	11	10†	4				6			9‡						0–0(0–0)7095	8
29. Celtic* 9.1	1		3			6		8	12	4	5	7	11	10‡	2							9						1–1(0–1)19,030	8
30. Falkirk 16.1	1		3†			6		8	14	4	5	7	11	10‡	2							9			12			0–3(0–1)4750	8
31. Hearts* 6.2	1		3						5			7	11		6			4				10	2	9				0–6(0–3)6659	8
32. Rangers 13.2	1		3			6	7	8	4	5	12	14			2			10				11†		9‡				0–4(0–2)41,664	8
33. Motherwell* 27.2	1		3				7		14	12	8		10†	4		6		5	11					9‡	2			0–0(0–0)5419	8
34. Dundee 1.3	1		3				12	9¹	8			7†	14	10‡	4	6		5	11						2			1–2(1–0)4265	—
35. Aberdeen* 5.3	1		3†				7		9	8		10	12	11	4	6		5							2			0–0(0–0)4858	8
36. Morton 19.3	1						7		9¹	4	10	8	11¹		3	6		5							2			2–0(2–0)3000	8
37. Hibernian* 26.3	1						7		9	8	3‡	10†	11¹	12	4	6		14	5						2			1–1(1–1)4655	8
38. Dundee U 30.3	1		3				9¹†	8‡	10		11	12		4		6		14	5						2			1–5(1–4)6294	—
39. Falkirk* 2.4	1		3				7		9			10	6	8†	11	4		5				12			2			0–0(0–0)4694	8
40. Celtic 5.4	1		3				7		9			10	6	14	11‡	12	4	5							2			0–2(0–0)45,465	—
41. Dunfermline A 16.4	1		3			6			9	8		14	11	12	4	2‡		5								10†		1–2(1–0)4390	9
42. Rangers* 23.4	1	2	3		5	6	9		8	4‡		11			14		12					10†				7		0–3(0–1)13,809	9
43. Hearts 30.4	1	2	3		5	6	9		8¹	4		11					10									7		1–0(0–0)8570	9
44. Dundee* 7.5	1	2	3			6	9		8	4‡			14	11†			10¹	5							12	7		1–0(1–0)5798	9
Apps(subs)/goals	41(0)0	31(4)0	19(0)0	9(0)0	26(0)2	27(0)1	18(7)2	26(4)10	24(2)1	28(1)0	25(1)12	36(5)8	22(2)1	16(8)0	18(1)3	8(5)0	7(0)0	24(0)0	18(0)0	0(2)0	3(0)0	9(0)1	1(0)0	3(0)0	1(0)0	3(0)0	12(0)0		

Final League Position: 9

STENHOUSEMUIR – LEAGUE RECORD 1987–88 (DIVISION TWO)

Match no/Opp/Date		S.Robertson	H.Cairney	D.Beaton	J.Waddell	G.Buchanan	H.Erwin	T.Condie	T.McCaffery	P.Quinn	J.Gillen	M.Jamieson	I.Thomson	S.McAra	P.Sexton	C.Walker	P.Russell	A.Maitland	G.McIntosh	A.Keith	A.Elliott	S.Hamill	FT(HT)Att Lge pos
1. Albion R*	8.8	1	2_1	3	4^1	5	6	7^1	8	9	10	11†		12									3–1(2–1)300 —
2. Stirling Albion*	15.8	1	2	3		5	6	7	8	9†	10	12	11	4									0–0(0–0)473 5
3. Queen's Park*	22.8	1	2	3		5	6	7	8	9	10†	12^2	11		4								2–3(0–1)350 7
4. East Stirling	29.8	1	2	3		5	6	7	8	9	11†	12	14		4	10‡							0–2(0–2)400 9
5. St Johnstone*	5.9	1	2	3	4		5	7	12	9			6	10		8	11†						0–0(0–0)600 9
6. Berwick R	12.9	1	2	3	4	12	5†	7	8	9^1		11^2	6			10							3–1(1–0)267 8
7. Arbroath*	15.9	1	2	3	4†	5^1		7	8	9		11	6			10	12						1–1(1–0)250 —
8. Stranraer*	19.9	1	2	3		5	7	12		9‡	6	11		8		10		4†	14				0–2(0–2)150 9
9. Montrose	26.9	1	2	3		5	7†	8	9	10	11		6			4		12					0–1(0–0)200 11
10. Ayr U*	3.10	1	2	5	4		6	7†	8	9		11		10		12				3			0–6(0–2)700 12
11. Alloa	10.10	1	2	5_1	4		6	7	8	9		11†		10			12			3			1–1(0–1)250 12
12. Brechin C	17.10	1	2	5	4	14	6	7	8‡	9		11	12	10†						3			0–2(0–0)350 12
13. Cowdenbeath*	24.10	1	2	5	4		6	7	8†	9		11		10			12			3			0–0(0–0)200 12
14. Albion R	31.10	1	2	5	4		6	7	•8	9		11‡	12	10						3			2–3(1–1)300 12
15. Stirling Albion	7.11	1	2	5	4		6		8	9^1		11^2		10		7				3			3–0(2–0)529 11
16. Queen's Park	14.11	1	2	5‡	4		6	14	8	9†		11	12	10^1		7				3			2–0(2–0)564 10
17. Montrose*	21.11	1	2	5	4		6†	14	8	9		11	12	10‡		7				3			0–2(0–2)250 11
18. Stranraer	28.11	1	2	5	4		6	12^1	8	9†		11^1		10		7				3			3–2(1–1)300 11
19. Arbroath	12.12	1	2	5	4		6	14	8	9‡		11	7	10†		12				3			0–3(0–2)356 11
20. Berwick R*	19.12	1	2	5	4		6	12	8	9†		11		10		7^1				3			1–2(0–1)250 11
21. St Johnstone	26.12	1	2	5	4		6^1		8	9	12	11		10		7†				3			1–4(0–1)2289 11
22. East Stirling*	2.1	1	2	5	4†		6‡	12^1	8	9	14	11		10		7				3	9^1		2–3(0–1)220 12
23. Alloa*	16.1	1	2	3	5		6	11	8	12		10	5†			7				3	9		0–1(0–1)300 12
24. Ayr U	23.1	1	2	3	4		5	7†	8			10			11	6	12	13		3	9		0–3(0–1)2714 12
25. Cowdenbeath	6.2	1	2	5	4		6	11	8			10				7†	12			3	9^1		1–1(0–0)200 12
26. Arbroath*	13.2	1	2	5	4		6	11^1	8			10				7				3	9		1–1(0–1)200 12
27. Albion R	20.2	1	2	5	4		6^1	11^1	8			10^1				7				3	9^1		4–0(2–0)300 12
28. Brechin C*	24.2	1	2	5	4		6	11^1	8			10‡				7†	12		14	3	9		1–2(0–2)250 —
29. Montrose	27.2	1	2	5_1	4		6	11	8			10†				7‡	12		14	3	9		1–1(0–0)250 12
30. St Johnstone*	5.3	1	2	5_1	4		6	11^1	8			10^1								3	9	7	3–0(1–0)406 11
31. Alloa*	12.3	1	2	5	4		6	11	8			10	12							3	9	7†	0–0(0–0)340 11
32. Berwick R	19.3	1	2	5^1	4		9^1	11	8			10	6^1							3		7	3–1(0–1)300 11
33. East Stirling	26.3	1	2	5^1	4		9	11^1	8			10†	6					12		3		7	2–1(2–1)300 10
34. Cowdenbeath*	2.4	1	2	5	4		9^1	11^1	8			10	6							3		7	2–0(1–0)200 10
35. Stirling Albion	9.4	1	2	5	4		9^1	11	8‡			10^1	6		14	12				3		7†	2–3(1–0)367 10
36. Brechin C*	16.4	1	2	5	4		9^1	11‡	8			10	6			12				3		7	2–1(2–0)240 10
37. Stranraer	23.4	1	2	5	4^1		9	11	8			10	6			12				3		7†	1–2(1–0)400 10
38. Ayr U*	30.4	1	2	5^1	4		9	11	8			10	6							3		7	1–0(0–0)1130 10
39. Queen's Park	7.5	1	2	5	4		9^1	11	8			10‡	12	6		14				3		7†	1–2(1–1) 463 10

Final League Position: 10

Apps(subs)/goals: 36(0)0 | 39(0)1 | 39(0)7 | 40(0)1 | 15(1)2 | 36(1)7 | 37(0)0 | 37(2)10 | 37(0)0 | 10(5)2 | 34(1)0 | 7(4)4 | 36(1)4 | 45(0)1 | 13(3)1 | 21(0)5 | 20(0)0 | 8(6)0 | 30(0)1 | 10(1)3 | 10(2)0

Own goal: N. Watt, match 18.

STIRLING ALBION – LEAGUE RECORD 1987-88 (DIVISION TWO)

Match no/Opp/Date	A Graham	T Aitchison	S Tennant	K Hoggan	G McTeague	T Spence	D Thompson	M Conway	C Gibson	B Kemp	J Brogan	S Gavin	A Gibson	S Maxwell	M Walsh	D Mills	J Ormond	J Cousin	M Murray	N Anderson	K Wilson	R Phillben	L Fridge	J McGill	FT(HT)Att	Lge pos
1. Montrose 8.8	1	2	3	4	5	6_1	7	8	9	10	11^2														3-1(2-0)771	—
2. Stenhousemuir 15.8	1	2		4	5	3	$7^\dagger$	8	9	10	11	12	6												0-0(0-0)473	6
3. Arbroath 22.8	1	2	$3^\ddagger$		5	6	7^1	4	$9^\dagger$	10	11^1	12	8	14											2-3(2-1)581	8
4. Alloa 29.8		2		12	5	3	7	8		10	11	$9^\ddagger$	$4^\dagger$	6		1	14								0-4(0-0)1000	10
5. Ayr U* 5.9	1	8		4	5	3	7	2	$9^\dagger$	10^1	11	12	6												1-1(1-0)2170	10
6. Albion R 12.9	1	8			5	3	4	2	9^1	10	$11^\dagger$	12	6			7									1-2(0-0)450	11
7. Brechin C* 15.9	1	8			5	3	7^2	2	9	10	$11^\dagger$		4	6		12									2-1(0-0)584	—
8. St Johnstone 19.9	1	8			5	3	$7^\dagger$	4	9	$10^\ddagger$	11		6	14		12^1			2						1-1(0-1)1521	10
9. Cowdenbeath* 26.9	1	4			5	3	7		$9^\dagger$	10	11^2		6			12		2	8						2-0(1-0)668	7
10. Berwick R* 3.10	1	4			5	3	7^1		9	$10^\dagger$	$11^\dagger$		6	14		12		2	8						1-0(1-0)628	6
11. Queen's Park 10.10	1	4			5	3	$7^\dagger$		9	10	11^1		6			12		2	8						1-1(0-0)631	6
12. East Stirling* 17.10	1	4			5	3	$7^\dagger$		9^2	$10^\ddagger$	$11^\dagger$		6	14		12		2	8						3-0(1-0)621	5
13. Stranraer 24.10	1	4			5		7	2	9	10	11		6			3			8						0-0(0-0)400	5
14. Montrose* 31.10	1	$4^\ddagger$			5		7	14	9	10	11		6			12	$3^\dagger$		8	2					0-2(0-1)587	5
15. Stenhousemuir* 7.11	1	12			5		7		9	10	11	4	6	14		3		$8^\ddagger$		2					0-3(0-2)529	7
16. Arbroath* 14.11	1	$4^\dagger$	3		5		7	12	9^1	10	11^2		6					8		2					3-0(3-0)434	5
17. Cowdenbeath 21.11	1	4^1	3		5		7		9^1	10	11^2		6					8		2					4-2(3-0)300	5
18. St Johnstone* 28.11	1	4			5	3	$7^\dagger$	12	9	10	11		6			14		$8^\dagger$		2					0-6(0-4)1201	5
19. Brechin C 12.12	1	8			5	3_1	7	4	9	10	11^1		6							2					2-1(0-0)500	5
20. Albion R* 19.12	1	8			5	3	7	4	9^1	10	11		6							2		1			1-0(0-0)310	5
21. Ayr U 26.12	1		14		5	3	7	4	9	10	$11^\dagger$	$8^\ddagger$	6			12				2					0-4(0-3)3658	5
22. Alloa* 2.1	1	8			5	3	7	4	$9^\dagger$	10	11^1		6			12^1				2					2-0(1-0)1208	5
23. Queen's Park* 16.1	1	8	14		5	3	7^1	4	9^1	$10^\ddagger$	$11^\dagger$		6			12				2					2-2(1-0)533	5
24. Berwick R 23.1	1	8	3		5^1		7	$4^\ddagger$	$9^{1\dagger}$	10	11^1		6			12^1	14			2					4-0(0-0)320	5
25. East Stirling 2.2	1	8	3		5	7^1	14		$9^\dagger$	10	11		6			12	$4^\ddagger$			2					1-2(0-1)600	—
26. Stranraer* 6.2	1	8	3		5	7^2		4	10	9			6			11				2					2-0(0-0)282	5
27. Montrose* 20.2	1	14	3		5		7	$4^\ddagger$	9	$10^\dagger$	11		6						8	2					0-2(0-1)381	5
28. Cowdenbeath 27.2	1	$5^\dagger$	3				7	8	9				6^1							2	4		12		1-0(1-0)300	5
29. St Johnstone 1.3	1		3		5		7		9	10	$11^\dagger$		6			12			8	2	4				0-1(0-0)1960	—
30. Alloa* 5.3	1	5	3				7	8	9^1	10^1	11^2		6			12				2	4				4-1(3-1)506	6
31. Berwick R* 12.3	1	5	3				7	8	9^1	10	11^1		6							2	4				2-0(1-0)297	6
32. Queen's Park 19.3	1	5	3				7	8	$9^\dagger$	10^1	11		6			12				2	4				1-1(0-1)626	6
33. Ayr U* 26.3	1	5	3				7	8	9^1	10	$11^\ddagger$		6							2	4				2-2(1-1)1796	6
34. Albion R 2.4	1		3				7	8	$9^\dagger$	10	11^1	14	6			12				2	4		$5^\ddagger$		1-3(1-1)310	6
35. Stenhousemuir* 9.4	1	5	3				7	$8^\dagger$	9	10	11		6			12^2				2	4				3-2(0-1)367	5
36. East Stirling 16.4	1	5	3			7^1		4	9^1	$10^\dagger$	8		6			11			12	2					3-1(2-1)363	5
37. Arbroath* 23.4	1	5	$3^\dagger$				7	4	9	12	10^1		6			11			8	2					2-0(0-0)375	5
38. Brechin C 30.4	1	5	3				7	8	9^1	10			6	2		11				4					1-1(1-0)400	5
39. Stranraer* 7.5	1	5	3				7	$4^\ddagger$	9	10	$8^{2\dagger}$	12	6			11	14			2					2-0(2-0)341	5
Apps(subs)/goals	37(0)0	34(2)1	20(2)0	3(1)0	27(0)1	18(0)2	39(0)0	29(4)0	37(0)13	37(1)4	39(0)23	4(1)0	38(0)1	1(2)0	1(0)0	6(20)4	3(3)1	5(0)0	10(0)0	18(2)0	19(1)0	1(0)0	2(1)0		Final League Position: 5	

Own goal: G. Buchanan, match 35.

STRANRAER – LEAGUE RECORD 1987-88 (DIVISION TWO)

Match no/Opp/Date		A Bryden	N Watt	G Hay	K Geals	J Carson	R Day	B McIntyre	J McNiven	B Cleland	F Campbell	J Creaney	G Wilson	E McQueen	J McDonald	K Knox	M McCabe	J Coyle	E McNab	A MacLean	A Bell	M McLafferty	C Hume	G Holt	J Edgar	M Dougan	N Armour	M Adams	D Henderson	L Lowe	P McGrath	FT(HT)Att Lge pos
1. Berwick R	8.8	1	2	3	4	5	6	7†	8[1]	9	10	11	12																			1-0(1-0)440 —
2. Arbroath*	15.8	1		3	4	5			8[1]	9[1]	6		2	7	10[1]	11																3-1(1-1)390 2
3. East Stirling	22.8	1		3	4	5			8	9	6		2	7	10[1]	11																1-1(1-1)170 3
4. Ayr U	29.8	1	12	3	4	5			8[1]	9†	6†	14	2	7	10	11																1-5(1-1)1948 5
5. Alloa*	5.9	1	5	3‡	4				14	8	12	6		2	7	10†		9														0-3(0-1)450 8
6. St Johnstone	12.9		4	3		5	12		8†	11	6‡		2	7	9		14	10														0-1(0-1)1252 9
7. Cowdenbeath*	15.9	1	4	3		5	6		8	11[1]†		12	14	7	9		2‡	10[1]														2-2(1-1)450 —
8. Stenhousemuir	19.9		4	3		5	6	8		11[2]				7	9		2	10														2-0(2-0)150 8
9. Brechin C*	26.9		4	3		5	6	8‡	14	11			7†	9[1]	12	2	10	12														1-1(0-0)400 8
10. Montrose*	3.10		4			5	3		8	11†			7	9	6	2	10	12														1-3(1-3)342 8
11. Albion R	10.10	1	4	3	14	5	10‡	2	8[1]	12			7	9	6		11†															1-2(1-1)250 11
12. Queen's Park	17.10	1	4			5	3	2	8†	12			7	9	10	6	11‡	14														0-3(0-1)529 11
13. Stirling Albion*	24.10		4	3	6	5		2		9		8	7		12		10	11†	1													0-0(0-0)400 11
14. Berwick R*	31.10	9	5			3	2		12			6	7	8†	4		10	11‡	1													0-2(0-1)250 11
15. Arbroath	7.11	4[1]	5	6		3	8				2	7	9‡		10†	12₁	14															2-3(0-2)369 12
16. East Stirling*	14.11	4			3	2		11₁		5	7	12	10	6[1]		8[1]†		9														3-3(3-1)350 12
17. Brechin C	21.11	4			3	2	14	9		5	7		8	6†	12	11		10‡	1													0-2(0-1)416 12
18. Stenhousemuir*	28.11	4			5	3	2	7†	9[2]	10‡		8		11	6		14	12		1												2-3(1-1)300 13
19. Cowdenbeath	12.12	6			5	3	2	8	9‡	12		4†	7	10	11	14				1												0-2(0-2)160 13
20. St Johnstone*	19.12	4			5	3	2	8	9†			12	7	10‡	11	6		14[1]		1												1-2(0-1)500 13
21. Alloa	30.12	4	3	5			2	10	9	8†		6	7‡		11	12	14			1												0-2(0-1)430 —
22. Ayr U*	2.1	4	3		5			2	8	9₁		6	7		11	12		10†		1												1-2(1-1)2080 13
23. Albion R*	16.1	4	3		5	11[1]†		8	9	6			7	12			1	2	10													1-2(1-1)400 13
24. Montrose	23.1	4			5	3	2	8	9†	6‡		7	10	11	12₁		1	14														1-3(0-2)300 13
25. Stirling Albion	6.2	4	3			5	2	8	6			7	9	11			1															0-2(0-0)282 13
26. Queen's Park	16.2	4	5		3‡	2	6†			7	8	11	14	12			1	9														0-2(0-1)394 —
27. Brechin C	20.2	6	3		5		2	7		4	8	9	11	10[1]			1															1-4(1-2)300 13
28. Cowdenbeath*	24.2	4	3	5		2	9		12	7‡		6	10	11†			14		1													0-4(0-2)250 —
29. Arbroath*	27.2	4	5	14		2	7†	6		9	11	8	12		10	3‡	1															0-3(0-1)300 14
30. East Stirling	5.3	4	3	14		2	7		9‡	11	6	12		10†	1	5																0-2(0-0)150 14
31. St Johnstone	12.3	12		6		3	2	7	4†	10		9‡	11	14		8[1]	1	5														1-3(1-0)900 14
32. Alloa	22.3		14	6		3	2	8	4	9†	7	12		5	11[1]	10‡	1															1-1(1-0)320 —
33. Berwick R	26.3	2		6	3‡		8	4	10†	7	12	14		5	9	11	1															0-2(0-1)300 14
34. Montrose*	2.4	4[1]	3			9	8	14	7	12	6		1	10†	5	11‡	2															1-1(1-1)400 14
35. Ayr U	9.4	5	3		6	8	4	7[1]	9†	10		1	12	11	2																	1-3(1-0)2967 14
36. Albion R*	16.4	5₁	3		6[1]	8	4†	9	7		10		1	11	2	12																2-2(0-2)350 14
37. Stenhousemuir*	23.4	4	3		11[1]	8	12	9	7		6		10†‡	2	5																	2-1(1-0)400 13
38. Queen's Park*	30.4	5	3		8[1]	4		10		1	12	6	11	2†	5																	1-4(0-3)450 13
39. Stirling Albion	7.5	4‡	3	14	11	6	9		7		1	12	10	2†	5																	0-2(0-2)341 14
Apps(subs)/goals		8(0)/0	34(2)/3	28(1)/0	12(4)/0	20(0)/3	24(1)/0	32(2)/5	19(4)/8	20(3)/0	6(3)/0	15(5)/0	31(0)/1	24(4)/3	22(2)/0	20(5)/1	12(1)/4	5(5)/2	20/0	20(0)/0	10/0	20/0	4(3)/1	20/0	5(0)/0	20/1	8(0)/1	6(0)/0	2(1)/0			Final League Position: 14

Own goal: D. Paterson, match 10. Also played: W. Mullen at 11 in match 5; J. Kapusciak at 1 in matches 6, 8, 9, 10; J. Pathak at 14 in match 14; I. McFarlane at 1 in matches 15, 16; P. Mackie at 11 in match 15; S. Kelly at 10 in match 26; M. Orr at 8 in match 28; D. Cree at 8 in match 30; A. McLean at 1 in match 31; M. Graham at 1 in matches 32, 33; P. Taylor at 7 in match 38; A. Ross at 9 in match 38; C. Wilson at 8 in match 39.

FINE FARE SCOTTISH LEAGUE FINAL TABLES 1987–88

PREMIER DIVISION

			Home				Away					
	P	W	D	L	F	A	W	D	L	F	A	GD	Pts
1 Celtic	44	16	5	1	42	11	15	5	2	37	12	+56	72
2 Hearts	44	13	8	1	37	17	10	8	4	37	15	+42	62
3 Rangers	44	14	4	4	49	17	12	4	6	36	17	+51	60
4 Aberdeen	44	11	7	4	27	11	10	10	2	29	14	+31	59
5 Dundee U	44	8	7	7	29	24	8	8	6	25	23	+7	47
6 Hibernian	44	8	8	6	18	17	4	11	7	23	25	−1	43
7 Dundee	44	9	5	8	31	25	8	2	12	39	39	+6	41
8 Motherwell	44	10	2	10	25	31	3	8	11	12	25	−19	36
9 St Mirren	44	5	11	6	22	28	5	4	13	19	36	−23	35
10 Falkirk	44	8	4	10	26	35	2	7	13	15	40	−34	31
11 Dunfermline Ath	44	6	6	10	23	35	2	4	16	18	49	−43	26
12 Morton	44	3	7	12	19	47	0	3	19	8	53	−73	16

DIVISION 1

			Home				Away					
	P	W	D	L	F	A	W	D	L	F	A	GD	Pts
1 Hamilton Acad	44	12	5	5	36	24	10	7	5	31	15	+28	56
2 Meadowbank Th	44	12	4	6	41	26	8	8	6	29	25	+19	52
3 Clydebank	44	13	2	7	32	25	8	5	9	27	36	−2	49
4 Forfar Ath	44	9	9	4	44	28	7	7	8	23	30	+9	48
5 Raith R	44	10	4	8	45	33	9	3	10	36	43	+5	45
6 Airdrieonians	44	11	4	7	34	28	5	9	8	31	40	−3	45
7 Queen of the S	44	8	7	7	23	28	6	8	8	33	39	−11	43
8 Partick Th	44	9	6	7	32	27	7	3	12	28	37	−4	41
9 Clyde	44	8	5	9	40	38	9	1	12	33	37	−2	40
10 Kilmarnock	44	8	6	8	30	30	5	5	12	25	30	−5	37
11 East Fife	44	8	5	9	34	34	5	5	12	27	42	−15	36
12 Dumbarton	44	4	8	10	23	30	8	4	10	28	40	−19	36

DIVISION 2

			Home				Away					
	P	W	D	L	F	A	W	D	L	F	A	GD	Pts
1 Ayr U	39	15	2	2	52	14	12	5	3	43	17	+64	61
2 St Johnstone	39	14	5	1	40	11	11	4	4	34	13	+50	59
3 Queen's Park	39	10	6	4	30	20	11	3	5	34	24	+20	51
4 Brechin C	39	12	3	5	33	20	8	5	6	23	20	+16	48
5 Stirling A	39	12	4	4	34	23	6	6	7	26	28	+9	46
6 East Stirling	39	8	5	6	25	23	7	8	5	26	24	+4	43
7 Alloa	39	10	4	6	30	19	6	4	9	20	27	+4	40
8 Montrose	39	6	4	9	21	25	6	7	7	24	26	−6	35
9 Arbroath	39	8	6	5	32	24	2	8	10	22	42	−12	34
10 Stenhousemuir	39	5	6	8	19	25	7	3	10	30	33	−9	33
11 Cowdenbeath	39	6	7	7	30	36	4	6	9	21	30	−15	33
12 Albion R	39	6	5	8	21	33	4	6	10	24	42	−30	31
13 Berwick R	39	3	4	13	18	38	3	0	16	14	39	−45	16
14 Stranraer	39	2	6	11	22	42	2	2	16	12	42	−50	16

SCOTTISH LEAGUE HONOURS SINCE 1890–91

Season	Max Pts	First	Pts	Second	Pts	Third	Pts
PREMIER DIVISION							
1975–76	72	Rangers	54	Celtic	48	Hibernian	43
1976–77	72	Celtic	55	Rangers	46	Aberdeen	43
1977–78	72	Rangers	55	Aberdeen	53	Dundee U	40
1978–79	72	Celtic	48	Rangers	45	Dundee U	44
1979–80	72	Aberdeen	48	Celtic	47	St Mirren	42
1980–81	72	Celtic	56	Aberdeen	49	Rangers	44
1981–82	72	Celtic	55	Aberdeen	53	Rangers	43
1982–83	72	Dundee U	56	Celtic	55	Aberdeen	55
1983–84	72	Aberdeen	57	Celtic	50	Dundee U	47
1984–85	72	Aberdeen	59	Celtic	52	Dundee U	47
1985–86	72	Celtic*	50	Hearts	50	Dundee U	47
1986–87	88	Rangers	69	Celtic	63	Dundee U	60
1987–88	88	Celtic	72	Hearts	62	Rangers	60

*Won on goal difference.

Season	Max Pts	First	Pts	Second	Pts	Third	Pts
FIRST DIVISION							
1975–76	52	Partick Th	41	Kilmarnock	35	Montrose	30
1976–77	78	St Mirren	62	Clydebank	58	Dundee	51
1977–78	78	Morton*	58	Hearts	58	Dundee	57
1978–79	78	Dundee	55	Kilmarnock	54	Clydebank	54
1979–80	78	Hearts	53	Airdrieonians	51	Ayr U	44
1980–81	78	Hibernian	57	Dundee	52	St Johnstone	51
1981–82	78	Motherwell	61	Kilmarnock	51	Hearts	50
1982–83	78	St Johnstone	55	Hearts	54	Clydebank	50
1983–84	78	Morton	54	Dumbarton	51	Partick Th	46
1984–85	78	Motherwell	50	Clydebank	48	Falkirk	45
1985–86	78	Hamilton Acad	56	Falkirk	45	Kilmarnock	44
1986–87	88	Morton	57	Dunfermline Ath	56	Dumbarton	53
1987–88	88	Hamilton Acad	56	Meadowbank Th	52	Clydebank	49

*Won on goal difference.

Season	Max Pts	First	Pts	Second	Pts	Third	Pts
SECOND DIVISION							
1975–76	52	Clydebank*	40	Raith R	40	Alloa	35
1976–77	78	Stirling A	55	Alloa	51	Dunfermline Ath	50
1977–78	78	Clyde*	53	Raith R	53	Dunfermline Ath	48
1978–79	78	Berwick R	54	Dunfermline Ath	52	Falkirk	50
1979–80	78	Falkirk	50	East Stirling	49	Forfar Ath	46
1980–81	78	Queen's Park	50	Queen of the S	46	Cowdenbeath	45
1981–82	78	Clyde	59	Alloa	50	Arbroath	50
1982–83	78	Brechin C	55	Meadowbank Th	54	Arbroath	49
1983–84	78	Forfar Ath	63	East Fife	47	Berwick R	43
1984–85	78	Montrose	53	Alloa	50	Dunfermline Ath	49
1985–86	78	Dunfermline Ath	57	Queen of the S	55	Meadowbank Th	49
1986–87	78	Meadowbank Th	55	Raith R	52	Stirling A	52
1987–88	78	Ayr U	61	St Johnstone	59	Queen's Park	51

*Won on goal difference.

Season	Max Pts	First	Pts	Second	Pts	Third	Pts
FIRST DIVISION TO 1974–75							
1890–91†	36	Dumbarton	29	Rangers	29	Celtic	24
1891–92	44	Dumbarton	37	Celtic	35	Hearts	30
1892–93	36	Celtic	29	Rangers	28	St Mirren	23
1893–94	36	Celtic	29	Hearts	26	St Bernard's	22
1894–95	36	Hearts	31	Celtic	26	Rangers	21
1895–96	36	Celtic	30	Rangers	26	Hibernian	24
1896–97	36	Hearts	28	Hibernian	26	Rangers	25
1897–98	36	Celtic	33	Rangers	29	Hibernian	22
1898–99	36	Rangers	36	Hearts	26	Celtic	24
1899–1900	36	Rangers	32	Celtic	25	Hibernian	24
1900–01	40	Rangers	35	Celtic	29	Hibernian	25
1901–02	36	Rangers	28	Celtic	26	Hearts	22
1902–03	44	Hibernian	37	Dundee	31	Rangers	29

SCOTTISH LEAGUE HONOURS

1903–04	52	Third Lanark	43	Hearts	39	Rangers	38
1904–05	52	Celtic‡	41	Rangers	41	Third Lanark	35
1905–06	60	Celtic	49	Hearts	43	Airdrieonians	38
1906–07	68	Celtic	55	Dundee	48	Rangers	45
1907–08	68	Celtic	55	Falkirk	51	Rangers	50
1908–09	68	Celtic	51	Dundee	50	Clyde	48
1909–10	68	Celtic	54	Falkirk	52	Rangers	46
1910–11	68	Rangers	52	Aberdeen	48	Falkirk	54
1911–12	68	Rangers	51	Celtic	45	Clyde	42
1912–13	68	Rangers	53	Celtic	49	Hearts	41
1913–14	76	Celtic	65	Rangers	59	Hearts	54
1914–15	76	Celtic	65	Hearts	61	Rangers	50
1915–16	76	Celtic	67	Rangers	56	Morton§	51
1916–17	76	Celtic	64	Morton	54	Rangers	53
1917–18	68	Rangers	56	Celtic	55	Kilmarnock	43
1918–19	68	Celtic	58	Rangers	57	Morton	47
1919–20	84	Rangers	71	Celtic	68	Motherwell	57
1920–21	84	Rangers	76	Celtic	66	Hearts	56
1921–22	84	Celtic	67	Rangers	66	Raith R	56
1922–23	76	Rangers	55	Airdrieonians	50	Celtic	46
1923–24	76	Rangers	59	Airdrieonians	50	Celtic	41
1924–25	76	Rangers	60	Airdrieonians	57	Hibernian	52
1925–26	76	Celtic	58	Airdrieonians	50	Hearts	50
1926–27	76	Rangers	56	Motherwell	51	Celtic	49
1927–28	76	Rangers	60	Celtic	55	Motherwell	55
1928–29	76	Rangers	67	Celtic	51	Motherwell	50
1929–30	76	Rangers	60	Motherwell	55	Aberdeen	53
1930–31	76	Rangers	60	Celtic	58	Motherwell	56
1931–32	76	Motherwell	66	Rangers	61	Celtic	48
1932–33	76	Rangers	62	Motherwell	59	Hearts	50
1933–34	76	Rangers	66	Motherwell	62	Celtic	47
1934–35	76	Rangers	55	Celtic	52	Hearts	50
1935–36	76	Celtic	66	Rangers	61	Aberdeen	61
1936–37	76	Rangers	61	Aberdeen	54	Celtic	52
1937–38	76	Celtic	61	Hearts	58	Rangers	49
1938–39	76	Rangers	59	Celtic	48	Aberdeen	46
1946–47	60	Rangers	46	Hibernian	44	Aberdeen	39
1947–48	60	Hibernian	48	Rangers	46	Partick Th	36
1948–49	60	Rangers	46	Dundee	45	Hibernian	39
1949–50	60	Rangers	50	Hibernian	49	Hearts	43
1950–51	60	Hibernian	48	Rangers	38	Dundee	38
1951–52	60	Hibernian	45	Rangers	41	East Fife	37
1952–53	60	Rangers*	43	Hibernian	43	East Fife	39
1953–54	60	Celtic	43	Hearts	38	Partick Th	35
1954–55	60	Aberdeen	49	Celtic	46	Rangers	41
1955–56	68	Rangers	52	Aberdeen	46	Hearts	45
1956–57	68	Rangers	55	Hearts	53	Kilmarnock	42
1957–58	68	Hearts	62	Rangers	49	Celtic	46
1958–59	68	Rangers	50	Hearts	48	Motherwell	44
1959–60	68	Hearts	54	Kilmarnock	50	Rangers	42
1960–61	68	Rangers	51	Kilmarnock	50	Third Lanark	42
1961–62	68	Dundee	54	Rangers	51	Celtic	46
1962–63	68	Rangers	57	Kilmarnock	48	Partick Th	46
1963–64	68	Rangers	55	Kilmarnock	49	Celtic	47
1964–65	68	Kilmarnock*	50	Hearts	50	Dunfermline Ath	49
1965–66	68	Celtic	57	Rangers	55	Kilmarnock	45
1966–67	68	Celtic	58	Rangers	55	Clyde	46
1967–68	68	Celtic	63	Rangers	61	Hibernian	45
1968–69	68	Celtic	54	Rangers	49	Dunfermline Ath	45
1969–70	68	Celtic	57	Rangers	45	Hibernian	44
1970–71	68	Celtic	56	Aberdeen	54	St Johnstone	44
1971–72	68	Celtic	60	Aberdeen	50	Rangers	44
1972–73	68	Celtic	57	Rangers	56	Hibernian	45
1973–74	68	Celtic	53	Hibernian	49	Rangers	48
1974–75	68	Rangers	56	Hibernian	49	Celtic	45

*Won on goal average/difference.   †Held jointly after a 2–2 draw in the deciding match
‡Won on deciding match.   §Morton v Hearts played only once.

SECOND DIVISION TO 1974–75

1893–94	36	Hibernian	29	Cowlairs	27	Clyde	24
1894–95	36	Hibernian	30	Motherwell	22	Port Glasgow	20
1895–96	36	Abercorn	27	Leith Ath	23	Renton	21
1896–97	36	Partick Th	31	Leith Ath	27	Kilmarnock	21
1897–98	36	Kilmarnock	29	Port Glasgow	25	Morton	22
1898–99	36	Kilmarnock	32	Leith Ath	27	Port Glasgow	25
1899–1900	36	Partick Th	29	Morton	26	Port Glasgow	20
1900–01	36	St Bernard's	26	Airdrieonians	23	Abercorn	21
1901–02	44	Port Glasgow	32	Partick Th	31	Motherwell	26
1902–03	44	Airdrieonians	35	Motherwell	28	Ayr U	27
1903–04	44	Hamilton Acad	37	Clyde	29	Ayr U	28
1904–05	44	Clyde	32	Falkirk	28	Hamilton Acad	27
1905–06	44	Leith Ath	34	Clyde	31	Albion R	27
1906–07	44	St Bernard's	32	Vale of Leven	27	Arthurlie	27
1907–08	44	Raith R	30	Dumbarton§	27	Ayr U	27
1908–09	44	Abercorn	31	Raith R	28	Vale of Leven	28
1909–10	44	Leith Ath‡	33	Raith R	33	St Bernard's	27
1910–11	44	Dumbarton	31	Ayr U	27	Albion R	25
1911–12	44	Ayr U	35	Abercorn	30	Dumbarton	27
1912–13	52	Ayr U	34	Dunfermline Ath	33	East Stirling	32
1913–14	44	Cowdenbeath	31	Albion R	27	Dunfermline Ath	26
1914–15	52	Cowdenbeath**	37	St Bernard's	37	Leith Ath	37
1921–22	76	Alloa	60	Cowdenbeath	47	Armadale	45
1922–23	76	Queen's Park	57	Clydebank†	50	St Johnstone†	45
1923–24	76	St Johnstone	56	Cowdenbeath	55	Bathgate	44
1924–25	76	Dundee U	50	Clydebank	48	Clyde	47
1925–26	76	Dunfermline Ath	59	Clyde	53	Ayr U	52
1926–27	76	Bo'ness	56	Raith R	49	Clydebank	45
1927–28	76	Ayr U	54	Third Lanark	45	King's Park	44
1928–29	72	Dundee U	51	Morton	50	Arbroath	47
1929–30	76	Leith Ath*	57	East Fife	57	Albion R	54
1930–31	76	Third Lanark	61	Dundee U	50	Dunfermline Ath	47
1931–32	76	East Stirling*	55	St Johnstone	55	Raith R	46
1932–33	68	Hibernian	54	Queen of the S	49	Dunfermline Ath	47
1933–34	68	Albion R	45	Dunfermline Ath	44	Arbroath	44
1934–35	68	Third Lanark	52	Arbroath	50	St Bernard's	47
1935–36	68	Falkirk	59	St Mirren	52	Morton	48
1936–37	68	Ayr U	54	Morton	51	St Bernard's	48
1937–38	68	Raith R	59	Albion R	48	Airdrieonians	47
1938–39	68	Cowdenbeath	60	Alloa	48	East Fife	48
1946–47	52	Dundee	45	Airdrieonians	42	East Fife	31
1947–48	60	East Fife	53	Albion R	42	Hamilton Acad	40
1948–49	60	Raith R*	42	Stirling A	42	Airdrieonians	41
1949–50	60	Morton	47	Airdrieonians	44	St Johnstone	36
1950–51	60	Queen of the S*	45	Stirling A	45	Ayr U	36
1951–52	60	Clyde	44	Falkirk	43	Ayr U	39
1952–53	60	Stirling A	44	Hamilton Acad	43	Queen's Park	37
1953–54	60	Motherwell	45	Kilmarnock	42	Third Lanark	36
1954–55	60	Airdrieonians	46	Dunfermline Ath	42	Hamilton Acad	39
1955–56	72	Queen's Park	54	Ayr U	51	St Johnstone	49
1956–57	72	Clyde	64	Third Lanark	51	Cowdenbeath	45
1957–58	72	Stirling A	55	Dunfermline Ath	53	Arbroath	47
1958–59	72	Ayr U	60	Arbroath	51	Stenhousemuir	40
1959–60	72	St Johnstone	53	Dundee U	50	Queen of the S	49
1960–61	72	Stirling A	55	Falkirk	54	Stenhousemuir	50
1961–62	72	Clyde	54	Queen of the S	53	Morton	44
1962–63	72	St Johnstone	55	East Stirling	49	Norton	48
1963–64	72	Morton	67	Clyde	53	Arbroath	46
1964–65	72	Stirling A	59	Hamilton Acad	50	Queen of the S	45
1965–66	72	Ayr U	53	Airdrieonians	50	Queen of the S	49
1966–67	72	Morton	69	Raith R	58	Arbroath	57
1967–68	72	St Mirren	62	Arbroath	53	East Fife	40
1968–69	72	Motherwell	64	Ayr U	53	East Fife	47
1969–70	72	Falkirk	56	Cowdenbeath	55	Queen of the S	50

SCOTTISH LEAGUE HONOURS

1970–71	72	Partick Th	56	East Fife	51	Arbroath	46
1971–72	72	Dumbarton*	52	Arbroath	52	Stirling A	50
1972–73	72	Clyde	56	Dunfermline Ath	52	Raith R	47
1973–74	72	Airdrieonians	60	Kilmarnock	59	Hamilton Acad	55
1974–75	76	Falkirk	54	Queen of the S	53	Montrose	53

*Won on goal average/difference.   †Two points deducted for fielding an ineligible player.   ‡Won on deciding match.
§Two points deducted for registration irregularities.   **Declared Champions after a three-team play-off.

The following clubs were elected to the First Division: Clyde (1894, 1906), Partick Thistle (1897, 1900, 1902), Kilmarnock (1899), Airdrieonians (1903), Falkirk (1905), Aberdeen (1905), Hamilton Academicals (1905), Raith Rovers (1910), Ayr United (1913). There was a Third Division in Scotland for three seasons (1923–24 to 1925–26) but it was disbanded as so many of its clubs were in financial difficulties. Arthurlie won it in 1924, Nithsdale Wanderers in 1925 and Helensburgh were leading when it was suspended in 1926. The division was briefly resurrected as Division C after the war. Stirling Albion won it in 1947, East Stirling in 1948 and Forfar in 1949. From 1946–47 to 1955–56 inclusive, Divisions 1 and 2 were called Divisions A and B. Renton were expelled after four games in 1890–91 for playing v Edinburgh Saints, who included professional players. They were later re-admitted but resigned in 1897–98, being replaced by Hamilton. Bathgate and Arthurlie resigned in 1929. Bo'ness and Armadale were expelled in November 1932 for being unable to meet their £50 match guarantees. Third Lanark, founder members, dropped out in 1967 and ceased to exist. The following 18 clubs (not counting the short-lived Third Division) either failed re-election or chose not to re-apply: Abercorn, Broxburn, Cambuslang, Clackmannan, Clydebank (not the current club), Cowlairs, Dundee Wanderers, Edinburgh City, Leith Athletic, Linthouse, Lochgelly, Johnstone (not St Johnstone), King's Park, Northern, Port Glasgow, St Bernard's, Thistle and Vale of Leven. Former Third Division clubs no longer in the League are: Peebles Rovers, Dykehead, Solway Star, Helensburgh, Beith, Nithsdale Wanderers, Royal Albert and Mid-Annandale.

RELEGATIONS

	FROM PREMIER DIVISION	FROM DIVISION ONE
1975–76	Dundee, St Johnstone	Clyde, Dunfermline Ath
1976–77	Hearts, Kilmarnock	Falkirk, Raith R
1977–78	Ayr U, Clydebank	Alloa Ath, East Fife
1978–79	Hearts, Motherwell	Montrose, Queen of the S
1979–80	Dundee, Hibernian	Arbroath, Clyde
1980–81	Hearts, Kilmarnock	Berwick R, StirlingA
1981–82	Airdrieonians, Partick Th	East Stirling, Queen of the S
1982–83	Kilmarnock, Morton	Dunfermline Ath, Queen's Park
1983–84	Motherwell, St Johnstone	Alloa, Raith R
1984–85	Dumbarton, Morton	Meadowbank Th, St Johnstone
1985–86	*League reorganised, no relegation*	Alloa, Ayr U
1986–87	Clydebank, Hamilton Acad	Brechin C, Montrose
1987–88	Dunfermline Ath, Falkirk, Morton	Dumbarton, East Fife

FROM DIVISION ONE TO 1973–74

1921–22*	Clydebank, Dumbarton, Queen's Park	1951–52	Morton, Stirling A
1922–23	Albion R, Alloa Ath	1952–53	Motherwell, Third Lanark
1923–24	Clyde, Clydebank	1953–54	Airdrieonians, Hamilton Acad
1924–25	Ayr U, Third Lanark	1954–55	*No relegation*
1925–26	Clydebank, Raith R	1955–56	Clyde, Stirling A
1926–27	Dundee U, Morton	1956–57	Ayr U, Dunfermline Ath
1927–28	Bo'ness, Dunfermline Ath	1957–58	East Fife, Queen'sPark
1928–29	Raith R, Third Lanark	1958–59	Falkirk, Queen of the S
1929–30	Dundee U, St Johnstone	1959–60	Arbroath, Stirling A
1930–31	East Fife, Hibernian	1960–61	Ayr U, Clyde
1931–32	Dundee U, Leith Ath	1961–62	St Johnstone, Stirling A
1932–33	East Stirling, Morton	1962–63	Clyde, Raith R
1933–34	Cowdenbeath, Third Lanark	1963–64	East Stirling, Queen of the S
1934–35	Falkirk, St Mirren	1964–65	Airdrieonians, Third Lanark
1935–36	Airdrieonians, Ayr U	1965–66	Hamilton Acad,Morton
1936–37	Albion R, Dunfermline Ath	1966–67	Ayr U, St Mirren
1937–38	Dundee, Morton	1967–68	Motherwell, Stirling A
1938–39	Queen's Park, Raith R	1968–69	Arbroath, Falkirk
1946–47	Hamilton Acad, Kilmarnock	1969–70	Partick Th, Raith R
1947–48	Airdrieonians, Queen's Park	1970–71	Cowdenbeath, St Mirren
1948–49	Albion R, Morton	1971–72	Clyde, Dunfermline Ath
1949–50	Queen of the S, Stirling A	1972–73	Airdrieonians, Kilmarnock
1950–51	Clyde, Falkirk	1973–74	East Fife, Falkirk

*Season 1921–22, only 1 club promoted, 3 relegated.

There were no relegations at the end of season 1974–75 as the Scottish League was reconstructed into three divisions. Further reorganistion, increasing the size of the Premier Division to 12 teams from 10, took place in the summer of 1986, but the Premier Division reverted to 10 teams for the start of season 1988–89.

LEADING SCOTTISH SCORERS 1987–88

Listed in order League, League Cup, Scottish Cup, Total.

PREMIER DIVISION

	L	LC	SC	T
A. McCoist (Rangers)	31	6	1	38
T. Coyne (Dundee)	33	4	0	37
J. Robertson (Hearts)	26	3	2	31
A. Walker (Celtic)	26	3	2	31
K. Wright (Dundee)	15	3	1	19
F. McAvennie (Celtic)	15	0	3	18
J. Colquhoun (Hearts)	15	0	1	16
I. Ferguson (Dundee U)	11	2	2	15
I. Durrant (Rangers)	10	3	2	15
D. Dodds (Aberdeen)	9	2	4	15
C. Robertson (Dunfermline Ath)	13	1	0	14
J. Bett (Aberdeen)	10	3	0	13
W. Stark (Celtic)	8	3	2	13
P. Kane (Hibernian)	10	2	0	12
M. Paatelainen (Dundee U)	9	0	2	11
P. Chalmers (St Mirren)	10	0	0	10
W. Falconer (Aberdeen)	8	1	1	10
J. Miller (Aberdeen)	7	3	0	10
(Inc. 3 Lge for Celtic)				
C. Baptie (Falkirk)	9	0	0	9
S. Cowan (Motherwell)	9	0	0	9

SECOND DIVISION

	L	LC	SC	T
J. Sludden (Ayr U)	31	0	1	32
H. Templeton (Ayr U)	23	1	3	27
J. Brogan (Stirling A)	23	1	0	24
T. Walker (Ayr U)	19	2	1	22
G. Buckley (Berwick R)	17	0	1	18
(Inc 15 Lge, 1 SC for Brechin C)				
P. O'Brien (Queen's Park)	17	1	0	18
W. Watters (St Johnstone)	16	0	2	18
P. Rutherford (Alloa)	14	0	0	14
A. McKenna (Arbroath)	13	1	0	14
S. Johnston (St Johnstone)	11	1	2	14
T. Coyle (St Johnstone)	13	0	0	13
C. Gibson (Stirling A)	13	0	0	13
S. Sorbie (Alloa)	12	1	0	13
R. Grant (Cowdenbeath)	11	1	1	13
T. Ward (East Stirling)	8	2	3	13
R. Forrest (Arbroath)	12	0	0	12
G. Murray (East Stirling)	9	0	3	12
B. Cleland (Stranraer)	8	0	4	12
H. Mackay (Montrose)	11	0	0	11
A. Graham (Albion R)	10	0	1	11

FIRST DIVISION

	L	LC	SC	T
G. Dalziel (Raith R)	25	1	0	26
C. Harris (Raith R)	20	2	0	22
(Inc. 6 Lge for Hamilton Acad)				
D. MacCabe (Airdrieonians)	20	1	0	21
K. Macdonald (Forfar Ath)	20	1	0	21
J. Hughes (Queen of the S)	17	1	0	18
C. McGlashan (Clyde)	16	0	2	18
D. Walker (Clyde)	16	2	0	18
E. Gallagher (Partick Th)	13	0	5	18
P. Hunter (East Fife)	17	0	0	17
C. Harkness (Kilmarnock)	16	0	1	17
G. Scott (Forfar Ath)	15	0	1	16
(Inc 4 Lge, 1 SC for Hamilton Acad)				
C. Campbell (Airdrieonians)	15	0	0	15
O. Coyle (Dumbarton)	14	0	0	14
J. McGachie (Meadowbank Th)	14	0	0	14
A. Willock (Clyde)	13	0	1	14
A. McGonigal (Meadowbank Th)	12	0	0	12
D. Roseburgh (Meadowban Th)	12	0	0	12
J. Mailer (Clyde)	11	1	0	12
T. Bryce (Clydebank)	10	1	1	12
M. Conroy (Clydebank)	11	0	0	11

LEADING LEAGUE SCORERS SINCE 1946–47

Figures not available for Division C 1946–47 to 1948–49.

1946–47 Division A: R. Mitchell (Third Lanark) 22. Division B: R. Flavell (Airdrieonians) 38.
1947–48 Division A: A. Aikman (Falkirk) 20. Division B: H. Morris (East Fife) 41.
1948–49 Division A: A. Stott (Dundee) 30. Division B: W. Penman (Raith R) 35.
1949–50 Division A: W. Bauld (Hearts) 30. Division B: N. Mochan (Morton) 24.
1950–51 Division A: L. Reilly (Hibernian) 22. Division B: P. McKay (Dundee U) 34.
1951–52 Division A: L. Reilly (Hibernian) 27. Division B: W. McPhail (Clyde) 36.
1952–53 Division A: L. Reilly (Hibernian) & C. Fleming (East Fife) 30. Division B: J. Cunningham (Alloa) 25.
1953–54 Division A: J. Wardhaugh (Hearts) 27. Division B: I. Rodger (St Johnstone) 30.
1954–55 Division A: W. Bauld (Hearts) 21. Division B: H. Baird (Airdrieonians) 34.
1955–56 Division A: J. Wardhaugh (Hearts) 28. Division B: J. Coyle (Dundee U) 41.
1956–57 Division 1: H. Baird (Airdrieonians) 33. Division 2: P. Keogh (Clyde) 35.
1957–58 Division 1: J. Wardhaugh & J. Murray (Hearts) 28. Division 2: P. Price (Ayr U) 46.
1958–59 Division 1: J. Baker (Hibernian) 25. Division 2: D. Easson (Arbroath) 45.
1959–60 Division 1: J. Baker (Hibernian) 42. Division 2: J. Liddell (St Johnstone) 28.
1960–61 Division 1: A. Harvey (Third Lanark) 42. Division 2: J. Coburn (Forfar Ath) & D. Moran (Falkirk) 29.
1961–62 Division 1: A. Gilzean (Dundee) 24. Division 2: P. Smith (Alloa) 29.
1962–63 Division 1: J. Millar (Rangers) 27. Division 2: A. McGraw (Morton) 30.
1963–64 Division 1: A. Gilzean (Dundee) 32. Division 2: K. Bowron (Berwick R) 34.
1964–65 Division 1: J. Forrest (Rangers) 30. Division 2: W. Forsyth (Hamilton Acad) 33.
1965–66 Division 1: J. McBride (Celtic) & A. Ferguson (Dunfermline Ath) 31. Division 2: T. Murray (Airdrieonians) 33.
1966–67 Division 1: S. Chalmers (Celtic) 21. Division 2: J. Mason (Morton) 35.
1967–68 Division 1: R. Lennox (Celtic) 32. Division 2: D. Bruce (Arbroath) 32.
1968–69 Division 1: K. Cameron (Dundee U) 26. Division 2: J. Deans (Motherwell) 29.
1969–70 Division 1: C. Stein (Rangers) 24. Division 2: J. Dickson (Cowdenbeath) 28.
1970–71 Division 1: H. Hood (Celtic) 22. Division 2: K. Wilson (Dumbarton) 28.
1971–72 Division 1: J. Harper (Aberdeen) 33. Division 2: K. Wilson (Dumbarton) 38.
1972–73 Division 1: A. Gordon (Hibernian) 27. Division 2: B. Third (Montrose) 28.
1973–74 Division 1: J. Deans (Celtic) 26. Division 2: I. Fleming (Kilmarnock) 32.
1974–75 Division 1: A. Gray (Dundee U) & W. Pettigrew (Motherwell) 20. Division 2: J. Reid (Queen of the S) 27.
1975–76 Premier Division: K. Dalglish (Celtic) 24. Division 1: J. Bourke (Dumbarton) & J. Whiteford (Falkirk) 17. Division 2: M. Lawson (Stirling A) 18.
1976–77 Premier Division: W. Pettigrew (Motherwell) 21. Division 1: W. Pirie (Dundee) 36. Division 2: J. F. Frye (Stranraer) 24.
1977–78 Premier Division: D. Johnstone (Rangers) 25. Division 1: W. Pirie (Dundee) 35. Division 2: J. F. Frye (Stranraer) 27.
1978–79 Premier Division: A. Ritchie (Morton) 22. Division 1: B. Millar (Clydebank) 28. Division 2: B. Cleland (Albion R) 24.
1979–80 Premier Division: D. Somner (St Mirren) 25. Division 1: A. Clark (airdrieonians) & J. Brogan (St Johnstone) 22. Division 2: I. M. Campbell (Brechin C) 25.
1980–81 Premier Division: F. McGarvey (Celtic) 23. Division 1: A. McCoist (St Johnstone) 22. Division 2: S. Hancock (Stenhousemuir) 20.
1981–82 Premier Division: G. McCluskey (Celtic) 21. Division 1: B. Millar (Clydebank) & W. Irvine (Motherwell) 20. Division 2: D. Masterton (Clyde) 23.
1982–83 Premier Division: C. Nicholas (Celtic) 29. Division 1: J. Brogan (St Johnstone) 26. Division 2: I. M. Campbell (Brechin C) 23.
1983–84 Premier Division: B. McClair (Celtic) 23. Division 1: I. M. Campbell (Brechin C) 19. Division 2: J. Liddle (Forfar Ath) 22.
1984–85 Premier Division: F. McDougall (Aberdeen) 22. Division 1: G. McCoy (Falkirk) 22. Division 2: B. Slaven (Albion R) 27.
1985–86 Premier Division: A. McCoist (Rangers) 24. Division 1: J. Brogan (Hamilton Acad) 23. Division 2: J. Watson (Dunfermline Ath) 24.
1986–87 Premier Division: B. McClair (Celtic) 35. Division 1: R. Alexander (Morton) 23. Division 2: J. Sludden (Ayr U) 26.
1987–88 Premier Division: T. Coyne (Dundee) 33. Division 1: G. Dalziel (Raith R) 25. Division 2: J. Sludden (Ayr U) 31.

SCOTTISH LEAGUE ATTENDANCES 1987–88

PREMIER DIVISION

Club	League Position	Home Average 1987–88	Home Average 1986–87	Difference
Aberdeen	4	13,460	12,595	+865
Celtic	1	33,199	25,311	+7,888
Dundee	7	8,595	7,513	+1,082
Dundee United	5	10,462	10,432	+30
Dunfermline Ath*	11	9,245	4,145	+5,100
Falkirk	10	6,659	6,274	+385
Heart of Midlothian	2	16,633	14,531	+2,102
Hibernian	6	11,589	9,154	+2,435
Morton*	12	4,933	1,932	+3,001
Motherwell	8	6,659	5,397	+1,262
Rangers	3	38,568	36,152	+2,416
St Mirren	9	7,386	5,865	+1,521

FIRST DIVISION

Club	League Position	Home Average 1987–88	Home Average 1986–87	Difference
Airdrieonians	6	1,414	1,430	−16
Clyde	9	1,051	914	+137
Clydebank†	3	1,063	3,181	−2,118
Dumbarton	12	836	1,077	−241
East Fife	11	980	1,250	−270
Forfar Athletic	4	739	877	+138
Hamilton Acad.†	1	2,043	4,238	−2,195
Kilmarnock	10	1,846	1,898	−52
Meadowbank Th*	2	734	411	+323
Partick Thistle	8	1,972	1,756	+216
Queen of the South	7	1,282	1,742	−460
Raith Rovers*	5	2,109	1,436	+673

*Promoted at the end of the previous season.
†Relegated at the end of the previous season.

SECOND DIVISION

Club	League Position	Home Average 1987–88	Home Average 1986–87	Difference
Albion Rovers	12	358	497	−139
Alloa	7	570	577	−7
Arbroath	9	587	475	+112
Ayr United	1	2,796	1,553	+1,243
Berwick Rangers	13	448	380	+68
Brechin City+	4	474	612	−138
Cowdenbeath	11	268	383	−115
East Stirlingshire	6	354	345	+9
Montrose+	8	420	648	−228
Queen'sPark	3	610	538	+72
St Johnstone	2	1,946	1,074	+872
Stenhousemuir	10	358	365	−7
Stirling Albion	5	760	725	+35
Stranraer	14	493	525	−32

SCOTTISH LEAGUE ATTENDANCES SINCE 1961–62

Season	Matches	Div 1	Div 2		Total
1961–62	648	3 411 129	576 659		3 987 788
1962–63	648	3 043 567	590 452		3 634 019
1963–64	648	2 962 114	498 309		3 460 423
1964–65	648	2 908 508	350 788		3 259 296
1965–66	648	2 667 380	346 432		3 013 812
1966–67	686	2 836 762	405 620		3 242 382
1967–68	648	2 869 815	345 280		3 215 095
1968–69	648	3 060 783	334 747		3 395 530
1969–70	648	3 045 994	371 919		3 417 913
1970–71	648	2 893 652	412 566		3 306 218
1971–72	648	3 132 141	484 241		3 616 382
1972–73	648	2 816 106	467 763		3 283 869
1973–74	648	2 452 562	451 107		2 903 669
1974–75	648	2 673 655	445 656		3 119 311

Season	Matches	Premier Div	Div 1	Div 2	Total
1975–76	544	2 422 833	451 153	140 391	3 014 377
1976–77	726	2 131 848	636 410	208 861	2 977 119
1977–78	726	2 356 440	790 111	268 830	3 415 381
1978–79	726	2 324 799	538 735	249 791	3 113 325
1979–80	726	2 225 650	599 958	205 452	3 031 060
1980–81	726	1 759 856	601 152	166 175	2 527 183
1981–82	726	1 704 140	512 242	151 675	2 368 057
1982–83	726	1 859 856	474 879	140 709	2 475 444
1983–84	726	2 019 949	321 749	156 078	2 497 776
1984–85	726	1 949 788	366 785	188 283	2 504 856
1985–86	726	2 260 411	351 610	255 831	2 837 852
1986–87	801	3 094 224	402 236	180 733	3 677 193
1987–88	801	3 682 604	353 578	203 481	4 239 663

SCOTTISH CUP 1987–88

FIRST ROUND

ALBION R (0)1 ST JOHNSTONE (0)1 (5.12.87, 800)
Albion R: Tracey; Lennon, McGowan, Ahern, Gallagher, Chapman, Teevan, Rodgers, Graham, D. McDonald, T. McDonald, Mearns. **Scorer:** Graham.
St Johnstone: Balavage; K. Thomson, Smith, Barron McKillop, Johnston, G. Thompson, Coyle, Powell (Gavin), Watters, Heddle. **Scorer:** Watters.

MONTROSE (0)0 AYR U (2)2 (5.12.87, 850)
Montrose: Larter; Wright, McLelland, Sheran, Halley, Wallace, Allan, Brown, Mackay, Robertson, Murray.
Ayr U: Watson; McIntyre, Hughes, Furphy, McCracken, Evans, Templeton, Scott, Walker, Sludden, Cowell. **Scorers:** Templeton (pen), Sludden.

STIRLING ALBION (1)1 COWDENBEATH (1)2 (5.12.87, 400)
Stirling Albion: Graham; Wilson, Spence, Aitchison (Conway), McTeague, Maxwell (Tennant), Thompson, Anderson, C. Gibson, Kemp, Brogan. **Scorer:** Thompson.
Cowdenbeath: Allan; Williamson, Burnside, McGovern, D. Grant, Muir, Cherry, Hutt, R. Grant, MacKenzie, Leetion. **Scorers:** Hutt, R. Grant.

THREAVE ROVERS (0)0 STRANRAER (1)6 (5.12.87, 520)
Threave Rovers: Shanks; Middleton, Houston, Thomson, Gallacher (Connelly), McKittie, Findlay, Little, Maxwell, Bendall, Prentice (Rudd).
Stranraer: McLafferty; McIntyre, Day, Watt, Carson, Wilson, McQueen, McNiven, Cleland, McDonald, Knox. **Scorers:** McNiven, McQueen, Cleland 3, McDonald.

VALE OF LEITHEN (1)2 BRECHIN C (3)3 (5.12.87, 200)
Vale of Leithen: McDermott; Gary Darling, Graham (Ross), Graham Darling, Bird, Smith, W. Cormack, Thorpe, Hogarth, Spence, B. Cormack (Myatt). **Scorers:** Spence, B. Cormack.
Brechin C: Lawrie; Watt, Candlish, Brown, Stevens, Taylor, Gallacher, Adam, Paterson (Lees), Scott, Buckley (Bourke). **Scorers:** Buckley, Candlish, Gallacher.

INVERNESS CAL (1)1 EAST STIRLING (1)1 (12.12.87, 1311)
Inverness Caledonian: Morrison; Davidson, Mann, Hercher, Summers, Bellshaw, Docherty, Lisle, Urquhart, Duff, Robertson (MacDonald). **Scorer:** Lisle.
East Stirling: C. Kelly; Gilchrist, Russell, D. Wilcox, P. Kelly (C. Grant), Woods, A. Grant, O'Brien, Ward, Harvey, Murray (Irvine). **Scorer:** Ward.

FIRST ROUND REPLAYS

ST JOHNSTONE (2)2 ALBION R (0)0 (8.12.87, 1447)
St Johnstone: Balavage; K. Thomson, Smith, Barron McKillop, Johnston, G. Thompson, Coyle, Powell (Maskrey) Watters, Heddle. **Scorers:** McKillop, Powell.
Albion R: Tracey; Lennon, McGowan, Ahern, Gallagher, Chapman, Teevan, Rodgers, Graham, McGuire, Mearns.

EAST STIRLING (1)2 INVERNESS CAL (1)1 (21.12.87, 400)
East Stirling: C. Kelly; Gilchrist, Russell, D. Wilcox, P. Kelly, Woods, A. Grant, O'Brien, Ward, Harvey, Murray.
Scorers: D. Wilcox (Pen), Murray.
Inverness Caledonian: Morrison; Davidson, Mann, Hercher, Summers, Bellshaw, Docherty, Gibson, Urquhart,

Duff, Robertson (MacDonald). **Scorer:** MacDonald.

SECOND ROUND

BERWICK R (0)0 BRECHIN C (0)1 (9.1.88, 300)
Berwick R: Donaldson; Moyes, Fleming, Marshall, Douglas, Leitch (K. Buckley), Cameron, Thompson, Sokoluk, Lytwyn, Alexander.
Brechin C: Lawrie; Watt, Candlish, Inglis, Stevens, Hamilton, Lees, Adam Paterson, Scott (Taylor), Buckley (Gallacher). **Scorer:** Taylor.

BUCKIE THISTLE (0)2 EAST STIRLING (0)3 (9.1.88, 650)
Buckie Th: Innes; Morrison (G. Anderson), Ewen, Pirie, Buchanan, McPherson, Mason, Barclay, Whyte, Yule, Loch (D. Anderson). **Scorers:** Buchanan, McPherson.
East Stirling: C. Kelly; C. Grant, Russell, D. Wilcox, G. Wilcox (Wilson), Woods, A. Grant, O'Brien, Ward, Harvey, Murray. **Scorers:** O'Brien, Murray, Ward.

FRASERBURGH (1)2 ST JOHNSTONE (1)5 (9.1.88, 1500)
Fraserburgh: Clark; Cormack, Sim, Young, A. Thomson, Ellis (Smith), J. Thomson, Duncan, Beagrie, B. Thomson, Chalmers. **Scorers:** J. Thomson, B. Thomson.
St Johnstone: Balavage; K. Thomson, McVicar, Barron, McKillop, Johnston, G. Thompson (McGurn), Coyle, Maskrey, Watters (Powell), Heddle. **Scorers:** Maskrey, Watters, Johnstone 2, Powell.

GALA FAIRYDEAN (0)3 CIVIL SERVICE STROLLERS (0)0 (9.1.88, 250)
Gala Fairydean: Miller; Mann, Loughran, Dick, Anderson, Thomson, R. Frizzell (Malone), Notman, Lothian, I. Frizzell, Ainslie. **Scorers:** Loughran, Malone, I. Frizzell.
Civil Service Strollers: Higgins; Dargo, Burns, McLelland, M. Tulloch, Wood, Keenan (Givan), L. Tulloch, Renwick, Turner, Hutton (Collins).

QUEEN'S PARK (0)2 AYR U (0)3 (9.1.88, 2739)
Queen's Park: Monaghan; Boyle, McLaughlin, P. McLean, McNamee, Hendry, Caven, Armstrong (Elliot), O'Brien, MacKenzie, Crooks (Martin). **Scorers:** Hendry, Martin.
Ayr U: Watson; McCann, Hughes, Furphy, McCracken, Evans (McAllister), Templeton, Scott, Walker, Sludden, Cowell (Wilson). **Scorers:** Templeton 2, McAllister.

STENHOUSEMUIR (1)1 ARBROATH (0)1 (9.1.88, 500)
Stenhousemuir: Keith; Cairney, Gillen, Buchanan, McAra, Erwin, Condie, McCafferty, Elliott, Thomson, Walker. **Scorer:** Elliott.
Arbroath: Jackson; Mitchell, Mackie, R. Anderson, Hill (Burnside), P. Anderson, Forrest, Brannigan, McKenna, Fotheringham, Richardson. **Scorer:** Mackie.

STRANRAER (3)6 KEITH (1)2 (9.1.88, 500)
Stranraer: McLafferty; McIntyre, Hay (Day), Watt, Carson, Wilson, McQueen, McNiven, Cleland, McDonald (McNab), Knox. **Scorers:** Knox, McNiven 2, McDonald, Cleland, McQueen.
Keith: Thain; McKay, Wilson, Masson, Wisely, Girling (Forbes), Maver, Matheson, Barbour, Cowie, Pirie (Yeats). **Scorer:** Masson 2.

ALLOA (0)0 COWDENBEATH (0)1 (10.1.88, 500)
Alloa: Lowrie; Marshall (Smith), Haggart, Millen, McCulloch, Love, Findley (Wilkie), Donaldson, Rutherford, Sorbie, Nelson.
Cowdenbeath: Allan; Williamson, Burnside, McGovern, D. Grant, Muir, Cherry, Hutt, R. Grant, MacKenzie, Hepburn. **Scorer:** MacKenzie.

SECOND ROUND REPLAY

ARBROATH (0)1 STENHOUSEMUIR (1)1 aet
(12.1.88, 575)
Arbroath: Jackson; Mitchell, Jack, Phillip, Burnside (Mackie), P. Anderson, Forrest, Brannigan, Kerr (McKenna), Fotheringham, Richardson. **Scorer:** Mackie.
Stenhousemuir: Keith; Cairney, Gillen, Buchanan, McAra, Erwin, McIntosh (Jamieson), McCafferty, Elliott, Condie, Walker (Quinn). **Scorer:** McAra.

SECOND ROUND, SECOND REPLAY

STENHOUSEMUIR (0)0 ARBROATH (0)1
(Muirton Park, 18.1.88, 707)
Stenhousemuir: Keith; Cairney, Gillen, Buchanan, Thomson, Erwin, Condie, McCafferty, Elliott, Beaton, Walker.
Arbroath: Jackson; Mitchell, Jack, R. Anderson, Mackie, P. Anderson, Forrest, Brannigan, Kerr, Fotheringham, Morrison. **Scorer:** Fotheringham.

THIRD ROUND

ARBROATH (0)0 DUNDEE U (3)7 (30.1.88, 5905)
Arbroath: Jackson; Mitchell, Laing, R. Anderson, Mackie, P. Anderson, Forrest, Brannigan, McKenna (Kerr), Fotheringham, Morrison (Burnside).
Dundee U: Thomson; Bowman, Malpas, McInally, Hegarty (Clark), Narey, Bannon, J. A. Irvine, Paatelainen (Ferguson), French, Redford. **Scorers:** Redford, Malpas, Paatelainen, J. A. Irvine 2, Bannon, French.

CELTIC (1)1 STRANRAER (0)0 (30.1.88, 21,625)
Celtic: Bonner; Morris, Whyte, Aitken, Baillie, Grant, Miller, McStay, McAvennie, Walker, Burns. **Scorer:** McAvennie.
Stranraer: McLafferty; McIntyre, Day, Watt, Carson, Wilson (McCabe), McQueen (Coyle), McNiven, Cleland, McDonald, Knox.

CLYDE (0)0 COWDENBEATH (0)0 (30.1.88, 965)
Clyde: Atkins; McFarlane, Napier, Donnelly, Flexney, Clark, Willock, Millar, McGlashan, Walker (McEntaggart), Mailer (Quinn).
Cowdenbeath: Allan; Williamson, Burnside, Herd, Young, Miller, Cherry, Leetion, R. Grant, MacKenzie, Hepburn.

DUMBARTON (0)0 HIBERNIAN (0)0 (30.1.88, 7000)
Dumbarton: Arthur; Montgomerie, Cranmer, Martin, McCahill, Cairns, Docherty (McGowan), J. Rooney, McCoy, Houston, Coyle.
Hibernian: Goram; Sneddon, Mitchell, Watson (May), Rae, Hunter, Kane, Orr, McCluskey (McGovern), Collins, Weir.

DUNDEE (0)0 BRECHIN C (0)0 (30.1.88, 5040)
Dundee: Geddes; Forsyth, McKinlay, Shannon, Smith, Glennie (MacFarlane), Harvey, Rafferty, Wright, Coyne, Angus (Campbell).
Brechin C: Lawrie; Watt, Candlish, Inglis, Stevens, Hamilton, Wilkie, Brown, Paterson, Scott, Buckley.

DUNFERMLINE ATH (0)1 AYR U (0)1 (30.1.88, 8484)
Dunfermline Ath: Westwater; Holt, R. Smith, McCathie, Riddell, Beedie (Morrison), M. Smith, Jack, T. Smith, C. Robertson, Kirkwood. **Scorer:** Jack.

Ayr U: Watson; McIntyre (Wilson), Hughes, Furphy, McAllister, Evans, Templeton, Scott, Walker, Sludden, Cowell. **Scorer:** Walker.

EAST FIFE (0)1 AIRDRIEONIANS (2)2 (30.1.88, 1484)
East Fife: Charles; Connor, Pittman, Perry, McDowall, McLaren, Blair, McCafferty, Hunter, McNaughton, Scott (Reid). **Scorer:** Perry.
Airdrieonians: Martin; MacKinnon, Black, McKeown, Lawrie, Moore, Parlane (Campbell), Hughes, MacCabe, McDonald, Christie. **Scorers:** Lawrie, Parlane.

FALKIRK (1)1 HEARTS (1)3 (30.1.88, 16,000)
Falkirk: Marshall; MacLeod, Dempsey (Grant), Romaines, Burgess, Manley, McWilliams, Nicol, Baptie, Conn, Stewart (McNair). **Scorer:** Romaines.
Hearts: Smith; Kidd (I. Jardine), Whittaker, Berry, Galloway, McPherson, MacKay, Black, Robertson, Colquhoun, Foster. **Scorers:** Robertson 2, Foster.

GALA FAIRYDEAN (2)3 EAST STIRLING (2)5 (30.1.88, 1351)
Gala Fairydean: Miller; Mann, Loughran, Dick, Anderson (Collins), Thomson, R. Frizzell, Notman, Lothian (Malone), I. Frizzell, Ainslie. **Scorers:** Lothian, Notman, I. Frizzell.
East Stirling: C. Kelly; Gilchrist, Russell, D. Wilcox, P. Kelly, Woods, Irvine, O'Brien, Ward, Harvey (G. Wilcox), Murray. **Scorers:** Murray, Irvine 3, Ward.

MOTHERWELL (0)0 KILMARNOCK (0)0 (30.1.88, 6488)
Motherwell: Duncan; Wishart, Philliben, Paterson, McAdam, Boyd, Smith, Farningham, Cowan, Kirk (Gahagan), Mair.
Kilmarnock: McCulloch; McLean, Robertson, Davidson, Martin, McConville, Houston (McInnes) Cuthbertson, Harkness, Gilmour, Bryson.

QUEEN OF THE S (0)1 MORTON (1)2 (30.1.88, 2454)
Queen of the S: Davidson; Bain, Sim, Docherty, Oliver, Mills, Reid, Sinclair, Hughes (Pelosi), Robertson, Moore. **Scorer:** Docherty (pen).
Morton: Wylie; O'Hara, Holmes, Hunter, MacDonald, Margaard, D. Robertson, Christensen, Alexander, John Boag, Jim Boag (J. Robertson). **Scorers:** D. Roberston, Alexander (pen).

ST JOHNSTONE (0)0 ABERDEEN (0)1 (30.1.88, 10,000)
St Johnstone: Balavage; K. Thomson, McVicar, Barron, McKillop, Johnston, G. Thompson, Coyle, Maskrey, Watters (Powell), Heddle (McGurn).
Aberdeen: Leighton; McKimmie, Falconer, Connor, McLeish, Miller, C. Nicholas, Bett, Hewitt (Jones), P. Nicholas, Hackett. **Scorer:** Connor.

ST MIRREN (0)0 CLYDEBANK (0)3 (30.1.88, 6142)
St Mirren: Money; Wilson, D. Hamilton, Fitzpatrick, B. Hamilton, Winnie, Lambert, Ferguson, Davies (Chalmers), McDowall (Conroy), Cameron.
Clydebank: Gallacher; Shanks, Rodger, Maher, Auld, Irons, Davies, Bryce (Harvey), Eadie, Wright, Charnley. **Scorers:** Eadie 2, Wright.

HAMILTON A (2)2 MEADOWBANK T (0)0 (31.1.88, 6142)
Hamilton A: Ferguson; McKee, Martin, Jamieson, Collins, Fairlie, Weir, Scott, Sprott, McCabe. **Scorers:** Scott, McCabe (pen).
Meadowbank T: McQueen; Irvine, Armstrong, Boyd, Tierney, Prentice, Logan, Park, Callachan (McGonigal), Roseburgh, McGachie.

FORFAR ATH (0)1 PARTICK T (0)1 (3.2.88, 1332)
Forfar Ath: Kennedy; Lorimer, Hamill, Brazil, Morris, Brewster, Blackie, S. Clarke, J. Clarke, Morton (Ward), Macdonald. Scorer: J. Clark.
Partick T: McLean; Dinnie, Workman, Purdie, McGhee, McCormack (Law), Kelly, McGuire (Logan), McNaught, Mitchell, McDonald. Scorer: McNaught.

RAITH R (0)0 RANGERS (0)0 (8.2.88, 9500)
Raith R: McAlpine; McStay, Harrow, Fraser, Brash, Gibson, Simpson, Coyle, Harris, Dalziel (Lloyd), Sweeney.
Rangers: Woods; Nicholl, Bartram, Roberts, Wilkins, Brown, Cooper (Souness), Ferguson, McCoist, Durrant, Walters.

THIRD ROUND REPLAYS

HIBERNIAN (1)3 DUMBARTON (0)0 (2.2.88, 8000)
Hibernian: Goram; McIntyre, Mitchell, May, Rae, Hunter, Weir (McGovern), Orr, Kane, Collins, McBride (Tortolano). Scorers: Docherty (og), Tortolano, Orr.
Dumbarton: Arthur; Montgomerie, Cranmer, Martin, McCahill, Cairns, Docherty (MacIver), McCoy, Houston, J. Rooney, Coyle (McGowan).

AYR U (0)0 DUNFERMLINE ATH (1)2 (3.2.88, 11,712)
Ayr U: Watson; Scott (McCann), Hughes, Furphy, McAllister, Evans, Templeton, Wilson (McKenzie), Walker, Sludden, Cowell.
Dunfermline Ath: Westwater; G. Robertson, R. Smith, McCathie, Riddell, Beedie, M. Smith (Morrison), Jack, T. Smith (Watson), C. Robertson, Kirkwood. Scorers: Jack, T. Smith (pen).

BRECHIN C (0)0 DUNDEE (2)3 (3.2.88, 3000)
Brechin C: Lawrie; Watt, Candlish, Inglis, Stevens, Hamilton, Wilkie, Brown, Paterson (Bourke), Scott, Buckley (Gallacher).
Dundee: Geddes; MacFarlane, McKinlay, Shannon, Smith, Mennie, Harvey, Rafferty, Wright, Coyne, Angus. Scorers: Harvey 2, Wright.

COWDENBEATH (0)0 CLYDE (0)1 (3.2.88, 951)
Cowdenbeath: Allan; Williamson, Burnside, Herd, Young, Muir, Cherry, Leetion, R. Grant, MacKenzie, Hepburn (Cavanagh).
Clyde: Atkins; McFarlane, Napier, Tait, Flexney, Clark, Murphy, Miller, McGlashan (Quinn), Henderson, Willock (Walker). Scorer: Napier.

KILMARNOCK (0)1 MOTHERWELL (0)3 (3.2.88, 7591)
Kilmarnock: McCulloch; McLean, Robertson, Davidson, Martin, McConville, McInnes, Cuthbertson, Harkness, Gilmour, Bryson. Scorer: Harkness.
Motherwell: Duncan; Wishart, Philliben (McBride), Paterson, McAdam, Boyd, Smith, Farningham (Kirk), Cowan, Russell, Mair. Scorers: Mair, Farningham, McBride.

PARTICK T (2)3 FORFAR ATH (0)0 (10.2.88, 2450)
Partick T: McLean; Dinnie, Mitchell, Purdie, McGhie, McCormack, Kelly, Law, Gallagher (McGuire), McDonald, Dodds (Workman). Scorers: Gallagher, Dodds 2.
Forfar Ath: Kennedy; Lorimer, Hamill, Brazil, Smith, Brewster (J. Clark), Ward, S. Clarke, Blackie, Morton (Morris), Macdonald.

RANGERS (1)4 RAITH R (0)1 (10.2.88, 35,144)
Rangers: Woods; Gough, Bartram, Roberts, Wilkins, Brown (Souness), Nisbet, D. Ferguson, McCoist (Cooper),

Durrant, Walters. Scorers: Durrant 2 (1 pen), McCoist, Walters.
Raith R: McAlpine; McStay, Harrow, Fraser, Brash, Gibson (MacLeod), Simpson, Coyle, Harris, Lloyd (Marshall), Sweeney. Scorer: Lloyd.

FOURTH ROUND

AIRDRIEONIANS (0)0 DUNDEE U (1)2 (20.2.88, 6500)
Airdrieonians: Martin; MacKinnon, Black, McKeown, Lawrie, Moore, Campbell (Hughes), Lindsay, MacCabe, Parlane (Christie), McDonald.
Dundee U: Thomson; Bowman, Malpas, McInally, Hegarty, Narey, Bannon, Gallacher, Paatelainen, French, Redford. Scorers: Bannon, Hegarty.

CLYDEBANK (2)2 PARTICK T (1)2 (20.2.88, 5397)
Clydebank: Gallacher; Shanks, Rodger, Maher, Auld, Irons, Davies, Wright, Eadie, Bryce (Harvey), Dickson. Scorers: Bryce, Eadie.
Partick T: McLean; Dinnie (Workman), Mitchell, Purdie, McGhie, McCormack, Kelly, Law, Gallagher, McNaught, Dodds. Scorer: Gallagher 2.

DUNDEE (2)2 MOTHERWELL (0)0 (20.2.88, 7243)
Dundee: Geddes; Forsyth, McKinlay, MacFarlane, Smith, Glennie (Lawrence), Mennie, Rafferty, Wright, Coyne, Angus. Scorers: Angus, Rafferty.
Motherwell: Duncan; Wishart, Griffin, Paterson, McAdam (McBride), Boyd, Smith, Farningham (Russell), Cowan, Kirk, Mair.

DUNFERMLINE ATH (1)2 RANGERS (0)0 (20.2.88, 19,000)
Dunfermline Ath: McKellar; G. Robertson, R. Smith, McCathie, Andersen, Holt, M. Smith, Jack (Ferguson), Watson, C. Robertson, Beedie. Scorers: M. Smith, Watson.
Rangers: Woods; Gough, Bartram, Roberts, Wilkins, Brown, Cooper (Nisbet), D. Ferguson, Souness (Francis), Durrant, Walters.

EAST STIRLING (2)2 CLYDE (2)3 (20.2.88, 2000)
East Stirling: C. Kelly; Gilchrist (Laughlan), Russell, D. Wilcox, P. Kelly (McColl) Woods, A. Grant, O'Brien, McNeill, G. Wilcox, Irvine. Scorers: McNeill, O'Brien.
Clyde: Atkins; McFarlane, Napier, Tait, Flexney, Clark, Willock, Millar, McGlashan, Mailer (Quinn), McEntaggart. Scorers: McGlashan 2, Willock.

HAMILTON A (0)0 ABERDEEN (0)2 (20.2.88, 7270)
Hamilton A: A. Ferguson; McKee, Kerr (McCabe), Martin, Jamieson, Collins, Fairlie, Taylor, Scott, Sprott, Thomson (McDonald).
Aberdeen: Leighton; McKimmie, Robertson (Hewitt), Connor, McLeish, Miller, Dodds, Hackett (Jones), C. Nicholas, P. Nicholas. Falconer. Scorers: C. Nicholas, Dodds.

HEARTS (1)2 MORTON (0)0 (20.2.88, 13,646)
Hearts: Smith; Berry, Whittaker, Black, Galloway, McPherson, MacKay, I. Jardine (Burns), Robertson, Colquhoun (Moore), Clark. Scorers: Clark, MacKay.
Morton: Wylie; Collins, Holmes, Hunter, MacDonald, John Boag, D. Robertson, Christensen (J. Robertson), Alexander, Turner, Verlaque (O'Hara).

CELTIC (0)0 HIBERNIAN (0)0 (21.2.88, 30,537)
Celtic: Bonner; Morris, Rogan, Aitken, McCarthy, Baillie, Miller, McStay, McAvennie, McGhee, Grant (Stark).
Hibernian: Goram; Sneddon, Mitchell, May, Rae, Hunter, Weir, Orr, Kane, Collins, Evans.

SCOTTISH CUP

FOURTH ROUND REPLAYS

PARTICK T (2)4 CLYDEBANK (0)1 (23.2.88, 5564)
Partick T: MacLean; Dinnie, Mitchell, Purdie, McGhie, McCormack, Kelly (McGuire), Law, Gallagher, McNaught, Dodds. **Scorers:** Kelly, Gallagher 2, McNaught.
Clydebank: Gallacher; Shanks, Rodger (Dickson), Maher, Auld, Irons, Davies, Wright, Eadie, Bryce, Charnley (Harvey). **Scorer:** Davies.

HIBERNIAN (0)0 CELTIC (0)1 (23.2.88, 24,000)
Hibernian: Goram; Sneddon, Mitchell, Milne (Tortolano), Rae, Hunter, Weir, Orr, Kane, Collins, Evans (May).
Celtic: Bonner; Morris, Whyte, Aitken, McCarthy, Grant, Stark, McStay, McAvennie, McGhee (Miller), Burns. **Scorer:** Stark.

QUARTER-FINALS

ABERDEEN (2)5 CLYDE (0)0 (12.3.88, 12,000)
Aberdeen: Leighton; Grant, Falconer, Simpson (Connor), Irvine, Miller, Dodds, Bett, C. Nicholas, P. Nicholas, Jones (Edwards). **Scorers:** Dodds 3, Falconer, Edwards.
Clyde: Atkins; McFarlane, Napier, Donnelly, Flexney (McEntaggart), Clark, Willock, Millar, McGlashan, Walker, Tait (Murphy).

DUNDEE (0)0 DUNDEE U (0)0 (12.3.88, 19,355)
Dundee: Carson; Forsyth, McKinlay, Shannon, Smith, Saunders, Mennie (Lawrence), Rafferty, Wright, Coyne, Angus.
Dundee U: Bowman, Malpas, McInally, Hegarty, Narey, Bannon, Gallacher (Clark), Paatelainen (Ferguson), French, Redford.

HEARTS (2)3 DUNFERMLINE ATH (0)0 (12.3.88, 21,900)
Hearts: Smith; Burns, Whittaker, Black, Berry, McPherson, MacKay, I. Jardine (Sandison), Robertson, Colquhoun, Foster. **Scorers:** Colquhoun, Foster, MacKay.
Dunfermline Ath: Segers; G. Robertson, R. Smith, McCathie, Andersen (Donnelly), Holt, M. Smith, Jack, Watson, Beedie, Morrison.

PARTICK T (0)0 CELTIC (1)3 (12.3.88, 16,800)
Partick T: McLean; Dinnie, Mitchell, Purdie, McGhie, McCormack, Kelly (McGuire), McNaught, Gallagher, Law, Dodds (Workman).
Celtic: Bonner; Morris, Rogan, Aitken, Whyte, Burns, Stark, McStay, McAvennie, Walker, Miller. **Scorers:** Walker, Burns, Stark.

QUARTER-FINAL REPLAY

DUNDEE U (2)2 DUNDEE (0)2 (aet)
(15.3.88, 19,102)
Dundee U: Main; Bowman, McGinnis, McInally, Hegarty, Narey, Bannon, Gallacher, Ferguson (Clark), French, Redford. **Scorer:** Bannon 2.
Dundee: Carson; Forsyth, McKinlay (Harvey), Shannon, Smith, Saunders, Mennie, Rafferty, Wright, Coyne, Angus. **Scorer:** Harvey 2.

QUARTER-FINAL, SECOND REPLAY

DUNDEE (0)0 DUNDEE U (1)3 (Dens Park, 28.3.88, 19,152)
Dundee: Geddes; Forsyth, Mennie, Shannon (Harvey), Smith, Saunders, Lawrence, Rafferty, Wright, Coyne, Angus.
Dundee U: Thomson; Bowman, Malpas, McInally, Hegarty, Narey, Bannon, Gallacher, Paatelainen (Ferguson), J. McLeod (Clark), Redford. **Scorers:** J. McLeod, Redford (pen), Ferguson.

SEMI-FINALS

CELTIC (0)2 HEARTS (0)1 (Hampden Park, 9.4.88, 65,886)
Celtic: Bonner; Morris, Rogan, Aitken, Whyte, Burns, Stark, McStay, McAvennie, Walker, Miller (McGhee). **Scorers:** McGhee, Walker.
Hearts: Smith; Murray, Whittaker, Black, Galloway, McPherson, MacKay (I. Jardine), Berry, Foster (Clark), Colquhoun, Robertson. **Scorer:** Whittaker.

ABERDEEN (0)0 DUNDEE U (0)0 (Dens Park, 9.4.88, 20,488)
Aberdeen: Leighton; McKimmie, Robertson, Simpson, McLeish, Miller, Dodds, Bett, C. Nicholas, P. Nicholas, Hewitt.
Dundee U: Thomson; Bowman, Malpas, McInally, Hegarty, Narey, Bannon, Gallacher, French (Ferguson), J. McLeod (Clark), Redford.

SEMI-FINAL REPLAY

ABERDEEN (0)1 DUNDEE U (0)1 (aet)
(Dens Park, 13.4.88, 17,288)
Aberdeen: Leighton; McKimmie, Robertson, Simpson, McLeish, Miller, Dodds, Bett (Gray), C. Nicholas, P. Nicholas, Hewitt. **Scorer:** C. Nicholas.
Dundee U: Thomson; Clark, Malpas, McInally, Hegarty, Narey, Bannon, Gallacher, Paatelainan (Ferguson), J. McLeod (McGinnis), Redford. **Scorer:** Paatelainan.

SEMI-FINAL, SECOND REPLAY

ABERDEEN (0)0 DUNDEE U (0)1
(Dens Park, 20.4.88, 19,048)
Aberdeen: Leighton; McKimmie, Robertson, Simpson, McLeish, Miller, Dodds (Falconer), Bett, C. Nicholas, P. Nicholas, Hewitt.
Dundee U: Thomson; Bowman, Malpas, McInally, Hegarty, Narey, Bannon, Gallacher, Paatelainan (Clark), Ferguson, Redford. **Scorer:** Ferguson.

FINAL

CELTIC (0)2 DUNDEE U (0)1
(Hampden Park, 14.5.88, 74,000)
Celtic: McKnight; Morris, Rogan, Aitken, McCarthy, Whyte (Stark), Miller, McStay, McAvennie, Walker (McGhee), Burns. **Scorer:** McAvennie.
Dundee U: Thomson; Bowman, Malpas, McInally, Hegarty, Narey, Bannon, Gallacher, Paatelainen (Clark), Ferguson, McKinlay. **Scorer:** Gallacher.
Referee: Mr G. B. Smith (Edinburgh).

SCOTTISH CUP FINALS SINCE 1874

1873–74: QUEEN'S PARK 2, CLYDESDALE 0 (First Hampden, 21.3.74, 2500)
Queen's Park: Dickson; Taylor, Neill, Thomson, Campbell, Weir, Leckie, W. McKinnon, Lawrie, McNeil, A. McKinnon. **Scorers:** W. McKinnon, Leckie.
Clydesdale: Gardner; Wotherspoon, McArley, Henry, Raeburn, Anderson, Gibb, Wilson, Lang, McPherson, Kennedy.

1874–75: QUEEN'S PARK 3, RENTON 0 (First Hampden, 10.4.75, 7000)
Queen's Park: Neill; Taylor, Phillips, Campbell, Dickson, McNeil, Highet, W. McKinnon, A. McKinnon, Lawrie, Weir. **Scorers:** A. McKinnon, Highet, W. McKinnon.
Renton: Turnbull; A. Kennedy, McKay, Scallion, McGregor, Melville, McRae, M. Kennedy, J. Brown, Glen, L. Brown.

1875–76: QUEEN'S PARK 1, THIRD LANARK RV 1 (Hamilton Crescent, 11.3.76, 10,000)
Queen's Park: Dickson; Taylor, Neill, Campbell, Phillips, Lawrie, McGill, Highet, W. McKinnon, A. McKinnon, McNeil. **Scorer:** Highet.
Third Lanark: Wallace; Hunter, Watson, White, Davidson, Crichton, W. Drinnan, Scoular, Walker, Millar, McDonald. **Scorer:** Drinnan.

REPLAY: QUEEN'S PARK 2, THIRD LANARK RV 0 (Hamilton Crescent, 18.3.76, 6000)
Queen's Park: Dickson; Taylor, Neill, Campbell, Phillips, Highet, W. McKinnon, Hillcote, McNeil, McGill, Smith. **Scorer:** Highet 2.
Third Lanark: Unchanged.

1876–77: VALE OF LEVEN 1, RANGERS 1 (Hamilton Crescent, 17.3.77, 12,000)
Vale of Leven: Wood; A. McIntyre, Michie, Jamieson, A. McLintock, J. Ferguson, R. Paton, J. McGregor, McDougall, J. Baird, Lindsay. **Scorer:** Paton.
Rangers: Watt; Vallance, Gillespie, Ricketts, W. McNeil, M. McNeil, Watson, Dunlop, P. Campbell, Marshall, Hill. **Scorer:** McDougall (og).

REPLAY: VALE OF LEVEN 1, RANGERS 1 (aet, Hamilton Crescent, 7.4.77, 15,000)
Vale of Leven: Unchanged. **Scorer:** McDougall.
Rangers: Unchanged. **Scorer:** Dunlop.

REPLAY: VALE OF LEVEN 3, RANGERS 2 (First Hampden, 13.4.77, 8000)
Vale of Leven: Unchanged. **Scorers:** Watson (og), Baird, Paton.
Rangers: Unchanged. **Scorers:** P.Campbell, W.O'Neill.

1877–78: VALE OF LEVEN 1, THIRD LANARK RV 0 (First Hampden, 30.4.78, 5000)
Vale of Leven: Parlane; A. McLintock, A. McIntyre, J. McPherson, Jamieson, J. Ferguson, McFarlane, J. McGregor, James Baird, McDougall, J. Baird. **Scorer:** McDougall.
Third Lanark: Wallace; Somers, J. Hunter, Kennedy, McKenzie, Miller, A. Hunter, Lang, Peden, McCririck, Kay.

1878–79: VALE OF LEVEN 1, RANGERS 1 (First Hampden, 19.4.79, 6000)
Vale of Leven: Parlane; A. McLintock, A. McIntyre, J. McIntyre, J. McPherson, McFarlane, J. Ferguson, James Baird, P. McGregor, J. Baird, McDougall. **Scorer:** Ferguson.
Rangers: Gillespie; A. Vallance, T. Vallance, J. Drinnan, H. McIntyre, Hill, Dunlop, Steel, Struthers, P. Campbell, M. McNeil. **Scorer:** Struthers.
Vale of Leven were awarded the Cup when Rangers failed to turn up for the replay on 26 April 1879.

1879–80: QUEEN'S PARK 3, THORNLIEBANK 0 (First Cathkin, 21.2.80, 7000)
Queen's Park: Graham; Somers, Neill, Campbell, Davidson, Richmond, Weir, Highet, Ker, Kay, McNeil. **Scorers:** Highet 2, Ker.
Thornliebank: Cadden; Jamieson, Marshall, Henderson, McFetridge, A.Brannan, Clark, Wham, Anderson, Hutton, T.Brannan.

1880–81: QUEEN'S PARK 2, DUMBARTON 1 (Kinning Park, 26.3.81, 10,000)
Queen's Park: McCallum; Watson, Holm, Campbell, Davidson, Anderson, Fraser, Ker, Smith, McNeil, Kay. **Scorers:** McNeil, Kay.
Dumbarton: Kennedy; Hutcheson, Paton, J. Miller, Anderson, Meikleham, Brown, Lindsay, McAulay, McKinnon, Kennedy. **Scorer:** McAulay.
Dumbarton protested against Kay's goal, and a replay was ordered.

REPLAY: QUEEN'S PARK 3, DUMBARTON 1 (Kinning Park, 9.4.81, 10,000)
Queen's Park: Allan for McNeil. **Scorers:** Smith 2, Ker.
Dumbarton: Unchanged. **Scorer:** Meikleham.

1881–82: QUEEN'S PARK 2, DUMBARTON 2 (First Cathkin, 18.3.82, 12,000)
Queen's Park: McCallum; Watson, A. Holm, Davidson, J. Holm, Fraser, Anderson, Ker, Harrower, Richmond, Kay. **Scorer:** Harrower 2.
Dumbarton: Kennedy; Hutcheson, Paton, P. Miller, McKinnon, Brown, Meikleham, McAulay, Lindsay, Kennedy, J. Miller. **Scorers:** Brown, Meikleham.

REPLAY: QUEEN'S PARK 4, DUMBARTON 1 (First Cathkin, 1.4.82, 15,000)
Queen's Park: McCallum; Watson, Holm, Davidson, Campbell, Fraser, Anderson, Ker, Harrower, Richmond, Kay. **Scorers:** Richmond, Ker, Harrower, Kay.
Dumbarton: Kennedy; Hutcheson, Paton, P. Miller, Watt, Brown, Meikleham, McAulay, Lindsay, Kennedy, J. Miller. **Scorer:** J.Miller.

SCOTTISH CUP

1882–83: DUMBARTON 2, VALE OF LEVEN 2 (First Hampden, 31.3.83, 15,000)
Dumbarton: McAulay; Hutcheson, Paton, P. Miller, Lang, L. Keir, R. Sparrow Brown, R. Plumber Brown, J. Miller, Lindsay, McArthur. **Scorers:** Paton, McArthur.
Vale of Leven: A. McLintock, A. McIntyre, Forbes, McLeish, McPherson, Gillies, McCrae, Johnstone, Friel, Kennedy, McFarlane. **Scorers:** Johnstone, McCrae.

REPLAY: DUMBARTON 2, VALE OF LEVEN 1 (First Hampden, 7.4.83, 8000)
Dumbarton: Anderson for Lang. **Scorers:** Anderson, Sparrow Brown.
Vale of Leven: Unchanged. **Scorer:** Friel.

1883–84: *Queen's Park were awarded the Cup when Vale of Leven failed to turn up for the final on 23 February 1884 at First Cathkin. Queen's Park played a friendly with Third Lanark, winning 4–0, and it is thought that those players (below) were awarded Cup–winners' medals.*
McCallum; Arnott, A. Holm, Campbell, Gow, Christie, Allan, Smith, Harrower, Anderson, Watt.

1884–85: RENTON 0, VALE OF LEVEN 0 (Second Hampden, 21.2.85, 2500)
Renton: Lindsay; Hannah, A. McCall, Kelso, McKechnie, Barbour, Kelly, A. McIntyre, J. McCall, Thomson, Grant.
Vale of Leven: James Wilson; A. McIntyre, Forbes, Abraham, J. Wilson, Galloway, D. McIntyre, Ferguson, Johnstone, Gillies, Kennedy.

REPLAY: RENTON 3, VALE OF LEVEN 1 (Second Hampden, 28.2.85, 3500)
Renton: Unchanged. **Scorers:** J. McCall, McIntyre 2.
Vale of Leven: McPherson for J. Wilson. **Scorer:** Gillies.

1885–86: QUEEN'S PARK 3, RENTON 1 (First Cathkin, 13.2.86, 7000)
Queen's Park: Gillespie; Arnott, Watson, Campbell, Gow, Christie, Somerville, Hamilton, Allan, Harrower, Lambie. **Scorers:** Hamilton, Christie, Somerville.
Renton: Lindsay; Hannah, A. McCall, Kelso, McKechnie, Thomson, Grant, Barbour, J. McCall, H. McIntyre, Kelly. **Scorer:** Kelso.

1886–87: HIBERNIAN 2, DUMBARTON 1 (Second Hampden, 12.2.87, 10,000)
Hibernian: Tobin; Lundy, Fagan, McGhee, McGinn, McLaren, Lafferty, Groves, Montgomery, Clark, Smith. **Scorers:** Smith, Groves.
Dumbarton: McAulay; Hutcheson, Fergus, Miller, McMillan, Kerr, Brown, Robertson, Madden, Aitken, Jamieson. **Scorer:** Aitken.

1887–88: RENTON 6, CAMBUSLANG 1 (Second Hampden, 4.2.88, 10,000)
Renton: Lindsay; Hannah, A. McCall, Kelso, Kelly, McKechnie, McCallum, J. Campbell, D. Campbell, J. McCall, McNee. **Scorers:** D. Campbell, McCallum, McNee, McCall 2, J. Campbell.
Cambuslang: Dunn; Smith, Semple, McKay, J. Gourlay, Jackson, James Buchanan, John Buchanan, Plenderleith, H. Gourlay, J. Gourlay. **Scorer:** H. Gourlay.

1888–89: THIRD LANARK 3, CELTIC 0 (Second Hampden, 2.2.89, 17,000)
Third Lanark: Downie; Thomson, Rae, Lochhead, Auld, McFarlane, Marshall, Oswald Jr, Oswald Sr, Hannah, Johnstone. **Scorers:** Oswald Jr 2, Hannah.
Celtic: John Kelly; Gallacher, McKeown, W. Maley, James Kelly, McLaren, McCallum, Dunbar, Groves, Coleman, T. Maley.
Both teams agreed in advance (unknown to the crowd) to treat the game as a friendly, due to the snowbound pitch, and the SFA agreed to a replay.

REPLAY: THIRD LANARK 2, CELTIC 1 (Second Hampden, 9.2.89, 16,000)
Third Lanark: Unchanged. **Scorers:** Marshall, Oswald Jr.
Celtic: Unchanged. **Scorer:** McCallum.

1889–90: QUEEN'S PARK 1, VALE OF LEVEN 1 (First Ibrox, 15.2.90, 10,000)
Queen's Park: Gillespie; Arnott, Smellie, McAra, Stewart, Robertson, Berry, Gulliland, J. Hamilton, Sellar, Allan. **Scorer:** Hamilton.
Vale of Leven: Wilson; Murray, Whitelaw, Sharp, McNicol, Osborne, McLachlan, Rankin, Paton, Bruce, McMillan. **Scorer:** McLachlan.

REPLAY: QUEEN'S PARK 2, VALE OF LEVEN 1 (First Ibrox, 22.2.90, 14,000)
Queen's Park: Unchanged. **Scorers:** Hamilton, Stewart.
Vale of Leven: Unchanged. **Scorer:** Bruce.

1890–91: HEART OF MIDLOTHIAN 1, DUMBARTON 0 (Second Hampden, 7.2.91, 14,000)
Hearts: Fairbairn; Adams, Goodfellow, Begbie, McPherson, Hill, Taylor, Mason, Russell, Scott, Baird. **Scorer:** Russell.
Dumbarton: McLeod; Watson, Miller, McMillan, Bøyle, Keir, Taylor, Galbraith, Mair; McNaught, Bell.

1891–92: CELTIC 1, QUEEN'S PARK 0 (First Ibrox, 12.3.92, 40,000)
Celtic: Cullen; Reynolds, Doyle, W. Maley, Kelly, Dowds, McCallum, Brady, Madden, McMahon, Campbell. **Scorer:** Campbell.
Queen's Park: Baird; Sillars, Smellie, Gillespie, Robertson, Stewart, Gulliland, Waddell, J. Hamilton, Sellar, Lambie.
Because of crowd encroachment, it was agreed to replay the match.

REPLAY: CELTIC 5, QUEEN'S PARK 1 (First Ibrox, 9.4.92, 20,000)
Celtic: Gallacher for Madden. **Scorers:** Campbell 2, McMahon 2, Sillars (og).
Queen's Park: Scott for Smellie. **Scorer:** Waddell.

1892–93: QUEEN'S PARK 0, CELTIC 1 (First Ibrox, 25.2.93, 20,000)
Queen's Park: Baird; Sillars, Smellie, Gillespie, Robertson, Stewart, Waddell, Gulliland, J. Hamilton, Lambie, Sellar.
Celtic: Cullen; Doyle, Reynolds, Dunbar, Kelly, W.Maley, Campbell, McMahon, Madden, Towie, Blessington. **Scorer:** Towie.
Because of the frozen pitch, it was agreed to replay the match.
REPLAY: QUEEN'S PARK 2, CELTIC 1 (First Ibrox, 25.2.93, 15,000)
Queen's Park: McFarlane for Robertson. **Scorer:** Sellar 2.
Celtic: Unchanged. **Scorer:** Blessington.
1893–94: RANGERS 3, CELTIC 1 (Second Hampden, 17.2.94, 15,000)
Rangers: Haddow; N. Smith, Drummond, Marshall, A.McCreadie, Mitchell, Steel, H.McCreadie, Gray, McPherson, Barker. **Scorers:** H.McCreadie, Barker, McPherson.
Celtic: Cullen; Reynolds, Doyle, Curran, Kelly, W.Maley, Blessington, Madden, Cassidy, Campbell, McMahon. **Scorer:** Maley.
1894–95: ST BERNARD'S 2, RENTON 1 (First Ibrox, 20.4.95, 13,500)
St Bernard's: Sneddon; Hall, Foyers, McManus, Robertson, Murdoch, Laing, Paton, Oswald, Crossan, Clelland. **Scorer:** Clelland 2.
Renton: Dickie; Ritchie, A. McCall, Glen, McColl, Tait, McLean, Murray, Price, Gilfillan, Duncan. **Scorer:** Duncan.
1895–96: HEART OF MIDLOTHIAN 3, HIBERNIAN 1 (Logie Green, 14.3.96, 16,034)
Hearts: Fairbairn; McCartney, Mirk, Begbie, Russell, Hogg, McLaren, Baird, Michael, King, Walker. **Scorers:** Baird, Walker, Michael.
Hibernian: McColl; Robertson, Macfarlane, Breslin, Neill, Murphy, Murray, Kennedy, Groves, Smith, O'Neill. **Scorer:** O'Neill.
1896–97: RANGERS 5, DUMBARTON 1 (Second Hampden, 20.3.97, 15,000)
Rangers: Dickie; N. Smith, Drummond, Gibson, A. McCreadie, Mitchell, Low, McPherson, Miller, Hyslop, A. Smith. **Scorers:** Miller 2, Hyslop, McPherson, A.Smith.
Dumbarton: Docherty; D. Thomson, Mauchlan, Miller, Gillan, Sanderson, Mackie, W. Speedie, Hendry, W.Thomson, Fraser. **Scorer:** W.Thomson.
1897–98: RANGERS 2, KILMARNOCK 0 (Second Hampden, 26.3.98, 14,000)
Rangers: Dickie; N. Smith, Drummond, Gibson, Neil, Mitchell, Miller, McPherson, Hamilton, Hyslop, A. Smith. **Scorers:** A. Smith, Hamilton.
Kilmarnock: McAllan; Busby, Brown, McPherson, Anderson, Johnstone, Muir, Maitland, Campbell, Reid, Finlay.
1898–99: CELTIC 2, RANGERS 0 (Second Hampden, 22.4.99, 25,000)
Celtic: McArthur; Welford, Storrier, Battles, Marshall, King, Hodge, Campbell, Divers, McMahon, Bell. **Scorers:** McMahon, Hodge.
Rangers: Dickie; N. Smith, Crawford, Gibson, Neill, Mitchell, Campbell, McPherson, Hamilton, Miller, A. Smith.
1899–1900: CELTIC 4, QUEEN'S PARK 3 (Ibrox, 14.4.1900, 17,000)
Celtic: McArthur; Storrier, Battles, Russell, Marshall, Orr, Hodge, Campbell, Divers, McMahon, Bell. **Scorers:** McMahon, Divers 2, Bell.
Queen's Park: Gourlay; D. Stewart, Swan, Irons, Christie, Templeton, W. Stewart, Wilson, McColl, Kennedy, Hay. **Scorers:** Christie, W. Stewart, Battles (og).
1900–01: HEART OF MIDLOTHIAN 4, CELTIC 3 (Ibrox, 6.4.01, 15,000)
Hearts: Philip; Allan, Baird, Key, Buick, Hogg, Porteous, Walker, Thomson, Houston, Bell. **Scorers:** Walker, Bell 2, Thomson.
Celtic: McArthur; Davidson, Battles, Russell, Loney, Orr, McOustra, Divers, Campbell, McMahon, Quinn. **Scorers:** McOustra 2, McMahon.
1901–02: HIBERNIAN 1, CELTIC 0 (Celtic Park, 26.4.02, 16,000)
Hibernian: Rennie; Gray, Glen, Breslin, Harrower, Robertson, McCall, McGeachan, Divers, Callaghan, Atherton. **Scorer:** McGeachan.
Celtic: McFarlane; Watson, Battles, Loney, Marshall, Orr, McCafferty, McDermott, McMahon, Livingstone, Quinn.
1902–03: RANGERS 1, HEART OF MIDLOTHIAN 1 (Celtic Park, 11.4.03, 28,000)
Rangers: Dickie; Fraser, Drummond, Gibson, Stark, Robertson, McDonald, Speedie, Hamilton, J. Walker, Smith. **Scorer:** Stark.
Hearts: McWattie; Thomson, Orr, Key, Buick, Hogg, Dalrymple, Walker, Porteous, Hunter, Baird. **Scorer:** Walker.
REPLAY: RANGERS 0, HEART OF MIDLOTHIAN 0 (Celtic Park, 18.4.03, 16,000)
Rangers: Unchanged.
Hearts: Unchanged.
REPLAY: RANGERS 2, HEART OF MIDLOTHIAN 0 (Celtic Park, 25.4.03, 32,000)
Rangers: Henderson for Gibson, Mackie for J. Walker. **Scorers:** Mackie, Hamilton.
Hearts: Anderson for Buick.
1903–04: CELTIC 3, RANGERS 2 (Hampden Park, 16.4.04, 64,323)
Celtic: Adams; McLeod, Orr, Young, Loney, Hay, Muir, McMenemy, Quinn, Somers, Hamilton. **Scorer:** Quinn 3.
Rangers: Watson; N. Smith, Drummond, Henderson, Stark, Robertson, Walker, Speedie, Mackie, Donnachie, A. Smith. **Scorer:** Speedie 2.

SCOTTISH CUP

1904–05: THIRD LANARK 0, RANGERS 0 (Hampden Park, 8.4.05, 55,000)
Third Lanark: Raeside, Barr, McIntosh, Comrie, Sloa!n, Neilson, Johnstone, Kidd, McKenzie, Wilson, Munro.
Rangers: Sinclair; Fraser, Craig, Henderson, Stark, Robertson, Hamilton, Speedie, McColl, Kyle, Smith.
REPLAY: THIRD LANARK 3, RANGERS 1 (Hampden Park, 15.4.05, 40,000)
Third Lanark: Unchanged. **Scorers:** Wilson 2, Johnstone.
Rangers: Low for Hamilton. **Scorer:** Smith.
1905–06: HEART OF MIDLOTHIAN 1, THIRD LANARK 0 (Ibrox, 28.4.06, 30,000)
Hearts: G. Philip; McNaught, D. Philip, McLaren, Thomson, Dickson, Cooper, Walker, Menzies, D. Wilson, G. Wilson.
Scorer: G. Wilson.
Third Lanark: Raeside; Barr, Hill, Cross, Neilson, Comrie, Johnstone, Graham, Reid, Wilson, Munro.
1906–07: CELTIC 3, HEART OF MIDLOTHIAN 0 (Hampden Park, 20.4.07, 50,000)
Celtic: Adams; McLeod, Orr, Young, McNair, Hay, Bennett, McMenemy, Quinn, Somers, Templeton. **Scorers:** Orr (pen), Somers 2.
Hearts: Allan; Reid, Collins, Philip, McLaren, Henderson, Bauchope, Walker, Axford, Yates, Wombwell.
1907–08: CELTIC 5, ST MIRREN 1 (Hampden Park, 18.4.08, 55,000)
Celtic: Adams; McNair, Weir, Young, Loney, Hay, Bennett, McMenemy, Quinn, Somers, Hamilton. **Scorers:** Bennett 2, Hamilton, Somers, Quinn.
St Mirren: Grant; Gordon, White, Key, Robertson, McAvoy, Clements, Cunningham, Wylie, Paton, Anderson. **Scorer:** Cunningham.
1908–09: CELTIC 2, RANGERS 2 (Hampden Park, 10.4.09, 70,000)
Celtic: Adams; McNair, Weir, Young, Dodds, Hay, Munro, McMenemy, Quinn, Somers, Hamilton. **Scorers:** Quinn, Munro.
Rangers: Rennie; Law, Craig, May, Stark, Galt, Bennett, Gilchrist, Campbell, McPherson, Smith. **Scorers:** Gilchrist, Bennett.
REPLAY: CELTIC 1, RANGERS 1 (Hampden Park, 17.4.09, 60,000)
Celtic: Kivlichan for Munro. **Scorer:** Quinn.
Rangers: Rennie; Law, Craig, Gordon, Stark, Galt, Bennett, McDonald, Reid, McPherson, Smith. **Scorer:** Gordon.
The Cup was withheld following a riot by spectators who were incensed by the decision not to play extra time.
1909–10: DUNDEE 2, CLYDE 2 (Ibrox, 9.4.10, 60,000)
Dundee: Crumley; Lawson, Chaplin, Lee, Dainty, Comrie, Bellamy, Langlands, Hunter, McFarlane, Fraser. **Scorers:** Blair (og), Langlands.
Clyde: McTurk; Watson, Blair, Walker, McAteer, Robertson, Stirling, McCartney, Chalmers, Jackson, Booth. **Scorers:** Chalmers, Booth.
REPLAY: DUNDEE 0, CLYDE 0 (aet, Ibrox, 16.4.10, 20,000)
Dundee: Neal for Lawson.
Clyde: Unchanged.
REPLAY: DUNDEE 2, CLYDE 1 (Ibrox, 20.4.10, 24,000)
Dundee: Neal for Lawson, McEwan for Chaplin. **Scorers:** Bellamy, Hunter.
Clyde: Wyllie for Stirling, Wyse for Jackson. **Scorer:** Chalmers.
1910–11: CELTIC 0, HAMILTON ACADEMICAL 0 (Ibrox, 8.4.11, 45,000)
Celtic: Adams; McNair, Dodds, Young, McAteer, Hay, Ki'vlichan, McMenemy, Quinn, Hastie, Hamilton.
Hamilton Acad: J. Watson; Davie, Miller, P. Watson, W. McLaughlin, Eglington, J. McLaughlin, Waugh, Hunter, Hastie, McNeil.
REPLAY: CELTIC 2, HAMILTON ACADEMICAL 0 (Ibrox, 15.4.11, 25,000)
Celtic: McAtee for Hastie. **Scorers:** Quinn, McAteer.
Hamilton Acad: Unchanged.
1911–12: CELTIC 2, CLYDE 0 (Ibrox, 6.4.12, 45,000)
Celtic: Mulrooney; McNair, Dodds, Young, Loney, Johnstone, McAtee, Gallagher, Quinn, McMenemy, Brown. **Scorers:** McMenemy, Gallagher.
Clyde: Grant; Gilligan, Blair, Walker, McAndrew, Collins, Hamilton, Jackson, Morrison, Carmichael, Stevens.
1912–13: FALKIRK 2, RAITH ROVERS 0 (Celtic Park, 12.4.13, 45,000)
Falkirk: Stewart; Orrock, Donaldson, McDonald, T. Logan, McMillan, McNaught, Gibbons, Robertson, Croal, Terris. **Scorers:** Robertson, T. Logan.
Raith R: McLeod; Morrison, Cumming, J. Gibson, J. Logan, Anderson, Cranston, Graham, Martin, Gourlay, F. Gibson.
1913–14: CELTIC 0, HIBERNIAN 0 (Ibrox, 11.4.14, 55,000)
Celtic: Shaw; McNair, Dodds, Young, Johnstone, McMaster, McAtee, Gallagher, Owers, McMenemy, Browning.
Hibernian: Allan; Girdwood, Templeton, Kerr, Paterson, Grossert, Wilson, Fleming, Hendren, Wood, Smith.
REPLAY:CELTIC 4, HIBERNIAN 1 (Ibrox, 16.4.14, 36,000)
Celtic: McColl for Owers. **Scorers:** McColl 2, Browning 2.
Hibernian: Unchanged. **Scorer:** Smith.
1919–20: KILMARNOCK 3, ALBION ROVERS 2 (Hampden Park, 17.4.20, 95,000)
Kilmarnock: Blair; Hamilton, Gibson, Bagan, Shortt, Neave, *(McNaught, M. Smith, J. Smith, Culley, McPhail. **Scorers:** Culley, Shortt, J. Smith.
Albion R: Short; Penman, Bell, Wilson, Black, Ford, Ribchester, James White, John White, Watson, Hillhouse. **Scorers:** Watson, Hillhouse.

1920–21: PARTICK THISTLE 1, RANGERS 0 (Celtic Park, 16.4.21, 28,294)
Partick Th: Campbell; Chrichton, Bullock, Harris, Wilson, Borthwick, Blair, Kinloch, Johnston, McMenemy, Salisbury. **Scorer:** Blair.
Rangers: Robb; Manderson, McCandless, Meiklejohn, Dixon, Bowie, Archibald, Cunningham, Henderson, Cairns, Morton.

1921–22: MORTON 1, RANGERS 0 (Hampden Park, 15.4.22, 75,000)
Morton: Edwards; McIntyre, R. Brown, Gourlay, Wright, McGregor, McNab, McKay, Buchanan, A. Brown, McMinn. **Scorer:** Gourlay.
Rangers: Robb; Manderson, McCandless, Meiklejohn, Dixon, Muirhead, Archibald, Cunningham, Henderson, Cairns, Morton.

1922–23: CELTIC 1, HIBERNIAN 0 (Hampden Park, 31.3.23, 80,100)
Celtic: Shaw; McNair, W. McStay, J. McStay, Cringan, McFarlane, McAtee, Gallagher, Cassidy, McLean, Connolly. **Scorer:** Cassidy.
Hibernian: Harper; McGinnigle, Dornan, Kerr, Miller, Shaw, Ritchie, Dunn, McColl, Halliagn, Walker.

1923–24: AIRDRIEONIANS 2, HIBERNIAN 0 (Ibrox, 19.4.24, 59,218)
Airdrie: Ewart; Dick, McQueen, Preston, McDougall, Bennie, Reid, Russell, Gallacher, McPhail, Sommerville. **Scorer:** Russell 2.
Hibernian: Harper; McGinnigle, Dornan, Kerr, Miller, Shaw, Ritchie, Dunn, McColl, Halligan, Walker.

1924–25: CELTIC 2, DUNDEE 1 (Hampden Park, 11.4.25, 75,137)
Celtic: Shevlin; W. McStay, Hilley, Wilson, J. McStay, McFarlane, Connolly, Gallagher, McGrory, Thomson, A. McLean. **Scorers:** Gallagher, McGrory.
Dundee: Britton; Brown, Thomson, Ross, W. Rankine, Irving, Duncan, A. McLean, Halliday, J. Rankine, Gilmour. **Scorer:** D. McLean.

1925–26: ST MIRREN 2, CELTIC 0 (Hampden Park, 10.4.26, 98,620)
St Mirren: Bradford; Findlay, Newbiggin, Morrison, Summers, McDonald, Morgan, Gebbie, McCrae, Howieson, Thomson. **Scorers:** McCrae, Howieson.
Celtic: Shevlin; W. McStay, Hilley, Wilson, J. McStay, McFarlane, Connolly, Thomson, McGrory, McInally, Leitch.

1926–27: CELTIC 3, EAST FIFE 1 (Hampden Park, 16.4.27, 80,070)
Celtic: J. Thomson; W. McStay, Hilley, Wilson, J. McStay, McFarlane, Connolly, A. Thomson, McInally, McMenemy, McLean. **Scorers:** Robertson (og), McLean, Connolly.
East Fife: Gilfillan; Robertson, Gillespie, Hope, Brown, Russell, Weir, Paterson, Wood, Barrett, Edgar. **Scorer:** Wood.

1927–28: RANGERS 4, CELTIC 0 (Hampden Park, 14.4.28, 118,115)
Rangers: T. Hamilton; Gray, R. Hamilton, Buchanan, Meiklejohn, Craig, Archibald, Cunningham, Fleming, McPhail, Morton. **Scorers:** Meiklejohn (pen), McPhail, Archibald 2.
Celtic: J. Thomson; W. McStay, Donoghue, Wilson, J. McStay, McFarlane, Connolly, A. Thomson, McGrory, McInally, McLean.

1928–29: KILMARNOCK 2, RANGERS 0 (Hampden Park, 6.4.29, 114,708)
Kilmarnock: Clemie; Robertson, Nibloe, Morton, McLaren, McEwan, Connell, Smith, Cunningham, Williamson, Aitken. **Scorers:** Aitken, Williamson.
Rangers: T. Hamilton; Gray, R. Hamilton, Buchanan, Meiklejohn, Craig, Archibald, Muirhead, Fleming, McPhail, Morton.

1929–30: RANGERS 0, PARTICK THISTLE 0 (Hampden Park, 12.4.30, 107,475)
Rangers: T. Hamilton; Gray, R. Hamilton, Buchanan, Meiklejohn, Craig, Archibald, Marshall, Fleming, McPhail, Nicholson.
Partick Th: Jackson; Calderwood, Rae, Elliot, Lambie, McLeod, Ness, Grove, Boardman, Ballantyne, Torbet.

REPLAY: RANGERS 2, PARTICK THISTLE 1 (Hampden Park, 16.4.30, 103,686)
Rangers: McDonald for Buchanan, Morton for Nicholson. **Scorers:** Marshall, Craig.
Partick Th: Unchanged. **Scorer:** Torbet.

1930–31: CELTIC 2, MOTHERWELL 2 (Hampden Park, 11.4.31, 105,000)
Celtic: J. Thomson; Cook, McGonagle, Wilson, McStay, Geatons, R. Thomson, A. Thomson, McGrory, Scarff, Napier. **Scorers:** McGrory, Craig (og).
Motherwell: McClory; Johnman, Hunter, Wales, Craig, Telfer, Murdoch, McMenemy, McFadyen, Stevenson, Ferrier. **Scorers:** Stevenson, McMenemy.

REPLAY: CELTIC 4, MOTHERWELL 2 (Hampden Park, 15.4.31, 98,579)
Celtic: Unchanged. **Scorers:** Thomson 2, McGrory 2.
Motherwell: Unchanged. **Scorers:** Murdoch, Stevenson.

1931–32: RANGERS 1, KILMARNOCK 1 (Hampden Park, 16.4.32, 111,982)
Rangers: Hamilton; Gray, McAuley, Meiklejohn, Simpson, Browm, Archibald, Marshall, English, McPhail, Morton. **Scorer:** McPhail.
Kilmarnock: Bell; Leslie, Nibloe, Morton, Smith, McEwan, Connell, Muir, Maxwell, Duncan, Aitken. **Scorer:** Maxwell.

REPLAY: RANGERS 3, KILMARNOCK 0 (Hampden Park, 20.4.32, 104,695)
Rangers: Fleming for Morton. **Scorers:** Fleming, McPhail, English.
Kilmarnock: Unchanged.

SCOTTISH CUP

1932–33: CELTIC 1, MOTHERWELL 0 (Hampden Park, 15.4.33, 102,339)
Celtic: Kennaway; Hogg, McGonagle, Wilson, McStay, Geatons, R. Thomson, A. Thomson, McGrory, Napier, H. O'Donnell. **Scorer:** McGrory.
Motherwell: McClory; Crapnell, Ellis, Wales, Blair, Mackenzie, Murdoch, McMenemy, McFadyen, Stevenson, Ferrier.

1933–34: RANGERS 5, ST MIRREN 0 (Hampden Park, 21.4.34, 113,403)
Rangers: Hamilton; Gray, McDonald, Meiklejohn, Simpson, Brown, Main, Marshall, Smith, McPhail, Nicholson. **Scorers:** Nicholson 2, McPhail, Main, Smith.
St Mirren: McCloy; Hay, Ancell, Gebbie, Wilson, Miller, Knox, Latimer, McGregor, McCabe, Phillips.

1934–35: RANGERS 2, HAMILTON ACADEMICAL 1 (Hampden Park, 20.4.35, 87,286)
Rangers: Dawson; Gray, McDonald, Kennedy, Simpson, Brown, Main, Venters, Smith, McPhail, Gillick. **Scorer:** Smith 2.
Hamilton Acad: Morgan; Wallace, Bulloch, Cox, McStay, Murray, King, McLaren, Wilson, Harrison, Reid. **Scorer:** Harrison.

1935–36: RANGERS 1, THIRD LANARK 0 (Hampden Park, 18.4.36, 88,859)
Rangers: Dawson; Gray, Cheyne, Meiklejohn, Simpson, Brown, Fiddes, Venters, Smith, McPhail, Turnbull. **Scorer:** McPhail.
Third Lanark: Muir; Carabine, Hamilton, Blair, Denmark, McInnes, Howe, Gallacher, Hay, Kennedy, Kinnaird.

1936–37: CELTIC 2, ABERDEEN 1 (Hampden Park, 24.4.37, 147,365)
Celtic: Kennaway; Hogg, Morrison, Geatons, Lyon, Paterson, Delaney, Buchan, McGrory, Crum, Murphy. **Scorers:** Crum, Buchan.
Aberdeen: Johnstone; Cooper, Temple, Dunlop, Falloon, Thomson, Benyon, McKenzie, Armstrong, Mills, Laing. **Scorer:** Armstrong.

1937–38: EAST FIFE 1, KILMARNOCK 1 (Hampden Park, 23.4.38, 80,091)
East Fife: Milton; Laird, Tait, Russell, Sneddon, Herd, Adams, McLeod, McCartney, Miller, McKerrell. **Scorer:** McLeod.
Kilmarnock: Hunter; Fyfe, Milloy, Robertson, Stewart, Ross, Thomson, Reid, Collins, McAvoy, McGrogan. **Scorer:** McAvoy.

REPLAY: EAST FIFE 4, KILMARNOCK 2 (aet, Hampden Park, 27.4.38, 92,716)
East Fife: Harvey for Herd. **Scorers:** McKerrell 2, McLeod, Miller.
Kilmarnock: Unchanged. **Scorers:** Thomson (pen), McGrogan.

1938–39: CLYDE 4, MOTHERWELL 0 (Hampden Park, 22.4.39, 94,799)
Clyde: Brown; Kirk, Hickie, Beaton, Falloon, Weir, Robertson, Noble, Martin, Wallace, Gillies. **Scorers:** Wallace, Martin 2, Noble.
Motherwell: Murray; Wales, Ellis, Mackenzie, Blair, Telfer, Ogilvie, Bremner, Mathie, Stevenson, McCulloch.

1946–47: ABERDEEN 2, HIBERNIAN 1 (Hampden Park, 19.4.47, 82,140)
Aberdeen: Johnstone; McKenna, Taylor, McLaughlin, Dunlop, Waddell, Harris, Hamilton, Williams, Baird, McCall. **Scorers:** Hamilton, Williams.
Hibernian: Kerr; Govan, Shaw, Howie, Aird, Kean, Smith, Finnigan, Cuthbertson, Turnbull, Ormond. **Scorer:** Cuthbertson.

1947–48: RANGERS 1, MORTON 1 (aet, Hampden Park, 17.4.48, 129,176)
Rangers: Brown; Young, Shaw, McColl, Woodburn, Cox, Rutherford, Gillick, Thornton, Findlay, Duncanson. **Scorer:** Gillick.
Morton: Cowan; Mitchell, Whigham, Campbell, Miller, Whyte, Hepburn, Murphy, Cupples, Orr, Liddell. **Scorer:** Whyte.

REPLAY: RANGERS 1, MORTON 0 (aet, Hampden Park, 21.4.48, 131,975)
Rangers: Williamson for Findlay. **Scorer:** Williamson.
Morton: Unchanged.

1948–49: RANGERS 4, CLYDE 1 (Hampden Park, 23.4.49, 108,435)
Rangers: Brown; Young, Shaw, McColl, Woodburn, Cox, Waddell, Duncanson, Thornton, Williamson, Rutherford. **Scorers:** Young (2 pens), Williamson, Duncanson.
Clyde: Cullan; Gibson, Mennie, Campbell, Milligan, Long, Davies, Wright, Linwood, Galletly, Bootland. **Scorer:** Galletly.

1949–50: RANGERS 3, EAST FIFE 0 (Hampden Park, 22.4.50, 118,262)
Rangers: Brown; Young, Shaw, McColl, Woodburn, Cox, Rutherford, Findlay, Thornton, Duncanson, Rae. **Scorers:** Findlay, Thornton 2.
East Fife: Easson; Laird, Stewart, Philp, Finlay, Aitken, Black, Fleming, Morris, Brown, Duncan.

1950–51: CELTIC 1, MOTHERWELL 0 (Hampden Park, 21.4.51, 131,943)
Celtic: Hunter; Fallon, Rollo, Evans, Boden, Baillie, Weir, Collins, J. McPhail, Peacock, Tully. **Scorer:** McPhail.
Motherwell: Johnstone; Kilmarnock, Shaw, McLeod, Paton, Redpath, Humphries, Forrest, Kelly, Watson, Aitkenhead.

1951–52: MOTHERWELL 4, DUNDEE 0 (Hampden Park, 19.4.52, 136,304)
Motherwell: Johnstone; Kilmarnock, Shaw, Cox, Paton, Redpath, Sloan, Humphries, Kelly, Watson, Aitkenhead. **Scorers:** Watson, Redpath, Humphries, Kelly.
Dundee: Henderson; Fallon, Cowan, Gallagher, Cowie, Boyd, Hill, Patillo, Flavell, Steel, Christie.

1952–53: RANGERS 1, ABERDEEN 1 (Hampden Park, 25.4.53, 129,861)
Rangers: Niven; Young, Little, McColl, Stanners, Pryde, Waddell, Grierson, Paton, Prentice, Hubbard. **Scorer:** Prentice.
Aberdeen: Martin; Mitchell, Shaw, Harris, Young, Allister, Rodger, Yorston, Buckley, Hamilton, Hather. **Scorer:** Yorston.
REPLAY: RANGERS 1, ABERDEEN 0 (Hampden Park, 29.4.53, 112,619)
Rangers: Woodburn for Stanners, Simpson for Prentice. **Scorer:** Simpson.
Aberdeen: Unchanged.

1953–54: CELTIC 2, ABERDEEN 1 (Hampden Park, 24.4.54, 129,926)
Celtic: Bonnar; Haughney, Meechan, Evans, Stein, Peacock, Higgins, Fernie, Fallon, Tully, Mochan. **Scorers:** Young (og), Fallon.
Aberdeen: Martin; Mitchell, Caldwell, Allister, Young, Glen, Leggat, Hamilton, Buckley, Clunie, Hather. **Scorer:** Buckley.

1954–55: CLYDE 1, CELTIC 1 (Hampden Park, 23.4.55, 106,111)
Clyde: Hewkins; Murphy, Haddock, Granville, Anderson, Laing, Divers, Robertson, Hill, Brown, Ring. **Scorer:** Robertson.
Celtic: Bonnar; Haughney, Meechan, Evans, Stein, Peacock, Collins, Fernie, W.McPhail, Walsh, Tully. **Scorer:** Walsh.
REPLAY: CLYDE 1, CELTIC 0 (Hampden Park, 27.4.55, 68,735)
Clyde: Unchanged. **Scorer:** Ring.
Celtic: Fallon for Collins.

1955–56: HEART OF MIDLOTHIAN 3, CELTIC 1 (Hampden Park, 21.4.56, 133,399)
Hearts: Cuff; Kirk, Mackenzie, Mackay, Glidden, Cumming, Young, Conn, Bauld, Wardhaugh, Crawford. **Scorers:** Crawford 2, Conn.
Celtic: Beattie; Meechan, Fallon, Smith, Evans, Peacock, Craig, Haughney, Mochan, Fernie, Tully. **Scorer:** Haughney.

1956–57: FALKIRK 1, KILMARNOCK 1 (Hampden Park, 20.4.57, 81,057)
Falkirk: Slater; Parker, Rae, Wright, Irvine, Prentice, Murray, Grierson, Merchant, Moran, O'Hara. **Scorer:** Prentice (pen).
Kilmarnock: Brown; Collins, J. Stewart, R. Stewart, Toner, Mackay, Mays, Harvey, Curlett, Black, Burns. **Scorer:** Curlett.
REPLAY: FALKIRK 2, KILMARNOCK 1 (aet, Hampden Park, 24.4.57, 79,785)
Falkirk: Unchanged. **Scorers:** Merchant, Moran.
Kilmarnock: Unchanged. **Scorer:** Curlett.

1957–58: CLYDE 1, HIBERNIAN 0 (Hampden Park, 26.4.58, 95,123)
Clyde: McCulloch; Murphy, Haddock, Walters, Finlay, Clinton, Herd, Currie, Coyle, Robertson, Ring. **Scorer:** Coyle.
Hibernian: Leslie; Grant, McClelland, Turnbull, Plenderleith, Baxter, Fraser, Aitken, Baker, Preston, Ormond.

1958–59: ST MIRREN 3, ABERDEEN 1 (Hampden Park, 25.4.59, 108,591)
St Mirren: Walker; Lapsley, Wilson, Neilson, McGugan, Leishman, Rodger, Bryceland, Baker, Gemmell, Miller. **Scorers:** Bryceland, Miller, Baker.
Aberdeen: Martin; Caldwell, Hogg, Brownlie, Clunie, Glen, Ewan, Davidson, Baird, Wishart, Hather. **Scorer:** Baird.

1959–60: RANGERS 2, KILMARNOCK 0 (Hampden Park, 23.4.60, 108 ,017)
Rangers: Niven; Caldow, Little, McColl, Paterson, Stevenson, Scott, McMillan, Millar, Baird, Wilson. **Scorer:** Millar 2.
Kilmarnock: Brown; Richmond, Watson, Beattie, Toner, Kennedy, Stewart, McInally, Kerr, Black, Muir.

1960–61: DUNFERMLINE ATHLETIC 0, CELTIC 0 (Hampden Park, 22.4.61, 113,618)
Dunfermline Ath: Connachan; Fraser, Cunningham, Mailer, Williamson, Miller, Peebles, Smith, Dickson, McLindon, Melrose.
Celtic: Haffey; McKay, Kennedy, Crerand, McNeill, Clark, Gallagher, Fernie, Hughes, Chalmers, Byrne.
REPLAY: DUNFERMLINE ATHLETIC 2, CELTIC 0 (Hampden Park, 26.4.61, 87,866)
Dunfermline Ath: Sweeney for Williamson, Thomson for McLindon. **Scorers:** Thomson, Dickson.
Celtic: O'Neill for Kennedy.

1961–62: RANGERS 2, ST MIRREN 0 (Hampden Park, 21.4.62, 126,930)
Rangers: Ritchie; Shearer, Caldow, Davis, McKinnon, Baxter, Henderson, McMillan, Millar, Brand, Wilson. **Scorers:** Brand, Wilson.
St Mirren: Williamson; Campbell, Wilson, Stewart, Clunie, McLean, Henderson, Bryceland, Kerrigan, Fernie, Beck.

1962–63: RANGERS 1, CELTIC 1 (Hampden Park, 4.5.63, 129,527)
Rangers: Ritchie; Shearer, Provan, Greig, McKinnon, Baxter, Henderson, McLean, Millar, Brand, Wilson. **Scorer:** Brand.
Celtic: Haffey; McKay, Kennedy, McNamee, McNeill, Price, Johnstone, Murdoch, Hughes, Divers, Brogan. **Scorer:** Murdoch.
REPLAY: RANGERS 3, CELTIC 0 (Hampden Park, 15.5.63, 120,263)
Rangers: McMillan for McLean. **Scorers:** Brand 2, Wilson.
Celtic: Craig for Johnstone, Chalmers for Brogan.

1963–64: RANGERS 3, DUNDEE 1 (Hampden Park, 25.4.64, 120,982)
Rangers: Ritchie; Shearer, Provan, Greig, McKinnon, Baxter, Henderson, McLean, Millar, Brand, Wilson. **Scorers:** Millar 2, Brand.
Dundee: Slater; Hamilton, Cox, Seith, Ryden, Stuart, Penman, Cousin, Cameron, Gilzean, Robertson. **Scorer:** Cameron.

SCOTTISH CUP

1964–65: CELTIC 3, DUNFERMLINE ATHLETIC 2 (Hampden Park, 24.4.65, 108,800)
Celtic: Fallon; Young, Gemmell, Murdoch, McNeill, Clark, Chalmers, Gallagher, Hughes, Lennox, Auld. **Scorers:** Auld 2, McNeill.
Dunfermline Ath: Herriot; W. Callaghan, Lunn, Thomson, McLean, T. Callaghan, Edwards, Smith, McLaughlin, Melrose, Sinclair. **Scorers:** Melrose, McLaughlin.
1965–66: RANGERS 0, CELTIC 0 (Hampden Park, 23.4.66, 126,552)
Rangers: Ritchie; Johansen, Provan, Grieg, McKinnon, Millar, Wilson, Watson, Forrest, Johnston, Henderson.
Celtic: Simpson; Young, Gemmell, Murdoch, McNeill, Clark, Johnstone, McBride, Chalmers, Gallagher, Hughes.
REPLAY: RANGERS 1, CELTIC 0 (Hampden Park, 27.4.66, 98,202)
Rangers: McLean for Forrest. **Scorer:** Johansen.
Celtic: Craig for Young, Auld for Gallagher.
1966–67: CELTIC 2, ABERDEEN 0 (Hampden Park, 29.4.67, 127,117)
Celtic: Simpson; Craig, Gemmell, Murdoch, McNeill, Clark, Johnstone, Wallace, Chalmers, Auld, Lennox. **Scorer:** Wallace 2.
Aberdeen: Clark; Whyte, Shewan, Munro, McMillan, Petersen, Wilson, Smith, Storrie, Melrose, Johnston.
1967–68: DUNFERMLINE ATHLETIC 3, HEART OF MIDLOTHIAN 1 (Hampden Park, 27.4.68, 56,366)
Dunfermline Ath: Martin; W. Callaghan, Lunn, McGarty, Barry, T. Callaghan, Lister, Paton, Gardner, Robertson, Edwards. **Scorers:** Gardner 2, Lister (pen).
Hearts: Cruikshank; Sneddon, Mann, Anderson, Thomson, Miller, Jensen (Moller), Townsend, Ford, Irvine, Traynor. **Scorer:** Lunn (og).
1968–69: CELTIC 4, RANGERS 0 (Hampden Park, 26.4.69, 132,870)
Celtic: Fallon; Craig, Gemmell, Murdoch, McNeill, Brogan (Clark), Connelly, Chalmers, Wallace, Lennox, Auld. **Scorers:** McNeill, Lennox, Connelly, Chalmers.
Rangers: Martin; Johansen, Mathieson, Greig, McKinnon, Smith, Henderson, Penman, Ferguson, Johnston, Persson.
1969–70: ABERDEEN 3, CELTIC 1 (Hampden Park, 11.4.70, 108,244)
Aberdeen: Clark; Boel, Murray, Hermiston, McMillan, M. Buchan, McKay, Robb, Forrest, Harper, Graham. **Scorers:** Harper (pen), McKay 2.
Celtic: Williams; Hay, Gemmell, Murdoch, McNeill, Brogan, Johnstone, Wallace, Connelly, Lennox, Hughes (Auld). **Scorer:** Lennox.
1970–71: CELTIC 1, RANGERS 1 (Hampden Park, 8.5.71, 120,027)
Celtic: Williams; Craig, Brogan, Connelly, McNeill, Hay, Johnstone, Lennox, Wallace, Callaghan, Hood. **Scorer:** Lennox.
Rangers: McCloy; Miller, Mathieson, Greig, McKinnon, Jackson, Henderson, Penman (D. Johnstone), Stein, A. MacDonald, W. Johnston. **Scorer:** M. Johnstone.
REPLAY: CELTIC 2, RANGERS 1 (Hampden Park, 12.5.71, 103,297)
Celtic: Macari for Wallace, Wallace came on for Hood. **Scorers:** Macari, Hood (pen).
Rangers: Denny for Miller, D. Johnstone came on for Penman. **Scorer:** Craig (og).
1971–72: CELTIC 6, HIBERNIAN 1 (Hampden Park, 6.5.72, 105,909)
Celtic: Willliams; Craig, Brogan, Murdoch, McNeill, Connelly, Johnstone, Deans, Macari, Dalglish, Callaghan. **Scorers:** McNeill, Deans 3, Macari 2.
Hibernian: Herriot; Brownlie, Schaedler, Stanton, Black, Blackley, Edwards, Hazel, Gordon, O'Rourke, Duncan (Auld). **Scorer:** Gordon.
1972–73: RANGERS 3, CELTIC 2 (Hampden Park, 5.5.73, 122,714)
Rangers: McCloy; Jardine, Mathieson, Greig, Johnstone, A. MacDonald, McLean, Forsyth, Parlane, Conn, Young. **Scorers:** Parlane, Conn, Forsyth.
Celtic: Hunter; McGrain, Brogan (Lennox), Murdoch, McNeill, Connelly, Johnstone, Deans, Dalglish, Hay, Callaghan. **Scorers:** Dalglish, Connelly (pen).
1973–74: CELTIC 3, DUNDEE UNITED 0 (Hampden Park, 4.5.74, 75,959)
Celtic: Connaghan; McGrain (Callaghan), Brogan, Murray, McNeill, McCluskey, Johnstone, Hood, Deans, Hay, Dalglish. **Scorers:** Hood, Murray, Deans.
Dundee U: Davie; Gardner, Kopel, Copland, D. Smith (Traynor), W. Smith, Payne (Rolland), Knox, Gray, Fleming, Houston.
1974–75: CELTIC 3, AIRDRIEONIANS 1 (Hampden Park, 3.5.75, 75,457)
Celtic: Latchford; McGrain, Lynch, Murray, McNeill, McCluskey, Hood, Glavin, RPDalglish, Lennox, Wilson. **Scorers:** Wilson 2, McCluskey (pen).
Airdrie: McWilliams; Jonquin, Cowan, Menzies, Black, Whiteford, McCann, Walker, McCulloch (March), Lapsley (Reynolds), Wilson.
1975–76: RANGERS 3, HEART OF MIDLOTHIAN 1 (Hampden Park, 1.5.76, 85,250)
Rangers: McCloy; Miller, Greig, Forsyth, Jackson, A. MacDonald, McKean, Hamilton (Jardine), Henderson, McLean, Johnstone. **Scorers:** Johnstone 2, MacDonald.
Hearts: Cruikshank; Brown, Burrell (Aird), Jeffries, Gallagher, Kay, Gibson (Park), Busby, Shaw, Callachan, Prentice. **Scorer:** Shaw.
1976–77: CELTIC 1, RANGERS 0 (Hampden Park, 7.5.77, 54,252)
Celtic: Latchford; McGrain, Lynch, Stanton, McDonald, Aitken, Dalglish, Edvaldsson, Craig, Conn, Wilson. **Scorer:** Lynch (pen).
Rangers: Kennedy; Jardine, Greig, Forsyth, Jackson, Watson (Robertson), McLean, Hamilton, Parlane, A. MacDonald, Johnstone.

1977–78: RANGERS 2, ABERDEEN 1 (Hampden Park, 6.5.78, 61,563)
Rangers: McCloy; Jardine, Greig, Forsyth, Jackson, A. MacDonald, McLean, Russell, Johnstone, Smith, Cooper (Watson). **Scorers:** MacDonald, Johnstone.
Aberdeen: Clark; Kennedy, Ritchie, McMaster, Garner, Miller, Sullivan, Fleming (Scanlon), Harper, Jarvie, Davidson. **Scorer:** Ritchie.

1978–79: RANGERS 0, HIBERNIAN 0 (Hampden Park, 12.5.79, 50,260)
Rangers: McCloy; Jardine, Dawson, Johnstone, Jackson, A. MacDonald (Miller), McLean, Russell, Parlane, Smith, Cooper.
Hibernian: McArthur; Brazil, Duncan, Bremner, Stewart, McNamara, Hutchison (Rae), McLeod, Campbell, Callachan, Higgins.

REPLAY: RANGERS 0, HIBERNIAN 0 (aet, Hampden Park, 16.5.79, 33,508)
Rangers: Unchanged. Miller came on for McLean.
Hibernian: Rae for Hutchison. Brown came on for Higgins.

REPLAY: RANGERS 3, HIBERNIAN 2 (aet, Hampden Park, 28.5.79, 30,602)
Rangers: Watson for Smith. Miller came on for Watson, Smith came on for McLean. **Scorers:** Johnstone 2, Duncan (og).
Hibernian: McArthur; Brazil, Duncan, Bremner, Stewart, McNamara, Rae, McLeod, Campbell, Callachan (Brown), Higgins (Hutchison). **Scorers:** Higgins, McLeod (pen).

1979–80: CELTIC 1, RANGERS 0 (aet, Hampden Park, 10.5.80, 70,303)
Celtic: Latchford; Sneddon, McGrain, Aitken, Conroy, MacLeod, Provan, Doyle (Lennox), McCluskey, Burns, McGarvey. **Scorer:** McCluskey.
Rangers: McCloy; Jardine, Dawson, Forsyth (Miller), Jackson, Stevens, Cooper, Russell, Johnstone, Smith, J. MacDonald (McLean).

1980–81: RANGERS 0, DUNDEE UNITED 0 (aet, Hampden Park, 9.5.81, 53,000)
Rangers: Stewart; Jardine, Dawson, Stevens, Forsyth, Bett, McLean, Russell, McAdam (Cooper), Redford, W. Johnston (J. MacDonald).
Dundee U: McAlpine; Holt, Kopel, Phillips (Stark), Hegarty, Narey, Bannon, Milne (Pettigrew), Kirkwood, Sturrock, Dodds.

REPLAY: RANGERS 4, DUNDEE UNITED 1 (Hampden Park, 12.5.81, 43,099)
Rangers: Stewart; Jardine, Dawson, Stevens, Forsyth, Bett, Cooper, Russell, D. Johnstone, Redford, J. MacDonald. **Scorers:** Cooper, Russell, MacDonald 2.
Dundee U: Unchanged. Stark came on for Phillips.

1981–82: ABERDEEN 4, RANGERS 1 (aet, Hampden Park, 22.5.82, 53,788)
Aberdeen: Leighton; Kennedy, Rougvie, McMaster (Bell), McLeish, Miller, Strachan, Cooper, McGhee, Simpson, Hewitt (Black). **Scorers:** McLeish, McGhee, Strachan, Cooper.
Rangers: Stewart; Jardine (McAdam), Dawson, McClelland, Jackson, Bett, Cooper, Russell, Dalziel (McLean), Miller, J. MacDonald. **Scorer:** MacDonald.

1982–83: ABERDEEN 1, RANGERS 0 (aet, Hampden Park, 21.5.83, 62,979)
Aberdeen: Leighton, Rougvie (Watson), McMaster, Cooper, McLeish, Miller, Strachan, Simpson, McGhee, Black, Weir (Hewitt). **Scorer:** Black.
Rangers: McCloy; Dawson, McClelland, McPherson, Paterson, Bett, Cooper (Davis), McKinnon, Clark, Russell, J. MacDonald (Dalziel).

1983–84: ABERDEEN 2, CELTIC 1 (aet, Hampden Park, 19.5.84, 58,900)
Aberdeen: Leighton; McKimmie, Rougvie (Stark), Cooper, McLeish, Miller, Strachan, Simpson, McGhee, Black, Weir (Bell). **Scorers:** Black, McGhee.
Celtic: Bonner, McGrain, Reid (Melrose), Aitken, W. McStay, MacLeod, Provan, P. McStay, McGarvey, Burns, McClair (Sinclair). **Scorer:** P. McStay.

1984–85: CELTIC 2, DUNDEE UNITED 1 (Hampden Park, 18.5.85, 60,346)
Celtic: Bonner; W. McStay, McGrain, Aitken, McAdam, MacLeod, Provan, P. McStay (O'Leary), Johnston, Burns (McClair), McGarvey. **Scorers:** Provan, McGarvey.
Dundee U: McAlpine; Malpas, Beedie (Holt), Gough, Hegarty, Narey, Bannon, Milne, Kirkwood, Sturrock, Dodds. **Scorer:** Beedie.

1985–86: ABERDEEN 3, HEART OF MIDLOTHIAN 0 (Hampden Park, 10.5.86, 62,841)
Aberdeen: Leighton; McKimmie, McQueen, McMaster (Stark), McLeish, W. Miller, Hewitt (J. Miller), Cooper, McDougall, Bett, Weir. **Scorers:** Hewitt 2, Stark.
Hearts: Smith; Kidd, Whittaker, W. Jardine, Berry, Levein, Colquhoun, Black, Clark, G. Mackay, Robertson.

1986–87: ST MIRREN 1, DUNDEE UNITED 0 (aet, Hampden Park, 16.5.87, 51,782)
St Mirren: Money; Wilson, D. Hamilton, Abercromby, Winnie, Cooper, McGarvey, Ferguson, McDowall (Cameron), B. Hamilton, Lambert (Fitzpatrick). **Scorer:** Ferguson.
Dundee U: Thomson; Holt, Malpas, McInally, Clark, Narey, Ferguson, Bowman, Bannon, Sturrock (Gallacher), Redford (Hegarty).

SCOTTISH CUP FINALS SINCE 1874

1874 Queen's Park 2, Clydesdale 0	1900 Celtic 4, Queen's Park 3	1949 Rangers 4, Clyde 1
1875 Queen's Park 3, Renton 0	1901 Hearts 4, Celtic 3	1950 Rangers 3, East Fife 0
1876 Queen's Park 1,	1902 Hibernian 1, Celtic 0	1951 Celtic 1, Motherwell 0
Third Lanark RV 1	1903 Rangers 1, Hearts 1	1952 Motherwell 4, Dundee 0
Replay Queen's Park 2,	Replay Rangers 0, Hearts 0	1953 Rangers 1, Aberdeen 1
Third Lanark RV 0	Replay Rangers 2, Hearts 0	Replay Rangers 1, Aberdeen 0
1877 Vale of Leven 0, Rangers 0	1904 Celtic 3, Rangers 2	1954 Celtic 2, Aberdeen 1
Replay Vale of Leven 1, Rangers 1	1905 Third Lanark 0, Rangers 0	1955 Clyde 1, Celtic 1
Replay Vale of Leven 3, Rangers 2	Replay Third Lanark 3, Rangers 1	Replay Clyde 1, Celtic 0
1878 Vale of Leven 1,	1906 Hearts 1, Third Lanark 0	1956 Hearts 3, Celtic 1
Third Lanark RV 0	1907 Celtic 3, Hearts 0	1957 Falkirk 1, Kilmarnock 1
1879 Vale of Leven 1, Rangers 1	1908 Celtic 5, St Mirren 1	Replay Falkirk 2, Kilmarnock 1
Replay Awarded Vale of Leven	1909 Celtic 2, Rangers 2	1958 Clyde 1, Hibernian 0
(Rangers failed to appear)	Replay Celtic 1, Rangers 1 (Cup with-	1959 St Mirren 3, Aberdeen 1
1880 Queen's Park 3,	held after riot)	1960 Rangers 2, Kilmarnock 0
Thornliebank 0	1910 Dundee 2, Clyde 2	1961 Dunfermline Ath 0, Celtic 0
1881 Queen's Park 2, Dumbarton 1	Replay Dundee 0, Clyde 0	Replay Dunfermline Ath 2, Celtic 0
Replay Queen's Park 3, Dumbarton 1	Replay Dundee 2, Clyde 1	1962 Rangers 2, St Mirren 0
(Replay after Dumbarton protested at	1911 Celtic 0, Hamilton Acad 0	1963 Rangers 1, Celtic 1
the result of first match)	Replay Celtic 2, Hamilton Acad 0	Replay Rangers 3, Celtic 0
1882 Queen's Park 2, Dumbarton 2	1912 Celtic 2, Clyde 0	1964 Rangers 3, Dundee 1
Replay Queen's Park 4, Dumbarton 1	1913 Falkirk 2, Raith R 0	1965 Celtic 3, Dunfermline Ath 2
1883 Dumbarton 2, Vale of Leven 2	1914 Celtic 0, Hibernian 0	1966 Rangers 0, Celtic 0
Replay Dumbarton 2, Vale of Leven 1	Replay Celtic 4, Hibernian 1	Replay Rangers 1, Celtic 0
1884 Queen's Park	1920 Kilmarnock 3, Albion R 2	1967 Celtic 2, Aberdeen 0
(Vale of Leven failed to appear)	1921 Partick Thistle 1, Rangers 0	1968 Dunfermline Ath 3, Hearts 1
1885 Renton 0, Vale of Leven 0	1922 Morton 1, Rangers 0	1969 Celtic 4, Rangers 0
Replay Renton 3, Vale of Leven 1	1923 Celtic 1, Hibernian 0	1970 Aberdeen 3, Celtic 1
1886 Queen's Park 3, Renton 0	1924 Airdrieonians 2, Hibernian 0	1971 Celtic 1, Rangers 1
1887 Hibernian 2, Dumbarton 1	1925 Celtic 2, Dundee 1	Replay Celtic 2, Rangers 1
1888 Renton 6, Cambuslang 1	1926 St Mirren 2, Celtic 0	1972 Celtic 6, Hibernian 1
1889 Third Lanark 3, Celtic 0	1927 Celtic 3, East Fife 1	1973 Rangers 3, Celtic 2
Replay Third Lanark 2, Celtic 1	1928 Rangers 4, Celtic 0	1974 Celtic 3, Dundee U 0
(Replay due to poor playing conditions	1929 Kilmarnock 2, Rangers 0	1975 Celtic 3, Airdrieonians 1
in first match)	1930 Rangers 0, Partick Th 0	1976 Rangers 3, Hearts 1
1890 Queen's Park 1,	Replay Rangers 2, Partick Th 1	1977 Celtic 1, Rangers 0
Vale of Leven 1	1931 Celtic 2, Motherwell 2	1978 Rangers 2, Aberdeen 1
Replay Queen's Park 2,	Replay Celtic 4, Motherwell 2	1979 Rangers 0, Hibernian 0
Vale of Leven 1	1932 Rangers 1, Kilmarnock 1	Replay Rangers 0, Hibernian 0
1891 Hearts 1, Dumbarton 0	Replay Rangers 3, Kilmarnock 0	Replay Rangers 3, Hibernian 2
1892 Celtic 1, Queen's Park 0	1933 Celtic 1, Motherwell 0	1980 Celtic 1, Rangers 0
Replay Celtic 5, Queen's Park 1	1934 Rangers 5, St Mirren 0	1981 Rangers 0, Dundee U 0
(Agreed to Replay after crowd en-	1935 Rangers 2, Hamilton Acad 1	Replay Rangers 4, Dundee U 1
croachment in first match)	1936 Rangers 1, Third Lanark 0	1982 Aberdeen 4, Rangers 1 (aet)
1893 Queen's Park 2, Celtic 1	1937 Celtic 2, Aberdeen 1	1983 Aberdeen 1, Rangers 0 (aet)
1894 Rangers 3, Celtic 1	1938 East Fife 1, Kilmarnock 1	1984 Aberdeen 2, Celtic 1 (aet)
1895 St Bernard's 2, Renton 1	Replay East Fife 4, Kilmarnock 2	1985 Celtic 2, Dundee U 1
1896 Hearts 3, Hibernian 1	1939 Clyde 4, Motherwell 0	1986 Aberdeen 3, Hearts 0
1897 Rangers 5, Dumbarton 1	1947 Aberdeen 2, Hibernian 1	1987 St Mirren 1, Dundee U 0 (aet)
1898 Rangers 2, Kilmarnock 0	1948 Rangers 1, Morton 1	1988 Celtic 2, Dundee U 1
1899 Celtic 2, Rangers 0	Replay Rangers 1, Morton 0	

WINS

28 – Celtic. 24 – Rangers. 10 – Queen's Park. 6 – Aberdeen. 5 – Hearts. 3 – Clyde, St Mirren, Vale of Leven. 2 – Dunfermline Ath, Falkirk, Hibernian, Kilmarnock, Renton, Third Lanark. 1 – Airdrieonians, Dumbarton, Dundee, East Fife, Morton, Motherwell, Partick Th, St Bernard's.

APPEARANCES IN FINAL

44 – Celtic. 39 – Rangers. 12 – Aberdeen, Queen's Park. 10 – Hearts, Hibernian. 7 – Kilmarnock, Vale of Leven. 6 – St Mirren, Third Lanark. 5 – Dundee U, Motherwell, Renton. 4 – Dundee. 3 – Dunfermline Ath, East Fife. 2 – Airdrieonians, Falkirk, Hamilton Acad, Morton, Partick Th. 1 – Albion R, Cambuslang, Clydesdale, Raith R, St Bernard's, Thornliebank.

SKOL CUP 1987–88

FIRST ROUND

STENHOUSEMUIR (0)1 EAST STIRLING (1)3 (aet)
(11.8.87, 600)
Stenhousemuir: Robertson; Cairney, Beaton, Waddell (McAra), Buchanan, Erwin, Condie, McCafferty, Quinn, Gillen, Jamieson (Thomson). **Scorer:** Erwin.
East Stirling: Kelly; Mackay, Harvey, D.Wilcox, Rennie, Woods, Tasker, Wylde, Ward, G.Wilcox (O'Brien), Henderson (McGonigal). **Scorers:** Ward, O'Brien, McGonigal.

ARBROATH (1)1 AYR UNITED (0)3 (aet)
(12.8.87, 740)
Arbroath: Jackson; Duff, Jack, Phillip, Hill, Steel, Morrison, Mitchell, McKenna, Cumming (Fotheringham), Brannigan. **Scorer:** McKenna.
Ayr United: Watson; Hughes, McCann, Furphy, McAllister, Evans, Templeton, McKenzie, Walker, Sludden, Cowell. **Scorers:** Walker 2, Templeton.

BERWICK RANGERS (1)1 STIRLING ALBION (0)2 (aet)
(12.8.87, 400)
Berwick Rangers: Thomson; McCann, Fleming, Douglas, Marshall, Oliver, Haig, Main (K. Buckley), G. Buckley, Cavenagh, Leitch (Alexander). **Scorer:** Main.
Stirling Albion: Graham; Aitchison, Spence, Hoggan (Tennant), McTeague, Maxwell (Gavin), Thompson, Conway, Gibson, Kemp, Brogan. **Scorers:** Spence, Brogan.

COWDENBEATH (1)1 QUEEN'S PARK (2)3
(12.8.87, 540)
Cowdenbeath: Allan; Baillie, Kirkcaldy, Muir, D. Grant, McGovern, Proudfoot (Leetion), Paxton, R. Grant, Cherry, Hepburn (K. McCullough). **Scorer:** R. Grant.
Queen's Park: Ross; P. McClean, McLaughlin, Boyle, Elder, McEntegart, Cavan, Elliot, O'Brien, MacKenzie, Hendry. **Scorers:** Hendry, O'Brien, MacKenzie.

ST JOHNSTONE (2)4 ALLOA (1)1
(12.8.87, 1313)
St Johnstone: Balavage; Wilson, McVicar, Barron, McKillop, Johnston (Coyle), Maskrey, McGurn, Lloyd, Brown, Heddle (Smith). **Scorers:** McKillop, Brown 2, Johnston.
Alloa: Lowrie; Haggart, Love, Thomson, Donaldson, Sullivan, Smith (MacDonald), Wilkie, Sorbie, Nelson, Torrance. **Scorer:** Sorbie.

STRANRAER (0)0 ALBION ROVERS (0)3
(12.8.87, 600)
Stranraer: Bryden; Watt, Hay (McIntyre), Geals, Carson, Day (Wilson), Campbell, McNiven, McNab, Know, Creaney.
Albion R: McCulloch; Edgar, McGowan, Ahern, Gallagher, T. McDonald, Teevan, Rodgers, Black, Houston, Chapman. **Scorers:** Teevan, Gallagher, Black.

SECOND ROUND

EAST STIRLING (0)1 DUNFERMLINE ATH (1)3
(18.8.87, 2600)
East Stirling: Kelly; Gilchrist, Harvey, G. Wilcox (Wilson), Rennie, Woods, O'Brien, Wylde, Ward, D. Wilcox, Grant. **Scorer:** Ward.
Dunfermline Ath: Westwater; G. Robertson, Forrest, McCathie, Young, C. Robertson, Beedie, Cowie, T. Smith

(Irvine), McCall, Morrison. **Scorers:** Cowie, C. Robertson, McCall pen.

HIBERNIAN (0)3 MONTROSE (1)2
(18.8.87, 5500)
Hibernian: Rough; Hunter, McIntyre, May, Chisholm, Mitchell, Kane, McGovern (McCluskey), Cowan, Collins, Tortolano. **Scorers:** Tortolano, May, McCluskey.
Montrose: Larter; Barr, McLelland, K. Brown, Sheran, Forbes, Allan, Lyons (Lees), Paterson, Wright (Robertson), McDonald. **Scorers:** Sheran, Brown pen.

MEADOWBANK THISTLE (0)1 HAMILTON ACADEMICAL (0)0 (aet)
(18.8.87, 750)
Meadowbank Th: McQueen; Hendrie, Roseburgh, Boyd, Tierney, Armstrong, Kasule (Liddle), Lawson, Callachan, Prentice (Park), McGachie. **Scorer:** Boyd.
Hamilton A: McKellar; McGrain, Sprott, Speirs, Martin, Collins (McKee), Taylor, Clarke, Jamieson, Caughey, McCabe (McDonald).

QUEEN OF THE SOUTH (0)2 FALKIRK (1)1
(18.8.87, 950)
Queen of the S: Davidson; Sinclair, Dickson, Docherty, Mackin, Hetherington, Pelosi (Robertson), Hughes, Frye (Moore), Cloy, Doherty. **Scorers:** Doherty, Hughes pen.
Falkirk: Marshall; MacLeod, Scrimgeour, Baptie (Manley), Dempsey, Burgess, Gilmour, Hill, Eadie, Nicol, Rae (Kerr). **Scorer:** Eadie.

QUEEN'S PARK (0)0 DUNDEE (2)3
(18.8.87, 1400)
Queen's Park: Ross; P. McLean, McLaughlin, Boyle, Elder, Elliot, O'Brien (Lennox), Caven, Armstrong, MacKenzie, Hendry.
Dundee: Geddes; Glennie, McKinlay, Shannon (Jack), Smith, Duffy, Forsyth, Brown (McGeachie), Wright, Coyne, Angus. **Scorers:** McKinlay, Wright, Coyne.

ST MIRREN (0)0 ST JOHNSTONE (1)1
(18.8.87, 3500)
St Mirren: Fridge; Dawson, Wilson, Abercromby, Winnie, Cooper, McGarvey, Ferguson, Lambert (McDowall), B. Hamilton, Chalmers (Cameron).
St Johnstone: Balavage; Wilson, McVicar, Barron, McKillop, McGurn, Maskrey, Coyle, Johnstone, Brown, Heddle. **Scorer:** Heddle.

ABERDEEN (1)5 BRECHIN CITY (0)1
(19.8.87, 9000)
Aberdeen: Leighton; McKimmie, D. Robertson, Simpson (Grant), Irvine, W. Miller, Dodds, Bett, J. Miller, Nicholas, Hewitt (Hackett). **Scorers:** J. Miller 3, Hewitt, Irvine.
Brechin C: Lawrie; Watt, Candlish, Inglis, Stevens, Taylor, Gallacher, Adam (Brown), Lees, Scott, Lyall (Bourke). **Scorer:** Candlish pen.

ALBION ROVERS (1)1 EAST FIFE (0)1 (aet)
(19.8.87, 950)
Albion R: McCullough; Edgar, McGowan, Ahern, Gallagher, Chapman, Teevan, Rodgers, Graham, Houston, Black (T. McDonald). **Scorer:** Rodgers pen.
East Fife: Banner; Connor, Pittman (Conroy), McCafferty, Halley, McLaren, Perry, Deas (Stead), Smith, Mitchell, Hunter. **Scorer:** McCafferty.
Albion R won 5–3 on penalties.

SCOTTISH LEAGUE CUP

AYR UNITED (0)0 DUMBARTON (0)1
(19.8.87, 2428)
Ayr U: Watson; McIntyre, McCann (Kennedy), Furphy, Hughes, Evans, Templeton, Scott, Walker, Sludden, Cowell.
Dumbarton: Arthur; Montgomerie, Martin, McCahill, D. McNeil, J. McNeil, McGowan, J. Rooney, O. Coyle, Houston, B. Rooney (Gow). **Scorer:** D. McNeil.

CELTIC (3)3 FORFAR ATHLETIC (1)1
(19.8.87, 15,000)
Celtic: Bonner; Morris, Rogan, Aitken, Whyte, McGugan, Stark, McStay, McGhee, Walker (Shepherd), Burns. **Scorers:** Walker 2, Stark.
Forfar Ath: Kennedy; W. Bennett, Hamill, Brazil (Morris), Smith, Clark, Blackie (Ward), M. Bennett, Scott, Brewster, Macdonald. **Scorer:** Macdonald pen.

DUNDEE UNITED (0)4 PARTICK THISTLE (0)1
(19.8.87, 6075)
Dundee U: Thomson; Holt, Malpas, McPhee, Hegarty, Narey, Ferguson, Bowman, Gallacher, Sturrock (J. A. Irvine), Redford. **Scorers:** Gallacher, Sturrock, McPhee, Ferguson.
Partick T: Brough; Pirie (Logan), Workman, Dinnie, Spittal, Rafferty, Kelly, Law, Gallagher, McDonald, Mitchell (Leyden). **Scorer:** Mitchell.

HEARTS (2)6 KILMARNOCK (1)1
(19.8.87, 7600)
Hearts: Smith; Kidd, Whittaker, W, Jardine, Berry, McPherson (I. Jardine), Colquhoun, Black, Clark (Foster), MacKay, Robertson. **Scorers:** McPherson, Clark 2, MacKay, Berry, Foster.
Kilmarnock: Holland; McLean, Bell, McVeigh, Davidson, Robertson, McInnes, Cuthbertson, Harkness, Reid, Bryson. **Scorer:** Bryson pen.

MORTON (1)1 CLYDE (1)5
(19.8.87, 2500)
Morton: Wylie; John Boag, Holmes, Hunter, Doak, McMaster, D. Robertson, Turner (Jim Boag), Alexander, Clinging, J. Robertson (McNeill). **Scorer:** J. Robertson.
Clyde: Latchford; McFarlane, Napier, Walker, Flexney, McDowall, Willock, Millar, Watters, Mailer (Murray), Henderson. **Scorers:** Mailer, Walker 2, 1 pen, Watters 2.

MOTHERWELL (0)3 AIRDRIEONIANS (0)1
(19.8.87, 2790)
Motherwell: Duncan; Wishart (Wright), Murray, Kennedy, McAdam, Boyd, Fairlie, Kirk, Smith, Russell, Mair (Gahagan). **Scorers:** Kirk, Fairlie, Boyd.
Airdrieonians: Martin; MacKinnon, Black, McKeown, Lawrie, Moore, Campbell, Docherty, MacCabe, Reilley (Hughes), Flood (Lindsay). **Scorer:** MacCabe.

RAITH ROVERS (1)2 CLYDEBANK (1)1
(19.8.87, 1200)
Raith R: McAlpine; Archibald, MacLeod, Kerr, Brash, McStay, Simpson, Marshall, Harris, Dalziel (Harrow), Sweeney (Gibson). **Scorers:** Dalziel, Harris.
Clydebank: Gallacher; Dickson, Rodger, Treanor, Auld, Sweeney, Shanks, Irons, Gordon (Conroy), Grant, Bryce. **Scorer:** Bryce.

STIRLING ALBION (0)1 RANGERS (1)2
(19.8.87, 13,000)
Stirling Albion: Graham; Aitchison, Spence, Hoggan,

McTeague, Maxwell, Thompson, Conway, Gibson, Kemp, Brogan (Gavin). **Scorer:** Thompson.
Rangers: Woods; Nicholl, Munro, Roberts, Souness, Butcher, Kirkwood (McGregor), Falco, McCoist, Durrant, Phillips. **Scorers:** Falco, McCoist.

THIRD ROUND

HEARTS (1)2 CLYDE (0)0
(25.8.87, 10,000)
Hearts: Smith; Kidd, Whittaker, W. Jardine, Berry, McPherson, Colquhoun, I. Jardine (Burns), Clark, MacKay, Robertson. **Scorer:** Robertson 2, 1 pen.
Clyde: Latchford; McFarlane, Napier (Watters), Walker, Flexney, McDowall, Willock, Millar, McGlashan, Mailer, Henderson.

HIBERNIAN (2)3 QUEEN OF THE SOUTH (1)1
(25.8.87, 7600)
Hibernian: Rough; Hunter, Mitchell, Bell (Tortolano), Orr, McIntyre, Weir, Chisholm, McCluskey (Cowan), Kane, Collins. **Scorers:** Orr, Kane 2, 1 pen.
Queen of the S: Davidson; Sinclair, Dickson (Frye), Docherty, Mackin, Hetherington, Reid, Hughes, Moore, Anderson (Cloy), Doherty. **Scorer:** Hughes.

RAITH ROVERS(1)1 DUNDEE UNITED (1)2
(25.8.87, 6500)
Raith R: McAlpine; Archibald, McStay, Kerr, Brash, Gibson, Simpson, Marshall, Harris, Dalziel (Harrow), MacLeod. **Scorer:** Harris pen.
Dundee U: Thomson; Holt, Malpas, McPhee, Hegarty, Narey, Ferguson, Kirkwood, Gallacher, Sturrock, Redford (Bannon). **Scorers:** Sturrock, Malpas.

ABERDEEN (1)3 ST JOHNSTONE (0)0
(26.8.87, 10,800)
Aberdeen: Leighton; McKimmie, D. Robertson, Simpson, Irvine, W. Miller, Dodds, Bett, J. Miller, Nicholas (Grant), Hewitt (Hackett). **Scorers:** Dodds 2, Bett.
St Johnstone: Balavage; Wilson, McVicar, Barron, McKillop, McGurn (Smith), Maskrey, Coyle, Johnston (Lloyd), Brown, Heddle.

DUMBARTON (0)1 CELTIC (2)5
(26.8.87, 10,000)
Dumbarton: Arthur; Montgomerie, Martin, McCahill, D. McNeil, J. McNeil (B. Rooney), McGowan, J. Rooney, O. Coyle, Houston (Gow), MacIver. **Scorer:** Martin.
Celtic: McKnight; Morris, Rogan, Aitken, McGugan, Grant, Stark (Archdeacon), Shepherd, McGhee, Walker, Burns (McGuire). **Scorers:** Burns, Stark 2, Walker, McGhee.

DUNFERMLINE ATHLETIC (1)1 RANGERS (2)4
(26.8.87, 18,070)
Dunfermline Ath: Westwater; G. Robertson, Cowie, McCathie, Young, C. Robertson, Beedie, Morrison, Ferguson, McCall, Jenkine (Irvine). **Scorer:** McCall pen.
Rangers: Woods; Nicholl, Phillips, Roberts, Souness (McGregor), Butcher, Ferguson (Fleck), Falco, McCoist, Durrant, Cooper. **Scorers:** McCoist 3, 1 pen, Falco.

MEADOWBANK THISTLE (0)0 DUNDEE (2)3
(26.8.87, 2744)
Meadowbank T: McQueen; Hendrie, Roseburgh, Boyd, Tierney, Armstrong, Park, Lawson (Prentice), Callachan, Kasule (Liddle), McGachie.
Dundee: Geddes; Forsyth, McKinlay, Glennie, Smith, Duffy, Mennie, Shannon, Wright, Coyne, Angus. **Scorers:** Coyne 2, Wright.

MOTHERWELL (2)4 ALBION ROVERS (0)0
(26.8.87, 2000)
Motherwell: Duncan; Wishart, Murray, Paterson, Kennedy, Boyd, Fairlie, Kirk (Wright), Smith, Russell (Gahagan), Mair. **Scorers:** Kirk, Russell 2, Fairlie.
Albion R: McCulloch, Lennon, McGowan, Ahern, Gallagher (Wilson), Chapman (McDonald), Rodgers, Edgar, Graham, Houston, Teevan.

QUARTER-FINALS

ABERDEEN (0)1 CELTIC (0)0
(1.9.87, 24,000)
Aberdeen: Leighton; McKimmie, D. Robertson, Connor, Irvine, W. Miller, Hewitt, Bett, J. Miller, Nicholas, Hackett. **Scorer:** Bett.
Celtic: McKnight; Morris, Rogan, Aitken, Whyte, Grant, Stark, McStay, McGhee, Walker, Burns.

MOTHERWELL (1)1 HIBERNIAN (0)0
(1.9.87, 9600)
Motherwell: Duncan; Wishart, Murray, Paterson, McAdam, Boyd, Fairlie (Russell), Farningham, Smith, Kirk (Wright), Mair. **Scorer:** Fairlie.
Hibernian: Rough; Hunter, Mitchell, May, Rae, McIntyre, Weir, Orr, McCluskey (Bell), Kane, Watson (Collins).

DUNDEE (0)2 DUNDEE UNITED (1)1 (aet)
(2.9.87, 19,800)
Dundee: Geddes; Forsyth, McKinlay, Glennie, Smith, Duffy, Mennie (Harvey), Shannon, Wright, Coyne (Jack), Angus. **Scorers:** Coyne, Wright.
Dundee U: W. Thomson; Holt, Malpas, McPhee (Bowman), Hegerty, Narey, Ferguson, Bannon, Gallacher, Sturrock (A. J. Irvine), Redford. **Scorer:** Ferguson.

RANGERS (3)4 HEARTS (0)1
(2.9.87, 39,303)
Rangers: Woods; Nicholl, Munro, Roberts, Phillips, McGregor, Ferguson (Cohen), Fleck, McCoist, Durrant, Cooper. **Scorers:** Durrant 2, McCoist 2, 1 pen.
Hearts: Smith; Kidd, Whittaker, W. Jardine, Berry McPherson, Colquhoun, I. Jardine (Black), Clark (Foster), MacKay, Robertson.
Scorer: Robertson.

SEMI-FINALS

ABERDEEN (2)2 DUNDEE (0)0
(23.9.87, Tannadice Park, 22,034)
Aberdeen: Leighton; McKimmie, D. Robertson, Connor, McLeish, W. Miller, Hewitt, Bett, J. Miller, Falconer, Irvine. **Scorers:** Connor, Irvine.
Dundee: Geddes; McGeachie, McKinlay, Mennie (Jack), Smith, Glennie, Harvey, Brown, Wright, Coyne, Angus.

RANGERS (2)3 MOTHERWELL (1)1 Hampden Park,
(23.9.87, 45,938)
Rangers: Woods; Nicholl, Phillips, Roberts, Souness, Butcher, Francis, Fleck, McCoist, Durrant, Cooper (Falco). **Scorers:** Kirk og, Fleck, Falco.
Motherwell: Duncan; Wishart (Fairlie), Philliben, Peterson, McAdam, Boyd, Farningham, Kirk (Mair), Smith, Russell, Gahagan. **Scorer:** Smith

FINAL

RANGERS (2)3 ABERDEEN (1)3 (aet)
(25.10.87, Hampden Park, 71,961)
Rangers: Walker; Nicholl, Munro, Roberts, Ferguson (Francis), Gough, McGregor (Cohen), Fleck, McCoist, Durrant, Cooper. **Scorers:** Cooper, Durrant, Fleck.
Aberdeen: Leighton; McKimmie, Connor, Simpson (Weir), McLeish, W. Miller, Hewitt, Bett, J. Miller, Nicholas, Falconer. **Scorers:** Bett pen, Hewitt, Falconer.
Rangers won 5–3 on penalties.

SCOTTISH LEAGUE CUP FINALS SINCE 1947

1946–47: RANGERS 4, ABERDEEN 0 (Hampden Park, 5.4.47, 82,584)
Rangers: Brown; Young, Shaw, McColl, Woodburn, Rae, Rutherford, Gillick, Williamson, Thornton, Duncanson. **Scorers:** Gillick, Williamson, Duncanson 2.
Aberdeen: Johnstone; Cooper, McKenna, McLaughlin, Dunlop, Taylor, Harris, Hamilton, Williams, Baird, McCall.
1947–48: EAST FIFE 4, FALKIRK 1 (after Replay) (Hampden Park, 1.11.47, 30,664)
East Fife: Niven; Laird, Stewart, Philp, Finlay, Aitken, Adams, D. Davidson, Morris, J. Davidson, Duncan. **Scorers:** Duncan 3, Adams.
Falkirk: J. Dawson; White, McPhee, Bolt, R. Henderson, Gallagher, Fiddes, Alison, Aikman, J. Henderson, K. Dawson. **Scorer:** Aikman.
1948–49: RANGERS 2, RAITH ROVERS 0 (Hampden Park, 12.3.49, 53,359)
Rangers: Brown; Young, Shaw, McColl, Woodburn, Cox, Gillick, Paton, Thornton, Duncanson, Rutherford. **Scorers:** Gillick, Paton.
Raith R: Westland; McKure, McNaught, Young, Colville, Leigh, Maule, Collins, Penman, Brady, Joyner.
1949–50: EAST FIFE 3, DUNFERMLINE ATHELETIC 0 (Hampden Park, 29.10.49, 38,897)
East Fife: McGarrity; Laird, Stewart, Philp, Finlay, Aitken, Black, Fleming, Morris, Brown, Duncan. **Scorers:** Fleming, Duncan, Morris.
Dunfermline Ath: Johnstone; Kirk, McLean, McCall, Clarkson, Whyte, Mayes, Cannon, Henderson, McGairy, Smith.
1950–51: MOTHERWELL 3, HIBERNIAN 0 (Hampden Park, 28.10.50, 63,074)
Motherwell: Johnstone; Kilmarnock, Shaw, McLeod, Paton, Redpath, Watters, Forrest, Kelly, Watson, Aitkenhead. **Scorers:** Kelly, Forrest, Watters.
Hibernian: Younger; Govan, Ogilvie, Buchanan, Paterson, Combe, Smith, Johnstone, Reilly, Ormond, Bradley.

SCOTTISH LEAGUE CUP

1951–52: DUNDEE 3, RANGERS 2 (Hampden Park, 27.10.51, 91,075)
Dundee: Brown; Fallon, Cowan, Gallacher, Cowie, Boyd, Toner, Pattillo, Flavell, Steel, Christie. **Scorers:** Flavell, Pattillo, Boyd.
Rangers: Brown; Young, Little, McColl, Woodburn, Cox, Waddell, Findlay, Thornton, Johnson, Rutherford. **Scorer:** Thornton 2.
1952–53: DUNDEE 2, KILMARNOCK 0 (Hampden Park, 25.10.52, 51,830)
Dundee: R. Henderson; Fallon, Frew, Ziesing, Boyd, Cowie, Toner, A. Henderson, Flavell, Steel, Christie. **Scorer:** Flavell 2.
Kilmarnock: Niven; Collins, Hood, Russell, Thyne, Middlemass, Henaughan, Harvey, Mayes, Jack, Murray.
1953–54: EAST FIFE 3, PARTICK THISTLE 2 (Hampden Park, 24.10.53, 38,529)
East Fife: Curran; Emery, S. Stewart, Christie, Finlay, McLennan, J. Stewart, Fleming, Bonthrone, Gardiner, Mathew.
Scorers: Gardiner, Fleming, Christie.
Partick T: Ledgerwood; McGowan, Gibb, Crawford, Davidson, Kerr, McKenzie, Howitt, Sharpe, Wright, Walker.
Scorers: Walker, McKenzie.
1954–55: HEART OF MIDLOTHIAN 4, MOTHERWELL 2 (Hampden Park, 23.10.54, 55,640)
Hearts: Duff; Parker, McKenzie, Mackay, Glidden, Cumming, Souness, Conn, Bauld, Wardhaugh, Urquhart. **Scorers:**
Bauld 3, Wardhaugh.
Motherwell: Weir; Kilmarnock, McSeveney, Cox, Paton, Redpath, Hunter, Aitken, Bain, Humphries, Williams. **Scorers:**
Redpath (pen), Bain.
1955–56: ABERDEEN 2, ST MIRREN 1 (Hampden Park, 22.10.55, 44,103)
Aberdeen: Martin; Mitchell, Caldwell, Wilson, Clunie, Glen, Leggat, Yorston, Buckley, Wishart, Hather. **Scorers:** Mallan
(og), Leggat.
St Mirren: Lornie; Lapsley, Mallan, Neilson, Telfer, Holmes, Rodger, Laird, Brown, Gemmell, Callan. **Scorer:** Holmes.
1956–57: CELTIC 3, PARTICK THISTLE 0 (after Replay) (Hampden Park, 31.10.56, 31,126)
Celtic: Beattie; Haughney, Fallon, Evans, Jack, Peacock, Tully, Collins, McPhail, Wilson, Mochan. **Scorers:** McPhail 2, Collins.
Partick T: Ledgerwood; Kerr, Gibb, Collins, Crawford, Mathers, McKenzie, Wright, Hogan, McParland, Ewing.
1957–58: CELTIC 7, RANGERS 1 (Hampden Park, 19.10.57, 82,293)
Celtic: Beattie; Donnelly, Fallon, Fernie, Evans, Peacock, Tully, Collins, McPhail, Wilson, Mochan. **Scorers:** Mochan 2,
McPhail 3, Wilson, Fernie (pen).
Rangers: Niven; Shearer, Caldow, McColl, Vallentine, Davis, Scott, Simpson, Murray, Baird, Hubbard. **Scorer:** Simpson.
1958–59: HEART OF MIDLOTHIAN 5, PARTICK THISTLE 1 (Hampden Park, 25.10.58, 59,960)
Hearts: Marshall; Kirk, Thomson, Mackay, Glidden, Cumming, Hamilton, Murray, Bauld, Wardhaugh, Crawford.
Scorers: Murray 2, Bauld 2, Hamilton.
Partick T: Ledgerwood; Hogan, Donlevy, Mathers, Davidson, Wright, McKenzie, Thomson, Smith, McParland, Ewing.
Scorer: Smith.
1959–60: HEART OF MIDLOTHIAN 2, THIRD LANARK 1 (Hampden Park, 24.10.59, 57,974)
Hearts: Marshall; Kirk, Thomson, Bowman, Cumming, Higgins, Smith, Crawford, Young, Blackwood, Hamilton.
Scorers: Hamilton, Young.
Third Lanark: Robertson; Lewis, Brown, Reilly, McCallum, Cunningham, McInnes, Craig, D. Hilley, Gray, I. Hilley.
Scorer: Gray.
1960–61: RANGERS 2, KILMARNOCK 0 (Hampden Park, 29.10.60, 82,063)
Rangers: Niven; Shearer, Caldow, Davis, Paterson, Baxter, Scott, McMillan, Millar, Brand, Wilson. **Scorers:** Brand, Scott.
Kilmarnock: Brown; Richmond, Watson, Beattie, Toner, Kennedy, Brown, McInally, Kerr, Black, Muir.
1961–62: RANGERS 3, HEART OF MIDLOTHIAN 1 (after Replay) (Hampden Park, 18.12.61, 47,552)
Rangers: Ritchie; Shearer, Caldow, Davis, Baillie, Baxter, Scott, McMillan, Millar, Brand, Wilson. **Scorers:** Millar, Brand,
McMillan.
Hearts: Cruickshank; Kirk, Holt, Cumming, Polland, Higgins, Ferguson, Davidson, Bauld, Blackwood, Hamilton. **Scorer:**
Davidson.
1962–63: HEART OF MIDLOTHIAN 1, KILMARNOCK 0 (Hampden Park, 27.10.62, 51,280)
Hearts: Marshall; Polland, Holt, Cumming, Barry, Higgins, Wallace, Paton, Davidson, W. Hamilton, J. Hamilton. **Scorer:**
Davidson.
Kilmarnock: McLaughlin; Richmond, Watson, O'Connor, McGrory, Beattie, Brown, Black, Kerr, McInally, McIlroy.
1963–64: RANGERS 5, MORTON 0 (Hampden Park, 26.10.63, 105,907)
Rangers: Ritchie; Shearer, Provan, Greig, McKinnon, Baxter, Henderson, Willoughby, Forrest, Brand, Watson. **Scorers:**
Forrest 4, Willoughby.
Morton: Brown; Boyd, Mallan, Reilly, Keirnan, Strachan, Adamson, Campbell, Stevenson, McGraw, Wilson.
1964–65: RANGERS 2, CELTIC 1 (Hampden Park, 24.10.64, 91,000)
Rangers: Ritchie; Provan, Caldow, Greig, McKinnon, Wood, Brand, Millar, Forrest, Baxter, Johnston. **Scorer:** Forrest 2.
Celtic: Fallon; Young, Gemmell, Clark, Cushley, Kennedy, Johnstone, Murdoch, Chalmers, Divers, Hughes. **Scorer:**
Johnstone.
1965–66: CELTIC 2, RANGERS 1 (Hampden Park, 23.10.65, 107,609)
Celtic: Simpson; Young, Gemmell, Murdoch, McNeill, Clark, Johnstone, Gallagher, McBride, Lennox, Hughes. **Scorer:**
Hughes 2 (2 pens).
Rangers: Ritchie; Johansen, Provan, Wood, McKinnon, Greig, Henderson, Willoughby, Forrest, Wilson, Johnston.
Scorer: Young (og).
1966–67: CELTIC 1, RANGERS 0 (Hampden Park, 29.10.66, 94,532)
Celtic: Simpson; Gemmell, O'Neil, Murdoch, McNeill, Clark, Johnstone, Lennox, McBride, Auld, Hughes (Chalmers).
Scorer: Lennox.

Rangers: Martin; Johansen, Provan, Greig, McKinnon, D. Smith, Henderson, Watson, McLean, A. Smith, Johnston

1967–68: CELTIC 5, DUNDEE 3 (Hampden Park, 28.10.67, 66,660)
Celtic: Simpson; Craig, Gemmell, Murdoch, McNeill, Clark, Chalmers, Lennox, Wallace, Auld (O'Neil), Hughes. **Scorers:** Chalmers 2, Hughes, Lennox, Wallace.
Dundee: Arrol; R. Wilson, Houston, Murray, G. Stewart, A. Stuart, Campbell, J. McLean, S. Wilson, G. McLean, Bryce. **Scorers:** G. McLean 2, J. McLean.

1968–69: CELTIC 6, HIBERNIAN 2 (Hampden Park, 5.4.69, 74,000)
Celtic: Fallon; Craig, Gemmell, Murdoch, McNeill, Brogan, Johnstone, Wallace, Chalmers, Auld, Lennox (Craig). **Scorers:** Lennox 3, Wallace, Auld, Craig.
Hibernian: Allan; Shevlane, Davis, Stanton, Madsen, Blackley, Marinello, Quinn, Cormack, O'Rourke, Stevenson. **Scorers:** O'Rourke, Stevenson.

1969–70: CELTIC 1, ST JOHNSTONE 0 (Hampden Park, 25.10.69, 73,067)
Celtic: Fallon; Craig, Hay, Murdoch, McNeill, Brogan, Johnstone, Hood, Hughes, Chalmers (Johnstone), Auld. **Scorer:** Auld.
St Johnstone: Donaldson; Lambie, Coburn, Gordon, Rooney, McPhee, Aird, Hall, McCarry (Whitelaw), Connolly, Aitken.

1970–71: RANGERS 1, CELTIC 0 (Hampden Park, 24.10.70, 106,263)
Rangers: McCloy; Jardine, Miller, Conn, McKinnon, Jackson, Henderson, MacDonald, D. Johnstone, Stein, W. Johnston. **Scorer:** D. Johnstone.
Celtic: Williams; Craig, Quinn, Murdoch, McNeill, Hay, Johnstone, Connelly, Wallace, Hood (Lennox), Macari.

1971–72: PARTICK THISTLE 4, CELTIC 1 (Hampden Park, 23.10.71, 62,740)
Partick T: Rough; Hansen, Forsyth, Glavin (Gibson), Campbell, Strachan, McQuade, Coulston, Bone, Rae, Lawrie. **Scorers:** Rae, Lawrie, McQuade, Bone.
Celtic: Williams; Hay, Gemmell, Murdoch, Connelly, Brogan, Johnstone (Craig), Dalglish, Hood, Callaghan, Macari. **Scorer:** Dalglish.

1972–73: HIBERNIAN 2, CELTIC 1 (Hampden Park, 9.12.72, 71,696)
Hibernian: Herriot; Brownlie, Schaedler, Stanton, Black, Blackley, Edwards, O'Rourke, Gordon, Cropley, Duncan. **Scorers:** Stanton, O'Rourke.
Celtic: Williams; McGrain, Brogan, McCluskey, McNeill, Hay, Johnstone (Callaghan), Connelly, Dalglish, Hood, Macari. **Scorer:** Dalglish.

1973–74: DUNDEE 1, CELTIC 0 (Hampden Park, 15.12.73, 27,974)
Dundee: Allan; Wilson, Gemmell, Ford, Stewart, Phillip, Duncan, Robinson, Wallace, Scott, Lambie. **Scorer:** Wallace.
Celtic: Hunter; McGrain, Brogan, McCluskey, McNeill, Murray, Hood (Johnstone), Hay (Connelly), Wilson, Callaghan, Dalglish.

1974–75: CELTIC 6, HIBERNIAN 3 (Hampden Park, 26.10.74, 53,848)
Celtic: Hunter; McGrain, Brogan, Murray, McNeill, McCluskey, Johnstone, Dalglish, Deans, Hood, Wilson. **Scorers:** Johnstone, Deans 3, Wilson, Murray.
Hibernian: McArthur; Brownlie (Smith), Bremner, Stanton, Spalding, Blackley, Edwards, Cropley, Harper, Munro, Duncan (Murray). **Scorer:** Harper 3.

1975–76: RANGERS 1, CELTIC 0 (Hampden Park, 25.10.75, 58,806)
Rangers: Kennedy; Jardine, Greig, Forsyth, Jackson, MacDonald, McLean, Stein, Parlane, Johnstone, Young. **Scorer:** MacDonald.
Celtic: Latchford; McGrain, Lynch, McCluskey, MacDonald, Edvaldsson, Hood (McNamara), Dalglish, Wilson (Glavin), Callagham, Lennox.

1976–77: ABERDEEN 2, CELTIC 1 (after extra time) (Hampden Park, 6.11.76, 69,268)
Aberdeen: Clark; Kennedy, Williamson, Smith, Garner, Miller, Sullivan, Scott, Harper, Jarvie (Robb), Graham. **Scorers:** Jarvie, Robb.
Celtic: Latchford; McGrain, Lynch, Edvaldsson, MacDonald, Aitken, Doyle, Glavin, Dalglish, Burns (Lennox), Wilson. **Scorer:** Dalglish (pen).

1977–78: RANGERS 2, CELTIC 1 (Hampden Park, 18.3.78, 60,168)
Rangers: Kennedy; Jardine, Greig, Forsyth, Jackson, MacDonald, McLean, Hamilton (Miller), Johnstone, Smith, Cooper (Parlane). **Scorers:** Cooper, Smith.
Celtic: Latchford; Sneddon, Lynch (Wilson), Munro, MacDonald, Dowie, Glavin (Doyle), Edvaldsson, McCluskey, Aitken, Burns. **Scorer:** Edvaldsson.

1978–79: RANGERS 2, ABERDEEN 1 (Hampden Park, 31.3.79, 54,000)
Rangers: McCloy; Jardine, Dawson, Johnstone, Jackson, MacDonald, McLean, Russell, Urquhart (Miller), Smith (Parlane), Cooper. **Scorers:** McMaster (og), Jackson.
Aberdeen: Clark; Kennedy, McLelland, McMaster, Rougvie, Miller, Strachan, Archibald, Harper, Jarvie (McLeish), Davidson. **Scorer:** Davidson.

1979–80: DUNDEE UNITED 3, ABERDEEN 0 (after Replay) (Dens Park, 12.12.79, 28,984) (Bell's)
Dundee U: McAlpine; Stark, Kopel, Fleming, Hegarty, Narey, Bannon, Sturrock, Pettigrew, Holt, Kirkwood. **Scorers:** Pettigrew 2, Sturrock.
Aberdeen: Clark; Kennedy, Rougvie, McLeish, Garner, Miller, Strachan, Archibald, McGhee (Jarvie), McMaster, Scanlon (Hamilton).

1980–81: DUNDEE UNITED 3, DUNDEE 0 (Dens Park, 6.12.80, 24,466) (Bell's)
Dundee U: McAlpine; Holt, Kopel, Phillip, Hegarty, Narey, Bannon, Payne, Pettigrew, Sturrock, Dodds. **Scorers:** Dodds, Sturrock 2.
Dundee: R. Geddes; Barr, Schaedler, Fraser, Glennie, McGeachie, Mackie, Stephen, Sinclair, Williamson, A. Geddes.

SCOTTISH LEAGUE CUP

1981–82: RANGERS 2, DUNDEE UNITED 1 (Hampden Park, 28.11.81, 53,795)
Rangers: Stewart; Jardine, Miller, Stevens, Jackson, Bett, Cooper, Johnstone, Russell, MacDonald, Dalziel (Redford). **Scorers:** Cooper, Redford.
Dundee U: McAlpine; Holt, Stark, Narey, Hegarty, Phillip, Bannon, Milne, Kirkwood, Sturrock, Dodds. **Scorer:** Milne.
1982–83: CELTIC 2, RANGERS 1 (Hampden Park, 4.12.82, 55,372)
Celtic: Bonner; McGrain, Sinclair, Aitken, McAdam, MacLeod, Provan, McStay (Reid), McGarvey, Burns, Nicholas. **Scorers:** Nicholas, MacLeod.
Rangers: Stewart; MacKinnon, Redford, McClelland, Paterson, Bett, Cooper, Prytz (Dawson), Johnstone, Russell (MacDonald), Smith. **Scorer:** Bett.
1983–84: RANGERS 3, CELTIC 2 (after extra time) (Hampden Park, 25.3.84, 66,369)
Rangers: McCloy; Nicholl, Dawson, McClelland, Paterson, McPherson, Russell, McCoist, Clark (McAdam), MacDonald (Burns), Cooper. **Scorer:** McCoist 3 (2 pens).
Celtic: Bonner; McGrain, Reid, Aitken, McAdam, MacLeod, Provan (Sinclair), McStay, McGarvey (Melrose), Burns, McClair. **Scorers:** McClair, Reid (pen).
1984–85: RANGERS 1, DUNDEE UNITED 0 (Hampden Park, 28.10.84, 44,698)
Rangers: McCloy; Dawson, McClelland, Fraser, Paterson, McPherson, Russel (Prytz), McCoist, Ferguson (Mitchell), Redford, Cooper. **Scorer:** Ferguson.
Dundee U: McAlpine; Holt (Clark), Malpas, Gough, Hegarty, Narey, Bannon, Milne (Beedie), Kirkwood, Sturrock, Dodds.
1985–86: ABERDEEN 3, HIBERNIAN 0 (Hampden Park, 27.10.85, 40,065)
Aberdeen: Leighton; McKimmie, Mitchell, Stark, McLeish, Miller, Black (Gray), Simpson, McDougall, Cooper, Hewitt. **Scorers:** Black 2, Stark.
Hibernian: Rough; Sneddon, Munro, Brazil (Harris), Fulton, Hunter, Kane, Chisholm, Cowan, Durie, McBride (Collins).
1986–87: RANGERS 2, CELTIC 1 (Hampden Park, 26.10.86, 74,219)
Rangers: Woods; Nicholl, Munro, Fraser (MacFarlane), Dawson, Butcher, D. Ferguson, McMinn, McCoist (Fleck), Durrant, Cooper. **Scorers:** Durrant, Cooper (pen).
Celtic: Bonner; Grant, MacLeod, Aitken, Whyte, McGhee (Archdeacon), McClair, P. McStay, Johnston, Shepherd, McInally. **Scorer:** McClair.
1987–88: RANGERS 3, ABERDEEN 3 (aet) (Hampden Park, 25.10.87, 71,961)
Rangers: Walker; Nicholl, Munro, Roberts, Ferguson (Francis), Gough, McGregor (Cohen), Fleck, McCoist, Durrant, Cooper. **Scorers:** Cooper, Durrant, Fleck.
Aberdeen: Leighton; McKimmie, Connor, Simpson (Weir), McLeish, W. Miller, Hewitt, Bett, J. Miller, P. Nicholas, Falconer. **Scorers:** Bett, Hewitt, Falconer.
Rangers won 5–3 on penalties.

SCOTTISH LEAGUE CUP FINALS SINCE 1946-57

1946–47	Rangers 4, Aberdeen 0	1960–61	Rangers 2, Kilmarnock 0	1974–75	Celtic 6, Hibernian 3
1947–48	East Fife 0,4, Falkirk 0,1	1961–62	Rangers 1,3, Hearts 1,1	1975–76	Rangers 1, Celtic 0
1948–49	Rangers 2, Raith R 0	1962–63	Hearts 1, Kilmarnock 0	1976–77	Aberdeen 2, Celtic 1
1949–50	East Fife 3, Dunfermline Ath 0	1963–64	Rangers 5, Morton 0	1977–78	Rangers 2, Celtic 1
1950–51	Motherwell 3, Hibernian 0	1964–65	Rangers 2, Celtic 1	1978–79	Rangers 2, Aberdeen 1
1951–52	Dundee 3, Rangers 2	1965–66	Celtic 2, Rangers 1	1979–80	Dundee U 0,3, Aberdeen 0,0
1952–53	Dundee 2, Kilmarnock 0	1966–67	Celtic 1, Rangers 0	1980–81	Dundee U 3, Dundee 0
1953–54	East Fife 3, Partick Th 2	1967–68	Celtic 5, Dundee 3	1981–82	Rangers 2, Dundee U 1
1954–55	Hearts 4, Motherwell 2	1968–69	Celtic 6, Hibernian 2	1982–83	Celtic 2, Rangers 1
1955–56	Aberdeen 2, St Mirren 1	1969–70	Celtic 1, St Johnstone 0	1983–84	Rangers 3, Celtic 2
1956–57	Celtic 0,3, Partick Th 0,0	1970–71	Rangers 1, Celtic 0	1984–85	Rangers 1, Dundee U 0
1957–58	Celtic 7, Rangers 1	1971–72	Partick Th 4, Celtic 1	1985–86	Aberdeen 3, Hibernian 0
1958–59	Hearts 5, Partick Th 1	1972–73	Hibernian 2, Celtic 1	1986–87	Rangers 2, Celtic 1
1959–60	Hearts 2, Third Lanark 1	1973–74	Dundee 1, Celtic 0	1987–88	Rangers 3, Aberdeen 3*

*Rangers won 5–3 on penalties

WINS

15 – Rangers. 9 – Celtic. 4 – Hearts. 3 – Aberdeen, Dundee, East Fife. 2 – Dundee U. 1 – Hibernian, Motherwell, Partick Th.

APPEARANCES IN FINAL

20 – Rangers. 19 – Celtic. 7 – Aberdeen. 5 – Dundee, Hearts, Hibernian. 4 – Dundee U, Partick Th. 3 – East Fife*, Kilmarnock. 2 – Motherwell. 1 – Dunfermline Ath, Falkirk, Morton, Raith R, St Johnstone, St Mirren, Third Lanark.
*Denotes undefeated

EUROPEAN CLUB FOOTBALL

EUROPEAN CHAMPIONS' CUP FINALS SINCE 1956

1955–56: REAL MADRID 4, STADE DE REIMS 3 (Paris, 13.6.56, 38,000)
Real: Alonso; Atienza, Lesmes, Munoz, Marquitos, Zarraga, Joseito, Marchal, Di Stefano, Rial, Gento. **Scorers:** Di Stefano, Rial 2, Marquitos.
Reims: Jacquet; Zimmy, Giraudo, Leblond, Jonquet, Siatka, Hidalgo, Glovacki, Kopa, Bliard, Templin. **Scorers:** Leblond, Templin, Hidalgo.

1956–57: REAL MADRID 2, FIORENTINA 0 (Madrid, 30.5.57, 124,000)
Real: Alonso; Torres, Lesmes, Munoz, Marquitos, Zarraga, Kopa, Mateos, Di Stefano, Rial, Gento. **Scorers:** Di Stefano (pen), Gento.
Fiorentina: Sarti; Magnini, Cervato, Scaramucci, Orzan, Segato, Julinho, Gratton, Virgili, Montuori, Bizzarri.

1957–58: REAL MADRID 3, AC MILAN 2 (aet, Brussels, 28.5.58, 67,000)
Real: Alonso; Atienza, Lesmes, Santisteban, Zarraga, Kopa, Joseito, Di Stefano, Rial, Gento. **Scorers:** DiStefano, Rial, Gento.
Milan: Soldan; Fontana, Beraldo, Bergamaschi, Maldini, Radice, Danova, Liedholm, Schiaffino, Grillo, Cucchiaroni. **Scorers:** Schiaffino, Grillo.

1958–59: REAL MADRID 2, STADE DE REIMS 0 (Stuttgart, 2.6.59, 80,000)
Real: Dominguez; Marquitos, Zarraga, Santisteban, Santamaria, Ruiz, Kopa, Mateos, Di Stefano, Rial, Gento. **Scorers:** Mateos, Di Stefano.
Reims: Colonna; Rodzik, Giraudo, Penverne, Jonquet, Leblond, Lamartine, Bliard, Fontaine, Piantoni, Vincent.

1959–60: REAL MADRID 7, EINTRACHT FRANKFURT 3 (Hampden Park, 18.5.60, 135,000)
Real: Dominguez; Marquitos, Pachin, Vidal, Santamaria, Zarraga, Canario, Del Sol, Di Stefano, Puskas, Gento. **Scorers:** Di Stefano 3, Puskas 4.
Eintracht: Loy; Lutz, Hoefer, Weilbacher, Eigenbrodt, Stinka, Kress, Lindner, Stein, Pfaff, Meier. **Scorers:** Kress, Stein 2.

1960–61: BENFICA 3, BARCELONA 2 (Berne, 31.5.61, 28,000)
Benfica: Costa Pereira; Joao, Angelo, Neto, Germano, Cruz, Augusto, Santana, Aguas, Coluna, Cavem. **Scorers:** Aguas, Ramallets (og), Coluna.
Barcelona: Ramallets; Foncho, Gracia, Verges, Gensana, Garay, Kubala, Kocsis, Evaristo, Suarez, Czibor. **Scorers:** Kocsis, Czibor.

1961–62: BENFICA 5, REAL MADRID 3 (Amsterdam, 2.5.62, 65,000)
Benfica: Costa Pereira; Joao, Angelo, Cavem, Germano, Cruz, Augusto, Eusebio, Aguas, Coluna, Simoes. **Scorers:** Aguas, Cavem, Coluna, Eusebio 2.
Real: Araquistain; Cassado, Miera, Felo, Santamaria, Pachin, Tejada, Del Sol, Di Stefano, Puskas, Gento. **Scorer:** Puskas 3.

1962–63: AC MILAN 2, BENFICA 1 (Wembley, 22.5.63, 45,000)
Milan: Ghezzi; David, Trebbi, Benitez, Maldini, Trapattoni, Pivatelli, Sani, Altafini, Rivera, Mora. **Scorer:** Altafini 2.
Benfica: Costa Pereira; Cavem, Cruz, Humberto, Raul, Coluna, Augusto, Santana, Torres, Eusebio, Simoes. **Scorer:** Eusebio.

1963–64: INTERNAZIONALE MILAN 3, REAL MADRID 1 (Vienna, 27.5.64, 74,000)
Inter: Sarti; Burgnich, Facchetti, Tagnin, Guarneri, Picchi, Jair, Mazzola, Milani, Suarez, Corso. **Scorers:** Mazzola 2, Milani.
Real: Vicente; Isidro, Pachin, Muller, Santamaria, Zoco, Amancio, Felo, Di Stefano, Puskas, Gento. **Scorer:** Felo.

1964–65: INTERNAZIONALE MILAN 1, BENFICA 0 (Milan, 28.5.65, 80,000)
Inter: Sarti; Burgnich, Facchetti, Bedin, Guarneri, Picchi, Jair, Mazzola, Peiro, Suarez, Corso. **Scorer:** Jair.
Benfica: Costa Pereira; Cavem, Cruz, Neto, Germano, Raul, Augusto, Eusebio, Torres, Coluna, Simoes.

1965–66: REAL MADRID 2, PARTIZAN BELGRADE 1 (Brussels, 11.5.66, 55,000)
Real: Araquistain; Pachin, Sanchis, Pirri, De Felipe, Zoco, Serena, Amancio, Grosso, Velazquez, Gento. **Scorers:** Amancio, Serena.
Partizan: Soskic; Jusufi, Mihailovic, Becejac, Rasovic, Vasovic, Bejic, Kovacevic, Hasanagic, Galic, Primajer. **Scorer:** Vasovic.

1966–67: CELTIC 2, INTERNAZIONALE MILAN 1 (Lisbon, 25.5.67, 56,000)
Celtic: Simpson; Craig, Gemmell, Murdoch, McNeill, Clark, Johnstone, Wallace, Chalmers, Auld, Lennox. **Scorers:** Gemmell, Chalmers.
Inter: Sarti; Burgnich, Facchetti, Bedin, Guarneri, Picchi, Bicicli, Mazzola, Cappellini, Corso, Domenghini. **Scorer:** Mazzola (pen).

1967–68: MANCHESTER UNITED 4, BENFICA 1 (aet, Wembley, 29.5.68, 100,000)
Manchester U: Stepney; Brennan, Dunne, Crerand, Foulkes, Stiles, Best, Kidd, Charlton, Sadler, Aston. **Scorers:** Charlton 2, Best, Kidd.
Benfica: Henrique; Adolfo, Humberto, Jacinto, Cruz, Graca, Coluna, Augusto, Eusebio, Torres, Simoes. **Scorer:** Graca.

1968–69: AC MILAN 4, AJAX AMSTERDAM 1 (Madrid, 28.5.69, 50,000)
Milan: Cudicini; Anquiletti, Schnellinger, Rosato, Malatrasi, Trapattoni, Hamrin, Lodetti, Sormani, Rivera, Prati. **Scorers:** Prati 3, Sormani.
Ajax: Bals; Suurbier, Hulshoff, Vasovic, van Duivenbode, Pronk, Groot, Swart, Cruyff, Danielsson, Keizer. **Scorer:** Vasovic (pen).

1969–70: FEYENOORD 2, CELTIC 1 (aet, Milan, 6.5.70, 50,000)
Feyenoord: Graafland; Romeyn (Haak), Laseroms, Israel, van Duivenbode, Hasil, Jansen, van Hanegem, Wery, Kindvall, Moulijn. **Scorers:** Israel, Kindvall.
Celtic: Williams; Hay, Gemmell, Murdoch, McNeill, Brogan, Johnstone, Lennox, Wallace, Auld (Connolly), Hughes. **Scorer:** Gemmell.

1970–71: AJAX AMSTERDAM 2, PANATHINAIKOS 0 (Wembley, 2.6.71, 90,000)
Ajax: Stuy; Vasovic, Suurbier, Hulshoff, Rijnders (Haan), Neeskens, Swart (Blankenburg), G.Muhren, Keizer, van Dijk, Cruyff. **Scorers:** van Dijk, Kapsis (og).
Panathinaikos: Economopoulos; Tomaros, Vlahos, Elefterakis, Kamaras, Sourpis, Grammos, Filokouris, Antoniadis, Domazos, Kapsis.

1971–72: AJAX AMSTERDAM 2, INTERNAZIONALE MILAN 0 (Rotterdam, 31.5.72, 67,000)
Ajax: Stuy; Suurbier, Blankenburg, Hulshoff, Krol, Neeskens, Haan, G.Muhren, Swart, Cruyff, Keizer. **Scorer:** Cruyff 2.
Inter: Bordon; Burgnich, Bellugi, Oriali, Facchetti, Bedin, Mazzola, Guibertoni (Bertini), Jair (Pellizarro), Boninsegna, Frustalupi.

1972–73: AJAX AMSTERDAM 1, JUVENTUS 0 (Belgrade, 30.5.73, 93,500)
Ajax: Stuy; Suurbier, Krol, Neeskens, Hulshoff, Blankenburg, Rep, Haan, Cruyff, G.Muhren, Keizer. **Scorer:** Rep.
Juventus: Zoff; Longobucco, Marchetti, Furino, Morini, Salvadore, Altafini, Causio (Cuccureddu), Anastasi, Capello, Bettega (Haller).

1973–74: BAYERN MUNICH 1, ATLETICO MADRID 1 (Brussels, 15.5.74, 65,000)
Bayern: Maier; Hansen, Breitner, Schwarzenbeck, Beckenbauer, Roth, Torstensson (Durnberger), Zobel, Muller, Hoeness, Kappellmann. **Scorer:** Schwarzenbeck.
Atletico: Reina; Melo, Capon, Adelardo, Heredia, Eusebio, Ufarte (Becerra), Luis, Garate, Irureta, Salcedo (Alberto). **Scorer:** Luis.

REPLAY: BAYERN MUNICH 4, ATLETICO MADRID 0 (Brussels, 17.5.74, 65,000)
Bayern: Unchanged (no subs). **Scorers:** Muller 2, Hoeness 2.
Atletico: Alberto for Irureta. Benegas came on for Adelardo, Becerra came on for Ufarte.

1974–75: BAYERN MUNICH 2, LEEDS UNITED 0 (Paris, 28.5.75, 50,000)
Bayern: Maier; Durnberger, Andersson (Weiss), Schwarzenbeck, Beckenbauer, Roth, Torstensson, Zobel, Muller, Hoeness (Wunder), Kapellmann. **Scorers:** Roth, Muller.
Leeds U: Stewart; Reaney, F.Gray, Bremner, Madeley, Hunter, Lorimer, Clarke, Jordan, Giles, Yorath (E.Gray).

1975–76: BAYERN MUNICH 1, ST ETIENNE 0 (Hampden Park, 12.5.76, 54,864)
Bayern: Maier; Hansen, Schwarzenbeck, Beckenbauer, Horsmann, Roth, Durnberger, Kapellmann, Rummenigge, Muller, Hoeness. **Scorer:** Roth.
St Etienne: Curkovic; Repellini, Piazza, Lopez, Janvion, Bathenay, Santini, Larque, P.Revelli, H.Revelli, Sarramanga (Rocheteau).

1976–77: LIVERPOOL 3, BORUSSIA MUNCHENGLADBACH 1 (Rome, 25.5.77, 57,000)
Liverpool: Clemence; Neal, Jones, Smith, Kennedy, Hughes, Keegan, Case, Heighway, Callaghan, McDermott. **Scorers:** McDermott, Smith, Neal (pen).
Borussia: Kneib; Vogts, Klinkhammer, Wittkamp, Bonhof, Wohlers(Hannes), Simonsen, Wimmer (Kulik), Stielike, Schaffer, Heynckes. **Scorer:** Simonsen.

1977–78: LIVERPOOL 1, FC BRUGES 0 (Wembley, 10.5.78, 92,000)
Liverpool: Clemence; Neal, Thompson, Hansen, Hughes, McDermott, Kennedy, Souness, Case (Heighway), Fairclough, Dalglish. **Scorer:** Dalglish.
Bruges: Jensen; Bastijns, Krieger, Leekens, Maes (Volders), Cools, De Cubber, van der Eycken, Ku (Sanders), Simoen, Sorensen.

EUROPEAN CUP

1978–79: NOTTINGHAM FOREST 1, MALMO 0 (Munich, 30.5.79, 57,500)
Nottingham F: Shilton; Anderson, Lloyd, Burns, Clark, Francis, McGovern, Bowyer, Robertson, Woodcock, Birtles. **Scorer:** Francis.
Malmo: Moller; Roland Andersson, Jonsson, Magnus Andersson, Erlandsson, Tapper (Malmberg), Ljungberg, Prytz, Kinnvall, Hansson (Tommy Andersson), Cervin.

1979–80: NOTTINGHAM FOREST 1, SV HAMBURG 0 (Madrid, 28.5.80, 50,000)
Nottingham F: Shilton; Anderson, Gray (Gunn), McGovern, Lloyd, Burns, O'Neill, Bowyer, Birtles, Mills (O'Hare), Robertson. **Scorer:** Robertson.
Hamburg: Kargus; Kaltz, Nogly, Jakobs, Buljan, Hieronymus (Hrubesch), Keegan, Memering, Milewski, Magath, Reimann.

1980–81: LIVERPOOL 1, REAL MADRID 0 (Paris, 27.5.81, 48,360)
Liverpool: Clemence; Neal, A.Kennedy, Thompson, R.Kennedy, Hansen, Dalglish (Case), Lee, Johnson, McDermott, Souness. **Scorer:** A.Kennedy.
Real: Rodriguez; Garcia Cortes, Camacho, Stielike, Sabido (Pineda), Del Bosque, Juanito, De Los Santos, Santillana, Navajas, Cunningham.

1981–82: ASTON VILLA 1, BAYERN MUNICH 0 (Rotterdam, 26.5.82, 46,000)
Aston Villa: Rimmer (Spink); Swain, Williams, Evans, McNaught, Mortimer, Bremner, Shaw, Withe, Cowans, Morley. **Scorer:** Withe.
Bayern: Muller; Dremmler, Horsmann, Weiner, Augenthaler, Kraus (Niedermayer), Durnberger, Breitner, D.Hoeness, Mathy (Guttler), Rummenigge.

1982–83: SV HAMBURG 1, JUVENTUS 0 (Athens, 25.5.83, 80,000)
Hamburg: Stein; Kaltz, Wehmeyer, Jakobs, Hieronymus, Rolff, Milewski, Groh, Hrubesch, Magath, Bastrup (von Heesen). **Scorer:** Magath.
Juventus: Zoff; Gentile, Cabrini, Bonini, Brio, Scirea, Bettega, Tardelli, Rossi (Marocchino), Platini, Boniek.

1983–84: LIVERPOOL 1, AS ROMA 1 (aet, Rome, 30.5.84, 69,693)
Liverpool: Grobbelaar; Neal, Kennedy, Lawrenson, Whelan, Hansen, Dalglish (Robinson), Lee, Rush, Johnston (Nicol), Souness. **Scorer:** Neal.
Roma: Tancredi; Nappi, Bonetti, Righetti, Nela, Di Bartolomei, Falcao, Cerezo (Strkelj), Conti, Pruzzo (Chierico), Graziani. **Scorer:** Pruzzo.
Liverpool won 4–2 on penalties.

1984–85: JUVENTUS 1, LIVERPOOL 0 (Brussels, 29.5.85, 58,000)
Juventus: Tacconi; Favero, Cabrini, Bonini, Brio, Scirea, Briaschi (Prandelli), Tardelli, Rossi (Vignola), Platini, Boniek. **Scorer:** Platini (pen).
Liverpool: Grobbelaar; Neal, Beglin, Lawrenson (Gillespie), Nicol, Hansen, Dalglish, Whelan, Rush, Walsh (Johnston), Wark.

1985–86: STEAUA BUCHAREST 0, BARCELONA 0 (aet, Seville, 7.5.86, 70,000)
Steaua: Ducadam; Belodedici, Iovan, Bombescu, Barbulescu, Balint, Balan (Ionescu), Boloni, Majearu, Lacatus, Piturca (Radu).
Barcelona: Urruti; Gerardo, Migueli, Alesanco, Julio Alberto, Victor, Marcos, Schuster (Moratalla), Pedraza, Archibald (Pichi Alonso), Carrusco.
Steaua won 2–0 on penalties.

1986–87: FC PORTO 2, BAYERN MUNICH 1 (Vienna, 27.5.87, 59,000)
Porto: Mlynarczyk; Joao Pinto, Eduardo Luis, Celso, Inacio (Frasco), Quim (Juary), Magalhaes, Sousa, Andre, Futre, Madjer, Juary. **Scorers:** Madjer, Juary.
Bayern: Pfaff; Winklhofer; Nachtwein, Eder, Pfluger, Flick (Lunde), Brehme, D.Hoeness, Matthaus, Kogl, M. Rummenigge. **Scorer:** Kogl.

EUROPEAN CUP 1987–88

FIRST ROUND, FIRST LEG

Aarhus (4)4 (Andersen 1, Bartram 4, Lundkvist 8,18), **Jeunesse d'Esch (0)1** (Seeholten 73)
Bayern Munich (2)4 (Wegmann 31,65, Dorfner 37, Brehme 56), **CSKA Sredets Sofia (0)0**
Benfica (1)4 (Hametaj og 35, Mozer 85, Rui Aguas 91,99 normal time), **Partizan Tirana (0)0**
Bordeaux (0)2 (Ferreri 47,58), **Dynamo Berlin (0)0**
Fram Reykjavik (0)0, **Sparta Prague (0)2** (Skuhavry 78, Musil 86)
Dynamo Kiev (0)1 (Mikhailichenko 72 pen), **Rangers (0)0**
Lillestrom (1)1 (Olsen 44), **Linfield (0)1** (Baxter 74)
Malmo (0)0, **Anderlecht (1)1** (Vervoort 37)
Neuchatal Xamax (3)5 (Van der Gijp 9,20,75, Hermann 31, B. Sutter 50), **Kuusysi Lahti (0)0**
Olympiakos Piraeus (1)1 (Alexiou 19), **Gornik Zabrze (1)1** (Klemenz 26)
FC Porto (1)3 (Madjer 13,85, Sousa 51), **Vardar Skopje (0)0**
PSV Eindhoven (0)3 (Gilhaus 51, R. Koeman 75, Koot 88), **Galatasaray (0)0**
Rapid Vienna (3)6 (Ktanjcar 9 pen, 43, Stojadinovic 29, 81, 88, Willfurth 78), **Hamrun Spartans (0)0**
Real Madrid (1)2 (Michel 18 pen, Tendillo 76), **Napoli (0)0**
Shamrock Rovers (0)0, **Omonia Nicosia (1)1** (Fanis Theophanous 10)
Steaua Bucharest (2)4 (Hagi 11,27, Boloni 63, Lacatus 82), **MTK/VM Budapest (0)0**

FIRST ROUND, SECOND LEG

Anderlecht (1)1 (Vervoort 29), **Malmo (0)1** (Engqvist 62)
CSKA Sredets Sofia (0)0, **Bayern Munich (1)1** (Kogl 69)
Dynamo Berlin (0)0, **Bordeaux (0)2** (Zlatko Vujovic 58, Ferreri 87)
Galatasaray (2)2 (Tanju 5, Nielsen og 42), **PSV Eindhoven (0)0**
Gornik Zabrze (2)2 (Cyron 24, Iwan 42), **Olympiakos Piraeus (0)1** (Kostikos 65 pen)
Hamrun Spartans (0)0, **Rapid Vienna (0)1** (Weber 70)
Jeunesse d'Esch (1)1 (Theis 7), **Aarhus (0)0**
Kuusysi Lahti (2)2 (Lius 7, Kousa 28), **Xamax Neuchatel (1)1** (C. Nielsen 10)
Linfield (1)2 (McGaughey 42,66), **Lillestrom (2)4** (Larsen 26,80, Haberg 44, Sognnes 81)
MTK/VM Budapest (2)2 (Hires 18, Szeibert 42), **Steaua Bucharest (0)0**
Napoli (1)1 (Francini 9), **Real Madrid (1)1** (Butragueno 43)
Omonia Nicosia (0)0, **Shamrock Rovers (0)0**
Partizan Tirana v Benfica – Walkover for Benfica, Partizan expelled by UEFA
Rangers (1)2 (Falco 24, McCoist 50), **Dynamo Kiev (0)0**
Sparta Prague (3)8 (P. Novak 14,56,64, Hasek 7,77, Griga 17, Cabala 59, Chovanec 73), **Fram Reykjavik (0)0**
Vardar Skopje (0)0, **FC Porto (1)3** (Sousa 38, Jaime Magalhaes 64, Madjar 66)

SECOND ROUND, FIRST LEG

Aarhus (0)0, **Benfica (0)0**
Lillestrom (0)0, **Bordeaux (0)0**
Rangers (3)3 (McCoist 6, Durrant 22, Falco 44), **Gornik Zabrze (0)1** (Urban 56)
Rapid Vienna (0)1 (Keinast 47 pen), **PSV Eindhoven (1)2** (Van Aerle 7, Gilhaus 77)
Real Madrid (0)2 (Sanchez 81, Sanchis 89), **FC Porto (0)1** (Madjer 58)
Sparta Prague (1)1 (Hasek 10), **Anderlecht (1)2** (Vervoort 27, Frimann 50)
Steaua Bucharest (2)3 (Hagi 14 pen,60, Iovan 43), **Omonia Nicosia (1)1** (Csurupas 44)
Xamax Neuchatel (1)2 (Luthi 27, Sutter 50), **Bayern Munich (0)1** (Matthaus 46)

SECOND ROUND, SECOND LEG

Anderlecht (1)1 (Nilis 12), **Sparta Prague (0)0**
Bayern Munich (0)2 (Pfluger 88, Wegmann 89), **Xamax Neuchatel (0)0**
Benfica (1)1 (Nunes 38), **Aarhus (0)0**
Bordeaux (1)1 (Ferreri 4), **Lillestrom (0)0**
Gornik Zabrze (0)1 (Orzeszek 63), **Rangers (1)1** (McCoist 41 pen)
Omonia Nicosia (0)0, **Steaua Bucharest (2)2** (Christofi 7 og, Lacatus 34)
FC Porto (1)1 (Sousa 23), **Real Madrid (0)2** (Michel 54,70)
PSV Eindhoven (1)2 (Lerby 15, Gilhaus 84), **Rapid Vienna (0)0**

EUROPEAN CUP

QUARTER–FINALS, FIRST LEG

Bayern Munich (2)3 (Pflugler 40, Eder 45, Wohlfarth 50), **Real Madrid (0)2** (Butragueno 88, Sanchez 90)
Benfica (2)2 (Magnusson 15, Chiquinho 20), **Anderlecht (0)0**
Bordeaux (1)1 (Toure 21), **PSV Eindhoven (1)1** (Kieft 40)
Steaua Bucharest (1)2 (Piturca 2, Iovan 66), **Rangers (0)0**

QUARTER–FINALS, SECOND LEG

Anderlecht (0)1 (Gudjohnsen 64), **Benfica (0)0**
PSV Eindhoven (0)0, Bordeaux (0)0 (PSV won on away goals)
Rangers (2)2 (Gough 16, McCoist 30 pen), **Steaua Bucharest (1)1** (Lacatus 3)
Real Madrid (2)2 (Jankovic 27, Michel 41), **Bayern Munich (0)0**

SEMI–FINALS, FIRST LEG

Real Madrid (1)1 (Sanchez 6 pen), **PSV Eindhoven (1)1** (Linskens 19)
Steaua Bucharest (0)0, Benfica (0)0

SEMI–FINALS, SECOND LEG

PSV Eindhoven (0)0, Real Madrid (0)0 (PSV won on away goals)
Benfica (2)2 (Rui Aguas 22,33), **Steaua Bucharest (0)0**

FINAL

PSV EINDHOVEN (0)0, BENFICA (0)0 (aet, Stuttgart, 25 May 1988, 70,000)
PSV: Van Breukelen; Gerets, Nielsen, Koeman, Heintze, Lerby, van Aerle, Vanenberg, Linskens, Kieft, Gillhaus (Jansson 107).
Benfica: Silvino; Veloso, Dito, Alvaro, Mozer, Elzo, Chiquinho, Pacheco, Aguas (Vando 57), Shew, Magnusson (Haijri 112).
PSV won 6–5 on penalties.

PSV Eindhoven pictured just before their closely-fought victory over Benfica in the European Cup final.
Photo: Bob Thomas Sports Photography

EUROPEAN CUP 1987–88 – BRITISH AND IRISH CLUBS

FIRST ROUND, FIRST LEG

DYNAMO KIEV (0)1, RANGERS (0)0 (16.9.87, 100,000)
Dynamo: Chanov; Bessonov, Baltacha, Kuznetsov, Demianenko, Rats, Yakovenko, Mikhailichenko, Yaremchuk, Yevtushenko, Blokhin. **Scorer:** Mikhailichenko 72 pen.
Rangers: Woods; Nicholl, Butcher, McGregor, Phillips, Roberts, Souness, Ferguson, Cohen, Durrant, McCoist.

LILLESTROM (1)1, LINFIELD (0)1 (16.9.87, 1,123)
Lillestrom: A. Amundsen; Schiller, Dyrstad, Olsen, Halle, Richardson, Erlandsen, F. Larsen, Sognnes, Haberg, Vaadal. **Scorer:** Olsen 44.
Linfield: Dunlop; Dornan, Kennedy, Doherty, Jerhey, McKeown, Grattan (Murray 46), Davies, McLeod (McCarthey 81), Baxter, Burrows. **Scorer:** Baxter 74.

SHAMROCK ROVERS (0)0, OMONIA NICOSIA (1)1 (16.9.87, 2,489)
Shamrock R: J. Byrne; Kenny (O'Connor 66), Brady, Eccles, D. Byrne, P. Byrne (Carlisle 46), Neville, Larkin, M. Byrne, Doolin, McCarthy.
Omonia: Charitou; Mavris (Iakovou 78), Tsikos, Christodolou, Christofi, Stefan, Kantilos, Kalotheou, Djevisov, Costas, F. Theophanous (Andreou 69). **Scorer:** Theophanous 10.

FIRST ROUND, SECOND LEG

RANGERS (1)2, DYNAMO KIEV (0)0 (30.9.87, 44,500)
Rangers: Woods; Nicholl, Phillips, McGregor, Souness, Butcher, Francis (Fleck 70), Falco, McCoist, Durrant, Cohen (Kirkwood 63). **Scorers:** Falco 24, McCoist 50.
Dynamo: Chanov; Bessonov, Baltacha, Kuznetsov, Yevseyev, Rats, Yakovenko (Shamatovenko 80), Mikhailichenko, Yaremchuk, Belanov (Yevtushenko 26), Blokhin.

LINFIELD (1)2, LILLESTROM (2)4 (30.9.87, 12,000)
Linfield: Dunlop; Dornan, Kennedy, Doherty, Jeffrey, McKeown, Murray, Davies, McGaughey, Baxter, Burrows. **Scorer:** McGaughey 42,66.
Lillestrom: A. Amundsen; Schiller, Dyrstad, Olsen, Halle, Richardson, Erlandsen, Larsen, Pendersen, Haberge, Sognnes. **Scorers:** Larsen 26,80, Haberg 44, Sognnes 81.

OMONIA NICOSIA (0)0, SHAMROCK ROVERS (0)0 (30.9.87, 20,000)
Omonia: Charitou; Mavris, Tsikos, Lahcsidy, Christofi, Christodolou, Kantilos, Kalotheou, Djevisov, Tersas (Andreou 75), Theophanous.

Shamrock R: J. Byrne; Kenny, Brady, Neville, Eccles (D. Byrne 65), P. Byrne, Carlisle, Larkin, M. Byrne, Doolin, McCarthy.

SECOND ROUND, FIRST LEG

RANGERS (3)3, GORNIK ZABRZE (0)1 (21.10.87, 41,366)
Rangers: Woods; Nicholl, Phillips, Roberts, Ferguson (Cohen 55), Butcher, Francis (Fleck 76), Falco, McCoist, Durrant, Souness. **Scorers:** McCoist 6, Durrant 22, Falco 44.
Gornik: Wandzik; Grembocki, Dankowski, Kostrzewa, Piotrowicz, Klemenz (Orzeszk 55), Iwan, Komornicki, Urban, Baran (Kolaczyk 73), Cyron. **Scorer:** Urban 56.

SECOND ROUND, SECOND LEG

GORNIK ZABRZE (0)1, RANGERS (1)1 (4.11.87, 23,250)
Gornik: Wandzik; Grembocki, Dankowski, Kostrzewa, Klemenz (Kolaczyk 76), Majka, Iwan, Komornicki, Urban, Barab (Orzeszk 60), Cyron. **Scorer:** Orzeszk 63.
Rangers: Woods; Nicholl, Phillips, Roberts, Souness, Butcher, McGregor, Durrant, Ferguson, McCoist (Fleck 80), Cooper. **Scorer:** McCoist 41 pen.

QUARTER-FINALS, FIRST LEG

STEAUA BUCHAREST (1)2, RANGERS (0)0 (3.3.88, 30,000)
Steaua: Stingaciu; Iovan, Bumbescu, Belodedici, Ungureanu, Rotariu (Balan 65), Stoica, Hagi, Majaru, Lacatus (Balint 40), Piturca. **Scorers:** Piturca 2, Iovan 66.
Rangers: Woods; Gough, Munro, Roberts, Wilkins, Nisbet (D. Ferguson 79), Nicholl, Souness, McCoist (Francis 86), Durrant, Cooper.

QUARTER–FINALS, SECOND LEG

RANGERS (2)2, STEAUA BUCHAREST (1)1 (16.3.88, 44,000)
Rangers: Woods; Nisbet (Francis 71), Munro, Roberts, Wilkins, Gough, D. Ferguson, Souness, McCoist, Durrant, Cooper. **Scorers:** Gough 16, McCoist 30 pen.
Steaua: Stingaciu (Lilac 58); Iovan, Ungureanu (Balan 85), Cireasa, Stoica, Belodedici, Lacatus, G. Popescu, Piturca, Hagi, Rotariu. **Scorer:** Lacatus 3.

EUROPEAN CUP-WINNERS' CUP FINALS SINCE 1961

1960–61 (2 legs): RANGERS 0, FIORENTINA 2 (Glasgow, 17.5.61, 80,000)
Rangers: Ritchie, Shearer, Caldow, Davis, Paterson, Baxter, Wilson, McMillan, Scott, Brand, Hume.
Fiorentina: Albertosi, Robotti, Castelletti, Gonfiantini, Orzan, Rimbaldo, Hamrin, Micheli, Da Costa, Milan, Petris.
Scorer: Milan 2.

2nd LEG: FIORENTINA 2, RANGERS 1 (Florence, 27.5.61, 40,000)
Fiorentina: Unchanged. **Scorers:** Milan, Hamrin.
Rangers: Millar for Hume. **Scorer:** Scott.

1961–62: ATLETICO MADRID 1, FIORENTINA 1 (Glasgow, 10.5.62, 27,389)
Atletico: Madinabeytia, Rivilla, Calleja, Ramirez, Griffa, Glaria, Jones, Adelardo, Mendonca, Peiro, Collar. **Scorer:** Peiro.
Fiorentina: Albertosi, Robotti, Castelletti, Malatrasi, Orzan, Marchesi, Hamrin, Ferretti, Milan, Dell'Angelo, Petris.
Scorer: Hamrin.

REPLAY: ATLETICO MADRID 3, FIORENTINA 0 (Stuttgart, 5.9.62, 45,000)
Atletico: Unchanged. **Scorers:** Jones, Mendonca, Peiro.
Fiorentina: Unchanged.

1962–63: TOTTENHAM HOTSPUR 5, ATLETICO MADRID 1 (Rotterdam, 15.5.63, 25,000)
Tottenham H: Brown, Baker, Henry, Blanchflower, Norman, Marchi, Jones, White, Smith, Greaves, Dyson. **Scorers:** Greaves 2, White, Dyson 2.
Atletico: Madinabeytia, Rivilla, Rodrigues, Ramiro, Griffa, Glaria, Jones, Adelardo, Chuzo, Mendonca, Collar. **Scorer:** Collar (pen).

1963–64: SPORTING LISBON 3, MTK BUDAPEST 3 (aet, Brussels, 13.5.64, 9000)
Sporting: Carvalho, Gomez, Perdis, Battista, Carlos, Geo, Mendes, Oswaldo, Mascarenhas, Figueiredo, Morais. **Scorers:** Figueiredo 2, Dansky (og).
MTK: Kovalik, Keszei, Dansky, Jenei, Nagy, Kovacs, Sandor, Vasas, Kuti, Bodor, Halapi. **Scorers:** Sandor 2, Kuti.

REPLAY: SPORTING LISBON 1, MTK BUDAPEST 0 (Antwerp, 15.5.64, 18,000)
Sporting: Unchanged. **Scorer:** Mendes.
MTK: Unchanged.

1964–65: WEST HAM UNITED 2, MUNICH 1860 0 (Wembley, 19.5.65, 100,000)
West Ham U: Standen, Kirkup, Burkett, Peters, Brown, Moore, Sealey, Boyce, Hurst, Dear, Sissons. **Scorer:** Sealey 2.
Munich: Radenkovic, Wagner, Kohlars, Bena, Reich, Luttrop, Heiss, Kuppers, Brunnenmeier, Grosser, Rebele.

1965–66: BORUSSIA DORTMUND 2, LIVERPOOL 1 (Glasgow, 5.5.66, 41,657)
Borussia: Tilkowski, Cyliax, Redder, Kurrat, Paul, Assauer, Libuda, Schmidt, Held, Sturm, Emmerich. **Scorers:** Held, Yeats (og).
Liverpool: Lawrence, Lawler, Byrne, Milne, Yeats, Stevenson, Callaghan, Hunt, St John, Smith, Thompson. **Scorer:** Hunt.

1966–67: BAYERN MUNICH 1, RANGERS 0 (aet, Nuremberg, 31.5.67, 69,480)
Bayern: Maier, Nowak, Kupferschmidt, Roth, Beckenbauer, Olk, Nafziger, Ohlhauser, Muller, Koulmann, Brenninger. **Scorer:** Roth.
Rangers: Martin, Johansen, Provan, Jardine, McKinnon, Greig, Henderson, A. Smith, Hynd, D. Smith, Johnston.

1967–68: AC MILAN 2, SV HAMBURG 0 (Rotterdam, 23.5.68, 54,000)
Milan: Cudicini, Anquilletti, Schnellinger, Trappatoni, Rosato, Scala, Hamrin, Lodetti, Sormani, Rivera, Prati. **Scorer:** Hamrin 2.
Hamburg: Ozcan, Sandmann, Kurbjuhn, Dieckmann, Horst, W. Schulz, B. Dorfel, Kramer, Seeler, Honig, G. Dorfel.

1968–69: SLOVAN BRATISLAVA 3, BARCELONA 2 (Basle, 21.5.69, 40,000)
Slovan: Vencel, Filo, Hrivnak, Jan Zlocha, Horvath, Hrdlicka, Cvetler, Moder, Josef Capkovic, Jokl, Jan Capkovic. **Scorers:** Cvetler, Hrivnak, Jan Capkovic.
Barcelona: Sadurni, Franch (Pereda), Eladio, Rife, Olivella, Zabalza, Pellicer, Castro (Mendoca), Zaluda, Fuste, Rexach. **Scorers:** Zaluda, Rexach.

1969–70: MANCHESTER CITY 2, GORNIK ZABRZE 1 (Vienna, 20.4.70, 10,000)
Manchester C: Corrigan, Book, Pardoe, Doyle (Bowyer), Booth, Oakes, Heslop, Bell, Lee, Young, Towers. **Scorers:** Young, Lee (pen).
Gornik: Kostka, Gorgan, Ozlizlo, Latogha, Forenski, Szoltyski, Wilczek, Olek, Banas, Lubanski, Szaryniski. **Scorer:** Ozlizlo.

1970–71: CHELSEA 1, REAL MADRID 1 (aet, Athens, 19.5.71, 42,000)
Chelsea: Bonetti, Boyle, Harris, Hollins, Dempsey, Webb, Weller, Hudson, Osgood, Cooke, Houseman. **Scorer:** Osgood.
Real: Borja, Luis, Zunzunegui, Pirri, Benito, Zoco, Perez, Amancio, Grosso, Velazquez, Gento. **Scorer:** Zoco.

REPLAY: CHELSEA 2, REAL MADRID 1 (Athens, 21.5.71, 24,000)
Chelsea: Baldwin for Hollins, Smethurst came on for Osgood. **Scorers:** Dempsey, Osgood.
Real: Fleitas for Perez, Bueno for Gento, Gento came on for Velazquez, Grande came on for Bueno. **Scorer:** Fleitas.

1971–72: RANGERS 3, DYNAMO MOSCOW 2 (Barcelona, 24.5.72, 35,000)
Rangers: McCloy, Jardine, Mathieson, Greig, Johnstone, Smith, McLean, Conn, Stein, MacDonald, Johnston. **Scorers:** Stein, Johnston 2.
Dynamo: Pilgui, Basalev, Dolmatov, Zykov, Dobbonosov (Gerschkovitch), Zhukov, Baidatchini, Jakubik (Estrekov), Sabo, Makovikov, Evryuzikhin. **Scorers:** Estrekov, Makovikov.

1972–73: AC MILAN 1, LEEDS UNITED 0 (Salonika, 16.5.73, 45,000)
Milan: Vecchi, Sabadini, Zigno, Anquilletti, Turone, Rosato (Dolci), Sogliano, Benetti, Bigon, Rivera, Chiarugi. **Scorer:** Chiarugi.
Leeds U: Harvey, Reaney, Cherry, Bates, Madeley, Hunter, Lorimer, Jordan, Jones, E. Gray, Yorath (McQueen).

1973–74: FC MAGDEBURG 2, AC MILAN 0 (Rotterdam, 8.5.74, 5000)
Magdeburg: Schulze, Enge, Zapf, Abraham, Gaube, Pommerenke, Seguin, Tyll, Raugust, Sparwasser, Hoffmann. **Scorers:** Lanzi (og), Seguin.
Milan: Pizzaballa, Anquilletti, Sabadini, Lanzi, Scnellinger, Maldera, Tresoldi, Benetti, Bigon, Rivera, Bergamaschi.

1974–75: DYNAMO KIEV 3, FERENCVAROS 0 (Basle, 14.5.75, 13,000)
Dynamo: Rudakov, Fomenko, Troshkin, Reshko, Matvienko, Muntian, Konkov, Burjak, Kolotov, Onischenko, Blokhin. **Scorers:** Onischenko 2, Blokhin.
Ferencvaros: Geczi, Pataki, Martos, Rab, Megyesi, Nyilasi (Onhaus), Juhasz, Mucha, Szabo, Mate, Magyar.

1975–76: RSC ANDERLECHT 4, WEST HAM UNITED 2 (Brussels, 5.5.76, 58,000)
Anderlecht: Ruiter, Lomme, Broos, van Binst, Thissen, Dockx, Coeck (Vercauteren), van der Elst, Ressel, Haan, Rensenbrink. **Scorers:** Rensenbrink 2 (1 pen), van der Elst 2.
West Ham U: Day, Coleman, Bonds, T. Taylor, Lampard (A. Taylor), McDowell, Brooking, Paddon, Holland, Jennings, Robson. **Scorers:** Holland, Robson.

1976–77: SV HAMBURG 2, RSC ANDERLECHT 0 (Amsterdam, 11.5.77, 65,000)
Hamburg: Kargus, Kaltz, Ripp, Nogly, Hidien, Memering, Magath, Steffenhagen, Reimann, Keller, Volkert. **Scorers:** Volkert (pen), Magath.
Anderlecht: Ruiter, van Binst, van den Daele, Broos, Thissen, van der Elst, Coeck, Haan, Dockx (van Poucke), Ressel, Rensenbrink.

1977–78: RSC ANDERLECHT 4, AUSTRIA WIEN 0 (Paris, 3.5.78, 48,679)
Anderlecht: De Bree, van Binst, Broos, Dusbaba, Thissen, van der Elst, Haan, Nielsen, Coeck, Vercauteren (Dockx), Rensenbrink. **Scorers:** Rensenbrink 2, van Binst 2.
Austria Wien: Baumgartner, Robert Sara, Josef Sara, Obermayer, Baumiester, Prohaska, Daxbacher (Martinez), Gasselich, Morales (Drazen), Pirkner, Parits.

1978–79: BARCELONA 4, FORTUNA DUSSELDORF 3 (aet, Basle, 16.5.79, 58,000)
Barcelona: Artola, Zuviria, Migueli, Costas (Martinez), Albaladejo (de le Cruz), Sanchez, Neeskens, Asensi, Rexach, Krankl, Carrasco. **Scorers:** Sanchez, Asensi, Rexach, Krankl.
Fortuna: Daniel, Baltes, Zewe, Zimmermann (Lund), Kohnen, Brei (Weikl), Schmitz, Bommer, Thomas Allofs, Klaus Allofs, Seel. **Scorers:** Klaus Allofs, Seel 2.

1979–80: VALENCIA 0, ARSENAL 0 (aet, Brussels, 14.5.80, 40,000)
Valencia: Pereira, Carrette, Botubot, Arias, Tendillo, Solsona, Saura, Bonhof, Kempes, Sbirates (Castellanos), Pablo.
Arsenal: Jennings, Rice, Nelson, Talbot, O'Leary, Young, Brady, Sunderland, Stapleton, Price (Hollins), Rix.
Valencia won 5–4 on penalties.

1980–81: DYNAMO TBILISI 2, CARL ZEISS JENA 1 (Dusseldorf, 13.5.81, 9000)
Dynamo: Gabelia, Kostava, Chivadze, Khisanishvili, Tavadze, Svanadze (Kakilashvili), Sulakvelidze, Daraselia, Gutsayev, Kipiani, Shengelia. **Scorers:** Gutsayev, Daraselia.
Carl Zeiss Jena: Grapenthin, Brauer, Kurbjuweit, Schnuphase, Schilling, Hoppe (Overmann), Krause, Lindemann, Bielau (Topfer), Raab, Vogel. **Scorer:** Hoppe.

EUROPEAN CUP-WINNERS' CUP

1981–82: BARCELONA 2, STANDARD LIEGE 1 (Barcelona, 12.5.82, 100,000)
Barcelona: Urruti, Gerardo, Migueli, Alesanco, Manolo, Sanchez, Moratalla, Esteban, Simonsen, Quini, Carrasco.
Scorers: Simonsen, Quini.
Standard: Preud'homme, Gerets, Poel, Meeuws, Plessers, Vandermissen, Daerden, Haan, Botteron, Tahamata, Wendt.
Scorer: Vandermissen.

1982–83: ABERDEEN 2, REAL MADRID 1 (Gothenburg, 11.5.83, 17,804)
Aberdeen: Leighton, Rougvie, Miller, McLeish, McMaster, Cooper, Strachan, Simpson, Weir, McGhee, Black (Hewitt).
Scorers: Black, Hewitt.
Real: Augustin, Metgod, Bonet, Camacho (San Jose), Juan Jose, Angel, Gallego, Stielike, Juanito, Santillana, Isidro
(Salguero). **Scorer:** Juanito (pen).

1983–84: JUVENTUS 2, FC PORTO 1 (Basle, 16.5.84, 60,000)
Juventus: Tacconi, Gentile, Brio, Scirea, Cabrini, Tardelli, Bonini, Vignola (Caricola), Rossi, Platini, Boniek. **Scorers:**
Vignola, Boniek.
Porto: Ze Beto, Joao Pinto, Lima Pereira, Eurico, Eduardo Luis (Costa), Jaime Megalhaes (Walsh), Frasco, Jaime
Pachecho, Sousa, Gomes, Vermelhinho. **Scorer:** Sousa.

1984–85: EVERTON 3, RAPID VIENNA 1 (Rotterdam, 15.5.85, 50,000)
Everton: Southall, Stevens, van den Hauwe, Ratcliffe, Mountfield, Reid, Steven, Gray, Sharp, Bracewell, Sheedy.
Scorers: Gray, Steven, Sheedy.
Rapid: Konsel, Kienast, Garger, Weber, Lainer, Hristic, Kranjcar, Weinhofer (Panenka), Brauneder, Pacult (Gross),
Krankl. **Scorer:** Krankl.

1985–86: DYNAMO KIEV 3, ATLETICO MADRID 0 (Lyon, 2.5.86, 39,300)
Dynamo: Chanov, Baltacha (Bal), Bessonov, Kuznetsov, Demianenko, Yaremchuk, Zavarov (Yevtushenko), Yakovenko,
Rats, Belanov, Blokhin. **Scorers:** Zavarov, Blokhin, Yevtushenko.
Atletico: Fillol, Tomas, Arteche, Ruiz, Clemente, Julio Prieto, Marina, Landaburu (Setien), Ramos, Cabrera, Da Silva.

1986–87: AJAX AMSTERDAM 1, LOKOMOTIV LEIPZIG 0 (Athens, 13.5.87, 35,000)
Ajax: Menzo, Silooy, Rijkaard, Verlaat, Boeve, Wouters, Winter, Muhren (Scholten), van't Schip, van Basten, Witschge
(Bergkamp). **Scorer:** van Basten.
Lokomotiv: Muller, Kreek, Baum, Lindner, Zotzsche, Scholz, Liebers (Kuhn), Bredon, Richter, Edmond (Leitzke),
Marschal.

EUROPEAN CUP-WINNERS' CUP 1987–88

PRELIMINARY ROUND

AEL Limassol (0)0, DAC Dunajska Streda (0)1 (Majoros 66)
DAC Dunajska Streda (4)5 (Micinec 6,39, Medgyes 20, Pavlik 27, Majoros 85 pen), AEL Limassol (0)1 (Aristodelos 69)

FIRST ROUND, FIRST LEG

Aalborg (0)1 (Boye 63), Hajduk Split (0)0
Ajax (0)4 (Rijkaard 65, Blind 73, Winter 81, Stapleton 84), Dundalk (0)0
Akranes (0)0, Kalmar (0)0
Avenir Beggen (0)0, SV Hamburg (2)5 (Labbadia 10, 69, Laubinger 44, Okonski 58, Dittmar 82)
DAC Dunajska Streda (2)2 (Micinec 9, Kaspar 38), Young Boys Berne (1)1 (Zuffi 22)
Lokomotiv Leipzig (0)0, Marseille (0)0
Mechelen (0)1 (Den Boer 49), Dinamo Bucharest (0)0
Merthyr Tydfil (1)2 (Rogers 34, Williams 82), Atalanta (1)1 (Progna 41)
Dynamo Minsk (0)2 (Zigmantovich 82, Gotsmanov 88), Genclerbirligi (0)0
Real Sociedad (0)0, Slask Wroclaw (0)0
RoPs Rovaniemi (0)0, Glentoran (0)0
St Mirren (1)1 (McDowall 3), Tromso (0)0
Sporting Lisbon (3)4 (Sealy 3, 42, Paulinho Cascavel 24 pen, 82), FC Tirol (0)0
Ujpest Dozsa (1)1 (Heredi 32 pen), Den Haag (0)0
Vllaznia Skoder (0)2 (Buchati 52, Jera 66), Sliema Wanderers (0)0
Vitosha (0)1 (Sirakov 88 pen), OFI Crete (0)0

FIRST ROUND, SECOND LEG

Atalanta (2)2 (Garlini 16, Cantarutti 20), Merthyr Tydfil (0)0
Den Haag (2)3 (Boerne 22,24, Varga og 82), Ujpest Dozsa (0)1 (Rostas 89)
Dinamo Bucharest (0)0, Mechelen (1)2 (Hofkens 40, Den Boer 72)
Dundalk (0)0, Ajax (0)2 (Newe og 72, Meijer 87)
Genclerbirligi (1)1 (Tuncay 30), Dynamo Minsk (0)2 (Derkach 69, Kondratiev 84)
Glentoran (0)1 (Caskey 65), RoPs Rovaniemi (0)1 (Kallio 63) (RoPs won on away goals)
Hajduk Split (1)1 (Asanovic 43 pen), Aalborg (0)0 (Hajduk won 4–2 on pens)
SV Hamburg (1)3 (Kroth 9, Kaltz 72, Labbadia 82), Avenir Beggen (0)0
Kalmar (0)1 (Alexandersson 102), Akranes (0)0 (aet)
Marseille (1)1 (Allofs 8), Lokomotiv Leipzig (0)0
OFI Crete (1)3 (Tsimbos 24, Marinakis 48, Haralambidis 69), Vitosha (0)1 (Curdov 71)
Slask Wroclaw (0)0, Real Sociedad (0)2 (Loren 75, Berguiristain 82)
Sliema Wanderers (0)0, Vllaznia Skoder (1)4 (Pashaj 15, Vukatana 59, Rragami 70 pen, Fakja 83)
FC Tirol (1)4 (Marko 16, Roscher 53, Prohaska 69, Linzmaier 85), Sporting Lisbon (0)2 (Sealy 57, Paulinho Cascavel 67)
Tromso (0)0, St Mirren (0)0

SECOND ROUND, FIRST LEG

Den Haag (1)2 (De Rhoode 3, Van den Hoogenband 71), Young Boys Berne (0)1 (Zuffi 62)
SV Hamburg (0)0, Ajax (0)1 (Meijer 52)
Kalmar (0)1 (T. Arvidsson 83), Sporting Lisbon (0)0
Marseille (1)4 (Papin 31, Diallo 47, Allofs 68, Giresse 89), Hajduk Split (0)0
Mechelen (0)0, St Mirren (0)0
OFI Crete (1)1 (Persias 17), Atalanta (0)0
Real Sociedad (0)1 (Gajate 86), Dynamo Minsk (1)1 (Kondratiev 5)
Vllaznia Skoder (0)0, RoPs Rovaniemi (1)1 (Pollack 27)

SECOND ROUND, SECOND LEG

Ajax (1)2 (A. Muhren 12, Meijer 82), SV Hamburg (0)0
Atalanta (1)2 (Nicolini 22, Garlini 73), OFI Crete (0)0
Hajduk Split (1)2 (Asanovic 19 pen, Bursac 82), Marseille (0)0
Dynamo Minsk (0)0, Real Sociedad (0)0 (Dynamo won on away goals)
RoPs Rovaniemi (0)1 (Pollack 47), Vllaznia Skoder (0)0
St Mirren (0)0, Mechelen (1)2 (Ohana 34, 50)
Sporting Lisbon (1)5 (Cascavel 34 pen, 53, 57, Sealy 62, Duilio 67), Kalmar (0)0
Young Boys Berne (0)1 (Fimian 68), Den Haag (0)0 (Young Boys Berne won on away goals)

EUROPEAN CUP-WINNERS' CUP

QUARTER-FINALS, FIRST LEG

Atalanta (1)2 (Nicolini 44 pen, Cantarutti 79), **Sporting Lisbon (0)0**
Mechelen (0)1 (Dewilde 86), **Dynamo Minsk (0)0**
RoPs Rovaniemi (0)0, Marseille (1)1 (Papin 26)
Young Boys Berne (0)0, Ajax (1)1 (Bosman 44)

QUARTER-FINALS, SECOND LEG

Ajax (1)1 (Larsson 39), **Young Boys Berne (0)0**
Dynamo Minsk (0)1 (Kistev 59), **Mechelen (1)1** (Ohana 29)
Marseille (2)3 (Genghini 18, Allofs 22, Papin 77 pen), **RoPs Rovaniemi (0)0**
Sporting Lisbon (0)1 (Houtman 66), **Atalanta (0)1** (Cantarutti 82)

SEMI-FINALS, FIRST LEG

Marseille (0)0, Ajax (2)3 (Witschge 12,42, Bergkamp 89)
Mechelen (1)2 (Ohana 7, Den Boer 82), **Atalanta (1)1** (Stromberg 9)

SEMI–FINALS, SECOND LEG

Ajax (1)1 (Larsson 22), **Marseille (0)2** (Papin 65, Allofs 89)
Atalanta (1)1 (Garlini 39 pen), **Mechelen (0)2** (Rutjes 56, Emmers 80)

FINAL

MECHELEN (0)1, AJAX AMSTERDAM (0)0 (Strasbourg, 11 May 1988, 40,000)
Mechelen: Preud'homme; Deferm, Clijsters, Rutjes, Emmers, De Wilde, Koeman, Hofkens (de Mesmaeker 80), Sanders, Ohana, Den Boer. **Scorer:** Den Boer.
Ajax: Menzo; Blind, Larsson, Verlaat (Meijer 80), Wouters, Scholten, Winter, Muhren, Van't Schip, Bosman, Witschge.

EUROPEAN CUP-WINNERS' CUP 1987–88
BRITISH AND IRISH CLUBS

FIRST ROUND, FIRST LEG

AJAX (0)4, DUNDALK (0)0 (16.9.87, 12,500)
Ajax: Menzo; Blind, Spelbos, Boeve, Wouters, Rijkaard, Bosman (Winter 65), A.Muhren, Van't Schip, Meijer (Stapleton 46), Roy. **Scorers:** Rijkaard 65, Blind 73, Winter 81, Stapleton 84.
Dundalk: O'Neill; Lawless (Gorman 60), McCue, Malone, Shelly, Wyse, Cleary, Murray, Kehoe, Eviston, Newe.

MERTHYR TYDFIL (1)2, ATALANTA (1)1 (16.9.87, 8,000)
Merthyr: Wager; Tong, Baird, Mullen, Evans, Rogers, French, Webley, Chris Williams (P. Jones 87), Beattie, Ceri Williams. **Scorers:** Rogers 34, Williams 82.
Atalanta: Piotti; Gentile, Pasciullo (Nicolini 46), Prandelli, Barcella, Progna, Stromberg, Icardi, Garlini, Fortunato, Incocciati (Cantarutti 75). **Scorer:** Progna 41.

RoPs ROVANIEMI (0)0, GLENTORAN (0)0 (16.9.87, 3,978)
RoPs: Martinassi; Autti, Oulla, Tolvanen, Illola, Hannola, Virtanen (Honkanen 27), Kallio, V. Tauriainen (Tegelberg 24), Pollack, Heaton.
Glentoran: Paterson; McGreevy, Stewart, Rogers, Moore, Cleary, Jameson, Caskey, Blackledge (Montgomery 57), McCartney, Harrison.

ST MIRREN (1)1, TROMSO (0)0 (16.9.87, 7,797)
St Mirren: Money; Dawson, Winnie, Abercromby, Godfrey, Cooper, McGarvey (McWhirter 57), Ferguson, Lambert (Chalmers 75), McDowall, Cameron. **Scorer:** McDowall 3.
Tromso: Flem; Solstad, Albertsen, Pedersen, Nilsen, Kraemer, B. Johansen, Jensen, Rismo, T. Johansen, Hogmo.

FIRST ROUND, SECOND LEG

DUNDALK (0)0, AJAX (0)2 (10.9.87, 5,000)
Dundalk: O'Neill; Lawless, Shelly, Murray, McCue, Malone, Wyse, Kehoe, Cleary, Gorman, Newe.
Ajax: Menzo; Blind, Spelbos, Scholten, Winter, Bosman, Van't Schip, Wouters, Stapleton, A. Muhren, Witschge (Meijer 70). **Scorers:** Newe og 72, Meijer 87.

ATALANTA (2)2, MERTHYR TYDFIL (0)0 (20.9.87, 14,000)
Atalanta: Piotti; Prandelli, Gentile, Fortunato, Progna, Icardi, Stromberg, Nicolini, Cantarutti, Incocciati (Barcella 83), Garlini. **Scorers:** Garlini 16, Cantarutti 20.
Merthyr: Wagner; Tong, Baird, Mullen, Evans, Rogers, French, Webley, Chris Williams, Beattie (Hopkins 87), Ceri Williams (S.Williams 83).

GLENTORAN (0)1, RoPs ROVANIEMI (0)1 (29.9.87, 2,000)
Glentoran: Paterson; McGreevy, Stewart, Bowers, Moore, Cleary, Montgomery, Caskey, Mullan, McCartney, Jameson. **Scorer:** Caskey 65.
RoPs: Martinassi; Autti, Oulla, Tolvanen, Illola, Kallio, V. Tauriainen, Hannola, P. Tauriainen, Pollack, Heaton. **Scorer:** Kallio 63.

TROMSO (0)0, ST MIRREN (0)0 (20.9.87, 5,114)
Tromso: Flem; Solstad, Albertsen, Pedersen, Nilsen, Forfang (K. Olsen 77), B. Johansen, Esperjord, Rismo (Andreassen 68), T. Johansen, Hogmo.
St Mirren: Money; Wilson, Godfrey, Cooper, Winnie, Walker, Ferguson, Abercromby (Fitzpatrick 19), Cameron, McDowall (Chambers 76), Lambert.

SECOND ROUND, FIRST LEG

MECHELEN (0)0, ST MIRREN (0)0 (21.10.87, 6,146)
Mechelen: Preud'homme; Cluytens, Rutjes, Clijsters, Koemans, Sanders, Theunis (De Wilde 46), De Mesmaeker, Hofkens, Den Boer, Ohana.
St Mirren: Money; Winnie, Godfrey, Cooper, Wilson, Walker (Dawson 77), Cameron, Fitzpatrick (Hamilton 59), Chambers, Lambert, Ferguson.

SECOND ROUND, SECOND LEG

ST MIRREN (0)0, MECHELEN (1)2 (4.11.87, 12,000)
St Mirren: Money; Dawson, Wilson, Fitzpatrick, Godfrey, Cooper, Lambert, Walker (Hamilton 63), Chalmers, McDowall (Shaw), Cameron.
Mechelen: Preud'homme; Cluytens, Jaspers, Rutjes, Hofkens, Theunis, Sanders, Mesmaeker, Koeman, Ohana, Den Boer. **Scorer:** Ohana 34,50.

UEFA CUP FINALS SINCE 1958 (Fairs Cup until 1971)

1955–58: LONDON 2, *BARCELONA 2 (Stamford Bridge, 5.3.58, 45,466)
London: Kelsey (Arsenal); P. Sillett (Chelsea), Langley (Fulham), Blanchflower, Norman (Tottenham H), Coote (Brentford), Groves (Arsenal), Greaves (Chelsea), Smith (Tottenham H), Haynes (Fulham), Robb (Tottenham H). **Scorers:** Greaves, Langley (pen).
Barcelona: Estrems; Olivella, Segarra, Gracia, Gensana, Ribelles, Basora, Evaristo, Martinez, Villaverde, Tejada. **Scorers:** Tejada, Martinez.
*Composite side, though 10 players were from FC Barcelona.

2nd LEG: BARCELONA 6, LONDON 0 (Barcelona, 1.5.58, 62,000)
Barcelona: Ramallets; Olivella, Segarra, Verges, Brugue, Gensana, Tejada, Evaristo, Martinez, Suarez, Basora. **Scorers:** Suarez 2, Evaristo 2, Martinez, Verges.
London: Kelsey (Arsenal); Wright, Cantwell (West Ham U), Blanchflower (Tottenham H), Brown (West Ham U), Bowen (Arsenal), Medwin (Tottenham H), Groves (Arsenal), Smith (Tottenham H), Bloomfield (Arsenal), Lewis (Chelsea).

1958–60: BIRMINGHAM CITY 0, BARCELONA 0 (Birmingham, 29.3.60, 40,500)
Birmingham C: Schofield; Farmer, Allen, Watts, Smith, Neal, Astall, Gordon, Weston, Orritt, Hooper.
Barcelona: Ramallets; Olivella, Gracia, Segarra, Rodri, Gensana, Coll, Kocsis, Martinez, Ribelles, Villaverde.

2nd LEG: BARCELONA 4, BIRMINGHAM CITY 1 (Barcelona, 4.5.60, 70,000)
Barcelona: Verges for Gensana, Kubala for Kocsis, Czibor for Villaverde. **Scorers:** Martinez, Czibor 2, Coll.
Birmingham C: Murphy for Orritt. **Scorer:** Hooper.

1960–61: BIRMINGHAM CITY 2, AS ROMA 2 (Birmingham, 27.9.61, 21,005)
Birmingham C: Schofield; Farmer, Sissons, Hennessey, Foster, Beard, Hellawell, Bloomfield, Harris, Orritt, Auld. **Scorers:** Hellawell, Orritt.
Roma: Cudicini; Fontana, Corsini, Giuliana, Losi, Carpanesi, Orlando, Da Costa, Manfredini, Angelillo, Menichelli. **Scorer:** Manfredini 2.

2nd LEG: AS ROMA 2, BIRMINGHAM CITY 0 (Rome, 11.10.61, 60,000)
Roma: Pestrin for Giuliana, Lojacono for Da Costa. **Scorers:** Farmer (og), Pestrin.
Birmingham C: Smith for Foster, Singer for Auld.

1961–62: VALENCIA 6, BARCELONA 2 (Valencia, 8.9.62, 65,000)
Valencia: Zamora; Piquer, Mestre, Sastre, Quincoces, Chicao, Nunez, Ribelles, Waldo, Guillot, Yosu. **Scorers:** Yosu 2, Guillot 3, Nunez.
Barcelona: Pesudo; Benitez, Rodri, Olivella, Verges, Gracia, Cubilla, Kocsis, Re, Villaverde, Camps. **Scorer:** Kocsis 21.

2nd LEG: BARCELONA 1, VALENCIA 1 (Barcelona, 12.9.62, 60,000)
Barcelona: Pesudo; Benitez, Garay, Fuste, Verges, Gracia, Cubilla, Kocsis, Goyvaerts, Villaverde, Camps. **Scorer:** Kocsis.
Valencia: Unchanged. **Scorer:** Guillot.

1962–63: DYNAMO ZAGREB 1, VALENCIA 2 (Zagreb, 12.6.63, 40,000)
Dynamo: Skoric; Belin, Braun, Biscam, Markovic, Perusic, Kobesnac, Zambata, Knez, Matus, Lamza. **Scorer:** Zambata.
Valencia: Zamora; Piquer, Chicao, Paquito, Quincoces, Sastre, Mano, Sanchez–Lage, Waldo, Ribelles, Urtiaga. **Scorers:** Waldo, Urtiaga.

2nd LEG: VALENCIA 2, DYNAMO ZAGREB 0 (Valencia, 26.6.63, 55,000)
Valencia: Nunez for Urtiaga. **Scorers:** Mano, Nunez.
Dynamo: Raus for Biscam.

1963–64: REAL ZARAGOZA 2, VALENCIA 1 (Barcelona, 24.6.64, 50,000)
Real: Yarza; Cartizo, Reija, Isasi, Santamaria, Pepin, Canario, Duca, Marcelino, Villa, Lapetra. **Scorers:** Villa, Marcelino.
Valencia: Zamora; Arnal, Videgany, Paquito, Quincoces, Roberto, Suco, Guillot, Waldo, Urtiaga, Ficha. **Scorer:** Urtiaga.

1964–65: FERENCVAROS 1, JUVENTUS 0 (Turin, 23.6.65, 25,000)
Ferencvaros: Gerzi; Novak, Horvath, Juhasz, Matrai, Orosz, Karaba, Varga, Albert, Rakosi, Fenyvesi. **Scorer:** Fenyvesi.
Juventus: Anzolin; Gori, Serti, Bercellini, Castano, Leoncini, Estacchini, Del Sol, Combin, Mazzia, Menichelli.

1965–66: BARCELONA 0, REAL ZARAGOZA 1 (Barcelona, 14.9.66, 70,000)
Barcelona: Sadurni; Benitez, Eladio, Montesinos, Gallego, Torres, Zaballa, Muller, Zaldua, Fuste, Vidal.
Real Zaragoza: Yarza; Irusquieta, Reija, Pais, Santamaria, Violeta, Canario, Santos, Marcelino, Villa, Lapetra. **Scorer:** Canario.

2nd LEG: REAL ZARAGOZA 2, BARCELONA 4 (Zaragoza, 21.9.66, 70,000)
Real: Unchanged. **Scorer:** Marcelino 2.
Barcelona: Sadurni; Foncho, Eladio, Montesinos, Gallego, Torres, Zaballa, Mas, Zaldua, Fuste, Pujol. **Scorers:** Pujol 3, Zaballa.

1966–67: DYNAMO ZAGREB 2, LEEDS UNITED 0 (Zagreb, 30.8.67, 40,000)
Dynamo: Skoric; Gracanin, Brncic, Belin, Ramljak, Blaskovic, Cercek, Piric, Zambata, Gucmirtl, Rora. **Scorers:** Cercek, Rora.
Leeds U: Sprake; Reaney, Cooper, Bremner, Charlton, Hunter, Bates, Lorimer, Belfitt, Gray, O'Grady.

561

UEFA CUP

2nd LEG: LEEDS UNITED 0, DYNAMO ZAGREB 0 (Leeds, 7.8.68. 35,268)
Leeds U: Sprake; Bell, Cooper, Bremner, Charlton, Hunter, Reaney, Belfitt, Greenhoff, Giles, O'Grady.
Dynamo: Unchanged.

1967–68: LEEDS UNITED 1, FERENCVAROS 0 (Leeds, 7.8.68, 25,168)
Leeds U: Sprake; Reaney, Cooper, Bremner, Charlton, Hunter, Lorimer, Madeley, Jones (Belfitt), Giles (Greenhoff), E.
Gray. **Scorer:** Jones.
Ferencvaros: Geczi; Novak, Pancsics, Havasi, Juhasz, Szucs, Szoke, Varga, Albert, Rakosi, Fenyvesi (Balint).

2nd LEG: FERENCVAROS 0, LEEDS UNITED 0 (Budapest, 11.9.68, 76,000)
Ferencvaros: Katona for Fenyvesi. Karaba came on for Szoke.
Leeds U: Hibbitt for Giles, O'Grady for Gray. Bates came on for Hibbitt.

1968–69: NEWCASTLE UNITED 3, UJPEST DOZSA 0 (Newcastle, 29.5.69, 60,000)
Newcastle U: McFaul; Craig, Clark, Gibb, Burton, Moncur, Scott, Robson, Davies, Arentoft, Sinclair (Foggon). **Scorers:**
Moncur 2, Scott.
Ujpest: Szentimihalyi; Kaposza, Solymosi, Bankuti, Nosko, E.Dunai, Fazekas, Gorocs, Bene, A.Dunai, Zambo.

2nd LEG: UJPEST DOZSA 2, NEWCASTLE UNITED 3 (Budapest, 11.6.69, 37,000)
Ujpest: Unchanged. **Scorers:** Bene, Gorocs.
Newcastle U: Unchanged. Foggon came on for Scott. **Scorers:** Moncur, Arentoft, Foggon.

1969–70: RSC ANDERLECHT 3, ARSENAL 1 (Brussels, 22.4.70, 37,000)
Anderlecht: Trappaniers; Heylens, Velkeneers, Nordahl, Kialunda, Cornelis (Peeters), Desanghere, Devrindt, Mulder,
van Himst, Puis. **Scorers:** Devrindt, Mulder 2.
Arsenal: Wilson; Storey, McNab, Kelly, McLintock, Simpson, Armstrong, Sammels, Radford, George (Kennedy),
Graham. **Scorer:** Kennedy.

2nd LEG: ARSENAL 3, RSC ANDERLECHT 0 (London, 28.4.70, 51,612)
Arsenal: Unchanged. **Scorers:** Kelly, Radford, Sammels.
Anderlecht: Maartens for Cornelis.

1970–71: JUVENTUS 2, LEEDS UNITED 2 (Turin, 29.5.71, 45,000)
Juventus: Piloni; Spinosi, Marchetti, Furino, Morini, Salvadore, Haller, Causio, Anastasi (Novellini), Capello, Battega.
Scorers: Bettega, Capello.
Leeds U: Sprake; Reaney, Cooper, Bremner, Charlton, Hunter, Lorimer, Clarke, Jones (Bates), Giles, Madeley. **Scorers:**
Madeley, Clarke.

2nd LEG: LEEDS UNITED 1, JUVENTUS 1 (Leeds, 2.6.71, 42,483)
Leeds U: Unchanged. Bates came on for Madeley. **Scorer:** Clarke.
Juventus: Tancredi for Piloni. **Scorer:** Anastasi.
Leeds United won on away goals.

1971–72: WOLVERHAMPTON WANDERERS 1, TOTTENHAM HOTSPUR 2 (Wolverhampton, 3.5.72, 45,000)
Wolverhampton W: Parkes; Shaw, Taylor, Hegan, Munro, McAlle, McCalliog, Hibbitt, Richards, Dougan, Wagstaffe.
Scorer: McCalliog.
Tottenham H: Jennings; Kinnear, Knowles, Mullery, England, Beal, Gilzean, Perryman, Chivers, Peters, Coates (Pratt).
Scorer: Chivers 2.

2nd LEG: TOTTENHAM HOTSPUR 1, WOLVERHAMPTON WANDERERS 1 (London, 17.5.72, 54,303)
Tottenham H: Unchanged. **Scorer:** Mullery.
Wolverhampton W: Unchanged. Bailey came on for Hibbitt, Curran came on for Dougan. **Scorer:** Wagstaffe.

1972–73: LIVERPOOL 3, BORUSSIA MOENCHENGLADBACH 0 (Liverpool, 10.5.73, 41,169)
Liverpool: Clemence; Lawler, Lindsay, Smith, Lloyd, Hughes, Keegan, Cormack, Toshack, Heighway (Hall), Callaghan.
Scorers: Keegan 2, Lloyd.
Borussia: Kleff; Vogts, Michalik, Danner, Bonhof, Kulik, Jensen, Wimmer, Rupp (Simonsen), Netzer, Heynckes.

2nd LEG: BORUSSIA MOENCHENGLADBACH 2, LIVERPOOL 0 (Moenchengladbach, 23.5.73, 35,000)
Borussia: Surau for Michalik. **Scorer:** Heynckes 2.
Liverpool: Unchanged. Boersma came on for Heighway.

1973–74: TOTTENHAM HOTSPUR 2, FEYENOORD 2 (Tottenham, 21.5.74, 46,281)
Tottenham H: Jennings; Evans, Naylor, Pratt, England, Beal, McGrath, Perryman, Chivers, Peters, Coates. **Scorers:**
England, van Hanegem (og).
Feyenoord: Treytel; Rijsbergen, van Daele, Israel, Vos, de Jong, Jansen, van Hanegem, Ressel, Schoenmaker, Kristensen.
Scorers: van Hanegem, de Jong.

2nd LEG: FEYENOORD 2, TOTTENHAM HOTSPUR 0 (Rotterdam, 29.5.74, 68,000)
Feyenoord: Ramljak for van Hanegem. Boskamp came on for Kristensen, Wery came on for Boskamp. **Scorers:**
Rijsbergen, Ressel.
Tottenham H: Unchanged. Holder came on for Pratt.

UEFA CUP

1974–75: BORUSSIA MOENCHENGLADBACH 0, TWENTE ENSCHEDE 0 (Dusseldorf, 7.5.75, 45,000)
Borussia: Kleff; Wittkamp, Stielike, Vogts, Surau, Bonhof, Wimmer, Danner (Del'Haye), Kulik (Schaeffer), Simonsen, Jensen.
Twente: Gross; Drost, van Ierssel, Overweg, Oranen, Thijssen, Pahlplatz, van der Vall, Bos, Jeuring (Achterberg), Zuidema.
2nd LEG: TWENTE ENSCHEDE 1, BORUSSIA MOENCHENGLADBACH 5 (Enschede, 21.5.75, 24,500)
Twente: Unchanged. Muhren came on for Bos, Achterberg came on for Pahlplatz. **Scorer:** Drost.
Borussia: Klinkhammer for Stielike, Heynckes for Kulik. Schaeffer came on for Surau, Koppel came on for Wimmer.
Scorers: Heynckes 3, Simonsen 2 (1 pen).

1975–76: LIVERPOOL 3, BRUGES 2 (Liverpool, 28.4.76, 56,000)
Liverpool: Clemence; Smith, Neal, Thompson, Kennedy, Hughes, Keegan, Fairclough, Heighway, Toshack (Case), Callaghan. **Scorers:** Kennedy, Case, Keegan (pen).
Bruges: Jensen; Bastyns, Krieger, Leekens, Volders, Cools, Vandereycken, de Cubber, van Gool, Lambert, le Fevre.
Scorers: Lambert, Cools.
2nd LEG: BRUGES 1, LIVERPOOL 1 (Bruges, 19.5.76, 32,000)
Bruges: Unchanged. Sanders came on for Lambert, Hinderyckx came on for de Cubber. **Scorer:** Lambert (pen).
Liverpool: Case for Fairclough, Fairclough came on for Toshack. **Scorer:** Keegan.

1976–77: JUVENTUS 1, ATHLETIC BILBAO 0 (Turin, 4.5.77, 75,000)
Juventus: Zoff; Cuccureddu, Gentile, Scirea, Morini, Tardelli, Furino, Benetti, Causio, Boninsegna (Gori), Bettega. **Scorer:** Tardelli.
Athletic: Iribar; Villar, Escalza, Guoicoechea, Guisasola, Quaderra, Irureta, Rojo II, Dani, Churruca, Rojo I.
2nd LEG: ATHLETIC BILBAO 2, JUVENTUS 1 (Bilbao, 18.5.77, 43,000)
Athletic: Iribar; Lasa (Carlos), Guisasola, Alesanco, Escalza, Villar, Churruca, Irureta, Amarrortu, Dani, Rojo I. **Scorers:** Irureta, Carlos.
Juventus: Unchanged. Spinosi came on for Boninsegna. **Scorer:** Bettega.
Juventus won on away goals.

1977–78: BASTIA 0, PSV EINDHOVEN 0 (Corsica, 26.4.78, 15,000)
Bastia: Hiard; Burkhard, Guesdon, Orlanducci, Cazes, Papi, Lacuseta (Felix), Larios, Rep, Krimau, Mariot.
PSV: van Beveren; van Kraay, Krijgh, Stevens, Brandts, Poortvliet, van der Kuylen, Willy van der Kerkhof, Deijkers, Rene van der Kerkhof, Lubse.
2nd LEG: PSV EINDHOVEN 3, BASTIA 0 (Eindhoven, 9.5.78, 27,000)
PSV: Unchanged. Deacy came on for van Kraay. **Scorers:** Willy van der Kerkhof, Deijkers, van der Kuylen.
Bastia: Marchioni for Burkhard. Weller came on for Hiard, de Zerbi came on for Mariot.

1978–79: RED STAR BELGRADE 1, BORUSSIA MOENCHENGLADBACH 1 (Belgrade, 9.5.79, 87,500)
Red Star: Stojanovic; Jovanovic, Miletovic, Jurisic, Jovin, Muslin (Krmpotic), Petrovic, Blagojevic, Miloslavjevic (Milovanovic), Savic, Sestic. **Scorer:** Sestic.
Borussia: Kneib; Vogts, Hannes, Schaeffer, Ringels, Schaefer, Kulik, Nielsen (Danner), Wohlers (Gores), Simonsen, Lienen. **Scorer:** Juristic (og).
2nd LEG: BORUSSIA MOENCHENGLADBACH 1, RED STAR BELGRADE 0 (Dusseldorf, 23.5.79, 45,000)
Borussia: Gores for Nielsen. Koppel came on for Kulik. **Scorer:** Simonsen (pen).
Red Star: Milovanovic for Sestic. Sestic came on for Milovanovic.

1979–80: BORUSSIA MOENCHANGLADBACH 3, EINTRACHT FRANKFURT 2 (Moenchengladbach, 7.5.80, 25,000)
Borussia: Kneib; Hannes, Schaefer, Schaeffer, Ringels, Matthaus, Kulik, Nielsen (Thychosen), Del'Haye (Boedeker), Harald Nickel, Lienen. **Scorers:** Kulik 2, Matthaus.
Eintracht: Pahl; Pezzey, Neuberger, Koerbel, Ehrmanntraut, Lorant, Holzenbein (Nachtweih), Borchers, Bernd Nickel, Tscha, Kargar (trapp). **Scorers:** Karger, Holzenbein.
2nd LEG: EINTRACHT FRANKFURT 1, BORUSSIA MOENCHENGLADBACH 0 (Frankfurt, 21.5.80, 60,000)
Eintracht: Nachtweih for Karker. Schaub came on for Nachtweih. **Scorer:** Schaub.
Borussia: Fleer for Schaeffer, Boedeker for Del'Haye. Thychosen came on for Mattheus, Del'Haye came on for Nielsen.
Eintracht Frankfurt won on away goals.

1980–81: IPSWICH TOWN 3, AZ 67 ALKMAAR 0 (Ipswich, 6.5.81, 27,532)
Ipswich T: Cooper; Mills, McCall, Thijssen, Osman, Butcher, Wark, Muhren, Mariner, Brazil, Gates. **Scorers:** Wark (pen), Thijssen, Mariner.
AZ 67: Treytel; van der Meer, Spelbos, Metgod, Hovenkamp, Peters, Jonker, Arntz, Nygaard (Welzl), Kist, Tol.
2nd LEG: AZ 67 ALKMAAR 4, IPSWICH TOWN 2 (Amsterdam, 20.5.81, 28,500)
AZ 67: Reynders for van der Meer, Welzl for Kist. Kist came on for Welzl. **Scorers:** Welzl, Metgod, Tol.
Ipswich T: Unchanged. **Scorers:** Thijssen, Wark.
1981–82: 1FK GOTHENBURG 1, SV HAMBURG 0 (Gothenburg, 5.5.82, 42,548)
Gothenburg: Wernersson; Svensson, Hysen, C. Karlsson, Fredriksson, Tord Holmgren, J. Karlsson, Stromberg, Corneliusson, Nilsson (Sandberg), Tommy Holmgren (Schiller). **Scorer:** Tord Holmgren.
Hamburg: Stein; Kaltz, Jakobs, Hieronymus, Groh, Hartwig, Wehmeyer, Magath, von Heesen (Memering), Bastrup, Hrubesch.

2nd LEG: SV HAMBURG 0, 1FK GOTHENBURG 3 (Hamburg, 19.5.82, 60,000)
Hamburg: Memering for Jakobs. Hidien came on for Kaltz.
Gothenburg: Unchanged. Sandberg came on for Corneliusson. **Scorers:** Corneliusson, Nilsson, Fredriksson (pen).

1982–83: RSC ANDERLECHT 1, BENFICA 0 (Brussels, 4.5.83, 60,000)
Anderlecht: Munaron; Olsen, Hofkens, Peruzovic, de Groote, Frimann, Lozano, Coeck, Vercauteren, van den Bergh (Czerniatynski), Brylle. **Scorer:** Brylle.
Benfica: Bento; Humberto, Pietra, Frederico (Lopes), Alvaro, Sheu, Carlos Manuel, Jose Luis, Chalana, Diamantino, Filipovic (Nene).

2nd LEG: BENFICA 1, RSC ANDERLECHT 1 (Lisbon, 18.5.83, 80,000)
Benfica: Bento; Humberto, Pietra, Lopes, Veloso, Carlos Manuel, Sheu (Filipovic), Stromberg, Chalana, Nene, Diamantino (Alves). **Scorer:** Sheu.
Anderlecht: de Greef for Hofkens, Broos for Brylle. Brylle came on for van den Bergh. **Scorer:** Lozano.

1983–84: RSC ANDERLECHT 1, TOTTENHAM HOTSPUR 1 (Brussels, 9.5.84, 40,000)
Anderlecht: Munaron; Grun, de Greef, Olsen, de Groote, Hofkens, Scifo, van den Bergh (Arnesen), Vandereycken, Czerniatynski (Vercauteren), Brylle. **Scorer:** Olsen.
Tottenham H: Parks; Thomas, Hughton, Roberts, Miller, Perryman, Stevens (Mabbutt), Archibald, Falco, Hazard, Galvin. **Scorer:** Miller.

2nd LEG: TOTTENHAM HOTSPUR 1, RSC ANDERLECHT 1 (aet, Tottenham, 23.5.84, 46,205)
Tottenham H: Mabbutt for Perryman. Ardiles came on for Miller. Dick came on for Mabbutt. **Scorer:** Roberts.
Anderlecht: Vercauteren for van den Bergh, Arnesen for Brylle. Brylle came on for Czerniatynski, Gudjohnsen came on for Arnesen. **Scorer:** Czerniatynski.
Tottenham Hotspur won 4–3 on penalties.

1984–85: VIDEOTON 0, REAL MADRID 3 (Szekesfehervar, 8.5.85, 30,000)
Videoton: P.Disztl; Csuhay, Horvath, L.Disztl, Vegh, Wittmann, Burcsa, Vadasz, Borsanyi, Palkovics, Novath (Gyenti).
Real: Migeul Angel; Chendo, Sanchis, Stielike, Camacho, San Jose, Michel, Gallego, Butragueno (Juanito), Santillana (Salguera), Valdano. **Scorers:** Michel, Santillana, Juanito.

2nd LEG: REAL MADRID 0, VIDEOTON 1 (Madrid, 22.5.85, 90,000)
Real: Unchanged. Same substitutions.
Videoton: P.Disztl; Csuhay, Horvath, L.Disztl, Vegh, Csongradi (Wittmann), Burcsa, Vadasz, Szabo, Majer, Novath (Palkovics). **Scorer:** Majer.

1985–86: REAL MADRID 5, COLOGNE 1 (Madrid, 30.4.86, 80,000)
Real: Agustin; Salguero, Solana, Camacho, Martin Vazquez (Santillana), Michel, Juanito, Gordillo, Butragueno, Sanchez, Valdano. **Scorers:** Sanchez, Gordillo, Valdano 2, Santillana.
Cologne: Schumacher; Gielchen, Steiner, Prestin, Geils, Geilenkirchen, Honerbach, Bein (Hassler), Janssen, Littbarski (Dickel), K. Allofs. **Scorer:** K. Allofs.

2nd LEG: COLOGNE 2, REAL MADRID 0 (Berlin, 6.5.86, 15,000)
Cologne: Unchanged. Schmitz came on for Geils, Pisanti came on for Janssen. **Scorers:** Bein, Geilenkirchen.
Real: Agustin; Chendo, Maceda, Solana, Camacho, Michel, Gallego, Gordillo, Butragueno (Juanito), Sanchez (Santillana), Valdano.

1986–87: 1FK GOTHENBURG 1, DUNDEE UNITED 0 (Gothenburg, 6.5.87, 50,023)
Gothenburg: Wernersson; Carlsson, Hysen, Larsson, Fredriksson, Johansson (R. Nilsson), Tord Holmgren (Zetterlund), Andersson, Tommy Holmgren, Pettersson, L. Nilsson. **Scorer:** Pettersson.
Dundee U: Thomson; Holt, Malpas, McInally, Hegarty (Clark), Narey, Kirkwood, Bowman, Bannon, Sturrock (Beaumont), Redford.

2nd LEG: DUNDEE UNITED 1, 1FK GOTHENBURG 1 (Dundee, 20.5.87, 20,911)
Dundee U: Thomson; Holt (Hegarty), Malpas, McInally, Clark, Narey, Ferguson, Gallagher, Kirkwood, Sturrock, Redford (Bannon). **Scorer:** Clark.
Gothenburg: R.Nilsson for Johansson. Johansson came on for R. Nilsson, Mordt came on for Tommy Holmgren. **Scorer:** L. Nilsson.

UEFA CUP 1987–88

FIRST ROUND, FIRST LEG

Barcelona (0)2 (Moratalla 87, Victor 89), **Belenenses (0)0**
Besiktas (0)0, Internazionale (0)0
Beveren (1)2 (Fairclough 15, 50), **Bohemians Prague (0)0**
Bohemians Dublin (0)0, Aberdeen (0)0
Borussia Moenchengladbach (0)0, Espanol (1)1 (Pineda 34)
Brondbyernes (1)2 (C. Nielsen 33, B. Christensen 79), **1FK Gothenburg (0)1** (L. Nilsson 77)
Celtic (1)2 (Walker 5, Whyte 89), **Borussia Dortmund (0)1** (Mill 63)
Coleraine (0)0, Dundee U (1)1 (Sturrock 39)
EPA Larnaca (0)0, Vitoria Bucharest (0)1 (Enne 50)
Feyenoord (2)5 (Blinker 16, Mitchell 37, 60, Van Herpen 72, Elstrup 76), **Spora Luxembourg (0)0**
FK Austria (0)0, Bayer Leverkusen (0)0
Flamurtari (1)2 (Djordjevic og 30, Iljadhi 83), **Partizan Belgrade (0)0**
Gijon (0)1 (Jaime Alvarez 69), **AC Milan (0)0**
Grasshoppers (0)0, Moscow Dynamo (2)4 (Borodyuk 22,44 pen, 58, Karatayev 80)
Honved (0)1 (Fodor 56), **Lokeren (0)0**
Linzer ASK (0)0, Utrecht (0)0
Lokomotiv Sofia (1)3 (Zlatimov 44 pen, Stoiev 50 pen, Todorov 82), **Dynamo Tbilisi (0)1** (Shengalia 75)
Mjondalen (0)0, Werder Bremen (1)5 (Riedle 6,86, Ordenwitz 53, Sauer 55, Wolter 63)
Panathinaikos (1)2 (Barret og 9, Vlachos 51), **Auxerre (0)0**
Pogon Szczecin (0)1 (Lesniak 60), **Verona (1)1** (Elkjaer 9)
Red Star Belgrade (0)3 (Radovanovic 57, Sabanadzovic 61, Cvetkovic 71), **Trakia Plovdiv (0)0**
Spartak Moscow (1)3 (Mostovoy 32, 81, Cherenkov 58), **Dynamo Dresden (0)0**
Sportul Studentesc (0)1 (Tirlea 46), **GKS Katowice (0)0**
Tatabanya (1)1 (Plotar 41), **Vitoria Guimaraes (0)1** (Caio 78)
Toulouse (2)5 (Passi 8, Stopyra 26, Rocheteau 48, Marcico 52, 87 pen), **Panionios (0)1** (Aposporis 64)
TPs Turun (0)0, Admira Wacker (1)1 (Rodax 14)
Uni. Craiova (0)3 (Ciurea 65 pen, Vancea 66, Ghita 87), **Chaves (1)2** (Gilberto 19, Vermelinho 52)
Valletta (0)0, Juventus (3)4 (Laudrup 26,44, Alessio 39, 70)
Velez Mostar (3)5 (Tuce 17, 32, 37, 62, Sisic 63), **Sion (0)0**
Vitkovice (0)1 (Staricny 77), **AIK Stockholm (0)1** (Kindvall 52)
Wismut Aue (0)0, Valur Reykjavik (0)0
Zenit Leningrad (1)2 (Chuklov 8, Zheludkov 70), **CS Bruges 0**

FIRST ROUND, SECOND LEG

Aberdeen (1)1 (Bett 2 pen), **Bohemians Dublin (0)0**
Admira Wacker (0)0, TPs Turun (1)2 (Altonen 39,75)
AIK Stockholm (0)0, Vitkovice (0)2 (Dostal 61, Houska 77)
Auxerre (2)3 (Dutuel 23, Cantona 41, Courtet 73), **Panathinaikos (2)2** (Vassilou 31, Sarakavos 44)
Bayer Leverkusen (1)5 (Rolff 24,60, Schreier 46, Horster 57, Cha 74), **FK Austria (1)1** (Vebora 31)
Belenenses (1)1 (Mapuata 4), **Barcelona (0)0**
Bohemians Prague (1)1 (Chaloupka 11), **Beveren (0)0**
Borussia Dortmund (0)2 (Dickel 74,87), **Celtic (0)0**
CS Bruges (3)5 (Brylle 20,39,56,69, Ceulemans 44), **Zenit Leningrad (0)0**
Chaves (1)2 (Slavkov 5, Vermelinho 62), **Uni. Craiova (0)1** (Sandoi 78) (Chaves won on away goals)
Dundee U (1)3 (Gallacher 28, Sturrock 73, Clark 80), **Coleraine (0)1** (Edgar 48)
Dynamo Dresden (1)1 (Minge 8), **Spartak Moscow (0)0**
Espanol (2)4 (Valverde 30, Perez 44, Golobart 50, Pineda 54), **Borussia Moenchengladbach (0)1** (Rahn 59)
1FK Gothenburg (0)0, Brondbyernes (0)0
Internazionale (2)3 (Altobelli 36, Serena 44,86), **Besiktas (1)1** (Feyyaz 15)
Juventus (1)3 (Magrin 23, Vignola 60, Rush 87), **Valletta (0)0**
GKS Katowice (1)1 (Koniarek 30), **Sportul Studentesc (2)2** (Tirlea 21, Cristea 27)
Lokeren (0)0, Honved (0)0
AC Milan (3)3 (Virdis 21 pen,44 pen, Gullit 43), **Gijon (0)0**
Moscow Dynamo (1)1 (Vasilyev 33), **Grasshoppers (0)0**
Panionios (0)0, Toulouse (0)1 (Rocheteau 57)
Partizan Belgrade (1)2 (Stevanovic 44 pen, Vokrii 61), **Flamurtari (0)1** (Perko 82)
Sion (3)3 (Bergy 4, Aziz Bouderbala 7, Balet 22), **Velez Mostar (0)0**
Spora Luxembourg (2)2 (Di Domenico 28, Jeitz 42), **Feyenoord (1)5** (Elstrup 24,80, Hoekstra 61, Wijnstekers 62, Hausch 65)
Dynamo Tbilisi (1)3 (Sulakvelidze 41, Gorili 73, Chivadze 79), **Lokomotiv Sofia (0)0**
Trakia Plovdiv (0)2 (Pashev 56 pen, Georgiev 67), **Red Star Belgrade (1)2** (Djurovic 11, Binic 82)
Utrecht (1)2 (Van Loen 23, Steinman 47), **Linzer ASK (0)0**
Valur Reykjavik (1)1 (Jon Gretar Jonsson 10), **Wismut Aue (0)1** (Weiss 80) (Wismut win on away goals)

Verona (3)3 (Elkjaer 32, 40, Di Gennaro 43 pen), **Pogon Szczecin (0)1** (Hawrylewicz 82)
Vitoria Bucharest (1)3 (Nuta 32,60 pen, Augustin 82), **EPA Larnaca (0)0**
Vitoria Guimaraes (0)1 (Kipulu 71), **Tatabanya (0)0**
Werder Bremen (0)0, **Mjondalen (0)1** (Markussen 78)

SECOND ROUND, FIRST LEG

Aberdeen (1)2 (Falconer 34, J. Miller 68), **Feyenoord (1)1** (Elstrup 21 pen)
Barcelona (2)2 (Amarilla 10, Schuster 30), **Moscow Dynamo (0)0**
Borussia Dortmund (0)2 (Hupe 68, Dickel 86), **Velez Mostar (0)0**
Brondbyernes (2)3 (L. Olsen 14, Steffensen 30 pen, Bent Christensen 84), **Sportul Studentesc (0)0**
Chaves (0)1 (Zdravkov 87), **Honved (0)2** (Kovacs, Fodor 81)
Dundee U (1)1 (Ferguson 24), **Vitkovice (1)2** (Dostal 13,77)
Internationale (0)0, **TPs Turun (1)1** (Altonen 11)
AC Milan (0)0, **Espanol (1)2** (Zubillaga 41, Oichi Alonso 49)
Panathinaikos (1)1 (Saravakos 6), **Juventus (0)0**
Red Star Belgrade (0)3 (Radovanovic 53, Cvetkovic 82, Stojkovic 89 pen), **CS Bruges (1)1** (Beyens 42)
Spartak Moscow (2)4 (Mostovoi 10, Rodionov 35,55, Pasulko 89), **Werder Bremen (0)1** (Burgsmuller 80)
Toulouse (0)1 (Tarantini 69 pen), **Bayer Leverkusen (1)1** (Schreier 32)
Utrecht (1)1 (Van Ginkel 44), **Verona (1)1** (Berthold 43)
Vitoria Bucharest (0)1 (Vaiscovici 67 pen), **Dynamo Tbilisi (2)2** (Shedia 3, Shengelia 20)
Vitoria Guimaraes (0)1 (Ademir 66 pen), **Beveren (0)0**
Wismut Aue (1)1 (Krauss 20), **Flamurtari (0)0**

SECOND ROUND, SECOND LEG

Bayer Leverkusen (0)1 (Schreier 80), **Toulouse (0)0**
Beveren (0)1 (Lemoine 66), **Vitoria Guimaraes (0)0** (Vitoria won 5–4 on pens)
CS Bruges (1)4 (Brylle 13, Ceulemans 47, Radovanovic og 49, Beyens 88), **Red Star Belgrade (0)0**
Espanol (0)0, **AC Milan (0)0**
Feyenoord (0)1 (Hoekstra 74), **Aberdeen (0)0** (Feyenoord won on away goals)
Flamurtari (1)2 (Taho 3, Vasil Ruci 72), **Wismut Aue (0)0**
Honved (1)3 (Sallai 22, Fitos 79, Kovaks 88), **Chaves (0)1** (Jorginho 77)
Juventus (0)3 (Cabrini 49,71 pen, Alessio 59), **Panathinaikos (0)2** (Saravakos 47, Dimopulos 53) (Panathinaikos won on away goals)
Moscow Dynamo (0)0, **Barcelona (0)0**
Sportul Studentesc (1)3 (Munreanu 7, Bozesan 78, Pana 89), **Brondbyernes (0)0** (Sportul won 3–0 on penalties)
Dynamo Tbilisi (0)0, **Vitoria Bucharest (0)0**
TPs Turun (0)0, **Internazionale (0)2** (Scifo 50, Altobelli 74)
Velez Mostar (0)2 (Kodro 65, Juric 89), **Borussia Dortmund (0)1** (Mill 88)
Verona (0)2 (Di Gennaro 69, Verrips og 89), **Utrecht (0)1** (De Knock 80)
Vitkovice (0)1 (Vik 76), **Dundee U (1)1** (Dostal og 37)
Werder Bremen (3)6 (Neubarth 3,10, Ordenwitz 25, Sauer 78, Riedle 100, Burgsmuller 108), **Spartak Moscow (0)2** (Cherenkov 71, Pasulko 109) (aet)

THIRD ROUND, FIRST LEG

Barcelona (1)4 (Urbano 43, Lineker 57,62, Carrasco 58), **Flamurtari (0)1** (Vasil Ruci 74 pen)
Borussia Dortmund (1)3 (Mill 12,64, Anderbruegge 77), **CS Bruges (0)0**
Feyenoord (2)2 (Been 39, Hoekstra 44), **Bayer Leverkusen (2)2** (Buncol 20, Falkenmeyer 32)
Honved (3)5 (Kalman Kovacs 2,33,59,63, Fodor 24 pen), **Panathinaikos (0)2** (Saravakos 66,88)
Internazionale (1)1 (Serena 32), **Espanol (0)1** (Lauridsen 80)
Verona (2)3 (Fontolan 25, Pacione 28, Elkjaer 82 pen), **Sportul Studentesc (0)1** (Coras 62)
Vitoria Guimaraes (0)2 (Kioma 60, Caio Junior 72), **Vitkovice (0)0**
Werder Bremen (2)2 (Neubarth 3, Riedle 18), **Dynamo Tbilisi (1)1** (Shengelia 20)

THIRD ROUND, SECOND LEG

Bayer Leverkusen (1)1 (Gotz 30), **Feyenoord (0)0**
CS Bruges (1)5 (Ceulemans 9, L. Van der Elst 48, 83, 107 pen, F. Van der Elst 97), **Borussia Dortmund (0)0** (aet)
Espanol (1)1 (Orejuela 22), **Internazionale (0)0**
Flamurtari (1)1 (Kushta 15), **Barcelona (0)0**
Panathinaikos (2)5 (Vlachos 22,37, Antoniou 55, Mavridis 65, Batsinilas 82), **Honved (0)1** (Fitos 59)
Sportul Studentesc (0)0, **Verona (0)1** (Elkjaer 67)
Dynamo Tbilisi (1)1 (Sulakvelidze 31), **Werder Bremen (0)1** (Schaaf 60)
Vitkovice (1)2 (Kovacik 33, Grussmann 88), **Vitoria Guimaraes (0)0**

UEFA CUP

QUARTER-FINALS, FIRST LEG

Bayer Leverkusen (0)0, **Barcelona** (0)0
Espanol (1)2 (Lauridsen 31, Pineda 69), **Vitkovice** (0)0
Panathinaikos (0)2 (Saravakos 54, Antoniou 65), **CS Bruges** (0)2 (Ceulemans 57, Degryse 83)
Verona (0)0, **Werder Bremen** (1)1 (Neubarth 49)

QUARTER-FINALS, SECOND LEG

Barcelona (0)0, **Bayer Leverkusen** (0)1 (Tita 59)
CS Bruges (1)1 (Brylle 43), **Panathinaikos** (0)0
Vitkovice (0)0, **Espanol** (0)0
Werder Bremen (1)1 (Sauer 32), **Verona** (0)1 (Volpecina 53)

SEMI-FINALS, FIRST LEG

Bayer Leverkusen (0)1 (Alois Reinhardt 61), **Werder Bremen** (0)0
CS Bruges (1)2 (Ceulemans 42, Gallart og 74), **Espanol** (0)0

SEMI-FINALS, SECOND LEG

Werder Bremen (0)0, **Bayer Leverkusen** (0)0
Espanol (1)3 (Orejuela 10, Losada 61, Pichi Alonso 119), **CS Bruges** (0)0 (aet)

FINAL

FIRST LEG: ESPANOL (1)3, BAYER LEVERKUSEN (0)0 (4 May 1988, 45,000)
Espanol: Nkono; Job, Miguel Angel, Inaki, Urquiaga, Orejuela (Golobart 66), Gallart, Valverde, Soler, Pichi Alonso (Lauridsen 71), Losada. **Scorers:** Losada 44,57, Soler 48.
Bayer: Vollborn; Hinterberger, Rolff, de Kayser, A. Reinhardt, Falkenmayer (K. Reinhardt 70), Buncol, Tita, Tauber, Cha (Gotz 18), Waas.
SECOND LEG: BAYER LEVERKUSEN (0)3, ESPANOL (0)0 (18 May 1988, 22,000)
Bayer: Vollborn; Rolff, Seckler, Alois, A. Reinhardt, K. Reinhardt, Buncol, Falkenmayer, Tita (Tauber 62), Cha, Schreier (Waas 46), Gotz. **Scorers:** Tita 56, Gotz 63, Cha 81.
Espanol: Nkono; Miguel Angel, Job, Gallart, Golobart (Zuniga 73), Inaki, Orejuela (Zubillaga 67), Soler, Uruquiaga, Pichi Alonso, Losada.
Bayer Leverkusen won 3-2 on penalties.

UEFA CUP 1987–88 – BRITISH AND IRISH CLUBS

FIRST ROUND, FIRST LEG

BOHEMIANS DUBLIN (0)0, ABERDEEN (0)0 (15.9.87, 10,000)
Bohemians: O'Neill; Kinsella, Duffy, B. Murphy, R. Murphy, O'Brien, Lawless, Murray (Byrne 76), Jameson, Swan, McGee.
Aberdeen: Leighton; McKimmie, Robertson, Connor, McLeish, W. Miller, Hewitt, Simpson (Weir 66), J. Miller (Hackett 76), P. Nicholas, Falconer.

CELTIC (1)2, BORUSSIA DORTMUND (0)1 (15.9.87, 41,400)
Celtic: McKnight; Morris, Rogan, Aitken, Whyte, Grant, Stark, McStay, McGhee, Walker, Burns (Archdeacon 77).
Scorers: Walker 5, Whyte 89.
Borussia: De Beer; Kleppinger, Kutowski, Pagelsdorf, Hupe, MacLeod, Helmer, Zorc, Dickel (Simmes 76), Radacanu, Mill. **Scorer:** Mill 63.

COLERAINE (0)0, DUNDEE UNITED (1)1 (16.9.87, 3,800)
Coleraine: Platt; Quigley, Edgar, Henry, Tabb, Wade, McGurnaghan, Robinson, McCreadie, Beggs, Doherty.
Dundee U: W.Thomson; McGinnis, Malpas, Brown, Hegarty, Narey, Ferguson, Bannon, Gallacher, Sturrock, Redford.
Scorer: Sturrock 39.

FIRST ROUND, SECOND LEG

ABERDEEN (1)1, BOHEMIANS DUBLIN (0)0 (30.9.87, 10,000)
Aberdeen: Leighton; McKimmie, Robertson (Grant 46), Connor, McLeish, W. Miller, Hewitt (Hackett 68), Bett, J. Miller, P. Nicholas, Falconer. **Scorer:** Bett 2 pen.
Bohemians: O'Neill; Kinsella, Duffy, B. Murphy, R. Murphy, O'Brien, Murray, Byrne, Jameson, Lawless, McGee.

BORUSSIA DORTMUND (0)2, CELTIC (0)0 (29.9.87, 54,000)
Borussia: De Beer; Kleppinger, Kutowski, Pagelsdorf, Hupe (Simmes 69), Macleod, Helmer, Zorc, Dickel, Radacanu, Mill. **Scorer:** Dickel 74, 87.
Celtic: McKnight; Morris, Rogan, Aitken, Whyte, McCarthy, Stark (McGuire 88), McStay, Grant, Walker (Mathie 83), Burns.

DUNDEE UNITED (1)3, COLERAINE (0)1 (30.9.87, 8,430)
Dundee U: W. Thomson; McGinnis, Malpas, Clark, Hegarty, Narey, Gallacher, J. A. Irvine, G. McLeod, Sturrock, McPhee. **Scorers:** Gallacher 28, Sturrock 73, Clark 80.
Coleraine: Platt; McCullogh, Edgar, Quigley, Tabb, Wade, McGurnaghan, Robinson, McCreadie, Kee, O'Neill. **Scorer:** Edgar 48.

SECOND ROUND, FIRST LEG

ABERDEEN (1)2, FEYENOORD (1)1 (21.10.87, 16,000)
Aberdeen: Leighton; McKimmie, Falconer, Connor, McLeish, W. Miller, Hewitt, Bett, J. Miller, C. Nicholas, Weir.
Scorers: Falconer 34, J. Miller 68.
Feyenoord: Hiele; Proost, Van Herpen, Wijnstekers, Molenaar, Hofman, Elstrup, Mitchell (Barendse 25) (Monkou 48), Been, Hoekstra, Blinker. **Scorer:** Elstrup 21 pen.

DUNDEE UNITED (1)1, VITKOVICE (1)2 (21.10.87, 8,938)
Dundee U: W. Thomson; Bowman, Malpas, McGinnis (Clark 60), Hegarty, Narey, Ferguson, Bannon, French, Kinnaird, McPhee (Sturrock 54). **Scorer:** Ferguson 24.
Vitkovice: Zapalka; Karas, Kadlec, Vlk, Grussmann, Chmela, Bartl, Houska (Sourek 85), Skarecky, Kovacik (Jerabek 81), Dostal. **Scorer:** Dostal 13, 77.

SECOND ROUND, SECOND LEG

FEYENOORD (0)1, ABERDEEN (0)0 (4.11.87, 22,000)
Feyenoord: Hiele; Monkou, Proost, Van Herpen, Hoekstra, Molenaar, Hofman, Elstrup, Mitchell, Been, Blinker. **Scorer:** Hoekstra 74.
Aberdeen: Leighton; Irvine, Connor, Simpson, McLeish, W. Miller, J. Miller (Hewitt 80), Bett, Falconer, Nicholas, Weir.

VITKOVICE (0)1, DUNDEE UNITED (1)1 (4.11.87, 15,000)
Vitkovice: Zapalka; Karas, Kadlec, Vlk, Grussmann, Chlema (Sourek 78), Bartl, Houska (Jerabek 59), Skarecky, Kovacik, Dostal. **Scorer:** Vlk 76.
Dundee U: W. Thomson; Bowman, Malpas, McInally, Hegarty, Beaumont, Ferguson, Bannon, Clark, McKinlay (McGinnis 63), McLeod (Kinnaird 74). **Scorer:** Dostal og 37.

WORLD CLUB CHAMPIONSHIP

Normally played annually between the winners of the European Cup and the South American Cup (Copa Libertadores). On occasions, European Cup winners have declined to participate. Played over two legs until 1980, since when a single match has been played in Tokyo. Line-ups given for matches involving British teams and the most recent final.

1960   Real Madrid 0,5, Penarol 0,1
1961   Penarol 0,5,2, Benfica 1,0,1
1962   Santos 3,5, Benfica 2,2
1963   Santos 2,4,1, AC Milan 4,2,0
1964   Inter-Milan 0,2,1, Independiente 1,0,0
1965   Inter-Milan 3,0, Independiente 0,0
1966   Penarol 2,2, Real Madrid 0,0

1967 CELTIC 1, RACING BUENOS AIRES 0
Celtic: Simpson; Craig, McNeill, Gemmell, Murdoch, Clark, Johnstone, Lennox, Wallace, Auld, Hughes. **Scorer:** McNeill.
Racing: Cejas; Martin, Perfumo, Basile, Diaz, Rulli, Mori, Maschio, Cardenas, Raffo, Rodriguez.

2nd LEG: RACING BUENOS AIRES 2, CELTIC 1
Racing: Cejas; Martin, Perfumo, Basile, Chabay, Rulli, Maschio, Cardoso, Cardenas, Rodriguez, Raffo. **Scorer:** Raffo 2.
Celtic: Fallon; Clark, Craig, McNeill, Gemmell, Murdoch, O'Neill, Johnstone, Wallace, Chalmers, Lennox. **Scorer:** Gemmell (pen).

PLAY-OFF: RACING BUENOS AIRES 1, CELTIC 0
(In Montevideo)
Racing: Cejas; Martin, Perfumo, Basile, Chabay, Rulli, Maschio, Cardoso, Cardenas, Rodriguez, Raffo. **Scorer:** Cardenas.
Celtic: Fallon; Clark, Craig, McNeill, Gemmell, Murdoch, Auld, Johnstone, Lennox, Wallace, Hughes.

1968 ESTUDIANTES 1, MANCHESTER UNITED 0
Estudiantes: Poletti; Suarez, Medina, Malbernat, Pachame, Madero, Ribaudo, Bilardo, Conigliaro, Togneri, Veron.
Manchester U: Stepney; Dunne, Foulkes, Sadler, Burns, Crerand, Stiles, Charlton, Morgan, Law, Best.

2nd LEG:
MANCHESTER UNITED 1, ESTUDIANTES 1
Manchester U: Stepney; Dunne, Foulkes, Sadler, Brennan, Crerand, Charlton, Morgan, Kidd, Law (Sartori), Best. **Scorer:** Morgan.
Estudiantes: Poletti; Malbernat, Suarez, Medina, Bilardo, Pachame, Madero, Ribaudo (Echecopar), Conigliaro, Togneri, Veron. **Scorer:** Veron.

1969   AC Milan 3,1, Estudiantes 0,2
1970   Feyenoord 2,1, Estudiantes 2,0
1971   Nacional 1,2, Panathinaikos 1,1
1972   Ajax 1,3, Independiente 1,0

1973   Independiente 1, Juventus 0
1974   Atletico Madrid 0,2, Independiente 1,0
1975   Not contested.
1976   Bayern Munich 2,0, Cruzeiro 0,0
1977   Boca Juniors 2,3, Bor. M'gladbach 2,0
1978   Not contested.
1979   Olimpia 1,2, Malmo 0,1

1980 NACIONAL 1, NOTTINGHAM FOREST 0
Nacional: Rodriguez; Moreira, Blanco, Enriquez, Gonzalez, Milar, Esparrago, Luzardo, Morales, Bica, Victorino. **Scorer:** Victorino.
Nottingham F: Shilton; Anderson, Lloyd, Burns, F.Gray, Ponte (Ward), O'Neill, S.Gray, Robertson, Francis, Wallace.

1981 FLAMENGO 3, LIVERPOOL 0
Flamengo: Raul; Leandro, Junior, Mozer, Marinho, Adilio, Tita, Andrade, Nunes, Zico, Lico. **Scorers:** Nunes 2, Adilio.
Liverpool: Grobbelaar; Neal, Lawrenson, Thompson, R.Kennedy, Hansen, Dalglish, Lee, Johnston, McDermott (Johnson), Souness.

1982 PENAROL 2, ASTON VILLA 0
Penarol: Fernandez; Olivera, Guitierrez, Diogo, Bossio, Morales, Ramos, Saralegui, Morena, Jair, Silva. **Scorers:** Jair, Silva.
Aston Villa: Rimmer; Jones, Williams, Evans, McNaught, Mortimer, Bremner, Cowans, Shaw, Withe, Morley.

1983   Gremio Porto Alegre 2, SV Hamburg 1

1984 INDEPENDIENTE 1, LIVERPOOL 0
Independiente: Goyen; Villaverde (Monzon), Enrique, Clausen, Trossero, Marangoni, Burruchaga, Giusti, Percudani, Bochini, Barberon. **Scorer:** Percudani.
Liverpool: Grobbelaar; Neal, Kennedy, Gillespie, Nicol, Hansen, Dalglish, Molby, Rush, Johnston, Wark (Whelan).

1985   Juventus 2, Argentinos Juniors 2
Juventus won 4–2 on penalties.
1986   River Plate 1, Steaua Bucharest 0

1987 FC PORTO 2, PENAROL 1
Porto: Mlynarczk; Joao Pinto, Geraldao, Lima Pereira, Inacio, Rui Barrow (Quim), Jaime Magalhaes, Andre, Sousa, Gomes, Madjer. **Scorers:** Gomes, Madjer.
Penarol: Pereira; Herrera, Goncalves, Rotti, Trasante, Dominguez, Perdomo, Viera, Aguirre, Cabrera, Matosas. **Scorer:** Viera.

EUROPEAN SUPER CUP

Normally played annually between the winners of the European Cup and the European Cup–Winners' Cup. Played over two legs until 1983, and as a single match thereafter.

1972　Ajax 3,3, Rangers 1,2
1973　Ajax 0,6, AC Milan 1,0
1974　Not contested.
1975　Dynamo Kiev 1,2, Bayern Munich 0,0
1976　Anderlecht 4,1, Bayern Munich 1,2
1977　Liverpool 1,6, SV Hamburg 1,0
1978　Anderlecht 3,1, Liverpool 1,2
1979　Nottingham Forest 1,1, Barcelona 0,1
*Won on away goals.

1980　*Valencia 1,1, Nottingham Forest 0,2
1981　Not contested.
1982　Aston Villa 0,3, Barcelona 1,0
1983　Aberdeen 0,2, Hamburg 0,0
1984　Juventus 2, Liverpool 0
1985　Juventus v Everton not contested due to UEFA ban on English clubs.
1986　Steaua Bucharest 1, Dynamo Kiev 0

1987: AJAX (0)0, FC PORTO (1)1 (Amsterdam, 24.11.87, 27,000)
Ajax: Menzo; Blind, Verlaat, Winter, Rob Witschge, Van't Schip, Bergkamp, Wouters (de Boer 68), Bosman, A. Muhren (Richard Witschge 46), Dick.
Porto: Mlynarczyk; Jaoa Pinto, Inacio, Geraldao, Lima Periera, Frasco (Quim 84), Jaime Magalhaes, Rui Barros, Gomes, Sousa, Andre. **Scorer:** Rui Barros 5.

2nd LEG: FC PORTO (0)1, AJAX (0)0 (Oporto, 13.1.88, 50,000)
Porto: Mlynarczyk; Joao Pinto, Lima Pereira, Geraldao, Inacio, Bandeirinha (Semedo 83), Jaime Magalhaes, Rui Barros, Sousa, Andre, Gomes (Jorge Placido 69). **Scorer:** Sousa 70.
Ajax: Menzo; Blind, Larsson, Wouters, Hesp, Van't Schip, A. Muhren, Winter, Bergkamp (Meijer 80), Bosman, Rob Witschge (Roy 64).

EUROPEAN LEAGUE TABLES 1987-88

ALBANIA

Championship Pool	P	W	D	L	F	A	Pts
17 Nentori	36	18	12	6	59	29	48
Flamurtari	36	15	11	10	55	38	41
Labinoti	36	14	11	11	31	33	39
Apolonia	36	16	6	14	51	43	38
Besa	36	11	13	12	38	36	35
Villaznia	36	13	8	15	40	42	34
Relegation Pool							
Lokomotiva	36	11	16	9	34	35	38
Beselidhja	36	12	14	10	38	42	38
Partizani	36	12	13	11	51	44	47
Skenderbeu	36	11	14	11	26	33	36
Dinamo	36	10	14	12	41	42	34
Luftetari	36	11	11	14	31	34	33

AUSTRIA

Promotion/ Relegation	P	W	D	L	F	A	Pts
Linz ASK	14	4	10	0	16	7	18
Austria Klagenfurt	14	6	6	2	18	12	18
St Poelten	14	6	5	3	30	17	17
Steyr	14	5	7	2	14	8	17
Voest Linz	14	5	5	4	17	16	15
Kremser	14	4	4	6	14	16	12
Austria Salzburg	14	4	1	9	10	20	9
Modling	14	2	2	10	14	35	6

Final Round	P	W	D	L	F	A	Pts
Rapid	36	22	10	4	81	40	54
Austria	36	19	8	9	83	47	46
Sturm Graz	36	15	12	9	55	48	42
Vienna	36	18	3	15	68	65	39
Admira Wacker	36	16	6	14	73	51	38
Tirol	36	11	15	10	47	49	37
Graz	36	11	13	12	50	66	35
Wiener SC	36	9	13	14	63	77	31

BELGIUM

	P	W	D	L	F	A	Pts
Club Brugge	34	23	5	6	74	34	51
Mechelen	34	21	7	6	50	24	49
Antwerp	34	20	9	5	75	40	49
Anderlecht	34	18	9	7	64	27	45
Liege	34	14	16	4	52	28	44
Waregem	34	16	7	11	50	43	39
Cercle	34	12	9	13	48	45	33
Charleroi	34	11	10	13	39	48	32
FC Kortrijk	34	11	9	14	40	54	31
Standard Liege	34	11	8	15	46	51	30
St Truiden	34	10	9	15	30	39	29
RWDM	34	8	12	14	33	48	28
Beerschot	34	10	7	17	39	49	27
Beveren	34	8	11	15	36	38	27
Winterslag	34	10	6	18	32	74	26
Lokeren	34	9	8	17	42	47	26
AA Ghent	34	8	9	17	34	60	25
Racing Jet	34	7	7	20	21	56	21

BULGARIA

	P	W	D	L	F	A	Pts
Vitosha	30	20	8	2	67	29	48
Sredets	30	20	6	4	76	32	46
Trakia	30	15	9	6	52	31	39
Slavia	30	14	10	6	48	30	38
Lokomotiv Sofia	30	12	8	10	47	47	32
Beroe	30	11	7	12	41	44	29
Lokomotiv Plovdiv	30	12	4	14	44	59	28
Sliven	30	11	5	14	35	43	27
Etur	30	10	6	14	44	41	26
Spartak Varna	30	10	6	14	36	52	26
Mineur	30	10	5	15	34	36	25
Pirin	30	7	11	12	32	37	25
Lokomotiv Gorna	30	11	3	16	41	57	25
Vratza	30	8	8	14	34	46	24
Tchernomoretz	30	9	3	18	27	50	21
Spartak Pleven	30	6	9	15	37	61	21

CYPRUS

	P	W	D	L	F	A	Pts
Pezoporikos	30	19	10	1	56	20	48
Apoel	30	22	3	5	66	23	47
Omonia	30	15	7	8	59	32	37
Paralimni	30	14	8	8	44	38	36
Apollon	30	13	9	8	46	24	35
AEL	30	15	5	10	46	33	35
Salamina	30	14	5	11	43	34	33
Anortosi	30	9	12	9	36	36	30
EPA	30	10	7	13	37	43	27
Apop	30	9	8	13	31	34	26
Aris	30	10	6	14	49	54	26
Olympiakos	30	9	7	14	32	48	25
Ethnikos	30	5	13	12	27	44	23
Apep	30	5	9	16	23	54	19
Alki	30	4	9	17	27	63	17
Anagennisis	30	5	6	19	26	68	16

CZECHOSLOVAKIA

	P	W	D	L	F	A	Pts
Sparta Prague	30	22	5	3	82	22	49
Dukla Prague	30	15	9	6	54	34	39
Dunajska Streda	30	13	9	8	39	36	35
Banik Ostrava	30	13	8	9	49	40	34
Olomouc	30	12	9	9	50	46	33
Slavia Prague	30	12	7	11	49	45	31
Nitra	30	13	4	13	46	45	30
Vitkovice	30	11	7	12	49	45	29
Banska Bystrica	30	12	5	13	44	46	29
Trnava	30	11	7	12	38	42	29
Cheb	30	9	11	10	31	36	29
Bohemians	30	13	3	14	41	54	29
Inter	30	11	5	14	50	54	27
Hradec Kralove	30	8	11	11	32	52	27
Zilina	30	7	7	16	32	54	21
Tatran Presov	30	3	4	23	29	64	10

DENMARK

	P	W	D	L	F	A	Pts
Brondby	26	22	3	1	63	17	47
Ikast	26	16	6	4	53	26	38
Aarhus	26	15	6	5	43	26	36
Odense	26	12	7	7	39	26	34
Vejle	26	13	4	9	53	39	30
Naestved	26	11	6	9	56	46	28
Bronshoj	26	10	7	9	32	33	27
Lyngby	26	9	8	9	42	38	26
B 1903	26	8	10	8	36	35	26
Aalborg	26	7	6	13	27	38	20
KB	26	6	6	14	30	43	18
Herfolge	26	5	5	16	17	53	15
Hvidovre	26	5	4	17	25	57	14
Kastrup	26	1	6	19	19	62	8

FINLAND

	P	W	D	L	F	A	Pts
HJK	22	15	3	4	38	14	33
Kuusysi	22	12	6	4	37	21	30
TPS	22	12	4	6	36	21	28
Iives	22	12	1	9	43	43	25
RoPs	22	9	6	7	30	25	24
Pori	22	9	5	8	39	32	23
Mikkell	22	8	6	8	27	21	22
KuPs	22	6	5	9	34	39	21
Kaka	22	7	5	10	30	36	19
Reipas L.	22	4	6	12	20	43	14
KePs	22	5	3	14	19	33	12
Koparit	22	1	10	11	17	42	12

EAST GERMANY

	P	W	D	L	F	A	Pts
Dynamo Berlin	26	15	7	4	59	30	37
Lokomotiv Leipzig	26	14	9	3	42	21	37
Dynamo Dresden	26	12	9	5	47	24	33
Brandenburg	26	12	5	9	44	37	29
Chemie Halle	26	7	12	7	33	33	26
Carl Zeiss Jena	26	8	10	8	26	29	26
Magdeburg	26	9	7	10	34	33	25
Karl Marx Stadt	26	8	9	9	40	45	25
Hansa Rostock	26	7	9	10	42	49	23
Wismut Aue	26	8	7	11	24	34	23
Union Berlin	26	7	8	11	35	54	22
Erfurt	26	8	5	13	40	49	21
Vorwaerts	26	6	9	11	33	43	21
Stahl Riesa	26	3	10	13	23	45	16

GREECE

	P	W	D	L	F	A	Pts
Larissa	30	18	7	5	50	22	43
AEK	30	15	10	5	50	31	40
PADK	30	17	5	8	62	27	39
OFI Crete	30	17	3	10	50	40	37
Panathinaikos	30	15	6	9	47	34	36
Iraklis	30	13	8	9	41	32	34
Ethnikos	30	12	8	10	30	25	32
Olympiakos	30	9	13	8	39	40	31
Aris	30	11	5	14	36	39	27
Panionios	30	8	10	12	33	35	26
Kalamaria	30	7	10	13	23	39	24
Diagoras	30	7	9	14	36	38	23
Levadiakos	30	7	9	14	33	44	23
Verria	30	7	9	14	24	53	23
Panserraikos	30	7	5	18	24	46	23
Panachaiki	30	9	5	16	35	50	20

FRANCE

	P	W	D	L	F	A	Pts
Monaco	38	20	12	6	53	29	52
Bordeaux	38	18	10	10	46	30	46
Montpellier	38	18	9	11	68	38	45
St Etienne	38	18	6	14	54	56	42
Toulon	38	14	13	11	41	26	41
Marseille	38	18	5	15	49	42	41
Racing Paris	38	12	17	9	35	42	41
Metz	38	16	8	14	46	40	40
Auxerre	38	12	15	11	37	29	39
Nantes	38	13	13	12	44	41	39
Lille	38	14	9	15	45	39	37
Cannes	38	13	11	14	42	52	37
Toulouse	38	14	7	17	35	47	35
Laval	38	12	10	16	38	38	34
Paris St Germain	38	12	10	16	36	45	34
Nice	38	15	3	20	42	47	33
Lens	38	13	7	18	40	62	33
Nioret	38	11	10	17	34	41	32
Brest	38	11	10	17	32	52	32
Le Havre	38	8	11	19	35	56	27

HUNGARY

	P	W	D	L	F	A	Pts
Honved	30	17	7	6	48	23	41
Tatabanya	30	13	11	6	58	35	37
Ujpest Dozsa	30	12	13	5	48	29	37
Raba ETO	30	14	7	9	49	43	35
Ferencvaros	30	12	9	9	48	32	33
MTK VM	30	14	4	12	53	50	32
Haladas	30	9	13	8	38	37	31
Pecs	30	11	9	10	31	34	31
Vasas	30	9	11	10	33	27	29
Izzo Vac	30	9	10	11	34	34	28
Videoton	30	6	15	9	28	32	27
Siofok	30	9	9	12	39	50	27
Bekescsaba	30	8	11	11	20	42	27
Zalaegerszeg	30	7	11	12	26	32	25
Debrecen	30	8	7	15	39	45	23
Kaposvar	30	4	9	17	25	63	17

EUROPEAN LEAGUE TABLES

ICELAND

	P	W	D	L	F	A	Pts
Valur	18	10	7	1	30	10	37
Fram	18	9	5	4	33	21	32
IA	18	9	3	6	36	30	30
Per	18	9	2	7	33	33	29
KR	18	7	4	7	28	22	25
KA	18	5	6	7	18	17	21
IBK	18	5	6	7	22	30	21
Valsungur	18	4	5	9	20	32	17
Vidir	18	3	8	7	20	33	17
FH	18	4	4	10	22	34	16

Note: 3 pts for a win, 1 pt for a draw.

MALTA

	P	W	D	L	F	A	Pts
Hamrun S	14	9	4	1	21	5	22
Sliema	14	8	3	3	19	7	19
Zurrieq	14	6	6	2	17	10	18
Valletta	14	4	5	5	9	16	13
Hibernians	14	4	3	7	11	15	11
Floriana	14	2	6	6	8	13	10
Birkirkara	14	2	6	6	8	17	10
Mosta	14	4	1	9	13	13	9

ITALY

	P	W	D	L	F	A	Pts
Milan	30	17	11	2	43	14	45
Napoli	30	18	6	6	55	27	42
Roma	30	15	8	7	39	26	38
Sampdoria	30	13	11	6	41	30	37
Inter	30	11	10	9	42	35	32
Juventus	30	11	9	10	35	30	31
Torino	30	8	15	7	33	30	31
Fiorentina	30	9	10	11	29	33	28
Cesena	30	7	12	11	23	32	26
Verona	30	7	11	12	23	30	25
Como	30	6	13	11	22	37	25
Ascoli	30	6	12	12	30	37	24
Pisa	30	6	12	12	23	30	24
Pescara	30	8	8	14	27	44	24
Avellino	30	5	13	12	19	39	23
Empoli	30	6	13	11	20	30	20

Juventus beat Torino on penalties after 0–0 draw in UEFA Cup place play-offs. Empoli minus 5 points.

NETHERLANDS

	P	W	D	L	F	A	Pts
PSV	34	27	5	2	177	28	59
Ajax	34	23	4	7	78	40	50
FC Twente	34	16	9	9	63	40	41
Willem II	34	14	10	10	60	46	38
VVV	34	13	12	9	43	35	38
Feyenoord	34	14	8	12	63	57	36
FC Den Bosch	34	15	6	13	46	46	36
Fortuna S	34	11	13	10	51	48	35
Haarlem	34	14	6	14	42	46	34
Utrecht	34	11	11	12	41	55	33
Groningen	34	13	6	15	54	52	32
Sparta	34	12	8	14	44	50	32
PEC Zwolle	34	10	9	15	40	64	29
Volendam	34	10	9	15	40	66	29
Roda JC	34	10	8	16	46	54	28
AZ	34	9	10	15	44	64	28
Den Haag	34	7	8	19	50	72	22
DS'79	34	2	8	24	41	100	12

LUXEMBOURG

First round	P	W	D	L	F	A	Pts
Jeunesse Esch	22	15	4	3	53	20	34
Spora	22	14	5	3	56	21	33
Avenir Beggen	22	11	6	5	48	25	28
Union	22	11	5	6	48	32	27
Red Boys	22	8	7	7	38	27	23
Olympique	22	7	7	8	24	35	21
Niedercorn	22	7	6	9	35	35	20
Grevenmacher	22	8	4	10	27	36	20
Hesperange	22	6	4	12	32	48	16
Alliance	22	6	4	12	24	40	16
Aris	25	5	6	11	33	54	16
Rumelange	22	2	6	14	20	63	10

NORWAY

	P	W	D	L	F	A	Pts
Moss	22	13	3	6	44	30	44
Molde	22	11	5	6	27	20	41
Kongsvinger	22	9	8	5	32	22	39
Rosenborg	22	8	11	3	33	25	39
Byrne	22	11	1	10	32	27	34
Tromso	22	5	9	8	19	31	31
Valerengen	22	8	5	9	26	27	30
Brann	22	7	6	9	25	28	30
Lillestrom	22	7	5	10	22	21	29
Hamkam	22	7	5	10	27	34	29
Myondalen	22	6	5	11	26	34	25
Start	22	6	5	11	30	44	25

Note: 3 pts for a win, 2 pts for a drawn match won on penalty shoot-out; 1 pt for draw and defeat in shoot-out.

POLAND

	P	W	D	L	F	A	Pts
Gornik Zabrze	30	19	7	4	65	30	51
Katowice	30	14	9	7	40	23	40
Legia	30	15	8	7	39	27	39
LKS Lodz	30	16	5	9	40	29	39
Widzew Lodz	30	8	15	7	28	24	31
Slask	30	9	11	10	31	32	29
Szombierki	30	10	10	10	28	29	29
Jagiellonia	30	11	7	12	24	25	29
Lech Poznan	30	10	9	11	29	30	28
Pogon Stettin	30	12	5	13	32	36	28
Zaglebie	30	8	11	11	23	25	26
Lech Danzig	30	6	14	10	18	26	26
Olimpia	30	7	11	12	36	46	24
Walbrzych	30	6	11	13	24	36	24
Baltyk Gdynia	30	9	6	15	27	41	21
Stal Stalowa	30	6	9	15	31	56	16

One extra point for victories over three goals; one deducted for defeats conceding over three goals.

PORTUGAL

	P	W	D	L	F	A	Pts
FC Porto	38	29	8	1	88	15	66
Benfica	38	19	13	6	59	25	51
Belenenses	38	18	12	8	52	38	48
Sporting	38	17	13	8	62	41	47
Boavista	38	16	14	8	42	25	46
Chaves	38	13	14	11	51	31	40
Setubal	38	15	10	13	56	43	40
Espinho	38	13	14	11	42	38	40
Maritimo	38	11	17	10	36	37	39
Penafiel	38	10	18	10	36	45	38
Braga	38	8	18	12	32	42	34
Farense	38	12	10	16	36	50	34
Portimonense	38	12	10	16	35	50	34
Guimaraes	38	11	11	16	48	50	33
Elvas	38	8	17	13	35	40	33
Academica	38	9	15	14	32	42	33
Varzim	38	7	16	15	31	52	30
Rio Ave	38	7	14	17	29	67	28
Salgueiros	38	6	13	19	31	62	25
Covilha	38	5	11	22	30	70	21

REPUBLIC OF IRELAND

	P	W	D	L	F	A	Pts
Dundalk	33	19	8	6	54	32	46
St Patrick's	33	18	9	6	52	25	45
Bohemians	33	17	11	5	57	32	45
Shamrock	33	16	9	8	53	30	41
Galway Utd	33	15	10	8	48	34	40
Cork City	33	12	10	11	41	47	34
Waterford Utd	33	10	14	9	40	31	34
Derry City	33	13	5	15	59	44	31
Limerick	33	9	7	17	33	60	25
Shelbourne	33	8	8	17	31	44	24
Bray Wanderers	33	4	10	19	27	65	18
Sligo Rovers	33	4	5	24	30	81	13

RUMANIA

	P	W	D	L	F	A	Pts
Steaua	34	30	4	0	114	18	64
Dinamo	34	30	3	1	107	25	63
Victoria	34	18	4	12	58	41	40
Otelul	34	18	3	13	49	46	39
Uni. Craiova	34	16	4	14	61	51	36
Flacara Moreni	34	13	7	14	40	48	33
Olt	34	13	4	17	41	62	30
Brasov	34	11	7	16	47	51	29
Arges	34	11	7	16	41	47	29
Uni. Cluj	34	11	7	16	39	54	29
Bacau	34	10	9	15	36	53	29
Rapid	34	10	9	15	36	58	29
Tirgu Mures	34	13	3	18	49	66	29
Sportul	34	10	8	16	43	50	28
Corvinul	34	12	4	17	49	63	28
Timisoara	34	10	6	18	35	53	26
Petrolul	34	10	6	18	24	51	26
Suceava	34	9	5	19	35	67	23

SPAIN

	P	W	D	L	F	A	Pts
Real Madrid	38	28	6	4	95	26	62
Real Sociedad	38	22	7	9	61	33	51
Atletico Madrid	38	19	10	9	60	38	48
Athletic Bilbao	38	17	12	9	50	43	46
Osasuna	38	15	10	13	40	34	40
Barcelona	38	15	9	14	49	44	39
Celta	38	14	11	13	43	40	39
Valladolid	38	13	12	13	31	34	38
Gijon	38	14	10	14	44	49	38
Sevilla	38	13	11	14	41	46	37
Zaragoza	38	11	14	13	54	56	36
Cadiz	38	11	13	14	47	54	35
Logrones	38	12	9	17	28	45	33
Valencia	38	10	13	15	44	53	33
Espanol	38	11	11	16	44	55	33
Betis	38	14	5	19	42	54	33
Murcia	38	9	13	16	31	42	31
Mallorca	38	9	12	17	35	50	30
Sabadell	38	9	11	18	27	48	29
Las Palmas	38	12	5	21	43	65	29

SWEDEN

	P	W	D	L	F	A	Pts
Malmo FF	22	14	6	2	50	21	34
IFK Norrkoping	22	11	7	4	33	19	29
IFK Goteborg	22	9	8	5	39	24	25
Oster IF	22	11	2	9	25	26	24
IK Brage	22	6	12	4	21	23	24
Hammarby IF	22	6	10	6	37	27	22
Frolunda	22	6	9	7	21	29	21
Orgryte G	22	5	10	7	32	33	20
AIK Solna	22	5	10	7	15	17	20
GIF Sundsvalt	22	5	7	10	25	31	17
Halmstad BK	22	4	9	9	22	23	17
IF Elfsborg	22	3	4	15	18	49	10

Championship title play-offs – Semi finals: Oster v Malmo 1–2, 1–2, IFK Goteborg v Norrkoping 3–0, 2–2. **Final:** IFK Goteborg v Malmo 1–0, 1–2. (Agg 2–2; IFK won on away goals rule).

EUROPEAN LEAGUE TABLES

SWITZERLAND – Final Round

	P	W	D	L	F	A	Pts
Neushatel.Xamax	14	6	4	4	29	19	32
Servette	14	7	4	3	38	23	30
Aarau	14	6	5	3	24	17	30
Grasshoppers	14	6	3	5	23	21	30
Lucerne	14	5	5	4	19	19	27
St Gallen	14	4	3	7	16	25	23
Lausanne	14	3	5	6	18	30	23
Young Boys	14	4	1	9	18	31	22

TURKEY

	P	W	D	L	F	A	Pts
Galatasaray	38	27	9	2	86	35	90
Besiktas	38	22	12	4	68	29	78
Malatyaspor	38	17	11	10	64	61	62
Samsunspor	38	17	9	12	43	41	60
Bursaspor	38	17	6	15	63	56	57
Trabzonspor	38	16	9	13	57	51	57
Karsiyaka	38	13	17	8	43	34	56
Fenerbahce	38	15	10	13	45	43	55
Sariyer	38	12	16	10	60	51	52
Adana d. spor	38	16	4	18	59	64	52
Sakaryaspor	38	14	9	15	54	67	51
Altay	38	13	9	16	60	57	48
Ankaragucu	38	11	13	14	46	47	46
Boluspor	38	13	7	18	45	52	46
Eskisehirspor	38	11	13	14	45	53	46
Rizespor	38	13	7	18	37	56	46
Denizlispor	38	12	9	17	35	46	45
Kocaelispor	38	6	16	16	44	61	34
Genclerbirligi	38	7	9	22	41	65	30
Zonguldakspor	38	6	9	23	37	61	27

USSR

	P	W	D	L	F	A	Pts
Spartak	30	16	11	3	49	26	42
Dnepr	30	15	9	6	42	22	39
Zalghiris	30	14	8	8	43	29	36
Torpedo	30	12	12	6	35	25	34
Minsk	30	12	9	9	33	25	33
Kiev	30	11	10	9	37	27	32
Shakthyor	30	10	10	10	29	31	30
Ararat	30	13	3	14	32	45	29
Neftchi	30	9	10	11	33	30	28
Moscow Dynamo	30	9	11	10	27	30	28
Metallist	30	10	7	13	23	32	27
Kairat	30	10	6	14	27	38	26
Tbillsl	30	9	7	14	31	40	25
Zenit	30	7	10	13	25	37	24
TSKA	30	7	11	12	26	36	24
Guria	30	5	8	17	18	38	18

Note: No points awarded for draws per team beyond the limit of ten.

WEST GERMANY

	P	W	D	L	F	A	Pts
Werder Bremen	34	22	8	4	61	22	52
Bayern Munich	34	22	4	8	83	45	48
Koln	34	18	12	4	57	28	48
Stuttgart	34	16	8	10	69	49	40
Nurnberg	34	13	11	10	47	40	37
Hamburg	34	13	11	10	63	68	37
Borussia Mg	34	14	5	15	55	53	33
Bayer Leverkusen	34	10	12	12	53	60	32
Eintracht Frankfurt	34	10	11	13	51	50	31
Hannover	34	12	7	15	59	60	31
Bayer Uerdingen	34	11	9	14	59	61	31
Bochum	34	10	10	14	47	51	30
Borussia Dortmund	34	9	11	14	51	54	29
Kaiserslautern	34	1	7	16	53	62	29
Karlsruhe	34	9	11	14	37	55	29
Waldhof-Mannheim	34	7	14	13	35	50	28
FC Homburg	34	7	10	17	37	70	24
Schalke	34	8	7	19	48	84	23

YUGOSLAVIA

	P	W	D	L	F	A	Pts
Red Star Belgrade	34	17	11	6	66	39	45
Partizan	34	17	10	7	62	37	44
Velez Mostar	34	15	12	7	61	34	42
Dynamo Zagreb	34	16	10	8	55	36	42
Sloboda	34	14	10	10	53	41	38
Vardar Skopje	34	15	7	12	37	40	37
Radnicki	34	14	4	16	48	46	32
Rijeka	34	9	14	11	33	39	32
Buducnost	34	10	12	12	40	48	32
Vojvodina	34	11	10	13	40	51	32
Osijek	34	10	11	13	44	61	31
Zeljeznicar	34	8	14	12	38	44	30
Sarajevo	34	11	8	15	37	47	30
Hajduk Split	34	8	14	12	40	50	30
Rad	34	11	8	15	44	56	30
Celik	34	12	5	17	39	45	29
Sutjeska	34	10	9	15	42	49	29
Pristina	34	10	7	17	43	59	27

INTERNATIONAL FOOTBALL

EUROPEAN CHAMPIONSHIP 1988

FINAL TOURNAMENT

GROUP 1

WEST GERMANY (0)1, ITALY (0)1
Dusseldorf, 10 June 1988, 68,400
West Germany: Immel; Buchwald, Brehme (Borowka 76), Kohler, Herget, Littbarski, Matthaus, Voller (Eckstein 82), Thon, Berthold, Klinsmann. **Scorer:** Brehme 56.
Italy: Zenga; Baresi, Bergomi, Ferri, Maldini, Ancelotti, de Napoli (de Agostini 85), Gianinni, Donadoni, Mancini, Vialli (Altobelli 89). **Scorer:** Mancini 51.

SPAIN (1)3, DENMARK (1)2
Hanover, 11 June 1988, 60,000
Spain: Zubizaretta; Tomas, Andrinua, Sanchis, Camacho (Soler 46), Gallego, Victor, Michel, Gordillo (Vasquez 87), Butragueno, Bakero. **Scorers:** Michel 6, Butragueno 52, Gordillo 67.
Denmark: Rasmussen; Sivebaek, Busk, M.Olsen (L.Olsen 66), Heintze, Helt (Jensen 46), Nielsen, Lerby, Poulsen, Laudrup, Elkjaer. **Scorers:** Laudrup 25, Poulsen 83.

WEST GERMANY (1)2, DENMARK (0)0
Gelsenkirchen, 14 June 1988, 60,800
West Germany: Immel; Buchwald (Borowka 33), Brehme, Kohler, Herget, Littbarski, Matthaus, Voller (Mill 74), Thon, Klinsmann, Rolff. **Scorers:** Klinsmann 9, Thon 85).
Denmark: Schmeichel; Sivebaek, M.Olsen, Nielsen, Lerby, Heintze, Elkjaer, Laudrup (Eriksen 63), L.Olsen, Poulsen, Vilfort (Berggren 73).

ITALY (0)1, SPAIN (0)0
Frankfurt, 14 June 1988, 51,790
Italy: Zenga; Baresi, Bergomi, Ferri, Maldini, Ancelotti, de Napoli, Gianinni, Donadoni, Mancini (Altobelli 70), Vialli (de Agostini 89). **Scorer:** Vialli 73.
Spain: Zubizaretta; Tomas, Genaro, Victor, Sanchis, Butragueno, Gordillo, Gallego (Vasquez 68), Bakero, Soler, Michel (Beguiristain 73).

WEST GERMANY (1)2, SPAIN (0)0
Munich, 17 June 1988, 72,308
West Germany: Immel; Brehme, Kohler, Herget, Borowka, Littbarski (Wuttke 63), Matthaus, Rolff, Thon, Klinsmann (Mill 86), Voller. **Scorer:** Voller 30, 51.
Spain: Zubizaretta; Tomas, Sanchis, Andrinua, Camacho, Victor, Martin Vasquez, Michel, Gordillo, Butragueno (Salinas 51), Bakero.

ITALY (0)2, DENMARK (0)0
Cologne, 17 June 1988, 60,500
Italy: Zenga; Bergomi, Baresi, Ferri, Maldini, Ancelotti, Gianinni, Donadoni (de Agostini 84), de Napoli, Vialli, Mancini (Altobelli 67). **Scorers:** Altobelli 67, de Agostini 86.
Denmark: Schmeichel; M.Olsen, L.Olsen, Kristensen, Nielsen, Jensen, Frimann, Heintze, Laudrup, Eriksen, Poulsen.

GROUP 2

REP. OF IRELAND (1)1, ENGLAND (0)0
Stuttgart, 12 June 1988, 53,000
Rep. of Ireland: Bonner; Morris, McCarthy, Moran, Hughton, Houghton, Whelan, McGrath, Galvin (Sheedy 77), Aldridge, Stapleton (Quinn 63). **Scorer:** Houghton 6.
England: Shilton; Stevens, Adams, Wright, Sansom, Waddle, Robson, Webb (Hoddle 60), Barnes, Lineker, Beardsley (Hateley 83).

USSR (0)1, NETHERLANDS (0)0
Cologne, 12 June 1988, 60,000
USSR: Dassaev; Bessonov, Demianenko, Khidiatulin, Kuznetsov, Zavarov (Sulakvelidze 89), Mikhailichenko, Litovchenko, Rats, Belanov (Aleinikov 79), Protasov. **Scorer:** Rats 54.
Netherlands: van Breukelen; van Tiggelen, R.Koeman, Rijkaard, van Aerle, Vanenburg (van Basten 57), Wouters, Muhren, van't Schip, Gullit, Bosman.

NETHERLANDS (1)3, ENGLAND (0)1
Dusseldorf, 15 June 1988, 65,000
Netherlands: van Breukelen; van Tiggelen, R.Koeman, van Aerle, Vanenburg (Kieft 61), Muhren, Gullit, van Basten (Suvrijn 86), E. Koeman, Rijkaard, Wouters. **Scorer:** van Basten 43, 72, 75.
England: Shilton; Sansom, Adams, Steven (Waddle 68), Wright, Stevens, Hoddle, Robson, Beardsley (Hateley 72), Lineker, Barnes. **Scorer:** Robson 53.

REP. OF IRELAND (1)1, USSR (0)1
Hanover, 15 June 1988, 45,298
Rep. of Ireland: Bonner; Morris, McCarthy, Moran, Hughton, Houghton, Whelan, Sheedy, Galvin, Stapleton (Cascarino 81), Aldridge. **Scorer:** Whelan 38.
USSR: Dassaev (Chanov 67); Sulakvelidze (Gotsmanov 46), Khidiatulin, Kuznetsov, Demianenko, Belanov, Aleinikov, Mikhailichenko, Zavarov, Rats, Protasov. **Scorer:** Protasov 75.

NETHERLANDS (0)1, REP. OF IRELAND (0)0
Gelsenkirchen, 18 June 1988, 70,000
Netherlands: van Breukelen; van Tiggelen, Rijkaard, R. Koeman, van Aerle, Vanenburg, Wouters, Gullit, Muhren, E. Koeman (Kieft 50), van Basten. **Scorer:** Kieft 82.
Rep. of Ireland: Bonner; Morris (Sheedy 46), McCarthy, Moran, Hughton, Houghton, McGrath, Whelan, Galvin, Stapleton (Cascarino 83), Aldridge.

USSR (2)3, ENGLAND (1)1
Frankfurt, 18 June 1988, 53,000
USSR: Dassaev; Bessonov, Khidiatulin, Kuznetsov, Aleinikov, Rats, Litovchenko, Zavarov (Gotsmanov 82), Belanov (Pasulko 46), Mikhailichenko, Protasov. **Scorers:** Aleinikov 3, Mikhailichenko 26, Pasulko 73.
England: Woods; Stevens, Watson, Adams, Sansom, Steven, Robson, McMahon (Webb 54), Barnes, Hoddle, Lineker (Hateley 69). **Scorer:** Adams 16.

FINAL TABLE	P	W	D	L	F	A	GD	Pts
WEST GERMANY	3	2	1	0	5	1	+4	5
ITALY	3	2	1	0	4	1	+3	5
Spain	3	1	0	2	3	5	−2	2
Denmark	3	0	0	3	2	7	−5	0

FINAL TABLE	P	W	D	L	F	A	GD	Pts
USSR	3	2	1	0	5	2	+3	5
NETHERLANDS	3	2	0	1	4	2	+2	4
Rep. of Ireland	3	1	1	1	2	2	0	3
England	3	0	0	3	2	7	−5	0

577

SEMI-FINALS

NETHERLANDS (0)2, WEST GERMANY (0)1
Hamburg, 21 June 1988, 61,330
Netherlands: van Breukelen; van Tiggelen, R. Koeman, van Aerle, Vanenburg, Muhren (Kieft 58), Gullit, van Basten, E. Koeman (Suvrijn 90), Rijkaard, Wouters. **Scorers:** R. Koeman pen 74, van Basten 88.
West Germany: Immel; Brehme, Kohler, Herget (Pfluegler 43), Borowka, Matthaus, Voller, Thon, Mill (Littbarski 85), Klinsmann, Rolff. **Scorer:** Matthaus pen 55.

USSR (0)2, ITALY (0)0
Stuttgart, 22 June 1988, 70,000
USSR: Dassaev; Khidiatulin, Bessonov (Demianenko 37), Kuznetsov, Rats, Zavarov, Aleinikov, Litovchenko, Mikhailichenko, Gotsmanov, Protasov. **Scorers:** Litovchenko 60, Protasov 63.
Italy: Zenga; Ferri, Baresi, Bergomi, Maldini (de Agostini 72), Ancelotti, de Napoli, Giannini, Donadoni, Mancini (Altobelli 46), Vialli.

FINAL

NETHERLANDS (1)2, USSR (0)0
Munich, 25 June 1988, 72,308
Netherlands: van Breukelen; Rijkaard, R.Koeman, van Tiggelen, van Aerle, Wouters, E.Koeman, Vanenburg, Muhren, Gullit, van Basten. **Scorers:** Gullit 34, van Basten 55.
USSR: Dassaev; Khidiatulin, Demianenko, Rats, Aleinikov, Litovchenko, Zavarov, Mikhailichenko, Gotsmanov (Baltacha 68), Protasov (Pasulko 71), Belanov.

EUROPEAN CHAMPIONSHIP 1988

QUALIFYING TOURNAMENT

Note: West Germany qualify automatically as host nation for the final tournament. They are joined by the winners of the following seven groups.

GROUP 1
(Albania, Austria, Rumania, Spain)

RUMANIA (1)4, AUSTRIA (0)0
Bucharest, 10.9.1986, 20,000
Rumania: Moraru; Iovan, Belodedici, Bumbescu, Rednic, Hagi, Mateut (Balaci 73), Boloni, Klein, Camataru, Piturca (Lacatus 46). **Scorers:** Iovan 44,63, Lacatus 61, Hagi 89.
Austria: Lindenberger; Weber, Messlender, Brauneder (Pacult 65), Lainer, Kienast (Werner 46), Baumeister, Turmer, Degeorgi, Schachner, Polster.

AUSTRIA (1)3, ALBANIA (0)0
Graz, 15.10.1986, 8000
Austria: Lindenberger; Weber, Piesinger, Messlender, Brauneder, Zsak, Linzmaier, Werner, Baumeister, Ogris, Polster. **Scorers:** Ogris 19, Polster 65, Linzmaier 76.
Albania: Musta; Cipi, Zmijani, Taho, Ocelli, Ferko (Omuri 71), Josa, Demollari, Ziaji, Kola, Minga.

SPAIN (0)1, RUMANIA (0)0
Seville, 12.11.1986, 47,500
Spain: Zubizarreta; Chendo, Sanchis, Arteche, Camacho, Victor, Michel, Gallego (Senor 72), Julio Alberto, Butragueno, Rincon (Eloy 46). **Scorer:** Michel 57.
Rumania: Lung; Iovan, Bumbescu, Belodedici, Ungureanu, Stoica (Rednic 82), Boloni, Klein, Hagi, Lacatus, Camataru (Balint 80).

ALBANIA (1)1, SPAIN (0)2
Tirana, 3.12.1986, 20,000
Albania: Musta; Omuri, Taho, Zmijani, Hodja, Ferko (Kola 70), Josa, Jera, Demollari, Muca, Minga. **Scorer:** Muca 27.
Spain: Zubizarreta; Chendo, Arteche, Sanchis, Camacho, Michel, Victor, Joaquin, Senor (Eloy 46), Butragueno, Rincon. **Scorers:** Arteche 66, Joaquin 83.

RUMANIA (3)5, ALBANIA (1)1
Bucharest, 25.3.1987, 15,000
Rumania: Lung; Iovan, Bumbescu, Belodedici, Ungureanu, Hagi (Rednic 67), Stoica, Boloni, Klein (Mateut 63), Lacatus, Piturca. **Scorers:** Piturca 1, Holoni 42, Hagi 44 pen, Belodedici 54, Bumbescu 69.
Albania: Musta; Hodja, Zmijani, Taho, Bilalli (Omuri 42), Demollari, Jera, Kushta (Ferko 73), Josa, Muca, Minga. **Scorer:** Muca 34.

AUSTRIA (1)2, SPAIN (1)3
Vienna, 1.4.1987, 41,000
Austria: Lindenberger; Pezzey, Piesinger, Zsak, Weinhofer (Roscher 70), Linzmaier, Kienast, Werner, Baumeister, Ogris, Polster. **Scorers:** Linzmaier 39, Polster 64.
Spain: Zubizarreta; Gallego, Chendo, Andrinua, Camacho, Michel, Roberto, Caldere, Victor, Butragueno (Eloy 13) (Sanchis 78), Carrasco. **Scorers:** Eloy 31,58, Carrasco 89.

ALBANIA (0)0, AUSTRIA (1)1
Tirana, 29.4.1987, 13,000
Albania: Musta; Zmijani, Hodja, Omuri, Gega, Jera, Josa, Demollari, Muca (Kushta 70), Minga, Bubeqi (Pano 64).
Austria: Lindenberger; Pezzey, Zsak, Brauneder, Piesinger, Linzmaier, Baumeister, Werner, Weinhofer (Frind 46), Ogris (Pacult 82), Polster. **Scorer:** Polster 7.

RUMANIA (3)3, SPAIN (0)1
Bucharest, 29.4.1987, 30,000
Rumania: Lung; Iovan (Negrila 78), Bumbescu, Belodedici, Ungureanu, Hagi, Boloni, Klein (Balint 89), Mateut, Lacatus, Piturca. **Scorers:** Piturca 37, Mateut 45, Ungureanu 48 (all in first half).
Spain: Zubizarreta; Camacho (Soler 37), Andrinua, Goicoechea (Joaquin 70), Sanchis, Caldere, Victor, Gallego, Michel, Eloy, Butragueno. **Scorer:** Caldere 81.

SPAIN (0)2, AUSTRIA (0)0
Seville, 14.10.1987, 70,410
Spain: Zubizarreta; Chendo, Julio Alberto, Andrinua, Sanchis, Gordillo, Carrasco (Baquer II 77), Michel (Caldere 77), Butragueno, Senor, Victor. **Scorers:** Michel 58 pen, Sanchis 63.
Austria: Lindenberger; Frind (Werner 46), Messlender, Brauneder, Pezzey, Zsak, Ogris, Kienast, Polster, Baumeister (Linzmaier 64), Willfurth.

ALBANIA (0)0, RUMANIA (0)1
Vlore, 28.10.1987, 18,000
Albania: S.Lekbello (Shkurti 65); Zmijani, Taho, F.Lekbello, Iljadhi, Ferko, Demollari (Zijal 46), Josa, Gjondeda, Bubeqi, Muca.
Rumania: Lung; Iovan, Belodedici, Andone, Ungureanu, Mateut, Boloni, Klein, Lacatus (Piturca 89), Hagi (Rednic 84), Camataru. **Scorer:** Klein 61.

SPAIN (3)5, ALBANIA (0)0
Seville, 18.11.1987, 50,000
Spain: Zubizarreta; Chendo, Julio Alberto (Quique Flores 63), Goicoechea, Sanchis, Victor, Baquero, Butragueno, Michel, Senor, Caldere (Llorente 46). **Scorers:** Baquero 5,31,74, Michel 36 pen, Llorente 67.
Albania: S.Lekbello; Ocello, Taho, Iljadhi, Gega, F.Lekbello, Demollari (Ferko 70), Josa (Ruci 69), Gjondeda, Minga, Bubeqi.

AUSTRIA (0)0, RUMANIA (0)0
Vienna, 18.11.1987, 6200
Austria: Lindenberger; Pezzey, Frind, Pecl, Brauneder, Artner, Baumeister, Willfurth, Rodax, Polster, Schachner.
Rumania: Lung; Belodedici, Iovan, Bumbescu, Ungureanu, Mateut, Klein, Boloni, Hagi, Lacatus, Camataru (Piturca 66).

FINAL TABLE	P	W	D	L	F	A	GD	Pts
SPAIN	6	5	0	1	14	6	+ 8	10
Rumania	6	4	1	1	13	3	+10	9
Austria	6	2	1	3	6	9	− 3	5
Albania	6	0	0	6	2	17	−15	0

GROUP 2
(Italy, Malta, Portugal, Sweden, Switzerland)

SWEDEN (1)2, SWITZERLAND (0)0
Stockholm, 24.9.1986, 27,751
Sweden: Moller; Fredriksson, Dahlkvist, P.Larsson, R.Nilsson, Eriksson, Prytz, Stromberg, Palmer (Engkvist 82), B.Nilsson, Ekstrom. **Scorer:** Ekstrom 19,79.
Switzerland: Brunner; Wittwer, In–Albon, Egli, Ryf, Mottiez (Sulser 57), Geiger, Hermann, Bickel (Bregy 72), Maissen, Halter.

PORTUGAL (0)1, SWEDEN (0)1
Lisbon, 12.10.1986, 15,000
Portugal: Ze Beto; Veloso, Eduardo Luis, Dito, Alberto, Fernando Mendes, Jaime, Nunes, Sheu (Coelho 62), Adao (Mario Jorge 72), Manuel Fernandes. **Scorer:** Coelho 66.
Sweden: Moller; R.Nilsson, Hysen, P.Larsson, Fredriksson, Eriksson (Engkvist 84), Stromberg, Prytz, Palmer (Magnusson 75), Ekstrom, B.Nilsson. **Scorer:** Stromberg 50.

SWITZERLAND (1)1, PORTUGAL (0)1
Berne, 29.10.1986, 11,000
Switzerland: Brunner; Marini, Ryf, Egli, Weber, Bregy, Geiger, Heinz Hermann, B.Sutter, Bickel (Maissen 62), A.Sutter (Cina 78). **Scorer:** Bregy 6.
Portugal: Ze Beto; Veloso, Eduardo Luis, Fernando Mendes, Dito, Sheu (Coelho 22), Jaime, Alberto, Manuel Fernandes, Nunes (Mario Jorge 31), Adao. **Scorer:** Manuel Fernandes 86.

ITALY (1)3, SWITZERLAND (1)2
Milan, 15.11.1986, 75,000
Italy: Zenga; Bergomi, Cabrini (Francini 8), F.Baresi, Bonetti, Bagni, Donadoni (Serena 40), Ancelotti, Altobelli, Dossena, Vialli. **Scorers:** Donadoni 1, Altobelli 52,85.
Switzerland: Brunner; Wittwer, Ryf, Weber, Geiger, Bamert, B.Sutter, Hermann, Brigger, Bregy, Halter (Zuffi 69). **Scorers:** Brigger 31, Weber 89.

MALTA (0)0, SWEDEN (1)5
Valletta, 16.11.1986, 15,000
Malta: Mifsud; Aquilina (Azzopardi 80), E.Cammilleri, Scicluna, Holland, Laferia, J.Cammilleri, Vella, Mizzi, Farrugia, Schembri (Cauchi 70).
Sweden: Moller; Andersson, Hysen, P.Larsson, Fredriksson, Eriksson, Engkvist, Prytz, B.Nilsson (Palmer 80), Ekstrom, Magnusson. **Scorers:** Hysen 38, Magnusson 67, Fredriksson 69, Ekstrom 81, Palmer 84.

MALTA (0)0, ITALY (2)2
Valletta, 6.12.1986, 30,000
Malta: Bonello; Scicluna, Mackay (Azzopardi 33), Laferia, Holland, Buttigieg, Busuttil, Vella, Gregory (Scerri 83), Farrugia, De Giorgio.
Italy: Zenga; Bergomi, Nela, F.Baresi, Ferri, Bagni (de Napoli 65), Donadoni, Dossena (Matteoli 74), Altobelli, Giannini, Vialli. **Scorers:** Ferri 11, Altobelli 19.

ITALY (5)5, MALTA (0)0
Bergamo, 24.1.1987, 35,000
Italy: Zenga; Bergomi, Cabrini, F.Baresi, Ferri, Bagni (de Napoli 56), Donadoni, Dossena (Matteoli 56), Altobelli, Giannini, Vialli. **Scorers:** Bagni 4, Bergomi 9, Altobelli 24,35, Vialli 44.
Malta: Bonello; Galea, Scicluna, Buttigieg, Holland,

Laferia, Busuttil, Vella, Gregory (Cauchi 66), Farrugia (Scerri 25), De Giorgio.

PORTUGAL (0)0, ITALY (1)1
Lisbon, 14.2.1987, 32,500
Portugal: Jesus; Veloso, Dito, Eduardo Luis, Alvaro, Frasco, Nascimento, Quim, Adao (Mario Jorge 30), Jaime, Manuel Fernandes (Coelho 46).
Italy: Zenga; Bergomi, F.Baresi, Ferri, Cabrini, Bagni, Donadoni (de Napoli 82), Dossena (Matteoli 75), Giannini, Altobelli, Vialli. **Scorer:** Altobelli 40.

PORTUGAL (1)2, MALTA (1)2
Funchal, Madeira, 29.3.1987, 12,000
Portugal: Jesus; Veloso, Dito, Eduardo Luis, Alvaro, Nascimento (Skoda 81), Frasco (Rui Barrios 46), Adao, Jaime, Manuel Fernandes, Jorge Placido. **Scorer:** Jorge Placido 12,76.
Malta: Cluett; Camilleri, Azzopardi, Laferia, Scicluna, Buttigieg, Busuttil (Schembri 87), Vella, Mizzi, Scerri, De Giorgio (Gregory 72). **Scorers:** Mizzi 23 pen, Busuttil 66.

SWITZERLAND (3)4, MALTA (0)1
Neuchatel, 15.4.1987, 5000
Switzerland: Brunner; Geiger, Weber (Bickel 75), Egli, Ryf, Marini (Perret 81), Hermann, Bregy, Cina, Brigger, A.Sutter. **Scorers:** Egli 5, Bregy 16,38 pen,87.
Malta: Cluett; Buttigieg, Camilleri, Scicluna, Vella, Azzopardi, Scerri, Laferia (Gregory 87), Busuttil, Mizzi, De Giorgio.

SWEDEN (1)1, MALTA (0)0
Gothenburg, 23.5.1987, 16,165
Sweden: T.Ravelli; A.Ravelli, Hysen, P.Larsson, Fredriksson, Eriksson (Pettersson 68), Prytz, Stromberg, Limpar, Ekstrom (Nielsson 68), Magnusson. **Scorer:** Ekstrom 13.
Malta: Cluett; Camilleri, Scicluna (Holland 78), Buttigieg, Azzopardi, Busuttil, Laferia, Vella, De Giorgio (Mackay 87), Mizzi, Gregory.

SWEDEN (1)1, ITALY (0)0
Stockholm, 3.6.1987, 40,070
Sweden: T.Ravelli; R.Nilsson, Hysen, P.Larsson, Fredriksson, Eriksson (A.Ravelli 79), Prytz, Stromberg (Limpar 88), Holmqvist, Ekstrom, L.Nilsson. **Scorer:** P.Larsson 25.
Italy: Zenga; Tricella, Bergomi, Ferri, Francini, de Napoli, Mancini (de Agostini 46), Giannini, Dossena, Altobelli, Vialli.

SWITZERLAND (0)1, SWEDEN (0)1
Lausanne, 17.6.1987, 7000
Switzerland: Brunner; Geiger, Marini, Weber, Ryf, Koller, Bregy (Bamert 75), Hermann, B.Sutter, Halter, Bonvin (A.Sutter 79). **Scorer:** Halter 58.
Sweden: T.Ravelli; R.Nilsson, A.Ravelli, Larsson, Fredriksson, Eriksson, Prytz, Stromberg, Holmqvist, Ekstrom, L.Nilsson (Magnusson 79). **Scorer:** Ekstrom 60.

SWEDEN (0)0, PORTUGAL (1)1
Stockholm, 23.9.1987, 28,916
Sweden: T.Ravelli; Fredriksson, Hysen, P.Larsson, T.Persson, R.Nilsson, Prytz (Limpar 74), Stromberg, B.Nilsson, Magnusson (L.Nilsson 57), Ekstrom.
Portugal: Pereira; Joao Pinto, Marques, Venancio, Alvaro, Jaime Magalhaes, Andre, Oceano, Sousa, Futre, Gomes (Barros 86). **Scorer:** Gomes 35.

580

EUROPEAN CHAMPIONSHIP

SWITZERLAND (0)0, ITALY (0)0
Berne, 17.10.1987, 35,000
Switzerland: Brunner; Geiger, Marini, Schallibaum, Weber, Bickel (Bamert 56), Bonvin (Zwicker 56), Brigger, Hermann, Koller, B.Sutter.
Italy: Zenga; F.Baresi, Ferrera, Ferri, Cabrini, Bagni (Ancelotti 77), de Napoli, Giannini, Donadoni, Altobelli (Mancini 83), Vialli.

PORTUGAL (0)0, SWITZERLAND (0)0
Oporto, 11.11.1987, 12,500
Portugal: Jesus; Joao Pinto, Frederico, Marques, Alvaro, Frasco (Parente 46), Coelho, Sousa, Rui Aguas (Adao 73), Futre, Andre.
Switzerland: Brunner; Marini, Schallibaum, Weber, Geiger, Koller (Perret 80), B.Sutter, Hermann, Brigger (Zwicker 66), Bickel, Bonvin.

ITALY (2)2, SWEDEN (1)1
Naples, 14.11.1987, 65,000
Italy: Zenga; Bergomi, Francini (de Agostini 26), F.Baresi, Ferrera, Bagni (Ancelotti 89), Donadoni, de Napoli, Altobelli, Giannini, Vialli. **Scorer:** Vialli 27,45.
Sweden: T.Ravelli; R.Nilsson (Limpar 70), Hysen, P.Larsson, Persson, Thern, Stromnerg, Prytz, B.Nilsson, Ekstrom (Corneliusson 70), Pettersson. **Scorer:** P.Larsson 38.

MALTA (0)1, SWITZERLAND (1)1
Valletta, 15.11.1987, 5000
Malta: Cluett; Buttigieg, Camilleri, Scicluna, Azzopardi, Gregory (Scerri 73), Vella, Laferia, Busuttil, Carabotto (Mizzi 73), Degiorgio. **Scorer:** Busuttil 89.
Switzerland: Brunner; Geiger, Marini, Weber, Schallibaum, Koller, Hermann, Bickel, Zwicker, Brigger (Mottiez 86), Sutter (Bonvin 75). **Scorer:** Zwicker 3.

ITALY (1)3, PORTUGAL (0)0
Milan, 5.12.1987, 20,000
Italy: Zenga; Bergomi, Francini, F.Baresi, Ferri, Bagni (de Agostini 60), Donadoni, de Napoli, Altobelli (Mancini 70), Giannini, Vialli. **Scorers:** Vialli 8, Giannini 88, de Agostini 89.
Portugal: Jesus (Lucio 75); Costeado, Miguel, Frederico, Dito, Carvalho, Hernani, Nascimento (Parente 55), Coelho, Adao, Gilberto.

MALTA (0)0, PORTUGAL (0)1
Valletta, 20.12.1987, 4000
Malta: Cluett; E.Camilleri, J.Camilleri, Laferia, Azzopardi, Buttigieg, Busuttil, Vella, Gregory, Carabotto, Mizzi (Degiorgio 70).
Portugal: Jesus; Costeado, Miguel, Frederico, Fernando Mendes, Dito, Gilberto (Aparicio 46), Rui Barros, Nascimento, Adao, Coelho (Carvalho 83).

FINAL TABLE	P	W	D	L	F	A	GD	Pts
ITALY	8	6	1	1	16	4	+12	13
Sweden	8	4	2	2	12	5	+ 7	10
Portugal	8	2	4	2	6	8	− 2	8
Switzerland	8	1	5	2	9	9	0	7
Malta	8	0	2	6	4	21	−17	2

GROUP 3
(East Germany, France, Iceland, Norway, USSR)

ICELAND (0)0, FRANCE (0)0
Reykjavik, 10.9.1986, 13,700
Iceland: Sigurdsson; Saevar Jonsson, Gislasson, Edvaldsson, A.Jonsson, Torfasson, Siggi Jonsson, Margiersson, Sigurvinsson, Gudjohnsson, Petursson.
France: Bats; Ayache, Boli, Battiston, Amoros, Fernandez, Tigana, Vercruysse, Genghini, Stopyra, Paille.

ICELAND (1)1, USSR (1)1
Reykjavik, 24.9.1986, 7000
Iceland: Sigurdsson; Gislasson, Saevar Jonsson, M.Jonsson, Edvaldsson, Torfasson, Margeirsson, Siggi Jonsson, Sigurvinsson, Gudjohnsson, Petursson. **Scorer:** Gudjohnsson 29.
USSR: Dassayev; Sulakvelidze, Larionov (Litovchenko 80), Kuznetsov, Demianenko, Bessonov, Rats, Aleinikov, Khidiatulin (Rodionov 46), Zavarov, Blokhin. **Scorer:** Sulakvelidze 44.

NORWAY (0) 0, EAST GERMANY (0)0
Oslo, 24.9.1986, 10,142
Norway: Thorstvedt; Mordt, Giske (Aas 74), Kojedal, Fjaelberg, Osvold, Sundby, Haaberg (Seland 70), Larsen Oekland, Herlovsen, Berg.
East Germany: Muller; Kreer, Rohde, Sanger, Zotzsche, Stubner, Ernst, Liebers, Thom, Kirsten, Pastor.

FRANCE (0)0, USSR (0)2
Paris, 11.10.1986, 40,496
France: Bats; Ayache, Boli (Vercruysse 87), Jeannol, Amoros, Tigana, Ferreri, Fernandez, Platini, Stopyra, Papin (Bellone 70).
USSR: Dassayev; Bessonov (Khidiatulin 33), Kuznetsov, Chivadze, Demianenko, Rats, Zavarov, Rodionov (Blokhin 82), Yakovenko, Aleinikov, Belanov. **Scorers:** Belanov 67, Rats 73.

USSR (3)4, NORWAY (0)0
Simferopol, 29.9.1986, 35,000
USSR: Dassayev; Bessonov, Khidiatulin, Kuznetsov, Demianenko, Rodionov, Aleinikov, Yakovenko, Zavarov (Blokin 22), Belanov, Litovchenko (Baltacha 82). **Scorers:** Litovchenko 25, Belanov 27 pen, Blokhin 32, Khidiatulin 52.
Norway: By Rise; Bratseth, Aas, Giske, Mordt (Haaberg 50), Davidsen, Herlovsen, Osvold, Sundby, Berg, Larsen Oekland (Halsen 80).

EAST GERMANY (1)2, ICELAND (0)0
Karl-Marx-Stadt, 29.10.1986, 18,000
East Germany: Muller; Schossler, Doschner, Rohde, Sanger (Stahmann 69), Stubner, Thom, Liebers, Ernst (Minge 85), Pastor, Kirsten. **Scorer:** Thom 4,89.
Iceland: Sigurdsson; A.Jonsson, Gislasson, Edvaldsson, Saevar Jonsson, St.Jonsson, O.Torfasson, Bergsson (G.Torfasson 79), Margeirsson, Ormslev, Gudjohnsson.

EAST GERMANY (0)0, FRANCE (0)0
Leipzig, 19.11.1986, 52,000
East Germany: Muller; Schossler, Rohde, Stahmann (Richter 62), Doschner, Stubner, Liebers, Steinmann, Pastor, Kirsten (Sammer 76), Thom.
France: Bats; Amoros, Ayache, Boli, Battiston, Le Roux, Tigana, Poullain, Stopyra, Platini, Papin (Bellone 83).

FRANCE (1)2, ICELAND (0)0
Paris, 29.4.1987, 30,000
France: Bats; Amoros, Thouvene, Boli, Domergue, Fernandez, Toure, Platini, Passi, Stopyra (Papin 67), Micciche. **Scorers:** Micciche 38, Stopyra 65.
Iceland: Sigurdsson; Saevar Jonsson, Mar Jonsson, Edvaldsson, Gislasson (Gretarsson 38), Sigurvinsson, Torfasson, Siggi Jonsson, Margeirsson, Petursson, Gudjohnsson.

USSR (1)2, EAST GERMANY (0)0
Kiev, 29.4.1987, 95,000
USSR: Dassayev; Bessonov, Khidiatulin, Kuznetsov, Demianenko, Rats, Aleinikov (Protasov 86), Rodionov, Zavarov, Mikhailichenko (Yakovenko 73), Belanov. **Scorers:** Zavarov 41, Belanov 49.
East Germany: Muller; Kreer, Rohde, Lindner, Zotzsche, Stubner (Wuckel 70), Liebers, Raab, Kirsten (Scholz 75), Ernst, Thom.

NORWAY (0)0, USSR (1)1
Oslo, 3.6.1987, 10,473
Norway: Thorstvedt; Bratseth (Henriksen 68), Giske, Kojedal, Mordt, Herlovsen, Ahlsen, Thoresen, Osvold (Seland 46), Sundby, Andersen.
USSR: Dassayev; Kuznetsov, Sulakvelidze, Khidiatulin, Rats, Rodionov, Yakovenko (Demianenko 68), Mikhailichenko, Aleinikov, Zavarov, Belanov (Protasov 78).
Scorer: Zavarov 16.

ICELAND (0)0, EAST GERMANY (2)6
Reykjavik, 3.6.1987, 10,000
Iceland: Sigurdsson; Siggi Jonsson, Saevar Jonsson, Edvaldsson, Gislasson, Sigurvinsson (Gudmundsen 71), Torfasson, Agust, Jonsson, Margeirsson (Arnthorsson 82), Gudjohnsson, Petursson.
East Germany: Muller; Dorschner, Rohde, Lindner, Kreer, Raab, Steinmann, Minge (Kirsten 82), Ernst, Doll (Scholz 78), Thom. **Scorers:** Minge 16, Thom 37,65,88, Doll 49, Dorschner 85.

NORWAY (0)2, FRANCE (0)0
Oslo, 16.6.1987, 8260
Norway: Thorstvedt; Henriksen, Kojedal, Giske, Ahlsen, Berg, Mordt, Sundby, Thoresen, Seland (Osvold 62), Andersen (Soler 89). **Scorers:** Mordt 72, Andersen 80.
France: Bats; Thouvene, Boli, Domergue, Amoros, Ferreri, Poullain (Delamontaigne 81), Tigana, Tassi, Stopyra, Micchiche (Fargeon 75).

USSR (0)1, FRANCE (1)1
Moscow, 9.9.1987, 100,000
USSR: Dassayev; Losev, Khidiatulin, Kuznetsov, Rats, Tishenko (Belanov 46), Litovchenko, Yakovenko, Aleinikov, Protasov, Dobrovolski (Mikhailichenko 66). **Scorer:** Mikhailichenko 77.
France: Bats; Amoros, Ayache, Vogel, Boli, Fernandez, Fargeon (Papin 89), Toure (Bijotat 75), Stopyra, Passi, Poullain. **Scorer:** Toure 13.

ICELAND (1)2, NORWAY (1)1
Reykjavik, 9.9.1987, 6500
Iceland: Sigurdsson; Saevar Jonsson, Edvaldsson, Gislasson, Thorkelsson, Siggi Jonsson, Ormslev, Thordarsson, Margeirsson (Arnthorsson 78), Torfasson, Petursson. **Scorers:** Petursson 28, Ormslev 60.
Norway: Thorstvedt; Solar (Fjaelestad 77), Kojedal, Soleid, Henriksen, Mordt, Herlovsen, Skogheim (Erlandsen 84), Veinstedt, Andersen, Osvold. **Scorer:** Andersen 11.

NORWAY (0)0, ICELAND (1)1
Oslo, 23.9.1987, 3540
Norway: Thorstvedt; Henriksen, Bratseth, Giske, Mordt, Soler, Herlovsen, Osvold, Skogheim (Moller 46), Sundby (Berg 77), Andersen.
Iceland: Sigurdsson; Gislasson, Edvaldsson, Arnthornsson, Thorkelsson, Saevar Jonsson, Bergsson, Thordarsson, Margeirsson, Torfasson, Gudmundsson (Askelsson 75).
Scorer: Edvaldsson 31.

EAST GERMANY (1)1, USSR (0)1
East Berlin, 10.10.1987, 25,000
East Germany: Muller; Kreer, Zotzsche, Schossler, Doschner, Pilz (Stubner 76), Liebers, Raab (Minge 82), Kirsten, Doll, Thom. **Scorer:** Kirsten 44.
USSR: Dassayev; Bessonov, Khidiatulin (Rats 70), Kuznetsov, Demianenko, Yaremchuk, Aleinikov, Mikhailichenko, Zavarov (Litovchenko 60), Protasov, Dobrovolski.
Scorer: Aleinikov 80.

FRANCE (0)1, NORWAY (0)1
Paris, 14.10.1987, 12,000
France: Martini; Sonor, Senac, Boli, Amoros, Fernandez, Toure, Anziani (Ferreri 53), Bijotat, Fargeon, Cantona. **Scorer:** Fargeon 63.
Norway: Thorstvedt; Henriksen, Kojedal, Bratseth, Mordt, Giske, Herlovsen (Soler 77), Osvold, Sundby, Berg (Skogheim 79), Meinseth. **Scorer:** Sundby 76.

USSR (1)2, ICELAND (0)0
Simferopol, 28.10.1987, 40,000
USSR: Dassayev; Bessonov, Demianenko, Khidiatulin, Bubnov, Rats (Yakovenko 80), Yaremchuk (Blokhin 72), Litovchenko, Aleinikov, Belanov, Protasov. **Scorers:** Belanov 15, Protasov 50.
Iceland: Sigurdsson; Gislasson (Orludsson 80), Edvaldsson, Torfasson, Askelsson, Saevar Jonsson, Bergsson, Thordarsson, Margeirsson, Torfasson, Gudmundsson (Kristiansson 70).

EAST GERMANY (2)3, NORWAY (1)1
Magdeburg, 28.10.1987, 10,000
East Germany: Muller; Kreer, Stahmann, Schlossler, Doschner, Liebers, Pilz, Thom, Doll, Kirsten, Raab. **Scorers:** Kirsten 15,53, Thom 34.
Norway: Boe; Soler, Kojedal, Giske, Bratseth, Mordt, Erlandsen, Fjaelestad, Meinseth, Moller (Berg 61), Sundby. **Scorer:** Fjaelestad 32.

FRANCE (0)0, EAST GERMANY (0)1
Paris, 18.11.1987, 20,000
France: Bats; Amoros, le Roux, Boli, Kastendeuch, Poullain, Germain, Zenier, Bijotat (Fargeon 76), Cantona, Bellone.
East Germany: Muller; Kreer, Zotzsche, Stahmann, Doschner, Liebers, Pilz, Minge (Ernst 62), Steinmann, Kirsten, Thom. **Scorer:** Ernst 89.

FINAL TABLE	P	W	D	L	F	A	GD	Pts
USSR	8	5	3	0	14	3	+11	13
East Germany	8	4	3	1	13	4	+ 9	11
France	8	1	4	3	4	7	− 3	6
Iceland	8	2	2	4	4	14	−10	6
Norway	8	1	2	5	5	12	= 7	4

EUROPEAN CHAMPIONSHIP

GROUP 4
(England, Northern Ireland, Turkey, Yugoslavia)

ENGLAND (1)3, NORTHERN IRELAND (0)0
Wembley, 15.10.1986, 35,300
England: Shilton; Anderson, Sansom, Hoddle, Watson, Butcher, Robson, Hodge, Lineker, Beardsley (Cottee 84), Waddle. **Scorers:** Lineker 33,80, Waddle 78.
Northern Ireland: Hughes; Fleming, McDonald, McClelland, Worthington, Donaghy, Whiteside (McIlroy 84), Penney (Quinn 74), Clarke, Campbell, Stewart.

YUGOSLAVIA (2)4, TURKEY (0)0
Split, 29.10.1986, 15,000
Yugoslavia: Ravnic; Zoran Vujovic, Baljic, Sabanadovic, Elsner, Jankovic, Skoro (Savicevic 55), Katanec, Mihajlovic (Tuce 65), Mlinaric, Zlatko Vujovic. **Scorers:** Zlatko Vujovic 25,35,84, Savicevic 75.
Turkey: Fatih; B.Ismail, Yusuf, K.Ismail, Erdogan, Savas, Ugur, Metin, Senol, Tanju (Semih 75), Erdal (K.Hasan 46).

ENGLAND (1)2, YUGOSLAVIA (0)0
Wembley, 12.11.1986, 60,000
England: Woods; Anderson, Wright, Butcher, Sansom, Hoddle, Mabbutt, Hodge (Wilkins 82), Lineker, Beardsley, Waddle (Steven 79). **Scorers:** Mabbutt 21, Anderson 57.
Yugoslavia: Ravnic; Zoran Vujovic, Baljic, Sabanadovic, Elsner, Hadzibegic, Katanec, Jankovic, Skoro (Tuce 71) (Juric 73), Sliskovic, Zlatko Vujovic.

TURKEY (0)0, NORTHERN IRELAND (0)0
Izmir, 12.11.1986, 25,000
Turkey: Fatih; B.Ismail, Yusuf, K.Ismail, Kadir, Savas, Ugur, Metin, Ridvan, Tanju (Erhan 10), Senol.
Northern Ireland: Hughes; Donaghy, McDonald, McClelland, Worthington (McNally 75), Penney, Wilson, McCreery, Quinn (Sanchez 46), Clarke, Campbell.

NORTHERN IRELAND (0)0, ENGLAND (2)2
Belfast, 1.4.1987, 23,000
Northern Ireland: Dunlop; Fleming, Donaghy, McClelland, McDonald, Ramsey, Campbell (D.Wilson 70), McCreery, K.Wilson, Whiteside, Worthington.
England: Shilton (Woods 46); Anderson, Sansom, Mabbutt, Wright, Butcher, Robson, Hodge, Beardsley, Lineker, Waddle. **Scorers:** Robson 19, Waddle 43.

NORTHERN IRELAND (1)1, YUGOSLAVIA (0)2
Belfast, 29.4.1986, 5000
Northern Ireland: Dunlop; Fleming, Donaghy, McClelland, McDonald, McCreery (Ramsey 46), Campbell (McCoy 76), K.Wilson, Clarke, Whiteside, Worthington. **Scorer:** Clarke 39.
Yugoslavia: Ivkovic; Zoran Vujovic, Baljic, Katanec (Vulic 46), Elsner, Hadzibegic, Stojkovic, Jankovic, Pancev, Asanovic (Smajic 77), Zlatko Vujovic. **Scorers:** Stojkovic 48, Zlatko Vujovic 79.

TURKEY (0)0, ENGLAND (0)0
Izmir, 29.4.1987, 25,000
Turkey: Fatih; D.Ismail, Semih, Ali Coban, Erhan, Riza, Ugur, Savas, Hasan Vezir (Feyyaz 85), Erdal, Iskender (Tufekci 78).

England: Woods; Anderson, Adams, Mabbutt, Sansom, Waddle, Hoddle, Robson, Hodge (Barnes 75), C.Allen (Hateley 75), Lineker.

YUGOSLAVIA (2)3, NORTHERN IRELAND (0)0
Sarajevo, 14.10.1987, 22,500
Yugoslavia: Ravnic; Zoran Vujovic, Baljic, Katanec, Hadzibegic, Radanovic, B.Cvetkovic, Mlinaric (Brnovic 76), Vokrri (Savicevic 76), Bazdarevic, Zlatko Vujovic. **Scorers:** Vokrri 13,35, Hadzibegic 73 pen.
Northern Ireland: McKnight; Ramsey, Worthington, Donaghy, McDonald, McCreery, Campbell (Rogan 55), D.Wilson, Clarke (Quinn 48), McNally, K.Wilson.

ENGLAND (4)8, TURKEY (0)0
Wembley, 14.10.1987, 42,528
England: Shilton; Stevens, Adams, Butcher, Sansom, Steven (Hoddle 46), Webb, Robson, Barnes, Beardsley (Regis 73), Lineker. **Scorers:** Barnes 1,28, Lineker 8,42,71, Robson 59, Beardsley 62, Webb 88.
Turkey: Fatih; Riza, Semih, Ali Coban, Erhan, Guilken (Savas 34), Ugur, Muhammed, Kayhan, Erdal, Iskender.

YUGOSLAVIA (0)1, ENGLAND (4)4
Belgrade, 11.11.1987, 70,000
Yugoslavia: Ravnic (Radac 46); Zoran Vujovic, Baljic, Katanec, Elsner (Jankovic 29), Hadzibegic, Stojkovic, Mlinaric, Vokrri, Bazdarevic, Zlatko Vujovic. **Scorer:** Katanec 80.
England: Shilton; Stevens, Sansom, Steven, Adams, Butcher, Robson (Reid 75), Webb (Hoddle 83), Beardsley, Lineker, Barnes. **Scorers:** Beardsley 4, Barnes 17, Robson 20, Adams 25.

NORTHERN IRELAND (0)1, TURKEY (0)0
Belfast, 11.11.1987, 5000
Northern Ireland: McKnight; Fleming, Worthington, McClelland, McDonald, Donaghy, D.Wilson (Campbell 46), Quinn, Clarke, Whiteside, K.Wilson (Doherty 75). **Scorer:** Quinn 47.
Turkey: Okan; D.Ismail, Semih, Gokham, Yusuf, Riza, Ugur, Savas, Metin (Hami 66), Tanju (Gokhan 81), Erdal.

TURKEY (0)2, YUGOSLAVIA (2)3
Izmir, 16.12.1987, 10,000
Turkey: Okan; Riza, Gokhan, Yusuf, Erhan, Unal, Ugur (Ali 46), Erdal (Savas 40), Feyyaz, Tanju, Iskender. **Scorers:** Yusuf 68, Feyyaz 73.
Yugoslavia: Radaca; Brnovic, Krivokapic, Katanec, Hadzibegic, Radanovic, Smajic (Janevski 75), Savicevic, Jakovijevic, Bazdarevic, Skoro (P.Juric 80). **Scorers:** Radanovic 5, Katanec 40, Hadzibegic 54 pen.

FINAL TABLE	P	W	D	L	F	A	GD	Pts
ENGLAND	6	5	1	0	19	1	+18	11
Yugoslavia	6	4	0	2	13	9	+ 4	8
Northern Ireland	6	1	1	4	2	10	− 8	3
Turkey	6	0	2	4	2	16	−14	2

GROUP 5
(Cyprus, Greece, Hungary, Netherlands, Poland)

HUNGARY (0)0, NETHERLANDS (0)1
Budapest, 15.10.1986, 15,000
Hungary: Szendrei; Sallai, Pinter, Preszeller, Kardos, Garaba, K.Kovacs, Roth (Koller 66), Boda (Szekeres 65), Detari, Esterhazy.
Netherlands: Van Breukelen; Silooy, Spelbos, Rijkaard, van Tiggelen, Wouters, van t'Schip, R.Koeman, van Basten, Gullit, Tahamata (Suvrijn 88). **Scorer:** van Basten 68.

POLAND (1)2, GREECE (1)1
Poznan, 15.10.1986, 32,500
Poland: Kazimierski; Pawlak, Krol, Ostrowski, Prusik, Karas, Matysik, Tarasiewicz, Dziekanowski (Urban 46), Lesniak, Smolarek (Baran 68). **Scorer:** Dziekanowski 5 pen,40 pen.
Greece: Minou; Xanthoupulos, Michos, Mavridis (Batsinilas 74), Manolas, Antoniou, Skartados (Apostolakis 88), Kofidis, Alavantas, Sarakavos, Anastopulos. **Scorer:** Anastopulos 22.

GREECE (1)2, HUNGARY (0)1
Athens, 12.11.1986, 15,000
Greece: Minou; Apostolakis, Vamvakulos, Manolas, Michos, Kofidis, Antoniou, Papaioannu (Skartados 64), Saravakos, Anastopulos, Mitropulos (Xanthoupulos 78). **Scorers:** Mitropulos 39, Anastopulos 65.
Hungary: Szendrei; Sallai, Roth, Garaba, Pinter, Csonka (Tzapfo 67), Burcsa, Nagy, Detari, Meszaros (Boda 46), Esterhazy. **Scorer:** Boda 72.

NETHERLANDS (0)0, POLAND (0)0
Amsterdam, 19.11.1986, 65,000
Netherlands: Van Breukelen; Silooy, Spelbos, Rijkaard, van Tiggelen, Wouters, van t'Schip, R.Koeman (Bosman 46), van Basten, Gullit, Tahamata (van der Gijp 74).
Poland: Kazimierski; Pawlak, Krol, Wdowczyk, Wojcicki, Rudy (Tarasiewicz 46), Karas, Prusik, Boniek, Dziekanowski (Urban 46), Smolarek.

CYPRUS (2)2, GREECE (1)4
Nicosia, 3.12.1986, 10,000
Cyprus: Charitou; Andrelis (Papadopulos 67), Miamiliotis, Misou, N.Pantzarias, Yiangudakis, Ioannou, Marangos, Savvides, Nicolau (Kantelos 77), Christofi. **Scorers:** Christofi 28, Savvides 41.
Greece: Minou; Apostolakis, Vamvakulas, Manolas, Mihos, Antoniou, Saravakos (Batsinilas 46), Kofidis, Anastopulos, Papaioannou, Mitropulos (Anastasiadis 73). **Scorers:** Antoniou 13, Papaioannou 48, Batsinilas 73, Anastopulos 86 pen.

CYPRUS (0)0, NETHERLANDS (1)2
Limassol, 21.12.1986, 10,000
Cyprus: Charitou; Tsikos, Mauliotis, Misos, Socratous, Yiangudakis, Savva, Marangos (Nicolau 84), Savvides, Ioannou (L.Mavroudis 46), Christofi.
Netherlands: Van Breukelen; van Tiggelen, Spelbos, Silooy, Rijkaard (Vanenburg 65), Wouters, van der Gijp, Muhren, Bosman, Gullit, Tahamata. **Scorers:** Gullit 19, Bosman 73.

GREECE (0)3, CYPRUS (0)1
Athens, 14.1.1987, 35,000
Greece: Papadopulos; Apostolakis, Vamvakulas, Manolas, Michos, Bonovas, Saravakos, Antonious, Anastopulos, Papaioannou (Mitropoulos 46), Kofidis (Batsinilas 46). **Scorers:** Anastopulos 54,66, Bonovas 63.
Cyprus: Charitou; Pitos, Miamiliotis, Misos, Pantzarias, Yiangudakis, L.Mavroudis (Georgiou 87), Marangos (Nicolau 84), Christofi, Savva, Savvides. **Scorer:** Savva 60.

CYPRUS (0)0, HUGARY (0)1
Nicosia, 8.2.1987, 8000
Cyprus: Charitou; Lemesios, Pitos, Socratous, Misos, Yiangudakis, Savva, Marangos (Floros 57), Savvides, Mavridis (Xiouroppas 52), Christofi.
Hungary: Szendrei; Sallai, Hires, Roth, Preszeller, Varga, Kardos, Hannich, Bognar (Garaba 80), Boda, K.Kovacs. **Scorer:** Boda 49.

NETHERLANDS (0)1, GREECE (1)1
Rotterdam, 25.3.1987, 56,000
Netherlands: Van Breukelen; Silooy, Spelbos, Rijkaard, R. Koeman (Bosman 71), Wouters, van der Gijp (Winter 82), A. Muhren, van Basten, Gullit, van t'Schip. **Scorer:** van Basten 55.
Greece: Manikos; Apostolakis (Xanthoupulos 68), Michos, Manolas, Vamvakulas, Bonovas (Skartados 83), Antoniou, Mitropulos, Kofidis, Saravakos, Anastopulos. **Scorer:** Saravakos 6.

POLAND (0)0, CYPRUS (0)0
Gdansk, 12.4.1987, 25,000
Poland: Kazimierski; Prusik, Krol, Wdowczyk, Urban, Wijas, Dziekanowski (L.Iwanicki 66), Karas, Okonski, Furtok (J.Bayer 46), Smolarek.
Cyprus: Charitou; Miamiliotis, Pittas, Pantzarias, Misos, Yiangudakis, Savva, Marangos, Savvides, Nicolau, Tsingis (K.Pantzarias 85).

GREECE (0)1, POLAND (0)0
Athens, 29.4.1987, 70,000
Greece: Papadopulos; Alavantas, Vamvakulas, Michos, Manolas, Bonovas, Skartados (Xanthopoulos 73), Kofidis, Anastopulos, Antoniou, Saravakos (Papaioannou 68). **Scorer:** Saravakos 57.
Poland: Kazimierski; Pawlak, Wojcicki, Krol, Wdowczyk, Matysik, Ostrowski (Prusik 58), Tarasiwicz, Dziekanowski, Furtok (Lesniak 66), Smolarek.

NETHERLANDS (2)2, HUNGARY (0)0
Rotterdam, 29.4.1987, 53,000
Netherlands: Heile; van Tiggelen, Rijkaard, R.Koeman, Silooy, Wouters, Gullit, A.Muhren, Vanenburg, van Basten, van t'Schip (van der Gijp 81). **Scorers:** Gullit 37, A.Muhren 40.
Hungary: Szendrei; Sallai (Vegh 40), Hires, Garaba, Preszeller, Hannicj, Kardos, Peter (Burcsa 70), Detari, Kiprich, K.Kovacs.

HUNGARY (1)5, POLAND (1)3
Budapest, 17.5.1987, 8000
Hungary: Gaspar; Vargas, Hires, Sallai, Peter (Preszeller 70), Rostas (Kekesi 46), Garaba, Detari, Fekeres, Kipric, Vincze. **Scorers:** Vincze 39, Detari 62 pen,76, Peter 66, Preszeller 83.
Poland: Wandzik; Pawlak, Wojcicki, Krol, Wdowczyk, Prusik, Tarasiewicz (Lesniak 46), Matysik, Urban (Przybys 60), Marziniak, Smolarek. **Scorers:** Marziniak 27, Smolarek 52, Wojkicki 81.

POLAND (1)3, HUNGARY (1)2
Warsaw, 23.9.1987, 10,000
Poland: Wandzik; Grembocki, Dankowski (Araskiewicz 46), Cisek (Jakolcewicz 66), Krol, Urban, Tarasiewicz, Prusik, Iwan, Dziekanowski, Lesniak. **Scorers:** Dziekanowski 6, Tarasiewicz 57, Lesniak 61.
Hungary: P.Disztl; Sallai, Toma, Peter, Ervin Kovacs, Garaba, Bognar (Fitos 79), Heredi, J.Meszaros, Detari, Szerekes (Handel 79). **Scorers:** Bognar 10, Meszaros 72.

HUNGARY (3)3, GREECE (0)0
Budapest, 14.10.1987, 8000
Hungary: P.Disztl; Sallai, Toma, Garaba, Peter, Heredi, Detari, Bognar, Hajszan (K.Kovacs 81), Kiprich, Meszaros. **Scorers:** Detari 4, Bognar 12, Meszaros 15.
Greece: Papadopulos; Xanthoupulos (Apostolakis 81), Bambakulas, Manolas, Michos, Bonovas, Saravakos, Antoniou (Mavridis 46), Anastopulos, Mitropulos, Kofidis.

POLAND (0)0, NETHERLANDS (2)2
Zabrze, 14.10.1987, 21,500
Poland: Szczech; Przybys, Krol, Prusik, Kostrzewa, Urban, Tarasiewicz, Iwan, Karas (Jakolcewicz 46), Dziekanowski, Araskiewicz (Robakiewicz 67).
Netherlands: Van Breukelen; van Tiggelen, Spelbos, Silooy, R.Koeman, van Aerle, Vanenburg, A.Muhren, Gullit, van Basten (Winter 78), van t'Schip. **Scorer:** Gullit 30,38.

NETHERLANDS (4)8, CYPRUS (0)0
Rotterdam, 28.10.1987, 55,000
Netherlands: Van Breukelen; van Tiggelen, Spelbos, R.Koeman, Silooy, van Aerle, Vanenburg, A.Muhren, Bosman, Gullit (Gilhaus 84), van t'Schip. **Scorers:** Bosman 1,38,52,60,67, Gullit 20, Spelbos 40, van t'Schip 46.
Cyprus: Charitou (K.Pantzarias 3); Pittas, Miamiliotis (Kleftis 72), Misos, Socratous, Yiangudakis, Savva, Christoforou, Savvides, L.Mavroudis, Christofi.

CYPRUS (0)0, POLAND (0)1
Limassol, 11.11.1987, 8000
Cyprus: Charitou; Pittas, Miamiliotis, Christoforou, Socratous, Yiangudakis, Savva, Nicolau (Tsingis 74), Savvides, L.Mavroudis, Xiourouppas (G.Mavroudis 60).
Poland: Wandzik; Prusik, Krol, Wdowczyk, Wenclewski, Rudy, Tarasiewicz, Urban (Wardzik 58), Araszkiewicz (K.Warzycha 50), Dziekanowski, Lesniak. **Scorer:** Lesniak 74.

HUNGARY (0)1, CYPRUS (0)0
Budapest, 2.12.1987, 2000
Hungary: P.Disztl; Sallai, Toma, E. Kovacs, Keller, Fitos, Detari (Vincze 80), Bognar, Meszaros (Hajszan 46), Kiprich, K. Kovacs. **Scorer:** Kiprich 89.
Cyprus: G.Pantzarias; Miamiliotis, Socratous, Misos, Pittas, Savva, Nicolau, Yiangudakis, L.Mavroudis (Christoforou 88), Xiouruppas (G.Mavroudis 70), Tsingis.

GREECE (0)0, NETHERLANDS (1)3
Rhodes, 16.12.1987, 7000
Greece: Michail; Georchamlis, Hatsiathansiou, Kalitzakis (Pachaturides 32), Mitsibonas, Vakalopulos, Ziogas, Kanaras, Pavlos, Papaioannou (Mavromatis 12), Samaras.
Netherlands: Van Breukelen; Lankhaar, van Tiggelen, R.Koeman, Troost (Gilhaus 46), van Aerle, Winter, Kruezen, Vanenburg, Bosman, van t'Schip.

FINAL TABLE	P	W	D	L	F	A	GD	Pts
NETHERLANDS	8	6	2	0	15	1	+14	14
Greece	8	4	1	3	12	13	− 1	9
Hungary	8	4	0	4	13	11	+ 2	8
Poland	8	3	2	3	9	11	− 2	8
Cyprus	8	0	1	7	3	16	−13	1

GROUP 6
(Czechoslovakia, Denmark, Finland, Wales)

FINLAND (1)1, WALES (0)1
Helsinki, 10.9.1986, 9840
Finland: Laukkanen; Pekkonen, Ukkonen, Ikalainen, Europaeus, Petaja, Tauriainen, Tornvall, Hjelm, Lipponen (Valvee 76), Rantanen. **Scorer:** Hjelm 11.
Wales: Thomas; Jackett, Ratcliffe, Charles, R.James, Nicholas, Blackmore (Lowndes 81), Aizlewood, Williams (Slatter 52), Rush, Saunders. **Scorer:** Slatter 68.

CZECHOSLOVAKIA (2)3, FINLAND (0)0
Brno, 15.10.1986, 26,000
Czechoslovakia: Miklosko; Levy, Straka, Fiala, Hasek, Kubik (Ondra 74), Janecka, Chovanec, Skuhravy (Griga 81), Kula, Knoflicek. **Scorers:** Janecka 38, Knoflicek 43, Kula 67.
Finland: Laukkanen; Pekkonen, Ikalainen, Rantanen, Petaja, Europaeus, Tornvall, Ukkonen, Tauriainen (Valvee 29), Lipponen, Hjelm (Ikainen 3).

DENMARK (0)1, FINLAND (0)0
Copenhagen, 29.10.1986, 40,300
Denmark: Rasmussen; Sivebaek, M.Olsen, I.Nielsen, Busk, Bertelsen, Molby, Lerby, Arnesen (H.Andersen 77), C.Nielsen (Thychosen 81), Eriksen. **Scorer:** Bertelsen 68.
Finland: Laukkanen; Pekkonen, Ikalainen, Europaeus, Petaja, Tiainen, Ukkonen, Tornvall (Tauriainen 70), Hjelm, Rantanen, Lipponen (Jalaskara 77).

CZECHOSLOVAKIA (0)0, DENMARK (0)0
Bratislava, 12.11.1986, 30,000
Czechoslovakia: Miklosko; Levy, Straka, Chovanec, Fiala, Kubic (Ondra 76), Hasek, Kula, Skuhravy (Griga 80), Knoflicek, Janecka.
Denmark: Rasmussen; Busk, M.Olsen, I.Nielsen, Lerby, Berggren, Bertelsen, Arnesen, Molby (Andersen 46), Elkjaer, Laudrup (J.Olsen 88).

WALES (2)4, FINLAND (0)0
Wrexham, 1.4.1987, 7696
Wales: Southall; Jackett, Blackmore, van den Hauwe (Aizlewood 11), Ratcliffe, Phillips, Nicholas, James, Hodges, Rush, A.Jones. **Scorers:** Rush 14, Hodges 28, Phillips 64, A.Jones 73.
Finland: Laukkanen; Pekonen, Ikalainen, Europaeus, Petaja, Turunen, Holmgren, Tauriainen, Rantanen, Tiainen, Hjelm.

FINLAND (0)0, DENMARK (0)1
Helsinki, 29.4.1987, 29,197
Finland: Laukkanen; Lahtinen, Europaeus, Ikalainen, Petaja, Pekonen, Ukkonen, Tiainen (Hjelm 66), Rantanen, Lipponen (Valvee 66), Lius.
Denmark: Rasmussen; M.Olsen, Busk, I.Nielsen, Heintze, Lerby (Lunde 42), Molby, Bertelsen, Arnesen, Berggren (Sivebaek 73), Eriksen. **Scorer:** Molby 53.

WALES (0)1, CZECHOSLOVAKIA (0)1
Wrexham, 29.4.1987, 14,150
Wales: Southall; Slatter, Ratcliffe, van den Hauwe, Blackmore, Phillips, James, Nicholas, Hodges, Rush, Hughes (A.Jones 78). **Scorer:** Rush 83.
Czechoslovakia: Miklosko; Hasek, Straka, Fiala, Novak, Kubik, Janecka (Luhovy 82), Chovanec, Skuhravy (Kadlec 80), Kula, Knoflicek. **Scorer:** Knoflicek 74.

DENMARK (1)1, CZECHOSLOVAKIA (0)1
Copenhagen, 3.6.1987, 46,600
Denmark: Rasmussen; M.Olsen, I.Nielsen, Busk, Sivebaek, Arnesen, Bertelsen, Lerby, Molby, Elkjaer (Eriksen 85), Poulsen (J.Olsen 67). **Scorer:** Molby 16.
Czechoslovakia: Miklosko; Hasek, Novak, Straka, Fiala, Kubik, Chovanec, Skuhravy (Jarolin 47), Kula (Bielik 82), Janecka, Knoflicek. **Scorer:** Hasek 48.

WALES (1)1, DENMARK (0)0
Cardiff, 9.9.1987, 20,535
Wales: Southall; Slatter, Blackmore, Ratcliffe, van den Hauwe, R.James (Horn 88), Phillips, Nicholas, A.Jones, Hughes, Hodges (Aizlewood 71). **Scorer:** Hughes 19.
Denmark: Rasmussen; Sivebaek, K.Nielsen, M.Olsen, I.Nielsen, Lerby, Berggren, Bertelsen, Poulsen (C.Nielsen 65), Elkjaer, Laudrup (Jensen 46).

FINLAND (1)3, CZECHOSLOVAKIA (0)0
Helsinki, 9.9.1987, 6430
Finland: Laukkanen; Lahtinen, Europaeus, Ikalainen, Petaja, Tianen, Rautiainen (Kanerva 63), Hjelm, Lius, Rantanen, Holmgren. **Scorers:** Hjelm 29, Lius 72, Tiainen 82.
Czechoslovakia: Miklosko; Straka, Chovanec, J.Nobak, Fiala, Kula (Chalouopka 72), K.Jarolim, Kubik (Hasek 63), Janecka, Skuhravy, Knoflicek.

DENMARK (0)1, WALES (0)0
Copenhagen, 14.10.1987, 44,500
Denmark: Rasmussen; M.Olsen, I.Nielsen, Sivebaek, Heintze (Poulsen 46), J.Jensen, Lerby, Frimann, J.Olsen, Elkjaer, Laudrup (L.Olsen 85). **Scorer:** Elkjaer 49.
Wales: Niedzwiecki; Slatter, Ratcliffe, van den Hauwe, Blackmore, R.James (A.Jones 72), Nicholas, Phillips, Jackett (Hodges 64), Rush, Hughes.

CZECHOSLOVAKIA (1)2, WALES (0)0
Prague, 11.11.1987, 70,000
Czechoslovakia: Miklosko; J.Novak, Kadlec, Straka, Levy, Hasek, Chovanec, Moravcik (Kula 71), Bilek, Skuhravy, Knofliczek. **Scorers:** Knoflicek 32, Bilek 89.
Wales: Southall; Slatter (A.Jones 46), Ratcliffe, van den Hauwe, Jackett, G.Williams, Blackmore (Hodges 66), Nicholas, Phillips, Rush, Hughes.

FINAL TABLE	P	W	D	L	F	A	GD	Pts
DENMARK	6	3	2	1	4	2	+2	8
Czechoslovakia	6	2	3	1	7	5	+2	7
Wales	6	2	2	2	7	5	+2	6
Finland	6	1	1	4	4	10	−6	3

GROUP 7
(Belgium, Bulgaria, Republic of Ireland, Luxembourg, Scotland)

SCOTLAND (0)0, BULGARIA (0)0
Hampden Park, 10.9.1986, 35,070
Scotland: Leighton; Gough, Malpas, P.McStay, Narey, Miller, Cooper, Aitken, Johnston, Strachan, Nicholas (Dalglish 53).
Bulgaria: Mikhailov; Nikolov, G.Dimitrov, P.Petrov, Iliev, Simeonov (Karashev 80), Kolev, Sadkov, Alexandrov (Tanev 89), Sirakov, Voinov.

BELGIUM (1)2, REP.OF IRELAND (1)2
Brussels, 10.9.1986, 22,212
Belgium: Pfaff; Grun, F. van der Elst, Clysters, Vervoort, Vercauteren, de Mol, Scifo, Claesen, Desmet, Ceulemans. **Scorers:** Claesen 14, Scifo 71.
Rep.of Ireland: Bonner; Langan, Hughton (Beglin 82), Lawrenson, Moran, Brady, Houghton, McGrath, Stapleton, Aldridge, Galvin (Whelan 80). **Scorers:** Stapleton 18, Brady 89 pen.

LUXEMBOURG (0)0, BELGIUM (3)6
Luxembourg, 14.10.1986, 15,000
Luxembourg: Van Rijswijck; Meunier, Bossi, Barboni, Schonkert, Girres, Weis, Saibene (Thome 73), Malget, Reiter (Scholten 58), Langers.
Belgium: Munaron; Gerets, Vervoort, de Mol (Grun 50), Clysters, Vercauteren, Scifo (L. van der Elst 55), Ceulemans, Vandenbergh, Claesen, Desmet. **Scorers:** Gerets 6, Claesen 9,55,88 pen, Vercauteren 41, Ceulemans 87.

REP.OF IRELAND (0)0, SCOTLAND (0)0
Dublin, 15.10.1986, 48,000
Rep.of Ireland: Bonner; Langan, Beglin, McCarthy, Moran (Daly 71), Brady, McGrath, Houghton, Stapleton, Aldridge, Sheedy.
Scotland: Leighton; Stewart, Narey, P.McStay, Gough, Hansen, Strachan, Sharp, Johnston, Aitken, MacLeod.

SCOTLAND (2)3, LUXEMBOURG (0)0
Hampden Park, 12.11.1986, 35,078
Scotland: Leighton; Stewart, MacLeod (McCoist 64), Aitken, Gough, Hansen (P. McStay 46), Nevin, McClair, Johnston, Dalglish, Cooper. **Scorers:** Cooper 24 pen, 38, Johnston 70.
Luxembourg: Van Rijswijck; Bossi, di Pentima, Meunier, Schonkert, Hellers, Barboni, Weiss, Scholten, Langers, Malget.

BELGIUM (0)1, BULGARIA (0)1
Brussels, 19.11.1986, 33,000
Belgium: Pfaff; Gerets, Clijsters (Renquin 46), Janssen, Vervoort, Vercauteren, de Mol, Claesen, Desmet (Grun 61), Scifo, Ceulemans. **Scorer:** Janssen 47.
Bulgaria: Mikhailov; Nikolov, Petkov, Iliev, Simeonov, Kolev, Sadkov, Alexandrov (Tanev 62), Sirakov, Iskrenov (Voinov 87). **Scorer:** Tanev 63.

SCOTLAND (0)0, REP. OF IRELAND (1)1
Hampden Park, 18.2.1987, 45,081
Scotland: Leighton; Stewart, Malpas, McCoist (Aitken 67), Gough, Hansen, Nevin, McClair, Johnston, Strachan, Cooper (McStay 46).
Rep. of Ireland: Bonner; McGrath, Whelan, McCarthy, Moran, Brady (Byrne 60), Lawrenson, Houghton, Stapleton, Aldridge, Galvin. **Scorer:** Lawrenson 8.

BELGIUM (1)4, SCOTLAND (1)1
Brussels, 1.4.1987, 26,650
Belgium: Pfaff; Grun, F. van der Elst, Vandermissen 89), Clijsters, Vervoort, Vercauteren, De Mol, Claesen, Vandenberg, Scifo (L.van der Elst 73), Desmet. **Scorers:** Claesen 8,55,85, Vercauteren 62.
Scotland: Leighton; Gough, Malpas, P. McStay, McLeish, Narey, Aitken, McInally, Bett (Nevin 80), McCoist, Sturrock. **Scorer:** McCoist 13.

BULGARIA (1)2, REP. OF IRELAND (0)1
Sofia, 1.4.1987, 38,000
Bulgaria: Mikhailov; Nikolov, Iliev, Bezinski, G.Dimitrov, Simeonov, (Voinov 63), Kolev, Sadkov, Tanev, Sirakov, Iskrenov (Alexandrov 60). **Scorers:** Sadkov 41, Tanev 82 pen.
Rep. of Ireland: Bonner; Anderson, Houghton, Moran, McCarthy, Whelan, McGrath, O'Brien, Galvin, Aldridge, Stapleton (Quinn 85). **Scorer:** Stapleton 52.

REP. OF IRELAND (0)0, BELGIUM (0)0
Dublin, 29.4.1987, 49,000
Rep. of Ireland: Bonner; Anderson, Whelan, McCarthy, Moran, Brady (Byrne 78), McGrath, Houghton, Stapleton, Aldridge, Galvin.
Belgium: Pfaff; Gerets, Grun, Clijsters, Vervoort, Vercauteren, Albert (Janssen 67), Claesen, Desmet, Scifo, Ceulemans.

LUXEMBOURG (0)1, BULGARIA (0)4
Luxembourg, 30.4.1987, 1500
Luxembourg: Van Rijswijck; Schonkert, Bossi, Weicas, Dresch (Jeitz 71), Girres (Juchem 87), Hellers, Barboni, Langers, Malget, Reiter. **Scorer:** Langers 59.

Bulgaria: Mikhailov; Nikolov, Iliev, Petrov, G. Dimitrov, Simeonov (Alexandrov 46), Kolev, Sadkov, Tanev, Sirakov, Iskrenov (Iordanov 60). **Scorers:** Sadkov 49, Sirakov 55, Tanev 62, Kolev 82.

BULGARIA (2)3, LUXEMBOURG (0)0
Sofia, 20.5.1987, 20,000
Bulgaria: Mikhailov; Nikolov, Iliev, Petrov, G.Dimitrov, Iordanov, Kolev, Sadkov (Voinov 12), Tanev, Sirakov, Penev. **Scorers:** Sirakov 35, Iordanov 41 pen, Kolev 57.
Luxembourg: Van Rijswijck; Schonkert, Meunier, Weis, Bossi, Girres, Hellers, Barboni, Langers, Malget, Reiter (Thome 80).

LUXEMBOURG (0)0, REP. OF IRELAND (1)2
Luxembourg, 28.5.1987, 4290
Luxembourg: Van Rijswijck; Meunier, Bossi, Weis, Schonkert, Girres (Dresch 87), Hellers, Barboni, Malget, Langers, Reiter (Jeitz 69).
Rep. of Ireland: Bonner; Anderson (Langan 62), McCarthy, Moran (J.Byrne 46), Whelan, Houghton, McGrath, Brady, Aldridge, Stapleton, Galvin. **Scorers:** Galvin 43, Whelan 64.

REP. OF IRELAND (1)2, LUXEMBOURG (1)1
Dublin, 9.9.1987, 18,000
Rep. of Ireland: Peyton; Langan, McGrath, Moran, Grimes, Houghton, Whelan, Brady, Galvin (Quinn 56), Stapleton, Byrne. **Scorers:** Stapleton 31, McGrath 74.
Luxembourg: Van Rijswijck; Schonkert, Meunier, Weiss, Bossi, Malget, Hellers, Barboni (Jeitz 83), Scholten, Langers, Krings. **Scorer:** Krings 28.

BULGARIA (1)2, BELGIUM (0)0
Sofia, 23.9.1987, 60,000
Bulgaria: Mikhailov; Nikolov, Ilievd, P. Petrov, G. Dimitrov, Simeonov, Stoichkov (Iordanov 68), Sadkov, Tanev, Sirakov, Iskrenov (Voinov 80). **Scorers:** Sirakov 19, Tanev 70.
Belgium: Pfaff; Gerets, Clijsters, Grun, Renquin, Vervoort, F. van der Elst (Veyt 61), Claesen, Degrijse, Scifo, Desmet (Vandersmissen 72).

SCOTLAND (1)2, BELGIUM (0)0
Hampden Park, 14.10.1987, 20,052
Scotland: Leighton; Clarke, Malpas (Whyte 53), P. McStay, McLeish, Gillespie, Johnston (Sharp 72), Aitken, McCoist, Durrant, Wilson. **Scorers:** McCoist 14, McStay 79.
Belgium: Preud'homme; Gerets, Grun, Clijsters, Vervoort, Vercauteren, F. van der Elst, Beyens (Desmet 55), Claesen, Degrijse, Ceulemans.

REP. OF IRELAND (0)2, BULGARIA (0)0
Dublin, 14.10.1987, 26,000
Rep. of Ireland: Bonner; McGrath, Whelan, Moran, McCarthy, Brady, Lawrenson, Houghton, Stapleton, Aldridge (J. Byrne 77), Galvin (Quinn 77). **Scorers:** McGrath 52, Moran 85.
Bulgaria: Ananiev (Velev 55); Nikolov, Iliev, Petrov, G.Dimitrov, Simeonov, Voinov (Alexandrov 65), Sadkov, Stoichkov, Sirakov, Iskrenov.

BELGIUM (1)3, LUXEMBOURG (0)0
Brussels, 11.11.1987, 15,000
Belgium: Preud'homme; Grun, Clijsters, Plovie (Dekenne 46), Mommens, Beyens (Creve 71), van der Linden, Ceulemaigns, de Mesmaeker, Degrijse, Claesen. **Scorers:** Ceulemans 17, Degrijse 55, Creve 81.
Luxembourg: Van Rijswijck; Schonkert (Meunier 65), Bossi, Weiss, Petry, Jeitz, Hellers, Barboni, Scholten (Girres 46), Langers, Reiter.

BULGARIA (0)0, SCOTLAND (0)1
Sofia, 11.11.1987, 60,000
Bulgaria: Mikhailov; Nikolov, Bezinski, Petrov, Iliev, Simeonov (Penev 88), Stoichkov, Sdakov, Alexandrov (Voinov 42), Sirakov, Iskrenov.
Scotland: Leighton; Clarke, Malpas, Aitken, McLeish, Gillespie, Nicol, P.McStay (Mackay 57), Sharp (Durie 71), McClair, Wilson. **Scorer:** Mackay 87.

LUXEMBOURG (0)0, SCOTLAND (0)0
Esch-sur-Alzette, 2.12.1987, 1999
Luxembourg: Van Rijswijck; Meunier, Bossi, Weiss, Petry, Girres, Jeitz, Barboni, Scholten, Langers, Reiter.
Scotland: Leighton; Malpas, Whyte (Mackay 60), Aitken, McLeish, W. Miller, Nevin (Black 60), P.McStay, Johnston, Sharp, Wilson.

FINAL TABLE	P	W	D	L	F	A	GD	Pts
REP. OF IRELAND	8	4	3	1	10	5	+ 5	11
Bulgaria	8	4	2	2	12	16	+ 6	10
Belgium	8	3	3	2	16	8	+ 8	9
Scotland	8	3	3	2	7	5	+ 2	9
Luxembourg	8	0	1	7	2	23	−21	1

Manager Bobby Robson and assistant physio Norman Medhurst *(left)* look bemused by it all, but physio Fred Street is in no doubt – England have slammed four past Yugoslavia and wrapped up their European Championship qualifying programme with a flourish. *Photo: Bob Thomas Sports Photography.*

EUROPEAN CHAMPIONSHIP PAST FINALS

(Formerly the European Nations' Cup)

1960: USSR (0)2, YUGOSLAVIA (1)1 (aet, Paris, 10.7.60, 17,966)
USSR: Yachin; Tchekeli, Kroutikov, Voinov, Maslenkin, Netto, Metreveli, Ivanov, Ponedelnik, Bubukin, Meshki. **Scorers:** Metreveli, Ponedelnik.
Yugoslavia: Vidinic; Durkovic, Jusufi, Zanetic, Miladinovic, Perusic, Sekularac, Jerkovic, Galic, Matus, Kostic. **Scorer:** Netto og.

1964: SPAIN (1)2, USSR (1)1 (Madrid, 21.6.64, 120,000)
Spain: Iribar; Rivilla, Calleja, Fuste, Olivella, Zoco, Amancio, Pereda, Marcellino, Suarez, Lapetra. **Scorers:** Pereda, Marcellino.
USSR: Yachin; Chustikov, Mudrik, Voronin, Shesternjev, Anitchkin, Chislenko, Ivanov, Ponedelnik, Kornaev, Khusainov. **Scorer:** Khusainov.

1968: ITALY (0)1, YUGOSLAVIA (1)1 (aet, Rome, 8.6.68, 75,000)
Italy: Zoff; Burgnich, Facchetti, Ferrini, Guarneri, Castano, Domenghini, Juliano, Anastasi, Lodetti, Prati. **Scorer:** Domenghini.
Yugoslavia: Pantelic; Fazlagic, Damjanovic, Pavlovic, Paunovic, Holcer, Petkovic, Acimovic, Musemic, Trivic, Dzajic. **Scorer:** Dzajic.

REPLAY: ITALY (2)2, YUGOSLAVIA (0)0 (Rome, 10.6.68, 60,000)
Italy: Zoff; Burgnich, Facchetti, Rosato, Guarneri, Salvadore, Domenghini, Mazzola, Anastasi, De Sisti, Riva. **Scorers:** Riva, Anastasi.
Yugoslavia: Hosic for Petkovic.

1972: WEST GERMANY (1)3, USSR (0)0 (Brussels, 18.6.72, 43,437)
West Germany: Maier; Hottges, Schwarzenbeck, Beckenbauer, Breitner, Hoeness, Wimmer, Netzer, Heynkes, Muller, Kremers. **Scorers:** Muller 2, Wimmer.
USSR: Rudakov; Dzodzuashvili, Khurtislava, Kaplichny, Istomin, Troshkin, Kolotov, Baidachni, Konkov (Dolmatov), Banishevski (Kozinkievits), Onishenko.

1976: CZECHOSLOVAKIA (2)2, WEST GERMANY (1)2 (aet, Belgrade, 20.6.76, 45,000)
Czechoslovakia: Viktor; Dobias (F.Vesely), Pivarnik, Ondrus, Capkovic, Gogh, Moder, Panenka, Svehlic (Jurkemic), Masny, Nehoda. **Scorers:** Svehlic, Dobias.
West Germany: Maier; Vogts, Beckenbauer, Schwarzenbeck, Dietz, Bonhof, Wimmer (Flohe), D.Muller, Beer (Bongartz), Hoeness, Holzenbein. **Scorers:** Muller, Holzenbein.
Czechoslovakia won 5–3 on penalties.

1980: WEST GERMANY (1)2, BELGIUM (0)1 (Rome, 22.6.80, 47,864)
West Germany: Schumacher; Briegel, K–H.Forster, Dietz, Schuster, Rummenigge, Hrubesch, Muller, Aloffs, Stielike, Kaltz. **Scorer:** Hrubesch 2.
Belgium: Pfaff; Gerets, Millecamps, Meeuws, Renquin, Cools, Van der Eycken, Van Moer, Mommens, Van der Elst, Ceulemans. **Scorer:** Van der Eycken.

1984: FRANCE (0)2, SPAIN (0)0 (Paris, 27.6.84, 80,000)
France: Bats; Battiston (Amoros), Le Roux, Bossis, Domergue, Giresse, Platini, Tigana, Fernandez, Lacombe (Genghini), Bellone. **Scorers:** Platini, Bellone.
Spain: Arconada; Urquiaga, Salva (Roberto), Gallego, Camacho, Francisco, Julio Alberto (Sarabia), Senor, Victor, Carrasco, Santillana.

FIFA WORLD CUP 1990 – QUALIFYING COMPETITION

Not all fixture dates were available at the time of going to Press.

EUROPE (UEFA)

34 members, 33 entries. Italy qualify automatically as hosts for the finals. The top two teams in five-team groups qualify, together with the top team from four-team groups, and the best two runners-up from the four-team groups. Best runners-up are decided as follows: a) number of points, b) goal difference, c) number of goals scored, d) play-off on a neutral ground.

GROUP 1 (Denmark, Bulgaria, Rumania, Greece)
19.10.88 Greece v Denmark, Bulgaria v Rumania. 2.11.88 Rumania v Greece, Denmark v Bulgaria. 26.4.89 Greece v Rumania, Bulgaria v Denmark. 17.5.89 Rumania v Bulgaria, Denmark v Greece. 11.10.89 Bulgaria v Greece, Denmark v Rumania. 15.11.89 Greece v Bulgaria, Rumania v Denmark.

GROUP 2 (England, Poland, Sweden, Albania)
19.10.88 England v Sweden, Poland v Albania. 5.11.88 Albania v Sweden. 8.3.89 Albania v England. 26.4.89 England v Albania. 7.5.89 Sweden v Poland. 3.6.89 England v Poland. 6.9.89 Sweden v England. 8.10.89 Sweden v Albania. 11.10.89 Poland v England. 25.10.89 Poland v Sweden. 15.11.89 Albania v Poland.

GROUP 3 (USSR, East Germany, Austria, Iceland, Turkey)
31.8.88 Iceland v USSR. 12.10.88 Turkey v Iceland. 19.10.88 USSR v Austria, East Germany v Iceland. 2.11.88 Austria v Turkey. 30.11.88 Turkey v East Germany. 12.4.89 East Germany v Turkey. 26.4.89 USSR v East Germany. 10.5.89 Turkey v USSR. 17.5.89 East Germany v Austria. 31.5.89 USSR v Iceland. 14.6.89 Iceland v Austria. 23.8.89 Austria v Iceland. 6.9.89 Austria v USSR, Iceland v East Germany. 20.9.89 Iceland v Turkey. 7/8.10.89 East Germany v USSR. 25.10.89 Turkey v Austria. 8.11.89 USSR v Turkey. 15.11.89 Austria v East Germany.

GROUP 4 (West Germany, Netherlands, Wales, Finland)
31.8.88 Finland v West Germany. 14.9.88 Netherlands v Wales. 19.10.88 Wales v Finland, West Germany v Netherlands. 26.4.89 Netherlands v West Germany. 31.5.89 Wales v West Germany, Finland v Netherlands. 6.9.89 Finland v Wales. 4.10.89 West Germany v Finland. 11.10.89 Wales v Netherlands. 15.11.89 West Germany v Wales, Netherlands v Finland.

GROUP 5 (France, Scotland, Yugoslavia, Norway, Cyprus)
14.9.88 Norway v Scotland. 28.9.88 France v Norway. 19.10.88 Scotland v Yugoslavia. 22.10.88 Cyprus v France. 2.11.88 Cyprus v Norway. 19.11.88 Yugoslavia v France. 11.12.88 Yugoslavia v Cyprus. 8.2.89 Cyprus v Scotland. 8.3.89 Scotland v France. 25.4.89 Scotland v Cyprus. 29.4.89 France v Yugoslavia. 16.5.89 Norway v Cyprus. 14.6.89 Norway v Yugoslavia. 5.9.89 Norway v France. 6.9.89 Yugoslavia v Scotland. 11.10.89 Yugoslavia v Norway, France v Scotland. 28.10.89 Cyprus v Yugoslavia. 15.11.89 Scotland v Norway. 18.11.89 France v Cyprus.

GROUP 6 (Spain, Hungary, Northern Ireland, Republic of Ireland, Malta)

NORTHERN IRELAND (3)3, MALTA (0)0
Belfast, 21 May 1988, 9,000
N. Ireland: McKnight; Donaghy, Worthington, McClelland, McDonald, O'Neill, Penney (McNally 81), D. Wilson, Clarke, Quinn, Dennison (Black 65). **Scorers:** Quinn 14, Penney 25, Clarke 26.
Malta: Cluett; Camilleri (Micallef 45), Azzopardi, Galea, Brincat, Buttigieg, Busuttil, Scerri, Carabott, Scicluna, Digiorgio (Caruana 60).
Remaining fixtures: 14.9.88 Northern Ireland v Rep.of Ireland, 19.10.88 Hungary v Northern Ireland, 16.11.88 Spain v Rep.of Ireland. 11.12.88 Malta v Hungary. 21.12.88 Spain v Northern Ireland. 22.1.89 Malta v Spain. 8.2.89 Northern Ireland v Spain. 8.3.89 Hungary v Rep.of Ireland. 22.3.89 Spain v Malta. 12.4.89 Hungary v Malta. 26.4.89 Malta v Northern Ireland, Rep.of Ireland v Spain. 28.5.89 Rep.of Ireland v Malta. 4.6.89 Rep.of Ireland v Hungary. 6.9.89 Northern Ireland v Hungary. 11.10.89 Hungary v Spain, Rep.of Ireland v Northern Ireland. 15.11.89 Spain v Hungary, Malta v Rep.of Ireland.

GROUP 7 (Belgium, Portugal, Czechoslovakia, Switzerland, Luxembourg)
21.9.88 Luxembourg v Switzerland. 19.10.88 Belgium v Switzerland, Luxembourg v Czechoslovakia. 16.11.88 Czechoslovakia v Belgium, Portugal v Luxembourg. 15.2.89 Portugal v Belgium. 26.4.89 Portugal v Switzerland. 29.4.89 Belgium v Czechoslovakia. 10.5.89 Czechoslovakia v Luxembourg. 31.5/1.6.89 Luxembourg v Belgium. 7.6.89 Switzerland v Czechoslovakia. 6.9.89 Belgium v Portugal. 20.9.89 Switzerland v Portugal. 6.10.89 Czechoslovakia v Portugal. 11.10.89 Luxembourg v Portugal, Switzerland v Belgium. 25.10.89 Czechoslovakia v Switzerland, Belgium v Luxembourg. 15.11.89 Portugal v Czechoslovakia, Switzerland v Luxembourg.

SOUTH AMERICA (CONMEBOL)

10 members, 10 entries. Argentina qualify automatically as Champions, plus the winners of Groups 1 and 3. The winners of Group 2 play off against the winners of the Oceania/Israel group for a place in the finals.

GROUP 1 – Uruguay, Peru, Bolivia.
GROUP 2 – Paraguay, Colombia, Ecuador.
GROUP 3 – Brazil, Chile, Venezuela.

WORLD CUP

OCEANIA/ISRAEL

6 + 1 members, 4 + 1 entries. The winners of the second round play off against the winners of South American Group 2 for a place in the finals.

FIRST ROUND (knock-out system).
GROUP 1: 11.12.88 Chinese Taipei v New Zealand. 18.12.88 New Zealand v Chinese Taipei.
GROUP 2: 26.11.88 Fiji v Australia. 3.12.88 Australia v Fiji.
SECOND ROUND (league system) Israel, winners Group 1, winners Group 2.

ASIA

35 members, 25 entries. Two teams qualify from the Second Round.

FIRST ROUND (league system)
WEST ASIA
GROUP 1 – Iraq, Qatar, Jordan, Oman.
GROUP 2 – Saudi Arabia, Syria, Bahrain, Yemen Arab Republic.
GROUP 3 – Kuwait, United Arab Emirates, Pakistan, Yemen PDR.
EAST ASIA
GROUP 4 – Korea Republic, Singapore, Malaysia, India.
GROUP 5 – China PR, Iran, Thailand, Bangladesh, Nepal.
GROUP 6 – Korea DPR, Japan, Indonesia, Hong Kong.
SECOND ROUND (league system)
To be played between the winners of the six groups.

NORTH AND CENTRAL AMERICA AND THE CARIBBEAN (CONCACAF)

24 members, 15 entries. Two teams qualify from the Third Round

FIRST ROUND
17.4.88 Guyana v Trinidad/Tobago. 30.4.88 Cuba v Guatemala. 8.5.88 Trinidad/Tobago v Guyana. 12.5.88 Jamaica v Puerto Rico. 15.5.88 G uatemala v Cuba. 29.5.88 Puerto Rico v Jamaica. 17.7.88 Antigua v Netherlands Antilles, Costa Rica v Panama. 29.7.88 Netherlands Antilles v Antigua. 31.7.88 Panama v Costa Rica.

SECOND ROUND
The five winners of the First Round home and away fixtures are joined by El Salvador, USA, Honduras, Mexico and Canada.

THIRD ROUND
The five Second Round winners play in a League system.

AFRICA

47 members, 24 entries. Two teams qualify from the Third Round

FIRST ROUND (cup system)
1 – 7.8.88 Angola v Sudan, 19.8.88 Sudan v Angola.
2 – 12.6.88 Lesotho v Zimbabwe, 26.6.88 Zimbabwe v Lesotho.
3 – Rwanda v Zambia. Rwanda withdrew. Zambia through to Second Round.
4 – 16.7.88 Uganda v Malawi, 30.7.88 Malawi v Uganda.
5 – 3.6.88 Libya v Burkina Faso, 3.7.88 Burkina Faso v Libya.
6 – 7.8.88 Ghana v Liberia, 21.8.88 Liberia v Ghana.
7 – 5.8.88 Tunisia v Guinea, 21.8.88 Guinea v Tunisia.
8 – 7.8.88 Togo v Gabon, 21.8.88 Gabon v Togo.
SECOND ROUND (league system)
GROUP A Algeria, Ivory Coast, winner 5, winner 2.
GROUP B Egypt, Kenya, winner 4, winner 6.
GROUP C Cameroon, Nigeria, winner 8, winner 1.
GROUP D Morocco, Zaire, winner 7, Zambia.
THIRD ROUND
Winner Group A v Winner Group B
Winner Group C v Winner Group D

WORLD CUP FINALS 1930–1986

1930: URUGUAY (1)4, ARGENTINA (2)2 (Montevideo, 30.7.30, 90,000)
Uruguay: Ballesteros; Nasazzi, Mascheroni, Andrade, Fernadnez, Gestido, Dorado, Scarone, Castro, Cea, Iriarte. **Scorers:** Dorado, Cea, Iriarte, Castro.
Argentina: Botasso; Della Torre, Paternoster, J. Evaristo, Monti, Suarez, Peucelle, Varallo, Stabile, Ferreira, M. Evaristo. **Scorers:** Peucelle, Stabile.

1934: ITALY (0)2, CZECHOSLOVAKIA (0)1 (aet, 90 mins 1–1, Rome, 10.6.34, 50,000)
Italy: Combi; Monzeglio, Allemandi, Ferraris IV, Monti, Bertolini, Guaita, Meazza, Schiavio, Ferrari, Orsi. **Scorers:** Orsi, Schiavio.
Czechoslovakia: Planicka; Zenisek, Ctyroky, Kostalek, Cambal, Krcil, Junek, Svoboda, Sobotka, Nejedly, Puc. **Scorer:** Puc.

1938: ITALY (3)4, HUNGARY (1)2 (Paris, 19.6.38, 45,000)
Italy: Olivieri; Foni, Rava, Serantoni, Andreolo, Locatelli, Biavati, Meazza, Piola, Ferrari, Colaussi. **Scorers:** Cloaussi 2, Piola 2.
Hungary: Szabo; Polgar, Biro, Szalay, Szucs, Lazar, Sas, Vincze, Sarosi, Szengeller, Titkos. **Scorers:** Titkos, Sarosi.

1950: URUGUAY (0)2, BRAZIL (0)1 (Rio de Janeiro, 16.7.50, 199,850*)
Uruguay: Maspoli; Gonzales, Tejera, Gambetta, Varela, Andrade, Ghiggia, Perez, Miguez, Schiaffino, Moran. **Scorers:** Schiaffino, Ghiggia.
Brazil: Barbosa; Augusto, Juvenal, Bauer, Danilo, Bigode, Friaca, Zizinho, Ademir, Jair, Chico. **Scorer:** Friaca.
*The 1950 World Cup was decided on a league basis, although the match between Uruguay and Brazil was effectively the decider and is normally referred to as the final.

1954: WEST GERMANY (2)3, HUNGARY (2)2 (Berne, 4.7.54, 60,000)
West Germany: Turek; Posipal, Kohlmeyer, Eckel, Liebrich, Mai, Rahn, Morlock, O. Walter, F. Walter, Schaefer. **Scorers:** Morlock, Rahn 2.
Hungary: Grosics; Buzansky, Lantos, Bozsik, Lorant, Zakarias, Czibor, Kocsis, Hidegkuti, Puskas, J. Toth. **Scorers:** Puskas, Czibor.

1958: BRAZIL (2)5, SWEDEN (1)2 (Stockholm, 29.6.58, 49,737)
Brazil: Gilmar; D. Santos, N. Santos, Zito, Bellini, Orlando, Garrincha, Didi, Vava, Pele, Zagalo. **Scorers:** Vava 2, Pele 2, Zagalo.
Sweden: Svensson; Bergmark, Axbom, Boerjesson, Gustavsson, Parliag, Hamrin, Gren, Simonsson, Liedholm, Skoglund. **Scorers:** Liedholm, Simonsson.

1962: BRAZIL (1)3, CZECHOSLOVAKIA (1)1 (Santiago, 17.6.62, 68,679)
Brazil: Gilmar; D. Santos, Mauro, Zozimo, N. Santos, Zito, Didi, Garrincha, Vava, Amarildo, Zagalo. **Scorers:** Amarildo, Zito, Vava.
Czechoslovakia: Schroiff; Tichy, Novak, Pluskal, Popluhar, Masopust, Pospichal, Scherer, Kvasniak, Kadraba, Jelinek. **Scorer:** Masopust.

1966: ENGLAND (1)4, WEST GERMANY (1)2 (aet, 90 mins 2–2, Wembley, 30.7.66, 93,802)
England: Banks; Cohen, Wilson, Stiles, J. Charlton, Moore, Ball, Hurst, Hunt, R. Charlton, Peters. **Scorers:** Hurst 3, Peters.
West Germany: Tilkowski; Hottges, Schulz, Weber, Schnellinger, Haller, Beckenbauer, Overath, Seeler, Held, Emmerich. **Scorers:** Haller, Weber.

1970: BRAZIL (1)4, ITALY (1)1 (Mexico City, 21.6.70, 107,412)
Brazil: Felix; Carlos Alberto, Brito, Piazza, Everaldo, Gerson, Clodoaldo, Jairzinho, Pele, Tostao, Rivelino. **Scorers:** Pele, Gerson, Jairzinho, Carlos Alberto.
Italy: Albertosi; Burgnich, Cera, Rosato, Facchetti, Bertini (Juliano), Riva, Domenghini, Mazzola, De Sisti, Boninsegna (Rivera). **Scorer:** Boninsegna.

1974: WEST GERMANY (2)2, NETHERLANDS (1)1 (Munich, 7.7.74, 77,833)
West Germany: Maier; Vogts, Schwarzenbeck, Beckenbauer, Breitner, Bonhof, Hoeness, Overath, Grabowski, Muller, Holzenbein. **Scorers:** Breitner pen, Muller.
Netherlands: Jongbloed; Suurbier, Rijsbergen (De Jong), Haan, Krol, Jansen, Van Hanegem, Neeskens, Rep, Cruyff, Rensenbrink (R. Van der Kerkhof). **Scorer:** Neeskens pen.

1978: ARGENTINA (1)3, NETHERLANDS (0)1 (aet, 90 mins 1–1, Buenos Aires, 25.6.78, 77,000)
Argentina: Fillol; Passarella, Olquin, L.Galvan, Tarantini, Ardiles (Larrosa), Gallego, Ortiz (Houseman), Bertoni, Luque, Kempes. **Scorers:** Kempes 2, Bertoni.
Netherlands: Jongbloed; Krol, Poortvliet, Brandts, Jansen (Suurbier), Haan, Neeskens, W. Van der Kerkhof, Rep (Nanninga), R. Van der Kerkhof, Rensenbrink. **Scorer:** Nanninga.

1982: ITALY (0)3, WEST GERMANY (0)1 (Madrid, 11.7.82, 90,089)
Italy: Zoff; Bergomi, Cabrini, Collovati, Scirea, Gentile, Oriali, Tardelli, Conti, Graziani (Altobelli) (Causio), Rossi.
Scorers: Rossi, Tardelli, Altobelli.
West Germany: Schumacher; Kaltz, K-H.Forster, Stielike, B. Forster, Breitner, Dremmler (Hrubesch), Littbarski, Brigel, Rummenigger (Muller), Fischer. **Scorer:** Breitner.

1986: ARGENTINA (1)3, WEST GERMANY (0)2 (Mexico City, 29.6.86, 114,580)
Argentina: Pumpido; Cuciuffo, Olarticoechea, Ruggeri, Brown, Giusti, Burruchaga (Trobbiani), Batista, Valdano, Maradona, Enrique. **Scorers:** Brown, Valdano, Burruchaga.
West Germany: Schumacher; Berthold, Briegel, Jakobs, K-H.Forster, Eder, Brehme, Matthaus, Allofs (Voller), Magath (Hoeness), Rummenigge. **Scorers:** Rummenigge, Voller.

England captain Bryan Robson shows off the Rous Cup after the draw with Colombia at Wembley, but will he have his hands on the World Cup in 1990?
Photo: Bob Thomas Sports Photography

OTHER BRITISH & IRISH INTERNATIONAL MATCHES 1987–88

SCOTLAND (1)2, HUNGARY (0)0
Hampden Park, 9.9.1987, 21,128
Scotland: Leighton; Clarke, Gough, Miller, Nicol, Strachan, McStay (Bett 77), Aitken, Durrant, Johnston (Black 71), McCoist. **Scorer:** McCoist, 34,62.
Hungary: P. Disztl; Csuhay, Toma, Peter, Sallai, Garaba, Gy Bognar, Keller, Meszaros, K. Kovacs (Lovasz 87), Hajszan.

WEST GERMANY (2)3, ENGLAND (1)1
Dusseldorf, 9.9.1987, 45,000
West Germany: Immel; Kohler, Herget, Buchwald, Brehme (Reuter 61), Littbarski, Thon, Dorfner, Frontzeck, Voller (Wuttke 78), K. Allofs. **Scorers:** Littbarski 24, 33, Wuttke 84.
England: Shilton; Anderson, Adams, Mabbutt, Sansom (Pearce 77), Waddle (Hateley 51), Hoddle (Webb 65), Reid, Barnes, Beardsley, Lineker. **Scorer:** Lineker 42.

REP.OF IRELAND (2)5, ISRAEL (0)0
Dublin, 10.11.1987, 9,500
Rep. of Ireland: O'Hanlon; C. Morris, Hughton, Moran, McCarthy, J. Byrne, Lawrenson, Houghton (L. O'Brien 74), N. Quinn, D. Kelly, Sheedy. **Scorers:** Byrne 13, Kelly 41, 56, 70 pen, Quinn 83.
Israel: Ginsburg; Avraham Cohen, E. Cohen, Klinger, Davidi, Shimonov, Amar, Malmilian, Ovadia (Eizenberg 46), Brialovsky, Tikva (Ovadi 46).

GREECE (0)3, NORTHERN IRELAND (1)2
Athens, 17.2.1988, 5,000
Greece: Minou (Gitsoudis 46); Apostolakis, Kolomitrousis, Manolas, Mihou (Mavridis 46), Karapialis, Saravakos, Skartados (Nioblias 46), Dimnitriadis (Borbokis 66), Mitropulos, Kofidis (Tsalouhides 46). **Scorers:** Manolas 62, 79, Mitropulos 89.
Northern Ireland: McKnight; Fleming, Rogan, McClelland, Donaghy, McNally (K. Wilson 77), D. Wilson, Michael O'Neill (Campbell 46), Clarke, Quinn, Worthington. **Scorer:** Clarke 32, 76.

ISRAEL (0)0, ENGLAND (0)0
Tel Aviv, 17.2.1988, 5,000
Israel: Ginsburg; Avraham Cohen, E. Cohen, Klinger, Avi Cohen, Shimonov, Alon, Malmilian, Drieks (Eizenberg 89), Ivanir (Ovadia 89), Tikva (Brialovsky 46).
England: Woods; Stevens, Pearce, Webb, Watson, Wright (Fenwick 74), C. Allen (Harford 67), McMahon, Beardsley, Barnes, Waddle.

SAUDI ARABIA (1)2, SCOTLAND (0)2
Riyadh, 17.2.1988, 20,000
Saudi Arabia: Abdullah Al-Diaye; Saleb Al-Nuameh, Ahmed Jamil, Mohammed Abdul Jawad, Zaki Saleh, Bassim Abu Daud, Khalid Said, Hathal Al-Dawseri, Majid Abdullah, Youssef Jaze, Fahd Al-Harifi. **Scorers:** Jaze 16, Majid 71.
Scotland: Leighton (Henry Smith 46); Clarke, Malpas, Aitken, Gough, Miller (McLeish 64), Nicol (Colquhoun 46), McStay (Mackay 75), Johnston, McAvennie (Connor 64), Collins. **Scorers:** Johnston 47, Collins 49.

MALTA (0)1, SCOTLAND (1)1
Valletta, 22.3.1988, 8,000
Malta: Cluett; Camilleri, A. Azzopardi, Zirncat, Scicluna, Buttigieg, Busuttil, Vella, Carabott, Micallef (Scerri 10), Degeorgio. **Scorer:** Busuttil 54.
Scotland: Leighton; Clarke, Malpas, Aitken, McLeish, Miller, I. Ferguson, Durrant, Sharp, McCoist (McClair 51), Mackay (McInally 55). **Scorer:** Sharp 21.

ENGLAND (1)2, NETHERLANDS (2)2
Wembley, 23.3.1988, 74,590
England: Shilton; Stevens, Sansom, Steven, Adams, Watson (Wright 72), Robson, Webb (Hoddle 69), Beardsley (Hateley 35), Lineker, Barnes. **Scorers:** Lineker 13, Adams 65.
Netherlands: Van Breukelen; Troost, Silooy, R. Koeman, Van Aerle, Wouters, Vanenburg, Muhren, Bosman, Gullit (Kruzen 62), Van't Schip (Koot 85). **Scorers:** Adams og 20, Bosman 25.

NORTHERN IRELAND (1)1, POLAND (1)1
Belfast, 23.3.1988, 5,000
Northern Ireland: McKnight; Fleming, Worthington, Donaghy, McDonald, D. Wilson, Penney (Campbell 70), Quinn (K. Wilson 78), Clarke, Whiteside, O'Neill (Rogan 60). **Scorer:** D. Wilson 1.
Poland: Wandzik; Kubicki, Boniek, Lukasik, Wdowczyk, Tarasiewicz (Karas 46), Komornicki (Cisek 83), Ziober (Araszkiewicz 69), Urban, Dziekanowski, Kosecki. **Scorer:** Dziekanowski 32.

REP.OF IRELAND (1)2, RUMANIA (0)0
Dublin, 23.3.1988, 15,000
Rep. of Ireland: Bonner; C. Morris, Grimes, McCarthy (Anderson 46), Moran, Sheridan, Galvin (L. O'Brien 70), J. Byrne, Stapleton (N. Quinn 52), D. Kelly, Sheedy. **Scorers:** Moran 20, Kelly 89.
Rumania: Moraru; M. Popa, Rednic, Andone, Stanescu, Mateut, Boloni, Coras, Sabau, Vaiscovici (Lasconi 46), Camataru.

WALES (1)1, YUGOSLAVIA (1)2
Swansea, 23.3.1988, 5,985
Wales: Southall; Horne (Hall 80), Blackmore, van den Hauwe, Jackett, Phillips, G. Williams, Nicholas, Rush, R. James (Bowen 68), Saunders. **Scorer:** Saunders 7.
Yugoslavia: Radaca; Vulic, Hadzibegic, Radanovic, Brnovic, Katanec (Krivokapic 85), Stojkovic, Bazdarevic, Savicevic, Jakoljevic, Skoro (Pancev 74). **Scorers:** Stojkovic 43, Jakoljevic 72.

HUNGARY (0)0, ENGLAND (0)0
Budapest, 27.4.1988, 25,000
Hungary: Szendrei; Kozma, Pinter, Sass, Balog, Roth (Varga 65), Kiprich (Kovacs 83), Garaba, Fitos, Detari, Vincze.
England: Woods; Anderson, Pearce (Stevens 45), Steven, Adams, Pallister, Robson, McMahon, Beardsley (Hateley 65), Lineker (Cottee 83), Waddle (Hoddle 65).

OTHER INTERNATIONALS

NORTHERN IRELAND (0)0, FRANCE (0)0
Belfast, 27.4.1988, 7,500
Northern Ireland: McKnight; Donaghy, McDonald, McClelland, Worthington, D. Wilson, Whiteside (Quinn 40), Penney, Clarke (K. Wilson 82), O'Neill, Dennison (Black 60).
France: Martini; Amoros, Sonor, Casoni, Kastendeuch, Fernandez, Durand, Bijotat, Vercruysse (Ferrerim 82), Stopyra, Garande (Fargeon 82).

REP. OF IRELAND (1)2, YUGOSLAVIA (0)0
Dublin, 27.4.1988, 12,000
Rep. of Ireland: Bonner; C. Morris, Hughton, McCarthy, Moran, Sheridan, McGrath, Houghton (Anderson 55), Stapleton, D. Kelly (J. Byrne 69), M. Kelly (L. O'Brien 89).
Scorers: McCarthy 24, Moran 64.
Yugoslavia: Lekovic; Miljus, Baljic, Hadzibegic, Elsner, Radanovic, Skoro, Jankovic (Boban 77), Mlinaric (Brnovic 67), Bazdarevic, Vujovic.

SPAIN (0)0, SCOTLAND (0)0
Madrid, 27.4.1988, 15,000
Spain: Zubizarreta; Tomas, Soler, Sanchis, Victor, Gordillo, J. Salinas, Michel, Butragueno, Gallego, M. Vazquez.
Scotland: Leighton; Gough, Nicol, Aitken, McLeish, Gillespie, McCoist (McClair 68), Miller, Johnston, McStay, Durrant.

SWEDEN (2)4, WALES (1)1
Stockholm, 27.4.1988, 11,656
Sweden: Ravelli; Nilsson, Hysen, Larssen, Schiller, Thern, Stromberg, Prytz, Lympar, Eskilsson, Holmquist.
Scorers: Holmquist 17, 56, Stromberg 24, Eskilsson 62.
Wales: Southall; Phillips, Aizlewood, Jackett, Blackmore, Nicholas (Horne 78), G. Williams, Hodges, Saunders (Lowndes 78), Rush, Hughes. **Scorer:** Hodges 26.

SCOTLAND (0)0, COLOMBIA (0)0
Hampden Park, 17 May 1988, 20,489 (Rous Cup)
Scotland: Leighton; Gough, Nicol, Aitken, McLeish, Miller, Gallacher (Walker 67), McStay, McCoist (D. Ferguson 58), MacLeod, Johnston.
Colombia: Higuita; Escobar, Herrera, Hoyos, Perea, Garcia, Valderrama, Redin, Iguaran, Trellez, Alvarez.

ENGLAND (1)1, SCOTLAND (0)0
Wembley, 21 May 1988, 70,480 (Rous Cup)
England: Shilton; Stevens, Sansom, Webb, Watson, Adams, Robson, Steven (Waddle 72), Beardsley, Lineker, Barnes. **Scorer:** Beardsley 12.
Scotland: Leighton; Gough, Nicol, Aitken, McLeish, Miller, Simpson (Burns 74), McStay, McCoist (Gallacher 77), MacLeod, Johnston.

REP. OF IRELAND (3)3, POLAND (0)1
Dublin, 22 May 1988, 18,500
Rep. of Ireland: Peyton; C. Morris, Hughton, McGrath (N. Quinn 54), Moran, Sheridan (M. Kelly 64), Whelan (J. Byrne 56), Aldridge, Galvin (L. O'Brien 64), Cascarino, Sheedy. **Scorers:** Sheedy 12, Cascarino 31, Sheridan 40.
Poland: Wandzik; Kubicki, Wojcicki, Cisek, Lukasik, Komornicki, Ziober, Urban, Prusik, Dziekanowski, Koseckiend.

ENGLAND (1)1, COLOMBIA (0)1
Wembley, 24 May 1988, 25,756 (Rous Cup)
England: Shilton; Anderson, Sansom, McMahon, Wright, Adams, Robson, Waddle (Hoddle 73), Beardsley (Hateley 73), Lineker, Barnes. **Scorer:** Lineker 22.
Colombia: Higuita; Escobar, Herrera, Hoyos, Arango (Trellez 65), Garcia, Valderrama, Redin, Alvarez, Perea, Iguaran. **Scorer:** Escobar 67.

SWITZERLAND (0)0, ENGLAND (0)1
Lausanne, 28 May 1988, 10,000
Switzerland: Corminboeuf; Tschuppert, Schallibaum, Weber, Geiger, Perret (Andermatt 46), Sutter, Hermann, Zwicker, Bickel (Mottiez 82), Bonvin (Turkyilmaz 66).
England: Shilton (Woods 46); Stevens, Sansom, Webb, Wright, Adams (Watson 46), Robson (Reid 80), Steven (Waddle 46), Beardsley, Lineker, Barnes. **Scorer:** Lineker 59.

MALTA (1)2, WALES (1)3
Valletta, 1 June 1988, 7,000
Malta: Cluett; Camilleri, Azzopardi, Galea, Brincat (Scicluna 75), Buggieg, Busuttil, Scerri, Carabott (Refalo 59), Micallef (Lowell 37), Degiorgio. **Scorer:** Busuttil 15, 22.
Wales: Norman; Hall, Blackmore, G. Williams, Aizlewood, Slatter, Saunders (Hodges 77), Horne, Rush, Hughes, Davies. **Scorers:** Horne 10, Hughes 54, Rush 75.

NORWAY (0)0, REP. OF IRELAND (0)0
Oslo, 1 June 1988, 9,494
Norway: Thorstvedt; Hansen, Johnsen, Bratseth, Halle, Osbold, Brandhaug, O. Berg, Petter (Backhe 75), Andersen (Sorloth 62), J. Berg.
Rep. of Ireland: Bonner; C. Morris, Hughton, McCarthy, Moran, McGrath, Whelan, Houghton, Aldridge, Stapleton (Cascarino 62), Galvin (Sheridan 75).

ITALY (0)0, WALES (1)1
Brescia, 4 June 1988, 18,931
Italy: Zenga; Bergomi, Baresi, Ferri, Maldini (de Agostini 56), de Napoli, Ancelotti, Donadoni (Rizzitelli 70), Giannini, Vialli (Altobelli 46), Mancini.
Wales: Norman; Hall, Blackmore, G. Williams (Saunders 60), Aizlewood, Slatter, Van den Hauwe, Horne (Hodges 60), Rush, Hughes, Davies. **Scorer:** Rush 37.

BRITISH & IRISH INTERNATIONAL RESULTS SINCE 1872

BRITISH INTERNATIONAL CHAMPIONSHIP 1883–1984

Season	Champions	Pts
1883–84	Scotland	6
1884–85	Scotland	5
1885–86	England	5
	Scotland	5
1886–87	Scotland	6
1887–88	England	6
1888–89	Scotland	5
1889–90	England	5
	Scotland	5
1890–91	England	6
1891–92	England	6
1892–93	England	6
1893–94	Scotland	5
1894–95	England	5
1895–96	Scotland	5
1896–97	Scotland	5
1897–98	England	6
1898–99	England	6
1899–1900	Scotland	6
1900–01	England	5
1901–02	Scotland	5
1902–03	England	4
	Ireland	4
	Scotland	4
1903–04	England	5
1904–05	England	5
1905–06	England	4
	Scotland	4
1906–07	Wales	5
1907–08	England	5
	Scotland	5
1908–09	England	6
1909–10	Scotland	4
1910–11	England	5
1911–12	England	5
	Scotland	5
1912–13	England	4
1913–14	Ireland	5
1919–20	Wales	4
1920–21	Scotland	6
1921–22	Scotland	4
1922–23	Scotland	5
1923–24	Wales	6
1924–25	Scotland	6
1925–26	Scotland	6
1926–27	England	4
	Scotland	4
1927–28	Wales	5
1928–29	Scotland	6
1929–30	England	6
1930–31	England	4
	Scotland	4
1931–32	England	6
1932–33	Wales	5
1933–34	Wales	5
1934–35	England	4
	Scotland	4
1935–36	Scotland	4
1936–37	Wales	6
1937–38	England	4
1938–39	England	4
	Scotland	4
	Wales	4
1946–47	England	5
1947–48	England	5
1948–49	Scotland	6
1949–50	England	6
1950–51	Scotland	6
1951–52	England	5
	Wales	5
1952–53	England	4
	Scotland	4
1953–54	England	6
1954–55	England	6
1955–56	England	3
	Scotland	3
	Wales	3
1956–57	England	5
1957–58	England	4
	N.Ireland	4
1958–59	England	4
	N.Ireland	4
1959–60	England	4
	Scotland	4
	Wales	4
1960–61	England	6
1961–62	Scotland	6
1962–63	Scotland	6
1963–64	England	4
	N.Ireland	4
	Scotland	4
1964–65	England	5
1965–66	England	5
1966–67	Scotland	5
1967–68	England	5
1968–69	England	6
1969–70	England	4
	Scotland	4
	Wales	4
1970–71	England	5
1971–72	England	4
	Scotland	4
1972–73	England	6
1973–74	England	4
	Scotland	4
1974–75	England	4
1975–76	Scotland	6
1976–77	Scotland	5
1977–78	England	6
1978–79	England	5
1979–80	N.Ireland	5
1980–81	Not completed	
1981–82	England	6
1982–83	England	5
1983–84	N.Ireland	3

Summary of outright wins: England 34, Scotland 24, Wales 7, Northern Ireland 2, Ireland 1.

In the following lists of results, * = European Championship. † = World Cup. Only official internationals, as defined by the British and Irish Football Associations, are included. WSCC = West of Scotland Cricket Ground, Glasgow (Hamilton Crescent).

ENGLAND v SCOTLAND

Date	Venue	E	S
30.11.1872	WSCC	0	0
8.3.1873	Kennington Oval	4	2
7.3.1874	WSCC	1	2
6.3.1875	Kennington Oval	2	2
4.3.1876	WSCC	0	3
3.3.1877	Kennington Oval	1	3
2.3.1878	First Hampden	2	7
5.4.1879	Kennington Oval	5	4
13.3.1880	First Hampden	4	5
12.3.1881	Kennington Oval	1	6
11.3.1882	First Hampden	1	5
10.3.1883	Brammall Lane	2	3
15.3.1884	First Cathkin	0	1
21.3.1885	Kennington Oval	1	1
31.3.1886	Second Hampden	1	1
19.3.1887	Blackburn	2	3
17.3.1888	Second Hampden	5	0
13.4.1889	Kennington Oval	2	3
5.4.1890	Second Hampden	1	1
6.4.1891	Blackburn	2	1
2.4.1892	Ibrox	4	1
1.4.1893	Richmond	5	2
7.4.1894	Parkhead	2	2
6.4.1895	Everton	3	0
4.4.1896	Parkhead	1	2
3.4.1897	Crystal Palace	1	2
2.4.1898	Parkhead	3	1
8.4.1899	Villa Park	2	1
7.4.1900	Parkhead	1	4
30.3.1901	Crystal Palace	2	2
3.5.1902	Villa Park	2	2
4.4.1903	Bramall Lane	1	2
9.4.1904	Parkhead	1	0
1.4.1905	Crystal Palace	1	0
7.4.1906	Hampden Pk	1	2
6.4.1907	Newcastle	1	1
4.4.1908	Hampden Pk	1	1
3.4.1909	Crystal Palace	2	0
2.4.1910	Hampden Pk	0	2

INTERNATIONAL FOOTBALL

1.4.1911	Everton	1	1	17.4.1937	Hampden Pk	1	3	15.4.1967	Wembley	2	3*
23.3.1912	Hampden Pk	1	1	9.4.1938	Wembley	0	1	24.2.1968	Hampden Pk	1	1*
5.4.1913	Stamford Bridge	1	0	15.4.1939	Hampden Pk	2	1	10.5.1969	Wembley	4	1
4.4.1914	Hampden Pk	1	3	12.4.1947	Wembley	1	1	25.4.1970	Hampden Pk	0	0
10.4.1920	Brammall Lane	5	4	10.4.1948	Hampden Pk	2	0	22.5.1971	Wembley	3	1
9.4.1921	Hampden Pk	0	3	9.4.1949	Wembley	1	3	27.5.1972	Hampden Pk	1	0
8.4.1922	Villa Park	0	1	15.4.1950	Hampden Pk	1	0†	14.2.1973	Hampden Pk	5	0
14.4.1923	Hampden Pk	2	2	14.4.1951	Wembley	2	3	19.5.1973	Wembley	1	0
12.4.1924	Wembley	1	1	5.4.1952	Hampden Pk	2	1	18.5.1974	Hampden Pk	0	2
4.4.1925	Hampden Pk	0	2	18.4.1953	Wembley	2	2	24.5.1975	Wembley	5	1
17.4.1926	Old Trafford	0	1	3.4.1954	Hampden Pk	4	2†	15.5.1976	Hampden Pk	1	2
2.4.1927	Hampden Pk	2	1	2.4.1955	Wembley	7	2	4.6.1977	Wembley	1	2
31.3.1928	Wembley	1	5	14.4.1956	Hampden Pk	1	1	20.5.1978	Hampden Pk	1	0
13.4.1929	Hampden Pk	0	1	6.4.1957	Wembley	2	1	26.5.1979	Wembley	3	1
5.4.1930	Wembley	5	2	19.4.1958	Hampden Pk	4	0	24.5.1980	Hampden Pk	1	0
28.3.1931	Hampden Pk	0	2	11.4.1959	Wembley	1	0	23.5.1981	Wembley	0	1
9.4.1932	Wembley	3	0	9.4.1960	Hampden Pk	1	1	29.5.1982	Hampden Pk	1	0
1.4.1933	Hampden Pk	1	2	15.4.1961	Wembley	9	3	1.6.1983	Wembley	2	0
14.4.1934	Wembley	3	0	14.4.1962	Hampden Pk	0	2	26.5.1984	Hampden Pk	1	1
6.4.1935	Hampden Pk	0	2	6.4.1963	Wembley	1	2	25.5.1985	Hampden Pk	0	1
4.4.1936	Wembley	1	1	11.4.1964	Hampden Pk	0	1	23.4.1986	Wembley	2	1
				10.4.1965	Wembley	2	2	23.5.1987	Hampden Pk	0	0
				2.4.1966	Hampden Pk	4	3	21.5.1988	Wembley	1	0

Summary: Played 106. England won 42. Scotland won 40. Drawn 24. Goals: England 186, Scotland 168.

ENGLAND v WALES

Date	Venue	E	W	Date	Venue	E	W	Date	Venue	E	W
18.1.1879	Kennington Oval	2	1	14.3.1910	Cardiff	1	0	10.10.1953	Cardiff	4	1†
15.3.1880	Wrexham	3	2	13.3.1911	Millwall	3	0	10.11.1954	Wembley	3	2
26.2.1881	Blackburn	0	1	11.3.1912	Wrexham	2	0	22.10.1955	Cardiff	1	2
13.3.1882	Wrexham	3	5	17.3.1913	Ashton Gate	4	3	14.11.1956	Wembley	3	1
3.2.1883	Kennington Oval	5	0	16.3.1914	Cardiff	2	0	19.10.1957	Cardiff	4	0
17.3.1884	Wrexham	4	0	15.3.1920	Highbury	1	2	26.11.1958	Villa Park	2	2
14.3.1885	Blackburn	1	1	14.3.1921	Cardiff	0	0	17.10.1959	Cardiff	1	1
29.3.1886	Wrexham	3	1	13.3.1922	Anfield	1	0	23.11.1960	Wembley	5	1
26.2.1887	Kennington Oval	4	0	5.3.1923	Cardiff	2	2	14.10.1961	Cardiff	1	1
4.2.1888	Crewe	5	1	3.3.1924	Blackburn	1	2	21.11.1962	Wembley	4	0
23.2.1889	Stoke	4	1	28.2.1925	Swansea	2	1	12.10.1963	Cardiff	4	0
15.3.1890	Wrexham	3	1	1.3.1926	Selhurst Park	1	3	18.11.1964	Wembley	2	1
7.3.1891	Sunderland	4	1	12.2.1927	Wrexham	3	3	2.10.1965	Cardiff	0	0
5.3.1892	Wrexham	2	0	28.11.1927	Burnley	1	2	16.11.1966	Wembley	5	1*
13.3.1893	Stoke	6	0	17.11.1928	Swansea	3	2	21.10.1967	Cardiff	3	0*
12.3.1894	Wrexham	5	1	20.11.1929	Stamford Bridge	6	0	7.5.1969	Wembley	2	1
18.3.1895	Kensington	1	1	22.11.1930	Wrexham	4	0	18.4.1970	Cardiff	1	1
16.3.1896	Cardiff	9	1	18.11.1931	Anfield	3	1	19.5.1971	Wembley	0	0
29.3.1897	Bramall Lane	4	0	16.11.1932	Wrexham	0	0	20.5.1972	Cardiff	3	0
28.3.1898	Wrexham	3	0	15.11.1933	Newcastle	1	2	15.11.1972	Cardiff	1	0†
20.3.1899	Ashton Gate	4	0	29.9.1934	Cardiff	4	0	24.1.1973	Wembley	1	1†
26.3.1900	Cardiff	1	1	5.2.1936	Wolverhampton	1	2	15.5.1973	Cardiff	3	0
18.3.1901	Newcastle	6	0	17.10.1936	Cardiff	1	2	11.5.1974	Cardiff	2	0
3.3.1902	Wrexham	0	0	17.11.1937	Middlesbrough	2	1	21.5.1975	Wembley	2	2
2.3.1903	Portsmouth	2	1	22.10.1938	Cardiff	2	4	24.3.1976	Wrexham	2	1
29.2.1904	Wrexham	2	2	13.11.1946	Maine Road	3	0	8.5.1976	Cardiff	1	0
27.3.1905	Anfield	3	1	18.10.1947	Cardiff	3	0	31.5.1977	Wembley	0	1
19.3.1906	Cardiff	1	0	10.11.1948	Villa Park	1	0	13.5.1978	Cardiff	3	1
18.3.1907	Fulham	1	1	15.10.1949	Cardiff	4	1†	23.5.1979	Wembley	0	0
16.3.1908	Wrexham	7	1	15.11.1950	Sunderland	4	2	17.5.1980	Wrexham	1	4
15.3.1909	Trent Bridge	2	0	20.10.1951	Cardiff	1	1	19.5.1981	Wembley	0	0
				12.11.1952	Wembley	5	2	27.4.1982	Cardiff	1	0
								23.2.1983	Wembley	2	1
								2.5.1984	Wrexham	0	1

Summary: Played 97. England won 62. Wales won 14. Drawn 21. Goals: England 239, Wales 90.

ENGLAND v IRELAND

To 1920. Ireland was then partitioned into the Irish Free State and Northern Ireland. The Irish Free State became the Republic of Ireland in 1937.

Date	Venue	E	I
18.2.1882	Belfast	13	0
24.2.1883	Liverpool	7	0
23.2.1884	Belfast	8	1
28.2.1885	Manchester	4	0
13.3.1886	Belfast	6	1
5.2.1887	Bramall Lane	7	0
7.4.1888	Belfast	5	1
2.3.1889	Anfield	6	1
15.3.1890	Belfast	9	1
7.3.1891	Wolverhampton	6	1
5.3.1892	Belfast	2	0
25.2.1893	Perry Barr	6	1
3.3.1894	Belfast	2	2
9.3.1895	Derby Racecourse	9	0
7.3.1896	Belfast	2	0
20.2.1897	Trent Bridge	6	0
5.3.1898	Belfast	3	2
18.2.1899	Roker Park	13	2
17.3.1900	Dublin	2	0
9.3.1901	Southampton	3	0
22.3.1902	Belfast	1	0
14.2.1903	Wolverhampton	4	0
12.3.1904	Belfast	3	1
25.2.1905	Middlesbro	1	1
17.2.1906	Belfast	5	0
16.2.1907	Everton	1	0
15.2.1908	Belfast	3	1
13.2.1909	Valley Parade	4	0
12.2.1910	Belfast	1	1
11.2.1911	Baseball Ground	2	1
10.2.1912	Dublin	6	1
15.2.1913	Belfast	1	2
14.2.1914	Middlesbrough	4	3
25.10.1919	Belfast	1	1
23.10.1920	Roker Park	2	0

Summary: Played 35. England won 30. Ireland won 1. Drawn 4. Goals: England 158, Ireland 25.

ENGLAND v NORTHERN IRELAND

Date	Venue	E	I
22.10.1921	Belfast	1	1
21.10.1922	West Bromwich	2	0
20.10.1923	Belfast	1	2
22.10.1924	Everton	3	1
24.10.1925	Belfast	0	0
20.10.1926	Anfield	3	3
22.10.1927	Belfast	0	2
22.10.1928	Everton	2	1
19.10.1929	Belfast	3	0
20.10.1930	Bramall Lane	5	1
17.10.1931	Belfast	6	2
17.10.1932	Blackpool	1	0
14.10.1933	Belfast	3	0
6.2.1935	Everton	2	1
19.10.1935	Belfast	3	1
18.11.1936	Stoke	3	1
23.10.1937	Belfast	5	1
16.11.1938	Maine Road	7	0
28.9.1946	Belfast	7	2
5.11.1947	Everton	2	2
9.10.1948	Belfast	6	2
16.11.1949	Maine Road	9	2†
7.10.1950	Belfast	4	1
14.11.1951	Villa Park	2	0
4.10.1952	Belfast	2	2
11.11.1953	Anfield	3	1†
2.10.1954	Belfast	2	0
2.11.1955	Wembley	3	0
6.10.1956	Belfast	1	1
6.11.1957	Wembley	2	3
4.10.1958	Belfast	3	3
18.11.1959	Wembley	2	1
8.10.1960	Belfast	5	2
22.11.1961	Wembley	1	1
20.10.1962	Belfast	3	1
20.11.1963	Wembley	8	3
3.10.1964	Belfast	4	3
10.11.1965	Wembley	2	1
22.10.1966	Belfast	2	0*
22.11.1967	Wembley	2	0*
3.5.1969	Belfast	3	1
21.4.1970	Wembley	3	1
15.5.1971	Belfast	1	0
23.5.1972	Wembley	0	1
12.5.1973	Everton‡	2	1
15.5.1974	Wembley	1	0
17.5.1975	Belfast	0	0
11.5.1976	Wembley	4	0
28.5.1977	Belfast	2	1
16.5.1978	Wembley	1	0
7.2.1979	Wembley	4	0*
19.5.1979	Belfast	2	0
17.10.1979	Belfast	4	0*
20.5.1980	Wembley	1	1
1981 fixture cancelled.			
23.2.1982	Wembley	4	0
28.5.1983	Belfast	0	0
4.4.1984	Wembley	1	0
27.2.1985	Belfast	1	0†
13.11.1985	Wembley	0	0†
15.10.1986	Wembley	3	0*
1.4.1987	Belfast	2	0*

Summary: Played 61. England won 45. Northern Ireland won 4. Drawn 12. Goals: England 164, Northern Ireland 54.
‡Switched from Belfast for security reasons.

SCOTLAND v WALES

Date	Venue	S	W
25.3.1876	WSCC	4	0
5.3.1877	Wrexham	2	0
23.3.1878	First Hampden	9	0
7.4.1879	Wrexham	3	0
3.4.1880	First Hampden	5	1
14.3.1881	Wrexham	5	1
25.3.1882	First Hampden	5	0
12.3.1883	Wrexham	3	0
29.3.1884	First Cathkin	4	1
23.3.1885	Wrexham	8	1
10.4.1886	Second Hampden	4	1
21.3.1887	Wrexham	2	0
10.2.1888	Easter Road	5	1
15.4.1889	Wrexham	0	0
22.3.1890	Paisley	5	0
21.3.1891	Wrexham	4	3
26.3.1892	Tynecastle	6	1
18.3.1893	Wrexham	8	0
24.3.1894	Kilmarnock	5	2
23.3.1895	Wrexham	2	2
21.3.1896	Carolina, Dundee	4	0
20.3.1897	Wrexham	2	2
19.3.1898	Motherwell	5	2
18.3.1899	Wrexham	6	0
3.2.1900	Aberdeen	5	2
2.3.1901	Wrexham	1	1
15.3.1902	Greenock	5	1
9.3.1903	Cardiff	1	0
12.3.1904	Dens Park	1	1
6.3.1905	Wrexham	1	3
3.3.1906	Tynecastle	0	2
4.3.1907	Wrexham	0	1
7.3.1908	Dens Park	2	1
1.3.1909	Wrexham	2	3
5.3.1910	Kilmarnock	1	0
6.3.1911	Cardiff	2	2
2.3.1912	Tynecastle	1	0
3.3.1913	Wrexham	0	0
28.2.1914	Parkhead	0	0
26.2.1920	Cardiff	1	1
12.2.1921	Aberdeen	2	1

INTERNATIONAL FOOTBALL

4.2.1922	Wrexham	1	2	23.10.1948	Cardiff	3	1	3.5.1969	Wrexham	5	3
17.3.1923	Paisley	2	0	9.11.1949	Hampden Pk	2	0†	22.4.1970	Hampden Pk	0	0
16.2.1924	Cardiff	0	2	21.10.1950	Cardiff	3	1	15.5.1971	Cardiff	0	0
14.2.1925	Tynecastle	3	1	14.11.1951	Hampden Pk	0	1	24.5.1972	Hampden Pk	1	0
31.10.1925	Cardiff	3	0	18.10.1952	Cardiff	2	1	12.5.1973	Wrexham	2	0
30.10.1926	Ibrox	3	0	4.11.1953	Hampden Pk	3	3†	14.5.1974	Hampden Pk	2	0
29.10.1927	Wrexham	2	2	16.10.1954	Cardiff	1	0	17.5.1975	Cardiff	2	2
27.10.1928	Ibrox	4	2	9.11.1955	Hampden Pk	2	0	6.5.1976	Hampden Pk	3	1
26.10.1929	Cardiff	4	2	20.10.1956	Cardiff	2	2	17.11.1976	Hampden Pk	1	0†
25.10.1930	Ibrox	1	1	13.11.1957	Hampden Pk	1	1	28.5.1977	Wrexham	0	0
31.10.1931	Wrexham	3	2	18.10.1958	Cardiff	3	0	12.10.1977	Anfield	2	0†
26.10.1932	Tynecastle	2	5	4.11.1959	Hampden Pk	1	1	17.5.1978	Hampden Pk	1	1
4.10.1933	Cardiff	2	3	22.10.1960	Cardiff	0	2	19.5.1979	Cardiff	0	3
21.11.1934	Pittodrie	3	2	8.11.1961	Hampden Pk	2	0	21.5.1980	Hampden Pk	1	1
5.10.1935	Cardiff	1	1	20.10.1962	Cardiff	3	2	15.5.1981	Swansea	0	2
2.12.1936	Dens Park	1	2	20.11.1963	Hampden Pk	2	1	24.5.1982	Hampden Pk	1	0
30.10.1937	Cardiff	1	2	3.10.1964	Cardiff	2	3	28.5.1983	Cardiff	2	0
9.11.1938	Tynecastle	3	2	24.11.1965	Hampden Pk	4	1	28.2.1984	Hampden Pk	2	1
19.10.1946	Wrexham	1	3	22.10.1966	Cardiff	1	1*	27.3.1985	Hampden Pk	0	1†
12.11.1947	Hampden Pk	1	2	22.11.1967	Hampden Pk	3	2*	10.9.1985	Cardiff	1	1†

Summary: Played 101. Scotland won 60. Wales won 18. Drawn 23. Goals: Scotland 238, Wales 111.

SCOTLAND v IRELAND

To 1920.

Date	Venue	S	I								
26.1.1884	Belfast	5	0	29.3.1890	Belfast	4	1	21.3.1903	Parkhead	0	2
14.3.1885	Second Hampden	8	2	28.3.1891	Parkhead	2	1	26.3.1904	Dublin	1	1
				19.3.1892	Cliftonville	3	2	18.3.1905	Parkhead	4	0
20.3.1886	Belfast	7	2	25.3.1893	Parkhead	6	1	17.3.1906	Dublin	1	0
19.2.1887	Second Hampden	4	1	31.3.1894	Cliftonville	2	1	16.3.1907	Parkhead	3	0
				30.3.1895	Parkhead	3	1	14.3.1908	Dublin	5	0
24.3.1888	Cliftonville	3	0	28.3.1896	Cliftonville	3	3	15.3.1909	Ibrox	5	0
9.3.1889	Ibrox	7	0	27.3.1897	Ibrox	5	1	19.3.1910	Belfast	0	1
				26.3.1898	Cliftonville	3	0	18.3.1911	Parkhead	2	0
				25.3.1899	Parkhead	9	1	16.3.1912	Belfast	4	1
				3.3.1900	Cliftonville	3	0	15.3.1913	Dublin	2	1
				23.2.1901	Parkhead	11	0	14.3.1914	Belfast	1	1
				1.3.1902	Belfast	5	1	13.3.1920	Parkhead	3	0

Summary: Played 32. Scotland won 27. Ireland won 2. Drawn 3. Goals: Scotland 131, Ireland 27.

SCOTLAND v NORTHERN IRELAND

Date	Venue	S	NI								
26.2.1921	Belfast	2	0	27.11.1946	Hampden Pk	0	0	16.11.1966	Hampden Pk	2	1*
4.3.1922	Parkhead	2	1	4.10.1947	Belfast	0	2	21.10.1967	Belfast	0	1*
3.3.1923	Belfast	1	0	17.11.1948	Hampden Pk	3	2	6.5.1969	Hampden Pk	1	1
1.3.1924	Parkhead	2	0	1.10.1949	Belfast	8	2†	18.4.1970	Belfast	1	0
28.2.1925	Belfast	3	0	1.11.1950	Hampden Pk	6	1	18.5.1971	Hampden Pk	0	1
27.2.1926	Ibrox	4	0	6.10.1951	Belfast	3	0	20.5.1972	Hampden Pk‡	2	0
26.2.1927	Belfast	2	0	5.11.1952	Hampden Pk	1	1	16.5.1973	Hampden Pk	1	2
25.2.1928	Partick	0	1	3.10.1953	Belfast	3	1†	11.5.1974	Hampden Pk‡	0	1
23.2.1929	Belfast	7	3	3.11.1954	Hampden Pk	2	2	20.5.1975	Hampden Pk	3	0
22.2.1930	Parkhead	3	1	8.10.1955	Belfast	1	2	8.5.1976	Hampden Pk‡	3	0
21.2.1931	Belfast	0	0	7.11.1956	Hampden Pk	1	0	1.6.1977	Hampden Pk	3	0
19.9.1931	Ibrox	3	1	5.10.1957	Belfast	1	1	13.5.1978	Hampden Pk‡	1	1
17.9.1932	Belfast	4	0	5.11.1958	Hampden Pk	2	2	22.5.1979	Hampden Pk	1	0
16.9.1933	Parkhead	1	2	3.10.1959	Belfast	4	0	17.5.1980	Belfast	0	1
20.10.1934	Belfast	1	2	9.11.1960	Hampden Pk	5	2	25.3.1981	Hampden Pk	1	1†
13.11.1935	Tynecastle	2	1	7.10.1961	Belfast	6	1	14.10.1981	Belfast	0	0†
31.10.1936	Belfast	3	1	7.11.1962	Hampden Pk	5	1	28.4.1982	Belfast	1	1
10.11.1937	Pittodrie	1	1	12.10.1963	Belfast	1	2	24.5.1983	Hampden Pk	0	0
8.10.1938	Belfast	2	0	25.11.1964	Hampden Pk	3	2	13.12.1983	Belfast	0	2
				2.10.1965	Belfast	2	3				

Summary: Played 59. Scotland won 33. Northern Ireland won 13. Drawn 13. Goals: Scotland 122, Northern Ireland 54.
‡*Switched from Belfast for security reasons.*

WALES v IRELAND

To 1921				7.2.1891	Belfast	2	7		21.3.1904	Bangor, Wales	0	1
				27.2.1892	Bangor, Wales	1	1		8.4.1905	Belfast	2	2
				8.4.1893	Belfast	3	4		2.4.1906	Wrexham	4	4
Date	*Venue*	*W*	*I*	24.2.1894	Swansea	4	1		23.2.1907	Belfast	3	2
25.2.1882	Wrexham	7	1	16.3.1895	Belfast	2	2		11.4.1908	Aberdare	0	1
17.3.1883	Belfast	1	1	29.2.1896	Wrexham	6	1		20.3.1909	Belfast	3	2
9.2.1884	Wrexham	6	0	6.3.1897	Belfast	3	4		11.4.1910	Wrexham	4	1
11.4.1885	Belfast	8	2	19.2.1898	Llandudno	0	1		28.1.1911	Belfast	2	1
27.2.1886	Wrexham	5	0	4.3.1899	Belfast	0	1		13.4.1912	Cardiff	2	3
12.3.1887	Belfast	1	4	24.2.1900	Llandudno	2	0		18.1.1913	Belfast	1	0
3.3.1888	Wrexham	11	0	23.3.1901	Belfast	1	0		19.1.1914	Wrexham	1	2
27.4.1889	Belfast	3	1	22.3.1902	Cardiff	0	3		14.2.1920	Belfast	2	2
8.2.1890	Shrewsbury	5	2	28.3.1903	Belfast	0	2		9.4.1921	Swansea	2	1

Summary: Played 35. Wales won 17. Ireland won 12. Drawn 6. Goals: Wales 97, Ireland 60.

WALES v NORTHERN IRELAND

Date	*Venue*	*W*	*NI*	16.4.1947	Belfast	1	2		30.3.1966	Cardiff	1	4
1.4.1922	Belfast	1	1	10.3.1948	Wrexham	2	0		12.4.1967	Belfast	0	0*
14.4.1923	Wrexham	0	3	9.3.1949	Belfast	2	0		28.2.1968	Wrexham	2	0*
15.3.1924	Belfast	1	0	8.3.1950	Wrexham	0	0†		10.5.1969	Belfast	0	0
18.4.1925	Wrexham	0	0	7.3.1951	Belfast	2	1		25.4.1970	Swansea	1	0
13.2.1926	Belfast	0	3	19.3.1952	Swansea	3	0		22.5.1971	Belfast	0	1
9.4.1927	Cardiff	2	2	15.4.1953	Belfast	3	2		28.5.1972	Wrexham	0	0
4.2.1928	Belfast	2	1	31.3.1954	Wrexham	1	2†		19.5.1973	Everton‡	0	1
2.2.1929	Wrexham	2	2	20.4.1955	Belfast	3	2		18.5.1974	Wrexham	1	0
1.2.1930	Belfast	0	7	11.4.1956	Cardiff	1	1		23.5.1975	Belfast	0	1
22.4.1931	Wrexham	3	2	10.4.1957	Belfast	0	0		14.5.1976	Swansea	1	0
5.12.1931	Belfast	0	4	16.4.1958	Cardiff	1	1		3.6.1977	Belfast	1	1
7.12.1932	Wrexham	4	1	22.4.1959	Belfast	1	4		19.5.1978	Wrexham	1	0
4.11.1933	Belfast	1	1	6.4.1960	Wrexham	3	2		25.5.1979	Belfast	1	1
27.3.1935	Wrexham	3	1	12.4.1961	Belfast	5	1		23.5.1980	Cardiff	0	1
11.3.1936	Belfast	2	3	11.4.1962	Cardiff	4	0		*1981 fixture cancelled*			
17.3.1937	Wrexham	4	1	3.4.1963	Belfast	4	1		27.5.1982	Wrexham	3	0
16.3.1938	Belfast	0	1	15.4.1964	Swansea	3	2		31.5.1983	Belfast	1	0
15.3.1939	Wrexham	3	1	31.3.1965	Belfast	5	0		22.5.1984	Swansea	1	1

Summary: Played 55. Wales won 26. Northern Ireland won 14. Drawn 15. Goals: Wales 86, Northern Ireland 66.
†*Switched from Belfast for security reasons.*

OTHER BRITISH AND IRISH INTERNATIONAL RESULTS
ENGLAND

v ARGENTINA

Date	*Venue*	*E*	*A*
9.5.1951	Wembley	2	1
17.5.1953	Buenos Aires	0	0
(abandoned after 21 minutes)			
2.6.1962	Rancagua	3	1†
6.6.1964	Rio de Janeiro	0	1
23.7.1966	Wembley	1	0†
22.5.1974	Wembley	2	2
12.6.1977	Buenos Aires	1	1
13.5.1980	Wembley	3	1
22.6.1986	Mexico City	1	2†

v AUSTRALIA

Date	*Venue*	*E*	*A*
31.5.1980	Sydney	2	1
11.6.1983	Sydney	0	0
15.6.1983	Brisbane	1	0
18.6.1983	Melbourne	1	1

v AUSTRIA

Date	*Venue*	*E*	*A*
6.6.1908	Vienna	6	1
8.6.1908	Vienna	11	1
1.6.1909	Vienna	8	1
14.5.1930	Vienna	0	0
7.12.1932	Stamford Bridge	4	3
6.5.1936	Vienna	1	2
28.11.1951	Wembley	2	2
25.5.1952	Vienna	3	2
15.6.1958	Boras	2	2†
27.5.1961	Vienna	1	3
4.4.1962	Wembley	3	1
20.10.1965	Wembley	2	3
27.5.1967	Vienna	1	0
26.9.1973	Wembley	7	0
13.6.1979	Vienna	3	4

v BELGIUM

Date	*Venue*	*E*	*B*
21.5.1921	Brussels	2	0
19.3.1923	Highbury	6	1
1.11.1923	Antwerp	2	2
8.12.1924	West Bromwich	4	0
24.5.1926	Antwerp	5	3
11.5.1927	Brussels	9	1
19.5.1928	Antwerp	3	1
11.5.1929	Brussels	5	1
16.5.1931	Brussels	4	1
9.5.1936	Brussels	2	3
21.9.1947	Brussels	5	2
18.5.1950	Brussels	4	1
26.11.1952	Wembley	5	0

17.6.1954	Basle	4	4†
(after extra time)			
21.10.1964	Wembley	2	2
25.2.1970	Brussels	3	1
12.6.1980	Turin	1	1*

v BOHEMIA

Date	Venue	E	B
13.6.1908	Prague	4	0

v BRAZIL

Date	Venue	E	B
9.5.1956	Wembley	4	2
11.6.1958	Gothenburg	0	0†
13.5.1959	Rio de Janeiro	0	2
10.6.1962	Vina del Mar	1	3†
8.5.1963	Wembley	1	1
30.5.1964	Rio de Janeiro	1	5
12.6.1969	Rio de Janeiro	1	2
7.6.1970	Guadalajara	0	1
23.5.1976	Los Angeles	0	1
8.6.1977	Rio de Janeiro	0	0
19.4.1978	Wembley	1	1
12.5.1981	Wembley	0	1
10.6.1984	Rio de Janeiro	2	0
19.5.1987	Wembley	1	1

v BULGARIA

Date	Venue	E	B
7.6.1962	Rancagua	0	0†
11.12.1968	Wembley	1	1
1.6.1974	Sofia	1	0
6.6.1979	Sofia	3	0*
22.11.1979	Wembley	2	0

v CANADA

Date	Venue	E	C
24.5.1986	Burnaby	1	0

v CHILE

Date	Venue	E	C
25.6.1950	Rio de Janeiro	2	0†
24.5.1953	Santiago	2	1
17.6.1984	Santiago	0	0

v COLOMBIA

Date	Venue	E	C
20.5.1970	Bogota	4	0
24.5.1988	Wembley	1	1

v CYPRUS

Date	Venue	E	C
16.4.1975	Wembley	5	0*
11.5.1975	Limassol	1	0*

v CZECHOSLOVAKIA

Date	Venue	E	C
16.5.1934	Prague	1	2
1.12.1937	Tottenham	5	4
29.5.1963	Bratislava	4	2
2.11.1966	Wembley	0	0
11.6.1970	Guadalajara	1	0†
27.5.1973	Prague	1	1

30.10.1974	Wembley	3	0*
30.10.1975	Bratislava	1	2*
29.11.1978	Wembley	1	0
20.6.1980	Bilbao	2	0†

v DENMARK

Date	Venue	E	D
26.9.1948	Copenhagen	0	0
2.10.1955	Copenhagen	5	1
5.12.1956	Wolver-hampton	5	2†
15.5.1957	Copenhagen	4	1
3.7.1966	Copenhagen	2	0
20.9.1978	Copenhagen	4	3*
12.9.1979	Wembley	1	0*
22.9.1982	Copenhagen	2	2*
21.9.1983	Wembley	0	1*

v EAST GERMANY

Date	Venue	E	EG
2.6.1963	Leipzig	2	1
25.11.1970	Wembley	3	1
29.5.1974	Leipzig	1	1
12.9.1984	Wembley	1	0

v ECUADOR

Date	Venue	E	Ec
24.5.1970	Quito	2	0

v EGYPT

Date	Venue	E	Eg
29.1.1986	Cairo	4	0

v FIFA

Date	Venue	E	F
26.10.1938	Highbury	3	0
21.10.1953	Wembley	4	4
21.10.1963	Wembley	2	1

v FINLAND

Date	Venue	E	F
20.5.1937	Helsinki	8	0
20.5.1956	Helsinki	5	1
26.6.1966	Helsinki	3	0
13.6.1976	Helsinki	4	1†
13.10.1976	Wembley	2	1†
3.6.1982	Helsinki	4	1
17.10.1984	Wembley	5	0†
22.5.1985	Helsinki	1	1†

v FRANCE

Date	Venue	E	F
10.5.1923	Paris	4	1
17.5.1924	Paris	3	1
21.5.1925	Paris	3	2
26.5.1927	Paris	6	0
17.5.1928	Paris	5	1
9.5.1929	Paris	4	1
14.5.1931	Paris	2	5
6.12.1933	Tottenham	4	1
26.5.1938	Paris	4	2
3.5.1947	Highbury	3	0
22.5.1949	Paris	3	1
3.10.1951	Highbury	2	2

15.5.1955	Paris	0	1
27.11.1957	Wembley	4	0
3.10.1962	Sheffield	1	1*
27.2.1963	Paris	2	5*
20.7.1966	Wembley	2	0†
12.3.1969	Wembley	5	0
16.6.1982	Bilbao	3	1†
29.2.1984	Paris	0	2

v GERMANY

Date	Venue	E	G
10.5.1930	Berlin	3	3
4.12.1935	Tottenham	3	0
14.5.1938	Berlin	6	3

v GREECE

Date	Venue	E	G
21.4.1971	Wembley	3	0*
1.12.1971	Athens	2	0*
17.11.1982	Athens	3	0*
30.3.1983	Wembley	0	0*

v HUNGARY

Date	Venue	E	H
10.6.1908	Budapest	7	0
29.5.1909	Budapest	4	2
31.5.1909	Budapest	8	2
10.5.1934	Budapest	1	2
2.12.1936	Highbury	6	2
25.11.1953	Wembley	3	6
23.5.1954	Budapest	1	7
22.5.1960	Budapest	0	2
31.5.1962	Rancagua	1	2†
5.5.1965	Wembley	1	0
24.5.1978	Wembley	4	1
6.6.1981	Budapest	3	1†
18.11.1982	Wembley	1	0†
27.4.1983	Wembley	2	0*
12.10.1983	Budapest	3	0*
27.4.88	Budapest	0	0

v ICELAND

Date	Venue	E	I
2.6.1982	Reykjavik	1	1

v REPUBLIC OF IRELAND

Date	Venue	E	I
30.9.1946	Dublin	1	0
21.9.1949	Everton	0	2
8.5.1957	Wembley	5	1†
19.5.1957	Dublin	1	1†
24.5.1964	Dublin	3	1
8.9.1976	Wembley	1	1
25.10.1978	Dublin	1	1*
6.2.1980	Wembley	2	0*
26.3.1985	Wembley	2	1
12.6.1988	Stuttgart	0	1*

v ISRAEL

Date	Venue	E	I
26.2.1986	Ramat Gan	2	1
17.2.1988	Tel Aviv	0	0

v ITALY

Date	Venue	E	I
13.5.1933	Rome	1	1
14.11.1934	Highbury	3	2
13.5.1939	Milan	2	2
16.5.1948	Turin	4	0
30.11.1949	Tottenham	2	0
18.5.1952	Florence	1	1
6.5.1959	Wembley	2	2
24.5.1961	Rome	3	2
14.6.1973	Turin	0	2
14.11.1973	Wembley	0	1
28.5.1976	New York	3	2
17.11.1976	Rome	0	2†
16.11.1977	Wembley	2	0†
15.6.1980	Turin	0	1*
6.6.1985	Mexico City	1	2

v KUWAIT

Date	Venue	E	K
25.6.1982	Bilbao	1	0†

v LUXEMBOURG

Date	Venue	E	L
21.5.1927	Luxembourg	5	2
19.10.1960	Luxembourg	9	0†
28.9.1961	Highbury	4	1†
30.3.1977	Wembley	5	0†
12.10.1977	Luxembourg	2	0†
15.12.1982	Wembley	9	0*
16.11.1983	Luxembourg	4	0*

v MALTA

Date	Venue	E	M
3.2.1971	Valletta	1	0*
12.5.1971	Wembley	5	0*

v MEXICO

Date	Venue	E	M
24.5.1959	Mexico City	1	2
10.5.1961	Wembley	8	0
16.7.1966	Wembley	2	0†
1.6.1969	Mexico City	0	0
9.6.1985	Mexico City	0	1
17.5.1986	Los Angeles	3	0

v MOROCCO

Date	Venue	E	M
6.6.1986	Monterrey	0	0†

v NETHERLANDS

Date	Venue	E	N
18.5.1935	Amsterdam	1	0
27.11.1946	Huddersfield	8	2
9.12.1964	Amsterdam	1	1
5.11.1969	Amsterdam	1	0
14.1.1970	Wembley	0	0
9.2.1977	Wembley	0	2
25.5.1982	Wembley	2	0
23.3.1988	Wembley	2	2
15.6.1988	Dusseldorf	1	3*

v NORWAY

Date	Venue	E	N
14.5.1937	Oslo	6	0
9.11.1938	Newcastle	4	0
18.5.1949	Oslo	4	1
29.6.1966	Oslo	6	1
10.9.1980	Wembley	4	0†
9.9.1981	Oslo	1	2†

v PARAGUAY

Date	Venue	E	P
18.6.1986	Mexico City	3	0†

v PERU

Date	Venue	E	P
17.5.1959	Lima	1	4
20.5.1962	Lima	4	0

v POLAND

Date	Venue	E	P
5.1.1966	Everton	1	1
5.7.1966	Chorzow	1	0
6.6.1973	Chorzow	0	2†
17.10.1973	Wembley	1	1†
11.6.1986	Monterrey	3	0†

v PORTUGAL

Date	Venue	E	P
25.5.1947	Lisbon	10	0
14.5.1950	Lisbon	5	3
19.5.1951	Everton	5	2
22.5.1955	Oporto	1	3
7.5.1958	Wembley	2	1
21.5.1961	Lisbon	1	1†
25.10.1961	Wembley	2	0†
17.5.1964	Lisbon	4	3
4.6.1964	Sao Paulo	1	1
26.7.1966	Wembley	2	1†
10.12.1969	Wembley	1	0
3.4.1974	Lisbon	0	0
20.11.1974	Wembley	0	0*
19.11.1975	Lisbon	1	1*
3.6.1986	Monterrey	0	1†

v RUMANIA

Date	Venue	E	R
24.5.1939	Bucharest	2	0
6.11.1968	Bucharest	0	0
15.1.1969	Wembley	1	1
2.6.1970	Guadalajara	1	0†
15.10.1980	Bucharest	1	2†
29.4.1981	Wembley	0	0†
1.5.1985	Bucharest	0	0†
11.9.1985	Wembley	1	1†

v SPAIN

Date	Venue	E	S
15.5.1929	Madrid	3	4
9.12.1931	Highbury	7	1
2.7.1950	Rio de Janeiro	0	1†
18.5.1955	Madrid	1	1
30.11.1955	Wembley	4	1
15.5.1960	Madrid	0	3
26.10.1960	Wembley	4	2
8.12.1965	Madrid	2	0
24.5.1967	Wembley	2	0
3.4.1968	Wembley	1	0*
8.5.1968	Madrid	2	1*
26.3.1980	Barcelona	2	0
18.6.1980	Naples	2	1*
25.3.1981	Wembley	1	2
5.7.1982	Madrid	0	0†
18.2.1987	Madrid	4	2

v SWEDEN

Date	Venue	E	S
21.5.1923	Stockholm	4	2
24.5.1923	Stockholm	3	1
17.5.1937	Stockholm	4	0
19.11.1947	Highbury	4	2
13.5.1949	Stockholm	1	3
16.5.1956	Stockholm	0	0
28.10.1959	Wembley	2	3
16.5.1965	Gothenburg	2	1
22.5.1968	Wembley	3	1
10.6.1979	Stockholm	0	0
10.9.1986	Stockholm	0	1

v SWITZERLAND

Date	Venue	E	S
20.5.1933	Berne	4	0
21.5.1938	Zurich	1	2
18.5.1947	Zurich	0	1
2.12.1948	Highbury	6	0
28.5.1952	Zurich	3	0
20.6.1954	Berne	2	0†
9.5.1962	Wembley	3	1
5.6.1963	Basle	8	1
13.10.1971	Basle	3	2*
10.11.1971	Wembley	1	1*
3.9.1975	Basle	2	1
7.9.1977	Wembley	0	0
19.11.1980	Wembley	2	1†
30.5.1981	Basle	1	2†
28.5.1988	Lausanne	1	0

v TURKEY

Date	Venue	E	T
14.11.1984	Istanbul	8	0†
16.10.1985	Wembley	5	0†
29.4.1987	Izmir	0	0*
14.10.1987	Wembley	8	0*

v USA

Date	Venue	E	US
29.6.1950	Belo Horizonte	0	1†
8.6.1953	New York	6	3
28.5.1959	Los Angeles	8	1
27.5.1964	New York	10	0
16.6.1985	Los Angeles	5	0

v URUGUAY

Date	Venue	E	U
31.5.1953	Montevideo	1	2
26.6.1954	Basle	2	4†
6.5.1964	Wembley	2	1
11.7.1966	Wembley	0	0†
8.6.1969	Montevideo	2	1
15.6.1977	Montevideo	0	0
13.6.1984	Montevideo	0	2

INTERNATIONAL FOOTBALL

v USSR

Date	Venue	E	SU
18.5.1958	Moscow	1	1
8.6.1958	Gothenburg	2	2†
17.6.1958	Gothenburg	0	1†
22.10.1958	Wembley	5	0
6.12.1967	Wembley	2	2
8.6.1968	Rome	2	0*
10.6.1973	Moscow	2	1
2.6.1984	Wembley	0	2
26.3.1986	Tbilisi	1	0
18.6.1988	Frankfurt	1	3*

v WEST GERMANY

Date	Venue	E	WG
1.12.1954	Wembley	3	1
26.5.1956	West Berlin	3	1
12.5.1965	Nuremberg	1	0
23.2.1966	Wembley	1	0
30.7.1966	Wembley	4	2†

(after extra time)

1.6.1968	Hanover	0	1
14.6.1970	Leon	2	3†

(after extra time)

29.4.1972	Wembley	1	3*
13.5.1972	West Berlin	0	0*
12.3.1975	Wembley	2	0
22.2.1978	Munich	1	2
29.6.1982	Madrid	0	0†
13.10.1982	Wembley	1	2
12.6.1985	Mexico City	3	0
9.9.1987	Dusseldorf	1	3

v YUGOSLAVIA

Date	Venue	E	Y
18.5.1939	Belgrade	1	2
22.11.1950	Highbury	2	2
16.5.1954	Belgrade	0	1
28.11.1956	Wembley	3	0
11.5.1958	Belgrade	0	5
11.5.1960	Wembley	3	3
9.5.1965	Belgrade	1	1
4.5.1966	Wembley	2	0
5.6.1968	Florence	0	1*
11.10.1972	Wembley	1	1
5.6.1974	Belgrade	2	2
12.11.1986	Wembley	2	0*
11.11.1987	Belgrade	4	1*

SCOTLAND

v ARGENTINA

Date	Venue	S	A
18.6.1977	Buenos Aires	1	1
2.6.1979	Hampden Pk	1	3

v AUSTRALIA

Date	Venue	S	A
20.11.1985	Hampden Pk	2	0†
4.12.1985	Sydney	0	0†

v AUSTRIA

Date	Venue	S	A
16.5.1931	Vienna	0	5
29.11.1933	Hampden Pk	2	2
9.5.1937	Vienna	1	1
13.12.1950	Hampden Pk	0	1
27.5.1951	Vienna	0	4
16.6.1954	Zurich	0	1†
19.5.1955	Vienna	4	1
2.5.1956	Hampden Pk	1	1
29.5.1960	Vienna	1	4
8.5.1963	Hampden Pk	4	1

(abandoned after 79 minutes)

6.11.1968	Hampden Pk	2	1†
5.11.1969	Vienna	0	2†
20.9.1978	Vienna	2	3*
17.10.1979	Hampden Pk	1	1

v BELGIUM

Date	Venue	S	B
18.5.1947	Brussels	1	2
28.4.1948	Hampden Pk	2	0
20.5.1951	Brussels	5	0
3.2.1971	Liege	0	3*
10.11.1971	Aberdeen	1	0*
2.6.74	Brussels	1	2
21.11.1979	Brussels	0	2*
19.12.79	Hampden Pk	1	3*
15.12.82	Brussels	2	3*
12.10.83	Hampden Pk	1	1*
1.4.87	Brussels	1	4*
14.10.1987	Hampden Pk	2	0*

v BRAZIL

Date	Venue	S	B
25.6.1966	Hampden Pk	1	1
5.7.1972	Rio de Janeiro	0	1
30.6.1973	Hampden Pk	0	1
18.6.1974	Frankfurt	0	0†
23.6.1977	Rio de Janeiro	0	2
18.6.1982	Seville	1	4†
26.5.1987	Hampden Pk	0	2

v BULGARIA

Date	Venue	S	B
22.2.1978	Hampden Pk	2	1
10.9.1986	Hampden Pk	0	0*
11.11.1987	Sofia	1	0*

v CHILE

Date	Venue	S	C
15.6.1977	Santiago	4	2

v COLOMBIA

Date	Venue	S	C
17.5.1988	Hampden Pk	0	0

v CYPRUS

Date	Venue	S	C
17.12.1968	Nicosia	5	0†
11.5.1969	Hampden Pk	8	0†

v CZECHOSLOVAKIA

Date	Venue	S	C
22.5.1937	Prague	3	1
8.12.1937	Hampden Pk	5	0
14.5.1961	Bratislava	0	4†
26.9.1961	Hampden Pk	3	2†
29.11.1961	Brussels	2	4†

(after extra time)

2.7.1972	Porto Alegre	0	0
26.9.1973	Hampden Pk	2	1†
17.10.1973	Prague	0	1†
13.10.1976	Prague	0	2†
21.9.1977	Glasgow	3	1†

v DENMARK

Date	Venue	S	D
12.5.1951	Hampden Pk	3	1
25.5.1952	Copenhagen	2	1
16.10.1968	Copenhagen	1	0
11.11.1970	Hampden Pk	1	0*
9.6.1971	Copenhagen	0	1*
18.10.1972	Copenhagen	4	1†
15.11.1972	Hampden Pk	2	0†
3.9.1975	Copenhagen	1	0*
29.10.1975	Hampden Pk	3	1*
4.6.1986	Nezahual-coyotl	0	1†

v EAST GERMANY

Date	Venue	S	EG
30.10.1974	Hampden Pk	3	0
7.9.1977	East Berlin	0	1
13.10.1982	Hampden Pk	2	0*
16.11.1983	Halle	1	2*
16.10.1985	Hampden Pk	0	0

v FINLAND

Date	Venue	S	F
25.5.1954	Helsinki	2	1
21.10.1964	Hampden Pk	3	1†
27.5.1965	Helsinki	2	1†
8.9.1976	Hampden Pk	6	0

v FRANCE

Date	Venue	S	F
18.5.1930	Paris	2	0
8.5.1932	Paris	3	1
23.5.1948	Paris	0	3
27.4.1949	Hampden Pk	2	0
27.5.1950	Paris	1	0
16.5.1951	Hampden Pk	1	0
15.6.1958	Orebro	1	2†
1.6.1984	Marseilles	0	2

v GERMANY

Date	Venue	S	G
1.6.1929	Berlin	1	1
14.10.1936	Ibrox	2	0

v HUNGARY

Date	Venue	S	H
7.12.1938	Ibrox	3	1
8.12.1954	Hampden Pk	2	4
29.5.1955	Budapest	1	3
7.5.1958	Hampden Pk	1	1
5.6.1960	Budapest	3	3
31.5.1980	Budapest	1	3
9.9.1987	Hampden Pk	2	0

v ICELAND

Date	Venue	S	I
17.10.1984	Hampden Pk	3	0†
28.5.1985	Reykjavik	1	0†

v IRAN

Date	Venue	S	I
7.6.1978	Cordoba	1	1†

v REPUBLIC OF IRELAND

Date	Venue	S	I
3.5.1961	Hampden Pk	4	1†
7.5.1961	Dublin	3	0†
9.6.1963	Dublin	0	1
21.9.1969	Dublin	1	1
15.10.1986	Dublin	0	0*
18.2.1987	Hampden Pk	0	1*

v ISRAEL

Date	Venue	S	I
25.2.1981	Tel Aviv	1	0†
28.4.1981	Hampden Pk	3	1†
28.1.1986	Tel Aviv	1	0

v ITALY

Date	Venue	S	I
20.5.1931	Rome	0	3
9.11.1965	Hampden Pk	1	0†
7.12.1965	Naples	0	3†

v LUXEMBOURG

Date	Venue	S	L
24.5.1947	Luxembourg	6	0
12.11.1986	Hampden Pk	3	0*
2.12.1987	Luxembourg	0	0*

v MALTA

Date	Venue	S	M
22.3.1988	Valletta	1	1

v NETHERLANDS

Date	Venue	S	N
4.6.1929	Amsterdam	2	0
21.5.1938	Amsterdam	3	1
27.5.1959	Amsterdam	2	1
11.5.1966	Hampden Pk	0	3
30.5.1968	Amsterdam	0	0
1.12.1971	Rotterdam	1	2
11.6.1978	Mendoza	3	2†
23.3.1982	Hampden Pk	2	1
29.4.1986	Eindhoven	0	0

v NEW ZEALAND

Date	Venue	S	NZ
15.6.1982	Malaga	5	2†

v NORWAY

Date	Venue	S	N
28.5.1929	Oslo	7	3
5.5.1954	Hampden Pk	1	0
19.5.1954	Oslo	1	1
4.6.1963	Bergen	3	4
7.11.1963	Hampden Pk	6	1
6.6.1974	Oslo	2	1
25.10.1978	Hampden Pk	3	2*
7.6.1979	Oslo	4	0*

v PARAGUAY

Date	Venue	S	P
11.6.1958	Norrkoping	2	3†

v PERU

Date	Venue	S	P
26.4.1972	Hampden Pk	2	0
3.6.1978	Cordoba	1	3†
12.9.1979	Hampden Pk	1	1

v POLAND

Date	Venue	S	P
1.6.1958	Warsaw	2	1
4.5.1960	Glasgow	2	3
23.5.1965	Chorzow	1	1†
13.10.1965	HampdenPk	1	2†
28.5.1980	Poznan	0	1

v PORTUGAL

Date	Venue	S	P
21.5.1950	Lisbon	2	2
4.5.1955	Hampden Pk	3	0
3.6.1959	Lisbon	0	1
18.6.1966	Hampden Pk	0	1
21.4.1971	Lisbon	0	2*
13.10.1971	Hampden Pk	2	1*
13.5.1975	Hampden Pk	1	0
29.11.1978	Lisbon	0	1*
26.3.1980	Hampden Pk	4	1*
15.10.1980	Hampden Pk	0	0†
18.11.1981	Lisbon	1	2†

v RUMANIA

Date	Venue	S	R
1.6.1975	Bucharest	1	1*
17.12.1975	Hampden Pk	1	1*
26.3.1986	Hampden Pk	3	0

v SAUDI ARABIA

Date	Venue	S	SA
17.2.1988	Riyadh	2	2

v SPAIN

Date	Venue	S	Sp
8.5.1957	Hampden Pk	4	2†
26.5.1957	Madrid	1	4†
13.6.1963	Madrid	6	2
8.5.1965	Hampden Pk	0	0

20.11.1974	Glasgow	1	2*
5.2.1975	Valencia	1	1*
24.2.1982	Valencia	0	3
14.11.1984	Hampden Pk	3	1†
27.2.1985	Seville	0	1†
27.4.1988	Madrid	0	0

v SWEDEN

Date	Venue	S	Sw
30.5.1952	Stockholm	1	3
6.5.1953	Hampden Pk	1	2
16.4.1975	Gothenburg	1	1
27.4.1977	Hampden Pk	3	1
10.9.1980	Stockholm	1	0†
9.9.1981	Hampden Pk	2	0†

v SWITZERLAND

Date	Venue	S	Sw
24.5.1931	Geneva	3	2
17.5.1948	Berne	1	2
26.4.1950	Hampden Pk	3	1
19.5.1957	Basle	2	1†
6.11.1957	Hampden Pk	3	2†
22.6.1973	Berne	0	1
7.4.1976	Hampden Pk	1	0
17.11.1982	Berne	0	2*
30.5.1983	Hampden Pk	2	2*

v TURKEY

Date	Venue	S	T
8.6.1960	Ankara	2	4

v URUGUAY

Date	Venue	S	U
19.6.1954	Basle	0	7†
2.5.1962	Hampden Pk	2	3
21.9.1983	Hampden Pk	2	0
13.6.1986	Nezahual-coyotl	0	0†

v USA

Date	Venue	S	US
30.4.1952	Hampden Pk	6	0

v USSR

Date	Venue	S	SU
10.5.1967	Hampden Pk	0	2
14.6.1971	Moscow	0	1
22.6.1982	Malaga	2	2†

v WEST GERMANY

Date	Venue	S	WG
22.5.1957	Stuttgart	3	1
6.5.1959	Hampden Pk	3	2
12.5.1964	Hanover	2	2
16.4.1969	Hampden Pk	1	1†
22.10.1969	Hamburg	2	3†
14.11.1973	Hampden Pk	1	1
27.3.1974	Frankfurt	1	2
8.6.1986	Queretaro	1	2†

INTERNATIONAL FOOTBALL

v YUGOSLAVIA

Date	Venue	S	Y
15.5.1955	Belgrade	2	2
21.11.1956	Hampden Pk	2	0
8.6.1958	Vasteras	1	1†
29.6.1972	Belo Horizonte	2	2
22.6.1974	Frankfurt	1	1†
12.9.1984	Hampden Pk	6	1

v ZAIRE

Date	Venue	S	Z
14.6.1974	Dortmund	2	0†

WALES

v AUSTRIA

Date	Venue	W	A
9.5.1954	Vienna	0	2
23.11.1955	Wrexham	1	2*
4.9.1974	Vienna	1	2*
19.11.1975	Wrexham	1	0

v BELGIUM

Date	Venue	W	B
22.5.1949	Liege	1	3
23.11.1949	Cardiff	5	1

v BULGARIA

Date	Venue	W	B
27.4.1983	Wrexham	1	0*
16.11.1983	Sofia	0	1*

v BRAZIL

Date	Venue	W	B
19.6.1958	Gothenburg	0	1†
12.5.1962	Rio de Janeiro	1	3
16.5.1962	Sao Paulo	1	3
14.5.1966	Rio de Janeiro	1	3
18.5.1966	Belo Horizonte	0	1
12.6.1983	Cardiff	1	1

v CANADA

Date	Venue	W	C
10.5.1986	Toronto	0	2
20.5.1986	Vancouver	3	0

v CHILE

Date	Venue	W	C
22.5.1966	Santiago	0	2

v CZECHOSLOVAKIA

Date	Venue	W	C
1.5.1957	Cardiff	1	0†
26.5.1957	Prague	0	2†
21.4.1971	Swansea	1	3*
27.10.1971	Prague	0	1*
30.3.1977	Wrexham	3	0†
16.11.1977	Prague	0	1†
19.11.1980	Cardiff	1	0†
9.9.1981	Prague	0	2†
29.4.1987	Wrexham	1	1*
11.11.1987	Prague	0	2*

v DENMARK

Date	Venue	W	D
21.10.1964	Copenhagen	0	1†
1.12.1965	Wrexham	4	2†
9.9.1987	Cardiff	1	0*
14.10.1987	Copenhagen	0	1*

v EAST GERMANY

Date	Venue	W	EG
19.5.1957	Leipzig	1	2†
25.9.1957	Cardiff	4	1†
16.4.1969	Dresden	1	2†
22.10.1969	Cardiff	1	3†

v FINLAND

Date	Venue	W	F
26.5.1971	Helsinki	1	0*
13.10.1971	Swansea	3	0*
10.9.1987	Helsinki	1	1*
1.4.1987	Wrexham	4	0*

v FRANCE

Date	Venue	W	F
25.5.1933	Paris	1	1
20.5.1939	Paris	1	2
14.5.1953	Paris	1	6
2.6.1982	Toulouse	1	0

v GREECE

Date	Venue	W	G
9.12.1964	Athens	0	2†
17.3.1965	Cardiff	4	1†

v HUNGARY

Date	Venue	W	H
8.6.1958	Sandviken	1	1†
17.6.1958	Stockholm	2	1†
28.5.1961	Budapest	2	3
7.11.1962	Budapest	1	3*
20.3.1963	Cardiff	1	1*
30.10.1974	Cardiff	2	0*
16.4.1975	Budapest	2	1*
16.10.1985	Cardiff	0	3

v ICELAND

Date	Venue	W	I
2.6.1980	Reykjavik	4	0†
14.10.1981	Swansea	2	2†
12.9.1984	Reykjavik	0	1†
14.11.1984	Cardiff	2	1†

v IRAN

Date	Venue	W	I
18.4.1978	Tehran	1	0

v REPUBLIC OF IRELAND

Date	Venue	W	I
28.9.1960	Dublin	3	2
11.9.1979	Swansea	2	1
24.2.1981	Dublin	3	1
26.3.1986	Dublin	1	0

v ISRAEL

Date	Venue	W	I
15.1.1958	Tel Aviv	2	0†
5.2.1958	Cardiff	2	0†
10.6.1984	Tel Aviv	0	0

v ITALY

Date	Venue	W	I
1.5.1965	Florence	1	4
23.10.1968	Cardiff	0	1†
4.11.1969	Rome	1	4†
4.6.1988	Brescia	1	0

v KUWAIT

Date	Venue	W	K
6.9.1977	Wrexham	0	0
20.9.1977	Kuwait	0	0

v LUXEMBOURG

Date	Venue	W	L
20.11.1974	Swansea	5	0*
1.5.1975	Luxembourg	3	1*

v MALTA

Date	Venue	W	M
25.10.1978	Wrexham	7	0*
2.6.1979	Valletta	2	0*
1.6.1988	Valletta	3	2

v MEXICO

Date	Venue	W	M
11.6.58	Stockholm	1	1†
22.5.1962	Mexico City	1	2

v NORWAY

Date	Venue	W	N
22.9.1982	Swansea	1	0*
21.9.1983	Oslo	0	0*
6.6.1984	Trondheim	0	1
26.2.1985	Wrexham	1	1
5.6.1985	Bergen	2	4

v POLAND

Date	Venue	W	P
28.3.1973	Cardiff	2	0†
26.9.1973	Katowice	0	3†

v PORTUGAL

Date	Venue	W	P
15.5.1949	Lisbon	2	3
12.5.1951	Cardiff	2	1

v RUMANIA

Date	Venue	W	R
11.11.1970	Cardiff	0	0*

| 24.11.1971 | Bucharest | 0 | 2* |
| 12.10.1983 | Wrexham | 5 | 0 |

v SAUDI ARABIA

Date	Venue	W	SA
25.2.1986	Dahran	2	1

v SPAIN

Date	Venue	W	S
19.4.1961	Cardiff	1	2†
18.5.1961	Madrid	1	1†
24.3.1982	Valencia	1	1
17.10.1984	Seville	0	3†
30.4.1985	Wrexham	3	0†

v SWEDEN

Date	Venue	W	S
15.6.1958	Stockholm	0	0†
27.4.1988	Stockholm	1	4

v SWITZERLAND

Date	Venue	W	S
26.5.1949	Berne	0	4

| 16.5.1951 | Wrexham | 3 | 2 |

v TURKEY

Date	Venue	W	T
29.11.1978	Wrexham	1	0*
21.11.1979	Izmir	0	1*
15.10.1980	Cardiff	4	0†
25.3.1981	Ankara	1	0†

v REST OF UK

Date	Venue	W	UK
5.12.1951	Cardiff	3	2
28.7.1969	Cardiff	0	1

v URUGUAY

Date	Venue	W	U
21.4.1986	Wrexham	0	0

v USSR

Date	Venue	W	SU
30.5.1965	Moscow	1	2†

27.10.1965	Cardiff	2	1†
30.5.1981	Wrexham	0	0†
18.11.1981	Tbilisi	0	3†
18.2.1987	Swansea	0	0

v WEST GERMANY

Date	Venue	W	WG
8.5.1968	Cardiff	1	1
26.3.1969	Frankfurt	1	1
6.10.1976	Cardiff	0	2
14.12.1977	Dortmund	1	1
2.5.1979	Wrexham	0	2*
17.10.1979	Cologne	1	5*

v YUGOSLAVIA

Date	Venue	W	Y
21.5.1953	Belgrade	2	5
22.11.1954	Cardiff	1	3
24.4.1976	Zagreb	0	2*
22.5.1976	Cardiff	1	1*
15.12.1982	Titograd	4	4*
14.12.1983	Cardiff	1	1*
23.3.1988	Swansea	1	2

NORTHERN IRELAND

‡Switched from Belfast for security reasons.

v ALBANIA

Date	Venue	NI	A
7.5.1965	Belfast	4	1†
24.11.1965	Tirana	1	1†
15.12.1982	Tirana	0	0*
27.4.1983	Belfast	1	0*

v ALGERIA

Date	Venue	NI	A
3.6.1986	Guadalajara	1	1†

v ARGENTINA

Date	Venue	NI	A
11.6.1958	Halmstad	1	3†

v AUSTRIA

Date	Venue	NI	A
1.7.1982	Madrid	2	2†
13.10.1982	Vienna	0	2*
21.9.1983	Belfast	3	1*

v AUSTRALIA

Date	Venue	NI	A
11.6.1980	Sydney	2	1
15.6.1980	Melbourne	1	1
18.6.1980	Adelaide	2	1

v BELGIUM

Date	Venue	NI	B
10.11.1976	Liege	0	2†
16.11.1977	Belfast	3	0†

v BRAZIL

Date	Venue	NI	B
12.6.1986	Guadalajara	0	3†

v BULGARIA

Date	Venue	NI	B
18.10.1972	Sofia	0	3†
26.9.1973	Hillsborough‡	0	0†
29.11.1978	Sofia	2	0*
2.5.1979	Belfast	2	0*

v CYPRUS

Date	Venue	NI	C
3.2.1971	Nicosia	3	0*
21.4.1971	Belfast	5	0*
14.2.1973	Nicosia	0	1†
8.5.1973	Fulham‡	3	0†

v CZECHOSLOVAKIA

Date	Venue	NI	C
8.6.1958	Halmstad	1	0†
17.6.1958	Malmo	2	1†

(after extra time)

v DENMARK

Date	Venue	NI	D
25.10.1978	Belfast	2	1*
6.6.1979	Copenhagen	0	4*
26.3.1986	Belfast	1	1

v FINLAND

Date	Venue	NI	F
27.5.1984	Pori	0	1†
14.11.1984	Belfast	2	1†

v FRANCE

Date	Venue	NI	F
12.5.1951	Belfast	2	2
11.11.1952	Paris	1	3

19.6.1958	Norrkoping	0	4†
24.3.1982	Paris	0	4
4.7.1982	Madrid	1	4†
26.2.1986	Paris	0	0
27.4.1988	Belfast	0	0

v GREECE

Date	Venue	NI	G
3.5.1961	Athens	1	2†
17.10.1961	Belfast	2	0†
17.2.1988	Athens	2	3

v HONDURAS

Date	Venue	NI	H
21.6.1972	Zaragoza	1	1†

v ICELAND

Date	Venue	NI	I
11.6.1977	Reykjavik	0	1†
21.9.1977	Belfast	2	0†

v REPUBLIC OF IRELAND

Date	Venue	NI	I
20.9.1978	Dublin	0	0*
21.11.1979	Belfast	1	0*

v ISRAEL

Date	Venue'	NI	I
10.9.1968	Jaffa	3	2
3.3.1976	Tel Aviv	1	1
26.3.1980	Tel Aviv	0	0†
18.11.1981	Belfast	1	0†
16.10.1984	Belfast	3	0
18.2.1987	Tel Aviv	1	1

INTERNATIONAL FOOTBALL

v ITALY

Date	Venue	NI	I
25.2.1957	Rome	0	1†
4.12.1957	Belfast	2	2
15.1.1958	Belfast	2	1†
25.4.1961	Bologna	2	3

v MALTA

Date	Venue	NI	M
21.5.1988	Belfast	3	0†

v MEXICO

Date	Venue	NI	M
22.6.1966	Belfast	4	1

v MOROCCO

Date	Venue	NI	M
23.4.1986	Belfast	2	1

v NETHERLANDS

Date	Venue	NI	N
9.5.1962	Rotterdam	0	4
17.3.1965	Belfast	2	1†
7.4.1965	Rotterdam	0	0†
13.10.1976	Rotterdam	2	2†
12.10.1977	Belfast	0	1†

v NORWAY

Date	Venue	NI	N
4.9.1974	Oslo	1	2*
29.10.1975	Belfast	3	0*

v POLAND

Date	Venue	NI	P
10.10.1962	Katowice	2	0*
28.11.1962	Belfast	2	0*
23.3.1988	Belfast	1	1

v PORTUGAL

Date	Venue	NI	P
16.1.1957	Lisbon	1	1†
1.5.1957	Belfast	3	0†
28.3.1973	Coventry‡	1	1†
14.11.1973	Lisbon	1	1†
19.11.1980	Lisbon	0	1†
29.4.1981	Belfast	1	0

v RUMANIA

Date	Venue	NI	R
12.9.1984	Belfast	3	2†
16.10.1985	Bucharest	1	0†

v SPAIN

Date	Venue	NI	S
15.10.1958	Madrid	2	6
30.5.1963	Bilbao	1	1
30.10.1963	Belfast	0	1
11.11.1970	Seville	0	3*
16.2.1972	Hull‡	1	1*
25.6.1982	Valencia	1	0†
27.3.1985	Palma	0	0
7.6.1986	Guadalajara	1	2†

v SWEDEN

Date	Venue	NI	S
30.10.1974	Solna	2	0*
3.9.1975	Belfast	1	2*
15.10.1980	Belfast	3	0†
3.6.1981	Solna	0	1†

v SWITZERLAND

Date	Venue	NI	S
14.10.1964	Belfast	1	0†
14.11.1964	Lausanne	1	2†

v TURKEY

Date	Venue	NI	T
23.10.1968	Belfast	4	1†
11.12.1968	Istanbul	3	0†
30.3.1983	Belfast	2	1*
12.10.1983	Ankara	0	1*
1.5.1985	Belfast	2	0†
11.9.1985	Izmir	0	0†
12.11.1986	Izmir	0	0*
11.11.1987	Belfast	1	0*

v URUGUAY

Date	Venue	NI	U
29.4.1964	Belfast	3	0

v USSR

Date	Venue	NI	SU
10.9.1969	Belfast	0	0†
22.10.1969	Moscow	0	2†
22.9.1971	Moscow	0	1*
13.10.1971	Belfast	1	1*

v WEST GERMANY

Date	Venue	NI	WG
15.6.1958	Malmo	2	2†
26.10.1960	Belfast	3	4†
10.5.1961	Hamburg	1	2†
7.5.1966	Belfast	0	2
27.4.1977	Cologne	0	5
17.11.1982	Belfast	1	0*
16.11.1983	Hamburg	1	0*

v YUGOSLAVIA

Date	Venue	NI	Y
16.3.1975	Belfast	1	0*
19.11.1975	Belgrade	0	1*
17.6.1982	Zaragoza	0	0†
29.4.1987	Belfast	1	2*
14.10.1987	Sarajevo	0	3*

REPUBLIC OF IRELAND

Including matches played by the Irish Free State 1921–37.

v ALGERIA

Date	Venue	RI	A
28.4.1982	Algiers	0	2

v ARGENTINA

Date	Venue	RI	A
13.5.1951	Dublin	0	1
29.5.1979	Dublin	0	0
16.5.1980	Dublin	0	1

v AUSTRIA

Date	Venue	RI	A
7.5.1952	Vienna	0	6
25.3.1953	Dublin	4	0
14.3.1958	Vienna	1	3
8.4.1962	Dublin	2	3
25.9.1963	Vienna	0	0*
13.10.1963	Dublin	3	2*
22.5.1966	Vienna	0	1
10.11.1968	Dublin	2	2
30.5.1971	Dublin	1	4*
10.10.1971	Linz	0	6*

v BELGIUM

Date	Venue	RI	B
12.2.1928	Liege	4	2
30.4.1929	Dublin	4	0
11.5.1930	Brussels	3	1
25.2.1934	Dublin	4	4†
24.4.1949	Dublin	0	2
10.5.1950	Brussels	1	5
24.3.1965	Dublin	0	2
25.5.1966	Liege	3	2
15.10.1980	Dublin	1	1†
25.3.1981	Brussels	0	1†
10.9.1986	Brussels	2	2*
29.4.1987	Dublin	0	0*

v BRAZIL

Date	Venue	RI	B
5.5.1974	Rio de Janeiro	1	2
27.5.1982	Uberlandia	0	7
23.5.1987	Dublin	1	0

v BULGARIA

Date	Venue	RI	B
1.6.1977	Sofia	1	2†
12.10.1977	Dublin	0	0†
19.5.1979	Sofia	0	1*
17.10.1979	Dublin	3	0*
1.4.1987	Sofia	1	2*
14.10.1987	Dublin	2	0*

v CHILE

Date	Venue	RI	C
30.3.1960	Dublin	2	0
21.6.1972	Recife	1	2

12.5.1974	Santiago	2	1
22.5.1982	Santiago	0	1

v CYPRUS

Date	Venue	RI	C
26.3.1980	Nicosia	3	2†
19.11.1980	Dublin	6	0†

v CZECHOSLOVAKIA

Date	Venue	RI	C
18.5.1938	Prague	2	2
5.4.1959	Dublin	2	0*
10.5.1959	Bratislava	0	4*
8.10.1961	Dublin	1	3†
29.10.1961	Prague	1	7†
21.5.1967	Dublin	0	2*
22.11.1967	Prague	2	1*
4.5.1969	Dublin	1	2†
7.10.1969	Prague	0	3†
26.9.1979	Prague	1	4
29.4.1981	Dublin	3	1
27.5.1986	Reykjavik	1	0

v DENMARK

Date	Venue	RI	D
3.10.56	Dublin	2	1†
2.10.1957	Copenhagen	2	0†
4.12.1968	Dublin	1	1†
(abandoned after 51 minutes.)			
27.5.1969	Copenhagen	0	2†
15.10.1969	Dublin	1	1†
24.5.1978	Copenhagen	3	3*
2.5.1979	Dublin	2	0*
14.11.1984	Copengahen	0	3†
13.11.1985	Dublin	1	4†

v ECUADOR

Date	Venue	RI	E
19.6.1972	Natal	3	2

v ENGLAND

Date	Venue	RI	E
30.9.1946	Dublin	0	1
21.9.1949	Everton	2	0
8.5.1957	Wembley	1	5†
19.5.1957	Dublin	1	1†
24.5.1964	Dublin	1	3
8.9.1976	Wembley	1	1
25.10.1978	Dublin	1	1*
6.2.1980	Wembley	0	2*
26.3.1985	Wembley	1	2
12.6.1988	Stuttgart	1	0*

v FINLAND

Date	Venue	RI	F
8.9.1949	Dublin	3	0†
9.10.1949	Helsinki	1	1†

v FRANCE

Date	Venue	RI	F
23.5.1937	Paris	2	0
16.11.1952	Dublin	1	1
4.10.1953	Dublin	3	5†
25.11.1953	Paris	0	1†
15.11.1972	Dublin	2	1†

19.5.1973	Paris	1	1†
17.11.1976	Paris	0	2†
30.3.1977	Dublin	1	0†
28.10.1980	Paris	0	2†
14.10.1981	Dublin	3	2†

v GERMANY

Date	Venue	RI	G
8.5.1935	Dortmund	1	3
17.10.1936	Dublin	5	2
23.5.1939	Bremen	1	1

v HUNGARY

Date	Venue	RI	H
15.12.1934	Dublin	2	4
3.5.1936	Budapest	3	3
6.12.1936	Dublin	2	3
19.3.1939	Cork	2	2
18.5.1939	Budapest	2	2
8.6.1969	Dublin	1	2†
5.11.1969	Budapest	0	4†

v ICELAND

Date	Venue	RI	I
12.8.1962	Dublin	4	2*
2.9.1962	Reykjavik	1	1*
13.10.1982	Dublin	2	0*
21.9.1983	Reykjavik	3	0*
25.5.1986	Reykjavik	2	1

v IRAN

Date	Venue	RI	I
18.6.1972	Recife	2	1

v NORTHERN IRELAND

Date	Venue	RI	NI
20.9.1978	Dublin	0	0*
21.11.1979	Belfast	0	1*

v ISRAEL

Date	Venue	RI	I
4.4.1984	Tel Aviv	0	3
10.11.1987	Dublin	5	0

v ITALY

Date	Venue	RI	I
21.3.1926	Turin	0	3
23.4.1927	Dublin	1	2
8.12.1970	Rome	0	3*
10.5.1971	Dublin	1	2*
5.2.1985	Dublin	1	2

v LUXEMBOURG

Date	Venue	RI	L
9.5.1936	Luxembourg	5	1
28.10.1953	Dublin	4	0†
7.3.1954	Luxembourg	1	0†
28.5.1987	Luxembourg	2	0*
9.9.1987	Dublin	2	1*

v MALTA

Date	Venue	RI	M
30.3.1983	Valletta	1	0*
16.11.1983	Dublin	8	0*

v NETHERLANDS

Date	Venue	RI	N
8.5.1932	Amsterdam	2	0
8.4.1934	Amsterdam	2	5
8.12.1935	Dublin	3	5
1.5.1955	Dublin	1	0
10.5.1956	Rotterdam	4	1
10.9.1980	Dublin	2	1†
9.9.1981	Rotterdam	2	2†
22.9.1982	Rotterdam	1	2*
12.10.1983	Dublin	2	3*
18.6.1988	Gelsenkirchen	0	1*

v NORWAY

Date	Venue	RI	N
10.10.1937	Oslo	2	3†
7.11.1937	Dublin	3	3†
26.11.1950	Dublin	2	2
30.5.1951	Oslo	3	2
8.11.1954	Dublin	2	1
25.5.1955	Oslo	3	1
6.11.1960	Dublin	3	1
13.5.1964	Oslo	4	1
6.6.1973	Oslo	1	1
24.3.1976	Dublin	3	0
21.5.1978	Oslo	0	0
17.10.1984	Dublin	0	1†
1.5.1985	Dublin	0	0†
1.6.1988	Oslo	0	0

v POLAND

Date	Venue	RI	P
22.5.1938	Warsaw	0	6
13.11.1938	Dublin	3	2
11.5.1958	Katowice	2	2
5.10.1958	Dublin	2	2
10.5.1964	Crakow	1	3
25.10.1964	Dublin	3	2
15.5.1968	Dublin	2	2
30.10.1968	Katowice	0	1
6.5.1970	Dublin	1	2
23.9.1970	Dublin	0	2
16.5.1973	Wroclaw	0	2
21.10.1973	Dublin	1	0
26.5.1976	Posnan	2	0
24.4.1977	Dublin	0	0
12.4.1978	Lodz	0	3
23.5.1981	Bydgoszcz	0	3
23.5.1984	Dublin	0	0
12.11.1986	Warsaw	0	1
22.5.1988	Dublin	3	1

v PORTUGAL

Date	Venue	RI	P
16.6.1946	Lisbon	1	3
4.5.1947	Dublin	0	2
23.5.1948	Lisbon	0	2
22.5.1949	Dublin	1	0
25.6.1972	Recife	1	2

v RUMANIA

Date	Venue	RI	R
23.3.1988	Dublin	2	0

INTERNATIONAL FOOTBALL

v SCOTLAND

Date	Venue	RI	S
3.5.1961	Hampden Pk	1	4†
7.5.1961	Dublin	0	3†
9.6.1963	Dublin	1	0
21.9.1969	Dublin	1	1
15.10.1986	Dublin	0	0*
18.2.1987	Hampden Pk	1	0*

v SPAIN

Date	Venue	RI	S
26.4.1931	Barcelona	1	1
13.12.1931	Dublin	0	5
23.6.1946	Madrid	1	0
2.3.1947	Dublin	3	2
30.5.1948	Barcelona	1	2
12.6.1949	Dublin	1	4
1.6.1952	Madrid	0	6
27.11.1955	Dublin	2	2
11.3.1964	Seville	1	5*
8.4.1964	Dublin	0	2*
5.5.1965	Dublin	1	0†
27.10.1965	Seville	1	4†
10.11.1965	Paris	0	1†
23.10.1966	Dublin	0	0*
7.12.1966	Valencia	0	2*
9.2.1977	Dublin	0	1
17.11.1982	Dublin	3	3*
27.4.1983	Zaragoza	0	2*
26.5.1985	Cork	0	0

v SWEDEN

Date	Venue	RI	S
2.6.1949	Stockholm	1	3†
13.11.1949	Dublin	1	3†
1.11.1959	Dublin	3	2
18.5.1960	Malmo	1	4

14.10.1970	Dublin	1	1*
28.10.1970	Malmo	0	1*

v SWITZERLAND

Date	Venue	RI	S
5.5.1935	Basle	0	1
17.3.1936	Dublin	1	0
17.5.1937	Berne	1	0
18.9.1938	Dublin	4	0
5.12.1948	Dublin	0	1
11.5.1975	Dublin	2	1*
21.5.1975	Berne	0	1*
30.4.1980	Dublin	2	0
11.9.1985	Berne	0	0

v TRINIDAD & TOBAGO

Date	Venue	RI	TT
30.5.1982	Port of Spain	1	2

v TURKEY

Date	Venue	RI	T
16.11.1966	Dublin	2	1*
22.2.1967	Ankara	1	2*
20.11.1974	Izmir	1	1*
29.10.1975	Dublin	4	0*
13.10.1976	Ankara	3	3
5.4.1978	Dublin	4	2

v URUGUAY

Date	Venue	RI	U
8.5.1974	Montevideo	0	2
23.4.1986	Dublin	1	1

v USA

Date	Venue	RI	US
29.10.1979	Dublin	3	2

v USSR

Date	Venue	RI	SU
18.10.1972	Dublin	1	2†
13.5.1973	Moscow	0	1†
30.10.1974	Dublin	3	0*
18.5.1975	Kiev	1	2*
12.9.1984	Dublin	1	0†
16.10.1985	Moscow	0	2†
15.6.1988	Hanover	1	1*

v WALES

Date	Venue	RI	W
28.9.1960	Dublin	2	3
11.9.1979	Swansea	1	2
24.2.1981	Dublin	1	3
26.3.1986	Dublin	0	1

v WEST GERMANY

Date	Venue	RI	WG
17.10.1951	Dublin	3	2
4.5.1952	Cologne	0	3
28.5.1955	Hamburg	1	2
25.11.1956	Dublin	3	0
11.5.1960	Dusseldorf	1	0
4.5.1966	Dublin	0	4
9.5.1970	West Berlin	1	2
22.5.1979	Dublin	1	3
21.5.1981	Bremen	0	3

(v West Germany 'B')

v YUGOSLAVIA

Date	Venue	RI	Y
19.9.1955	Dublin	1	4
27.4.1988	Dublin	2	0

BRITISH & IRISH INTERNATIONAL APPEARANCES

The following list of international appearances includes only those matches recognised by the relevant Football Associations as full internationals. For England and Northern Ireland, the years stated are calendar years, whereas for Scotland, Wales and the Republic of Ireland, the years stated are seasons (e.g. 1988 indicates season 1987-88).

Key: A, Austria; Alb, Albania; Alg, Algeria; Arg, Argentina; Aus, Australia; B, Bohemia; Bel, Belgium; Bra, Brazil; Bul, Bulgaria; Can, Canada; Ch, Chile; Chn, China; Col, Colombia; Cyp, Cyprus; Cz, Czechoslovakia; Den, Denmark; Ec, Ecuador; GDR, East Germany; Eg, Egypt; F, France; Fin, Finland; G, Germany (pre-war): Gr, Greece; H, Hungary; Hon, Honduras; I, Italy; Ic, Iceland; Ir, Iran; Ire, Ireland (pre-1921); Is, Israel; K, Kuwait; Lux, Luxembourg; Mex, Mexico; Ma, Malta; Mor, Morocco; Neth, Netherlands; Nor, Norway; NI, Northern Ireland; NZ, New Zealand; P, Portugal; Par, Paraguay; Pe, Peru; Pol, Poland; Rum, Rumania; RI, Republic of Ireland; EUR, Rest of Europe; WXI, Rest of World XI; S. Ar, Saudi Arabia; S, Scotland; Sp, Spain; Swe, Sweden; Swz, Switzerland; T, Turkey; TT, Trinidad & Tobago; U, Uruguay; UK, Rest of United Kingdom; USA, United States of America; USSR; W, Wales; FRG, West Germany, Y, Yugoslavia.

Includes matches to end of June 1988.

ENGLAND

Abbott, W. (1) (Everton), 1902 v W

A'Court, A. (5) (Liverpool), 1957 v NI; 1958 v Bra, A, USSR; 1959 v W

Adams, T. A. (14) (Arsenal), 1987 v Sp, T, Bra, FRG, T, Y; 1988 v Neth, H, S, Col, Swz, RI, Neth, USSR

Adcock, H. (5) (Leicester C), 1929 v F, Bel, Sp, NI, W

Alcock, C. W. (1) (Wanderers), 1875 v S

Alderson, J. T. (1) (C Palace), 1923 v F

Aldridge, A, (2) (WBA), 1888 v Ire; (Walsall Town Swifts), 1889 v Ire

Allen, A. (3) (Stoke C) 1959 v W, Swe, NI

Allen, A. (1) (Aston Villa), 1888 v Ire

Allen, C. (5) (QPR), 1984 v Bra, U, Ch; (Tottenham H), 1987 v T; 1988 v Is

Allen, H. (5) (Wolverhampton W), 1888 v S, W, Ire; 1889 v S; 1890 v S

Allen, J. P. (2) (Portsmouth), 1933 v NI, W

Allen, R, (5) (WBA), 1952 v Swz; 1954 v Y, S, FRG, W

Alsford, W. J. (1) (Tottenham H), 1935 v S

Amos, A. (2) (Old Carthusians), 1885 v S; 1886 v W

Anderson, R. D. (1) (Old Etonians), 1879 v W

Anderson, S. (2) (Sunderland), 1962 v A, S

Anderson, V. (30) (Nottingham F), 1978 v Cz; 1979 v Swe, Bul; 1980 v Sp, Nor, Rum; 1981 v W, S; 1982 v NI, Ic; 1984 v NI, (Arsenal) T; 1985 v NI, RI, Rum, Fin, S, Mex, USA; 1986 v USSR, Mex, Swe, NI, Y; 1987 v Sp, NI, T, (Manchester U) FRG; 1988 v H, Col

Angus, J. (1) (Burnley), 1961 v A

Armfield, J. C. (43) (Blackpool), 1959 v Bra, Pe, Mex, USA; 1960 v S, Y, Sp, H, NI, Lux, Sp, W; 1961 v S, Mex, P, I, A, Lux, W, P, NI; 1962 v A, S, Swz, Pe, H, Arg, Bul, Bra, F, NI, W; 1963 v F, S, Bra, GDR, Swz, W, WXI, NI; 1964 v S; 1966 v Y, Fin

Armitage, G. H. (1) (Charlton Ath), 1925 v NI

Armstrong, D. (3) (Middlesbrough), 1980 v Aus; (Southampton), 1982 v FRG; 1984 v W

Armstrong, K. (1) (Chelsea), 1955 v S

Arnold, J. (1) (Fulham), 1933 v S

Arthur, J. W. H. (7) (Blackburn R), 1885 v S, W, Ire; 1886 v S, W; 1887 v W, Ire

Ashcroft, J. (3) (Woolwich Arsenal), 1906 v Ire, W, S

Ashmore, G. S. (1) (WBA), 1926 v Bel

Ashton, C. T. (1) (Corinthians), 1925 v NI

Ashurst, W. (5) (Notts Co), 1923 v Swe, Swe; 1924 v Bel; 1925 v W, S

Astall, G. (2) (Birmingham C), 1956 v Fin, FRG

Astle, J. (5) (WBA), 1969 v W; 1969 v P; 1970 v S, Bra, Cz

Aston, J. (17) (Manchester U), 1948 v Den, W, Swz; 1949 v S, Swe, Nor, F, RI, W, NI, I; 1950 v S, P, Bel, Ch, USA, NI

Athersmith, W. C. (12) (Aston Villa), 1892 v Ire, 1897 v S, W, Ire; 1898 v S, W, Ire; 1899 v S, W, Ire; 1900 v S, W

Atyeo, P. J. W. (6) (Bristol C), 1955 v Sp; 1956 v Bra, Swe, Den; 1957 v RI, RI

Austin, S. W. (1) (Manchester C), 1925 v NI

Bach, P. (1) (Sunderland), 1899 v Ire

Bache, J. W. (7) (Aston Villa), 1903 v W; 1904 v W, Ire; 1905 v S; 1907 v Ire; 1910 v Ire; 1911 v S

Baddeley, T. (5) (Wolverhampton W), 1903 v S, Ire; 1904 v S, W, Ire

Bagshaw, J. J. (1) Derby Co), 1919 v Ire

Bailey, G. R. (2) (Manchester U), 1985 v RI, Mex

Bailey, H. P. (5) (Leicester Fosse), 1908 v W, A (2), H, B

Bailey, M. A. (2) (Charlton Ath), 1964 v USA, W

Bailey, N. C. (19) (Clapham Rovers), 1878 v S; 1879 v S, W; 1880 v S; 1881 v S; 1882 v S, W; 1883 v S, W; 1884 v S, W, Ire; 1885 v S, W, Ire; 1886 v S, W; 1887 v S, W

Baily, E. F. (9) (Tottenham H), 1950 v Sp, Y, NI, W; 1951 v A, W; 1952 v A, Swz, NI

Bain, J. (1) (Oxford University), 1887 v S

Baker, A (1) (Arsenal), 1927 v W

Baker, B. H. (2) (Everton), 1921 v Bel; (Chelsea), 1925 v NI

Baker, J. H. (8) (Hibernian), 1959 v NI; 1960 v S, Y, Sp, H; (Arsenal), 1965 v Sp, NI; 1966 v Pol

Ball, A. J. (72) (Blackpool), 1965 v Y, FRG, Swe, Sp; 1966 v Pol, FRG, S, Fin, Den, Pol, (Everton) U, Arg, P, FRG, NI, Cz, W; 1967 v S, Sp, A, W, USSR; 1968 v S, Sp, Sp, FRG, Y, Rum; 1969 v Rum, NI, W, S, Mex, U, Bra, P; 1970 v Bel, W, S, Col, Ec, Rum, Bra, Cz, FRG, GDR; 1971 v Ma, Gr, Ma, NI, S, Swz, Gr; (Arsenal) 1972 v FRG, FRG, S, Y, W; 1973 v W, S, NI, W, S, Cz, Pol; 1974 v P; 1975 v FRG, Cyp, Cyp, NI, W, S

Ball, J. (1) (Bury), 1927 v NI

Balmer, W. (1) (Everton), 1905 v Ire

Bamber, J. (1) (Liverpool), 1921 v W

Bambridge, A. L. (3) (Swifts), 1881 v W; 1883 v W; 1884 v Ire

Bambridge, E. C. (18) (Swifts), 1879 v S; 1880 v S; 1881 v S; 1882 v S, W, Ire; 1883 v W; 1884 v S, W, Ire; 1885 v S, W, Ire; 1886 v S, W; 1887 v S, W, Ire

Bambridge, E. H. (1) (Swifts), 1876 v S

Banks, G. (73) (Leicester C), 1963 v S, Bra, Cz, GDR, W, WXI, NI; 1964 v S, U, P, USA, P, Arg, NI; 1965 v S, H, Y, FRG, Swe, NI, Sp; 1966 v Pol, FRG, S, Y, Fin, Pol, U, Mex, F, Arg, P, FRG, NI, Cz, W; 1967 v S, W, NI, USSR; 1968 v S, Sp, FRG, Y, USSR, Rum; 1969 v Rum, F, NI, S, U, Bra; 1970 v Neth, Bel, W, NI, S, Col, Ec, Rum, Bra, Cz, FRG; 1971 v Ma, Gr, Ma, NI, S, Swz, Gr; 1972 v FRG, FRG, W, S

Banks, H. E. (1) (Millwall), 1901 v Ire

Banks, T. (6) (Bolton W), 1958 v USSR, USSR, Bra, A, USSR, NI

Bannister, W. (2) (Burnley), 1901 v W; (Bolton W), 1902 v Ire

Barclay, R. (3) (Sheffield W), 1932 v S, NI; 1936 v S

Barham, M. (2) (Norwich C), 1983 v Aus, Aus

Barkas, S. (5) (Manchester C), 1936 v Bel; 1937 v S, W, NI, Cz

Barker, J. (11) (Derby Co), 1934 v W, I; 1935 v NI, S, Neth, NI, G; 1936 v W, S, A, W

Barker, R. (1) (Herts Rangers), 1872 v S

Barker, R. R. (1) (Casuals), 1895 v W

Barlow, R. J. (1) (WBA), 1954 v NI

Barnes, J. C. B. (42) (Watford), 1983 v NI, Aus, Aus, Aus, Den, Lux; 1984 v F, S, USSR, Bra, U, Ch, GDR, Fin, T; 1985 v NI, Rum, Fin, S, I, Mex, FRG, USA, Rum; 1986 v Is, Mex, Can, Arg, Swe; 1987 v T, Bra, (Liverpool) FRG, T, Y; 1988 v Is, Neth, S, Col, Swz, RI, Neth, USSR

Barnes, P. S. (22) (Manchester C), 1977 v I; 1978 v FRG, Bra, W, S, H, Den, RI, Cz; 1979 v NI, NI, S, Bul, A, (WBA) Den; 1980 v W; 1981 v Sp, Bra, W, Swz, (Leeds U) Nor; 1982 v Neth

Barnet, H. H. (1) (Royal Engineers), 1882 v NI

Barrass, M. W. (3) (Bolton W), 1951 v W, NI; 1953 v S

Barrett, A. F. (1) (Fulham), 1929 v NI

Barrett, J. W. (1) (West Ham U), 1928 v NI

Barry, L. (5) (Leicester C), 1928 v F, Bel; 1929 v F, Bel, Sp

Barson, F. (1) (Aston Villa), 1920 v W

Barton, J. (1) (Blackburn R), 1890 v Ire

Barton, P. H. (7) (Birmingham), 1921 v Bel, NI; 1923 v F, Bel; 1924 v W, S, NI

Bassett, W. I. (16) (WBA), 1888 v Ire; 1889 v S, W; 1890 v S, W; 1891 v S, Ire; 1892 v S; 1893 v S, W; 1894 v S; 1895 v S, Ire; 1896 v S, W, Ire

Bastard, S. R. (1) (Upton Park), 1880 v S

Bastin, C. S. (21) (Arsenal), 1931 v W; 1932 v I; 1933 v Swz, NI, W; 1934 v S, H, Cz, I; 1935 v S, NI, G; 1936 v S, W, A, W, NI; 1938 v S, G, Swz, F

Baugh, R. (2) (Stafford Road), 1886 v Ire; (Wolverhampton W) 1890 v Ire

Bayliss, A. E. J. M. (1) (WBA), 1891 v Ire

Baynham R. L. (3) (Luton T), 1955 v Den, NI, Sp

Beardsley, P. A. (26) (Newcastle U), 1986 v Eg, Is,

USSR, Mex, Can, P, Pol, Par, Arg, NI, Y; 1987 v Sp, Bra, S, (Liverpool) FRG, T, Y; 1988 v Is, Neth, H, S, Col, Swz, RI, Neth

Beasley, A. (1) (Huddersfield T), 1939 v S

Beats, W. E. (2) (Wolverhampton W), 1901 v W; 1902 v S

Beattie, T. K. (9) (Ipswich T), 1975 v Cyp, Cyp, S, Swz, P; 1976 v Fin, I; 1977 v Neth, Lux

Becton, F. (2) (Preston NE), 1895 v Ire; (Liverpool), 1897 v W

Bedford, H. (2) (Blackpool), 1923 v Swe; 1924 v NI

Bell, C. (48) (Manchester C), 1968 v Swe, FRG, Bul; 1969 v F, W, U, Bra, Neth, P; 1970 v Neth, NI, Bra, Cz, FRG; 1971 v Gr; 1972 v FRG, FRG, W, NI, S, Y, W; 1973 v W, S, NI, W, S, Cz, Pol, A, Pol, I; 1974 v W, NI, S, Arg, GDR, Bul, Y, Cz, P; 1975 v FRG, Cyp, Cyp, NI, S, Swz, Cz

Bennett, W. (2) (Sheffield U), 1901 v S, W

Benson, R. W. (1) (Sheffield U), 1913 v Ire

Bentley, R. T. F. (12) (Chelsea), 1949 v Swe; 1950 v S, P, Bel, Ch, USA; 1952 v W, Bel; 1954 v W, FRG; 1955 v Sp, P

Beresford, J. (1) (Aston Villa), 1934 v Cz

Berry, A. (1) (Oxford University), 1909 v Ire

Berry, J. J. (4) (Manchester U), 1953 v Arg, Ch, U; 1956 v Swe

Bestall, J. G. (1) (Grimsby T), 1935 v NI

Betmead, H. A. (1) (Grimsby T), 1937 v Fin

Betts, M. P. (1) (Old Harrovians), 1877 v S

Betts, W. (1) (Sheffield W), 1889 v W

Beverley, J. (3) (Blackburn R), 1884 v S, W, Ire

Birkett, R. H. (1) (Clapham Rovers), 1879 v S

Birkett, R. J. E. (1) (Middlesbrough), 1935 v NI

Birley, F. H. (2) (Oxford University), 1874 v S; (Wanderers), 1875 v S

Birtles, G. (3) (Nottingham F), 1980 v Arg, I, Rum

Bishop, S. M. (4) (Leicester C), 1927 v S, Bel, Lux, F

Blackburn, F. (3) (Blackburn R), 1901 v S; 1902 v Ire; 1904 v S

Blackburn, G. F. (1) (Aston Villa), 1924 v F

Blenkinsop, E. (26) (Sheffield W), 1928 v F, Bel, NI, W; 1929 v S, F, Bel, Sp, NI, W; 1930 v S, G, A, NI, W; 1931 v S, F, Bel, NI, W, Sp; 1932 v S, NI, W, A; 1933 v S

Bliss, H. (1) (Tottenham H), 1921 v S

Blissett, L. (14) (Watford), 1982 v FRG, Lux; 1983 v W, Gr, H, NI, S, Aus, Aus, (AC Milan) Den, H; 1984 v W, S, USSR

Blockley, J. P. (1) (Arsenal), 1972 v Y

Bloomer, S. (23) (Derby Co), 1895 v S, Ire; 1896 v W, Ire; 1897 v S, W, Ire; 1898 v S; 1899 v S, W, Ire; 1900 v S; 1901 v S, W; 1902 v S, W, Ire; 1904 v S; 1905 v S, W, Ire; (Middlesbrough), 1907 v S, W

Blunstone, F. (5) (Chelsea), 1954 v W; 1955 v S, F, P; 1956 v Y

Bond, R. (8) (Preston NE), 1905 v Ire, W; 1906 v S, W, Ire; (Bradford C), 1910 v S, W, Ire

Bonetti, P. P. (7) (Chelsea), 1966 v Den; 1967 v Sp, A; 1968 v Sp; 1969 v Neth, P; 1970 v FRG

Bonsor, A. G. (2) (Wanderers), 1873 v S; 1875 v S

Booth, F. (1) (Manchester C), 1905 v Ire

Booth, T. (2) (Blackburn R), 1898 v W; (Everton), 1903 v S

Bowden, E. R. (6) (Arsenal), 1934 v W, I; 1935 v NI; 1936 v W, A, H

Bower, A. G. (5) (Corinthians), 1923 v NI, Bel; 1924 v Bel; 1925 v W; 1927 v W

Bowers, J. W. (3) (Derby Co), 1933 v NI, W; 1934 v S

Bowles, S. (5) (QPR), 1974 v P, W, NI; 1976 v I; 1977 v Neth

Bowser, S. (1) (WBA), 1919 v Ire

Boyer, P. J. (1) (Norwich C), 1976 v W

Boyes, W. (3) (WBA), 1935 v Neth; (Everton), 1938 v W, WXI

Boyle, T. W. (1) (Burnley), 1913 v Ire

Brabrook, P. (3) (Chelsea), 1958 v USSR; 1958 v NI; 1960 v Sp

Bracewell, P. W. (3) (Everton), 1985 v FRG, USA, NI

Bradford, G. R. W. (1) (Bristol R), 1955 v Den

Bradford, J. (12) (Birmingham), 1923 v NI; 1924 v Bel; 1928 v S, NI, W; 1929 v F, Sp, NI; 1930 v S, G, A, W

Bradley, W. (3) (Manchester U), 1959 v I, Mex, USA

Bradshaw, F. (1) (Sheffield W), 1908 v A

Bradshaw, T. H. (1) (Liverpool), 1897 v Ire

Bradshaw, W. (4) (Blackburn R), 1910 v W, Ire; 1912 v Ire; 1913 v W

Brann, G. (3) (Swifts), 1886 v S, W; 1891 v W

Brawn, W. F. (2) (Aston Villa), 1904 v W, Ire

Bray, J. (6) (Manchester C), 1934 v W; 1935 v NI, G; 1936 v W, S; 1937 v S

Brayshaw, E. (1) (Sheffield W), 1887 v Ire

Bridges, B. J. (4) (Chelsea), 1965 v S, H, Y, A

Bridgett, A. (11) (Sunderland), 1905 v S; 1908 v S, A, A, H, B; 1909 v Ire, W, H, H, A

Brindle, T. (2) (Darwen), 1880 v S, W

Brittleton, J. T. (5) (Sheffield W), 1912 v S, W, Ire; 1913 v S, 1914 v W

Britton, C. S. (9) (Everton), 1934 v W, I; 1935 v S, NI; 1936 v NI, H; 1937 v S, Nor, Swe

Broadbent, P. F. (7) (Wolverhampton W), 1958 v USSR, W, NI; 1959 v S, I, Bra; 1960 v S

Broadis, I. A. (14) (Manchester C), 1951 v A; 1952 v S, I; 1953 v S, Arg, Ch, U, USA, (Newcastle U), 1954 v S, Y, H, Bel, Swz, U

Brockbank, J. (1) (Cambridge University), 1872 v S

Brodie, J. B. (3) (Wolverhampton W), 1889 v S, Ire; 1891 v Ire

Bromilow, T. G. (5) (Liverpool), 1921 v W; 1922 v S, W; 1923 v Bel; 1925 v NI

Bromley-Davenport, W. E. (2) (Oxford University), 1884 v S, W

Brook, E. F. (18) (Manchester C), 1929 v NI; 1933 v Swz, NI, W, F; 1934 v S, H, Cz, W, I; 1935 v NI, S, NI; 1936 v W, S, H; 1937 v NI, W

Brooking, T. D. (47) (West Ham U), 1974 v P, Arg, GDR, Bul, Y, Cz, P; 1975 v P; 1976 v W, Bra, I, Fin, RI, Fin, I; 1977 v Neth, NI, W, I; 1978 v FRG, W, S, H, Den, RI; 1979 v NI, W, S, Bul, Swe, A, Den, NI; 1980 v Arg, W, NI, S, Bel, Sp, Swz; 1981 v Sp, Rum, H, H; 1982 v S, Fin, Sp

Brooks, J. (3) (Tottenham H), 1956 v W, Y, Den

Broome, F. H. (7) (Aston Villa), 1938 v G, Swz, F, Nor; 1939 v I, Y, Rum

Brown, A, (3) (Aston Villa), 1882 v S, W, Ire

Brown, A. (1) (WBA), 1971 v W

Brown, A. S. (2) (Sheffield U), 1904 v W; 1906 v Ire

Brown, G. (9) (Huddersfield T), 1926 v NI; 1927 v W, S, Bel, Lux, F, W; 1929 v S; (Aston Villa), 1932 v W

Brown, J. (5) (Blackburn R), 1881 v W; 1882 v Ire; 1885 v S, W, Ire

Brown, J. H. (6) (Sheffield W), 1927 v W, S, Bel, Lux, F; 1929 v NI

Brown, K. (1) (West Ham U), 1959 v NI

Brown, W. (1) (West Ham U), 1923 v Bel

Bruton, J. (3) (Burnley), 1928 v F, Bel; 1929 v S

Bryant, W. I. (1) (Clapton); 1925 v F

Buchan, C. M. (6) Sunderland), 1913 v Ire; 1920 v W; 1921 v W, Bel; 1923 v F; 1924 v S

Buchanan, W. S. (1) (Clapham Rovers), 1876 v S

Buckley, F. C. (1) (Derby Co), 1914 v Ire

Bullock, F. E. (1) (Huddersfield T), 1920 v Ire

Bullock, N. (3) (Bury), 1923 v Bel; 1926 v W, NI

Burgess, H. (4) (Manchester C), 1904 v S, W, Ire; 1906 v S

Burgess, H. (4) (Sheffield W), 1930 v NI; 1931 v S, F, Bel

Burnup, C. J. (1) (Cambridge University), 1896 v S

Burrows, H. (3) (Sheffield W), 1934 v H, Cz; 1935 v Neth

Burton, F. E. (1) (Nottingham F), 1889 v Ire

Bury, L. (2) (Cambridge University), 1877 v S; (Old Etonians), 1879 v W

Butcher, T. (54) (Ipswich T), 1980 v Aus; 1981 v Sp; 1982 v W, S, F, Cz, FRG, Sp, Den, FRG, Lux; 1983 v W, Gr, H, NI, S, Aus, Aus, Aus, Den, H, Lux; 1984 v F, NI, GDR, Fin, T; 1985 v NI, RI, Rum, Fin, S, I, FRG, USA, 1986 v Is, USSR, S, Mex, Can, P, Mor, Pol, Par, Arg, (Rangers), Swe, NI, Y; 1987 v Sp, NI, Bra, S, T, Y

Butler, J. D. (1) (Arsenal), 1924 v Bel

Butler, W. (1) (Bolton W), 1924 v S

Byrne, G. (2) (Liverpool), 1963 v S, 1966 v Nor

Byrne, J. J. (11) (C Palace), 1961 v NI; (West Ham U), 1963 v Swz; 1964 v S, U, P, RI, Bra, P, Arg, W; 1965 v S

Byrne, R. W. (33) (Manchester U), 1954 v S, Y, H, Bel, Swz, U, NI, W, FRG; 1955 v S, F, Sp, P, Den, W, NI, Sp; 1956 v S, Bra, Swe, Fin, FRG, NI, W, Y, Den; 1957 v S, RI, Den, RI, W, NI, F

Callaghan, I. R. (4) (Liverpool), 1966 v Fin, F; 1977 v Swz, Lux

Calvey, J. (1) (Nottingham F), 1902 v Ire

Campbell, A. F. (8) (Blackburn R), 1928 v NI, W; (Huddersfield T), 1930 v NI, W; 1931 v S, NI, W, Sp

Camsell, G. H. (9) (Middlesbrough), 1929 v F, Bel, NI, W; 1933 v F; 1935 v G; 1936 v S, A, Bel

Capes, A. I. (1) (Stoke C), 1903 v S

Carr, J. (2) (Middlesbrough), 1919 v Ire; 1923 v W

Carr, J. (2) (Newcastle U), 1905 v Ire; 1907 v Ire

Carr, W. H. (1) (Owlerton, Sheffield), 1875 v S

Carter, H. S. (13) (Sunderland), 1934 v S, H; 1935 v G; 1936 v NI, H; 1937 v S; (Derby Co), 1946 v NI, RI, W, Neth; 1947 v S, F, Swz

Carter, J. H. (3) (WBA), 1926 v Bel; 1929 v Bel, Sp

Catlin, A. E. (5) (Sheffield W), 1936 v W, NI, H; 1937 v Nor, Swe

Chadwick, A. (2) (Southampton), 1900 v S, W

Chadwick, E. (7) (Everton), 1891 v S, W; 1892 v S; 1893 v S; 1894 v S; 1896 v Ire; 1897 v S

Chamberlain, M. (8) (Stoke C), 1982 v Lux; 1983 v Den; 1984 v S, USSR, Bra, U, Ch; 1984 v Fin

Chambers, H. (8) (Liverpool), 1921 v W, S, Bel; 1922 v NI; 1923 v W, Bel, S, NI

Channon, M. R. (46) (Southampton), 1972 v Y; 1973 v S, NI, W, S, Cz, USSR, I, A, Pol, I; 1974 v P, W, NI, S, Arg, GDR, Bul, Y, Cz, P; 1975 v FRG, Cyp, Cyp, NI, W, S, Swz, Cz, P; 1976 v W, NI, S, Bra, I, Fin, Fin, I; 1977 v Lux, NI, W, S, Bra, Arg, U, (Manchester C), Swz

Charlton, J. (35) (Leeds U), 1965 v S, H, Y, FRG, Swe, W, A, NI, Sp; 1966 v Pol, FRG, S, Y, Fin, Den, Pol, U, Mex, F, Arg, P, FRG, NI, Cz, W; 1967 v S, W, Sp; 1969 v Rum, F, W, Neth, P; 1970 v Neth, Cz

Charlton, R. (106) (Manchester U), 1958 v S, P, Y, NI, USSR, W; 1959 v S, I, Bra, Pe, Mex, USA, W, Swe; 1960 v S, Y, Sp, H, NI, Lux, Sp, W; 1961 v S, Mex, P, I, A, Lux, W, P, NI; 1962 v A, S, Swz, Pe, H, Arg, Bul, Bra; 1963 v F, S, Bra, Cz, GDR, Swz, W, WXI, NI; 1964 v S, U, P, RI, USA, Bra, Arg, NI, Neth; 1965 v S, W, A, NI, Sp; 1966 v FRG, S, Y, Fin, Nor, Pol, U, Mex, F, Arg, P, FRG, NI, CZ, W; 1967 v S, W, NI, USSR; 1968 v S, Sp, Sp, Swe, Y, USSR, Rum, Bul; 1969 v Rum, NI, W, S, Mex, Bra, Neth, P; 1970 v Neth, W, NI, Col, Ec, Rum, Bra, Cz, FRG

Charnley, R. O. (1) (Blackpool), 1963 v F

Charsley, C. C. (1) (Small Heath), 1893 v Ire

Chedgzoy, S. (8) (Everton), 1920 v W, Ire; 1921 v W, S, NI; 1923 v S; 1924 v W, NI

Chenery, C. J. (3) (C Palace), 1872 v S; 1873 v S; 1874 v S

Cherry, T. J. (27) (Leeds U), 1976 v W, S, Bra, Fin, RI, I; 1977 v Lux, NI, S, Bra, Arg, U, Swz, Lux, I; 1978 v Bra, W, Cz; 1979 v W, Swe; 1980 v RI, Arg, W, NI, S, Aus, Sp

Chilton, A. (2) (Manchester U), 1950 v NI; 1951 v F

Chippendale, H. (1) (Blackburn R), 1894 v Ire

Chivers, M. (24) (Tottenham H), 1971 v Ma, Gr, Ma, NI, S, Swz, Swz, Gr; 1972 v FRG, FRG, NI, S, W; 1973 v W, S, NI, W, S, Cz, Pol, USSR, I, A, Pol

Christian, E, (1) (Old Etonians), 1879 v S

Clamp, E. (4) (Wolverhampton W), 1958 v USSR, USSR, Bra, A

Clapton, D. R. (1) (Arsenal), 1958 v W

Clare, T. (4) (Stoke C), 1889 v Ire; 1892 v Ire; 1893 v W; 1894 v S

Clarke, A. J. (19) (Leeds U), 1970 v Cz, GDR; 1971 v Ma, NI, W, S; 1973 v S, W, S, Cz, Pol, USSR, I, A, Pol, I; 1974 v P; 1975 v Cz, P

Clarke, H. A. (1) (Tottenham H), 1954 v S

Clay, T. (4) (Tottenham H), 1920 v W; 1921 v Ire; 1922 v W, S

Clayton, R. (35) (Blackburn R), 1955 v NI, Sp; 1956 v Bra, Swe, Fin, FRG, NI, W, Y, Den; 1957 v S, RI, Den, RI, W, NI, F; 1958 v S, P, Y, USSR, NI, USSR, W; 1959 v S, I, Bra, Pe, Mex, USA, W, Swe, NI; 1960 v S, Y

Clegg, J. C. (1) (Sheffield W), 1872 v S

Clegg, W. E. (2) (Sheffield W), 1873 v S; (Sheffield Albion), 1879 v W

Clemence, R. N. (61) (Liverpool), 1972 v W; 1973 v W; 1974 v GDR, Bul, Y, Cz, P; 1975 v FRG, Cyp, NI, W, S, Swz, CZ, P; 1976 v W, W, NI, S, Bra, Fin, RI, Fin, I; 1977 v Neth, Lux, S, Bra, Arg, U, Swz, Lux, I; 1978 v FRG, NI, S, Den, RI; 1979 v NI, NI, S, Bul, A, Den, Bul; 1980 v RI, Arg, W, S, Bel, Sp, Rum; 1981 v Sp, Bra, Swz, H, (Tottenham H) Nor; 1982 v NI, Fin, Lux; 1983 v Lux

Clement, D. T. (5) (QPR), 1976 v W, W, I; 1976 v I; 1977 v Neth

Clough, B. H. (2) (Middlesbrough), 1959 v W, Swe

Coates, R. (4) (Burnley), 1970 v NI; 1971 v Gr; (Tottenham H), Ma, W

Cobbold, W. N. (9) (Cambridge University), 1883 v S, Ire; 1885 v S, Ire; 1886 v S, W; (Old Carthusians), 1887 v S, W, Ire

Cock, J. G. (2) (Huddersfield T), 1919 v Ire; (Chelsea) 1920 v S

Cockburn, H. (13) (Manchester U), 1946 v NI, RI, W; 1948 v S, I; 1948 v Den, NI, Swz; 1949 v S, Swe; 1951 v Arg, P; 1951 v F

Cohen, G. R. (37) (Fulham), 1964 v U, P, RI, USA, Bra, NI, Bel, W, Neth; 1965 v S, H, Y, FRG, Swe, W, A, NI, Sp; 1966 v Pol, FRG, S, Nor, Den, Pol, U, Mex, F, Arg, P, FRG, NI, Cz, W; 1967 v S, Sp, W, NI

Coleclough, H. (1) (C Palace), 1914 v W

Coleman, E. H. (1) (Dulwich Hamlet), 1921 v W

Coleman, J. (1) (Woolwich Arsenal), 1907 v Ire

Common, A. (3) (Sheffield U), 1904 v W, Ire; (Middlesbrough), 1906 v W

Compton, L. H. (2) (Arsenal), 1950 v W, Y

Conlin, J. (1) (Bradford C), 1906 v S

Connelly, J. M. (20) (Burnley), 1959 v W, Swe, NI; 1960 v S; 1961 v W, P; 1962 v A, Swz, W; 1963 v F; (Manchester U), 1965 v H, Y, Swe, W, A, NI; 1966 v S, Nor, Den, U

Cook, T. E. R. (1) (Brighton), 1925 v W

Cooper, N. C. (1) (Cambridge University), 1893 v Ire

Cooper, T. (15) (Derby Co); 1927 v NI; 1928 v NI, W; 1929 v S, F, Bel, Sp; 1931 v F; 1931 v W, Sp; 1933 v S; 1934 v S, H, Cz; 1934 v W

Cooper, T. (20) (Leeds U), 1969 v F, W, S, Mex; 1970 v Neth, Bel, Col, Ec, Rum, Bra, Cz, FRG, GDR; 1971 v Ma, NI, W, S, Swz, Swz; 1974 v P

Coppell, S. J. (42) (Manchester U), 1977 v I; 1978 v FRG, Bra, W, NI, S, H, Den, RI, Cz; 1979 v NI, NI, W, S, Bul, A, Den, NI; 1980 v RI, Sp, Arg, W, S, Bel, I, Rum, Swz; 1981 v Rum, Bra, W, S, Swz, H, H; 1982 v S, Fin, F, Cz, K, FRG, Lux; 1983 v Gr

Copping, W. (20) (Leeds U), 1933 v I, Swz, NI, W, F; 1934 v S, I; (Arsenal), 1935 v NI; 1936 v A, Bel; 1937 v Nor, Swe, Fin, NI, W, Cz; 1938 v S, W, EUR; 1939 (LeedsU), Rum

Corbett, B. O. (1) (Corinthians), 1901 v W

Corbett, R. (1) (Old Malvernians), 1903 v W

Corbett, W. S. (3) (Birmingham), 1908 v A, H, B

Corrigan, J. T. (9) (Manchester C), 1976 v I; 1978 v Bra; 1979 v W; 1980 v NI, Aus; 1981 v W, S; 1982 v W, Ic

Cottee, A. R. (3) (West Ham U), 1986 v Swe, NI; 1988 v H

Cotterill, G. H. (4) (Cambridge University), 1891 v Ire; (Old Brightonians), 1892 v W; 1893 v S, Ire
Cottle, J. R. (1) (Bristol C), 1909 v Ire
Cowan, S. (3) (Manchester C), 1926 v Bel; 1930 v A; 1931 v Bel
Cowans, G. (9) (Aston Villa), 1983 v W, H, NI, S, Aus, Aus, Aus; (Bari), 1986 v Eg, USSR
Cowell, A. (1) (Blackburn R), 1910 v Ire
Cox, J. (3) (Liverpool), 1901 v Ire; 1902 v S; 1903 v S
Cox, J. D. (1) (Derby Co), 1892 v Ire
Crabtree, J. W. (14) (Burnley), 1894 v Ire; 1895 v Ire, S; (Aston Villa), 1896 v W, S, Ire; 1899 v S, W, Ire; 1900 v S, W, Ire; 1901 v W; 1902 v W
Crawford, J. F. (1) (Chelsea), 1931 v S
Crawford, R. (2) (Ipswich T), 1961 v NI; 1962 v A
Crawshaw, T. H. (10) (Sheffield W), 1895 v Ire; 1896 v S, W, Ire; 1897 v S, W, Ire; 1901 v Ire; 1904 v W, Ire
Crayston, W. J. (8) (Arsenal), 1935 v G; 1936 v W, S, A, Bel; 1937 v NI, W, Cz
Creek, F. N. S. (1) (Corinthians), 1923 v F
Cresswell, W. (7) (South Shields), 1921 v W; (Sunderland), 1923 v F; 1923 v Bel; 1924 v NI; 1926 v W, NI; (Everton), 1929 v NI
Crompton, R. (41) (Blackburn R), 1902 v S, W, Ire; 1903 v S, W; 1904 v S, W, Ire; 1906 v S, W, Ire; 1907 v S, W, Ire; 1908 v S, W, Ire, A (2), H, B; 1909 v S, W, Ire, H (2), A; 1910 v S, W; 1911 v S, W, Ire; 1912 v S, W, Ire; 1913 v S, W, Ire; 1914 v S, W, Ire
Crooks, S. D. (26) (Derby Co), 1930 v S, G, A, NI, W; 1931 v S, F, Bel, NI, W, Sp; 1932 v S, NI, W, A; 1933 v NI, W, F; 1934 v S, H, Cz; 1935 v NI; 1936 v W, S, W, H
Crowe, C. (1) (Wolverhampton W), 1962 v F
Cuggy, F. (2) (Sunderland), 1913 v Ire; 1914 v Ire
Cullis, S. (12) (Wolverhampton W), 1937 v NI, W, Cz; 1938 v S, F, EUR, Nor, NI; 1939 v S, I, Y, Rum
Cunliffe, A. (2) (Blackburn R), 1932 v NI, W
Cunliffe, D. (1) (Portsmouth), 1900 v Ire
Cunliffe, J. N. (1) (Everton), 1936 v Bel
Cunningham, L. (6) (WBA), 1979 v W, Swe, A; (Real Madrid), 1980 v RI, Sp; 1980 v Rum
Currey, E. S. (2) (Oxford University), 1890 v S, W
Currie, A. W. (17) (Sheffield U), 1972 v NI; 1973 v USSR, I, A, Pol, I; 1976 v Swz; (Leeds U), 1978 v Bra, W, NI, S, H, Cz; 1979 v NI, NI, W, Swe
Cursham, A. W. (6) (Notts Co), 1876 v S; 1877 v S; 1878 v S; 1879 v W; 1883 v S, W
Cursham, H. A. (8) (Notts Co), 1880 v W; 1882 v S, W, Ire; 1883 v S, W, Ire; 1884 v Ire

Daft, H. B. (5) (Notts Co), 1889 v Ire; 1890 v S, W; 1891 v Ire; 1892 v Ire
Danks, T. (1) (Nottingham F), 1885 v S
Davenport, P. (1) (Nottingham F), 1985 v RI
Davenport, J. K. (2) (Bolton W), 1885 v W; 1890 v Ire
Davis, G. (2) (Derby Co), 1904 v W, Ire
Davis, H. (3) (Sheffield W), 1903 v S, W, Ire
Davison, J. E. (1) (Sheffield W), 1922 v W
Dawson, J. (2) (Burnley), 1921 v Ire, 1922 v S
Day, S. H. (3) (Old Malvernians), 1906 v Ire, W, S
Dean, W. R. (16) (Everton), 1927 v W, S, Bel, Lux, F, W, NI; 1928 v S, F, Bel, NI, W; 1929 v S; 1931 v S, Sp; 1932 v NI

Deeley, N. V. (2) (Wolverhampton W), 1959 v Bra, Pe
Devey, J. H. G. (2) (Aston Villa), 1892 v Ire, 1894 v Ire
Devonshire, A. (8) (West Ham U), 1980 v NI, Aus; 1982 v Neth, Ic, FRG; 1983 v W, Gr, Lux
Dewhurst, F. (9) (Preston NE), 1886 v W, Ire; 1887 v S, W, Ire; 1888 v S, W, Ire; 1889 v W
Dewhurst, G. P. (1) (Liverpool Ramblers), 1895 v W
Dickinson, J. W. (48) (Portsmouth), 1949 v Nor, F, RI, W; 1950 v S, P, Bel, Ch, USA, Sp, NI, W, Y; 1951 v W, NI, A; 1952 v S, I, A, Swz, NI, W, Bel; 1953 v S, Arg, Ch, U, USA, W, EUR, NI, H; 1954 v S, Y, H, Bel, Swz, U; 1955 v Sp, P, Den, W, NI, Sp; 1956 v S, W, Y, Den
Dimmock, J. H. (3) (Tottenham H), 1921 v S; 1926 v W, Bel
Ditchburn, E. G. (6) (Tottenham H), 1948 v Swz; 1949 v Swe; 1953 v USA; 1956 v W, Y, Den
Dix, R. W. (1) (Derby Co), 1938 v Nor
Dixon, J. A. (1) (Notts Co), 1885 v W
Dixon, K. M. (8) (Chelsea), 1985 v Mex, FRG, USA, NI; 1986 v Is, Mex, Pol, Swe
Dobson, A. T. C. (4) (Notts Co), 1882 v Ire; 1884 v S, W, Ire
Dobson, C. F. (1) (Notts Co), 1886 v Ire
Dobson, J. M. (5) (Burnley), 1974 v P, GDR, Bul, Y, (Everton) Cz
Doggart, A. G. (1) (Corinthians), 1923 v Bel
Dorrell, A. R. (4) (Aston Villa), 1924 v Bel; 1925 v W, F, NI
Douglas, B. (36) (Blackburn R), 1957 v W, NI, F; 1958 v S, P, Y, USSR, USSR, Bra, A, USSR; 1959 v S; 1960 v Y, H, NI, Lux, Sp, W; 1961 v S, Mex, P, I, A, Lux, W, P, NI; 1962 v S, Pe, H, Arg, Bul, Bra; 1963 v S, Bra, Swz
Downs, R. W. (1) (Everton), 1920 v Ire
Doyle, M. (5) (Manchester C), 1976 v W, S, Bra, I; 1977 v Neth
Drake, E. J. (5) (Arsenal), 1934 v I; 1935 v NI; 1936 v W, H; 1938 v F
Ducat, A. (6) (Woolwich Arsenal), 1910 v S, W, Ire; (Aston Villa), 1920 v W, S, Ire
Dunn, A. T. B. (4) (Cambridge University), 1883 v Ire; 1884 v Ire; (Old Etonians), 1892 v S, W
Duxbury, M. (10) (Manchester U), 1983 v Lux; 1984 v F, W, S, USSR, Bra, U, Ch, GDR, Fin

Earle, S. G. J. (2) (Clapton), 1924 v F; (West Ham U), 1927 v NI
Eastham, G. (19) (Arsenal), 1963 v Bra, Cz, GDR, W; 1964 v WXI, NI, S, U, P, RI, USA, Bra, Arg; 1965 v H, FRG, Swe, Sp; 1966 v Pol, Den
Eastham, G. R. (1) (Bolton W), 1935 v Neth
Eckersley, W. (17) (Blackburn R), 1950 v Sp, Y; 1951 v S, Arg, P, A; 1952 v A, Swz, NI; 1953 v Arg, Ch, U, USA, W, EUR, NI, H
Edwards, D. (18) (Manchester U), 1955 v S, F, Sp, P; 1956 v S, Bra, Swe, Fin, FRG, NI, Den; 1957 v S, RI, Den, RI, W, NI, F
Edwards, J. H. (1) (Shropshire Wanderers), 1874 v S
Edwards, W. (16) (Leeds U), 1926 v W, S, NI; 1927 v W, S, Bel, Lux, F; 1928 v S, F, Bel, NI, W; 1929 v S, NI, W
Ellerington, W. (2) (Southampton), 1949 v Nor, F

Elliott, G. W. (3) (Middlesbrough), 1913 v Ire; 1914 v Ire; 1920 v W

Elliott, W. H. (5) (Burnley), 1952 v I, A, NI, W, Bel

Evans, R. E. (4) (Sheffield U), 1911 v S, W, Ire; 1912 v W

Ewer, F. H. (2) (Casuals), 1924 v F, Bel

Fairclough, P. (1) (Old Foresters), 1878 v S

Fairhurst, D. (1) (Newcastle U), 1933 v F

Fantham, J. (1) (Sheffield W), 1961 v Lux

Felton, W. (1) (Sheffield W), 1925 v F

Fenton, M. (1) (Middlesbrough), 1938 v S

Fenwick, T. (20) (QPR), 1984 v W, S, USSR, Bra, U, Ch, Fin; 1985 v S, Mex, USA, Rum, T, NI; 1986 v Eg, Mex, P, Mor, Pol, Arg; (Tottenham H) 1988 v Is

Field, E. (2) (Clapham Rovers), 1876 v S; 1881 v S

Finney, T. (76) (Preston NE), 1946 v NI, RI, W, Neth; 1947 v F, P, Bel, W, NI, Swe; 1948 v S, I, NI, W; 1949 v S, Swe, Nor, F, RI, W, NI, I; 1950 v S, P, Bel, Ch, USA, Sp, W; 1951 v S, Arg, P, F, W, NI; 1952 v S, I, A, Swz, NI, W, Bel; 1953 v S, Arg, Ch, U, USA, W; 1954 v S, Y, H, Bel, Swz, U, FRG; 1955 v Den, W, NI, Sp; 1956 v S, W, Y, Den; 1957 v S, RI, Den, RI, W, F; 1958 v S, P, Y, USSR, USSR, NI, USSR

Fleming, H. J. (11) (Swindon T), 1909 v S, H (2); 1910 v W, Ire; 1911 v W, Ire; 1912 v Ire; 1913 v S, W; 1914 v S

Fletcher, A. (2) (Wolverhampton W), 1889 v W; 1890 v W

Flowers, R. (49) (Wolverhampton W), 1955 v F; 1958 v I, W; 1959 v S, Bra, Pe, Mex, USA, W, Swe, NI; 1960 v S, Y, Sp, H, NI, Lux, Sp, W; 1961 v S, Mex, P, I, A, Kux, W, P, NI; 1962 v A, S, Swz, Pe, H, Arg, Bul, Bra, F, NI, W; 1963 v F, S, Swz; 1964 v RI, USA; P, W, Neth; 1965 v FRG; 1966 v N

Forman, Frank (9) (Nottingham F), 1898 v S, Ire; 1899 v S, W, Ire; 1901 v S; 1902 v S, Ire; 1903 v W

Forman, F. R. (3) (Nottingham F), 1899 v S, W, Ire

Forrest, J. H. (11) (Blackburn R), 1884 v W; 1885 v S, W, Ire; 1886 v S, W; 1887 v S, W, Ire; 1889 v S; 1890 v Ire

Fort, J. (1) (Millwall), 1921 v Bel

Foster, R. E. (5) (Oxford University), 1900 v W; (Corinthians), 1901 v W, Ire, S; 1902 v W

Foster, S. (3) (Brighton & HA), 1982 v NI, Neth, K

Foulke, W. J. (1) (Sheffield U), 1897 v W

Foulkes, W. A. (1) (Manchester U), 1954 v NI

Fox, F. S. (1) (Gillingham), 1925 v F

Francis, G. C. J. (12) (QPR), 1974 v Cz, P; 1975 v W, S, Swz, Cz, P; 1976 v W, NI, S, Bra, Fin

Francis, T. (52) Birmingham C), 1977 v Neth, Lux, S. Bra, Swz, Lux, I; 1978 v FRG, Bra, W, S, H; (Nottingham F), 1979 v Bul, Swe, A, NI, Bul; 1980 v Sp; 1981 v Sp, Rum, Swz, (Manchester C) Nor; 1982 v NI, W, S, Fin, F, Cz, K, FRG, Sp, (Sampdoria) Den, Gr; 1983 v H, NI, S, Aus, Aus, Aus, Den; 1984 v NI, USSR, GDR, T; 1985 v NI, Rum, Fin, S, I, Mex; 1986 v S

Franklin, C. F. (27) (Stoke C), 1946 v NI, RI, W, Neth; 1947 v S, F, Swz, P, Bel, W, NI, Swe; 1948 v S, I, Den, NI, W, Swz; 1949 v S, Swe, Nor, F, RI, W, NI, I; 1950 v S

Freeman, B. C. (5) (Everton), 1909 v S, W; (Burnley), 1912 v S, W, Ire

Froggatt, J. (13) (Portsmouth), 1949 v NI, I; 1951 v S, A; 1952 v S, I, A, Swz, NI, W, Bel; 1953 v S, USA

Froggatt, R. (4) (Sheffield W), 1952 v W, Bel; 1953 v S, USA

Fry, C. B. (1) (Corinthians), 1901 v Ire

Furness, W. I. (1) (Leeds U), 1933 v I

Galley, T. (2) (Wolverhampton W), 1937 v Nor, Swe

Gardner, T. (2) (Aston Villa), 1934 v Cz; 1935 v Neth

Garfield, B. (1) (WBA), 1898 v Ire

Garratty, W. (1) (Aston Villa), 1903 v W

Garrett, T. (3) (Blackpool), 1952 v S, I; 1953 v W

Gates, E. (2) (Ipswich T), 1980 v Nor, R

Gay, L. H. (3) (Cambridge University), 1893 v S; (Old Brightonians), 1894 v S, W

Geary, F. (2) (Everton), 1890 v Ire; 1891 v S

Geaves, R. L. (1) (Clapham Rovers), 1875 v S

Gee, C. W. (3) (Everton), 1931 v W, Sp; 1936 v NI

Geldard, A. (4) (Everton), 1933 v I, Swz; 1935 v S; 1937 v NI

George, C. (1) (Derby Co), 1976 v RI

George, W. (3) (Aston Villa), 1902 v S, W, Ire

Gibbins, W. V. T. (2) (Clapton), 1924 v F; 1925 v F

Gidman, J. (1) (Aston Villa), 1977 v Lux

Gillard, I. T. (3) (QPR), 1975 v FRG, W, Cz

Gilliat, W. E. (1) (Old Carthusians), 1893 v Ire

Goddard, P. (1) (West Ham U), 1982 v Ic

Goodall, F. R. (25) (Huddersfield T), 1926 v S; 1927 v S, Bel, Lux, F, W; 1928 v S, F, Bel; 1930 v S, G, A, NI, W; 1931 v S, Bel, NI; 1932 v NI, W, A; 1933 v I, Swz, NI, W, F

Goodall, J. (14) (Preston NE), 1888 v S, W; 1889 v S, W; (Derby Co), 1891 v S, W; 1892 v S; 1893 v W; 1894 v S; 1895 v S, Ire; 1896 v S, W; 1898 v W

Goodhart H. C. (3) (Old Etonians), 1883 v S, W, Ire

Goodwyn, A, G. (1) (Royal Engineers), 1873 v S

Goodyer, A. C. (1) (Nottingham F), 1879 v S

Gosling, R. C. (5) (Old Etonians), 1892 v W; 1893 v S; 1894 v W; 1895 v W, S

Gosnell, A. A (1) (Newcastle U), 1906 v Ire

Gough, H. C. (1) (Sheffield U), 1921 v S

Goulden, L. A. (14) (West Ham U), 1937 v Nor, Swe, NI, W, Cz; 1938 v G, Swz, F, W, EUR; 1939 v S, I, Y, Rum

Graham, L. (2) (Millwall), 1925 v W, S

Graham, T. (2) (Nottingham F), 1931 v F, NI

Grainger, C. (7) (Sheffield U), 1956 v Bra, Swe, Fin, FRG, NI, W; (Sunderland), 1957 v S

Greaves, J. (57) (Chelsea), 1959 v Pe, Mex, USA, W, Swe; 1960 v Y, Sp, NI, Lux, Sp, W; 1961 v S, P, I, A; (Tottenham H), 1962 v S, Swz, Pe, H, Arg, Bul, Bra, F, NI, W; 1963 v F, S, Bra, Cz, Swz, W, WXI, NI; 1964 v U, P, RI, Bra, P, Arg, NI, Bel, Neth; 1965 v S, H, Y, W, A; 1966 v Y, Nor, Den, Pol, U, Mex, F; 1967 v S, Sp, A

Green, F. T. (1) (Wanderers), 1876 v S

Green, G. H. (8) (Sheffield U), 1925 v F, W; 1926 v S, Bel, NI; 1927 v W; 1928 v F, Bel

Greenhalgh, E. H. (2) (Notts Co), 1872 v S; 1873 v S

Greenhoff, B. (18) (Manchester U), 1976 v W, NI, RI,

Fin, I; 1977 v Neth, NI, W, S, Bra, Arg, U; 1978 v Bra, W, NI, S, H; (Leeds U), 1980 v Aus

Greenwood, D. H. (2) (Blackburn R), 1882 v S, Ire

Gregory, J. (6) (QPR), 1983 v Aus, Aus, Aus, Den, H; 1984 v W

Grimsdell, A. (6) (Tottenham H), 1920 v W, S, Ire; 1921 v S; 1922 v NI; 1923 v W

Grosvenor, A. T. (3) (Birmingham), 1933 v NI, W, F

Gunn, W. (2) (Notts Co), 1884 v S, W

Gurney, R. (1) (Sunderland), 1935 v S

Hacking, J. (3) (Oldham Ath), 1928 v NI, W; 1929 v S

Hadley, N. (1) (WBA), 1903 v Ire

Hagan, J. (1) (Sheffield U), 1948 v Den

Haines, J. T. W. (1) (WBA), 1948 v Swz

Hall, A. E. (1) (Aston Villa), 1910 v Ire

Hall, G. W. (10) (Tottenham H), 1933 v F; 1937 v NI, W, Cz; 1938 v S, EUR, NI; 1939 v S, I, Y

Hall, J. (17) (Birmingham C), 1955 v Den, W, NI, Sp; 1956 v S, Bra, Swe, Fin, FRG, NI, W, Y, Den; 1957 v S, RI, Den, RI

Halse, H. J. (1) (Manchester U), 1909 v A

Hammond, H. E. D. (1) (Oxford University), 1889 v S

Hampson, J. (3) (Blackpool), 1930 v NI, W; 1932 v A

Hampton, H. (4) (Aston Villa), 1913 v S, W; 1914 v S, W

Hancocks, J. (3) (Wolverhampton W), 1948 v Swz; 1949 v W; 1950 v Y

Hapgood, E. (30) (Arsenal), 1933 v I, Swz, NI, W; 1934 v S, H, CZ, W, I; 1935 v NI, S, Neth, NI, G; 1936 v W, S, A, Bel; 1937 v Fin; 1938 v S, G, Swz, F, W, WXI, Nor, NI; 1939 v S, I, Y

Hardinge, H. T. W. (1) (Sheffield U), 1910 v S

Hardman, H. P. (4) (Everton), 1905 v W; 1907 v S, Ire; 1908 v W

Hardwick, G. F. M. (13) (Middlesbrough), 1946 v NI, RI, W, Neth; 1947 v S, F, Swz, P, Bel, W, NI, Swe; 1948 v S

Hardy, H. (1) (Stockport Co), 1924 v Bel

Hardy, S. (21) (Liverpool), 1907 v S, W, Ire; 1908 v S; 1909 v S, W, Ire, H, H, A; 1910 v S, W, Ire; 1912 v Ire; (Aston Villa), 1913 v S; 1914 v Ire, W, S; 1919v Ire; 1920 v S, W

Harford, M. G. (1) (Luton T) 1988 v Is

Hargreaves, F. W. (3) (Blackburn R), 1880 v W; 1881 v W; 1882 v Ire

Hargreaves, J. (2) (Blackburn R), 1881 v S, W

Harper, E.C. (1) (Blackburn R), 1926 v S

Harris, G. (1) (Burnley), 1966 v Pol

Harris, P. P. (2) (Portsmouth), 1949 v RI; 1954 v H

Harris, S. S. (6) (Cambridge University), 1904 v S; (Old Westminsters), 1905 v Ire, W; 1906 v S, W, Ire

Harrison, A. H. (2) (Old Westminsters), 1893 v S, Ire

Harrison, G. (2) (Everton), 1921 v Bel, NI

Harrow, J. H. (2) (Chelsea), 1922 v NI; 1923 v Swe

Hart, E. (8) (Leeds U), 1928 v W; 1929 v NI, W; 1932 v A; 1933 v S; 1934 v S, H, Cz

Hartley, F. (1) (Oxford C), 1923 v F

Harvey, A. (1) (Wednesbury Strollers), 1881 v W

Harvey, J. C. (1) (Everton), 1971 v Ma

Hassall, H. W. (5) (Huddersfield T), 1951 v S, Arg, P, F (Bolton W); 1953 v NI

Hateley, M. (31) (Portsmouth), 1984 v USSR, Bra, U,

Ch, (AC Milan), GDR, Fin; 1985 v NI, RI, Fin, S, I, Mex, Rum, T; 1986 v Eg, S, Mex, Can, P, Mor, Par; 1987 v T, Bra, S (Monaco) FRG; 1988 v Neth, H, Col, RI, Neth, USSR

Haworth, G. (5) (Accrington), 1887 v Ire, W, S; 1888 v S; 1890 v S

Hawtrey, J. P. (2) (Old Etonians), 1881 v S, W

Hawkes, R. M. (5) (Luton T), 1907 v Ire; 1908 v A, A, H, B

Haygarth, E. B. (1) (Swifts), 1875 v S

Haynes, J. N. (56) (Fulham), 1954 v NI; 1955 v NI, Sp; 1956 v S, Bra, Swe, Fin, FRG, W, Y; 1957 v RI, Den, RI, W, NI, F; 1958 v S, P, Y, USSR, USSR, Bra, A, USSR, NI, USSR; 1959 v S, I, Bra, Pe, Mex, USA, NI; 1960 v Y, Sp, H, NI, Lux, Sp, W; 1961 v S, Mex, P, I, A, W, P, NI; 1962 v A, S, Swz, Pe, H, Arg, Bul, Bra

Healless, H. (2) (Blackburn R), 1924 v NI; 1928 v S

Hector, K. J. (2) (Derby Co), 1973 v Pol, I

Hedley, G. A. (1) (Sheffield U), 1901 v Ire

Hegan, K. E: (4) (Corinthians), 1923 v Bel, F, NI, Bel

Hellawell, M. S. (2) (Birmingham C), 1962 v F, NI

Henfrey, A. G. (5) (Cambridge University), 1891 v Ire; (Corinthians), 1892 v W; 1895 v W; 1896 v S, W

Henry, R. P. (1) (Tottenham H), 1963 v F

Heron, F. (1) (Wanderers), 1876 v S

Heron, G. H. H. (5) (Uxbridge), 1873 v S; 1874 v S; (Wanderers), 1875 v S; 1876 v S; 1878 v S

Hibbert, W. (1) (Bury), 1910 v S

Hibbs, H. E. (25) (Birmingham), 1929 v W; 1930 v S, A, G, NI, W; 1931 v S, NI, W, Sp, NI, W, A; 1933 v S, I, Swz, NI, W, F; 1934 v W; 1935 v NI, S, Neth, G; 1936 v W

Hill, F. (2) (Bolton W), 1962 v NI, W

Hill, G. A. (6) (Manchester U), 1976 v I, RI, Fin; 1977 v Lux, Swz, Lux

Hill, J. H. (11) (Burnley), 1925 v W; 1926 v S, NI; 1927 v S, Bel, F, NI, W; 1929 v F, Bel, Sp

Hill, R. (3) (Luton T), 1982 v Den, FRG; 1986 v Eg

Hill, R. H. (1) (Millwall), 1926 v Bel

Hillman, J. (1) (Burnley), 1899 v Ire

Hills, A. F. (1) (Old Harrovians), 1879 v S

Hilsdon, G. R. (8) (Chelsea), 1907 v Ire; 1908 v S, W, Ire, A, H, B; 1909 v Ire

Hine, E. W. (6) (Leicester C), 1928 v NI, W; 1929 v NI, W; 1931 v NI, W

Hinton, A. T. (3) (Wolverhampton W), 1962 v F; (Nottingham F), 1964 v Bel, W

Hitchens, G. A. (7) (Aston Villa), 1961 v Mex, I, A; (Inter Milan), 1962 v Swz, Pe, H, Bra

Hobbis, H. H. F. (2) (Charlton Ath), 1936 v A, Bel

Hoddle, G. (53) (Tottenham H), 1979 v Bul; 1980 v W, Aus, Sp; 1981 v Sp, W, S, Nor; 1982 v NI, W, Ic, Cz, K, Lux; 1983 v NI, S, H, Lux; 1984 v F; 1985 v RI, S, I, Mex, FRG, USA, Rum, T, NI; 1986 v Is, USSR, S, Mex, Can, P, Mor, Pol, Par, Arg, Swe, NI, Y; 1987 v Sp, T, S (Monaco) FRG, T, Y; 1988 v Neth, H, Col, RI, Neth, USSR

Hodge, S. B. (15) (Aston Villa), 1986 v USSR, S, Can, P, Mor, Pol, Par, Arg, Swe, NI, Y; (Tottenham H), 1987 v Sp, NI, T, S

Hodgets, D, (6) (Aston Villa), 1888 v S, W, Ire; 1892 v S, Ire; 1894 v Ire

BRITISH & IRISH INTERNATIONAL APPEARANCES

Hodgkinson, A, (5) (Sheffield U), 1957 v S, RI, Den, RI; 1960 v W

Hodgson, G. (3) (Liverpool), 1930 v NI, W; 1931 v S

Hodkinson, J. (3) (Blackburn R), 1913 v W, S; 1919 v Ire

Hogg, W. (3) (Sunderland), 1902 v S, W, Ire

Holdcroft, G. H. (2) (Preston NE), 1936 v W, NI

Holden, A. D. (5) (Bolton W), 1959 v S, I, Bra, Pe, Mex

Holden, G. H. (4) (Wednesbury OA), 1881 v S; 1884 v S, W, Ire

Holden-White, C. (2) (Corinthians), 1888 v W, S

Holford, T. (1) (Stoke), 1903 v Ire

Holley, G. H. (10) (Sunderland), 1909 v S, W, H, H, A; 1910 v W; 1912 v S, W, Ire; 1913 v S

Holliday, E. (3) (Middlesbrough), 1959 v W, Swe, NI

Hollins, J. W. (1) (Chelsea), 1967 v Sp

Holmes, R. (7) (Preston NE), 1888 v Ire; 1891 v S; 1892 v S; 1893 v S, W; 1894 v Ire; 1895 v Ire

Holt, J. (10) (Everton), 1890 v W; 1891 v S, W; 1892 v S, Ire; 1893 v S; 1894 v S, Ire; 1895 v S; (Reading), 1900 v Ire

Hopkinson, E. (14) (Bolton W), 1957 v W, NI, F; 1958 v S, P, Y; 1959 v S, I, Bra, Pe, Mex, USA, W, Swe

Hossack, A. H. (2) (Corinthians), 1892 v W; 1894 v W

Houghton, W. E. (7) (Aston Villa), 1930 v NI, W; 1931 v F, Bel, NI; 1932 v S, A

Houlker, A. E. (5) (Blackburn R), 1902 v S; (Portsmouth), 1903 v S, W; (Southampton), 1906 v W, Ire

Howarth, R. H. (5) (Preston NE), 1887 v Ire; 1888 v S, W; 1891 v S; (Everton), 1894 v Ire

Howe, D. (23) (WBA), 1957 v W, NI, F; 1958 v S, P, Y, USSR, USSR, Bra, A, USSR, NI, USSR, W; 1959 v S, I, Bra, Pe, Mex, USA, W, Swe, NI

Howe, J. R. (3) (Derby Co), 1948 v I, NI; 1949 v S

Howell, L. S. (1) (Wanderers), 1873 v S

Howell, R. (2) (Sheffield U), 1895 v Ire; (Liverpool), 1899 v S

Hudson, A. A. (2) (Stoke C), 1975 v FRG, Cyp

Hudson, J. (1) (Sheffield), 1883 v Ire

Hudspeth, F. C. (1) (Newcastle U), 1925 v NI

Hufton, A. E. (6) (West Ham U), 1923 v Bel; 1927 v NI; 1928 v S; 1929 v F. Bel, Sp

Hughes, E. W. (62) (Liverpool), 1969 v Neth, P; 1970 v Bel, W, NI, S, GDR; 1971 v Ma, Gr, Ma, W, Gr, Swz; 1972 v FRG, FRG, W, NI, S, W; 1973 v W, S, W, S, Pol, USSR, I, A, Pol, I; 1974 v W, NI, S, Arg, GDR, Bul, Y, Cz, P; 1975 v Cyp, NI; 1976 v I; 1977 v Lux, W, S, Bra, Arg, U, Swz, Lux, I; 1978 v FRG, NI, S, H, Den, RI; 1979 v NI, W, Swe; (Wolverhampton W), 1980 v Sp, NI, S

Hughes, L. (3) (Liverpool), 1950 v Ch, USA, Sp

Hulme, J. H. A. (9) (Arsenal), 1927 v S, Bel, F, NI, W; 1928 v S, NI, W; 1933 v S

Humphreys, P. (1) (Notts Co), 1903 v S

Hunt, G. S. (3) (Tottenham H), 1933 v S, I, Swz

Hunt, Rev K. R. G. (2) (Leyton), 1911 v S, W

Hunt, R. (34) (Liverpool), 1962 v A; 1963 v GDR; 1964 v S, USA, P; 1964 v W; 1965 v Sp; 1966 v Pol, FRG, S, Fin, Nor, Pol, U, Mex, F, Arg, P, FRG, NI, Cz, W; 1967 v Sp, A, W, NI, USSR; 1968 v Sp, Sp, Swe, Y, USSR, Rum; 1969 v Rum

Hunt, S. (2) (WBA), 1984 v S, USSR

Hunter, J. (7) (Sheffield Heeley), 1878 v S; 1880 v S, W; 1881 v S, W; 1882 v S, W

Hunter, N. (28) (Leeds U), 1965 v Sp; 1966 v FRG, Y, Fin; 1967 v A; 1968 v Sp, Swe, FRG, Y, USSR; 1969 v Rum, W; 1970 v Neth, FRG; 1971 v Ma; 1972 v FRG, FRG, W, NI, S, W; 1973 v W, USSR, A, Pol; 1974 v NI, S, Cz

Hurst, G. C. (49) (West Ham U), 1966 v FRG, S, Y, Fin, Den, Arg, P, FRG, NI, Cz, W; 1967 v S, Sp, A, W, NI, USSR; 1968 v S, Swe, FRG, USSR, Rum, Bul; 1969 v Rum, F, NI, S, Mex, U, Bra, Neth; 1970 v Neth, Bel, W, NI, S, Col, Ec, Rum, Bra, FRG, GDR; 1971 v Gr, W, S, Swz, Swz, Gr; 1972 v FRG

Iremonger, J. (2) (Nottingham F), 1901 v S; 1902 v Ire

Jack, D. N. B. (9) (Bolton W), 1924 v W, S; 1928 v F, Bel; (Arsenal), 1930 v S, G, A; 1932 v W, A

Jackson, E. (1) (Oxford University), 1891 v W

Jarrett, B. G. (3) (Cambridge University), 1876 v S; 1877 v S; 1878 v S

Jefferis, F. (2) (Everton), 1912 v S, W

Jezzard, B. A. G. (2) (Fulham), 1954 v H; 1955 v NI

Johnson, D. E. (8) (Ipswich T), 1975 v W, S, Swz; (Liverpool), 1980 v RI, Arg, NI, S, Bel

Johnson, E. (2) (Saltley College), 1880 v W; (Stoke C), 1884 v Ire

Johnson, J. A. (5) (Stoke C), 1936 v NI; 1937 v S, Nor, Swe, Fin

Johnson, T. C. F. (5) (Manchester C), 1926 v Bel; 1929 v W; (Everton), 1931 v Sp; 1932 v S, NI

Johnson, W. H. (6) (Sheffield U), 1900 v S, W, Ire; 1903 v S, W, Ire

Johnston, H. (10) (Blackpool), 1946 v Neth; 1947 v S; 1951 v S; 1953 v Arg, Ch, U, USA; 1953 v W, NI, H

Jones, A. (3) (Walsall Town Swifts), 1882 v S, W; (Great Lever), 1883 v S

Jones, H. (6) (Blackburn R), 1927 v S, Bel, Lux, F, NI; 1928 v S

Jones, H. (1) (Nottingham F), 1923 v F

Jones, M. D. (3) (Sheffield U), 1965 v FRG, Swe; (Leeds U), 1970 v Neth

Jones, W. (1) (Bristol C), 1901 v Ire

Jones, W. H. (2) (Liverpool), 1950 v P, Bel

Joy, B. (1) (Casuals), 1936 v Bel

Kail, E. I. L. (3) (Dulwich Hamlet), 1929 v F, Bel, Sp

Kay, A. H. (1) (Everton), 1963 v Swz

Kean, F. W. (9) (Sheffield W), 1923 v Bel, S; 1924 v W, NI; 1925 v NI; 1926 v Bel; 1927 v Lux; (Bolton W), 1929 v F, Sp

Keegan, J. K. (63) (Liverpool), 1972 v W; 1973 v W; 1974 v W, NI, Arg, GDR, Bul, Y, Cz; 1975 v FRG, Cyp, Cyp, NI, S, Swz, Cz, P; 1976 v W, W, NI, S, Bra, Fin, RI, Fin, I; 1977 v Neth, Lux, (SV Hamburg) W, Bra, Arg, U, Swz, I; 1978 v FRG, Bra, H, Den, RI, Cz; 1979 v NI, W, S, Bul, Swe, A, Den, NI; 1980 v RI, Sp, Arg, Bel, I, Sp, (Southampton) 1981 v Sp, Swz, H, Nor, H; 1982 v NI, S, Fin, Sp

Keen, E. R. L. (4) (Derby Co), 1932 v A; 1936 v W, NI, H

Kelly, R. (14) (Burnley), 1920 v S, Ire; 1921 v W, S; 1922 v W, S; 1923 v S, NI; 1924 v NI; 1925 v W, S;

(Sunderland) 1926 v W; (Huddersfield T) 1927 v Lux; 1928 v S

Kennedy, A. (2) (Liverpool), 1984 v NI, W

Kennedy, R. (17) (Liverpool), 1976 v W, W, NI, S; 1977 v Lux, W, S, Bra, Arg, Swz, Lux; 1979 v Bul; 1980 v Sp, Arg, W, Bel, I

Kenyon-Slaney, W. S. (1) (Wanderers), 1873 v S

Kevan, D. T. (14) (WBA), 1957 v S, W, NI; 1958 v S, P, Y, USSR, USSR, Bra, A, USSR; 1959 v Mex, USA; 1961 v Mex

Kidd, B. (2) (Manchester U), 1970 v NI, Ec

King, R. S. (1) (Oxford University), 1882 v Ire

Kingsford, R. K. (1) (Wanderers), 1874 v S

Kingsley, M. (1) (Newcastle U), 1901 v W

Kinsey, G. (4) (Wolverhampton W), 1892 v W; 1893 v S; (Derby Co), 1896 v W, Ire

Kirchen, A. J. (3) (Arsenal), 1937 v Nor, Swe, Fin

Kirton, W. J. (1) (Aston Villa), 1921 v NI

Knight, A. E. (1) (Portsmouth), 1919 v Ire

Knowles, C. (4) (Tottenham H), 1967 v USSR; 1968 v Sp, Swe, FRG

Labone, B. L. (26) (Everton), 1962 v NI, W; 1963 v F; 1967 v Sp, A; 1968 v S, Sp, Swe, Y, FRD, USSR, Rum, Bul; 1969 v NI, S, Mex, U, Bra; 1970 v Bel, W, S, Col, Ec, Rum, Bra, FRG

Lampard, F. R. G. (2) (West Ham U), 1972 v Y; 1980 v Aus

Langley, E. J. (3) (Fulham), 1958 v S, P, Y

Langton, R. (11) (Blackburn R), 1946 v NI, RI, W, Neth; 1947 v F, Swz, Swe; (Preston NE), 1948 v Den; 1949 v Swe; (Bolton W), 1950 v S, NI

Latchford, R. D. (12) (Everton), 1977 v I; 1978 v Bra, W, Den, RI, Cz; 1979 v NI, NI, W, S, Bul, A

Latheron, E. G. (2) (Blackburn R), 1913 v W; 1914 v Ire

Lawler, C. (4) (Liverpool), 1971 v Ma, W, S, Swz

Lawton, T. (23) (Everton), 1938 v W, EUR, Nor, NI; 1939 v S, I, Y, Rum; (Chelsea), 1946 v NI, RI, W, Neth; 1947 v S, F, Swz, P, Bel, W, NI, Swe; (Notts Co), 1948 v S, I, Den

Leach, T. (2) (Sheffield W), 1930 v NI, W

Leake, A, (5) (Aston Villa), 1904 v S, Ire; 1905 v S, W, Ire

Lee, E. A. (1) (Southampton), 1904 v W

Lee, F. H. (27) (Manchester C), 1968 v Bul; 1969 v F, NI, W, S, Mex, U, Neth, P; 1970 v Neth, Bel, W, Col, Ec, Rum, Bra, FRG, GDR; 1971 v Gr, Ma, NI, W, S, Swz, Swz, Gr; 1972 v FRG

Lee, J. (1) (Derby Co), 1950 v NI

Lee, S. (14) (Liverpool), 1982 v Gr, Lux; 1983 v W, Gr, H, S, Aus, Den, H, Lux; 1984 v F, NI, W, Ch

Leighton, J. E. (1) (Nottingham F), 1886 v Ire

Lilley, H. E. (1) (Sheffield U), 1892 v W

Linacre, H. J. (2) (Nottingham F), 1905 v W, S

Lindley, T. (13) (Cambridge University), 1886 v S, W, Ire, 1887 v S, W, Ire; 1888 v S, W, Ire; (Nottingham F), 1889 v S; 1890 v S, W; 1891 v Ire

Lindsay, A. (4) (Liverpool), 1974 v Arg, GDR, Bul, Y

Lindsay, W. (1) (Wanderers), 1877 v S

Lineker, G. (35) (Leicester C), 1984 v S; 1985 v RI, Rum, S, I, FRG, USA; (Everton), Rum, T, NI; 1986

v Eg, USSR, Can, P, Mor, Pol, Par, Arg; (Barcelona) NI, Y; 1987 v Sp, NI, T, Bra, FRG, T, Y; 1988 v Neth, H, S, Col, Swz, RI, Neth, USSR

Lintott, E. H. (7) (QPR), 1908 v S, W, Ire; (Bradford C), 1909 v S, Ire, H, H

Lipsham, H. B. (1) (Sheffield U), 1902 v W

Little, B. (1) (Aston Villa), 1975 v W

Lloyd, L. V. (4) (Liverpool), 1971 v W, Swz; 1972 v NI; (Nottingham F), 1980 v W

Lockett, A. (1) (Stoke C), 1903 v Ire

Lodge, L. V. (5) (Cambridge University), 1894 v W; 1895 v S, W; (Corinthians), 1896 v S, Ire

Lofthouse, J. M. (7) (Blackburn R), 1885 v S, W, Ire; 1887 v S, W; (Accrington), 1889 v Ire; (Blackburn R), 1890 v Ire

Lofthouse, N. (33) (Bolton W), 1950 v Y; 1951 v W, NI, A; 1952 v S, I, A, Swz, NI, W, Bel; 1953 v S, Arg, Ch, U, USA, W, EUR, NI; 1954 v Bel, U, NI; 1955 v S, F, Sp, P, Den, W, Sp; 1956 v S, Fin; 1958 v USSR, W

Longworth, E. (5) (Liverpool), 1920 v S; 1921 v Bel; 1923 v W, Bel, S

Lowder, A. (1) (Wolverhampton W), 1889 v W

Lowe, E, (3) (Aston Villa), 1947 v F, Swz, P

Lucas, T. (3) (Liverpool), 1921 v NI; 1924 v F; 1926 v Bel

Luntley, E. (2) (Nottingham F), 1880 v S, W

Lyttelton, Hon. A. (1) (Cambridge University), 1877 v S

Lyttelton, Hon, E. (1) (Cambridge University), 1878 v S

McCall, J. (5) (Preston NE), 1913 v S, W; 1914 v S; 1920 v S; 1921 v Ire

McDermott, T. (25) (Liverpool), 1977 v Swz, Lux; 1979 v NI; W, Swe, Den, NI; 1980 v RI, NI, S, Bel, Sp, Nor, Rum, Swz; 1981 v Rum, Bra, Swz, H, Nor, H; 1982 v W, Neth, S, Ic

McDonald, C. A. (8) (Burnley), 1958 v USSR, USSR, Bra, A, USSR, NI, USSR, W

McFarland, R. L. (28) (Derby Co), 1971 v Ma, Gr, Ma, NI, S, Swz, Gr; 1972 v FRG, W, S, W; 1973 v W, NI, W, S, Cz, Pol, USSR, I, A, Pol, I; 1974 v W, NI; 1975 v Cz; 1976 v S, RI, I

McGarry, W. H. (4) (Huddersfield T), 1954 v Swz, U; 1955 v Den, W

McGuinness, W. (2) (Manchester U), 1958 v NI; 1959 v Mex

McInroy, A. (1) (Sunderland), 1926 v NI

McMahon, S. (4) (Liverpool) 1988 v Is, H, Col, USSR

McNab, R. (4) (Arsenal), 1968 v Rum, Bul; 1969 v Rum, NI

McNeal, R. (2) (WBA), 1914 v S, W

McNeil, M. (9) (Middlesbrough), 1960 v NI, Lux, Sp, W; 1961 v S, Mex, P, I, Lux

Mabbutt, G. (13) (Tottenham H), 1982 v FRG, Gr, Lux; 1983 v W, Gr, H, NI, S, H; 1986 v Y; 1987 v NI, T, FRG

Macaulay, R. H. (1) (Cambridge University), 1881 v S

Macdonald, M. (14) (Newcastle U), 1972 v W, NI, S; 1973 v USSR; 1974 v P, S, Y; 1975 v FRG, Cyp, Cyp, NI, Swz, Cz, P

Macrae, S. (6) (Notts Co), 1883 v S, W, Ire; 1884 v S, W, Ire

Maddison, F. B. (1) (Oxford University), 1872 v S

Madeley, P. E. (24) (Leeds U), 1971 v NI, Swz, Swz, Gr; 1972 v FRG, FRG, W, S; 1973 v S, Cz, Pol, USSR, I, A, Pol, I; 1974 v Cz, P; 1975 v Cyp, Cz, P; 1976 v Fin, RI; 1977 v Neth

Magee, T. P. (5) (WBA), 1923 v W, Swe; 1924 v Bel; 1925 v S, F

Makepeace, H. (4) (Everton), 1906 v S; 1910 v S; 1910 v S; 1912 v S, W

Male, C. G. (19) (Arsenal), 1934 v I; 1935 v NI, S, Neth, NI, G; 1936 v W, S, A, Bel, NI, H; 1937 v S, Nor, Swe, Fin; 1939 v I, Y, Rum

Mannion, W. J. (26) (Middlesbrough), 1946 v NI, RI, W, Neth; 1947 v S, F, Swz, P, Bel, W, NI, Swe; 1948 v I; 1949 v Nor, F, RI; 1950 v S, P, Bel, Ch, USA, NI, W, Y; 1951 v S, F

Mariner, P. (35) (Ipswich T), 1977 v Lux, NI, Lux; 1978 v W, S; 1980 v W, NI, S, Aus, I, Sp, Nor, Swz; 1981 v Sp, Swz, H, Nor, H; 1982 v Neth, S, Fin, F, Cz, K, FRG, Swz, Den, FRG, Gr; 1983 v W, Den, H, Lux; (Arsenal), 1984 v GDR; 1985 v Rum

Marsden, J. T. (1) (Darwen), 1891 v Ire

Marsden, W. (3) (Sheffield W), 1929 v W; 1930 v S, G

Marsh, R. W. (9) (QPR), 1971 v Swz; (Manchester C), 1972 v FRG, FRG, W, NI, S, Y, W; 1973 v W

Marshall, T. (2) (Darwen), 1880 v W; 1881 v W

Martin, A. (17) (West Ham U), 1981 v Bra, S, H; 1982 v Fin, Gr, Lux; 1983 v W, Gr, H, H, Lux; 1984 v W; 1985 v NI; 1986 v Is, Can, Par, Swe

Martin, H. (1) (Sunderland), 1914 v Ire

Maskrey, H. M. (1) (Derby Co), 1908 v Ire

Mason, C. (3) (Wolverhampton W), 1887 v Ire; 1888 v W; 1890 v Ire

Matthews, R. D. (5) (Coventry C), 1956 v S, Bra, Swe, FRG, NI

Matthews, S. (54) (Stoke C), 1934 v W, I; 1935 v G; 1937 v S, W, Cz; 1938 v S, G, Swz, F, W, EUR, Nor, NI; 1939 v S, I, Y; 1947 v S, (Blackppool) Swz, P, Bel, W, NI; 1948 v S, I, Den, NI, W, Swz; 1949 v S; 1950 v Sp, NI; 1951 v S; 1953 v EUR, NI, H; 1954 v Bel, U, NI, W, FRG; 1955 v S, F, Sp, P; 1955 v W; 1956 v Bra, NI, W, Y, Den; 1957 v S, RI, Den

Matthews, V. (2) (Sheffield U), 1928 v F, Bel

Maynard, W. J. (2) (1st Surrey Rifles), 1872 v S; 1876 v S

Meadows, J. (1) (Manchester C), 1955 v S

Medley, L. D. (6) (Tottenham H), 1950 v W, Y; 1951 v F, W, NI, A

Meechan, T. (1) (Chelsea), 1923 v NI

Melia, J. (2) (Liverpool), 1963 v S, Swz

Mercer, D. W. (2) (Sheffield U), 1922 v NI; 1923 v Bel

Mercer, J. (5) (Everton), 1938 v NI; 1939 v S, I, Y, Rum

Merrick, G. H. (23) (Birmingham C), 1951 v NI, A; 1952 v S, I, A, Swz, NI, W, Bel; 1953 v S, Arg, Ch, U, W, EUR, NI, H; 1954 v S, Y, H, Bel, Swz, U

Metcalfe V. (2) (Huddersfield T), 1951 v Arg, P

Mew, J. W. (1) (Manchester U), 1920 v Ire

Middleditch, B. (1) (Corinthians), 1897 v Ire

Milburn, J. E. T. (13) (Newcastle U), 1948 v NI, W, Swz; 1949 v S, W; 1950 v P, Bel, Sp, W; 1951 v Arg, P, F; 1955 v Den

Miller, B. G. (1) (Burnley), 1961 v A

Miller, H. S. (1) (Charlton Ath), 1923 v Swe

Mills, G. R. (3) (Chelsea), 1937 v NI, W, Cz

Mills, M. D. (42) (Ipswich T), 1972 v Y; 1976 v W, W, NI, S, Bra, I, Fin, Fin, I; 1977 v NI, W, S; 1978 v FRG, Bra, W, NI, S, H, Den, RI; 1979 v NI, NI, S, Bul, A, Den, NI; 1980 v Sp, Sp, Swz; 1981 v Swz, H, Nor, H; 1982 v S, Fin, F, Cz, K, FRG, Sp

Milne, G. (14) (Liverpool), 1963 v Bra, Cz, GDR, W, WXI, NI; 1964 v S, U, P, RI, Bra, Arg, NI, Bel

Milton, C. A. (1) (Arsenal), 1951 v A

Milward, A. (4) (Everton), 1891 v S, W; 1897 v S, W

Mitchell, C. (5) (Upton Park), 1880 v W; 1881 v S; 1883 v S, W; 1885 v W

Mitchell, J. F. (1) (Manchester C), 1924 v NI

Moffat, H. (1) (Oldham Ath), 1913 v W

Molyneux, G. (4) (Southampton), 1902 v S; 1903 v S, W, Ire

Moon, W. R. (7) (Old Westminsters), 1888 v S, W; 1889 v S, W, 1890 v S, W; 1891 v S

Moore, H. T. (2) (Notts Co), 1883 v Ire; 1885 v W

Moore, J. (1) (Derby Co), 1923 v Swe

Moore, R. F. (108) (West Ham U), 1962 v Pe, H, Arg, Bul, Bra, F, NI, W; 1963 v F, S, Bra, Cz, GDR, Swz, W, WXI, NI; 1964 v S, U, P, RI, Bra, P, Arg, NI, Bel; 1965 v S, H, Y, FRG, Swe, W, A, NI, Sp; 1966 v Pol, FRG, S, Nor, Den, Pol, U, Mex, F, Arg, P, FRG, NI, Cz, W; 1967 v S, Sp, A, W, NI, USSR; 1968 v S, Sp, Sp, Swe, FRG, Y, USSR, Rum, Bul; 1969 v F, NI, W, S, Mex, U, Bra, Neth, P; 1970 v Bel, W, NI, S, Col, Ec, Rum, Bra, Cz, FRG, GDR; 1971 v Gr, Ma, NI, S, Swz, Swz, Gr; 1972 v FRG, FRG, W, S, Y, W; 1973 v W, S, NI, W, S, Cz, Pol, USSR, I, I

Moore, W. G. B. (1) (West Ham U), 1923 v Swe

Mordue, J. (2) (Sunderland), 1912 v Ire; 1913 v Ire

Morice, C. J. (1) (Barnes), 1872 v S

Morley, A. (6) (Aston Villa), 1981 v H; 1982 v NI, W, Ic, Den, Gr

Morley, H. (1) (Notts Co), 1910 v Ire

Morren, T. (1) (Sheffield U), 1898 v Ire

Morris, F. (2) (WBA), 1920 v S, Ire

Morris, J. (3) (Derby Co), 1949 v Nor, F, RI

Morris, W. W. (3) (Wolverhampton W), 1938 v NI; 1939 v S, Rum

Morse, H. (1) (Notts Co), 1879 v S

Mort, T. (3) (Aston Villa), 1924 v W, F; 1926 v S

Morten, A. (1) (Crystal Palace), 1873 v S

Mortensen, S. H. (25) (Blackpool), 1947 v P, Bel, W, NI, Swe; 1948 v S, I, NI, W; 1949 v S, Swe, Nor, W, NI, I; 1950 v S, P, Bel, Ch, USA, Sp; 1951 v S, Arg; 1953 v EUR, H

Morton, J. R. (1) (West Ham U), 1937 v Cz

Mosforth, W. (9) (Sheffield W), 1877 v S; (Sheffield Albion), 1878 v S; 1879 v S, W; 1880 v S, W; (Sheffield W), 1881 v W; 1882 v S, W

Moss, F. (4) (Arsenal), 1934 v S, H, Cz, I

Moss, F. (5) (Aston Villa), 1921 v NI; 1922 v S, NI; 1923 v Bel; 1924 v S

Mosscrop, E. (2) (Burnley), 1914 v S, W

Mozley, B. (3) (Derby Co), 1949 v RI, W, NI

Mullen, J. (12) (Wolverhampton W), 1947 v S; 1949 v Nor, F; 1950 v Bel, Ch, USA; 1953 v W, EUR, NI; 1954 v S, Y, Swz

Mullery, A. P. (35) (Tottenham H), 1964 v Neth; 1967 v Sp, A, W, NI, USSR; 1968 v S, Sp, Sp, Swe, Y, Rum,

Bul; 1969 v F, NI, S, Mex, U, Bra, Neth, P; 1970 v Neth, W, NI, S, Col, Ec, Rum, Bra, Cz, FRG, GDR; 1971 v Ma, Gr, Swz

Neal, P. G. (50) (Liverpool), 1976 v W, I; 1977 v W, S, Bra, Arg, U, Swz, I; 1978 v FRG, NI, S, H, Den, RI; 1979 v NI, NI, S, Bul, A, Den, NI; 1980 v Sp, Arg, W, Bel, I, Rum, Swz; 1981 v Sp, Bra, H, Nor, H; 1982 v W, Neth, Ic, F, KDen, Gr, Lux; 1983 v W, Gr, H, NI, S, Aus, Aus, Den

Needham, E. (16) (Sheffield U), 1894 v S; 1895 v S; 1897 v S, W, Ire; 1898 v S, W; 1899 v S, W, Ire; 1900 v S, Ire; 1901 v S, W, Ire; 1902 v W

Newton, K. R. (27) (Blackburn R), 1966 v FRG, S; 1967 v Sp, A, W; 1968 v S, Sp, Swe, FRG, Y, Rum, Bul; 1969 v F, NI, W, S, Mex, U, Bra; (Everton), 1970 v Neth, NI, S, Col, Ec, Rum, Cz, FRG

Nicholls, J. (2) (WBA), 1954 v S, Y

Nicholson, W. E. (1) (Tottenham H), 1951 v P

Nish, D. J. (5) (Derby Co), 1973 v NI; 1974 v P, W, NI, S

Norman, M. (23) (Tottenham H), 1962 v Pe, H, Arg, Bul, Bra, F; 1963 v S, Bra, Cz, GDR, W, WXI, NI; 1964 v S, U, P, USA, Bra, P, Arg, NI, Bel, Neth

Nuttall, H. (3) (Bolton W), 1927 v NI, W; 1929 v S

Oakley, W. J. (16) (Oxford University), 1895 v W; 1896 v S, W, Ire; (Corinthians), 1897 v S, W, Ire; 1898 v S, W, Ire; 1900 v S, W, Ire; 1901 v S, W, Ire

O'Dowd, J. P. (3) (Chelsea), 1932 v S, NI; 1933 v Swz

O'Grady, M. (2) (Huddersfield T), 1962 v NI; (Leeds U), 1969 v F

Ogilvie, R. A. M. M. (1) (Clapham Rovers), 1874 v S

Oliver, L. F. (1) (Fulham), 1929 v Bel

Olney, B. A. (2) (Aston Villa), 1928 v F, Bel

Osborne, F. R. (4) (Fulham), 1922 v NI; 1923 v F; (Tottenham H), 1924 v Bel; 1926 v Bel

Osborne, R. (1) (Leicester C), 1927 v W

Osgood, P. L. (4) (Chelsea), 1970 v Bel, Rum, Cz; 1973 v I

Osman, R. (11) (Ipswich T), 1980 v Aus; 1981 v Sp, Rum, Swz, Nor; 1982 v Ic, Den; 1983 v Aus, Aus, Aus, Den

Ottaway, C. J. (2) (Oxford University), 1872 v S; 1874 v S

Owen, J. R. B. (1) (Sheffield), 1874 v S

Owen, S. W. (3) (Luton T), 1954, v Y, H, Bel

Page, L. A. (7) Burnley), 1927 v W, S, Bel, Lux, F, NI, W

Paine, T. L. (19) (Southampton), 1963 v Cz, GDR, W, WXI, NI; 1964 v S, U, USA, P, NI; 1965 v H, Y, FRG, Swe, W, A; 1966 v Y, Nor, Mex

Pallister, G. A. (1) (Middlesbrough) 1988 v H

Pantling, H. H. (1) (Sheffield U), 1923 v NI

Paravacini, P. J. de (3) (Cambridge University), 1883 v S, W, Ire

Parker, T. R. (1) (Southampton), 1925 v F

Parkes, P. B. (1) (QPR), 1974 v P

Parkinson, J. (2) (Liverpool), 1910 v S, W

Parr, P. C. (1) (Oxford University), 1882 v W

Parry, E. H. (3) (Old Carthusians), 1879 v W; 1882 v W, S

Parry, R. A. (2) (Bolton W), 1959 v NI; 1960 v S

Patchitt, B. C. A. (2) (Corinthians), 1923 v Swe, Swe

Pawson, F. W. (2) (Cambridge University), 1883 v Ire; (Swifts), 1885 v Ire

Payne, J. (1) (Luton T), 1937 v Fin

Peacock, A. (6) (Middlesbrough), 1962 v Arg, Bul, NI, W; (Leeds U), 1965 v W, NI

Peacock, J. (3) (Middlesbrough), 1929 v F, Bel, Sp

Pearce, S. (5) (Nottingham F), 1987 v Bra, S, FRG; 1988 v Is, H

Pearson, H. F. (1) (WBA), 1932 v S

Pearson, J. H. (1) (Crewe Alex), 1892 v Ire

Pearson, J. S. (15) (Manchester U), 1976 v W, NI, S, Bra, Fin, RI; 1977 v Neth, W, S, Bra, Arg, U, I; 1978 v FRG, NI

Pearson, S. C. (8) (Manchester U), 1948 v S, NI; 1949 v S, NI, I; 1951 v P; 1952 v S, I

Pease, W. H. (1) (Middlesbrough), 1927 v W

Pegg, D. (1) (Manchester U), 1957 v RI

Pejic, M. (4) (Stoke C), 1974 v P, W, NI, S

Pelly, F. R. (3) (Old Foresters), 1893 v Ire; 1894 v S, W

Pennington, J (25) (WBA), 1907 v S, W; 1908 v S, W, Ire, A; 1909 v S, W, H, H, A; 1910 v S, W; 1911 v S, W, Ire; 1912 v S, W, Ire; 1913 v S, W; 1914 v S, Ire; 1920 v S, W

Pentland, F. B. (5) (Middlesbrough), 1909 v S, W, H, H, A

Perry, C. (3) (WBA), 1890 v Ire; 1891 v Ire; 1893 v W

Perry, T. (1) (WBA), 1898 v W

Perry, W. (3) (Blackpool), 1955 v NI, Sp; 1956 v S

Perryman, S. (1) (Tottenham H), 1982 v Ic (1)

Peters, M. (67) (West Ham U), 1966 v Y, Fin, Pol, Mex, F, Arg, P, FRG, NI, Cz, W; 1967 v S, W, NI, USSR; 1968 v S, Sp, Sp, Swe, Y, USSR, Rum, Bul; 1969 v F, NI, S, Mex, U, Bra, Neth, P; 1970 v Neth, Bel, (Tottenham H) W, NI, S, Col, Ec, Rum, Bra, Cz, FRG, GDR; 1971 v Ma, Gr, Ma, NI, W, S, Swz, Gr; 1972 v FRG, FRG, NI ; 1973 v S, NI, W, S, Cz, Pol, USSR, I, A, Pol, I; 1974 v P, S

Phillips, L. H. (3) (Portsmouth), 1951 v NI; 1954 v W, FRG

Pickering, F. (3) (Everton), 1964 v USA, NI, Bel

Pickering, N. (1) (Sunderland), 1983 v Aus

Pickering, J. (1) (Sheffield U), 1933 v S

Pike, T. M. (1) (Cambridge University), 1886 v Ire

Pilkington, B. (1) (Burnley), 1954 v NI

Plant, J. (1) (Bury), 1900 v S

Plum, S. L. (1) (Charlton Ath), 1923 v F

Pointer, R. (3) (Burnley), 1961 v Lux, W, P

Porteous, T. S. (1) (Sunderland), 1891 v W

Priest, A. E. (1) (Sheffield U), 1900 v Ire

Prinsep, J. F. M. (1) (Clapham Rovers), 1879 v S

Puddefoot, S. C. (2) (Blackburn R), 1925 v NI; 1926 v S

Pye, J. (1) (Wolverhampton W), 1949 v RI

Pym, R.H. (3) (Bolton W), 1925 v W, S; 1926 v W

Quantrill, A. (4) (Derby Co), 1920 v W, S, Ire; 1921 v W

Quixall, A. (5) (Sheffield W), 1953 v W, EUR, NI; 1955 v Sp, P

Radford, J. (2) (Arsenal), 1969 v Rum; 1971 v Swz

Raikes, G. B. (4) (Oxford University), 1895 v W; 1896 v W, Ire, S

Ramsey, A. E. (32) (Southampton), 1948 v Swz; (Tottenham H), 1949 v I; 1950 v S, P, Bel, Ch, USA, Sp, NI, W, Y; 1951 v S, Arg, P, F, W, NI, A; 1952 v S, I, A, Swz, NI, W, Bel; 1953 v S, Arg, Ch, U, USA, EUR, H

Rawlings, A. (1) (Preston NE), 1921 v Bel

Rawlings, W. E. (2) (Southampton), 1922 v W, S

Rawlingson, J. F. P. (1) (Cambridge University), 1882 v Ire

Rawson H. E. (1) (Royal Engineers), 1875 v S

Rawson, W. S. (2) (Oxford University), 1875 v S; 1877 v S

Read, A. (1) (Tufnell Park), 1921 v Bel

Reader, J. (1) (WBA), 1894 v Ire

Reaney, P. (3) (Leeds U), 1968 v Bul; 1969 v P; 1971 v Ma

Reeves, K. (2) (Norwich C), 1979 v Bul; (Manchester C), 1980 v NI

Regis, C. (5) (WBA), 1982 v NI, W, Ic; 1982 v FRG; (Coventry C) 1987 v T

Reid, P. (13) (Everton), 1985 v Mex, FRG, USA, Rum; 1986 v S, Can, Pol, Par, Arg; 1987 v Bra, FRG, Y; 1988 v Swz

Revie, D. G. (6) (Manchester C), 1954 v NI; 1955 v S, F, Den, W; 1956 v NI

Reynolds, J. (8) (WBA), 1892 v S; 1893 v S, W; (Aston Villa), 1894 v S, Ire; 1895 v S; 1897 v S, W

Richards, C. H. (1) (Nottingham F), 1898 v Ire

Richards, G. H. (1) (Derby Co), 1909 v A

Richards, J. P. (1) (Wolverhampton W), 1973 v NI

Richardson, J. R. (2) (Newcastle U), 1933 v I, Swz

Richardson, W. G. (1) (WBA), 1935 v Neth

Rickaby, S, (1) (WBA), 1953 v NI

Rigby, A. (5) (Blackburn R), 1927 v S, Bel, Lux, F, W

Rimmer, E. J. (4) (Sheffield W), 1930 v S, G, A; 1931 v Sp

Rimmer, J. J. (1) (Arsenal), 1976 v I

Rix, G. (17) (Arsenal), 1980 v Nor, Rum, Swz; 1981 v Bra, W, S; 1982 v Neth, Fin, F, Cz, K, FRG, Sp, Den, FRD; 1983 v Gr; 1984 v NI

Robb, G. (1) (Tottenham H), 1953 v H

Roberts, C. (3) (Manchester), 1905 v Ire, W, S

Roberts, F. (4) (Manchester C), 1924 v Bel; 1925 v W, S, F

Roberts, G. (6) (Tottenham H), 1983 v NI, S; 1984 v F, NI, S, USSR

Roberts, H. (1) (Arsenal), 1931 v S

Roberts, H. (1) (Millwall), 1931 v Bel

Roberts, R. (3) (WBA), 1887 v S; 1888 v Ire; 1890 v Ire

Roberts, W. T. (2) (Preston NE), 1923 v Bel; 1924 v W

Robinson, J. (4) (Sheffield W), 1937 v Fin; 1938 v G, Swz, W

Robinson, J. W. (11) (Derby Co), 1897 v S, Ire; (New Brighton Tower), 1898 v S, W, Ire; (Southampton), 1899 v W, S; 1900 v S, W, Ire; 1901 v Ire

Robson, B. (69) (WBA), 1980 v RI, Aus, Nor, Rum, Swz; 1981 v Sp, Rum, Bra, W, S, Swz, H, Nor, (Manchester U), H; 1982 v NI, W, Neth, S, Fin, F, Cz, FRG, Sp, Den, Gr, Lux; 1983 v S, H, Lux; 1984 v F, NI, S, USSR, Bra, U, Ch, GDR, Fin, T; 1985 v RI, Rum, Fin, S, I, Mex, FRG, USA, Rum, T; 1986 v Is, Mex, P, Mor, NI; 1987 v NI, Sp, T, Bra, S, T, Y; 1988 v Neth, H, S, Col, Swz, RI, Neth, USSR

Robson, R. (20) (WBA), 1957 v F; 1958 v USSR, USSR, Bra, A; 1960 v Sp, H, NI, Lux, Sp, W; 1961 v S, Mex, P, I, Lux, W, P, NI; 1962 v Swz

Rose, W. C. (5) (Wolverhampton W), 1884 v S, W, Ire; (Preston NE), 1886 v Ire; (Wolverhampton W), 1891 v Ire

Rostron, T. (2) (Darwen), 1881 v S, W

Rowe, A. (1) (Tottenham H), 1933 v F

Rowley, J. F. (6) (Manchester U), 1948 v Swz; 1949 v Swe, F, NI, I; 1952 v S

Rowley, W. (2) (Stoke C), 1889 v Ire; 1892 v Ire

Royle, J. (6) (Everton), 1971 v Ma; 1972 v Y; (Manchester C), 1976 v NI, I, Fin; 1977 v Lux

Ruddlesdin, H. (3) (Sheffield W), 1904 v W, Ire; 1905 v S

Ruffell, J. W. (6) (West Ham U), 1926 v S, NI; 1928 v NI, W; 1929 v S, W

Russell, B. B. (1) (Royal Engineers), 1883 v W

Rutherford, J. (11) Newcastle U), 1904 v S; 1907 v S, Ire, W; 1908 v S, Ire, W, A, A, H, B

Sadler, D. (4) (Manchester U), 1967 v NI, USSR; 1970 v Ec, GDR

Sagar, C. (2) (Bury), 1900 v Ire; 1902 v W

Sagar, E. (4) (Everton), 1935 v NI; 1936 v S, A, Bel

Sandford, E. A. (1) (WBA), 1932 v W

Sandilands, R. R. (5) (Old Westminsters), 1892 v W; 1893 v Ire; 1894 v W; 1895 v W; 1896 v W

Sands, J. (1) (Nottingham F), 1880 v W

Sansom, K. (86) (C Palace), 1979 v W, Bul; 1980 v RI, Arg, W, NI, S, Bel, I, (Arsenal) Nor, Rum, Swz; 1981 v Sp, Rum, Bra, W, S, Swz; 1982 v NI, W, Neth, S, Fin, F, Cz, FRG, Sp, Den, FRG, Gr, Lux; 1983 v Gr, H, NI, S, Den, H, Lux; 1984 v F, USSR, Bra, U, Ch, GDR, Fin, T; 1985 v NI, RI, Rum, Fin, S, I, Mex, FRG, USA, Rum, T; NI; 1986 v Eg, Is, USSR, S, Mex, Can, P, Mor, Pol, Par, Arg, Swe, NI, Y; 1987 v Sp, NI, T, FRG, T, Y; 1988 v Neth, S, Col, Swz, RI, Neth, USSR

Saunders, F. E. (1) (Swifts), 1888 v W

Savage, A. H. (1) (C Palace), 1876 v S

Sayer, J. (1) (Stoke C), 1887 v Ire

Scattergood, E. (1) (Derby Co), 1913 v W

Schofield, J. (3) Stoke C), 1892 v W; 1893 v W; 1895 v Ire

Scott, L. (17) (Arsenal), 1946 v NI, RI, W, Neth; 1947 v S, F, Swz, P, Bel, W, NI, Swe; 1948 v S, I, Den, NI, W

Scott, W. R. (1) (Brentford), 1936 v W

Seddon, J. (6) (Bolton W), 1923 v F, Swe, Swe, Bel; 1927 v W; 1929 v S

Seed, J. M. (5) (Tottenham H), 1921 v Bel; 1922 v NI; 1923 v W, Bel; 1925 v S

Settle, J. (6) (Bury), 1899 v S, W, Ire; (Everton), 1902 v S, Ire; 1903 v Ire

Sewell, J. (6) (Sheffield W), 1951 v NI; 1952 v A, Swz, NI; 1953 v H; 1954 v H

Sewell, W. R. (1) (Blackburn R), 1924 v W

Shackleton, L. F. (5) (Sunderland), 1948 v Den, W; 1949 v W; 1954 v W, FRG

Sharp, J. (2) (Everton), 1903 v Ire; 1905 v S

Shaw, G. E. (1) (WBA), 1932 v S
Shaw, G. L. (5) (Sheffield U), 1958 v USSR, W; 1959 v
S, I; 1962 v W
Shea, D. (2) (Blackburn R), 1914 v W, Ire
Shellito, K. J. (1) (Chelsea), 1963 v Cz
Shelton, A. (6) (Notts Co), 1889 v Ire; 1890 v S, W;
1891 v S, W; 1892 v S
Shelton, C. (1) (Notts Rangers), 1888 v Ire
Shepherd, A. (2) (Bolton W), 1906 v S; (Newcastle U),
1911 v Ire
Shilton, P. L. (100) (Leicester C), 1970 v GDR; 1971 v
W, Swz; 1972 v NI, Y; 1973 v S, NI, W, S, Cz, Pol,
USSR, I, A, Pol, I; 1974 v W, NI, S, Arg; (Stoke C),
1975 v Cyp; 1977 v NI, W; (Nottingham F), 1978 v
W, H, Cz; 1979 v Swe, A, NI; 1980 v Sp, I, Nor, Swz;
1981 v Rum, H; 1982 v Neth, S, F, Cz, K, FRG, Sp,
(Southampton), Den, FRG, Gr; 1983 v W, Gr, H,
NI, S, Aus, Aus, Aus, Den, H; 1984 v F, NI, W, S,
USSR, Bra, U, Ch, GDR, Fin, T; 1985 v NI, Rum,
Fin, S, I, FRG, Rum, T, NI; 1986 v Eg, Is, USSR, S,
Mex, Can, P, Mor, Pol, Par, Arg, Swe, NI; 1987 v Sp,
NI, Bra, (Derby Co) FRG, T, Y; 1988 v Neth, S, Col,
Swz, RI, Neth
Shimwell, E. (1) (Blackpool), 1949 v Swe
Shutt, G. (1) (Stoke C), 1886 v Ire
Silcock, J. (3) (Manchester U), 1921 v W, S; 1923 v Swe
Sillett, R. P. (3) (Chelsea), 1955 v F, Sp, P
Simms, E. (1) (Luton T), 1921 v NI
Simpson, J. (8) (Blackburn R), 1911 v S, W, Ire; 1912 v
S, W, Ire; 1913 v S; 1914 v W
Slater, W. J. (12) (Wolverhampton W), 1954 v W, FRG;
1958 v S, P, Y, USSR, USSR, Bra, A, USSR,
USSR; 1960 v S
Smalley, T. (1) (Wolverhampton W), 1936 v W
Smart, T. (5) (Aston Villa), 1921 v S; 1924 v W, S; 1925
v NI; 1929 v W
Smith, A. (3) (Nottingham F), 1891 v S, W; 1893 v Ire
Smith, A. K: (1) (Oxford University), 1872 v S
Smith, B. (2) (Tottenham H), 1921 v S; 1922 v W
Smith, C. E. (1) (C Palace), 1876 v S
Smith, G. O. (20) (Oxford University), 1893 v Ire; 1894
v W, S; 1895 v W; 1896 v Ire, W, S; (Old
Carthusians), 1897 v Ire, W, S; 1898 v Ire, W, S;
(Corinthians), 1899 v Ire, W, S; 1899 v Ire, W, S;
1901 v S
Smith, H. (4) (Reading), 1905 v W, S; 1906 v W, Ire
Smith J. (2) (WBA), 1919 v Ire; 1922 v NI
Smith, Joe (5) (Bolton W), 1913 v Ire; 1914 v S, W;
1920 v W, Ire
Smith, J. C. R. (2) (Millwall), 1938 v Nor, NI
Smith, J. W. (3) (Portsmouth), 1931 v NI, W, Sp
Smith, Leslie (1) (Brentford), 1939 v Rum
Smith, Lionel (6) (Arsenal), 1950 v W; 1951 v W, NI;
1952 v W, Bel; 1953 v S
Smith, R. A. (15) (Tottenham H), 1960 v NI, Lux, Sp,
W; 1961 v S, P; 1962 v S; 1963 v F, S, Bra, Cz, GDR,
W, WXI, NI
Smith, S. (1) (Aston Villa), 1895 v S
Smith, S. C. (1) (Leicester C), 1935 v NI
Smith, T. (2) (Birmingham C), 1959 v W, Swe
Smith, T. (1) (Liverpool), 1971 v W
Smith, W. H. (3) (Huddersfield T), 1922 v W, S; 1928 v
S

Sorby, T. H. (1) (Thursday Wanderers, Sheffield),
1879 v W
Southworth, J. (3) (Blackburn R), 1889 v W; 1891 v W;
1892 v S
Sparks, F. J. (3) (Herts Rangers), 1879 v S; (Clapham
Rovers), 1880 v S, W
Spence, J. W. (2) (Manchester U), 1926 v Bel, NI
Spence, R. (2) (Chelsea), 1936 v A, Bel
Spencer, C. W. (2) (Newcastle U), 1924 v S; 1925 v W
Spencer, H. (6) (Aston Villa), 1897 v S, W; 1900 v W;
1903 v Ire; 1905 v W, S
Spiksley, F. (7) (Sheffield W), 1893 v S, W; 1894 v S,
Ire; 1896 v Ire, 1898 v S, W
Spilsbury, B. W. (3) (Cambridge University), 1885 v
Ire; 1886 v Ire, S
Spink, N. (1) (Aston Villa), 1983 v Aus
Spouncer, W. A. (10 (Nottingham F), 1900 v W
Springett, R. D. G. (33) (Sheffield W), 1959 v NI; 1960
v S, Y, Sp, H, NI, Lux, Sp; 1961 v S, Mex, P, I, A,
Lux, W, P, NI; 1962 v A, S, Swz, Pe, H, Arg, Bul,
Bra, F, NI, W; 1963 v F, Swz; 1965 v W, A; 1966 v
Nor
Sproston, B. (11) (Leeds U), 1936 v W; 1937 v NI, W,
Cz; 1938 v S, G, Swz, F, (Tottenham H), W, EUR,
(Manchester C) Nor
Squire, R. T. (3) (Cambridge University), 1886 v S, W,
Ire
Stanbrough, M. H. (1) (Old Carthusians), 1895 v W
Staniforth, R. (8) (Huddersfield T), 1954 v S, Y, H, Bel,
Swz, U, W, FRG
Starling, R. W. (2) (Sheffield W), 1933 v S; (Aston
Villa), 1937 v S
Statham, D. (3) (WBA), 1983 v W, Aus, Aus
Steele, F. C. (6) (Stoke C), 1936 v W, NI; 1937 v S,
Nor, Swe, Fin
Stein, B. (1) (Luton T), 1984 v F
Stephenson, C. (1) (Huddersfield T), 1924 v W
Stephenson, G. T. (3) (Derby Co), 1928 v F, Bel;
(Sheffield W), 1931 v F
Stephenson, J. E. (2) (Leeds U), 1938 v S, NI
Stepney, A. C. (1) (Manchester U), 1968 v Swe
Steven, T. M. (24) (Everton), 1985 v NI, RI, Rum, Fin,
I, USA, T; 1986 v Eg, USSR, Mex, Pol, Par, Arg,
Swe, Y; 1987 v Sp, T, Y; 1988 v Neth, H, S, Swz,
Neth, USSR
Stevens, G. A. (7) (Tottenham H), 1984 v Fin, T; 1985
v NI; 1986 v S, Mex, Mor, Par
Stevens, M. G. (26) (Everton), 1985 v I, FRG, Rum, T,
NI; 1986 v Eg, Is, S, Can, P, Mor, Pol, Par, Arg; 1987
v Bra, S, T, Y; 1988 v Is, Neth, H, S, Swz, RI, Neth,
USSR
Stewart, J. (3) (Sheffield W), 1907 v S, W; (Newcastle
U), 1911 v S
Stiles, N. P. (28) (Manchester U), 1965 v S, H, Y, Swe,
W, NI, Sp, A; 1966 v Pol, FRG, S, Nor, Den, Pol, U,
Mex, F, Arg, P, FRG, NI, Cz, W; 1967 v S; 1968 v
USSR; 1969 v Rum; 1970 v NI, S
Stoker, J. (3) (Birmingham), 1933 v W; 1934 v S, H
Storer, H. (2) (Derby Co), 1924 v F; 1927 v NI
Storey, P. E. (19) (Arsenal), 1971 v Gr, NI, S, Swz;
1972 v FRG, W, NI, S, Y, W; 1973 v W, S, NI, W, S,
Cz, Pol, USSR, I
Storey-Moore, I. (1) (Nottingham F), 1970 v Neth

Strange, A. H. (20) (Sheffield W), 1930 v S, G, A, NI, W; 1931 v S, F, Bel, NI, W, Sp; 1932 v S, NI, A; 1933 v S, I, Swz, NI, W, F

Stratford, A. H. (1) (Wanderers), 1874 v S

Streten, B. (1) (Luton T), 1949 v NI

Sturgess, A. (2) (Sheffield U), 1911 v Ire; 1914 v S

Summerbee, M. G. (8) (Manchester C), 1968 v S, Sp, FRG; 1971 v Swz; 1972 v FRG, W, NI; 1973 v USSR

Sunderland, A. (1) (Arsenal), 1980 v Aus

Sutcliffe, J. W. (5) (Bolton W), 1893 v W; 1895 v S, Ire; 1901 v S; (Millwall), 1903 v W

Swan, P. (19) (Sheffield W), 1960 v Y, Sp, H, NI, Lux, Sp, W; 1961 v S, Mex, P, I, A, Lux, W, P, NI; 1962 v A, S, Swz

Swepstone, H. A. (6) (Pilgrims), 1880 v S; 1882 v S, W; 1883 v S, W, Ire

Swift, F. V. (19) (Manchester C), 1946 v NI, RI, W, Neth; 1947 v S, F, Swz, P, Bel, W, NI, Swe; 1948 v S, I, Den, NI, W; 1949 v S, Nor

Tait, G. (1) (Birmingham Excelsior), 1881 v W

Talbot, B. (6) (Ipswich T), 1977 v NI, S, Bra, Arg, U; (Arsenal), 1980 v

Aus

Tambling, R. V. (3) (Chelsea), 1962 v W; 1963 v F; 1966 v Y

Tate, J. T. (3) (Aston Villa), 1931 v F, Bel; 1932 v W

Taylor, E. (1) (Blackpool), 1954 v H

Taylor, E. H. (8) (Huddersfield T), 1922 v NI; 1923 v W, Bel, S, NI; 1924 v S, F; 1926 v S

Taylor, J. G. (2) (Fulham), 1951 v Arg, P

Taylor, P. J. (4) (Crystal Palace), 1976 v W, W, NI, S

Taylor, P. H. (3) (Liverpool), 1947 v W, NI, Swe

Taylor, T. (19) (Manchester U), 1953 v Arg, Ch, U; 1954 v Bel, Swz; 1956 v S, Bra, Swe, Fin, FRG, NI, Y, Den; 1957 v RI, Den, RI, W, NI, F

Temple, D. W. (1) (Everton), 1965 v FRG

Thickett, H. (2) (Sheffield U), 1899 v S, W

Thomas, D. (2) (Coventry C), 1983 v Aus, Aus

Thomas, D. (8) (QPR), 1974 v Cz, P; 1975 v Cyp, Cyp, W, S, Cz, P

Thompson, P. (16) (Liverpool), 1964 v P, RI, USA, Bra, P, Arg, NI, Bel, W, Neth; 1965 v S, NI; 1967 v NI; 1968 v FRG; 1969 v Neth; 1970 v S

Thompson, P. B. (42) (Liverpool), 1976 v W, W, NI, S, Bra, I, Fin, Fin; 1978 v RI, Cz; 1979 v NI, S, Bul, Swe, A, Den, NI, Bul; 1980 v RI, Sp, Arg, W, S, Bel, I, Sp, Nor, Rum; 1981 v H, Nor, H, 1982 v W, Neth, S, Fin, F, Cz, K, FRG, Sp, FRG, Gr

Thompson, T. (2) (Aston Villa), 1951 v W; (Preston NE), 1957 v S

Thomson, R. A. (8) (Wolverhampton W), 1963 v NI; 1964 v USA, P, Arg, NI, Bel, W, Neth

Thornewell, G. (4) (Derby Co), 1923 v Swe, Swe; 1924 v F; 1925 v F

Thornley, I. (1) (Manchester C), 1907 v W

Tilson, S. F. (4) (Manchester C), 1934 v H, Cz, W; 1935 v NI

Titmuss, F. (2) (Southampton), 1922 v W; 1923 v W

Todd, C. (27) (Derby Co), 1972 v NI; 1974 v P, W, NI,

S, Arg, GDR, Bul, Y, P; 1975 v FRG, Cyp, Cyp, NI, W, S, Swz, Cz, P; 1976 v NI, S, Bra, Fin, RI, Fin; 1977 v Neth, NI

Toone, G. (2) (Notts Co), 1892 v S, W

Topham, A. G. (1) (Casuals), 1894 v W

Topham, R. (2) (Wolverhampton W), 1893 v Ire; (Casuals) 1894 v W

Towers, M. A. (3) (Sunderland), 1976 v W, NI, I

Townley, W. J. (2) (Blackburn R), 1889 v W; 1890 v Ire

Townrow, J. E. (2) (Clapton Orient), 1925 v S; 1926 v W

Tremelling, D. R. (1) (Birmingham), 1927 v W

Tresadern, J. (2) (West Ham), 1923 v S, Swe

Tueart, D. (6) (Manchester C), 1975 v Cyp, NI; 1976 v Fin; 1977 v NI, W, S

Tunstall, F. E. (7) (Sheffield U), 1923 v S, NI; 1924 v W, S, F, NI; 1925 v S

Turnbull, R. J. (1) (Bradford), 1919 v Ire

Turner, A. (2) (Southampton), 1900 v Ire; 1901 v Ire

Turner, H. (2) (Huddersfield T), 1931 v F, Bel

Turner, J. A. (3) (Bolton W), 1893 v W; (Stoke C), 1895 v Ire; (Derby Co), 1898 v Ire

Tweedy, G. J. (1) (Grimsby T), 1936 v H

Ufton, D. G. (1) (Charlton Ath), 1953 v EUR

Underwood A. (2) (Stoke C), 1891 v Ire; 1892 v Ire

Urwin, T. (4) (Middlesbrough), 1923 v Swe, Swe; (Newcastle U), 1923 v Bel; 1926 v W

Utley, G. (1) (Barnsley), 1913 v Ire

Vaughton, O. H. (5) (Aston Villa), 1882 v S, W, Ire; 1884 v S, W

Veitch, C. C. M. (6) (Newcastle U), 1906 v S, W, Ire; 1907 v S, W; 1909 v W

Veitch, J. G. (1) (Old Westminsters), 1894 v W

Venables, T. F. (2) (Chelsea), 1964 v Bel, Neth

Vidal, R. W. S. (1) (Oxford University), 1873 v S

Viljoen, C. (2) (Ipswich T), 1975 v NI, W

Viollet, D. S. (2) (Manchester U), 1960 v H; 1961 v Lux

Von Donop (2) (Royal Engineers), 1873 v S; 1875 v S

Wace, H. (3) (Wanderers), 1878 v S; 1879 v S, W

Waddle, C. R. (36) (Newcastle U), 1985 v RI, Rum, Fin, S, I, Mex, FRG, USA, (Tottenham H), Rum, T, NI; 1986 v Is, USSR, S, Mex, Can, P, Mor, Pol, Arg, Swe, NI, Y; 1987 v Sp, NI, T, Bra, S, FRG; 1988 v Is, H, S, Col, Swz, RI, Neth

Wadsworth, S. J. (9) (Huddersfield T), 1922 v S; 1923 v Bel, S, NI; 1924 v S, NI; 1925 v S; 1926 v W, NI

Wainscoat, W. R. (1) (Leeds U), 1929 v S

Waiters, A. K. (5) (Blackpool), 1964 v RI, Bra, Bel, W, Neth

Walden, F. I. (2) (Tottenham H), 1914 v S; 1922 v W

Walker, W. H. (18) (Aston Villa), 1920 v Ire; 1921 v NI, 1922 v W, S; 1923 v Swe, Swe; 1924 v S, NI, Bel; 1925 v W, S, F, NI; 1926 v W, S, NI; 1927 v W; 1932 v A

Wall, G. (7) (Manchester U), 1907 v W; 1908 v Ire; 1909 v S; 1910 v W, S; 1912 v S; 1913 v Ire

Wallace, C. W. (3) (Aston Villa), 1913 v W; 1914 v Ire, 1920 v S

Wallace, D. L. (1) (Southampton), 1986 v Eg

Walsh, P. (3) (Luton T), 1983 v Aus, Aus, Aus

Walters, A. M. (9) (Cambridge University), 1885 v S, Nor; 1886 v S; 1887 v S, W; (Old Carthusians), 1889 v S, W; 1890 v S, W

Walters, P. M. (13) (Oxford University), 1885 v S, Ire; (Old Carthusians), 1886 v S, W, Ire; 1887 v S, W; 1888 v S, Ire; 1889 v S, W; 1890 v S, W

Walton, N. (1) (Blackburn R), 1890 v Ire

Ward, J. T. (1) (Blackburn Olympic), 1885 v W

Ward, P. (1) (Brighton & HA), 1980 v Aus

Ward T. V. (2) (Derby Co), 1947 v Bel; 1948 v W

Waring, T. (5) (Aston Villa), 1931 v F, Bel, NI, W; 1932 v S

Warner, C. (1) (Upton Park), 1878 v S

Warren, B. (22) (Derby Co), 1906 v S, W, Ire; 1907 v S, W, Ire; 1908 v S, W, Ire, A (2), H, B; 1909 v S, Ire, W, H (2), A; 1911 v S, Ire, W

Waterfield, G. S. (1) (Burnley), 1927 v W

Watson, D. (12) (Norwich C), 1984 v Bra, U, Ch; 1985 v Mex, USA; 1986 v S, (Everton), NI; 1988 v Is, Neth, S, Swz, USSR

Watson, D. V. (65) (Sunderland), 1974 v P, S, Arg, GDR, Bul, Y, Cz, P; 1975 v FRG, Cyp, Cyp, NI, W, S, (Manchester C) Swz, Cz, P; 1977 v Neth, Lux, NI, W, S, Bra, Arg, U, Swz, Lux, I; 1978 v FRG, Bra, W, NI, S, HDen, RI, Cz; 1979 v NI, NI, W, S, Bul, Swe, A, (Werder Bremen), Den, (Southampton) NI, Bul; 1980 v RI, Sp, Arg, NI, S, Bel, I, Sp, Nor, Rum, Swz; 1981 v Rum, W, S, Swz, H; (Stoke C), 1982 v NI, Ic

Watson, V. M. (5) (West Ham U), 1923 v W, S; 1930 v S, G, A

Watson, W. (3) (Burnley), 1913 v S; 1914 v Ire; 1919 v Ire

Watson, W. (4) (Sunderland), 1949 v NI, I; 1950 v W, Y

Weaver, S. (3) (Newcastle U), 1932 v S, NI; 1933 v S

Webb, G. W. (2) (West Ham U), 1911 v S, W

Webb, N.J. (9) (Nottingham F) 1987 v FRG, T, Y; 1988 v Is, Neth, S, Swz, RI, USSR

Webster, M. (3) (Middlesbrough), 1930 v S, G, A

Wedlock, W. J. (26) (Bristol C), 1907 v S, Ire, W; 1908 v S, Ire, W, A, A, H, B; 1909 v S, W, Ire, H, H, A; 1910 v S, W, Ire; 1911 v S, W, Ire; 1912 v S, W, Ire; 1914 v W

Weir, D. (2) (Bolton W), 1889 v S, Ire

Welch, R. de C. (2) (Wanderers), 1872 v S; (Harrow Chequers), 1874 v S

Weller, K. (4) (Leicester C), 1974 v W, NI, S, Arg

Welsh, D. (3) (Charlton Ath), 1938 v G, Swz; 1939 v Rum

West, G. (3) (Everton), 1968 v Bul; 1969 v W, Mex

Westwood, R. W. (6) (Bolton W), 1934 v W; 1935 v S, Neth, NI, G; 1936 v W

Whateley, O. (2) (Aston Villa), 1883 v S, Ire

Wheeler, J. E. (1) (Bolton W), 1954 v NI

Wheldon, G. F. (4) (Aston Villa), 1897 v Ire; 1898 v S, W, Ire

White, T. A. (1) (Everton), 1933 v I

Whitehead, J. (2) (Accrington), 1893 v W; (Blackburn R), 1894 v Ire

Whitfield, H. (1) (Old Etonians), 1879 v W

Witham, M. (1) (Sheffield U), 1892 v Ire

Whitworth, S. (7) (Leicester C), 1975 v FRG, Cyp, NI, W, S, Swz, P

Whymark, T. J. (1) (Ipswich T), 1977 v Lux

Widdowson, S. W. (1) (Nottingham F), 1880 v S

Wignall, F. (2) (Nottingham F), 1964 v W, Neth

Wilkes, A. (5) (Aston Villa), 1901 v S, W; 1902 v S, W, Ire

Wilkins, R. G. (84) (Chelsea), 1976 v I, RI, Fin; 1977 v NI, Bra, Arg, U, Swz, Lux, I; 1978 v FRG, W, NI, S, H, Den, RI, Cz; 1979 v NI, W, S, Bul, Swe, A, (Manchester U), Den, NI, Bul; 1980 v Sp, Arg, W, NI, S, Bel, I, Sp; 1981 v Sp, Rum, Bra, W, S, Swz, H; 1982 v NI, W, Neth, S, Fin, F, Cz, K, FRG, Sp, Den, FRG; 1983 v Den; 1984 v NI, W, S, USSR, Bra, U, Ch, (AC Milan), GDR, Fin, T; 1985 v NI, RI, Rum, Fin, S, I, Mex, T, NI; 1986 v Eg, Is, USSR, S, Mex, Can, P, Mor, Swe, Y

Wilkinson, B. (1) (Sheffield U), 1904 v S

Wilkinson, L, R. (1) (Oxford University), 1891 v W

Williams, B. F. (24) (Wolverhampton W), 1949 v F, RI, W, I; 1950 v S, P, Bel, Ch, USA, Sp, NI, W, Y; 1951 v S, Arg, P, F, W; 1954 v FRG; 1955 v S, F, Sp, P, W

Williams, O. (2) (Clapton Orient), 1922 v NI; 1923 v W

Williams, S. (6) (Southampton), 1983 v Aus, Aus; 1984 v F, GDR, Fin, T

Williams, W. (6) (WBA), 1897 v Ire; 1898 v W, Ire, S; 1899 v W, Ire

Williamson, E. C. (2) (Arsenal), 1923 v Swe

Williamson, R. G. (7) (Middlesbrough), 1905 v Ire; 1911 v Ire, S, W; 1912 v S, W; 1913 v Ire

Willingham, C. K. (12) (Huddersfield T), 1937 v Fin; 1938 v S, G, Swz, F, W, EUR, Nor, NI; 1939 v S, I, Y

Willis, A. (1) (Tottenham H), 1951 v F

Wilshaw, D. J. (12) (Wolverhampton W), 1953 v W; 1954 v Swz, U; 1955 v S, F, Sp, P, W, NI; 1956 v Fin, FRG, NI

Wilson, C. P. (2) (Hendon), 1884 v S, W

Wilson, C. W. (2) (Oxford University), 1879 v W; 1881 v S

Wilson, G. (12) (Sheffield W), 1921 v W, S, Bel, NI; 1922 v S, NI; 1923 v W, Bel, S, NI; 1924 v W, F

Wilson, G. P. (2) (Corinthians), 1900 v S, W

Wilson, R. (63) (Huddersfield T), 1960 v S, Y, Sp, H; 1961 v W, P, NI; 1962 v A, S, Swz, Pe, H, Arg, Bul, Bra, F, NI; 1963 v Bra, Cz, GDR, Swz, W, WXI; 1964 v S, U, P, RI, Bra, P, Arg; (Everton), 1965 v S, H, Y, FRG, Swe, W, A, NI, Sp; 1966 v Pol, FRG, Y, Fin, Den, Pol, U, Mex, F, Arg, P, FRG, NI, Cz, W; 1967 v S, A, NI, USSR; 1968 v S, Sp, Sp, Y, USSR

Wilson, T. (1) (Huddersfield T), 1928 v S

Winckworth, W. N. (2) (Old Westminsters), 1892 v W; 1893 v Ire

Windridge, J. E. (8) (Chelsea), 1908 v S, W, Ire, A (2), H, B; 1909 v Ire

Wingfield-Stratford, C. V. (1) (Royal Engineers), 1877 v S

Withe, P. (11) (Aston Villa), 1981 v Bra, W, S, Nor; 1982 v W, Ic; 1983 v H, NI, S, H; 1984 v T

Wollaston, C. H. R. (4) (Wanderers), 1874 v S; 1875 v S; 1877 v S; 1880 v S

Wolstenholme, S. (3) (Everton), 1904 v S; (Blackburn R), 1905 v W, Ire

Wood, H. (3) (Wolverhampton W), 1890 v S, W; 1896 v S

Wood, R. E. (3) (Manchester U), 1954 v NI, W; 1956 v Fin

BRITISH & IRISH INTERNATIONAL APPEARANCES

Woodcock, A. S. (42) (Nottingham F), 1978 v NI, RI, Cz; 1979 v Bul, Swe, NI, (Cologne), Bul; 1980 v RI, Sp, Arg, Bel, I, Sp, Nor, Rum, Swz; 1981 v Rum, W, S; 1982 v NI, Neth, Fin, FRG, Sp, (Arsenal), FRG, Gr, Lux; 1983 v Gr, Lux; 1984 v F, NI, W, S, Bra, U, GDR, Fin, T; 1985 v NI, Rum, T; 1986 v Is

Woodger, G. (1) (Oldham Ath), 1911 v Ire

Woodhall, G. (2) (WBA), 1888 v S, W

Woodley, V. R. (19) Chelsea), 1937 v S, Nor, Swe, Fin, NI, W, Cz; 1938 v S, G, Swz, F, W, EUR, Nor, NI; 1939 v S, I, Y, Rum

Woods, C. C. E. (13) (Norwich C), 1985 v USA; 1986 v Eg, Is, Can, (Rangers), Y; 1987 v Sp, NI, T, S; 1988 v Is, H, Swz, USSR

Woodward, V. J. (23) (Tottenham H), 1903 v S, W, Ire; 1904 v S, Ire, 1905 v S, W, Ire; 1907 v S; 1908 v S, W, Ire, A (2), H, B; 1909 v W, Ire, H (2), A; (Chelsea), 1910 v Ire; 1911 v W

Woosnam, M. (1) (Manchester C), 1922 v W

Worrall, F. (2) (Portsmouth), 1935 v Neth; 1936 v NI

Worthington, F. S. (8) (Leicester C), 1974 v NI, S, Arg, GDR, Bul, Y, Cz, P

Wreford-Brown, C. (4) (Oxford University), 1889 v Ire; (Old Carthusians), 1894 v W; 1895 v W; 1898 v S

Wright, E. G. D. (1) (Cambridge University), 1906 v W

Wright, J. D. (1) (Newcastle U), 1938 v Nor

Wright, M. (22) (Southampton), 1984 v W, GDR, Fin, T; 1985 v RI, Rum, I, FRG, Rum, T, NI; 1986 v Eg, USSR, Y; 1987 v NI, S; (Derby Co) 1988 v Is, Neth, Col, Swz, RI, Neth

Wright, T. J. (11) (Everton), 1968 v USSR, Rum; 1969 v Rum, Mex, U, Bra, Neth; 1970 v Bel, W, Rum, Bra

Wright, W. A. (105) (Wolverhampton W), 1946 v NI, RI, W, Neth; 1947 v S, F, Swz, P, Bel, W, NI, Swe; 1948 v S, I, Den, NI, W, Swz; 1949 v S, Swe, Nor, F, RI, W, NI, I; 1950 v S, P, Bel, Ch, USA, Sp, NI; 1951 v S, Arg, F, W, NI, A; 1952 v S, I, A, Swz, NI, W, Bel; 1953 v S, Arg, Ch, U, USA, W, EUR, NI, H; 1954 v S, Y, H, Bel, Swz, U, NI, W, FRG; 1955 v S, F, Sp, P, Den, W, NI, Sp; 1956 v S, Bra, Swe, Fin, FRG, NI, W, Y, Den; 1957 v S, RI, Den, RI, W, NI, F; 1958 v S, P, Y, USSR, USSR, Bra, A, USSR, NI, USSR, W; 1959 v S, I, Bra, Pe, Mex, USA

Wylie, J. G. (1) (Wanderers), 1878 v S

Yates, J. (1) (Burnley), 1889 v Ire

York, R. E. (2) (Aston Villa), 1922 v S; 1926 v S

Young, A. (9) (Huddersfield T), 1932 v W; 1936 v H; 1937 v S, Nor, Swe; 1938 v G, Swz, F, W

Young, G. M. (1) (Sheffield W), 1964 v W

R. E. Evans also played for Wales v England, Northern Ireland and Scotland, and J. Reynolds also played for Ireland against England, Wales and Scotland.

NORTHERN IRELAND

Note: Prior to 1921, teams were all-Ireland.

Aherne, T. (4) (Belfast C), 1946 v E; 1947 v S; 1949 v W; (Luton T), 1950 v W

Alexander, A. (1) (Cliftonville), 1895 v S

Allen, C. A. (1) (Cliftonville), 1935 v E

Allen, J. (1) (Limavady), 1887 v E

Anderson, T. (22) (Manchester U), 1973 v Cyp, E, S, W, Bul, P; (Swindon T), 1975 v S; 1976 v Is, Neth, Bel; 1977 v FRG, E, S, W, Ic, Ic, Neth, Bel; (Peterborough U), 1978 v S, E, W, Den

Anderson, W. (4) (Linfield), 1898 v W, E, S; 1899 v S

Andrews, W. (3) (Glentoran), 1908 v S; (Grimsby T), 1913 v E, S

Armstrong, G. (63) (Tottenham H), 1977 v FRG, E, W, Ic, Bel; 1978 v S, E, W, RI, Den; 1979 v Bul, E; Bul, E, S, W, Den, E, RI; 1980 v Is, S, E, W, Aus, Aus, Aus, Swe, (Watford), P; 1981 v S, P, S, Swe, S, Is; 1982 v E, F, W, Y, Hon, Sp, A, F, A; 1983 v T, Alb, S, E, W, (Real Mallorca), A, FRG; 1984 v E, W, Fin, Rum, Fin; 1985 v E, Sp, (WBA), T, Rum, E; 1986 v F; (Chesterfield), Den, Bra

Baird, G. (3) (Distillery), 1896 v S, E, W

Baird, H. (1) (Huddersfield T), 1938 v E

Balfe, J. (2) (Shelbourne), 1909 v E; 1910 v W

Bambrick, J. (11) (Linfield), 1928 v E; 1929 v W, S, E; 1930 v W, S; 1931 v W; (Chelsea), 1934 v W; 1935 v E, S; 1938 v W

Banks, S. J. (1) (Cliftonville), 1937 v W

Barr, H. H. (3) (Linfield), 1961 v E; (Coventry C), 1962 v Pol, E

Barron, H. (7) (Cliftonville), 1894 v E, W, S; 1895 v S; 1896 v S; 1897 v E, W

Barry, H. (1) (Bohemians), 1900 v S

Baxter, R. A. (2) (Cliftonville), 1887 v S, W

Bennett, L. V. (1) (Dublin University), 1889 v W

Berry, J. (3) (Cliftonville), 1888 v S, W; 1889 v E

Best, G. (37) (Manchester U), 1964 v W, U, E, Swz, Swz, S; 1965 v Neth, Neth, Alb, S, E, Alb; 1966 v E; 1967 v S; 1968 v T; 1969 v E, S, W, USSR; 1970 v S, E, W, Sp; 1971 v Cyp, Cyp, E, S, W, USSR; 1972 v Sp, Bul; 1973 v P; (Fulham), 1976 v Neth, Bel; 1977 v FRG, Ic, Neth

Bingham, W. L. (56) (Sunderland), 1951 v F, S, E; 1952 v W, E, S, F; 1953 v W, S, E; 1954 v W, E, S; 1955 v W, S, E; 1956 v W, E, S; 1957 v P, W, I, P, S, E, I; 1958 v I, W, Cz, Arg, FRG, Cz, F; (Luton T), E, Sp, S; 1959 v W, S, E; 1960 v W, E, FRG, S; (Everton), 1961 v I, Gr, FRG, Gr, E; 1962 v Pol, E, S, Pol; 1963 v Sp, (Port Vale), S, Sp, E

Black, J. (1) (Glentoran), 1901 v E

Black, K. (2) (Luton T), 1988 v F, Ma

Blair, H. (3) (Portadown), 1931 v S, S; (Swansea T), 1933 v S

Blair, J. (5) (Cliftonville), 1907 v W, E, S; 1908 v E, S

Blair, R. V. (5) (Oldham Ath), 1974 v Swe; 1975 v S, W, Swe; 1976 v Is

Blanchflower, R. D. (56) (Barnsley), 1949 v S; 1950 v W, E, S; (Aston Villa), 1951 v F; 1952 v W, E, S, F; 1953 v W, S, E; 1954 v W, (Tottenham H), E, S;

1955 v W, S, E; 1956 v W, E, S; 1957 v P, W, I, P, S, E, I; 1958 v I, W, Cz, Arg, FRG, Cz, F, E, Sp, S; 1959 v W, S, E; 1960 v W, E, FRG, S; 1961 v W, FRG, S, Gr, E; 1962 v W, Neth, Pol, E, S, Pol

Blanchflower, J. (12) (Manchester U), 1954 v W, E, S; 1955 v S; 1956 v W, E, S; 1957 v P, S, E, I; 1958 v I

Bookman, L. O. (4) (Bradford C), 1914 v W; (Luton T), 1921 v S, W, E

Bothwell, A. W. (5) (Ards), 1925 v E; 1926 v W, S; 1927 v E, W

Bowler, G. C. (3) (Hull C), 1949 v S, E; 1950 v W

Boyle, P. (5) (Sheffield U), 1901 v E; 1902 v E; 1903 v S, W; 1904 v E

Braithwaite, R. S. (10) (Linfield), 1962 v W, Pol; 1963 v Sp; (Middlesbrough), 1964 v W, U, E, Swz, Swz, S; 1965 v Neth

Breen, T. (9) (Belfast C), 1934 v E, W; 1936 v S, E; (Manchester U), 1937 v W, E, S; 1938 v S; 1939 v W

Brennan, B. (1) (Bohemians), 1912 v W

Brennan, R. A. (5) (Luton T), 1949 v W, (Birmingham C), S, E; 1950 v W, (Fulham), E

Briggs, W. R. (2) (Manchester U), 1962 v W; (Swansea T), 1965 v Neth

Brisby, D. (1) (Distillery), 1891 v S

Brolly, T. (4) (Millwall), 1937 v W; 1938 v W, E; 1939 v W

Brookes, E. A. (1) (Shelbourne), 1920 v S

Brotherston, N. (27) (Blackburn R), 1980 v S, E, W, Aus, Aus, Aus, Swe, P; 1981 v S, Is; 1982 v E, F, S, W, Hon, A, A, FRG, Alb; 1983 v T, Alb, S, E, W, T; 1984 v Is; 1985 v T

Brown, J. (3) (Glenavon), 1921 v W; (Tranmere R), 1923 v E; 1924 v W

Brown, J. (10) (Wolverhampton W), 1934 v E, W; 1935 v E; (Coventry C), 1936 v E; 1937 v W, S; 1938 v W, S, E; (Birmingham C), 1939 v W

Brown, W. G. (1) (Glenavon), 1926 v W

Brown, W. M. (1) (Limavady), 1887 v E

Browne, F. (5) (Cliftonville), 1887 v E, S, W; 1888 v E, S

Browne, R. J. (6) (Leeds U), 1935 v E; 1936 v W; 1937 v E; 1938 v W, S, E

Bruce, W. (2) (Glentoran), 1960 v S; 1967 v W

Buckle, H. (1) (Cliftonville), 1882 v E

Buckle, H. R. (2) (Sunderland), 1904 v E; (Bristol R), 1908 v W

Burnett, J. (5) (Distillery), 1894 v E, W, S; (Glentoran), 1895 v E, W

Burnison, J. (2) (Distillery), 1901 v E, W

Burnison, S. (8) (Distillery), 1908 v E; 1910 v E, S; (Bradford PA), 1911 v E, S, W; (Distillery), 1912 v E; 1913 v W

Burns, J. (1) (Glenavon), 1922 v E

Butler, M. P. (1) (Blackpool), 1939 v W

Campbell, A. C. (2) (Crusaders), 1963 v W; 1964 v Swz

Campbell, D. A. (10) (Nottingham F), 1986 v Mor, Bra, E, T; 1987 v E, Y, Y, (Charlton Ath), T; 1988 v Gr, Pol

Campbell, J. (15) (Cliftonville), 1896 v W; 1897 v E, S, W; (Distillery), 1898 v E, S, W; (Cliftonville), 1899 v

E; 1900 v E, S; 1901 v S, W; 1902 v S; 1903 v E; 1904 v S

Campbell, J. P. (2) (Fulham), 1950 v E, S

Campbell, R. (2) (Bradford C), 1982 v S, W

Campbell, W. G. (6) (Dundee), 1967 v S, E; 1968 v T; 1969 v USSR; 1970 v S, W

Carey, J. J. (7) (Manchester U), 1946 v E, S; 1947 v W, E; 1948 v E, S; 1949 v W

Carroll, E. (1) (Glenavon), 1925 v S

Casey, T. (12) (Newcastle U), 1955 v W; 1956 v W, E, S; 1957 v P, W, I, P; 1958 v FRG, F, (Portsmouth), E, Sp

Cashin, M. (1) (Cliftonville), 1898 v S

Caskey, W. (7) (Derby Co), 1979 v Bul, E, Bul, E, Den, E; (Tulsa R), 1982 v F

Cassidy, T. (24) (Newcastle U), 1971 v E, USSR; 1973 v Bul; 1974 v S, E, W, Nor; 1976 v S, E, W; 1977 v FRG; 1979 v E, RI; 1980 v Is, S, E, W, Aus, Aus, Aus, (Burnley), Swe, P; 1981 v Is; 1982 v Sp

Caughey, M. (2) (Linfield), 1986 v F, Den

Chambers, J. (12) (Distillery), 1921 v W; (Bury), 1927 v E; 1928 v W, S, E; 1929 v W, S; 1930 v W, S; (Nottingham F), 1931 v E, S, W

Chatton, H. A. (3) (Partick T), 1924 v E; 1925 v S, E

Christian, J. (1) (Linfield), 1889 v S

Clarke, C. J. (15) (Bournemouth), 1986 v F, Den, Mor, Alg, Sp, Bra, (Southampton), E, T; 1987 v Y, Y, T; 1988 v Gr, Pol, F, Ma

Clarke, R. (2) (Belfast C), 1901 v E, S

Cleary, J. (5) (Glentoran), 1982 v S, W; 1983 v W, T; 1984 v Is

Clements, D. (48) (Coventry C), 1965 v Neth, W; 1966 v Mex, S; 1967 v W, S, E; 1968 v T, T; 1969 v S, W, USSR, USSR; 1970 v S, E, W, Sp; 1971 v Cyp, E, S, W, (Sheffield W), USSR, USSR; 1972 v Sp, S, E, W, Bul; 1973 v Cyp, P, Cyp, E, S, W, (Everton), Bul, P; 1974 v S, E, W, Nor; 1975 v Y, E, S, W, Swe, Y; (New York Cosmos), 1976 v E, W

Clugston, J. (14) (Cliftonville), 1888 v 1889 v W, S, E; 1890 v E, S; 1891 v E, W; 1892 v E, S, W; 1893 v E, S, W

Cochrane, D. (12) (Leeds U), 1938 v E; 1939 v W; 1946 v E, S; 1947 v W, S, E; 1948 v W, S; 1949 v W, S, E

Cochrane, M. (8) (Distillery), 1898 v S, W, E; 1899 v E; 1900 v E, S, W; (Leicester Fosse), 1901 v S

Cochrane, T. (26) (Coleraine), 1975 v Nor; (Burnley), 1978 v S, E, W, RI, (Middlesbrough), Den; 1979 v Bul, E, Bul, E; 1980 v Is, E, W, Aus, Aus, Aus, Swe, P; 1981 v S, P, S, Swe; 1982 v E, F; (Gillingham), 1983 v S; 1984 v Fin

Collins, F. (1) (Glasgow C), 1922 v S

Condy, J. (3) (Distillery), 1882 v W; 1886 v E, S

Connell, T. (1) (Coleraine), 1978 v W

Connor, J. (13) (Glentoran), 1901 v S, E; (Belfast C), 1905 v E, S, W; 1907 v E, S; 1908 v E, S; 1909 v W; 1911 v S, E, W

Connor, M. J. (3) (Brentford), 1903 v S, W; (Fulham), 1904 v E

Cook, W. (15) (Celtic), 1932 v E, W, S; (Everton), 1934 v E; 1935 v S; 1936 v W, S, E; 1937 v W, E, S; 1938 v W, S, E; 1939 v W

Cooke, S. (3) (Belfast YMCA), 1889 v E; (Cliftonville), 1890 v E, S

BRITISH & IRISH INTERNATIONAL APPEARANCES

Coulter, J. (11) (Belfast C), 1933 v E, S, W; (Everton), 1934 v E, S, W; 1936 v S; 1937 v W, (Grimsby T), S; 1938 v W, (Chelmsford C), S

Cowan, J. (1) (Newcastle U), 1970 v E

Cowan, T. S. (1) (Queen's Island), 1925 v W

Coyle, F. (4) (Coleraine), 1955 v S, E; 1957 v P (Nottingham F); 1958 v Arg

Coyle, R. I: (5) (Sheffield W), 1973 v P, Cyp, W, Bul, P

Craig, A. B. (9) (Rangers), 1908 v E, S, W; 1909 v S; (Morton), 1912 v S, W; 1914 v E, S, W

Craig, D. J. (25) (Newcastle U), 1967 v W; 1968 v W, T, T; 1969 v E, S, W, USSR; 1970 v S, E, W, Sp; 1971 v Cyp, Cyp, S, USSR; 1972 v S; 1973 v Cyp, Cyp, E, S, W, Bul, P; 1974 v Nor

Crawford, S. (7) (Distillery), 1889 v E, W; (Cliftonville), 1891 v E, S, W; 1893 v E, W

Croft, T. (1) (Queen's Island), 1923 v E

Crone, R. (4) (Distillery), 1889 v S; 1890 v E, S, W

Crone, W. (12) (Distillery), 1882 v W; 1884 v E, S, W; 1886 v E, S, W; 1887 v E; 1888 v E, W; 1889 v S; 1890 v W

Crooks, W. (1) (Manchester U), 1922 v W

Crossan, E. (3) (Blackburn R), 1949 v S; 1950 v E; 1955 v W

Crossan, J. A. (24) (Sparta Rotterdam), 1959 v E; (Sunderland), 1962 v Pol; 1963 v W, Sp, S, Sp, E; 1964 v W, U, E, Swz, Swz, S; (Manchester C), 1965 v Neth, W, Neth, Alb, S, E, Alb; 1966 v FRG, E, S; (Middlesbrough), 1967 v S

Crothers, C. (1) (Distillery), 1907 v W

Cumming, L. (3) (Huddersfield T), 1929 v W, S, (Oldham Ath), E

Cunningham R. (4) (Ulster), 1892 v S, E, W; 1893 v E

Cunningham, W. E. (30) (St Mirren), 1951 v W; 1952 v E; 1953 v S; 1954 v S; (Leicester C), 1955 v S, E; 1956 v W, E, S; 1957 v P, W, I, P, S, I; 1958 v W, Cz, Arg, FRG, Cz, F, E, S; 1959 v W, S, E; 1960 v W; (Dunfermline Ath), 1961 v W; 1962 v W, Neth

Curran, S. (3) (Belfast C), 1926 v W, S; 1928 v S

Curran, J. J. (4) (Glenavon), 1922 v W, (Pontypridd), E; 1923 v S, (Glenavon), E

Cush, W. W. (26) Glenavon), 1950 v E, S; 1955 v S, E; 1957 v P, W, I, P, (Leeds U), I; 1958 v I, W, Cz, Arg, FRG, Cz, F, E, Sp, S; 1959 v W, S, E; 1960 v W, (Portadown), FRG; 1961 v Gr, Gr

Dalton, W. (11) (YMCA), 1888 v S; (Linfield), 1890 v S, W; 1891 v S, W; 1892 v E, S, W; 1894 v E, S, W

D'Arcy, S. D. (5) (Chelsea), 1952 v W, E, (Brentford), S, F; 1953 v W

Darling, J. (21) (Linfield), 1897 v E, S; 1900 v S; 1902 v E, S, W; 1903 v E, S, W; 1905 v E, S, W; 1906 v E, S, W; 1908 v W; 1909 v E; 1910 v E, S, W; 1912 v S

Davey, H. H. (5) (Reading), 1925 v E; 1926 v E; 1927 v S, E; (Portsmouth), 1929 v W

Davis, T. L. (1) (Oldham Ath), 1936 v E

Davison, J. R. (8) (Cliftonville), 1882 v E, W; 1883 v E, W; 1884 v E, W, S; 1885 v E

Dennison, R. (2) (Wolverhampton W), 1988 v F, Ma

Devine, W. (4) (Limavady), 1886 v E, W; 1887 v W; 1888 v W

Dickson, D. (4) (Coleraine), 1970 v S, W; 1973 v Cyp, P

Dickson, T. A. (1) (Linfield), 1956 v S

Dickson, W. (12) (Chelsea), 1951 v W, F, E, S; 1952 v W, E, S, F; 1953 v F, (Arsenal), E; 1954 v W, E

Diffin, W, (1) (Belfast C), 1931 W

Dill, A. H. (9) (Knock and Down Ath), 1882 v E, W; (Cliftonville), 1883 v W; 1884 v E, S, W; 1885 v E, S, W

Doherty, I. (1) (Belfast C), 1901 v E

Doherty, J. (2) (Cliftonville), 1932 v E, W

Doherty, L. (2) (Linfield), 1984 v Is; 1988 v T

Doherty, M. (1) (Derry C), 1937 v S

Doherty, P. D. (16) (Blackpool), 1934 v E, W; 1935 v E, S; (Manchester C), 1936 v E; 1937 v W, E, S; 1938 v E; 1939 v W; (Derby Co), 1946 v E; (Huddersfield T), 1947 v W, E; 1948 v W, S; (Doncaster R), 1950 v S

Donaghy, M. (56) (Luton T), 1980 v S, E, W, Swe, P; 1981 v S, S, Is; 1982 v E, F, S, W, Y, Hon, Sp, F, A, FRG, Alb; 1983 v T, Alb, S, E, W, A, T, FRG, S; 1984 v E, W, Fin, Rum, Fin; 1985 v E, Sp, T, T, Rum, E; 1986 v F, Den, Mor, Alg, Sp, Bra, E, T; 1987 v Is, E, Y, Y, T; 1988 v Gr, Pol, F, Ma

Donnelly, L. (1) (Distillery), 1913 v W

Doran, J. F. (3) (Brighton & HA), 1920 v E; 1921 v E; 1922 v W

Dougan, A. D. (43) (Portsmouth), 1958 v Cz; (Blackburn R), 1959 v S; 1960 v E; 1961 v W, I, Gr; (Aston Villa), 1962 v P, S, P; (Leicester C), 1965 v S, E, Alb; 1966 v W, FRG, Mex, E, S; (Wolverhampton W), 1967 v W, S; 1968 v W, Is, T, T; 1969 v E, S, W, USSR, USSR; 1970 v S, E, Sp; 1971 v Cyp, Cyp, E, S, W, USSR, USSR; 1972 v S, E, W, Bul; 1973 v Cyp

Douglas, J. P. (1) (Belfast C), 1946 v E

Dowd, H. O. (3) (Glenavon), 1974 v W, Nor, Swe

Duggan, H. A. (8) (Leeds U), 1929 v E; 1930 v E; 1931 v W; 1932 v E; 1933 v E; 1934 v S, W; 1935 v S

Dunlop, G. (3) (Linfield), 1984 v Is; 1987 v E, Y

Dunne, J. (7) (Sheffield U), 1928 v W; 1930 v E; 1931 v W; 1931 v E, S; 1932 v E, W

Eames, W. L. E. (3) (Dublin U), 1885 v E, S, W

Eglington, T. J. (6) (Everton), 1946 v S; 1947 v W, S, E; 1948 v W, E

Elder, A. R. (40) (Burnley), 1960 v W, E, FRG, S; 1961 v W, Gr, FRG, S, Gr, E; 1962 v P, E, S, P; 1963 v W, Sp; 1964 v W, U, E, Swz, Swz, S; 1965 v Neth, W, Neth, Alb, S, E, Alb; 1966 v W, Mex, E, S; 1967 v W, (Stoke C), E; 1968 v W; 1969 v E, S, W, USSR

Elleman, A. R. (2) (Cliftonville), 1889 v W; 1890 v E

Elwood, J. H. (2) (Bradford), 1929 v E

Emerson, W. (11) (Glentoran), 1919 v E; 1920 v W, S, E; 1921 v E; 1922 v S, (Burnley), W, E; 1923 v S, W, E

English, S. (2) (Glasgow R), 1932 v W, S

Enright, J. (1) (Leeds C), 1912 v S

Falloon, E. (2) (Aberdeen), 1931 v S; 1932 v S

Farquharson, T. G. (7) (Cardiff C), 1923 v S, W, E; 1924 v S, W, E; 1925 v S

Farrell, P. (2) (Distillery), 1901 v S, W

Farrell, P. (1) (Hibernian), 1938 v W

Farrell, P. D. (7) (Everton), 1946 v S; 1947 v W, E, S; 1948 v W, E; 1949 v W

Feeney, J. M. (2) (Linfield), 1946 v S; (Swansea T), 1949 v E

Feeney, W. (1) (Glentoran), 1976 v Is

Ferguson, W. (2) (Linfield), 1966 v Mex, E

Ferris, J. (5) (Belfast Celtic), 1919 v E; 1920 v W, E; (Chelsea), 1921 v S; (Belfast C), 1928 v S

Ferris, R. O. (3) (Birmingham), 1949 v S; 1951 v F, S

Finney, T. (15) (Sunderland), 1974 v Nor; 1975 v E, S, W, Nor, Y; 1976 v Is, S; (Cambridge U), 1979 v E; 1980 v Is, S, E, W, Aus, Aus

Fitzpatrick, J. C. (2) (Bohemians), 1896 v E, S

Flack, H. (1) (Burnley), 1929 v S

Fleming, J. G. (7) (Nottingham F), 1986 v E; 1987 v Is, E, Y, T; 1988 v Gr, Pol

Forbes, G. (3) (Limavady), 1888 v W; (Distillery), 1891 v E, S

Forde, J. T. (4) (Ards), 1958 v Sp; 1960 v E, FRG, S

Foreman, T. A. (1) (Cliftonville), 1899 v S

Forsyth, J. (2) (YMCA), 1888 v E, S

Fox, W. (2) (Ulster), 1887 v E, S

Fulton, R. P. (20) (Belfast C), 1930 v W, E; 1931 v S, W; 1931 v E, W; 1932 v S, E; 1933 v S, E, W; 1934 v S, E, W; 1935 v S; 1936 v W, S, E; 1937 v W; 1938 v W

Gaffikin, J. (15) (Linfield Ath), 1890 v S, W; 1891 v S, W; 1892 v E, S, W; 1893 v E, S, W; 1894 v E, S, W; 1895 v E, W

Galbraith, W. (1) (Distillery), 1890 v W

Gallagher, P. (11) (Celtic), 1919 v E; 1920 v S; 1922 v S; 1923 v S, W; 1924 v S, W, E; 1925 v S, W; (Falkirk), 1927 v S

Gallogly, C. (2) (Huddersfield T), 1950 v E, S

Gara, A. (3) (Preston NE), 1902 v E, S, W

Gardiner, A. (5) (Cliftonville), 1930 v W, S; 1931 v S, E

Garrett, J. (1) (Distillery), 1925 v W

Gaston, R. (1) (Oxford U), 1968 v Is

Gaukrodger, G. (1) (Linfield), 1895 v W

Gaussen, A. W. (6) (Moyala Park), 1884 v E, S; 1888 v E, W; 1889 v E, W

Geary, J. (2) (Glentoran), 1931 v S, S

Gibb, J. T. (10) (Wellington Park) 1884 v S, W; 1885 v S, E, W; 1886 v S; 1887 v S, E, W; 1889 v S

Gibb, T. J. (1) (Cliftonville), 1936 v W

Gibson, W. K. (13) (Cliftonville), 1894 v S, W, E, 1895 v S; 1897 v W; 1898 v S, W, E; 1901 v S, W, E, 1902 v S, W

Gillespie, R. (6) (Hertford), 1886 v E, S, W; 1887 v E, S, W

Gillespie, W. (25) (Sheffield U), 1913 v E, S; 1914 v E, W; 1920 v W, S, E, 1921 v E; 1922 v S, W, E; 1923 v S, W, E; 1924 v S, W, E; 1925 v S; 1926 v W, S, E, 1927 v W,E; 1928 v E; 1930 v E

Gillespie, W. (1) (West Down), 1889 v W

Goodall, A. L. (10) (Derby Co), 1899 v S, W; 1900 v E, W; 1901 v E; 1902 v S; 1903 v E, W; (Glossop), 1904 v E, W

Goodbody, M. F. (2) (Dublin University), 1889 v E; 1891 v W

Gordon, H. (11) (Linfield), 1891 v S; 1892 v E, S, W; 1893 v E, S, W; 1895 v E, W; 1896 v E, S

Gordon, T. (2) (Linfield), 1894 v W; 1895 v E

Gorman, W. C. (4) (Brentford), 1946 v E, S; 1947 v W; 1948 v W

Gowdy, J. (6) (Glentoran), 1919 v E; (Queen's Island), 1924 v W; (Falkirk), 1925 v E; 1926 v S, E; 1927 v S

Gowdy, W. A. (6) (Hull C), 1931 v S; (Sheffield W), 1932 v S; (Linfield), 1935 v S, E, W; (Hibernian), 1936 v W

Graham, W. G. L. (14) (Doncaster R), 1951 v W, F, S, E; 1952 v W, S, F; 1953 v E; 1954 v W, S; 1955 v W, S, E; 1958 v E

Greer, W, (3) (QPR), 1909 v E, S, W

Gregg, H. (25) (Doncaster R), 1954 v W; 1956 v E, S; 1957 v P, W, I, P, E, I; (Manchester U), 1958 v W, Cz, Arg, FRG, F, E; 1959 v W, S, E; 1960 v W, E, S; 1961 v S, Gr; 1963 v S, E

Hall, G. (1) (Distillery), 1897 v E

Halligan, W. (2) (Derby Co), 1911 v W; (Wolverhampton W), 1912 v E

Hamill, M. (7) (Manchester U), 1912 v E; 1914 v E, S; (Belfast C), 1919 v E; 1920 v S, W; (Manchester C), 1921 v S

Hamilton, B. (50) (Linfield), 1968 v T; 1971 v Cyp, Cyp, E, S, W, (Ipswich T), USSR, USSR, 1972 v Sp, Bul; 1973 v Cyp, P, Cyp, E, S, W, Bul; 1974 v S, E, W, Nor, Swe; 1975 v Y, E, Swe, Nor, Y; (Everton), 1976 v Is, S, E, W, Neth, Bel; 1977 v FRG, E, S, W, Ic; (Millwall), 1978 v S, E, W, RI; (Swindon T), 1979 v Bul, Bul, E, S, W, Den; 1980 v Aus, Aus

Hamilton, J. (2) (Knock), 1882 v E, W

Hamilton, R. (1) (Distillery), 1908 v W

Hamilton, R. (5) (Glasgow R), 1928 v S, E; 1929 v E; 1930 v S; 1931 v S

Hamilton, W. (41) (QPR), 1978 v S; (Burnley), 1980 v S, E, W, Aus, Aus, Swe, P; 1981 v S, P, S, Swe, S, Is; 1982 v E, W, Y, Hon, Sp, A, F, A, FRG, Alb; 1983 v Alb, S, E, W, A, T, FRG, S; 1984 v E, W, Fin, (Oxford U), Rum; 1985 v Sp; 1986 v Mor, Alg, Sp, Bra

Hamilton, W. Den. (1) (Dublin Association), 1885 v W

Hamilton, W. J. (1) (Dublin Association), 1885 v W

Hampton, H. (9) (Bradford C), 1911 v E, S, W; 1912 v E, W; 1913 v E, S, W; 1914 v E

Hanna, D. R. A. (1) (Portsmouth), 1899 v W

Hanna, J. (2) (Nottingham F), 1912 v S, W

Hannon, D. J. (6) (Bohemian), 1908 v E, S; 1911 v E, S; 1912 v W; 1913 v E

Harkin, J. T. (5) (Southport), 1968 v W, T, (Shrewsbury T), 1969 v W, USSR, 1970 v Sp

Harland, A. I. (1) (Linfield), 1922 v E

Harris, J. (1) (Cliftonville), 1921 v W

Harris, V. (20) (Shelbourne), 1906 v E, 1907 v E, W; 1908 v E, W, S; (Everton), 1909 v E, W, S; 1910 v E, S, W; 1911 v E, S, W; 1912 v E; 1913 v E, S; 1914 v S, W

Harvey, M. (34) (Sunderland), 1961 v I, 1962 v Neth; 1963 v W, Sp, S, Sp, E; 1964 v W, U, E, Swz, Swz, S; 1965 v Neth, W, Neth, Alb, S, E, Alb; 1966 v W, FRG, Mex, E, S; 1967 v E; 1968 v W, Is. T, T; 1969 v E, USSR; 1971 v Cyp, W

Hastings, J. (7) (Knock), 1882 v E, W; (Ulster), 1883 v W; 1884 v E, S; 1886 v E, S

Hatton, S, (2) (Linfield), 1962 v S, Pol

Hayes, W. E. (4) (Huddersfield T), 1937 v E, S; 1938 v S, E

BRITISH & IRISH INTERNATIONAL APPEARANCES

Healy, F. (4) (Coleraine), 1982 v S, W, Hon, (Glentoran), A

Hegan, D. (7) (WBA), 1969 v USSR; (Wolverhampton W), 1971 v USSR; 1972 v S, E, W, Bul; 1973 v Cyp

Henderson, A. W. (3) (Ulster), 1885 v E, S, W

Hewison, G. (2) (Moyola Park), 1885 v E, S

Hill, M. J. (7) (Norwich C), 1959 v W; 1960 v W, FRG; 1961 v S; (Everton), 1963 v S, Sp, E

Hinton, E. (7) (Fulham), 1946 v S; 1947 v W, S, E; 1948 v W; (Millwall), 1951 v W, F

Hopkins, J. (1) (Brighton), 1925 v E

Houston, J. (6) (Linfield), 1912 v S, W; 1913 v W; (Everton), 1913 v E, S; 1914 v S

Houston, W. (1) (Linfield), 1932 v W

Houston, W. G. (2) (Moyola Park), 1885 v E, S

Hughes, P. (3) (Bury), 1986 v E, T; 1987 v Is

Hughes, W. (1) (Bolton W), 1951 v W

Humphries, W. (14) (Ards), 1962 v W, (Coventry C), Neth, E, S, Pol; 1963 v W, Sp, S, Sp, E; 1964 v S; (Swansea T), 1965 v W, Neth, Alb

Hunter, A. (53) (Blackburn R), 1969 v USSR; 1971 v Cyp, Cyp, E, S, W, (Ipswich T), USSR, USSR; 1972 v Sp, S, E, W, Bul; 1973 v Cyp, P, Cyp, E, S, W, Bul; 1974 v S, E, W, Nor, Swe; 1975 v Y, E, S, W, Swe, Nor, Y; 1976 v Is, S, E, W, Neth, Bel; 1977 v FRG, E, S, W, Ic, Ic, Neth, Bel; 1978 v RI, Den; 1979 v S, W, Den, E, RI

Hunter, A. (8) (Distillery), 1905 v W; 1906 v W, E, S; (Belfast C), 1908 v W; 1909 v W, E, S

Hunter, R. J. (3) (Cliftonville), 1884 v E, S, W,

Hunter, (2) (Coleraine), 1961 v E; 1963 v Sp

Irvine, R. W. (15) (Everton), 1922 v S, E; 1923 v W, E; 1924 v S, E; 1925 v E; 1926 v E; 1927 v W, E; 1928 v S, (Portsmouth), E; 1930 v S, (Connah's Quay), E; (Derry C), 1931 v W

Irvine, R. J. (8) (Linfield), 1962 v Neth, Pol, E, S, Pol; 1963 v W, Sp; (Stoke C), 1965 v W

Irvine, W. J. (23) (Burnley), 1963 v W, Sp, Swz, S; 1965 v Neth, W, Neth, Alb, S, E, Alb; 1966 v W, Mex, E, S; 1967 v E; 1968 v W, (Preston NE), Is, T; 1969 v E; (Brighton & HA), 1972 v S, E, W

Irving, S. J. (18) (Dundee), 1923 v S, W, E; 1924 v S, W, E; 1925 v S, W; 1926 v W, S, E; (Cardiff C), 1927 v S, W, E; 1928 v S, W, (Chelsea), E; 1931 v W

Jackson, T. (35) (Everton), 1968 v Is; 1969 v E, S, W, USSR, USSR; (Nottingham F), 1970 v Sp; 1972 v S, E, W; 1973 v Cyp, E, S, W, Bul, P; 1974 v S, E, W, Nor, Swe; 1975 v Y, E, S, W, (Manchester U); Swe, Nor, Y; 1976 v Neth, Bel; 1977 v FRG, E, S, W, Ic

Jamison, J. (1) (Glentoran), 1975 v Nor

Jennings, P. A. (119) (Watford), 1964 v W, U, (Tottenham H), E, Swz, Swz, S, 1965 v Neth, Alb, S, E, Alb; 1966 v W, FRG, S, E; 1967 v S, E; 1968 v W, Is, T; 1969 v E, S, W, USSR, USSR; 1970 v S, E; 1971 v Cyp, Cyp, E, S, W, USSR; 1972 v Sp, S, E, W, Bul; 1973 v Cyp, P, E, S, W, P; 1974 v S, E, W, Nor, Swe; 1975 v Y, E, S, W, Swe, Nor, Y; 1976 v Is, S, E, W, Neth, Bel; 1977 v FRG, E, S, W, Ic, (Arsenal), Ic, Neth, Bel; 1978 v RI, Den; 1979 v Bul, E, Bul, E, S, W, Den, E, RI; 1980 v Is; 1981 v S, P, S, Swe, S, Is; 1982 v E, W, Y, Hon, Sp, F; 1983 v Alb, S, E, W, A,

T, FRG, S; 1984 v W, Fin, Rum, Fin; 1985 v E, Sp, T, (Tottenham H), T, Rum, E; 1986 v F. Den, Mor, Alg, Sp, Bra

Johnston, H. (1) (Portadown), 1927 v W

Johnston, R. (2) (Old Park), 1885 v S, W

Johnston, S. (4) (Distillery), 1882 v W; 1884 v E; 1886 v E, S

Johnston, S. (4) (Linfield), 1890 v W; 1893 v S, W; 1894 v E

Johnston, S. (1) (Distillery), 1905 v W

Johnston, W. C. (2) (Glenavon), 1962 v W; (Oldham Ath), 1966 v Mex

Jones, J. (23) (Linfield), 1930 v W, S, E; 1931 v S, W, S, E; 1932 v S, E, W; 1933 v S, E, W; 1934 v S, E, W; 1935 v E, S; (Hibernian), 1936 v W, S, E; 1937 v W, (Glenavon), E

Jones, J. (3) (Glenavon), 1956 v W, E; 1957 v W

Jones S. (2) (Distillery), 1933 v E, (Blackpool), W

Jordan, T. (2) (Linfield), 1895 v E, W

Kavanagh, P. J. (1) (Glasgow C), 1929 v E

Keane, T. R. (1) (Swansea T), 1948 v S

Kearns, A. (6) (Distillery), 1900 v E, S, W; 1902 v E, S, W

Keith, R. M. (23) (Newcastle U), 1957 v E, I; 1958 v W, Cz, Arg, FRG, Cz, F, E, Sp, S; 1959 v W, S, E; 1960 v E, FRG, S; 1961 v W, I, Gr, FRG; 1962 v W, Neth

Kelly, H. R. (4) (Fulham), 1949 v E; 1950 v W, (Southampton), E, S

Kelly, J. (1) (Glentoran), 1896 v E

Kelly, J. (11) (Derry C), 1931 v E, W; 1932 v E, W, S; 1933 v W; 1935 v E, S; 1936 v W, S, E

Kelly, P. (1) (Manchester C), 1920 v E

Kelly, P. M. (1) (Barnsley), 1949 v S

Kennedy, A. L. (2) (Arsenal), 1923 v W; 1924 v E

Kernaghan, N. (3) (Belfast C), 1936 v W, S; 1937 v E

Kirkwood, H. (1) (Cliftonville), 1904 v W

Kirwan, J. (17) (Tottenham H), 1900 v W; 1902 v E, W; 1903 v E, S, W; 1904 v E, S, W; 1905 v E, S, W; (Chelsea), 1906 v E, S, W; 1907 v W; (Clyde), 1909 v S

Lacey, W. (23) (Everton), 1909 v E, S, W; 1910 v E, S, W; 1911 v E, S, W; 1912 v E; (Liverpool), 1913 v W; 1914 v E, S, W; 1919 v E; 1920 v W, S, E; 1921 v S, W, E; 1922 v S; (New Brighton), 1924 v E

Lawther, W. I. (4) (Sunderland), 1960 v W; 1961 v I, (Blackburn R), S; 1962 v Neth

Leatham, J. (1) (Belfast C), 1939 v W

Ledwidge, J. J. (2) (Shelbourne), 1906 v S, W

Lemon, J. (3) (Glentoran), 1886 v W; 1888 v S; (Belfast YMCA), 1889 v W

Leslie, W. (1) (YMCA), 1887 v E

Lewis, J. (4) (Glentoran), 1899 v S, E, W; (Distillery), 1900 v S

Little, J. (1) (Glentoran), 1898 v W

Lockhart, H. (1) (Rossall School), 1884 v W

Lockhart, N. (8) (Linfield), 1946 v E; (Coventry C), 1950 v W; 1951 v W; 1952 v W; (Aston Villa), 1953 v S, E; 1955 v W; 1956 v W

Lowther, R. (2) (Glentoran), 1888 v E, S
Loyal, J. (1) (Clarence), 1891 v S
Lutton, R. J. (6) (Wolverhampton W), 1970 v S, E; (West Ham U), 1973 v Cyp, S, W, P
Lyner, D. (6) (Glentoran), 1919 v E; 1920 v W; 1922 v S, W, (Manchester U), E; (Kilmarnock), 1923 v W

McAdams, W. J. (15) (Manchester C), 1954 v W, S; 1956 v E; 1957 v S, I; (Bolton W), 1960 v E, FRG, S; 1961 v W, I, Gr, FRG, Gr, E; (Leeds U), 1962 v Neth
McAlery, J. M. (2) (Cliftonville), 1882 v E, W
McAlinden, J. (4) (Belfast C), 1937 v S; 1938 v S; (Portsmouth), 1946 v E; (Southend U), 1948 v E
McAllen, J. (9) Linfield), 1898 v E; 1899 v E, S, W; 1900 v E, S, W; 1901 v W; 1902 v S
McAlpine, W. J. (1) (Cliftonville), 1901 v S
McArthur, A. (1) (Distillery), 1886 v W
McAuley, J. L. (6) (Huddersfield T), 1911 v E, W; 1912 v E, S; 1913 v E, S
McAuley, P. (1) (Belfast C), 1900 v S
McCabe, J. J. (6) (Leeds U), 1948 v S; 1949 v W, E; 1951 v W; 1953 v W, S
McCabe, W. (1) (Ulster), 1891 v E
McCambridge, J. (4) (Ballymena), 1930 v W, S; (Cardiff C), 1931 v W, E
McCandless, J. (5) (Bradford), 1912 v W; 1913 v W; 1920 v W, S, E
McCandless, W. (9) (Linfield), 1919 v E; 1920 v W, E; (Rangers), 1921 v W; 1922 v S; 1924 v S, W; 1925 v S; 1929 v W
McCann, P. (7) (Belfast C), 1910 v E, S, W; 1911 v E; (Glentoran), 1911 v S; 1912 v E; 1913 v W
McCashin, J. (4) (Cliftonville), 1896 v W; 1898 v S, W; 1899 v S
McCavana, W. T. (3) (Coleraine), 1954 v S; 1955 v S, E
McCaw, D. (1) (Distillery), 1882 v E
McCaw, J. H. (5) (Linfield), 1927 v W; 1930 v S, E; 1931 v W, E
McClatchey, J. (3) (Distillery), 1886 v E, S, W
McClatchey, R. (1) (Distillery), 1895 v S
McCleary, J. W. (1) (Cliftonville), 1955 v W
McCleery, W. (9) (Cliftonville), 1929 v E; 1930 v W, E; 1931 v S, W, S, W; 1932 v E, W
McClelland, J. (6) (Arsenal), 1960 v FRG; 1961 v W, I, Gr, FRG; (Fulham), 1966 v Mex
McClelland, J. (47) (Mansfield T), 1980 v S, Aus, Aus, Aus, Swe; 1981 v S, (Rangers), S, Swe; 1982 v S, W, Y, Hon, Sp, A, F, A, FRG, Alb; 1983 v T, Alb, S, E, W, A, T, FRG, S; 1984 v E, W, Fin, Rum, (Watford), Is, Fin; 1985 v E, Sp, T, T; 1986 v F, E; 1987 v E, T, Is, Y, T; 1988 v Gr, F, Ma
McCluggage, A. (12) (Bradford), 1923 v E; (Burnley), 1927 v S, W, E; 1928 v W, S, E; 1929 v W, S; 1930 v W, E; 1931 v W
McClure, G. (4) (Cliftonville), 1907 v S, W; 1908 v E; (Distillery), 1909 v E
McConnell, E. (12) (Cliftonville), 1904 v S, W; (Glentoran), 1905 v S; (Sunderland), 1906 v E; 1907 v E; 1908 v S, W; (Sheffield W), 1909 v S, W; 1910 v S, W, E
McConnell, P. (2) (Doncaster R), 1928 v W; (Southport), 1931 v E

McConnell, W. G. (6) (Bohemians), 1912 v W; 1913 v E, S; 1914 v E, S, W
McConnell, W. H. (8) (Reading), 1925 v W, E; 1926 v W, E; 1927 v S, W, E; 1928 v W
McCourt, F. J. (6) (Manchester C), 1951 v E; 1952 v W, E, S, F; 1953 v W
McCoy, J. (1) (Distillery), 1896 v W
McCoy, R. (1) (Coleraine), 1987 v Y
McCracken, R. (4) (C Palace), 1920 v E; 1921 v E; 1922 v S, W
McCracken, W. (15) (Distillery), 1902 v E, W; 1903 v E; 1904 v E, S, W; (Newcastle U), 1905 v E, S, W; 1907 v E, 1920 v E; 1922 v E, S, W; (Hull C), 1923 v S
McCreery, D. (60) (Manchester U), 1976 v S, E, W, Neth, Bel; 1977 v FRG, E, S, W, Ic, Ic, Neth, Bel; 1978 v S, E, W, RI, Den; 1979 v Bul, E, Bul, W, Den, (QPR) E, RI; 1980 v S, E, W, Aus, Aus, Swe, P; (Tulsa Roughnecks), 1981 v S, P, Swe, S, Is; 1982 v E, F, Y, Hon, Sp, A, F, (Newcastle U), A; 1983 v T; 1984 v Rum; 1985 v Sp, T, Rum, E; 1986 v F, Den, Alg, Sp, Bra, T; 1987 v E, Y, Y
McCrory, S. (1) (Southend), 1957 v E
McCullough, K. (5) (Belfast C), 1934 v W, E; (Manchester C), 1935 v S; 1936 v S, E
McCullough, W. J. (10) (Arsenal), 1961 v I; 1963 v Sp, S, Sp, E; 1964 v W, U, E, Swz; (Millwall), 1966 v E
McCurdy, C. (1) (Linfield), 1980 v Aus
McDonald, A. (10) (QPR), 1985 v Rum, E; 1986 v F, Den, Mor, Alg, Sp, Bra, E, T; 1987 v Is, E, Y, Y, T; 1988 v Pol, Fr, Ma
McDonald, R. (2) (Glasgow R), 1930 v S; 1931 v E
McDonnell, J. (4) (Bohemians), 1911 v E, S; 1912 v W; 1913 v W
McElhinney, G. (6) (Bolton W), 1983 v FRG, S; 1984 v E, W, Fin, Rum
McFaul, W. S. (6) (Linfield), 1966 v E; (Newcastle U), 1970 v W, Sp; 1971 v USSR; 1973 v Cyp, Bul
McGarry, J. K. (3) (Cliftonville), 1950 v S; 1951 v W, F
McGaughey, M. (1) (Linfield), 1984 v Is
McGee, G. (3) (Wellington Park), 1885 v E, S, W
McGrath, R. C. (21) (Tottenham H), 1974 v S, E, W, Nor; 1976 v Is, Neth, (Manchester U), Bel; 1977 v FRG, E, S, W, Ic, Ic, Neth, Bel; 1978 v S, E, W; 1979 v Bul, E, E
McGregor, S. (1) (Glentoran), 1921 v S
McGrillen, J. (2) (Clyde), 1924 v S; (Belfast C), 1927 v S
McGuire, E. (1) (Distillery), 1907 v S
McIlroy, H. (1) (Cliftonville), 1906 v E
McIlroy, J. (55) (Burnley), 1951 v S, E; 1952 v W, E, S; 1953 v W, S, E; 1954 v W, E, S; 1955 v W, S, E; 1956 v W, E, S; 1957 v P, W, I, P, S, E, I; 1958 v I, W, Cz, Arg, FRG, Cz, F, E, Sp, S; 1959 v W, S, E; 1960 v W, E, FRG; 1961 v W, Gr, FRG, S, Gr, E; 1962 v Neth, Pol, E, S, Pol; (Stoke C), 1963 v W; 1965 v S, E, Alb
McIlroy, S. B. (88) (Manchester U), 1972 v Sp, S; 1974 v S, E, W, Nor, Swe; 1975 v Y, E, S, W, Swe, Nor, Y; 1976 v S, E, W, Neth, Bel; 1977 v E, S, W, Ic, Ic, Neth, Bel; 1978 v S, E, W, RI, Den; 1979 v Bul, E, Bul, E, S, W, Den, E, RI; 1980 v Is, S, E, W, Swe, P; 1981 v S, P, S, Swe, S, Is; (Stoke C), 1982 v E, F, S, W, Y, Hon, Sp, A, F, A, FRG, Alb; 1983 v T, Alb, S,

E, W, A, T, S; 1984 v E, W, Fin, Fin; 1985 v E, T, (Manchester C), T, Rum, E; 1986 v F, Den, Mor, Alg, Sp, Bra, E

McIlvenny, J. (2) (Distillery), 1890 v E; 1891 v E

McIlvenny, P. (1) (Distillery), 1924 v W

McKeag, W. (2) (Glentoran), 1967 v S; 1968 v W

McKee, F. W. (5) (Cliftonville), 1906 v S, W; (Belfast C), 1914 v E, S, W

McKelvie, H. (1) (Glentoran), 1901 v W

McKenna, J. (7) (Huddersfield T), 1949 v S, E; 1950 v W, S, E; 1951 v F, E

McKenzie, H. (1) (Distillery), 1923 v S

McKenzie, R. (1) (Airdrie), 1967 v W

McKeown, H. (7) (Linfield), 1892 v E, S, W; 1893 v S, W; 1894 v S, W

McKie, H. (3) (Cliftonville), 1895 v E, S, W

McKinney, D. (2) (Hull C), 1921 v S; (Bradford C), 1924 v S

McKinney, V. J. (1) (Falkirk), 1966 v FRG

McKnight, A. (6) (Celtic), 1987 v Y, T; 1988 v Gr, Pol, F, Ma

McKnight, J. (2) (Preston NE), 1912 v S; (Glentoran) 1913 v S

McLaughlin, J. C. (12) (Shrewsbury T), 1961 v S, Gr, E; 1962 v W; 1963 v W; (Swansea T), 1964 v W, U, E, Swz, Swz; 1965 v W; 1966 v W

McLean, T. (1) (Limavady), 1885 v S

McMahon, J. (1) (Bohemians), 1933 v S

McMaster, G. (3) (Glentoran), 1897 v E, S, W

McMichael, A. (40) (Newcastle U), 1949 v S, E; 1950 v E, S; 1951 v F, E; 1952 v S, W, E, S, F; 1953 v W, S, E; 1954 v W, E; 1955 v W; 1956 v W, E, S; 1957 v P, W, I, P, S, E, I; 1958 v I, W, Cz, Arg, FRG, Cz, F, Sp, S; 1959 v W, S, E; 1960 v W

McMillan, G. (2) (Distillery), 1903 v E; 1905 v W

McMillan, S. (2) (Manchester U), 1962 v E, S

McMillen, W. S. (7) (Manchester U), 1933 v E; 1934 v S; 1936 v S; (Chesterfield), 1937 v S; 1938 v W, S, E

McMordie, A. S. (21) (Middlesbrough), 1968 v Is, T, T; 1969 v S, W, USSR; 1970 v S, E, W; 1971 v Cyp, Cyp, E, S, W, USSR; 1972 v Sp, S, E, W, Bul

McMorran, E. J. (15) (Belfast C), 1946 v E; (Barnsley), 1950 v S, E; 1951 v W, S, E; 1952 v W, E, S, F; (Doncaster R), 1953 v W, E; 1956 v W; 1957 v I, P

McMullan, D. (3) (Liverpool), 1925 v E; 1926 v W; 1927 v S

McNally, B.A. (5) (Shrewsbury T), 1986 v Mor, T; 1987 v Y; 1988 v Gr, Ma

McNinch, J. (3) (Ballymena), 1931 v S, S, W

McParland, P. J. (34) (Aston Villa), 1954 v W, E, S; 1955 v S, E; 1956 v E, S; 1957 v W, P, S, E, I; 1958 v I, W, Cz, Arg, FRG, Cz, F, E, Sp, S; 1959 v W, S, E; 1960 v W, E, FRG, S; 1961 v W, I, Gr, FRG; (Wolverhampton W), 1962 v Neth

McShane, J. (4) (Cliftonville), 1899 v S; 1900 v E, S, W

McVickers J. (2) (Glentoran), 1888 v E; 1889 v S

McWha, W. B. R. (7) (Knock), 1882 v E, W; (Cliftonville), 1883 v E, W; 1884 v E; 1885 v E, W

Macartney, A: (15) (Ulster), 1903 v S, W; (Linfield), 1904 v S, W; (Everton), 1905 v E, S; (Belfast C), 1907 v E, S, W; 1908 v E, S, W; (Glentoran), 1909 v E, S, W

Mackie, J. (3) (Arsenal), 1923 v W; (Portsmouth), 1934 v S, W

Madden, O. (1) (Norwich C), 1937 v E

Magill, E. J. (26) (Arsenal), 1961 v S, Gr, E; 1962 v Pol, E, S, Pol; 1963 v W, Sp, S, Sp, E; 1964 v W, U, E, Swz, Swz, S; 1965 v Neth, Alb, S, E, (Brighton & HA), Alb; 1966 v W, FRG, Mex

Maginnis, H. (8) (Linfield), 1900 v E, S, W; 1903 v S, W; 1904 v E, S, W

Maguire, E. (1) (Distillery), 1907 v S

Mahood, J. (9) (Belfast C), 1926 v S; 1927 v E; 1928 v W, S, E; 1929 v W, S; 1930 v W; (Ballymena), 1933 v S

Manderson, R. (5) (Glasgow R), 1920 v W, S; 1924 v E; 1925 v S; 1926 v S

Mansfield, J. (1) (Dublin Freebooters), 1901 v E

Martin, C. J. (6) (Glentoran), 1946 v S; (Leeds U), 1947 v S, E; 1948 v W, (Aston Villa), E; 1950 v W

Martin, D. (1) (Bo'ness), 1925 v S

Martin, D. C. (3) (Cliftonville), 1882 v E, W; 1883 v E

Martin, D. K. (10) (Belfast C), 1933 v E, S, W; 1934 v S, (Wolverhampton W), E; 1936 v W, (Nottingham F), S; 1937 v E, S; 1938 v S

Mathieson, A. (2) (Luton T), 1921 v W, E

Maxwell, J. (7) (Linfield), 1902 v W; 1903 v W, E; (Glentoran), 1905 v W, S; (Belfast C), 1906 v W; 1907 v S

Meek, H. L. (1) (Glentoran), 1925 v W

Mehaffy, J. A. C. (1) (Queen's Island), 1922 v W

Meldon, J. (2) (Dublin Freebooters), 1899 v S, W

Mercer, H. V. A. (1) (Linfield), 1908 v E

Mercer, J. T. (11) (Distillery), 1898 v E, S, W; 1899 v E; (Linfield), 1902 v E, W; (Distillery), 1903 v S, W; (Derby Co), 1904 v E, W; 1905 v S

Millar, W. (2) (Barrow), 1931 v W; 1932 v S

Miller, J. (3) (Middlesbrough), 1929 v W, S, E

Milligan, D. (1) (Chesterfield), 1939 v W

Milne, R. G. (27) (Linfield), 1894 v E, S, W; 1895 v E, W; 1896 v E, S, W; 1897 v E, S; 1898 v E, S, W; 1899 v E, W; 1901 v W; 1902 v E, S, W; 1903 v E, S; 1904 v E, S, W; 1906 v E, S, W

Mitchell, C. (1) (Glentoran), 1933 v W

Mitchell, E. J. (1) (Cliftonville), 1932 v S

Mitchell, W. (15) (Distillery), 1931 v E, W; 1932 v E, W; (Chelsea), 1933 v W, S; 1934 v S, E; 1935 v E, S; 1936 v S, E; 1937 v W, E, S

Molyneux, T. B. (11) (Ligoniel), 1883 v E, W; (Cliftonville), 1884 v E, W, S; 1885 v E, W; 1886 v E, S; 1888 v S

Montgomery, F. J: (1) (Coleraine), 1954 v E

Moore, C. (1) (Glentoran), 1949 v W

Moore, J. (3) (Linfield Ath), 1891 v E, S, W

Moore, P. (1) (Aberdeen), 1932 v E

Moore, T. (2) (Ulster), 1887 v S, W

Moore, W. (1) (Falkirk), 1923 v S

Moorhead, F. W. (1) (Dublin University), 1885 v E

Moorhead, G. (3) (Linfield), 1923 v S; 1928 v S; 1929 v S

Moran, J. (1) (Leeds C), 1912 v S

Moreland, V. (6) (Derby Co), 1979 v Bul, Bul, E, S, E, RI

Morgan, F. G. (7) (Linfield), 1922 v E; (Nottingham F), 1924 v S; 1926 v E; 1927 v E; 1928 v W, S, E

Morgan, S. (18) (Port Vale), 1972 v Sp, Bul; 1973 v P, Cyp, E, S, W, (Aston Villa), Bul, P; 1974 v S, E, Swe; 1975 v Swe, Nor, Y; (Brighton & HA), 1976 v S, W; (Sparta Rotterdam), 1978 v Den

Morrison, J. (2) (Linfield Ath), 1891 v E, W

Morrison, T. (7) (Glentoran), 1895 v E, S, W; (Burnley), 1899 v W; 1900 v W; 1902 v E, S

Morrogh, E. (1) (Bohemians), 1896 v S

Morrow, W. J. (3) (Moyola Park), 1883 v E, W; 1884 v S

Muir, R. (2) (Oldpark), 1885 v S, W

Mullan, G. (4) (Glentoran), 1983 v Alb, S, E, W

Mulholland, S. (2) (Celtic), 1906 v S, E

Mulligan, J. (1) (Manchester C), 1921 v S

Murphy, J. (3) (Bradford C), 1910 v E, S, W

Murphy, N. (3) (QPR), 1905 v E, S, W

Murray, J. M. (3) (Motherwell), 1910 v E, S; (Sheffield W), 1910 v W

Napier, R. J. (1) (Bolton W), 1966 v FRG

Neill, W. J. T. (59) (Arsenal), 1961 v I, Gr, FRG, S, Gr, E; 1962 v W, E, Pol; 1963 v W, Sp, S, Sp, E; 1964 v W, U, E, Swz, S; 1965 v Neth, W, Neth, Alb, S, E, Alb; 1966 v W, FRG, Mex, S; 1967 v W, S, E, Is, T, T; 1969 v E, S, W, USSR, USSR; 1970 v S, E, W, (Hull C), Sp; 1971 v Cyp, USSR, USSR; 1972 v Sp, S, E, W, Bul; 1973 v Cyp, P, Cyp, E, S, W

Nelis, P. (1) (Nottingham F), 1922 v E

Nelson, S. (51) (Arsenal), 1970 v E, W, Sp; 1971 v Cyp, E, S, W, USSR, USSR; 1972 v Sp, S, E, W, Bul; 1973 v Cyp, P; 1974 v S, E, Swe; 1975 v Y, Swe, Nor; 1976 v Is, E, Bel; 1977 v FRG, W, Ic, Ic, Neth, Bel; 1978 v RI, Den; 1979 v Bul, E, Bul, E, S, W, Den, E, RI; 1980 v Is; 1981 v S, P, S, Swe; (Brighton & HA), 1982 v E, S, Sp, A

Nicholl, C. J. (51) (Aston Villa), 1974 v Swe; 1975 v Y, E, S, W, Swe, Nor, Y; 1976 v S, E, W; 1977 v W, (Southampton), Bel; 1978 v S, E, W, RI; 1979 v Bul, E, Bul, E, W, RI; 1980 v Is, S, E, W, Aus, Aus, Aus, Swe, P; 1981 v S, P, S, Swe, S, Is; 1982 v E, F, W, Y, Hon, Sp, A, F; 1983 v S, E, W, (Grimsby T), A, T

Nicholl, H. (3) (Belfast C), 1902 v E, W; 1905 v E

Nicholl, J. M. (73) (Manchester U), 1976 v Is, W, Neth, Bel; 1977 v E, S, W, Ic, Ic, Neth, Bel; 1978 v S, E, W, RI, Den; 1979 v Bul, E, Bul, E, S, W, Den, E, RI; 1980 v Is, S, E, W, Aus, Aus, Aus, Swe, P; 1981 v S, P, S, Swe, S, Is; 1982 v E, (Toronto B), F, W, Y, Hon, Sp, A, F, (Sunderland), A, FRG, Alb; 1983 v T, Alb, (Toronto B), S, E, W, (Rangers), T, FRG, S; 1984 v E, (Toronto B), Fin, Rum, (WBA), Fin; 1985 v E, Sp, T, T, Rum, E; 1986 v F, Alg, Sp, Bra

Nicholson, J. J. (41) (Manchester U), 1960 v S; 1961 v W, Gr, E; 1962 v W, Neth, Pol, E, S, Pol; (Huddersfield T), 1965 v Neth, W, Neth, Alb, S, E, Alb; 1966 v W, Mex, S; 1967 v W, S, E; 1968 v W, T, T; 1969 v E, S, W, USSR, USSR; 1970 v S, E, W; 1971 v Cyp, Cyp, E, S, W, USSR, USSR

Nixon, R. (1) (Linfield), 1914 v S

Nolan-Whelan, J. V. (4) (Dublin Freebooters), 1901 v E, W; 1902 v S, W

O'Brien, M. T. (10) (QPR), 1921 v S; (Leicester C), 1922 v S, W; 1924 v S, W, (Hull C), E; 1925 v S, W; 1926 v W; (Derby Co), 1927 v W

O'Connell, P. (5) (Sheffield W), 1912 v E, S; (Hull C), 1914 v E, S, W

O'Doherty, A. (2) (Coleraine), 1970 v E, W

O'Driscoll, J. F. (3) (Swansea T), 1948 v E, S; 1949 v W

O'Hagan, C. (11) (Tottenham H), 1905 v S, W; 1906 v S, W, E; (Aberdeen), 1907 v E, S, W; 1908 v S, W; 1909 v E

O'Hagan, W. (2) (St Mirren), 1919 v E; 1920 v W

O'Hehir J. C. (1) (Bohemians), 1910 v W

O'Kane, W. J. (20) (Nottingham F), 1970 v S, E, W, Sp; 1971 v E, S, W, USSR, USSR; 1973 v P, Cyp, Bul, P; 1974 v S, E, W, Nor, Swe; 1975 v E, S

O'Mahoney, M. T. (1) (Bristol R), 1938 v S

O'Neill, J. (39) (Leicester C), 1980 v Is, S, E, W, Aus, Aus, Aus, P; 1981 v S, P, S, Swe, S, Is; 1982 v E, F, S, F, A, FRG, Alb; 1983 v T, Alb, S, S; 1984 v Is, Fin; 1985 v E, Sp, T, T, Rum, E; 1986 v F, Den, Mor, Alg, Sp, Bra

O'Neill, J. (1) (Sunderland), 1962 v W

O'Neill, M. H. (64) (Distillery), 1971 v USSR; (Nottingham F), 1972 v Sp, W; 1973 v P, Cyp, E, S, W, Bul, P; 1974 v E, W, Swe; 1975 v Y, E, S, Y; 1977 v E, S, Ic, Neth; 1978 v S, E, W, RI, Den; 1979 v Bul, E, Bul, Den, RI; 1980 v Is, Aus, Aus, Aus, Swe, P; (Norwich C), 1981 v P, S, Swe, (Manchester C); S, (Norwich C), 1982 v E, F, S, Y, Hon, Sp, A, F, A, FRG, Alb; 1983 v T, Alb, S, E, (Notts Co), A, T, FRG; 1984 v E, W, Fin, Rum, Fin

O'Neill, M. A. (4) (Newcastle U), 1988 v Gr, Pol, F, Ma

O'Reilly, H. (3) (Dublin Freebooters), 1901 v S, W; 1904 v S

Parke, J. (14) Linfield), 1963 v S, (Hibernian), Sp, E; (Sunderland), 1964 v Swz, S; 1965 v Neth, W, Neth, Alb; 1966 v FRG, E, S; 1967 v S, E

Peacock, R. (31) (Celtic), 1951 v S; 1952 v F; 1954 v W, E, S; 1955 v S, E; 1957 v W, I, P, S, E, I; 1958 v I, W, Cz, Arg, FRG, Cz, E, S; 1959 v W, S, E; 1960 v E, FRG, S; 1961 v I, Gr, FRG, (Coleraine), S

Peden, J. (24) (Linfield), 1887 v S, W; 1888 v W, E; 1889 v S, E, 1890 v W, S; 1891 v W, E; 1892 v W, E, 1893 v E, S, W; (Distillery), 1896 v W, E, S; 1897 v W, S; 1898 v W, E, S; (Linfield), 1899 v W

Penney, S. (15) (Brighton & HA), 1984 v Is; 1985 v T, Rum, E; 1986 v F, Den, Mor, Alg, Sp, E, T; 1987 v Is; 1988 v Pol, F, Ma

Percy, J. C. (1) (Belfast YMCA), 1889 v W

Platt, J. A. (23) (Middlesbrough), 1976 v Is; 1978 v S, E, W; 1980 v S, E, W, Aus, Aus, Aus, Swe, P; 1982 v F, S, W, A, A, FRG, Alb; 1983 v T; (Ballymena U), 1984 v E, W; (Coleraine), 1986 v Mor

Ponsonby, J. (8) (Distillery), 1895 v S; 1896 v E, S, W; 1897 v E, S, W; 1899 v E

Potts, R. M. C. (2) (Cliftonville), 1883 v E, W

Priestley, T. J. (2) (Coleraine), 1932 v S; (Chelsea), 1933 v E

Pyper, Jas. (7) (Cliftonville), 1897 v S, W; 1898 v S, E, W; 1899 v S; 1900 v E

Pyper, John (9) (Cliftonville), 1897 v E, S, W; 1899 v E, W; 1900 v E, W, S; 1902 v S

Pyper, M. (1) (Linfield), 1931 v W

Quinn, J. M. (18) (Blackburn R), 1984 v Is, Fin; 1985 v

E, Sp, T, T, Rum, E; 1986 v F, Den, Mor, E, T; (Swindon T), 1987 v Y, T; 1988 v Gr, Pol, Ma
Quinn, M. (1) (Portsmouth), 1988 v F

Rafferty, P. (1) (Linfield), 1980 v E
Ramsey, P. (13) (Leicester C), 1983 v A, FRG, S; 1984 v Is; 1985 v E, Sp, T, T; 1986 v Mor; 1987 v Is, E, Y, Y
Rankine, J. (2) (Alexander), 1883 v E, W
Raper, E. O. (1) (Dublin University), 1886 v W
Rattray, D. (3) (Avoniel), 1882 v E; 1883 v E, W
Rea, B. (1) (Glentoran), 1901 v E
Redmond, J. (1) (Cliftonville), 1884 v W
Reid, G. H. (1) (Cardiff C), 1923 v S
Reid, J. (6) (Ulster), 1883 v E; 1884 v W; 1887 v S; 1889 v W; 1890 v S, W
Reid, S, E. (3) (Derby Co), 1933 v E, W; 1935 v E
Reid, W. (1) (Hearts), 1930 v E
Reilly, J. (2) (Portsmouth), 1900 v E; 1902 v E
Renneville, W. T. (4) (Leyton), 1910 v S, E, W; (Aston Villa), 1911 v W
Reynolds, J. (5) (Distillery), 1890 v E, W; (Ulster), 1891 v E, S, W
Reynolds, R. (1) (Bohemians), 1905 v W
Rice, P. J. (49) (Arsenal), 1968 v Is; 1969 v USSR; 1971 v E, S, W, USSR; 1972 v Sp, S, E, W, Bul; 1973 v Cyp, E, S, W, Bul, P; 1974 v S, E, W, Nor; 1975 v Y, E, S, W, Swe, Nor, Y; 1976 v Is, S, E, Neth, Bel; 1977 v FRG, E, S, Ic, Ic, Neth, Bel; 1978 v RI, Den; 1979 v E, E, S, W, Den, E
Roberts, F. C. (1) (Glentoran), 1931 v S
Robinson, P. (2) (Distillery), 1920 v S; (Blackburn R), 1921 v W
Rogan, A. (3) (Celtic), 1987 v Y; 1988 v Gr, Pol
Rollo, D. (16) (Linfield), 1912 v W; 1913 v W; 1914 v W, E; (Blackburn R), 1920 v W, S, E; 1921 v S, W, E; 1922 v E; 1924 v S, W; 1925 v W, E; 1926 v E
Rosbotham, A. (7) (Cliftonville), 1887 v E, S, W; 1888 v E, S, W; 1889 v E
Ross, W. E. (1) (Newcastle U), 1968 v Is
Rowley, R. W. M. (6) (Southampton), 1929 v W, S, E; 1930 v W; (Tottenham H), 1931 v W, S
Russell, A. (1) (Linfield), 1946 v E
Russell, S, R: (3) (Bradford C), 1929 v E; 1930 v S; (Derry C), 1931 v E
Ryan, R. A. (1) (WBA), 1950 v W

Sanchez, L. P. (1) (Wimbledon), 1987 v T
Scott, E. (31) (Liverpool), 1920 v S, E; 1921 v S, W, E; 1925 v W, E; 1926 v S, W, E; 1927 v S, W, E; 1928 v S, W, E; 1929 v W, S, E; 1930 v E; 1931 v W; 1932 v E, S, W; 1933 v E, S, W; (Belfast C), 1934 v S; 1935 v E, S; 1936 v W
Scott, J. (2) (Grimsby), 1958 v Cz, F
Scott, J. E. (1) (Cliftonville), 1901 v S
Scott, L. J. (2) (Dublin University), 1895 v S, W
Scott, P. W. (10) (Everton), 1975 v W, Y; (York C), 1976 v Is, S, E, W; 1978 v S, E, W; (Aldershot), 1979 v S
Scott, T. (13) (Cliftonville), 1894 v E, S; 1895 v S, W; 1896 v S, E, W; 1897 v E, W; 1898 v E, S, W; 1900 v W
Scott, W. (25) (Linfield), 1903 v E, S, W; 1904 v E, S,

W; (Everton), 1905 v E, S; 1907 v E, S; 1908 v E, S, W; 1909 v E, S, W; 1910 v E, S; 1911 v E, S, W; 1912 v E; (Leeds C), 1913 v E, S, W
Scraggs, M. J. (2) (Glentoran), 1921 v W, E
Seymour, H. C. (1) (Bohemians), 1914 v W
Seymour, J. (2) (Cliftonville), 1907 v W; 1909 v W
Shanks, T. (3) (Woolwich Arsenal), 1903 v S; 1904 v W; (Brentford), 1905 v E
Sharkey, P. (1) (Ipswich T), 1976 v S
Sheehan, Dr G. (3) (Bohemians), 1899 v S; 1900 v E, W
Sheridan, J. (6) (Everton), 1903 v W, E, S; 1904 v E, S; (Stoke C), 1905 v E
Sherrard, J. (3) (Limavady), 1885 v S; 1887 v W; 1888 v W
Sherrard, W. (3) (Cliftonville), 1895 v E, W, S
Sherry, J. J. (2) (Bohemians), 1906 v E; 1907 v W
Shields, J. (1) (Southampton), 1956 v S
Silo, M. (1) (Belfast YMCA), 1888 v E
Simpson, W. J. (12) (Glasgow R), 1951 v W, F; 1953 v S, E; 1954 v E; 1957 v I, P, S, E, I; 1958 v W, S
Sinclair, J. (2) (Knock), 1882 v E, W
Slemin, J. C. (1) (Bohemians), 1909 v W
Sloan, A. S. (1) (London Caledonians), 1925 v W
Sloan, D. (2) (Oxford U), 1968 v Is; 1970 v Sp
Sloan, H. A. de B. (8) (Bohemians), 1903 v E; 1904 v S; 1905 v E; 1906 v W; 1907 v E, W; 1908 v W; 1909 v S
Sloan, J. W. (1) (Arsenal), 1947 v W
Sloan, T. (11) (Cardiff C), 1925 v E; 1926 v W, S; 1927 v S, W, E; 1928 v W, E; (Linfield), 1930 v W, S; 1931 v S
Sloan, T. (3) (Manchester U), 1979 v S, W, Den
Small, J. (1) (Clarence), 1887 v E
Small, J. M. (3) (Cliftonville), 1893 v E, S, W
Smith, E. E. (4) (Cardiff C), 1921 v S; 1922 v E; 1923 v W, E
Smith, J. (2) (Distillery), 1901 v S, W
Smyth, R. H. (1) (Dublin University), 1886 v W
Smyth, S. (9) (Wolverhampton W), 1947 v S, E; 1948 v W, S; 1949 v W, S, E; 1950 v W; (Stoke C), 1951 v E
Smyth, W. (4) (Distillery), 1948 v E, S; 1953 v S, E
Snape, A. (1) (Airdrie), 1919 v E
Spence, Den. W: (29) (Bury), 1975 v Y, E, S, W, Swe; 1976 v Is, S, E, W, (Blackpool), Neth; 1977 v FRG, E, S, W, Ic; 1978 v RI, Den; 1979 v E, Bul, E, S, W, Den, RI; (Southend U), 1980 v Is, Aus; 1981 v S, Swe; 1982 v F
Spencer, S. (6) (Distillery), 1890 v E, S; 1892 v E, S, W, 1893 v E
Spiller, E. A. (5) (Cliftonville), 1883 v E, W; 1884 v E, W, S
Stanfield, O. M. (30) (Distillery), 1887 v E, S, W; 1888 v E, S, W; 1889 v E, S, W; 1890 v E, S; 1891 v E, S, W; 1892 v E, S, W; 1893 v E, W; 1894 v E, S, W; 1895 v E, S; 1896 v E, S, W; 1897 v E, S, W
Steele, A. (4) (Charlton Ath), 1926 v W, S; (Fulham), 1929 v W, S
Stevenson, A. E. (17) (Rangers), 1933 v E, S, W; (Everton), 1934 v E, S; 1935 v S; 1936 v W, E; 1937 v W, E; 1938 v W, S, E; 1939 v W; 1946 v S; 1947 v W, S
Stewart, A. (7) (Glentoran), 1967 v W, S, E; (Derby Co), 1968 v W, Is, T, T
Stewart, D. C. (1) (Hull C), 1977 v Bel
Stewart, I. (31) (QPR), 1982 v F, A, FRG, Alb; 1983 v

T, Alb, S, E, W, A, T, FRG, S; 1984 v E, W, Fin, Rum, Is, Fin; 1985 v E, Sp, T, (Newcastle U), Rum, E; 1986 v Den, Mor, Alg, Sp, Bra, E; 1987 v Is
Stewart, R. H. (11) (St Columb's Court), 1890 v E, S, W; (Cliftonville), 1892 v E, S, W; 1893 v E, W; 1894 v E, S, W
Stewart, T. C. (1) (Linfield), 1961 v W
Swan, S. (1) (Linfield), 1899 v S

Taggart, J. (1) (Walsall), 1899 v W
Thompson, F. W. (12) (Cliftonville), 1910 v E, S, W; (Bradford C), 1911 v E; (Linfield), v W; 1912 v E, W; 1913 v E, S, W; (Clyde), 1914 v E, S
Thompson, J. (1) (Distillery), 1897 v S
Thompson, J. (1) (Belfast Ath), 1889 v S
Thunder, P. J. (1) (Bohemians), 1911 v W
Todd, S. J. (11) (Burnley), 1966 v Mex, E; 1968 v W; 1969 v E, S, W, USSR; 1970 v S, (Sheffield W), Sp; 1971 v Cyp, Cyp
Toner, J. (8) (Arsenal), 1922 v W; 1923 v W, E; 1924 v W, E; 1925 v S; (St Johnstone), 1926 v E; 1927 v S
Torrans, R. (1) (Linfield), 1893 v S
Torrans, S. (26) (Linfield), 1889 v S; 1890 v S, W; 1891 v S, W; 1892 v E, S, W; 1893 v E, S; 1894 v E, S, W; 1895 v E; 1896 v E, S, W; 1897 v E, S, W; 1898 v E, S; 1899 v E, W; 1901 v S, W
Trainor, D. (1) (Crusaders), 1967 v W
Tully, C. P. (10) (Glasgow C), 1948 v E; 1949 v E; 1951 v S; 1952 v E, S, F; 1953 v W, S; 1955 v E; 1958 v Sp
Turner, E. (2) (Cliftonville), 1896 v E, W
Turner, W. (3) (Cliftonville), 1886 v E; 1886 v S; 1888 v S
Twoomey, J. F. (2) (Leeds U), 1938 v W, E

Uprichard, W. N. M. C. (18) (Swindon T), 1951 v S, E; 1952 v W, E, S, (Portsmouth), F; 1953 v W; 1954 v E, S; 1955 v W, S, E; 1956 v W; 1957 v S, I; 1958 v Cz, Sp, S

Vernon, J. (17) (Belfast C), 1946 v E, S; (WBA), 1947 v W, S, E; 1948 v W, E, S; 1949 v W, E, S; 1950 v S, E; 1951 v W, F, S, E

Waddell, T. M. R. (1) (Cliftonville), 1906 v S
Walker, J. (1) (Doncaster R), 1955 v W
Walker, T. (1) (Bury), 1911 v S
Walsh, D. J. (9) (WBA), 1946 v S; 1947 v W, S, E; 1948 v W, E, S; 1949 v W; 1950 v W

Walsh, W. (5) (Manchester C), 1947 v S, E; 1948 v W, E, S,
Waring, R. (1) (Distillery), 1899 v E
Warren, P. (2) (Shelbourne), 1913 v E, S
Watson, J. (9) (Ulster), 1883 v E, W; 1886 v E, S, W; 1887 v S, W; 1889 v E, W
Watson, P. (1) (Distillery), 1971 v Cyp
Watson, T. (1) (Cardiff C), 1926 v S
Wattle, J. (1) (Distillery), 1899 v E
Webb, C. G. (3) (Brighton), 1909 v S, W; 1911 v S
Weir, E. (1) (Clyde), 1939 v W
Welsh, E. (4) (Carlisle U), 1966 v W, FRG, Mex; 1967 v W
Whiteside, N. (36) (Manchester U), 1982 v Y, Hon, Sp, A, F, FRG, Alb; 1983 v T, A, T, FRG, S; 1984 v E, W, Fin, Rum, Is, Fin; 1985 v E, Sp, T, Rum, E; 1986 v F, Den, Mor, Alg, Sp, Bra, E; 1987 v Is, E, Y, T; 1988 v Pol, F
Whiteside, T. (1) (Distillery), 1891 v E
Whitfield, E. R. (1) (Dublin University), 1886 v W
Williams, J. R. (2) (Ulster), 1886 v E, S
Williamson, J. (3) (Cliftonville), 1890 v E; 1892 v S; 1893 v S
Willigham, T. (2) (Burnley), 1932 v W; 1933 v S
Willis, G. (4) (Linfield), 1906 v S, W; 1907 v S; 1912 v S
Wilson, D. J. (9) (Brighton & HA), 1986 v T; 1987 v Is, E, (Luton T) Y, T; 1988 v Gr, Pol, F, Ma
Wilson, H. (1) (Linfield), 1925 v W
Wilson, K. J. (8) (Ipswich T), 1987 v Is, E, Y, (Chelsea) Y, T; 1988 v Gr, Pol, F
Wilson, M. (3) (Distillery), 1884 v E, S, W
Wilson, R. (1) (Cliftonville), 1888 v S
Wilson, S. J. (12) (Glenavon), 1961 v S; 1963 v S, (Falkirk), Sp, E; 1964 v W, U, E, Swz; (Dundee), 1966 v W, FRG, S; 1967 v E
Wilton, J. M. (7) (St Columb's Court), 1888 v E, W; 1889 v S; (Cliftonville), 1890 v E; (St Columb's Court), 1892 v W; 1893 v S
Worthington, N. (21) (Sheffield W), 1984 v W, Fin, Is; 1985 v Sp, T, Rum, E; 1986 v Den, Alg, Sp, E, T; 1987 v E, Is, Y, Y, T; 1988 v Gr, Pol, F, Ma
Wright, J. (6) (Cliftonville), 1906 v E, S, W; 1907 v E, S, W

Young, S. (9) (Linfield), 1907 v E, S; 1908 v E, S; (Airdrie), 1909 v E; 1912 v S; (Linfield), 1914 v E, S, W

SCOTLAND

Adams, J. (3) (Hearts), 1889 v Ire; 1892 v W; 1893 v Ire
Agnew, W. B. (3) (Kilmarnock), 1907 v Ire; 1908 v W, Ire
Aird, J. (4) (Burnley), 1954 v Nor, Nor, A, U
Aitken, A. (14) (Newcastle U), 1901 v E; 1902 v E; 1903 v E, W; 1904 v E; 1905 v E, W; 1906 v E; (Middlesbrough), 1907 v E, W; 1908 v E; (Leicester Fosse), 1910 v E; 1911 v E, Ire
Aitken, G. G. (8) (East Fife), 1949 v E, F; 1950 v W, NI, Swz; (Sunderland), 1953 v W, NI; 1954 v E
Aitken, R. (2) (Dumbarton), 1886 v E; 1888 v Ire
Aitken, R. (39) (Celtic), 1980 v Pe, Bel, W, E, Pol; 1983

v Bel, Can, Can; 1984 v Bel, Ni, W; 1985 v E, Ic; 1986 v W, GDR, Aus, Aus, Is, Rum, E, Den, FRG, U; 1987 v Bul, RI (2) Lux, Bel, E, Bra, H, Bel, Bul, Lux; 1988 v S.Ar, Ma, Sp, Col, E
Aitkenhead, W. A. C. (1) (Blackburn R), 1912 v Ire
Albiston, A. (14) (Manchester U), 1982 v NI; 1984 v U, Bel, GDR, W, E; 1985 v Y, Ic, Sp, Sp, W; 1986 v GDR, Neth, U
Alexander, D. (2) (East Stirlingshire), 1894 v W, Ire
Allan, D. S. (3) (Queen's Park), 1885 v E, W; 1886 v W
Allan, G. (1) (Liverpool), 1897 v E
Allan, H. (1) (Hearts), 1902 v W

BRITISH & IRISH INTERNATIONAL APPEARANCES

Allan, J. (2) (Queen's Park), 1887 v E, W
Allan, T. (2) (Dundee), 1974 v FRG, N
Ancell, R. F. D. (2) (Newcastle U), 1937 v W, NI
Anderson, A. (23) (Hearts), 1933 v E; 1934 v A, E, W, NI; 1935 v E, W, NI; 1936 v E, W, NI; 1937 v G, E, W, NI, A; 1938 v E, W, NI, Cz, Neth; 1939 v W, H
Anderson, F. (1) (Clydesdale), 1874 v E
Anderson, G. (1) (Kilmarnock), 1901 v Ire
Anderson, H. A. (1) (Raith R), 1914 v W
Anderson, J. (1) (Leicester C), 1954 v Fin
Anderson, K. (3) (Queen's Park), 1896 v Ire; 1898 v E, Ire
Anderson, W. (6) (Queen's Park), 1882 v E; 1883 v E, W; 1884 v E, 1885 v E, W
Andrews, P. (1) (Eastern), 1875 v E
Archibald, A. (8) (Rangers), 1921 v W; 1922 v W, E; 1923 v NI; 1924 v E, W; 1931 v E; 1932 v E
Archibald, S, (27) (Aberdeen), 1980 v P; (Tottenham H), NI, Pol. H; 1981 v Swe, Is, NI, Is, NI, E; 1982 v NI, P, Sp, Neth, NZ, Bra, USSR; 1983 v GDR, Swz, Bel; 1984 v GDR, E, F; (Barcelona), 1985 v Sp, E, Ic; 1986 v FRG
Armstrong, M. W. (3) (Aberdeen), 1936 v W, NI; 1937 v G
Arnott, W. (14) (Queen's Park), 1883 v W; 1884 v E, Ire; 1885 v E, W; 1886 v E; 1887 v E, W; 1888 v E; 1889 v E; 1890 v E; 1891 v E; 1892 v E; 1893 v E
Auld J. R. (3) (Third Lanark), 1887 v E, W; 1889 v W
Auld, R. (3) (Celtic), 1959 v H, P; 1960 v W

Baird, A. (2) (Queen's Park), 1892 v Ire; 1894 v W
Baird, D. (3) (Hearts), 1890 v Ire; 1891 v E; 1892 v W
Baird, H. (1) (Airdrie), 1956 v A
Baird, J. C. (3) (Vale of Leven), 1876 v E; 1878 v W; 1880 v E
Baird, S. (7) (Rangers), 1957 v Y, Sp, Sp, Swz, FRG; 1958 v F, NI
Baird, W. U. (1) (St Bernard), 1897 v Ire
Bannon, E. (11) (Dundee U), 1980 v Bel; 1983 v NI, W, E, Can; 1984 v GDR; 1986 v Is, Rum, E, Den, FRG
Barbour, A. (1) (Renton), 1885 v Ire
Barker, J. B. (2) (Rangers), 1893 v W; 1894 v W
Barrett, F. (2) (Dundee), 1894 v Ire; 1895 v W
Battles, B. (3) (Celtic), 1901 v E, W, Ire
Battles, B. Jnr. (1) (Hearts), 1931 v W
Bauld, W. (3) (Hearts), 1950 v E, Swz, P
Baxter, J. C. (34) (Rangers), 1961 v NI, RI, RI, Cz; 1962 v NI, W, E, Cz, Cz, U; 1963 v W, NI, E, A, Nor, RI, Sp; 1964 v W, E, Nor, FRG; 1965 v W, NI, Fin; (Sunderland), 1966 v P, Bra, NI, W, E, I; 1967 v W, E, USSR; 1968 v W
Baxter, R. D. (3) (Middlesbrough), 1939 v E, W, H
Beattie, A. (7) (Preston NE), 1937 v E, A, Cz; 1938 v E; 1939 v W, NI, H
Beattie, R. (1) (Preston NE) 1939 v W
Begbie, I. (4) (Hearts), 1890 v Ire; 1891 v E; 1892 v W; 1894 v E
Bell, A. (1) (Manchester U), 1912 v Ire
Bell, J. (10) (Dumbarton), 1890 v Ire; 1892 v E; (Everton), 1896 v E; 1897 v E; 1898 v E; (Celtic), 1899 v E, W, Ire; 1900 v E, W

Bell, M. (1) (Hearts), 1901 v W
Bell, W. J. (2) (Leeds U), 1966 v P, Bra
Bennett, A. (11) (Celtic), 1904 v W; 1907 v Ire; 1908 v W; (Rangers), 1909 v W, Ire, E; 1910 v E, W; 1911 v E, W; 1913 v Ire
Bennie, R. (3) (Airdrieonians), 1925 v W, NI; 1926 v NI
Berry, D. (3) (Queen's Park), 1894 v W; 1899 v W, Ire
Berry, W. H. (4) (Queen's Park), 1888 v E; 1889 v E; 1890 v E; 1891 v E
Bett, J. (18) (Rangers), 1982 v Neth; 1983 v Bel; (Lokeren), 1984 v Bel, W, E, F; 1985 v Y, Ic, Sp, Sp, W, E, Ic; (Aberdeen), 1986 v W, Is, Neth; 1987 v Bel, H
Beveridge, W. W. (3) (Glasgow University), 1879 v E, W; 1880 v W
Black, A. (3) (Hearts), 1938 v Cz, Neth; 1939 v H
Black, D. (1) (Hurlford), 1889 v Ire
Black, E. (2) (Aberdeen), 1987 v H, Lux
Black, I. H. (1) (Southampton), 1948 v E
Blackburn, J. E. (1) (Royal Engineers), 1873 v E
Blacklaw, A. S. (3) (Burnley), 1963 v Nor, Sp; 1966 v I
Blackley, J. (7) (Hibernian), 1974 v Cz, E, Bel, Z; 1976 v Swz; 1977 v W, Swe
Blair, D. (3) (Clyde), 1929 v W, NI; 1931 v E, A, I; 1932 v W, NI; (Aston Villa), 1933 v W
Blair, J. (8) (Sheffield W), 1920 v E, Ire; (Cardiff C), 1921 v E; 1922 v E; 1923 v E, W, NI; 1924 v W
Blair, J. (1) (Motherwell), 1934 v W
Blair, J. A. (1) (Blackpool), 1947 v W
Blair, W. (1) (Third Lanark), 1896 v W
Blessington, J. (4) (Celtic), 1894 v E, Ire; 1896 v E, Ire
Blyth, J. A. (2) (Coventry C), 1978 v Bul, W
Bone, J. (2) (Norwich C), 1972 v Y; 1973 v D
Bowie, J. (2) (Rangers), 1920 v E, Ire
Bowie, W. (1) (Linthouse), 1891 v Ire
Bowman, G. A. (1) (Montrose), 1892 v Ire
Boyd, J. M. (1) (Newcastle U), 1934 v NI
Boyd, R. (2) (Mossend Swifts), 1889 v Ire; 1891 v W
Boyd, W. G. (2) (Clyde), 1931 v I, Sw
Brackenbridge, T. (1) (Hearts), 1888 v Ire
Bradshaw, T. (1) (Bury), 1928 v E
Brand, R. (8) (Rangers), 1961 v NI, Cz, RI, RI; 1962 v NI, W, Cz, U
Branden, T. (1) (Blackburn R), 1896 v E
Brazil, A. (13) (Ipswich T), 1980 v Pol, H; 1982 v Sp, Neth, NI, W, E, NZ, USSR; 1983 v GDR, Swz, W, E
Bremner, D. (1) (Hibernian), 1976 v Sw
Bremner, W. J. (54) (Leeds U), 1965 v Sp; 1966 v E, Pol, P, Bra, I, I; 1967 v W, NI, E, 1968 v W, E; 1969 v W, E, NI, Den, A, FRG, Cyp, Cyp; 1970 v RI, FRG, A; 1971 v W, E; 1972 v P, Bel, Neth, NI, W, E, Y, Cz, Bra; 1973 v Den, Den, E, E, NI, Swz, Bra; 1974 v Cz, FRG, NI, W, E, Bel, Nor, Z, Bra, Y; 1975 v Sp, Sp; 1976 v Den
Brennan, F. (7) (Newcastle U), 1947 v W, NI; 1953 v W, NI, E; 1954 v NI, E
Breslin, B. (1) (Hibernian), 1897 v W
Brewster, G. (1) (Everton), 1921 v E
Brogan, J. (4) (Celtic), 1971 v W, NI, P, E
Brown, A. (1) (Middlesbrough), 1904 v E
Brown, A. (2) (St Mirren), 1890 v W; 1891 v W
Brown, A. D. (14) (East Fife), 1950 v Swz, P, F; (Blackpool), 1952 v USA, Den, Swe; 1953 v W; 1954 v W, E, Nor, Nor, Fin, A, U

Brown, G. C. P. (19) (Rangers), 1931 v W; 1932 v E, W, NI; 1933 v E; 1935 v A, E, W; 1936 v E, W; 1937 v G, E, W, NI, Cz; 1938 v E, W, Cz, Neth

Brown, H. (3) (Partick T), 1947 v W, Bel, Lux

Brown, J. (1) (Cambuslang), 1890 v W

Brown, J. B. (1) (Clyde), 1939 v W

Brown, J. G. (1) (Sheffield U), 1975 v R

Brown, R. (2) (Dumbarton), 1884 v W, Ire

Brown, R. (3) (Rangers), 1947 v NI; 1949 v NI; 1952 v E

Brown, R. Jnr. (1) (Dumbarton), 1885 v W

Brown, W. D. F. (28) (Dundee), 1958 v F; 1959 v E, W, NI; (Tottenham H), 1960 v W, NI, Pol, A, H, T; 1962 v NI, W, E, Cz; 1963 v W, NI, E, A; 1964 v NI, W, Nor; 1965 v E, Fin, Pol, Sp; 1966 v NI, Pol, I

Browning, J. (1) (Celtic), 1914 v W

Brownlie, J. (7) (Hibernian), 1971 v USSR; 1972 v Pe, NI, E; 1973 v Den, Den; 1976 v R

Brownlie, J. (16) (Third Lanark), 1909 v E, Ire; 1910 v E, W, Ire; 1911 v W, Ire; 1912 v W, Ire, E; 1913 v W, Ire, E; 1914 v W, Ire, E

Bruce, D. (1) (Vale of Leven), 1890 v W

Bruce, R. F. (1) (Middlesbrough), 1934 v A

Buchan, M. M. (34) (Aberdeen), 1972 v P, Bel; (Manchester U), W, Y, Cz, Bra; 1973 v Den, Den, E; 1974 v FRG, NI, W, Nor, Bra, Y; 1975 v GDR, Sp, P; 1976 v Den, Rum; 1977 v Fin, Cz, Ch, Arg, Bra; 1978 v GDR, W, NI, Pe, Ir, Neth; 1979 v A, Nor, P

Buchanan, J. (1) (Cambuslang), 1889 v Ire

Buchanan, J. (2) (Rangers), 1929 v E; 1930 v E

Buchanan, P. S. (1) (Chelsea), 1938 v Cz

Buchanan, R. (1) (Abercorn), 1891 v W

Buckley, P. (3) (Aberdeen), 1954 v Nor; 1955 v W, NI

Buick, A. (2) (Hearts), 1902 v W, Ire

Burley, G. (11) (Ipswich T), 1979 v W, NI, E, Arg, Nor; 1980 v P, NI, E, Pol; 1982 v W, E

Burns, F. (1) (Manchester U), 1970 v A

Burns, K. (20) (Birmingham C), 1974 v FRG; 1975 v GDR, Sp, Sp; 1977 v Cz, W, Swe, W; (Nottingham F), 1978 v NI, W, E, Pe, Ir; 1979 v Nor; 1980 v Pe, A, Bel; 1981 v Is, NI, W

Burns, T. (8) (Celtic), 1981 v NI; 1982 v Neth, W; 1983 v Bel, NI, Can, Can; 1988 v E

Busby, M. W. (1) (Manchester C), 1934 v W

Cairns, T. (8) (Rangers), 1920 v W; 1922 v E; 1923 v E, W; 1924 v NI; 1925 v W, E, NI

Calderhead, D. (1) (Queen of the South), 1889 v Ire

Calderwood, R. (3) (Cartvale), 1885 v Ire, E, W

Caldow, E. (40) (Rangers), 1957 v Sp, Sp, Swz, FRG, E; 1958 v NI, W, Swz, Par, H, Pol, Y, F; 1959 v W, NI, FRG, Neth, P; 1960 v E, W, NI, A, H, T; 1961 v E, W, NI, RI, RI, Cz; 1962 v NI, W, E, Cz, Cz, U; 1963 v W, NI, E

Callaghan, P. (1) (Hibernian), 1900 v Ire

Callaghan, W. (2) (Dunfermline Ath), 1970 v EI, W

Cameron, J. (2) (St Mirren), 1904 v Ire; (Chelsea), 1909 v E

Cameron, J. (1) (Queen's Park), 1896 v Ire

Cameron, J. (1) (Rangers), 1886 v Ire

Campbell, C. (13) (Queen's Park), 1874 v E; 1876 v W; 1877 v E, W; 1878 v E; 1879 v E; 1880 v E; 1881 v E; 1882 v E, W; 1884 v E; 1885 v E; 1886 v E

Campbell, H. (1) (Renton), 1889 v W

Campbell, Jas. (1) (Sheffield W), 1913 v W

Campbell, J. (1) (South Western), 1880 v W

Campbell, J. (2) (Kilmarnock), 1891 v Ire; 1892 v W

Campbell, John (12) (Celtic), 1893 v E, Ire; 1898 v E, Ire; 1900 v E, Ire; 1901 v E, W, Ire; 1902 v W, Ire; 1903 v W

Campbell, John (4) (Rangers), 1899 v E, W, Ire; 1901 v Ire

Campbell, K. (8) (Liverpool), 1920 v E, W, Ire; (Partick T), 1921 v W, Ire; 1922 v W, NI, F

Campbell, P. (2) (Rangers), 1878 v W; 1879 v W

Campbell, P. (1) (Morton), 1898 v W

Campbell, R. (5) (Falkirk), 1947 v Bel, Lux; (Chelsea), 1950 v Swz, P, F

Campbell, W. (5) (Morton), 1947 v NI; 1948 v E, Bel, Swz, F

Carabine, J. (3) (Third Lanark), 1938 v Neth; 1939 v E, NI

Carr, W. M. (6) (Coventry C), 1970 v NI, W, E; 1971 v Den; 1972 v Pe; 1973 v Den

Cassidy, J. (4) (Celtic), 1921 v W, Ire; 1923 v NI; 1924 v W

Chalmers, S. (5) (Celtic), 1965 v W, Fin; 1966 v P, Bra; 1967 v NI

Chalmers, W. (1) (Rangers), 1885 v Ire

Chalmers, W. S. (1) (Queen's Park), 1929 v NI

Chambers, T. (1) (Hearts), 1894 v W

Chaplin, G. D. (1) (Dundee), 1908 v W

Cheyne, A. G. (5) (Aberdeen), 1929 v E, Nor, G, Neth; 1930 v F

Christie, A. J. (3) (Queen's Park), 1898 v W; 1899 v E, Ire

Christie, R. M. (1) (Queen's Park), 1884 v E

Clark, J. (4) (Celtic), 1966 v Bra; 1967 v W, NI, USSR

Clark, R. B. (17) (Aberdeen), 1968 v W, Neth; 1970 v NI; 1971 v W, NI, E, Den, P, USSR; 1972 v Bel, NI, W, E, Cz, Bra; 1973 v Den, E

Clarke, S. (5) (Chelsea), 1987 v H, Bel, Bul; 1988 v S.Ar, Ma

Cleland, J. (1) (Royal Albert), 1891 v Ire

Clements, R. (1) (Leith Ath), 1891 v Ire

Clunas, W. L. (2) (Sunderland), 1924 v E; 1926 v W

Collier, W. (1) (Raith R), 1922 v W

Collins, R. Y. (31) (Celtic), 1951 v W, NI, A; 1955 v Y, A, H; 1956 v NI, W; 1957 v E, W, Sp, Sp, Swz, FRG; 1958 v NI, W, Swz, H, Pol, Y, F, Par; (Everton), 1959 v E, W, NI, FRG, Neth, P; (Leeds U), 1965 v E, Pol, Sp

Collins, J. (1) (Hibernian), 1988 v S.Ar

Collins, T. (1) (Hearts), 1909 v W

Colman, D. (4) (Aberdeen), 1911 v E, W, Ire; 1913 v Ire

Colquhoun, E. P. (9) (Sheffield U), 1972 v P, Neth, Pe, Y, Cz, Bra; 1973 v Den, Den, E

Colquhoun, J. (1) (Hearts), 1988 v S.Ar

Combe, J. R. (3) (Hibernian), 1948 v E, Bel, Swz

Conn, A. (1) (Hearts), 1956 v A

Conn, A. (2) (Tottenham H), 1975 v NI, E

Connachan, E. D. (2) (Dunfermline Ath), 1962 v Cz, U

Connelly, G. (2) (Celtic), 1974 v Cz, FRG

Connolly, J. (1) (Everton), 1973 v Swz

Connor, J. (1) (Airdrieonians), 1886 v Ire

Connor, J. (4) (Sunderland), 1930 v F; 1932 v NI; 1934 v E; 1935 v NI

BRITISH & IRISH INTERNATIONAL APPEARANCES

Dowds, P. (1) (Celtic), 1892 v Ire

Downie, R. (1) (Third Lanark), 1892 v W

Doyle, D. (8) (Celtic), 1892 v E; 1893 v W; 1894 v E; 1895 v E, Ire; 1897 v E; 1898 v E, Ire

Doyle, J. (1) (Ayr U), 1976 v R

Drummond, J. (14) (Falkirk), 1892 v Ire; (Rangers), 1894 v Ire; 1895 v Ire, E; 1896 v E, Ire; 1897 v Ire; 1898 v E; 1900 v E; 1901 v E; 1902 v E, W, Ire; 1903 v Ire

Dunbar, M. (1) (Cartvale), 1886 v Ire

Duncan, A. (6) (Hibernian), 1975 v P, W, NI, E, Rum; 1976 v Den

Duncan, D. (14) (Derby Co), 1933 v E, W; 1934 v A, W; 1935 v E, W; 1936 v E, W, NI; 1937 v G, E, W, NI; 1938 v W

Duncan, D. M. (3) (East Fife), 1948 v Bel, Swz, F

Duncan, J. (2) (Alexandra Ath), 1878 v W; 1882 v W

Duncan, J. (1) (Leicester C), 1926 v W

Duncanson, J. (1) (Rangers), 1947 v NI

Dunlop, J. (1) (St Mirren), 1890 v W

Dunlop, W. (1) (Liverpool), 1906 v E

Dunn, J. (6) (Hibernian), 1925 v W, NI; 1927 v NI; 1928 v NI, E; (Everton), 1929 v W

Durie, G. S. (1) (Chelsea), 1987 v Bul

Durrant, I. (4) (Rangers), 1987 v H, Bel; 1988 v Ma, Sp

Dykes, J. (2) (Hearts), 1938 v Neth; 1939 v NI

Easson, J. F. (3) (Portsmouth), 1931 v A, Swz; 1934 v W

Ellis, J. (1) (Mossend Swifts), 1892 v Ire

Evans, A. (4) (Aston Villa), 1982 v Neth, NI, E, NZ

Evans, R. (48) (Celtic), 1949 v E, W, NI, F; 1950 v W, NI, Swz, P; 1951 v E, A; 1952 v NI; 1953 v Swe; 1954 v NI, W, E, Nor, Fin; 1955 v NI, P, Y, A, H; 1956 v E, NI, W, A; 1957 v FRG, Sp; 1958 v NI, W, E, Swz, H, Pol, Y, Par, F; 1959 v E, FRG, Neth, P; 1960 v E, NI, W, Pol; (Chelsea), 1960 v A, H, T

Ewart, J. (1) (Bradford C), 1921 v E

Ewing, T. (2) (Partick T), 1958 v W, E

Farm, G. N. (10) (Blackpool), 1953 v W, NI, E, Swe; 1954 v NI, W, E; 1959 v FRG, Neth, P

Ferguson, D. (2) (Rangers), 1988 v Ma, Col

Ferguson, J. (6) (Vale of Leven), 1874 v E; 1876 v E, W; 1877 v E, W; 1878 v W

Ferguson, R. (7) (Kilmarnock), 1966 v W, E, Neth, P, Bra; 1967 v W, NI

Fernie, W. (12) (Celtic), 1954 v Fin, A, U; 1955 v W, NI; 1957 v E, NI, W, Y; 1958 v W, Swz, Par

Findlay, R. (1) (Kilmarnock), 1898 v W

Fitchie, T. T. (4) (Woolwich Arsenal), 1905 v W; 1906 v W, Ire; (Queen's Park), 1907 v W

Flavell, R. (2) (Airdrieonians), 1947 v Bel, Lux

Fleming, C. (1) (East Fife), 1954 v NI

Fleming, J. W. (3) (Rangers), 1929 v G, Neth; 1930 v E

Fleming, R. (1) (Morton), 1886 v Ire

Forbes, A. R. (14) (Sheffield U), 1947 v Bel, Lux, E; 1948 v W, NI; (Arsenal), 1950 v E, P, F; 1951 v W, NI, A; 1952 v W, Den, Swe

Forbes, J. (5) (Vale of Leven), 1884 v E, W, Ire; 1887 v W, E

Ford, D. (3) (Hearts), 1974 v Cz, FRG, W

Forrest, J. (5) (Rangers), 1966 v W, I; (Aberdeen), 1971 v Bel, Den, USSR

Forrest, J. (1) (Motherwell), 1958 v E

Forsyth, A. (10) (Partick T), 1972 v Y, Cz, Bra; 1973 v Den; (Manchester U), E; 1975 v Sp, NI, Rum, GDR; 1976 v Den

Forsyth, C. (4) (Kilmarnock), 1964 v E; 1965 v W, NI, Fin

Forsyth, T. (22) (Motherwell), 1971 v Den; (Rangers), 1974 v Cz; 1976 v Swz, NI, W, E; 1977 v Fin, Swe, W, NI, E, Ch, Arg, Bra; 1978 v Cz, W, NI, W, E, Pe, Ir, Neth

Foyers, R. (2) (St Bernard's), 1893 v W; 1894 v W

Fraser, D. M. (2) (WBA), 1968 v Neth; 1969 v Cyp

Fraser, J. (1) (Moffat), 1891 v Ire

Fraser, M. J. E. (5) (Queen's Park), 1880 v W; 1882 v W, E; 1883 v W, E

Fraser, J. (1) (Dundee), 1907 v Ire

Fraser, W. (2) (Sunderland), 1955 v W, NI

Fulton, W. (1) (Abercorn), 1884 v Ire

Fyfe, J. H. (1) (Third Lanark), 1895 v W

Gabriel, J. (2) (Everton), 1961 v W; 1964 v Nor

Gallacher, H. K. (20) (Airdrieonians), 1924 v NI; 1925 v E, W, NI, 1926 v W; (Newcastle U), 1926 v E, NI; 1927 v E, W, NI; 1928 v E, W; 1929 v E, W, NI; 1930 v W, NI, F; (Chelsea), 1934 v E; (Derby Co), 1935 v E

Gallacher, K. (2) (Dundee U), 1988 v Col, E

Gallacher, P. (1) (Sunderland), 1935 v NI

Galt, J. H. (2) (Rangers), 1908 v W, Ire

Gardiner, I. (1) (Motherwell), 1958 v W

Gardner, D. R. (1) (Third Lanark), 1897 v W

Gardner, R. (5) (Queen's Park), 1872 v E; 1873 v E; (Clydesdale), 1874 v E; 1875 v E; 1878 v E

Gemmell, T. (2) (St Mirren), 1955 v P, Y

Gemmell, T. (18) (Celtic), 1966 v E; 1967 v W, NI, E, USSR; 1968 v NI, E; 1969 v W, NI, E, Den, A, FRG, Cyp; 1970 v E, RI; 1971 v Bel

Gemmill, A. (43) (Derby Co), 1971 v Bel; 1972 v P, Neth, Pe, NI, W, E; 1976 v Den, Rum, NI, W, E; 1977 v Fin, Cz, W, W, NI, E, Ch, Arg, Bra; 1978 v GDR; (Nottingham F), Bul, NI, W, E, Pe, Ir, Neth; 1979 v A, Nor, P, Nor; (Birmingham C), 1980 v A, P, NI, W, E, H; 1981 v Swe, P, Is, NI

Gibb, W. (1) (Clydesdale), 1873 v E

Gibson, D. W. (7) (Leicester C), 1963 v A, Nor, RI, Sp; 1964 v NI; 1965 v W, Fin

Gibson, J. D. (8) (Partick T), 1926 v E; 1927 v E, W, NI; (Aston Villa), 1928 v E, W; 1930 v W, NI

Gibson, N. (14) (Rangers), 1895 v E, Ire; 1896 v E, Ire; 1897 v E, Ire; 1898 v E; 1899 v E, W, Ire; 1900 v E, Ire; 1901 v W; (Partick T), 1905 v Ire

Gilchrist, J. E. (1) (Celtic), 1922 v E

Gilhooley, M. (1) (Hull C), 1922 v W

Gillespie, G. (7) (Rangers), 1880 v W; 1881 v E, W; 1882 v E; (Queen's Park), 1886 v W; 1890 v W; 1891 v Ire

Gillespie, G. T. (3) (Liverpool), 1987 v Bel, Bul; 1988 v Sp

Gillespie, Jas. (1) (Third Lanark), 1898 v W

Gillespie, John. (1) (Queen's Park), 1896 v W

Gillespie, R. (4) (Queen's Park), 1927 v W; 1931 v W; 1932 v F; 1933 v E

Gillick, T. (5) (Everton), 1937 v A, Cz; 1939 v W, NI, H

Gilmour, J. (1) (Dundee), 1931 v W

Gilzean, A. J. (22) (Dundee), 1964 v W, E, Nor, FRG; 1965 v NI; (Tottenham H), Sp; 1966 v NI, W, Pol, I; 1968 v W; 1969 v W, E, FRG, Cyp, Cyp, A; 1970 v NI, E, FRG, A; 1971 v P

Glavin, R. (1) (Celtic), 1977 v Swe

Glen, A. (2) (Aberdeen), 1956 v E, NI

Glen, R. (3) (Renton), 1895 v W; 1896 v W; (Hibernian), 1900 v Ire

Goram, A. L. (4) (Oldham Ath), 1986 v GDR, Rum, Neth; 1987 v Bra

Gordon, J. E. (10) (Rangers), 1912 v E, Ire; 1913 v E, Ire, W; 1914 v E, Ire; 1920 v W, E, Ire

Gossland, J. (1) (Rangers), 1884 v Ire

Goudie, J. (1) (Abercorn), 1884 v Ire

Gough, C. R. (38) (Dundee U), 1983 v Swz, NI, W, E, Can, Can, Can; 1984 v U, Bel, GDR, NI, W, E, F; 1985 v Sp, E, Ic; 1986 v W, GDR, Aus, Is, Rum, E, Den, FRG, U; (Tottenham H), 1987 v Bul, RI, RI, Bel, E, Bra, H; (Rangers), 1988 v S.Ar, Sp, Col, E

Gourlay, J. (2) (Cambuslang), 1886 v Ire; 1888 v W

Govan, J. (6) (Hibernian), 1948 v E, W, Bel, Swz, F; 1949 v NI

Gow, D. R. (1) (Rangers), 1888 v E

Gow, J. J. (1) (Queen's Park), 1885 v E

Gow, J. R. (1) (Rangers), 1888 v Ire

Graham, A. (10) (Leeds U), 1978 v GDR; 1979 v A, Nor, W, NI, E, Arg, Nor; 1980 v A; 1981 v W

Graham G. (12) (Arsenal), 1972 v P, Neth, NI, Y, Cz, Bra; 1973 v Den, Den; (Manchester U), E, W, NI, Bra

Graham, J. (1) (Annbank), 1884 v Ire

Graham J. A. (1) (Arsenal), 1921 v Ire

Grant, J. (2) (Hibernian), 1959 v W, NI

Gray, A. (1) (Hibernian), 1903 v Ire

Gray, A. M. (20) (Aston Villa), 1976 v Rum, Swz; 1977 v Fin, Cz; 1979 v A, Nor; (Wolverhampton W), 1980 v P, E; 1981 v Swe, P, Is, NI; 1982 v Swe, NI; 1983 v NI, W, E, Can, Can; (Everton), 1985 v Ic

Gray, D. (10) (Rangers), 1929 v W, NI, G, Neth; 1930 v W, E, NI; 1931 v W; 1933 v W, NI

Gray, E. (12) (Leeds U), 1969 v E, Cyp, 1970 v FRG, A; 1971 v W, NI; 1972 v Bel, Neth; 1976 v W, E, 1977 v Fin, W

Gray, F. T. (32) (Leeds U), 1976 v Swz; 1979 v Nor, P, W, NI, E, Arg; (Nottingham F) 1980 v Bel; 1981 v Swe, P, Is, NI, is, W, (Leeds U), NI; E; 1982 v Swe, NI, P, Sp, Neth, W, NZ, Bra, USSR; 1983 v GDR, Swz, Bel, Swz, W, E, Can

Gray, W. (1) (Pollokshields Ath), 1886 v E

Green, A. (6) (Blackpool), 1971 v Bel, P, NI, E; 1972 v W, E

Greig, J. (44) (Rangers), 1964 v E, FRG; 1965 v W, NI, E, Fin, Fin, Sp, Pol; 1966 v NI, W, E, Pol, I, I, P, Neth, Bra; 1967 v W, NI, E; 1968 v NI, W, E, Neth; 1969 v W, NI, E, Den, A, FRG, Cyp, Cyp; 1970 v W, E, RI, FRG, A; 1971 v Den, Bel, W, NI, E; 1976 v Den

Groves, W. (3) (Hibernian), 1888 v W; (Celtic), 1889 v Ire; 1890 v E

Guilliland, W. (4) (Queen's Park), 1891 v W; 1892 v Ire; 1894 v E; 1895 v E

Haddock, H. (6) (Clyde), 1955 v E, H, H, P, Y; 1958 v E

Haddow, D. (1) (Rangers), 1894 v E

Haffey, F. (2) (Celtic), 1960 v E; 1961 v E

Hamilton, A. (4) (Queen's Park), 1885 v E, W; 1886 v E; 1888 v E

Hamilton, A. W. (24) (Dundee), 1962 v Cz, U, W, E; 1963 v W, NI, E, A, Nor, RI; 1964 v NI, W, E, Nor, FRG; 1965 v NI, W, E, Fin, Fin, Pol, Sp; 1966 v Pol, NI

Hamilton, G. (5) (Aberdeen), 1947 v NI; 1951 v Bel, A; 1954 v Nor, Nor

Hamilton, G. (1) (Port Glasgow Ath), 1906 v Ire

Hamilton, J. (3) (Queen's Park), 1892 v W; 1893 v E, Ire

Hamilton, J. (1) (St Mirren) 1924 v NI

Hamilton, R. C. (11) (Rangers), 1899 v E, W, Ire; 1900 v W; 1901 v E, Ire; 1902 v W, Ire; 1903 v E; 1904 v Ire; (Dundee), 1911 v W

Hamilton, T. (1) (Hurlford), 1891 v Ire

Hamilton, T. (1) (Rangers), 1932 v E

Hamilton, W. M. (1) (Hibernian), 1965 v Fin

Hannah, A. B. (1) (Renton), 1888 v W

Hannah, J. (1) (Third Lanark), 1889 v W

Hansen, A. D. (26) (Liverpool), 1979 v W, Arg; 1980 v Bel, P; 1981 v Swe, P, Is; 1982 v Swe, NI, P, Sp, NI, W, E, NZ, Bra, USSR; 1983 v GDR, Swz, Bel, Swz; 1985 v W; 1986 v Rum; 1987 v RI, RI, Lux

Hansen, J. (2) (Partick T), 1972 v Bel, Y

Harkness, J. D. (11) (Queen's Park), 1927 v E, NI; 1928 v E; (Hearts), 1929 v W, E, NI; 1930 v E, W; 1932 v W, F; 1934 v NI

Harper, J. M. (4) (Aberdeen), 1973 v Den, Den; (Hibernian), 1976 v Den; (Aberdeen), 1978 v Ir

Harper, W. (11) (Hibernian), 1923 v E, NI, W; 1924 v E, NI, W; 1925 v E, NI, W; (Arsenal), 1926 v E, NI

Harris, J. (2) (Partick T), 1921 v W, Ire

Harris, N. (1) (Newcastle U), 1924 v E

Harrower, W. (3) (Queen's Park), 1882 v E; 1884 v Ire; 1886 v W

Hartford, R. A. (50) (WBA), 1972 v Pe, W, E, Y, Cz, Bra; (Manchester C), 1976 v Den, Rum, NI; 1977 v Cz, W, Swe, W, NI, E, Ch, Arg, Bra; 1978 v GDR, Cz, W, Bul, W, E, Pe, Ir, Neth; 1979 v A, Nor, P, W, NI, E, Arg, Nor; (Everton), 1980 v Pe, Bel; 1981 v NI, is, W, NI, E; 1982 v Swe; (Manchester C), NI, P, Sp, NI, W, E, Bra

Harvey, D. (16) (Leeds U), 1973 v Den, 1974 v Cz, FRG, NI, W, E, Bel, Z, Bra, Y; 1975 v GDR, Sp, Sp; 1976 v Den, Den; 1977 v Fin

Hastings, A. C. (2) (Sunderland), 1936 v NI; 1938 v NI

Haughney, M. (1) (Celtic), 1954 v E

Hay, D. (27) (Celtic), 1970 v NI, W, E; 1971 v Den, Bel, W, P, NI; 1972 v P, Bel, Neth; 1973 v W, NI, E, Swz, Bra; 1974 v Cz, Cz, FRG, NI, W, E, Bel, Nor, Z, Bra, Y

Hay, J. (11) (Celtic), 1905 v Ire; 1909 v Ire; 1910 v W, Ire, E; 1911 v Ire, E; (Newcastle U), 1912 v E, W; 1914 v E, Ire

Hegarty, P. (8) (Dundee U), 1979 v W, NI, E, Arg, Nor; 1980 v W, E; 1983 v NI

Heggie, C. (1) (Rangers), 1886 v Ire

Henderson, G. H. (1) (Rangers), 1904 v Ire

Henderson, J. G. (7) (Portsmouth), 1953 v Swe; 1954 v NI, E, Nor; 1956 v W; (Arsenal), 1959 v W, NI

Henderson, W. (29) (Rangers), 1963 v W, NI, E, A, Nor, RI, Sp; 1964 v W, NI, E, Nor, FRG; 1965 v Fin, Pol, E, Sp; 1966 v NI, W, Pol, I, Neth; 1967 v W, NI; 1968 v Neth; 1969 v NI, E, Cyp; 1970 v RI; 1971 v P

Hepburn, J. (1) (Alloa Ath), 1891 v W

Hepburn, R. (1) (Ayr U), 1932 v NI

Herd, A. C. (1) (Hearts), 1935 v NI

Herd, D. G. (5) (Arsenal), 1959 v E, W, NI; 1961 v E, Cz

Herd, G. (5) (Clyde), 1958 v E; 1960 v H, T; 1961 v W, NI

Herriot, J. (8) (Birmingham C), 1969 v NI, E, Den, Cyp, Cyp, W; 1970 v RI, FRG

Hewie, J. D. (19) (Charlton Ath), 1956 v E, A; 1957 v E, NI, W, Y, Sp, Sp, Swz, FRG; 1958 v H, Pol, Y, F; 1959 v Neth, P; 1960 v NI, W, Pol

Higgins, A. (1) (Kilmarnock), 1885 v Ire

Higgins, A. (4) (Newcastle U), 1910 v E, Ire; 1911 v E, Ire

Highet, T. C. (4) (Queen's Park), 1875 v E; 1876 v E, W; 1878 v E

Hill, D. (3) (Rangers), 1881 v E, W; 1882 v W

Hill, D. A. (1) (Third Lanark), 1906 v Ire

Hill, F. R. (3) (Aberdeen), 1930 v F; 1931 v W, NI

Hill, J. (2) (Hearts), 1891 v E; 1892 v W

Hogg, G. (2) (Hearts), 1896 v E, Ire

Hogg, J. (1) (Ayr U), 1922 v NI

Hogg, R. M. (1) (Celtic), 1937 v Cz

Holm, A. H. (3) (Queen's Park), 1882 v W; 1883 v E, W

Holt, D. D. (5) (Hearts), 1963 v A, Nor, RI, Sp; 1964 v FRG

Holton, J. A. (15) (Manchester U), 1973 v W, NI, E, Swz, Bra; 1974 v Cz, FRG, NI, W, E, Nor, Z, Bra, Y; 1975 v GDR

Hope, R. (2) (WBA), 1968 v Neth; 1969 v Den

Houliston, W. (3) (Queen of the South), 1949 v E, NI, F

Houston, S. M. (1) (Manchester U), 1976 v Den

Howden, W. (1) (Partick T), 1905 v Ire

Howe, R. (2) (Hamilton A), 1929 v Nor, Neth

Howie, J. (3) (Newcastle U), 1905 v E; 1906 v E; 1908 v E

Howie, H. (1) (Hibernian), 1949 v W

Howieson, J. (1) (St Mirren), 1927 v NI

Hughes, J. (8) (Celtic), 1965 v Pol, Sp; 1966 v NI, I, I; 1968 v E; 1969 v A; 1970 v RI

Hughes, W. (1) (Sunderland), 1975 v Swe

Humphries, W. (1) (Motherwell), 1952 v Swe

Hunter, A. (4) (Kilmarnock), 1972 v Pe, Y; (Celtic), 1973 v E; 1974 v Cz

Hunter, J. (1) (Dundee), 1909 v W

Hunter, J. (4) (Third Lanark), 1874 v E; (Eastern), 1875 v E; (Third Lanark), 1876 v E; 1877 v W

Hunter, R. (1) (St Mirren), 1890 v Ire

Hunter, W. (3) (Motherwell), 1960 v H, T; 1961 v W

Husband, J. (1) (Partick T), 1947 v W

Hutchison, T. (17) (Coventry C), 1974 v Cz, Cz, FRG, FRG, NI, W, Bel, Nor, Z, Y; 1975 v GDR, Sp, Sp, P, E, R; 1976 v Den

Hutton, J. (10) (Aberdeen), 1923 v E, W, NI; 1924 v NI; 1926 v W, E, NI; (Blackburn R), 1927 v NI; 1928 v W, NI

Hutton, J. (1) (St Bernard's), 1887 v Ire

Hyslop, T. (2) (Stoke C), 1896 v E; (Rangers), 1897 v E

Imlach, J. J. S. (4) (Nottingham F), 1958 v H, Pol, Y, F

Imrie, W. N. (2) (St Johnstone), 1929 v Nor, G

Inglis, J. (1) (Kilmarnock Ath), 1884 v Ire

Inglis, J. (2) (Rangers), 1883 v E, W

Irons, J. H. (1) (Queen's Park), 1900 v W

Jackson, A. (2) (Cambuslang), 1886 v W; 1888 v Ire

Jackson, A. (17) (Aberdeen), 1925 v E, W, NI; (Huddersfield T), 1926 v E, W, NI; 1927 v W, NI; 1928 v E, W; 1929 v E, W, NI; 1930 v E, W, NI F

Jackson, C. (8) (Rangers), 1975 v Swe, P, W; 1976 v Den, Rum, NI, W, E

Jackson, J. (8) (Partick T), 1931 v A, I, Swz; 1933 v E; (Chelsea), 1934 v E; 1935 v E; 1936 v W, NI

Jackson, T. A. (6) (St Mirren), 1904 v W, E, Ire; 1905 v W; 1907 v W, Ire

James, A. W. (8) (Preston NE), 1926 v W; 1928 v E, 1929 v E, NI; (Arsenal), 1930 v E, W, NI, 1933 v W

Jardine, A. (38) (Rangers), 1971 v Den; 1972 v P, Bel, Neth; 1973 v E, Swz, Bra; 1974 v Cz, Cz, FRG, FRG, NI, W, E, Bel, Nor, Z, Bra, Y; 1975 v GDR, Sp, Sp, Swe, P, W, NI, E; 1977 v Swe, Ch, Bra; 1978 v Cz, W, NI, Ir; 1980 v Pe, A, Bel, Bel

Jarvie, A. (3) (Airdrieonians), 1971 v P, NI, E

Jenkinson, T. (1) (Hearts), 1887 v Ire

Johnston, L. H. (2) (Clyde), 1948 v Bel, Swz

Johnston, M. (20) (Watford), 1984 v W, E, F; (Celtic), 1985 v Y, Ic, Sp, Sp, W; 1986 v GDR; 1987 v Bul, RI, RI, Lux, H, Bel, Lux; 1988 v S.Ar, Sp, Col, E

Johnston, R. (1) (Sunderland), 1938 v Cz

Johnston, W. (22) (Rangers), 1966 v W, E, Pol, Neth; 1968 v W, E; 1969 v NI; 1970 v NI; 1971 v Den; (WBA), 1977 v Swe, W, NI, E, Ch, Arg, Bra; 1978 v GDR, Cz, W, W, E, Pe

Johnstone, D. (14) (Rangers), 1973 v W, NI, E, Swz, Bra; 1975 v GDR, Swe; 1976 v Swz, NI, E; 1978 v Bul, NI, W; 1980 v Bel

Johnstone, J. (1) (Abercorn), 1888 v W

Johnstone, J. (23) (Celtic), 1965 v W, Fin; 1966 v E; 1967 v W, USSR; 1968 v W; 1969 v A, FRG; 1970 v E, FRG; 1971 v Den, E; 1972 v P, Bel, Neth, NI, E; 1974 v W, E, Bel, Nor; 1975 v GDR, Sp

Johnstone, Jas (1) (Kilmarnock), 1894 v W

Johnstone, J. A. (3) (Hearts), 1930 v W; 1933 v W, NI

Johnstone, R. (17) (Hibernian), 1951 v E, Den, F; 1952 v NI, E; 1953 v E, Swe; 1954 v W, Nor, Fin; 1955 v NI, H; (Manchester C), 1955 v E; 1956 v E, NI, W

Johnstone, W. (3) (Third Lanark), 1887 v Ire, 1889 v W; 1890 v E

Jordan, J. (52) (Leeds U), 1973 v E, Swz, Bra; 1974 v Cz, Cz, FRG, NI, W, E, Bel, Nor, Z, Bra, Y; 1975 v GDR, Sp, Sp; 1976 v NI, W, E; 1977 v Cz, W, NI, E; 1978 v GDR, Cz, W; (Manchester U), Bul, NI, E, Pe, Ir, Neth; 1979 v A, P, W, NI, E, Nor; 1980 v Bel, NI, W, E, Pol; 1981 v Is, W, E; (AC Milan), 1982 v Swe, Neth, W, E, USSR

Kay, J. L. (6) (Queen's Park), 1880 v E, 1882 v E, W; 1883 v E, W; 1884 v W

Keillor, A. (6) (Montrose), 1891 v W; 1892 v Ire (Dundee), 1894 v Ire; 1895 v W; 1896 v W; 1897 v W

Keir, L. (5) (Dumbarton), 1885 v W; 1886 v Ire; 1887 v E, W; 1888 v E

BRITISH & IRISH INTERNATIONAL APPEARANCES

Kelly, H. T. (1) (Blackpool), 1952 v USA
Kelly, J. (8) (Renton), 1888 v E; (Celtic), 1889 v E; 1890 v E; 1892 v E; 1893 v E, Ire; 1894 v W; 1896 v Ire
Kelly, J. C. (2) (Barnsley), 1949 v W, NI
Kelso, R. (8) (Renton), 1885 v W, Ire; 1886 v W; 1887 v E, W; 1888 v E, Ire; (Dundee), 1898 v Ire
Kelso, T. (1) (Dundee), 1914 v W
Kennaway, J. (2) (Celtic), 1934 v A, W
Kennedy, A. (6) (Eastern), 1875 v E; 1876 v E, W; (Third Lanark), 1878 v E; 1882 v W; 1884 v W
Kennedy, J. (6) (Celtic), 1964 v W, E, FRG; 1965 v W, NI, Fin
Kennedy, J. (1) (Hibernian), 1897 v W
Kennedy, S. (8) (Aberdeen), 1978 v Bul, W, E, Pe, Neth; 1979 v A, P; 1982 v P
Kennedy, S. (1) (Partick T), 1905 v W
Kennedy, S. (5) (Rangers), 1975 v Swe, P, W, NI, E
Ker, G. (5) (Queen's Park), 1880 v E; 1881 v E, W; 1882 v W, E
Ker, W. (2) (Granville), 1872 v E; (Queen's Park), 1873 v E
Kerr, A. (2) (Partick T), 1955 v A, H
Kerr, P. (1) (Hibernian), 1924 v NI
Key, G. (1) (Hearts), 1902 v Ire
Key, W. (1) (Queen's Park), 1907 v Ire
King, A. (6) (Hearts), 1896 v E, W; (Celtic), 1897 v Ire; 1898 v Ire; 1899 v Ire, W
King, J. (2) (Hamilton A), 1933 v NI; 1934 v NI
King, W. S. (1) (Queen's Park), 1929 v W
Kinloch, J. D. (1) (Partick T), 1922 v NI
Kinnaird, A. F. (1) (Wanderers), 1873 v E
Kinnear, D. (1) (Rangers), 1939 v Cz

Lambie, J. A. (3) (Queen's Park), 1886 v Ire; 1887 v Ire; 1888 v E
Lambie, W. A. (9) (Queen's Park), 1892 v Ire; 1893 v W; 1894 v E; 1895 v E, Ire; 1896 v E, Ire; 1897 v E, Ire
Lamont, D. (1) (Pilgrims), 1885 v Ire
Lang, A. (1) (Dumbarton), 1880 v W
Lang, J. J. (2) (Clydesdale), 1876 v W; (Third Lanark), 1878 v W
Latta, A. (2) (Dumbarton), 1888 v W; 1889 v E
Law, D. (55) (Huddersfield T), 1959 v W, NI, Neth, P; 1960 v NI, W; (Manchester C), 1960 v E, Pol, A; 1961 v E, NI; (Torino), 1962 v Cz, Cz, E; (Manchester U), 1963 v W, NI, E, A, Nor, RI, Sp; 1964 v W, E, Nor, FRG; 1965 v W, NI, E, Fin, Fin, Pol, Sp; 1966 v NI, E, Pol; 1967 v W, E, USSR; 1968 v NI; 1969 v NI, A, FRG; 1972 v Pe, NI, W, E, Y, Cz, Bra; (Manchester C), 1974 v Cz, Cz, FRG, FRG, NI, Z
Law, G. (3) (Rangers), 1910 v E, Ire, W
Law, T. (2) (Chelsea), 1928 v E, 1930 v E
Lawrence, J. (1) (Newcastle U), 1911 v E
Lawrence, T. (3) (Liverpool), 1963 v RI; 1969 v W, FRG
Lawson, D. (1) (St Mirren), 1923 v E
Leckie, R. (1) (Queen's Park), 1872 v E
Leggat, G. (18) (Aberdeen), 1956 v E; 1957 v W; 1958 v NI, H, Pol, Y, Par; (Fulham), 1959 v E, W, NI, FRG, Neth; 1960 v E, NI, W, Pol, A. H
Leighton, J. (44) (Aberdeen), 1983 v GDR, Swz, Bel, Swz, W, E, Can, Can; 1984 v U, Bel, NI, W, E, F;

1985 v Y, Ic, Sp, Sp, W, E, Ic; 1986 v W, GDR, Aus, Aus, Is, Den, FRG, U; 1987 v Bul, RI, RI, Lux, Bel, E, H, Bel, Bul, Lux; 1988 v S.Ar, Ma, Sp, (Manchester U), Col, E
Lennie, W. (2) (Aberdeen), 1908 v W, Ire
Lennox, R. (10) (Celtic), 1967 v NI, E, USSR; 1968 v W, Lux; 1969 v Den, A, FRG, Cyp; 1970 v W
Leslie, L. G. (5) (Airdrieonians), 1961 v W, NI, RI, RI, Cz
Liddell, W. (28) (Liverpool), 1947 v W, NI; 1948 v E, W, NI; 1950 v E, W, P, F; 1951 v W, NI, E, A; 1952 v W, NI, E, USA, Den, Swe; 1953 v W, NI, E; 1954 v W; 1955 v P, Y, A, H; 1956 v NI
Liddle, D. (3) (East Fife), 1931 v A, I, Swz
Lindsay, D. (1) (St Mirren), 1903 v Ire
Lindsay, J. (8) (Dumbarton), 1880 v W; 1881 v W, E; 1884 v W; E; 1885 v W, E; 1886 v E
Lindsay, J. (3) (Renton), 1888 v E; 1893 v E, Ire
Linwood, A. B. (1) (Clyde), 1950 v W
Little, R. J. (1) (Rangers), 1953 v Swe
Livingstone, G. T. (2) (Manchester C), 1906 v E; (Rangers), 1907 v W
Lochhead, A. (1) (Third Lanark), 1889 v W
Logan, J. (1) (Ayr U), 1891 v W
Logan, T. (1) (Falkirk), 1913 v Ire
Logie, J. T. (1) (Arsenal), 1953 v NI
Loney, W. (2) (Celtic), 1910 v W, Ire
Long, H. (1) (Clyde), 1947 v NI
Longair, W. (1) (Dundee), 1894 v Ire
Lorimer, P. (21) (Leeds U), 1970 v A; 1971 v W, NI; 1972 v NI, W, E; 1973 v Den, Den, E, E; 1974 v FRG, E, Bel, Nor, Z, Bra, Y; 1975 v Sp; 1976 v Den, Den, R
Love, A. (3) (Aberdeen), 1931 v A, I, Sw
Low, A. (1) (Falkirk), 1934 v NI
Low, T. P. (1) (Rangers), 1897 v Ire
Low, W. L. (5) (Newcastle U), 1922 v E, W; 1912 v Ire; 1920 v E, Ire
Lowe, J. (1) (Cambuslang), 1891 v Ire
Lowe, J. (1) (St Bernard's), 1887 v Ire
Lundie, J. (1) (Hibernian), 1886 v W
Lyall, J. (1) (Sheffield W), 1905 v E

McAdam, J. (1) (Third Lanark), 1880 v W
McArthur, D. (3) (Celtic), 1895 v E, Ire; 1899 v W
McAtee, A. (1) (Celtic), 1913 v W
McAulay, J. (2) (Dumbarton), 1882 v W; (Arthurlie), 1884 v Ire
McAulay, J. (8) (Dumbarton), 1883 v E, W; 1884 v E; 1885 v E, W; 1886 v E; 1887 v E, W
McAuley, R. (2) (Rangers), 1932 v NI, W
McAvennie, F. (5) (West Ham U), 1986 v Aus (2), Den, FRG; (Celtic), 1988 v S.Ar
McBain, E. (1) (St Mirren), 1894 v W
McBain, N. (3) (Manchester U), 1922 v E; (Everton), 1923 v NI; 1924 v W
McBride, J. (2) (Celtic), 1967 v W, NI
McBride, P. (6) (Preston NE), 1904 v E; 1906 v E; 1907 v E, W; 1908 v E; 1909 v W
McCall, J. (5) (Renton), 1886 v W; 1887 v E, W; 1888 v E; 1890 v E
McCalliog, J. (5) (Sheffield W), 1967 v E, USSR; 1968 v NI; 1969 v Den; (Wolverhampton W), 1971 v P

McCallum, N. (1) (Renton), 1888 v Ire
McCann, R. J. (5) (Motherwell), 1959 v FRG; 1960 v E, NI, W; 1961 v E
McCartney, W. (1) (Hibernian), 1902 v Ire
McClair, B. (7) (Celtic), 1987 v Lux, RI, E, Bra, (Manchester U), Bul; 1988 v Ma, Sp
McClory, A. (3) Motherwell), 1927 v W; 1928 v NI; 1935 v W
McCloy, P. (2) (Ayr U), 1924 v E; 1925 v E
McCloy, P. (4) (Rangers), 1973 v W, NI, Swz, Bra
McCoist, A. (12) (Rangers), 1986 v Neth; 1987 v Lux, RI, Bel, E, Bra, H, Bel; 1988 v Ma, Sp, Col, E
McColl, A. (1) (Renton), 1888 v Ire
McColl, I. M. (14) (Rangers), 1950 v E, F; 1951 v W, NI, Bel; 1957 v E, NI, W, Y, Sp, Swz, FRG; 1958 v NI, E
McColl, R. S. (13) (Queen's Park), 1896 v W, Ire; 1897 v Ire; 1898 v Ire; 1899 v Ire, E, W; 1900 v E, W; 1901 v E, W; (Newcastle U), 1902 v E; (Queen's Park), 1908 v Ire
McColl, W. (1) (Renton), 1895 v W
McCombie, A. (4) (Sunderland), 1903 v E, W; (Newcastle U), 1905 v E, W
McCorkindale, J. (1) (Partick T), 1891 v W
McCormick, R. (1) (Abercorn), 1886 v W
McCrae, D. (2) (St Mirren), 1929 v Nor, G
McCreadie, A. (2) (Rangers), 1893 v W; 1894 v E
McCreadie, E. G. (23) (Chelsea), 1965 v E, Sp, Fin, Pol; 1966 v P, NI, W, Pol, I; 1967 v E, USSR; 1968 v NI, W, E, Neth; 1969 v W, NI, E, Den, A, FRG, Cyp, Cyp
McCulloch, D. (7) (Hearts), 1935 v W; (Brentford), 1936 v E; 1937 v W, NI; 1938 v Cz; (Derby Co), 1939 v H, W
MacDonald, A. (1) (Rangers), 1976 v Swz
McDonald, J. (1) (Edinburgh University), 1886 v E
McDonald, J. (2) (Sunderland), 1956 v W, NI
MacDougall, E. J. (7) (Norwich C), 1975 v Swe, P, W, NI, E; 1976 v Den, R
McDougall, J. (2) (Liverpool), 1931 v I, A
McDougall, J. (1) (Airdrieonians), 1926 v NI
McDougall, J. (5) (Vale of Leven), 1877 v E, W; 1878 v E; 1879 v E, W
McFadyen, W. (2) (Motherwell), 1934 v A, W
Macfarlane, A. (5) (Dundee), 1904 v W; 1906 v W; 1908 v W; 1909 v Ire; 1911 v W
McFarlane, R. (1) (Greenock Morton), 1896 v W
Macfarlane, W. (1) (Hearts), 1947 v Lux
McGarr, E. (2) (Aberdeen), 1970 v RI, A
McGarvey, F. P. (7) (Liverpool), 1979 v NI, Arg; (Celtic), 1984 v U, Bel, GDR, NI, W
McGeoch, A. (4) (Dumbreck), 1876 v E, W; 1877 v E, W
McGhee, J. (1) (Hibernian), 1886 v W
McGhee, M. (4) (Aberdeen), 1983 v Can, Can; 1984 v NI, E
McGonagle, W. (6) (Celtic), 1933 v E; 1934 v A, E, NI; 1935 v NI, W
McGrain, D. (62) (Celtic), 1973 v W, NI, E, Swz, Bra; 1974 v Cz, Cz, FRG, W, E, Bel, Nor, Z, Bra, Y; 1975 v Sp, Swe, P, W, NI, E, Rum; 1976 v Den, Den, Swz, NI, W, E; 1977 v Fin, Cz, W, W, Swe, NI, E, Ch, Arg, Bra; 1978 v GDR, Cz; 1980 v Bel, P, NI, W, E, Pol,

H; 1981 v Swe, P, Is, NI, Is, W, NI, E; 1982 v Swe, Sp, Neth, NI, E, NZ, USSR
McGregor, J. C. (4) (Vale of Leven), 1877 v E, W; 1878 v E; 1880 v E
McGrory, J. E. (3) (Kilmarnock), 1965 v NI, Fin; 1966 v P
McGrory, J. (7) (Celtic), 1928 v NI; 1931 v E; 1932 v NI, W; 1933 v E, NI; 1934 v NI
McGuire, W. (2) (Beith), 1881 v E, W
McGurk, F. (1) (Birmingham), 1934 v W
McHardy, H. (1) (Rangers), 1885 v Ire
McInally, J. (3) (Dundee U), 1987 v Bel, Bra; 1988 v Ma
McInally, T. B. (2) (Celtic), 1926 v NI; 1927 v W
McInnes, T. (1) (Cowlairs), 1889 v Ire
McIntosh, W. (1) (Third Lanark), 1905 v Ire
McIntyre, A. (2) (Vale of Leven), 1878 v E; 1882 v E
McIntyre, H. (1) (Rangers), 1880 v W
McIntyre, J. (1) (Rangers), 1884 v W
McKay, D. (14) (Celtic), 1959 v E, FRG, Neth, P; 1960 v E, Pol, A, H, T; 1961 v W, NI; 1962 v NI, Cz, U
Mackay, D. C. (22) (Hearts), 1957 v Sp; 1958 v F; 1959 v W, NI; (Tottenham H), 1959 v FRG, E; 1960 v W, NI, A, Pol, H, T; 1961 v W, NI, E; 1963 v E, A, Nor; 1964 v NI, W, Nor; 1966 v NI
MacKay, G. (4) (Hearts) 1987 v Bul, Lux; 1988 v S.Ar, Ma
McKay, J. (1) (Blackburn R), 1924 v W
McKay, R. (1) (Newcastle U), 1928 v W
McKean, R. (1) (Rangers), 1976 v Sw
McKenzie, D. (1) (Brentford), 1938 v NI
Mackenzie, J. A. (9) (Partick T), 1954 v W, E, Nor, Fin, A, U; 1955 v E, H; 1956 v A
McKeown, M. (2) (Celtic), 1889 v Ire; 1890 v E
McKie, J. (1) (East Stirling), 1898 v W
McKillop, T. R. (1) (Rangers), 1938 v Neth
McKinlay, D. (2) (Liverpool), 1922 v W, NI
McKinnon, A. (1) (Queen's Park), 1874 v E
McKinnon, R. (28) (Rangers), 1966 v W, E, I, I, Neth, Bra; 1967 v W, NI, E; 1968 v NI, W, E, Neth; 1969 v Den, A, FRG, Cyp; 1970 v NI, W, E, RI, FRG, A; 1971 v Den, Bel, P, USSR, Den
MacKinnon, W. (4) (Dumbarton), 1883 v E, W; 1884 v E, W
MacKinnon, W. W. (9) (Queen's Park), 1872 v E; 1873 v E; 1874 v E; 1875 v E; 1876 v E, W; 1877 v E; 1878 v E; 1879 v E
McLaren, A. (5) (St Johnstone), 1929 v Nor, G, Neth; 1933 v W, NI
McLaren, A. (4) (Preston NE), 1947 v E, Bel, Lux; 1948 v W
McLaren, J. (3) (Hibernian), 1888 v W; (Celtic), 1889 v E; 1890 v E
McLean, A. (4) (Celtic), 1926 v W, NI; 1927 v W, E
McLean, D. (2) (St Bernard's), 1896 v W; 1897 v Ire
McLean, D. (1) (Sheffield W), 1912 v E
McLean, G. (1) (Dundee), 1968 v Neth
McLean, T. (6) (Kilmarnock), 1969 v Den, Cyp; W; 1970 v NI, W; 1971 v Den
McLeish, A. (55) (Aberdeen), 1980 v F, NI, W, E, Pol, H; 1981 v Swe, Is, NI, Is, NI, E; 1982 v Swe, Sp, NI, Bra; 1983 v Bel, Swz, W, E, Can, Can, Can; 1984 v U, Bel, GDR, NI, W, E, F; 1985 v Y, Ic, Sp, Sp, W, E, Ic; 1986 v W, GDR, Aus, Aus, E, Neth, Den; 1987

BRITISH & IRISH INTERNATIONAL APPEARANCES

v Bel, E, Bra, Bel, Bul, Lux; 1988 v S.Ar, Ma, Sp, Col, E

McLeod, D. (4) (Celtic), 1905 v Ire; 1906 v E, W, Ire

McLeod, J. (5) (Dumbarton), 1888 v Ire; 1889 v W; 1890 v Ire; 1892 v E; 1893 v W

MacLeod, J. M. (4) (Hibernian), 1961 v E, RI, RI, Cz

MacLeod, M. (7) (Celtic), 1985 v E; 1987 v RI, Lux, E, Bra; 1988 v Col, E

McLeod, W. (1) (Cowlairs), 1886 v Ire

McLintock, A. (3) (Vale of Leven), 1875 v E; 1876 v E; 1880 v E

McLintock, F. (9) (Leicester C), 1963 v Nor, RI, Sp; (Arsenal), 1965 v NI; 1967 v USSR; 1970 v NI; 1971 v W, NI, E

McLuckie, J. S. (1) (Manchester C), 1934 v W

McMahon, A. (6) (Celtic), 1892 v E; 1893 v E, Ire; 1894 v E; 1901 v Ire; 1902 v W

McMenemy, J. (12) (Celtic), 1905 v Ire; 1909 v Ire; 1910 v E, W; 1911 v Ire, W, E; 1912 v W; 1914 v W, Ire, E; 1920 v Ire

McMenemy, J. (1) (Motherwell), 1934 v W

McMillan, J. (1) (St Bernard's), 1897 v W

McMillan, I. L. (6) (Airdrieonians), 1952 v E, USA, Den; 1955 v E; 1956 v E; (Rangers), 1961 v Cz

McMillan, T. (1) (Dumbarton), 1887 v Ire

McMullan, J. (16) (Partick T), 1920 v W; 1921 v W, Ire, E; 1924 v E, NI; 1925 v E; 1926 v W; (Manchester C), 1926 v E; 1927 v E, W; 1928 v E, W; 1929 v W, E, NI

McNab, A. (2) (Morton), 1921 v E, Ire

McNab, A. (2) (Sunderland), 1937 v A; (WBA), 1939 v E

McNab, C. D. (6) (Dundee), 1931 v E, W, A, I, Swz; 1932 v E

McNab, J. S. (1) (Liverpool), 1923 v W

McNair, A. (15) (Celtic), 1906 v W; 1907 v Ire; 1908 v E, W; 1909 v E; 1910 v W; 1912 v E, W, Ire; 1913 v E; 1914 v E, Ire; 1920 v E, W, Ire

McNaught, W. (5) (Raith R), 1951 v A, W, NI; 1952 v E; 1955 v NI

McNeil, H. (10) (Queen's Park), 1874 v E; 1875 v E; 1876 v E, W; 1877 v W; 1878 v E; 1879 v E, W; 1881 v E, W

McNeill, W. (29) (Celtic), 1961 v E, Ire, RI, RI, Cz; 1962 v NI, E, Cz, U; 1963 v RI, Sp; 1964 v W, E, FRG; 1965 v E, Fin, Pol, Sp; 1966 v NI, Pol; 1967 v USSR; 1968 v E; 1969 v Cyp, W, E, Cyp; 1970 v FRG; 1972 v NI, W, E

McPhail, J. (5) (Celtic), 1950 v W; 1951 v W, NI, A; 1954 v NI

McPhail, R. (17) (Airdrieonians), 1927 v E; (Rangers), 1929 v W; 1931 v E, NI; 1932 v W, NI, F; 1933 v E, NI; 1934 v A, NI; 1935 v E; 1937 v G, E, Cz; 1938 v W, NI

McPherson, D. (1) (Kilmarnock), 1892 v Ire

McPherson, J. (9) (Kilmarnock), 1888 v W; (Cowlairs), 1889 v E; 1890 v Ire, E; (Rangers), 1892 v W; 1894 v E; 1895 v E, Ire; 1897 v Ire

McPherson, J. (1) (Clydesdale), 1875 v E

McPherson, J. (8) (Vale of Leven), 1879 v E, W; 1880 v E; 1881 v W; 1883 v E, W; 1884 v E; 1885 v N

McPherson, J. (1) (Hearts), 1891 v E

McPherson, R. (1) (Arthurlie), 1882 v E

McQueen, G. (30) (Leeds U), 1974 v Bel; 1975 v Sp, Sp, P, W, NI, E, Rum; 1976 v Den; 1977 v Cz, W, W, NI, E; 1978 v GDR, Cz, W; (Manchester U), Bul, NI, W; 1979 v A, Nor, P, NI, E, Nor; 1980 v Pe, A, Bel; 1981 v W

McQueen, M. (2) (Leith Ath), 1890 v W; 1891 v W

McRorie, D. M. (1) (Morton), 1931 v W

McSpadyen, A. (2) (Partick T), 1939 v E, H

McStay, P. (29) (Celtic), 1984 v U, Bel, GDR, NI, W, E; 1985 v Ic, Sp, Sp, W; 1986 v GDR, Aus, Is, U; 1987 v Bul, RI, RI, Lux, Bel, E, Bra, H, Bel, Bul, Lux; 1988 v S.Ar, Sp, Col, E

McStay, W. (13) (Celtic), 1921 v W, Ire; 1925 v E, NI, W; 1926 v E, NI, W; 1927 v E, NI, W; 1928 v W, NI

McTavish, J. (1) (Falkirk), 1910 v Ire

McWhattie, G. C. (2) (Queen's Park), 1901 v W, Ire

McWilliam, P. (8) (Newcastle U), 1905 v E; 1906 v E; 1907 v E, W; 1909 v E, W; 1910 v E; 1911 v W

Macari, L. (24) (Celtic), 1972 v W, E, Y; Cz, Bra; 1973 v Den; (Manchester U), E, E, W, NI; 1975 v Swe, P, W, E, Rum; 1977 v NI, E, Ch, Arg; 1978 v GDR, W, Bul, Pe, Ir

Macauley, A. R. (7) (Brentford), 1947 v E; (Arsenal), 1948 v E, W, NI, Bel, Swz, F

Madden, J. (2) (Celtic), 1893 v W; 1895 v W

Main, F. R. (1) (Rangers), 1938 v W

Main, J. (1) (Hibernian), 1909 v Ire

Maley, W. (2) (Celtic), 1893 v E, Ire

Malpas, M. (20) (Dundee U), 1984 v F; 1985 v E, Ic; 1986 v W, Aus, Aus, Is, Rum, E, Neth, Den, FRG; 1987 v Bul, RI, Bel, Bel, Bul, Lux; 1988 v S.Ar, Ma

Marshall, H. (2) (Celtic), 1899 v W; 1900 v Ire

Marshall, J. (3) (Rangers), 1932 v E; 1933 v E; 1934 v E

Marshall, J. (7) (Middlesbrough), 1921 v E, W, Ire; 1922 v E, W, NI; (Llanelly), 1924 v W

Marshall, J. (4) (Third Lanark), 1885 v Ire; 1886 v W; 1887 v E, W

Marshall, R. W. (2) (Rangers), 1892 v Ire; 1894 v Ire

Martin, F. (6) (Aberdeen), 1954 v Nor, Nor, A, U; 1955 v E, H

Martin, N. (3) (Hibernian), 1965 v Fin, Pol; (Sunderland), 1966 v I

Martis, J. (1) (Motherwell), 1961 v W

Mason, J. (7) (Third Lanark), 1949 v E, W, NI; 1950 v NI; 1951 v NI, Bel, A

Massie, A. (18) (Hearts), 1932 v NI, W, F; 1933 v NI; 1934 v E, NI; 1935 v E, NI, W; 1936 v W, NI; (Aston Villa), 1936 v E; 1937 v G, E, W, NI, A; 1938 v W

Masson, D. S. (17) (QPR), 1976 v NI, W, E; 1977 v Fin, Cz, W, NI, E; Ch, Arg, Bra; 1978 v GDR, Cz, W; (Derby Co), NI, E, Pe

Mathers, D. (1) (Partick T), 1954 v Fin

Maxwell, W. S. (1) (Stoke C), 1898 v E

May, J. (5) (Rangers), 1906 v W, Ire; 1908 v E, Ire; 1909 v W

Meechan, P. (1) (Celtic), 1896 v Ire

Meiklejohn, D. D. (15) (Rangers), 1922 v W; 1924 v W; 1925 v W, NI; 1928 v W, NI; 1929 v E, NI; 1930 v E, NI; 1931 v E; 1932 v W, NI; 1934 v A

Menzies, A. (1) (Hearts), 1906 v E

Mercer, R. (2) (Hearts), 1912 v W; 1913 v Ire

Middleton, R. (1) (Cowdenbeath), 1930 v NI

Millar, J. (3) (Rangers), 1897 v E; 1898 v E, W

Millar, J. (2) (Rangers), 1963 v A, RI

Millar, A. (1) (Hearts), 1939 v W

Miller, J. (5) (St Mirren), 1931 v E, I, Swz; 1932 v F; 1934 v E

Miller, P. (3) (Dumbarton), 1882 v E; 1883 v E, W

Miller, T. (3) (Liverpool), 1920 v E; (with Manchester U), 1921 v E, Ire

Miller, W. (1) (Third Lanark), 1876 v E

Miller, W. (6) (Celtic), 1947 v E, W, Bel, Lux; 1948 v W, NI

Miller, W. (61) (Aberdeen), 1975 v Rum; 1978 v Bul; 1980 v Bel, W, E, Pol, H; 1981 v Swe, P, Is, NI, W, NI, E; 1982 v NI, P, Neth, Bra, USSR; 1983 v GDR, Swz, Swz, W, E, Can, Can, Can; 1984 v U, Bel, GDR, W, E, F; 1985 v Y, Ic, Sp, Sp, W, E, Ic; 1986 v W, GDR, Aus, Aus, Is, Rum, E, Neth, Den, FRG, U; 1987 v Bul, E, Bra, H, Lux; 1988 v S.Ar, Ma, Sp, Col, E

Mills, W. (3) (Aberdeen), 1936 v W, NI; 1937 v W

Milne, J. V. (2) (Middlesbrough), 1938 v E; 1939 v E

Mitchell, D. (5) (Rangers), 1890 v Ire; 1892 v E; 1893 v E, Ire; 1894 v E

Mitchell, J. (3) (Kilmarnock), 1908 v Ire; 1910 v Ire, W

Mitchell, R. C. (2) (Newcastle U), 1951 v Den, F

Mochan, N. (3) (Celtic), 1954 v Nor, A, U

Moir, W (1) (Bolton W), 1950 v E

Moncur, R. (16) (Newcastle U), 1968 v Neth; 1970 v NI, W, E, RI; 1971 v Den, Bel, W, P, NI, E, Den; 1972 v Pe, W, E

Morgan, H. (2) (St Mirren), 1898 v W; (Liverpool), 1899 v E

Morgan, W. (21) (Burnley), 1968 v NI; (Manchester U) 1972 v Pe, Y, Cz, Bra; 1973 v Den, Den, E, E, W, NI, Swz, Bra; 1974 v Cz, Cz, FRG, FRG, NI, Bel, Bra, Y

Morris, D. (6) (Raith R), 1923 v NI; 1924 v E, NI; 1925 v E, W, NI

Morris, H. (1) (East Fife), 1950 v NI

Morrison, T. (1) (St Mirren), 1927 v E

Morton, A. L. (31) (Queen's Park), 1920 v W, Ire; (Rangers), 1921 v E; 1922 v E, W; 1923 v E, W; 1924 v E, W, NI; 1925 v E, W, NI; 1927 v E, NI; 1928 v E, W, NI; 1929 v E, W, NI; 1930 v E, W, NI; 1931 v E, W, NI; 1932 v E, W, F

Morton, H. A. (2) (Kilmarnock), 1929 v G, Neth

Mudie, J. K. (17) (Blackpool), 1957 v W, NI, E, Y, Swz, Sp, Sp, FRG; 1958 v NI, E, W, Swz, H, Pol, Y, Par, F

Muir, W. (1) (Dundee), 1907 v Ire

Muirhead, T. A. (8) (Rangers), 1922 v NI; 1923 v E; 1924 v W; 1927 v NI; 1928 v NI; 1929 v W, NI; 1930 v W

Mulhall, G. (3) (Aberdeen), 1960 v NI; (Sunderland), 1963 v NI; 1964 v NI

Munro, A. D. (3) Hearts), 1937 v W, NI; (Blackpool), 1938 v Neth

Munro, F. M. (9) Wolverhampton W), 1971 v NI, E, Den, USSR; 1975 v Swe, W, NI, E, R

Munro, I. (7) (St Mirren), 1979 v Arg, Nor; 1980 v Pe, A, Bel, W, E

Munro, N. (2) (Abercorn), 1888 v W; 1889 v E

Murdoch, J. (1) (Motherwell), 1931 v NI

Murdoch, R. (12) (Celtic), 1966 v W, E, I (2); 1967 v NI; 1968 v NI; 1969 v W, NI, E, FRG, Cyp; 1970 v A

Murphy, F. (1) (Celtic), 1938 v Neth

Murray, J. (1) (Renton), 1895 v W

Murray, J. (5) (Hearts), 1958 v E, H, Pol, Y, F

Murray, J. W. (1) (Vale of Leven), 1890 v W

Murray, P. (2) (Hibernian), 1896 v Ire; 1897 v W

Murray, S. (1) (Aberdeen), 1972 v Bel

Mutch, G. (1) (Preston NE), 1938 v E

Napier, C. E. (5) (Celtic), 1932 v E; 1935 v E, W; (Derby Co), 1937 v NI, A

Narey, D. (33) (Dundee U), 1977 v Swe; 1979 v P, NI, Arg; 1980 v P, NI, Pol, H; 1981 v W, E; 1982 v Neth, W, E, NZ, Bra, USSR; 1983 v GDR, Swz, Bel, NI, W, E, Can, Can, Can; 1986 v Is, Rum, Neth, FRG, U; 1987 v Bul, E, Bel

Neil, R. G. (2) (Hibernian), 1896 v W; (Rangers), 1900 v W

Neill, R. W. (5) (Queen's Park), 1876 v W; 1877 v E, W; 1878 v W; 1880 v E

Neilles, P. (2) (Hearts), 1914 v W, Ire

Nelson, J. (4) (Cardiff C), 1925 v W, NI; 1928 v E; 1930 v F

Nevin, P. K. F. (6) (Chelsea), 1986 v Rum, E; 1987 v Lux, RI, Bel, Lux

Niblo, T. D. (1) (Aston Villa), 1904 v E

Nibloe, J. (11) (Kilmarnock), 1929 v E, Nor, Neth; 1930 v W; 1931 v E, NI, A, I, Swz; 1932 v E, F

Nicholas, C. (19) (Celtic), 1983 v Swz, NI, E, Can, Can, Can; (Arsenal), 1984 v Bel, F; 1985 v Y, Ic, Sp, W; 1986 v Is, Rum, E, Den, U, 1987 v Bul, E

Nicol, S. (17) (Liverpool), 1985 v Y, Ic, Sp, W; 1986 v W, GDR, Aus, E, Den, FRG, U, H, Bul; 1988 v S.Ar, Sp, Col, E

Nisbet, J. (3) (Ayr U), 1929 v Nor, G, Neth

Niven, J. B. (1) (Moffatt), 1885 v Ire

O'Donnell, F. (6) (Preston NE), 1937 v E, A, Cz; 1938 v E, W; (Blackpool), Neth

Ogilvie, D. H. (1) (Motherwell), 1934 v A

O'Hare, J. (13) (Derby Co), 1970 v W, NI, E; 1971 v Den, Bel, W, NI; 1972 v P, Bel, Neth, Pe, NI, W

Ormond, W. E. (6) (Hibernian), 1954 v E, Nor, Fin, A, U; 1959 v E

O'Rourke, F. (1) (Airdrieonians), 1907 v Ire

Orr, J. (1) (Kilmarnock), 1892 v W

Orr, R. (2) (Newcastle U), 1902 v E; 1904 v E

Orr, T. (2) (Morton), 1952 v NI, W

Orr, W. (3) (Celtic), 1900 v Ire; 1903 v Ire; 1904 v W

Orrock, R. (1) (Falkirk), 1913 v W

Oswald, J. (3) (Third Lanark), 1889 v E; (St Bernard's), 1895 v E; (Rangers), 1897 v W

Parker, A. H. (15) (Falkirk), 1955 v P, Y, A; 1956 v E, NI, W, A; 1957 v NI, W, Y; 1958 v NI, W, E, Swz; (Everton), Par

Parlane, D. (12) (Rangers), 1973 v W, Swz, Bra; 1975 v Sp, Swe, P, W, NI, E, Rum; 1976 v Den; 1977 v W

Parlane, R. (3) (Vale of Leven), 1878 v W; 1879 v E, W

Paterson, G. D. (1) (Celtic), 1939 v NI

Paterson, J. (1) (Leicester C), 1920 v E

Paterson, J. (3) (Cowdenbeath), 1931 v A, I, Sw

Paton, A. (2) (Motherwell), 1952 v Den, Swe

Paton, D. (1) (St Bernard's), 1896 v W

BRITISH & IRISH INTERNATIONAL APPEARANCES

Paton, M. (5) (Dumbarton), 1883 v E; 1884 v W; 1885 v W, E; 1886 v E
Paton, R. (2) (Vale of Leven), 1879 v E, W
Patrick, J. (2) (St Mirren), 1897 v E, W
Paul, H. McD. (3) (Queen's Park), 1909 v E, W, Ire
Paul, W. (3) (Partick T), 1888 v W; 1889 v W; 1890 v W
Paul, W. (1) (Dykebar), 1891 v Ire
Pearson, T. (2) (Newcastle U), 1947 v E, Bel
Penman, A. (1) (Dundee), 1966 v Neth
Pettigrew, W. (5) (Motherwell), 1976 v Swz, NI, W; 1977 v W, Swe
Phillips, J. (3) (Queen's Park), 1877 v E, W; 1878 v W
Plenderleith, J. B. (1) (Manchester C), 1961 v NI
Porteous, W. (1) (Hearts), 1903 v Ire
Pringle, C. (1) (St Mirren), 1921 v W
Provan, D. (5) (Rangers), 1964 v NI, Nor; 1966 v I, I, Neth
Provan, D. (10) (Celtic), 1980 v Bel, Bel, P, NI; 1981 v Is, W, E; 1982 v Swe, P, NI
Pursell, P. (1) (Queen's Park), 1914 v W

Quinn, J. (11) (Celtic), 1905 v Ire; 1906 v Ire, W; 1908 v Ire, E; 1909 v E; 1910 v E, Ire, W; 1912 v E, W
Quinn, P. (4) (Motherwell), 1961 v E, RI (2); 1962 v U

Rae, J. (2) (Third Lanark), 1889 v W; 1890 v Ire
Raeside, J. S. (1) (Third Lanark), 1906 v W
Raisbeck, A. G. (8) (Liverpool), 1900 v E; 1901 v E; 1902 v E; 1903 v E, W; 1904 v E; 1906 v E; 1907 v E
Rankin, G. (2) (Vale of Leven), 1890 v Ire; 1891 v E
Rankin, R. (3) (St Mirren), 1929 v Nor, G, Neth
Redpath, W. (9) (Motherwell), 1949 v W, NI; 1951 v E, Den, F, Bel, A; 1952 v NI, E
Reid, J. G. (3) (Airdrieonians), 1914 v W; 1920 v W; 1924 v NI
Reid, R. (2) (Brentford), 1938 v E, NI
Reid, W. (9) (Rangers), 1911 v E, W, Ire; 1912 v Ire; 1913 v E, W, Ire; 1914 v E, Ire
Reilly, L. (38) (Hibernian), 1949 v E, W, F; 1950 v W, NI, Swz, F; 1951 v W, E, Den, F, Bel, A; 1952 v NI, W, E, USA, Den, Swe; 1953 v NI, W, E, Swe; 1954 v W; 1955 v H, H, P, Y, A, E; 1956 v E, W, NI, A; 1957 v E, NI, W, Y
Rennie, H. G. (13) (Hearts), 1900 v E, Ire; (Hibernian), 1901 v E; 1902 v E, Ire, W; 1903 v Ire, W; 1904 v Ire; 1905 v W; 1906 v Ire; 1908 v Ire, W
Renny-Tailyour, H. W. (1) (Royal Engineers), 1873 v E
Rhind, A. (1) (Queen's Park), 1872 v E
Richmond, A. (1) (Queen's Park), 1906 v W
Richmond, J. T. (3) (Clydesdale), 1877 v E; (Queen's Park), 1878 v E; 1882 v W
Ring, T. (12) (Clyde), 1953 v Swe; 1955 v W, NI, E, H; 1957 v E, Sp, Sp, Swz, FRG; 1958 v NI, Swz
Rioch, B. D. (24) (Derby Co), 1975 v P, W, NI, E, Rum; 1976 v Den, Den, R, NI, W, E; 1977 v Fin, Cz, W; (Everton), W, NI, E, Ch, Bra; 1978 v Cz (Derby Co), NI, E, Pe, Neth
Ritchie, A. (1) (East Stirlingshire), 1891 v W
Ritchie, H. (2) (Hibernian), 1923 v W; 1928 v NI
Ritchie, J. (1) (Queen's Park), 1897 v W
Ritchie, W. (1) (Rangers), 1962 v U
Robb, D. T. (5) (Aberdeen), 1971 v W, E, P, Den, USSR

Robb, W. (2) (Rangers), 1926 v W; (Hibernian), 1928 v W
Robertson, A. (5) (Clyde), 1955 v P, A, H; 1958 v Swz, Par
Robertson, G. (4) (Motherwell), 1910 v W; (Sheffield W), 1912 v W; 1913 v E, Ire
Robertson, G. (1) (Kilmarnock), 1938 v Cz
Robertson, H. (1) (Dundee), 1962 v Cz
Robertson, J. (2) (Dundee), 1931 v A, I
Robertson, J. N. (28) (Nottingham F), 1978 v NI, W, Ir; 1979 v P, Nor; 1980 v Pe, A, Bel, Bel, P; 1981 v Swe, P, Is, NI, Is, NI, E; 1982 v Swe, NI, NI, E, NZ, Bra, USSR; 1983 v GDR, Swz; (Derby Co), 1984 v U, Bel
Robertson, J. G. (1) (Tottenham H), 1965 v W
Robertson, J. T. (16) (Everton), 1898 v E; (Southampton), 1899 v E; (Rangers), 1900 v E, W; 1901 v W, Ire, E; 1902 v W, Ire, E; 1903 v E, W; 1904 v E, W, Ire; 1905 v W
Robertson, P. (1) (Dundee), 1903 v Ire
Robertson, T. (4) (Queen's Park), 1889 v Ire; 1890 v E; 1891 v W; 1892 v Ire
Robertson, T. (1) (Hearts), 1898 v Ire
Robertson, W. (2) (Dumbarton), 1887 v E, W
Robinson, R. (4) (Dundee), 1974 v FRG; 1975 v Swe, NI, R
Rough, A. (53) (Partick T), 1976 v Swz, NI, W, E; 1977 v Fin, Cz, W, W, Swe, NI, E, Ch, Arg, Bra; 1978 v Cz, W, NI, E, Pe, Ir, Neth; 1979 v A, P, W, Arg, Nor; 1980 v Pe, A, Bel, Bel, P, W, E, Pol, H; 1981 v Swe, P, Is, NI, Is, W, E; 1982 v Swe, NI, Sp, Neth, W, E, NZ, Bra, USSR; (Hibernian), 1986 v W, E
Rougvie, D. (1) (Aberdeen), 1984 v NI
Rowan, A. (2) (Caledonian), 1880 v E; (Queen's Park), 1882 v W
Russell, D. (6) (Hearts), 1895 v E, Ire; (Celtic), 1897 v W; 1898 v Ire; 1901 v W, Ire
Russell, J. (1) (Cambuslang), 1890 v Ire
Russell, W. F. (2) (Airdrieonians), 1924 v W; 1925 v E
Rutherford, E. (1) (Rangers), 1948 v F

St John, I. (21) (Motherwell), 1959 v FRG; 1960 v E, NI, W, Pol, A; 1961 v E; (Liverpool), 1962 v NI, W, E, Cz, Cz, U; 1963 v W, NI, E, Nor, RI, Sp; 1964 v NI; 1965 v E
Sawers, W. (1) (Dundee), 1895 v W
Scarff, P. (1) (Celtic), 1931 v NI
Schaedler, E. (1) (Hibernian), 1974 v FRG
Scott, A. S. (16) (Rangers), 1957 v NI, Y, FRG; 1958 v W, Swz; 1959 v P; 1962 v NI, W, E, Cz, U; (Everton), 1964 v W, Nor; 1965 v Fin; 1966 v P, Bra
Scott, J. (1) (Hibernian), 1966 v Neth
Scott, J. (2) (Dundee), 1971 v Den, USSR
Scott, M. (1) (Airdrieonians), 1898 v W
Scott, R. (1) (Airdrieonians), 1894 v Ire
Scoular, J. (9) (Portsmouth), 1951 v Den, F, A; 1952 v E, USA, Den, Swe; 1953 v W, NI
Sellar, W. (9) (Battlefield), 1885 v E; 1886 v E; 1887 v E, W; 1888 v E; (Queen's Park), 1891 v E; 1892 v E; 1893 v E, Ire
Semple, W. (1) (Cambuslang), 1886 v W
Shankly, W. (5) (Preston NE), 1938 v E; 1939 v E, W, NI, H

Sharp, G. M. (12) (Everton), 1985 v Ic; 1986 v W, Aus, Aus, Is, Rum, U; 1987 v RI, Bel, Bul, Lux; 1988 v Ma

Sharp, J. (5) (Dundee), 1904 v W; (Woolwich Arsenal), 1907 v W, E; 1908 v E; (Fulham), 1909 v W

Shaw, D. (8) (Hibernian), 1947 v W, NI; 1948 v E, Bel, Swz, F; 1949 v W, NI

Shaw, F. W. (2) (Pollokshields Ath), 1884 v E, W

Shaw, J. (4) (Rangers), 1947 v E, Bel, Lux; 1948 v NI

Shearer, R. (4) (Rangers), 1961 v E, RI, RI, Cz

Sillars, D. C. (5) (Queen's Park), 1891 v Ire; 1892 v E; 1893 v W; 1894 v E; 1895 v W

Simpson, J. (3) (Third Lanark), 1895 v E, W, Ire

Simpson, J. (14) (Rangers), 1935 v E, W, NI; 1936 v E, W, NI; 1937 v G, E, W, NI, A, Cz; 1938 v W, NI

Simpson, N. (4) (Aberdeen), 1983 v NI; 1984 v F; 1987 v F; 1988 v E

Simpson, R. C. (5) (Celtic), 1967 v E, USSR; 1968 v NI, E; 1969 v A

Sinclair, G. L. (3) (Hearts), 1910 v Ire; 1912 v W, Ire

Sinclair, J. W. E. (1) (Leicester C), 1966 v P

Skene, L. H. (1) (Queen's Park), 1904 v W

Sloan, T. (1) (Third Lanark), 1904 v W

Smellie, R. (6) (Queen's Park), 1887 v Ire; 1888 v W; 1889 v E; 1891 v E; 1893 v E, Ire

Smith, A. (20) (Rangers), 1898 v E; 1900 v E, Ire, W; 1901 v E, Ire, W; 1902 v E, Ire, W; 1903 v E, Ire, W; 1904 v Ire; 1905 v W; 1906 v E, Ire; 1907 v W; 1911 v E, Ire

Smith, D. (2) (Aberdeen), 1966 v Neth; (Rangers), 1968 v Neth

Smith, G. (18) (Hibernian), 1947 v E, NI; 1948 v W, Bel, Swz, F; 1952 v E, USA; 1955 v P, Y, A, H; 1956 v E, NI, W; 1957 v Sp, Sp, Swz

Smith, H. (1) (Hearts), 1988 v S.Ar

Smith, J. (2) (Rangers), 1935 v NI; 1938 v NI

Smith, J. (1) (Ayr U), 1924 v E

Smith, J. (4) (Aberdeen), 1968 v Neth; (Newcastle U), 1974 v FRG, NI, W

Smith, J. E. (2) (Celtic), 1959 v H, P

Smith, Jas. (1) (Queen's Park), 1872 v E

Smith, John. (10) (Mauchline), 1877 v E. W; 1879 v E, W; (Edinburgh University), 1880 v E; (Queen's Park), 1881 v W, E; 1883 v E; W; 1884 v E

Smith, N. (12) (Rangers), 1897 v E; 1898 v W; 1899 v E, W, Ire; 1900 v E, W, Ire; 1901 v Ire, W; 1902 v E, Ire

Smith, R. (2) (Queen's Park), 1872 v E; 1873 v E

Smith, T. M. (2) (Kilmarnock), 1934 v E; (Preston NE), 1938 v E

Somers, P. (4) (Celtic), 1905 v E, Ire; 1907 v Ire; 1909 v W

Somers, W. S. (3) (Third Lanark), 1879 v E, W; (Queen's Park), 1880 v W

Somerville, G. (1) (Queen's Park), 1886 v E

Souness, G. J. (54) (Middlesbrough), 1975 v EG, Sp, Swe; (Liverpool), 1978 v Bul, W, E, Neth; 1979 v A, Nor, W, NI, E; 1980 v Pe, A, Bel, P, NI; 1981 v P, Is, Is; 1982 v NI, P, Sp, W, E, NZ, Bra, USSR; 1983 v GDR, Swz, Bel, Swz, W, E, Can, Can; 1984 v U, NI, W; (Sampdoria), 1985 v Y, Ic, Sp, Sp, W, E, Ic; 1986 v GDR, Aus, Aus, Rum, E, Den, FRG

Speedie, D. R. (5) (Chelsea), 1985 v E; 1986 v W, GDR, Aus, E

Speedie, F. (3) (Rangers), 1903 v E, W, Ire

Speirs, J. H. (1) (Rangers), 1908 v W

Stanton, P. (16) (Hibernian), 1966 v Neth; 1969 v NI; 1970 v RI, A; 1971 v Den, Bel, P, USSR, Den; 1972 v P, Bel, Neth, W; 1973 v W, NI; 1974 v FRG

Stark, J. (2) (Rangers), 1909 v E, Ire

Steel, W. (30) (Morton), 1947 v E, Bel, Lux; (Derby Co), 1948 v F, E, W, NI; 1949 v E, W, NI, F; 1950 v E, W, NI, Swz, P, F; (Dundee), 1951 v W, NI, E, A, A, Den, F, Bel; 1952 v W; 1953 v W, E. NI, Swe

Steele, D. M. (3) (Huddersfield), 1923 v E, W, NI

Stein, C. (21) (Rangers), 1969 v W, NI, Den, E, Cyp, Cyp; 1970 v A, NI, W, E, RI, FRG; 1971 v Den, USSR, Bel, Den; 1972 v Cz; (Coventry C), 1973 v E, W, NI

Stephen, J. F. (2) (Bradford), 1947 v W; 1948 v W

Stevenson, G. (12) (Motherwell), 1928 v W, NI; 1930 v NI, E, F; 1931 v E, W; 1932 v W, NI, 1933 v NI; 1934 v E; 1935 v NI

Stewart, A. (2) (Queen's Park), 1888 v Ire; 1889 v W

Stewart, A. (1) (Third Lanark), 1894 v W

Stewart, D. (1) (Dumbarton), 1888 v Ire

Stewart, D. (3) (Queen's Park), 1893 v W; 1894 v Ire; 1897 v Ire

Stewart, D. S. (1) (Leeds U), 1978 v GDR

Stewart, G. (4) (Hibernian), 1906 v W, E; (Manchester C), 1907 v E, W

Stewart, J. (2) (Kilmarnock), 1977 v Ch; (Middlesbrough), 1979 v N

Stewart, R. (10) (West Ham U), 1981 v W, NI, E; 1982 v NI, P. W; 1984 v F; 1987 v RI, RI, Lux

Stewart, W. E. (2) (Queen's Park), 1898 v Ire; 1900 v Ire

Storrier, D. (3) (Celtic), 1899 v E, W, Ire

Strachan, G. (41) (Aberdeen), 1980 v NI, W, E, Pol, H; 1981 v Swe, P; 1982 v NI, P, Sp, Neth, NZ, Bra, USSR; 1983 v GDR, Swz, Bel, Swz, NI, W, E, Can, Can; 1984 v GDR, NI, E, F; (Manchester U), 1985 v Sp, E, Ic; 1986 v W, Aus, Rum, Den, FRG, U; 1987 v Bul, RI, RI, H

Sturrock, P. (20) (Dundee U), 1981 v W, NI, E; 1982 v P, NI, W, E; 1983 v GDR, Swz, Bel, Can, Can, Can; 1984 v W; 1985 v Y; 1986 v Is, Neth, Den, U; 1987 v Bel

Summers, W. (1) (St Mirren), 1926 v E

Symon, J. S. (1) (Rangers), 1939 v H

Tait, T. S. (1) (Sunderland), 1911 v W

Taylor, J. (6) (Queen's Park), 1872 v E; 1873 v E; 1874 v E; 1875 v E; 1876 v E, W

Taylor, J. D. (4) (Dumbarton), 1892 v W; 1893 v W; 1894 v Ire; (St Mirren), 1895 v Ire

Taylor, W. (1) (Hearts), 1892 v E

Telfer, W. (2) (Motherwell), 1933 v NI; 1934 v NI

Telfer, W. D. (1) (St Mirren), 1954 v W

Templeton, R. (11) (Aston Villa), 1902 v E; (Newcastle U), 1903 v E, W; 1904 v E; (Woolwich Arsenal), 1905 v W; (Kilmarnock), 1908 v Ire; 1910 v E, Ire; 1912 v E, Ire; 1913 v W

Thomson, A. (1) (Arthurlie), 1886 v Ire

Thomson, A. (1) (Airdrieonians), 1909 v Ire

Thomson, A. (3) (Celtic), 1926 v E; 1932 v F; 1933 v W

Thomson, A. (1) (Third Lanark), 1889 v W

Thomson, C. (21) (Hearts), 1904 v Ire; 1905 v E, Ire, W; 1906 v W, Ire; 1907 v E, W, Ire; 1908 v E, W, Ire;

(Sunderland), 1909 v W; 1910 v E; 1911 v Ire; 1912 v E, W; 1913 v E, W; 1914 v E, Ire
Thomson, C. (1) (Sunderland), 1937 v Cz
Thomson, D. (1) (Dundee), 1920 v W
Thomson, J. (4) (Celtic), 1930 v F; 1931 v E, W, NI
Thomson, J. J. (3) (Queen's Park), 1872 v E; 1873 v E; 1874 v E
Thomson, J. R. (1) (Everton), 1933 v W
Thomson, R. (1) (Celtic), 1932 v W
Thomson, R. W. (1) (Falkirk), 1927 v E
Thomson, S. (2) (Rangers), 1884 v W, Ire
Thomson, W. (4) (Dumbarton), 1892 v W; 1893 v W; 1898 v Ire, W
Thomson, W. (1) (Dundee), 1896 v W
Thomson, W. (7) (St Mirren), 1980 v NI; 1981 v NI, NI; 1982 v P; 1983 v NI, Can; 1984 v GDR
Thornton, W. (7) (Rangers), 1947 v W, NI; 1948 v E, NI; 1949 v F; 1952 v Den, Swe
Toner, W. (2) (Kilmarnock), 1959 v W, NI
Townsley, T. (1) (Falkirk), 1926 v W
Troup, A. (5) (Dundee), 1920 v E; 1921 v W, Ire; 1922 v NI; (Everton), 1926 v E
Turnbull, E. (8) (Hibernian), 1948 v Bel, Swz; 1951 v A; 1958 v H, Pol, Y, Par, F
Turner, T. (1) (Arthurlie), 1884 v W
Turner, W. (2) (Pollokshields), 1885 v Ire; 1886 v Ire

Ure, J. F. (11) (Dundee), 1962 v W, Cz; 1963 v W, NI, E, A, Nor, Sp; (Arsenal), 1964 v NI, Nor; 1968 v NI
Urquhart, D. (1) (Hibernian), 1934 v W

Vallance, T. (7) (Rangers), 1877 v E, W; 1878 v E; 1879 v E, W; 1881 v E, W
Venters, A. (3) (Cowdenbeath), 1934 v NI; (Rangers), 1936 v E; 1939 v E

Waddell, T. S. (6) (Queen's Park), 1891 v Ire; 1892 v E; 1893 v E, Ire; 1895 v E, Ire
Waddell, W. (17) (Rangers), 1947 v W; 1949 v E, W, NI, F; 1950 v E, NI; 1951 v E, Den, F, Bel, A; 1952 v NI, W; 1954 v NI; 1955 v W, NI
Wales, H. M. (1) (Motherwell), 1933 v W
Walker, A. (1) (Celtic), 1988 v Col
Walker, F. (1) (Third Lanark), 1922 v W
Walker, G. (4) (St Mirren), 1930 v F; 1931 v NI, A, Swz
Walker, J. (5) (Hearts), 1895 v Ire; 1897 v W; 1898 v Ire; (Rangers), 1904 v W, Ire
Walker, J. (9) (Swindon T), 1911 v E, W, Ire; 1912 v E, W, Ire; 1913 v E, W, Ire
Walker, R. (29) (Hearts), 1900 v E, Ire; 1901 v E, W; 1902 v E, W, Ire; 1903 v E, W, Ire; 1904 v E, W, Ire; 1905 v E, W, Ire; 1906 v Ire; 1907 v E, Ire; 1908 v E, W, Ire; 1909 v E, W; 1912 v E, W, Ire; 1913 v E, W
Walker, T. (20) (Hearts), 1935 v E, W; 1936 v E, W, NI; 1937 v G, E, W, NI, A, Cz; 1938 v E, W, NI, Cz, Neth; 1939 v E, W, NI, H
Walker, W. (2) (Clyde), 1909 v Ire; 1910 v Ire
Wallace, I. A. (3) (Coventry C), 1978 v Bul; 1979 v P, W
Wallace, W. S. B. (7) (Hearts), 1965 v NI; 1966 v E, Neth; (Celtic), 1967 v E, USSR; 1968 v NI; 1969 v E
Wardhaugh, J. (2) (Hearts), 1955 v H; 1957 v NI
Wark, J. (29) (Ipswich T), 1979 v W, NI, E, Arg, Nor; 1980 v Pe, A, Bel, Bel; 1981 v Is, NI; 1982 v Swe, Sp,

Neth, NI, NZ, Bra, USSR; 1983 v GDR, Swz, Swz, NI, E; 1984 v U, Bel, GDR; (Liverpool), E, F; 1985 v Y
Watson, A. (3) (Queen's Park), 1881 v E, W; 1882 v E
Watson, J. (6) (Sunderland), 1903 v E, W; 1904 v E; 1905 v E; (Middlesbrough), 1909 v E, Ire
Watson, J. (2) (Motherwell), 1948 v NI; (Huddersfield T), 1954 v NI
Watson, J. A. K. (1) (Rangers), 1878 v W
Watson, P. R. (1) (Blackpool), 1934 v A
Watson, R. (1) (Motherwell), 1971 v USSR
Watson, W. (1) (Falkirk), 1898 v W
Watt, F. (4) (Kilbirnie), 1889 v W, Ire; 1890 v W; 1891 v E
Watt, W. W. (1) (Queen's Park), 1887 v Ire
Waugh, W. (1) (Hearts), 1938 v Cz
Weir, A. (6) (Motherwell), 1959 v FRG; 1960 v E, P, A, H, T
Weir, J. (1) (Third Lanark), 1887 v Ire
Weir, J. B. (4) (Queen's Park), 1872 v E; 1874 v E; 1875 v E; 1878 v W
Weir, P. (6) (St Mirren), 1980 v Nor, W, Pol, H; (Aberdeen), 1983 v Swz; 1984 v NI
White, John (2) (Albion R), 1922 v W; (Hearts), 1923 v NI
White, J. A. (22) (Falkirk), 1959 v FRG, Neth, P; 1960 v NI; (Tottenham H), 1960 v W, Pol, A, T; 1961 v W; 1962 v NI, W, E, Cz, Cz; 1963 v W, NI, E; 1964 v NI, W, E, Nor, FRG
White, W. (2) (Bolton W), 1907 v E; 1908 v E
Whitelaw, A. (2) (Vale of Leven), 1887 v Ire; 1890 v W
Whyte, D. (2) (Celtic), 1987 v Bel, Lux
Wilson, A. (6) (Sheffield W), 1907 v E; 1908 v E; 1912 v E; 1913 v E, W; 1914 v Ire
Wilson, A: (1) (Portsmouth), 1954 v Fin
Wilson, A. N. (12) (Dunfermline), 1920 v E, W, Ire; 1921 v E, W, Ire; (Middlesbrough), 1922 v E, W, NI; 1923 v E, W, NI
Wilson, D. (1) (Queen's Park), 1900 v W
Wilson, D. (1) (Oldham Ath), 1913 v E
Wilson, D. (22) (Rangers), 1961 v E, W, NI, RI, RI, Cz; 1962 v NI, W, E, Cz, U; 1963 v W, E, A, Nor, RI, Sp; 1964 v E, FRG; 1965 v NI, E, Fin
Wilson, G. W. (6) (Hearts), 1904 v W; 1905 v E, Ire; 1906 v W; (Everton), 1907 v E; (Newcastle U), 1909 v E
Wilson, Hugh, (4) (Newmilns), 1890 v W; (Sunderland), 1897 v E; (Third Lanark), 1902 v W, 1904 v Ire
Wilson, I. A. (5) (Leicester C), 1987 v E, Bra, (Everton), Bel, Bul, Lux
Wilson, J. (4) (Vale of Leven), 1888 v W, 1889 v E; 1890 v E; 1891 v E
Wilson, P. (4) (Celtic), 1926 v NI; 1930 v F; 1931 v NI; 1933 v E
Wilson, P. (1) (Celtic), 1975 v Sp
Wilson, R. P. (2) (Arsenal), 1972 v P, Neth
Wiseman, W. (2) (Queen's Park), 1927 v W; 1930 v NI
Wood, G. (4) (Everton), 1979 v NI, E, Arg; (Arsenal), 1982 v NI
Woodburn, W. A. (24) (Rangers), 1947 v E, Bel, Lux; 1948 v W, NI; 1949 v E, F; 1950 v E, W, NI, P, F; 1951 v E, W, NI, A, A, Den, F, Bel; 1952 v E, W, NI, USA

Wotherspoon, D. N. (2) (Queen's Park), 1872 v E; 1873 v E

Wright, T. (3) (Sunderland), 1953 v W, NI, E

Wylie, T. G. (1) (Rangers), 1890 v Ire

Yeats, R. (2) (Liverpool), 1965 v W; 1966 v I

Yorston, B. C. (1) (Aberdeen), 1931 v NI

Yorston, H. (1) (Aberdeen), 1955 v W

Young, A. (8) (Hearts), 1960 v E, A, H, T; 1961 v W, NI; (Everton), RI; 1966 v P

Young, A. (2) (Everton), 1905 v E; 1907 v W

Young, G. L. (53) (Rangers), 1947 v E, NI, Bel, Lux; 1948 v E, NI, Bel, Swz, F; 1949 v E, W, NI, F; 1950 v E, W, NI, Swz, P, F; 1951 v E, W, NI, A, A, Den, F, Bel; 1952 v E, W, NI, USA, Den, Swe; 1953 v W, E, NI, Swe; 1954 v NI, W; 1955 v W, NI, P, Y; 1956 v NI, W, E, A; 1957 v E, NI, W, Y, Sp, Swz

Young, J. (1) (Celtic), 1906 v Ire

Younger, T. (24) (Hibernian), 1955 v P, Y, A, H; 1956 v E, NI, W, A; (Liverpool), 1957 v E, NI, W, Y, Sp, Sp, Swz, FRG; 1958 v NI, W, E, Swz, H, Pol, Y, Par

WALES

Adams, H. (4) (Berwyn R), 1882 v Ire, E; (Druids), 1883 v Ire, E

Aizlewood, M. (10) (Charlton Ath), 1986 v S.Ar, Can, Can; 1987 v Fin (Leeds U); USSR, Fin, Den; 1988 v Swe, Ma, I

Allchurch, I. J. (68) (Swansea T), 1951 v E, NI, P, Swz; 1952 v E, S, NI, UK; 1953 v S, E, NI, F, Y; 1954 v S, E, NI, A; 1955 v S, E, NI, Y; 1956 v E, S, NI, A; 1957 v E, S; 1958 v NI, Is, Is, H, H, Mex, Swz, Bra; (Newcastle U), 1959 v E, S, NI; 1960 v E, S; 1961 v NI, H, Sp, Sp; 1962 v E, S, Bra, Bra, Mex; (Cardiff C), 1963 v S, E, NI, H, H; 1964 v E; 1965 v S, E, NI, Gr, I, USSR; (Swansea T), 1966 v USSR, E, S, Den, Bra, Bra, Ch

Allchurch, L. (11) (Swansea T), 1955 v NI; 1956 v A; 1958 v S, NI, GDR, Is; 1959 v S; Sheffield U), 1962 v S, NI, Bra; 1964 v E

Allen, B. W. (2) (Coventry C), 1951 v S, E

Allen, M. (3) (Watford), 1986 v S.Ar, Can, Can

Arridge, S. (8) (Bootle), 1892 v S, Ire; (Everton), 1894 v Ire; 1895 v Ire; 1896 v E; (New Brighton Tower), 1898 v E, Ire; 1899 v E

Astley, D. J. (13) (Charlton Ath), 1931 v NI; (Aston Villa), 1932 v E; 1933 v E, S, NI; 1934 v E, S; 1935 v S; 1936 v E, NI; (Derby Co), 1939 v E, S; (Blackpool), F

Atherton, R. W. (9) (Hibernian), 1899 v E, Ire; 1903 v E, S, Ire; (Middlesbrough), 1904 v E, S, Ire; 1905 v Ire

Bailiff, W. E. (4) (Llanelly), 1913 v E, S, Ire; 1920 v Ire

Baker, C. W. (7) (Cardiff C), 1958 v Mex; 1960 v S, NI; 1961 v S, E, RI; 1962 v S

Baker, W. G. (1) (Cardiff C), 1948 v NI

Bamford, T. (5) (Wrexham), 1931 v E, S, NI; 1932 v NI; 1933 v F

Barnes, W. (22) (Arsenal), 1948 v E, S, NI; 1949 v E, S, NI; 1950 v E, S, NI, Bel; 1951 v E, S, NI, P; 1952 v E, S, NI, UK; 1954 v E, S; 1955 v S, Y

Bartley, T. (1) (Glossop NE), 1898 v E

Beadles, G. H. (2) (Cardiff C), 1925 v E, S

Bell, W. S. (5) (Shrewsbury Engineers), 1881 v E, S; (Crewe Alex), 1886 v E, S, Ire

Bennion, S. R. (10) (Manchester U), 1926 v S; 1927 v S; 1928 v S, E, NI; 1929 v S, E, NI; 1930 v S; 1932 v NI

Berry, G. F. (5) (Wolverhampton W), 1979 v FRG; 1980 v RI, FRG, T; (Stoke C), 1983 v E

Blackmore, C. G. (17) (Manchester U), 1985 v Nor;

1986 v S, H, S.Ar, RI, U; 1987 v Fin, Fin, USSR, Cz, Den, Den, Cz; 1988 v Y, Swe, Ma, I

Blew, H. (22) (Wrexham), 1899 v E, S, Ire; 1902 v S, Ire; 1903 v E, S; 1904 v E, S, Ire; 1905 v S; Ire; 1906 v E, S, Ire; 1907 v S; 1908 v E, S, Ire; 1909 v E, S; 1910 v E

Boden, T. (1) (Wrexham), 1880 v E

Bostock, A. M. (1) (Shrewsbury), 1892 v Ire

Boulter, L. M. (1) (Brentford), 1939 v NI

Bowdler, H. E. (1) (Shrewsbury), 1893 v S

Bowdler, J. C. H. (4) (Shrewsbury), 1890 v Ire; (Wolverhampton W), 1891 v S; 1892 v Ire; (Shrewsbury), 1894 v E

Bowen, D. L. (19) (Arsenal), 1955 v S, Y; 1957 v NI, Cz, GDR; 1958 v E, S, NI, GDR, Is, Is, H, H, Mex, Swe, Bra; 1959 v E, S, NI

Bowen, E. (2) (Druids), 1880 v S; 1883 v S

Bowen, M. R. (3) (Tottenham H), 1986 v Can, Can; (Norwich C), 1988 v Y

Bowsher, S. J. (1) (Burnley), 1929 v NI

Boyle, T. (2) (C Palace), 1981 v RI, S

Britten, T. J. (2) (Parkgrove), 1878 v S; (Presteigne), 1880 v S

Brookes, S. J. (2) (Llandudno), 1900 v E, Ire

Brown, A. I. (1) (Aberdare Ath), 1926 v NI

Bryan, T. (2) (Oswestry), 1886 v E, Ire

Buckland, T. (1) (Bangor), 1899 v E

Burgess, W. A. R. (32) (Tottenham H), 1947 v E, S, NI; 1948 v E, S; 1949 v E, S, NI, P, Bel, Swz; 1950 v E, S, NI, Bel; 1951 v S, NI, P, Swz; 1952 v E, S, NI, UK; 1953 v S, E, NI, F, Y; 1954 v S, E, NI, A

Burke, T. (8) (Wrexham), 1883 v E; 1884 v S; 1885 v E, S, Ire; (Newton Heath), 1887 v E, S; 1888 v S

Burnett, T. B. (1) (Ruabon), 1877 v S

Burton, A. D. (9) (Norwich C), 1963 v NI, H; (Newcastle U), 1964 v E; 1969 v S, E, NI, I, GDR; 1972 v Cz

Butler, A. (2) (Druids), 1900 v S, Ire

Butler, J. (3) (Chirk), 1893 v E, S, Ire

Cartwright, L. (7) (Coventry C), 1974 v E, S, NI; 1976 v ' S; 1977 v FRG; (Wrexham), 1978 v Ir; 1979 v Ma

Carty, T. (1) (Wrexham), 1889 v Ire

Challen, J. B. (4) (Corinthians), 1887 v E, S; 1888 v E; (Wellingborough GS), 1890 v E

Chapman, T. (7) (Newtown), 1894 v E, S, Ire; 1895 v S, Ire; (Manchester C), 1896 v E; 1897 v E

Charles, J. M. (19) (Swansea C), 1981 v Cz, T, S, USSR; 1982 v Ic; 1983 v Nor, Y, Bul, S, NI, Bra;

1984 v Bul, (QPR), Y, S; (Oxford U), 1985 v Ic, Sp, Ic; 1986 v RI; 1987 v Fin

Charles, M. (31) (Swansea T), 1955 v NI; 1956 v E, S, A; 1957 v E, NI, Cz, Cz, GDR; 1958 v E, S, GDR, Is, Is, H, H, Mex, Swe, Bra; 1959 v E, S; (Arsenal), 1961 v NI, H, Sp, Sp; 1962 v E, S; (Cardiff C), 1962 v Bra, NI; 1963 v S, H

Charles, W. J. (38) (Leeds U), 1950 v NI; 1951 v Swz; 1953 v NI, F, Y; 1954 v E, S, NI, A; 1955 v S, E, NI, Y; 1956 v E, S, A, NI; 1957 v E, S, NI, Cz, Cz, GDR; (Juventus), 1958 v Is, Is, H, H, Mex, Swe; 1960 v S; 1962 v E, Bra, Bra, Mex; (Leeds U), 1963 v S; (Cardiff C), 1964 v S; 1965 v S, USSR

Clarke, R. J. (22) (Manchester C), 1949 v E; 1950 v S, NI, Bel; 1951 v E, S, NI, P, Swz; 1952 v S, E, NI, UK; 1953 v S, E; 1954 v E, S, NI; 1955 v Y, S, E; 1956 v NI

Collier, D. J. (1) (Grimsby T), 1921 v S

Collins, W. S. (1) (Llanelly), 1931 v S

Conde, C. (3) (Chirk), 1884 v E, S, Ire

Cook, F. C. (8) (Newport Co), 1925 v E, S; (Portsmouth), 1928 v E, S; 1930 v E, S, NI; 1932 v E

Crompton, W. (3) (Wrexham), 1931 v E, S, NI

Cross, E. A. (2) (Wrexham), 1876 v S; 1877 v S

Cross, K. (3) (Druids), 1879 v S; 1881 v E, S

Crowe, V. H. (16) (Aston Villa), 1959 v E, NI; 1960 v E, NI; 1961 v S, E, NI, RI, H, Sp, Sp; 1962 v E, S, Bra, Mex; 1963 v H

Cumner, R. H. (3) (Arsenal), 1939 v E, S, NI

Curtis, A. (35) (Swansea C), 1976 v E, Y, S, NI, Y, E; 1977 v FRG, S, NI; 1978 v FRG, E, S; 1979 v FRG, S; (Leeds U), E, NI, Ma; 1980 v RI, FRG, T; (Swansea C), 1982 v Cz, Ic, USSR, Sp, E, S, NI; 1983 v Nor; 1984 v Rum, (Southampton), S; 1985 v Sp. Nor, Nor; 1986 v H; (Cardiff C), 1987 v USSR

Curtis, E. R. (3) (Cardiff C), 1928 v S; (Birmingham), 1932 v S; 1934 v NI

Daniel, R. W. (21) (Arsenal), 1951 v E, NI, P; 1952 v E, S, NI, UK; 1953 v S, E, NI, F, Y; (Sunderland), 1954 v E, S, NI; 1955 v E, NI; 1957 v S, E, NI, Cz

Darvell, S. (2) (Oxford University), 1897 v S, Ire

Davies, A. (8) (Manchester U), 1983 v NI, Bra; 1984 v E, NI; 1985 v Ic; (Newcastle U), 1986 v H; (Swansea C), 1988 v Ma, I

Davies, A. (2) (Wrexham), 1876 v S; 1877 v S

Davies, A. (1) (Shrewsbury), 1891 v Ire

Davies, A. (2) (Druids), 1904 v S; (Middlesbrough), 1905 v S

Davies, A. O. (9) (Barmouth), 1885 v Ire; 1886 v E, S; (Swifts), 1887 v E, S; 1888 v E, Ire; (Wrexham), 1889 v S; (Crewe Alex), 1890 v E

Davies, C. (2) (Brecon), 1899 v Ire; (Hereford), 1900 v Ire

Davies, C. (1) (Charlton Ath), 1972 v R

Davies, D. (3) (Bolton W), 1904 v S, Ire; 1908 v E

Davies, D. W. (2) (Treharris), 1912 v Ire; (Oldham Ath), 1913 v Ire

Davies, E. Lloyd, (16) (Stoke C), 1904 v E; 1907 v E, S, Ire; (Northampton T), 1908 v S; 1909 v Ire; 1910 v Ire; 1911 v E, S; 1912 v E, S; 1913 v E, S; 1914 v Ire, E, S

Davies, E. R. (6) (Newcastle U), 1953 v S, E; 1954 v E, S; 1958 v E, GDR

Davies, G. (18) (Fulham), 1980 v T, Ic; 1982 v Sp, F; 1983 v E, Bul, S, NI, Bra; 1984 v Rum, S, E, NI; 1985 v Ic, Ic, (Chelsea), Nor; (Manchester C), 1986 v S.Ar, RI

Davies, Rev. H. (1) (Wrexham), 1928 v NI

Davies, Idwal (1) (Liverpool Marine), 1923 v S

Davies, J. E. (1) (Oswestry), 1885 v E

Davies, Jas. (1) (Wrexham), 1878 v S

Davies, John. (1) (Wrexham), 1879 v S

Davies, Jos. (11) (Everton), 1889 v S, Ire; (Chirk), 1891 v Ire; (Ardwick), v E, S; (Sheffield U), 1895 v E, S, Ire; (Manchester C), 1896 v E; (Millwall), 1897 v E; (Reading), 1900 v E

Davies, Jos. (7) (Newton Heath), 1888 v E, S, Ire; 1889 v S; 1890 v E; (Wolverhampton W), 1892 v E; 1893 v E

Davies, J. P. (2) (Druids), 1883 v E, Ire

Davies, Ll. (13) (Wrexham), 1907 v Ire; 1910 v Ire, S, E; (Everton), 1911 v S, Ire; 1912 v Ire, S, E; 1913 v Ire, S, E; 1914 v Ire

Davies, L. S. (23) (Cardiff C), 1922 v E, S, NI; 1923 v E, S, NI; 1924 v E, S, NI; 1925 v S, NI; 1926 v E, NI; 1927 v E, NI; 1928 v S, NI, E; 1929 v S, NI, E; 1930 v E, S

Davies, O. (1) (Wrexham), 1890 v S

Davies, R. (3) (Wrexham), 1883 v Ire; 1884 v Ire; 1885 v Ire

Davies, R. (1) (Druids), 1885 v E

Davies, R. L. (1) (Wrexham), 1892 v Ire

Davies, R. O. (2) (Wrexham), 1892 v Ire, E

Davies, R. T. (29) (Norwich C), 1964 v NI; 1965 v E; 1966 v Bra, Bra, Ch; (Southampton), 1967 v S, E, NI; 1968 v S, NI, FRG; 1969 v S, E, NI, I, FRG, UK; 1970 v E, S, NI; 1971 v Cz, S, E, NI; 1973 v Rum, E, S, Nor; (Portsmouth), 1974 v E

Davies, R. W. (34) (Bolton W), 1964 v E; 1965 v E, S, NI, Den, Gr, USSR; 1966 v E, S, NI, USSR, Den, Bra, Bra, Ch; 1967 v S; (Newcastle U). E; 1968 v S, NI, FRG; 1969 v S, E, NI, I; 1970 v GDR; 1971 v Rum, Cz (Manchester C), 1972 v E, S, NI; (Manchester U), 1973 v E, S, NI; (Blackpool), 1974 v Pol

Davies, Stanley (18) (Preston NE), 1920 v E, S, Ire; (Everton), 1921 v E, S, Ire; (WBA), 1922 v E, S, NI; 1923 v S; 1925 v S, NI; 1926 v S, NI; 1927 v S; 1928 v S; (Rotherham U), 1930 v NI

Davies, T. (1) (Oswestry), 1886 v E

Davies, T. (4) (Druids), 1903 v E, Ire, S; 1904 v S

Davies, W. (17) (Swansea T), 1924 v E, S, NI; (Cardiff C), 1925 v E, S, NI; 1926 v E, S, NI; 1927 v S; 1928 v NI; (Notts Co), 1929 v E, S, NI; 1930 v E, S, NI

Davies, W. (1) (Wrexham), 1884 v Ire

Davies, William (11) (Wrexham), 1903 v Ire; 1905 v Ire; (Blackburn R), 1908 v E, S; 1909 v E, S, Ire; 1911 v E, S, Ire; 1912 v Ire

Davies, W. C. (4) (C Palace), 1908 v S; (WBA), 1909 v E; 1910 v S; (C Palace), 1914 v E

Davies, W. D. (52) (Everton), 1975 v H, Lux, S, E, NI; 1976 v Y, Y, E, NI; 1977 v FRG, S, S, Cz, E, NI; 1978 v K; (Wrexham), S, Cz, FRG, Ir, E, S, NI; 1979 v Ma, T, FRG, S, E, NI, Ma; 1980 v RI, FRG, T, E,

S, NI, Ic; 1981 v T, Cz, RI, T, S, E, USSR; (Swansea C) 1982 v Cz, Ic, USSR, Sp, E, S, F; 1983 v Y

Davies, W. H. (4) (Oswestry), 1876 v S; 1877 v S; 1879 v E; 1880 v E

Davies, W. O. (5) (Millwall Ath), 1913 v E, S, Ire; 1914 v S, Ire

Davis, G. (3) (Wrexham), 1978 v Ir, E, NI

Day, A. (1) (Tottenham H), 1934 v NI

Deacy, N. (12) (PSV Eindhoven), 1977 v Cz, S, E, NI; 1978 v K, S, Cz, FRG, Ir, S, NI; (Beringen), 1979 v T

Dearson, D. J. (3) (Birmingham), 1939 v S, NI, F

Derrett, S. C. (4) (Cardiff C), 1969 v S, FRG; 1970 v I; 1971 v Fin

Dewey, F. T. (2) (Cardiff Corinthians), 1931 v E, S

Dibble, A. (2) (Luton T), 1986 v Can, Can

Doughty, J. (8) (Druids), 1886 v S; (Newton Heath), 1887 v S, Ire; 1888 v E, S, Ire; 1889 v S; 1890 v E

Doughty, R. (3) (Newton Heath and Druids), 1888 v S, Ire; 1890 v E

Durban, A. (27) (Derby Co), 1966 v Bra; 1967 v NI; 1968 v E, S, NI, FRG; 1969 v GDR, S, E, NI, FRG; 1970 v E, S, NI, GDR, I; 1971 v Rum, S, E, NI, Cz, Fin; 1972 v Fin, Cz, E, S, NI

Dwyer, P. (10) (Cardiff C), 1978 v Ir, E, S, NI; 1979 v T, S, E, NI, Ma; 1980 v FRG

Edwards, C. (1) (Wrexham), 1878 v S

Edwards, G. (12) (Birmingham C), 1947 v E, S, NI; 1948 v E; S, NI; (Cardiff C), 1949 v NI, P, Bel, Swz; 1950 v E, S

Edwards, H. (7) (Wrexham Civil Service), 1878 v S; 1880 v E; 1882 v E, S, 1883 v S; 1884 v Ire; 1887 v Ire

Edwards, J. H. (4) (Oswestry), 1895 v Ire; 1897 v E, Ire; (Aberystwyth), 1898 v Ire

Edwards, J. H. (1) (Wanderers), 1876 v S

Edwards, L. T. (2) (Charlton Ath), 1957 v NI, GDR

Edwards, R. I. (4) (Chester), 1978 v K; 1979 v Ma, FRG; (Wrexham), 1980 v T

Edwards, T. (1) (Linfield), 1932 v S

Egan, W. (1) (Chirk), 1892 v S

Ellis, B. (6) (Motherwell), 1932 v E; 1933 v E, S; 1934 v S; 1936 v E; 1937 v S

Ellis, E. (3) (Nunhead), 1931 v E; (Oswestry), S; 1932 v NI

Emanuel, W. J. (2) (Bristol C), 1973 v E, NI

England, H. M. (44) (Blackburn R), 1962 v NI, Bra, Mex; 1963 v NI, H; 1964 v E, S, NI; 1965 v E, Den, Gr, Gr, USSR, NI, I; 1966 v S, NI, USSR, Den; (Tottenham H), 1967 v S, E; 1968 v E, NI, FRG; 1969 v GDR; 1970 v UK, GDR, E, S, NI, I; 1971 v Rum; 1972 v Fin, E, S, NI, 1973 v E, E, E, S; 1974 v Pol; 1975 v H. Lux

Evans, B. C. (7) (Swansea C), 1972 v Fin, Cz; 1973 v E, E, Pol, S; (Hereford U), 1974 v Pol

Evans, D. G. (4) (Reading), 1926 v NI; 1927 v NI, E; (Huddersfield T), 1929 v S

Evans, H. P. (6) (Cardiff C), 1922 v E, S, NI; 1924 v E, S, NI

Evans, I. (13) (Crystal Palace), 1976 v A, E, Y, Y, E, NI; 1977 v FRG, S, S, Cz, E, NI; 1978 v K

Evans, J. (8) (Cardiff C), 1912 v Ire; 1913 v Ire; 1914 v S; 1920 v S, Ire; 1922 v NI; 1923 v E, NI

Evans, J. (3) (Oswestry), 1893 v Ire; 1894 v E, Ire

Evans, J. H. (4) (Southend U), 1922 v E, S, NI; 1923 v S

Evans, Len (3) (Cardiff C), 1931 v E, S; (Birmingham), 1934 v NI

Evans, L. H. (1) (Aberdare Ath), 1927 v NI

Evans, M. (1) (Oswestry), 1884 v E

Evans, R. (1) (Clapton) 1902 v Ire

Evans, R. E. (10) (Wrexham), 1906 v E, S; (Aston Villa), Ire; 1907 v E; 1908 v E, S; (Sheffield U), 1909 v S; 1910 v E, S, Ire

Evans, R. O. (10) (Wrexham), 1902 v Ire; 1903 v E, S, Ire; (Blackburn R), 1908 v Ire; (Coventry C), 1911 v E, Ire; 1912 v E, S, Ire

Evans, R. S. (1) (Swansea T), 1964 v NI

Evans T. J. (4) (Clapton Orient), 1927 v S; 1928 v E, S; (Newcastle U), NI

Evans, W. (6) (Tottenham H), 1933 v NI; 1934 v E, S; 1935 v E; 1936 v E, NI

Evans, W. A. W. (2) (Oxford University), 1876 v S; 1877 v S

Evans, W. G. (3) (Bootle), 1890 v E; 1891 v E (Aston Villa), 1892 v E

Evelyn, E. C. (1) (Crusaders), 1887 v E

Eyton-Jones, J. A. (4) (Wrexham), 1883 v Ire; 1884 v Ire, E, S

Farmer, G. (2) (Oswestry), 1885 v E, S

Felgate, D. (1) (Lincoln C), 1984 v R

Finnigan, R. J. (1) (Wrexham), 1930 v NI

Flynn, B. (66) (Burnley), 1975 v Lux, Lux, H, S, E, NI; 1976 v A, E, Y, Y, E, NI; 1977 v FRG, S, S, Cz, E, NI; 1978 v K, K, S; (Leeds U), Cz, FRG, Ir, E, S, NI; 1979 v Ma, T, S, E, NI, Ma; 1980 v RI, FRG, E, S, NI, Ic; 1981 v T, Cz, RI, T, S, E, USSR; 1982 v Cz, USSR, E, S, NI, F; 1983 v Nor, (Burnley), Y, E, Bul, S, NI, Bra; 1984 v Nor, Rum, Bul, Y, S, Nor, Is

Ford, T. (38) (Swansea T), 1947 v S; (Aston Villa), 1947 v NI; 1948 v S, NI; 1949 v E, S, NI, P, Bel, Swz; 1950 v E, S, NI, Bel; 1951 v S; (Sunderland), 1951 v E, NI, P, Swz; 1952 v E, S, NI, UK; 1953 v S, E, NI, F, Y; (Cardiff C), 1954 v A; 1955 v S, E, NI, Y; 1956 v S, NI, E, A; 1957 v S

Foulkes, H. E. (1) (WBA), 1932 v NI

Foulkes, W. I. (11) (Newcastle U), 1952 v E, S, NI, UK; 1953 v S, E, S, F, Y; 1954 v E, S, NI

Foulkes, W. T. (2) (Oswestry), 1884 v Ire; 1885 v S

Fowler, J. (6) (Swansea T), 1925 v E; 1926 v E, NI; 1927 v S; 1928 v S; 1929 v E

Garner, J. (1) (Aberystwyth), 1896 v S

Giles, D. (12) (Swansea C), 1980 v E, S, NI, Ic; 1981 v T, Cz, T, E, USSR; (C Palace), 1982 v Sp; 1983 v NI, Bra

Gillam, S. G. (5) (Wrexham), 1889 v S, Ire; (Shrewsbury), 1890 v E, Ire; (Clapton), 1894 v S

Glascodine, G. (1) (Wrexham), 1879 v E

Glover, E. M. (7) (Grimsby T), 1932 v S; 1934 v NI; 1936 v S; 1937 v E, S, NI; 1939 v NI

Godding, G. (2) (Wrexham), 1923 v S, NI

Godfrey, B. C. (3) (Preston NE), 1964 v NI; 1965 v Den, I

Goodwin, U. (1) (Ruthin), 1881 v E

Gough, R. T. (1) (Oswestry White Star), 1883 v S

Gray, A. (24) (Oldham Ath), 1924 v E, S, NI; 1925 v E, S, NI; 1926 v E, S; 1927 v S; (Manchester C), 1928 v E, S; 1929 v E, S, NI; (Manchester Central), 1930 v S; (Tranmere R), 1932 v E, S, NI; (Chester), 1937 v E, S, NI; 1938 v E, S, NI

Green, A. W. (8) (Aston Villa), 1901 v Ire; (Notts Co), 1903 v E; 1904 v S, Ire; 1906 v Ire, E; (Nottingham F), 1907 v E; 1908 v S

Green, C. R. (15) (Birmingham C), 1965 v USSR, I; 1966 v E, S, USSR, Bra, Bra; 1967 v E; 1968 v E, S, NI, FRG; 1969 v S, I, NI

Green, G. H. (4) (Charlton Ath), 1938 v NI; 1939 v E, NI, F

Grey, Dr W. (2) (Druids), 1876 v S, 1878 v S

Griffiths, A. T. (17) (Wrexham), 1971 v Cz; 1975 v A, H, H, Lux, Lux, E, NI; 1976 v A, E, S, E, NI, Y, Y; 1977 v FRG, S

Griffiths, F. J. (2) (Blackpool), 1900 v E, S

Griffiths, G. (1) (Chirk), 1887 v Ire

Griffiths, J. H. (1) (Swansea T), 1953 v NI

Griffiths, M. W. (11), (Leicester C), 1947 v NI; 1949 v P, Bel; 1950 v E, S, Bel; 1951 v E, NI, P, Swz, 1954 v A

Griffiths, P. (6) (Chirk), 1884 v E, Ire; 1888 v E; 1890 v S, Ire; 1891 v Ire

Griffiths, S. (1) (Wrexham), 1902 v S

Griffiths, T. P. (21) (Everton), 1927 v E, NI; 1929 v E; 1930 v E; 1931 v NI; 1932 v NI, S, E; (Bolton W), 1933 v F, E, S, NI; (Middlesbrough), 1934 v E, S; 1935 v E, NI, 1936 v S; (Aston Villa), NI; 1937 v E, S, NI

Hall, G. D. (3) (Chelsea), 1988 v Y, Ma, I

Hallam, J. (1) (Oswestry), 1889 v E

Hanford, H. (7) (Swansea T), 1934 v NI; 1935 v S; 1936 v E; (Sheffield W), 1936 v NI; 1938 v E, S; 1939 v F

Harrington, A. C. (11) (Cardiff C), 1956 v NI, 1957 v E, S, 1958 v S, NI, Is, Is; 1961 v S, E; 1962 v E, S

Harris, C. S. (24) (Leeds U), 1976 v E, S; 1978 v WG, Ir, E, S, NI; 1979 v Ma, T, FRG, E, Ma; 1980 v NI, Ic; 1981 v T, Cz, RI, T, S, E, USSR; 1982 v Cz, Ic, E

Harris, W. C. (6) (Middlesbrough), 1954 v A; 1957 v GDR, Cz; 1958 v E, S, GDR

Harrison, W. C. (5) (Wrexham), 1899 v E, 1900 v E, S, Ire; 1901 v Ire

Hayes, A. (2) (Wrexham), 1890 v Ire, 1894 v Ire

Hennessey, W. T. (39) (Birmingham C), 1962 v NI, Bra, Bra; 1963 v S, E, H, H; 1964 v E, S; 1965 v S, E, Den, Gr, USSR; 1966 v E, USSR; (Nottingham F), 1966 v S, NI, Den, Bra, Bra, Ch; 1967 v S, E; 1968 v E, S, NI; 1969 v FRG, GDR, UK, GDR (Derby Co), 1970 v E, S, NI; 1972 v Fin, Cz, E, S; 1973 v E

Hersee, A. M (2) (Bangor), 1886 v S, Ire

Hersee, R. (1) (Llandudno), 1886 v Ire

Hewitt, R. (5) (Cardiff C), 1958 v NI, Is, Swe, H. Bra

Hewitt, T. J. (8) (Wrexham), 1911 v E, S, Ire; (Chelsea), 1913 v E, S, Ire; (South Liverpool), 1914 v E, S

Heywood, D. (1) (Druids), 1879 v E

Hibbott, H. (2) (Newtown Excelsior), 1880 v E, S

Hibbott, R. (1) (Newtown), 1885 v S

Higham, G. G. (2) (Oswestry), 1878 v S; 1879 v E

Hill, M. R. (2) (Ipswich T), 1972 v Cz, Rum

Hockey, T. (9) (Sheffield U), 1972 v Fin, Rum; 1973 v E (2); (Norwich C), Pol, S, E, NI; (Aston Villa), 1974 v Pol

Hoddinott, T. F. (2) (Watford), 1921 v E, S

Hodges, G. (11) (Wimbledon), 1984 v Nor, Is; 1987 v USSR, Fin, Cz, (Newcastle U), Den, (Watford), Den, Cz; 1988 v Swe, Ma, I

Hodgkinson, A. V. (1) (Southampton), 1908 v Ire

Holden, A. (1) (Chester C), 1984 v Is

Hole, B. G. (30) (Cardiff C), 1963 v NI; 1964 v NI, 1965 v S, E, NI, Den, Gr (2), USSR, I; 1966 v E, S, NI, USSR, Den, Bra, Bra, Ch; (Blackburn R), 1967 v S, E, NI; 1968 v E, S, NI, FRG; (Aston Villa), 1969 v I, FRG, GDR; 1970 v I; (Swansea C), 1971 v Rum

Hole, W. J. (9) (Swansea T), 1921 v Ire, 1922 v E; 1923 v E, NI; 1928 v E, S, NI; 1929 v E, S

Hollins, D. M. (11) (Newcastle U), 1962 v Bra, Mex; 1963 v NI, H; 1964 v E; 1965 v NI, Gr, I; 1966 v S, Den, Bra

Hopkins, I. J. (12) (Brentford), 1935 v S, NI; 1936 v E, NI, 1937 v E, S, NI; 1938 v E, NI, 1939 v E, S, NI

Hopkins, J. (14) (Fulham), 1983 v NI, Bra; 1984 v Nor, Rum, Bul, Y, S, E, NI, Nor, Is; 1985 v Ic, Ic, N

Hopkins, M. (34) (Tottenham H), 1956 v NI, 1957 v NI, S, E, Cz, Cz, GDR; 1958 v S, NI, GDR, Is, Is, H, H, Mex, Swe, Bra; 1959 v E, S, NI, 1960 v E, S; 1961 v NI, H, Sp, Sp; 1962 v NI, Bra, Bra, Mex; 1963 v S, NI, H

Horne, B. (5) (Portsmouth), 1987 v Den; 1988 v Y, Swe, Ma, I

Howell, E. G. (3) (Builth), 1888 v Ire; 1890 v E; 1891 v E

Howells, R. G. (2) (Cardiff C), 1954 v E, S

Hugh, A. R. (1) (Newport Co), 1930 v NI

Hughes, A. (2) (Rhos), 1894 v E, S

Hughes, A. (1) (Chirk), 1907 v Ire

Hughes, A. J. (1) (Aberystwyth), 1879 v S

Hughes, E. (14) (Everton), 1899 v S, Ire; (Tottenham H), 1901 v E, S, 1902 v Ire; 1904 v E, Ire, S; 1905 v E, Ire, S; 1906 v E, Ire; 1907 v E

Hughes, E. (16) (Wrexham), 1906 v S; (Nottingham F), 1906 v Ire, 1908 v S, E; 1910 v Ire, E, S; 1911 v Ire, E, S; (Wrexham), 1912 v Ire, E, S; (Manchester C), 1913 v E, S; 1914 v N

Hughes, F. W. (6) (Northwich Victoria), 1882 v E, Ire; 1883 v E, Ire, S; 1884 v S

Hughes, I. (4) (Luton T), 1951 v E, NI, P, Sw

Hughes, J. (1) (Cambridge University), 1877 v S

Hughes, J. (3) (Liverpool), 1905 v E, S, Ire

Hughes, J. I. (1) (Blackburn R), 1935 v NI

Hughes, L. M. (20) (Manchester U), 1984 v E, NI; 1985 v Ic, Sp, Ic, Nor, S, Sp, Nor; 1986 v S, H, U; (Barcelona), 1987 v USSR, Cz, (Bayern Munich on loan), Den, Den, Cz; 1988 v Swe, Ma, I

Hughes, P. W. (3) (Bangor), 1887 v Ire, 1889 v Ire, E

Hughes, W. (3) (Bottle), 1891 v E; 1892 v S, Ire

Hughes, W. A. (5) (Blackburn R), 1949 v E, NI, P. Bel, Sw

Hughes, W. M. (10) (Birmingham), 1938 v E, NI, S; 1939 v E, NI, S, F; 1947 v E, S, NI

Humphreys, J. V. (1) (Everton), 1947 v NI

Humphreys, R. (1) (Druids), 1888 v Ire

Hunter, W. H. (1) (North End, Belfast), 1887 v Ire

Jones, T. (4) (Manchester U), 1926 v NI, 1927 v E, NI; 1930 v NI

Jones, T. D. (1) (Aberdare), 1908 v Ire

Jones, T. G. (17) (Everton), 1938 v NI; 1939 v E, S, NI; 1947 v E, S; 1948 v E, S, NI; 1949 v E, NI, P, Bel, Swz; 1950 v E, S, Bel

Jones, T. J. (2) (Sheffield W), 1932 v NI; 1933 v F

Jones, W. (1) (Druids), 1899 v E

Jones, W. E. A. (4) (Swansea T), 1947 v E, S; (Tottenham H), 1949 v E, S

Jones, W. J. (4) (Aberdare), 1901 v E, S; (West Ham U), 1902 v E, S

Jones, W. Lot (20) (Manchester C), 1905 v E, Ire; 1906 v E, S, Ire; 1907 v E, S, Ire; 1908 v S; 1909 v E, S, Ire; 1910 v E; 1911 v E; 1913 v E, S; 1914 v S, Ire; (Southend U), 1920 v E, Ire

Jones, W. P. (4) (Druids), 1889 v E, Ire; (Wynstay), 1890 v S, Ire

Jones, W. R. (1) (Aberystwyth), 1897 v S

Keenor, F. C. (32) (Cardiff C), 1920 v E, Ire; 1921 v E, Ire, S; 1922 v NI; 1923 v E, NI, S; 1924 v E, NI, S; 1925 v E, NI, S; 1926 v S; 1927 v E, NI, S; 1928 v E, NI, S; 1929 v E, NI, S; 1930 v E, NI, S; 1931 v E, NI, S; (Crewe Alex), 1933 v S

Kelly, F. C. (3) (Wrexham), 1899 v S, Ire; (Druids), 1902 v Ire

Kelsey, A. J. (41) (Arsenal), 1954 v NI, A; 1955 v S, NI, Y; 1956 v E, NI, S, A; 1957 v E, NI, S, Cz, Cz, GDR; 1958 v E, S, NI, Is, Is, H, H, Mex, Swe, Bra; 1959 v E, S; 1960 v E, NI, S; 1961 v E, NI, S, H, Sp, Sp; 1962 v E, S, NI, Bra, Bra

Kenrick, S. L. (5) (Druids), 1876 v S, 1877 v S; (Oswestry), 1879 v E, S; (Shropshire Wanderers), 1881 v E

Ketley, C. F. (1) (Druids), 1882 v Ire

King, J. (1) (Swansea T), 1955 v E

Kinsey, N. (7) (Norwich C), 1951 v NI, P, Swz; 1952 v E; (Birmingham C), 1954 v NI, 1956 v E, S

Krzywicki, R. L. (8) (Huddersfield T), 1970 v E, S; (WBA), NI, GDR, I; 1971 v Rum, Fin; 1972 v Cz

Lambert, R. (5) (Liverpool), 1947 v S; 1948 v E; 1949 v P, Bel, Swz

Lathom, G. (10) (Liverpool), 1905 v E, S; 1906 v S; 1907 v E, S, Ire, 1908 v E, 1909 v Ire; (Southport Central), 1910 v E; (Cardiff C), 1913 v Ire

Lawrence. E. (2) (Clapton Orient), 1930 v NI; (Notts Co), 1932 v S

Lawrence, S. (8) (Swansea T), 1932 v NI; 1933 v F; 1934 v S, E, NI; 1935 v E, S; 1936 v S

Lea, A. (4) (Wrexham), 1889 v E; 1891 v S, Ire; 1893 v Ire

Lea, C. (2) (Ipswich T), 1965 v NI, I

Leary, P. (1) (Bangor), 1889 v Ire

Leek, K. (13) (Leicester C), 1961 v S, E, NI, H, Sp, Sp; (Newcastle U), 1962 v S; (Birmingham C), v Bra, Mex; 1963 v E; 1965 v S, Gr; (Northampton T), 1965 v Gr

Lever, A. R. (1) (Leicester C), 1953 v S

Lewis, B. (10) (Wrexham), 1891 v Ire; 1892 v S, E, Ire; (Middlesbrough), 1893 v S, E; (Wrexham), 1894 v S, E, Ire; 1895 v S

Lewis, D. (3) (Arsenal), 1927 v E; 1928 v NI; 1930 v E

Lewis, D. J. (2) (Swansea T), 1933 v E, S

Lewis, D. (1) (Swansea C), 1983 v Bra

Lewis, J. (1) (Bristol R), 1906 v E

Lewis, J. (1) (Cardiff C), 1926 v S

Lewis, T. (2) (Wrexham), 1881 v E, S

Lewis, W. L. (6) (Swansea T), 1927 v E, NI; 1928 v E, NI; 1929 v S; (Huddersfield T), 1930 v E

Lewis, W. (30) (Bangor), 1885 v E; 1886 v E, S; 1887 v E, S; 1888 v E; 1889 v E, Ire, S; (Crewe Alex), 1890 v E, Ire, S; 1891 v E, Ire; S; 1892 v E, S, Ire; 1894 v E, S, Ire; (Chester), 1895 v S, Ire, E; 1896 v E, S, Ire; (Manchester C), 1897 v E, S; (Chester), 1898 v Ire

Lloyd, B. W. (3) (Wrexham), 1976 v A, E, S

Lloyds, J. W. (2) (Wrexham), 1879 v S, (Newtown), 1885 v S

Lloyds, R. A. (2) (Ruthin), 1891 v Ire; 1895 v S

Lockley, A. (1) (Chirk), 1898 v Ire

Lovell, S. (6) (C Palace), 1982 v USSR; (Millwall), 1985 v Nor; 1986 v S, H, Can, Can

Lowrie, G. (4) (Coventry C), 1948 v E, S, NI; (Newcastle U), 1949 v P

Lowndes, S. (10) (Newport Co), 1983 v S, Bra; (Millwall), 1985 v Nor; 1986 v S.Ar, RI, U, Can, Can; (Barnsley), 1987 v Fin; 1988 v Swe

Lucas, P. M. (4) (Leyton Orient), 1962 v NI, Mex; 1963 v S, E

Lucas, W. H. (7) (Swansea T), 1949 to S, NI; P, Bel, Swz; 1950 v E; 1951 v E

Lumberg, A. (4) (Wrexham), 1929 v NI; 1930 v E, S; (Wolverhampton W), 1932 v S

McMillan, R. (2) (Shrewbury Engineers), 1881 v E, S

Mahoney, J. F. (51) (Stoke C), 1968 v E; 1969 v GDR; 1971 v Cz; 1973 v E, E, Pol, S, NI; 1974 v Pol, E, S, NI; 1975 v A, H, H, Lux, Lux, S, E, NI; 1976 v A, Y, Y, E, NI; 1977 v FRG, Cz, S, E, NI; (Middlesbrough), 1978 v K, K, S, Cz, Ir, E, S, NI; 1979 v FRG, S, E, NI, Ma; (Swansea C), 1980 v RI, FRG, T; 1982 v Ic, USSR; 1983 v Y, E

Martin, T. J. (1) (Newport Co), 1930 v NI

Marustik, C. (6) (Swansea C), 1982 v Sp, E, S, NI, F; 1983 v N

Mates, J. (3) (Chirk), 1891 v Ire; 1897 v E, S

Mathews, R. W. (3) (Liverpool), 1921 v Ire, (Bristol C), 1923 v E; (Bradford), 1926 v NI

Matthews W. (2) (Chester), 1905 v Ire, 1908 v E

Matthias, J. S. (5) (Brymbo), 1896 v S, Ire; (Shrewsbury), 1897 v E, S; (Wolverhampton W), 1899 v S

Matthias, T. J. (12) (Wrexham), 1914 v S, E, 1920 v Ire, S, E; 1921 v S, E, Ire; 1922 v S, E, NI; 1923 v S

Mays, A. W. (1) (Wrexham), 1929 v NI

Medwin, T. C. (29) (Swansea T), 1953 v NI, F, Y; (Tottenham H), 1957 v E, S, NI, Cz, Cz, GDR; 1958 v E, S, NI, Is, Is, H, H, Mex. Bra; 1959 v E, S, NI; 1960 v E, S, NI; 1961 v S, RI, Sp; 1963 v E, H

Meredith, S. (8) (Chirk), 1900 v S; 1901 v S, Ire; (Stoke C), 1902 v E; 1903 v Ire; 1904 v E; (Leyton), 1907 v E

Meredith, W. H. (48) (Manchester C), 1895 v E, Ire; 1896 v E, Ire; 1897 v E, Ire, S; 1898 v E, Ire; 1899 v E; 1900 v E, Ire; 1901 v E, Ire; 1902 v E, S; 1903 v E, S, Ire; 1904 v E, 1905 v E, S; (Manchester U), 1907 v E, S, Ire; 1908 v E, Ire; 1909 v E, S, Ire; 1910 v E, S,

Ire; 1911 v E, S, Ire; 1912 v E, S, Ire; 1913 v E, S, Ire; 1914 v E, S, Ire; 1920 v E, S, Ire
Mielczarek, R. (1) (Rotherham U), 1971 v Fin
Millership, H. (6) (Rotherham Co), 1920 v E, S, Ire; 1921 v E, S, Ire
Millington, A. H. (21) (WBA), 1963 v S, E, H; (C Palace), 1965 v E, USSR; (Peterborough U), 1966 v Ch, Bra; 1967 v E, NI, 1968 v NI, FRG; 1969 v I, GDR; (Swansea) 1970 v E, S, NI; 1971 v Cz, Fin; 1972 v Fin, Cz, R
Mills, T. J. (4) (Clapton Orient), 1934 v E, NI; (Leicester C), 1935 v E, S
Mills-Roberts, R. H. (8) (St Thomas' Hospital), 1885 v E, S, Ire; 1886 v E, 1887 v E; (Preston NE), 1888 v E, Ire; (Llanberis), 1892 v E
Moore, G. (21) (Cardiff C), 1960 v E, S, NI; 1961 v RI, Sp; (Chelsea), 1962 v Bra; 1963 v NI, H; (Manchester U), 1964 v S, NI; (Northampton T), 1966 v NI, Ch; (Charlton Ath), 1969 v S, E, NI, UK; 1970 v E, S, NI, I; 1961 v Rum
Morgan, J. R. (10) (Cambridge University), 1877 v S; (Swansea), 1879 v S; (Derby School Staff), 1880 v E, S; 1881 v E, S; 1882 v E, S, Ire; (Swansea), 1883 v E
Morgan, J. T. (1) (Wrexham), 1905 v Ire
Morgan-Owen, H. (6) (Oxford University), 1901 v E, S; 1902 v S; 1906 v E, Ire; (Welshpool), 1907 v S
Morgan-Owen, M. M. (11) (Oxford University), 1897 v S, Ire; 1989 v E, S, 1899 v S; 1900 v E; (Corinthians), 1903 v S; 1906 v S, E, Ire; 1907 v E
Morley, E. J. (4) (Swansea T), 1925 v E; (Clapton Orient), 1929 v E, S, NI
Morris, A. G. (21) (Aberystwyth), 1896 v E, Ire; S; (SwindonT), 1897 v E; 1898 v S; (Nottingham F), 1899 v E, S; 1903 v E, S; 1905 v E, S; 1907 v E, S; 1908 v E; 1910 v E, S, Ire; 1911 v E, S; Ire; 1912 v E
Morris, C. (28) (Chirk), 1900 v E, S, Ire; (Derby Co), 1901 v E, S, Ire; 1902 v E, S; 1903 v E, S, Ire; 1904 v Ire; 1905 v E, S, Ire; 1906 v S; 1907 v S, 1908 v E, S; 1909 v E, S, Ire; 1910 v E, S, Ire; (Huddersfield T); 1911 v E, S, Ire
Morris, E. (3) (Chirk), 1893 v E, S, Ire
Morris, H. (3) (Sheffield U), 1894 v S; (Manchester C), 1896 v E, (Grimsby T), 1897 v E
Morris, J. (1) (Oswestry), 1887 v S
Morris, J. (1) (Chirk), 1898 v Ire
Morris, R. (6) (Chirk), 1900 v E, Ire; 1901 v Ire; 1902 v S, (Shrewsbury T), 1903 v E, Ire
Morris, R. (11) (Druids), 1902 v E, S; (Newtown), 1902 v Ire; (Liverpool), 1903 v S, Ire; 1904 v E, S, Ire; (Leeds C), 1906 v S, (Grimsby T), 1907 v Ire, (Plymouth Arg), 1908 v Ire
Morris, S. (5) (Birmingham), 1937 v E, S; 1938 v E, S; 1939 v F
Morris, W. (5) (Burnley), 1947 v NI; 1949 v E; 1952 v S, NI, UK
Moulsdale, J. R. B. (1) (Corinthians), 1925 v NI
Murphy, J. P. (15) (WBA), 1933 v F, E, NI; 1934 v E, S; 1935 v E, S, NI; 1936 v E, S, NI; 1937 v S, NI; 1938 v E, S

Nardiello, D. (2) (Coventry C), 1978 v Cz, FRG
Neal, J. E. (2) (Colwyn Bay), 1931 v E, S
Newnes, J. (1) (Nelson), 1926 v NI

Newton, L. F. (1) (Cardiff Corinthians), 1912 v Ire
Nicholas, D. S. (3) (Stoke C), 1923 v S; (Swansea T), 1927 v E, NI
Nicholas, P. (54) (C Palace), 1979 v S, NI, Ma; 1980 v RI, FRG, T, E, S, NI, Ic; 1981 v T, Cz, E; (Arsenal), T, S, E, USSR; 1982 v Cz, Ic, USSR, Sp, E, S, NI, F, 1983 v Y, Bul, S, NI; 1984 v Nor, Bul, Nor, Is; (C Palace); 1985 v Sp; (Luton T), Nor, S, Sp, Nor; 1986 v S, H, S.Ar, RI; U, Can, Can; 1987 v Fin, Fin, USSR, Cz, (Aberdeen), Den, Den, Cz; 1988 v Y, Swe
Nicholls, J. (4) (Newport Co), 1924 v E, NI; (Cardiff C), 1925 v E, S
Niedzwiecki, E. A. (2) (Chelsea), 1985 v Nor; 1987 v Den
Nock, W. (1) (Newtown), 1897 v Ire
Norman, A. J. (5) (Hull C), 1986 v RI, U, Can; 1988 v Ma, I
Nurse, M. T. G. (12) (Swansea T), 1960 v E, NI; 1961 v S, E, H, NI, RI, Sp, Sp; (Middlesbrough), 1963 v E. H; 1964 v S

O'Callaghan, E. (11) (Tottenham H), 1929 v NI; 1930 v S; 1932 v S, E; 1933 v NI, S, E; 1934 v NI, S, E; 1935 v E
Oliver, A. (2) (Blackburn R), 1905 v E; (Bangor), S
O'Sullivan, P. A. (3) (Brighton & HA), 1973 v S; 1976 v S; 1979 v Ma
Owen, D. (1) (Oswestry), 1879 v E
Owen, E. (3) (Ruthin Grammar School), 1884 v E, Ire, S
Owen, G. (5) (Chirk), 1888 v S; (Newton Heath), 1889 v S, Ire; 1892 v E; 1893 v Ire
Owen, T. (1) (Oswestry), 1879 v E
Owen, Trevor (2) (Crewe Alex), 1899 v E, S
Owen, W. (16) (Chirk), 1884 v E; 1885 v Ire; 1887 v E; 1888 v E; 1889 v E, Ire, S; 1890 v S, Ire; 1891 v E, S, Ire; 1892 v E, S; 1893 v S, Ire
Owen, W. P. (12) (Ruthin), 1880 v E, S; 1881 v E, S; 1882 v E, S, Ire; 1883 v E, S; 1884 v E, S, Ire
Owens, J. (1) (Wrexham), 1902 v S

Page, M. E. (28) (Birmingham C), 1971 v Fin; 1972 v S, NI; 1973 v E, S, NI; 1974 v S, NI; 1975 v H, Lux, S, E, NI; 1976 v E, Y, Y, E, NI, 1977 v FRG, S, 1978 v K, K, FRG, Ir, E, S; 1979 v Ma, FRG
Palmer, D. (3) (Swansea T), 1957 v Cz; 1958 v E, GDR
Parris, J. E. (1) (Bradford), 1932 v NI
Parry, B. J. (1) (Swansea T), 1951 v S
Parry, C. (13) (Everton), 1891 v E, S; 1893 v E; 1894 v E; 1895 v E, S; (Newtown), 1896 v E, S, Ire, 1897 v Ire; 1898 v E, S, Ire
Parry, E. (5) (Liverpool), 1922 v S, 1923 v E, NI; 1925 v NI; 1926 v NI
Parry, H. (1) (Newtown), 1895 v Ire
Parry, M. (16) (Liverpool), 1901 v E, S, Ire; 1902 v E, S, Ire; 1903 v E, S; 1904 v E, Ire; 1906 v E, 1908 v E, S, Ire; 1909 v E, S
Parry, T. D. (7) (Oswestry), 1900 v E, S, Ire; 1901 v E, S, Ire; 1902 v E
Pascoe, C. (2) (Swansea C), 1984 v Nor, Is
Paul, R. (33) (Swansea T), 1949 v E, S, NI, P, Swz;

1950 v E, S, NI, Bel; (Manchester C), 1951 v S, E, NI, P, Swz; 1952 v E, S, NI, UK; 1953 v S, E, NI, F, Y; 1954 v E, S, NI; 1955 v S, E, Y; 1956 v E, NI, S, A

Peake, E. (11) (Aberystwyth), 1908 v Ire; (Liverpool), 1909 v Ire, S, E; 1910 v S, Ire; 1911 v Ire; 1912 v E; 1913 v E, Ire; 1914 v Ire

Peers, E. J. (12) (Wolverhampton W), 1914 v Ire, S, E; 1920 v E, S; 1921 v S, Ire, E; (Port Vale), 1922 v E, S, NI; 1923 v E

Perry, E. (3) (Doncaster R), 1938 v E, S, NI

Phennah, E. (1) (Civil Service), 1878 v S

Phillips, C. (13) (Wolverhampton W), 1931 v NI; 1932 v E; 1933 v S; 1934 v E, S, NI; 1935 v E, S, NI; 1936 v S; (Aston Villa), 1936 v E, NI; 1938 v S

Phillips, D. (20) (Plymouth Arg), 1984 v E, NI, Nor; (Manchester C), 1985 v Sp, Ic, S, Sp, Nor; 1986 v S, H, S.Ar, RI, U; (Coventry C) 1987 v Fin, Cz, Den, Den, Cz; 1988 v Y, Swe

Phillips, L. (58) (Cardiff C), 1971 v Cz, S, E, NI; 1972 v Cz, Rum, S, NI; 1973 v E; 1974 v Pol, NI; 1975 v A; (Aston Villa), H, H, Lux, Lux, S, E, NI; 1976 v A, E, Y, Y, E, NI; 1977 v FRG, S, S, Cz, E; 1978 v K, K, S, Cz, FRG, E, S; 1979 v Ma; (Swansea C), T, FRG, S, E, NI, Ma; 1980 v RI, FRG, T, S, NI, Ic; 1981 v T, Cz, T, S, E, USSR; (Charlton Ath), 1982 v Cz, USSR

Phillips, T. J. S. (4) (Chelsea), 1973 v E; 1974 v E; 1975 v H; 1978 v K

Phoenix, H. (1) (Wrexham), 1882 v S

Poland, G. (2) (Wrexham), 1939 v NI, F

Pontin, K. (2) (Cardiff C), 1980 v E, S

Powell, A. (8) (Leeds U), 1947 v E, S; 1948 v E, S, NI; (Everton), 1949 v E; 1950 v Bel; (Birmingham C), 1951 v S

Powell, D. (11) (Wrexham), 1968 v FRG; (Sheffield U), 1969 v S, E, NI, I, FRG; 1970 v E, S, NI, GDR; 1971 v Rum

Powell, I. V. (8) (QPR), 1947 v E; 1948 v E, S, NI; (Aston Villa), 1949 v Bel; 1950 v S, Bel; 1951 v S

Powell, J. (15) (Druids), 1878 v S; 1880 v E, S; 1882 v E, S, Ire; 1883 v E, S, Ire; (Bolton W), 1884 v E; (Newton Heath), 1887 v E, S; 1888 v E, S, Ire

Powell, Seth (7) (WBA), 1885 v S; 1886 v E, Ire; 1891 v E, S; 1892 v E, S

Price, H. (5) (Aston Villa), 1907 v S; (Burton U), 1908 v Ire; (Wrexham), 1909 v S, E, Ire

Price, J. (12) (Wrexham), 1877 v S; 1878 v S; 1879 v E; 1880 v E, S; 1881 v E, S; (Druids), 1882 v S, E, Ire; 1883 v S, Ire

Price, P. (25) (Luton T), 1980 v E, S, NI, Ic; 1981 v T, Cz, RI, T, S, E, USSR; (Tottenahm H), 1982 v USSR, Sp, F; 1983 v Nor, Y, E, Bul, S, NI; 1984 v Nor, Rum, Bul, Y, S

Pring, K. D. (3) (Rotherham U), 1966 v Ch, Den; 1967 v NI

Pritchard, H. K. (1) (Bristol C), 1985 v Nor

Pryce-Jones, A. W. (1) (Newtown), 1895 v E

Pryce-Jones, W. E. (5) (Cambridge University), 1887 v S; 1888 v S, E, Ire; 1890 v Ire

Pugh, A. (1) (Rhostyllen), 1889 v S

Pugh, D. H. (7) (Wrexham), 1896 v S, Ire; 1897 v S, Ire; (Lincoln C), 1900 v S; 1901 v S, E

Pugsley, J. (1) (Charlton Ath), 1930 v NI

Pullen, W. . (1) (Plymouth Arg), 1926 v E

Rankmore, F. E. J. (1) (Peterborough), 1966 v Ch

Ratcliffe, K. (43) (Everton), 1981 v Cz, RI, T, S, E, USSR; 1982 v Cz, Ic, USSR, Sp, E; 1983 v Y, E, Bul, S, NI, Bra; 1984 v Nor, Rum, Bul, Y, S, E, NI, Nor, Is; 1985 v Ic, Sp, Ic, Nor, S, Sp; 1986 v S, H, S.Ar, U; 1987 v Fin, Fin, USSR, Cz, Den, Den, Cz

Rea, J. C. (9) (Aberystwyth), 1894 v Ire, S, E; 1895 v S; 1896 v S, Ire; 1897 v S, Ire; 1898 v Ire

Reece, G. I. (29) (Sheffield U), 1966 v E, S, NI, USSR; 1967 v S; 1969 v UK; 1970 v I; 1971 v S, E, NI, Fin; 1972 v Fin, Rum, E, S, NI; (Cardiff C), 1973 v E, NI; 1974 v Pol, E, S, NI; 1975 v A, H, H, Lux, Lux, S, NI

Reed, W. G. (2) (Ipswich T), 1955 v S, Y

Rees, A. (1) (Birmingham C), 1984 v Nor

Rees, R. R. (39) (Coventry C), 1965 v S, E, NI, Den, Gr, Gr, I, R; 1966 v E, S, NI, Rum, Den, Bra, Bra, Ch; 1967 v E, NI; 1968 v E, S, NI; (WBA), FRG; 1969 v I; (Nottingham F), 1969 v FRG, GDR, S, UK; 1970 v E, S, NI, GDR, I; 1971 v Cz, Rum, E, NI, Fin; 1972 v Cz, R

Rees, W. (4) (Cardiff C), 1949 v NI, Bel, Swz; (Tottenham H), 1950 v NI

Richards, A. (1) (Barnsley), 1932 v S

Richard, D. (21) (Wolverhampton W), 1931 v NI; 1933 v E, S, NI; 1934 v E, S, NI; 1935 v E, S, NI; 1936 v S; (Brentford), 1936 v E, NI; 1937 v S, E; (Birmingham), 1937 v NI; 1938 v E, S, NI; 1939 v E, S

Richards, G. (6) (Druids), 1899 v E, S, Ire; (Oswestry), 1903 v Ire; (Shrewsbury), 1904 v S, 1905 v Ire

Richards, R. W. (9) (Wolverhampton W), 1920 v E, S; 1921 v Ire; 1922 v E, S; (West Ham U), 1924 v E, S, NI; (Mold), 1926 v S

Richards, S. V. (1) (Cardiff C), 1947 v E

Richards, W. E. (1) (Fulham), 1933 v NI

Roach, J. (1) (Oswestry), 1885 v Ire

Robbins, W. W. (11) (Cardiff C), 1931 v E, S; 1932 v NI, E, S; (WBA), 1933 v F, E, S, NI; 1934 v S; 1936 v S

Roberts, D. F. (17) (Oxford U), 1973 v Pol, E, NI; 1974 v E, S; 1975 v A; (Hull C), Lux, NI; 1976 v S, NI, Y; 1977 v E, NI, 1978 v K, K, S, NI

Roberts, J. G. (22) (Arsenal), 1971 v S, E, NI; Fin; 1972 v Fin, E, NI; (Birmingham C), 1973 v E, E, Pol, S, NI; 1974 v Pol, E, S, NI; 1976 v A, H, S, E; 1976 v E, S

Roberts, J. H. (1) (Bolton), 1949 v Bel

Roberts, J. (7) (Corwen), 1879 v S; 1880 v E, S; 1882 v E, S, Ire; (Berwyn R); 1883 v E

Roberts, J. (2) (Ruthin), 1881 v S; 1882 v S

Roberts, J. (2) (Bradford C), 1906 v Ire; 1907 v Ire

Roberts, Jas. (1) (Chirk), 1898 v S

Roberts, Jas (2) (Wrexham), 1913 v S, Ire

Roberts, P. S. (4) (Portsmouth), 1974 v E; 1975 v A, H, Lux

Roberts, R. (2) (Rhos), 1891 v Ire; (Crewe Alex), 1893 v E

Roberts, R. (9) (Druids), 1884 v S; (Bolton W), 1887 v S; 1888 v S, E; 1889 v S, E; 1890 v S; 1892 v Ire; (Preston NE), S

Roberts, R. (3) (Wrexham), 1886 v Ire; 1887 v Ire; 1891 v Ire

Roberts, W. (7) (Llangollen), 1879 v E, S; 1880 v E, S; (Berwyn R), 1881 v S; 1883 v E, S
Roberts W. (4) (Wrexham), 1886 v E, S, Ire; 1887 v Ire
Roberts, W. H. (6) (Ruthin), 1882 v E, S; 1883 v E, S, Ire; (Rhyl), 1884 v S
Rodrigues, P. J. (40) (Cardiff C), 1965 v NI, Gr, Gr; 1966 v USSR, E, S, Den; (Leicester C), v NI, Bra, Bra, Ch; 1967 v S; 1968 v E, S, NI; 1969 v E, NI, GDR, UK; 1970 v E, S, NI, GDR; (Sheffield W), 1971 v Rum, E, S, Cz, NI; 1972 v Fin, Cz, Rum, E, NI; 1973 v E, E, E, Pol, S, NI; 1974 v Pol
Rogers, J. P. (3) (Wrexham), 1896 v E, S, Ire
Rogers, W. (2) (Wrexham), 1931 v E, S
Roose, L. R. (24) (Aberystwyth), 1900 v Ire; (London Welsh), 1901 v E, S, Ire; (Stoke C), 1902 v E, S; 1904 v E, (Everton), 1905 v S, E; (Stoke C), 1906 v E, S, Ire; 1907 v E, S, Ire; (Sunderland), 1908 v E, S; 1909 v E, S, Ire; 1910 v E, S, Ire; 1911 v S
Rouse, R. V. (1) (C Palace), 1959 v NI
Rowlands, A. C. (1) (Tranmere R), 1959 v NI
Rush, I. (38) (Liverpool), 1980 v S, NI; 1981 v E; 1982 v Ic, USSR, E, S, NI, F; 1983 v Nor, Y, E, Bul; 1984 v Nor, Rum, Bul, Y, S, E, NI; 1985 v Ic, Nor, S, Sp; 1986 v S, S.Ar, RI, U; 1987 v Fin, Fin, USSR, Cz, (Juventus), Den, Cz; 1988 v Y, Swe, Ma, I
Russell, M. R. (23) (Merthyr T), 1912 v S, Ire; 1914 v E; (Plymouth Arg), 1920 v E, S, Ire; 1921 v E, S, Ire; 1922 v E, NI; 1923 v E, S, NI; 1924 v E, S, NI; 1925 v E, S; 1926 v E, S; 1928 v S, 1929 v E

Sabine, H. W. (1) (Oswestry), 1887 v Ire
Saunders, D. (9) (Brighton & HA), 1986 v RI, Can, Can; 1987 v Fin, USSR; (Oxford U), 1988 v Y, Swe, Ma, I
Savin, G. (1) (Oswestry), 1878 v S
Sayer, P. (7) (Cardiff C), 1977 v Cz, S, E, NI; 1978 v K, K, S
Scrine, F. H. (2) (Swansea T), 1950 v E, NI
Sear, C. R. (1), (Manchester C), 1963 v E
Shaw, E. G. (3) (Oswestry), 1882 v Ire; 1884 v S, Ire
Sherwood, A. T. (41) (Cardiff C), 1947 v E, NI; 1948 v S, NI; 1949 v E, S, NI; P, Swz; 1950 v E, S, NI; Bel; 1951 v E, S, NI; P, Swz; 1952 v E, S, NI, UK; 1953 v S, E, NI, F, Y; 1954 v E, S, NI, A; 1955 v S, E, Y, NI; 1956 v E, S, NI; A; (Newport Co), 1957 v E, S
Shone, W. W. (1) (Oswestry), 1879 v E
Shortt, W. W. (12) (Plymouth Arg), 1947 v NI; 1950 v Ni, Bel; 1952 v E, S, NI, UK; 1953 v S, E, NI; F; Y
Showers, D. (2) (Cardiff C), 1975 v E, NI
Sidlow, C. (7) (Liverpool), 1947 v E, S; 1948 v E, S, NI; 1949 v S; 1950 v E
Sisson, H. (3) (Wrexham Olympic), 1885 v Ire; 1886 v S, Ire
Slatter, N. (21) (Bristol R), 1983 v S; 1984 v N, Is; 1985 v Ic, Sp, Ic, Nor, S, Sp, Nor; (Oxford U), 1986 v H, S.Ar, Can, Can; 1987 v Fin, Cz, Den, Den, Cz; 1988 v Ma, I
Smallman, D. P. (7) (Wrexham), 1974 v E, S, NI; (Everton), 1975 v H, E, NI; 1976 v A
Southall, N. (34) (Everton), 1982 v NI; 1983 v Nor, E, Bul, S, NI, Bra; 1984 v Nor, Rum, Bul, Y, S, E, NI,

Nor, Is; 1985 v Ic, Sp, Ic, Nor, S, Sp, Nor; 1986 v S, H, S.Ar, RI; 1987 v USSR, Fin, Cz, Den, Cz; 1988 v Y, Swe
Sprake, G. (37) (Leeds U), 1964 v S, NI; 1965 v S, Den, Gr; 1966 v E, NI, USSR; 1967 v S; 1968 v E, S; 1969 v S, E, NI, FRG, UK; 1970 v GDR, 1; 1971 v Rum, S, E, NI; 1972 v Fin, E, S, NI; 1973 v E (2), Pol, S, NI; 1974 v Pol; (Birmingham C), S, NI; 1975 v A, H, Lux
Stansfield, F. (1) (Cardiff C), 1949 v S
Stevenson B. (15) (Leeds U), 1978 v NI; 1979 v Ma, T, S, E, NI, Ma; 1980 v FRG, T, Ic; 1982 v Cz; (Birmingham C), Sp, S, NI, F
Stevenson, N. (4) (Swansea C), 1982 v E, S, NI; 1983 v Nor
Stitfall, R. F. (2) (Cardiff C), 1953 v E; 1957 v Cz
Sullivan, D. (17) (Cardiff C), 1953 v NI, F, Y; 1954 v NI; 1955 v E, NI; 1957 v E, S; 1958 v NI; H, H, Swe, Bra; 1959 v S, NI; 1960 v E, S

Tapscott, D. R. (14) (Arsenal), 1954 v A; 1955 v S, E, NI, Y; 1956 v E, NI, S, A; 1957 v NI, Cz, GDR; (Cardiff C), 1959 v E, NI
Taylor, J. (1) (Wrexham), 1898 v E
Taylor, O. D. S. (4) (Newtown), 1893 v S, Ire; 1894 v S, Ire
Thomas, C. (2) (Druids), 1899 v Ire; 1900 v S
Thomas, D. A. (2) (Swansea T), 1957 v Cz; 1958 v GDR
Thomas, D. S. (4) (Fulham), 1948 v E, S, NI; 1949 v S
Thomas, E. (1) (Cardiff Corinthians), 1925 v E
Thomas, G. (2) (Wrexham), 1885 v E, S
Thomas, H. (1) (Manchester U), 1927 v E
Thomas, M. (51) (Wrexham), 1977 v FRG, S, S, NI; 1978 v K, S, Cz, Ir, E, NI; 1979 v Ma; (Manchester U), T, FRG, Ma; 1980 v RI, FRG, T, E, S, NI; 1981 v Cz, S, E, USSR; (Everton), 1982 v Cz, (Brighton & HA), USSR, Sp, E, S, NI; 1983 (Stoke C), v Nor, Y, E, Bul, S, NI, Bra; 1984 v Rum, Bul, Y; (Chelsea), S, E; 1985 v Ic, Sp, Ic, S, Sp, Nor; 1986 v S; (WBA), H, S.Ar
Thomas, M. R. (1) (Newcastle U), 1987 v Fin
Thomas, R. J. (50) (Swindon T), 1967 v NI; 1968 v FRG; 1969 v E, NI, I, FRG, UK; 1970 v E, S, NI, GDR, I; 1971 v S, E, NI, Rum, Cz; 1972 v Fin, Cz, Rum, S, NI; 1973 v E, E, E, Pol, S, NI; 1974 v Pol; (Derby Co), E, S, NI; 1975 v H, H, Lux, Lux, S, E, NI; 1976 v A, Y, E; 1977 v Cz, S, E, NI; 1978 v K, S; (Cardiff C), Cz
Thomas, T. (2) (Bangor), 1898 v S, Ire
Thomas, W. R. (2) (Newport Co), 1931 v E, S
Thomson D. (1) (Druids), 1876 v S
Thomson, G. F. (2) (Druids), 1876 v S; 1877 v S
Toshack, J. B. (40) (Cardiff C), 1969 v S, E, NI, FRG, GDR, UK; 1970 v GDR, I; (Liverpool), 1971 v S, E, NI, Fin; 1972 v Fin, E; 1973 v E, E, E, Pol, S; 1975 v A, H, H, Lux, Lux, S, E; 1976 v Y, Y, E; 1977 v S; 1978 v K, K, S, Cz; (Swansea C), 1979 v FRG, S, E, NI, Ma; 1980 v FRG
Townsend, W. (2) (Newtown), 1887 v Ire; 1893 v Ire
Trainer, H. (3) (Wrexham), 1895 v E, S, Ire
Trainer, J. (20) (Bolton W), 1887 v S; (Preston NE), 1888 v S; 1889 v E; 1890 v S; 1891 v S; 1892 v Ire, S;

1893 v E; 1894 v Ire, E; 1895 v Ire, E, 1896 v S; 1897 v Ire, S, E; 1898 v S, E; 1899 v Ire, S

Turner, H. G. (8) (Charlton Ath), 1937 v E, S, NI; 1938 v E, S, NI; 1939 v NI, F

Turner, J. (1) (Wrexham), 1892 v E

Turner, R. E. (2) (Wrexham), 1891 v E, Ire

Turner, W. H. (5) (Wrexham), 1887 v E, Ire; 1890 v S; 1891 v E, S

Van Den Hauwe, P. W. R. (11) (Everton), 1985 v Sp; 1986 v S, H; 1987 v USSR, Fin; Cz, Den, Den, Cz; 1988 v Y, I

Vaughan, Jas (4) (Druids), 1893 v E, S, Ire; 1899 v E

Vaughan, John (11) (Oswestry), 1879 v S; 1880 v S; 1881 v E, S; 1882 v E, S, Ire; 1883 v E, S, Ire; (Bolton W), 1884 v E

Vaughan, J. O. (4) (Rhyl), 1885 v Ire; 1886 v Ire, E, S

Vaughan, N. (10) (Newport Co), 1983 v Y, Bra; 1984 v Nor; (Cardiff C), Rum, Bul, Y, NI, Nor, Is; 1985 v Sp

Vaughan, T. (1) (Rhyl), 1885 v E

Vearncombe, G. (2) (Cardiff C), 1958 v GDR, 1961 v RI

Vernon, T. R. (32) (Blackburn R), 1957 v NI, Cz, Cz, GDR; 1958 v E, S, GDR, Swe; 1959 v S; (Everton), 1960 v NI; 1961 v S, E, RI; 1962 v NI, Bra, Bra, Mex; 1963 v S, E, H; 1964 v E, S; (Stoke C), 1965 v NI, Gr, I; 1966 v E, S, NI, USSR, Den; 1967 v NI; 1968 v E

Villars, A. K. (3) (Cardiff C), 1974 v E, S, NI

Vizard, E. T. (22) (Bolton W), 1911 v E, S, Ire; 1912 v E, S; 1913 v S; 1914 v E, Ire; 1920 v E; 1921 v E, S, Ire; 1922 v E, S; 1923 v E, NI; 1924 v E, S, NI; 1926 v E, S; 1927 v S

Walley, J. T. (1) (Watford), 1971 v Cz

Walsh, I. (18) (C Palace), 1980 v RI, T, E, S, Ic; 1981 v T, Cz, RI, T, S, E, USSR; 1982 v Cz, Ic; (Swansea C), Sp, S, NI, F

Ward, D. (2) (Bristol R), 1959 v E; (Cardiff C), 1962 v E

Warner, J. (2) (Swansea T), 1937 v E; (Manchester U), 1939 v F

Warren, F. W. (6) (Cardiff C), 1929 v NI; (Middlesbrough), 1931 v NI; 1933 v F, E; (Hearts), 1937 v NI; 1938 v NI

Watkins, A. E. (5) (Leicester Fosse), 1898 v E, S; (Aston Villa), 1900 v E, S; (Millwall), 1904 v Ire

Watkins, W. M. (10) (Stoke C), 1902 v E; 1903 v E, S; (Aston Villa), 1904 v E, S, Ire; (Sunderland), 1905 v E, S, Ire; (Stoke C); 1908 v Ire

Webster, C. (4) (Manchester U), 1957 v Cz; 1958 v H, M, Bra

Whatley, W. J. (2) (Tottenham H), 1939 v E, S

White, P. F. (1) (London Welsh), 1896 v Ire

Wilcocks, A. R. (1) (Oswestry), 1890 v Ire

Wilding, J. (9) (Wrexham O), 1885 v E, S, Ire; 1886 v E, Ire; (Bootle), 1887 v E; 1888 v S, Ire; (Wrexham), 1892 v S

Williams, A. L. (1) (Wrexham), 1931 v E

Williams, B. D. (10) (Swansea T), 1928 v NI; E; 1930 v

E, S; (Everton), 1931 v NI; 1932 v E; 1933 v E, S, NI; 1935 v NI

Williams, B. (1) (Bristol C), 1930 v NI

Williams, D. G. (5) (Derby Co), 1987 v Cz; 1988 v Y, Swe, Ma, I

Williams, D. M. (5) (Norwich C), 1986 v S.Ar, U, Can, Can; 1987 v Fin

Williams, D. R. (8) (Merthy T), 1921 v E, S; (Sheffield W), 1923 v S; 1926 v S; 1927 v E, NI; (Manchester U); 1929 v E, S

Williams, E. (2) (Crewe Alex), 1893 v E, S

Williams, E. (5) (Druids), 1901 v E, Ire, S; 1902 v E, Ire

Williams, G. (6) (Chirk), 1893 v S; 1894 v S; 1895 v E, S, Ire; 1898 v Ire

Williams, G. E. (26) (WBA), 1960 v NI; 1961 v S, E, RI; 1963 v NI, H; 1964 v E, S, NI; 1965 v S, E, NI, Den, Gr, Gr, USSR, I; 1966 v NI; Bra, Bra, Ch; 1967 v S, E, NI; 1968 v NI; 1969 v I

Williams, G. G. (5) (Swansea T), 1961 v NI, H, Sp, Sp; 1962 v E

Williams, G. J. J. (1) (Cardiff C), 1951 v Swz

Williams, G. O. (1) (Wrexham), 1907 v Ire

Williams, H. J. (3) (Swansea), 1965 v Gr, Gr; 1972 v R

Williams, H. T. (4) (Newport Co), 1949 v NI, Swz; (Leeds U); 1950 v NI; 1951 v S

Williams, J. H. (1) (Oswestry), 1884 v E

Williams, J. T. (1) (Wrexham), 1939 v F

Williams, J. T. (1) (Middlesbrough), 1925 v NI

Williams, J. W. (2) (C Palace), 1912 v S, Ire

Williams, R. (2) (Newcastle U), 1935 v S, E

Williams, R. P. (1) (Caernarvon), 1886 v S

Williams, S. G. (43) (WBA), 1954 v A; 1955 v E, NI; 1956 v E, S, A; 1958 v E, S, NI, Is, Is, H, H, Mex, Swe, Bra; 1959 v E, S, NI; 1960 v E, S, NI; 1961 v NI, RI, H, Sp, Sp; 1962 v E, S, NI, Bra, Bra, Mex; (Southampton), 1963 v S, E, H, H; 1964 v E, S; 1965 v S, E, Den; 1966 v Den

Williams W. (12) (Druids), 1876 v S; 1878 v S; (Oswestry), 1879 v E, S; (Druids), 1880 v E, S; 1881 v E, S; 1882 v E, S, Ire; 1883 v Ire

Williams, W. (1) (Northampton) T), 1925 v S

Witcomb, D. F. (3) (WBA), 1947 v E, S; (Sheffield W), 1947 v NI

Woosnam, A. P. (17) (Leyton Orient), 1959 v S; (West Ham U), v E; 1960 v E, S, NI; 1961 v S, E, NI, RI, Sp, H; 1962 v E, S, NI, Bra; (Aston Villa), 1963 v NI, H

Woosnam, G. (1) (Newton White Star), 1879 v S

Worthington, T. (1) (Newtown), 1894 v S

Wynn, G. A. (12) (Chirk), 1903 v Ire; (Wrexham), 1909 v E, S, Ire; (Manchester City), 1910 v E; 1911 v Ire; 1912 v E, S, 1913 v E, S; 1914 v E, S

Yorath, T. C. (59) (Leeds U), 1970 v Is; 1971 v S, E, NI; 1972 v Cz, E, S, NI; 1973 v E, Pol, S, 1974 v Pol, E, S, NI; 1975 v A, H, H, Lux, Lux, S; 1976 v A, E, S, Y, Y, E, NI; (Coventry C), 1977 v FRG, S, S, Cz, E, NI; 1978 v K, K, S, Cz, FRG, Ir, E, S, NI; 1979 v T, FRG, S, E, NI; (Tottenham H) 1980 v RI, T, E, S, NI, Ic; 1981 v T, Cz; (Vancouver W), RI, T, USSR

REPUBLIC OF IRELAND

Aherne, T. (16) (Belfast Celtic), 1946 v P, Sp; (Luton T), 1950 v Fin, E, Fin, Swe, Bel; 1951 v Nor, Arg, Nor; 1952 v FRG, FRG, A, Sp; 1953 v F; 1954 v F

Aldridge, J. W. (18) (Oxford U), 1986 v W, U, Ic, Cz; 1987 v Bel, S, Pol (Liverpool), S, Bul, Bel, Bra, Lux; 1988 v Bul, Pol, Nor, E, USSR, Neth

Ambrose, P. (5) (Shamrock R), 1955 v Nor, Neth; 1964 v Pol, Nor, E

Anderson, J. (15) (Preston NE), 1980 v Cz, USA; 1982 v Ch, Bra, TT; (Newcastle U), 1984 v Chn; 1986 v W, Ic, Cz; 1987 v Bul, Bel, Bra, Lux; 1988 v Rum, Y

Andrews, P. (1) (Bohemians), 1936 v Neth

Arrigan, T. (1) (Waterford), 1938 v N

Bailham, E. (1) (Shamrock R), 1964 v E

Barber, E. (2) (Shelbourne), 1966 v Sp; (Birmingham C), 1966 v Bel

Barry, P. (2) (Fordsons), 1928 v Bel; 1929 v Bel

Beglin, J. (15) (Liverpool), 1984 v Chn; 1985 v Mex, Den, I, Is, E, Nor, Swz; 1986 v Swz, USSR, Den,W; 1987 v Bel, S, Pol

Bermingham, J. (1) (Bohemians), 1929 v Bel

Bermingham, P. (1) (St. James' Gate), 1935 v H

Bonner, P. (26) (Celtic), 1981 v Pol; 1982 v Alg; 1984 v Ma, Is, Chn; 1985 v I, Is, E, Nor; 1986 v U, Ic; 1987 v Bel, Bel, S, S, Pol, Bul, Bra, Lux; 1988 v Bul, Rum, Y, Nor, E, USSR, Neth

Braddish, S. (1) (Dundalk), 1978 v Pol

Bradshaw, P. (5) (St James' Gate), 1939 v Swz, Pol, H, H, G

Brady, F. (2) (Fordsons), 1926 v I; 1927 v I

Brady, T. R. (6) (QPR), 1964 v A, A, Sp, Sp, Pol, N

Brady, W. L. (67) (Arsenal), 1975 v USSR, T, Swz, USSR, Swz; 1976 v T, Nor, Pol; 1977 v E, T, F, F, Sp, Bul; 1978 v Bul, Nor; 1979 v NI, E, Den, Bul, FRG, Arg; 1980 v W, Bul, E, Cyp; (Juventus), 1981 v Neth, Bel, F, Cyp, Bel; 1982 v Neth, F, Ch, Bra, TT; 1983 (Sampdoria), v Neth, Sp, Ic, Ma; 1984 v Ic, Neth, Ma, Pol, Is; (Internazionale), 1985 v USSR, Nor, Den, I, E, Nor, Sp, Swz; 1986 v Swz, USSR, Den, W; (Ascoli), 1987 v Bel, S, S, Pol, (West Ham U), Bul, Bel, Bra, Lux; 1988 v Lux, Bul

Breen, T. (5), (Manchester U), 1937 v Swz, F; (Shamrock R), 1947 v E, Sp, P

Brennan, F. (1) (Drumcondra), 1965 v Bel

Brennan, S. A. (19) (Manchester U), 1965 v Sp; 1966 v Sp, A, Bel; 1967 v Sp, T, Sp; 1969 v Cz, Den, H; 1970 v S, Cz, Den, H, Pol, FRG (Waterford), 1971 v Pol, Swe, I

Brown, J. (2) (Coventry C), 1937 v Swz, F

Browne, W. (3) (Bohemians), 1964 v A, Sp, E

Buckley, L. (2) (Shamrock R), 1984 v Pol; (Waregem), 1985 v Mex

Burke, F. (1) (Cork), 1934 v Bel

Burke, F. (1) (Cork Ath), 1952 v FRG

Burke, J. (1) (Shamrock R), 1929 v Bel

Byrne, A. B. (14) (Southampton), 1970 v Den, Pol, FRG; 1971 v Pol, Swe, Swe, I, I, A; 1973 v F, USSR, F, Nor; 1974 v Pol

Byrne, D. (3) (Shelbourne), 1929 v Bel; (Shamrock R), 1932 v Sp; (Coleraine), 1934 v Bel

Byrne, J. (1) (Bray Unknowns), 1928 v Bel

Byrne, J. (13) (QPR), 1985 v I, E, Sp; 1987 v S, Bel, Bra, Lux; 1988 v Lux, Bul, Is, Rum, Y, Pol

Byrne, P. (8) (Shamrock R), 1984 v Pol, Chn; 1985 v Mex, I; 1986 v Den, W, U, Cz

Byrne, P. (3) (Shelbourne), 1931 v Sp; 1932 v Neth; (Drumcondra), 1934 v Neth

Byrne, S. (1) (Bohemians), 1931 v Sp

Campbell, A. (3) (Santander), 1985 v I, Is, Sp

Campbell, N. (10) (St Patrick's Ath), 1971 v A; (Fortuna, Cologne), 1972 v Ir, Ec, Ch, P; 1973 v USSR, F; 1976 v Nor; 1977 v Sp, Bul

Cannon, H. (2) (Bohemians), 1926 v I; 1928 v Bel

Cantwell, N. (36), (West Ham U), 1954 v Lux; 1956 v Sp, Neth; 1957 v Den, FRG; E, E; 1958 v Den, Pol, A; 1959 v Pol, Cz, Cz; 1960 v Swe, Ch, Swe; 1961 v Nor; (Manchester U), 1961 v S, S; 1962 v Cz, Cz, A; 1963 v Ic, Ic, S; 1964 v A, Sp, E; 1965 v Pol, Sp; 1966 v Sp, Sp, A, Bel; 1967 v Sp; T

Carey, J. J. (29) (Manchester U), 1938 v Nor, Cz, Pol; 1939 v Swz, Pol, H, H, G; 1946 v P, Sp; 1947 v E, Sp, P; 1948 v P, Sp; 1949 v Swz, Bel, P, Swe, Sp; 1950 v Fin, E, Fin, Swe; 1951 v Nor, Arg, Nor; 1953 v F, A

Carolan, J. (2) (Manchester U), 1960 v Swe, Ch

Carroll, B. (2) (Shelbourne), 1949 v Bel; 1950 v Fin

Carroll, T. R. (17) (Ipswich T), 1968 v Pol; 1969 v Pol, A, Den; 1970 v Cz, Pol, FRG; 1971 v Swe; (Birmingham C), 1972 v Ir, Ec, Ch, P; 1973 v USSR, USSR, Pol, F, N

Cascarino, A. G. (7) (Gillingham), 1986 v Swz, USSR, Den; (Millwall), 1988 v Pol, Nor, USSR, Neth

Chandler, J. (2) (Leeds U), 1980 v Cz, USA

Chatton, H. A. (3) (Shelbourne), 1931 v Sp; (Dumbarton), 1932 v Sp; (Cork), 1934 v Neth

Clarke, J. (1) (Drogheda U), 1978 v Pol

Clarke, K. (2), (Drumcondra), 1948 v P, Sp

Clarke, M. (1) (Shamrock R), 1950 v Bel

Clinton, T. J. (3) (Everton), 1951 v Nor; 1954 v F, Lux

Coad, P. (11) (Shamrock R), 1947 v E, Sp, P; 1948 v P, Sp; 1949 v Swz, Bel, P, Swe; 1951 v Nor; 1952 v Sp

Coffey, T. (1) (Drumcondra), 1950 v Fin

Colfer, M. D. (2) (Shelbourne), 1950 v Bel; 1951 v N

Collins, F. (1) (Jacobs), 1927 v I

Conmy, O. M. (5) (Peterborough U), 1965 v Bel; 1967 v Cz; 1968 v Cz, Pol; 1970 v Cz

Connolly, J. (1) (Fordsons), 1926 v I

Connolly, N. (1) (Cork), 1937 v G

Conroy, G. A. (26) (Stoke C), 1970 v Cz, Den, H, Pol, FRG; 1971 v Pol, Swe, Swe, I; 1973 v USSR, F, USSR, Nor; 1974 v Pol, Bra, U, Ch; 1975 v T, Swz, USSR, Swz; 1976 v T, Pol; 1977 v E, T, Pol

Conway, J. P. (19) (Fulham), 1967 v Sp, T, Sp; 1968 v Cz; 1969 v A, H; 1970 v S, Cz, Den, H, Pol, FRG; 1971 v I, A; 1974 v U, Ch, 1976 v Nor, Pol; (Manchester C), 1977 v Pol

Corr, P. J. (4) (Everton), 1949 v P, Sp; 1950 v E, Swe

Courtney, E. (1) (Cork U), 1946 v P

Cummins, G. P. (19) (Luton T), 1954 v Lux, Lux; 1955 v Nor, Nor, FRG; 1956 v Y, Sp; 1958 v Den, Pol, A; 1959 v Pol, Cz, Cz; 1960 v Swe, Ch, FRG, Swe; 1961 v S, S

Cuneen, T. (1) (Limerick), 1951 v N

Curtis, D. P. (17) (Shelbourne), 1957 v Den, FRG; (Bristol C), 1957 v E, E; 1958 v Den, Pol, A; (Ipswich T), 1959 v Pol; 1960 v Swe, Ch, FRG, Swe; 1961 v Nor, S; 1962 v A; 1963 v Ic (Exeter C), 1964 v A

Cusack, S. (1) (Limerick), 1953 v F

Daly, G. A. (46) (Manchester U), 1973 v Pol, Nor; 1974 v Bra, U; 1975 v Swz; 1977 v E, T, F; (Derby Co), F, Bul; 1978 v Bul, T, Den; 1979 v NI, E, Den, Bul; 1980 v NI, E, Cyp, Swz, Arg; (Coventry C), 1981 v Neth, Bel, Cyp, W, Bel, Cz, Pol; 1982 v Alg, Ch, Bra, TT; 1983 v Neth, Sp, Ma; 1984 v Is; (Birmingham C), 1985 v Mex, Nor, Sp, Swz; 1986 v Swz; (Shrewbury T), U, Ic, Cz; 1987 v S

Daly, J. (2) (Shamrock R), 1932 v Neth; 1935 v Sw

Daly, M. (2) (Wolverhampton W), 1978 v T, Pol

Daly, P. (1) (Shamrock R), 1950 v Fin

Davis, T. L. (4) (Oldham Ath), 1937 v G, H; (Tranmere R), 1938 v Cz, Pol

Deacy, E. (4) (Aston Villa), 1982 v Alg, Ch, Bra, TT

De Mange, K. J. P. P. (1) (Liverpool), 1987 v Bra

Dempsey, J. T. (19) (Fulham), 1967 v Sp, Cz; 1968 v Cz; Pol; 1969 v Pol, A, Den; (Chelsea), 1969 v Cz, Den, 1970 v H, FRG; 1971 v Pol, Swe, Swe, I; 1972 v Ir, Ec, Ch, P

Dennehy, J. (10) (Cork Hibernians), 1972 v Ec, Ch; (Nottingham F), 1973 v USSR, Pol, F, Nor; 1974 v Pol; 1975 v T; (Walsall), 1976 v Pol; 1977 v Pol

Desmond, P. (4) (Middlesbrough), 1950 v Fin, E, Fin, Swe

Devine, J. (12) (Arsenal), 1980 v Cz, NI; 1981 v Cz; 1982 v Neth, Alg; 1983 v Sp, Ma; (Norwich C), 1984 v Ic, Neth, Is; 1985 v USSR, N

Donnelly, J. (10) (Dundalk), 1935 v H, Swz, G; 1936 v Neth, Swz, H, Lux; 1937 v G, H; 1938 v Nor

Donnelly, T. (2) (Drumcondra), 1938 v Nor; (Shamrock R), 1939 v Swz

Donovan, D. C. (5) (Everton), 1955 v Nor, Neth, Nor, FRG, 1957 v E

Donovan, T. (1) (Aston Villa), 1980 v Cz

Dowdall, C. (3) (Fordsons), 1928 v Bel; (Barnsley), 1929 v Bel; (Cork), 1931 v Sp

Doyle, C. (1) (Shelbourne), 1959 v Cz

Doyle, D. (1) (Shamrock R), 1926 v I

Doyle, L. (1) (Dolphin), 1932 v Sp

Duffy, B. (1) (Shamrock R), 1950 v Bel

Duggan, H. A. (5) (Leeds U), 1927 v I; 1930 v Bel; 1936 v H, Lux; (Newport Co), 1938 v Nor

Dunne, A. P. (32) (Manchester U), 1962 v A; 1963 v Ic, S; 1964 v A, Sp, Pol, Nor, E; 1965 v Pol, Sp; 1966 v Sp, Sp, A, Bel; 1967 v Sp, T, Sp; 1969 v Pol, Den, H; 1970 v H; 1971 v Swe, I, A; (Bolton W), 1974 v Bra, U, Ch; 1975 v T, Swz, USSR, Swz; 1976 v T

Dunne, J. (15) (Sheffield U), 1930 v Bel, (Arsenal), 1936 v Swz, H, Lux; (Southampton), 1937 v Swz, F; (Shamrock R), 1938 v Nor, Nor, Cz, Pol; 1939 v Swz, Pol, H, G

Dunne, J. C. (1) (Fulham), 1971 v A

Dunne, L. (2) (Manchester C), 1935 v Swz, G

Dunne, P. A. J. (5) (Manchester U), 1965 v Sp; 1966 v Sp, Sp, FRG; 1967 v T

Dunne, S. (15) (Luton T), 1953 v F, A; 1954 v F, Lux; 1956 v Sp, Neth; 1957 v Den, FRG, E; 1958 v Den, Pol, A; 1959 v Pol; 1960 v FRG, Swe

Dunne, T. (3) (St Patrick's Ath), 1956 v Neth; 1957 v Den, FRG

Dunning, P. (2) (Shelbourne), 1971 v Swe, I

Dunphy, E. M. (23) (York C), 1966 v Sp; (Millwall), 1966 v FRG; 1967 v T, Sp, T, Cz; 1968 v Cz, Pol; 1969 v Pol, A, Den, Den, H; 1970 v Den, H, Pol, FRG; 1971 v Pol, Swe, Swe, I, I, A

Dwyer, N. M. (14) (West Ham U), 1960 v Swe, Ch, FRG, Swe; (Swansea T), 1961 v W, Nor, S, S; 1962 v Cz, Cz; 1964 v Pol, Nor, E; 1965 v Pol

Eccles, P. (1) (Shamrock R), 1986 v U

Egan, R. (1) (Dundalk), 1929 v Bel

Eglington, T. J. (24) (Shamrock R), 1946 v P, Sp; (Everton), 1947 v E, Sp, P; 1948 v P; 1949 v Swz, P, Swe; 1951 v Nor, Arg; 1952 v FRG, FRG, A, Sp; 1953 v F, A; 1954 v F, Lux, F; 1955 v Nor, Neth, FRG; 1956 v Sp

Ellis, P. (7) (Bohemians), 1935 v Swz, G; 1936 v Neth, Swz, Lux; 1937 v G, H

Fagan, E. (1) (Shamrock R), 1973 v Nor

Fagan, F. (8) (Manchester C), 1955 v Nor; 1960 v Swe; (Derby Co), 1960 v Ch, FRG, Swe; 1961 v W, Nor, S

Fagan, K. (1) (Shamrock R), 1926 v I

Fairclough, M. (2) (Dundalk), 1982 v Ch, TT

Fallon, S. (8) (Celtic), 1951 v Nor; 1952 v FRG, FRG, A, Sp; 1953 v F; 1955 v Nor, FRG

Fallon, W. J. (9) (Notts Co), 1935 v H; 1936 v H; 1937 v H, Swz, F; 1939 v Swz, Pol; (Sheffield W), 1939 v H, G

Farquharson, T. G. (4) (Cardiff C), 1929 v Bel; 1930 v Bel; 1931 v Sp; 1932 v Sp

Farrell, P. (2) (Hibernian), 1937 v Swz, F

Farrell, P. D. (28) (Shamrock R), 1946 v P, Sp; (Everton), 1947 v Sp, P; 1948 v P, Sp; 1949 v Swz, P, Sp; 1950 v E, Fin, Swe; 1951 v Arg, Nor; 1952 v FRG, FRG, A, Sp; 1953 v F, A; 1954 v F, F; 1955 v Nor, Neth, FRG; 1956 v Y, Sp; 1957 v E

Feenan, J. J. (2) (Sunderland), 1937 v Swz, F

Finucane, A. (11) (Limerick), 1967 v T, Cz; 1969 v Cz, Den, H; 1970 v S, Cz; 1971 v Swe, I, I; 1972 v A

Fitzgerald, F. J. (2) (Waterford), 1955 v Neth; 1956 v Neth

Fitzgerald, P. J. (5) (Leeds U), 1961 v W, Nor, S; 1962 v Cz, Cz

Fitzpatrick, K. (1) (Limerick), 1970 v Cz

Fitzsimons, A. G. (26) (Middlesbrough), 1950 v Fin, Bel; 1952 v FRG, FRG, A, Sp; 1953 v F, A; 1954 v F, Lux, F; 1955 v Neth, Nor, FRG; 1956 v Y, Sp, Neth; 1957 v Den, FRG, E, E; 1958 v Den, Pol, A; 1959 v Pol; (Lincoln C), 1959 v Cz

Flood, J. J. (5) (Shamrock R), 1926 v I; 1929 v Bel; 1930 v Bel; 1931 v Sp; 1932 v Sp

Fogarty, A. (11) (Sunderland), 1960 v FRG, Swe; 1961 v S; 1962 v Cz, Cz; 1963 v Ic, Ic, S; 1964 v A, A; (Hartlepools U), Sp

Foley, J. (7) (Cork), 1934 v Bel, Neth; (Celtic), 1935 v H, Swz, G; 1937 v G, H

Foley, M. (1) (Shelbourne), 1926 v I
Foley, T. C. (9) (Northampton T), 1964 v Sp, Pol, Nor; 1965 v Pol, Bel; 1966 v Sp, Sp, FRG; 1967 v Cz
Foy, T. (2) (Shamrock R), 1938 v Nor; 1939 v H
Fullam, J. (11) (Preston NE), 1961 v Nor; (Shamrock R), 1964 v Sp, Pol, Nor; 1966 v A, Bel; 1968 v Pol; 1969 v Pol, A, Den; 1970 v Cz
Fullam, R. (2) (Shamrock R), 1926 v I; 1927 v I

Gallagher, C. (2) (Celtic), 1967 v T, Cz
Gallagher, M. (1) (Hibernian), 1954 v Lux
Gallagher, P. (1) (Falkirk), 1932 v Sp
Galvin, A. (27) (Tottenham H), 1983 v Neth, Ma; 1984 v Neth, Is; 1985 v Mex, USSR, Nor, Den, I, Nor, Sp; 1986 v U, Ic, Cz; 1987 v Bel, Bel, S, Bul, Lux; (Sheffield W), 1988 v Lux, Bul, Rum, Pol, Nor, E, USSR, Neth
Gannon, E. (14) (Notts Co). 1949 v Swz; (Sheffield W), 1949 v Bel, P, Swe, Sp; 1950 v Fin; 1951 v Nor; 1952 v G, A; 1954 v Lux, F; 1955 v Nor; (Shelbourne), 1955 v Nor, FRG
Gannon, M. (1) (Shelbourne), 1972 v A
Gaskins, P. (7) (Shamrock R), 1934 v Bel, Neth; 1935 v H, Swz, G, (St James' Gate), 1938 v Cz, Pol
Gavin, J. T. (7) (Norwich C), 1950 v Fin, Fin; 1953 v F; 1954 v Lux; (Tottenham H), 1955 v Neth, FRG; (Norwich C), 1957 v Den
Geoghegan, M. (2) (St. James' Gate), 1937 v G, 1938 v N
Gibbons, A. (4) (St. Patrick's Ath), 1952 v FRG; 1954 v Lux; 1956 v Y, Sp
Gilbert, R. (1) (Shamrock R), 1966 v FRG
Giles, C. (1) (Doncaster R), 1951 v N
Giles, M. J. (60) (Manchester U), 1960 v Swe, Ch; 1961 v W, Nor, S, S; 1962 v Cz, Cz, A; 1963 v Ic, S; (Leeds U), 1964 v A, A, Sp, Sp, Pol, Nor, E; 1965 v Sp; 1966 v Sp, Sp, A, Bel; 1967 v Sp, T, T; 1969 v A, Den, Cz; 1970 v S, Pol, FRG; 1971 v I; 1973 v F, USSR; 1974 v Bra, U, Ch; 1975 v USSR, T, Swz, USSR, Swz; (WBA), 1976 v T; 1977 v E, T, F, F, Pol, Bul; (Shamrock R), 1978 v Bul, T, Pol, Nor, Den; 1979 v NI, Den, Bul, FRG, Arg
Givens, D. J. (56) (Manchester U), 1969 v Den, H; 1970 v S, Cz, Den, H; (Luton T), 1970 v Pol, FRG; 1971 v Swe, I, I, A, 1972 v Ir, Ec, P; (QPR), 1973 v F, USSR, Pol, F, Nor; 1974 v Pol, Bra, U, Ch, 1975 v USSR, T, Swz, USSR, Swz; 1976 v T, Nor, Pol; 1977 v E, T, F, F, Sp, Bul; 1978 v Bul, Nor, Den; (Birmingham C), 1979 v NI, E, Den, Bul, FRG, Arg; 1980 v USA, NI, E, Den, Bul, FRG, Arg; 1981 v Neth, Bel, Cyp, W; (Neuchatel X), 1982 v F
Glen, W. (8) (Shamrock R), 1927 v I; 1929 v Bel; 1930 v Bel; 1932 v Sp; 1936 v Neth, Swz, H, Lux
Glynn, D. (2) (Drumcondra), 1952 v FRG; 1955 v N
Godwin, T. F. (13) (Shamrock R), 1949 v P, Swe, Sp; 1950 v Fin, E, (Leicester C), 1950 v Fin, Swe, Bel; 1951 v Nor; (Bournemouth & Boscombe Ath), 1956 v Neth; 1957 v E; 1958 v Den, Pol
Golding, L. (2) (Shamrock R), 1928 v Bel; 1930 v Bel
Gorman, W. C. (13) (Bury), 1936 v Swz, H, Lux; 1937 v G, H; 1938 v Nor, Cz, Pol; 1939 v Swz, Pol, H; (Brentford), 1947 v E, P
Grace, J. (1) (Drumcondra), 1926 v I
Grealish, A. (44) (Orient), 1976 v Nor, Pol, Den; 1979 v

NI, E, FRG, Arg; (Luton T), 1980 v W, Cz, Bul, USA, NI, E, Cyp, Swz, Arg; 1981 v Neth, Bel, F, Cyp, W, Bel, Pol; (Brighton & HA), 1982 v Neth, Alg, Ch, Bra, TT; 1983 v Neth, Sp, Ic, Sp; 1984 v Ic, Neth (WBA), Pol, Chn; 1985 v Mex, USSR, Nor, Den, Sp, Swz; 1986 v USSR, Den
Gregg, E. (9) (Bohemians), 1978 v Pol, Den; 1979 v E, Den, Bul, FRG, Arg; 1980 v W, Cz
Griffith, R. (1) (Walsall), 1935 v H
Grimes, A. A. (17) (Manchester U), 1978 v T, Pol, Nor; 1980 v Bul, USA, NI, E, Cyp; 1981 v Cz, Pol; 1982 v Alg; 1983 v Sp, Sp; (Coventry C), 1984 v Pol, Is; (Luton T), 1988 v Lux, Rum

Hale, A. (13) (Aston Villa), 1962 v A; (Doncaster R), 1963 v Ic; 1964 v Sp, Sp; (Waterford), 1967 v Sp; 1968 v Pol; 1969 v Pol, A, Den; 1970 v S, Cz; 1971 v Pol; 1972 v A
Hamilton, T. (2) (Shamrock R), 1959 v Cz, Cz
Hand, E. K. (19) (Portsmouth), 1969 v Cz; 1970 v Pol, FRG; 1971 v Pol, A; 1973 v USSR, F, USSR, Pol, F; 1974 v Pol, Bra, U, Ch; 1975 v T, Swz, USSR, Swz; 1976 v T
Harrington, W. (4) (Cork), 1936 v Neth, Swz, H, Lux
Hartnett, J. B. (2) (Middlesbrough), 1949 v Sp; 1954 v Lux
Harverty, J. (32) (Arsenal), 1956 v Neth, 1957 v Den, FRG, E, E; 1958 v Den, Pol, A; 1959 v Pol; 1960 v Swe, Ch; 1961 v W, Nor, S, S; (Blackburn R), 1962 v Cz, Cz; (Millwall), 1963 v S; 1964 v A, Sp, Pol, Nor, E; (Celtic), 1965 v Pol; (Bristol R), 1965 v Sp; (Shelbourne), 1966 v Sp, Sp, FRG, A, Bel; 1967 v T, Sp
Hayes, A. W. P. (1) (Southampton), 1979 v Den
Hayes, W. E. (2) (Huddersfield T), 1947 v E, P
Hayes, W. J. (1) (Limerick), 1949 v Bel
Healey, R. (2) (Cardiff C), 1977 v Pol; 1980 v E
Heighway, S. D. (33) (Liverpool), 1971 v Pol, Swe, Swe, I, A; 1973 v USSR; 1975 v USSR, T, USSR; 1976 v T, Nor; 1977 v E, F, F, Sp, Bul; 1978 v Bul, Nor, Den; 1979 v NI, Bul; 1980 v Bul, USA, NI, E, Cyp, Arg; 1981 v Bel, F, Cyp, W, Bel; (Minnesota K), 1982 v Neth
Henderson, B. (2) (Drumcondra), 1948 v P, Sp
Hennessy, J. (5) (Shelbourne), 1956 v Pol, B, Sp; 1966 v FRG; (St Patrick's Ath), 1969 v A
Herrick, J. (3) (Cork Hibernians), 1972 v A, Ch; (Shamrock R), 1973 v F
Higgins, J. (1) (Birmingham C), 1951 v Arg
Holmes, J. (30) (Coventry C), 1971 v A; 1973 v F, USSR, Pol, F, Nor; 1974 v Pol, Bra; 1975 v USSR, Swz; 1976 v T, Nor, Pol; 1977 v E, T, F, Sp; (Tottenham H), F, Pol, Bul; 1978 v Bul, T, Pol, Nor, Den; 1979 v NI, E, Den, Bul; 1981 (Vancouver W), v W
Horlecher, A. F. (6) (Bohemians), 1930 v Bel; 1932 v Sp, Neth; 1935 v H; 1936 v Neth, Sw
Houghton, R. J. (18) (Oxford U), 1986 v W, U, Ic, Cz; 1987 v Bel, Bel, S, S, Pol, Lux; 1988 v Lux, Bul, (Liverpool), Is, Y, Nor, E, USSR, Neth
Howlett, G. (1) (Brighton & HA), 1984 v Chn
Hoy, M. (6) (Dundalk), 1938 v Nor; 1939 v Swz, Pol, H, H, G
Hughton, C. (39) (Tottenham H), 1980 v USA, E, Swz, Arg; 1981 v Neth, Bel, F, Cyp, W, Bel, Pol; 1982 v F;

1983 v Neth, Sp, Ma, Sp; 1984 v Ic, Neth, Ma; 1985 v Mex, USSR, Nor, I, Is, E, Sp; 1986 v Swz, USSR, U, Ic; 1987 v Bel, Bul; 1988 v Is, Y, Pol, Nor, E, USSR, Neth

Hurley, C. J. (40) (Millwall), 1957 v E; 1958 v Den, Pol, A; (Sunderland), 1959 v Cz, Cz; 1960 v Swe, Ch, FRG, Swe; 1961 v W, Nor, S, S; 1962 v Cz, Cz, A; 1963 v Ic, Ic, S; 1964 v A, A, Sp, Sp, Pol, Nor; 1965 v Sp; 1966 v FRG, A, Bel; 1967 v T, Sp, T, Cz; 1968 v Cz, Pol (2); (Bolton W), 1969 v Den, Cz, H

Hutchinson, F. (2) (Drumcondra), 1935 v Swz, G

Jordan, D. (2) (Wolverhampton W), 1937 v Swz, F
Jordan, W. (2) (Bohemians), 1934 v Neth; 1938 v N

Kavanagh, P. J. (2) (Celtic), 1931 v Sp; 1932 v Sp
Keane, T. R. (4) (Swansea T), 1949 v Swz, P, Swe, Sp
Kearin, M. (1) (Shamrock R), 1972 v A
Kearns, F. T. (1) (West Ham U), 1954 v Lux
Kearns, M. (18) (Oxford U), 1970 v Pol; (Walsall), 1974 v Pol, U, Ch; 1976 v Nor, Pol; 1977 v E, T, F, F, Sp, Bul; 1978 v Nor, Den; 1979 v NI, E; (Wolverhampton W), 1980 v USA, NI
Kelly, D. T. (3) (Walsall), 1988 v Is, Rum, Y
Kelly, J. (4) (Derry C), 1932 v Neth; 1934 v Bel; 1936 v Swz, Lux
Kelly, J. A. (47) (Drumcondra), 1957 v FRG, E; (Preston NE), 1962 v A; 1963 v Ic, Ic, S; 1964 v A, A, Sp, Sp, Pol; 1965 v Bel; 1966 v A, Bel; 1967 v Sp, Sp, T, Cz, Cz, Pol; 1968 v Pol, A, Den, Cz, Den, H; 1970 v S, Den, H, Pol, FRG; 1971 v Pol, Swe, Swe, I, I, A, 1972 v Ir, Ec, Ch, P; 1973 v USSR, F, USSR, Pol, F, N
Kelly, J. P. V. (5) (Wolverhampton W), 1961 v W, Nor, S; 1962 v Cz, Cz
Kelly, M. J. (2) (Portsmouth), 1988 v Y, Pol
Kelly, N. (1) (Nottingham F), 1954 v Lux
Kendrick, J. (4) (Everton), 1927 v I; 1934 v Bel, Neth; 1936 v Neth
Kennedy, M. F. (2) (Portsmouth), 1986 v Ic, Cz
Kennedy, W. (3) (St James's Gate), 1932 v Neth; 1934 v Bel, Neth
Keogh, J. (1) (Shamrock R), 1966 v FRG
Keogh, S. (1) (Shamrock R), 1959 v Pol
Kiernan, F. W. (5) (Shamrock R), 1951 v Arg, Nor; (Southampton), 1952 v FRG, FRG, A
Kinnear, J. P. (25) (Tottenham H), 1967 v T; 1968 v Cz, Pol; 1969 v A, 1970 v Cz, Den, H, Pol; 1971 v Swe, I; 1972 v Ir, Ec, Ch, P; 1973 v USSR, F; 1974 v Pol, Bra, U, Ch; 1975 v USSR, T, Swz, USSR; (Brighton & HA), 1976 v T
Kinsella, J. (1) (Shelbourne), 1928 v Bel
Kinsella, P. (2) (Shamrock R), 1932 v Neth; 1938 v N
Kirkland, A. (1) (Shamrock R), 1927 v I

Lacey, W. (3) (Shelbourne), 1927 v I; 1928 v Bel; 1930 v Bel
Langan, D. (25) (Derby Co), 1978 v T, Nor; 1980 v Swz, Arg; (Birmingham C), 1981 v Neth, Bel, F, Cyp, W, Bel, Cz, Pol; 1982 v Neth, F; (Oxford U), 1985 v Nor, Sp, Swz; 1986 v W, U; 1987 v Bel, S, Pol, Bra, Lux; 1988 v Lux
Lawler, J. F. (8) (Fulham), 1953 v A; 1954 v Lux, F; 1955 v Nor, H, Nor, FRG; 1956 v Y

Lawlor, J. C. (3) (Drumcondra), 1949 v Bel; (Doncaster R), 1951 v Nor, Arg
Lawlor, M. (5) (Shamrock R), 1971 v Pol, Swe, Swe, I; 1973 v Pol
Lawrenson, M. (38) (Preston NE), 1977 v Pol; (Brighton & HA), 1978 v Bul, Pol, Nor; 1979 v NI, E; 1980 v E, Cyp, Swz; 1981 v Neth, Bel, F, Cyp, Pol; (Liverpool), 1982 v Neth, F, 1983 v Neth, Sp, Ic, Ma, Sp; 1984 v Ic, Neth, Ma, Is; 1985 v USSR, Nor, Den, I, E, Nor; 1986 v Swz, USSR, Den; 1987 v Bel, S; 1988 v Bul, Is
Leech, M. (8) (Shamrock R), 1969 v Cz, Den, H; 1972 v A, Ir, Ec, P; 1973 v USSR
Lennon, C. (3) (St James's Gate), 1935 v H, Swz, G
Lennox, G. (2) (Dolphin), 1931 v Sp; 1932 v Sp
Lowry, D. (1) (St Patrick's Ath), 1962 v A
Lunn, R. (2) (Dundalk), 1939 v Swz, Pol
Lynch, J. (1) (Cork Bohemians), 1934 v Bel

McAlinden, J. (2) (Portsmouth), 1946 v P, Sp
McCann, J. (1) (Shamrock R), 1957 v FRG
McCarthy, J. (3) (Bohemians), 1926 v I; 1928 v Bel; 1930 v Bel
McCarthy, M. (30) (Manchester C), 1984 v Pol, Chn; 1985 v Mex, Den, I, Is, E, Sp, Swz; 1986 v Swz, USSR, W, U, Ic, Cz; 1987 v S, S, Pol, Bul, Bel, Bra, Lux; (Celtic) 1988 v Bul, Is, Rum, Y, Nor, E, USSR, Neth
McCarthy, M. (1) (Shamrock R), 1932 v Neth
McConville, T. (6) (Dundalk), 1972 v A, (Waterford), 1973 v USSR, F, USSR, Pol, F
McDonagh, J. (24) (Everton), 1981 v W, Bel, Cz; (Bolton W), 1982 v Neth, F, Ch, Bra; 1983 v Neth, Sp, Ic, Ma, Sp; (Notts Co), 1984 v Ic, Neth, Pol; 1985 v Mex, USSR, Nor, Den, Sp, Swz; 1986 v Swz, USSR, Den
McDonagh, Joe (3) (Shamrock R), 1984 v Pol, Ma; 1985 v Mex
McEvoy, M. A. (17) (Blackburn R), 1961 v S, S; 1963 v S; 1964 v A, Sp, Sp, Pol, Nor, E; 1965 v Pol, Bel, Sp; 1966 v Sp, Sp; 1967 v Sp, T, Cz
McGee, P. (16) (QPR), 1978 v T, Nor, Den; 1979 v NI, E, Den, Bul, Arg; 1980 v Cz, Bul; (Preston NE), USA, NI, Cyp, Swz, Arg; 1981 v Bel
McGowan, D. (3) (West Ham U), 1949 v P, Swe, Sp
McGowan, J. (1) (Cork U), 1947 v Sp
McGrath M. (22) (Blackburn R), 1958 v A; 1959 v Pol, Cz, Cz; 1960 v Swe, FRG, Swe; 1961 v W; 1962 v Cz, Cz; 1963 v S; 1964 v A, A, E; 1965 v Pol, Bel, Sp; 1966 v Sp; (Bradford), 1966 v FRG, A, Bel; 1967 v T
McGrath, P. (25) (Manchester U), 1985 v I, Is, E, Nor, Swz; 1986 v Swz, Den, W, Ic, Cz; 1987 v Bel, Bel, S, S, Pol, Bul, Bra, Lux; 1988 v Lux, Bul, Y, Pol, Nor, E, Neth
McGuire, W. (1) (Bohemians), 1936 v Neth
McKenzie, G. (9) (Southend U), 1938 v Nor, Nor, Cz, Pol; 1939 v Swz, Pol, H, H, G
Mackey, G. (3) (Shamrock R), 1957 v Den, FRG, E
McLoughlin, F. (2) (Fordsons), 1930 v Bel; (Cork), 1932 v Sp
McMillan, W. (2) (Belfast Celtic), 1946 v P, Sp
McNally, J. B. (3) (Luton T), 1959 v Cz; 1961 v Sp; 1963 v Ic

Macken, A. (1) (Derby Co), 1977 v Sp
Madden, O. (1) (Cork), 1936 v H
Maguire, J. (1) (Shamrock R), 1929 v Bel
Malone, G. (1) (Shelbourne), 1949 v Bel
Mancini, T. J. (5) (QPR), 1974 v Pol, Bra, U, Ch; (Arsenal), 1975 v USSR
Martin, C. (1) (Bo'ness), 1927 v I
Martin, C. J. (30) (Glentoran), 1946 v P, Sp; 1947 v E; (Leeds U), 1947 v Sp; 1948 v P, Sp; (Aston Villa), 1949 v Swz, Bel, P, Swe, Sp; 1950 v Fin, E, Fin, Swe, Bel; 1951 v Arg; 1952 v FRG, A, Sp; 1954 v F, F, Lux; 1955 v Nor, Neth, Nor, FRG; 1956 v Y, Sp, Neth
Martin, M. P. (51) (Bohemians), 1972 v A, Ir, Ec, Ch, P; 1973 v USSR; (Manchester U), 1973 v USSR, Pol, F, Nor; 1974 v Pol, Bra, U, Ch; 1975 v USSR, T, Swz, USSR, Swz; (WBA), 1976 v T, Nor, Pol; 1977 v E, T, F (2), Sp, Pol, Bul; (Newcastle U), 1979 v Den, Bul, FRG, Arg; 1980 v W, Cz, Bul, USA, NI; 1981 v F, Bel, Cz; 1982 v Neth, F, Alg, Ch, Bra, TT; 1983 v Neth, Sp, Ma, Sp
Meagen, M. K. (17) (Everton), 1961 v S; 1962 v A; 1963 v Ic; 1964 v Sp; (Huddersfield T), 1965 v Bel; 1966 v Sp, Sp, A, Bel; 1967 v Sp, T, Sp, T, Cz; 1968 v Cz, Pol; (Drogheda), 1970 v S
Meehan, P. (1) (Drumcondra), 1934 v Neth
Monahan, P. (2) (Sligo R), 1935 v Swz, G
Mooney, J. (2) (Shamrock R), 1965 v Pol, Bel
Moore, P. (9) (Shamrock R), 1931 v Sp; 1932 v Neth; (Aberdeen), 1934 v Bel, Neth; 1935 v H, G, (Shamrock R), 1936 v Neth; 1937 v G, H
Moran, K. (38) (Manchester U), 1980 v Swz, Arg; 1981 v Bel, F, Cyp, W, Bel, Cz, Pol; 1982 v F, Alg; 1983 v Ic; 1984 v Ic, Neth, Ma, Is; 1985 v Mex; 1986 v Den, Ic, Cz; 1987 v Bel, Bel, S, S, Pol, Bul, Bra, Lux; 1988 v Lux, Bul, Is, Rum, Y, Pol, Nor, E, USSR, Neth
Moroney, T. (12) (West Ham U), 1948 v Sp; 1949 v P, Swe, Sp; 1950 v Fin, E, Fin, Bel; 1951 v Nor, Nor; 1952 v FRG; 1954 v F
Morris, C. (8) (Celtic), 1988 v Is, Rum, Y, Pol, Nor, E, USSR, Neth
Moulson, C. (5) (Lincoln C), 1936 v H, Lux; (Notts Co), 1937 v H, Swz, F
Moulson, G. B. (3) (Lincoln C), 1948 v P, Sp; 1949 v Sw
Mucklan, C. (1) (Drogheda U), 1978 v Pol
Muldoon, T. (1) (Aston Villa), 1927 v I
Mulligan, P. M. (51) (Shamrock R), 1969 v Cz, Den, H; 1970 v S, Cz, Den; (Chelsea), 1970 v H, Pol, FRG; 1971 v Pol, Swe, I; 1972 v A, Ir, Ec, Ch, P; (Crystal Palace), 1973 v F, USSR, Pol, F, Nor; 1974 v Pol, Bra, U, Ch; 1975 v USSR, T, Swz, USSR, Swz; (WBA), 1976 v T, Pol; 1977 v E, T, F, F, Pol, Bul; 1978 v Bul, Nor, Den; 1979 v E, Den, Bul, FRG, Arg; (Shamrock R), 1980 v W, Cz, Bul, USA
Munroe, L. (1) (Shamrock R), 1954 v Lux
Murphy, A. (1) (Clyde), 1956 v Y
Murphy, B. (1) (Bohemians), 1986 v U
Murphy, J. (3) (Crystal Palace), 1980 v W, USA, Cyp
Murray, T. (1) (Dundalk), 1950 v Bel

Newman, W. (1) (Shelbourne), 1969 v Den
Nolan, R. (10) (Shamrock R), 1957 v Den, FRG, E;

1958 v Pol; 1960 v Ch, FRG, Swe; 1962 v Cz, Cz; 1963 v Ic

O'Brien, F. (4) (Philadelphia F), 1980 v Cz, E, Cyp, Arg
O'Brien, L. (6) (Shamrock R), 1986 v U; (Manchester U), 1987 v Bra; 1988 v Is, Rum, Y, Pol
O'Brien, M. T. (4) (Derby Co), 1927 v I; (Walsall), 1929 v Bel, (Norwich C), 1930 v Bel; (Watford), 1932 v Neth
O'Brien, R. (4) (Notts Co), 1976 v Nor, Pol; 1977 v Sp, Pol
O'Byrne, L. B. (1) (Shamrock R), 1949 v Bel
O'Callaghan, B. R. (7) (Stoke C), 1979 v FRG, Arg; 1980 v W, USA; 1981 v W; 1982 v Bra, TT
O'Callaghan, K. (20) (Ipswich T), 1981 v Cz, Pol; 1982 v Alg, Ch, Bra, TT; 1983 v Sp, Ic, Ma, Sp; 1984 v Ic, Neth, Ma; 1985 v Mex, Nor, Den, E; (Portsmouth), 1986 v Swz, USSR; 1987 v Bra
O'Connell, A. (2) (Dundalk), 1967 v Sp; (Bohemians), 1971 v Pol
O'Connor, T. (4) (Shamrock R), 1950 v Fin, E, Fin, Swe
O'Connor, T. (7) (Fulham), 1968 v Cz; (Dundalk), 1972 v A, Ir, Ec, Ch; (Bohemians), 1973 v F, Pol
O'Driscoll, J. F. (3) (Swansea T), 1949 v Swz, Bel, Swe
O'Driscoll, S. (3) (Fulham), 1982 v Ch, Bra, TT
O'Farrell, F. (9) (West Ham U), 1952 v A; 1953 v A; 1954 v F; 1955 v Neth, Nor; 1956 v Y, Neth; (Preston NE), 1958 v Den; 1959 v Cz
O'Flanagan, K. P. (10) (Bohemians), 1938 v Nor, Cz, Pol, Pol, H, H, G; (Arsenal), 1947 v E, Sp, P
O'Flanagan, M. (1) (Bohemians), 1947 v E
O'Hanlon, K. G. (1) (Rotherham U), 1988 v Is
O'Kane, P. (3) (Bohemians), 1935 v H, Swz, G
O'Keefe, E. (5) (Everton), 1981 v W; (Port Vale), 1984 v Chn; 1985 v Mex, USSR, E
O'Keefe, T. (3) (Cork), 1934 v Bel; (Waterford), 1938 v Cz, Pol
O'Leary, D. (40) (Arsenal), 1977 v E, F, F, Sp, Bul; 1978 v Bul, Nor, Den; 1979 v E, Bul, FRG, Arg; 1980 v W, Bul, NI, E, Cyp; 1981 v Neth, Cz, Pol; 1982 v Neth, F; 1983 v Neth, Ic, Sp; 1984 v Pol, Is, Chn; 1985 v USSR, Nor, Den, Is, E, Nor, Sp, Swz; 1986 v Swz, USSR, Den, W
O'Leary, P. (7) (Shamrock R), 1980 v Bul, USA, NI, E, Cz, Arg; 1981 v Neth
O'Mahoney, M. T. (6) (Bristol R), 1938 v Cz, Pol; 1939 v Swz, Pol, H. G
O'Neill, F. S. (20) (Shamrock R), 1962 v Cz, Cz; 1965 v Pol, Bel, Sp; 1966 v Sp, Sp, FRG, A; 1967 v Sp, T, Sp, T; 1969 v Pol, A, Den, Cz Den, H; 1972 v A
O'Neill, J. (17) (Everton), 1952 v Sp; 1953 v F, A; 1954 v F, Lux, F; 1955 v Nor, Neth; Nor, FRG; 1956 v Y, Sp; 1957 v Den; 1958 v Pol; 1959 v Pol, Cz, Cz
O'Neill, J. (1) (Preston NE), 1961 v W
O'Neill, W. (11) (Dundalk), 1936 v Neth, Swz, H, Lux; 1937 v G, H, Swz, F; 1938 v Nor; 1939 v H, G
O'Regan, K. (4) (Brighton & HA), 1984 v Ma, Pol; 1985 v Mex, Sp
O'Reilly, J. (20) (Brideville), 1932 v Neth; (Aberdeen), 1934 v Bel, Neth; (Brideville), 1936 v Neth, Swz, H, Lux; (St. James's Gate), 1937 v G, H, Swz, F; 1938 v Nor, Nor, Cz, Pol; 1939 v Swz, Pol, H, H, G

O'Reilly, J. (2) (Cork U), 1946 v P, Sp

Peyton, G. (25) (Fulham), 1977 v Sp; 1978 v Bul, T, Pol; 1979 v Den, Bul, FRG, Arg; 1980 v W, Cz, Bul, E, Cyp, Swz, Arg; 1981 v Neth; Bel, F, Cyp; 1982 v TT; 1985 v Mex; 1986 v W, Cz; (Bournemouth), 1988 v Lux, Pol

Peyton, N. (6) (Shamrock R), 1957 v FRG; (Leeds U), 1960 v FRG, Swe; 1961 v W; 1963 v Ic, S

Quinn, N. J. (9) (Arsenal), 1986 v Ic, Cz; 1987 v Bul; 1988 v Lux, Bul, Is, Rum, Pol, E

Reid, C. (1) (Brideville), 1931 v Sp
Richardson, D. J. (3) (Shamrock R), 1972 v A; (Gilling-ham), 1973 v Nor; 1980 v Cz
Rigby, A. (3) (St James' Gate), 1935 v H, Swz, G
Ringstead, A. (20) (Sheffield U), 1951 v Arg, Nor; 1952 v FRG, FRG, A, Sp; 1953 v A; 1954 v F; 1955 v Nor; 1956 v Y, Sp, Neth; 1957 v E, E; 1958 v Den, Pol, A; 1959 v Pol, Cz, Cz
Robinson, J. (2) (Bohemians), 1928 v Bel; (Dolphin), 1931 v Sp
Robinson, M. (23) (Brighton & HA), 1981 v F, Cyp, Bel, Pol; 1982 v Neth, F, Alg, Ch; 1983 v Neth, Sp, Ic, Ma; (Liverpool), 1984 v Ic, Neth, Is; 1985 v USSR, Nor, (QPR), Nor, Sp, Swz; 1986 v Den, W, Cz
Roche, P. J. (7) (Shelbourne), 1972 v A, (Manchester U), 1975 v USSR, T, Swz, USSR, Swz; 1976 v T
Rogers, E. (19) (Blackburn R), 1968 v Cz, Pol; 1969 v Pol, A, Den, Cz, Den, H; 1970 v S, Den, H; 1971 v I, I, A; (Charlton Ath), 1972 v Ir, Ec, Ch, P; 1973 v USSR
Ryan, G. (16) (Derby Co), 1978 v T; (Brighton & HA) 1979 v E, FRG; 1980 v W, Cyp, Swz, Arg; 1981 v F, Pol; 1982 v Neth, Alg, Ch, TT; 1984 v Pol, Chn; 1985 v Mex
Ryan, R. A. (16) (WBA), 1950 v Swe, Bel; 1951 v Nor, Arg, Nor; 1952 v FRG, FRG, A, Sp; 1953 v F, A; 1954 v F, Lux, F; 1955 v Nor; (Derby Co), 1956 v Sp

Saward, P. (18) (Millwall), 1954 v Lux; (Aston Villa), 1957 v E, E; 1958 v Den, Pol, A; 1959 v Pol, Cz; 1960 v Swe, Ch, FRG, Swe; 1961 v W, Nor; (Huddersfield T), 1961 v S; 1962 v A; 1963 v Ic, Ic
Scannell, T. (1) (Southend U), 1954 v Lux
Sheedy, K. (16) (Everton), 1984 v Neth, Ma; 1985 v Den, I, Is, Swz; 1986 v Swz, Den; 1987 v S, Pol; 1988 v Is, Rum, Pol, E, USSR, Neth
Sheridan, J. J. (4) (Leeds U), 1988 v Rum, Y, Pol, Nor
Sloan, J. W. (2) (Arsenal), 1946 v P, Sp
Smyth, M. (1) (Shamrock R), 1969 v Pol
Squires, J. (1) (Shelbourne), 1934 v Neth
Stapleton, F. (66) (Arsenal), 1977 v T, F, Sp, Bul; 1978 v Bul, Nor, Den; 1979 v NI, E, Den, FRG, Arg; 1980 v W, Bul, NI, E, Cyp; 1981 v Neth, Bel, F, Cyp, Bel, Cz, Pol; (Manchester U), 1982 v Neth, F, Alg; 1983 v Neth, Sp, Ic, Ma, Sp; 1984 v Ic, Neth, Ma, Pol, Is, Chn; 1985 v Nor, Den, I, Is, E, Nor, Swz; 1986 v Swz, USSR, Den, U, Ic, Cz; 1987 v Bel, Bel, S, S, Pol, Bul, Lux; (Ajax), 1988 v Lux, Bul, (Derby Co), Rum, Y, Nor, E, USSR, Neth

Stevenson, A. E. (7), (Dolphin), 1932 v Neth; (Everton), 1947 v E, Sp, P; 1948 v P, Sp; 1949 v Swz
Strahan, F. (5) (Shelbourne), 1964 v Pol, Nor, E; 1965 v Pol; 1966 v FRG
Sullivan, J. (1) (Fordsons), 1928 v Bel
Swan, M. M. G. (1) (Drumcondra), 1960 v Swe
Synnott, N. (3) (Shamrock R), 1978 v T, Pol; 1979 v NI

Thomas, P. (2) (Waterford), 1974 v Pol, Bra
Traynor, T. J. (8) (Southampton), 1954 v Lux; 1962 v A; 1963 v Ic, Ic, S; 1964 v A, A, Sp
Treacy, R. C. P. (42) (WBA), 1966 v FRG; 1967 v Sp, Cz; 1968 v Cz; (Charlton Ath), 1968 v Pol; 1969 v Pol, Cz, Den; 1970 v S, Den, H, Pol, FRG; 1971 v Pol, Swe, Swe, I, A; (Swindon T), 1972 v Ir, Ec, Ch, P; 1973 v USSR, F, USSR, Pol, F, Nor; 1974 v Pol; (Preston NE), 1974 v Bra; 1975 v USSR; Swz, Swz; 1976 v T, Nor, Pol; (WBA), 1977 v F, Pol; 1978 (Shamrock R), v T, Pol, Pol; 1980 v Cz
Tuohy, L. (8) (Shamrock R), 1956 v Y; 1959 v Cz, Cz; (Newcastle U), 1962 v A, 1963 v Ic, Ic; (Shamrock R), 1964 v A; 1965 v Bel
Turner, A. (2) (Celtic), 1963 v S; 1964 v Sp
Turner, C. J. (10) (Southend U), 1936 v Swz; 1937 v G, H, Swz, F; (West Ham U), 1938 v Nor, Nor, Cz, Pol; 1939 v H

Vernon, J. (2) (Belfast Celtic), 1946 v P, Sp

Waddock, G. (18) (QPR), 1980 v Swz, Arg; 1981 v W, Pol; 1982 v Alg; 1983 v Ic, Ma, Sp, Neth; 1984 v Ic, Neth, Is; 1985 v I, Is, E, Nor, Sp; 1986 v USSR
Walsh, D. J. (20) (WBA), 1956 v P, Sp; 1947 v Sp, P; 1948 v P, Sp; 1949 v Swz, P, Swe, Sp; 1950 v E, Fin, Swe; 1951 v Nor; (Aston Villa), v Arg, Nor; 1952 v Sp; 1953 v A; 1954 v F, F
Walsh, J. (1) (Limerick), 1982 v TT
Walsh, M. (22) (Blackpool), 1976 v Nor, Pol; 1977 v F, Pol; (Everton), 1979 v NI; (QPR), Den, Bul, FRG, Arg; (Porto), 1981 v Bel, Cz; 1982 v Alg; 1983 v Sp, Neth, Sp; 1984 v Ic, Ma, Pol, Chn; 1985 v USSR, Nor, Den
Walsh, M. (5) (Everton), 1982 v Ch, Bra, TT; 1983 v Sp (Norwich C), Ic
Walsh, W. (9) (Manchester C), 1947 v E, Sp, P; 1948 v P, Sp; 1949 v Bel; 1950 v E, Swe, Bel
Waters, J. (2) (Grimsby T), 1977 v T; 1980 v NI
Watters, F. (1) (Shelbourne), 1926 v I
Weir, E. (3) (Clyde), 1939 v H, H, G
Whelan, R. (29) (Liverpool), 1981 v Cz; 1982 v Neth, F; 1983 v Ic, Ma, Sp; 1984 v Is; 1985 v USSR, Nor, I, Is, E, Nor, Swz; 1986 v USSR, W; 1987 v Bel, S, Bul, Bel, Bra, Lux; 1988 v Lux, Bul, Pol, Nor, E, USSR, Neth
Whelan, W. (4) (Manchester U), 1956 v Neth; 1957 v Den, E, E
White, J. J. (1) (Bohemians), 1928 v Bel
Whittaker, R. (1) (Chelsea), 1959 v Cz
Williams, J. (1) (Shamrock R), 1938 v N

BRITISH INTERNATIONAL GOALSCORERS

Note: Four of Scotland's goalscorers in their 10–2 win v Ireland in 1888 and one of their goalscorers v Wales in their 9–0 win in 1878 are unknown. Only goals scored in recognised full internationals have been counted. Data compiled to 30.6.1988.

ENGLAND

A'Court, A.	1	Brown, J.	3	Freeman, B. C.	3
Adams, T. A.	3	Brown, W.	1	Froggatt, J.	2
Adcock, H.	1	Buchan, C. M.	4	Froggatt, R.	2
Alcock, C. W.	1	Bullock, N.	2	Galley, T.	1
Allen, A.	3	Burgess, H.	4	Geary, F.	3
Allen, R.	2	Butcher, T.	3	Gibbins, W. V. T.	3
Anderson, V.	2	Byrne, J. J.	8	Gilliatt, W. E.	3
Astall, G.	1	Camsell, G. H.	18	Goddard, P.	1
Athersmith, W. C.	3	Carter, H. S.	7	Goodall, J.	12
Atyeo, P. J. W.	5	Carter, J. H.	4	Goodyer, A. C.	1
Bache, J. W.	4	Chadwick, E.	3	Gosling, R. C.	2
Bailey, N. C.	2	Chamberlain, M.	1	Goulden, L. A.	4
Baily, E. F.	5	Chambers, H.	6	Grainger, C.	3
Baker, J. H.	4	Channon, M. R.	21	Greaves, J.	44
Ball, A. J.	8	Charlton, J.	6	Grosvenor, A. T.	2
Bambridge, A. L.	1	Charlton, R.	49	Gunn, W.	1
Bambridge, E. C.	12	Chenery, C. J.	1	Haines, J. T. W.	2
Barclay, R.	2	Chivers, M.	13	Hall, G. W.	9
Barnes, J. C. B.	6	Clarke, A. J.	10	Halse, H. J.	2
Barnes, P. S.	4	Cobbold, W. N.	7	Hampson, J.	5
Barton, J.	1	Cock, J. G.	2	Hampton, H.	2
Bassett, W. I.	7	Common, A.	2	Hancocks, J.	2
Bastin, C. S.	12	Connelly, J. M.	7	Hardman, H. P.	1
Beardsley, P. A.	5	Coppell, S. J.	7	Harris, S. S.	2
Beasley, A.	1	Cotterill, G. H.	2	Hassall, H. W.	4
Beattie, T. K.	1	Cowans, G.	2	Hateley, M.	9
Becton, F.	2	Crawford, R.	1	Haynes, J. N.	17
Bedford, H.	1	Crawshaw, T. H.	1	Hegan, K. E.	4
Bell, C.	9	Crayston, W. J.	1	Henfrey, A. G.	2
Bentley, R. T. F.	9	Creek, F. N. S.	1	Hilsdon, G. R.	14
Bishop, S. M.	1	Crooks, S. D.	7	Hine, E. W.	4
Blackburn, F.	1	Currey, E. S.	2	Hinton, A. T.	1
Blissett, L.	3	Currie, A. W.	3	Hitchens, G. A.	5
Bloomer, S.	28	Cursham, A. W.	2	Hobbis, H. H. F.	1
Bond, R.	2	Cursham, H. A.	5	Hoddle, G.	8
Bonsor, A. G.	1	Daft, H. B.	3	Hodgetts, D.	1
Bowden, E. R.	1	Davenport, J. K.	2	Hodgson, G.	1
Bowers, J. W.	2	Davis, G.	1	Holley, G. H.	8
Bowles, S.	1	Davis, H.	1	Houghton, W. E.	5
Bradford, G. R. W.	1	Day, S. H.	2	Howell, R.	1
Bradford, J.	7	Dean, W. R.	18	Hughes, E. W.	1
Bradley, W.	2	Devey, J. H. G.	1	Hulme, J. H. A.	4
Bradshaw, F.	3	Dewhurst, F.	11	Hunt, G. S.	1
Bridges, B. J.	1	Dix, W. R.	1	Hunt, R.	18
Bridgett, A.	3	Dixon, K. M.	4	Hunter, N.	2
Brindle, T.	1	Douglas, B.	11	Hurst, G. C.	24
Britton, C. S.	1	Drake, E. J.	6	Jack, D. N. B.	3
Broadbent, P. F.	2	Ducat, A.	1	Johnson, D. E.	5
Broadis, I. A.	8	Dunn, A. T. B.	2	Johnson, E.	2
Brodie, J. B.	1	Eastham, G.	2	Johnson, J. A.	2
Bromley-Davenport, W. E.	2	Edwards, D.	5	Johnson, T. C. F.	5
Brook, E. F.	10	Elliott, W. H.	3	Johnson, W. H.	1
Brooking, T. D.	5	Evans, R. E.	1	Kail, E. I. L.	2
Brooks, J.	2	Finney, T.	30	Kay, A. H.	1
Broome, F. H.	3	Fleming, H. J.	9	Keegan, J. K.	21
Browne, A.	5	Flowers, R.	10	Kelly, R.	8
Brown, A. S.	1	Forman, Frank	1	Kennedy, R.	3
Brown, G.	5	Forman, Fred	3	Kenyon–Slaney, W. S.	2
		Foster, R. E.	3	Kevan, D. T.	8
		Francis, G. C. J.	3	Kidd, B.	1
		Francis, T	12	Kingsford, R. K.	1

BRITISH INTERNATIONAL GOALSCORERS

Kirchen, A. J.	2
Kirton, W. J.	1
Langton, R.	1
Latchford, R. D.	5
Latheron, E. G.	1
Lawler, C.	1
Lawton, T.	22
Lee, F.	10
Lee, J.	1
Lee, S.	2
Lindley, T.	15
Lineker, G.	26
Lofthouse, J. M.	3
Lofthouse, N.	30
Hon. A. Lyttleton	1
McCall, J.	1
McDermott, T.	3
Mabbutt, G. V.	1
Macdonald, M.	6
Mannion, W. J.	11
Mariner, P.	14
Marsh, R. W.	1
Matthews, S.	11
Matthews, V.	1
Medley, L. D.	1
Melia, J.	1
Mercer, D. W.	1
Milburn, J. E. T.	9
Miller, H. S.	1
Mills, G. R.	3
Milward, A.	3
Mitchell, C.	5
Moore, J.	1
Moore, R. F.	2
Moore, W. G. B.	2
Morren, T.	1
Morris, F.	1
Morris, J.	3
Mortensen, S. H.	24
Morton, J. R.	1
Mosforth, W.	3
Mullen, J.	6
Mullery, A. P.	1
Neal, P. G.	5
Needham, E.	3
Nicholls, J.	1
Nicholson, W. E.	1
O'Grady, M.	3
Osborne, F. R.	3
Own goals by opponents	20
Page, L. A.	1
Paine, T. L.	7
Parry, E. H.	1
Parry, R. A.	1
Pawson, F. W.	1
Payne, J.	2
Peacock, A.	3
Pearson, J. S.	5
Pearson, S. C.	5
Perry, W.	2
Peters, M.	20
Pickering, F.	5
Pointer, R.	2
Quantrill, A.	1

Ramsey, A. E.	3
Revie, D. G.	4
Reynolds, J.	3
Richardson, J. R.	2
Rigby, A.	3
Rimmer, E. J.	2
Roberts, H.	1
Roberts, W. T.	4
Robinson, J.	3
Robson, B.	22
Robson, R.	4
Rowley, J. F.	6
Royle, J.	2
Rutherford, J.	3
Sagar, C.	1
Sandilands, R. R.	2
Sansom, K.	1
Schofield, J.	1
Seed, J. M.	1
Settle, J.	6
Sewell, J.	3
Shackleton, L. F.	1
Sharp, J.	1
Shepherd, J.	2
Simpson, J.	1
Smith, G. O.	12
Smith, Joe	1
Smith, J. R.	2
Smith, J. W.	4
Smith, R.	13
Smith, S.	1
Sorby, T. H.	1
Southworth, J.	3
Sparks, F. J.	3
Spence, J. W.	1
Spiksley, F.	5
Spilsbury, B. W.	5
Steele, F. C.	8
Stephenson, G. T.	2
Steven, T. M.	3
Stewart, J.	2
Stiles, N. P.	1
Storer, H.	1
Summerbee, M. G.	1
Tambling, R. V.	1
Taylor, P. J.	2
Taylor, T.	16
Thompson, P. B.	1
Thornewell, G.	1
Tilson, F. S.	6
Townley, W. J.	2
Tueart, D.	2
Vaughton, O. H.	6
Veitch, J. G.	1
Viollet, D. S.	1
Waddle, C. R.	4
Walker, W. H.	9
Wall, G.	2
Wallace, D.	1
Walsh, P.	1
Waring, T.	4
Warren, B.	2
Watson, D. V.	4
Watson, V. M.	4
Webb, G. W.	1
Webb, N. J.	1

Wedlock, W. J.	2
Weir, D.	2
Weller, K.	1
Welsh, D.	1
Whateley, O.	2
Wheldon, G. F.	6
Whitfield, H.	1
Wignall, F.	2
Wilkes, A.	1
Wilkins, R. G.	3
Willingham, C. K.	1
Wilshaw, D. J.	10
Wilson, G. P.	1
Winckworth, W. N.	1
Windridge, J. E.	7
Withe, P.	1
Wollaston, C. H. R.	1
Wood, H.	1
Woodcock, T.	16
Woodhall, G.	1
Woodward, V. J.	29
Worrall, F.	2
Worthington, F. S.	2
Wright, W. A.	3
Wylie, J. G.	1
Yates, J.	3

NORTHERN IRELAND

(Includes All-Ireland teams prior to 1921).

Anderson, T.	4
Armstrong, G.	12
Bambrick, J.	12
Barr, H. H.	1
Barron, H.	3
Best, G.	9
Bingham, W. L.	10
Blanchflower, D.	2
Blanchflower, J.	1
Brennan, B.	1
Brennan, R. A.	1
Brotherston, N.	3
Brown, G. C. P.	1
Browne, F.	2
Campbell, J.	1
Campbell, W. G.	1
Casey, T.	2
Caskey, W.	1
Cassidy, T.	1
Chambers, J.	3
Clarke, C. J.	6
Clements, D.	2
Cochrane, T.	1
Condy, J.	1
Connor, M. J.	1
Coulter, J.	1
Croft, T.	1
Crone, W.	1
Crossan, E.	1
Crossan, J. A.	10
Curran, S.	2
Cush, W. W.	5
Dalton, W.	6
D'Arcy, S. D.	1

Darling, J.	1	McMordie, A. S.	3	Aitkenhead, W. A. C.	2
Davey, H. H.	1	McMorran, E. J.	4	Alexander, D.	1
Davis, T. L.	1	McParland, P. J.	10	Allan, D. S.	4
Dill, A. H.	1	McWha, W. B. R.	1	Allan, J.	2
Doherty, L.	1	Mahood, J.	2	Anderson, F.	1
Doherty, P. D.	3	Martin, D. K.	3	Anderson, W.	4
Dougan, A. D.	8	Maxwell, J.	2	Andrews, P.	1
Dunne, J.	4	Meldon, J.	1	Archibald, A.	1
Elder, A. R.	1	Mercer, J. T.	1	Archibald, S.	4
Emerson, W.	1	Millar, W.	1	Baird, D.	2
English, S.	1	Milligan, D.	1	Baird, J. C.	2
Ferguson, W.	1	Milne, R. G.	2	Baird, S.	2
Ferris, J.	1	Molyneux, T. B.	1	Bannon, E.	1
Ferris, R. O.	1	Moreland, V.	1	Barbour, A.	1
Finney, T.	2	Morgan, S.	3	Barker, J. B.	4
Gaffikin, J.	5	Morrow, W. J.	1	Battles, B. Jr	1
Gara, A.	3	Murphy, N.	1	Bauld, W.	2
Gawkrodger, G.	1	Neill, W. J. T.	2	Baxter, J. C.	3
Gibb, J. T.	2	Nelson, S.	1	Bell, J.	5
Gibb, T. J.	1	Nicholl, C. J.	3	Bennett, A.	2
Gibson, W. K.	1	Nicholl, J. M.	1	Berry, D.	1
Gillespie, W.	12	Nicholson, J. J.	6	Bett, J.	1
Goodall, A. L.	2	O'Hagan, C.	2	Beveridge, W. W.	1
Halligan, W.	1	O'Kane, W. J.	1	Black, A.	3
Hamill, M.	1	O'Neill, J.	1	Black, D.	1
Hamilton, B.	4	O'Neill, M. H.	9	Bone, J.	1
Hamilton, W.	5	Own goals by opponents	5	Boyd, R.	2
Hannon, D. J.	1	Peacock, R.	2	Boyd, W. G.	1
Harkin, J. T.	2	Peden, J.	7	Brackenridge, T.	1
Harvey, M.	3	Penney, S. A.	2	Brand, R.	8
Humphries, W.	1	Pyper, James	2	Brazil, A.	1
Hunter, A. (Belfast C)	1	Pyper, John	1	Bremner, W. J.	3
Hunter, A. (Ipswich T)	1	Quinn, J. M.	5	Brown, A. D.	6
Irvine, R. W.	3	Reynolds, J.	1	Buchanan, P. S.	1
Irvine, W. J.	8	Rowley, R. W. M.	2	Buchanan, R.	1
Johnston, H.	2	Sheridan, J.	2	Buckley, P.	1
Johnston, S.	2	Sherrard, J.	3	Buick, A.	2
Johnston, W. C.	1	Simpson, W. J.	5	Burns, K.	1
Jones, S.	1	Sloan, H. A. de B.	4	Cairns, T.	1
Jones, J.	1	Smyth, S.	5	Calderwood, R.	2
Kelly, J.	4	Spence, D. W.	3	Caldow, E.	4
Kernaghan, N.	2	Stanfield, O. M.	9	Campbell, C.	1
Kirwan, J.	2	Stevenson, A. E.	5	Campbell, H.	2
Lacey, W.	3	Stewart, I.	2	Campbell, J. (South Western)	1
Lemon, J.	2	Thompson, F. W.	2	Campbell, John (Celtic)	7
Lockhart, N.	3	Tully, C. P.	3	Campbell, P.	2
McAdams, W. J.	7	Turner, E.	1	Campbell, R.	1
McAllen, J.	1	Walker, J.	1	Cassidy, J.	1
McAuley, J. L.	1	Walsh, D. J.	5	Chalmers, S.	3
McCandless, J.	3	Welsh, E.	1	Chambers, T.	1
McCaw, J. H.	1	Whiteside, N.	8	Cheyne, A. G.	4
McClelland, J.	1	Whiteside, T.	1	Christie, A. J.	1
McCluggage, A.	2	Williams, J. R.	1	Clunas, W. L.	1
McCracken, W.	1	Williamson, J.	1	Collins, J.	1
McCrory, S.	1	Wilson, D.	1	Collins, R. Y.	10
McCurdy, C.	1	Wilson, S. J.	7	Combe, J. R.	1
McDonald, A.	1	Wilton, J. M.	2	Conn, A.	1
McGarry, J. K.	1	Young, S.	2	Cooper, D.	6
McGrath, R. C.	4			Craig, J.	1
McIlroy, J.	10	**SCOTLAND**		Craig, T.	1
McIlroy, S. B.	5			Cunningham, A. N.	5
McKnight, J.	2	Aitken, R.	2	Curran, H. P.	1
McLaughlin, J. C.	6			Dalglish, K.	30
				Davidson, D.	1
				Davidson, J. A.	1
				Delaney, J.	3

BRITISH INTERNATIONAL GOALSCORERS

Devine, A.	1	Howie, J.	2	McLean, A.	1
Dewar, G.	1	Hughes, J.	1	McLean, T.	1
Dewar, N.	4	Hunter, W.	1	McLintock, F.	1
Dickson, W.	1	Hutchison, T.	1	McMahon, A.	6
Divers, J.	1	Hutton J.	1	McMenemy, J.	5
Docherty, T. H.	1	Hyslop, T.	1	McMillan, I. L.	2
Dodds, D.	1	Imrie, W. N.	1	McNeil, H.	5
Donaldson, A.				McNeill, W.	3
Donnachie, J.	1	Jackson, A,	8	McPhail, J.	3
Dougall, J.	1	Jackson, C.	1	McPhail, R.	7
Drummond, J.	2	James. A. W.	3	McPherson, J.	8
Dunbar, M.	1	Jardine, A.	1	McPherson, R.	1
Duncan, D.	7	Jenkinson, T.	1	McQueen, G.	5
Duncan, D. M.	1	Johnston, L. H.	1	McStay, P.	5
Duncan, J.	1	Johnston, M.	6	Macari, L.	5
Dunn, J.	2	Johnstone, D.	2	MacDougall, E. J.	3
Easson, J. F.	1	Johnstone, J.	4	Mackay, D. C.	4
Ellis, J.	1	Johnstone, Jas.	1	MacKay, G.	1
Ferguson, J.	6	Johnstone, R.	9	MacKenzie, J. A.	1
Fernie, W.	1	Johnstone, W.	1	Madden, J.	5
Fitchie, T. T.	1	Jordan, J.	11	Marshall, H.	1
Flavell, R.	2	Kay, J. L.	5	Marshall, J.	1
Fleming, C.	2	Kaillor, A.	3	Mason, J.	4
Fleming, J. W.	3	Kelly, J.	1	Massie, A.	1
Fraser, M. J. E.	4	Kelso, R.	1	Masson, D. S.	5
Gallacher, H. K.	23	Ker, G.	10	Meiklejohn, D. D.	3
Gallacher, P.	1	King, A.	1	Millar, J.	2
Galt, J. H.	1	King, J.	1	Miller, T.	2
Gemmell, T. (St Mirren)	1	Kinnear, D.	1	Miller, W.	1
Gemmell, T. (Celtic)	1	Lambie, W. A.	5	Mitchell, R. C.	1
Gemmill, A.	8	Lang, J. J.	1	Morgan, W.	1
Gibb, W.	1	Law, D.	30	Morris, D.	1
Gibson, D. W.	3	Leggat, G.	8	Morris, H.	3
Gibson, J. D.	2	Lennie, W.	1	Morton, A. L.	5
Gibson, N.	1	Lennox, R.	3	Mudie, J. K.	9
Gillespie, Jas.	3	Liddell, W.	6	Mulhall, G.	1
Gillick, T.	3	Lindsay, J.	6	M'unro, A. D.	1
Gilzean, A. J.	10	Linwood, A. B.	1	Munro, N.	1
Gossland, J.	2	Logan, J.	1	Murdoch, R.	5
Goudie, J.	1	Lorimer, P.	4	Murphy, F.	1
Gough, C. R.	3	Love, A.	1	Murray, J.	1
Gourlay, J.	1	Lowe, J. (Cambuslang)	1	Napier, C. E.	3
Graham, A.	2	Lowe, J. (St Bernards)	1	Narey, D.	1
Graham, G.	3	McAdams, J.	3	Neil, R. G.	2
Gray, A.	7	McAulay, J.	1	Nicholas, C.	5
Gray, E.	3	McAvennie, F.	1	Nisbet, J.	2
Gray, F.	1	McCall, J.	1	O'Donnell, F.	2
Greig, J.	5	McCalliog, J.	1	O'Hare, J.	5
Groves, W.	4	McCallum, N.	1	Ormond, W. E.	1
Hamilton, G.	4	McCoist, A.	3	O'Rourke, F.	1
Hamilton, J.	3	McColl, R. S.	13	Orr, R.	1
Hamilton, R. C.	14	McCulloch, D.	3	Orr, T.	1
Harper, J. M.	2	McDougall, J.	4	Oswald, J.	4
Harrower, W.	5	McFarlane, A.	1	Own goals by opponents	14
Hartford, R. A.	4	McFayden, W.	2	Parlane, D.	1
Heggie, C.	5	McGhee, M.	2	Paul, H. McD.	2
Henderson, J. G.	1	McGregor, J. C.	1	Paul, W.	6
Henderson, W.	5	McGrory, J.	6	Pettigrew, W.	2
Herd, D. G.	4	McGuire, W.	1	Provan, D.	1
Hewie, J. D.	2	McInnes, T.	2	Quinn, J.	7
Higgins, A. (Newcastle U)	1	McKie, J.	2	Quinn, P.	1
Higgins, A. (Kilmarnock)	4	McKinnon, A.	1	Rankin, G.	2
Highet, T. C.	1	McKinnon, R.	1	Rankin, R.	2
Holton, J. A.	2	McKinnon, W. W.	5	Reid, W.	4
Houliston, W.	2	McLaren, A.	4	Reilly, L.	22
Howie, H.	1	McLaren, J.	1		

Renny-Tailyour, H. W.	1	
Ric)hmond, J. T.	1	
Ring, T.	2	
Rioch, B. D.	6	
Ritchie, J.	1	
Robertson, A.	2	
Robertson, J.	8	
Robertson, J. T.	2	
Robertson, T.	1	
Robertson, W.	1	
Russell, D.	1	
Scott, A. S.	5	
Sellar, W.	4	
Sharp, G. M.	1	
Shaw, F. W.	1	
Simpson, J.	1	
Smith, A.	5	
Smith, G.	4	
Smith, J.	1	
Smith, John	12	
Somerville, G.	1	
Souness, G. J.	3	
Speedie, F.	2	
St John, I.	9	
Steel, W.	12	
Stein, C.	10	
Stevenson, G.	4	
Stewart, R.	1	
Stewart, W. E.	1	
Strachan, G. D.	4	
Sturrock, P.	3	
Taylor, J. D.	1	
Templeton, R.	1	
Thomson, A.	1	
Thomson, C.	4	
Thomson, R.	1	
Thomson, W.	1	
Thornton, W.	1	
Waddell, T. S.	1	
Waddell, W.	6	
Walker, J.	2	
Walker, R.	7	
Walker, T.	9	
Wallace, I. A.	1	
Wark, J.	7	
Watson, J. A. K.	1	
Watt, F.	2	
Watt, W. W.	1	
Weir, A.	1	
Weir, J. B.	2	
White, J. A.	3	
Wilson, A.	2	
Wilson, A. N.	13	
Wilson, D. (Queen's Park)	2	
Wilson, D. (Rangers)	9	
Wilson, H.	1	
Wylie, T. G.	1	
Young, A.	5	

WALES

Allchurch, I. J.	23
Allen, M.	1
Astley, D. J.	12
Atherton, R. W.	2
Bamford, T,.	1
Barnes, W.	1
Boulter, L. M.	1
Bowdler, J. C. H.	3
Bowen, D. L.	1
Boyle, T.	1
Bryan, T.	1
Burgess, W. A. R.	1
Burke, T.	1
Butler, A.	1
Chapman, T.	2
Charles, J.	1
Charles, M.	6
Charles, W. J.	15
Clarke, R. J.	5
Collier, D. J.	1
Cross, K.	1
Cumner, R. H.	1
Curtis, A.	6
Curtis, E. R.	3
Davies, D. W.	1
Davies, E. Lloyd	1
Davies, G.	2
Davies, L. S.	6
Davies,. R. T.	7
Davies, R. W.	8
Davies, S.	5
Davies, W.	6
Davies, W. H.	1
Davies, William	5
Davies, W. O.	1
Deacy, N.	4
Doughty, J	6
Doughty, R.	2
Durban, A.	2
Dwyer, P.	2
Edwards, G.	2
Edwards, R. J.	4
England, H. M.	3
Evans, I.	1
Evans, J.	1
Evans, R. E.	2
Evans, W.	1
Eyton-Jones, J. A.	1
Flynn, B.	7
Ford, T.	23
Foulkes, W. I.	1
Fowler, J.	3
Giles, D.	2
Glover, E. M.	7
Godfrey, B. C.	2
Green, A. W.	3
Griffiths, A. T.	6
Griffiths, M. W.	2
Griffiths, T. P.	3
Harris, C. S.	1
Hersee, R.	1
Hewitt, R.	1
Hockey, T.	1
Hodges, G. P.	2
Hole, W. J.	1
Hopkins, I. J.	2
Horne, B.	1
Howell, E. G.	3
Hughes, M.	8
James, E.	2
James, L.	10
James, R.	7
Jarrett, R. H.	3
Jenkyns, C. A.	1
Jones, A.	1
Jones, Bryn	6
Jones, B. S.	2
Jones, Cliff	15
Jones, C. W.	1
Jones, D. E.	1
Jones, Evan	1
Jones, H.	1
Jones, I.	1
Jones, J. O.	2
Jones, J. P.	1
Jones, Leslie J.	1
Jones, R. A.	2
Jones, W. L.	6
Keenor, F. C.	2
Kryzwicki, R. L.	1
Leek, K.	5
Lewis, B.	3
Lewis, J.	1
Lewis, W.	11
Lewis, W. L.	2
Lovell, S.	1
Lowrie, G.	2
Mahoney, J. F.	1
Mays, A. W.	1
Medwin, T. C.	6
Meredith, W. H.	11
Mills, T. J.	1
Moore, G.	1
Morgan, J. R.	2
Morgan-Owen, H.	1
Morgan-Owen, M. M.	2
Morris, A. G.	9
Morris, H.	2
Morris, R.	3
Nicholas, P.	2
O'Callaghan, E.	3
O'Sullivan, P. A.	1
Owen, G.	2
Owen, W.	4
Owen, W. P.	6
Own goals by opponents	10
Palmer, D.	3
Parry, T. D.	3
Paul, R.	1
Peake, E.	1
Perry, E.	1
Phillips, C.	5
Phillips, D.	1
Powell, A.	1
Powell, D.	1
Price, J.	4
Price, P.	1
Pryce-Jones, W. E.	3
Pugh, D. H.	2
Reece, G. I.	2
Rees, R. R.	3
Richards, R. W.	1
Roach, J.	2

BRITISH INTERNATIONAL GOALSCORERS

Robbins, W. W.	4	Shaw, E. G.	2	Vernon, T. R.	8
Roberts, J. (Corwen)	1	Sisson, H.	4	Vizard, E. T.	1
Roberts, Jas. (Wrexham)	1	Slatter, N.	2	Walsh, I.	7
Roberts, P. S.	1	Smallman, D. P.	1	Warren, F. W.	3
Roberts, R. (Druids)	1			Watkins, W. M.	4
Roberts, W. (Llangollen)	2	Tapscott, D. R.	4	Wilding, J.	4
Roberts, W. (Wrexham)	1	Thomas, M.	4	Williams, G. E.	2
Roberts, W. H.	1	Thomas, T.	1	Williams, R.	2
Rush, I.	16	Toshack, J. B.	13	Williams, W.	7
Russell, M. R.	1	Trainer, H.	2	Woosnam, A. P.	4
				Wynn, G. A.	1
Sabine, H. W.	1				
Saunders, D.	3	Vaughan, John	2	Yorath, T. C.	2

ENGLAND UNDER-21 INTERNATIONAL RESULTS 1976–88

* = European Under-21 Championship.

v BULGARIA

Date	Venue	E	B
5.6.1979	Pernik	3	1*
20.11.1979	Leicester	5	0*

v DENMARK

Date	Venue	E	D
19.9.1978	Hvidovre	2	1*
11.9.1979	Watford	1	0*
21.9.1982	Hvidovre	4	1*
20.9.1983	Norwich	4	1*
12.3.1986	Copenhagen	1	0*
26.3.1986	Manchester	1	1*

v EAST GERMANY

Date	Venue	E	EG
16.4.1980	Sheffield	1	2*
23.4.1980	Jena	0	1*

v FINLAND

Date	Venue	E	F
26.5.1977	Helsinki	1	0*
12.10.1977	Hull	8	1*
16.10.1984	Southampton	2	0*
21.5.1985	Mikkeli	1	3*

v FRANCE

Date	Venue	E	F
28.2.1984	Sheffield	6	1*
28.3.1984	Rouen	1	0*
11.6.1987	Toulon	0	2
13.4.1988	Besancon	2	4*
27.4.1988	Highbury	2	2*
12.6.1988	Toulon	2	4

v GREECE

Date	Venue	E	G
16.11.1982	Piraeus	0	1*
29.3.1983	Portsmouth	2	1*

v HUNGARY

Date	Venue	E	H
5.6.1981	Keszthely	2	1*
17.11.1981	Nottingham	2	0*
26.4.1983	Newcastle	1	0*
11.10.1983	Nyiregyhaza	2	0*

v ITALY

Date	Venue	E	I
8.3.1978	Manchester	2	1*
5.4.1978	Rome	0	0*
18.4.1984	Manchester	3	1*

2.5.1984	Florence	0	1*
9.4.1986	Pisa	0	2*
23.4.1986	Swindon	1	1*

v ISRAEL

Date	Venue	E	I
27.2.1985	Tel Aviv	2	1

v MEXICO

Date	Venue	E	M
5.6.1988	Toulon	2	1

v MOROCCO

Date	Venue	E	M
7.6.1987	Toulon	2	0
9.6.1988	Toulon	1	0

v NORWAY

Date	Venue	E	N
1.6.1977	Bergen	2	1*
6.9.1977	Brighton	6	0*
9.9.1980	Southampton	3	0
8.9.1981	Drammen	0	0

v POLAND

Date	Venue	E	P
17.3.1982	Warsaw	2	1*
7.4.1982	West Ham	2	2*

v PORTUGAL

Date	Venue	E	P
13.6.1987	Toulon	0	0

v REPUBLIC OF IRELAND

Date	Venue	E	RI
25.2.1981	Liverpool	1	0
25.3.1985	Portsmouth	3	2

v RUMANIA

Date	Venue	E	R
14.10.1980	Ploesti	0	4*
28.4.1981	Swindon	3	0*
30.4.1985	Brasov	0	0*
10.9.1985	Ipswich	3	0*

v SCOTLAND

Date	Venue	E	S
27.4.1977	Sheffield	1	0
12.2.1980	Coventry	2	1*
4.3.1980	Aberdeen	0	0*

19.4.1982	Glasgow	1	0*
28.4.1982	Manchester	1	1*
16.2.1988	Aberdeen	1	0*
22.3.1988	Nottingham	1	0*

v SPAIN

Date	Venue	E	S
17.5.1984	Seville	1	0*
24.5.1984	Sheffield	2	0*
18.2.1987	Burgos	2	1

v SWEDEN

Date	Venue	E	S
9.6.1979	Vasteras	2	1
9.9.1986	Ostersund	1	1

v SWITZERLAND

Date	Venue	E	S
18.11.1980	Ipswich	5	0*
31.5.1981	Neuenburg	0	0*

v TURKEY

Date	Venue	E	T
13.11.1984	Bursa	0	0*
15.10.1985	Bristol	3	0*
28.4.1987	Izmir	0	0*
13.10.1987	Sheffield	1	1*

v USSR

Date	Venue	E	SU
9.6.1987	Toulon	0	0
7.6.1988	Six-Fours	1	0

v WALES

Date	Venue	E	W
15.12.1976	Wolverhampton	0	0
6.2.1979	Swansea	1	0

v WEST GERMANY

Date	Venue	E	WG
21.9.1982	Sheffield	3	1*
12.10.1982	Bremen	2	3*
8.9.1987	Dusseldorf	0	2

v YUGOSLAVIA

Date	Venue	E	Y
19.4.1978	Novi Sad	1	2*
2.5.1978	Manchester	1	1*
11.11.1986	Peterborough	1	1*
10.11.1987	Belgrade	5	1*

UEFA UNDER-21 CHAMPIONSHIPS 1986–88

GROUP 1
Rumania (1)1, Austria (0)0 — Ploesti, 9.9.1986
Austria (0)1, Albania (0)0 — Kapfenberg, 14.10.1986
Spain (0)1, Rumania (0)0 — Cordoba, 12.11.1986
Albania (0)0, Spain (0)0 — Berat, 2.12.1986
Rumania (3)3, Albania (2)2 — Pitesti, 24.3.1987
Austria (1)1, Spain (1)1 — Vienna, 1.4.1987
Albania (0)1, Austria (1)1 — Tirana, 28.4.1987
Rumania (0)0, Spain (0)1 — Bucharest, 29.4.1987
Spain (1)3, Austria (0)0 — Cadiz, 13.10.1987
Albania (1)1, Rumania (1)2 — Berat, 27.10.1987
Austria (0)2, Rumania (1)1 — Stockerau, 17.11.1987
Spain (2)3, Albania (0)0 — Jerez, 18.11.1987

FINAL TABLE	P	W	D	L	F	A	GD	Pts
SPAIN	6	4	2	0	9	1	+8	10
Rumania	6	3	0	3	7	7	0	6
Austria	6	2	2	2	5	7	−2	6
Albania	6	0	2	4	4	10	−6	2

GROUP 2
Sweden (0)0, Switzerland (0)0 — Norrkoping, 23.9.1986
Portugal (1)2, Sweden (0)0 — Lisbon, 11.10.1986
Switzerland (2)3, Portugal (0)1 — Entlebuch, 28.10.1986
Italy (1)1, Switzerland (0)1 — Empoli, 19.11.1986
Portugal (0)1, Italy (0)2 — Lisbon, 11.2.1987
Sweden (1)2, Italy (0)2 — Stockholm, 4.6.1987
Switzerland (0)0, Sweden (0)0 — Basle, 16.6.1987
Sweden (4)4, Portugal (1)2 — Uppsala, 22.9.1987
Switzerland (0)0, Italy (1)3 — Neuchatel, 16.10.1987
Portugal (1)2, Switzerland (0)0 — Oporto, 10.11.1987
Italy (0)0, Sweden (0)0 — Perugia, 12.11.1987
Italy (1)6, Portugal (0)0 — Piacenza, 2.12.1987

FINAL TABLE	P	W	D	L	F	A	GD	Pts
ITALY	6	3	3	0	14	4	+10	9
Sweden	6	1	4	1	6	6	0	6
Switzerland	6	1	3	2	4	7	−3	5
Portugal	6	2	0	4	8	15	−7	4

GROUP 3
Norway (0)0, East Germany (0)0 — Hamar, 23.9.1986
France (1)2, USSR (0)1 — Le Havre, 10.10.1986
USSR (1)1, Norway (0)0 — Simferopol, 28.10.1986
East Germany (0)1, France (0)0 — Halle, 18.11.1986
USSR (1)2, East Germany (0)1 — Kiev, 28.4.1987
Norway (0)0, USSR (1)2 — Trondheim, 2.6.1987
Norway (0)1, France (0)2 — Oslo, 15.6.1987
USSR (0)0, France (1)1 — Moscow, 8.9.1987
East Germany (3)5, USSR (0)1 — Ludwigsfelde, 9.10.1987
France (0)1, Norway (0)1 — Villeneuve d'Ascq, 13.10.1987
East Germany (1)1, Norway (0)1 — Schoenebeck, 27.10.1987
France (1)2, East Germany (0)2 — Besancon, 17.11.1987

FINAL TABLE	P	W	D	L	F	A	GD	Pts
FRANCE	6	3	2	1	8	6	+2	8
East Germany	6	2	3	1	10	6	+4	7
USSR	6	3	0	3	7	9	−2	6
Norway	6	0	3	3	7	7	−4	3

GROUP 4
Yugoslavia (2)3, Turkey (0)0 — Sibenik, 28.10.1986
England (1)1, Yugoslavia (1)1 — Peterborough, 11.11.1986
Turkey (0)0, England (0)0 — Izmir, 28.4.1987
England (0)1, Turkey (1)1 — Sheffield, 13.10.1987
Yugoslavia (1)1, England (3)5 — Belgrade, 10.11.1987
Turkey (2)3, Yugoslavia (1)2 — Izmir, 15.12.1987

FINAL TABLE	P	W	D	L	F	A	GD	Pts
ENGLAND	4	1	3	0	7	3	+4	5
Turkey	4	1	2	1	4	6	−2	4
Yugoslavia	4	1	1	2	7	9	−2	3

GROUP 5
Poland (1)1, Greece (0)0 — Gorzow Wiel, 14.10.1986
Greece (1)2, Hungary (0)0 — Corfu, 11.11.1986
Cyprus (0)0, Greece (3)4 — Nicosia, 2.12.1986
Greece (4)5, Cyprus (0)1 — Rhodes, 13.1.1987
Cyprus (2)2, Hungary (1)1 — Nicosia, 7.2.1987
Poland (0)3, Cyprus (0)0 — Starograd, 11.4.1987
Greece (2)2, Poland (0)0 — Athens, 28.4.1987
Hungary (1)3, Poland (0)0 — Kecskemet, 16.5.1987
Poland (0)0, Hungary (0)1 — Bialystok, 22.9.1987
Hungary (2)2, Greece (2)2 — Budapest, 13.10.1987
Cyprus (0)0, Poland (1)1 — Paphos, 10.11.1987
Hungary (1)4, Cyprus (1)1 — Budapest, 1.12.1987

FINAL TABLE	P	W	D	L	F	A	GD	Pts
GREECE	6	4	1	1	15	5	+10	9
Hungary	6	3	1	2	12	7	+5	7
Poland	6	3	0	3	5	6	−1	6
Cyprus	6	1	0	5	4	18	−14	2

GROUP 6
Finland (1)2, Iceland (0)0 — Kemi, 4.9.1986
Iceland (0)0, Czechoslovakia (1)4 — Akureyri, 25.9.1986
Czechoslovakia (1)2, Finland (0)0 — Oloumouc, 14.10.1986
Denmark (3)4, Finland (1)1 — Slagelse, 28.10.1986
Czechoslovakia (1)1, Denmark (0)1 — Trnava, 11.11.1986
Finland (0)0, Denmark (1)1 — Tampere, 28.4.1987
Denmark (0)0, Czechoslovakia (0)1 — Copenhagen, 2.6.1987
Iceland (0)0, Denmark (0)0 — Akureyri, 24.6.1987
Iceland (2)2, Finland (0)2 — Akureyri, 5.8.1987
Denmark (0)1, Iceland (2)3 — Copenhagen, 26.8.1987
Finland (3)3, Czechoslovakia (1)2 — Pori, 8.9.1987
Czechoslovakia (2)4, Iceland (3)4 — Cheb, 14.10.1987

FINAL TABLE	P	W	D	L	F	A	GD	Pts
CZECHOSLOVAKIA	6	3	2	1	14	8	+6	8
Denmark	6	2	2	2	7	6	+1	6
Finland	6	2	1	3	8	11	−3	5
Iceland	6	1	3	2	9	13	−4	5

GROUP 7
Belgium (0)0, Rep.of Ireland (0)0 — Lokeren, 9.9.1986
Rep. of Ireland (0)1, Scotland(0)2 — Dundalk, 14.10.1986
Scotland (2)4,Rep.of Ireland (1)1 — Edinburgh, 17.2.1987
Belgium (0)0, Scotland (0)0 — Bruges,31.3.1987
Rep.of Ireland (1)1,Belgium (0)1 — Dublin, 28.4.1987
Belgium forfeited the match3–0 for fielding 3 over-age players
Scotland (0)1, Belgium (0)0 — Falkirk,13.10.1987

FINAL TABLE	P	W	D	L	F	A	GD	Pts
SCOTLAND	4	3	1	0	7	2	+5	7
Rep. of Ireland	4	1	1	2	5	6	−1	3
Belgium	4	0	2	2	0	4	−4	2

GROUP 8

West Germany (0)2,Bulgaria (0)0   Koblenz, 29.10.1986
Bulgaria (0)1, Netherlands (0)0   Sofia, 19.11.1986
Luxembourg (0)0, Netherlands (0)2   Luxembourg, 3.12.1986
West Germany (2)4,Luxembourg (1)1   Koblenz, 24.3.1987
Bulgaria (0)1, Luxembourg(0)0   Kyustendil, 31.3.1987
Netherlands (2)3, WestGermany (1)1   Venlo, 28.4.1987
Luxembourg (0)0, Bulgaria (0)1   Esch-sur-Alzette, 29.4.1987
Netherlands (1)1, Luxembourg (0)0   Middelburg, 13.10.1987
Luxembourg (0)1, W Germany (0)4 Luxembourg, 28.10.1987
West Germany (0)0, Netherlands (1)2   Munster, 17.11.1987
Bulgaria (1)2, West Germany(0)1   Sofia, 2.12.1987
Netherlands (1)4, Bulgaria(2)3   Nijmegen, 15.12.1987

FINAL TABLE	P	W	D	L	F	A	GD	Pts
NETHERLANDS	6	5	0	1	12	5	+7	10
Bulgaria	6	4	0	2	8	7	+1	8
West Germany	6	3	0	3	12	9	+3	6
Luxembourg	6	0	0	6	2	13	−11	0

QUARTER-FINALS, First Leg

Aberdeen, 16.2.1988, 8,000
Scotland (0)0, England (0)1 (Porter 83)

Murcia, 24.2.1988, 7,000
Spain (0)0, Netherlands (0)1 (Plomp, 89 pen)

Athens, 2.3.1988, 3,000
Greece(0)1 (Borbokis 49), **Czechoslovakia (0)1** (Niemecek 65)

Nancy, 16.3.1988, 13,462
France(0)2 (Paille81, Sauzee 89), **Italy (0)1** (Maldini 51)

QUARTER-FINALS, Second Leg

Nottingham, 22.3.1988, 11,284
England (0)1 (White 82), **Scotland (0)0**

Utrecht, 23.3.1988, 5,500 (aet)
Netherlands (0)2 (Van Leon 100, Viscaal 103), **Spain (1)1** (Loren 21)

Ceske Budejovice, 23.3.1988, 4,500
Czechoslovakia (0)2 (Vacalopulos og 77, Litos 84), **Greece (1)2** (Karasavides 20, Kapuranis 86)
(Greece won on away goals)

San Benedetto del Tronto, 23.3.1988, 15,000
Italy (1)2(Rizzitelli 32, Ciocci 84), **France (0)2** (Paille 84,89)

SEMI-FINALS, First Leg

Besancon, 13.4.1988, 22,000
France (1)4 (Angloma 23, Cantona 49, Dogon 78, Paille 83), **England (1)2** (Parker 24, Stewart 76)

Athens, 13.4.1988, 5,000
Greece (3)5 (Karasavides 10, 41, 73, 88, Oikonomides 13), **Netherlands (0)0**

SEMI-FINALS, Second Leg

Highbury, 27.4.1988, 5,661
England (1)2 (Gascoigne 5, Carr 59), **France (0)2** (Cantona 56, 78)

Utrecht, 27.4.1988
Netherlands (0)2 (Fraeser 60, RobWitschge 88), **Greece (0)0**

FINAL, First Leg

Athens, 24.5.1988, 15,000
Greece (0)0, France (0)0

FINAL, Second Leg

To be played in France on October 12 1988.

YOUTH INTERNATIONAL FOOTBALL

FIFA/COCA-COLA WORLD YOUTH CHAMPIONSHIP

GROUP 1 (in Santiago)
Yugoslavia (2)4, Chile (1)2	10.10.87, 70,000	
Australia (2)2, Togo (0)0	11.10.87, 15,000	
Chile (2)3, Togo (0)0	13.10.87, 40,000	
Yugoslavia (2)4, Australia (0)0	14.10.87, 8,000	
Chile (1)2, Australia (0)0	17.10.87, 75,000	
Yugoslavia (2)4, Togo (0)1	18.10.87, 10,000	

FINAL TABLE	P	W	D	L	F	A	Pts
YUGOSLAVIA	3	3	0	0	12	3	6
CHILE	3	2	0	1	7	4	4
Australia	3	1	0	2	2	6	2
Togo	3	0	0	3	1	9	0

GROUP 2 (in Concepcion)
Brazil (3)4, Nigeria (0)0	11.10.87, 30,000
Italy (0)2, Canada (2)2	12.10.87, 13,560
Italy (0)1, Brazil (0)0	14.10.87, 17,500
Nigeria (2)2, Canada (1)2	15.10.87, 6,500
Brazil (0)1, Canada (0)0	17.10.87, 8,300
Italy (2)2, Nigeria (0)0	18.10.87, 9,000

FINAL TABLE	P	W	D	L	F	A	Pts
ITALY	3	2	1	0	5	2	5
BRAZIL	3	2	0	1	5	1	4
Canada	3	0	2	1	4	5	2
Nigeria	3	0	1	2	2	8	1

GROUP 3 (in Valparaiso)
Scotland (2)2, East Germany (1)1	11.10.87, 6,000
Colombia (1)1, Bahrain (0)0	12.10.87, 5,000
East Germany (2)3, Colombia (0)1	14.10.87, 3,500
Scotland (0)1, Bahrain (1)1	15.10.87, 6,000
East Germany (0)2, Bahrain (0)0	17.10.87, 2,000
Scotland (0)2, Colombia (0)2	18.10.87, 4,000

FINAL TABLE	P	W	D	L	F	A	Pts
EAST GERMANY	3	2	0	1	6	3	4
SCOTLAND	3	1	2	0	5	4	4
Colombia	3	1	1	1	4	5	3
Bahrain	3	0	1	2	1	4	1

GROUP 4 (in Antofagasta)
Bulgaria (1)1, USA (0)0	11.10.87, 5,000
West Germany (3)3, Saudi Arabia (0)0	12.10.87, 10,000
USA (0)1, Saudi Arabia (0)0	14.10.87, 5,000
West Germany (0)3, Bulgaria (0)0	15.10.87, 6,000
West Germany (1)2, USA (1)1	17.10.87, 3,000
Bulgaria (2)2, Saudi Arabia (0)0	18.10.87, 3,000

FINAL TABLE	P	W	D	L	F	A	Pts
WEST GERMANY	3	3	0	0	8	1	6
BULGARIA	3	2	0	1	3	3	4
USA	3	1	0	2	2	3	2
Saudi Arabia	3	0	0	3	0	6	0

QUARTER-FINALS
Yugoslavia (0)2, Brazil (1)1	Santiago, 21.10.87, 60,000
Chile (0)1, Italy (0)0	Concepcion, 21.10.87, 35,000
East Germany (0)2, Bulgaria (0)0	Valparaiso, 21.10.87, 3,000

West Germany (1)1, Scotland (1)1 Antofagasta, 21.10.87, 4,000
(aet, West Germany won 4–3 on penalties)

SEMI-FINALS
Yugoslavia (1)2, East Germany (0)1 Santiago, 23.10.87, 35,000
West Germany (3)4, Chile (0)0 Concepcion, 23.10.87, 36,000

THIRD PLACE MATCH
East Germany (0)1, Chile (0)1 Santiago, 25.10.87, 68,000
(aet, East Germany won 3–1 on penalties)

FINAL
YUGOSLAVIA (0)1, WEST GERMANY (0)1 (aet, Santiago, 25.10.87, 68,000)
Yugoslavia: Lekovic; Jankovic, Brnovic, Pavlicic, Jarni, Pavlovic (Zirojevic 88), Boban, Petric, Skoric, Mijucic, Suker. **Scorer:** Boban 85.
West Germany: Brunn; Luginger, Spyrka, Metz, Strehmel, Schnieder, Reinhardt, Moller, Dammeier (Heidenreich 106), Eichenauer (Epp 74), Witeczek. **Scorer:** Witeczek 87 pen.
Yugoslavia won 5–4 on penalties.

UEFA UNDER-18 CHAMPIONSHIP 1986–88

GROUP 1
France (0)0, Portugal (0)0	Amiens, 26.11.86
France (0)3, Switzerland (0)0	Besancon, 22.4.87
Portugal (0)1, Switzerland (0)0	Lisbon, 6.5.87
Switzerland (0)0, West Germany (2)3	Berne-Neufeld, 20.5.87
Switzerland (0)1, France (1)1	Yverdon, 14.10.87
West Germany (1)3, Portugal (3)3	Dusseldorf, 4.11.87
Portugal (1)2, France (0)0	Lisbon, 25.11.87
West Germany (1)1, France (0)0	Kaiserslautern, 9.12.87
Portugal (0)0, West Germany (0)0	Loule, 17.2.88
France (1)2, West Germany (1)1	Mulhouse, 13.4.88
Switzerland (0)0, Portugal (2)2	Renens, 4.5.88
West Germany (0)3, Switzerland (0)1	Ampfing, 11.5.88

FINAL TABLE	P	W	D	L	F	A	Pts
PORTUGAL	6	3	3	0	8	3	9
West Germany	6	3	2	1	11	6	8
France	6	2	2	2	6	5	6
Switzerland	6	0	1	5	2	13	1

GROUP 2
Luxembourg (0)0, Spain (4)4	Ettelbruck, 26.11.86
Malta (0)0, Italy (4)4	Ta'Qali, 4.2.87
Italy (0)0, Spain (0)1	Barletta, 11.3.87
Malta (1)2, Luxembourg (2)2	Ta'Qali, 22.3.87
Italy (2)6, Luxembourg (0)0	Campobasso, 25.3.87
Spain (3)6, Malta (0)0	Alcala d. Henares, 29.4.87
Spain (4)7, Luxembourg (0)0	Tortosa, 4.11.87
Italy (1)4, Malta (0)0	Siracusa, 8.12.87
Spain (0)1, Italy (0)0	Alcira, 27.1.87
Malta (0)0, Spain (0)2	Ta'Qali, 9.3.88
Luxembourg (1)1, Italy (1)1	Esch-sur-Alzette, 23.3.88
Luxembourg (0)2, Malta (0)1	Verlorenkost, 6.4.88

FINAL TABLE	P	W	D	L	F	A	Pts
SPAIN	6	6	0	0	21	0	12
Italy	6	3	1	2	15	3	7
Luxembourg	6	1	2	3	5	21	4
Malta	6	0	1	5	3	20	1

YOUTH INTERNATIONAL FOOTBALL

GROUP 3

Norway (0)0, Scotland (0)0	Fredrikstad, 22.10.86
Scotland (1)1, Wales (0)1	Dundee, 3.2.87
Scotland (0)2, Northern Ireland (2)2	Dumfries, 3.3.87
Northern Ireland (0)1, Wales (1)2	Belfast, 24.3.87
Wales (0)0, Norway (0)2	Newport, 5.5.87
Northern Ireland (0)0, Norway (2)2	Bangor, 7.5.87
Norway (3)5, Northern Ireland (1)1	Porsgrunn, 15.9.87
Scotland (1)1, Norway (2)3	Aberdeen, 22.9.87
Norway (2)2, Wales (0)2	Stavanger, 13.10.87
Wales (0)2, Scotland (3)3	Cardiff, 24.11.87
Northern Ireland (0)0, Scotland (0)2	Belfast, 19.2.88
Wales (0)1, Northern Ireland (2)4	Newtown, 23.2.88

FINAL TABLE	P	W	D	L	F	A	Pts
NORWAY	6	4	2	0	14	4	10
Scotland	6	2	3	1	9	8	7
Wales	6	1	2	3	8	13	4
Northern Ireland	6	1	1	4	8	14	3

GROUP 4

Belgium (1)1, Denmark (1)1	Ekeren, 26.11.86
Denmark (1)1, Iceland (0)1	Ronne, 28.4.87
Belgium (0)0, Poland (1)1	Beveren, 6.5.87
Iceland (1)2, Belgium (1)3	Gardabaer, 26.5.87
Iceland (0)0, Denmark (1)2	Reykjavik, 8.6.87
Iceland (2)2, Poland (2)3	Reykjavik, 8.9.87
Poland (0)0, Iceland (0)0	Varsovie, 22.9.87
Belgium (0)0, Iceland (1)2	Bastogne, 25.9.87
Denmark (1)2, Poland (0)0	Copenhagen, 7.10.87
Denmark (0)3, Belgium (0)0	Holstebro, 21.10.87
Poland (0)2, Denmark (0)0	Jastrzebie Zdroj, 19.4.88
Poland (1)1, Belgium (2)2	Radom, 11.5.88

FINAL TABLE	P	W	D	L	F	A	Pts
DENMARK	6	3	2	1	9	4	8
Poland	6	3	1	2	7	6	7
Belgium	6	2	1	3	6	10	5
Iceland	6	1	2	3	7	9	4

GROUP 5

Sweden (0)1, East Germany (2)4	Trelleborg, 1.10.86
East Germany (0)0, Finland (0)0	Weimar, 25.10.86
East Germany (2)4, Rep.of Ireland (0)0	Lauchhammer, 11.4.87
Finland (1)1, Sweden (1)3	Hanko, 16.5.87
Sweden (0)1, Rep.of Ireland (0)0	Nynasham, 6.6.87
Finland (0)0, Rep.of Ireland (0)1	Valkeakoski, 9.6.87
Sweden (0)1, Finland (0)1	Halmstad, 16.9.87
Finland (0)0, East Germany (0)3	Hyvinkaa, 30.9.87
Rep.of Ireland (1)2, Sweden (2)2	Dublin, 6.10.87
Rep.of Ireland (0)0, East Germany (0)0	Dublin, 4.11.87
Rep.of Ireland (0)1, Finland (0)1	Dublin, 10.5.88
East Germany (0)2, Sweden (1)2	Greifswald, 14.5.88

FINAL TABLE	P	W	D	L	F	A	Pts
EAST GERMANY	6	3	3	0	13	3	9
Sweden	6	2	3	1	10	10	7
Rep. of Ireland	6	1	3	2	4	8	5
Finland	6	0	3	3	3	9	3

GROUP 6

Rumania (1)3, Turkey (1)1	Plopeni, 13.5.87
Rumania (1)4, USSR (1)1	Brasov, 26.6.87

Turkey (0)0, USSR (0)1	Ankara, 5.9.87
USSR (2)3, Austria (0)0	Moscow, 30.9.87
Austria (2)2, Turkey (0)3	Kapfenberg, 28.10.87
USSR (0)2, Rumania (0)0	Gori-Tbilisi, 28.10.87
Rumania (1)2, Austria (0)1	Brasov, 11.11.87
Turkey (0)1, Austria (0)1	Bursa, 6.12.87
USSR (3)7, Turkey (1)1	Kishinev, 23.4.88
Austria (0)1, Rumania (1)1	Vienna, 27.4.88
Austria (0)1, USSR (1)1	Kuchl, 11.5.88
Turkey (1)3, Rumania (0)2	Canakkale, 14.5.88

FINAL TABLE	P	W	D	L	F	A	Pts
USSR	6	4	1	1	15	6	9
Rumania	6	3	1	2	12	9	7
Turkey	6	2	1	3	6	16	5
Austria	6	0	3	3	6	11	3

GROUP 7

Albania (0)1, Netherlands (1)1	Tirana, 31.3.87
Albania (0)1, Hungary (0)0	Elbasan, 23.5.87
Netherlands (1)1, Bulgaria (1)1	Hoogeveen, 7.4.87
Bulgaria (3)4, Hungary (0)1	Kjustendil, 7.6.87
Hungary (1)7, Bulgaria (0)1	Budapest, 6.9.87
Bulgaria (1)4, Albania (0)0	Kyustendil, 14.10.87
Hungary (0)0, Netherlands (0)1	Budapest, 20.10.87
Bulgaria (1)1, Netherlands (0)0	Sandanski, 17.2.88
Albania (0)1, Bulgaria (0)0	Shkodra, 23.3.88
Netherlands (0)2, Albania (0)0	Delft, 20.4.88
Netherlands (0)0, Hungary (0)0	Deventer, 10.5.88
Hungary (1)3, Albania (0)0	Kalosca, 25.5.88

FINAL TABLE	P	W	D	L	F	A	Pts
NETHERLANDS	6	2	3	1	5	3	7
Bulgaria	6	3	1	2	11	10	7
Hungary	6	2	1	3	11	7	5
Albania	6	2	1	3	3	10	5

GROUP 8

Yugoslavia (2)5, Cyprus (0)0	Valjevo, 1.4.87
Czechoslovakia (1)2, Greece (0)0	Trebechovice, 16.4.87
Yugoslavia (1)4, Greece (0)0	Leskovac, 29.4.87
Yugoslavia (0)1, Czechoslovakia (0)2	Slavonska, 13.5.87
Greece (0)1, Yugoslavia (2)2	Alexandroupoli, 7.10.87
Czechoslovakia (0)1, Yugoslavia (0)0	Hlinsko, 18.10.87
Cyprus (0)1, Greece (0)0	Paralimni, 4.11.87
Cyprus (0)0, Czechoslovakia (0)0	Larnaca, 29.11.87
Greece (0)1, Cyprus (1)2	Piraeus, 24.2.88
Cyprus (0)1, Yugoslavia (0)3	Larnaca, 23.3.88
Czechoslovakia (4)5, Cyprus (0)1	Cesky Brod, 7.4.88
Greece (0)0, Czechoslovakia (1)1	Corinth, 27.4.88

FINAL TABLE	P	W	D	L	F	A	Pts
CZECHOSLOVAKIA	6	5	1	0	11	2	11
Yugoslavia	6	4	0	2	15	5	8
Cyprus	6	2	1	3	5	14	5
Greece	6	0	0	6	2	12	0

The final tournament was scheduled for July 22 to 27, 1988, in Czechoslovakia.

YOUTH INTERNATIONAL FOOTBALL

UEFA UNDER-16 CHAMPIONSHIP 1988

GROUP 1
Portugal (0)1, Bulgaria (0)0 — Lisbon, 9.3.88
Bulgaria (0)1, Portugal (1)2 — Sandanski, 23.3.88

GROUP 2
Luxembourg (0)0, Belgium (1)3 — Luxembourg, 18.11.87
Belgium (1)3, Luxembourg (0)0 — Tirlemont, 9.12.87

GROUP 3
Cyprus (1)1, East Germany (0)0 — Aradippou, 18.11.87
East Germany (1)3, Cyprus (0)0 — Hettstedt, 8.12.87

GROUP 4
Netherlands (0)0, France (1)1 — Den Helder, 9.3.88
France (0)4, Netherlands (0)0 — Tours, 23.3.88

GROUP 5
Greece (1)2, Austria (1)1 — Veri, 2.12.87
Austria (0)2, Greece (0)0 — Koeflach, 30.3.88

GROUP 6
Finland (1)3, Norway (0)0 — Lohja, 17.9.87
Norway (1)1, Denmark (1)1 — Aarnes, 29.9.87
Norway (1)1, Finland (0)1 — Strommen, 1.10.87
Finland (1)2, Denmark (0)0 — Parainen, 13.10.87
Denmark (0)1, Norway (3)4 — Vejle, 24.10.87
Denmark (2)5, Finland (1)1 — Horsens, 3.11.87

FINAL TABLE	P	W	D	L	F	A	Pts
FINLAND	4	2	1	1	7	6	5
NORWAY	4	1	2	1	6	6	4
Denmark	4	1	1	2	7	8	3

GROUP 7
West Germany (0)1, Scotland (0)1 — Oldenburg, 2.3.88
Scotland (0)0, West Germany (0)0 — Edinburgh, 24.3.88

GROUP 8
Hungary (0)1, Czechoslovakia (0)0 — Solgatavjan, 25.10.87
Czechoslovakia (1)2, Hungary (1)1 — Pisek, 26.3.88

GROUP 9
Iceland (1)3, Sweden (1)3 — Reykjavik, 30.9.87
Sweden (1)5, Iceland (0)0 — Mariestad, 17.10.87

GROUP 10
Northern Ireland (0)0, Rep. of Ireland (0)0 — Belfast, 17.11.87
Rep. of Ireland (2)2, Northern Ireland (0)0 — Cork, 8.3.88

GROUP 11
Poland (1)1, Turkey (0)1 — Mirkow, 15.10.87
Turkey (0)1, Poland (0)1 — Kocaeli, 23.3.88
(Turkey won 5–4 on penalties.)

GROUP 12
Switzerland (2)3, Italy (0)0 — Kreuzlingen, 25.11.87
Italy (1)3, Switzerland (0)0 — Sassari, 16.3.88
(Switzerland won 9–8 on penalties.)

GROUP 13
Saint Marin (0)2, Rumania (5)6 — San Marino, 11.11.87
Rumania (2)5, Saint Marin (0)1 — Arad, 25.11.87

GROUP 14
Yugoslavia (1)3, USSR (0)0 — Pancevo, 15.11.87
USSR (1)2, Yugoslavia (1)1 — Baku, 28.3.88

FINAL TOURNAMENT IN SPAIN

GROUP A
Finland (1)1, Austria (0)0 — Alicante, 11.5.88
Norway (1)1, West Germany (0)1 — Elche, 11.5.88
Finland (0)0, Norway (1)2 — Santa Pola, 13.5.88
Austria (0)0, West Germany (1)3 — Benidorm, 13.5.88
Finland (0)1, West Germany (0)2 — Alicante, 15.5.88
Austria (0)1, Norway (0)0 — Elda, 15.5.88

FINAL TABLE	P	W	D	L	F	A	Pts
WEST GERMANY	3	2	1	0	6	2	5
Norway	3	1	1	1	3	2	3
Finland	3	1	0	2	2	4	2
Austria	3	1	0	2	1	4	2

GROUP B
Rumania (1)1, East Germany (1)1 — Caceres, 11.5.88
Sweden (1)1, Yugoslavia (0)0 — Don Benito, 11.5.88
Rumania (0)1, Sweden (1)1 — Almendralejo, 13.5.88
East Germany (0)1, Yugoslavia (0)0 — Badajoz, 13.5.88
Rumania (0)1, Yugoslavia (0)1 — Santos de Maimona, 15.5.88
East Germany* (0)1, Sweden (0)1 — Merida, 15.5.88
*East Germany won 6–5 on penalties.

FINAL TABLE	P	W	D	L	F	A	Pts
EAST GERMANY	3	1	2	0	3	2	4
Sweden	3	1	2	0	3	2	4
Rumania	3	0	3	0	3	3	3
Yugoslavia	3	0	1	2	1	3	1

GROUP C
Hungary (0)0, Spain (0)0 — Antequera, 11.5.88
Turkey (0)0, France (1)1 — Arroyo de la Miel, 11.5.88
Hungary (0)1, Turkey (0)0 — Malaga, 13.5.88
Spain (1)1, France (0)0 — Marbella, 13.5.88
Hungary (1)1, France (0)1 — Marbella, 15.5.88
Spain (1)4, Turkey (0)2 — Malaga, 15.5.88

FINAL TABLE	P	W	D	L	F	A	Pts
SPAIN	3	2	1	0	5	2	5
Hungary	3	1	2	0	2	1	4
France	3	1	1	1	2	2	3
Turkey	3	0	0	3	2	6	0

GROUP D
Rep. of Ireland (0)0, Portugal (0)0 — Basauri, 11.5.88
Switzerland (0)1, Belgium (1)2 — Bilbao, 11.5.88
Rep. of Ireland (2)2, Switzerland (0)2 — Santurce, 13.5.88
Portugal (0)1, Belgium (0)0 — Baracaldo, 13.5.88
Rep. of Ireland (1)1, Belgium (0)0 — Getxo, 15.5.88
Portugal (0)1, Switzerland (0)0 — Sestao, 15.5.88

FINAL TABLE	P	W	D	L	F	A	Pts
PORTUGAL	3	2	1	0	2	0	5
Rep. of Ireland	3	1	2	0	3	2	4
Belgium	3	1	0	2	2	3	2
Switzerland	3	0	1	2	3	5	1

SEMI-FINALS
West Germany (0)0, Spain(1)3 — Getafe, 18.5.88
East Germany (0)0, Portugal (1)4 — Valdemoro, 18.5.88

THIRD-PLACE MATCH
West Germany (0)0, East Germany (0)0 — Rayo Vallecano, 21.5.88
East Germany won 5–4 on penalties.

FINAL
Spain (0)0, Portugal (0)0 — Madrid, 21.5.88
Spain won 4–2 on penalties.

GM VAUXHALL CONFERENCE RESULTS 1987–88

	Altrincham	Barnet	Bath City	Boston United	Cheltenham Town	Dagenham	Enfield	Fisher Athletic	Kettering Town	Kidderminster H	Lincoln City	Macclesfield Town	Maidstone United	Northwich Victoria	Runcorn	Stafford Rangers	Sutton United	Telford United	Wealdstone	Welling United	Weymouth	Wycombe Wanderers
Altrincham	—	1-1	2-0	4-1	1-0	3-2	1-1	3-2	1-2	4-1	5-0	1-0	2-2	1-2	1-1	3-0	2-1	1-0	0-0	0-1	1-0	1-0
Barnet	1-1	—	4-0	1-0	0-2	3-2	2-0	2-2	1-1	1-1	2-2	2-1	2-1	4-1	2-1	2-1	2-1	0-1	0-6	0-2	2-0	0-7
Bath City	2-0	4-0	—	2-0	3-3	1-1	1-3	2-0	1-1	3-2	3-0	0-2	3-0	2-1	2-1	1-0	3-1	3-1	1-1	2-1	3-1	2-2
Boston United	4-1	1-0	2-1	—	1-5	4-2	3-2	0-0	3-0	1-0	5-1	2-1	1-2	6-0	3-0	3-4	1-2	2-1	1-1	3-1	3-1	1-2
Cheltenham T	1-1	1-1	1-1	4-1	—	1-3	0-1	1-0	1-1	3-2	5-1	1-0	2-2	0-0	2-2	2-2	3-0	0-1	1-4	0-1	1-1	5-3
Dagenham	6-0	3-2	4-2	1-0	5-1	—	2-2	5-1	3-0	1-1	3-0	3-1	2-0	1-0	2-1	4-0	1-1	1-0	2-3	6-1	1-0	2-1
Enfield	5-1	3-0	0-1	2-3	1-1	1-2	—	2-3	2-1	4-0	4-0	0-3	3-2	1-1	2-2	3-1	3-3	4-0	1-1	1-1	1-3	1-5
Fisher Athletic	2-3	2-0	1-3	2-1	2-0	1-5	0-0	—	2-1	1-1	3-0	2-4	2-2	1-2	5-1	3-2	2-0	2-1	2-1	1-1	1-1	2-3
Kettering Town	2-2	4-0	2-0	0-2	1-2	0-5	2-0	1-1	—	2-1	2-0	2-3	0-1	1-0	2-1	2-2	2-3	0-2	3-1	2-1	2-1	0-3
Kidderminster H	0-2	1-1	3-3	1-0	2-2	1-2	5-2	3-1	1-1	—	5-3	1-2	1-2	1-1	2-0	0-2	2-0	4-3	1-1	1-2	1-1	0-1
Lincoln City	0-0	4-2	2-1	1-2	3-3	0-3	0-0	1-1	2-0	3-3	—	2-0	1-2	2-3	4-1	1-4	4-1	0-1	0-0	1-4	3-0	1-2
Macclesfield T	1-3	2-1	3-4	0-2	1-0	0-0	1-2	1-2	3-2	3-2	3-0	—	2-0	2-1	1-2	0-1	2-3	0-0	1-1	3-1	1-1	5-0
Maidstone U	0-0	2-0	1-3	3-3	2-2	0-3	2-4	0-3	0-2	2-1	1-1	1-0	—	2-3	3-2	2-3	5-1	1-0	1-3	0-1	2-1	1-5
Northwich Vic	2-0	4-1	0-0	0-1	1-1	1-0	0-1	0-0	3-1	1-1	3-2	5-0	1-1	—	2-1	3-0	1-1	1-1	2-2	0-0	1-1	2-0
Runcorn	2-0	1-2	0-1	2-2	0-0	1-4	1-3	0-2	0-3	1-1	1-0	4-0	3-0	2-0	—	2-1	2-2	0-1	1-1	0-0	2-2	0-0
Stafford Rangers	2-0	2-2	0-3	4-1	2-3	2-4	0-0	1-2	1-0	0-0	2-1	2-3	4-2	1-1	1-1	—	2-0	1-2	4-2	0-5	2-0	0-2
Sutton United	0-1	6-2	0-4	0-0	1-1	0-1	2-3	1-1	2-2	2-2	1-1	1-1	2-4	1-4	1-0	2-0	—	3-3	0-0	1-4	2-1	1-1
Telford United	0-3	0-2	1-2	1-1	3-0	0-1	1-4	0-1	1-0	2-4	0-0	1-1	2-4	1-2	2-1	1-1	2-1	—	2-2	4-1	1-0	2-1
Wealdstone	1-0	5-1	0-0	0-1	1-1	1-2	5-2	3-1	3-2	2-1	3-0	3-2	1-1	0-0	1-0	5-2	1-1	1-1	—	4-0	2-1	1-0
Welling United	1-0	5-2	0-0	1-2	2-2	1-2	1-0	1-0	1-0	5-2	2-1	3-2	0-1	0-0	4-0	2-0	1-1	2-0	1-1	—	4-0	1-0
Weymouth	3-0	3-2	3-1	1-0	2-1	0-3	3-2	1-0	3-0	1-0	0-0	1-2	2-1	2-1	2-1	0-0	0-1	1-0	0-2	0-2	—	2-1
Wycombe Wan	4-2	1-1	2-1	4-0	2-2	2-1	3-2	0-0	3-0	0-2	2-0	1-1	0-1	2-1	1-2	3-0	2-2	0-0	0-0	1-0	0-0	—

GM VAUXHALL CONFERENCE 1987–88

ATTENDANCE FIGURES

Club	Position	Average Home Gate 1986–87	Average Home Gate 1987–88	% Difference
Altrincham	14	1,476	1,349	−8
Barnet	2	1,712	2,644	+54
Bath C	20	501	597	+19
Boston U	16	1,237	1,546	+25
Cheltenham T	13	1,029	1,332	+29
Dagenham	22	554	527	−4
Enfield	12	810	776	−4
Fisher Ath	15	*	592	*
Kettering T	3	939	1,381	+47
Kidderminster H	7	1,092	1,345	+23
Lincoln C	1	2,022	3,762	+86
Macclesfield T	11	485	1,200	+147
Maidstone U	9	1,107	980	−11
Northwich Vic	17	773	785	+2
Runcorn	4	619	700	+13
Stafford R	6	1,103	1,231	+12
Sutton U	8	657	682	+4
Telford U	5	1,488	1,480	0
Wealdstone	21	636	733	+15
Welling U	19	704	873	+24
Weymouth	10	890	1,491	+68
Wycombe W	18	1,128	1,460	+30

*Figures not available.

Aggregate 1986–87: 424,493.
Aggregate 1987–88: 576,839.
Difference: +36%.

LEADING GOALSCORERS 1987–88

Listed in order of Conference goals.

Player (Club)	GMV Conference	FA Cup	FA Trophy	GMAC Cup	Total
Steve Norris (Telford U)	24	0	6	5	35
Phil Derbyshire (Stafford R)	24	3	3	2	32
Paul Davies (Kidderminster H)	24	2	1	0	27
Steve Butler (Maidstone U)	22	3	4	0	29
Mark Carter (Runcorn)	22	1	2	0	25
Nicky Evans (Barnet)	22	7	0	1	30
Nicky Francis (Enfield)	21	1	4	3	29
Steve Burr (Macclesfield T)	19	9	4	0	32
Lenny Dennis (Sutton U)	19	4	0	2	25
Dave Sansom (Barnet)	19	3	2	3	27
Kim Casey (Kidderminster H)	17	2	2	0	21
Phil Brown (Lincoln C)	16	1	2	1	20
Mark Smith (Kettering T)	16	0	2	1	19
Paul Wilson (Boston U)	16	2	3	0	21
Brett Angell (Cheltenham T)	15	5	1	0	21
Steve Biggins (Telford U)	15	1	3	1	20
John McGinley (Lincoln C)	15	3	0	2	20
Paul McKinnon (Sutton U)	15	2	0	2	19

SPONSORSHIP AWARDS 1987–88

Club	Sponsorship	GM Monthly Jackpot	Vauxhall Championship Awards	GMV GMAC Cup	Total
Lincoln C	2,000	3,250	5,000	–	10,250
Barnet	2,000	2,625	3,000	–	7,625
Kettering T	2,000	1,125	2,000	–	5,125
Enfield	2,000	2,000	–	1,000	5,000
Maidstone U	2,000	1,875	–	–	3,875
Stafford R	2,000	1,875	–	–	3,875
Kidderminster H	2,000	1,625	–	–	3,625
Runcorn	2,000	1,625	–	–	3,625
Weymouth	2,000	–	–	1,500	3,500
Sutton U	2,000	875	–	500	3,375
Telford U	2,000	500	–	500	3,000
Boston U	2,000	875	–	–	2,875
Fisher Ath	2,000	500	–	–	2,500
Northwich Vic	2,000	–	–	500	2,500
Welling U	2,000	–	–	500	2,500
Altrincham	2,000	375	–	–	2,375
Bath C	2,000	375	–	–	2,375
Macclesfield T	2,000	375	–	–	2,375
Wycombe W	2,000	125	–	–	2,125
Cheltenham T	2,000	–	–	–	2,000
Dagenham	2,000	–	–	–	2,000
Wealdstone	2,000	–	–	–	2,000

THE GM CHALLENGE CUP (For the Bob Lord Trophy)

QUALIFYING ROUND

Beazer Homes League

Burton A v Worcester C 2–2,2–6
Corby T v Redditch U 2–1
Gosport Bor v Crawley T 2–2,3–2
Dorchester T v Fareham T 2–1
Shepshed Ch v Leicester U 0–1
VS Rugby v Alvechurch 5–0
Willenhall T v Bedworth U 2–3
Witney T v Ashford T 1–2

Byes to First Round: Aylesbury U, Bromsgrove R, Cambridge C, Chelmsford C, Dartford, Nuneaton Bor.

Northern Premier League

Buxton v Frickley Ath 3–2
Caernarfon T v Southport 2–0
Chorley v Matlock T 2–3
Marine v Barrow 1–0
Mossley v Hyde U 0–1
Rhyl v Bangor C 1–0
S Liverpool v Horwich RMI 1–1,1–2
Witton A v Gainsborough Tr 4–0

Byes to First Round: Gateshead, Goole T, Morecambe, Oswestry T, Workington, Worksop T.

Vauxhall–Opel League

Barking v Bromley 0–1
Dulwich H v Farnborough T 0–2
Hayes v Bishops Stortford 2–2,2–1
Leyton–Wingate v Hitchin T 5–1
St Albans C v Leytonstone–Ilford 1–2
Tooting & Mitcham v Basingstoke T 0–2
Windsor & Eton v Carshalton Ath 2–3
Wokingham T v Kingstonian 1–0

Byes to First Round: Bognor Regis T, Croydon, Harrow Bor, Hendon, Slough T, Yeovil T.

FIRST ROUND

Altrincham v Runcorn 1–0
Aylesbury U v Leytonstone–Ilford 2–3
Bromsgrove R v Kidderminster H 1–0
Buxton v Goole T 3–4
Carshalton Ath v Barnet 1–2
Chelmsford C v Sutton U 1–3
Cambridge C v Stafford R 1–3
Cheltenham T v Slough T 1–2
Corby T v Bedworth U 1–4
Croydon v Welling U 0–1
Dagenham v Hayes 1–0
Dorchester T v Weymouth 1–1,1–2
Enfield v Ashford T 4–1
Farnborough T v Yeovil T 1–2
Fisher Ath v Bromley 1–4
Gateshead v Marine 2–3

Gosport Bor v Bath C 0–1
Harrow Bor v Hendon 2–1
Hyde U v Macclesfield T 3–4
Kettering T v VS Rugby 1–0
Leicester U v Boston U 0–1
Leyton–Wingate v Dartford 1–4
Lincoln C v Matlock T 2–1
Maidstone U v Wealdstone 4–1

Morecambe v Caernarfon T 2–1
Northwich Vic v Worksop T 4–2
Nuneaton Bor v Telford U 1–3
Rhyl v Witton A 4–0
Wokingham T v Basingstoke T 3–2
Worcester C v Oswestry T 2–1
Workington v Horwich RMI 1–2
Wycombe W v Bognor Regis T 0–1

SECOND ROUND

Bath C v Weymouth 1–5
Boston U v Bromsgrove R 0–2
Dagenham v Harrow Bor 1–1, 0–1
Dartford v Barnet 1–3
Goole T v Morecambe 0–0, 1–3
Horwich RMI v Marine 1–0
Lincoln C v Bedworth U 4–1
Macclesfield T v Altrincham 0–1

Maidstone U v Enfield 0–2
Northwich Vic v Rhyl 1–0
Slough T v Bognor Regis T 2–3
Stafford R v Kettering T 0–1
Sutton U v Leytonstone–Ilford 2–0
Telford U v Worcester C 4–
Welling U v Bromley 0–0, 2–1
Yeovil T v Wokingham T 2–1

THIRD ROUND

Altrincham v Horwich RMI 1–2
Enfield v Barnet 2–1
Kettering T v Northwich Vic 2–3
Morecambe v Bromsgrove R 3–0

Sutton U v Bognor Regis T 2–1
Telford U v Lincoln C 2–1
Welling U v Yeovil T 1–0
Weymouth v Harrow Bor 2–0

QUARTER-FINALS

Enfield v Sutton U 1–1, 3–1
Northwich Vic v Horwich RMI 1–1, 2–3

Morecambe v Telford U 1–1, 2–0
Welling U v Weymouth 0–2

SEMI-FINALS

Horwich RMI v Enfield 3–1

Morecambe v Weymouth 1–2

FINAL

HORWICH RMI 2, WEYMOUTH 0 (Horwich RMI FC, 8.5.88, 1,149)
Horwich: Allison (Schofield*); Hart, Mitchell, Booth, Howard, Senior, Walmsley, Street, Power, Page, McLachlan.
Scorers: Page, McLachlan.
Weymouth: Smeulders; Pugh, Gibson, Teale, Compton, Conning, Myers, Roberts, Iannone, Nardiello, Lewis.
*Hart played in goal after the substitution.

NORTHERN PREMIER LEAGUE RESULTS 1987-88

	Worksop T	Workington	Witton A	Southport	S Liverpool	Rhyl	Oswestry T	Mossley	Morecambe	Matlock T	Marine	Hyde U	Horwich	Goole T	Gateshead	Gainsborough Tr	Frickley Ath	Chorley	Caernarfon T	Buxton	Barrow	Bangor C
Bangor C	2-3	5-0	4-0	1-1	0-1	3-0	2-2	3-1	2-4	2-0	2-0	3-4	0-0	2-1	1-3	1-0	3-2	1-1	0-0	2-2	1-0	—
Barrow	0-1	2-0	1-0	0-1	1-1	2-4	4-0	3-2	0-0	5-0	3-2	2-1	2-0	5-0	2-1	4-1	3-0	1-2	0-1	3-1	—	2-3
Buxton	2-2	3-1	1-4	0-1	0-0	2-2	3-3	1-0	1-1	2-1	1-1	5-1	2-1	2-4	1-1	0-0	1-2	1-2	1-3	—	2-0	2-4
Caernarfon T	1-0	3-0	0-0	2-1	2-2	2-1	3-0	3-2	1-0	3-1	1-0	1-1	2-4	2-1	3-0	0-0	0-1	2-1	—	1-3	0-2	1-0
Chorley	0-1	9-0	1-1	2-1	4-2	2-1	5-1	1-1	2-1	0-0	2-1	1-1	1-0	1-1	4-0	2-1	0-3	—	1-0	1-0	1-0	1-0
Frickley Ath	3-0	2-1	1-0	2-1	2-1	0-1	3-1	4-1	0-2	1-0	1-1	4-2	0-0	3-3	0-0	3-1	—	1-2	2-1	1-3	0-4	1-2
Gainsborough Tr	1-3	1-2	1-1	1-1	1-2	0-1	2-1	1-2	2-3	0-2	4-1	1-1	1-0	0-3	1-0	—	1-0	1-6	0-0	0-6	1-1	0-0
Gateshead	3-5	4-0	1-1	1-0	0-2	0-1	4-0	0-3	1-1	2-0	1-3	0-1	1-0	3-1	—	4-1	2-0	0-2	0-1	3-2	0-0	1-1
Goole T	1-2	8-1	3-0	0-1	4-0	3-1	3-2	4-2	2-1	4-0	0-1	0-5	1-1	—	1-0	2-2	1-1	1-0	1-0	0-0	0-2	1-2
Horwich	2-0	2-0	1-0	1-1	1-2	0-0	2-1	1-0	0-1	2-0	0-0	1-4	—	0-2	3-2	1-0	1-2	0-1	0-1	1-0	1-1	3-2
Hyde U	1-1	6-0	2-3	5-1	3-3	0-0	2-0	4-1	2-1	2-0	1-0	—	2-0	3-1	2-1	3-0	0-0	2-1	2-1	4-2	2-1	2-0
Marine	1-1	3-0	0-1	3-1	1-0	4-2	1-0	0-1	1-1	1-3	—	1-0	1-0	2-1	2-1	5-1	0-0	1-0	0-0	1-0	0-1	2-2
Matlock T	2-2	2-1	1-3	2-1	2-2	1-1	2-2	2-3	1-3	—	1-2	2-3	0-4	2-3	2-0	4-2	2-4	1-1	0-2	3-3	5-1	2-3
Morecambe	2-1	2-0	0-0	0-1	1-0	0-1	4-1	4-1	—	1-0	3-2	4-1	3-2	2-2	2-1	0-0	0-0	1-2	2-0	2-2	0-0	0-2
Mossley	1-1	2-1	0-2	0-0	1-0	1-3	1-2	—	2-2	1-1	1-3	0-4	0-2	2-1	4-1	1-0	1-1	0-1	1-1	1-1	1-1	1-2
Oswestry T	1-1	2-0	2-2	2-0	0-0	0-3	—	1-2	1-1	0-2	1-7	0-2	2-3	1-0	4-1	3-2	3-3	1-1	1-1	2-3	1-1	0-3
Rhyl	2-4	3-1	2-2	1-2	1-2	—	5-0	1-1	0-0	4-0	0-1	1-1	0-1	1-0	1-1	5-0	2-1	2-3	0-4	0-1	1-2	2-0
S Liverpool	2-1	0-2	0-3	1-1	—	1-3	2-2	6-3	1-1	4-2	1-0	1-1	1-1	1-1	2-1	1-2	2-0	1-1	1-1	3-2	1-1	0-0
Southport	0-2	3-0	0-4	—	1-1	2-2	1-2	1-1	2-0	2-0	0-0	1-0	1-0	3-1	4-1	1-2	1-2	1-2	1-1	2-1	1-2	2-3
Witton A	0-0	3-2	—	0-1	0-0	0-0	2-1	3-2	0-1	4-0	2-2	1-1	0-1	0-2	1-2	0-1	1-3	0-0	0-2	2-3	1-0	3-1
Workington	5-1	—	1-0	0-1	2-2	0-8	5-0	2-1	0-1	0-2	0-4	0-2	2-2	0-1	1-0	2-3	2-2	1-2	1-4	0-1	0-4	0-1
Worksop T	—	4-1	1-0	2-0	2-2	1-1	1-1	1-0	2-3	2-4	2-0	0-2	1-2	1-2	3-2	3-1	2-2	2-0	2-0	5-2	1-0	4-1

BEAZER HOMES LEAGUE PREMIER DIVISION RESULTS 1987–88

	Alvechurch	Ashford T	Aylesbury U	Bedworth U	Bromsgrove R	Burton A	Cambridge C	Chelmsford C	Corby T	Crawley T	Dartford	Dorchester T	Fareham T	Gosport Bor	Leicester U	Nuneaton Bor	Redditch U	Shepshed Ch	VS Rugby	Willenhall T	Witney T	Worcester C
Worcester C	2-2	1-3	1-0	0-1	2-1	2-3	5-0	2-0	1-0	2-1	3-1	0-2	2-1	2-3	2-0	0-1	1-1	2-3	2-0	0-4	0-0	—
Witney T	2-0	0-0	1-0	2-1	4-0	2-1	4-0	3-1	3-0	4-3	3-0	1-0	0-3	1-0	3-3	2-2	1-1	1-0	4-0	2-2	—	1-0
Willenhall T	3-0	0-0	3-0	2-2	0-0	2-2	3-1	5-0	1-0	2-2	4-1	1-1	4-2	0-2	0-1	2-2	2-1	1-0	1-0	—	1-0	2-1
VS Rugby	0-0	1-0	2-0	2-0	5-2	1-1	3-3	1-1	2-0	3-2	1-0	0-4	1-1	0-0	1-1	2-1	0-0	1-1	—	2-1	0-2	2-1
Shepshed Ch	2-1	1-0	1-0	2-2	0-2	2-2	0-2	1-0	3-0	0-1	5-1	1-3	1-0	2-0	3-3	1-3	2-1	—	1-4	2-1	1-1	4-1
Redditch U	2-1	2-4	2-0	0-0	1-0	0-3	1-0	1-2	0-1	0-1	3-2	1-1	0-0	0-0	1-1	2-2	—	2-0	3-0	2-5	4-1	1-0
Nuneaton Bor	1-0	4-2	1-1	2-2	1-0	1-1	6-1	3-1	3-2	0-0	3-1	2-5	3-1	0-0	5-3	—	2-3	3-0	1-2	0-3	2-1	3-2
Leicester U	0-0	1-1	0-2	1-1	2-2	3-1	2-0	2-2	0-4	2-0	1-0	0-0	2-1	1-5	—	2-2	2-3	1-0	1-1	0-2	1-2	0-2
Gosport Bor	1-1	0-0	1-0	3-2	0-1	0-0	1-1	2-1	2-0	1-1	2-2	4-1	1-1	—	1-1	0-2	3-1	1-1	1-0	1-0	1-0	1-0
Fareham T	4-0	1-0	6-0	1-0	1-0	1-3	2-0	2-2	2-1	0-1	2-0	1-0	—	1-1	2-3	1-1	3-3	0-2	2-1	1-3	1-0	2-0
Dorchester T	1-3	1-0	5-1	1-1	0-0	3-1	0-0	3-0	2-0	3-2	2-1	—	2-0	0-0	2-2	4-0	1-2	2-2	0-0	2-2	0-1	0-1
Dartford	1-2	1-1	3-1	2-1	2-1	0-1	0-1	3-0	1-2	0-0	—	1-0	0-0	1-0	1-0	2-3	1-1	1-2	1-2	1-3	1-3	1-2
Crawley T	1-1	2-3	3-2	0-3	4-0	2-3	2-0	1-1	2-2	—	4-1	1-1	0-2	1-1	3-1	0-1	1-2	2-4	1-4	1-1	1-3	3-2
Corby T	4-1	0-0	3-1	1-1	1-0	2-1	5-2	1-3	—	4-3	1-0	3-0	2-1	2-2	1-1	0-1	1-2	1-1	0-0	0-5	1-1	3-1
Chelmsford C	2-0	4-3	3-1	1-1	2-1	3-0	4-1	—	4-1	2-1	3-1	1-1	2-0	4-1	4-2	1-0	1-1	1-0	2-2	2-0	2-0	2-0
Cambridge C	2-1	0-1	2-1	0-1	1-2	1-4	—	0-3	2-1	2-2	0-1	4-2	1-0	4-3	1-2	0-2	0-3	1-3	0-3	1-2	0-0	0-0
Burton A	6-1	1-0	3-3	2-2	1-1	—	1-4	3-0	2-1	2-3	0-1	3-1	1-3	0-0	3-1	1-1	0-3	1-3	1-1	3-3	2-1	2-3
Bromsgrove R	3-1	3-0	1-0	4-1	—	3-0	1-2	1-2	1-0	0-3	2-1	0-0	1-0	0-1	2-2	1-0	1-0	0-2	1-1	0-0	4-0	2-1
Bedworth U	4-1	0-0	3-1	—	4-1	2-2	1-2	3-2	1-3	1-2	3-1	1-2	1-1	2-1	2-0	2-2	0-0	1-2	2-0	3-1	0-1	0-1
Aylesbury U	0-0	2-0	—	3-1	1-0	3-3	1-1	2-3	1-2	2-1	3-1	5-1	6-0	1-0	0-2	1-1	0-0	3-0	2-0	3-0	1-0	1-0
Ashford T	1-1	—	1-4	0-0	3-0	1-0	1-0	1-0	0-0	3-0	3-0	1-0	1-0	0-0	1-1	1-1	2-4	3-1	1-0	2-0	0-0	1-3
Alvechurch	—	1-1	0-0	3-1	3-1	6-1	0-0	1-1	0-1	1-2	4-0	2-0	1-1	0-0	0-2	2-1	3-0	0-2	0-1	2-1	1-2	3-1

BEAZER HOMES LEAGUE MIDLAND DIVISION RESULTS 1987-88

	Atherstone U	Banbury U	Bilston T	Bridgnorth T	Buckingham T	Coventry Sp	Dudley T	Forest Green R	Gloucester C	Grantham T	Halesowen T	Hednesford T	King's Lynn	Merthyr Tydfil	Mile Oak R	Moor Green	Paget Rangers	Rushden T	Stourbridge	Sutton Coldfield T	Trowbridge T	Wellingborough T
Atherstone U	—	0-2	4-0	4-0	2-1	6-0	0-1	0-3	2-3	3-0	3-2	3-0	1-0	1-1	1-1	2-1	4-0	3-1	2-2	2-0	6-0	4-2
Banbury U	0-2	—	3-0	0-0	1-0	2-0	1-3	0-1	1-1	1-0	0-2	2-1	1-1	0-1	0-1	2-0	3-0	1-1	0-2	0-2	2-0	2-0
Bilston T	2-4	0-2	—	1-4	2-3	4-0	0-4	2-1	1-2	0-3	1-4	2-2	3-0	1-5	0-1	1-1	1-1	3-0	2-3	2-1	1-0	0-2
Bridgnorth T	2-1	2-0	1-0	—	3-4	3-1	2-2	2-2	3-2	3-0	0-2	2-0	2-1	0-1	3-0	1-4	4-5	4-2	2-0	2-0	2-3	0-4
Buckingham T	1-2	0-3	1-2	2-2	—	2-2	3-2	1-1	1-1	2-4	0-2	2-1	2-0	3-0	1-0	1-2	3-1	3-3	7-1	0-1	1-0	2-0
Coventry Sp	1-0	1-0	1-5	1-2	3-1	—	1-1	3-3	0-0	2-1	4-1	2-0	0-2	0-1	1-0	0-3	2-3	1-1	3-1	0-1	2-3	1-4
Dudley T	2-2	1-0	2-0	1-0	1-0	2-3	—	1-1	0-0	2-0	5-0	2-0	3-2	0-1	2-1	1-0	3-1	8-2	1-0	0-2	2-0	1-2
Forest Green R	2-3	1-1	3-0	0-0	1-1	2-1	1-2	—	1-1	1-4	2-2	4-0	4-0	1-2	2-2	0-1	2-2	4-1	2-0	1-1	0-1	3-0
Gloucester C	4-1	1-0	1-1	1-2	2-2	5-0	1-2	0-0	—	2-2	2-2	5-0	3-1	0-3	3-1	1-3	2-2	2-1	5-0	1-0	2-1	5-1
Grantham T	4-2	3-0	4-1	6-0	4-1	1-1	5-1	2-3	1-1	—	2-1	1-1	4-1	3-1	3-1	2-3	1-0	3-1	7-3	1-0	3-1	4-0
Halesowen T	2-2	2-0	1-1	1-1	1-0	2-0	3-0	0-0	3-3	1-0	—	5-2	1-2	2-2	2-2	1-1	1-0	0-0	2-1	2-1	2-0	2-1
Hednesford T	1-3	3-1	2-3	1-0	5-3	2-0	0-2	3-1	2-2	0-4	1-2	—	1-1	0-1	1-1	1-4	1-0	1-2	1-1	1-3	0-2	0-0
King's Lynn	3-1	0-3	0-1	4-0	0-1	2-1	2-1	3-2	0-1	0-3	2-2	1-0	—	2-5	3-2	1-1	3-1	1-2	1-1	3-0	2-0	1-0
Merthyr Tydfil	1-3	1-1	8-0	5-1	3-0	2-0	2-0	3-0	3-1	3-0	0-2	6-1	2-1	—	1-0	1-4	1-2	11-0	1-0	3-1	3-0	3-1
Mile Oak R	3-1	1-3	2-2	1-0	2-1	3-0	3-0	1-2	2-0	0-1	1-4	2-2	0-3	0-1	—	1-1	6-1	1-2	2-0	2-6	0-5	1-1
Moor Green	1-0	1-0	1-0	3-1	1-1	1-0	1-0	1-0	1-3	1-3	1-1	1-3	1-1	3-2	0-0	—		0-1	4-0	2-1	4-2	4-3
Paget Rangers	0-3	3-2	0-3	2-0	1-1	7-2	3-0	1-1	1-6	2-3	1-6	0-1	2-1	0-2	1-1	1-1	—	1-0	3-1	0-0	3-3	2-2
Rushden T	1-1	6-1	2-0	0-1	0-3	1-1	2-0	0-1	2-0	1-3	6-2	1-2	0-1	3-1	1-1	2-4	4-1	—	3-1	0-0	3-1	1-0
Stourbridge	1-0	1-3	6-0	2-1	4-6	1-3	3-1	0-2	2-4	2-0	1-1	1-1	1-1	0-2	1-1	2-4	1-0	2-0	—	0-2	2-0	1-2
Sutton Coldfield T	3-3	0-0	1-3	0-0	1-1	0-0	0-3	4-1	3-1	5-1	2-1	2-1	2-0	0-1	0-2	0-2	1-0	1-0	0-2	—	3-2	3-2
Trowbridge T	1-2	0-1	1-1	1-0	3-1	2-1	2-1	0-3	5-2	0-2	2-1	1-1	0-2	2-1	1-1	1-3	1-0	0-3	2-0	2-5	—	0-3
Wellingborough T	0-0	1-3	5-1	5-1	5-3	0-1	2-1	2-2	4-0	0-1	2-2	1-2	3-0	2-2	1-0	0-0	1-2	1-1	1-6	1-0	4-2	—

BEAZER HOMES LEAGUE SOUTHERN DIVISION RESULTS 1987–88

	Andover	Baldock	Burnham & Hillingdon	Bury T	Canterbury C	Chatham T	Corinthian	Dover Ath	Dunstable	Erith & Belvedere	Folkestone	Gravesend & Northfleet	Hastings T	Hounslow	Poole T	Ruislip	Salisbury	Sheppey U	Thanet U	Tonbridge AFC	Waterlooville
Andover	—	3-0	3-3	2-5	2-0	2-1	1-0	1-0	2-1	1-0	3-1	1-0	2-1	2-1	0-0	3-1	0-0	5-1	0-2	2-2	2-2
Baldock	0-0	—	0-2	0-2	2-1	3-0	0-1	2-2	0-3	0-1	1-1	1-0	3-1	2-2	1-1	0-0	1-1	0-1	1-0	1-0	3-4
Burnham and Hillingdon	2-1	0-1	—	0-2	5-0	3-0	3-1	0-1	2-2	4-3	1-2	1-1	2-0	1-0	1-0	0-0	0-1	0-0	1-1	2-0	1-4
Bury T	1-2	3-2	2-4	—	4-1	4-2	4-1	2-3	2-2	2-1	3-2	1-2	4-2	0-1	1-0	8-3	0-0	4-0	0-1	3-0	0-0
Canterbury C	0-0	1-4	1-0	1-5	—	0-0	1-2	1-3	1-2	1-2	3-1	0-1	2-0	1-2	0-2	0-0	0-1	0-4	1-3	3-2	0-2
Chatham T	2-3	3-0	2-3	3-2	2-0	—	1-7	0-4	1-0	1-2	5-0	0-1	2-1	1-3	0-1	0-1	1-5	1-6	1-1	0-1	0-0
Corinthian	0-3	1-0	0-3	3-1	3-0	1-1	—	0-1	0-3	4-1	0-0	2-2	1-1	1-3	1-3	0-0	0-1	2-0	0-0	0-2	2-2
Dover Ath	1-0	4-0	2-1	4-0	1-0	1-1	3-1	—	3-0	1-0	2-0	2-2	2-0	1-0	3-0	2-2	2-3	2-0	1-1	1-1	3-1
Dunstable	2-3	2-1	0-0	3-3	5-0	1-0	3-3	0-3	—	3-0	1-1	2-2	4-2	2-2	3-1	3-0	2-1	1-1	1-3	3-2	0-3
Erith & Belvedere	1-1	1-0	1-1	3-0	1-1	1-0	1-1	1-1	3-1	—	2-2	0-2	1-1	1-1	2-0	1-0	1-1	2-1	0-2	2-2	0-1
Folkestone	2-2	4-0	1-1	2-1	5-1	2-0	1-1	0-1	1-1	0-2	—	1-5	2-5	3-2	3-4	6-4	1-2	2-2	0-2	2-1	0-2
Gravesend & Northfleet	1-0	0-0	0-3	2-1	5-1	2-1	4-1	1-2	2-1	2-0	2-0	—	1-2	2-0	2-0	5-0	0-0	0-1	0-0	3-1	1-0
Hastings T	4-4	1-4	3-0	2-3	4-2	1-1	2-1	0-3	0-0	0-0	3-0	2-0	—	1-0	4-1	2-0	1-1	1-1	3-1	3-1	1-1
Hounslow	3-1	0-0	1-3	1-2	0-3	1-0	2-1	2-5	1-7	1-3	1-0	0-2	1-2	—	1-1	2-1	2-6	0-1	0-2	2-1	1-1
Poole T	2-2	2-0	1-1	3-2	1-2	3-1	2-2	1-2	3-4	2-2	2-0	1-2	1-0	6-0	—	6-4	1-2	4-2	3-2	1-2	1-2
Ruislip	1-0	2-2	0-0	0-2	1-2	3-0	1-3	1-2	0-5	2-2	1-0	1-0	2-3	6-0	2-0	—	0-0	1-0	1-1	1-3	1-0
Salisbury	2-2	1-0	1-0	2-3	2-0	3-0	2-0	2-4	1-1	1-3	3-0	1-0	2-0	0-0	2-1	6-0	—	1-0	1-1	3-0	2-3
Sheppey U	5-1	2-2	1-3	2-0	0-1	3-0	2-1	1-1	0-2	1-0	5-1	1-1	3-2	0-0	4-2	3-0	2-3	—	1-2	1-2	0-1
Thanet U	1-1	1-3	1-0	2-0	0-0	8-0	2-1	0-2	0-2	4-0	3-0	0-0	5-0	2-1	1-4	1-0	0-2	3-1	—	1-1	1-2
Tonbridge AFC	4-1	0-2	1-0	1-0	2-0	2-0	2-1	0-0	1-2	3-0	1-2	0-0	5-0	2-1	1-4	0-0	0-2	0-3	0-0	—	1-3
Waterlooville	3-0	1-1	3-1	1-1	8-1	3-0	2-1	0-0	1-0	2-3	3-1	1-0	4-1	6-0	1-1	4-1	2-0	3-0	2-1	2-1	—

VAUXHALL-OPEL LEAGUE PREMIER DIVISION RESULTS 1987–88

	Barking	Basingstoke	B Stortford	Bognor Regis	Bromley	Carshalton Ath	Croydon	Dulwich Hamlet	Farnboro T	Harrow Bor	Hayes	Hendon	Hitchin T	Kingstonian	Leytonstone-Ilford	Leyton-Wingate	St Albans C	Slough T	Tooting & Mitcham	Windsor & Eton	Wokingham T	Yeovil T
Yeovil T	1-2	1-0	1-2	2-1	2-1	0-0	1-2	1-1	0-1	1-0	0-0	0-0	0-4	2-3	1-0	2-1	1-2	2-2	1-2	3-1	3-0	—
Wokingham T	2-2	0-2	2-0	1-1	3-0	0-0	1-1	1-2	1-2	1-0	2-1	1-1	2-3	2-5	1-2	3-2	1-2	3-1	0-1	2-0	—	1-0
Windsor & Eton	1-0	2-2	2-1	0-1	2-1	2-3	0-0	1-1	0-0	1-1	1-1	1-1	0-1	0-1	3-1	3-0	2-1	1-0	0-0	—	1-1	2-0
Tooting & Mitcham	2-2	1-1	0-1	2-0	2-0	1-0	1-2	3-3	2-2	4-0	0-0	1-0	0-1	3-0	1-2	3-1	2-4	4-1	—	2-2	1-2	2-3
Slough T	1-0	0-3	1-1	0-2	2-1	1-1	0-1	1-0	4-1	1-3	3-1	1-4	1-6	1-0	3-0	1-1	1-3	—	2-0	1-0	0-3	2-1
St Albans C	1-0	1-1	2-3	1-0	1-2	1-1	1-0	1-0	3-1	1-1	1-1	0-3	1-0	2-1	1-1	3-0	—	1-0	3-0	3-2	0-0	2-1
Leyton-Wingate	2-1	1-1	1-2	2-1	2-2	2-3	1-0	1-3	0-0	0-1	5-1	3-1	3-1	1-2	3-2	—	2-1	1-3	3-1	3-0	3-2	2-0
Leytonstone-Ilford	0-1	0-2	0-2	1-1	1-2	0-1	2-1	4-0	1-2	4-0	0-1	1-2	0-0	0-1	—	0-1	3-4	3-2	0-0	1-1	0-0	2-1
Kingstonian	1-3	2-1	5-1	1-0	2-0	1-1	0-1	0-0	1-0	0-1	3-1	2-0	1-1	—	0-1	0-1	1-3	3-1	0-0	2-0	2-1	2-0
Hitchin T	3-1	1-1	0-0	4-2	3-2	5-0	0-0	5-0	2-0	1-0	1-0	3-2	—	2-0	0-1	2-0	2-1	1-0	4-3	2-1	2-3	1-1
Hendon	3-0	2-0	1-0	1-0	1-0	1-1	1-3	1-2	2-3	2-2	3-2	—	4-1	1-1	1-3	0-2	2-1	0-0	2-0	1-1	2-3	3-0
Hayes	1-2	1-3	0-3	0-2	1-1	0-1	2-2	0-1	0-1	2-3	—	1-0	0-5	2-0	2-0	0-0	2-1	1-1	5-3	4-1	2-0	2-0
Harrow Bor	0-1	1-3	2-1	1-1	1-0	2-0	1-2	1-2	2-1	—	1-0	5-1	2-2	2-2	2-2	1-1	0-1	3-1	0-2	5-2	2-0	2-0
Farnborough T	5-0	2-2	1-5	0-2	4-2	0-0	3-0	1-4	—	1-1	1-2	5-2	4-1	1-1	2-0	1-2	3-2	3-1	3-0	1-2	0-1	2-0
Dulwich Hamlet	2-1	1-1	0-1	3-0	0-0	2-2	2-2	—	1-1	2-1	0-2	0-2	1-0	2-2	4-0	0-1	4-1	2-0	1-0	2-1	2-1	4-0
Croydon	0-0	1-1	2-1	1-2	2-0	0-1	—	0-1	2-1	1-1	2-1	3-0	2-1	0-0	3-1	2-4	3-0	1-0	2-2	1-1	1-2	3-1
Carshalton Ath	0-1	1-2	1-0	0-3	2-0	—	1-0	0-1	1-1	0-1	0-2	2-2	2-0	0-2	3-0	3-1	0-1	1-1	1-1	2-0	4-1	4-1
Bromley	0-1	2-1	5-3	0-3	—	0-3	2-1	3-0	1-0	1-0	2-0	0-3	0-0	3-1	0-0	0-0	1-0	1-0	1-0	1-0	3-0	0-1
Bognor Regis T	0-1	0-1	3-0	—	0-3	0-3	1-2	3-0	0-2	1-1	0-1	1-0	4-2	1-0	1-1	1-0	1-0	0-2	2-0	0-1	1-1	2-1
Bishops Stortford	1-1	2-0	—	3-0	5-3	1-0	2-1	0-1	3-1	2-1	0-3	1-0	0-0	5-1	0-2	1-2	2-3	1-1	0-1	2-1	2-0	1-2
Basingstoke	1-1	—	3-1	1-1	2-1	2-0	1-1	1-1	1-1	2-2	3-1	2-0	0-0	2-1	0-2	0-3	1-1	0-3	1-1	2-2	0-2	1-0
Barking	—	0-0	1-0	1-3	5-1	2-0	1-1	0-1	4-1	1-0	2-3	1-0	0-0	1-1	1-1	1-1	5-2	2-0	5-2	1-0	2-0	0-0

VAUXHALL OPEL LEAGUE 1987–88

LEADING GOALSCORERS

PREMIER DIVISION	Lge	AC	GMAC	Total
Mark Graves (Hayes)	23	6	1	30
Jimmy Brown (Slough Town)	23	0	1	24
Allan Cockram (St Albans City)	21	2	0	23
Paul Randall (Yeovil Town)	21	2	0	23
Carl Zachhau (Bishops Stortford)	17	3	1	21
Micky Dingwall (Leytonstone-Ilford)	20	0	0	20
Simon Read (Farnborough Town)	19	0	1	20
Dave Pearce (Wokingham Town)	16	2	1	19
Sean Baker (Leyton-Wingate)	16	1	1	18
Iain Dowie (Hendon)	16	1	0	17
Paul Wilson (Barking)	15	2	0	17
Ronnie Murrock (Bromley)	13	1	3	17
Murray Jones (Carshalton Athletic)	12	2	1	15
Andy Nunn (Wokingham Town)	11	2	2	15
Dave Flint (Tooting & Mitcham)	14	1	0	15,

DIVISION ONE	Lge	AC		Total
Pip Parris (Lewes)	30	0		30
Marc Smelt (Leatherhead)	28	1		29
Steve Jenkins (Oxford City)	29	0		29
Steve Conroy (Chesham United)	25	2		27
Kevin Stone (Marlow)	26	1		27
Godfrey Cordice (Marlow)	27	0		27
Gurstel Gulfer (Kingsbury Town)	19	3		22
(including 14 Lge for Haringey Bor)				
Steve Russell (Walton & Hersham)	22	0		22
(including 6 Lge for Dorking)				
Tony Mahoney (Grays Athletic)	20	1		21
Alan Gregory (Staines Town)	19	1		20
Tim Buzaglo (Woking)	20	0		20

DIVISION TWO NORTH	Lge	AC		Total
Paul Harrison (Wivenhoe Town)	38	1		39
Keith Pope (Wivenhoe Town)	30	0		30
Tony Liddle (Harlow Town)	27	1		28
Mark Watkins (Tring Town)	28	0		28
Steve Hudspith (Berkhamsted Town)	20	4		24
Bobby Moyce (Rainham Town)	22	1		23
Barry Steele (Berkhamsted Town)	19	1		20
Steve Newing (Finchley)	17	0		17
Allan Brett (Hornchurch)	15	2		17
Rawling Simon (Letchworth Garden City)	17	0		17

DIVISION TWO SOUTH	Lge	AC		Total
Raoul Sam (Yeading)	22	4		26
Andy Bushnell (Dorking)	24	0		24
John Regan (Chalfont St Peter)	22	2		24
Trevor Smith (Whyteleafe)	23	0		23
Tommy Hewitt (Chertsey Town)	22	0		22
Paul Clarke (Feltham)	22	0		22
Steven Milton (Whyteleafe)	22	0		22
Nick Matthew (Metropolitan Police)	22	0		22
Mark Butler (Egham Town)	20	1		21

AC DELCO CUP 1987–88

FIRST ROUND

Barking v Woking	2–0	Berkhamsted T v Chertsey T	2–0
Basildon U v Maidenhead U	1–2	Billericay T v Met.Police	2–1
Basingstoke T v Kingstonian	0–2	Bracknell v Ruislip Manor	0–3
		Bromley v Egham T	3–1

VAUXHALL-OPEL LEAGUE

Carshalton Ath v Leatherhead	2–1	Hayes v Haringey Bor	7–0
Chesham U v Worthing	5–1	Kingsbury T v Hendon	2–1
Croydon v Bishops Stortford	0–1	Kingstonian v Leyton-Wingate	3–1
Dulwich Hamlet v Wokingham T	0–1	Leytonstone Ilford v St Albans C	1–0
Harefield U v Hampton	0–2	Marlow v Wembley	1–2
Haringey Bor v Hitchin T	3–2	Royston T v Carshalton Ath	1–5
Harlow T v Bognor Regis T	0–0, 0–3	Ruislip Manor v Wokingham T	2–3
Harrow Bor v Grays Ath	1–2	Staines T v Southwick	2–1
Hayes v Newbury T	6–0	Tooting & Mitcham v Bromley	0–4
Hemel Hempstead v Wembley	0–2		
Hornchurch v Kingsbury T	0–1	**THIRD ROUND**	
Lewes v Hendon	0–3	Barking v Wembley	5–2
Leytonstone Ilford v Witham T	3–0	Berkhamsted T v Wokingham T	0–0, 1–3
Leyton-Wingate v Petersfield U	6–1	Billericay T v Bognor Regis T	2–4
Oxford C v Marlow	0–1	Hampton v Carshalton Ath	3–2
Royston T v Clapton	2–1	Hayes v Bromley	5–4
Saffron Walden T v Farnborough T	0–3	Kingsbury T v Staines T	1–1, 4–3
St Albans C v Dorking	7–0	Kingstonian v Bishops Stortford	1–0
Southwick v Slough T	3–1	Yeovil T v Leytonstone Ilford	2–0
Stevenage Bor v Chalfont St P.	1–2		
Tooting & Mitcham v Yeading	3–2	**QUARTER-FINALS**	
Walthamstow Avenue v Yeovil T	0–5	Barking v Hayes	0–3
Walton & Hersham v Boreham Wood	1–0	Bognor Regis T v Kingstonian	1–2
Windsor & Eton v Uxbridge	2–1	Hampton v Yeovil T	0–2
Wolverton T v Staines T	0–2	Kingsbury T v Wokingham T	0–3
SECOND ROUND		**SEMI-FINALS (2 legs)**	
Barking v Farnborough T	3–0	Wokingham T v Hayes	1–1, 0–3
Berkhamsted T v Maidenhead U	1–0	Yeovil T v Kingstonian	2–0, 1–0
Billericay T v Windsor & Eton	5–2		
Bognor Regis T v Chalfont St P.	2–1	**FINAL**	
Chesham U v Yeovil T	0–3	Yeovil T v Hayes	3–1
Grays Ath v Bishops Stortford	0–0, 1–3	(at Basingstoke Town FC)	
Hampton v Walton & Hersham	4–3		

HUNTING GATE HOMES LTD MANAGER OF THE MONTH AWARDS

September
Premier Division	Ted Pearce (Farnborough Town)
Division One	Fred Saxton (Grays Athletic)
Division Two North	Colin Norman (Heybridge Swifts)
Division Two South	Bruce Butler (Egham Town)

October
Premier Division	John Lacy (St Albans City)
Division One	Mike Keen (Marlow)
Division Two North	Brian Lambert (Letchworth G.C.)
Division Two South	Martin Collins (Dorking)

November
Premier Division	Micky Janes (Hendon)
Division One	Mike Keen (Marlow)
Division Two North	Brian Lambert (Letchworth G.C.)
Division Two South	Clive Howse (Chertsey Town)

December
Premier Division	Brian Hall (Yeovil Town)
Division One	Fred Saxton (Grays Athletic)
Division Two North	Bill Baldry (Vauxhall Motors)
Division Two South	Brian Lang (Feltham)

January
Premier Division	Trevor Ford (Bromley)
Division One	Geoff Chapple (Woking)
Division Two North	John Godleman (Ware)
Division Two South	Andy McElwee (Met.Police)

February
Premier Division	Eddie Presland (Dulwich Hamlet)
Division One	Larry Pritchard (Walton & Hersham)
Division Two North	Alan Marson (Collier Row)
Division Two South	Clive Howse (Chertsey Town)

March
Premier Division	Ted Hardy (Leytonstone Ilford)
Division One	Fred Saxton (Grays Athletic)
Division Two North	John Ryan (Saffron Walden T)
Division Two South	Steve Kember (Whyteleafe)

April
Premier Division	Chris Kelly (Kingstonian)
Division One	Mike Keen (Marlow)
Division Two North	Geoff Bennett (Wivenhoe Town)
Division Two South	Laurie Craker (Chalfont St P)

Manager of the Season: BRIAN HALL (Yeovil Town).

OTHER LEAGUE TABLES 1987–88

GM VAUXHALL CONFERENCE

	P	W	D	L	F	A	W	D	L	F	A	Pts
Lincoln City	42	16	4	1	53	13	8	6	7	33	35	82
Barnet	42	15	4	2	57	23	8	7	6	36	22	80
Kettering Town	42	13	5	3	37	20	9	4	8	31	28	75
Runcorn	42	14	4	3	42	20	7	7	7	26	27	74
Telford United	42	11	5	5	33	23	9	5	7	32	27	70
Stafford Rangers	42	12	4	5	43	25	8	5	8	36	33	69
Kidderminster H.	42	11	8	2	42	28	7	7	7	33	38	69
Sutton United	42	9	8	4	41	25	7	10	4	36	29	66
Maidstone United	42	8	5	8	38	33	10	4	7	41	31	63
Weymouth	42	13	7	1	33	13	5	2	14	20	30	63
Macclesfield Town	42	10	5	6	36	27	8	4	9	28	35	63
Enfield	42	8	5	8	35	34	7	5	9	33	44	55
Cheltenham Town	42	6	11	4	36	32	5	9	7	28	35	53
Altrincham	42	11	5	5	41	21	3	5	13	18	38	52
Fisher Athletic	42	8	7	6	28	23	5	6	10	30	38	52
Boston United	42	9	5	7	33	25	5	2	14	27	50	49
Northwich Victoria	42	8	6	7	30	25	2	11	8	16	32	47
Wycombe Wanderers	42	8	5	8	32	43	3	8	10	18	33	46
Welling United	42	8	4	9	33	32	3	5	13	17	40	42
Bath City	42	7	5	9	27	32	2	5	14	21	44	37
Wealdstone	42	3	11	7	20	33	2	6	13	19	43	32
Dagenham	42	4	3	14	20	46	1	3	17	17	58	21

NORTHERN PREMIER LEAGUE

PREMIER DIVISION

	P	W	D	L	F	A	Pts
Chorley	42	26	10	6	78	35	88
Hyde U	42	25	10	7	91	52	85
Caernarfon T	42	22	10	10	56	34	76
Morecambe	42	19	15	8	61	41	72
Barrow	42	21	8	13	70	41	71
Worksop T	42	20	11	11	74	55	71
Bangor C	42	20	10	12	72	55	70
Rhyl	42	18	13	11	70	42	67
Marine	42	19	10	13	67	45	67
Frickley Ath	42	18	11	13	61	55	65
Witton A	42	16	12	14	61	47	60
Goole T	42	17	9	16	71	61	60
Horwich	42	17	9	16	46	42	60
Southport	42	15	12	15	43	48	57
S Liverpool	42	10	19	13	56	64	49
Buxton	42	11	14	17	72	76	47
Mossley	42	11	11	20	54	75	44
Gateshead	42	11	7	24	52	71	40
Matlock T	42	10	8	24	58	89	38
Gainsborough T	42	8	10	24	38	81	34
Oswestry T	42	6	10	26	44	101	*28
Workington	42	6	3	33	28	113	21

FIRST DIVISION

	P	W	D	L	F	A	Pts
Fleetwood	36	22	7	7	85	45	73
Stalybridge C	36	22	6	8	72	42	72
Leek T	36	20	10	6	63	38	70
Accrington Stanley	36	21	6	9	71	39	69
Farsley C	36	18	9	9	64	48	60
Droylsden	36	16	10	10	63	48	†58
Eastwood Hanley	36	14	12	10	50	37	54
Winsford U	36	15	6	15	59	47	51
Congleton T	36	12	16	8	43	39	*51
Harrogate T	36	13	9	14	51	50	48
Alfreton T	36	13	8	15	53	54	47
Radcliffe Bor	36	11	13	12	66	62	46
Irlam T	36	12	10	14	39	45	46
Penrith	36	11	11	14	46	51	44
Sutton T	36	11	5	20	51	96	38
Lancaster C	36	10	6	20	45	72	36
Eastwood T	36	8	10	18	45	65	34
Curzon Ashton	36	8	4	24	43	73	28
Netherfield	36	4	4	28	35	93	16

*One point deducted for breach of rule.
†Three points deducted for breach of rule.

BEAZER HOMES LEAGUE

PREMIER DIVISION

	P	W	D	L	F	A	Pts
Aylesbury U	42	27	8	7	79	35	89
Dartford	42	27	8	7	79	39	89
Cambridge C	42	24	8	10	84	43	80
Bromsgrove R	42	22	11	9	65	39	77
Worcester C	42	22	6	14	58	48	72
Crawley T	42	17	14	11	73	63	65
Alvechurch	42	17	13	12	54	52	64
Leicester U	42	15	14	13	68	59	59
Fareham T	42	16	11	15	51	59	59
Corby T	42	16	8	18	61	64	56
Dorchester T	42	14	14	14	51	57	56
Ashford T	42	12	16	14	45	54	52
Shepshed Ch	42	13	11	18	53	62	50
Bedworth U	42	12	14	16	49	64	50
Gosport Bor	42	10	17	15	39	49	47
Burton A	42	11	14	17	62	74	47
V.S. Rugby	42	10	16	16	52	57	46
Redditch U	42	10	13	19	55	63	43
Chelmsford C	42	11	10	21	60	75	43
Willenhall T	42	9	12	21	39	76	39
Nuneaton Bor	42	8	13	21	58	77	37
Witney T	42	8	11	23	45	71	35

MIDLAND DIVISION

	P	W	D	L	F	A	Pts
Merthyr Tydfil	42	30	4	8	102	40	94
Moor Green	42	26	8	8	91	49	86
Grantham T	42	27	4	11	97	53	85
Atherstone U	42	22	10	10	93	56	76
Sutton Coldfield T	42	22	6	14	71	47	72
Halesowen T	42	18	15	9	75	59	69
Gloucester C	42	18	14	10	86	62	68
Dudley T	42	20	5	17	64	55	65
Forest Green R	42	14	16	12	67	54	58
Banbury U	42	17	7	18	48	46	58
Bridgnorth T	42	16	7	19	59	75	55
Buckingham T	42	15	9	18	74	75	54
King's Lynn	42	16	6	20	53	63	54
Wellingborough T	42	14	10	18	67	70	52
Rushden T	42	14	9	19	69	85	51
Trowbridge T	42	14	3	25	53	82	45
Bilston T	42	12	8	22	52	87	44
Hednesford T	42	11	10	21	50	81	43
Mile Oak R	42	9	14	19	43	65	41
Coventry Sporting	42	11	8	23	46	83	41
Stourbridge	42	10	10	22	46	79	40
Paget R	42	10	9	23	49	89	39

SOUTHERN DIVISION

	P	W	D	L	F	A	Pts
Dover Ath	40	28	10	2	81	28	94
Waterlooville	40	27	10	3	88	33	91
Salisbury	40	24	11	5	71	33	83
Gravesend & N'fleet	40	20	12	8	60	32	72
Thanet U	40	17	13	10	60	38	64
Andover	40	17	13	10	64	58	64
Dunstable	40	17	12	11	78	56	63
Burnham	40	17	10	13	61	45	61
Bury T	40	17	7	16	80	67	58
Erith & Belvedere	40	16	9	15	52	56	57
Sheppey U	40	14	10	16	58	52	52
Hastings T	40	14	10	16	62	70	52
Tonbridge A.F.C.	40	14	8	18	51	56	50
Poole T	40	13	10	17	69	70	49
Baldock T	40	12	12	16	44	53	48
Hounslow	40	11	8	21	41	76	41
Folkestone	40	9	11	20	47	76	38
Corinthian	40	9	10	21	49	67	37
Ruislip	40	5	13	22	33	80	28
Canterbury C	40	7	6	27	33	87	27
Chatham T	40	7	5	28	39	88	26

VAUXHALL-OPEL LEAGUE

PREMIER DIVISION

	P	W	D	L	F	A	Pts
Yeovil T	42	24	9	9	66	34	81
Bromley	42	23	7	12	68	40	76
Slough T	42	21	9	12	67	41	72
Leytonstone Ilford	42	20	11	11	59	43	71
Wokingham T	42	21	7	14	62	52	70
Hayes	42	20	9	13	62	48	69
Windsor & Eton	42	16	17	9	59	43	65
Farnborough T	42	17	11	14	63	60	62
Carshalton Ath	42	16	13	13	49	41	61
Hendon	42	16	12	14	62	58	60
Tooting & Mitcham U	42	15	14	13	57	59	59
Harrow Bor	42	15	11	16	53	58	56
Bishop's St	42	15	10	17	55	58	55
Kingstonian	42	14	12	16	47	53	54
St. Albans C	42	15	6	21	60	69	51
Bognor Regis T	42	14	9	19	41	57	51
Leyton-Wingate	42	14	8	20	58	64	50
Croydon	42	11	13	18	40	52	46
Barking	42	11	12	19	44	57	45
Dulwich Hamlet	42	10	11	21	46	64	41
Hitchin T	42	10	8	24	46	79	38
Basingstoke T	42	6	17	19	37	71	35

DIVISION ONE

	P	W	D	L	F	A	Pts
Marlow	42	32	5	5	100	44	101
Grays Ath	42	30	10	2	74	25	100
Woking	42	25	7	10	91	52	82
Boreham Wood	42	21	9	12	65	45	72
Staines T	42	19	11	12	71	48	68
Wembley	42	18	11	13	54	46	65
Basildon U	42	18	9	15	65	58	63
Walton & Hersham	42	15	16	11	53	44	61
Hampton	42	17	10	15	59	54	61
Leatherhead	42	16	11	15	64	53	59
Southwick	42	13	12	17	59	63	51
Oxford C	42	13	12	17	70	77	51
Worthing	42	14	8	20	67	73	50
Kingsbury T	42	11	17	14	62	69	50
Walthamstow Ave	42	13	11	18	53	63	50
Lewes	42	12	13	17	83	77	49
Uxbridge	42	11	16	15	41	47	49
Chesham U	42	12	10	20	69	77	46
Bracknell T	42	12	9	21	54	80	45
Billericay T	42	11	11	20	58	88	44
Stevenage Bor	42	11	9	22	36	64	42
Wolverton T	42	3	3	36	23	124	12

DIVISION TWO NORTH

	P	W	D	L	F	A	Pts
Wivenhoe T	42	26	10	6	105	42	88
Collier Row	42	22	13	7	71	39	79
Tilbury	42	18	15	9	61	40	69
Berkhamsted T	42	19	12	11	71	53	69
Harlow T	42	17	16	9	67	36	67
Ware	42	17	15	10	63	58	66
Witham T	42	17	14	11	69	47	65
Vauxhall Motors	42	16	17	9	56	42	65
Heybridge Swifts	42	17	13	12	56	50	64
Tring T	42	18	6	18	69	67	60
Letchworth Gardens C	42	18	5	19	59	64	59
Finchley	42	16	10	16	67	54	58
Clapton	42	14	15	13	50	62	57
Hornchurch	42	13	15	14	56	65	54
Barton R	42	13	10	19	43	60	49
Rainham T	42	12	12	18	63	66	48
Royston T	42	13	8	21	49	70	47
Saffron Walden T	42	13	7	22	34	67	46
Hemel Hempstead	42	11	12	19	38	71	45
Haringey Bor	42	11	8	23	54	78	41
Aveley	42	8	13	21	42	65	37
Hertford T	42	8	4	30	45	92	28

DIVISION TWO SOUTH

	P	W	D	L	F	A	Pts
Chalfont St Peter	42	26	9	7	81	35	87
Met Police	42	23	17	2	80	32	86
Dorking	42	25	11	6	86	39	86
Feltham	42	21	12	9	74	41	75
Epsom & Ewell	42	21	11	10	71	49	74
Chertsey T	42	22	7	13	63	47	73
Whyteleafe	42	20	11	11	84	55	71
Hungerford T	42	21	7	14	66	54	70
Ruislip Manor	42	21	5	16	74	57	68
Yeading	42	19	10	13	83	56	67
Maidenhead U	42	18	12	12	69	54	66
Eastbourne U	42	18	10	14	67	57	64
Harefield U	42	18	6	18	59	60	60
Egham T	42	12	12	18	45	55	48
Horsham	42	12	10	20	45	66	46
Southall	42	13	7	22	45	72	46
Molesey	42	11	11	20	42	63	44
Newbury T	42	8	13	21	40	81	37
Camberley T	42	9	9	24	51	94	36
Flackwell Heath	42	6	8	28	42	96	26
Banstead Ath	42	6	7	29	34	81	25
Petersfield U	42	6	7	29	45	102	25

BANKS'S BREWERY LEAGUE

PREMIER DIVISION

	P	W	D	L	F	A	Pts
Tamworth	34	27	3	4	98	31	57
Oldbury U	34	25	6	3	91	39	56
Lye Town	34	22	8	4	65	27	52
Gresley R	34	20	10	4	74	36	50
Chasetown	34	22	4	8	74	40	48
Halesowen Har	34	18	6	10	66	40	42
Malvern T	34	15	6	13	59	47	36
Wednesfield Soc	34	14	7	13	43	43	35
Rushall Olympic	34	13	7	14	43	44	33
Hinckley Ath	34	11	9	14	58	58	31
Harrisons	34	13	5	16	54	61	31
Blakenall	34	11	7	16	42	49	29
Tividale	34	11	5	18	40	68	27
Westfields	34	10	6	18	60	64	26
Tipton T	34	7	9	18	38	56	23
GKN Sankey	34	7	7	20	46	73	21
Wolverhampton U	34	4	4	26	25	88	12
Oldswinford	34	1	1	32	16	128	3

DIVISION ONE

	P	W	D	L	F	A	Pts
Rocester	36	28	6	2	91	27	62
Stourport Swifts	36	22	7	7	79	40	51
Millfields	36	20	11	5	60	38	51
Wolverhampton Cas	36	20	8	8	74	48	48
Great Wyrley	36	19	8	9	76	48	46
Ettingshall HT	36	17	12	7	58	43	46
Newport T	36	15	11	10	68	46	41
Donnington Wood	36	16	7	13	62	60	39
Nuneaton Bor Res	36	13	11	12	53	46	37
Aero Lucas	36	14	5	17	51	62	33
Springvale-Tranco	36	12	7	17	54	53	31
Cradley T	36	12	7	17	45	62	31
Pelsall Villa	36	12	6	18	61	70	30
Ludlow T	36	12	6	18	39	57	30
Brewood	36	8	13	15	44	51	29
Bilston U	36	7	10	19	49	79	24
Cannock Chase	36	8	8	20	51	92	24
Gornal Ath	36	5	8	23	35	83	18
Darlaston	36	4	5	27	43	88	13

CENTRAL LEAGUE

DIVISION ONE

	P	W	D	L	F	A	Pts
Nottingham F	34	25	2	7	81	37	77
Liverpool	34	23	3	8	91	31	72
Derby Co	34	21	3	10	79	41	66
Manchester C	34	20	4	10	74	51	64
Sheffield U	34	17	6	11	68	55	57
Leeds U	34	15	5	14	58	56	50
Sunderland	34	14	8	12	51	54	50
Everton	34	14	5	15	57	46	47
Sheffield W	34	13	8	13	54	52	47
Manchester U	34	13	8	13	49	48	47
Coventry C	34	11	13	10	51	37	46
Leicester C	34	14	3	17	61	55	45
Huddersfield T	34	13	6	15	44	63	45
Aston Villa	34	13	5	16	62	69	44
Hull C	34	12	6	16	53	61	42
Bradford C	34	12	6	19	45	77	33
Grimsby T	34	6	3	25	29	100	21
Blackpool	34	3	6	25	23	97	15

DIVISION TWO

	P	W	D	L	F	A	Pts
Blackburn R	34	21	7	6	69	24	70
Newcastle U	34	20	7	7	81	42	67
Barnsley	34	20	6	8	82	50	66
WBA	34	18	7	9	75	39	61
Scunthorpe U	34	15	8	11	47	48	53
Oldham Ath	34	15	5	14	47	44	50
Bolton W	34	14	8	12	55	58	50
Wigan Ath	34	13	8	13	46	60	47
Port Vale	34	12	10	12	56	50	46
Rotherham U	34	11	10	13	52	55	43
Preston NE	34	13	4	17	44	58	43
Notts Co	34	12	6	16	39	46	42
Stoke C	34	11	8	15	30	44	41
Doncaster R	34	10	8	16	51	77	38
Darlington	34	10	7	17	46	74	37
Middlesbrough	34	10	6	18	44	56	36
York C	34	10	4	20	43	65	34
Mansfield T	34	8	7	19	40	57	31

BUILDING SCENE EASTERN LEAGUE

	P	W	D	L	F	A	Pts
March Town U	42	28	11	3	92	33	67
Braintree T	42	27	10	5	96	34	64
Sudbury T	42	26	11	5	94	44	63
Great Yarmouth T	42	22	10	10	53	31	54
Histon	42	21	9	12	63	52	51
Wisbech T	42	18	13	11	62	41	49
Chatteris T	42	18	9	15	64	60	45
Lowestoft T	42	16	12	14	72	68	44
Watton U	42	18	7	17	51	62	43
Haverhill R	42	16	10	16	58	51	42
Tiptree U	42	13	15	14	50	49	*39
Clacton T	42	15	8	19	54	66	38
Harwich & Parkeston	42	14	10	18	47	61	38
Colchester U Res	42	12	13	17	61	52	37
Newmarket T	42	12	13	17	49	58	37
Thetford T	42	14	7	21	70	82	35
Felixstowe T	42	12	11	19	64	76	35
Gorleston	42	13	7	22	56	95	*31
Stowmarket T	42	10	10	22	44	66	30
Brantham Ath	42	11	6	25	50	93	28
Soham Town R	42	8	10	24	42	78	26
Ely City	42	7	10	25	34	74	24

*Two points deducted for playing an unregistered player.

EAST OF SCOTLAND LEAGUE

PREMIER DIVISION

	P	W	D	L	F	A	Pts
Whitehill Welfare	18	9	7	2	41	17	25
Vale of Leithen	18	8	6	4	43	32	22
Gala Fairydean	18	8	6	4	26	15	22
Civil Service Strollers	18	10	2	6	28	21	22
Kelso U	18	6	8	4	32	25	20
Edinburgh C	18	6	6	6	25	32	18
Craigroyston	18	6	4	8	25	31	16
Spartans	18	5	5	8	23	23	15
Hawick Royal Albert	18	4	4	10	17	43	12
Pencaitland	18	3	2	13	18	39	8

FIRST DIVISION

	P	W	D	L	F	A	Pts
Annan Ath	18	12	5	1	57	33	29
Eyemouth U	18	11	3	4	46	22	25
Peebles R	18	10	4	4	39	27	24
Coldstream	18	8	6	4	34	22	22
Berwick Rangers A	18	6	8	4	27	23	20
Easthouses MW	18	6	6	6	28	32	18
Tollcross	18	7	3	8	32	34	17
Edinburgh Uni	18	4	2	12	18	42	10
Selkirk	18	2	5	11	23	44	9
Heriot Watt	18	2	2	14	18	42	6

GREAT MILLS LEAGUE

PREMIER DIVISION

	P	W	D	L	F	A	Pts
Liskeard Ath	42	29	10	3	98	33	68
Saltash U	42	27	6	9	116	41	60
Mangotsfield U	42	25	10	7	99	38	60
Plymouth Arg	42	26	8	8	105	46	60
Weston Super Mare	42	21	8	13	81	62	50
Exmouth T	42	19	10	13	61	55	48
Bristol C	42	16	15	11	76	53	47
Bristol Manor Farm	42	17	14	11	66	52	*47
Taunton T	42	15	15	12	49	48	45
Bideford	42	17	9	16	60	61	43
Swanage & Herston	42	16	10	16	73	63	42
Barnstable T	42	17	6	19	62	72	40
Clevedon T	42	13	12	17	42	56	38
Paulton R	42	13	10	19	46	72	36
Dawlish T	42	14	6	22	49	77	34
Radstock T	42	13	9	20	44	57	*33
Torrington	42	12	7	23	49	83	31
Frome T	42	9	13	20	36	69	*30
Minehead	42	10	10	22	47	87	30
Chippenham T	42	10	8	24	35	62	28
Melksham T	42	7	14	21	45	84	28
Clandown	42	5	12	25	33	102	22

FIRST DIVISION

	P	W	D	L	F	A	Pts
Welton R	36	21	12	3	74	36	54
Chard T	36	21	11	4	75	41	53
Tiverton T	36	21	7	8	82	46	49
Bath City	36	18	11	7	61	46	47
Larkhall Ath	36	17	8	11	72	49	42
Devizes T	36	15	9	12	44	38	39
Keynsham T	36	16	7	13	53	54	39
Westbury U	36	15	7	14	61	56	37
Ottery St Mary	36	16	5	15	43	41	37
Backwell U	36	11	13	12	49	52	35
Warminster T	36	15	5	16	46	55	35
Wellington	36	14	6	16	60	67	34
Calne T	36	11	10	15	45	59	32
Odd Down	36	10	11	15	51	62	31
Ilfracombe T	36	11	7	18	45	59	29
Heavitree U	36	11	6	19	49	62	28
Yeovil T	36	7	11	18	39	57	25
Elmore	36	7	6	23	46	81	20
Glastonbury	36	5	8	23	39	73	18

* Points deducted for fielding ineligible players.

HALLS BREWERY HELLENIC LEAGUE

PREMIER DIVISION

	P	W	D	L	F	A	W	D	L	F	A	Pts
Yate T	34	14	3	0	37	11	11	4	2	36	9	82
Abingdon T	34	13	3	1	45	15	9	5	3	31	16	74
Shortwood U	34	12	5	0	46	15	8	3	6	32	30	68
Abingdon U	34	11	4	2	34	17	6	7	4	24	19	62
Didcot T	34	7	6	4	29	20	6	6	5	26	27	51
Penhill	34	9	4	4	24	20	5	5	7	23	24	51
Sharpness	34	7	5	5	39	25	6	6	5	24	23	50
Fairford T	34	7	6	4	25	20	5	4	8	19	18	46
Thame U	34	7	5	5	28	24	4	8	5	26	31	46
Bicester T	34	8	3	6	23	17	4	5	8	19	26	44
Viking Sports	34	7	3	7	26	31	4	5	8	18	33	41
Moreton T	34	6	4	7	23	25	5	1	11	18	32	38
Rayners Lane	34	6	5	6	23	21	3	3	11	19	43	35
Morris Motors	34	4	7	6	15	24	4	4	9	21	39	35
Supermarine	34	5	5	7	25	28	3	4	10	21	30	33
Bishops Cleeve	34	5	5	7	25	32	2	6	9	17	38	32
Pegasus Juniors	34	6	3	8	27	30	3	0	14	19	31	30
Wallingford T	34	3	3	11	14	30	2	3	12	12	39	21

DIVISION ONE

	P	W	D	L	F	A	W	D	L	F	A	Pts
Cheltenham T Res	30	12	2	1	42	14	8	4	3	28	9	66
Wantage T	30	11	4	0	35	7	6	3	6	20	22	58
Kintbury R	30	8	4	3	29	16	8	5	2	19	10	57
Almondsbury P'sons	30	8	4	3	28	15	8	3	4	23	18	55
Lambourn Sports	30	9	2	4	33	27	6	3	6	20	25	50
Kidlington	30	7	3	5	29	24	6	4	5	22	21	46
Highworth T	30	7	4	4	27	21	5	2	8	25	36	42
Clanfield	30	8	0	7	28	24	5	2	8	23	35	41
Cirencester T	30	5	4	6	18	21	6	3	6	25	30	40
Carterton T	30	4	4	7	19	23	6	5	4	27	31	39
Chipping Norton T	30	7	5	3	33	19	1	6	8	16	26	35
Purton	30	5	4	6	21	17	4	4	7	19	22	35
The Herd	30	7	3	5	25	17	2	4	9	22	30	34
Cheltenham Saracens	30	5	2	8	13	17	2	2	11	9	37	25
Easington Sports	30	3	6	6	13	31	2	4	9	13	29	25
Avon Bradford	30	3	5	7	24	28	0	2	13	10	36	16

LEICESTERSHIRE SENIOR LEAGUE

PREMIER DIVISION

	P	W	D	L	F	A	Pts
Holwell Works	30	20	6	4	73	39	46
Stapenhill	30	18	6	6	97	43	42
St Andrews SC	30	18	5	7	71	43	41
Lutterworth T	30	16	8	6	48	29	40
Wigston Fields	30	17	5	8	71	46	39
N'brough & L'thorpe	30	16	6	8	54	47	38
Kirby Muxloe SC	30	13	9	8	59	55	35
Birstall U	30	13	7	10	50	43	33
Wigston T	30	11	10	9	49	41	32
Oadby T	30	10	7	13	47	48	27
Anstey Nomads	30	9	5	16	52	69	23
Newfoundpool WMC	30	6	9	15	31	46	21
Friar Lane OB	30	6	9	15	34	51	21
Thringstone	30	5	10	15	39	64	20
Rolls Royce (M'Sorrel)	30	5	5	20	33	72	15
Sileby T	30	1	5	24	24	96	7

DIVISION ONE

	P	W	D	L	F	A	Pts
Quorn	30	24	6	—	78	20	54
Syston St Peters	30	17	7	6	54	30	41
Barwell Athletic	30	18	4	8	59	39	40
Pedigree Petfoods	30	16	7	7	58	32	39
Barlestone St Giles	30	14	8	8	50	37	36
Whetstone Ath	30	12	9	9	33	32	33
Earl Shilton A	30	14	4	12	52	51	32
Houghton R	30	10	11	9	46	38	31
Barrow T	30	11	6	13	35	43	28
Downes Sports	30	8	10	12	45	48	26
Ibstock Wel	30	8	8	14	50	53	24
Harborough T	30	8	6	16	35	50	22
Anstey T	30	10	2	18	39	57	22
Leicester YMCA	30	8	5	17	23	50	21
Hillcroft	30	7	6	17	49	68	20
North Kilworth	30	5	1	24	37	85	11

NENE GROUP UNITED COUNTIES LEAGUE

PREMIER DIVISION

	P	W	D	L	F	A	Pts
Spalding	40	28	6	6	97	35	90
Rothwell	40	23	7	10	81	56	76
Raunds	40	21	8	11	72	46	71
Potton	40	19	12	9	76	38	69
Stotfold	40	20	9	11	72	49	69
S & L Corby	40	18	13	9	95	60	67
Desborough	40	18	9	13	71	55	63
N'ton Spencer	40	19	5	16	65	53	62
Arlesey	40	17	9	14	60	65	60
Long Buckby	40	17	8	15	70	65	59
Cogenhoe	40	15	10	15	58	64	55
Stamford	40	13	14	13	59	56	53
Irthlingborough	40	12	14	14	53	52	50
Brackley	40	14	7	19	52	57	49
Baker Perkins	40	12	12	16	68	70	48
Eynesbury	40	12	12	16	56	72	48
Wootton	40	10	11	19	41	66	41
St Neots	40	9	8	23	35	84	35
Kempston	40	6	15	19	46	82	33
Holbeach	40	8	7	25	47	118	31
Bourne	40	6	10	24	40	71	28

DIVISION ONE

	P	W	D	L	F	A	Pts
Timken Duston	38	29	4	5	123	27	91
M Blackstone	38	26	6	6	99	31	84
Blisworth	38	25	8	5	85	40	83
Burton P W	38	22	6	10	73	36	72
Sharnbrook	38	22	5	11	80	40	71
Ramsey	38	22	4	12	95	64	70
St Ives	38	19	10	9	71	49	67
Irchester	38	21	4	13	67	45	67
Higham	38	20	5	13	76	56	65
Timken Ath	38	20	3	15	70	68	63
Cottingham	38	18	8	12	68	50	62
Olney	38	12	9	17	60	70	45
Thrapston	38	12	5	21	48	80	41
Whitworths	38	12	5	21	51	86	41
O N Chenecks	38	9	5	24	42	72	32
Bugbrooke	38	10	2	26	48	101	32
Towcester	38	9	5	24	55	117	32
Newport Pagnell	38	7	9	22	36	68	30
Ampthill	38	5	5	28	41	117	20
Ford Sports	38	2	8	28	33	104	14

McEWANS MIDLAND FOOTBALL COMBINATION

PREMIER DIVISION

	P	W	D	L	F	A	Pts
Racing Club Warwick	36	22	12	2	74	23	56
Boldmere St Michaels	36	22	6	8	69	30	50
Ashtree Highfield	36	20	10	6	70	44	50
Stratford T	36	20	8	8	65	40	48
Evesham U	36	20	6	10	81	47	46
West Midlands Police	36	20	3	13	77	57	43
Coleshill T	36	16	10	10	61	41	42
Princes End U	36	16	9	11	55	55	41
Northfield T	36	14	12	10	48	40	40
Kings Heath	36	12	12	12	45	50	36
Solihull Bor	36	14	6	16	62	65	34
Bolehall Swifts	36	11	8	17	40	53	30
Walsall Wood	36	10	9	17	51	61	29
Knowle	36	10	8	18	40	60	28
Leamington	36	8	11	17	37	59	27
Polesworth N Warwick	36	8	8	20	53	85	24
Highgate U	36	9	6	21	44	80	24
Wilmcote	36	5	8	23	28	65	18
Bloxwich AFC	36	7	4	25	45	90	18

NORTH WEST COUNTIES LEAGUE

DIVISION ONE

	P	W	D	L	F	A	Pts
Colne Dynamoes	34	24	7	3	71	14	55
Rossendale U	34	24	7	3	68	23	55
Clitheroe	34	18	10	6	51	20	46
Colwyn Bay	34	20	7	7	60	42	*45
St Helens T	34	18	6	10	61	36	42
Ellesmere Port & N	34	17	5	12	55	48	39
Darwen	34	14	10	10	55	45	38
Warrington T	34	16	5	13	68	47	37
Kirkby T	34	11	13	10	57	54	35
Burscough	34	14	7	13	45	51	35
Leyland Motors	34	10	11	13	53	53	31
Prescot Cables	34	10	11	13	34	45	*29
Bootle	34	12	5	17	43	61	29
Formby	34	6	10	18	32	63	22
Salford	34	8	6	20	33	66	22
Skelmersdale U	34	4	11	19	34	64	19
Atherton LR	34	4	7	23	31	78	15
Glossop	34	5	4	25	30	71	14

DIVISION TWO

	P	W	D	L	F	A	Pts
Ashton U	42	32	6	4	107	30	70
Flixton	42	27	10	5	94	38	64
Wren R	42	26	9	7	92	51	61
Newcastle T	42	26	7	9	81	39	59
Maine Road	42	23	4	15	74	48	50
Maghull	42	18	11	13	73	66	47
Vauxhall GM	42	15	16	11	58	50	46
Atherton Col	42	20	6	16	63	63	46
Whitworth Valley	42	15	12	15	50	60	42
Ashton T	42	17	8	17	64	70	*40
Oldham T	42	13	11	18	44	51	37
Cheadle T	42	13	11	18	47	62	*35
Chadderton	42	13	9	20	55	71	35
Great Harwood T	42	14	8	20	52	66	*34
Blackpool Mech	42	12	10	20	57	77	34
Nelson	42	12	10	20	49	76	34
Ford Motors	42	12	9	21	59	70	33
Daisy Hill	42	12	8	22	55	66	32
Padiham	42	10	14	18	53	76	*32
Newton	42	10	12	20	47	84	*30
Nantwich T	42	8	13	21	41	68	29
Bacup Bor	42	8	8	26	38	71	*22

*Points deducted for breach of rule.

NORTHERN COUNTIES EAST LEAGUE

PREMIER DIVISION

	P	W	D	L	F	A	Pts
Emley	32	20	8	4	57	21	68
Armthorpe Wel	32	21	5	6	56	36	68
Denaby U	32	19	4	9	61	46	61
Bridlington T	32	18	5	9	63	25	59
Thackley	32	16	8	8	50	37	56
North Ferriby	32	12	11	9	49	41	47
Guiseley	32	14	5	13	52	51	47
Pontefract Col	32	11	10	11	42	42	43
Grimethorpe MW	32	11	9	12	46	49	42
Hallam	32	11	6	15	48	53	39
Hatfield Main	32	11	6	15	52	59	39
Harrogate Railway	32	9	9	14	40	56	36
Bridlington Tr	32	8	9	15	52	68	33
Long Eaton U	32	9	6	17	24	44	33
Brigg T	32	8	8	16	40	57	32
Belper T	32	5	12	15	32	52	27
Ossett A	32	4	9	19	31	58	21

DIVISION ONE

	P	W	D	L	F	A	Pts
York RI	30	22	2	6	66	29	68
Rowntree Mackintosh	30	20	5	5	74	35	65
Maltby MW	30	18	6	6	61	32	60
Parkgate	30	18	4	8	52	34	58
Bradley R	30	15	9	6	64	45	54
Woolley MW	30	14	8	8	69	39	50
Eccleshill U	30	13	8	9	49	50	47
Sheffield	30	13	4	13	38	34	43
Immingham T	30	9	10	11	41	40	37
Frecheville CA	30	8	10	12	40	51	34
Kiveton Park	30	10	4	16	29	51	34
Staveley	30	9	5	16	42	65	32
Pilkington Rec	30	6	7	17	30	65	25
Garforth T	30	6	6	18	29	51	24
Mexborough T	30	6	5	19	38	62	23
Dronfield U	30	3	7	20	36	75	16

NORTHERN LEAGUE

DIVISION ONE

	P	W	D	L	F	A	Pts
Blyth Spartans	38	28	8	2	106	36	92
Newcastle Blue Star	38	28	3	7	79	33	87
Billingham Synth	38	23	8	7	76	41	77
Whitley Bay	38	22	9	7	60	27	75
Guisborough T	38	18	12	8	63	41	66
Bishop Auckland	38	19	7	12	70	48	64
Gretna	38	17	6	15	69	46	57
Tow Law T	38	16	6	16	65	72	54
North Shields	38	16	5	17	62	59	53
Brandon U	38	15	7	16	64	61	52
Spennymoor U	38	15	7	16	57	57	52
Shildon	38	14	7	17	61	59	49
Whitby T	38	12	10	16	57	74	46
Ferryhill Ath	38	12	7	19	58	75	43
Easington Coll	38	12	6	20	65	85	42
South Bank	38	10	11	17	34	48	41
Crook T	38	8	9	21	45	84	33
Chester-le-Street T	38	7	9	22	38	73	30
Ryhope Community	38	5	10	23	40	89	25
Consett	38	5	9	24	44	105	24

DIVISION TWO

	P	W	D	L	F	A	Pts
Stockton	34	21	10	3	78	31	73
Seaham Red Star	34	21	8	5	63	32	71
Durham C	34	19	6	9	55	37	63
Billingham T	34	14	13	7	60	43	55
Esh Winning	34	14	7	13	47	49	49
Alnwick T	34	12	9	13	53	47	45
Bedlington Terr	34	11	11	12	49	46	44
Peterlee Newtown	34	11	11	12	37	34	44
Northallerton T	34	13	5	16	49	49	44
Norton & S'ton Acc	34	11	10	13	49	58	43
Horden Colliery Wel	34	10	13	11	48	65	43
Langley Park Wel	34	11	9	14	52	57	42
Willington	34	11	7	16	44	53	40
Darlington Cleveland B	34	11	7	16	45	57	40
Ashington	34	10	9	15	45	62	39
Evenwood T	34	10	8	16	42	56	38
West Auckland T	34	9	8	17	46	62	35
Shotton Comrades	34	7	9	18	33	57	30

SOUTH MIDLANDS LEAGUE

PREMIER DIVISION

	P	W	D	L	F	A	Pts
Shillington	32	21	7	4	48	17	70
Selby	32	21	6	5	74	35	69
Langford	32	21	3	8	58	26	66
Totternhoe	32	18	7	7	58	34	61
Hoddesdon T	32	17	8	7	63	38	59
Leighton T	32	16	5	11	58	38	53
The 61 FC (Luton)	32	13	9	10	54	40	48
Electrolux	32	13	6	13	42	37	45
Welwyn G C	32	12	9	11	49	44	45
Shefford T	32	13	6	13	41	65	45
Milton Keynes Bor	32	10	8	14	40	55	38
New Bradwell St Peter	32	8	5	19	40	59	29
Pirton	32	7	8	17	40	59	29
Winslow U	32	6	10	16	37	51	28
Biggleswade T	32	4	14	14	35	58	26
Cranfield U	32	5	8	19	31	62	23
Knebworth	32	6	3	23	32	82	21

DIVISION ONE

	P	W	D	L	F	A	Pts
Pitstone & Ivinghoe	24	19	2	3	67	23	59
Brache Sparta	24	13	5	6	46	35	44
Caddington	24	13	4	7	46	30	43
Walden R	24	12	7	5	45	33	43
Stony Stratford T	24	12	6	6	43	32	42
Milton Keynes T	24	9	6	9	34	30	33
Welwyn Garden U	24	9	5	10	41	40	32
Ashcroft Co-op	24	7	5	12	28	41	26
Buckingham Ath	24	7	4	13	24	39	25
Sandy A	24	7	4	13	34	52	25
Harpenden T	24	6	6	12	34	52	24
Delco Products	24	5	7	12	30	37	22
Ickleford	24	5	3	16	26	54	18

SUNDAY MIRROR COMBINATION

	P	W	D	L	F	A	Pts
Tottenham H	38	25	3	10	92	43	53
Watford	38	21	7	10	71	37	49
Norwich C	38	18	13	7	69	41	49
Southampton	38	16	14	8	76	46	46
Luton T	38	19	8	11	76	61	46
Ipswich T	38	17	10	11	67	46	44
QPR	38	18	8	12	68	54	44
Arsenal	38	19	5	14	77	48	43
West Ham U	38	17	7	14	62	52	41
Chelsea	38	16	8	14	60	54	40

	P	W	D	L	F	A	Pts
Charlton Ath	38	16	8	14	58	62	40
Portsmouth	38	16	7	15	64	73	39
Swindon T	38	15	8	15	64	72	38
Brighton & HA	38	15	8	15	58	72	38
Millwall	38	13	9	16	49	48	35
Oxford U	38	10	6	22	61	95	26
Fulham	38	8	9	21	48	91	25
Reading	38	10	4	24	51	85	24
Crystal Palace	38	8	7	23	38	78	23
Bristol R	38	4	9	25	52	103	17

SOUTH OF SCOTLAND LEAGUE

	P	W	D	L	F	A	Pts
Newton Stewart	18	12	5	1	48	23	29
Threave R	18	12	3	3	61	18	27
Stranraer	18	9	4	5	37	24	22
Annan Ath	18	9	4	5	45	32	22
Dalbeattie Star	18	8	5	5	53	23	21
St Cuthbert W	18	7	5	6	52	36	19
Wigtown & Bladnoch	18	6	3	9	40	54	15
Tarff R	18	5	1	12	29	57	11
Girvan	18	3	3	12	24	66	9
Creetown	18	2	1	15	19	75	5

WINSTONLEAD KENT LEAGUE

DIVISION ONE

	P	W	D	L	F	A	Pts
Greenwich Bor	36	26	5	5	111	50	83
Faversham	36	23	7	6	92	36	76
Whitstable	36	20	8	8	57	37	68
Sittingbourne	36	17	11	8	68	53	62
Hythe T	36	19	4	13	70	58	61
Kent Police	36	16	8	12	69	66	56
Cray Wanderers	36	16	7	13	72	51	55
Beckenham	36	16	5	15	61	55	53
Tunbridge Wells	36	14	10	12	57	50	52
Ramsgate	36	14	8	14	55	53	50
Darenth Heathside	36	11	11	14	57	58	44
Alma Swanley	36	11	11	14	41	47	44
Met Police (Hayes)	36	11	8	17	45	61	41
Slade Green	36	10	9	17	54	60	39
Danson	36	10	9	17	44	68	39
Deal T	36	11	5	20	40	67	38
Thames Poly	36	10	8	18	37	65	38
Herne Bay	36	9	8	19	35	69	35
Crockenhill	36	4	6	26	21	82	18

DIVISION TWO

	P	W	D	L	F	A	Pts
Fisher Ath	34	27	4	3	111	21	85
Ashford	34	23	5	6	77	25	74
Faversham	34	21	4	9	71	38	67
Dover Ath	34	19	6	9	64	47	63
Sittingbourne	34	19	5	10	72	52	62
Darenth Heathside	34	16	11	7	63	43	59
Snowdown CW	34	16	9	9	59	47	57
Whitstable	34	13	7	14	31	44	46
Sheppey U	34	14	3	17	57	53	45
Hastings T	34	13	6	15	60	69	45
Ramsgate	34	13	2	19	54	56	41
Deal T	34	11	6	17	59	75	39
Folkestone	34	12	3	19	47	80	39
Beckenham	34	10	3	21	54	74	33
Thames Poly	34	10	3	21	39	73	33
Thanet U	34	7	9	18	36	68	30
Hythe T	34	8	4	22	41	85	28
Herne Bay	34	8	2	24	41	86	26

McEWANS NORTHERN ALLIANCE

	P	W	D	L	F	A	Pts
Seaton Deleval S T	28	20	3	5	66	35	43
Prudhoe East End	28	18	3	7	81	48	39
Gosforth St Nicholas	28	16	7	5	61	39	39
West Allotment Celtic	28	17	6	6	75	49	39
Forest Hall	28	11	7	10	55	53	29
Dudley Wel	28	12	5	11	58	57	29
Heaton Stannington	28	12	4	12	42	43	28
Seaton Delaval Am	28	10	7	11	50	57	27
Morpeth T	28	11	4	13	51	52	26
Wigton	28	11	3	14	48	52	25
Percy Main Am	28	8	6	14	42	64	22
Newbiggin Central Wel	28	8	5	15	65	86	21
Ponteland U	28	9	2	17	41	66	20
Swalwell	28	7	4	17	39	62	18
Dunston Tyne Sports	28	6	3	19	37	70	15

SMIRNOFF IRISH LEAGUE

	P	W	D	L	F	A	Pts
Glentoran	26	19	5	2	48	15	62
Linfield	26	19	3	4	51	15	60
Coleraine	26	16	4	6	53	28	52
Newry	26	15	5	6	34	22	50
Larne	26	12	4	10	35	35	40
Glenavon	26	11	5	10	28	27	38
Ballymena	26	9	9	8	34	34	36
Portadown	26	10	5	11	31	27	35
Crusaders	26	8	6	12	29	35	30
Cliftonville	26	6	8	12	18	38	26
Ards	26	6	7	13	29	38	25
Bangor	26	7	4	15	24	47	25
Carrick	26	5	5	16	25	44	20
Distillery	26	3	2	21	19	53	11

FA CHALLENGE TROPHY 1987–88

THIRD ROUND

Altrincham 1,0,1,1 Fisher Athletic 1,0,1,0
Cheltenham Town 2, Bromsgrove Rovers 1
Leyton-Wingate 1, Macclesfield Town 2
Lincoln City 2, Maidstone United 1
Runcorn 0, Barrow 1
Telford United 1,3, Stafford Rangers 1,2
Witton Albion 1, Enfield 2
Wokingham Town 3, Spennymoor United 0

QUARTER-FINALS

Altrincham 0,1, Barrow 0,2
Cheltenham Town 2, Telford United 4
Enfield 1, Lincoln City 0
Wokingham Town 2, Macclesfield Town 0

SEMI-FINALS (2 legs)

Barrow 1,1, Enfield 2,0,
Telford United 2,1, Wokingham Town 0,0

FINAL

ENFIELD 0, TELFORD 0
(aet, Wembley, 7 May 1988, 20,061)
Enfield: Pape; Cooper, Sparrow (Hayzleden 112), Howell, Keen, Francis, Lewis (Edmonds 104), Cottington, Furlong, Harding, King.
Telford: Charlton; McGinty, Wiggins, Mayman, Nelson, Storton, Joseph, Biggins, Norris, Sankey, Stringer (Griffiths 28).

Replay: ENFIELD 3, TELFORD 2
(West Bromwich, 12 May 1988, 17,500)
Enfield: Unchanged. **Scorers:** Howell, Furlong 2 (1 pen).
Telford: Unchanged. **Scorers:** Biggins, Norris.

FA CHALLENGE VASE

FIFTH ROUND

Atherstone United 1, Colne Dynamoes 2
Bashley 2, Hounslow 0
Clevedon Town 2, Corinthian 1
Chertsey Town 0,2, Falmouth Town 0,1
Durham City 4, Tamworth 2
Gresley Rovers 0, Emley 1
North Ferriby United 1, Farsley Celtic 2
Sudbury Town 1, Braintree Town 0

QUARTER-FINALS

Chertsey Town 1, Bashley 3
Colne Dynamoes 2, Farsley Celtic 0
Durham City 2, Emley 4
Sudbury Town 2, Clevedon Town 0

SEMI-FINALS (2 legs)

Bashley 1,0, Emley 1,1
Sudbury Town 1,0, Colne Dynamoes 1,2

FINAL

COLNE DYNAMOES 1, EMLEY 0
(aet, Wembley, 23.4.88, 15,146)
Colne: Mason; McFadyen, Dunn, Westwell, Bentley, Whitehead (Burke 59), Roscoe, Anderson, Wood (Coates 74), Rodaway, Diamond. **Scorer:** Anderson 97.
Emley: Dennis; Hirst (Burrows 78), Fielding, Mellor, Codd, Green, Bramald, Francis, Devine, Carmody, Gartland (Cook 108).

FA YOUTH CUP 1987–88

FOURTH ROUND

Crewe Alexandra 0,0,1, Middlesbrough 0,0,0
Leyton Orient 0, Manchester City 1
Liverpool 1, Derby County 0
Nottingham Forest 1,3,2, Everton 1,3,1
Plymouth Argyle 3, Doncaster Rovers 6
Southampton 1, Arsenal 2
Southend United 0, Reading 3
Tottenham Hotspur 6, Chelsea 0

QUARTER-FINALS

Crewe Alexandra 1,0, Arsenal 1,3
Doncaster Rovers 2, Manchester City 1
Liverpool 3,0, Nottingham Forest 3,3
Reading 0,1, Tottenham Hotspur 0,2

SEMI-FINALS (2 legs)

Arsenal 1,3, Nottingham Forest 1,0
Doncaster Rovers 2,1, Tottenham Hotspur 1,1

FINAL

First Leg: DONCASTER ROVERS 0, ARSENAL 5
(29 April 1988, 6,451)
Doncaster R: Lamont; Hall, Brevett, Raffell, Raven, Snowball, peckett, Rankine, Morris, Winship, Gaughan.
Arsenal: Miller; Francis, Carstairs, Hiller, Hannigan, Morrow, Heaney, Cagigao, Campbell, Ball, McKeown (Lee). **Scorers:** Campbell 3, Ball pen, Lee.

Second Leg: ARSENAL 1, DONCASTER ROVERS 1
(3 May 1988, 4,843)
Arsenal: Unchanged. Lee came on for Ball. **Scorer:** McKeown.
Doncaster R: Slingsby for Morris, Stewart for Winship. Morris came on for Snowball, Winship came on for Stewart. Scorer: Peckett.

FA CHALLENGE TROPHY FINALS 1970–88

1970	Macclesfield T 2, Telford U 0	1980	Dagenham 2, Mossley 1
1971	Telford U 3, Hillingdon Bor 2	1981	Bishop's Stortford 1, Sutton U 0
1972	Stafford R 3, Barnet 0	1982	Enfield 1, Altrincham 0 (aet)
1973	Scarborough 2, Wigan Ath 1 (aet)	1983	Telford U 2, Northwich Vic 1
1974	Morecambe 2, Dartford 1	1984	Northwich Vic 1,2, Bangor City 1,1
1975	Matlock 4, Scarborough 0	1985	Wealdstone 2, Boston U 1
1976	Scarborough 3, Stafford R 2 (aet)	1986	Altrincham 1, Runcorn 0
1977	Scarborough 2, Dagenham 1	1987	Kidderminster H 0,2, Burton A 0,1
1978	Altrincham 3, Leatherhead 1	1988	Enfield 0,3, Telford U 0,2
1979	Stafford R 2, Kettering T 0		

FA CHALLENGE VASE FINALS 1975–88

1975	Hoddesdon T 2, Epsom & Ewell 1	1982	Forest Green R 3, Rainworth MW 0
1976	Billericay T 1, Stamford 0 (aet)	1983	VS Rugby 1, Halesowen T 0
1977	Billericay T 1,2, Sheffield 1,1	1984	Stansted 3, Stamford 2
1978	Blue Star 2, Barton R 1	1985	Halesowen T 3, Fleetwood T 1
1979	Billericay T 4, Almondsbury G 1	1986	Halesowen T 3, Southall 0
1980	Stamford 2, Guisborough T 0	1987	St Helens T 3, Warrington T 2
1981	Whickham 3, Willenhall T 2 (aet)	1988	Colne Dynamoes 1, Emley 0

FA YOUTH CUP FINALS 1953–88 (Aggregate scores)

1953	Manchester U 9, Wolverhampton W 3	1971	Arsenal 2, Cardiff C 0
1954	Manchester U 5, Wolverhampton W 4	1972	Aston Villa 5, Liverpool 2
1955	Manchester U 7, WBA 1	1973	Ipswich T 4, Bristol C 1
1956	Manchester U 4, Chesterfield 3	1974	Tottenham H 2, Huddersfield T 1
1957	Manchester U 8, West Ham U 2	1975	Ipswich T 5, West Ham U 1
1958	Wolverhampton W 7, Chelsea 6	1976	WBA 5, Wolverhampton W 0
1959	Blackburn R 2, West Ham U 1	1977	Crystal Palace 1, Everton 0
1960	Chelsea 5, Preston NE 2	1978	Crystal Palace 1, Aston Villa 0 (Single game)
1961	Chelsea 5, Everton 3	1979	Millwall 2, Manchester C 0
1962	Newcastle U 2, Wolverhampton W 1	1980	Aston Villa 3, Manchester C 2
1963	West Ham U 6, Liverpool 5	1981	West Ham U 2, Tottenham H 1
1964	Manchester U 5, West Ham U 2	1982	Watford 7, Manchester U 6
1965	Everton 3, Arsenal 2	1983	Norwich C 6, Everton 5 (Including replay)
1966	Arsenal 5, Sunderland 3	1984	Everton 4, Stoke C 2
1967	Sunderland 2, Birmingham C 0	1985	Newcastle U 4, Watford 1
1968	Burnley 3, Coventry C 2	1986	Manchester C 3, Manchester U 1
1969	Sunderland 6, WBA 3	1987	Coventry C 2, Charlton Ath 1
1970	Tottenham H 4, Coventry C 3	1988	Arsenal 6, Doncaster R 1

FA SUNDAY CUP FINALS 1965–88

1965	London 6, Staffordshire 2 (Aggregate score)	1977	Langley Park RH 2, Newtown Unity 0
1966	Unique U 1, Aldridge F 0	1978	Arras 2,2, Lion Rangers 2,1
1967	Carlton U 2, Stoke W 0	1979	Lobster 3, Carlton U 2
1968	Drovers 2, Brook U 0	1980	Fantail 1, Twin Foxes 0
1969	Leigh Park 3, Loke U 1	1981	Fantail 1, Mackintosh 0
1970	Vention U 1, Unique U 0	1982	Dingle Rail 2, Twin Foxes 1
1971	Beacontree R 2, Saltley U 0	1983	Eagle 1,2, Lee Chapel North 1,1
1972	Newtown Unity 4, Springfield C 0	1984	Lee Chapel North 4, Eagle 3
1973	Carlton U 2, Wear Valley 1 (aet)	1985	Hobbies 1,2,2, Avenue 1,2,1
1974	Newtown Unity 3, Brentford E 0	1986	Avenue 1, Glenn Sports 0
1975	Fareham TC 1, Players Ath E 0	1987	Lodge Cottrell 1, Avenue 0
1976	Brandon U 2, Evergreen 1	1988	Nexday 2, Sunderland HP 0

FA CHARITY SHIELD 1908–87

1908 Manchester U 1, QPR 1	1954* Wolverhampton W 4, WBA 4
Replay Manchester U 4, QPR 0	1955 Chelsea 3, Newcastle U 0
1909 Newcastle U 2, Northampton T 0	1956 Manchester U 1, Manchester C 0
1910 Brighton & Hove A 1, Aston Villa 0	1957 Manchester U 4, Aston Villa 0
1911 Manchester U 8, Swindon T 4	1958 Bolton W 4, Wolverhampton W 1
1912 Blackburn R 2, QPR 1	1959 Wolverhampton W 3, Nottingham F 1
1913 Professionals 7, Amateurs 2	1960* Burnley 2, Wolverhampton W 2
1919 WBA 2, Tottenham H 0	1961 Tottenham H 3, FA XI 2
1920 Tottenham H 2, Burnley 0	1962 Tottenham H 5, Ipswich T 1
1921 Huddersfield T 1, Liverpool 0	1963 Everton 4, Manchester U 0
1922 Not played	1964* Liverpool 2, West Ham U 2
1923 Professionals 2, Amateurs 0	1965* Manchester U 2, Liverpool 2
1924 Professionals 3, Amateurs 1	1966 Liverpool 1, Everton 0
1925 Amateurs 6, Professionals 1	1967* Manchester U 3, Tottenham H 3
1926 Amateurs 6, Professionals 3	1968 Manchester C 6, WBA 1
1927 Cardiff C 2, Corinthians 1	1969 Leeds U 2, Manchester C 1
1928 Everton 2, Blackburn R 1	1970 Everton 2, Chelsea 1
1929 Professionals 3, Amateurs 0	1971 Leicester C 1, Liverpool 0
1930 Arsenal 2, Sheffield W 1	1972 Manchester C 1, Aston Villa 0
1931 Arsenal 1, WBA 0	1973 Burnley 1, Manchester C 0
1932 Everton 5, Newcastle U 3	1974 †Liverpool 1, Leeds U 1
1933 Arsenal 3, Everton 0	1975 Derby Co 2, West Ham U 0
1934 Arsenal 4, Manchester C 0	1976 Liverpool 1, Southampton 0
1935 Sheffield W 1, Arsenal 0	1977* Liverpool 0, Manchester U 0
1936 Sunderland 2, Arsenal 1	1978 Nottingham F 5, Ipswich T 0
1937 Manchester C 2, Sunderland 0	1979 Liverpool 3, Arsenal 1
1938 Arsenal 2, Preston NE 1	1980 Liverpool 1, West Ham U 0
1948 Arsenal 4, Manchester U 3	1981* Aston Villa 2, Tottenham H 2
1949* Portsmouth 1, Wolverhampton W 1	1982 Liverpool 1, Tottenham H 0
1950 World Cup Team 4, Canadian Touring Team 2	1983 Manchester U 2, Liverpool 0
1951 Tottenham H 2, Newcastle U 1	1984 Everton 1, Liverpool 0
1952 Manchester U 4, Newcastle U 2	1985 Everton 2, Manchester U 0
1953 Arsenal 3, Blackpool 1	1986* Everton 1, Liverpool 1

1987: EVERTON (1)1, COVENTRY CITY (0)0 (Wembley, 1.8.87, 88,000)
Everton: Mimms; Harper, Power, Ratcliffe, Watson, Reid, Steven, Clarke, Sharp, Heath, Sheedy (Pointon).
Scorer: Clarke.
Coventry C: Ogrizovic; Phillips, Downs, McGrath (Sedgley), Kilcline, Peake, Bennett, Gynn (Borrows), Speedie, Houchen, Pickering.
*Trophy shared.   †Won on penalties.

Everton's Wayne Clarke fires the winner past Coventry keeper Steve Ogrizovic in last season's Charity Shield match at Wembley. *Photo: Bob Thomas Sports Photography.*

SOUTH AMERICAN FOOTBALL

SOUTH AMERICAN CLUB CHAMPIONSHIP (COPA LIBERTADORES) 1987

KEY: Arg – Argentina, Bol – Bolivia, Bra – Brazil, Chi – Chile, Col – Colombia, Ecu – Ecuador, Par – Paraguay, Per – Peru, Uru – Uruguay

SEMI-FINAL – GROUP 1

Cobreola (Chi) (2)3, Barcelona (Ecu) (0)0   1.9.87
Cobreola (Chi) (0)2, America (Col) (0)2   4.9.87
Barcelona (Ecu) (0)0, America (Col) (1)2   9.9.87
Barcelona (Ecu) (0)0, Cobreola (Chi) (0)2   15.9.87
America (Col) (0)1, Cobreola (Chi) (1)1   18.9.87
America (Col) (2)4, Barcelona (Ecu) (0)0   23.9.87

FINAL TABLE	P	W	D	L	F	A	Pts
AMERICA	4	2	2	0	9	3	6
Cobreola	4	2	2	0	8	3	6
Barcelona	4	0	0	4	0	11	0

SEMI-FINAL – GROUP 2

River Plate (Arg)* (0)0, Independiente (Arg) (0)0   26.8.87
Penarol (Uru) (2)3, Independiente (Arg) (0)0   3.9.87
Penarol (Uru) (0)0, River Plate (Arg) (0)0   16.9.87
Independiente (Arg) (0)2, River Plate (Arg) (1)1   23.9.87
Independiente (Arg) (0)2, Penarol (Uru) (0)4   30.9.87
River Plate (Arg) (1)1, Penarol (Uru) (0)0   8.10.87
*Qualified automatically as holders.

FINAL TABLE	P	W	D	L	F	A	Pts
PENAROL	4	2	1	1	7	3	5
River Plate	4	1	2	1	2	2	4
Independiente	4	1	1	2	4	8	3

FINAL 1st LEG

AMERICA (2)2, PENAROL (0)0
Cali, 21.10.87, 45,000
America: Falcioni; Valencia, Espinosa, Aponte, Porras, Luna, Santin, Hernan Herrera (Alex Escobar), Cabanas, Gareca (Maturana), Bataglia. **Scorers:** Bataglia, Cabanas.
Penarol: Pereyra; Jose Herrera, Trasante, Rotti, Dominguez, Perdomo, Matosas (Da Silva), Viera, Vidal (Villar), Aguirre, Cabrera.

FINAL 2nd LEG

PENAROL (0)2, AMERICA (1)1
Montevideo, 28.10.87, 70,000
Penarol: Unchanged. Goncalves came on for Rotti, Villar came on for Cebrera. **Scorers:** Aquirre, Villar.
America: Ortiz for Herrera. Herrera came on for Ortiz.
Scorer: Cabanas.

PLAY-OFF
(Goal difference is not calculated)

PENAROL (0)1, AMERICA (0)0
Santiago, 31.10.87, 30,000
Penarol: Pereyra; Rotti, Trasante, Dominguez, Da Silva, Perdomo, Goncalves, Viera, Vidal (Villar), Aguirre, Cabrera. **Scorer:** Aguirre.
America: Falcioni; Valencia, Espinosa, Aponte, Ampudia, Luna, Santin, Cabanas, Ortiz, Gareca (Esterilla), Bataglia.

PAN-AMERICAN GAMES

INDIANAPOLIS, INDIANA, August 9-21, 1987

GROUP A
Argentina (1)1, El Salvador (0)0
USA (2)3, Trinidad & Tobago (1)1
Argentina (3)6, Trinidad & Tobago (0)0
USA (0)0, El Salvador (0)0
El Salvador (1)1, Trinidad & Tobago (0)0
Argentina (0)1, USA (0)0

GROUP B
Brazil (2)4, Canada (1)1
Chile (0)1, Cuba (0)0
Canada (0)2, Chile (1)2
Brazil (1)3, Cuba (0)1
Brazil (0)0, Chile (0)0
Cuba (2)2, Canada (0)0

GROUP C
Mexico (1)1, Guatemala (0)0
Colombia (0)0, Paraguay (0)0

Mexico (4)7, Paraguay (0)0
Guatemala (1)2, Colombia (0)0
Mexico (1)2, Colombia (1)1
Guatemala (1)1, Paraguay (1)1

Semi-finals
Chile (3)3, Argentina (1)2
Brazil (0)1, Mexico (0)0

Third Place Match
Argentina (0)0, Mexico (0)0
Argentina won 5–4 on penalties.

FINAL
BRAZIL (0)2, CHILE (0)0 (aet, att. 14,000)
Brazil: Tafarel; Geraldao, I.Ricardo, Nelsinho (Meneres), Andre Cruz, Evair, Careca, Valdo, Edu, Pita, Joao Paulo (Washington). **Scorers:** Washington 104, Evair 115)
Chile: Fournier; Ceballos, Figueroa, Enriquez, Medina, Tamayo, Hormann (Pinto), Perez, Gonzalez, Francino, Pino (Gonzalez).

OLYMPIC FOOTBALL

PAST FINALS

1908 (LONDON): Great Britain 2, Denmark 0	1956 (MELBOURNE): USSR 1, Yugoslavia 0
1912 (STOCKHOLM): Great Britain 4, Denmark 2	1960 (ROME): Yugoslavia 3, Denmark 1
1920 (ANTWERP): Belgium 2, Czechoslovakia 0	1964 (TOKYO): Hungary 2, Czechoslovakia 1
1924 (PARIS): Uruguay 3, Switzerland 0	1968 (MEXICO CITY): Hungary 4, Bulgaria 1
1928 (AMSTERDAM): Uruguay 2, Argentina 1	1972 (MUNICH): Poland 2, Hungary 1
1932 (LOS ANGELES): No football tournament	1976 (MONTREAL): East Germany 3, Poland 1
1936 (BERLIN): Italy 2, Austria 1	1980 (MOSCOW): Czechoslovakia 1, East Germany 0
1948 (LONDON): Sweden 3, Yugoslavia 1	1984 (LOS ANGELES): France 2, Brazil 0
1952 (HELSINKI): Hungary 2, Yugoslavia 0	

SEOUL 1988 – QUALIFYING COMPETITION

EUROPE

One qualifier from each group. France qualify automatically as holders.

PRELIMINARY ROUND

Group 1
Liechtenstein 0, Switzerland 10	10.9.86
Switzerland 9, Liechtenstein 0	23.9.86

Group 2
Cyprus 1, Greece 2	12.11.86
Greece 2, Cyprus 0	10.12.86

FINAL ROUND

Group A
Rumania 1, West Germany 0	18.4.87
Greece 0, Denmark 5	20.5.87
Rumania 0, Poland 0	20.5.87
Denmark 8, Rumania 0	10.6.87
Rumania 1, Denmark 2	3.9.87
West Germany 3, Greece 0	22.9.87
West Germany 5, Poland 1	13.10.87
Poland 2, Denmark 0	28.10.87

(Denmark won 2–0, but result reversed by FIFA as Denmark fielded an ineligible player)

Denmark 0, West Germany 1	18.11.87
Greece 0, Poland 1	18.11.87
Greece 0, West Germany 2	18.2.88
Poland 5, Greece 1	16.3.88
West Germany 1, Denmark 1	22.3.88
Poland 1, Rumania 0	30.3.88
Rumania 0, Greece 1	6.4.88
Denmark 4, Greece 0	20.4.88
Poland 1, West Germany 1	27.4.88
Denmark 3, Poland 0	18.5.88
Greece 2, Rumania 3	18.5.88
West Germany 3, Rumania 0	31.5.88

FINAL TABLE	P	W	D	L	F	A	GD	Pts
WEST GERMANY	8	5	2	1	16	4	+12	12
Denmark	8	5	1	2	23	5	+18	11
Poland	8	4	2	2	11	10	+1	10
Rumania	8	2	1	5	5	17	−12	5
Greece	8	1	0	7	4	23	−19	2

Group B
Netherlands 0, East Germany 1	3.12.86
Italy 1, Portugal 0	18.2.87
Portugal 1, Netherlands 1	25.2.87
East Germany 0, Italy 0	25.3.87
Italy 2, Iceland 0	15.4.87
Portugal 0, East Germany 0	28.4.87
Iceland 2, Netherlands 2	26.5.87
Iceland 2, East Germany 0	2.9.87
East Germany 4, Netherlands 2	22.9.87
Portugal 2, Iceland 1	7.10.87
Italy 1, East Germany 1	18.11.87
Portugal 0, Italy 0	24.2.88
Netherlands 0, Italy 1	9.3.88
Netherlands 0, Portugal 0	30.3.88
East Germany 3, Portugal 0	13.4.88
Italy 3, Netherlands 0	13.4.88
Netherlands 1, Iceland 0	27.4.88
East Germany 3, Iceland 0	30.4.88
Iceland 0, Portugal 1	24.5.88
Iceland 0, Italy 3	29.5.88

FINAL TABLE	P	W	D	L	F	A	GD	Pts
ITALY	8	5	3	0	11	1	+10	13
East Germany	8	4	3	1	12	5	+ 7	11
Portugal	8	2	4	2	4	6	−2	8
Netherlands	8	1	3	4	6	12	−6	5
Iceland	8	1	1	6	5	14	−9	3

Group C
Spain 1, Sweden 1	19.11.86
Rep. of Ireland 1, Hungary 2	19.11.86
Rep. of Ireland 2, Spain 2	4.2.87
France 0, Hungary 2	28.4.87
Sweden 1, Rep. of Ireland 0	5.5.87
Hungary 2, Spain 1	13.5.87
Hungary 2, Sweden 1	3.6.87
Sweden 4, France 2	16.6.87
France 1, Rep. of Ireland 1	12.8.87
Rep. of Ireland 0, Sweden 1	25.8.87
Sweden 1, Hungary 0	9.9.87
Sweden 2, Spain 0	23.9.87
Spain 1, France 2	14.10.87
Rep. of Ireland 3, France 0	18.11.87
Spain 1, Hungary 0	18.11.87
France 1, Spain 1	23.3.88
Hungary 2, France 2	27.4.88
Hungary 3, Rep. of Ireland 1	4.5.88
Spain 2, Rep. of Ireland 2	18.5.88
France 1, Sweden 2	26.5.88

FINAL TABLE	P	W	D	L	F	A	GD	Pts
SWEDEN	8	6	1	1	13	6	+7	13
Hungary	8	5	1	2	13	8	+5	11
Spain	8	1	4	3	9	12	−3	6
Rep. of Ireland	8	1	3	4	10	12	−2	5
France	8	1	3	4	9	16	−7	5

Group D

Norway 0, USSR 0	14.10.86
Switzerland 1, Norway 0	8.11.86
Turkey 3, Switzerland 2	3.12.86
Turkey 0, USSR 2	15.4.87
Switzerland 1, Bulgaria 1	16.4.87
Norway 1, Turkey 1	6.5.87
Bulgaria 0, USSR 1	7.5.87
Norway 0, Bulgaria 0	26.5.87
USSR 1, Norway 0	12.8.87
Norway 0, Switzerland 0	26.8.87
Switzerland 2, Turkey 0	7.10.87
Switzerland 2, USSR 4	28.10.87
Bulgaria 4, Norway 0	14.11.87
Turkey 0, Norway 0	18.11.87
Turkey 0, Bulgaria 3	9.12.87
USSR 2, Turkey 0	6.4.88
Bulgaria 2, Switzerland 0	13.4.88
USSR 2, Bulgaria 0	27.4.88
USSR 0, Switzerland 0	10.5.88
Bulgaria 3, Turkey 1	25.5.88

FINAL TABLE	P	W	D	L	F	A	GD	Pts
USSR	8	6	2	0	12	2	+10	14
Bulgaria	8	4	2	2	13	5	+8	10
Switzerland	8	2	3	3	8	10	−2	7
Norway	8	0	5	3	1	7	−6	5
Turkey	8	1	2	5	5	15	−10	4

Group E

Finland 0, Belgium 2	14.10.86
Czechoslovakia 2, Belgium 0	29.10.86
Belgium 2, Austria 3	18.11.86
Austria 2, Czechoslovakia 0	14.4.87
Finland 2, Austria 1	12.5.87
Austria 0, Yugoslavia 1	3.6.87
Finland 0, Czechoslovakia 2	10.6.87
Yugoslavia 2, Austria 1	26.8.87
Yugoslavia 5, Finland 0	2.9.87
Czechoslovakia 2, Finland 0	23.9.87
Belgium 2, Yugoslavia 2	24.9.87
Belgium 0, Czechoslovakia 2	7.10.87
Belgium 1, Finland 0	28.10.87
Czechoslovakia 1, Yugoslavia 0	28.10.87
Austria 0, Belgium 1	11.11.87
Yugoslavia 4, Belgium 0	2.12.87
Czechoslovakia 1, Austria 0	12.4.88
Yugoslavia 1, Czechoslovakia 0	27.4.88
Finland 1, Yugoslavia 2	18.5.88
Austria 0, Finland 2	31.5.88

FINAL TABLE	P	W	D	L	F	A	GD	Pts
YUGOSLAVIA	8	6	1	1	17	5	+12	13
Czechoslovakia	8	6	0	2	10	3	+7	12
Belgium	8	3	1	4	8	13	−5	7
Austria	8	2	0	6	7	11	−4	4
Finland	8	2	0	6	4	15	−11	4

ASIA

One qualifier from each area

WEST ASIA, FINAL ROUND

Saudi Arabia 0, Kuwait 0	4.12.87
Qatar 0, Kuwait 0	4.12.87
Qatar 1, Iraq 3	11.12.87
Kuwait 1, Saudi Arabia 0	11.12.87
Kuwait 2, Iraq 1	18.12.87
Saudi Arabia 1, Qatar 1	18.12.87
Iraq 1, Saudi Arabia 1 (in Tokyo)	1.1.88
Kuwait 0, Qatar 0	1.1.88
Iraq 4, Qatar 1 (in Tokyo)	8.1.88
Saudi Arabia 0, Kuwait 0	8.1.88
Iraq 1, Kuwait 0 (in Tokyo)	15.1.88
Qatar 1, Saudi Arabia 0	15.1.88

FINAL TABLE	P	W	D	L	F	A	GD	Pts
IRAQ	6	3	2	1	10	5	+5	8
Kuwait	6	2	3	1	3	2	+1	7
Qatar	6	1	3	2	4	8	−4	5
Saudi Arabia	6	0	4	2	2	4	−2	4

EAST ASIA, FINAL ROUND

Thailand 0, Japan 0	2.9.87
Japan 5, Nepal 0	15.9.87
Nepal 0, Japan 9 (in Tokyo)	18.9.87
China 8, Nepal 0	23.9.87
Japan 1, Thailand 0	26.9.87
Nepal 0, China 12 (in Shenyan, China)	26.9.87
Thailand 3, Nepal 0	1.10.87
Nepal 1, Thailand 2 (in Bangkok)	4.10.87
China 0, Japan 1	4.10.87
Thailand 0, China 1	11.10.87
China 2, Thailand 0	18.10.87
Japan 0, China 2	26.10.87

FINAL TABLE	P	W	D	L	F	A	GD	Pts
CHINA	6	5	0	1	25	1	+24	10
Japan	6	4	1	1	16	2	+14	9
Thailand	6	2	1	3	5	5	0	5
Nepal	6	0	0	6	1	39	−38	0

OCEANIA/ISRAEL

One qualifier.

Group 1

Papua New Guinea withdrew.

Taiwan 0, Australia 3	15.11.87
Australia 3, Taiwan 0	26.2.88

Group 2

Fiji withdrew

Western Samoa 0, New Zealand 7	7.11.87
New Zealand 12, Western Samoa 0	14.11.87

Play-off match

Taiwan 5, Western Samoa 0	2.3.88

FINAL ROUND

In Australia:

Taiwan 0, New Zealand 1	6.3.88
Australia 2, Israel 0	6.3.88

OLYMPIC FOOTBALL

Israel 2, New Zealand 0	9.3.88		New Zealand 1, Australia 1		23.3.88
Australia 3, Taiwan 2	9.3.88		Taiwan 0, Australia 3		27.3.88
Israel 5, Taiwan 0	13.3.88		New Zealand 0, Israel 1		27.3.88
Australia 3, New Zealand 1	13.3.88				

In New Zealand:

Israel 0, Australia 0	20.3.88
New Zealand 2, Taiwan 0	20.3.88
Taiwan 0, Israel 9	23.3.88

FINAL TABLE	P	W	D	L	F	A	GD	Pts
AUSTRALIA	6	4	2	0	12	4	+8	10
Israel	6	4	1	1	17	3	+14	9
New Zealand	6	2	1	3	5	7	−2	5
Taiwan	6	0	0	6	3	23	−20	0

AFRICA

Three qualifiers.

FINAL ROUND

Algeria 1, Nigeria	15.1.88
Nigeria 2, Algeria 0	30.1.88

Tunisia 1, Morocco 0	17.1.88
Morocco 2, Tunisia 2	30.1.88
Zambia 2, Ghana 0	17.1.88
Ghana 1, Zambia 0	31.1.88

TUNISIA, ZAMBIA, NIGERIA QUALIFY

CONMEBOL

Two qualifiers

Tournament in Bolivia

Group A

Peru 0, Colombia 1	18.4.87
Brazil 3, Paraguay 1	18.4.87
Peru 0, Uruguay 1	20.4.87
Brazil 0, Colombia 2	20.4.87
Peru 0, Paraguay 2	22.4.87
Uruguay 0, Colombia 0	22.4.87
Paraguay 0, Colombia 1	24.4.87
Brazil 1, Uruguay 1	24.4.87
Uruguay 0, Paraguay 1	26.4.87
Brazil 1, Peru 1	26.4.87

Group B

Chile 1, Argentina 1	19.4.87
Bolivia 3, Venezuela 0	19.4.87
Ecuador 0, Argentina 0	21.4.87
Bolivia 1, Chile 0	21.4.87
Chile 2, Ecuador 1	23.4.87

Venezuela 0, Argentina 2	23.4.87
Venezuela 1, Chile 3	25.4.87
Ecuador 0, Bolivia 1	25.4.87
Ecuador 1, Venezuela 0	27.4.87
Bolivia 0, Argentina 3	27.4.87

FINAL ROUND

Argentina 2, Brazil 0	29.4.87
Colombia 1, Bolivia 2	29.4.87
Colombia 1, Brazil 2	1.5.87
Argentina 0, Bolivia 0	1.5.87
Brazil 2, Bolivia 1	3.5.87
Colombia 1, Argentina 0	3.5.87

FINAL TABLE	P	W	D	L	F	A	GD	Pts
BRAZIL	3	2	0	1	4	4	0	4
ARGENTINA	3	1	1	1	2	1	+1	3
Bolivia	3	1	1	1	3	3	0	3
Colombia	3	1	0	2	3	4	−1	2

CONCACAF

Two qualifiers.

FINAL ROUND

Group A

USA 4, Trinidad & Tobago 1	6.9.87
Trinidad & Tobago 0, USA 1	20.9.87
El Salvador 2, USA 4	18.10.87
USA 4, El Salvador 1	25.5.88
El Salvador 0, Trinidad & Tobago 1	15.5.88
Trinidad & Tobago v El Salvador (match cancelled)	

USA QUALIFY

Group B

Guatemala 6, Guyana 0	18.10.87
Guyana 0, Guatemala 3	25.10.87
Guyana 0, Mexico 9	2.12.87
Mexico v Guyana – walkover for Mexico	
Mexico 2, Guatemala 1	3.2.88
Guatemala 0, Mexico 3	14.2.88

MEXICO QUALIFY

FOOTBALL AWARDS

THE PFA AWARDS

Player of the Year 1988: John Barnes (Liverpool)
Past winners

1974	Norman Hunter (Leeds United)	1981	John Wark (Ipswich Town)
1975	Colin Todd (Derby County)	1982	Kevin Keegan (Southampton)
1976	Pat Jenning (Tottenham Hotspur)	1983	Kenny Dalglish (Liverpool)
1977	Andy Gray (Aston Villa)	1984	Ian Rush (Liverpool)
1978	Peter Shilton (Nottingham Forest)	1985	Peter Reid (Everton)
1979	Liam Brady (Arsenal)	1986	Gary Lineker (Everton)
1980	Terry McDermott (Liverpool)	1987	Clive Allen (Tottenham Hotspur)

Young Player of the Year 1988: Paul Gascoigne (Newcastle United)
Past winners

1974	Kevin Beattie (Ipswich Town)	1981	Gary Shaw (Aston Villa)
1975	Mervyn Day (West Ham United)	1982	Steve Moran (Southampton)
1976	Peter Barnes (Manchester City)	1983	Ian Rush (Liverpool)
1977	Andy Gray (Aston Villa)	1984	Paul Walsh (Luton Town)
1978	Tony Woodcock (Nottingham Forest)	1985	Mark Hughes (Manchester United)
1979	Cyrille Regis (West Bromwich Albion)	1986	Tony Cottee (West Ham United)
1980	Glenn Hoddle (Tottenham Hotspur)	1987	Tony Adams (Arsenal)

PFA Merit Award 1988: Billy Bonds MBE
Past winners

1974	Bobby Charlton CBE, Cliff Lloyd OBE	1981	John Trollope MBE
1975	Denis Law	1982	Joe Mercer OBE
1976	George Eastham OBE	1983	Bob Paisley OBE
1977	Jack Taylor OBE	1984	Bill Nicholson
1978	Bill Shankly OBE	1985	Ron Greenwood
1979	Tom Finney OBE	1986	England's 1966 World Cup team, Sir Alf Ramsey, Harold Shepherdson
1980	Sir Matt Busby CBE	1987	Sir Stanley Matthews

John Barnes with the PFA Player of the Year Trophy after the annual awards dinner, sponsored by Panini, at the Grosvenor House Hotel. With John are Panini Publishing's managing director Manlio Guidetti *(left)* and managing editor Peter Dunk. *Photo: Bob Thomas Sports Photography*

FOOTBALL AWARDS

FOOTBALL WRITERS' ASSOCIATION

Footballer of the Year 1988: John Barnes (Liverpool)
Past winners

1948	Stanley Matthews (Blackpool)	1968	George Best (Manchester United)
1949	Johnny Carey (Manchester United)	1969	Dave Mackay (Derby County)
1950	Joe Mercer (Arsenal)	1970	Billy Bremner (Leeds United)
1951	Harry Johnston (Blackpool)	1971	Frank McLintock (Arsenal)
1952	Billy Wright (Wolverhampton W)	1972	Gordon Banks (Stoke City)
1953	Nat Lofthouse (Bolton Wanderers)	1973	Pat Jennings (Tottenham Hotspur)
1954	Tom Finney (Preston North End)	1974	Ian Callaghan (Liverpool)
1955	Don Revie (Manchester City)	1975	Alan Mullery (Fulham)
1956	Bert Trautmann (Manchester City)	1976	Kevin Keegan (Liverpool)
1957	Tom Finney (Preston North End)	1977	Emlyn Hughes (Liverpool)
1958	Danny Blanchflower (Tottenham H)	1978	Kenny Burns (Nottingham Forest)
1959	Syd Owen (Luton Town)	1979	Kenny Dalglish (Liverpool)
1960	Bill Slater (Wolverhampton W)	1980	Terry McDermott (Liverpool)
1961	Danny Blanchflower (Tottenham H)	1981	Frans Thijssen (Ipswich Town)
1962	Jimmy Adamson (Burnley)	1982	Steve Perryman (Tottenham H)
1963	Stanley Matthews (Stoke City)	1983	Kenny Dalglish (Liverpool)
1964	Bobby Moore (West Ham United)	1984	Ian Rush (Liverpool)
1965	Bobby Collins (Leeds United)	1985	Neville Southall (Everton)
1966	Bobby Charlton (Manchester United)	1986	Gary Lineker (Everton)
1967	Jackie Charlton (Leeds United)	1987	Clive Allen (Tottenham Hotspur)

THE SCOTTISH PFA AWARDS

Player of the Year 1988: Paul McStay (Celtic)
Past winners

1978	Derek Johnstone (Rangers)	1983	Charlie Nicholas (Celtic)
1979	Paul Hegarty (Dundee United)	1984	Willie Miller (Aberdeen)
1980	Davie Provan (Celtic)	1985	Jim Duffy (Morton)
1981	Sandy Clark (Airdrieonians)	1986	Richard Gough (Dundee United)
1982	Mark McGhee (Aberdeen)	1987	Brian McClair (Celtic)

Young Player of the Year 1988: John Collins (Hibernian)
Past winners

1978	Graeme Payne (Dundee United)	1983	Pat Nevin (Clyde)
1979	Graham Stewart (Dundee United)	1984	John Robertson (Hearts)
1980	John MacDonald (Rangers)	1985	Craig Levein (Hearts)
1981	Frank McAvennie (St Mirren)	1986	Craig Levein (Hearts)
1982	Charlie Nicholas (Celtic)	1987	Robert Fleck (Rangers)

SCOTTISH FOOTBALL WRITERS' ASSOCIATION

Player of the Year 1988: Paul McStay (Celtic)
Past winners

1965	Billy McNeill (Celtic)	1977	Danny McGrain (Celtic)
1966	John Grieg (Rangers)	1978	Derek Johnstone (Rangers)
1967	Ronnie Simpson (Celtic)	1979	Andy Ritchie (Morton)
1968	Gordon Wallace (Raith Rovers)	1980	Gordon Strachan (Aberdeen)
1969	Bobby Murdoch (Celtic)	1981	Alan Rough (Partick Thistle)
1970	Pat Stanton (Hibernian)	1982	Paul Sturrock (Dundee United)
1971	Martin Buchan (Aberdeen)	1983	Charlie Nicholas (Celtic)
1972	Dave Smith (Rangers)	1984	Willer Miller (Aberdeen)
1973	George Connelly (Celtic)	1985	Hamish McAlpine (Dundee United)
1974	Scotland's World Cup Squad	1986	Sandy Jardine (Hearts)
1975	Sandy Jardine (Rangers)	1987	Brian McClair (Celtic)
1976	John Grieg (Rangers)		

BELL'S FOOTBALL MANAGER AWARDS

Manager of the Year 1987–88: Kenny Dalglish (Liverpool)

Divisional Managers of the Season 1987–88: Division 2 – John Docherty (Millwall), Division 3 – Denis Smith (Sunderland), Division 4 – Graham Turner (Wolves).

FOOTBALL AWARDS

Divisional Managers of the Month 1987–88:
August: Manager of the Month – Jim Smith (QPR), Division 2 – Dave Smith (Plymouth Argyle), Division 3 – Tommy Coakley (Walsall), Division 4 – Cyril Knowles (Torquay United).
September: Manager of the Month – Kenny Dalglish (Liverpool), Division 2 – Terry Dolan (Bradford City), Division 3 – Harry McNally (Chester City), Division 4 – John Bird (Hartlepool).
October: Manager of the Month – George Graham (Arsenal), Division 2 – Graham Taylor (Aston Villa), Division 3 – Denis Smith (Sunderland), Division 4 – Mike Walker (Colchester United).
November: Manager of the Month – Kenny Dalglish (Liverpool), Division 2 – Mel Machin (Manchester City), Division 3 – Sam Ellis (Blackpool), Division 4 – Frank Clark (Leyton Orient).
December: Manager of the Month – Brian Clough (Nottingham Forest), Division 2 – Billy Bremner (Leeds United), Division 3 – Terry Cooper (Bristol City), Division 4 – Roger Brown (Colchester United).
January: Manager of the Month – Kenny Dalglish (Liverpool), Division 2 – Graham Taylor (Aston Villa), Division 3 – Denis Smith (Sunderland), Division 4 – Graham Taylor (Wolves).
February: Manager of the Month – George Graham (Arsenal), Division 2 – Don Mackay (Blackburn Rovers), Division 3 – Barry Lloyd (Brighton & Hove Albion), Division 4 – John Bird (Hartlepool).
March: Manager of the Month – Ian Branfoot (Reading), Division 1 – Colin Harvey (Everton), Division 3 – Gerry Francis (Bristol Rovers), Division 4 – Dixie McNeill (Wrexham).
April: Manager of the Month – John Docherty (Millwall), Division 1 – Ray Harford (Luton Town), Division 3 – Barry Lloyd (Brighton & Hove Albion), Division 4 – Frank Burrows (Cardiff City).

EUROPEAN FOOTBALLER OF THE YEAR

(Based on a poll by France Football magazine)

European Footballer of the Year 1987: Ruud Gullit (AC Milan)
Past winners

1956	Stanley Matthews (Blackpool)	1972	Franz Beckenbauer (Bayern Munich)
1957	Alfredo di Stefano (Real Madrid)	1973	Johan Cruyff (Barcelona)
1958	Raymond Kopa (Real Madrid)	1974	Johan Cruyff (Barcelona)
1959	Alfredo di Stefano (Real Madrid)	1975	Oleg Blokhin (Dynamo Kiev)
1960	Luis Suarez (Barcelona)	1976	Franz Beckenbauer (Bayern Munich)
1961	Omar Sivori (Juventus)	1977	Allan Simonsen (Borussia MG)
1962	Josef Masopust (Dukla Prague)	1978	Kevin Keegan (SV Hamburg)
1963	Lev Yachin (Moscow Dynamo)	1979	Kevin Keegan (SV Hamburg)
1964	Denis Law (Manchester United)	1980	Karl-Heinz Rummenigge (Bayern Munich)
1965	Eusebio (Benfica)	1981	Karl-Heinz Rummenigge (Bayern Munich)
1966	Bobby Charlton (Manchester United)	1982	Paolo Rossi (Juventus)
1967	Florian Albert (Ferencvaros)	1983	Michel Platini (Juventus)
1968	George Best (Manchester United)	1984	Michel Platini (Juventus)
1969	Gianni Rivera (AC Milan)	1985	Michel Platini (Juventus)
1970	Gerd Muller (Bayern Munich)	1986	Igor Belanov (Dynamo Kiev)
1971	Johan Cruyff (Ajax)		

WORLD PLAYER OF THE YEAR

(Based on a poll by World Soccer magazine)

World Player of the Year 1987: Ruud Gullit (AC Milan)
Past winners

1982	Paolo Rossi (Juventus)	1985	Michel Platini (Juventus)
1983	Zico (Udinese)	1986	Diego Maradona (Napoli)
1984	Michel Platini (Juventus)		

FOOTBALL LEAGUE TRANSFERS 1987–88

Player	*From*	*To*
MAY 1987		
1 Dennis, Mark E.	Southampton	Queen's Park Rangers
21 McCarthy, Michael J.	Manchester City	Celtic
18 Smyth, John M.	Dundalk	Liverpool
26 Winterburn, Nigel	Wimbledon	Arsenal
LOANS		
19 Hill, Richard W.	Northampton T	Watford
LOANS REVERTING		
13 Cawley, Peter	Bristol Rovers	Wimbledon
8 Hood, Derek	Lincoln City	York City
20 Joseph, Francis	Wimbledon	Brentford
JUNE 1987		
19 Barnes, John C.B.	Watford	Liverpool
25 Beckford, Darren	Manchester City	Port Vale
22 Brooks, Shaun	Leyton Orient	AFC Bournemouth
23 Cascarino, Anthony C.	Gillingham	Millwall
18 Coney, Dean H.	Fulham	Queens Park Rangers
19 Rosenior, Leroy de Graft	Queens Park Rangers	Fulham
24 Foley, Steven	Sheffield United	Swindon Town
19 Ford, Gary	York City	Leicester City
29 Gallagher, Jackie C.	Peterborough United	Wolverhampton W.
17 Glover, Dean V.	Aston Villa	Middlesbrough
30 Hart, Paul A.	Birmingham City	Notts County
18 Irvine, James A.	Crystal Palace	Dundee United
24 James, Robert M.	Queens Park Rangers	Leicester City
24 Kelly John	Chester City	Swindon Town
30 Langley, Kevin J.	Everton	Manchester City
26 Lowe, David A.	Wigan Athletic	Ipswich Town
18 McCall, Stephen H.	Ipswich Town	Sheffield Wednesday
30 Mackenzie, Steven	West Bromwich Albion	Charlton Athletic
22 Maddy, Paul M.	Brentford	Chester City
25 Morgan, Trevor J.	Bristol City	Bolton Wanderers
5 O'Callaghan, Kevin	Portsmouth	Millwall
24 Oghani, George	Bolton Wanderers	Burnley
18 Parker, Paul A.	Fulham	Queens Park Rangers
16 Ratcliffe, Simon	Manchester United	Norwich City
26 Rougvie, Douglas	Chelsea	Brighton & Hove A
23 Senior, Stephen	York City	Northampton Town
3 Simmonds, Robert L.	Leeds United	Rochdale
9 Sims, Steven F.	Watford	Aston Villa
8 Thomas, Geoffrey R.	Crewe Alexandra	Crystal Palace
23 Tomlinson, Paul	Sheffield United	Bradford City
8 Wakenshaw, Robert A.	Rochdale	Crewe Alexandra
11 Whitehead, Clive R.	West Bromwich Albion	Portsmouth
25 Wilson, Kevin J.	Ipswich Town	Chelsea
17 Wood, Stephen A.	Reading	Millwall
JULY 1987		
1 Adcock, Anthony C.	Colchester United	Manchester City
9 Anderson, Vivian A.	Arsenal	Manchester United
10 Barham, Mark F.	Norwich City	Huddersfield Town
24 Barrett, Scott	Wolverhampton W	Stoke City
24 Beardsley, Peter A.	Newcastle United	Liverpool
21 Bellamy, Gary	Chesterfield	Wolverhampton W
23 Bowen, Mark R.	Tottenham Hotspur	Norwich City
8 Bremner, Kevin J.	Reading	Brighton & Hove A
27 Brown, Anthony J.	Doncaster Rovers	Scunthorpe United
20 Cadette, Richard R.	Southend United	Sheffield United
9 Caldwell, Anthony	Bolton Wanderers	Bristol City
15 Carr, Clifford P.	Fulham	Stoke City
28 Chamberlain, Alec F.R.	Colchester United	Everton
31 Chandler, Jeffrey G.	Derby County	Bolton Wanderers
8 Childs, Gary P.C.	Walsall	Birmingham City
2 Clayton, Gary	Doncaster Rovers	Cambridge United
1 Connor, Terence F.	Brighton & Hove A	Portsmouth

16	Cornwell, John A.	Leyton Orient	Newcastle United
21	Day, Keith	Colchester United	Leyton Orient
3	Dorigo, Anthony R.	Aston Villa	Chelsea
3	Fairclough, Courtney H.	Nottingham Forest	Tottenham Hotspur
17	Falco, Mark P.	Watford	Rangers
31	Francis, Joseph	Brentford	Reading
3	Franklin, Paul L.	Watford	Reading
17	Gage, Kevin W.	Wimbledon	Aston Villa
22	Gittens, Jon	Southampton	Swindon
29	Goodyear, Clive	Plymouth Argyle	Wimbledon
17	Gordon, Colin K.	Wimbledon	Reading
16	Hackett, Gary S.	Shrewsbury Town	Aberdeen
21	Harbey, Graham K.	Derby County	Ipswich Town
27	Halsall, Michael	Grimsby Town	Peterborough United
21	Hetherston, Peter	Falkirk	Watford
15	Hodges, Glyn P.	Wimbledon	Newcastle United
17	Horne, Barry	Wrexham	Portsmouth
17	Jones, Linden	Newport County	Reading
22	Kay, John	Wimbledon	Sunderland
13	Kelly, Anthony G.	Stoke City	West Bromwich Albion
8	Ketteridge, Stephen J.	Crystal Palace	Leyton Orient
29	Lawrence, George R.	Southampton	Millwall
21	Lee, Colin	Chelsea	Brentford
3	Longhurst, David J.	Halifax Town	Northampton Town
3	Loram, Mark J.	Queen's Park Rangers	Torquay United
30	McClair, Brian J.	Celtic	Manchester United
28	McInally, Alan	Celtic	Aston Villa
31	MacPhail, John	Bristol City	Sunderland
13	May, Andrew M.	Manchester City	Huddersfield Town
22	Metgod, Johannes A.B.	Nottingham Forest	Tottenham Hotspur
23	Millar, John	Chelsea	Blackburn Rovers
21	Morris, Mark J.	Wimbledon	Watford
17	Nelson, Garry P.	Plymouth Argyle	Brighton & Hove A
27	O'Neill, John P.	Leicester City	Queen's Park Rangers
14	Pearce, Christopher L.	Wrexham	Burnley
29	Phelan, Terry	Swansea City	Wimbledon
13	Pike, Geoffrey A.	West Ham United	Notts County
21	Rathbone, Michael J.	Blackburn Rovers	Preston North End
31	Redfearn, Neil D.	Doncaster Rovers	Crystal Palace
21	Rees, Melvyn J.	Cardiff City	Watford
29	Robinson, Martin J.	Gillingham	Southend United
3	Robinson, Philip J.	Aston Villa	Wolverhampton W
17	Robson, Mark A.	Exeter City	Tottenham Hotspur
17	Russell, Kevin J.	Portsmouth	Wrexham
16	Scales, John R.	Bristol Rovers	Wimbledon
28	Senior, Trevor	Reading	Watford
24	Shelton, Gary	Sheffield Wednesday	Oxford United
7	Shilton, Peter L.	Southampton	Derby County
23	Sinnott, Lee	Watford	Bradford City
28	Smith, Mark C.	Sheffield Wednesday	Plymouth Argyle
31	Snodin, Glynn	Sheffield Wednesday	Leeds United
23	Speedie, David R.	Chelsea	Coventry City
29	Thomas, John W.	Preston North End	Bolton Wanderers
3	Walwyn, Keith I.	York City	Blackpool
28	Williams, Brian	Bristol City	Shrewsbury Town
31	Williams, Gary	Aston Villa	Leeds United
16	Wilson, Daniel	Brighton & Hove A	Luton Town
23	Wilson, Paul A.	Huddersfield Town	Norwich City
29	Young, Eric	Brighton & Hove A	Wimbledon

LOANS

28	Riley, David S.	Nottingham Forest	Peterborough United
23	Storer, Stuart J.	Everton	Wigan Athletic

LOANS UPGRADED TO FULL TRANSFER

3	Hill, Richard W.	Northampton Town	Watford

AUGUST 1987

10	Anderson, Douglas E.	Tranmere Rovers	Plymouth Argyle
12	Baird, Ian J.	Leeds United	Portsmouth
22	Barnes, David	Wolverhampton W	Aldershot
6	Bowden, John	Port Vale	Wrexham

FOOTBALL LEAGUE TRANSFERS

13 Brock, Kevin S.	Oxford United	Queens Park Rangers
13 Bromage, Russell	Port Vale	Bristol City
11 Burridge, John	Sheffield United	Southampton
3 Charles, Stephen	Wrexham	Mansfield Town
14 Clark, Jonathan	Bury	Carlisle United
12 Clegg, Tony	Bradford City	York City
7 Comstive, Paul T.	Wrexham	Burnley
14 Coyle, Ronald P.	Middlesbrough	Rochdale
4 Cunningham, Anthony E.	Newcastle United	Blackpool
21 Curbishley, Llewellyn C.	Charlton Athletic	Brighton & Hove A
11 Dawson, Alistair	Rangers	Blackburn Rovers
11 Dixon, Kevin L.	Hartlepool United	Scunthorpe United
14 Dublin, Keith B.L.	Chelsea	Brighton & Hove A
7 Farrell, Andrew J.	Colchester United	Burnley
29 Galvin, Anthony	Tottenham Hotspur	Sheffield Wednesday
14 Gavin, Mark W.	Bolton Wanderers	Rochdale
27 Gibson, Terence B.	Manchester United	Wimbledon
3 Godden, Anthony L.	Chelsea	Birmingham City
13 Gooding, Michael C.	Rotherham United	Peterborough United
21 Holloway, Ian S.	Brentford	Bristol Rovers
28 Irvine, Alan J.	Liverpool	Dundee United
14 Jones, Joseph P.	Huddersfield Town	Wrexham
14 Keeley, Glenn M.	Blackburn Rovers	Oldham Athletic
14 Knill, Alan R.	Halifax Town	Swansea City
13 Lowey, John A.	Wigan Athletic	Preston North End
14 Mills, Gary R.	Nottingham Forest	Notts County
3 Moore, Thomas K.	Oldham Athletic	Southampton
10 Morris, Christopher B.	Sheffield Wednesday	Celtic
6 Moss, Ernest	Stockport County	Scarborough
10 Nicholas, Peter	Luton Town	Aberdeen
25 Orr, Neil I.	West Ham United	Hibernian
14 Pearson, Lawrence	Bristol City	Port Vale
27 Poole, Kevin	Aston Villa	Middlesbrough
14 Ramsey, Christopher L.	Swindon Town	Southend United
26 Richardson, Kevin	Watford	Arsenal
14 Ritchie, Andrew T.	Leeds United	Oldham Athletic
3 Salmon, Michael B.	Bolton Wanderers	Wrexham
7 Shipley, George M.	Charlton Athletic	Gillingham
28 Shotton, Malcolm	Oxford United	Portsmouth
14 Stannard, James	Southend United	Fulham
19 Statham, Derek	West Bromwich Albion	Southampton
3 Steele, Eric G.	Derby County	Southend United
21 Taylor, Steven J.	Preston North End	Burnley
24 Turnbull, Lee M.	Middlesbrough	Aston Villa
28 Vaughan, Nigel M.	Cardiff City	Wolverhampton W
8 Walsh, Mario M.	Torquay United	Colchester United
13 Wilson, Philip	Huddersfield Town	York City
28 Wood, Paul A.	Portsmouth	Brighton & Hove A
3 Woods, Neil S.	Rangers	Ipswich Town
27 Wright, Mark	Southampton	Derby County
19 Young, Richard A.	Notts County	Southend United

LOANS

28 Batty, Lawrence	Fulham	Crystal Palace
14 Benstead, Graham M.	Norwich City	Colchester United
22 Chandler, Ian	Barnsley	Stockport County
29 Cook, Michael J.	Coventry City	York City
11 Gray, Andrew M.	Aston Villa	Notts County
27 Greygoose, Dean	Crystal Palace	Crewe Alexandra
14 Hardwick, Steven	Oxford United	Sunderland
12 Howlett, Gary P.	AFC Bournemouth	Aldershot
3 McGuire, Michael J.	Oldham Athletic	Blackpool
14 McLoughlin, Alan	Swindon Town	Torquay United
5 North, Mark V.	Luton Town	Grimsby Town
29 Prudhoe, Mark	Walsall	Hartlepool United
7 Slack, Trevor C.	Rotherham United	Grimsby Town
13 Thompson, Niogel D.	Leeds United	Rochdale
25 Walton, Mark A.	Luton Town	Colchester United

SEPTEMBER 1987

18 Bardsley, David J.	Watford	Oxford United
24 Branagan, James P.	Preston North End	York City

23	Broddle, Julian R.	Scunthorpe United	Barnsley
23	Edwards, Keith	Leeds United	Aberdeen
23	Gabbiadini, Marco	York City	Sunderland
10	Galliers, Steven	Wimbledon	Bristol City
18	Hill, Richard W.	Watford	Oxford United
26	Jones, Andrew M.	Port Vale	Charlton Athletic
3	Jones, Keith A.	Chelsea	Brentford
4	Lillis, Mark A.	Derby County	Aston Villa
25	De Mange, Kenneth J.P.P.	Liverpool	Leeds United
25	Melrose, James M.	Charlton Athletic	Leeds United
25	Murray, James G.	Brentford	Cambridge United
16	Newell, Michael C.	Luton Town	Leicester City
3	Proctor, Mark G.	Sunderland	Sheffield Wednesday
10	Savage, Robert J.	Bradford City	Bolton Wanderers
25	Seagraves, Mark	Liverpool	Manchester City
1	Tait, Michael P.	Portsmouth	Reading
4	Trewick, John	Oxford United	Birmingham City
11	Weir, Michael G.	Hibernian	Luton Town
7	West, Colin	Rangers	Sheffield Wednesday
20	Wilson, Ian W.	Leicester City	Everton
25	Wilson, Robert J.	Luton Town	Fulham

LOANS UPGRADED TO FULL TRANSFER
4	North, Mark V.	Luton Town	Grimsby Town
10	Slack, Trevor C.	Rotherham	Grimsby Town

LOANS
3	Allen, Malcolm	Watford	Aston Villa
23	Buchanan, David	Sunderland	York City
28	Burke, Steven J.	Doncaster Rovers	Stockport County
17	Burrows, Adrian M.	Plymouth Argyle	Southend United
14	Colville, Robert J.	Bury	Stockport County
10	Cooper, Mark D.	Tottenham Hotspur	Shrewsbury Town
28	Crichton, Paul A.	Nottingham Forest	Darlington
10	Dodds, William	Chelsea	Partick Thistle
11	Gray, Andrew W.	Aston Villa	West Bromwich Albion
11	Harvey, James	Bristol City	Wrexham
4	Hughes, Darren J.	Brighton & Hove A	Port Vale
25	Hutchinson, Robert	Walsall	Blackpool
24	Mimms, Robert A.	Everton	Manchester City
10	Muggleton, Carl D.	Leicester Cityy	Chesterfield
17	Nogan, Lee M.	Oxford United	Southend United
14	Parks, Anthony	Tottenham Hotspur	Gillingham
24	Phillips, Stephen E.	Peterborough United	Exeter City
11	Riley, Glyn	Bristol City	Torquay United
3	Stowell, Michael	Everton	Chester City
12	Stubbs, William	Nottingham Forest	Doncaster Rovers
25	Taylor, Martin J.	Derby County	Carlisle United
25	Wilson, Robert J.	Luton Town	Fulham
18	Withe, Peter	Sheffield United	Birmingham City

OCTOBER 1987
16	Allinson, Ian J.R.	Stoke City	Luton Town
16	Barnes, David O.	Aldershot	Swindon Town
29	Benjamin, Ian T.	Northampton Town	Cambridge United
9	Birch, Alan	Scunthorpe United	Stockport County
9	Burke, David I.	Huddersfield Town	Crystal Palace
9	Campbell, David A.	Nottingham Forest	Charlton Athletic
9	Cooper, Mark D.	Tottenham Hotspur	Gillingham
10	Culpin, Paul	Coventry City	Northampton Town
23	Curle, Keith	Bristol City	Reading
6	Ellis, Anthony J.	Oldham Athletic	Preston North End
8	Gaynor, Thomas	Doncaster Rovers	Nottingham Forest
9	Goram, Andrew L.	Oldham Athletic	Hibernian
2	Gough, C.Richard	Tottenham Hotspur	Rangers
8	Harvey, James	Bristol City	Tranmere Rovers
1	Hodges, Glyn P.	Newcastle United	Watford
19	Houghton, Raymond J.	Oxford United	Liverpool
23	Humphries, Glenn	Doncaster Rovers	Bristol City

FOOTBALL LEAGUE TRANSFERS

16	Joyce, Warren G.	Bolton Wanderers	Preston North End
19	Kimble, Garry L.	Cambridge United	Doncaster Rovers
26	Lewis, John	Newport County	Swansea City
3	McAvennie, Francis	West Ham United	Celtic
15	McGugan, Paul	Celtic	Barnsley
30	Moyes, David W.	Bristol City	Shrewsbury Town
6	Murray, Stephen	Nottingham Forest	Celtic
23	O'Neill, Michael A.	Coleraine	Newcastle United
16	Pearson, Nigel G.	Shrewsbury Town	Sheffield Wednesday
30	Pender, John P.	Charlton Athletic	Bristol City
19	Riley, David S.	Nottingham Forest	Port Vale
23	Riley, Glyn	Bristol City	Aldershot
28	Ryan, John B.	Oldham Athletci	Mansfield Town
30	Senior, Stephen	Northampton Town	Wigan Athletic
9	Shearer, David J.	Gillingham	AFC Bournemouth
30	Shutt, Carl S.	Sheffield Wednesday	Bristol City
9	Taylor, Kevin	Crystal Palace	Scunthorpe United
20	Thompson, David S.	Notts County	Wigan Athletic
28	Warren, Lee A.	Leeds United	Rochdale
2	Withe, Christopher	Bradford City	Notts County

LOANS UPGRADED TO FULL TRANSFER

16	Gray, Andrew M.	Aston Villa	West Bromwich Albion
2	Hughes, Darren J.	Brighton & Hove A	Port Vale
13	Walker, Clive	Queen's Park Rangers	Fulham
23	Berry, Steven A.	Swindon Town	Aldershot

LOANS

24	Alleyne, Robert A.	Leicester City	Wrexham
8	Barnes, Peter S.	Manchester City	Bolton Wanderers
12	Berry, Steven A.	Swindon Town	Aldershot
17	Buckley, John W.	Leeds United	Doncaster Rovers
30	Carr, Darren	Bristol Rovers	Newport County
16	Clark, William R.	AFC Bournemouth	Bristol Rovers
3	Davis, Steven P.	Crewe Alexandra	Burnley
26	Eves, Melvyn J.	Gillingham	mansfield Town
23	Fairbrother, Ian	Bury	Wrexham
16	Hansbury, Roger	Birmingham City	Sheffield United
2	Jeffels, Simon	Barnsley	Preston North End
20	Judge, Alan G.	Oxford United	Cardiff City
22	Langan, David	Oxford United	Leicester City
16	Leworthy, David J.	Oxford United	Shrewsbury Town
31	Marker, Nicholas R.T.	Exeter City	Plymouth Argyle
20	Miller, Paul	Wimbledon	Newport County
9	Mooney, Brian J.	Liverpool	Preston North End
5	Peacock, Gavin K.	Queen's Park Rangers	Gillingham
24	Purdie, Jon	Wolverhampton W	Cambridge United
2	Redfern, David	Rochdale	Wigan Athletic
16	Reeves, David	Sheffield Wednesday	Scunthorpe United
31	Rowbotham, Darran	Plymouth Argyle	Exeter City
20	Russell, Colin	Doncaster Rovers	Scarborough
2	Ryan, John B.	Oldham Athletic	Mansfield Town
29	Walford, Stephen J.	West Ham United	Huddersfield Town
9	Walker, Clive	Queen's Park Rangers	Fulham
9	Walker, Colin	Sheffield Wednesday	Torquay United
23	Wassall, Darren P.J.	Nottingham Forest	Hereford United
20	Williams, Paul A.	Charlton Athletic	Brentford

LOANS REVERTING

27	Batty, Lawrence	Crystal Palace	Fulham
14	Cook, Michael J.	York City	Coventry City
8	Harvey, James	Wrexham	Bristol City
9	Mimms, Robert A.	Manchester City	Everton
9	Parks, Anthony	Gillingham	Tottenham Hotspur
16	Riley, David S.	Peterborough United	Nottingham Forest
28	Stubbs, William	Doncaster Rovers	Nottingham Forest

NOVEMBER 1987

27	Barrett, Earl D.	Manchester City	Oldham Athletic
19	Buckley, John W.	Leeds United	Rotherham United
5	Caldwell, David W.	Chesterfield	Torquay United
7	Crown, David I.	Cambridge United	Southend United
27	Davison, Robert	Derby County	Leeds United

20	Eckhardt, Jeffrey E.	Sheffield United	Fulham
18	Galloway, Michael	Halifax Town	Heart of Midlothian
27	Gormley, Edward J.	Bray Wanderers	Tottenham Hotspur
25	Gray, Andrew A.	Crystal Palace	Aston Villa
25	Gray, Stuart	Barnsley	Aston Villa
7	Hughes, Philip	Bury	Wigan Athletic
13	Kelly, John	Swindon Town	Oldham Athletic
20	Mann, Adrian G.	Northampton Town	Newport County
13	Moran, Stephen J.	Leicester City	Reading
10	Patterson, Mark	Carlisle United	Derby County
12	Singleton, Martin D.	West Bromwich Albion	Northampton Town
21	Steel, William J.	Wrexham	Tranmere Rovers
28	Steggles, Kevin P.	West Bromwich Albion	Port Vale
6	Thorpe, Adrian	Bradford City	Notts County
2	Turnbull, Lee M.	Aston Villa	Doncaster Rovers

LOANS UPGRADED TO FULL TRANSFER

6	Marker, Nicholas R.T.	Exeter City	Plymouth Argyle
13	Mooney, Brian J.	Liverpool	Preston North End
7	Rowbotham, Darran	Plymouth Argyle	Exeter City
19	Russell, Colin	Doncaster Rovers	Scarborough

LOANS

4	Batty, Lawrence	Fulham	Crystal Palace
20	Chamberlain, Alec F.R.	Everton	Tranmere Rovers
20	Collins, Eamonn A.S.	Portsmouth	Exeter City
6	Cottington, Brian A.	Fulham	Aldershot
5	Cowling, David R.	Huddersfield Town	Scunthorpe United
20	Davison, Robert	Derby County	Leeds United
6	Duggan, Andrew J.	Barnsley	Rochdale
13	Flowers, Timothy D.	Southampton	Swindon Town
27	Grayson, Simon D.	Sheffield United	Chesterfield
3	Hogg, Graeme J.	Manchester United	West Bromwich Albion
2	Hughes, Philip	Bury	Wigan Athletic
9	Kelly, John	Swindon Town	Oldham Athletic
30	Langan, David	Oxford United	AFC Bournemouth
19	Lowe, Simon	Colchester United	Scarborough
20	Milton, Simon C.	Ipswich Town	Exeter City
19	Muggleton, Carl D.	Leicester City	Chesterfield
6	Prudhoe, Mark	Walsall	Bristol City
20	Reeves, David	Sheffield Wednesday	Burnley
19	Scott, Christopher	Northampton Town	Darlington
19	Segers, Johannes C.A.	Nottingham Forest	Sheffield United
7	Singleton, Martin D.	West Bromwich Albion	Northampton Town
13	Staunton, Stephen	Liverpool	Bradford City
5	Walton, Mark A.	Luton Town	Colchester United
27	Worthington, Frank S.	Preston North End	Stockport County

LOANS REVERTING

12	Buchanan, David	York City	Sunderland

DECEMBER 1987

26	Bell, Douglas	Hibernian	Shrewsbury Town
18	Bruce, Stephen R.	Norwich City	Manchester United
3	Bunn Frankie S.	Hull City	Oldham Athletic
23	Burke, Mark S.	Aston Villa	Middlesbrough
24	Carter, Timothy D.	Bristol Rovers	Sunderland
16	Colville, Robert J.	Bury	Stockport County
11	Cooke, Robert L.	Brentford	Millwall
11	Coughlin, Russell	Plymouth Argyle	Blackpool
23	Cusack, David S.	Doncaster Rovers	Rotherham United
3	Davis, Stephen P.	Crewe Alexandra	Burnley
31	Fenwick, Terence W.	Queen's Park Rangers	Tottenham Hotspur
17	Fleck, Robert	Rangers	Norwich City
3	Greygoose, Dean	Crystal Palace	Crewe Alexandra
10	Henry, Anthony	Oldham Athletic	Stoke City
4	Hutchings, Christopher	Brighton & Hove A	Huddersfield Town
30	Johns, Nicholas P.	Charlton Athletic	Queens Park Rangers
22	Keane, Thomas J.	AFC Bournemouth	Colchester United
24	Kearns, Oliver A.	Hereford United	Wrexham
19	McNaught, John	Chelsea	Partick Thistle
24	Mills, Simon A.	York City	Port Vale
16	O'Neill, John P.	Queens Park Rangers	Norwich City

FOOTBALL LEAGUE TRANSFERS

16	Peacock, Gavin K.	Queens Park Rangers	Gillingham
3	Pennyfather, Glenn J.	Southend United	Crystal Palace
23	Stephens, Arthur	Middlesbrough	Carlisle United
17	Turner, Robert P.	Bristol Rovers	Wimbledon
31	Walters, Mark	Aston Villa	Rangers
22	Walton, Mark A.	Luton Town	Colchester United

LOANS UPGRADED TO FULL TRANSFER

17	Langan, David	Oxford United	AFC Bournemouth
23	Lowe, Simon	Colchester United	Scarborough

LOANS

17	Angell, Darren J.	Portsmouth	Colchester United
19	Barnes, Peter S.	Manchester City	Port Vale
17	Birch, Paul A.	Portsmouth	Brentford
17	Brannigan, Kenneth	Sheffield Wednesday	Doncaster Rovers
18	Burke, Mark S.	Aston Villa	Middlesbrough
14	Carter, Timothy D.	Bristol Rovers	Newport County
31	Clement, Andrew D.	Wimbledon	Newport County
24	Cowling, David R.	Huddersfield Town	Reading
19	Coyle, Robert D.	Everton	Linfield
24	Crichton, Paul A.	Nottingham Forest	Swindon Town
27	Digweed, Perry M.	Brighton & Hove A.	Newcastle United
11	Downs, Walter J.	Wimbledon	Newport County
24	Endersby, Scott A.G.	York City	Cardiff City
4	Falco, Mark P.	Rangers	Queens Park Rangers
31	Ford, Gary	Leicester City	Port Vale
31	Granger, Keith W.	Southampton	Darlington
17	Heathcote, Michael	Sunderland	Halifax Town
10	Howlett, Gary P.	AFC Bournemouth	Chester City
20	Johns, Nicholas P.	Charlton Athletic	Queens Park Rangers
11	Kerr, John J.	Portsmouth	Peterborough United
23	MacDonald, Kevin D.	Liverpool	Leicester City
23	McEwan, Stanley	Hull City	Wigan Athletic
24	Neal, Dean J.	Southend United	Cambridge United
31	North, Stacey S.	Luton Town	West Bromwich Albion
23	Nuttell, Michael J.	Peterborough United	Crewe Alexandra
11	Ogley, Mark A.	Barnsley	Aldershot
3	Osvold, Kjetil	Nottingham Forest	Leicester City
18	Owen, Gordon	Bristol City	Hull City
4	Parkin, Brian	Crewe Alexandra	Crystal Palace
10	Powell, Clifford G.	Watford	Hereford United
11	Prudhoe, Mark	Walsall	Carlisle United
17	Pugh, Daral J.	Rotherham United	Cambridge United
23	Rix, Graham	Arsenal	Brentford
31	Rogers, Lee	Bristol City	York City
31	Stainrod, Simon A.	Aston Villa	Stoke City
24	Storer, Stuart J.	Everton	Bolton Wanderers
24	Stowell, Michael	Everton	York City
30	Suckling, Perry J.	Manchester City	Chelsea
17	Taylor, Martin J.	Derby County	Scunthorpe United
27	Whellans, Robert	Bradford City	Hartlepool United
9	White, Dale	Sunderland	Peterborough United

LOANS REVERTING

11	Carr, Darren	Newport County	Bristol Rovers
23	Carter, Timothy D.	Newport County	Bristol Rovers
21	Hogg, Graeme J.	West Bromwich Albion	Manchester United
5	Miller, Paul A.	Newport County	Wimbledon
15	Taylor, Martin J.	Carlisle United	Derby County
4	Williams, Paul A.	Brentford	Charlton Athletic

JANUARY 1988

25	Adcock, Anthony C.	Manchester City	Northampton Town
28	Carr, Darren	Bristol Rovers	Newport County
21	Clark, William R.	AFC Bournemouth	Bristol Rovers
8	Coyle, Ronald P.	Rochdale	Raith Rovers
22	Cross, Nicholas J.R.	Walsall	Leicester City
29	Dixon, Lee M.	Stoke City	Arsenal
22	Howlett, Gary P.	AFC Bournemouth	York City
15	Kasule, Victor	Meadowbank Thistle	Shrewsbury Town
12	Kennedy, Michael F.	Portsmouth	Bradford City
22	Morley, Trevor W.	Northampton Town	Manchester City

12	Morris, Andrew D.	Rotherham United	Chesterfield
7	Nicholas, Charles	Arsenal	Aberdeen
13	Owen, Gordon	Bristol City	Mansfield Town
22	Robinson, Colin R.	Shrewsbury Town	Birmingham City
14	Suckling, Perry J.	Manchester City	Crystal Palace
22	Talbot, Brian E.	Stoke City	West Bromwich Albion
11	Wark, John	Liverpool	Ipswich Town
14	Weir, Michael G.	Luton Town	Hibernian
14	Weir, Peter	Aberdeen	Leicester City

LOANS UPGRADED TO FULL TRANSFER

15	Birch, Paul A.	Portsmouth	Brentford
11	Falco, Mark	Rangers	Queens Park Rangers
6	Ford, Gary	Leicester City	Port Vale
22	James, Robert M.	Leicester City	Swansea City
6	North, Stacey S.	Luton Town	West Bromwich Albion
15	Prudhoe, Mark	Walsall	Carlisle United
7	Stainrod, Simon A.	Aston Villa	Stoke City
19	Storer, Stuart J.	Everton	Bolton Wanderers

LOANS

21	Brush, Paul	Crystal Palace	Southend United
7	Caldwell, Anthony	Bristol City	Chester City
16	Campbell, Raymond M.J.	Nottingham Forest	Hereford United
30	Carson, Thomas	Dundee	Ipswich Town
16	Close, Shaun C.	Tottenham Hotspur	AFC Bournemouth
15	Cole, Michael W.	Ipswich Town	Port Vale
8	Coles, David A.	Aldershot	Newport County
19	Coombe, Mark A.	Bristol City	Carlisle United
14	Danskin, Jason	Mansfield Town	Hartlepool United
14	Goulet, Brent	AFC Bournemouth	Crewe Alexandra
8	Harbottle, Mark S.	Notts County	Doncaster Rovers
21	Hildersley, Ronald	Preston North End	Cambridge United
27	Hucker, Peter I.	Oxford United	West Bromwich Albion
22	Hutchinson, Robert	Walsall	Carlisle United
16	James, Robert M.	Leicester City	Swansea City
22	Joseph, Francis	Reading	Bristol Rovers
28	Langley, Kevin J.	Manchester City	Chester City
23	McDonagh, James M.	Scarborough	Huddersfield Town
13	Marks, Michael	Millwall	Mansfield Town
21	Milne, Ralph	Charlton Athletic	Bristol City
8	Moore, John	Sunderland	Rochdale
22	Neenan, Joseph P.	Peterborough United	Scarborough
15	O'Donnell, Christopher	Ipswich Town	Northampton Town
21	Phillips, Stephen E.	Peterborough United	Chesterfield
25	Thorpe, Andrew	Tranmere Rovers	Stockport County
21	Vaughan, John	Fulham	Bristol City
14	Williams, Brett	Nottingham Forest	Northampton Town
30	Wood, George	Crystal Palace	Cardiff City
27	Wright, Thomas J.	Linfield	Newcastle United

LOANS REVERTING

20	Alleyne, Robert A.	Wrexham	Leicester City
22	Digweed, Perry M.	Newcastle United	Brighton & Hove A
8	Downes, Walter J.	Newport County	Wimbledon
13	Owen, Gordon	Hull City	Bristol City
4	Staunton, Stephen	Bradford City	Liverpool
14	Suckling, Perry J.	Chelsea	Manchester City

FEBRUARY 1988

19	Agana, Patrick A.O.	Watford	Sheffield United
12	Butler, Peter J.	Cambridge United	Southend United
19	Cunnington, Shaun G.	Wrexham	Grimsby Town
26	Currie, David N.	Darlington	Barnsley
6	Evans, Gareth J.	Rotherham United	Hibernian
3	Gavin, Mark W.	Rochdale	Heart of Midlothian
15	Greenall, Colin A.	Gillingham	Oxford United
19	Hetherston, Peter	Watford	Sheffield United
12	Irvine, Alan J.	Dundee United	Shrewsbury Town
19	Jobling, Kevin A.	Leicester City	Grimsby Town
19	Kuhl, Martin	Sheffield United	Watford
19	McClaren, Stephen	Derby County	Bristol City
26	McEwan, Stanley	Hull City	Wigan Athletic

FOOTBALL LEAGUE TRANSFERS

25	McStay, William	Huddersfield Town	Notts County
23	Marks, Michael	Millwall	Leyton Orient
25	Mimms, Robert A.	Everton	Tottenham Hotspur
2	Platt, David	Crewe Alexandra	Aston Villa
12	Pratley, Richard G.	Derby County	Shrewsbury Town
19	Saddington, Nigel	Sunderland	Carlisle United
12	Saunders, Wesley	Carlisle United	Dundee
12	Shearer, David J.	AFC Bournemouth	Scunthorpe United
16	Shotton, Malcolm	Portsmouth	Huddersfield Town
10	Slack, Trevor C.	Grimsby Town	Northampton Town
19	Turner, Philip	Grimsby Town	Leicester City
16	Walsh, Paul A.	Liverpool	Tottenham Hotspur
12	Whitehurst, William	Oxford United	Reading

LOANS UPGRADED TO FULL TRANSFER

25	Milne, Ralph	Charlton Athletic	Bristol City

LOANS

26	Bedford, Kevin E.	Wimbledon	Aldershot
26	Close, Shaun C.	Tottenham Hotspur	AFC Bournemouth
16	Coleman, David H.	AFC Bournemouth	Colchester United
2	Digweed, Perry M.	Brighton & Hove A	Chelsea
3	Fishenden, Paul	Wimbledon	Crewe Alexandra
26	Guthrie, Peter J.	Tottenham Hotspur	Swansea City
11	Holdsworth, Dean C.	Watford	Carlisle United
3	Keeley, Glenn M.	Oldham Athletic	Colchester United
19	McDonald, Robert W.	Leeds United	Wolverhampton W
23	McStay, William	Huddersfield Town	Notts County
6	Melrose, James M.	Leeds United	Shrewsbury Town
26	Mendonca, Clive P.	Sheffield United	Doncaster Rovers
22	Mimms, Robert A.	Everton	Tottenham Hotspur
12	Muggleton, Carl D.	Leicester City	Blackpool
5	Reeves, David	Sheffield Wednesday	Burnley
6	Sayer, Andrew C.	Wimbledon	Cambridge United
5	Shaw, Gary R.	Aston Villa	Blackpool
13	Stewart, Ian	Portsmouth	Brentford
2	Stowell, Michael	Everton	Manchester City
5	Swain, Kenneth	Portsmouth	West Bromwich Albion
26	Whellans, Robert	Bradford City	Hartlepool United
12	Wilson, Paul A.	Norwich City	Northampton Town

LOANS REVERTING

26	Carson, Thomas	Ipswich Town	Dundee
29	Cole, Michael W.	Port Vale	Ipswich Town
5	Coombe, Mark A.	Carlisle United	Bristol City
19	Marks, Michael	Mansfield Town	Millwall
29	Neenan, Joseph P.	Scarborough	Peterborough United

MARCH 1988

18	Alleyne, Robert A.	Leicester City	Chesterfield
4	Baird, Ian J.	Portsmouth	Leeds United
25	Baker, Stephen	Southampton	Leyton Orient
10	Bannister, Gary	Queen's Park Rangers	Coventry City
4	Barnes, Peter S.	Manchester City	Hull City
24	Bodak, Peter J.	Crewe Alexandra	Swansea City
7	Bodin, Paul J.	Newport County	Swindon Town
25	Branagan, Keith G.	Cambridge United	Millwall
25	Brook, Gary	Newport County	Scarborough
4	Brush, Paul	Crystal Palace	Southend United
29	Bull, Gary W.	Southampton	Cambridge United
10	Carr, Darren	Newport County	Sheffield United
29	Chapple, Philip R.	Norwich City	Cambridge United
23	Chard, Phillip J.	Northampton Town	Wolverhampton W
18	Chivers, Gary P.S.	Watford	Brighton & Hove A
4	Clayton, Paul S.	Norwich City	Darlington
17	Clements, Kenneth H.	Manchester City	Bury
25	Cole, Michael W.	Ipswich Town	Fulham
24	Cranson, Ian	Ipswich Town	Sheffield Wednesday
4	De Mange, Kenneth J.P.P.	Leeds United	Hull City
25	Dicks, Julian A.	Birmingham City	West Ham United
25	Doig, Russell	Leeds United	Hartlepool
25	Edwards, Keith	Aberdeen	Hull City
25	Gibbins, Roger G.	Newport County	Torquay United

25	Gourlay, Archibald M.	Morton	Newcastle United
3	Granger, Keith W.	Southampton	Darlington
11	Hackett, Gary S.	Aberdeen	Stoke City
29	Hamilton, Ian R.	Southampton	Cambridge United
1	Hetzke, Stephen E.R.	Chester City	Colchester United
25	Hitchcock, Kevin	Mansfield Town	Chelsea
25	Hodson, Simeon P.	Newport County	West Bromwich Albion
24	Holden, Richard W.	Halifax Town	Watford
10	Horrix, Dean V.	Reading	Millwall
25	Jacobs, Wayne G.	Sheffield Wednesday	Hull City
24	Jemson, Nigel B.	Preston North End	Nottingham Forest
24	Kendall, Paul S.	Scarborough	Halifax Town
25	Langley, Kevin J.	Manchester City	Birmingham City
4	Linighan, Andrew	Oldham Athletic	Norwich City
23	Lowey, John A.	Preston North End	Chester City
28	McDonagh, James M.	Scarborough	Charlton Athletic
11	Maddy, Paul M.	Chester City	Hereford United
24	Marshall, Ian P.	Everton	Oldham Athletic
25	Marwood, Brian	Sheffield Wednesday	Arsenal
25	Mendonca, Clive P.	Sheffield United	Rotherham United
25	Ogley, Mark A.	Barnsley	Carlisle United
24	Parker, Garry S.	Hull City	Nottingham Forest
8	Parkinson, Philip J.	Southampton	Bury
25	Pascoe, Colin J.	Swansea City	Sunderland
24	Pemberton, John M.	Crewe Alexandra	Crystal Palace
4	Phillips, Stewart G.	Hereford United	West Bromwich Albion
10	Powell, Clifford G.	Watford	Sheffield United
9	Rees, Anthony A.	Birmingham City	Barnsley
11	Rhodes, Andrew C.	Doncaster Rovers	Oldham Athletic
18	Rimmer, Stuart A.	Chester City	Watford
24	Robinson, Leslie	Stockport County	Doncaster Rovers
29	Sansome, Paul E.	Millwall	Southend United
24	Senior, Trevor	Watford	Middlesbrough
9	Thompson, Nigel D.	Leeds United	Chesterfield
31	Thorpe, Andrew	Tranmere Rovers	Stockport County
22	Venus, Mark	Leicester City	Wolverhampton W
25	Walker, Alan	Millwall	Gillingham
22	Webster, Simon P.	Huddersfield Town	Sheffield United
23	Williams, David P.	Oldham Athletic	Burnley
24	Willis, James A.	Stockport County	Darlington
9	Worthington, Frank S.	Preston North End	Stockport County
24	Wright, Thomas J.	Linfield	Newcastle United

LOANS UPGRADED TO FULL TRANSFER

11	Close, Shaun C.	Tottenham Hotspur	AFC Bournemouth
29	Fishenden, Paul	Wimbledon	Crewe Alexandra
25	Melrose, James M.	Leeds United	Shrewsbury Town
25	Rosenior, Leroy De Graft	Fulham	West Ham United

LOANS

24	Ardiles, Osvaldo C.	Tottenham Hotspur	Blackburn Rovers
24	Atkins, Ian L.	Ipswich Town	Birmingham City
1	Beasley, Andrew	Mansfield Town	Scarborough
22	Benstead, Graham M.	Norwich City	Sheffield United
18	Blair, Andrew	Aston Villa	Barnsley
18	Carter, Timothy D.	Sunderland	Carlisle United
8	Corner, David E.	Sunderland	Peterborough United
24	Craig, Albert H.	Newcastle United	Hamilton Academical
9	Crichton, Paul A.	Nottingham Forest	Rotherham United
11	Downes, Christopher B.	Sheffield United	Scarborough
7	Duffield, Peter	Sheffield United	Halifax Town
25	Farrell, Sean P.	Luton Town	Colchester United
24	Ferdinand, Leslie	Queen's Park Rangers	Brentford
3	Forrest, Craig L.	Ipswich Town	Colchester United
24	Gordon, Colin K.	Reading	Bristol City
18	Holdsworth, Dean C.	Watford	Port Vale
24	Joseph, Francis	Reading	Aldershot
11	Leonard, Gary A.	Shrewsbury Town	Hereford United
31	McAllister, Kevin	Chelsea	Falkirk
11	McGuire, Douglas	Celtic	Sunderland
11	Marshall, Ian P.	Everton	Oldham Athletic
24	May, Andrew	Huddersfield Town	Bolton Wanderers
3	Milton, Simon C.	Ipswich Town	Torquay United

FOOTBALL LEAGUE TRANSFERS

11	Moss, Ernest	Scarborough	Rochdale
24	Nixon, Eric W.	Manchester City	Tranmere Rovers
29	Plummer, Calvin A.	Nottingham Forest	Derry City
16	Powell, David R.	West Bromwich Albion	Stoke City
25	Puckett, David C.	AFC Bournemouth	Stoke City
4	Rees, Anthony A.	Birmingham City	Barnsley
24	Robson, Mark A.	Tottenham Hotspur	Reading
18	Rosenior, Leroy De Graft	Fulham	West Ham United
24	Sansome, Paul E.	Millwall	Southend United
24	Scott, Martin	Rotherham United	Nottingham Forest
5	Segers, Johannes C.A.	Nottingham Forest	Dunfermline Athletic
7	Starbuck, Philip M.	Nottingham Forest	Birmingham City
24	Steele, Eric G.	Southend United	Mansfield Town
15	Stimson, Mark	Tottenham Hotspur	Leyton Orient
3	Stubbs, William	Nottingham Forest	Grimsby Town
18	Venus, Mark	Leicester City	Wolverhampton W
18	Webster, Simon P.	Huddersfield Town	Sheffield United
24	Wegerle, Roy C.	Chelsea	Swindon Town
7	Williams, Paul A.	Newport County	Sheffield United
10	Wylde, Rodger J.	Barnsley	Rotherham United

LOANS REVERTING

24	Beasley, Andrew	Scarborough	Mansfield Town
24	Coleman, David H.	Colchester United	AFC Bournemouth
24	Digweed, Perry M.	Chelsea	Brighton & Hove A
21	Hildersley, Ronald	Cambridge United	Preston North End
25	Hucker, Peter I.	West Bromwich Albion	Oxford United
24	Langley, Kevin J.	Chester City	Manchester City
19	Phillips, Steven E.	Chesterfield	Peterborough United
24	Sayer, Andrew C.	Cambridge United	Wimbledon
28	Swain, Kenneth	West Bromwich Albion	Portsmouth

APRIL 1988

21	Atkins, Ian L.	Ipswich Town	Birmingham City
22	Grayson, Simon D.	Sheffield United	Hartlepool United
28	Robertson, John G.	Heart of Midlothian	Newcastle United
11	Wilson, Paul A.	Norwich City	Northampton Town

LOANS REVERTING

14	Carter, Timothy D.	Carlisle United	Sunderland
22	Scott, Martin	Nottingham Forest	Rotherham United

MAY 1988 (Up to 21 May only)

18	Smith, Kevan	Coventry City	York City

LOANS

9	Craig, Albert H	Hamilton Academical	Newcastle United
4	Gorton, Andrew W	Oldham Athletic	Tranmere Rovers

LOANS REVERTING

11	Gorton, Alndrew W	Tranmere Rovers	Oldham Athletic
11	McAllister, Kevin	Falkirk	Chelsea

SCOTTISH LEAGUE TRANSFERS 1987–88

	Player	*From*	*To*

MAY 1987

21	McCarthy, Michael J.	Manchester City	Celtic
15	Walker, Keith	Stirling Albion	St Mirren

LOANS REVERTING

11	Allan, Gerard	East Stirlingshire	Motherwell
16	Burns, Hugh	Hamilton Academical	Rangers
5	Kean, Stephen	Swansea City	Celtic
16	McKnight, Allen	Albion Rovers	Celtic
16	Millar, John	Ayr United	Airdrieonians

JUNE 1987

5	Dawson, Robert McQ.	Stirling Albion	St Mirren

16	Conn, Samuel C.	Clydebank	Falkirk
20	Fairlie, James	Clydebank	Motherwell
18	Irvine, Alan J.	Crystal Palace	Dundee United
27	McKillop, Alan	Forfar Athletic	St Johnstone
8	McWalter, Mark N.	Arbroath	St Mirren
12	Maskrey, Stephen W.	Queen of the South	St Johnstone
18	Powell, Daniel	Brechin City	St Johnstone
27	Richardson, Alexander S.	Morton	Arbroath
5	Romaines, Stuart	Berwick Rangers	Falkirk

JULY 1987

8	Bateman, Alan	Stenhousemuir	Morton
29	Blackie, William	Cowdenbeath	Forfar Athletic
1	Burgess, Stuart	East Fife	Falkirk
29	Burns, Hugh	Rangers	Heart of Midlothian
31	Cowie, George A.	Heart of Midlothian	Dunfermline Athletic
17	Falco, Mark P.	Watford	Rangers
16	Hackett, Gary S.	Shrewsbury Town	Aberdeen
21	Hetherston, Peter	Falkirk	Watford
6	McClair, Brian J.	Celtic	Manchester United
28	McInally, Alan	Celtic	Aston Villa
29	McPherson, David	Rangers	Heart of Midlothian
29	Morris, Christopher B.	Sheffield Wednesday	Celtic
31	Robertson, Craig P.	Raith Rovers	Dunfermline Athletic
31	Robertson, Graeme W.T.	Queen of the South	Dunfermline Athletic
13	Stark, William	Aberdeen	Celtic
1	Walker, Andrew	Motherwell	Celtic

AUGUST 1987

6	Bryce, Thomas	Queen of the South	Clydebank
12	Coyle, Thomas	Dumbarton	St Johnstone
28	Dall, Robert I.	Alloa	Cowdenbeath
11	Dawson, Alistair	Rangers	Blackburn Rovers
28	Irvine, Alan J.	Liverpool	Dundee United
29	McCall, Ian	Dunfermline Athletic	Rangers
28	McCulloch, Keith G.	Cowdenbeath	Alloa
15	McPhee, Ian	Forfar Athletic	Dundee United
7	Nicholas, Peter	Luton Town	Aberdeen
25	Orr, Neil I.	West Ham United	Hibernian
29	Paxton, William D.	Cowdenbeath	Partick Thistle
15	Sinnet, James W.	Stenhousemuir	Cowdenbeath
8	Templeton, Henry	Airdrieonians	Ayr United
28	Thomson, Kenneth A.	Alloa	St Johnstone
3	Woods, Neil S.	Rangers	Ipswich Town

LOANS

22	Carson, Thomas	Dundee	Partick Thistle
27	McWilliams, Derek	Dundee	Falkirk
21	Millen, Andrew	St Johnstone	Alloa

LOAN UPGRADED TO FULL TRANSFER

28	Millen, Andrew	St Johnstone	Alloa

SEPTEMBER 1987

26	Anderson, Norman	Queen of the South	Stirling Albion
5	Cavanagh, Paul	Berwick Rangers	Cowdenbeath
25	Chisholm, Gordon	Hibernian	Dundee
23	Edwards, Keith	Leeds United	Aberdeen
12	Gordon, Stuart L.	Clydebank	Hamilton Academical
5	Herd, William	Raith Rovers	Cowdenbeath
19	Holt, John W.	Dundee United	Dunfermline Athletic
12	Kirkwood, William J.	Dundee United	Dunfermline Athletic
15	Lloyd, David A.	St Johnstone	Raith Rovers
29	Logan, Stephen	Clyde	Meadowbank Thistle
26	MacDonald, Roderick D.W.	Heart of Midlothian	Morton
18	Murray, Stephen	Nottingham Forest	Celtic
23	Paterson, Ian A.	Montrose	Brechin City
19	Riddell, Gary E.	Aberdeen	Dunfermline Athletic
12	Scrimgeour, Brian	Falkirk	Partick Thistle
19	Thompson, Gary	Dunfermline Athletic	St Johnstone
1	Watson, Andrew	Heart of Midlothian	Hibernian

SCOTTISH LEAGUE TRANSFERS

11	Weir, Michael G.	Hibernian	Luton Town
7	West, Colin	Rangers	Sheffield Wednesday
3	Wylde, Gordon T.	East Stirlingshire	Kilmarnock

LOANS

12	Dodds, William	Chelsea	Partick Thistle
11	Kapusciak, John	Alloa	Stranraer
4	McConville, Robert	Kilmarnock	East Stirlingshire
29	Maxwell, Alistair E.	Motherwell	Clydebank
16	Murray, Malcolm	Heart of Midlothian	Stirling Albion

LOANS REVERTING

22	Carson, Thomas	Partick Thistle	Dundee
4	McWilliams, Derek	Falkirk	Dundee
30	Maxwell, Alistair E.	Clydebank	Motherwell

OCTOBER 1987

7	Bain, Alan	Clydebank	Queen of the South
3	Buckley, Graham	Berwick Rangers	Brechin City
27	Caughey, Mark	Hamilton Academical	Motherwell
9	Cowan, Steven J.	Hibernian	Motherwell
27	Fairlie, James	Motherwell	Hamilton Academical
31	Gavin, Stephen	Stirling Albion	St Johnstone
9	Gilmour, James	Falkirk	Kilmarnock
9	Goram, Andrew L.	Oldham Athletic	Hibernian
2	Gough, C.Richard	Tottenham Hotspur	Rangers
7	Grant, Alexander	Clydebank	Falkirk
21	Halley, Kenneth	East Fife	Montrose
24	Jack, J.Ross	Dundee	Dunfermline Athletic
6	Kerr, James	Falkirk	Hamilton Academical
1	Lytwyn, Charles	Brechin City	Berwick Rangers
3	McAvennie, Francis	West Ham United	Celtic
17	McCormack, John D.	Airdrieonians	Partick Thistle
15	MacDonald, Innes J.	Montrose	Airdrieonians
16	McDowall, Paul	Clyde	East Fife
15	McGonigal, Allan	East Stirlingshire	Meadowbank Thistle
15	McGugan, Paul	Celtic	Barnsley
9	McVeigh, John	Kilmarnock	Falkirk
7	McWilliams, Derek	Dundee	Falkirk
6	Reid, Grant J.	Dunfermline Athletic	East Fife
3	Scott, Ronald	Meadowbank Thistle	East Fife
10	Smith, Mark	Celtic	Dunfermline Athletic
7	Stewart, Ian B.	Meadowbank Thistle	Forfar Athletic
31	Wilson, Kenneth S.	St Johnstone	Stirling Albion
10	Wright, Brian	Motherwell	Clydebank
16	Young, David	Dunfermline Athletic	Airdrieonians

LOANS

10	Carson, Thomas	Dundee	Queen of the South
20	Ferguson, Riccardo R.	Hamilton Academical	Partick Thistle
31	Moffat, James	Forfar Athletic	East Fife
27	Stevenson, Hugh	Dumbarton	Partick Thistle

LOANS REVERTING

24	Ferguson, Riccardo R.	Partick Thistle	Hamilton Academical
12	Kapusciak, John	Stranraer	Alloa
4	McConville, Robert	East Stirlingshire	Kilmarnock
21	Murray, Malcolm	Stirling Albion	Heart of Midlothian

NOVEMBER 1987

20	Clarke, Stephen	Hamilton Academical	Forfar Athletic
21	Forrest, Robert	Dunfermline Athletic	Arbroath
18	Galloway, Michael	Halifax Town	Heart of Midlothian
12	Hamilton, Rowan	Dunfermline Athletic	Brechin City
14	Miller, Joseph	Aberdeen	Celtic
23	Scott, Gordon C.	Forfar Athletic	Hamilton Academical
11	Watters, William	Clyde	St Johnstone

LOANS

27	Irvine, Neil D.	Heart of Midlothian	Meadowbank Thistle

LOANS REVERTING

10	Carson, Thomas	Queen of the South	Dundee
2	Moffat, James	East Fife	Forfar Athletic

| 2 | Stevenson, Hugh | Partick Thistle | Dumbarton |

DECEMBER 1987

26	Bell, Douglas	Hibernian	Shrewsbury Town
31	Cairns, William R.	Partick Thistle	Dumbarton
12	Conroy, Michael K.	Clydebank	St Mirren
17	Fleck, Robert W.	Rangers	Norwich City
19	Findlay, Ronald	Dunfermline Athletic	Alloa
19	McNaught, John	Chelsea	Partick Thistle
19	Purdie, Bryan	Raith Rovers	Partick Thistle
31	Walters, Mark	Aston Villa	Rangers

LOANS

12	Carson, Thomas	Dundee	Dunfermline Athletic
4	Donnelly, John	Dunfermline Athletic	East Fife
4	Falco, Mark P.	Rangers	Queen's Park Rangers
23	Ferguson, Eric	Dunfermline Athletic	Clydebank
10	Henderson, Alan	Rangers	Albion Rovers
19	MacFarlane, David	Rangers	Kilmarnock
29	Robertson, Robert C.G.	Dunfermline Athletic	Alloa
31	Walker, J.Nichol	Rangers	Dunfermline Athletic

LOANS REVERTING

| 30 | Carson, Thomas | Dunfermline Athletic | Dundee |

JANUARY 1988

15	Brown, John	Dundee	Rangers
27	Brown, William	St Johnstone	Forfar Athletic
8	Coyle, Ronald P.	Rochdale	Raith Rovers
16	Eadie, Kenneth W.	Falkirk	Clydebank
11	Falco, Mark P.	Rangers	Queen's Park Rangers
16	Grant, Derek	Cowdenbeath	Airdrieonians
28	Jenkins, Grant R.	Dunfermline Athletic	St Johnstone
15	Kasule, Victor P.A.	Meadowbank Thistle	Shrewsbury Town
27	McKellar, David	Hamilton Academical	Dunfermline Athletic
7	Nicholas, Charles	Arsenal	Aberdeen
23	Taylor, David	Heart of Midlothian	Cowdenbeath
14	Weir, Michael G.	Luton Town	Hibernian
14	Weir, Peter R.	Aberdeen	Leicester City
16	Young, David	Airdrieonians	Cowdenbeath

LOAN UPGRADED TO FULL TRANSFER

| | Irvine, Neil D. | Heart of Midlothian | Meadowbank Thistle |

LOANS

30	Carson, Thomas	Dundee	Ipswich Town
15	MacFarlane, David	Rangers	Dundee
15	Spiers, Charles	Hamilton Academical	Queen of the South

LOANS REVERTING

8	Donnelly, John	East Fife	Dunfermline Athletic
4	Falco, Mark P.	Queen's Park Rangers	Rangers
31	Ferguson, Eric	Clydebank	Dunfermline Athletic
14	MacFarlane, David	Kilmarnock	Rangers
6	Walker, J.Nichol	Dunfermline Athletic	Rangers

FEBRUARY 1988

26	Anderson, Norman	Stirling Albion	Clyde
10	Cadden, Stephen	Motherwell	Albion Rovers
26	Carson, Joseph	Stranraer	Dumbarton
6	Evans, Gareth J.	Rotherham United	Hibernian
15	Ferguson, Ian	St Mirren	Rangers
3	Gavin, Mark W.	Rochdale	Heart of Midlothian
12	Irvine, Alan J.	Dundee United	Shrewsbury Town
27	Kirkwood, William J.	Dunfermline Athletic	Dundee
27	Martin, Brian	Hamilton Academical	St Mirren
29	Nelson, Martin	Alloa	Hamilton Academical
5	Reid, Joseph	Kilmarnock	Cowdenbeath
5	Reilly, Robert P.	Airdrieonians	Meadowbank Thistle
12	Saunders, Wesley	Carlisle United	Dundee

LOANS

| 12 | Candlish, Neil G. | Motherwell | Kilmarnock |

SCOTTISH LEAGUE TRANSFERS

| 8 | Fridge, Leslie F. | St Mirren | Arbroath |
| 12 | McGuire, Douglas | Celtic | Dumbarton |

LOANS REVERTING

26	Carson, Thomas	Ipswich Town	Dundee
24	Robertson, Robert C.G.	Alloa	Dunfermline Athletic
13	Spiers, Charles	Queen of the South	Hamilton Academical

MARCH 1988

31	Blackie, William	Forfar Athletic	Dumbarton
5	Bourke, John F.	Brechin City	Kilmarnock
24	Edwards, Keith	Aberdeen	Hull City
31	Gallagher, Anthony	Albion Rovers	Stranraer
24	Gourlay, Archibald M.	Morton	Newcastle United
11	Hackett, Gary S.	Aberdeen	Stoke City
19	Harris, Colin	Raith Rovers	Hamilton Academical
17	Henderson, Darren	Clyde	Stranraer
31	Holmes, James B.	Morton	Falkirk
2	Irons, David J.	Clydebank	Dunfermline Athletic
5	Kinnaird, Paul	Dundee United	Motherwell
16	Knox, Keith	Stranraer	Clyde
25	McIntyre, Brendan	Stranraer	Falkirk
31	McNaught, John	Partick Thistle	Hamilton Academical
5	Powell, Daniel	St Johnstone	Montrose
3	Shanks, David T.	Clydebank	Motherwell

LOANS

5	Armour, Neil	Morton	Stranraer
2	Carson, Thomas	Dundee	Dunfermline Athletic
18	Clark, Robert	Kilmarnock	Albion Rovers
25	Craig, Albert H.	Newcastle United	Hamilton Academical
31	McAllister, Kevin	Chelsea	Falkirk
31	McCabe, Gerald	Hamilton Academical	Dumbarton
9	McGuire, Douglas	Celtic	Sunderland
12	Ritchie, Paul	Dundee	Brechin City
5	Segers, Hans	Nottingham Forest	Dunfermline Athletic

LOANS REVERTING

12	Candlish, Neil G.	Kilmarnock	Motherwell
4	Carson, Thomas	Dunfermline Athletic	Dundee
5	Fridge, Leslie F.	Arbroath	St Mirren
4	Henderson, Alan	Albion Rovers	Rangers
18	MacFarlane, David	Dundee	Rangers
7	McGuire, Douglas	Dumbarton	Celtic

APRIL 1988

| 28 | Robertson, John G. | Heart of Midlothian | Newcastle United |

LOANS REVERTING

6	Armour, Neil	Stranraer	Morton
10	McGuire, Douglas	Sunderland	Celtic
2	Segers, Hans	Dunfermline Athletic	Nottingham Forest

MAY 1988

| 17 | Arthur, Gordon G. | Dumbarton | Raith Rovers |
| 31 | Sorbie, Stuart G. | Alloa | St Johnstone |

LOANS REVERTING

9	Clark, Robert R.	Albion Rovers	Kilmarnock
9	Craig, Albert H.	Hamilton Academical	Newcastle United
8	Dodds, William	Partick Thistle	Chelsea
10	McAllister, Kevin	Falkirk	Chelsea
15	McCabe, Gerald	Dumbarton	Hamilton Academical
1	Ritchie, Paul	Brechin City	Dundee

MAJOR BRITISH SOCCER RECORDS

HIGHEST SCORES

FIRST CLASS MATCH	Arbroath 36, Bon Accord 0 (Scottish Cup First Round)	12.9.1885
INTERNATIONAL	England 13, Ireland 0	18.2.1882
FA CUP	Preston NE 26, Hyde U 0	15.10.1887
LEAGUE CUP	West Ham U 10, Bury 0	25.10.1983
	Liverpool 10, Fulham 0	23.9.1986

FOOTBALL LEAGUE (HOME)

Division One	WBA 12, Darwen 0	4.4.1892
	Nottingham F 12, Leicester Fosse 0	21.4.1909
Division Two	Newcastle U 13, Newport Co 0	5.10.1946
Division Three	Gillingham 10, Chesterfield 0	5.9.1987
Division Four	Oldham Ath 11, Southport 0	26.12.1962
Division Three (S)	Luton T 12, Bristol R 0	13.4.1936
Division Three (N)	Stockport Co 13, Halifax T 0	6.1.1934

FOOTBALL LEAGUE (AWAY)

Division One	Newcastle U 1, Sunderland 9	5.12.1908
	Cardiff C 1, Wolverhampton W 9	3.9.1955
Division Two	Burslem PV 0, Sheffield U 10	10.12.1892
Division Three	Halifax T 0, Fulham 8	16.9.1969
Division Four	Crewe Alex 1, Rotherham U 8	8.9.1973
Division Three (S)	Northampton T 0, Walsall 8	2.2.1947
Division Three (N)	Accrington S 0, Barnsley 9	3.2.1934

SCOTTISH LEAGUE (HOME)

Premier Division	Aberdeen 8, Motherwell 0	26.3.1979
Division One	Celtic 11, Dundee 0	26.10.1895
Division Two	East Fife 13, Edinburgh C 2	11.12.1937

SCOTTISH LEAGUE (AWAY)

Premier Division	Kilmarnock 1, Rangers 8	20.9.1980
Division One	Airdrieonians 1, Hibernian 11	24.10.1950
Division Two	Alloa Ath 0, Dundee 10	8.3.1947

MOST LEAGUE GOALS IN A SEASON (TEAMS)

FOOTBALL LEAGUE

		Games	Goals	Season
Division One	Aston Villa	42	128	1930-31
Division Two	Middlesbrough	42	122	1926-27
Division Three	QPR	46	111	1961-62
Division Four	Peterborough U	46	134	1960-61
Division Three (S)	Millwall	42	127	1927-28
Division Three (N)	Bradford C	42	128	1928-29

SCOTTISH LEAGUE

		Games	Goals	Season
Premier Division	Dundee U	36	90	1982-83
	Celtic	36	90	1982-83
	Celtic	44	90	1986-87
Division One	Hearts	34	132	1957-58
Division Two	Raith R	34	142	1937-38

MOST LEAGUE GOALS IN A SEASON (PLAYERS)

FOOTBALL LEAGUE

		Games	Goals	Season
Division One	W. R. 'Dixie' Dean (Everton)	39	60	1927-28
Division Two	George Camsell (Middlesbrough)	37	59	1926-27
Division Three	Derek Reeves (Southampton)	46	39	1959-60
Division Four	Terry Bly (Peterborough U)	46	52	1960-61
Division Three (S)	Joe Payne (Luton T)	39	55	1936-37
Division Three (N)	Ted Harston (Mansfield T)	41	55	1936-37

MAJOR BRITISH SOCCER RECORDS

SCOTTISH LEAGUE

Premier Division	Brian McClair (Celtic)	44	35	1986-87
Division One	William McFadyen (Motherwell)	34	52	1931-32
Division Two	Jim Smith (Ayr U)	38	66	1927-28

FEWEST LEAGUE GOALS AGAINST IN A SEASON

FOOTBALL LEAGUE
(minimum 42 games)

		Games	Goals	Season
Division One	Liverpool	42	16	1978-79
Division Two	Manchester U	42	23	1924-25
Division Three	Middlesbrough	46	30	1986-87
Division Four	Lincoln C	46	25	1980-81
Division Three (S)	Southampton	42	21	1921-22
Division Three (N)	Port Vale	46	21	1953-54

SCOTTISH LEAGUE
(minimum 30 games)

Premier Division	Aberdeen	36	21	1983-84
Division One	Celtic	38	14	1913-14
Division Two	Morton	38	20	1966-67

MOST LEAGUE POINTS IN A SEASON

FOOTBALL LEAGUE
(2 points for a win)

		Games	Points	Season
Division One	Liverpool	42	68	1978-79
Division Two	Tottenham H	42	70	1919-20
Division Three	Aston Villa	46	70	1971-72
Division Four	Lincoln C	46	74	1975-76
Division Three (S)	Nottingham F	46	70	1950-51
	Bristol C	46	70	1954-55
Division Three (N)	Doncaster R	42	72	1946-47

FOOTBALL LEAGUE
(3 points for a win)

		Games	Points	Season
Division One	Everton	42	90	1984-85
	Liverpool	40	90	1987-88
Division Two	Luton T	42	88	1981-82
	Chelsea	42	88	1983-84
	Sheffield W	42	88	1983-84
Division Three	Bournemouth	46	97	1986-87
Division Four	Swindon T	46	102	1985-86

SCOTTISH LEAGUE

Premier Division	Aberdeen	36	59	1984-85
	Celtic	44	72	1987-88
Division One	Rangers	42	76	1920-21
Division Two	Morton	38	69	1966-67

MOST LEAGUE WINS IN A SEASON

FOOTBALL LEAGUE

		Games	Wins	Season
Division One	Tottenham H	42	31	1960-61
Division Two	Tottenham H	42	32	1919-20
Division Three	Aston Villa	46	32	1971-72
Division Four	Lincoln C	46	32	1975-76
	Swindon T	46	32	1985-86
Division Three (S)	Bristol C	46	30	1954-55
	Cardiff C	42	30	1946-67
	Millwall	42	30	1927-28
	Nottingham F	46	30	1950-51
	Plymouth Arg	42	30	1929-30
Division Three (N)	Doncaster R	42	33	1946-47

SCOTTISH LEAGUE

Premier Division	Aberdeen	36	27	1984-85
	Rangers	44	31	1986-87
	Celtic	44	31	1987-88
Division One	Rangers	42	35	1920-21
Division Two	Morton	38	33	1966-67

FEWEST LEAGUE DEFEATS IN A SEASON

FOOTBALL LEAGUE
(minimum 20 games)

		Games	Defeats	Season
Division One	Preston NE	22	0	1888-89
	Leeds U	42	2	1968-69
	Liverpool	44	2	1987-88
Division Two	Liverpool	28	0	1893-94
	Burnley	30	2	1897-98
	Bristol C	38	2	1905-06
	Leeds U	42	3	1963-64
Division Three	QPR	46	5	1966-67
Division Four	Lincoln C	46	4	1975-76
	Sheffield U	46	4	1981-82
Division Three (S)	Southampton	42	4	1921-22
	Plymouth Arg	42	4	1929-30
Division Three (N)	Port Vale	46	3	1953-54
	Doncaster R	42	3	1946-47
	Wolverhampton W	42	3	1923-24

SCOTTISHLEAGUE
(minimum 20 games)

Premier Division	Celtic	44	3	1987-88
Division One	Rangers	42	1	1920-21
Division Two	Clyde	36	1	1956-57
	Morton	36	1	1962-63
	St Mirren	36	1	1967-68

MOST GOALS IN A GAME

FOOTBALL LEAGUE

Division One	Ted Drake (Arsenal)	7	v Aston Villa	14.12.1935
Division Two	Tommy Briggs (Blackburn R)	7	v Bristol R	5.2.1955
	Neville Coleman (Stoke C)	7	v Lincoln C	23.2.1957
Division Three	Tony Caldwell (Bolton W)	5	v Walsall	10.9.1983
	Steve Earl (Fulham)	5	v Halifax T	16.9.1969
	Keith East (Swindon T)	5	v Mansfield T	20.11.1965
	Andy Jones (Port Vale)	5	v Newport Co	4.5.1987
	Barrie Thomas (Scunthorpe)	5	v Luton T	24.4.1965
	Alf Wood (Shrewsbury T)	5	v Blackburn R	2.10.1971
Division Four	Herbert Lister (Oldham Ath)	6	v Southport	26.12.1962
Division Three (S)	Joe Payne (Luton T)	10	v Bristol R	13.4.1936
Division Three (N)	Robert Bell (Tranmere R)	9	v Oldham Ath	26.12.1935

FA CUP — Ted MacDougall (Bournemouth) — 9 — v Margate — 20.11.1971

SCOTTISH LEAGUE

Premier Division	Paul Sturrock (Dundee U)	5	v Morton	17.11.1984
Division One	Jimmy McGrory (Celtic)	8	v Dunfermline	14.9.1928
Division Two	John Calder (Morton)	8	v Raith R	18.4.1936
	Jim Dyet (King's Park)	8	v Forfar Ath	2.1.1930
	Owen McNally (Arthurlie)	8	v Armadale	1.10.1927

SCOTTISH CUP — John Petrie (Arbroath) — 13 — v Bon Accord — 12.9.1885

MAJOR BRITISH SOCCER RECORDS

MOST LEAGUE GOALS IN A CAREER

	Team	Games	Goals	Seasons
FOOTBALL LEAGUE				
Arthur Rowley	WBA	24	4	1946-48
	Fulham	56	27	1948-50
	Leicester C	303	251	1950-58
	Shrewsbury T	236	152	1958-65
		Total 619	434	
SCOTTISH LEAGUE				
Jimmy McGrory	Celtic	3	1	1922-23
	Clydebank	30	13	1923-24
	Celtic	375	396	1924-38
		Total 408	410	

MOST GOALS IN AN INTERNATIONAL CAREER

		Games	Goals	Seasons
England	Bobby Charlton	106	49	1957-70
Ireland	Gerry Armstrong	63	12	1976-86
	Joe Bambrick	11	12	1928-38
	Billy Gillespie	25	12	1912-31
Scotland	Denis Law	55	30	1958-74
	Kenny Dalglish	102	30	1971-87
Wales	Ivor Allchurch	68	23	1950-66
	Trevor Ford	38	23	1946-57

MOST GOALS IN AN INTERNATIONAL MATCH

				Venue	Date
England	Steve Bloomer (Derby Co)	5	v Wales	Cardiff	16.3.1896
	Willie Hall (Tottenham H)	5	v Ireland	Old Trafford	16.11.1938
	Malcolm Macdonald (Newcastle U)	5	v Cyprus	Wembley	16.4.1975
	G. O. Smith (Corinthians)	5	v Ireland	Sunderland	18.2.1899
Ireland	Joe Bambrick (Linfield)	6	v Wales	Belfast	1.2.1930
Scotland	Charles Heggie (Rangers)	5	v Ireland	Belfast	20.3.1886
Wales	Mel Charles (Cardiff C)	4	v Ireland	Cardiff	11.4.1962
	Ian Edwards (Chester)	4	v Malta	Wrexham	25.10.1978
	James Price (Wrexham)	4	v Ireland	Wrexham	25.2.1882

RECORD ATTENDANCES

	Att.	Match	Venue	Date
Football League	83,260	Manchester U v Arsenal	Maine Road	17.1.1948
Scottish League	118,567	Rangers v Celtic	Ibrox	2.1.1939
FA Cup Final	126,047	Bolton W v West Ham U	Wembley	28.4.1923
(Official figure - unofficial estimates nearer to 200,000)				
Scottish Cup Final	147,365	Celtic v Aberdeen	Hampden Park	24.4.1937
European Cup Semi-Final	135,826	Celtic v Leeds U	Hampden Park	15.4.1970
World Cup Final	199,850	Uruguay v Brazil	Rio de Janeiro	16.7.1950

LONGEST RUNS WITHOUT DEFEAT

- Nottingham Forest hold the Football League record for the longest undefeated run - 42 First Division games between November 1977 and December 1978.
- Burnley hold the Football League record for the longest undefeated run in a single season - 30 First Division games in season 1920-21.
- Leeds United and Liverpool share the record for the longest undefeated run from the start of a First Division season - 29 games. Leeds achieved this in 1973-74, Liverpool in 1987-88.
- Brazil hold the record for the longest undefeated run in the World Cup - 13 matches in the finals of 1958 and 1962. Their 3-1 defeat by Hungary in the 1966 tournament ended the run.
- Real Madrid had a run of 122 League games without defeat between February 1957 and March 1965. Of the 122, they won 114.
- England's longest run without defeat is 20 matches, between 1889 and 1896.
- Scotland's longest run without defeat is 21 matches, between 1880 and 1888.

APPEARANCES

- The record for the greatest number of League appearances is held by Peter Shilton, with a total of 826 between 1966 and 1988, surpassing the previous record of 824 held by Terry Paine. He is also the only England goalkeeper to have won 100 caps, a feat he achieved in England's match v the Netherlands on 15 June 1988, during the European Championships. He is only the fourth England player in all to reach that target, the others being Bobby Moore (108), Bobby Charlton (106) and Billy Wright (105).
- The record for most consecutive League appearances is held by Harold Bell, who played 401 games for Tranmere Rovers in the Third Division (North) between 1946 and 1955.
- The record for the number of League appearances with a single club is held by John Trollope, who played 770 times for Swindon Town between 1960 and 1980.
- The most League appearances for a single club in Scotland were the 626 made by Bob Ferrier for Motherwell between 1918 and 1937.
- Billy Wright set a world record by making 70 consecutive appearances for England in full internationals between 1951 and 1959.
- Pat Jennings has made more international appearances than any other player in the world. His 119th and final cap for Northern Ireland was awarded for the game v Brazil in Guadalajara on 12 June 1986 - his 41st birthday.

USEFUL ADDRESSES

Federation Internationale de Football Association (FIFA) FIFA House, Hitzigweg 11, CH–8032 Zurich, Switzerland. Telephone 01–555400. Telex 817240.

Union of European Football Associations (UEFA) PO Box 16, CH–3000 Berne 15, Switzerland. Telephone 031–321735. Telex 912037. Fax 031–321838.

The Football Association 16 Lancaster Gate, London W2 3LW. Telephone 01–262 4542.

The Football League Lytham St Annes, Lancs FY8 1JG. Telephone 0253–729421. Telex 67675. **Commercial and Marketing Department** Wembley Conference Centre, London HA9 0DW. Telephone 01–902 1233. Fax 01–903 5625.

The Scottish Football Association 6 Park Gardens, Glasgow G3 7YE. Telephone 041–332 6372.

The Scottish Football League 188 West Regent Street, Glasgow G2 4RY. Telephone 041–248 384415.

The Football Association of Wales 3 Westgate Street, Cardiff CF1 1JF. Telephone 0222–372325.

The Welsh League 39 Ty Newydd, Whitchurch, Cardiff CF4 1NQ. Telephone 0222–627722.

The Irish Football Association 20 Windsor Avenue, Belfast BT9 6EG. Telephone 0232–669458.

The Irish League 87 University Street, Belfast BT7 1HP. Telephone 0232–242888.

The Football Association of Ireland 80 Merrion Square South, Dublin 2. Telephone 0001–766864.

The Football League of Ireland 80 Merrion Square South, Dublin 2. Telephone 0001–765120.

GM–Vauxhall Conference c/o P. D. Hunter, 24 Barnehurst Road, Bexleyheath, Kent DA7 6EZ. Telephone 0322–521116.

Northern Premier League c/o R. D. Bayley, 22 Woburn Drive, Hale, Altrincham, Cheshire WA15 8LZ. Telephone 061–980 7007.

Beazer Homes (Southern) League c/o D. J. Strudwick, 11 Welland Close, Durrington, Worthing, West Sussex BN13 3NR. Telephone 0903–67788.

Vauxhall–Opel League c/o N. R. Robinson, 226 Rye Lane, Peckham, London SE15 4NL. Telephone 01–653 3903.

The Professional Footballers' Association 2 Oxford Court, Bishopsgate, Lower Mosley Street, Manchester M2 3WQ. Telephone 061–236 0575.

The Scottish Professional Footballers' Association Fountain House, 1–3 Woodside Crescent, Glasgow G3 7UJ. Telephone 041–332 8641.

English Schools Football Association 4a Eastgate Street, Stafford ST16 2NN. Telephone 0785–51142.

The Football Trust c/o Scott & Jones Communications, 6A Adam & Eve Mews, Kensington, London W8 6UJ. Telephone 01–938 4566. Fax 01–938 1525.

The Women's Football Association c/o Miss L. Whitehead, 11 Portsea Mews, Portsea Place, London W2 2BN. Telephone 01–402 9388.

The Association of Football Statisticians c/o R. J. Spiller, 22 Breton, Basildon, Essex. Telephone 0268–416020.

The Football Programme Directory c/o David Stacey, The Beeches, 66 Southend Road, Wickford, Essex SS11 8EN.

The Ninety–Two Club 104 Gilda Crescent, Whitchurch, Bristol BS14 9LD.

LAWS OF THE GAME

LAW 1 – THE FIELD OF PLAY

The Field of Play and appurtenances shall be as shown in the following plan:

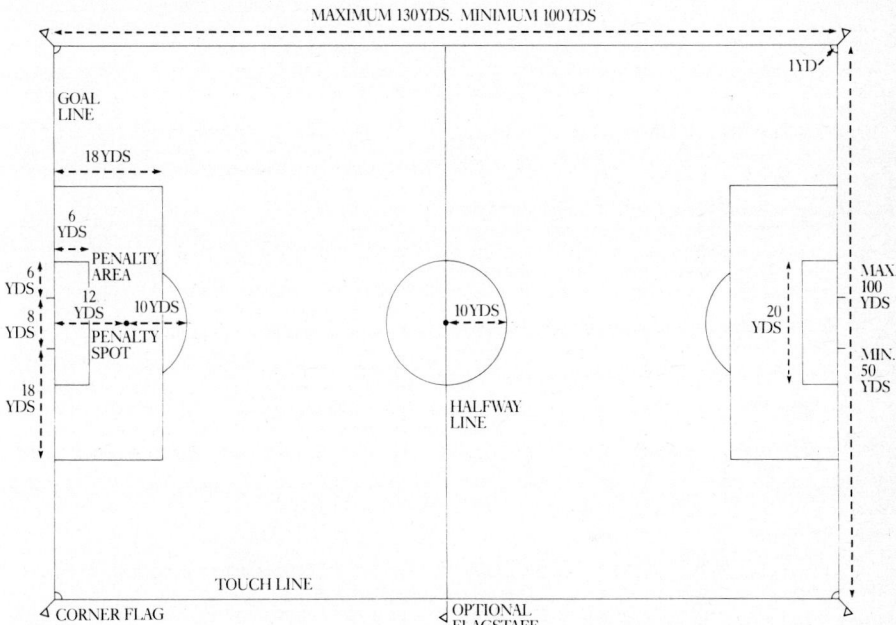

1. Dimensions. The field of play shall be rectangular, its length being not more than 130 yards nor less than 100 yards, and its breadth not more than 100 yards nor less than 50 yards. (In International Matches the length shall be not more than 120 yards nor less than 110 yards and the breadth not more than 80 yards nor less than 70 yards.) The length shall in all cases exceed the breadth.

2. Marking. The field of play shall be marked with distinctive lines, not more than 5 inches in width, not by a V-shaped rut, in accordance with the plan, the longer boundary lines being called the touch-lines and the shorter the goal-lines. A flag on a post not less than 5ft high and having a non-pointed top, shall be placed at each corner; a similar flag-post may be placed opposite the half-way line on each side of the field of play, not less than 1 yard outside the touch-line. A half-way-line shall be marked out across the field of play. The centre of the field of play shall be indicated by a suitable mark and a circle with a 10 yards radius shall be marked round it.

3. The Goal-Area. At each end of the field of play two lines shall be drawn at right-angles to the goal-line, 6 yards from each goal-post. These shall extend into the field of play for a distance of 6 yards and shall be joined by a line drawn parallel with the goal-line. Each of the

spaces enclosed by these goal-lines and the goal-line shall be called a goal-area.

4. The Penalty-Area. At each end of the field of play two lines shall be drawn at right angles to the goal-line, 18 yards from each goal-post. These shall extend into the field of play for a distance of 18 yards and shall be joined by a line drawn parallel with the goal-line. Each of the spaces enclosed by these lines and the goal-line shall be called a penalty-area. A suitable mark shall be made within each penalty area 12 yards from the mid-point of the goal-line, measured along an undrawn line at right-angles thereto. These shall be the penalty-kick marks. From each penalty-kick mark an arc of a circle, having a radius of 10 yards, shall be drawn outside the penalty-area.

5. The Corner Area. From each corner-flag post a quarter circle, having a radius of 1 yard, shall be drawn inside the field of play.

6. The Goals. The goals shall be placed on the centre of each goal-line and shall consist of two upright posts, equidistant from the corner-flags and 8 yards apart (inside measurement), joined by a horizontal cross-bar the lower edge of which shall be 8ft from the ground. The width and depth of the goal-posts and the width and depth of the cross-bars shall not exceed 5 inches.

The goal-posts and the cross-bars shall have the same width.

Nets may be attached to the posts, cross-bars and ground behind the goals. They should be appropriately supported and be so placed as to allow the goal-keeper ample room.

Goal nets. The use of nets made of hemp, jute or nylon is permitted. The nylon strings may, however, not be thinner than those made of hemp or jute.

Decisions of the International Board

1. In International Matches the dimensions of the field of play shall be: maximum 110×75 metres; minimum 100×64 metres.

2. National Associations must adhere strictly to these dimensions. Each National Association organising an International Match must advise the visiting Association, before the match, of the place and the dimensions of the field of play.

3. The Board has approved this table of measurements for the Laws of the Game:

130 yd	– 120 m	8 ft	– 2.44 m
120 yd	– 110 m	5 ft	– 1.5 m
110 yd	– 100 m	28 in	– 0.71 m
100 yd	– 90 m	27 in	– 0.68 m
80 yd	– 75 m	9 in	– 0.22 m
70 yd	– 64 m	5 in	– 0.12 m
50 yd	– 45 m	3/4 in	– 0.019 m
18 yd	– 16.5 m	1/2 in	– 0.0127 m
12 yd	– 11 m	3/8 in	– 0.01 m
10 yd	– 9.15 m	14 oz	– 396 grm
8 yd	– 7.32 m	16 oz	– 453 grm
6 yd	– 5.5 m	15 lb/sq in	– 1 kg/cm^2
1 yd	– 1 m		

4. The goal-line shall be marked the same width as the depth of the goal-posts and the cross-bar, so that the goal-line and goal-post will conform to the same interior and exterior edges.

5. The 6 yards (for the outline of the goal-area) and the 18 yards (for the outline of the penalty-area) which have to be measured along the goal-line, must start from the inner sides of the goal-posts.

6. The space within the inside areas of the field of play includes the width of the lines marking these areas.

7. All Associations shall provide standard equipment, particularly in International Matches, when the Laws of the Game must be complied with in every respect and especially with regard to the size of the ball and other equipment which must conform to the regulations. All cases of failure to provide standard equipment must be reported to FIFA.

8. In a match played under the Rules of a Competition, if the cross-bar becomes displaced or broken, play shall be stopped and the match abandoned unless the cross-bar has been repaired and replaced in position or a new one provided without such being a danger to the players. A rope is not considered to be a satisfactory substitute for a cross-bar.

In a Friendly Match, by mutual consent, play may be resumed without the cross-bar provided it has been removed and no longer constitutes a danger to the players. In these circumstances, a rope may be used as a substitute for a cross-bar. If a rope is not used and the ball crosses the goal-line at a point which in the opinion of the Referee is below where the cross-bar should have been he shall award a goal.

The game shall be restarted by the Referee dropping the ball at the place where it was when play was stopped.

9. National Associations may specify such maximum and minimum dimensions for the cross-bars and goal-posts, within the limits laid down in Law 1, as they consider appropriate.

10. Goal-posts and cross-bars must be made of wood, metal or other approved material as decided from time to time by the International FA Board. They may be square, rectangular, round, half-round or elliptical in shape. Goal-posts and cross-bars made of other materials and in other shapes are not permitted.

11. 'Curtain-raisers' to International Matches should only be played following agreement on the day of the match, and taking into account the condition of the field of play, between representatives of the two Associations and the Referee (of the International Match).

12. National Associations, particularly in International Matches, should

- restrict the number of photographers around the field of play.
- have a line ('photographers' line') marked behind the goal-lines at least two metres from the corner flag going through a point situated at least 3.5 metres behind the intersection of the goal-line with the line marking the goal area to a point situated at least six metres behind the goal-posts.
- prohibit photographers from passing over these lines.
- forbid the use of artificial lighting in the form of 'flashlights'.

LAW 2 – THE BALL

The ball shall be spherical; the outer casing shall be of leather or other approved materials. No material shall be used in its construction which might prove dangerous to the players.

The circumference of the ball shall not be more than 28in and not less than 27in. The weight of the ball at the start of the game shall not be more than 16oz nor less than 14oz. The pressure shall be equal to 0.6–1.1 atmospheres (=600–1100gr/cm^2) at sea level. The ball shall not be changed during the game unless authorised by the Referee.

Decisions of the International Board

1. The ball used in any match shall be considered the property of the Association or Club on whose ground the match is played, and at the close of play it must be returned to the Referee.

2. The International Board, from time to time, shall decide what constitutes approved materials. Any approved material shall be certified as such by the International Board.

3. If the ball bursts or becomes deflated during the course of a match, the game shall be stopped and restarted by dropping the new ball at the place where the first ball became defective.

4. If this happens during a stoppage of the game (place-kick, goal-kick, corner-kick, free-kick, penalty-kick or throw-in) the game shall be restarted accordingly.

LAW 3 – NUMBER OF PLAYERS

1. A match shall be played by two teams, each consisting of not more than eleven players, one of whom shall be the goalkeeper.

2. Substitutes may be used in any match played under the rules of an official competition at FIFA, Confederation or National Association level, subject to the following conditions:

a) that the authority of the international association(s) or national association(s) concerned, has been obtained.

b) that, subject to the restriction contained in the following paragraph (c), the rules of a competition shall state how many, if any, substitutes may be used, and

c) that a team may not be permitted to use more than two substitutes in any match, who must be chosen from not more than five players whose names shall be given to the referee prior to the commencement of the match.

3. Substitutes may be used in any other match, provided that the two teams concerned reach agreement on a maximum number, not exceeding five, and that the terms of such agreement are intimated to the Referee, before the match. If the Referee is not informed, or if the teams fail to reach agreement, no more than two substitutes shall be permitted. In all cases, the substitutes must be chosen from not more than five players whose names shall be given to the referee prior to the commencement of the game.

4. Any of the other players may change places with the goalkeeper, provided that the Referee is informed before the change is made, and provided also, that the change is made during a stoppage in the game.

5. When a goalkeeper or any other player is to be replaced by a substitute, the following conditions shall be observed.

a) the Referee shall be informed of the proposed substitution, before it is made.

b) the substitute shall not enter the field of play until the player he is replacing has left, and then only after having received a signal from the Referee.

c) he shall enter the field during a stoppage in the game, and at the half-way line.

d) a player who has been replaced shall not take any further part in the game.

e) a substitute shall be subject to the authority and jurisdiction of the Referee whether called upon to play or not.

f) the substitution is completed when the substitute enters the field of play, from which moment he becomes a player and the player whom he is replacing ceases to be a player.

Punishment:

a) Play shall not be stopped for an infringement of paragraph 4. The players concerned shall be cautioned immediately when the ball goes out of play.

b) If a substitute enters the field of play without the authority of the Referee, play shall be stopped. The substitute shall be cautioned or sent off according to the circumstances. The game shall be restarted by the Referee dropping the ball at the place where it was when play was stopped, unless it was within the goal area at that time, in which case it shall be dropped on the part of the goal area line which runs parallel to the goal-line, at the point nearest to where the ball was when play was stopped.

c) For any other infringement of the Law, the player concerned shall be cautioned, and if the game is stopped by the Referee, to administer the caution, it shall be restarted by an indirect free-kick, to be taken by a player of the opposing team from the place where the ball was, when play was stopped. If the free-kick is awarded to a team within its own goal-area, it may be taken from any point within that half of the goal-area in which the ball was when play was stopped.

Decisions of the International Board

1. The minimum number of players in a team is left to the discretion of National Associations.

2. The Board is of the opinion that a match should not be considered valid if there are fewer than seven players in either of the teams.

3. A player who has been ordered off before play begins may be replaced only by one of the named substitutes. The kick-off must not be delayed to allow the substitute to join his team.

A player who has been ordered off after play has started may not be replaced.

A named substitute who has been ordered off, either before or after play has started, may not be replaced (this decision relates only to players who are ordered off under Law 12. It does not apply to players who have infringed Law 4).

4. For any offence committed on the field of play a substitute shall be subject to the same punishment as any other player whether called upon or not.

LAW 4 – PLAYERS' EQUIPMENT

A player shall not wear anything which is dangerous to another player. Footwear (boots or shoes) must conform to the following standard.

a) Bars shall be made of leather or rubber and shall be transverse and flat, not less than half an inch in width and shall extend the total width of the sole and be rounded at the corners.

b) Studs which are independently mounted on the sole and are replaceable shall be made of leather, rubber, aluminium, plastic or similar material and shall be solid. With the exception of that part of the stud forming the base, which shall not protrude from the sole more than one quarter of an inch, studs shall be round in plan and not less than half an inch in diameter. Where studs are tapered, the minimum diameter of any section of the stud must not be less than half an inch. Where metal seating for the screw type is used, this seating must be embedded in the sole of the footwear and any attachment screw shall be part of the stud. Other than the metal seating for the screw-type of stud, no metal plates even though covered with leather or rubber shall be worn, neither studs which are threaded to allow them to be screwed on to a base screw that is fixed by nails or otherwise to the soles of footwear, nor studs which, apart from the base, have any form of protruding edge rim or relief marking or ornament should be allowed.

c) Studs which are moulded as an integral part of the sole and are not replaceable shall be made of rubber, plastic, polyurethene or similar soft materials. Provided that there are no fewer than ten studs on the sole, they shall have a minimum diameter of three-eighths of an inch (10mm). Additional supporting material to stabilise studs of soft materials, and ridges which shall not protrude more than 5mm from the sole and moulded to strengthen it, shall be permitted provided that they are in no way dangerous to other players. In all other respects they shall conform to the general requirements of this Law.

d) Combined bars and studs may be worn, provided the whole conforms to the general requirements of this Law. Neither bars nor studs on the soles or heels shall project more than three-quarters of an inch. If nails are used they shall be driven in flush with the surface.

The goalkeeper shall wear colours which distinguish him from the other players and from the Referee.

Punishment: For any infringement of this Law, the player at fault shall be sent off the field of play to adjust his equipment and he shall not return without first reporting to the Referee, who shall satisfy himself that the player's equipment is in order; the player shall only re-enter the game at a moment when the ball has ceased to be in play.

Decisions of the International Board

1. The usual equipment of a player is a jersey or shirt, shorts, stockings, and footwear. In a match played under the rules of a competition, players need not wear boots or shoes, but shall wear jersey or shirt, shorts, or track suit or similar trousers, and stockings.

2. The Law does not insist that boots or shoes must be worn. However, in competition matches Referees should not allow one or a few players to play without footwear when all the other players are so equipped.

3. In International Matches, International Competitions, International Club Competitions, and friendly matches between clubs of different National Associations, the Referee, prior to the start of the game, shall inspect the players' footwear, and prevent any player whose footwear does not conform to the requirements of the Law from playing until such time as it does comply.

The rules of any competition may include a similar provision.

4. If the Referee finds that a player is wearing articles not permitted by the Laws and which may constitute a danger to other players, he shall order him to take them off. If he fails to carry out the Referee's instruction, the player shall not take part in the match.

5. A player who has been prevented from taking part in the game or a player who has been sent off the field for infringing Law 4 must report to the Referee during a stoppage of the game and may not enter or re-enter the field of play unless and until the Referee has satisfied himself that the player is no longer infringing Law 4.

6. A player who has been prevented from taking part in a game or who has been sent off because of an infringement of Law 4, and who enters or re-enters the field of play to join or rejoin his team, in breach of the conditions of Law 12(j), shall be cautioned. If the Referee stops the game to administer the caution, the game shall be restarted by an indirect free-kick, taken by a player of the opposing side, from the place where the ball was when the Referee stopped the game. If the free-kick is awarded to a side within its own goal-area, it may be taken from any point within that half of the goal-area in which the ball was when play was stopped.

LAW 5 – REFEREES

A Referee shall be appointed to officiate in each game. The authority and the exercise of the powers granted to him by the Laws of the Game commence as soon as he enters the field of play.

His power of penalising shall extend to offences committed when play has been temporarily suspended, or when the ball is out of play. His decision on points of fact connected with the play shall be final, so far as the result of the game is concerned. He shall:

a) Enforce the Laws.

b) Refrain from penalising in cases where he is satisfied that, by doing so, he would be giving an advantage to the offending team.

c) Keep a record of the game, act as time-keeper and allow the full or agreed time, adding thereto all time lost through accident or other cause.

d) Have discretionary power to stop the game for any infringement of the Laws and to suspend or terminate the game whenever, by reason of the elements, interference by spectators, or other cause, he deems such stoppage necessary. In such a case he shall submit a detailed report to the competent authority, within the stipulated time, and in accordance with the provisions set up by the National Association under whose jurisdiction the match was played. Reports will be deemed to be made when received in the ordinary course of post.

e) From the time he enters the field of play, caution any player guilty of misconduct or ungentlemanly behaviour and, if he persists, suspend him from further participation in the game. In such cases the Referee shall send the name of the offender to the competent authority, within the stipulated time, and in accordance with the provisions set up by the National Association under whose jurisdiction the match was played. Reports will be deemed to be made when received in the ordinary course of post.

f) Allow no person other than the players and linesmen to enter the field of play without his permission.

g) Stop the game if, in his opinion, a player has been seriously injured, have the player removed as soon as possible from the field of play, and immediately resume the game. If a player is slightly injured, the game shall not be stopped until the ball has ceased to be in play. A player who is able to go to the touch or goal-line for attention of any kind, shall not be treated on the field of play.

h) Send off the field of play, any player who, in his opinion, is guilty of violent conduct, serious foul play, or the use of foul or abusive language.

i) Signal for recommencement of the game after all stoppages.

j) Decide that the ball provided for a match meets with the requirements of Law 2.

Decisions of the International Board

1. Referees in International Matches shall wear a blazer or blouse the colour of which is distinct from the colours worn by the contesting teams.

2. Referees for International Matches will be selected from a neutral country unless the countries concerned agree to appoint their own officials.

3. The Referee must be chosen from the official list of International Referees. This need not apply to Amateur and Youth International Matches.

4. The Referee shall report to the appropriate authority misconduct or any misdemeanour on the part of spectators, officials, players, named substitutes or other persons which take place either on the field of play or in its vicinity at any time prior to, during, or after the match in question so that appropriate action can be taken by the authority concerned.

5. Linesmen are assistants of the Referee. In no case shall the Referee consider the intervention of a Linesman if he himself has seen the incident and from his position on the field, is better able to judge. With this

reserve, and the Linesman neutral, the Referee can consider the intervention and if the information of the Linesman applies to that phase of the game immediately before the scoring of a goal, the Referee may act thereon and cancel the goal.

6. The Referee, however, can only reverse his first decision so long as the game has not been restarted.

7. If the Referee has decided to apply the advantage clause and to let the game proceed, he cannot revoke his decision if the presumed advantage has not been realised, even though he has not, by any gesture, indicated his decision. This does not exempt the offending player from being dealt with by the Referee.

8. The Laws of the Game are intended to provide that games should be played with as little interference as possible, and in this view it is the duty of Referees to penalise only deliberate breaches of the Law. Constant whistling for trifling and doubtful breaches produces bad feeling and loss of temper on the part of the players and spoils the pleasure of spectators.

9. By paragraph (d) of Law 5 the Referee is empowered to terminate a match in the event of grave disorder, but he has no power or right to decide, in such event, that either team is disqualified and thereby the loser of the match. He must send a detailed report to the proper authority who alone has power to deal further with the matter.

10. If a player commits two infringements of a different nature at the same time, the Referee shall punish the more serious offence.

11. It is the duty of the Referee to act upon the information of neutral Linesmen with regard to incidents that do not come under the personal notice of the Referee.

12. The Referee shall not allow any person to enter the field until play has stopped, and only then, if he has given him a signal to do so, nor shall he allow coaching from the boundary lines.

LAW 6 – LINESMEN

Two Linesmen shall be appointed, whose duty (subject to the decision of the Referee) shall be to indicate when the ball is out of play, which side is entitled to the corner-kick, goal-kick or throw-in, and when a substitute is desired. They shall also assist the Referee to control the game in accordance with the Laws. In the event of undue interference or improper conduct by a Linesman, the Referee shall dispense with his services and arrange a substitute to be appointed. (The matter shall be reported by the Referee to the competent authority.) The Linesmen should be equipped with flags by the Club on whose ground the match is played.

Decisions of the International Board

1. Linesmen, where neutral, shall draw the Referee's attention to any breach of the Laws of the Game of which they become aware if they consider that the

LAWS OF THE GAME

Referee may not have seen it, but the Referee shall always be the judge of the decision to be taken.

2. National Associations are advised to appoint official Referees of neutral nationality to act as Linesmen in International Matches.

3. In International Matches, Linesmen's flags shall be of a vivid colour, bright reds and yellows. Such flags are recommended for use in all other matches.

4. A Linesman may be subject to disciplinary action only upon a report of the Referee for unjustified interference or insufficient assistance.

LAW 7 – DURATION OF THE GAME

The duration of the game shall be two equal periods of 45 minutes, unless otherwise mutually agreed upon, subject to the following: (a) Allowance shall be made in either period for all time lost through substitution, the transport from the field of injured players, time-wasting or other cause, the amount of which shall be a matter for the discretion of the Referee; (b) Time shall be extended to permit a penalty-kick being taken at or after the expiration of the normal period in either half.

At half time the interval shall not exceed five minutes except by consent of the Referee.

Decisions of the International Board

1. If a match has been stopped by the Referee, before the completion of the time specified in the rules, for any reason stated in Law 5 it must be replayed in full unless the rules of the competition concerned provide for the result of the match at the time of such stoppage to stand.

2. Players have a right to an interval at half-time.

LAW 8 – THE START OF PLAY

a) At the beginning of the game, choice of ends and the kick-off shall be decided by the toss of a coin. The team winning the toss shall have the option of choice of ends or the kick-off. The Referee having given a signal, the game shall be started by a player taking a place-kick (i.e. a kick at the ball while it is stationary on the ground in the centre of the field of play) into his opponents' half of the field of play. Every player shall be in his own half of the field and every player of the team opposing that of the kicker shall remain not less than 10 yards from the ball until it is kicked-off; it shall not be deemed in play until it has travelled the distance of its own circumference. The kicker shall not play the ball a second time until it has been touched or played by another player.

b) After a goal is scored, the game shall be restarted in like manner by a player of the team losing the goal.

c) After half-time: when restarting after half-time, ends shall be changed and the kick-off shall be taken by a player of the opposite team to that of the player who started the game.

Punishment: For any infringement of this Law, the kick-off shall be retaken, except in the case of the kicker playing the ball again before it has been touched or played by another player; for this offence, an indirect free-kick shall be taken by a player of the opposing team from the place where the infringement occurred, unless the offence is committed by a player in his opponents' goal-area, in which case the free-kick shall be taken from a point anywhere within that half of the goal-area in which the offence occurred. A goal shall not be scored direct from a kick-off.

d) After any other temporary suspension: when restarting the game after a temporary suspension of play from any cause not mentioned elsewhere in these Laws, provided that immediately prior to the suspension the ball has not passed over the touch or goal-lines, the Referee shall drop the ball at the place where it was when play was suspended, unless it was within the goal area at that time, in which case it shall be dropped on that part of the goal area line which runs parallel to the goal-line, at the point nearest to where the ball was when play was stopped. It shall be deemed in play when it has touched the ground; if, however, it goes over the touch or goal-lines after it has been dropped by the Referee, but before it is touched by a player, the Referee shall again drop it. A player shall not play the ball until it has touched the ground. If this section of the Law is not complied with the Referee shall again drop the ball.

Decisions of the International Board

1. If, when the Referee drops the ball, a player infringes any of the Laws before the ball has touched the ground, the player concerned shall be cautioned or sent off the field according to the seriousness of the offence, but a free-kick cannot be awarded to the opposing team because the ball was not in play at the time of the offence. The ball shall therefore be again dropped by the Referee.

2. Kicking-off by persons other than the players competing in a match is prohibited.

LAW 9 – BALL IN AND OUT OF PLAY

The ball is out of play.

a) When it has wholly crossed the goal-line or touch-line, whether on the ground or in the air.

b) When the game has been stopped by the Referee.

The ball is in play at all other times from the start of the match to the finish including:

a) If it rebounds from a goal-post, cross-bar or corner-flag post into the field of play.

b) If it rebounds off either the Referee or Linesmen when they are in the field of play.

c) In the event of a supposed infringement of the Laws, until a decision is given.

Decisions of the International Board

1. The lines belong to the area of which they are the boundaries. In consequence, the touch-lines and the goal-lines belong to the field of play.

LAW 10 – METHOD OF SCORING

Except as otherwise provided by these Laws, a goal is scored when the whole of the ball has passed over the goal-line, between the goal-posts and under the cross-bar, provided it has not been thrown, carried or intentionally propelled by hand or arm, by a player of the attacking side, except in the case of a goalkeeper, who is within his own penalty area.

The team scoring the greater number of goals during a game shall be the winner; if no goals, or an equal number of goals are scored, the game shall be termed a 'draw'.

Decisions of the International Board

1. Law 10 defines the only method according to which a match is won or drawn; no variation whatsoever can be authorised.

2. A goal cannot in any case be allowed if the ball has been prevented by some outside agent from passing over the goal-line. If this happens in the normal course of play, other than at the taking of a penalty-kick, the game must be stopped and restarted where the ball came into contact with the interference.

3. If, when the ball is going into goal, a spectator enters the field before it passes wholly over the goal-line, and tries to prevent a score, a goal shall be allowed if the ball goes into goal unless the spectator has made contact with the ball or has interfered with play, in which case the Referee shall stop the game and restart it by dropping the ball at the place where the contact or interference occurred.

LAW 11 – OFF-SIDE

1. A player is in an off-side position if he is nearer to his opponents' goal-line than the ball *unless:*

a) He is in his own half of the field of play, or

b) There are at least two of his opponents nearer their own goal-line than he is.

2. A player shall only be declared off-side and penalised for being in an off-side position, if, at the moment the ball touches, or is played by, one of his team, he is, in the opinion of the Referee

a) interfering with play or with an opponent, or

b) seeking to gain an advantage by being in that position.

3. A player shall not be declared off-side by the Referee

a) merely because of his being in an off-side position, or

b) if he receives the ball, direct, from a goal-kick, a corner-kick, a throw-in, or when it has been dropped by the Referee.

4. If a player is declared off-side, the Referee shall award an indirect free-kick, which shall be taken by a player of the opposing team from the place where the infringement occurred, unless the offence is committed by a player in his opponents' goal-area, in which case, the free-kick shall be taken from a point anywhere within that half of the goal-area in which the offence occurred.

Decisions of the International Board

1. Off-side shall not be judged at the moment the player in question receives the ball, but at the moment when the ball is passed to him by one of his own side. A player who is not in an off-side position when one of his colleagues passes the ball to him or takes a free-kick, does not therefore become off-side if he goes forward during the flight of the ball.

LAW 12 – FOULS AND MISCONDUCT

A player who intentionally commits any of the following nine offences:

a) Kicks or attempts to kick an opponent;

b) Trips an opponent, i.e. throwing or attempting to throw him by the use of the legs or by stooping in front of or behind him;

c) Jumps at an opponent;

d) Charges an opponent in a violent or dangerous manner;

e) Charges an opponent from behind unless the latter be obstructing;

f) Strikes or attempts to strike an opponent;

g) Holds an opponent;

h) Pushes an opponent;

i) Handles the ball, i.e. carries, strikes or propels the ball with his hand or arm. (This does not apply to the goalkeeper within his own penalty-area);

shall be penalised by the award of a direct free-kick to be taken by the opposing side from the place where the offence occurred, unless the offence is committed by a player in his opponents' goal-area in which case, the free-kick shall be taken from a point anywhere within that half of the goal-area in which the offence occurred.

Should a player of the defending side intentionally commit one of the above nine offences within the penalty-area he shall be penalised by a *penalty-kick*.

A penalty-kick can be awarded irrespective of the position of the ball, if in play, at the time an offence within the penalty-area is committed.

A player committing any of the five following offences:

1. Playing in a manner considered by the Referee to be dangerous, e.g. attempting to kick the ball while held by the goalkeeper.

2. Charging fairly, i.e. with the shoulder, when the ball is not within playing distance of the players concerned and they are definitely not trying to play it;

3. When not playing the ball, intentionally obstructing an opponent, i.e. running between the opponent and the ball, or interposing the body so as to form an obstacle to an opponent;

4. Charging the goalkeeper except when he

    a) is holding the ball;

    b) is obstructing an opponent;

    c) has passed outside the goal-area;

5. When playing as goalkeeper and within his own penalty area.

    a) from the moment he takes control of the ball with his hands, he takes more than four steps in any direction whilst holding, bouncing or throwing the ball in the air and catching it again, without releasing it into play, or, having released the ball into play before, during or after the four steps, he touches it again with his hands, before it has been touched or played by another player of the same team outside of the penalty area or by a player of the opposing team either inside or outside of the penalty area, or

    b) indulges in tactics which, in the opinion of the Referee, are designed merely to hold up the game and thus waste time and so give an unfair advantage to his own team;

shall be penalised by the award of an *indirect free-kick* to be taken by the opposing side from the place where the infringement occurred, unless the offence is committed by a player in his opponents' goal-area, in which case the free-kick shall be taken from a point anywhere within that half of the goal-area in which the offence occurred.

A player shall be *cautioned* if:

    j) he enters or re-enters the field of play to join or rejoin his team after the game has commenced, or leaves the field of play during the progress of the game (except through accident) without, in either case, first having received a signal from the Referee showing him that he may do so. If the Referee stops the game to administer the caution the game shall be restarted by an indirect free-kick taken by a player of the opposing team from the place where the ball was when the Referee stopped the game. If the free-kick is awarded to a side within its own goal-area it may be taken from any point within the half of the goal-area in which the ball was when play was stopped. If, however, the offending player has committed a more serious offence he shall be penalised according to that section of the law he infringed.

    k) he persistently infringes the Laws of the Game;

    l) he shows by word or action, dissent from any decision given by the Referee;

    m) he is guilty of ungentlemanly conduct.

For any of these last three offences, in addition to the caution, an *indirect free-kick* shall also be awarded to the opposing side from the place where the offence occurred unless a more serious infringement of the Laws of the Game was committed. If the offence is committed by a player in his opponents' goal-area, a free-kick shall be taken from a point anywhere, within that half of the goal-area in which the offence occurred.

A player shall be *sent off* the field of play, if:

    n) in the opinion of the Referee he is guilty of violent conduct or serious foul play;

    o) he uses foul or abusive language;

    p) he persists in misconduct after having received a caution.

If play be stopped by reason of a player being ordered from the field for an offence without a separate breach of the Law having been committed, the game shall be resumed by an *indirect free-kick* awarded to the opposing side from the place where the infringement occurred, unless the offence is committed by a player in his opponents' goal-area, in which case, the free-kick shall be taken from a point anywhere within that half of the goal-area in which the offence occurred.

Decisions of the International Board

1. If the goalkeeper either intentionally strikes an opponent by throwing the ball vigorously at him or pushes him with the ball while holding it, the Referee shall award a penalty-kick, if the offence took place within the penalty-area.

2. If a player deliberately turns his back to an opponent when he is about to be tackled, he may be charged but not in a dangerous manner.

3. In case of body-contact in the goal-area between an attacking player and the opposing goalkeeper not in possession of the ball, the Referee, as sole judge of intention, shall stop the game if, in his opinion, the action of the attacking player was intentional, and award an indirect free-kick.

4. If a player leans on the shoulders of another player of his own team in order to head the ball, the Referee shall stop the game, caution the player for ungentlemanly conduct and award an indirect free-kick to the opposing side.

5. A player's obligation when joining or rejoining his team after the start of the match to 'report to the Referee' must be interpreted as meaning 'to draw the attention of the Referee from the touch-line'. The signal from the Referee shall be made by a definite gesture which makes the player understand that he may come into the field of play; it is not necessary for the Referee to wait until the game is stopped (this does not apply in respect of an infringement of Law 4), but the Referee is the sole judge of the moment in which he gives his signal of acknowledgement.

6. The letter and spirit of Law 12 do not oblige the Referee to stop a game to administer a caution. He may, if he chooses, apply the advantage. If he does apply the advantage, he shall caution the player when play stops.

7. If a player covers up the ball without touching it in an endeavour not to have it played by an opponent, he obstructs but does not infringe Law 12 paragraph 3 because he is already in possession of the ball and covers it for tactical reasons whilst the ball remains within playing distance. In fact, he is actually playing the ball and does not commit an infringement; in this case, the player may be charged because he is in fact playing the ball.

8. If a player intentionally stretches his arms to obstruct an opponent and steps from one side to the other moving his arms up and down to delay his opponent, forcing him to change course, but does not make 'bodily contact' the Referee shall caution the player for ungentlemanly conduct and award an indirect free-kick.

9. If a player intentionally obstructs the opposing goalkeeper, in an attempt to prevent him from putting the ball into play in accordance with Law 12, 5(a), the Referee shall award an indirect free-kick.

10. If after a Referee has awarded a free-kick a player protests violently by using abusive or foul language and is sent off the field, the free-kick should not be taken until the player has left the field.

11. Any player, whether he is within or outside the field of play, whose conduct is ungentlemanly or violent, whether or not it is directed towards an opponent, a colleague, the Referee, a Linesman or other person, or who uses foul or abusive language, is guilty of an offence, and shall be dealt with according to the nature of the offence committed.

12. If, in the opinion of the Referee a goalkeeper intentionally lies on the ball longer than is necessary, he shall be penalised for ungentlemanly conduct and

a) be cautioned and an indirect free-kick awarded to the opposing team;

b) in case of repetition of the offence, be sent off the field.

13. The offence of spitting at opponents, officials or other persons, or similarly unseemly behaviour shall be considered as violent conduct within the meaning of section (n) of Law 12.

14. If, when a Referee is about to caution a player, and before he has done so, the player commits another offence which merits a caution, the player shall be sent off the field of play.

LAW 13 – FREE-KICK

Free-kicks shall be classified under two headings: 'Direct' (from which a goal can be scored direct against the offending side), and 'Indirect' (from which a goal cannot be scored unless the ball has been played or touched by a player other than the kicker before passing through the goal).

When a player is taking a direct or an indirect free-kick inside his own penalty-area, all of the opposing players shall be at least 10 yards from the ball and shall remain outside the penalty area until the ball has been kicked out of the area. The ball shall be in play immediately it has travelled the distance of its own circumference and is beyond the penalty-area. The goalkeeper shall not receive the ball into his hands, in order that he may thereafter kick it into play. If the ball is not kicked direct into play, beyond the penalty-area, the kick shall be retaken.

When a player is taking a direct or an indirect free-kick outside his own penalty-area, all of the opposing players shall be at least ten yards from the ball, until it is in play, unless they are standing on their own goal-line, between the goal-posts. The ball shall be in play when it has travelled the distance of its own circumference.

If a player of the opposing side encroaches into the penalty-area, or within ten yards of the ball, as the case may be, before a free-kick is taken, the Referee shall delay the taking of the kick, until the Law is complied with.

The ball must be stationary when a free-kick is taken, and the kicker shall not play the ball a second time, until it has been touched or played by another player.

Notwithstanding any other reference in these Laws to the point from which a free-kick is to be taken:

1. Any free kick awarded to the defending team, within its own goal area, may be taken from any point within that half of the goal area in which the free kick has been awarded.

2. Any indirect free kick awarded to the attacking team within its opponents' goal area shall be taken from that part of the goal area line which runs parallel to the goal-line, at the point nearest to where the offence was committed.

Punishment: If the kicker, after taking the free-kick, plays the ball a second time before it has been touched or played by another player an indirect free-kick shall be taken by a player of the opposing team from the spot where the infringement occurred, unless the offence is committed by a player in his opponents' goal area, in which case the free kick shall be taken from a point anywhere within that half of the goal area in which the offence occurred.

Decisions of the International Board

1. In order to distinguish between a direct and indirect free-kick, the Referee, when he awards an indirect free-kick, shall indicate accordingly by raising an arm above his head. He shall keep his arm in that position until the kick has been taken and retain the signal until the ball has been played or touched by another player or goes out of play.

2. Players who do not retire to the proper distance when a free-kick is taken must be cautioned and on any repetition be ordered off. It is particularly requested of Referees that attempts to delay the taking of a free-kick by encroaching should be treated as serious misconduct.

3. If, when a free-kick is being taken, any of the players dance about or gesticulate in a way calculated to distract their opponents, it shall be deemed ungentlemanly conduct for which the offender(s) shall be cautioned.

LAW 14 – PENALTY-KICK

A penalty-kick shall be taken from the penalty-mark and, when it is being taken, all players with the exception of the player taking the kick, properly identified, and the opposing goalkeeper, shall be within the field of play but outside the penalty-area, and at least 10 yards from the penalty-mark. The opposing goalkeeper must stand (without moving his feet) on his own goal-line, between the goal-posts, until the ball is kicked. The player taking the kick must kick the ball forward; he shall not play the ball a second time until it has been touched or played by another player. The ball shall be deemed in play directly it is kicked, i.e., when it has travelled the distance of its circumference. A goal may be scored directly from a penalty-kick. When a penalty-kick is being taken during the normal course of play, or when time has been extended at half-time or full-time to allow a penalty-kick to be taken or re-taken, a goal shall not be nullified if, before passing between the posts and under the cross-bar, the ball touches either or both of the goal-posts or the cross-bar, or the goalkeeper, or any combination of these agencies, providing that no other infringement has occurred.

Punishment: For any infringement of this Law:

a) by the defending team, the kick shall be retaken if a goal has not resulted.

b) by the attacking team other than by the player taking the kick, if a goal is scored it shall be disallowed and the kick retaken.

c) by the player taking the penalty-kick, committed after the ball is in play, a player of the opposing team shall take an indirect free-kick from the spot where the infringement occurred. If, in the case of paragraph (c), the offence is committed by the player in his opponents' goal-area, the free-kick shall be taken from a point anywhere within that half of the goal-area in which the offence occurred.

Decisions of the International Board

1. When the Referee has awarded a penalty-kick, he shall not signal for it to be taken, until the players have taken up position in accordance with the Law.

2. **a)** If, after the kick has been taken, the ball is stopped in its course towards goal, by an outside agent, the kick shall be retaken.

b) If, after the kick has been taken, the ball rebounds into play, from the goalkeeper, the cross-bar or a goal-post, and is then stopped in its course by an outside agent, the Referee shall stop play and restart it by dropping the ball at the place where it came into contact with the outside agent.

3. **a)** If, after having given the signal for a penalty-kick to be taken, the Referee sees that the goalkeeper is not in his right place on the goal-line, he shall, nevertheless, allow the kick to proceed. It shall be retaken if a goal is not scored.

b) If, after the Referee has given the signal for a penalty-kick to be taken, and before the ball has been kicked, the goalkeeper moves his feet, the Referee shall, nevertheless, allow the kick to proceed. It shall be retaken, if a goal is not scored.

c) If, after the Referee has given the signal for a penalty-kick to be taken, and before the ball is in play, a player of the defending team encroaches into the penalty-area, or within ten yards of the penalty-mark, the Referee shall, nevertheless, allow the kick to proceed. It shall be retaken if a goal is not scored.

The player concerned shall be cautioned.

4. **a)** If, when a penalty-kick is being taken, the player taking the kick is guilty of ungentlemanly conduct, the kick, if already taken, shall be retaken, if a goal is scored.

The player concerned shall be cautioned.

b) If, after the Referee has given the signal for a penalty-kick to be taken, and before the ball is in play, a colleague of the player taking the kick encroaches into the penalty-area or within ten yards of the penalty-mark, the Referee shall, nevertheless, allow the kick to proceed. If a goal is scored, it shall be disallowed, and the kick retaken.

The player concerned shall be cautioned.

c) If, in the circumstances described in the foregoing paragraph, the ball rebounds into play from the goalkeeper, the crossbar or a goal-post and a goal has not been scored, the Referee shall stop the game, caution the player and award an indirect free-kick to the opposing team from the place where the infringement occurred, subject to the over-riding conditions imposed in Law 13.

5. **a)** If, after the Referee has given the signal for a penalty-kick to be taken, and before the ball is in play, the goalkeeper moves from his position on the goal-line, or moves his feet, and a colleague of the kicker encroaches into the penalty-area or within 10 yards of the penalty mark, the kick, if taken, shall be retaken.

The colleague of the kicker shall be cautioned.

b) If, after the Referee has given the signal for a penalty-kick to be taken, and before the ball is in play, a player of each team encroaches into the penalty area, or within 10 yards of the penalty-mark, the kick, if taken, shall be retaken.

The players concerned shall be cautioned.

6. When a match is extended, at half-time or full-time, to allow a penalty-kick to be taken or retaken, the extension shall last until the moment that the penalty-kick has been completed, i.e. until the referee has decided whether or not a goal is scored, and the game shall terminate immediately the Referee has made his decision. After the player taking the penalty-kick has put the ball into play, no player other than the defending goalkeeper may play or touch the ball before the kick is completed.

A goal is scored when the ball passes wholly over the goal-line.

a) direct from the penalty-kick.

b) having rebounded from either goal-post or the cross-bar, or

c) having touched or been played by the goalkeeper.

The game shall terminate immediately the Referee has made his decision.

7. When a penalty-kick is being taken in extended time:

a) the provisions of all of the foregoing paragraphs, except paragraphs (2)(b) and (4)(c) shall apply in the usual way, and

b) in the circumstances described in paragraphs (2)(b) and (4)(c) the game shall terminate immediately the ball rebounds from the goalkeeper, the cross-bar or the goal-post.

LAW 15 – THROW-IN

When the whole of the ball passes over a touchline, either on the ground or in the air, it shall be thrown in from the point where it crossed the line, in any direction, by a player of the team opposite to that of the player who last touched it. The thrower at the moment of delivering the ball must face the field of play and part of each foot shall be either on the touch-line or on the ground outside the touch-line. The thrower shall use both hands and shall deliver the ball from behind and over his head. The ball shall be in play immediately it enters the field of play, but the thrower shall not again play the ball until it has been touched or played by another player. A goal shall not be scored direct from a throw-in.

Punishment:

a) If the ball is improperly thrown in, the throw-in shall be taken by a player of the opposing team.

b) If the thrower plays the ball a second time before it has been touched or played by another player, an indirect free-kick shall be taken by a player of the opposing team from the place where the infringement occurred, unless the offence is committed by a player in his opponents' goal-area, in which case, the free-kick shall be taken from a point anywhere within that half of the goal-area in which the offence occurred.

Decisions of the International Board

1. If a player taking a throw-in, plays the ball a second time by handling it within the field of play before it has been touched or played by another player, the Referee shall award a direct free-kick.

2. A player taking a throw-in must face the field of play with some part of his body.

3. If, when a throw-in is being taken, any of the opposing players dance about or gesticulate in a way calculated to distract or impede the thrower, it shall be deemed ungentlemanly conduct for which the offender(s) shall be cautioned.

4. A throw-in taken from any position other than the point where the ball passed over the touch-line shall be considered to have been improperly thrown.

LAW 16 – GOAL-KICK

When the whole of the ball passes over the goal-line excluding that portion between the goal-posts, either in the air or on the ground, having last been played by one of the attacking team, it shall be kicked direct into play beyond the penalty-area from a point within that half of the goal-area nearest to where it crossed the line, by a player of the defending team. A goalkeeper shall not receive the ball into his hands from a goal-kick in order that he may thereafter kick it into play. If the ball is not kicked beyond the penalty-area, i.e. direct into play, the kick shall be retaken. The kicker shall not play the ball a second time until it has touched—or been played by—another player. A goal shall not be scored direct from such a kick. Players of the team opposing that of the player taking the goal-kick shall remain outside the penalty-area whilst the kick is being taken.

Punishment: If a player taking a goal-kick plays the ball a second time after it has passed beyond the penalty-area, but before it has touched or been played by another player, an indirect free-kick shall be awarded to the opposing team, to be taken from the place where the infringement occurred, unless the offence is committed by a player in his opponents' goal-area, in which case, the free-kick shall be taken from a point anywhere within that half of the goal-area in which the offence occurred.

Decisions of the International Board

1. When a goal-kick has been taken and the player who has kicked the ball touches it again before it has left the penalty-area, the kick has not been taken in accordance with the Laws and must be retaken.

LAW 17 – CORNER-KICK

When the whole of the ball passes over the goal-line, excluding that portion between the goal-posts, either in the air or on the ground, having last been played by one of the defending team, a member of the attacking team shall take a corner-kick, i.e. the whole of the ball shall be placed within the quarter circle at the nearest corner-flag post, which must not be moved, and it shall be kicked from that position. A goal may be scored direct from such a kick. Players of the team opposing that of the player taking the corner-kick shall not approach within 10 yards of the ball until it is in play, i.e. it has travelled the distance of its own circumference, nor shall the kicker play the ball a second time until it has been touched or played by another player.

Punishment:

a) If the player who takes the kick plays the ball a second time before it has been touched or played by another player, the Referee shall award an indirect free-kick to the opposing team, to be taken from the place where the infringement occurred, unless the offence is committed by a player in his opponents' goal-area, in which case the free-kick shall be taken from a point anywhere within that half of the goal-area in which the offence occurred.

b) For any other infringement the kick shall be retaken.

BARCLAYS LEAGUE FIXTURES 1988–89

SATURDAY 27 AUGUST

Division 1
Aston Villa v Millwall
Charlton Ath v Liverpool
Derby Co v Middlesbrough
Everton v Newcastle U
Manchester U v Queen's Park R
Norwich C v Nottingham F
Sheffield W v Luton T
Southampton v West Ham U
Tottenham H v Coventry C
Wimbledon v Arsenal

Division 2
Brighton & Hove A v Bradford C
Chelsea v Blackburn R
Hull C v Manchester C
Leeds U v Oxford U
Leicester C v West Bromwich A
Oldham Ath v Barnsley
Shrewsbury T v Portsmouth
Stoke C v Ipswich T
Sunderland v AFC Bournemouth
Swindon T v Crystal Palace
Walsall v Plymouth Arg
Watford v Birmingham C

Division 3
Brentford v Huddersfield T
Bristol R v Wigan Ath
Bury v Wolverhampton W
Cardiff C v Fulham
Chester C v Blackpool
Chesterfield v Aldershot
Gillingham v Swansea C
Mansfield T v Northampton T
Notts Co v Bristol C
Preston NE v Port Vale
Reading v Sheffield U
Southend U v Bolton W

Division 4
Burnley v Rochdale
Cambridge U v Grimsby T
Carlisle U v Peterborough U
Colchester U v York C
Darlington v Stockport Co
Exeter C v Wrexham
Leyton Orient v Crewe Alex
Lincoln C v Hartlepool U
Rotherham U v Doncaster R
Scarborough v Tranmere R
Scunthorpe U v Hereford U
Torquay U v Halifax T

MONDAY 29 AUGUST

Division 2
Barnsley v Swindon T
Bradford C v Stoke C
Manchester C v Oldham Ath
Oxford U v Hull C

Portsmouth v Leicester C
West Bromwich A v Watford

TUESDAY 30 AUGUST

Division 2
Crystal Palace v Chelsea

FRIDAY 2 SEPTEMBER

Division 4
Tranmere R v Colchester U

SATURDAY 3 SEPTEMBER

Division 1
Arsenal v Aston Villa
Coventry C v Everton
Liverpool v Manchester U (12 noon)
Luton T v Wimbledon
Middlesbrough v Norwich C
Millwall v Derby Co
Newcastle U v Tottenham H
Nottingham F v Sheffield W
Queen's Park R v Southampton
West Ham U v Charlton Ath

Division 2
AFC Bournemouth v Chelsea
Barnsley v Stoke C
Birmingham C v Leicester C
Blackburn R v Oldham Ath
Bradford C v Shrewsbury T
Crystal Palace v Watford
Ipswich T v Sunderland
Manchester C v Walsall
Oxford U v Brighton & Hove A
Plymouth Arg v Hull C
Portsmouth v Leeds U
West Bromwich A v Swindon T

Division 3
Aldershot v Gillingham
Blackpool v Notts Co
Bolton W v Cardiff C
Bristol C v Chesterfield
Fulham v Southend U
Huddersfield T v Preston NE
Northampton T v Brentford
Port Vale v Chester C
Sheffield U v Bristol R
Swansea C v Bury
Wigan Ath v Mansfield T
Wolverhampton W v Reading

Division 4
Crewe Alex v Scunthorpe U
Doncaster R v Exeter C
Grimsby T v Torquay U
Halifax T v Burnley

Hartlepool U v Darlington
Hereford U v Cambridge U
Peterborough U v Scarborough
Rochdale v Rotherham U
Stockport Co v Leyton Orient
Wrexham v Lincoln C
York C v Carlisle U

FRIDAY 9 SEPTEMBER

Division 3
Southend U v Swansea C (7.45 pm)

Division 4
Colchester U v Doncaster R

SATURDAY 10 SEPTEMBER

Division 1
Aston Villa v Liverpool
Charlton Ath v Millwall
Derby Co v Newcastle U
Everton v Nottingham F
Manchester U v Middlesbrough
Norwich C v Queen's Park R
Sheffield W v Coventry C
Southampton v Luton T
Tottenham H v Arsenal
Wimbledon v West Ham U

Division 2
Brighton & Hove A v AFC
Bournemouth
Chelsea v Oxford U
Hull C v Barnsley
Leeds U v Manchester C
Leicester C v Ipswich T
Oldham Ath v Birmingham C
Shrewsbury T v West Bromwich A
Stoke C v Blackburn R
Sunderland v Bradford C
Walsall v Crystal Palace
Watford v Plymouth Arg

Division 3
Brentford v Wigan Ath
Bristol R v Aldershot
Bury v Port Vale
Cardiff C v Huddersfield T
Chester C v Bristol C
Chesterfield v Wolverhampton W
Gillingham v Sheffield U
Mansfield T v Fulham
Notts Co v Northampton T
Preston NE v Blackpool
Reading v Bolton W

Division 4
Burnley v York C
Cambridge U v Stockport Co
Carlisle U v Tranmere R
Darlington v Peterborough U

Exeter C v Halifax T
Leyton Orient v Hereford U
Lincoln C v Crewe Alex
Rotherham U v Wrexham
Scarborough v Rochdale
Scunthorpe U v Grimsby T
Torquay U v Hartlepool U

SUNDAY 11 SEPTEMBER

Division 2
Swindon T v Portsmouth

FRIDAY 16 SEPTEMBER

Division 4
Halifax T v Carlisle U
Stockport Co v Burnley
Tranmere R v Cambridge U
Wrexham v Colchester U

SATURDAY 17 SEPTEMBER

Division 1
Arsenal v Southampton
Coventry C v Charlton Ath
Liverpool v Tottenham H
Luton T v Manchester U
Middlesbrough v Wimbledon
Millwall v Everton
Newcastle U v Norwich C
Nottingham F v Derby Co
Queen's Park R v Sheffield W
West Ham U v Aston Villa

Division 2
AFC Bournemouth v Leeds U
Barnsley v Chelsea
Birmingham C v Sunderland
Blackburn R v Swindon T
Bradford C v Oldham Ath
Crystal Palace v Shrewsbury T
Ipswich T v Watford
Manchester C v Brighton & Hove A
Oxford U v Leicester C
Plymouth Arg v Stoke C
Portsmouth v Hull C
West Bromwich A v Walsall

Division 3
Aldershot v Southend U
Blackpool v Mansfield T
Bolton W v Bristol R
Bristol C v Preston NE
Fulham v Bury
Huddersfield T v Gillingham
Northampton T v Chesterfield
Port Vale v Cardiff C
Sheffield U v Chester C
Swansea C v Brentford
Wigan Ath v Reading
Wolverhampton W v Notts Co

Division 4
Crewe Alex v Darlington
Doncaster R v Torquay U
Grimsby T v Rotherham U
Hartlepool U v Leyton Orient
Hereford U v Scarborough
Peterborough U v Lincoln C
Rochdale v Exeter C
York C v Scunthorpe U

MONDAY 19 SEPTEMBER

Division 3
Port Vale v Chesterfield

Division 4
Stockport Co v Halifax T
Tranmere R v Peterborough U

TUESDAY 20 SEPTEMBER

Division 2
Chelsea v Manchester C
Hull C v Blackburn R
Oldham Ath v Oxford U
Shrewsbury T v Ipswich T
Stoke C v Portsmouth
Sunderland v Crystal Palace
Swindon T v AFC Bournemouth (7.45 pm)
Walsall v Birmingham C
Watford v Bradford C (7.45 pm)

Division 3
Blackpool v Bristol C
Bolton W v Fulham
Cardiff C v Bury (7.45 pm)
Huddersfield T v Notts Co
Mansfield T v Gillingham
Preston NE v Chester C
Sheffield U v Northampton T
Wigan Ath v Swansea C
Wolverhampton W v Aldershot

Division 4
Cambridge U v Lincoln C
Colchester U v Scarborough
Darlington v Exeter C
Rochdale v Doncaster R
Rotherham U v Leyton Orient
Scunthorpe U v Carlisle U
Torquay U v Burnley
Wrexham v Grimsby T
York C v Hartlepool U

WED. 21 SEPTEMBER

Division 2
Brighton & Hove A v West Bromwich A

Leeds U v Barnsley
Leicester C v Plymouth Arg (7.45 pm)

Division 3
Bristol R v Brentford (7.45 pm)
Reading v Southend U (8.00 pm)

Division 4
Hereford U v Crewe Alex

FRIDAY 23 SEPTEMBER

Division 4
Crewe Alex v Stockport Co
Halifax T v Tranmere R
Leyton Orient v Darlington (7.45 pm)

SATURDAY 24 SEPTEMBER

Division 1
Aston Villa v Nottingham F
Charlton Ath v Newcastle U
Derby Co v Queen's Park R
Everton v Luton T
Manchester U v West Ham U
Norwich C v Millwall
Sheffield W v Arsenal
Southampton v Liverpool
Tottenham H v Middlesbrough
Wimbledon v Coventry C

Division 2
AFC Bournemouth v Oxford U
Barnsley v Manchester C
Blackburn R v Birmingham C
Ipswich T v Bradford C
Leeds U v Chelsea
Leicester C v Watford
Oldham Ath v Hull C
Plymouth Arg v West Bromwich A
Portsmouth v Crystal Palace
Shrewsbury T v Sunderland
Swindon T v Brighton & Hove A
Walsall v Stoke C

Division 3
Aldershot v Bolton W
Brentford v Sheffield U
Bristol C v Port Vale
Bury v Mansfield T
Chester C v Huddersfield T
Chesterfield v Blackpool
Fulham v Wigan Ath
Gillingham v Reading
Northampton T v Bristol R
Notts Co v Preston NE
Southend U v Cardiff C
Swansea C v Wolverhampton W

BARCLAYS LEAGUE FIXTURES 1988–89

Division 4

Burnley v Colchester U
Carlisle U v Rotherham U
Doncaster R v Wrexham
Exeter C v Scunthorpe U
Grimsby T v Rochdale
Hartlepool U v Cambridge U
Lincoln C v Hereford U
Peterborough U v York C
Scarborough v Torquay U

FRIDAY 30 SEPTEMBER

Division 3

Wigan Ath v Blackpool

Division 4

Cambridge U v Carlisle U
Tranmere R v Hartlepool U

SATURDAY 1 OCTOBER

Division 1

Coventry C v Middlesbrough
Liverpool v Newcastle U
Millwall v Queen's Park R
Norwich C v Charlton Ath
Nottingham F v Luton T
Sheffield W v Aston Villa
Southampton v Derby Co
Tottenham H v Manchester U
West Ham U v Arsenal
Wimbledon v Everton

Division 2

Birmingham C v Barnsley
Bradford C v Portsmouth
Brighton & Hove A v Leeds U
Chelsea v Leicester C
Crystal Palace v Plymouth Arg
Hull C v Walsall
Manchester C v Blackburn R
Oxford U v Shrewsbury T
Stoke C v AFC Bournemouth
Sunderland v Oldham Ath
Watford v Swindon T
West Bromwich A v Ipswich T

Division 3

Bolton W v Sheffield U
Brentford v Gillingham
Bristol C v Swansea C
Cardiff C v Bristol R
Chesterfield v Bury
Huddersfield T v Fulham
Mansfield T v Notts Co
Northampton T v Aldershot
Preston NE v Southend U
Reading v Chester C
Wolverhampton W v Port Vale

Division 4

Colchester U v Lincoln C
Darlington v Burnley
Hereford U v Grimsby T
Rochdale v Crewe Alex
Rotherham U v Exeter C
Scunthorpe U v Scarborough
Stockport Co v Doncaster R
Torquay U v Leyton Orient
Wrexham v Peterborough U
York C v Halifax T

MONDAY 3 OCTOBER

Division 3

Port Vale v Huddersfield T

TUESDAY 4 OCTOBER

Division 2

Birmingham C v Plymouth Arg
Chelsea v Walsall
Crystal Palace v Ipswich T (7.45 pm)
Hull C v Leicester C
Stoke C v Shrewsbury T
Sunderland v Leeds U
Watford v Oldham Ath (7.45 pm)

Division 3

Aldershot v Wigan Ath
Blackpool v Northampton T
Bury v Reading
Gillingham v Bristol C (7.45 pm)
Notts Co v Chesterfield
Southend U v Mansfield T (7.45 pm)
Swansea C v Bolton W

Division 4

Burnley v Rotherham U
Carlisle U v Colchester U
Crewe Alex v Cambridge U
Doncaster R v Hereford U
Grimsby T v Tranmere R
Halifax T v Wrexham
Hartlepool U v Rochdale
Leyton Orient v York C (7.45 pm)

WED. 5 OCTOBER

Division 2

Bradford C v Blackburn R
Brighton & Hove A v Barnsley

Manchester C v Portsmouth
Oxford U v Swindon T
West Bromwich A v AFC
Bournemouth

Division 3

Bristol R v Preston NE (7.45 pm)
Chester C v Brentford
Fulham v Wolverhampton W

Division 4

Exeter C v Torquay U
Lincoln C v Scunthorpe U
Peterborough U v Stockport Co
Scarborough v Darlington

FRIDAY 7 OCTOBER

Division 4

Tranmere R v York C

SATURDAY 8 OCTOBER

Division 1

Arsenal v Millwall
Aston Villa v Wimbledon
Charlton Ath v Tottenham H
Derby Co v Norwich C
Everton v Southampton
Luton T v Liverpool
Manchester U v Sheffield W
Middlesbrough v West Ham U
Newcastle U v Coventry C
Queen's Park R v Nottingham F

Division 2

AFC Bournemouth v Birmingham C
Barnsley v West Bromwich A
Blackburn R v Crystal Palace
Ipswich T v Manchester C
Leeds U v Watford
Leicester C v Brighton & Hove A
Oldham Ath v Stoke C
Plymouth Arg v Bradford C
Portsmouth v Oxford U
Shrewsbury T v Hull C
Walsall v Sunderland

Division 3

Bolton W v Blackpool
Bristol C v Fulham
Cardiff C v Reading
Gillingham v Chesterfield
Mansfield T v Bristol R
Northampton T v Huddersfield T
Preston NE v Bury
Sheffield U v Wolverhampton W
Wigan Ath v Port Vale

Division 4

Burnley v Exeter C
Cambridge U v Halifax T
Colchester U v Scunthorpe U
Darlington v Rotherham U
Doncaster R v Hartlepool U
Grimsby T v Peterborough U
Hereford U v Carlisle U
Rochdale v Stockport Co
Scarborough v Leyton Orient
Torquay U v Lincoln C
Wrexham v Crewe Alex

SUNDAY 9 OCTOBER

Division 2

Swindon T v Chelsea

Division 3

Aldershot v Swansea C
Brentford v Southend U
Notts Co v Chester C

FRIDAY 14 OCTOBER

Division 4

Halifax T v Rochdale

SATURDAY 15 OCTOBER

Division 1

Charlton Ath v Aston Villa
Coventry C v Millwall
Everton v Derby Co
Luton T v Arsenal
Manchester U v Norwich C
Newcastle U v Middlesbrough
Nottingham F v Liverpool
Queen's Park R v West Ham U
Sheffield W v Wimbledon
Tottenham H v Southampton

Division 2

Birmingham C v West Bromwich A
Blackburn R v Barnsley
Bradford C v Crystal Palace
Hull C v Sunderland
Ipswich T v Oxford U
Leicester C v Stoke C
Oldham Ath v Chelsea
Plymouth Arg v Manchester C
Portsmouth v AFC Bournemouth
Shrewsbury T v Walsall
Watford v Brighton & Hove A

Division 3

Blackpool v Sheffield U
Bristol R v Notts Co
Bury v Brentford
Chester C v Cardiff C

Chesterfield v Preston NE
Fulham v Aldershot
Huddersfield T v Bristol C
Port Vale v Bolton W
Reading v Mansfield T
Southend U v Gillingham
Swansea C v Northampton T
Wolverhampton W v Wigan Ath

Division 4

Carlisle U v Torquay U
Crewe Alex v Doncaster R
Exeter C v Grimsby T
Hartlepool U v Wrexham
Leyton Orient v Colchester U
Lincoln C v Scarborough
Peterborough U v Burnley
Rotherham U v Tranmere R
Scunthorpe U v Cambridge U
Stockport Co v Hereford U
York C v Darlington

SUNDAY 16 OCTOBER

Division 2

Swindon T v Leeds U

FRIDAY 21 OCTOBER

Division 2

AFC Bournemouth v Shrewsbury T

Division 4

Colchester U v Cambridge U
Doncaster R v Halifax T

SATURDAY 22 OCTOBER

Division 1

Arsenal v Queen's Park R
Aston Villa v Everton
Derby Co v Charlton Ath
Liverpool v Coventry C
Middlesbrough v Luton T
Millwall v Nottingham F
Norwich C v Tottenham H
Southampton v Sheffield W
West Ham U v Newcastle U
Wimbledon v Manchester U

Division 2

Barnsley v Ipswich T
Brighton & Hove A v Oldham Ath
Chelsea v Plymouth Arg
Crystal Palace v Hull C
Leeds U v Leicester C
Manchester C v Birmingham C
Oxford U v Blackburn R
Stoke C v Watford
Sunderland v Swindon T
Walsall v Portsmouth
West Bromwich A v Bradford C

Division 3

Aldershot v Huddersfield T
Blackpool v Port Vale
Bolton W v Wolverhampton W
Brentford v Preston NE
Bristol R v Chester C
Gillingham v Bury
Mansfield T v Cardiff C
Northampton T v Bristol C
Notts Co v Reading
Sheffield U v Wigan Ath
Southend U v Chesterfield
Swansea C v Fulham

Division 4

Burnley v Leyton Orient
Exeter C v Carlisle U
Grimsby T v York C
Hartlepool U v Crewe Alex
Lincoln C v Darlington
Peterborough U v Hereford U
Rochdale v Scunthorpe U
Scarborough v Stockport Co
Torquay U v Rotherham U
Wrexham v Tranmere R

MONDAY 24 OCTOBER

Division 3

Port Vale v Sheffield U

Division 4

Stockport Co v Hartlepool U
Tranmere R v Lincoln C

TUESDAY 25 OCTOBER

Division 2

Birmingham C v Stoke C
Crystal Palace v Oxford U (7.45 pm)
Hull C v Chelsea
Ipswich T v Portsmouth (7.45 pm)
Oldham Ath v AFC Bournemouth
Plymouth Arg v Shrewsbury T
Sunderland v Blackburn R
Watford v Barnsley (7.45 pm)

Division 3

Bristol C v Aldershot (7.45 pm)
Bury v Southend U
Cardiff C v Notts Co (7.45 pm)
Chesterfield v Brentford
Fulham v Northampton T
Huddersfield T v Swansea C
Preston NE v Gillingham
Wigan Ath v Bolton W
Wolverhampton W v Blackpool

BARCLAYS LEAGUE FIXTURES 1988–89

Division 4

Cambridge U v Scarborough
Carlisle U v Burnley
Crewe Alex v Grimsby T
Darlington v Torquay U
Halifax T v Peterborough U
Leyton Orient v Exeter C (7.45 pm)
Rotherham U v Colchester U
Scunthorpe U v Wrexham
York C v Doncaster R

WED. 26 OCTOBER

Division 2

Bradford C v Leeds U
Brighton & Hove A v Walsall
Leicester C v Swindon T (7.45 pm)
West Bromwich A v Manchester C

Division 3

Chester C v Mansfield T
Reading v Bristol R (8.00 pm)

Division 4

Hereford U v Rochdale

FRIDAY 28 OCTOBER

Division 3

Southend U v Wigan Ath (7.45 pm)

Division 4

Colchester U v Stockport Co

SATURDAY 29 OCTOBER

Division 1

Arsenal v Coventry C
Aston Villa v Tottenham H
Charlton Ath v Sheffield W
Derby Co v Wimbledon
Everton v Manchester U
Luton T v Queen's Park R
Middlesbrough v Millwall
Newcastle U v Nottingham F
Norwich C v Southampton
West Ham U v Liverpool

Division 2

AFC Bournemouth v Ipswich T
Barnsley v Plymouth Arg
Blackburn R v West Bromwich A
Chelsea v Brighton & Hove A
Leeds U v Hull C
Manchester C v Sunderland
Oxford U v Bradford C
Portsmouth v Oldham Ath
Shrewsbury T v Leicester C

Stoke C v Crystal Palace
Swindon T v Birmingham C
Walsall v Watford

Division 3

Aldershot v Chester C
Blackpool v Cardiff C
Bolton W v Chesterfield
Brentford v Port Vale
Bristol R v Huddersfield T
Gillingham v Wolverhampton W
Mansfield T v Bristol C
Northampton T v Reading
Notts Co v Fulham
Sheffield U v Bury
Swansea C v Preston NE

Division 4

Burnley v Cambridge U
Doncaster R v Leyton Orient
Exeter C v Crewe Alex
Grimsby T v Halifax T
Hartlepool U v Hereford U
Lincoln C v Carlisle U
Peterborough U v Scunthorpe U
Rochdale v Darlington
Scarborough v Rotherham U
Torquay U v Tranmere R
Wrexham v York C

TUESDAY 1 NOVEMBER

Division 3

Sheffield U v Cardiff C

WED. 2 NOVEMBER

Division 2

Oxford U v Sunderland

FRIDAY 4 NOVEMBER

Division 4

Cambridge U v Exeter C
Crewe Alex v Colchester U
Halifax T v Hartlepool U
Tranmere R v Rochdale

SATURDAY 5 NOVEMBER

Division 1

Coventry C v West Ham U
Liverpool v Middlesbrough
Manchester U v Aston Villa
Millwall v Luton T
Nottingham F v Arsenal
Queen's Park R v Newcastle U
Sheffield W v Everton
Southampton v Charlton Ath
Tottenham H v Derby Co
Wimbledon v Norwich C

Division 2

Birmingham C v Portsmouth
Bradford C v AFC Bournemouth
Brighton & Hove A v Shrewsbury T
Crystal Palace v Barnsley
Hull C v Swindon T
Ipswich T v Leeds U
Leicester C v Manchester C
Oldham Ath v Walsall
Plymouth Arg v Blackburn R
Sunderland v Stoke C
Watford v Chelsea
West Bromwich A v Oxford U

Division 3

Bristol C v Bolton W
Bury v Notts Co
Cardiff C v Gillingham
Chester C v Swansea C
Chesterfield v Bristol R
Fulham v Blackpool
Huddersfield T v Sheffield U
Port Vale v Aldershot
Preston NE v Mansfield T
Reading v Brentford
Wigan Ath v Northampton T
Wolverhampton W v Southend U

Division 4

Carlisle U v Scarborough
Darlington v Doncaster R
Hereford U v Wrexham
Leyton Orient v Peterborough U
Rotherham U v Lincoln C
Scunthorpe U v Burnley
Stockport Co v Grimsby T
York C v Torquay U

MONDAY 7 NOVEMBER

Division 4

Tranmere R v Hereford U

TUESDAY 8 NOVEMBER

Division 2

Ipswich T v Walsall (7.45 pm)

Division 3

Aldershot v Sheffield U
Brentford v Notts Co (7.45 pm)
Bristol C v Wolverhampton W (7.45 pm)
Bury v Chester C
Chesterfield v Cardiff C
Fulham v Reading
Gillingham v Blackpool (7.45 pm)
Huddersfield T v Bolton W
Northampton T v Port Vale
Preston NE v Wigan Ath
Southend U v Bristol R (7.45 pm)
Swansea C v Mansfield T

Division 4

Burnley v Lincoln C
Darlington v Cambridge U
Grimsby T v Doncaster R
Halifax T v Colchester U
Leyton Orient v Carlisle U (7.45 pm)
Rotherham U v Scunthorpe U
Torquay U v Rochdale
Wrexham v Stockport Co
York C v Crewe Alex

WED. 9 NOVEMBER

Division 4

Exeter C v Scarborough
Peterborough U v Hartlepool U

FRIDAY 11 NOVEMBER

Division 2

Shrewsbury T v Oldham Ath

Division 4

Colchester U v Torquay U
Stockport Co v York C

SATURDAY 12 NOVEMBER

Division 1

Charlton Ath v Everton
Coventry C v Luton T
Derby Co v Manchester U
Liverpool v Millwall
Middlesbrough v Queen's Park R
Newcastle U v Arsenal
Norwich C v Sheffield W
Southampton v Aston Villa
Tottenham H v Wimbledon
West Ham U v Nottingham F

Division 2

AFC Bournemouth v Crystal Palace
Barnsley v Bradford C
Blackburn R v Brighton & Hove A
Chelsea v Sunderland
Leeds U v West Bromwich A
Manchester C v Watford
Oxford U v Birmingham C
Portsmouth v Plymouth Arg
Swindon T v Ipswich T
Walsall v Leicester C

Division 3

Blackpool v Aldershot
Bolton W v Bury
Bristol R v Gillingham

Cardiff C v Northampton T
Chester C v Chesterfield
Mansfield T v Brentford
Notts Co v Southend U
Port Vale v Swansea C
Reading v Preston NE
Sheffield U v Fulham
Wigan Ath v Bristol C
Wolverhampton W v Huddersfield T

Division 4

Cambridge U v Rotherham U
Carlisle U v Darlington
Crewe Alex v Tranmere R
Doncaster R v Peterborough U
Hartlepool U v Grimsby T
Hereford U v Halifax T
Lincoln C v Exeter C
Rochdale v Wrexham
Scarborough v Burnley
Scunthorpe U v Leyton Orient

SUNDAY 13 NOVEMBER

Division 2

Stoke C v Hull C

SATURDAY 19 NOVEMBER

Division 1

Arsenal v Middlesbrough
Aston Villa v Derby Co
Everton v Norwich C
Luton T v West Ham U
Manchester U v Southampton
Millwall v Newcastle U
Nottingham F v Coventry C
Queen's Park R v Liverpool
Sheffield W v Tottenham H
Wimbledon v Charlton Ath

Division 2

AFC Bournemouth v Manchester C
Bradford C v Chelsea
Crystal Palace v Leicester C
Hull C v Birmingham C
Ipswich T v Brighton & Hove A
Oldham Ath v Leeds U
Oxford U v Plymouth Arg
Portsmouth v Barnsley
Shrewsbury T v Watford
Stoke C v Swindon T
Sunderland v West Bromwich A
Walsall v Blackburn R

TUESDAY 22 NOVEMBER

Division 2

Birmingham C v Leeds U
Blackburn R v Shrewsbury T

FRIDAY 25 NOVEMBER

Division 4

Colchester U v Darlington
Crewe Alex v Peterborough U
Stockport Co v Tranmere R

SATURDAY 26 NOVEMBER

Division 1

Charlton Ath v Nottingham F
Coventry C v Aston Villa
Derby Co v Arsenal
Liverpool v Wimbledon
Middlesbrough v Sheffield W
Newcastle U v Manchester U
Norwich C v Luton T
Southampton v Millwall
Tottenham H v Queen's Park R
West Ham U v Everton

Division 2

Barnsley v AFC Bournemouth
Birmingham C v Ipswich T
Blackburn R v Portsmouth
Brighton & Hove A v Sunderland
Chelsea v Shrewsbury T
Leeds U v Stoke C
Leicester C v Bradford C
Manchester C v Oxford U
Plymouth Arg v Oldham Ath
Swindon T v Walsall
Watford v Hull C
West Bromwich A v Crystal Palace

Division 3

Blackpool v Swansea C
Bolton W v Northampton T
Bristol R v Bury
Cardiff C v Brentford
Chester C v Southend U
Mansfield T v Aldershot
Notts Co v Gillingham
Port Vale v Fulham
Reading v Chesterfield
Sheffield U v Bristol C
Wigan Ath v Huddersfield T
Wolverhampton W v Preston NE

Division 4

Cambridge U v Leyton Orient
Carlisle U v Grimsby T
Doncaster R v Burnley
Hartlepool U v Exeter C
Hereford U v Rotherham U
Lincoln C v Halifax T
Rochdale v York C
Scarborough v Wrexham
Scunthorpe U v Torquay U

748

BARCLAYS LEAGUE FIXTURES 1988–89

FRIDAY 2 DECEMBER

Division 3
Southend U v Port Vale (7.45 pm)

Division 4
Halifax T v Crewe Alex
Torquay U v Cambridge U
Tranmere R v Doncaster R

SATURDAY 3 DECEMBER

Division 1
Arsenal v Liverpool
Aston Villa v Norwich C
Everton v Tottenham H
Luton T v Newcastle U
Manchester U v Charlton Ath
Millwall v West Ham U
Nottingham F v Middlesbrough
Queen's Park R v Coventry C
Sheffield W v Derby Co
Wimbledon v Southampton

Division 2
AFC Bournemouth v Blackburn R
Bradford C v Birmingham C
Crystal Palace v Manchester C
Hull C v Brighton & Hove A
Ipswich T v Plymouth Arg
Oldham Ath v Leicester C
Oxford U v Barnsley
Portsmouth v West Bromwich A
Shrewsbury T v Swindon T
Stoke C v Chelsea
Sunderland v Watford
Walsall v Leeds U

Division 3
Aldershot v Notts Co
Brentford v Bolton W
Bristol C v Reading
Bury v Wigan Ath
Chesterfield v Mansfield T
Fulham v Bristol R
Gillingham v Chester C
Huddersfield T v Blackpool
Preston NE v Cardiff C
Swansea C v Sheffield U

Division 4
Burnley v Hartlepool U
Darlington v Scunthorpe U
Exeter C v Colchester U
Grimsby T v Scarborough
Leyton Orient v Lincoln C
Peterborough U v Rochdale
Rotherham U v Stockport Co
Wrexham v Carlisle U
York C v Hereford U

SUNDAY 4 DECEMBER

Division 3
Northampton T v Wolverhampton W (12 noon)

TUESDAY 6 DECEMBER

Division 2
Plymouth Arg v Brighton & Hove A

SATURDAY 10 DECEMBER

Division 1
Charlton Ath v Queen's Park R
Coventry C v Manchester U
Derby Co v Luton T
Liverpool v Everton
Middlesbrough v Aston Villa
Newcastle U v Wimbledon
Norwich C v Arsenal
Southampton v Nottingham F
Tottenham H v Millwall
West Ham U v Sheffield W

Division 2
Barnsley v Walsall
Birmingham C v Crystal Palace
Blackburn R v Ipswich T
Brighton & Hove A v Stoke C
Chelsea v Portsmouth
Leeds U v Shrewsbury T
Leicester C v Sunderland
Manchester C v Bradford C
Plymouth Arg v AFC Bournemouth
Swindon T v Oldham Ath
Watford v Oxford U
West Bromwich A v Hull C

FRIDAY 16 DECEMBER

Division 2
Birmingham C v Chelsea
Ipswich T v Oldham Ath (7.45 pm)

Division 4
Crewe Alex v Torquay U
Halifax T v Scarborough
Rochdale v Colchester U
Tranmere R v Darlington
Wrexham v Cambridge U
York C v Rotherham U

SATURDAY 17 DECEMBER

Division 1
Arsenal v Manchester U
Coventry C v Derby Co
Liverpool v Norwich C
Luton T v Aston Villa

Middlesbrough v Charlton Ath
Millwall v Sheffield W
Newcastle U v Southampton
Queen's Park R v Everton
West Ham U v Tottenham H

Division 2
AFC Bournemouth v Walsall
Barnsley v Leicester C
Blackburn R v Watford
Bradford C v Swindon T
Crystal Palace v Leeds U
Manchester C v Shrewsbury T
Portsmouth v Brighton & Hove A

Division 3
Blackpool v Bristol R
Bolton W v Chester C
Bristol C v Cardiff C
Fulham v Preston NE
Huddersfield T v Bury
Port Vale v Reading
Sheffield U v Southend U
Swansea C v Chesterfield
Wolverhampton W v Mansfield T

Division 4
Doncaster R v Scunthorpe U
Grimsby T v Leyton Orient
Hartlepool U v Carlisle U
Hereford U v Burnley
Peterborough U v Exeter C
Stockport Co v Lincoln C

SUNDAY 18 DECEMBER

Division 1
Nottingham F v Wimbledon

Division 2
Plymouth Arg v Sunderland
West Bromwich A v Stoke C

Division 3
Aldershot v Brentford (11.30 am)
Northampton T v Gillingham (2.00 pm)
Wigan Ath v Notts Co (12 noon)

MONDAY 26 DECEMBER

Division 1
Aston Villa v Queen's Park R
Charlton Ath v Arsenal (11.30 am)
Derby Co v Liverpool
Everton v Middlesbrough
Manchester U v Nottingham F
Norwich C v West Ham U
Sheffield W v Newcastle U (12 noon)
Southampton v Coventry C
Tottenham H v Luton T (11.30 am)
Wimbledon v Millwall (11.30 am)

Division 2

Brighton & Hove A v Crystal Palace
Chelsea v Ipswich T (12 noon)
Hull C v Bradford C
Leeds U v Blackburn R
Leicester C v AFC Bournemouth (11.30 am)
Oldham Ath v West Bromwich A
Shrewsbury T v Birmingham C (11.30 am)
Stoke C v Manchester C
Sunderland v Barnsley
Swindon T v Plymouth Arg
Walsall v Oxford U
Watford v Portsmouth (12 noon)

Division 3

Brentford v Blackpool (11.30 am)
Bristol R v Wolverhampton W
Bury v Bristol C
Cardiff C v Swansea C
Chester C v Wigan Ath
Chesterfield v Huddersfield T
Gillingham v Fulham
Mansfield T v Port Vale (11.30 am)
Notts Co v Sheffield U
Preston NE v Bolton W (11.00 am)
Reading v Aldershot
Southend U v Northampton T (11.30 am)

Division 4

Burnley v Wrexham
Cambridge U v Doncaster R
Carlisle U v Rochdale
Colchester U v Peterborough U
Darlington v Halifax T
Exeter C v Hereford U (12 noon)
Leyton Orient v Tranmere R (12 noon)
Lincoln C v Grimsby T
Rotherham U v Crewe Alex
Scarborough v York C
Scunthorpe U v Hartlepool U
Torquay U v Stockport Co

WED. 28 DECEMBER

Division 4

Lincoln C v Doncaster R

FRIDAY 30 DECEMBER

Division 2

Oldham Ath v Crystal Palace

Division 3

Cardiff C v Wigan Ath (7.45 pm)
Gillingham v Port Vale (7.45 pm)
Reading v Blackpool (8.00 pm)

Division 4

Cambridge U v Rochdale
Colchester U v Hartlepool U

SATURDAY 31 DECEMBER

Division 1

Aston Villa v Arsenal
Charlton Ath v West Ham U
Derby Co v Millwall
Everton v Coventry C
Manchester U v Liverpool
Norwich C v Middlesbrough
Sheffield W v Nottingham F
Southampton v Queen's Park R
Tottenham H v Newcastle U
Wimbledon v Luton T

Division 2

Brighton & Hove A v Birmingham C
Chelsea v West Bromwich A
Hull C v Ipswich T
Leeds U v Plymouth Arg
Leicester C v Blackburn R
Shrewsbury T v Barnsley
Stoke C v Oxford U
Sunderland v Portsmouth
Swindon T v Manchester C
Walsall v Bradford C
Watford v AFC Bournemouth

Division 3

Brentford v Wolverhampton W
Bristol R v Swansea C
Bury v Aldershot
Chester C v Northampton T
Chesterfield v Fulham
Mansfield T v Huddersfield T
Notts Co v Bolton W
Preston NE v Sheffield U
Southend U v Bristol C

Division 4

Burnley v Grimsby T
Carlisle U v Stockport Co
Darlington v Hereford U
Exeter C v York C
Leyton Orient v Wrexham
Rotherham U v Halifax T
Scarborough v Crewe Alex
Scunthorpe U v Tranmere R
Torquay U v Peterborough U

MONDAY 2 JANUARY, 1989

Division 1

Arsenal v Tottenham H
Coventry C v Sheffield W
Liverpool v Aston Villa

Luton T v Southampton
Middlesbrough v Manchester U (12 noon)
Millwall v Charlton Ath
Newcastle U v Derby Co
Nottingham F v Everton
Queen's Park R v Norwich C
West Ham U v Wimbledon

Division 2

AFC Bournemouth v Brighton & Hove A
Barnsley v Hull C
Birmingham C v Oldham Ath
Blackburn R v Stoke C
Bradford C v Sunderland
Crystal Palace v Walsall
Ipswich T v Leicester C
Manchester C v Leeds U (2.00 pm)
Oxford U v Chelsea
Plymouth Arg v Watford
Portsmouth v Swindon T
West Bromwich A v Shrewsbury T

Division 3

Aldershot v Cardiff C
Blackpool v Bury
Bolton W v Mansfield T
Bristol C v Bristol R
Fulham v Brentford
Huddersfield T v Southend U
Northampton T v Preston NE
Port Vale v Notts Co
Sheffield U v Chesterfield
Swansea C v Reading
Wigan Ath v Gillingham
Wolverhampton W v Chester C

Division 4

Crewe Alex v Carlisle U
Doncaster R v Scarborough
Grimsby T v Colchester U
Halifax T v Scunthorpe U
Hartlepool U v Rotherham U
Hereford U v Torquay U
Peterborough U v Cambridge U
Rochdale v Leyton Orient
Stockport Co v Exeter C
Tranmere R v Burnley
Wrexham v Darlington
York C v Lincoln C

FRIDAY 6 JANUARY

Division 4

Tranmere R v Exeter C
Wrexham v Torquay U

BARCLAYS LEAGUE FIXTURES 1988–89

SATURDAY 7 JANUARY

Division 3
Aldershot v Preston NE
Blackpool v Southend U
Bolton W v Gillingham
Bristol C v Brentford
Fulham v Chester C
Huddersfield T v Reading
Northampton T v Bury
Port Vale v Bristol R
Sheffield U v Mansfield T
Swansea C v Notts Co
Wigan Ath v Chesterfield
Wolverhampton W v Cardiff C

Division 4
Crewe Alex v Burnley
Doncaster R v Carlisle U
Grimsby T v Darlington
Halifax T v Leyton Orient
Hartlepool U v Scarborough
Hereford U v Colchester U
Peterborough U v Rotherham U
Rochdale v Lincoln C
Stockport Co v Scunthorpe U
York C v Cambridge U

Division 3
Brentford v Northampton T
Bristol R v Sheffield U
Bury v Swansea C
Cardiff C v Bolton W
Chester C v Port Vale
Chesterfield v Bristol C
Gillingham v Aldershot
Mansfield T v Wigan Ath
Notts Co v Blackpool
Preston NE v Huddersfield T
Reading v Wolverhampton W

Division 4
Burnley v Halifax T
Cambridge U v Hereford U
Carlisle U v York C
Darlington v Hartlepool U
Exeter C v Doncaster R
Leyton Orient v Stockport Co
Lincoln C v Wrexham
Rotherham U v Rochdale
Scarborough v Peterborough U
Scunthorpe U v Crewe Alex
Torquay U v Grimsby T

Division 3
Aldershot v Bristol R
Blackpool v Preston NE
Bolton W v Reading
Bristol C v Chester C
Fulham v Mansfield T
Huddersfield T v Cardiff C
Northampton T v Notts Co
Port Vale v Bury
Sheffield U v Gillingham
Swansea C v Southend U
Wigan Ath v Brentford
Wolverhampton W v Chesterfield

Division 4
Crewe Alex v Leyton Orient
Doncaster R v Rotherham U
Grimsby T v Cambridge U
Hartlepool U v Lincoln C
Hereford U v Scunthorpe U
Peterborough U v Carlisle U
Rochdale v Burnley
Tranmere R v Scarborough
Wrexham v Exeter C
York C v Colchester U

FRIDAY 13 JANUARY

Division 3
Southend U v Fulham (7.45 pm)

Division 4
Colchester U v Tranmere R

SATURDAY 14 JANUARY

Division 1
Aston Villa v Newcastle U
Charlton Ath v Luton T
Derby Co v West Ham U
Everton v Arsenal
Manchester U v Millwall
Norwich C v Coventry C
Sheffield W v Liverpool
Southampton v Middlesbrough
Tottenham H v Nottingham F
Wimbledon v Queen's Park R

Division 2
Brighton & Hove A v Plymouth Arg
Chelsea v Crystal Palace
Hull C v AFC Bournemouth
Leeds U v Birmingham C
Leicester C v Portsmouth
Oldham Ath v Manchester C
Shrewsbury T v Blackburn R
Stoke C v Bradford C
Sunderland v Oxford U
Swindon T v Barnsley
Walsall v Ipswich T
Watford v West Bromwich A

FRIDAY 20 JANUARY

Division 4
Halifax T v Torquay U
Stockport Co v Darlington

SATURDAY 21 JANUARY

Division 1
Arsenal v Sheffield W
Coventry C v Wimbledon
Liverpool v Southampton
Luton T v Everton
Middlesbrough v Tottenham H
Millwall v Norwich C
Newcastle U v Charlton Ath
Nottingham F v Aston Villa
Queen's Park R v Derby Co
West Ham U v Manchester U

Division 2
AFC Bournemouth v Sunderland
Barnsley v Oldham Ath
Birmingham C v Watford
Blackburn R v Chelsea
Bradford C v Brighton & Hove A
Crystal Palace v Swindon T
Ipswich T v Stoke C
Manchester C v Hull C
Oxford U v Leeds U
Plymouth Arg v Walsall
Portsmouth v Shrewsbury T
West Bromwich A v Leicester C

FRIDAY 27 JANUARY

Division 4
Colchester U v Wrexham

SATURDAY 28 JANUARY

Division 3
Brentford v Swansea C
Bristol R v Bolton W
Bury v Fulham
Cardiff C v Port Vale
Chester C v Sheffield U
Chesterfield v Northampton T
Gillingham v Huddersfield T
Mansfield T v Blackpool
Notts Co v Wolverhampton W
Preston NE v Bristol C
Reading v Wigan Ath
Southend U v Aldershot

Division 4
Burnley v Stockport Co
Cambridge U v Tranmere R
Carlisle U v Halifax T
Darlington v Crewe Alex
Exeter C v Rochdale
Leyton Orient v Hartlepool U
Lincoln C v Peterborough U
Rotherham U v Grimsby T
Scarborough v Hereford U
Scunthorpe U v York C
Torquay U v Doncaster R

FRIDAY 3 FEBRUARY

Division 3
Southend U v Preston NE (7.45 pm)
Swansea C v Bristol C

SATURDAY 4 FEBRUARY

Division 1
Arsenal v West Ham U
Aston Villa v Sheffield W
Charlton Ath v Norwich C
Derby Co v Southampton
Everton v Wimbledon
Luton T v Nottingham F
Manchester U v Tottenham H
Middlesbrough v Coventry C
Newcastle U v Liverpool
Queen's Park R v Millwall

Division 2
AFC Bournemouth v West Bromwich A
Barnsley v Brighton & Hove A
Blackburn R v Bradford C
Ipswich T v Crystal Palace
Leeds U v Sunderland
Leicester C v Hull C
Oldham Ath v Watford
Plymouth Arg v Birmingham C
Portsmouth v Manchester C
Shrewsbury T v Stoke C
Walsall v Chelsea

Division 3
Aldershot v Northampton T
Blackpool v Wigan Ath
Bristol R v Cardiff C
Bury v Chesterfield
Chester C v Reading
Fulham v Huddersfield T
Gillingham v Brentford
Port Vale v Wolverhampton W
Sheffield U v Bolton W

Division 4
Burnley v Torquay U
Carlisle U v Scunthorpe U
Crewe Alex v Hereford U
Doncaster R v Rochdale
Exeter C v Darlington
Grimsby T v Wrexham
Halifax T v Stockport Co
Hartlepool U v York C
Leyton Orient v Rotherham U
Lincoln C v Cambridge U
Peterborough U v Tranmere R
Scarborough v Colchester U

SUNDAY 5 FEBRUARY

Division 2
Swindon T v Oxford U

Division 3
Notts Co v Mansfield T

FRIDAY 10 FEBRUARY

Division 4
Colchester U v Burnley
Stockport Co v Crewe Alex
Tranmere R v Halifax T

SATURDAY 11 FEBRUARY

Division 1
Coventry C v Newcastle U
Liverpool v Luton T
Millwall v Arsenal
Norwich C v Derby Co
Nottingham F v Queen's Park R
Sheffield W v Manchester U
Southampton v Everton
Tottenham H v Charlton Ath
West Ham U v Middlesbrough
Wimbledon v Aston Villa

Division 2
Birmingham C v AFC Bournemouth
Bradford C v Plymouth Arg
Brighton & Hove A v Leicester C
Chelsea v Swindon T
Crystal Palace v Blackburn R
Hull C v Shrewsbury T
Manchester C v Ipswich T
Oxford U v Portsmouth
Stoke C v Oldham Ath
Sunderland v Walsall
Watford v Leeds U
West Bromwich A v Barnsley

Division 3
Bolton W v Swansea C
Brentford v Chester C
Bristol C v Gillingham
Cardiff C v Sheffield U
Chesterfield v Notts Co
Huddersfield T v Port Vale
Mansfield T v Southend U
Northampton T v Blackpool
Preston NE v Bristol R
Reading v Bury
Wigan Ath v Aldershot
Wolverhampton W v Fulham

Division 4
Cambridge U v Hartlepool U
Darlington v Leyton Orient
Hereford U v Lincoln C
Rochdale v Grimsby T
Rotherham U v Carlisle U
Scunthorpe U v Exeter C
Torquay U v Scarborough
Wrexham v Doncaster R
York C v Peterborough U

TUESDAY 14 FEBRUARY

Division 2
AFC Bournemouth v Hull C

FRIDAY 17 FEBRUARY

Division 3
Southend U v Brentford (7.45 pm)

Division 4
Crewe Alex v Wrexham
Halifax T v Cambridge U
Stockport Co v Rochdale

SATURDAY 18 FEBRUARY

Division 1
Charlton Ath v Derby Co
Coventry C v Liverpool
Everton v Aston Villa
Luton T v Middlesbrough
Manchester U v Wimbledon
Newcastle U v West Ham U
Nottingham F v Millwall
Queen's Park R v Arsenal
Sheffield W v Southampton
Tottenham H v Norwich C

Division 2
Birmingham C v Manchester C
Blackburn R v Oxford U
Bradford C v West Bromwich A
Hull C v Crystal Palace
Ipswich T v Barnsley
Leicester C v Leeds U
Oldham Ath v Brighton & Hove A
Plymouth Arg v Chelsea
Portsmouth v Walsall
Shrewsbury T v AFC Bournemouth
Swindon T v Sunderland
Watford v Stoke C

Division 3
Blackpool v Bolton W
Bristol R v Mansfield T
Bury v Preston NE
Chester C v Notts Co
Chesterfield v Gillingham
Fulham v Bristol C
Huddersfield T v Northampton T
Port Vale v Wigan Ath
Reading v Cardiff C
Wolverhampton W v Sheffield U

BARCLAYS LEAGUE FIXTURES 1988–89

Division 4
Carlisle U v Hereford U
Exeter C v Burnley
Hartlepool U v Doncaster R
Leyton Orient v Scarborough
Lincoln C v Torquay U
Peterborough U v Grimsby T
Rotherham U v Darlington
Scunthorpe U v Colchester U
York C v Tranmere R

SUNDAY 19 FEBRUARY
Division 3
Swansea C v Aldershot

FRIDAY 24 FEBRUARY
Division 3
Wigan Ath v Wolverhampton W

Division 4
Colchester U v Leyton Orient
Darlington v York C
Doncaster R v Crewe Alex

SATURDAY 25 FEBRUARY
Division 1
Arsenal v Luton T
Aston Villa v Charlton Ath
Derby Co v Everton
Liverpool v Nottingham F
Millwall v Coventry C
Norwich C v Manchester U
Southampton v Tottenham H
West Ham U v Queen's Park R
Wimbledon v Sheffield W

Division 2
AFC Bournemouth v Portsmouth
Barnsley v Blackburn R
Brighton & Hove A v Watford
Chelsea v Oldham Ath
Crystal Palace v Bradford C
Leeds U v Swindon T
Manchester C v Plymouth Arg
Oxford U v Ipswich T
Stoke C v Leicester C
Sunderland v Hull C
Walsall v Shrewsbury T
West Bromwich A v Birmingham C

Division 3
Aldershot v Fulham
Bolton W v Port Vale
Brentford v Bury
Bristol C v Huddersfield T
Cardiff C v Chester C
Gillingham v Southend U
Mansfield T v Reading
Northampton T v Swansea C

Notts Co v Bristol R
Preston NE v Chesterfield
Sheffield U v Blackpool

Division 4
Burnley v Peterborough U
Cambridge U v Scunthorpe U
Grimsby T v Exeter C
Hereford U v Stockport Co
Rochdale v Halifax T
Scarborough v Lincoln C
Torquay U v Carlisle U
Tranmere R v Rotherham U
Wrexham v Hartlepool U

SUNDAY 26 FEBRUARY
Division 1
Middlesbrough v Newcastle U (12 noon)

TUESDAY 28 FEBRUARY
Division 2
AFC Bournemouth v Oldham Ath
Barnsley v Watford
Blackburn R v Sunderland
Chelsea v Hull C
Portsmouth v Ipswich T
Shrewsbury T v Plymouth Arg
Stoke C v Birmingham C
Swindon T v Leicester C (7.45 pm)
Walsall v Brighton & Hove A

Division 3
Aldershot v Bristol C
Blackpool v Wolverhampton W
Bolton W v Wigan Ath
Brentford v Chesterfield (7.45 pm)
Gillingham v Preston NE (7.45 pm)
Mansfield T v Chester C
Northampton T v Fulham
Notts Co v Cardiff C
Sheffield U v Port Vale
Southend U v Bury (7.45 pm)
Swansea C v Huddersfield T

Division 4
Burnley v Carlisle U
Colchester U v Rotherham U
Doncaster R v York C
Grimsby T v Crewe Alex
Hartlepool U v Stockport Co
Rochdale v Hereford U
Torquay U v Darlington
Wrexham v Scunthorpe U

WED. 1 MARCH
Division 2
Leeds U v Bradford C
Manchester C v West Bromwich A
Oxford U v Crystal Palace

Division 3
Bristol R v Reading (7.45 pm)

Division 4
Exeter C v Leyton Orient
Lincoln C v Tranmere R
Peterborough U v Halifax T
Scarborough v Cambridge U

FRIDAY 3 MARCH
Division 2
Oldham Ath v Shrewsbury T

Division 4
Halifax T v Doncaster R
Tranmere R v Wrexham

SATURDAY 4 MARCH
Division 1
Coventry C v Arsenal
Liverpool v West Ham U
Manchester U v Everton
Millwall v Middlesbrough
Nottingham F v Newcastle U
Queen's Park R v Luton T
Sheffield W v Charlton Ath
Southampton v Norwich C
Tottenham H v Aston Villa
Wimbledon v Derby Co

Division 2
Birmingham C v Oxford U
Bradford C v Barnsley
Brighton & Hove A v Blackburn R
Crystal Palace v AFC Bournemouth
Hull C v Stoke C
Ipswich T v Swindon T
Leicester C v Walsall
Plymouth Arg v Portsmouth
Sunderland v Chelsea
Watford v Manchester C

Division 3
Bristol C v Northampton T
Bury v Gillingham
Cardiff C v Mansfield T
Chester C v Bristol R
Chesterfield v Southend U
Fulham v Swansea C
Huddersfield T v Aldershot
Port Vale v Blackpool
Preston NE v Brentford
Reading v Notts Co
Wigan Ath v Sheffield U
Wolverhampton W v Bolton W

Division 4

Carlisle U v Exeter C
Crewe Alex v Hartlepool U
Darlington v Lincoln C
Hereford U v Peterborough U
Leyton Orient v Burnley
Rotherham U v Torquay U
Scunthorpe U v Rochdale
Stockport Co v Scarborough
York C v Grimsby T

SUNDAY 5 MARCH

Division 2
West Bromwich A v Leeds U

Division 4
Cambridge U v Colchester U

FRIDAY 10 MARCH

Division 3
Southend U v Wolverhampton W
(7.45 pm)

Division 4
Colchester U v Crewe Alex
Doncaster R v Darlington
Torquay U v York C

SATURDAY 11 MARCH

Division 1
Arsenal v Nottingham F
Aston Villa v Manchester U
Charlton Ath v Southampton
Derby Co v Tottenham H
Everton v Sheffield W
Luton T v Millwall
Middlesbrough v Liverpool
Newcastle U v Queen's Park R
Norwich C v Wimbledon
West Ham U v Coventry C

Division 2
AFC Bournemouth v Bradford C
Barnsley v Crystal Palace
Blackburn R v Plymouth Arg
Chelsea v Watford
Leeds U v Ipswich T
Manchester C v Leicester C
Oxford U v West Bromwich A
Portsmouth v Birmingham C
Shrewsbury T v Brighton & Hove A
Stoke C v Sunderland
Swindon T v Hull C
Walsall v Oldham Ath

Division 3
Aldershot v Port Vale
Blackpool v Fulham

Bolton W v Bristol C
Brentford v Reading
Bristol R v Chesterfield
Gillingham v Cardiff C
Mansfield T v Preston NE
Northampton T v Wigan Ath
Notts Co v Bury
Sheffield U v Huddersfield T
Swansea C v Chester C

Division 4
Burnley v Scunthorpe U
Exeter C v Cambridge U
Grimsby T v Stockport Co
Hartlepool U v Halifax T
Lincoln C v Rotherham U
Peterborough U v Leyton Orient
Rochdale v Tranmere R
Scarborough v Carlisle U
Wrexham v Hereford U

MONDAY 13 MARCH

Division 3
Port Vale v Brentford

Division 4
Stockport Co v Colchester U
Tranmere R v Torquay U

TUESDAY 14 MARCH

Division 2
Birmingham C v Swindon T
Crystal Palace v Stoke C
Hull C v Leeds U
Ipswich T v AFC Bournemouth
(7.45 pm)
Oldham Ath v Portsmouth
Plymouth Arg v Barnsley
Sunderland v Manchester C
Watford v Walsall (7.45 pm)

Division 3
Bristol C v Mansfield T (7.45 pm)
Bury v Sheffield U
Cardiff C v Blackpool (7.45 pm)
Chesterfield v Bolton W
Fulham v Notts Co
Huddersfield T v Bristol R
Preston NE v Swansea C
Wigan Ath v Southend U
Wolverhampton W v Gillingham

Division 4
Cambridge U v Burnley
Carlisle U v Lincoln C

Crewe Alex v Exeter C
Darlington v Rochdale
Halifax T v Grimsby T
Leyton Orient v Doncaster R (7.45
pm)
Rotherham U v Scarborough
Scunthorpe U v Peterborough U
York C v Wrexham

WED. 15 MARCH

Division 2
Bradford C v Oxford U
Brighton & Hove A v Chelsea
Leicester C v Shrewsbury T (7.45
pm)
West Bromwich A v Blackburn R

Division 3
Chester C v Aldershot
Reading v Northampton T (8.00 pm)

Division 4
Hereford U v Hartlepool U

FRIDAY 17 MARCH

Division 4
Halifax T v Exeter C
Stockport Co v Cambridge U
Tranmere R v Carlisle U

SATURDAY 18 MARCH

Division 1
Arsenal v Wimbledon
Coventry C v Tottenham H
Liverpool v Charlton Ath
Luton T v Sheffield W
Middlesbrough v Derby Co
Millwall v Aston Villa
Newcastle U v Everton
Nottingham F v Norwich C
Queen's Park R v Manchester U
West Ham U v Southampton

Division 2
AFC Bournemouth v Swindon T
Barnsley v Leeds U
Birmingham C v Walsall
Blackburn R v Hull C
Bradford C v Watford
Crystal Palace v Sunderland
Ipswich T v Shrewsbury T
Manchester C v Chelsea
Oxford U v Oldham Ath
Plymouth Arg v Leicester C
Portsmouth v Stoke C
West Bromwich A v Brighton &
Hove A

BARCLAYS LEAGUE FIXTURES 1988–89

Division 3

Aldershot v Chesterfield
Blackpool v Chester C
Bolton W v Southend U
Bristol C v Notts Co
Fulham v Cardiff C
Huddersfield T v Brentford
Northampton T v Mansfield T
Port Vale v Preston NE
Sheffield U v Reading
Wigan Ath v Bristol R
Wolverhampton W v Bury

Division 4

Crewe Alex v Lincoln C
Doncaster R v Colchester U
Grimsby T v Scunthorpe U
Hartlepool U v Torquay U
Hereford U v Leyton Orient
Peterborough U v Darlington
Rochdale v Scarborough
Wrexham v Rotherham U
York C v Burnley

SUNDAY 19 MARCH

Division 3

Swansea C v Gillingham

FRIDAY 24 MARCH

Division 2

Oldham Ath v Blackburn R
Watford v Crystal Palace

Division 3

Brentford v Fulham
Gillingham v Wigan Ath (7.45 pm)

Division 3

Colchester U v Grimsby T (7.30 pm)

SATURDAY 25 MARCH

Division 1

Aston Villa v West Ham U
Charlton Ath v Coventry C
Derby Co v Nottingham F
Everton v Millwall
Manchester U v Luton T
Norwich C v Newcastle U
Sheffield W v Queen's Park R
Southampton v Arsenal
Tottenham H v Liverpool
Wimbledon v Middlesbrough

Division 2

Brighton & Hove A v Oxford U
Chelsea v AFC Bournemouth
Hull C v Plymouth Arg
Leeds U v Portsmouth

Leicester C v Birmingham C
Shrewsbury T v Bradford C
Stoke C v Barnsley
Sunderland v Ipswich T
Swindon T v West Bromwich A
Walsall v Manchester C

Division 3

Bristol R v Bristol C
Bury v Blackpool
Cardiff C v Aldershot
Chester C v Wolverhampton W
Chesterfield v Sheffield U
Mansfield T v Bolton W
Notts Co v Port Vale
Preston NE v Northampton T
Reading v Swansea C
Southend U v Huddersfield T

Division 4

Burnley v Tranmere R
Cambridge U v Peterborough U
Carlisle U v Crewe Alex
Darlington v Wrexham
Exeter C v Stockport Co
Leyton Orient v Rochdale
Lincoln C v York C
Rotherham U v Hartlepool U
Scarborough v Doncaster R
Scunthorpe U v Halifax T
Torquay U v Hereford U

MONDAY 27 MARCH

Division 1

Arsenal v Charlton Ath
Coventry C v Southampton
Liverpool v Derby Co
Luton T v Tottenham H
Middlesbrough v Everton
Millwall v Wimbledon
Newcastle U v Sheffield W
Nottingham F v Manchester U
Queen's Park R v Aston Villa
West Ham U v Norwich C

Division 2

AFC Bournemouth v Leicester C
Barnsley v Sunderland
Birmingham C v Shrewsbury T
Blackburn R v Leeds U
Bradford C v Hull C
Crystal Palace v Brighton & Hove A
Manchester C v Stoke C
Oxford U v Walsall
Plymouth Arg v Swindon T
Portsmouth v Watford
West Bromwich A v Oldham Ath

Division 3

Aldershot v Reading
Blackpool v Brentford
Bolton W v Preston NE
Bristol C v Bury
Fulham v Gillingham

Huddersfield T v Chesterfield
Northampton T v Southend U
Port Vale v Mansfield T (7.30 pm)
Sheffield U v Notts Co
Swansea C v Cardiff C
Wigan Ath v Chester C
Wolverhampton W v Bristol R

Division 4

Crewe Alex v Rotherham U
Doncaster R v Cambridge U
Grimsby T v Lincoln C
Halifax T v Darlington
Hartlepool U v Scunthorpe U
Hereford U v Exeter C
Peterborough U v Colchester U
Rochdale v Carlisle U
Stockport Co v Torquay U
Tranmere R v Leyton Orient
Wrexham v Burnley
York C v Scarborough

TUESDAY 28 MARCH

Division 2

Ipswich T v Chelsea (7.45 pm)

FRIDAY 31 MARCH

Division 2

Southend U v Sheffield U (7.45 pm)

Division 4

Cambridge U v Wrexham
Colchester U v Rochdale
Torquay U v Crewe Alex

SATURDAY 1 APRIL

Division 1

Aston Villa v Luton T
Charlton Ath v Middlesbrough
Derby Co v Coventry C
Everton v Queen's Park R
Manchester U v Arsenal
Norwich C v Liverpool
Sheffield W v Millwall
Southampton v Newcastle U
Tottenham H v West Ham U
Wimbledon v Nottingham F

Division 2

Brighton & Hove A v Manchester C
Chelsea v Barnsley
Hull C v Portsmouth
Leeds U v AFC Bournemouth
Leicester C v Oxford U
Oldham Ath v Bradford C
Shrewsbury T v Crystal Palace
Stoke C v Plymouth Arg
Sunderland v Birmingham C
Swindon T v Blackburn R
Walsall v West Bromwich A
Watford v Ipswich T

Division 3

Brentford v Aldershot
Bristol R v Blackpool
Bury v Huddersfield T
Cardiff C v Bristol C
Chester C v Bolton W
Chesterfield v Swansea C
Gillingham v Northampton T
Mansfield T v Wolverhampton W
Notts Co v Wigan Ath
Preston NE v Fulham
Reading v Port Vale

Division 4

Burnley v Hereford U
Carlisle U v Hartlepool U
Darlington v Tranmere R
Exeter C v Peterborough U
Leyton Orient v Grimsby T
Lincoln C v Stockport Co
Rotherham U v York C
Scarborough v Halifax T
Scunthorpe U v Doncaster R

TUESDAY 4 APRIL

Division 2

Chelsea v Birmingham C
Hull C v Oxford U
Oldham Ath v Ipswich T
Shrewsbury T v Manchester C
Stoke C v West Bromwich A
Sunderland v Plymouth Arg
Swindon T v Bradford C (7.45 pm)
Walsall v AFC Bournemouth
Watford v Blackburn R (7.45 pm)

Division 3

Brentford v Bristol C (7.45 pm)
Bury v Northampton T
Cardiff C v Wolverhampton W (7.45 pm)
Chesterfield v Wigan Ath
Gillingham v Bolton W (7.45 pm)
Mansfield T v Sheffield U
Notts Co v Swansea C
Preston NE v Aldershot
Southend U v Blackpool (7.45 pm)

Division 4

Burnley v Crewe Alex
Cambridge U v York C
Carlisle U v Doncaster R
Colchester U v Hereford U
Darlington v Grimsby T
Leyton Orient v Halifax T (7.45 pm)
Rotherham U v Peterborough U
Scunthorpe U v Stockport Co
Torquay U v Wrexham

WED. 5 APRIL

Division 2

Brighton & Hove A v Portsmouth
Leeds U v Crystal Palace
Leicester C v Barnsley (7.45 pm)

Division 3

Bristol R v Port Vale (7.45 pm)
Chester C v Fulham
Reading v Huddersfield T (8.00 pm)

Division 4

Exeter C v Tranmere R
Lincoln C v Rochdale
Scarborough v Hartlepool U

FRIDAY 7 APRIL

Division 3

Wigan Ath v Cardiff C

Division 4

Halifax T v Rotherham U
Stockport Co v Carlisle U

SATURDAY 8 APRIL

Division 1

Arsenal v Everton
Coventry C v Norwich C
Liverpool v Sheffield W (11.30 am)
Luton T v Charlton Ath
Middlesbrough v Southampton
Millwall v Manchester U
Newcastle U v Aston Villa
Nottingham F v Tottenham H
Queen's Park R v Wimbledon
West Ham U v Derby Co

Division 2

AFC Bournemouth v Watford
Barnsley v Shrewsbury T
Birmingham C v Brighton & Hove A
Blackburn R v Leicester C
Bradford C v Walsall
Crystal Palace v Oldham Ath
Ipswich T v Hull C
Manchester C v Swindon T
Oxford U v Stoke C
Portsmouth v Sunderland
West Bromwich A v Chelsea

Division 3

Aldershot v Bury
Blackpool v Reading
Bolton W v Notts Co
Bristol C v Southend U
Fulham v Chesterfield
Huddersfield T v Mansfield T
Northampton T v Chester C

Port Vale v Gillingham
Sheffield U v Preston NE
Swansea C v Bristol R
Wolverhampton W v Brentford

Division 4

Crewe Alex v Scarborough
Doncaster R v Lincoln C
Grimsby T v Burnley
Hartlepool U v Colchester U
Hereford U v Darlington
Peterborough U v Torquay U
Rochdale v Cambridge U
Tranmere R v Scunthorpe U
Wrexham v Leyton Orient
York C v Exeter C

SUNDAY 9 APRIL

Division 2

Plymouth Arg v Leeds U (11.00 am)

FRIDAY 14 APRIL

Division 3

Southend U v Reading (7.45 pm)

Division 4

Crewe Alex v Rochdale
Halifax T v York C

SATURDAY 15 APRIL

Division 1

Arsenal v Newcastle U
Aston Villa v Southampton
Everton v Charlton Ath
Luton T v Coventry C
Manchester U v Derby Co
Millwall v Liverpool
Nottingham F v West Ham U
Queen's Park R v Middlesbrough
Sheffield W v Norwich C
Wimbledon v Tottenham H

Division 2

AFC Bournemouth v Stoke C
Barnsley v Birmingham C
Blackburn R v Manchester C
Bradford C v Ipswich T
Crystal Palace v Portsmouth
Leeds U v Brighton & Hove A
Leicester C v Chelsea
Oldham Ath v Sunderland
Shrewsbury T v Oxford U
Swindon T v Watford
Walsall v Hull C
West Bromwich A v Plymouth Arg

BARCLAYS LEAGUE FIXTURES 1988–89

Division 3

Aldershot v Wolverhampton W
Brentford v Bristol R
Bristol C v Blackpool
Bury v Cardiff C
Chesterfield v Port Vale
Fulham v Bolton W
Gillingham v Mansfield T
Huddersfield T v Chester C
Northampton T v Sheffield U
Preston NE v Notts Co
Swansea C v Wigan Ath

Division 4

Burnley v Darlington
Carlisle U v Cambridge U
Doncaster R v Stockport Co
Exeter C v Rotherham U
Grimsby T v Hereford U
Hartlepool U v Tranmere R
Leyton Orient v Torquay U
Lincoln C v Colchester U
Peterborough U v Wrexham
Scarborough v Scunthorpe U

TUESDAY 18 APRIL

Division 3

Northampton T v Bolton W

FRIDAY 21 APRIL

Division 3

Port Vale v Bristol C

Division 4

Colchester U v Carlisle U
Stockport Co v Peterborough U
Wrexham v Halifax T

SATURDAY 22 APRIL

Division 1

Charlton Ath v Manchester U
Coventry C v Queen's Park R
Derby Co v Sheffield W
Liverpool v Arsenal
Middlesbrough v Nottingham F
Newcastle U v Luton T
Norwich C v Aston Villa
Southampton v Wimbledon
Tottenham H v Everton
West Ham U v Millwall

Division 2

Birmingham C v Blackburn R
Brighton & Hove A v Swindon T
Chelsea v Leeds U
Hull C v Oldham Ath

Ipswich T v West Bromwich A
Manchester C v Barnsley
Oxford U v AFC Bournemouth
Plymouth Arg v Crystal Palace
Portsmouth v Bradford C
Stoke C v Walsall
Sunderland v Shrewsbury T
Watford v Leicester C

Division 3

Blackpool v Chesterfield
Bolton W v Aldershot
Bristol R v Northampton T
Cardiff C v Southend U
Chester C v Preston NE
Mansfield T v Bury
Notts Co v Huddersfield T
Reading v Gillingham
Sheffield U v Brentford
Wigan Ath v Fulham
Wolverhampton W v Swansea C

Division 4

Cambridge U v Crewe Alex
Darlington v Scarborough
Hereford U v Doncaster R
Rochdale v Hartlepool U
Rotherham U v Burnley
Scunthorpe U v Lincoln C
Torquay U v Exeter C
Tranmere R v Grimsby T
York C v Leyton Orient

FRIDAY 28 APRIL

Division 3

Gillingham v Bristol R (7.45 pm)
Southend U v Notts Co (7.45 pm)

Division 4

Torquay U v Scunthorpe U
Tranmere R v Stockport Co

SATURDAY 29 APRIL

Division 1

Arsenal v Norwich C
Aston Villa v Middlesbrough
Everton v Liverpool
Luton T v Derby Co
Manchester U v Coventry C
Millwall v Tottenham H
Nottingham F v Southampton
Queen's Park R v Charlton Ath
Sheffield W v West Ham U
Wimbledon v Newcastle U

Division 2

AFC Bournemouth v Barnsley
Bradford C v Leicester C
Crystal Palace v West Bromwich A
Hull C v Watford

Ipswich T v Birmingham C
Oldham Ath v Plymouth Arg
Oxford U v Manchester C
Portsmouth v Blackburn R
Shrewsbury T v Chelsea
Stoke C v Leeds U
Sunderland v Brighton & Hove A
Walsall v Swindon T

Division 3

Aldershot v Blackpool
Brentford v Mansfield T
Bristol C v Wigan Ath
Bury v Bolton W
Chesterfield v Chester C
Fulham v Sheffield U
Huddersfield T v Wolverhampton W
Northampton T v Cardiff C
Preston NE v Reading
Swansea C v Port Vale

Division 4

Burnley v Doncaster R
Darlington v Colchester U
Exeter C v Hartlepool U
Grimsby T v Carlisle U
Halifax T v Lincoln C
Leyton Orient v Cambridge U
Peterborough U v Crewe Alex
Rotherham U v Hereford U
Wrexham v Scarborough
York C v Rochdale

MONDAY 1 MAY

Division 2

Barnsley v Oxford U
Birmingham C v Bradford C
Blackburn R v AFC Bournemouth (7.30 pm)
Brighton & Hove A v Hull C
Chelsea v Stoke C
Leeds U v Walsall
Leicester C v Oldham Ath (7.45 pm)
Manchester C v Crystal Palace
Plymouth Arg v Ipswich T
Swindon T v Shrewsbury T
Watford v Sunderland
West Bromwich A v Portsmouth

Division 3

Blackpool v Gillingham
Bolton W v Huddersfield T
Bristol R v Southend U
Cardiff C v Chesterfield
Chester C v Bury
Notts Co v Brentford (7.30 pm)
Port Vale v Northampton T (7.30 pm)
Reading v Fulham
Sheffield U v Aldershot
Wigan Ath v Preston NE
Wolverhampton W v Bristol C

BARCLAYS LEAGUE FIXTURES 1988–89

Division 4

Carlisle U v Leyton Orient
Colchester U v Halifax T
Crewe Alex v York C
Doncaster R v Grimsby T (11.00 am)
Hartlepool U v Peterborough U
Hereford U v Tranmere R
Lincoln C v Burnley
Rochdale v Torquay U
Scarborough v Exeter C
Scunthorpe U v Rotherham U
Stockport Co v Wrexham

TUESDAY 2 MAY

Division 3

Mansfield T v Swansea C

Division 4

Cambridge U v Darlington

FRIDAY 5 MAY

Division 4

Colchester U v Exeter C
Crewe Alex v Halifax T

SATURDAY 6 MAY

Division 1

Charlton Ath v Wimbledon
Coventry C v Nottingham F
Derby Co v Aston Villa
Liverpool v Queen's Park R
Middlesbrough v Arsenal
Newcastle U v Millwall
Norwich C v Everton
Southampton v Manchester U
Tottenham H v Sheffield W
West Ham U v Luton T

Division 2

Barnsley v Portsmouth
Birmingham C v Hull C
Blackburn R v Walsall
Brighton & Hove A v Ipswich T
Chelsea v Bradford C
Leeds U v Oldham Ath
Leicester C v Crystal Palace
Manchester C v AFC Bournemouth
Plymouth Arg v Oxford U
Swindon T v Stoke C
Watford v Shrewsbury T
West Bromwich A v Sunderland

Division 3

Blackpool v Huddersfield T
Bolton W v Brentford
Bristol R v Fulham
Cardiff C v Preston NE
Chester C v Gillingham
Mansfield T v Chesterfield
Notts Co v Aldershot
Port Vale v Southend U
Reading v Bristol C
Sheffield U v Swansea C
Wigan Ath v Bury
Wolverhampton W v Northampton T

Division 4

Cambridge U v Torquay U
Carlisle U v Wrexham
Doncaster R v Tranmere R
Hartlepool U v Burnley
Hereford U v York C
Lincoln C v Leyton Orient
Rochdale v Peterborough U
Scarborough v Grimsby T
Scunthorpe U v Darlington
Stockport Co v Rotherham U

SATURDAY 13 MAY

Division 1

Arsenal v Derby Co
Aston Villa v Coventry C

Everton v West Ham U
Luton T v Norwich C
Manchester U v Newcastle U
Millwall v Southampton
Nottingham F v Charlton Ath
Queen's Park R v Tottenham H
Sheffield W v Middlesbrough
Wimbledon v Liverpool

Division 2

AFC Bournemouth v Plymouth Arg
Bradford C v Manchester C
Crystal Palace v Birmingham C
Hull C v West Bromwich A
Ipswich T v Blackburn R
Oldham Ath v Swindon T
Oxford U v Watford
Portsmouth v Chelsea
Shrewsbury T v Leeds U
Stoke C v Brighton & Hove A
Sunderland v Leicester C
Walsall v Barnsley

Division 3

Aldershot v Mansfield T
Brentford v Cardiff C
Bristol C v Sheffield U
Bury v Bristol R
Chesterfield v Reading
Fulham v Port Vale
Gillingham v Notts Co
Huddersfield T v Wigan Ath
Preston NE v Wolverhampton W
Southend U v Chester C
Swansea C v Blackpool

Division 4

Burnley v Scarborough
Darlington v Carlisle U
Exeter C v Lincoln C
Grimsby T v Hartlepool U
Halifax T v Hereford U
Leyton Orient v Scunthorpe U
Peterborough U v Doncaster R
Rotherham U v Cambridge U
Torquay U v Colchester U
Tranmere R v Crewe Alex
Wrexham v Rochdale
York C v Stockport Co

SCOTTISH (B&Q) LEAGUE FIXTURES 1988–89

SATURDAY 13 AUGUST

Premier Division
Celtic v Hearts
Dundee v Aberdeen
Hamilton Acad v Rangers
Hibernian v Motherwell
St. Mirren v Dundee U

Division 1
Ayr U v Clydebank
Falkirk v Airdrieonions
Forfar Ath v Meadowbank Th
Morton v Clyde
Partick Th v Dunfermline Ath
Queen of the S v Kilmarnock
St. Johnstone v Raith R

Division 2
Albion R v East Stirling
Brechin C v Alloa
Cowdenbeath v Montrose
Dumbarton v East Fife
Queens Park v Berwick R
Stirling A v Stenhousemuir
Stranraer v Arbroath

SATURDAY 20 AUGUST

Premier Division
Aberdeen v St. Mirren
Dundee U v Celtic
Hearts v Hamilton Acad
Motherwell v Dundee
Rangers v Hibernian

Division 1
Airdrieonians v Morton
Clyde v Forfar Ath
Clydebank v Falkirk
Dunfermline Ath v St. Johnstone
Kilmarnock v Partick Th
Meadowbank Th v Ayr U
Raith R v Queen of the S

Division 2
Alloa v Cowdenbeath
Arbroath v Brechin C
Berwick R v Stranraer
East Fife v Albion R
East Stirling v Queens Park
Montrose v Stirling A
Stenhousemuir v Dumbarton

SATURDAY 27 AUGUST

Premier Division
Dundee U v Aberdeen
Hamilton Acad v Motherwell
Hibernian v Hearts

Rangers v Celtic
St. Mirren v Dundee

Division 1
Airdrieonians v Queen of the S
Clyde v Partick Th
Dunfermline Ath v Raith R
Forfar Ath v St. Johnstone
Kilmarnock v Ayr U
Meadowbank Th v Falkirk
Morton v Clydebank

Division 2
Arbroath v Alloa
Dumbarton v Queens Park
East Fife v Cowdenbeath
Montrose v Brechin C
Stenhousemuir v East Stirling
Stirling A v Berwick R
Stranraer v Albion R

SATURDAY 3 SEPTEMBER

Premier Division
Aberdeen v Hibernian
Celtic v Hamilton Acad
Dundee v Dundee U
Hearts v St. Mirren
Motherwell v Rangers

Division 1
Ayr U v Forfar Ath
Clydebank v Kilmarnock
Falkirk v Dunfermline Ath
Partick Th v Morton
Queen of the S v Meadowbank Th
Raith R v Clyde
St. Johnstone v Airdrieonians

Division 2
Albion R v Dumbarton
Alloa v Stenhousemuir
Berwick R v Arbroath
Brechin C v Stirling A
Cowdenbeath v Stranraer
East Stirling v East Fife
Queens Park v Montrose

SATURDAY 10 SEPTEMBER

Division 1
Airdrieonians v Kilmarnock
Ayr U v Falkirk
Clyde v Clydebank
Dunfermline Ath v Queen of the S
Forfar Ath v Partick Th
Meadowbank Th v Raith R
Morton v St. Johnstone

Division 2
Albion R v Brechin C
Dumbarton v Stranraer

East Fife v Alloa
East Stirling v Berwick R
Montrose v Arbroath
Stenhousemuir v Cowdenbeath
Stirling A v Queens Park

SATURDAY 17 SEPTEMBER

Premier Division
Celtic v Aberdeen
Dundee U v Hibernian
Hamilton Acad v Dundee
Hearts v Rangers
St. Mirren v Motherwell

Division 1
Clydebank v Dunfermline Ath
Falkirk v Morton
Kilmarnock v Clyde
Partick Th v Ayr U
Queen of the S v Forfar Ath
Raith R v Airdrieonians
St. Johnstone v Meadowbank Th

Division 2
Alloa v East Stirling
Arbroath v Stenhousemuir
Berwick R v Montrose
Brechin C v Dumbarton
Cowdenbeath v Albion R
Queens Park v East Fife
Stranraer v Stirling A

SATURDAY 24 SEPTEMBER

Premier Division
Aberdeen v Hearts
Dundee v Celtic
Hibernian v Hamilton Acad
Motherwell v Dundee U
Rangers v St Mirren

Division 1
Airdrieonians v Partick Th
Ayr U v St. Johnstone
Clyde v Falkirk
Dunfermline Ath v Kilmarnock
Forfar Ath v Raith R
Meadowbank Th v Clydebank
Morton v Queen of the S

Division 2
Albion R v Queens Park
Dumbarton v Alloa
East Fife v Arbroath
East Stirling v Brechin C
Montrose v Stranraer
Stenhousemuir v Berwick R
Stirling A v Cowdenbeath

SCOTTISH LEAGUE FIXTURES

TUESDAY 27 SEPTEMBER

Premier Division
Dundee U v Rangers
Hamilton Acad v Aberdeen

WEDNESDAY 28 SEPTEMBER

Premier Division
Celtic v Motherwell
Hearts v Dundee
St. Mirren v Hibernian

SATURDAY 1 OCTOBER

Premier Division
Dundee U v Hearts
Hibernian v Celtic
Motherwell v Aberdeen
Rangers v Dundee
St. Mirren v Hamilton Acad

Division 1
Airdrieonians v Meadowbank Th
Clyde v Dunfermline Ath
Clydebank v Forfar Ath
Kilmarnock v Morton
Queen of the S v Falkirk
Raith R v Ayr U
St. Johnstone v Partick Th

Division 2
Alloa v Albion R
Arbroath v Stirling A
Berwick R v Dumbarton
Cowdenbeath v East Stirling
Montrose v Stenhousemuir
Queens Park v Brechin City
Stranraer v East Fife

SATURDAY 8 OCTOBER

Premier Division
Aberdeen v Rangers
Celtic v St. Mirren
Dundee v Hibernian
Hamilton Acad v Dundee U
Hearts v Motherwell

Division 1
Ayr U v Queen of the S
Dunfermline Ath v Airdrieonians
Falkirk v St. Johnstone
Forfar Ath v Kilmarnock
Meadowbank Th v Clyde
Morton v Raith R
Partick Th v Clydebank

Division 2
Albion R v Berwick R
Brechin C v Cowdenbeath
Dumbarton v Arbroath
East Fife v Montrose
East Stirling v Stranraer
Stenhousemuir v Queens Park
Stirling A v Alloa

TUESDAY 11 OCTOBER

Premier Division
Hamilton Acad v Hearts

WEDNESDAY 12 OCTOBER

Premier Division
Celtic v Dundee U
Dundee v Motherwell
Hibernian v Rangers
St. Mirren v Aberdeen

SATURDAY 15 OCTOBER

Division 1
Airdrieonians v Clyde
Ayr U v Dunfermline Ath
Forfar Ath v Morton
Meadowbank Th v Kilmarnock
Partick Th v Falkirk
Raith R v Clydebank
St. Johnstone v Queen of the S

Division 2
Albion R v Arbroath
Alloa v Berwick R
Brechin C v Stranraer
Dumbarton v Stirling A
East Fife v Stenhousemuir
East Stirling v Montrose
Queens Park v Cowdenbeath

SATURDAY 22 OCTOBER

Premier Division
Aberdeen v Dundee
Dundee U v St. Mirren
Hearts v Celtic
Motherwell v Hibernian
Rangers v Hamilton Acad

Division 1
Clyde v St. Johnstone
Clydebank v Airdrieonians
Dunfermline Ath v Meadowbank Th
Falkirk v Forfar Ath
Kilmarnock v Raith R
Morton v Ayr U
Queen of the S v Partick Th

Division 2
Arbroath v East Stirling
Berwick R v East Fife
Cowdenbeath v Dumbarton
Montrose v Alloa
Stenhousemuir v Brechin C
Stirling A v Albion R
Stranraer v Queens Park

SATURDAY 29 OCTOBER

Premier Division
Celtic v Dundee
Dundee U v Motherwell
Hamilton Acad v Hibernian
Hearts v Aberdeen
St. Mirren v Rangers

Division 1
Ayr U v Clyde
Falkirk v Raith R
Forfar Ath v Airdrieonians
Morton v Dunfermline Ath
Partick Th v Meadowbank Th
Queen of the S v Clydebank
St. Johnstone v Kilmarnock

Division 2
Albion R v Montrose
Brechin C v Berwick R
Cowdenbeath v Arbroath
Dumbarton v East Stirling
Queens Park v Alloa
Stirling A v East Fife
Stranraer v Stenhousemuir

TUESDAY 1 NOVEMBER

Premier Division
Motherwell v St. Mirren
Rangers v Hearts

WEDNESDAY 2 NOVEMBER

Premier Division
Aberdeen v Celtic
Dundee v Hamilton Acad
Hibernian v Dundee U

SATURDAY 5 NOVEMBER

Premier Division
Dundee U v Dundee
Hamilton Acad v Celtic
Hibernian v Aberdeen
Rangers v Motherwell
St. Mirren v Hearts

Division 1
Airdrieonians v Ayr U
Clyde v Queen of the S
Clydebank v St. Johnstone
Dunfermline Ath v Forfar Ath
Kilmarnock v Falkirk
Meadowbank Th v Morton
Raith R v Partick Th

Division 2
Alloa v Stranraer
Arbroath v Queens Park
Berwick R v Cowdenbeath
East Fife v Brechin C
East Stirling v Stirling A
Montrose v Dumbarton
Stenhousemuir v Albion R

SATURDAY 12 NOVEMBER

Premier Division
Aberdeen v Dundee U
Celtic v Rangers
Dundee v St. Mirren
Hearts v Hibernian
Motherwell v Hamilton Acad

Division 1
Clydebank v Clyde
Falkirk v Ayr U
Kilmarnock v Airdrieonians
Partick Th v Forfar Ath
Queen of the S v Dunfermline Ath
Raith R v Meadowbank Th
St. Johnstone v Morton

Division 2
Albion R v East Fife
Brechin C v Arbroath
Cowdenbeath v Alloa
Dumbarton v Stenhousemuir
Queens Park v East Stirling
Stirling A v Montrose
Stranraer v Berwick R

SATURDAY 19 NOVEMBER

Premier Division
Aberdeen v Motherwell
Celtic v Hibernian
Dundee v Rangers
Hamilton Acad v St. Mirren
Hearts v Dundee U

Division 1
Airdrieonians v Raith R
Ayr U v Partick Th
Clyde v Kilmarnock

Dunfermline Ath v Clydebank
Forfar Ath v Queen of the S
Meadowbank Th v St. Johnstone
Morton v Falkirk

Division 2
Alloa v Brechin C
Arbroath v Stranraer
Berwick R v Queens Park
East Fife v Dumbarton
East Stirling v Albion R
Montrose v Cowdenbeath
Stenhousemuir v Stirling A

SATURDAY 26 NOVEMBER

Premier Division
Dundee U v Hamilton Acad
Hibernian v Dundee
Motherwell v Hearts
Rangers v Aberdeen
St. Mirren v Celtic

Division 1
Clydebank v Meadowbank Th
Falkirk v Clyde
Kilmarnock v Dunfermline Ath
Partick Th v Airdrieonians
Queen of the S v Morton
Raith R v Forfar Ath
St. Johnstone v Ayr U

Division 2
Alloa v East Fife
Arbroath v Montrose
Berwick R v East Stirling
Brechin C v Albion R
Cowdenbeath, v Stenhousemuir
Queens Park v Stirling A
Stranraer v Dumbarton

SATUDAY 3 DECEMBER

Premier Division
Aberdeen v Hamilton Acad
Dundee v Hearts
Hibernian v St. Mirren
Motherwell v Celtic
Rangers v Dundee U

Division 1
Ayr U v Meadowbank Th
Falkirk v Clydebank
Forfar Ath v Clyde
Morton v Airdrieonians
Partick Th v Kilmarnock
Queen of the S v Raith R
St. Johnstone v Dunfermline Ath

SATURDAY 10 DECEMBER

Premier Division
Celtic v Aberdeen
Dundee U v Hibernian
Hamilton Acad v Dundee
Hearts v Rangers
St. Mirren v Motherwell

Division 1
Airdrieonians v Forfar Ath
Clyde v Ayr U
Clydebank v Queen of the S
Dunfermline Ath v Morton
Kilmarnock v St. Johnstone
Meadowbank Th v Partick Th
Raith R v Falkirk

Division 2
Albion R v Cowdenbeath
Dumbarton v Brechin C
East Fife v Queens Park
East Stirling v Alloa
Montrose v Berwick R
Stenhousemuir v Arbroath
Stirling A v Stranraer

SATURDAY 17 DECEMBER

Premier Division
Aberdeen v St. Mirren
Dundee U v Celtic
Hearts v Hamilton Acad
Motherwell v Dundee
Rangers v Hibernian

Division 1
Airdrieonians v Clydebank
Ayr U v Morton
Forfar Ath v Falkirk
Meadowbank Th v Dunfermline Ath
Partick Th v Queen of the S
Raith R v Kilmarnock
St. Johnstone v Clyde

Division 2
Alloa v Dumbarton
Arbroath v East Fife
Berwick R v Stenhousemuir
Brechin C v East Stirling
Cowdenbeath v Stirling A
Queens Park v Albion R
Stranraer v Montrose

SATURDAY 24 DECEMBER

Division 1
Clyde v Airdrieonians
Clydebank v Raith R
Dunfermline Ath v Ayr U
Falkirk v Partick Th
Kilmarnock v Meadowbank Th
Morton v Forfar Ath
Queen of the S v St. Johnstone

SCOTTISH LEAGUE FIXTURES

Division 2
Albion R v Stenhousemuir
Brechin C v East Fife
Cowdenbeath v Berwick R
Dumbarton v Montrose
Queens Park v Arbroath
Stirling A v East Stirling
Stranraer v Alloa

SATURDAY 31 DECEMBER

Premier Division
Celtic v Hearts
Dundee v Aberdeen
Hamilton Acad v Rangers
Hibernian v Motherwell
St. Mirren v Dundee U

Division 1
Airdrieonians v St. Johnstone
Clyde v Raith R
Dunfermline Ath v Falkirk
Forfar Ath v Ayr U
Kilmarnock v Clydebank
Meadowbank Th v Queen of the S
Morton v Partick Th

Division 2
Alloa v Queens Park
Arbroath v Cowdenbeath
Berwick R v Brechin C
East Fife v Stirling A
East Stirling v Dumbarton
Montrose v Albion R
Stenhousemuir v Stranraer

TUESDAY 3 JANUARY, 1989

Premier Division
Dundee U v Aberdeen
Hamilton Acad v Motherwell
Hibernian v Hearts
Rangers v Celtic
St. Mirren v Dundee

Division 1
Ayr U v Kilmarnock
Clydebank v Morton
Falkirk v Meadowbank Th
Partick Th v Clyde
Queen of the S v Airdrieonians
Raith R v Dunfermline Ath
St. Johnstone v Forfar Ath

Division 2
Albion R v Stranraer
Alloa v Arbroath
Berwick R v Stirling A

Brechin C v Montrose
Cowdenbeath v East Fife
East Stirling v Stenhousemuir
Queens Park v Dumbarton

SATURDAY 7 JANUARY

Premier Division
Aberdeen v Hibernian
Celtic v Hamilton Acad
Dundee v Dundee U
Hearts v St. Mirren
Motherwell v Rangers

Division 1
Ayr U v Airdrieonians
Falkirk v Kilmarnock
Forfar Ath v Dunfermline Ath
Morton v Meadowbank Th
Partick Th v Raith R
Queen of the S v Clyde
St. Johnstone v Clydebank

SATURDAY 14 JANUARY

Premier Division
Aberdeen v Rangers
Celtic v St. Mirren
Dundee v Hibernian
Hamilton Acad v Dundee U
Hearts v Motherwell

Division 1
Airdrieonians v Falkirk
Clyde v Morton
Clydebank v Ayr U
Dunfermline Ath v Partick Th
Kilmarnock v Queen of the S
Meadowbank Th v Forfar Ath
Raith R v St. Johnstone

Division 2
Arbroath v Berwick R
Dumbarton v Albion R
East Fife v East Stirling
Montrose v Queens Park
Stenhousemuir v Alloa
Stirling A v Brechin C
Stranraer v Cowdenbeath

SATURDAY 21 JANUARY

Premier Division
Dundee U v Hearts
Hibernian v Celtic
Motherwell v Aberdeen
Rangers v Dundee
St. Mirren v Hamilton Acad

Division 1
Airdrieonians v Dunfermline Ath
Clyde v Meadowbank Th
Clydebank v Partick Th
Kilmarnock v Forfar Ath
Queen of the S v Ayr U
Raith R v Morton
St. Johnstone v Falkirk

Division 2
Arbroath v Albion R
Berwick R v Alloa
Cowdenbeath v Queens Park
Montrose v East Stirling
Stenhousemuir v East Fife
Stirling A v Dumbarton
Stranraer v Brechin C

SATURDAY 28 JANUARY

Division 2
Albion R v Stirling A
Alloa v Montrose
Brechin C v Stenhousemuir
Dumbarton v Cowdenbeath
East Fife v Berwick R
East Stirling v Arbroath
Queens Park v Stranraer

SATURDAY 4 FEBRUARY

Division 1
Ayr U v Raith R
Dunfermline Ath v Clyde
Falkirk v Queen of the S
Forfar Ath v Clydebank
Meadowbank Th v Airdrieonians
Morton v Kilmarnock
Partick Th v St. Johnstone

Division 2
Alloa v Stirling A
Arbroath v Dumbarton
Berwick R v Albion R
Cowdenbeath v Brechin C
Montrose v East Fife
Queens Park v Stenhousemuir
Stranraer v East Stirling

SATURDAY 11 FEBRUARY

Premier Division
Celtic v Motherwell
Dundee U v Rangers
Hamilton Acad v Aberdeen
Hearts v Dundee
St. Mirren v Hibernian

Division 1

Airdrieonians v Forfar Ath
Clydebank v Queen of the S
Dunfermline Ath v St. Johnstone
Kilmarnock v Clyde
Meadowbank Th v Raith R
Morton v Falkirk
Partick Th v Ayr U

Division 2

Albion R v Alloa
Brechin C v Queens Park
Dumbarton v Berwick R
East Fife v Stranraer
East Stirling v Cowdenbeath
Stenhousemuir v Montrose
Stirling A v Arbroath

SATURDAY 18 FEBRUARY

Division 2

Alloa v Arbroath
Berwick R v Stirling A
Cowdenbeath v Stenhousemuir
Dumbarton v East Fife
East Stirling v Brechin C
Montrose v Stranraer
Queens Park v Albion R

SATURDAY 25 FEBRUARY

Premier Division

Aberdeen v Hearts
Dundee v Celtic
Hibernian v Hamilton Acad
Motherwell v Dundee U
Rangers v St. Mirren

Division 1

Ayr U v Meadowbank Th
Clyde v Clydebank
Falkirk v Dunfermline Ath
Forfar Ath v Morton
Queen of the S v Partick Th
Raith R v Airdrieonians
St. Johnstone v Kilmarnock

Division 2

Albion R v Montrose
Arbroath v Berwick R
Brechin C v Alloa
East Fife v Cowdenbeath
Stenhousemuir v East Stirling
Stirling A v Queens Park
Stranraer v Dumbarton

SATURDAY 4 MARCH

Premier Division

Clyde v Ayr U
Clydebank v Dunfermline Ath

Falkirk v Meadowbank Th
Forfar Ath v St. Johnstone
Kilmarnock v Airdrieonians
Morton v Partick Th
Raith R v Queen of the S

Division 2

Albion R v East Fife
Alloa v Stenhousemuir
Berwick R v East Stirling
Brechin C v Arbroath
Cowdenbeath v Dumbarton
Queens Park v Montrose
Stranraer v Stirling A

SATURDAY 11 MARCH

Premier Division

Aberdeen v Dundee
Dundee U v St. Mirren
Hearts v Celtic
Motherwell v Hibernian
Rangers v Hamilton Acad

Division 1

Airdrieonians v Clyde
Ayr U v Kilmarnock
Dunfermline Ath v Raith R
Meadowbank Th v Clydebank
Partick Th v Falkirk
Queen of the S v Forfar Ath
St. Johnstone v Morton

Division 2

Arbroath v Stranraer
Dumbarton v Queens Park
East Fife v Alloa
East Stirling v Albion R
Montrose v Cowdenbeath
Stenhousemuir v Berwick R
Stirling A v Brechin C

SATURDAY 18 MARCH

Division 1

Falkirk v Ayr U
Kilmarnock v Forfar Ath
Meadowbank Th v Clyde
Morton v Clydebank
Partick Th v Airdrieonians
Queen of the S v Dunfermline Ath
Raith R v St. Johnstone

Division 2

Albion R v Stranraer
Arbroath v East Fife
Berwick R v Alloa
Brechin C v Stenhousemuir
Cowdenbeath v Queens Park
Dumbarton v Montrose
Stirling A v East Stirling

SATURDAY 25 MARCH

Premier Division

Celtic v Dundee U
Dundee v Motherwell
Hamilton Acad v Hearts
Hibernian v Rangers
St. Mirren v Aberdeen

Division 1

Airdrieonians v Morton
Ayr U v Raith R
Clyde v Partick Th
Clydebank v Falkirk
Dunfermline Ath v Kilmarnock
Forfar Ath v Meadowbank Th
St. Johnstone v Queen of the S

Division 2

Alloa v Cowdenbeath
East Fife v Stirling A
East Stirling v Dumbarton
Montrose v Brechin C
Queens Park v Arbroath
Stenhousemuir v Albion R
Stranraer v Berwick R

SATURDAY 1 APRIL

Premier Division

Aberdeen v Dundee U
Celtic v Rangers
Dundee v St. Mirren
Hearts v Hibernian
Motherwell v Hamilton Acad

Division 1

Airdrieonians v Queen of the S
Clydebank v St. Johnstone
Forfar Ath v Ayr U
Kilmarnock v Falkirk
Morton v Meadowbank Th
Partick Th v Dunfermline Ath
Raith R v Clyde

Division 2

Berwick R v Queens Park
Brechin C v Albion R
Cowdenbeath v Arbroath
East Stirling v East Fife
Stenhousemuir v Montrose
Stirling A v Dumbarton
Stranraer v Alloa

SATURDAY 8 APRIL

Premier Division

Dundee U v Dundee
Hamilton Acad v Celtic
Hibernian v Aberdeen
Rangers v Motherwell
St. Mirren v Hearts

SCOTTISH LEAGUE FIXTURES

Division 1
Ayr U v Clydebank
Clyde v Forfar Ath
Dunfermline Ath v Airdrieonians
Falkirk v Raith R
Meadowbank Th v Kilmarnock
Queen of the S v Morton
St. Johnstone v Partick Th

Division 2
Albion R v Cowdenbeath
Alloa v Stirling A
Arbroath v Stenhousemuir
Dumbarton v Berwick R
East Fife v Stranraer
Montrose v East Stirling
Queens Park v Brechin C

SATURDAY 15 APRIL

Premier Division
Aberdeen v Hamilton Acad
Dundee v Hearts
Hibernian v St. Mirren
Motherwell v Celtic
Rangers v Dundee U

Division 1
Airdrieonians v St. Johnstone
Dunfermline Ath v Morton
Falkirk v Clyde
Forfar Ath v Clydebank
Kilmarnock v Raith R
Partick Th v Meadowbank Th
Queen of the S v Ayr U

Division 2
Berwick R v Cowdenbeath
Dumbarton v Brechin C
East Fife v Stenhousemuir
East Stirling v Alloa
Montrose v Arbroath
Sitrling A v Albion R
Stranraer v Queens Park

SATURDAY 22 APRIL

Premier Division
Celtic v Dundee
Dundee U v Motherwell
Hamilton Acad v Hibernian
Hearts v Aberdeen
St. Mirren v Rangers

Division 1
Ayr U v Dunfermline Ath
Clyde v Queen of the S
Clydebank v Partick Th
Meadowbank Th v Airdrieonians
Morton v Kilmarnock
Raith R v Forfar Ath
St. Johnstone v Falkirk

Division 2
Albion R v Dumbarton
Alloa v Montrose
Arbroath v East Stirling
Brechin C v Berwick R
Cowdenbeath v Stranraer
Queens Park v East Fife
Stenhousemuir v Stirling A

SATURDAY 29 APRIL

Premier Division
Aberdeen v Celtic
Dundee v Hamilton Acad
Hibernian v Dundee U
Motherwell v St. Mirren
Rangers v Hearts

Division 1
Airdrieonians v Falkirk
Clyde v Morton
Forfar Ath v Dunfermline Ath
Kilmarnock v Partick Th
Queen of the S v Meadowbank Th
Raith R v Clydebank
St. Johnstone v Ayr U

Division 2
Alloa v Albion R
Arbroath v Dumbarton
Cowdenbeath v Brechin C
East Fife v Berwick R
East Stirling v Queens Park
Montrose v Stirling A
Stenhousemuir v Stranraer

SATURDAY 6 MAY

Premier Division
Aberdeen v Motherwell

Celtic v Hibernian
Dundee v Rangers
Hamilton Acad v St. Mirren
Hearts v Dundee U

Division 1
Ayr U v Airdrieonians
Clydebank v Kilmarnock
Dunfermline Ath v Clyde
Falkirk v Queen of the S
Meadowbank Th v St. Johnstone
Morton v Raith R
Partick Th v Forfar Ath

Division 2
Albion R v Arbroath
Berwick R v Montrose
Brechin C v East Fife
Dumbarton v Stenhousemuir
Queens Park v Alloa
Stirling A v Cowdenbeath
Stranraer v East Stirling

SATURDAY 13 MAY

Premier Division
Dundee U v Hamilton Acad
Hibernian v Dundee
Motherwell v Hearts
Rangers v Aberdeen
St. Mirren v Celtic

Division 1
Ayr U v Morton
Clyde v St. Johnstone
Clydebank v Airdrieonians
Dunfermline Ath v Meadowbank Th
Forfar Ath v Falkirk
Queen of the S v Kilmarnock
Raith R v Partick Th

Division 2
Albion R v Berwick R
Arbroath v Stirling A
Dumbarton v Alloa
East Fife v Montrose
East Stirling v Cowdenbeath
Stenhousemuir v Queens Park
Stranraer v Brechin C

SCOTTISH INTERNATIONAL AND CUP FIXTURES 1988–89

AUGUST 1988

Wed 10   Skol Cup, 1st Round
Wed 17   Skol Cup, 2nd Round
Wed 24   Skol Cup, 3rd Round
Wed 31   Skol Cup, 4th Round

SEPTEMBER 1988

Wed 14   NORWAY v SCOTLAND
          (World Cup)
Wed 21   Skol Cup, Semi-finals

OCTOBER 1988

Wed 19   SCOTLAND v YUGOSLAVIA
          (World Cup)
Sun 23   Skol Cup, Final

DECEMBER 1988

Sat 3   Scottish Cup, 1st Round

JANUARY 1989

Sat 7   Scottish Cup, 2nd Round
Sat 28   Scottish Cup, 3rd Round

FEBRUARY 1989

Wed 8   CYPRUS v SCOTLAND
          (World Cup)
Sat 18   Scottish Cup, 4th Round

MARCH 1989

Wed 8   SCOTLAND v FRANCE
          (World Cup)
Sat 18   Scottish Cup, Quarter-finals

APRIL 1989

Sat 15   Scottish Cup, Semi-finals
Tue 25   SCOTLAND v CYPRUS
          (World Cup)

MAY 1989

Sat 20   Scottish Cup, Final

INTERNATIONAL & CUP FIXTURES 1988–89

AUGUST 1988

Sat 20   FA Charity Shield
Sat 27   League season starts
Wed 31   Littlewoods Cup 1st Rd, 1st leg

SEPTEMBER 1988

Sat 3   FA Cup Preliminary Rd
Wed 7   Littlewoods Cup 1st Rd, 2nd leg
             European Cups 1st Rd, 1st leg
Sat 10   FA Vase Extra Preliminary Rd
             FA Youth Cup Preliminary Rd
Wed 14   ENGLAND v DENMARK (Friendly)
Sat 17   FA Cup 1st Qualifying Rd
Sat 24   FA Trophy 1st Qualifying Rd
Wed 28   Littlewoods Cup 2nd Rd, 1st leg

OCTOBER 1988

Sat 1   FA Cup 2nd Qualifying Rd
             FA Youth Cup 1st Qualifying Rd
Wed 5   European Cups 1st Rd, 2nd leg
Sat 8   FA Vase Preliminary Rd
Sun 9   FA Sunday Cup 1st Rd
Wed 12   Littlewoods Cup 2nd Rd, 2nd leg
Sat 15   FA Cup 3rd Qualifying Rd
Wed 19   ENGLAND v SWEDEN (World Cup)
Sat 22   FA Trophy 2nd Qualifying Rd
             FA Youth Cup 2nd Qualifying Rd
             FA County Youth Cup 1st Rd
Wed 26   European Cups 2nd Rd, 1st leg
Sat 29   FA Cup 4th Qualifying Rd

NOVEMBER 1988

Wed 2   Littlewoods Cup 3rd Rd
Sat 5   FA Vase 1st Rd
Wed 9   European Cups 2nd Rd, 2nd leg
Sun 13   FA Sunday Cup 2nd Rd
Wed 16   ENGLAND INTERNATIONAL (To be announced)
Sat 19   FA Cup 1st Rd
             FA Youth Cup 1st Rd
Wed 23   UEFA Cup 3rd Rd, 1st leg
Sat 26   FA Vase 2nd Rd
Wed 30   Littlewoods Cup 4th Rd

DECEMBER 1988

Sat 3   FA Trophy 3rd Qualifying Rd
             FA County Youth Cup 2nd Rd
Wed 7   UEFA Cup 3rd Rd, 2nd leg
Sat 10   FA Cup 2nd Rd
Sat 17   FA Vase 3rd Rd
             FA Youth Cup 2nd Rd
Sun 18   FA Sunday Cup 3rd Rd

JANUARY 1989

Sat 7   FA Cup 3rd Rd
Sat 14   FA Trophy 1st Rd
             FA Youth Cup 3rd Rd
Wed 18   Littlewoods Cup 5th Rd

Sat 21   FA Vase 4th Rd
             FA County Youth Cup 3rd Rd
Sun 22   FA Sunday Cup 4th Rd
Sat 28   FA Cup 4th Rd

FEBRUARY 1989

Sat 4   FA Trophy 2nd Rd
Wed 8   ENGLAND INTERNATIONAL (to be announced)
Sat 11   FA Vase 5th Rd
             FA Youth Cup 4th Rd
Wed 15   Littlewoods Cup Semi-finals, 1st leg
Sat 18   FA Cup 5th Rd
Sun 19   FA Sunday Cup 5th Rd
Wed 22   Littlewoods Cup Semi-finals, 2nd leg
Sat 25   FA Trophy 3rd Rd
             FA County Youth Cup 4th Rd

MARCH 1989

Wed 1   European Cups Quarter-finals, 1st leg
Sat 4   FA Vase 6th Rd
             FA Youth Cup 5th Rd
Wed 8   ALBANIA v ENGLAND (World Cup)
Sat 11   FA Trophy 4th Rd
Wed 15   European Cups Quarter-finals, 2nd leg
Sat 18   FA Cup Quarter-finals
Sun 19   FA Sunday Cup Semi-finals
Sat 25   FA Vase Semi-finals, 1st leg
             FA County Youth Cup Semi-finals

APRIL 1989

Sat 1   FA Vase Semi-finals, 2nd leg
             FA Youth Cup Semi-finals
Wed 5   European Cups Semi-finals, 1st leg
Sat 8   FA Trophy Semi-finals, 1st leg
Sun 9   Littlewoods Cup Final
Sat 15   FA Cup Semi-finals
             FA Trophy Semi-finals, 2nd leg
Wed 19   European Cups Semi-finals, 2nd leg
Wed 26   ENGLAND v ALBANIA (World Cup)
Sat 29   FA County Youth Cup Final
Sun 30   FA Sunday Cup Final

MAY 1989

Wed 3   UEFA Cup Final, 1st leg
Sat 6   FA Vase Final
             FA Youth Cup Final
Wed 10   European Cup-Winners' Cup Final
Sat 13   FA Trophy Final
Wed 17   UEFA Cup Final, 2nd leg
Sat 20   FA Cup Final
Tue 23   Rous Cup
Wed 24   European Cup Final
Sat 27   Rous Cup
Tue 30   Rous Cup

JUNE 1989

Sat 3   ENGLAND v POLAND (World Cup)